TECHNIQUES FOR WILDLIFE INVESTIGATIONS AND MANAGEMENT

Edited by

Clait E. Braun

Grouse Inc.

and

School of Natural Resources

University of Arizona

Tucson, Arizona

The Wildlife Society

Bethesda, Maryland, USA

2005

This book is the sixth in a series on wildlife techniques published by The Wildlife Society

Editor, Henry S. Mosby
  Manual of Game Investigational Techniques
      (1) First Edition—May 1960
          Second Printing—February 1961
  Wildlife Investigational Techniques
      (2) Second Edition—May 1963
          Second Printing (Revised)—March 1965
          Third through Sixth Printing—March 1966 to September 1968

Editor, Robert H. Giles, Jr.
  Wildlife Management Techniques
      (3) Third Edition—June 1969
          Second Printing (Revised)—January 1971
          Third Printing—May 1972

Editor, Sanford D. Schemnitz
  Wildlife Management Techniques Manual
      (4) Fourth Edition—September 1980

Editor, Theodore A. Bookhout
  Research and Management Techniques for Wildlife and Habitats
      (5) Fifth Edition—January 1994
          Second Printing (Revised)—April 1996
          Third Printing—August 1999

Editor, Clait E. Braun
  Techniques for Wildlife Investigations and Management
      (6) Sixth Edition—March 2005   _____

Suggested citation formats:

Entire book

Braun, C. E., editor. 2005. Techniques for wildlife investigations and management. Sixth edition. The Wildlife Society, Bethesda, Maryland, USA.

Chapter of the book

Young, J. R. 2005. Animal behavior: its role in wildlife biology. Pages 616–631 *in* C. E. Braun, editor. Techniques for wildlife investigations and management. Sixth edition. The Wildlife Society, Bethesda, Maryland, USA.

_____

This book was produced in QuarkXpress for Windows, printed as Adobe Postscript files, resaved as high-resolution Adobe PDF files, and imaged direct-to-plate to a Creo VLF platesetter. The text is Adobe Times Roman. The text paper is 50 pound Accent Opaque (acid free). The Arrestox cloth cover was screen printed and the case binding was done by Advantage Bookbinding in Baltimore, Maryland. This book was printed on a Timson full-sized heat-set web press by Port City Press (a division of Cadmus) in Baltimore, Maryland.

ISBN 0-933564-15-5
Library of Congress Catalog Card Number: 2004117702

Contents

WILDLIFE MANAGEMENT TECHNIQUES

WILDLIFE HABITAT MANAGEMENT

FOREWORD

This book is the sixth edition in a series published by The Wildlife Society (TWS). Founded in 1937, TWS is an international, nonprofit, scientific and educational association dedicated to excellence in wildlife stewardship through science and education. TWS's mission is to enhance the ability of wildlife professionals to conserve diversity, sustain productivity, and ensure responsible use of wildlife resources for the benefit of society. This book is a significant addition to the toolbox wildlife biologists use to accomplish that mission. Over the years this book has been affectionately called the "Wildlife Techniques Manual," because it contained just about everything a practicing wildlife biologist must know about the tools of the trade. It is *the* most comprehensive and complete volume of its kind available anywhere in the world. All practicing wildlife biologists worth their salt must have a copy on their desk or in their bookcase as a ready reference. The tools and techniques in this manual are essential to the practice of conservation and management of our rich wildlife heritage.

In the *Foreword* of the 1960 edition, it states that the limited number of the first version of a "techniques manual," which was published in 1938 (Wight, H. M. 1938. Field and laboratory technic in wildlife management. University of Michigan Press, Ann Arbor, USA.), a year after The Wildlife Society was formed, was soon sold out due to "...a great interest in wildlife management techniques." Interest was keen nearly 70 years ago, and has not waned since. The 2005 sixth edition contains 34 chapters, 919 pages, thousands of citations, and was electronically prepared for publication. In contrast, the first edition was 107 pages long, was typed on a typewriter, and was multilithed.

It is astounding to see how far the field has come in about one biologist's lifespan. The rate of progress has been rapid in the 10 years since the previous edition, and in some specialty areas has likely eclipsed all previous advancements combined. A quick search of the fifth edition published in 1994 reveals that geographic information systems were just showing up. Global positioning systems (GPS) were brand new and researchers only dreamed of placing GPS units on animals. DNA analyses and AIC statistical procedures, now common in the vernacular of wildlife biologists and researchers, were nowhere to be found in the 1994 index. New chapters in the sixth edition on spatial technologies, radar, animal behavior, conservation genetics, and contaminants reflect current concerns not present 10 years earlier. Finally, an entirely new section on teaching and communication skills, reflecting the significance of further development of the profession, appears in the sixth edition.

The breadth of material covered in this edition demonstrates just how diverse the wildlife field has become. Historically, wildlife biologists were principally engaged in game species and habitat management. A continued perception of this categorization is an anachronistic vestige of the past, far removed from reality. Yet many laymen and professionals still perceive wildlife biologists as game managers. All one has to do is pick up this edition and thumb through the pages to quickly dispel that misperception.

Authors contributing to this work are all experts in their fields, nationally and internationally recognized for their experience and technical publications. Many have unique personal stories that go along with scholarly contribution to this work. Numerous anecdotes can be related that underscore the discipline and dedication of authors. For example, one chapter was completed after the senior author had a major medical problem. The material for another chapter (and other scientific equipment) was stolen while a senior author was overseas. Many interesting (and sometimes comical) "incidents" occurred in the real life of the scientists and biologists during the period they helped make the sixth edition reality.

The wildlife profession owes a sincere thanks to these "volunteer" authors (many were actually solicited and/or drafted) who added the responsibility for preparing a chapter to their already full professional life. The same is true for the dedicated referees for each chapter who were asked to critically evaluate up to several hundred manuscript pages and respond to the editor within 30 days or less. So in addition to the science, there is a significant personal underpinning to this book.

Special thanks must go to Clait E. Braun, editor of the sixth edition. Clait's tireless attention to detail, relentless pursuit of excellence, and an uncompromising standard of quality and professionalism all have worked together to ensure that this edition is an immense contribution to the body of wildlife literature.

Richard A. Lancia
President, TWS
2004–2005

PREFACE

The Wildlife Society has a 40-year history of developing and publishing a "Techniques Manual." I am pleased to have the good fortune of being selected as the editor of the sixth edition. Preparation of the sixth edition was initiated in 2001 with a survey of interested users concerning the content. Selection of senior authors was initiated for continuing and completely new chapters with the understanding they could select junior authors. My preference was to work with senior authors but I also expressed interest in authors experienced in working with management agencies and also "younger" junior authors. This could help continuity if there is a seventh edition some time in the future. Senior authors developed outlines, which were reviewed for content and possible overlap with other chapters. Initial drafts of each chapter were requested by 1 September 2002 and most were in hand by late 2002. Reviews of each chapter by 2 experienced subject matter referees were requested, although some chapters received 3 reviews. This process took time as did initial edits. We used a mixture of U.S. Postal Service mail and electronic correspondence with the latter being most efficient. All initial edits were on paper copy with the final editorial cleanup being done electronically. All manuscripts went through the editing process at least twice. By March 2004, all chapters had been fully processed and sent to the publications unit of The Wildlife Society in Bethesda, Maryland. This explains the "nuts and bolts" of how the process worked.

The above does not sound exciting but it worked. I enjoyed reading and editing each chapter and am indebted to all of the senior and junior authors who provided the initial drafts and then endured my editing, which occasionally was "severe." I am also indebted to all of those who served as reviewers as they were exceedingly important in providing useful suggestions. Gavin R. Bieber of Tucson, Arizona served as chief literature checker and his patience, endurance in the library, careful attention to detail, and service as an occasional critic were important to identifying problems and inconsistencies. He has my effusive praise as his work improved the Literature Cited of each chapter. Julie L. Moore of Wildlife Information Service, Las Cruces, New Mexico served as the Indexer for the sixth edition and her great care and attention to detail improved the usefulness of the final product. She is commended for excellent work on this edition. Don Radovich of Ouray, Colorado, and Tucson, Arizona prepared the artwork for the cover and his talent contributed to the overall appearance.

Many other people, especially authors and reviewers, made useful comments that were helpful to me at different stages in the preparation of the sixth edition. I thank all who directly and indirectly helped in some manner. Real life events also happened during preparation of the sixth edition. These included several major medical issues with senior authors, and a major theft of research and manuscript materials. Junior authors of several chapters became far more involved than I am sure they initially intended. I sincerely thank them for stepping forward to help us reach our goal. Two referees died during preparation of the Sixth Edition and both Beth Williams and Alan Woolf made important contributions to the chapters they reviewed. The editorial staff at the Bethesda office of The Wildlife Society, Susan Monseur, Gene Pozniak, and Bill Rooney, was helpful in bringing this edition of the "Techniques Manual" to a successful conclusion. I also thank Richard A. Lancia, who served as liaison with Council of The Wildlife Society, and Harry E. Hodgdon and Thomas M. Franklin, Executive Directors of The Wildlife Society, for their support of my role as editor and of the overall project. My wife Nancy tolerated my use of every available space and both computers for this project during the last 4+ years and I am greatly appreciative of her support.

During the initial survey of those who used the Techniques Manual, it became clear that inclusion of new material was needed, as were serious updates of chapters in the Fifth Edition. We invited new chapters on animal behavior, communications, coastal wetland management, conservation genetics, contaminants, impacts of wildland recreation, radar biology, teaching of wildlife techniques, and wildlife diseases. Other major changes were the inclusion of material on Habitat Conservation Plans and managing small populations. Authors were receptive to new ideas and all chapters included were either updated or largely rewritten. Several of The Wildlife Society's Working Groups undertook revision of previous chapters or preparation of new chapters. I especially thank those groups as they greatly expedited the process of preparation of some chapters. I am really pleased by all of the chapters and especially the broader coverage.

One of my goals in this project was to not lose the "flavor" of the individual writing styles of the authors while maintaining consistency. I also tried to organize the presentation of the chapters in a logical sequence. Many of the authors of the individual chapters helped in this process but the final decision was mine as I tried to group chapters based on their relatedness and or perceived (by myself) importance. For those who find the chapter sequence different from what they would have preferred, I accept full responsibility for the organization. I also accept responsibility for any editing lapses although I am not fully responsible for any factual issues.

A friend asked me if I knew what I was getting into when I was selected as editor for the sixth edition. My response was that I knew exactly what I was getting into and I looked forward to it. In truth, I learned a lot about many different topics and I enjoyed almost every minute of it. I appreciate the opportunity to be of service to The Wildlife Society and the wildlife profession.

Clait E. Braun
Editor, Sixth Edition
February 2005

CHAPTER AUTHORS

Lowell W. Adams
Natural Resources Management Program
University of Maryland
College Park, MD 20742

J. Richard Alldredge
Department of Statistics
Washington State University
Pullman, WA 99164

Stanley H. Anderson
U. S. Department of the Interior
Geological Survey
Wyoming Cooperative Fish and Wildlife Research Unit
University of Wyoming
Laramie, WY 82071

Keith E. Aune
Montana Department of Fish, Wildlife and Parks
Helena, MT 59620

William T. Barker
Department of Animal and Range Sciences
North Dakota State University
Fargo, ND 58105

Charley Barrett
Northwest Habitat Institute
Corvallis, OR 97339

Jonathan R. Bart
U. S. Department of the Interior
Geological Survey
Forest and Rangeland Ecosystem Science Center
Boise, ID 83706

Susan Bernatas
Vision Air Research
904 East Washington Street
Boise, ID 83712

Pete Bettinger
Daniel B. Warnell School of Forest Resources
University of Georgia
Athens, GA 30602

Vernon C. Bleich
Sierra Nevada Bighorn Sheep Recovery Program
California Department of Fish and Game
Bishop, CA 93514

Mark S. Boyce
Department of Biological Sciences
University of Alberta
Edmonton, AB T6G 2E9
Canada

Howard J. Bruner
Department of Forest Science
Oregon State University
Corvallis, OR 97331

Henry Campa, III
Department of Fisheries and Wildlife
Michigan State University
East Lansing, MI 48824

Robert H. Chabreck
School of Renewable Natural Resources
Louisiana State University
Baton Rouge, LA 70808

Kevin E. Church
Idaho Conservation Data Center
Idaho Department of Fish and Game
Boise, ID 83707

Gary K. Clambey
Department of Botany/Biology
North Dakota State University
Fargo, ND 58105

David N. Cole
Aldo Leopold Wilderness Research Institute
P. O. Box 8089
Missoula, MT 59807

John W. Connelly
Idaho Department of Fish and Game
1345 Barton Road
Pocatello, ID 83204

F. Joshua Dein
U. S. Department of the Interior
Geological Survey
National Wildlife Health Center
Madison, WI 53711

Stephen J. Dinsmore
Department of Wildlife and Fisheries
Mississippi State University
Mississippi State, MS 39762

Richard A. Dolbeer
U. S. Department of Agriculture
Wildlife Services
Plum Brook Station
Sandusky, OH 44870

Wallace P. Erickson
Western EcoSystems Technology, Inc.
2003 Central Avenue
Cheyenne, WY 82001

Leigh H. Fredrickson
U. S. Department of the Interior
Geological Survey
Northern Prairie Wildlife Research Center
Jamestown, ND 58401

Mark R. Fuller
U. S. Department of the Interior
Geological Survey
Forest and Rangeland Ecosystem Science Center
Boise, ID 83706

James H. Gammonley
Wildlife Research Center
Colorado Division of Wildlife
Fort Collins, CO 80526

Edward O. Garton
Department of Fish and Wildlife Resources
University of Idaho
Moscow, ID 83844

Eric M. Gese
U. S. Department of Agriculture
Wildlife Services
National Wildlife Research Center
Utah State University
Logan, UT 84322

John H. Giudice
Farmland Wildlife Research Group
Minnesota Department of Natural Resources
Madelia, MN 56062

Kevin J. Gutzwiller
Department of Biology
Baylor University
Waco, TX 76798

John D. Harder
Department of Evolution, Ecology, and Organismal
    Biology
The Ohio State University
Columbus, Ohio 43210

Eric C. Hellgren
Department of Zoology
Oklahoma State University
Stillwater, OK 74078

Kenneth F. Higgins
U. S. Department of the Interior
Geological Survey
South Dakota Cooperative Fish and Wildlife Research Unit
South Dakota State University
Brookings, SD 57007

Elwood F. Hill
P. O. Box 1615
Gardnerville, NV 89410

Catherine L. Hoffman
Department of Natural Resources and Environmental
Sciences
University of Illinois
Urbana, IL 61801

Susan K. Jacobson
Department of Wildlife Ecology and Conservation
University of Florida
Gainesville, FL 32611

Kurt J. Jenkins
U. S. Department of the Interior
Geological Survey
Forest and Rangeland Ecosystem Science Center
Port Angeles, WA 98362

Douglas H. Johnson
U. S. Department of the Interior
Geological Survey
Northern Prairie Wildlife Research Center
Jamestown, ND 58401

William L. Kendall
U. S. Department of the Interior
Geological Survey
Patuxent Wildlife Research Center
Laurel, MD 20708

Kevin P. Kenow
U. S. Department of the Interior
Geological Survey
Upper Midwest Environmental Sciences Center
La Crosse, WI 54603

Robert E. Kenward
Natural Environment Research Council
Centre for Ecology and Hydrology
Winfrith Technology Centre
Dorchester DT2 8ZD
United Kingdom

John G. Kie
U. S. Department of Agriculture
Forest Service
La Grande, OR 97850

Sammy L. King
U. S. Department of the Interior
Geological Survey
Louisiana Cooperative Fish and Wildlife Research Unit
Louisiana State University
Baton Rouge, LA 70803

Gregory T. Koeln
Environmental and GIS Services
Earth Satellite Corporation
6011 Executive Blvd., Suite 400
Rockville, MD 20852

Kyran Kunkel
Turner Endangered Species Fund
1875 Gateway South
Gallatin Gateway, MT 59730

Richard A. Lancia
Fisheries and Wildlife Program
Department of Forestry
North Carolina State University
Raleigh, NC 27607

viii

Ronald P. Larkin
Center for Wildlife Ecology
Illinois Natural History Survey
Champaign, IL 61820

Murray K. Laubhan
U. S. Department of the Interior
Geological Survey
Northern Prairie Wildlife Research Center
Jamestown, ND 58401

Paul L. Leberg
Department of Biology
University of Louisiana
Lafayette, LA 70504

Eric R. Loft
Habitat Conservation Division
California Department of Fish and Game
Sacramento, CA 95814

Roel R. Lopez
Department of Wildlife and Fisheries Sciences
Texas A&M University
College Station, TX 77843

Maciej Luniak
Museum and Institute of Zoology
Polish Academy of Sciences
Warsaw, Poland

B. Wayne Luscombe
Spatial Information Systems and International
Development
464 Skyline Crest Road
Portland, OR 97229

Carolyn G. Mahan
Department of Biology
Pennsylvania State University-Altoona
Altoona, PA 16601

Bruce G. Marcot
U. S. Department of Agriculture
Forest Service
Pacific Northwest Research Station
Portland, OR 97205

Lyman L. McDonald
Western EcoSystems Technology, Inc.
2003 Central Avenue
Cheyenne, WY 82001

Scott R. McWilliams
Wildlife and Conservation Biology Program
Department of Natural Resources Science
University of Rhode Island
Kingston, RI 02881

Alvin L. Medina
U. S. Department of Agriculture
Forest Service
Rocky Mountain Research Station
Flagstaff, AZ 86001

L. Scott Mills
Wildlife Biology Program
College of Forestry and Conservation
University of Montana
Missoula, MT 59812

Joshua J. Millspaugh
Department of Fisheries and Wildlife Sciences
University of Missouri
Columbia, MO 65211

David E. Naugle
Wildlife Biology Program
College of Forestry and Conservation
University of Montana
Missoula, MT 59812

James D. Nichols
U. S. Department of the Interior
Geological Survey
Patuxent Wildlife Research Center
Laurel, MD 20708

Jack E. Norland
Department of Animal and Range Sciences
North Dakota State University
Fargo, ND 58105

William I. Notz
Department of Statistics
The Ohio State University
Columbus, OH 43210

John A. Nyman
School of Renewable Natural Resources
Louisiana State University
Baton Rouge, LA 70803

Michael W. Oehler, Sr.
U. S. Department of the Interior
National Park Service
Theodore Roosevelt National Park
Medora, ND 58645

Thomas A. O'Neil
Northwest Habitat Institute
P. O. Box 855
Corvallis, OR 97339

Sara J. Oyler-McCance
U. S. Department of the Interior
Geological Survey
Rocky Mountain Center for Conservation Genetics and
    Systematics
Department of Biological Sciences
University of Denver
Denver, CO 80208

James M. Peek
Department of Fish and Wildlife Resources
University of Idaho
Moscow, ID 83844

Markus J. Peterson
Department of Wildlife and Fisheries Sciences
Texas A&M University
College Station, TX 77843

Jennifer A. Pollock
U. S. Department of the Interior
Geological Survey
Center for Biological Informatics
Denver Federal Center
Denver, CO 80225

Kenneth H. Pollock
Fisheries and Wildlife Program
Departments of Zoology and Statistics
North Carolina State University
Raleigh, NC 27695

John T. Ratti
Department of Fish and Wildlife Resources
University of Idaho
Moscow, ID 83844

Leslie A. Robb
P. O. Box 1077
Bridgeport, WA 98813

Amanda D. Rodewald
School of Natural Resources
The Ohio State University
Columbus, OH 43210

Thomas J. Roffe
U. S. Department of the Interior
Fish and Wildlife Service
Mountain-Prairie Region
Bozeman, MT 59718

Mark R. Ryan
Department of Fisheries and Wildlife Sciences
University of Missouri
Columbia, MO 65211

Sanford D. Schemnitz
Department of Fishery and Wildlife Sciences
New Mexico State University
Las Cruces, NM 88003

Michael A. Schroeder
Washington Department of Fish and Wildlife
P. O. Box 1077
Bridgeport, WA 98813

J. Michael Scott
U. S. Department of the Interior
Geological Survey
Idaho Cooperative Fish and Wildlife Research Unit
University of Idaho
Moscow, ID 83844

Frederick A. Servello
Department of Wildlife Ecology
University of Maine
Orono, ME 04469

Steven R. Sheffield
Department of Environmental Science and Policy
George Mason University
Fairfax, VA 22030

Nova J. Silvy
Department of Wildlife and Fisheries Sciences
Texas A&M University
College Station, TX 77843

Thomas R. Stephenson
Sierra Nevada Bighorn Sheep Recovery Program
California Department of Fish and Game
Bishop, CA 93514

Katherine M. Strickler
Department of Fish and Wildlife Resources
University of Idaho
Moscow, ID 83844

Joseph P. Sullivan
Ardea Consulting
10 First Street
Woodland, CA 95695

Steven J. Sweeney
U. S. Department of Agriculture
Animal and Plant Health Inspection Service
Veterinary Services
Bozeman, MT 59715

Stanley A. Temple
Department of Wildlife Ecology
University of Wisconsin
Madison, WI 53706

Dale E. Toweill
Idaho Department of Fish and Game
Boise, ID 83707

Joe C. Truett
Turner Endangered Species Fund
P.O. Box 211
Glenwood, NM 88039

Daniel W. Uresk
U. S. Department of Agriculture
Forest Service
Rocky Mountain Research Station
Rapid City, SD 57702

Larry W. VanDruff
College of Environmental Science and Forestry
State University of New York
Syracuse, NY 13210

Kurt C. VerCauteren
U. S. Department of Agriculture
Wildlife Services
National Wildlife Research Center
Fort Collins, CO 80521

Jeffery W. Walk
Illinois Natural History Survey
One Natural Resources Way
Springfield, IL 62702

Richard E. Warner
Department of Natural Resources and Environmental
  Sciences
University of Illinois
Urbana, IL 61801

Thierry M. Work
U. S. Department of the Interior
Geological Survey
National Wildlife Health Center
Hawaii Field Station
Honolulu, HI 96850

Richard H. Yahner
School of Forest Resources
The Pennsylvania State University
University Park, PA 16802

Jessica R. Young
Department of Natural and Environmental Sciences
Western State College
Gunnison, CO 81231

Marilet A. Zablan
U. S. Department of the Interior
Fish and Wildlife Service
Pacific Islands Fish and Wildlife Office
Honolulu, HI 96850

CHAPTER REFEREES

Gordon R. Batcheller
New York State Department of Environmental
    Conservation
Division of Fish, Wildlife, and Marine Resources
Albany, NY 12233

Robert C. Beason
U. S. Department of Agriculture
Wildlife Services
National Wildlife Research Center
Ohio Field Station
Sandusky, OH 44870

Robert E. Bennetts
U. S. Department of the Interior
National Park Service
Greater Yellowstone Network
Bozeman. MT 58717

Louis B. Best
Department of Natural Resource Ecology and Management
Iowa State University
Ames, IA 50011

William M. Block
U. S. Department of Agriculture
Forest Service
Rocky Mountain Research Station
Flagstaff, AZ 86001

William W. Bowerman
Department of Forestry and Natural Resources
Clemson University
Clemson, SC 29634

Clait E. Braun
Grouse Inc.
5572 North Ventana Vista Road
Tucson, AZ 85750

Brian S. Cade
U. S. Department of the Interior
Geological Survey
Fort Collins Science Center
Fort Collins, CO 80526

Michael R. Conover
Berryman Institute
Department of Forest, Range, and Wildlife Sciences
Utah State University
Logan, UT 84322

Robert R. Cox, Jr.
U. S. Department of the Interior
Geological Survey
Northern Prairie Wildlife Research Center
Jamestown, ND 58401

Duane R. Diefenbach
U. S. Department of the Interior
Geological Survey
Pennsylvania Cooperative Fish and Wildlife Research Unit
Pennsylvania State University
University Park, PA 16802

Ralph W. Dimmick
Department of Forestry, Wildlife, and Fisheries
University of Tennessee
Knoxville, TN 37901

Rod C. Drewien
Hornocker Institute
University of Idaho
Rigby, ID 83442

Cindy P. Driscoll
Maryland Department of Natural Resources
Fish and Wildlife Health Program
Oxford, MD 21654

Thomas C. Edwards, Jr.
U. S. Department of the Interior
Geological Survey
Utah Cooperative Fish and Wildlife Research Unit
Utah State University
Logan, UT 84322

Robert L. Eng
Fish and Wildlife Program
Department of Ecology
Montana State University
Bozeman, MT 59717

Ned H. Euliss, Jr.
U. S. Department of the Interior
Geological Survey
Northern Prairie Wildlife Research Center
Jamestown, ND 58401

James R. Fazio
Department of Resource Recreation and Tourism
University of Idaho
Moscow, ID 83844

Lester D. Flake
Department of Wildlife and Fisheries Sciences
South Dakota State University
Brookings, SD 57007

Erik K. Fritzell
College of Agricultural Sciences
Oregon State University
Corvallis, OR 97331

Robert J. Gates
School of Natural Resources
The Ohio State University
Columbus, OH 43210

Sidney A. Gauthreaux, Jr.
Department of Biological Sciences
Clemson University
Clemson, SC 29634

James R. Gilbert
Department of Wildlife Ecology
University of Maine
Orono, ME 04469

James W. Hardin
College of Natural Resources
University of Wisconsin
Stevens Point, WI 54481

William M. Healy
Owl Run Farm
P. O. Box 187
Smithville, WV 26178

David G. Hewitt
Caesar Kleberg Wildlife Research Institute
Texas A&M University-Kingsville
Kingsville, TX 78363

Elwood F. Hill
P. O. Box 1615
Gardnerville, NV 89410

Jon K. Hooper
Department of Recreation and Parks Management
California State University-Chico
Chico, CA 95929

George F. Hubert, Jr.
P. O. Box 728
Hinckley, IL 60520

Jerry W. Hupp
U. S. Department of the Interior
Geological Survey
Alaska Science Center
Anchorage, AK 99503

Laura S. Jackson
Oregon Department of Fish and Wildlife
Roseburg, OR 97470

David A. Jessup
Marine Wildlife Veterinary Care and Research Center
California Department of Fish and Game
Santa Cruz, CA 95060

Douglas H. Johnson
U. S. Department of the Interior
Geological Survey
Northern Prairie Wildlife Research Center
Jamestown, North Dakota 58401

William H. Karasov
Department of Wildlife Ecology
University of Wisconsin
Madison, WI 53706

Roy L. Kirkpatrick
Department of Fisheries and Wildlife Sciences
College of Natural Resources
Virginia Tech
Blacksburg, VA 24061

Scott D. Klopfer
Conservation Management Institute
Virginia Tech
Blacksburg, VA 24061

Paul R. Krausman
School of Natural Resources
The University of Arizona
Tucson, AZ 85721

Terry J. Kreeger
Wyoming Game and Fish Department
Wheatland, WY 82201

John A. Litvaitis
Department of Natural Resources
University of New Hampshire
Durham, NH 03824

Jerry R. Longcore
U. S. Department of the Interior
Geological Survey
Patuxent Wildlife Research Center
Orono, ME 04469

Richard J. Mackie
Fish and Wildlife Program
Department of Ecology
Montana State University
Bozeman, MT 59717

R. William Mannan
School of Natural Resources
The University of Arizona
Tucson, AZ 85721

R. Larry Marchinton
Wildlife Ecology and Management
Daniel B. Warnell School of Forest Resources
University of Georgia
Athens, GA 30602

Jeffery L. Marion
U. S. Department of the Interior
Geological Survey
Patuxent Wildlife Research Center
Virginia Tech
Blacksburg, VA 24061

Kathy Martin
Centre for Applied Conservation Biology
University of British Columbia
Vancouver, B.C., Canada V6T 1Z4

L. Scott Mills
Wildlife Biology Program
College of Forestry and Conservation
University of Montana
Missoula, MT 59812

Karen Mock
Department of Forest, Range, and Wildlife Sciences
Utah State University
Logan, UT 84322

Clinton T. Moore
U. S. Department of the Interior
Geological Survey
Patuxent Wildlife Research Center
Daniel B. Warnell School of Forest Resources
University of Georgia
Athens, GA 30602

Barry R. Noon
Department of Fishery and Wildlife Biology
Colorado State University
Fort Collins, CO 80523

Gail S. Olson
Department of Fisheries and Wildlife
Oregon State University
Corvallis, OR 97331

Thomas E. Olson
Biological Consulting
104 South "C" Street, Suite G
Lompoc, CA 93436

Eric T. Reed
Environment Canada
Canadian Wildlife Service
Gatineau, Quebec, K1A 0H3
Canada

Kerry P. Reese
Department of Fish and Wildlife Resources
University of Idaho
Moscow, ID 83844

Samuel K. Riffell
Department of Zoology
Michigan State University
East Lansing, MI 48824

Glen A. Sargeant
U. S. Department of the Interior
Geological Survey
Northern Prairie Wildlife Research Center
Jamestown, ND 58401

Charles C. Schwartz
U. S. Department of the Interior
Geological Survey
Northern Rocky Mountain Science Center
Montana State University
Bozeman, MT 59717

Sara H. Schweitzer
Wildlife Ecology and Management
Daniel B. Warnell School of Forest Resources
University of Georgia
Athens, GA 30602

Nova J. Silvy
Department of Wildlife and Fisheries Sciences
Texas A&M University
College Station, TX 77843

Warren D. Snyder
Colorado Division of Wildlife
Sterling, CO 80751

Dean F. Stauffer
Department of Fisheries and Wildlife Science
College of Natural Resources
Virginia Tech
Blacksburg, VA 24061

Richard B. Stiehl
Alice Lloyd College
Pippa Passes, KY 41844

Laurence L. Strong
U. S. Department of the Interior
Geological Survey
Northern Prairie Wildlife Research Center
Jamestown, ND 58401

W. Daniel Svedarsky
Northwest Research and Outreach Center
University of Minnesota
Crookston, MN 56718

W. Fred Taylor, Jr.
U. S. Department of the Interior
Bureau of Land Management
Hines, OR 97738

Ronald M. Thom
Battelle Marine Sciences Laboratory
Pacific Northwest National Laboratory
Sequim, WA 98382

Robert M. Timm
Hopland Research and Extension Center
University of California
Hopland, CA 95449

Mark C. Wallace
Department of Range, Wildlife, and Fisheries
    Management
Texas Tech University
Lubbock, TX 79409

Milton W. Weller
Department of Wildlife and Fisheries Sciences
Texas A&M University
College Station, TX 77843

Gary C. White
Department of Fishery and Wildlife Biology
Colorado State University
Fort Collins, CO 80523

Margaret A. Wild
U. S. Department of the Interior
National Park Service
Biological Resource Management Division
Fort Collins, CO 80525

Elizabeth S. Williams
Department of Veterinary Sciences
University of Wyoming
Laramie, WY 82070

Gary A. Wobeser
Department of Veterinary Pathology
University of Saskatchewan
Saskatoon, SK S7N 5B4 Canada

Michael L. Wolfe, Jr.
Department of Forest, Range, and Wildlife Sciences
Utah State University
Logan, UT 84322

Alan Woolf
Cooperative Wildlife Research Laboratory
Southern Illinois University
Carbondale, IL 62901

1

TEACHING WILDLIFE RESEARCH AND MANAGEMENT TECHNIQUES

Mark R. Ryan and Henry Campa, III

THE LEARNING PROCESS

Professional Expectations

The working environments of wildlife professionals are at least as dynamic as the ecosystems they manage. This is what makes the profession of wildlife management exciting and challenging. As students become wildlife professionals they will be confronted with new problems, they may need to establish research hypotheses, plan and conduct fieldwork, analyze complex data sets, develop policy recommendations, create educational programs, or respond to multiple stakeholders concerning environmental issues. The problems facing wildlife biologists of the future will be complex and will not be addressed successfully without considering linkages among ecological, cultural, and economic factors (Kessler and Eastland 1995). Working in a setting with these challenges will require a strong knowledge of ecology and natural resource management principles; life-long learning of new concepts and techniques; well-developed higher order thinking abilities; interpersonal communication, problem-solving, and team-working skills; and the ability to adapt to new ideas and conservation paradigms (Schmidly et al. 1990).

The objectives of this chapter are to explore teaching and learning processes, and review and critique active learning strategies used to teach wildlife research and management techniques. Many of the approaches discussed are presented in a problem-based learning format that creates meaningful contexts in which students learn. Problem-based learning is the process of exposing students first to meaningful, relevant problems to engage them and subsequently make them accountable for their own learning by collecting, learning, and teaching information (Woods 1994, Wilkerson and Gijselaers 1996, Duch et al. 2001). This approach to teaching wildlife research and management techniques mirrors approaches used by Aldo Leopold (Meine 1988).

Box 1A. Traditional problem-solving process or subject-based learning (modified from Woods [1994] and Smith [1995]).

Goals and Objectives

Evaluation-What was learned?

Problem Identification

Apply the information to the problem or take management actions

Be given the critical information

Learn the information

Box 1B. Problem-based learning (modified from Woods [1994] and Smith [1995]) or the "Desk of a Working Wildlife Professional."

Problem Identification—What shows up on your desk?

Evaluation—What was learned?

What do you need to know—identify goals and objectives for learning

Apply the information to the problem or take management actions

Collect the necessary information

Learn the information

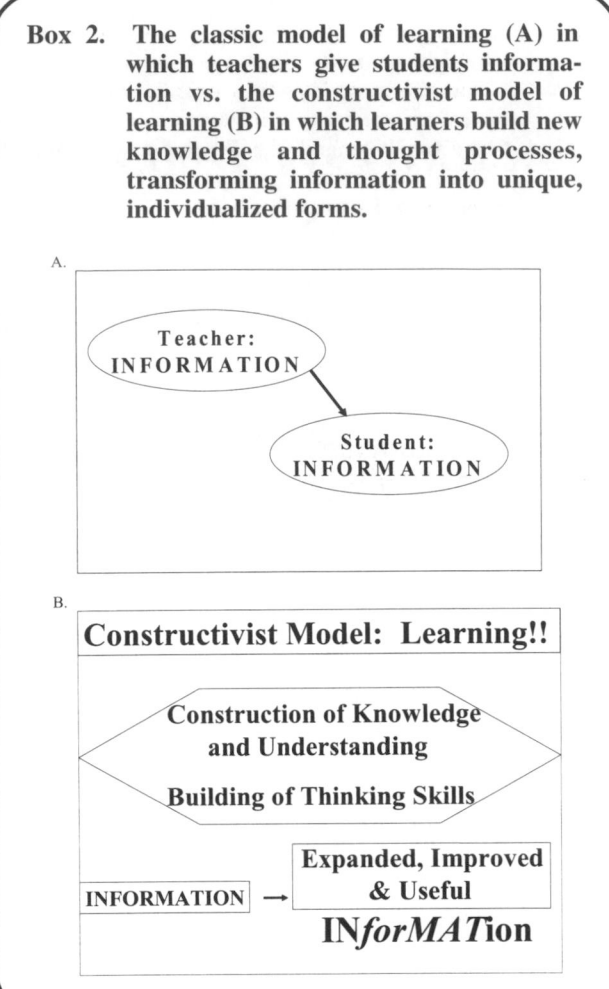

Box 2. The classic model of learning (A) in which teachers give students information vs. the constructivist model of learning (B) in which learners build new knowledge and thought processes, transforming information into unique, individualized forms.

A.

Teacher: INFORMATION

Student: INFORMATION

B.

Constructivist Model: Learning!!

Construction of Knowledge and Understanding

Building of Thinking Skills

INFORMATION → **Expanded, Improved & Useful** **IN*forMA*Tion**

In introductory natural resource management courses (e.g., Introduction to Fisheries and Wildlife) freshman are taught about the problem solving process. While there are many variations, the process generally starts with setting objectives and ends with evaluating results (Box 1A). While this is a good theoretical model, it does not represent the working environment of wildlife professionals in the 21st century.   An alternative model starts with being assigned a problem, learning or synthesizing the necessary information to address the problem, and ending with evaluating your management effectiveness (Box 1B).

Knowledge and How People Learn

In the early 20th century, knowledge was thought to exist as discrete blocks of information that existed outside the minds of individuals and as such could be transferred, unaltered, from one person to another (e.g., Thorndike 1913) (Box 2A). Thus, teachers *gave* pieces of knowledge to students, who learned it through rote, repetitive process. If adequate repetition was practiced, the learner retained the unmodified knowledge.

In the contemporary paradigm of cognitive psychology, learning is a constructive, not repetitive, process (Gijselaers 1996) (Box 2B). In constructivist theory, students *interpret* information presented to them, modifying it based on prior knowledge, previous experience, and their own idiosyncratic perception process (Byrnes 2001:5–6) to build new knowledge (Box 3). This model suggests that learners extract parts or pieces of information from a lec-

ture, and use that partial understanding to construct more complete knowledge and deeper understanding. Knowledge grows over time, only with repeated, *meaningful* encounters with the same material. The concept of "knowing" has changed in the last 100 years from the simple ability to remember information to that of being able to effectively use it (H. Simon in Bransford et al. 2000:5).

Learning psychologists (e.g., Anderson 1995, Byrnes 2001:45) refer to, at least, 4 types of knowledge. *Declarative* knowledge refers to factual information; *procedural* knowledge includes fixed sets of actions and flexible processes of thought, such as problem solving; *conceptual* knowledge is the understanding of underlying principles; and *episodic* knowledge is the temporal and spatial memory of events. Knowledge is thought to be the outcome of a developmental process involving learning and thinking.

The best-known model for the development of thinking is Bloom's Taxonomy (Bloom et al. 1956) (Box 4). Bloom et al. characterized learners as moving from lower to higher orders of thinking as they develop. Thus, knowledge and comprehension were prerequisites for application, analysis, synthesis, and evaluation. Because application, analysis, and synthesis can be done well or poorly, mastery of these levels was a prerequisite to evaluation.

Box 3. The 3 phases of constructivist learning in which students filter new information, transforming it as they encode it in their brains; rehearse with and elaborate on the newly encoded material to transfer it to long-term memory, and make it useful in future situations.

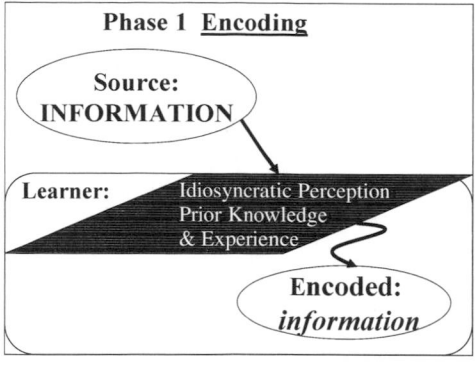

Phase 1 <u>Encoding</u>

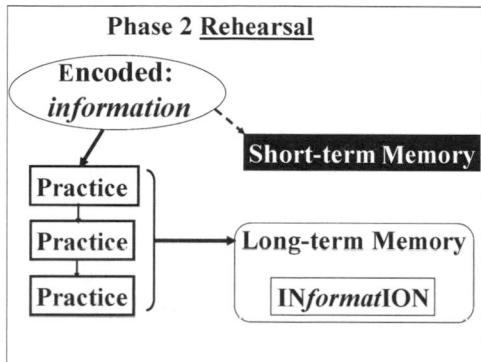

Phase 2 <u>Rehearsal</u>

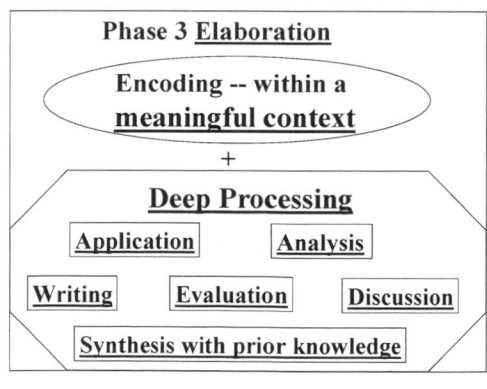

Phase 3 <u>Elaboration</u>

Box 4. Bloom's taxonomy of thinking (adapted from Bloom et al. [1956] and Byrnes [2001]).

Knowledge.—Facts, concepts, procedures known only through associative or rote-learning process (declarative or "what" knowledge).
Comprehension.—Understanding knowledge in a deeper, more elaborative way (conceptual or "why" knowledge).
Application.—Taking declarative knowledge and using it to identify or classify things, and especially to solve problems (procedural or "how" knowledge).
Analysis.—Understanding interrelationships among ideas; dividing complex information into component parts.
Synthesis.—Taking a set of ideas or concepts and creating something more complex; (creative problem solving, not simply applying a problem-solving technique, but devising a new one).
Evaluation.—Judging something against a standard of quality; explaining why one solution is better than another.

of solid lower-order thinking. The development of creative or critical thinking involves learning problem-solving techniques (i.e., problem identification, brainstorming alternative solutions), regular practice, and refinement and extension of the techniques.

Teaching must be the process of aiding students in building knowledge and knowing how to apply it to meaningful situations throughout life. Effective teaching will encompass helping students build a large, readily retrievable store of information, and giving them practice using it in professionally relevant circumstances. This requires teachers to understand how people build knowledge (i.e., facts, concepts, procedures), retain it, and develop higher-order thinking skills (i.e., application, analysis, synthesis, evaluation; Bloom et al. 1956).

Building Content Knowledge

Information processing theory suggests that learning is the process of "attending to information" in a manner that results in knowledge being transferred from short to long-term memory. The process involves *encoding*, *rehearsal*, and *elaboration*. The learner encodes new information encountered; then via meaningful repetition and elaboration (e.g., application) information is processed resulting in storage in permanent memory banks (Byrnes 2001:50–53) (Box 3). In the *encoding process*, students interpret new experiences and construct a unique mental representation of it (Anderson 1995), which is then initially stored in short-term memory (Phase 1 in Box 3). Unless individuals continue to "re-experience" this new information, via *rehearsal*, the material will be quickly lost from short-term memory (Phase 2 in Box 3). In the *elaboration* phase, learners embellish the initial encoded message with details. The combined rehearsal and elaboration efforts

Experts are recognized as those who have a substantial base of well-understood content knowledge and who are skilled in its flexible application in different real-life contexts (Bransford et al. 2000:31, Byrnes 2001:77–79). The key lesson of current learning research is the need for "straightforward connection[s] between school tasks and tasks in the real world" (Byrnes 2001:91).

Bloom's taxonomy does not imply that higher-order thinking processes cannot be *used* in the rehearsal process necessary to build knowledge and comprehension, but that mastery of advanced thinking will come after development result in *deep processing* of information, which strengthens the long-term memory and associates cues with the memory that aids in retrieval (Anderson 1995, Byrnes 2001:50–53) (Phase 3 in Box 3). A learner takes in information and new knowledge is built. New knowledge is created that provides expanded information and enhanced thinking skills useful to the learner and society.

Encoding is understood to be selective and interpretive (Byrnes 2001:50). Teachers can promote effective encoding by presenting material in organized groups or subgroups (Byrnes 2001:30–32). Delivering information in small, linked packages with time for rehearsal and elaboration will promote movement of knowledge from short- to long-term memory (Anderson 1995). Multiple delivery mechanisms also enhance the formation of mental representations of information. To address diverse learning styles and multiple forms of intelligence, presentations that combine multiple auditory, visual, and tactile formats will increase the likelihood of deeper, more accurate encoding by all students.

A large body of learning research indicates that recall of information is strongly dependent on the amount of *practice*. Studies (e.g., Anderson 1995) have demonstrated that practice distributed over time is important to forming permanent memory. This applies not only to student study habits, but also to repetition of material by instructors within a term, and to planned redundancy among courses. Knowledge grows over time, only with repeated, meaningful encounters with similar material.

Elaboration is thought to strengthen memory by imposing meaning on any kind of knowledge (Byrnes 2001:59–61). Particularly powerful elaboration techniques include presentation of material in real-world contexts. When students can understand how material might be applied, their level of engagement is enhanced, their emotions involved, associations between new and prior knowledge highlighted, and personal relevancy made apparent.

By combining numerous different experiences with the same information to promote rich encoding, repeated distributed practice, and use of the information in meaningful contexts, deep processing will occur and long-term memory of the newly created knowledge will be enhanced. Associations of emotion or modest levels of intellectual dissonance or stress with new material have been shown to promote knowledge retention (Byrnes 2001:61–62).

Developing Higher-order Thinking

Beyond retention of information, learning involves the development of what is widely referred to as critical or higher-order thinking. The apex of Bloom's higher-order thinking is evaluation: the ability to discriminate effective versus ineffective strategies for desired outcomes. Successful evaluation is predicated on the ability to generate such strategies by synthesizing facts, concepts, and analytical products and creatively applying them under different constraints.

Resnick (1987) defined higher-order thinking as requiring the creation of paths of action; application of mental energy; consideration of multiple, possible solutions; making subtle judgments; the application of multiple, and sometimes conflicting criteria in making judgments; self-regulation; and the imposition of meaning. These are fundamental thinking skills that define effective professionals.

Another aspect of higher-order thought is the ability to *transfer* or extend knowledge (including problem-solving skills) from one context to another (Byrnes 2001:86–90). This is especially important in professional education where the goal is to develop the ability to transfer information learned in school to real-life situations. When employers complain that recent graduates cannot think, they are usually identifying the inability of those graduates to transfer what was learned in formal education to the workplace (Byrnes 2001:87).

The ability to transfer knowledge is largely a function of how the information was learned. Transfer is rare when facts are learned in a rote fashion, but is promoted when deep conceptual understanding is achieved (Singley and Anderson 1989, Bransford et al. 2000:55). Educational strategies, such as simulation of real world contexts in the classroom, that link formal learning and professional contexts will promote transfer (Byrnes 2001:91). Transfer also can be diminished when too much material is covered too quickly, or when material is poorly organized (i.e., not linked to prior knowledge and to relevant contexts) (Bransford et al. 2000:58). A large body of research also suggests that when students build knowledge in only one context, transfer to other contexts will be limited (e.g., Singley and Anderson 1989). Learning psychologists stress the importance of having students solve several realistic problems that are superficially different, but nearly identical with respect to underlying principles and problem-solving strategies (Byrnes 2001:91).

Motivation and Learning

A growing research literature emphasizes the importance of student motivation to building knowledge and higher-order thinking skills. Within any college classroom, students differ on goals, personal standards of achievement, ability, beliefs, interests, self-monitoring skills, and values. These differences translate into substantial variation in engagement, effort, and persistence (Byrnes 2001:93–119). Teachers can improve motivation by helping students see the relevance of material, creating a challenging atmosphere, allowing for establishment of social relationships, using numerous teaching methods, grading on effort and individual improvement as well as overall mastery, and encouraging the view that errors are an inherent aspect of learning (Bransford et al. 2000:60–61, Byrnes et al. 2001:93–119).

Active Learning

The overriding theme that emerges from contemporary research in cognitive psychology is that knowledge is built and critical thinking developed when students are actively engaged with learning material in relevant, meaningful contexts. Teaching methods that strive to create such engagement are collectively known as *active learning strategies* (Meyers and Jones 1993, Sutherland and Bonwell 1996, Handelsman et al. 2004). These strategies share numerous characteristics. There is recognition that different people learn in different ways and using multiple strategies will be more effective than any single technique. Learning is fostered in a social context involving multilevel interactions between students and instructors, *and* among students. Learning is student-centered rather than teacher-centered and students are encouraged to assume responsibility for their own learning. Students learn best by *doing*, especially in contexts relevant to them as individuals.

The successful application of active learning techniques requires creating an energized, supportive, and inviting atmosphere in the classroom. Because active learning presupposes students taking responsibility for their own learning, it is initially riskier for students than passive learning environments. Establishing a psychologically safe classroom environment that provides a sense of social connectedness is important. Research indicates a high correlation between students believing the teacher cares about them and academic success. "Perhaps the single most important act that faculty can do to improve the climate in the classroom is to learn student names" (Bonwell and Eison 1991:22). We add the corollary that students need to know each other, even if it is just the people sitting near them. It also is essential to communicate expectations (Groccia and Miller 1996). Fear of looking foolish, uncertainty about responsibilities, and differences in learning styles make many students initially uncomfortable or resistant to active learning situations (Brookfield 1990:151–152). For students new to active learning classrooms, it is important they understand why lecturing will be minimized, how they will contribute to the learning process, what they can expect to gain from participating in active learning, the ground rules for participation, and how they will be evaluated.

Regular and varied use of numerous active learning techniques maintains motivation (Byrnes 2001:118–119) and stimulating learning and teaching environments (Brookfield 1990, Groccia and Miller 1996). Sporadic use of student-centered learning activities may be ineffectual, as students may not get comfortable with the new approaches. Relying excessively on any one technique may result in loss of attention and concentration. Active learning techniques must promote the relevancy of the material to be learned (Bruer 1993). Discussion or small group activities in which students cannot grasp the significance of the material in relation to their personal or professional lives are likely to be no more effective than traditional lectures.

THE TEACHING PROCESS
Choosing to Be an Educator

The teaching process does not start with developing a syllabus or selecting a textbook for your course. The first step is accepting the responsibilities and opportunities that come with being an educator. Arguably, the first step of the teaching process is what Wilcox (1998:72) describes as "helping faculty see themselves as educators...." Faculty "must CHOOSE to become educators—only then can they really learn the role." As faculty or biologists take on the role of an educator they must also demonstrate authenticity and credibility if they hope to develop connections with their students (Wilcox 1998). This is another critical step in the teaching process that will create a community of learners comfortable with taking risks and asking questions in class (Tidwell and Heston 1998). The result of creating this type of teaching and learning environment is that educators may more easily get feedback on student learning and instructional quality. Upon developing connections with students, educators may also become more

accessible to students searching for information on professional development opportunities, how to look for jobs, or how to apply to graduate school.

Dealing with Resistance to Learning

Because learning involves change and most people find change threatening, it is not surprising that students often resist learning. Even learning that is in their best interest. What is perceived by the instructor as apathy may be resistance.

We regularly encounter students that accept the idea of habitat preservation, but strongly resist the concept of habitat management. Some students seem reluctant to learn that not all harvest management can be justified by the biological need for population control. Brookfield (1990:150–154) identified several reasons why people resist learning and offered strategies for overcoming resistance.

Poor Self Image as Learner/Fear of Looking Foolish

Many students, even those with good academic histories, have been humiliated in the past by experiences that leave them uncertain about their capacity to learn or make them unwilling to participate in a class discussion. Excellent students in mammalogy may have poor images of themselves as learners in population ecology. Students that memorize well may be doubtful of their ability to learn in a problem-solving course or to contribute to a group project developing a habitat management plan.

Instructors should initially reflect on what is good about a student's performance, especially before providing critical feedback. Acknowledge the effort made, even in a disastrous result. This is important to keep students from giving up and for building a supportive, learning environment.

Instructors should create situations in which students can succeed. Start with simple problems and build complexity. Be sure that students have ample opportunity to practice using the information. Repetition will enhance learning and build self-confidence. Using peer-learning/teaching activities, especially in small groups, can reduce fear of making mistakes in front of the entire class and the instructor.

Fear of the Unknown

Brookfield (1990:150) called this "the single greatest cause of resistance to learning." This is especially an issue for students early in their college experience. It also can be important in classes that introduce students to new teaching methods. There are usually students who have not been exposed to cooperative learning, facilitated discussions, or group problem-solving experiences. These students are often uncomfortable and resistant to the non-lecture format.

Overcoming this resistance starts with explaining your intentions clearly and linking them to the students' professional development. Students need to understand the importance and relevance of the course material and what is expected of them and *why*. Brookfield (1990:159) stressed to not push too fast with new teaching techniques. Students need the opportunity to become comfortable with new ideas, new expectations of them, and new learning environments. Opportunities to reflect, via writing or discussion, on new material may be useful.

Lack of Clear Instructions

When students are unsure of what is expected and the criteria by which they will be judged, their anxiety rises and with it the likelihood of resistance. Explicit presentation of evaluation criteria can reduce resistance and substantially improve student performance. We occasionally model an assignment to demonstrate how the task can be accomplished. For example, if students are expected to give an oral presentation on results of a habitat analysis and management plan the instructor may provide examples of good or inadequate presentations while students use the teacher's grading sheet to evaluate strengths and weakness of the presentations. Following the presentation, the instructor could discuss what went well and what could be improved. This process will clarify what could be accomplished in the assignment and provide a framework for student groups to evaluate their own assignment as it is being developed.

Class syllabi or assignment grading sheets that detail what a given grade signifies helps students better understand their obligations. For example: A = paper adequately states and defends an argument and answers all counter arguments; provides evidence to support argument; no serious factual errors; few, minor errors in writing. B = Argument and supporting evidence presented, counter arguments weakly developed. C = paper states argument, but supporting evidence is minimal, and counter arguments not developed. D = Paper only lists or describes data, several factual errors. F = paper is dishonest; ignores question posed in the assignment; is incomprehensible in language use (adapted from B. E. Walvoord, undated).

Apparent Irrelevance of the Learning Activity

Not understanding the significance of course content to their lives and careers is a major factor affecting student resistance to learning. The more students see the relevance of the material and the learning format, the less likely they are to express passive or active resistance. Case studies, examples, stories from your own experience, problem sets that use the concepts in actual conservation scenarios can all promote relevance and breakdown resistance.

Disjunction of Learning and Teaching Styles

A teacher's personality is reflected in their teaching style. Teachers should avoid inappropriate humor, sexist or racist remarks, and the appearance of being arrogant, aloof, or cynical. Reliance on any one teaching method will likely result in a disconnection with some segment of the student audience. Building a positive rapport and using a variety of teaching strategies can help overcome student resistance.

It also may be helpful to conduct regular, informal evaluations of the class-learning environment. Ask students about their learning preferences and invite feedback about your behaviors in class writing assignments. Difficult as it is, it is worthwhile to ask yourself whether resistance is justified. Giving students the opportunity, anonymously, to raise issues, make complaints, or identify frustrating aspects of a course gives the instructor information to act on and involves students in creating the learning atmosphere. By having students contribute to the learning objectives of a course, specific content to be addressed, teaching styles to be used, or the evaluation processes reduces student fear of the unknown, makes them feel respected and valued, and promotes their own responsibility for learning.

TECHNIQUES TO PROMOTE ACTIVE LEARNING

Normal Lecturing

Lecturing is the most pervasive, and typically least effective, teaching style in higher education (Blackburn et al. 1980). Perhaps one reason it is used most frequently is that it allows an instructor to *cover* large amounts of material. However, coverage of material often does not equate with learning. Weaknesses of lectures are numerous (Cashin 1985, Johnson et al. 1991, Bonwell 1996); some key problems are discussed below.

Too Passive

Students are not easily engaged with the material when listening passively. This reduces motivation and encoding for long-term memory. Passive listening rarely effectively links new material to professional context.

Requires Long Attention Span

Student attention and focus typically decline after 15–20 minutes (Stuart and Rutherford 1978). Pollio (1984) reported that individuals did not pay attention 40% of the time during lectures. Students retain about 70% of material heard in the first 10 minutes of a lecture, but only 20% in the last 10 minutes of a typical hour-long lecture (McKeachie et al. 1986) (Box 5).

Promotes Rote Learning

Rote learning results in little transfer of information to long-term memory and limited ability to transfer that knowledge to other situations.

Does Not Promote Higher-order Thinking

Passive lectures provide little or no opportunity for application, analysis, synthesis, or evaluation. Students who are only taught facts will not intuitively understand when or how to use them. Hearing how someone else does it is not sufficient (Byrnes 2001).

Hard to Convey Complex, Abstract Ideas

Understanding complex ideas is difficult for most students without opportunities for elaboration, such as application to authentic scenarios. For students to progress to more logical, abstract thinking requires *practice* using the material.

Does Not Effectively Engage All Learning Styles

Students that benefit from lectures usually have more background upon which to build new knowledge or are primarily auditory learners. Visual learners may benefit if instructors present information with visual aids. Lecturing tends to be most problematic to tactile learners who need to move around, write, or work with tools and easily distracted learners. Lectures do not allow students to learn at their own pace. In classrooms with students of different experience, knowledge, and ability, it is difficult to deliver lectures at a pace that keeps everyone engaged.

No Feedback for Instructor About Student Learning

Passive lectures yield little opportunity for teachers to gage comprehension of material by students. Feedback is essential if students are to learn. If students do not under-

>100 (Allen et al. 1996, Shipman and Duch 2001). In large, predominantly lecture courses, beginning a series of lectures with a problem case creates context and provides a template for discussion. Pausing during lectures for small-group consideration of how lecture content applies to the case reinforces content learning and provides practice in problem solving. Lectures can demonstrate how information presented could be used in solving the problem. Class writing assignments also can be restructured from literature reviews to problem case resolutions or stakeholder analyses.

Building Effective Problem Cases

To be effective vehicles for student learning, problem cases should have several key attributes (White 1995, Duch et al.1998, Duch 2001*b*).

- *Engaging.* Problems based on real or, at least realistic, conservation issues better capture student interest and motivate them to seek new information and understanding. Cases should be used that invoke controversy and elicit strong emotional connections that draw students into taking an active role in their own education.
- *Complex.* Problem cases will be more authentic if they depict the complexity that characterizes most real-world conservation issues. Cases should be sufficiently complicated to require cooperation among team members (Duch 2001*b*). Our experience with wildlife undergraduates and graduate students suggests teams of 4 works best for complex problems (see **Working in Teams**). Larger groups make it easier for some students to be less than fully engaged, whereas smaller teams can be overwhelmed by the workload. Simple problems that focus on building knowledge and comprehension of facts, concepts, and principles can be used in large classes (Allen et al. 1996).
- *Open-ended.* Solutions to problems should not be cut-and-dried. Problems with multiple, reasonable resolutions challenge students to consider costs and benefits of alternatives. This puts a premium on justifying the proposed solution rather than deriving the correct answer. Good problem cases should not provide all the information needed initially.
- *Require making decisions or judgments.* Cases should require students to make evaluations and decide on a course of action. Students often are reluctant to make final decisions. We routinely remind them that professionals must be proactive in decision-making. Not reaching a decision does not mean that nothing will happen. Most likely someone else will make a decision that could threaten the natural resource in question. Problems should necessitate definition of underlying assumptions, examination of what information is relevant, and identification of what procedures are needed to solve the problem (Duch 2001*b*).
- *Connect to previous knowledge.* Cases should be constructed so they integrate content objectives into the problem. New concepts, facts, or procedures should be linked to previous knowledge.

Explicit identification of the facts, principles, concepts, or procedures that students should master during the case process should be done prior to writing the case. Teachers can fine-tune the delivery of a case by identifying which higher-order thinking abilities will be the focus of the exercise and which process skills will be honed. Basing cases on personal experiences is most efficient and better assures authenticity.

Constructive Controversies and Problem-based Learning

Why would a wildlife educator want to introduce controversies into their classroom or workshop? Because biologists and students alike may be able to learn wildlife management principles and their applications more effectively by examining and discussing the controversies that challenge them. By teaching with controversies you identify the increasingly complex work atmosphere of professionals.

Teaching with constructive controversies (Johnson and Johnson 1992) is one method that promotes learner-based education by requiring students to work in cooperative teams; learn, synthesize, and integrate information; develop and defend a position for a stakeholder group; and cooperatively develop the best approach for managing the controversy. The goal is for students to gain an understanding of the types of information needed from stakeholders to develop the best collective solution to the controversy. Johnson and Johnson (1992), Campa et al. (1996), and Johnson et al. (1996) provide discussions of how to use this teaching technique and what types of supportive materials are needed to teach concepts as well as demonstrate how information can be synthesized to address controversies.

Our Maasai Mara National Reserve example (Box 7) also can illustrate using constructive controversies as a cooperative learning technique. The instructor first selects a controversy and then develops general background material describing the controversy and involved stakeholders. Campa et al. (1996) recommended selecting controversies that are current, have not been well publicized, or perhaps are occurring in another state or country. Thus, students will not know as much about the issues involved and will not bring as many preconceived ideas into the exercise.

The general controversy description should only provide information that all stakeholders normally would know or have access to through newspapers or other periodicals. Students requiring information about the case must seek out the necessary information from other stakeholders, thereby developing interpersonal communication skills. When students ask the instructor questions—our response is frequently, that is an excellent question, you should find a wildlife biologist who knows something about that topic. This creates an excellent opportunity to enhance a professional skill. We also encourage student stakeholder groups to gather and/or analyze additional data through personal research (Campa et al. 1996).

Students in each respective stakeholder group are asked to learn who they are and how they might address the controversy based on class materials and their own research. We encourage students to write questions they have for other stakeholders and their responses. Stakeholder groups are then divided, with an equal number of representatives from each group placed in multidisciplinary groups. The goal for these groups is to identify the best information available from all stakeholders to address the controversy and its solution. To promote positive interdependence among team members, we inform students that we will randomly select representatives from each group to make a presentation of their findings and recommendations. This encourages all students to be engaged in the discussion because they may be called upon to speak. Throughout this exercise, we typically have individual or group-writing assignments depending on class size, the complexity of the controversy, and the desired learning objectives (Ryan and Campa 2000).

After multidisciplinary group representatives report to the class, the instructor summarizes the applicability of positions presented by all groups and discusses current activities being implemented by natural resource professionals. The challenge of requiring students to integrate material presented in earlier class periods to a controversy will give them an opportunity to test their knowledge and application of those concepts.

Writing-to-Learn

The writing process is a potent technique for developing critical thinking and promoting retention of discipline-based information (Emig 1977, Young and Fulwiler 1986, Moore 1993, Rivard 1994). Writing is especially helpful in bringing order and understanding to complex and confusing ideas.

Writing-to-learn emphasizes the writer being engaged with material in meaningful contexts. The process becomes the exploration, synthesis, and evaluation of ideas and creating a message about those ideas, rather than passive reporting on the thoughts of others (Bean 1996). Drafting and redrafting a solution to a problem requires building new knowledge and application of intuition and creative thought. These efforts promote discovery of linkages among existing ideas, reshaping and reorganization of old ideas, and creation of new ones. In this process, principles, facts, or procedures are actively sought, absorbed, and understood (Ryan and Campa 2000).

Writing as active learning is a tool to foster thinking not just communication of a separate thinking process (Britton et al. 1975, Emig 1977). The emphasis is on ideas, not writing mechanics, although through the revision process improvements in grammar, style, etc. are likely (Ryan and Campa 2000).

Developing Good Writing Assignments

Writing assignments will be more effective if presented in relevant contexts (Fulwiler 1986). By having students address problems that require selection of techniques, descriptions of how the tools work, and justification of their reasoning, student learning goes beyond rote memory of procedures. They develop understanding of the limitations of the technique and hone professionally relevant thinking skills (Ryan and Campa 2000). Poor student writing is often the result of a lack of understanding about what is expected (Fulwiler 1986). Context helps provide the purpose of the document. Discuss the assignment with students making clear the problem to be addressed, your expectations about the format, general length, depth of coverage, resources to be used, evaluation standards and procedures, and audience to whom the paper is addressed (Fulwiler 1986). Having students write for different audiences helps them think differently about and, therefore,

develop deeper understanding of data, principles, procedures, or problem solutions.

Different writing assignments foster different levels of knowledge building and critical thinking. Short (1–3 minute), in-class papers can help students organize new material and promote knowledge retention and understanding. Such papers also give the instructor feedback about misunderstandings or lack of comprehension (Mosteller 1989).

Informal writing, short essays, or free-writing assignments (Elbow 1981) in class can benefit formal out-of-class assignments as students understand writing as a way of learning (Bishop and Fulwiler 1997). When using free-writing assignments in class, Bishop and Fulwiler (1997) recommend that instructors write with their class, demonstrating to students the credibility and value of the assignment.

Writing short papers that summarize lectures, readings, or laboratory outcomes, especially in the context of a question or problem, builds knowledge and comprehension, and offers practice in synthesis. Having students share their papers with each other in small groups can add to the learning experience.

Longer writing assignments should be framed around a question or problem. Writing that requires use of new content material, provides practice, which promotes deep processing and stronger retention.

Regardless of the writing assignment, there are techniques that can improve the learning experience for students. Allow ample time for thoughtful composing (Fulwiler 1986). Encourage drafts for review by the writer, peers, or the instructor. It is critical that students learn that writing is an iterative process that cannot be done over a short period of time. Instructors are more likely to get a return on their time investment in evaluation if they give students constructive critiques on drafts (Ryan and Campa 2000).

Dubrow (1984) suggested sharing models of student writing (anonymously) to help establish expectations for an assignment. He also encouraged taking time to explain why some passages were, or were not, effective so that students could see why revisions are needed and what direction changes should take. Showing well-written and poorly written material (from previous classes) and asking students to judge which is which, and why, is an effective technique (Fulwiler 1986). Students also will more quickly grasp grammatical errors by seeing contrasting forms than if instructors simply reference rules. Fulwiler (1986) stated that students who see examples of good writing would be more likely to recognize that they are capable of it and be motivated to strive for success.

Most experts on writing-to-learn (e.g., Fulwiler 1986) suggest that a series of short papers (3–4 pages) is more effective than one long one (ca. 20 pages). Students can learn progressively from one paper, or revision, to the next, thinking and writing more crisply, and eliminating technical problems, as they draw on constructive feedback from earlier papers (Fulwiler 1986, Bishop and Fulwiler 1997).

How writing assignments are evaluated also affects the learning process. When teachers' critiques probe for deeper analysis, synthesis, or justification the revision process becomes one of rethinking, and not simple editing. Evaluation also offers insight into student command of the material and their ability to use that information in specific contexts (Ryan and Campa 2000).

When evaluating papers, MacAllister (1982) and Fulwiler (1986) recommended responding to content rather than mechanics first. Focusing on ideas helps in suggesting revisions, including technical changes, which will improve clarity and focus. Fulwiler (1986) made a case against separate grades for mechanics and content, arguing that poor writing is often the result of insufficient knowledge and understanding. We believe, however, that good thinking, even that obscured by poor grammar, should be rewarded (Ryan and Campa 2000). Students with weak preparation in writing mechanics can be easily discouraged by low grades. Separate grades for mechanics and content can bolster student motivation.

Because student self-confidence about writing is often weak, they can be easily overwhelmed by too many negative comments (Lamberg 1980). Identifying effective passages while suggesting changes to improve others, encourages and motivates students. When papers have numerous problems, Fulwiler (1986) recommended singling out 1 or 2 key issues for correction and addressing others in later drafts.

Whereas specific comments regarding problems are preferable (Fulwiler 1986) to vague notations, instructors should not correct errors. The "minimal marking technique" (Haswell 1983) suggests detailed editing takes responsibility away from the writer and takes too long for the evaluator. Teachers should demonstrate ways to restructure passages for clarity, brevity, style, or proper grammatical form on the first few paragraphs or pages and then have students edit the remainder themselves using the examples provided (MacAllister 1982, Haswell 1983, Fulwiler 1986).

Writing experts differ on the appropriateness of grading drafts versus only grading final versions of an assignment. Fulwiler (1986) argued that students equate grades with completed products and that grading drafts reduces motivation for revision. Others (e.g., Dubrow 1984) prefer assigning some grade to works in progress to remind students that a serious effort on early drafts is important. We stress that failure to do "best effort" drafts does not take full advantage of the revision process and results in weaker final papers. We also prefer the term "versions" to "drafts" in our writing assignments, hoping to disabuse students of the notion that first drafts are unimportant and, therefore, not worth the effort (Ryan and Campa 2000).

Cooperative Learning

Learning information and solving complex problems is often best accomplished when working in supportive groups and exchanging information. The practice of using groups to enhance the learning of all individuals within a group, in a supportive manner, is referred to as cooperative learning. In all cooperative learning environments, instructors emphasize teaching students how to learn on their own as they work together towards a common goal (Johnson et al. 1991, Meyers and Jones 1993, Ryan and Campa 2000, Miller 2002). Our experience has shown that you cannot just put students together in a group and expect them to work effectively together. The learning environment of a course must be established with cooperative learning activities and assignments that entail the elements of cooperative learning.

After creating a cooperative learning environment, instructors need to consider the basic elements of cooperative learning as they develop materials and assignments for their course. These elements include: positive interdependence, promotive interaction, individual accountability, interpersonal and small-group skills, and group processing (Johnson and Johnson 1992, Smith and Waller 1997).

Positive interdependence (Johnson et al. 1993, Smith and Waller 1997:193) occurs in a classroom when students' success in learning is dependent upon others succeeding in tasks. This approach to learning is in contrast to more traditional approaches where individual students take responsibility for only their own learning.

Perhaps the truest test of understanding new material is being able to effectively teach it to someone else. This process demonstrates promotive interaction. As students explain material they have mastered to other students, they are assisting others while gaining confidence in their own learning.

Instructors must also build individual accountability into their classes. Each student in a cooperative learning group must be evaluated for their own learning and evaluations shared with students so areas of deficiencies can be improved. We use essay exam questions or randomly call on student group members to make short oral presentations to promote individual accountability.

Because one individual rarely makes wildlife management decisions, it is essential for students to develop interpersonal and small-group skills. As students learn to work in cooperative learning groups, they build leadership, communication, and conflict management skills.

Group processing in cooperative learning activities is also critical so students receive feedback on their individual contributions to the group; this facilitates students enhancing their collaborative skills. Smith and Waller (1997:194) recommended this may be accomplished by asking groups to respond to questions such as: 1) "what is something each member did that was helpful for the group?" and 2) "what is something each member could do to make the group even better tomorrow?"

Cooperative learning activities also place more responsibility on students for learning and instructors have different responsibilities than in traditional lecture-based classes. We recommend instructors adhere to specific cooperative learning guidelines: 1) ensure individual and group accountability (Slavin 1991), 2) monitor group function (Campa et al. 2003), 3) keep assignments of similar lengths for all groups (O'Conner and Jenkins 1996), and 4) communicate and monitor a cooperation ethic in class as well as results of not cooperating (Campa et al. 2003). We believe instructors who use cooperative learning are able to more effectively assess student learning, be more responsive to the diversity of learning styles in a classroom, and increase student self-esteem as they become more capable of learning, applying, and communicating course material. For example, we recommend using different types of groups, such as informal, formal, and base groups throughout a course or workshop to enhance learning.

Informal Groups

These groups can be used relatively easily to achieve numerous academic objectives including: focusing attention on material, facilitating an atmosphere for learning, providing a framework for material to be covered, helping students process material, and concluding a body of material or a discussion (Johnson et al. 1991).

Formal Groups

The jigsaw technique (Aronson et al. 1978) is often used with formal groups to meet 4 academic objectives: act as an alternative way to introduce new material, create information interdependence among members, ensure that participants orally rehearse information learned, and provide an example of high performance teamwork. This technique is commonly used in association with cases and constructive controversies.

When using the jigsaw technique, students are initially assigned to a group. Each member is then assigned a different part of the material to learn. After working individually, all students learning the same material meet to discuss and master the material and decide how they will teach it to others. Students then return to their original groups and teach what they have learned.

The jigsaw approach facilitates student-centered learning, but instructors have crucial roles in the success or failure of this learning experience for students. The instructor must decide what material will be learned with the process, who will be in what group, how many groups will be used, how groups will be monitored to evaluate learning, and what will be done to help students synthesize and summarize information (Smith and Waller 1997).

The Group Investigation technique described by Sharan and Sharan (1976, 1994) is another cooperative learning technique that can be used with formal groups. In this process, problems are posed to the class, student groups develop subtopics they will investigate, members plan their investigation, students carry out their research plan, each group presents to the entire class, and then students and teachers cooperatively evaluate the work done by all.

Cooperative Base Groups

These groups usually have long-term relationships with stable membership with the primary responsibility to provide support, encouragement, and assistance in completing large tasks (Johnson et al. 1991). The benefits of using base groups are that they may enhance learning and improve attendance especially in larger courses and institutions or when the material to be learned is relatively complex. An instructor may develop base groups at the beginning of a semester for the purpose of developing questions regarding unclear material presented in previous readings, lectures, or labs prior to exams. These questions are then used for the focus of subsequent lecture or lab periods or review sessions. The secondary benefit of requiring base groups to go through this exercise is that students may realize the benefits of meeting regularly to discuss course material and develop informal study groups that can also be used in subsequent courses.

Working in Teams

Teams constitute the predominant problem-solving environment in which wildlife professionals work. Learning to work effectively in a team structure is a basic professional skill students need to master before entering the workplace. Benefits of cooperative learning can only be maximized if students know how to function effective-

ly in team-learning environments (Johnson et al. 1991).

Professional skills and learning aptitude will be enhanced when students are taught how to be an effective team member. Team functioning has been characterized (Tuckman 1965) as a 4-part process (forming-norming-storming-performing).

In the formation phase, students first buy-in to the team concept. Students must believe they need each other to succeed (Johnson et al. 1991:16–18). Providing examples of why and how wildlife professionals work in team environments is important. Ecosystem management teams, such as the Forest Ecosystem Management Team (1993) that developed an ecological, economic, and social assessment on logging alternatives in the Pacific Northwest, are increasingly common in state, federal, and provincial agencies. It is essential that team assignments be sufficiently complex to require collaboration for successful completion. Members need time to get to know and trust one another (Johnson et al. 1991) and appreciate what each person can contribute. Instructors should ensure that teams take time to identify common interests. Johnson et al. (1991) and Bosworth (1994) argued convincingly that students should be taught the social skills necessary for teams to work effectively.

Bosworth (1994) presented a "taxonomy" of 5 collaborative social skills. Interpersonal skills are needed to establish rapport among team members. Team members should practice congeniality, positive communication, focused listening skills, making eye contact, and clear communications. Group building and management skills include being organized, staying on task, showing empathy to others, and participating in group reflection on individual effectiveness in team functions. Inquiry skills include the ability to probe assumptions and evaluate evidence, critique the value of information, be able to clarify statements or analyses of information, assess the implications and consequences of recommended actions, and seek alternative viewpoints or perspectives. Team members should also practice conflict resolution skills, including efforts to prevent needless conflict, mediation of conflicts among other team members, and resolution. Teamwork also requires presentation skills such as the ability to synthesize and summarize information, the creation of presentations, speaking in front of groups, and report writing. Bosworth (1994) suggested identifying these important skills to the team functioning process and to practice their use.

Instructors should help students learn the different roles of team members and allow time to allocate roles among members (Yamane 1996, Ferreri et al. 1998). Possible team roles include those of discussion leader, who keeps the team on task by developing an agenda and keeping the group focused. A meeting recorder keeps the minutes of each team meeting, paying attention to work assignments, deadlines, etc. and distributing this information to all members. The devil's advocate checks group thinking for assumptions, generates alternatives, or tries to find holes in recommendations or justifications. Before this role is assigned, a class discussion will help set ground rules for tactful application of this team task. This is a good opportunity to distinguish between making a difference and making a point, and help students understand the subtle difference in thinking critically and being critical. An intermediary represents the team in meetings with the instructor or with other teams, reporting on team progress, asking clarifying questions, or being a conduit for the flow of other information. The team coordinator may be responsible for identifying times and places for meetings and can serve as a clearinghouse for team information exchanges. It may be valuable for these roles to rotate among team members throughout the semester so that students learn basic team skills. Regardless of the specific tasks assigned, it is essential that each member knows and understands their role. Group achievement is notably increased when each member can identify and takes responsibility for their contributions to the final product (Johnson et al. 1991).

During the norming period, teams should evolve rules for conducting a meeting, dealing with absenteeism, failure to meet deadlines, and settling disagreements. Class discussion or readings related to conflict resolution may be appropriate at this time.

Storming happens to most teams as they struggle with identifying goals and processes, personality clashes, or divergent values. It can be helpful if students are taught to expect these rough spots in the team process. Too often, students are surprised by the storming period and retreat into attempts to solve the problem on their own, or in subgroups. Group processing (Johnson et al. 1991) in which teams meet to reflect on how they are functioning, what is working, and what is not can improve group achievement. Instructors have the responsibility of monitoring team functioning and being ready to facilitate resolutions. Preemptive efforts during norming, such as consideration of conflict resolution strategies, are beneficial.

If the first 3 phases are successfully negotiated, teams can reach the performing stage where the benefits of effective teams are realized. It is important that students have positive performing experiences so they are open to team work environments when they begin professional careers.

There are several ways to form student teams for projects or activities. The basis for how teams are formed should be affected by an instructor's learning objectives, size of the class, and what can be implemented to facilitate students working together. Methods for forming teams include: *self-selected*, *assigned*, or *random*—each of which has advantages and disadvantages.

Students in self-selected teams work with individuals they know they can work with, students with similar schedules for out-of-class-work, or those with similar interests. One advantage of this method is students should not complain about whom they had to work with because they picked their group members. However, working with friends is not always productive. Working with others with the same interests and background may not broaden an individual's perspective. If students self-select their team members, we recommend that they should "apply" to work together by writing a letter of application. The benefit of their application serves as a contract that students will work cooperatively and uses a professional skill (Campa et al. 2003).

Instructors can also develop assigned teams of students. For example, an instructor can stratify students putting some with an ecological and social science background on each team. In this setting, students learn to work with people they do not know. We tell students what our rationale is for using the methods selected for placing them on teams

such as they will be working with individuals they do not know as professionals or they will have to communicate their expertise to individuals with different educational backgrounds. However, incompatible personalities and schedules for working during out-of-class times may make it difficult for an assigned team to work cooperatively.

Randomly selecting teams is an excellent method of putting groups together for informal cooperative group activities because it can be done relatively quickly. Another advantage of this is that it may facilitate students working with others they have not worked with previously or with those from other majors. However, using this method of organizing formal or base cooperative learning groups, especially where there may be a lot of out-of-class work, may cause conflicts within groups because of diverse work and class schedules or family obligations.

An alternative approach to forming teams (Yamane 1996, Ferreri et al. 1998) is to first survey student audiences regarding logistic issues, disciplinary interests, expertise, and complementary learning styles (Miller et al. 1994). Structuring teams around focal interests and expertise can serve multiple purposes. By forming teams with divergent expertise, students get a better sense of how teams can be more effective in addressing complex problems. Surveying previous course history can assess student expertise or by asking students to qualitatively self evaluate themselves on knowledge of specific subject areas (Ferreri et al. 1998).

Student motivation and achievement in team learning environments can be affected by lack of understanding of how they will be evaluated. Strong academic students may be concerned their grades will be negatively affected by weak performances of other team members. Less accomplished students may perceive little incentive to work hard if the team seems to function well without their involvement (Ferreri et al. 1998). Assigning some grading weight to effort or to individual's performance in team roles may partially alleviate both of these problems. Other alternatives are to use groups to brainstorm solutions, but require individually authored recommendations or resolutions, or having individual team members take primary responsibility for sections of final reports and assigning both overall and individual segment grades. In no case, however, should peers' evaluation be incorporated into final grades without being filtered by the instructor.

We recommend instructors have a plan for managing teams to ensure learning objectives are met; this plan should be communicated to the groups. If teams are managed effectively, instructors should not be surprised by the quality of groups' final products.

Our experience is that if the process for managing groups follows a professional work experience, students are more likely to work cooperatively, take the assignment seriously, and perform at a higher level. For example, students should be given deadlines throughout the semester and at each deadline, be expected to present oral and written progress reports. This process is similar to how researchers may have to provide summaries of progress to funding organizations, or how management personnel may have to periodically address a natural resource commission on an on-going controversial issue.

Requiring students to prepare progress reports accomplishes an academic objective for students and several team management objectives for the instructor. The progress reports divides the large, apparently daunting task into definable and accomplishable components that students can complete over several weeks. This process of intellectual scaffolding (Harley et al. 1998) where a single large task is divided into several more easily accomplishable components fosters students' mastery of material and helps them gain confidence.

Managing teams should promote individual and group accountability, and positive interdependence. While managing teams, instructors should be aware that successful team projects will require periodic intensive schedules of instruction, occur primarily due to the use of cooperative teams not because of peer tutoring, and may enhance student attitudes for learning (Slavin 1978).

Peer Teaching

One way to test one's comprehension of material is to teach it. By presenting and explaining information to your peers one participates in the process of peer teaching. Whitman (1988) identified 5 types of peer teaching: teaching assistants, peer tutors, peer counselors, partnerships, and working groups.

Serving as a teaching assistant with an instructor is an excellent way to demonstrate comprehension of material and experiment with teaching and learning techniques to meet different learning objectives. Just because an individual has presented research findings at conferences as a graduate student does not mean they can teach the same material to college freshman. Teaching requires an understanding and willingness to try active learning strategies that best meet the diversity of student learning styles and objectives of your class. A benefit of getting "teaching experience" is that all wildlife professionals teach—within agencies, academia, and in private organizations.

Peer tutoring involves working with students one-on-one in a predefined academic area. Miller (2002:236) describes this learning environment as teachers assigning "one student as the tutor and the other as the tutee." Some students may do better with this approach because of their need for a structured learning environment. If this method is used in class, Miller (2002) recommends that specific guidelines are followed, such as: (1) tutors and tutees should be trained in what the tutoring process involves, (2) develop rewards and performance contingencies, (3) avoid assigning tasks for the tutee that are too simplistic, and (4) have 3 or 4 tutoring sessions per week. Cohen et al. (1982) commented that with a student-teacher relationship, the tutor benefits from the teaching process because they are expected to explain concepts and principles to others. This forces the tutor to learn the material and identify how to "uncover it" for the student.

Whitman (1988) described peer counselors as individuals who advise students over broad areas. Stromei (2000) observed that traditionally, mentoring associated with academic institutions has focused on enhanced learning and has not emphasized career development activities. A failure to facilitate students' career development may make the transition between school and a career problematic (Hoerner and Wehrley 1995). All students need good counselors or mentors.

Partnerships are developed to gain a greater understanding of potentially complex information. In this relationship, students switch teacher-student roles (Whitman 1988). McGill University researchers demonstrated the effectiveness of learning with partnerships by placing students in pairs or "learning cells" (Goldschmid and Goldschmid 1976). In this relationship, students would prepare for classes by individually reading assigned material and developing lists of questions on the major points of the material. All students would then be randomly assigned to pairs in class and alternatively ask each other questions, getting assistance from the instructor when necessary. When this approach to learning was evaluated in relation to other techniques, students in learning cells had higher test scores and liked the approach in comparison with other teaching-learning techniques.

Working groups are groups of individuals that work collaboratively on a common topic or problem to help individual performance (Whitman 1988). For example, working groups within The Wildlife Society collectively work together giving workshops, writing technical reviews, or preparing symposia while they individually gain a broader understanding of a subject area. A benefit of learning in a working group is that individuals are exposed to a breadth of information that can be applied to their individual jobs.

Regardless of the peer teaching strategy used, it should be encouraged and facilitated because it promotes positive interdependence among students, and better retention and application of material. The specific method(s) used should be based on class learning and teaching objectives and prior experiences.

SUMMARY

The effectiveness of future wildlife biologists to deal with complex issues will be affected by their educational foundation and ability to be life-long learners. A student's ability to put techniques in this volume into practice may be limited depending upon how well their instructors present the material. Did the instructor cover a lot of material or did they uncover the material (K. A. Smith, University of Minnesota, personal communication) so students can use it throughout their career? It is oftentimes easier to cover information than uncover it. As you prepare to teach wildlife research and management techniques to college students or wildlife biologists, you are urged to think as much about how you will present material as what you will present. Using active learning strategies will aid in the students' understanding and future applications of research and management concepts and techniques to address the future complex issues facing wildlife resources. Student learning and professional development can be most enhanced when instructors use relevant contexts to present new material, provide opportunities for meaningful practice using information, teach high-order thinking not just facts, and get students actively involved in the learning process.

ACKNOWLEDGMENTS

The following colleagues greatly influenced our thinking about teaching and learning: (for MRR) C. A. Mertensmeyer, H. Campa, III, J. J. Dinsmore, G. A. Atchison, E. K. Fritzell, J. R. Jones, J. J. Millspaugh, J. E. Groccia, M. A. Townsend, M. D. Patton, N. E. Gardner, and the CAFNR Faculty Teaching Scholars group at the University of Missouri; (for HC) M. R. Ryan, S. R. Winterstein, K. F. Millenbah, K. A. Smith, T. G. Coon, J. B. Haufler, and colleagues associated with the Michigan State University Lilly Fellows Teaching Program (e.g., L. S. Julier, N. H. Pogel, and R. F. Banks).

LITERATURE CITED

ALBANESE, M. A., AND S. MITCHELL. 1993. Problem-based learning: a review of literature on its outcomes and implementation issues. Academic Medicine 68:52–81.

ALLEN, D. E., B. J. DUCH, AND S. E. GROH. 1996. The power of problem-based learning in teaching introductory science courses. Pages 43–52 in L. Wilkerson and W. H. Gijselaers, editors. Bringing problem-based learning to higher education: theory and practice. New directions for teaching and learning. Number 68. Jossey-Bass Publishers, San Francisco, California, USA.

ANDERSON, J. R. 1995. Learning and memory: an integrated approach. John Wiley and Sons, New York, USA.

ARONSON, E., N. BLANEY, C. STEPHAN, J. SIKES, AND M. SNAPP. 1978. The jigsaw classroom. Sage Publishers, Beverly Hills, California, USA.

BARROWS, H. S., AND R. M. TAMBLYN. 1980. Problem-based learning: an approach to medical education. Springer-Verlag Publishing, New York, USA.

BEAN, J. C. 1996. Using writing to promote thinking. Pages 1–12 in J. C. Bean, editor. Engaging ideas. Jossey-Bass Publications, San Francisco, California, USA.

BISHOP, W., AND T. FULWILER. 1997. The braiding of classroom voices: learning to write by learning to learn. Pages 37–50 in W. E. Campbell and K. A. Smith, editors. New paradigms for college teaching. Interaction Book Company, Edina, Minnesota, USA.

BLACKBURN, R. T., G. PELLINO, A. BOBERG, AND C. O'CONNEL. 1980. Are instructional improvement programs off-target. Current Issues in Higher Education 1:32–48.

BLIGH, D. A., editor. 1986. Teach thinking by discussion. Society for Research into Higher Education and NFER-NELSON, Guildford, Surrey, United Kingdom.

BLOOM, B. S., M. B. ENGLEHART, E. J. FURST, W. H. HILL, AND D. R. KRATHWOHL. 1956. Taxonomy of educational objectives: the classification of educational goals. Handbook 1: the cognitive domain. Longmans, Green, and Co., New York, USA.

BONWELL, C. C. 1996. Enhancing the lecture: revitalizing a traditional format. Pages 31–44 in T. E. Sutherland and C. C. Bonwell, editors. Using active learning in college classrooms: a range of options for faculty. Jossey-Bass Publishers, San Francisco, California, USA.

———, AND J. A. EISON. 1991. Active learning: creating excitement in the classroom. ASHE-ERIC Higher Education Report 1. George Washington University, Washington, D.C., USA.

BOSWORTH, K. 1994. Developing collaborative skills in college students. Pages 25–31 in K. Bosworth and S. J. Hamilton, editors. Collaborative learning: underlying processes and effective techniques. New directions for teaching and learning. Number 59. Jossey-Bass Publishers, San Francisco, California, USA.

BOUD, D., AND G. FELETTI, editors. 1991. The challenge of problem-based learning. St. Martin's Press, New York, USA.

BRANSFORD, J. R., A. L. BROWN, AND R. R. COCKING, editors. 2000. How people learn: brain, mind, experience, and school. National Academy Press, Washington, D. C., USA.

BRINKLEY, A., B. DESSANTS, M. FLAMM, C. FLEMING, C. FORCEY, AND E. ROTHSCHILD. 1999. The Chicago handbook for teachers: a practical guide to the college classroom. University of Chicago Press, Chicago, Illinois, USA.

BRITTON, J. N., T. BURGESS, N. MARTINE, A. MCCLEOD, AND H. ROSEN. 1975. The development of writing abilities: school's council project on writing language of 11–18 year-olds. MacMillan Publishers, London, United Kingdom.

BROOKFIELD, S. D. 1990. The skillful teacher: on technique, trust, and responsiveness in the classroom. Jossey-Bass Publishers, San Francisco, California, USA.

BRUER, J. T. 1993. Schools for thought: a science of learning in the classroom. Massachusetts Institute of Technology Press, Cambridge, USA

BYRNES, J. P. 2001. Cognitive development and learning in instructional contexts. Second edition. Allyn and Bacon, Boston, Massachusetts, USA.

CAMPA, III, H., K. F. MILLENBAH, AND C. P. FERRERI. 1996. Lessons learned from fisheries and wildlife management: using constructive controversies in the classroom. Pages 235–244 in J. C. Finley and K. C. Steiner, editors. Proceedings of the First Biennial Conference on University Education in Natural Resources. Pennsylvania State University, University Park, USA.

———, D. F. RAYMER, AND C. HANABAUGH. 2003. Ecosystem management education: teaching and learning principles and applications with problem-based learning. Pages 370–383 in A. R. Berkowitz, C. H. Nilon, K. S. Hollweg, editors. Understanding urban ecosystems: a new frontier for science and education. Springer-Verlag Publishers, New York, USA.

CASHIN, W. E. 1985. Improving lectures. Idea Paper Number 14. Center for Faculty Evaluation and Development, Kansas State University, Manhattan, USA.

CHERIF, A. H., AND C. H. SOMERVILL. 1995. Maximizing learning: using role playing in the classroom. American Biology Teacher 57:28–33.

CHRISTENSEN, C. R., AND A. J. HANSEN. 1987. Teaching and the case method: text, cases, and readings. Harvard Business School Publishing, Boston, Massachusetts, USA.

COHEN, P. A., J. A. KULIK, AND C. C. KULIK. 1982. Educational outcomes of tutoring: a meta-analysis of findings. American Educational Research Journal 19:237–248.

CREED, T. 1997. Extending the classroom walls electronically. Pages 149–182 in W. E. Campbell and K. A. Smith, editors. New paradigms for college teaching. Interaction Book Company, Edina, Minnesota, USA.

DALE, E. 1954. Audio-visual methods in teaching. Holt, Rinehart, and Winston, New York, USA.

DILLON, J. T. 1984. Research on questioning and discussion. Educational Leadership 42 (3):50–56.

DUBROW, H. 1984. Teaching essay writing in a liberal arts curriculum. Pages 88–102 in M. M. Gullette, editor. The art and craft of teaching. Harvard University Press, Cambridge, Massachusetts, USA.

DUCH, B. J. 2001a. Models for problem-based instruction in undergraduate courses. Pages 39–46 in B. J. Duch, S. E. Groh, and D. E. Allen, editors. The power of problem-based learning. Stylus Publishing, Sterling, Virginia, USA.

———. 2001b. Writing problems for deeper understanding. Pages 47–58 in B. J. Duch, S. E. Groh, and D. E. Allen, editors. The power of problem-based learning. Stylus Publishing, Sterling, Virginia, USA.

———, D. E. ALLEN, AND H. B. WHITE, III. 1998. Problem-based learning: preparing students to succeed in the 21st century. Chalkboard 18:3–4.

———, S. E. GROH, AND D. E. ALLEN, editors. 2001. The power of problem-based learning. Stylus Publishing, Sterling, Virginia, USA.

EDENS, K. M. 2000. Preparing problem solvers for the 21st century through problem-based learning. College Teaching 48:55–60.

ELBOW, P. 1981. Writing with power: techniques for mastering the writing process. Oxford University Press, Oxford, United Kingdom.

ELLNER, C. L., AND C. P. BARNES. 1983. Studies of college teaching. Lexington Books, Lexington, Massachusetts, USA.

EMIG, J. 1977. Writing as a mode of learning. College Composition and Communication 28:122–128.

FERRERI, C. P., C. E. GLOTFELTY, AND J. C. FINLEY. 1998. Student team projects and natural resources education: are we achieving educational objectives. Pages 72–80 in C. G. Heister, compiler. Proceedings of the Second Biennial Conference on University Education in Natural Resources. Natural resources and environmental issues. Vol. II. Utah State University, Logan, USA.

FERRIER, B. M. 1990. Problem-based learning: does it make a difference? Journal of Dental Education 54:550–551.

FISHER, C. F. 1978. Being there vicariously by case studies. Pages 258–285 in O. Milton and Associates. On college teaching: a guide to contemporary practices. Jossey-Bass Publishers, San Francisco, California, USA.

FOREST ECOSYSTEM MANAGEMENT ASSESSMENT TEAM. 1993. Forest ecosystem management: an ecological, economic, and social assessment. U. S. Departments of Agriculture,Commerce, and Interior, and the Environmental Protection Agency. Washington, D. C., USA.

FULWILER, T. 1986. The argument for writing across the curriculum. Pages 21–32 in A. Young and T. Fulwiler, editors. Writing across the disciplines: research into practice. Boynton-Cook, Upper Montclair, New Jersey, USA.

GAKAHU, C. G., editor. 1992. Tourist attitudes and use impacts in Maasai

Mara National Reserve. Wildlife Conservation International, Nairobi, Kenya.

GIJSELAERS, W. H. 1996. Connecting problem-based practices with educational theory. Pages 13–21 *in* L. Wilkerson and W. H. Gijselaers, editors. Bringing problem-based learning to higher education: theory and practice. New directions for teaching and learning. Number 68. Jossey-Bass Publishers, San Francisco, California, USA.

GILBERT, D. L. 1976. Professionalism and the professional. Fisheries 1:4–6.

GOLDSCHMID, B., AND M. L. GOLDSCHMID. 1976. Peer teaching in higher education: a review. Higher Education 5:9–33.

GROCCIA, J. E., AND M. MILLER. 1996. Creating active learning environments. Program for Excellence in Teaching. University of Missouri, Columbia, USA.

HAMMARLUND-UDENAES, M., M. HOGLUND, AND D. MARTENSON. 1993. Experience of problem-based learning in a new course in pharmacotherapeutics for undergraduate pharmacy students. Pages 183–189 *in* P. A. J. Bouhuijs, H. G. Schmidt, H. J. M. van Berkel, editors. Problem-based learning as an educational strategy. Network Publications, Maastricht, The Netherlands.

HANDELSMAN, J., D. EBERT-MAY, R. BEICHNER, P. BRUNS, A. CHANG, R. DEHAAN, J. GENTILE, S. LAUFFER, J. STEWART, S. M. TILGHMAN, AND W. B. WOOD. 2004. Scientific teaching. Science 304:521–522.

HANSEN, A. J. 1987. Reflections of a case writer: writing teaching cases. Pages 264–270 *in* C. R. Christensen, editor. Teaching and the case method. Harvard Business School, Boston, Massachusetts, USA.

HANSEN, W. L., AND M. K. SALEMI. 1990. Improving classroom discussions in economics courses. Pages 96–110 *in* P. Saunders and W. Walstad, editors. The principles of economics course: a handbook for instructors. McGraw-Hill Publishing, New York, USA.

HARLEY, H. D., C. D. SEALS, AND M. B. ROSSON. 1998. A formative evaluation of scenario-based tools for learning object-oriented design. ACM Crossroads (Winter):10–13.

HASWELL, R. H. 1983. Minimal marking. College English 45:600–604.

HAWKINS, D. 1973. How to plan for spontaneity. Pages 486–503 *in* C. E. Silberman, editor. The open classroom reader. Vintage Books, New York, USA.

HOERNER, J. L., AND J. B. WEHRLEY. 1995. Work-based learning: the key to school-to-work transition. McGraw-Hill Publishing, New York, USA.

JOHNSON, D. W., AND R. T. JOHNSON. 1992. Creative controversy: intellectual challenge in the classroom. Interaction Book Company, Edina, Minnesota, USA.

———, ———, AND E. HOLUBEC. 1993. Cooperation in the classroom. Sixth edition. Interaction Book Company, Edina, Minnesota, USA.

———, ———, AND K. A. SMITH. 1991. Active learning: cooperation in the college classroom. Interaction Book Company, Edina, Minnesota, USA.

———, ———, AND ———. 1996. Academic controversy: enriching college instruction through intellectual conflict. ASHE-ERIC Higher Education Report 25 (3). George Washington University, Graduate School of Education and Human Development, Washington, D.C., USA.

KESSLER, W. B., AND W. G. EASTLAND. 1995. Strategies to sustain human and wildlife communities. Pages 1–3 *in* J. A. Bissonnette and P. R. Krausman, editors. Integrating people and wildlife for a sustainable future. Proceedings of the First International Wildlife Management Congress. The Wildlife Society, Bethesda, Maryland, USA.

LAMBERG, W. 1980. Self-provided and peer-provided feedback. College Composition and Communication 31:63–69.

LIEUX, E. M. 2001. A skeptic's look at PBL. Pages 223–236 *in* B. J. Duch, S. E. Groh, and D. E. Allen, editors. The power of problem-based learning. Stylus Publishing, Sterling, Virginia, USA.

LIGHT, R. J. 2001. Making the most of college: students speak their minds. Harvard University Press, Cambridge, Massachusetts, USA.

MACALLISTER, J. 1982. Responding to student writing. Pages 59–65 *in* C. W. Griffin, editor. Teaching writing in all disciplines. New directions for teaching and learning. Number 12. Jossey-Bass Publishers, San Francisco, California, USA.

MCKEACHIE, W. J. 2002. Teaching tips: strategies, research, and theory for college and university teachers. Eleventh edition. D. C. Heath and Co., Lexington, Massachusetts, USA.

———, P. R. PINTRICH, Y. LIN, AND D. A. SMITH. 1986. Teaching and learning in the college classroom: a review of the research literature. The Regents of the University of Michigan, Ann Arbor, USA.

MCTIGHE, J. 1985. Questioning for quality thinking. Maryland State Department of Education, Division of Instruction, Baltimore, USA.

———, and F. Lyman 1988. Cueing thinking in the classroom: the promise of theory embedded tools. Educational Leadership 45 (7):18–24.

MEINE, C. 1988. Aldo Leopold: his life and work. University of Wisconsin Press, Madison, USA.

MEYERS, C., AND T. B. JONES. 1993. Promoting active learning: strategies for the college classroom. Jossey-Bass Publishers, San Francisco, California, USA.

MILLER, J. E., J. TRIMBUR, AND J. M. WILKES. 1994. Group dynamics: understanding group success and failure in collaborative learning. Pages 33–44 *in* K. Bosworth and S. J. Hamilton, editors. Collaborative learning: underlying processes and effective techniques. New directions for teaching and learning. Number 59. Jossey-Bass Publishers, San Francisco, California, USA.

MILLER, S. P. 2002. Validated practices for teaching students with diverse needs and abilities. Allyn and Bacon, Boston, Massachusetts, USA.

MOORE, R. 1993. Does writing about science improve learning about science? Journal of College Teaching 22:212–217.

MOSTELLER, F. 1989. The muddiest point in the lecture as a feedback device. On Teaching and Learning 3 (April):10–21.

MWAISAKA, P. E. 1992. Forward. Page ix *in* C. G. Gakahu, editor. Tourist attitudes and use impacts in Maasai Mara National Reserve. Wildlife Conservation International, Nairobi, Kenya.

NELSON, C. 1997. Tools for tampering with teaching's taboos. Pages 51–77 *in* W. E. Campbell and K. A. Smith, editors. New paradigms for college teaching. Interaction Book Company, Edina, Minnesota, USA.

NODDINGS, N. 1997. The use of stories in teaching. Pages 19–35 *in* W. E. Campbell and K. A. Smith, editors. New paradigms for college teaching. Interaction Book Company, Edina, Minnesota, USA.

NUHFER, E. B. 1997. Student management teams—the heretic's path to teaching success. Pages 101–126 *in* W. E. Campbell and K. A. Smith, editors. New paradigms for college teaching. Interaction Book Company, Edina, Minnesota, USA.

O'CONNER, R. E., AND J. R. JENKINS. 1996. Cooperative learning as an inclusion strategy: a closer look. Exceptionality 6:29–51.

PENNER, J. G. 1984. Why many college teachers cannot lecture: how to avoid communication breakdown in the classroom. Charles C. Thomas Publisher, Springfield, Illinois, USA.

PIAGET, J. 1952. The origins of intelligence in children. International Universities Press, New York, USA.

POLLIO, H. R. 1984. What students think about and do in college lecture classes. Teaching and Learning Issues. Number 53. Learning Research Center, University of Tennessee, Knoxville, USA.

RESNICK, L. B. 1987. Education and learning to think. National Academy Press, Washington, D.C., USA.

RIVARD, L. P. 1994. A review of writing to learn in science: implications for practice and research. Journal of Research in Science Teaching 31:969–983.

ROWE, M. B. 1980. Pausing principles and their effects on reasoning in science. Pages 27–34 *in* F. B. Brawer, editor. Teaching the sciences. New Directions for Community Colleges. Number 31. Jossey-Bass Publishers, San Francisco, California, USA.

ROYSE, D. D. 2001. Teaching tips for college and university instructors: a practical guide. Allyn and Bacon, Boston, Massachusetts, USA.

RUHL, K. L., C. A. HUGHES, AND P. J. SCHLOSS. 1987. Using the pause procedure to enhance lecture recall. Teacher Education and Special Education 10:14–18.

RYAN, M. R., AND H. CAMPA, III. 2000. Application of learner-based teaching innovations to enhance education in wildlife conservation. Wildlife Society Bulletin 28:168–179.

SCHMIDLY, D. J., I. R. ADELMAN, AND J. S. GREENE. 1990. Educational content of university fish and wildlife programs based on expressed needs of federal and state agency employers. Transactions of the North American Wildlife and Natural Resources Conference. 55:133–143.

SHARAN, S., AND Y. SHARAN. 1976. Small group teaching. Educational Technology Publications, Englewood Cliffs, New Jersey, USA.

SHARAN, Y., AND S. SHARAN. 1994. Group investigations in the cooperative classroom. Pages 97–114 *in* S. Sharan, editor. Handbook of cooperative learning methods. Greenwood Press, Westport, Connecticut, USA.

SHIPMAN, H. L., AND B. J. DUCH. 2001. Problem-based learning in large and very large classes. Pages 149–164 *in* B. J. Duch, S. E. Groh, and D. E. Allen, editors. The power of problem-based learning. Stylus Publishing, Sterling, Virginia, USA

SINGLEY, M. K., AND J. R. ANDERSON. 1989. The transfer of cognitive skill. Harvard University Press, Cambridge, Massachusetts, USA.

SLAVIN, R. E. 1978. Student teams and achievement divisions. Journal of Research and Development in Education. 12:39–49.

———. 1991. Synthesis of research on cooperative learning. Educational Leadership 48(5):71–82.

SMITH, K. A. 1995. Cooperative learning: effective teamwork for engineer classrooms. IEEE Education Society. ASEE Electrical Engineering Division. April Newsletter. Piscataway, New Jersey, USA.

———, AND A. A. WALLER. 1997. Cooperative learning for new college teachers. Pages 185–209 in W. E. Campbell and K. A. Smith, editors. New paradigms for college teaching. Interaction Book Company, Edina, Minnesota, USA.

STINSON, J. E., AND R. G. MILTER. 1996. Problem-based learning in business education: curriculum design and implementation issues. Pages 33–42 in L. Wilkerson and W. H. Gijselaers, editors. Bringing problem-based learning to higher education: theory and practice. New directions for teaching and learning. Number 68. Jossey-Bass Publishers, San Francisco, California, USA.

STOMEI, L. K. 2000. Increasing retention and success through mentoring. Pages 55–62 in S. Aragon, editor. Beyond access: methods and models for increasing retention and learning success for minority students. New Directions for Community Colleges. Number 112. Jossey-Bass Publishers, San Francisco, California, USA.

STUART, J., AND R. RUTHERFORD. 1978. Medical student concentration during lectures. Lancet 2:514–516.

SUTHERLAND, T. E., AND C. C. BONWELL, editors. 1996. Active learning: lessons from practice and emerging issues. New directions for teaching and learning. Number 67. Jossey-Bass Publishers, San Francisco, California, USA.

THOMAS, J. W. 1986. Effectiveness—the hallmark of the natural resources management professional. Transactions of the North American Wildlife and Natural Resources Conference 51:27–38.

THORNDIKE, E. L. 1913. Educational psychology. Teachers College Press, New York, USA.

TIDWELL, D., AND M. HESTON. 1998. Self-study through use of the practical argument. Pages 45–66 in M. L. Hamilton, S. Pinnegar, T. Russell, J. Loughran, and V. LaBoskey, editors. Reconceptualizing teaching practice: self-study in teacher education. Falmer Press, Bristol, Pennsylvania, USA.

TUCKMAN, B. W. 1965. Developmental sequence in small groups. Psychological Bulletin 63:384–399.

UNIVERSITY OF MISSOURI. 2001. MU medical students out-perform national average. News release, University of Missouri Health Care. Available online at http://www.hsc.missouri.edu/~news/USMLE01.shtml (accessed 15 July 2003).

VERNER, C., AND G. DICKINSON. 1967. The lecture: an analysis and review of literature. Adult Education 17:85–100.

VERNER, D. T., AND R. L. BLAKE. 1993. Does problem-based learning work? A meta-analysis of evaluative research. Academic Medicine 68:550–563.

WALVOORD, B. E. Undated. Establishing and communicating standards and criteria for higher order learning. Kaneb Center for Teaching and Learning, University of Notre Dame, Indiana, USA.

WELTY, W. M. 1989. Discussion method teaching. Change (July/August):41–49.

WHITE, H. 1995. "Creating problems" for PBL. About Teaching 47: www.udel.edu/pbl/cte/spr96-phys (accessed 22 December 2004).

WHITMAN, N. A. 1988. Peer teaching: to teach is to learn twice. ASHE-ERIC. Higher Education Report 4. Association for the Study of Higher Education, Washington, D.C., USA.

WILCOX, S. 1998. Claiming to understand educational development. Pages 67–76 in M. L. Hamilton, S. Pinnegar, T. Russell, J. Loughran, and V. LaBoskey, editors. Reconceptualizing teaching practice: self-study in teacher education. Falmer Press, Bristol, Pennsylvania, USA.

WILKERSON, L., AND W. H. GIJSELAERS, editors. 1996. Bringing problem-based learning to higher education: theory and practice. New directions for teaching and learning. Number 68. Jossey-Bass Publishers, San Francisco, California, USA.

WOODS, D. R. 1994. Problem-based learning: how to gain the most from PBL. McMaster University Bookstore, Hamilton, Ontario, Canada.

———. 1996. Problem-based learning for large classes in chemical engineering. Pages 91–100 in L. Wilkerson and W. H. Gijselaers, editors. Bringing problem-based learning to higher education: theory and practice. New directions for teaching and learning. Number 68. Jossey-Bass Publishers, San Francisco, California, USA.

YAMANE, D. 1996. Collaboration and its discontents: steps toward overcoming barriers to successful group projects. Teaching Sociology 24:378–383.

YOUNG, A., AND T. FULWILER, editors. 1986. Writing across the disciplines: research into practice. Boynton-Cook, Upper Montclair, New Jersey, USA.

2

COMMUNICATIONS FOR WILDLIFE PROFESSIONALS

Susan K. Jacobson

INTRODUCTION

Reintroducing endangered panthers (*Puma concolor coryi*) in Florida is not only a biological challenge, but also a social one. People decide whether to allocate funds to translocate animals, legislate protected habitat, or tolerate the large carnivores nearby. The panther's fate depends on how wildlife managers communicate with public groups and policy-makers to raise concern and support for panther conservation. Between 1988 and 1995, 26 animals were experimentally released in Osceola National Forest in northern Florida to test habitat suitability for reintroduction. The experiment was a biological success (the habitat was good and the recovery goal of reestablishing panthers in north Florida was feasible) but was a social failure. Poor communication by the agencies fueled local landowner opposition. A vocal minority caught media attention with their own more successful communication campaign: "Kids not Cougars" (Fig. 1). They halted panther recovery efforts in north Florida (Sunquist and Sunquist 2002).

Half a century ago Aldo Leopold, considered the father of wildlife management, suggested that wildlife management is comparatively easy but that human management was difficult (Meine 1988). Think of a challenging wildlife problem you have encountered—protecting a rare butterfly, managing bears in the suburbs, or setting sustainable hunting limits. More than likely people are part of the problem and communication will be part of the solution.

Effective communication is essential for influencing conservation policy, changing people's behaviors, garnering funds, or recruiting volunteers. The fate of our wildlands and wildlife resources depends on successful communication with a variety of audiences—from anglers to zoo visitors, in a variety of places—from agricultural lands to the legislative floor.

This chapter describes the communication process. It provides a systematic plan for identifying communication goals, targeting specific audiences, selecting appropriate

Fig. 1. A handmade billboard slyly declares, "Kids not Cougars," in a local effort to prevent reintroduction of Florida panthers (photograph by S. K. Jacobson).

24

Fig. 2. Human conflicts with wildlife range from concerns about diseases and safety to opportunities for ecotourism. Effective communication is needed to better manage wildlife and people (photograph by S. K. Jacobson).

media and messages, and evaluating your results. The following guidelines will help ensure your effectiveness at using common communication techniques needed by wildlife professionals. Whether giving an interview or public presentation or designing a brochure or scientific poster, follow a game plan for success.

WHY COMMUNICATE?

The public affects the success or failure of wildlife management efforts. Yaffee et al. (1996) found that public opposition was the major constraint to implementing ecosystem management plans. In the case of reintroduction of the gray wolf (*Canis lupus*) in Yellowstone National Park, biologists working with the recovery plan concluded that many recovery issues have more to do with people's deeply held personal values about the government and perceptions of nature rather than about wolves themselves (Fritts and Carbyn 1995). In essence, researchers could spend years designing plans or studying the biology of gray wolves, but wildlife goals may not be achieved without adequate public support. In such cases, failure to accurately assess and target public opinion can result in opposition to wildlife initiatives and costly political battles.

The need for improved communications about wildlife grows as more people use public lands and conflicts over natural resources increase (Fig. 2). Imagine the varying viewpoints on a proposed wildlife refuge from just 3 stakeholder groups (parties whose actions affect, or are affected by an issue): local landowners concerned with increased traffic or crime, business people interested in tourism revenue, and hunters seeking recreational opportunities. Stakeholders are diverse and their concerns may overlap or conflict.

The public is exposed to wildlife issues through print media, radio, television, and the Internet. Public opinion polls show interest and concern for wildlife are increasing. An ABC News/*Washington Post* poll found that 70% of the public thought the government had not gone far enough to protect the environment (ABC News 1995). The National Opinion Research Center (1995) found that 61% of survey respondents recognized that humans were the main cause of species extinctions. Yet, public knowledge about wildlife is minimal. The views of most North Americans are emotionally charged but woefully lacking in basic ecolog-

ical understanding (Gigliotti 1990). Concern for wildlife is largely confined to attractive and emotionally appealing species. Sociologist Stephen Kellert (1996) found that although 89% of the people he surveyed agreed that endangered bald eagles (*Haliaeetus leucocephalus*) should be protected, only 24% believed the endangered Kauai wolf spider (*Adelocosa anops*) deserved protection. Kellert found most people view invertebrates with indifference, aversion, and disdain.

As a wildlife professional, your communication skills must include the ability to promote your program's products—its mission, policies, services, and goods—for spiders as well as eagles. Promotion entails sparking public interest by showing people how the objectives of wildlife management relate to their needs and wants. Communicating with the public and decision makers helps increase their long-term support and leads to appropriate behavior and sound wildlife conservation policy. One of The Wildlife Society's 4 principal objectives is to increase awareness and appreciation of wildlife values (Case 1989). Researchers have shown that appropriate communications can improve public support for and behavior toward wildlife, reduce vandalism and poaching, improve compliance with regulations, increase recreation carrying capacities, and influence policies and decisions that affect public lands and wildlife resources (e.g., Jacobson 1990, 1999; Knudson et al. 1995). Can we afford not to communicate?

WHAT IS COMMUNICATION?

Communication is a process of exchanging ideas and imparting information. We do it all day long. It involves making yourself understood to others and understanding others in return. If you send a message—verbal, visual, or written—that the intended receiver does not understand, communication has not occurred. The only way to make sure the message has been received and properly understood is to incorporate feedback into the process. Consider a great public relations success story—the U.S. Forest Service's wildfire prevention campaign. Their message, "Only YOU can prevent forest fires," is unambiguous on a poster with Smokey Bear dousing a campfire. They used a catchy slogan, a charismatic "spokesperson," and media targeting specific audiences to ensure that most U.S. citizens remember Smokey Bear and his message that we not only can, but also should, prevent forest fires. In one public poll, 95% of those surveyed could recognize Smokey Bear, whereas only two-thirds could recognize the U.S. president (Jacobson 1999).

Communication involves both interpersonal and mass media approaches. Interpersonal techniques use face-to-face dialogue, group interaction, speeches, and participatory demonstrations. Mass media approaches use newspapers, magazines, radio, television, billboards, mail, films, publications, the Internet, and satellite conferences. The public receives much of its environmental information through mass media channels. A survey of teenagers revealed that mass media—not school—was the most important source of information about environmental issues (Blum 1987). Although mass media are a primary source of information, interpersonal and hands-on activities can be more effective in influencing attitudes and behaviors. Selecting the appropriate communication

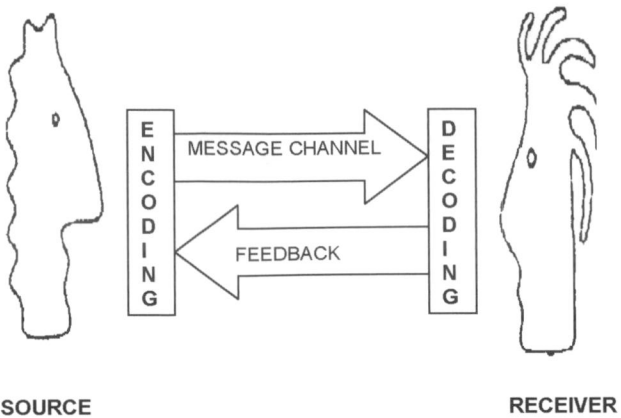

SOURCE   **RECEIVER**

Fig. 3. Simplified model of the communication process.

Fig. 4. How can you interest your audience in an endangered beach mouse (photograph by Florida Fish and Wildlife Conservation Commission)?

medium based on your goals and audience is critical. Below, theories and approaches are described that apply to all forms of effective communication about wildlife.

Communication Theory

Communication theory borrows from the fields of psychology, education, and sociology. Models of communication include an encoding stage, in which the source (in this case, you, the wildlife professional) sends a message that is translated and conveyed via a medium (Cutlip et al. 1985). Your message is decoded by the receiver (your audience or stakeholder group) who possibly responds, thereby, providing feedback (Fig. 3). Both encoding and decoding are critical stages in the communication process, no matter your media—interview, speech, brochure, scientific poster, website, or outreach program.

Gatekeepers regulate the flow of information from source to receiver and can introduce additional changes or noise into the communication. Different media have different gatekeepers. For example, suppose you speak to a reporter about your organization's new project to save endangered beach mice (*Peromyscus polionotus*). The reporter encodes your message in the form of a newspaper article. A gatekeeper in the form of an editor must accept the story for publication. Perhaps the last 3 paragraphs will be cut due to a shortage of space. Perhaps the headline is misleading. Ultimately, the receiver—individuals perusing the paper over their morning coffee—will decode the article based on their own experience. Why should rodents interest them? If you do not catch their attention by addressing their interests or concern, they will not read it (Fig. 4).

Feedback from receivers allows the source to adjust the message; thus, receivers also are senders if their response is captured in some way. Sources must be listening or observing, however, to modify their communication on the basis of the receivers' feedback. For example, an agency that fails to respond to constituent anger about changes in a hunting policy will have more problems than an agency that listens and understand the needs of their constituents. Researchers in upstate New York found the communication process in itself—whether through individual conversations, group surveys, or a citizens' task force—improved satisfaction with the wildlife management agency, even when the management outcome was the same (Stout et al. 1997). Wildlife organizations fueled by tax dollars or pri-

vate donations must understand and respond to their audiences' needs.

ELEMENTS OF COMMUNICATION

Understanding the vital organs of the communication system (source, message and medium, receiver, feedback loop) can help you design effective wildlife communications. Failure of any one organ dooms the entire effort.

Source

The source of the message is the central person or organization doing the communicating. For example, an agency director gives a public speech on changes in hunting regulations to a hunt club, a scientist explains the release of endangered California condors (*Gymnogyps californianus*) to media representatives, or an organization publishes a colorful, fund-raising brochure for members. The source knows how it wants the message to be received, yet it often cannot guarantee how the message is encoded or how it will be decoded by the receiver. During a speech, the speaker's body language, voice tone, and vocabulary influence how the audience receives the message. For environmental issues, source credibility is important. Most audiences will scrutinize a speech or advertisement by an oil company spokesperson regarding the status of oil development in the Arctic National Wildlife Refuge differently than an announcement by a government agency or environmental organization. It is important that your message is delivered by a source credible to the audience you are trying to reach. Credibility usually involves trustworthiness, expertise, and power.

Message and Medium

Once the source's ideas are encoded or translated, they are transmitted in the form of a message. The content of the message, its medium, and its source all influence the perception of the message. Simple messages are most easily understood.

"Where's the beef?" was a popular slogan used by Wendy's fast food restaurants to draw attention to the lack of hamburger meat in their competitors' buns.

"Can you hear me now?" asks a man on a cell phone wandering in a desert in an advertisement demonstrating the clear range of the Verizon Wireless system.

Fig. 5. Woodsy Owl received a makeover by the U.S. Forest Service.

"A fed bear is a dead bear," is the blunt message of the New Hampshire Fish and Game Department to discourage the public from feeding bears and creating potential conflicts.

"Lend a hand—care for the land," replaced the U.S. Forest Service's Woodsy Owl's original slogan: Give a hoot, don't pollute," in the 1990s. Woodsy was directed at kids ages 5–8, when youngsters begin to form their views about the environment and how they should interact with it. Woodsy also received a makeover with his new slogan. He now sports a backpack, hiking shoes, and field pants to appeal to modern children (Fig. 5).

Messages dealing with more complex issues may be harder to transmit to the public. The concept of prescribed fire as a management tool goes against many people's early indoctrination by Smokey Bear. In a survey of west Florida residents, only 12% knew that regular fires are a natural process maintaining their native pine forests (Jacobson and Marynowski 1997). Slogans to promote prescribed burning have been difficult to design. "Rx Fire: Prescription for Forest Health," is the title of a Division of Forestry's brochure in the southwestern United States. It seems to be more cumbersome than catchy. Personal experience with fire-adapted ecosystems or coverage of wildfires in mass media may stimulate public interest in prescribed burning and create a need for more information (Jacobson et al. 2001). Framing your message and strategically selecting media to reach your target audience is the key to successful communications.

How do you choose the medium that will effectively reach the target audience? Different channels offer different advantages (Box 1). For example, mass media has a powerful role in setting the public agenda and reinforcing opinions. However, more detailed publications or interpersonal methods are generally needed to change an audience's fundamental knowledge or shift their opinions. The adoption of new behaviors, such as recycling or composting, frequently occurs as a result of friends, family members, or colleagues introducing people to them (McKenzie-Mohr and Smith 1999). Communications that foster this type of social diffusion of the message provide opportunities to effectively reach your audience.

Target audiences can be segmented by factors such as age, education, occupation, recreation activities, or geographic location. Using a variety of media may be the answer to sufficiently reach each audience. Different audience characteristics may call for techniques such as speeches and demonstrations or direct mailings and placement of messages in specialized newsletters. Knowing the media habits of your audience is one obvious way to target a message. For example, an article in the *Washington Post* may effectively reach policy-makers' eyes, but few farmers may ever read it. An article in an agricultural newsletter may better target farmers.

The use of more than one channel increases the likelihood of reaching a greater audience and reinforces the message. When selecting media to communicate about wildlife, one must evaluate such factors as potential impact, production and dissemination expense, and audience size (Table 1). Television ads may be beyond your budget,

---

Box 1. Media channels for reaching audiences.

Personal dialogue	Telephone
Speech	Magazine
Public conference	Newsletter
Advisory group meeting	Exhibit
Demonstration	Guided program
Direct mail	Website

Table 1. Factors that influence decisions regarding appropriate messages and media.

Factors	Questions to ask
Background and habits of the audience	What are the interests and media sources of your target audiences?
Attributes of the message	Does it require background knowledge, maps, graphics, color, or sound?
Urgency of the message	Do you need a response today or next month?
Complexity of the message	Is a 30-second sound bite adequate for the message or is a lengthy educational publication necessary?
Frequency of the message	Is repetition needed regularly, seasonally, infrequently? Do new people keep joining the target audience?
Personnel required	Is staff time available for personal contact, developing materials, providing outreach activities, interfacing with media, or training volunteers?
Cost	How many in your target audience can be reached, for how long, with what detail, at what price?

periodic newsletters may be too sluggish for your scheduling needs, or lack of staff may turn a special event into a nightmare. A realistic view of the resources and constraints of time, personnel, and money provides the foundation for a successful media strategy.

Receiver

A communication may bomb or blossom. It may do nothing, or it may make the receiver aware of an issue, shift the receiver's attitude, or, more rarely, change the receiver's behavior. An understanding of the receiving audiences is vital in designing messages and selecting media to produce an effective program. Without knowledge of your audiences' needs and concerns, programs often are doomed. Wildlife communicators can be more effective by dividing their audiences into segments according to their specific wants and needs, interests, habits, or other useful characteristics. To succeed, messages must be directed to your target audience, whether it is hunters using the resource, homeowners living at the wildland interface, or wealthy urbanites who support your programs.

Audience research can help orient your wildlife communication program to meet your audiences' needs and to promote the products of your organization. Methods for identifying and targeting audiences include collecting data through public surveys, interviews, group meetings, direct observation, census reports, Internet sources, case studies, and networks with organizations that already serve the audience. Researchers in the field of human dimensions of wildlife use sociodemographic information, psychological profiles, consumer behaviors, geographic residence, and a host of other variables to help wildlife agencies tailor messages to audience needs. Audience research allows you to assess alternative strategies for communication channels and messages. It provides a foundation for building support for a program or influencing audience behaviors. Research also provides baseline information to evaluate the results of your wildlife communication efforts.

The Yukon Department of Renewable Resources developed a communication campaign to reduce the number of female grizzly bears (*Ursus arctos*) killed by hunters (Smith 1995). Their program targeted outfitters and hunting guides. Their baseline research about this audience suggested messages and media to be used. The most critical message for the campaign was information that gave guides the ability to judge the gender and age of a grizzly bear. This information was delivered using a videotaped workshop by a respected Alaskan bear guide. He convincingly demonstrated that guides could judge bear gender and age, leading clients to kill only male bears. The videotape also took advantage of motivational factors for the outfitters by including the symbolic value of the bear as a lone, powerful, wild figure, an image the agency found greatly appealed to their audience. In a similar manner, natural resource managers at Eglin Air Force Base in Florida used their knowledge of their hunting constituents to craft messages regarding feral hog (*Sus scrofa*) control. The managers stressed the need to reduce hog populations to reduce competition with deer and other game species that hunters valued. The importance of reducing hog damage to preserve endangered pitcher plant (*Sarracenia leucophylla*) bogs was not a compelling message for this audience (Jacobson 1999).

Thus, a wildlife organization or agency needs to be able to communicate with many audiences, each with its own beliefs, self-interests, and concerns. Communication theories portray information spreading through society from opinion leaders to informed people and finally to uninformed people, like ripples emanating from a rock thrown into a pond. Studies of how ideas diffuse through society show groups of early, average, and late adopters of information (Brown 1981). Knowledge of your target audience can facilitate diffusion of wildlife information to opinion leaders or critical members of your audience. This will improve the likelihood of obtaining the response you want from your audience.

Feedback

Was your message received as intended? Feedback will help you evaluate whether you achieved objectives to increase your audience's awareness about a wildlife issue, shifted their attitudes, or changed their behaviors. Feedback will help identify whether your program worked and how it can be improved. Feedback from local residents targeted in an environmental communication program in Senegal, Africa revealed they were more confused about conservation objectives of the government after the program. Not surprisingly, no conservation action occurred (IIED 1994). Without systematically obtaining feedback for evaluation, failed programs can be continued or replicated, instead of improved.

Methods to evaluate your communication range from formal before-and-after surveys to direct observations of the target audience or their impacts on the environment. To measure the effectiveness of a communication program to conserve a rare wildlife species, you might count new members joining your organization, funds donated to purchase key habitat, legislators' votes to pass protective measures, increases in public awareness after your campaign and, ultimately, status of the wildlife population after a certain time period. Continuous assessment allows you to modify activities based on timely feedback and new information. Evaluation of products and outcomes tells whether your message and media strategy worked. It allows you to make decisions about the fate of the program—should it be continued, cut, or expanded.

Feedback and evaluation during program implementation allows you to change direction and chart a more productive course. The Florida Wildlife Federation avoided financial heartache by collecting feedback from their members about a new way of communicating with that audience. Before the Federation embarked on a new magazine for its members, they wisely collected information. They sent a sample of 240 members a trial magazine with a written survey. The survey asked members what they liked most and least about the publication and how much they might pay to receive such a magazine. Based on the negative responses to the survey and the high cost of the project, the Federation rejected the entire activity of publishing a magazine (Manley Fuller, Director, Florida Wildlife Federation, personal communication).

GAME PLAN FOR COMMUNICATION PROGRAMS

Communication programs help wildlife organizations solve management problems or fulfill needs of their audiences. To succeed, organizations and agencies must under-

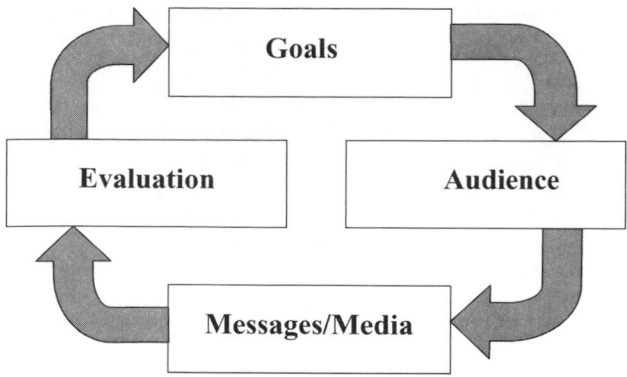

Fig. 6. A GAME plan to guide wildlife communications involves an iterative process to identify your Goals and objectives, Audiences, Message and Media strategy, and Evaluation techniques.

stand and respond to their audiences' existing interests and behaviors. Some communication programs target a broad audience with a public awareness campaign, such as providing information about recycling to all homeowners in Colorado. Other programs target groups practicing specific behaviors the organization wishes to change, such as providing information about new hunting regulations to deer hunters. To assess the nature of communication needs for a wildlife initiative, organizations must have a G-A-M-E plan. They must identify their **g**oals and objectives, **a**udiences, **m**essage and media strategy, and **e**valuation techniques (Fig. 6). This iterative process leads to a communication program that avoids common problems such as targeting the wrong audience or using an inappropriate message or medium.

Box 2 outlines a GAME plan for guiding just about any wildlife communications program. Most wildlife concerns are urgent. These guidelines help avoid wasting time on ineffective practices or programs. The first step in planning a communication program is identifying the goals and objectives. Once the goals are established, objectives specific to target audiences can be identified and you are ready to plan an interview, public presentation, brochure, scientific poster, or any other communication activity.

IDENTIFYING COMMUNICATION GOALS AND OBJECTIVES

Goals of wildlife agencies or organizations may be to protect endangered species, sustain game animals, conserve land, manage a reserve, or restore a forest. Communication goals generally address problems. Conversely, identifying problems is a good way to formulate goals. An analysis of the context and situation helps focus the specific conservation problem to be addressed. One of the Save the Manatee Club's goals, for example, is the recovery of manatees (*Trichechus manatus*) in the wild. The more clearly the problem is stated, the more targeted a goal will be. The problem, "Manatees are an endangered species," is less helpful for identifying potential communication-based solutions than: "Collisions with motorboats cause manatee deaths in Florida." This problem statement helps identify a specific goal: "Reduce boat collisions with manatees." It also helps identify specific audiences, such as boat owners, marina operators, or water management

Box 2. Planning guidelines for a communication program.

Goal: *What is your goal?* Identify your wildlife problem or issue you want to address. Identify the specific objectives associated with your audiences.

Audience: *What audiences or stakeholders are involved in the issues to be communicated? For each audience, what changes or actions are desired?* The audience should be defined using socioeconomic, psychographic, or demographic analyses to gain insight into the nature of the audience, their needs and interests, and their behaviors. Audience involvement is necessary to develop objectives regarding expected changes in knowledge, attitudes, or behaviors that will result from the communication program.

Message/Media Strategy: *What messages must be sent? What channels will most efficiently result in the desired behaviors?* The interests, needs, and motivations of the stakeholder groups must be addressed, and media must be selected that will efficiently and effectively deliver the message to the audience.

Evaluation: *How will you know if the strategy worked?* Changes in the environment or in audience knowledge levels, attitudes, or behaviors should be monitored and assessed.

district regulators. Now specific objectives can be identified for each audience (Fig. 7).

Communication objectives may be related to changing a target audience's knowledge, attitudes, or behaviors. Commercial advertisers view objectives in the form of a staircase leading up to their goal of selling their product. The first step is building consumer awareness—the consumer's ability to recognize and remember the product. The next step piques the consumer's interest. This increases their desire to learn about some of the features of the product and to evaluate these attributes. The remaining steps lead to the consumer's first purchase, and, if all goes according to plan, the repeated purchase and continued use of the product.

This same process can be duplicated in wildlife communications where each objective may focus on one or several steps. An initial message may try only to increase awareness about a wildlife issue or agency service. A further objective may focus on increasing concern or shifting

Fig. 7. A researcher interviews boaters to obtain baseline information for a communication program promoting safe boating in areas frequented by manatees (photograph by S. Aipunjiguly).

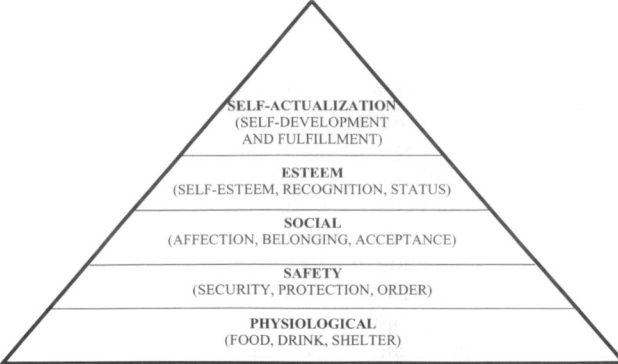

Fig. 8. Maslow's hierarchy of needs suggests people must first address their physiological needs before striving for self-esteem and, ultimately, self-fulfillment.

an attitude, and a final objective may encourage conservation action. However, increasing general awareness about a problem or product does not guarantee action.

To ascertain whether your communications objectives are met, they must be measurable. Often objectives specify the number of people that will display the desired concern or behavior and the dates by which these changes will be achieved (e.g., a 10% increase in visitors to a wildlife reserve per month or 100 new donors to a conservation organization in a year). All objectives should identify the audience, the media and message, desired effect, and timeframe for a communications strategy to be implemented and results attained. When objectives are specific, the program results can be compared with anticipated outcomes to judge success and make decisions about program continuation. Wildlife biologists may want to write objectives in terms of what they hope their intended audience will do. Consider the manatee example: "As a result of receiving a safe boating booklet in the mail, 90% of Tampa Bay boaters will obey voluntary speed zones by the end of the year."

Influencing Attitudes

Attitudes are predispositions to think in a specific way about a specific subject and are mediated by the situation. For example, a homeowner might enjoy watching woodpeckers and other cavity-nesting birds in his yard, but because he finds dead trees ugly, be unwilling to leave a snag standing to provide a nest site. People hold a positive, negative, or neutral attitude toward a particular issue, such as an endangered species. Most people (the silent majority!) are neutral or don't care. A small percentage will express strong support or opposition. People whose attitudes can be influenced most easily are those who hold a neutral view or do not care (Seitel 1995). Influencing people who strongly oppose a subject is difficult, whereas reinforcing someone who already agrees with an issue or individual is easy. The success of communications lies primarily in winning support from the indifferent public and building on positive opinion.

Social psychologists have noted that opinion is affected by self-interest. A communication will affect public opin-

ion primarily if its relationship to the audience member's interests is clear (Cantril 1972). A wildlife organization wishing to influence public opinion must ask, what's in this for the individuals whose opinions we are trying to change?

People are motivated by a variety of needs and desires. The psychologist Abraham Maslow (1954) developed a hierarchy of people's needs, or drives. His theory suggests that people will first fulfill their physiological needs for food, health, safety, and security. Human needs then progress to personal drives for a sense of belonging, self esteem, and, ultimately, self-fulfillment (Fig. 8). As people satisfy one level of needs, they move up the hierarchy. Maslow believed that fewer than 10% of people satisfy lower needs and become self-actualized. Knowing where your target audience fits in this hierarchy can help you develop appropriate messages to influence their attitudes. For example, a wildlife refuge may offer recreational opportunities that appeal to hikers seeking to meet needs for esteem or fulfillment, while opportunities for hunting may appeal to desires for a sense of belonging or esteem in hunting clubs. Framing messages to appeal to people's specific needs can reinforce positive attitudes about your wildlife agenda (Box 3).

Box 3. Humor or excitement appeals to the public by implying that a product or service is more fun than an alternative. Humor can be used to lighten critical messages or to just catch an audience's attention.

In an advertisement appearing in a January issue of their magazine, The Nature Conservancy presented a tongue-in-cheek list of suggested New Year's resolutions. The ad was displayed on a scrap of paper.

My New Year's Resolutions
1. *Get in shape*
2. *Take more hikes*
3. *Eat more fruits and vegetables*
4. ***Include The Nature Conservancy in my will***

A bequest to The Nature Conservancy will make you feel great, too!

The values and uses to people of ecosystem services can be viewed according to Maslow's (1954) hierarchy of needs. These values are useful for communicators to use when trying to promote conservation of natural systems. People's basic physiological and security needs are fulfilled when natural systems provide material uses such as food, clothing, shelter, water, and medicine. Also basic are the life support or ecosystem services that natural systems provide such as clean water, degradation of wastes, and natural pest and pathogen control.

Nonmaterial uses of natural resources and ecological systems address people's higher needs for a sense of belonging, esteem, and fulfillment. These include the value of nature for religious beliefs and ceremonial uses, spiritual and aesthetic uses, scientific and educational uses, and physical and emotional recreation. For some people, preserving or delaying use of natural systems for future generations also may meet their need for fulfillment.

Although some argue that nature has values independent of human needs, most people find it difficult to relate to an argument about the intrinsic value of natural systems. The belief that nonhuman species and ecosystems have values unrelated to human desires is rare, although perhaps more prevalent among readers of this book. Communicators must deal with the real needs and desires of their target audiences if they expect to achieve their wildlife management goals.

Over the years, researchers have developed lists of values that all people seek. Political scientist Harold Lasswell (1971) listed 8 base values: power, enlightenment, wealth, well being, skill, affection, respect, and rectitude. People seek to gratify these desires but, similar to Maslow's hierarchy of needs, different needs are pursued more vigorously at different times. Communicators must understand, for example, that some individuals may perceive the Endangered Species Act or other environmental regulation threatens their base values of wealth or power. Conversely, an intact forest that provides habitat for endangered species may satisfy individuals' base values of well-being or wealth. Communicating how wildlife initiatives satisfy basic human values is one key to achieving the goal of shifting audience attitudes.

Influencing Behavior

The goal of many wildlife communications programs is to affect long-term behavior—a difficult task. Researchers continue to debate the influence of people's knowledge and attitudes on their behaviors. Increased awareness of a wildlife problem in no way guarantees meaningful behavioral changes in support of conservation. Environmental educators initially suggested the learning process necessary for conservation action progresses from ignorance to awareness, understanding, concern, and finally action (Henderson 1984). Following this awareness-to-action model, communications programs should first deliver information to increase knowledge and shift attitudes about a wildlife problem, and then seek to influence future behaviors.

However, changing behaviors related to environmental protection is complex. The consequences of wildlife problems are often long term, and delayed or intangible benefits provide little incentive for people facing urgent day-to-day concerns. Many conservation problems seem national or global in scope, so individuals believe they can do little to help. Personal actions fail to have noticeable effects because of broader political and economic factors. People often misbehave despite knowledge of the environmentally correct thing to do. They poach wildlife; they do not carpool; they harvest trees unsustainably. Giving people new information will not necessarily change their behavior. People might be aware of the problem, but may not have the knowledge or skills to identify alternatives to their current behaviors or the motivation to comply.

Studies of environmental behavior reveal many factors affect conservation action. Educators believe that environmental behavior depends on cognitive factors, such as an individual's knowledge of environmental issues and action strategies, and skills in performing conservation-oriented activities. Personality factors, such as the extent of responsibility and commitment felt toward the environment, attitudes toward the environment, and perception of the ability to affect change also influence an individual's intention to act in an environmentally responsible manner (Hines et al. 1986/87). Obviously, if someone does not believe they can make a difference, they are unlikely to act.

Marketing specialists use psychological factors to predict behavior change. They examine an individual's perception of benefits and barriers to practicing a new behavior (e.g., Smith 1995, Byers 1996). Marketers believe you must offer people a benefit they want in exchange for their behavioral change. Thus, the benefits must outweigh any costs of engaging in a new behavior. Other researchers focus on social influences or norms regarding the new behavior; for example, who does the individual care about and trust on this topic and what do they think that person would want them to do (Fishbein and Ajzen 1975)? The individual's intention to behave in a certain way is mediated by how they think their family or friends might want them to respond. All of these factors influence a person's desire and ability to act in accordance with the objectives of your wildlife program.

WWF-International, a leading environmental organization formerly called the World Wildlife Fund, conducted audience research to better understand the public in the many countries in which they have national members. They wanted to examine people's attitudes and behaviors with respect to the environment and their willingness to support WWF initiatives. They conducted a series of small focus groups and broad public surveys in 25 countries. The results allowed WWF to understand the wide range of attitudes and support within and across nations. It helped them design a 2-pronged approach for promoting sustainable environmental behaviors.

For countries where environmental awareness was relatively low (e.g., Greece, Italy, Spain), WWF developed 30-second television advertisements with light-hearted messages that conveyed the need to curb consumption and wasteful habits such as leaving the tap running or lights on. One ad depicts an elderly woman, in comical fast motion, knitting a sweater to stay warm, rather than continuing to turn up a thermostat. In contrast, for countries where their research showed high levels of environmental awareness (e.g., The Netherlands, New Zealand, Sweden), WWF used more sophisticated advertising to convey an environmental message. They focused on issues such as tropical forest protection, which they found to be of high public concern (Klingemann and Rommele 2002). For countries where

Fig. 9. Families participate in the "Great Air Potato Round-up," sponsored by the Nature Operations Division in Gainesville, Florida (photograph by M. Spalding).

the ad was shown, their research suggested that people already were aware that rain forest destruction contributes to global warming and reduction in biodiversity, and that this audience would not require an explanation. Rather, they needed a reminder, or prompt, to examine their own consumer behavior to avoid buying furniture made from tropical hardwood that was unsustainably harvested (Box 4).

Communication programs may follow a variety of strategies to achieve the goal of changing behaviors to conserve wildlife resources. Programs must influence not only their audience's knowledge about the environment, but also attitudes and behaviors that can promote environmentally responsible actions in the future. It follows that techniques for wildlife communications must be multifaceted to influence knowledge, attitudes, and behaviors. Understanding the elements of communication and following a systematic GAME plan will help ensure your success.

Identifying your goals is the first step in following a GAME plan. Successive steps include: audience identification, message and media strategy development, and evaluation. The following sections provide plans for developing specific types of communications for wildlife professionals. These include interpersonal communication, such as giving an interview and presenting a public or scientific talk, and the use of print media, such as the production of brochures and scientific posters. For any activity, carefully identifying the goals, audiences, messages, and evaluation techniques, will help ensure your success.

PLANNING SUCCESSFUL NEWS INTERVIEWS

Many wildlife professionals fear a close encounter with the press, perhaps envisioning a ruthless or ignorant reporter barging into their office. Yet, the consequences of

not harnessing the power of mass media—newspapers, magazines, radio, television, and the Internet—are dire! What if you planned a special event and nobody came? What if you took a stand on a controversial wildlife issue or designated new hunting regulations without publicity?

Mass communication approaches can help you disseminate your wildlife message. Different types of media transmit messages of varying complexity to different audiences. Your situation and message will dictate the right media approach for achieving your objectives. The GAME plan for preparing for news interviews follows the general framework that can be used for most mass communication approaches, from advertisements and public service announcements to press kits and news conferences. Following the GAME plan's 4 successive steps should help you put your best foot forward at an interview, rather than stumbling through it.

Defining Communication Goals and Objectives

Your overall goal may be to accomplish tasks associated with your organizational mission, such as gaining protection for a particular wildlife species or raising public awareness of an issue to influence legislative actions. Whatever the medium for your interview—print or electronic—you must keep in mind your communication objectives. To be effective, your message must be interesting, informative, and persuasive. In advance, you must identify 1 or 2 specific messages that are most important for achieving your communication goal.

For example, your objective might be that a majority of the readers of a local newspaper understand your message: "Exotic air potato (*Dioscorea bulbifera*) vines are killing native plants." A more ambitious objective would be to expect significant changes in behavior, for example, that 5% of the readers act on your message and pull air potato vines out of their yards or join a field day to assist your site in removing the vines (Fig. 9). Depending on your objective, you will need to carefully craft your message to achieve the desired result.

Identifying Audiences

Identify who is important to achieving your goals. Who are the stakeholders? You may need to research your audience to identify their relevant needs, concerns, and inter-

Box 5. Typical questions asked in a feature interview.

What are you trying to achieve?
What is the purpose of your program?
What problems have you had?
What obstacles do you still face?
How have you handled past (and future) problems?
When did your program start?
Who started it?
How did you get interested in it?

ests. What will motivate your audience to retain and accept your message or to shift their attitude or change their behavior? Before participating in an interview, ask in advance about the audience that listens to the station or reads the publication. Knowledge of the audience will guide your specific objectives for your presentation. It will allow you to put your story in a context relevant to the audience by emphasizing values and results that resonate with their lives. For a specialist audience, such as scientists, you obviously will describe your work or program with different words or visual props than for a general audience.

Mass media implies a diverse audience, but even mass media channels have segmented audiences. For example, the audience of a top-40 radio show will be different from the listeners of a classical music station. An understanding of the audience's backgrounds and common interests will improve your likelihood of a successful interview.

Developing Message and Media Strategies

Once you have identified your audience, develop and write your messages in advance to help organize your thoughts. Practice saying your key message 3 or 4 different ways—use action verbs, pithy phrases, and vivid images. During the interview, take every opportunity to make your point. Focus on components of the questions that allow you to deliver and repeat your message. You should be able to state your message in 1 or 2 sentences and deliver it in one breath. For example, Marjorie Stoneman Douglas, a venerated crusader for the Florida Everglades, is remembered for this sound bite: "The Everglades is a test. If we pass it, we get to keep the planet."

Other examples of effective messages include: "If you care about clean drinking water, you'll help us preserve the Jeffrey County Marsh." or, "Better protection of this rare wildlife species now will give you more land-use options in the future." The Nature Conservancy reminds people: "A world that can sustain nature will be a healthier and happier place for our children and their grandchildren." Note how these messages relate directly to people's interests and lives.

Identify where your target audiences get their information. Broadcast interviews with you or other experts in your organization might complement messages transmitted through specialized newsletters for a specific audience. Ensure that your media approaches enhance each other. In addition to understanding the audience, learn about the interview format and the background of the interviewer. If the interviewer has little knowledge of your subject, you can plan in advance the detail and explanations that you will provide. Before you give the interview, monitor the paper or show. Study the editorial style of the program in advance. Does the interviewer grill subjects or is he or she friendly? How long will you have? Will others with opposing viewpoints appear with you?

At times, an interviewer is looking for a response to some national or regional event, such as an oil spill; new policy, such as property rights legislation; or new study, such as data regarding declining animal populations. You may have 30 seconds to get your point across on an evening news broadcast or 30 minutes on a radio talk show interview. You can prepare for the interview by anticipating the kinds of questions that might be asked (Box 5). Most reporters ask the 5 "W"s: who, what, where, when, and why. Be prepared to briefly answer these questions about your organization or wildlife issue. Always remember your communication objectives—the 1 or 2 messages you want to deliver about your project or position, whether asked about them or not. To help advance your message, be prepared to give specific data. Do not be vague. For example, the answer: "250 landowners signed the petition," is better than "Lots of people support us."

Interviewers for print and broadcast media have varying time constraints and deadlines. News broadcasts are brief. Public relations experts suggest anticipating questions you may be asked and imagining a 15-second reply in the form of a newspaper headline. Use each question as a launching pad for your key messages. If the interview will be taped and edited, your replies must be self-contained statements that can be aired without any of your preceding or following replies.

For longer interviews, it is necessary not only to decide your message and to repeat it, but also to support your message with data and examples. You can supply written background material to the reporter in advance of the interview. This could include fact sheets about the program or issue and background documents about your organization. Not all interviewers will have the time or interest to take advantage of it, but background material will help them prepare for an effective interview based on your agenda.

Interviewers will probe to discover your program goals, obstacles you have faced, solutions found, and the roots of your activities. Make your point with data and information that supports what you have to say. Use a few good examples or anecdotes to vividly dramatize your point. Stories are an effective method for ensuring your message is remembered. Politicians litter their campaign speeches with personal stories to help the audience relate to their message. You should too.

Evaluating and Monitoring Your Performance

Using mass communication successfully requires an understanding of what makes your activities or events newsworthy. Your organization is newsworthy when you do things that are socially useful, fill a public need, or are just plain interesting (Fig. 10). To be newsworthy, a story must appeal to people's concerns and desires. Monitoring can help you evaluate whether you have reached your audience and addressed their interests. Monitoring allows you to modify your program as you go along. You can assess the outcomes of your communications activity—press coverage, audience members contacted, impacts on natural resources—to identify what did and did not work. Without monitoring, you risk duplicating failure rather than success.

Fig. 10. The stinky, 2.5-m blossom of this rare corpse flower (*Titan arum*) attracted 20,000 visitors to the University of Wisconsin botany greenhouse. Many more visited the university's web site that featured a web cam broadcasting the plant's astounding growth. The volume of hits temporarily halted the university's servers for the first time ever (photograph by M. F. Rothbart, UW-Madison, University Communications).

People will read or watch only what interests them. Your topic must concern or touch the audience in some way. Capitalizing on the audience's self-interest, a quality called relevance, will increase the audience's attention. Whether you are conducting and publishing a wildlife study or protecting an endangered species or parcel of land, you must convey the relevance of your work to your audience.

Monitoring techniques to measure the impacts of your interview can range from informal feedback from colleagues to tallies of additional press coverage or specific actions taken by members of your audience, such as votes generated, numbers of participants in an activity, and funds garnered. Regular monitoring helps you assess whether you are achieving your objectives.

Few people are natural stars. Following a GAME plan reminds you to identify your audience, develop your message, and learn exactly what the reporter wants and the format for the interview. This will go a long way toward a successful encounter.

PLANNING A PUBLIC TALK

Some people are more afraid of speaking in public than dying, according to psychologists. Yet, much of daily life revolves around oral communication. You greet people. You give and receive information. Your voice, tone, body language, and appearance combine to communicate information to others. This is also true of speaking to the public. Public presentations are delivered in a variety of settings such as auditoriums, outdoor theatres, classrooms, extension program sites, campfire circles, park trams, zoos, and almost anywhere visitors or organized groups can gather. Unlike a media interview, you usually have more control over the content and duration of your presentation. The principles of effective public talks, not surprisingly, follow the GAME plan for all effective communication. Once you've established your goals, you must identify your audience and address their needs and interest. By following your plan, you can be an effective public speaker, whether talking to small groups of people or giving scientific presentations to large audiences. Like any successful communication, a good presentation is interesting, targeted to the audience, and organized around your main idea or theme (Box 6).

In planning your talk, first clarify in your mind exactly what you hope to accomplish. If your goal is to inform the audience, what are the major themes and points you want them to learn? Do you want to change the way your audience thinks or behaves? What specific actions do you want them to take?

When preparing a talk, think about the content and organization of the subject matter. But don't just think about the major points you want to make—think about what your listeners want to hear and to what they will pay attention. Professional public speakers, like politicians, never recite only dry facts and figures to an audience. Their secret is to transform the information into a story. They make their major points through stories and follow each story with a punchy statement of fact or opinion. Translating abstract facts and data into stories or relevant life situations makes them matter to people. Try it!

Introduction

The introduction provides a succinct explanation of your presentation and defines the purpose of your talk for the audience. It reveals your theme, or main message, and why your subject is important. Audiences that are given the theme at the beginning of a talk will have better recall of it later (Thorndyke 1977). Your introduction presents a road map to help your audience follow the talk. It presents the organization of the talk and any ground rules, such as: "Please hold your questions until the end of the show." In the introduction, you can enhance your rapport with the audience by describing what you share in common. You also may wish to establish your credibility by letting your audience know why you are qualified to talk about the subject.

The introduction should create a supportive atmosphere for learning and capture the audience's attention by describing how your subject relates to the audience's needs. Acknowledge your audience and grab their attention with questions, a quotation, an illustration, a story, a picture, or an attention-getting generalization. Why should the audience listen? Tell them something that affects them directly, for example, "We all drink water from Blues Reservoir, but do you know where the water originates?" Or give an illustration that relates the subject to your audience. A provocative statement beginning your talk may help convince the audience to stay. "Picture yourself in a situation where the only food you can eat must be gathered from the forest...."

Or grab audience attention with a startling fact: "These golden toads (*Bufo periglenes*) may now be extinct" (Fig. 11).

Body

The body of the talk presents the factual support for your theme. As the theme is developed, key points are made in a logical sequence and the audience follows along as you elaborate. People only make sense of 5 to 9 new ideas at one time (Miller 1956). Limiting your talk to 5 or fewer main points that illustrate or support your message will help ensure that people will remember them. The amount of information you include in the body depends on the amount of time you have. The use of stories and anecdotes can illustrate your meaning and keep the audience's attention.

Conclusion

The conclusion of your speech is the climax. Reemphasize your theme or take home messages and tie the conclusion back to the opening of your talk. The conclusion should suggest what you want the audience to do—how to learn more about the topic and/or take action on the issue. You might want to finish the talk in a memorable way with an anecdote, poem, visual image, or quote. When you finish your talk, don't fade away. Conclude!

Transitions

Do not forget to use smooth transitions between the opening, body, and conclusion of the speech. Transitions provide continuity and make the talk easy to understand. Transitions also are needed between each main point you are making. A good transition should summarize the preceding idea, establish the relationship between the preceding and following ideas, and preview the next idea (Lewis 1980). For example: "Now that we know how frogs reproduce, let's see what happens to their eggs."

Visual Props

Once you have identified your goals and audiences and developed your talk, think about visual props to illustrate your points. Visual aids can increase audience understanding and retention of information by 50 to 200% (Bunnell and Mock 1990). Many wildlife talks occur outdoors or in settings where a variety of visual props can enhance the presentations. Props can be actual artifacts, such as plant parts, live animals or animal specimens, soil samples, rocks, scientific equipment, or other objects that you want the audience to see. Props also can be 3-dimensional models that illustrate things that are barely visible or difficult to witness. For example, you can show an enormous model grasshopper with clearly visible chewing mouthparts. Staff at the Monterey Bay Aquarium show their audience a

---

Box 6. Tips for effective talks.

Practice ahead of time. As Mark Twain said, "It takes three weeks to prepare a good ad-lib speech."

Make sure your talk is the proper length of time. Thirty to 45 minutes is the maximum length for an auditorium program. Orientation presentations should be only 5–15 minutes long.

Adapt your talk to your audience's background and interests. Simplify things and do not give unneeded detail. Stick to your theme.

Talk to the audience. Do not hide behind a podium. Stand where the audience can see you and talk directly to them. If you need to write on the board, or point at a slide, stop talking while your back is turned. Then continue.

Make eye contact with the audience. Some speakers like to pick out a few people in the audience in different areas of the room to focus on during their talk.

Talk at a rate of about 125 words per minute. Talk clearly, do not mutter. Vary the pitch and tone of your voice.

Avoid saying "uhmm," and other filler words. Use a microphone if it is provided.

Use hand gestures and body language to help tell your story and keep the audience's attention. Put your whole body into your presentation. Facial expressions and body movements can show pleasure, enthusiasm, pain, and sorrow. Gesture with your hands and arms to show shape and location or to emphasize an important point.

Record or videotape your practice talk to evaluate how you do. Watch politicians as they deliver speeches, and see how gestures may work for you.

Use visual aids to complement your talk. If your props are small, like a rock or leaf, have several specimens that you can quickly pass around the audience. Use your props actively—move them around, have people touch or smell them.

Use slides, PowerPoint or overhead projections and other visual cues. Use birdcalls, music, or other audio cues to make presentations more interesting and memorable.

Make sure charts and graphs are simple and clear if you use them, and make sure the entire audience can see or hear the aids you use.

Do not worry if you are nervous. Most people feel a sense of anxiety before a talk. This can make you seem enthusiastic and help you stay focused on the presentation. Your own interest in and enthusiasm for the subject will be contagious.

End on time.

Leave time for questions or discussion.

Fig. 11. Grab audience attention with a startling fact and interesting photograph (photograph by S. K. Jacobson).

Fig. 12. An interpreter at the Monterey Bay Aquarium demonstrates jellyfish anatomy using a plastic model (photograph by S. K. Jacobson).

Box 7. Evaluation checklist for your public presentation.

Voice and Body
 Suitable voice volume
 Understandable speaking rate
 Varied vocal pitch
 Pleasant voice tone
 Clear articulation
 Language appropriate for audience
 Expressive body language
 Appropriate dress
 Confident manner (your audience will think you
   are confident if you appear confident)
 Good eye contact with audience

Content
 Addressed audience's needs and interests
 Attention-getting beginning
 Organized, logical flow of ideas
 Points supported by examples
 Effective transitions between points
 Effective conclusion
 Clear message
 Precise words
 Vivid mental images
 Good use of illustrations and/or anecdotes
 Visual aids enhance message and points
 Visual aids clear and easily seen

---

model of a jellyfish to explain its unusual biology (Fig. 12). Then, they hold up a clear plastic bag and let the audience see for themselves why sea turtles (Family Cheloniidae) mistake plastic trash for their jellyfish prey. The audience clearly sees how their litter endangers sea turtles.

Evaluation

Once your talk is over, breathe a sigh of relief. But don't forget the last step in your GAME plan: evaluation. The best way to improve your presentation skills is to carefully evaluate them. Before the actual performance, you can make a videotape of your practice talk and review it, or ask your colleagues to provide feedback (Box 7). Feedback from your audience, by using comment forms or other methods, will provide direct evidence of the success of your talk and will help improve your next one. Informal feedback from the audience, such as people looking alert during the talk, asking questions, coming up to you at the end of the talk, or contacting your organization at a later date, provides valuable feedback. For many audiences, particularly children, asking questions about the presentation content or their behavioral intentions after the talk will let you know if your main points were retained and well-received.

PLANNING A SCIENTIFIC PRESENTATION

The GAME plan for most scientific presentations is obvious. The goal is to convey scientific information and the audience is generally other scientists. A good presentation can help you accomplish a variety of objectives, such as making professional contacts, establishing your reputation in the field, exchanging information about research findings with similar researchers, and promoting your department or agency. Typical media used for scientific presentations include computer graphic programs and slide shows. These easily illustrate a scientific subject with a succession of pictures, graphs, tables, and text. Not sur-

prising, all of the guidelines outlined for public presentations also apply to scientific talks.

Most scientific presentations fall into 2 categories, 1-hour research seminars for job interviews or departmental colloquia and 15- to 20-minute presentations at scientific meetings. Generally, leaving the last 15 minutes of an hour-long presentation and 3 minutes of a 15-minute presentation to answer questions and interact with the audience is standard. Ironically, the shorter the talk, the more preparation is required to ensure you make your main points succinctly in the given time. Similar to public talks, use of slides, PowerPoint or other electronic media, and other visual images should help you introduce your study, explain your methods and results, and discuss the findings. The sequence of visual images and accompanying narration should have a cohesive introduction, body, and conclusion to help you weave a unified story.

Knowing the composition of your audience (students, faculty, researchers, administrators, field practitioners) and the number expected to attend is helpful to design a GAME plan for your presentation. It will help dictate how much time you need to spend introducing the scientific context of your presentation or the details of your methods.

Generally, the introduction of a scientific talk lets you set the stage by describing the theoretical or applied context for your research question and the main topics you will cover in the rest of your talk. This focuses the audience on your subject and allows them to understand the logical structure of what they are about to hear. An introductory slide listing the main topics you will cover should adequately orient your listeners. The aphorism for giving talks—"Tell 'em what you're going to say; say it; tell 'em what you said."—isn't bad advice as you introduce your talk at the beginning, present your information, and reiterate your key findings at the end.

The body of your talk will briefly explain your study site, subjects, and methods. It will focus on your results and the implications of your findings. Planning the body of the talk depends on the time available. In a 10-minute presentation, details must be jettisoned and only your most important results described. For longer talks, a more complete discussion of the results and their ramifications is in order. Although this is a "scientific" talk, you are still obligated to present information clearly, in an interesting manner, and to make your findings relevant to the audience. This is just as important for an audience of scientists as any other audience.

The conclusion of a scientific presentation reviews the key findings and ends with your take-home message. The outline for your talk should be built by putting flesh and muscle around the backbone of your take-home message. Your conclusion should logically follow from the introduction and body. The conclusion also can stimulate further interest in the subject by suggesting unanswered questions raised by the results or future lines of research.

It is easy to lull an audience to sleep with an electronic presentation or slide-show: just dim the lights, speak in a monotonous tone, and show graphics that are hard to see, out of focus, repetitive, or irrelevant to your main topic. Too much text per image and too many images for your allotted time also will lose the attention of your audience.

Tips

There are many ways to ensure a quality scientific presentation.

- Arrive early. Arrange in advance for someone to operate the lights and projector and to trouble-shoot problems so that you can remain in front of the audience. If no one is available, familiarize yourself with the equipment before your talk; test your computer files or slide carousel on the equipment. Be sure to discuss computer compatibility issues with your host in advance.
- Talk to the audience before showing slides to establish rapport before plunging the room in darkness or hiding behind your computer monitor. During the presentation, face your audience (not the image). Stand to the side of the screen and don't block it.
- Always preview slides to ensure none is backward or upside down. Make sure they will show clearly in the darkened room. Make sure computer images are legible and colors contrast well for easy viewing.
- Images should be organized in sequences to develop a single idea. For example, if your point is to describe forest growth, a wide view of a pine forest will orient the audience. Follow this by closer shots of pine trees, pine cones, and finally pine seedlings. Slide sequences are especially good at showing before and after conditions, and cause and effect images. Grouping of images on computer presentations can serve this purpose well.
- Use sequences of images to reveal the complex nature of a specific topic, such as adding more

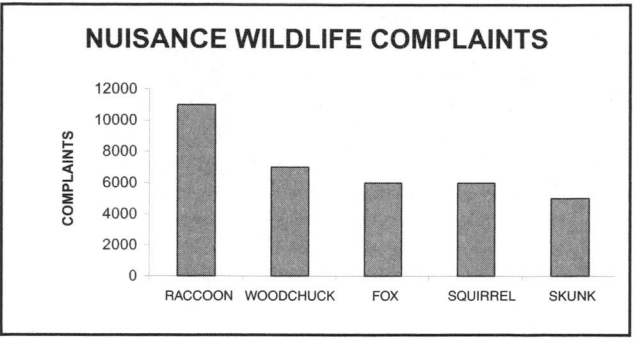

We evaluated data from Maryland, Vermont, and New Hampshire consisting of approximately 48,000 nuisance wildlife contacts. The top 5 nuisance species based on number of contacts are raccoons (*Procyon lotor*) with 11,000 complaints, woodchucks (*Marmota monax*) with 7,000 complaints, red fox (*Vulpes vulpes*) and gray squirrels (*Sciurus carolinensis*) each with 6,000 complaints, and striped skunks (*Mephitis mephitis*) with 5,000 complaints.

Fig. 13. The top slide depicts results visually and avoids displaying extraneous information (data from Organ and Ellingwood 2000).

details to a diagram or additional items to a list. Revealing information progressively also adds an air of mystery and interest to your talk.

- Use high-quality images: clear, focused subjects with good composition and color. Include people in some of your images, where appropriate, such as the researcher collecting data at a field site. People like to look at other people.
- For text slides use symbols and bullets to minimize the number of words. Use simple fonts and large lettering. Choose colors that have good contrast: yellow text on blue background is easily seen. Let the colors help emphasize the organization of the talk.
- Avoid crowding too much information on a slide. Leave spaces between lines and use indentations to help your audience follow along. Graphs, like bar graphs and pie charts, are easier to read than tables or text (Fig. 13). The International Congress of Zoology strictly limits slides to 8 lines of text or tabulated material for presentation at their annual meeting (Hailman and Strier 1997). Eight lines are probably too much for most presentations. Don't frustrate your audience by showing a riot of material they cannot read or comprehend.
- Vary the length of time you leave each image illuminated, from a few seconds to a minute or more, depending on the text or image. On average, plan to show images at a rate of one slide per 15 seconds. This may vary greatly depending on your topic, style, audience, and objectives. Once the image no longer pertains to your narration, change it. Don't let the audience contemplate the image for longer than is necessary to illustrate your particular point.
- Do not introduce each image, for example, "This is a giant panda (*Ailuropoda melanoleuca*)." Instead,

make your point: "The giant panda is one of the world's most imperiled mammals." The image should enhance your narration.

- Change your voice inflection to keep the audience's attention. If you are showing slides, they cannot see your enthusiastic hand gestures in the dark.
- Your narration should anticipate the next image and provide a smooth transition to it in advance of flashing it on the screen.
- Additional equipment to add sounds to your narration or animation to your PowerPoint presentation will make your talk more interesting and entertaining.
- Practice your talk in front of sympathetic colleagues to get feedback on the content, transitions, clarity, graphics, timing, and delivery. Then, practice your talk. Again!
- End on time, reiterating your take-home message and let everyone know you have concluded. You might want to finish your conclusion with the room lights on to reestablish rapport with the audience.
- Allow enough time for questions. Don't be alarmed if it takes the audience a few seconds to blink and muster some questions. Repeat questions before answering if the acoustics are poor. Answer questions briefly and directly. If you don't know an answer, say so. If time permits, you can sidestep a question and remark, "That's a good question, does anyone have a response to that?" Deflect the question to your audience and stimulate some discussion.

Evaluation

Few scientists start out as gifted public speakers. Feedback from your friends during practice talks is helpful for improving your presentation. Just like a rehearsal before a theatre production, trying out your talk on colleagues allows you to fine tune your performance. Ask them for feedback using the checklist for successful talks (Box 6).

Observing other peoples' presentations also helps. What delivery styles do you like? What annoying behaviors—repeating "uhhm," jingling pocket change, clicking a ballpoint pen, not speaking into the microphone—can you avoid? The ultimate evaluation for your scientific presentation is whether you're offered a job, asked to submit your work for publication, provided with additional funding for your study, and the many other beneficial kinds of feedback you can reap from being a good communicator.

PLANNING PRINT COMMUNICATIONS— DEVELOPING A BROCHURE

Wildlife professionals create a mountain of print communications over a lifetime. It starts with your first research proposal as a student and, with luck, expands into a thesis, research reports, professional papers, book chapters, books, newsletter articles, presentation abstracts, and scientific posters.

Wildlife professionals also commonly use print media for reaching audiences that visit their refuges or for offsite audiences ranging from legislators to school groups. Brochures, booklets, magazines, guidebooks, and other printed material can provide your target audience with information, ideas, and illustrations. Publications are easy

to disseminate to target audiences, and can be used how and when the audience desires. Printed materials also are relatively easy to produce and revise.

The GAME plan for creating effective print materials follows similar guidelines for any effective communication. This section explores the design of a brochure for popular audiences. The next section describes the development of a professional poster for a scientific meeting. Although the goals and audiences for these 2 types of print media differ, most of the concepts for effective print communication are similar. If you make your material attractive, brief, clear, and dynamic—the A, B, C, and D's of print communication—you will be successful (Ham 1992, Jacobson 1999). There are a number of tips for writing briefly and clearly (Box 8). Good writing is a prerequisite for accomplishing communication goals using print media.

Design Elements

Brochures are the most commonly used written format for interpretation at parks and refuges. They are used for many purposes and disseminated as handouts at sites, exhibits, and trails, mailed to groups planning a visit, and used for fund-raising or membership drives. Brochures also are dispensed at nearby hotels and at other public lands or agencies. For much of the lay public audience, if the cover of a brochure does not look inviting, few will make the effort to delve into the text, no matter how scintillating the writing.

Following a GAME plan, your communication goal and specific audience will dictate the design and content for your brochure. Think about the main goal of the brochure and what you want your readers to know or do. To attract most audiences, a brochure should have a catchy title, bright colors, and an inviting layout (e.g., Brigham 1991, Fazio and Gilbert 2000). Brochures for a general audience are written

---

Box 8. Tips for effective writing.

Write with nouns and verbs. Adjectives and adverbs seldom add vigor to a story. For example, "Bob yelled," is more compelling than, "Bob said loudly."

Use active, not passive, voice. (e.g., *Good*: "Biologist Bob darted the grizzly." *Bad*: "The grizzly was darted by biologist Bob.")

Write simple, ordinary English. Avoid jargon and elaborate words. (e.g., write "use" not "utilize," and "now" not "at the present time")

Avoid using qualifiers, such as "very," "rather," and "little." They sap strength from your statements.

Be clear. As Mark Twain admonished: "Choose the right word, not its second cousin."

Relay your message using elements of interest to the reader.

Be specific and provide details; do not be vague.

Be concise. Use short sentences and paragraphs; they are easier to read.

Rewrite, rewrite, rewrite. Particularly when you are starting out, the wastebasket or delete button is your best friend.

Fig. 14. A brief title and single, interesting photograph attract readers to this brochure for the Royal Society for the Protection of Birds.

for an 8th grade reading level. If your audience speaks English as a second language or is not familiar with your subject, visual images may relay your message better than text. Collect and study brochures that catch your eye from other organizations before deciding on a design for your brochure. Your budget and the number of copies you need will limit some choices, such as glossy paper or full-color graphics. An attractive brochure does not have to be expensive.

Catchy Covers

Keep the title brief and thematic. Short titles of less than 10 words get read more. For example, "Insects—We Can't Live Without Them" or "Water—Lifeblood of the Everglades" give a snappy overview of the theme of the brochure. Keep your target audience in mind. If the brochure is for hikers, hunters, boaters, or other specific audiences, mention them in the title. For example: Insect Ecology for Successful Flyfishing" or "Boater's Guide to Seeing and Protecting Manatees." Draw readers in with an emphasis on their personal interest.

A single photograph or illustration on the cover is usually more effective than multiple visuals (Fig. 14). Make the visual interesting by showing something happening. Action shots of a bear eating berries or people hiking through a forest have more appeal than an inactive bear or a forest setting. Use bright colors or a high contrast design to attract people. Select colors that help emphasize your theme, such as red for a brochure on prescribed fire or blue for marine ecology. Resist the urge to fill the cover with your agency logo. This identifying mark should not distract from the main message and illustration.

Body and Content

The body of the brochure should make use of subtitles, photographs, and other graphics to break up the writing. Many people will only read the headlines, so you need to make it obvious why the reader should continue. Some tips for ease of reading are below.

- Use wide margins and extra white space (empty areas) around the headlines and between sections to make the brochure look casual and easy to read. Empty areas attract the reader's attention.
- Use a simple font to make the page look inviting. Try a bold, sans serif font (e.g., Helvetica or Futura) for the headings and subheadings and a serif font, (e.g., this print) which is easier to read, for the text.
- Consider using direct quotes or question and answer approaches. These often entice people to continue reading.
- Use bullets or check boxes to add interest and help organize the text.
- Use simple graphics, maps, and charts. Your photographs or illustrations should be sharp and compelling.
- Put captions (in a different size or font from the text) under photos and graphics. People often read captions, second only to headlines.
- Ensure that your layout, colors, text, font, type size, and visual images all reinforce your overall message. The headings, captions, and images should create a visual order so the audience can easily follow the information in a logical sequence.
- Follow the tips for effective writing (Box 8). You need relevant and interesting content to hold attention and accomplish your communication goal.

Evaluation

All communications benefit from evaluation. Have members of your target audience evaluate your brochure before you invest in publication. Ask a dozen members of your audience, as well as other experts in your field, to review the draft brochure. Have several versions of the theme, content, and design from which to select. Their feedback can help you avoid the common mistakes in brochure design that reduce readership. The problem ABC's of the brochure reader are listed below.

- **A**ggravation—The page is too jammed with information. The type is hard to read or too close together. Organization is poor or nonexistent. The page lacks white spaces and does not provide breathing space for the reader.

- **B**oredom—Nothing in the brochure stands out; it looks like a page of gray. Headlines are too small. Columns are too wide. Articles are too long. Paragraphs and sentences are too long or complex. Pictures or visual interest is lacking.
- **C**onfusion—The reader cannot follow the flow of the text, visuals interrupt reading, or the headings and subheadings are indistinguishable.

Once you have received feedback, you are ready to revise your brochure. Get more feedback if revisions are extensive. If not, you are ready to go to press.

PLANNING A SCIENTIFIC POSTER

The advancement of scientific knowledge depends on effective communication of research findings to the scientific community as well as the wider public. Poster sessions are an important form of communication at many scientific meetings. Poster sessions allow you to highlight the main message—your research findings. Viewers can study your poster at their own pace and discuss the results with you in an informal and interactive setting. The Wildlife Society meeting held in North Dakota in 2002 had over 150 posters on display. Scientists attending the Ecological Society of America's meeting in Arizona the same year presented almost 800 posters.

The GAME plan for a poster follows the usual guidelines of identifying your **g**oal, **a**udience, **m**essage, and **e**valuation process. The goal of a poster is to convey scientific information in a visual format to an audience primarily of other scientists. Similar to a good oral presentation, an effective poster can help you make professional contacts, exchange information about research findings with other researchers, and promote your organization. With some planning and preparation you can create an effective poster presentation and a great impression.

Attracting Viewers

How do you attract viewers to your poster? The type of meeting you are attending allows you to identify your probable audience. You'll be competing with scores of other posters and often a concurrent social gathering. The same principles for designing an effective brochure apply to posters. Qualities of attractiveness, brevity, clarity, and dynamism are crucial to hook your audience. The audience will want to briskly scan the important points of the your poster to see how it relates to them. An inviting title, enticing graphics, and clear layout will entice your audience to give your poster a closer look. Study other scientific posters that catch your eye before deciding on a design for your poster.

Content

The conference organizers will often dictate the format of a poster. Posters may be required to include a title, authors, and authors' affiliations, abstract, introduction, methods, results, discussion, conclusions, and literature cited. A good poster is organized around an introduction, body, and conclusion, similar to an oral presentation. The title should concisely communicate your main message. It should catch the attention of the audience and arouse their interest in your subject.

The introduction should briefly indicate why the topic is important, placing it in the context of other scientific literature. It should state the hypotheses and objectives of your study and briefly explain your methods. A photograph of your study organism or site helps illustrate this section. If a separate methods section is needed, you can briefly describe your experimental equipment, techniques, and statistical analysis. Often a flow chart or brief table can be used to illustrate the research design.

You should illustrate the most important results, visually, if possible, using graphs, photos, and other illustrations. Describe briefly whether the study supported your hypothesis and whether the experiment worked. The figures illustrating your results should have legends that concisely state your major findings. This may be all many viewers read. The main conclusions and implications should be discussed. This section should summarize the hypothesis and results, and tell everyone why they are noteworthy relative to other studies and to the real world. Literature citations can be placed at the bottom of the poster because only the most dedicated will want to peruse them.

Keep in mind that most people will spend about 10 seconds gazing at your poster, so you must catch their interest with your title and graphics. Few will spend more than a few minutes. This limits your total text to 200–300 words. It is important to curb the urge to tell the viewer everything about your study. Instead, you must be satisfied if your main messages are successfully communicated. Colleagues who are involved in related research will no doubt spend time chatting with you at the poster session—then you can tell them the details. It's a good idea to have your business card or an abstract of your study available next to the poster for viewers that want to request more information later.

Layout

Your poster is made up of 3 components: text, graphics, and empty space. A rule of thumb is to have equal parts of these 3 elements. Just as in the brochure design, the empty space helps make the poster look inviting and easy to read. Visual material, such as photographs, drawings, diagrams, charts, graphs, and tables will make the poster attractive and emphasize your main points. Charts and graphs are usually easier to absorb at a glance than tables. These should be simplified to enable the reader to understand the main points quickly. To create more empty space, avoid extraneous text and distracting graphics. Colors, graphics, and text should work together to make the poster easy to read. The size of the text and the colors selected for text and graphics help orient the reader and emphasize the main points. Larger text for headings and subheadings will indicate the organization of the poster and can be used to emphasize important points. Choosing a light, unifying color for the background and 2 or 3 dark, contrasting colors for your various-sized text and graphics will make your poster stand out and can highlight your photographs and other visual materials. Color can be used to associate related text and graphics, and to separate sections. However, too many colors can confuse the viewer.

Conference organizers will usually specify the size of the posters. A vertical format that is about 120 cm high by

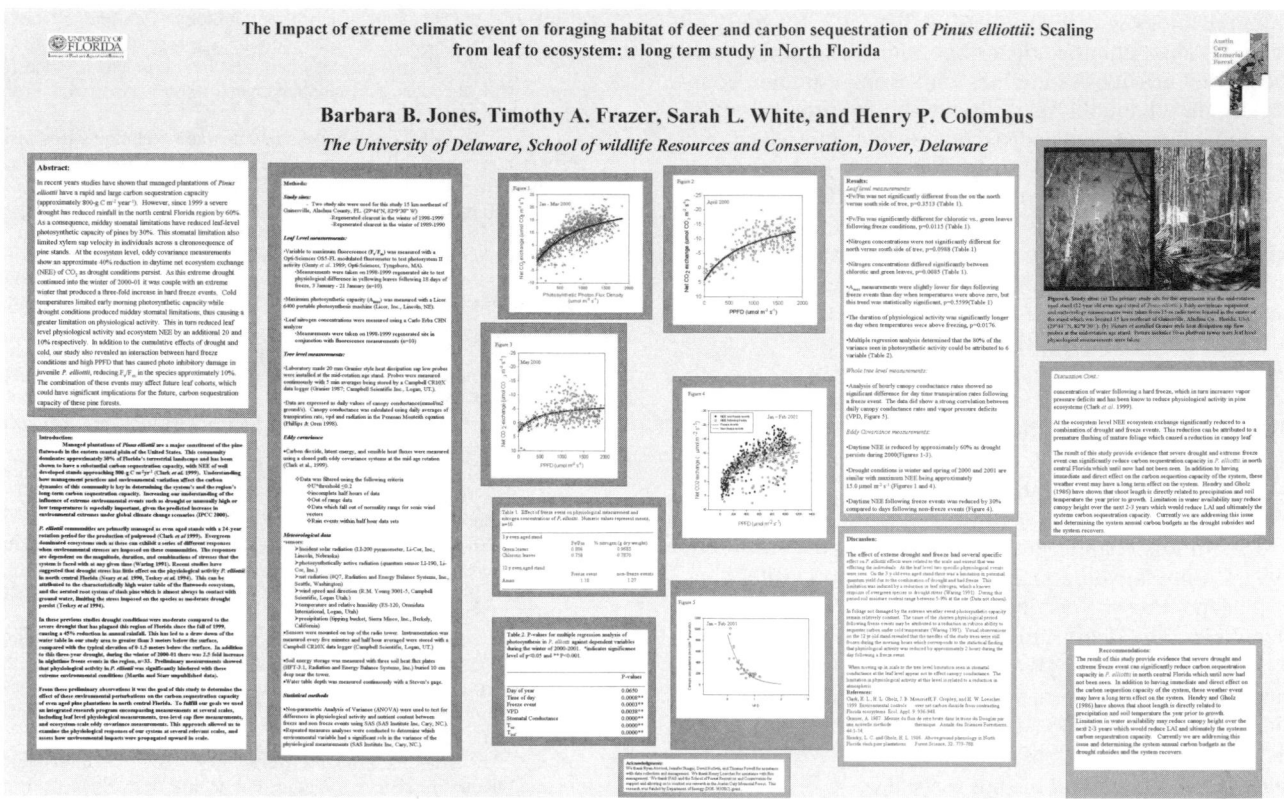

Fig. 15. Poor posters such as this one share common design faults, including: title too long and font too small; text too long and continuous; graphic material and text crowded together; varying column widths create a jagged appearance; directional flow of material unclear; material placed too low to read; and inconsistent use of blank space between elements confuses viewers.

100 cm wide is common. The poster title should have lettering large enough to be read from 4 m away to reel in prospective viewers. Poster text should be legible from a distance of 2 m. This requires font sizes of 90–110 point for the title, 48–72 point for section headings, and 24–36 pt for the text. Some scientific posters use a minimum text font size of 18 pt, but see what **you** can read from 2 m distance. If you can't read it, no one else can. Only the least important information, such as literature citations should be printed in smaller fonts. The headings and subheadings form different levels to emphasize your main points and lead the reader to the conclusion.

The layout should follow how people usually view material. English-speakers are used to reading from left to right and from top to bottom. Their first glance at your poster will be at the center. Attract them with your succinct title and effective graphics. Then, don't confuse them. Your overall format should proceed from left to right and from top to bottom. If the allowable poster size is large, think carefully before you fill all the space. Few people will squat to read your conclusions if they are printed at knee height.

Most of the design elements for posters are common sense if you keep in mind the audience. Posters often display text and graphics in 3 vertical columns because of the size of the text font and the number of words (about 11) that fit across each column and make it easy to read. Lower-case print is more legible than all capital letters. Using all capitals reduces reading comprehension by 25% and reduces speed by 14% (Tinker 1963, Ham 1992). This means capitalize only the first letters in your title and headings to maximize ease of reading. Bulleted lists are easier

to read than full sentences or numbered items. A clear graph or chart is more succinct than a lengthy table.

Evaluation

Similar to other communication materials, it is imperative to pilot-test your poster with members of the target audience. Feedback is critical. See if you can identify all the problems with the poster example (Fig. 15). Before you print your poster, make a small mock-up and ask your colleagues to critique it. Are they confused? Can some verbiage be eliminated? Do they understand your main points? Are your graphics clear? Fix it before you waste time and money printing your final poster. Once you are at your meeting, observe viewers as they pass your poster to see if they read any or all of it, react to the information, talk to each other about the information, ask you questions about it, and ask for any follow-up information. You also should ask colleagues and experts in your field for additional feedback about your poster—what could be changed or improved in future posters. Also, take advantage of the opportunity to study other posters that attract many viewers. Can you identify common elements that are interesting or stimulating? Similar to all forms of communication, if people don't read or can't understand your message, have you really communicated?

SUMMARY

Effective communications are essential for influencing conservation policy, changing people's behaviors, garnering funds, and sharing scientific advances. The fate of our wildlands and wildlife resources depends on effective communications with a variety of audiences in a variety of places. This chapter describes the communications process and provides guidelines for several common communication channels used by wildlife professionals, including interpersonal approaches, such as interviews and public talks, and the design of brochures and scientific posters. Following a GAME plan that includes identifying goals and objectives, analyzing audiences, selecting media and message strategies, and evaluating your activities will help ensure your communication success. As the National Outreach Strategy drafted in 1997 by the U.S. Fish and Wildlife Service stated, "It is our job to speak up for the wild creatures that cannot speak for themselves." By following a systematic plan, all communications by wildlife professionals should be effective and efficient.

ACKNOWLEDGMENTS

Ideas in this chapter are adapted from S. K. Jacobson, 1999. Communication skills for conservation professionals. Island Press, Washington, D.C., USA; http://www.islandpress.org. I am grateful to C. M. Browne-Nunez, J. N. Solomon, and S. A. Espinosa for helpful review of this manuscript. C. E. Braun, J. K. Hooper, and E. Main provided excellent editorial review and suggestions. I thank J. K. Morris for research assistance and J. X. Wu and M. O. Siegel for computer and design assistance.

LITERATURE CITED

ABC News/Washington Post. 1995. ABC News/Washington Post Poll, 11–14 May 1995. ABC News, New York, USA.

Blum, A. 1987. Students' knowledge and beliefs concerning environmental issues in four countries. Journal of Environmental Education 18 (3):7–13.

Brigham, N. 1991. How to do leaflets, newsletters, & newspapers. PEP Publishers, Detroit, Michigan, USA.

Brown, L.A. 1981. Innovation diffusion: a new perspective. Methuen Publishers, New York, USA.

Bunnell, P., and T. Mock. 1990. A guide for the preparation and use of overhead and slide visuals. Ministry of Forests, Research Branch Publication, Victoria, British Columbia, Canada.

Byers, B. A. 1996. Understanding and influencing behaviors in conservation and natural resources management. African Biodiversity Series 4, Biodiversity Support Program, Washington, D.C., USA

Cantril, H. 1972. Gauging public opinion. Princeton University Press, Princeton, New Jersey, USA.

Case, D. J. 1989. Are we barking up the wrong trees? Illusions, delusions, and realities of communications in the natural resource management mix. Transactions of the North American Wildlife and Natural Resources Conference 54:630–639.

Cutlip, S. M., A. H. Center, and G. M. Broom. 1985. Effective public relations. Sixth edition. Prentice-Hall, Inc., Upper Saddle River, New Jersey, USA.

Fazio, J. R., and D. L. Gilbert. 2000. Public relations and communications for natural resource managers. Kendall/Hunt Publishing Company, Dubuque, Iowa, USA.

Fishbein, M., and I. Ajzen. 1975. Belief, attitude, intention and behavior: an introduction to theory and research. Addison-Wesley Publishing Co., Reading, Massachusetts, USA.

Fritts, S. H., and L. N. Carbyn. 1995. Population viability, nature reserves, and the outlook for gray wolf conservation in North America. Restoration Ecology 3:26–38.

Gigliotti, L. M. 1990. Environmental education: what went wrong? What can be done? Journal of Environmental Education 21(2):9–12.

Hailman, J. P., and K. B. Strier. 1997. Planning, proposing, and presenting science effectively: a guide for graduate students and re-searchers in the behavioral sciences and biology. Cambridge University Press, Cambridge, United Kingdom.

Ham, S. H. 1992. Environmental interpretation: a practical guide for people with big ideas and small budgets. North American Press, Golden, Colorado, USA.

Henderson, C. L. 1984. Publicity strategies and techniques for Minnesota's nongame wildlife checkoff. Transactions of the North American Wildlife and Natural Resources Conference 49:181–189.

Hines, J. M., H. R. Hungerford, and A. N. Tomera. (1986/87) Analysis and synthesis of research on responsible environmental behavior: a meta-analysis. Journal of Environmental Education 18(2):1–8.

International Institute for Environment and Development (IIED). 1994. Who's Eden is it anyway? IIED Publication, London, United Kingdom.

Jacobson, S. K. 1990. A model for using a developing country's park system for conservation education. Journal of Environmental Education 22(1):19–25.

———. 1999. Communications skills for conservation professionals. Island Press, Washington, D.C., USA.

———, and S. B. Marynowski. 1997. Public attitudes and knowledge about ecosystem management on Department of Defense lands in Florida. Conservation Biology 11:770–781.

———, M. C. Monroe, and S. Marynowski. 2001. Fire at the wildland interface: the influence of experience and mass media on public knowledge, attitudes, and behavioral intentions. Wildlife Society Bulletin 29:929–937.

Kellert, S. R. 1996. The value of life: biological diversity and human society. Island Press, Washington, D.C., USA.

Klingemann, H. D., and A. Rommele. 2002. Public information campaigns & opinion research. Sage Publications Ltd., Thousand Oaks, California, USA.

Knudson, D. M., T. T. Cable, and L. Beck. 1995. Interpretation of cultural and natural resources. Venture Publishing, Inc., State College, Pennsylvania, USA.

Lasswell, H. D. 1971. A pre-view of policy sciences. American Elsevier Publishing Co., New York, USA.

Lewis, W. J. 1980. Interpreting for park visitors. Eastern Acorn Press and Eastern National Park and Monument Association, Philadelphia, Pennsylvania, USA.

Maslow, A. H. 1954. Motivation and personality. Harper and Row, New York, USA.

Meine, C. 1988. Aldo Leopold: his life and work. University of Wisconsin Press, Madison, USA

McKenzie-Mohr, D., and W. Smith. 1999. Fostering sustainable behavior: an introduction to community based social marketing. New Society Publishers, Gabriola Island, British Columbia, Canada.

Miller, G. 1956. The magical number seven, plus or minus two. The Psychological Review 63:81–97.

National Opinion Research Center. 1995. Environmental and scientific knowledge around the world. National Opinion Research Center, University of Chicago, Illinois, USA.

Organ, J. F., and M. R. Ellingwood. 2000. Wildlife stakeholder acceptance capacity for black bears, beavers, and other beasts in the East. Human Dimensions of Wildlife 5:63–75.

Seitel, F. P. 1995. The practice of public relations. Sixth edition. Prentice Hall, Englewood Cliffs, New Jersey, USA.

Smith, W. A. 1995. Behavior, social marketing and the environment. Pages 9–20 in J. Palmer, W. Goldstein, and A. Curnow, editors. Planning education to care for the earth. International Union for Conservation of Nature and Natural Resources, Gland, Switzerland.

Stout, R. J., D. J. Decker, B. A. Knuth, J. C. Proud, and D. H. Nelson. 1997. Comparison of three public-involvement approaches for stakeholder input into deer management decisions: a case study. Wildlife Society Bulletin 24:312–317.

Sunquist, M. E., and F. C. Sunquist. 2002. Wild cats of the world. University of Chicago Press, Chicago, Illinois, USA.

Thorndyke, P. W. 1977. Cognitive structures in comprehension and memory of narrative discourse. Cognitive Psychology 9:77–110.

Tinker, M. A. 1963. Legibility of print. Iowa State University Press, Ames, USA.

Yaffee, S. L., A. F. Phillips, I. C. Frentz, P. W. Hardy, S. M. Maleki, and B. E. Thorpe. 1996. Ecosystem management in the United States. Island Press, Washington, D.C, USA.

3

RESEARCH AND EXPERIMENTAL DESIGN

Edward O. Garton, John T. Ratti, and John H. Giudice

INTRODUCTION

Management programs must be based on quality scientific investigations that produce objective, relevant information—and quality science is dependent upon carefully designed experiments, comparisons, and models. This chapter provides an overview of the fundamental concepts of wildlife research and study design, and is a revision of Ratti and Garton (1994).

Emergence of Rigor in Wildlife Science

Wildlife science is a term the wildlife profession has only recently nurtured. Our profession of wildlife conservation and management was built on natural-history observations and conclusions from associations of wildlife population changes with environmental factors such as weather, habitat loss, or harvest. Thus, we have a long tradition of wildlife management based on "laws of association" rather than on experimental tests of specific hypotheses (Romesburg 1981).

Although Romesburg (1981) and others have been critical of wildlife research and resulting management, the wildlife biologist is confronted with tremendous natural variation that might confound results and conclusions of an investigation. Scientists conducting experiments in physics and chemistry have the ability to control variables associated with an experiment, isolating the key components, and can repeat these experiments under the exact same conditions to confirm their results. They also have the ability to systematically alter the nature or level of specific variables to examine cause and effect.

The wildlife scientist often conducts investigations in natural environments over large geographic areas. It is usually difficult to control potentially causal factors. Responses, such as density of the species in question, are simultaneously subject to the influences of factors such as weather, habitat, predators, and competition, which change spatially and temporally. Thus, rigorous scientific investigation in wildlife ecology is challenging and requires careful design. An early step that moved wildlife investigators from descriptive natural-history studies toward rigorous examination of processes was application of statistics to wildlife data. In the past 30 years the profession has evolved from testing differences among sample means with simple *t*-tests to complex computer models and multivariate analyses. This transition continues as important, new methods emerge.

Scientific inquiry involves a systematic series of steps; wildlife research prior to the last 2 decades had taken only the initial steps in the process. Realization of this problem became more prominent after Romesburg (1981:293) recommended that we move from "unreliable knowledge" to management based on a series of carefully tested hypotheses and conclusions based on sound scientific inquiry.

Experimental vs. Descriptive Research

Most wildlife research prior to 1985 was descriptive. Experimental research is the most powerful tool for identifying causes and should be used more in wildlife studies. However, descriptive natural-history studies, field studies, and carefully designed comparisons based on probability sampling continue to be useful. Descriptive research is an essential, initial phase of wildlife science, which can produce answers to important questions.

Descriptive research often involves broad objectives rather than tests of specific hypotheses. For example, we might have a goal to describe and analyze gray partridge (*Perdix perdix*) breeding ecology. Thus, we might measure characteristics of nesting habitat, clutch size, hatching success, brood use of habitat, food habits of chicks and adult hens, and mortality due to weather events and predators. From this information, we can learn details of partridge biology that will help us understand and manage the species. If we observe that 90% of gray partridge nests are in habitat "A," 10% in habitat "B," with none in "C" and "D," we are tempted to manage for habitat "A" to increase nesting density. However, many alternatives must be investigated. Possibly habitat "A" is the best available habitat, but partridge experience high nest mortality in this type. Maybe habitat "X" would be the best habitat for nesting, but it is not available on our study area. What habitat types do gray partridge in other regions use? How does nest success and predation differ among regions and habitats? With answers to these questions we can begin to see that defining quality nesting habitat is complex. Nest success may be related not only to a specific habitat type, but also to the spatial and proportional distribution of habitat types, species of predators present, partridge density, and climatic conditions.

Combining descriptive studies with other studies published in the scientific literature should provide sufficient information to develop a research hypothesis (theory or conceptual model, Fig. 1) that attempts to explain the relationship between habitat and nesting success of partridge. Such descriptive models are general, but can help define specific predictions to be tested to examine validity of the model. These predictions can be stated as hypotheses. We can test hypotheses by gathering more descriptive observations or by conducting an experiment (Fig. 1) in which manipulated treatments are compared with controls (no treatment) to measure magnitude of change (+ or −) resulting from experimental treatments. An alternative approach based on building predictive models is often easier and

more feasible than an experimental approach to hypothesis testing. However, it does not provide as firm a basis for drawing conclusions concerning causes of observed differences. Random assignment of plots to treatment and control groups dramatically increases our certainty that measured differences are due to treatment effects rather than some ancillary factor.

Consider again the partridge study and assume we developed a theory (Fig. 1) that partridge adapted to be most successful at nesting in areas resembling their native habitat in Eurasia with its natural complement of predators, food sources, and vegetation cover. From this theory we predict that partridge nesting success in grasslands in North America would be highest in undisturbed native prairie, resembling native, Eurasian partridge habitat and least successful in highly modified agricultural monocultures of corn, wheat, etc. We then formulate the hypothesis that gray partridge nesting density and nest success are higher in areas dominated (e.g., >75% of the available habitat) by pasture than in areas dominated by cultivated fields. The strongest test of this hypothesis we could perform would involve an experiment (Fig. 1) for which we must establish a series of control and experimental study plots. Our study plots would be randomly chosen from large blocks of land where agricultural practices have not changed in recent years, which contain the types of agricultural practices common to the region where we want to apply our findings. Some of these study plots (commonly half of them) will be randomly selected to act as control plots and will not change throughout the duration of the study. On the experimental plots (the remaining randomly selected plots within the same region as our control plots), cultivated fields will be planted to pasture grass to test the validity of our hypothesis and predictions regarding the effect of habitat on partridge nesting.

This process is difficult, because it requires large blocks of habitat, cooperation from landowners, several years to establish pasture grass on the experimental plots, and additional years of study to measure the response of birds to vegetative changes. The comparison between control and experimental plots will provide a basis to reject the null hypothesis of no effect so we can draw a firm conclusion that increasing cover of pasture or conservation reserve program (CRP) habitat in agricultural areas will increase nesting density and success of gray partridge. In addition, we should be able to estimate the magnitude of effects from management efforts directed at partridge production. If we fail to reject the null hypothesis we cannot draw a firm conclusion since it might be due to insufficient sample size.

Some questions concerning wildlife biology are not amenable to experimentation (e.g., effects of weather on populations, or differences in survival rates between gender or age classes). Other potential treatment effects are too expensive or difficult to accomplish. Some treatments may require substantial efforts to convince interested publics of the value of applying them in any single treatment area. Finally, the need to evaluate effects of many habitat or population factors simultaneously may preclude experimentation. In such cases, an alternative to hypothesis testing is modeling. Information theoretic methods provide powerful tools to evaluate potential models (Burnham and Anderson 2002). Incorporating modeling into the management process is a powerful strategy for predicting

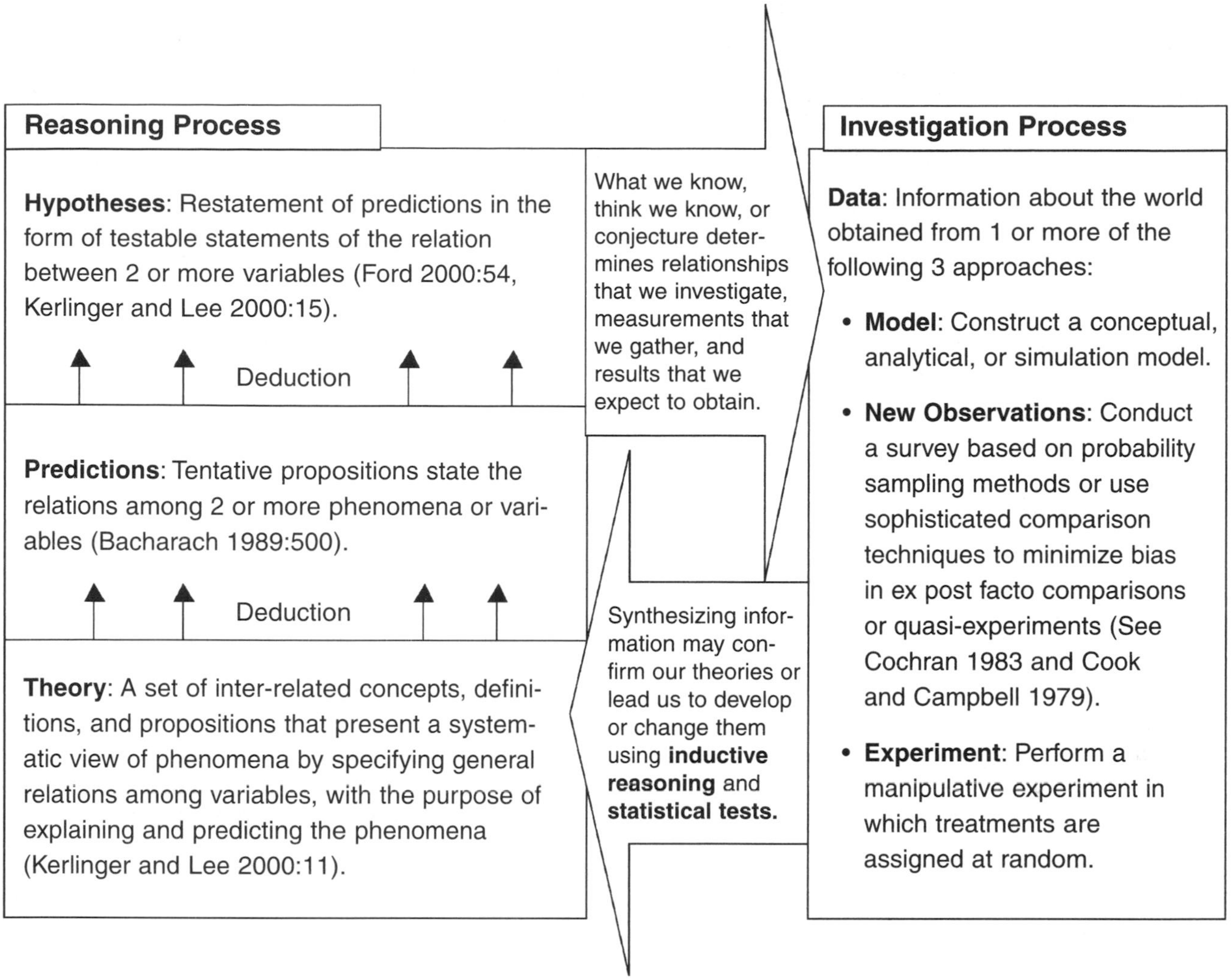

Reasoning Process

Hypotheses: Restatement of predictions in the form of testable statements of the relation between 2 or more variables (Ford 2000:54, Kerlinger and Lee 2000:15).

↑ ↑ Deduction ↑ ↑

Predictions: Tentative propositions state the relations among 2 or more phenomena or variables (Bacharach 1989:500).

↑ ↑ Deduction ↑ ↑

Theory: A set of inter-related concepts, definitions, and propositions that present a systematic view of phenomena by specifying general relations among variables, with the purpose of explaining and predicting the phenomena (Kerlinger and Lee 2000:11).

What we know, think we know, or conjecture determines relationships that we investigate, measurements that we gather, and results that we expect to obtain.

Synthesizing information may confirm our theories or lead us to develop or change them using **inductive reasoning** and **statistical tests**.

Investigation Process

Data: Information about the world obtained from 1 or more of the following 3 approaches:

- **Model**: Construct a conceptual, analytical, or simulation model.

- **New Observations**: Conduct a survey based on probability sampling methods or use sophisticated comparison techniques to minimize bias in ex post facto comparisons or quasi-experiments (See Cochran 1983 and Cook and Campbell 1979).

- **Experiment**: Perform a manipulative experiment in which treatments are assigned at random.

Fig. 1. Circular nature of the scientific method where data are synthesized inductively to develop theories which form the basis for deductively derived predictions and hypotheses that can be tested empirically by gathering new data with experiments, new observations, or models (modified from Ford 2000:6).

consequences of management actions while simultaneously learning about key processes affecting wildlife populations and their habitats (Walters 1986). A key requirement for this process to be successful is the need to monitor consequences of management actions through an adaptive management process (Walters 1986). This adaptive learning process can be facilitated by application of Bayesian statistics, which use additional observations to improve estimates of key relationships assumed prior to the management action (Gelman et al. 1995).

SCIENTIFIC METHOD

One of the early papers published on the scientific method in *Science* in 1890 (Chamberlin 1965) emphasized the need to examine "multiple working hypotheses" to explain an observation. This method is commonly referred to as the hypothetico-deductive method and was formalized in classic contributions by Popper (1959, 1968). The method is a circular process in which previous information is synthesized into a theory, predictions are deduced from the theory, the predictions are stated explicitly in the form of hypotheses, hypotheses are tested through an investiga-

tion involving experimentation, observation, or quantitative models, the theory is supported, modified, or expanded on the basis of the results of these tests, and the process starts again (Fig. 1). Platt (1964) reemphasized the importance of multiple competing hypotheses and proposed a systematic pattern of inquiry, referred to as strong inference, in which the investigator devises alternate hypotheses, develops an experimental design to reject as many hypotheses as possible, conducts the experiment to achieve unambiguous results, and repeats the procedure on the remaining hypotheses. Other major works that provide detailed discussions of the scientific method include Dewey (1938), Bunge (1967), Newton-Smith (1981), Ford (2000), and Gauch (2003).

The most successful applications of the hypothetico-deductive method have been in physics, chemistry, and molecular biology where experiments can isolate the results from all but a small number of potentially causal factors. The classic methods of natural history observation in wildlife biology and other natural sciences have expanded to include experimentation, hypothesis testing, and quantitative modeling. James and McCulloch (1985:1) described this transition for avian biologists: "traditional ornithologists accumulated facts but did not make generalizations or formulate causal hypotheses...modern ornithologists formulate hypotheses, make predictions, check the predictions with new data sets, perform experiments, and do statistical tests." This statement is equally applicable to wildlife research. In addition to James and McCulloch (1985), other excellent reviews include Romesburg (1981), Quinn and Dunham (1983), Diamond (1986), Eberhardt and Thomas (1991), Murphy and Noon (1991), Sinclair (1991), Boitani and Fuller (2000), Morrison et al. (2001), and Williams et al. (2001).

The first step in the scientific method is a clear statement of the problem (Box 1), which includes a careful review of literature on the topic and preliminary observations or data collection. Published studies and preliminary data should be evaluated and synthesized by exploratory data analysis (Tukey 1977) to develop a conceptual model (theoretical framework or general research hypothesis). This conceptual model is essentially a broad theory (Fig. 1) that offers explanations and possible solutions, and places the problem in a broader context (Box 1). The next step is to develop predictions from the conceptual model; i.e., statements that would be true if the conceptual model were true. These predictions are then stated as multiple testable

---

Box 1. Systematic outline of sequential events in scientific research.

1. Identify the research problem.
2. Conduct literature review of relevant topics.
3. Identify broad and basic research objectives.
4. Collect preliminary observations and data as necessary.
5. Conduct exploratory data analysis.
6. Formulate a theory (conceptual model or research hypothesis).
7. Formulate predictions from conceptual model as testable hypotheses (Fig. 1).
8. Design research and methodology for each hypothesis with assistance from a statistical consultant to estimate required sample sizes and anticipate analysis procedures.
9. Prepare written research proposal that reviews the problem, objectives, hypotheses, methodology, and procedures for data analysis.
10. Obtain peer review of the research proposal from experts on the research topic and revise if necessary.
11. Perform experiments, collect observational data, or construct model.
12. Conduct data analysis.
13. Evaluate, interpret, and draw conclusions from the data.
14. Speculate on results and formulate new hypotheses.
15. Submit manuscript describing the research for peer-reviewed journal publication, agency publication, and/or presentation at scientific meetings.
16. Repeat the process with new hypotheses (starting at step 6 or 7).

---

hypotheses. Research should be designed to test these hypotheses; ideally experimentation should be used whenever possible. Included in the design is calculation of sample sizes required to detect the hypothesized effects. Peers and a statistician should review the proposed design before data collection begins. This is also the appropriate time to decide how the data will be analyzed. Data analysis with appropriate statistical procedures leads to rejection of, or failure to reject, hypotheses. Final conclusions usually result in further speculation, modification of the original conceptual model and hypotheses, and formulation of new hypotheses. The publication process is the last, but essential, step, and peer-review comments should be considered carefully before research on new hypotheses is designed.

Problem Identification

The initial step in most wildlife research is problem identification. Most research is either applied or basic. Applied research usually is related to a management problem; e.g., proper habitat management or identification of critical habitat for a declining species. Some problems that require research stem from political controversy or public demand. For example, we may study specific populations because the hunting public has demanded greater hunting success. Other applied studies may be politically supported due to projected loss of habitat by development or concerns over environmental problems such as contamination from agricultural chemicals.

Unfortunately, few wildlife research projects are basic. We rarely have the luxury of studying wildlife populations to gain knowledge for the sake of knowledge and a more complete understanding of factors that affect behavior, reproduction, density, competition, mortality, habitat use, and population fluctuations. However, once there is political support for research on species of concern (e.g., declining raptor populations), there may be a period when research funding is relatively abundant and allows for basic studies. Research on management questions can often be designed so basic research on underlying principles can be conducted for minimal extra cost as data are gathered to solve the immediate management problem.

Once objectives are identified, research should begin with a thorough literature review followed by a descriptive phase. This phase can be omitted if descriptive work has been completed on the specific problem. Descriptive phases amass natural history observations, previous data, and information relevant to the specific study objectives. An important aspect of this phase is exploratory data analysis (Tukey 1977, James and McCulloch 1985). During this process data are quantitatively analyzed in terms of means, medians, modes, standard deviations, and frequency distributions for important groups as well as scatter plots of potential relationships. Exploration of the data should be as complete and biologically meaningful as possible, which may include comparison of data categories (e.g., mean values, proportions, ratios), multivariate analysis, correlation analysis, and regression. The "basic aim of exploratory data analysis is to look at patterns to see what the data indicate" (James and McCulloch 1985:21). If the research topic has received extensive previous investigation, the exploratory phase might even take the form of a meta-analysis of previous data gathered on the question (Osenberg et al. 1999). This phase often involves extensive discussions with other investigators with field or experimental experience on the topic.

Theory, Predictions, and Hypotheses

Exploratory data analysis and perceived associations should lead to development of a theoretical framework (conceptual model) of the problem. Kerlinger and Lee (2000:11) defined theory as "a set of interrelated constructs (concepts), definitions, and propositions that present a systematic view of phenomena by specifying general relations among variables, with the purpose of explaining and predicting the phenomena." Ford (2000:43) identifies 2 parts of a theory consisting of a working part providing information and logical basis for making generalizations and a motivational or speculative component that defines a general direction for investigation. Predictions or deductive consequences of theory form the basis for hypotheses, which are assertions subject to verification (Fig. 1) (Dolby 1982, James and McCulloch 1985). Normally, the primary research hypothesis is what we initially consider to be the most likely explanation but, if the question has been placed into the proper theoretical framework, several alternate hypotheses are presented as possible explanations for facts observed.

We take an important step from descriptive natural history when we formulate research hypotheses. Interpretation of exploratory data analysis, creation of a theoretical framework, deducing predicted consequences, and formulation of testable hypotheses are difficult aspects of science that require creativity and careful reasoning but they are essential to the future of wildlife science.

Study Design and Statistical Inference

Many different research options are available for answering questions about the biology and management of wildlife species (Fig. 2) (Eberhardt and Thomas 1991, Morrison et al. 2001). These options differ dramatically in terms of 2 criteria: how certain are the conclusions reached and how widely applicable are the conclusions? No single option is perfect. The biologist must weigh the available options carefully to find the best choice that fits within constraints of time and resources.

Experiments consisting of manipulative trials are underused in wildlife science. Laboratory experiments, in which most extraneous factors are controlled, provide the cleanest results with the most certainty, but results generally have only narrow application to free-ranging wildlife populations. Their demonstrated power and applicability to studies of basic processes in animal physiology, biochemistry, and molecular biology do not easily translate to studies of wildlife habitat and populations. Natural experiments (Diamond 1986), in which large-scale perturbations such as wildfires, disease outbreaks, and hurricanes affect populations and landscapes naturally, provide only weak conclusions because of lack of replication and inability to control extrinsic factors through random assignment of treatments. Results from studies of natural events (quasi-experiments) are applicable to a variety of populations, especially where multiple similar natural events are analyzed. Field experiments (Hurlbert 1984), in which manipulative treatments are applied in the field, combine some of the advantages of laboratory and natural experiments (Fig. 2). Field experiments span a range from pseudoreplicated field experiments (Hurlbert 1984) in which no true replication is used

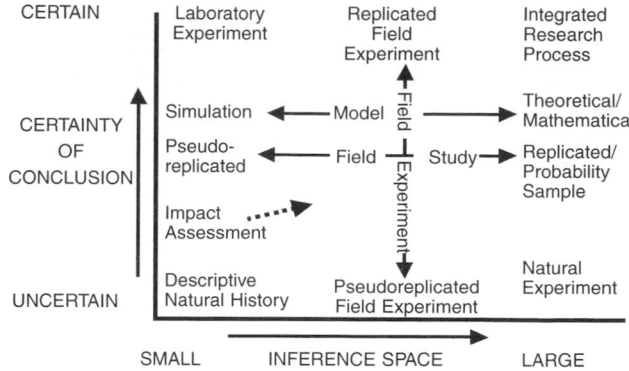

Fig. 2. The potential for wildlife study designs to produce conclusions with high certainty (few alternative hypotheses likely) and widespread applicability (a diversity of research populations where inferences apply).

(or possible) and conclusions are not certain, to replicated field experiments in which conclusions are relatively certain (Johnson 2002). Replicated field experiments provide conclusions that are broadly applicable to free-ranging wildlife populations.

Case studies consisting of unreplicated, natural history descriptions (Fig. 2) are most useful at early stages in development of the research process. Pseudoreplicated field studies are only slightly better than descriptive natural history studies. At the other extreme are replicated field studies wherein no manipulation or randomization of treatments occurs, but true replication occurs within a probability sampling framework and information is gathered to evaluate alternate hypotheses. Conclusions from replicated field studies are broadly applicable, but are less certain than those from replicated field experiments. Some questions of importance in wildlife biology and management are not appropriate for experimentation. For example, we may be interested in the effects of weather on a particular animal population, but we cannot manipulate weather. In addition, we may be interested in the relative importance of factors such as predation, habitat, and food limitations on population changes (Quinn and Dunham 1983). In these cases we should formulate primary and alternate hypotheses in the form of models that can be tested statistically or evaluated using likelihood methods to estimate parameters and likelihood ratios or information criteria for comparisons (Burnham and Anderson 2002).

Designing good field studies is more difficult than designing good experiments because of the potential for extraneous factors to invalidate tests or comparisons. One key step for both experiments and field studies is designing a sampling procedure to draw observations (experimental units or sample units) from the populations of interest. Only if this is done properly can conclusions of the tests be applied to these populations. Survey sampling (Cochran 1963) provides methods that are helpful in designing such sampling procedures. These methods are particularly important for field studies, but are also useful in field experiments for drawing experimental units and subsamples (samples within one experimental unit).

Careful planning of the actual testing process can proceed once a research option has been chosen for each hypothesis. For each hypothesis we must identify exactly what data will be collected and when, how, how much, and for how long. Further, how will these data be treated statistically? Will the data meet assumptions of the statistical test? Is the sample size adequate? Will the statistical hypothesis provide information directly related to the theory or model? Do biases exist in data collection, research design, or data analysis that might lead to a spurious conclusion? These questions must be considered carefully for each hypothesis before fieldwork begins. Consulting a statistician is important, and the statistician should understand the basic biological problem, the overall objectives, and the research hypotheses.

Peer review of the proposed research should be obtained from several people with expertise and experience with the research topic. Peer review will usually improve a research design, and may disclose serious problems that can be solved during the planning stage. Unfortunately, most peer reviews occur too late, after data collection when the final report or publication manuscript is written.

Sample Size and Power

One of the more challenging steps prior to starting actual data collection is to set goals for sample size using a prospective power analysis. The power of any hypothesis test is defined as the probability of rejecting the null hypothesis when, in fact, it is false. Power depends upon the magnitude of the effect (e.g., magnitude of difference between treatment and control or bound on estimate), variation in the characteristic, significance level (α), and sample size. Zar (1999) provides formulas to calculate power and sample size for hypothesis tests but a statistician should be consulted for complicated experimental designs and analyses. Many statistical packages (e.g., SAS by Statistical Analysis Systems) or specialized analysis software (e.g., CAPTURE and MARK) provide capability to generate sample data for analysis to identify in advance how large the sample size should be to detect effects expected.

Effect size (magnitude of effect) is an important factor influencing sample-size requirements and power of a test. However, power and sample-size calculations should be based on a biologically meaningful effect size. Identifying a biologically significant effect usually involves expressing the conceptual model as a quantitative model plus value judgments about the importance of a biological response. Estimating power of the test and calculating sample size requirements forces the investigator to evaluate the potential significance of the research prior to beginning fieldwork. Sample size analysis may lead to substantial revision of the goals and objectives of the research.

Data Collection

All data should be recorded on preprinted data sheets or entered directly into a hand-held data logger, computer, or personal digital assistant. This ensures that each field person collects exactly the same data as consistent collection of data simplifies analysis. Data sheets should be duplicated after each field day (e.g., computer entry, photocopies, or transcribed) and stored in a separate location from the original data set. Data entered electronically in the field should be downloaded daily and backed up for storage at another location. Transcription of data (including computer data entry) must be followed by careful proofreading, which is greatly facilitated by use of error-checking programs. All field personnel should receive

careful instructions regarding data collection, and the principal researcher must check periodically to see that each person has similar skills and uses the same methods for observation, measurement, and recording (Kepler and Scott 1981). The principal researcher has responsibility for quality control and the validity of research results depends upon quality of research design and data collection.

Most novice research biologists are anxious to initiate data collection because of the attractiveness of working out-of-doors and the pleasure derived from observing wildlife-related phenomena. The design phase should not be rushed to initiate fieldwork more quickly. Successful research biologists often spend about 40% of their time in design and planning phases, 20% in actual fieldwork, and 40% in data analysis and writing publications. Data collection can be physically difficult and highly repetitious. Often the most enjoyable and rewarding portion of research comes during the data-analysis phase when the biologist begins to see results from several years of planning and fieldwork.

Data Analysis

Analysis of data should be an enjoyable phase. Frequently this stage takes longer than anticipated because substantial effort must be expended preparing data for analysis. An excellent way to accelerate this part of the process is to begin analyzing the data once a moderately sized portion of it, such as one third, has been gathered. This also facilitates finding major errors in measurement or recording methods before a large amount of effort is wasted. Performing exploratory data analyses to summarize distributions, calculate basic descriptive statistics, and plot preliminary relationships enables the researcher to provide positive feedback to field workers that their work is making a solid contribution while it helps the researcher identify any problems. Analysis methods are covered by Bart and Notz (2005) and in standard statistical references such as Milliken and Johnson (1984), Johnson and Wichern (1988), and Zar (1999). The researcher is cautioned not to lose track of the magnitude of effects or differences in a rush to test their statistical significance. Statistical tests are not the results, but facilitate evaluating the meaning of effects or differences measured. If adequate effort was devoted to planning analysis in cooperation with a statistician during the design phase and quality control was exercised during data collection, data analysis will proceed rapidly.

Evaluation and Interpretation

Evaluation and interpretation is a creative phase, similar to hypothesis formulation. The quality of conclusions drawn is dependent upon the biologist's past educational and professional experience as well as willingness to consider standard and less-traditional interpretations. One great danger in wildlife science (and other fields) is that researchers often have a conscious or unconscious expectation of results. This bias might begin with development of the overall research objective and carry through to the interpretation phase. This danger is so great that in some fields, such as medicine, experiments are performed with a double-blind approach in which neither researcher nor subjects know membership of treatment and non-treatment groups. A scientist must not design research or interpret data in a way that is more likely to support preconceived explanations of biological systems. Biologists who are consciously aware of their own biases and strive to keep an open mind to new ideas are most likely to make revolutionary discoveries.

The first objective is to organize, clearly and concisely, the results of data collection, exploratory data analysis, and specific statistical analyses. These results must be transformed from a collection of specific information into a synthesis explaining the biological system. Do specific statistical tests support one or more of the theories and hypotheses and clearly reject others? Do the results provide a reasonable explanation of the biological system? Are there alternative explanations of the data and statistical tests? Are there specific problems with the data that should be identified, such as inadequate sample sizes or unusual variation in specific variables measured? What could have introduced bias into the estimates? Are additional data required? These questions must be considered carefully and, if concerns are identified, they must be noted in reports and publications.

During this phase, the biologist usually reaches some conclusions based on the data and results of statistical tests. If the data support the hypothesis, we cannot conclude the theory (model) is true, but only that it has not been rejected (James and McCulloch 1985). The central issue is that we do not prove a research hypothesis or theory to be correct. The credibility of the hypothesis increases as more of its predictions are supported and alternative hypotheses are rejected. The goal of science is knowledge and, in wildlife science, we attempt to explain processes within biological systems and to predict how changes will affect specific wildlife populations.

We can assist other biologists by carefully considering how broadly our conclusions can be generalized to other areas or populations. A relatively common problem is that conclusions often go beyond the data. Interpretation of research data must clearly separate conclusions and inferences based on data from speculation. For example, if we demonstrate that droppings from spruce grouse (*Falcipennis canadensis*) are most abundant under lodgepole pine (*Pinus contorta*) and Engelmann spruce (*Picea engelmannii*), we can conclude that grouse use both tree species for some behaviors, but the type of behavior (e.g., roosting or feeding) is speculation without additional data (e.g., observations of feeding activity, and crop or fecal analyses). Likewise, replication of studies across space and time "provides us greater confidence that certain relationships are general and not specific to the circumstances that prevailed during a single study" (Johnson 2002: 930).

Speculation and New Hypotheses

Rarely does a single research project provide the last word on any problem (Johnson 2002). More commonly, research will generate more questions than it answers. Speculation, based on inconclusive or incomplete evidence, is one of the most important aspects of science. Speculation must be identified and should not be confused with conclusions based on data. But speculation is the fuel for future research. Many facts of nature have been discovered by accident—an unexpected result from some associated research effort. However, most research is directional; i.e., it attempts to support or falsify a theory reached by speculating from facts.

New hypotheses can be considered a form of speculation, which is verbalized in a more formal fashion and has a specific, testable format. For example, considering spruce grouse, we can formulate a basically untestable hypothesis that "spruce grouse have evolved a preference for use of lodgepole pine and Engelmann spruce trees." This statement is too vague and requires historical data that cannot be collected. However, we can hypothesize that spruce grouse use lodgepole pine and Engelmann spruce trees for (1) feeding or (2) roosting. Testing these hypotheses we might learn that 80% of the spruce grouse diet is lodgepole pine even though Engelmann spruce is more abundant. We may then hypothesize that needles from lodgepole pine have higher nutritional quality than needles from Engelmann spruce.

Publication

The final step of the scientific method is publication of the research. Unfortunately, many research dollars are wasted because the knowledge gained was not published, and the information is buried in file cabinets or boxes of data sheets. The publication process is the most difficult phase for many biologists. Clear, concise scientific writing is difficult because most biologists have little formal training and inclination in this activity. Peer review may also be damaging to a person's ego, because we must subject our work to anonymous critiques used by editors to judge whether the manuscript is acceptable for publication.

Agency administrators often do not encourage or reward employees for publishing their work and discourage publication in some instances. Administrators are pressured with calls for immediate answers to management problems; thus, they devalue the long-term benefits of the publication process. Effective administrators recognize that peer review and publication will (1) correct errors and possibly lead to a better analysis, (2) help authors reach the most sound conclusions from their data, (3) make it easier to defend controversial policies, (4) help their personnel grow as scientists by responding to critical comments and careful consideration of past errors (which may have been overlooked without peer review), and (5) make a permanent contribution to wildlife management by placing results in a literature format available to other agencies, researchers, and students.

Publication is essential to science. Peer reviews normally improve the quality of a manuscript, but some research may not be suitable for publication. This emphasizes the importance of careful planning, design, data collection, etc. Rarely would any research effort that is properly planned, designed, and executed (including a well-written manuscript) be unpublishable. However, the revision process (i.e., responding to criticisms from the editor and referees) may be painful and frustrating to authors. Overall, the system is necessary to insure quality publications, and authors should not be discouraged by the necessity to defend their work and revise manuscripts. Research is not complete and does not make a contribution to knowledge and sound management of wildlife resources until results are published in a way that effectively communicates to the scientific community and user groups (e.g., wildlife managers). In addition to publication in peer-reviewed journals, research findings will improve wildlife management immediately if they are communicated in other forums such as professional meetings, workshops, seminars, general technical reports, informational reports, and articles in the popular press.

MAJOR COMPONENTS OF RESEARCH
Biological and Statistical Populations

The wildlife profession works with 3 types of populations: biological, political, and research populations. Mayr (1970:424) defined a population as a group "of potentially interbreeding individuals at a given locality," and species as "a reproductively isolated aggregate of interbreeding populations." This biological population is an aggregation of individuals of the same species that occupy a specific locality, and often the boundaries can be described with accuracy. For example, the dusky Canada goose (*Branta canadensis*) population breeds within a relatively small area on the Copper River delta of Alaska and winters in the Willamette Valley near Corvallis, Oregon (Chapman et al. 1969). Between the breeding and wintering grounds of the dusky Canada goose is the more-restricted range of the relatively nonmigratory Vancouver Canada goose (Ratti and Timm 1979). Although these 2 populations are contiguous with no physical barriers between their boundaries, they remain reproductively isolated and independent. The Yellowstone National Park elk (*Cervus elaphus*) herds are additional examples of biological populations with separate boundaries (Houston 1982). Biological populations for other species may not be so geographically distinct as Canada geese and Yellowstone elk, in which case the researcher will have to carefully consider from which biological aggregation their samples are selected and to which their findings will apply. Carefully specifying this biological population is essential in the planning phase of an investigation and may require thorough investigation of existing literature on the species, geographic resources, and reviews of literature on biological aggregations (Mayr 1970, Selander 1971, Stebbins 1971, Ratti 1980, Wells and Richmond 1995, Garton 2002).

The political population has artificial constraints of political boundaries, such as county, state, or international entities. For example, a white-tailed deer (*Odocoileus virginianus*) population within an intensively farmed agricultural region in the Midwest might be closely associated with a river drainage system due to permanent riparian cover and food critical for winter survival. The biological population may extend the entire length of the river drainage but, if the river flows through 2 states, the biological population is often split into 2 political populations that are subjected to different management strategies and harvest regulations. Traditionally, this has been a common wildlife management problem. When biological populations have a political split, it is best to initiate cooperative studies, in which research personnel and funding resources can be pooled to benefit both agencies.

Research populations are usually only a segment of a biological population. From this segment we take a sample resulting in the research population commonly being referenced as the sample frame (Scheaffer et al. 1996). In rare instances, a population may be studied that represents all individuals of a species; e.g., endangered species with few individuals, such as whooping cranes (*Grus americana*). Or, our research population might represent an entire biological population, such as one of the elk herds in Yellowstone National Park. However, the research population usually is only a portion of the biological population and a small segment of the species. Thus, sampling methodology is critical, for it provides the only link between our samples and the research population.

Conclusions from research are directly applicable only to the population from which the sample was drawn, the research population. However, biologists usually have goals to obtain knowledge and solve problems regarding biological populations and species. The key questions are: (1) is the sample an unbiased representation of the research population, (2) is the research population an unbiased representation of the biological population, and (3) is the biological population representative of the species? Because traits among segments of biological populations (and among populations of a species) often differ, broad conclusions relative to a research hypothesis should be avoided until several projects from different populations and geographic locations provide similar results. Combining and synthesizing replicate studies across large spatial extents should be a long-term goal, but may require use of new techniques such as meta-analysis (Osenberg et al. 1999).

Approaches to Evaluating Hypotheses

Descriptive natural-history studies are important for gathering basic information and formulating questions but we must go further by placing these questions within the context of theory and using the theory to turn our questions into testable hypotheses (Fig. 1). Three approaches are available to investigate hypotheses: perform a manipulative experiment, gather new observations, or construct a model (Ford 2000:487). We illustrate the application of these approaches with published studies of wildlife questions.

Managers, biologists, hunters, and conservationists have expressed concern about the long-term effects of hunting, predation, and habitat conversion on elk populations from the Lochsa River drainage in northern Idaho to the northern range of Yellowstone National Park. Large scale wildfires such as occurred in the Yellowstone Ecosystem in 1988 raise concerns of park visitors for their potential negative impacts on elk populations, but they probably are a primary cause of some exceptional elk populations such as the Lochsa elk herd which developed following an enormous fire burning across the northern Rocky Mountains in 1910 (Mohler et al. 1958). Do stand replacing wildfires and similar management activities such as clear-cutting harm or benefit elk populations?

Lyon and Christensen (2002) suggest that fire and logging effects are complex. An observational approach to evaluating effects of fire and logging on elk would be the simplest to conduct. For example we might measure changes in forage resources for elk following wildfires, clearcuts, or prescribed burns following Leege and Hickey (1971). This habitat work shows potential effects but responses of elk must be also documented. DelGiudice et al. (1991) used chemical analysis (N and P to creatinine ratios) of elk urine in snow to provide evidence of nutritional stress in elk on the northern range of Yellowstone National Park following the fires in 1988. Better evidence comes from Singer et al. (1997) who estimated survival rates of radiocollared elk calves before and after the large fires. Their work demonstrated the complexity of effects of fire on large mammals because "density-dependent mortality of calves during winter due to malnutrition and summer mortality of calves due to predation were partially compensatory, but severe environmental conditions produced largely additive components of both summer (increased predation) and winter (increased malnutrition) mortality" (Singer et al. 1997:12).

DelGiudice et al. (2001) used simulation modeling for elk in Yellowstone National Park in combination with snow-urine nitrogen to creatinine ratio analyses to predict more severe nutritional conditions for animals on the Madison-Firehole range than on the northern range immediately following the fires in 1988. Turner et al. (1994) developed a spatially explicit individual-based simulation model to explore the effects of fire scale and pattern on the winter foraging dynamics and survival of free-ranging elk on the northern range. Their simulated elk survival for the winters before, during, and after the fires agreed with observed data and provided the basis for a factorial simulation experiment to "explore effects on ungulate survival of fire size, fire pattern, and winter severity during an initial post fire winter (when no forage was available in burned areas) and a later post fire winter (when forage was enhanced in burned areas)" (Turner et al. 1994:1).

Field experiments to evaluate effects of fires and logging are the most difficult and expensive to conduct but their power to provide insightful results is demonstrated by the work of Cook et al. (1998) who tested the widely held assumption that thermal cover enhances winter survival and reproduction of elk. They placed small groups of young cow elk in 12 pens at the center of 2.3-ha treatment units assigned 1 of 4 levels of thermal cover from dense overstory to clearcuts. They found no significant positive effect of thermal cover on condition of elk during 4 winter and 2 summer experiments. "Dense cover provided a costly energetic environment, resulting in significantly greater over winter mass loss, fat catabolism, and (in one winter) mortality" (Cook et al. 1998:1). Experimental investigations often provide clean results but the value of observational studies and models should be also considered.

Pilot Study

A pilot study is a preliminary, short-term trial through all phases of a research project. Pilot studies are an important but often neglected step in the research process. Information can be obtained that will help the researcher avoid potentially disastrous problems during or after the formal research phase. Pilot studies often will disclose hidden costs or identify costs that were over- or underestimated. Optimal sample allocation (Scheaffer et al. 1996) incorporates cost estimates to maximize benefit from limited research budgets. Use of a pilot study should reveal basic logistical problems; e.g., travel time among study plots might have been underestimated or expectations for overall sample sizes might not be feasible without additional personnel and funding. Statistical procedures for estimating needed sample sizes require variance estimates of variables that will be measured, and these variance estimates often are available only from data gathered in a pilot study. These preliminary data might disclose the variance of the population is so large that obtaining adequate sample sizes will be difficult. It is far better to discover these problems before time, energy, personnel, and critical research dollars

A. Unbiased and precise = accurate   B. Unbiased but not precise = not accurate

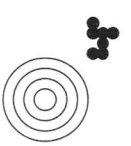 

C. Biased and precise = not accurate   D. Biased and not precise = not accurate

Fig. 3. Concepts of bias, precision, and accuracy illustrated with targets and a shot pattern [modified from Overton and Davis (1969) and White et al. (1982)].

are committed to a formal research project. If the research is part of an ongoing project, or if much research on the topic has been published, costs, methodology, and variance estimates may already be firmly established.

Precision, Bias, and Accuracy

One measure of quality of estimates is their precision. Precision refers to the closeness to each other of repeated measurements of the same quantity (Cochran 1963, Krebs 1999, Zar 1999). Precision of an estimate depends on variation in the population and size of the sample. Indicators of precision of an estimator are standard error and confidence intervals. Larger variation in the population leads to lower precision in an estimate, whereas a larger sample size produces higher precision in the estimator. Another measure of quality of an estimator is termed bias. Bias describes how far the average value of the estimator is from the true population value. An unbiased estimator centers on the true value for the population. If an estimate is both unbiased and precise, we say that it is accurate (defined as an estimator with small mean-squared error, Cochran 1963). Accuracy is the ultimate measure of the quality of an estimate (Fig. 3) and refers to the small size of deviations of the estimator from the true population value (Cochran 1963).

Let us illustrate these concepts with a typical population survey. Suppose we were interested in estimating density of elk on a large winter range. One approach might be to divide the area into a large number of count units of equal size and draw a sample of units to survey from a helicopter. This would define our research population in terms of a geographic area rather than animals. The elements of our target population are count units, and we select a sample of these units using an objective sampling design (a probability sample). Using the helicopter we search each of the sampled units, attempting to count all elk present in each unit. We divide the number of elk counted in each unit by the size of that unit to obtain a density estimate for each unit (Fig. 4A). The histogram suggests little variation in density on this winter range, as most spatial-units (80%) have densities between 1.5 and 2.3 elk/km^2. We need a

A. Area 1

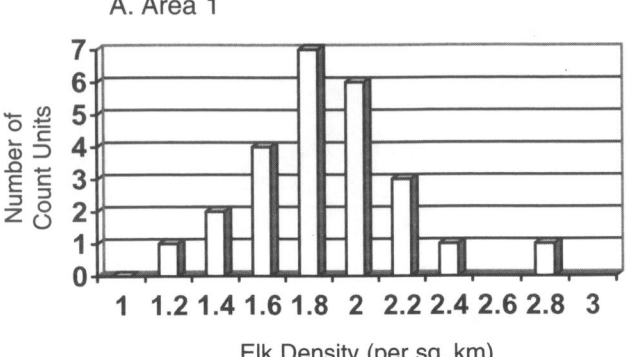

B. Area 2

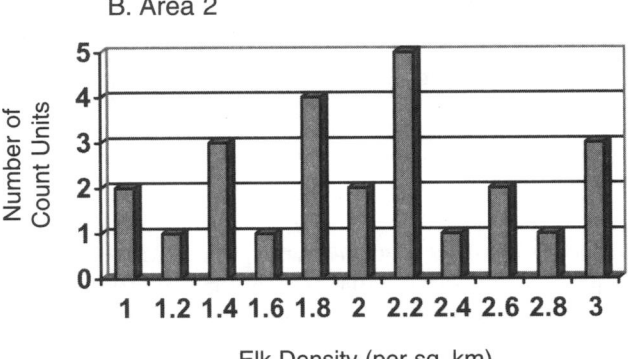

Fig. 4. Hypothetical example of elk counts and density estimates in Areas 1 and 2.

single value that is representative of the entire winter range, and we choose the mean from our sample as the best estimate of the mean for the winter range. The variation from one unit to the next is small, thus the mean from our sample is a fairly precise estimate. But suppose we had obtained different results (Fig. 4B). Now the variation from one unit to the next is great, and the sample mean is less precise and not as reliable as the previous estimate. Thus, for a given sample size, the former estimate is more precise because of less variation in the population.

Would the mean from the sample in Area A (Fig. 4A) be an accurate estimate of the mean density of elk on this winter range? To answer this question, we must evaluate the bias in the estimate. If the winter range was partially forested or had tall brush capable of hiding elk from view, aerial counts in each unit would underestimate the true number of elk present (Samuel et al. 1987). In this example the mean density from the sample would be a biased estimate of elk density on the winter range and, therefore, not highly accurate. If the winter range was a mixture of open brush fields and grasslands where all animals would be visible, mean density from the sample could be an accurate estimate of elk density on the entire winter range. We strive for accuracy in our estimates by selecting the approach with the least bias and most precision, applying a valid sampling or experimental design, and obtaining a sufficiently large sample size to provide precise estimates.

Evaluating bias in an estimate is difficult and, in the past, has been based on the researcher's biological knowledge and intuition. If bias is constant, the estimate can be used to make relative comparisons and detect changes (Caughley 1977). Usually bias is not constant (Anderson

2001), but its magnitude often can be measured so that a procedure to correct estimates can be developed (Rosenstock et al. 2002, Thompson 2002). For example, Samuel et al. (1987) measured visibility bias in aerial surveys of elk from helicopters, and Steinhorst and Samuel (1989) developed a procedure to correct aerial surveys for this bias.

Replication

Sample size refers to the number of independent, random sample units drawn from the research population. In experiments, sample size is the number of replicates to which a treatment is assigned. For logistical reasons, we may measure numerous subsamples closely spaced in a single sample unit. However, we must be careful to distinguish these subsamples from independent, random samples. Subsamples are not independent random sample units because they typically are more similar to each other than are widely spaced samples. Similarly, subsamples in experiments are not true replicates if they cannot be independently assigned to a treatment category. The precision of a statistic is measured by its standard error. Standard error is calculated from the variation among the true sample units or replicates and the number of samples. If subsamples are mistakenly treated as true sample units or replicates, sample variance will underestimate actual amount of variation in the populations, sample size will overestimate true sample size, and precision of the estimate will be overestimated.

To illustrate this point, suppose we wanted to evaluate the effect of prescribed fire on northern bobwhite (*Colinus virginianus*) habitat in a large valley (1,000 km²). We might conduct research on a habitat improvement project that involves burning 1 km² of grassland and brush (e.g., Wilson and Crawford 1979). We could place 20 permanent plots within the area to be burned and 20 in an adjacent unburned area. Measurements before and after the fire on the burned and unburned plots could be compared to examine effects of fire on bobwhite habitat. However, the 20 plots on the burned area are not really replicates but merely subsamples or pseudoreplicates (Hurlbert 1984). In fact, we have only one observation because we have only one fire in a 1-km² plot within the 1,000-km² valley. What would happen if we were to redesign the study to conduct 20 burns on 20 randomly chosen areas scattered throughout the valley. We would expect to see more variation among these plots than among 20 plots in a single burned area. The fallacy of the first design is obvious. A statistical test would evaluate only whether the burned 1-km² area differed from the unburned 1-km² area and could lead to false conclusions about effects of burning on bobwhite habitat in this area. A more appropriate design would require randomly selecting 40 sites from throughout the entire valley and randomly assigning 20 to be burned (treatments) and 20 to be control (unburned) sites. Each burned and control site would be sampled with 5 plots to measure bobwhite habitat before and after the treatment, and data would be analyzed by analysis of variance; the 40 sites are samples and the 5 plots per site are subsamples. Thus, the 20 sites of each type would be true replicates. Treating the 100 burned and 100 unburned plots as experimental replicates would be an example of pseudoreplication. Pseudoreplication is a common problem and investigators must understand the concept of replication and its importance in ecological research (Hurlbert 1984, Johnson 2002).

Table 1. Possible outcomes (4) of a statistical test for declining production in a deer herd. Counts of 500 antlerless deer (adult does and fawns) were obtained each year, and tests of the null hypothesis of no change in the fawn: doe ratio were performed at the 5% level of significance ($\alpha = 0.05$).

| | Fawns per 100 does | | | | | | | |
| | Actual herd values | | | Count values | | | | |
Case	1988	1989	Change	1988	1989	Conclusion from test	Result of test	Likelihood of this result
1	60	60	None	61	59	No change	No error	95% $(1 - \alpha)$
2	60	60	None	65	50	Declined	Type I error	5% (α)
3	65	50	Declined	65	50	Declined	No error	50% $(1 - \beta)$
4	65	50	Declined	62	57	No change	Type II error	50% (β)

Sample Size and Power of a Test

In descriptive studies, sample size required to obtain an estimate of desired precision can be calculated after an estimate of population variance is obtained from previous studies or a pilot study. Formulas for sample size are available for standard survey designs (Scheaffer et al. 1996, Thompson et al. 1998) and for typical hypothesis tests (Zar 1999).

In studies involving experiments or other types of comparisons, sample size is increased to improve the power of the test (defined as probability of detecting a real difference) and to prevent erroneous conclusions. To illustrate power of a test, consider the following example. Suppose we were using fawn: doe ratio as an indicator of production for a mule deer (*Odocoileus hemionus*) herd (i.e., our research population). We want to know if the fawn: doe ratio has declined. There are 4 possible outcomes from sampling the herd and testing for a decline in the fawn: doe ratio (the null hypothesis is that there is no change, Table 1). We evaluate whether the fawn: doe ratio has declined by comparing the test statistic we calculate from our data to a value for this statistic at our chosen level of significance (α). The level of significance represents the chance of concluding the ratio changed when in fact it did not. An α of 0.05 indicates that we would make this error only 5 times if the population really did not decline and we tested it by drawing a sample 100 times. This is referred to as Type I error. But we could make another error. We could conclude the ratio had not changed when in fact it had declined. For the situation (Table 1) where we count 500 deer, we would fail to detect the decline in the fawn: doe ratio 50% of the time. This type of error is referred to as Type II error, and its likelihood is measured by β. When we perform a test, we typically set α low to minimize Type I errors. But Type II errors might be as important (Alldredge and Ratti 1986, 1992) or even more important than Type I errors. Obviously we want to detect a change when it occurs; the probability of detecting a change is called the power of the test. The power of the test is calculated as the probability of not making the Type II error $(1 - \beta)$.

The power of the test depends on several factors including sample size, level of significance (α), variance in the populations, effect size (the true change that occurred), and efficiency of the test or design (Steidl et al. 1997). We cannot control natural variation within the population or the actual change that occurred, but we can control the other 3 factors. Parametric tests (based on standard distributions such as normal distribution; e.g., *t*-tests, *F*-tests, *Z*-tests) have the highest efficiency for normally distributed populations and for large samples. Nonparametric tests (based on ranks of values rather than their actual numerical value; e.g., Mann-Whitney, Wilcoxon signed-ranks test) are superior when sample sizes are small (<30) and populations are not normally distributed (Johnson 1995, Cherry 1998). The power of a test declines as the level of significance is made more stringent (decreasing α). In the example (Table 1), this is a critical problem because the Type II error (failing to detect declining production) is the more serious error. It would be preferable to increase α so that power of the test could be increased. In other situations the Type I error will be more serious and α must be kept low. Increasing sample size increases power of the test. Calculating sample size necessary for a desired level of power is essential to designing a high quality study (Toft and Shea 1983, Forbes 1990, Peterman 1990). However, such calculations should be based on meaningful effect sizes; i.e., what constitutes a biologically significant result (Reed and Blaustein 1997, Cherry 1998, Johnson 1999).

Controls

Observations on control sites are especially important in research design. In nonexperimental research, observations from randomly selected control sites can be compared with observations associated with a particular variable. For example, we may wish to know if habitat used by snowshoe hares (*Lepus americanus*) is different than general habitat availability. To examine this question, we can make observations (e.g., measure vegetation) at habitat-use sites and compare those observations with a series of random sites (controls) that we assume represent general habitat availability. If use sites differ from random control sites, we conclude habitat selection occurred (Pietz and Tester 1983).

In experimental research, controls may be defined as parallel observations used to verify effects of experimental treatments. Control units are the same as experimental units except they are not treated; they are used to eliminate effects of confounding factors that could potentially influence conclusions or results. Creative use of controls would improve many wildlife studies. Experimental studies in wildlife that involve repeated measurements through time must include controls because of the importance of weather and other factors that vary through time (Morrison et al. 2001). Without adequate controls, distinguishing treatment effects from other sources of variation is difficult.

For example, in the bobwhite study, control sites were required to distinguish the effects of burning from effects of rainfall and other weather characteristics that affect plant productivity. There might be an increase in grass production in the year following burning because the rainfall was higher that year. Without control sites we cannot tell whether increased grass production resulted from increased rainfall, from burning, or from a combination of both factors. Thus, we cannot evaluate the relative importance of each factor.

SAMPLING

Most information gathered by wildlife biologists is used to meet descriptive rather than experimental objectives. Examples include estimates of population size, recruitment, herd composition, annual production of forage species, hunter harvest, and public attitudes. In these efforts biologists attempt to obtain estimates of characteristics that are important for management decisions. We want to obtain the best estimates possible within the constraints of our resources of time and money. A large body of statistical literature exists to help; these types of studies are referred to as surveys and the topic is known as survey sampling (Cochran 1963, 1983; Scheaffer et al. 1996) or finite population sampling.

The research population is typically synonymous with the statistical population but may differ when we define the statistical population geographically in terms of units of space or habitat. Defining our statistical population as drainages, forest stands, individual ponds, or square-km blocks often facilitates estimating total numbers of animals and composition of a population. Sampling smaller units of habitat is more likely to be logistically feasible. Likewise this redefinition of our research (statistical) population makes it feasible to apply the powerful tools for sampling from finite populations.

Sampling is also a critical part of experimental research and the test of formal statistical hypotheses. All field studies and most field experiments require creative sampling designs to reduce variation between observations in our treatment or comparison categories. For example, stratification and clustering can sharpen comparisons, but data collected using these methods require analysis by more complicated designs (e.g., block or split-plot designs) (Zar 1999). Choice of specific sampling methods is dependent on the objectives or hypotheses being addressed, the nature of the population being sampled, and many other factors such as species, weather conditions, topography, equipment, personnel, time constraints, and desired sample sizes. A variety of sampling designs is available for biologists to use in wildlife surveys and experimental research (Scheaffer et al. 1996, Thompson et al. 1998, Morrison et al. 2001).

Sampling Design

Simple Random

A simple random sample requires that every sample unit in the population has an equal chance of being drawn in the sample and the procedure for selecting units is truly random. This can be accomplished by assigning each member of the population a number and then picking numbers, to identify members to sample, from a table of random numbers or a random number generator on a computer

or calculator. For example, suppose we wanted to estimate the number of successful hunters in a special hunt where a limited number of permits was issued. We might decide to contact a sample of permit buyers by telephone after the season to measure their hunting success. A survey design checklist (Box 2) helps us design such a survey properly. The population that we want to make statements about is all persons who obtained a permit. The list of the members of the population is usually called the sampling frame (Scheaffer et al. 1996). It is used to draw a random sample from the population. The sampling frame must be developed carefully or the resulting estimates may be biased. For example, if a portion of our permit buyers did not have telephones and we decided to drop them from the list, the results could be biased if such hunters had different hunting success than permit buyers with telephones. To draw a random sample for our survey we could assign each person who purchased a permit a number and select the numbers to be contacted from a random-numbers table or by using a random-number generator.

In other types of surveys, obtaining a truly random sample of the population might be difficult. In such instances another method such as systematic sampling should be used. One approach, when the research population consists of animals that would be difficult to sample randomly, is to change the design. We do this by making small geographic units, such as plots or stands, our sample units (or experimental units if we are developing a sampling design for an experimental treatment) and making our measurement on each plot a number or density of animals. Thus, we can take a random sample and use it to infer abundance across our entire study area sampled. A valid random sampling procedure must be independent of investigator decisions. For example, an excellent procedure to locate plots randomly in a study area would be to use a Landsat image of the study area stored in a Geographic Information System (GIS) program which allows us to select random locations within the boundary of our study area using Universal Transverse Mercator (UTM) coordinates (Fig. 5A). The UTM coordinates of these selected plot locations can be entered into a hand-held GPS (Global Positioning System) unit that will guide us to the exact location. Random-like methods, referred to as haphazard or representative, have been used in place of truly random designs, but should be avoided because they are subject to investigator bias. An example of these methods is the technique of facing in a random direction and throwing a pin over the shoulder to obtain the center for a vegetation plot. Although this sounds random, the odds of a field crew randomly facing away from a dense stand of thorny shrubs such as multiflora rose (*Rosa multiflora*) and throwing the pin into the middle of such a patch is practically zero. Truly random samples occasionally produce poor estimates by chance due to poor spatial coverage of the area or population of interest (e.g., in an area with a small number of important habitat patches, all of the patches may be missed by a truly random approach) (Hurlbert 1984, Johnson 2002).

Systematic

A systematic sample is taken by selecting elements (sampling units) at regular intervals as they are encountered. This method is easier to perform and less subject to investigator errors than simple random sampling. For

Box 2.   Survey design checklist.

Question	Example
1. What is the survey objective?	Estimate the percentage of successful hunters
2. What is the best technique or method?	Telephone survey of permit holders
3. To which population do we want to make inferences?	Everyone who has a permit for this hunting period
4. What will be the sample unit?	Individual permit holders
5. What is the size of the population (N) to be sampled?	$N = 350$ (for special permit hunt)
6. Which sample design is best?	Simple random sample[a]
7. How large should the sample (n) be?	$n = \dfrac{Np(1-p)}{(N-1)\,B^2/4\ +\ p(1-p)}$
	where:
	$N =$ population size (350)
	$p =$ proportion of permit holders who harvested deer (from pilot survey = 0.24)
	$B =$ bound on the estimate = 0.05 (we want an estimate with $p \pm 0.05$ confidence)
	Therefore
	$n = \dfrac{350(0.24)(1-0.24)}{(350-1)(0.05)^2/4 + 0.24(1-0.24)}$
	$n = 159$; i.e., we should contact approximately 160 permit holders
8. Have you contacted a statistician to review design?	Yes!

[a] Scheaffer et al. (1996:99).

example, if we wanted to sample bird-watchers leaving a wildlife management area it would be difficult to draw a truly random sample. However, it would be easy to draw a systematic sample of 10% of the population by sampling every tenth person leaving the area. Systematic sampling is also used extensively in vegetation measurements because of its ease of use in the field. Systematic sampling is almost exclusively used in geographic sampling because it makes possible evaluation of the spatial pattern of variability (e.g., spatial autocorrelation), which is used for most modern spatial modeling. A valid application requires random placement of the first plot followed by systematic placement of subsequent plots, usually along a transect or in a grid pattern (Fig. 5B). This approach often provides greater information per unit cost than simple random sampling because the sample is distributed uniformly over the entire population or study area. For random populations (i.e., no serial correlation, cyclic pattern, or long-period trend), systematic samples give estimates with the same variance as simple random samples.

The major danger with systematic samples is that they may give biased estimates with periodic populations (i.e., with regular or repeating cycles). For example, if we were interested in estimating the number of people using a wildlife management area, we might establish a check station and take a systematic sample of days during the season. This procedure could yield extremely biased results if we chose to take a sample of one-seventh of the days. If our sample day fell during the work week, we could obtain different results than if it was during the weekend. Additionally, our estimate of variance would likely be too small,

leading us to conclude that our estimate was much more precise than in reality. In this situation the population sampled obviously is periodic; in other situations the periodicity might be quite subtle. Thus, systematic sampling must be used with caution. The formal procedure is conducted by randomly selecting one of the first k elements to sample and every kth element thereafter. For example, if we wanted to sample 10% of our population, k would equal 10 and we would draw a random number between 1 and 10. Suppose we selected 3, we would then sample the third element and every tenth element thereafter (i.e., 13th, 23rd, 33rd, . . .). At a check station we might use this approach to sample 10% of the deer hunters or bird watchers that came through the station. When locating plots along a transect, we would randomly locate the starting point of the transect and then place plot centers at fixed intervals along the transect such as every 100 m. Advantages and disadvantages of random and systematic sampling have been reviewed by Thompson et al. (1998), Krebs (1999), and Morrison et al. (2001).

Stratified Random

In many situations, obvious subpopulations exist within one total population. For example, tourists, bird-watchers, and hunters are readily divided into residents and nonresidents. A study area can be divided into habitats. A population of animals can be divided into age or gender groups. If members of these subpopulations are similar in terms of the characteristics we are estimating and the subpopulations themselves differ from each other in the characteristic of interest, a powerful design to use is stratified random

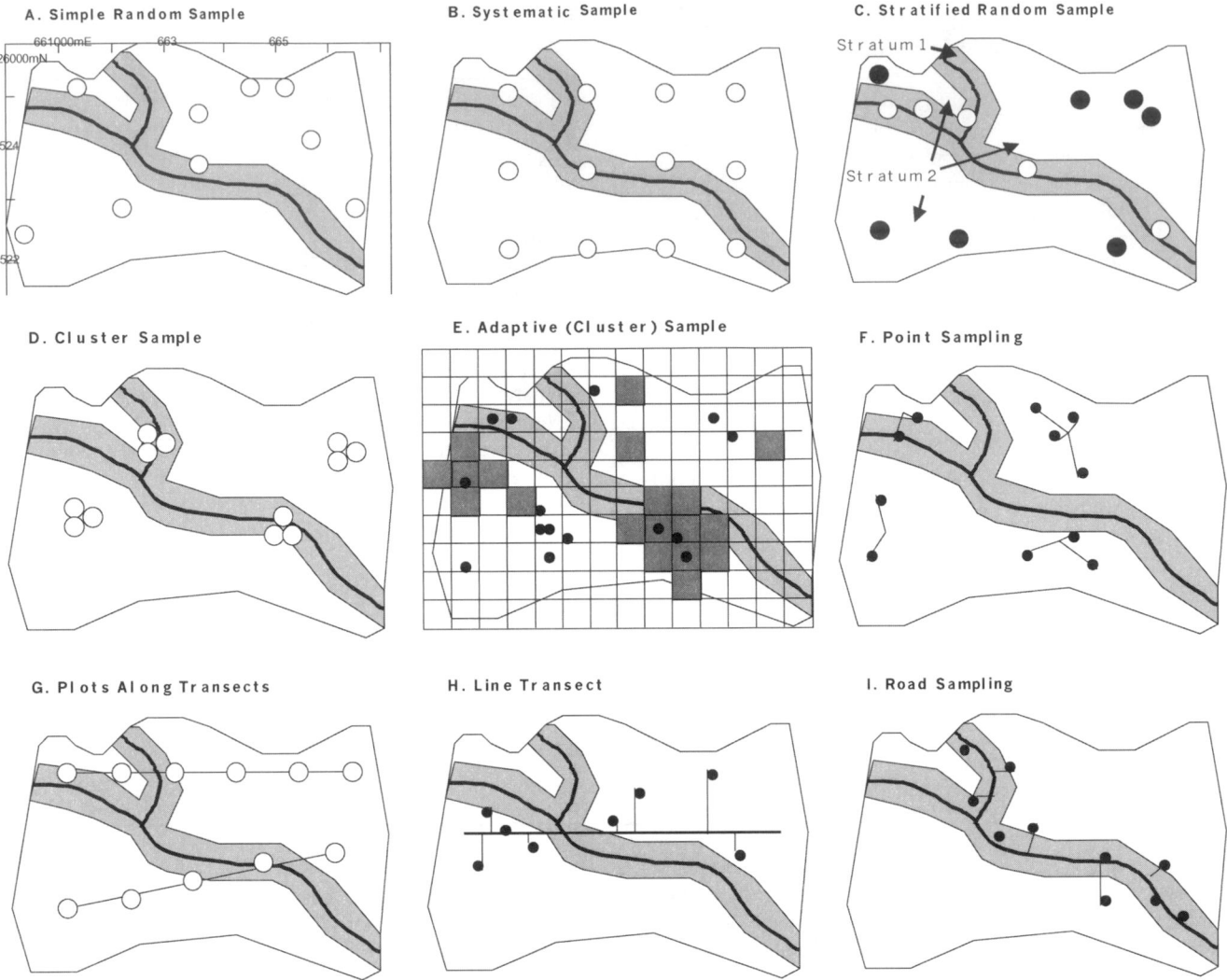

Fig. 5. Examples of sampling methods: A = simple random sample, B = systematic sample, C = stratified random sample, D = cluster sample, E = adaptive cluster sampling, F = point sampling, G = plots along transects, H = line transect, and I = road sampling.

sampling. Subpopulations are referred to as "strata," and we draw a simple random sample of members from each of these strata. Stratified random sampling is also useful if we are particularly interested in the estimates for the sub-populations themselves. The strata are chosen so they contain units of identifiably different sample characteristics, usually with lower variance within each stratum.

For example, if the objective of a study of moose (*Alces alces*) is to estimate moose density, we might define strata on the basis of habitats (e.g., bogs and riparian willow [*Salix* spp.] patches, unburned forests, and burned forest). We then draw a simple random sample from each of these strata (Fig. 5C). If moose density is different among strata, variation in each stratum will be less than the overall variation. Thus, we will obtain a better estimate of moose density for the same or less cost. If strata are not different, stratified estimators may not be as precise as simple random estimators. In some instances, cost of sampling is less for stratified random sampling than for simple random sampling. A final advantage of stratified random sampling is that separate estimates for each stratum (e.g., moose density in willows and in forests) are obtained at no extra cost. The formal procedure for stratified random sampling

consists of 3 steps: (1) clearly specify the strata—they must be mutually exclusive and exhaustive, (2) classify all sampling units into their stratum, and (3) draw a simple random sample from each stratum. Formulas are available to calculate the sample size and optimal allocation of effort to strata (Scheaffer et al. 1996, Krebs 1999). A pilot survey can be analyzed using analysis of variance (ANOVA) to learn if stratification is indicated. If cover types define strata, most GIS software will automatically select random coordinates within cover types making stratified random samples easy to select.

Cluster Sampling

A cluster sample is a simple random sample in which each sample unit is a cluster or collection of observations (Fig. 5D). This approach has wide application in wildlife biology because many birds and mammals occur in groups during all or part of the year. When we draw samples from such populations we draw clusters of observations; i.e., groups of animals. Likewise, many wildlife user groups (e.g., waterfowl hunters, park visitors) occur in clusters (e.g., boats in wetlands, vehicles along highways). Cluster sampling is also useful where cost or time to travel from

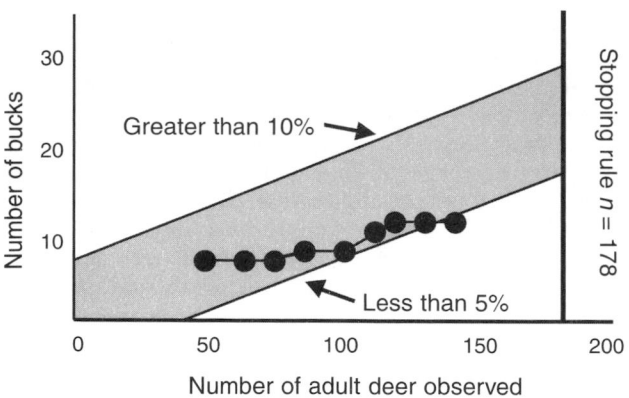

Fig. 6. Sequential sampling for percentage bucks in a deer herd.

one sample unit to the next is prohibitive. This is commonly the situation in surveys of animals and habitat. The formal procedure for cluster sampling consists of 3 steps: (1) specify the appropriate clusters and make a list of all clusters, (2) draw a simple random sample of clusters, and (3) measure all elements of interest within each cluster selected.

Making a formal list of clusters is rarely possible or essential. Instead, we emphasize obtaining a random sample of clusters. If the sample units are animals, which naturally occur in groups, the size of the clusters will vary from group to group depending on the social behavior of the species. Cluster sampling of habitat is performed by choosing a random sample of locations and then locating multiple plots in a cluster at each location. In this case, the researcher sets cluster size. The optimal number of plots (cluster size) depends upon the pattern of variability in habitat. If plots in a cluster tend to be similar (little variability within a cluster), cluster size should be small. If plots in a cluster tend to be heterogeneous (high variability within a cluster), cluster size should be large. For other types of cluster samples such as groups of animals or people in vehicles, cluster size is not under control but is a characteristic of the population. For example, aerial surveys of elk and deer on winter ranges result in samples of animals in clusters. Estimates of herd composition (e.g., fawn: doe or bull: cow ratios) are readily obtained by treating these data as cluster samples (Bowden et al. 1984).

Adaptive Sampling

Adaptive sampling is a recent development in sampling design. It differs from earlier methods because the sample size is not set at the start of the sampling effort, but rather depends upon the results obtained during sampling. Thompson and Ramsey (1983) pioneered adaptive cluster sampling for gathering information on rare animals and plants, which often are clustered in occurrence. In adaptive cluster sampling, an initial sample of units is drawn by a random or other standard design and neighboring units are also sampled for any unit that satisfies a criterion such as having more than *x* individuals present (Thompson and Seber 1996). The initial sampling unit and neighbors (where sampled) form neighborhoods analogous to clusters and are treated similar to cluster sampling. Size of clusters does not need to be constant nor is it known in advance. For spatially clustered animals or plants, the

neighborhood consists of adjacent spatial sample units (Fig. 5E). Smith et al. (1995) showed that adaptive cluster sampling would be relatively more efficient than simple random sampling for estimating densities of some species of wintering waterfowl if the right sample unit size and criterion for further sampling in the neighborhood were chosen. The species for which it would be superior show more highly clustered distributions. For other species, conventional sampling designs with fixed sample sizes were superior. Thompson and Seber (1996) provided numerous examples of applications of adaptive sampling under conventional sampling designs and estimation methods, as well as applications based on maximum likelihood methods and Bayesian approaches. Thompson et al. (1998) and Morrison et al. (2001) also review the basic concept and provide simple examples.

Sequential Sampling

Another recent development is use of sequential sampling, which differs from the classical statistical approach in that sample size is not fixed in advance. Instead, samples are drawn one at a time and, after each sample is taken, the researcher decides whether a conclusion can be reached. Sampling is continued until either the null hypothesis is rejected or the estimate has adequate precision. This type of sampling is applicable to wildlife studies where sampling is performed serially; i.e., the result of each sample is known before the next sample is drawn (Krebs 1999). The major advantage of this approach is that it usually minimizes sample size saving time and money. After an initial sample of moderately small size is obtained, successive samples are added until the desired precision is met, the null hypothesis can be rejected, or a maximum sample size under a stopping rule has been reached. This approach typically requires < one-third the sample size required in a standard design (Krebs 1999:304). For example, if we wanted to survey deer on a winter range to ensure that harvest had not reduced buck abundance below a management guideline of 5% bucks, we would develop a graph (Fig. 6) and plot the results of successive samples as shown (Krebs 1999:312). We must choose a level of significance for our test (e.g., $\alpha = 0.10$) and a power for the test $(1 - \beta = 0.90)$ and specify an upper rejection region (>10% bucks) above, which we assume the population has not been adversely impacted by buck-only harvests. Once an initial sample of 50 deer has been obtained, sequential groups of deer encountered are added and totals plotted on the graph until the line crosses one of the upper or lower lines or the stopping rule is reached. For example, (Fig. 6) the lower rejection line was reached at a sample size of 140. At this point the null hypothesis that bucks were >5% would be rejected and the conclusion would be there were <5% bucks remaining. An important constraint is the sample must be distributed throughout the entire population so that a simple random sample of deer groups is obtained. This would be most feasible using aerial surveys from helicopter or fixed-wing aircraft.

Other Sampling Methods

Many other sampling designs are available. For example, 2-stage cluster sampling involves surveying only a portion of the members of each cluster drawn in the sample. This approach is efficient when clusters are large.

Cluster sampling is one version of the more general method referred to as ratio estimation (Cochran 1963). Related methods are regression estimation and double sampling (Scheaffer et al. 1996), which have wide potential for application to wildlife research. The interested reader should consult a standard reference on sampling techniques (Scheaffer et al. 1996) and work with a statistician experienced in survey sampling.

Sampling Methodology

Plots

Plots are used widely to sample habitat characteristics and count animal numbers and sign. Plots represent small geographic areas (circular, square, or rectangular) that are the elements of the geographically defined population. The research population size is the number of these geographic areas (plots) that would cover the entire study area. Sufficient time, money, and personnel to study an entire area are usually not available, and a subset of plots is used with the assumption that it is representative of the area. Any of the survey designs (simple random, systematic, stratified random, cluster, etc.), or more complicated designs such as 2-stage designs may be applied (Cochran 1963). Selecting the best design requires insight into characteristics and patterns of distribution of species across the landscape. One advantage of this approach is that size of the population is known and totals can be estimated (Seber 1982). Selection of plot size and shape, also an important consideration, has been reviewed by Krebs (1999).

Point Sampling

In point sampling, a set of points is established throughout the population and measurements are taken from each sample point (Fig. 5F). A common measurement is distance from the point to a member of the population (e.g., plant or calling bird). Examples include point quarter and nearest neighbor methods used widely to estimate density of trees and shrubs (Mueller-Dombois and Ellenberg 1974), and the variable circular plot method of estimating songbird density (Reynolds et al. 1980). If observers doing point counts for birds record the distance to each bird detected, as in the variable circular plot approach, transforming distances to areas makes it easy to apply the extensive methods and algorithms developed for line transects (Buckland et al. 1993, Laake et al. 1994). Selection of sample points usually follows a systematic design, but other sample designs can be used as long as points are spaced sufficiently that few members of the population are sampled more than once. Necessary sample size can be estimated from formulas even if population size is assumed to be large or unknown (Zar 1999).

Transects

A transect is a straight line or series of straight-line segments placed in the area to be sampled. Transects are used to organize or simplify establishment of a series of sample points or plots, and as a sample unit themselves. Transects are used widely to obtain systematic samples of spatially distributed populations (e.g., plants). In these situations, plots along transects are actual sample units (Fig. 5G), and should be treated as described under systematic sampling. Plots can also be placed along transects at random intervals. When transects are used as sample units, they are commonly referred to as line transects (Burnham et al. 1980). Measurements of perpendicular distance, or sighting distance and angle, to the sampled elements (e.g., flushing animals, groups of animals, carcasses, snags, etc.) are recorded (Fig. 5H). These distances are used to estimate effective width of the area sampled by the transect (Seber 1982, Buckland et al. 1993). Each transect is treated as an independent observation, and transects should be non-overlapping according to established sampling designs (e.g., simple random, systematic, stratified random). Transects are often easier to establish in rough terrain than are plots, but they must be established carefully with compass or transit and measuring tape or with a GPS unit. Use of transects is becoming more widespread in aerial survey work because of development of precise navigational systems (Patric et al. 1988, Anthony and Stehn 1994). The critical assumptions for transect methods for sampling mobile objects such as animals (i.e., 100% detection for objects directly on the line, no movement toward or away from the observer before detection) must be examined carefully before this sampling method is selected (Burnham et al. 1980). In certain cases, more sophisticated methods may be used to adjust counts for less than perfect detection on the line (Buckland et al. 1993, Manly et al. 1996, Quang and Becker 1996). A strip transect appears similar, but it is really a long, thin plot, because the method assumes all animals or objects in the strip are counted (Krebs 1999).

Road Sampling

Sampling from roads is a widely used method for obtaining observations of species sparsely distributed over large areas, or for distributing observations of abundant species over a large geographic area. This sampling method is usually the basis for spotlight surveys of nocturnal species such as white-tailed deer (Boyd et al. 1986), black-tailed jackrabbits (*Lepus californicus*) (Chapman and Willner 1986), brood and call counts of upland game birds (Kozicky et al. 1952), scent-station surveys (Nottingham et al. 1989), and the Breeding Bird Survey (Robbins et al. 1986). This approach involves drawing a sample from a population defined as that population occupying an area within a distance x of a road (Fig. 5I). The distance x is generally unknown and varies with any factor that would affect detection of an animal, such as conspicuousness, density, type of vegetation cover, or background noise for surveys based on aural cues.

Roads rarely provide unbiased estimates for a region because they are generally placed along ridges or valleys and avoid steep or wet areas. Further, roads modify habitat for many species and may attract some wildlife. For example, during snow periods some bird species will come to roads for grit and spilled grain. Thus, sampling along roads rarely provides a representative sample of habitat (e.g., Hanowski and Niemi 1995). Although this bias is well known, it is often ignored in exchange for the cost efficient and easy method. As with all indices, every effort should be made to standardize counting conditions along fixed, permanently located routes (Caughley 1977); however, this alone does not guarantee reliable counts (Anderson 2001, Thompson 2002). Sampling along roads can be an efficient approach if it is designed as a random sample from a stratum adjacent to roads that is one element of a

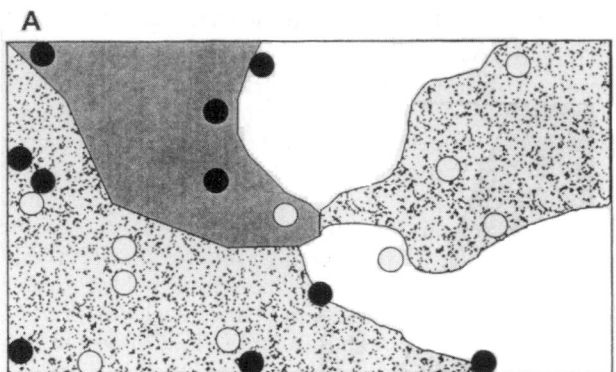 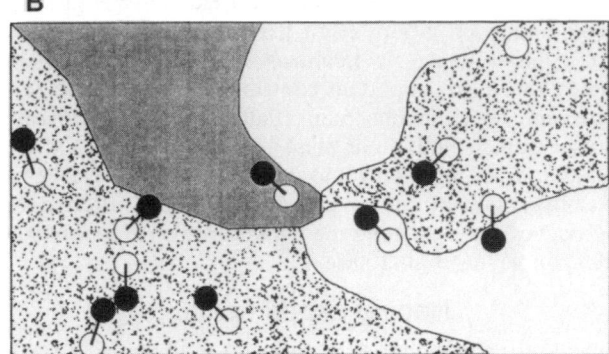

Fig. 7. Illustrative examples of (A) use (O) and random plots (●), and (B) use plots paired with random plots.

stratified random sample of the entire area including other strata distant from roads (Bate et al. 1999).

Dependent (Paired) and Independent Observations

If we wish to make population comparisons, pairing observations is a powerful tool for detecting differences. If there is a correlation between members of a pair, treating them as dependent or paired observations can improve the power of tests for differences. For example, to compare diets of adult female mountain sheep (*Ovis canadensis*) and lambs, we might treat a ewe with a lamb as a pair and measure the diet of each animal by counting the number of bites of each plant they eat while foraging together. Treating these observations as pairs would sharpen comparison between age classes because it would compare animals foraging together and experiencing the same availability of plants. Pairing is a powerful technique in other contexts in which there is dependency between the observations. Pairing should be used only if an association really exists, otherwise power of comparison will be decreased.

Pairing also can be used to help answer a different question. For example, studies of habitat selection are often made by locating areas used by a species (i.e., nest sites or radio locations) and measuring habitat characteristics at these use sites with sample plots. Available habitats are measured from random sample plots throughout the study area (Fig. 7A). A comparison of use and random plots is used to identify characteristics of areas selected by the species. An alternative approach involves pairing use and random plots by selecting a random plot within a certain distance of the use plot (Fig. 7B). For analysis, use and random plots are paired (i.e., random plot locations are dependent on use sites). This comparison could produce different results from the unpaired comparison because it would be testing for habitat differences within areas used by the species (microhabitat selection), whereas the unpaired comparison (e.g., independent plots) would be testing for habitat differences between areas used by the species and typical habitat available within the general study area (macrohabitat selection). Choosing a paired or unpaired design will depend on the objectives of the study but both may be useful in applying a hierarchical approach to studying habitat selection (Wiens 1973, Johnson 1980).

STUDY DESIGN

Hypothesis testing incorporates 1 or more of 4 basic research options: field studies, natural experiments, field experiments (Hurlbert 1984), and laboratory experiments (Fig. 2). Wildlife field studies are common, but interpretation of the results has severe limitations. Experiments span a continuum from natural experiments over which we have no control to completely controlled laboratory experiments (Table 2).

Field Studies

Field studies, sometimes called mensurative or observational experiments, are similar to experiments in that they are conducted to test hypotheses, but they differ because treatments are not assigned at random. Making inferences from field studies is difficult because we make *ex post facto* (Kerlinger 1973) or after the fact comparisons between groups. Drawing firm conclusions is difficult, because these groups also differ in many other aspects. For example, in a field study of dietary selection by Canada geese we might randomly select plots where flocks of geese have fed and those where they have not fed to examine if geese chose areas with vegetation that is more nutritious. If they did, a weak inference would be that geese are choosing nutritious food, but numerous alternative explanations remain untested (e.g., maybe geese preferred hilltop sites where visibility was good, and coincidentally these were also sites farmers fertilized most heavily to compensate for wind–soil erosion from previous years of

Table 2. Strengths and weaknesses of different types of experiments (modified from Diamond 1986).

	Experiment		
	Laboratory	Field	Natural
Control of independent variables[a]	Highest	Medium	Low
Ease of inference	High	Medium	Low
Potential scale (time and space)	Lowest	Medium	Highest
Scope (range of manipulations)	Lowest	Medium	High
Realism	Low	High	Highest
Generality	Low	Medium	High

[a] Active regulation and /or site matching.

tillage). The important aspect of a field study is that we have comparison groups (e.g., fed upon vs. non-fed upon plots), but we have no treatments. Well-designed field studies can make important contributions to wildlife science and management (e.g., Paltridge and Southgate 2001), but their limitations must not be overlooked. Many statisticians strongly object to performing hypothesis tests on observational data and recommend alternative approaches for evaluating the data (Cherry 1998, Johnson 1999, Anderson et al. 2000).

Natural Experiments

Natural experiments are similar to field studies except that we study the effects of uncontrolled treatments such as wildfires, hurricanes, mass mortality from diseases, agricultural practices, and range expansions by animals or plants. A key problem in evaluating natural experiments is that we cannot assign treatments randomly. In natural experiments the treatment precedes the hypothesis and most comparisons must be made after the fact. In laboratory and field experiments the treatment follows the hypothesis. Many hypotheses of interest to wildlife biologists can be tested only with natural experiments, yet it is difficult to draw inferences from such experiments. The applied nature of wildlife management makes the realism and generality of natural experiments an important advantage. With our Canada goose example, a natural experiment might be to survey farmers in the region to locate pastures that have been fertilized and those that have not been fertilized in recent years. If our observations of feeding geese show more use of pastures that had been fertilized, we have more evidence indicating they select more nutritious forage. However, many alternative explanations remain. For example, perhaps those pastures that were fertilized were grazed later in the summer, and geese preferred fields with the shortest grass where ability to detect approaching predators was greatest.

Field Experiments

Field experiments offer advantages over natural experiments in terms of ease of inference and control but disadvantages of restricted scale and lower generality (Table 2). Compared to laboratory experiments, field experiments have greater scope and realism. Their main advantage is that we can randomly assign treatments. In field experiments, manipulations are conducted, but other factors are not subject to control (e.g., weather). In many situations in wildlife science, field experiments offer the best compromise between the limitations of laboratory experiments and natural experiments (Wiens 1989). In our Canada goose example, a subsequent field experiment would be to select random pairs of plots in known foraging areas. One member of each pair would be randomly assigned to be fertilized to learn if geese select the fertilized plots more than nonfertilized control plots. If they did, a stronger inference about selection of nutritious foods could be made, because random assignment of a large number of plots to fertilization and control groups should have canceled the effects of extraneous confounding factors. Interspersion of treatment and control plots (Hurlbert 1984, Johnson 2002) in fields naturally used by geese strengthens our belief that our conclusion would apply in systems where geese typically forage.

Impact Assessment

The most basic form of impact assessment compares measurements of wildlife and other characteristics at a site potentially affected by development to similar measurements at an unaffected reference site (Fig. 2). This most simple form of impact assessment provides almost no basis for inference because the reference site may differ for a multitude of reasons besides absence of the development. Green (1979) noted the potential improvement in this design that results from making measurements before and after development at both reference and development sites. The basic before-after/control-impact (BACI) design has become standard in impact assessment studies (Morrison et al. 2001) and has also been used in predator-removal studies (e.g., Risbey et al. 2000). However, differences from before to after at reference (control) and impacted (treatment) sites is confounded by natural variation and may not be produced by the impact itself (Hurlbert 1984, Underwood 1994). In contrast to a well-designed field experiment, neither reference nor impacted site is chosen randomly over space and the treatments are not assigned randomly. These severely limit certainty of conclusions and inferences to other areas. The goal is not to make inferences to all possible sites (Stewart-Oaten et al. 1986) for a power plant, for example, but to the particular power plant site developed. For larger impact studies where the goal is to make inferences with more certainty and to more sites (Fig. 2), the basic BACI design must be improved through addition of replication and randomization (Skalski and Robson 1992, Underwood 1994). Stewart-Oaten et al. (1986) emphasized the value of expanding the BACI design to include temporal replication and noted the advantage of taking samples at nonregular time intervals rather than on a fixed schedule. Hurlbert (1984) emphasized that comparing abundances of wildlife from repeated surveys at one impact and one reference site constitutes pseudoreplication that is only eliminated by having several replicated impact and reference sites. Replicated reference sites with environmental characteristics similar to the impact site are quite possible and highly desirable; however, replicated impact sites are only feasible in large-scale impact studies, typically involving meta-analysis of many single impact-site studies.

Laboratory Experiments

Drawing inferences from laboratory experiments is easy because of the high level of control, yet this advantage must be weighed against their disadvantages (Table 2) in terms of (1) scale —laboratory experiments are restricted to small spatial scales and short time periods, (2) scope — only a restricted set of potential manipulations is possible in the laboratory, (3) realism —the laboratory environment places many unnatural stresses and constraints on animals, and (4) generality—some laboratory results cannot be extrapolated to natural communities. Laboratory experiments in biology have been most useful in studying basic molecular or biochemical processes common to all organisms of a class. Laboratory experiments have also provided valuable information on emerging issues such as wildlife diseases (e.g., Cooke and Berman 2000), efficacy of fertility control (Chambers et al. 1999), and interactions between exotic and native species (e.g., Komak and Crossland 2000). In a continuation of our example, laboratory experiments could be designed to examine if geese really can select the most nutritious forage when given several alternatives in a cafeteria-feeding trial.

Identifying one research option as best for all situations is not possible. All options should be considered as possibilities when a hypothesis test is designed. Sometimes the best evaluation of a hypothesis involves using a combination of field studies and several types of experiments. For example, Takekawa and Garton (1984) obtained field observations of birds feeding heavily on western spruce budworm (*Choristoneura occidentalis*) during a budworm outbreak, which suggested that birds were a major source of budworm mortality. Field experiments were conducted to test this hypothesis by placing netting over trees to exclude birds. Survival of budworms on trees with netting was 3–4 times higher than on the control trees exposed to bird predation (Takekawa and Garton 1984). Field observations by Ratti et al. (1984) indicated spruce grouse fed exclusively on certain trees while ignoring numerous other similar trees of the same species. This led to a laboratory experiment with captive birds by Hohf et al. (1987) that tested the hypothesis that trees selected for feeding had higher nutritional content than random trees. Diamond (1986) provided examples of the 3 types of experiments and excellent suggestions for improving each type. Other examples and discussion of experiments were provided by Cook and Campbell (1979), Milliken and Johnson (1984), Kamil (1988), Hairston (1989), and Underwood (1997).

Integrated Research Process

The integrated research process (Fig. 2) builds on a solid base of natural history observations. Field observations should lead to experiments, and the results of natural experiments should lead to field and laboratory experiments. The level of certainty increases as many predictions from the research hypothesis are supported and alternate hypotheses are rejected in successively more rigorous tests that use replicated research options. After such findings are repeated over broad geographic areas or throughout the range of the species, the research hypothesis may become a principle of wildlife science (Johnson 2002). The integrated research process should be the goal of wildlife science.

Outstanding examples of integrated research programs include long-term research on red grouse (*Lagopus lagopus scoticus*) in Scotland (Jenkins et al. 1963, Watson and Moss 1972, Moss et al. 1984, Watson et al. 1994), red deer on the Isle of Rhum (Scotland) (Lowe 1969, Guinness et al. 1978, Clutton-Brock et al. 1985, Coulson et al. 1997), and snowshoe hares in North America (Keith 1963, 1974; Windberg and Keith 1976; Keith and Windberg 1978; Keith et al. 1984). Research on red grouse and snowshoe hares has focused on hypothesized causes of population cycles, while research on red deer has focused on population regulation and density-dependent effects on survival, fecundity, reproductive success, spacing behavior, and emigration. In all 3 examples, descriptive studies and field observations formed the groundwork for subsequent research that included a series of innovative field studies and experiments (natural, field, and laboratory).

Preliminary studies of red grouse in Scotland (Jenkins et al. 1963) provided information on fundamental population parameters: births, deaths, immigration, and emigra-tion. This information was used to form research hypotheses about causes of population fluctuations. Postulated causes initially included food quality, breeding success, spacing behavior, and genetics (Watson and Moss 1972). Using data from long-term field studies coupled with field and laboratory experiments, Watson and Moss (1972) concluded that quality of spring and summer foods [heather (*Calluna vulgaris*) shoots and flowers] affected egg quality, breeding success (viability of young), and spacing behavior of males and females, but territory size ultimately affected recruitment and population density [but see Bergerud (1988) for a critique of the self-regulation hypothesis and inferences based on red grouse research].

The level of certainty increases as predictions from a research hypothesis are supported and alternate hypotheses are rejected via replicated research and successively more rigorous observational, experimental, and modeling tests. Watson, Moss and co-workers took these findings into innovative field experiments in which they (1) fertilized fields to assess grouse response to increased nutritional quality of the heather (Watson et al. 1984b) and (2) implanted males with time-release hormones to monitor changes in territory size associated with aggressiveness induced by higher or lower levels of androgens and estrogens (Watson 1967). Additional and more rigorous research rejected hypotheses that nutrition, genetics, and parasitism were causal factors (although Dodson and Hudson [1992] make a counter argument for the role of the parasite *Trichostrongylus tenuis*), and instead focused on emigration as the key factor in population declines (Moss et al. 1984, Watson et al. 1984a, Moss et al. 1990). These findings led to more research because the mechanisms underlying density-dependent relationships, including summer and winter emigration, were unclear. Recent research has focused on the hypothesis of kin selection and differential aggression between kin and non-kin to explain cyclic changes in red grouse (Moss and Watson 1991, Watson et al. 1994) and synchronization of cycles across large regions by weather (Watson et al. 2000). Thus, the integrated research process continues.

A Checklist for Experimental Design

The design of any experiment must be developed carefully or the conclusions reached will be subject to doubt. Four particularly critical elements in the design of a manipulative experiment are: (1) specification of the research population, (2) replication, (3) proper use of controls, and (4) random assignment of treatments to experimental units. An experimental design checklist is useful to provide a series of questions to assist in addressing these critical elements. Many of the questions will be helpful with design of data gathering for studies involving nonexperimental hypothesis testing. Some experimental designs may address several hypotheses simultaneously; in other designs, each hypothesis may require independent experimental testing.

1. **What is the hypothesis to be tested?** The hypothesis developed from the conceptual model must be stated clearly before any experiment can be designed. For example, we could test the hypothesis that nest predation on forest songbirds is higher at sharp edges, such as occur at typical forest clearcuts, than at feathered edges (partial timber

removal), such as occur at the boundary of selectively-logged areas (Ratti and Reese 1988).

2. **What is the response or dependent variable(s) and how should it be measured?** The response variable should be clear from the hypothesis (e.g., nest predation), but selecting the best technique to measure it might be more difficult. We must consider all possible methods and identify one that will simultaneously maximize precision and minimize cost and bias. It is often helpful to contact others who have used the techniques, examine the assumptions of the techniques, and conduct a pilot study to test the potential techniques. In our example, we might search for naturally occurring nests along forest edges and use a generalized Mayfield estimator (Heisey and Fuller 1985) of mortality rate. This response variable is continuous and we could apply any of a variety of designs termed general linear models (GLM) (e.g., ANOVA, linear regression, analysis of covariance). Alternately, we could measure our response for each nest as successful (at least one young fledged) or unsuccessful and use appropriate analysis methods such as chi-squared statistics applied to contingency tables or log-linear models (Fienberg 1970, 1980).

3. **What is the independent or treatment variable(s) and what levels of the variable(s) will we test?** The independent variable(s) should be clear from the hypothesis (sharp and feathered forest edges in our example), but selecting levels to test will depend upon the population to which we want to make inferences. If we want to test the effects of our independent variable at any level, we must select the levels to test at random (random effects or Model II ANOVA, Zar 1999). If we are interested in only a few levels that our independent variable could take, we use only those levels in our experiment and make inferences only to the levels tested (fixed effects or Model I ANOVA, Zar 1999). For example, if we wanted to evaluate effects of forest edges of any type on predation rates, we would select types of forest edges at random from all types that occur and apply a random effects or Model II ANOVA to analyze the data. In our example we are interested only in the 2 types categorized as sharp and feathered. Additionally, our independent variable must be identified and classified clearly or measured precisely. Finally, how can we use controls to expand our understanding? In our example, comparing nest predation in undisturbed forests to predation at the 2 types of edges might be enlightening and we would analyze the data with fixed-effects or Model I ANOVA. Our final conclusions would not apply to predation rates in all types of forest edges but only to the 2 types that we compared to undisturbed forest. An alternative approach to the design would be to treat the independent (treatment) variable as being continuous and use regression for the analysis rather than ANOVA. Under this design we might specify the treatment would consist of some level of overstory removal on one side of the forest edge and we would apply regression forms of GLM. The response could be measured as the difference in predation rates between the 2 sides of the boundary, which would be regressed on percent of overstory removed. Here it becomes critical to select treatment levels (percent overstory removed) across the full range of forest treatments to which we want to apply our conclusions.

4. **To which population do we want to make inferences?** If the results of the experiment are to be applied to the real world, our experimental units must be drawn from some definable portion of that world, the research population. The dependent and independent variables chosen should define the relationship(s) examined and place constraints on the definition of this population. Finally, we must consider the impact of potential extraneous factors in selecting the population of interest. If the population is defined so broadly that many extraneous factors impact the results, the variation might be so large that we cannot test the hypothesis (low internal validity). If the population is defined so narrowly that we have essentially a laboratory experiment, application of the results might be severely limited (low generality or external validity).

Reaching the proper balance between internal and external validity takes thought and insight. For example, we might want to compare nest-predation rates in sharp and feathered forest edges throughout the northern Rocky Mountains, but the logistics and cost would make the study difficult. Thus, we might restrict our population to one national forest in this region. Next we need to consider the types of forests. We might want to test the hypothesis for the major forest types, but we know the species of birds nesting in these forests and their nest predators differ among forest types. Thus, we may need to restrict our population to one important type of forest to remove extraneous factors that could impact our results if we sampled a large variety of forest types. We need to ask what types of sharp and feathered edges occur to decide which ones we will sample. Sharp edges are commonly produced by clearcuts, power line rights-of-way, and road rights-of-way. These 3 types differ dramatically in factors such as size, shape, human access, and disturbance after treatment. Additionally, our ability to design a true experiment involving random assignment of treatments is severely limited for all but the clearcuts. Therefore, we might restrict our populations to sharp edges created by clearcuts and feathered edges created by selective harvests.

5. **What will be our experimental unit?** What is the smallest unit that is independent of other units, which will allow random assignment of a treatment? This must be identified correctly or the resulting experiment might not have true replication, but represent a case of pseudoreplication (Hurlbert 1984). For example, we might erroneously decide the experimental unit for our nest-predation study will be an individual nest. The resulting design might entail selecting 3 areas and randomly assigning them to be clearcut, control, and the other to be selectively logged. By intensive searching we find 20 nests along the edge of each area and monitor them for predation. The resulting data would suggest 20 replicates of each treatment but, in fact, only a single area was given each treatment. Only one area was randomly assigned each treatment and the 20 nests are subsamples. Thus, pseudoreplication restricts our potential inferences. In effect, we have sampled from populations consisting only of 2 logged areas and one unlogged area, and our inferences can be made only to those 3 areas, not to clearcuts, selective cuts, or undisturbed forests in general.

In some situations, pseudoreplicated designs are unavoidable, but interpretation of their results is severely restricted because, without replication, confounding factors rather than the treatment could have caused the results. For example, in our nest predation experiment if one of the areas was within the home range of a pair of common ravens (*Corvus corax*) and the other areas were not, this single confounding factor could affect the results regardless of which treatment was in which area. A more reliable experiment would require that we identify several areas with potential to be logged, perhaps 15, sufficiently far apart to be independent of each other, and that we randomly assign 5 to be clearcut, 5 to be selectively harvested, and 5 to be controls. We would locate and monitor several nests in each area. The nests in a single area would be correctly treated as subsamples and their overall success treated as the observation for that area. This approach attempts to remove effects of confounding factors and allow development of a conclusion with general application to the populations sampled; i.e., edges created by clearcuts and selective cuts within this habitat type in this region. Including control stands without an edge provides invaluable information for assessing the biological significance of the difference between the 2 types of edges.

6. **Which experimental design is best?** A few of the most widely used designs are described, but we advise consulting texts on experimental design and a statistician before making the final selection. The choice depends primarily upon the type of independent and dependent variables (categorical, discrete, or continuous), number of levels of each, ability to block experimental units together, and type of relationship hypothesized (additive or with interactions). For our study of nest predation along 2 types of forest edges, a single-factor design would be appropriate, but Hurlbert's (1984) argument for interspersion of treatments and controls could be incorporated using a more sophisticated design. For example, 3 adjacent stands in 5 different areas might be randomly assigned to treatment and controls, with areas cast as blocks resulting in a randomized complete blocks design (Zar 1999).

7. **How large should the sample size be?** Estimating sample size needed for proper analysis is essential. If the necessary sample size were too costly or difficult to obtain, it would be better to redesign the project or work on a different question that can be answered. Sample size depends upon the magnitude of the effect to be detected, variation in the populations, type of relationship that is hypothesized, and desired power for the test. Typically some preliminary data from a pilot test or from the literature are required to estimate variances. These estimates are used in the appropriate formulas available in statistical texts (e.g., Zar 1999) and incorporate a prospective power analysis through which we are assured that we have a high (80–90%) chance of detecting biologically meaningful differences between our treatment and control categories.

8. **Have you consulted a statistician and received peer review on your design?** Obtaining review by a statistician before the data are gathered is essential. The statistician will not be able to help salvage an inadequate design after a study is completed. Peer review by other biologists with experience on similar studies could also prevent wasted effort if measurements or treatments are proposed that will not work on a large scale in the field. Now is the time to get these comments!

Single-factor vs. Multifactor Designs

Single-factor analyses are simplest because they involve only comparisons between 2 or more levels of one factor. Evaluating the simultaneous effect of 2 or more independent variables (factors) at once requires use of complicated statistical methods, which should be discussed with a statistician. Under many conditions we can test 2 factors at once without expending more effort than would be required to test either of the factors alone. A complicating issue is the potential for interaction between factors (Steel and Torrie 1980). An interaction occurs if the effects of one factor on the response variable are not the same at different levels of the second factor. For example, if we are interested in the effect of snowmelt date on nest success by arctic nesting, polymorphic snow geese (*Chen caerulescens*), we might discover an interaction between color phase and the onset of spring snow melt. Thus, darker blue-phase birds would have higher nesting success during early snowmelt years because they are more cryptically colored once snow has melted and experience less nest predation. During late snowmelt years white-phase birds are more cryptically colored and experience less nest predation. Many observations might be required to clarify possible relationships in these situations.

Dependent Experimental Units

Special designs have been developed to handle many types of dependency in experimental units. A common design involves pairing. In a paired design we match experimental units in pairs that are as similar as possible. The treatment is then applied to one member of each pair at random. If there is a confounding factor, which we succeed in matching in the pairs, this approach will lead to a more powerful test than if pairing is not performed. For example, if we were studying the effects of spring burning on bobwhite habitat, we could place pairs of plots throughout our study area, being careful to place each pair in a homogeneous stand of vegetation. We would then randomly assign one member of each pair to be burned in spring. The analysis would then examine the differences between the members of a pair and test for a consistent improvement or decline in the burned portion of the pair. Pairing would remove the effects of vegetation difference from one part of the study area to another and result in a more sensitive experiment. If members of pairs are not more similar than members of the general population, the test will be less powerful because of the pairing.

When more than 2 levels of a factor are compared, pairing is referred to as blocking. A block is a set of similar experimental units. Treatments are randomly assigned to units within each block, and the effectiveness of blocking can be tested during the analysis. For example, if we expanded our study of burning to include spring and autumn burning as treatments, a block design would be appropriate. Three adjacent plots would be placed in homogeneous vegetation stands, and spring and autumn burning would be applied randomly to 2 of the 3 plots. The analysis would entail a randomized block ANOVA.

Another common form of dependency occurs when repeated measurements are taken on the same experimental unit through time. This is common in wildlife research wherein the effects of treatments may change over time and must be monitored over a series of years. For example, in our study of spring and autumn burning the effects may be different in the first, second, and third growing seasons after treatment. The plots should be monitored over several years to measure these effects. The measurements are repeated on the same plots, so they are not independent. This must be treated correctly in the analysis by using repeated measures or multivariate analysis of variance (Milliken and Johnson 1984, Johnson and Wichern 1988). Dependency is also common in count data, especially when animals occur in groups (Eberhardt 1970). This lack of independence is often referred to as over dispersion. To properly cope with significant over dispersion the dependency should be modeled. Unless the biologist has extensive training in this topic, close cooperation with a consulting statistician is essential in designing and analyzing experiments involving such complicated designs.

Crossover Experiments

Crossover experiments provide a powerful tool to evaluate treatments that do not produce a long-lasting effect. Selecting pairs of experimental units and randomly assigning one member of each pair to be treated during the first treatment period initiates a crossover experiment. The second member of each pair serves as the control during this treatment period. In the second treatment period, the control unit becomes the treatment and the former treatment becomes the control. In this way the effects of any underlying characteristics of experimental units are prevented from influencing the results. This technique is valid only if treatment effects do not persist into the second treatment period.

Consider the following example. Suppose we wanted to test the hypothesis that mowing hay before 4 July decreases ring-necked pheasant (*Phasianus colchicus*) nest success. We could test this by dividing our study area into 5 homogeneous hayfield regions and then dividing each region into 2 portions. In one randomly selected portion of each region we could pay farmers not to mow their hay fields until after 4 July (treatments). In the other portion of each region, hay mowing would proceed as in most years, with the first cutting during mid-June; these portions will serve as controls. To monitor nest success, we locate nests by systematic field searches, being sure to search treatment and control areas with identical methodology; e.g., search intensity and seasonal timing. Nest success will be measured with standard techniques. After one year, we might measure significantly higher nesting success in the treatment portions; i.e., those areas with delayed hay mowing. However, the number of treatments is small and we are not able to conclude with confidence if higher nest success resulted from the treatment or from some undetected, inherent differences in treated portions of each region, such as nest predators. We implement the crossover experiment by switching in the second year so the original control portions of the study regions now have mowing delayed until after 4 July (new treatments), and the original treatment portions revert to the standard practice of first cutting in mid-June (new controls). If the portions with late cutting treatments again have higher nest success, we have better evidence that delayed mowing is responsible for higher nest success than we had at the end of the

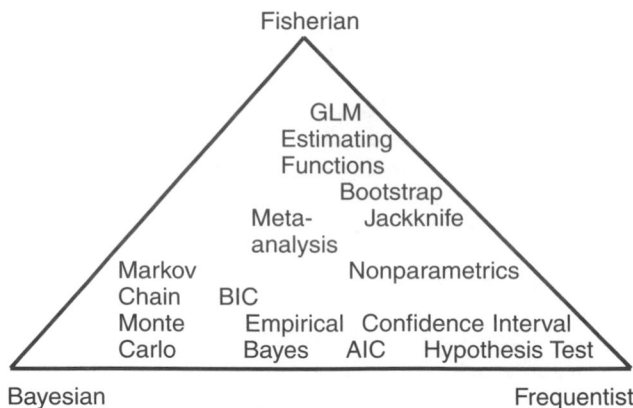

Fig. 8. Selecting analysis methods from 3 dominant statistical philosophies (GLM = General Linear Model, BIC = Bayesian Information Criterion, AIC = Akaike's Information Criterion) (modified from Efron 1998).

first year (i.e., we have better evidence for a cause-and-effect relationship). If even stronger support for the hypothesis is desired, the crossover experiment might be repeated in the same region and in other farming regions.

Fixed, Random, Mixed, and Nested Effects

One of the most critical decisions we must make in design concerns choosing the population to which we want to make inferences. If only a few levels of a treatment factor are relevant or would occur in the future, we set a limited number of values at which the treatment would be applied and the factor is termed a fixed effect or Model I ANOVA. If we want the conclusion to apply to any level of a treatment factor, we must select the treatment levels as a random sample from the population of potential values so a conclusion drawn about the effect of this factor applies across all levels at which it occurs. This design is termed a random effect or Model II ANOVA. A mixed model (Model III) includes both fixed and random effects. In simple 2-factor or multi-factor designs all levels of each factor are applied to all levels of other factors and the design is considered to be a crossed design. When this is not possible, the design must use approaches in which one factor is nested within another factor. A nested design can be described as a hierarchical design, which occurs most commonly where certain levels of one factor only occur within some of the levels of another factor. For example, a study evaluating the effect of vegetation treatment on bird communities might have 3 plant communities with treatments of clearcut, burn, partial-cut, and controls. These factors would need to be nested if one of the plant communities was a shrub community where timber harvest does not occur. Decisions about design of experiments must be reflected correctly in the analysis, as different measures of variance are appropriate for fixed, random, mixed, or nested effects.

ALTERNATIVES TO HYPOTHESIS TESTING

Many of the questions that wildlife biologists and managers wish to answer are not amenable to experimental manipulation and testing. Answers to these questions rely on field studies and natural experiments (Fig. 2). Applying hypothesis testing to such comparisons is invalid under a frequentist philosophy (Fig. 8, Efron 1998), but treating them as quasi-experiments (Cook and Campbell 1979) is done widely in the social sciences. Unfortunately the strength of causal inferences is weak because of high potential for confounding other factors with the measured "treatment" or comparison factor. Alternatives to hypothesis testing are available and have recently become more accepted and feasible through development of powerful computer algorithms.

Regression and General Linear Models

One of the most flexible approaches to identifying predictive and potentially causal relationships between wildlife and environmental or management characteristics involves use of ordinary least squares to estimate parameters of regression or general linear models (GLM) (Fig. 8). Experimental manipulations that produce different levels of predictor variables are more readily analyzed by ANOVA, regression, or analysis of covariance versions of general linear models under a Fisherian philosophy (Fig. 8), named after R. A. Fisher who pioneered a "spirit of reasonable compromise, cautious but not overly concerned with pathological situations" (Efron 1998:99) in the analysis of experiments. Designing a study to gather data on a variety of potential causal variables rather than manipulating those variables through a designed experiment is an appealing alternative but yields inferences of much lower certainty (Fig. 2). Performing hypothesis tests on such data (e.g., testing point null hypotheses) is easily performed with modern regression programs. However, it may not be justified as an inferential approach and may readily lead into a "fishing-expedition" doomed to failure due to high Type I errors. Many statisticians refuse to analyze such data using hypothesis tests and instead encourage biologists to apply maximum likelihood and information-theoretical approaches under a modeling perspective; i.e., identifying the most parsimonious model with good predictive ability (Milliken and Johnson 1984, Anderson et al. 2000, Burnham and Anderson 2002).

It is essential in designing manipulative or observational studies to estimate linear models to strive to obtain observations throughout the full range of the predictive variables. It is especially important to obtain observations at both low and high values of the predictive variable because these set limits for the range of values that can be used later for prediction. The values at the ends of this range have the most leverage on slope estimates. If too narrow a range is measured, a significant relationship may not be detected among the variability. However, a relationship may be linear only through a portion of its range such that beyond a certain level an increasing effect may turn into a negative effect at progressively higher levels. Such situations should be apparent from exploratory data analyses (Anderson 2001, Johnson 2002).

Model Building vs. Hypothesis Testing

Rigorously evaluating ideas concerning wildlife habitats and populations using experimental manipulations may be difficult because we cannot randomly assign treatments and the high cost of treatments precludes adequate replication. However, modeling methods (Shenk and Franklin 2001) and information-theoretic approaches to evaluating competing models can be useful (Burnham and Anderson 2002). A biologist's goal should be to build the

Table 3. Modeling strategy based on objectives (A) and complexity (B).

A. Objectives		
Empirical		
	Statistical estimation	Sampling
		Fixed effects models
		Random effects models
	Forecasting	Adaptive management
	Projection	
	General principles	
Theoretical		

B. Complexity		
Simple		Complex
Conceptual (verbal)	---Quantification---	Quantitative
Linear	---Relationships---	Non-linear
Deterministic	---Variability---	Stochastic
Time-specific	---Time scale---	Dynamic
Single	---Factors---	Multifactor
Single site	---Spatial---	Multi-site
Single species	---Number of species---	Multi-species

simplest model that describes the relationships between causative factors and the effects they produce. The biologist or manager is most likely to select a modeling strategy at the simple, empirical ends of the continua in terms of model objectives and complexity (Table 3). Long-term monitoring data provide the basis for more complex models. In most cases the goal is to model the responses of wildlife populations or habitats with the smallest number of predictors necessary to make good predictions. Likelihood methods are used to compare how well a number of potential models perform against each other. Akaike (1973) developed one of the most popular measures, Akaike's Information Criterion (AIC). This criterion penalizes the likelihood of the model based on how many parameters are required to estimate from the observed data. The model with the lowest AIC (Burnham and Anderson 2002) is the most parsimonious model that gives the best predictions. Burnham and Anderson (2002) contend that information theoretic methods, such as using AIC to assess the information content of a model, should be applied where we cannot experimentally manipulate causes or predictors. Unfortunately, information theoretic approaches do not provide guidance for key issues during the design phase such as necessary sample sizes, which are best addressed by a prospective power analysis. After data are gathered, AIC does not identify how well any model performs but does provide an objective basis for choosing the best model among the models evaluated. One of the limitations of using AIC is that the results are dependent upon the models chosen for the analysis, which may differ between biologists.

Bayesian Statistics

Bayesian data analysis is described as "practical methods for making inferences from data using probability models for quantities we observe and for quantities about which we wish to learn" (Gelman et al. 1995:3). One of the primary appeals of Bayesian statistics is that after sampling a population and calculating statistics such as the mean, variance, and confidence interval for the mean, Bayesian analysis allows us to state we are 95% certain the true mean for the population is within this 95% confidence interval. Johnson (1999) provided an easily understood description of the conceptual differences between the frequentist and Bayesian approaches (Fig. 8). A Bayesian analysis requires performing 3 basic steps (Gelman et al. 1995).

1. **Specify a probability distribution for all quantities** [i.e., use prior studies and creative thinking to specify a particular "**prior**" probability for the parameter(s)]. We begin by stating what is the range of all possible values for the characteristics that we are attempting to measure and make our best guess, from earlier studies and clear thinking, if any of the values are more likely than others. This step is controversial because it introduces subjective decisions into the process and has potential for misuse if one's goal is to "cook the books" to produce a particular result (Dennis 1996). However, well-designed research should gather historical data so that knowledge is available on the probability distribution of the parameter(s) (Box 1).

2. **Use the observed data to calculate a posterior distribution for the parameter of interest as a conditional probability distribution.** This second step in Bayesian analysis follows data collection. We improve our prior guess of the value of the characteristic by combining it with the new data we gathered to state conclusively our best "posterior" guess of the value of the characteristic. This step is performed using Bayes' rule and this Bayesian estimate might be considered as a weighted average estimate based on the sample data and the assumed prior value where weights are proportional to the precision of the observed and prior values (Gelman 1995:43). As sample size increases, the Bayesian value approaches the maximum likelihood estimate and any influence of the prior probability vanishes. Markov chain Monte Carlo methods are used widely for these calculations (Fig. 8).

3. **Evaluate the fit of the model and the implications of the resulting posterior distribution.** The third step in Bayesian analysis (Gelman et al. 1995:3) consists of "evaluating the fit of the model and the implications of the resulting posterior distribution: does the model fit the data, are the substantive conclusions reasonable, and how sensitive are the results to the modeling assumptions?"

COMMON PROBLEMS

Sample Size and Power

The importance of sample size cannot be overemphasized. Sample size and experimental design are the major factors under the control of the biologist that strongly influence power of the test; i.e., the likelihood of detecting a significant difference when one really occurs. Inadequate sample size usually results from (1) inadequate consideration of population variance, (2) inability to collect data (e.g., observe a rare species), or (3) insufficient funding, time, or personnel. Often a sample-size problem is overlooked initially because of failure to consider sample-size reduction throughout the study; i.e., we focus mostly on the initial sample size and not on the final sample size that represents the most important data for consideration of

a hypothesis. For example, in a study of mallard (*Anas platyrhynchos*) brood movements almost 10 times as many nests were required to be found as the sample size of broods indicated because of an 89% sample size reduction from nests located to actual brood data (Rotella and Ratti 1992*a*, *b*).

Another common problem is fairly large overall data sets that are not sufficiently similar among years (or seasons) to combine, resulting in annual sample sizes that are too small for analysis. At the beginning of a research project we often set our desired sample size based on combining data collected over several continuous years. However, if the characteristic of interest was different among years of the study, combining the data would not be valid. For example, in a study of habitat selection by red fox (*Vulpes vulpes*), habitat use might differ between mild and severe winters with heavy snow cover. In this example, combining the data would not be valid, yet the sample size in each year may be too small to detect selection (Alldredge and Ratti 1986, 1992).

A primary defense against weak tests of hypotheses is to perform a prospective power analysis at the start of the research following a pilot study. Zar (1999:559) provided simple ways to estimate the required sample size for most common sampling and experimental designs. In contrast to this essential prospective power analysis during the design phase, performing a retrospective power analysis after the data are collected, during the analysis phase, is controversial or contraindicated (Thomas 1996, Steidl et al. 1997). Retrospective power analysis is uninformative unless effect sizes are set independently of the observed effect (Steidl et al. 1997).

Procedural Inconsistency

Procedural inconsistency is another common problem that can be prevented with proper research design. Problems of this type occur from seemingly minor variations or alterations in methodology. For example, if a project is dependent upon field personnel to accurately identify songs of forest passerine birds, the data set may be biased by identification errors (Cyr 1981). In this situation, magnitude of the bias will depend upon the rate of errors by individuals, difference in the rate of errors among individuals, and relative proportion of data collected by each individual. Research methodology should be defined with great detail, and all individuals collecting data should have similar skills and knowledge of methods used (Kepler and Scott 1981). If inconsistencies cannot be eliminated through selection and training of field workers, the design must incorporate double-sampling or similar procedures to remove inherent biases (Farnsworth et al. 2002). One unfortunate aspect of biases of this type is that they are often overlooked (or ignored) as potential problems and are seldom reported in research publications.

Non-uniform Treatments

A third common bias is non-uniform treatments. This problem is illustrated by considering 2 previous research examples. In the discussion of crossover experiments, we described a 2-year study in which mowing on the treatment areas was delayed until after 4 July. Assume that in the first year of this study, all treatment areas were mowed between 4 and 7 July, as planned. But during year 2 of the study, a 3-day rainstorm began on 4 July, and the treatment areas were not cut until 9–12 July. Although this 5-day difference in mowing of the treatment areas may seem insignificant, the impact on the results and interpretation of our experiment is really unknown—and may be serious. Thus, the second year of the experiment should be repeated. Since dates of pheasant nesting and plant growth vary from year to year in response to temperature and rainfall patterns, a better way to set the date for the mowing treatment might be based on the cumulated degree-days widely published in farm journals.

In the second example, consider again our field experiment to evaluate effects of sharp and feathered edges on nest success of forest birds. If we had used both clearcuts and roadways as sharp edges, we might have hopelessly confused our treatment results because of differences in attractiveness of sharp edges near roads where carrion is an abundant attractant to generalist predators like ravens. High variability between replicates in non-uniform treatments substantially reduces our power to detect biologically significant effects.

Pseudoreplication

Pseudoreplication occurs when sample or experimental units are not independent; i.e., they are really subsamples rather than replicates, but are treated as though they are independent samples or experimental units. This is a widespread problem in field ecology (Hurlbert 1984) that should be avoided wherever possible. In manipulative experiments, experimental units are independent only if we can randomly assign treatments to each unit. In field studies, a simple test for pseudoreplication is to ask if the values for 2 successive observations are more similar than values for 2 observations drawn completely at random from the research population. If so, the successive observations are probably not true replicates and the research should be redesigned or this lack of independence must be treated correctly in the analysis through use of cluster sampling or adjustments in degrees of freedom for tests.

There must be a direct tie between the sample or experimental unit and the research population. If the research population consists of one meadow in Yellowstone National Park, then 2 or more samples drawn from that meadow would be replicates. In this example, our inferences or conclusions would apply only to that single meadow. If our research population consisted of all meadows in Yellowstone National Park, then 2 plots in the same meadow would not constitute true replicate samples. Also, repeated sampling of the same radiomarked animal often constitutes a form of pseudoreplication; e.g., if our research population consisted of moose in one ecoregion, repeated observations of habitat use by a single animal would not be true replicates (and a similar problem would arise if 2 radiomarked animals were traveling together, thus, their habitat selection would not be truly independent). The data would have to be summarized into a single value such as the proportion of the observations in a certain habitat for statistical analysis. This would reduce sample size to the number of radio-marked moose. Treating repeated observations as replicates is strictly justified only when the individual animal is the research population. In this situation, tests for serial correlation (Swihart and Slade 1985) should be conducted to assure the observations are not repeated so frequently that they are still pseudoreplicates.

THE RESEARCH-MANAGEMENT CONNECTION

Wildlife management programs should be developed from application of scientific knowledge; i.e., we should apply scientific facts and principles resulting from research on specific topics such as population ecology, habitat selection, or behavior. Initially, this is a sound practice for development of a new management program. The logic behind formulation of a management program is similar to formulation of a research hypothesis; both provide opportunity for predictive statements. Our management prediction is that our plan of action will achieve a desired result. However, a major problem with nearly all wildlife management programs throughout the world is the lack of research on the effectiveness of programs (Macnab 1983, Gill 1985). Seldom is the question "does our management lead to the desired result?" addressed in formal, well designed, long-term research projects. For example, disparate gender ratios are common among North American mallard populations (i.e., more males than females, Bellrose et al. 1961). Our long-term management response (with monogamous species) is to set hunting regulations that direct more harvest pressure on males. Initially this management plan seems appropriate, the assumption being that we shift harvest to the "surplus" segment of the population that adds little to overall recruitment. However, several important questions should be considered. Does reduction of excess males in the mallard population affect overall recruitment? For example, unpaired males often fertilize females attempting to renest. Is there an evolutionary adaptation to disparate gender ratios? With given levels of harvest, mallard population levels may not be maximized by disproportional harvest of the male segment. No research to date has adequately addressed these questions. If these basic biological questions cannot be answered, hunting regulations to increase male harvest may not be justified because of expensive public education and enforcement problems they create.

A second common example is prescribed burning as a management practice to increase deer and elk populations. The effectiveness of this management has not been addressed, and most evaluations have only noted increases in browse forage species and changes in animal distributions. Increased population levels in response to prescribed burning have not been adequately documented or thoroughly studied (Peek 1989).

A third example is the use of population indices to monitor changes in population levels (e.g., ring-necked pheasant crowing counts). The primary assumption for use of a population index is that the index is directly related to density. Although nearly every wildlife management agency uses trend data from population indices for management decisions, only a few rare examples of index validation exist (e.g., Rotella and Ratti 1986, Crête and Messier 1987). Some studies have disclosed that index values are not related to density (Smith et al. 1984, Rotella and Ratti 1986, Nottingham et al. 1989).

Walters (1986) proposed a systematic solution to these problems, which he called adaptive management. It involves a more formal specification of management goals and responses to management actions through the use of predictive models (Table 3), which can be compared to actual system responses through detailed monitoring (Thompson et al. 1998). Management actions are treated as experiments, which must be monitored carefully to ascertain if goals were met and to identify errors in understanding the dynamics of the natural systems that we manage. Actual responses to management actions are compared to predictions from our models based on current knowledge and assumptions (e.g., adaptive harvest management, Williams and Johnson 1995, Williams et al. 1996). Some management actions are taken to intentionally disturb the system to learn more about system response and its determinants. System disturbances can be problematic if there is considerable public interest in a particular issue and strongly held opinions as to preferred management action.

If wildlife agencies have the responsibility for management of wildlife populations, they also have the responsibility to conduct research on the effectiveness of management programs. Wildlife agency administrators should strive to develop well-designed, long-term management-research programs as a basic component of annual agency operations.

SUMMARY

Carefully designed wildlife research will improve the reliability of knowledge that is the basis of wildlife management. Research biologists must rigorously apply the scientific method and make use of powerful techniques in survey sampling and experimental design. Modeling offers powerful tools to predict consequences of management choices, especially when it is based on carefully designed field studies, long-term monitoring, and management experiments designed to increase understanding. More effort should be dedicated to the design phase of research, including obtaining critiques from other biologists and statisticians, and avoiding common problems such as insufficient sample sizes, procedural inconsistencies, non-uniform treatments, and pseudoreplication. Wherever possible, we must move from observational studies to experimental studies that provide a more reliable basis for interpretation and conclusions; these studies need to be replicated across space and time. Wildlife biologists have a tremendous responsibility associated with management of animal species experiencing increasing environmental-degradation problems, loss of habitat, and declining populations. We must face these problems armed with knowledge from quality scientific investigations.

ACKNOWLEDGMENTS

We thank J. R. Alldredge, J. L. Aycrigg, J. H. Bassman, R. A. Black, W. R. Clark, W. C. Conway, F. W. Davis, T. DeMeo, R. A. Fischer, T. K. Fuller, G. D. Hayward, D. J. Johnson, S. L. Johnson, J. A. Kadlec, S. T. Knick, J. A. Manning, D. G. Miquelle, L. S. Mills, D. M. Montgomery, J. M. Peek, K. P. Reese, D. L. Roberts, J. J. Rotella, D. J. Schill, J. M. Scott, D. F. Stauffer, R. K. Steinhorst, G. C. White, wildlife students at The Ohio State University, University of Montana, and University of Idaho, and official reviewers D. H. Johnson and D. F. Stauffer for valuable review comments.

LITERATURE CITED

AKAIKE, H. 1973. Information theory and an extension of the maximum likelihood principle. Pages 267–281 *in* B. N. Petran and F. Csaki, editors. Second international symposium on information theory. Akadeemiai Kiadi, Budapest, Hungary.

ALLDREDGE, J. R., AND J. T. RATTI. 1986. Comparison of some statistical techniques for analysis of resource selection. Journal of Wildlife Management 50:157–165.

———, AND ———. 1992. Further comparison of some statistical techniques for analysis of resource selection. Journal of Wildlife Management 56:1–9.

ANDERSON, D. R. 2001. The need to get the basics right in wildlife field studies. Wildlife Society Bulletin 29:1294–1297.

———, K. P. BURNHAM, AND W. L. THOMPSON. 2000. Null hypothesis testing: problems, prevalence, and an alternative. Journal of Wildlife Management 64:912–923.

ANTHONY, R. M., AND R. A. STEHN. 1994. Navigating aerial transects with a laptop computer map. Wildlife Society Bulletin 22:674–676.

BACHARACH, S. B. 1989. Organizational theories: some criteria for evaluation. Academy of Management Review 14:496–515.

BART, J. R., AND W. I. NOTZ. 2005. Analysis of data in wildlife biology. Pages 72–105 *in* C. E. Braun, editor. Techniques for wildlife investigations and management. Sixth edition. The Wildlife Society, Bethesda, Maryland, USA.

BATE, L. J., E. O. GARTON, AND M. J. WISDOM. 1999. Estimating snag and large tree densities and distributions on a landscape for wildlife management. U.S. Department of Agriculture, Forest Service, General Technical Report PNW-GTR-425.

BELLROSE, F. C., T. G. SCOTT, A. S. HAWKINS, AND J. B. LOW. 1961. Sex ratios and age ratios in North American ducks. Illinois Natural History Survey Bulletin 27:391–474.

BERGERUD, A. T. 1988. Population ecology of grouse. Pages 578–685 *in* A. T. Bergerud and M. W. Gratson, editors. Adaptive strategies and population ecology of northern grouse. Volume II. Theory and synthesis. University of Minnesota Press, Minneapolis, USA.

BOITANI, L., AND T. K. FULLER, editors. 2000. Research techniques in animal ecology: controversies and consequences. Columbia University Press, New York, USA.

BOWDEN, D. C., A. E. ANDERSON, AND D. E. MEDIN. 1984. Sampling plans for mule deer sex and age ratios. Journal of Wildlife Management 48:500–509.

BOYD, R. J., A. Y. COOPERRIDER, P. C. LENT, AND J. A. BAILEY. 1986. Ungulates. Pages 519–564 *in* A. Y. Cooperrider, R. J. Boyd, and H. R. Stuart, editors. Inventory and monitoring of wildlife habitat. U.S. Department of the Interior, Bureau of Land Management, Service Center, Denver, Colorado, USA.

BUCKLAND, S. T., D. R. ANDERSON, K. P. BURNHAM, AND J. L. LAAKE. 1993. Distance sampling: estimating abundance of biological populations. Chapman and Hall, New York, USA.

BUNGE, M. 1967. Scientific research. I. The search for system. Springer-Verlag, New York, USA.

BURNHAM, K. P., AND D. R. ANDERSON. 2002. Model selection and inference: a practical information–theoretic approach. Second edition. Springer-Verlag, New York, USA.

———, ———, AND J. L. LAAKE. 1980. Estimation of density from line transect sampling of biological populations. Wildlife Monographs 72.

CAUGHLEY, G. 1977. Analysis of vertebrate populations. John Wiley and Sons, New York, USA.

CHAMBERLIN, T. C. 1965. The method of multiple working hypotheses. Science 148:754–759.

CHAMBERS, L. K., G. R. SINGLETON, AND L. A. HINDS. 1999. Fertility control of wild mouse populations: the effects of hormonal competence and an imposed level sterility. Wildlife Research 26:579–591.

CHAPMAN, J. A., AND G. R. WILLNER. 1986. Lagomorphs. Pages 453–473 *in* A.Y. Cooperrider, R. J. Boyd, and H. R. Stuart, editors. Inventory and monitoring of wildlife habitat. U.S. Department of the Interior, Bureau of Land Management, Service Center, Denver, Colorado, USA.

———, C. J. HENNY, AND H. M. WIGHT. 1969. The status, population dynamics, and harvest of the dusky Canada goose. Wildlife Monographs 18.

CHERRY, S. 1998. Statistical tests in publications of The Wildlife Society. Wildlife Society Bulletin 26:947–953.

CLUTTON-BROCK, T. H., M. MAJOR, AND F. E. GUINNESS. 1985. Population regulation in male and female red deer. Journal of Animal Ecology 54:831–846.

COCHRAN, W. G. 1963. Sampling techniques. Second edition. John Wiley and Sons, New York, USA.

———. 1983. Planning and analysis of observational studies. John Wiley and Sons, New York, USA.

COOK, J. G., L. L. IRWIN, L. D. BRYANT, R. A. RIGGS, AND J. W. THOMAS. 1998. Relations of forest cover and condition of elk: a test of the thermal cover hypothesis in summer and winter. Wildlife Monographs 141.

COOK, T. D., AND D. T. CAMPBELL. 1979. Quasi-experimentation: design and analysis issues for field settings. Houghton Mifflin, Boston, Massachusetts, USA.

COOKE, B. D., AND D. BERMAN. 2000. Effect of inoculation rate and ambient temperature on the survival time of rabbits, *Oryctolagus cuniculus* (L.), infected with the rabbit haemorrhagic disease virus. Wildlife Research 27:137–142.

COULSON, T., S. ALBON, F. GUINNESS, J. PEMBERTON, AND T. CLUTTON-BROCK. 1997. Population substructure, local density, and calf winter survival in red deer (*Cervus elaphus*). Ecology 78:852–863.

CRÊTE, M., AND F. MESSIER. 1987. Evaluation of indices of gray wolf, *Canis lupis*, density in hardwood–conifer forests of southwestern Quebec. Canadian Field-Naturalist 101:147–152.

CYR, A. 1981. Limitation and variability in hearing ability in censusing birds. Studies in Avian Biology 6:327–333.

DELGIUDICE, G. D., F. J. SINGER, AND U. S. SEAL. 1991. Physiological assessment of winter nutritional deprivation in elk of Yellowstone National Park. Journal of Wildlife Management 55:653–664.

———, R. A. MOEN, F. J. SINGER, AND M. R. RIGGS. 2001. Winter nutritional restriction and simulated body condition of Yellowstone elk and bison before and after the fires of 1988. Wildlife Monographs 147.

DENNIS, B. 1996. Discussion: should ecologists become Bayesians? Ecological Applications 6:1095–1103.

DEWEY, J. 1938. Scientific method: induction and deduction. Pages 419–441 *in* J. Dewey, editor. Logic—the theory of inquiry. Henry Holt and Company, New York, USA.

DIAMOND, J. 1986. Overview: laboratory experiments, field experiments and natural experiments. Pages 3–22 *in* J. Diamond and T. J. Case, editors. Community ecology. Harper and Row, New York, USA.

DODSON, A. P., AND P. J. HUDSON. 1992. Regulation and stability of a free-living host-parasite system: *Trichostrongylus tenuis* in red grouse. II. Population models. Journal of Animal Ecology 61:487–498.

DOLBY, G. R. 1982. The role of statistics in the methodology of the life sciences. Biometrics 38:1069–1083.

EBERHARDT, L. L. 1970. Correlation, regression, and density dependence. Ecology 51:306–310.

———, AND J. M. THOMAS. 1991. Designing environmental field studies. Ecological Monographs 61:53–73.

EFRON, B. 1998. R. A. Fisher in the 21st century. Statistical Science 13:95–122.

FARNSWORTH, G. L., K. H. POLLOCK, J. D. NICHOLS, T. R. SIMONS, J. E. HINES, AND J. R. SAUER. 2002. A removal model for estimating detection probabilities from point-count surveys. Auk 119:414–425.

FIENBERG, S. E. 1970. The analysis of multidimensional contingency tables. Ecology 51:419–433.

———. 1980. The analysis of cross-classified categorical data. Massachusetts Institute of Technology Press, Cambridge, USA.

FORBES, L. S. 1990. A note on statistical power. Auk 107:438–439.

FORD, E. D. 2000. Scientific method for ecological research. Cambridge University Press, Cambridge, United Kingdom.

GARTON, E. O. 2002. Mapping a chimera? Pages 663–666 *in* J. M. Scott, P. J. Heglund, M. L. Morrison, J. B. Haufler, M. G. Raphael, W. A. Wall, and F. B. Sampson, editors. Predicting species occurrences: issues of accuracy and scale. Island Press, Washington, D.C., USA.

GAUCH, JR., H. G. 2003. Scientific method in practice. Cambridge University Press, Cambridge, United Kingdom.

GELMAN, A. B., J. B. CARLIN, H. S. STERN, AND D. B. RUBIN. 1995. Bayesian data analysis. Chapman and Hall, Boca Raton, Florida, USA.

GILL, R. B. 1985. Wildlife research—an endangered species. Wildlife Society Bulletin 13:580–587.

GREEN, R. H. 1979. Sampling design and statistical methods for environmental biologists. John Wiley and Sons, New York, USA.

GUINNESS, F. E., T. H. CLUTTON-BROCK, AND S. D. ALBON. 1978. Factors affecting calf mortality in red deer (*Cervus elaphus*). Journal of Animal Ecology 47:817–832.

HAIRSTON, N. G. 1989. Ecological experiments: purpose, design, and execution. Cambridge studies in ecology. Cambridge University Press, New York, USA.

HANOWSKI, J. M., AND G. J. NIEMI. 1995. A comparison of on- and off-road bird counts: do you need to go off road to count birds accurately? Journal of Field Ornithology 66:469–483.

HEISEY, D. M., AND T. K. FULLER. 1985. Evaluations of survival and cause-specific mortality rates using telemetry data. Journal of Wildlife Management 49:668–674.

HOHF, R. S., J. T. RATTI, AND R. CROTEAU. 1987. Experimental analysis of winter food selection by spruce grouse. Journal of Wildlife Management 51:159–167.

HOUSTON, D. B. 1982. The northern Yellowstone elk: ecology and management. Macmillan Publishing Company, New York, USA.

HURLBERT, S. H. 1984. Pseudoreplication and the design of ecological field experiments. Ecological Monographs 54:187–211.

JAMES, F. C., AND C. E. MCCULLOCH. 1985. Data analysis and the design of experiments in ornithology. Pages 1–63 *in* R. F. Johnston, editor. Current Ornithology. Volume 2. Plenum Press, New York, USA.

JENKINS, D., A. WATSON, AND G. R. MILLER. 1963. Population studies on red grouse, *Lagopus lagopus scoticus* (Lath.) in north-east Scotland. Journal of Animal Ecology 32:317–376.

JOHNSON, D. H. 1980. The comparison of usage and availability measurements for evaluating resource preference. Ecology 61:65–71.

———. 1995. Statistical sirens: the allure of nonparametrics. Ecology 76:1998–2000.

———. 1999. The insignificance of statistical significance testing. Journal of Wildlife Management 63:763–772.

———. 2002. The importance of replication in wildlife research. Journal of Wildlife Management 66:919–932.

JOHNSON, R. A., AND D. W. WICHERN. 1988. Applied multivariate statistical analysis. Second edition. Prentice-Hall, Englewood Cliffs, New Jersey, USA.

KAMIL, A. C. 1988. Experimental design in ornithology. Pages 313–346 *in* R. F. Johnston, editor. Current ornithology. Volume 5. Plenum Press, New York, USA.

KEITH, L. B. 1963. Wildlife's ten-year cycle. University of Wisconsin Press, Madison, USA.

———. 1974. Some features of population dynamics in mammals. Proceedings of the International Congress of Game Biologists 11:17–58.

———, AND L. A. WINDBERG. 1978. A demographic analysis of the snowshoe hare cycle. Wildlife Monographs 58.

———, J. R. CARY, O. J. RONGSTAD, AND M. C. BRITTINGHAM. 1984. Demography and ecology of a declining snowshoe hare population. Wildlife Monographs 90.

KEPLER, C. B., AND J. M. SCOTT. 1981. Reducing bird count variability by training observers. Studies in Avian Biology 6:366–371.

KERLINGER, F. N. 1973. Foundations of behavioral research. Second edition. Holt, Rinehart, and Winston, Inc., New York, USA.

———, AND H. B. LEE. 2000. Foundations of behavioral research. Fourth edition. Harcourt College Publishers, New York, USA.

KOMAK, S., AND M. R. CROSSLAND. 2000. An assessment of the introduced mosquito fish (*Gambusia affinis holbrooki*) as a predator of eggs, hatchlings and tadpoles of native and non-native anurans. Wildlife Research 27:185–189.

KOZICKY, E. L., G. O. HENDERSON, P. G. HOMEYER, AND E. B. SPEAKER. 1952. The adequacy of the fall roadside pheasant census in Iowa. Transactions of the North American Wildlife Conference 17:293–305.

KREBS, C. J. 1999. Ecological methodology. Second edition. Harper and Row, New York, USA.

LAAKE, J. L., S. T. BUCKLAND, D. R. ANDERSON, AND K. P. BURNHAM. 1994. DISTANCE user's guide V2.1. Colorado Cooperative Fish and Wildlife Research Unit, Colorado State University, Fort Collins, USA.

LEEGE, T. A., AND W. O. HICKEY. 1971. Sprouting of northern Idaho shrubs after prescribed burning. Journal of Wildlife Management 35:508–515.

LOWE, V. P. W. 1969. Population dynamics of red deer (*Cervus elaphus* L.) on Rhum. Journal of Animal Ecology 38:425–457.

LYON, L. J., AND A. G. CHRISTENSEN. 2002. Elk and land management. Pages 557–581 *in* D. E. Toweill and J. W. Thomas, editors. North American elk: ecology and management. Smithsonian Institution Press, Washington, D.C., USA.

MACNAB, J. 1983. Wildlife management as scientific experimentation. Wildlife Society Bulletin 11:397–401.

MANLY, B. F. J., L. L. MCDONALD, AND G. W. GARNER. 1996. Maximum likelihood estimation for the double-count method with independent observers. Journal of Agricultural, Biological, and Environmental Statistics 1:170–189.

MAYR, E. 1970. Populations, species, and evolution: an abridgement of animal species and evolution. Harvard University Press, Cambridge, Massachusetts, USA.

MILLIKEN, G. A., AND D. E. JOHNSON. 1984. Analysis of messy data: designed experiments. Volume I. Van Nostrand Reinhold, New York, USA.

MOHLER, L. L., P. D. DALKE, AND W. M. SHAW. 1958. Elk and elk hunting in Idaho. Transactions of the North American Wildlife Conference 23:491–501.

MORRISON, M. L., W. M. BLOCK, M. D. STRICKLAND, AND W. L. KENDALL, editors. 2001. Wildlife study design. Springer-Verlag, New York, USA.

MOSS, R., AND A. WATSON. 1991. Population cycles and kin selection in red grouse *Lagopus lagopus scoticus*. Ibis 133:113–120.

———, ———, AND P. ROTHERY. 1984. Inherent changes in the body size, viability, and behavior of a fluctuating red grouse (*Lagopus lagopus scoticus*) population. Journal of Animal Ecology 53:171–189.

———, I. B. TRENHOLM, A. WATSON, AND R. PARR. 1990. Parasitism, predation and survival of hen red grouse *Lagopus lagopus scoticus* in spring. Journal of Animal Ecology 59:631–642.

MUELLER-DOMBOIS, D., AND H. ELLENBERG. 1974. Aims and methods of vegetation ecology. John Wiley and Sons, New York, USA.

MURPHY, D. D., AND B. D. NOON. 1991. Coping with uncertainty in wildlife biology. Journal of Wildlife Management 55:773–782.

NEWTON-SMITH, W. H. 1981. The rationality of science. Routledge and Kegan Paul, Boston, Massachusetts, USA.

NOTTINGHAM, JR., B. G., K. G. JOHNSON, AND M. R. PELTON. 1989. Evaluation of scent-station surveys to monitor raccoon density. Wildlife Society Bulletin 17:29–35.

OSENBERG, C. W., O. SARNELLE, S. D. COOPER, AND R. D. HOLT. 1999. Resolving ecological questions through meta-analysis: goals, metrics, and models. Ecology 80:1105–1117.

OVERTON, W. S., AND D. E. DAVIS. 1969. Estimating the numbers of animals in wildlife populations. Pages 403–455 *in* R. H. Giles, Jr., editor. Wildlife management techniques. Third edition. The Wildlife Society, Washington, D.C., USA.

PALTRIDGE, R., AND R. SOUTHGATE. 2001. The effect of habitat type and seasonal conditions on fauna in two areas of the Tanami Desert. Wildlife Research 28:247–260.

PATRIC, E. F., T. P. HUSBAND, C. G. McKIEL, AND W. M. SULLIVAN. 1988. Potential of LORAN-C for wildlife research along coastal landscapes. Journal of Wildlife Management 52:162–164.

PEEK, J. M. 1989. Another look at burning shrubs in northern Idaho. Pages 157–159 *in* D. M. Baumgartner, D. W. Breuer, and B. A. Zamora, editors. Proceedings of the symposium on prescribed fire in the Intermountain Region: forest site preparation and range improvement. Washington State University, Pullman, USA.

PETERMAN, R. M. 1990. Statistical power analysis can improve fisheries research and management. Canadian Journal of Fisheries and Aquatic Sciences 47:2–15.

PIETZ, P. J., AND J. R. TESTER. 1983. Habitat selection by snowshoe hares in north central Minnesota. Journal of Wildlife Management 47:686–696.

PLATT, J. R. 1964. Strong inference. Science 146:347–353.

POPPER, K. R. 1959. The logic of scientific discovery. Hutchinson and Co., London, United Kingdom.

———. 1968. Conjectures and refutations: the growth of scientific knowledge. Second edition. Harper and Row, New York, USA.

QUANG, P. X., AND E. F. BECKER. 1996. Combining line transect and double count sampling techniques for aerial surveys. Journal of Agricultural, Biological, and Environmental Statistics 2:230–242.

QUINN, J. F, AND A. E. DUNHAM. 1983. On hypothesis testing in ecology and evolution. American Naturalist 122:602–617.

RATTI, J. T. 1980. The classification of avian species and subspecies. American Birds 34:860–866.

———, AND E. O. GARTON. 1994. Research and experimental design. Pages 1–23 *in* T. A. Bookhout, editor. Research and management techniques for wildlife and habitats. Fifth edition. The Wildlife Society, Bethesda, Maryland, USA.

———, AND K. P. REESE. 1988. Preliminary test of the ecological trap hypothesis. Journal of Wildlife Management 52:484–491.

———, AND D. E. TIMM. 1979. Migratory behavior of Vancouver Canada geese: recovery rate bias. Pages 208–212 *in* R. L. Jarvis and J. C. Bartonek, editors. Proceedings, management and biology of Pacific Flyway geese: a symposium. Northwest Section, The Wildlife Society, Portland, Oregon, USA.

———, D. L. MACKEY, AND J. R. ALLDREDGE. 1984. Analysis of spruce grouse habitat in north-central Washington. Journal of Wildlife Management 48:1188–1196.

REED, J. M., AND A. R. BLAUSTEIN. 1997. Biologically significant population declines and statistical power. Conservation Biology 11:281–282.

REYNOLDS, R. T., J. M. SCOTT, AND R. A. NUSSBAUM. 1980. A variable circular-plot method for estimating bird numbers. Condor 82:309–313.

RISBEY, D. A., M. C. CALVER, J. SHORT, J. S. BRADLEY, AND I. W. WRIGHT. 2000. The impact of cats and foxes on the small vertebrate fauna of Heirisson Prong, Western Australia. II. A field experiment. Wildlife Research 27:223–235.

ROBBINS, C. S., D. BYSTRAK, AND P. H. GEISSLER. 1986. The breeding bird survey: its first 15 years, 1965–1979. U.S. Department of the Interior, Fish and Wildlife Service, Resource Publication 157.

ROMESBURG, H. C. 1981. Wildlife science: gaining reliable knowledge. Journal of Wildlife Management 45:293–313.

ROTELLA, J. J., AND J. T. RATTI. 1986. Test of a critical density index assumption: a case study with gray partridge. Journal of Wildlife Management 50:532–539.

———, AND ———. 1992a. Mallard brood movements and wetland selection in southwestern Manitoba. Journal of Wildlife Management 56:508–515.

———, AND ———. 1992b. Mallard brood survival and wetland habitat conditions in southwestern Manitoba. Journal of Wildlife Management 56:499–507.

ROSENSTOCK, S. S., D. R. ANDERSON, K. M. GIESEN, T. LEUKERING, AND M. F. CARTER. 2002. Landbird counting techniques: current practices and an alternative. Auk 119:46–53.

SAMUEL, M. D., E. O. GARTON, M. W. SCHLEGEL, AND R. G. CARSON. 1987. Visibility bias during aerial surveys of elk in northcentral Idaho. Journal of Wildlife Management 51:622–630.

SCHEAFFER, R. L., W. MENDENHALL, AND L. OTT. 1996. Elementary survey sampling. Fifth edition. Duxbury Press. Boston, Massachusetts, USA.

SEBER, G. A. F. 1982. The estimation of animal abundance and related parameters. Second edition. Charles Griffin, London, United Kingdom.

SELANDER, R. K. 1971. Systematics and speciation in birds. Pages 57–147 *in* D. S. Farner and J. R. King, editors. Avian biology. Volume I. Academic Press, New York, USA.

SHENK, T. M., AND A. B. FRANKLIN, editors. 2001. Modeling in natural resource management: development, interpretation, and application. Island Press, Washington, D.C., USA.

SINCLAIR, A. R. E. 1991. Science and the practice of wildlife management. Journal of Wildlife Management 55:767–773.

SINGER, F. J., A. HARTING, K. K. SYMONDS, AND M. B. COUGHENOUR. 1997. Density dependence, compensation, and environmental effects on elk calf mortality in Yellowstone National Park. Journal of Wildlife Management 61:12–25.

SKALSKI, J. R., AND D. S. ROBSON. 1992. Techniques for wildlife investigations: design and analysis of capture data. Academic Press, San Diego, California, USA.

SMITH, D. R., M. J. CONROY, AND D. H. BRAKHAGE. 1995. Efficiency of adaptive cluster sampling for estimating density of wintering waterfowl. Biometrics 51:777–788.

SMITH, L. M., I. L. BRISBIN, JR., AND G. C. WHITE. 1984. An evaluation of total trapline captures as estimates of furbearer abundance. Journal of Wildlife Management 48:1452–1455.

STEBBINS, G. L. 1971. Processes of organic evolution. Second edition. Prentice-Hall, Englewood Cliffs, New Jersey, USA.

STEEL R. G. D., AND J. H. TORRIE. 1980. Principles and procedures of statistics: a biometrical approach. Second edition. McGraw-Hill Book Company, New York, USA.

STEIDL, R. J., J. P. HAYES, AND E. SCHAUBER. 1997. Statistical power analysis in wildlife research. Journal of Wildlife Management 61:270–279.

STEINHORST, R. K., AND M. D. SAMUEL. 1989. Sightability adjustment methods for aerial surveys of wildlife populations. Biometrics 45:415–425.

STEWART-OATEN, A., W. M. MURDOCH, AND K. R. PARKER. 1986. Environmental impact assessment: pseudoreplication in time? Ecology 67:929–940.

SWIHART, R. K., AND N. A. SLADE. 1985. Testing for independence of observations in animal movements. Ecology 66:1176–1184.

TAKEKAWA, J. Y., AND E. O. GARTON. 1984. How much is an evening grosbeak worth? Journal of Forestry 82:426–428.

THOMAS, L. 1997. Retrospective power analysis. Conservation Biology 11:276–280.

THOMPSON, S. K., AND F. L. RAMSEY. 1983. Adaptive sampling of populations. Department of Statistics, Technical Report 82. Oregon State University, Corvallis, USA.

———, AND G. A. F. SEBER. 1996. Adaptive sampling. John Wiley and

Sons, New York, USA.

THOMPSON, W. L. 2002. Towards reliable bird surveys: accounting for individuals present but not detected. Auk 119:18–25.

———, G. C. WHITE, AND C. GOWAN. 1998. Monitoring vertebrate populations. Academic Press, San Diego, California, USA.

TOFT, C. A., AND P. J. SHEA. 1983. Detecting community-wide patterns: estimating power strengthens statistical inference. American Naturalist 122:618–625.

TUKEY, J. W. 1977. Exploratory data analysis. Addison-Wesley Publishing Company, Reading, Massachusetts, USA.

TURNER, M. G., Y. WU, L. L. WALLACE, W. H. ROMME, AND A. BRENKERT. 1994. Simulating winter interactions among ungulates, vegetation, and fire in northern Yellowstone Park. Ecological Applications 4:472–496.

UNDERWOOD, A. J. 1994. On beyond BACI: sampling designs that might reliably detect environmental disturbances. Ecological Applications 4:3–15.

———. 1997. Experiments in ecology: their logical design and interpretation using analysis of variance. Cambridge University Press, Cambridge, United Kingdom.

WALTERS, C. J. 1986. Adaptive management of renewable resources. MacMillan Publishing Company, New York, USA.

WATSON, A. 1967. Social status and population regulation in the red grouse (*Lagopus lagopus scoticus*). Royal Society Population Study Group 2:22–30.

———, AND R. MOSS. 1972. A current model of population dynamics in red grouse. Proceedings of the International Ornithological Congress 15:134–149.

———, AND R. PARR. 1984a. Effects of food enrichment on numbers and spacing behavior of red grouse. Journal of Animal Ecology 53:663–678.

———, ———, AND P. ROTHERY. 2000. Weather and synchrony in 10-year population cycles of rock ptarmigan and red grouse in Scotland. Ecology 81:2126–2136.

———, ———, ———, AND R. PARR. 1984b. Demographic causes and predictive models of population fluctuation in red grouse. Journal of Animal Ecology 53:639–662.

———, ———, R. PARR, M. D. MOUNTFORD, AND P. ROTHERY. 1994. Kin landownership, differential aggression between kin and non-kin, and population fluctuations in red grouse. Journal of Animal Ecology 63:39–50.

WELLS, J. V., AND M. E. RICHMOND. 1995. Populations, metapopulations, and species populations: what are they and who should care? Wildlife Society Bulletin 23:458–462.

WHITE, G. C., D. R. ANDERSON, K. P. BURNHAM, AND D. L. OTIS. 1982. Capture–recapture and removal methods for sampling closed populations. Report LA-8787-NERP, UC-11, Los Alamos National Laboratory, Los Alamos, New Mexico, USA.

WIENS, J. A. 1973. Pattern and process in grassland bird communities. Ecological Monographs 43:237–270.

———. 1989. The ecology of bird communities: foundations and patterns. Volume I. Cambridge University Press, New York, USA.

WILLIAMS, B. K., AND F. A. JOHNSON. 1995. Adaptive management and the regulation of waterfowl harvests. Wildlife Society Bulletin 23:430–436.

———, ———, AND K. WILKINS. 1996. Uncertainty and the adaptive management of waterfowl harvests. Journal of Wildlife Management 60:223–232.

———, J. D. NICHOLS, AND M. J. CONROY. 2001. Analysis and management of animal populations. Academic Press, San Diego, California, USA.

WILSON, M. M., AND J. A. CRAWFORD. 1979. Response of bobwhites to controlled burning in south Texas. Wildlife Society Bulletin 7:53–56.

WINDBERG, L. A., AND L. B. KEITH. 1976. Snowshoe hare population response to artificial high densities. Journal of Mammalogy 57:523–553.

ZAR, J. H. 1999. Biostatistical analysis. Fourth edition. Prentice-Hall, Upper Saddle River, New Jersey, USA.

4

ANALYSIS OF DATA IN WILDLIFE BIOLOGY

Jonathan R. Bart and William I. Notz

INTRODUCTION

This chapter describes general procedures for analyzing data collected during wildlife studies. We try to provide the level of quantitative detail about each topic that will be most useful to readers. Statistical analyses are now conducted almost exclusively with statistical packages. The user should understand which procedures to use, the assumptions, and the products but they do not need to understand—and few non-statisticians do understand—the mathematical details. Thus, we concentrate on explaining which procedures to use and how to interpret the results but do not dwell on mechanics of how the estimates are produced. Design of projects is discussed in this manual by Garton et al. (2005). Specialized methods widely used by wildlife biologists are discussed in several other chapters including Lancia et al. (2005) (estimating population size), Dinsmore and Johnson (2005) (population analysis), Connelly et al. (2005) (harvest

management), and Higgins et al. (2005) (vegetation sampling). General accounts of statistical methods widely used by wildlife biologists include Cochran (1977) (sampling); Snedecor and Cochran (1980), Steel and Torrie (1980), McCullagh and Nelder (1989) (multivariate methods); Kutner et al. (1996) (regression); Wichern and Johnson (2002) (multivariate methods); Sokal and Rohlf (1995), Zar (1998), Hicks and Turner (1999) (analysis of variance including mixed effects models); and Hosmer and Lemeshow (2000) (logistic regression). General accounts that emphasize wildlife include Bart et al. (1998), McGarigal et al. (2000) (multivariate methods), Burnham and Anderson (2002) (model selection), and Williams et al. (2002).

GRAPHICS

One of the simplest yet most powerful ways of summarizing data is by means of charts, graphs, and tables. This

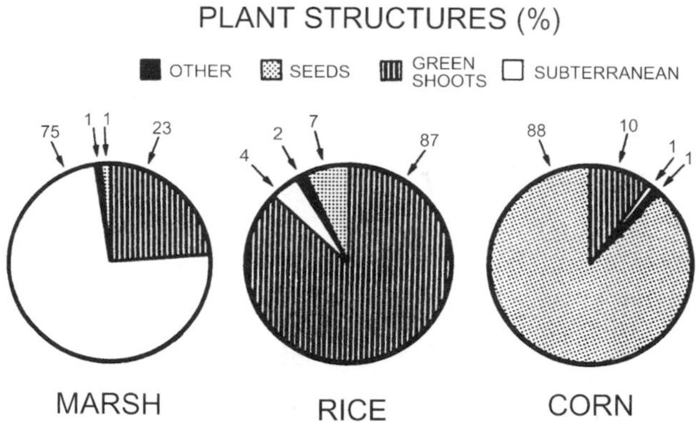

PLANT STRUCTURES (%)

■ OTHER ▨ SEEDS ▥ GREEN SHOOTS □ SUBTERRANEAN

MARSH   RICE   CORN

Fig. 1. Pie-chart showing relative proportions (%) of a composition of winter diets of lesser snow geese on the basis of the plant structures consumed during 1983–1984 in coastal marshes (MARSH), rice prairies (RICE), and areas near the Missouri River Valley (CORN) (from Alisauskas et al. 1988).

is also one of the best techniques for misrepresenting data, either intentionally or unintentionally. Most articles in the wildlife literature contain at least one chart, graph, or table pertaining to the data collected or subsequent statistical analyses. With increasing popularity of desktop computers has come a proliferation of software (computer programs), such as spreadsheets, graphics, and statistical packages, for handling data. Most software has some capability for creating high-quality charts, graphs, and tables. Although certain types of charts, graphs, and tables are standard, there is room for creativity and presenting complex data clearly is an art. Good graphics allow the reader to see the salient features of the data at a glance. Graphic displays are also a powerful tool for exploring data, i.e., seeing what the data appear to indicate before proceeding to more formal analyses. Using graphic displays in this way is sometimes referred to as exploratory data analysis, and the ease with which graphic displays can be created with modern software makes exploration simple.

Before specific types of graphic displays are discussed, a few general principles should be considered. First, strive for clarity and honesty. This includes labeling displays clearly, avoiding distortion, and scaling properly. Second, give the source of the data. Third, tables are generally preferable to graphics for displaying exact numerical values and for small data sets. For large data sets, where one wishes to display trends or overall relationships, graphics are preferable to tables. These principles and common sense will carry one a long way. One of the best ways to decide how to make a chart, graph, or table of a set of data is to examine similar examples in wildlife journals. Another excellent source of examples is the *Statistical Abstract of the United States* available in most libraries. This yearly compilation of data contains a variety of tables and graphs. Finally, Tufte (1983) is an excellent reference for good graphics.

Charts

Among the most commonly used graphics are pie charts, histograms, and bar charts. All are used to display characteristics of data that have been subdivided into classes. The pie chart is a circle (pie) divided into slices to display the relative sizes of different classes. Each slice cor-

responds to a class, and the size of the slice represents the proportion of the data in that class. Alisauskas et al. (1988) used pie charts to display the composition of winter diets (relative sizes of classes of plant structures comprising the diet) of lesser snow geese (*Chen caerulescens*) based on the type of region in which the geese fed (Fig. 1). It is immediately clear from the charts that one plant structure predominated in the diet of the geese, but this predominating structure differed in each region.

Histograms and bar charts convey information analogous to that in a pie chart. A histogram is appropriate for numerical data and a bar chart for categorical (non-numerical) data, but in other respects these 2 types of graphs are nearly identical. A histogram is constructed by first dividing data into classes, each class consisting of a value or range of values of the data. Classes must be defined so that each data value belongs to one and only one class. A histogram is then constructed by drawing horizontal and vertical axes. The horizontal axis is marked in the units of measurement of the data with a uniform scaling along the axis. The horizontal axis is then divided into segments corresponding to the range of values defining the different classes. The vertical axis represents frequencies (counts) or relative frequencies (proportions). Vertical bars are drawn above each class so the area of the bar is proportional to the frequency or relative frequency of observations in the class. If classes correspond to ranges of values of equal length, one may draw the bars to have heights equal to frequencies or relative frequencies, and areas of bars will automatically be in the correct proportions. If class widths vary, heights must be adjusted to keep the area of the bars proportional to frequencies. Thus, heights of bars represent frequencies or relative frequencies per unit length of the classes.

To illustrate how one might construct a histogram when classes are of differing lengths, we consider an example. O'Gara and Harris (1988) constructed charts of the number of deaths (frequencies) of deer (*Odocoileus* spp.) in several age classes due to a variety of causes (a separate graph for each cause) (Fig. 2). In these charts, the authors treated age as a categorical variable and, technically, these charts are bar charts. Because age is actually a numerical variable, histograms might be more appropriate here. To view how these charts might be redrawn as histograms, consider the All Causes chart. The last 2 age categories are each 3 times as wide as the others. If we construct a proper histogram, the horizontal axis should be marked in years and the bars for the last 2 categories should have heights that are one-third those displayed in the bar chart so the areas of bars are proportional to frequencies (Fig. 3). The heights of the last 2 bars now represent the average number of deaths per year over the interval covered by the class.

By redrawing this bar chart we altered the visual impression it makes. First, we see the last 2 bars cover a wider age class than the other bars. Second, the original chart gives a false impression of a sudden large increase in the death rate when deer are >3 years of age. After adjustment (Fig. 3), the last 2 bars have heights comparable to the bars above the 1-, 2-, and 3-year classes. The increase in death rate does not appear as dramatic. For the remaining charts (Fig. 2), the appropriate adjustment for converting the age class charts to histograms would be to reduce the height of the bar above the 1-6 class by a factor of 6. In

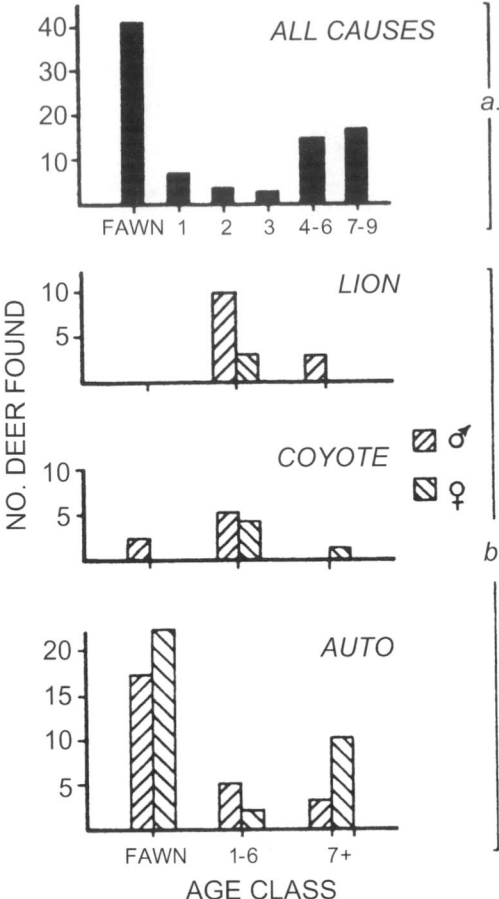

Fig. 2. Bar chart showing age structure of deer killed by mountain lions (*Puma concolor*), coyotes (*Canis latrans*), and automobiles combined (a) and separately (b) in western Montana during winters 1969–1981 (from O'Gara and Harris 1988).

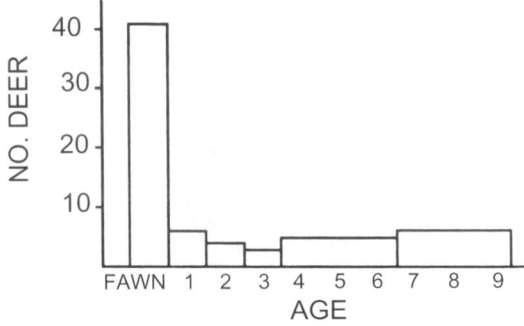

Fig. 3. Properly drawn histogram for age structure of deer killed by mountain lions, coyotes, and automobiles combined. Notice the lack of vertical lines between ages 4, 5, and 6. This suggests these ages are not separated in the data. One might consider labeling the bar above 4, 5, and 6 as 4–6. Similar comments apply to the bar above 7, 8, and 9.

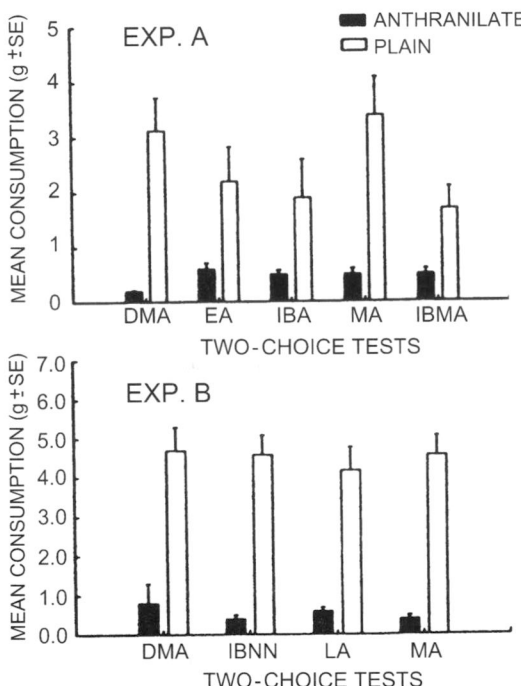

Fig. 4. Bar charts representing the consumption of anthranilate and plain Purina Flight Bird Conditioner (PFBC) in 2 experiments (A and B) when European starlings were given both as a choice. Dark bars represent consumption of anthranilate PFBC. Open bars represent consumption of plain PFBC. Capped vertical lines represent standard errors of the means. DMA = methyl-N-methyl anthranilate, EA = ethyl anthranilate, IBA = isobutyl anthranilate, MA = methyl anthranilate, IBMA = isobutyl methyl anthranilate, IBNN = isobutyl-N-N-dimethyl anthranilate, LA = linalyl anthranilate (from Mason et al. 1989).

the 7+ age class, one would need to know the oldest observed age to make the proper adjustment. The All Causes chart suggests the oldest age is 9; if correct, the bar height would be reduced by a factor of 3.

Bar charts are similar to histograms and are appropriate when data are categorical. The horizontal axis is marked with category labels, and bars are drawn above each category. Additionally, the vertical axis can be used to display characteristics (such as means) of the classes instead of frequencies or relative frequencies. Mason et al. (1989) used bar charts to represent the mean consumption of anthranilate and plain Purina Flight Bird Conditioner (PFBC) when European starlings (*Sturnus vulgaris*) were given both as a choice. The classes correspond to different types of anthranilate used in the anthranilate PFBC. Heights of bars (Fig. 4) represent means rather than frequencies or relative frequencies. By displaying pairs of bars, the authors essentially superimposed 2 separate bar charts. This allows display of extra information in a single graph, and comparisons are readily made. The plain PFBC was clearly preferred to the anthranilate PFBC in all tests. One extra feature of this chart is that the authors have also provided information about standard errors of the means by including capped vertical lines atop each bar. This feature is not unusual in bar charts representing means. Although such charts appear often in publications, bar charts are typically used to represent frequencies of categorical variables rather than means. A better graphic for means than the bar chart (Fig. 4) could be constructed by replacing each bar by a point whose vertical coordinate corresponds to the mean of the categorical variable with capped vertical lines that represent 95% confidence limits extending above and below this point.

Although pie charts, histograms, and bar charts convey similar information, pie charts are probably best used, if at all, when classes are few and are merely categorical. Histograms and bar charts are usually appropriate, espe-

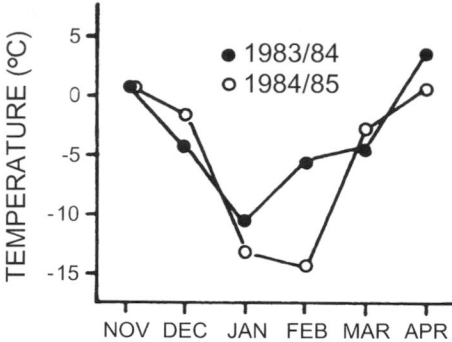

Fig. 5. Line graph showing temperatures in southeastern Norway during winters, 1984 and 1985 (from Sæther and Gravem 1988).

Table 1. Number of observations, mean amount of kidney fat (g) of moose calves from southeastern Norway, SE of the mean, and range of the observations by gender for winters 1984 and 1985 (from Sæther and Gravem 1988).

| Winter | Gender | n | Kidney fat | | |
			Mean	SE	Range
1984	M	9	2.9	0.34	1.1–4.4
	F	14	3.5	0.36	1.6–7.3
1985	M	7	3.2	0.31	2.5–4.5
	F	13	3.0	0.23	1.9–4.0
Both winters	M	16	3.0	0.23	1.1–4.5
	F	27	3.3	0.22	1.6–7.3

cially when number of classes is large. If the data are numerical and classes represent ranges of values of the variable, use of a horizontal axis marked in equal increments displays the ordering of the data. By displaying this ordering, the histogram conveys more information than the corresponding pie chart. Some authors (i.e., Tufte 1983) advocate use of tables instead of pie charts to display small data sets, in keeping with our third general principle. However, pie charts remain a popular and familiar graphic.

Graphs

Perhaps the most commonly used graphics are line graphs and scatterplots. In both types, the objective is to view how some measured response (usually plotted on the vertical axis of the graph) varies as a function of some independent variable (usually plotted on the horizontal axis). Scatterplots are described later (Scatterplots and Correlation). Line graphs are generally used to display measurements taken in sequence, usually over a period of time. The vertical axis of the graph is marked in the units of the measurements. The horizontal axis is marked at 1, 2, 3, 4,... or, if the measurements are merely ordered, 1st, 2nd, 3rd, 4th,... If measurements are taken over time, the horizontal axis is scaled in units of time. Measurements are plotted as points, and consecutive measurements are connected with lines, hence the name line graph. This type of graph is particularly useful for viewing trends in measurements over time. Sæther and Gravem (1988) plotted temperature measurements (C) recorded over time (Nov–Apr) in Norway for winter 1983/84 and 1984/85 (Fig. 5). Not surprisingly, temperatures decreased until January or February, after which they began to increase. It is easy to note the 1984/85 winter was colder than 1983/84 in the January–March period.

Two points are important in preparation of graphs. The first is to use a uniform scaling of the axes. Changing the scale along an axis distorts the appearance of the trend in the graph. The second involves location of zero points, particularly when the zero point represents the absence of some property. Generally one assumes the intersection of the horizontal and vertical axes occurs at the zero point of both scales, and one may unconsciously extrapolate trends in a graph to the zero point by extrapolating to the intersection of the axes. Thus, consideration of whether the intersection should represent zero for one or both axes is important. In wildlife studies, displaying population size on the vertical axis and year or some other temporal vari-

able on the horizontal axis is especially common. In these cases, proportional change is usually more relevent than absolute change but is hard to visualize if the vertical axis does not start at zero. Changes in population size will appear to be larger—perhaps larger than they should—if the vertical axis does not begin at zero. Often, however, the range of measurements is far from zero and it becomes difficult to use a reasonable scaling of an axis while including the zero point and fitting the graph into a small space. In these situations axes must be labeled clearly to alert the reader that the intersection of the axes is not the zero point.

Tables

Tables are the most common means of displaying or summarizing information in the wildlife literature. No one style predominates, but all have elements in common. Typically rows (or groups of rows) correspond to classes, i.e., different categories or ranges of values of some variable. Columns present summary information corresponding to these classes. As an example, Sæther and Gravem (1988) provided summary statistics (number of animals and the mean, standard error, and range of kidney fat) for a sample of male and female moose (*Alces alces*) for the 1984 and 1985 winters in southeastern Norway (Table 1).

The important principles to consider when tables are constructed are, as for all graphics, to be clear (label clearly) and to provide the source of the data. In the example above (Table 1), the authors make it clear how the data were collected in the text of the paper. The table itself provides sufficient information for the reader to understand the meaning of the numbers.

An important advantage of tables is that they provide exact values of data, which can be used by other researchers for further analysis. Perhaps the main drawback of tables is that they do not make as forceful an impression as other graphics. For example, consider Fig. 6, also from Sæther and Gravem (1988), which gives information on fat content in moose femurs. This graphic presents the same kind of information as in Table 1. However, in this graphic one more readily sees patterns (such as the change from 1984 to 1985) than one would in a table.

Graphics Software

Many statistical software packages now have the capability for preparing interactive graphics. Familiar packages include S-PLUS, Minitab, SPSS-X, SYSTAT, Data

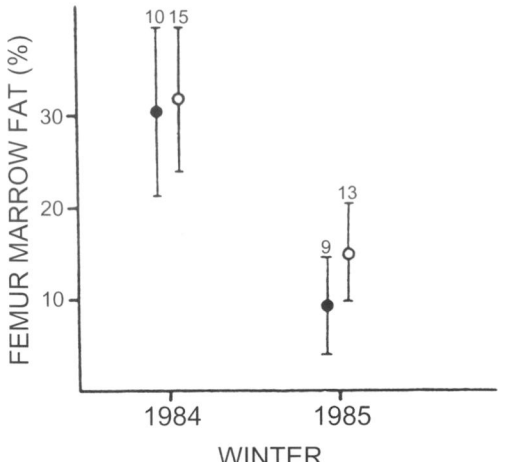

Fig. 6. Graphic representing femur fat content (%) (mean ± SE) for male (black circles) and female (open circles) moose calves in southeastern Norway, 1984–1985 (sample size is indicated above SE) (from Sæther and Gravem 1988).

Desk Professional, and JMP (distributed by SAS™). Besides enabling the user to interactively work to produce the best possible graphic (for example, one could interactively construct histograms with greater or fewer bars, or scale axes differently to construct the histogram that most clearly displays important characteristics of the data), these programs allow the user to use graphics as a means of exploring what the data appear to indicate. Velleman and Hoaglin (1981) discuss graphical methods that can be used for such exploratory data analysis in more detail and this can be particularly useful for identifying hidden patterns or trends in "messy" data sets. Because creating graphs is not truly formal analysis, the apparent patterns should be taken as suggestive, rather than as strong evidence of characteristics or relationships. Follow-up experiments or studies can be designed to confirm any unusual features one finds through interactive analyses. Another approach is to randomly divide one's data into 2 groups. Graphic displays can be used to investigate the data in one group, and the other group can be used to confirm any patterns found in the first group. This approach is sometimes called cross validation. The interested reader can find more information about interactive graphical methods for data analysis in manuals for these packages, as well as in Chambers et al. (1983).

QUANTITATIVE ANALYSIS

The remainder of this chapter is concerned with quantitative, largely statistical analysis. We have divided the material into 3 main sections: estimating a single quantity of interest, comparing 2 estimates, and investigating relationships between 2 or more quantities of interest. We begin by defining terms used repeatedly in the rest of the chapter.

Population Units and Response Variables

The *population unit* is what we measure, or "the thing about which we record data." It is usually a plant or animal, a trap or recording device, or an area. The population unit often has a temporal dimension (e.g., a trap-night, an animal watched for 1 hour). In telemetry and behavior stud-

ies, instantaneous observations are often made on several animals. We refer to this type of population unit as "animal-time." *Sample units* are the population units selected for inclusion in the sample.

Variables are the measurements recorded for each sample unit. *Response variables,* also called *dependent variables,* are the attributes we are interested in estimating or studying. *Explanatory variables,* also known as *independent variables,* are used to obtain information about the response or dependent variables. Variables also may be classified according to how many different values they may take and by whether the values are labels or imply size or some other ordered relationship. *Continuous variables* take on an infinite number of values, such as all real numbers in an interval. *Dichotomous or binomial variables* can have only 2 values. Common examples in wildlife studies include male/female, young/adult, alive/dead, present/not present in a given habitat. Such data are often coded as 1s and 0s. The mean of 1s and 0s equals the proportion of units in one category. One reason for distinguishing between dichotomous and continuous variables is that different statistical methods are used for these 2 types of data. In practice, methods for continuous data are usually applied when data have 3 or more different values (Snedecor and Cochran 1980). *Label, categorical or nominal* variables may take any number of values, but larger values do not imply larger size or any other ordering; they designate different conditions. Common examples include gender, which is also a dichotomous variable, study site, year, and age. Year and age might be used as either label or continuous variables according to whether trends through time or age are being estimated. The critical issue is whether the values of the variable are *ordered.* Some examples will help illustrate these terms.

In a study of habitat relationships of stream amphibians, Welsh and Lind (2002) surveyed clusters of plots in 39 streams in southwest Oregon. Each plot covered a 5-m reach of stream. The authors recorded a variety of habitat measurements and number of amphibians in each plot. The population unit was a 5-m reach of stream. The population was all potential 5-m reaches in the 39 streams the authors studied. The response variables were the number of amphibians of each species. The explanatory variables were the habitat measurements.

Santillo et al. (1989) studied response of small mammals to herbicide treatment. For one of their objectives, they counted the number of hardwood stems on small, circular plots. The population unit, for this part of the study, was the area covered by one plot; the response variable was the number of stems, which was treated as a continuous variable. Note that technically a count is not continuous, but if the counts take on a wide range of values they are often treated as though continuous in statistical analyses. The authors also measured small mammal abundance by setting snap traps and checking them once each day. The results were expressed as captures per trap-night. The population unit was one trap set for 24 hours (1 trap-night). The response variable was the number of captures, 0 or 1, a dichotomous variable.

"Population" in the small mammal example refers to the set of all possible trap-nights, not the set of all small mammals that might have been captured. Nearly any time animals are captured or surveyed, the statistical population is defined in terms of capture or survey effort (e.g., trap-nights, mist-net days, observer-hours, survey-miles). The animals captured or counted constitute the response variable. If this seems confusing, it may be helpful to distinguish between the statistical population, defined as above, and the biological population, which is the group of animals being studied.

Types of Error

Error, in statistical terminology, refers to the difference between an estimate and the quantity being estimated, usually referred to as the *parameter.* Error may be divided into *sampling error,* caused by random selection of the items in the sample, and *bias,* a consistent tendency to over or underestimate the parameter. More specifically, bias is any error that would have occurred even if we had selected a large sample so that effects of random selection were negligible.

Measurement bias is the result of errors occurring as the data are recorded; *statistical bias* is caused by the way the data are analyzed. Measurement bias is possible whenever measurements are not recorded on some units selected for the sample or when measurements are recorded inaccurately. Statistical bias is usually zero or negligible when standard, widely recognized analytic methods are used. When newer methods, especially those developed by the investigator, are used, careful consideration should be given to whether statistical bias exists. Some examples will make the 3 types of error clearer.

Leuschner et al. (1989) selected a random sample of hunters in the southeastern United States and asked them whether tax dollars should be spent on wildlife. The purpose was to estimate what proportion of all hunters in the study area would answer yes to this question. Sampling error was probably present in the study because, by chance, the proportion of respondents in the sample who believed that tax dollars should be spent on wildlife was probably not equal to the proportion of all hunters who felt this way. Measurement bias could have been present, because 42% of the people selected for the sample were unreachable, gave unusable answers, or did not answer at all. These people might have felt differently, as a group, than those who did answer the question; thus, the proportion of yes answers in the responses obtained might have differed from the proportion that would have been obtained had everyone provided a usable answer. The authors used standard, widely accepted methods to analyze their results, and it is unlikely that any serious statistical bias was present in the estimates. These 3 sources of error, sampling error, measurement bias, and statistical bias are entirely separate from one another. Stating, as in the example, that no statistical bias was present in the estimates does not reveal anything about the magnitude of sampling error or measurement bias.

Otis et al. (1978) developed methods for estimating population size when animals are captured, marked, and released, and then some of them are recaptured one or more times. The quantity of interest (the parameter) is the total number of animals in the population (assumed, in these particular models, to remain constant during the study). Sampling error would occur because the estimates depend on which animals are captured and this, in turn, depends on numerous factors not under the biologists' control. Measurement bias would occur if animals lost their marks (this was assumed not to occur). The methods were

relatively new, so the authors studied statistical bias with computer simulations. They reported little statistical bias under some conditions, but under others the estimates were consistently too high or too low. These errors occurred even if they assumed that no marks were lost and the data were collected properly in all other ways (i.e., no measurement bias).

One reason for distinguishing these types of error is that statistical analyses usually provide estimates of sampling error, but usually do not provide any information about the effects of bias. This point is often not stressed by introductory statistics texts because the authors assume that bias will be negligible. In many wildlife studies, however, this is not a reasonable assumption. For example, wildlife populations are often monitored with methods that do not detect all individuals in the sample plots. If the results are used to estimate density, the estimate is biased by undercounting. Statistical analysis of the counts reveals the effects of sampling error but not the effects of the undercounting. Furthermore, if detection rates change, the counts may suggest a change in abundance when none has occurred or may miss a real change in abundance. Because the effects of bias are not estimated or accounted for in most statistical analyses, a great deal of effort in wildlife studies is directed towards reducing bias and placing upper bounds on the magnitude of the bias that remains despite the investigators' best efforts.

Sampled Population and Population of Interest

Investigators usually wish to extrapolate their findings beyond the limits of the population they studied. For example, most studies are confined to relatively small areas and are conducted during a small number of years. Investigators hope, however, that their results are applicable to a much wider region and other years. Most questionnaire studies, for example, are made on smaller populations than the investigator is really interested. Thus, in the study of attitudes toward spending tax money for wildlife, Leuschner et al. (1989) wished to examine the views of foresters as well as hunters. The sample was selected from the 1985 Virginia membership list of the Society of American Foresters, but the main population of interest included all foresters in the southeastern United States.

In examples such as these, distinguishing between the sampled population, the group from which samples were selected, and the larger population of interest is sometimes helpful. Two reasons exist for making this distinction. Conclusions about the sampled population have the force of statistical analysis behind them, whereas extrapolation to a larger population of interest must usually be justified primarily on nonstatistical grounds. In addition, the limits of the sampled population are usually well defined, whereas the limits of the population of interest usually are not. Thus, the term "forester" may be difficult to define rigorously, and conclusions from a banding study probably apply best to birds that were in the area at the time the banding was done, less well to birds in the area in other years, and even less well to birds farther from the study area.

Probability Models

Statisticians use special types of mathematical equations, called probability models, to describe variables observed when we sample from a population. To introduce the concept of a probability model, we first need to discuss the concepts of distribution and probability density functions.

The process of collecting data involves observing a sample of units from a population and recording some numerical characteristic (variable) for each unit observed. A measured variable (e.g., the weight of an animal) is associated with each unit (an animal) in the population. The value of this variable varies from unit to unit in the population. The (relative) frequency with which different values of the variable occur in the population is called the distribution of the variable. A histogram is one way to display this distribution. The highest bars in a histogram correspond to values that occur most frequently in the population. Statisticians use equations, called probability density functions, to describe distributions. Probability density functions are curves that approximate the shape of the histogram and summarize the distribution of a variable. For example, the normal distribution is a bell-shaped curve that approximates the distribution of variables in many studies. Values of a variable for which the probability density function is large are those that occur frequently in the population. Values of a variable for which the probability density function is small are those that occur infrequently.

The concepts of distribution and probability density function are important in statistics. Statisticians use probability density functions to describe the distribution of a variable in a population. They consider the probability density function to be a complete description of the values of a variable in a population, and the probability density function may be referred to as though it was the population.

In practice, we usually do not exactly know the distribution of a variable in the population of interest. When we begin a study, our scientific judgment allows us to make some assumptions about the nature of this population. However, there are certain features of this population about which we are uncertain and the purpose of the study is to gain information about these features. Statisticians use probability density functions to express knowledge about a population. These probability density functions are mathematical equations that contain unknown quantities, called parameters. The purpose of the study is to estimate the parameters and, thus, have a complete description of the population. For example, a probability density function that is often used to describe a population is the normal distribution. The equation of the normal probability density function $f(y)$ is

$$f(y) = \frac{1}{\sqrt{2\pi}\sigma} \exp\left(-\frac{(y-\mu)^2}{2\sigma^2}\right).$$

This formula is somewhat intimidating (exp stands for the number 2.7183...raised to the exponent indicated by the number in parentheses), but it tells us something about the frequency with which the value y occurs in the population, and is sometimes interpreted as the likelihood that the variable of interest has value y. The quantities denoted m and σ^2 represent the mean and variance of the population. Typically, the mean and variance of the population are unknown and the goal is to estimate these parameters.

In many research studies, the variable of interest is called the response variable. The probability density function that describes the distribution of the response depends on known quantities associated with each unit (independent variables) and on (unknown) parameters. For example, in simple linear regression we measure both a response (that we denote by y) and an independent variable (that we denote by x) on each unit. In some cases, it is plausible to assume the probability distribution for y is normal with mean $\beta_0 + \beta_1 x$ and variance σ^2. The formula for the probability density function is

$$f(y) = \frac{1}{\sqrt{2\pi}\sigma} \exp\left(-\frac{(y-\beta_0-\beta_1 x)^2}{2\sigma^2}\right),$$

and the parameters that we need to estimate are β_0, β_1, and σ^2.

A probability density function for a response variable is often called a probability model for the response. Such models can be specified in a number of equivalent ways. We describe an alternative formulation for simple linear regression later in the chapter. Researchers often talk about "modeling" a response, and by this they mean the process of specifying a probability density function for the response in terms of parameters and possibly independent variables. The goal is to use data from a research study to estimate the parameters and, thus, completely specify the model for the response. Once the model is specified, we have a complete description of the population. This provides scientific insight (often the parameters have scientific meaning), and the model can be used to make predictions about future observations from the population.

Selecting appropriate independent variables is an important aspect of modeling. Recall that independent variables are characteristics of sample units that are thought to explain variation in the response. Thus, as the value of the independent variable changes, the value of the response also changes in a systematic way. Of course, in any study one can think of many characteristics of units that might be associated with variation in the response. Some of these may account for sizeable variation and others for only small amounts of variation. For purposes of modeling, only those that are known or thought to be important sources of variation should be included. For example, if the sample units are animals and there is reason to believe the response varies considerably as a function of age, one would include age as an independent variable in modeling the response. Almost any way in which animals differ (coloring, size) might be associated with variation in the response, but most will be associated with minor variation. Independent variables should be included in a model because there are good scientific or empirical reasons to believe they explain substantial amounts of variation in the response. If independent variables are included because they are shown empirically to explain significant variation in the response, it will be important to consider the scientific reasons why this is the case. Ultimately, a model should make good scientific sense if it is to be meaningful, and this should be kept in mind when specifying the independent variables to be included.

Model Selection

In the previous section, we introduced the concept of a probability model. How do researchers develop the equation of a probability model? Scientific knowledge about the population, perhaps based on previous studies or scientific theory, has an important role in developing a model that adequately describes the distribution of a response in a population. In some cases, scientific knowledge leads to several possible models. In such cases, we use data from our research study to estimate the parameters in each of the candidate models and then to decide which of these models is most reasonable based on our data. The process of choosing between several candidate models is called model selection. Later in this chapter we discuss methods for selecting regression models. Here, we consider the case where we wish to choose between 2 possible models.

How does one use data to choose between 2 candidate models? When one of these models is a special case of the other, formal methods exist for choosing between the models. By special case, we mean that one of the models can be obtained from the other by setting one or more of the parameters equal to specific values. An example is the 1-sample t-test described in most elementary statistics textbooks. The object is to decide whether our data can be modeled as having a normal distribution with arbitrary mean or with mean equal to 0. Obviously, having mean 0 is a special case of having an arbitrary mean (i.e., it is obtained from the model that assumes the mean is arbitrary by setting the mean equal to the specific value 0). Unfortunately, when we wish to compare 2 models where neither is a special case of the other, there is no formal, universal method that is accepted by all statisticians. Anderson and Burnham (2002) and Burnham and Anderson (2002) discuss the problem of model selection in detail, including the comparison of 2 models where neither is a special case of the other, and the interested reader should consult these references.

When choosing between 2 models, there are 3 issues to consider. First, we consider which model is most consistent with the data. By consistent, we mean "most likely to have produced the data we actually observed" or "does the best job of predicting the values we actually observed." There are several ways to compute a number that measures this and several rules for choosing between models based on these measures (Burnham and Anderson 2002). We will discuss some of these (R^2, comparing the sums of squares for regression) later in this chapter when we consider multiple regression. Here we note there are 2 important ways that models can be inconsistent with data. One is that a model consistently misrepresents the data in the same way. For example, the model may consistently predict values that are too small. This type of inconsistency is called bias or model bias. It sometimes arises when the model does not account for an important independent variable. Another way that a model can be inconsistent with data is that it gives inaccurate predictions, but in no consistent way. Sometimes it gives predictions that are much too large and other times much too small. The predictions vary too much from the actual data. This type of inconsistency is referred to as variance. It often arises when a complex phenomena is being modeled by a relatively simple model (one with only a few parameters). A good model should have both low bias and low variance. Whatever measure and rule we use, we want to identify which model is most consistent with the data (best fits the data).

The second issue is the complexity of the model. If a simple model is almost as consistent with the data as a much more complex model (one with many parameters), we should prefer the simpler model, even though the more complex model fits the data slightly better. This is some-times referred to as the principle of parsimony and has been an important issue in the history of science. In philosophy, it is sometimes referred to as Occam's razor.

The third issue is whether one model makes more scientific sense than the other. In choosing between 2 models that are comparable in terms of how well they fit the data and their complexity, we should prefer the model that makes the most sense scientifically.

Researchers should strive to find parsimonious models that are scientifically sensible. Relying solely on statistical measures of how well a model fits the data can lead to statistical "fishing expeditions" that result in complicated models that appear to fit the data well but make little scientific sense. Ultimately, the issue of model selection involves using statistical measures of how consistent models are with data, the complexity of the models, and scientific judgment. Finding an appropriate balance between these issues continues to be an important, but controversial, topic.

Point and Interval Estimates

By "point and confidence interval estimates" we mean, "what is our best guess about the parameter's value?" and "how accurate is our guess?" For example, Koehler and Hornocker (1989) studied habitat preferences of bobcats (*Lynx rufus*). They reported their animals spent 10.3% of their time in alpine areas, and the 90% confidence interval (CI) for the estimate was 6.2–14.4%. To define the phrases best guess (or point estimate) and CI rigorously, we must imagine taking a large number of additional samples from the same population, using the same sampling plan (except that a different random sample would be drawn each time), and calculating the estimate and CI for each one. If we assume the estimates are unbiased, the average of all the point estimates would exactly equal the true value. This is the sense in which the method used to analyze the sample data provides our "best guess" about the parameter's value. Furthermore, if the assumptions of the analysis are met, 90% of the CIs obtained in a large series of samples would include the true value and 10% would not. This interpretation of point and interval estimates relies heavily on the estimates being unbiased. If any bias exists, the average of all possible point estimates does not equal the parameter and the proportion of all possible 90% CIs that include the percentage parameter does not equal 90%.

Construction of a CI begins with deciding how confident one wants to be that the parameter is included in the CI. The most common level of confidence is 95%, but any level can be selected and, in management applications, a lower level is often appropriate. The estimate can be nearly any quantity of interest. Typical examples include sample means, estimated population totals, survival rates, and estimates of relationship such as the slope from a regression analysis. In reporting estimates, one commonly provides the standard error (SE) rather than CIs. Confidence intervals can then be constructed at whatever level believed appropriate. The accuracy of an estimate can also be described by the coefficient of variation (CV) which is the SE divided by the estimate. CVs are often multiplied by 100, which expresses them as percentages. Using the CV, one can quickly identify how large the CI is compared to the estimate. For example, in many situations an approximate 95% CI is given by the expression 95% CI = $y \pm 2\text{SE}(y)$ where y and $\text{SE}(y)$ are the estimate and its SE respectively. If the CV is 10% we may infer the 95% CI is the mean plus and minus 20% of the mean (because the CI $= y \pm 2SE = y[1 \pm 2SE/y] = y[1 \pm 2 \cdot CV]$). This gives a different picture of how accurate the estimate is than, say, a CV of 40%, which tells us the 95% CI equals the mean plus and minus 80% of the mean. The CV also provides a useful way to describe several estimates briefly. An investigator may report, for example, that all CVs were <15%.

Describing Variability in the Population

The CI, SE, and CV describe the accuracy of the point estimate, but tell us little about variability of the measurements. We may be interested in both the mean of the observations and in their variability. For example, Golightly and Hofstra (1989) studied the time required to immobilize elk (*Cervus elaphus*) with different chemicals. Investigators want this time to be as short as possible because animals may injure themselves or escape if the chemical requires a long time to take effect. In evaluating different chemicals, one must estimate the mean immobilization time but also must know how consistent the time is from animal to animal.

Two approaches are commonly used to analyze and describe how variable measurements were in a random sample. The investigator may report the sample size and range, thereby informing readers of the extreme values. Golightly and Hofstra (1989) used this approach, reporting the mean immobilization time for ketamine used on 23 elk was 8.7 minutes and the range was 5–14 minutes. The second approach is to calculate intervals that contained some proportion of the observations. Thus, Golightly and Hofstra might have stated that two-thirds of the immobilization times were between 7.3 and 9.6 minutes or that 80% of them were between 5.8 and 12.7 minutes. A common variation of this approach is to examine whether the distribution of the measurements is about the same as a normal distribution. If it is, the standard deviation (SD) may be used to calculate the width of any desired interval. For example, in a sample that has a normal distribution, 65% of the observations lie within 1 SD of the mean and 80% of them lie within 1.28 SD of the mean. This approach was used by Anthony and Isaacs (1989) in studying nest sites used by bald eagles (*Haliaeetus leucocephalus*). One of their objectives was to describe how much variation occurred in the heights of trees used as nest sites by the eagles. They measured 53 ponderosa pines (*Pinus ponderosa*) used by eagles as nest sites, showed the distribution of the measurements did not differ significantly from a normal distribution, and reported the mean height was 38.0 m and its SD was 5.3 m. Given this information, one can construct intervals that included (approximately) any desired proportion of the measurements. For example, about 80% of the tree heights were probably between 31 and 45 m [$38 \pm (1.28)(5.3)$]. Methods for examining whether observations follow a normal distribution and for calculating intervals estimated to contain any given proportion of the observations in the population are presented in many statistics texts (e.g., Moore and McCabe 2002).

The CV can also be used to express variability in observations. Its formula, for this purpose, is SD/mean rather than SE/mean. A report that the CV was 15% indicates that approximately 65% of the measurements were within 15% of the mean and approximately 80% were within 19% ($1.28 \times 15\%$) of the mean.

Changing the Scale at Which Results are Reported

Investigators frequently record data at one scale of measurement and then need to report the results in a different scale. This is especially common when the population units are plots and the response value is a mean or count. For example, Wood (1988) studied effects of prescribed fire on deer forage and nutrients. He measured the dry weight of vegetation in 1-m^2 plots before burning. Results were converted to weight per hectare for comparison with other variables.

Conversion to the new scale, in this study, involved multiplying the original estimate by a constant. By the word constant, we mean a number that would be the same regardless of what value was obtained for the point estimate. The constant is multiplied by the SE of the mean when conversion is accomplished in this manner. The constant in this example was 10,000 (the number of m^2 in 1 ha), so the SE of the mean/ha would be 10,000 times the SE of the mean/m^2. CIs would be obtained in the usual way (mean/ha $\pm$ *t*-value $\times$ SE of the mean/ha).

This principle also provides a general way of obtaining estimated totals from estimated means. Suppose the estimated mean number of animals per plot is 2.0, and the study area contains 100 plots. An obvious estimate of population size is $100 \times 2.0 = 200$. The 100 in this example is a constant; its value would be the same regardless of what estimate we obtained for the mean per plot. We can therefore apply the "change of scale" rule to obtain the SE and, thus, CIs, for the estimated population total.

ESTIMATING ONE QUANTITY OF INTEREST

This section discusses methods for estimating means, proportions, and totals. Examples include average height, proportion of females that are lactating, and total number of animals present in a study area. Several variables can be measured for each population unit, but we assume they are analyzed one at a time. Thus, we may estimate average weight, then average age, then proportion of individuals more than 2 years old, etc. Methods for comparing estimates or studying the relationship between 2 or more variables are discussed in later sections.

We may record several quantities, but need only one from each population unit for the analysis. For example, condition indices may require several measurements from each animal. If we are estimating the average condition index, only one number per animal—its condition index—is needed for the estimate. Thus, methods discussed in this section may be used for the analysis.

The Finite Population Correction

Formulas for calculating SEs and CIs include a term called the finite population correction (fpc), which considers how much of the population is included in the sample. Including the fpc makes the SE smaller or, if only a tiny fraction of the population is included in the sample, has virtually no effect on the SE. In most studies, the sampled population is much larger than the sample, so the fpc can be ignored (and most formulas in standard statistics texts do not include the fpc). Even if a substantial fraction of the sampled population is included in the sample, the fpc should still not be used if the *population of interest* is large. For example, McAuley and Longcore (1988) estimated survival rates of young ring-necked ducks (*Aythya collaris*) on 3 study areas in Maine. On each study area they found most broods, so their overall fpc was substantial, and, if used in their statistical analysis, would have decreased their SEs by an appreciable amount. The purpose of their study, however, was to characterize survival rates of ring-necked ducks over a much larger area. The fpc was therefore not appropriate, and they did not include it.

One case does arise frequently in wildlife studies in which the fpc should be included. If a small population is being studied, and investigators are interested in some attribute of the population actually present rather than the biological process that produced these individuals, the fpc may be appropriate and may have a major influence on SEs. For example, suppose that an agency needs to monitor the number of falcons (*Falco* spp.) nesting in a canyon. Resources are available to survey about one-half of the canyon. The fpc is appropriate in this case because the goal is to estimate the number of birds actually present not to make inferences about other areas or about the biological process that resulted in birds being present.

Widely Used Sampling Methods

The formulas required for estimates and statistical tests vary according to the sampling plan used to collect the data. In most wildlife studies, the formulas developed for simple random sampling can be used.

Simple Random Sampling

Suppose that a simple random sample of n animals has been selected, we measure an attribute such as weight, age, or gender (coded as 0 = male/1 = female), and wish to estimate the mean (which in the case of gender equals the proportion of individuals that were female) and its SE. Let the measurements be y_i, $i = 1,..., n$. The formulas for the mean and SE (ignoring the fpc) are

$$\overline{y} = \sum_{i=1}^{n} y_i \qquad (1)$$

and

$$\mathrm{SE}(\overline{y}) = \frac{\mathrm{SD}(y_i)}{\sqrt{n}} = \sqrt{\frac{\sum_{i=1}^{n}(y_i - \overline{y})^2}{n(n-1)}}, \qquad (2)$$

respectively. Selecting units with known but unequal probabilities is unusual in wildlife studies, and is not discussed in this chapter. If unequal probability sampling has been used, a statistician should be consulted before the analysis is undertaken because some of the required analytical methods are complex (Cochran 1977).

Nonrandom Sampling

Although nonrandom sampling is often unavoidable for practical reasons, inferences based on nonrandom sampling are often subject to error whose magnitude is difficult to estimate. With random selection we obtain 3 benefits: unbiased estimates of the parameter, unbiased estimates of the SE, and extrapolation of the results to a well-defined population. When random sampling is not possible, we may lose any or all of these benefits. Biased estimation of the parameter is especially likely when population units are

animals and are difficult to catch. The sampling method may tend to capture animals that are young or nonterritorial, for example, and these individuals may differ from older or territorial individuals with respect to the response variable. If all animals in one area are studied, they may be more like one another than a random sample from the region due to effects of habitat. In this situation, SEs and, thus, CIs will be too small. Instances in which the SE will be over-estimated can also be imagined. Extrapolation of the results to a larger population of interest—the whole point of statistical analysis in these studies—is also often difficult if all data come from a small area or time interval, or if capture methods are more effective for certain animals than for others. We may believe the analysis applies to some larger group, but deciding which areas, times, or animals the results characterize may be difficult, and different investigators may have different views.

Nonrandom samples are usually analyzed as though they are simple random samples. In some situations, however, one can make different assumptions about what stages of the sample selection were equivalent to random selection. These choices generally lead to different formulas for the SE, and the resulting estimates of precision may differ widely. A final problem with nonrandom sampling is that investigators may be tempted to explore different options and take that producing the smallest SE. Nonrandom samples should be avoided whenever possible. Investigators who use nonrandom sampling should be aware that rigorous statistical analysis of the resulting data often will be difficult.

Systematic Sampling

Systematic samples are usually analyzed in the same way as simple random samples. This practice is so widespread that investigators usually do not report they used formulas for simple random sampling. Systematic samples, however, are not equivalent to simple random samples, and several points should be understood. First, the point estimates (of means, totals, or proportions) are unbiased if the first unit for the sample is selected randomly. Second, in many situations, systematic selection leads to estimates that are actually more precise (have smaller true SEs) than estimates obtained from simple random sampling although occasionally the reverse is true. Third, a peculiar point, *the estimated* SEs (calculated with the simple random sampling formula) are often biased. In particular, if systematic selection gives a more precise estimate than simple random selection (because the systematic sample covers the population uniformly and does not coincide with any periodicity in the population), the simple random sampling formula overestimates the true SE. This leads to CIs larger than they should be. Thus, if one has used systematic selection, 2 options are available: use the simple random sampling formulas for analysis and accept the fact the CIs will probably be too large, or consult a statistician for advice on whether some more complex method might be used to estimate the SE.

Multiple-stage Sampling

Multiple-stage sampling means that groups of population units are first selected and then some or all of the units in each group are measured. We refer to the initial groups selected as primary sampling units, or just primary units. In habitat studies, a common design is to select plots and then several subplots in each plot. The population unit in this example is a subplot and the plots are the primary sampling units. In questionnaire studies, investigators often select a simple random sample of families and then record the views of each member of the family. The population unit is a person, and the family is the primary sampling unit. In telemetry or behavior studies, investigators frequently mark several animals and record several observations on each animal. The population unit is an animal-time, and the set of all possible measurements that might be recorded on one animal is the primary sampling unit. For simplicity, we often refer to each animal as a primary sampling unit. Multiple-stage sampling is quite common in wildlife studies.

In multiple-stage sampling the number of population units in a primary unit is defined as the "size" of the primary unit. In estimating means, proportions, or totals, one must know whether all of the primary units are of equal size and, if sizes vary, the size of each must be known. In some studies, size is not well defined, but we consider sizes to be the same for all primary units. For example, when animals are the primary units and the population unit is an instant in time, the "size" of the primary unit is not well defined, but investigators usually weight results from different animals equally which amounts to considering them to be of the same size.

Analysis of data from multiple-stage samples with equal-sized primary units is particularly easy because formulas for simple random sampling are used. The quantity of interest is calculated for each primary unit and these numbers are used in the formulas for simple random sampling. Thus, in expressions (1) and (2), y_i would be the mean (or other quantity of interest) from the ith primary unit and n would be the number of primary units.

In most wildlife studies that use this method, selection of population units within primary sampling units is by one-stage sampling. Occasionally, however, a more complex sampling scheme is used within primary units. In telemetry or behavioral studies, for example, observations may be selected in several stages (animal, season, day, hour, instant-in-time), and the stages may differ in length or size. Thus, the seasons may be pre-breeding, breeding, and post-breeding and they may differ in length and in how much data were collected in each. In such situations, estimating the mean per animal may be complicated because the results from each stage of the sampling must be weighted properly. In making the calculations, the goal is to obtain unbiased estimates for each animal (or other primary unit). By unbiased, we mean that if a much larger sample had been taken, with the same sampling plan, the mean per animal would have equaled the true mean for that animal.

Stratified Sampling

The procedure for estimating means and SEs with stratified sampling is: make a separate estimate of $\bar{y}_i$, the estimated mean per population unit in the ith stratum, and of $SE(\bar{y}_i)$, and combine these using

$$\bar{y} = \sum_{i=1}^{L} W_i \bar{y}_i$$

(3)

$$SE(\bar{y}) = \sqrt{\sum_{i=1}^{L} W_i^2 [SE(\bar{y}_i)^2]},$$

where W_i is the proportion of the population in stratum i and L is the number of strata and we again ignore fpcs. In wildlife studies that use stratified sampling, the sampling plan within strata is usually one-stage sampling or multiple-stage with equal-sized primary sampling units, so that $\bar{y}_i$ and $SE(\bar{y}_i)$ are easily obtained using expressions (1) and (2). Note that stratum sizes must be known so that W_i can be calculated.

One advantage of stratification is that sampling intensity can vary among strata. Here is an example showing how valuable this technique can be. We once encountered a biologist studying habitat preferences of radio-collared gray foxes (*Urocyon cinereoargenteus*). He wanted to monitor their behavior throughout a 24-hour period. During the night he checked each animal once every 4 hours and felt comfortable with the resulting data. During the day, however, this sampling intensity seemed too labor-intensive because foxes used the same resting areas each day and seldom moved during the day. The biologist was concerned, however, that he should standardize procedures, so he continued to record locations every 4 hours during the day. If he had defined day and night strata, he could have greatly reduced sampling intensity during the daytime period because there was virtually no variation in habitat use during the day. His $SE(\bar{y}_{day})$ would have been small despite the smaller sample size. Furthermore, if habitat use during day and night differed, the SE of his overall estimate would probably have been even smaller than the estimate he actually obtained because, in stratified sampling, the overall SE comes from the variance within strata as indicated in expression (3).

Problems in Defining Primary Sampling Units

Deciding how primary sampling units should be defined can be difficult. For example, suppose we record territory size during the breeding season for 100 animals in each of 2 years. Should we view the 100 animals as comprising a one-stage sample from a large, hypothetical population, or should we consider the data set to be a 2-stage sample in which years are the primary sampling units, and we have a sample of animals from each primary unit? The answer to this question is important because with the first plan our t-value (for a 5% level of significance) for tests or CIs will be 1.98 ($n = 100$), whereas if the data are viewed as a 2-stage sample, we have only one degree of freedom (df) and the t-value will be 12.7 ($n = 2$). As a result, the CI will probably be much wider and tests will have far less power.

If possible, situations with only a few primary units should be avoided. If this is not possible, consider conducting a whole analysis in each primary unit and report the results for each primary unit separately. Some investigators test for a significant difference between primary unit means, or between the distribution of observations in primary units. If primary units are not significantly different, the data are treated as a simple random sample. If the units are significantly different, the multiple-stage sampling formulas are used for the analysis. This approach has the weakness that failing to find a difference does not mean that none exists. Furthermore, if one does exist, the investigator is more likely to detect it with a large sample than with a small sample. This leads to the paradoxical situation that one may be better off collecting only a small sample within primary units because one is less likely to have to use less powerful, multiple-stage sampling formulas.

Despite these drawbacks, testing for significant differences at least provides an objective decision-making process.

Importance of Independent Sampling

The formulas given above for multiple-stage and stratified sampling are appropriate only if sampling is independent in different primary sampling units or strata. This means that a completely separate sampling effort is conducted in each group and that selection of units in one group has no effect on which units are selected in any other group.

Acknowledging dependence between strata or primary sampling units can be important. For example, Andres (1989) surveyed shorebirds migrating through the Colville River delta in northern Alaska. He stratified the study area using habitats to delineate strata borders. The population unit was a plot-time, and the response variable was number of shorebirds. Andres visited all of the habitats in 20% of the study area on one day; the next day he visited all the habitats in the next 20% of the study area, and so on. Sampling was therefore not independent (in time) in different strata (habitats); areas close together, but in different habitats, were counted on the same day far more frequently than would happen with independent selection. In some studies, this might not have mattered, but shorebirds migrating through the area were strongly influenced by weather, so 2 plots in different strata that were sampled on the same day were likely to be much more similar to each other than the same 2 plots sampled on different days. It therefore became important to include the effects of sampling different strata at the same time. When the lack of independence was ignored, the CV of the estimated density was 0.06. When effects of the lack of independence were included, the CV increased to 0.11. Thus, the assumption of independence should be examined carefully and, when it is not satisfied, a statistician should be consulted for assistance in developing the correct formula to estimate SEs. In addition, the assumption of independence should be met whenever possible, because the formula for the SE can be complex if the assumption is not met. Andres (1989), for example, had to calculate more then 200 covariance terms in his analysis.

Estimating Quantities Other Than Means, Totals, and Proportions

The quantities of interest discussed thus far are all calculated from the means per sample or per group. Occasionally, more complex calculations are needed to obtain the point estimate—as in capture-recapture studies—and formulas for the SE may be quite complex. The SE of a diversity index provides another example of this problem. SEs can usually be calculated, although the advice of a statistician may be needed. If multiple-stage sampling with equal-sized primary units has been used, however, and if the quantity of interest is the mean of the results for each primary unit, the calculations above apply for obtaining the SE of the final estimate. An example should make this point clear. Thill and Martin (1989:541) calculated Kulcyznski's coefficient of similarity for the diets of "4 gentle cows and 3 tame deer." The authors calculated these coefficients during each of several periods. The coefficient is a complex quantity, and its SE could not be derived with methods in this section. The authors, however, were not primarily interested in the coefficient for any single period, rather they were interested in the mean of the coefficients from several periods. They therefore calculated the coefficient for each period and used these values as the y_i in expressions (1) and (2) to calculate the average coefficient and its SE.

COMPARING TWO ESTIMATES

Comparing 2 estimates is probably the most common statistical analysis conducted by wildlife biologists. The general objective in such analyses is to make inferences about the parameters (i.e., the quantities of interest) in the 2 populations being studied. Two questions may be addressed in a 2-sample comparison: do the data show that one of the parameters is larger than the other, and, if so, how much larger? The first question is answered by testing the hypothesis of no difference between the parameters; the second question is answered by constructing a CI for the estimated difference between the parameters. Three examples in which the hypothesis of no difference was tested in a 2-sample comparison follow.

Quinn and Thompson (1987) studied Canada lynx (*Lynx canadensis*) in Ontario, Canada. One of their objectives was to compare the physical condition of males and females of the same age. They collected carcasses from trappers and used renal fat as an index to condition. They considered the animals to be a random sample from a large population and tested the null hypothesis that, in this population, the renal fat indices of males and females were equal. They used a *t*-test to evaluate the differences.

Cowan et al. (1987) studied the acceptance by European rabbits (*Oryctolagus cuniculus*) of baits containing Rhodamine B dye. The authors captured male and female rabbits during several periods after baits were placed in the field. Carcasses were examined for presence of the dye to learn what fraction of the rabbits had eaten the bait. One purpose was to examine whether males and females accepted the baits at different rates. They used ferrets (*Mustela* spp.) to drive the rabbits into nets and considered the resulting catch of males and females to comprise random samples from large hypothetical populations of males and females. They tested the null hypothesis that the proportions of males and females consuming bait in these hypothetical populations were equal, using a chi-square analysis.

Holl and Bleich (1987) compared the chemical content of soils from sites used as mineral licks by mountain sheep (*Ovis canadensis*) and from randomly selected sites to examine which chemicals might be important to the sheep. They collected soil from 12 mineral licks and 12 adjacent control sites, considered the pairs of samples to constitute a simple random sample from a large population, and tested the null hypothesis that average concentrations of Na, K, Ca, Mg, and Cl were the same in the licks and control sites in the study area. They used a Wilcoxon signed-rank test for the analysis.

The main use of hypothesis testing in these and most wildlife studies is to help guard against unwarranted conclusions. One estimate may be substantially larger than the other, but statistical analysis may indicate that such a difference might readily occur even if the 2 populations were identical. In these situations, the data should not be taken as providing evidence that the populations differ with respect to the quantity being estimated.

One- and Two-tailed Tests

In most 2-sample comparisons, the null hypothesis is that the 2 population means are equal, and the alternative hypothesis is that they are not equal. Under the alternative hypothesis, either population mean may be larger. Occasionally, however, one has more information about the difference between the parameters. For example, in comparing survival rates of animals with radio transmitters (test animals) and without radio transmitters (control animals), the investigator might assume that, at most, the survival rate of the test individuals equaled that of controls. In such a situation, the true difference (survival of test animals minus survival of control animals) would be zero or negative, but it could not be positive. When positive (or negative) values of the true difference can be ruled out *a priori*, it is permissible to use a "one-tailed *t*-test" that recognizes the value of this information. Specifically, one adjusts the threshold value of the *t* statistic at which the null hypothesis will be rejected. This approach, however, is appropriate only if one is certain that the true difference cannot be positive (or negative). For this reason one-tailed tests are rarely used in wildlife studies.

Cautions About the Two-sample Comparison

Several points should be considered when one makes comparisons. The hypothesis test is useful in examining which population has the larger mean (or other quantity of interest), but it does not provide any indication of the size of the difference between populations. Furthermore, it does not indicate whether the difference is sufficiently large to be of biological importance.

Failure to detect a statistically significant difference does not mean that no difference exists. Population means are usually different; we may have too small a sample to detect the difference. In addition, failing to find a significant difference does not mean the 2 populations are sufficiently similar to each other that no difference of biological importance exists. It is entirely possible for 2 populations, for example males and females, to differ in biologically important ways, but for this difference to be undetectable from the data collected.

A final, frequently misunderstood point concerns deducing whether 2 estimates are significantly different by examination of plots that show the means (or other estimates) and error bars. The error bars usually represent 1 SE or the 95% CI, and biologists often assume the estimates are not significantly different if the bars overlap and are different if the bars do not overlap. Neither of these claims is true. It is easy to find published data in which the means are significantly different even though the CIs overlap and to find data that are not significantly different even though the SE bars do not overlap. Only the *t*-test tells for certain.

Multiple Comparisons

In most wildlife studies, investigators are interested in making comparisons between several populations and drawing overall conclusions from these multiple comparisons. Weights of males and females may be compared at each of several times, home range size may be compared in several different cohorts (e.g., older vs. younger, paired vs. unpaired), density of a species may be compared before and after a treatment on each of several plots, etc. Several issues warrant consideration in such cases. First, investigators must guard against reaching unwarranted conclusions simply because of the number of tests conducted. Even if no differences actually exist, we would expect about 1 in 20 comparisons (at the 5% significance level) to be statistically significant. That is the meaning of the 5% significance level: even if populations are not different, there is a 5% probability of (incorrectly) rejecting the null hypothesis. Thus, there is a difference between the level of significance for each individual comparison (i.e., 5%) and the overall level of significance or probability of incorrectly deciding that one or more of several comparisons are statistically significant when, in fact, none of them differ. When many comparisons are to be made, the overall level of significance can be substantially higher than the level of significance used for individual comparisons.

To further complicate matters, the overall level of significance can be defined in several ways. It might be defined as the probability of incorrectly deciding that one or more of the comparisons made are statistically significant when, in fact, none of the populations differ. If some, but not all, of the populations differ, it could be defined as the probability of incorrectly deciding that one or more of the comparisons between those populations that do not differ are statistically significant. In the first definition, we are protecting against incorrectly deciding that 2 of the populations differ when in fact no populations differ. In the second definition we are only interested in protecting against incorrectly deciding that 2 populations differ among those subsets of the populations that do not differ. The difference between these (and other possible) definitions is subtle, but many of the methods for multiple comparisons differ in the overall level of significance they guarantee.

A second issue is the ability of a procedure to detect differences that actually exist, that is, the power of the procedure. Several methods (described later) guarantee the overall level of significance (when in fact no populations differ) will be less than or equal to a prespecified value such as 5%. However, these methods differ in their overall power and, generally, we would prefer to use the method with the highest power.

Many different procedures have been suggested for maintaining the overall significance level when several comparisons are made. Some of the most widely used methods are Tukey's procedure, the Student-Newman-Keuls procedure, Duncan's multiple range test, and the Bonferroni procedure. These and other methods differ in a number of ways, including the assumptions they make, type of overall level of significance they provide, and the power of the procedure (in other words, how much protection they provide against a variety of errors). Because of these differences, some of which are quite subtle, it is difficult to compare the methods. We believe many wildlife biologists would welcome a simple and general guideline as to which multiple comparison procedure to use. With this in mind, we describe 2 approaches.

The simplest method, and that requiring the fewest assumptions, is the Bonferroni method. If M comparisons (hypothesis tests) are to be made and one wishes to guarantee the overall level of significance is no more than α, conduct each comparison using a significance level of α/M. This method is general and works regardless of the nature of the individual comparisons. For example, some of these may be *t*-tests, some may involve nonparametric procedures, and some may be exact binomial tests. The drawback is that the actual overall level of significance is usually less than α and the power is low if more than a few tests are made. However, the overall level of significance associated with the Bonferroni test is the second definition above which is preferred by many statisticians.

A second approach is to begin with a comprehensive test of whether all populations are equal. This test is often made using a one-way analysis of variance (ANOVA), a chi-square test (sometimes referred to as a goodness-of-fit test) if one is comparing population proportions, or the Kruskal-Wallis test. If the result is nonsignificant, no further tests are conducted and the investigator concludes the samples do not permit detections of any differences between the populations. If the comprehensive test statistic is significant, then pairwise tests are made using the same level of significance as was used in the comprehensive test.

If the level of significance used for the overall test of equality is α, then we are guaranteed the overall level of significance of this method is also α. This is because the overall test will be significant with a probability of α if none of the populations differ. Thus, if none of the populations differ, we will only proceed to conduct the pair wise comparisons (and perhaps incorrectly reject one or more of the null hypotheses) with a probability of α. The method is referred to as the "protected" least significant difference (LSD) method.

Occasionally in behavioral ecology, the pairwise tests of interest are independent. When this is true, the comprehensive test may be conducted using a simple procedure based on the binomial distribution. The procedure may have smaller power than an ANOVA or chi-square test, but it may be easier to apply if a complex sampling design was used to obtain the point estimates. The procedure makes use of the fact that if all null hypotheses are true in the pairwise tests of interest, the probability of achieving a significant result in each test is α. Suppose that we conduct n tests and that k of them yield significant results. The probability of achieving exactly k significant results, when the probability of a significant result is α on each test, is

$$\binom{n}{k}\alpha^k(1-\alpha)^{n-k},$$

and the probability of achieving k or more significant results is

$$\sum_{k^*=k}^{n}\binom{n}{k^*}\alpha^{k^*}(1-\alpha)^{n-k^*}. \tag{4}$$

Thus, expression (4) may be used as the test statistic for the comprehensive test. If it were large, we would be inclined to view the significant results (pairs declared significantly different) as arising by chance. If expression (4) is small, less than α, we may regard the comprehensive test as having been rejected and the pairwise tests may be interpreted in the same way as if we had conducted a comprehensive test such as an ANOVA and obtained a significant result. We emphasize this approach may be invalid if the tests are not independent. Consultation with a statistician to decide whether this requirement is satisfied in a particular application is advisable.

Biologists often combine the 2 approaches described here, first applying a comprehensive test and then, if results are significant, using the Bonferroni approach to adjust α for the pairwise comparison. However, if the Bonferroni approach is used, there is no need to conduct an initial comprehensive test. This point is important because conducting the comprehensive test, when complex survey designs have been used, can be quite difficult. Use of the Bonferroni approach avoids this difficulty.

In specific situations, a particular multiple comparison procedure (such as Tukey's procedure) may be preferred to either of the procedures described here. However, because of the many subtleties associated with multiple comparisons, we refrain from making further recommendations about other procedures, and recommend consultation with a statistician. Review of Steward-Oaten (1995), who questions the utility of most multiple comparisons in ecological studies, and of a comprehensive treatment of the subject such as Hsu (1996), may also help provide a deeper understanding of how to select a multiple comparison procedure.

Confidence Intervals

When a single comparison is of particular interest, calculating a CI on the difference is often useful. The meaning of the interval may be difficult to grasp at first, but it has exactly the same interpretation as the CI for a point estimate. Each of the 2 populations has a true but unknown mean (or other quantity of interest); we are estimating the difference between these means and may refer to it as the "true difference." A 95% CI on the differences tells us, with 95% probability (if all assumptions are met), that the true difference lies within the computed interval. More precisely, if we were to repeat the sampling and calculations a large number of times, 95% of the computed CIs would include the true difference and 5% would not include it.

The CI has 2 practical uses. When the null hypothesis of no difference has been rejected, the CI tells us the largest and smallest value that is realistic for the true difference. Such a conclusion can be of great value. For example, suppose the mean weights of males and females were 12 and 8 kg, respectively, and the difference was statistically significant. Given only this information, a reader cannot ascertain whether the average weight of females is much smaller than the average for males or only slightly smaller. Suppose that, in addition, we were told the CI on the difference (4) was ± 3.5 kg. This shows the average weight of females may be only slightly less than the average for males (the difference may be as small as 0.5). In contrast, a CI of ± 0.7 would show the average for females was probably (i.e., with 95% certainty) at least 3.3 kg smaller than the average for males. Thus, providing the CI helps the reader, and perhaps the investigator, evaluate the biological importance of the observed difference.

CIs can also be useful when the estimates are not significantly different. Suppose, for example, the weights above were 12 kg for males and 11.5 kg for females and the result was not significant. Do these results show that males and females have about the same average weight? The reader cannot answer this question without additional information. But if the CI on the difference was ± 6 kg, the interval within which the true difference lies (with 95% certainty) would be -5 to $+7$ kg, and we might conclude that not a great deal had been learned about similarities of the average weights of males and females. Conversely, if the CI was ± 0.7, the interval would be -0.2 to $+1.2$ kg and we might conclude the average weights were fairly similar. This analysis—construction of CIs when the null hypothesis is not rejected—is similar to conducting a power calculation. It tells us how large a difference could have been detected with high probability given the data collected.

The CI and hypothesis test are similar in that if the CI on a difference does not cross 0.0, the significance test will reject the null hypothesis. This rejection is reasonable, because the CI tells us the region within which it is plausible to assume the true difference falls. If this region does not include 0.0, one population parameter must (with probability $1 - \alpha$) be larger than the other. Care must be taken, however, in applying this principle of the equivalence of CIs and hypothesis tests. CIs and hypothesis tests derived under the same assumptions yield equivalent results. Differences may occur, however, when the 2 are derived under different assumptions. In testing the null hypothesis of no difference between population means, investigators usually assume, under the null hypothesis, the variances are also equal. As a result, only one variance must be estimated. If the null hypothesis of equal population means is rejected, and a CI is being calculated, the investigator usually assumes that population variances are unequal, because in ecological data, means and variances are usually correlated. Thus, a second variance usually must be estimated in CI calculations, so a loss of precision, compared to the initial test, occurs. As a result, the confidence interval may cross 0.0 even though the null hypothesis was rejected.

Analyzing Paired Data With Parametric Tests

The phrase "paired data" means that 2 observations were collected on every population unit in the sample. The quantity of interest usually is the difference between the means of the 2 data sets. Typical examples in wildlife studies include recording the number of some event (such as activity level) before and after some treatment (such as presentation of food), and measuring the habitat at several sites of interest (such as dens) and at a randomly selected location near to each site of interest. In these examples, the data are clearly paired in the sense that we have only a single random sample from the population of interest, we collect 2 observations on each sampled item, and our goal is to estimate the difference between the means of the 2 observed variables.

Occasionally, some observations are paired and others are not. For example, abundance may be estimated in 2 years with the same survey routes, but some routes might not be used each year, or data might be collected on animals in summer and winter to estimate effects of season, but some of the animals might die before winter. Numerous other examples could be cited in which the observations are largely, but not completely, paired. Several approaches are available for analyzing such data. We recommend consulting a statistician for advice.

Choosing Between Parametric and Nonparametric Tests

In comparing 2 estimates based on continuous data, one has a choice of using t-tests or nonparametric tests. The t-test evaluates whether the population means are equal; the equivalent nonparametric test evaluates whether the population medians are equal. Nonparametric tests are generally regarded as requiring fewer assumptions and as having less power. The choice between the 2 approaches involves a number of issues, including personal preference. In many specific situations the outcome is nearly the same regardless of which test is used. In certain situations, however, one test may be much more appropriate than the other. The most commonly used nonparametric tests are the Wilcoxon signed-rank test for paired data and the Mann-Whitney rank sum test for independent estimates.

At least 3 issues warrant attention in choosing between parametric and nonparametric methods. First, and perhaps most important, t-tests lead naturally to estimates of the smallest likely difference between population *means*, either by construction of a CI or by inspection of the estimates and SEs. CI procedures are available for most nonparametric methods (Randles and Wolfe 1979), but they are rarely used in wildlife studies. This may be because the interpretation of nonparametric confidence intervals is slightly more complex. They indicate how much one of the populations is shifted from the other (often this is interpreted as how much the population medians differ). If the quantity of interest is a population mean, t-tests are probably a better choice than nonparametric tests. Many biologists are concerned that t-tests may be invalid because the observations are not normally distributed. Unless sample sizes are small and there is strong evidence of nonnormality, this problem is rarely serious enough to preclude use of t-tests.

If the goal is restricted to learning whether the data demonstrate a difference between populations, and the sign of the difference, nonparametric tests may be quite useful. However, nonparametric methods test whether the medians, not the means, are equal. This point is important because the mean from one population might be larger and the median from the other population might be larger. Thus, the conclusion about which population is "larger" could depend on whether a t-test or a nonparametric test was used.

One other point about nonparametric tests should be mentioned. With large samples, the distribution of the test statistic is approximately normal and tables for parametric tests can be used to detect significance. Some biologists mistakenly believe that if these tables are used in the analysis, one must assume the underlying population has a normal distribution, or that the nonparametric test is equivalent to a t-test. Neither of these views is correct. No assumption about normality of the observations is required and the nonparametric test is testing the null hypothesis that medians—not means—are equal. The nonparametric test statistic, evaluated with the large sample normal approximation, is much less affected by extreme values than is the parametric test statistic.

STUDYING THE RELATIONSHIP BETWEEN TWO OR MORE VARIABLES

When 2 or more variables are recorded for each sample unit, we are said to have *multivariate* data. One can calculate point estimates, construct CIs, or test hypotheses for each variable separately. However, one is often interested in exploring relationships between or among variables measured in a multivariate data set. For example, Franzmann and Schwartz (1988) analyzed blood samples from 298 black bears (*Ursus americanus*), and measured 26 blood parameters in each of the summer, autumn, and winter seasons. Age, gender, and several "condition" variables also were recorded. The bears represented the sample units, and 75 measurements were recorded for each

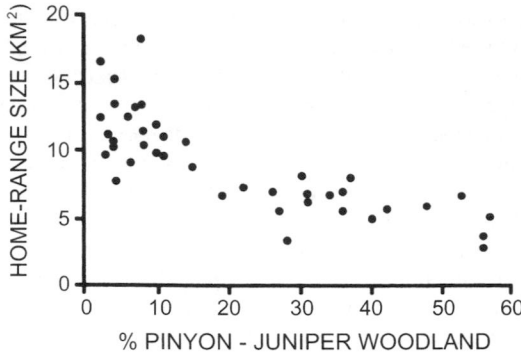

Fig. 7. Scatterplot showing coyote home-range size versus percent available pinyon-juniper habitat (from Gese et al. 1988).

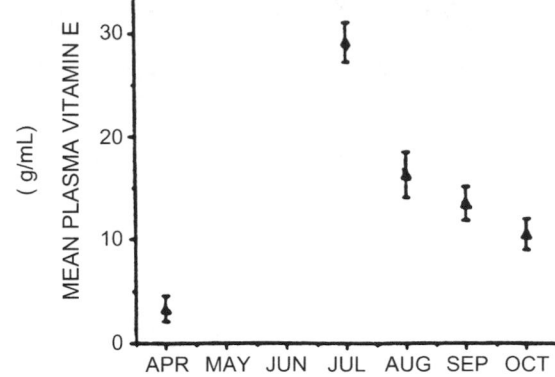

Fig. 8. Scatterplot involving a categorical independent variable. The plot displays both the mean of plasma vitamin E per month and a bar representing the standard error of the means in captive peregrine falcons (from Dierenfeld et al. 1989).

bear. The objective was to examine which blood parameters were useful in assessing condition of the bears; this was to be accomplished by investigating the relation between blood parameters and change in condition.

In studying relationships between or among variables, we must answer some preliminary questions. Are we interested in relationships between *categorical* variables (variables that are essentially labels indicating several classes of interest, such as gender or race), between *quantitative* variables (variables that take numerical values and for which quantities such as means are useful), or between mixtures of categorical and quantitative variables? Different statistical techniques are appropriate for studying relationships between different types of variables. Another question we must ask is whether we wish to establish the existence of some relationship, often for purposes of prediction, or to show that changes in some of the variables, called *explanatory or independent* variables, explain or cause changes in other of the variables, called *response or dependent* variables? In the Franzmann and Schwartz (1988) study, interest seemed to be more in exploring the relation between blood parameters and change in condition (for purposes of prediction) rather than establishing a causal relation between blood parameters and changes in condition. Conover (1988) measured rye biomass in January and again in April, and whether Canada geese (*Branta canadensis*) grazed on several plots (the sample units) on which rye was being grown. The objective was to show that grazing by geese caused changes in rye biomass.

A final question that must be addressed concerns the purpose of the study. In some studies the purpose is to make inferences, i.e., test formally posed hypotheses about, or estimate parameters that describe, the underlying population from which the data were collected. In other studies the purpose is descriptive or exploratory. One is informally using the data to learn if relationships appear to exist between variables, explore the possible form of such relationships, and gain some information about the population from which the data were drawn. Informal studies are useful for posing formal questions to be answered in a future, more carefully designed investigation.

Scatterplots and Correlation

Among the simplest and most commonly used methods for studying the relationship between 2 quantitative variables are scatterplots and correlations. A scatterplot is pro-

duced by plotting the pair of measurements recorded for each sample unit as a point on a graph, the vertical axis representing one of the variables (the dependent variable if one of the variables is so designated) and the horizontal axis the other (the independent variable if one is so designated). The result is a plot that looks like a scattering of points. Gese et al. (1988) made a scatterplot (Fig. 7) of coyote home-range size (the dependent variable) versus percent available pinyon-juniper (*Pinus* spp.–*Juniperus* spp.) habitat (the independent variable) to investigate the relationship between these 2 variables. The scatterplot suggests that home-range size decreases as percentage of available pinyon-juniper habitat increases.

When a categorical variable is used to explain changes in a quantitative variable, a scatterplot also can be constructed. The categories of the categorical variable are represented as equally spaced points on the horizontal axis, and the resulting scatterplot looks like a series of vertical bars of points. One may wish to display the mean or median of the quantitative variable at each value of the qualitative variable on the plot. For example, Dierenfeld et al. (1989) plotted the mean of plasma vitamin E (the dependent variable) of peregrine falcons (*Falco peregrinus*) versus the categorical independent variable month (Fig. 8). The individual data points were suppressed, and only the mean and a bar representing the SE of the data points for a given month were shown to keep the plot from appearing too cluttered.

It is customary to attempt to quantify any relationships that appear in a scatterplot. The simplest relationship is when the points in a scatterplot appear to be centered along a straight line. When above-average values of one variable tend to accompany above-average values of the other variable, the variables are *positively associated*. When above-average values of one variable tend to accompany below-average values of the other, and vice versa, the variables are *negatively associated*. Scatterplots of variables that appear to be centered on a positively (negatively) sloping line are positively (negatively) associated. The more tightly the points appear to be clustered about a straight line, the more highly associated they are. A numerical measure of this association is the (Pearson product moment) *correlation coefficient*. If we have a sample of n observations on 2 variables X and Y denoted

$$(X_1, Y_1), (X_2, Y_2),\ldots, (X_n, Y_n),$$

the correlation coefficient r is defined to be

$$r = \frac{1}{n-1} \sum_{i=1}^{n} \left(\frac{X_i - \overline{X}}{\mathrm{SD}(X)} \right) \left(\frac{Y_i - \overline{Y}}{\mathrm{SD}(Y)} \right),$$

where $\mathrm{SD}(X)$ and $\mathrm{SD}(Y)$ are the SDs of X_i and Y_i, respectively. If, when X is above its mean, $\overline{X}$, the corresponding value of Y tends also to be above its mean, $\overline{Y}$, the products of the terms in parentheses in the summation tend to be positive and r will be positive. Likewise, if, when X takes on a value above its mean, the corresponding value of Y tends to be below its mean, the products of the terms in parentheses in the summation tend to be negative and r will be negative. Positively (negatively) associated variables will therefore have a positive (negative) correlation. A mathematician can show the correlation coefficient must take on a value between -1 and $+1$, achieving the values ± 1 only if all observations are exactly on a straight line. Data perfectly on a horizontal line are defined to have correlation 0 *(Y* has constant value independent of the value of *X)*. The correlation coefficient is undefined for data perfectly on a vertical line (*X* has constant value). In these latter examples, either *X* or *Y* remains constant and questions concerning how changes in one variable relate to changes in the other cannot be answered, because one of the variables does not change. Sample scatterplots and the associated value of r are shown in Fig. 9.

Two subtle points about the relation between scatterplots and the correlation coefficient should be considered. First, the equation for the correlation coefficient actually implies that how tightly points are scattered about a straight line is affected by their *vertical* distance to the line rather than their perpendicular distance to the line. The discrepancy between these 2 distances can be large if the line is steep. Thus, 2 scatterplots may appear to be equally tightly clustered (in the sense of perpendicular distance) about a line yet have quite different values of r because the lines have quite different slopes. Second, a scatterplot can show a distinct trend or pattern and yet the correlation can be 0. This is because the correlation coefficient indicates only whether there is a *straight-line re*lation between 2 variables. When a scatterplot displays a relationship other than a straight line, the "strength" of the relationship can be measured through other measures such as the coefficient of multiple determination in multiple regression or by investigating whether a straight-line relation exists between transformations (functions) of the 2 variables.

A few words of caution concerning correlation should be considered. The presence of correlation between 2 variables, even a substantial correlation (near $+1$ or -1), does not imply that a cause-and effect relationship exists between the 2 variables. The correlation may be present because both variables are responding to changes in some third variable. For example, changes in the purchase of charcoal briquettes and wearing of shorts may be positively correlated because both are responding to changes in outdoor temperature. Correlation may be present but difficult to interpret when a cause-and-effect relation exists between 2 variables, but this effect is "mixed up" or "confounded" as changes in several other factors may also be causing changes in the 2 variables. Understanding why an observed correlation is actually present can be difficult, and the researcher must be careful whenever attempting to interpret a correlation.

Additional features of scatterplots that one should be aware of are *outliers* and *influential points*. An outlier is a point that lies well above or below the "band" or "cloud" of the vast majority of the points. An influential point is one that has a strong effect on the impression that a trend is present in the data, i.e., removal of this point would have a significant effect on our impression of the trend present. Isolated points to the extreme left or right of a scatterplot are often influential.

In the scatterplot (Fig. 10) from Fryxell et al. (1988), the circled point would be considered an outlier, because it lies well above the "band" of the other points. In the scatterplot (Fig. 11), adapted from Renecker and Hudson (1989) (we retained only the points corresponding to moose #727), the circled point is influential. The trend suggested by the plot with the point present is much steeper than when the point is removed. When outliers are present, it is worth investigating whether the observation corresponding to the point is special in any way. If it is, analyzing it separately from the remaining data may be worthwhile. When a point is influential, the data should be analyzed twice, once with the point present and once with the point absent. Conclusions based on analysis with the point

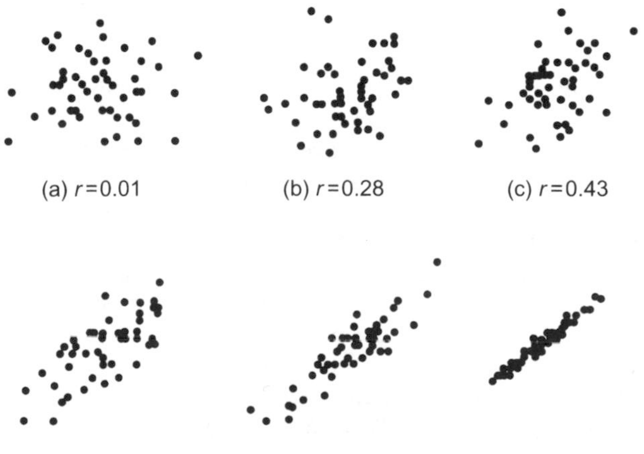

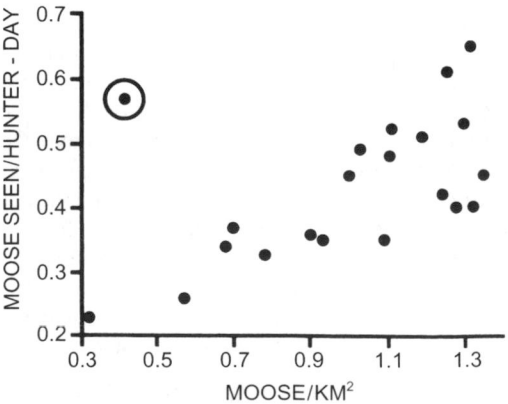

Examples of scatterplots:

(a) $r=0.01$ (b) $r=0.28$ (c) $r=0.43$

(d) $r=0.73$ (e) $r=0.91$ (f) $r=0.99$

Fig. 9. Examples of scatterplots and their associated correlations (r).

Fig. 10. Example of an outlier (circled) in a scatterplot. The plot displays moose density (per km^2) versus moose seen per hunter-day (from Fryxell et al. 1988).

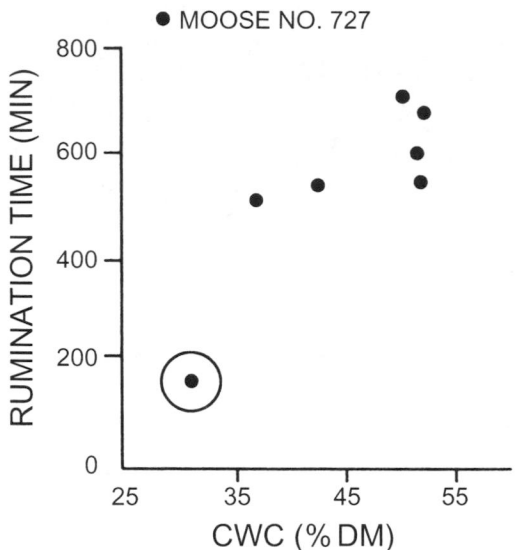

Fig. 11. Example of an influential observation (circled) in a scatterplot. The plot displays the time a female moose spent ruminating cell wall constituents (CWC) in the diet dry matter (DM) for selected times from December 1982 to January 1984 at the Ministik Wildlife Research Station, Alberta, Canada (from Renecker and Hudson 1989).

present must be regarded with caution if they differ from those based on analysis with the point absent. Conclusions whose validity rests on a single observation cannot be made with confidence.

Simple Linear Regression

Formal Models

If the scatterplot or correlation coefficient suggests the relation between *bivariate data* (i.e., data in which 2 variables are measured on each sample unit) is a straight-line trend (recall the equation of a straight line is $Y = b_0 + b_1 X$, where b_0 is the Y-intercept and b_1 is the slope), often one will want to explore this apparent relation further. The method for such exploration is called *simple linear regression*. The word "regression" was coined by the English scientist Francis Galton (1822–1911) and was based on his study of the relation between the heights of fathers and their sons. He observed that tall parents tended to produce offspring that were taller than average, but not as tall as their parents and called this phenomenon "regression toward mediocrity."

In the wildlife literature, the question most commonly of interest is whether the apparent straight-line trend indicates that a true straight-line trend exists in the population from which the data were drawn. To answer this question, one must think about the population from which the sample $(X_1, Y_1), (X_2, Y_2), \ldots, (X_n, Y_n)$ is drawn. If one thinks of X_i as independent variables and Y_i as dependent variables, a formal regression analysis assumes that for a given value of X, the distribution of the values of Y for all population units having the given value of X is normal with mean $\beta_0 + \beta_1 X$ and variance σ^2. This is sometimes expressed by writing the simple linear regression model as

$$Y = \beta_0 + \beta_1 X + \varepsilon$$

where ε is a normally distributed random variable with mean 0 and variance σ^2. Thus, the population units are

scattered around the line $Y = \beta_0 + \beta_1 X$ (with ε representing the departure from the line), and σ^2 describes how tightly the points cluster around the line. In particular, the proportion of population units within a given band about the line $Y = \beta_0 + \beta_1 X$ is affected by the normal distribution, the distribution of ε. The variance σ^2 of the population of Y-values for a given X is independent of X. This is referred to as the assumption of *homogeneity of variance*. One makes no assumptions about the distribution of the values of X in the population. If neither the X_i nor Y_i is regarded as an independent variable, the population is regarded as being described by a *bivariate normal* distribution, wherein for a given value of X the distribution of the values of Y is normal with mean $= \beta_0 + \beta_1 X$ and variance σ^2. In addition, the values of X are assumed to be normally distributed in the population, and in the population of all units the correlation coefficient between the X and Y values is assumed to be ρ. Discussion of the bivariate normal distribution is beyond the scope of this chapter. The interested reader is referred to Kutner et al. (1996) for additional discussion of regression in this context. Although this description of the population is complicated, the validity of any formal inference one makes depends on the extent to which this description holds. When this adequately describes the population, we see the line $Y = \beta_0 + \beta_1 X$, the variance σ^2, and the correlation ρ (when the population is bivariate normal) describe the relation between the variables X and Y.

Inference

In the wildlife literature, researchers usually wish to make inferences about the slope β_1, generally testing whether the slope is 0 (which is interpreted as equivalent to testing whether the relation between Y and X in the population is better described by a straight line with some nonzero slope than by a horizontal line). One may also wish to make inferences about the intercept β_0, the variance σ^2, the correlation ρ (when the population is bivariate normal), and predictions of future values of Y for a given X based on the line $Y = \beta_0 + \beta_1 X$. The first step is to obtain estimates of the slope, β_1, and intercept, β_0. This is generally done by the *method of least squares*. This method finds the equation of the straight line (called the least squares regression line) having the property that minimizes the sum of the squares of the vertical distances of the individual data points from the line. If we have n observations on 2 variables X and Y, denoted $(X_1, Y_1), (X_2, Y_2), \ldots, (X_n, Y_n)$, using calculus one can show the least squares line has the equation $Y = b_0 + b_1 X$, where

$$b_1 = \frac{\sum_{i=1}^{n}(X_i - \bar{X})(Y_i - \bar{Y})}{\sum_{i=1}^{n}(X_i - \bar{X})^2}$$

and

$$b_0 = \bar{Y} - b_1 \bar{X}$$

where $\bar{X}$ and $\bar{Y}$ are the means of X_i and Y_i, respectively. Notice in the denominator of b_1 that if all X_i are the same, then all X_i will equal $\bar{X}$ and the denominator will be 0. We must take observations at 2 or more different values of X_i (and hence at least 2 observations) to estimate the 2 quantities b_0 and b_1. At least 3 observations involving at least 2 different values of X_i are necessary to estimate variances and for statistical inference. If the pairs (X_1, Y_1), (X_2, Y_2), ..., (X_n, Y_n) in the sample are independent (this will be true if sample units were selected from some population by simple random sampling), one can show that unbiased estimates of β_0 and β_1 are given by the least squares estimates b_0 and b_1.

An unbiased estimate of σ^2 is given by the mean square error (MSE)

$$\frac{1}{n-2}\sum_{i=1}^{n}(Y_i - b_0 - b_1 X_i)^2$$

and, if appropriate, ρ is estimated by the correlation coefficient, r, for the sample data. In addition, b_0 and b_1 have normal distributions with means β_0 and β_1 and SEs

$$\sigma(b_0) = \sigma\sqrt{\frac{1}{n} + \frac{\overline{X}^2}{\sum_{i=1}^{n}(X_i - \overline{X})^2}}$$

$$\sigma(b_1) = \frac{\sigma}{\sqrt{\sum_{i=1}^{n}(X_i - \overline{X})^2}},$$

respectively. Estimates of these SEs, denoted $SE(b_0)$ and $SE(b_1)$, are obtained by replacing σ by its estimate, $\sqrt{MSE}$. $\sqrt{MSE}$, $SE(b_0)$, and $SE(b_1)$ all have 2 degrees of freedom. CIs and hypothesis tests for β_0 and β_1 based on normal theory are applicable, and the general procedures discussed previously can be used. For example, a $(1 - \alpha) \times 100\%$ CI for the true slope β_1 of the regression line is

$$b_1 \pm t_{n-2,\alpha/2}SE(b_1)$$

and an α-level test of the hypotheses $H_0:\beta_1 = 0$ versus $H_1:\beta_1: \neq 0$; i.e., a test of whether the slope differs from 0, is to reject H_0 if

$$|b_1| > t_{n-2,\alpha/2}SE(b_1).$$

Rejection of H_0 implies there is evidence of a straight-line relation between X and Y and the correlation, ρ, is nonzero. One can show the test of $H_0:\beta_1 = 0$ versus $H_1:\beta_1 \neq 0$ is equivalent to testing $H_0:\rho = 0$ versus $H_1:\rho \neq 0$. Let us return again to the study of coyote home range. Gese et al. (1988) reported the slope of the simple linear regression between coyote home-range size and the square root of percent available pinyon–juniper habitat to be –1.52 and that it was significant at $\alpha < 0.01$, i.e., the hypothesis $H_0:\beta_1 = 0$ would have been rejected at $\alpha = 0.01$.

Examining Assumptions

The validity of any inference one makes depends on the extent to which our formal model describes the population from which the data were drawn. Thus, a complete regression analysis should include examining the assumption the data follow a normal distribution, have homogeneity of

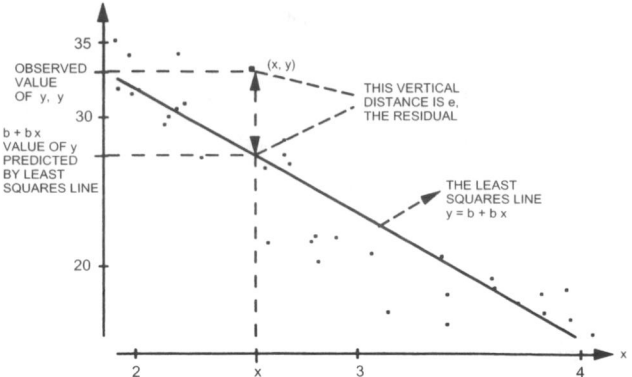

Fig. 12. The least squares line superimposed on a scatterplot. Also shown for a particular point are the observed value of y, the predicted value of y, and the residual as the vertical distance from a point to the regression line.

variance, do not follow a trend other than a straight line, and are independent. "Unusual" observations, such as outliers or influential points, should also be identified and given careful scrutiny. Examination of assumptions is often conducted by examining the residuals $\varepsilon_i = Y_i - b_0 - b_1 X_i$. Notice the residual is the difference between the value of Y actually observed and the value Y would have if it were exactly on the least squares line (Fig. 12).

Two ways in which residuals are used to examine assumptions are worth considering. First, recall the scatter of the population units (of which our data are a sample) about a line is affected by the normal distribution. In particular, the proportion within a given band about this line is affected by the normal distribution. One consequence is that the residuals, which measure how far a particular observation is from the least squares line, should behave approximately as though they have a normal distribution with mean 0. If one calculates all the residuals (many statistical software packages that do regression will calculate residuals), one can use statistical procedures to investigate whether the residuals, in fact, appear to follow a normal distribution. Second, the homogeneity of variance assumption implies the population units should display the same magnitude of variability about a line. As a consequence, the magnitude of the residuals should not display any tendency to increase or decrease as the associated value of X increases or decreases. Such tendencies may indicate a violation of the homogeneity of variance assumption.

Corrective action may be necessary if the assumptions are not valid. For example, if the data do not appear normal or do not satisfy the homogeneity of variance assumption (violations of these 2 assumptions often occur together), one may try replacing (transforming) the values of $Y_1, \ldots, Y_n$ by some function of these values, i.e., by $f(Y_1), \ldots, f(Y_n)$. Common functions of f are the logarithm, square root, reciprocal, or arcsin. Often, the transformed Y-values will satisfy the assumptions of normality or homogeneity of variance, and regression can proceed on the pairs $[X_1, f(Y_1)], \ldots, [X_n, f(Y_n)]$. One must proceed with caution, however, because conclusions will now refer to the *transformed* data. For example, if a reciprocal transformation is used and one calculates the relation between $1/Y$ and X is $1/Y = -2X$, it is incorrect to conclude that increases in X produce decreases in Y. The relation between Y and X is Y

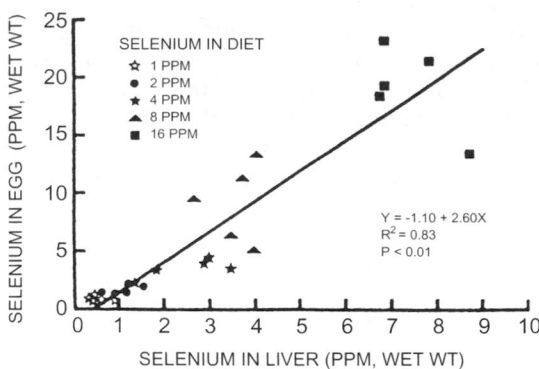

Fig. 13. Example of a violation of the homogeneity of variance assumption. The scatterplot displays the relationship between the concentration of selenium in the liver of female mallards and the concentration in the eighth eggs for females fed diets containing 1, 2, 4, 8, or 16 ppm selenium as selenomethionine (from Heinz et al. 1989).

$= -0.5(1/X)$ and Y increases (becomes less negative) as X increases.

Heinz et al. (1989), studying impaired reproduction of mallards (*Anas platyrhynchos*) fed an organic form of selenium, observed that data in their study that were measured as percentages were made to appear more normal by a transformation. The scatterplot (Fig. 13) of the measured concentration of selenium in the eighth eggs of females fed diets of selenium versus the concentration in their liver suggests a violation of the homogeneity of variance assumption. Notice that variation about the regression line increases as selenium in the diet increases.

Although a formal discussion concerning the effects of violations of assumptions on the resulting inference is quite mathematical, a few comments can be made. If the expected value of Y at a given X is in fact $\beta_0 + \beta_1 X$ (i.e., on average the value of Y at a given X is $\beta_0 + \beta_1 X$), the least squares estimates of β_0 and β_1 are unbiased even if the assumptions of homogeneity of variance, normality, and independence do not hold. If the expected value of Y at a given X is $\beta_0 + \beta_1 X$ and the assumptions of homogeneity of variance and independence hold, MSE is an unbiased estimate of the variance even if the assumption of normality does not hold. For testing hypotheses or constructing CIs all assumptions must hold, although these procedures are felt to be "robust" to departures from the assumption of normality, i.e., these inferences are still valid even if the assumption of normality is somewhat suspect.

The above discussion of simple linear regression is brief. It is important to remember that simple linear regression is a statistical tool for studying possible straight-line relationships between pairs of variables. A thorough discussion of simple linear regression, including checking of assumptions, can be found in any book on regression analysis (e.g., Neter et al. 1983). Many introductory texts on statistics also discuss simple linear regression (e.g., Moore and McCabe 2002).

Multiple Regression
Formal Models

The techniques used in simple linear regression can be extended to provide methods for examining relationships, other than straight-line relationships, between sets of variables. The method for examining these relationships is called *multiple regression analysis* and applies to so-called *linear models*. Suppose a sample of n units is selected from some population, and for each of these units one records a dependent variable Y and p independent variables $X_1, \ldots, X_p$. Some of the X_i may be functions of the others; for example, one might allow X_2 to be the square of X_1. Let Y_i and $X_{1i}, \ldots, X_{pi}$ be the variables associated with unit i. One is said to have a linear model if the population from which the units are drawn and the method of selecting units are such that the relationship between Y and the Xs can be written as

$$Y_i = \beta_0 + \beta_1 X_{1i} + \beta_2 X_{2i} + \ldots + \beta_p X_{pi} + \varepsilon_i.$$

The ε_i represent the cumulative effects of measurement error and independent variables not included in the model whose individual effects are considered to be small relative to those of the Xs. The Y_i are assumed to be independent (this is reasonable if units are selected by simple random sampling), and each Y_i is assumed to have mean $\beta_0 + \beta_1 X_{1i} + \beta_2 X_{2i} + \ldots + \beta_p X_{pi}$, have variance denoted by σ^2 (this is called the homogeneity of variance assumption because this variance is the same regardless of the values of Xs), and be normally distributed. These last 3 assumptions concern the population from which the data are drawn. $\beta_0, \beta_1, \ldots, \beta_p$ are unknown constants (parameters) that one wishes to make inferences about. These assumptions imply that the ε_i are independent and have mean 0, variance σ^2, and are normally distributed. Thus, a given value, Y_i, of the dependent variable will generally not equal $\beta_0 + \beta_1 X_{1i} + \beta_2 X_{2i} + \ldots + \beta_p X_{pi}$, exactly, but the average discrepancies, over all units in the population for which the independent variables are $X_{1i}, \ldots, X_{pi}$, is 0. In mathematical language, one says the expected value of Y_i is $\beta_0 + \beta_1 X_{1i} + \beta_2 X_{2i} + \ldots + \beta_p X_{pi}$. $\beta_0 + \beta_1 X_{1i} + \beta_2 X_{2i} + \ldots + \beta_p X_{pi}$ is the multiple regression function. As with simple linear regression, the validity of any inference one makes in multiple regression depends on the extent to which the above assumptions hold. An important component of any analysis involves checking that these assumptions are reasonable.

The β_i are often interpreted as the "effects" of the X_i in the sense that a unit change in X_k, holding the other X_i fixed, produces a change of size β_k in Y, on average. This change may be directly caused by X_i or may occur because a change in X_i causes changes in other variables, which in turn cause a change in Y. Obviously if β_k is 0, changes in X_k, with the other X_i fixed, produce no change in Y and X_k has no "effect" on Y. Testing hypotheses as to whether β_k is 0 is one way to examine whether X_k has an "effect" on Y. In practice, however, one may encounter the following problem. In many experiments, the researcher has little or no control over the values of X_i. This occurs in observational studies, for example, when units are selected from some population by simple random sampling and the X_i are characteristics of the unit (i.e., age, gender, weight). In such instances, the X_i are likely to be correlated and so a change in X_k is associated with changes in other of the X_i, which in turn affect Y through the other β_i. One does not observe a set of units for which all the X_i, except, X_k, remain fixed and only X_k varies. This means that we get no "direct" information about β_k, only "indirect" information subject to the additional variation in the other X_i. If the correlation among the X_i is large, this additional variation is large and one's uncertainty about β_k is increased. This state is called *multicollinearity* and can lead to rather uncertain inferences about β_k, i.e., estimates with large SEs.

The term "linear" in linear model means the model is a sum of terms of the form (parameter) × (some function of the independent variables). It does not mean that Y is a straight-line function of the X_i. For example, if only a single independent variable X is measured, one can define $X_j = X^j$, so the linear model is

$$Y_i = \beta_0 + \beta_1 X_i + \beta_2 X^2_i + \ldots + \beta_p X^p_i + \varepsilon_i,$$

i.e., Y is a polynomial in X. Models that are not linear in the β_i, such as

$$Y_i = \beta_0 + \beta_1 X_i^{\beta_2}$$

are called *nonlinear* models.

Inference and Interpretation

Analysis of a linear model proceeds in a manner analogous to that used for simple linear regression. The method of least squares can be used to obtain estimates of β_i. At least $p + 1$ sets of values of the independent variables (and at least $p + 1$ observations) are needed to estimate the $p + 1$ parameters $\beta_0, \beta_1, \ldots, \beta_p$. At least $p + 2$ observations and at least $p + 1$ sets of values of the independent variables are needed to estimate variances. To evaluate the fit of the model (Kutner et al. 1996), at least one repeat observation is needed at a fixed set of values of the independent variables. The more observations taken, the better and, for purposes of inference, the wider the range of values of the independent variables at which observations are obtained (with several repeat observations at several sets of values of the independent variables), the better. Unfortunately, cost or difficulty of obtaining observations may place severe limits on the number of observations one can obtain. Giving guidelines concerning how many observations to take is therefore difficult, and perhaps the best advice is to consult a statistician knowledgable in design of experiments.

If β_i can be estimated and if errors ε_i are assumed to be normal, formulas for the SEs of these estimates can be derived and used to construct CIs and test hypotheses with normal methods discussed previously. Unfortunately, these formulas are rather complex, and knowledge of matrix algebra is necessary for their derivation (Kutner et al. 1996). In practice these estimates and SEs are obtained with statistical software.

Interpretation of results can be complicated. For example, Bergerud and Ballard (1988) used multiple regression to study the effect of snow depth (mean depth in cm over an 8-month winter period), gray wolf (*Canis lupus*) numbers (in winter after birth), and total caribou (*Rangifer tarandus*) numbers on an index of caribou recruitment in south-central Alaska. The index of caribou recruitment used was the percentage of 2.5-year-old caribou among all caribou ≥2.5 years old. Several multiple regression models were conducted. One result was recruitment = 20.980 + 0.128 snow − 0.064 wolves. This model would predict that for a mean snow depth of 50 cm and 200 wolves in the

winter after birth, recruitment would be 20.980 + 0.128 × 50 − 0.064 × 200 = 14.58%. This model has a positive coefficient for the snow-depth term, which would seem to suggest that increased snow depth (indicating a more severe winter) increases recruitment. This is counterintuitive and undoubtedly due to multicollinearity, i.e., number of wolves and snow depth may be correlated and the coefficients are somewhat difficult to interpret. The presence of multicollinearity is further indicated by a simple linear regression of recruitment on snow depth that yielded the model: recruitment = 23.261 − 0.166 snow. In this model, the coefficient for snow is negative, i.e., less snow yields higher recruitment, which would seem more sensible. When the coefficient of a term in a multiple regression model changes sign or changes in size dramatically when other independent variables are added to the model, multicollinearity is often present and interpretation of individual coefficients must be done with care, if at all.

In a multiple regression analysis one often reports more than least squares estimates and SEs of parameters. Several measures of how well the model fits the data and generalizations of the correlation coefficient discussed in simple linear regression are also reported. For the model

$$Y_i = \beta_0 + \beta_1 X_{1i} + \beta_2 X_{2i} + \ldots + \beta_p X_{pi} + \varepsilon_i$$

several items are noted.

1. The sum of squares total (SSTO or SST). This measures the total variation in the dependent variable Y and is given by the formula

$$\text{SSTO} = \sum (Y_i - \bar{Y})^2,$$

where $\bar{Y}$ is the mean of the Y_i.

2. The sum of squares for error (SSE). This measures how much the actual values of the dependent variables vary about the fitted multiple regression model $b_0 + b_1 X_{1i} + \ldots + b_p X_{pi}$, where b_k is the least squares estimate of β_k. The formula for SSE is

$$\text{SSE} = \sum (Y_i - b_0 - b_1 X_{1i} - \ldots - b_p X_{pi})^2.$$

Additionally, one can define the mean sum of squares for error (MSE) to be $\text{SSE}/(n - p - 1)$, where n is the number of observations. MSE is an unbiased estimate of σ^2, the variance of the errors ε_i, and provides a measure of how well the model fits the data; the smaller the MSE the better the fit. The number of observations (n) must exceed $p + 1$ for MSE to be defined. If $n < p + 1$, one is dividing SSE by 0 or a negative number. Estimating variances by negative numbers makes no sense.

3. The sum of squares for regression (SSR). This measures how much of the variation in the dependent variable is accounted for by the multiple regression model and is given by the formula

$$\text{SSR} = \text{SSTO} - \text{SSE}.$$

4. The coefficient of multiple determination, denoted R^2. This measures the fraction of the variation in the dependent variable accounted for by the multiple regression model and is given by the formula

$$R^2 = \text{SSR/SSTO}.$$

R^2 is between 0 and 1 and is similar to SSR in interpretation. SSR must be interpreted relative to SSTO. R^2 accomplishes this automatically by taking the ratio of SSR and SSTO. Thus, it is a unitless quantity. In simple linear regression, one can compute R^2 and it turns out to equal the square of the usual correlation coefficient. For this reason R, the positive square root of R^2 is often perceived as the generalization of the correlation coefficient from simple linear regression to multiple regression and is called the *multiple correlation coefficient.*

These 4 measures are routinely reported by statistical software for regression and form the basis for comparing multiple regression models. To learn whether the "full" regression model

$$Y_i = \beta_0 + \beta_1 X_{1i} + \beta_2 X_{2i} + \ldots + \beta_p X_{pi} + \varepsilon_i$$

is necessary to explain the variation in the dependent variable Y, or if the "reduced" model

$$Y_i = \beta_0 + \beta_1 X_{1i} + \beta_2 X_{2i} + \ldots + \beta_q X_{qi} + \varepsilon_i$$

involving only the independent variables $X_1, X_2, \ldots, X_q$ ($q < p$), which are a subset of $X_1, X_2, \ldots, X_p$, is adequate to explain the variation in the dependent variable, calculate SSR and SSE for the full model and for the reduced model. Let $\text{SSR}(X_1, \ldots, X_p)$ and $\text{SSE}(X_1, \ldots, X_p)$ denote SSR and SSE for the full model and $\text{SSR}(X_1, \ldots, X_q)$ and $\text{SSE}(X_1, \ldots, X_q)$ denote SSR and SSE for the reduced model. The quantity

$$\text{SSR}(X_{q+1}, \ldots, X_p \mid X_1, \ldots, X_q) = \text{SSR}(X_1, \ldots, X_p) - \text{SSR}(X_1, \ldots, X_q)$$

is called the *extra sum of squares* and measures how much better the full model fits the dependent variable than does the reduced model. If this is sufficiently large, or more precisely, if $(\text{SSR}[X_{q+1}, \ldots, X_p \mid X_1, \ldots, X_q] / [p - q]) / (\text{SSE}[X_1, \ldots, X_p] / [n - p])$ exceeds the appropriate critical value of the F statistic with $p - q$ numerator and $n - p$ denominator df, then one decides that the full model is necessary. Otherwise one decides the reduced model is adequate. Formally this tests the hypothesis that the independent variables X_{q+1}, X_p have a significant effect on the dependent variable after accounting for the effects of the independent variables $X_1, \ldots, X_q$. This method is purely statistical and does not take into account the scientific "reasonableness" of the full or reduced model. The statistical decision must be modified by scientific considerations in any final decision concerning an appropriate model.

An informal test of the above hypothesis is often conducted by comparing the R^2 values for the full and reduced models and selecting the full model if the R^2 is appreciably higher, although how much higher is "appreciably higher" is subjective. The formal hypothesis test is probably the better way to make comparisons.

For the Bergerud and Ballard (1988) study, the 2 multiple regression models mentioned above, recruitment = 23.261 − 0.166 snow and recruitment = 20.980 + 0.128 snow − 0.064 wolves, have R^2 values of 0.10 and 0.79, respectively. These values suggest that snow depth is not a partic-

ularly significant predictor of recruitment, but wolf numbers, when added to a model containing snow depth, seem to be a significant predictor of recruitment. The authors also fit a model using only wolf numbers as an independent variable and obtained recruitment = 24.379 − 0.057 wolves with $R^2 = 0.75$. This suggests that wolf numbers are a significant predictor of recruitment but that addition of snow depth to a model containing wolf numbers is not particularly significant (R^2 increases only to 0.79). Unfortunately, no information about formal tests of hypotheses is mentioned in the paper, so these conclusions are somewhat subjective.

Several general observations can be made from this example. First, the value of R^2 increased in the above models when an additional independent variable was added. This occurs in multiple regression, i.e., the addition of an independent variable causes R^2 to increase (or stay the same). This is intuitively plausible. Addition of independent variables provides extra information and cannot reduce predictive ability. Because R^2 can be inflated by adding independent variables, one must be careful to avoid adding extra independent variables to increase R^2. A balance between a reasonable R^2 and relatively few independent variables (simplicity of the model and ease in interpretation) is the goal. As noted earlier, this balance is called parsimony.

Second, the interpretations were awkward. For example, in comparing the model with snow depth and wolf numbers as independent variables to the model with only snow as an independent variable, we concluded that wolf numbers added predictive power to a model already containing snow depth as an independent variable. This "conditional" interpretation is different than saying wolf numbers are a significant predictor of recruitment. This illustrates the care that one must take in interpreting results of a multiple regression analysis.

Third, we mentioned the model with only snow depth as an independent variable had an R^2 of 0.10, which did not seem particularly significant. It is possible in multiple regression to have a low R^2 (any value >0, even 0.000001) and have statistical significance in a formal hypothesis test. Conversely, it is possible to have a large value of R^2 and not have statistical significance. For this reason it is important to conduct formal tests of hypotheses in addition to reporting R^2 values.

Fourth, again examining the model with only snow depth as an independent variable, we were tempted to conclude snow depth was not useful as a predictor of recruitment. Technically one can conclude only that a straight-line relationship between snow depth and recruitment does not exist. In theory, one might find that a multiple regression model like recruitment = constant + $\beta_1 \times$ snow + $\beta_2 \times$ snow^2 + $\beta_3 \times$ snow^3 has a fairly high R^2 and is statistically significant, indicating snow depth is useful for predicting recruitment, but the prediction relation is more complicated (here a cubic polynomial) than a simple straight-line relation. Bergerud and Ballard (1988) reported that a 3-way ANOVA was conducted and that snow depth as a main effect and in interactions was not significant. This analysis does suggest that snow depth is not useful as a predictor of recruitment. In general, multiple regression tends to provide information about the specific way in which an independent variable may be useful for predicting a dependent variable. ANOVA (or regression with indicator variables) is more suitable for answering the question of whether an independent variable is useful in some way (no specific functional form specified) for prediction.

Fifth, notice the dependent variable, being a percentage, is constrained to lie between 0 and 100%. For the model with snow depth as the only independent variable, a snow depth of 150 cm would predict recruitment at –1.639% which is nonsense. Examination of the authors' data shows that actual snow depth did not exceed 75 cm. Substituting a value of 150 cm, therefore, involves extrapolating to data outside the range used to estimate the multiple regression model. Such extrapolation should be avoided, and multiple regression models should be considered valid only for the range of data used to establish the model.

Partial Correlation

The *coefficient of partial correlation* is often reported in multiple regression analyses. Consider once again the multiple regression model

$$Y_i = \beta_0 + \beta_1 X_{1i} + \beta_2 X_{2i} + \ldots, + \beta_p X_{pi} + \varepsilon_i.$$

The amount of additional variability explained by adding X_j to a model already containing the r variables X_{k_1}, $\ldots$, X_{k_r}, is called the *coefficient of partial determination* between Y and X_j given $X_{k_1}, \ldots, X_{k_r}$, and is defined as

$$r^2_{j.k_1 \ldots k_r} = \text{SSR}(X_j \mid X_{k_1 \ldots k_r}) / \text{SSE}(X_{k_1 \ldots k_r}).$$

The corresponding coefficient of partial correlation is the square root of $r^2_{j.k_1 \ldots k_r}$ with sign equal to that of b_j in the fitted model

$$Y = b_0 + b_j X_j + b_{k_1} X_{k_1} + \ldots + b_{k_r} X_{k_r}.$$

The relationship between the coefficient of partial determination and the coefficient of partial correlation is analogous to that between the coefficient of multiple determination (R^2) and the correlation coefficient (r) in regression. In particular, the coefficient of partial determination is easier to interpret than the coefficient of partial correlation. Compton et al. (1988) fitted a multiple regression model with number of deer (ND) observed at locations along the lower Yellowstone River as the dependent variable. Amount of riparian cover in hectares (RC) and amount of riparian cover with cattle in hectares (GR) were the independent variables. The fitted model was

$$\text{ND} = -3.69 + 0.92\text{RC} - 0.50\text{GR},$$

with an R^2 of 0.57. The coefficient of partial correlation of GR for a model already containing RC was –0.53. Notice the sign matches that of the coefficient of GR in the fitted model. The coefficient of partial determination is $(-0.53)^2$ = 0.28. We conclude that addition of GR to a model already containing RC accounts for an additional 28% of the variance (SSE [RC]).

Examining Assumptions

In any multiple regression one should thoroughly check whether the model assumptions seem reasonable, i.e., whether the errors are normally distributed with mean 0 and constant variance σ^2. For example, in Bergerud and Ballard (1988), the plot (Fig. 14) of the observed and calculated

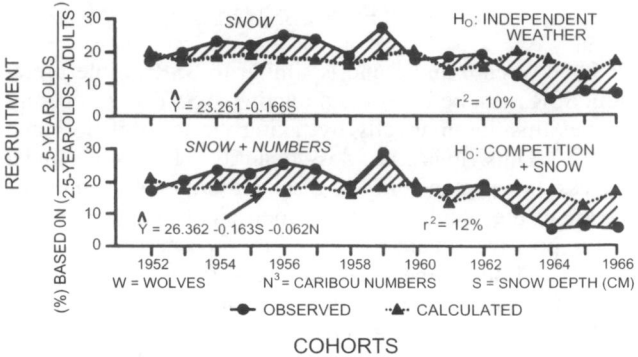

Fig. 14. Example of a possible violation of the assumptions of multiple regression. The plots display actual recruitment at 2.5 years of age in the Nelchina caribou herd, south-central Alaska, versus predicted recruitment using first snow depth and then both snow depth and caribou numbers as independent variables, for the years 1952–1966 (from Bergerud and Ballard 1988).

(from the fitted model) values of the dependent variable shows the early data tended to have observed values above those predicted by the model, whereas in later years the observed values were below the predicted values. This suggests the errors do not have mean 0, but a mean dependent on time. Time should probably be included in the model as an additional independent variable. This is good practice for any data collected over time and may require use of time-series analysis for a thorough statistical investigation.

Because the dependent variable in the Bergerud and Ballard (1988) models is constrained to lie between 0 and 100%, it cannot technically be considered normally distributed. This problem may not be serious if the values of the dependent variable do not tend to cluster near the extremes of 0 or 100% and appear approximately normal over the range of values observed. In such a situation, the multiple regression analysis is probably satisfactory.

A multiple regression analysis may be statistically valid in the sense that all assumptions seem reasonable and the calculations are done properly, but it may be criticized on other grounds. For example, Van Ballenberghe (1989) criticized the multiple regressions of Bergerud and Ballard (1988) on the basis that wolf numbers were obtained artificially, and the apparent relation between recruitment and wolf numbers may have been partly due to something in the artificial method of estimating wolf numbers rather than actual wolf numbers, which were not measured. This possibility deserves further consideration and, to address this issue it may be necessary to conduct a study in which actual wolf numbers are estimated and compared to values based on this artificial method.

Categorical Independent Variables

Categorical variables can be incorporated into multiple regression models in a number of ways. As an illustration, suppose one records eye colors of human subjects as brown, blue, or other. Eye color is thus a categorical variable with 3 categories. A naive way (that should be avoided as we explain below) to quantify this variable might be to denote it by the letter Z and write $Z = 1$ if eye color is brown, $Z = 2$ if eye color is blue, and $Z = 3$ if eye color is other. Suppose we now use multiple regression to examine the relation between eye color and blood pressure (Y). Treating eye color Z as the independent variable and blood pressure Y as the dependent variable, we would get a regression equation of the form

$$Y = b_0 + b_1 Z.$$

Unfortunately, this equation predicts that blood pressure for brown-eyed people is $b_0 + b_1$, that blood pressure for blue-eyed people is $b_0 + 2b_1$, and that blood pressure for other eye colors is $b_0 + 3b_1$. Regardless of the values of b_0 and b_1, our coding scheme used to define Z forces the predicted value of blood pressure Y, for blue-eyed individuals, as given by the regression equation, to take on a value between that for brown-eyed individuals and that for individuals with other eye colors, even if the data indicate otherwise. Furthermore, the difference in predicted blood pressure, based on the regression equation, between brown- and blue-eyed individuals is automatically the same as that between blue-eyed individuals and those with other eye colors. The way in which Z was defined automatically imposes these relations (possibly incorrect) between eye color and blood pressure as predicted by the regression equation. The above way of quantifying eye color leads to poor results in multiple regression and should not be used.

The best way to quantify eye color in the example is to define 2 variables, Z_1 and Z_2. Let

$Z_1 = 1$ if the subject has brown eyes,
    $= 0$ if the subject does not have brown eyes,
and let
$Z_2 = 1$ if the subject has blue eyes,
    $= 0$ if the subject does not have blue eyes.

A variable such as Z_1 or Z_2 that takes on only the values 0 and 1, 1 if a certain characteristic is present and 0 if the characteristic is not present, is called an indicator variable. Notice that for a brown-eyed subject $Z_1 = 1$ and $Z_2 = 0$, for a blue-eyed subject $Z_1 = 0$ and $Z_2 = 1$, and for a subject with some other eye color $Z_1 = 0$ and $Z_2 = 0$. There is thus a unique pair of values for each eye color and no need to define a third variable Z_3. Fitting a multiple regression model as before yields an equation of the form

$$Y = b_0 + b_1 Z_1 + b_2 Z_2.$$

If a subject has brown eyes, the regression equation predicts a blood pressure of $b_0 + b_1$. If the subject has blue eyes, the regression equation predicts a blood pressure of $b_0 + b_2$. For subjects with other eye colors, the regression equation predicts a blood pressure of b_0. Notice b_1 and b_2, the coefficients of Z_1 and Z_2, respectively, represent the difference in the effects of brown and blue eyes, respectively, from the effect of other eye colors on blood pressure, and thus b_0, the effect of other eye colors, becomes a reference value. Because b_0, b_1, and b_2 can take on any values, the equation has the flexibility to predict any blood pressures for the different eye colors.

The example above indicates that one must exercise care in quantifying the values of a categorical variable. The second method indicated is the better way to proceed. In general, if a categorical variable is an independent variable, it is quantified for use in multiple regression by means of indicator or 0–1 variables. If a categorical vari-

able can take on c possible values, the c minus 1 indicator variables are defined as

$Z_i = 1$ if the categorical variable has the ith possible value,
    $= 0$ otherwise

for $i = 1, \dots, c - 1$. If $Z_1, \dots, Z_{c-1}$ are all 0, the categorical variable has value c. There is no need to define Z_c because it is redundant. Notice the ith indicator variable "indicates" whether the categorical variable takes on the ith value. The $c - 1$ indicator variables are all added to the multiple regression equation to represent the (main) effects of the categorical variable. If the coefficient of any of these indicator variables in the fitted multiple regression model is found, in a hypothesis test, to be significantly different from 0, the effect of that value of the categorical variable differs significantly from that of the cth value. The cth value becomes the reference value. By clever use of indicator variables and their cross products, one can represent ANOVA models as multiple regression models and test all standard hypotheses of ANOVA. In particular, in ANOVA models all factors are categorical. One recodes these factors (categorical variables) as indicator variables. The set of indicator variables derived from a particular factor correspond to the main effect of the factor. The products of the indicator variables for one factor with the indicator variables of another factor correspond to the interaction between the factors. Higher order interactions correspond to collections of products of multiple indicator variables, each indicator variable in the product corresponding to a different factor. The resulting regression model has many independent variables, but is equivalent to an ANOVA model. Full and reduced models are compared to examine if the collection of indicator variables correspond to a particular main effect or interaction.

To illustrate, consider a 2-factor ANOVA model. Suppose each factor has 3 levels. Thus, each factor is a categorical variable with 3 values. Let X_1 and X_2, be the 2 indicator variables representing the 3 values of the first factor. Let Z_1 and Z_2, be the 2 indicator variables representing the 3 values of the second factor. The multiple regression model,

$$Y = \beta_0 + \beta_1 X_1 + \beta_2 X_2 + \beta_3 Z_1 + \beta_4 Z_2 + \beta_5 X_1 Z_1 + \beta_6 X_1 Z_2 + \beta_7 X_2 Z_1 + \beta_8 X_2 Z_2 + \varepsilon,$$

is equivalent to the full 2-factor ANOVA model. $\beta_1 X_1 + \beta_2 X_2$ corresponds to the main effect of the first factor, $\beta_3 Z_1 + \beta_4 Z_2$ to the main effect of the second factor, and $\beta_5 X_1 Z_1 + \beta_6 X_1 Z_2 + \beta_7 X_2 Z_1 + \beta_8 X_2 Z_2$ to the interaction between the factors. Comparing the full model to the reduced model

$$Y = \beta_0 + \beta_1 X_1 + \beta_2 X_2 + \beta_3 Z_1 + \beta_4 Z_2 + \varepsilon$$

is equivalent to testing for interactions.

Mixing quantitative independent variables with indicator variables allows one to represent analysis of covariance models as multiple regression models. Additional discussion of the regression approach to ANOVA and analysis of covariance is in Neter et al. (1983). Use of indicator variables makes multiple regression models more general than might first appear and illustrates the fact that regression, ANOVA, and analysis of covariance have much in common. They are all special cases of general linear models for which extensive theory exists.

Logistic Regression

In some biological problems, the response variable is categorical, taking on only 2 values; success or failure, presence or absence, survival or death, etc. When the response takes on only 2 values we say the response is binary. In this case, one can define an indicator variable Y to represent these 2 values, and treat this indicator variable as the response. For example, if the actual response is whether an animal survives or fails to survive, we can represent this by defining Y to be 1 if the animal survives and 0 if the animal fails to survive. Formally, one can then fit a regression model that predicts this response (now a number taking on either the value 0 or the value 1) from a set of independent variables. However, a little thought should convince the reader this is not a reasonable approach. First, because Y can take on only values 0 and 1, the assumption that for given values of the independent variables, repeated observations of the response follow a normal distribution cannot hold. A plot of the residuals after fitting a regression model to Y will clearly reveal this is incorrect and any formal inference will be invalid. Second, the regression model that we fit to the data will not give predictions that are either 0 or 1 for any value of the independent variables. If the predicted value is -3.7, 0.2, or 5.8, how are we to interpret it, given the response can only be 0 or 1?

Logistic regression is the method used to build a model that relates a binary response (represented by an indicator variable Y) to a set of independent variables. Rather than trying to find a formula that predicts Y from the independent variables, we try to find a formula for predicting the probability p that $Y = 1$. To see why this is sensible, consider a simple example. Suppose we are studying how various factors affect the survival of animals. The response is whether an animal survives ($Y = 1$) or dies ($Y = 0$). The independent variables are factors we believe affect survival (for example, these factors might include the animal's age and gender). For given values of the independent variables, not all animals will survive ($Y = 1$) nor will all die ($Y = 0$). A prediction that $Y = 1$ would suggest that all animals with the given values of the independent variables will survive. We know this is not true and we are likely to interpret a prediction that $Y = 1$ to mean that an animal is likely to survive. Thus, instead of trying to predict whether or not an animal will survive (i.e., whether $Y = 1$ or $Y = 0$) it may make more sense to predict the probability that a randomly chosen animal having a given set of values of the independent variables will survive.

Because probabilities must be between 0 and 1, we must be careful what prediction equations we allow. For example, the formula $p = 7 - 5X$ would not work. When $X = 2$, this equation predicts that $p = -3$, which is not meaningful. To solve this problem, instead of trying to find a formula for predicting p, we try and predict $\ln[p/(1 - p)]$, where ln denotes the natural logarithm. We denote $p/(1 - p)$ the odds ratio, and $\ln[p/(1 - p)]$ the logit of the odds ratio. When $p = 0$, $\ln[p/(1 - p)]$ is taken to be negative infinity. When $p = 1$, $\ln[p/(1 - p)]$ is taken to be positive infinity. We can verify that as p varies from 0 to 1, $\ln[p/(1 - p)]$ varies from negative infinity to positive infinity. When $p = 1/2$, $\ln[p/(1 - p)]$ is 0. The prediction formula, $\ln[p/(1 - p)] = 7 - 5X$ is meaningful. When $X = 2$, this

equation predicts that $\ln[p/(1 - p)] = -3$. We can solve this for p and we find $p = 0.047$.

Logistic regression uses the method of maximum likelihood to find a multiple regression model that predicts $\ln[p/(1 - p)]$. Many statistical packages will perform logistic regression including SAS, SPSS-X, and Minitab. The product includes standard errors for the regression coefficients and tests of whether these coefficients differ from 0. Those that do are considered useful for predicting $\ln[p/(1 - p)]$. Interpretation is much like that in multiple regression.

Hosmer and Lemeshow (2000) discuss logistic regression in some detail. Because many statistical packages will do logistic regression, this has become a popular method for exploring the relationship between a binary response and several independent variables. When the response is categorical and takes more than 2 values, multinomial logit models are used. The idea is to build a formula that predicts the probabilities the response takes on the possible values. The mathematics for fitting such models is more complicated than for logistic regression and software packages that fit multinomial logit models are less common. SAS will fit multinomial logit models.

More generally, logistic regression and multinomial logistic regression are special cases of generalized linear models. Generalized linear models allow one to model data that follow distributions other than normal. In generalized linear models, some function (called the link function) of the expected value of the response is modeled by a multiple regression model. In the case of logistic regression, the expected value of the response is p and the link function is the $\ln[p/(1 - p)]$, the logit of the odds ratio. The other components of a generalized linear model are the form of the variance of the response and the probability distribution of the response (Bernoulli in the case of logistic regression). McCullagh and Nelder (1989) discuss generalized linear models in more detail.

Stepwise Regression and Methods of Model Selection

Often in multiple regression many independent variables are measured. Some of these variables may be significantly correlated, and part of the goal of the analysis is to produce a model that makes scientific sense and fits the data well (has high R^2 or small value of MSE for example) while retaining only a relatively small number of independent variables. The best way to find such a model is to fit every possible regression model with some or all of the independent variables and choose the one that strikes the desired balance among scientific sense, good fit, and small number of independent variables. Several rules of thumb are available for deciding what constitutes a desirable balance (Kutner et al. 1996), but ultimately the choice is somewhat subjective. For example, Nixon et al. (1988) examined the effect of 24 habitat variables (the independent variables) on presence or absence of deer (the dependent variable). After examining all possible regression models on the basis of R^2, the authors decided a model involving only 5 of the independent variables was satisfactory. Because the dependent variable was categorical with 2 values, a logistic regression might have been more appropriate.

If one has p independent variables, there are $2^p - 1$ possible models involving at least one independent variable, so the number of models rapidly gets large. For example, with $p = 24$ (Nixon et al. 1988), one must examine $2^{24} - 1$, or 16,777,215 models. Even on modern computers, examining this many models is time consuming. For large p, therefore, algorithms have been developed that "cleverly" search for models with good fit while examining only a fraction of the possible models. These algorithms have been implemented in computer packages and are called *stepwise regressions*. The *forward stepwise regression* algorithm starts by trying all models with a single independent variable and selecting the one with highest R^2 or highest value of the F-statistic for testing whether the model fits. If this highest R^2 or value of F exceeds a pre-specified cut-off, the algorithm accepts this model and continues. It now adds the independent variables not currently in the multiple regression equation to the one it has just accepted and finds the variable that increases R^2 the most or has highest value of F. If this exceeds the cut-off, the algorithm accepts this model and proceeds. The algorithm continues to add variables until there is inadequate improvement, at which point the computer stops and prints the final model accepted as best. Changing the user-specified cut-off values can change the final model produced by the algorithm.

Backward stepwise regression works just the reverse of forward stepwise regression. It begins with all variables in the model and identifies which one decreases R^2 or F the least. If this decrease does not exceed a user-specified cut-off, the variable is dropped from the model and the algorithm is repeated. This process continues until no more variables can be removed, at which point it ceases and the final model is printed. The model resulting from a backward stepwise regression may vary as one changes the cut-off values and may not produce the model produced by a forward stepwise regression.

The most popular stepwise procedure is the *full stepwise regression,* which alternates between a forward and backward stepwise approach. Variables added at a given stage may be removed at a later stage, and those removed at a given stage may be replaced later. The user must supply 2 cut-off values (one for the forward part and one for the backward part), and the choice will affect the final result. The result of a full stepwise regression need not agree with either a forward or backward stepwise regression. Johnson et al. (1989) used stepwise regression (presumably the full stepwise algorithm) to examine the effects of 15 land use variables on a variable measuring bird damage to grapefruit in southern Texas. The final model involved only 3 of the independent variables.

Although a stepwise regression will generally lead to a model with reasonably good fit, some words of caution are offered. These algorithms do not examine all possible models, so they may miss models with better fit and possibly fewer variables than those produced by the stepwise procedure. Models produced by these algorithms need not make scientific sense nor need they satisfy our regression assumptions. Any model produced by a stepwise procedure should therefore be investigated further. In addition to checking model assumptions, one may wish to add or delete variables to produce a model that achieves a better balance among scientific sense, good fit, and small number of independent variables. One may also wish to compare the model produced by a stepwise procedure to other models. Use of a stepwise procedure does not eliminate the need for additional investigation before one decides on a

final regression model. Examination of all possible models is therefore recommended when feasible; i.e., when the number of independent variables is not too large. Stepwise procedures should be used only when this is not the case.

Because of the problems associated with stepwise procedures (for example, the dependence of the model selected on the cut-off values specified), other methods for model selection have been proposed. Many are based on measures of how well a given model predicts the observed data but at the same time include a penalty for having a large number of parameters. Some of these measures are derived from so-called information theoretic approaches. Two popular measures are the Akaike's Information Criterion (AIC) and the Bayes Information Criterion (BIC). The latter is also sometimes referred to as the Schwartz Criterion. In cases where models are fit by maximum likelihood (for example, in logistic regression), AIC and BIC are a function of the negative of the logarithm of the likelihood (small values of this term indicate good model fit) plus a term that increases as the number of parameters in the model increases. Small values of AIC or BIC indicate good fit. Further discussion of these criteria is beyond the scope of this chapter, but the interested reader is referred to Hastie et al. (2001) and Burnham and Anderson (2002) who discuss issues of model assessment and selection using a variety of criteria, including AIC and BIC.

Other Methods in Regression Analysis

Recall that our multiple regression model is

$$Y_i = \beta_0 + \beta_1 X_{1i} + \beta_2 X_{2i} + \ldots + \beta_p X_{pi} + \varepsilon_i.$$

The Y_i are assumed to be independent and random, which will be the case if the data were collected by simple random sampling. The multiple regression function is the mean of the Y_i and the independent variables are regarded as nonrandom fixed quantities. In some applications, for example when the observations are the result of stratified random sampling or multi-stage sampling, it may not be reasonable to assume that observations are independent. In situations in which several animals are studied and more than one observation is taken on an animal, observations on different animals may be regarded as independent, but observations on the same animal are likely to be dependent.

One can incorporate dependency into linear models by regarding some of the independent variables as random. As a simple example, suppose we study 5 animals and have multiple observations on each. Let Z_j be the effect of animal j. Consider the regression model

$$Y_{ij} = \beta_0 + \beta_1 X_{1ij} + \beta_2 X_{2ij} + \ldots + \beta_p X_{pij} + Z_j + \varepsilon_{ij}$$

where Y_{ij} is the i-th observation on animal j and X_{kij} is the value of the k-th independent variable for the i-th observation on animal j. If we regard Z_j as random (one often regards Z_j as having a normal distribution with mean 0 and unknown variance), then Z_j is the same for all observations on animal j and this makes all observations on animal j correlated. As animals vary, Z_j represents the animal to animal variation. In this way, mixed effects models allow us to model both the means of data as well as the vaiances and covariances.

When some of the independent variables in a linear model are treated as random, one is said to have a mixed effects model. Adding appropriate random independent variables to a linear model allows one to account for some observations that may not be independent. Discussion of the analysis of mixed effects models is beyond the scope of this chapter, but most statistical packages (e.g., SAS, SPSS-X, Minitab) allow one to fit mixed effects models to data. Hicks and Turner (1999) discuss mixed effects models, including how to fit such models in SAS. Because such models allow us to incorporate features of the sampling design, repeated measures on subjects, etc. into the model, these models are of great utility in wildlife studies.

Additional topics in regression beyond the scope of the present discussion include analysis of nonlinear models (Gallant 1987, Kutner et al. 1996), inverse regression or calibration (Kutner et al. 1996), path analysis which provides a method for detecting cause and effect relationships (Namboodiri et al. 1975, Sokal and Rohlf 1995), and response surface methodology (Box and Draper 1987).

Factor Analysis and Principal Components

Investigators collect multivariate data in essentially all real experiments, usually with a fairly large number of variables measured on each unit. Browsing through issues of the *Journal of Wildlife Management* or the *Wildlife Society Bulletin* will quickly convince one of this fact. For example, Cruz (1988) measured the frequency of use of 20 foraging categories for 11 species of birds. Thus, for each species (basic experimental unit), there were 20 measured variables resulting in 11 multivariate measurements.

When many variables are measured on each unit, often these variables are correlated with each other. In fact, "redundancies" may exist in the variables, i.e., the information in one variable is essentially contained in a subset of the other variables. In multiple regression terms, this one variable could be predicted fairly precisely with a multiple regression equation involving a subset of the other variables and eliminated from the data without much loss of information. For multivariate data, the following question may be worth investigating. "Is it possible to replace the set of variables actually measured with a much smaller set of artificial variables without sacrificing much of the information contained in the original measurements?" *Principal components analysis* provides a means of answering this question.

Suppose $X_1, \ldots, X_n$ are the n variables measured on each experimental unit. A *linear combination* or (linear) *score* of these variables is any function of the form $a_1 X_1 + a_2 X_2 + \ldots + a_n X_n$ where the a_k are known constants (some may be 0). Principal components analysis attempts to find the set of m linear combinations or scores of the X_i, such as

$$
\begin{aligned}
&a_{11} X_1 + \ldots + a_{1n} X_n, \\
&a_{21} X_1 + \ldots + a_{2n} X_n, \\
&a_{m1} X_1 + \ldots + a_{mn} X_n,
\end{aligned}
$$

with m much smaller than n, which "best" replaces the original variables $X_1, \ldots, X_n$. Here "best" has the following meaning. The sum of the sample variances of these m linear combinations or scores is the largest possible for any set of m scores. The set with largest variance accounts for as much of the variability in the original data as possible

by use of only m scores, and "best" explains the variation in the original data. The goal of most studies is to understand why the data vary, so this set of m scores is the "best" way to replace the original variables by a smaller subset of m new variables for purposes of investigating the variation. These best m scores are called the *first m principal components*. The $a_{11}, a_{12}, \ldots, a_{mn}$ in the above linear combinations are called *factor loadings*.

One reason for using principal components is to replace a large, unwieldy set of measurements with a much smaller set without sacrificing too much of the information in the original measurements. Smaller sets of data are generally easier to analyze and interpret. In Cruz (1988), it was important to reduce the number of variables. Recall in the discussion of multiple regression we mentioned the method of least squares required at least $p + 1$ observations to estimate the $p + 1$ parameters and $p + 2$ observations to estimate variances in the multiple regression equation. The Cruz (1988) data consisted of 11 multivariate observations, each containing 20 variables. For reasons similar to those in multiple regression, one needs at least 21 (and preferably more) observations to jointly investigate correlations among the 20 variables without problems. With only 11 observations one is capable of examining correlations among only 10 variables. Thus, in the Cruz data, the number of variables must be reduced before investigation of relationships among the variables can proceed. Principal components provides a method for doing this while retaining as much information as possible. Cruz (1988) reduced the number of variables from 20 to the best 5 scores, or first 5 principal components, using principal components analysis.

Selecting m, i.e., the number of scores to include in a principal components analysis is somewhat subjective. The mathematics of a principal components analysis guarantees that if one chooses $m = n$, i.e., the number of scores equals the number of original variables (in this case one is said to have selected all n principal components), the resulting scores will not be the original variables but rather a set of uncorrelated scores that can be ordered so that the first one is the best single score (first principal component), the first 2 are the best pair of scores (first 2 principal components), the first 3 are the best set of 3 scores (first 3 principal components), etc. The fact these scores are uncorrelated suggests they can be interpreted as being independent. Associated with each score is a number (called an eigenvalue) that is proportional to the additional variance explained by the score. The sum of all $m = n$ eigenvalues equals the total variance in the data, and the eigenvalue of a particular score divided by this total indicates the fraction of the total variability explained by the score. The sum of the eigenvalues of the first j principal components divided by the total variability indicates the fraction of the total variability accounted for by these j scores. One wants to keep the number of scores included fairly small while explaining a reasonable fraction of the total variability. Adding scores increases this fraction and there is a trade-off between these 2 objectives. In the Cruz (1988) paper, the first 5 principal components accounted for 0.75 of the total variability, and this was believed to be a reasonable compromise. Thompson and Capen (1988) measured 13 habitat variables for each of 24 species of birds. They used a principal components analysis to reduce the number of habitat variables and found the best 3 scores, or first 3 principal components, accounted for 0.886 of the variation. This was believed to be satisfactory. The ideal would be to have the first 1–2 scores account for 0.90 or greater of the variability; this rarely happens in practice. Generally there is no point in adding additional principal components when the addition of the next one increases the fraction of the variability explained by only a small amount.

Having identified the first m principal components, one commonly attempts to attach subject matter interpretations to them. This is generally a subjective undertaking. For example, suppose one had 10 variables, say $X_1, \ldots, X_{10}$, and the first principal component was

$$0.87X_1 + 0.12X_2 + 0.09X_3 - 0.17X_4 + 0.75X_5 - 0.06X_6 + 0.84X_7 + 0.29X_8 + 0.18X_9 - 0.22X_{10}.$$

The coefficients or loadings of X_1, X_5, and X_7 are considerably larger in absolute value than the rest and are of the same order of magnitude. One might say, therefore, that the first principal component is essentially the mean or total of X_1, X_5, and X_7 because it is basically an equally weighted sum of these values. If X_1, X_5, and X_7 share some common characteristic and this characteristic is not shared by the other variables, this principal component might further be interpreted as measuring this characteristic. In the Cruz (1988) data, the first principal component had large, positive loadings (coefficients) for the variables "gleaning" and "probing," large negative loadings for several "sally" or "hovering" variables, and somewhat smaller loadings for all other variables. This component was therefore interpreted as a variable that distinguished between species that sally or hover and species that mainly glean or probe for food.

If a small number of principal components can be found that explain a high fraction of the variability in the data, and if reasonable subject matter interpretations can be attached to these components, one is tempted to conclude these principal components represent "unmeasurable" factors (i.e., quantities that cannot be directly measured) that are responsible for generating the values of the variables actually measured. In an education context, one might believe that grades in math courses and scores on math achievement tests are all basically driven by a single "unmeasurable" factor called innate math ability. Although the results of a principal components analysis may suggest that a large collection of variables can be "explained" by a relatively small number of "unmeasurable" factors, a formal attempt to answer such a question involves conducting a *factor analysis*.

Discussion of factor analysis requires advanced mathematics (knowledge of linear algebra), and will not be presented in detail here. Wichern and Johnson (2002) present a detailed discussion of factor analysis as well as principal components analysis. A readable, nontechnical discussion can also be found in Hair et al. (1998). In essence, a formal factor analysis involves writing a model, not unlike a regression model, that relates a large quantity of measured variables to a small quantity of (unmeasurable) factors. Some statistical method (maximum likelihood and least squares are 2 that are used) is used to fit the model (estimate parameters). The results are used to examine if the factor model adequately describes the data, if fewer factors are needed, or if additional factors are necessary. Formal statistical tests can be performed to answer these questions

if the method of maximum likelihood is used and errors (discrepancies between the fitted model and the actual data) appear to be normally distributed. A typical factor analysis also involves attempts to find the model that relates the measured variables to the factors in the manner that makes interpretation of the factors most clear. This is accomplished using means of so-called methods for *rotating* solutions. Fitting these models, rotating them, and conducting statistical tests require using a statistical package such as SAS, SPSS, or LISREL. This, along with the difficulties of interpretation, suggests that one should not attempt to use factor analysis without first consulting a statistician. Rexstad et al. (1988) reported some of the pitfalls that can occur when these procedures are used without sufficient care.

In practice, many researchers use principal components analysis to identify a small number of "unmeasurable" factors that "explain" a large collection of measured variables. Although not a formal factor analysis, this use of principal components is a popular and acceptable substitute and is presented as factor analysis in some texts.

Classification and Discriminant Analysis

Occasionally, experiments are designed or data are collected for the purpose of ascertaining how to classify an experimental unit into one of several groups on the basis of measurements of several independent variables. In the example of Nixon et al. (1988), the authors investigated how 24 habitat variables could be used to classify sites into areas with deer during the winter versus areas with no deer during the winter. In another example, Crabtree et al. (1989) investigated the effectiveness of 15 habitat variables for classifying gadwall (*Anas strepera*) nests as likely or unlikely to be destroyed by mammalian predators.

The 2 basic objectives in a classification analysis are to learn which of several variables are useful for purposes of classification and to devise a classification rule based on these variables. Several methods are available for achieving these objectives; all require that for each experimental unit one measures the independent variables of interest and knows how to classify the unit. Obviously not knowing to which group a unit belongs prevents identifying the relation between the independent variables and groups for the unit and, thus, the unit provides no useful information for the classification analysis.

The most widely used method for classification is *discriminant analysis*. For a discriminant analysis to be appropriate, all independent variables must be jointly normally distributed (more precisely, the independent variables must have a multivariate normal distribution). In addition, if the variances and correlations between the variables do not depend on the group from which the unit came (called homogeneity of covariance matrices or the assumption of equal covariance matrices), one can develop a classification rule as follows: (1) form a linear combination or score, as defined in principal components analysis, involving the independent variables; (2) for each unit, calculate this score from the observed data; and (3) conduct a one-way ANOVA using these scores, computing the F statistic for testing the hypothesis that the groups do not differ with respect to this score. As one changes the formula for the score, one produces different values of this F statistic. Using calculus one can calculate the score that maximizes this F statistic and best displays differences in the groups. This score, called *Fisher's* linear discriminant function, best differentiates among the groups and can be used for classification. If the *F* statistic associated with Fisher's linear discriminant function is sufficiently large [a formal hypothesis test can be constructed following Wichern and Johnson 2002)], one concludes the independent variables are useful for purposes of classification. This analysis is called a *discriminant analysis*. Hypothesis tests can also be constructed for testing whether a given variable significantly improves the discriminant function, and stepwise algorithms, not unlike those discussed in multiple regression, can be developed for identifying a good subset of independent variables for purposes of classification. Such procedures have been implemented in many computer packages. Nixon et al. (1988) used a stepwise discriminant analysis and concluded a linear discriminant function involving only 2 of the 24 habitat variables classified variables satisfactorily.

When variances or correlations among variables depend on the groups, i.e., the assumption of homogeneity of covariance matrices fails, a variation on the above analysis, also called a discriminant analysis, can be conducted. Techniques borrowed from advanced calculus and probability can be used to select the rule for classifying units into groups that minimizes the number of incorrect classifications for the data collected (Wichern and Johnson 2002). Because one knows to which groups the units in the sample belong, any candidate rule can be tried on the data; its performance can be evaluated by comparing the results of the rule to the actual classifications. This procedure actually yields Fisher's linear discriminant function when the covariance matrices are equal. Formal hypothesis tests concerning whether the classification rule is adequate are not available when the assumption of homogeneity of the covariance matrices fails. Adequacy is subjectively based on the number of correct classifications when the rule is applied to the data. One drawback of this measure is that the rule was constructed to maximize the number of correct classifications in the data used to construct the rule and, not surprisingly, it will appear to perform well on these data. For purposes of evaluating rules produced by this method, it is better to divide the data into 2 sets. One set is used to derive the discriminant function and the other is used to evaluate it. This procedure will give a truer measure of the performance of the classification rule. The set used to construct the rule should generally be larger than that used to evaluate the rule, because one typically wants most of the information in the data to be used to construct the rule.

Many statistical software packages (for example, SAS, SPSS-X, and BMDP) do both of the above discriminant analyses, including testing for equality of covariance matrices. They also allow the user to test the resulting rule on a portion of the data set that has been set aside for that purpose.

When the independent variables are decidedly non-normal (this would occur if several of them were categorical), the above classification methods may not be appropriate. However, if the assumption of homogeneity of covariance matrices holds, the analysis is thought to be somewhat insensitive to departures from normality. Other methods exist for conducting classification analysis when discriminant analysis is inappropriate. One possibility is to use a categorical variable to represent the groups, treat this as the dependent variable, and conduct a logistic regression or fit a multinomial logit model to the data. Another possibility is to use Classification and Regression Trees (CART). This is a nonparametric method for identifying which of a set of variables is useful for classification or prediction and for developing classification or prediction rules based on these variables. Because this method can be used for developing prediction equations, CART can be used in place of multiple regression when the assumptions of multiple regression are violated. Breiman et al. (1984) describe CART and the software that is available for conducting this analysis. Hastie et al. (2001) discuss extensions of CART.

Discriminant analysis is by far the most common method of classification analysis, perhaps in part because other classification methods are not well known to nonstatisticians. Also, software for other analyses is not as widely available as that for discriminant analysis. Researchers should be aware, however, that discriminant analysis may not be appropriate for some classification analysis and that more appropriate methods may exist. The interested reader should consult Hair et al. (1998) for a more detailed, readable description of discriminant analysis. Rexstad et al. (1988) discussed some of the pitfalls associated with discriminant analysis. The best advice is to consult a statistician before doing classification analysis.

Bayesian Analysis

Bayesian methods have been popular among many statisticians for a long time. With advances in computational power, researchers are now finding ways to apply these methods to complex scientific problems. Thus, these methods are becoming an important tool in wildlife biology.

We previously introduced the concept of probability density functions. Probability density functions completely describe the distribution of a variable in a population, i.e., they summarize our knowledge about the values of the variable in the population. These probability density functions contain (unknown) parameters, and the goal of a research study is to estimate these parameters. In classical statistics, these parameters are considered unknown constants. However, in practice, we often know something about these parameters based on scientific theory and past data. For example, if the weights of animals in a population are believed to follow a normal distribution with (unknown) mean μ, it is not true that we know nothing about μ. Obviously, μ must be positive if it represents a mean weight. We are also likely to be able to specify a range of plausible values for μ based on what we know about the animal of interest. If the animals are mice, a mean weight of 1,000 kg is not plausible. In Bayesian methodology, we use probability density functions to specify what we know about parameters. In particular, we associate a probability density function with each parameter in our probability model. Large values of this density function correspond to values of the parameter that we believe are likely to be true. Small values of this density function correspond to values that we believe are unlikely. We call this probability density function the prior distribution for the parameter. It summarizes our knowledge about the parameter prior to collecting data. Specifying a density function *a priori* that realistically reflects our knowledge is a nontrivial task, and is one of the more challenging aspects of using Bayesian methods.

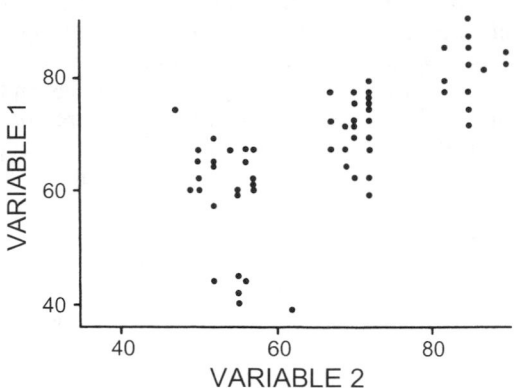

Fig. 15. Scatterplot displaying clustering. There appear to be 4 clusters in this plot.

The purpose of a research study is to gain information about parameters. In Bayesian methods, the data we collect allow us to update or refine our prior knowledge about parameters. The distribution that represents our knowledge about a parameter after observing data, i.e., after updating our prior knowledge, is called the posterior distribution. It summarizes our knowledge about a parameter after observing data. For example, suppose we believe the distribution of the weights of an animal is normal with unknown mean m and known variance σ^2. Suppose our prior distribution for μ is that μ is equally likely to be any value between 0.5 and 5 kg. If our data gives a mean weight of 3 kg. we might revise our prior distribution so the values near 3 kg arc now more likely to be correct than values near 0.5 or 5 kg. This revised prior knowledge is the posterior distribution. Bayesian methodology consists of mathematical formulas for revising the prior distribution (modifying the formula of the probability density function) to produce the posterior distribution based on the data we observe. Only in special cases can these formulas be evaluated in closed form. Recent advances in computational methods now allow researchers to numerically compute posteriors in complicated situations, increasing the extent to which Bayesian methods can be applied in practice. Bayesian methods are further discussed by Lindley (1971), Cohen (1988) and Press (1989). For an example of use of Bayesian methods in wildlife studies, readers are referred to Woodward et al. (1999), who apply Bayesian analyses to wild turkey (*Meleagris gallopavo*) harvests.

Other Methods

Numerous additional statistical methods exist that have not been mentioned. In the interest of space we mention some of these below with a brief, simplified description of the methods and references for additional information.

Canonical Correlation Analysis

The standard correlation coefficient allows one to measure correlations between pairs of variables. This is extended to R^2, the coefficient of multiple determination, in multiple regression and gives a measure of how a group of (independent) variables "correlates" with a single (dependent) variable. The next level of generalization would be to examine a measure of how one group of several variables correlates with another group of several variables. This is the goal of canonical correlation analysis.

Suppose one labels the variables in one set X_1, ..., X_q and the variables in the other set Y_1, ..., Y_q. The *first canonical correlation* is defined to be the correlation between the pair of linear combinations or scores of the X and Y variables having the largest possible correlation coefficient. Because a linear combination of the X (Y) variables reduces the set of variables to a single variable, the 2 sets reduce to a pair of variables, and one can calculate the correlation coefficient between them. The scores producing the first canonical correlation are called the *first canonical variates*. The *second canonical correlation* is the largest correlation possible between a score in the X variables that is statistically independent of the first canonical variate in the Xs and a score in the Y variables that is statistically independent of the first canonical variate in the Ys. The scores producing the second canonical correlation are called the *second canonical variates*. One proceeds to define additional canonical correlations and variates by calculating the scores of the X and Y variables that are independent of all previous canonical variates and have maximum correlation. Most statistical software packages have routines for computing canonical correlations and variates.

Canonical correlations provide information concerning the strength of the relationship ("correlation") between the set of X variables and the set of Y variables. One can test for statistical significance of the canonical correlations (i.e., do they differ from 0). The form of the scores making up the canonical variates may also provide subject-matter interpretations concerning why the sets are correlated. Interpretation of these scores is similar to the "art" of interpretation in a principal components analysis and is somewhat subjective.

Wichern and Johnson (2002) describe details of canonical correlation analysis and Hair et al. (1998) present a readable discussion of canonical correlation analysis. Rexstad et al. (1988) discussed pitfalls associated with canonical correlation analysis.

Cluster Analysis

The basic objective of a cluster analysis is to "classify" or "cluster" n units into k groups where variables X_1, ..., X_p are measured for each of the n experimental units. All units in a group are assumed to be "similar" or "close" to one another. Units in different groups are "dissimilar" or "far apart." For example, suppose one measures 2 variables on each unit and makes a scatterplot of the data. If the points in the scatterplot separated into several "clouds" of points (Fig. 15), these "clouds" could be taken as clusters. Unfortunately, this graphical approach is possible only when 1, 2, or 3 variables are measured for each unit and the variables measured are quantitative. In general, k is usually not known in advance and is calculated by the analysis. Also, there is no way of calculating whether the groupings are "correct." The groupings derived in a cluster analysis are decided on subjective grounds, and one is seeking to find evidence that some units are more alike than others.

To conduct a cluster analysis, one first needs a criterion for deciding whether a pair of units is similar or close. Many measures of similarity or closeness are possible. Two common measures are the usual geometric or Euclidean distance and a "statistical" version of distance

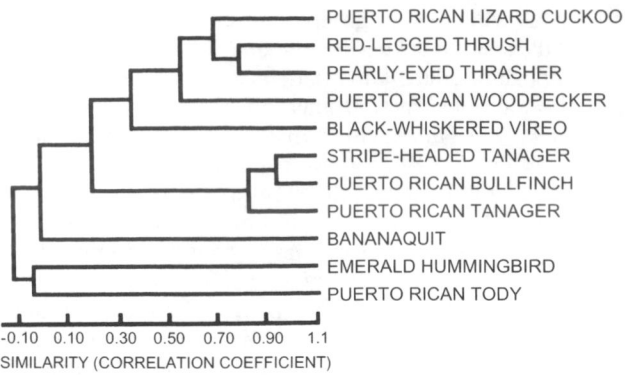

Fig. 16. Dendrogram indicating similarity in foraging relationships based on a correlation coefficient matrix of 11 species in the Cubuy Caribbean pine avifaunal assemblage, Luquilo Experimental Forest, Puerto Rico, March–August 1981–1986 (from Cruz 1988).

called the Mahalanobis distance. Whatever measure of distance is used, one must also decide how to use this quantity to measure the distance between 2 collections of observations. One possibility is to define this to be the distance between the means of the 2 collections. Many others are possible.

Having decided on a measure of closeness, one next needs to develop an algorithm for "grouping" the observations. If only 1, 2, or 3 variables are measured on each unit and the measure of distance is geometric, one can plot the measurements on each unit as points on a 1, 2, or 3-dimensional graph, examine the graph, and decide on groupings from the appearance of the plot. This fails when more than 3 measurements are taken on each unit. In this situation some algorithm that can be programmed on a computer is typically used and the computer is allowed to define groupings. Several algorithms are possible. One popular method is called hierarchical clustering. One begins by treating each unit (more precisely the set of measurements on the unit) as a separate cluster. A series of steps is then followed. In step 1, for every pair of existing clusters [initially there are *n,* one for each unit, and hence $n(n - 1)/2$ pairs], the distance between each pair is calculated with the measure of distance decided upon. In step 2, the pair of clusters having the smallest distance (i.e., closest together) is merged to form a new cluster, thus reducing the number of existing clusters by one. This set of clusters is printed and steps 1 and 2 are repeated. This continues until all units have been merged into a single cluster. The results at each stage are usually summarized in a graph called a *dendrogram.*

Cruz (1988) applied a hierarchical cluster analysis to examine how 11 species might produce a cluster based on 20 foraging variables measured for each species (Fig. 16). The first species joined into a single cluster were the striped-headed tanager (*Spindalis zena*) and the Puerto Rican bullfinch (*Loxigilla portoricensis*). At the next step, the Puerto Rican tanager (*Nesospingus speculiferus*) was added to this group. Next, the red-legged thrush (*Turdus plumbeus*) and pearly-eyed thrasher (*Margarops fuscatus*) were joined into a single cluster. At the next-to-last stage, the species were divided into 2 clusters. The emerald hummingbird (*Chlorostilbon maugaeus*) and Puerto Rican tody (*Todus mexicanus*) (both sally-hoverers) formed one cluster, and all other species [Puerto Rican woodpecker (*Melanerpes*

portoricensis), Puerto Rican lizard cuckoo (*Saurothera vielioti*), black-whiskered vireo (*Vireo altiloquus*) bananaquit (*Coereba flaveola*)] formed the other (Fig. 16).

Cluster analysis should be regarded as a descriptive method useful for identifying interesting features of the data. Because of the large (essentially infinite) number of possible distance measures and clustering algorithms, a set of data can be subjected to a large number of cluster analyses yielding different clusterings, none of which may be particularly dramatic or informative. One does not know if some untried measure might have yielded a clustering that would truly clarify the data or if the clustering obtained is biologically "correct." Cluster analysis and related issues are discussed by Wichern and Johnson (2002), including use of pictures to suggest clusters and a discussion of a technique called *multidimensional scaling.* Hair et al. (1998) provided a readable introduction to cluster analysis and multidimensional scaling.

Spatial Analysis

Spatial analysis involves a large body of techniques that allows one to examine whether units are uniformly separated or distributed in space with respect to the distance measure, or if they display some other interesting spatial distribution. In other instances, one simply estimates features of the spatial distribution. Buskirk et al. (1989) investigated the ecology of resting sites of American marten (*Martes americana*) in the central Rocky Mountains during 2 winters. Because winter resting sites are often associated with coarse woody debris, the authors estimated spatial density of coarse woody debris on the forest floor. Those interested in spatial analyses should consult Upton and Fingleton (1985).

Time Series

Measurements taken over time often exhibit a periodic or "fluctuating" behavior. Common examples include meteorological and economic data. In such data, it may be of interest to study characteristics of the relationship between the measurements (dependent variable) and time (independent variable). At times this can be accomplished with multiple regression. For purposes of studying periodicities (how often certain features repeat themselves) a more appropriate approach is to use time series analysis. Among other things, a time series analysis allows one to identify periodicities in data, identify what portion of the fluctuations in data is due to "noise" (random error) and what is due to more systematic sources, identify trends in data, and fit models to the data. The results can be used for forecasting (prediction) or simply for clarifying the behavior of the data. To understand the methodology of time series, one must have some knowledge of mathematical analysis (including Fourier series) and stochastic processes. Many statistical software packages will conduct time series analyses. Two references containing more information on time series are Box and Jenkins (1976) and Cryer (1986).

Botsford et al. (1988) plotted numbers of adult, juvenile, and juvenile/adult California quail (*Callipepla californica*) from 1958 to 1980. The resulting plots (Fig. 17) were time series and provide evidence of periodic or fluctuating behavior of the data. Peaks seem to repeat roughly every 4 or 5 years, and the height of the peaks appears to decline gradually over time. As part of the analysis, the

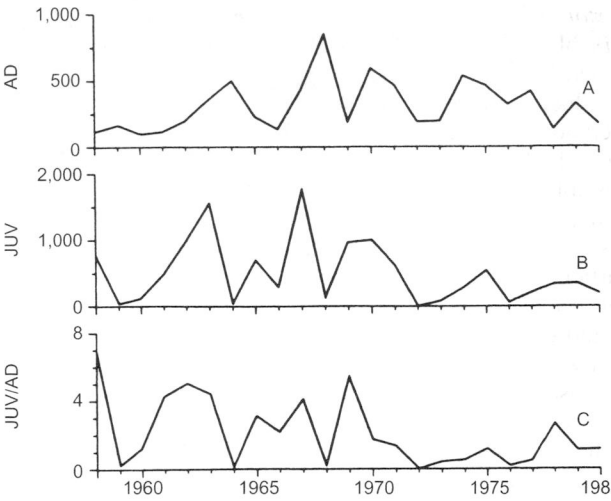

Fig. 17. Examples of time series, displaying numbers of California quail adults (A), juveniles (B), and computed juveniles/adults (C) from annual counts in the Panoche Management Area, California, 1958–1980 (from Botsford et al. 1988).

authors tried to relate this behavior to precipitation (also time series data).

Directional Data

Occasionally experimenters are interested in recording a direction (angle from 0 to 359°) or day of year (1 to 365, leap years ignored) as part of their data. One oddity of such data is that the 2 most extreme values (0 and 359° or day 1 and day 365) are actually adjacent. Absolute differences in values do not necessarily indicate how far apart 2 measurements lie. Diefenbach et al. (1988) recorded day of year of band recoveries for American black ducks (*Anas rubripes*) and mallards. They were interested, among other things, in distribution patterns of recoveries throughout the winter.

Data such as those described have a cyclical structure and can be thought as lying in a circle. Such data are called *directional data,* and several special procedures have been developed for analysis in view of some peculiarities of these data. The interested reader should consult Mardia (1972) for further information.

Miscellaneous Topics

Additional procedures one may encounter in the wildlife literature include MANOVA or multivariate analysis of variance (ANOVA methods applied to situations in which several dependent variables are measured on each unit [Hair et al. 1998, Wichern and Johnson 2002]), and survival analysis (methods for investigating the effects of factors on survival of experimental units [Lee 1980]). We have not mentioned numerous other statistical procedures. The best advice we can give is to consult a statistician before analyzing data from an experiment.

SUMMARY

Statistical methods that wildlife biologists use frequently are reviewed in this chapter. Graphical methods should present the data clearly, use proper scaling, and provide the source of the data. Quantitative analysis requires clear specification of the population and the sampling plan and,

for formal inference, the probability model that describes the variable of interest. Analysis is used to compute point estimates and estimates of accuracy, usually described using SE, CI, or CV. Error in estimates may be divided into bias, a consistent tendency to under- or over-estimate the quantity of interest, and sampling error, caused by which population units happen to enter the sample. Sampling plans widely used in wildlife biology include simple random, systematic, stratified, and multiple-stage. Formulas for simple random sampling are used in systematic samples, within strata in stratified sampling, and with multiple-stage sampling if the primary units are of equal size. In comparing estimates, 2-tailed, rather than one-tailed, tests should generally be used; hypothesis tests should be viewed as investigating which population has the larger parameter, not whether the 2 parameters are different; statistical significance should be sharply distinguished from biological or management importance. Confidence intervals, rather than tests, should be used as the basis for conclusions and recommendations.

The most commonly used methods in studying the relationship between variables are scatterplots and correlations, and simple and multiple regression. Scatterplots should be analyzed both with and without outliers and influential points. Regression analysis is useful for quantifying relationships such as how much the dependent variable tends to change with changes in independent variables. Forms of regression useful in wildlife biology include logistic regression, stepwise regression, and regression with categorical variables. Multivariate methods that wildlife biologists should be familiar with include path analysis, which distinguishes between causal and correlative relationships; factor analysis and principal components, which help reduce the number of independent variables and identify underlying variables; classification, discriminant, and cluster analysis, which assign population units to categories; canonical correlation analysis, useful for exploring relationships between independent variables and sets of dependent variables; time series analysis, for detecting cyclic or periodic behavior in response variables; and methods for directional data. Early consultation with a statistician is recommended to insure that analytic methods are properly applied.

ACKNOWLEDGMENTS

Helpful comments on this Chapter were received from B. S. Cade, J. E. Kautz, E. T. Reed, and D. R. Diefenbach. Many of the ideas in this chapter were developed while J. R. Bart was a member of the Zoology Department at The Ohio State University. He benefited from discussions with T. A. Bookhout, S. L. Earnst, T. C. Grubb, Jr., J. D. Harder and their graduate students. The U.S. Department of the Interior, Geological Survey, Forest and Rangeland Ecosystem Science Center, and the U.S. Fish and Wildlife Service supported the work of the senior author.

LITERATURE CITED

ALISAUSKAS, R. T., C. D. ANKNEY, AND E. E. KLAAS. 1988. Winter diets and nutrition of midcontinental lesser snow geese. Journal of Wildlife Management 52: 403–414.

ANDERSON, D. R., AND K. P. BURNHAM. 2002. Avoiding pitfalls when using information–theoretic methods. Journal of Wildlife

Management 66:912–918.

ANDRES, B. 1989. Littoral zone use by post-breeding shorebirds on the Colville River delta, Alaska. Thesis, Ohio State University, Columbus, USA.

ANTHONY, R. G., AND F. B. ISAACS. 1989. Characteristics of bald eagle nest sites in Oregon. Journal of Wildlife Management 53:148–159.

BART, J., M. A. FLIGNER, AND W. I. NOTZ. 1998. Sampling and statistical methods for behavioral ecologists. Cambridge University Press, New York, USA.

BERGERUD, A. T., AND W. B. BALLARD. 1988. Wolf predation on caribou: the Nelchina herd case history, a different interpretation. Journal of Wildlife Management 52:344–357.

BOTSFORD, L. W., T. C. WAINWRIGHT, J. T. SMITH, S. MASTRUP, AND D. F. LOTT. 1988. Population dynamics of California quail related to meteorological conditions. Journal of Wildlife Management 52:469–477.

BOX, G. E. P., AND N. R. DRAPER. 1987. Empirical model-building and response surfaces. John Wiley and Sons, New York, USA.

——, AND G. M. JENKINS. 1976. Time series analysis. Holden-Day, San Francisco, California, USA.

BREIMAN, L. J., D. FRIEDMAN, R. OLSHEN, AND C. STONE. 1984. Classification and regression trees. Wadsworth International Group, Belmont, California, USA.

BURNHAM, K. P., AND D. R. ANDERSON. 2002. Model selection and multi-model inference. Springer Verlag, Inc., New York, USA.

BUSKIRK, S. W., S. C. FORREST, M. G. RAPHAEL, AND H. J. HARLOW. 1989. Winter resting site ecology of marten in the central Rocky Mountains. Journal of Wildlife Management 53:191–196.

CHAMBERS, J. M., W. S. CLEVELAND, B. KLEINER AND P. A. TUKEY. 1983. Graphical methods for data analysis. Wadsworth International Group, Belmont, California, USA.

COCHRAN, W. G. 1977. Sampling techniques. John Wiley and Sons, New York, USA.

COHEN, Y. 1988. Bayesian estimation of clutch size for scientific and management purposes. Journal of Wildlife Management 52:787–793.

COMPTON, B. B., R. J. MACKIE, AND G. L. DUSEK. 1988. Factors influencing distribution of white-tailed deer in riparian habitats. Journal of Wildlife Management 52:544–548.

CONNELLY, J. W., J. H. GAMMONLEY, AND J. M. PEEK. 2005. Harvest management. Pages 658–690 in C. E. Braun, editor. Techniques for wildlife investigations and management. Sixth edition. The Wildlife Society, Bethesda, Maryland, USA.

CONOVER, M. R. 1988. Effect of grazing by Canada geese on the winter growth of rye. Journal of Wildlife Management 52:76–80.

COWAN, D. P., J. A. VAUGHAN, AND W. G. CHRISTER. 1987. Bait consumption by the European rabbit in southern England. Journal of Wildlife Management 51:386–392.

CRABTREE, R. L., L. S. BROOME, AND M. L. WOLFE. 1989. Effects of habitat characteristics on gadwall nest predation and nest-site selection. Journal of Wildlife Management 53:129–137.

CRUZ, A. 1988. Avian resource use in a Caribbean pine plantation. Journal of Wildlife Management 52:274–279.

CRYER, J. D. 1986. Time series analysis. Duxbury Press, Boston, Massachusetts, USA.

DIEFENBACH, D. R., J. D. NICHOLS, AND J. E. HINES. 1988. Distribution patterns of American black duck and mallard winter band recoveries. Journal of Wildlife Management 52:704–710.

DIERENFELD, E. S., C. E. SANDFORT, AND W. C. SATTERFIELD. 1989. Influence of diet on plasma vitamin E in captive peregrine falcons. Journal of Wildlife Management 53:160–164.

DINSMORE, S. J., AND D. H. JOHNSON. 2005. Population analysis in wildlife biology. Pages 154–184 in C. E. Braun, editor. Techniques for wildlife investigations and management. Sixth edition. The Wildlife Society, Bethesda, Maryland, USA.

FRANZMANN, A. W., AND C. C. SCHWARTZ. 1988. Evaluating condition of Alaskan black bears with blood profiles. Journal of Wildlife Management 52:63–70.

FRYXELL, J. M., W. E. MERCER, AND R. B. GELLATELY. 1988. Population dynamics of Newfoundland moose using cohort analysis. Journal of Wildlife Management 52:14–21.

GALLANT, A. R. 1987. Nonlinear statistical models. John Wiley and Sons, New York, USA.

GARTON, E. O., J. T. RATTI, AND J. H. GIUDICE. 2005. Research and experimental design. Pages 43–71 in C. E. Braun, editor. Techniques for wildlife investigations and management. Sixth edition. The Wildlife Society, Bethesda, Maryland, USA.

GESE, E. M., O. J. RONGSTAD, AND W. R. MYTTON. 1988. Home range and habitat use of coyotes in southeastern Colorado. Journal of Wildlife Management 52:640–646.

GOLIGHTLY, JR., R. T., AND T. D. HOFSTRA. 1989. Immobilization of elk with a ketamine-xylazine mix and rapid reversal with yohimbine hydrochloride. Wildlife Society Bulletin 17:53–58.

HAIR, JR., J. F., R. E. ANDERSON, R. L. TATHAM, AND W. C. BLACK. 1998. Multivariate data analysis. Prentice-Hall, Upper Saddle River, New Jersey, USA.

HASTIE, T., R. TIBSHIRANI, AND J. FRIEDMAN. 2001. The elements of statistical learning. Springer Verlag, Inc., New York, USA.

HEINZ, G. H., D. J. HOFFMAN, AND L. G. GOLD. 1989. Impaired reproduction of mallards fed an organic form of selenium. Journal of Wildlife Management 53:418–428.

HICKS, C. R., AND K. V. TURNER. 1999. Fundamental concepts in the design of experiments. Fifth edition. Oxford University Press, Oxford, United Kingdom.

HIGGINS, K. F., K. J. JENKINS, G. K. CLAMBEY, D. W. URESK, D. E. NAUGLE, J. E. NORLAND, AND W. T. BARKER. 2005. Vegetation sampling and measurement. Pages 524–553 in C. E. Braun, editor. Techniques for wildlife investigations and management. Sixth edition. The Wildlife Society, Bethesda, Maryland, USA.

HOLL, S. A., AND V. C. BLEICH. 1987. Mineral lick use by mountain sheep in the San Gabriel Mountains, California. Journal of Wildlife Management 51:383–385.

HOSMER, JR., D.W., AND S. LEMESHOW. 2000. Applied logistic regression. John Wiley and Sons, New York, USA.

HSU, J. C. 1996. Multiple comparisons: theory and methods. Chapman & Hall/CRC Press, New York, USA.

JOHNSON, D. B., F. S. GUTHERY, AND N. E. KOERTH. 1989. Grackle damage to grapefruit in the lower Rio Grande Valley. Wildlife Society Bulletin 17:46–50.

KOEHLER, G. M., AND M. G. HORNOCKER. 1989. Influences of seasons on bobcats in Idaho. Journal of Wildlife Management 53:197–202.

KUTNER, M. H., C. J. NACHTSCHIEM, W. WASSERMAN, AND J. NETER. 1996. Applied linear statistical models. McGraw-Hill Book Co., New York, USA.

LANCIA, R. A., W. L. KENDALL, K. H. POLLOCK, AND J. D. NICHOLS. 2005. Estimating the number of animals in wildlife populations. Pages 106–153 in C. E. Braun, editor. Techniques for wildlife investigations and management. Sixth edition. The Wildlife Society, Bethesda, Maryland, USA.

LEE, E. T. 1980. Statistical methods for survival data analysis. Lifetime Learning Publications, Belmont, California, USA.

LEUSCHNER, W. A., V. P. RITCHIE, AND D. F. STAUFFER. 1989. Options on wildlife: responses of resource managers and wildlife users in the southeastern United States. Wildlife Society Bulletin 17:24–29.

LINDLEY, D. V. 1971. Making decisions. Wiley-Interscience, New York, USA.

MARDIA, K. V. 1972. Statistics and directional data. Academic Press, London, United Kingdom.

MASON, J. R., M. A. ADAMS, AND L. CLARK. 1989. Anthranilate repellency to starlings: chemical correlates and sensory perception. Journal of Wildlife Management 53:55–64.

MCAULEY, D. G., AND J. R. LONGCORE. 1988. Survival of juvenile ring-necked ducks on wetlands of different pH. Journal of Wildlife Management 52:169–176.

MCCULLAGH, P., AND J. A. NELDER. 1989. Generalized linear models. Second edition. Chapman & Hall, London, United Kingdom.

MCGARIGAL, K., S. CUSHMAN, AND S. STAFFORD. 2000. Multivariate statistics for wildlife ecology and research. Springer Verlag, Inc., New York, USA.

MOORE, D. S., AND G. P. MCCABE. 2002. Introduction to the practice of statistics. Fourth edition. W. H. Freeman Co., San Francisco, California, USA.

NAMBOORDIRI, N. K., L. F. CARTER, AND H. M. BLALOCK. 1975. Applied multivariate analysis and experimental designs. McGraw-Hill Book Co., New York, USA.

NETER, J., W. WASSERMAN, AND M. H. KUTNER. 1983. Applied linear regression models. Richard D. Irwin, Homewood, Illinois, USA.

NIXON, C. M., L. P. HANSEN, AND P. A. BREWER. 1988. Characteristics of winter habitats used by deer in Illinois. Journal of Wildlife Management 52:552–555.

O'GARA, B. W., AND R. B. HARRIS. 1988. Age and condition of deer killed by predators and automobiles. Journal of Wildlife Management 52:316–320.

OTIS, D. L., K. P. BURNHAM, G. C. WHITE, AND D. R. ANDERSON. 1978. Statistical inference from capture data on closed animal populations.

Wildlife Monographs 62.

PRESS, S. J. 1989. Bayesian statistics. John Wiley and Sons, New York, USA.

QUINN, N. W. S., AND J. E. THOMPSON. 1987. Dynamics of an exploited Canada lynx population in Ontario. Journal of Wildlife Management 51:297–305.

RANDLES, R. H., AND D. A. WOLFE. 1979. Introduction to the theory of nonparametric statistics. John Wiley and Sons, New York, USA.

RENECKER, L. A., AND R. J. HUDSON. 1989. Seasonal activity budgets of moose in aspen-dominated boreal forests. Journal of Wildlife Management 53:296–302.

REXSTAD, E. A., D. D. MILLER, C. H. FLATHER, E. M. ANDERSON, J. W. HUPP, AND D. R. ANDERSON. 1988. Questionable multivariate statistical inference in wildlife habitat and community studies. Journal of Wildlife Management 52:794–798.

SÆTHER, B. -E., AND A. J. GRAVEM. 1988. Annual variation in winter body condition of Norwegian moose calves. Journal of Wildlife Management 52:333–336.

SANTILLO, D. J., D. M. LESLIE, JR., AND P. W. BROWN. 1989. Responses of small mammals and habitat to glyphosate application on clearcuts. Journal of Wildlife Management 53:164–172.

SNEDECOR, G. W., AND W. G. COCHRAN. 1980. Statistical methods. Seventh edition. Iowa State University Press, Ames, USA.

SOKAL, R. R., AND F. J. ROHLF. 1995. Biometry. Third edition. W. H. Freeman, New York, USA.

STEEL, R. G. D., AND J. H. TORRIE. 1980. Principles and procedures of statistics. Second edition. McGraw-Hill Book Co., New York, USA.

STEWART-OATEN, A. 1995. Rules and judgments in statistics: three examples. Ecology 76:2001–2009.

THILL, R. E., AND A. MARTIN, JR. 1989. Deer and cattle diets on heavily grazed pine-bluestem range. Journal of Wildlife Management 53:40–548.

THOMPSON, III, F. R., AND D. E. CAPEN. 1988. Avian assemblages in several stages of a Vermont forest. Journal of Wildlife Management 52:771–777.

TUFTE, E. R. 1983. The visual display of quantitative information. Graphics Press, Cheshire, Connecticut, USA.

UPTON, G. J. G., AND B. FINGLETON. 1985. Spatial data analysis by example. John Wiley and Sons, New York, USA.

VAN BALLENBERGHE, V. 1989. Wolf predation on the Nelchina caribou herd: a comment. Journal of Wildlife Management 53:243–250.

VELLEMAN, P. F., AND D. C. HOAGLIN. 1981. Applications, basics, and computing of exploratory data analysis. Duxbury Press, Boston, Massachusetts, USA.

WELSH, JR., H. H., AND A. J. LIND. 2002. Multiscale habitat relationships of stream amphibians in the Klamath-Siskiyou region of California and Oregon. Journal of Wildlife Management 66:581–602.

WICHERN, D. W., AND R. A. JOHNSON. 2002. Applied multivariate statistical analysis. Prentice Hall, Englewood Cliffs, New Jersey, USA.

WILLIAMS, B. K., J. D. NICHOLS, AND M. J. CONROY. 2002. Analysis and management of animal populations. Academic Press, New York, USA.

WOOD, G. W. 1988. Effects of prescribed fire on deer forage and nutrients. Wildlife Society Bulletin 16:180–186.

WOODARD, R., D. SUN, Z. HE, AND S. L. SHERIFF. 1999. Estimating hunting success rates via Bayesian generalized linear models. Journal of Agricultural, Biological and Environmental Statistics 4:456–472.

ZAR, J. H. 1998. Biostatistical analysis. Third edition. Prentice Hall, Englewood Cliffs, New Jersey, USA.

5

ESTIMATING THE NUMBER OF ANIMALS IN WILDLIFE POPULATIONS

Richard A. Lancia, William L. Kendall, Kenneth H. Pollock, and James D. Nichols

INTRODUCTION

In 1938, Howard M. Wight devoted 9 pages, which was an entire chapter in the first wildlife management techniques manual, to what he termed "census" methods (Wight 1938). As books (Seber 1982, Thompson et al. 1998, Williams et al. 2002) and chapters such as this attest, the volume of literature on this subject has grown tremendously. Abundance estimation remains an active area of biometrical research, as reflected in the many differences between this chapter and the similar contribution in the previous manual (Lancia et al. 1994). Our intent in this chapter is to present an overview of the basic and most widely used population estimation techniques and to provide an entree to the relevant literature.

Several possible approaches could be taken in writing a chapter dealing with population estimation. For example, we could provide a detailed treatment focusing on statistical models and on derivation of estimators based on these models. Although a chapter using this approach might provide a valuable reference for quantitative biologists and biometricians, it would be of limited use to many field biologists and

wildlife managers. Another approach would be to focus on details of actually applying different population estimation techniques. This approach would include both field application (e.g., how to set out a trapping grid or conduct an aerial survey) and detailed instructions on how to use the resulting data with appropriate estimation equations. We are reluctant to attempt such an approach, however, because of the tremendous diversity of real-world field situations defined by factors such as the animal being studied, habitat, available resources, and because of our resultant inability to provide detailed instructions for all possible cases.

We believe it is more useful to provide the reader with the conceptual basis underlying estimation methods. Thus, we have tried to provide intuitive explanations for how basic methods work. In doing so, we present relevant estimation equations for many methods and provide citations of more detailed treatments covering both statistical considerations and field applications. We have chosen to present methods that are representative of classes of estimators, rather than address every available method. Our hope is that this chapter will provide the reader with enough background to make an informed decision about what general method(s) will likely perform well in any particular field situation. Readers with a more quantitative background may then be able to consult detailed references and tailor the selected method to suit their particular needs. Less quantitative readers should consult a biometrician, preferably one with experience in wildlife studies, for this "tailoring," with the hope they will be able to do so with a basic understanding of the general method, thereby permitting useful interaction and discussion with the biometrician.

Why Estimate Population Size?

The goals of managing natural animal populations are frequently expressed in terms of population size. When dealing with rare or endangered species, for example, wildlife managers often try to increase population size, whereas for undesirable (pest) species, we try to reduce population size. For harvested populations, we attempt to maintain population size at a desired level, while permitting a harvest. Population size is thus the currency by which success of many management programs is ultimately judged. Even in cases where population size is not the primary quantity of interest, it is often functionally related to the variables of interest. For example, probability of extinction over some finite time period is sometimes of interest, and population size affects this probability. Population size is thus a natural choice as a variable, which reflects change, in models developed for management purposes.

Most formal approaches to management of animal populations include a monitoring program as an important component, and monitoring is usually focused on abundance (Walters 1986, Williams et al. 2002). Resulting estimates of population size are used for 3 primary purposes in formal management programs. First, abundance estimates are needed to make state-dependent management decisions. These decisions depend heavily on whether we would like the population to increase or decrease relative to current abundance. The second use of abundance estimates is to assess the performance of management. Is the population changing in the desired direction or not, and how close are we coming to management objectives? The third use of abundance estimates is to judge the predictive abilities of our models of the managed system. A management decision is made at each decision point, and competing models of the managed system are used to predict abundance following the management action. Differences between the single estimate of abundance and different model-based predictions provide new information about the relative faith we should place in the different models. This third use of abundance estimates in management programs is equivalent to the conduct of science (Hilborn and Mangel 1997, Nichols 2001), where our goal is to learn how populations respond to management actions.

Perhaps because of these clear roles of abundance estimates in well-conceived wildlife management programs, there is a tendency for managers to express unthinking interest in population size, even in cases where abundance estimates are not likely to be useful. For example, a manager who professes interest in the "health" or status of a particular population might decide to estimate population size as a way of assessing status. However, a single estimate of population size at one point in space and time is usually of limited value, and provides much less information about status than commonly thought. Any biologist/manager

considering expending the effort to estimate population size properly should carefully consider the need for an estimate, and the manner in which the estimate would be used. We recommend the biologist/manager ask the following question: "what will I do with the estimate once I get it?" For example, if a population estimate of 400 deer versus one of 700 deer is not likely to lead to different management responses, then devoting a lot of effort to achieve an accurate population estimate might not be necessary.

Finally, even when estimates of population size are useful, as when abundance monitoring is a component of a formal management program, they seldom provide all answers to management questions. Estimates of population size can be compared with model predictions to help discriminate among competing models of system response to management actions. But a more fundamental, mechanistic explanation of exactly how and why the population responds to the manipulation (Gavin 1989) frequently does not emerge from such comparisons. Our models are often likely to be more useful (to make better predictions) if they incorporate mechanistic explanations of population response to management actions. For example, all changes in population size result from the action of 4 fundamental demographic variables: mortality, reproduction, emigration, and immigration. In addition to estimates of population size, we will want to obtain estimates of these rates and of parameters describing the relationship between these rates and both environmental covariates and management actions. These estimates will be important components of our management models.

Definitions

The following definitions are used throughout this chapter. These terms, defined in relation to population estimation to help the reader understand the material in our chapter, are based on Overton (1969), Caughley (1977), White et al. (1982), Verner (1985), and Thompson et al. (1998).

Populations

(1) A *population* is a group of animals that occupy a certain area at a certain time as defined by the people interested in the group. A population could be white-tailed deer (*Odocoileus virginianus*) on Chesapeake Farms, grizzly bears (*Ursus arctos*) in Yellowstone National Park, northern spotted owls (*Strix occidentalis caurina*) in the Pacific Northwest, or the continental mallard (*Anas platyrhynchos*) population. We emphasize this is an operational definition for this chapter and that it is not adequate from ecological or genetic perspectives.

(2) *Abundance or population size* refers to the number of individual animals; e.g., 49 white-footed mice (*Peromyscus leucopus*). This is sometimes referred to as *absolute abundance* for the purpose of distinguishing number of animals from the concept of *relative abundance*.

(3) *Relative abundance* refers to the ratio of abundances. For example, we might refer to the relative abundance of a species at 2 points in space or time, or to the relative abundance of 2 different species in the same area at the same time.

(4) *Population density* is the number of individuals per unit area; e.g., 1.2 squirrels/ha or 1 deer/km^2. Both abundance and area are relevant to density; consequently, density is frequently difficult to estimate. For example, trapping grids are commonly used to estimate the abundance of small mammals, but density estimates are more difficult

to obtain because the effective area (i.e., the area from which trapped animals are drawn) of the trapping grid must also be estimated. Abundance is often much easier to estimate than density and will be sufficient for many management decisions. At times, *population density* is defined more generally as the number of animals per unit of resource, where the resource need not be land area.

(5) *Relative density* refers to the ratio of population densities. For example, if relative density of mice at location A to location B is 1.4, then location A has 40% more mice/unit area than location B.

(6) A *census* is a complete count of an entire population of animals. True censuses are relatively rare in wildlife research and management.

(7) A *population estimate* is a numerical approximation of true population size calculated from sample data collected from a sampled population of animals. Sampling methods often involve capturing or observing animals, or combinations of both processes. Estimates of quantities of interest are denoted by a small caret or "hat" over the symbol for the quantity of interest. For example, N represents true population size, and $\hat{N}$ represents either an estimator or an estimate of population size calculated from sample data.

(8) A *population estimator* is a mathematical formula or expression used to compute a population estimate. Estimators are also denoted by a small caret or "hat" over the symbol for the quantity of interest.

(9) *Population closure* refers to the absence of births, deaths, emigration, and immigration over the period of interest (usually the period of sampling). Population closure has 2 components: *demographic closure*, where there are no births (natality) or deaths (mortality) occurring over the period of interest, and *geographic closure*, where there are no movements into (immigration) or out of (emigration) a population between sample periods. Thus, neither abundance nor identities of specific individuals in the population change for a population that is demographically and geographically closed. Population closure is a basic assumption for some population estimation procedures that are based on repeated observations of individuals over time such as those involving capture and marking or removal of individuals. In practice it is difficult to know if the closure assumption is met. For counts that are essentially snapshots in time, such as an aerial count of kangaroos (Macropodidae) on a transect, the closure assumption is not a concern.

(10) An *open population* is one that is not closed.

(11) A *population index* is a statistic that is related to population size (Caughley 1977). Indices are used to draw comparative inferences about populations at different times and/or locations. Because the exact relationship between the index and true population size frequently is not known, there is typically uncertainty about the validity of resulting comparisons.

(12) *Observability* is the probability that a member of a sampled population is detected. It is more properly referred to as *probability of detection* or *detection probability*. Other synonyms in the literature are *sightability*, *catchability*, or *detectability*.

Statistical

(1) *Frequency of occurrence* is a count of units, such as traps or plots, which have a particular attribute. An example would be the number of bait stations disturbed by bears, the number of traps that caught animals, or number of traps that caught 5 mice, 4 mice, etc. over a number of trap nights.

(2) An *expected value* of a population estimator is the average value of the estimate that would be obtained if the estimation procedure were repeated many times under exactly the same conditions. The notation E(C) represents the expected value of random variable C.

(3) *Accuracy* is a measure of how close an estimate (e.g., a population estimate) tends to be to the true quantity of interest (e.g., abundance).

(4) Accuracy can be measured by *mean squared error (MSE),* which is the expected value of the squared deviations between the true quantity of interest and the corresponding estimate.

(5) *Bias* is the difference between the expected value of an estimator and the true quantity of interest. If the expected value of a population estimator is equal to true population size, the estimator is unbiased.

(6) *Precision* refers to the variation in estimates obtained from repeated samples. Precision is often expressed in terms of distance of estimates from their expected value.

(7) Precision can be measured by *variance (VAR)*, which is the average of the squared deviations between a population estimate repeated many times and its expected value. The relationship between MSE, VAR, and bias is $\text{MSE} = \text{VAR} + \text{bias}^2$.

(8) *Standard error* is the square root of the variance and is another measure of precision. One use of the standard error is to calculate confidence intervals. The *confidence interval* reflects the reliability of an estimate and is usually written as P $[a \leq q \leq b] = 1 - \alpha$, where a and b are the upper and lower bounds of the interval, q is the parameter of interest, and $1 - \alpha$ is the confidence level. If the estimator, $\hat{q}$, is normally distributed, the 95% (i.e., $1 - 0.05$) confidence interval would be $\hat{q} \pm 1.96\ \widehat{\text{SE}}(\hat{q})$, where $\hat{q}$ is the estimate and $\widehat{\text{SE}}(\hat{q})$ is the standard error of the estimate. The confidence interval implies that if the estimation were repeated many times, then 95% of the confidence intervals corresponding to each estimate would include the true value of the parameter q.

(9) A *model* is an abstraction and simplification of reality that contains relevant features needed to serve a specific purpose. Models are often used to develop a population estimator and are often constructed so that unknown quantities such as population size are expressed in terms of known quantities such as observations or captures of animals.

(10) A *parameter* is usually an unknown quantity or constant characterizing a population. Parameters are frequently incorporated into estimation models. As an example, capture probability is usually an unknown parameter.

(11) A *statistic* is a quantity derived from observed values taken from a sampled population.

Estimator Properties

Several of the definitions describe estimator properties that are not easy to visualize. The following analogy of a rifle firing at a target, taken from the third edition of the *Wildlife Management Techniques Manual* (Overton 1969), should help illustrate these definitions. The bull's eye is analogous to the value of the parameter being estimated (Fig. 1). The process of aiming and firing under a particular set of conditions is analogous to the process of collecting data and calculating an estimate under a particular set of conditions. The location of the bullet strike is analogous to the value of an estimate.

Now, imagine a large number of shots fired at the target. The average or mean point of impact is analogous to the expected value of the estimator. This is where the rifle is firing, on the average. The precision of the estimator is analogous to the spread of the group about the mean point of impact. The greater the spread, the poorer the precision. Variance (VAR) is used to measure precision; the smaller the spread, the smaller the variance, and the better the precision. Accuracy, measured as the mean squared error (MSE) of the estimator, is analogous to the spread of the group about the bull's eye; i.e., the smaller the MSE, the better the accuracy of the estimator. Last, the distance from the mean point of impact to the bull's eye is analogous to the bias of the estimator. Bias reflects the extent of incorrect sighting of the rifle for the conditions during firing. Thus, an unbiased estimate would be analogous to a rifle that is correctly sighted-in.

In practice population estimates need to be accurate to be useful. If an experiment could be replicated many times, perhaps precision would not be as great a concern because averaging the replicates would tend to counteract a lack of precision. However, a biologist rarely has the luxury of being able to replicate a population estimate many times (e.g., in the same field season). In any event, accuracy is still crucial. One should not fall into the trap of using precision as a surrogate for accuracy. Often the variance of an estimate is readily computed, but measuring accuracy of estimators based on field surveys is difficult.

Estimation and Model Selection Concepts
Maximum Likelihood Estimation

Estimation of parameters can be complex because we often have to fit complex models to our data. The most widely used method of estimation is maximum likelihood. For this method we calculate the probability distribution of the observed data as a function of the parameters $p(x; \theta)$, where x denotes the data and θ denotes the parameters. This probability distribution is viewed as a function of the parameters given the data and is called the likelihood function $L(\theta; x)$. We need to find the values of the parameters that maximize

this function; that is, given the underlying model, for what values of the parameters are these data most likely? These values are the maximum likelihood estimators (MLEs).

A simple example of a likelihood function involves a tag loss study. Suppose you held 10 animals in a cage to evaluate immediate tag loss and after 1 day found that the 10 tags had the following fates:

RRLRLRRRL,

where *R* denotes an animal that retained its tag and *L* denotes an animal that lost its tag. If all tags and animals are viewed as having been identical with respect to tag loss, the likelihood is given by

$$P(RRLRLRRRRL) = p^7(1-p)^3$$

where p is the probability the tag is retained and $(1-p)$ is the probability the tag is lost. The likelihood is maximized at

$$\hat{p} = x/n = 7/10 = 0.7$$

where $x = 7$ is the number of tags that were retained, and $n = 10$ is the total number of tags on day 1. For this likelihood it was easy to find the maximum, but general methods of maximizing a function need to be used in practice, as the likelihood may be complex. One approach is to use calculus and set the partial derivatives of the likelihood with respect to each parameter equal to zero, and then solve the resulting equations. Another general approach is to use a computer package that may use any of a variety of numerical algorithms to find the maximum. This is often necessary, as the likelihoods are frequently complex with many parameters. Programs such as DISTANCE (Buckland et al. 2001) and MARK (White and Burnham 1999) use this approach.

Model Selection and AIC (Akaike's Information Criterion)

For most estimation problems we will have multiple competing models describing the processes that give rise to the data, and the investigator must select a particular model or models for use in estimation. Current ideas of

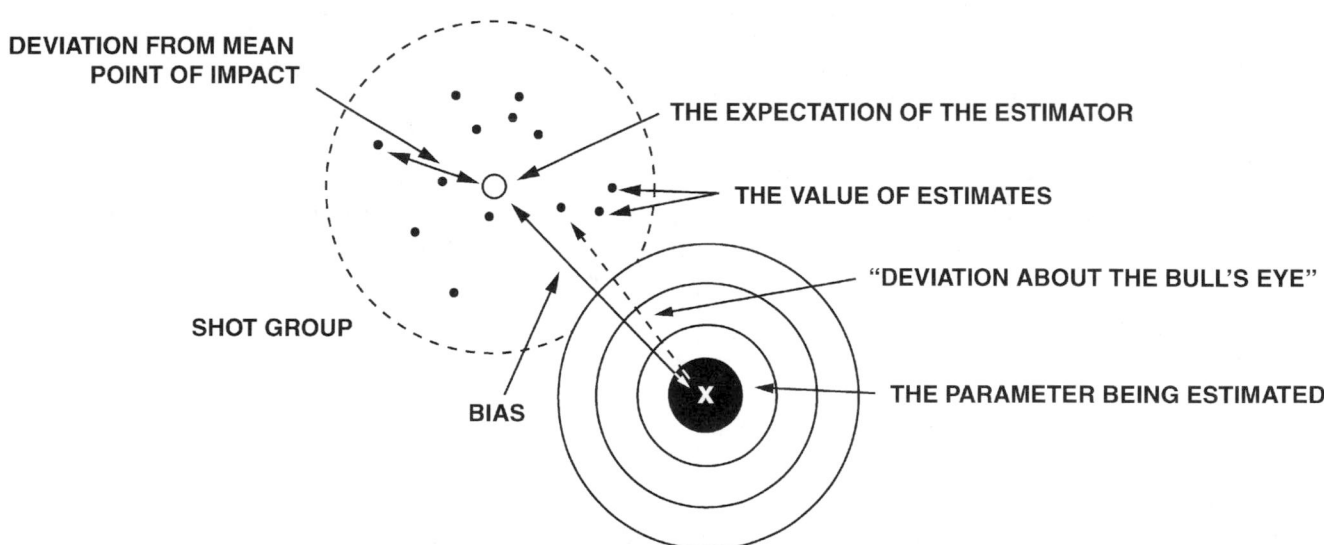

Fig. 1. The analogy of precision, bias, and accuracy in estimation and firing a rifle (from Overton 1969:405).

model selection are based on the "principle of parsimony." This can be summarized (Fig. 2) as a tradeoff between fitting realistic, complex models with a large numbers of parameters but estimated with poor precision versus fitting simpler, less realistic models where the parameters are estimated with better precision. There is need for a way of trading off realism (i.e., using more parameters) versus precision (i.e., using fewer parameters).

The **Akaike's Information Criterion (AIC)** (Akaike 1973) is just such a model selection criterion. We minimize

$$AIC = -2 \log L + 2(\# \text{ pars}).$$

The first term is $-2 \log L$ where L is the likelihood function evaluated at the MLE values and reflects the adequacy of model fit; the second term, twice the number of parameters, [2(#pars)], can be viewed as a penalty for over parameterization. AIC weights can also be calculated which represent a weight of evidence of a certain model versus competing models. In some cases instead of selecting a "best" model based on minimum AIC, one can use model-averaged estimates where the estimates of individual models are weighted based on the AIC weights (Buckland et al. 1997). This is a brief treatment of a rich and important topic, and there are many important refinements (Burnham and Anderson 2002, Williams et al. 2002).

Other Sources of Information

There are numerous technical papers and reviews on population estimation procedures. Some of the more significant and recent ones are identified below; other important papers are cited to support discussion of particular techniques. *The Estimation of Animal Abundance and Related Parameters* (Seber 1982) is a classic source for mathematical and statistical models of population estimation. Caughley (1977) devoted several excellent chapters in his book, *Analysis of Vertebrate Populations*, to population estimation techniques, as did Krebs (1989) in a book, *Ecological Methodology*, a decade later. The book by Thompson et al. (1998), *Monitoring Vertebrate Populations*, provides an excellent introductory overview. The recent book by Williams et al. (2002), *Analysis and Management of Animal Populations*, devotes substantial attention to abundance estimation. Books by Skalski and Robson (1992) and Morrison et al. (2001) provide excellent advice on design of studies directed at temporal and spatial differences in animal abundance.

Other references are more specific and focus on classes of abundance estimation methods. Books by Buckland et al. (1993, 2001) provide excellent descriptions of distance sampling (including line transects) methods. Otis et al. (1978), White et al. (1982) and, more recently, Chao and Huggins (2004) reviewed capture–recapture and removal methods for closed animal populations. Pollock et al. (1990) detailed the design, analysis, and interpretation of capture–recapture studies, emphasizing open populations. There are also population estimation reviews that emphasize specific groups of animals (e.g., Ralph and Scott [1981], Verner [1985], and Bibby et al. [2000] for birds; Wilson et al. [1996] for mammals; Eberhardt et al. [1979] for marine mammals; and Heyer et al. [1993] for amphibians).

As a final introductory note, we attempt to retain the notation that is traditional in the literature for particular methods. Consequently, notation may not be consistent among the methods discussed. We will, however, define the notation as it is used in each method.

A CONCEPTUAL FRAMEWORK

We make an effort to present a unified view of population estimation. The methods discussed form a diverse group of field applications and statistical estimation methods. It is easy to be caught in the details of the approaches and to be overwhelmed and confused by their diversity. Rather than present different methods as unrelated entries in a cookbook, we emphasize the features they share.

Two basic problems confront any biologist who wants to estimate population size—probability of detection and sampling. All methods discussed represent solutions to one, or both, of these basic problems. Thus, superficially diverse solutions can all be expressed in a single general form.

Probability of Detection

Most methods of surveying animals, such as direct observation or capture in traps, do not result in counts or captures of all animals present on an area. Instead, the probability (β) of seeing or catching an animal will generally be less than 1. We can write this relationship between a count of animals, denoted as the random variable C, and the true population size, N, as:

$$E(C) = \beta N \qquad (1)$$

where $E(C)$ denotes the expected value of the count C. Thus, to translate a count resulting from any survey method into an estimate of population size, we must estimate the probability of detecting an animal (equivalent to the expected proportion of animals counted), β, and then divide our count by this estimate:

$$\hat{N} = \frac{C}{\hat{\beta}}. \qquad (2)$$

For example, if 20 birds are seen in a woodlot and we estimate the birds we see are only 25% of the total number of birds actually present, then $C = 20$, $\hat{\beta} = 0.25$, and $\hat{N} = 20/0.25 = 80$. Most of the effort in developing population estimation methods for animal populations has involved ways of estimating the probability of detection (β) from counts of animals.

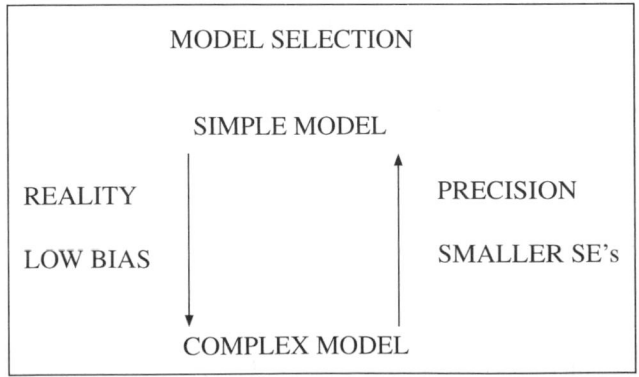

Fig. 2. Tradeoffs in reality versus precision; parsimony as a basis for model selection.

Sampling

The second basic problem is that time and money are usually limited, so a particular survey method cannot be applied to the entire area of interest. In this case, sample area(s) must be selected that represent a fraction, α, of the total area of interest. Unlike β, this sampling fraction is frequently known with reasonable accuracy. If $\hat{N}'$ represents the estimated number of animals in a representative sample area, the population size of the entire area, $\hat{N}$, can be estimated as:

$$\hat{N} = \frac{\hat{N}'}{\alpha}, \tag{3}$$

where α again is the proportion of the total area to which $\hat{N}'$ pertains. For example, if 32 animals were estimated on sample plots representing 10% of the total area of interest, then $\hat{N}' = 32$, $\alpha = 0.10$, and $\hat{N} = 32/0.10 = 320$, which is our estimate of the number of animals in the entire area of interest.

We use the term "sampling design" to refer to the manner in which sample units are selected from the entire area of interest. Sampling designs can range from simple random sampling to more involved designs such as stratified random sampling or double sampling (Thompson 1992, Williams et al. 2002, Garton et al. 2005). The objective of these designs is to provide a means of selecting sample units (units on which to conduct animal counts) so that information from sampled units can be used to estimate the numbers of animals on units not selected for counting. Stated differently, we want to select sample units in a manner that permits inference about the entire area of interest.

Thus, probability of detection (equations 1 and 2) and sampling (equation 3) are 2 basic concerns involved with estimating populations of animals. Combining equations (2) and (3) yields the following general population size estimator:

$$\hat{N} = \frac{C}{\alpha\hat{\beta}} \tag{4}$$

where $\hat{N}$ is the estimate of population size, C is the total count of animals over all sampling units, α is the proportion of the entire area that is surveyed, and $\hat{\beta}$ is the estimated detection probability or proportion of the animals counted. Virtually all estimators of population size can be expressed in the form of equation (4). We have made simplifying assumptions for heuristic reasons. For example, expression (4) contains no quantities with subscripts corresponding to the different individual sampling units, implying the estimated detection probability, $\hat{\beta}$, applies to all sampling units on which counts were obtained. It may be that different detection probabilities pertain to the different sampling units, and estimators for this situation represent straightforward generalizations of equation (4) (Thompson 1992, Skalski 1994).

If there is no sampling correlation between C and $\hat{\beta}$, the variance of the estimator (equation 4) is:

$$\text{var}(\hat{N}) = (N^2)\left\{\left[\frac{\text{var}(C)}{C^2}\right] + \left[\frac{\text{var}(\hat{\beta})}{\beta^2}\right]\right\}, \tag{5}$$

where var denotes sampling variance. The 2 additive terms within the square brackets of equation (5) are the central components of variation contributing to the variance of $\hat{N}$. The component associated with var($\hat{\beta}$) depends on the method of estimating β, and it can be large. The component associated with var(C) depends on the variation in true abundance over the area of interest, survey procedure, and the proportion of area sampled, α. The var(C) component is smaller when animals are distributed uniformly and larger when animals are distributed in a patchy or clumped manner. This geographic component of variation is best estimated from replicate samples (subareas) within the total area (e.g., Thompson 1992, Williams et al. 2002). The var(C) component, and hence the variance of $\hat{N}$, also becomes smaller as α becomes larger; i.e., approaches 1. This corresponds to the intuitive idea that var($\hat{N}$) decreases as the proportion of the total area sampled becomes large. The magnitude of β is also important, with lower var($\hat{N}$) associated with larger β. This corresponds with our intuition that the greater the proportion of the population counted, the less variable the population estimate. Finally, if there is correlation (i.e., a measure of the joint variation of 2 variables) between C and β, an additional term (covariance) must also be included in equation (5) (Mood et al. 1974).

This discussion provides a brief, but fundamental, framework for the estimators of population size described in this chapter. Although our focus is on population size, we sometimes refer to the closely related quantity, population density. Density is generally defined as the number of animals per unit area. If we estimate population size (N) at some specified location of total area, A, density is estimated as:

$$\hat{D} = \frac{\hat{N}}{A}. \tag{6}$$

If A is known exactly, then var($\hat{D}$) can be estimated as:

$$\text{var}(\hat{D}) = \left(\frac{1}{A}\right)^2 \text{var}(\hat{N}), \tag{7}$$

where var($\hat{N}$) is the estimated variance of $\hat{N}$. At times, the exact area to which an estimate of population size applies is not known but must be estimated. For example, capture–recapture studies of small mammals on trapping grids can be used to estimate population size, but the area to which such an estimate applies is often larger than the area covered by the grid. If A is not known but must be estimated, equation (7) must be modified (e.g., Williams et al. 2002:314–316) to incorporate this additional source of variation in var($\hat{D}$).

The organization of this chapter is presented diagrammatically (Fig. 3). Indices are separated from population estimation methods because they are a special case for which no population estimate is intended. The application of indices to make inferences about differences in population size principally requires assumptions about probability of detection. We divided population estimation methods into 2 major categories depending on whether all individuals, or only a portion of the individuals, can be observed. In the former category, which is not common in wildlife studies, sampling concerns predominate, and in the more common latter case, probability of detection is also important. We have further subdivided these major categories into methods that involve capture of animals and those that involve only observing animals. For some readily observable species, estimation methods based on actual counts should be useful. For animals that are not easily seen but can be captured, capture methods might be the only feasible alternative.

INDICES

Animal ecologists have long dealt with statistics that do not actually estimate animal abundance but are believed to be correlated with abundance. For example, the number of birds seen or heard singing in a woodlot, the number of small mammals caught in a grid of traps set in an old field, and the number of deer pellets counted in a plot of woods are all thought to provide some information on animal abundance. Few people would claim these statistics are good estimators of abundance, but they should be related to abundance in some manner. Caughley (1977:12) defined a density index as "any measurable correlative of density" and proceeded to describe several possible functional relationships between a density index and absolute density (Eberhardt 1978).

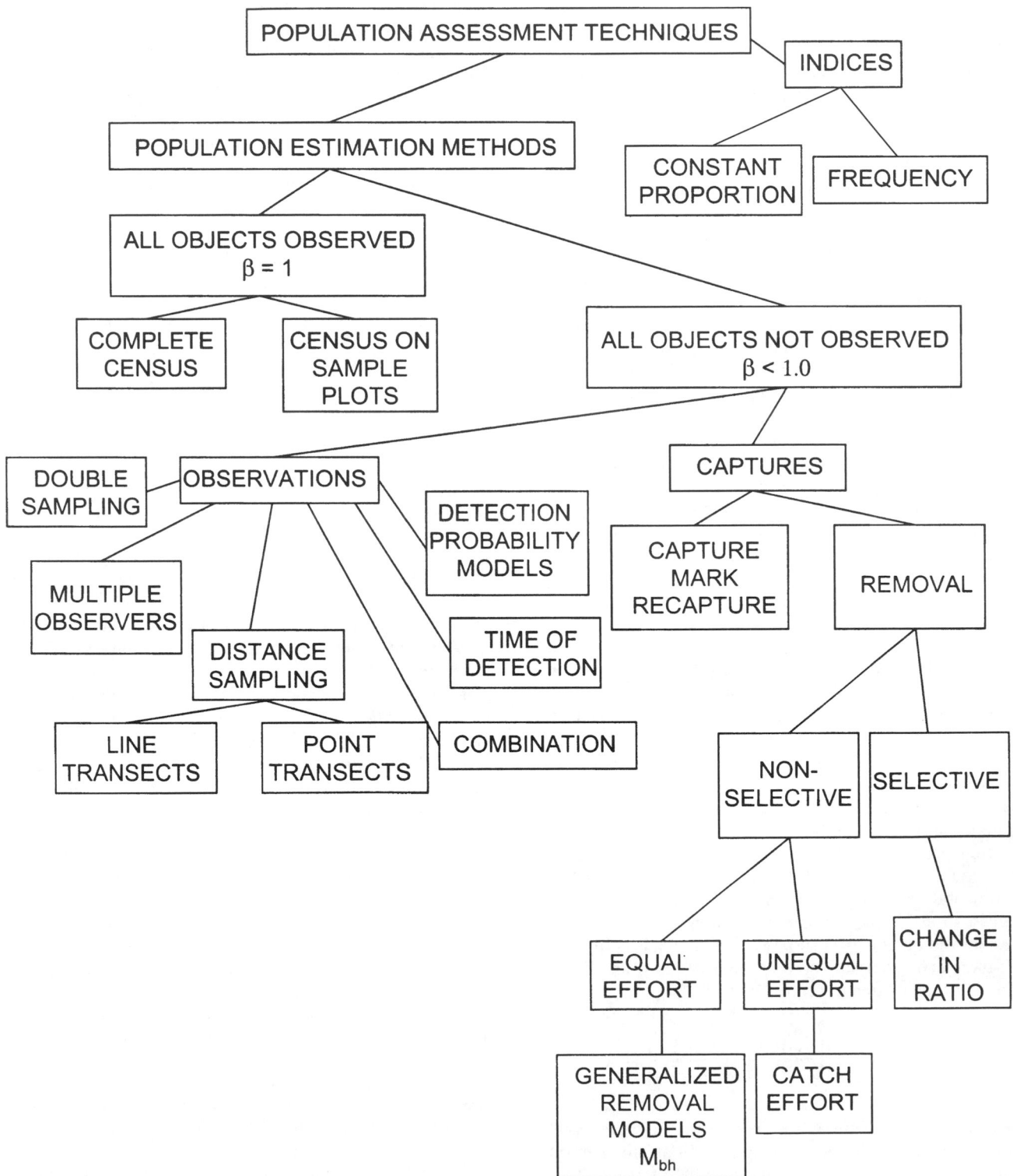

Fig. 3. The relationship among population estimation approaches.

Most uses of indices of either abundance or density involve comparisons between populations from the same location at different times or between populations from different locations at the same time. Thus, indices are used to indicate relative differences in abundance. Indices that are best suited to such uses are related to abundance as in the equation (which is the same as equation 1) below:

$$E(C) = \beta N \qquad (8)$$

where E(C) denotes the expected value of the count statistic (C), here viewed as an index, N denotes true abundance (the number of animals in some specified area), and β is a proportionality constant relating C and N. In our discussion of equation (1), β was defined as the probability of detection and was equated with the expected proportion of animals in the area of interest that is observed. Thus, β lies in the interval $0 \le \beta \le 1$. This definition corresponds to the usual situation in population estimation where the count is of animals themselves. In this discussion of indices, however, we interpret β more generally to correspond not only to counts of animals but also to counts of animal sign (scats, tracks, nests, etc.). In such cases, β is still a constant relating counts and true abundance, but β is no longer a detection probability and is not constrained to lie between 0 and 1. We refer to indices that are related to true abundance as in equation (8), as constant-proportion indices. They are, by far, the most useful indices for comparative population studies and will be the subject of most of our subsequent discussion. However, we briefly discuss other indices at the end of this section.

Constant-proportion Indices

The key to reasonable use of any statistic thought to be a constant–proportion index is to ensure that equation (8) holds true for the intended comparison. For example, assume we are considering using the number of muskrats (*Ondatra zibethicus*) caught during 2 nights of trapping with 100 traps as a possible index to abundance in a marsh. We are interested in estimating the rate of change in population size (i.e., the finite rate of increase λ) between sampling periods in 2 consecutive years, 1 and 2. We would thus like to estimate $\lambda = N_2/N_1$, using C_2/C_1, where the subscripts denote year. We can approximate the expected value of our estimator, $E(C_2/C_1)$, as:

$$\frac{E(C_2)}{E(C_1)} \approx \frac{\beta_2 N_2}{\beta_1 N_1} \qquad (9)$$

where β_i is the capture probability or the proportion of the population caught in the sampling effort of year i. If the same proportion of the muskrat population is captured in the 2 different years of the study (i.e., if $\beta_1 = \beta_2 = \beta$), the β_i in equation (9) cancel, and C_2/C_1 is a reasonable (but still not unbiased [Barker and Sauer 1992]) estimator for population change. However, if $\beta_1 \ne \beta_2$, we are not catching the same fraction of the population each year, and C is not a good index. In this latter case our estimate of λ is a function of the change in detection probability between years as well as the change in population size; i.e., changes in detection probability and population size are confounded. Thus, the estimator should not be used to draw inferences about population change.

When count statistics are obtained for many consecutive time periods (e.g., years) and interest is in an average rate of change over time (trend), then variation in β over time can be tolerated as long as the β_i can be viewed as random selections from some overall distribution that does not change over time. More specifically, we must specify that $E(\beta_i)$ does not change over time. This assumption is violated, for example, whenever there is a temporal trend in β_i.

The question of whether some statistic, C_i, is a reasonable index of abundance for a specific comparative purpose thus involves a test of the hypothesis that the same proportion of the population is being sampled; i.e., that $\beta_i = \beta$ for all i's being compared, where i might denote year or geographic location. We can separate constant-proportion indices of abundance into 2 categories depending on whether they are collected as part of a formal method for estimating population size (i.e., whether the data are available for drawing inferences about N_i).

Indices Associated with Formal Population Estimation Methods

All of the formal methods developed for estimating population size we describe (except change-in-ratio estimators) can be viewed in the context of equation (8). They all involve some observation-based statistic, C, and additional information that can be used to estimate the proportionality constant, β, relating C and population size, N. Estimation of N is then accomplished as in equation (10) (which is the same as equation 2):

$$\hat{N} = \frac{C}{\hat{\beta}}. \qquad (10)$$

In capture–recapture studies, for example, C is the number of animals caught, and β is the capture probability, or the proportion of the population represented by C. In this case, β is estimated from data on the capture histories of marked animals. In the simplest case β is estimated as the proportion of marked animals that are recaptured. Similarly, in removal studies in which constant effort is applied such as on a trapping grid, C is the total number of animals captured, and β again represents the capture probability and is estimated from information on the change in number of new individuals caught in successive sampling periods. In catch-per-unit-effort removal studies, C is essentially the catch of animals standardized for variable effort (i.e., catch-per-unit-effort), and β is a "probability of catch constant" estimated from cumulative removals in relation to the numbers of animals caught in each time period. In line transect studies, C is the number of animals actually seen by observers on the transect, and β can be thought of as the average probability of observing an animal from the transect. Here, β is estimated from the distribution of right-angle distances of animals observed along the transect line. Aerial surveys of animals sometimes use a double-sampling approach in which complete ground counts are obtained for subsamples of the entire surveyed area. In this situation, C is the total aerial count. The ratio of the mean aerial count on the subsampled area to the mean ground count on this area then estimates β, the proportion of animals seen from the air.

Change-in-ratio (CIR) estimators are a unique class of population estimation techniques in which detection probabilities are not estimated directly. Instead, detection probabilities for different types of animals appear as ratios in CIR models. Under some reduced-parameter models, detection probabilities for different classes of animals are assumed to be equal, so they cancel out and do not appear in CIR equations. In more general models (e.g., Udevitz and Pollock 1991), detection probabilities for different classes of animals (for example, males and females) are expressed relative to one another using parameters for "relative probability of detection."

For most of these formal estimation methods, statistical tests of the hypothesis of constant β can be developed. For example, Skalski et al. (1983) and Skalski and Robson (1992) presented both likelihood ratio and conditional contingency table tests of the null hypothesis of equal capture probabilities for 2 times or locations sampled with 2-sample capture–recapture experiments. If the null hypothesis is not rejected, (i.e., if capture probabilities are not found to be different), Skalski et al. (1983) recommended using total animals captured to index abundance, and basing comparative tests on this index. Skalski et al. (1984) provided a similar test for populations being compared with constant-effort removal sampling. For capture–recapture experiments on open populations, the null hypothesis of constant capture probability for a single population over time can be tested (Jolly 1982, Brownie et al. 1986). Aerial surveys of animals often use a double-sampling approach to estimate β. Contingency tables can be used to test hypotheses about variation in these β_i over time and space.

Why should the hypothesis of equal β_i be tested when indices are obtained in conjunction with a formal population estimation method? The biological hypothesis of interest can be tested with the actual population estimates themselves, $\hat{N}_i$ (e.g., from equation 10), rather than the statistics, C_i, on which they are based. The reason for using the statistics in the case of equal β_i's is that index statistics will generally have smaller variances than their associated population estimators (Eberhardt and Simmons 1987, Skalski and Robson 1992). This can be seen by examining equation (5) and recalling the variance of N includes 2 main components, one associated with the statistic, C, and the other associated with the estimation of β. The variance of C alone, however, does not include variation associated with estimation of β.

An important consequence of the smaller relative variance of C than $\hat{N}$ is that hypothesis tests using C will tend to have greater power than tests using $\hat{N}$. Similarly, estimates of rate of change (when comparisons involve a single population at different points in time) and proportional or relative abundance (when comparisons involve different populations at one point in time) tend to be more precise when based on C_i than when based on $\hat{N}_i$. For example, estimates of proportional abundance (N_2/N_1) based on the total number of animals captured in 2, 2-sample capture–recapture experiments (C_2/C_1) are from 2 to 20 times more efficient than estimates based on Lincoln–Petersen estimates ($\hat{N}_2/\hat{N}_1$) (Skalski et al. 1983).

However, there is danger in using (C_2/C_1) to estimate relative abundance based on a standard test of the null hypothesis that $\beta_1 = \beta_2$. If the true difference between β_1 and β_2 is sufficiently large, the estimate of relative abundance based on indices will be biased. Following MacKenzie and Kendall (2002), we recommend handling this

potential problem using either of 2 approaches. The first approach uses equivalence tests (Manly 2001), rather than standard hypothesis tests, to examine differences between detection probabilities. Under equivalence testing, the investigator specifies the difference between detection probabilities that can be practically tolerated. The hypothesis tested is that 2 detection probabilities are substantially different, with the alternative the true difference lies within a specified interval of practical tolerance (Mackenzie and Kendall 2002). Specification of an acceptable difference can be based on the amount of bias that can be tolerated in the relative abundance estimator.

The other approach to estimation of relative abundance is to use model-averaging (Buckland et al. 1997, Burnham and Anderson 2002) and compute a weighted average relative abundance estimate using estimates from one model that assumes equal detection probabilities and another that retains separate parameters for the different detection probability parameters. This approach should properly incorporate the uncertainty associated with model selection (constant β vs. separate β_i) while balancing the trade-off in bias and precision associated with these 2 models (MacKenzie and Kendall 2002).

Indices Not Associated with Formal Population Estimation Methods

Many statistics considered as potential indices of abundance are not obtained with a formal estimation model in mind. Data needed to estimate and test hypotheses about β_i generally are not obtained as part of the standard, data-collection process. Inferences about β_i require special efforts to estimate the true population size to which the index is thought to apply and then to "calibrate" the index to population size (Eberhardt and Simmons 1987, Diefenbach et al. 1994, Conroy 1996). If estimates of population size can be obtained for several time periods or locations (depending on the intended comparative use of the index), a regression of population estimates on index values permits inferences about β. If the selected statistic is a true constant-proportion index, the relationship between the population estimates and index values will be linear, the intercept will be zero, and the slope of the regression will estimate β. Each ratio of the index statistic to the population size estimate, $C_i/\hat{N}_i$, will also estimate β_i, and it is often possible to use these ratios to devise tests of the hypothesis that the β_i's are equal. If tests indicate the β_i's are equal, the index is calibrated. In this case, index proponents frequently claim the index has been "validated" and that future index use is justified. However, "validation" at a small number of points in time and space does not necessarily provide justification for index use at other times and locations. When comparison of population estimates and potential index statistics leads to the conclusion that the β_i's are not constant, the selected statistic, C_i, does not meet the critical criterion of a constant–proportion index.

There are 3 basic approaches used in attempts to deal with variation in detection probability in index surveys (e.g., Conroy and Nichols 1996, Pollock et al. 2002). The first is standardization and can be used for factors identified as potential sources of variation in detection probability that are under the control of the investigator. For example, sampling methods and effort can be standardized (e.g., bait all small mammal traps with the same type and amount of bait, spend the same amount of time listening for birds at all sample locations, conduct surveys only with observers who have undergone a training program, conduct bird surveys only during early-mid morning), as can weather conditions in which surveys are conducted (e.g., conduct avian point counts only on days with little wind and no rain).

The second approach to dealing with variation in detection probability involves use of covariates in analyses of index statistics. For example, it may be that measurable, exogenous variables, such as weather conditions or observer identity, account for most of the variation in β_i. Thus, models can be developed for estimating change in population size as a function of the index statistic and relevant exogenous variables (Overton 1969; Craig et al. 1997; Link and Sauer 1997, 1998, 2002). An important caveat for this approach is that covariates selected for use in modeling cannot be associated with both detection probability and true abundance. For example, habitat is a potentially important covariate affecting detection probability. However, because it can also influence abundance itself, incorporation of habitat as a covariate affecting detection probability would not be appropriate.

The third approach is to acknowledge that detection probability is not likely to be constant over space or time and that not all covariates can be measured, modeled, or even perceived. This acknowledgment leads to implementation of study designs that collect data in a manner that permits direct estimation of detection probability. This is the approach discussed with indices associated with formal estimation methods. We believe this is the only approach of the 3 that is scientifically defensible, and we strongly recommend that developers of future surveys and monitoring programs follow this approach. Burnham (1981), Lancia et al. (1994), Conroy and Nichols (1996), Thompson et al. (1998), Nichols et al. (2000), Anderson (2001), Morrison et al. (2001), Yoccoz et al. (2001), Karanth and Nichols (2002), Pollock et al. (2002), Rosenstock et al. (2002), Thompson (2002), and Williams et al. (2002) have developed additional discussion of this perspective.

Despite this recommendation, index use is common in wildlife surveys and monitoring programs throughout the world (e.g., Thompson et al. 1998). Indices in animal surveys are generally based on actual counts of animals seen, heard, caught, or harvested. The North American Breeding Bird Survey (Robbins et al. 1986, Peterjohn et al. 1997), now coordinated by the U.S. Geological Survey, the mourning dove (*Zenaida macroura*) call-count survey (Dolton 1993), and the American woodcock (*Scolopax minor*) singing-ground survey (Tautin 1982, Tautin et al. 1983), the latter 2 coordinated by the U.S. Fish and Wildlife Service, are large-scale surveys based on birds seen and heard at established stops along permanent, roadside routes. Detailed written instructions are provided to observers in these surveys, and counts are "standardized" to the extent possible with respect to season, time of day, and weather. Information on observer identity is also recorded.

Possible sources of variation in the proportion of populations counted in these and similar bird surveys include species, observer, and environmental influences including season, time of day, habitat, and weather (e.g., Ralph and Scott 1981, Wilson and Bart 1985). There is strong evidence in Breeding Bird Survey data of variation in detection probability associated with observer experience and identity (Sauer et al. 1994, Kendall et al. 1996), and these covariates are included in most serious analyses of these data (e.g., Geissler and Sauer 1990; Link and Sauer 1997, 1998, 2002). Previous work on the Breeding Bird Survey has also provided evidence of variation in detection probability as a function of species (Nichols et al. 2000) and density (Bart and Schoultz 1984).

Baskett et al. (1978) considered the utility of indices resulting from the mourning dove call-count survey and reviewed results of research on potential effects on detection probability of various factors, including dove pair status, position in the nesting cycle, time of day, population density, and weather. They concluded these variables can influence call-count results and speculated that problems would be more serious for local studies than for the nationwide call-count survey. Efforts to evaluate possible variation in detection probability for the woodcock singing-ground survey have yielded variable results (Tautin et al. 1983). In an important study on Moosehorn National Wildlife Refuge in Maine, Dwyer et al. (1988) concluded the proportion of adult males in the population that had singing grounds varied over time (i.e., that β varied over time).

In addition to extensive national surveys, counts of birds seen and heard are used to index local abundance of raptors, ring-necked pheasants (*Phasianus colchicus*), ruffed grouse (*Bonasa umbellus*), and northern bobwhites (*Colinus virginianus*) (Bull 1981, Fuller and Mosher 1981). Spotlight counts at night of white-tailed deer (e.g., Storm et al. 1992), American alligators (*Alligator mississippiensis*) (Chabreck 1966, 1973; Taylor and Neal 1984) and other animals are sometimes used as indices. Woodward and Marion (1978) studied sources of variation in alligator night counts and identified water level, water temperature, and moonlight as factors influencing the proportion of animals seen. Packard et al. (1985) provided evidence that detection probability for aerial counts of manatees (*Trichechus manatus*) during winter in Florida varied over surveys, likely in response to a number of different factors including habitat, observer, and weather. Roadside counts of eastern cottontail rabbits (*Sylvilagus floridanus*) at night and in early morning have been used to monitor statewide population trends in Illinois (Preno and Labisky 1971). Observations of red foxes (*Vulpes vulpes*) by rural mail carriers have been used to index fox abundance in North Dakota (Allen and Sargeant 1975). Fox observations were correlated with abundance estimates based on aerial surveys, leading Allen and Sargeant (1975) to conclude the index was useful. Thus, statistics based on direct counts may provide reasonable indices to abundance. For the majority of such indices, however, the question of constancy of the proportion of the population seen or heard has not been adequately addressed.

The number of animals caught in trapping efforts is a commonly used population index in studies of small mammals (e.g., Dice 1941, Keller and Krebs 1970), and recommendations have been made for establishing standardized trap lines to obtain such statistics (Calhoun 1948). However, capture–recapture studies of small mammals using model-based estimators typically show evidence of variation in capture probability over time (Nichols and Pollock 1983) and between species (Nichols 1986). The number of animals caught on traplines has also been used to index furbearer abundance (e.g., Wood 1959, Wood and Odum

1964).   Recent capture–recapture studies of furbearers, however, have provided strong evidence of year-to-year variation in capture probability (Smith et al. 1984). Camera-trap photographs of tigers (*Panthera tigris*) have been proposed as an index to tiger abundance (Carbone et al. 2001), but use of this index has been criticized (Jennelle et al. 2002). We suspect the number of animals caught generally will not represent a constant proportion of the population, and this statistic will typically be a poor index.

The number of animals harvested has been used to index the size of animal populations exposed to open hunting, fishing, or trapping seasons. For harvests to be a reasonable index, the proportion of the total population that is harvested (harvest rate) must be a constant for areas or time periods being compared. Investigations of harvest rate, however, usually find evidence of variation over both time and space (e.g., Anderson 1975, Clark 1987, Johnson et al. 1997), indicating that harvest generally does not provide a good population index.

In addition to counts of animals seen, heard, trapped, or harvested, there are many indirect indices based on signs of animal presence and activity (reviewed by Scattergood 1954, Overton 1969). Counts of animal tracks crossing roads or trails have been used to index abundance for various species such as tigers (Smirnov and Miquelle 1999) and especially deer (Tyson 1959, Connolly 1981). Downing et al. (1965) compared track counts with known numbers of deer in an enclosure and the results indicated variation in the relationship between tracks and deer number.

Fecal or pellet counts have been used as an abundance index for deer and other ungulates (reviewed by Neff 1968, Karanth and Kumar 2002), rabbits (Cochran and Stains 1961), and even birds (Bull 1981). Ancillary information on rates of defecation and fecal decomposition can be used to estimate β, and hence to estimate population size from fecal counts (Eberhardt and Van Etten 1956, Neff 1968, Hiby and Lovell 1991, Karanth and Kumar 2002). Neff (1968) reviewed studies comparing pellet-count estimates of deer abundance with known numbers of deer and reported evidence of variation in β over time. More recently, Fuller (1991) found no relationship between pellet counts and aerial survey counts corrected for probability of detection estimated using radio-marked deer. However, the power of his test was low so his conclusion should be viewed with caution (White 1992).

Counts of conspicuous structures made by animals are also used as population indices. For example, indices have been based on counts of muskrat houses (Dozier et al. 1948), American beaver (*Castor canadensis*) lodges (Hay 1958), and nests of gray squirrels (*Sciurus carolinensis*) (Uhlig 1956), American alligators (Chabreck 1966, Taylor and Neal 1984), and various bird species (e.g., Nettleship 1976, Bull 1981, Fuller and Mosher 1981). Independent estimates of beaver population size did not show a constant relationship to number of active lodges across colonies (Hay 1958), indicating that lodge counts do not provide an adequate index. Efforts to relate counts of bird nests to independent estimates of bird abundance are few. However, variation in age structure of the population, proportion of breeding-age birds that nest, timing of the breeding season, and tendency to renest can easily result in substantial variation in β, the birds-per-nest ratio. When counts of animal structures are used to index animal abundance, a common assumption is these structures are detected with probability of 1.0; i.e., all existing structures are seen. A study of nest counts in white-winged dove (*Zenaida asiatica*) colonies indicated the proportion of nests seen by observers ranged from 0.93 to only 0.57 (Nichols et al. 1986). Formal estimation methods may be necessary to properly estimate the number of animal structures in many situations (Magnusson et al. 1978, Nichols et al. 1986).

Although the focus of this chapter is on abundance estimation, we comment briefly on the related concept of population "trend" and data-analytic approaches for its estimation. We define "trend" in a general manner as a descriptive statistic reflecting change in abundance over time. Index statistics are commonly used to estimate trend. However, methods used have generated much controversy (e.g., for birds see Sauer and Droege 1990, James et al. 1996, Link and Sauer 1997). Many current approaches to modeling count data resulting from index surveys are based on the Poisson distribution, with modification because counts are typically overdispersed, or more variable than indicated by the Poisson (Link and Sauer 1997, 1998, 2002). Link and Sauer (2002) present an overdispersed Poisson regression model that accommodates trend and year effects as well as nuisance parameters for observer and start-up (new observer) effects. In addition, the hierarchical modeling approach of Link and Sauer (2002) permits the view of population parameters at different geographic scales as random variables.

Model fitting and estimation are accomplished using Markov Chain Monte Carlo methods (Link and Sauer 2002, Link et al. 2002). Craig et al. (1997) used a hierarchical modeling approach to estimate manatee population trend for Florida's Atlantic Coast with a model that included not only the observation process (detection probability), but also manatee movement between surveys. Similar efforts have been made to incorporate measurement error into hierarchical models that include parameters for trend and other processes (e.g., density-dependence) (Bjornstad et al. 1999, Stenseth et al. 1999, Bjornstad and Grenfell 2001). These models represent the state of the art with respect to statistical modeling and the best that can be done to estimate trend and related parameters from index surveys. However, potential users should be aware that they require assumptions about the detection process that usually translate to an average detection probability that does not change over time, except for changes induced by measured covariates (observer, weather, etc.) that are incorporated into the model.

Many different statistics not collected in conjunction with a formal population estimation method have been proposed as possible constant-proportion indices. Although the assumption of constant β [or at least constant $E(\beta)$] is required for the reasonable use of such indices to compare population sizes, data required to test this assumption are not routinely collected. In many cases the assumption of constant β is not tested. When special efforts have been made to test this assumption, they have typically identified sources of variation in β. Some sources of variation can be adequately addressed by standardizing data collection procedures and by using covariates in the analysis. However, many other sources either cannot be handled in these ways or cannot even be identified. Thus, we recommend caution and skepticism when using and interpreting these indices.

FREQUENCY DENSITY RELATIONSHIP

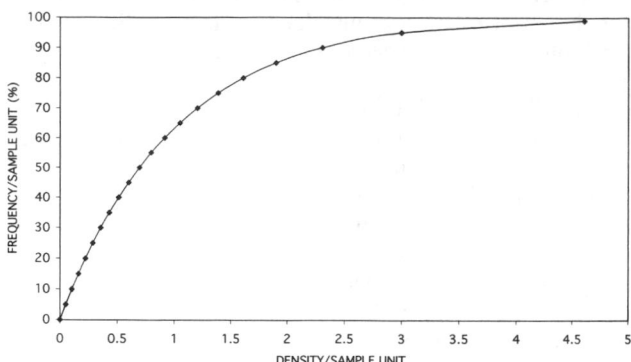

Fig. 4. The relationship between frequency and density when animals are distributed randomly (from Caughley 1977).

When population changes estimated from indices are used in population management, the assumption of constant β probably merits detailed study. Our preference is to incorporate data collection needed to estimate β directly into the sampling program.

Frequency Indices

Although constant-proportion indices are the most useful type for estimating rate of population change, there are situations when other indices have some utility, depending on whether something is known about the relationship between population size and the index. This represents a "Catch-22" because the only way to obtain knowledge of the relationship is to estimate detection probability directly or to estimate population size and "calibrate" the index. However, the reason for considering use of an index may be because cost and effort involved in estimating population size are thought to be prohibitive.

Conroy (1996) discussed use of indices that are related to abundance in ways other than that described by equation (8). The only index we discuss in this category is the frequency index. Frequency indices are based on the proportion of sample units that contain at least one item of interest such as an animal or sign of animal activity (Scattergood 1954, Caughley 1977, Seber 1982). Frequency indices generally are not related linearly to abundance or density as in equation (8). In the best situations, the relationship between an index and true population size is positive, but nonlinear (Fig. 4). Comparative uses are thus restricted to ranking density or abundance and, in general, neither rate of change nor proportional abundance can be estimated. However, Caughley (1977:22) noted that for frequencies less than about 0.2, the frequency-density relationship is nearly linear and may provide useful comparisons.

Frequency indices have been used in conjunction with several different sampling methods. For example, direct counts of animals on quadrats or other sampling units, numbers of animals caught in a specified number of traps, and counts of animal tracks or other sign on a specific number of sampling units have all been used to compute frequency indices. The proportion of transects on which groups of howler monkeys (*Alouatta* spp.) were seen provided a useful frequency index (Subcommittee on Conser-

vation of Natural Populations 1981). Wood (1959) concluded the number of trapline stations catching at least one fox provided a reasonable frequency index to fox abundance, but this conclusion was not supported by Smith et al. (1984). The proportion of established scent stations where animal activity is detected by the presence of tracks provides an often-used frequency index to abundance of many furbearer species (Wood 1959, Conner et al. 1983, Diefenbach et al. 1994). Conner et al. (1983) compared scent-station indices to abundance estimates and concluded that indices accurately reflected trends in the population abundance of bobcats (*Lynx rufus*), raccoons (*Procyon lotor*), and gray foxes (*Urocyon cinereoargenteus*), but not Virginia opossums (*Didelphis virginiana*).

In an exemplary evaluation of index utility, Diefenbach et al. (1994) obtained scent station indices at various known abundances of bobcats following bobcat introductions to Cumberland Island, Georgia. They found a positive relationship between indices and abundance, and recommended specific data transformations to handle frequency index data. Predictions of abundance based on data from single scent station surveys had poor precision, although 4 replicate surveys were predicted to have adequate power to detect rather large differences in abundance at high bobcat densities (Diefenbach et al. 1994).

Assumptions underlying reasonable use of frequency indices are similar to those required for more useful constant-proportion indices. The probability of catching, counting, or otherwise detecting an animal in sample units from 2 areas or time periods being compared should be similar. As Seber (1982) noted, the statistical distribution of animals over space should also be similar for areas or time periods being compared. For example, if direct counts are used to ascertain presence or absence on sample quadrats, a population with a highly clumped distribution will yield a lower frequency index (proportion of quadrats with at least one animal) than a population of similar density that exhibits a more uniform distribution over space. We recommend collecting data in a manner that permits inference about detection probability and whether this probability varies over time and/or space. Various kinds of spatial and temporal replication (e.g., multiple visits to sample plots) permit direct estimation of the probability of detecting animal sign or animals themselves, given presence on the sample plot (e.g., MacKenzie et al. 2002, Nichols and Karanth 2002). Although frequency data are usually treated as indices, adequate replication permits direct estimation of the proportion of sample units occupied by the species of interest (e.g., MacKenzie et al. 2002, Nichols and Karanth 2002). The combination of replication and certain distributional assumptions permits direct estimation of population size in some cases (Royle and Nichols 2003).

ESTIMATES OF ABUNDANCE AND DENSITY
Complete Counts

Seldom, if ever, will it be possible to obtain a total count of animals over an entire area of interest. If the count is purported to be a total census of all the animals, then inferential statistics such as variance and confidence interval are not needed because the entire population is counted; no sampling is used. In such situations, both α and β in equation (4) equal 1, so $N = C$, and the count represents population size. However, an error-free census is unlikely, so "... a census datum should be accompanied by a critical evaluation of its accuracy and by an explicit statement of the constraints and definitions under which it was collected" (Overton 1969:419).

Total counts on small areas can be derived from intensive surveys, from a known number of marked individuals, or other ingenious means. These total counts are assumed to be accurate and are used to calibrate (i.e., estimate probability of detection) extensive field surveys.

Drive counts (Morse 1943) of deer or other ungulates have been purported to permit accurate population counts, but most workers using this method concede that an unknown number of animals is likely missed (e.g., Tyson 1959, McCullough 1979). Aerial photography can be used to obtain nearly complete counts of animals in certain special situations. For example, Haramis et al. (1985) used 35-mm photography from low-flying aircraft to count canvasback (*Aythya valisineria*) flocks throughout Chesapeake Bay and coastal North Carolina. We give brief descriptions of several complete count methods below and refer the reader to reviews by Scattergood (1954), Overton (1969), Eberhardt et al. (1979), Seber (1982), and Miller (1984).

Drive Counts

As the name implies, counters drive animals to census the total number of animals in a defined area. The technique is suited to species such as deer and pheasants that inhabit relatively open habitat. Overton (1969) gave a brief overview of the technique. Drivers, spaced along a line, sweep across an area with well-defined boundaries. Additional observers may be placed along the boundaries to count animals that move in or out of the census area. The census is the sum of the number of animals moving out of the area ahead of the line of drivers, plus those moving from ahead of observers back through the line, minus any moving into the area ahead of the drivers.

McCullough (1979) used drive counts to census a fenced-in deer population on the George Reserve in Michigan. He compared drive counts with the "known" population that was reconstructed from the age of death of individuals in the population. He concluded that at low populations drive counts underestimated the true population, and at high populations they overestimated the true population. Errors could be as large as 20–30%. Thus, drive counts are probably best viewed as an index of population size. As with other indices, efforts to test hypotheses about possible variation in probability of detection (β) should precede serious use of drive-count data for management purposes.

Total Mapping of Bird Territories

This approach is similar to spot mapping except that an effort is made to color band breeding birds and follow all marked individuals to delineate their territories or home ranges. In most total mapping studies, however, population estimation is not the primary objective of the study. Verner (1985:266) believed that, when thoroughly executed, total mapping is probably the most accurate method of estimating population density of breeding birds, and "... total mapping should be used as a standard for evaluating the accuracy of other methods of estimating the densities of birds."

However, others note, "This view is not always justified" (Bibby et al. 2000:42). This method only estimates the population of relatively conspicuous birds holding territories, not nonterritorial birds (i.e., floaters) or transients.

Spot Mapping or Territory Mapping

Spot mapping (Verner 1985, Bibby et al. 2000) gives estimates of breeding bird population density. The technique is most suited to birds that regularly sing or call within exclusive territories. Floaters and young of the year are usually not surveyed by this technique.

Spot mapping involves plotting locations of individual birds on a grid map during repeated visits to a study area. Most information comes from individuals of a species that can be seen or heard simultaneously (Bibby et al. 2000). Clusters of locations, assumed to represent centers of activity of individual territories during the breeding season, are identified on the map. The total number of clusters in the study area equals the number of clusters completely inside the area plus the sum of fractional parts of clusters on the boundaries. Total number of birds is estimated by multiplying the number of clusters by mean number of birds per cluster, which is normally 2, assuming birds breed in pairs.

Assumptions of the method (after Verner 1985, Bibby et al. 2000) are (1) populations are constant, and birds remain within exclusive spaces or territories during the sampling period; (2) birds on territories produce cues frequently enough to permit repeated location on successive observational visits; (3) estimated proportions of territories along boundaries are accurate; (4) the estimated mean number of birds represented by each cluster is accurate; and (5) observers are skilled, record data accurately, and are consistent.

There are many problems with meeting the assumptions of the method. For example, interpretation of the spatial arrangement of clusters for some species varies considerably among observers (Best 1975, O'Conner and Marchant 1981). Verner and Milne (1990) provided strong evidence that spot mapping results should not be considered to be complete counts as these results can vary substantially among observers and map analysts. At best, spot mapping yields an index; the variation in detectability (β) among observers and analysts suggests caution in using this method.

Point Counts

Point counts are typically used to estimate bird density. An observer proceeds to a sample point and might or might not allow a rest period of specified duration for equilibration of bird activity (Reynolds et al. 1980). The observer then detects birds (by both sight and sound) for a specified count period. Although the assumption is that all birds are detected at a point, typically point counts have been viewed as indices of abundance when standardized protocols are emphasized (Ralph et al. 1995). In fixed radius point transects where all the birds are detected then

$$\hat{D} = N/a = N/k\pi w^2,$$

where D denotes density, N denotes the number of birds in the sampled area, and w is the radius of the circle around the point. The area surveyed is therefore $a = k\pi w^2$, if k points are surveyed. This is unrealistic in practice because it is virtually impossible to detect all birds within the sampled area.

The importance of trying to estimate detection probability during point counts has been noted for some time (Ramsey and Scott 1979, Reynolds et al. 1980, Burnham 1981, Barker and Sauer 1992, Buckland 1987, Buckland et al. 1993, Johnson 1995, Pendleton 1995, Nichols et al. 2000, Buckland et al. 2001, Farnsworth et al 2002). Two recent overview papers by Rosenstock et al. (2002) and Thompson (2002) stress the importance of estimation of detection probability to sound inference based on point counts.

Thermal Scanners

Thermal infrared (IR) scanners that detect wavelengths (3–12 mm) emitted by homeotherms and natural vegetation have been proposed as a technique to census animal populations (O'Neil et al. 2005). As early as the 1970s Parker and Driscoll (1972) suggested that thermal scanning for wildlife was feasible, but appropriate equipment needed to be developed. Wiggers and Beckerman (1993) used a Forward Looking Infrared (FLIR) scanner mounted on a fixed-wing aircraft to count a known deer population in pens. Thermal scans were displayed in real-time on a monitor in the cockpit that could be viewed by the surveyor and were recorded on videotape. Scenes were viewed by biologists, and deer were identified by gender and age. Most recently, Haroldson et al. (2004) compared detection rates for thermal imaging surveys to replicated aerial mark–recapture surveys and estimated detection rates for thermal imaging to range from 31 to 89%. They concluded that "Until the capabilities of thermal imaging are more fully understood …detection rates may be too variable to provide reliable counts of animal abundance" (Haroldson et al. 2004:1188).

In a different application of thermal scanners, Gill et al. (1997) used a direct view thermal imager on the ground to observe red deer (*Cervus elaphus*) on transects on mainland Britain. Rather than attempting a census, they used a line transect approach to estimate density. Bontaites et al. (2000) used FLIR to estimate moose (*Alces alces*) numbers in New Hampshire. They obtained information on detection probability (β) by reflying survey units at a lower speed, and estimated detectability to be 88%. As with other methods that purport to be a census, we recommend designing an experiment to estimate detection probability (β) of the scanner rather than assuming the count is complete.

Radar

High-frequency marine radar has been used to study movements and to estimate populations of marbled murrelets (*Brachyramphus marmoratus*) in the Pacific Northwest (Burger 2001, Larkin 2005). As with other techniques, the proportion of the population that is detected (β) should be estimated. Otherwise changes in population size could be confounded with changes in probability of detection. Without estimates of β, these estimates should be treated as an index.

Population Reconstruction

If all dead animals from a population can be located or otherwise known, and if the year and age at death can be identified with certainty, the population can be "reconstructed" based on how long each individual was known to be in the population. Thus, population size can be reconstructed for a given year in the past only after all the individuals alive in that year have died. This technique has more potential for populations of short-lived individuals, than for long lived ones. The reconstructed population is essentially the minimum possible number of individuals that were alive in a given cohort in a given year, summed over all possible cohorts. Population reconstruction is distinct from life table analysis (Dinsmore and Johnson 2005) where the relative numbers of animals dying (surviving) in different age classes are used to estimate survival rates, not population size directly. However, many big-game surveys in the western United States estimate population size through post-hoc life table methods based on herd composition (Rabe et al. 2002). McCullough (1979) used population reconstruction to measure the size of the George Reserve deer herd. Roseberry and Woolf (1991:22) compared reconstruction with a modeled population and found that reconstruction estimates were low when harvests were low, and high when harvests were high. Gove et al. (2002) used maximum likelihood approaches to analyze age-at-harvest data, supplemented with auxiliary information on harvest and survival probabilities estimated from radiotelemetry, to estimate abundance and other population demographic rates simultaneously.

Aerial Photography

Low altitude photography of flocks of birds (or other groups of animals) is often used as a census technique. The entire assemblage of animals is photographed and later counted to give a complete census. However, it is often difficult to ascertain if all individuals are "visible" to be photographed, and errors in counting undoubtedly are made (Bajzak and Piatt 1990). This approach is distinct from aerial surveys where the population is sampled by counting animals seen on a transect or on quadrats as the observer flies over.

Haramis et al. (1985) conducted a photographic census of the wintering population of canvasbacks in Chesapeake Bay and North Carolina. The authors believed the photographic survey represented "... nearly a complete census of open water habitats in this region" (Haramis et al. 1985:449). A sequence of photos was often necessary to cover an entire flock clearly. Slides were projected on paper, and ducks were identified by species and gender. Bajzak and Piatt (1990) used a computer-aided procedure to increase the precision of waterfowl counts from aerial photographs.

Total Counts on Sample Plots

It may be possible to obtain complete counts of animals on suitable-sized (relative to the organism being considered) sample plots within some larger area of interest. Because all individuals are counted, there is no variation associated with estimating the proportion of animals seen on sample plots. Instead, only geographic (plot to plot) variation is a concern. Derivation of estimates is based on standard sampling theory (Cochran 1977). The following are some representative examples. Kufeld et al. (1980) used complete counts on sample plots to estimate mule deer (*Odocoileus hemionus*) abundance in Colorado. Kraft et al. (1995) presented a thorough analysis of sampling plans for aerial surveys to estimate pronghorn (*Antilocapra americana*) populations and compared them to preliminary "counts [that] were virtually exact" (Kraft et al. 1995:130).

Cordts et al. (2002) used traditional ground surveys and experimental helicopter surveys to estimate abundance of ducks breeding on prairie potholes in Iowa.

Estimation Based on Incomplete Counts

Incomplete counts (rather than actual captures) of animals are common due to the high cost of capturing animals; typically, we cannot assume that all animals present are observed. Instead, the observers count some fraction, β, of the total animals present, and this fraction must be estimated to translate the incomplete counts into estimates of population size (as in equation 2). Several approaches are available for estimating β in conjunction with animal counts. Some of these approaches were developed for ground surveys whereas others were developed for aerial surveys. Although the general estimation methods are applicable regardless of the observer's location (air or ground), our description of each method is based on the survey methodology most commonly applied.

Complete Counts on a Subsample—Double Sampling

Complete counts of animals based on intensive field surveys can be made in small subsamples of a larger area where incomplete counts based on less intensive techniques are made. In this case the "complete counts" in the subsample areas are used to estimate β, which can be thought of as the probability of detection of animals in the less intensive field survey. The less intensive, incomplete counts are calibrated with the information from the intensive survey method. In a typical wildlife application (e.g., Smith 1995), incomplete counts are made over an extensive area, for example from the air (via fixed-wing airplane or helicopter), and complete counts are made on the ground. In many aerial surveys, the airplane flies along a predetermined flight path or transect line, and an observer counts animals seen in the strip extending from the transect line to some specified distance on either side of the line. Ground sampling involves an intensive search of the surveyed strip on some smaller sample of transects. Ideally, ground and air counts should be made simultaneously. If this is not possible, the 2 counts should be separated by as little time as possible to minimize the chance of movement changing the number of animals in the sampled area.

The natural estimator for β, the proportion of animals seen from the air, is the ratio of the mean aerial count ($\bar{y}$) to the mean ground count ($\bar{x}$) on the air-ground subsample

$$\hat{\beta} = \frac{\bar{y}}{\bar{x}}. \qquad (11)$$

It follows that total number of animals present on the transects surveyed from the air can be estimated by using equation (2)

$$\hat{N}_{air} = \frac{C}{\hat{\beta}},$$

where $\hat{\beta}$ is from equation (11) and C is the total number of animals seen from the air. To estimate population size for the entire area, we can use equation (4)

$$\hat{N} = \frac{C}{\alpha\hat{\beta}},$$

where $\hat{\beta}$ and C were defined above, and α is the fraction of the total area sampled from the air (Box 1). Jolly (1969a,b) and Pollock and Kendall (1987) presented an estimator for the variance of this estimator.

In another example, Bart and Earnst (2002) used direct calibration to "adjust" rapidly surveyed avian point counts, which can be used to estimate bird abundance, by intensively surveying a subsample of the same point count plots. In this subsample "actual" abundance is measured by intensive searches. The ratio between the rapidly surveyed point counts and the intensive searches on the same plots estimates the adjustment; i.e., β, the probability of detection of birds in the point counts. They used this method to estimate breeding shorebird abundance in Alaska.

The most critical consideration in the practical application of direct calibration is the accuracy of the "actual count" used to calibrate the survey method, because the method assumes that "actual counts" are accurate. If all animals in subsampled areas are not counted, estimates of detection probability (β) will be too large, and estimates of population size will be too low. Additionally, the timing of the "actual" and survey counts must coincide so they reflect the same population of animals. Jolly (1969a,b) discussed other considerations relevant to this approach.

Marked Subsample

It is also possible to use marked subpopulations to estimate the probability of detection. In this approach animals are marked so that at the time of the survey a known number of marked animals is in the area being surveyed. During the survey, marked and unmarked animals are counted.

Assume that we are dealing with an aerial or ground survey and define the following notation: N = total population size in the surveyed area, n_1 = number of marked animals present in the area at the time of the survey, n_2 = num-

---

Box 1. Hypothetical example of using double sampling (direct calibration) to estimate probability of detection (β).

In a subsample of 4 transects we saw 25 breeding waterfowl from the air (6+5+9+5) and 30 from the ground (7+6+10+7) so that (equation 11) $\hat{\beta}$ = 25/30 = 0.8333, which is the proportion of breeding waterfowl seen from the air. If we had seen 54 breeding waterfowl from the air in the entire survey which consisted of 10 transects (the 4 surveyed from the ground and the air plus 6 additional not surveyed from the ground), we then would estimate population size in the surveyed area as (equation 2):

$$\hat{N}_{air} = 54/0.8333 = 64.8.$$

If the area covered by the aerial survey comprised only 10% (α = 0.10) of the total area of interest, we would estimate (equation 4)

$$\hat{N} = 64.8/0.10$$
$$\hat{N} = 648$$

breeding waterfowl in the total area of interest.

ber of animals (both marked and unmarked) seen during the survey, and m = number of marked animals seen during the survey. The probability of detection (β) can be estimated by the proportion of the marked individuals that are observed such as

$$\hat{\beta} = \frac{m}{n_1}. \tag{12}$$

Our estimator for population size based on equation (2) is thus:

$$\hat{N} = \frac{n_2}{\hat{\beta}} = \frac{n_1 n_2}{m}. \tag{13}$$

This estimator (equation 13) is simply the Lincoln–Petersen estimator from capture–recapture (Lincoln 1930). In practice we recommend use of the bias-adjusted modification of this estimator and the associated variance estimator provided by Chapman (1951).

Although this approach appears straightforward, the practical aspects of application to any particular situation require careful consideration. The nature of the mark, for example, is important. The mark must be visible so the observer knows whether each animal that is seen is marked, and yet marked and unmarked individuals must have the same probability of being observed. Thus, the mark must be distinct and readily visible so that no marked animals are seen but recorded as unmarked, but not so obvious that it draws attention to marked animals, making them more visible than unmarked animals. Radiotelemetry can be used to ascertain the number of radio-marked animals in the surveyed area at the time of the survey (e.g., Packard et al. 1985) and a receiver can be used to detect whether each animal seen is marked. If radio-marked individuals cannot be positively identified in this manner, these animals will require some additional, visible mark.

A major advantage of using radio-marked animals as the marked subpopulation is that ascertaining the number of marked animals in the surveyed area at the time of the aerial survey is relatively easy (but see DeYoung et al. 1989). If other markers are used (e.g., identification collars on deer or other ungulates), then different considerations become important. If animals are marked and released just before (e.g., within a few days) the count, it may be reasonable to assume that all released animals are available to be seen. With some exceptions, it is not necessary to have individually identifiable animals, and "batch" marks (e.g., collars with no alphanumeric identification code) will suffice. However, capturing and marking an adequate number of animals in a relatively short period of time is often difficult, necessitating introduction of marked animals to the population over an extended period (e.g., several weeks or even months). In these situations, marked animals could die or emigrate from the survey area before the survey is conducted. Special efforts, such as using radio telemetry, may be necessary to locate marked animals immediately before and/or after the survey to establish which marked animals are known to have been present at the time of the survey. Thus, n_1 in equations (12) and (13) is the number of marked animals known to be present from efforts to locate marked animals and not necessarily the total number of marked animals released. Similarly, m is the number of these n_1 animals seen in the

survey. Marked animals seen during the survey, but not "known" to be present from earlier efforts on the ground, are not included in n_1. They are treated as unmarked in the survey data so they are included in n_2 but not in m.

The above method can be extended to the case of multiple resighting events, conducted over a short period of time. Equation 13 could be applied to each resighting event and those Lincoln–Petersen estimates of population size could be averaged. A better approach would be to model all resighting events concurrently, to arrive at the best estimate of N, with precision increasing with each additional resighting survey. Program NOREMARK (White 1996) (http://www.cnr.colostate.edu/~gwhite/software.html) provides a computing tool for this approach, including a simulation capability for anticipating estimator performance and calculating necessary sample sizes. For example, this simulation provides a method for calculating the relative effort to put into marking versus resighting.

Program NOREMARK includes 4 estimators. The first uses a joint hypergeometric distribution to estimate the number of animals in the study area (Bartmann et al. 1987, White and Garrott 1990, Neal et al. 1993). This estimator assumes that all animals in the study area have the same resighting probability on a specific occasion, but resighting probabilities can vary across occasions. The second is an extension of the first, permitting animals to move in and out of the study area completely randomly, and estimates either the average number in the study area at any given sampling occasion, or the total size of the population moving in and out of the study area (Neal et al. 1993). This method requires the number of marked animals in and out of the study area at each time is known (using radiotelemetry). It uses this information to implicitly model both detection probability given presence in the study area, and the probability an animal is available to be detected at that time (Box 2).

The third estimator uses bootstrapping based on sighting frequencies of marked animals (Minta and Mangel 1989). This method requires that marked animals be individually identifiable (i.e., no batch marks), but permits individuals to have differing resighting probabilities (i.e., individual heterogeneity exists in the population). The fourth estimator, by Bowden and Kufeld (1995), is an improved version of the Minta and Mangel estimator, deriving its confidence interval from the variance of resighting frequencies of marked animals (White 1993).

Arnason et al. (1991) developed a mark–resighting method and software for the case where the number of marked animals in the population must be estimated. This would be appropriate where the time between marking and resighting is too long to assume closure to deaths or emigration. Their approach also requires that animals be individually identifiable.

These mark–resight methods have been applied in the field in various ways. Marking with telemetry permits knowing how many marked animals are on and off the study area during resighting (e.g., Hein and Andelt 1995, Miller et al. 1997). Resighting is often done from the air (e.g., Bartmann et al. 1987, Neal et al. 1993), especially in habitats with relatively sparse cover. However, for more secretive animals the ratio of marked to unmarked animals can also be obtained from methods such as camera trapping (e.g., Mace et al. 1994, Sweitzer et al. 2000). Finally, these methods have been applied extensively to medi-

Box 2. An example of using a marked subpopulation and sequential surveys to estimate probability of detection and population size using program NOREMARK.

Hein and Andelt (1995) used aerial surveys in conjunction with a marked subsample to estimate coyote (*Canis latrans*) numbers on the Rocky Mountain Arsenal, a 70-km^2 federal installation near Commerce City, Colorado. Coyotes were captured during July 1990 to January 1991 and fitted with radio collars. Marked and unmarked animals were then counted systematically from ground vehicles during 7 snow-covered mornings in December 1990–January 1991. The first of the 7 counts yielded 11 coyotes, 3 of which were marked. At the time, telemetry indicated there were 10 marked coyotes on the study area. These statistics ($n_1 = 10$, $n_2 = 11$, $m = 3$) yield a bias-adjusted Lincoln-Petersen estimate (equation 28) of 32 animals (95% profile likelihood interval of 13.2–50.8) in program NOREMARK (White 1996). The probability of detection (β) in this case was estimated to be 0.3 ($m/n_1 = 3/10$). Hein and Andelt (1995) found that 0–25% of the radiomarked coyotes were off the survey area during any given survey. Therefore they used the immigration/emigration version of the joint hypergeometric estimator (Neal et. al. 1993) in program NOREMARK to estimate the average number of coyotes on the study area at any given time (49.7 with 95% profile likelihood interval of 34.4–80.7). This approach also yielded an estimate of the total number of coyotes that used the study area during the surveys (73 with 95% profile likelihood interval of 49.9–120.8). Using simulations in NOREMARK to consider future study design, Hein and Andelt (1995) reported that if ≥20% of their population is marked, it would be more cost effective to decrease bias and improve precision by conducting additional surveys, rather than by capturing and marking more animals.

um-size and large mammals (e.g., Bartmann et al. 1987, Mace et al. 1994, Bowden and Kufeld 1995, Hein and Andelt 1995, Miller et al. 1997, Sweitzer et al. 2000) and birds (e.g., Arnason et al. 1991, Collazo and Bonilla-Martinez 2001, Ganter and Madsen 2001).

Multiple Observers–Aerial

Multiple observer approaches were developed initially for aerial surveys (Cook and Jacobson 1979), but more recently have been applied to ground surveys as well (e.g., Nichols et al. 2000). These approaches can be divided into 2 categories—independent and dependent observers.

Two independent observers in the same airplane might be able to record the sighting location of individual animals on a map even if the animals are not individually marked. If the 2 observers do not communicate and if they observe animals independently, the mapped locations can be used with the Lincoln–Petersen estimator (the bias-adjusted version of equation 13 [equation 28]) to estimate total number of animals in the surveyed area (Grier et al. 1981, Caughley and Grice 1982, Pollock and Kendall 1987). In this situation, n_1 of equation (13) is the total number of animals seen by one observer, n_2 is the number seen by the other observer, and m is the number seen by both observers. This method requires precise and detailed maps of locations to ensure no ambiguity about whether one or both observers saw a particular animal. Independence of sightings between the observers is also an important requirement that may be difficult to achieve. For example, the independence assumption will be violated if some activity of one observer, such as speaking into a tape recorder microphone or writing on a map, alerts the other observer to the possibility of an animal nearby. Another assumption is that all animals have equal detection probabilities for a particular observer, but they can differ between the 2 observers. If certain animals are much more visible than others, the resulting heterogeneity will produce negative bias in the Lincoln–Petersen estimator.

When mobile animals are considered, mapping of locations must occur at the same time to be reasonably confi-

dent of animal identification. However, this general approach can also be used with immobile objects such as muskrat lodges, bird nests, or alligator nests (Box 3) because their location does not change, and the 2 observers need not be in the same aircraft at the same time. To ensure independence of the 2 observers, either 2 separate aerial surveys or an aerial survey and corresponding ground survey could be conducted. Different observers should be used for the 2 surveys, and locations are mapped for identification as before. The bias-adjusted version of equation (13) [equation 28] can be used with n_1 and n_2 corresponding to the total number of objects counted by observers 1 and 2, respectively, and m corresponding to the number of objects seen by both observers. Henny et al. (1977) used

Box 3. An example of using 2 independent observers with the bias adjusted Lincoln–Petersen estimator to estimate size of a population of immobile objects—alligator nests.

Two independent observers were used to estimate the number of alligator nests on Orange Lake, Florida, in summer 1986. The unpublished work was conducted by A. R. Woodward and M. L. Jennings of the Florida Game and Fresh Water Fish Commission, and H. F. Percival of the Florida Cooperative Fish and Wildlife Research Unit. Two helicopter surveys with different observers were conducted during the early incubation period and nest locations were mapped, permitting unambiguous identification. The number of nests seen by the first and second observers was $n_1 = 34$ and $n_2 = 37$, respectively, and the number of nests seen by both observers was $m = 20$. Use of these data in conjunction with the bias-adjusted Lincoln–Petersen estimator yielded $\hat{N} = 62 (\widehat{SE} = 5.7)$ total nests.

this general approach to estimate numbers of osprey (*Pandion haliaetus*) nests, Magnusson et al. (1978) used it to estimate the number of crocodile (*Crocodylus porosus*) nests, and Estes and Jameson (1988) used it to estimate a probability of detection for sea otters (*Enhydra lutris*).

The other approach involves 2 dependent observers in the same plane or at the same sample point who communicate with each other. One is designated as the "primary" observer, the other as the "secondary" observer. Here, we are interested in the number of animals seen by the primary observer and the number of additional animals (i.e., in addition to those seen by the primary observer) seen by the secondary observer. Under the assumption of equal detection probabilities of the 2 observers, these 2 statistics permit estimation of population size under the 2-sample removal model (Pollock and Kendall 1987). Heterogeneous detection probabilities again produce negatively biased estimates of population size.

Cook and Jacobson (1979) developed a similar approach that does not require the assumption of equal detection probabilities of the 2 observers. Under this design, the primary observer records animals seen, and the secondary observer records additional animals seen. However, the 2 observers switch roles halfway through the survey. We assume the detection probability associated with observers does not change with their role as primary or secondary observer. Cook and Jacobson (1979) presented the estimators associated with this method.

Multiple Observers–Ground

In fixed radius point counts, which are typically used to estimate bird abundance, one can use 2 independent observers at each point to estimate detection probability based on the Lincoln–Petersen method (Seber 1982). This approach is analogous to the aerial approach and can be divided into categories of independent and dependent observers. For independent observers the approach has 4 assumptions.

(1) There are no matching errors between the 2 observers so assignments as to which individuals were seen by observer A only, or observer B only, or both observers are accurate.

(2) Detection probabilities may differ between observers but are equal for all individuals for each observer.

(3) There is no undetected movement into or out of the fixed radius circle.

(4) Observers accurately assign individuals to within or beyond the radius used for the fixed radius circle.

Generalizations using program MARK (White and Burnham 1999) or DOBSERV (www.mbr-pwrc.usgs.gov/software.html) give the researcher the option to fit generalized Lincoln–Petersen models which allow for detection probability to depend on covariates such as species, wind speed, distance, etc. MARK and DOBSERV use AIC (Burnham and Anderson 1998, 2002) to pick the most parsimonious model that explains the data adequately.

Nichols et al. (2000) suggested applying a dependent double-observer method, originally used for aerial surveys by Cook and Jacobson (1979), to estimate bird abundance from fixed-radius point counts. At each point, a designated "primary" observer indicates to another ("secondary") observer all birds detected. The secondary observer records all detections of birds not detected by the primary observer.

Observers alternate primary and secondary roles during the course of the survey. The approach permits estimation of observer-specific detection probabilities and bird abundance. The model can be fitted using DOBSERV (Nichols et al. 2000) and MARK (White and Burnham 1999).

The dependent double-observer approach can be viewed as an extension of the removal method (Zippin 1958, Otis et al. 1978, Seber 1982:309). The advantage of this approach occurs when there are practical and logistical reasons why it is difficult to conduct the method with 2 independent observers. The disadvantage is that if the independent double-observer approach works, the dependent approach is less efficient (capture–recapture methods are more efficient than removal methods) (Seber 1982:324).

Observation Probability Models

The preceding methods for estimating population size from incomplete count data involve (either explicitly or implicitly) efforts to estimate detection probability (β) during the survey. Incomplete counts and data to estimate detection probabilities associated with those counts are obtained concurrently.

An alternative approach is to conduct experimental surveys designed to identify variables likely to influence detection probability and to use these variables to develop a model for predicting detection probability (e.g., Caughley et al. 1976, Samuel et al. 1987). A known population, in most cases radio-marked individuals, is observed using operational survey methods while simultaneously recording data on variables thought to influence detection such as habitat, group size, weather, etc. The combination of known animals, the proportion detected, and variables influencing detection is used to develop the model. During subsequent surveys, variables used to develop the models are measured and used to predict detection probability. These detection probability estimates are used with incomplete counts from these subsequent surveys to estimate population size.

An excellent example is provided by Samuel et al. (1987) who used data from radio-marked elk to develop a detection probability model for use with aerial surveys in Idaho. Prior to each experimental survey flight, Samuel et al. (1987) located radio-marked individuals and measured variables they believed affected probability of detection. They then recorded whether each animal was seen during the subsequent survey. The resulting data were used with binary regression analysis to develop models for predicting detection probability. They found that group size and percent vegetation cover were the factors most important in affecting detection probability. The model based on these 2 variables was used to compute a detection probability for each group of elk observed during operational surveys. The number of groups of a given size and in a given cover class was adjusted using the estimated detection probability, as in equation (2). The total population estimate for the surveyed area was computed as the sum of group estimates. Unsworth et al. (1990:115) used presumably complete counts of elk by ground personnel to validate the Samuel et al. (1987) model and concluded the detection model "compared favorably" with independent ground counts.

The appeal of a model-based approach is the often-costly process of estimating detection probabilities is done only once during the initial, experimental period of model development. After the model has been developed and satisfactorily tested, operational survey efforts require only recording information on the model variables; detection probabilities are not directly estimated in subsequent surveys. A limitation is the possibility the model works well only under the exact conditions when the model was developed. We believe it is better to estimate the detection detectability for each specific survey wherever possible.

Distance Sampling

Distance sampling is a comprehensive approach encompassing study design, data collection, and statistical analyses (Buckland et al. 2001). When properly applied and when critical assumptions are met, distance data yield direct estimates of density (and not simply abundance) that take probability of detection into account (Rosenstock et al. 2002). Density estimates can be expanded to yield estimates of total number of individuals by multiplying density by a known area of interest. Distance sampling is based on developing a function that models the fact that the probability of detection decreases with increasing distance from the observer. This function is used to estimate the probability of detection $\hat{\beta}$. In the simplest case density ($\hat{D}$) is estimated as:

$$\hat{D} = \frac{n}{a\hat{\beta}}, \qquad (14)$$

where n is the total number of detections and a is the total area sampled. This relationship is analogous to equation (4).

Line Transects.—In line transect methods, a transect or line of length L is located randomly within some area to be sampled. The observer traveling along this line then makes counts of all animals seen. In some instances, a maximum observation distance, w (perpendicular to the line on each side), beyond which no animals are counted, is established. In other applications, all animals are counted regardless of distance from the line.

The term line transect or, more commonly, strip transect, has been used to refer to transects of fixed half-width, w, for which counts within the strip are assumed to be complete (i.e., the observer sees all animals actually present within the strip). Strip transects are a special case of complete counts on sample plots, where the plot is a long rectangular strip.

In line transect methods considered here, counts are assumed to be incomplete. Thus, the proportion of animals present that are actually seen (β) must be estimated, and actual counts must be corrected by these detection probabilities. Perpendicular distance data, or less commonly both detection distance and angle data, are required to estimate detection probabilities. These data are defined as $x_i =$ the perpendicular distance from the line to the detected animal i (or to a nest or center of a group of animals), $r_i =$ distance from the observer to detected animal i at the moment of detection, and $q_i =$ the angle between the line of travel and the line of sight to detected animal i at the moment of detection. Data resulting from any line transect survey are the total number of animals detected, n, and either the corresponding perpendicular distances, x_i, or both the observation distances, r_i, and angles, q_i. Estimation proceeds with these data and the known transect length, L, and width, $2w$. Recall that w is the maximum observation distance; hence the width of the surveyed strip is $2w$.

The use of line transect methodology requires 5 assumptions (Buckland et al. 2001, Thomas and Karanth 2002) listed from most to least critical: (1) transect lines are located randomly with respect to the distribution of animals (for example, typically lines should not be along roads, trails, levees, ridge tops or linear water bodies such as rivers); (2) all animals directly on the line are detected (i.e., detection probability on the line is 1); (3) animals are detected at their initial location (i.e., they do not move in response to the observer before being observed) and no animals are counted twice; (4) distances (and angles if recorded) are measured exactly; and (5) observations are independent events (e.g., the flushing of one animal does not cause another to flush).

The basis for estimation from line transect data, or similar "distance sampling" approaches, is that probability of detecting an animal decreases with increasing distance from the line; i.e., increasing x. Distance data, x_i, are used to estimate the specific shape of this function, $g(x)$, relating detection probability to distance from the transect. We can define the detection function, g(x), as the conditional probability of observing an animal, given that it is located at distance x from the line, or mathematically: g(x) = Pr{animal observed | x}.

To examine what $g(x)$ looks like, we can plot a histogram of detections grouped by small distance intervals from the center of the transect to the maximum observation distance. If our sample size is large and we detect a large number of animals, n, we can approximate the shape of $g(x)$ by drawing a smooth curve through the histogram. In practice, sample sizes are often too small, and this procedure does not work well. In addition to the actual number of animals present to be counted, sample size, n, also reflects 3 factors (Anderson et al. 2001:584): (1) environmental variables (e.g., vegetation, topography, etc.), (2) observer variables (e.g., interest, training, fatigue, skill, etc.), and (3) variables related to the animals (e.g., color, size, orientation, etc.). Some of these variables can be controlled (e.g., training).

Even if we know $g(x)$, we must still estimate population size. This involves estimating an average detection probability, P_w, which is equivalent to β in our general equation (2). Thus, the number of detected objects and P_w are used to estimate N:

$$\hat{N}_w = \frac{n}{\hat{P}_w}, \text{ and} \qquad (15)$$

$$\hat{D}_w = \frac{n}{a\hat{P}_w} = \frac{n}{L2w\hat{P}_w},$$

where $\hat{N}_w$ is the estimated number of animals present in the strip defined by length L and width $2w$ (where w is the predetermined maximum observation distance). $\hat{D}_w$ is density in the strip defined above, which is estimated by dividing $\hat{N}_w$ by the area $a = L2w$. Because of the random placement of the transect line, animals are equally likely to be located (not detected) at all distances between zero and w. Thus, we can estimate the average detection probability, P_w as:

$$\hat{P}_w = \frac{\int_0^w g(x)dx}{w}. \qquad (16)$$

Those who prefer not to think in terms of integrals of functions may prefer to think of $g(x)$ as a histogram of detection frequencies at different distances. Equation (16) is roughly equivalent to computing the average of the probabilities for different distance categories of the histogram, or the probability of detecting an animal that is within distance w of the line.

Both parametric and nonparametric estimation models have been proposed for use in line transect estimation. Rather than review these models and estimators, we recommend the excellent book by Buckland et al. (2001). Distance sampling can be organized and analyzed with the program DISTANCE (Thomas et al. 1998), available at http://www.rupwa.st-and.ac.uk/distance (Box 4). Program DISTANCE allows for the fitting of complex detection functions of the form:

$$g(r) = key(r)[1 + series(r)]; \qquad (17)$$

i.e., there is a key function (half normal, uniform, or hazard rate) plus a series adjustment (cosine, simple polynomial, or hermite polynomial). Data analysis involves 3 steps: (1) data examination via graphical displays, (2) model selection using the AIC criterion, and (3) inference under the chosen model (Box 4) (Fig. 5).

Actual application of line transect methods involves many decisions and considerations specific to a particular situation. For example, many animals exhibit gregarious behavior and tend to occur in groups. The density of groups can be estimated with distance measurements taken from the line to the geometric center of each observed group (Buckland et al. 2001). The number of animals in each detected group must also be recorded to estimate density or population size. Drummer and McDonald (1987)

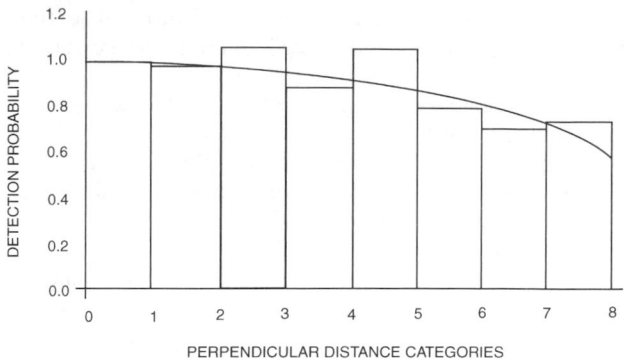

Fig. 5. The detection function for the uniform plus one term detection function for duck nest data (from Anderson and Pospahala 1970).

and Otto and Pollock (1990) discussed models for use when detection probability for fixed distance depends on group size. Line transects are ideal for stationary objects that can be viewed over some distance (Box 4). Other special considerations involve the possible existence of extreme values (sightings at extreme distances) or outliers. Buckland et al. (2001) recommended truncation of data at distances greater than some distance, w^*, beyond which observations seem likely to be outliers.

Another consideration involves grouping of data. Accurate measurement of distances in the field may not be possible, but detections may be grouped by distance categories. Even when direct distance measurements are recorded, anomalous patterns may be apparent, such as few objects detected at short distances, clumped detections at commonly rounded measurements, or a relatively large number of detections near the boundary distance, w. In

---

Box 4. An example of the use of the line transect method to estimate density of duck nests.

Anderson and Pospahala (1970) used line transect methods during spring–summer 1967–1968 to estimate the density of duck nests on Monte Vista National Wildlife Refuge, Colorado. Perpendicular distance data were obtained for 534 nests and were grouped into 8 intervals for plotting (Fig. 5). The data were reanalyzed by K. H. Pollock in program DISTANCE (Buckland et al. 2001) allowing for the fitting of complex detection functions of the form: $g(x) = key(x)[1 + series(x)]$; that is there is a key function (half normal, uniform, or hazard rate) plus a series adjustment (cosine, simple polynomial, or hermite polynomial). We can use the DISTANCE program to perform complex computations to fit such models to detection distance data. An important part of the process is model selection using AIC criteria to decide which of the detection functions is best to use in terms of the trade off between reality and simplicity.

For simplicity, we present the results of fitting using a uniform key function plus a series of polynomial adjustment terms.

Model fitted	Delta AIC	Estimate (95% CI)
Uniform/ 1 term	0.00	126.01 (112.19–141.53)
Uniform/ 2 terms	1.99	126.80 (109.38–146.99)
Uniform/ 3 terms	3.25	124.44 (104.09–148.77)
Uniform/ unadjusted	7.04	110.14 (101.17–119.90)

The best model is that with the uniform key function plus one adjustment term because it has the lowest AIC value. This detection function can be plotted with the observed data (Fig. 5). The model fits the data well ($\chi^2 = 3.63$, df = 6, and $p = 0.73$). The density estimate is 126.01 duck nests per 2.59 km^2. If we had pretended perfect detection (uniform with no adjustment terms), we would have obtained 110.14 duck nests per 2.59 km^2. This is clearly not a good estimate because population density is underestimated by about 10% compared to the estimate from program DISTANCE.

these situations, data may be grouped into a histogram before analysis as a "smoothing" technique (Buckland et al. 2001).

We recommend those planning to conduct a line transect study consult Buckland et al. (2001) and, if available, published recommendations for specific field situations (e.g., Karanth et al. 2002). We also suggest that L be selected to provide a minimum of 40 animals detected, and preferably 60–80 (Buckland et al. 2001).

Anderson et al. (2001) used field trials to estimate the abundance of artificial desert tortoise (*Gopherus agassizi*) models to test whether assumptions that underlie distance sampling were met. They found the density estimate of adult tortoise models was relatively unbiased, while the estimate for subadult (small) tortoise models was biased low (about 20%), which they attributed to failure to detect models on, or near, the centerline. They present ideas to better train observers before commencing the survey.

Point Transects.—Distances can be measured to animals (usually landbirds) that are counted around a point rather than along a transect. These points, sometimes called point transects, can be thought of as transects of zero length; distance data can be analyzed the same as line transect data. For line transects, distances are perpendicular to the transect line, while for points they are radial distances (r). There are advantages and disadvantages associated with use of points rather than line transects. For example, a line transect can yield more data per unit field time than points when relatively less time is spent traveling between transects than between points (Bibby et al. 2000, Rosenstock et al. 2002). Scale is important as a typical transect generally covers more spatial area than a typical set of points; thus the scale of spatial habitat diversity must be commensurate with the scale of transects or points. Points are often preferred to transects in habitats with a variety of small patches of habitat relative to the home range of an animal (Bibby et al. 2000).

The main disadvantage with points according to Bibby et al. (2000:92) is that the area surveyed is proportional to the square of the distance from the observer, whereas in transects, the area is proportional to lateral distance from the transect line. Thus, density estimates from point data are more susceptible to errors arising from inaccurate distance measurements or from violation of assumptions about detecting animals. Reynolds et al. (1980) noted that observers traveling along line transects in structurally complex vegetation and rough terrain tended to watch the path of travel reducing their ability to detect birds. Consequently, they recommended establishing equally spaced observer stations positioned along a transect, or points could be located randomly. Burnham et al. (1980) and Buckland et al. (1993, 2001) provide details for sampling designs of point transects.

Standard transect theory, based on the premise that detection probability is a decreasing function of distance and that nothing else influences detection, can be applied to point transects (Buckland et al. 2001:55) so that:

$$\hat{D} = \frac{n}{a\hat{p}_d} = \frac{n}{k\pi w^2 \hat{p}_d} \qquad (18)$$

where $a = k\pi w^2$ is area covered by the set of points (k is the number of points and πw^2 is the area covered by a single point with survey radius w), $\hat{p}_d$ is the probability of detection, and

$$p_d = 2\int_0^w rg(r)dx/r^2 . \qquad (19)$$

This latter expression is the probability of detection in a circle of radius w and depends on the detection function $g(r)$ which is the probability of detecting an animal given it is distance r from the central point where the count is conducted. We can use program DISTANCE to perform complex computations to fit such models to distance data.

The assumptions of point transect sampling are: (1) points are located randomly with respect to the distribution of animals, (2) all objects at the center point are detected, (3) objects are detected at their initial location prior to any movement in response to the observer, (4) distances are measured accurately (ungrouped data), or objects are counted in the proper distance category (grouped data), and (5) objects are detected independently. Violation of the second assumption is a critical assumption failure and is probably common when conducting bird surveys. This violation will result in negatively biased estimates of density.

Density of species other than landbirds can also be estimated with point transects. Koenen et al. (2002) used point transects to estimate seasonal density and group size of desert mule deer by gender and age class on the Buenos Aires National Wildlife Refuge in southeastern Arizona. The authors believed their survey design balanced the often conflicting objectives of random placement of transects and detecting animals before they moved. Distances were measured accurately with a rangefinder.

Time of Detection

Time of detection is a modification of removal methods used in capture–mark–recapture that has recently been applied to estimate detection probabilities for birds on point count surveys. Following Farnsworth et al. (2002), the simplest application of the time of detection approach to point counts can be illustrated with just 2 time intervals of equal duration. Suppose an observer records all birds seen/heard in the interval $(0, t)$ and continues the point count, recording any additional birds detected in the interval $(t, 2t)$. At the end of the point count, we define x_1 as the number of birds counted in the first time interval, and x_2 as the number of new birds (not detected in the first period) detected in the second time interval. The expected value of the random variable x_1 is

$$E(x_1) = Np_1, \qquad (20)$$

where N is the total number of birds within the detection radius of the observer and p_1 is the detection probability for an individual bird in the first time period. The expected value of x_2 is

$$E(x_2) = N(1 - p_1)p_2, \qquad (21)$$

where p_2 is the detection probability in the second time period. The $(1 - p_1)$ term is needed because, for a bird to be first counted in the second time interval, it must have been missed in the first time interval.

Let us assume the detection probability for the 2 intervals is the same (i.e., $p_1 = p_2 = p$) because the duration of each interval is the same. Solving the above equations produces the following moment estimators for p and N (Zippin 1958):

$$\hat{p} = \frac{x_1 - x_2}{x_1} \qquad (22)$$

and

$$\hat{N} = \frac{x_1^2}{x_1 - x_2} = \frac{x_1}{\hat{p}} . \qquad (23)$$

The estimators can fail if $x_1 \leq x_2$, which is possible when p is small. We present this 2-sample removal estimator to illustrate the approach with the simplest possible situation. In addition, we note the canonical form (as in equation 2) of equation (23).

In practice, we recommend using more than 2 intervals, which permits us to relax the assumption of equal detection for different species. Program CAPTURE can produce maximum likelihood estimates for N, as well as the estimated variance of $\hat{N}$, using model M_b or M_{bh} (Otis et al. 1978, White et al. 1982), as long as each of the time intervals is the same length.

Farnsworth et al. (2002) present a more general model that allows for 3 count intervals to have variable lengths (i.e., the detection probabilities in the different intervals need not be the same). They also allow for heterogeneity of detection among individual birds. This is done by assuming there are 2 groups of individuals in an unknown proportion and that all members of the first group are detected in the first time interval. This model is a slight restriction of model M_{bh} of Norris and Pollock (1996) and Pledger (2000), which is necessary because there are only 3 sampling periods. With 4 time intervals one can have 2 groups of birds in unknown proportions with different unknown detection probabilities.

Assumptions of the general Farnsworth et al. (2002) model are: (1) there is no change in the population of birds within the detection radius during the point count (i.e., the population is closed and birds do not move in or out), (2) there is no double counting of individuals, (3) all members of group 1 are detected in the first interval, (4) all members of group 2 that have not yet been detected have a constant per minute probability of being detected, and (5) observers accurately assign birds to within or beyond the radius used for the fixed radius circle.

Farnsworth et al. (2002) incorporated a removal framework because only the interval of the first detection of each bird was used. They kept track of individual birds; thus, when a bird is detected in sampling interval 2 or 3, it must be identified as an individual that either was or was not detected in a previous interval. A more efficient approach would use a K sample closed capture–recapture model based on a detection history by noting, for the set of K time intervals, the time intervals when a particular bird was detected and the time intervals when that same bird was not detected. Heterogeneity of detection probabilities can be modeled more efficiently in a capture–recapture setting than in a removal setting.

Combination Methods

Alpizar-Jara and Pollock (1996), Manly et al. (1996), and Borchers et al. (1998*a*,*b*) developed a method for line transects with 2 independent observers. This combination method, along with others, can be adapted to point transects and is currently an intense and exciting area of research. The advantage of combining methods is 2-fold. First, if assumptions of all the methods are met it will increase precision of the estimates. Second, if some assumptions are not met it might give us the ability to infer which assumption violations are occurring and are most important. This will also lead to clearer recommendations as to which methods are best to use. We believe that in the near future point transects will routinely be used to collect information on distance and time of detection. We recommend such data collection for any new point transect survey design. We also believe that 2 observer data will be routinely collected, but perhaps only on a small subset of points. Given fixed resources of time and money, one difference between using 2 observers and using the other methods of estimating probability of detection is that only half the number of points can be surveyed.

Estimation Based on Capture Methods

Capture methods typically involve handling animals in some way. Many of these methods require the assumption of a closed population (i.e., a population in which the individuals do not change while the population estimate is being made, thus no births, deaths, emigration, or immigration are assumed), but open population models have been developed as well. Biologists usually resort to capture methods when animals are difficult to observe and count, but there is a reasonable chance of capturing them.

Removal Methods

Removal methods of population estimation are old and have been analyzed by numerous investigators. These methods are attractive because someone other than the investigator, such as hunters, can often collect removal data. Thus, the investigator may not have to actually capture animals to develop population estimates based on removals, which often makes these methods inexpensive to implement in the field.

Removal methods can be categorized according to whether the removals are "selective" (Fig. 3). If the proportions of "types" (e.g., genders, age classes, species) of animals in the removals are substantially different from the proportions of the same types in the pre–removal population, then change-in-ratio (CIR) estimators can be used. If removals are not selective, then either standard removal models or catch-per-unit-effort (C/E) models can be used. Standard removal models assume equal effort is expended on catching/removing animals at each sampling occasion, whereas C/E models can be applied when sampling effort varies among sampling periods, but is known (or can be estimated). Change-in-ratio and C/E estimators are covered in this section and standard removal models are discussed under K-sample Closed Population Models in the Capture–Mark–Recapture Methods section.

Single-stage Change-in-ratio.—We briefly describe the equations used to estimate population size with change-in-ratio (CIR). These equations are algebraic solutions to simultaneous equations relating population sizes of classes of animals before and after known removals (Overton 1969, Paulik and Robson 1969, Seber 1982).

The basic CIR method assumes a closed population with 2 classes of animals, x- and y-types. These could be male and female pheasants, antlered and antlerless deer, adults and juveniles, or even 2 different species. If the proportion of x- and y-type animals in the population changes due to removal of a known number of animals, then we can write the new (post-removal) proportion of x-type animals as:

$$P_2 = \frac{X_1 - R_x}{N_1 - R} = \frac{P_1 N_1 - R_x}{N_1 - R},$$

where R_x = the number of x-types removed (known), R_y = the number of y-types removed (known), $R = R_x + R_y$ = the total number of animals removed (known), X_1 = the number of x-type animals in the initial (pre-removal) population, and Y_1 = the number of y-type animals in the initial (pre-removal) population. Thus, $P_1 = X_1/N_1$ = the proportion of x-type animals before the removal (where N_1 is the total population size before the removal) and $P_2 = X_2/N_2$ = the proportion of x-type animals after the removal (where N_2 is the total population size after the removal). Solving for N_1 yields the following estimator of total population size before the removal:

$$\hat{N}_1 = \frac{(R_x - RP_2)}{(P_1 - P_2)}. \tag{24}$$

Note that P_1 and P_2 are estimated by some sampling scheme, such as road counts of antlered and antlerless deer, as $\hat{P}_1$ and $\hat{P}_2$ and, together with the numbers removed, are substituted into equation (24) to estimate the pre-removal population size. The number of x-type animals in the initial (pre-removal) population is estimated by:

$$\hat{X}_1 = \hat{P}_1 \hat{N}_1. \tag{25}$$

If independent estimates of P_1 and P_2 are assumed, variance estimates for N_1 and X_1 can be calculated (Seber 1982, Lancia et al. 1994). From the estimates of N_1 and X_1, and the removals, $\hat{Y}_1 = \hat{N}_1 - \hat{X}_1$, $\hat{X}_2 = \hat{X}_1 - R_x$, $\hat{Y}_2 = \hat{Y}_1 - R_y$, $\hat{N}_2 = \hat{X}_2 + \hat{Y}_2$, or $\hat{N}_2 = \hat{N}_1 - R$. There are 5 assumptions of the CIR method.

(1) The observed proportions of x- and y-type animals are unbiased estimates of the true proportions in the population. Thus, x- and y-type animals have an equal probability of being sampled; i.e., they are equally observable.

(2) The CIR method can be used when only a single type is removed such as x-types being removed in an antlered-males-only hunt. In this special case, the population estimate of the type removed (males) is appropriate regardless of whether x- and y-types are equally observable (Seber 1982). This relationship is exploited in the 2-stage CIR.

(3) The population is closed except for the removals. This assumption can best be met by keeping the removal period and the time between the 2 estimates of the P ratios as short as possible.

(4) The number of removals of x- and y-type animals is known. The method can still be applied if unknown removals can be estimated (Paulik and Robson 1969, Seber 1982).

(5) The proportion of x-types in the harvest is different from that in the population. If x-types are removed in the same proportion that they occur in the population, the P ratios do not change from before to after the removal.

Therefore $P_1 = P_2$, the denominator in equation (24) is zero, and the method fails. This can be a shortcoming in the technique if the management objective is to maintain a balanced ratio of x- to y-types in the population such as in quality deer herd management (Lancia et al. 1988). However, the 2-stage CIR circumvents this problem.

Several authors have investigated the effect of sample size and variability in samples used to estimate the P ratios on accuracy and precision of CIR estimates (Paulik and Robson 1969, Seber 1982, Pollock et al. 1985, Conner et al. 1986). The initial P ratio (P_1), the change in P ratios ($\Delta P = P_1 - P_2$), and the number of animals that are observed to estimate the P ratios all affect the accuracy and precision of CIR estimates. In general, CIR is most accurate when ΔP is large. Computer simulations (J. W. Bishir, personal communication) suggest that removing 70–80% or more of x-types in a single-type removal from populations of 50 to 1,000 animals, with a large number observed to estimate the P ratios, yielded accurate CIR population estimates. Removals of this magnitude, for example, could occur where antlered deer only are removed (Box 5).

Box 5.   The change-in-ratio method to estimate population size of antlered and antlerless deer.

Conner et al. (1986) reported that antlered (x-type) and antlerless (y-type) deer were observed during 54 prehunt and 52 posthunt road counts on Remington Farms, Maryland (now Chesapeake Farms). One hundred and twenty x-type and 1,126 y-type animals were observed before 56 antlered deer (R_x) and 54 antlerless deer (R_y) were removed by hunters during a 1-week season. After the season, 43 x-type and 1,086 y-type deer were observed. Therefore,

$$\hat{P}_1 = \frac{x_1}{n_1} = 120/1246 = 0.0963, \text{ and}$$

$$\hat{P}_2 = \frac{x_2}{n_2} = 43/1,129 = 0.0381.$$

$$\hat{N}_1 = \frac{R_x - R\hat{P}_2}{\hat{P}_1 - \hat{P}_2}$$

$$= \{(56 - 110(0.0381)\}/ (0.0963 - 0.0381),$$
$$= 51.809 / 0.0582,$$
$$= 890 \ (SE = 149).$$

$$\hat{X}_1 = \hat{P}_1 \hat{N}_1 = 0.0963(890),$$

$$= 86 \ (SE = 14).$$

In this example, both x- and y-types were removed. Because y-type (antlerless) animals were probably more observable than x-type animals, λ was probably >1.0, and the population estimates are likely to be biased high.

In practice, the assumption of equal detection probability (assumption 1) is most difficult to meet. Relative probability of detection of the 2 types of animals (λ) can be expressed mathematically as λ = detection probability of y-type animals / detection probability of x-type animals. When both types are equally detectable, then $\lambda = 1$. For deer populations, antlerless deer are usually more easily observed than antlered animals (Conner et al. 1986), and detection of antlered males probably varies with age of the animal, etc. If λ is known or can be estimated, the P ratios can be adjusted to reflect λ, yielding unbiased CIR estimates (Conner et al. 1986). Alternative methods include the 2–stage CIR that relaxes the equal probability of detection assumption, single-type removals that are not affected by unequal probability of detection, or brief removal periods that limit the time over which changes in detection could occur.

Two-stage Change-in-ratio.—Consider a closed population in which the relative probability of detection of x- and y-type animals is not equal ($\lambda \neq 1.0$) (Pollock et al. 1985). If animals are removed in 2 separate, single-type hunts, then λ and the size of the x- and y-type portions of the population before and after the removals can be estimated. The observed proportions of x-type animals in the population at 3 times (t_1, t_2, t_3), separated by the 2 single-type removals, and the numbers removed are used to estimate population size (Pollock et al. 1985). A typical application would be removing antlered and antlerless deer in 2 separate single-type hunts. The observed proportions (P) of antlered deer in the population before and after the removals can be represented algebraically and solved for X_1, Y_1, and λ. Udevitz and Pollock (1991, 1992) provide variance estimates for X_1, Y_1, and λ.

The assumptions of the 2-stage CIR are the same as in the traditional CIR with one exception. In the traditional CIR, detection probabilities of the x- and y-types must be equal. In the 2-stage CIR, detection probabilities need only to be constant from t_1 to t_3. Thus, λ must be constant from before the first to after the last removal. This assumption could be difficult to meet, but it is much less severe than the assumption of equal detection probability that is required for the traditional CIR method. An additional advantage is that λ can also be estimated.

Pollock et al. (1985) evaluated the accuracy and precision of the 2-stage CIR. In general, larger changes in P ratios yield better estimates. Also, large sample sizes to estimate the P ratios increase the accuracy of the 2-stage CIR estimates (Pollock et al. 1985). Udevitz and Pollock (1991, 1992) present extensions of the CIR method.

Catch-per-unit-effort.—Catch-per-unit-effort (C/E) estimators have been examined by many individuals including Leslie and Davis (1939), Chapman (1954), Ricker (1958), Seber (1982), Bishir and Lancia (1996), and Lancia et al. (1996). Overton (1969) provided a clear description of the derivation of the basic C/E estimator.

Catch-per-unit-effort is based on the premise that as more and more animals are removed from a population, fewer are available to be "caught," and catch per unit of effort should decline. For example, fewer animals can be seen per hour or fewer can be harvested per hunter-day as more animals are removed. Eventually, if all animals could be removed, the expected catch would be zero and the total number of animals removed would be equivalent to the initial population size. Because it is generally not desirable (or possible) to remove all individuals in a population, the C/E method estimates the cumulative catch (total animals removed) at which the expected catch-per-unit-effort is zero, which corresponds to the initial population size. An advantage of C/E is that population estimates can be derived from removals that are a part of a routine management activity such as hunter harvests.

The traditional C/E method (Leslie and Davis 1939) involves developing a linear regression of catch-per-unit-effort on the cumulative total number of animals removed. Repeated observations of catch-per-unit-effort (where effort may be expressed as trap nights, hunter days, etc.) and cumulative number removed are used to derive the linear regression. Thus,

$$y_i = A + Bx_i$$

where y_i = observations of catch-per-unit-effort at time i, A = y-intercept estimated by the regression equation, B = the slope of the regression, and x_i = the observed cumulative removals prior to time i.

The probability a given animal is "caught" (K) in a given unit of effort (sometimes expressed as a period of effort, such as 1 day, 1 week) is equal to $-B$. The estimated pre-removal population size, N, is the cumulative catch (population size) for which the expected catch-per-unit-effort is zero ($y = 0$), or the x-intercept. Thus,

$$N = \frac{A}{-B}, \text{ or}$$

$$N = \frac{A}{K}.$$

The y-intercept (A) represents a "count" of the animals in the pre-removal population (i.e., the initial catch standardized for variable effort), and the slope of the regression ($K = -B$) represents β the "probability of detection."

Although maximum likelihood and weighted least-squares estimators for the C/E method have been presented (e.g., Seber 1982:297, Pollock et al. 1984), the traditional regression method has typically been used to implement the C/E method for closed populations. Novak et al. (1991) used an open C/E model and maximum likelihood estimates (Dupont 1983) to estimate the size of a deer population. Methods based on equal effort can be analyzed with the generalized removal methods in CAPTURE (models M_b or M_{bh}), MARK, or in SURVIV.

The meanings of "removed" and "caught" require elaboration. Removed animals can be physically taken from the population by being killed or livetrapped and removed, or animals can be figuratively "removed" by being marked (e.g., as when using closed capture–mark–recapture models M_b and M_{bh}). In the latter case, observations of marked animals would be ignored in subsequent catches. Removals can be by any means; they do not have to correspond to the effort used in the estimator. For example, removals can be hunter kills and effort can be animals seen per day (Box 6) (Fig. 6). All sources of removals, such as accidental road kills, poached animals, or unretrieved kills, are included in the cumulative total removed. Finally, animals "caught" during the catch-per-unit-effort can be shot, trapped, or seen. They do not have to be physically taken or removed to be "caught."

Box 6.   Removal methods can be used in conjunction with harvests of hunted species.   In this example, the intent of management was to control a deer herd.   An attempt to estimate population size began after (rather than before) the hunt was undertaken.

White-tailed deer were harvested in a special hunt to control a nuisance population.   Deer were hunted for 10 days in 1999, divided into 3 short periods (18–20 and 25–29 Oct, 8–9 Nov).   Hunters were required to harvest a doe before a buck was taken, so the harvest was primarily antlerless deer (about 90% in 1999).   This requirement violates the assumption of equal vulnerability of all deer, because antlered bucks would be less likely to be harvested than were antlerless deer.   Thus, using deer killed per day alone as "catch" to estimate the population is suspect.   However, because most of the deer harvested were not antlered bucks it probably did not make that much difference.   Using deer observed per day as "catch" might be a better choice because we assume there was no intentional choice by the hunters not to "see" a certain class of deer.

Effort was recorded as the number of hunters per day.   It was assumed that each hunter hunted for 5 hours per day so that a day correctly represented equal hunting effort for each hunter.   But, if individual hunters hunted different numbers of hours, then a measure of effort in days would be inappropriate to use.   Unless it is assured that each hunter actually hunted the same amount each day, it would have been much better to record effort on an hourly basis than on a daily basis.

The catch-per-unit-effort estimate from kill data only using all 10 days is 456 and SE = 363.   The large SE indicates that the estimate is not precise.   The upward trend in kill/hunter and observed/hunter on the last 2 days (Fig. 6) indicates a problem, perhaps a violation of the equal probability of detection or closure assumptions.   If we exclude the last 2 days and calculate the kill only model, the population estimate is 203 (SE = 77).   Estimates using observation data only and joint observation-kill data (the first 8 days only) are 152 and 154, respectively.   The latter 3 estimates are probably biased low.

Although the form of the C/E regression equation looks familiar, it is not a typical regression because y, the catch-per-unit-effort, and x, the cumulative removals, can depend on the same removals.   This lack of independence makes calculation of variances and confidence intervals difficult.   Bishir and Lancia (1996) have shown that estimates of N do not follow a normal distribution and, therefore, standard variance equations are not appropriate.   The assumptions of the C/E method are similar to those of CIR.

(1) The population is closed (except for the removals).   This assumption can best be met by keeping the removal period as short as possible.   Some models (e.g., Dupont 1983) permit relaxation of this assumption.

(2) For each period (e.g., day, week), all individual animals have an equal probability (K) of being caught by a unit of effort, and K is constant over time.   This is the equal probability of detection assumption.   A qualitative test of this assumption can be conducted by examining the trajectory of the plot of catch-per-unit-effort on the cumulative removals.   If it is not linear, the equal probability of detection assumption is violated, and the technique should be abandoned (Caughley 1977).

(3) If the units of effort are constant, such as the same number of traps being set each night or the same number of hunters each day and the units of effort are trap-nights or hunter-days, respectively, the catch-per-unit-effort is the number of new animals caught on successive occasions.   The CAPTURE program models M_b and M_{bh}, which are constant-effort models, can be used to estimate population size.   Model M_{bh} relaxes the assumption of equal probability of detection and allows individual differences in detection probability.   The M_{bh} model is a generalized removal model that can be used to estimate population size when constant effort is used.   Program MARK provides general models that can incorporate covariates and more sophisticated models of changes in detection probabilities.

(4) All the removals are known.   The likelihood of violating this assumption can be minimized by keeping the removal period as short as possible and by searching the study area for unreported removals.

Bishir and Lancia (1996) used computer simulation to examine the accuracy and precision of C/E estimates.   The method can fail if the slope of the regression line (B) is positive, resulting in a negative population estimate (negative x-intercept) (Overton 1969).   Similarly, excessively large estimates result if $\hat{B}$ is negative but close to zero.   These occasional large values skew distributions of C/E estimates towards larger values.   Consequently, the mean and variance are often unreliable indicators of central tendency and dispersion, respectively.   Both model failures and excessively large estimates are more likely to occur if a small proportion of the population is removed.   Catch-per-

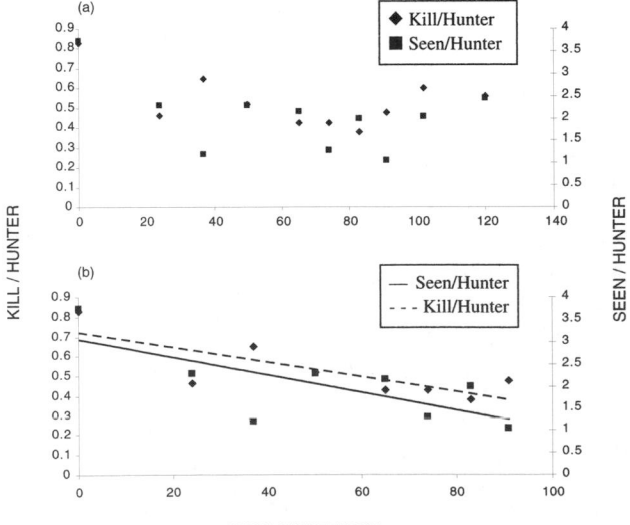

Fig. 6. Catch-per-unit-effort regressions for white-tailed deer during a special hunt in Maryland; (a) = all 10 days and (b) = only days 1–8.

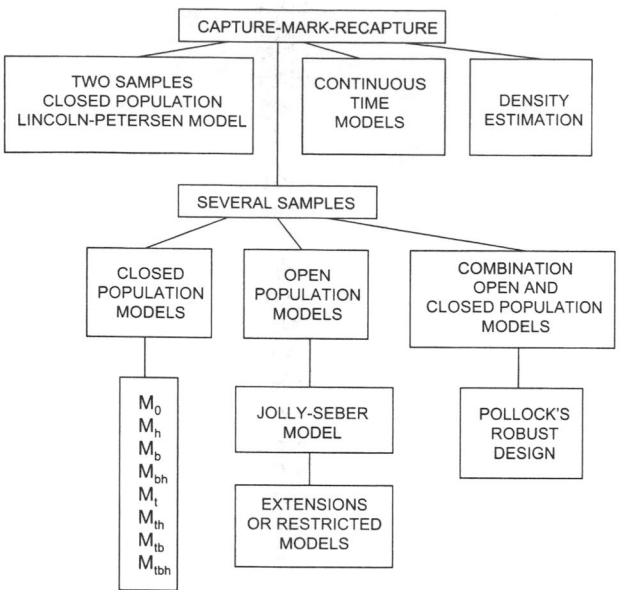

Fig. 7. The relationship among classes of capture–mark–recapture models.

unit-effort estimates are likely to be accurate and precise if greater than 70–80% of the population is removed.

Capture–Mark–Recapture Methods

Capture–mark–recapture (CMR) methods have a long history of use in ecology (LeCren 1965), resulting in a large body of literature on the statistics of capture–recapture sampling models. Reviews include Cormack (1979), Nichols et al. (1981), Pollock (1981*b*), Seber (1982), Pollock et al. (1990), Schwarz and Seber (1999), Williams et al. (2002), and Manly et al. (2004). Skalski and Robson (1992) considered the design and analysis of CMR methods for field studies and environmental impact assessment. The following section closely follows the presentation in Pollock et al. (1990).

In CMR studies the population is sampled 2 or more times, generally by live trapping, or in some cases by re-observation without actual recapture (Fig. 7). Each time, every unmarked animal that is captured is uniquely marked, previously marked animals are recorded, and all animals are released into the population so at the end of the study each animal has a complete capture history. Batch marks, wherein individual animals cannot be distinguished, do not provide individual capture histories and should be avoided, except perhaps for Lincoln–Petersen estimates.

There is no need to ever physically capture an animal if it can be uniquely identified without doing so. Examples include taking pictures of animals that have unique natural patterns (e.g., tiger stripes) (Karanth and Nichols 1998, 2002), jaguar (*Panthera onca*) spots (Trolle and Kery 2003), or acquired marks (e.g., scars on manatees [Langtimm et al. 1998], scars or callosity patterns of whales [Caswell et al. 1999, Fujiwara and Caswell 2001]). Photographic sampling has its own set of important design issues. For example, when using remote photography (e.g., camera-trapping), unambiguous identification is important; thus, for terrestrial mammals cameras are usually deployed in pairs to assure that both flanks of an animal (e.g., tiger or jaguar) are photographed whenever possible. In species for which scar acquisition is a frequent phenomenon (e.g., Florida mana-

tees), investigators must consider the evolution of scar patterns and guard against the possibility that new scars will cause a previously identified animal to not be recognized as previously seen. When large numbers of animals have been identified, it is frequently necessary to develop computer software to aid in matching of photographs (e.g., Langtimm et al. 1998, Kelly 2001). The noninvasive nature of remote photography makes this approach attractive for capture–recapture analyses; despite the special design considerations, we expect this approach to have increasing use in the future.

Another noninvasive method of sampling individuals uses DNA fingerprinting from hair, feathers, or feces. For example, this approach has been successfully used for capture–recapture studies of black bears (*Ursus americanus*) and brown bears (e.g., Woods et al. 1999, Mowat and Strobek 2000, Boulanger and McClellan 2001). In the case of bears, sampling is done by hair traps, consisting of barbed wire (and sometimes wire brushes nailed to logs) coupled with a scent lure (e.g., fish oil, rotted cow blood, beaver castor) suspended off the ground (e.g., Woods et al. 1999, Mowat and Strobek 2000). Hair is removed from the wire periodically (each removal period constitutes a capture occasion), and DNA is extracted from the hair roots.

Capture–recapture models were developed based on the assumption that individual identity is known, but use of DNA for identification can result in at least 2 kinds of errors. One is termed *probability of identity* and refers to the fact that different individuals may share the same genes at the surveyed loci, thus appearing to the investigator to be a single individual (e.g., Woods et al. 1999, Mills et al. 2000). The other problem involves errors in the genotyping process. Hair samples and feces frequently yield low quality and quantities of DNA such that resulting microsatellite genotypes contain false alleles ("misprinting"), and other alleles may fail to amplify ("allelic dropout") (e.g., Taberlet et al. 1999, Creel et al. 2003). Creel et al. (2003) suggest methods for dealing with these problems, and P. M. Lukacs and K. P. Burnham (personal communications) are developing approaches for formally handling DNA genotyping uncertainties in capture–recapture models. We believe that capture–recapture based on noninvasive DNA sampling (Oyler-McCance and Leberg 2005) holds promise for some species and sampling situations.

The need to precisely define the population of interest (i.e., target population) is especially important with CMR studies. Estimates from CMR statistical models are based on data collected over time, whether short- or long-term. Animals can move in or out of the study area during that time, and the nature of that movement will affect the population of animals that is subject to being counted. The nature of this movement can vary. For example, live traps (e.g., for small mammals) may be placed over a subset of the area occupied by a biological population (Fig. 8). Based on home range movements, animals may move in and out of the study area. In other cases, the movement has a specific biological interpretation such as where a subset of the population is unavailable for capture because it is underground (Fig. 8). For example, some small mammals will go into torpor (Kendall et al. 1997) or salamanders can go underground to avoid desiccation or predators (Bailey et al. 2004). If the study area is a breeding site, those unavailable for capture in a given year can be classified as the nonbreeding component of the same biological population (e.g., Kendall and Nichols 1995, Schwarz and Stobo 1997, Kendall and Bjorkland 2001, Lindberg et al. 2001). In some cases, animals that occupy a given study area are just one component of a metapopulation that includes one or more other sites. Those sites may or may not be part of the CMR study.

Before designing a CMR study to estimate population size, the investigator should decide whether the population of interest is the collection of animals occupying an area at a given time or the larger population that moves in and out of that area over time. For a metapopulation, the investigator should identify whether it is the number of animals occupying a patch, or the size of the entire metapopulation that is of interest. Answers to these questions will greatly affect how the study is designed and how data are analyzed.

Data collection frequently is based on a "snapshot in time" where counts (either adjusted for detection probability or not) in an area are done instantaneously (e.g., point counts), or over a short period of time. When a CMR study is conducted in a short time, we often assume it is a closed-population study. That is, for the duration of the study the population of interest is closed to its 4 potential sources of change: births, deaths, immigration, and emigration. Studies that are conducted over longer periods of time are called open-population studies and, depending on the length of time between successive capture occasions, we assume that several sources of change can occur. A long-term study can also consist of a collection of short-term studies and, hence, have both open and closed population components (Pollock 1982). Whatever method is used, it is important to identify which population, the one occupying the study site at the time of a specific sample or the larger population that is moving in and out of an area, is being assessed.

Lincoln–Petersen.—The Lincoln–Petersen model dates to Laplace who, in 1786, used it to estimate the human population of France (Seber 1982). It has great flexibility and sets the stage for more complex models that follow.

Let's assume a sample of n_1 animals is captured, marked, and released. Later, a second sample of n_2 animals is captured some of which, m_2, are marked. Intuitively, the proportion of marked animals in the second sample should be equivalent to the proportion of marked animals in the total population (assuming that capture probability is independent of marking status) so that

$$m_2 / n_2 \approx n_1 / N, \qquad (26)$$

where N is the total population size. Rearranging terms yields the estimator

$$\hat{N} = n_1 n_2 / m_2 = n_2 / \hat{\beta}. \qquad (27)$$

Chapman (1951) originally developed a modified version with less bias where

$$\hat{N}_c = \left[\frac{(n_1 + 1)(n_2 + 1)}{(m_2 + 1)} \right] - 1. \qquad (28)$$

The variance of $\hat{N}_c$ is (Seber 1982:60):

$$\text{var}(\hat{N}_c) = \frac{(n_1 + 1)(n_2 + 1)(n_1 - m_2)(n_2 - m_2)}{(m_2 + 1)^2 (m_2 + 2)}. \qquad (29)$$

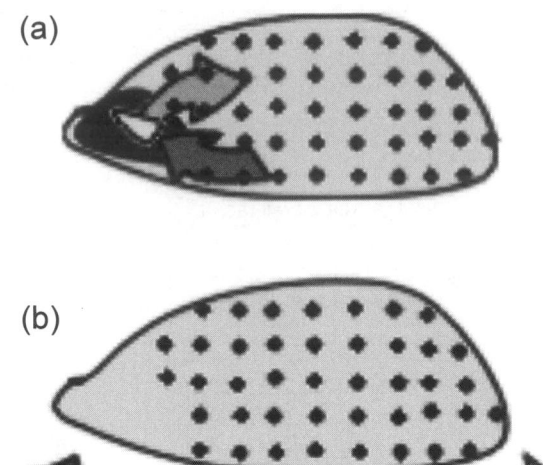

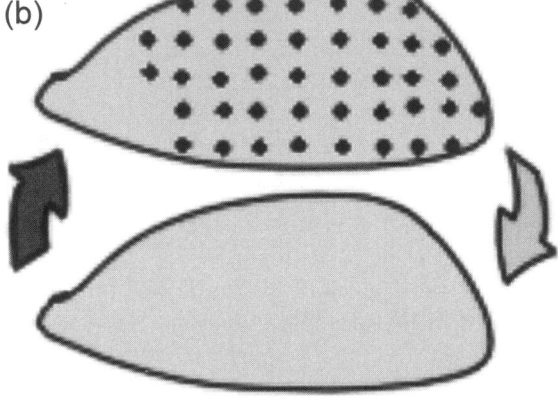

Fig. 8. Examples where there is movement in and out of the study area. In (a) the grid of traps does not enclose the movements of the entire population. In (b) some of the population is underground and therefore unavailable for detection at a given time (from Kendall 2001).

The Lincoln–Petersen model is based on the following assumptions: (1) the population is closed, (2) all animals are equally likely to be captured in each sample, and (3) marks are not lost, gained, or overlooked. The first assumption usually can be met if the interval between samples is short. The second assumption, equal probability of capture, is relaxed in models presented later. The last assumption can also be met if an appropriate marking technique is used (Silvy et al. 2005). If marks are lost, then m_2 would be too small and $\hat{N}$ too large, yielding a positively biased estimate. If tag loss is a serious problem, then corrections based on a double marking scheme (Caughley 1977, Seber 1982) could be used.

The closure assumption can be violated in 1 of 4 ways. If the entire population of interest is present in the first sample but there is death or emigration between samples, $\hat{N}$ tends to be an unbiased estimator for N_1 if marked and unmarked animals leave with equal probability. Similarly, if the entire population of interest is present during the second sample but not the first, $\hat{N}$ still tends to be unbiased for that population (Seber 1982). If members of the population move randomly in and out of the study area during the 2 sampling occasions, $\hat{N}$ tends to be unbiased (Kendall 1999) when the population of interest includes all animals with a chance of being in the study area during any sample. However, if there is nonrandom ingress (births or immigration) and egress (deaths or emigration), $\hat{N}$ will tend to be biased (Seber 1982, Kendall 1999).

The assumption of equal probability of capture is unlikely to be true for many wildlife populations because individual animals might differ in movement patterns or in behavioral responses to traps or baits. When the probability of capture is a property of individual animals and each

Box 7.   Examples of the Lincoln–Petersen mark–recapture method.   In both examples, different methods were used to initially "capture" the animals and then to "recapture" them.

In August 1974, a sample of 87 Nuttall's cottontail rabbits (*Sylvilagus nuttallii*) was livetrapped and marked with picric acid dye on their tails and hind legs (Skalski et al. 1983). About 1 month later, rabbits were counted on a drive. Fourteen rabbits were seen, 7 of which were marked. Chapman's estimate from equation (28) is

$$\hat{N}_C = \left[\frac{(n_1 + 1)(n_2 + 1)}{(m_2 + 1)} \right] - 1$$

$$= \left[\frac{(88)(15)}{(8)} \right] - 1$$

$$= 164$$

and the variance estimate is

$$\text{var}(\hat{N}_C) = \frac{(n_1 + 1)(n_2 + 1)(n_1 - m_2)(n_2 - m_2)}{(m_2 + 1)^2 (m_2 + 2)}$$

$$= \frac{(88)(15)(80)(7)}{(8)^2 (9)}$$

$$= 1{,}283.33.$$

An approximate 95% CI (normality for $\hat{N}_C$ is assumed) is

$$\hat{N}_C \pm 1.965 \sqrt{\text{var}(\hat{N}_C)}$$

$$164 \pm 1.965 \sqrt{1283.33}$$

$$164 \pm 70.$$

The approximate 95% confidence interval would be from 94 to 234, a rather wide range. Precision would improve if more animals had been seen on the drive count. Because 2 different sampling techniques were used, concern for heterogeneity or trap response of the capture probabilities should have been minimal.

In northern Florida, Conner et al. (1983) captured 48 raccoons in live traps. An unusual marking scheme was used; the animals were injected with a small amount of radioactive isotope. The "recapture" sample involved an intensive search of the study area for scats, and scats that were "marked" were detected with a special scintillation counter. Both this and the previous study provide examples of batch marking, which restricts analysis to the Lincoln–Petersen method only.

Conner et al. (1983) searched for scats for 5 weeks and treated each week separately, so they obtained 5 different Lincoln–Petersen estimates. With 5 estimates they could consider variation in the estimates during the study.

Week of collection	Number marked, (n_1)	Number of scats, (n_2)	Number of marked scats (m_2)	Lincoln–Petersen $\hat{N}$
1	48	71	31	109.9
2	48	22	11	96.0
3	48	74	35	101.5
4	48	28	9	149.3
5	48	35	19	88.4

If we assume these were 5 independent, normally distributed estimates of *N*, then 109 (SE = 10.6) is a reasonable point estimate (obtained as the arithmetic mean of the 5 weekly estimates of *N*), with a 95% confidence interval of 82–136.

animal has a unique capture probability, the situation is termed heterogeneity. Variation in capture probabilities among individuals could be due to many factors such as gender, age, social status, spatial distribution of animals, and capture efforts. If heterogeneity is present, individuals with high capture probabilities tend to be captured in the first sample and recaptured in the second sample. Thus, m_2 is too large and, hence, $\hat{N}$ is too small. Therefore, $\hat{N}$ is negatively biased when capture probabilities are heterogeneous.

A solution to the heterogeneity problem is to use a different trapping method in each period, so that capture probability for an individual in period 1 is independent of that in period 2. This serves to neutralize effects of heterogeneity (Seber 1982) (Box 7).

Another possibility is that capture probabilities may depend on whether an animal has been captured previously. For example, marked animals may become "trap shy" and have a lower capture probability, or they may become "trap happy" and have a higher capture probability than unmarked (not previously captured) individuals. If animals are trap happy, m_2 will be too large and $\hat{N}$ too small, whereas the converse is true for a population with trap shy individuals. Thus, a trap or behavioral response in capture probabilities can result in population estimates that are either negatively biased (too low) due to trap happy animals or positively biased (too high) due to trap shy animals.

K-sample Closed Population Models.—The 2-sample Lincoln–Petersen approach can be extended to *K* samples (i.e., >1 recapture occasions) and can be generalized to include other sources of variation in capture probability besides time. Otis et al. (1978), White et al. (1982), Chao (2001), Williams et al. (2002), and Chao and Huggins (2004) presented excellent reviews of closed models. Because closed population models do not permit unknown changes in size of the population while the estimation procedure is being implemented, these methods are generally conducted over a relatively short period (e.g., 5–10 days). Capture histories of every animal caught are needed for obtaining estimates with closed models that allow relaxation of the equal probability of capture assumption. Pollock (1974) prepared an early

> **Box 8.   Using program CAPTURE to estimate population size of meadow voles (*Microtus pennsylvanicus*) on a live-trapping grid.**
>
>   Nichols and Pollock (Nichols et al. 1984*b*) established a small mammal live-trapping grid in old-field habitat at the Patuxent Wildlife Research Center in Laurel, Maryland in 1981. The grid contained a 10×10 matrix of Fitch live traps (Rose 1973) at 7.6-m intervals. Hay and dried grass were placed in the nest box section of the traps, and whole corn was used as bait. Traps were set each evening and checked each morning for 5-day periods once each month from June 1981 through January 1982. Captured animals were marked with ear tags and released at the capture site.
>
>   Five consecutive trapping days from October 1981 are used as an example of the model selection procedure and population estimation from program CAPTURE. Data are the capture histories of adult meadow voles. Model selection results are presented below.
>
> | Model | M_0 | M_h | M_b | M_{bh} | M_t | M_{th} | M_{tb} | M_{tbh} |
> |---|---|---|---|---|---|---|---|---|
> | Criteria | 0.80 | 1.00 | 0.38 | 0.59 | 0.00 | 0.32 | 0.52 | 0.98 |
>
>   The highest value for the model selection procedure indicates the most appropriate model for these data. High values for M_h and M_{tbh} suggest they are better models than the others. The best is the jackknife estimator corresponding to M_h (Table 1). The estimated average capture probability, $\hat{p} = 0.44$, is high (Table 1) and precision of the population estimate is good.

synthetic treatment of these models followed by Otis et al. (1978), White et al. (1982), and Pollock and Otto (1983).

Closed population models differ in the way capture probabilities are modeled in that 3 basic sources of variation are considered: heterogeneity, trap response or behavior, and time. Heterogeneity and trap response were discussed under the Lincoln–Petersen method. Variability in time means that capture probabilities are different for each occasion (e.g., day) of trapping. For example, different weather conditions might change capture probabilities.

The following models have been developed to account for different sources of variation in capture probabilities: equal probability of capture (M_0), heterogeneity (M_h), behavior (M_b), time (M_t), behavior-heterogeneity (M_{bh}), time-heterogeneity (M_{th}), time-behavior (M_{tb}), and time-behavior-heterogeneity (M_{tbh}). Program CAPTURE (Rexstad and Burnham 1991) was developed to estimate population size under these models. It also provides a model selection procedure that chooses the model to best use for a particular data set. This program can be accessed directly, or through program MARK (White and Burnham 1999)

Table 1. Estimates from the jackknife estimator for the heterogeneity model (M_h) of program CAPTURE for meadow vole data collected at Patuxent Wildlife Research Center, Laurel, Maryland, 1981 (adapted from Nichols et al. 1984*b*).

Frequencies of capture[a]					
i	1	2	3	4	5
$f(i)$	29	15	15	16	27

Number of animals captured = 102[b]

Average $\hat{p}$ = 0.44

Interpolated population estimate = 139 (SE = 10.85)

Approximate 95% CI = 117–161

[a] Frequencies of capture are the number of animals captured 1, 2, 3 times, up to the number of capture occasions.
[b] Number of different individuals captured one or more times.

at http://www.cnr.colostate.edu/~gwhite/software.html (Box 8). Program MARK can also be used to compute some estimators under these models.

M_0 Equal Probability of Capture Model.—This model is unlikely to be realistic because it assumes that every animal in the population has the same probability of capture (p) for each sampling period in the study. However, it may provide a reasonable approximation for some situations and might be the only useful model if data are limited. Finally, it is useful for pedagogic reasons to provide a basis for generalizations.

The M_0 model uses a Maximum Likelihood (ML) estimator of N (and an approximate standard error) that is computed iteratively by CAPTURE, or by MARK. This estimator can be highly biased if the equal probability of capture assumption is violated. Otis et al. (1978) found it to be reasonably robust to changes in capture probabilities over time. Thus, model M_0 can give reasonable estimates even if capture probabilities vary over time. When recaptures are infrequent, the M_0 model is usually chosen by the model selection procedure in CAPTURE as the most appropriate estimator. Few recaptures provide only limited information about different sources of variation in capture probability and, hence, little evidence of the need for other models.

M_h Heterogeneity Model.—The heterogeneity model assumes each animal has a unique capture probability (p_j, where $j = 1, \ldots, N$ animals in the population) that remains constant over all trapping occasions. Because under this model some individuals are unlikely to enter a trap, ignoring heterogeneity will tend to produce a large negative bias in $\hat{N}$. Assuming the capture probabilities of those captured to be a random sample from all individuals in the population, the number of animals captured 1, 2, 3, . . . K times contains all the information used for estimating N.

The M_h model was first considered by Burnham (1972) and later by Burnham and Overton (1978, 1979), who developed a jackknife estimation procedure. Chao (1988) proposed a moment estimator under the heterogeneity model. Based on computer simulation, her moment estimator was superior to the jackknife procedure when capture probabilities were so small that most animals were recaptured only 1 or 2 times. Both methods are now implemented in program CAPTURE. Chao and Lee (1992), Chao et al. (1992), and Lee and Chao (1994) developed sample coverage approaches to this problem, and Chao and Huggins (2004) outlined an estimating equation approach.

A disadvantage of the above approaches is they are not based on maximum likelihood estimation. Therefore, they do not lend themselves to comparison with estimators from other models using common approaches such as likelihood ratio tests or information theory (e.g., Akaike's Information Criterion, or AIC).

Two alternative approaches to estimation are likelihood based. One assumes there is an unidentified mixture of groups within the population, where each group has its own capture probability that is constant for individuals within the group. Norris and Pollock (1995, 1996) considered estimation where the number of these groups is to be estimated, along with the detection probability for each group. Pledger (2000) found that when only 2 groups were assumed, this model produced estimators with good properties based on simulated and real data. If capture probability for an individual can be viewed as a function only of a set of known and measurable attributes (e.g., body mass at first capture), this relationship can be modeled within a likelihood framework (e.g., p_j as a linear-logistic function of mass, m_j):

$$p_j = \frac{e^{\beta_0 + \beta_1 m_j}}{1 + e^{\beta_0 + \beta_1 m_j}} \; , \qquad (30)$$

where β_0 and β_1 are intercept and slope parameters (on the logit scale) for which ML estimators are derived (Pollock et al. 1984; Huggins 1989, 1991; Alho 1990). The mixture model of Pledger (2000) and covariate models have been implemented in program MARK (White and Burnham 1999), which also permits comparison of models using likelihood ratio tests and AIC. Program LINLOGN (Hines et al. 1984) is also available where covariate values can be grouped into discrete classes.

None of the above methods is guaranteed to produce reasonable estimates of abundance (Link 2003). All of these methods, as well as additional ones such as a bootstrap approach by Smith and van Belle (1984), have been found through simulations to perform well in some scenarios and not so well in others (Otis et al. 1978, Norris and Pollock 1996). In general, simulation results indicate the jackknife estimator (Burnham and Overton 1979), which is available in program CAPTURE, is the most robust to various patterns of heterogeneity. This is especially true when the study consists of at least 5 capture occasions (Otis et al. 1978).

No statistical procedure will remedy the case where a substantial proportion of the population is essentially uncatchable (Link 2003). The only solution is to change field methods to make that component of the population catchable, if possible. More generally, making capture probability for each individual independent over time by varying capture methods used across capture periods, can help neutralize the effect of heterogeneity on the estimation of N.

M_b Trap Response Model.—Model M_b allows a change in capture probabilities caused by a response to trapping. The model assumes every unmarked (not previously captured) individual in the population has the same initial capture probability (p) for all trapping occasions, and every marked individual has the same probability of recapture (c) for all trapping occasions after its initial capture. These capture probabilities p and c need not be equal.

The M_b model is essentially a constant effort, catch-per-unit-effort removal model, because all of the information needed to estimate N is contained in the initial capture data. The "removed" individuals need not be physically taken out of the population. Rather, marked individuals are ignored in subsequent samples, and only initial capture data are used to estimate the population. An assumption of model M_b is the initial capture probability for all animals is the same.

Programs CAPTURE and MARK use a MLE of N rather than the traditional catch-per-unit-effort regression technique. There appears to be little difference between the ML and regression estimates (J. W. Bishir, personal communication).

M_{bh} Behavior-heterogeneity Model.—The M_{bh} model is based on the assumption that each animal has its own unique pair of potential capture probabilities, p_j and c_j ($j = 1, \ldots, N$ animals in the population), where p_j is the initial capture probability and c_j is the recapture probability. The capture probabilities are assumed to remain constant for all trapping occasions. This model was first considered by Pollock (1974). Subsequently, Otis et al. (1978) developed a "generalized removal method" and Pollock and Otto (1983) developed a jackknife method; both of these are now implemented in program CAPTURE.

As with model M_h, a sample coverage estimator (Lee and Chao 1994) is available for this model. This estimator performed better (based on mean square error) than the generalized removal estimator in simulations, but not as well as the jackknife approach. As with model M_h, MLE's have been developed from finite mixture models (Norris and Pollock 1995, 1996; Pledger 2000). Simulations suggest their performance is competitive, and they are derived in a likelihood context permitting comparison using likelihood ratio tests or AIC. MLE's can also be computed if capture probabilities can be modeled as a function of individual covariates.

M_t Time Variation (Schnabel) Model.—The M_t model is a direct extension of the Lincoln–Petersen model, based on the assumption that every individual in the population has the same capture probability for a given sampling occasion but these probabilities can vary at each sampling time. Thus, the capture probabilities are p_i, $i = 1, 2, \ldots, K$ sampling occasions. This is the classic closed population model allowing temporal variation first developed by Schnabel (1938).

Programs CAPTURE and MARK use a ML estimator to calculate N. Although Schnabel estimates are easy to compute manually, these programs should be used because they can also help select the most appropriate model for a given data set. Model M_t estimates can be highly biased if capture probabilities are not equal for all individuals within a given time period. The effect is similar to the bias created by unequal capture probability when model M_0 is used.

M_{th} Time-heterogeneity Model.—Otis et al. (1978) developed this model as an extension of model M_h, but provided no estimators due to the large number of parameters. They conceptualized capture probability p_{ij} of animal j at time i to be a product of 2 factors operating independently: one reflecting random variation among animals and one reflecting variation in environmental conditions over time.

Chao et al. (1992) developed a sample coverage estimator for this model, which is included in program CAPTURE. Likelihood-based methods are also possible. Pledger (2000) applied a finite mixture approach, which can be implemented in program MARK. In MARK it is also possible to model p_{ij} as a function of individual or time-dependent covariates.

M_{tb} Time-behavioral Response Model.—This model is an extension of model M_b where each animal that has previously been marked has a different capture probability (c_i) than those not previously captured (p_i), but capture probabilities for both previously marked and unmarked vary by time i.

Unfortunately, an ML approach cannot be taken with this model without additional constraints. This can be resolved if some relationship is assumed between c_i and p_i. Otis et al. (1978) considered $c_i = \theta p_i$, and it was implemented by Chao et al. (2000) in program CARE-2. Rexstad and Burnham (1991) incorporated $c_i = p_i^{1/\theta}$ into CAPTURE. In MARK, a constant relationship between c_i and p_i can be established on the logit scale:

$$p_i = \frac{e^{\beta_{0i}}}{1+e^{\beta_{0i}}} \; , \; c_i = \frac{e^{\beta_{0i}+\beta_1}}{1+e^{\beta_{0i}+\beta_1}} \; , \qquad (31)$$

where β_1 represents the constant trap effect (Kendall 2001).

M_{tbh} Time-behavior-heterogeneity Model.—This model combines all 3 types of variation in capture probability, making it the most realistic of the available set of models. However, its large number of parameters makes it the most difficult statistically. Nevertheless Lee and Chao (1994), viewing the capture process as a variable catch-effort problem (initial capture probabilities considered a product of inherent variability among individuals and known variability in capture effort), used a sample coverage approach to estimate N. Chao et al. (2001) used estimating equations to estimate N by viewing the process in the same way as Lee and Chao (1994). They also assumed that heterogeneity among animals could be characterized by the mean and coefficient of variation of their capture probabilities.

Pledger (2000) developed an estimator based on this model by combining finite mixture and a linear logistic approach that uses time, trap response, and heterogeneity as main effects, with interactions. It is possible to model capture and recapture probabilities over time as functions of covariates.

Variance and Confidence Interval Estimation.—Methods based on ML estimation also generate asymptotic (i.e., large sample assumed) variances. Similarly, asymptotic confidence intervals are based on a normal distribution (e.g., a 95% confidence interval for N is represented by $\hat{N} \pm 1.96$ SE[$\hat{N}$]). An alternative, especially for small sample sizes, is a parametric bootstrap approach (Buckland and Garthwaite 1991), where capture histories are simulated based on the available sample sizes and estimated parameters. This generates an empirical distribution of $\hat{N}$. An estimate of SE($\hat{N}$) is computed as the standard deviation of this distribution, and a confidence interval is constructed from percentiles of this distribution (e.g., the 2.5th and 97.5th percentiles for a 95% confidence interval).

Program CAPTURE computes 2 alternative confidence intervals for N. The first is based on the assumption the difference between $\hat{N}$ and the total number of individuals captured (this difference is the estimated number of animals in the population that are not captured) is log-normally distributed (Burnham et al. 1987, Chao 1989). This approach prevents the confidence interval from including values less than the number of animals encountered. For models M_0, M_t, M_b, M_{tb}, and M_{bh} a confidence interval based on profile likelihoods can also be computed (Rexstad and Burnham 1991).

Model Selection.—Program CAPTURE (Rexstad and Burnham 1991) includes a procedure to choose the best model based on goodness-of-fit tests and tests between models. The model selection procedure should be used with caution, however, because the tests often have low power, especially for small populations (Chapman 1980, Menkens and Anderson 1988). In some cases, a Lincoln–Petersen estimate based on pooling samples into an early versus late sample might be preferable to the estimator based on CAPTURE's model choice (Menkens and Anderson 1988).

For those models where ML estimates are available, likelihood ratio tests are feasible for comparing specific pairs of models. Alternatively, information criteria such as the AIC can be used to select among models and to generate weights for averaging values of $\hat{N}$ across models.

Although statistical methods can be used to select among candidate models, biological information should also be used to guide the selection of candidate models. This should keep the number of candidates from becoming unwieldy, and will reduce the probability that a completely unreasonable model biologically is selected by chance. For example, evidence may exist, based on the behavior of a particular species and the trapping method used, that trap response is unlikely and models that allow trap response should not be considered.

Assumption Violations.—If closure is maintained during the K-period study, the population being assessed is geographically defined by the area enclosed by the set of sampling stations (e.g., traps), with some additional area outside the perimeter to allow for home ranges that partially overlap the sampled area. This is also true with the 2-sample Lincoln–Petersen method. Violation of geographic closure during the study can cause additional bias problems. However, if the animals in the study area can be viewed as a random sample from a larger "superpopulation" (i.e., animals move in and out of the study area completely randomly), the estimate of N would apply to the larger "superpopulation" from which the animals are drawn (Kendall 1999).

Two other scenarios permit unbiased estimation of N, and both require that M_t or M_0 be the appropriate underlying model. First, if the entire population is present at the first sampling occasion, but marked and unmarked animals emigrate with equal probability (e.g., a migratory breeding or wintering population) during the rest of the sampling periods, N can be estimated by pooling all but the first sampling occasions and applying the Lincoln–Petersen method. Conversely, if sampling begins before all animals have arrived, but all have arrived by the last sampling period, then all occasions but the last (or up to the occasion where all have arrived) can be pooled into one, and the Lincoln–Petersen method applied.

Tests of the closure assumption do exist. The test in program CAPTURE is based on the observed times between first and last capture (Otis et al. 1978). However, it is overly sensitive to behavioral response or time variation in capture probability, and relatively insensitive to temporary emigration. Stanley and Burnham (1999) developed a composite test for closure based on earlier work by Pollock et al. (1974). If a closure violation is detected, this test can be evaluated to discover whether this is due to recruitment or mortality. This test is not sensitive to time variation in capture probability, but is sensitive to trap response and heterogeneity. Stanley and Burnham (1999) recommended using their test, available in program CLOSTEST, in conjunction with the test in CAPTURE.

In capture–recapture methods when tags are lost over time, a positive bias in $\hat{N}$ can develop because a trap-shy response is mimicked. The probability of recapture is reduced because an animal must be marked before it can be recaptured. If tags are lost the population appears to have fewer marked animals that are available for recapture. Therefore, a trap-response model might be appropriate. The rate of loss can be estimated by placing more than one mark on an animal that is captured (Seber 1982), and the effect of loss can be adjusted directly.

Continuous Time Models.—Chao and Huggins (2004) outlined and reviewed models where there are no discrete sampling periods, but encounters with individuals can occur at any time during the period of interest and time of detection is recorded for each animal. Boyce et al. (2001) presented a case where searches for grizzly bears occurred from May through September. They developed a method that allows for heterogeneity in capture probability.

Wilson and Anderson (1995) considered whether using a continuous time approach to model M_t might be helpful even where sampling periods are well defined and discrete (i.e., whether recording time of capture provides an advantage). They found these models did not offer any particular advantage over discrete time models.

Density Estimation.—Although this chapter is devoted to estimation of population size, the closely related concept of density is important also. Density generally can be defined as number of animals per unit resource, or commonly animals per unit area. The key question to translate population size into density is: "how large is the area that is being sampled?" It has been traditional (e.g., Dice 1938) to consider a boundary strip of constant width extending beyond the area in which the sampling efforts actually occur. For example in grid trapping, the boundary strip extends beyond the traps along the periphery of the trapping grid including the area from which animals trapped on the grid were drawn. The area used by the population of animals exposed to grid trapping is the sum of the areas of the grid itself and of the boundary strip. We consider 2 methods that adopt this approach for CMR data. Another approach is to estimate density directly with distance methods.

Movement Distances from Trapping Data.—The effective size of the study area is derived by establishing a strip of width W along the periphery of the grid of traps. Width W is estimated as half the average maximum distance an individual moves during the study, based on individuals captured more than once (Wilson and Anderson 1985b). Jett and Nichols (1987) modified this approach because the apparent maximum distance an individual moves is partly an artifact of the number of times it is captured. The greater the number of captures per animal, the

less bias in the final estimate of density (Wilson and Anderson 1985b). This approach is best where the study area is within a larger expanse of habitat similar to that within the grid, and can be especially useful where the study area is irregularly shaped (Karanth and Nichols 1998). Problems can occur with this method when animals outside the trapping grid are artificially drawn into the grid (e.g., due to baiting).

Nested Grids.—This method of estimating density was developed by Otis et al. (1978) for use in conjunction with closed population capture–mark–recapture models. They noted that population size associated with a trapping grid can be written as a function of 2 known parameters—grid area and perimeter—and 2 unknown parameters—boundary strip width and true animal density. Data from a single grid do not permit estimation of the 2 unknown parameters, but if population size estimates are available for several grids of different size, then density estimation is possible. A single trapping grid can be viewed as a series of nested grids. For example, assume that we have a 10×10 square-trapping grid. If we omit captures from the outermost 2 squares, data correspond to an 8×8 grid. Similarly, we can omit the outermost 4 and 6 squares of traps to yield 6 $\times$ 6 and 4 $\times$ 4 grids, respectively.

To estimate density, Otis et al. (1978) first used closed population models to estimate population size in each nested grid within the overall trapping grid (4 grids in the 10×10 example). They wrote their "naive density" estimate (i.e., population size estimate divided by area covered by the grid) as a function of the 2 quantities of interest, true density and boundary strip width. The naive density estimates are successively less biased as grid size increases. Estimates from the different grids are used (in conjunction with generalized nonlinear least squares) to estimate both true density and boundary strip width.

Simulation studies by Wilson and Anderson (1985b) showed large positive biases and estimated variances associated with density estimates based on the nested grid approach. However, when capture probabilities are high and sample sizes are large, the nested grid approach can perform relatively well (Jett and Nichols 1987).

Trapping Web.—This method of density estimation relies on captures of animals, but is free of specific assumptions about sources of variation in capture probabilities (Anderson et al. 1983). The method is not based on underlying models of capture history data and differs conceptually from capture–mark–recapture models. Distance sampling is the conceptual basis for estimation with the trapping web, which is analogous to formal transect models and point transects.

With line and point transect sampling, detection probabilities decrease with distance from the transect line or center of the circular plot. The trapping web is a configuration of traps designed to yield a similar gradient of detection (capture) probabilities. The web consists of some number (e.g., 16) of equally spaced lines of equal length radiating from a randomly chosen center point. Traps (e.g., 20 per line) are placed on the radial lines at fixed distances from the center point (the center of the web), with a constant distance separating successive traps on a particular line. The design yields a series of concentric rings, each having the same number of traps. The ring nearest the web center has traps spaced close together, and the distance between traps of the

Box 9. Using the Jolly–Seber CMR method to estimate births, survival, and population size.

We analyzed data from a 2-year study of gray squirrels in a mature oak (*Quercus* spp.) woodland in Surrey, England, by A. Duboek (Pollock et al. 1990). Squirrels were captured at approximately monthly intervals from November 1972 until September 1974. Multiple–capture traps, dispersed throughout the woodland, were baited with grain. Captured squirrels were uniquely marked by toe clipping.

Jolly–Seber estimates are calculated (Table 2) except there were no estimates for September through November 1973 because the small number of captures would give misleading estimates. Survival rate estimates that were >1.0 were recorded as 1.0, and some birth number estimates that were negative were recorded as zero.

The estimates in this example were precise because of high capture and survival probabilities. Once a squirrel was captured and marked, it tended to stay in the population a long time and was recaptured often. Consequently, recaptures provided substantial information for the estimation procedures. However, the precision of the estimates varied considerably during the study due to changes in capture probabilities. Even when capture probabilities remained nearly constant, precision was highest during the middle of the study because the

marked population gradually increased, and many sampling periods remained for obtaining recapture data. Thus, r_i needs to be large for highly precise estimates.

Many factors affected the accuracy of the estimates. Duboek believed movement in and out of the population was negligible and interpreted the estimates of survival and births to reflect only mortality and reproduction. Because of possible differences in capture and survival probabilities for the different gender and age classes in the population (heterogeneity) and because the animals were probably trap happy (trap response), capture probabilities were probably not equal among individuals as assumed in the model. Both of these departures could cause negatively biased population size estimates and, to a lesser extent, underestimation of survival rates.

Young animals should have been joining the catchable population in April and May. This showed as a high estimate of the number of births during these months in 1974 but not in 1973. Duboek predicted that 1973 would be a bad year for squirrel production. After a large number of squirrels joined the population in spring 1974, survival dropped substantially. Unfortunately, this occurred at the end of the study so the estimates may be unreliable.

---

same ring on adjacent radial lines increases with increasing distance of the ring from the web center. Trap density, and the probability that an animal in a particular area will be caught, decreases with distance from the web center producing a gradient in detection probabilities similar to that of line transect and point transect sampling situations. Traps are checked for several consecutive days (e.g., 5), and the concentric ring of initial capture is recorded for each animal. Because only initial capture data are used, the method will work with "removal" data. Actual removal is not recommended, however, because in some species adjacent individuals may quickly fill vacated spaces.

Rings, defined by points halfway between adjacent traps on a radial line, are used to compute the area trapped by a particular ring of traps. Data on area trapped and number of animals caught are available for each ring and form the basis for estimation of $f(c)$, the probability density function of the area sampled. After estimating $f(c)$, density is estimated in a manner similar to that used for line transects:

$$\hat{D} = M_{t+1}\hat{f}(0), \qquad (32)$$

where M_{t+1} denotes the total number of animals captured during web operation. The various estimators from program DISTANCE (Buckland et al. 2001) can be used to estimate density. The variance [VAR($\hat{D}$)] can be estimated using DISTANCE in conjunction with the estimator of Wilson and Anderson (1985*a*).

Four assumptions underlie estimating density with the trapping web: (1) all animals at the web center are caught with probability 1.0, (2) animal movements are "stable" (i.e., there are no preferential movements toward or away from the web center), (3) distances from the web center to

each trap are measured accurately when the web is established, and (4) animal captures are independent events (required for variance estimation). Computer simulation studies led Wilson and Anderson (1985*a*) to conclude the trapping web performed well. Examples are given by Anderson et al. (1983), Jett and Nichols (1987), Parmenter et al. (1989), and Corn and Conroy (1998). Parmenter et al. (2003) presented evidence that web estimates performed well in field tests on populations of known density. Link and Barker (1994) took a different approach to analyzing data from the trapping web. Their analysis focused on how the geometry of the web affects the traps in which animals are eventually captured. Whereas distance methods focus on the web center, their approach focuses on the location of each trap. Their approach raises a question about optimal configuration of trap placement.

Open Population Models.—The basic open population model used to estimate population size, survival rates, and births is the Jolly–Seber model (Jolly 1965, Seber 1965). Cormack (1973) gave a brief intuitive description of this model and its estimators, and Seber (1982) gave a detailed presentation. Computer programs that calculate Jolly–Seber estimates of population size include POPAN (Arnason and Schwarz 1999), JOLLY (Pollock et al. 1990), and MARK (White and Burnham 1999).

The Jolly–Seber Model.—The Jolly–Seber model allows estimation of population size at each sampling time as well as "survival" rates and "births" between sampling occasions (Box 9). The mathematical complement of "survival rate" (i.e., 1 – survival) includes mortality and permanent emigration, and "births" include immigration. The following discussion closely follows Seber (1982). Assumptions of the Jolly-Seber model are below.

Table 2. Capture–recapture data (collected by A. Duboek), Jolly–Seber estimates, and approximate standard errors[a] for a gray squirrel population at Alice Hold Forest Research Station, Surrey, England, November 1972 to September 1974 (from Pollock et al. 1990).

Date	n_i	m_i	R_i	r_i	z_i	$\hat{N}_i$	$\widehat{SE}$	$\hat{\phi}_i$	$\widehat{SE}$	$\hat{B}_i$	$\widehat{SE}$
Nov	46		46	43				0.94	0.03		
Dec	46	42	46	44	1	47.1	0.4	0.96	0.03	6.3	0.7
Jan	48	42	48	48	3	51.3	0.7	1.00	0.00	4.5	1.3
Feb	46	42	46	45	9	56.0	1.2	0.99	0.02	5.1	1.5
Mar	51	46	50	46	8	60.5	1.5	0.94	0.04	0.0	1.1
Apr	37	37	37	35	17	54.9	1.2	0.95	0.04	0.0	0.0
May	41	41	41	40	11	52.3	0.6	1.00	0.03	3.9	1.2
May–Jun	42	39	42	37	12	56.5	2.1	0.90	0.05	3.7	1.4
Jun	47	43	47	40	6	54.6	1.6	0.92	0.07	8.7	3.3
Jul	31	26	31	26	20	58.9	4.6	0.84	0.07	2.2	6.6
Aug	8	7	8	8	39	51.8	6.0	1.00	0.00	0.0	6.0
Sep	2	2	2	2	45						
Oct	1	0	1	1	47						
Nov	4	3	4	3	45						
Dec	9	8	9	8	40	58.3	9.2	0.93	0.12	1.0	6.6
Jan	19	17	18	17	31	55.3	4.3	0.98	0.07	13.1	8.2
Feb	19	14	19	18	34	66.4	8.1	1.00	0.07	6.8	10.1
Mar	27	20	27	24	32	74.5	7.9	0.93	0.07	0.0	6.3
Apr	36	36	36	32	20	58.4	2.1	0.99	0.07	18.2	4.2
May	45	34	44	33	18	76.0	6.1	1.00	0.17	33.9	8.9
Jul	74	46	73	15	5	110.3	18.1	0.21	0.05	0.0	2.2
Aug	22	20	22	2	0	21.9	0.0				
Sep	3	2	2								

[a] $\widehat{SE}(\hat{N}_i)$ includes only sampling variation or "error of estimation;" $\widehat{SE}(\hat{\phi}_i)$ and $\widehat{SE}(\hat{B}_i)$ were obtained using the full variance estimators of Jolly (1965).

(1) Every animal present in the population at the time of the ith sample, where $i = 1, 2, 3, ... , K$ trapping occasions, has the same probability of capture, p_i. Thus, the Jolly–Seber model requires the assumption of equal probability of capture.

Table 3. Notation for the Jolly–Seber model.

M_i	=	number of marked animals in the population at time of the ith sample ($i = 1, 2, ..., K$; $M_1 = 0$).
N_i	=	total number of animals in the population at time of the ith sample ($i = 1, 2, ..., K$).
B_i	=	total number of new animals entering the population between the ith and $i + 1$th sample and still in the population at time of the $i + 1$th sample ($i = 2, ..., K - 1$).
ϕ_i	=	survival probability for all animals between the ith and $i + 1$th sample ($i = 1, 2, ..., K - 1$).
p_i	=	capture probability in the ith sample ($i = 2, 3, ..., K$) for all animals in the population.
m_i	=	number of marked animals captured in the ith sample ($i = 1, 2, ..., K$; $m_1 = 0$).
u_i	=	number of unmarked animals captured in the ith sample ($i = 1, 2, ..., K$).
n_i	=	$m_i + u_i$, total number of animals captured in the ith sample ($i = 1, 2, ..., K$).
R_i	=	number of the n_i animals released after the ith sample ($i = 1, 2, ..., K - 1$). This might not include all n_i because of losses during capture.
r_i	=	number of R_i animals released at i that are captured again ($i = 2, ..., K - 1$).
z_i	=	number of animals captured before i that are not captured at i, but are captured again later ($i = 2, 3, ..., K - 1$).

(2) Every marked animal present in the population immediately after the ith sample has the same probability of survival, ϕ_i, until the next sampling time, $i + 1$, where $i = 1, 2, 3, . . . , K - 1$ trapping occasions.

(3) Marks are not lost or overlooked.

(4) All samples are instantaneous and each release is made immediately after the sample.

(5) Every animal in the population is equally likely to emigrate and all emigration from the population is permanent.

Assumptions 1 and 3 are required under the Lincoln–Petersen model. Only marked animals are used to estimate survival rates; an assumption that marked and unmarked animals have equal survival is not necessary. However, in practice survival estimates are interpreted as though they apply to the entire population and this assumption is needed to estimate the number of new recruits.

In the Jolly–Seber model (Table 3), imagine the number of marked animals in the population, M_i, just before the ith sample is known for all values of i from $i = 2, ..., K$, where K is the number of sampling occasions. There are no marked animals before the first sample, so $M_1 = 0$. We will discuss below how to estimate M_i's, which are unknown in an open population because some mortality (and/or emigration) can occur.

An intuitive estimator, N_i, of population size at time i, is the Lincoln–Petersen estimator. Thus,

$$m_i / n_i \approx M_i / N_i, \tag{33}$$

where m_i is the number of marked animals recaptured in the ith sample and n_i is the total number of animals captured in the ith sample. Solving for N_i yields the estimator

$$\hat{N}_i = n_i \hat{M}_i \: / \: m_i. \qquad (34)$$

Estimates of N_i are defined only for $i = 2, \ldots, K - 1$ sampling times.

The survival rate is the ratio of the number of marked animals in the population at the time of the $i + 1$th sample to the number of marked animals in the population just following the ith sample. The number of marked animals in the population just following the ith sample is the number of marked animals in the population just prior to the ith sample, M_i, plus the unmarked animals, u_i, that are newly marked in the ith sample. Because some animals may be captured but not released back into the population (due to trap mortality for example), we write the number of marked animals in the population following release in period i as: $M_i - m_i$ (the number of marked animals available at period i that were not caught) plus R_i (the number of animals caught in period i *and* released following i; this includes members of both m_i and u_i that were released). The number of animals still alive in the population just before the $i + 1$th sample is $M_{i + 1}$. The survival rate at sampling time i is estimated as:

$$\hat{\phi}_i = \hat{M}_{i + 1} \: / \: (\hat{M}_i - m_i + R_i). \qquad (35)$$

Parameters ϕ_i are defined only for $i = 1, \ldots, K - 1$ sampling times. Under the standard Jolly–Seber model, $\phi_{K - 1}$ and p_K cannot be separately estimated.

The number of "births" or recruitment in time interval i to $i + 1$ is estimated as the difference between the size of the population at time $i + 1$, which is $N_{i + 1}$, and the expected number of survivors from i to $i + 1$, which is the product of the survival rate and the number of animals at time i or $\phi_i N_i$. In the presence of trap mortality, the expected number of survivors can be written as $\phi_i \: (N_i - n_i + R_i)$ (note that $n_i = R_i$ if there are no trap mortalities). Thus, the number of births at sampling time i is estimated as:

$$\hat{B}_i = \hat{N}_{i + 1} - \hat{\phi}_i \: (\hat{N}_i - n_i + R_i). \qquad (36)$$

Under the Jolly–Seber model, estimates of B_i are defined only for $i = 2, \ldots, K - 2$ sampling times.

The probability of capture, p_i, can be estimated as the proportion of marked animals alive at time i captured at time i or the proportion of the total (marked + unmarked) animals alive at time i that are captured at time i. Thus,

$$\hat{p}_i = m_i \: / \: \hat{M}_i = n_i \: / \: \hat{N}_i. \qquad (37)$$

Estimates of p_i are defined only for $i = 2, \ldots, K - 1$ sampling times under the Jolly–Seber model.

Finally, M_i is unknown in an open population and must be estimated by equating the 2 ratios

$$z_i \: / \: (M_i - m_i) = r_i \: / \: R_i, \qquad (38)$$

which are the future recapture rates of 2 distinct groups of marked animals in the population at sampling period i. $M_i - m_i$ are the marked animals not captured at time i, and R_i are the animals captured at time i, marked (if they do not already have a mark), and then released for possible recapture. Both z_i and r_i are animals from the groups $M_i - m_i$ and R_i, respectively, that are captured again at least once. Thus, r_i is the number of animals recaptured later from animals released at time i (i.e., R_i), and z_i is the number of animals captured before time i that are not recaptured at time i (i.e., they are members of $M_i - m_i$) but are recaptured during a subsequent capture session. The estimator of M_i is

$$\hat{M}_i = m_i + R_i z_i \: / \: r_i. \qquad (39)$$

Estimates of M_i are defined only for $i = 2, \ldots, K - 1$ sampling times. Seber (1982) presented approximately unbiased versions of these estimators and gave equations for variances and covariances.

The above estimators can be computed directly by program JOLLY (Pollock et al. 1990) (http://www.mbr-pwrc.usgs.gov/software.html). Program POPAN-5 (Arnason and Schwarz 1999) (http://www.cs.umanitoba.ca/~popan/) is based on a different approach to the Jolly–Seber model (Crosbie and Manly 1985, Schwarz and Arnason 1996). It includes estimation of the total number of individuals that are in the population at any time during the study, and from that computes N_i as defined above (plus survival rate and recruitment). To achieve this, one must make some assumptions about the values of parameters at the beginning and end of the study (Schwarz and Arnason 1996).

A concern when using the Jolly–Seber model is whether the equal probability of capture assumption can be met. Heterogeneity or trap response in capture probabilities can have a large effect on population size estimates because the sample ratio, m_i / n_i, will not accurately reflect the population ratio, M_i / N_i. Heterogeneity and some forms of trap response will also affect survival estimates to a lesser extent than population size estimates. This is because survival is estimated from ratios of only marked animals so that variation in capture probabilities tends to cancel out. In the case of a permanent trap response, survival estimates are not affected (Nichols et al. 1984*a*).

If assumption 5 holds, the animals occupying the study area and the population being assessed are equivalent. If there is movement in and out of the study area by the same individuals across periods (e.g., Fig. 8), the Jolly–Seber method is assessing the superpopulation that supplies animals to the study area (Kendall et al. 1997). If that movement is completely random (e.g., each member of the superpopulation has the same probability γ_i of being in the study area during sampling period i), then $\hat{N}_i$ is an unbiased estimator of the size of the superpopulation (Burnham 1993, Kendall et al. 1997). If the probability of being in the study area at time i depends on whether or not the animal was in the study area at time $i - 1$, then $\hat{N}_i$, as well as the Jolly–Seber estimates for other parameters of interest, will be biased (Kendall et al. 1997).

Extensions and Restrictions of the Jolly–Seber Model.—A variety of restricted versions of the Jolly–Seber model is available in the literature (Pollock et al. 1990). For populations in which births and immigration are negligible, a model that allows only for losses (deaths and emigration) may be useful (Darroch 1959, Jolly 1965). Darroch (1959) and Jolly (1965) also proposed a model for which only additions (births and immigration) are allowed. Other restricted models that are useful are constant survival and capture rate models described by Jolly (1982) and developed further by Brownie et al. (1986).

Generalizations of the Jolly–Seber model include allowing for a short-term effect of trapping on survival and capture rates (Robson 1969, Pollock 1975, Cormack 1981, Sandland and Kirkwood 1981, Brownie and Robson 1983, Lebreton et al. 1992, Pradel 1993). In addition, Buckland (1982) and Loery et al. (1987) described a cohort Jolly–Seber model for animals marked at a known age.

Other generalizations can be characterized as allowing for an animal to occupy one of a number of states. This state might be static, where the animal must remain in it for the duration of the study (e.g., male or female). Other states can be viewed as dynamic, where the animal can transition between states over time. For these dynamic states, transitions can be viewed as deterministic (obligatory) or probabilistic. Age is an example of a dynamic state with deterministic transitions. Pollock (1981a) and Stokes (1984) developed models with age-dependency in survival rate and capture probability for a specified number of age classes (e.g., 2 classes: juvenile and adult).

There are many possibilities for modeling individuals as occupying a dynamic state with probabilistic transitions. These could include size classes (e.g., as in stage-based projection models), location (e.g., as in metapopulation models), breeding status, etc. Arnason (1972, 1973), followed by Hestbeck et al. (1991), Brownie et al. (1993), Schwarz et al. (1993), and Nichols et al. (1994) developed multi-state capture–mark–recapture models that permit estimation of state-specific capture, survival, and transition probabilities, for the case where each state is sampled.

Further generalizations include allowing for some previously unmarked animals to be composed of a mixture of residents and transients (Pradel et al. 1997), whereas animals marked in previous periods are assumed to be residents. One can also allow for detection probability for an individual to be a function of one or more covariates (McDonald and Amstrup 2001).

Several computer programs can be used to estimate population size under these restrictions and generalizations of the Jolly–Seber model. Program JOLLY estimates population size for the case where survival or capture probabilities are constant over time, and JOLLYAGE permits 2 age classes (Pollock et al. 1990) (http://www.mbr-pwrc.usgs.gov/software.html). Program POPAN-5 (Arnason and Schwarz 1999) (http://www.cs.umanitoba.ca/~popan/) is flexible and estimates population size and other parameters for a variety of models.

An alternative approach is to estimate capture probability for a given period, and from that estimate N_i^s, the population size for a given state at time i, using the canonical approach described above:

$$\hat{N}_i^s = \frac{n_i^s}{\hat{p}_i^s}, \qquad (40)$$

where n_i^s and p_i^s are sample size and capture probability at time i for state S. Williams et al. (2002) outlined how this can be done for each type of model. For some of these models p_i^s can be estimated using programs SURGE (Pradel and Lebreton 1999) (http://www.phidot.org/software/surge/), MSSURVIV or TMSURVIV (http://www.mbr-pwrc.usgs.gov/software.html). Program MARK (White and Burnham 1999) (http://www.cnr.colostate.edu/~gwhite/software.html) will compute estimates of p_i^s under

any of these models. Although an expression for the approximate variance of $\hat{N}_i^s$ can be written, it involves cov $(n_i^s, \hat{p}_i^s)$, which is sometimes difficult to derive. A parametric bootstrap approach to variance estimation (Buckland and Garthwaite 1991) is often a good alternative.

Combination of Open and Closed Models-Pollock's Robust Design.—The distinction between open and closed populations is made to simplify the models used to estimate population parameters of interest. The simplifications are a result of assumptions that may or may not be met in field applications. Biologists must be aware of the assumptions that underlie these models and design studies that satisfy the assumptions as closely as possible.

Pollock (1982) was motivated by the desire to find a design for a long-term study that was robust to heterogeneity and/or trap response in capture probabilities. He proposed a design that combined both open and closed population models to exploit the advantages and minimize the shortcomings of both. For example, some closed-population models (e.g., CAPTURE models) relax the assumption of equal probability of capture, and the Jolly–Seber open-population model allows for changes in the size of the population. An experimental design in which short-term studies are used to estimate population size with closed population models, combined with Jolly–Seber open-population model estimates of survival in between the short-term studies, appears to be a robust design for many long-term field applications.

Kendall and Pollock (1992) confirmed the robustness of this method over the Jolly–Seber model alone. They also outlined several additional advantages of the robust design: population size and other parameters can be estimated for all time periods, density-dependent modeling of survival rate is more reasonable because there is little sampling correlation between $\hat{N}_i$ and $\hat{\phi}_i$, recruitment can be separated into immigration and births when there are only 2 age classes (also Nichols and Pollock 1990), and 2 levels of sampling adds another dimension to controlling sampling design. Kendall et al. (1995) placed the robust design into a formal model where within- and between-period information is used simultaneously to estimate parameters, permitting trap response (temporary or permanent) and time variation in capture probability, but not heterogeneity.

Kendall et al. (1997) discovered another advantage of the robust design; it permits estimation of the rate of movement in and out of the study area. Although the Jolly–Seber method purports to estimate population size in the study area, in the case of temporary emigration, it comes closer to estimating the size of the superpopulation from which the population in the study area is derived.

Estimation of Population Parameters.—Consider a capture–mark–recapture sampling study where we have K primary sampling periods, such as seasons or years (Fig. 9). Within each primary period i we have l_i secondary sampling periods over a short time, such as l_i consecutive days of trapping. Assuming the closure assumption applies to the animals in the study area over those l_i days of trapping, closed population models can be used to compute ($\hat{N}_i^{cl}$), which is the estimated size of the population in the study area for each primary sampling period ($N_1, N_2, ..., N_K$).

Further assume the probability of movement in and out of the study area between primary periods is completely random (i.e., each individual in the superpopulation is equally likely [γ_i] to be in the study area in period i), and there is no undescribed heterogeneity in capture probabilities. By pooling capture histories within each primary period into whether or not an animal was captured at all in that period, we can compute estimates under the Jolly–Seber model. Because the expected value of $\hat{p}_i^{JS}$ under this open model is the product of the probability an animal is available for capture and its probability of capture given availability ($\gamma_i p_i$), the expected value of $\hat{N}_i^{JS}$ under the Jolly–Seber model is N_i^0, the size of the superpopulation. The probability that an animal is not a temporary emigrant can be estimated as $\hat{\gamma}_i = \hat{p}_i^{JS} / \hat{p}_i^{cl}$ (Kendall et al. 1997).

When there is heterogeneity in capture probability within a primary period, estimation of parameters is more complicated. Kendall and Pollock (1992) provided alternatives for estimating ϕ_i and Kendall et al. (1997) described the estimation of γ_i. It is also necessary to estimate N_i^0 from $\hat{N}_i^{cl}$ and $\hat{\gamma}_i$:

$$\hat{N}_i^0 = \frac{\hat{N}_i^{cl}}{\hat{\gamma}_i} . \qquad (41)$$

The advantage of the ability to account for temporary emigration from the study area is evident when the movement has biological meaning. For example, when the study is conducted in areas where only breeders go (e.g., a nesting beach for sea turtles [Cheloniidae]), N_i represents the breeding component of the population, γ_i represents the probability that a member of the superpopulation is a breeder, and N_i^0 represents the size of the entire population (or at least the adult female component in the case of sea turtles). We illustrate a similar case for salamanders (Box 10). In this model $\hat{\phi}_i$ under the Jolly–Seber model is still unbiased as long as ϕ_i is the same for all animals in the superpopulation.

In addition to this ad hoc approach, programs RDSUR-VIV (Kendall and Hines 1999) (www.mbr-pwrc.usgs.gov/software.html) and MARK (White and Burnham 1999, Kendall 2001) can estimate availability, capture, and survival probabilities for all time periods simultaneously, except for the case of heterogeneity in capture probability. Program MARK will also estimate N_i using 1 of 2 options, whereas with RDSURVIV, N_i must be estimated as

$$\hat{N}_i = n_i / \hat{p}_i^*, \qquad (42)$$

where $\hat{p}_i^* = 1 - \prod_{j=1}^{l_i}(1 - \hat{p}_{ij})$

and p_{ij} is the probability that an animal is captured during secondary sampling occasion j of primary period i, given it is in the study area. The size of the superpopulation is estimated as in equation (41).

A recent extension of the robust design is to relax the closure assumption within primary periods to permit one entry into and one exit from (although no true birth or mortality) the study area (Schwarz and Stobo 1997, Kendall and Bjorkland 2001). Thus, within-season captures are modeled as a secondary Jolly–Seber model using the approach of Schwarz and Arnason (1996). Schwarz and Stobo (1997) estimated N_i directly, whereas with program ORDSURVIV (Kendall and Bjorkland 2001) (http://www.mbr-pwrc.usgs.gov/software.html), N_i is estimated as in equation (42), except the denominator is replaced by a function of entry, capture, and exit probabilities from the secondary sampling occa-

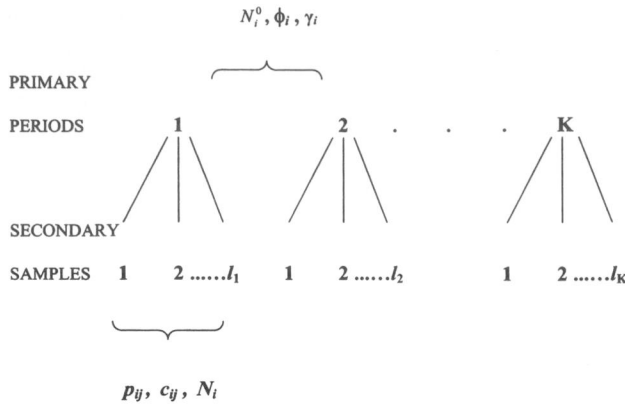

Fig. 9. The relationship between primary and secondary sampling periods in Pollock's robust design (after Pollock 1982), where N_i^0, ϕ_i, and γ_i are derived from information across primary periods, and p_{ij}, c_{ij}, and N_i are derived from information within a primary period.

sions. Under completely random movement, N_i^0 is estimated as in equation (41).

It may be more reasonable to assume the probability of being in the study area in any primary period is not completely random, but is dependent on whether the animal was in (γ_i') or out (γ_i'') of the study area in the previous primary period, as N_i can still be estimated. Detection, movement, and survival probabilities can be estimated using programs MARK, RDSURVIV or, when closure is relaxed, ORDSURVIV. However, unbiased estimation of the superpopulation can only occur if there is no recruitment or recruitment is directly to the study area and capture probability is 1.0 (W. L. Kendall, unpublished manuscript). This problem, combined with the requirement that survival rate must be the same in and out of the study area, underlines the disadvantage of a major component of the population being absent from the study area at any point in time. If a way can be found to observe these "unobservable" locations, multi-state models can be used and population size can be estimated based on equation (40).

An additional advantage recently developed for the robust design is to correct for mis-classifying an animal to the wrong state. For example, a female manatee is classified as a breeder when a first-year calf is observed with her. There is a chance the female will be observed but the calf will be missed (i.e., the detection probability of a calf is <1.0, even when the mother is observed). If missed at each encounter within a season, the mother would be mis-classified as a nonbreeder. Thus, state-specific abundance estimates based on equation (40) would be biased. Kendall et al. (2003) used observation histories of mothers and calves from 2 sampling occasions within a season to estimate the detection probability of a calf, given detection of the mother. This permits correction for the misclassification in a multistate model (with breeding status as the state).

INTEGRATED MODELING OF POPULATION DYNAMICS

Abundance is frequently the variable of interest in wildlife management. Thus, models of population dynamics have been developed that focus on population response to environmental conditions and especially to management

Box 10. An example of Pollock's Robust Design that combines both open and closed population models.

Bailey et al. (2004) trapped and marked plethodontid salamanders (Plethodontidae) in Great Smoky Mountains National Park in 1999–2001 using the robust design. The authors marked salamanders each year in each plot during 4 primary periods from early April to mid-June. The primary periods consisted of 3–4 consecutive days of trapping, and were separated by 6–10 days. Salamanders come to the surface to forage, but spend much of their time underground and are, therefore, unavailable for capture.

Primary period	Category	Secondary period (day)			
		1	2	3	4
1	Animals caught[a]	17	9	4	4
	Animals newly caught[b]	17	5	4	3
	Frequency[c]	24	5	0	0
2	Animals caught	8	5	2	5
	Animals newly caught	8	5	1	5
	Frequency	18	1	0	0
3	Animals caught	2	3	3	4
	Animals newly caught	2	3	3	3
	Frequency	10	1	0	0
4	Animals caught	5	0	1	1
	Animals newly caught	5	0	1	1
	Frequency	7	0	0	0

[a] Number of animals caught on each day of trapping.

[b] Number of animals caught for the first time within that primary period.

[c] Number of animals caught 1, 2, 3, or 4 times within that primary period.

Bailey et al. (2004) used program MARK to estimate parameters and select the best fitting models, using small sample AIC. The most parsimonious model included parameters that were constant over time. Models permitting temporary emigration from the study area (i.e., surface) fit better than models that ignored this movement, but Markovian emigration (i.e., probability of movement

dependent on presence/absence on the surface in the previous period) was not supported by the data. Because the study was sufficiently short within a given year, the authors assumed $\phi_i = 1$, and it was conducted when births were unlikely. Thus, the best-fitting model included a constant population size of 31 at the surface.

Rates of availability, $\gamma'(.)$ and $\gamma(.)$, and recapture probability, $c(..)$, were estimated for salamanders on one disturbed site in the Great Smoky Mountains National Park in 2001. In this case, $p(..)$ is considered conditional capture probability for Model 1 (random temporary emigration) and the Markovian model, and resembles an effective capture probability for Model 2 (no temporary emigration). $N(.)$ is interpreted as surface population for Model 1 and the Markovian model. Apparent survival rate is fixed at $\phi(.) = 1$ and all parameters are constant across primary sampling periods (from Bailey et al. 2004).

	Model 2 : $\gamma(.) = 1.0$[a]		Model 1: $\gamma(.)$[b]		Markovian, $\gamma'(.)$[c]	
Parameter	Est.	SE	Est.	SE	Est.	SE
$\gamma(.)$	0.08	0.03	0.09			0.04
$\gamma'(.)$					0.07	0.03
$p(..)$	0.02	0.01	0.44	0.06	0.44	0.06
$c(..)$	0.05	0.02	0.05	0.02	0.05	0.02
$N(.)$	209.10	67.36	30.06	1.07	30.06	1.07

[a] $\Delta AIC_c = 30.38$.

[b] $\Delta AIC_c = 0.0$.

[c] $\Delta AIC_c = 2.01$.

Using equation (41), they computed the size of the entire population, at and below the surface combined, as $\hat{N}/\hat{\gamma} = 30.06/0.08 = 375$ salamanders. Because MARK includes N_i as part of the likelihood, it provides an estimate of $cov(\hat{N}, \hat{\gamma})$, and they derived an approximate standard error for $\hat{N}^0 = 401.05$. This number is quite large in relation to $\hat{N}^0$, but not surprising given that only 8% of the animals were available for capture at any point in time.

actions. For example, if abundance at time i is estimated as $\hat{N}_i$, and if a specific management action is applied during the interval i to $i + 1$, what abundance, N_{i+1} would be expected at time $i + 1$?" All population change can be viewed as resulting from one or more of the 4 fundamental demographic parameters: mortality, reproduction, immigration, and emigration. Management actions must influence one or more of these parameters to bring about changes in abundance. In addition, development of population-dynamic models frequently requires estimates of demographic parameters (Dinsmore and Johnson 2005).

Pradel (1996) presented a parameterization of open-population capture–recapture models that permits direct estimation of the finite rate of population increase, $\lambda_i = \lambda(N_{i+1}/N_i)$. This parameterization is discussed further by Nichols and Hines (2002) and Williams et al. (2002) and can be viewed as an extension of abundance estimation. Lambda, λ_i, can be writ-

ten as a function of the fundamental demographic parameters. For example, assume an island population closed to movement, so that no emigration or immigration is possible. In the absence of age-specificity, if we define survival (ϕ_i) as the probability that an animal alive in period i is still alive in period $i + 1$, and reproductive recruitment (f_i) as the expected number of new recruits in year $i + 1$ produced by each animal in year i, we can write an expression for population change as:

$$N_{i+1} = N_i(\phi_i + f_i); \lambda_i = N_{i+1}/N_i = \phi_i + f_i. \quad (43)$$

Thus, the finite rate of population increase can be written as the sum of survival probability and expected reproductive recruitment. This relationship emphasizes the obvious point that information about the fundamental demographic parameters is relevant to abundance and changes in abundance and vice versa.

In cases where multiple data types are available, it may be possible to combine them in joint likelihoods that exploit the above relationship to obtain increased precision in estimates of abundance and demographic parameters (Nichols and Hines 2002, Williams et al. 2002). Consider a multi-year study in which a population is sampled by observation-based methods (e.g., distance sampling, multiple observer point counts, temporal removal point counts) for the purpose of estimating abundance and by open-population capture–mark–recapture methods to estimate survival rate and λ_i. In the usual case where the 2 data sets are independent, a joint likelihood can be developed by multiplying the 2 separate likelihoods (the observation-based model and the capture–recapture model). The usual parameterization for observation-based modeling requires detection probability parameters and either abundance, N_i or density, D_i. We suggest reparameterizing by including the initial abundance parameter, N_1, and then writing each subsequent abundance as:

$$N_i = N_1 \prod_{j=1}^{i-1} \lambda_j. \qquad (44)$$

We can substitute D_i for N_i in the above expression if the observation-based method yields density estimates directly (e.g., as with distance sampling [Buckland et al. 2001]). The λ_i are also parameters of the capture–recapture portion of the model and are shared by both portions of the likelihood. Thus, we acknowledge that both sources of information are relevant to population change and permit both sources to contribute to estimation of λ_i.

Multiple data sets can provide information about either abundance or fundamental demographic parameters. Combining these data with population-dynamic models permits different sources of information to contribute to the estimation. Several data sources permit independent estimation of λ_i but, in the general case, we might have a data source that contributes only to the estimation of a single demographic parameter (e.g., survival or reproduction). State-space models for projecting abundance as a function of demographic parameters can be combined with sampling models discussed in this chapter that directly link the data to parameters. Estimation under the resulting joint models can be accomplished by maximum likelihood (e.g., Besbeas et al. 2002, Gove et al. 2002), least squares (White and Lubow 2002), or using Bayesian approaches (e.g., Elliott and Little 2000, Millar and Meyer 2000, Trenkel et al. 2000). This general approach has been used for several years by fisheries scientists (e.g., Schnute 1994, Gallucci et al. 1996, Quinn and Deriso 1999) and is beginning to be used in wildlife investigations (Trenkel et al. 2000, Besbeas et al. 2002, Gove et al. 2002, White and Lubow 2002).

SELECTION AND COMPARISON OF METHODS

Although selection of a method is the first task a biologist has to consider, we have left this topic until all the methods were presented. We believe that a biologist must be aware of the breadth of options and the underlying assumptions before selecting a population estimation method.

Selection of a method for estimating population size involves both the probability of detection and sampling considerations (equation 4). The first sampling consideration is whether the area of interest is sufficiently large that sampling is required. When sampling is necessary, the investigator must make decisions about the size of the sample plots (or transects). These decisions will depend largely on logistical considerations associated with the method selected for solving detection concerns.

The number of sample plots, and hence the sampling proportion, α, must be decided. Here, as in all sampling problems, the investigator must balance the desirability of increased precision (the variance of the estimate decreases as α increases) with the costs of sampling. A sampling scheme must also be decided. If plot-to-plot variation in animal abundance is thought to be large, and if the investigator has (or can readily obtain) some *a priori* information about relative abundances over the entire study area, then stratified, random sampling will often be advisable. However, if there is no basis for stratification, then simple, random sampling will be the most reasonable approach. In some situations, logistical considerations or ancillary objectives involving distribution patterns may dictate a systematic, rather than a random sampling scheme. For relatively rare, clustered animals, adaptive cluster sampling approaches may prove useful (e.g., Thompson and Seber 1994, 1996). For multi-period samples of relatively rare organisms that tend to use the same areas over time, dual-frame sampling (Hartley 1962, 1974) may prove useful (e.g., Haines and Pollock 1998). We have not considered sampling approaches in detail because that goes beyond the scope of this chapter. We recommend Cochran (1977), Thompson (1992), Morrison et al. (2001), and Garton et al. (2005) for further information. Jolly (1969*a*,*b*), Jolly and Watson (1979), Hankin (1984), Hankin and Reeves (1988), Skalski and Robson (1992), Skalski (1994), Thompson and Seber (1994, 1996), Smith et al. (1996), Haines and Pollock (1998), and Buckland et al. (2001) discuss sampling issues for specific kinds of animal surveys. These discussions are relevant to problems of estimating animal abundance.

Although the investigator interested in estimating animal abundance can obtain guidance on sampling considerations from traditional statistical work on sampling problems (e.g., Cochran 1977), some sampling issues are peculiar to animal estimation problems. In particular, issues involving the interplay between sampling and probability of detection had received inadequate attention when the Lancia et al. (1994) chapter was prepared. This issue has been considered over the last decade (Skalski and Robson 1992, Thompson 1992, Skalski 1994, Pollock et al. 2002), but there is still great need for additional statistical research. Examination of our general expression for the variance of a population estimate (equation 5) shows that both sampling [$\text{var}(C)$] and probability of detection [$\text{var}(\hat{\beta})$] components are important determinants of precision. Because we face resource limitations, the tradeoffs between these components must be considered. Should, for example, α be increased at the expense of obtaining a smaller β estimated with less precision?

One issue associated with this tradeoff involves double sampling—the approach of obtaining a count statistic, C, on all sample plots, and then estimating detection probability, β, on a subset of these sample plots (see Thompson 1992, Pollock et al. 2002). On a given plot, estimation of β is typically more expensive in time, effort, and money than obtaining the count statistic. Therefore, an obvious question is: on how many sample plots must β be estimated? In many cases, the precision of β on a sample plot is a function of effort expended on its estimation; thus, another question involves how much effort to expend on each sample plot. Extremely useful considerations of expenditure of effort in double sampling problems for animal populations have been presented by Jolly (1969a,b) and Jolly and Watson (1979) for aerial survey work, Hankin (1984) and Hankin and Reeves (1988) for stream fish surveys, and Skalski (1985a,b) for capture–recapture surveys (with a small mammal example). Despite different specific examples considered by these authors, a common conclusion involves the importance of geographic variation among sample plots relative to variation associated with estimation of β within plots. Skalski (1985a,b), Skalski and Robson (1992), and Pollock et al. (2002) considered the development of cost functions as a means of exploring optimal sampling designs. We believe this work is extremely important and merits much more attention.

In cases where all animals can be observed, total counts (either on sample plots or on the entire study area) are recommended. It is our experience, however, that even the most visible animals in the most open habitat can seldom be detected with probability 1.0, and we strongly recommend that investigators intending to use total counts first test the hypothesis that $\beta = 1.0$.

In situations involving large areas and animals that are observable from the air, aerial surveys provide an excellent means of counting animals and obtaining C. Of several methods for estimating β in conjunction with aerial surveys, we do not recommend an obvious "front runner." In different situations they all have limitations and advantages. Where total ground counts are possible, the double sampling approach of estimating β from ground counts on a subset of sample plots should be useful. However, we emphasize that this method depends on the detection of all animals in ground counts and that this assumption should be tested. Use of a marked subpopulation also enables estimation of β from aerial surveys, although the requirements of this approach will prohibit its use in many situations. Implementation depends upon whether the number of marked animals available to be counted is known. If so, the methods of Bartmann et al. (1987), White and Garrott (1990), White (1993), and Neal et al. (1993) can be used. Unknown numbers of marked animals with multiple observation surveys require use of the approach developed by Arnason et al. (1991).

Methods involving development of a probability of detection model show good promise for use with mobile animals. Although model development could be expensive, subsequent use of the model involves little work in addition to the actual counting. For this reason, we believe this approach will be especially useful in operational management surveys. The greatest potential problem is that conditions affecting detection probability when the model was developed may differ from those affecting detection probability when the model is applied.

Finally, counts from repeated surveys of the same sampling units contain information about abundance in the case of populations closed to gains and losses between surveys. Modeling and estimation using such data are new and topics of active research (Royle and Nichols 2003; J. A. Royle,

personal communication; K. H. Pollock, personal commuication). Projected applications include aerial surveys of waterfowl and ground surveys of waterfowl broods.

When aerial surveys are not used, but when animals are readily visible from the ground, "distance sampling methods" (e.g., line and point transects) provide a rigorous means of estimating density and population size. Line transect methods should be useful for highly visible animals inhabiting relatively open habitat. The primary limitations are (1) the assumption that all animals on the line are seen and (2) the practicality of measuring or estimating perpendicular distances from the line to observed animals. Line transects are useful for estimating population size in many circumstances.

Point transects have been used extensively in bird population surveys. The main advantages of point transects over line transects are increased safety and ease of use in rough terrain, decreased chance of missing animals close to the observer, and increased ability to define habitat variables associated with each observation station. The relative disadvantages are that less area is covered (and sample size is often reduced), and the opportunity to count animals more than once is greater. Point transects were developed for use in structurally complex vegetation, but in these situations it may be difficult to accurately record distances, especially when birds are identified only by song or call. However, use of the method in extensive surveys of Hawaiian birds (Mountainspring and Scott 1985, Scott et al. 1986) provides a good demonstration of its utility. In situations where distance measurement is sufficiently difficult to preclude reasonable use of distance sampling methods, multiple observer approaches and time of detection modeling may be useful for avian point count data. Recent advances include the development of models that use multiple sources of information (e.g., distance and time of first detection) to estimate detection probability and hence abundance and density.

When animals are readily observable, observation-based methods are generally preferred. Managers and biologists have generally recognized this and have tended to use observation-based methods for estimating population size of birds and large mammals. However, other smaller and more secretive vertebrates and most invertebrates are not readily observed. For these animals, capture–mark–recapture and removal methods will frequently be the most reasonable means of estimating population size.

When population size is the only parameter of interest, capture–mark–recapture studies should be conducted over a short period of time (e.g., trapping small mammals on a grid for 5 consecutive days) thereby increasing the likelihood that the population is closed to gains and losses of animals over the study period. Closure is desirable because a variety of available closed, capture–mark–recapture models permit various sources of variation in capture probability. If tests indicate failure of the closure assumption, then partially and completely open models could be used. Studies involving several (>4) different capture periods are desirable because tests of assumptions about closure and variation in capture probability can be made. These tests then lead to selection of the most appropriate model to fit the data.

Historically, 2-sample capture–mark–recapture studies have been popular, relying on the Lincoln–Petersen estimator. However, data from 2-sample studies (i.e., 2 trapping occasions) are not adequate to test the assumptions on which the method is based. However, if the recapture (or reobservation) method is different from, and independent of, the initial capture method, the 2-sample capture–mark–recapture method is recommended. Different capture and recapture methods were used in both of our examples (Box 7) of the Lincoln–Petersen estimator. In such situations, heterogeneous capture probabilities and trap response are not likely to present problems, and resulting estimates should be reasonable.

In many investigations of animal population dynamics, the investigator will be interested in periodic estimates not only of population size, but also survival and recruitment rates. Open capture–mark–recapture models can be used to estimate gains and losses to the population. For long-term, capture–mark–recapture studies of animal population dynamics, we recommend the combined use of closed and open models (i.e., Pollock's [1982] Robust Design). This design enables estimation of population size with a variety of flexible, closed population models. Survival rate is then estimated with capture–recapture data for the primary sampling periods, and recruitment is estimated from these population size and survival estimates. The incorporation of these modeling approaches in a single model (e.g., Kendall et al. 1995, 1997) permits flexible modeling and efficient estimation. This design offers great potential for studying long-term population dynamics.

For species heavily exploited by hunting, trapping, or other means of population reduction, removal methods might be useful for estimating population size. These methods require data on the numbers of animals removed and lend themselves to application in controlled, local situations such as deer hunting on a management area, trapping a specific marsh, etc., in which harvested animals are brought through check stations or otherwise tallied. Statistics reflecting "effort," for example the number of hunters per unit of time, the number of trap-nights, the number of animals seen per unit of time, etc., are also frequently available in these controlled situations, permitting use of catch-effort models and, perhaps, the special-case, constant-effort removal models. Catch-effort models have been used extensively in fisheries applications and we believe they offer potential for use in wildlife studies associated with closely monitored harvests.

If exploitation in controlled situations is likely to be selective for different types of animals (e.g., antlered-bucks-only deer hunting, size–selective alligator hunting), then change-in-ratio methods could be useful. These methods require additional surveys to estimate the proportions of the different types of animals in the population. When the different types of animals are equally observable in these ancillary surveys, then only 2 surveys are necessary—one before and one after the removal period. When detection probabilities of the different types are not equal, other approaches can be used such as single-type removals, the 2-stage change-in-ratio, or direct estimation of detection probabilities and "correction" of the standard change-in-ratio technique. We doubt that change-in-ratio methods will have the general applicability of catch-effort models, but they do seem to offer good potential in some special cases of controlled, selective exploitation.

It makes no sense to speak of a single, "best" method for estimating population size. If we believed that one method was universally preferable, this chapter would be considerably shorter. Rather, virtually all the methods are useful in certain situations. Selection of the most reasonable method will depend upon details of the particular situation. These details, which must come from a wildlife biologist or manager, include information on the biology and habits of the animal species under study. In addition, because of the variety and complexity of methods available for estimating animal population size, a statistician or quantitative population biologist should be consulted.

Our goal has been to provide biologists and managers with a sufficient understanding of the concepts underlying population estimation methods to enable useful dialog between them and a statistician. This dialogue is essential, not only to method selection (and frequently tailoring the method to a particular set of circumstances), but also to study design. We believe this collaboration will become more common and will lead to a better understanding of animal populations.

SUMMARY

Estimating the abundance or density of animals in wild populations is not a trivial matter. Virtually all techniques involve the basic problem of estimating the probability of seeing, capturing, or otherwise detecting animals during some type of survey and, in many cases, sampling concerns as well. In the case of indices, the detection probability is assumed to be constant (but unknown). We caution against use of indices unless this assumption can be verified for the comparison(s) of interest. In the case of population estimation, many methods have been developed over the years to estimate the probability of detection associated with various kinds of count statistics (Figs. 3, 7). Techniques range from complete counts, where sampling concerns often dominate, to incomplete counts where detection probabilities are also important. Some examples of the latter are multiple observers, removal methods, and capture–recapture.

Before embarking on a survey to estimate the size of a population, one must understand clearly what information is needed and for what purpose the information will be used. The key to deriving population abundance estimates is to choose a method that fits a particular application. If necessary, techniques can be adapted to meet a particular need. Generally, a biometrician familiar with population estimation literature should be consulted

ACKNOWLEDGMENTS

We acknowledge the multitude of individuals who have grappled with population estimation over many generations and who have contributed to the development of this important field of wildlife biology. Jon D. Klimstra helped check literature citations. Thomas J. Maier contributed to the section on trapping webs, and Gary C. White provided helpful suggestions on an early draft of the manuscript.

LITERATURE CITED

AKAIKE, H. 1973. Information theory and extension of the maximum likelihood principle. Pages 267–281 *in* B. N. Petrou and F. Csaki, editors. Second international symposium on information theory. Akadeemiai Kiadi, Budapest, Hungary.

ALHO, J. M. 1990. Logistic regression in capture–recapture models. Biometrics 46:623–635.

ALLEN, S. H., AND A. B. SARGEANT. 1975. A rural mail-carrier index of North Dakota red foxes. Wildlife Society Bulletin 3:74–77.

ALPIZAR-JARA, R., AND K. H. POLLOCK. 1996. A combination line transect and capture–recapture sampling model for multiple observers in aerial surveys. Environmental Ecology and Statistics 3:311–327.

ANDERSON, D. R. 1975. Population ecology of the mallard. V. Temporal and geographic estimates of survival, recovery and harvest rates. U.S. Department of the Interior, Fish and Wildlife Service, Resource Publication 125.

———. 2001. The need to get the basics right in wildlife field studies. Wildlife Society Bulletin 29:1294–1297.

———, AND R. S. POSPAHALA. 1970. Correction of bias in belt transect studies of immotile objects. Journal of Wildlife Management 34:141–146.

———, K. P. BURNHAM, G. C. WHITE, AND D. L. OTIS. 1983. Density estimation of small-mammal populations using a trapping web and distance sampling methods. Ecology 64:674–680.

———, B. C. LUBOW, L. THOMAS, P. S. CORN, P. A. MEDICA, AND R. W. MARLOW. 2001. Field trials of line transect methods applied to estimation of desert tortoise abundance. Journal of Wildlife Management 65:583–597.

ARNASON, A. N. 1972. Parameter estimates from mark–recapture experiments on two populations subject to migration and death. Researches on Population Ecology 13:97–113.

———. 1973. The estimation of population size, migration rates, and survival in a stratified population. Researches on Population Ecology 15:1–8.

———, AND C. J. SCHWARZ. 1999. Using POPAN-5 to analyse banding data. Bird Study 46:S157–168.

———, ———, AND J. M. GERRARD. 1991. Estimating closed population size and number of marked animals from sighting data. Journal of Wildlife Management 55:716–730.

BAILEY, L. L, T. R. SIMONS, AND K. H. POLLOCK. 2004. Estimating detection probability parameters for plethodon salamanders using the robust capture–recapture design. Journal of Wildlife Management 68:1–13.

BAJZAK, D., AND J. F. PIATT. 1990. Computer-aided procedure for counting waterfowl on aerial photographs. Wildlife Society Bulletin 18:125–129.

BARKER, R. J., AND J. R. SAUER. 1992. Modeling population change from time series data. Pages 182–194 in D. R. McCullough and R. H. Barrett, editors. Wildlife 2001: populations. Elsevier Scientific Publishers, London, United Kingdom.

BART, J., AND S. EARNST. 2002. Double sampling to estimate density and population trends in birds. Auk 119: 36-45.

———, AND J. D. SCHOULTZ. 1984. Reliability of singing bird surveys: changes in observer efficiency with avian density. Auk 101:307–318.

BARTMANN, R. M., G. C. WHITE, L. H. CARPENTER, AND R. A. GARROTT. 1987. Aerial mark–recapture estimates of confined mule deer in pinyon–juniper woodland. Journal of Wildlife Management 51:41–46.

BASKETT, T. S., M. J. ARMBRUSTER, AND M. W. SAYRE. 1978. Biological perspectives for the mourning dove call-count survey. Transactions of the North American Wildlife and Natural Resources Conference 43:163–180.

BESBEAS, P., S. N. FREEMAN, B. J. T. MORGAN, AND E. A. CATCHPOLE. 2002. Integrating mark–recapture–recovery and census data to estimate animal abundance and demographic parameters. Biometrics 58:540–547.

BEST, L. B. 1975. Interpretational errors in the "mapping method" as a census technique. Auk 92:452–460.

BIBBY, C. J., N. D. BURGESS, D. A. HILL, AND S. MUSTOE. 2000. Bird census techniques. Second edition. Academic Press, London, United Kingdom.

BISHIR, J. W., AND R. A. LANCIA. 1996. On catch-effort methods of estimating animal abundance. Biometrics 52:1457–1466.

BJØRNSTAD, O. N., AND B. T. GRENFELL. 2001. Noisy clockwork: time series analysis of population fluctuations in animals. Science 293:638–643.

———, J.-M. FROMENTIN, N. C. STENSETH, AND J. GJØSAETER. 1999. Cycles and trends in cod populations. Proceedings of the National Academy of Science 96:5066–5071.

BONTAITES, K. M., K. A. GUSTAFSON, AND R. MAKIN. 2000. A Gasaway-type moose survey in New Hampshire using infrared thermal imagery: preliminary results. Alces 36:69–75.

BORCHERS, D. L., W. ZUCCHINI, AND R. M. FEWSTER. 1998a. Mark–recapture models for line transect surveys. Biometrics 54:1207–1220.

———, S. T. BUCKLAND, P. W. GOEDHART, E. D. CLARKE, AND S. L. HEDLEY. 1998b. Horvitz-Thompson estimators for double-platform line transect surveys. Biometrics 54:1221–1237.

BOWDEN, D. C., AND R. C. KUFELD. 1995. Generalized mark-sight population size estimation applied to Colorado moose. Journal of Wildlife Management 59:840–851.

BOULANGER, J., AND B. MCLELLAN. 2001. Closure violation in DNA-based mark-recapture estimation of grizzly bear populations. Canadian Journal of Zoology 78:642–651.

BOYCE, M. S., D. I. MACKENZIE, B. F. J. MANLY, M. A. HAROLDSON, AND D. MOODY. 2001. Negative binomial models for abundance estimation of multiple closed populations. Journal of Wildlife Management 65:498–509.

BROWNIE, C., AND D. S. ROBSON. 1983. Estimation of time-specific survival rates from tag–resighting samples: a generalization of the Jolly–Seber model. Biometrics 39:437–453.

———, J. E. HINES, AND J. D. NICHOLS. 1986. Constant-parameter capture–recapture models. Biometrics 42:561–574.

———, ———, K. H. POLLOCK, AND J. B. HESTBECK. 1993. Capture–recapture studies for multiple strata including non-Markovian transition probabilities. Biometrics 49:1173–1187.

BUCKLAND, S. T. 1982. A mark–recapture survival analysis. Journal of Animal Ecology 51:833–847.

———. 1987. On the variable circular plot method of estimating animal density. Biometrics 43:363–384.

———, AND P. H. GARTHWAITE. 1991. Quantifying precision of mark–recapture estimates using the bootstrap and related methods. Biometrics 47:255–268.

———, K. P. BURNHAM, AND N. H. AUGUSTIN. 1997. Model selection: an integral part of inference. Biometrics 53:603–618.

———, D. R. ANDERSON, K. P. BURNHAM, AND J. L. LAAKE. 1993. Distance sampling: estimating abundance of biological populations. Chapman and Hall, New York, USA.

———, ———, ———, D. L. BORCHERS, AND L. THOMAS. 2001. Introduction to distance sampling: estimating abundance of biological populations. Oxford University Press, Oxford, United Kingdom.

BULL, E. L. 1981. Indirect estimates of abundance of birds. Studies in Avian Biology 6:76–80.

BURGER, A. E. 2001. Using radar to estimate populations and assess habitat associations of marbled murrelets. Journal of Wildlife Management 65:696–715.

BURNHAM, K. P. 1972. Estimation of population size in multiple capture–recapture studies when capture probabilities vary among animals. Dissertation. Oregon State University, Corvallis, USA.

———. 1981. Summarizing remarks: environmental influences. Studies in Avian Biology 6:324–325.

———. 1993. A theory for combined analysis of ring recovery and recapture data. Pages 199–213 in J. D. Lebreton and P. M. North, editors. Marked individuals in the study of bird populations. Birkhäuser Verlag, Basel, Switzerland.

———, AND D. R. ANDERSON. 1976. Mathematical models for nonparametric inferences from line transect data. Biometrics 32:325–336.

———, AND ———. 1998. Model selection and inference: a practical information–theoretic approach. Springer-Verlag, Inc., New York, USA.

———, AND ———. 2002. Model selection and inference: a practical information–theoretic approach. Second edition. Springer-Verlag, Inc., New York, USA.

———, AND W. S. OVERTON. 1978. Estimation of the size of a closed population when capture probabilities vary among animals. Biometrika 65:625–633.

———, AND ———. 1979. Robust estimation of population size when capture probabilities vary among animals. Ecology 60:927–936.

———, D. R. ANDERSON, AND J. L. LAAKE. 1980. Estimation of density from line transect sampling of biological populations. Wildlife Monographs 72.

———, ———, G. C. WHITE, C. BROWNIE, AND K. H. POLLOCK. 1987. Design and analysis of methods for fish survival experiments based on release–recapture. Monograph 5. American Fisheries Society, Bethesda, Maryland, USA.

CALHOUN, J. B. 1948. North American census of small mammals. Rodent Ecology Program Release 1. Johns Hopkins University, Baltimore, Maryland, USA.

CARBONE, C., CHRISTIE, K. CONFORTI, T. COULSON, N. FRANKLIN, J. R. GINSBERG, M. GRIFFITHS, J. HOLDEN, K. KAWANISHI, M. KINNAIRD, R. LAIDLAW, A. LYNAM, D. W. MCDONALD, D. MARTYR, C. MCDOUGAL, L. NATH, T. O'BRIEN, J. SEIDENSTICKER, D. J. L. SMITH, M. SUNQUIST, R. TILSON, AND W. N. W. SHAHRUDDIN. 2001. The use of photographic rates to estimate densities of tigers and other cryptic mammals. Animal Conservation 4:75–79.

CASWELL, H., M. FUJIWARA, AND S. BRAULT. 1999. Declining survival probability threatens the North Atlantic right whale. Proceedings of the National Academy of Science 96:3308–3313.

CAUGHLEY, G. 1977. Analysis of vertebrate populations. John Wiley and Sons, New York, USA.

———, AND D. GRICE. 1982. A correction factor for counting emus from the air and its application to counts in western Australia. Australian Wildlife Research 9:253–259.

———, R. SINCLAIR, AND D. SCOTT-KEMMIS. 1976. Experiments in aerial survey. Journal of Wildlife Management 40:290–300.

CHABRECK, R. H. 1966. Methods of determining the size and composition of alligator populations in Louisiana. Proceedings of the Annual Conference of the Southeastern Association of Game and Fish Commissioners 20:105–112.

———. 1973. Population status surveys of the American alligator in the southeastern United States. Pages 14-21 *in* Crocodiles. IUCN Publication New Series Supplement 41. Gland, Switzerland.

CHAO, A. 1988. Estimating animal abundance with capture frequency data. Journal of Wildlife Management 52:295–300.

———. 1989. Estimating population size for sparse data in capture–recapture experiments. Biometrics 45:427–438.

———. 2001. An overview of closed capture–recapture models. Journal of Agricultural, Biological, and Environmental Statistics 6:158–175.

———, AND R. M. HUGGINS. 2005. Modern closed population models. *In* B. F. J. Manly, T. McDonald, and S. Amstrup, editors. Handbook of capture–recapture methods. Princeton University Press, Princeton, New Jersey, USA.

———, AND S.-M. LEE. 1992. Estimating the number of classes via sample coverage. Journal of the American Statistical Association 87: 210–217.

———, W.-T. CHU, AND C.-H. HSU. 2000. Capture–recapture when time and behavioral response affect capture probabilities. Biometrics 56:427–433.

———, S.-M. LEE, AND S. L. JENG. 1992. Estimating population size for capture–recapture data when capture probabilities vary by time and individual animal. Biometrics 48:201–216.

———, P. S. F. YIP, S.-M. LEE, AND W.-T. CHU. 2001. Population size estimation based on estimating functions for closed capture–recapture models. Journal of Statistical Planning and Inference 92:213–232.

CHAPMAN, D. G. 1951. Some properties of the hypergeometric distribution with applications to zoological censuses. University of California Publications in Statistics 1 (7):131–159.

———. 1954. The estimation of biological populations. Annals of Mathematical Statistics 25:1–15.

———. 1980. Review of statistical inference from capture data on closed animal populations. Biometrics 36:362.

CLARK, W. R. 1987. Effects of harvest on annual survival of muskrats. Journal of Wildlife Management 51:265–272.

COCHRAN, G. A., AND H. J. STAINS. 1961. Deposition and decomposition of fecal pellets by cottontails. Journal of Wildlife Management 25:432–435.

COCHRAN, W. G. 1977. Sampling techniques. Third edition. John Wiley and Sons, New York, USA.

COLLAZO, J. A., AND G. BONILLA-MARTINEZ. 2001. Population size, survival and movements of white-cheeked pintails in eastern Puerto Rico. Caribbean Journal of Science 37:194–201.

CONNER, M. C., R. F. LABISKY, AND D. R. PROGULSKE, JR. 1983. Scent-station indices as measures of population abundance for bobcats, raccoons, gray foxes, and opossums. Wildlife Society Bulletin 11:146–152.

———, R. A. LANCIA, AND K. H. POLLOCK. 1986. Precision of the change-in-ratio technique for deer population management. Journal of Wildlife Management 50:125–129.

CONNOLLY, G. E. 1981. Assessing populations. Pages 287–345 *in* O. C. Wallmo, editor. Mule and black-tailed deer of North America. University of Nebraska Press, Lincoln, USA.

CONROY, M. J. 1996. Abundance indices. Pages 179–192 *in* D. E. Wilson, F. R. Cole, J. D. Nichols, R. Rudran, and M. S. Foster, editors. Measuring and monitoring biological diversity: standard methods for mammals. Smithsonian Institution Press, Washington, D.C., USA.

———, AND J. D. NICHOLS. 1996. Designing a study to assess mammalian diversity. Pages 41–49 *in* D. E. Wilson, F. R. Cole, J. D. Nichols, R. Rudran, and M. S. Foster, editors. Measuring and monitoring biological diversity: standard methods for mammals. Smithsonian Institution Press, Washington, D.C., USA.

COOK, R. D., AND J. O. JACOBSON. 1979. A design for estimating visibility bias in aerial surveys. Biometrics 35:735–742.

CORDTS, S. D., G. G. ZENNER, AND R. R. KOFORD. 2002. Comparison of helicopter and ground counts for waterfowl in Iowa. Wildlife Society Bulletin 30:317–326.

CORMACK, R. M. 1973. Common sense estimates from capture–recapture studies. Pages 225–234 *in* M. S. Bartlett and R. W. Hiorns, editors. The mathematical theory of the dynamics of biological populations. Academic Press, New York, USA.

———. 1979. Models for capture–recapture. Pages 217–255 *in* R. M. Cormack, G. P. Patil, and D. S. Robson, editors. Sampling biological populations. Volume 5. Statistical Ecology Series, International Cooperative Publishing House, Fairland, Maryland, USA.

———. 1981. Loglinear models for capture–recapture experiments on open populations. Pages 217–235 *in* R. W. Hiorns and D. Cooke, editors. The mathematical theory of the dynamics of biological populations. II. Academic Press, New York, USA.

CORN, J. L., AND M. J. CONROY. 1998. Estimation of density of mongooses with capture–recapture and distance sampling. Journal of Mammalogy 79:1009–1015.

CRAIG, B. A., M. A. NEWTON, R. A. GARROTT, J. E. REYNOLDS, III, AND J. R. WILCOX. 1997. Analysis of aerial survey data on Florida manatee using Markov Chain Monte Carlo. Biometrics 53:524–541.

CREEL, S., G. SPONG, J. L. SANDS, J. ROTELLA, J. ZEIGLE, L. JOE, K. M. MURPHY, AND D. SMITH. 2003. Population size estimation in Yellowstone wolves with error-prone noninvasive microsatellite genotypes. Molecular Ecology 12:2003–2009.

CROSBIE, S. F., AND B. F. J. MANLY. 1985. Parsimonious modeling of capture–mark–recapture studies. Biometrics 41:385–398.

DARROCH, J. N. 1959. The multiple recapture census. II. Estimation when there is immigration or death. Biometrika 46:336–351.

DEYOUNG, C. A., F. S. GUTHERY, S. L. BEASOM, S. P. COUGHLIN, AND J. R. HEFFELFINGER. 1989. Improving estimates of white-tailed deer abundance from helicopter surveys. Wildlife Society Bulletin 17:275–279.

DICE, L. R. 1938. Some census methods for mammals. Journal of Wildlife Management 2:119–130.

———. 1941. Methods for estimating populations of mammals. Journal of Wildlife Management 5:398–407.

DIEFENBACH, D. R., M. J. CONROY, R. J. WARREN, W. E. JAMES, L. A. BAKER, AND T. HON. 1994. A test of the scent-station technique for bobcats. Journal of Wildlife Management 58:10–17.

DINSMORE, S. J., AND D. H. JOHNSON. 2005. Population analysis in wildlife biology. Pages 154–184 *in* C. E. Braun, editor. Techniques for wildlife investigations and management. Sixth edition. The Wildlife Society, Bethesda, Maryland, USA.

DOLTON, D. D. 1993. Call-count survey: historical development and current procedures. Pages 233–252 *in* T. S. Baskett, M. W. Sayre, R. E. Tomlinson, and R. E. Mirarchi, editors. Ecology and management of the mourning dove. Stackpole Books, Harrisburg, Pennsylvania, USA.

DOWNING, R. L., W. H. MOORE, AND J. KIGHT. 1965. Comparison of deer census techniques applied to a known population in a Georgia enclosure. Proceedings of the Annual Conference of the Southeastern Association of Fish and Wildlife Commissioners 19:26–30.

DOZIER, H. L., M. H. MARKLEY, AND L. M. LLEWELLYN. 1948. Muskrat investigations on the Blackwater National Wildlife Refuge, Maryland, 1941–1945. Journal of Wildlife Management 12:177–190.

DRUMMER, T. D., AND L. L. MCDONALD. 1987. Size bias in line transect sampling. Biometrics 43:13–21.

DUPONT, W. D. 1983. A stochastic catch-effort method for estimating animal abundance. Biometrics 39:1021–1033.

DWYER, T. J., G. F. SEPIK, E. L. DERLETH, AND D. G. MCAULEY. 1988. Demographic characteristics of a Maine woodcock population and effects of habitat management. U.S. Department of the Interior, Fish and Wildlife Service, Wildlife Research 4. Washington, D.C., USA.

EBERHARDT, L. L. 1978. Appraising variability in population studies. Journal of Wildlife Management 42:207–238.

———, AND M. A. SIMMONS. 1987. Calibrating population indices by double sampling. Journal of Wildlife Management 51:665–675.

———, AND R. C. VAN ETTEN. 1956. Evaluation of the pellet group count as a deer census method. Journal of Wildlife Management 20:70–74.

———, D. G. CHAPMAN, AND J. R. GILBERT. 1979. A review of marine mammal census methods. Wildlife Monographs 63.

ELLIOTT, M. R., AND R. J. A. LITTLE. 2000. A Bayesian approach to combining information from a census, a coverage measurement survey, and demographic analysis. Journal of the American Statistical Association 95:351–362.

ESTES, J. A., AND R. J. JAMESON. 1988. A double-survey estimate for sighting probability of sea otters in California. Journal of Wildlife Management 52:70–76.

FARNSWORTH, G. L., K. H. POLLOCK, J. D. NICHOLS, T. R. SIMONS, J. E. HINES, AND J. R. SAUER. 2002. A removal model for estimating detection probabilities from point–count surveys. Auk 119:414–425.

FUJIWARA, M., AND H. CASWELL. 2001. Demography of the endangered North Atlantic right whale. Nature 414:537–541.

FULLER, M. R., AND J. A. MOSHER. 1981. Methods of detecting and counting raptors: a review. Studies in Avian Biology 6:235–246.

FULLER, T. K. 1991. Do pellet counts index white-tailed deer numbers and population change? Journal of Wildlife Management 55:393–396.

GALLUCCI, V. F., S. B. SAILA, D. J. GUSTAFSON, AND B. J. ROTHSCHILD, editors. 1996. Stock assessment: quantitative methods and applications for small-scale fisheries. CRC/Lewis Publishers, New York, USA.

GANTER, B., AND J. MADSEN. 2001. An examination of methods to estimate population size in wintering geese. Bird Study 48:90–101.

GARTON, E. O., J. T. RATTI, AND J. H. GIUDICE. 2005. Research and experimental design. Pages 43–71 in C. E. Braun, editor. Techniques for wildlife investigations and management. Sixth edition. The Wildlife Society, Bethesda, Maryland, USA.

GAVIN, T. A. 1989. What's wrong with the questions we ask in wildlife research? Wildlife Society Bulletin 17:345–351.

GEISSLER, P. H., AND J. R. SAUER. 1990. Topics in route-regression analysis. Pages 54–57 in J. R. Sauer and S. Droege, editors. Survey designs and statistical methods for the estimation of avian population trends. U.S. Department of the Interior, Fish and Wildlife Service, Biological Report 90(1).

GILL, R. M. A., M. L. THOMAS, AND D. STOCKER. 1997. The use of portable thermal imaging for estimating deer population density in forest habitats. Journal of Applied Ecology 34:1273–1286.

GOVE, N. E., J. R. SKALSKI, P. ZAGER, AND R. L. TOWNSEND. 2002. Statistical models for population reconstruction using age-at-harvest data. Journal of Wildlife Management 66:310–320.

GRIER, J. W., J. M. GERRARD, G. D. HAMILTON, AND P. A. GRAY. 1981. Aerial-visibility bias and survey techniques for nesting bald eagles in northwestern Ontario. Journal of Wildlife Management 45:83–92.

HAINES, D. E., AND K. H. POLLOCK. 1998. Estimating the number of active and successful bald eagle nests: an application of the dual frame method. Environmental and Ecological Statistics 5:245–256.

HANKIN, D. G. 1984. Multistage sampling designs in fisheries research: application in small streams. Canadian Journal of Fisheries and Aquatic Sciences 41:1575–1591.

———, AND G. H. REEVES. 1988. Estimating total fish abundance and total habitat area in small streams based on visual estimation methods. Canadian Journal of Fisheries and Aquatic Sciences 45:834–844.

HARAMIS, G. M., J. R. GOLDSBERRY, D. G. MCAULEY, AND E. L. DERLETH. 1985. An aerial photographic census of Chesapeake Bay and North Carolina canvasbacks. Journal of Wildlife Management 49:449–454.

HAROLDSON, B. S., E. P. WIGGERS, J. BERINGER, L. P. HANSEN, AND J. B. MCANINCH. 2004. Evaluation of aerial thermal imaging for detecting white-tailed deer in a deciduous forest environment. Wildlife Society Bulletin 31:1188–1197.

HARTLEY, H. O. 1962. Multiple frame surveys. Pages 203–206 in Proceedings of the Social Statistics Section, American Statistical Association, Minneapolis, Minnesota, USA.

———. 1974. Multiple frame methodology and selected applications. Sankhya (The Indian Journal of Statistics) 36:99–118.

HAY, K. G. 1958. Beaver census methods in the Rocky Mountain region. Journal of Wildlife Management 22:395–402.

HEIN, E. W., AND W. F. ANDELT. 1995. Estimating coyote density from mark–resight surveys. Journal of Wildlife Management 59:164–169.

HENNY, C. J., M. A. BYRD, J. A. JACOBS, P. D. MCLAIN, M. R. TODD, AND B. F. HALLA. 1977. Mid-Atlantic coast osprey population: present numbers, productivity, pollutant contamination, and status. Journal of Wildlife Management 41:254–265.

HESTBECK, J. B., J. D. NICHOLS, AND R. A. MALECKI. 1991. Estimates of movement and site fidelity using mark–resight data of wintering Canada geese. Ecology 72:523–533.

HEYER, W. R., M. A. DONNELLY, R. W. MCDIARMID, L. C. HAYEK, AND M. S. FOSTER, editors. 1993. Measuring and monitoring biological diversity: standard methods for amphibians. Smithsonian Institution Press, Washington, D.C., USA.

HIBY, L., AND P. LOVELL. 1991. DUNGSURV—a program for estimating elephant density from dung density without assuming "steady state." Pages 73–80 in U. Ramakrishnan, J. A. Santosh, and R. Sukumar, editors. Proceedings of the Workshop for Censusing Elephants in Forests. Asian Elephant Conservation Center, Bangalore, India.

HILBORN, R., AND M. MANGEL. 1997. The ecological detective: confronting models with data. Princeton University Press, Princeton, New Jersey, USA.

HINES, J. E., K. H. POLLOCK, AND J. D. NICHOLS. 1984. Program LINLOGN users' instructions. Institute of Statistics Mimeograph Series 1651. North Carolina State University, Raleigh, USA.

HUGGINS, R. M. 1989. On the statistical analysis of capture experiments. Biometrika 76:133–140.

———. 1991. Some practical aspects of conditional likelihood approach to capture experiments. Biometrics 47:725–732.

JAMES, F. C., C. E. MCCULLOCH, AND D. A. WIEDENFIELD. 1996. New approaches to the analysis of population trends in land birds. Ecology 77:13–27.

JENNELLE, C. S., M. C. RUNGE, AND D. I. MACKENZIE. 2002. The use of photographic rates to estimate densities of tigers and other cryptic mammals: a comment on misleading conclusions. Animal Conservation 5:119–120.

JETT, D. A., AND J. D. NICHOLS. 1987. A field comparison of nested grid and trapping web density estimators. Journal of Mammalogy 68:888–892.

JOHNSON, D. H. 1995. Point counts of birds: what are we estimating? Pages 117–123 in C. J. Ralph, J. R. Sauer, and S. Droege, editors. Monitoring bird populations by point counts. U.S. Department of Agriculture, Forest Service, General Technical Report PSW-GTR-149.

JOHNSON, F. A., C. T. MOORE, W. L. KENDALL, J. A. DUBOSKY, D. F. CAITHAMER, J. R. KELLEY, JR., B. K. WILLIAMS. 1997. Uncertainty and the management of mallard harvests. Journal of Wildlife Management 61:202–216.

JOLLY, G. M. 1965. Explicit estimates from capture–recapture data with both death and immigration–stochastic model. Biometrika 52:225–247.

———. 1969a. Sampling methods for aerial censuses of wildlife populations. East African Agriculture and Forestry Journal 34:46–49.

———. 1969b. The treatment of errors in aerial counts of wildlife populations. East African Agriculture and Forestry Journal 34:50–56.

———. 1982. Mark–recapture models with parameters constant in time. Biometrics 38:301–321.

———, AND R. M. WATSON. 1979. Aerial sample survey methods in the quantitative assessment of ecological resources. Pages 203–216 in R. M. Cormack, G. P. Patil, and D. S. Robson, editors. Sampling biological populations. Volume 5. Statistical Ecology Series, International Cooperative Publishing House, Fairland, Maryland, USA.

KARANTH, K. U., AND N. S. KUMAR. 2002. Field surveys: assessing relative abundance of tigers and prey. Pages 71–85 in K. U. Karanth and J. D. Nichols, editors. Monitoring tigers and their prey: a manual for wildlife managers, researchers, and conservationists in tropical Asia. Centre for Wildlife Studies, Bangalore, India.

———, AND J. D. NICHOLS. 1998. Estimation of tiger densities in India using photographic captures and recaptures. Ecology 79:2852–2862.

———, AND ———, editors. 2002. Monitoring tigers and their prey: a manual for researchers, managers, and conservationists in tropical Asia. Centre for Wildlife Studies, Bangalore, India.

———, L. THOMAS, AND N. S. KUMAR. 2002. Field surveys: estimating absolute densities of prey species using line transect sampling. Pages 111–120 in K. U. Karanth and J. D. Nichols, editors. Monitoring tigers and their prey: a manual for wildlife managers, researchers, and conservationists in tropical Asia. Centre for Wildlife Studies, Bangalore, India.

KELLER, B. L., AND C. J. KREBS. 1970. *Microtus* population biology. III. Reproductive changes in fluctuating populations of *M. ochrogaster* and *M. pennsylvanicus* in southern Indiana, 1965–67. Ecological Monographs 40:263–294.

KELLY, M. J. 2001. Computer-aided photograph matching in studies using individual identification: an example from Serengeti cheetahs. Journal of Mammalogy 82:440–449.

KENDALL, W. L. 1999. Robustness of closed capture–recapture methods to violations of the closure assumption. Ecology 80:2517–2525.

———. 2001. The robust design for capture–recapture studies: analysis using program MARK. Proceedings of the International Wildlife Management Congress 2:279–282.

———, AND R. BJORKLAND. 2001. Using open robust design models to estimate temporary emigration from capture–recapture data. Biometrics 57:1113-1122.

———, AND J. E. HINES. 1999. Program RDSURVIV: an estimation tool for capture–recapture data collected under Pollock's robust design. Bird Study 46:S32–38.

————, AND J. D. NICHOLS. 1995. On the use of secondary capture–recapture samples to estimate temporary emigration and breeding proportions. Journal of Applied Statistics 22:751–762.

————, AND K. H. POLLOCK. 1992. The robust design in capture–recapture studies: a review and evaluation by Monte Carlo simulation. Pages 31–43 *in* D. R. McCullough and R. H. Barrett, editors. Wildlife 2001: populations. Elsevier Scientific Publishers, New York, USA.

————, J. E. HINES, AND J. D. NICHOLS. 2003. Adjusting multi-state capture–recapture models for misclassification bias: manatee breeding proportions. Ecology 84:1058–1066.

————, J. D. NICHOLS, AND J. E. HINES. 1997. Estimating temporary emigration using capture–recapture data with Pollock's robust design. Ecology 78:563–578.

————, B. G. PETERJOHN, AND J. R. SAUER. 1996. First-time observer effects in the North American Breeding Bird Survey. Auk 113:823–829.

————, K. H. POLLOCK, AND C. BROWNIE. 1995. A likelihood-based approach to capture–recapture estimation of demographic parameters under the robust design. Biometrics 51:293–308.

KOENEN, K. K. G., S. DeSTEFANO, AND P. R. KRAUSMAN. 2002. Using distance sampling to estimate seasonal densities of desert mule deer in a semidesert grassland. Wildlife Society Bulletin 30:53–63.

KRAFT, K. M., D. H. JOHNSON, J. M. SAMUELSON, AND S. H. ALLEN. 1995. Using known populations of pronghorn to evaluate sampling plans and estimators. Journal of Wildlife Management 59:129–137.

KREBS, C. J. 1989. Ecological methodology. Harper and Row Publishing, New York, USA.

KUFELD, R. C., J. H. OLTERMAN, AND D. C. BOWDEN. 1980. A helicopter quadrat census for mule deer on the Uncompahgre Plateau, Colorado. Journal of Wildlife Management 44:632–639.

LANCIA, R. A., J. D. NICHOLS, AND K. H. POLLOCK. 1994. Estimating the number of animals in wildlife populations. Pages 215–253 *in* T. A. Bookhout, editor. Research and management techniques for wildlife and habitats. Fifth edition. The Wildlife Society, Bethesda, Maryland, USA.

————, J. W. BISHIR, M. C. CONNER, AND C. S. ROSENBERRY. 1996. Use of catch–effort to estimate population size. Wildlife Society Bulletin 24:731–737.

————, K. H. POLLOCK, J. W. BISHIR, AND M. C. CONNER. 1988. A white-tailed deer harvesting strategy. Journal of Wildlife Management 52:589–595.

LANGTIMM, C. A., T. J. O'SHEA, R. PRADEL, AND C. A. BECK. 1998. Estimates of annual survival probabilities for adult Florida manatees (*Trichecus manatus latirostris*). Ecology 79:981–997.

LARKIN, R. P. 2005. Radar techniques for wildlife biology. Pages 448–464 *in* C. E. Braun, editor. Techniques for wildlife investigations and management. Sixth edition. The Wildlife Society, Bethesda, Maryland, USA.

LEBRETON, J.-D., K. P. BURNHAM, J. CLOBERT, AND D. R. ANDERSON. 1992. Modeling survival and testing biological hypotheses using marked animals: a unified approach with case studies. Ecological Monographs 62:67–118.

LeCREN, E. D. 1965. A note on the history of mark–recapture population estimates. Journal of Animal Ecology 34:453–454.

LEE, S.-M., AND A. CHAO. 1994. Estimating population size via sample coverage for closed capture–recapture models. Biometrics 50:88–97.

LESLIE, P. H., AND D. H. S. DAVIS. 1939. An attempt to determine the absolute number of rats on a given area. Journal of Animal Ecology 8:94–113.

LINCOLN, F. C. 1930. Calculating waterfowl abundance on the basis of banding returns. U.S. Department of Agriculture, Circular Number 118.

LINDBERG, M. S., W. L. KENDALL, J. E. HINES, AND M. G. ANDERSON. 2001. Combining band recovery data and Pollock's robust design to model temporary and permanent emigration. Biometrics 57:273–281.

LINK, W. A. 2003. Nonidentifiability of population size from capture–recapture data with heterogeneous detection probabilities. Biometrics 59:1123–1130.

————, AND R. J. BARKER. 1994. Density estimation using the trapping web design: a geometric analysis. Biometrics 50:733–745.

————, AND J. R. SAUER. 1997. Estimation of population trajectories from count data. Biometrics 53:488–497.

————, AND ————. 1998. Estimating population change from count data: application to the North American Breeding Bird Survey. Ecological Applications 8:258–268.

————, AND ————. 2002. A hierarchical analysis of population change with application to Cerulean warblers. Ecology 83:2832–2840.

————, E. CAM, J. D. NICHOLS, AND E. G. COOCH. 2002. Of bugs and birds: Markov chain Monte Carlo for hierarchal modeling in wildlife research. Journal of Wildlife Management 66:277–291.

LOERY, G., K. H. POLLOCK, J. D. NICHOLS, AND J. E. HINES. 1987. Age-specificity of black-capped chickadee survival rates: analysis of capture–recapture data. Ecology 68:1038–1044.

MACE, R. D., S. C. MINTA, T. L. MANLEY, AND K. E. AUNE. 1994. Estimating grizzly bear population size using camera sightings. Wildlife Society Bulletin 22:74–83.

MacKENZIE, D. I., AND W. L. KENDALL. 2002. How should detection probability be incorporated into estimates of relative abundance? Ecology 83:2387–2393.

————, J. D. NICHOLS, G. B. LACHMAN, S. DROEGE, J. A. ROYLE, AND C. A. LANGTIMM. 2002. Estimating site occupancy rates when detection probabilities are less than one. Ecology 83:2248–2255.

MAGNUSSON, W. E., G. J. CAUGHLEY, AND G. C. GRIGG. 1978. A double-survey estimate of population size from incomplete counts. Journal of Wildlife Management 42:174–176.

MANLY, B. F. J. 2001. Statistics for environmental science and management. Chapman and Hall/CRC, Boca Raton, Florida, USA.

————, L. L. McDONALD, AND G. W. GARNER. 1996. Maximum likelihood estimation for the double count method with independent observers. Journal of Agricultural, Biological, and Environmental Statistics 1:170–189.

————, T. McDONALD, AND S. AMSTRUP, editors. 2004. Handbook of capture–recapture methods. Princeton University Press, Princeton, New Jersey, USA.

McCULLOUGH, D. R. 1979. The George Reserve deer herd: population ecology of a *k*-selected species. University of Michigan Press, Ann Arbor, USA.

McDONALD, T. L., AND S. C. AMSTRUP. 2001. Estimation of population size using open capture–recapture models. Journal of Agricultural, Biological, and Environmental Statistics 6:206–220.

MENKENS, JR., G. E., AND S. H. ANDERSON. 1988. Estimation of small-mammal population size. Ecology 69:1952–1959.

MILLAR, R. B., AND R. MEYER. 2000. Bayesian state-space modeling of age-structured data: fitting a model is just the beginning. Canadian Journal of Fisheries and Aquatic Sciences 57:43–50.

MILLER, S. A. 1984. Estimation of animal production numbers for national assessments and appraisals. U.S. Department of Agriculture, Forest Service, General Technical Report RM-105.

MILLER, S. D., G. C. WHITE, R. A. SELLERS, H. V. REYNOLDS, J. W. SCHOEN, K. TITUS, V. G. BARNES, R. B. SMITH, R. R. NELSON, W. B. BALLARD, AND C. C. SCHWARTZ. 1997. Brown and black bear density estimation in Alaska using radiotelemetry and replicated mark–resight techniques. Wildlife Monographs 133.

MILLS, L. S., J. J. CITTA, K. P. LAIR, M. K. SCHWARTZ, AND D. A. TALLMON. 2000. Estimating animal abundance using noninvasive DNA sampling: promise and pitfalls. Ecological Applications 10:283–294.

MINTA, S., AND M. MANGEL. 1989. A simple population estimate based on simulation for capture–recapture and capture–resight data. Ecology 70:1738–1751.

MOOD, A. M., F. A. GRAYBILL, AND D. C BOES. 1974. Introduction to the theory of statistics. Third edition. McGraw-Hill Book Co., New York, USA.

MORRISON, M. L., W. M. BLOCK, M. D. STRICKLAND, AND W. L. KENDALL. 2001. Wildlife study design. Springer-Verlag, Inc., New York, USA.

MORSE, M. A. 1943. Technique for reducing man-power in the deer drive census. Journal of Wildlife Management 7:217–220.

MOUNTAINSPRING, S., AND J. M. SCOTT. 1985. Interspecific competition among Hawaiian forest birds. Ecological Monographs 55:219–239.

MOWAT, G., AND C. STROBECK. 2000. Estimating population size of grizzly bears using hair capture, DNA profiling, and mark–recapture analysis. Journal of Wildlife Management 64:183–193.

NEAL, A. K., G. C. WHITE, R. B. GILL, D. F. REED, AND J. H. OLTERMAN. 1993. Evaluation of mark–resight model assumptions for estimating mountain sheep numbers. Journal of Wildlife Management 57:436–450.

NEFF, D. J. 1968. The pellet-group count technique for big-game trend, census, and distribution: a review. Journal of Wildlife Management 32:597–614.

NETTLESHIP, D. N. 1976. Census techniques for seabirds of arctic and eastern Canada. Occasional Paper 25. Canadian Wildlife Service, Ottawa, Ontario, Canada.

NICHOLS, J. D. 1986. On the use of enumeration estimators for interspecific comparisons, with comments on a "trappability" estimator. Journal of Mammalogy 67:590–593.

————. 2001. Using models in the conduct of science and management of natural resources. Pages 11–34 *in* T. M. Shenk and A. B. Franklin, editors. Modeling in natural resource management: development, interpretation, and application. Island Press, Washington, D.C., USA.

————, AND J. E. HINES. 2002. Approaches for the direct estimation of λ, and demographic contributions to λ, using capture–recapture data. Journal of Applied Statistics 29:539-568.

————, AND K. U. KARANTH. 2002. Statistical concepts: assessing spatial distributions. Pages 29–38 *in* K. U. Karanth and J. D. Nichols, editors. Monitoring tigers and their prey: a manual for researchers, managers, and conservationists in tropical Asia. Centre for Wildlife Studies, Bangalore, India.

————, AND K. H. POLLOCK. 1983. Estimation methodology in contemporary small mammal capture–recapture studies. Journal of Mammalogy 64:253–260.

————, AND ————. 1990. Estimation of recruitment from immigration versus *in situ* reproduction using Pollock's robust design. Ecology 71:21–26.

————, J. E. HINES, AND K. H. POLLOCK. 1984a. Effects of permanent trap response in capture probability on Jolly–Seber capture–recapture model estimates. Journal of Wildlife Management 48:289–294.

————, K. H. POLLOCK, AND J. E. HINES. 1984b. The use of a robust capture–recapture design in small mammal population studies: a field example with *Microtus pennsylvanicus*. Acta Theriologica 29(26–3):357–365.

————, R. E. TOMLINSON, AND G. WAGGERMAN. 1986. Estimating nest detection probabilities for white-winged dove nest transects in Tamaulipas, Mexico. Auk 103:825–828.

————, B. R. NOON, S. L. STOKES, AND J. E. HINES. 1981. Remarks on the use of mark–recapture methodology in estimating avian population size. Studies in Avian Biology 6:121–136.

————, J. E. HINES, K. H. POLLOCK, R. L. HINZ, AND W. A. LINK. 1994. Estimating breeding proportions and testing hypotheses about costs of reproduction with capture–recapture data. Ecology 75:2052–2065.

————, ————, J. R. SAUER, F. W. FALLON, J. E. FALLON, AND P. J. HEGLUND. 2000. A double-observer approach for estimating detection probability and abundance from point counts. Auk 117:393–408.

NORRIS, III, J. L., AND K. H. POLLOCK. 1995. A capture–recapture model with heterogeneity and behavioral response. Environmental and Ecological Statistics 2:305–313.

————, AND ————. 1996. Nonparametric MLE under two closed capture–recapture models with heterogeneity. Biometrics 52:639–649.

NOVAK, J. M., K. T. SCRIBNER, W. D. DUPONT, AND M. H. SMITH. 1991. Catch-effort estimation of white-tailed deer population size. Journal of Wildlife Management 55:31–38.

O'CONNER, R. J., AND J. H. MARCHANT. 1981. A field validation of some common bird census techniques. Report from the British Trust for Ornithology to the Nature Conservancy Council, Huntingdon, United Kingdom.

O'NEIL, T. A., P. BETTINGER, B. G. MARCOT, B. W. LUSCOMBE, G. T. KOELN, H. J. BRUNER, C. BARRETT, J. A. POLLOCK, AND S. BERNATAS. 2005. Application of spatial technologies in wildlife biology. Pages 418–447 *in* C. E. Braun, editor. Techniques in wildlife investigations and management. Sixth edition. The Wildlife Society, Bethesda, Maryland, USA.

OTIS, D. L., K. P. BURNHAM, G. C. WHITE, AND D. R. ANDERSON. 1978. Statistical inference from capture data on closed animal populations. Wildlife Monographs 62.

OTTO, M. C., AND K. H. POLLOCK. 1990. Size bias in line transect sampling: a field test. Biometrics 46:239–245.

OVERTON, W. S. 1969. Estimating the numbers of animals in wildlife populations. Pages 403–455 *in* R. H. Giles, Jr., editor. Wildlife management techniques manual. Third edition. The Wildlife Society, Washington, D.C., USA.

OYLER-MCCANCE, S. J., AND P. L. LEBERG. 2005. Conservation genetics in wildlife biology. Pages 632–657 *in* C. E. Braun, editor. Techniques in wildlife investigations and management. Sixth edition. The Wildlife Society, Bethesda, Maryland, USA.

PACKARD, J. M., R. C. SUMMERS, AND L. B. BARNES. 1985. Variation of visibility bias during aerial surveys of manatees. Journal of Wildlife Management 49:347–351.

PARKER, JR., H. D., AND R. S. DRISCOLL. 1972. An experiment in deer detection by thermal scanning. Journal of Range Management 25:480–481.

PARMENTER, R. R., J. A. MACMAHON, AND D. R. ANDERSON. 1989. Animal density estimation using a trapping web design: field validation experiments. Ecology 70:169–179.

————, T. L. YATES, D. R. ANDERSON, K. P. BURNHAM, J. L. DUNNUM, A. B. FRANKLIN, M. T. FRIGGENS, B. L. LUBOW, M. MILLER, G. S. OLSON, C. A. PARMENTER, J. POLLARD, E. REXSTAD, T. M SHENK, T. R. STANLEY, AND G. C. WHITE. 2003. Small-mammal density estimation: a field comparison of grid-based vs. web-based density estimators. Ecological Monographs 73:1–26.

PAULIK, G. J., AND D. S. ROBSON. 1969. Statistical calculations for change-in-ratio estimators of population parameters. Journal of Wildlife Management 33:1–27.

PENDLETON, G. W. 1995. Effects of sampling strategy, detection probability, and independence of counts on the use of point counts. Pages 131–133 *in* C. J. Ralph, J. R. Sauer, and S. Droege, editors. Monitoring bird populations by point counts. U.S. Department of Agriculture, Forest Service, General Technical Report PSW-GTR-149.

PETERJOHN, B. G., J. R. SAUER, AND W. A. LINK. 1997. The 1994 and 1995 summary of the North American Breeding Bird Survey. Bird Populations 3:48–66.

PLEDGER, S. 2000. Unified maximum likelihood estimates for closed capture–recapture models using mixtures. Biometrics 56:434–442.

POLLOCK, K. H. 1974. The assumption of equal catchability of animals in tag–recapture experiments. Dissertation. Cornell University, Ithaca, New York, USA.

————. 1975. A K-sample tag–recapture model allowing for unequal survival and catchability. Biometrika 62:577–583.

————. 1981a. Capture–recapture models allowing for age-dependent survival and capture rates. Biometrics 37:521–529.

————. 1981b. Capture–recapture models: a review of current methods, assumptions and experimental design. Studies in Avian Biology 6:426–435.

————. 1982. A capture–recapture design robust to unequal probability of capture. Journal of Wildlife Management 46:752–757.

————, AND W. L. KENDALL. 1987. Visibility bias in aerial surveys: a review of estimation procedures. Journal of Wildlife Management 51:502–510.

————, AND M. C. OTTO. 1983. Robust estimation of population size in closed animal populations from capture–recapture experiments. Biometrics 39:1035–1049.

————, J. E. HINES, AND J. D. NICHOLS. 1984. The use of auxiliary variables in capture–recapture and removal experiments. Biometrics 40:329–340.

————, D. L. SOLOMON, AND D. S. ROBSON. 1974. Tests for mortality and recruitment in a K-sample tag–recapture experiment. Biometrics 30:77–87.

————, R. A. LANCIA, M. C. CONNER, AND B. L. WOOD. 1985. A new change-in-ratio procedure robust to unequal catchability of types of animal. Biometrics 41:653–662.

————, J. D. NICHOLS, C. BROWNIE, AND J. E. HINES. 1990. Statistical inference for capture–recapture experiments. Wildlife Monographs 107.

————, ————, T. R. SIMONS, G. L. FARNSWORTH, L. L. BAILEY, AND J. R. SAUER. 2002. Large scale wildlife monitoring studies: statistical methods for design and analysis. Environmetrics 13:105–119.

PRADEL, R. 1993. Flexibility in survival analysis from recapture data: handling trap-dependence. Pages 29–37 *in* J.-D. Lebreton and P. M. North, editors. Marked individuals in the study of bird populations. Birkhäuser Verlag, Basel, Switzerland.

————. 1996. Utilization of capture–mark–recapture for the study of recruitment and population growth rate. Biometrics 52:703–709.

————, AND J.-D. LEBRETON. 1999. Comparison of different approaches to the study of local recruitment of breeders. Bird Study 46:S74–81.

————, J. E. HINES, J.-D. LEBRETON, AND J. D. NICHOLS. 1997. Capture–recapture survival models taking account of transients. Biometrics 53:60–72.

PRENO, W. L., AND R. F. LABISKY. 1971. Abundance and harvest of doves, pheasants, bobwhites, squirrels, and cottontails in Illinois, 1956–69. Technical Bulletin 4. Illinois Department of Conservation, Springfield, USA.

QUINN, II, T. J., AND R. B. DERISO. 1999. Quantitative fish dynamics. Oxford University Press, Oxford, United Kingdom.

RABE, M. J., S. S. ROSENSTOCK, AND J. C. DEVOS, JR. 2002. Review of big-game survey methods used by wildlife agencies of the western United States. Wildlife Society Bulletin 30:46–52.

RALPH, C. J., AND J. M. SCOTT, editors. 1981. Estimating the numbers of terrestrial birds. Studies in Avian Biology 6.

————, J. R. SAUER, AND S. DROEGE. 1995. Monitoring bird populations by point counts. U.S. Department of Agriculture, Forest Service, General Technical Report PSW-GTR-149.

RAMSEY, F. L., AND J. M. SCOTT. 1979. Estimating population densities from variable circular plot surveys. Pages 155–181 *in* R. M. Cormack, G. P. Patil, and D. S. Robson, editors. Sampling biological populations. Volume 5. Statistical Ecology Series, International Cooperative Publishing House, Fairland, Maryland, USA.

REXSTAD, E., AND K. P. BURNHAM. 1991. User's guide for interactive program CAPTURE. Colorado Cooperative Fish and Wildlife Research Unit, Colorado State University, Fort Collins, USA.

REYNOLDS, R. T., J. M. SCOTT, AND R. A. NUSSBAUM. 1980. A variable circular-plot method for estimating bird numbers. Condor 82:309–313.

RICKER, W. E. 1958. Handbook of computations for biological statistics of fish populations. Fisheries Research Board of Canada Bulletin 119.

ROBBINS, C. S., D. BYSTRAK, AND P. H. GEISSLER. 1986. The breeding bird survey: its first fifteen years, 1965–1979. U.S. Department of the Interior, Fish and Wildlife Service, Resource Publication 157.

ROBSON, D. S. 1969. Mark–recapture methods of population estimation. Pages 120–140 *in* N. L. Johnson and H. Smith, Jr., editors. New developments in survey sampling. John Wiley and Sons, New York, USA.

ROSE, R. K. 1973. A small mammal live trap. Transactions of the Kansas Academy of Science 76:14–17.

ROSEBERRY, J. L., AND A. WOOLF. 1991. A comparative evaluation of techniques for analyzing white-tailed deer harvest data. Wildlife Monographs 117.

ROSENSTOCK, S. S., D. R. ANDERSON, K. M. GIESEN, T. LEUKERING, AND M. F. CARTER. 2002. Landbird counting techniques: current practices and an alternative. Auk 119:46–53.

ROYLE, J. A., AND J. D. NICHOLS. 2003. Estimating abundance from repeated presence absence data or point counts. Ecology 84:777–790.

SAMUEL, M. D., E. O. GARTON, M. W. SCHLEGEL, AND R. G. CARSON. 1987. Visibility bias during aerial surveys of elk in northcentral Idaho. Journal of Wildlife Management 51:622–630.

SANDLAND, R. L., AND G. P. KIRKWOOD. 1981. Estimation of survival in marked populations with possibly dependent sighting probabilities. Biometrika 68:531–541.

SAUER, J. R., AND S. DROEGE, editors. 1990. Survey designs and statistical methods for the estimation of avian population trends. U.S. Department of the Interior, Fish and Wildlife Service, Biological Report 90(1).

———, B. G. PETERJOHN, AND W. A. LINK. 1994. Observer differences in the North American Breeding Bird Survey. Auk 111:50–62.

SCATTERGOOD, L. W. 1954. Estimating fish and wildlife populations: a survey of methods. Pages 273–285 *in* O. Kempthorne, T. A. Bancroft, J. W. Gowen, and J. L. Lush, editors. Statistics and mathematics in biology. Iowa State College Press, Ames, USA.

SCHNABEL, Z. E. 1938. The estimation of the total fish population of a lake. American Mathematical Monthly 45:348–352.

SCHNUTE, J. T. 1994. A general framework for developing sequential fisheries models. Canadian Journal of Fisheries and Aquatic Sciences 51:1676–1688.

SCHWARZ, C. J., AND A. N. ARNASON. 1996. A general methodology for the analysis of capture–recapture experiments in open populations. Biometrics 52:860–873.

———, AND G. A. F. SEBER. 1999. Estimating animal abundance: review. III. Statistical Science 14:427–456.

———, AND W. T. STOBO. 1997. Estimating temporary migration using the robust design. Biometrics 53:178–194.

———, J. F. SCHWEIGERT, AND A. N. ARNASON. 1993. Estimating migration rates using tag-recovery data. Biometrics 49:177–193.

SCOTT, J. M., S. MOUNTAINSPRING, F. L. RAMSEY, AND C. B. KEPLER. 1986. Forest bird communities of the Hawaiian islands: their dynamics, ecology, and conservation. Studies in Avian Biology 9.

SEBER, G. A. F. 1965. A note on the multiple-recapture census. Biometrika 52:249–259.

———. 1982. The estimation of animal abundance and related parameters. Second edition. MacMillian Publishing Company, New York, USA.

SILVY, N. J., R. R. LOPEZ, AND M. J. PETERSON. 2005. Wildlife marking techniques. Pages 339–376 *in* C. E. Braun, editor. Techniques for wildlife investigations and management. Sixth edition. The Wildlife Society, Bethesda, Maryland, USA.

SKALSKI, J. R. 1985*a*. Construction of cost functions for tag–recapture research. Wildlife Society Bulletin 13:273–283.

———. 1985*b*. Use of capture data to quantify change and test for effects on the abundance of wild populations. Dissertation. Cornell University, Ithaca, New York, USA.

———. 1994. Estimating wildlife populations based on incomplete area surveys. Wildlife Society Bulletin 22:192–203.

———, AND D. S. ROBSON. 1992. Techniques for design and analysis of wildlife investigations: statistical inferences based on capture data. Academic Press, San Diego, California, USA.

———, ———, AND M. A. SIMMONS. 1983. Comparative census procedures using single mark–recapture methods. Ecology 64:752–760.

———, M. A. SIMMONS, AND D. S. ROBSON. 1984. The use of removal

sampling in comparative censuses. Ecology 65:1006–1015.

SMIRNOV, E. N., AND D. G. MIQUELLE. 1999. Population dynamics of the Amur tiger in Sikhote-Alin Zapovednik, Russia. Pages 61–70 *in* J. Seidensticker, S. Christie, and P. Jackson, editors. Riding the tiger: tiger conservation in human-dominated landscapes. Cambridge University Press, Cambridge, United Kingdom.

SMITH, D. R., M. J. CONROY, AND D. H. BRAKHAGE. 1996. Efficiency of adaptive cluster sampling for estimating density of wintering waterfowl. Biometrics 51:777–788.

SMITH, E. P., AND G. VAN BELLE. 1984. Nonparametric estimation of species richness. Biometrics 40:119–129.

SMITH, G. W. 1995. A critical review of the aerial and ground surveys of breeding waterfowl in North America. U.S. Department of the Interior, Biological Science Report 5. Washington, D.C., USA.

SMITH, L. M., I. L. BRISBIN, JR., AND G. C. WHITE. 1984. An evaluation of total trapline captures as estimates of furbearer abundance. Journal of Wildlife Management 48:1452–1455.

STANLEY, T. R., AND K. P. BURNHAM. 1999. A closure test for time-specific capture–recapture data. Environmental and Ecological Statistics 6:197–209.

STENSETH, N. C., O. N. BJØRNSTAD, W. FALCK, J.-M. FROMENTIN, J. GJØSÆTER, AND J. S. GRAY. 1999. Dynamics of coastal cod populations: intra- and intercohort density dependence and stochastic processes. Proceedings of the Royal Society of London Biological Sciences 266:1645–1654.

STOKES, S. L. 1984. The Jolly–Seber method applied to age stratified populations. Journal of Wildlife Management 48:1053–1059.

STORM, G. L., D. F. COTTAM, R. H. YAHNER, AND J. D. NICHOLS. 1992. A comparison of 2 techniques for estimating deer density. Wildlife Society Bulletin 20:197–203.

SUBCOMMITTEE ON CONSERVATION OF NATURAL POPULATIONS. 1981. Techniques for the study of primate population ecology. National Academy Press, Washington, D.C., USA.

SWEITZER, R. A., D. VAN VUREN, I. A. GARDNER, W. M. BOYCE, AND J. D. WAITHMAN. 2000. Estimating sizes of wild pig populations in the North and Central Coast regions of California. Journal of Wildlife Management 64:531–543.

TABERLET, P., L. P. WAITS, AND G. LUIKART. 1999. Noninvasive genetic sampling: look before you leap. TREE 14:323–327.

TAUTIN, J. 1982. Assessment of some important factors affecting the singing-ground survey. Pages 6–11 *in* T. J. Dwyer and G. L. Storm, editors. Woodcock ecology and management. U.S. Department of the Interior, Fish and Wildlife Service, Wildlife Research Report 14.

———, P. H. GEISSLER, R. E. MUNRO, AND R. S. POSPAHALA. 1983. Monitoring the population status of American woodcock. Transactions of the North American Wildlife and Natural Resources Conference 48:376–388.

TAYLOR, D., AND W. NEAL. 1984. Management implications of size-class frequency distributions in Louisiana alligator populations. Wildlife Society Bulletin 12:312–319.

THOMAS, L., AND K. U. KARANTH. 2002. Statistical concepts: estimating absolute densities of prey species using line transect sampling. Pages 87–109 *in* K. U. Karanth and J. D. Nichols, editors. Monitoring tigers and their prey: a manual for wildlife managers, researchers, and conservationists in tropical Asia. Centre for Wildlife Studies, Bangalore, India.

———, J. F. DERRY, S. T. BUCKLAND, D. L. BORCHERS, D. R. ANDERSON, K. P. BURNHAM, S. STRINDBERG, S. L. HEDLEY, M. L. BURT, F. F. C. MARQUES, J. H. POLLARD, AND R. M. FEWSTER. 1998. DISTANCE 3.5. Research Unit for Wildlife Population Assessment, University of St. Andrews, Scotland, United Kingdom.

THOMPSON, S. K. 1992. Sampling. John Wiley and Sons, New York, USA.

———, AND G. A. F. SEBER. 1994. Detectability in conventional and adaptive sampling. Biometrics 50:712–724.

———, AND ———. 1996. Adaptive sampling. John Wiley and Sons, New York, USA.

THOMPSON, W. L. 2002. Towards reliable bird surveys: accounting for individuals present but not detected. Auk 119:18–25.

———, G. C. WHITE, AND C. GOWAN. 1998. Monitoring vertebrate populations. Academic Press, San Diego, California, USA.

TRENKEL, V. M., D. A. ELSTON, AND S. T. BUCKLAND. 2000. Fitting population dynamics models to count and cull data using sequential importance sampling. Journal of the American Statistical Association 95:363–374.

TROLLE, M., AND M. KERY. 2003. Estimation of ocelot density in the Pantanal using capture–recapture analysis of camera-trapping data. Journal of Mammalogy 84:607–614.

TYSON, E. L. 1959. A deer drive vs. track census. Transactions of the North American Wildlife Conference 24:457–464.

UDEVITZ, M. S., AND K. H. POLLOCK. 1991. Change-in-ratio estimators for populations with more than two subclasses. Biometrics 47:1531–1546.

———, AND ———. 1992. Change-in-ratio methods for estimating population size. Pages 90–101 *in* D. R. McCullough and R. H. Barrett, editors. Wildlife 2001: populations. Elsevier Scientific Publishers, New York, USA.

UNSWORTH, J. W., L. KUCK, AND E. O. GARTON. 1990. Elk sightability model validation at the National Bison Range, Montana. Wildlife Society Bulletin 18:113–115.

UHLIG, H. G. 1956. The gray squirrel in West Virginia. Division of Game Management Bulletin 3. West Virginia Conservation Commission, Charleston, USA.

VERNER, J. 1985. Assessment of counting techniques. Current Ornithology 2:247–302.

———, AND K. A. MILNE. 1990. Analyst and observer variability in density estimates from spot mapping. Condor 92:313-325.

WALTERS, C. J. 1986. Adaptive management of renewable resources. MacMillan Publishing Company, New York, USA.

WHITE, G. C. 1983. Numerical estimation of survival rates from band-recovery and biotelemetry data. Journal of Wildlife Management 47:716–728.

———. 1992. Do pellet counts index white-tailed deer numbers and population change?: a comment. Journal of Wildlife Management 56:611–612.

———. 1993. Evaluation of radio tagging, marking, and sighting estimators of population size using Monte Carlo simulations. Pages 91–103 *in* J.-D. Lebreton and P. M. North, editors. Marked individuals in the study of bird populations. Birkhäuser Verlag, Basel, Switzerland.

———. 1996. NOREMARK: population estimation from mark-resighting surveys. Wildlife Society Bulletin 24:50–52.

———, AND K. P. BURNHAM. 1999. Program MARK: survival rate estimation from both live and dead encounters. Bird Study 46:S120–139.

———, AND R. A. GARROTT. 1990. Analysis of wildlife radio-tracking data. Academic Press, San Diego, California, USA.

———, AND B. C. LUBOW. 2002. Fitting population models to multiple sources of observed data. Journal of Wildlife Management 66:300–309.

———, D. R. ANDERSON, K. P. BURNHAM, AND D. L. OTIS. 1982. Capture–recapture and removal methods for sampling closed populations. Los Alamos National Laboratory LA-8787-NERP, Los Alamos, New Mexico, USA.

WIGGERS, E. P., AND S. F. BECKERMAN. 1993. Use of thermal infrared sensing to survey white-tailed deer populations. Wildlife Society Bulletin 21:263–268.

WIGHT, H. M. 1938. Field and laboratory technic in wildlife management. University of Michigan Press, Ann Arbor, USA.

WILLIAMS, B. K., J. D. NICHOLS, AND M. J. CONROY. 2002. Analysis and management of animal populations. Academic Press, San Diego, California, USA.

WILSON, D. E., F. R. COLE, J. D. NICHOLS, R. RUDRAN, AND M. S. FOSTER, editors. 1996. Measuring and monitoring biological diversity: standard methods for mammals. Smithsonian Institution Press, Washington, D.C., USA.

WILSON, D. M., AND J. BART. 1985. Reliability of singing bird surveys: effects of song phenology during the breeding season. Condor 87:69–73.

WILSON, K. R., AND D. R. ANDERSON. 1985*a*. Evaluation of a density estimator based on a trapping web and distance sampling theory. Ecology 66:1185–1194.

———, AND ———. 1985*b*. Evaluation of a nested grid approach for estimating density. Journal of Wildlife Management 49:675–678.

———, AND ———. 1995. Continuous time capture–recapture population estimation when capture probabilities vary by time. Environmental Ecology and Statistics 2:55–69.

WOOD, J. E. 1959. Relative estimates of fox population levels. Journal of Wildlife Management 23:53–63.

———, AND E. P. ODUM. 1964. A nine-year history of furbearer populations on the AEC Savannah River Plant area. Journal of Mammalogy 45:540–551.

WOODS, J. G., D. PAETKAU, D. LEWIS, B. N. MCLELLAN, M. PROCTOR, AND C. STROBECK. 1999. Genetic tagging of free-ranging black and brown bears. Wildlife Society Bulletin 27:616–627.

WOODWARD, A. R., AND W. R. MARION. 1978. An evaluation of factors affecting night-light counts of alligators. Proceedings of the Annual Conference of the Southeastern Association of Fish and Wildlife Agencies 32:291–302.

YOCCOZ, N. G., J. D. NICHOLS, AND T. BOULINIER. 2001. Monitoring of biological diversity in space and time. Trends in Ecology and Evolution 16:446–453.

ZIPPEN, C. 1958. The removal method of population estimation. Journal of Wildlife Management 22:82–90.

6

POPULATION ANALYSIS IN WILDLIFE BIOLOGY

Stephen J. Dinsmore and Douglas H. Johnson

INTRODUCTION

Wildlife ecologists frequently ask questions about wildlife populations—how many individuals are there, what are estimates of vital rates (birth rate, survival rate) of that population, and, ultimately, is the population increasing or decreasing? A *population*, defined here as a group of organisms of the same species living in a particular space at a particular time (Krebs 1985:157), involves concepts such as birth rate, death rate, sex ratio, and age structure (Cole 1957). These concepts lack meaning for lower levels of biological organization (individuals) or at higher levels (communities or ecosystems). Populations are composed of individual organisms; thus, the study of population dynamics includes the concepts of survival, immigration, and emigration. It is these topics that form the basis for this chapter.

Population analysis also involves the study of population dynamics: the changes that occur over time and the causes of those changes. The population could be the number of aphids on a plant, the number of white-tailed deer (*Odocoileus virginianus*) in a woodlot, or the number of snow geese (*Chen caerulescens*) in North America.

Population-level questions are of obvious interest to wildlife managers and scientists. For species that are economic pests, ways of reducing numbers are sought. For game species, managers desire to maintain populations at levels that provide surpluses for harvest. For threatened or endangered species, the goal is to increase their numbers to avoid extinction. To meet any of these objectives, an understanding of the species' population dynamics is the first priority.

The subject of population dynamics includes the number of individuals in a population and the factors that affect that population size: 1) survival of those individuals, 2) their reproduction, and 3) their movements into and out of a population (immigration and emigration). If all factors were known for a population, understanding its dynamics would be straightforward. This is rarely achieved, however, and biologists are forced to make decisions based on an incomplete understanding.

Examples used in this chapter are based on several species, but disproportionate attention is given to a few, especially mallards (*Anas platyrhynchos*), mountain plover (*Charadrius montanus*), and white-tailed deer. This emphasis reflects our own experience and, in all cases, the amount of work that has been done on the species. It is worth recalling Durward Allen's remark that "numbers phenomena tend to be universal. They change only in detail as we shift from fish to fur to fowl" (Allen 1962:36).

A single chapter can only touch lightly on the diversity of techniques used in population analysis. References for further reading are given at appropriate places throughout. For general reference, 3 books stand out. Seber (1982) (and 2 updates; 1986, 2001) provided near-encyclopedic coverage of methods used to estimate numbers of wild animals as well as their survival and related parameters. Caughley (1977) described his practical views on population analysis. Williams et al. (2002) provided a detailed overview of contemporary population analysis tools and techniques, and the serious student is advised to carefully study that volume.

This chapter presents material in several sections. We begin by introducing theoretical models of population growth, which form the basis for a discussion of population analyses. We then discuss concepts of parameter estimation and population modeling, population viability analyses and, ultimately, how we make inferences from population data. In each section, we introduce the basic concepts and appropriate formulae, and illustrate them with biological examples. The purpose of showing simple calculations is only to demonstrate them. We acknowledge that today's population analyst will rarely do these calculations by hand and will instead use a computer. The material provides a general overview of the subject matter and the reader is encouraged to refer to the specific references in each section for more detailed coverage of that topic.

THEORETICAL MODELS OF POPULATION GROWTH

The growth (or decline) of a population (Box 1) can be described by following the number of individuals in the population through time. In the simplest context, the number of individuals (N) in a population at some future time (time $t + 1$) depends on the number of individuals present now (time t) and any gains (births [B] and immigrants [I]) and losses (deaths [D] and emigrants [E]) that occur between times t and $t + 1$. This can be written as a simple difference equation, $N_{t+1} = N_t + B_t + I_t - D_t - E_t$. Although this model is simplistic, it forms an important foundation for building more complex models of population growth. What happens if we place constraints on the relationship between N_t and N_{t+1}? We could consider population growth that is *density-independent* (unimpeded population

growth) or *density-dependent* (population growth depends directly on population density). From this simple equation, we can also discuss concepts of population growth as measured by lambda (λ). The population rate of growth from time t to time $t + 1$ is simply $\lambda = N_{t+1}/N_t$.

Population analysis increasingly requires a modeling approach, especially to bridge gaps in knowledge. A *model* is an abstraction of a real system that enables us to think more clearly about the real one. Any model must sacrifice at least 1 of 3 desiderata: generality, realism, or precision (Levins 1966). A model may be a complex mathematical exercise, incorporating thousands of variables and equations, and requiring hours of computer time to analyze. Or it may be a simple heuristic concept, such that barn owls (*Tyto alba*) lay larger clutches of eggs in years when food resources are abundant. Which kind of model is appropriate to a scientific or management application depends on the objectives of the model.

This chapter presents a variety of models, from simple, involving only a single parameter, to complex, involving numerous rates and relationships. A *parameter* is something that describes a population, e.g., the annual survival rate of male mallards. However, we can rarely measure all individuals in the population. Thus, a parameter is an unknown numerical characteristic of the entire population. There is a general trade-off between model complexity and realism. Simple models are relatively easy to interpret but lack a sense of realism when applied to actual biological situations. Conversely, complex models may be more realistic but suffer because we seldom have sufficient data to support them.

In addition to varying in complexity, models of populations may vary in other attributes. In *discrete-time models*, events, such as births, occur only at certain times, such as a short breeding season within a year. In *continuous-time models*, events can occur throughout time. Or, as Starfield and Bleloch (1991:9) expressed it, time jumps in a discrete model; time flows in a continuous one. Another distinction is whether random components are included in a model. In a *deterministic model*, parameter values are fixed through time and the result from the model depends only on the values of the variables. In a *stochastic model*, certain parameters vary randomly; their statistical distributions rather than exact values are specified. If the variation of the system is important, stochastic models are usually more suitable than deterministic ones. In the following sections we discuss ways of estimating population change under these and other scenarios.

Populations with Unimpeded Growth

The simplest model assumes the number of animals in a population (N) goes up (or down) by a constant ratio, say λ, during each unit of time (which we will assume is a year). That is, at time $t + 1$ the population size is λ times its value at time t:

$$N_{t+1} = \lambda N_t .$$

The population is increasing if $\lambda > 1$, constant if $\lambda = 1$, and declining if $\lambda < 1$. Sometimes λ is called the *finite rate of population increase*. This formulation is geared toward organisms that reproduce during a short breeding season (discrete growth, *birth-pulse fertility* of Caughley 1977).

Box 1. The behavior of small populations—the Allee Effect.

We have assumed density-dependence will increase mortality rates or decrease birth rates or both as populations become large. Conversely, as populations become small, mortality rates should decline and birth rates increase, according to the model. In reality, small populations may not enjoy favorable demographic rates. Birth rates especially may decline, rather than increase, as populations dwindle. This may happen because it is difficult to find mates when the population is small, or because breeding requires social stimulation. Another possibility is illustrated by colonial-nesting birds, in which larger colonies provide greater protection from predators and greater reproductive success (Birkhead 1977). The phenomenon of increased mortality rates or decreased birth rates at low population levels is known as the *Allee Effect*, after W. C. Allee, who documented numerous situations in which it was manifested (Allee 1931).

Table 1. Counts of wintering whooping cranes, Aransas National Wildlife Refuge, Texas, USA, 1938–2001 (from Boyce 1987; W. G. Jobman, U. S. Fish and Wildlife Service, personal communication).

Year	Adults	Young	Year	Adults	Young
1938	14	4	1970	51	6
1939	15	7	1971	54	5
1940	21	5	1972	46	5
1941	14	2	1973	47	2
1942	15	4	1974	47	2
1943	16	5	1975	49	8
1944	15	3	1976	57	12
1945	18	4	1977	62	10
1946	22	3	1978	68	7
1947	25	6	1979	70	6
1948	27	3	1980	72	6
1949	30	4	1981	71	2
1950	26	5	1982	67	6
1951	20	5	1983	68	7
1952	19	2	1984	71	15
1953	21	3	1985	81	16
1954	21	0	1986	89	21
1955	20	8	1987	109	25
1956	22	2	1988	116	18
1957	22	4	1989	126	20
1958	23	9	1990	133	13
1959	31	2	1991	124	8
1960	30	6	1992	121	15
1961	34	5	1993	127	16
1962	32	0	1994	125	8
1963	26	7	1995	130	28
1964	32	10	1996	144	16
1965	36	8	1997	152	30
1966	38	5	1998	165	18
1967	39	9	1999	171	17
1968	44	6	2000	171	9
1969	48	8	2001	161	15

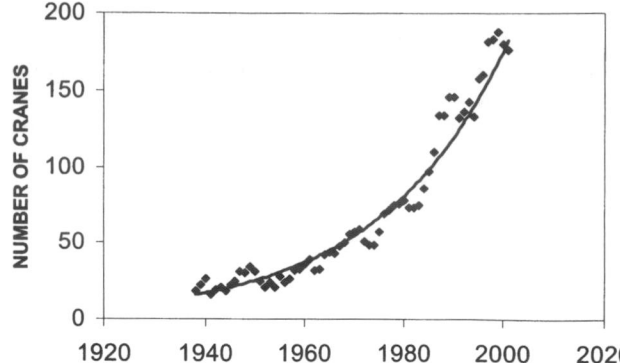

Fig. 1. Counts of wintering whooping cranes at Aransas National Wildlife Refuge, Texas, USA, 1938–2001, fitted to an exponential curve.

If N_0 is population size at some initial year, then repeating the above equation t times gives:

$$N_t = \lambda^t N_0. \tag{1}$$

Consider the natural population of whooping cranes (*Grus americana*), which has been monitored on its wintering ground since 1938. Virtually the entire natural population congregates near Aransas National Wildlife Refuge in Texas. The actual counts (Table 1) during 1938–2001 were fitted to Equation 1, where year t has been recoded so that 1938 is year 0 and $\hat{\lambda} = 1.0363$ is an estimate of λ (the hat symbol denotes an estimator of a parameter). Thus, the crane population was growing similarly to a bank deposit with an interest rate of 3.63%, compounded annually (Fig. 1). Binkley and Miller (1980, 1988), Boyce and Miller (1985), Boyce (1987), and Nedelman et al. (1987) have presented more detailed analyses of this population.

An alternative expression for population growth has some advantages. If we replace λ by e^r, then $\lambda^t = e^{rt}$. Here e is the base of natural logarithms and r is the *instantaneous rate of increase*. Among the advantages of the expo-

nential formulation (Caughley 1977:52) is the ability to convert easily between time units; e.g., if the growth rate of a population per year is 0.10, the growth rate per day is 0.10/365. Also, the time it takes a population to double is $(\log 2)/r = 0.69315/r$ (note: throughout this chapter natural logarithms are used). This formulation is particularly appropriate for continuously growing populations (*birth-flow fertility* of Caughley 1977), but it works if the times (t) when the population is counted represent comparable times in the life cycle, such as the beginning of the breeding season. Then r is $\log(\lambda)$, and Equation 1 becomes:

$$N_t = N_0 e^{rt}. \tag{2}$$

For the whooping crane population, we get $\hat{r} = \log(\hat{\lambda}) = \log(1.0363) = 0.03566$, on an annual basis. Thus, the population is growing 3.566% per year and will double every 19.4 years (0.69315/0.03566), should growth continue at this rate.

This model is termed the *exponential growth model*, and may be realistic when growth is unhindered (i.e., resources are ample, competition is not a factor). Such situations often occur when a species initially invades an optimal habitat or, as with whooping cranes, when a population rebounds from near extinction and the habitat is adequate. It can also be useful for short-term forecasts (Eberhardt 1987). This approach is deterministic, that is, no allowance is made for variation caused by randomness or by variables not included in the model. It can be made stochastic (incorporating random events) by considering chance variations in births and deaths (Pielou 1969:13–16).

Estimating r from Counts

The simplest way to estimate the growth rate r in Equation 2 from population counts is to take logarithms of both sides, giving:

$$\log(N_t) = \log(N_0) + rt. \tag{3}$$

Linear regression of $\log(N_t)$ on t for a series of years provides estimates of the regression coefficient (slope, equal to r) and the intercept. These values can be transformed by exponentiating to provide estimates of λ and, if desired, N_0. As an example, consider the whooping crane counts during 1938–2001 (Table 1). A linear regression of the logs of the counts (adults plus young) against year (recoded so that 1938 = 0) provides a slope of $\hat{r} = 0.03880$ (the estimated standard error [SE] = 0.00112) and an intercept of 2.7638 (SE = 0.0408). Thus, $\hat{N}_0 = e^{2.7638} = 15.9$ (SE = 0.6471 by the delta method, a procedure for obtaining estimated standard errors of functions of random variables) (Seber 1982:7).

An alternative to linear regression on transformed variables is to use nonlinear regression directly on Equation 2. Using the whooping crane data gives $\hat{r} = 0.0421$ (SE = 0.00123) and $\hat{N}_0 = 14.0$ (SE = 0.9129). These estimates differ from those given previously because the analytic methods are based on different assumptions. Because errors in estimated population sizes are likely to increase with true population size, the assumption of constant error variance, used in ordinary least squares regression, is more likely to be met with the linearized form of the model represented by Equation 3 than by Equation 2. For this reason, the linear approach is usually preferred.

Estimating r from Changes in Population Size

The form of the exponential growth model lends itself to another method for estimating r. Consider the ratio of population sizes in successive years. From Equation 2, this is:

$$\frac{N_t}{N_{t-1}} = \frac{N_0 e^{rt}}{N_0 e^{r(t-1)}} = e^r = \lambda.$$

Thus, the logarithms of the average of these ratios can be used to estimate r. For the whooping crane example, counts for 1938–2001 provided 63 ratios N_t/N_{t-1}, which averaged 1.0454 (SE = 0.0164). The logarithm of this average gives the estimate $\hat{r} = 0.0444$ (SE = 0.0157).

In a comparison of the 3 estimates of whooping crane population growth (not shown here), the fit provided by the linearized model (Equation 3) was second best, that of the nonlinear fit (Equation 2) was best, and that of the ratios in successive years was worst. Eberhardt (1987) discussed other estimation methods for this model, including ratio estimators with various weights. He also considered variance estimators. McCullough (1982, 1983) and Van Ballenberghe (1983) present a spirited discussion of the estimation of population growth of a white-tailed deer herd.

Populations with Density-dependent Growth

Continuous-time Formulation

We now consider the number of bison (*Bison bison*) on the National Bison Range, Montana during 1909–22 when no harvesting occurred (Table 2). Fitting the linearized model (Equation 3) to the first 10 years of data gives $\hat{N}_0 = 53.45$ (SE = 1.53) and $\hat{r} = 0.216$ (SE = 0.00535). The observed number of bison at the end of each of those years fits the exponential curve nicely (Fig. 2). Projections for 1919–22, however, are consistently higher than actual numbers (Fig. 2). It is conceivable the slowdown in population growth can be attributed to a density-dependent response. The proportional annual change in population ($\hat{R}$) is negatively correlated with population size ($r = -0.77$, $P = 0.001$; here r denotes the correlation coefficient, not the population growth rate, a distinction between usages that should be clear from the context) (Fig. 3).

Table 2. Counts of bison on the National Bison Range, Montana, USA, 1909–22 (from Fredin 1984).

Year	Number at start of year	Young born	Deaths	Number at end of year
1909	37	11	0	48
1910	51[a]	19	0	70
1911	70	16	1	85
1912	85	19	0	104
1913	104	26	0	130
1914	130	34	0	164
1915	164	32	2	194
1916	194	47	1	240
1917	240	56	1	295
1918	295	73	1	367
1919	367	58	5	420
1920	420	68	9	479
1921	479	82	7	554
1922	554	85	4	635

[a] Three animals added to the existing herd.

It is impossible for any population to continue to grow indefinitely at a constant rate. Most likely, growth will slow as the population becomes large and some limiting factor exerts an influence. Density-dependence is likely to operate (Box 2). How can density-dependence be included in the model to make it more realistic and useful? In the model of Equation 2, the population growth rate per animal,

$$\frac{1}{N_t} \frac{dN_t}{dt} = r,$$

is constant, regardless of population size. One way to make it depend on population size is to multiply it by a factor that has negligible effect when the population is small, but reduces the growth rate to zero as the population approaches some limit, K (which we might call the carrying capacity). The term $(K - N)/K$ does just that (this is the simplest way; there are many others, reviewed by May [1973:80–81]). It is nearly 1 when N is small, and converges to 0 as N approaches K. If we use this factor, the per capita growth rate becomes:

$$\frac{1}{N_t} \frac{dN_t}{dt} = r_m \frac{K - N_t}{K}, \qquad (4)$$

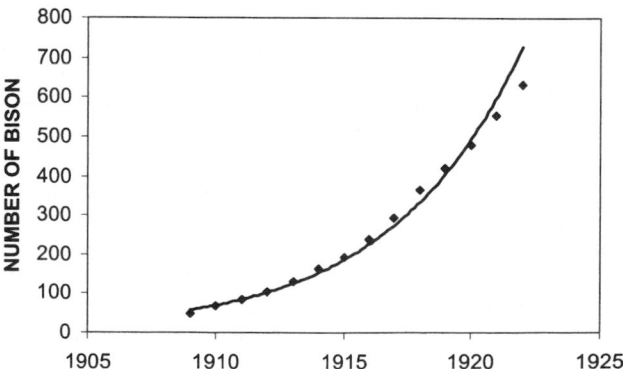

Fig. 2. Bison counts on the National Bison Range, Montana, USA, 1909-22, fitted to exponential curve.

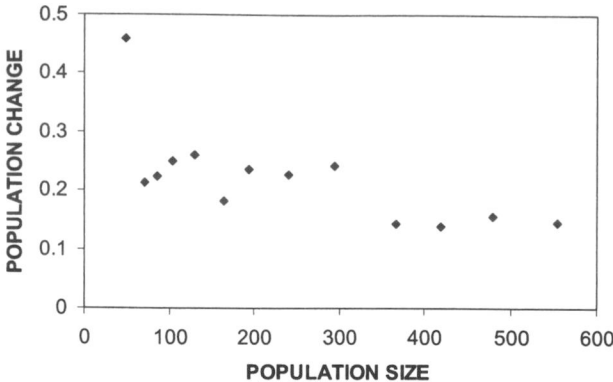

Fig. 3. Proportional change in bison population, $(N_{t+1} - N_t) / N_t$, versus population size, N_t, on the National Bison Range, Montana, USA, 1909–22.

where r_m, the maximum rate of growth, replaces r. Equivalently,

$$\frac{dN_t}{dt} = r_m N_t \frac{K - N_t}{K},$$

which can be interpreted (Krebs 1985:213) as rate of increase per unit of time, dN_t/dt, equals maximum rate of population growth per capita, r_m, times population size, N_t, times unused opportunity for growth, $(K - N_t)/K$. Note the factor modifying growth rate depends both on population size (through N) and the environment (through K). The equation has the solution

$$N_t = \frac{K}{1 + e^{a - r_m t}},$$ (5)

which is known as the logistic equation. K is the asymptote or carrying capacity and r_m is the maximum rate of population growth, the rate that would result if the population was free of constraints caused by the density of the population. The value of the parameter a depends on the time origin used; it measures the size of the population at time 0 relative to the asymptotic (infinite time) population size. Setting $t = 0$ in Equation 5, we find $a = \log[(K - N_0)/N_0]$.

The logistic equation has a rich history (Hutchinson 1978, Kingsland 1995) and is a mathematically convenient model that describes growth of a variety of populations. It is not, however, any sort of law of population growth. Among the assumptions (e.g., Pielou 1969:30, Poole 1974:63, Krebs 1985:220) are: 1) all individuals, regardless of age, gender, or genotype, are equivalent with respect to survival, reproduction, and susceptibility to crowding; 2) carrying capacity (K) is constant; 3) growth rate of the population responds instantaneously to population size; and 4) the effect of population size on growth rate is linear. Each of these restrictive assumptions can be relaxed, but with a loss of mathematical tractability. Models in which assumptions 1 and 2 are eased are discussed later. Assumption 3 can be modified either with discrete-time formulations or by introducing time lags into the continuous-time model (e.g., May 1973, Krebs 1985:224). One extension that overcomes assumption 4 is the generalized logistic equation (Gilpin and Ayala 1973, Eberhardt 1987). Pielou (1969:22–30) and others have considered stochastic versions of the logistic model.

Discrete-time Formulation

The logistic formulation specifically applies to continuously reproducing organisms, although it suffices for populations with discrete breeding seasons if population size is measured at the same time each year, as with the bison example. Otherwise, for animals with discrete breeding seasons, the discrete counterpart of Equation 4 is:

$$\frac{N_{t+1} - N_t}{N_t} = r_m \frac{K - N_t}{K},$$

with solution

$$N_{t+1} = N_t + r_m \left(1 - \frac{N_t}{K}\right) N_t.$$ (6)

This discrete version implicitly has a time delay; the population growth rate at time $t + 1$ depends on population size at time t. In contrast, Equation 4 assumes the rate of population change responds instantaneously to changes in the size of the population. Because of the time delay in the discrete version, the behavior of the modeled population depends strikingly on the values of the parameters. The

---

Box 2. How does density dependence work?

The exact role of density dependence in population regulation has long been a source of controversy (e.g., Krebs 1985:327–347). Density may influence survival or reproduction rates only at extreme densities (e.g., Strong 1986), exact values of which depend on the quantity and quality of the habitat available.

Knowlton (1972) presented evidence suggesting a relation between population density and fertility when he compared the average number of uterine swellings per female coyote (*Canis latrans*), an index to fertility, with intensity of efforts used to control coyotes in 7 counties in south Texas. Although sample sizes were limited and levels of coyote control were not randomly assigned to counties, there is a suggestion of an effect of population density on this index of fertility.

Control effort	County	Sample size	Average number of uterine swellings per female	Average number of uterine swellings per treatment
Intensive	Zavala	8	8.9	7.2
	Dimmit	12	6.4	
	Uvalde	10	6.2	
Moderate	Jim Wells	21	5.3	4.5
	Hildago	11	3.7	
Light	Jim Hogg	17	4.2	3.5
	Duval	11	2.8	

population can smoothly approach the asymptote, approach it in an oscillatory manner, cycle indefinitely, or fluctuate chaotically, depending on the value of r_m (May 1974, May and Oster 1976). That model, along with the realization that a simple deterministic mechanism could produce such a striking array of random-appearing behavior, was one of the early discoveries of what has now become the study of chaos.

Nonlinear least squares can be used directly on Equation 5 to estimate the parameters of the logistic equation. Using the bison data for 1909–22 gave estimates of $\hat{K} = 1{,}172$ (SE = 77.4) for the asymptote, $\hat{r}_m = 0.2479$ (SE = 0.0078) for the rate parameter, and $\hat{a} = 3.069$ (SE = 0.046) for the origin parameter.

An alternative is to use the discrete form of the logistic model. From Equation 6, we have:

$$N_{t+1} = N_t + r_m \left(1 - \frac{N_t}{K}\right) N_t = N_t \left(1 + r_m\right) + N_t^2 \left(\frac{-r_m}{K}\right)$$

and can perform a regression of N_{t+1} on N_t and N_t^2, excluding an intercept term. The coefficient of N_t will be an estimate of $(1 + r_m)$ and the coefficient of N_t^2 will estimate $-r_m/K$. For the bison example, we obtain $\widehat{(1+r_m)} = 1.2669$ (SE = 0.0266) and $\hat{r}_m = 0.2669$ (SE = 0.0266). The estimate of $-r_m/K$ is -0.000238 (SE = 0.000061) and $\hat{K} = 0.2669/0.000238 = 1{,}121.43$ (SE = 183.24).

One statistical difficulty with this regression approach is the assumption that explanatory variables, in this case N_t and N_t^2, are measured without error (Walters 1986:136). This is not a problem in the present case, because we believe the bison counts are exact, but the problem arises in most situations. We can illustrate the effect of measurement errors by reanalyzing the bison data, except that we include a small multiplicative error (each count is multiplied by e^z, where z is a normal random deviate with mean zero and standard deviation = 0.1) (Table 3). Results from this analysis give $\hat{r}_m = 0.4295$ (SE = 0.1138) and $\hat{K} = 594.88$ (SE = 72.43), values far different from estimates obtained using values measured without error (0.2669 and 1,121.43).

Of the 2 estimation techniques applied to the bison data, the nonlinear regression applied to Equation 5 gave a better fit (higher r^2 value) than linear regression of N_{t+1} on N_t and N_t^2. That superiority may not hold in general.

Some Dangers of Detecting Density Dependence

Discovering density dependence in a series of counts of a population is less straightforward than it might appear. First, population size and change in population tend to be negatively correlated, even if the change occurs independently of population size (e.g., Maelzer 1970, St. Amant 1970). Second, any uncertainty in estimating population size tends to add to the appearance of density dependence.

Consider a hypothetical example (Table 4), in which we started with $N_0 = 1{,}000$ animals; $\ln (N_0) = \log(1{,}000) = 6.91$. Adding a random number to the logarithm of the previous population generated the population in each successive year:

$$\log(N_{t+1}) = \log(N_t) + z,$$

where z is a random deviate with mean zero and standard deviation = 0.1. Although z was generated independently of N_t, a negative correlation between the 2 variables was induced; in the example shown (Table 4) we have $r = -0.62$ ($P = 0.055$). The reason for this surprising result is that, even in an irregular sequence of numbers, an unusually high value tends to be followed by a decrease (if it was more likely followed by an increase then it would no longer be an unusually high value), and vice versa (St. Amant 1970). Thus, a negative correlation between population change and previous population size cannot be construed as evidence for density dependence.

If the counts had been made subject to error, the situation is even worse. The appearance of density dependence increases, as the following illustrates. Suppose the population was underestimated in a particular year, this error will make the observed population size in that year more likely to be small than large. Also, it will make the change in observed population size larger than it should be, unless the population is underestimated again the following year.

Table 3. Actual counts of bison on the National Bison Range, Montana, USA, 1909–22, and counts with multiplicative error.

Year	Actual count	Count with error
1909	48	48
1910	70	64
1911	85	84
1912	104	100
1913	130	144
1914	164	178
1915	194	199
1916	240	227
1917	295	292
1918	367	389
1919	420	387
1920	479	496
1921	554	598
1922	635	553

Table 4. Hypothetical example illustrating the appearance of density dependence from annual counts of a population that varies randomly from year to year. N_t is actual population size in year t, O_t is observed population size, $\Delta_t = \log(N_t / N_{t-1})$ is actual change in population size, and $\Delta_t = \log(O_t / O_{t-1})$ is observed change in population size.

Year (t)	$\log(N_t)$	Δ_t	$\log(O_t)$	Δ_t
0	6.91		6.76	
1	7.15	0.24	6.95	0.19
2	7.18	0.03	7.58	0.63
3	7.12	−0.06	7.03	−0.55
4	7.10	−0.02	7.19	0.16
5	7.03	−0.07	7.23	0.04
6	7.06	0.03	7.12	−0.11
7	6.96	−0.10	6.94	−0.18
8	6.87	−0.09	6.89	−0.05
9	7.02	0.15	6.77	−0.12
10	7.12	0.10	7.22	0.45

Thus, a smaller-than-expected population size will be associated with a larger-than-expected population change, and a negative correlation will be induced. Consider again the hypothetical example (Table 4), except that now the counts were measured with error rather than exactly (call the observed counts O_t):

$$\log(O_t) = \log(N_t) + y,$$

where y is another random deviate, normally distributed with mean zero and standard deviation = 0.2. The correlation between observed population change and observed population size is stronger ($r = -0.73$, $P = 0.017$) than the correlation between true values.

From this we conclude that density-dependence should not be inferred from regression analysis on counts of populations, even if they are measured exactly. The same problem arises when performing a regression of $\log(N_{t+1})$ on $\log(N_t)$; regression coefficients <1.0 are expected even if there is no density dependence (Maelzer 1970). Eberhardt (1970), Slade (1977), Solow (1990), and especially Pollard et al. (1987) presented additional cautions. The converse problem also arises; Gaston and Lawton (1987) found that methods for detecting density dependence from census data consistently failed to do so, even for populations known (from independent evidence) to be subject to density-dependent processes.

Immigration and Emigration

Dispersal is a critical process that allows individuals to persist despite degradation of the habitat they currently occupy. Virtually all plant and animal species exhibit dispersal during at least one life stage. Caughley (1977:57) defined *dispersal* as the movement an animal makes from its point of origin to the place where it reproduces. He distinguished it from other types of movements, namely local movement within a home range, and migration (back-and-forth movements between discrete locations). Although dispersal is important in population dynamics, it is hard to detect and harder yet to measure. A biologist conducting a population analysis typically ignores dispersal, assumes it to be nonexistent, or hopes that immigration and emigration cancel one another.

Several texts (e.g., Pielou 1969, Poole 1974, Caughley 1977) discussed models of dispersal, but its estimation has received little attention. Most techniques for detecting or estimating dispersal rely on observations and recaptures of marked animals. Recently, other tools such as genetic markers have been used to address dispersal in animals (see Clobert et al. 2001).

Observation of marked animals has provided most of the evidence of dispersal, including direction, distance, time of occurrence, and length of time between sightings. Fortuitous records, such as a coyote being trapped a long distance from where it had been marked, are interesting and informative but reveal little about the dispersal patterns of coyotes in general. For a more complete picture, telemetry studies are needed in which all radio-equipped animals can be followed.

Mark–recapture studies can provide estimates of losses or gains to the population between trapping occasions, although they ordinarily are used to estimate size of a population. With certain designs, losses can be partitioned into deaths and emigration, and gains can be separately estimated as births and immigration (Jackson 1939, Krebs 1985:169, Manly 1985:41–43). Nichols and Pollock (1990) presented a procedure for separately estimating births and immigrants from a robust design mark–recapture study involving primary periods of trapping (well separated in time) and secondary trapping periods (closely spaced in time). Zeng and Brown (1987) proposed a method for distinguishing emigration from death in mark–recapture studies, but it requires recapture of all animals that are still alive and have not dispersed. By comparing estimated survival rates based on local mark–recapture studies (which incorporate probabilities of surviving and returning to the study area) with survival rates from banding studies (which incorporate only survival), one can estimate the return rate (e.g., Anderson and Sterling 1974, Hepp et al. 1987) as 1 minus the probability of permanent dispersal from an area.

Hestbeck et al. (1991) developed models for resighting of individually marked Canada geese (*Branta canadensis*) in the Atlantic Flyway, USA. In 3 years nearly 29,000 geese were marked and 102,000 resightings were made. The models included survival and resighting probabilities, and the probability of movement from one region to another in successive winters. They found that annual changes in movement probabilities corresponded to variation in the severity of winter. A model incorporating memory and tradition better fit the data, indicating that wintering location of a goose depended not only on where it spent the previous winter, but also where it had been 2 years before.

Birth and Death Models

We first recognize that population growth is the net result of births and deaths in the population (ignoring emigration and immigration), and refer again to the simple difference equation $N_{t+1} = N_t + B_t + I_t - D_t - E_t$. From this equation, birth rate ($b = B_t / N_t$) and death rate ($d = D_t / N_t$) can be defined as simple proportions. In many cases we can analyze birth and death processes separately, because they may be affected by different environmental variables. Consider again the bison example used earlier. Counts of bison can be divided into young of the year and adult age classes (Table 2), and the count of young of the year can be considered the final outcome of the birth process, birth here including not only parturition, but also survival until fall. The number of deaths of adults was also recorded.

Estimates of annual birth and death rates (defined per individual in the bison population at the start of the year) varied. Birth rates were lower when the population was larger (Fig. 4), and death rates increased with population size (Fig. 5). If birth and death rates are similar functions of population size, as appears to be true for the bison data, we can work with their difference rather than with individual components. It may be that only one or the other of birth and death rates is density-dependent, or that the nature of the relationship differs for the 2 processes. Thus, we should treat the 2 processes separately. Suppose for example that instantaneous birth rates (logarithms of finite birth rates) varied with density, say

$$b = b_0 + b_1 N,$$

but that instantaneous death rates were independent of density:

$$d = d_0 .$$

The population rate of increase $r = b - d$ is thus

$$r = (b_0 - d_0) + b_1N$$

and depends on the population size N. That is, population growth is density dependent, but an analysis of population size alone would not indicate which of the 2 processes, birth or death, was density-dependent.

Pielou (1969), among others, provided an introduction to stochastic birth and death processes. De Angelis (1976) applied these models to a population of Canada geese.

Estimating Birth Rates

The *fertility* of a population is the number of live births produced over some period of time, generally a year. Because it usually suffices to study the female segment of a population, fertility is often expressed as young females produced per female in the population. A related parameter is *fecundity*, the potential level of reproductive performance of a population, which is ordinarily much greater than the realized reproduction (fertility) (the terms fertility and fecundity are not used consistently). A related term, *recruitment*, refers to the addition of new individuals (typically only breeding individuals) to the population through reproduction. To calculate fertility in mammals, for example, we need to know average litter size, average number of litters produced per time interval (year), and the sex ratio at birth (Caughley 1977).

Estimation of fertility rate has received only scattered attention. Typically, rates are based on different criteria for different species groups. For mammals, number of live births is an appropriate measure. For fish, reptiles, and birds, the number of eggs laid or that hatch is often used. It is ordinarily difficult to see newborn young of many species. Thus, fertility is often assessed by the number of young produced that attain a particular life stage or size. In waterfowl studies, some measures of reproduction involve counts of ducklings nearly ready to fledge, or as members of the fall (hunted) population. For populations with synchronized, seasonal breeding (birth-pulse fertility), we calculate the number of births for females in a given age *class*. For more-or-less continuous breeders (birth-flow fertility), the number of births for females in a specified age *interval* is appropriate.

Estimation of birth rate, especially by age class, is dif-

ficult. Three general approaches are discussed. The first uses age ratios based on direct counts. The second uses mark–recapture methods, and the third involves a potpourri of indirect measures. In addition, change-in-ratio techniques may be applicable in some limited circumstances (e.g., Hanson 1963, Seber 1982:382).

Age Ratios Based on Direct Counts.—With whooping cranes or bison, we could count exactly the young produced (and surviving until time of census). More generally, biologists often relate number of young seen to number of adults seen and obtain an index to fertility. For example, ratios of fawns to does may be used for white-tailed deer, or number of placental scars in harvested fox squirrels (*Sciurus niger*), or number of successful nests or broods for birds or American crocodiles (*Crocodylus acutus*). For hunted species, the age ratio in the harvest is an index to recruitment, which must be adjusted for differential vulnerability of age classes (e.g., Martin et al. 1979). A variety of errors can creep into calculations of fertility. For example, does without fawns may be less conspicuous than those with fawns, or squirrels that had borne young may be more likely to be shot (and fertility thus measured) than those that did not, or successful bird nests may be more likely found than unsuccessful ones (Mayfield 1961).

More fundamentally, all the components of reproduction should be considered to gain a full understanding of the process. These include age at which animals first breed, incidence of nonbreeding among adults of breeding age, number of breeding cycles per year, size of clutch or litter, and survival to adult stage. For management purposes, a consistent index to reproduction, along with its standard error, will often suffice.

Mark–recapture Methods.—These methods have been described for both *closed populations* (which do not change during the period of interest) and *open populations* (which allow births, deaths, emigration, and immigration) (Lancia et al. 2005). The primary method for open populations involves the Jolly-Seber model, although the more restrictive Cormack-Jolly-Seber model is often used in practice. This model yields estimates not only of population size, but also of the number of individuals added to the population between trapping occasions (which includes births and immigrants) and the number removed from the population (which includes deaths and emigrants). If one can safely assume that no immigration has occurred, the estimated number of additions to the population is a meas-

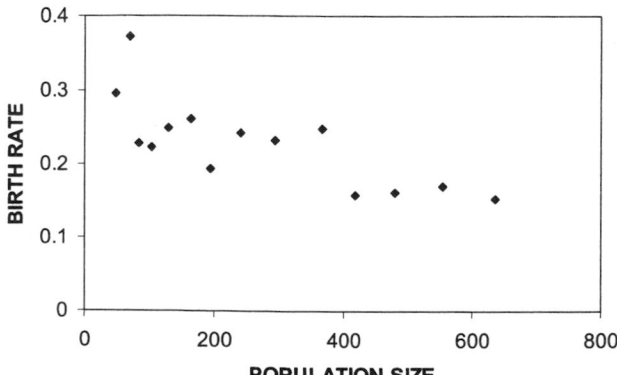

Fig. 4. Bison birth rates versus population size at start of year on the National Bison Range, Montana, USA, 1909-22.

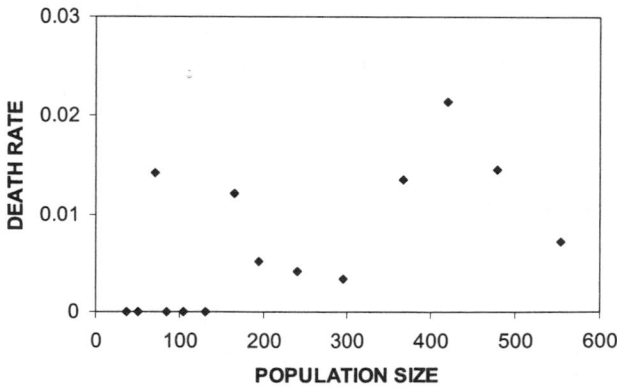

Fig. 5. Bison death rates versus population size at start of year on the National Bison Range, Montana, USA, 1909-22.

ure of births, although standard errors are usually large. Another approach is to estimate the recruitment rate (f_i) of the population using a reparameterized Jolly-Seber model (Pradel 1996) and program MARK. Here, f_i is defined as the number of new animals in the population at time i per animal in the population at time $i -1$ and is calculated using information about population size and apparent survival (ϕ_i, see section on Estimating Survival Rates) as

$$f_i = \frac{N_{i+1} - N_i\phi_i}{N_i}.$$

Indirect Measures.—Reproductive success of a population is often evaluated in terms of some component of reproduction. For example, clutch size and nest success are commonly used as measures in bird studies. Among mammals, characteristics of female reproductive tracts may be used (e.g., Harder and Kirkpatrick 1994). These measures might be perfectly adequate indices to reproduction, but they are only part of the picture. Other factors must be considered, for by focusing on only 1 or 2 of the components of reproduction, we implicitly assume the others vary only slightly, if at all.

Consider how duck productivity might be monitored on a refuge, for example. Counts of breeding pairs are used to estimate the size of the population and studies of nests give an estimate of nest success rate (Cowardin and Blohm 1992) (Box 3). These 2 variables may be key components in reproduction, but other variables could have a major or even a dominant role (Johnson et al. 1992). Some members of the population might not breed, for example. Some might renest after a nest failure while others do not. Clutch size can differ, and individual eggs may be depredated from nests or not hatch for other reasons. Finally, of the ducklings that hatch from a successful nest, the proportion that ultimately fledges may vary from 0 to 100%. Hence, reliance on only a subset of the components can cause misleading conclusions.

Estimating Survival Rates

In addition to recruitment, survival is an important component of population growth and decline. Here, we first distinguish between *true survival* (the real probability of living) and *apparent survival* (the product of true survival and fidelity). Only if fidelity is 100% will apparent survival equal true survival. Relative to true survival, apparent survival will be biased low when there is permanent emigration. Due largely to the design of the studies we conduct, apparent survival is much easier to estimate than true survival because our studies are limited in space and we may not be able to account for permanent emigrants that tend to bias survival estimates low. Furthermore, we

---

Box 3. A common bias in estimating nest success.

Among birds, one of the most important factors affecting size of a population is the percentage of nests from which young are successfully fledged. Fortunately, it is a parameter that managers often can influence by manipulating habitat or predation rates.

Many studies and monitoring programs of nest success fell victim to a serious bias. Biologists reported nest success rate to be the percentage of the successful nests among the sample of nests they found. This intuitively reasonable procedure is acceptable if all nests can be found at initiation, or if destroyed nests are as likely to be found as successful ones. Many species of birds, however, are secretive when nesting, and biologists are likely to find mostly nests when tended by an adult. Once destroyed, a nest will be abandoned by the adults and may be difficult to detect by usual nest-searching methods (e.g., Klett et al. 1986). An adult, in contrast, will tend a successful nest from initiation until the young leave. For that reason, it will more likely be found. This disparity in chances of detecting failed and successful nests introduces a major bias into the usual nest success rate. Harold Mayfield (1961) was among the first to recognize this problem, and he proposed a solution: He recommended computing a *daily mortality rate* for nests, based on the number of nests destroyed, divided by the total number of days nests were under observation. Subtracting this value from 1.0 gives a daily survival rate, which, when raised to a power equal to the number of days needed for a nest to proceed from initiation to success, gives a much better estimate of the true nest success rate. For example, Dinsmore et al. (2002) studied the nesting success of mountain plovers in Montana. Their apparent nesting success estimate was 0.58. The Mayfield daily survival estimate was 0.9740 (SE = 0.0021). The incubation period is 29 days for this species, so the estimated proportion of successful nests was $0.9740^{29} = 0.47$. Johnson (1979) presented a statistical model and standard errors for the Mayfield procedure. Johnson and Shaffer (1990) outlined situations in which the Mayfield method performed better than the apparent method.

The Mayfield method is clearly superior to estimates of apparent nest success but is not always biologically reasonable. In natural settings, daily survival of nests would hardly be expected to be constant in time. Instead, nest survival probably varies as a result of season, habitat, experience of the incubating adult, and other factors. Johnson (1979), Bart and Robson (1982), and Klett and Johnson (1982) discussed models that relax the assumption of constant nest survival. Additional developments in nest survival modeling include random individual nest effects (Natarajan and McCulloch 1999), daily nest survival across nest stages (for example, the transition between incubation and nestling stages) where the exact transition date between stages is unknown (Stanley 2000), and the effects of nest checks on the daily nest survival rate following a visit (Rotella et al. 2000). The Bart and Robson (1982) nest survival model is now incorporated into program MARK (Dinsmore et al. 2002) and offers greater flexibility to explore factors affecting daily nest survival rates of birds. Shaffer (2004) discusses how flexible models can be fit using logistic regression.

seldom are able to observe the fates of all individuals in a population and use this information as a measure of survival. Increasingly, we rely on estimates of survival from a sample of marked individuals. Thus, there are 5 basic approaches to estimating a survival rate (many involve estimating the complement of survival, the mortality rate that is equal to 1 – survival rate); each requires a different sort of data.

Observed Survival.—In some studies survival can be observed directly when deaths in the population are known. For captive or other closely watched populations, survival rates can be calculated without difficulty. In other studies, markers attached to animals allow biologists to observe a subset of a population. Radiotelemetry especially affords an opportunity to monitor animals closely and record instances of mortality. Fuller et al. (2005) describe methods for estimating survival rates from radiomarked animals. The same methods can be used for animals marked in other ways, as long as markers are retained and marked individuals can readily be found. Particularly troublesome are instances in which an animal's signal or marker cannot be located, so the observer is not sure if the transmitter failed, the animal (along with its transmitter) was destroyed, or the animal left the study area. Also, radio packages (Fuller et al. 2005) or other markers (e.g., Brodsky 1988, Kinkel 1989) may influence behavior and survival. Further, telemetry studies usually have been limited by small samples of animals and relatively short durations.

Ratios of Population Sizes or Indices.—If no movement into or out of a population occurs, the mortality between times t and $t + 1$ is the population size at time t minus the number of those that still remain at time $t + 1$. If those survivors can be distinguished from the young that were added to the population, survival can be computed directly. Consider the whooping crane example again. This is a rare example where all individuals in the population are known, so there were no immigrants. Adults counted in one winter thus represent the survivors of the total population (adults plus young) in the previous winter. From ratios of these counts, survival rates can be computed. In 1938, for instance, there were 18 birds (14 adults and 4 young) (Table 1). Of these, 15 were still alive in 1939, giving a survival rate of 15/18 = 0.83 (SE = 0.09, as a binomial variate). Survival rates for other years can be similarly calculated.

It is unusual to have exact counts from which survival rates can be calculated, such as we have for the cranes. Often, however, indices to population size are available; if these are representative of a constant proportion of the population, they can be used equally as well. Consider as an example results from a banding study of female mallards in Minnesota (Table 5). In 1968, 338 adult females were banded. Assume that hunters took equal proportions of the banded populations in the 1968 and 1969 hunting seasons (a conclusion supported by a more rigorous analysis in Johnson [1974: Table 3]). Thus, the 16 recoveries in 1968 represent the same fraction of the 1968 population that the 9 recoveries in 1969 represent of the 1969 population. From this, we can estimate the survival between hunting seasons to be 9/16 = 0.56, albeit with a large standard error (SE = 0.23, as a ratio of 2 multinomial variates).

Table 5. Recoveries of female mallards banded as adults in Minnesota, USA, 1968–70 (from Johnson 1974).

Year	Number banded	Number of recoveries 1968	1969	1970
1968	338	16	9	5
1969	67		6	5
1970	93			12

Survival can also be estimated if indices do not represent constant fractions of the population, but are known to be in certain proportions. Such methods are based on *catch-effort models.* Suppose it is somehow known that recovery rates of female mallards banded in Minnesota varied during 1968–70 in the proportions 0.058, 0.056, and 0.100 (Johnson 1974: Table 3). The numbers of birds banded in 1968 and recovered in 1968, 1969, and 1970 were 16, 9, and 5. The ratios 16/0.058, 9/0.056, and 5/0.100 should represent the same proportion of the population in each of the 3 years. These ratios, 275.86, 160.71, and 50.00, suggest that survival from 1968 to 1969 was 160.71/275.86 = 0.58 (minimum SE = 0.24, assuming that effort is known exactly) and survival from 1969 to 1970 was 50.00/160.71 = 0.31 (minimum SE = 0.17). Catch-effort models are most often applied to fisheries problems, in which fishing effort is well known, or to populations of small mammals where trapping effort can be calculated.

A similar technique produces estimates of the survival of young animals from ratios of sizes of litters or broods at different ages. For example, Stoudt (1971) computed mortality of canvasback (*Aythya valisineria*) ducklings between young (Class I) and older (Class II) stages to be 1.2 ducklings per brood, based on average brood sizes in those 2 classes. It is necessary, however, to account for the possibility that some litters or broods may have been lost completely. Further, among young waterfowl it is not uncommon for broods to split into 2 or more groups, or for 2 or more broods to combine into a larger aggregation. These processes can bias estimates of survival rate from brood counts.

Change-in-ratio Methods.—The change-in-ratio technique, usually applied to estimating population size, can be used to estimate the rate of mortality due to exploitation (Paulik and Robson 1969:16, Seber 1982:380). To do so requires 2 distinguishable types of animals (male and female, or young and adult) and estimates of the fraction of each type in the population before harvest, in the harvest, and in the population after harvest. Assumptions required to give good estimates are stringent, however, and should be carefully considered before the method is adopted (Downing 1980:251–252).

Mark–recapture Methods.—These methods are the most widely used approaches for estimating survival. A large class of models exists, each emphasizing particular assumptions or a combination of survival and other parameters.

Consider a study involving J occasions on which animals are captured, marked, and returned to the population. Suppose that all animals are alike in having the same chance of being captured on a particular occasion, call this probability c_i for the ith occasion, and in having the same probability of surviving from occasion i to occasion $i + 1$, say S_i. Define N_i to be the number of animals in the population on occasion i. Suppose that M_i of these had been marked previously. On the ith occasion, n_i animals are captured, of which m_i had been marked already and the remaining u_i had not been marked previously. From these values we can estimate the population size on occasions 2 through J-1, as well as the number of combined births and immigrants (B_i) between occasions i and $i + 1$ for $i = 2$ through J-2. Of special concern, survival rates S_i, $i = 1$ through J-2, can be estimated. These are:

$$\hat{S}_i = \frac{\hat{M}_{i+1}}{\hat{M}_i - m_i + R_i},$$

where

$$\hat{M}_i = m_i + \frac{R_i z_i}{r_i}$$

and R_i is the number of the n_i animals that are released after the ith sampling occasion (normally this will be n_i minus any losses during capture), r_i is the number of the R_i animals released at i that are captured again, and z_i is the number of animals that were captured before i, not captured at i, but captured again later. Estimated standard errors of survival rates are available (e.g., Seber 1982:202, Pollock et al. 1990:21–22). Methods for estimating N_i, B_i, and c_i are given in Lancia et al. (2005). Cormack (1973) presented a readable justification for the Jolly-Seber model. Program MARK can be used to estimate parameters of the Jolly-Seber model. Seber (1982) described a variety of alternative models, while Pollock et al. (1990) discussed mark–recapture methods and developed several new models.

Recently, the Jolly-Seber model has been reparameterized (Pradel 1996) to allow estimation of parameters other than survival, including *seniority* (γ_i, the probability that an animal alive at time i had not entered the population between times $i - 1$ and i, which is useful for estimating recruitment), a recruitment rate into the population (f_i), and the rate of population change (λ). Estimating seniority becomes important because it can be used to estimate the proportion of population change that is due to recruitment (births and immigration) and survival (Franklin 2001). In terms of the Jolly-Seber model, seniority can also be written as

$$\gamma_i = 1 - \frac{B_i}{N_{i+1}}$$

and λ can be computed as

$$\lambda_i = \frac{S_i}{\gamma_{i+1}}.$$

As an example consider the data in Table 6, derived from a mark–recapture study of meadow voles (*Microtus pennsylvanicus*). There were 6 trapping occasions from late June through December. From these recapture statistics, we can calculate estimates of survival rate from one occasion to the next (for the first 4 occasions). We can estimate survival from occasion 1 to occasion 2 from

$$\hat{M}_1 = m_1 + \frac{R_1 z_1}{r_1}$$

$$= 0 + 105\left(\frac{0}{87}\right)$$

$$= 0$$

$$\hat{M}_2 = m_2 + \frac{R_2 z_2}{r_2}$$

$$= 84 + 121\left(\frac{5}{76}\right)$$

$$= 91.96,$$

thus,

$$\hat{S}_1 = \frac{\hat{M}_2}{\hat{M}_1 - m_1 + R_1}$$

$$= \frac{91.96}{0 - 0 + 105}$$

$$= 0.88,$$

and likewise for the remaining values. Pollock et al. (1990:30) also presented estimates of population size and the number of births.

It should be emphasized that births include all animals added to a population, whether by actual birth or by immigration. Also, the survival rate reflects not only actual survival, but also permanent emigration from the study area; the measure is thus of apparent survival. This method can be used with different kinds of capture on different occasions. Of particular interest is marking animals on the first occasion and using resightings of marked animals on subsequent occasions.

There are other methods of estimating survival rates using mark–recapture data; these approaches have become varied and sophisticated. A class of models called multistate or multi-stratum models (Arnason 1973, Nichols et al. 1992) at times may be used to estimate survival rates, although they are more appropriate for estimating transition probabilities between specific stages (e.g., the rate at which individuals in a population transition between life stages or age classes or the rate of movement between different sites).

Table 6. Mark–recapture statistics for a population of meadow voles trapped in 1981, Maryland, USA (Pollock et al. 1990:29).[a]

Period	Dates	n_i	m_i	R_i	r_i	z_i	$\hat{S}_i$	SE
1	27 Jun–1 Jul	108	0	105	87	0	0.88	0.039
2	1 Aug–5 Aug	127	84	121	76	5	0.66	0.048
3	29 Aug–2 Sep	102	73	101	68	8	0.69	0.049
4	3 Oct–7 Oct	103	73	102	63	3	0.63	0.049
5	31 Oct–4 Nov	102	61	100	84	5		
6	4 Dec–8 Dec	149	89	148				

[a] For the ith occasion, n_i animals are captured, of which m_i were already marked; R_i is the number of n_i animals released after the ith sampling occasion; r_i is the number of R_i animals released at i that are captured again; z_i is the number of animals that were captured before i, not captured at i, but captured again later; and $\hat{S}_i$ is the estimated survival rate.

The robust design (Pollock 1982; Kendall and Nichols 1995; Kendall et al. 1995, 1997) incorporates features of both open and closed capture–recapture models and offers several advantages over the traditional Jolly-Seber model. A limitation of the Jolly-Seber model is that it estimates parameters associated with the general population (N_i^0) and not with the subset of the population that is exposed to sampling (N_i) (Kendall et al. 1997). Consideration of this sampling issue is necessary because some individuals may occasionally not be exposed to sampling efforts, effectively making them temporary emigrants. This relationship is clarified by the formula:

$$E(N_i) = (1 - \gamma_i)N_i^0,$$

where γ_i is the probability that an individual is not exposed to capture in period i and is thus a temporary emigrant (note: this is not the same γ_i used earlier to indicate seniority; notation used in mark–recapture models is sometimes confusing!). Furthermore, the relationship between the probability of temporary emigration (γ_i) and the capture probabilities of animals that are exposed to sampling (p_i^*, a pooled capture probability for each sampling period) and those of all individuals in the population (p_i^0) is

$$p_i^0 = (1 - \gamma_i)p_i^*.$$

The probability of temporary emigration is then estimated as

$$\hat{\gamma}_i = 1 - \frac{\hat{p}_i^0}{\hat{p}_i^*}.$$

A robust design study includes i primary sampling periods, each with l_i secondary sampling periods. The number of secondary sampling periods in each primary sampling period need not be equal. Closure (no births, deaths, immigration, or emigration) is assumed during the secondary sampling periods within each primary sampling period. The population is "open" to births, deaths, immigration, and emigration in the time interval between primary sampling periods. Information from secondary sampling periods is used to estimate conditional capture (p_{ij}) and recapture (c_{ij}) probabilities, and population size (N_i). A pooled capture probability (p_i^*) is then calculated for each primary sampling period as

$$p_i^* = 1 - \prod_{j=1}^{l_i}\left(1 - p_{ij}\right)$$

and is the probability that an animal is captured in at least one of the l_i secondary sampling periods in primary sampling period i. The pooled capture probabilities are used to estimate apparent survival and temporary emigration. Temporary emigration is defined by 2 parameters, γ_i'' and γ_i'. Here, γ_i'' is the probability that an animal is a temporary emigrant in period i, given that it was alive and available for sampling in primary sampling period $i - 1$. This contrasts with γ_i', which is the probability that an animal that was a temporary emigrant in primary sampling period $i - 1$ remains a temporary emigrant in primary sampling period i. This design allows estimation of apparent survival ($\phi_1, ..., \phi_{k-1}$) and population size ($N_1, ..., N_k$) in the presence of temporary emigration. By estimating capture probabilities separately for each secondary sampling peri-

Table 7. Bandings and recoveries of wood ducks in 1964 and 1965 (from Brownie et al. 1985:22).

Year	Number banded	Number of recoveries	
		1964	1965
1964	1,603	127	44
1965	1,595		62

od, this approach is robust to heterogeneity and trap response in capture probability (Pollock et al. 1990). The advantages of the robust design are many and include the ability to estimate temporary emigration, population size, and apparent survival simultaneously with a single study. Other variations of the robust design permit use of individual covariates (a unique characteristic of each individual such as its body mass or total length) on capture and recapture probabilities (Huggins 1989, 1991).

Methods Based on Tag Recoveries.—An important class of models, called tag or band recovery models, is similar to mark–recapture methods but typically involves recoveries of dead, rather than live, marked animals. Many of these models were developed to use with data from banding programs for game birds, although they are also widely used with other taxa. In those programs, large numbers of birds are captured each year and banded with individually identifiable bands. Hunters who recover a banded bird are encouraged to report the identification number. The situation is a mark–recapture study with many marking occasions (typically one per year for a series of years), but for an individual bird only a single recapture is possible. Consider a simple example. Suppose that wood ducks (*Aix sponsa*) are banded for 2 years, just prior to the hunting season of each year (Table 7). Define c_1 to be the recovery rate, the probability that a bird is shot and its band reported during the first year. Similarly, c_2 is the probability that a bird, alive at the beginning of the hunting season in year 2, is shot and its band reported. Let S_1 be the probability that a bird survives from the beginning of the first hunting season to the beginning of the second; this is the survival rate we wish to estimate. If 1,603 birds are banded in year 1, we expect $1,603 \times c_1$ to be shot and reported the first year (Table 8); the actual number was 127. From this we calculate an estimate of c_1: $\hat{c}_1 = 127/1,603 = 0.0792$. We also calculate an estimate of c_2: $\hat{c}_2 = 62/1,595 = 0.0389$. Of the 1,603 birds banded the first year, we expect $1,603 \times S_1$ to survive to the beginning of the hunting season in the second year, and a

Table 8. Expected numbers of bandings and recoveries of wood ducks in 1964 and 1965.[a]

Year	Number banded	Expected number of recoveries	
		1964	1965
1964	N_1	N_1c_1	$N_1S_1c_2$
1965	N_2		N_2c_2

[a] c_1 is the recovery rate in the ith hunting season and S_i is the probability that a bird survives from the beginning of the ith hunting season to the beginning of the next.

fraction c_2 of them to be shot and reported. The actual number was 44. Thus, $44 = 1{,}603 \times \hat{S}_1 \times 0.0389$, or $\hat{S}_1 = 0.7056$.

This procedure of equating observed to expected values works only when the number of parameters to be estimated equals the number of equations, but it does illustrate the principle behind the construction of modern banding models.

Suppose that only adults are banded and released in the program. It may be reasonable to assume that recovery and survival rates vary annually but do not depend on the year when the bird originally was banded. This is Seber's (1970) model, termed Model 1 in Brownie et al. (1985).

We illustrate this procedure with an example from Brownie et al. (1985:14) involving male wood ducks (Table 9). From the summary statistics, we get $\hat{c}_1 = 0.0792$, $\hat{c}_2 = 0.0401$, $\hat{c}_3 = 0.0688$, $\hat{S}_1 = 0.6512$, and $\hat{S}_2 = 0.6311$. Calculated standard errors were SE $(\hat{c}_1) = 0.00674$, SE $(\hat{c}_2) = 0.00415$, SE $(\hat{c}_3) = 0.00608$, SE $(\hat{S}_1) = 0.0675$, and SE $(\hat{S}_2) = 0.0647$. An approximate 95% confidence interval is the sample value minus and plus 1.96 times the standard error. For the first-year recovery rate, for example, we get $0.0792 - 1.96 \times 0.00674 = 0.0660$ as a lower limit, and $0.0792 + 1.96 \times 0.00674 = 0.0924$ as an upper limit. Hence, a 95% confidence interval for c_1 is (0.0660–0.0924).

It is possible that more restrictive models fit a particular data set adequately, in which case the relevant parameters may be estimated more precisely. A likely candidate is the model in which survival rates are assumed to be the same each year, but recovery rates vary. This model (Model 2 of Brownie et al. 1985) often fits data sets well, perhaps because true survival rates do not vary much, and the ability of actual banding data to detect those differences is weak. The most restrictive model assumes that both survival rates and recovery rates are the same each year. This model (Model 0 of Brownie et al. 1985) might fit small data sets, but is likely actually to be true only in rare circumstances.

Both young and adult birds are often banded in the same program. One cannot safely assume that birds of the 2 age groups have the same survival and recovery rates, so they must be treated differently. Yet, if the young birds survive long enough, they become adults, subject to adult survival and recovery patterns. Several useful models have been developed for this situation. One of the most general is that of Brownie and Robson (1976), termed Model H_1 by Brownie et al. (1985). As before, survival and recovery rates are assumed to vary by year, and young have different

survival and recovery rates for their first year only. Estimators are presented in Brownie et al. (1985:60) and are calculated by the recoveries-only model in program MARK. An example is presented in Tables 10 and 11.

More restrictive models can give more precise estimates, if they fit the data adequately. Another reasonable model allows survival rates for both young and adults to vary from year to year, but assumes that rates for the 2 age groups fluctuate in parallel. This model, proposed by Johnson (1974), has no closed-form solution and is not included in program BROWNIE but can be fitted with program MARK or with general maximum-likelihood programs. In addition, one can fit models that allow survival rates for 2 age classes to vary from year to year in parallel, but with recovery rates varying independently, or vice versa.

Table 9. Banding and recovery data for male wood ducks (from Brownie et al. 1985:22).[a]

Year banded (i)	Number banded	Year of recovery (j)					
		1964 1	1965 2	1966 3	1967 4	1968 5	R_i
1964	1,603	127	44	37	40	17	265
1965	1,595		62	76	44	28	210
1966	1,157			82	61	24	167
		$C_j = 127$	106	195	145	69	
		$T_j = 265$	348	409	214	69	

[a] R_i are row totals, C_j are column totals, and T_j are block totals, of the number of recoveries.

Table 10. Data from a banding study of juvenile and adult male mallards banded preseason in the San Luis Valley, Colorado, USA, 1963–71.

Year banded	Number banded	Year of recovery								
		1963	1964	1965	1966	1967	1968	1969	1970	1971
		Banded as adults								
1963	231	10	13	6	1	1	3	1	2	0
1964	649		58	21	16	15	13	6	1	1
1965	885			54	39	23	18	11	10	6
1966	590				44	21	22	9	9	3
1967	943					55	39	23	11	12
1968	1,077						66	46	29	18
1969	1,250							101	59	30
1970	938								97	22
1971	312									21
		Banded as juveniles								
1963	962	83	35	18	16	6	8	5	3	1
1964	702		103	21	13	11	8	6	6	0
1965	1,132			82	36	26	24	15	18	4
1966	1,201				153	39	22	21	16	8
1967	1,199					109	38	31	15	1
1968	1,155						113	64	29	22
1969	1,131							124	45	22
1970	906								95	25
1971	353									38

Table 11. Estimated survival and recovery rates for juvenile and adult male mallards fitted to Model H_1. Estimated standard errors are in parentheses.

Year	Survival rate		Recovery rate	
	Adult	Juvenile	Adult	Juvenile
1963	0.576 (0.113)	0.471 (0.059)	0.0433 (0.0134)	0.0863 (0.0091)
1964	0.636 (0.076)	0.506 (0.070)	0.0856 (0.0092)	0.1467 (0.0134)
1965	0.666 (0.079)	0.589 (0.072)	0.0590 (0.0061)	0.0724 (0.0077)
1966	0.805 (0.098)	0.591 (0.072)	0.0628 (0.0067)	0.1274 (0.0096)
1967	0.650 (0.072)	0.478 (0.061)	0.0520 (0.0050)	0.0909 (0.0083)
1968	0.552 (0.058)	0.652 (0.072)	0.0633 (0.0055)	0.0978 (0.0087)
1969	0.572 (0.066)	0.464 (0.068)	0.0789 (0.0061)	0.1096 (0.0093)
1970	0.542 (0.129)	0.393 (0.113)	0.0888 (0.0080)	0.1049 (0.0102)
1971	0.0673 (0.0142)	0.1076 (0.0165)		

Other restrictions include assuming that survival rates remain the same from year to year (Model H_{02} of Brownie et al. 1985), or that both survival and recovery rates are constant (Model H_{01} of Brownie et al. 1985). Further, the procedure can be generalized to 3 age classes, if birds can be distinguished by age class, and some members from each age class are banded. This situation may pertain to geese, for example.

Two thoughts should be considered when planning a banding program to estimate survival. First, adults need to be included. If only young are banded, little can be estimated from the resulting recovery data unless some strong assumptions are made (e.g., Burnham and Anderson 1979, Anderson et al. 1981). Second, sample size must be large to obtain meaningful estimates. The program BAND2 (Wilson et al. 1989) estimates required sample sizes for different models. That program should be used, and the handbook by Brownie et al. (1985) carefully reviewed, prior to embarking on a banding program.

Populations With Age-dependent Birth and Death Rates

Fertility Tables

Both fertility and survival (Box 4) are known to vary by age for many species, and considerable effort has been expended in developing models with age-dependent birth and death rates. Consider an age-structured population with a maximum of i age classes, recorded in years. Suppose females of age x produce an average of m_x young females per year. The table giving the number of female offspring per year per female of age x is called the *fertility table* (e.g., see Table 12 for a population of white-tailed deer in central Michigan). Average fertility rates vary with age and are zero for young of the year, nearly zero for yearlings, and increase up to age 6, after which they decline.

Life Tables

Analogous to the fertility table is the mortality schedule, which describes the pattern of deaths by age class. The probability of a female surviving from the beginning of age class x to the beginning of age class $x + 1$ is defined to be s_x. The survival data (Table 12) for the central Michigan deer population (Eberhardt 1969) suggested the survival rate of age classes 1 and above did not differ from one another and the average rate was 0.70.

Consider a cohort of animals (a group born at roughly

the same time) that begins with 1,000 individuals at age 0. Thus, there will be $1,000 \times s_0$ individuals the next year (at age 1), $1,000 \times s_0 \times s_1$ members the following year (at age 2), and so forth. The number of individuals surviving from birth to age class x will be termed n_x:

$$n_x = 1,000 s_0 s_1 ... s_{x-1}.$$

Often the mortality rate, rather than the survival rate, is expressed: $q_x = 1 - s_x$.

A *life table* gives these and other relevant values. A life table is basically a summary of the survivorship of a population. It can also be used to calculate or estimate mortality rates, by age, under certain assumptions. Life tables were developed for human populations, especially for insurance applications, but have also been applied to wildlife populations. Human life tables generally involve large numbers of individuals for which exact times of death can be ascertained, whereas information for wild animals is typically incomplete. For most animal populations, information is based on a sample; thus, a life table provides *estimates* of relevant parameters that are less exact than values for humans.

Box 4. Age variation in survival rates.

For vertebrate populations it is the norm that survival (or, conversely, mortality) rates vary by age. Typical patterns involve low survival of young animals, higher survival of animals in their prime, and decreasing survival with advancing age. Deviations from this pattern can occur, especially if reproduction imposes an added mortality risk. For the analysis of a population, the difference in survival between young animals and prime-age animals is usually important. The difference between prime and older years may be less important, especially in exploited populations in which few animals reach advanced ages.

Consider a simple example of the age-specific survival of the mountain plover (Dinsmore et al. 2003). These birds have 2 distinct age classes: juveniles (hatch to first birthday) and adult (>1 year old). A simple model with no age differences produced an estimate of annual survival of $\hat{S} = 0.59$ (SE = 0.02). When age effects were considered, the corresponding estimates of annual survival were $\hat{S}_{adult} = 0.68$ (SE = 0.03) and $\hat{S}_{juvenile} = 0.46$ (SE = 0.07). The model with age effects received far more support than the no-age-effects model using AIC model selection criteria, suggesting that survival differed by age. This result was expected, and the large differences in annual survival by age class are an indication of the importance of modeling age effects in survival.

Table 12. Survival and reproduction data for white–tailed deer in central Michigan, USA (from Eberhardt 1969).

Age (x)	Survival rate (s_x)	Fertility rate (m_x)
0	0.58	0
1	0.70	0.047
2	0.70	0.503
3	0.70	0.663
4	0.70	0.733
5	0.70	0.743
6	0.70	0.771
>6	0.70	0.644

Table 13. Example of a life table based on known deaths of 42 gray squirrels (*Sciurus carolinensis*) born in 1954 (from Downing 1980:256).

Age (years) (x)	Number in population (n_x)	Number of deaths (d_x)	Mortality rate (q_x)	Survival rate (s_x)
0–1	42	22	22/42 = 0.52	20/42 = 0.48
1–2	20	10	10/20 = 0.50	10/20 = 0.50
2–3	10	7	7/10 = 0.70	3/10 = 0.30
3–4	3	2	2/3 = 0.67	1/3 = 0.33
4–5	1	1	1/1 = 1.00	0/1 = 0

For many animals, survival and fertility rates differ more sharply by size or life stage than by age. Some life table methods can be used with size classes or stages. Lefkovitch (1965) developed population projection methods for such situations. Usher (1972), Kirkpatrick (1984), Sauer and Slade (1987), and Caswell (2000) provided further details and some applications.

A life table consists of 6 basic columns:

x: age, measured in years or some other convenient unit or interval, $[x, x + 1)$;

n_x: the number of individuals surviving to the beginning of age x from an initial cohort of n_0 members;

d_x: the number of deaths in the age class $[x, x + 1)$, $d_x = n_x - n_{x+1}$;

q_x: the mortality rate at age x, $q_x = d_x / n_x$;

s_x: the survival rate at age x, $s_x = 1 - q_x$; and

l_x: the cumulative survival rate from birth until age x, $l_x = s_0 \times s_1 \times ... \times s_{x-1} = n_x / n_0$.

The definition of survival rates in the mortality table pertains to the period from the beginning of one age class to the beginning of the next. The fertility table describes reproduction per female in an age class. To use survival and reproductive rates in combination, one must define the age classes similarly in the 2 tables. That is, if reproduction is categorized by number of young produced and surviving to autumn, survival of adults should be assessed from autumn to autumn.

We provide an example of a life table (Table 13) and note that examples are given only to illustrate the method, as sample sizes are too small to draw reliable conclusions. Note that d_x can be computed from values of n_x by subtraction, and n_x can be calculated by adding entries in the d_x column from the bottom. Also, q_x is based on d_x and n_x; conversely, the table of n_x for $x > 0$ can be constructed from q_x values. Thus, there is only one independent column and all others can be calculated from any one of them. Depending on the type of data available and the assumptions that can realistically be made, a variety of life tables can be constructed.

Graphs of cohort size or cumulative survivorship (on a logarithmic scale) against age often approximate 1 of 3 characteristic shapes (Fig. 6), but possibly with a down-

ward jag reflecting lower survival of newborns (Pearl 1928). Type I survivorship curves have low mortality early in life but higher rates among older individuals. Female elk (*Cervus elaphus*) in the northern Yellowstone herd exemplify this pattern, with the exception of a depressed survival rate of young (Fig. 7). Type II survivorship curves have mortality rates roughly constant with age, leading to a straight-line relation on a log scale. Adult songbirds are suggested to have similar patterns (Krebs 1985). The Type III survivorship curve involves high mortality among young and decreasing mortality as individuals age. Many invertebrates and fish display Type III survivorship; they are vulnerable when they are young and small, but age and growth impart greater security. Siler (1979) and Eberhardt (1985) discussed how survivorship functions might be decomposed into functions representing 3 stages of life: early life, maturity, and senescence.

The Stable Age Distribution

The *age distribution* of a population is the number of individuals of each age class in the population at a particular time. If age-dependent survival and fertility rates remain constant for a fairly long period of time, the proportion of animals in each age class will stabilize. This is true even if the population itself is not constant in size; that is, a population can be expanding or declining and still have constant proportions in each age class. The resulting fractions comprise what is termed the *stable age distribution*. The fraction of the population in age class x will equal C_x:

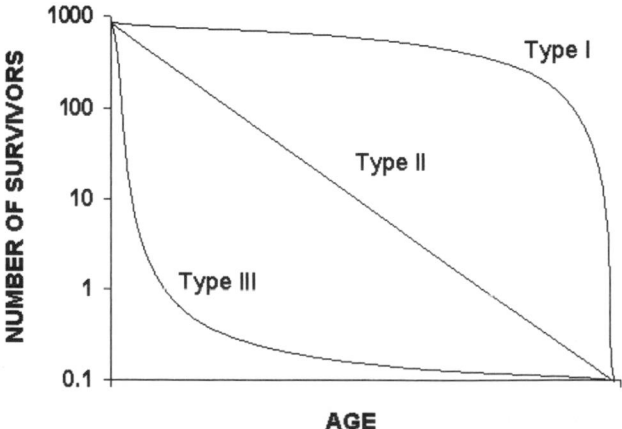

Fig. 6. Three characteristic survivorship curves.

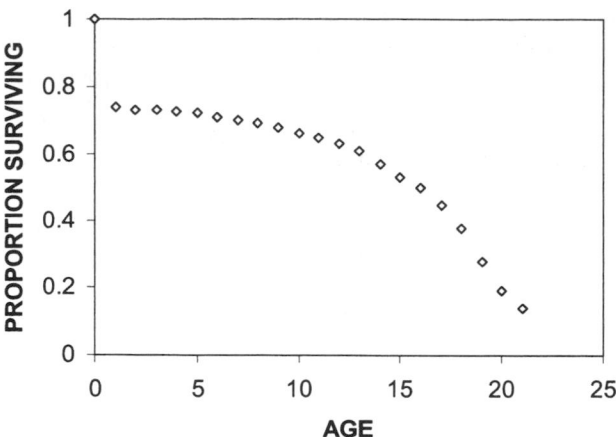

Fig. 7. Survivorship curve of female elk in the Northern Yellowstone herd (Houston 1982:55).

Table 14. Stable age distribution calculated from survival and reproduction data for white-tailed deer in central Michigan, USA (from Eberhardt 1969).

Age (x)	Survival to age (l_x)	Fraction in age (C_x)
0	1.0000	0.3214
1	0.5800	0.1913
2	0.4060	0.1375
3	0.2842	0.0988
4	0.1989	0.0709
5	0.1392	0.0510
6	0.0974	0.0366
7	0.0682	0.0263
8	0.0478	0.0189
9	0.0334	0.0136
>9	$0.58(0.70)^{x-1}$	0.0337

$$C_x = \frac{e^{-rx}l_x}{\sum_i e^{-ri}l_i}. \tag{7}$$

where r is the growth rate of the population once it attains a stable age distribution.

Suppose a population was constant in size at N members. The stable age distribution at any time t would contain members in each age class proportional to the survivorship, i.e., $N \times l_0$ of age class 0, $N \times l_1$ of age class 1, and so on. But, if the population has been changing at an annual rate λ, the number of members in age class x at time t would be the number born x years earlier ($N_{t-x}l_0$) times the survivorship of those members (l_x/l_0). Because of population growth, $N_t = N_{t-x}e^{-\lambda x}$. Thus, in year t the fraction of the population in age class x will be $N_{t-x}l_0 \times l_x/l_0 = N_t e^{-\lambda x}l_x$, which is proportional to the numerator of Equation 7. The denominator is the sum of such values over all ages, which scales the numbers so they total 1.0.

Alternatively, the size of the age class x relative to that of newborn (Caughley 1977:114) is:

$$C_x = \frac{e^{-rx}l_x}{\sum_i e^{-ri}l_i}.$$

The value of r can be calculated from age-dependent survival and fertility rates according to the following equation:

$$1 = \sum_x e^{-rx}l_x m_x. \tag{8}$$

This is the discrete version of *Lotka's equation* (sometimes called Euler's equation) (e.g., Mertz [1970], Wilson and Bossert [1971:116], or Caughley [1977:107]). This equation requires that survival and reproduction schedules remain constant for a long period of time, often an unlikely presumption. It is strictly appropriate only for a "birth pulse" population in which births occur instantaneously and the age structure is observed at the same time (Michod and Anderson 1980).

Equation 8 can be solved for r from a schedule of age-dependent cumulative survival rates (l_x) and fertility rates

(m_x). For the white-tailed deer data (Table 12), the estimated value of r is $\hat{r} = -0.026$. This suggests, because $e^{-0.026} = 1 - 0.0257$, that the deer population was declining (since the rate is negative) at about 2.6% each year.

With this estimate of r, we can now calculate the asymptotic age structure of the deer population from Equation 7. The number in age class x is proportional to $e^{-rx}l_x$, which gives the C_x values (Table 14). This distribution can be compared to the actual age distribution, if known, to test whether or not the underlying assumptions are met.

Projecting the Population: Leslie Matrices

If a population has attained a stable age distribution, and we were fortunate enough to know the age-dependent survival and fertility rates, we could learn a lot about the population from studying those rates. Consider an age-structured population (with M age classes) that breeds seasonally, and has survival and fertility rates that vary with age, but not annually. Suppose the population is surveyed for several years at the same time each year, say immediately after the birth season. Let $n_{x,t}$ be the number of individuals of age x in year t. The number of 1-year-olds in year $t + 1$ ($n_{1,t+1}$) will be the number that were born in year t ($n_{0,t}$) times the survival rate of 0-year-olds (s_0):

$$n_{1,t+1} = s_0 n_{0,t}.$$

Similarly, the number of 2-year-olds in year $t + 1$ equals the number of 1-year-olds in the previous year times their survival rate:

$$n_{2,t+1} = s_1 n_{1,t},$$

or, in general,

$$n_{i+1,t+1} = s_i n_{i,t}. \tag{9}$$

Consider next the number of births, which can be allocated according to the different age classes that reproduce. The number of 0-year-olds (births) in year $t + 1$ ($n_{0,t+1}$) represents the number of 1-year-olds in that year ($n_{1,t+1}$)

times the fertility rate of 1-year-olds (m_1), plus the number of 2-year-olds in that year ($n_{2,t+1}$) times their fertility rate, and so forth. That is:

$$n_{0,t+1} = m_1 n_{1,t+1} + m_2 n_{2,t+1} + \ldots + m_M n_{M,\,t+1} \, .$$

We want to express this number in terms of the population in the previous year and, in light of Equation 9, we get:

$$
\begin{aligned}
n_{0,t+1} &= m_1(s_0 n_{0,t}) + m_2(s_1 n_{1,t}) + \ldots + m_M(s_{M-1} n_{M-1,t}) \\
&= (m_1 s_0) n_{0,t} + (m_2 s_1) n_{1,t} + \ldots + (m_M s_{M-1}) n_{M-1,t} \\
&= g_0 n_{0,t} + g_1 n_{1,t} + \ldots + g_{M-1} n_{M-1,t} \, ,
\end{aligned}
\tag{10}
$$

where

$$g_i = m_{i+1}\, s_i \, , \text{ for } i = 0, \ldots, M-1. \tag{11}$$

Equation 10 expresses the production of young (number of 0-year-olds) as a linear combination of the number in each age class in the previous year. The values of g_i indicate the number of young that are produced per individual of age i in year t that will be alive in year $t + 1$. We can combine Equation 9 for $I = 0, \ldots, M - 1$ and Equation 10 into a single equation involving matrices:

$$
\begin{bmatrix} n_o \\ n_1 \\ n_2 \\ \cdot \\ \cdot \\ n_M \end{bmatrix}_{t+1}
=
\begin{bmatrix}
g_0 & g_1 & g_2 & \cdots & g_{M-1} & g_M \\
s_0 & 0 & 0 & \ldots & 0 & 0 \\
0 & s_1 & 0 & \ldots & 0 & 0 \\
\cdot & \cdot & \cdot & \cdots & \cdot & \cdot \\
\cdot & \cdot & \cdot & \cdots & \cdot & \cdot \\
0 & 0 & 0 & \ldots & s_{M-1} & s_M
\end{bmatrix}
\times
\begin{bmatrix} n_0 \\ n_1 \\ n_2 \\ \cdot \\ \cdot \\ n_M \end{bmatrix}_t
$$

or, in matrix notation, $\mathbf{n}_{t+1} = \mathbf{L} \times \mathbf{n}_t$. $\mathbf{L}$ is called the *population projection matrix*, or *Leslie matrix*. The term in any particular row and column can be considered the contribution of an individual in the age class represented by that *column* in year t to the age class represented by that *row* in year $t + 1$ (Jenkins 1988). Note that we assumed survival and fertility rates were the same each year. This formulation was developed by Bernadelli (1941), Lewis (1942), and Leslie (1945, 1948). Van Groenendael et al. (1988) reviewed the method and applications, and Caswell (2000) gave an excellent overview of the technique. It allows several interesting interpretations. For example, we can project the population from one year to the next or, by repeating the process, k years into future:

$$\mathbf{n}_{t+1} = \mathbf{L} \times \mathbf{n}_t \, .$$

Thus,

$$
\begin{aligned}
\mathbf{n}_{t+2} &= \mathbf{L} \times \mathbf{n}_{t+1} \\
&= \mathbf{L} \times \mathbf{L} \times \mathbf{n}_t \, ,
\end{aligned}
$$

and in general

$$\mathbf{n}_{t+k} = \mathbf{L}^k \mathbf{n}_t \, .$$

We can also derive useful properties mathematically from this formulation, including the stable age distribution and population rate of change (e.g., Leslie [1945], Pielou [1969]).

The population projection matrix approach has occasionally been misused, generally by using fertility data as g_i values; Wethey (1985) and Jenkins (1988, 1989) presented examples. The parameter g_i is somewhat odd, incorporating both fertility and survival, and measuring the fertility of a cohort of age $i + 1$ times the survival rate from age i to age $i + 1$ (Equation 11).

We described this formulation with surveys occurring immediately following the birth season. If counts are conducted at another time, the definition of g_i must be changed to incorporate survival from birth until the time of the census (e.g., Michod and Anderson 1980). In practice, the estimation of g_i is difficult (Taylor and Carley 1988).

Age- and Density-dependent Models

Birth and death models in which the rates depend on both age and density can be constructed (Leslie 1948, 1959; Williamson 1959; Cooke and Leon 1976; Caswell 2000), but they do not have ready mathematical solutions and their properties are not well understood. Pennycuick et al. (1968) developed a computer program that allowed elements of a Leslie matrix to be density-dependent and also to have time lags. Little is known about how density dependence actually operates, however. More likely to be useful are models that decompose birth and death rates into meaningful components. These components can be related to age, density, or environmental factors, as appropriate.

Estimating Age-dependent Death Rates

Earlier we discussed ways of estimating mortality rates not specifically related to age. We now turn to the common problem of estimating mortality rates by age. Several methods are available, based either on following a cohort of animals or on examining the age distribution of a population. The appropriateness of estimators depends on the assumptions they require, how they are met by the population under study, and on how the data are collected.

Estimating Survival by Following a Cohort

Knowing All the Deaths.—Suppose we knew the complete death history of a cohort of 42 gray squirrels born in 1954 (d_x column, Table 13). Specifically, we knew that 22 died during their first year, 10 died during their second year, 7 died during their third year, 2 died during their fourth year, and 1 died in its fifth year. From this information, we can calculate exact mortality rates by age. If q_i is the probability of dying during year i (which also is during age i), then $q_0 = 22/42 = 0.52$, since 22 of the 42 squirrels died before their first birthday. Likewise, $q_1 = 10/20 = 0.50$, since 10 of the 20 survivors from the first year died during the second. Similarly, $q_2 = 7/10 = 0.70$, $q_3 = 2/3 = 0.67$, and $q_4 = 1/1 = 1.00$. Thus, age-dependent mortality rates can be computed exactly for this known population.

If the 42 animals can be considered a random sample from some larger population, statistical estimation is possible. Since q_0 is the mortality rate of animals in their first year of life, the number of animals expected to die by the beginning of the second year is $42\, q_0$. That number was actually 22, hence $\hat{q}_0 = 22/42 = 0.52$. Also, the number of animals alive at the beginning of each year is known at that time and, if we assume that individual animals live or die independently of one another, the number dying during year i can be treated as a binomial variate, with n_i representing the number of animals alive at the beginning of the year and rate = q_i. From this, the standard error of $\hat{q}_i$ is estimated by:

$$\sqrt{\frac{\hat{q}_i\left(1-\hat{q}_i\right)}{N_i}}.$$

In our example, SE($\hat{q}_0$) = 0.52 × 0.48/42 = 0.077. Similarly, SE($\hat{q}_1$) = 0.112, SE($\hat{q}_2$) = 0.145, SE($\hat{q}_3$) = 0.272, and SE($\hat{q}_4$) = 0.

Knowing All the Living.—Suppose that instead of knowing the age at which the individual squirrels died, we had surveyed the cohort at the beginning of each year. This information forms the basis of the n_x column (Table 13). There were 42 at the beginning of year 0 and 20 at the beginning of year 1. Thus, the survival rate during that year was 20/42 = 0.48 and the mortality rate was 1 − 0.48 = 0.52. Mortality rates for the other years also coincide with those calculated from the information on age of death. Likewise, if the sample of animals is representative of a larger population, we can treat the process as binomial and calculate the same estimates of standard errors.

Life tables based on information from following a specific cohort are termed *cohort*, or sometimes *dynamic* or *age-specific life tables*. Unfortunately, only for closely monitored or captive populations do we have situations with such ideal knowledge, either of the ages at death or exactly how the size of a cohort changes over time.

Following More than One Cohort.—If more than one cohort is followed, an age-specific table can be generated for each of them. Survival rates can then be estimated that vary both by age and by year, although limited sample sizes usually preclude accurate estimates. Alternatively, estimates can be pooled across years to get age-dependent estimates (e.g., Downing 1980: Table 15.6), or pooled across ages to get year-dependent estimates. Which pooling is more appropriate depends on whether survival rates vary more by age or by year. Loery et al. (1987) presented an example of estimating survival rates by both age and year for black-capped chickadees (*Poecile atricapilla*), based on a long-term mark–recapture study.

Estimating Survival from Age Distributions

Suppose that we do not have complete information from following one or more cohorts through time, but that we have the age composition of a sample of animals from the population at a particular time. That sample must accurately reflect either these members *dying* or *living*. We also require the population to have achieved a stable age distribution and to be constant in size (although the method can be adapted if the population is increasing or decreasing at a known rate). These are stringent assumptions that must be carefully considered, and the methods that follow work better in theory than in practice.

The Age Distribution of the Living.—Suppose that we have the age distribution of a sample from the living members of the population at a particular time in year t. The number of individuals of age x in year t ($n_{x,t}$) is the number that were of age $x-1$ in year $t-1$ ($n_{x-1,t-1}$) times the survival rate for those animals ($s_{x-1,t-1}$):

$$n_{x,t} = n_{x-1,t-1}\, s_{x-1,t-1},$$

from which we could estimate $s_{x-1,t-1}$ as:

$$\hat{s}_{x-1,t-1} = n_{x,t}\, / \,n_{x-1,t-1}.$$

This can be done only if we have accurate age distribution data for successive years. By assuming the population is stationary, however, we can obtain estimates from a sample in a single year. Stationarity implies that survival rates (and fertility rates) are constant from year to year ($s_{x,t}$ is independent of t) and that population size and age structure are the same from year to year. That is, $n_{x,t}$ is independent of t. (This is a *critical assumption*.) Hence we have

$$\hat{s}_{x-1} = n_x\, / \,n_{x-1}.$$

Chapman and Robson (1960) recommended adding 1 to the denominator to reduce bias. Life tables formed this way are called *time-specific life tables* and represent a cross-section of ages at a specific time.

A statistical model for these data can be developed. In a sample of n_* animals in a particular year, the number of individuals of age x can be considered a multinomial variate. The probability ϕ_x that an individual will be in age class x is proportional to $n_0 s_0 s_1 ... s_{x-1}$. This proportion depends on sampling intensity. These probabilities are estimated by $\hat{\phi}_x = n_x / n_*$. Also, due to the multinomial nature of the data,

$$E(\hat{\phi}_x) = \phi_x,$$

$$\text{Var}\left(\hat{\phi}_x\right) = \frac{\phi_x\left(1-\phi_x\right)}{n_*},$$

and the covariance between 2 survival rates is

$$\text{Cov}\left(\hat{\phi}_x, \hat{\phi}_y\right) = -\frac{\phi_x \phi_y}{n_*}.$$

Survival rates are estimated by the ratio of successive $\hat{\phi}_x$ values:

$$\hat{s}_x = \frac{\hat{\phi}_{x+1}}{\hat{\phi}_x},$$

with standard error estimated from

$$\text{SE}^2\left(\hat{s}_x\right) = \frac{\phi_{x+1}\left(\hat{\phi}_x + \hat{\phi}_{x+1}\right)}{n_* \phi_x^3}$$

$$= \frac{\hat{s}_x\left(1+\hat{s}_x\right)}{n_* \hat{\phi}_x}.$$

The mortality rate, $\hat{q}_x$, will have the same standard error as the survival rate $\hat{s}_x$.

We illustrate the procedure with the age distribution of male white-tailed deer on the George Reserve in Michigan, just before the 1956 hunting season (n_x, Table 15). These values (n_x) can be used to generate a life table with estimated survival rate (Table 15). These estimates appear unrealistic, especially the higher survival rate for younger animals than for older individuals. These aberrancies might in part reflect large sampling errors due to small

172 | Population Analysis

Table 15. Life table based on age distribution of male white-tailed deer alive in 1956 (data from McCullough 1979:36).

Age (years)$_x$	n_x	$\hat{d}_x$	$\hat{s}_x$	SE($\hat{s}_x$)
0	40	17	0.575	0.150
1	23	17	0.261	0.120
2	6	2	0.667	0.430
3	4	3	0.250	0.280
4	1	1	0.000	0
>4	0	—	—	—

sample sizes, but more likely result from the population not being stationary because of year-to-year variation in reproduction (McCullough 1979).

The Age Distribution of the Dying.—Consider the example (Table 16) representing ages of white-tailed deer found dead in surveys of carcasses. These data reflect the age distribution of dying members of the population. Suppose the studied population is stationary; the age distribution can then be used as the d_x column of a life table (Table 16). From these values we can estimate the n_x column by adding the d_x entries from the bottom up. The ratio of d_x to $\hat{n}_x$ gives an estimate of q_x, the age-dependent mortality rate (Table 16). Note the mortality rate for the last age class will always be 1.0.

Is the Sample of the Living or the Dying?—Surprisingly, the age composition of dead animals may not provide a suitable estimate of the age structure of animals dying (Caughley 1966). For example, if animals are shot unselectively with respect to age, the resulting sample will reflect the population *alive* at the beginning of the collection period, and will not reflect the age structure of all animals that died (unless the shooting was the only mortality source). Such data would most appropriately be used in the n_x column of a life table. In contrast, if carcass pickups were made of *all* animals that died during a year (Table 16), the resulting data would truly reflect mortality and could be used in the d_x column.

The 3 main kinds of data (Seber 1982:401–402) that can be used to construct a time-specific life table are: 1) number of animals of each age for a representative sample of live animals, used as the n_x column; 2) number of animals of each age at death for a representative sample of

animals killed by an agent independent of age (nonselective collection, natural catastrophe), also used as the n_x column; or 3) number of animals of each age at death for a representative sample of carcasses, used as the d_x column. Biased estimates can arise if younger age classes are less vulnerable to sampling, possibly because when they are alive, they are less detectable, and when they die their softer bones do not persist as long. Survival estimates for older age classes are unaffected by this bias (Caughley 1966, Seber 1982:402).

Is the Population Stationary?—We indicated that age distribution data can be used to estimate survival if the population has a stable age distribution and is constant in size (i.e., the population is stationary). The method can be modified if the population is increasing or decreasing at a *known* rate (Caughley 1977:92, Eberhardt 1988). Knowing this requires independent information, such as estimates of population trend. The requirement of stable age distributions remains. Survival rates can also be estimated from data for a stable-age distribution if appropriate fertility rates are available (Michod and Anderson 1980).

One cannot examine a single age distribution and learn whether the population is stationary or not (Caughley 1966, Seber 1982:403). However, Tait and Bunnell (1980) provided a possible exception if the age at death is known for a large number of animals. A series of age distributions at different times may be used to examine if a population is stable.

It is tempting to assume a population is stationary and to estimate survival rates from age structure data, concluding from those results that the population is stable. Despite warnings to the contrary about this circular argument (Caughley and Birch 1971), the practice has persisted (Lancia and Bishir 1985, Jenkins 1989).

Pooling Ages for Survival Estimation.—Because of variation due to small samples, it is often necessary to smooth either the observed age frequencies or the resulting estimators; Caughley (1977:96–97) illustrated the former, and we mention the latter.

If we believe that mortality is constant for ages in a specified interval, pooled estimates of the rate can be obtained. Eberhardt (1985) noted that pooled mortality estimates are biased high if older animals survive at a lower rate than animals of prime age. For example, it seems reasonable the mortality rate of the deer in one example (Table 16) is roughly constant for individuals greater than 1 year of age. A pooled estimator of that adult mortality rate is:

$$\frac{d_1 + d_2 + \ldots}{n_1 + n_2 + \ldots} = \frac{(n_1 - n_2) + (n_2 - n_3) + \ldots}{n_1 + n_2 + \ldots}$$

$$= \frac{n_1}{\sum\limits_{j \geq 1} n_j},$$

which in the present example is:

$$\frac{18 + 14 + \ldots + 8}{92 + 74 + \ldots + 8} = \frac{92}{383} = 0.240.$$

Average, rather than pooled, estimators also can be formed (Seber 1982:397). More importantly, the unbiased estimator of adult survival rate with smallest variance (Chapman

Table 16. Life table based on age distribution of female white–tailed deer found dead (data from Eberhardt 1969:488).

Age (years)$_x$	$\hat{n}_x$	d_x	$\hat{q}_x$
0–1	198	106	0.535
1–2	92	18	0.196
2–3	74	14	0.189
3–4	60	18	0.300
4–5	42	9	0.214
5–6	33	5	0.152
6–7	28	6	0.214
7–8	22	8	0.364
8–9	14	4	0.286
9–10	10	2	0.200
>10	8	8	1.000

and Robson 1960, Robson and Chapman 1961) is:

$$\hat{s}_{CR} = \frac{T}{n+T-1},$$

where

$$n = \sum_{j\geq 1} n_j$$

and

$$T = \sum_{j\geq 1} jn_j.$$

Its standard error can be estimated from:

$$\text{SE}^2\left(\hat{s}_{CR}\right) = \hat{s}_{CR}\left(\hat{s}_{CR} - \frac{T-1}{n+T-2}\right).$$

In the example (Table 16), we have $n = 92 + 74 + \ldots + 8 = 383$, $T = 1 \times 92 + 2 \times 74 + 3 \times 60 + \ldots + 11 \times 8 = 1365$, so $\hat{s}_{CR} = 1365/(383+1365 - 1) = 0.781$, and $\hat{q} = 1 - \hat{s} = 0.219$. Its standard error is calculated from:

$$\text{SE}^2\left(\hat{q}\right) = \text{SE}^2\left(\hat{s}_{CR}\right) = 0.78134\left(0.78134 - \frac{1365}{383+1365-2}\right)$$

$$= 0.0000983,$$

so $\text{SE} = \sqrt{0.0000983} = 0.0099$.

Comments on Life Tables.—Because age composition is typically measured from samples, rather than from entire populations, the entries in the life table are estimates, subject to sampling variation. Caughley (1977:95) suggested that life tables based on fewer than 150 age determinations were unlikely to be sufficiently accurate for any purpose. Polacheck (1985) found with simulation that analyses based on even larger samples often provided misleading estimates of survival rate.

McCullough (1979:221) analyzed one of the best available sets of data on age structure of white-tailed deer and concluded: "Although numerous attempts have been made to apply life-table methods to the analysis of kill data, ... most of these methods have not proven to be useful at the practical level." The major problem he identified was meeting the assumption of a stable age distribution as variable environmental factors had differential effects on different age classes. He suggested that time-specific life tables, although clearly not meeting the assumptions necessary to estimate survival rates, are valuable to the manager of exploited populations because they show the existence of strong year classes, indicative of good reproduction in a particular year. Seber (1982:393) cautioned that life tables may give an overall picture of a population but have limited accuracy and should be supported by other methods of estimation. Jenkins (1989) also cautioned about the limited value of age distribution data, in light of the ease with which they can be obtained, especially by wildlife management agencies that monitor harvests.

Estimating Population Growth from Birth and Death Rates

Knowing the birth and death rates of a population should allow us to examine whether the population was increasing, holding steady, or declining. We can indeed calculate the growth rate of the population from such information. We discuss 2 approaches, a simplified one applicable when birth and death rates are not segregated into many age classes, and the Lotka equation for when they are segregated. The population projection matrix can also be used to measure the growth rate of a population (Leslie 1945, Pielou 1969).

A Direct Method.—Consider, following Martin et al. (1979), the female segment of the North American population of mallards. For the 1961–74 period, the average survival rate for adult females was 0.555 and the average survival rate for immature females was 0.563. Survival was estimated between anniversary dates of 1 September in successive years. Suppose the recruitment rate, measured as young females per adult female on this anniversary date, averaged 1.03. From these survival and fertility rates we can estimate the average annual change in the population of female mallards. The number of adult females on 1 September of year $t + 1$ represents the adults from the previous year that survived, plus the immatures that survived. That is:

$$A_{t+1} = A_t(0.0555) + Y_t(0.563),$$

where A_t is the number of adult females in year t and Y_t is the number of young females in year t. We also have from the recruitment rate:

$$Y_t = A_t(1.03),$$

so

$$A_{t+1} = A_t(0.555) + A_t(1.03)(0.563),$$

or

$$A_{t+1} = A_t(1.135).$$

From this we can conclude 1 of 3 things: 1) the female segment of the mallard population was growing at a rate of 13.5% per year ($\lambda = 1.135$), 2) the estimates of survival and/or recruitment are wrong, or 3) the model is incorrect. Evidence from annual surveys of mallards during 1961–74 led Martin et al. (1979) to reject the first possibility, and the simplicity of the model argues against the third. Thus, the authors concluded that certain estimates of survival or recruitment were the problem and they used this approach as a check on the consistency of their parameter estimates.

Lotka's Equation.—If age-dependent schedules of survival (l_x) and fertility (m_x) are available, the growth rate implied by those schedules can be computed from Lotka's formula (Equation 8) in an iterative procedure. Caughley (1977:215) presented a short Fortran computer program to perform the necessary calculations. We illustrate use of this equation with the white-tailed deer data (Tables 12, 14). Using a value of $r = 0$, indicative of a steady population and values of l_x (Table 14) and m_x (Table 12) in the right-hand-side of Equation 8, we get (since $e^0 = 1$):

$$1.000 \times 0 + 0.5800 \times 0.047 + 0.4060 \times 0.503 + \text{etc.},$$

which sums to 0.89. This value is less than 1, which indicates $r = 0$ is too high. Using $r = -0.10$ in Equation 8 gives 1.44, which is also too large. The value of the sum that we want is 20% of the way between 0.89 and 1.44. We then try a value for r that is 20% of the way between 0 and -0.10, that is, $r = -0.02$. Use of $r = -0.02$ gives 0.97, which is too small, but $r = -0.026$ results in a sum of 0.9995; close enough to stop the iteration. Since $e^{-0.026} = 1 - 0.0257$, this value suggests the deer population was declining by about 2.57% each year.

This approach could also be used with the mallard data. Age-dependent survival and fertility rates give:

$$l_0 = 1,$$
$$l_x = 0.563(0.555)^{x-1} \quad x > 0,$$

and

$$m_0 = 0,$$
$$m_x = 1.03 \quad x > 0.$$

Using these values with $r = \log \lambda = \log (1.135) = 0.1266$ in the right-hand side of Equation 8 yields 0.99987, negligibly different from 1.0.

Another useful statistic is the *net reproductive rate*, the average number of young produced by an individual during its lifetime:

$$R_0 = \sum l_x m_x.$$

Values of $R_0 < 1$ indicate that members of the population are not replacing themselves and the population is declining. Conversely, $R_0 > 1$ denotes an increasing population, and $R_0 = 1$ indicates a stable population.

For the deer population, we get $R_0 = 0.89$, indicating a declining population. For the mallard example, we have:

$$\begin{aligned} R_0 &= 1 \times 0 + 0.563 \times 1.03 + 0.563 \times 0.555 \times 1.03 + ... \\ &= 0 + 0.580 + 0.322 + 0.179 + 0.099 + 0.055 \\ &\quad + 0.031 + 0.017 + 0.009 + 0.005 \\ &= 1.300, \end{aligned}$$

adding through age class 10 (note that terms become small for older age classes, indicating the few old individuals have little effect on the size of the population). This value also suggests an increasing population.

Models With Components of Survival or Birth

The models presented thus far are rather simple as they really depend only on time. Given the features of a model and the current status of a population, we can predict exactly what will happen at any future time (if the model was correct). This is unrealistic, but simple models have nonetheless proven useful. Their major advantage lies in the way they can be treated mathematically. We now turn to models that are more complex but actually often simpler to construct and analyze. The trade-off is that as we gain realism and complexity, we lose the ability to analyze the model mathematically, requiring use of a computer. For that reason, most of these models are simulation models. Some of the most useful population analyses today are based on simulation models.

A population goes up or down during a year depending on its annual survival and birth rates. The annual survival rate is an overall measure, encompassing the risks encountered by a population, which may vary season to season, day to day, among individuals in the population, and from place to place (Box 5). It is often worthwhile to examine survival rate in closer detail, such as by parts of the year. Likewise, fertility rates incorporate a multiplicity of components, which may be treated individually. For example, the measure of births for our whooping crane example is the number of young recorded in the winter population. This reflects the number of adults that are paired, the proportion of those that successfully lay eggs, clutch size, proportion of eggs that hatch, survival of young until fledging, and survival from fledging until the winter survey.

By reducing survival and fertility rates into finer components, we gain several advantages. First, we can consider environmental and other factors, beyond the density of conspecifics, that influence individual components. For

---

Box 5.   Estimating population trends using life-history traits.

In many situations, the biologist is ultimately interested in answering the question, "Is the population stable, increasing, or decreasing?" To fully answer this question, the trend in the population must be estimated. We can use a wide range of tools to estimate population trends, from simple changes in observed count data to complex models that attempt to explain temporal patterns in populations. An example of a contemporary approach to modeling population changes is that of Franklin et al. (2000) who estimated annual population trends of the northern spotted owl (*Strix occidentalis caurina*) in California.

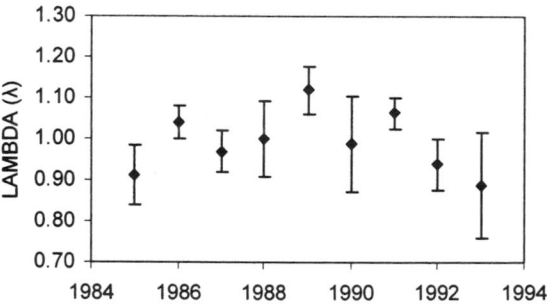

Using capture–recapture data, they built models to explain variation in life history traits (e.g., annual survival) that ultimately affected the rate of population change. They then estimated the annual rate of population change (λ) as a function of annual rates of survival and recruitment, and further suggested that yearly climate changes best explained annual variation in this species. The study focused on understanding the processes that influence annual population changes in this species and provided a template for how wildlife biologists should model life history traits and incorporate this information into estimates of population change.

example, clutch size of mallards depends primarily on age of the female and date the clutch is initiated. Thus, it can be modeled as a function of those factors. Nest success, however, depends mostly on nesting habitat and predator numbers, and these features can be used to model nest success. The second potential advantage is that we can often obtain better estimates of individual components and the factors that influence them. For example, clutch size can be studied either passively or experimentally, and studies that manipulate clutch size might give good insight into that parameter but poor information about overall nest success. A third advantage is that we may gain a clearer understanding of the relationships involved in each component by their separate study. This is especially important for management applications, in which one or more components may be altered; the effect on the entire system needs to be understood or else the population response may not be the one desired.

We illustrate this procedure with a model of the production of mallards in the prairie pothole region (Johnson et al. 1992). Only females are considered and 2 age classes of breeding females, yearling and older, are identified. Let F_i ($i = 1, 2$) be the number of yearling females and older females, respectively, in the breeding population, and F_0 be the number produced. F_0 can be apportioned according to age class of the adult:

$$F_0 = F_1 R_1 + F_2 R_2 ,$$

where R_i is the production rate for females in age class i. This value can be further decomposed according to nesting attempts, giving

$$R_i = D_i (Q_{i1} + Q_{i2} + Q_{i3} + Q_{i4} + Q_{i5}),$$

where D_i is the proportion of females of age class i that attempt to breed, and Q_{ij} is the production from the jth nesting attempt of females in age class i. This allows a maximum of 5 nesting efforts in a breeding season.

The production from a particular nesting attempt itself involves several factors, and can be expressed as the product:

$$Q_{ij} = A_{ij} C_{ij} HEB,$$

where A_{ij} is the probability that a female of age i will make the jth nesting attempt in a breeding season, C_{ij} is the average clutch size of the jth nesting attempt by a female of age i, H is the nest success rate, E is the survival rate of eggs in successful nests, and B is the survival rate of young.

Most parameters are indexed by age of the female and nesting attempt, because age and attempt are known to influence them. Effects of age and attempt on nest success rate (H), survival rate as eggs (E), and survival rate as young (B) have not been demonstrated clearly. The rates of incidence of breeding (D_i) vary most strongly with wetland conditions. Nesting probabilities were formulated to be higher for older females than yearlings, to be higher when wetland conditions were good, to decline with nesting attempt, and to be lower when nest success is high (because nests are more likely to be destroyed later, when the female is in poorer condition). Clutch size was modeled to decline with nesting attempt and to be 1 egg smaller for yearling than for older females.

Nest success of mallards is highly variable and is a component amenable to management. It varies according to the condition of the nesting habitat and predator abundance. Egg survival is generally high and in the model does not vary as a function of any environmental variable. Survival of young after hatch is lower, however, and likely depends on weather, predators, food supplies for ducklings, and possibly disease; some of these factors may operate in a density-dependent manner.

Johnson et al. (1992) executed the model described above by allowing the parameters to vary about as widely as they seem to do in natural populations. They contrasted results from the model for mallards with results for other species. They concluded that recruitment of mallards was most dependent on wetland conditions and predation. Similar models (e.g., Johnson et al. 1987, Cowardin et al. 1988) have been used to evaluate management options in terms of expected production of mallards anticipated by manipulating various parameters.

Simulation models have been applied to many wildlife species, often to assess the effect of harvest strategies. Useful references on the construction of models for wildlife management include texts by Starfield and Bleloch (1991), Grant et al. (1997), and Williams et al. (2002).

It is easy to build models, perhaps too easy in this day of ready access to computing power. It is harder to evaluate them (Johnson 2001). One should compare model results with real data, independent of information used to construct the model, and preferably obtained by direct experimentation. If that test is not feasible, a comparison with other models, built on different assumptions, is worthwhile, as is a comparison to analytic solutions.

Competition Models

Let us briefly consider populations not of a single species but of 2 species that interact. Here we assume they compete for some resource, such as food. If that resource is limited, the habitat will support fewer of species 1 when species 2 is common than when species 2 is rare. Let α ($\alpha > 0$) be the relative impact of an individual of species 2 on the population growth rate of species 1. That is, αN_2 individuals of species 2 have the same effect on species 1 as do N_1 individuals of species 1, or $N_1 = \alpha N_2$ in terms of effect on species 1. Then, generalizing the logistic model of Equation 5, and writing $N_1(t)$ and $N_2(t)$ as the sizes of the 2 populations at time t, the per capita growth rate of population 1 is modified, not just by

$$\frac{K_1 - N_1(t)}{K_1},$$

but by

$$\frac{K_1 - N_1(t) - \alpha N_2(t)}{K_1},$$

where $K_1 - \alpha N_2(t)$ can be considered the carrying capacity for species 1, as reduced by the presence of N_2 animals of species 2. From this we have:

$$\frac{1}{N_1(t)} \frac{dN_1(t)}{dt} = r_1 \frac{K_1 - N_1(t) - \alpha N_2(t)}{K_1},$$

where r_1 and K_1 are the parameters of logistic growth for species 1 in the absence of species 2. Analogously, if β ($\beta > 0$) is the relative effect of an individual of species 1 on the population growth rate of species 2, we obtain

$$\frac{1}{N_2(t)}\frac{dN_2(t)}{dt} = r_2\frac{K_2 - N_2(t) - \beta N_1(t)}{K_2},$$

where r_2 and K_2 are defined correspondingly. Many of the results can be obtained without recourse to logistic formulation (Maynard Smith 1974:62), but it is a convenience. Parameters α and β are termed the *competition coefficients* of the model, which was developed by Lotka (1925) and Volterra (1926). This system has been the basis of substantial theoretical work in competition (e.g., Levins 1968; MacArthur 1968, 1972; Vandermeer 1972; Pianka 1974; Berryman 1981), but has received little use in wildlife studies, in part because of the inherent difficulty of estimating the relevant parameters.

Mathematical results from the equations above follow from the values of K_1, K_2, α, and β. Only if $K_1/\alpha > K_2$ and $K_2/\beta > K_1$ is it possible for the 2 species to coexist. Basically, this indicates that coexistence is possible only if the growth rate of each species is inhibited more by a member of its own species than by an individual of the other species. Their own density-dependent controls must cause growth to stop before they eliminate the competitor. One way this can happen is if the 2 species do not overlap completely in resource use. While results such as these are useful theoretically, most actual populations probably do not exhibit behavior similar to that predicted by this simple competition model, but are affected by a variety of other phenomena. For example, patchiness in resources reduces competition by favoring the first species in one kind of habitat and the second species in another kind. Also, because the environment changes with time, the relative competitive abilities of the species may vary.

Predator-prey Models

A second kind of interaction involves predation. Predator-prey models in a variety of forms have seen extensive use in wildlife studies. Suppose that species 1 serves as prey for species 2, and the population growth rate of species 1 is inhibited in direct proportion to the number of predators. Then

$$\frac{1}{N_1(t)}\frac{dN_1(t)}{dt} = r_1 - \gamma N_2(t),$$

where the *predation coefficient*, γ, indicates the removal rate of prey per predator. This model includes no inhibitory effects of the population of species 1; that is, in the absence of predators, the prey population would grow exponentially. Also, each predator consumes a number of prey proportional to the abundance of the prey. For predators (species 2), the per capita population growth rate is assumed to be

$$\frac{1}{N_2(t)}\frac{dN_2(t)}{dt} = \delta N_1(t) - d_2,$$

where d_2 is the death rate of predators, which is assumed to be independent of the population of prey. The coefficient δ represents the *conversion rate* of prey to predators.

This model also was developed by Lotka (1925) and Volterra (1926).

The model assumes (e.g., Ricklefs 1979:602): 1) exponential growth by the prey species in the absence of predators; i.e., numbers of prey are limited only by predation; 2) exponential decay by predators in the absence of prey—mortality is independent of the density of predators; and 3) the rate at which prey are consumed is directly proportional to the product of the 2 species' densities (which can be construed as the chance of encountering one another if movements are random). The first 2 assumptions indicate that population growth of each species is controlled by the other species; these assumptions can be relaxed by including a logistic-type self-inhibitory restraint on population growth rates. The third assumption can be replaced by any of a variety of choices (May 1973:81–84, Maynard Smith 1974:25–33).

This model can be analyzed mathematically under the assumption there is no random variation. Depending on the values of the parameters, 2 outcomes of the model are feasible: either populations of both species reach an equilibrium point and remain there, or populations of both species oscillate over time, with increases in the predator species lagging behind increases in the prey species. Most investigations of actual populations of predators and prey involved invertebrate species in controlled laboratory situations; Tanner (1975) offered an exception that dealt with vertebrates. He concluded that vertebrate predator-prey systems were stable only if the prey species limited its own population or if it had lower (intrinsic) growth rate than the predator species. Populations of snowshoe hares (*Lepus americanus*) and Canada lynx (*Lynx canadensis*), which have roughly equal growth rates, oscillate in a cyclic fashion. Caughley and Krebs (1983) provided a more general view of this issue.

Powell (1979) applied predator-prey modeling to a community involving fisher (*Martes pennanti*) and its primary prey, the porcupine (*Erethizon dorsatum*). He prudently examined 5 variations and extensions of the basic predator-prey model, so the conclusions he drew would be less susceptible to assumptions underlying any single model. He also considered the effects of 2 alternative prey species. Although space does not permit a detailed treatment of the models here, Powell's results suggested the community was stable, but that only small increases in fisher mortality could cause local extinction of that predator.

These general predator-prey models, like other models, are unrealistically simplistic. Nonetheless, they offer useful insight into the general behavior of predator-prey systems, lead to more realistic models, and form the foundation for managing populations for optimal yield. Connelly et al. (2005) discussed situations where the predator is human.

PARAMETER ESTIMATION

In the previous discussion, we introduced theoretical models of population growth under a range of conditions and assumptions. Once the proper model is chosen for an analysis, it is desirable to estimate the parameters of the model; we denote such estimates with a "hat" symbol (thus, $\hat{\lambda}$ is an estimate of λ) and an appropriate measure of uncertainty (typically a standard error). In the discussion of theoretical models, we illustrated some simple calculations of parameter estimates, but in practice these calculations are complicated and require use of a computer for all but the simplest models. How do we use a computer to estimate the parameters of a particular model?

To estimate a population parameter, say a survival rate *S*, we first sample the population of interest and then use statistical procedures to derive the estimate. Parameter estimation has seen considerable growth in the past 5–10 years, evolving from simplistic and often inflexible computer programs to more comprehensive programs. Several computer programs are available to aid parameter estimation, and new developments occur regularly. In this section, we outline a general approach to parameter estimation, briefly discuss how to examine if a model "fits" the data, and introduce the reader to key computer programs to estimate certain parameters.

Key Steps to Parameter Estimation

Once an underlying theoretical model is chosen for an analysis, there are several steps to obtain estimates of parameters. *Modeling* logically precedes the process of parameter estimation because it can identify important variables. Earlier, we introduced the concept of a population model. Because we are often interested in predicting population responses to one or more variables, there is a need to develop and evaluate competing models to describe a population process.

Modeling is an iterative process where multiple models to explain the same phenomenon are compared, and a decision is made regarding the appropriateness of one or more of these models to describe the process (Williams et al. 2002 provided a thorough review). The first and arguably most important step involves thinking about the process and developing a short list of *a priori* biological hypotheses (Lebreton et al. 1992, Anderson and Burnham 2001, Burnham and Anderson 2002). These hypotheses should be based on whatever biological information is available, should address the specific factors of interest, and will form the basis for specific models. The building of meaningful models should be guided by the desire to answer "Why?" questions about the population of interest. For example, it might be relatively easy to estimate an annual survival rate for a particular species. It is more difficult to understand factors that might influence annual survival such as the health or condition of the animal, its age, the habitat where it resides, etc. It is imperative that model development be guided by these questions, and that analyses seek to understand processes rather than simply describe patterns.

Once this list of hypotheses is formulated, we rely on computers to help us choose one or more of these models for inference and generate parameter estimates. Many models used in population analyses are based on the multinomial distribution and use procedures such as the method of maximum likelihood to estimate the parameters (Williams et al. 2002), although other distributions and estimation procedures are sometimes used. Finally, the parameter estimates, whether survival rates or rates of population change, are obtained. Because different models often result in different parameter estimates, a key question is, "Which model do I use for inference?" Should the estimates come from a single (best) model or from a number of potential models?

The process of deciding which model or models to use for inference is known as *model selection*. Model selection in itself is a complex process (Franklin et al. 2001). Model selection methods vary from traditional hypothesis-testing approaches (e.g., likelihood ratio tests) to more complex methods based on information theory (e.g., Akaike's Information Criterion [AIC]; Akaike 1973). The most popular model selection tool in wildlife science is probably AIC (Burnham and Anderson 2002), which optimizes the trade-off between model fit and parsimony. In some cases, a "best" model may be chosen for inference and parameter estimates from that model are used. However, in many situations, it may be desirable to use parameter estimates that reflect the uncertainty associated with selecting the "best" model. In such cases, parameter estimates may be weighted by the strength of evidence for each model followed by computation of the parameter estimates (Buckland et al. 1997, Burnham and Anderson 2002). This is termed *model averaging,* which is used increasingly often to present parameter estimates that incorporate the uncertainty that is present in the model selection process (Box 6).

Factors Affecting Parameter Estimates

Biologists should not be satisfied with simply estimating a parameter without gaining some understanding of *why* the parameter varies and what it means. We are particularly interested in answering the question, "What affects the parameter?" There are several types of factors, called covariates, that can affect a parameter.

Some covariates are characteristics that apply at a group level. Gender (male vs. female) or geographic location (site A vs. site B) are examples of group variables that may influence some parameters, such as survival. Some factors can vary in time, such as weather events. If rainfall is believed to influence survival, then models incorporating some measure of precipitation (e.g., total annual rainfall or daily rainfall) could be used to address this question. Both group and temporal sources of variation can be easily incorporated into a population analysis using MARK and certain other software.

In addition to group covariates, some factors that vary among individuals may influence a parameter of interest, such as survival or reproduction (Franklin 2001, Pollock 2002). The possible types of these variables, called individual covariates, is almost endless, including measures of body condition, size metrics, breeding history, genetic characteristics, and many more. Each of these captures some of the inherent variation among individuals in any population and can be used to model the parameter of interest. Program MARK handles individual covariates easily. The inclusion of individual covariates allows a more thorough exploration of mechanisms affecting the dynamics of a population (Franklin 2001).

Goodness-of-fit Tests

Another key step in population analysis involves answering the question, "Does my model fit the data?" To properly answer this question, we must somehow "test" to see if the statistical model is appropriate for the data. Generally, this is done using a *goodness-of-fit test*. There are many goodness-of-fit tests available, each suited for a

Box 6.   The process of modeling and parameter estimation.

To illustrate the concept of population modeling, we refer to a simple example: modeling the daily nest survival of the mountain plover (Dinsmore et al. 2002). The mountain plover is a ground-nesting bird of the Great Plains and has a mating system where males and females incubate separate nests. The nesting season spans mid-May to early August. Of primary interest was whether male- and female-tended nests had different patterns of daily nest survival. Researchers were also interested in describing the within-season variation in nest survival, believing that early nests survived better because they were tended by older, more experienced adults. This a priori knowledge forms the basis for a set of 4 competing models:

(1) daily nest survival of male- and female-tended nests differs (S_{gender} model);
(2) daily nest survival of male- and female-tended nests differs, and within-year variation follows a linear time trend ($S_{gender + T}$ model);
(3) daily nest survival of male- and female-tended nests differs, and within-year variation follows a quadratic time trend ($S_{gender + TT}$ model); and
(4) daily nest survival is constant, both within years and between genders ($S_.$ model).

Each of these competing models was fitted using the nest survival model in program MARK (below) including model ranking by AIC and delta AIC and the AIC weight (w_i), number of parameters (K), and deviance for each model (see Burnham and Anderson 2002).

Model	AIC	Delta AIC	w_i	K	Deviance
$S_{gender + TT}$	1132.50	0.00	0.65	4	1124.46
$S_{gender + T}$	1134.96	2.45	0.19	3	1128.94
S_{gender}	1136.40	3.90	0.09	2	1132.39
$S_.$	1137.02	4.52	0.07	1	1135.02

On the basis of these results, what can we conclude about nest survival? Gender appears to have an effect because the best 3 models contain this effect and their AIC weights sum to 0.93. There also appears to be evidence of within-year variation in nest survival, and the form of that variation appears to be quadratic (this model has most of the weight, $w_i = 0.65$). There does not appear to be strong evidence supporting similar nest survival rates by gender, or that these rates are constant across the nesting season.

Last, we are interested in estimates of the daily nest survival rates. What is the probability that a nest will survive a day? Because the best 2 models contain temporal variation, it makes sense that daily nest survival rates vary over time. In the best model ($S_{gender + TT}$), daily nest survival rates begin at about 0.977 at the beginning of the nesting season, slowly decrease to a low of about 0.966 in mid-season, and then gradually climb to peak at about 0.995 at the end of the nesting season. In the model with only gender effects (S_{gender}), the daily nest survival rates are 0.971 for female-tended nests and 0.977 for male-tended nests. The model with neither gender effects nor temporal variation ($S_.$) produces an estimate of daily nest survival of 0.975.

How are we to choose which parameter estimate is best? In this example, we would be reasonably safe in basing inference on the best model, although a better approach would be to "average" the daily nest survival rates by allowing each model to influence the estimate proportional to its AIC weight. In this example, the model-averaged estimate of the first daily survival rate is $\hat{S}_1 = 0.974$, which compares to the estimates generated from each model: $S_{gender + TT}$ ($\hat{S}_1 = 0.977$), $S_{gender + T}$ ($\hat{S}_1 = 0.963$), S_{gender} ($\hat{S}_1 = 0.971$), and $S_.$ ($\hat{S}_1 = 0.975$). The model-averaged estimate is "close" to the estimate from the best model, reflecting the influence of its model weight.

particular class of models. The general procedure with any of these tests is to compare the data against the expectations under a particular model. For example, a band recovery study would include releases and recoveries of birds in multiple years. The underlying band recovery model (described earlier) can be used to compute the expected number of recoveries each year, given the assumptions of the model. The expected recoveries are compared to the actual recoveries using a chi-square goodness-of-fit test. The model is judged to "fit" the data adequately if the test result is clearly nonsignificant (e.g., the P value associated with the test statistic is much greater than the critical value of $\alpha = 0.05$); there is "lack of fit" otherwise. If the model "fits", the analysis can proceed. If there is a lack of model fit, the analyst should scrutinize study design and model assumptions, try to uncover the source of the lack of fit, and make adjustments to ensure future adherence to model assumptions.

Methods for testing model goodness-of-fit are limited to the simpler population models; there are no goodness-of-fit tests for complex models such as the robust design. Computer programs can compute goodness-of-fit tests for band recovery models (program ESTIMATE, Brownie et al. [1985]) and the Jolly-Seber model (program RELEASE, Burnham et al. [1987]). For other models, goodness-of-fit tests are either lacking or fit must be assessed using *ad hoc* methods or by techniques such as bootstrapping.

Computer Programs for Population Analyses

Computer programs to estimate population parameters have become more sophisticated, providing biologists with tools to estimate parameters such as population size and rates of survival, fecundity, immigration and emigration, population change, etc. There have been major advances in computer programs to facilitate these complex analyses. Formerly, biologists might have been responsible for learning multiple computer programs (e.g., programs JOLLY, JOLLYAGE, SURVIV, and others) to complete a population analysis. Many of these programs are now unified in program MARK (White and Burnham 1999, White et al. 2001). Program MARK is a powerful and flexible program that allows most population parameters to be estimated, provided the study is designed well and includes a sufficient sample of marked individuals. This program requires knowledge of basic mathematical and statistical concepts, and the serious population analyst should carefully study the user's guide (Cooch and White 2002).

Program MARK offers a wide range of modeling features, including: 1) the ability to model group (e.g., gender or age class) effects, 2) the ability to include individual (e.g., a measure of body mass) or time-varying (e.g., daily precipitation) covariates (see Pollock 2002), 3) model selection using Akaike's Information Criterion (AIC; Akaike 1973), 4) the ability to model-average parameter estimates across competing models to reflect model-selection uncertainty (see Burnham and Anderson 2002), and 5) goodness-of-fit testing for some models. Program MARK is available free at http://www.cnr.colostate.edu/~gwhite/ mark/mark.htm. The detailed user's guide for MARK is also available from the same link.

Program MARK is certainly the most comprehensive computer program for population analyses, although other programs like POPAN (Arnason and Schwarz 1995, 2002; useful for the analysis of open populations) and M-SURGE (Choquet et al. 2003) are widely used.

POPULATION VIABILITY ANALYSIS

A culmination of our knowledge of population biology is the ability to predict future population viability (Lande 1988, 1993; Noon et al. 1999). The process of making such predictions using available population data is called *population viability analysis*, or PVA for short (Boyce 1992). Two general approaches are used to make predictions: 1) the probability is estimated that a population of a specified size will persist for a certain time period (PVA), or 2) the minimum viable population (MVP) needed for a population to persist for a certain time period is estimated (Shaffer 1987). In either case, an underlying population model is used to make predictions about future behavior of the population.

While appealing to biologists, good population viability analyses present many challenges (see White 2000). Making meaningful predictions requires a thorough knowledge of the population process, including detailed information on survival, reproduction, and other facets of population growth, all based on studies that are replicated in space and time. Given expense and time commitments, few such studies exist. Most studies are hampered by sparse data, collected for a few years and at one or a few sites. Should these types of studies form the basis for population viability analyses? The answer depends on the desired predictions. If only a general idea about population persistence is sought, then predictions based on simpler studies might be useful, but only for planning purposes. If detailed predictions are sought, for example the conservation of an endangered species, then only data from long-term, replicated studies should be used. Computer programs such as RAMAS Metapop 4.0 and VORTEX are available commercially and can perform many of the calculations associated with a population viability analysis.

As with all analyses discussed in this chapter, a thorough understanding of assumptions is necessary to do a PVA. In PVA, the behavior of the population is influenced by demographic parameters of the population (e.g., survival), environmental variation (temporal and spatial variation), and individual heterogeneity (e.g., the genetic makeup of an individual). These sources of variation collectively constitute *process variance*, which refers to the real underlying variation in the population growth process. Making predictions about population persistence would be much easier if such analyses were not confounded by *sampling variation*. Sampling variation results from stochasticity (random events) in our measures of these sources of variation and from having only samples, not the entire population, measured.

To realistically model population persistence, all of these sources of variation must be included in the population model. In addition, the underlying statistical distribution of demographic parameters (e.g., annual survival rate) across all individuals in the population must be included (White 2000), resulting in increased persistence times for most populations. This is a common omission in many PVA analyses and yields results that are often too pessimistic.

As interest in making long-term population predictions increases, use of population viability analysis is likely to increase. The models themselves are appealing and offer useful predictions necessary for management decisions. However, many PVAs are plagued by too few data and a lack of rigorous estimates of demographic, environmental, and individual variation, thus reducing their real utility to managers and conservationists (Box 7).

INFERENCE

Once a population analysis is complete, we often desire to draw conclusions from the data. The process of formulating hypotheses, testing those hypotheses with data, and then making conclusions based on the study results is a logical scientific process. Typically, we use inductive inference to use the results from localized studies to make broader statements about a larger population of interest. For example, we may estimate the annual survival of mal-

Box 7. An example of population viability analysis.

A population viability analysis (PVA) is used to predict the future behavior of a population, usually related to specific management or conservation goals. As an example, consider the population viability analysis for the California gnatcatcher (*Polioptila californica*), an endangered songbird of the Pacific Coast (Akçakaya and Atwood 1997). Using multiple field studies, the authors gathered information on vital rates (survival, dispersal, fecundity, etc.), habitat use, known range of the species, and characteristics of the habitat "patches" the species occupied to build a detailed model for predicting future population behavior. The metapopulation model incorporated spatial and stochastic variation and predicted sharp population declines and a high risk of extinction for this species. However, some parameters were poorly understood, leading to variation in estimates of persistence and uncertainty in the interpretation of some of the results. Modeling results could be used to suggest possible conservation strategies, and the authors suggested that such an exercise may prove useful for evaluating future management activities and conservation measures.

This example provides a template for thinking about PVAs. Emphasis should be placed on estimating demographic parameters well, including multiple sources of population variation in the PVA model, and on a careful interpretation of the results. Models built in this manner can be informative and will provide a useful tool for wildlife biologists.

Box 8. Metapopulations.

Many animals occur in distinct patches of suitable habitat, rather than in a large continuous area. If they move freely among patches, we can treat them as a single population, since the dynamics are likely to be similar in all patches. If there is virtually no movement among patches, the population in each patch should be treated separately, because they can display completely different dynamics. If there is limited movement among patches, the dynamics of the patches may differ and extinction of a population in a patch can be overcome (rescued) by immigration from another patch. This is the situation in which metapopulation theory applies. A metapopulation is basically a population of populations.

Richard Levins coined the term metapopulation around 1970 (Levins 1970). Interest in the topic has flourished, however, as exemplified by 2 recent edited volumes (McCullough 1996, Hanski and Gilpin 1997).

Metapopulation dynamics clearly apply to populations that occupy naturally occurring patches of habitat. Moreover, increasing human-induced fragmentation of once-continuous habitats has made metapopulation theory more generally applicable. What used to be large expanses of forest, for example, have been reduced to smaller stands of trees, surrounded by a landscape matrix of habitats unsuitable for many forest-dwelling species. Metapopulation theory has largely replaced island biogeography as a theoretical framework for thinking about fragmentation (Wiens 1996).

Metapopulation theory resides at the intersection of numerous topics of interest to modern wildlife biologists, including landscape ecology, corridors that connect habitat patches, and source-sink population dynamics (Pulliam 1988). Further, it is key to population viability analysis; an important consequence is that, because the dynamics of populations in separate patches may differ, metapopulation structure may enhance the viability of populations (Wiens 1996).

Unfortunately, empirical studies involving metapopulations, and methods to analyze them, lag far behind the theory. However, acknowledging that many populations may occur as metapopulations, it is important to consider this topic and recognize that conclusions based on treating a population as continuous may be flawed.

lards from a localized study in the Great Plains, but really desire to infer those results to all mallards in the Great Plains. How, then, do we correctly interpret the results of a population analysis?

In a population analysis, emphasis is typically placed on modeling one or more parameters of interest, and different hypotheses about how the population behaves are imbedded in different (competing) models. We then use model selection procedures to come to some conclusion(s) about the system, whether it is that adult and juvenile survival differs or that increased body condition results in greater survival. We seldom use controlled experiments, although such studies offer more powerful results and increase the scope of inference.

Results of a population analysis can be interpreted in several contexts, each directed at answering a different question. How, for example, could we infer that increased body condition resulted in greater survival in male mallards? Ideally, we would conduct a manipulative experiment in which body condition was experimentally controlled, and then measure the resulting effect(s) on survival. This would allow us to infer causation; we could then say that increased body condition *does* result in greater survival in male mallards. But what happens if we

can't conduct a manipulative experiment? In this example, we would probably attempt to mark a sample of male mallards of known body condition, and then estimate survival in the presence of that variable. We could build models with and without a body condition effect on survival, and then compare those models to see which receives better support. In this example, we could not infer causation, but would instead demonstrate a correlative relationship between body condition and survival, the strength of which would depend on sample size and study design.

SUMMARY

This chapter introduces numerous methods for analysis of wildlife population data. From the simplest (but often biased) estimate of observed survival to complex models to estimate survival as it relates to biological processes, today's wildlife biologist has many tools to estimate parameters of interest. We began by introducing theoretical models of population growth, including concepts such as exponential and logistic growth, birth and death processes, age effects, etc. We considered situations in which growth also depended on numbers of another species, either a competitor, or a prey or predator. Next, we discussed parameter estimation. Given data and a set of models, how do we generate an estimate of a parameter of interest? We emphasized computer-based modeling of population processes and the need to model complex biological processes as a function of a variety of variables, including environmental factors, age or gender differences, and variables particular to an individual. We briefly covered methods for predicting the long-term viability of a population and concluded with a section on inference, or how we draw conclusions from data. Each of these components is vital to a proper analysis of population data, and the entire process is intended to contribute to our collective scientific knowledge.

Given the diversity of approaches that can be taken, how is a wildlife biologist to choose? The choice ultimately depends on the specific objectives of the study. An analysis should include those relationships and variables suspected of being most influential to the dynamics of the population under study. Parameters are of interest because they can help describe complex population processes and lead to a better understanding of factors that influence the population. The trade-off between simple and complex models is difficult; simple models are tractable but may overlook key processes, whereas a complex model may satisfy only its builder.

Wildlife management in essence is based on only 2 primary tools, manipulation of habitat and control of harvest. These activities are effective only if they influence in the desired manner the population dynamics of the target species. To evaluate their actions and know they are doing the right thing, managers must understand those dynamics.

Methods for analyzing population data are changing rapidly, and this process is likely to continue in the future. Some topics have seen great advances in the last decade—model selection, numerical approaches to parameter estimation, and model averaging, to name a few. But other topics like individual heterogeneity and goodness-of-fit testing are still somewhat poorly understood and await the development of new approaches. With frequent methodological and technological advances, approaches to population analysis continue to evolve rapidly to make this an exciting and important discipline of wildlife biology.

ACKNOWLEDGMENTS

We are grateful to W. R. Clark and G. C. White for initial suggestions on the organization of this chapter. K. P.

Reese and an anonymous reviewer provided useful comments on this chapter. W. G. Jobman (U. S. Fish and Wildlife Service) kindly provided data on whooping crane numbers after 1984. D. R. Anderson, T. A. Bookhout, J. D. Carlson, Jr., M. J. Conroy, L. L. Eberhardt, G. Caughley, J. D. Nichols, T. L. Shaffer, D. R. Smith, and B. S. Bowen provided comments on earlier drafts of this chapter.

LITERATURE CITED

AKAIKE, H. 1973. Information theory and an extension of the maximum likelihood principle. Pages 267–281 *in* B. N. Petran and F. Csaki, editors. International symposium on information theory. Second edition. Budapest, Hungary.

AKÇAKAYA, H. R., AND J. L. ATWOOD. 1997. A habitat-based metapopulation model of the California gnatcatcher. Conservation Biology 11: 422–434.

ALLEE, W. C. 1931. Animal aggregations: a study in general sociology. University of Chicago Press, Illinois, USA.

ALLEN, D. L. 1962. Our wildlife legacy. Revised edition. Funk and Wagnalls Co., Inc., New York, USA.

ANDERSON, D. R., AND K. P. BURNHAM. 2001. Commentary on models in ecology. Bulletin of the Ecological Society of America 82: 160–161.

———, AND R. T. STERLING. 1974. Population dynamics of molting pintail drakes banded in south-central Saskatchewan. Journal of Wildlife Management 38:266–274.

———, A. P. WYWIALOWSKI, AND K. P. BURNHAM. 1981. Tests of the assumptions underlying life table methods for estimating parameters from cohort data. Ecology 62:1121–1124.

ARNASON, A. N. 1973. The estimation of population size, migration rates, and survival in a stratified population. Research in Population Ecology 15:1–8.

———, AND C. J. SCHWARZ. 1995. POPAN 4. Enhancements to a system for the analysis of mark-recapture data from an open population. Journal of Applied Statistics 22:785–800.

———, AND ———. 2002. POPAN-6: exploring convergence and estimate properties with SIMULATE. Journal of Applied Statistics 29: 649–668.

BART, J., AND D. S. ROBSON. 1982. Estimating survivorship when the subjects are visited periodically. Ecology 63:1078–1090.

BERNADELLI, H. 1941. Population waves. Journal of the Burma Research Society 31:1–18.

BERRYMAN, A. A. 1981. Population systems: a general introduction. Plenum Press, New York, USA.

BINKLEY, C. S., AND R. S. MILLER. 1980. Survivorship of the whooping crane, *Grus americana*. Ecology 61:434–437.

———, AND ———. 1988. Recovery of the whooping crane *Grus americana*. Biological Conservation 45:11–20.

BIRKHEAD, T. R. 1977. The effect of habitat and density on breeding success in the common guillemot (*Uria aalge*). Journal of Animal Ecology 46:751–764.

BOYCE. M. S. 1987. Time-series analysis and forecasting of the Aransas/Wood Buffalo whooping crane population. Pages 1–9 *in* J. C. Lewis, editor. Proceedings of the 1985 Crane Workshop. Whooping Crane Maintenance Trust, Grand Island, Nebraska, USA.

———. 1992. Population viability analysis. Annual Review of Ecology and Systematics 23:481–506.

———, AND R. S. MILLER. 1985. Ten-year periodicity in whooping crane census. Auk 102:658–660.

BRODSKY, L. M. 1988. Ornament size influences mating success in male rock ptarmigan. Animal Behavior 36:662–667.

BROWNIE, C., AND D. S. ROBSON. 1976. Models allowing for age-dependent survival rates for band-return data. Biometrics 32:305–323.

———, D. R. ANDERSON, K. P. BURNHAM, AND D. S. ROBSON. 1985. Statistical inference from band recovery data—a handbook. Second edition. U. S. Department of the Interior, Fish and Wildlife Service, Resource Publication 156.

BUCKLAND, S. T., K. P. BURNHAM, AND N. H. AUGUSTIN. 1997. Model selection: an integral part of inference. Biometrics 53:603–618.

BURNHAM, K. P., AND D. R. ANDERSON. 1979. The composite dynamic method as evidence for age-specific waterfowl mortality. Journal of Wildlife Management 43:356–366.

———, AND ———. 2002. Model selection and multi-model inference. Springer-Verlag, Inc., New York, USA.

———, ———, G. C. WHITE, C. BROWNIE, AND K. H. POLLOCK. 1987. Design and analysis methods for fish survival experiments based on release-recapture. American Fisheries Society Monograph 5.

CASWELL, H. 2000. Matrix population models: construction, analysis, and interpretation. Sinauer Associates, Inc., Sunderland, Massachusetts, USA.

CAUGHLEY, G. 1966. Mortality patterns in mammals. Ecology 47: 906–918.

———. 1977. Analysis of vertebrate populations. John Wiley and Sons, New York, USA.

———, AND L. C. BIRCH. 1971. Rate of increase. Journal of Wildlife Management 35:658–663.

———, AND C. J. KREBS. 1983. Are big mammals simply little mammals writ large? Oecologia 59:7–17.

CHAPMAN, D. G., AND D. S. ROBSON. 1960. The analysis of a catch curve. Biometrics 16:354–368.

CHOQUET, R., A. M. REBOULET, R. PRADEL, O. GIMENEZ, AND J. D. LEBRETON. 2003. User's manual for M-SURGE 1.01. Mimeographed document, CEFE/CNRS, Montpellier, France (ftp://ftp.cefe.cnrs-mop.fr/biom/Soft-CR).

CLOBERT, J., E. DANCHIN, A. A. DHONT, AND J. D NICHOLS. 2001. Dispersal. Oxford University Press, Oxford, United Kingdom.

COLE, L. C. 1957. Sketches of general and comparative demography. Quantitative Biology 22:1–15.

CONNELLY, J. W., J. H. GAMMONLEY, AND J. M. PEEK. 2005. Harvest management. Pages 658–690 in C. E. Braun, editor. Techniques for wildlife investigations and management. Sixth edition. The Wildlife Society, Bethesda, Maryland, USA.

COOCH, E., AND G. C. WHITE. 2002. Using MARK—A gentle introduction. Second edition. Available online at http://www.phidot.org/software/mark/docs/book/ (accessed 15 January 2004).

COOKE, D., AND J. A. LEON. 1976. Stability of population growth determined by 2 × 2 Leslie matrix with density-dependent elements. Biometrics 32:435–442.

CORMACK, R. M. 1973. Common sense estimates from capture-recapture studies. Pages 225–234 in M. S. Bartlett and R. W. Hiorns, editors. The mathematical theory of the dynamics of biological populations. Academic Press, New York, USA.

COWARDIN, L. M., AND R. J. BLOHM. 1992. Breeding population inventories and measures of recruitment. Pages 423–445 in B. D. J. Batt, A. D. Afton, M. G. Anderson, C. D. Ankeny, D. H. Johnson, J. A. Kadlec, and G. L. Krapu, editors. Ecology and management of breeding waterfowl. University of Minnesota Press, Minneapolis, USA.

———, D. H. JOHNSON, T. L. SHAFFER, AND D. W. SPARLING. 1988. Application of a simulation model to decisions in mallard management. U. S. Department of the Interior, Fish and Wildlife Service, Technical Report 17.

DE ANGELIS, D. L. 1976. Application of stochastic models to a wildlife population. Mathematical Biosciences 31:227–236.

DINSMORE, S. J., G. C. WHITE, AND F. L. KNOPF. 2002. Advanced techniques for modeling avian nest survival. Ecology 83:3476–3488.

———, ———, AND ———. 2003. Annual survival and population estimates of mountain plovers in southern Phillips County, Montana. Ecological Applications 13:1013–1026.

DOWNING, R. L. 1980. Vital statistics of animal populations. Pages 247–267 in S. D. Schemnitz, editor. Wildlife management techniques manual. Fourth edition. The Wildlife Society, Washington, D. C., USA.

EBERHARDT, L. L. 1969. Population analysis. Pages 457–495 in R. H. Giles, Jr., editor. Wildlife management techniques. Third edition. The Wildlife. Society, Washington, D. C., USA.

———. 1970. Correlation, regression, and density dependence. Ecology 51:306–310.

———. 1985. Assessing the dynamics of wild populations. Journal of Wildlife Management 49:997–1012.

———. 1987. Population projections from simple models. Journal of Applied Ecology 24:103–118.

———. 1988. Using age structure data from changing populations. Journal of Applied Ecology 25:373–378.

FRANKLIN, A. B. 2001. Exploring ecological relationships in survival and estimating rates of population change using program MARK. Pages 350–356 in R. Field, R. J. Warren, H. Okarma, and P. R. Sievert, editors. Wildlife, land, and people: priorities for the 21st century. Proceedings of the Second International Wildlife Management Congress. The Wildlife Society, Bethesda, Maryland, USA.

———, D. R. ANDERSON, R. J. GUTIERREZ, AND K. P. BURNHAM. 2000. Climate, habitat quality, and fitness in northern spotted owl populations in northwestern California. Ecological Monographs 70: 539–590.

———, T. M. SHENK, D. R. ANDERSON, AND K. P. BURNHAM. 2001. Statistical model selection: an alternative to null hypothesis testing. Pages 75–90 in T. M. Shenk and A. B. Franklin, editors. Modeling in natural resource management: development, interpretation, and application. Island Press, Washington, D. C., USA.

FREDIN, R. A. 1984. Levels of maximum net productivity in populations of large terrestrial mammals. Pages 381–387 in W. F. Perrin, R. L. Brownell, Jr., and D. P. DeMaster, editors. Special Issue 6. Reports of the International Whaling Commission, Cambridge, United Kingdom.

FULLER, M. R., J. J. MILLSPAUGH, K. E. CHURCH, AND R. E. KENWARD. 2005. Wildlife radiotelemetry. Pages 377–417 in C. E. Braun, editor. Techniques for wildlife investigations and management. Sixth edition. The Wildlife Society, Bethesda, Maryland, USA.

GASTON, K. J., AND J. H. LAWTON. 1987. A test of statistical techniques for detecting density dependence in sequential censuses of animal populations. Oecologia 74: 404–410.

GILPIN, M. E., AND F. J. AYALA. 1973. Global models of growth and competition. Proceedings of the National Academy of Science of the United States 70:3590-3593.

GRANT, W. E., E. K. PEDERSON, AND S. L. MARIN. 1997. Ecology and natural resource management: systems analysis and simulation. John Wiley and Sons, New York, USA.

HANSKI, I., AND M. E. GILPIN, editors. 1999. Metapopulation biology: ecology, genetics, and evolution. Academic Press, San Diego, California, USA.

HANSON, W. R. 1963. Calculation of productivity, survival, and abundance of selected vertebrates from sex and age ratios. Wildlife Monographs 9.

HARDER, J. D., AND R. L. KIRKPATRICK. 1994. Physiological methods in wildlife research. Pages 275–306 in T. H. Bookhout, editor. Fifth edition. Research and management techniques for wildlife and habitats. The Wildlife Society, Bethesda, Maryland, USA.

HEPP, G. R., R. T. HOPPE, AND R. A. KENNAMER. 1987. Population parameters and philopatry of breeding female wood ducks. Journal of Wildlife Management 51:401–404.

HESTBECK, J. B., J. D. NICHOLS, AND R. A. MALECKI. 1991. Estimates of movement and site fidelity using mark-resight data of wintering Canada geese. Ecology 72:523–533.

HOUSTON, D. B. 1982. The northern Yellowstone elk: ecology and management. Macmillan Publishing Company, New York, USA.

HUGGINS, R. M. 1989. On the statistical analysis of capture-recapture experiments. Biometrika 76:133–140.

———. 1991. Some practical aspects of a conditional likelihood approach to capture experiments. Biometrics 47:725–732.

HUTCHINSON, G. E. 1978. An introduction to population ecology. Yale University Press, New Haven, Connecticut, USA.

JACKSON, C. H. N. 1939. The analysis of an animal population. Journal of Animal Ecology 8:238–246.

JENKINS, S. H. 1988. Use and abuse of demographic models of population growth. Bulletin of the Ecological Society of America 69: 201–207.

———. 1989. Comments on an inappropriate population model for feral burros. Journal of Mammalogy 70:667–670.

JOHNSON, D. H. 1974. Estimating survival rates from banding of adult and juvenile birds. Journal of Wildlife Management 38:290–297.

———. 1979. Estimating nest success: the Mayfield method and an alternative. Auk 96:651–661.

———. 2001. Validating and evaluating models. Pages 105–119 *in* T. M. Shenk and A. B. Franklin, editors. Modeling in natural resource management: development, interpretation, and application. Island Press, Washington, D. C., USA.

———, AND T. L. SHAFFER. 1990. Estimating nest success: when Mayfield wins. Auk 107:595–600.

———, J. D. NICHOLS, AND M. D. SCHWARTZ. 1992. Population dynamics of breeding waterfowl. Pages 446–485 *in* B. D. J. Batt, A. D. Afton, M. G. Anderson, C. D. Ankeny, D. H. Johnson, J. A. Kadlec, and G. L. Krapu, editors. Ecology and management of breeding waterfowl. University of Minnesota Press, Minneapolis, USA.

———, D. W. SPARLING, AND L. M. COWARDIN. 1987. A model of the productivity of the mallard duck. Ecological Modelling 38:257–275.

KENDALL, W. L., AND J. D. NICHOLS. 1995. On the use of secondary capture-recapture samples to estimate temporary emigration and breeding proportions. Journal of Applied Statistics 22:751–762.

———, ———, AND J. E. HINES. 1997. Estimating temporary emigration using capture-recapture data with Pollock's robust design. Ecology 78:563–578.

———, K. H. POLLOCK, AND C. BROWNIE. 1995. A likelihood-based approach to capture-recapture estimation of demographic parameters under the robust design. Biometrics 51:293–308.

KINGSLAND, S. E. 1995. Modeling nature: episodes in the history of population ecology. Second edition. University of Chicago Press, Illinois, USA.

KINKEL, L. K. 1989. Lasting effects of wing tags on ring-billed gulls. Auk 106:619–624.

KIRKPATRICK, M. 1984. Demographic models based on size, not age, for organisms with indeterminate growth. Ecology 65:1874–1884.

KLETT, A. T., AND D. H. JOHNSON. 1982. Variability in nest survival rates and implications to nesting studies. Auk 99:77–87.

———, H. F. DUEBBERT, C. A. FAANES, AND K. F. HIGGINS. 1986. Techniques for studying nest success of ducks in upland habitats in the prairie pothole region. U. S. Department of the Interior, Fish and Wildlife Service, Resource Publication 158.

KNOWLTON, F. F. 1972. Preliminary interpretations of coyote population mechanics with some management implications. Journal of Wildlife Management 36:369–382.

KREBS, C. J. 1985. Ecology: the experimental analysis of distribution and abundance. Third edition. Harper and Row, New York, USA.

LANCIA, R. A., AND J. W. BISHIR. 1985. Mortality rates of beaver in Newfoundland—a comment. Journal of Wildlife Management 49:879–881.

———, W. L. KENDALL, K. H. POLLOCK, AND J. D. NICHOLS. 2005. Estimating the number of animals in wildlife populations. Pages 106–153 *in* C. E. Braun, editor. Techniques for wildlife investigations and management. Sixth edition. The Wildlife Society, Bethesda, Maryland, USA.

LANDE, R. 1988. Demographic models of the northern spotted owl (*Strix occidentalis caurina*). Oecologia 75:601–607.

———. 1993. Risks of population extinction from demographic and environmental stochasticity and random catastrophes. American Naturalist 142:911–927.

LEBRETON, J. D., K. P. BURNHAM, J. CLOBERT, AND D. R. ANDERSON. 1992. Modeling survival and testing hypotheses using marked animals: a unified approach with case studies. Ecological Monographs 62:67–118.

LEFKOVITCH, L. P. 1965. The study of population growth in organisms grouped by stages. Biometrics 21:1–18.

LESLIE, P. H. 1945. On the use of matrices in certain population mathematics. Biometrika 33:183–212.

———. 1948. Some further notes on the use of matrices in population mathematics. Biometrika 35:213–245.

———. 1959. The properties of a certain lag type of population growth and the influence of an external random factor on a number of such populations. Physiological Zoology 32:151–159.

LEVINS, R. 1966. The strategy of model building in population biology. American Scientist 54:421–431.

———. 1968. Evolution in changing environments. Princeton University Press, Princeton, New Jersey, USA.

———. 1970. Extinction. Pages 77–107 in M. Gerstenhaber, editor. Some mathematical questions in biology. American Mathematical Society, Providence, Rhode Island, USA.

LEWIS, E. G. 1942. On the generation and growth of a population. Sankhya 6:93–96.

LOERY, G., K. H. POLLOCK, J. D. NICHOLS, AND J. E. HINES. 1987. Age-specificity of black-capped chickadee survival rates: analysis of capture-recapture data. Ecology 68:1038–1044.

LOTKA, A. J. 1925. Elements of physical biology. Williams and Wilkins, Baltimore, Maryland, USA.

MACARTHUR, R. H. 1968. The theory of the niche. Pages 159–176 *in* R. C. Lewontin, editor. Population biology and evolution. Syracuse University Press, Syracuse, New York, USA.

———. 1972. Geographical ecology: patterns in the distribution of species. Harper and Row, New York, USA.

MAELZER, D. A. 1970. The regression of log N_{n+1} on log N_n as a test of density dependence: an exercise with computer-constructed density-independent populations. Ecology 51:810–822.

MANLY, B. F. J. 1985. The statistics of natural selection on animal populations. Chapman and Hall, New York, USA.

MARTIN, F. W., R. S. POSPAHALA, AND J. D. NICHOLS. 1979. Assessment and population management of North American migratory birds. Pages 187–239 *in* J. Cairns, Jr., G. P. Patil, and W. E. Waters, editors. Environmental biomonitoring, assessment, prediction, and management—certain case studies and related quantitative issues. International Cooperative Publishing House, Fairland, Maryland, USA.

MAY, R. M. 1973. Stability and complexity in model ecosystems. Princeton University Press, Princeton, New Jersey, USA.

———. 1974. Biological populations with nonoverlapping generations: stable points, stable cycles, and chaos. Science 186:645–647.

———, AND G. F. OSTER. 1976. Bifurcations and dynamic complexity in simple ecological models. American Naturalist 110:573–599.

MAYFIELD, H. 1961. Nesting success calculated from exposure. Wilson Bulletin 73:255–261.

MAYNARD SMITH, J. 1974. Models in ecology. Cambridge University Press, New York, USA.

MCCULLOUGH, D. R. 1979. The George Reserve deer herd. University of Michigan Press, Ann Arbor, USA.

———. 1982. Population growth rate of the George Reserve deer herd. Journal of Wildlife Management 46:1079–1083.

———. 1983. Rate of increase of white-tailed deer on the George Reserve: a response. Journal of Wildlife Management 47:1248–1250.

———, editor. 1996. Metapopulations and wildlife conservation. Island Press, Washington, D. C., USA.

MERTZ, D. B. 1970. Notes on methods used in life-history studies. Pages 4–17 *in* J. H. Connell, D. B. Mertz, and W. W. Murdoch, editors. Readings in ecology and ecological genetics. Harper and Row, New York, USA.

MICHOD, R. E., AND W. W. ANDERSON. 1980. On calculating demographic parameters from age frequency data. Ecology 61:265–269.

NATARAJAN, R., AND C. E. MCCULLOCH. 1999. Modeling heterogeneity in nest survival data. Biometrics 55:553–559.

NEDELMAN, J., J. A. THOMPSON, AND R. J. TAYLOR. 1987. The statistical demography of whooping cranes. Ecology 68:1401–1411.

NICHOLS, J. D., AND K. H. POLLOCK. 1990. Estimation of recruitment from immigration versus in situ reproduction using Pollock's robust design. Ecology 71:21–26.

———, J. R. SAUER, K. H. POLLOCK, AND J. B. HESTBECK. 1992. Estimating transition probabilities for stage-based population matrices using capture-recapture data. Ecology 73:306–312.

NOON, B. R., R. H. LAMBERSON, M. S. BOYCE, AND L. L. IRWIN. 1999. Population viability analysis: a primer on its principal technical concepts. Pages 87–134 *in* N. C. Johnson, A. J. Malk, W. T. Sexton, and R. Szaro, editors. Ecological stewardship: a common reference for ecosystem management. Elsevier Science Limited, Oxford, United Kingdom.

PAULIK, G. J., AND D. S. ROBSON. 1969. Statistical calculations for change-in-ratio estimators of population parameters. Journal of Wildlife Management 33: 1–27.

PEARL, R. 1928. The rate of living. Alfred A. Knopf, Inc., New York, USA.

PENNYCUICK, C. J., R. M. COMPTON, AND L. BECKINGHAM. 1968. A computer model for simulating the growth of a population, or of two interacting populations. Journal of Theoretical Biology 18: 316–329.

PIANKA, E. R. 1974. Evolutionary ecology. Harper and Row, New York, USA.

PIELOU, E. C. 1969. An introduction to mathematical ecology. John Wiley and Sons, New York, USA.

POLACHECK, T. 1985. The sampling distribution of age-specific survival estimates from an age distribution. Journal of Wildlife Management 49: 180–184.

POLLARD, E., K. H. LAKHANI, AND P. ROTHERY. 1987. The detection of density-dependence from a series of annual censuses. Ecology 68: 2046–2055.

POLLOCK, K. H. 1982. A capture-recapture design robust to unequal probability of capture. Journal of Wildlife Management 46: 757–760.

———. 2002. The use of auxiliary variables in capture-recapture modeling: an overview. Journal of Applied Statistics 29: 85–102.

———, J. D. NICHOLS, C. BROWNIE, AND J. E. HINES. 1990. Statistical inference for capture–recapture experiments. Wildlife Monographs 107.

POOLE, R. W. 1974. An introduction to quantitative ecology. McGraw-Hill Book Co., New York, USA.

POWELL, R. A. 1979. Fishers, population models, and trapping. Wildlife Society Bulletin 7: 149–154.

PRADEL, R. 1996. Utilization of capture-mark-recapture for the study of recruitment and population growth rate. Biometrics 52: 703–709.

PULLIAM, H. R. 1988. Sources, sinks, and population regulation. American Naturalist 132: 652–661.

RICKLEFS, R. E. 1979. Ecology. Second edition. Chiron Press, New York, USA.

ROBSON, D. S., AND D. G. CHAPMAN. 1961. Catch curves and mortality rates. Transactions of the American Fisheries Society 90: 181–189.

ROTELLA, J. J., M. L TAPER, AND A. J. HANSEN. 2000. Correcting nesting-success estimates for observer effects: maximum likelihood estimates of daily survival rates with reduced bias. Auk 117: 92–109.

SAUER, J. R., AND N. A. SLADE. 1987. Size-based demography of vertebrates. Annual Review of Ecology and Systematics 18: 71–90.

SEBER, G. A. F. 1970. Estimating time-specific survival and reporting rates for adult birds from band returns. Biometrika 57: 313–318.

———. 1982. The estimation of animal abundance and related parameters. Second edition. Macmillan Publishing Company, Inc., New York, USA.

———. 1986. A review of estimating animal abundance. Biometrics 42: 267–292.

———. 2001. Some new directions in estimating animal population parameters. Journal of Agricultural, Biological, and Environmental Statistics 6: 140–151.

SHAFFER, M. L. 1987. Minimum viable populations: coping with uncertainty. Pages 69–86 *in* M. E. Soulé, editor. Viable populations for conservation. Cambridge University Press, Cambridge, United Kingdom.

SHAFFER, T. L. 2004. A unified approach to analyzing nest success. Auk 121: 526–540

SILER, W. 1979. A competing-risk model for animal mortality. Ecology 60: 750–757.

SLADE, N. A. 1977. Statistical detection of density dependence from a series of sequential censuses. Ecology 58: 1094–1102.

SOLOW, A. R. 1990. Testing for density dependence: a cautionary note. Oecologia 83: 47–49.

ST. AMANT, J. L. S. 1970. The detection of regulation in animal populations. Ecology 51: 823–828.

STANLEY, T. R. 2000. Modeling and estimation of stage-specific daily survival probabilities of nests. Ecology 81: 2048–2053.

STARFIELD, A. M., AND A. L. BLELOCH. 1991. Building models for conservation and wildlife management. Second edition. The Burgess Press, Edina, Minnesota, USA.

STOUDT, J. H. 1971. Ecological factors affecting waterfowl production in the Saskatchewan parklands. U. S. Department of the Interior, Fish and Wildlife Service, Resource Publication 99.

STRONG, D. R. 1986. Density vagueness: abiding the variance in the demography of real populations. Pages 257–268 *in* J. Diamond and T. J. Case, editors. Community ecology. Harper and Row, New York, USA.

TAIT, D. E. N., AND R. L. BUNNELL. 1980. Estimating rate of increase from age at death. Journal of Wildlife Management 44: 296–299.

TANNER, J. T. 1975. The stability and the intrinsic growth rates of prey and predator populations. Ecology 56: 855–867.

TAYLOR, M., AND J. S. CARLEY. 1988. Life table analysis of age structured populations in seasonal environments. Journal of Wildlife Management 52: 366–373.

USHER, M. B. 1972. Developments in the Leslie matrix model. Pages 29–60 *in* J. N. R. Jeffers, editor. Mathematical models in ecology. Blackwell Scientific Publishing, Oxford, United Kingdom.

VAN BALLENBERGHE, V. 1983. Rate of increase of white-tailed deer on the George Reserve: a re-evaluation. Journal of Wildlife Management 47: 1245–1247.

VANDERMEER, J. H. 1972. Niche theory. Annual Review of Ecology and Systematics 3: 107–132.

VAN GROENENDAEL, J., H. DE KROON, AND H. CASWELL. 1988. Projection matrices in population biology. Trends in Ecology and Evolution 3: 264–269.

VOLTERRA, V. 1926. Fluctuations in the abundance of a species considered mathematically. Nature 118: 558–560.

WALTERS, C. J. 1986. Adaptive management of renewable resources. Macmillan Publishing Company, New York, USA.

WETHEY, D. S. 1985. Catastrophe, extinction, and species diversity: a rocky intertidal example. Ecology 66: 445–456.

WHITE, G. C. 2000. Population viability analysis: data requirements and essential analyses. Pages 288–331 *in* L. Boitani and T. K. Fuller, editors. Research techniques in animal ecology: controversies and consequences. Columbia University Press, New York, USA.

———, AND K. P. BURNHAM. 1999. Program MARK: survival estimation from populations of marked animals. Bird Study 46: 120–139.

———, ———, AND D. R. ANDERSON. 2001. Advanced features of program MARK. Pages 368–377 *in* R. Field, R. J. Warren, H. Okarma, and P. R. Sievert, editors. Wildlife, land, and people: priorities for the 21st century. Proceedings of the Second International Wildlife Management Congress. The Wildlife Society, Bethesda, Maryland, USA.

WIENS, J. A. 1996. Wildlife in patchy environments: metapopulations, mosaics, and management. Pages 53–84 in D. R. McCullough, editor. Metapopulations and wildlife conservation. Island Press, Washington, D. C., USA.

WILLIAMS, B. K., J. D. NICHOLS, AND M. J. CONROY. 2002. Analysis and management of animal populations. Academic Press, San Diego, California, USA.

WILLIAMSON, M. H. 1959. Some extensions of the use of matrices in population theory. Bulletin of Mathematical Biophysics 21: 13–17.

WILSON, E. O., AND W. H. BOSSERT. 1971. A primer of population biology. Sinauer Associates, Inc., Sunderland, Massachusetts, USA.

WILSON, K. R., J. D. NICHOLS, AND J. E. HINES. 1989. A computer program for sample size computations for banding studies. U. S. Department of the Interior, Fish and Wildlife Service, Technical Report 23.

ZENG, Z., AND J. H. BROWN. 1987. A method for distinguishing dispersal from death in mark-recapture studies. Journal of Mammalogy 68: 656–665.

7

CARE AND USE OF WILDLIFE IN FIELD RESEARCH

F. Joshua Dein, Dale E. Toweill, and Kevin P. Kenow

INTRODUCTION

Scientists operate in an arena with responsibilities to the organisms they study and to society. Further, professional scientists must consider the effects of their activities on the organisms under study, the validity of study results, and the values and uses of these organisms by other segments of society. The Wildlife Society recognizes these relationships and supports sound application of responsible methods for conduct of animal research in all field and laboratory investigations. This position reflects our ethical and moral concerns regarding human interactions with each other and with other species, and recognizes the scientific benefits of investigations that are not compromised by the manner in which animals are handled or maintained. These concerns are the foundation for our philosophy that responsible methods of animal investigations must include all animal species. Wildlife professionals are urged to apply high standards of animal care and maintenance, and responsible methods of experimental procedures based on written and reviewed Study Plans, when conducting each animal investigation. It is now the policy of most scientific journals to publish only articles reporting research for which appropriate animal care and use can be assured. This chapter provides guidelines for research involving wild animals, and promotes the humane care of experimental subjects. The variety of wild vertebrates investigated and conditions encountered precludes provision of specific information applicable to each situation. While the focus of this chapter is on research procedures, we suggest that, to the extent possible, these guidelines be applied to management activities as well.

BACKGROUND

The Animal Welfare Act (AWA) (7 U.S.C. 2131, et seq.) was originally enacted in 1966 (Public Law 89-544) and amended in 1970, 1976, 1985, 1990, and 2002 (U.S. Department of Agriculture 2002). Animal Care Regulations derived from the AWA (U.S. Department of Agriculture 2002) established definitions of terms (Part 1) used in the regulations (Part 2) and standards (Part 3) for humane handling, care, treatment, and transportation of regulated animals used for research, exhibition, or teaching purposes, sold as pets, or transported in commerce. Excluded from the provisions of the Act are ectotherms, birds, rats *(Rattus)*, and mice *(Mus)* bred for use in research, horses and other farm animals used or intended for use as food and fiber, and livestock and poultry used or intended for use in improving animal nutrition, breeding, management, or production efficiency, or for improving the quality of food or fiber. Field studies, defined as "a study conducted on free-living wild animals in their natural habitat," may not fall under AWA regulation (U.S. Department of Agriculture 2002:9). However, this exemption also states, "this term excludes any study that involves an invasive procedure, harms, or materially alters the behavior of an animal under study" (U.S. Department of Agriculture 2002:9). These terms are subject to interpretation, and institutional Animal Care and Use Committees (ACUC) should review and make any final determination whether a study is covered.

Exclusion of animal species under the U.S. Animal Welfare Act removes reporting requirements and reduces oversight by the U.S. Department of Agriculture, but does not negate inclusion of these species under guidelines

Box 1.   Sources of assistance for technical information and interpretation of the Animal Welfare Act in the United States.

Animal Welfare Information Center
National Agricultural Library
Beltsville, Maryland 20705
Phone: 301-504-6212
Fax: 301-504-7125
E-mail: awic@nal.usda.gov
http://www.nal.usda.gov/awic/

Institute for Laboratory Animal Research
National Academy of Sciences
500 Fifth Street, NW, NA 687
Washington, D.C. 20001
Phone: 202-334-2590
Fax: 202-334-1687
E-mail: ILAR@nas.edu
http://dels.nationalacademies.org/ilar/index.asp?id=index

Office of Laboratory Animal Welfare
National Institutes of Health
RKL1, Suite 360, MSC 7982
6705 Rockledge Drive

Bethesda, Maryland 20892-7982
E-mail: olaw@od.nih.gov
Fax: 301-402-7065
http://grants1.nih.gov/grants/olaw/olaw.htm

Scientists Center for Animal Welfare
7833 Walker Drive, Suite 410
Greenbelt, Maryland 20770
Phone: 301-345-3500
Fax: 301-345-3503
E-mail: info@scaw.com
http://www.scaw.com

USDA/APHIS/AC
4700 River Road, Unit 84
Riverdale, Maryland 20737-1232
Phone 301-734-7833
Fax: 301-734-4978
E-mail: ace@aphis.usda.gov
http://www.aphis.usda.gov/ac/

established by other agencies. Fish, amphibians, reptiles, birds, and mammals are covered by National Science Foundation and Public Health Service (NSF/PHS) policy "Guidelines" (Office of Laboratory Animal Welfare 2002). These policies rely on the *Guide for the Care and Use of Laboratory Animals* for specific information (Institute of Laboratory Animal Resources 1996). Coverage is extended to research grants funded by these agencies and to federal agencies, such as the U.S. Fish and Wildlife Service, that follow the U.S. government's *Principles for the Utilization and Care of Vertebrate Animals Used in Testing, Research, and Training*, formulated by the Interagency Research Animal Committee (Office of Science and Technology Policy 1985). A number of sources (Box 1) are available for consultation on the AWA in the United States. In Canada, the Canadian Council on Animal Care has produced an extensive 2-volume general set of guidelines (Canadian Council on Animal Care 1984, 1993), and an additional volume specifically focused on wildlife (Canadian Council on Animal Care 2003). Similar guidelines and policies have been produced in other countries, and the United Nations Food and Agriculture Organization provides a web gateway to much of this information (Food and Agriculture Organization 2003). This chapter refers mainly to procedures in the United States.

Many professional societies have produced guidelines for use of animals in field research specifically focused on their species of interest (American Society of Ichthyologists and Herpetologists 1997, American Society of Mammalogists 1998, Gaunt et al. 1999, Animal Behavior Society/Association for the Study of Animal Behavior 2003). While these guidelines may provide a useful review of current practices in that field, they are only suggested, not definitive, reference points. Assessment of appropriate animal care and use can only be made after proposal

review by the institutional Animal Care and Use Committee (ACUC). All proposed procedures and care should be consistent with principles of the AWA and the *Guide for the Care and Use of Laboratory Animals*.

ANIMAL CARE AND USE COMMITTEES

A major requirement of the AWA and NSF/PHS guidelines is establishment of institutional ACUCs. The function of ACUCs is critical to the conduct of scientific investigations. Each ACUC must consist of at least 3 members, one of whom is the attending veterinarian of the research facility (or another veterinarian with delegated program responsibility), and one who does not conduct animal research, and is not affiliated in any way with the facility, other than as a committee member. Extensive information about formation and operation of effective ACUC's is readily available (Orlans et al. 1987, Allen 2000, Pitts 2002). The purpose of the ACUC is to evaluate the care, treatment, housing, and use of animals and to promote compliance with the AWA regulations. This process involves evaluation of experimental protocols to ensure that animal pain and distress are minimized. ACUC oversight includes laboratory and field studies. Orlans (1988) first provided application of AWA principles to wildlife and field studies. The topic has since been addressed by others (Michener 1989, Elliott 1995, Peck and Simmonds 1995, Putnam 1995, Waples and Stagoll 1997, Williams 1999, Mulcahy 2003). Differences between laboratory and field studies (Orlans 1988, Mulcahy 2003) do not negate the need for application of responsible methods for care and use of animals during field research activities. ACUCs and field investigators must work together in reaching agreement on appropriate protocols and methods for specific circumstances of the field research to be undertaken. "Standards for humane treatment of wild vertebrates must continue to be constantly developed, applied, and reexamined. Practices that are acceptable today may well prove unacceptable to tomorrow's scientific community, and/or to society in general" (Canadian Council on Animal Care 1984:192).

Wildlife professionals are strongly encouraged to serve on ACUCs and contribute their specific knowledge about the needs of free-living wildlife to help guide committee actions involving protocol reviews for field investigations. Wildlife professionals are also encouraged to publish manuscripts that document the proper care and maintenance of free-living wildlife species during field investigations. Development of this information by knowledgeable field biologists provides specific species information for guiding ACUC decisions involving protocol reviews. Irrespective of the species or circumstances involved, wildlife professionals should satisfy 7 conditions for all research studies. Written assurance that these conditions will be met is a prerequisite for project consideration and funding by many granting agencies. These conditions also are principal points for evaluation by the ACUC.

(1) Wildlife professionals must approach all projects involving use of wildlife for research, management, testing or teaching with a commitment to making a contribution to improving understanding of biological principles, or obtaining knowledge expected to benefit wildlife populations, ecosystems, or humans.

(2) Procedures used should avoid or minimize distress to animals consistent with sound research design.

(3) Procedures that may cause more than momentary or slight distress to animals should be performed with appropriate sedation, analgesia, or anesthesia, except when justified for scientific reasons in writing by the investigator in advance, and approved by the institutional ACUC.

(4) Animals that otherwise would experience severe or chronic distress that cannot be relieved will be euthanized at the end of the procedure or, if appropriate, during the procedure.

(5) Methods of euthanasia should be consistent with recommendations of the American Veterinary Medical Association (AVMA) Panel on Euthanasia (Andrews et al. 1993, AVMA 2001) unless deviation is justified for scientific reasons in writing by the investigator. However, species differences must be considered. "The AVMA recommendations cannot be taken rigidly for ectotherms; the methods suggested for endotherms are often not applicable to ectotherms with significant anaerobic capacities" (American Society of Ichthyologists and Herpetologists 1997:2). Other guidelines and resources are also available (Cooper et al. 1989, Institute of Laboratory Animal Resources 1992, Kreeger 1997).

(6) Living conditions of animals held in captivity at field sites should be appropriate for that species and contribute to their health and well being. Specific considerations include appropriate standards of hygiene, nutrition, group composition and numbers, provisions for refuge and seclusion, and protection from weather and other forms of environmental stress. Housing, feeding, and nonmedical care of these animals must be directed by a scientist trained and experienced in the proper care, handling, and use of the species being maintained or studied. Some experiments (e.g., competition studies) may require housing of mixed species, possibly in the same enclosure.

Mixed housing also is appropriate for holding or displaying certain species.

(7) Post-release monitoring of animals involved in experimental procedures should be conducted to examine effects on individuals and populations.

WILDLIFE OBSERVATIONS AND COLLECTIONS

Before initiating field research, investigators must be familiar with the target species and its response to disturbance, sensitivity to capture and restraint and, if necessary, requirements for captive maintenance. To the extent feasible, animals with dependent young should not be removed from the wild unless the young are also collected or removed alive, and provided for in a manner that facilitates their survival beyond the period of dependency. Whenever possible, voucher specimens of animals, their tissues, and parasitic and microbial fauna collected during field investigations should be deposited in catalogued scientific collections available to others within the scientific community to provide for maximum use of animals collected. The number of animals required for investigations depends on questions being investigated, but provision of adequate sample size is essential to assure scientific validity of results and avoid unnecessary repetition of studies. Removal of animals from a population (either for translocation or by lethal means) should be restricted to the fewest animals necessary to achieve established goals, but must not jeopardize the population's well being.

Investigator Disturbance and Impacts

Potential gains in knowledge from field investigations must be balanced against the potential adverse consequences associated with conduct of the study (Animal Behavior Society/Association for the Study of Animal Behavior 2003). A high level of sensitivity to the potential, indirect effects of investigator presence and study procedures must be maintained, and appropriate steps must be taken to minimize these effects. Examples of secondary impacts associated with field investigations may include nest desertion, abandonment of young, increased vulnerability to predation, traumatic injuries and mortality resulting from panic escape response, cessation of breeding activities, increased energy use by disrupted species, altered feeding behavior, habitat abandonment, long-term marring of fragile habitats, increased vulnerability to hunting, introduction of disease, and spread of disease. These effects may impact either research (target) or other (non-target) species. Investigators should use available information on secondary impacts as a basis for taking appropriate precautions to minimize known potential impacts. Such factors as frequency and timing of investigator presence can greatly influence research effects on target and non-target species. When applicable, remote methods of data collection should be used to minimize disturbance. Investigators must be constantly aware of and minimize the impacts of even remote activities, since the use of aircraft and vehicles may cause significant stress on wild animals, and repeated disturbances may lead to detrimental changes in habitat use. Habitat conservation should be practiced rigorously during all field investigations, and every reasonable effort should be made to leave the study area and access to it as undisturbed as possible.

Museum Collections and Other Specimens

Collection of animals often is an essential component of field investigations. These collections may involve systematic zoology, comparative anatomy, disease assessment or control in localized areas, food preference studies, environmental contaminant evaluations, and numerous other justifiable causes and scientific needs. Assessment of the need should involve appropriate evaluations to demonstrate the proposed collections will provide scientific data that are not duplicative of information already available in the scientific literature (unless confirmation of these data is needed), or that are presently available in accessible scientific collections and repositories. These evaluations also should assess whether suitable information can be obtained from alternative methods that do not require taking live animals. Methods of collection must be responsible, minimize the potential for the taking of nontarget species, and not compromise the purpose of the study. In some instances, it is possible and practical to capture animals and then apply approved euthanasia methods (Andrews et al. 1993, AVMA 2001). However, for many field studies the only practical means of animal collection are those involving direct collection as the initial step in the process. Under these conditions, methods of vertebrate collection must be as species or age–class specific as possible.

Methods must not be used that compromise data evaluation. Appropriate provisions also must be made for proper collection and preservation of biological materials associated with the purpose of the study. Improperly collected or preserved specimens that fail as useful and valid sources of scientific information negate the purpose of collecting the animals. In some circumstances, such as efforts to reduce populations of potentially infected species within a localized geographic area to prevent the spread of disease, it may be necessary to use a variety of methods (lethal and nonlethal) to remove wildlife. In these situations, investigators must identify the geographic region targeted, select the most humane and efficient methods of targeting the species of concern, use the organisms removed to the greatest extent practical to further knowledge of the species and disease, and communicate their findings to the scientific and local communities affected.

When shooting is the collection method, the firearm and ammunition should be appropriate for the species and purpose of the study. The shooter should be sufficiently skilled to be able to kill the animal cleanly. If an animal is wounded, immediate attention must be given to kill it quickly. Attention also must be given to the animal's location to assure it can be killed cleanly and that it will be readily accessible for retrieval and data collection. For game animals, harvest via public hunting may be used to collect samples of interest when participants are made aware of potential human health risks (if any) and means of minimizing risk, hunt area boundaries are clearly identified, protocols are established for collection and use of pertinent data, and measures are in place to prevent inadvertent spread of transmissible diseases.

Kill traps, with attendant baits and attractants, are acceptable and effective for animal collection when used in a manner that minimizes the potential for collecting nontarget species. All traps should be checked regularly, at least daily, to prevent specimen loss from scavengers and predators and should be nonfunctional when not in use.

Live traps for nocturnal species should be set before dusk, checked as soon as possible after dawn, and closed during the day to prevent capture of nontarget species. Live traps for diurnal species should be shaded or positioned to avoid full exposure to the sun. Live traps for non-fossorial mammals should enclose a volume of space adequate for movement within the trap; for fossorial mammals, trap diameter should approximate that of the burrow. The live-trap mechanism should not cause serious injury to the animal, and trap doors should be effective in preventing the captive animal from becoming stuck or partially held in the door opening (American Society of Mammalogists 1998). Pitfalls used as live traps should contain adequate food to last until the next trap check and should be covered to keep out rain or punctured to permit drainage.

Blood and Tissue Collections

Only properly trained individuals proficient in the required techniques should attempt to take tissue samples from live animals. Collection of tissue samples requires proper animal restraint to avoid traumatic injuries to the animal and to the investigator taking the samples. Use of anesthetics is required when the sample procedure will cause more than slight or momentary pain. The institution/facility ACUC is the proper source for evaluating collection methods and use of anesthetics for noninvasive and invasive procedures for tissue collections from live animals.

Blood is the most common tissue sampled from live animals. A conservative rule of thumb is that the amount of blood drawn at one time from a healthy animal that is to be kept alive should be no more than 0.5–1% of its body weight, depending on taxa. However, the amount of blood taken should be limited to actual needs, rather than the maximum amount that can be safely taken to reduce stress from handling. Appropriate equipment (e.g., syringe and needle size) and sample site should be selected to provide the amount of blood needed for the species involved (McGuill and Rowan 1989, Jacobson 1993, Morton and Jennings 1993, Green 2002, Dein 2003)

Obtaining blood samples from amphibians can be relatively simple such as collecting from the lingual venous plexus and the midline abdominal vein in some frogs and toads, to the more difficult latter procedure in salamanders. Cardiac puncture can also be used, although concerns about sample quality, and safety to the animal must be considered. Toe clipping for blood collection is not recommended. These techniques are well covered by Whitaker and Wright (2001) and Green (2002).

Jacobson (1993) and Campbell (1996) provide guidance and references on blood and tissue sample collection from reptiles. The jugular vein, scapular vein, brachial vein, orbital sinus and heart can be used for sampling chelonians, while the ventral coccygeal vein can be used in lizards and snakes. The supervertebral vein is commonly used for crocodilians.

The 3 most common sites for obtaining blood from birds arc the right jugular vein of the neck, medial-metatarsal vein of the leg, and brachial vein of the wing. Needle pricks at vessel extremities are preferable to toenail clips for small samples (Dein 2003). The jugular is preferred for bleeding most birds because of its accessibility and size and because large samples can be taken relatively easily. The medial–metatarsal vein is not recommended for use in raptors, nor is the brachial vein in large birds such as cranes. Feathers should not be plucked to locate these veins. Birds have also been bled from a variety of other sites including the heart and occipital venous sinus. However, there is seldom reason to assume the risk associated with these sites for nonlethal sampling, even though successful application of these techniques has been demonstrated.

Multiple sites also are available for drawing blood samples from mammals. Venipuncture of the cephalic, femoral, or jugular vein, the orbital sinus, or various venous plexuses are common procedures. Small samples may be quickly and easily taken from the marginal ear vein in small mammals. If an animal will be killed immediately thereafter, cardiac bleeding also is acceptable. Need for anesthesia with any of these procedures depends upon methods of restraint, species being bled, physical condition of the animal, and volume of blood needed.

RESTRAINT AND HANDLING

Safety of wild animals, and scientists who are studying them, should be the primary consideration when physical contact is judged to be necessary and unavoidable. Non-domesticated animals usually try to elude capture, handling, and restraint. The means by which a particular animal may try to prevent capture will vary with the species, gender, physiologic condition, and temperament of the individual. In attempts to elude capture, wild animals are capable of inflicting severe damage to themselves and their potential captors.

Investigators should make every effort to minimize the amount of handling time and associated stress to captured animals. Many mammals and birds become highly agitated at the sight and sound of humans in their immediate proximity. Handlers should consider use of eye masks suitable to the species being handled, reduce human conversation during handling, and provision of darkened holding facilities away from human activity to minimize undue stress on wildlife during periods of handling and restraint.

Behavioral characteristics of wild animals may be used to assist the potential captor. For instance, animals in a small pen or cage voluntarily may enter a smaller container to hide and evade capture. If that container provides adequate restraint, the potentially dangerous work of securing the animal can be accomplished more easily. Every effort involving contact between wild animals and humans should be carefully conceived and skillfully executed. Personnel involved must know the habits and behaviors of the animal to be handled; the plan must have suitable alternatives; and a genuine regard for the physical, physiological, and psychological welfare of the animal must be of deep concern to those actually handling the animals. If the planned and alternate procedures do not appear to be satisfactory, or if unforeseen circumstances arise associated with project personnel, weather, or potential predators in the immediate proximity of capture/handling, or release sites, the responsible thing to do is cease immediately and return to the planning stage. Trying to force unworkable procedures in a particular situation is a virtual guarantee of injury to either the animals or the humans involved.

Physical Restraint

For many situations, physical restraint is the most appropriate method of animal handling, because of risks from chemical immobilization to the animal and humans when potentially toxic drugs are used (Roffe et al. 2005). When physical restraint is selected, an adequate number of sufficiently trained and equipped personnel must be available to complete the task safely. Location and type of capture, as well as procedures to be performed and time required to accomplish them, will influence the particular type of physical restraint. Gloves, catch poles, ropes, nets, body bags, holding boxes, corrals, squeeze chutes, or more sophisticated mechanical holding devices may be required for specific situations.

For some highly excitable or anatomically fragile species, prolonged physical restraint (minutes or hours depending on species) without some chemical tranquilization may result in self-inflicted trauma, physiological disturbances or, occasionally, death. Investigators have an obligation to make every effort to avoid physical restraint procedures that result in cardiogenic shock, capture myopathy, and other stress-induced causes of mortality in their animal subjects. Stress-related damage may not be immediately apparent but may lead to physiological damage or death after release. Release of animals following restraint should be made at or near the site of capture or near the appropriate social group depending on the species and its social behavior. Post-release monitoring will help assess the short-and long-term effects of these procedures.

Chemical Restraint

Use of drugs to restrain a wild and potentially dangerous animal for handling has many applications in wildlife research and management (Roffe et al. 2005). The use of anesthetics, analgesics, and sedatives is mandatory for control of pain and distress before potentially painful procedures such as surgery are performed on animals. As all tranquilizing drugs do not provide pain relief, they must be selected carefully. Use of drugs and "tranquilizer guns," however, is not the panacea to wild-animal restraint. Chemicals used for tranquilization and immobilization, if not correctly handled and delivered, may be dangerous to the target animals and humans. In addition, during the drug induction phase or during recovery, an unrestrained animal may be subject to increased potential for accidental injury or death (including predation). While under the effects of the drug, the animal may become hyper- or hypothermic, depending on chemicals used and ambient temperature, it may vomit and aspirate the vomitus, or pregnant females may abort. A darted animal may be able to elude its captors and hide before being completely anesthetized, a particularly acute hazard when chemicals are used that require administration of an antidote. Metabolic disturbances (e.g., "capture myopathy") may not be apparent during a procedure, but may lead to an animal's death after release. All of these circumstances and possibilities must be understood and evaluated by the researcher before a chemical is selected as the best method of restraint in a given instance.

If chemical restraint is selected, it is imperative for all members of the capture team to have a working knowledge of the chemical or drugs being used, even if they are to be handled and delivered by a veterinarian. It also is the responsibility of researchers to know the effects, side effects, advantages, and disadvantages of the drugs being used, and to have knowledge of such factors as minimum and maximum induction times and potential for adverse drug reactions. This type of information is necessary to evaluate the danger to target animals, and to humans that might be exposed to the drugs.

Researchers should be capable of monitoring the condition of anesthetized animals and be able to apply resuscitative routines in a life-threatening emergency. Electronic equipment such as thermometers, cardiac monitors, and pulse oximetry units can make animal monitoring convenient and efficient. Specific recommendations for drug use and their dosage, drug delivery systems, and physical restraint techniques applicable to the specific species are available in the published literature (reviewed by Roffe et al. 2005). The use of paralytic agents without the addition of other anesthetic drugs is not considered acceptable. Additional information on use of these methods exists in some of the guidelines on acceptable field techniques published by professional societies.

ANIMAL MARKING

Developing means of reliably identifying individual animals to achieve field research objectives often is necessary. In addition to requiring individual identification, researchers may need information on nonconspicuous aspects of physiology or movements, or other aspects of animal ecology that can be examined directly or indirectly through specially designed markers. However, before initiating any marking procedure for wild animals, researchers should demonstrate whether marking is required and appropriate for the particular situation (Silvy et al. 2005). If the marking process causes pain or distress, as defined by the AWA, appropriate analgesics or anesthetics should be used.

Criteria for Marking

Researchers must search among a wide array of potential techniques with varying strengths and weaknesses to select the method(s) most suited to their particular project. Technological and methodological constraints and available resources can vary widely from project to project and will require researchers to examine each potential marking technique in terms of a standard set of criteria. Specific criteria (below) relate to impacts of marking on the organism, validity of the study, and other constraints such as legal requirements.

(1) Marks should have minimal effect on the anatomy and physiology of the organism; i.e., no immediate or long-term physical hindrance.

(2) Marks should not influence the organism's behavior; i.e., they should not reduce an organism's ability to secure food, shelter, or inhibit breeding activity (unless the marks are intended as a reproductive inhibitor).

(3) Marks that make an organism more conspicuous must be evaluated carefully to ensure they neither cause others of the same species to react differently to it than to other conspecifics nor subject it to increased selection by potential predators (unless this is a purpose of the study).

(4) Marks should be retained for the minimal period required to achieve project goals.

(5) Unambiguous marks that are quick and easy to apply should be selected to avoid extensive handling or error potential.

(6) Marks must comply with federal, state, and other agency rules and regulations.

The first 3 criteria focus on the well being of the organism being studied and the potential for marks to influence research results by affecting the fitness or behavior of the organisms. Criteria 4 and 5 may affect the validity of the research design, and criterion 6 reflects other constraints placed upon the researcher. Violation of any of the first 5 criteria may result in biased research results and researchers must specifically address these criteria in any evaluation of research resulting from a sample of marked organisms.

Although marks that may be applied to organisms are commonly perceived as passive and visual, some markers are active and visual (lights), auditory, use radiotelemetry, or rely on electronic chemical detection. The wide availability of inplantable transponders (PIT tags, etc.) now expands the possibility for minimally invasive and positive marking methods. A vast literature exists of techniques and potential concerns regarding the marking of organisms from insects to whales (Silvy et al. 2005).

Other Professional and Ethical Considerations

Organisms of interest to wildlife professionals are free ranging and may be enjoyed by other segments of society in many ways, from observation or photography to harvest as meat or trophies. Professional ethics dictate that other potential uses of organisms be considered and accommodated if possible. Wild animals and birds are valued in part because they are wild, and the presence of human-caused marks may detract from that value. Accordingly, short-lived and inconspicuous marks should be selected whenever they can meet the objectives of proposed research. Scientists have an ethical responsibility to attempt to remove collars or other external markers at the conclusion of their research if possible and feasible. Furthermore, professional and ethical considerations dictate that permanent markers that injure or change the appearance of an animal (e.g., toe-clipping, branding, and tattooing) be used only under the most humane conditions and when alternate methods are not available to achieve desired research objectives.

HOUSING AND MAINTENANCE AT FIELD SITES

Proper care and responsible treatment of captive animals must depend on scientific and professional judgment, concern for the animal, knowledge of animal behavior and animal husbandry, and familiarity with the species. Investigators working with species unfamiliar to them should obtain all pertinent information before confining those animals. Curatorial staffs at zoological institutions are excellent resources for information (American Zoo and Aquarium Association 2003) and may be a good starting point for collecting information. It also may be necessary to test and compare several methods of housing to identify the most appropriate one for the well being of the animal and the purpose of the study. Findings should be part of a permanent record system and animal logbook associated with the study and the maintenance facility.

Housing

Housing for wild vertebrates should approximate natural conditions as closely as possible and provide safety and comfort for the animal as well as meet the study objectives. Housing should provide for behavioral needs, safety, adequate exercise and rest, and conditions for the general well being of the animal. Considerations depend on the animal involved and include isolation or refuge areas, natural materials, dust and water baths, natural foods, sunlight, and fresh air. Housing should incorporate as many aspects of natural living as possible, such as brushy areas for escape, resting cover, shade and protection from environmental elements, a natural stream traversing the pen, rocky areas for hoofed animals that need to wear down their hooves, and social groups of animals kept together. Housing of compatible species in a common pen also will provide for social interaction. Frequency of cleaning should be a compromise between level of cleanliness necessary to prevent disease and amount of stress imposed by cleaning. Provision of adequate veterinary care is a critical component of appropriate housing standards, and should be arranged in advance of need.

In general, housing must be of adequate size to allow for the physical and behavioral needs of the animals, while allowing scientists to collect appropriate data. For many housing situations, the pen can be large and natural, with a smaller internal or attached catch pen to restrain animals for experimental techniques. Pen construction materials must provide for the safety of the animals, as well as prevent the animals from escaping. Materials should be of sufficient durability to last for the intended period of confinement. When long-term confinement (weeks or longer) is necessary, or pens are to be reused, materials with impervious surfaces should be used to facilitate sanitation and minimize the potential for survival of animal pathogens. All animals that are inherently dangerous, are environmentally injurious, or have a propensity for escape require special attention. Double walls, double enclosures, double doors, covered tops of enclosures, and construction with metal bars or chain link may be required, depending on the species, with locks to deter unauthorized access. Mesh size and spacing between fencing materials must be sufficiently small to prevent the head of an animal from extending through the fence. Smaller fencing mesh also is more visible to animals. Colored flagging material may be necessary for animals to visualize fencing until they become accustomed to it. Animals should be released into the housing in a calm and unstressed manner so that initial mortality and morbidity from fence encounters are minimal. A small dose of sedative may reduce the immediate flight response when an animal is released into the housing and may help prevent initial injuries. Once animals have investigated the limits of the housing, injury occurrence is minimized if investigators do not cause undue flight reactions.

Adequacy of housing often can be judged by normal behavior patterns, weight gains and growth, survival rates, reproductive success, and physical appearance of the animals involved in the research project. Established guidelines for housing laboratory, farm, and wild animals are provided by the Canadian Council on Animal Care (1984, 1993, 2003). Additional guidelines for housing requirements of fish, amphibians, reptiles, wild birds, and small mammals have been reported by the appropriate professional societies and also appear in the Animal Care Regulations (U.S. Department of Agriculture 2001). Crawford et al. (2001) and the U.S. Department of Agriculture (2003) have made information available on resources for the management of nondomestic species.

Maintenance

Maintenance must meet the needs of the animal unless deviations are an approved purpose of the investigation. Researchers are responsible for calculating the appropriate nutritional needs of study animals prior to placing them in confinement and for obtaining adequate food supplies to sustain them during the period of confinement (Robbins 1993). Feeding and watering should be under the direct supervision of an individual trained and experienced in animal care for the species being maintained. Animal care personnel must be familiar with the animals being studied so abnormalities in appearance and behavior that may be indicative of nutritional deficiencies can be recognized quickly. Support for nutritional decisions can easily be found at zoological institutions (Nutrition Advisory Group 2003) and feed manufacturers. Formulated diet lines specifically designed for nondomestic species are readily available (Box 2).

TRANSPORTATION

Shipment

A variety of vehicles such as conventional motor vehicles, all-terrain vehicles, snow machines, rotary and fixed-wing aircraft, and boats has been used to transport wild animals. The species involved, method of transportation selected, and length of time an animal is to be transported are important factors regarding type of care and conditions of confinement required to maintain the animal in a state of well-being. Selection of transportation vehicles should include maintenance of the animal in a comfortable environment. Veterinary assistance may be required to prescribe and administer appropriate sedatives or other drugs when conditions of transportation are likely to result in a high level of stress to the animal due to its behavioral and physiological characteristics, restrictions of confinement, engine noise, and rigors of the trip. The transportation process should be as brief as possible. This can be expedited by proper and adequate planning to assure that transportation vehicles and housing units in appropriate numbers and size are available and ready for use as needed; that food, water, bedding, etc. are available to provide for the animals; that individuals involved in the transportation process are trained in the procedures to be used in confinement and transportation of the animals; and that all permits, health certificates, and other paperwork have been completed to the extent possible. Consideration must be given to the possibility of vehicle breakdown during transportation, and provisions provided, either through a following backup vehicle or communications equipment to rapidly summon assistance.

Box 2. Diet sources for captive wildlife.

Marion Zoological: http://www.marion-zoological.com/
Mazuri: http://www.mazuri.com
Nebraska Brand: http://www.nebraskabrand.com/
PetAg: http://www.petag.com/wildlife/wildlife.htm
Reliable Protein Products: http://www.zoofood.com
Zupreem: http://www.zupreem.com

When interstate movement of animals or shipment by commercial carriers is involved, scheduling of transportation segments to minimize the number of transfers and delays between transfers, having someone involved with the project meet the shipment at each transfer point, and, when appropriate, arranging for prompt clearance of animals by veterinary and customs inspectors can result in major reductions in transit time. The receiving party should be on-site when the animals reach their destination.

For some species, rest periods are required to allow the animals to feed undisturbed. Other species are best transported when they are normally inactive and do not feed. Ventilation and temperature controls within the confinement unit and transportation vehicle should provide adequate air movement, avoid buildup of exhaust gases, and limit temperature extremes. Appropriate shading in open vehicles may be required to reduce overheating due to direct sunlight. Subdued lighting and visual barriers between animals and humans and between animals and their transportation environment should be provided to help keep the animals calm. The U.S. Fish and Wildlife Service has published rules for the *Importation, Exportation, and Transportation of Wildlife* (U.S. Department of Interior 1985). The International Air Transport Association publishes an annual guide detailing construction of shipping containers for specific taxa (International Air Transport Association 2002).

Confinement During Shipping

Animal containers should be inspected to assure they have no sharp edges, protrusions, or rough surfaces that could cause injury during transport. When appropriate, containers also should be padded to help prevent injury. The floor of shipping containers should allow reasonable footing to prevent falling due to a slippery surface. Also, containers should not have coatings or be constructed of materials that are toxic and could be consumed by the animal through licking or chewing during transportation. Confinement units of porous materials, such as cardboard boxes, should not be reused; all other containers used to house animals should be suitably disinfected between uses. That portion of the transportation vehicle used to contain the confinement units also should be disinfected.

Grouping or separation of animals being transported at the same time should take into consideration the species, age, gender, and other appropriate factors. Direct contact generally should be maintained between females and their dependent young, particularly if abandonment may result (unless the young are to be maintained by some other means). Birds should be isolated in separate cells within the shipping container; if this cannot be done, each individual should have sufficient space to assume normal postures and engage in comfort and maintenance activities unimpeded by other birds (Gaunt et al. 1999).

Health Aspects

For short-term transportation (<30 minutes), basic considerations are to prevent pain, injury, and undue stress. Thermoregulation capabilities of the species must be considered when an animal is removed from its existing environment and transported. During transport, animals should be protected from exposure to inclement weather, harsh environmental conditions, and major temperature fluctuations and extremes.

Bedding, feed, and water should be provided, as appropriate, and the animals should be observed periodically, at least once every 4 hours, to examine their state of well being during transportation. On-site veterinary assistance may be warranted to monitor animals and to provide life-support assistance should a medical emergency occur during transportation or at the release or field study site. As within any discipline, specialization is common, thus, selection of veterinary assistance should focus on the individual's knowledge and experience with the wildlife species involved. Animals that die during transit should be removed as soon as practical from detection by other animals being transported. These carcasses should be retained for examination regarding cause of death. Similarly, animals that become severely injured or clinically ill should be removed and responsibly euthanized. Euthanasia should not take place in the presence by other live animals. A pathologist should examine sick animals. Cause of death is needed to assess whether the remaining animals are at risk from pathogens associated with the dead animals.

SURGICAL AND MEDICAL PROCEDURES

Wildlife field research can involve surgical and medical procedures such as implanting radio transmitters and gender identification. Wildlife should be subjected to surgical procedures only if proper justification has been established in the research protocol. Biologists must consider the potential impacts of the surgical procedure (e.g., attaching or implanting a transmitter) as it relates to the objectives of their study and fully describe these impacts in their interpretation of results. Every effort must be made to document or provide evidence to estimate the impact of the surgical procedure used in published results. Investigators should consult with appropriate veterinary and wildlife professionals to assist with selection of techniques. Surgical and medical techniques used should be based on accepted protocols for the studied species or for a closely related species. The Canadian Council on Animal Care's (1984, 2003) *Guide to the Care and Use of Experimental Animals* is a good source of such information. Incorporation of surgical techniques into a research protocol should follow the guidelines below.

(1) Protocols should be developed in collaboration with a veterinarian with experience with the species and techniques involved.

(2) Protocols must be reviewed carefully by the ACUC for appropriate care and handling of the animal, consideration of alternate procedures, and training documentation with special attention to limiting pain during the actual procedure and post-procedure period. Only properly trained personnel, conversant in all techniques necessary, should conduct the procedures. Only experienced individuals should conduct surgical procedures after they have received proper training, practiced and demonstrated competence in the technique, and have the necessary equipment and supplies. Investigators should arrange for oversight during the project by a qualified and species-knowledgeable veterinarian. Adequate anesthesia and/or analgesia must be provided. A plan should be developed for record keeping on each individual animal that undergoes the surgical procedure, including duration of anesthesia, reaction to anesthesia, description of any anesthetic problems and how they were

handled, duration of surgery, description of significant events during the surgical procedure, and notes on the recovery/postoperative period.

(3) Whenever possible, an evaluation component, including post-release monitoring, should be developed and incorporated into study proposals.

Minor Procedures

Minor medical procedures such as collection of blood, administration of drugs intravenously or intramuscularly, skin response assays, biopsies of superficial structures such as skin, and sutured attachment of radio transmitters usually can be performed safely and responsibly in the field without complicated equipment. However, it is the researcher's responsibility to choose the most effective, least invasive and least painful technique, minimize the duration of the procedure, use the most appropriate equipment and aseptic technique, and provide analgesia or sedation when indicated.

Major Procedures

As defined by the Animal Welfare Act (U.S. Department of Agriculture 2002:10, Part 1), major operative procedures are "any surgical intervention that penetrates and exposes a body cavity or any procedure which produces permanent impairment of physical or physiological functions." When survival of the animal is intended, major surgical procedures should be performed only under proper anesthesia and with sterile technique. The Animal Care Regulations (U.S. Department of Agriculture 2001:22, Part 2) also state "Major operative procedures on non-rodents will be conducted only in facilities intended for that purpose which shall be operated and maintained under aseptic conditions." Examples of major procedures used in wildlife research include radio transmitter implantation, laparotomy, surgical flight restraint, and sterilization. These procedures should be performed only in a clean space set aside for sterile surgery, with surgical instruments and drapes of the proper type, and with anesthesia protocols judged to be safe and appropriate for the species involved. Adequate monitoring equipment, operated by personnel well trained in its use, should be used during all procedures. Necessary equipment and trained personnel to deal with surgery or anesthesia-related emergencies (i.e., severe blood loss, cessation of breathing or cardiac function, severe hypo- or hyperthermia, acid-base imbalances) should be available at all times. This will maximize the success and subsequent scientific return from these often costly procedures and, therefore, minimize the number of animals needed and amount of animal distress. Acquiring adequate training to provide the required anesthetic, surgical, monitoring, and post-surgical skills necessitates a time commitment that would be a burden for most researchers and support staff. Therefore, it is highly recommended that the attending veterinarian, or other veterinarian with species expertise, be contracted to perform these functions.

MEDICAL CONSIDERATIONS

Wildlife field researchers should have access to appropriate veterinary consultation and take responsibility to prepare them to deal with any health problems that might arise in their study population. At times, intervention and control of a natural disease process may not be advisable

and may interfere with study goals. However, if an animal health problem arises due to the researcher's work, or if it will interfere with the study, the researcher must be ready to respond. Preparations should include gaining familiarity with the common diseases and health problems of the species under study, establishing a contact with a veterinary consultant with species expertise prior to study initiation, instituting a sampling regime to assist with identification of infectious agent(s), and having appropriate treatment or control equipment and drugs on hand or easily accessible. If drugs are prescribed, the investigator needs to ensure that physiologic changes that result from the treatment do not interfere with effects assessed in the study (e.g., pharmacokinetics of substances, appetite suppression, or altered growth rate). The researcher also is responsible for evaluating the possible impact of disease in the study animals on the larger population or ecosystem, and for making the maintenance of their welfare a priority. This is especially true when release or translocation of animals is part of the study; disease must be considered when evaluating the advisability of the program (Viggers et al. 1993, Waples and Stagoll 1997, Friend et al. 2000).

Euthanasia

Euthanasia is defined under the Animal Welfare Act as "the humane destruction of an animal accomplished by a method that produces rapid unconsciousness and subsequent death without evidence of pain or distress, or a method that utilizes anesthesia produced by an agent that causes painless loss of consciousness and subsequent death." Euthanasia may not be an approved component of a field study, but it may become a necessary option in a study involving capture, restraint, or surgical procedures. Thus, all wildlife researchers involved in studies must be familiar with approved euthanasia methods for their study species (Cooper et al. 1989, Institute of Laboratory Animal Resources 1992, Andrews et al. 1993, Kreeger 1997, American Veterinary Medical Association 2001) and have the appropriate equipment and drugs so euthanasia can be performed quickly. Even with the abundance of guidelines for euthanasia, there are legitimate differences of opinion as to what constitutes an appropriate procedure. Therefore, each ACUC has an important role in reviewing the methods contained in a protocol.

Animal Medicinal Drug Use Clarification Act

Use of drugs for a species that has not been approved by the U.S. Food and Drug Administration (extra-label use) is covered under the 1994 Animal Medicinal Drug Use Clarification Act (U.S. Food and Drug Administration 1996). This Act and regulations requires a number of conditions be established before use, including the involvement of a veterinarian (Drew 1998). One of the most important aspects of this Act, with regard to fish and wildlife, is to ensure there is appropriate time for any administered drugs to be cleared from an animal before the public potentially consumes the animal. *A Model Protocol for Purchase, Distribution and Use of Pharmaceuticals in Wildlife* has been prepared by the Western Wildlife Health Committee (available from J. C. DeVos, Arizona Game and Fish Department, 2221 West Greenway Road, Phoenix, 85203), which provides useful guidance for the application of these regulations in wildlife management.

DISEASE CONSIDERATIONS

Field investigators need to be fully aware of disease concepts so they may avoid introduction of new disease problems into animal populations, or the spread of disease to other populations and locations, as a result of their studies (Viggers et al. 1993; Friend et al. 1999, 2000). Disease introductions and spread may occur as a result of animals brought to the field research site to serve as biological sentinels, as decoys to lure and capture other animals, species introductions or releases to supplement existing populations, behavioral studies, assistance in tracking or retrieving animals, and other purposes. All of these uses of animals involve acceptable methods for scientific research and wildlife management. However, under no circumstances should the well being of free-ranging wildlife populations be unduly jeopardized by disease risks associated with animal use in field research. Field investigators have ethical and professional obligations to take appropriate actions for minimizing introduction of (a) new disease agents; (b) vectors (e.g., ticks and internal parasites) capable of efficiently transmitting indigenous, dormant diseases or those not currently being effectively transmitted; and (c) species that can serve as amplification hosts for transmitting indigenous diseases to other species. In addition, animals that are highly susceptible to diseases indigenous to the study location should not be released into the wild without using applicable prophylactic measures, unless these animals are to serve as biological sentinels for disease investigations. Biological sentinels should be monitored closely and euthanized by approved, responsible methods as soon as is practical after study objectives have been met.

Disease introduction and spread can result from mechanical means such as contaminated personnel, supplies, and equipment in addition to biological processes. Actions (below) taken to address disease prevention are far more cost effective than disease-control activities initiated after a problem has developed.

(1) Appropriate health certification is required for all animals being brought to the site of field investigations. State veterinary officials should be contacted to certify what specific testing is to be done when animals are moved into their jurisdiction.

(2) Appropriate disinfection and biosecurity procedures should be used for investigators and their equipment when disease risks are present. Toxic and infectious substances or material should be properly disposed.

(3) Prior knowledge of disease activity at the study site should be obtained to guide actions involving the research study.

(4) The source for any animals brought to a field investigation site (captive-reared and relocated wild stock) should be evaluated for inherent disease problems, and appropriate steps should be taken to avoid disease introductions.

(5) To the extent possible without inducing additional distress, animals should be held under surveillance for 15–30 days prior to their release into the wild, and only healthy animals should be released. These animals should not be mixed with other species during transportation and should be isolated from other animals during the surveillance period.

(6) Any animals that die should be examined by a disease diagnostic laboratory having competency for identify-ing cause of death in the species involved; these findings should be used to guide appropriate actions.

(7) Animals that become clinically ill should be examined by disease specialists, and their counsel should be used to protect the well being of other animals within the study area.

Human Health Considerations

Researchers working with free-ranging wildlife are subject to enhanced levels of exposure to wildlife diseases transmissible to humans. Disease transmission may involve direct contact with infected animals such as those with rabies, contact with disease vectors such as ticks transmitting Lyme disease, or contact with contaminated environments such as bird roosts and histoplasmosis. Field investigators should become familiar with the common diseases of wildlife species they are working with and the relative prevalence of those diseases in the populations being studied. Consultation with a physician specializing in infectious diseases, regarding immunization or other preventative treatment is advised when serious diseases for humans commonly occur in the populations being studied. The U.S. Centers for Disease Control and Prevention (Centers for Disease Control and Prevention 2003) and local public health officials can also provide useful information. Investigators who become ill should seek medical assistance and advise their physicians of their exposure to potentially hazardous animals, diseases, and environmental conditions.

ANIMAL DISPOSITION

When live animals are in the possession of investigators or under their control at the time of study completion, an evaluation must be made as to whether these animals can be released to a free-ranging existence, maintained under controlled conditions, or euthanized. Field-captured animals should be released only (a) at the site of the original capture, unless conservation efforts or safety considerations dictate otherwise; (b) when the released animal can be reasonably expected to function normally within the population; (c) when local and seasonal conditions are conducive to survival; (d) when the ability to survive in nature has not been irreversibly impaired; and (e) when release is not likely to spread pathogens or contribute to disease processes in other ways. Prior approval for releases at noncapture sites should be obtained from appropriate state/federal agencies. Relocation release sites should be within the native range of the species, or established range for introduced species, and be in habitat suitable for species survival.

The decision of whether to release captive-reared animals into the wild after completion of a field research project demands more rigorous evaluation than for field-captured animals. In addition to evaluating the future well being of the animal being released, impacts on other animals of the same species as well as competition and risks for other species sharing that environment also must be considered. Rarely, if ever, will releases of captive-reared animals at the completion of research studies be justified on the basis of animal welfare considerations. When animals are to be released, efforts should be made to enhance their chances of survival. Animals should be in good physical condition and released when weather conditions are favorable and at a time of day when they are able to locate food and cover that meet survival needs. Animals that cannot be released should be considered for distribution to other scientists for further study. However, if the animal was subject to a major invasive procedure, it may not be appropriate for additional experimentation. Animals not suitable for research may be suitable display animals that can be donated to a zoo or other type of educational institution.

When animals must be euthanized, responsible methods appropriate for the species and circumstances must be used. Care must be taken to assure that the animal is dead before disposal of the carcass. Disposal procedures must prevent carcasses containing toxic substances or drugs from the research investigations or euthanasia procedures to enter the food web of other animals. To the extent feasible, euthanized animals should be properly preserved and used as voucher specimens or for teaching purposes.

SUMMARY

All wildlife biologists, managers, and researchers must be aware of, and understand, the complex set of laws, rules, policies, and guidelines that relate to the proper care and use of animals in field and laboratory studies. There are a wide range of attitudes toward the value of wildlife, and the ethical principals that may apply to their study and use. Wildlife professionals must recognize and consider many viewpoints so their work is accepted within the multiple communities in which they operate. This chapter presents a broad review of these areas, providing guidance on major issues and references that should be consulted when planning and executing study protocols involving wild species.

ACKNOWLEDGMENTS

We acknowledge the substantial efforts of the authors (M. Friend, D. E. Toweill, R. L. Brownell, Jr., V. F. Nettles, D. S. Davis, and W. J. Foreyt) of this chapter in the fifth edition (*Research and management techniques for wildlife and habitats*). The assistance of M. Quesada C. and E. Lark is also appreciated.

LITERATURE CITED

ALLEN, T. 2000. Information resources for institutional animal care and use committees, 1985–Animal Welfare Information Center Resource Series 7. Available online at http://www.nal.usda.gov/awic/pubs/IACUC/iacuc.htm (accessed 14 January 2005).

AMERICAN SOCIETY OF ICHTHYOLOGISTS AND HERPETOLOGISTS. 1997. Guidelines for use of live amphibians and reptiles in field research. American Society of Ichthyologists and Herpetologists. Available online at http://www.asih.org/pubs/herpcoll.html (accessed 14 January 2005).

AMERICAN SOCIETY OF MAMMALOGISTS. 1998. Guidelines for the capture, handling and care of mammals as approved by the American Society of Mammalogists. Journal of Mammalogy 79:1416–1431.

AMERICAN VETERINARY MEDICAL ASSOCIATION. 2001. 2000 Report of the AVMA panel on euthanasia. Journal of the American Veterinary Medical Association 218:669–696.

AMERICAN ZOO AND AQUARIUM ASSOCIATION. 2003. American zoo and aquarium association zoo and aquarium directory: printable list of members. American Zoo and Aquarium Association, Silver Spring, Maryland, USA. Available online at http://www.aza.org/FindZooAquarium/ (accessed 14 January 2005).

ANDREWS, E. J., J. D. CLARK, P. J. PASCOE, J. R. BOYCE, B. T. BENNETT, K. A. HOUPT, AND G. W. ROBINSON. 1993. Report of the AVMA panel on euthanasia. Journal of the American Veterinary Medical Association 202:229–249.

ANIMAL BEHAVIOR SOCIETY/ASSOCIATION FOR THE STUDY OF ANIMAL BEHAVIOUR. 2003. Guidelines for the treatment of animals in behavioral research and teaching. Animal Behavior 65:249–265.

CAMPBELL, T. W. 1996. Clinical pathology. Page 248 in D. R. Mader, editor. Reptile medicine and surgery. W. B. Saunders, Philadelphia, Pennsylvania, USA.

CANADIAN COUNCIL ON ANIMAL CARE. 1984. Guide to the care and use of experimental animals. Volume 2. Second edition. Canadian Council on Animal Care, Ottawa, Ontario, Canada. Available online at http://www.ccac.ca/ english/gui_pol/guides/english/TOC_V2.htm (accessed 14 January 2005).

———. 1993. Guide to the care and use of experimental animals. Volume 1. Canadian Council on Animal Care, Ottawa, Ontario, Canada. Available online at http://www.ccac.ca/english/gui_pol/guides/english/v2_84/CH22_1.htm (accessed 14 January 2005).

———. 2003. Guidelines on the care and use of wildlife. Canadian Council on Animal Care, Ottawa, Ontario, Canada. Available online at http://www.ccac.ca/english/gdlines/wildlife/Wildlife.pdf (accessed 14 January 2005).

CENTERS FOR DISEASE CONTROL AND PREVENTION. 2003. Health topics A to Z. Centers for Disease Control and Prevention, Atlanta, Georgia, USA. Available online at http://www.cdc.gov/health/default.htm (accessed 14 January 2005).

COOPER, J. E., R. EWBANK, C. PLATT, AND C. WARWICK. 1989. Euthanasia of amphibians and reptiles. Report of a Joint Working Party. Universities Federation for Animal Welfare and World Society for the Protection of Animals, Wheathampstead, Hertsfordshire, United Kingdom.

CRAWFORD, R. L., D. JENSEN, AND T. ALLEN, compilers. 2001. Information resources on amphibians, fish and reptiles used in biomedical research. Animal Welfare Information Center Resource Series 10. Available online at http://www.nal.usda.gov/awic/pubs/amphib.htm (accessed 14 January 2005).

DEIN, F. J. 2003. Blood collection from birds: digital revised edition. U.S. Department of the Interior, Geological Survey, National Wildlife Health Center, Madison, Wisconsin, USA. Available online at http://wildlifedisease.nbii.gov/ (accessed 14 January 2005).

DREW, M. L. 1998. Update of the Animal Medicinal Drug Use Clarification Act of 1994: regulations for wildlife veterinarians. Pages 163–167 in C. K. Baer, editor. Proceedings of the American Association of Zoo Veterinarians and American Association of Wildlife Veterinarians Joint Conference. Omaha, Nebraska, USA.

ELLIOTT, C. L. 1995. Meeting animal care obligations in wildlife education. Wildlife Society Bulletin 23:631–634.

FOOD AND AGRICULTURE ORGANIZATION. 2003. Animal welfare gateway: international information. Food and Agriculture Organization of the United Nations, Rome, Italy. Available online at http://www.fao.org/ag/AGA/AW/awmatrix.htm (accessed 14 January 2005).

FRIEND, M., J. F. FRANSON, AND E. A. CIGANOICH, editors. 1999. Field manual of wildlife diseases: general procedures and diseases in birds. U.S. Department of the Interior, Geological Survey, Biological Resources Division, Information Technology Report 1999–2001. Available online at http://www.nwhc.usgs.gov/pub_metadata/field_manual/field_manual.html (accessed 14 January 2005).

———, R. G. MCLEAN, AND F. J. DEIN. 2000. Disease emergence in birds: challenges for the 21st century. Auk 118:290–303.

GAUNT, A. S., L. S. ORING, K. P. ABLE, D. W. ANDERSON, L. F. BAPTISTA, J. C. BARLOW, AND J. C. WINGFIELD. 1999. Guidelines to the use of wild birds in research. The Ornithological Council, Washington, D.C., USA. Available online at http://www.nmnh.si.edu/BIRDNET/GuideToUse/index.html (accessed 14 January 2005).

GREEN, E. D. 2002. Collection of blood samples from adult amphibians. Amphibian research and monitoring initiative standard operating procedure 101. U.S. Department of the Interior, Geological Survey, National Wildlife Health Center, Madison, Wisconsin, USA. Available online at http://www.nwhc.usgs.gov/research/amph_dc/sop_bloodcollect.html (accessed 14 January 2005).

INSTITUTE OF LABORATORY ANIMAL RESOURCES. 1992. Euthanasia. Pages 102–116 in Recognition and alleviation of pain and distress in laboratory animals. Institute of Laboratory Animal Resources, Commission on Life Sciences, National Research Council. National Academy Press, Washington, D.C., USA. Available online at http://www.nap.edu/

books/0309042755/html/ (accessed 14 January 2005).
———. 1996. Guide for the care and use of laboratory animals. National Academy Press, Washington, D.C., USA. Available online at http://books.nap.edu/books/0309053773/html/index.html (accessed 14 January 2005).

INTERNATIONAL AIR TRANSPORTATION ASSOCIATION. 2002. Live animals regulations. Twenty-ninth edition. International Air Transportation Association, Montreal, Quebec, Canada.

JACOBSON, E. R. 1993. Blood collection techniques in reptiles: laboratory investigations. Page 144 in M. E. Fowler, editor. Zoo and wild animal medicine: current therapy 3. W. B. Saunders, Philadelphia, Pennsylvania, USA.

KREEGER, M. D. 1997. Animal euthanasia. Animal Welfare Information Center Special Reference Brief Series SRB93-06. U.S. Department of Agriculture, National Agricultural Library, Beltsville, Maryland, USA. Available online at http://www.nal.usda.gov/awic/pubs/oldbib/srb9801.htm (accessed 14 January 2005).

McGUILL, M. W., AND A. N. ROWAN. 1989. Biological effects of blood loss: implications for sampling volumes and techniques. Institute of Laboratory Animal Resources News 31:5–18.

MICHENER, G. R. 1989. Ethical issues in the use of wild animals in behavioral and ecological studies. Pages 37–43 in J. W. Driscoll, editor. Animal care and use in behavioral research: regulations, issues, and applications. U.S. Department of Agriculture, National Agricultural Library, Beltsville, Maryland, USA.

MORTON, D. B., AND M. JENNINGS. 1993. Removal of blood from laboratory mammals and birds. Laboratory Animals 27:1–22.

MULCAHY, D. M. 2003. Does the Animal Welfare Act apply to free-ranging animals? Institute of Laboratory Animal Resources Journal 44:252–258. Available online at http://dels.nas.edu/ilar/jour_online/44_4/44_4.asp (accessed 14 January 2005).

NUTRITION ADVISORY GROUP. 2003. Scientific advisory group to the American Zoo and Aquarium Association, Silver Spring, Maryland, USA. Available online at http://nagonline.net/index.html (accessed 14 January 2005).

OFFICE OF LABORATORY ANIMAL WELFARE. 2002. Public Health Service policy on humane care and use of laboratory animals. National Institutes of Health, Bethesda, Maryland, USA. Available online at http://grants.nih.gov/grants/olaw/references/phspol.htm (accessed 14 January 2005).

OFFICE OF SCIENCE AND TECHNOLOGY POLICY. 1985. Interagency Research Animal Committee's U.S. government principles for the utilization and care of vertebrate animals used in testing, research, and training. Federal Register 50:20864–20865. Available online at http://grants2.nih.gov/grants/olaw/references/phspol.htm#USGovPrinciples (accessed 14 January 2005).

ORLANS, F. B., editor. 1988. Field research guidelines: impact on animal care and use committees. Scientist's Center for Animal Welfare, Bethesda, Maryland, USA.

———, R .C. SIMMONDS, AND W. J. DODDS, editors. 1987. Effective animal care and use committees. Scientist's Center for Animal Welfare, Bethesda, Maryland, USA.

PECK, F. R., AND R. C. SIMMONDS. 1995. Understanding animal research regulations: obligations of wildlife departments and field researchers. Wildlife Society Bulletin 23:279–282.

PITTS, M., editor. 2002. Institutional animal care and use committee

guidebook. Second edition. Office of Laboratory Animal Welfare, National Institutes of Health, Bethesda, Maryland, USA. Available online at http://grants.nih.gov/grants/olaw/Guidebook.pdf (accessed 14 January 2005).

PUTMAN, R. J. 1995. Ethical considerations and animal welfare in ecological field studies. Biodiversity and Conservation 4:903–915.

ROBBINS, C. T. 1993. Wildlife feeding and nutrition. Second edition. Academic Press, San Diego, California, USA.

ROFFE, T. J., S. J. SWEENEY, AND K. E. AUNE. 2005. Chemical immobilization of North American mammals. Pages 286–302 in C. E. Braun, editor. Techniques for wildlife investigations and management. Sixth edition. The Wildlife Society, Bethesda, Maryland, USA.

SILVY, N. J., R. R. LOPEZ, AND M. J. PETERSON. 2005. Wildlife marking techniques. Pages 339–376 in C. E. Braun, editor. Techniques for wildlife investigations and management. Sixth edition. The Wildlife Society, Bethesda, Maryland, USA.

U.S. DEPARTMENT OF AGRICULTURE. 2001. Animals and animal products. Code of Federal Regulations, Title 9, Volume 1, Chapter 1, Subchapter A—Animal Welfare. Pages 1–122. Part 1- Definitions [available online at http://www.aphis.usda.gov/ac/cfr/9cfr1.html]. Part 2- Regulations [available online at http://www.aphis.usda.gov/ac/cfr/9cfr2.html]. Part 3- Standards [available online at http://www.aphis.usda.gov/ac/cfr/9cfr3.html] (accessed 14 January 2005).

———. 2002. Transportation, sale, and handling of certain animals (Animal Welfare Act). Chapter 54, 7 United States Code 2131–59. Available online at http://www.aphis.usda.gov/ac/awa.html (accessed 14 January 2005).

———. 2003. Zoos, circuses and wildlife publications. Animal Welfare Information Center, National Agricultural Library. U.S. Department of Agriculture, Beltsville, Maryland, USA. Available online at http://www.nal.usda.gov/awic/zoo/zoopubs.htm (accessed 14 January 2005).

U.S. DEPARTMENT OF INTERIOR. 1985. Importation, exportation, and transportation of wildlife. Pages 51–76 in Code of Federal Regulations, Title 50, Chapter 1, Part 14. Available online at http://www.access.gpo.gov/nara/cfr/waisidx_02/50cfr14_02.html (accessed 14 January 2005).

U.S. FOOD AND DRUG ADMINISTRATION. 1996. Extralabel drug use in animals. 21 Code of Federal Regulations 530. Available online at http://www.fda.gov/cvm/index/amducca/amducafr.htm (accessed 14 January 2005).

VIGGERS, K. L., D. B. LINDENMEYER, AND D. M. SPRATT. 1993. The importance of disease in reintroduction programmes. Wildlife Research 20:687–698.

WAPLES, K. A., AND C. S. STAGOLL. 1997. Ethical issues in the release of animals from captivity. BioScience 47:115–120.

WHITAKER, B. R., AND K. M. WRIGHT. 2001. Clinical techniques. Page 102 in B. R. Whitaker and K. M. Wright, editors. Amphibian medicine and captive husbandry. Krieger Publishing Company, Malabar, Florida, USA.

WILLIAMS, B. 1999. Wildlife research and the Institutional Animal Care and Use Committee. Animal Welfare Information Center Bulletin 10. U.S. Department of Agriculture, National Agricultural Library, Beltsville, Maryland, USA. Available online at http://www.nal.usda.gov/awic/newsletters/v10n1/10n1will.htm (accessed 14 January 2005).

WILDLIFE HEALTH AND DISEASE INVESTIGATIONS

Thomas J. Roffe and Thierry M. Work

BACKGROUND

Wildlife diseases are increasingly important in wildlife conservation, particularly when endangered species or human health is involved (Daszak et al. 2000). Of 175 newly identified infectious threats to humans, 132 (75%) are zoonoses (diseases that can be transmitted between humans and animals) (Taylor et al. 2001). Overall, zoonotic pathogens are twice as likely to be associated with emerging human diseases than nonzoonotic agents (Taylor et al. 2001). Recent national concerns over West Nile virus, chronic wasting disease, and tuberculosis and the continuing concern over rabies and Lyme disease have sensitized people to the role wildlife may have in their own well-being. Timely and efficient investigation of wildlife diseases is also important for implementation of effective management for mitigation or prevention of further wildlife losses. However, biologists often ignore wildlife mortality episodes for several reasons. Diseases are often considered part of the "natural" ecology. Many biologists are unfamiliar with exactly how to approach and resolve wildlife mortality issues, or have the perception of "why bother?" because little can be done about wildlife mortality. This is unfortunate, because mortality, like recruitment and immigration/emigration, is 1 of the 3 fundamental demographic factors that affect success or failure of wildlife populations. Gaining a better understanding of this demographic component can help biologists more effectively manage populations, particularly when it becomes apparent that certain management methods enhance wildlife diseases. Furthermore, some wildlife diseases can be managed with the most basic of methods.

Even if the perception is that disease can be important, biologists frequently ask "when is disease important?" and "when is intervention warranted?" The definition of disease is varied and dictionaries provide a broad definition of a "condition that impairs the performance of a vital function." We prefer a definition of disease as "a disturbance that inhibits biological systems returning to homeostasis." Thus, with these broad definitions even something as simple as a broken leg would be classified as disease. A broken leg would be significant to that specific individual, but would it warrant intervention? The answer depends on your perspective. We suggest that several perspectives be considered in making a decision as to whether intervention is warranted. On the ecological scale, disease that causes mortality affecting population characteristics, perhaps even population survival, may present an unambiguous signal for intervention by most biologists and wildlife management agencies. Another perspective, though, might value conservation of "natural systems" exclusive of human intervention. Thus, low-level endemic diseases that do not threaten populations and are not the consequence of human activities might not warrant intervention. However, under this perspective, a disease that does not threaten population survival but is caused by, or exacerbated by, human wildlife management may warrant intervention.

Today wildlife is frequently managed on small, segregated tracts of habitat. Such management may lead to disease exacerbation (e.g., avian cholera or botulism) that may warrant intervention. Other perspectives are equally valid for some people and should be considered in making a decision whether to intervene to control disease. These may include considerations for public relations and public education regarding wildlife ecology, involvement of endangered/threatened species where loss of a single individual may be important, diseases that are economically important to domestic animals, diseases transmissible to humans, exotic (not native to the area of occurrence) diseases, diseases poorly characterized for their effect on populations, etc.

Decisions on disease intervention are based on a multiplicity of factors involving biology, politics, economics, resources, mission, management philosophy, and other perspectives. The simplistic view of only intervening when a disease is known to have a detrimental effect on populations is in the minority. There would be no need for the multiplicity of wildlife management agencies managing for different values if there was general agreement in the public at large for a single wildlife management perspective. Regardless of perspective, the only way to make informed decisions about intervention is to have a knowledge base of existing diseases, their prevalence and distribution as well as information on their effects on wildlife.

There are many general references available for biologists to learn about the broad array of wildlife diseases. The broadest general references include Wobeser (1994), Fairbrother et al. (1996), and Williams and Barker (2001) on wildlife diseases, noninfectious diseases of wildlife, and infectious diseases of wild mammals, respectively. Other references cover a wide breadth of species in specific geographic areas, such as Davidson and Nettles (1997) (southeast United States), Dieterich (1981) (Alaska), Thorne et al. (1982) (Wyoming), and Fowler (1981) (Pacific Basin). However, the diseases described in these references are applicable to those species across a much wider geographic area. Some references are restricted to certain species groups (Wobeser 1981, Geraci and Lounsbury 1993, Friend and Franson 1999, Noga 1999). Adrian (1992) provided background on forensic techniques and guidelines for evidence handling of law enforcement cases.

Wildlife diseases and mortality are most effectively investigated when there is a close partnership between wildlife disease specialists and biologists. Wildlife disease specialists are scientists trained in biomedical and epidemiological techniques applicable to wildlife populations. During wildlife mortality investigations, the wildlife disease specialist provides the disease expertise, access to specialized laboratories, and ability to interpret diagnostic findings for the biologist. The biologist has expertise on the habitats of the animals, and their ecology and behavior, all of which can provide valuable clues to cause of the mortality.

Biologists are often the first to observe dead and dying wildlife in free-ranging populations and frequently have background information on recent events that may have affected the population in question. This partnership between wildlife disease specialists and biologists is critical to successfully addressing the impacts of disease on wild populations. The interrelationship between field and laboratory findings to eventually arrive at a diagnosis and plan a strategy for management cannot be overemphasized. Each provides pieces of a puzzle; neither provides the complete picture. To be effective, this process requires a rapid dissemination and 2-way exchange of information between biologists and disease specialists. Such communications build confidence, efficiency, and accuracy.

Where can biologists turn for assistance on wildlife mortality events? In the United States and Canada, biologists have access to multiple resources and organizations

---

Box 1. Examples of national and regional wildlife health programs in North America.

UNITED STATES
- National Wildlife Health Center, 6006 Schroeder Road, Madison, WI 53711. Tel: 608-270-2400; Fax: 608-270-2415.
- Southeast Cooperative Wildlife Disease Study, The University of Georgia, Athens, GA 30602-7393. Tel: 706-542-1741; Fax: 706-542-5865
- Wildlife Health Center, University of California, TB128, Old Davis Road, Davis, CA 95616. Tel: 530-752-4167.

CANADA
- Canadian Cooperative Wildlife Health Centre, WCVM Vet Pathology, University of Saskatchewan, 52 Campus Drive, Saskatoon, SK S7N 5B4. Tel: 306-966-5099, Fax: 306-966-7439.

---

that can provide technical assistance on wildlife health related issues (Box 1). These organizations provide a good starting point for inquiry. However many other local, state, provincial, and regional sources of technical and diagnostic assistance exist and biologists are encouraged to develop local relationships. Assistance provided can range from phone consultations to on-site assistance by a wildlife disease specialist. However, because many wildlife mortality events occur in remote areas, it is likely the biologist will need to take the initiative and actively participate in the investigation including taking field samples and notes, discussing management options, and collaborating with the disease specialist to evaluate laboratory findings. This process will be more productive if the biologist is conversant on methods used to investigate wildlife diseases and the wildlife disease specialist is conversant on ecology of wildlife resources being affected.

Enhancing the skills of the biologist in wildlife disease investigation is the primary goal of this chapter. We realize that many techniques in this chapter are described as if implemented under ideal conditions frequently not encountered by biologists. The exact tools, containers, preservatives, etc. may not be available. However, in most circumstances field samples collected under less than ideal conditions are better than none at all and can provide important clues to the cause of the mortality event.

Before embarking on investigation of wildlife mortality events, it is important to recognize that some diseases of wildlife are zoonotic (transmissible between, and capable of causing diseases in, animals and humans). These diseases can be transmitted through aerosols (inhalation), ingestion (including food or hand-mouth contact), or contact through mucus membranes (eyes, mouth), cuts on the skin, or insect bites. While risk of this happening is most significant with mammals because of closer similarity to humans, birds, reptiles, fish, and invertebrates can also, at times, carry pathogens transmissible to humans. Another consideration is the potential for toxins that can pose a risk to investigators. Investigation of wildlife diseases, while potentially rewarding from a management standpoint, can be risky.

To limit potential exposure to pathogens and toxins, biologists and disease specialists must implement appropriate protective measures including involvement of qualified medical personnel in decisions on personnel vaccination, if warranted. At a minimum, when handing dead animals or animal tissues, personnel should wear protective clothing, and manipulation of specimens should be done with gloves that are impervious to body fluids. Biologists should be knowledgeable about the zoonotic diseases in their area. This information can be obtained from the local public health department. Many zoonotic diseases have nonspecific lingering "flu-like" symptoms, and some, if left untreated, can have serious long-term complications. Most physicians have little knowledge of zoonotic disease. Therefore, if the biologist suspects they have contacted a zoonotic disease, they may need to participate in education of their physician, impress upon them the possibility of a zoonotic disease, and remain closely involved in medical management of their case to ensure successful resolution of the illness.

DISEASES OF WILDLIFE

Three factors need to be present for disease to occur in wildlife populations: the agent, the host, and the environment. These must interact in a manner that disease can be expressed. The agent must be *capable* of producing disease in the host. For example, rabies virus is not capable of producing gastroenteritis but is capable of producing encephalitis in mammals. Some agents are obligate pathogens—that is, under appropriate circumstances, and for propagation of the disease agent, expression of disease is required. Other agents may be opportunistic. An opportunist may or may not produce disease depending on host or environmental characteristics. The host must be *susceptible* to that agent. For example, a mammal would generally be susceptible to rabies but a vaccinated individual may mount an effective immune response preventing disease. Only birds in the Order Anseriformes are susceptible to the viral agent that causes duck plague. An animal with nutritional insufficiency or deficiency may be susceptible to many disease agents to which it otherwise would not be susceptible. Lastly, a *suitable* environment for disease expression must be present. For example, with the disease brucellosis the suitable environment is one in which the bacteria can survive in an aborted fetus for sufficient time for another animal to ingest an infective dose. Sunlight and drying may rapidly inactivate an agent. If environmental conditions prevent contact of another animal with an abortion (unsuitable environment), the disease does not perpetuate.

Several basic terms are used to describe disease characteristics in populations.

Epidemic/Epizootic. This term describes a level of disease in populations that is above "normal" expected baseline values (see "endemic"). An example of epidemic disease is the occurrence of large die-offs of waterfowl in wildlife refuges. However, a single case of a foreign animal disease (one not found historically in a particular location) can be considered an epidemic.

Endemic/Enzootic. This describes a disease that is present in an animal community over the long term and frequently refers to the "usual" frequency of disease in a population or the constant presence of disease in a population. Presence of rabies in some populations of wild carnivores is a good example.

Prevalence. This is the number of *existing* cases of a disease in a known population (or sample size) at a specific time. Prevalence calculations are static indicators and are used to describe the existing status of disease in populations.

Incidence. This is the number of *new* cases of a disease in a known population over a specified period of time. Incidence calculations are dynamic indicators and are used to describe the progression of disease in a population over time.

Wildlife diseases are most notable when they cause catastrophic mortalities of large numbers of animals over a short period of time. These large mortality episodes may have a detrimental impact on wildlife populations and can have grave consequences when the species affected are endangered or threatened. An example of such a disease is avian cholera; a bacterial disease that is rapidly disseminated from bird to bird and that can cause large mortalities of waterfowl in wetlands. Avian malaria, a protozoan-caused disease transmitted by mosquitoes, has been associated with extensive mortalities of endangered Hawaiian forest birds and has been implicated in the disappearance of several species of native birds. Other wildlife diseases are more chronic and insidious. These diseases may affect demographic factors such as reproductive success or recruitment of young. An example of this is marine turtle fibropapillomatosis, a tumor disease that causes progressive wasting of predominantly immature green turtles (*Chelonia mydas*). Noninfectious agents can also cause significant disease in wildlife. Severe acute mortalities of birds and mammals have been traced to ingestion of toxins produced by fungi present in moldy grain. Lead poisoning from ingested lead shot was a significant cause of chronic mortalities in endangered bald eagles (*Haliaeetus leucocephalus*) and waterfowl until lead shot was banned for use in hunting migratory waterfowl in the United States.

Investigation of wildlife diseases is largely a deductive and iterative process. When confronted with wildlife mortality, the investigators (biologists and disease specialists) must initially consider a wide variety of possible causes both infectious (e.g., viruses, bacteria, parasites, fungi) and noninfectious (e.g., trauma, toxicants). Using a combination of field and laboratory observations, the investigators systematically eliminate the less plausible causes of the mortality and eventually arrive at a subset of the most likely cause(s). In many cases, the investigation will not point to a single cause; this is often a point of frustration for the biologist. However, in most cases, it is just as valuable to know for certain what did ***not*** cause the mortality as this information alone can help managers focus on management options. There are many potential causes to consider at the outset of the investigation and an investigator must keep an open mind as to the possibilities. An easy to remember acronym that captures most causes of disease is "DAMN IT." Specifically: D (degenerative and developmental conditions), A (allergic and autoimmune conditions), M (metabolic conditions), N (neoplastic [cancer] and nutritional conditions), I (infectious and idiopathic [unknown] conditions), and T (traumatic and toxic conditions). Interactions among these classes of disease may also occur, such as toxic insults resulting in neoplasia, or immune deficiency allowing an opportunistic infectious agent to cause disease.

While wildlife can be affected by all the above etiologies, those most commonly encountered fall into the nutrition, idiopathic, toxic, infectious, traumatic, and sometimes neoplastic categories. Some diseases will affect particular age groups of animals. For example, it is common to see large numbers of immature seabirds die from starvation shortly before or during fledging because a certain percent were unable to forage adequately or were abandoned by inexperienced parents. Brucellosis, a bacterial disease of ungulates, affects principally females that manifest disease through abortions or infertility. Certain diseases are more likely to occur in certain habitats. Wetlands are common areas where diseases of waterfowl such as botulism or duck plague are encountered. Other diseases depend on presence of insects for transmission and spread, and are absent where the vectors are absent. The absence of the insect vector for bluetongue virus explains the absence of this disease in deer in certain areas of the United States.

It is the basic understanding of these "epidemiological" relationships that helps narrow the list of possible causes and guides laboratory testing. The science of epidemiology is the study of the elements that contribute to occurrence or nonoccurrence of disease in a population. The wildlife disease specialist uses knowledge of these relationships to avoid unnecessary, sometimes expensive, testing and to guide further field investigation.

Investigation of chronic wildlife disease proceeds in a similar manner as acute diseases; however, there is more dependence on longer-term observations. Surveys of wildlife populations for pathogens involve capturing animals and taking biological samples including blood, feces, urine, and biopsies, or doing necropsies of dead animals over long time periods. Marking animals and following presence of disease over time can be valuable to clarify complex disease patterns. Use of geographic information systems and mathematical models are also becoming important in studying behavior of disease in wildlife populations and offering management options.

TOOLS AND METHODS TO INVESTIGATE WILDLIFE DISEASE

Field Observations

Careful recording of field observations and conditions is the first, most important tool in addressing wildlife disease and mortality. The clues provided by a detailed and accurate history of the event can narrow the possibilities for diagnosis. Some of the parameters associated with the disease outbreak that should be recorded are below.

Magnitude: is the morbidity/mortality unusual? How many?
Onset: when and how rapidly did the situation develop?
Environment: are there unusual or novel circumstances? Habitat types? Human uses and what type? Nearby land uses? Spatial distribution of mortality?
Species affected and species at risk: what species are

dying/sick compared to what species appear to be at risk for the disease?
Population at risk: what is the size of the population that is affected?
Population movement: where did the animals come from and where do they go?
Age and gender: do affected animals tend to be an age or gender specific?
Mortality and morbidity: are both dead and sick animals observed? What is the approximate ratio of sick to dead?
Clinical signs: if sick animals are seen, what physical or behavior abnormalities are apparent?

Documenting field observations is critical and can be done using write-in-the-rain notebooks and pencils to palm and laptop computers. The critical step is to carefully annotate events and their temporal sequence. Photographs can be useful in wildlife disease investigations. The advent of digital cameras has made it possible to instantly send photographs anywhere in the world for immediate consultations. However, photos must suitably depict the subject. Most importantly the subject should be recorded with sufficient image size and depth of field for identification of what is being viewed. Thus, a long distance view of a sick bird might provide information on the environment affected, but a close-up will be needed to assess clinical signs. When photographing lesions during field necropsies, the organ with the lesion rather than the entire carcass should predominantly occupy the field of view. It is sometimes helpful to take several exposures that vary in distance from the subject. Photos should be labeled so they can refer to specific animals/specimens. Digital videos of sick animals can also provide valuable information and complement field descriptions of clinical signs.

Magnitude and Onset

One of the most difficult issues is when to call a wildlife mortality event "unusual" and when to assign the time of onset. Unless the population is closely monitored and the biologist understands the background mortality in that population, assigning time of onset and whether the mortality is unusual is problematic. Many wildlife species, when ill, seek cryptic locations complicating the discovery of carcasses. Regular (monthly) patrols and cataloguing mortalities by location, species affected, and estimated status of decomposition provide valuable background information that can be used to make decisions as to whether or not mortality is unusual. Developing knowledge about normal behaviors and movements of wildlife facilitates detection of sick or abnormal animals. In reality, true onset of wildlife mortalities is seldom detected.

Environment

Establishing potential links between changes in the physical environment and wildlife mortality is important. If disease is occurring where previously there was none, something has changed in the environment. Many possibilities with regard to animal population and environmental changes should be considered.

Temporal Distribution

Assessing the temporal scale of the wildlife mortality can provide critical information on the potential cause(s) of the event. Spills of toxicants or natural toxins may kill large numbers of animals over short periods of time (days to weeks). Examples include avian botulism or organophosphate insecticide mortality. Certain infectious diseases, particularly when introduced where animals are concentrated, may kill many animals over several weeks. Mortalities diminish when immune animals remain, when animals emigrate from the area of disease transmission, or the source of the infectious agent is no longer available. An example is mortality due to acute aspergillosis that ceases once the grain pile containing high amounts of the fungus is no longer available. Other diseases cause losses over longer periods of time (months), and mortalities can increase and decrease depending on demographic and environmental factors. For example, brucellosis occurs in a narrow part of the reproductive cycle, and primarily in first pregnancy post-exposure animals. Losses to the population thus only occur at certain times of year, in only certain populations, and at varying rates depending on exposure history. Phocine distemper causes periodic mortalities in seals (Phocidae) in the eastern United States and Europe; seals tend to be particularly prone to disease when concentrated. Some diseases are only detectable when animals congregate in particular areas. For example, acute lead poisoning is most evident when waterfowl are staging for migration in wetlands contaminated with lead shot. Consequently mortalities due to ingestion are most likely to be detected when large numbers of animals are exposed. In contrast, chronic lead poisoning can be inapparent as slowly debilitating animals seek refuge before death, are killed by predators or disperse to other areas.

Species, Age, and Gender

Species, age, and gender of animals affected can also provide valuable indicators as to what may or may not be causing mortality. Starvation tends to disproportionately affect young or old animals. Some species are more sensitive to certain diseases than others. For example, northern shovelers (*Anas clypeata*) tend to be highly efficient sifters of sediments for invertebrates. Because botulism toxin is concentrated in invertebrates, shovelers are one of the first animals to be affected during botulism outbreaks. Other causes of wildlife mortality, such as pesticides, are more indiscriminate and will affect several species. Raptors, for example, can die from consuming smaller birds that die from organophosphate poisoning. Younger animal have a less developed immune system or different behaviors than adults and can be more susceptible or receive higher exposure to certain infectious agents; thus, they may be over-represented during certain disease outbreaks. Other diseases may affect one gender preferentially either because of behavioral or physiologic differences. Avian cholera affects female common eiders (*Somateria mollissima*) more than males because, during disease outbreaks on nesting grounds, males are at sea (Korschgen et al. 1978). Brucellosis, a pathogen of the reproductive tract in mammals, tends to affect females more severely and manifests as abortions.

Clinical Signs

Clinical signs of sick animals should be carefully documented and, if possible, videotaped. Animals with poor hair or feather appearance with large burdens of ectopara-sites are clearly abnormal. Many diseases cause neurological abnormalities such as inability to turn right side up, tremors, improper posture of limbs, abnormal gait or flight, or inability to keep the head upright. Clinical signs can also be characteristic. For example, brown pelicans (*Pelecanus occidentalis*) affected by the marine toxin domoic acid exhibit scratching behavior alternating between the left and right legs. Other diseases induce changes in temperament. Rabies will often make normally wary wild carnivores more docile or aggressive. At times, sick animals will be in unusual locations or apart from others. Absence of sick animals during wildlife mortality episodes can be just as an important clue as presence.

Geographic Distribution

Potential causes of wildlife disease can be gleaned from spatial patterns of wildlife mortalities. Carcasses in one particular area could suggest they were concentrated there by wind or current, or there was a point source of mortality in that area. Presence of severely decomposed carcasses along with fresher specimens would indicate mortality has been ongoing. Daily movement patterns of animal populations should be recorded as well as location of common foraging and loafing areas. Particular notation should be made of movement from a mortality area to other areas as this can help investigators map disease spread and take pre-emptive management actions. This information can help managers identify the source of disease outbreaks or alter the course of disease at locations to which wildlife may move. Knowing population movement patterns also affects timing and feasibility of intervention strategies. For example, in an attempt to eliminate chronic wasting disease from the first site of discovery on the western slope of the Rocky Mountains in Colorado, managers had a limited window of opportunity in which to take action before spring migration dispersed cervids to higher, inaccessible areas. Changes in ratios of animals affected (gender, age, or species) can provide valuable clues to wildlife disease specialists. At a minimum, location of carcasses should be plotted on a map. These locations should be by date of observation so that spread of the epizootic can be followed. Global position satellite technologies now allow users to add information about location including weather, diagnostic findings, etc. that can be later used to evaluate characteristics such as movement, distribution, and incidence of disease in the population.

Laboratory

Detailed field observations provide an invaluable starting point to initiate disease investigations. Proper collection and submittal of samples to appropriate laboratories is the next logical step. For many biologists, this process is a "black box" from which emerge results that are often presented in arcane language and format with little apparent management value. Poor communications between laboratory and field can easily derail the disease investigation and make management ineffective. This section is designed to aid biologists in their understanding of the basic principles used in laboratory investigations. Our intent is to help biologists understand the limitations, advantages, and requirements of each discipline. This knowledge will help biologists discuss laboratory results with wildlife disease specialists, collect the most useful specimens, and make better decisions based on laboratory findings for assessing and managing the field situation. These laboratory tools are designed to identify infectious and noninfectious agents that could be potential causes of observed mortalities.

Pathology

Wildlife disease investigations in the laboratory typically begin with an examination of dead animals. In pathology, a complete external and internal exam of the carcass (gross necropsy, postmortem or autopsy – generally autopsy is used in conjunction with human postmortems) is conducted and samples of animal tissues are preserved for further examination under the microscope (histopathology) or for tests in other laboratories. During the external exam, the animal is weighed and measured, and the presence of any evident abnormalities (emaciation, skin abnormalities, etc.) is recorded. All major internal organs are examined and changes in their color, consistency, appearance, number, distribution, and size are noted. Pathology and histopathology can only detect morphologic change in organ systems, organs, tissues, and cells. Biochemical, submicroscopic, and other nonanatomic changes cannot be visualized and detected by pathology. Electron microscopy can enhance detection of microorganisms such as viruses, but the technique is limited to having a sample with the offending organism present.

Tissue samples for histopathology are stored in 10% buffered neutral formalin (a mix of salts and formaldehyde) and formaldehyde or ethanol. Tissues from a single animal can be stored in one jar, the size of the tissue fragments should be sufficiently thin (6-8 mm) and the volume of formalin sufficient (at least 10 × the volume of formalin to tissues) to allow adequate penetration and fixation of tissues. Tissue should be collected with a sharp knife or scalpel and crushing the tissue when handling with forceps should be avoided. If a lesion is seen, it is critical the tissue section contain both tissue with the lesion and adjacent unaffected tissue because many pathologic diagnoses are based on observation of the transition between normal and abnormal tissue. Normal lung tissue will float in formalin and it is important to note if they sink. Tissue sections should not be so large as to curl during fixation. Only wide mouth containers should be used because tissues that easily slide into containers when fresh can be difficult to remove once fixed if the mouth is narrow. Tissues fixed in formalin should be stored at room temperature and kept from freezing. Inadvertent freezing, such as leaving the samples in a truck overnight during winter, can ruin samples for histopathology.

Samples are later sent to the laboratory where they are embedded in paraffin, trimmed into thin slices, placed on microscope slides, stained, and examined under the microscope by a pathologist who looks for abnormalities at the cell and tissue level. The findings may indicate the need for specialized techniques, such as use of stains that increase the visibility of bacteria, fungi, or internal parasites. Pathology can provide a wealth of information on what did or did not cause death in an animal and the results can be used to focus additional laboratory and field investigations.

The main limitation of pathology is condition of tissues. Decomposition, freezing, or improper fixation damages tissues and cells. The more damage by these postmortem factors, the less the pathologist can accurately interpret as the effect of disease. Severely altered tissue will allow a pathologist to find only the most obvious, but not necessarily the most significant, disease-caused changes. Biologists have a critical role in ensuring that specimens (carcasses) collected for pathology are as fresh as possible. The ideal specimens for pathologic exam are fresh, chilled unopened carcasses, individually wrapped and submitted to the diagnostic laboratory. A rule of thumb is to send fresh specimens if they can be rapidly chilled after discovery and delivered to the diagnostic laboratory within 24 hours (48 if the timing of death is known to be in the past 6 hours). If this is not possible, frozen carcasses can be submitted although freezing limits pathologic interpretation. When the carcass is large or when the location is remote, the biologist must do the gross examination, take careful notes of findings, and preserve tissues in formalin. Because gross pathology is an inherently low-technology tool, it lends itself to remote field situations. With practice, field biologists can become adept at recognizing normal from abnormal during gross exams. Necropsy kits can be assembled at minimal costs; tissues can be stored in formalin at room temperature and later sent to the laboratory. Several resources exist explaining the details of how to conduct necropsies and collect and preserve tissues of ungulates and birds (Roffe et al. 1994, Friend and Franson 1999), sea turtles (Rainey 1981), fish (Meyer and Barclay 1990), and marine mammals (Dierauf and Gage 1990).

Bacteriology/Mycology

In these disciplines, tissues, fluids or swabs from tissues taken during necropsy are processed in the laboratory to culture bacteria or fungi that may be responsible for the mortality. Bacteriology/mycology can document the presence of living microorganisms, assay samples for evidence that the nucleic acid of a suspected pathogen is present (e.g., through polymerase chain reactions) or assay for biotoxins produced by these microorganisms. If the submitted sample does not contain the causative agent, its toxin, or the causative agent/toxin has degraded; the laboratory will provide a negative finding. A living microorganism or intact toxin must be present in the sample for the usual techniques to be effective. A negative finding may lead to an erroneous conclusion that a particular bacteria or fungus was not responsible for the mortality. Interpretation of the findings has to be made in view of field events and known sampling limitations.

Typically, tissues for bacteriology are collected using sterile techniques and placed individually in sterile plastic bags. Alternatively, sterile swabs can be inserted in the tissues and fluids can be aspirated or swabbed. Swabs or tissues should be refrigerated (not frozen) and sent to the laboratory as soon as possible. However, many bacteria, fungi and their toxins survive freezing quite well. These samples are better than decomposed specimens. In the laboratory, tissues or swabs are placed in special media that encourage growth of bacteria or fungi. Media used are chosen based on their ability to selectively grow certain microorganisms and inhibit growth of others. Once bacteria or fungi are cultured in the laboratory, those thought to be significant are identified with a battery of biochemical tests. Repeated sampling may be needed during an outbreak to confirm the original agent is still responsible for continued mortality or to track the pathogen into other populations. This information allows managers to maintain or alter management response for optimum effect.

The main limitation of bacteriology/mycology is the condition of specimens relative to postmortem decomposition and preservation. A variety of opportunistic microorganisms will rapidly colonize a carcass and the number and variety of these contaminant organisms increase with time of decomposition. Colonization by contaminant organisms in tissues can hinder laboratory interpretation of results, mask the presence of the original pathogen, or kill the pathogen. Thus, it is critical that samples for bacteriology be taken using sterile techniques and immediately shipped to the laboratory. Poor sampling techniques or leaving samples refrigerated for long periods of time (days) prior to culture in the laboratory increases chances for secondary contamination.

Virology

Virology is similar to bacteriology in that tissues are processed in the laboratory in attempts to grow viruses from tissues or detect fragments of their nucleic acids. Typically, tissue samples are collected using sterile techniques and placed individually in labeled, sealed plastic bags where they are stored frozen (−70 C optimal). In the laboratory, tissues are homogenized in special media and placed in cell cultures. Because viruses use and kill animal cells to replicate, their effect can be detected in the culture. Laboratories may also use special staining techniques directly on samples for examination under the electron microscope to look for viruses. Additional molecular and immunologic tests are used to specifically identify the virus. As with bacteriology, virology will provide a positive response only if the sample contains virus particles that can be detected by the method of choice. Inactivated ("dead") viruses will not be detected on cell cultures and the result will be negative. False negative findings are even more common in virology than bacteriology because of the more fragile nature of viruses, greater susceptibility to handling errors, and because many viruses disappear after causing initial organ damage.

Virology requires that tissues be freshly refrigerated or rapidly frozen to ensure viruses are properly preserved in the sample. When freezing tissues, it is critical that tissues remain frozen until they arrive at the laboratory (however, the carbon dioxide produced by dry ice can inactivate some viruses). Viable viruses are less likely to be found in tissues that are decomposed or that have been repeatedly thawed and frozen. Unfortunately, because virology is expensive and requires particular expertise, relatively few laboratories are equipped to do these assays. Thus, virology is usually attempted only if there is evidence (based on gross and microscopic pathology) that viruses may be responsible for the animal mortality.

Parasitology

Parasitology is the study of organisms such as worms, protozoa, mites, and ticks. Some parasites can be visible to the naked eye and others can only be seen using microscopes. Parasites frequently occur in wildlife and may be a cause of mortality. If parasites are the causative agent for wildlife morbidity/mortality, they occur in large numbers and with associated tissue changes. Knowledge of "nor-

mal" parasite loads is important to interpreting findings. The mere presence of worms in lungs or intestine does not mean that organ was significantly compromised. As with other diagnostic disciplines, positive findings are conclusive but negative findings can be false negatives. False negative results are less common in parasitology than other disciplines, and considerably less likely to happen for metazoan (multicellular) parasites.

Some macroparasites (round worms, tapeworms, lice, fleas, and ticks) are preserved in labeled vials containing 70% ethanol. Other parasites (spiny-headed worms, flukes) are best preserved in alcohol-formalin-acetic acid. Parasites preserved in this way should be stored at room temperature and submitted to specialists for identification. Detection of microparasites such as blood parasites or skin mites requires examination of blood smears or skin scrapings under a microscope. A variety of specialized techniques are used to culture and identify protozoa, or to detect larval stages of worms or parasite eggs (Box 2).

Box 2. Worm egg flotation.

Numerous methods exist to detect parasites, but fecal flotation for nematode (round worms) eggs is the most common. This technique relies on thoroughly mixing fecal samples in a liquid with specific gravity higher than that of the eggs. Eggs then float to the top and can be collected. Nematode eggs have a specific gravity just slightly higher than water; thus a liquid with a specific gravity of 1.1–1.2 is used. In contrast, trematode (fluke) eggs have a much higher specific gravity and this technique will not detect these parasites.

Materials needed
- fecal sample
- flotation solution (generally saturated salt, sugar or magnesium sulfate)
- test tube and holder
- slides and cover slips
- stirring instrument (stick)
- compound microscope

Procedure
1. Place test tube in rack and fill the bottom one-third with feces.
2. Fill the remainder of the test tube with flotation solution leaving sufficient room for stirring.
3. Using the wooden stirring stick, thoroughly mix the solution and feces.
4. Immediately top off the test tube with flotation solution sufficient to bulge slightly above the rim.
5. Place cover slip on top of test tube.
6. Allow to sit for one half-hour. Eggs will float to the top and stick to the cover slip.
7. Gently lift cover slip, place on glass slide and examine under the microscope.

Toxicology/Toxinology

Toxicology uses a variety of techniques to identify the presence of particular chemicals in animal tissues or fluids. Toxicology refers specifically to the detection of man-made chemicals (e.g., insecticides, and rodenticides) while toxinology refers to detection of natural poisons (e.g., botulinum toxin or marine toxins). Laboratory assays for chemicals are complex and require expensive equipment. There are specific requirements to sample and package tissues for submittal to the laboratory. For example, tissues to be analyzed for heavy metals (e.g., lead, cadmium) are typically stored frozen in sterile plastic bags and should not contact metal objects. Wrapping the tissue in aluminum foil is desirable for certain other chemicals prior to freezing. Some chemicals are more resistant to decomposition than others, and some are more likely to be detected in one type of tissue or organ. There may be additional requirements to procure environmental samples (water, soil, and food) to trace the source of the chemical in the environment (Sheffield et al. 2005).

Toxicology results can be relied on more when a negative finding is reported. However, tests for some toxins (e.g., botulinum type E) are frequently negative even when they are the actual cause of mortality. The behavior of many toxins in biological samples and the environment is well characterized so a reasonable prediction can be made about the reliability of negative findings. The ability to detect a positive sample frequently depends on the sensitivity of the assay used. Generalized techniques (or assays) for toxicants are uncommon. Thus, questions must be more specific and assays must be for specific toxins. Because of the expense of testing, analyses for chemical toxins are rarely done before a thorough field investigation and postmortem examination suggest a particular toxin may be involved (Sheffield et al. 2005). The best approach for collection of tissues for toxicology is to have preliminary information suggesting the possibility of a specific toxin. The laboratory used for testing should be consulted for the best method of sample collection, handling, and shipping.

Molecular Biology

Use of the polymerase chain reaction (PCR) has revolutionized the detection of microorganisms and augments standard bacteriology, virology, and parasitology techniques. Polymerase chain reaction is a laboratory technique for amplification of DNA. Amplification permits detection of DNA that otherwise would be missed. For example, a single strand of DNA from a virus in a tissue sample can be amplified by 1,000. This powerful technique has enhanced the sensitivity of many assays for a wide variety of micro-organisms and an increasing number of laboratories have or are establishing capabilities to do PCR. Tissues for this assay can be individually wrapped in labeled plastic bags and stored frozen, preferably at –70 C.

The limitations of PCR are quite different from other techniques. First, the technique detects only genetic material and not viable organisms. Hence, the presence of DNA from a virus in a tissue sample does not necessarily indicate the virus was viable and replicating or even causing disease. Second, because the technique depends on the amplification of known sequences of DNA, an investigator must decide which virus or bacteria to seek. Third, if samples are contaminated with genetic material not originally found in the specimen of interest, a false positive finding may occur. Contamination can occur through specimen handling, instruments used for specimen collection, and packaging of multiple specimens, among other ways for cross-contaminating specimens. However, amplification and detection of a known genetic sequence is confirmation that the suspect organism was present at some time in the host's environment. Polymerase chain reaction technology is best used once field investigation and pathology have suggested the likelihood of a particular microorganism or if there is a high need to eliminate or confirm the presence of a specific pathogen. This technology is generally used to confirm the identity of pathogens that have been detected by other methods.

Serology

When microorganisms infect animals, the animals usually develop an antibody response towards that organism. The ability to generate antibody and the level of antibody production is host-agent specific. Serology is the technique used to detect and measure levels of antibodies in serum. Blood is collected (Fig. 1) from animals and centrifuged to separate cells from liquid. It is important not to freeze the blood before centrifugation. The cell-free liquid portion of the blood (serum) is removed and stored frozen in labeled vials for later analysis for antibodies. A variety of serologic assays exist to detect antibodies. Some can be used directly in the field while others are more complicated and must be done in specialized laboratories. Many assays are developed specifically for use in domestic livestock or small animals (dogs and cats) but are often used in wildlife species. However, validation of techniques developed in domestic animals for wildlife is frequently lacking.

Serologic assays detect exposure to an infectious agent (or similar micro-organism) but do not detect presence of disease. This is an important distinction because it is often assumed that presence of antibodies to an infectious agent indicates that disease from this organism is present. Most "serosurvey" results only reflect historical exposure and provide no evidence of disease or disease impact on the population. However, properly used serology can infer presence or absence of particular microorganisms, and inferences regarding disease can be made. As examples, brucellosis antibodies have been shown to be positively correlated with presence of the organism in bison (*Bison*

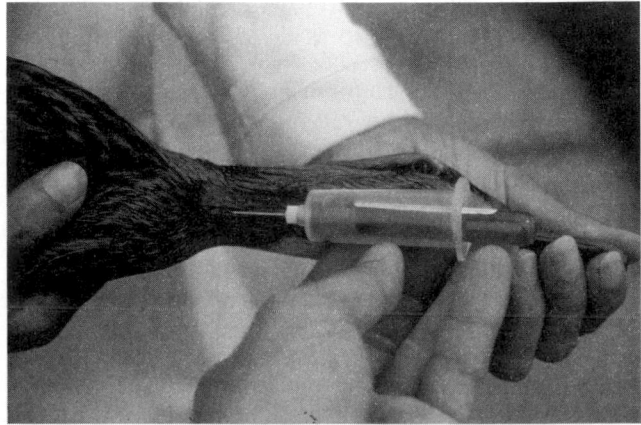

Fig. 1. Blood sample collection from a duck using jugular venipuncture and vacutainer system (photograph courtesy of T. J. Roffe).

bison) and elk (*Cervus elaphus*) (Roffe et al. 1999). Higher antibody levels correspond with a higher likelihood of being infected; high levels are often a good predictor of impending abortion. In comparison, low levels of parainfluenza antibodies are frequently found in ungulate populations and are probably meaningless relative to population effects. In individual animals, a 4-fold rise in titer of specific antibodies using paired serum samples is considered a reasonable indication the specific agent is present and replicating at the time of mortality or morbidity.

The timing of the rise in antibodies relative to disease and specificity of the test for antibodies are critical to make this inference about a disease agent. Whether that agent can be implicated as the cause of mortality or morbidity also depends on whether the field investigation and pathology corroborate the effects that agent would be expected to produce. Many serological tests developed for domestic animals use strains of pathogens or reagents specific for that animal. When used in wildlife species that are often infected with different strains of the organism, these tests can give misleading results (false positives and false negatives) or can lead to confusion as to what exactly constitutes a positive or negative result. In addition, some serologic tests measure antibody to the microorganism of concern and closely related microorganisms. Thus, knowledge of the specificity of the test is essential for interpretation. Serological tests can prove useful to trace the presence of a microorganism in animal populations.

Clinical Chemistry and Hematology

Clinical chemistry is the analysis of serum or plasma for proteins, enzymes, metabolites, and minerals. Whole blood is collected and the serum or plasma is separated, stored frozen, and subsequently chemically analyzed using automated analyzers. Damage to or improper function of internal organs (e.g., liver, kidney, pancreas, and muscle) will lead to changes in levels of specific proteins, enzymes, and minerals in the blood. The change may be an increase or decrease in a particular serum constituent depending on which organ is affected; however, interpretation is difficult because normal values for many species are unknown. Elevated levels of a particular enzyme might suggest liver disease while elevated levels of a particular mineral could suggest kidney disease. More frequently, the combination of elevations and decreases in multiple parameters may suggest a disease entity. Clinical chemistry is routinely used by clinicians to obtain an idea of how internal organs are functioning in living animals but is not useful for dead animals because of changes in parameters associated with decomposition.

Hematology is analysis of whole blood for quantification and morphologic evaluation of cellular components and, like clinical chemistry, is only useful in living animals. Whole blood collected in anticoagulants is necessary for cell counts. A drop of blood is placed on a microscope slide and stained to permit enumeration of the different types of cells or detection of blood parasites. The percentage of whole blood that is red cells (hematocrit) can be measured through centrifugation. Other assays can be used to detect hemoglobin content and morphology of red cells. Automated hematology analyzers are available for domestic animals. Some inflammatory processes will lead to elevation of specific types of white blood cells or decreased numbers of red cells; this can be detected through hematology.

Hematology and clinical chemistries can be useful to assist disease investigators in assessing which organ systems are likely affected by the disease agent, but they rarely provide a specific diagnosis. The goal with these tools is to narrow the list of suspect agents by detecting changes in the animal's physiology that are consistent with a limited number of agents. These tests require blood samples taken by trained personnel and generally require live, captured animals. Some hematology tests must be conducted shortly after blood collection making them impractical to use in remote field settings.

Most laboratories operate on and provide normal values for domestic animals. They do not have the expertise to assess hematology findings from wildlife species. Thus, interpretation of results must be done with care and in consultation with appropriate experts.

Epidemiology/Epizootiology

These terms are frequently interchanged in regard to animal populations. Epizootiology originated in reference to the science of epidemiology as applied to animals. Dictionary definitions of epidemiology refer to human communities. However, the origin of the term epidemiology is derived from the Greek for "study of something prevalent" and is equally applied to people and other animals. Epidemiology is the study of the relationship of factors affecting the frequency and distribution of disease in animal populations. A good general reference for the biologist is Thrusfield (1997). Epidemiology brings together laboratory findings and field observation using mathematical/statistical methods to detect trends and patterns in diseases of wildlife populations. At its most basic, epidemiology is the summarization of percent of animals affected by a particular agent. Or it may be complex, involving elaboration of mathematical models and spatial analysis to explain or predict behavior of disease in animal populations.

FIELD NECROPSY TECHNIQUES

When it is not possible to submit carcasses directly to a diagnostic laboratory, it will be necessary for the biologist to conduct necropsies in the field. Wildlife biologists contemplating doing so should obtain formal instruction from trained individuals. A variety of institutions provide guidance and training on necropsy procedures and sampling. A few institutions (e.g., National Wildlife Health Center, U.S. Geological Survey; Southeast Cooperative Wildlife Disease Study, University of Georgia) have specific training programs for teaching biologists about wildlife disease investigation techniques and necropsy procedures. While variations exist on the anatomy of different species of animals, the principles of necropsy remain the same. The first step is obtaining a detailed history of the circumstances surrounding the death of the animal. Thus, the animal should be observed *in-situ* for clues in the environment that could help explain the mortality.

Once this information is noted, the carcass can be moved to a suitable location (Fig. 2). The area where the necropsy is done should be as comfortable as possible,

Fig. 2. Using heavy equipment to transport a dead bison before necropsy (photograph courtesy of T. J. Roffe).

Fig. 3. Modified pit burning disposal of waterfowl carcasses. Use of a grate allows for more rapid and complete burning (photograph courtesy of T. J. Roffe).

well ventilated, and should have access to running water. Tools appropriate to the carcass to be examined should be available (Table 1). If the carcass cannot be moved to a suitable location, the necropsy must be done on site. However, it is important to check with local authorities to

Table 1. Components of a field necropsy kit.

Essential items	No.	Other useful items	No.
Scalpel handles	3	Bone snips	1
Large scissors	2	Hemostat	1
Toothed forceps	3	18G 1 ½" needles	100
Shears	1	20G 1 ½" needles	100
Scalpel blades	12 dz	22G 1 ½" needles	100
Sm whirl-pack bags	150	5-cc syringe	50
Various plastic bags	100	10-cc syringe	50
Ties for plastic bags	100	35-cc syringe	5
Bottles with 10%		Instrument tray with cover	1
buffered Formalin	2	Microscope slides	1 gr
Plastic bottle undiluted		Coverslips	1 bx
Roccal	1	Face masks	100
Waterproof markers	3	Clipboard	1
Pens	3	Dissecting pans	2
Pencils	3	Zip-loc bags	100
Necropsy sheets	100	Paper towels	100
Specimen bottles	2	Large whirl-pack bags	100
Dry ice shipping labels		Labels	1 gr
and instructions	2	Clear tape	1 roll
Nondisposable gloves	6 pr	Ringing sticks	1 gr
Disposable gloves	6 pr	Test tube racks	2
Ruler	1	Centrifuge tubes	100
Strapping tape	2 rolls	Gauze	1 roll
Aluminum foil	1 roll	Slide boxes	2
Straight butcher knife	1	Vials with screw caps	144
Curved butcher knife	1	Swabs	100
Blue ice packs	10	Hatchet	1
		Alcohol lamp	1
		Lighter	1
		Bottle fuel for lamp	1
		Boot brush	1
		Label tape	2 rolls
		Bone saw	1

ensure compliance with any ordinances, to warn them of possible complications, and/or to make arrangements for proper disposal of remains (Fig. 3). Assuming the carcass is small enough to permit relocation, efforts should be made to prevent contamination of the area with body fluids. The best facility is one designed for necropsy with a drain and stainless steel tables. On other surfaces plastic sheets and tarps can provide a barrier against contamination.

Prior to opening the carcass, it should be weighed, if possible, and an external exam completed. The key element to a postmortem exam is proceeding in a systematic manner (head to tail or vice versa) so that details are not overlooked. Mouth, nose, and eyes should be evaluated for discharge (blood, froth, and excessive mucus). Limbs should be palpated for broken bones (palpating both limbs on each side simultaneously helps in detecting abnormalities). Hair/feather/scale coat should be examined for abrasions, trauma, or ectoparasites. If no abnormalities are seen, this should be noted because absence of written records can imply the observation was not done.

The internal exam must be done in a systematic manner (Box 3) with all organs examined in a consistent order. Usually it is best to leave examination of the gastrointestinal tract until the end of the necropsy to minimize contamination of other organs with ingesta (and gut bacterial flora). During the internal exam, abnormalities in color, shape, size, texture, and number of organs should be noted. Recognizing normal from abnormal is challenging for the beginner and an appreciation of the difference can only be gained through practice and examination of many animals. If in doubt, it is better to record what appears to be abnormal than to record nothing at all. Photographs of suspected lesions can be electronically sent to the pathologist or enclosed with the gross necropsy report. More detail is better than less detail in the necropsy report, as this will aid the pathologist during the microscopic examination of tissues.

Thorough decontamination of the necropsy area and tools should be done after the necropsy to minimize risks of disease transmission. Scrubbing the area and tools with soap and water followed by rinse with 10% bleach or commercial disinfectant is usually sufficient to eliminate infectious organisms.

Box 3. General internal postmortem exam procedures.

1. Ungulates, small carnivores, and other laterally compressed species.
   a. Place in left lateral recumbency (on left side, places rumen down).
   b. By cutting with a knife, reflect right fore and hind legs over body.
   c. Make midline skin incision from tip of lower jaw to pubis.
   d. Reflect right side of skin over the back exposing all muscle and subcutis from head and face to pubis.
   e. Reflect penis or mammary gland downward, toward the left rear leg.
   f. Open small window into abdomen just behind last right rib by cutting through the abdominal wall. View internally for abnormal fluid, blood or exudate.
   g. Extend this window by cutting away the right lateral abdomen wall as a flap that remains attached along the midline. Make the window large enough to view all organs but not so large as to allow viscera to spill (Fig. 4).

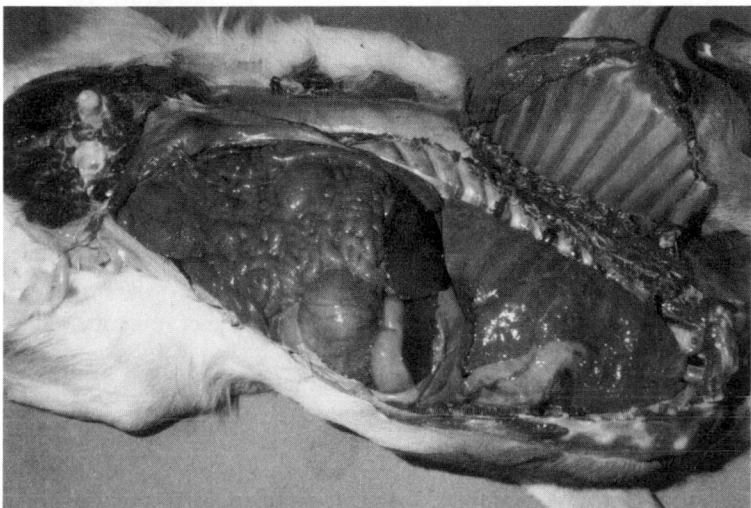

Fig. 4. *In-situ* internal organs of a properly prosected large ungulate during necropsy (photograph by T. J. Roffe).

   h. Reach under ribs; cut away diaphragm from right rib wall.
   i. At the head, cut the chin to separate the lower jaw.
   j. Cut all muscular attachments of the right lower jaw.
   k. Break the jaw outward and backward toward the right ear. The internal structures of the mouth and pharynx should be visible.
   l. Remove the tongue keeping it attached to the trachea and esophagus. This will require separating or cutting the hyoid bones at the back of the throat.
   m. Extend cut, separating tongue/trachea/esophagus to the chest.
   n. Mark muscles of right side ribs from the abdomen near the spine to the tongue/trachea/esophagus. Use rib cutters along this line to cut ribs.
   o. Mark muscles of right side ribs from the abdomen near the ventral midline to the tongue/trachea/esophagus. Use rib cutters along this line to cut ribs and remove right rib cage.
   p. Examine all organs in position.
   q. Remove thoracic organs by grasping trachea/esophagus near lungs, cutting along the spine, cutting along the sternum, and cutting structures along the diaphragm (aorta, esophagus, and caudal vena cava). Consider tying the esophagus before cutting if stomach is full.
   r. Remove liver by cutting gastrointestinal, kidney, and diaphragmatic attachments.
   s. Remove GI tract and spleen by cutting the distal descending colon, the diaphragmatic attachments, and the root of the mesentery.
   t. Separate the spleen from GI tract (located along stomach or rumen).
   u. For full exposure, remove the right (upside) half pelvis by cutting bone (ilium, ischium, and pubis) and soft tissue attachments. The entire urogenital tract and descending colon will be visible.
   v. Loosen urogenital tract and colon by first freeing kidneys, ureters, and ovary and uterine attachments. In males the reproductive tract is examined externally.
   w. Remove urogenital tract by grasping all organs and cutting soft tissue attachments in the pelvic canal.
2. Rotund or torpedo shaped mammals (bears, marine mammals, small furbearers).
   a. Place in dorsal recumbency (on their back).

Continued next page.

Box 3 (*continued*).   **General internal postmortem exam procedures.**

    b. Make midline incision as above from chin to pubis.
    c. Reflect skin laterally from both sides of carcass.
    d. Open the abdomen by making 2 flaps via a midline incision and creating one flap attached to each side.
    e. Cut the mid lower jaw (chin) and remove tongue keeping attachments to esophagus and trachea.
    f. Extend tongue/trachea/esophagus to chest as in 1.l and 1.m.
    g. Mark muscles on both sides of the ribs from the abdomen, along the midsection of the ribs, to trachea/esophagus.
    h. Remove ventral rib cage and sternum by cutting ribs along these lines.
    i. Remove the remainder of organs as described in 1.q to 1.u.
    j. Remove the ventral pelvis by cutting bone on both sides of the pubis and removing section of bone.
    k. Remove urogenital tract as in 1.v through 1.w.

3. Birds
    a. Generally necropsy in dorsal recumbency and as above.
    b. Use blunt dissection to remove skin.
    c. Do not have diaphragm.
    d. Have air sacs.
    e. To remove rib cage must also cut coracoid and furcula, 2 bones attaching wings and breast muscle to main body. Use poultry shears.
    f. GI tract may include a gizzard, large paired ceca, and cloaca.
    g. Remove heart independent of lungs.
    h. Lungs are adhered to ribs and must be "peeled" from body wall.
    i. Some organ shapes differ from mammals.
    j. Reproductive organs vary greatly in appearance depending on stage of reproduction.
    k. Female reproductive system is unilateral, generally left side.
    l. Kidneys are long, 3 lobed, and tightly recessed in bony structures of the pelvis.

4. Organ Examination.
    a. Lungs.
        i. The esophagus is generally opened before examining the lungs.
        ii. Thorough palpation is more important than visualization when examining the lungs.
        iii. Open trachea and mainstem bronchi lengthwise starting at the larynx.
        iv. Continue opening distal bronchi until very small airways are reached.
        v. Cross section several areas of lung.
        vi. Content and mucosal surface both important to examine.
    b. Heart.
        i. Examine and open the pericardium first.
        ii. Open the heart in direction of flowing blood—Right atrium, right ventricle, left atrium, left ventricle.
        iii. Examine 3 surfaces (epicardium, endocardium, and myocardium) and 3 structures (valves, cords anchoring the valves, and the muscular ridges lining the ventricles).
        iv. The ratio of left to right ventricular free-wall is approximately 3:1 in most normal mammal hearts.
        v. Bird hearts are best opened by first cutting off the end of the heart to observe the relative size and shape of the 2 ventricles. The right ventricle will be a thin crescent around the cylindrical left ventricle.
    c. Liver and spleen.
        i. Examine surfaces.
        ii. Examine biliary tract and gall bladder, if present.
        iii. "Bread-slice" (series of parallel slices not quite through the organ) the liver and spleen and examine cut surfaces.
        iv. Bird spleens can be spherical or triangular. A single section through the organ is generally sufficient.
    d. GI tract.
        i. Open lengthwise along entire length or spot check at different points.
        ii. Esophagus and colon are part of the GI tract.
        iii. Examine all 4 stomachs of ruminants, single stomach of monogastrics.
        iv. Examine some section of duodenum, jejunum, ileum, and colon.
        v. In ruminants the colon is complex. Examine ascending colon, spiral colon, and descending colon.
        vi. GI parasites can be removed individually or by washing GI content through a sieve.
        vii. Gizzard malfunction can be estimated by the degree of excessive keratin on the surfaces.
    e. Urogenital tract.
        i. Adrenals are located at the front end of the kidneys. Cut in half to examine.
        ii. Slice kidneys lengthwise in half to visualize all structures.
        iii. Open bladder by making a small incision then inverting the bladder over gloved fingers.
        iv. Preserve ovaries and testes either whole or sectioned in fixative. Distal descending colon is usually examined with urogenital tract.

Table 2. Sample selection and preservation from field necropsy when entire carcass cannot be submitted and circumstances/necropsy findings suggest specific causes may be involved.

Sample	Projected tests	Method of preservation	Comments
When microbial infections are expected			
Observed lesions	Microbiology	Frozen	Lesions (abnormal-appearing tissue): a portion of each should be saved frozen and fixed.
Heart	Bacteriology	Frozen	Entire heart from birds and small mammals; selected portions from larger animals.
Liver	Bacteriology	Frozen	Entire lobe from birds and small mammals; several pieces up to 2 cm^2 or larger in larger animals.
Blood/serum	Bacteriology/virology	Frozen	Serum also useful for serology.
Spleen	Bacteriology/virology	Frozen	Entire spleen from birds and small mammals; selected portions from larger mammals. Fix remainder.
Intestine (small fragment)	Bacteriology/virology	Frozen	Segments from middle or distal (ileum) of the small intestine.
Brain	Bacteriology/virology	Frozen	If animal exhibited abnormal behavior, save entire head; submit intact head to laboratory for removal of brain by laboratory personnel.
When toxicants are suspected			
Lesions	As appropriate	Frozen	Lesions (abnormal-appearing tissue): a portion of each lesion should be saved frozen. Fixed tissue important.
Liver	Heavy metals (Pb, Tl)	Frozen	Entire liver from birds and small mammals; selected portions from larger mammals. Fixed tissue important.
Kidney	Heavy metals (Pb, Hg, Tl, Fe, Cd, Cr)	Frozen	Entire kidneys from birds and small mammals; selected portions from larger mammals. Fixed tissue important.
Stomach contents	Organophosphates, carbamates, plant poisons, strychnine, cyanide, mycotoxins	Frozen	Save entire contents. Samples to be checked for cyanide or H_2S must be placed in airtight container to prevent loss of these toxic gasses into the air.
Brain	Brain cholinesterase, organochloride residues, organomercuric compounds	Frozen	If brain is removed for chemical analysis, the brain must be wrapped in clean aluminum foil then placed inside a chemically clean glass bottle. Fixed tissue important.
Blood	Lead, cyanide, H_2S, nitrites	Frozen	Samples to be checked for cyanide or H_2S must be placed in airtight container to prevent loss of these toxic gasses into the air.
Lungs	H_2S, cyanide	Frozen	Samples to be checked for cyanide or H_2S must be placed in airtight container to prevent loss of these toxic gasses into the air.

Continued next page.

Table 2 (*continued*). Sample selection and preservation from field necropsy when entire carcass cannot be submitted and circumstances/necropsy findings suggest specific causes may be involved.

Sample	Projected tests	Method of preservation	Comments
		For microscopic study	
Lesions	Specimen is fixed, sectioned, and stained for microscopic study	10% Formalin	Lesions (abnormal-appearing tissue): a portion of each lesion should be saved frozen.
Liver	Specimen is fixed, sectioned, and stained for microscopic study	10% Formalin	Specimen portions should not exceed 6 mm in thickness.
Kidney	Specimen is fixed, sectioned, and stained for microscopic study	10% Formalin	Specimen portions should not exceed 6 mm in thickness.
Gonads	Specimen is fixed, sectioned, and stained for microscopic study	10% Formalin or Bouin's	Specimen portions should not exceed 6 mm in thickness.
Intestinal tract	Specimen is fixed, sectioned, and stained for microscopic study	10% Formalin or Bouin's	Snippet of stomach at the ileocecal junction, piece of duodenum (near the pancreas), and colon.
Brain, nervous tissues, eyes	Formalin-fixed material will be sectioned and stained	10% Formalin	Divide brain in half (sagittal); place one half in Formalin and save the other half frozen.
Impression smear	Can be made by touching glass slide to cut surface of any organ	Air-dry	Air-dried side can be used for many laboratory tests.
Heart, lung, skeletal muscle, lymph nodes, spleen, thymus	Specimen is fixed, sectioned, and stained for microscopic study	10% Formalin	Specimen portions should not exceed 6 mm in thickness.

SPECIMEN COLLECTION AND PRESERVATION

Timely response to wildlife disease outbreaks is important. Equally important is proper sample collection (Table 2, Box 4). The ability to identify the cause of mortality is highly dependent on sample quality. Great effort should be expended in locating the freshest carcasses possible. An example for collection of high priority species would be application of radio-transmitters with mortality sensors to facilitate location of fresh carcasses. Another method for obtaining the freshest possible specimens might include humane euthanasia of sick animals for postmortem exam. These specimens also provide the opportunity to collect fresh blood for analyses. Regular patrols to locate newly dead or sick animals should be a top priority during epidemic mortalities. If practical, fresh, unopened carcasses should be submitted to the laboratory chilled, generally using chemical ice packs. However, frozen specimens are better than no specimens at all. Several (>5) specimens over different time intervals need to be examined for many reasons. First, animals die of many causes. Some specimens may reflect diseases unrelated to what is causing epidemic mortality. Sufficient samples need to be obtained to identify the dominant mortality factors. Second, limitations of laboratory analysis may result in the offending

agent not being found in every specimen that died. Many wildlife mortalities involve multiple factors that can only be detected over time. When possible, examining both sick and dead animals can provide a more complete picture of the disease event. Early signs of disease can be detected more readily in sick animals while dead animals may show late stage disease and opportunistic infections that, if examined solely, may complicate the picture.

In some cases, unaffected animals from unaffected areas may need to be examined for comparison. Attempts should be made to sample these animals in a nonlethal manner. However, should euthanasia be necessary, it should be conducted by qualified personnel in accordance with American Veterinary Medical Association approved guidelines (Beaver et al. 2001). Care should be taken to properly label all samples with a unique identification as well as location and collection date. If field necropsies are done, it is essential the labeling system ensure that laboratory results from samples can be referred to the specific specimen from which it was collected at necropsy. Strict hygiene should be used during sample collection to ensure personal safety and minimize exposure to potential zoonotic agents. At a minimum, protective clothing, footwear, and gloves should be used when handling carcasses or tissues. Biologists should thoroughly wash with water and soap after working with dead animals (Fig 5).

Box 4. Specimen collection.

1. Collect freshest specimens possible.
2. Use sharp knife or scalpel for tissue pieces, swab for surfaces and exudates, needle and syringe for fluids.
3. Collect all samples in separate containers except histopathology.
4. Prevent cross-contamination.
5. Use sterile sample plastic bags or tubes. Non-additive blood tubes (red top) can be used.
6. In general, freeze specimens unless they will get to the laboratory within 48 hours EXCEPT histopathology and parasitology samples.
7. Allow blood to clot. Centrifuge and remove serum. Freeze serum.
8. Label all samples from one specimen with the same unique number. Use indelible ink or pencil and labels that stay on in the freezer.

SPECIMEN SHIPMENT

There has been increased emphasis on security for shipment of air cargo. Thus, it is essential that biologists and receiving laboratories be familiar with U.S. Department of Transportation (DOT) and public health regulations involving shipment of biological samples by ground or air. Centers for Disease Control (CDC) and DOT regulations generally permit movement of "diagnostic specimens" although certain restrictions on packaging and select agents may be required. The Code of Federal Regulations is available by Internet (http://www.access.gpo.gov/nara/cfr/) and covers DOT shipping requirements for biological material (49 CFR 178) and "select agent" interstate movement and public health issues (42 CFR 72). Select agents are a unique list of pathogens provided by the CDC for agents considered a high risk for bioterrorism.

The first step in proper shipment of samples is to ensure they are properly packaged to avoid leakage and, in case of chilled or frozen samples, thawing or heating (Box 5). The best method is to work directly with the shipper to ensure samples are appropriately packaged and labeled. Some shippers will permit certain shipments whereas others forbid them. Although shippers will have the final word on acceptability of a particular shipment, knowledge of federal and state transportation regulations can assist in gaining their acceptance. Overnight shipment is the only practical method for perishable material. Time of shipping should ensure the package would arrive at the laboratory on a workday. Collection permits may need to be enclosed with the specimens. In other cases close coordination with appropriate law enforcement authorities may be necessary to avoid delays, particularly for international shipments. If the case is a legal matter, chain-of-custody forms will need to accompany the specimens. Under no circumstances should specimens be shipped without prior coordination with and consent of the receiving laboratory.

SUMMARY

Wildlife population management requires knowledge of factors that affect population sustainability. Mortality is one of the most important of those factors. Without a clear understanding of the causes of mortality, decisions by managers of whether or how to intercede may be inappropriate. Wildlife biologists are usually the first to discover, assess, and respond to wildlife mortality. Biologists who make accurate, complete and timely field investigations, and proper collection and shipment of samples to a diagnostic facility are essential for an accurate diagnosis. In

Fig. 5. Typical field equipment used when investigating wildlife mortality (photograph courtesy of T. J. Roffe).

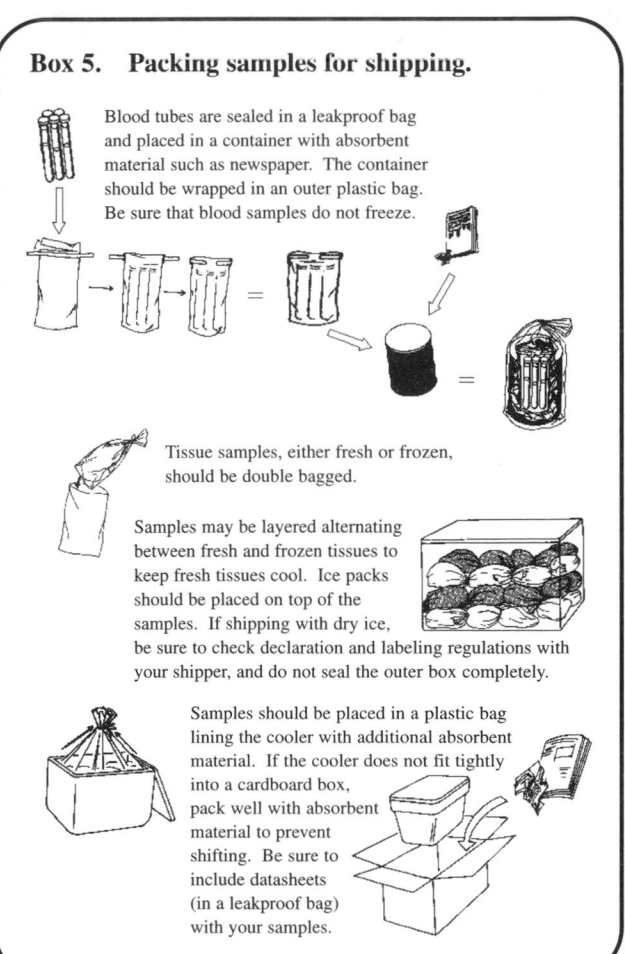

Box 5. Packing samples for shipping.

Blood tubes are sealed in a leakproof bag and placed in a container with absorbent material such as newspaper. The container should be wrapped in an outer plastic bag. Be sure that blood samples do not freeze.

Tissue samples, either fresh or frozen, should be double bagged.

Samples may be layered alternating between fresh and frozen tissues to keep fresh tissues cool. Ice packs should be placed on top of the samples. If shipping with dry ice, be sure to check declaration and labeling regulations with your shipper, and do not seal the outer box completely.

Samples should be placed in a plastic bag lining the cooler with additional absorbent material. If the cooler does not fit tightly into a cardboard box, pack well with absorbent material to prevent shifting. Be sure to include datasheets (in a leakproof bag) with your samples.

combination with wildlife disease specialists, biologists can identify causes of wildlife mortality, detect long-term patterns in factors that affect the survival of populations, and take appropriate corrective action to minimize the impact of some mortality factors on wildlife populations.

ACKNOWLEDGMENTS

We appreciate the insight and editorial help provided by C. E. Braun and 2 anonymous reviewers of this chapter.

LITERATURE CITED

ADRIAN, W., editor. 1992. Wildlife forensic field manual. Association of Midwest Fish and Game Law Enforcement Officers, Colorado Division of Wildlife, Fort Collins, USA.

BEAVER, B. V., W. REED, S. LEARY, B. MCKIERNAN, F. BAIN, R. SCHULTZ, B. T. BENNETT, P. PASCOE, E. SHULL, L. C. CORK, R. FRANCIS-FLOYD, K. D. AMASS, R. JOHNSON, R. H. SCHMIDT, W. UNDERWOOD, G. THORNTON, AND B. KOHN. 2001. 2000 report of the American Veterinary Medical Association panel on euthanasia. Journal of the American Veterinary Medical Association. 218:669–696.

DASZAK, P., A. A. CUNNINGHAM, AND A. D. HYATT. 2000. Emerging infectious diseases of wildlife: threats to biodiversity and human health. Science 287:443–449.

DAVIDSON, W. R., AND V. F. NETTLES. 1997. Field manual of wildlife diseases in the southeastern United States. Second edition. Southeast Cooperative Wildlife Disease Study, University of Georgia, Athens, USA.

DIERAUF, L. A., AND L. J. GAGE. 1990. Gross necropsy of cetaceans and pinnipeds. Pages 449–469 in L. A. Dierauf, editor. Handbook of marine mammal medicine: health, disease and rehabilitation. CRC Press, Boca Raton, Florida, USA.

DIETERICH, R. A., editor. 1981. Alaskan wildlife diseases. University of Alaska, Fairbanks, USA.

FAIRBROTHER, A., L. N. LOCKE, AND G. L. HUFF, editors. 1996. Noninfectious diseases of wildlife. Iowa State University Press, Ames, USA.

FOWLER, M. E., editor. 1981. Wildlife diseases of the Pacific basin and other countries. Proceedings of the Fourth International Conference of the Wildlife Disease Association, Sydney, Australia.

FRIEND, M., AND J. C. FRANSON, editors. 1999. Field manual of wildlife diseases, general field procedures and diseases of birds. U.S. Department of the Interior, Geological Survey, Biological Resources Division, Information and Technology Report 1999–001. Madison, Wisconsin, USA.

GERACI, J. R., AND V. J. LOUNSBURY. 1993. Marine mammals ashore: a field guide for strandings. Texas A & M Sea Grant Publication, Galveston, USA.

KORSCHGEN, C. E., H. C. GIBBS, AND H. L. MENDALL. 1978. Avian cholera in eider ducks in Maine. Journal of Wildlife Diseases 14: 254–258.

MEYER, F. P., AND L. A. BARCLAY, editors. 1990. Field manual for the investigation of fish kills. U.S. Department of the Interior, Fish and Wildlife Service, Resource Publication 177.

NOGA, E. J. 1999. Fish diseases. Iowa State University Press, Ames, USA.

RAINEY, W. E. 1981. Guide to sea turtle visceral anatomy. U.S. Department of Commerce, National Oceanic and Atmospheric Administration, National Marine Fisheries Service Publication 82.

ROFFE, T. J., M. FRIEND, AND L. N. LOCKE. 1994. Evaluation of causes of wildlife mortality. Pages 324–348 in T. E. Bookhout, editor. Research and management techniques for wildlife and habitats. Fifth Edition. The Wildlife Society, Bethesda, Maryland, USA.

———, J. C. Rhyan, K. Aune, L. M. Philo, D. R. Ewalt, T. Gidlewski, and S. G. HENNAGER. 1999. Brucellosis in Yellowstone National Park bison: quantitative serology and infection. Journal of Wildlife Management 63:1132–1137.

SHEFFIELD, S. R., J. P. SULLIVAN, AND E. F. HILL. 2005. Identifying and handling contaminant-related wildlife mortality/morbidity. Pages 213–238 in C. E. Braun, editor. Techniques for wildlife investigations and management. Sixth edition. The Wildlife Society, Bethesda, Maryland, USA

TAYLOR, L. H., S. M. LATHAM, AND M. E. WOOLHOUSE. 2001. Risk factors for human disease emergence. Philosophical Transactions of the Royal Society of London 365(1411):983–989.

THORNE, E. T., N. KINGSTON, W. R. JOLLEY, AND R. C. BERGSTROM. 1982. Diseases of wildlife in Wyoming. Second edition. Wyoming Game and Fish Department, Laramie, USA.

THRUSFIELD, M. 1997. Veterinary epidemiology. Blackwell Science Ltd, Cambridge University Press, London, United Kingdom.

WILLIAMS, E. S., AND I. BARKER, editors. 2001. Infectious diseases of wild mammals. Iowa State University Press, Ames, USA.

WOBESER, G. 1981. Diseases of wild waterfowl. Plenum Press, New York, USA.

———. 1994. Investigation and management of disease in wild animals. Plenum Press, New York, USA.

9

IDENTIFYING AND HANDLING CONTAMINANT-RELATED WILDLIFE MORTALITY/MORBIDITY

Steven R. Sheffield, Joseph P. Sullivan, and Elwood F. Hill

INTRODUCTION

Wildlife biologists have potential for field encounters with wildlife mortality/morbidity incidents as a result of routine monitoring of an area or a call from the general public. Wildlife mortality/morbidity can be due to natural or accidental causes, disease, or exposure to environmental contaminants. Every year, species of wildlife are subject to exposure to a myriad of different chemical contaminants that make their way into the environment. These chemical contaminants include pesticides, metals/metalloids, organics, inorganics, pharmaceuticals, and a wide variety of other compounds in air, soil, sediment, water, plants as well as in wild and domestic animals. If organisms are exposed to contaminants, there may be no resulting visible effects suggesting either there were no effects of exposure, or that if there was a negative effect, it was not apparent. However, there may be visible effects from exposure to chemical contaminants indicating either that it caused sickness or was lethal to wildlife species.

Understanding contaminant impacts on wildlife include parameters such as species (or higher taxa) involved, trophic level of the species involved, chemical(s) involved, route(s) of exposure, signs of intoxication, fate and transport (movement) through the environment, environmental compartment (media), and environmental persistence. Not all classes of contaminants pose the same level of risk to all taxonomic groups of animals. For example, mammals may be relatively less sensitive than birds or reptiles to environmental contaminants due to their evolutionarily more advanced detoxification enzyme system. The physical and chemical properties of the chemical (e.g., lipid solubility, water solubility, environmental persistence, volatility, etc.), differing toxicity, route(s) of exposure, and trophic level of the animal all affect which taxonomic groups may be more susceptible to different classes of contaminants. The trophic level at which the animal feeds is a major factor in contaminant exposure, with higher trophic level animals susceptible to biomagnification of contaminants. Herbivorous species may be less susceptible to the effects of contaminant exposure as they are better adapted for detoxifying foreign chemicals (xenobiotics) because they routinely encounter natural plant toxins (secondary plant compounds) in their diet that require similar detoxification (Vangilder 1983, Ray 1991).

Species that feed on soil invertebrates will be more susceptible to exposure to contaminants such as metals that remain in soil for long periods of time. The behavior of sick or intoxicated animals and where or how many animals are found may be indicative of different classes of contaminants. Once the class of contaminants is identified, characteristics of the class or the specific contaminant will affect what type, where, or how many environmental samples should be collected, and how long after the incident has been discovered the site should be monitored.

Upon discovery of a field mortality/morbidity incident suspected to be caused by environmental contaminants, there generally is little time to plan and conduct a research study of the incident. The available time for collecting evidence such as tissue samples and/or other environmental media (plants, soil, water, sediment, air) is often a matter of hours to a few days. Chemicals degrade, tissues decay/desiccate, and carcasses are readily scavenged, all of which greatly affect time available for sampling.

Box 1. Recommended fish and wildlife mortality/morbidity references.

ADRIAN, W. J., editor. 1996. Wildlife forensic field manual. Second edition. Association of Midwest Fish and Game Law Enforcement Officers, Denver, Colorado, USA.

AMERICAN SOCIETY FOR TESTING AND MEASUREMENT. 1997. Standard guide for fish and wildlife incident monitoring and reporting. Pages 1355–1382 in Biological effects and environmental fate; biotechnology; pesticides. ASTM E 1849-96. American Society for Testing and Measurement, Philadelphia, Pennsylvania, USA.

BRIGGS, S. A. 1992. Basic guide to pesticides: their characteristics and hazards. Hemisphere Publishing Corporation, Washington, D.C., USA.

CANADIAN COOPERATIVE WILDLIFE HEALTH CENTRE. 1975. Wildlife disease investigation manual. Canadian Cooperative Wildlife Health Centre, University of Saskatchewan, Saskatoon, Canada.

DIERAUF, L. A., AND F. M. D. GULLAND, editors. 2001. CRC handbook of marine mammal medicine. Second edition. CRC Press, Boca Raton, Florida, USA.

FAIRBROTHER, A., L. N. LOCKE, AND G. L. HUFF, editors. 1996. Noninfectious diseases of wildlife. Second edition. Iowa State University Press, Ames, USA.

FRIEND, M., AND J. C. FRANSON, editors. 1999. Field manual of wildlife diseases: general field procedures and diseases of birds. U.S. Department of the Interior, Geological Survey, Biological Resources Division, Information and Technology Report 1999-001.

HOFFMAN, D. J., B. A. RATTNER, G. A. BURTON, JR., AND J. CAIRNS, JR., editors. 2003. Handbook of ecotoxicology. Second edition. Lewis Publishers, Boca Raton, Florida, USA.

HUDSON, R. H., R. K. TUCKER, AND M. A. HAEGELE. 1984. Handbook of toxicity of pesticides to wildlife. Second edition. U.S. Department of the Interior, Fish and Wildlife Service, Resource Publication 163.

MEYER, F. P., AND L. A. BARCLAY, editors. 1990. Field manual for the investigation of fish kills. U.S. Department of the Interior, Fish and Wildlife Service, Resource Publication 177.

SMITH, G. J. 1987. Pesticide use and toxicology in relation to wildlife: organophosphorus and carbamate compounds. U.S. Department of the Interior, Fish and Wildlife Service, Resource Publication 170.

STROUD, R. K., AND W. J. ADRIAN. 1966. Forensic investigational techniques for wildlife law enforcement investigations. Pages 3–18 in A. Fairbrother, L. N. Locke, and G. L. Huff, editors. Noninfectious diseases of wildlife. Second edition. Iowa State University Press, Ames, USA.

U.S. DEPARTMENT OF THE INTERIOR. 1998. Fish and wildlife mortality incident information workshop. U.S. Department of the Interior, Geological Survey, National Wildlife Health Center, Madison, Wisconsin, USA.

———. 1999. Wildlife mortality database resource directory. U.S. Department of the Interior, Geological Survey, National Wildlife Health Center, Madison, Wisconsin, USA.

———. 2002. Environmental contaminants: field and laboratory techniques. U.S. Department of the Interior, Fish and Wildlife Service, National Conservation Training Center, Shepardstown, West Virginia, USA.

WORK, T. W. 2000a. Avian necropsy manual for biologists in remote refuges. U.S. Department of the Interior, Geological Survey, National Wildlife Health Center, Hawaii Field Station, Honolulu, USA.

———. 2000b. Sea turtle necropsy manual for biologists in remote refuges. U.S. Department of the Interior, Geological Survey, National Wildlife Health Center, Hawaii Field Station, Honolulu, USA.

The objective of this chapter is to provide guidelines for field biologists to assess wildlife mortality/morbidity incidents and sampling techniques useful in detection and documentation of environmental contaminants impacting wildlife. Presently, there is difficulty in finding published procedures for handling wildlife mortality/morbidity incidents. Few specific criteria are available for conclusive diagnosis of wildlife poisoning other than correlation of effects with chemical residues in critical tissues. We include safe, proper field techniques for collecting, handling, and preserving environmental samples for biological assays or chemical analyses as well as where to look for assistance with wildlife mortality/morbidity (Box 1). Because time is short and field data and samples are critical, assistance from others with experience in handling contaminant-related issues can be important to a full understanding of the entire incident. Careful documentation of the mortality/morbidity incident is necessary including appearance of affected individuals, species involved, and likely scenarios leading to the incident.

ENVIRONMENTAL CONTAMINANTS

Human activities have resulted in the pervasive and dynamic nature of contaminants in our environment. Although environmental contamination increased sharply with the rise of the Industrial Revolution in the mid- to late 1800s, the presence of contaminants in the environment has accelerated greatly since the 1940s. For example, pesticide use in the United States increased more than 10-fold, and chemical and mining industries continued high productivity during the post-war economic growth. The United States is the major producer, user, and exporter of pesticides in the world. In 1999, 2.27 billion kg of active

ingredient of toxic chemicals were used as pesticides in the United States (Donaldson et al. 2002). The United States is also the major producer, user, and exporter of organic and inorganic chemicals. In 1995, the amount of the top 50 chemicals produced by the chemical industry in the United States was over 340 billion kg (Chemical and Engineering News 1996). The United States produces or imports about 3,000 different organic chemicals of >454,000 kg each on an annual basis; 43% of these chemicals have no data on basic toxicity and only 7% have a full set of basic toxicity data (U.S. Environmental Protection Agency 1998b). The United States is also a major world producer of metals and minerals. In 2001, there were 13,925 active mines in the United States, and the annual per capita consumption rate of newly mined metals and minerals reached 20,870 kg in 2002 (National Mining Association 2004). The high level of production of these industries in the United States resulted in 2.8 billion kg of toxic chemicals released into the air, land, water, and underground in 2001 (U.S. Environmental Protection Agency 2003), 34,360 chemical and oil spills in 2001 (U.S. Department of Transportation 2004), 1,240 Superfund hazardous waste sites (U.S. Environmental Protection Agency 2004), and an estimated 450,000 contaminated commercial/industrial sites across the United States (U.S. Environmental Protection Agency 1996). Because of this great potential for chemical contaminants in the environment, it is inevitable that individuals of a variety of different wildlife species will be exposed and some will become sick and either recover or die.

The U.S. Environmental Protection Agency reports that state wildlife agencies in the United States annually receive about 3,800 reports of pesticide-related fish, wildlife, and plant incidents (American Society for Testing and Measurement 1997). These reports indicate that pesticide use can pose considerable risk to nontarget species, particularly birds and fishes. Most reported incidents are a result of exposure to insecticides and rodenticides, and not herbicides, fungicides, and other pesticides. The greatest number of wildlife mortality/morbidity incidents has been reported for anticholinesterase (organophosphorus and carbamate) insecticides and anticoagulant rodenticides. There is evidence from field investigations that many pesticides (mainly anticholinesterase insecticides) still on the market today have caused confirmed bird mortalities and that avian mortality occurs regularly and frequently in agricultural fields across North America (Mineau 2002).

In Europe, a large investigation of terrestrial wildlife mortality incidents involving pesticides in 18 countries was conducted from 1990 to 1994 (deSnoo et al. 1999). There were a high number of wildlife mortality incidents in France, The Netherlands, and the United Kingdom, all countries with intensive agricultural programs. Most reported incidents were due to deliberate abuse of pesticides with few mortality incidents reported for normal agricultural use (deSnoo et al. 1999). Their conclusion, that reporting of wildlife mortality incidents was not a reliable tool for obtaining an understanding of the occurrence of wildlife mortality incidents from agricultural pesticide use, is most likely valid worldwide.

Deleterious effects of pesticides on wildlife include death from direct exposure and secondary poisoning from consuming contaminated prey; reduced survival, growth, and reproductive rates from exposure to sublethal dosages; and habitat reduction through elimination of food resources and refuges. In the United States, approximately 3 kg of pesticide/ha are applied to about 160 million ha of land annually (Pimentel et al. 1997). With a large portion of the land area subjected to large quantities of pesticide applications, the impact of pesticides on wildlife could be predicted to be substantial (Pimentel et al. 1992). However, few attempts have been made to estimate the overall magnitude of pesticide impacts on wildlife species over a large geographic scale. An existing estimate for impacts on birds is substantial (Pimentel et al. 1992) but does not include such factors as bird losses caused by poisoning of invertebrate prey, eggs or chicks left to die when adults are killed and those birds suffering neurological effects that move from the area to places where they cannot reproduce or survive their exposure(s). The occurrence of these effects has been documented (Pimentel et al. 1992, Hill 1999) following pesticide application, but their importance to a population at the species or regional level has not been quantified.

In addition to pesticides, exposure to other chemicals can also serve as major sources of wildlife mortality and morbidity. These chemicals include metals/metalloids (Fairbrother et al. 1996, Goyer and Clarkson 2001, Hoffman et al. 2003), organic chemicals (Friend and Franson 1999, Bruckner and Warren 2001, Rice et al. 2003), cyanide associated with gold mining (Henny et al. 1994, Eisler et al. 1999), white phosphorus associated with military use (Sparling 2003), pharmaceutical drugs (Friend and Franson 1999, Oaks et al. 2004), and natural plant/animal toxins (Norton 2001, Russell 2001).

The full extent of wildlife mortality from contaminants is difficult to assess because wildlife species are often secretive, camouflaged, highly mobile, and live in dense habitat. Typical field studies of the effects of pesticides often obtain low estimates of mortality because carcasses disappear rapidly, well before they can be found and counted. Field studies rarely account for animals that die away from treated areas and many individuals often hide and die in inconspicuous locations. Studies have demonstrated that only 50% of dead or moribund birds are recovered even when their location is known (Mineau and Collins 1988). Carcass searches are rarely done and, even more rarely, done properly. Most carcasses disappear within 24–48 hours post-spray, making documentation difficult (Vyas 1999). When known numbers of bird carcasses were placed in identified locations in the field, 62–92% disappeared overnight due to scavengers (Balcomb 1986). Kostecke et al. (2001), using remote cameras, documented heavy scavenging of experimentally placed bird carcasses by mammals, particularly striped skunks (*Mephitis mephitis*), and to a lesser extent by birds. This study demonstrated the potential hazard of secondary poisoning and the need for careful searches for wildlife mortality/morbidity following pesticide applications.

The full extent of wildlife morbidity from contaminants can be even more difficult to assess because sick animals may move from the area of exposure or otherwise disappear (i.e., fly from the area, retreat to a burrow), may not demonstrate visible signs of morbidity, and/or may become more vulnerable to predation or other mortality factor as a result of exposure. Sublethal effects, those that serve to debilitate an exposed organism, are often subtle, and exposure to chemical contaminants can impact all internal body systems (i.e., biochemical, physiological, immunological, etc.), which in turn can reduce the fitness and/or survival of exposed individuals. For example, many chemical contaminants including pesticides, pharmaceuticals, and even natural plant chemicals that have the ability to disrupt normal endocrine function in animals are of particular concern and can have major implications for reproduction in wildlife species (Yamamoto et al. 1996, Gross et al. 2003). Although some sublethal effects can be apparent (i.e., tumors, developmental malformations), many are not and animals suspected of sublethal poisoning often require close examination and laboratory testing. A formidable problem in identifying and understanding sublethal effects is that baseline data for normal (unexposed) individuals are largely unavailable (Hill 1999).

CLASSES OF CONTAMINANTS
Metals/Metalloids

Metals are natural substances and, in most cases, only become significant contaminants where human activity such as mining and smelting releases them from the rocks in which they were deposited during volcanic activity or subsequent erosion and relocates them into situations where they can cause environmental problems (anthropogenic enrichment). Metals are nonbiodegradable and, unlike organic compounds, cannot decompose into less harmful components. Detoxification consists of "hiding" active metal ions within a protein (e.g., metallothionein) or depositing them in an insoluble form in intracellular granules for long-term storage or excretion in feces. The term "heavy metals" generally has been used to refer to metals that are environmental contaminants. However, true heavy metals have a density relative to water >5, which excludes some important contaminants such as aluminum.

The term metalloid is used for elements such as arsenic and selenium, which are transitory in nature between metals and non-metals. In the environment, metals and metalloids occur as organic or inorganic complexes; there are several factors that affect which form is more toxic than the other. For example, inorganic arsenic compounds generally are more toxic to wildlife than organic arsenic compounds, whereas the opposite is true for mercury and lead where the organic forms are more toxic than inorganic forms.

Essential Metals/Metalloids

All animals require 7 major metal minerals including sodium, calcium, phosphorus, potassium, magnesium, and sulfur for ionic balance and as integral parts of amino acids, nucleic acids, and structural compounds. All animals also require 12 trace metals/metalloids that are essential micronutrients including zinc, copper, manganese, iron, selenium, chromium (Cr^{+3}), nickel, cobalt, molybdenum, vanadium, and silicon as essential components of enzymes, enzyme cofactors, and other biochemical functions. Presently, there is insufficient information available to ascertain whether metals such as silver, tin, aluminum, lithium, and boron are essential. All essential metals/metalloids can be toxic to wildlife species if sufficiently concentrated. Selenium is an excellent example of an essential metalloid that has caused notable toxicity problems in wildlife species in the United States.

Selenium.—Major environmental sources of selenium are coal-fired and other fossil fuel-burning power plants, and mining and smelting operations. Selenium is a naturally occurring component of soils (Ohlendorf 2003) and an essential micronutrient for wildlife and an integral component of the glutathione detoxifying enzyme system. However, there is a fine line between selenium deficiency and selenium toxicosis. Selenium can become concentrated at relatively high levels from mining activities and agricultural runoff. Although occasionally implicated in mortalities of adult animals, it is more likely to produce sublethal effects, such as developmental abnormalities, or embryonic death (Eisler 1985b, Ohlendorf et al. 1986). It has been shown to be highly teratogenic (producing malformations) in aquatic birds, causing widespread reproductive failure through decreased egg weight, decreased egg production and hatching success, anemia, and a high incidence of grossly malformed embryos with missing or distorted eyes, beaks, wings, and feet (Eisler 1985b). Excess selenium also causes behavioral modifications, intestinal lesions, chronic liver damage, and impacts the immune system (Eisler 1985b). Signs of selenium poisoning include vomiting, lethargy/weakness, diarrhea, increased urination, panting, central nervous system depression, paresis (partial paralysis), and prostration, and death can result due to respiratory failure (Osweiler et al. 1985). Selenium is readily bioaccumulated in aquatic and terrestrial food chains, but is not biomagnified through food chains. In the early to mid-1980s at Kesterson National Wildlife Refuge in central California, selenium was the causative agent in numerous cases of waterfowl and wading bird nesting failure (Ohlendorf et al. 1986). In this situation, selenium from irrigation drain water accumulated in waters of Kesterson where it caused massive reproductive failure through embryonic mortality and developmental abnormalities of aquatic birds (Ohlendorf et al. 1986). Selenium was deposited in eggs and caused severe developmental abnormalities in chicks. Mean selenium concentrations

in livers and kidneys were about 95 ppm dry weight, about 10 × higher than levels in birds from a reference area (Eisler 1985b, Ohlendorf et al. 1986).

Nonessential Metals/Metalloids

Some metals have no known biological function and serve to replace essential metals of like valance in animals. These metals include mercury, lead, cadmium, chromium (Cr^{+6}), and arsenic. All tend to be highly toxic and may exert toxicity through the induction of deficiencies of essential metals through competition at active sites in biologically significant molecules. Examples include lead replacing calcium in bone and arsenic replacing phosphorus in DNA. Metals/metalloids with no biological function tend to be those of greatest environmental concern, particularly if they are anthropogenically concentrated in a given area.

Mercury.—Major environmental sources of mercury have been chlor-alkali (plastics) manufacturing; mining and smelting operations; mercurial seed dressings; mercury-based fungicides; coal-fired power plants; thermometer, battery, and fluorescent bulb manufacture; switches; paints; pulp and paper industry; and dental amalgam (Wiener et al. 2003). The use of mercury in agriculture has been largely curtailed in the United States; sources related to energy production and mining are now of greatest concern. About 25–30% of total atmospheric mercury is anthropogenic (Eisler 1987a). Under certain environment conditions (e.g., anoxic sediments), inorganic mercury can be readily transformed by anaerobic bacteria into methylmercury, which is extremely toxic.

Mercury deposition since industrial times (mid-1880s) and subsequent biotransformation to methylmercury in aquatic systems has created areas where mercury poses a relatively high risk to wildlife, particularly long-lived, piscivorus species (Henny et al. 2002, Wiener et al. 2003). Methylmercury readily crosses biological membrane barriers whereas inorganic mercury does not. However, once absorbed, both forms of mercury are highly cytotoxic (toxic to cells), causing histopathological lesions in tissues of the nervous, hepatic, renal, and immune systems (Heinz 1996). The most observable sign of organo-mercury poisoning is central nervous system dysfunction leading to respiratory stress and lack of coordination. Other common signs of mercury poisoning in wildlife species include anorexia (and resulting emaciation), ataxia (loss of coordination), progressive paralysis, tremors/spasms, and loss of sight (Heinz 1996, Wiener et al. 2003).

Mercury is readily bioaccumulated in wildlife and biomagnified through food chains. For birds and mammals that regularly consume fish and other aquatic organisms, total mercury concentrations in prey items should not exceed 100-μg/kg fresh weight for birds and 1,100 μg/kg for small and medium-sized mammals (Eisler 1987a). In wildlife, concentrations of mercury >1,100-μg/kg fresh weight of tissue (liver, kidney, blood, brain, hair/feathers) should be considered as presumptive evidence of an environmental mercury problem (Eisler 1987a). Although mortality/morbidity from mercury is more of an insidious event involving scattered individuals, a substantial number of mercury-related wildlife mortality/morbidity incidents have been reported. Many of these have involved mortality in grebes (Podicipedidae) in the western United States (Eisler 1987a), common loons (*Gavia immer*) and turkey vultures (*Cathartes aura*) in Canada (Friend and Franson 1999), and reproductive impairment in bald eagles (*Haliaeetus leucocephalus*) in the United States (Friend and Franson 1999).

Lead.—Major environmental sources of lead have been leaded gasoline, paints, pesticides, batteries, mining and smelting operations, metal finishing, petroleum refineries, and hunting, fishing, and shooting sports (e.g., trap, skeet, target shooting) as well as firearms training activities (Pattee and Pain 2003). Although leaded gasoline, paints, and pesticides are not as prevalent now, lead from these sources continues to persist in the environment. In animals, <10% of dietary lead is absorbed, but >90% of that absorbed is retained in bones. Lead causes anemia and inhibition of the enzyme D-ALAD (D-aminolevulinic acid dehydratase), and has been demonstrated to cause severe neurotoxic effects in young animals and humans (Pattee and Pain 2003). The exposure and effects of tetraethyl lead, an anti-knock agent formerly added to gasoline, have been examined along highways (Grue et al. 1984) while lead shot deposition has also been examined, particularly in wetlands (DiGiulio and Scanlon 1984), around trap/skeet shooting ranges (Stansley and Roscoe 1996), and at firearms training facilities (Lewis et al. 2001).

Lead poisoning is most commonly observed in birds, particularly waterfowl. The first documented report of lead poisoning in waterfowl came from Texas in 1894 and Bellrose (1951, 1959) reported widespread waterfowl mortality and illness associated with ingestion of lead shot in the 1950s. In the United States, an estimated 1.6–2.4 million ducks, geese, and swans died annually as a direct result of lead shot ingestion before widespread use of nontoxic shot in the early 1990s (Pattee and Pain 2003). Sanderson and Bellrose (1986) and Beyer et al. (1998) reviewed the problem of lead poisoning in waterfowl. Signs of lead poisoning include gross lesions, impactions of the upper gastrointestinal tract, submandibular edema (accumulation of fluid), myocardial necrosis, and biliary discoloration in the liver (Friend and Franson 1999). Field signs include inability/reluctance to fly, weak and/or erratic flight, poor landings and, as conditions worsen, birds become flightless and hold their wings in a characteristic "roof-shaped" position that progresses to wing droop as birds become more moribund (Friend 1987). About 95% of waterfowl diagnosed with lead poisoning had liver lead concentrations of at least 38 ppm (dry weight) (Friend and Franson 1999).

Ingestion of lead shot by both predatory and scavenging raptors feeding on hunter-killed carcasses has been reported for bald and golden eagles (*Aquila chrysaetos*), red-tailed hawks (*Buteo jamaicensis*), vultures (turkey and black [*Coragyps atratus*] vultures, and California condor [*Gymnogyps californianus*]) (Janssen et al. 1986, Craig et al. 1990). Vultures and eagles appear to be highly susceptible to poisoning from ingesting small quantities of lead shot (Eisler 1988*b*). In addition to lead shot, lead fishing sinkers have contributed to lead-caused mortalities in a number of aquatic birds and mammals, particularly common loons (Pokras and Chafel 1992, Scheuhammer and Norris 1996, Stone and Okoniewski 2001, Sidor et al. 2003). Lead is readily bioaccumulated in wildlife, but does not appear to be biomagnified in food chains. At least 6 endangered or formerly endangered species, including bald eagle, peregrine falcon (*Falco peregrinus*), California condor, brown pelican (*Pele-*

canus occidentalis), Mississippi sandhill crane (*Grus canadensis pulla*), and whooping crane (*G. americana*) have been victims of lead poisoning (Friend and Franson 1999).

Cadmium.—Major environmental sources of cadmium include electroplating, zinc and lead mining and smelting, paint and pigments, batteries, plastics, coal-fired power plants, and municipal wastewater and sewage sludge. Cadmium is a known teratogen and affects calcium metabolism causing excess calcium excretion, which negatively impacts both skeletal and cardiovascular systems (Eisler 1985*a*). In addition, growth retardation, anemia, and testicular damage occur in cadmium-exposed wildlife (Eisler 1985*a*). Cadmium is readily bioaccumulated and data are available suggesting that it is biomagnified through food chains (Larison et al. 2000). White-tailed ptarmigan (*Lagopus leucura*) in Colorado were poisoned by cadmium due to biomagnification (hyper accumulation) in willow (*Salix* spp.), a primary food plant for these birds (Larison et al. 2000). Cadmium residues in vertebrate kidney or liver that are >10 ppm fresh weight or 2 ppm whole body fresh weight should be viewed as evidence of probable cadmium toxicity; residues of 200 ppm kidney (fresh weight), or >5 ppm whole animal fresh weight are indicative of cadmium poisoning. Wildlife, especially migratory birds, which feed on crops growing in fields fertilized with municipal sewage sludge, may be at considerable risk from cadmium toxicity (Eisler 1985*a*).

Chromium.—Major environmental sources of chromium include production of stainless steel (ferrochrome) which includes electroplating and metal finishing industries, pigments (paint, ink), tanning leather, wood preservatives, coal-fired power plants, municipal incinerators and publicly owned treatment plants, cement-producing plants, and from anticorrosives in cooling systems and boilers. Chromium is most frequently found in the environment as trivalent (Cr^{+3}) and hexavalent (Cr^{+6}) forms. The biological effects of chromium (Cr^{+6}) is thought to be related to reduction to Cr^{+3} and formation of complexes with intracellular macromolecules that, if it occurs in genetic material, leads to mutagenesis. Chromium (Cr^{+6}) is toxic to embryos, teratogenic, and causes alterations of blood and serum chemistry, liver and kidney lesions (including acute renal tubular necrosis), and ulcerations in mucous membranes. In wildlife, tissue levels in excess of 4.0 mg total chromium/kg dry weight is presumptive evidence of an environmental chromium problem, although the significance of tissue chromium residues is not known. Chromium is readily bioaccumulated in wildlife, but concentrations are usually highest at the lower trophic levels and it is not known to be biomagnified in food chains (Eisler 1986*a*). Wildlife mortality/morbidity as a result of chromium exposure generally is infrequent (Eisler 1986*a*).

Arsenic.—Major environmental sources of arsenic include copper, zinc, and lead mining and smelting; glass and chemical manufacturing, particularly wood preservatives and arsenic-based herbicides; and coal-fired power plants. There are many different arsenic compounds and their environmental chemistry is quite complex, but trivalent (As^{+3}) and pentavalent (As^{+5}) forms predominate and both organic and inorganic forms are common. Arsenic is a teratogen and can traverse placental barriers and produce fetal death and malformations in wildlife (Eisler 1988*a*). It is highly cytotoxic, affecting mitochondrial enzymes and impairing tissue respiration. Chronic exposure leads to neurotoxicity of peripheral and central nervous systems, liver damage, and peripheral vascular disease (Eisler 1988*a*). Arsenic is bioaccumulated by wildlife but is not biomagnified in food chains. Despite its high toxicity, wildlife mortality/morbidity as a result of arsenic exposure generally is infrequent (Eisler 1988*a*).

Organic/Inorganic Chemicals

Organic Chemicals

Organic chemicals are based on carbon–hydrogen pairs that range from single carbon chains to multiple aromatic rings. Organic chemicals can be released from refineries, oil/gas spills, incinerators, sewage effluent, wood treating, chemical plants, military sites, and other industrial sites. Many pesticides are organic chemicals; pesticides are treated separately and this section pertains only to nonpesticide organic chemicals. Generally, organic chemicals are more hazardous to wildlife than are inorganic chemicals. A number of organic chemicals are of concern to wildlife including organic solvents, petroleum products, polychlorinated biphenyls (PCBs), dioxins, and furans.

Solvents.—Organic solvents generally are refined from petroleum and are used to dissolve, dilute, or disperse other chemicals (including pesticides) that are not soluble in water. They are used widely as degreasers and as constituents of paints, varnishes, lacquers, inks, aerosol sprays, dyes, and adhesives. They are also used as intermediates in chemical synthesis and as fuels and fuel additives. Organic solvents include widely-used chemicals such as chlorinated hydrocarbons (e.g., trichloroethylene, perchloroethylene, methylene chloride, carbon tetrachloride); aromatic hydrocarbons (e.g., benzene, toluene, xylene, styrene, ethylbenzene); alcohols (e.g., ethanol, methanol); aldehydes (e.g., formaldehyde); ketones (e.g., acetone); glycols (e.g., ethylene glycol, propylene glycol); glycol ethers; phenols (e.g., phenol, chlorophenol); carbon disulfide; and fuel and fuel additives (e.g., gasoline, methyl tertiary-butyl ether [MTBE], jet fuel, kerosene). Because of their widespread use, organic solvents are ubiquitous in the environment (Bruckner and Warren 2001). Generally highly lipophilic, extremely volatile, and of relatively small molecular size and lacking charge, organic solvents are rapidly absorbed across lungs, gastrointestinal tract, and skin. The most notable negative effect of this group is central nervous system depression (Bruckner and Warren 2001). Other negative effects include carcinogenesis and damage to the hematopoietic system (bone marrow), liver, and kidney (Bruckner and Warren 2001). Organic solvents tend to readily bioaccumulate but are not known to biomagnify through food chains.

Ethylene Glycol.—A major ingredient in antifreeze and de-icing solutions, ethylene glycol is responsible for numerous wildlife deaths in the United States and Canada each year (U.S. Environmental Protection Agency 1998*a*). It is an oily liquid with a mild odor and a sweet taste, which makes it attractive to wildlife. Puddles of antifreeze or brake fluid can accumulate on roads or parking lots, and their color and smell attracts many wildlife species. The vast majority of ethylene glycol is released directly into the environment as airport and runway runoff from de-icing activities. An annual release of over 26 million kg of ethylene glycol occurs during icing conditions at the 17

busiest airports in the United States (U.S. Environmental Protection Agency 1998*a*). Ethylene glycol is also used in polyester compounds and as a solvent in the paint and plastics industries, photographic developing solutions, hydraulic brake fluids, and inks.

Wildlife poisoned by ethylene glycol appear intoxicated; signs including depression, ataxia, and reluctance to move appear as soon as 2 to 4 hours following exposure (Stowe et al. 1981). Ethylene glycol metabolizes to oxalic acid and binds to calcium to form calcium oxalate crystals that block renal tubules with death resulting from acute kidney failure (MacNeill and Barnard 1978, Stowe et al. 1981). Kidneys should be collected from carcasses if ethylene glycol poisoning is suspected. Canids and felids are particularly susceptible to ethylene glycol; as little as 4–5 ml/kg is lethal to domestic dogs and 2–4 ml/kg is lethal to domestic cats (Osweiler et al. 1985). Waterfowl, vultures, and birds of the Family Corvidae (jays, crows, ravens, magpies) occasionally are victims of ethylene glycol poisoning. There is at least one record each of a California condor (Murnane et al.1995) and a polar bear (*Ursus maritimus*) (Amstrup et al. 1989) being lethally poisoned by ethylene glycol.

Petroleum Products.—Petroleum products, including crude oil, diesel, gasoline, kerosene, and others are ubiquitous in the environment. Every year, an average of 53 million liters of oil from more than 10,000 accidental spills flow into fresh and saltwater environments in the United States (Friend and Franson 1999). However, accidental releases account for a small fraction of all oil entering the environment; most oil is introduced through intentional discharges from normal transport and refining operations, industrial and municipal discharges, used lubricant and other waste oil disposal, urban runoff, river runoff, atmospheric deposition, and natural seeps (Eisler 1987*b*, Jessup and Leighton 1996, Albers 2003). Wildlife exposed to petroleum products can be impacted both externally and internally. Oil contamination of hair and feathers disrupts their normal structure and function, resulting in a loss of insulation and waterproofing (Eisler 1987*b*). Birds and mammals can also ingest, inhale, and absorb petroleum products when exposed during spill events while preening/grooming contaminated feathers/hair. In birds, hatching success is reduced when adults are exposed to fuel oil during incubation and transfer oil to their eggs (Jessup and Leighton 1996).

Polycyclic aromatic hydrocarbons contribute heavily to the toxicity of crude and refined petroleum products, but amounts of these compounds in petroleum products vary widely. Polycyclic aromatic hydrocarbons are semivolatile, and occur in the environment from many sources in addition to the petrochemical industry, including from natural sources. Lower molecular weight polycyclic aromatic hydrocarbons exhibit significant acute toxicity and other adverse effects to wildlife but are not carcinogenic. However, high molecular weight polycyclic aromatic hydrocarbons usually are less acutely toxic, but may be carcinogenic, mutagenic, or teratogenic to a wide variety of wildlife (Eisler 1987*b*). Polycyclic aromatic hydrocarbons, although highly lipid soluble, generally are rapidly metabolized and tend not to bioaccumulate in wildlife; there is little evidence for biomagnification in food chains. Polycyclic aromatic hydrocarbons such as benzo(a)pyrene, naphthalene, anthracene, styrene, and others have been investigated for wildlife impacts (Eisler 1987*b*). There are no specific regulations regarding the protection of wildlife species from polycyclic aromatic hydrocarbons other than laws governing petroleum products (Eisler 1987*b*). There is little evidence to indicate that polycyclic aromatic hydrocarbons are likely to produce large numbers of wildlife deaths or sicknesses except when associated with oil spills.

Polychlorinated Biphenyls.—Polychlorinated biphenyls (PCBs) were introduced in 1929 for use in dielectric (insulating) fluids. They were used extensively in the electricity generating industry as insulating or cooling agents in transformers and capacitors. Although their manufacture was banned by the U.S. Environmental Protection Agency in 1977, products containing PCBs made prior to that date can still be found. PCBs are still released from hazardous waste sites, illegal or improper disposal of industrial wastes and consumer products, leaks from old electrical transformers, burning of some wastes in incinerators, and aquatic sediments (Eisler 1986*c*, Eisler and Belisle 1996). The estimated environmental burden of PCBs from these sources is almost 400 million kg (Tanabe 1988, Eisler and Belisle 1996). PCBs bind strongly to organic particles in soil and sediment-forming PCB sinks where local concentrations can be high. PCBs are transported globally through atmospheric and oceanic processes. There are 209 different PCB congeners (forms), but only 100–150 are represented in PCB formulations (Eisler 1986*a*, Rice et al. 2003).

Some PCB congeners are of greater environmental concern than others. In general, PCB congeners with high K_{ow} (a physical characteristic of a chemical correlated with lipid solubility) values and high numbers of substituted chlorines in adjacent positions constitute the greatest environmental threat to wildlife. This includes planar PCBs, a group of about 20 PCB congeners that closely resemble dioxins (Eisler and Belisle 1996, Rice et al. 2003). PCBs cause a wide variety of biological effects including death, developmental abnormalities, reproductive failure, liver damage, tumors, and a wasting syndrome (Eisler and Belisle 1996). Effects on reproduction, endocrine and immune systems, and behavior may have the greatest impacts on wildlife populations. Mink (*Mustela vison*) are one of the most susceptible species to PCBs and dietary levels as low as 100 µg PCBs/kg fresh weight cause reproductive failure and death (Aulerich and Ringer 1977, Aulerich et al. 1987). Signs of PCB toxicity in mink include anorexia; bloody stools; disrupted molting patterns; and thickened, elongated, and deformed nails (Aulerich and Ringer 1977). In birds, total PCB levels (µg/kg fresh weight) of 3,000 in the diet, 16,000 in the egg, or 54,000 in the brain were associated with PCB poisoning (Eisler 1986*c*). PCBs have been shown to have severe effects on avian reproduction, mainly decreased productivity and hatching success (embryo mortality), and abnormal breeding behavior (Eisler 1986*c*, Eisler and Belisle 1996, Rice et al. 2003).

PCBs are highly lipid soluble and readily bioaccumulated in wildlife and biomagnified in both aquatic and terrestrial food chains. Some wildlife species such as long-lived fishes and common snapping turtles (*Chelydra serpentina*) can bioaccumulate and store high levels of PCBs in their tissues posing a potential hazard for predators, particularly avian piscivores (Eisler 1986*c*, Eisler and Belisle 1996). While much of the environmental burden of PCBs is localized, PCBs continue to represent a considerable hazard to exposed wildlife species (Eisler 1986*c*, Tanabe 1988, Rice et al. 2003). However, continuing impacts of PCBs on wildlife are likely to be related to reproductive impairment and other sublethal effects. Mortality from chronic exposure is unlikely except in sensitive species with high risk feeding habits (e.g., piscivores) (Eisler and Belisle 1996).

Dioxins and Furans.—Dioxins and furans have no commercial use and are released into the environment as contaminants from combustion, incineration, synthesis of phenoxy herbicides and wood preservatives, and industrial and municipal processes such as paper manufacturing (Bradbury 1996, Rice et al. 2003). There are approximately 75 different forms of dioxins with tetrachlorodibenzo-p-dioxin (2,3,7,8-TCDD) being most prevalent in the environment and of most concern to wildlife. There are approximately 135 different forms of furans. Most dioxins and furans are resistant to environmental and biologic degradation and, once formed, disperse throughout the atmosphere, soil, and water. Environmental dioxins and furans have resulted in deaths of many wildlife species and domestic animals (Bradbury 1996, Rice et al. 2003).

Exposure to dioxins and furans can result in a wide range of negative effects, from acute and delayed mortality to teratogenic, histopathological, immunological, and reproductive effects (Rice et al. 2003). Exposure to even minute quantities of 2,3,7,8-TCDD has been shown to result in reproductive failure in mink (Hochstein et al. 1988), wood ducks (*Aix sponsa*) (White and Seginak 1994) and ring-necked pheasants (*Phasianus colchicus*) (Nosek et al. 1992). Signs of dioxin toxicity include a "wasting syndrome," subcutaneous edema, alterations in lipid metabolism and gluconeogenesis, reproductive effects (teratogenicity, fetotoxicity), decreased immunocompetence, and thymic atrophy (Bradbury 1996). As with PCBs, dioxins and furans are highly lipid soluble and readily bioaccumulated in wildlife and biomagnified in both aquatic and terrestrial food chains. Wildlife that bioaccumulate and store high levels of dioxins and furans in their tissues pose a potential hazard for predators, particularly avian and mammalian piscivores. It is recommended that 2,3,7,8-TCDD concentrations in water should not exceed 0.01 ppt (parts per trillion) to protect aquatic wildlife species or 10–12 ppt in food of terrestrial wildlife (Eisler 1986*b*). Currently, there are no regulations governing dioxins and furans to protect wildlife (Eisler 1986*b*, Eisler and Belisle 1996).

Inorganic Chemicals

Inorganic chemicals are a diverse group that includes those that do not have carbon and its derivatives as their principal elements. This includes 4 general groups: alkalis and chlorine, industrial gases, inorganic pigments, and industrial inorganic chemicals. Examples of industrial inorganic chemicals include acids; bases; metallic compounds; catalysts; ammonia; and salts derived from sodium, phosphorus, potassium, and sulfur. Inorganic chemicals generally are disposed in hazardous waste streams and do not pose a great threat to wildlife. However, some chemicals are used in processes such as mining and military activities and can leak or spill from storage where they can occur in large volumes in the environment and pose substantial hazards to wildlife. Two inorganic chemicals that pose a particular hazard to wildlife include cyanide and white phosphorus.

Cyanide.—Cyanides are highly toxic chemicals widely used in mining and other industrial processes. Cyanide levels tend to be elevated in the vicinity of metal processing operations, electroplaters, gold-mining facilities, oil refineries, power plants, and solid waste combustion facilities (Eisler 1991). The most common form of cyanide is hydrocyanic acid, which is used in electroplating and for fumigation. Other chemical forms include sodium cyanide, used in extracting precious metals from raw ore and for predator control (M-44 ejector device), potassium cyanide, and calcium cyanide. Cyanides are readily absorbed through oral, dermal, and inhalation routes and are distributed throughout the body via the blood. Cyanide is a potent and rapid-acting asphyxiant, inducing tissue anoxia through inactivation of cytochrome oxidase causing cytotoxic hypoxia (lack of oxygen) in the presence of normal hemoglobin oxygenation. Diagnosis of acute lethal cyanide poisoning is difficult because symptoms are nonspecific and numerous factors modify its toxicity. The most consistent changes in acute cyanide poisoning are inhibition of brain cytochrome oxidase activity and changes in electrical activity in heart and brain.

Birds, mammals, and other wildlife in the vicinity of gold mining operations are particularly prone to cyanide exposure. Cyanide associated with gold mining activities in Nevada leached into nearby ponds and killed large numbers of migratory birds (Henny et al. 1994) and mammals (Clark and Hothem 1991). In a sampling of Nevada mines, more than 90 avian species (mainly waterfowl, shorebirds, and passerines), 28 mammalian species (mainly rodents, bats, and lagomorphs), and several reptilian and amphibian species were reported poisoned by cyanide solution ponds between 1986 and 1991 (Henny et al. 1994). For birds and bats, most mortality incidents associated with exposure to cyanide at mining operations are reported in spring and fall during migration (Clark 1991, Clark and Hothem 1991, Henny et al. 1994). Eisler et al. (1999) reviewed the specific environmental hazard for wildlife species at gold mining operations. In addition to mining, cyanide is used in M-44 predator control devices mainly in the western United States where mammalian (mainly coyotes [*Canis latrans*]) and avian (mainly golden eagles) predators are subject to cyanide poisoning. From 1986 through 1995, more than 3,000 cyanide-related mortalities involving about 75 species of birds representing 23 Families were reported to the National Wildlife Health Center in Madison, Wisconsin. Waterbirds and passerines were the 2 groups of birds most impacted by cyanide.

White Phosphorus.—White phosphorus (P_4) is a highly toxic, incendiary munition extensively used by the military for marking artillery impacts (target practice) and as an obscurant. Areas in and around active (and inactive) military artillery and bombing ranges can concentrate white phosphorus which can runoff into surface waters and move to areas away from military ranges. White phosphorus caused the death of an estimated 1,000 to 2,000 migrating dabbling ducks (*Anas* spp.) and 10 to 50 swans (*Cygnus buccinator* and *C. columbianus*) per year in the late 1980s and early 1990s at Eagle River Flats, a 1,000 ha estuarine salt marsh at Fort Richardson, Alaska used for artillery training by the U.S. Army (Racine et al. 1992, Sparling 2003). Signs of white phosphorus poisoning observed in wild waterfowl include lethargy, repeated drinking, and head shaking and rolling with convulsions prior to death (Racine et al. 1992). While no direct mortality of predators at Eagle River Flats was found, secondary exposure and poisoning of predators and scavengers such as bald eagles, herring gulls (*Larus argentatus*), and common ravens (*Corvus corax*) was noted (Roebuck et al. 1994). White phosphorus has been shown to cause significant changes in a wide range of blood parameters in mallards (*Anas platyrhynchos*) (Sparling et al. 1998) and mute swans (*Cygnus olor*) (Sparling et al. 1999), and to cause secondary poisoning in American kestrels (*Falco sparverius*) (Sparling and Federoff 1997).

Pharmaceuticals

There is a wide diversity of pharmaceutical drugs, hormones, and other related organic wastewater contaminants present in waterways of the United States that pose a potential hazard to wildlife. In 1999–2000, a U.S. Geological Survey monitoring effort found 82 of 95 different pharmaceutical drugs tested for in water samples from a network of 139 streams across 30 states (Kolpin et al. 2002). A wide range of residential, industrial, and agricultural drugs and chemicals was found in 80% of all streams tested. Little is known about the potential impact of these drugs/chemicals on wildlife, particularly the potential interactive effects that may occur from complex mixtures of these and other chemicals in the environment. Numerous wildlife mortality/morbidity incidents occurring from widely used pharmaceutical drugs such as sodium pentobarbital and diclofenac provide evidence of the hazard posed by this group of chemicals.

Sodium Pentobarbital.—Sodium pentobarbital and related barbiturates are used extensively in veterinary medicine, especially for euthanasia of domestic animals, and result in the deaths of numerous wildlife species across the United States and Canada each year (Friend and Franson 1999). The use of highly concentrated solutions for euthanasia of domestic animals (e.g., cats, dogs, horses, etc.) is routine practice in veterinary medicine. Carcasses that are not incinerated or otherwise properly disposed are subject to scavenging by wildlife, which can result in exposure to this family of chemicals. Any wildlife species that scavenges food potentially is at risk from these chemicals. Mortality of wildlife from bald and golden eagles to grizzly bears (*Ursus arctos*) has been reported from landfills and other improper burial sites where animal carcasses were either left in the open or not disposed of properly. In recent years, the National Wildlife Health Center in Madison, Wisconsin and the National Fish and Wildlife Forensic Laboratory in Ashland, Oregon had verifiable reports of at least 133 eagle deaths resulting from secondary pentobarbital poisoning, most likely only a fraction of the real total.

Diclofenac.—Diclofenac is a nonsteroidal, anti-inflammatory drug used extensively in veterinary medicine and is administered to livestock and other domestic animals for pain and arthritis in many countries around the world. Diclofenac was identified as the most likely cause of a mass mortality of 3 species of vultures in Pakistan (Oaks et al. 2004). Vultures consuming dead livestock containing diclofenac were exposed to high levels of the drug in livestock tissues. Necropsies revealed that exposed animals had visceral gout and histopathological lesions including acute renal tubular necrosis and uric acid crystal formation in the kidneys and other tissues, which led to acute kidney failure and death. Populations of the 3 species of vultures, Oriental white-backed vulture (*Gyps bengalensis*), long-billed vulture (*G. indicus*), and slender-billed vulture (*G. tenuirostris*) were decimated by as much as 95% in some cases (Oaks et al. 2004). Although this incident occurred in Asia, it clearly demonstrates the potential hazard of pharmaceutical drugs to wildlife.

Pesticides

A pesticide is any substance or mixture of substances intended for preventing, destroying, repelling, or mitigating any pest. The term pesticide is a generic name for a variety of agents classified more specifically on the basis of the pattern of use and organism killed. Pesticides include chemicals designed to kill specific groups of organisms, such as insecticides, herbicides, fungicides, rodenticides, miticides, acaricides, larvicides, and molluscicides. They also function as attractants (pheromones), defoliants, desiccants, plant growth regulators, repellents, and fumigants for purposes of reducing numbers of pest species.

Pesticides are a unique category of environmental contaminants as they are intentionally released into the environment. Thus, regulations for monitoring pesticide usage and the likelihood of detecting pesticide-related mortality events are enhanced. Insecticides are among the most acutely toxic contaminants in the environment and can produce dramatic mortality and morbidity incidents. Target species selectivity of pesticides is not well developed and nontarget species frequently are affected because they possess physiological and/or biochemical systems similar to those of the target organisms. Specific classes of pesticides of major concern to wildlife include insecticides, herbicides, fungicides, fumigants, and vertebrate pest control chemicals such as rodenticides and avicides.

Insecticides

Most chemical insecticides in use today are neurotoxicants and act by poisoning the nervous system of the target organisms. The central nervous system of insects is highly developed and not unlike that of the vertebrate central nervous system. Generally, insecticides are not selective and affect nontarget as readily as target organisms. Target sites and/or mechanism(s) of action may be similar in all species; only the level of exposure (dosage and duration of contact with toxic receptors) affects the intensity of biological effects. Four distinct groups of insecticides, including chlorinated hydrocarbons, anticholinesterases (organophosphorus and carbamate), synthetic pyrethroids, and other botanicals are discussed as they pose a significant threat to wildlife.

Chlorinated Hydrocarbons.—Chlorinated hydrocarbon (organochlorine) insecticides are a diverse group belonging to 3 distinct chemical classes: dichlorodiphenylethanes (e.g., DDT, dicofol, methoxychlor), cyclodienes (e.g., heptachlor, dieldrin, aldrin), and chlorinated benzenes (e.g., lindane) (Smith 1991, Blus et al. 1996, Blus 2003). DDT was used extensively in all aspects of agriculture and forestry, in building and structural protection, and in human health situations from the mid-1940s to the early 1970s. The chemical properties of chlorinated hydrocarbon insecticides (e.g., low volatility, chemical stability, lipid solubility, slow rate of biotransformation and degradation) that made them effective brought about their demise due to per-

sistence in the environment and bioaccumulation and biomagnification within food chains. Registration for DDT was cancelled in the United States and several other countries in 1972, and cancellation/restriction of registration for other chlorinated hydrocarbon insecticides followed. Despite the ban on their use in North America and Europe, chlorinated hydrocarbon insecticides are used extensively in developing countries. This occurs because they are inexpensive to manufacture, highly effective, relatively safe, few substitutes are available, and the risk-benefit ratio is highly weighted in favor of their continued use for control of insects causing devastation to crops and human health (Smith 1991, Blus et al. 1996, Blus 2003). The ramifications of continued heavy use of chlorinated hydrocarbons are that they become airborne and are transported globally in the atmosphere with deposition occurring on a global basis, particularly at high latitudes (Bidleman et al. 1990).

Definitive studies both in wildlife and laboratory species have demonstrated potent estrogenic and enzyme-inducing properties of chlorinated hydrocarbon insecticides, which interfere directly or indirectly with fertility and reproduction in wildlife. In avian species, this interference due to DDE exposure is related to steroid metabolism and the inability of the bird to mobilize calcium to produce sufficiently strong eggshells to withstand incubation (cracking allows bacteria to enter and kill developing embryos) (Blus et al. 1996, Blus 2003).

Chlorinated hydrocarbons act as diffuse stimulants or depressants of the central nervous system. Signs of acute toxicity occur within minutes to a few days following exposure, usually within 24 hours, may be progressively severe in nature, and can include muscle spasms, seizures, loss of coordination, abnormal walking/posturing, and excess salivation (Osweiler et al. 1985). Exposed animals may become comatose and remain so for several hours prior to death or may regain consciousness and fully recover. Pathologic changes associated with acute poisoning by chlorinated hydrocarbons usually are minimal and nonspecific, and include pulmonary congestion, hemorrhages, and edema, particularly in the central nervous system (Osweiler et al. 1985). Chronic exposure to chlorinated hydrocarbons results in alteration of hepatocytes (liver cells) (Osweiler et al. 1985).

The highly lipid-soluble nature of chlorinated hydrocarbon insecticides results in crossing of the normally protective placental and blood-brain barriers in mammals, leading to direct embryonic/fetal and central nervous system exposure. It also results in these chemicals being sequestered in body tissues (liver, kidney, nervous system, and fat tissue) having a high lipid content where the residues either elicit some biological effect or, as in the case of adipose tissue, remain stored and undisturbed until mobilized. Elimination rate and depletion of body storage sites may be enhanced by fasting resulting in mobilization of fat depots and any insecticide contained therein. However, with a high-chlorinated hydrocarbon body burden, there is a possibility of enhanced toxicity from the circulating agent being redistributed to target organs. The most serious effects, such as mortality, reduced reproductive success, population decline, and even extirpation occurred in birds, particularly raptors, seabirds, and waterbirds in the orders Strigiformes, Falconiformes, Pelecaniformes, Ciconiformes, and Podicipediformes (Blus et al. 1996, Blus 2003).

Anticholinesterases.—Organophosphorus and carbamate insecticides are commonly grouped together and referred to as anticholinesterases (anti-ChE's) (Mineau 1991, Hill 2003). These insecticides have a common mechanism of action, inhibition of the neurotransmitting enzyme cholinesterase (Baron 1991, Gallo and Lawryk 1991). However, they arise from 2 distinctly different chemical classes: the esters of phosphoric or phosphorothioic acid and those of carbamic acid. Currently, there are some 200 different organophosphorus and about 50 carbamate pesticides (mainly insecticides) on the market, formulated into thousands of different products (Hill 2003). Anti-ChE insecticides are applied mainly on terrestrial landscapes but are also used extensively in wetlands and coastal areas for mosquito control. The mechanism by which these insecticides elicit toxicity is identical and is associated with inhibition of the neurotransmitting enzyme acetylcholinesterase. This enzyme is responsible for the destruction and termination of the biological activity of the neurotransmitter acetylcholine. With accumulation of free, unbound acetylcholine at nerve endings of all cholinergic nerves, there is continual stimulation of electrical activity. Following lethal exposure, death results from acute respiratory failure (Hill 2003).

Organophosphorus and carbamate insecticide intoxication has become more complicated in recent years with recognition of additional and persistent signs of neurotoxicity not previously associated with acute exposure to these chemicals. One condition, an "intermediate syndrome," is a potentially lethal paralytic condition of the neck, limbs, and respiratory muscles. The other condition, where neuropathic conditions persist indefinitely, is referred to as organophosphorus-induced delayed neuropathy (Ecobichon 2001, Hill 2003).

Most widely used anti-ChE insecticides are highly toxic but relatively short-lived in the environment (usually 2–4 weeks) and are readily metabolized and excreted by birds and mammals (Hill 2003). Carbamates are direct cholinesterase inhibitors that do not require metabolic activation for full potency. Many organophosphorus insecticides are known to become more toxic as a result of metabolism (e.g., chlorpyrifos, diazinon, parathion, etc.) because the metabolites (the "oxon" form) are more potent inhibitors of cholinesterase (Matsumura 1985, Smith 1987). Thus, there may be some delayed toxicity (and onset of signs) associated with organophosphorus insecticide poisoning. Dietary toxicity experiments have shown that birds that die from carbamate insecticide poisoning do so within a few hours of exposure but mortality from organophosphorus insecticide poisoning may extend over 5 days (Hill 2003).

Organophosphorus and carbamate insecticides are responsible for more reported wildlife mortality/morbidity incidents than any other category of environmental contaminant. However, only a relatively small number of these pesticides are responsible for the majority of large-scale incidents of wildlife mortality/morbidity. Birds are highly sensitive to most organophosphorus and carbamate insecticides, and are particularly susceptible to granular formulations. As few as one granule (0.1–5 mg/kg) of some anti-ChE insecticides such as carbofuran may be lethal in <5 minutes to waterfowl and songbirds (Hill 2003). Extensive records of bird mortality/morbidity from exposure to organophosphorus and carbamate insecticides exist (Smith

1987, Sheffield 1997, Friend and Franson 1999, Mineau et al. 1999). One of the most notable mass mortalities in recent years involved the death of upwards of 10,000 or more Swainson's hawks (*Buteo swainsoni*) on their wintering grounds in the pampas of Argentina in the mid-1990s (Goldstein et al. 1996, Goldstein et al. 1999). In this case, hawks were poisoned through consumption of grasshoppers and other prey items in alfalfa fields sprayed with the organophosphorus insecticide monocrotophos. Although mammals generally are less sensitive than birds to organophosphorus and carbamate insecticides, many mammalian mortality incidents have also been reported (Smith 1987). Intensive field research with mammalian exposure to organophosphorus insecticides has documented reproductive and other sublethal effects at environmentally relevant levels (Sheffield and Lochmiller 2001, Sheffield et al. 2001).

Signs of acute exposure to anti-ChE insecticides include lethargy, excess salivation, lacrimation, urination, and defecation; vomiting may occur along with muscle fasciculation (brief spontaneous contractions of a few muscle fibers) and weakness, dyspnea (difficulty breathing), excessive bronchial secretion, and bradycardia (slowed heart rate) (Fairbrother 1996). In severe cases, prostration and convulsions precede death. These signs are useful when sick animals are found on or near an area of recent anticholinesterase insecticide application. However, these signs are not uniquely different from poisoning by other neurotoxic chemicals. Inhibition of brain cholinesterase activity by 20% (i.e., activity at 80% of normal) is considered diagnostic of sublethal poisoning and dead birds with a >50% reduction in activity generally is diagnostic of anti-ChE poisoning. Activity reductions of 70–95% are commonly reported for birds killed by organophosphorus insecticides (Hill and Fleming 1982, Hill 2003). Conclusive diagnosis depends on biochemical and chemical analyses for brain cholinesterase activity and organophosphorus residues in the carcass (Hill 1999, Hill 2003).

A wide diversity of sublethal effects has been documented to occur following exposure to anticholinesterase insecticides, including biochemical, physiological, behavioral, and others that impact survival and fitness of exposed animals (Mineau 1991, Hill 1999, Hill 2003). Many of these effects may be lethal, but may also mask pesticide exposure as the cause of mortality. For example, a group of exposed animals that has become disoriented and less vigilant may become more susceptible to predation or other mortality factors.

Anti-ChE insecticides generally do not bioaccumulate in organisms and do not biomagnify in food chains (Hill 2003). However, prey items such as arthropods and animal carcasses can contain sufficiently high levels of anticholinesterase insecticides to cause secondary poisoning in predatory and scavenging birds (particularly raptors) and mammals (Sheffield, 1997, Mineau et al. 1999, Shore and Rattner 2001). Bald eagles and red-tailed hawks in British Columbia were found poisoned by consuming unabsorbed pesticide in the stomachs of dead animals up to 6 months following its application (Elliott et al. 1996).

Synthetic Pyrethroids.—Synthetic pyrethroids are the newest major class of insecticides, entering the market in 1980. By 1982, they accounted for about 30% of the worldwide insecticide usage. These synthetics arise from a much older class of botanical insecticides, pyrethrum, which is a mixture of 6 insecticide esters extracted from dried pyrethrum or *Chrysanthemum* flowers (Ray 1991). The increasing demand for pyrethrum has exceeded the limited world production. This led chemists to focus attention on synthesis of new analogs with better stability in light and air, better persistence, more selectivity to target species, and low mammalian and avian toxicity. In addition to extensive agricultural use, synthetic pyrethroids are components of household sprays, flea dips and sprays, and plant sprays for home and greenhouse use. Studies on intact animals have not yielded conclusive, fundamental information concerning the mechanism of action of pyrethroids (Ray 1991, Ecobichon 2001).

Synthetic pyrethroids alter sodium channels in nerve membranes, causing repetitive (sensory, motor) neuronal discharge and a prolonged negative after-potential with the effects being similar to those produced by DDT. Other impacts noted for synthetic pyrethroids include inhibition of Ca- and Mg-ATPase, the effect of which would increase intracellular calcium levels accompanied by increased neurotransmitter release and post-synaptic depolarization (Matsumura 1985, Ray 1991).

There have been relatively few reports of wildlife mortality/morbidity as a result of synthetic pyrethroid exposure and little is known about their sublethal effects on wildlife. The available evidence suggests that synthetic pyrethroids elicit little chronic toxicity to wildlife. In addition, there is little storage or bioaccumulation of pyrethroids because they are readily biotransformed by the mixed-function oxidase system. However, piperonyl butoxide (an inhibitor of cytochrome P-450s which is an important family of detoxification enzymes) is a synergist added to many synthetic pyrethroid formulations for increased toxicity (10- to 300-fold increase in toxicity) (Ray 1991, Ecobichon 2001).

Other Botanical Insecticides.—Nicotine and rotenone are among the more widely used botanical insecticides. These compounds are natural plant alkaloids whose toxic properties have been recognized for hundreds of years (Ray 1991). Nicotine usually is obtained from the dried leaves of the tobacco plant (*Nicotiana tabacum*) and rotenone is derived from the roots of the derris (*Derris* spp.) (South America) and Cubé (*Lonchocarpus* spp.) (southeast Asia) plants. Used as an insecticide and piscicide, rotenone is extremely toxic to aquatic vertebrates, particularly fishes. Because use of rotenone as a piscicide is so widespread, there is concern about the potential negative effects of rotenone on amphibian (frogs, salamanders) and aquatic reptile (turtles, snakes) species, particularly neotenic salamanders that use aquatic respiration (Fontenot et al. 1994). The most frequent signs of rotenone poisoning in wildlife include vomiting, anorexia, dermatitis, irritation of the gastrointestinal tract, and lack of coordination, muscle tremors, and convulsions with death occurring through respiratory failure (Osweiler et al. 1985).

Herbicides

Herbicides are any compound capable of either killing or severely injuring plants and may be used for elimination of plant growth or killing of plant parts. Many of the early herbicides contained forms of arsenic and were difficult to handle, highly toxic, relatively nonspecific, or phytotoxic

to crops as well as undesirable plants. However, currently used herbicides generally have a much lower hazard to wildlife than those used earlier and are more likely to result in sublethal effects rather than cause wildlife mortality/morbidity (Stevens and Sumner 1991).

Over the past 2 decades, herbicides have represented the most rapidly growing section of the agrochemical pesticide business due in part to (1) monoculture practices where risk of weed infestation has increased because fallowing and crop rotation are no longer standard practices, and (2) mechanization of agricultural practices (planting, cultivating, harvesting) due to increased labor costs. The result has been a plethora of chemically diverse compounds rivaling the innovative chemistry of insecticides. The goal of herbicide application has been to protect desirable crops and obtain high yields by selectively eliminating unwanted plant species, thereby reducing competition for nutrients, water, and space (Stevens and Sumner 1991).

There are at least 6 different broad classes and 22 or more different chemical groups of herbicides, including: (1) germination inhibitors such as dinitroanilines (e.g., trifluralin) and chloroacetamides (e.g., alachlor, metolachlor); (2) photosynthesis inhibitors such as triazines (e.g., atrazine, simazine, metribuzin); (3) meristem inhibitors such as sulfonylureas (e.g., chlorsulfuron) and imidazolinones (e.g., imazethapyr, imazapyr); (4) contact action such as bipyridylium (e.g., paraquat, diquat) and arsenicals (e.g., MSMA); (5) auxin growth regulators such as phenoxy acids (e.g., 2, 4-D); and (6) foliar grass killers such as phosphono-amino acids (e.g., glyphosate).

Herbicide classification is based on how and when they are applied. Preplanting herbicides are applied to the soil before a crop is seeded, pre-emergent herbicides are applied to the soil before the usual time of appearance of the unwanted vegetation, and post-emergent herbicides are applied to the soil or foliage after germination of the crop and/or weeds.

The chlorphenoxy (e.g., 2, 4-D; 2, 4, 5-T) and bipyridyl (e.g., paraquat, diquat) herbicides are acutely toxic to wildlife and humans. Paraquat is a contact herbicide and one of the most specific pulmonary toxicants known. Many countries have banned or severely restricted use of these herbicides (Ecobichon 2001). Another group, the triazines, although considered less acutely toxic, are of concern for wildlife due to their widespread and high volume use. There is also evidence of sublethal effects such as endocrine disruption, with subsequent impacts on reproduction and development (Hayes et al. 2003).

Herbicides show a broad range of persistence (Stevens and Sumner 1991). Some, such as paraquat may persist for years while others persist for only days or months. Most herbicides occur either in plants or the soil. Because they are not as persistent as organics such as PCBs or some organochlorine insecticides such as DDT, they tend not to move via the atmosphere to distant locations. However, herbicides such as atrazine and metolachlor with high volume use throughout the midwestern United States can result in high atmospheric concentrations and movement. Most herbicides do not bioaccumulate in animal tissue of any class of animals. Because of the overall limited persistence or tendency to bind to soil particles, there is generally limited movement through the environment. The most frequent signs of herbicide poisoning in wildlife include anorexia, diarrhea, edema, ataxia, inflammation of the gastrointestinal tract, and congestion of the lungs, liver, and kidneys (Osweiler et al. 1985).

Fungicides

Fungicides are derived from a wide variety of chemicals ranging from simple inorganic compounds, such as sulfur and copper sulfate, through the aryl- and alkyl-mercurial compounds and chlorinated phenols to metal-containing derivatives of thiocarbamic acid. There are at least 36 different chemical groups of fungicides, a direct result of the great diversity of fungi (Edwards et al. 1991, Ecobichon 2001).

There are 3 general types of fungicides: (1) foliar, which are applied as liquids or powders to the aerial green parts of plants producing a protective barrier on the cuticular surface and causing systemic toxicity in developing fungus; (2) soil, which are applied as liquids, dry powders, or granules, acting either through the vapor phase or by systemic properties; and (3) dressings, which are applied to seeds prior to planting and to the post-harvest crop (cereal grains, tubers, etc.) as liquids or dry powders to prevent fungal infestation of the seed and crop (particularly if it is stored under less than optimal conditions of temperature and humidity).

Most fungicides have low acute toxicity to mammals and birds. However, all fungicides are cytotoxic and almost all produce positive results in microbial mutagenicity and animal carcinogenicity tests (Ecobichon 2001). Many fungicides are also teratogenic, embryotoxic, and endocrine disruptors (Edwards et al. 1991). Fungicide groups of current environmental concern to wildlife include benzimidazoles (e.g., benomyl, carbendazim, thiabendazole), dithiocarbamates (e.g., maneb, mancozeb, zineb), aromatics (e.g., chlorothalonil), dinitrophenols (e.g., dinocap), and dicarboximides (e.g., captan, vinclozolin) (Ecobichon 2001). Others, that were heavily used in the past but have largely been discontinued in the United States due to the environmental hazard they pose, include the organo-mercurials, hexachlorobenzene, pentachlorophenol, captafol, and folpet (Ecobichon 2001). The most frequent signs of fungicide poisoning in wildlife include anorexia and weight loss, lethargy and depression, impaired liver function, and reproductive impairment (Osweiler et al. 1985).

Fumigants

Fumigants are agents used to kill insects, nematodes, weed seeds, and fungi in soil as well as in stored cereal grains, fruit, and vegetables, clothes, and other products. They are normally used in enclosed spaces due to high volatility of the compounds. Chemicals used as fumigants include acrylonitrile, carbon disulfide, carbon tetrachloride, ethylene dibromide, chloropicrin, methyl bromide, and ethylene oxide. These can be liquids that readily vaporize at ambient temperatures, solids that can release a toxic gas on reacting with water or with acid, or gases. They generally are nonselective, highly reactive, and cytotoxic. Fumigants of environmental concern include phosphine (used heavily in grains), ethylene dibromide, and 1,2-dibromo-3-chloropropane; the latter 2 are known animal carcinogens (Ecobichon 2001).

Vertebrate Pest Control Chemicals

Rodenticides.—Rodenticides were developed to control pest small mammals (particularly rodents), which cause agricultural damage, carry disease, and are considered by some to be nuisance species. Chemicals used as rodenticides constitute a diverse range of compounds having a variety of mechanisms of action, which are partially successful at attaining species selectivity. Design of some rodenticides has taken advantage of unique physiological and biochemical characteristics of rodents. The sites of action are common to most mammals but advantage is taken of the habits of the pest animal and/or dosage minimizing impacts to nontarget species. A number of inorganic compounds, including thallium sulfate, arsenic oxide and other arsenicals, barium carbonate, yellow phosphorus, aluminum phosphide, and zinc phosphide have been used as rodenticides. A number of insecticides have been used as rodenticides, including DDT. In addition, a number of natural plant toxins, such as strychnine, red squill, ricin, and sodium monofluoroacetate (Ray 1991, Eisler 1995), have been used as rodenticides or to control other mammalian species. Sodium monofluoroacetate (compound 1080) has been used extensively in prepared baits to control rodents and predators, particularly coyotes. Most mammals are fatally poisoned by <1 mg/kg body weight of sodium monofluoroacetate (Eisler 1995). Domestic sheep have experienced toxic effects from wearing compound 1080-impregnated livestock protection collars (Burns and Connelly 1995).

Currently, anticoagulants are the most significant class of rodenticides in terms of wildlife mortality/morbidity incidents. The basis of efficacy of anticoagulant rodenticides is coumadin (warfarin), which was isolated from spoiled sweet clover (*Melilotus* spp.) and acted as an anticoagulant by antagonizing the actions of vitamin K in the synthesis of clotting factors. Warfarin has been in use since the 1920s and some rodent populations developed resistance to it by the 1950s. Since then, the next generation of "super warfarins" has appeared (e.g., brodifacoum, bromadiolone, diphenacoum, diphacinone, and others). These "super warfarins", particularly brodifacoum, have caused a substantial number of wildlife mortality incidents across the United States (Sheffield 1997, Stone et al. 1999). Brodifacoum has been documented to poison nontarget wildlife. Secondary poisoning of raptors (particularly red-tailed hawks and great horned owls [*Bubo virginianus*]) made up 50% of the cases. Gray squirrels (*Sciurus carolinensis*), raccoons (*Procyon lotor*), and white-tailed deer (*Odocoileus virginianus*) were the most frequently poisoned mammals (Stone et al. 1999).

Avicides.—Avicides were developed to control pest birds, particularly species that flock such as European starlings (*Sturnus vulgaris*), blackbirds (Family Icteridae), and rock pigeons (*Columba livia*), which cause agricultural damage or are considered nuisance species. Several chemicals with avicidal properties have been used including avitrol, chloralose, endrin, fenthion, methiocarb, and strychnine. Most of these chemicals are no longer registered for avicidal uses. One currently used avicide, DRC-1339, was developed specifically to kill starlings. Although designed to be specific to starlings, there is evidence that it is nonspecific because it has been shown to pose a hazard to nontarget seed-eating species such as ring-necked pheasants (Avery et al. 1998).

Because of the great potential for these compounds to kill nontarget vertebrates that may come in contact with them, they were designed to degrade fairly rapidly. Many are unstable and degrade rapidly in water. However, compounds such as avitrol (Kamrin 1997), some anticoagulants, and compound 1080 require months to decompose in soil. Many of these compounds, such as DRC-1339, are stable in water as well (Kimball and Mishalanie 1994). Soil degradation can last from hours to months depending on the compound and climatic conditions. Avitrol degrades slowly in sunlight under dry conditions and in flooded soils, but 2.5 cm of rain will wash it away (Betts et al. 1976). Not only is environmental degradation important, but also persistence within the target species. For example, the half-life of bromadiolone in Norway rats (*Rattus norvegicus*) is up to 58 hours (Kamil 1987) allowing for potential exposure to predators and scavengers.

Secondary poisoning has been documented or considered possible for many vertebrate pest control compounds. Barn owls (*Tyto alba*) are particularly sensitive to DRC-1339, but the residues present in dead birds are usually too low to cause secondary poisoning (Johnston et al. 1999). However, bromadiolone and chlorophacinone have been implicated in secondary poisoning of many predators and scavengers (Berny et al. 1997, McDonald et al. 1998). Avitrol has been shown to be a potential hazard to sharp-shinned hawks (*Accipiter striatus*) and American kestrels (Holler and Schafer 1982).

Vertebrate pest control chemicals include a wide range of compounds with a wide range of behavior in different environmental compartments. Anticoagulants and acute toxicants tend to be nonvolatile whereas fumigants are highly volatile. Fumigants generally are unstable in water, anticoagulants are stable in water, and acute toxicants vary in their water stability. All are fairly stable in dry soil, but fumigants degrade quickly in wet soil. For example, both aluminum and zinc phosphides release highly toxic phosphine gas when in contact with water (Kamrin 1997).

Pest control chemicals vary greatly in mobility in general and specific media alter their mobility. Anticoagulant rodenticides generally are not mobile in any environmental media, while fumigants are mobile in air, but not in water (Kamrin 1997). Acute toxicants are not mobile in air and vary in their mobility in water. Compound 1080 is highly mobile in water because it is highly soluble. However, because of its high adsorption onto soil particles, it does not penetrate deeply into soil (Irwin et al. 1996). Other acute toxicants such as avitrol exhibit moderate water solubility and are not highly mobile in water.

Natural Plant/Animal Toxins

Natural toxins are toxic chemicals produced by living organisms, such as bacteria, blue-green algae, fungi, marine invertebrates and fishes, vascular plants, and poisonous aquatic and terrestrial animal species. Exposure to certain natural toxins, especially natural plant toxins, may have significant impacts on wildlife. There are many different natural plant toxins, also known as secondary plant compounds, which can be highly toxic to wildlife causing mortality and morbidity. Some plant toxins are used as the basis for pesticides (e.g., nicotine, pyrethrum, rotenone, etc.) demonstrating their acute toxicity (Ray 1991). Several factors are involved in exposure of wildlife to natural plant toxins. For example, different portions of the plant (root, stem, leaves, seeds) often contain different concentrations of a chemical. Plant age, climate, soil, and genetic differences within a plant species are also important factors. Examples of natural plant toxin chemical groups that can be highly toxic are alkaloids, tannins, phenols, lectins, glycosides, and terpenes. Generally, wild herbivorous animals have adapted to avoid or efficiently detoxify endemic toxic plants and are not impacted by exposure to these toxins (Vangilder 1983). However, there have been a number of documented cases of poisoning of wildlife by plant toxins (Ray 1991, Wickstrom 1999, Norton 2001).

Three groups of microscopic organisms, bacteria, algae and fungi, are capable of producing some of the most deadly toxins known. Probably the most significant natural toxin in terms of wildlife mortality/morbidity is botulinum toxin from the bacteria *Clostridium botulinum* (types C and E). Type C botulism causes mortality and morbidity in thousands of waterfowl across the United States and Canada each year, while Type E botulism has largely been restricted to causing mortality of fish-eating birds (bald eagles, loons, grebes, gulls) in the Great Lakes (Friend and Franson 1999, Roffe and Work 2005). The botulinum toxin generally is formed under conditions of low environmental oxygen and is considered to be the most toxic substance known. Waterfowl, especially dabbling ducks, are most susceptible to Type C botulism, but American coots (*Fulica americana*), gulls, and shorebirds (Order Charadriiformes) are also commonly killed during an outbreak. In Canada, annual losses of waterfowl in the prairie provinces can reach 100,000–1,000,000 birds (Wickstrom 1999). The neurotoxins produced by *C. botulinum* cause a paralytic effect in birds, which show signs of weakness, dizziness, inability to fly, muscular paralysis, and respiratory distress (Friend and Franson 1999, Roffe and Work 2005)

Blue-green algae (cyanobacteria) blooms commonly occur in fresh and brackish water worldwide. Wildlife that inhabit stagnant, eutrophic, water bodies especially during warm, sunny weather are most susceptible to algal toxins. Algae in the genera *Nostoc*, *Oscillatoria*, *Anabaena*, and *Microcystis* produce hepatotoxic cyclic peptides that disrupt the structure of liver cells, causing massive hemorrhage and necrosis leading to shock and death within hours. Algae in the genera *Anabaena*, *Aphanizomenon*, and some *Oscillatoria* produce potent, rapid-acting alkaloid neurotoxins. Anatoxin-a is a potent cholinesterase inhibitor, which causes permanent depolarization of post-synaptic membranes and disrupts nerve conduction, leading to muscle tremors, rigidity, paralysis, and death by respiratory failure within minutes. Exposure to this toxin could be confounding to analysis of cholinesterase activity due to organophosphorus or carbamate insecticide exposure.

Aphanitoxins, another group of neurotoxins, act by blocking sodium channels, which disrupts nerve conduction leading to muscle tremors, rigidity, paralysis, and death. This group appears to be identical to saxitoxin and neosaxitoxin, the causative agents of paralytic shellfish poisoning in humans. In marine systems, harmful algal blooms produced by phytoplankton containing protozoans (mainly dinoflagellates) together produce some of the most potent toxins known including domoic acid, brevetoxins, and saxitoxins. These compounds are concentrated in shellfish, are highly neurotoxic, and are commonly lethal to mammals at levels of 1 µg/kg (ppb) or less. In North America, harmful algal blooms have been responsible for the death of wildlife in freshwater and marine systems including waterfowl, colonial waterbirds, and other bird species, wild canids, white-tailed deer, sea turtles, manatees (*Trichechus manatus*), pinnipeds, and whales (Friend and Franson 1999, Wickstrom 1999, Dierauf and Gulland 2001).

Fungi are also known to produce extremely toxic substances collectively known as mycotoxins (O'Hara 1996). Generally, wildlife is exposed to mycotoxins through contaminated feed. Although effects on wildlife can be significant, reports of poisoning by mycotoxins are relatively rare because it is difficult to establish a diagnosis in the field. Aflatoxins, produced by the fungus *Aspergillus flavus* (or *A. parasiticus*), are among the most toxic of the mycotoxins and are common contaminants of corn, peanuts, and other cereal and oil seeds. Wildlife is at risk from eating waste grain, especially during times of restricted access to other feed or forage. The trichothecenes is another group of mycotoxins produced by fungi in the genera *Fusarium*, *Cephalosporium*, *Myrothecium*, and *Trichoderma*. These sesquiterpene compounds include T-2 toxin, diacetoxyscirpenol, and vomitoxin and act to inhibit protein synthesis, targeting rapidly dividing cell types in the skin, intestine, hematopoetic (bone marrow), and lymphoid tissues. These toxins are known to cause anorexia, dermal, oral, and gastrointestinal necrosis and ulceration, hemorrhage, and impairments of the reproductive and immune systems. Other mycotoxins that may have adverse effects on wildlife include fumonisins, zearalenone, ochratoxin A, ergot alkaloids, and sporidesmin. Although data on the role of mycotoxins in wildlife mortality/morbidity are rare, *Fusarium* (trichothecene) mycotoxins on waste peanuts were implicated in a mass mortality of sandhill cranes involving 9,500 birds in New Mexico and Texas between 1982 and 1987 (Windingstad et al. 1989, Friend and Franson 1999). In this case, the most common visible sign was an inability to hold the head erect while standing or flying. Multiple muscle hemorrhages and submandibular edema were the predominant lesions at necropsy (Windingstad et al. 1989).

CONTAMINANT DIAGNOSTICS

Safety

Personal safety is a primary concern in a wildlife mortality/morbidity incident. Field investigators should not handle carcasses, collect environmental samples, or enter the area of the incident until adequate safety precautions have been taken. If the causative contaminant is known, a Material Safety Data Sheet (MSDS) or other Occupational Safety and Health Administration (OSHA) safety publications can provide the level of personal protective equipment required. For pesticides, the product label will provide the necessary information. Since some environmental contaminants may produce cancer, reproductive impairment, or birth defects in humans, which would not become immediately apparent, the results of not adequately protecting investigators can be severe and long lasting.

Field biologists should take safety precautions when investigating possible wildlife contaminant or disease mortality/morbidity incidents. If contaminants are suspected, proper protective clothing for the contaminant type should be worn. As a general rule, impermeable gloves and protective footwear (generally rubber boots) should be worn at incident sites. Some contaminants are readily dissolved in water and can readily penetrate the skin. Therefore, field investigators should keep bare skin protected and should not wade into shallow water. When retrieving carcasses or debilitated animals from water, impermeable gloves and rubber boots should be worn.

Short pants or short-sleeved shirts should not be worn, bare skin should be protected, and dust or fumes should not be inhaled. In wet conditions, waterproof pants may be required. Dust masks or respirators may also be required as well as impermeable clothing (e.g., TYVEK® coveralls or full suit), depending on the situation. In hot or humid weather, this type of equipment can be problematic to the person(s) wearing it, so common sense is needed to prevent heat stress or dehydration. If clothing becomes contaminated, once the contaminant type has been confirmed, it should be washed or discarded. For some contaminants, washing is not sufficient to allow continued wearing.

If disease, rather than contaminants is suspected, caution is still required, but the precautions are not as extensive (Roffe and Work 2005). It must be remembered that many contaminants in the environment are toxic to many different taxa, including humans. Further, some wildlife diseases can be transmitted to humans, but diseases generally are more species-specific than contaminants. This species-specificity may provide some support and clues as to whether an incident was contaminant- or infectious disease-mediated.

Initial Site Reconnaissance

Three rules govern initiation of any wildlife mortality/morbidity investigation: (1) protect yourself and others involved, (2) obtain the best case history possible, and (3) collect the best specimens possible. Handling and collection of specimens in the field will affect what the laboratory can (and cannot) do with them. Whenever possible, notify a wildlife veterinarian or other trained personnel and wait for their arrival before initiating the incident investigation. If this is not practical prior to starting the incident investigation, an initial reconnaissance of the site can direct the subsequent investigation and save time and money. During the initial reconnaissance, it is critical to assume there will be legal implications of the investigation and that the cause may be a highly toxic or contagious agent. Field notes and documentation that begin with the initial stages of the investigation are critically important and impact the entire investigation that follows.

An initial identification of the agent causing the incident should be attempted. (1) Is there reason to believe contaminants are the source? The approach to investigate and collect samples from a disease or contaminant incident differs. (2) Is the incident centralized and is it down slope, downstream, or downwind from a likely point source? (3) Is the incident on or near agricultural lands? In an agricultural setting, the crops in the area would be a starting point for what pesticides might have been applied. Early identification of the contaminant can dictate the safety precautions needed and direct the types of samples that should be collected and how they should be handled. If the source and cause of the incident are not immediately obvious, the field investigator should err on the side of safety and collect samples in the most inclusive manner within the constraints of time and expertise.

As a starting point to decide whether the cause is a disease or contaminant, the species affected should be considered. If a single species or group of species is affected, it is more likely disease. For example, botulism may be indicated if only ducks are found dead or debilitated while other species appear unaffected. However, if many unrelated species are affected, it is more likely a contaminant. Field biologists should carry an immediate response kit with them at all time. This would include protective (e.g., TYVEK®) coveralls, respirator or dust mask, plastic or rubber gloves, rubber boots, dark glass collection bottles or jars, and plastic bags. This kit could be kept in a waterproof container that can be securely closed to prevent contamination.

Upon initial discovery of the wildlife mortality/morbidity site, the nearest wildlife contaminant or disease expert should be contacted immediately. Experts in these areas may be at a teaching/research wildlife hospital or state or federal agency. In the case of pesticides, a county extension agent may be helpful.

Mortality

Personal safety must be the primary consideration before attempting to collect carcasses, samples, or spending any time at the site of the incident. If an environmental contaminant is present in sufficient concentrations to kill or debilitate wildlife species, it may also pose a health hazard to the field biologist.

Locating carcasses, especially of small, secretive species, can be difficult. Therefore, finding one or a few carcasses should not preclude the possibility that many additional animals could have been poisoned and either removed by scavengers or moved to another area prior to death. Once dead animals are found, the immediate goals are to prevent further deaths and to identify the cause and source of the environmental contaminant(s) involved. It may not be possible to accomplish the former without first determining the latter. An immediate search of the area for intoxicated/sick animals can be instructive in identifying the cause by observing their appearance, movements, and behavior. Detailed observations may also provide an opportunity to provide care for their recovery.

In many cases, exposure to environmental contaminants is obvious. Most likely, dying birds and mammals observed drinking irrigation runoff water from a field recently sprayed with an organophosphorus insecticide were poisoned. Aquatic birds, mammals, or other wildlife species found dead in a containment pond from a cyanide leaching process most likely died from exposure to cyanide. However, no matter how obvious these causal associations may seem, it is imperative that both carcasses and samples of the apparent source of exposure be chemically analyzed for evidence of environmental toxicants. In other cases, exposure to environmental contaminants is not as obvious. A colonial waterbird rookery with almost complete nesting failure the spring following a severe winter may not be due to the colony being exposed to applications of pesticides in the area but to exposure of the adults to organic chemicals remobilized in the environment. This could result from severe scouring of nearby river sediments during heavy winter flows (American Society for Testing and Measurement 1997).

The risk of chemical contaminants to wildlife is dependent on toxicity, concentration, and route of exposure. Acute toxicity of insecticides and vertebrate pest control chemicals (rodenticides, avicides) to wildlife is high, whereas the acute toxicity of herbicides is low. Exposure routes in wildlife include oral, dermal (including ocular, or through the eyes), and inhalation as well as from maternal sources (deposited in eggs, pass through the placenta). For mammals and birds, the most common route of exposure is oral, where contaminants are ingested through the mouth. In addition to consumption of contaminated food items, birds and mammals sprayed directly or exposed to an aerosol suspension of a pesticide would result in oral exposure through preening and grooming behaviors, respectively, which would result in oral ingestion. Secondary poisoning through consumption of contaminated prey items by predatory and scavenging wildlife species is a relatively common occurrence. Mammals and birds can also readily absorb pesticides directly through their feet by standing or perching on a contaminated substrate. This has been shown with red-tailed hawks foraging in orchards during the winter following applications of organophosphorus insecticide dormant sprays (Hooper et al. 1989). Perching behavior in birds has been exploited by avian pest control operators who target perches with toxic chemicals specifically for dermal exposure through the feet. Mortality incidents in birds and mammals through inhalation are difficult to document and relatively uncommon.

Morbidity

Discovering intoxicated or sick (morbid) animals presents the field biologist with a situation where action has to be taken. Species of wildlife that are intoxicated or sick from exposure to environmental contaminants may be able to fully recover. Depending upon the environmental contaminant involved and the concentration, duration, and route of exposure, the negative effects on wildlife may or may not be reversible. However, during a wildlife mortality or morbidity incident, there is the chance that exposed animals have been seriously poisoned and may need to be euthanized (Friend and Franson 1999, Dein et al. 2005).

Treatment or transport of many wildlife species, particularly birds, requires one or more permits. Additionally, a salvage permit is often required to collect dead animals. Before collecting either carcasses or live animals, the necessary permit(s) must be obtained as well as knowledge as to how to transport specimens or animals. It is also important to know where the specimens or animals are to be taken, particularly if the animals are still alive. Treatment of intoxicated or sick animals by wildlife rehabilitators requires specific permits. Most veterinarians are not equipped to accept and treat wildlife species, as they do not have the facilities to hold animals apart from their routine domestic patients. Wildlife rehabilitators generally are registered with state wildlife agencies, which can provide a list of wildlife rehabilitators for a given area. Prior to collecting morbid animals, the destination must be identified and appropriate transport containers obtained that will safely hold the animals and provide comfortable conditions. Allowing animals to die from improper care during transport is not acceptable. It may be better to humanely euthanize an animal than to subject it to unnecessary stress because it is not possible to provide adequate care during transport.

Wildlife species that are intoxicated or otherwise sick from exposure to environmental contaminants invariably demonstrate clinical signs of the poisoning (Table 1). Although many clinical signs from exposure to environ-

Table 1. Overview of clinical signs exhibited by wildlife species by general environmental contaminant group.

Clinical signs	Metals	Organic chemicals	Anti-ChE insecticides	Anti-coagulant rodenticides
Ataxia (loss of coordination)	X	X	X	X
Muscular weakness			X	
Tremors	X	X		
Convulsions		X	X	X
Lethargy	X	X	X	X
Hyperactivity	X			
Reproductive effects	X	X	X	
Developmental abnormalities	X	X	X	
Reduced fertility	X	X	X	
Spontaneous abortions	X	X		
Excretory effects		X	X	
Excess defecation			X	
Bloody feces		X		X
Diarrhea			X	
Spasmodic contraction of anal sphincter			X	
Emesis (vomiting)		X	X	
Anorexia (weight loss/emaciation)		X	X	
Excessive thirst			X	
Nasal secretions			X	
Epistaxis (bleeding from nares)			X	X
Salivation		X		
Edema	X	X	X	
Anemia	X	X		X
Skin lesions		X		
Immunotoxic response		X	X	
Depressed ChE			X	
Behavioral effects		X	X	
Altered behavior			X	
Unkempt appearance		X		
Hypothermia			X	
Coma		X	X	X
Paralysis			X	X
Internal bleeding				X
Dyspnea (labored breathing)		X	X	X
Tachypnea (rapid breathing)			X	
Eye/vision problems	X	X	X	
Blindness	X	X	X	
Contraction of pupils			X	
Dilation of pupils			X	
Ptosis (drooping of eyelids)		X	X	
Protrusion of eyes			X	
Lacrimation (excessive tears)			X	
Head and limbs arched back			X	
Piloerection (erection of contour feathers)			X	

mental contaminants are somewhat general in nature, the suite of responses exhibited in a given situation can be quite useful as a piece of the puzzle in diagnosing the group of contaminants responsible for the intoxication or sickness.

The Wildlife Contaminant Investigation

Circumstances involved in a contaminant-related wildlife mortality/morbidity incident and appearance of exposed wildlife are difficult to distinguish from those caused by disease or natural causes. For example, certain wildlife diseases may resemble wildlife mortality/morbidity caused by con-

taminants, including botulism, salmonella, trichomoniasis, mycotoxicosis, and duck virus enteritis (American Society for Testing and Measurement 1997). Investigators should rely on a wildlife disease specialist to obtain a definitive diagnosis if disease is suspected (Roffe and Work 2005). Investigations of wildlife mortality/morbidity suspected to be caused by contaminants should proceed as though the cause was unknown. All factors must be checked or eliminated unless there is solid evidence to support specific conclusions.

If only a few carcasses are involved, external examination is necessary to rule out natural (e.g., predation) or accidental causes. Thus, it is important to be able to differentiate between evidence left by scavenging and true predation. This may not be possible, but should be attempted. It is possible that predation was successful because the animal was impaired from disease or exposure to an environmental contaminant. Thus, overall condition of the carcass can be important. A wasted or unkempt appearance could be indicative of impairment prior to predation. Large numbers of carcasses are likely related to either disease or environmental contaminants, but could be the result of an accidental mortality (e.g., bird collisions with communication towers or other man-made structures, road kills). Therefore, accidents should be considered before assigning the cause to disease or environmental contaminants.

The initial decision as to whether or not a wildlife mortality/morbidity incident is likely contaminant-related is a process of elimination. If there are no other plausible explanations for the incident, the site should be investigated for contaminants or diseases. Locating and contacting someone with experience in differentiating between disease- and contaminant-related mortality is highly desirable. Thus, it is essential to document the incident with detailed field notes and photographs.

The investigator(s) often can obtain a substantial amount of information from the individual(s) reporting the incident, including the extent, whether a field response is necessary, and whether the contaminant(s) may cause more widespread wildlife mortality/morbidity. Important factors in interpretation of the incident scene include location, time and date of incident, species involved, number of dead and/or sick animals, rate of deaths (e.g., did they occur over a short or long period of time), chance of continuing mortality/morbidity, clinical signs observed, climatic conditions (e.g., precipitation, temperature, winds) preceding the incident, and any recent change that has occurred. Recent changes in land use, agricultural practices, insect outbreaks, evidence of recent pesticide applications, or other factor in the area of the incident should be noted as well as other similar incidents in this area and the observations of the person(s) reporting the incident. This information should allow the investigator to decide whether or not the incident warrants a field investigation. A specific case number should be assigned to each investigation and used on all labels, tags, data sheets, photographs, and other records related to the incident. The investigator must rely upon their best professional judgment as to the intensity of the field investigation and the individuals and agencies to contact.

The investigator's interpretation of the wildlife mortality/morbidity incident scene will affect the type, number, and location of samples taken and the analyses performed. The first few hours after arrival on the scene are most critical and information should be collected as soon as possible. This is especially important when an incident occurs in association with flowing waters of ditches and streams. One reason is that some chemical contaminants, such as most organophosphorus and carbamate insecticides degrade relatively quickly and chemical and diagnostic signs present at the site (e.g., sick or dying animals and water conditions) may rapidly disappear.

Wildlife mortality/morbidity incidents may be a result of illegal activities, such as a pesticide applied to intentionally kill wildlife and, thus, have the potential to become a legal case. In any investigation, chain-of-custody documen-

tation is required to demonstrate that evidence can be accounted for at all times (American Society for Testing and Measurement 1997). Chain of custody is defined as the witnessed, written record of all individuals who have maintained unbroken control over the evidence since acquisition. The chain of custody begins with the collection of an item of evidence and is maintained until its final disposal. Each individual in the chain of custody is responsible for items of evidence to include care, safekeeping, and preservation while under their control. Because it is possible that any item or specimen acquired during the investigation of a wildlife mortality/morbidity incident may have value as evidence, it is important to treat all specimens as evidence and follow chain-of-custody procedures.

FIELD PROCEDURES
Sample Documentation and Transport

It is critical that samples collected in the field are handled properly to ensure that useable information can be obtained for the best understanding of what may have caused the wildlife mortality/morbidity incident. All samples should be double bagged with a label on the inner bag or placed between the bags. By labeling the inner bag, if the label somehow becomes detached, the outer bag will keep the label with the sample. If adhesive labels are not available, the information can be recorded on notebook paper and included between the bags. Double bagging will help reduce dehydration and protect against loss of a sample should a bag inadvertently open during shipping or storage. Each specimen should be labeled with sample type, for example tissue type, species, plant, soil, etc. The sample location (both overall site name and location within the site), sample date and time, and the person's name that collected the sample must be included. This information is extremely important for subsequent follow-up and interpretation of the sample analysis.

Labels should be written clearly with indelible felt-tipped pens or other ink that will not smear when it comes in contact with water. Field biologists commonly use pencils for field notes because a lead pencil does not smudge when wet. However, when samples are being tracked for possible litigation, pencil is not acceptable as permanent labeling is required for all sample logs and sample labels. If permanent ink is not available for field records, it is best to make a photocopy of the sample log as soon as possible.

Samples should be placed on ice in the field as some contaminants can degrade quickly, for example in hours, and tissues or carcasses can deteriorate quickly at warm field temperatures. Once the samples are taken from the field, they should be hard frozen. When multiple specimens are available, some samples should be placed on ice for preliminary pathology analysis while the remaining specimens are frozen. The only exception would be animals that may have succumbed to disease. These should be cooled and shipped to a pathologist within 48 hours of collection (Box 2). Samples for contaminant analysis should be transported frozen or on dry ice. It is important that samples not thaw during shipment, because this may compromise subsequent contaminant or disease analyses.

Handling

The manner of handling field-collected samples can differ according to the likely contaminant type. Metals gen-

Box 2. Recommended laboratories for fish and wildlife mortality/morbidity incidents.

USA

New York State Department of Environmental
Conservation
Wildlife Resources Center/Wildlife Pathology Unit
108 Game Farm Road
Delmar, NY12054
T 518-478-3032; http://www.dec.state.ny.us/webvsite/
dfwmr/habitat/wpu/htm

Southeastern Cooperative Wildlife Disease Study
Wildlife Health Building
College of Veterinary Medicine
University of Georgia
Athens, GA 30602
T 706-542-1741; FAX 706-542-5865
http://www.uga.edu/scwds

U.S. Department of Agriculture
Animal and Plant Health Inspection Service (APHIS)
National Wildlife Research Center
4101 La Porte Avenue
Fort Collins, CO 80521
T 970-266-6000; FAX 970-266-6032
http://www.aphis.usda.gov/ws/nwrc

U.S. Department of Commerce
National Oceanic and Atmospheric Administration
National Marine Fisheries Service
1315 East-West Highway
Silver Spring, MD 20910
T 301-713-2332; FAX 301-713-0376
http://www.nmfs.noaa.gov/strandings.htm

U.S. Department of the Interior
Geological Survey
National Wildlife Health Center
6006 Schroeder Road
Madison, WI 53711
T 608-270-2400; FAX 608-270-2415
http://www.nwhc.usgs.gov,
http://www.nwhc.usgs.gov/best/index.html

U.S. Department of the Interior
Fish and Wildlife Service
National Fish and Wildlife Forensic Laboratory
Ashland, OR 97520
T 541-482-4191; FAX 541-482-4989
http://www.lab.fws.gov

U.S. Environmental Protection Agency
National Health and Environmental Effects Research
Laboratory (NHEERL)
109 TW Alexander Drive
Durham, NC 27709
T 919-541-4577; FAX 919-541-1831
http://www.epa.gov/nheer, http://www.epa.gov/ecotox

CANADA

Canadian Cooperative Wildlife Health Centre
Western College of Veterinary Medicine, Veterinary
Pathology
University of Saskatchewan
Saskatoon, SK, S7N 5B4 Canada
T 306-966-5099, 800-567-2033 (Canada);
FAX 306-966-7439
http://wildlife1.usask.ca/ccwhc2003

Environment Canada
Canadian Wildlife Service
National Wildlife Research Centre
Wildlife Toxicology Division
Carleton University
Ottawa, ON K1A 0H3 Canada
T 819-997-2800, 800-668-6767 (Canada);
FAX 819-953-2225
http://www.cws.ec.gc.ca/nwrc-cnrf/toxic/index_e.cfm

erally do not tend to adhere to plastics, nor will storage in plastics interfere with the analysis by the chemist. It is acceptable to use polyethylene bottles for sample shipping and storage with a 1 L bottle an appropriate size. It is important to acidify water samples to prevent degradation, but only when it is known that metals are the contaminant. Acidification can make other water sample types useless.

Organics, including pesticides, can readily adsorb onto or absorb into plastic and plasticizers can leach from the container into a water sample confounding the subsequent chemical analysis. Thus, it is best to use glass when sampling organics, including pesticides. Depending on the type of organic contaminant present, at least 40 ml and up to 2 L should be collected. If freezing without damaging the container is not possible, the sample should be cooled to 4°C for storage and shipping. At least 186 g of soil should be collected and frozen. Some pesticides may have a tenden-

cy to migrate down through soil. If this is considered likely, a soil core of up to 1 m in depth should be collected.

When animal tissues are collected, great care should be taken to prevent cross-contamination either from other samples or sources. Thus, only individuals experienced in dissecting animals for subsequent chemical analysis should do so. If the incident is legally contested and untrained individuals dissect the samples, damage can be done to the legal acceptability of the sample analyses. It is best to freeze the samples and allow specialists to perform the dissections.

Tissues can be placed into plastic bags or small glass sample jars that have sterile interiors and larger samples can be placed in zip-lock bags. Smoky-colored (dark) glass sampling jars should be used for soil, water, and sediment samples, particularly if pesticides or organics are involved. Using dark-colored glass is especially important when handling chemicals that undergo photodegradation. Plastic containers should be avoided for samples that could contain pesticides or organics, as they tend to adsorb onto the plastic. Sampling equipment should be cleaned between processing and collecting samples to prevent cross-contamination. Gloves should be changed between samples or between groups of samples of similar contamination levels to present cross-contamination.

Record Keeping

A field log will be useful to make entries regarding each sample collected for analysis. Entries should include the sample identification number, type of sample collected, site name where collected, date, and the name or initials of the sample collector. These entries provide backup identification in case sample labels are damaged or lost, or if confusion ensues over when and where certain samples were taken.

Accurate record keeping is critical in documenting wildlife mortality/morbidity incidents. Detailed incident reports (Appendix) are essential to identification and confirmation of ecological risks associated with a particular chemical contaminant. Over time, incident reports provide information regarding those chemicals or agricultural practices that are involved most often in wildlife mortality/morbidity incidents as well as identifying species that are particularly sensitive to certain chemicals. Incident reports can also identify geographic areas or landscape variables most frequently impacted by specific chemicals. The more detailed information provided on the field data sheet, the better the chances the investigator(s) of the incident will be able to understand what happened. The importance of detail in the field data sheet, both to enhance accurate diagnosis and to assure that appropriate information is provided for forensic purposes, cannot be overemphasized. It is imperative to learn if the contaminant threat is still present and if there is a continuing threat of wildlife mortality/morbidity.

Sample Collection

In addition to wildlife tissue samples that are critical for identifying the cause of the mortality/morbidity incident, other environmental samples are also critical. Some contaminants may be metabolized quickly within an animal and the environmental samples may be the only place where the unaltered contaminant will be found. It is also possible the contaminants were encountered in a location some distance from where the carcasses were discovered. If the exposure occurs off-site, the actual contamination source must be located. Depending on the specific conditions of the situation, soil, water, and vegetation should be sampled. If possible, advice should be pursued on the proper sampling techniques for different sample types and for different contaminants.

Environmental samples should be collected from the immediate area of where dead or debilitated animals are found. Additionally, samples should be collected from areas where the contamination may have moved or have originated. It is possible that dead or debilitated animals are first found in a highly visible location, but that contamination may be greater elsewhere. Those experienced with site and contaminant types can provide advice on number of samples required and how far the samples should be collected from the original site.

Many contaminants act as an emetic when ingested. If vomitus or regurgitated material is found with the specimens, it should be collected. This will often contain high concentrations of the contaminant, possibly higher than in the carcass or gastrointestinal (GI) tract. In acute poisonings, contaminant residues are usually higher in the anterior GI tract than in the post-absorptive tissues.

Animal Tissues.—Animal tissues can be taken directly from necropsies while vomitus, urine/feces, blood, and hair/feathers can be collected at or around the mortality/morbidity site. Collecting samples from carcasses becomes more difficult as time elapses. Time since death is a critical factor as the onset of rigor mortis, decomposition, and scavenging by predators make tissue samples more difficult to obtain. Ideally, whole, fresh carcasses available for sampling tissues would be present at the incident scene, but this frequently is not the case. For instances where the whole carcass cannot be submitted and evidence suggests specific causes may be involved, tissue samples can be strategically taken and preserved during necropsy (Table 2). The best materials for establishing oral exposure to an acute toxicant are in the GI tract (crop and gizzard/stomach in birds, stomach in mammals and other wildlife species). Liver tissue, lipid (fat) deposits, and brain tissue generally are considered best for identifying the presence of toxic levels of many lipid-soluble contaminants such as organochlorine insecticides and PCBs, and for trace metals (lead, mercury). Brain tissue also is important for diagnosing anticholinesterase insecticide poisoning through measurement of cholinesterase activity. Keratin structures (hair, feathers, scales) are often used as nonlethal samples to detect chronic exposure to heavy metals, which may be contributing to an overall decline in fitness of the animals making them more susceptible to disease or other environmental conditions. Analysis of samples from other environmental media can also assist in establishment of routes of exposure and to identify occurrences of exposure to multiple toxic chemicals. In the case of predators and scavengers, it may be necessary to collect local prey species or scavenged carcasses to examine possible exposure.

If the animals are not dead but are intoxicated or otherwise sick, nondestructive techniques can be used to collect tissue samples, specifically blood, hair/feather/scale, and biopsies or other types of samples, such as foot washes (Fossi and Leonzio 1994). Waste materials such as urine, feces, and vomitus can be collected from debilitated animals found at the site by holding them in clean, ventilated containers for a period of time. Fecal and urinary products are useful for analysis of contaminants and can be evaluated for disease as well. For living birds, a foot wash with methanol or isopropyl alcohol and analysis of feathers can be useful for establishing exposure to an aerosolized chemical application, such as a pesticide. Typically, a foot wash must be performed within 48–72 hours of exposure to detect the presence of the chemical. After that time, most or the entire chemical will have been absorbed through the skin (Fossi and Leonzio 1994, Friend and Franson 1999, Millam et al. 2000).

If the cause of the incident is unclear or if causes in addition to contaminants are possible, animal carcasses need to be handled in different ways. Freezing animal tissues can cause damage to tissues that make disease identification by a pathologist difficult or impossible. However, failure to freeze tissues for contaminant analysis may allow the contaminant to degrade to the extent they will not appear to be present.

Table 2. Sample selection and preservation from necropsy when whole carcasses cannot be submitted and evidence suggests specific causes may be involved (adapted from Friend and Franson 1999).

Sample	Suggested tests	Preservation	Comments
Lesions	As appropriate	Frozen	Lesions are abnormal-appearing tissues; a portion of each lesion should be saved frozen; fixed tissue important.
Lesions[a]	Specimen is fixed, sectioned, and stained for microscopic study	10% formalin	A portion of each lesion should be saved frozen.
Liver	Metals, organics	Frozen	Entire liver of birds and small mammals, selected portions from larger species; fixed tissue important.
Liver[a]	Specimen is fixed, sectioned, and stained for microscopic study	10% formalin	Specimen portions should not exceed 6 mm in thickness.
Kidney	Metals	Frozen	Entire kidneys from birds and small mammals, selected portions from larger species; fixed tissue important.
Kidney[a]	Specimen is fixed, sectioned, and stained for microscopic study	10% formalin	Specimen portions should not exceed 6 mm in thickness.
Stomach contents	OP and carbamate insecticides, plant toxins, mycotoxins, strychnine, cyanide	Frozen	Save entire contents; samples to be checked for cyanide or other toxic gases must be placed in airtight containers.
GI tract[a]	Specimen is fixed, sectioned, and stained for microscopic study	10% formalin or Bouin's stain	Small piece of stomach at the ileocecal junction, piece of duodenum (near pancreas), and colon.
Brain	Cholinesterase activity, OC insecticide residues, organomercuric compounds	Frozen	For chemical analysis of brain, it must be wrapped in clean aluminum foil and placed inside a clean glass bottle; fixed tissue important.
Brain, nervous tissue, eyes[a]	Specimen is fixed, sectioned, and stained for microscopic study	10% formalin	Divide brain in half (sagittal); place ½ in formalin, save other ½ frozen.
Blood	Lead, cyanide, H_2S, nitrites	Frozen	Samples to be checked for cyanide or other toxic gases must be placed in airtight containers.
Gonads[a]	Specimen is fixed, sectioned, and stained for microscopic study	10% formalin or Bouin's stain	Specimen portions should not exceed 6 mm in thickness.
Lungs	Cyanide, H_2S	Frozen	Samples to be checked for cyanide or other toxic gases must be placed in airtight containers.
Heart, lungs, skeletal muscle, lymph nodes, spleen, thymus[a]	Specimen is fixed, sectioned, and stained for microscopic study	10% formalin	Specimen portions should not exceed 6 mm in thickness.

[a] Histopathological examination (microscopic).

If there are many specimens, some should be frozen (with dry ice) and others kept cool (with ice or refrigeration). Those set aside for disease evaluation should be kept cool and transported to a trained pathologist within 48 hours or less of collection. If transportation will require more than 48 hours, it is best to freeze all specimens. It is best to freeze carcasses that are already deteriorating or have become putrid to prevent contamination. None of the carcasses should be dissected prior to sending them to the pathologist.

Plant Tissues.—Plant residues may be important in identifying how exposure may have occurred and the extent of the contamination. Some contaminants may accumulate in plants via uptake from the roots; however, many others may be present primarily as surface residues. For those contaminants that are most likely to be deposited on plant surfaces, care must be taken not to dislodge the residues from plant surfaces during collection. Contamination during collection of plant samples is a greater concern if surface residues are present.

When collecting plant samples, the plants should be handled as little as possible to prevent dislodging any contaminant residues. If possible, the entire plant including the roots should be collected as they may contain the highest residues making identification of the contaminant more likely. Samples should be collected from both on- and off-site areas. Cross-contamination among samples can be reduced by starting in the least contaminated areas. Consideration should be given to separating animal food items, such as seeds or fruits, from leaves and stems if it will help with the follow-up investigation. Samples should be frozen as soon as possible and remain frozen during shipping and storage until contaminant analysis.

Soil.—Soil samples can be useful for measuring the extent and levels of environmental contamination. Samples should be collected from the immediate vicinity where dead or debilitated animals were found. Depending on the specifics of the incident, soil should be collected at different distances from the site. Samples should be collected off-site if movement is possible, particularly up or down hill (or up or down wind). Some contaminants have a tendency to move down through soil and may contaminate groundwater. If possible and appropriate, collect soil core samples to a depth of 1 m. Samples should be collected first from areas thought to be least contaminated and then in those areas of highest contamination. It is surprisingly easy to contaminate samples from sampling equipment and even clothing and footwear. All soil samples should be frozen, if possible, at time of collection. If prompt freezing is not possible, the soil should be placed on ice and frozen as soon as practical.

Water/Sediment.—Water samples are useful for identifying the extent and levels of environmental contamination. Glass containers should be used to sample water as some contaminants adhere to or absorb into plastics. Samples should be protected from light and glass should either be brown or wrapped in aluminum foil. Samples should be collected from the immediate incident area (e.g., pond) and up or downstream. Samples can be collected from nearby surface water as appropriate. However, care should be taken that water samples contain no soil or other debris. Containers should be about half-full to prevent cracking from expansion during freezing, labeled, and placed in a plastic bag. Samples should be frozen immediately, if possible, but can be cooled to 4 C for shipping. During freezing, glass containers should be stored upright. Containers should be shipped upright, and frozen or cooled to 4 C.

Air.—Air might be the most difficult environmental factor to sample in the field. For soil, water, or vegetation as long as adequate sample amounts are collected, only portions of the sample are required for subsequent analyses. It is impractical to collect a sample of the air to provide to a chemist for analysis. Since air cannot be taken from the field, contaminants must be extracted from the air or measured during a field visit.

The concentration of a contaminant in the air is measured from a known volume of air sampled in the field. This requires a calibrated air pump or detector. Faulty calibration or leaks will produce inaccurate measurement of the volume sampled and inaccurate reporting of the concentrations of contaminants. Monitoring equipment must be checked for air leaks and proper calibration prior to monitoring for contaminants in the field.

Direct measurement of aerial contaminants in the field requires an instrument capable of detecting the presence and concentration of the specific contaminant of concern. If the contaminant of concern is not known before attempting air monitoring, selection of the proper detector will be difficult. Also, some detectors are designed for human health and safety and report only if a contaminant exceeds safe levels for humans. This might not be helpful when the level harmful to wildlife often is not known. Other detectors are designed for monitoring organic compounds and might not detect inorganics well and vice versa.

It is also possible to extract the contaminant from the air and provide the media to a chemist for analysis. Since concentration is based on the volume of air sampled, it is critical that the volume be accurately measured and recorded by using a pump calibrated to move a known volume of air during a specific time period (e.g., ml air/second) for a known period of time. The air being sampled must be pushed or pulled through a filter or liquid capable of extracting the contaminant. For many organic compounds, bubbling air through a solvent like hexane can be an effective sampling procedure. Filters also are available to remove many organic or inorganic compounds. However, the filter must be capable of capturing all the contaminant from the sampled air. The concentration will be under reported if the capacity of a filter is exceeded. Assistance from someone with experience in air quality monitoring will likely be necessary to ensure that measured air concentrations are accurate.

Chemical Residue Analysis.—Residue analysis is expensive and there are many aspects to consider including detection limits, quality assurance and control, how to read and evaluate a laboratory chemical analysis report, and how to interpret the toxicological data. There are 2 types of detection limits to be considered: instrument and method detection limits. Differences between instrument detection limits are a result of detector sensitivity, chromatograph system that precedes it, and the injection method. Method detection limits represent the best performance consistently achievable from a method in a particular laboratory with a given set of instrumentation. Method detection limits are a function of the clean-up and extractive procedure and, thus, more closely allied to the chemist's standard operating procedures and technical abilities. Standard operating procedures vary by detector and chemical based on the relative polarity of the chemical and the environmental media in which it is found.

Interpretation of residue analysis data can be frustrating. Overall, we know relatively little about how body residue levels of environmental contaminants correlate to corresponding effects seen in wildlife species. One excellent source of information on interpretation of residue analysis data is Beyer et al. (1996). This is the first major attempt to make sense of residue analysis data as related to accompanying effects.

SUMMARY

A wide variety and substantial volume of chemical contaminants as well as natural plant and animal toxins are present in the environment and frequently have been shown to have negative impacts on wildlife. As a result, wildlife mortality and morbidity incidents will occur. Thus, there is a strong need for field biologists to be able to adequately identify and handle these incidents. Few biologists receive training in the field of environmental or wildlife toxicology as this area of interest is relatively specialized. Thus, it is important that field biologists understand and have a source for standard operating procedures for successfully handling wildlife mortality/morbidity incidents. The goal of this chapter is to provide wildlife biologists with guidance on understanding wildlife toxicology and procedures that should be followed when confronted with a wildlife mortality/morbidity event. It is also important for biologists to have additional sources of information as well as locations of wildlife mortality/morbidity incident databases.

ACKNOWLEDGMENTS

This chapter evolved in part through development of educational tools by the Wildlife Toxicology Working Group of The Wildlife Society to assist field biologists in properly responding to wildlife mortality/morbidity events. We thank present and past members of the working group for their assistance. We thank the National Wildlife Health Center in Madison, Wisconsin, and the National Fish and Wildlife Forensic Laboratory in Ashland, Oregon, for helpful discussions on wildlife mortality/morbidity incidents and their experiences/procedures for processing them, K. A. Fagerstone, K. L. Ford, M. I. Goldstein, J. C. Franson, and M. L. Parker for valuable discussions, and 2 anonymous referees and the editor for chapter review and helpful comments.

LITERATURE CITED

ALBERS, P. H. 2003. Petroleum and individual polycyclic aromatic hydrocarbons. Pages 341–371 in D. J. Hoffman, B. A. Rattner, G. A. Burton, Jr., and J. Cairns, Jr., editors. Handbook of ecotoxicology. Second edition. Lewis Publishers, Boca Raton, Florida, USA.

AMERICAN SOCIETY FOR TESTING AND MEASUREMENT. 1997. Standard guide for fish and wildlife incident monitoring and reporting. Pages 1355–1382 in Biological effects and environmental fate; biotechnology; pesticides. ASTM E 1849-96. American Society for Testing and Measurement, Philadelphia, Pennsylvania, USA.

AMSTRUP, S. C., C. GARDNER, K. C. MYERS, AND F. W. OEHME. 1989. Ethylene glycol (antifreeze) poisoning in a free-ranging polar bear. Veterinary and Human Toxicology 31:317–319.

AULERICH, R. J., AND R. K. RINGER. 1977. Current status of PCB toxicity to mink, and effect on their reproduction. Archives of Environmental Contamination and Toxicology 6:279–292.

———, S. J. BURSIAN, M. G. EVANS, J. R. HOCHSTEIN, K. A. KOUDELE, B. A. OLSEN, AND A. C. NAPOLITANO. 1987. Toxicity of 3, 4, 5, 3', 4', 5'-hexachlorobiphenyl to mink. Archives of Environmental Contamination and Toxicology 16:53–60.

AVERY, M. L., M. J. KENYON, G. M. LINZ, D. L. BERGMAN, D. G. DECKER, AND J. S. HUMPHREY. 1998. Potential risk to ring-necked pheasants from application of toxic bait for blackbird control in South Dakota. Journal of Wildlife Management 62:388–394.

BALCOMB, R. 1986. Songbird carcasses disappear rapidly from agricultural fields. Auk 103:817–820.

BARON, R. L. 1991. Carbamate insecticides. Pages 1125–1189 in W. J. Hayes and E. R. Laws, Jr., editors. Handbook of pesticide toxicology. Volume 3. Classes of pesticides. Academic Press, San Diego, California, USA.

BELLROSE, F. C. 1951. Effects of ingested lead shot upon waterfowl populations. Transactions of the North American Wildlife Conference 16:125–135.

———. 1959. Lead poisoning as a mortality factor in waterfowl populations. Illinois Natural History Survey Bulletin 27:235–288.

BERNY, P. J., T. BURONFOSSE, F. BURONFOSSE, F. LAMARQUE, AND G. LORGUE. 1997. Field evidence of secondary poisoning of foxes (*Vulpes vulpes*) and buzzards (*Buteo buteo*) by bromadiolone, a 4-year survey. Chemosphere 35:1817–1829.

BETTS, P. M., C. W. GIDDINGS, AND J. R. FLEEKER. 1976. Degradation of 4-aminopyridine in soil. Journal of Agriculture and Food Chemistry 24:571–574.

BEYER, W. N., G. H. HEINZ, AND A. W. REDMON-NORWOOD. 1996. Environmental contaminants in wildlife: interpreting tissue concentrations. Lewis Publishers, Boca Raton, Florida, USA.

———, J. C. FRANSON, L. N. LOCKE, R. K. STROUD, AND L. SILEO. 1998. Retrospective study of the diagnostic criteria in a lead-poisoning survey of waterfowl. Archives of Environmental Contamination and Toxicology 35:506–512.

BIDLEMAN, T. F., G. W. PATTON, D. A. HINCKLEY, M. D. WALLA, W. E. COTHAM, AND B. T. HARGRAVE. 1990. Chlorinated pesticides and polychlorinated biphenyls in the atmosphere of the Canadian arctic. Pages 347–372 in D. A. Kurtz, editor. Long range transport of pesticides. Lewis Publishers, Boca Raton, Florida, USA.

BLUS, L. J. 2003. Organochlorine pesticides. Pages 313–339 in D. J. Hoffman, B. A. Rattner, G. A. Burton, Jr., and J. Cairns, Jr., editors. Handbook of ecotoxicology. Second edition. Lewis Publishers, Boca Raton, Florida, USA.

———, S. N. WIEMEYER, AND C. J. HENNY. 1996. Organochlorine pesticides. Pages 61–70 in A. Fairbrother, L. N. Locke, and G. L. Huff, editors. Noninfectious diseases of wildlife. Second edition. Iowa State University Press, Ames, USA.

BRADBURY, S. P. 1996. 2,3,7,8-Tetrachlorodibenzo-p-dioxin. Pages 87–98 in A. Fairbrother, L. N. Locke, and G. L. Huff, editors. Noninfectious diseases of wildlife. Second edition. Iowa State University Press, Ames, USA.

BRUCKNER, J. V., AND D. A. WARREN. 2001. Toxic effects of solvents and vapors. Pages 869–916 in C. D. Klaassen, editor. Casarett and Doull's toxicology: the basic science of poisons. Sixth edition. McGraw-Hill Book Co., New York, USA.

BURNS, R. J., AND G. E. CONNOLLY. 1995. Toxicity of compound 1080 livestock protection collars to sheep. Archives of Environmental Contamination and Toxicology 28:141–144.

CHEMICAL AND ENGINEERING NEWS. 1996. Production by the U.S. chemical industry. Available online at http://pubs.acs.org/hotartcl/cenear/960624/prod.html.

CLARK, JR., D. R. 1991. Bats, cyanide, and gold mining. Bats 9:17–18.

———, AND R. L. HOTHEM. 1991. Mammal mortality at Arizona, California, and Nevada gold mines using cyanide extraction. California Fish and Game 77:61–69.

CRAIG, T. H., J. W. CONNELLY, E. H. CRAIG, AND T. L. PARKER. 1990. Lead concentrations in golden and bald eagles. Wilson Bulletin 102:130–133.

DEIN, F. J., D. E. TOWEILL, AND K. P. KENOW. 2005. Care and use of wildlife in field research. Pages 185–196 in C. E. Braun, editor. Techniques for wildlife investigations and management. Sixth edition. The Wildlife Society, Bethesda, Maryland, USA.

DESNOO, G. R., N. M. I. SCHEIDEGGER, AND F. M. W. DEJONG. 1999. Vertebrate wildlife incidents with pesticides: a European survey. Pesticide Science 55:47–54.

DIERAUF, L. A., AND F. M. D. GULLAND, editors. 2001. CRC handbook of marine mammal medicine. Second edition. CRC Press, Boca Raton, Florida, USA.

DIGIULIO, R. T., AND P. F. SCANLON. 1984. Heavy metals in tissues of waterfowl from the Chesapeake Bay, USA. Environmental Pollution (Series A) 35:29–48.

DONALDSON, D., T. KIELY, AND A. H. GRUBE. 2002. Pesticides industry sales and usage: 1998 and 1999 market estimates. U.S. Environmental Protection Agency, Biological and Economic Analysis Division, Office of Pesticide Programs, Washington, D.C., USA.

ECOBICHON, D. J. 2001. Toxic effects of pesticides. Pages 763–810 in C. D. Klaassen, editor. Casarett and Doull's toxicology: the basic science of poisons. Sixth edition. McGraw-Hill Book Co., New York, USA.

EDWARDS, I. R., D. G. FERRY, AND W. A. TEMPLE. 1991. Fungicides and related compounds. Pages 1409–1470 in W. J. Hayes and E. R. Laws, Jr., editors. Handbook of pesticide toxicology. Volume 2. Classes of pesticides. Academic Press, San Diego, California, USA.

EISLER, R. 1985a. Cadmium hazards to fish, wildlife, and invertebrates: a synoptic review. U.S. Department of the Interior, Fish and Wildlife Service, Biological Report 85(1.2).

———. 1985b. Selenium hazards to fish, wildlife, and invertebrates: a synoptic review. U.S. Department of the Interior, Fish and Wildlife Service, Biological Report 85(1.5).

———. 1986a. Chromium hazards to fish, wildlife, and invertebrates: a synoptic review. U.S. Department of the Interior, Fish and Wildlife Service, Biological Report 85(1.6).

———. 1986b. Dioxin hazards to fish, wildlife, and invertebrates: a synoptic review. U.S. Department of the Interior, Fish and Wildlife Service, Biological Report 85(1.8).

———. 1986c. Polychlorinated biphenyls hazards to fish, wildlife, and invertebrates: a synoptic review. U.S. Department of the Interior, Fish and Wildlife Service, Biological Report 85(1.7).

———. 1987a. Mercury hazards to fish, wildlife, and invertebrates: a synoptic review. U.S. Department of the Interior, Fish and Wildlife Service, Biological Report 85(1.10).

———. 1987b. Polycyclic aromatic hydrocarbon hazards to fish, wildlife, and invertebrates: a synoptic review. U.S. Department of the Interior, Fish and Wildlife Service, Biological Report 85(1.11).

———. 1988a. Arsenic hazards to fish, wildlife, and invertebrates: a synoptic review. U.S. Department of the Interior, Fish and Wildlife Service, Biological Report 85(1.12).

———. 1988b. Lead hazards to fish, wildlife, and invertebrates: a synoptic review. U.S. Department of the Interior, Fish and Wildlife Service, Biological Report 85(1.14).

———. 1991. Cyanide hazards to fish, wildlife, and invertebrates: a synoptic review. U.S. Department of the Interior, Fish and Wildlife Service, Biological Report 85(1.23).

———. 1995. Monosodium fluoroacetate hazards to fish, wildlife, and invertebrates: a synoptic review. U.S. Department of the Interior, Fish and Wildlife Service, Biological Report 85(1.30).

———, AND A. A. BELISLE. 1996. Planar PCBs hazards to fish, wildlife, and invertebrates: a synoptic review. U.S. Department of the Interior, Fish and Wildlife Service, Biological Report 85(1.31).

———, D. R. CLARK, JR., S. N. WIEMEYER, AND C. J. HENNY. 1999. Sodium cyanide hazards to fish and other wildlife from gold mining operations. Pages 55–67 in J. M. Azcue, editor. Environmental impacts of mining activities: emphasis on mitigation and remedial measures. Environmental Sciences Series. Springer-Verlag, Inc., Berlin, Germany.

ELLIOTT, J. E., K. M. LANGELIER, P. MINEAU, AND L. K. WILSON. 1996. Poisoning of bald eagles and red-tailed hawks by carbofuran and fensulfothion in the Fraser Delta of British Columbia, Canada. Journal of Wildlife Diseases 32:486–491.

FAIRBROTHER, A. 1996. Cholinesterase-inhibiting pesticides. Pages 52–60 in A. Fairbrother, L. N. Locke, and G. L. Huff, editors. Noninfectious diseases of wildlife. Second edition. Iowa State University Press, Ames, USA.

———, L. N. LOCKE, AND G. L. HUFF, editors. 1996. Noninfectious diseases of wildlife. Second edition. Iowa State University Press, Ames, USA.

FONTENOT, L. W., G. P. NOBLET, AND S. G. PLATT. 1994. Rotenone hazards to amphibians and reptiles. Herpetological Review 25:150–156.

FOSSI, M. C., AND C. LEONZIO, editors. 1994. Nondestructive biomarkers in ecotoxicology. Lewis Publishers, Boca Raton, Florida, USA.

FRIEND, M. 1987. Field guide to wildlife diseases. Volume 1. General field procedures and diseases of migratory birds. U.S. Department of the Interior, Fish and Wildlife Service, Resource Publication 167.

———, AND J. C. FRANSON, editors. 1999. Field manual of wildlife diseases: general field procedures and diseases of birds. U.S. Department of the Interior, Geological Survey, Biological Resources Division, Information and Technology Report 1999-001.

GALLO, M. A., AND N. J. LAWRYK. 1991. Organic phosphorus pesticides. Pages 917–1123 in W. J. Hayes and E. R. Laws, Jr., editors. Handbook of pesticide toxicity. Volume 3. Classes of pesticides. Academic Press, San Diego, California, USA.

GOLDSTEIN, M. I., B. WOODBRIDGE, M. E. ZACCAGNINI, S. B. CANAVELLI, AND A. LANUSSE. 1996. An assessment of mortality to Swainson's hawks on wintering grounds in Argentina. Journal of Raptor Research 30:106–107.

———, T. E. LACHER, B. WOODBRIDGE, M. J. BECHARD, S. B. CANAVELLI, M. E. ZACCAGNINI, G. P. COBB, E. J. SCOLLON, R. TRIBOLET, AND M. J. HOOPER. 1999. Monocrotophos-induced mass mortality of Swainson's hawks in Argentina, 1995–96. Ecotoxicology 8:201–214.

GOYER, R. A., AND T. W. CLARKSON. 2001. Toxic effects of metals. Pages 811–867 in C. D. Klaassen, editor. Casarett and Doull's toxicology: the basic science of poisons. Sixth edition. McGraw-Hill Book Co., New York, USA.

GROSS, T. S., B. S. ARNOLD, M. S. SEPÚLVEDA, AND K. McDONALD. 2003. Endocrine disrupting chemicals and endocrine active agents. Pages 1033–1098 in D. J. Hoffman, B. A. Rattner, G. A. Burton, Jr., and J. Cairns, Jr., editors. Handbook of ecotoxicology. Second edition. Lewis Publishers, Boca Raton, Florida, USA.

GRUE, C. E., T. J. O'SHEA, AND D. J. HOFFMAN. 1984. Lead concentrations and reproduction in highway-nesting barn swallows. Condor 86:383–389.

HAYES, T. B., H. HASTON, M. TSUI, A. HOANG, C. HAEFFELE, AND A. VONK. 2003. Atrazine-induced hermaphroditism at 0.1 ppb in American leopard frogs (Rana pipiens): laboratory and field evidence.

Environmental Health Perspectives 111:568–575.

HEINZ, G. H. 1996. Mercury poisoning in wildlife. Pages 118–127 in A. Fairbrother, L. N. Locke, and G. L. Huff, editors. Noninfectious diseases of wildlife. Second edition. Iowa State University Press, Ames, USA.

HENNY, C. J., R. J. HALLOCK, AND E. F. HILL. 1994. Cyanide and migratory birds at gold mines in Nevada, USA. Ecotoxicology 3:45–58.

———, E. F. HILL, D. J. HOFFMAN, M. G. SPALDING, AND R. A. GROVE. 2002. Nineteenth century mercury: hazard to wading birds and cormorants of the Carson River, Nevada. Ecotoxicology 11:213–231.

HILL, E. F. 1999. Wildlife toxicology. Pages 1327–1363 in B. Ballantyne, T. C. Marrs, and T. Syversen, editors. General and applied toxicology. Volume 2. Second edition. MacMillan Publishers. London, United Kingdom.

———. 2003. Wildlife toxicology of organophosphorus and carbamate pesticides. Pages 281–312 in D. J. Hoffman, B. A. Rattner, G. A. Burton, Jr., and J. Cairns, Jr., editors. Handbook of ecotoxicology. Second edition. Lewis Publishers, Boca Raton, Florida, USA.

———, AND W. J. FLEMING. 1982. Anticholinesterase poisoning of birds: field monitoring and diagnosis of acute poisoning. Environmental Toxicology and Chemistry 1:27–38.

HOCHSTEIN, J. R., R. J. AULERICH, AND S. J. BURSIAN. 1988. Acute toxicity of 2,3,7,8-tetrachlorodibenzo-p-dioxin to mink. Archives of Environmental Contamination and Toxicology 17:33–37.

HOFFMAN, D. J., B. A. RATTNER, G. A. BURTON, JR., AND J. CAIRNS, JR., editors. 2003. Handbook of ecotoxicology. Second edition. Lewis Publishers, Boca Raton, Florida, USA.

HOLLER, N. R., AND E. W. SCHAFER, JR. 1982. Potential secondary hazards of Avitrol baits to sharp-shinned hawks and American kestrels. Journal of Wildlife Management 46:457–462.

HOOPER, M. J., P. J. DETRICH, C. P. WEISSKOPF, AND B. W. WILSON. 1989. Organophosphorus insecticide exposure in hawks inhabiting orchards during winter dormant spraying. Bulletin of Environmental Contamination and Toxicology 42:651–659.

IRWIN, K. C., R. T. PODOLL, R. I. STARR, AND D. J. ELIAS. 1996. The mobility of [^{14}C] 3-chloro-p-toluidine hydrochloride in a loam soil profile. Environmental Toxicology and Chemistry 15:1671–1675.

JANSSEN, D. L., J. E. OOSTERHUIS, J. L. ALLEN, M. P. ANDERSON, D. G. KELTS, AND S. N. WIEMEYER. 1986. Lead poisoning in free-ranging California condors. Journal of the American Veterinary Medical Association 189:1115–1117.

JESSUP, D. A., AND F. A. LEIGHTON. 1996. Oil pollution and petroleum toxicity to wildlife. Pages 141–156 in A. Fairbrother, L. N. Locke, and G. L. Huff, editors. Noninfectious diseases of wildlife. Second edition. Iowa State University Press, Ames, USA.

JOHNSTON, J. J., D. B. HURLBUT, M. L. AVERY, AND J. C. RHYAN. 1999. Methods for the diagnosis of acute 3-chloro-p-toluidine hydrochloride poisoning in birds and the estimation of secondary hazards to wildlife. Environmental Toxicology and Chemistry 18:2533–2537.

KAMIL, N. 1987. Kinetics of bromadiolone, anticoagulant rodenticide, in the Norway rat (Rattus norvegicus). Pharmacological Research Communications 19:767–775.

KAMRIN, M. A. 1997. Pesticide profiles: toxicity, environmental impact, and fate. CRC Press, Boca Raton, Florida, USA.

KIMBALL, B. A., AND E. A. MISHALANIE. 1994. Stability of 3-chloro-p-toluidine hydrochloride in buffered aqueous solutions. Environmental Science and Technology 28:419–422.

KOLPIN, D. W., E. T. FURLONG, M. T. MEYER, E. M. THURMAN. S. D. ZAUGG, L. B. BARBER, AND H. T. BUXTON. 2002. Pharmaceuticals, hormones, and other organic wastewater contaminants in U.S. streams, 1999–2000: a national reconnaissance. Environmental Science and Technology 36:1202–1211.

KOSTECKE, R. M., G. M. LINZ, AND W. J. BLEIER. 2001. Survival of avian carcasses and photographic evidence of predators and scavengers. Journal of Field Ornithology 72:439–447.

LARISON, J. R., G. E. LIKENS, J. W. FITZPATRICK, AND J. G. CROCK. 2000. Cadmium toxicity among wildlife in the Colorado Rocky Mountains. Nature 406:181–183.

LEWIS, L. A., R. J. POPPENGA, W. R. DAVISON, J. R. FISCHER, AND K. A. MORGAN. 2001. Lead toxicosis and trace element levels in wild birds and mammals at a firearms training facility. Archives of Environmental Contamination and Toxicology 41:208–214.

MACNEILL, A. C., AND T. BARNARD. 1978. Necropsy results in free-flying and captive Anatidae in British Columbia. Canadian Veterinary Journal 19:17–21.

MATSUMURA, F. 1985. Toxicology of insecticides. Second edition. Plenum Press, New York, USA.

McDONALD, R. A., S. HARRIS, G. TURNBULL, P. BROWN, AND M. FLETCHER.

1998. Anticoagulant rodenticides in stoats (*Mustela erminea*) and weasels (*Mustela nivalis*) in England. Environmental Pollution 103:17–23.

MILLAM, J. R., M. J. DELWICHE, C. B. CRAIG-VEIT, J. D. HENDERSON, AND B. W. WILSON. 2000. Noninvasive characterization of the effects of diazinon on pigeons. Bulletin of Environmental Contamination and Toxicology 64:534–541.

MINEAU, P., editor. 1991. Cholinesterase-inhibiting insecticides: their impact on wildlife and the environment. Elsevier Scientific Publishers, Amsterdam, The Netherlands.

———. 2002. Estimating the probability of bird mortality from pesticide sprays on the basis of the field study record. Environmental Toxicology and Chemistry 21:1497–1506.

———, AND B. T. COLLINS. 1988. Avian mortality in agro-ecosystems - 2. Methods of detection. Pages 13–27 *in* M. P. Greaves, B. D. Smith, and P. W. Greig-Smith, editors. Field methods for the study of environmental effects of pesticides. British Crop Protection Council, Croydon, United Kingdom.

———, M. R. FLETCHER, L. C. GLASER, N. J. THOMAS, C. BRASSARD, L. K. WILSON, J. E. ELLIOTT, L. A. LYON, C. J. HENNY, T. BOLLINGER, AND S. L. PORTER. 1999. Poisoning of raptors with organophosphorus and carbamate pesticides with emphasis on Canada, U.S. and U.K. Journal of Raptor Research 33:1–37.

MURNANE, R. D., G. MEERDINK, B.A. RIDEOUT, AND M. P. ANDERSON. 1995. Ethylene glycol toxicosis in a captive bred released California condor (*Gymnogyps californianus*). Journal of Zoo and Wildlife Medicine 26:306–310.

NATIONAL MINING ASSOCIATION. 2004. Mining in the United States: national statistics. Available online at http://www.nma.org.

NORTON, S. 2001. Toxic effects of plants. Pages 965–976 *in* C. D. Klaassen, editor. Casarett and Doull's toxicology: the basic science of poisons. Sixth edition. McGraw-Hill Book Co., New York, USA.

NOSEK, J. A., S. R. CRAVEN, J. R. SULLIVAN, S. S. HURLEY, AND R. E. PETERSON. 1992. Toxicity and reproductive effects of 2,3,7,8-tetrachlorodibenzo-p-dioxin in ring-necked pheasants. Journal of Toxicology and Environmental Health 35:187–198.

OAKS, J. L., M. GILBERT, M. Z. VIRANI, R. T. WATSON, C. U. METEYER, B. A. RIDEOUT, H. L. SHIVAPRASAD, S. AHMED, M. J. I. CHAUDHRY, M. ARSHAD, S. MAHMOOD, A. ALI, AND A. A. KHAN. 2004. Diclofenac residues as the cause of vulture population decline in Pakistan. Nature 427:630–633.

O'HARA, T. M. 1996. Mycotoxins. Pages 24–30 *in* A. Fairbrother, L. N. Locke, and G. L. Huff, editors. Noninfectious diseases of wildlife. Second edition. Iowa State University Press, Ames, USA.

OHLENDORF, H. M. 2003. Ecotoxicology of selenium. Pages 465–500 *in* D. J. Hoffman, B. A. Rattner, G. A. Burton, Jr., and J. Cairns, Jr., editors. Handbook of ecotoxicology. Second edition. Lewis Publishers, Boca Raton, Florida, USA.

———, D. J. HOFFMAN, M. K. SAIKI, AND T. W. ALDRICH. 1986. Embryonic mortality and abnormalities of aquatic birds: apparent impacts of selenium from irrigation drainwater. Science of the Total Environment 52:49–63.

OSWEILER, G. D., T. L. CARSON, W. B. BUCK, AND G. A. VAN GELDER. 1985. Clinical and diagnostic veterinary toxicology. Third edition. Kendall-Hunt Publishing, Dubuque, Iowa, USA.

PATTEE, O. H., AND D. J. PAIN. 2003. Lead in the environment. Pages 373–408 *in* D. J. Hoffman, B. A. Rattner, G. A. Burton, Jr., and J. Cairns, Jr., editors. Handbook of ecotoxicology. Second edition. Lewis Publishers, Boca Raton, Florida, USA.

PIMENTEL, D., A. GREINER, AND T. BASHORE. 1997. Economic and environmental costs of pesticide use. Pages 121–150 *in* J. Rose, editor. Environmental toxicology. Gordon and Breach, London, United Kingdom.

———, H. ACQUAY, M. BILTONEN, P. RICE, M. SILVA, J. NELSON, V. LIPNER, S. GIODANO, A. HOROWITZ, AND M. D'AMORE. 1992. Environmental and economic costs of pesticide use. BioScience 42:750–760.

POKRAS, M. S., AND R. CHAFEL. 1992. Lead toxicosis from ingested fishing sinkers in adult common loons (*Gavia immer*) in New England. Journal of Zoo and Wildlife Medicine 23:92–97.

RACINE C. H., M. E. WALSH, B. D. ROEBUCK, C. M. COLLINS, D. J. CALKINS, L. R. REITSMA, P. J. BUCHLI, AND G. GOLDFARB. 1992. White phosphorus poisoning of waterfowl in an Alaskan salt marsh. Journal of Wildlife Diseases 28:669–673.

RAY, D. E. 1991. Pesticides derived from plants and other organisms. Pages 585–636 *in* W. J. Hayes and E. R. Laws, Jr., editors. Handbook of pesticide toxicology. Volume 2. Classes of pesticides. Academic Press, San Diego, California, USA.

RICE, C. P., P. W. O'KEEFE, AND T. J. KUBIAK. 2003. Sources, pathways,

and effects of PCBs, dioxins, and dibenzofurans. Pages 501–573 *in* D. J. Hoffman, B. A. Rattner, G. A. Burton, Jr., and J. Cairns, Jr., editors. Handbook of ecotoxicology. Second edition. Lewis Publishers, Boca Raton, Florida, USA.

ROEBUCK, B. D., M. E. WALSH, C. H. RACINE, L. R. REITSMA, B. B. STEELE, AND S. I. NAM. 1994. Predation of ducks poisoned by white phosphorus: exposure and risks to predators. Environmental Toxicology and Chemistry 13:1613–1618.

ROFFE, T. J., AND T. M. WORK. 2005. Wildlife health and disease investigations. Pages 197–212 *in* C. E. Braun, editor. Techniques for wildlife investigations and management. Sixth edition. The Wildlife Society, Bethesda, Maryland, USA.

RUSSELL, F. E. 2001. Toxic effects of terrestrial animal venoms and poisons. Pages 945–964 *in* C. D. Klaassen, editor. Casarett and Doull's toxicology: the basic science of poisons. Sixth edition. McGraw-Hill Book Co., New York, USA.

SANDERSON, G. C., AND F. C. BELLROSE. 1986. A review of the problem of lead poisoning in waterfowl. Special Publication 4. Illinois Natural History Survey, Urbana, USA.

SCHEUHAMMER, A. M., AND S. L. NORRIS. 1996. The ecotoxicology of lead shot and lead fishing weights. Ecotoxicology 5:279–295.

SHEFFIELD, S. R. 1997. Owls as biomonitors of environmental contamination. Pages 383–398 *in* J. R. Duncan, D. H. Johnson, and T. H. Nicholls, editors. Biology and conservation of owls of the northern hemisphere. U.S. Department of Agriculture, Forest Service, General Technical Report NC-190.

———, AND R. L. LOCHMILLER. 2001. Effects of field exposure to diazinon on small mammals inhabiting a semi-enclosed prairie grassland ecosystem. I. Ecological and reproductive effects. Environmental Toxicology and Chemistry 20:284–296.

———, K. SAWICKA-KAPUSTA, J. B. COHEN, AND B. A. RATTNER. 2001. Rodents and lagomorphs. Pages 215–314 *in* R. F. Shore and B. A. Rattner, editors. Ecotoxicology of wild mammals. John Wiley and Sons, London, United Kingdom.

SHORE, R. F., AND B. A. RATTNER, editors. 2001. Ecotoxicology of wild mammals. John Wiley and Sons, London, United Kingdom.

SIDOR, I. F., M. A. POKRAS, A. R. MAJOR, R. H. POPPENGA, K. M. TAYLOR, AND R. M. MICONI. 2003. Mortality of common loons in New England, 1987 to 2000. Journal of Wildlife Diseases 39:306–315.

SMITH, A. G. 1991. Chlorinated hydrocarbon insecticides. Pages 731–915 *in* W. J. Hayes and E. R. Laws, Jr., editors. Handbook of pesticide toxicology. Volume 2. Classes of pesticides. Academic Press, San Diego, California, USA.

SMITH, G. J. 1987. Pesticide use and toxicology in relation to wildlife: organophosphorus and carbamate compounds. U.S. Department of the Interior, Fish and Wildlife Service, Resource Publication 170.

SPARLING, D. W. 2003. White phosphorus at Eagle River flats, Alaska: a case history of waterfowl mortality. Pages 767–786 *in* D. J. Hoffman, B. A. Rattner, G. A. Burton, Jr., and J. Cairns, Jr., editors. Handbook of ecotoxicology. Second edition. Lewis Publishers, Boca Raton, Florida, USA.

———, AND N. E. FEDEROFF. 1997. Secondary poisoning of kestrels by white phosphorus. Ecotoxicology 6:239–247.

———, D. DAY, AND P. KLEIN. 1999. Acute toxicity and sublethal effects of white phosphorus in mute swans, *Cygnus olor*. Archives of Environmental Contamination and Toxicology 36:316–322.

———, S. VANN, AND R. A. GROVE. 1998. Blood changes in mallards exposed to white phosphorus. Environmental Toxicology and Chemistry 17:2521–2529.

STANSLEY, W., AND D. E. ROSCOE. 1996. The uptake and effects of lead in small mammals and frogs at a trap and skeet range. Archives of Environmental Contamination and Toxicology 30:220–226.

STEVENS, J. T., AND D. D. SUMNER. 1991. Herbicides. Pages 1317–1408 *in* W. J. Hayes and E. R. Laws, Jr., editor. Handbook of pesticide toxicology. Volume 3. Classes of pesticides. Academic Press, San Diego, California, USA.

STONE, W. B., AND J. C. OKONIEWSKI. 2001. Necropsy findings and environmental contaminants in common loons from New York. Journal of Wildlife Diseases 37:178–184.

———, ———, AND J. R. STEDELIN. 1999. Poisoning of wildlife with anticoagulant rodenticides in New York. Journal of Wildlife Diseases 35:187–193.

STOWE, C. M., D. M. BARNES, AND T. D. ARENDT. 1981. Ethylene glycol intoxication in ducks. Avian Diseases 25:538–541.

TANABE, S. 1988. PCB problems in the future: foresight from current knowledge. Environmental Pollution 50:5–28.

U.S. DEPARTMENT OF TRANSPORTATION. 2004. National response center statistics: incident by type per year. U.S. Department of Transportation and U.S. Coast Guard, National Response Center, Washington, D.C., USA. Available online at http://www.nrc.usge.mil/incident.htm.

U.S. ENVIRONMENTAL PROTECTION AGENCY. 1996. The facts speak for themselves: a fundamentally different Superfund program. U.S. Environmental Protection Agency, Office of Solid Waste and Emergency Response, Washington, D.C., USA. Available online at http://www.epa.gov/superfund/whatissf/sf_fact4.

———. 1998a. Emergency planning and community right to know. Section 313. Toxic release inventory reporting. Notice of receipt of petition. Federal Register 63:6691–6698.

———. 1998b. U.S. high production volume chemical hazard data availability study. U.S. Environmental Protection Agency, Washington, D.C., USA.

———. 2003. 2001 toxic release inventory: executive summary. U.S. Environmental Protection Agency, Office of Environmental Information, EPA 260-S-03-001. Washington, D.C., USA.

———. 2004. EPA Superfund-final national priorities list sites. U.S. Environmental Protection Agency, Washington, D.C., USA. Available online at http://www.epa.gov/superfund/sites/query/queryhtm/hp/fin1.htm.

VANGILDER, L. D. 1983. Reproductive effects of toxic substances on wildlife: an evolutionary view. Pages 250–259 in Czechoslovak-American symposium on toxic effects and reproductive ability in free-living animals. Strblke Pleso, Czechoslovakia.

VYAS, N. B. 1999. Factors influencing estimation of pesticide-related wildlife mortality. Toxicology and Industrial Health 15:186–191.

WHITE, D. H., AND J. T. SEGINAK. 1994. Dioxins and furans linked to reproductive impairment in wood ducks. Journal of Wildlife Management 58:100–106.

WICKSTROM, M. 1999. Natural toxins and wildlife. Canadian Cooperative Wildlife Health Centre short course: wildlife toxicology. Canadian Cooperative Wildlife Health Centre, Saskatoon, Saskatchewan, Canada. Available online at http://wildlife.usask.ca/english/tox-6.htm.

WIENER, J. G., D. P. KRABBENHOFT, G. H. HEINZ, AND A. M. SCHEUHAMMER. 2003. Exotoxicology of mercury. Pages 373–408 in D. J. Hoffman, B. A. Rattner, G. A. Burton, Jr., and J. Cairns, Jr., editors. Handbook of ecotoxicology. Second edition. Lewis Publishers, Boca Raton, Florida, USA.

WINDINGSTAD, R. M., R. J. COLE, P. E. NELSON, T. J. ROFFE, R. R. GEORGE, AND J. W. DORNER. 1989. *Fusarium* mycotoxins from peanuts suspected as a cause of sandhill crane mortality. Journal of Wildlife Diseases 25:38–46.

YAMAMOTO, J. T., R. M. DONOHOE, D. M. FRY, M. S. GOLUB, J. M. DONALD. 1996. Environmental estrogens: implications for reproduction in wildlife. Pages 31–51 in A. Fairbrother, L. N. Locke, and G. L. Huff, editors. Noninfectious diseases of wildlife. Second edition. Iowa State University Press, Ames, USA.

(Appendix on next page.)

APPENDIX

Sample Wildlife Mortality/Morbidity Incident Field Data Sheet (modified from Friend and Franson 1999).

Date: _____

Submitter's name: _____

Submitter's affiliation: _____

Submitter's contact information: _____

Date collected: _____

Method of collection:_____
   (found dead, euthanized; if euthanized, technique used)

Incident scene biologist: _____

Incident location: State: _____ County: _____ Lat/Long: _____

Specific incident location: _____

Incident area description: _____
   (land use, habitat types, etc.)

Environmental factors at incident site: _____
   (climatic conditions, description of waterbodies, evidence of chemicals, etc.)

Time of onset of incident (date and time): _____
   (best estimate)

Species affected: _____

Species that appear unaffected (if known): _____

Age/sex of species affected: _____

Number known dead of each species: _____

Mortality/Morbidity ratio: _____
   (#dead/#sick)

Estimated dead: _____
   (consider scavengers, other removal)

Clinical signs: _____

_____

Species at risk: _____

Additional information and observations/comments:_____

_____

10

CAPTURING AND HANDLING WILD ANIMALS

Sanford D. Schemnitz

INTRODUCTION

The art of capturing wild animals for food and clothing is as old as human existence on earth. However, in today's world, reasons for catching wild species are more diverse. Millions of wild animals are captured each year as part of damage and disease control programs, population regulation activities, wildlife management efforts, and research studies. Many aspects of animal capture, especially those associated with protected wildlife species, are highly regulated by both state and federal governmental agencies. Animal welfare concerns are important regardless of the reason for capture. In addition, efficiency (the rate at which a device or system catches the intended species) is a critical aspect of wild animal capture systems.

Successful capture programs result from the efforts of experienced wildlife biologists and technicians who have planned, studied, and tested methods prior to starting any new program. Researchers must have valid trapping or banding permits or both before undertaking wildlife capture. Also, capture and handling protocols used should be approved by an institutional animal care and use committee, if appropriate, to insure compliance with the Federal Animal Welfare Act (P.L. 89-554, 1966) and its amendments. Researchers are encouraged to consult Littell (1993) and Gaunt et al. (1997) concerning guidelines and procedures relating to capture and handling permits.

CAPTURING BIRDS

Major review sources on bird capture techniques

239

Table 1. Box and cage traps used to capture birds.

Group/Species	References
Waterfowl	Kutz 1945, Hunt and Dahlka 1953, McCall 1954, Schierbaum and Talmage 1954, Addy 1956, Schierbaum et al. 1959, DuBois and Palmisano 1974, Mauser and Mensik 1992, Evrard and Bacon 1998, Harrison et al. 2000
Raptors	Ward and Martin 1968, Buck and Craft 1995
Ruffed grouse (*Bonasa umbellus*)	Tanner and Bowers 1948, Chambers and English 1958
Sharp-tailed grouse (*Tympanuchus phasianellus*)	Hamerstrom and Truax 1938
Greater prairie-chicken (*T. cupido*)	Hamerstrom and Truax 1938
Ring-necked pheasant	Hicks and Leedy 1939, Kutz 1945, Flock and Applegate 2002
Northern bobwhite	Schultz 1950, Smith et al. 1981
Scaled quail (*Callipepla squamata*)	Schemnitz 1961, Smith et al. 1981
Wild turkey	Baldwin 1947, Bailey 1976, Davis 1994
Puffin (*Fratercula* spp.)	Nettleship 1969
Burrowing owl (*Athene cunicularia*)	Martin 1971, Ferguson and Jorgensen 1981, Plumpton and Lutz 1992
Mourning dove (*Zenaida macroura*)	Reeves et al. 1968
Band-tailed pigeon (*Patagioenas fasciata*)	Drewien et al. 1966, Smith 1968, Braun 1976
Chihuahuan raven (*Corvus cryptoleucus*)	Aldous 1936
American magpie	Alsager et al. 1972
House finch (*Carpodacus mexicanus*)	Larsen 1970
House sparrow (*Passer domesticus*)	Therrien 1996

include Canadian Wildlife Service and U.S. Department of Interior (1977), Day et al. (1980), Davis (1981), Keyes and Grue (1982), Bloom (1987), Bub (1991), Schemnitz (1994), and Gaunt et al. (1997).

Baited Traps

Harrison et al. (2000) described a trap designed to accommodate tidal water level fluctuations by providing a 1,500-cm² floating platform in the trap to curtail mortality from drowning. Mauser and Mensik (1992) constructed a portable swim-in bait trap to capture ducks. The trap panels were covered with plastic netting to minimize injuries. A floating catch box allowed trap operation in a variety of water depths. They suggested a loafing platform for birds in the trap.

Wang and Trost (2000) used baited traps (Table 1) with a 50-cm long funnel entrance with a chicken wire open hoop 20 cm high at the end to catch American magpies (*Pica hudsonia*). This trap required the magpie to jump over the hoop to reach the bait.

Buck and Craft (1955) had success catching great horned owls (*Bubo virginianus*) and red-tailed hawks (*Buteo jamaicensis*) with 2 designs of walk-in traps. One type had a welded-wire funnel entrance. The other was activated with a monofilament trip wire that released a trap door. Rock pigeons (*Columba livia*), domestic chickens, or captive-bred northern bobwhites (*Colinus virginianus*) were enclosed in wire cages and served as live bait.

Use of Nets

Cannon and Rocket Nets

Grand and Fondell (1994) compared decoy traps and rocket netting for capturing northern pintails (*Anas acuta*) in spring. Male pintails were captured at similar rates using both methods. Baited rocket nets were more efficient than decoy traps for capturing females. Captive-reared female pintails were used as decoys. A portable platform for setting rocket nets in open-water habitats was perfected by Cox and Afton (1994). Incidence of mortality (1%) and escape (3%) of captured birds was low. Mahan et al. (2002) modified nets and net boxes to

enhance capture of wild turkeys (*Meleagris gallopavo*). They rotated a 12 × 12 m² drop net 45° so that it resembled a baseball diamond and attached 3 rockets. One set of drag weights rather than 3 was used. Their system was quicker and easier to prepare, transport, and set up. Flock and Applegate (2002) compared trapping methods for ring-necked pheasants (*Phasianus colchicus*) in Kansas. They reported that rocket nets had the highest capture rate and were the most effective trapping method. They recommended 3.2-cm mesh netting to minimize injury and expedite removal of pheasants from the net. Walk in bait traps were their second choice. King et al. (1998) successfully captured American white pelicans (*Pelecanus erythrorhynchos*) and great blue herons (*Ardea herodias*) with a modified rocket-net system consisting of an aluminum box (containing the net) set in 2–4 cm deep water (Table 2).

Drop Nets

Nastase (1982) captured flightless Canada geese (*Branta canadensis*) by herding them under an 18 × 18 m, 5.0-cm mesh drop-net. Lockowandt (1993) designed an electromagnetic trigger for drop-nets that worked well in cold weather with high winds and ice (Table 3).

Mist Nets

Mist nets continue to be an effective method for sampling bird populations. Remsen and Good (1996) urged caution in direct use of mist-net data to estimate relative bird abundance. Corrections should be based on detailed knowledge of the ecology and behavior of the birds involved. Ralph et al. (1993) emphasized the importance of setting nets in locations of similar vegetation density and terrain. Jenni et al. (1996) reported the proportion of birds avoiding mist nets without entering a net shelf depended on the extent of shading and net-shelf height but not on species, wind speed, or habitat. Dunn et al. (1997) reported that annual capture indices of 13 songbird species based on standardized autumn mist netting were significantly and positively correlated with breeding bird survey data from Michigan and Ontario. Their results suggested

Table 2. Cannon and rocket nets used to capture wildlife.

Group/Species	References
Birds	
American white pelican	King et al. 1998
Waterfowl	Dill and Thornsberry 1950, Turner 1956, Marquardt 1960, Funk and Grieb 1965, Raveling 1966, Moses 1968, Wunz 1984, Zahm et al. 1987, Cox and Afton 1994, Grand and Fondell 1994, Merendino and Lobpries 1998
Great blue heron	King et al. 1998
White ibis (*Eudocimus albus*)	Heath and Frederick 2003
Blue grouse (*Dendragapus obscurus*)	Lacher and Lacher 1964
Greater sage-grouse (*Centrocercus urophasianus*)	Lacher and Lacher 1964, Giesen et al. 1982
Sharp-tailed grouse	Peterle 1956
Greater prairie-chicken	Silvy and Robel 1968
Ring-necked pheasant	Flock and Applegate 2002
Wild turkey	Austin 1965; Bailey 1976; Wunz 1984, 1987; Davis 1994; Eriksen et al. 1995; Pack et al. 1996; Mahan et al. 2002
Bald eagle (*Haliaeetus leucocephalus*)	Grubb 1988, 1991
Ruddy turnstone (*Arenaria interpres*)	Thompson and DeLong 1967
Ring-billed gull (*Larus delawarensis*)	Southern 1972
Band-tailed pigeon	Smith 1968, Pederson and Nish 1975, Braun 1976
American crow (*Corvus brachyrhynchos*)	Caffrey 2001
Brown-headed cowbird (*Molothrus ater*)	Arnold and Coon 1972
Mammals	
White-tailed deer (*Odocoileus virginianus*)	Hawkins et al. 1968, Palmer et al. 1980, Beringer et al. 1996, Cromwell et al. 1999, Haulton et al. 2001
Fallow deer (*Dama dama*)	Nall et al. 1970
Mountain sheep (*Ovis canadensis*)	Jessup et al. 1984
Dall sheep (*O. dalli*)	Heimer et al. 1980

Table 3. Drop nets used to capture wildlife.

Group/Species	References
Birds	
Canada goose	Nastase 1982
Greater prairie-chicken	Jacobs 1958
Wild turkey	Baldwin 1947, Glazener et al. 1964
Band-tailed pigeon	Wooten 1955, Drewien et al. 1966
Shorebirds	Peyton and Shields 1979
Mammals	
White-tailed deer	Ramsey 1968, Conner et al. 1987, DeNicola and Swihart 1997, Lopez et al. 1998
Mule deer (*Odocoileus hemionus*)	White and Bartmann 1994, D'Eon et al. 2003
Mountain sheep	Fuller 1984, Kock et al. 1987

were suspended from a support cable and pulled along the cable by a control cord and pulley. This system allowed comparisons of mist net capture rates between forest canopy and understory levels. Albanese and Piaskowski (1999) perfected an inexpensive ($35.00) elevated mist net apparatus that sampled birds in vegetation strata from ground level to a height of 8.5 m. The equipment consisted of metallic tubs, "clothesline cord," single and double pulleys, and required only one person to operate the system. Meyers (1994) captured orange-winged parrots (*Amazona amazonica*) using mist nets in a circular configuration around roost trees. Live parrot decoys were placed within the circle of mist nets and supplemented with playback vocalizations. Catch rate was increased by flushing parrots as the observer rushed toward the nets. Wilson and Allan (1996) captured prothonotary warblers (*Prothonotaria citrea*) and Acadian flycatchers (*Empidonax virescens*) in a forested wetland by placing a mist net in a V-shaped configuration, mounted in a boat. A decoy study mount was placed close to a mist net pole. Barred owls (*Strix varia*) were successfully captured by Elody and Sloan (1984) using 3 mist nets set in an "A" configuration with a live barred owl placed in the center as a decoy, along with an outdoor megaphone speaker and cassette tape player broadcasting a barred owl recorded call.

Lesage et al. (1997) modified mist net techniques to capture breeding adult and young surf scoters (*Melanitta perspicillata*). They placed 2 nets at scoter feeding sites, extending perpendicular from the shore using copper poles painted black and pushed firmly into the lake bottom. A boat was used to herd the scoters into the net. Capture success occurred with nets placed both above and below the water surface. Breault and Cheng (1990) used submerged mist nets to capture eared grebes (*Podiceps nigricollis*). They set the nets in waist-deep (1.5 m) water and used 7-g fishing weights attached to the net bottom at 1.5-m intervals to sink the net. Nets were attached to wooden poles. Grebes were driven into the nets by walking or canoeing from behind the birds toward the submerged nets. Avoidance of drowning was achieved by immediate removal of any captured birds from the nets. Bacon and Evrard (1990) successfully captured upland nesting ducks by holding a mist net in a horizontal position over the nest. When the hen flushed, she became entangled in the net mesh. The net was attached between 3-m sections of conduit. Kaiser et al. (1995) placed an array of 3 mist nets floating on rafts to catch marbled

that mist netting could be a useful population-monitoring tool. Wang and Finch (2002) noted consistency between results of mist netting and point counts in assessing land bird species richness and relative abundance during migration in central New Mexico.

Meyers and Pardieck (1993) developed a lightweight, low canopy (1.8–7.3 m) mist-net system using adjustable aluminum telescoping poles. Stokes et al. (2000) perfected a method to deploy mist nests horizontally from a canopy platform in 30-m tall forests. A connecting wooden bridge can be built between platforms. The nets and net poles

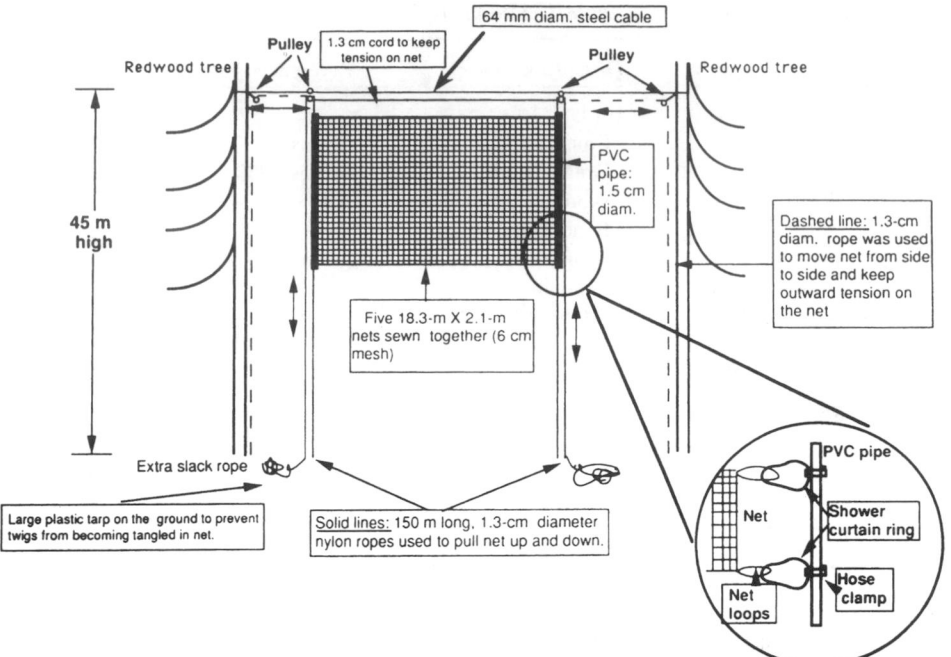

Fig. 1. Schematic of mist net used to capture marbled murrelets in the forests of northern California. Branches were on all sides of both trees and not removed. Diagram not drawn to scale (from Paton et al. 1991).

murrelets (*Brachyramphus marmoratus*) as they flew through narrow coastal channels. They used aluminum tubing to support the nets. Nets were set against a forested background to reduce their visibility to approaching murrelets. Paton et al. (1991) used a large mist net consisting of 5 nets sewn together, elevated with pulleys 45 m into the forest canopy (Fig. 1) to capture marbled murrelets. Netting sessions were conducted during the main activity periods, 60 minutes before to 60 minutes after sunrise. When not in use, the net was wrapped with a plastic tarp to avoid entanglement with woody debris.

Hilton (1989) used taped fledgling alarm calls along with mist nets near active blue jay (*Cyanocitta cristata*) nests to successfully capture blue jays. The taped calls were broadcast from a portable tape recorder placed beneath the center of the net.

Skinner et al. (1998) combined pointing dogs and mist nets attached to galvanized pipe poles to capture juvenile willow ptarmigan (*Lagopus lagopus*). After the dogs located and pointed the birds, the mist nets were arranged in a V pattern ahead of the covey. The ptarmigan were then flushed into the nets and captured. Geering (1998) used playback tapes during the breeding season to attract birds to be captured in mist nets. Bull and Cooper (1996) presented 4 new techniques for capturing pileated woodpeckers (*Drycopus pileatus*) and Vaux's swifts (*Chaetura vauxi*) in roost trees. They camouflaged traps with tree bark or lichens set above the entrance hole. A person on the ground released the trap by pulling a taut line as soon as the bird entered the hole. The lichen-covered trap closed to the side of the hole. Both the bark and the lichen-covered plastic netting were taped to a frame. They also used 2 designs, a mist net on a frame and a mist net suspended between 2 trees (Fig. 2) and positioned 3–5 m in front of a nest cavity to capture swifts.

Blackshaw (1994) devised a method to secure closed and rolled mist nets that prevented unrolling, tangling, and sag-

ging. She used a 61-cm length of sisal or braided non-slick twine attached to the net and to a long stick placed vertically in the ground near the center of the net. Sykes (1989) used strips of asphalt-saturated, 13.6-kg roofing felt under each tightly furled mist net to prevent accidental capture of birds, small mammals, and large insects, such as beetles, in unattended nets. A chain saw was used to cut rolls of roofing felt at 22.9-cm intervals.

Nets and Night-lighting

Earle (1988) combined night lighting and a cast-net to capture nightjars (Caprimulgidae) along gravel roads. The 85-cm diameter, circular cast-net had handles to facilitate throwing it.

Drewien and Clegg (1991) had great success capturing sandhill (*Grus canadensis*) and whooping (*G. americana*) cranes using a portable generator mounted on an aluminum back-pack frame and a 28-volt spotlight mounted on a helmet to locate them. Cranes were then captured using long-handled (3–3.6 m in length) nets with best success on dark, overcast nights when they were roosting in small flocks during summer. Drewien et al. (1999) captured trumpeter swans (*Cygnus buccinator*) using night lighting to locate them from a lightweight (180 kg) airboat during severe winter weather. King et al. (1994) successfully captured roosting double-crested cormorants (*Phalacrocorax auritus*) using night lighting from a boat at winter roosts in cypress trees (Fig. 3). Cormorants were captured with a long-handled net in shallow water.

Bowman et al. (1994) successfully used night lighting to survey, capture, and band island nesting American white pelicans, double-crested cormorants, and California gulls (*Larus californicus*). Disturbances to birds while night lighting were minimal with no predation by gulls on eggs or chicks. Night lighting was more effective for capturing young than adults. Snow et al. (1990) night-lighted com-

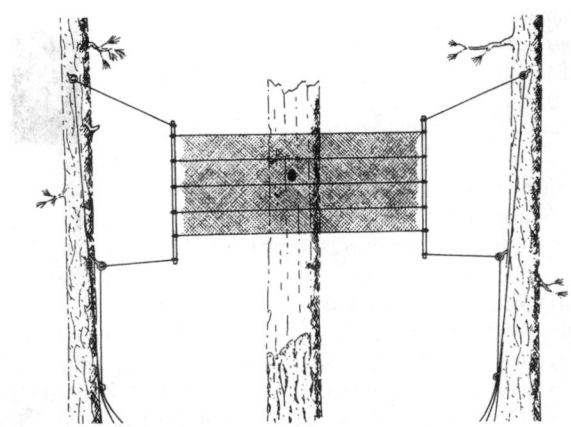

Fig. 2. Mist net erected between 2 live trees and positioned in front of a nest cavity (from Bull and Cooper 1996).

Table 4. Night-lighting methods and equipment used to capture wildlife.

Group/Species	References
Birds	
Greater rhea	Martella and Navarro 1992
American white pelican	Bowman et al. 1994
Double-crested cormorant	Bowman et al. 1994; King et al. 1994, 2000
Waterfowl	Glasgow 1957, Lindmeier and Jessen 1961, Cummings and Hewitt 1964, Drewien et al. 1967, Bishop and Barratt 1969, Merendino and Lobpries 1998
Trumpeter swan	Drewien et al. 1999
Common eider	Snow et al. 1990
Ruffed grouse	Huempfener et al.1975
Greater sage-grouse	Giesen et al. 1982, Wakkinen et al. 1992
Greater prairie-chicken	Labisky 1968
Northern bobwhite	Labisky 1968
Ring-necked pheasant	Drewien et al. 1967, Labisky 1968
Shorebirds	Potts and Sordahl 1979
Sandhill crane	Drewien and Clegg 1991
Whooping crane	Drewien and Clegg 1991
Yellow rail (*Coturnicops noveboracensis*)	Robert and Laporte 1997
American woodcock (*Scolopax minor*)	Rieffenberger and Ferrigno 1970, Shuler et al. 1986
California gull	Bowman et al. 1994
Common nighthawk (*Chordeiles minor*)	Swenson and Swenson 1977
Mammals	
Cottontail rabbit (*Silvilagus* spp.)	Drewien et al. 1967, Labisky 1968
Jackrabbit (*Lepus* spp.)	Griffith and Evans 1970
Muskrat (*Ondatra zibethicus*)	McCabe and Elison 1986
Mule deer	Steger and Neal 1981

Table 5. Drive and drift traps used to capture wildlife.

Group/Species	References
Birds	
Canada goose	Robards 1960, Heyland 1970, Timm and Bromley 1976, Costanzo et al. 1995
Snow goose (*Chen caerulescens*)	Cooch 1953
Wood duck (*Aix sponsa*)	Tolle and Bookhout 1974
Diving ducks	Cowan and Hatter 1952
Blue grouse	Tomlinson 1963, Pelren and Crawford 1995
Ruffed grouse	Liscinsky and Bailey 1955
Greater sage-grouse	Giesen et al. 1982
Greater prairie-chicken	Toepfer et al. 1988, Schroeder and Braun 1991
Lesser prairie-chicken	Haukos et al. 1990
Scaled quail	Schemnitz 1961
Sandhill crane	Logan and Chandler 1987
Clapper rail (*Rallus longirostris*)	Stewart 1951
Black rail	Flores and Eddleman 1993
Virginia rail	Kearns et al. 1998
Sora	Kearns et al. 1998
American coot (*Fulica americana*)	Glasgow 1957, Crawford 1977
Shorebirds	Low 1935
American woodcock	Liscinsky and Bailey 1955, Martin and Clark 1964
Mammals	
Snowshoe hare (*Lepus americanus*)	Keith et al. 1968
White-tailed deer	Stafford et al. 1966, Silvy et al. 1975, DeYoung 1988, Sullivan et al. 1991
Mule deer	Beasom et al. 1980, Thomas and Novak 1991
Himalayan musk deer (*Moschus moschiferus*)	Kattell and Alldredge 1991
Mountain sheep	Kock et al. 1987

mon eiders (*Somateria mollissima*) during the summer in shoal waters using deep hoop nets 46–61 cm in diameter attached to 3.7–4.3-m long handles (Table 4).

Fig. 3. Jon-boat showing positioning of night-lighting equipment (bow rails, lights, converter box, and generator) and personnel (from King et al. 1994).

Wakkinen et al. (1992) modified night spotlighting techniques by using binoculars in conjunction with a spotlight to locate greater sage-grouse. Binoculars allowed greater detection in 55 of 58 (95%) instances. Capture success increased >40%.

Martella and Navarro (1992) devised a novel method for capturing greater rheas (*Rhea americana*). They blinded the birds using a spotlight at night and captured them using a "boleadoras," a device consisting of 2–3 balls of round stone covered with leather and attached to a long strap of braided leather, 7-mm diameter and 1-m long. When the bird began to run, the 'boleadoras' was thrown toward the bird's legs. The straps wound around the rhea's legs, causing the bird to fall allowing hand capture.

Drive and Drift Traps

Costanzo et al. (1995) successfully herded large flocks of flightless Canada geese into a moveable catch pen comprised of 6 attached panels (Table 5). Each panel was 3.4 × 1.5 m made of nylon netting attached to a conduit frame. This trap was inexpensive, portable, and simple to assemble.

Flores and Eddleman (1993) placed drop-door traps

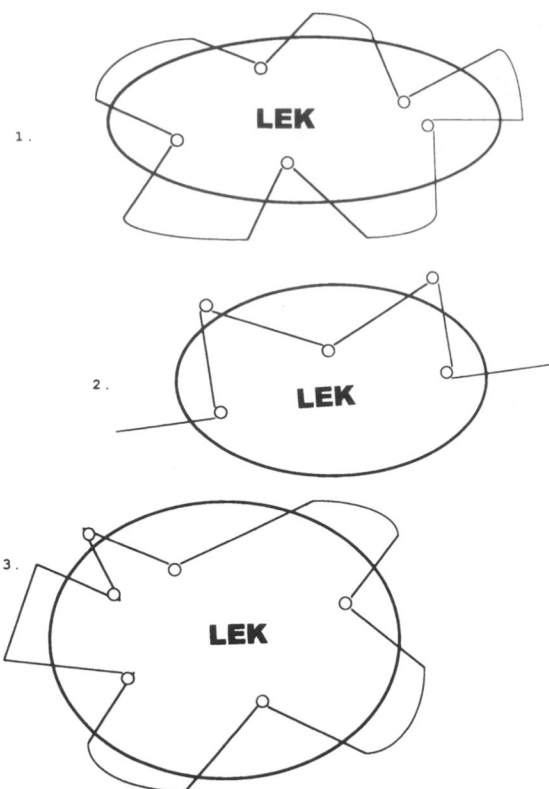

Fig. 4. Overhead view of lek walk-in designs used to capture lesser prairie-chickens (from Haukos et al. 1990).

along 1-m tall drift fences of 1.8 cm mesh black plastic bird netting to capture black rails (*Laterallus jamaicensis*). The netting was stapled to wooden surveyor's stakes. Kearns et al. (1998) combined 2.5-cm mesh welded wire cloverleaf traps with ramped funnel entrances with an attached catch box to catch sora (*Porzana carolina*) and Virginia rails (*Rallus limicola*). Drift fences deflected the rails into the traps. Capture rate was increased by using playback of rail vocalizations. The sound system was powered by solar panels. Fuertes et al. (2002) used a modified fish net trap in the shape of a funnel in pairs with a deflecting drift net in between to capture small rails. They added fruits, vegetables, and cat food as bait. Their traps were easy to transport and place, and had a low injury rate.

Haukos et al. (1990) recommended walk-in drift traps (Fig. 4) over rocket nets and baited walk-in traps for capture of lesser prairie-chickens (*Tympanuchus pallidicinctus*) on leks in spring. Advantages of walk-in drift traps included minimal capture stress, no need for observer presence, and the entire lek could be trapped. Pelren and Crawford (1995) successfully captured blue grouse with walk-in style traps that intercepted moving birds with 60-cm tall mesh wire fences. The fences guided the grouse into funnels connected to trap boxes made of plastic netting with fish netting tops to minimize injury to trapped birds.

Nest Traps

Blums et al. (2000) perfected a multi-capture nest box for cavity-nesting ducks (Table 6). This trap featured a swinging false floor, entrance baffle, and counter balance. A scaled-down version of this trap can be used to capture smaller cavity nesting birds. Plice and Balgooyen (1999)

Table 6. Nest traps used to capture birds.

Group	References
Cavities	
Hooded merganser (*Lophodytes cucullatus*)	Blums et al. 2000
Wood duck	Blums et al. 2000
Acorn woodpecker (*Melanerpes erythrocephalus*)	Stanback and Koenig 1994
Red-cockaded woodpecker (*Picoides borealis*)	Jackson and Parris 1991
Pileated woodpecker	Bull and Pedersen 1978
Red-bellied woodpecker (*Melanerpes carolinus*)	Bull and Pedersen 1978
Tree swallow	Rendell et al. 1989
Bank swallow (*Riparia riparia*)	Rendell et al. 1989
Nest boxes	
American kestrel	Plice and Balgooyen 1999
Tree swallow	Lombardo and Kemly 1983, Cohen and Hayes 1984, Cohen 1985, Stutchbury and Robertson 1986
Bluebird (*Sialia* spp.)	Kibler 1969, Pinkowski 1978
House sparrow	Mock et al. 1999
House wren	Pribil 1997
European starling (*Sturnus vulgaris*)	DeHaven and Guarino 1969, Lombardo and Kemly 1983
Other passerine birds	Dhondt and van Outryve 1971, Stewart 1971, Yunick 1990
Waterfowl	Harris 1952, Sowls 1955, Addy 1956, Weller 1957, Coulter 1958, Miller 1962, Salyer 1962, Doty and Lee 1974, Zicus 1975, Shaiffer and Krapu 1978, Blums et al. 1983, Zicus 1989, Bacon and Evrard 1990, Dietz et al. 1994, Yerkes 1997, Loos and Rohwer 2002
Other birds	
Pied-billed grebe (*Podilymbus podiceps*)	Otto 1983
Egrets and herons	Jewell and Bancroft 1991, Mock et al. 1999
White ibis	Frederick 1986
American coot	Crawford 1977
American avocet (*Recurvirostra americana*)	Sordahl 1980
Black-necked stilt (*Himantopus mexicanus*)	Sordahl 1980
Mountain plover (*Charadrius montanus*)	Graul 1979
Snowy plover (*C. alexandrinus*)	Conway and Smith 2000
Wilson's phalarope (*Phalaropus tricolor*)	Kagarise 1978
Herring gull (*Larus argentatus*)	Weaver and Kadlec 1970
Mourning dove	Swank 1952, Stewart 1954, Harris and Morse 1958, Blockstein 1985
White-winged dove (*Zenaida asiatica*)	Swanson and Rappole 1994
Raptors	Jacobs and Proudfoot 2002
Osprey (*Pandion haliaetus*)	Ewins and Miller 1993
Short-eared owl (*Asio flammeus*)	Leasure and Holt 1991
Belted kingfisher (*Ceryle alcyon*)	Thiel 1985

(Continued)

Table 6 (*continued*). Nest traps used to capture birds.

Group	References
Other birds (*continued*)	
Passerines	Gartshore 1978
Cliff swallow	Wolinski and Pike 1985
(*Petrochelidon pyrrhonota*)	
Barn swallow	Wolinski and Pike 1985
(*Hirundo rustica*)	
Blue jay	Hilton 1989

designed a remotely operated trap to capture American kestrels (*Falco sparverius*) using nest boxes. Kestrels were trapped during prey delivery to nestlings. Cohen and Hayes (1984) perfected a simple device to block the entrance to nest boxes. They used a wooden clothespin or a similar shaped Plexiglas™ version of a clothespin attached to a monofilament line. After the bird entered the nest box, the line was pulled, and the entrance was closed. Cohen (1985) used feathers to lure male tree swallows (*Tachycineta bicolor*) into nest boxes where they were subsequently captured.

Pribil (1997) developed a clever nest trap for house wrens (*Troglodytes aedon*). The trap consisted of a nest box containing a grass nest with 1 egg (Fig. 5). The egg was glued to a lever connected to a spring that closed a door over the entrance hole. The pecking action of the bird pushed the egg down releasing the lever. The lever pulled by a rubber band pulled a string which closed the door over the entry hole, thereby capturing the wren. The wren-trapping box should be placed 15 to 25 m from an active house wren nest. The author had her best trapping success early in the spring breeding season. Stanback and Koenig (1994) developed techniques for capturing acorn woodpeckers inside natural cavities. They reached the tree hole with the aid of basic rock-climbing gear and extension ladders. They then cut a triangular door below the cavity entrance using a folding pruning saw for the main cuts and held the door in place with nails. The cavity entrance was blocked with a plastic bobber, after the bird entered the nest, and the captured bird was removed.

Dietz et al. (1994) designed an inexpensive walk-in duck nest trap with a funnel entrance, and lily-pad shape, made of welded wire with a top of garden netting. The trap worked most effectively in dense vegetation where researchers could make a concealed approach to block the entrance. Yerkes (1997) described a portable, inexpensive trap for capturing incubating female mallards (*Anas platyrhynchos*) and redheads (*Aythya americana*) that used cylindrical, artificial nesting structures. The wire-covered trap doors at each end of the nesting cylinder were manually triggered with ropes. Loos and Rohwer (2002) found long-handled nets to be more efficient than nest traps for capturing upland nesting ducks. Trapping injuries were far less frequent when long-handled nets were used in comparison to nest traps. Netted females returned to their nest more rapidly than those captured with nest traps. Netting ducks required only one trip to the nest, disturbing females less often than with nest traps.

A self-tripping nest trap was designed by Frederick (1986) to capture white ibis and other colonial nesting birds. His trap design had the advantage of being suitable for cap-

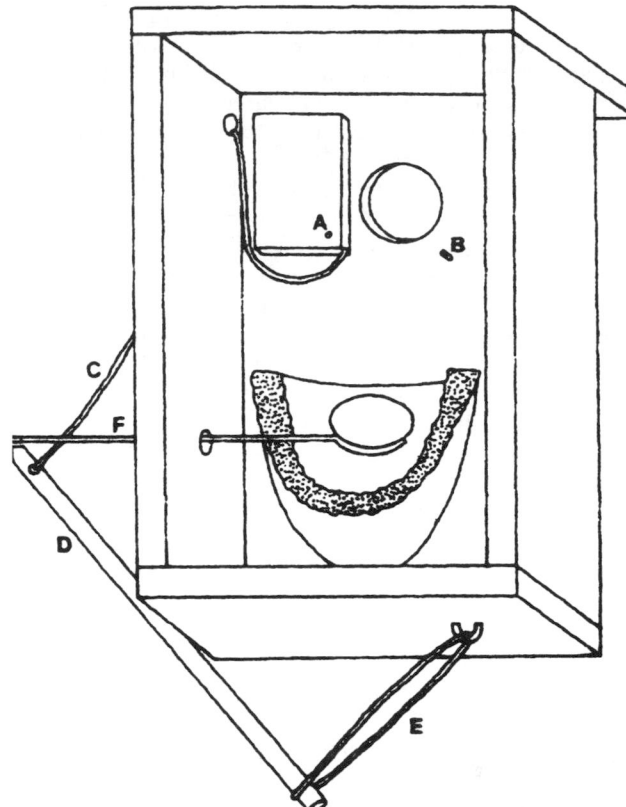

Fig. 5. Trapping box viewed from the rear with the back wall removed. A portion of the nest is removed to illustrate the position of the metal lever and the placement of the egg. A = pin around which the wooden door revolves; B = nail protruding from the wall which keeps the door aligned over the entrance; C = string; D = wooden lever (from Pribil 1997).

turing large numbers of birds in a dense nesting site with minimum disturbance where traps were left unattended. A similar automatic trap was developed by Otto (1983) to catch pied-billed grebes. Mock et al. (1999) developed a nest trap that featured a wire door that prevented escape. An electronic-release triggering mechanism allowed the researcher to control the capture at distances up to 200 m. The remote control system was battery operated and inexpensive.

Monofilament nooses of 15-kg test line, 5 cm in diameter, were attached to a 1-m diameter chicken wire dome and placed over the nest by Ewins and Miller (1993) to capture nesting ospreys. They secured the dome with cords around the base of the nest. Thiel (1985) placed a 20–25 cm monofilament fish-line snare into nest burrows of belted kingfishers. The snare was anchored to a tent stake inserted into the sand bank near the nest burrow entrance.

Yunick (1990) suggested blocking the entrance to nest boxes with a broom or rake handle upon approach to prevent escape of the incubating bird. He also described a simple, effective nest box trap of semi-rigid plastic film that hung inside the box entrance. The trap worked on the principle of a hinged flap that could be pushed like a swinging door. The "U" shaped film was pinned in place.

Rendell et al. (1989) perfected a manually operated "basket trap" consisting of a wire skeleton covered with mist netting attached by tape or line. The basket was attached to the end of a lightweight extendable pole and raised to enclose the entrance of a cavity containing a hole-nesting bird such as a tree or bank swallow. Their trap was simple for one person to use, flexible, portable, lightweight, easy to construct, and required few materials.

Hilton (1989) described a unique "double halo" nest trap to capture blue jays. The trap consisted of a black metal hanger bent into a "dog-bone shape." Halos at each end had a diameter of 12.5 cm and were connected by a 15-cm wire. Clear nylon, 4–5 kg test monofilament fishing line was tied into nooses similar to those used on bal-chatri and other noose traps. Elliptical nooses, 7 × 5 cm, were most successful. The bottom halo was anchored to the branch supporting the nest with 7–8 kg monofilament tied to a metal washer. The double-halo trap was designed to catch a bird by its neck as it arrived or left the nest. It was necessary for the bird trapper to remain nearby to prevent strangulation of the bird. The trap was deployed several days after incubation had begun to avoid nest desertion.

Swanson and Rappole (1994) modified a hoop-net trap, described by Nolan (1961), by attaching mist netting to an aluminum frame from a fishing dip net to capture nesting white-winged doves in subtropical thorn forest habitat. Conway and Smith (2000) designed a nest trap for snowy plovers. The trap consisted of 1.83-m lengths (2) of 1.25-cm electrical conduit, 16-cm pieces (4) of 1-cm wooden dowels, and 2 medium-weight strap hinges. The 2 pieces of conduit were bent into equal "U" shapes and attached to hinges to form the trap frame. Mesh netting was attached to the frame with twine, and black paint was sprayed on the aluminum conduit frame. The trap was anchored and activated with a 50-m long pull cord by an observer when the incubating bird returned to the nest. The pull cord was attached to the top piece of conduit. After the bird was caught, the trap was removed to facilitate rapid return of the incubating plover to the nest.

Decoy Traps and Enticement Lures

Thorstrom (1996) reviewed the methodology he used for capturing birds of prey in tropical forests. Baited bal-chatri traps (Fig. 6) were the most effective and versatile and the simplest to set. He described a modified bal-chatri, called an envelope trap, which used as bait the food left behind by a flushed raptor. The bait was enclosed on a semi-flat, wire cage with nooses that were tied to the ground. Jacobs (1996) reported high trapping success (overall 69%) with mist nets set next to a mechanical, mounted great horned owl decoy used to attract red-shouldered (*Buteo lineatus*), Cooper's (*Accipiter cooperii*), and sharp-shinned (*A. striatus*) hawks (Table 7).

Jacobs and Proudfoot (2002) designed an elevated dho-gaza net assembly that they used in combination with a great horned owl decoy to capture 5 species of nesting raptors. The owl decoy had a moveable head as described by Jacobs (1996). The net trap was attached to a 2–8-m telescoping pole to allow adjustment to nest-site height and was set within 50 m of the nest tree. Great horned owl vocalizations were also used to attract nesting raptors to the net system.

Bloom et al. (1992) evaluated the effectiveness of the dho-gaza net trap baited with a live, tethered great horned owl (Fig. 7) as a lure for 11 species of diurnal raptors and 3 species of owls. The technique was most successful when targeting a territorial pair during the reproductive

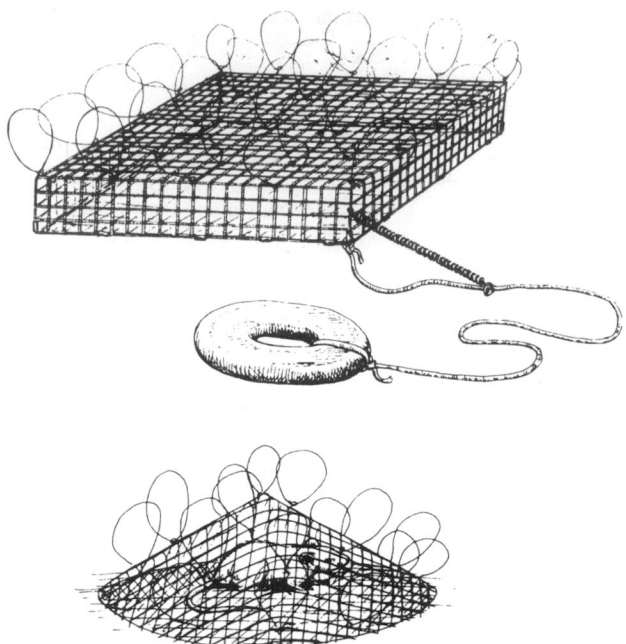

Fig. 6. Bal-chatri traps can be made in a variety of shapes. The box-shaped bal-chatri functions well for accipiters, buteos, and owls while the cone-shaped trap functions best for kestrels and burrowing owls (from Bloom 1987).

cycle. Playback of audiotaped recordings of great horned owls reduced the time necessary for capture. Net poles should be concealed with the owl lure placed in the shade. Knittle and Pavelka (1994) simplified attaching a dho-gaza net to poles by using fabric hooks and self-adhesive Velcro® as loop fasteners.

Morrison and McGehee (1996) set a Q-net similar to a bow net next to a live crested caracara tethered within 100 m of an active nest. The territorial and aggressive resident caracara moved toward the lure bird and was caught in the Q-net when the observer pulled the trigger wire.

Wang and Trost (2000) caught American magpies with a bal-chatri trap baited with a female magpie and placed under a nest tree. A mounted great horned owl next to a mist net placed 5–10 m from a nest tree was also successful in attracting nesting magpies for capture. A live, tethered mouse attached to a board surrounded by a monofilament noose lured spotted owls for capture (Johnson and Reynolds 1998). The noose was manually tightened when the owl landed on the mouse. Redpath and Wyllie (1994) captured territorial tawny owls by using a live, tethered tawny owl as an attractant in a large modified Chardoneret trap (Fig. 8). The territorial owl entered an open lid and lit on a perch that released the trigger closing the entrance lid.

McCloskey and Dewey (1999) reported improved success trapping northern goshawks using a mounted great horned owl decoy that was moved manually while held upright within 1 m of a dho-gaza net trap. The trapper, covered with camouflage netting, holding the mounted owl, uttered the 5-note territorial hoot of the great horned owl.

Gard et al. (1989) reported that breeding American kestrels responded less aggressively to taxidermy mounts of great horned owls than to live owls. Steenhof et al. (1994) successfully used a tethered great horned owl 1 m behind 2 mist nets to capture American kestrels. Nets were

Table 7. Decoys and enticement lures used to capture birds.

Group/Species	References
Waterfowl	
Mallard	Sharp and Lokemoen 1987
Gadwall (*Anas strepera*)	Blohm and Ward 1979
Northern pintail	Grand and Fondell 1994, Guyn and Clark 1999
Northern shoveler (*A. clypeata*)	Seymour 1974
Blue-winged teal (*A. discors*)	Garrettson 1998
Canvasback (*Aythya valisineria*)	Anderson et al. 1980
Lesser scaup (*A. affinis*)	Rogers 1964
Barrow's goldeneye (*Bucephala albeola*)	Savard 1985
Galliformes	
Ruffed grouse	Chambers and English 1958, Naidoo 2000
Greater prairie-chicken	Anderson and Hamerstrom 1967, Silvy and Robel 1967
Sharp-tailed grouse	Artmann 1971
Northern bobwhite	Smith et al. 2001
Ring-necked pheasant	Smith et al. 2001
Raptors	Berger and Hamerstrom 1962, Bloom 1987, Bloom et al. 1992, Plumpton et al. 1995, Jacobs 1996
Northern goshawk (*Accipiter gentilis*)	Meng 1971, McCloskey and Dewey 1999
Cooper's hawk	Rosenfield and Bielefeldt 1993
Red-tailed hawk	Buck and Craft 1995
Northern harrier (*Circus cyaneus*)	Hamerstrom 1963
Crested caracara (*Caracara cheriway*)	Morrison and McGehee 1996
American kestrel	Bryan 1988, Gard et al. 1989, Steenhof et al. 1994
Merlin (*Falco columbarius*)	Clark 1981
Other birds	
Yellow rail	Robert and Laporte 1997
Virginia rail	Kearns et al. 1998
Sora	Kearns et al. 1998
American woodcock	Norris et al. 1940
Band-tailed pigeon	Drewien et al. 1966
Northern saw-whet owl (*Aegolius cicadicus*)	Whalen and Watts 1999
Tawny owl (*Strix aluco*)	Redpath and Wyllie 1994
Spotted owl (*S. occidentalis*)	Bull 1987, Johnson and Reynolds 1998
Pileated woodpecker	York et al. 1998
Brown-headed cowbird	Burtt and Giltz 1976
American robin (*Turdus migratorius*)	Dykstra 1968
Loggerhead shrike (*Lanius ludovianus*)	Kridelbaugh 1982
Red-winged blackbird (*Agelaius phoeniceus*)	Burtt and Giltz 1970, 1976; Picman 1979
American magpie	Wang and Trost 2000
Regent honeyeater (*Xanthomyza phrygia*)	Geering 1998

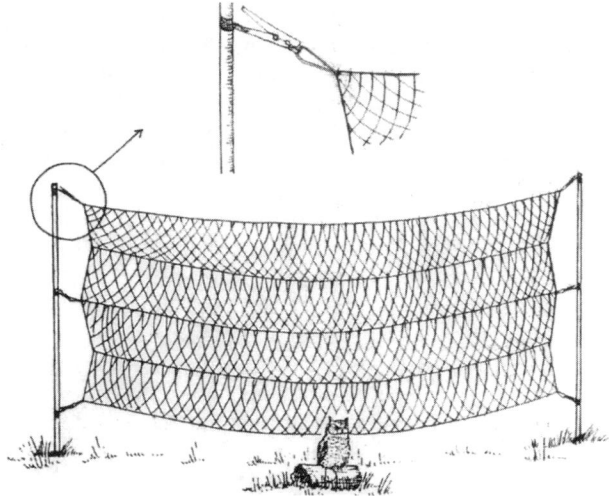

Fig. 7. A large dho-gaza trap with a tethered great horned owl as an attractant may be used to catch territorial adult raptors. The inset shows a clothespin attachment to a tape tab on a mist net loop (from Bloom 1987).

owl. Rosenfield and Bielefeldt (1993) suggested modifications to Bloom et al. (1992) methods for trap-shy breeding Cooper's hawks. They advised using an elevated great horned owl set, 10–13 m above ground, rather than at or within 0.5 m of the ground, to enhance trapping success. They also advised pre-incubation trapping at or near dawn. Hawks were trapped in mist nets, bow nets or bal-chatris baited with European starlings or ringed turtle-doves (*Streptopelia risoria*).

Plumpton et al. (1995) successfully used padded and weakened foothold traps to capture red-tailed, ferruginous

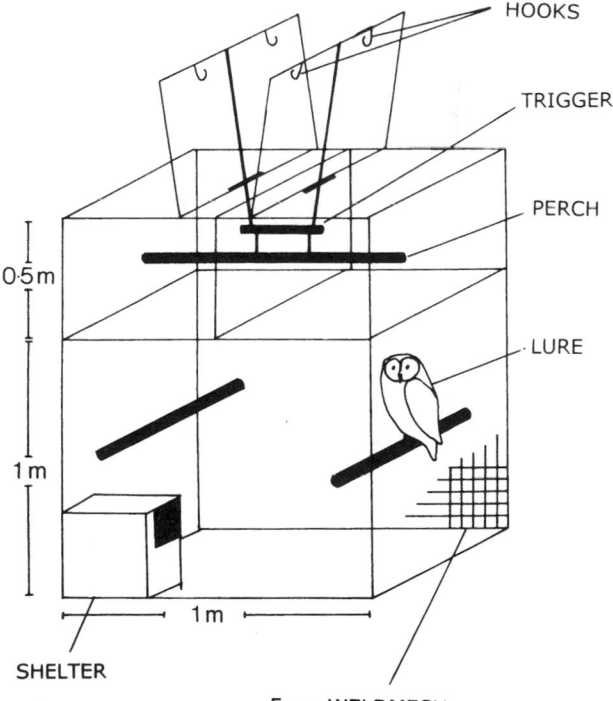

Fig. 8. Modified Chardoneret using a captive owl as lure. Owls flew from an external perch into one of the top compartments, landing on the internal perch and releasing the trigger, allowing the lid to close (from Redpath and Wyllie 1994).

placed 20 m from nest boxes occupied by American kestrels with >5-day-old young. They recommended placement of the nets and a live owl near trees whenever possible to provide shade to reduce heat stress to the lure

(*Buteo regalis*), and Swainson's (*B. swainsoni*) hawks along roads. Trap springs were weakened by repeatedly hitting them with a hammer. Jaws of size 3 and 3N double-spring foothold traps were padded with 5-mm thick adhesive-backed foam rubber and then wrapped with cloth friction tape. Traps were baited with a live mouse held in a harness in the form of a 24-ga. steel wire loop. The loop was placed over the head and behind the ears of the mouse. Traps were hidden with a thin covering of sifted soil or snow.

Whalen and Watts (1999) assessed the influence of audio lures on capture patterns of northern saw-whet owls. They found a general pattern of decreasing capture frequency with increasing distance from the audio lure. They suggested that capture rates may be maximized by using more lures, each with a small number of nets.

Breeding male ruffed grouse readily responded to playbacks of recordings of drumming display sounds by approaching to within 2–9 m of the observer (Naidoo 2000). Playback of recordings of male display sounds near a stuffed decoy could be used to lure ruffed grouse into noosing range for capture. Taped calls and "drums" of pileated woodpeckers were combined with a mist net by York et al. (1998) to rapidly capture this species with minimum stress to the birds.

Evrard and Bacon (1998) tested 4 duck trap designs. In spring, traps with a live female mallard decoy and traps with a similar decoy and bait were more successful than bait traps without a decoy. Spring trapping was more successful than autumn trapping. Floating bait traps were largely unsuccessful in capturing waterfowl.

Snares and Noose Poles

Benson and Suryan (1999) described a circular noose (Table 8) that allowed safe capture of specific individual black-legged kittiwakes (*Rissa tridactyla*). The leg noose was fitted to the rim of the nest and was remotely triggered. Launay et al. (1999) attached snares at 10-cm intervals to a 50-m long main line at male houbara bustard (*Chlamydotis undulata*) display areas. They also placed female bustard decoys surrounded by snares at display sites. Nesting females were attracted to dummy eggs made of wood painted to resemble houbara bustard eggs and caught with adjacent snares.

Cooper et al. (1995) described a noose trap arrangement used to capture pileated woodpeckers at nest and roost cavities. Foot nooses of clear monofilament line were spaced at 1-cm intervals along a main support line and fence staples were used to secure the line to the tree.

Thorstrom (1996) devised a noose pole trap for removing incubating and nestling birds from tree cavities. Young that were out of view in 2-m deep nest cavities were safely extracted. Kramer (1988) designed a noosing apparatus made of wire, plastic straws, and monofilament fishing line that he used to remove nestling bank swallows from their burrows for banding. Thiel (1985) built a similar noosing device to capture adult belted kingfishers as they entered their nesting burrows.

Frenzel and Anthony (1982) and Cain and Hodges (1989) described floating-fish snares with 2 and 4 nooses for capturing bald eagles. Jackman et al. (1993) described a modified floating-fish snare that achieved 40% capture success. They inserted a Styrofoam™ plug in the anterior

Table 8. Snares and noose poles used to capture birds.

Group	References
Galliformes	
Greater prairie-chicken	Berger and Hamerstrom 1962
Spruce grouse (*Falcipennis canadensis*)	Schroeder 1986
Blue grouse	Zwickel and Bendell 1967
Willow ptarmigan	Hoglund 1968
Raptors	Berger and Mueller 1959, Berger and Hamerstrom 1962, Ward and Martin 1968, Jenkins 1979, Dunk 1991
White-tailed kite (*Elanus leucurus*)	Dunk 1991
Rough-legged hawk (*Buteo lagopus*)	Watson 1985
Bald eagle	Frenzel and Anthony 1982; Cain and Hodges 1989; Jackman et al. 1993, 1994
Golden eagle	Jackman et al. 1994; McGrady and Grant 1994, 1996
Osprey	Frenzel and Anthony 1982, Prevost and Baker 1984, Ewins and Miller 1993
Crested caracara	Morrison and McGehee 1996
American kestrel	Wegner 1981, Toland 1985
Prairie falcon (*Falco mexicanus*)	Beauvais et al. 1992
Barn owl (*Tyto alba*)	Colvin and Hegdal 1986
Short-eared owl	Kahn and Millsap 1978
Eastern screech-owl	Smith and Walsh 1981
Tropical screech-owl (*Megascops choliba*)	Thorstrom 1996
Burrowing owl	Barrentine and Ewing 1988, Winchell and Turman 1992
Flammulated owl (*Otus flammeolus*)	Reynolds and Linkhart 1984
Spotted owl	Bull 1987
Other	
Colonial seabirds	Edgar 1968
Double-crested cormorant	Foster and Fitzgerald 1982, Hogan 1985
Black-legged kittiwake	Benson and Suryan 1999
Houbara bustard	Launay et al. 1999
Passerines	
Common nighthawk	McNicholl 1983
Belted kingfisher	Thiel 1985
Pileated woodpecker	Cooper et al. 1995
Loggerhead shrike	Yosef and Lohrer 1992, Collister and Fisher 1995, Doerr et al. 1998
American magpie	Scharf 1985
Bank swallow	Barrentine and Ewing 1988, Kramer 1988
Chipping sparrow (*Spizella passerina*)	Gartshore 1978

portion of the fish bait, allowing the tail of the fish to dip more deeply below the water surface. Nooses consisted of 18-kg test, light green monofilament tied with a slip knot. Two 10–12 cm nooses were placed in an alternate/lateral position. Sucker (*Catostomus* sp.) or catfish (*Ictalurus* sp.) approximately 40-cm long were used for bait. Fish were anchored and placed in shaded areas during early morning when the monofilament was less visible to eagles.

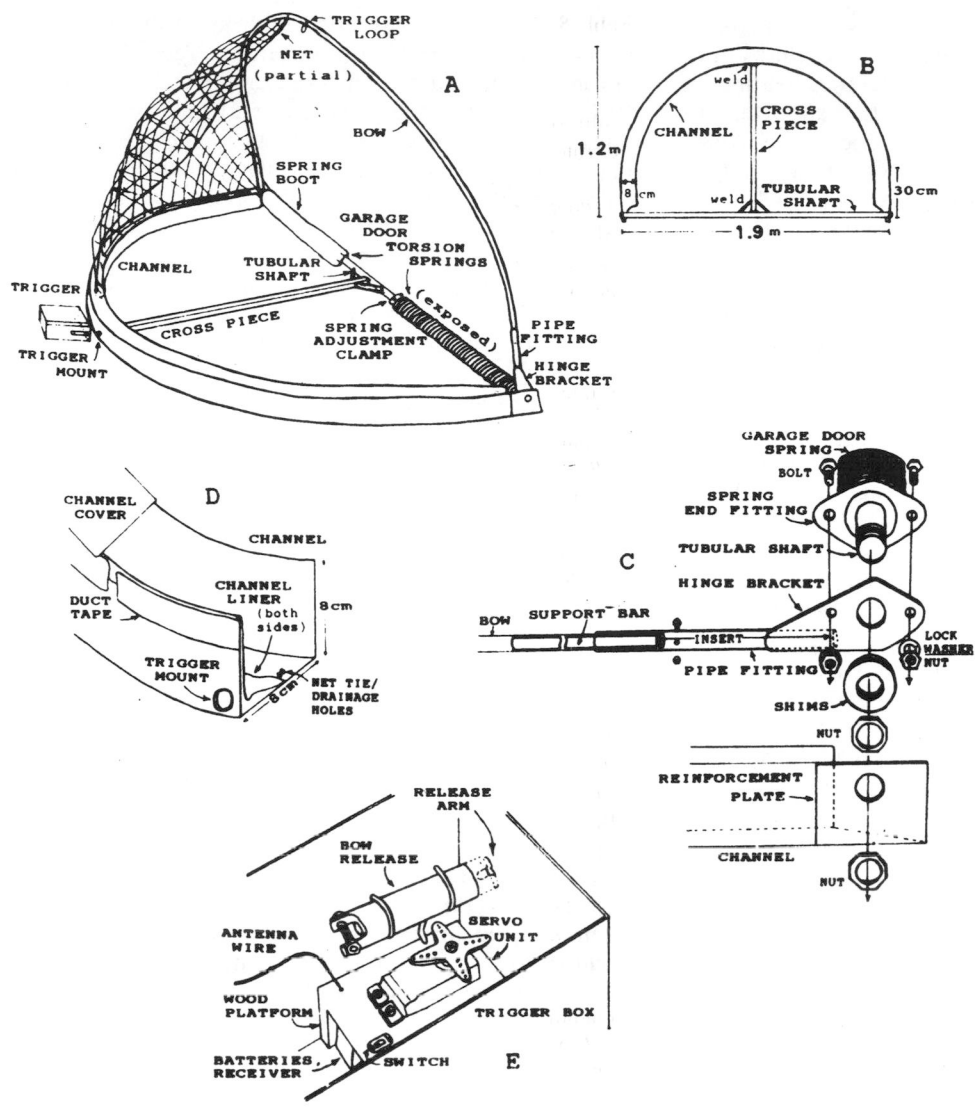

Fig. 9. Radio-controlled eagle bow net. A = bow net opening, showing position of principal components; B = top view, no springs; C = detail of spring-hinge-bow-channel attachment; D = cross section detail of channel at trigger mount; and E = interior detail of trigger box (from Jackman et al. 1994).

Jackman et al. (1994) devised a successful radio-controlled bow net and power snare (Fig. 9) to selectively capture bald and golden (*Aquila chrysaetos*) eagles. The net was completely concealed in loose soil and operated from distances up to 400 m. A recognizable marker was placed just outside the perimeter of the net trap to verify the eagle was in the center of the trap and feeding with its head down before triggering the trap.

McGrady and Grant (1996) designed a radio-controlled power snare similar to that described by Jackman et al. (1994) to capture nesting golden eagles. A nest anchor was used to keep the captured eagle on the nest to avoid injury. Nestlings were isolated in a small chicken-wire cage to avoid fouling the trap snare before firing. A video camera facilitated a clear view of the trap. Territorial golden eagles were caught on the nest efficiently and safely using their design.

Smith and Walsh (1981) modified a bal-chatri trap for eastern screech-owls (*Megascops asio*) by placing a 3-mm Plexiglas™ top on a rectangular hardware cloth base. Taped calls were used to attract owls to the mouse-baited trap. Small holes were drilled in the Plexiglas™ in which

nooses were tied. Blakeman (1990) increased the capture success rate of bal-chatri traps by spraying them with flat dark paint. Nylon monofilament used for nooses was soaked for a day in black fabric dye. Both treatments helped camouflage the traps.

Winchell and Turman (1992) used a combination of monofilament nooses and wooden dowel rods to capture burrowing owls during the fledging season when owls were extremely wary of any change near their burrows or roosts. Several noose rods were placed outside the burrow, and a dowel and weight were inserted beneath the soil surface.

Toland (1985) designed a leather harness with 15 monofilament slip nooses that he attached to house sparrows to capture trap-wary American kestrels. One end of a monofilament line was attached to a wooden dowel or stick and the other end to the edge of the harness. The wooden weight functioned as a drag when the kestrel attempted to fly away with the harnessed sparrow. Bloom (1987) provided details on use of a harnessed rock pigeon for the capture of raptors. Nylon monofilament nooses were tied or cemented to a leather harness that was attached to a pigeon tied on a line to a weight or a nearby shrub. Reynolds and Linkhart (1984) used a telescoping noose pole with an attached 12.5-cm diameter loop of coated stainless steel line (Zwickel and Bendell 1967) to capture flammulated owls from trees. Scharf (1985) used noose-covered wickets placed around a live male American magpie decoy to capture territorial magpies.

Use of Oral Drugs

Stouffer and Caccamise (1991) successfully captured American crows with alpha-chloralose inserted in fresh chicken eggs. However, McGowan and Caffrey (1994) expressed concern about high mortality of crows captured with alpha-chloralose. Caccamise and Stouffer (1994) explained the possible cause of mortality and justified the continued use of alpha-chloralose.

Woronecki et al. (1992) conducted safety, efficacy, and clinical trials required by U.S. Food and Drug Administration (FDA) to register alpha-chloralose (A-C). They reported the most effective dose to be 30 and 60 mg of A-C/kg of body weight for capturing waterfowl and rock pigeons. They concluded that A-C was a safe capture drug for waterfowl and pigeons. In 1992, the U.S. Department of Agriculture (USDA), Animal and Plant Health Inspection Service (APHIS), Wildlife Services (WS) was granted approval by the FDA to use A-C nationwide for capturing nuisance waterfowl, American coots, and rock pigeons (Woronecki and Thomas 1995). Wildlife Services personnel must complete a 12-hour training course and pass a written examination to be certified to use A-C (Belant et al. 1999). The use of A-C 30 days prior to and during the legal waterfowl season for populations that are hunted is prohibited.

Initial use of 60 mg/kg of A-C in field operations yielded a low (6%) capture rate of rock pigeons. Belant and Seamans (1999) reevaluated doses of A-C used for pigeons and recommended treating corn with 3 mg A-C/corn kernel and 180 mg/kg as an effective dose. Mean time of first effects and mean time to capture at the 180 mg/kg dose rate were significantly less than with lower dosages. Belant and Seamans (1997) also assessed the effectiveness of alpha-chloralose formulations for immobilizing Canada geese. Alpha-chloralose in tablet form was as effective as A-C in margarine and in corn oil in bread baits. Male and female geese responded similarly to A-C immobilization. Seamans and Belant (1999) recommended alpha-chloralose over DRC-1339 as a gull population management chemical because it was fast acting, humane, and could be used as a nonlethal capture agent.

Scientists at the National Wildlife Research Center (USDA, APHIS, WS), Fort Collins, Colorado, have recently developed and tested a tablet form of alpha-chloralose. These new tablets will be available in 3 sizes so that combinations of pellets can be used to achieve accurate dose levels for a variety of birds. Tablets should be administered to birds inside bread cube bits. The tablet formulation provides a safer and simple alternative to the current formulation, which requires mixing a powder prior to use and a syringe for injection of the solution into the bread bait.

Janovsky et al. (2002) tested tiletamine/zolazepam, another oral drug for bird immobilization, at a dosage of 80 mg/kg (in powdered form applied to the surface of fresh meat) on common buzzards (*Buteo buteo*) in Austria. The deepest anesthesia was produced by fresh-drugged bait administered immediately after preparation. This drug combination had a wide safety margin with little lethal risk from overdosing to nontarget birds that might accidentally feed on the bait.

Miscellaneous Capture Methods

Ostrowski et al. (2001) captured steppe eagles (*Aquila nipalensis*) in Saudi Arabia by vehicle pursuit. Their method was limited to open habitat but was effective on trap-shy individuals. Eagle chases were restricted to a maximum of 15 minutes. Similarly, Ellis et al. (1998) used a helicopter to pursue and capture sandhill cranes in open habitat.

Winchell (1999) designed a simplified, efficient push-door, wire mesh trap that readily captured complete broods of burrowing owls. Botelho and Arrowood (1995) constructed a trap for burrowing owls consisting of a 61-cm long and 10-cm diameter PVC pipe. A hinged, one-way Plexiglas™ door was inserted midway in the PVC pipe, which was placed in the owl burrows. Trapped owls were removed through a hinged door that opened on top of the PVC pipe. Plumpton and Lutz (1992) made multiple captures of burrowing owls by modifying large Sherman traps placed in burrow entrances by replacing one end with 2.5-cm wire mesh. They also captured young nestlings by quietly approaching the burrow and grabbing the birds by hand before they retreated completely into the tunnel. Banuelos (1997) advocated using a one-way Plexiglas™ door trap for burrowing owls. The ease of constructing and setting the trap, potential high capture rate, and lack of trapping injuries made this simple trap ideal. The one-way door trap captured owls twice as fast as bal-chatri and noose carpet attempts.

King et al. (1998) captured American white pelicans and great blue herons with modified No. 3 padded-jaw foothold traps by replacing both factory coil springs with weaker No. 1.5 coil springs. They also substituted the factory chain with a 20-cm length of aircraft cable and a 30-cm electric shock cord to minimize injury to captured birds. Cormorants have also been captured with padded foothold traps placed in trees with the aid of an 18-m extension ladder. The trap was camouflaged with a flour-water mixture to simulate cormorant guano (King et al. 2000). Hines and Custer (1995) collected great blue heron eggs from nests in tall trees using an extendable net-pole. The device consisted of 4 collapsible 2-m sections with an 11-cm wire loop and attached 9-cm deep basket made from nylon stocking material.

Folk et al. (1999) devised a safe, efficient daylight capture technique for cranes. They used a unique capture blind made from a cattle feed trough baited with corn. They grabbed the crane's leg through armholes in the side of the trough while the cranes were feeding on the corn in the trough.

Proudfoot and Jacobs (2001) combined 2-way radios with a conventional home security switch to develop an inexpensive, alarm equipped bow net. The radio alarm eliminated the need to periodically inspect automatic bow nets. The bow net was used to signal capture of owls, hawks, and loggerhead shrikes. Larkin et al. (2003) perfected an electronic signaling system for prompt removal of an animal from a trap. Collister and Fisher (1995) tested 4 trap types for capturing loggerhead shrikes. They had a higher percent trapping success with a modified Tordoff bow trap.

Kautz and Seamans (1992) described several methods to expedite capture of rock pigeons. They caught pigeons mainly at night by hand at roost sites in barns and silos by closing the roosting sites using burlap drop window covers to prevent birds from escaping. They also designed a "catch window" consisting of a net bag of 2.5 × 2.5 cm mesh nylon gill netting. They developed a "stuff" sack that allowed placing birds into a burlap bag with one hand, a necessity, while holding on to a supporting structure. Noose poles were used successfully in silos but not in barns. Headlamps with an on-off switch and a rheostat were used to help hand capture rock pigeons.

Caffrey (2001) discussed capture methods for American crows and emphasized that crows are extremely wary and difficult to catch. Unsuccessful methods included a "noose" carpet (Fig. 10), foothold and glue traps, and a net agricultural products, and naturally occurring and artificial scents have been used as attractants. Because of the diversity of habitats and species, no universal attractant successfully works for all animals. Consequently, wildlife biologists may need to evaluate several baits or lures before finding those that attract different species in a specific geographical area.

Baits

Pre-baiting is generally an important prerequisite to, and baiting an essential part of, any successful trapping program. Carnivores may be attracted to traps by bait made from chunks of meat that is fresh or tainted. For example, holes can be punched in a container of sardines to make a long-lasting attractant. Bluett (2000) reported that selectivity for certain species, such as raccoons (*Procyon lotor*), was enhanced by using "sweet" baits such as fruit or marshmallows. Saunders and Harris (2000) evaluated bait preferences of captive red fox (*Vulpes vulpes*). Whole mice were the most preferred and horsemeat the least preferred of the 6 animal baits tested. Travaini et al. (2001) simultaneously tested a variety of scented meat baits and 3 ways of delivering these baits to culpeo (*Pseudalopex culpaeus*) and Argentine gray (*P. griseus*) foxes in Patagonia. All 4 types of baits used were equally attractive to both species of fox. The percentage of the different types of baits consumed by the 2 species did not differ among bait type, and no differences were detected in visitation rates to the 3 types of bait delivery systems. Andrzejewski and Owadowska (1994) successfully captured bank voles (*Clethrionomys glareolus*) at a significantly greater rate by using conspecific odor foam cube baits rather than food as bait.

Morgan and Dusek (1992) had success capturing white-tailed deer in Clover traps on summer range using salt blocks as bait. Alfalfa hay was a successful bait in winter. Naugle et al. (1995) had better deer trapping success using corn rather than salt in summer in agriculture-wetland habitats. Bean and Mason (1995) evaluated the attractiveness of liquid baits to white-tailed deer. Apple juice was preferred to cyclamate or saccharin solutions. Volatile apple extract also was an effective lure. Hakim et al. (1996) found the greatest use of liquid bait was in May. They suggested that spring was the best season to attract and capture deer in Virginia. Ballard et al. (1998) reported that white cedar (*Thuja occidentalis*) browse was the best bait for trapping white-tailed deer in winter.

Scents

Fur trappers have used a variety of scents to attract furbearing mammals to traps. These lures can be divided into 3 basic categories: gland, food, and curiosity scents. Gland scents are made of different parts of animals such as the reproductive tract and anal glands. Examples of food scents include extracts of honey and anise, and fish oil. Curiosity scents are typically blends of essential oils, exotic musk, and American beaver (*Castor canadensis*) and muskrat scent glands. Mason and Blom (1998) listed the common ingredients in lure formulations as well as their sources, methods of preparation, and common uses (Table 9).

A variety of scents, including those composed from rotten eggs, decomposed meat, and fish oil have been used to increase trapping success rates. Other items, such as seal oil, Siberian musk oil, anal glands from foxes and skunks,

Fig. 10. Noose carpets may be applied to branches and around burrowing owl nests (from Bloom 1987).

gun. She modified the Australian crow trap (Aldous 1936) by adding a drop-door at one end. Other successful capture methods included camouflaged rocket and cannon nets and a net launcher. Bait on trapping days should not be large food items that can be picked up and carried away easily. In all cases, pre-baiting and habituating crows to trapping methods were required. Recaptures were infrequent.

CAPTURING MAMMALS

Readers of this chapter are encouraged to review previous major detailed coverage of mammal capture methods. These include publications by Day et al. (1980), Novak et al. (1987), Schemnitz (1994), Wilson et al. (1996), American Society of Mammalogists (1998), and Proulx (1999a). Mammal capture usually becomes more difficult as animal size increases. Thus, observational techniques and mammalian sign are often better for obtaining both inventory and density information (Jones et al. 1996). Several new techniques to capture mammals ranging in size from small rodents to large carnivores have been developed in recent years. Some of these represent either improved or modified versions of traditional capture methods. Most animals are captured by hand, mechanical devices, remote injection of drugs, or drugs administered orally in baits. The emphasis in this chapter is on methods and equipment other than remotely injected drugs used for capture.

Use of Attractants

Success of most animal trapping operations depends on a suitable bait or lure to attract animals to traps. Numerous native and commercial foods, artificial and visual lures,

Table 9. Common ingredients in lure formations, methods of preparation, and common applications (adapted from Mason and Blom 1998).

Ingredient	Source	Preparation	Use
Muskrat glands/musk	Small glands on either side of vent of males during spring breeding season	Fresh ground, preserved, tinctured	Acids in musk are attractive to coyotes
Beaver castor	Large flat glands on each side of vent of both males and females	Fresh ground, preserved, dried, rasped to a powder; tinctured (castorium)	Phenols attractive to coyotes, serve to fix, preserve other ingredients in lures
Beaver sac oil	Long oval-shaped, whitish glands next to the castors	Fresh ground, preserved, oil squeezed from glands	Used alone or mixed with castors and used as a fixative
Mink glands/musk	Glands on either side of vent of males in breeding season	Ground fresh, preserved, tinctured	Contains sulfides, attractive to coyotes
Glands/urine from canids/felids/mustelids	Fox, bobcat, dog, badger, etc.	Ground fresh, preserved, rotted	Curiosity lures
Asafetida	Plant	Gum or powdered or tinctured	Contains sulfides, attractive to coyotes
Garlic, onion	Plant	Powders, salts, oils	Contains sulfides, attractive to coyotes
Valerian root	Plant	Powder, oil, extract or salt (i.e., zinc valerate)	Valeric acid, attractive to coyotes
Rue oil	Plant	Oil, 3–5 drops per 1/2 L	Methyl ketones impart a cheesy odor
Skunk musk	Glands on either side of vent in males	Oil, 3-5 drops per 1/2 L used as component, 6–10 drops per 1/2 L as dominant odor	Powerful sulfide (mercaptan) odor attractive to coyotes
Orris root	Plant	Powder, oil, tincture, 1/2 tsp of oil/tincture or 1/8 tsp to powder per 1/2 L	Fixative, contains acids attractive to coyotes
Oakmoss	Plant	Resin, tincture, 3–5 drops resin, or 1/4 tsp of tincture per 1/2 L	Fixative
Phenyl acetic acid	Synthetic chemical	Tincture or crystals	Honey-like odor, also found in urines and scent glands
Cilantro oil (coriander leaf oil)	Plant	Oil, 2–4 drops per 1/2 L	Aldehydes attractive to coyotes
Anise oil	Plant	Oil, 3–5 drops per 1/2 L	Licorice odor.

and mink (*Mustela vison*) musk also are widely used. Clapperton et al. (1994) tested a variety of attractants for feral cats (*Felis catus*) in New Zealand. Catnip (*Nepeta cataria*) and matatabi (*Actinidia polygama*) were the most promising scent lures tried.

Phillips et al. (1990*a*) evaluated seasonal responses of captive coyotes (*Canis latrans*) to 9 chemical attractants, and tested 26 additional attractants during summer to examine the efficacy of traps, M-44s (a tube-like spring-loaded device designed to deliver a lethal dose of sodium cyanide into the mouth of a coyote), and placed baits. Of the 9 attractants tested throughout the year, FAS (fatty acid scent) and W-U lure (trimethylammonium decanoate plus sulfides) ranked highest in overall attractiveness. FAS and W-U lure also ranked highest among the 35 attractants tested only during the summer. Kimball et al. (2000) formulated 7 new synthetic coyote attractants using representative compounds from commercially available attractants with the intention of developing relatively simple synthetic alternatives. Bioassays with captive coyotes were conducted to compare 9 behavioral responses elicited by the 7 new attractants. Results indicated that each attractant elicited a different behavioral profile. No significant differences among attractants in regard to urinating, sniffing, and licking behaviors were detected, but differences among the attractants existed for rubbing, rolling, scratching, defecating, digging, and pulling behaviors. Saunders and Harris (2000) evaluated 9 chemical attractants for red fox. They reported the strongest preferences were for 2 gustatory additives, sugar and a combination of beef and sugar, and the olfactory attractant, synthetic fermented egg.

Andelt and Woolley (1996) tested the attractiveness of a variety of odors to urban mammals including cats, dogs (*Canis familiaris*), fox squirrels (*Sciurus niger*), striped skunks (*Mephitis mephitis*), and raccoons. Deep-fried cornmeal added to bait increased the rate of visitation to scent stations. Harrison (1997) field-tested the attractiveness of 4 scents (Hawbaker's Wildcat 2, synthetic fatty acid, bobcat [*Lynx rufus*] urine, and catnip) to wild felids, canids, and Virginia opossum (*Didelphis virginiana*). No differences were noted in visitations to scent stations. McDaniel et al. (2000) tested scent lures to attract Canada lynx (*Lynx canadensis*) and found beaver castoreum and catnip oil to be most effective.

Fur trappers, especially those who focus on foxes and coyotes, often use urine at trap sets to enhance their success. Young and Henke (1999) assessed trap response of eastern cottontail rabbits (*Sylvilagus floridanus*) using wooden cage traps baited with food, block salt and minerals, and urine from non-pregnant female domestic European rabbits (*Oryctolagus cuniculus*). They captured significantly more cottontails in traps baited with rabbit urine.

Plant extractions may also be added to scents. The root of the Asiatic plant asafetida (*Ferula assafoetida*) imparts a strong, persistent odor to scents. The oils from the herbs anise (*Pimpinella anisum*) and valerian (*Valeriana officinalis*) also have been added to scent mixtures.

Scents are used primarily to attract carnivores, but other mammals are also attracted to them. Large rodents such as beaver and muskrats can be attracted with scent mixtures containing castoreum from beaver and oil sacs from muskrats. Mason et al. (1993) evaluated salt blocks and several olfactory lures as potential lures for use in attracting white-tailed deer. Odor stimuli such as acorn, apple, and peanut butter significantly enhanced the effectiveness of salt blocks. Mineral blocks were more attractive to deer than salt, molasses, and mineral-molasses blocks; all were scented with apple extract.

Visual Attractants

Visual attractants can enhance trapping success for species such as bobcats that rely heavily on their sense of sight when hunting. Bobcats can be attracted to traps by a piece of fur or feathers suspended 90–120 cm above the wire or string. However, in many states, use of visual attractants by trappers is illegal since they may attract protected raptors. Knight (1994) and Virchow and Hogeland (1994) described the use of visual attractants in trapping mountain lion (*Puma concolor*) and bobcats, respectively.

Foot Traps and Snares

Fur trappers, nuisance wildlife control agents, and researchers have used commercial and hand-made traps to capture a variety of mammals including carnivores, rodents, lagomorphs, and marsupials. These mechanical devices can be divided into 2 broad categories—restraining (live) and killing traps. However, certain trap designs can be included in either category depending on how they are deployed in the field.

Trap Types

Restraining traps are those designed to capture an animal alive. Three basic types are used to capture mammals. Cage/box traps are manufactured in an array of sizes for small insectivores, rodents, lagomorphs, carnivores, and ungulates. They are constructed of wire or nylon mesh, wood, plastic, or metal. The functional components include the cage/box, 1 or 2 self-closing doors, a door lock mechanism, a trigger, and a treadle or trip pan. Foothold traps are commonly used to capture medium-sized mammals such as wild canids and felids (Fig. 11). A typical foothold trap has 2 jaws open at 180° when in the set position, and closing 90° upon each other when released. Another foothold design includes foot-encapsulating devices such as the EGG™ trap (Proulx et al. 1993*d*, Hubert et al. 1996) and Duffer's trap (IAFWA 2000) which have a pull trigger that releases a small striking bar to block an animal's paw as well as a plastic or metal housing that protects the captured limb from torsion or self-inflicted injuries. These traps are species-specific, considered relatively "dog proof," and used to capture raccoons and opossums. Foot snares such as the Aldrich (Poelker and Hartwell 1973), Åberg (Englund 1982), Fremont (Skinner and Todd 1990), and Belisle (Shivik et al. 2000) are spring-powered cables used to capture and hold medium and large animals by a limb (Fig. 12). Modified manual neck snares (McKinstry and Anderson 1998, Pruss et al. 2002) and specialized cable restraints such as the Collarum™ (Shivik et al. 2000) also can function as restraining traps.

Killing traps have one or more striking jaws (or a snare noose) activated by one or many springs upon firing by a trigger mechanism. Killing traps come in a variety of sizes, and their method of action varies. Mousetrap-type devices, where one jaw closes 180° upon a flat surface, are commonly used to capture commensal and other small rodents. Killing boxes, pincher- and spear-type traps, and

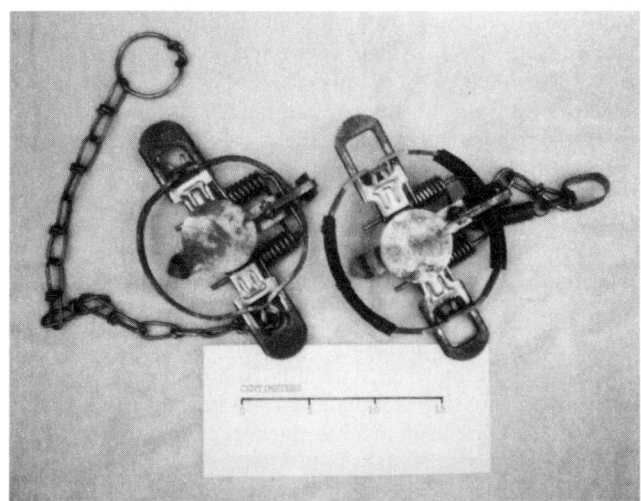

Fig. 11. Foothold restraining traps used to capture mammals; Victor™ No. 1½ coil spring foothold trap (left), Victor™ No. 1½ soft-catch™ foothold trap with padded jaws (right) (photograph by G. F. Hubert, Jr.).

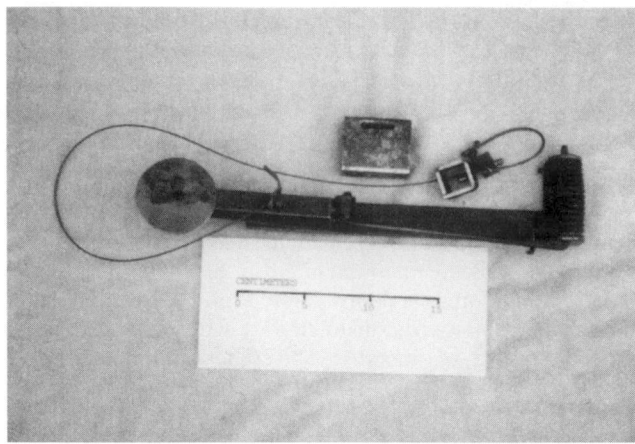

Fig. 12. The Novak™ foot snare (photograph by G. F. Hubert, Jr.).

Table 10. Snares and neck collars used to capture mammals.

Group/Species	References
Snowshoe hare	Keith 1965, Brocke 1972, Proulx et al. 1994*a*
Ground squirrel (*Spermophilus* spp.)	Lishak 1976
American beaver	Collins 1976, Mason et al. 1983, Weaver et al. 1985, Riedel 1988, McKinstry and Anderson 1998
Nutria (*Myocastor coypus*)	Evans et al. 1971
Gray wolf (*Canis lupus*)	Van Ballenberghe 1984, Schultz et al. 1996
Coyote	Nellis 1968, Guthery and Beasom 1978, Onderka et al. 1990, Phillips et al. 1990*b*, Skinner and Todd 1990, Phillips 1996, Sacks et al. 1999, Shivik et al. 2000, Pruss et al. 2002
Red fox	Berchielli and Tullar 1980, Novak 1981*b*, Rowsell et al. 1981, Englund 1982, Proulx and Barrett 1990, Bubela et al. 1998
Gray fox (*Urocyon cinereoargenteus*)	Berchielli and Tullar 1980
African lion (*Panthera leo*)	Frank et al. 2003
Amur (Siberian) tiger (*P. tigris*)	Goodrich et al. 2001
Snow leopard (*Uncia uncia*)	Jackson et al. 1990
Mountain lion	Pittman et al. 1995, Logan et al. 1999
Canada lynx	Mowat et al. 1994
Black bear (*Ursus americanus*)	Poelker and Hartwell 1973, Johnson and Pelton 1980
Raccoon	Berchielli and Tullar 1980
Skunk (Mustelidae)	Novak 1981*b*
Feral hog (*Sus scrofa*)	Anderson and Stone 1993
White-tailed deer	Verme 1962, DelGiudice et al. 1990
Mule deer	Ashcraft and Reese 1956
Guanaco (*Lama guanicoe*)	Jefferson and Franklin 1986
Pronghorn (*Antilocapra americana*)	Beale 1966

certain body-gripping devices are used to capture fossorial rodents and moles. The cage/box and foothold restraining traps can also be used as killing devices by placing them in or near water so the captured animal is submerged and drowns. This is a common technique used by fur trappers when harvesting aquatic and semi-aquatic mammals such as beaver, mink, muskrat, and northern river otter (*Lontra canadensis*). Planar traps, where a spring functions as a killing bar, are used to catch rat-sized rodents and small carnivores (e.g., Mustelidae). Rotating-jaw or body gripping traps have a scissor-like closing action, and are used for a variety of mammals ranging in size from tree squirrels to beaver. Finally, manual locking neck and power snares are used to catch and kill medium-sized carnivores such as foxes, coyotes, and bobcats (Table 10).

Trap Research, Performance Standards, and Evaluation

Traps have been and continue to be important and traditional tools for wildlife management and research (Boggess et al. 1990). Nevertheless, use of these capture devices is not without controversy (Gentile 1987, Andelt et al. 1999). Most concerns are related to animal welfare. Consequently, professional wildlife biologists have expressed the need to reduce injury and pain inflicted on animals by trapping (Schmidt and Brunner 1981, Proulx and Barrett 1989). Novak (1987) reviewed traps and trap research related to furbearers.

Recent efforts to improve welfare of animals captured in traps by developing humane trapping standards have met with mixed success. Endeavors through the International Organization of Standardization led to adoption of 2 international standards—one of methods for testing killing trap systems used on land or underwater (International Organization of Standardization 1999*a*), and another of methods for testing restraining traps (International Organization of Standardization 1999*b*). The Canadian General Standards Board first published a national killing trap standard in 1984 based on a 180-second time-to-unconsciousness interval (Canadian General Standards Board 1984). Twelve years later this interval was relaxed to 300 seconds for some species (Canadian General Standards Board 1996). However, there are several killing traps currently available which have been shown to kill certain species quicker than the Conibear™ body-

gripping series listed as state-of-the-art in 1996. Examples include the C120 Magnum with pitchfork trigger for American marten (*Martes americana*) (Proulx et al. 1989*a*), the C120 Magnum with pan trigger and the Bionic™ for mink (Proulx et al. 1990, Proulx and Barrett 1991), and the Sauvageau™ 2001-8 for arctic fox (*Alopex lagopus*) (Proulx et al. 1993*c*).

Numerical scores often have been used to quantify the extent of injury incurred by a trapped animal (e.g., Olsen et al. 1986, Linhart et al. 1988, Olsen et al. 1988, Onderka et al. 1990, Phillips et al. 1992, Hubert et al. 1996). Although Linhart and Linscombe (1987) recommended establishment of a standardized numerical system to rank trap-caused injuries, the issue is complicated by existence of a variety of scoring systems (Proulx 1999*a*). Engeman et al. (1997) criticized use of injury scores for judging acceptability of restraining traps. In contrast, Onderka (1999) indicated that numerical scoring reflecting the severity of injuries tended to be consistent and appropriate to assess live-holding devices. The current international standard that describes methods for testing restraining traps contains 2 trauma scales (International Organization for Standardization 1999*b*). One assigns point scores to 34 injury types; the other places these 34 injury types into 4 trauma classes that may be combined to provide an overall measure of animal welfare.

Most recently 2 international agreements, designed to further improve the welfare of trapped animals, have been developed. The United States and the European Union adopted a non-binding understanding in 1997; the other was signed by Canada, Russia, and the European Union in 1997 and 1998 (Andelt et al. 1999). Since that time, activities in the United States have focused on development of Best Management Practices (BMPs) for trapping furbearers under the auspices of the International Association of Fish and Wildlife Agencies (IAFWA) (1997). As part of this project, the best performing killing traps consider time to death, effectiveness, selectivity, safety, and practicality of field use. Similarly, the best restraining traps will be those based on reduced physical damage to the animal, effectiveness, selectivity, safety, and practicality. The first BMP was completed in 2003 and addresses use of restraining traps for coyotes in the eastern United States (IAFWA 2003). Best management practices for all other major furbearer species are under development (IAFWA 1997).

Trap Performance Data

Currently, 2 comprehensive reviews of trap performance data for use in mammal capture programs are available. The International Association of Fish and Wildlife Agencies (1997) included a list of trap-related publications along with a brief summary of the findings reported for each of 21 mammal species, primarily North American furbearers. Proulx (1999*a*) defined state-of-the-art killing and restraining traps for mammals based on welfare criteria and listed which currently available traps are acceptable for 18 mammals species based on published scientific literature (Table 11). Both reports included recommendations for future trap-related research as well as trap testing protocols. Canadian General Standards Board (1996) contained a list of killing traps designated as state-of-the-art along with their mechanical performance criteria (Table 12). Supplemental information, based on field tests conducted as part of the BMP project, was presented by the IAFWA (2000).

Species-specific Traps and Performance

American Badger

Limited research in Wyoming indicated that No.1½ coil spring foothold traps with unpadded, laminated, or padded jaws can be used to capture American badgers (*Taxidea taxus*) with only minor injuries (Kern et al. 1994). Also, 78% of 45 badgers captured for a telemetry study in Illinois using Victor™ No. 3 Soft-Catch™ padded foothold traps had no visible injuries (R. E. Warner, University of Illinois, unpublished data). Injuries recorded for the remaining 10 (22%) were minor (e.g., claw loss, mild edema, small lacerations). No data on performance of killing traps for badgers are available.

American Beaver

Limited data on restraining traps for beaver are available. Clamshell-type traps such as the Bailey, Hancock, and Scheffer-Couch have been used successfully to capture beaver alive (Couch 1942, Hodgdon and Hunt 1953) for research and management, but are relative inefficient, bulky, and expensive. Using Hancock and Bailey traps, Collins (1976) caught over 100 beaver with no mortalities. McKinstry and Anderson (1998) reported 2.38 mm (3/32 inch) locking snares could be used to efficiently live-capture beaver but recorded a mortality rate of 5.3%.

Research in Canada, performed under controlled conditions, has shown that beaver can be killed in $\leq$6.1 minutes using standard Conibear® 330 and modified (jaws bent inward) Conibear® 280 and 330 traps in terrestrial sets (Novak 1981*a*). Gilbert (1992) reported that Conibear® 330 traps with clamping bars rendered 14 beaver unconscious in $\leq$3 minutes. However, consistent positioning of juvenile beaver in a proper manner was an apparent problem. When captured underwater in locking snares or in drowning sets using No. 3 and 4 Victor™ foothold traps, beaver died in 5.5 to 10.5 minutes due to CO_2 narcosis or asphyxiation (Novak 1981*a*, Gilbert and Gofton 1982). Novak (1981*a*) reported that beaver trapped underwater in modified Conibear® 330 traps were killed in 7.0 to 9.25 minutes. In addition, tests on anesthetized beaver measured the minimum energy forces required to cause death when delivered via a blow to the head, neck, thorax, or chest (Gilbert 1976, Zelin et al. 1983).

Bobcat

Relatively few studies have investigated the performance of restraining traps for bobcats. Research in the western United States (Linscombe and Wright 1988, Olsen et al. 1988) and Michigan (Earle et al. 1996) has shown the Victor™ No. 3 Soft-Catch™ foothold trap with padded jaws was effective in capturing bobcats with minimal injuries compared to unpadded foothold traps. Modifications to the No. 3 Soft-Catch™, such as heavier springs, improved trapping success (Earle et al. 1996). Woolf and Nielson (2002) reported live capture of 96 bobcats in wire cage and No. 3 Soft-Catch™ traps. Trap-related injuries were uncommon with both devices and included only minor cuts and bruises. They captured 1.6 bobcats per 100 trap-nights in the cage trap compared with 0.8 per 100 trap-nights using the Soft-Catch™ trap.

Coyote

More restraining trap research has been conducted on coyotes than any other North American mammal. Andelt et al. (1999) summarized injury scores and capture rates for 8 coyote traps tested by the Denver Wildlife Research Center. Other investigations of trap performance for coyotes include Linhart et al. (1986,1988), Linscombe and Wright (1988), Olsen et al. (1988), Onderka et al. (1990), Skinner and Todd (1990), Linhart and Dasch (1992), Phillips et al. (1992, 1996), Gruver et al. (1996), Phillips and Mullis (1996), Hubert et al. (1997), and Shivik et al. (2000). Although Phillips et al. (1996) and Hubert et al. (1997) suggested that laminated traps are likely to be less injurious than standard unpadded foothold traps, differences in mean injury scores they observed were not significant. Houben et al. (1993) found no significant difference in mean injury scores assigned to limbs of coyotes captured in modified (heavier springs) No. 3 Soft-Catch™ padded foothold traps and No. 3 Northwoods™ foothold traps with laminated, offset jaws. Padded foothold traps such as the No. 3 Soft-Catch™ modified (Gruver et al. 1996) and the No. 3½ E-Z

Table 11. Classification of traps that meet state-of-the-art animal welfare performance criteria or are most acceptable in the interim by individual furbearer species (Proulx 1999*a*).

Group/Species	State-of-the-art traps		Acceptable interim traps	
	Killing	Restraining	Killing	Restraining
American marten	C120 Magnum, Kania 2000, Bionic™			
Arctic fox	Sauvageau™ 2001-8	No. 1 steel-jawed foothold		
American badger				Padded foothold
American beaver	Conibear® 330 with clamping bars			
Bobcat		No. 3 padded foothold		
Coyote		Nos. 3 and 3½ padded foothold, Fremont foot snare		
Fisher (*Martes pennanti*)	Bionic			
Gray fox			Power snare	No. 1½ padded foothold
Canada lynx	Conibear® 330 with clamping bars	Fremont foot snare		
Mink	C120 Magnum, Bionic			
Muskrat	C120 Magnum			
Raccoon		EGG™		
Red fox		No. 1½ padded foothold, Åberg (Swedish) foot snare, Novak™ foot snare	Power snare	
Red squirrel (*Tamiasciurus hudsonicus*)	Kania 1000			
Northern river otter		Modified No. 1½ padded foothold		
Virginia opossum		EGG™		
Weasels			C120 Magnum, Bionic	
Gray wolf			Power snare	Foot snare

Grip® (Phillips et al. 1996) have performed best in terms of both animal welfare and efficiency.

Way et al. (2002) tested 4 models of Tomahawk™ wire cage traps (models 610A, 610B, 610C, and 109) as an alternative capture technique for coyotes in a suburban environment in Massachusetts. These traps proved undesirable for capturing coyotes due to trap expense, time involved in baiting and conditioning coyotes to traps, a

Table 12. State-of-the-art killing traps used at the time of the implementation of the 1996 Canadian National Standard for animal (mammal) traps—mechanically powered, trigger-activated killing traps for use on land (Canadian General Standards Board 1996).

Group/Species	Trap window (cm)	Commercial trap identification
Rats (*Rattus* spp.)	8 × 5	Victor™ rat trap
Weasels	8 × 5	Victor™ rat trap
	10 × 11	Woodstream™ No. 1½ long-spring foothold
Squirrels (Sciuridae)	8 × 5	Victor™ rat trap
	10 × 11	Woodstream™ No. 1½ long spring foothold
Muskrat	11 × 11	Conibear® 120
Mink	11 × 11	Conibear® 120
American marten	11 × 11	Conibear® 120
Skunk	11 × 11	Conibear® 120
Raccoon	15 × 15	Conibear® 160
Arctic fox	18 × 18	Conibear® 220
Fisher	18 × 18	Conibear® 220
Northern river otter	18 × 18	Conibear® 220
American badger	20 × 20	Conibear® 280
American beaver	25 × 25	Conibear® 330
Canada lynx	25 × 25	Conibear® 330
Bobcat	5 × 25	Conibear® 330
Wolverine (*Gulo gulo*)	5 × 25	Conibear® 330

high rate of nontarget captures, and difficulty in capturing >1 adult in a social group. On the positive side, coyotes caught sustained few injuries.

Phillips (1996) tested 3 types of killing neck snares for coyotes. He found 94% of the coyotes snared by the neck with Kelley locks were dead when snares were checked versus 71 and 68% for the Gregerson and Denver Wildlife Research Center locks. However, the interval between trap checks was not specified. Phillips et al. (1990*b*) evaluated 7 types of breakaway snares for use in coyote control. Maximum tension before breakage for individual snares ranged from 64.5 to 221 kg. They indicated the differences in tension loads among coyotes and nontarget species should allow for development of snares that will consistently hold coyotes and release most large nontarget animals.

Phillips and Gruver (1996) evaluated performance of the Paws-I-Trip™ pan tension device on 3 types of foothold traps commonly used to capture coyotes. This device reduced capture of nontarget animals without reducing effectiveness of the traps for catching coyotes. The mean overall exclusion rates for combined nontarget species in the No. 3 Soft-Catch™, Victor™ 3NM, and No. 4 Newhouse™ foothold traps were 99.1, 98.1, and 91%, respectively. Kamler et al. (2002) effectively used modified No. 3 Soft-Catch™ foothold traps equipped with the Paws-I-Trip™ device set at 2.15 kg to capture coyotes while excluding swift foxes (*Vulpes velox*).

Feral Cat

Wire mesh traps (40 × 40 × 60 cm) and Victor™ No. 1½ Soft-Catch™ padded jaw foothold traps have been used to trap feral cats in Australia (Molsher 2001). No difference was found in capture efficiency between trap types. Injuries suffered by cats in cage traps were generally minor and usually involved self-inflicted abrasions to the face. Only 1 of 12 cats (8.3%) caught in Soft-Catch™ traps was more seriously injured. Meek et al. (1995) and Fleming et al. (1998) also used Soft-Catch™ traps (No. 1½ and 3) to capture feral cats. These researchers reported 100 and 68.6%, respectively, of the cats trapped had no visible trap-related injuries or only slight foot or leg edema or both.

Fisher

Fur trappers commonly use cage traps to capture fisher in Massachusetts, but efficiency and animal welfare data for this and other restraining traps are not available. Researchers in Canada have evaluated a variety of killing traps for capturing fisher. Controlled testing on captive animals has shown the Bionic™ trap cocked to 8 notches consistently killed fisher in <60 seconds (Proulx and Barrett 1993*b*). The mechanical characteristics of the Sauvageau™ 2001-8 and modified (stronger springs) Conibear® 220 traps surpassed the kill threshold established for fisher, but the standard Conibear® 220 and AFK Kania traps did not (Proulx 1990). Double strikes (head/neck and thorax) with a modified Conibear® 220 trap equipped with 280-size springs killed 5 of 6 fisher in an average of 51 seconds (Proulx and Barrett 1993*a*).

Arctic Fox

Two studies in Canada focused on the Sauvageau™ 2001-8 (a rotating-jaw killing trap) and the standard Victor™ No. 1½ coil spring foothold trap. Compound testing revealed that 9 arctic foxes caught in the Savageau™ 2001-8 set in a wire mesh cubby lost consciousness in an average of 74 seconds (Proulx et al. 1993*c*). During field tests on trap lines in the Northwest Territories, most arctic foxes captured in the No. 1½ coil spring trap had only minor injuries when traps were checked daily (Proulx et al. 1994*b*).

Gray Fox

Berchielli and Tullar (1980) found no difference in trap-related injuries of gray foxes caught in Victor™ No. 1½ coil spring foothold traps versus those captured with Ezyonem ™ leg snares. However, the leg snare was less effective in capturing foxes than the coil spring foothold trap. Other researchers in the eastern United States have compared the unpadded Victor™ No. 1½ coil spring with the padded Victor™ No. 1½ Soft-Catch™ for gray fox. These studies found no difference in capture efficiency between trap types (Tullar 1984, Linscombe and Wright 1988) and a reduction in injuries for foxes captured in padded traps (Tullar 1984, Olsen et al. 1988). Gray fox can be captured in rotating jaw killing traps, (e.g., Conibear® 220-2) as well as cage type restraining traps, but performance data are lacking.

Red Fox

The Victor™ No. 1½ coil spring is the most common restraining trap used to capture red fox in the United States (IAFWA 1992). Several studies have compared the performance of this trap to the No. 1½ Soft-Catch™ foothold trap with padded jaws (Tullar 1984, Linscombe and Wright 1988, Olsen et al. 1988, Kreeger et al. 1990, Kern et al. 1994). The No. 1½ Soft-Catch™ proved to be as efficient as its unpadded counterparts, and caused fewer and less serious injuries to trapped foxes. Kern et al. (1994) also reported that No. 1½ coil spring traps with laminated or offset jaws were less injurious than those with standard jaws. Some foot snares have been found to be effective restraining traps for foxes under certain conditions (Novak 1981*b*, Englund 1982). During field tests in southern Ontario and powder snow conditions in northern Sweden, the Novak™ and Åberg™ (Swedish) foot snares virtually eliminated trap-related injuries. However, Berchielli and Tullar (1980) reported the Ezyonem™ foot snare was less effective than No. 1½ coil spring foothold traps for capturing foxes, and both devices produced similar trap-related injuries. Researchers in Australia found a particular treadle (i.e., foot) snare difficult to set and inefficient; 3 of 71 red fox they captured using this device had broken legs (Bubela et al. 1998).

Few published data on the performance of killing traps for red fox exist. Limited testing of neck snares indicated that red fox become unconscious within 6 minutes using power snares, but manual snares may not be suitable killing devices for this species (Rowsell et al. 1981, Proulx and Barrett 1990).

Swift Fox

Baited single door Havahart™ wire cage traps (25.4 × 30.5 × 81.3 cm) have been successfully used to capture swift foxes in Texas (Kamler et al. 2002). The capture rate of swift foxes was 48% higher in reverse double sets (which used 2 traps set in opposite directions) than in single sets. No data on trap-related injuries were presented.

Gray Wolf

A variety of foothold restraining traps, including the Aldrich™ foot snare, have been evaluated for capturing gray wolves (Van Ballenberghe 1984, Kuehn et al. 1986, Schultz et al. 1996). Van Ballenberghe (1984) reported on trap related injuries to wolves caught in 3 types of long spring foothold traps and the Aldrich™ foot snare, but small sample sizes precluded comparison of injuries among trap types. However, suggested methods for reducing injury included shortened chains, center mounting of the chain, and use of tranquilizer tabs. Gray wolves captured in Minnesota using a custom-made No. 14 foothold trap with serrated jaws offset 0.7 cm had fewer injuries than those caught in No. 4 double long spring traps (with smooth jaws either not offset or offset 0.2 cm) and another No. 14 trap with a smaller offset (Kuehn et al. 1986). Schultz et al. (1996) equipped all their wolf traps with drags, and checked their sets at least once every 24 hours. They found 15% of the wolves captured in foothold traps with modified No. 14 Newhouse™ jaws had moderate to severe injuries and recommended use of the No. 4 Newhouse™ trap with modified jaws for capturing wolf pups. Schultz et al. (1996) noted a pan tension system (Paws-I-Trip™) was effective in reducing unwanted captures of other species. No data on the performance of killing traps for wolves are available.

Canada Lynx

Three restraining traps and 2 killing traps have been evaluated for capturing lynx in Canada. When tested in the Yukon at temperatures ranging from –40 to 0 C, modified Fremont™ foot snares caused less injury than the Victor™ No. 3 Soft-Catch™ foothold trap with padded jaws (Mowat et al. 1994). Proulx et al. (1995) reported a modified 330 Conibear® trap could consistently kill lynx in ≤3 minutes.

American Marten

The initial research to evaluate performances of killing traps for capturing marten was conducted in Canada using captive animals (Gilbert 1981*a, b*). Additional comparative testing revealed that standard Conibear® 110 and 120 traps could not consistently kill marten in <5 minutes (Novak 1981*a*, Proulx et al. 1989*b*). Proulx et al. (1989*a*) reported 13 of 14 marten caught in the C120 Magnum trap equipped with a pitchfork trigger had an average time to unconsciousness of ≤68 seconds. Field tests in Alberta indicated the C120 Magnum placed in elevated box sets was as efficient as foothold traps for harvesting marten (Barrett et al. 1989). During additional field tests in Ontario, Naylor and Novak (1994) found wire box traps and the Conibear® 120 had similar selectivity, but box traps were less efficient. Novak (1990) experimented with a variety of sets and traps, and reported the most efficient and selective set for marten used a killing trap placed in a "Trapper's Box" on a horizontal pole. Proulx et al. (1994*a*) designed a snare system that successfully captured snowshoe hares but allowed snared marten to escape. Their 0.02 gauge stainless steel wire snare was set with a 10.2-cm diameter loop and equipped with a release device, a 12 gauge high tensile fence wire shaped into a 5-coil spiral used as a snare anchor.

Mink

Restraining trap research on mink is lacking. Research in Canada under controlled conditions has shown that mink can be killed in terrestrial sets in ≤180 seconds using the C120 Magnum trap with a pan trigger (Proulx et al. 1990, Proulx et al. 1993*b*), the Bionic™ trap with a 6-cm bait cone (Proulx and Barrett 1991, Proulx et al. 1993*b*), and the C180 trap with a pan trigger (Novak 1981*a*). In contrast, the standard Conibear® 110 and 120 failed to consistently kill mink in <300 seconds when used on land (Gilbert 1981*b*, Novak 1981*a*). Mink died in <240 seconds when captured in drowning sets using foothold traps, but most "wet" drown (Gilbert and Gofton 1982). During field tests in Canada, the C120 Magnum with a pan trigger was as efficient for capturing mink as standard foothold traps and the Conibear® 120 (Proulx and Barrett 1993*c*).

Muskrat

Lacki et al. (1990) compared the efficiency of 2 cage type live traps with double doors for capturing muskrats; the Tomahawk was more effective than the Havahart™. Killing traps for muskrat have been evaluated in Louisiana, New Jersey, and Canada (Palmisano and Dupuie 1975, Linscombe 1976, Penkala 1978, Parker 1983). Tests on anesthetized animals have measured the minimum energy forces required to cause death when delivered via a blow to the head, neck, thorax, and abdomen (Gilbert 1976, Zelin et al. 1983). Novak (1981*a*) reported muskrats die in ≤4 minutes if caught in Conibear® 110 traps set underwater, but standard Conibear® 110 and 120 traps failed to consistently kill muskrats in ≤5 minutes when used on land. However, muskrats captured in modified (18-kg springs) Conibear® 110 traps set on land died in ≤200 seconds. Controlled experiments have shown muskrats taken in drowning sets using No. 1½ long spring foothold traps died in ≤315 seconds (Novak 1981*a*), and about half had no injuries (Gilbert and Gofton 1982). Based on a field study in New Jersey using drowning sets, McConnell et al. (1985) reported the Victor™ No. 1 VG Stoploss with padded jaws caused significantly less damage to limbs of trapped muskrats compared with the unpadded Victor™ No. 1 VG Stoploss; both traps captured and held muskrats equally well in drowning sets. Conibear® 110 traps (standard and modified) set at den entrances were more efficient for capturing muskrats than a variety of No. 1 size foothold traps placed in similar locations (Penkala 1978). Parker (1983) found that Conibear® 110 traps were more humane (i.e., killed a higher percentage of the muskrats caught) and selective for harvesting muskrats than Victor™ No. 1 Stoploss and Victor™ No. 1½ long spring footholds.

Nutria

Four field studies, 3 in Louisiana and the other in Great Britain, have evaluated the efficiency of nutria traps. In Great Britain, cage traps set on rafts caught significantly more nutria than traps set on land as well as 50% fewer non-target animals (Baker and Clarke 1988). Victor™ Nos. 1½ and 2 long spring foothold restraining traps proved more efficient for capturing nutria in Louisiana marshes than either the Conibear® 220, a killing trap, and the Tomahawk™ 206, a cage trap (Palmisano and Dupuie 1975, Linscombe 1976, Robicheaux and Linscombe 1978). The Conibear® trap failed to kill about 10% of the nutria caught.

Virginia Opossum

Restraining traps for Virginia opossum have been evaluated on a limited basis, primarily in the eastern United States. Berchielli and Tullar (1980) failed to observe any injuries in 67% of the opossum caught in standard, unpadded No. 1½ coil spring traps, but 20% had fractures. Other reports which contained data on restraining trap performance for this species included Turkowski et al. (1984), Linscombe and Wright (1988), and Philips and Gruver (1996). Hubert et al. (1999) examined injuries of opossums captured in the EGG ™ trap, a foot-encapsulating device, and found severe injuries such as bone fractures were limited to animals weighing ≤1.9 kg. Warburton (1982, 1992) examined the performance of several restraining traps for capturing Australian brush-tailed opossum (*Trichosurus vulpecula*). Hill (1981) noted certain killing traps appeared to be more efficient for catching Virginia opossum when placed in boxes on the ground rather than above ground level.

Pocket Gopher

Witmer et al. (1999) described a variety of killing and cage/box restraining traps for pocket gophers (Geomyidae). They noted over 100 killing trap designs have been developed and tried over the last 140 years, but only a few types remain in common use in North America. Few cage/box restraining type "live" traps are available because of a limited market; rectangular box traps of metal construction have been produced by Sherman Traps, Inc., Tallahassee, Florida and Don Sprague Sales, Inc., Woodburn, Oregon (Witmer et al. 1999). Sargeant (1966) and Baker and Williams (1972) described cylindrical cage/box restraining traps made of wire mesh and plastic, respectively.

Proulx (1997) evaluated the efficiency of 4 types of killing traps for gophers during the fall in alfalfa fields. The ConVerT™ box trap was most successful, and was followed, in decreasing success, by the Black Hole, Guardian, and Victor Easyset. Proulx (1999*b*) tested the experimental PG killing trap and found 9 of 9 northern pocket gophers (*Thomomys talpoides*) unconscious in ≤78 seconds. He also reported that pocket gophers caught in ConVerT™ and Sidman killing traps sometimes remained alive if captured in the lower thorax or abdominal regions. Pipas et al. (2000) evaluated the efficiency of 3 types of traps (Cinch, Macabee, and Black Hole) for capturing pocket gophers with the Macabee trap being most effective.

Porcupine

Single-door cage traps baited with sliced apples and placed at the base of occupied trees have been used successfully to capture porcupines (*Erethizon dorsatum*) (Griesemer et al. 1999). Traps have also been used to capture porcupines by other researchers (Brander 1973, Craig and Keller 1986). However, injury and efficiency data are lacking for this species. The performance of killing traps for porcupines has not been evaluated.

Mountain Lion

Logan et al. (1999) used modified foot snares (Schimetz-Aldrich) to trap mountain lions in New Mexico. Most captures (93.3%) resulted in minor or non-detectable injuries except for swelling of the capture foot, which ranged from none to >1/5 times normal girth. Mountain lions sustained severe, life-threatening injuries in 2.4% of 209 captures; 4 mountain lions (1.9%) subsequently died. Some problems with mortality of nontarget captures, especially mule deer and oryx (*Oryx gazella*), also were encountered.

Raccoon

Numerous studies of restraining traps for raccoons have been conducted. Most research has focused on comparing the capture rate and injuries associated with different trap types. In some instances, injury data from these investigations are difficult to compare because scoring systems have varied, and several studies reported only injuries to the trapped limb. However, a significant conclusion has been that most serious injuries observed are due to self-mutilation (e.g., Proulx et al. 1993*d*, Hubert et al. 1996).

Berchielli and Tullar (1980) reported the Blake & Lamb™ No. 1½ coil spring trap was more efficient for capturing raccoons than the Ezyonem™ leg snare. They observed self-mutilation in 39% of the raccoons caught in the No. 1½ coil spring, but were unable to compare injuries between trap types due to the small sample size for the Ezyonem™ (*n* = 2). However, raccoons caught in the No. 1½ coil spring had fewer injuries when the traps were covered with sifted soil. Similarly, Novak (1981*b*) reported a raccoon capture rate of 57% (*n* = 113) for the Novak™ foot snare compared with 76% (*n* = 34) for No. 2 coil spring and No. 4 double long spring traps, both with offset jaws. He noted 82% of the raccoons caught in the foot snare (*n* = 49), and 50% of those taken in the foothold traps (*n* = 22) had no injuries.

Tullar (1984) was the first researcher to report on the performance of padded foothold traps for raccoons. His data indicated injury scores failed to differ between the unpadded Victor™ No.1½ coil spring and a padded proto-type No. 1½ coil spring. However, 89% (*n* = 9) of the rac-coons caught in the padded trap had injury scores ≤15 compared with 50% (*n* = 14) for the unpadded trap. Self-mutilation was observed in 24% (*n* = 17) of the raccoons caught in the unpadded trap.

Most reports published since Tullar (1984) indicated padded traps failed to preclude self-mutilation behavior in raccoons and did not significantly reduce injury scores compared with unpadded traps (Olsen et al. 1988, Hubert et al. 1991, Kern et al. 1994). However, Saunders et al. (1988) and Heydon et al. (1993) provided data contrary to this generalization. Padded traps also appeared to be less efficient for capturing raccoons than unpadded versions (Linscombe and Wright 1988, Hubert et al. 1991). Smaller foothold traps seemed to reduce injuries without sacrific-ing efficiency. The only restraining trap tested to date that has significantly reduced the frequency of self-mutilation and the severity of injuries to trapped raccoons compared with padded and unpadded jaw-type foothold traps is the EGG™ (Proulx et al. 1993*d*, Hubert et al. 1996). Based on a field study in Illinois, Hubert et al. (1996) reported the mean total injury score (based on a modified Olsen scale) assigned to raccoons caught in EGG™ foothold traps was 68 compared to 116 for those trapped with the No. 1 coil spring trap. They reported the EGG™ trap had a raccoon capture efficiency that exceeded that of the unpadded No. 1 coil spring. Proulx (1991) found the raccoon capture efficiency of the EGG™ was similar to that of cage traps in British Columbia, but was less efficient than the Conibear® 220 during the latter part of the fur trapping season in Quebec.

Cage-type restraining traps are commonly used to cap-ture raccoons. Preliminary data contained in a progress report (IAFWA 2000) indicated 52% (*n* = 112) of the rac-coons caught in Tomahawk™ #108 wire cage traps sus-tained no injuries. Moore and Kennedy (1985) used Tomahawk™ and Havahart™ wire cage traps during a pop-ulation study and found capture success was highest in autumn/winter, higher with higher temperatures, and nega-tively correlated with precipitation. Gehrt and Fritzell (1996) reported a gender-biased response of raccoons when using Tomahawk™ cage traps in Texas. Adult males were consistently captured more frequently than adult females.

Controlled lab tests have been conducted on anes-thetized raccoons to measure the minimum energy forces a killing trap must deliver to cause death via a blow to the head and neck (Gilbert 1976, Zelin et al. 1983). Limited data about the effects of clamping force have also been obtained (Zelin et al. 1983). Other research on killing traps conducted in enclosures indicated raccoons can not be con-sistently killed in <5 minutes using standard Conibear® 220, 280 (with pan trigger), and 330 traps (Novak 1981*a*). However, about 60% of the raccoons captured in the Conibear® 220 and 280 traps died in <4 minutes. Proulx and Drescher (1994) reported the Sauvageau™ 2001-8 and a modified (extra clamping bar) Conibear® 280 have the potential to consistently immobilize raccoons irreversibly unconscious in ≤4 minutes, but not in ≤3 minutes. In a sep-arate lab study, the average time to unconsciousness for 4 of 5 immobilized raccoons caught in the BMI 160 (a rotating-jaw trap similar to the Conibear®) was 172±16 seconds; the remaining animal was euthanized after 5 minutes (Sabean

and Mills 1994). Proulx (1999*a*) recommended future research should focus on killing systems for raccoons that differ from the rotating-jaw trap type.

The raccoon capture efficiency of the Conibear® 220 may be comparable to or better than some restraining traps under certain environmental conditions but, in other instances, it may not (Proulx 1991). Linscombe (1976) reported the Victor™ No. 2 long spring trap was more effi-cient than the Conibear® 200 for capturing raccoons in brackish marshes. In contrast, Hill (1981) caught a similar number of raccoons per trap night in No. 2 coil spring traps placed in dirt-hole sets and Conibear® 220 traps in boxes placed on the ground.

Northern River Otter

A variety of restraining traps for live-capture of river otters have been evaluated in Canada and the United States. Capture success with Hancock traps has varied depending on season and setting techniques (Northcott and Slade 1976; Melquist and Hornocker 1979, 1983; Route and Peterson 1988). In Newfoundland, Bailey traps proved ineffective (Northcott and Slade 1976). Shirley et al. (1983) reported a modified Victor™ No. 11 double long spring trap was a practical and efficient live trap for otters in Louisiana marsh habitat, but they failed to catch any otters in No. 208 Tomahawk™ cage traps. Serfass et al. (1996) compared unpadded Victor™ No. 11 double long spring modified (heavier spring added) traps with Victor™ No. 1½ Soft-Catch™ traps with padded jaws for catching otters for relocation. Fewer severe injuries were noted in animals captured with the Soft-Catch™ trap, but there was no difference in frequency or severity of dental injuries between trap types. More recently, Blundell et al. (1999) compared Hancock and No. 11 Sleepy Creek double-jaw foothold traps with long springs for live-capture of river otter using blind sets at latrines. They found Hancock traps had slightly lower efficiency, a higher escape rate, a lower rate of malfunction, and much lower use than the No. 11 Sleepy Creek foothold trap. Otters captured in Hancock traps had significantly more serious injuries to their teeth than animals captured in foothold traps. Although more serious injuries to appendages were observed for otters caught in foothold traps compared with Hancock traps, the difference was not significant. No pub-lished research on killing traps for river otter is available.

Gray and Fox Squirrel

Huggins (1999) presented a detailed review of trapping techniques and equipment for gray (*Sciurus carolinensis*) and fox squirrels. Based on limited comparative research, cage traps and jaw-type foothold traps were relatively non-selective; rotating-jaw and tunnel type killing traps were relatively selective for these species. Research needs included welfare and effectiveness testing of killing traps, and additional comparative studies of trap types.

Red Squirrel

The Kania 1000, a mouse-type killing trap with a strik-ing bar powered by a coil spring, can reliably cause uncon-sciousness in red squirrels in ≤90 seconds (Proulx et al. 1993*a*). When set under conifer branches, it is unlikely the Kania would attract and capture birds (Currie and Robertson 1992). Preliminary field tests showed this trap had the potential to capture red squirrels during the regular harvest season (G. Proulx, Alpha Wildlife Research & Management, Ltd., unpublished data).

Striped Skunk

The restraining trap research conducted on striped skunks indicated leg injuries of animals caught in unpadded and padded foothold traps were often severe due to high incidence of self-mutilation (Berchielli and Tullar 1980, Novak 1981b,). Novak (1981b) reported skunks can be captured with few injuries in the Novak™ foot snare, but this device has a low capture rate and an unacceptable level of efficiency. Numerous pan tension devices have been used on a variety of coyote traps; all have been effective in reducing accidental skunk captures (Turkowski et al. 1984, Phillips and Gruver 1996). The performance of killing traps on striped skunks has not been evaluated.

Weasel

Research information on traps commonly used for harvesting weasels in North American is not available. During a field study in New Zealand, King (1981) concluded correctly set Fenn traps killed weasels more humanely than Gin traps. Typically, North American trapping technique manuals recommend use of small foothold or rotating-jaw traps as killing traps for weasels.

Belant (1992) tested the efficiency of double-door Havahart™, single-door National, and single-door wooden cage/box traps for capturing long-tailed (*Mustela frenata*) and short-tailed (*M. erminea*) weasels in New York. Overall success for all 3 types was similar. Trap-related injuries of long-tailed weasels caught in Havahart™ traps included skin abrasions and broken canines.

Wolverine

Copeland et al. (1995) used a specialized log trap to live capture wolverine in Idaho. No injuries were noted on individuals captured, but 3 wolverines escaped by chewing holes in the traps. No data are available on the performance of killing traps for wolverines.

Evaluation and Status of Tranquilizer Trap Devices

Balser (1965) used tranquilizer trap devices (TTDs) containing diazepam, a controlled substance not registered for such use by the U.S. Drug Enforcement Administration (Savarie et al. 1993) to reduce injuries to coyotes. Another drug, propiopromazine hydrochloride (PPZH), that acted as a tranquilizer and depressed the central nervous system was tested on captive coyotes by Savarie and Roberts (1979). Foot injuries to coyotes and other animals caught in foothold traps were reduced substantially when they ingested tranquilizers from tabs attached to trap jaws (Balser 1965).

Linhart et al. (1981) used TTDs containing PPZH to reduce foot and leg injuries to wild coyotes captured in foothold traps. Preliminary data reported by Zemlicka et al. (1997) suggested significant reduction in trap related injuries to the feet and legs of 37 gray wolves captured in traps using TTDs containing PPZH. None of 33 nontarget animals captured in traps with TTDs loaded with PPZH succumbed from ingestion of the tranquilizer, and injuries tended to be less severe than among nontarget captures in

traps without PPZH TTDs. Sahr and Knowlton (2000) demonstrated that TTDs containing PPZH effectively reduced injuries to limbs of wolves captured in foothold traps, but failed to reduce the severity of tooth injuries. Pruss et al. (2002) evaluated a modified locking neck snare equipped with a diazepam tab for coyotes in an effort to decrease stress, injuries, and unwanted animal captures. This device successfully reduced the incidence of lacerations experienced by captured coyotes without compromising capture efficiency or increasing capture of nontarget species.

The 2 drugs (diazepam and PPZH), used in conjunction with TTDs, are not available for widespread use. Pruss et al. (2002) reported future use of diazepam in Canada would require a researcher to submit a special request to the Drug Strategy and Controlled Substances Programme, Office of Controlled Substances, Ottawa, Ontario, Canada, and non-research use would require cooperation of a veterinarian. In the United States, diazepam (Valium®) is a Class IV controlled substance (Seal and Kreeger 1987), and has not been authorized as a tranquilizer for traps. Currently, only the U.S. Department of Agriculture (USDA), Animal and Plant Health Inspection Service (APHIS), Wildlife Services (WS) is authorized to use PPZH in TTDs as part of its wildlife damage control operations under a special permit issued by the U.S. Food and Drug Administration (T. J. Deliberto, USDA, APHIS, WS, National Wildlife Research Center, Fort Collins, Colorado, personal communication).

Box and Cage Traps

Haulton et al. (2001) evaluated 4 methods (Stephenson box traps, Clover traps, rocket nets, and dart guns) to capture deer. They found that smaller deer captured with Clover traps were more susceptible to capture mortality. Anderson and Nielsen (2002) described a modified Stephenson trap to capture deer that featured lightweight panels that were easily set up and readily movable. They recommended their trap for capturing deer in urban areas. Ballard et al. (1998) used Clover traps and darting from tree stands to capture white-tailed deer. They bolted U-clamps to keep the drop doors on the Clover traps closed to avoid deer escapes and substituted nuts and bolts for welds that broke at sub-zero temperatures (Table 13).

Bull et al. (1996) covered wire cage traps with black plastic to protect American marten from rain and snow to reduce the risk of mortality from hypothermia. They also placed clumps of wool for insulation in wood boxes to provide warm, dry shelter during winter trapping. Baited culvert traps (Fig. 13) have been widely used to capture and transplant nuisance bears (Erickson 1957).

Carey et al. (1991) placed a single door, collapsible wire box trap, 1.5 m above ground in large trees to capture arboreal mammals such as northern flying squirrels (*Glaucomys sabrinus*) and Townsend's chipmunks (*Tamias townsendii*). A nest box was inserted behind the trap treadle to minimize stress and hypothermia. Hayes et al. (1994) described a simple and inexpensive modification (Fig. 14) of the technique of Carey et al. (1991) to attach live traps to small-diameter trees, 8.5 to 30-cm diameter at breast height (dbh), using a triangular plywood bracket. The bracket was set tangential to the tree trunk, and 2 aluminum nails were driven through the plywood and into the

Table 13. Box and cage traps used to capture mammals.

Group	References
Nine-banded armadillo (*Dasypus novemcinctus*)	Bergman et al. 1999
Snowshoe hare	Aldous 1946, Libby 1957, Cushwa and Burnham 1974, Litvaitis et al. 1985
Northern flying squirrel	Carey et al. 1991
Gray squirrel	Huggins and Gee 1995
Fox squirrel	Huggins and Gee 1995
Abert's squirrel (*Sciurus aberti*)	Patton et al. 1976, Dodd et al. 2003
Townsend's chipmunk	Carey et al. 1991
Woodchuck (*Marmota monax*)	Trump and Hendrickson 1943, Ludwig and Davis 1975
California ground squirrel (*Spermophilus beecheyi*)	Horn and Fitch 1946
Pocket gopher	Howard 1952, Sargeant 1966, Baker and Williams, 1972, Witmer et al. 1999
American beaver	Couch 1942, Hodgdon and Hunt 1953, Collins 1976
Muskrat	Takos 1943, Snead 1950, Stevens 1953, Robicheaux and Linscombe 1978, McCabe and Elison 1986, Lacki et al. 1990
Nutria	Norris 1967, Evans et al. 1971, Palmisano and Dupuie 1975, Linscombe 1976, Robicheaux and Linscombe 1978, Baker and Clarke 1988
Porcupine	Brander 1973, Craig and Keller 1986, Griesemer et al. 1999
Coyote	Foreyt and Rubenser 1980, Way et al. 2002
Kit fox (*Vulpes macrotis*)	Zoellick and Smith 1986
Swift fox	Kamler et al. 2002
Mountain lion	Shuler 1992
Canada lynx	Mowat et al. 1994
Bobcat	Woolf and Nielson 2002
Black bear	Erickson 1957, Black 1958
Brown/grizzly bear (*Ursus arctos*)	Craighead et al. 1960, Troyer et al. 1962
Raccoon	Robicheaux and Linscombe 1978, Moore and Kennedy 1985, Proulx 1991, Gehrt and Fritzell 1996
American marten	Naylor and Novak 1994, Bull et al. 1996
Fisher	Arthur 1988, Frost and Krohn 1994
Striped skunk	Allen and Shapton 1942
Northern river otter	Northcott and Slade 1976; Melquist and Hornocker 1979, 1983; Shirley et al. 1983; Route and Peterson 1988; Serfass et al. 1996; Blundell et al. 1999
Long-tailed weasel	Belant 1992
Short-tailed weasel	Belant 1992
Feral hog	Matschke 1962, Williamson and Pelton 1971, Saunders et al. 1993, Jamison 2002
Collared peccary (*Pecari tajacu*)	Neal 1959
Elk (*Cervus elaphus*)	Thompson et al. 1989
White-tailed deer	Bartlett 1938; Ruff 1938; McBeath 1941; Webb 1943; Glazener 1949; Clover 1954, 1956; Hawkins et al. 1967; Sparrowe and Springer 1970; Runge 1972; McCullough 1975; Foreyt and Glazener 1979; Palmer et al. 1980; Rongstad and McCabe 1984; Morgan and Dusek 1992; Naugle et al. 1995; Beringer et al. 1996; Ballard et al. 1998; VerCauteren et al. 1999; DelGiudice et al. 2001; Haulton et al. 2001; Anderson and Nielsen 2002
Mule deer	Lightfoot and Maw 1963, Roper et al. 1971, D'Eon et al. 2003

tree. Nylon twine was tied around the trap and secured to 2 additional nails. Malcolm (1991), Vieira (1998), and Kays (1999) described an arboreal mammal box trap system that could be hoisted to sample arboreal mammal communities. Huggins and Gee (1995) tested 4 cage trap sets for gray and fox squirrels, and found traps set at eye-level on a platform attached to tree trunks resulted in the highest rate of capture.

Szaro et al. (1988) assessed the effectiveness of pitfalls and Sherman live-traps in measuring small mammal community structure. They found that live-traps and pitfalls provided different estimates of species composition and relative abundance. However, live trapping was significantly more successful than pitfalls in number of new captures per trap night. They recommended use of both pitfalls and live traps, particularly when it is essential that shrews (Soricidae), which are not readily caught in live traps, be sampled. Slade et al. (1993) advised using a combination of trap types for sampling diverse small mammal faunas.

Fitzgerald et al. (1999) tested the capture rate of buried and non-buried folding Sherman live traps in desert grasslands and desert shrub communities. Traps were set in pairs for 3 consecutive nights. The non-buried trap capture rate was significantly greater than for buried traps. Burying traps may be a cost-effective method of reducing trap fatalities related to temperature fluctuations in desert environments.

Standardization of traps and trapping procedures are needed to adequately sample small mammal populations. Kirkland and Sheppard (1994) proposed a standard protocol for sampling small mammal populations with emphasis on shrews. They suggested using Y-shaped arrays of 10 pitfall traps and drift fences. Each arm, which was anchored on a central pitfall, consisted of 3 pitfalls separated by 5 m sections of drift fence. Pitfalls not less than 14-cm diameter and 19-cm deep should be filled half full of water to quickly drown captured animals. They recommended that arrays be operated for 10 consecutive days. This totaled 100 trap nights of sampling effort per array, per sampling period and allowed easy calculation of relative abundance as percentage capture success. Handley and Varn (1994) suggested using a small, easily set pitfall array in the form of a triangle with 2.5-m sides and set in a transect for capturing shrews. Two people set 2 arrays per hour. They used 2-liter, heavy-gauge plastic soft drink bottles with the tops cut off as pitfalls. The plastic bottles were 20-cm deep and 11-cm in diameter. At the center of the array, they used a 4-liter plastic bottle 18-cm deep and 15-cm in diameter. Pitfalls were arranged with 120° between arms and joined with 1.2 m in length by 30-cm high drift fence. Tew et al. (1994) tested 2 trap spacings, 24 and 48 m, using 184 Longworth live-traps set in a rectangular grid covering an area of 10 ha. They found the 2 spacings were equally effective in capturing wood

Fig. 13. Culvert trap for capturing bears (photograph by New Mexico Department of Game and Fish).

mice (*Apodemus sylvaticus*). They suggested that projects with limited numbers of traps should consider wider trap spacing with an increased trapping period. A study by Mitchell et al. (1993) in saturated forested wetlands showed that pitfalls in conjunction with drift fences captured significantly greater numbers of small mammals than isolated pitfall can traps in the same general area. They recommended that different researchers should use the same technique and sampling effort for the same taxa.

Hays (1998) devised a new method for live trapping shrews by inserting small 10-cm Sherman live traps into

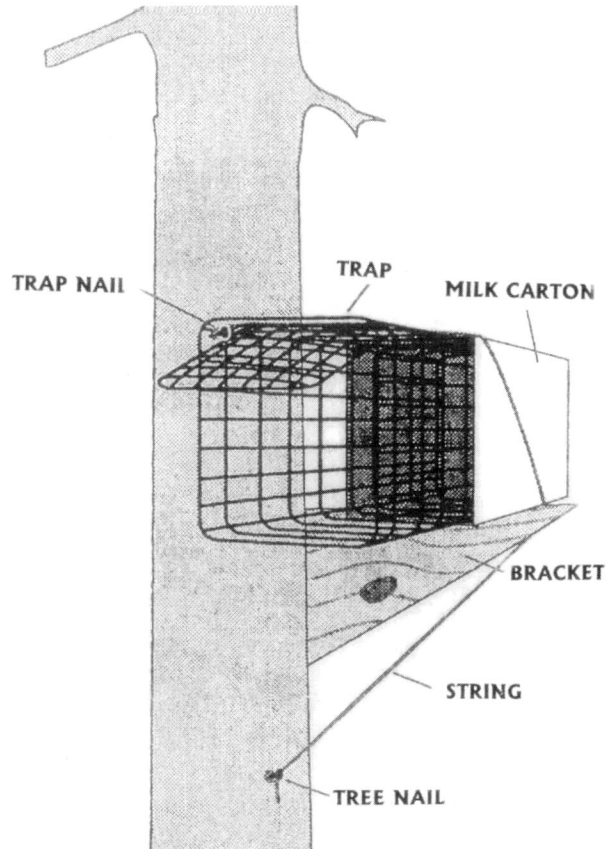

Fig. 14. Tomahawk™ live trap attached to a small-diameter tree by a bracket (from Hayes et al. 1994).

holes cut in Nalgene plastic jars (25-cm high × 15-cm diameter). The trap entrance was covered with 12-mm wire mesh to exclude mice. Traps were baited with mealworms and cotton batting. Traps were checked daily and trap mortality was only 1%. Yunger et al. (1992) greatly decreased the mortality of masked shrews (*Sorex cinereus*) (77.5% survival) caught in pitfall traps by providing 7 g of whitefish (*Coregonus* sp.) per pitfall.

Whittaker et al. (1998) evaluated captures of mice in 2 sizes of Sherman live traps. Small Sherman traps captured significantly more white-footed (*Peromyscus leucopus*) and cotton mice (*P. gossypinus*). More rice rats (*Oryzomys palustris*) were caught in large Sherman traps. Jorgensen et al. (1994) set paired Sherman and wire-mesh box traps. More rodents were consistently caught in the Sherman traps made of sheet metal. They attributed the capture rate difference to less frequent entry by rodents into wire-mesh traps and a more sensitive treadle in the Sherman traps. In contrast, O'Farrell et al. (1994) experimented with similar size Sherman and wire mesh live traps. Captures were significantly greater in mesh traps than Sherman traps. They surmised that an open trap that can be seen through was preferred to an enclosed box. Their estimates of small mammal density at different sites using wire mesh traps were 15–37% higher than estimates with Sherman traps. They concluded that composition of communities of small mammals might be inaccurately represented based on type of trap used. McComb et al. (1991) compared capture rates of small mammals and amphibians between pitfall and Museum Special snap traps in mature forests in Oregon. Fewer small mammal and amphibian species were caught with Museum Special traps than with pitfalls. However, 2 species of salamander were captured only in pitfall traps. Museum Specials baited with peanut butter were more effective than traps baited with meat paste. Pearson and Ruggiero (2003) examined trap arrangement in forested areas by comparing transect and grid trapping of small mammals. Transects yielded more total and individual captures and more species than grid arrangements.

Mitchell et al. (1996) reported that use of an ant insecticide (Dursban®) did not affect overall capture yield or probability of capture of 12 species of small mammals and that mutilation rates by ants were lower. Gettinger (1990) reported use of chemical insect repellents increased capture rates.

Yunger and Randa (1999) immersed Sherman live traps for 5 minutes in a 10% bleach solution (sodium hypochlorite) to decontaminate them from Sin Nombre Hantavirus. No effect on small mammal capture rate was observed. Cross et al. (1999) tested bleach treatment and found no effect on trap success. Van Horn and Douglass (2000) used a Lysol® disinfectant followed by a fresh water rinse to clean traps. This treatment did not influence subsequent deer mouse (*Peromyscus maniculatus*) capture rates.

Heske (1987) recommended use of non-soiled live traps to obtain an unbiased demographic sample of small mammals. He observed that using soiled traps might cause possible violations of the assumptions of equal catch success of all individuals. He documented that *Microtus* samples were more accurate demographically if all traps were kept clean. Jones et al. (1996) advised cleaning all traps with soap and water after each trapping session to increase consistency in trapping success.

Live trapping bias of small mammals varies with gender, age, and species. Results of capture rates to previous trap occupancy depended on gender and age (Gurnell and Little 1992). Wolf and Batzli (2002) reported that white-footed mice were less likely to be captured in live traps that previously held short-tailed shrews (*Blarina brevicauda*). Adult white-footed mice were more likely to be captured in traps previously occupied by conspecific individuals of the opposite gender than in traps previously occupied by the same gender. In contrast, Gurnell and Little (1992) reported no evidence of breeding males or females being attracted to traps containing odor of the opposite gender. Their studies involved various wood rodents—wood mice, bank voles, and yellow-necked mice (*Apodemus flavicollis*).

Corral Traps

Sweitzer et al. (1997) designed a modified steel mesh panel trap for capturing multiple wild hogs with a minimum (5%) of injury. Their traps included a gate entrance with a runway leading to an enlarged corral with a trip line activating a side-hinged squeeze gate. Saunders et al. (1993) suggested attaching fine mesh wire on the inside of trap drop gates to prevent hogs caught inside the trap from gripping the gate with their teeth and lifting it, allowing others to escape. They set traps using a trip wire placed in a back corner of the trap 20 cm above the floor of the trap. Jamison (2002) described effective traps for feral hog capture. He emphasized the need for a strong, portable trap the width and length of an average pickup truck bed to facilitate transporting live hogs. Choquenot et al. (1993) used estrous sows as a lure, but no hogs were attracted or captured.

Cancino et al. (2002) designed a modified corral trap (Table 14) consisting of a 70-ha enclosure and an adjacent observation tower. A 4-ha area within the enclosure was irrigated to attract pronghorn. A gate at one end was closed to confine the animals that gradually moved toward the end of the exclosure attracted by captive pronghorn, mobile feeders, and water where another gate was closed to confine them. Lee et al. (1998) summarized other pronghorn capture methods. Perez et al. (1997) perfected a corral trap for capturing Spanish ibexes. The trap consisted of a 3-m high metallic net fence with a 3-m high net inside. The 2 nets were 1 m apart with salt blocks as bait.

Table 14. Corral traps used to capture wildlife.

Group/Species	References
Canvasback	Haramis et al. 1987
Jackrabbit	Henke and Demarais 1990
Collared peccary	Neal 1959
Feral hog	Sweitzer et al. 1997
Deer	Lightfoot and Maw 1963, Hawkins et al. 1967, Rempel and Bertram 1975
Elk	Couey 1949, Mace 1971
Moose (*Alces alces*)	Pimlott and Carberry 1958, LeResche and Lynch 1973
Pronghorn	Spillett and Zobell 1967, Cancino et al. 2002
Spanish ibex (*Capra pyrenaica*)	Perez et al. 1997

Net Traps

Rosell and Hovde (2001) combined a spotlight and use of nylon mesh landing nets from boats on rivers and on foot on land to catch beaver. The net, when used in the water, was closed with a drawstring to prevent escape. The netting method resulted in no mortalities in contrast to 5.3% mortality with snares (McKinstry and Anderson 1998). Okarma and Jedrzejewski (1997) and Musiani and Visalberghi (2001) used fladry to help capture wolves. Fladry consists of red flags attached to nylon ropes 60 cm above ground placed along roads or trails in forested areas. Beaters, spaced at 250-m intervals, drove the wolves into nets where they became entangled and were captured. Drive nets have been widely used to capture large mammals but also are useful for trapping small mammals. Vernes (1993) devised a drive fence with attached wire cage traps set parallel to forest edges. Lentle et al. (1997) further refined a chicken wire drive fence by attaching a nylon drop net (Fig. 15).

Thomas and Novak (1991) described procedures contributing to successful helicopter drive-net captures of mule deer. Netting was dyed a dull green or brown color to reduce its visibility. Whenever possible, nets should be placed in or near a drainage bottom where deer could be herded downhill into the net which was concealed by terrain. Net sites that provided close hiding cover for observers that allowed quick access to entangled animals were essential. Ideal weather conditions consisted of high overcast that reduced glare and net visibility. A steady breeze of 9–18 km/hour blowing downwind from the helicopter toward the deer and net reduced the possibility of animals scenting and avoiding the capture site.

Sullivan et al. (1991) compiled data on captures of 430 white-tailed deer using the drive-net technique. The observed capture-related mortality and overall mortality

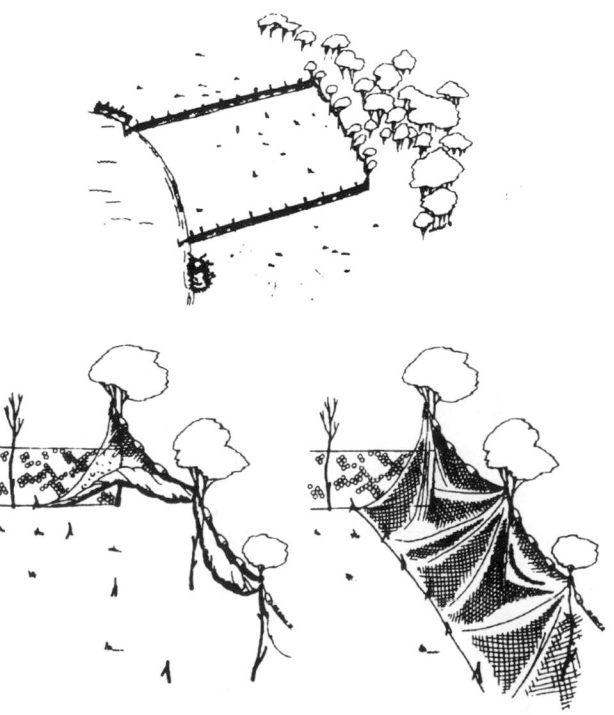

Fig. 15. Lake edge trap, showing secured drop net in raised and lowered position (from Lentle et al. 1997).

rates were 1.1 and 0.9%, respectively. These rates were lower than reported for other common capture methods. Kattell and Alldredge (1991) used 3 to 6-m long, 1.8 to 2-m high nets to capture Himalayan musk deer in Nepal. After the nets were set, 2 people slowly drove the deer towards the nets where they became entangled.

Kelly (1996) captured ringed seals (*Phoca hispida*) with nets set at breathing holes in the ice. He designed a net that lined a breathing hole and closed below the surface with a weighted, triggering device. Three wire hoops were attached to the net to hold it open. He increased seal visitation by cutting holes in the ice.

Net Guns

Carpenter and Innes (1995) used net guns fired from helicopters to capture moose with a mortality rate of less than 1%. White and Bartmann (1994) reported net gunning (Table 15) was a more economical, efficient, and safe capture method than drop nets for mule deer fawns. Use of net guns from a helicopter was the most effective method for winter capturing of yearling and adult white-tailed deer in non-yarding populations (Ballard et al. 1998).

Miscellaneous Capture Methods

Bergman et al. (1999) captured nine-banded armadillo by following a trained tracking dog to a burrow. They then placed a 30-cm high wire fence around the burrow and a cage live trap at the burrow entrance.

Godfrey et al. (2000) described a detailed protocol for safe entry into black bear tree dens for capture purposes that minimized risks to biologists and minimized bear mortality.

Karraker (2001) attached a string to hang from the cover board over pitfall traps allowing small mammals to escape. Amphibian (primarily salamanders) capture rates were not affected, but reptile capture rates were lower in pitfalls with escape strings. Perkins and Hunter (2002) reduced small mammal capture by placing wooden sticks in pitfall traps. The rate of amphibian capture was not

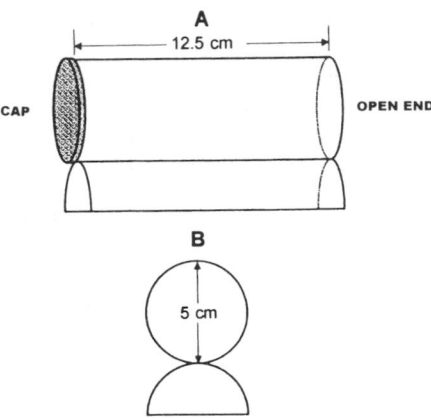

Fig. 16. Side (A) and front (B) view of the assembled rodent safe-house constructed with 5-cm diameter PVC pipe. (from Padgett-Flohr and Jennings 2001).

reduced. Padgett-Flohr and Jennings (2001) perfected a simple and inexpensive small mammal "safe-house" that is placed in the bottom of pitfall traps (Fig.16). The safe house was constructed of 5-cm diameter PVC pipe in 12.5-cm lengths and capped at one end. The center of the safe house was one-third filled with 100% cotton batting, and the "house" was glued to a base of PVC pipe cut in half to a length of 12 cm.

Francis (1989) compared mist nets and 2 designs of harp traps for capturing bats (Chiroptera). Large bats, megachiropterans, were captured at similar rates in harp traps and mist nets, but microchiropterans were captured nearly 60 times more frequently in traps. He noted that small bats have teeth with sharp cutting edges and often chewed part of the net around them and escaped. He recommended use of 4-bank harp traps over 2-bank harp traps for capture efficiency. Tidemann and Loughland (1993) devised a trap for capturing large bats featuring wire cables stretched between rigid uprights. Vertical strings were strung between the cables. Waldien and Hayes (1999) designed a hand-held portable "H" net used to capture bats that roosted at night under bridges. The H-net consisted of a mist net attached to PVC pipe and "T" couplers. Palmeirim and Rodrigues (1993) described an improved harp trap for bats that was inexpensive and lightweight (4.5 kg) that could be assembled by one person in less than 2 minutes. Kuenzi and Morrison (1998) suggested combining mist-net capture with ultrasonic detection to identify bat species presence. Cotterill and Fergusson (1993) described a new trapping device (Fig. 17) to capture African free-tailed bats (*Tadarida fulminans*) as they left their daylight roosts. They used polyethylene plastic sheeting attached to a rectangular frame of aluminum tubing. Bicycle wheels were attached to each corner of the frame to carry the assembled trap into position below the roost exit. Two people elevated the trap with ropes and pulleys. Bats were caught in a plastic bag and easily removed with a minimum of stress in contrast to mist nets. Kunz et al. (1996) provided an in-depth review of bat capture methods.

Karanth (1995) identified individual Siberian tigers on film from distinctive body stripe patterns. He used TrailMaster® camera-traps along regular travel routes to acquire photographs. He suggested the camera-trap method could be used on other secretive animals with dis-

Table 15. Net guns used for capturing wildlife.

Group/Species	References
Birds	
Waterfowl	Mechlin and Shaiffer 1980
Golden eagle	O'Gara and Getz 1986
Mammals	
Coyote	Barrett et al. 1982, Gese et al. 1987
Moose	Carpenter and Innes 1995
White-tailed deer	Barrett et al. 1982, De Young 1988, Potvin and Breton 1988, Ballard et al. 1998, DelGiudice et al. 2001, Haulton et al. 2001
Mule deer	Barrett et al. 1982, Krausman et al. 1985, White and Bartmann 1994
Caribou (*Rangifer tarandus*)	Valkenburg et al. 1983
Pronghorn	Barrett et al. 1982, Firchow et al. 1986
Mountain sheep	Andryk et al. 1983, Krausman et al. 1985, Kock et al. 1987, Jessup et al. 1988
Dall sheep	Barrett et al. 1982

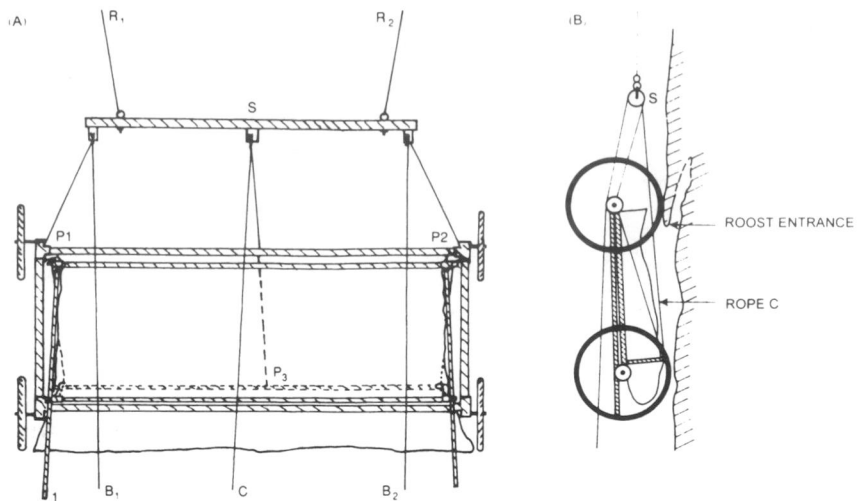

Fig. 17. Trap arrangement for catching bats. A = assembled trap with ropes and their points of attachment and B = lateral view of the assembled trap. Aluminum frames are cross-hatched (from Cotterill and Fergusson 1993).

tinctive natural markings, including leopard (*Panthera pardus*, jaguar (*P. onca*), snow leopard, and clouded leopard (*Neofelis nebulosa*).

Hernandez et al. (1997) reviewed the successful use of TrailMaster® cameras for identifying ground-nest predators and recommended the active infrared unit (TM1500). Additional summaries of the use of camera systems to identify marked individual animals include those by Kucera and Barrett (1993), Peterson and Thomas (1998), Cutler and Swann (1999), and Moruzzi et al. (2002). Remotely triggered cameras have been widely used to delineate species distribution, monitor presence-absence, identify nest predators, study feeding ecology, document

corridor use, examine activity patterns, and estimate population size.

Scotton and Pletscher (1998) jumped from a hovering helicopter to hand capture neonatal Dall sheep. They advocated using smaller, less noisy helicopters to minimize disturbance of ewes and their lambs.

An efficient technique for capturing swimming deer (Fig. 18) was developed by Boroski and McGlaughlin (1994) for use in lakes and reservoirs. They made a "head bag" from the upper half of a pants leg with a hole for insertion of pipe insulation for flotation. Other materials included a canvas pack cinch, a leather latigo strap, a nylon "piggin" string, and a 1.4 kg weight. A 3-person crew included a boat handler and 2 deer handlers. The "piggin" string was placed around the deer's neck and the "head bag" was placed to calm the deer. The latigo strap was positioned in front of the rear legs. After attachment of a radio-collar to the deer, the restraints and head bag were removed, and the deer previously kept in the water was released and allowed to swim freely. Handling time of captured deer averaged 5.5 minutes.

Ballard et al. (1998) decided that intensive grid ground searching was the most effective method for locating and capturing neonate white-tailed deer fawns. Franklin and Johnson (1994) hand captured South American guanacos within 30–60 minutes of birth before the neonates could escape by running. Care was taken to avoid separation of the mother from her offspring. Only 5 (1.2%) of 435 captured young guanacos failed to unite or were abandoned by

Fig. 18. Restraint and radio collar attachment for deer captured while swimming (from Boroski and McGlaughlin 1994).

their mothers. They suggested that hand capture and tagging of precocial newborns had potential application to a variety of African, Asian, and North American ungulates that live in open habitats.

Glennon et al. (2002) tested baited track tubes as an alternative technique for assessing populations of small mammals. They found a high correlation between live trapping and track tubes. When compared with live trapping, track tubes were less expensive and much less labor intensive. Woods et al. (1999) and Mowat and Strobeck (2000) used baited hair collection sites to "capture" grizzly and black bears. Bear hair was collected on barbed wire at bait sites and DNA sampling was used to identify individual bears. McDaniel et al. (2000) used hair snares with scented lures to detect presence of Canada lynx. Belant (2003) attached currycombs to cage trap doors for snaring hair samples from forest carnivores.

CAPTURING AMPHIBIANS AND REPTILES

Scott (1982), Heyer et al. (1994), Olson et al. (1997), and Simmons (2002) have compiled comprehensive capture references for amphibians

Amphibians

Nadorozny and Barr (1997) designed a side-flap pail to capture amphibians that were not readily captured in conventional pitfall traps due to their climbing and jumping ability. This trap design, when used with funnels and drift fencing, was effective for capturing amphibians in terrestrial habitats. Murphy (1993) captured tree frogs (*Hyla* spp.) with a modified drift fence (Fig. 19) of clear plastic suspended from PVC pipe joined in a T configuration. Boughton and Staiger (2000) caught hylid tree frogs in white 3.81-cm diameter PVC pipe capped at the bottom and hung vertically in hard-

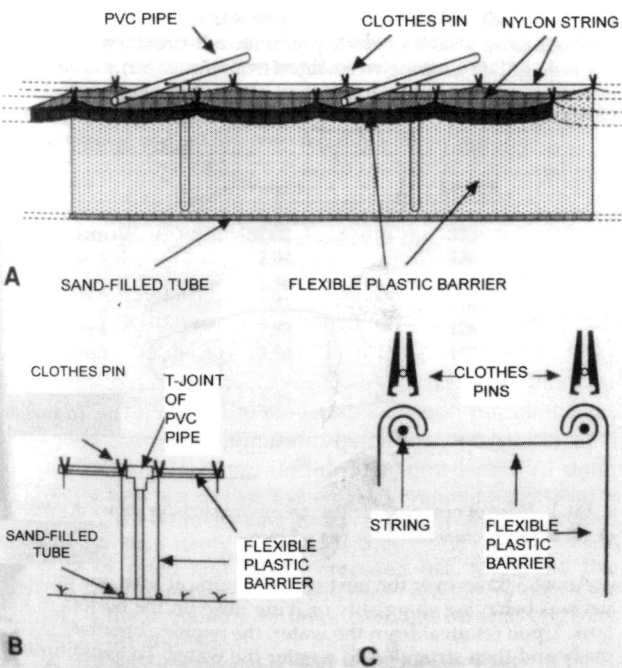

Fig. 19. Fence for capturing tree frogs as they enter and leave ponds. A = front view of the fence. Only a portion of the fence and only one of the plastic barriers are shown. B = side view of the fence showing both plastic barriers. C = enlarged side view of the fence showing method of attachment of flexible plastic barrier to strings (from Murphy 1993).

wood trees, 2 and 4 m above the ground. The 60-cm-long pipe caught more frogs than the 30-cm pipe. Daoust (1991) suggested placing moistened sponges ($10 \times 5 \times 7$ cm) in funnel traps along drift fences to minimize mortality of wood frogs (*Rana sylvatica*) from dehydration.

Adams and Freedman (1999) evaluated catch efficiency of 4 amphibian-sampling methods: pitfall transects, pitfall array, quadrat searches, and time-constrained searches in terrestrial habitats. Pitfall arrays sampled the greatest relative abundance and species richness of amphibians.

Smith and Rettig (1996) sampled amphibian larvae with an aquatic funnel trap made of 5-cm diameter PVC pipe with funnels at each end held in place with a large rubber band. Barr and Babbitt (2001) compared 2 techniques for sampling larval stream salamanders. More larvae were captured at high densities using 0.5-m^2 quadrats. Time-constrained sampling for 0.5 hours was more successful at low densities. Wilson and Maret (2002) reported timed dip net collections of 5 minutes provided reliable estimates of aquatic amphibian abundance and were superior to drop box sampling. Welsh and Lind (2002) sampled amphibians by searching streambed substrates with hardware-cloth catch nets placed downstream and from bank to bank to capture escaping individuals. Fronzuto and Verrell (2000) tested capture efficiency of wire and plastic funnel traps for aquatic salamanders. Plastic funnel traps with a maximum diagonal mesh of 5 mm were superior to 10-mm mesh hardware-cloth wire minnow traps. Mushet et al. (1997) designed a funnel trap for sampling salamanders in wetlands. They connected a 200-cm drift fence that directed free-swimming salamanders to the opening of the trap. This trap captured more salamanders than a minnow trap in the same area. Casazza et al. (2000) captured aquatic amphibians and reptiles using baited wire funnel entrance eel pots with Styrofoam™ blocks. This allowed the traps to float partly out of the water avoiding trap mortality from drowning. Richter (1995) used baited aquatic funnel traps made from plastic soda pop bottles attached to a steel rod baited with salmon (Salmonidae) eggs. He captured tadpoles and adult amphibians. Smith and Rettig (1996) increased the catch rate of tadpoles by putting glow sticks at night in 3 different funnel trap designs. Jenkins et al. (2002) compared 2 aquatic surveying techniques to sample marbled salamander (*Ambystoma opacum*) larvae. Nocturnal visual surveys were less intrusive and expensive and more accurate at detecting presence than bottle funnel traps described by Richter (1995).

Campbell and Christman (1982) developed and described a standardized amphibian and reptile trapping system. Their system included pitfalls and double-ended funnel traps placed in conjunction with drift fences that diverted moving animals into traps. Data obtained using their technique allowed estimates of species richness and an index of relative abundance of most common terrestrial amphibians and reptiles. Dodd (1991) warned that drift fences used with pitfalls were biased in sampling amphibians. Frogs, in particular, readily cross drift fences by climbing over. Other species burrow under drift fences. Brown (1997) also found drift fences allowed frogs to escape. She tested pitfall traps and reported that <1% of the individuals placed in pitfall traps escaped.

Corn and Bury (1990) described time-constrained searches for amphibians and reptiles that were immediately captured by hand. Equal effort was expended in each area searched. They described another hand collection method for amphibians (surveys of coarse woody debris) and advised searching 30 downed logs per forest stand.

Trapping methods for herpetofauna are time and labor intensive, and can result in injury to captured individuals due to physical stress such as overheating, desiccation, drowning, or predation. Cover boards ("boards" placed on the ground under which herpetofauna may hide) avoid these problems. Grant et al. (1992) evaluated cover boards in detail. They recommended that both metal and wood cover boards be used and a wait of at least 2 months before beginning the survey program. They suggested that checks of cover boards be made at different times of day and weather conditions to sample all taxa in residence. They advised that if encounter rates are to be compared among sites, time and weather conditions should be identical.

DeGraaf and Yamasaki (1992) used cover boards to simulate fallen timber to attract and evaluate terrestrial salamander abundance during daylight hours. Their procedure avoided laborious installation of pit traps as they placed a cluster of 3 boards along transects. They lifted boards 8 times during June–August in a variety of different age forest stands. Use of the boards avoided degradation of salamander habitat by turning or breaking existing logs or disrupting forest litter.

Pearman et al. (1995) evaluated day and night transects, artificial cover, and plastic washbasins with added leaf litter as sampling methods for amphibians. Significantly more species were found during nocturnal searches than with other methods. Parris et al. (1999) compared 3 techniques for sampling amphibians in forests. Nocturnal stream searches were the most sensitive, and pitfall trapping was the least sensitive sampling technique. A minimum of 4 nights of stream searching was recommended to detect the number of amphibian species present at a site. Crawford and Kurta (2000) tested capture success of black and white plastic pitfall traps on anurans and masked shrews. Both were caught significantly more often in pitfalls with a black interior than in those with a white interior. Hyde and Simons (2001) investigated 4 common sampling techniques to examine variability of salamander catches. They found natural cover transects and artificial cover boards to be the most effective sampling techniques for detecting long-term salamander population trends because of lower sampling variability, good capture success, and ease of use. They associated higher capture rates and lower variability with fewer but larger plots. An evaluation of cover boards for sampling terrestrial salamanders by Houze and Chandler (2002) found that most species were sampled in lower numbers (0.8/grid search) than under natural cover (2.3 salamanders/grid search). Temperatures were more variable under cover boards than under natural cover.

Williams et al. (1981) used electroshocking methods in the Allegheny River, Pennsylvania, to capture hellbenders (*Crytobranchus alleganiensis*) and reported it was superior to search and seizure, potato rake, and seine herding as a capture method. Soule and Lindberg (1994) used a peavey to move large rocks to locate and catch hellbenders. The peavey was hooked to the bottom of the rock, which was then manually moved. This technique required a 3-person crew to move rocks and capture hellbenders. The peavey was much less expensive than electroshocking equipment. Camp and Lovell (1989) caught blackbelly salamanders (*Desmognathus quadramaculatus*) using a "fishing pole" made from metal coat hangers with barbless hooks baited with earthworms.

Reptiles

Hobbs et al. (1994) tested a variety of pitfall trap designs. A straight line of pit traps with buckets approximately 7 m apart was most effective for sampling reptiles in arid Australia. Use of shade covers reduced heat related-mortality. Hobbs and James (1999) reported that foil covers placed inside and at the bottom of buckets reduced pitfall temperature and had minimal influence on trap success. Foil covers were superior to cardboard and plastic. Above ground covers reduced capture success for mammals but increased snake captures.

Vogt and Hine (1982) advocated use of drift fences combined with traps as a practical way to uniformly census reptiles and amphibians. Aluminum drift fences (50 cm high) caught more animals per 15 m of fence than those made of either screening or galvanized metal. A system of 18.9-L traps, 7.6-L traps with funnel rims, and funnel traps was necessary to capture the entire spectrum of amphibians and reptiles in the communities sampled. Funnel traps were more effective for catching lizards than pit traps and effective for catching snakes. They recommended at least 4 trapping periods of 3–5 days during April–mid June.

Moseby and Read (2001) recommended 5 nights of pitfall trapping as the most efficient duration for reptiles and 8 nights for mammals. Pitfalls should be at least 40 cm deep for small mammals and 60 cm for agile species such as hopping mice (*Notomys* spp.).

Greenberg et al. (1994) compared sampling effectiveness of pitfalls and single- and double-ended funnel traps used with drift fences. All 3-trap types yielded similar estimates of lizards and frogs but not snakes. Estimates of relative abundance of large snakes were higher in double-ended funnel traps than pitfalls or single-ended funnel traps. Captures of snakes were restricted to funnel traps. More surface-active lizards and frogs were captured in pitfalls. They advised that choice of trap type(s) depended on target species and sampling goals. Enge (2001) presented a detailed assessment of the effectiveness of pitfall versus funnel traps. He concluded that salamanders, anurans, lizards, and snakes were captured significantly more often in funnel traps than in pitfall traps. He added that studies that found funnel traps to be less effective than pitfall traps used smaller or poorly constructed or installed funnels. He also reported herpetofaunal mortality rates were generally higher in funnel traps than pitfall traps. Enge (2001) recommended that traps be checked at least every 3 days to minimize mortality.

Fair and Henke (1997) evaluated the efficiency of capture methods for a low-density population of Texas horned lizards (*Phrynosoma cornutum*). Road cruising yielded the highest capture rates with systematic searches second. Searching resulted in a higher rate of capture than pitfall and funnel traps. Sutton et al. (1999) compared pitfalls and drift fences with cover boards for sampling sand skinks (*Neoseps reynoldsi*). They reported that cover boards were more efficient in detecting the presence of skinks and were less costly and labor intensive. Allan et al. (2000) developed a successful "habitat" trap. The trap consisted of an artificial replica of a preferred habitat placed on a large sheet of camouflaged plastic. Two people lifted the plastic sheet at all edges once lizards began to occupy the artificial habitat, and the animals were trapped. The "habitat" consisted of a rock pile or woodpile built and placed in an excavated shallow pit 15 cm deep in an area of 1 m².

Doan (1997) captured large lizards by using large (88.5 × 31 × 31 cm), collapsible aluminum Sherman live traps. Traps were camouflaged with green mosquito netting and fallen branches and leaves. Zani and Vitt (1995) attached a wire-mesh minnow trap over holes in trees while Paterson (1998) used a mesh barrier of bridal veil fabric wrapped around a tree trunk to facilitate hand capture of arboreal lizards.

Gluesenkamp (1995) designed a simple snake rake consisting of 120-cm long, 19-mm diameter aluminum pipe, and 2 pieces of 25-cm long, 6.5-mm round steel. The 2 pieces were bent 90° and welded together at a 25° angle, and attached with hose clamps to the end of the aluminum pipe.

Franklin and Hartdegen (1997) sprayed large reptiles in the face with a fine mist of water to safely capture American crocodiles (*Crocodylus acutus*), American alligators (*Alligator mississipiensis*), pythons (*Python* spp.) and iguanas (*Iguana* spp.).

Lannom (1962) dangled a barbless dry fly from a support over a buried 1-L glass jar to attract and catch desert lizards. Whitaker (1967) increased his rate of capture of small lizards in pitfall traps by using canned fruits as bait. He also suggested using captive lizards in pitfall traps to attract other curious lizards. Serena (1980) used a fishing pole with a line attached to edible palm fruit to attract and capture whiptail (*Cnemidophorus* spp.) lizards. Durden et al. (1995) caught skinks using crickets threaded onto fishing line attached to a fishing rod. They also baited small Sherman small mammal traps with crickets tied inside the trap. Small, smooth scaled lizards were captured by Durtsche (1996) using a combination of a pole (fishing pole or collapsible car antenna) with a piece of sticky pad fastened to the end. The sticky pad was touched to the back of the lizard allowing capture. Bauer and Sadleir (1992) used mouse glue traps to capture lizards. Corn oil was used to release the lizards. Whiting (1998) increased lizard capture success by baiting glue traps with insects and figs. Downes and Borges (1998) captured small lizards with commercial packing tape by creating "sticky traps." However, Vargas et al. (2000) cautioned that sticky trapping of lizards had a higher fatality rate than capture with a noose or rubber band but yielded less reliable gender-biased capture information.

Witz (1996) coated the prongs of a bolt retriever (total length 60 cm) with liquid plastic. This "lizard grabber" grabs the pelvic girdle firmly with minimal chance of escape or injury to the lizard. Strong et al. (1993) caught small, fast-moving lizards by chasing them into PVC pipes covered at one end (Fig. 20). Brattstrom (1996) used a plastic wastebasket or garbage can as a "skink scooper." When he sighted a skink, he held the plastic container 15–30 cm away and swept the leaf litter and the skink into the "skink scooper" for capture. Sievert et al. (1999) made

Fig. 20. A method for catching lizards by chasing them into tubes placed beneath a bush. The tubes have one end covered with tape (from Strong et al. 1993).

a "herp scoop" (Fig. 21) of pliable plastic for safely capturing herpetofauna from roads at night. They used a 1-, 2-, or 3-L clear soft drink bottle with the bottom removed and a V-shaped notch 3–5 cm wide and 2 cm deep cut into the bottom lip of the bottle and a flashlight.

Recht (1981) modified a rat trap to block the entrance of burrows of desert (*Gopherus agassizii*) and Bolson (*G. flavomarginatus*) tortoises to facilitate hand-capture as they attempted to re-enter their burrow. Bryan et al. (1991)

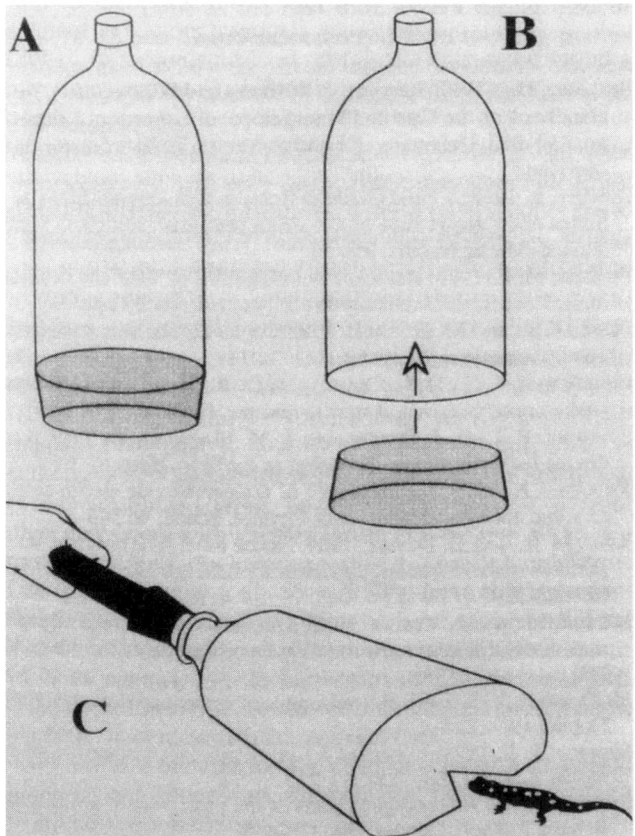

Fig. 21. Amphibia scoop made from a polyethylene soft drink bottle (A) with the base cut off and inverted to act as a lid (B). A V-shaped notch and a flashlight (C) were added to make the scoop more useful (from Sievert et al. 1999).

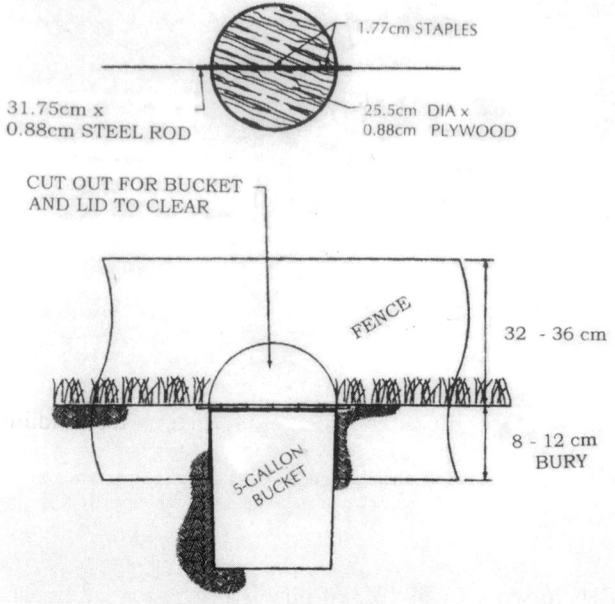

Fig. 22. Specifications of flip-top lid on 19-L (5 gallon) bucket set in a drift fences (from Christiansen and Vandewalle 2000).

designed a trap with a spring-loaded arm released by a trigger mechanism activated by a gopher tortoise (*G. polyphemus*) as it exited its burrow. A net was attached to the trigger to restrain the tortoise.

Graham and Georges (1996) modified collapsible turtle funnel traps by adding PVC pipe as struts to keep the funnels open and in place. They also used a piece of foam as a buoy to expedite trap retrieval. Mansfield et al. (1998) had success capturing spotted turtles (*Clemmys guttata*) in funnel traps using turtle-shaped decoys of cement poured in plaster of Paris casts. Decoys were painted to resemble turtle markings and color. Christiansen and Vandewalle (2000) perfected pitfall traps with wooden flip-top lids (Fig. 22) along drift fences that were effective in capturing terrestrial turtles. Their traps were more effective in capturing adult terrestrial turtles than either wire box traps or open pitfalls. Feuer (1980) modified the chicken wire turtle trap described by Iverson (1979) by using oval, galvanized hoops with nylon netting. He attached lines to hold the throats of hoop nets in place.

Vogt (1980) used fyke and trammel nets to catch aquatic turtles. A "carphorn" device was used to drive the turtles into the trammel nets. The fyke net was set parallel to a basking log. Braid (1974) used a bal-chatri trap with snares similar in design to a bird trap to capture basking turtles. Unlike bal-chatri traps used to catch birds, bait was not necessary. Nooses should be kept upright, and the chicken wire base should be tied to a log.

Fitch (1992) found that artificial shelters were superior to live-traps and random encounters for capturing snakes during a 12-year study. Kjoss and Litvaitis (2001) used black plastic sheets to capture snakes. Their cover sheet method was cheap, limited injuries, required less frequent checks, and was effective in open-canopy habitats. Lutterschmidt and Schaefer (1996) used mist netting with enclosed bait to capture semi-aquatic snakes.

Fritts et al. (1989) successfully captured brown tree snakes (*Boiga irregularis*) using bird odors. Their funnel traps were baited with chicken and quail manure. Shivik and Clark (1997) found that brown tree snakes were attracted to carrion and entered traps baited with dead mice as readily as traps baited with live mice. Engeman (1998) devised a simple method for capturing brown tree snakes in trees. He used a branch or stick with a fork at one end that was placed in the middle of the snake, and the stick was twirled to "wind" the snake on the stick. The snake would coil around the stick enabling time to bring the stick and snake from the tree for hand capture. Lindberg et al. (2000) tested a variety of lures for capturing brown tree snakes. They found that visual lures lacking movement were ineffective. Lures combining movement and prey odors were most effective (Shivik 1998). Engeman and Linnell (1998) used modified crawfish traps of 10-mm wire mesh with one-way flaps installed at the entrance and baited with a live mouse to capture brown tree snakes. Engeman et al. (1999) recommended placing a horizontal bar at the top of chain link fences to facilitate capture of brown tree snakes. Captures of brown tree snakes by trapping exceeded those by spotlight searches of fences (Engeman and Vice 2001).

Miscellaneous Capture Methods

Bertram and Cogger (1971) described a noose gun for live lizard captures. The noose gun was made of copper-coated welding wire and used rubber bands to tension the noose and trigger. Lohoefener and Wolfe (1984) designed a "pipe-trap" consisting of aluminum window screening, black PVC pipe, and 3 wooden disks. Pipe traps were used with drift fences and were more efficient in capturing salamanders, lizards, and snakes than pitfall traps. Frogs and toads were more likely to be captured in pitfall traps. A wire hook with a blunt end was placed around the tail of lizards by Bedford et al. (1995) to extract lizards from tree and rock crevices. They grasped the lizard by the head with forceps as it emerged from the crevice. Bending the wire at a 90° angle made a handle, and a flashlight was used to help position the wire hook. Enge (1997) recommended silt fencing over aluminum or galvanized drift fencing as less expensive, easy to install, and durable. Silt fence is a woven polypropylene material used to control sediment runoff at construction sites.

HANDLING CAPTURED ANIMALS

Clark et al. (1992) and Fowler (1995) are excellent sources of information on restraint and handling of wild animals. Nonchemical handling and restraint of captured animals is inexpensive and usually causes lower mortality rates.

Birds

Cox and Afton (1998) advised that holding times of waterfowl be minimized when large numbers are captured with rocket nets. To minimize subsequent mortality, ducks should be released immediately after they are processed and their plumage is dry. Maechtle (1998) described the Aba (cloak) made from rectangular cotton cloth for restraining raptors and other large birds. Wing pockets were stitched, and a strip of elastic tape was sewn onto the back of the cloth to be wrapped around the bird's tarsi. The Aba allows measurements and blood samples to be taken with a minimum of handling. A 4-pronged pick-up tool was used by Richardson et al. (1998) to remove red-cockaded woodpecker nestlings >8 days old from tree cavities. The 4-prongs must be blunted by bending or covered with liquid rubber to avoid injury to the young woodpeckers. Hess et al. (2001) questioned the feasibility of the Richardson et al. (1998) technique because of a high injury rate to red-cockaded woodpecker nestlings. Proudfoot (2002) perfected the use of a flexible fiberscope and noose to successfully remove ferruginous pygmy-owl (*Glaucidium brasilianum*) nestlings from oak (*Quercus* spp.) nest cavities without injury. He also suggested using a miniature camera system to assist with nestling removal from cavities.

Cardoza et al. (1995) suggested delaying capture attempts for wild turkeys that appear to be wet on arrival at a bait site if a soaking rain had recently occurred. If turkeys become wet from snow or rain during the capture process, they should be allowed to dry in transport boxes before handling to avoid excessive defeathering. Patterson et al. (1993) facilitated handling of mourning doves by designing a modified restraining device similar to one described by DeMaso and Peoples (1993) for northern bobwhite. Time of handling, stress, and struggling of captured doves was minimized while leg bands and radio transmitters were attached.

Blood sampling of birds from the brachial and jugular veins did not influence survival, movements, or reproduction (Colwell et al. 1988, Gratto-Trevor et al. 1991, Lanctot 1994).

Mammals

Swann et al. (1997) reviewed the effects of orbital sinus sampling of blood on survival of small mammals and found the results to be variable. White-throated woodrats (*Neotoma albigula*) and deer mice survival estimates were not adversely affected, but desert pocket mice (*Chaetodipus* spp.) and prairie vole (*Microtus ochrogaster*) survival rates were lower. Douglass et al. (2000) found no difference in handling mortality of 7 species of nonanesthetized wild rodents that were bled versus similar species of non-bled rodents. They concluded that bleeding in the absence of anesthesia did not affect immediate mortality or subsequent recapture. Parmenter et al. (1998) verified that handling/bleeding procedures for hantavirus had no adverse effect on survival and trap rates of murid rodents (including deer mice, woodrats, and prairie voles) and cottontail rabbits.

Mills et al. (1995) provided guidelines for personal safety while trapping, handling, and releasing rodents that might be infected with hantavirus. Special consideration is essential to provide respiratory protection from aerosolized virus. Protective gloves and clothing and suitable disinfectant are also necessary.

Yahner and Mahan (1992) used a polyvinyl Centrap™ cage as a restraining device for red squirrels. They used a mesh bag with a cone to minimize mortality from handling shock. Koprowski (2002) safely handled >3,500 squirrels of 7 species with a mortality of <0.01% using a cloth cone and without using an anesthesia as suggested by Arenz (1997).

Frost and Krohn (1994) described the care and handling of fisher. Serfass et al. (1996) successfully transported immobilized northern river otters in a well-ventilated tube made from 1-m sections of 40-cm diameter PVC pipe. Davis et al. (1996) designed a lightweight noose device attached to ski poles to safely remove mountain lions and bears from trees and cliffs.

Beringer et al. (1996) evaluated 2 capture methods, rocket-nets and Clover traps, as they influence capture myopathy in white-tailed deer. All deer mortality attributable to capture myopathy was associated with rocket-net captures. Mortality attributable to capture myopathy can be reduced by using Clover traps instead of rocket-nets whenever possible. If rocket-nets are used, they suggested that capture be limited to 3 deer, or fewer, per capture. They advised that handling time be minimized to reduce stress to captured deer.

Byers (1997) described proper precautions for handling young pronghorn including avoidance of handling until 6 hours after birth or when coyotes or golden eagles were in sight or known to be within 1 km. Handling time should be brief and avoided during crepuscular hours when coyotes are active. Byers (1997) concluded that methods he described did not increase mortality risk.

Thompson et al. (2001) concluded that direct release of mountain sheep from vehicles was advisable rather than transporting via helicopter to holding pens. Expenses were less, survival was lower for the sheep kept in holding pens, and no difference was evident in dispersal and group cohesion.

Amphibians

McCallum et al. (2002) made a "frog box" to hold frogs by cutting a round hole in the lid of a Styrofoam™ ice chest. They then inserted a Styrofoam™ cup with the bottom removed into the hole, and a second intact cup was inserted inside the first cup to close the hole. The "frog box" allowed quick collection and secure containment of large numbers of anurans in the field.

Reptiles

Rivas et al. (1995) described a safe method for handling large non-venomous snakes such as anacondas (*Eumcetes* spp.). They placed a cotton sock over the snake's head and then wrapped several layers of plastic electrician's tape around the sock. The tape could be removed to release the snake into cloth bags for transport or release. Gregory et al. (1989) developed a portable device made of aluminum tubing to safely restrain rattlesnakes (*Crotalis* spp.) in the field. Walczak (1991) safely handled venomous snakes by immersion in a plastic trash barrel partially filled with water. He then placed a clear plastic tube over the snake's head and gently submerged the snake. After the snake entered the tube, the snake's body and tube end were then grasped firmly with one hand. This method increased handler safety and decreased trauma.

Mauldin and Engeman (1999) restrained snakes using a wire mesh cable holder. Cross (2000) described a new design for a lightweight squeezebox to allow safe handling of venomous snakes. His squeezebox was made of Plexiglas™ with a foam rubber lining, sliding doors, and portholes at each end. The squeezebox allowed measurements with a minimum of direct handling of snakes.

Jones and Hayes-Odum (1994) used white PVC pipe with an inside diameter of 0.31 m cut in 3 m lengths to restrain and transport crocodilians. Holes of a diameter sufficient for a rope to move freely were drilled at 15 cm intervals in the PVC pipe. One rope was looped around the head and another in front of the hind legs. Pipe diameter and length were chosen to accommodate a variety of sizes of alligators.

Tucker (1994) described an "easy" method to remove snapping turtles (*Chelydra serpentina*) from Legler hoop traps. He grasped the turtle by the tail and the posterior edge of the carapace. The turtle was then upended with the head down. With the turtle in a vertical position it was pressed down over the substrate, forcing the turtle to retract its head. The turtle's hind limbs were held, and the turtle was removed from the trap. A 10.16-cm diameter, ca. 60 cm in length, PVC pipe was placed over the head of snapping turtles for restraining and safe handling by Quinn and Pappas (1997).

SUMMARY

Many new and innovative capture and handling methods, techniques, and equipment have been described in the lengthy list of literature citations (746) in the current chapter in comparison to the previous chapter (274 citations) published in 1994. A more in-depth coverage of amphibian and reptile capture and handling methods is included in this chapter in comparison to previous editions. Humane capture and handling techniques continue to be of paramount importance. Tranquilizer trap devices show promise to minimize injuries to nontarget captures but unfortunately are restricted and limited in use and availability by the U.S. Food and Drug Administration and a similar agency in Canada. Although complex electronic and mechanized devices have been recently developed to expedite successful and efficient capture, simple variations of existing equipment such as nets, and methods, such as use of live and mounted decoys, continue to be widely described in the literature. Use of different net types and configurations (e.g., mist, drop, drift, rocket, and cannon) continue to be the predominant technique for capturing birds. Mammals are captured primarily with snares and foothold, box, and cage traps. Wild animals may be captured for a variety of purposes including subsistence, animal damage control, population management, disease control, enhancement of other species, economic benefits, and research. Regardless of the reasons for capture, it is imperative the most humane devices and techniques be used. Finally, all untested capture devices should be evaluated using standardized, scientifically-sound protocols which include the documentation of capture-related injuries via whole body necropsies.

ACKNOWLEDGMENTS

George F. Hubert, Jr. made substantial and essential contributions to the sections on carnivore capture. I am greatly indebted to D. F. Caccamise, Head, Department of Fishery and Wildlife Sciences, New Mexico State University, Las Cruces for expediting the completion of this chapter by arranging for manuscript preparation. I thank D. J. Morgan, L. E. Maes, and R. R. Delgado for the excellence of their computer skills in helping complete drafts of this chapter, J. V. Espinosa, Department of Agricultural Communications, New Mexico State University, Las Cruces for providing valuable assistance with preparation of figures, and T. I. McKimmie, Science Librarian, New Mexico State University, for his expertise in locating obscure references. J. L. Moore, Bibliographer, Wildlife Information Service, Las Cruces provided helpful editorial suggestions.

I thank my wife, M. M. Schemnitz for patience, support, encouragement, and direct assistance in contributing to the completion of this chapter. I also thank G. Proulx for reviewing a preliminary draft of the section on trapping and providing several excellent suggestions as well as G. R. Batcheller and an anonymous referee for their useful suggestions.

LITERATURE CITED

ADAMS, J. D., AND B. FREEDMAN. 1999. Comparative catch efficiency of amphibian sampling methods in terrestrial habitats in southern New Brunswick. Canadian Field-Naturalist 113:493–496.

ADDY, C. E. 1956. Guide to waterfowl banding. U.S. Department of the Interior, Fish and Wildlife Service, Laurel, Maryland, USA.

ALBANESE, G., AND V. D. PIASKOWSKI. 1999. An inexpensive elevated mist net apparatus. North American Bird Bander 24:129–134.

ALDOUS, C. M. 1946. Box trap for snowshoe hares and small rodents. Journal of Wildlife Management 10:71–72.

ALDOUS, S. E. 1936. A cage trap useful in the control of white-necked ravens. U.S. Department of Agriculture, Bureau of Biological Survey, Wildlife Research and Management Leaflet BS-27.

ALLAN, G. M., C. J. PRELYPCHAN, AND P. T. GREGORY. 2000. "Habitat trap" for the capture of small- to medium-sized lizards. Herpetological Review 31:160–161.

ALLEN, D. L., AND W. W. SHAPTON. 1942. An ecological study of winter dens, with special reference to the eastern skunk. Ecology 23:60–68.

ALSAGER, D. E., J. B. STENRUE, AND R.L. BOYLES. 1972. Capturing black-billed magpies with circular live traps. Journal of Wildlife Management 36:981–983.

AMERICAN SOCIETY OF MAMMALOGISTS. 1998. Guidelines for the capture, handling and care of mammals as approved by the American Society of Mammalogists. Journal of Mammalogy 79:1416–1431.

ANDELT, W. F., AND T. P. WOOLLEY. 1996. Responses of urban mammals to odor attractants and a bait-dispensing device. Wildlife Society Bulletin 24:111–118.

————, R. L. PHILLIPS, R. H. SCHMIDT, AND R. B. GILL. 1999. Trapping furbearers: an overview of the biological and social issues surrounding a public policy controversy. Wildlife Society Bulletin 27:53–64.

ANDERSON, M. G., R. D., SAYLER, AND A. D. AFTON. 1980. A decoy trap for diving ducks. Journal of Wildlife Management 44:217–219.

ANDERSON, R. G., AND C. K. NIELSEN. 2002. Modified Stephenson trap for capturing deer. Wildlife Society Bulletin 30:606–608.

ANDERSON, R. K., AND F. HAMERSTROM. 1967. Hen decoys aid in trapping prairie chickens with bownets and noose carpets. Journal of Wildlife Management 31:829–832.

ANDERSON, S. J., AND C. P. STONE. 1993. Snaring to control feral pigs, *Sus scrofa*, in a remote Hawaiian rain forest. Biological Conservation 63:195–201.

ANDRYK, T. A., L. R. IRBY, D. L. HOOK, J. J. McCARTHY, AND G. OLSON. 1983. Comparison of mountain sheep capture techniques: helicopter darting versus net-gunning. Wildlife Society Bulletin 11:184–187.

ANDRZEJEWSKI, R., AND E. OWADOWSKA. 1994. Use of odour bait to catch bank voles. Acta Theriologica 39:221–225.

ARENZ, C. L. 1997. Handling fox squirrels: ketamine hydrochloride versus a simple restraint. Wildlife Society Bulletin 25:107–109.

ARNOLD, K. A., AND D. W. COON. 1972. Modifications of the cannon net for use with cowbird studies. Journal of Wildlife Management 36:153–155.

ARTHUR, S. M. 1988. An evaluation of techniques for capturing and radiocollaring fishers. Wildlife Society Bulletin 16:417–421.

ARTMANN, J. W. 1971. Capturing sharp-tailed grouse hens using taped chick distress calls. Journal of Wildlife Management 35:557–559.

ASHCRAFT G., AND D. REESE. 1956. An improved device for capturing deer. California Fish and Game 43:193–199.

AUSTIN, D. H. 1965. Trapping turkeys in Florida with the cannon net. Proceedings of the Annual Conference of the Southeastern Association of Game and Fish Commissioners 19:16–22.

BACON, B. R., AND J. O. EVRARD. 1990. Horizontal mist net for capturing upland nesting ducks. North American Bird Bander 15:18–19.

BAILEY, R. W. 1976. Live-trapping wild turkeys in North Carolina. North Carolina Wildlife Resources Commission, Raleigh, USA.

BAKER, R. J., AND S. L. WILLIAMS. 1972. A live trap for pocket gophers. Journal of Wildlife Management 36:1320–1322.

BAKER, S. J., AND C. N. CLARKE. 1988. Cage trapping coypus (*Myocaster coypus*) on baited rafts. Journal of Applied Ecology 25: 41–48.

BALDWIN, W. P. 1947. Trapping wild turkeys in South Carolina. Journal of Wildlife Management 11:24–36.

BALLARD, W. B., H. A. WHITLAW, D. L. SABINE, R. A. JENKINS, S. J. YOUNG, AND G. F. FORBES. 1998. White-tailed deer, *Odocoileus virginianus*, capture techniques in yarding and non-yarding populations in New Brunswick. Canadian Field-Naturalist 112:254–261.

BALSER, D. S. 1965. Tranquilizer tabs for capturing wild carnivores. Journal of Wildlife Management 29:438–442.

BANUELOS, G. 1997. The one-way door trap: an alternative trapping technique for burrowing owls. Journal of Raptor Research Report 9: 122–124.

BARR, G. E., AND K. J. BABBITT. 2001. A comparison of 2 techniques to sample larval stream salamanders. Wildlife Society Bulletin 29: 1238–1242.

BARRENTINE, C. D., AND K. D. EWING. 1988. A capture technique for burrowing owls. North American Bird Bander 13:107.

BARRETT, M. W., J. W. NOLAN, AND L. D. ROY. 1982. Evaluation of a hand-held net-gun to capture large mammals. Wildlife Society Bulletin 10:108–114.

———, G. PROULX, D. HOBSON, D. NELSON, AND J. W. NOLAN. 1989. Field evaluation of the C120 magnum trap for marten. Wildlife Society Bulletin 17:299–306.

BARTLETT, I. H. 1938. White-tails—presenting Michigan's deer problem. Michigan Conservation 8(2):4–5, 7; 8(7):8–11.

BAUER, A. M., AND R. A. SADLEIR. 1992. The use of mouse glue traps to capture lizards. Herpetological Review 23:112–113.

BEALE, D. M. 1966. A self-collaring device for pronghorn antelope. Journal of Wildlife Management 30:209–211.

BEAN, N. J., AND J. R. MASON. 1995. Attractiveness of liquid baits containing natural and artificial sweeteners to white-tailed deer. Journal of Wildlife Management 59:610–613.

BEASOM, S. L., W. EVANS, AND L. TEMPLE. 1980. The drive net for capturing western big game. Journal of Wildlife Management 44: 478–480.

BEAUVAIS, G., J. H. ENDERSON, AND A. J. MAGRO. 1992. Home range, habitat use and behavior of prairie falcons wintering in east-central Colorado. Journal of Raptor Research 26:13–18.

BEDFORD, G. S., K. CHRISTIAN, AND B. BARRETTE. 1995. A method for catching lizards in trees and rock crevices. Herpetological Review 26: 21–22.

BELANT, J. L. 1992. Efficacy of three types of live traps for capturing weasels, *Mustela* spp. Canadian Field-Naturalist 106:394–397.

———. 2003. A hairsnare for forest carnivores. Wildlife Society Bulletin 31:482–485.

———, AND T. W. SEAMANS. 1997. Comparisons of three formulations of alpha-chloralose for immobilization of Canada geese. Journal of Wildlife Diseases 33:606–610.

———, AND ———. 1999. Alpha-chloralose immobilization of rock doves in Ohio. Journal of Wildlife Diseases 35:239–242.

———, L. A. TYSON, AND T. W. SEAMANS. 1999. Use of alpha-chloralose by the Wildlife Services program to capture nuisance birds. Wildlife Society Bulletin 27:938–942.

BENSON, J., AND R. M. SURYAN. 1999. A leg-noose for capturing adult kittiwakes at the nest. Journal of Field Ornithology 70:393–399.

BERCHIELLI, JR., L. T., AND B. F. TULLAR, JR. 1980. Comparison of a leg snare with a standard leg-gripping trap. New York Fish and Game Journal 27:63–71.

BERGER, D. D., AND F. HAMERSTROM. 1962. Protecting a trapping station from raptor predation. Journal of Wildlife Management 26:203–206.

———, AND H. C. MUELLER. 1959. The bal-chatri: a trap for the birds of prey. Bird-Banding 30:18–26.

BERGMAN, D. L., R. D. BLUETT, AND A. R. TIPTON. 1999. An alternative method for capturing armadillos. Southwestern Naturalist 40: 414–416.

BERINGER, J., L. P. HANSEN, W. WILDING, J. FISCHER, AND S. L. SHERRIF. 1996. Factors affecting capture myopathy in white-tailed deer. Journal of Wildlife Management 60:373–380.

BERTRAM, B. P., AND H. G. COGGER. 1971. A noosing gun for live captures of small lizards. Copeia 1971:371–373.

BISHOP, R. A., AND R. BARRATT. 1969. Capturing waterfowl in Iowa by nightlighting. Journal of Wildlife Management 33:956–960.

BLACK, H. C. 1958. Black bear research in New York. Transactions of the North American Wildlife Conference 23:443–461.

BLACKSHAW, S. R. 1994. Tie ups and tie downs: a method for securing rolled nets. North American Bird Bander 19:99.

BLAKEMAN, J. A. 1990. Improvement in bal-chatri trap. North American Bird Bander 15:26.

BLOCKSTEIN, D. E. 1985. Active netting to capture nesting mourning doves. North American Bird Bander 10:117–118.

BLOHM, R. J., AND P. WARD. 1979. Experience with a decoy trap for male gadwalls. Bird-Banding 50:45–48.

BLOOM, P. H. 1987. Capturing and handling raptors. Pages 99–123 *in* B. A. G. Pendleton, B. A. Millsap, K. W. Cline, and D. M. Bird, editors. Raptor management techniques manual. National Wildlife Federation, Washington, D.C., USA.

———, J. L. HENCKEL, E. H. HENCKEL, J. K. SCHMUTZ, B. WOODBRIDGE, J. R. BRYAN, R. L. ANDERSON, P. J. DETRICH, T. L. MAECHTLE, J. O. MCKINLEY, M. D. MCCRARY, K. TITUS, AND P. F. SCHEMPF. 1992. The dho-gaza with great horned owl lure: an analysis of its effectiveness in capturing raptors. Journal of Raptor Research 26:167–178.

BLUETT, B. 2000. Trapper education student manual. Illinois Department of Natural Resources, Division of Wildlife Resources, Springfield, USA.

BLUMS, P., C. W. SHAIFFER, AND L. H. FREDRICKSON. 2000. Automatic multi-capture nest box trap for cavity-nesting ducks. Wildlife Society Bulletin 28:592–596.

———, V. K. REDERS, A. A. MEDNIS, AND J. A. BAUMANIS. 1983. Automatic drop-door traps for ducks. Journal of Wildlife Management 47:199–203.

BLUNDELL, G. M., J. W. KERN, R. T. BOWYER, AND L. K. DUFFY. 1999. Capturing river otters: a comparison of Hancock and leg-hold traps. Wildlife Society Bulletin 27:184–192.

BOGGESS, E. K., G. R. BATCHELLER, R. G. LINSCOMBE, J. W. GREER, M. NOVAK, S. B. LINHART, D. W. ERICKSON, A. W. TODD, D. C. JUVE, AND D. A. WADE. 1990. Traps, trapping, and furbearer management. Technical Review 90–1. The Wildlife Society, Bethesda, Maryland, USA.

BOROSKI, B. B., AND P. L. MCGLAUGHLIN. 1994. An efficient technique for capturing swimming deer. California Fish and Game 80:36–42.

BOTELHO, E. S., AND P. C. ARROWOOD. 1995. A novel, simple, safe and effective trap for burrowing owls and other fossorial animals. Journal of Field Ornithology 66:380–384.

BOUGHTON, R. G., AND J. STAIGER. 2000. Use of PVC pipe refugia as a sampling technique for hylid treefrogs. American Midland Naturalist 144:168–177.

BOWMAN, T. D., S. P. THOMPSON, C. A. JANIK, AND L. J. DUBUC. 1994. Nightlighting minimizes investigator disturbance in bird colonies. Colonial Waterbirds 17:78–82.

BRAID, M. R. 1974. A bal-chatri trap for basking turtles. Copeia 1974: 539–540.

BRANDER, R. B. 1973. Life-history notes on the porcupine in a hardwood-hemlock forest in Upper Michigan. The Michigan Academician 5:425–433.

BRATTSTROM, B. H. 1996. The "skink scooper": a device for catching leaf litter skinks. Herpetological Review 27:189.

BRAUN, C. E. 1976. Methods for locating, trapping, and banding band-tailed pigeons in Colorado. Special Report 39. Colorado Division of Wildlife, Fort Collins, USA.

BREAULT, A. M., AND K. M. CHENG. 1990. Use of submerged mist nets to capture diving birds. Journal of Field Ornithology 61:328–330.

BROCKE, R. H. 1972. A live snare for trap-shy snowshoe hares. Journal of Wildlife Management 36:988–991.

BROWN, L. J. 1997. An evaluation of some marking and trapping techniques currently used in the study of anuran population dynamics. Journal of Herpetology 31:410–419.

BRYAN, J. R. 1988. Radio-controlled bow-net for American kestrels. North American Bird Bander 13:30–32.

BRYAN, T. W., E. L. BLANKENSHIP, AND C. GUYER. 1991. A new method of trapping gopher tortoises (*Gopherus polyphemus*). Herpetological Review 22:19–21.

BUB, H. 1991. Bird trapping and bird banding: a handbook for trapping methods all over the world. Cornell University Press, Ithaca, New York, USA.

BUBELA, T. M., R. BARTELL, AND W. J. MULLER. 1998. Factors affecting the trappability of red foxes in Kosciusko National Park. Wildlife

Research 25:199–208.

BUCK, J. A., AND R. A. CRAFT. 1995. Two walk-in trap designs for great horned owls and red-tailed hawks. Journal of Field Ornithology 66: 133–139.

BULL, E. L. 1987. Capture techniques for owls. Pages 291–294 *in* Biology and conservation of northern forest owls. U.S. Department of Agriculture, Forest Service, General Technical Report RM-142.

———, AND H. D. COOPER. 1996. New techniques to capture pileated woodpeckers and Vaux's swifts. North American Bird Bander 21: 138–142.

———, AND R. J. PEDERSEN. 1978. Two methods of trapping adult pileated woodpeckers at their nest cavities. North American Bird-Bander 3:95–99.

———, T. W. HEATER, AND F. G. CULVER. 1996. Live-trapping and immobilizing American martens. Wildlife Society Bulletin 24: 55–558.

BURTT, H. E., AND M.L. GILTZ. 1970. A study of blackbird repeats at a decoy trap. Ohio Journal of Science 70:162–170.

———, AND ———. 1976. Sex differences in the tendency for brown-headed cowbirds and red-winged blackbirds to re-enter a decoy trap. Ohio Journal of Science 76:264–267.

BYERS, J. A. 1997. Mortality risk to young pronghorns from handling. Journal of Mammalogy 78:894–899.

CACCAMISE, D. F., AND P. C. STOUFFER. 1994. Risks of using alpha-chloralose to capture crows. Journal of Field Ornithology 65:458–460.

CAFFREY, C. 2001. Catching crows. North American Bird Bander 26: 137–145.

CAIN, S. L., AND J. I. HODGES. 1989. A floating-fish snare for capturing bald eagles. Journal of Raptor Research 23:10–13.

CAMP, C. D., AND D. G. LOVELL. 1989. Fishing for "spring lizards": a technique for collecting blackbelly salamanders. Herpetological Review 20:47.

CAMPBELL, H. W., AND S. P. CHRISTMAN. 1982. Field techniques for herpetofaunal community analysis. Pages 193–200 *in* N. J. Scott, Jr., editor. Herpetological communities. Symposium of the Society for the Study of Amphibians and Reptiles and the Herpetologist's League. U.S. Department of the Interior, Fish and Wildlife Service, Wildlife Research Report 13.

CANADIAN GENERAL STANDARDS BOARD. 1984. Animal traps – humane, mechanically powered, trigger-activated. Report CAN2–144.1-M84. Canadian General Standards Board, Ottawa, Ontario, Canada.

———. 1996. Animal (mammal) traps—mechanically powered, trigger-activated killing traps for use on land. Report CAN/CGSB-144. 1–96. Canadian General Standards Board, Ottawa, Ontario, Canada.

CANADIAN WILDLIFE SERVICE AND U.S. DEPARTMENT OF INTERIOR. 1977. North American bird banding techniques. Volume II. Canadian Wildlife Service, Ottawa, Ontario, Canada, and U.S. Department of the Interior, Fish and Wildlife Service, Washington, D.C., USA.

CANCINO, J., V. SANCHEZ-SOTOMAYOR, AND R. CASTELLANOS. 2002. Alternative capture technique for the peninsular pronghorn. Wildlife Society Bulletin 30:256–258.

CARDOZA, J., B. ERIKSEN, AND H. KILPATRICK. 1995. Procedures and guidelines for handling and transporting wild turkeys. Technical Bulletin 3. National Wild Turkey Federation, Edgefield, South Carolina, USA.

CAREY, A. B., B. L. BISWELL, AND J. W. WITT. 1991. Methods for measuring populations of arboreal rodents. U.S. Department of Agriculture, Forest Service, General Technical Report PNW-273.

CARPENTER, L. H., AND J. I. INNES. 1995. Helicopter netgunning: a successful moose capture technique. Alces 31:181–184.

CASAZZA, M. L., G. D. WYLIE, AND C. J. GREGORY. 2000. A funnel trap modification for surface collection of aquatic amphibians and reptiles. Herpetological Review 31:91–92.

CHAMBERS, R. E., AND P. F. ENGLISH. 1958. Modifications of ruffed grouse traps. Journal of Wildlife Management 22:200–202.

CHOQUENOT, D., R. J. KILGOUR, AND B. S. LUKINS. 1993. An evaluation of feral pig trapping. Wildlife Research 20:15–22.

CHRISTIANSEN, J. L., AND T. VANDEWALLE. 2000. Effectiveness of three trap types in drift fence surveys. Herpetological Review 31:158–160.

CLAPPERTON, B. K., C. T. EASON, R. J. WESTON, A. D. WOOLHOUSE, AND D. R. MORGAN. 1994. Development and testing of attractants for feral cats, *Felis catus* L. Wildlife Research 21:389–399.

CLARK, R. K., A. W. FRANZMANN, D. A. JESSUP, M. D. KOCK, N. D. KOCK, R. A. KOCK, AND P. MORKEL. 1992. Wildlife restraint series. Revised edition. International Wildlife Veterinary Service, Salinas, California, USA.

CLARK, W. S. 1981. A modified dho-gaza trap for use at a raptor banding station. Journal of Wildlife Management 45:1043–1044.

CLOVER, M. R. 1954. A portable deer trap and catch-net. California Fish and Game 40:367–373.

———. 1956. Single-gate deer trap. California Fish and Game 42:199–201.

COHEN, R. R. 1985. Capturing breeding male tree swallows with feathers. North American Bird Bander 10:18–21.

———, AND D. J. HAYES. 1984. A simple unattached nest-box trapping device. North American Bird Bander 9(1):10–11.

COLLINS, T. C. 1976. Population characteristics and habitat relationships of beavers, *Castor canadensis,* in northwest Wyoming. Dissertation. University of Wyoming, Laramie, USA.

COLLISTER, D. M., AND R. G. FISHER. 1995. Trapping techniques for loggerhead shrikes. Wildlife Society Bulletin 23:88–91.

COLVIN, B. A., AND P. L. HEGDAL. 1986. Techniques for capturing common barn-owls. Journal of Field Ornithology 57:200–207.

COLWELL, M. A., C. L. GROTTO, L. W. ORING, AND A. J. FIVIZZANI. 1988. Effects of blood sampling on shorebirds: injuries, return rates and clutch desertions. Condor 90:942–945.

CONNER, M. C., E. C. SOUTIERE, AND R. A. LANCIA. 1987. Drop-netting deer: costs and incidence of capture myopathy. Wildlife Society Bulletin 15:434–438.

CONWAY, W. C., AND L. M. SMITH. 2000. A nest trap for snowy plovers. North American Bird Bander 25:45–47.

COOCH, G. 1953. Techniques for mass capture of flightless blue and lesser snow geese. Journal of Wildlife Management 17:460–465.

COOPER, H. D., C. M. RALEY, AND K. B. AUBRY. 1995. A noose trap for capturing pileated woodpeckers. Wildlife Society Bulletin 23: 208–211.

COPELAND, J. P., E. CESAR, J. M. PEEK, C. E. HARRIS, C. D. LONG, AND D. L. HUNTER. 1995. A live trap for wolverines and other forest carnivores. Wildlife Society Bulletin 23:535–538.

CORN, P. S., AND R. B. BURY. 1990. Sampling methods for terrestrial amphibians and reptiles. U.S. Department of Agriculture, Forest Service, General Technical Report PNW-256.

COSTANZO, G. R., R. A. WILLIAMSON, AND D. E. HAYES. 1995. An efficient method for capturing flightless geese. Wildlife Society Bulletin 23:201–203.

COTTERILL, F. P. D., AND R. A. FERGUSSON. 1993. Capturing free-tailed bats (Chiroptera: Molossidae): the description of a new trapping device. Journal of Zoology (London) 231:645–651.

COUCH, L. K. 1942. Trapping and transplanting live beavers. Conservation Bulletin 30. U.S. Department of the Interior, Fish and Wildlife Service, Washington, D.C., USA.

COUEY, F. M. 1949. Review and evaluation of big game trapping techniques. Proceedings of the Western Association of State Game and Fish Commissioners 29:110–116.

COULTER, M. W. 1958. A new waterfowl nest trap. Bird-Banding 29: 236–241.

COWAN, I. M., AND J. HATTER. 1952. A trap and technique for the capture of diving waterfowl. Journal of Wildlife Management 16:438–441.

COX, JR., R. R., AND A. D. AFTON. 1994. Portable platforms for setting rocket nets in open-water habitats. Journal of Field Ornithology 65: 551–555.

———, AND ———. 1998. Effects of capture and handling on survival of female northern pintails. Journal of Field Ornithology 69:276–287.

CRAIG, E. H., AND B. L. KELLER. 1986. Movements and home range of porcupines, *Erethizon dorsatum,* in Idaho shrub desert. Canadian Field-Naturalist 100:167–173.

CRAIGHEAD, J. J., M. HORNOCKER, W. WOODGERD, AND F. C. CRAIGHEAD, JR. 1960. Trapping, immobilizing, and color-marking grizzly bears. Transactions of the North American Wildlife and Natural Resources Conference 25:347–363.

CRAWFORD, E., AND A. KURTA. 2000. Color of pitfall affects trapping success for anurans and shrews. Herpetological Review 31:222–224.

CRAWFORD, R. D. 1977. Comparison of trapping methods for American coots. Bird-Banding 48:309–313.

CROMWELL, J. A., R. J. WARREN, AND D. W. HENDERSON. 1999. Live capture and small-scale relocation of urban deer on Hilton Head Island, South Carolina. Wildlife Society Bulletin 27:1025–1031.

CROSS, C. L. 2000. A new design for a lightweight squeeze box for snake field studies. Herpetological Review 31:34.

CROSS, T. J., A. W. REED, B. T. RUTLEDGE, B. R. LASETER, S. A. MARIS, AND C. N. DOOLITTLE. 1999. A comparison of disinfected and untreated traps for sampling small mammal populations. Journal of the Tennessee Academy of Science 73:35.

CUMMINGS, G. E., AND O. H. HEWITT. 1964. Capturing waterfowl and marsh birds at night with light and sound. Journal of Wildlife Management 28:120–126.

CURRIE, D., AND E. ROBERTSON. 1992. Alberta wild fur management study guide. Alberta Forestry, Lands and Wildlife, Edmonton, Canada.

CUSHWA, C. T., AND K. P. BURNHAM. 1974. An inexpensive live trap for snowshoe hares. Journal of Wildlife Management 38:939–941.

CUTLER, T. L., AND D. E. SWANN. 1999. Using remote photography in wildlife ecology: a review. Wildlife Society Bulletin 27:571–581.

DAOUST, J.-L. 1991. Coping with dehydration of trapped terrestrial anurans. Herpetological Review 22:95.

DAVIS, J. L., C-L. B. CHETKIEWICZ, V. C. BLEICH, G. RAYGORODETSKY, B. M. PIERCE, J. W. OSTERGARD, AND J. D. WEHAUSEN. 1996. A device to safely remove immobilized mountain lions from trees and cliffs. Wildlife Society Bulletin 24:537–539.

DAVIS, P. G. 1981. Trapping methods for bird ringers. British Trust of Ornithology, Tring, United Kingdom.

DAVIS, R. D. 1994. A funnel trap for Rio Grande turkey. Proceedings of the Annual Conference of the Southeastern Association of Fish and Wildlife Agencies 48:109–116.

DAY, G. I., S. D. SCHEMNITZ, AND R. D. TABER. 1980. Capturing and marking wild animals. Pages 61–88 in S. D. Schemnitz, editor. Wildlife management techniques manual. Fourth edition. The Wildlife Society. Washington, D.C., USA.

DEGRAAF, R. M., AND M. YAMASAKI. 1992. A nondestructive technique to monitor the relative abundance of terrestrial salamanders. Wildlife Society Bulletin 20:260–264.

DEHAVEN, R. W., AND J. L. GUARINO. 1969. A nest-box trap for starlings. Bird-Banding 40:49–50.

DELGIUDICE, G. D., K. E. KUNKEL, L. D. MECH, AND U. S. SEAL. 1990. Minimizing capture-related stress on white-tailed deer with a capture collar. Journal of Wildlife Management 54:299–303.

———, B. A. MANGIPANE, B. A. SAMPSON, AND C. O. KOCHANNY. 2001. Chemical immobilization, body temperature, and post-release mortality of white-tailed deer captured by clover trap and net-gun. Wildlife Society Bulletin 29:1147–1157.

DEMASO, S. J., AND A. D. PEOPLES. 1993. A restraining device for handling northern bobwhites. Wildlife Society Bulletin 21:45–46.

DENICOLA, A. J., AND R. K. SWIHART. 1997. Capture-induced stress in white-tailed deer. Wildlife Society Bulletin 25:500–503.

D'EON, R. G., G. PAVAN, AND P. LINDGREN. 2003. A small drop-net versus clover traps for capturing mule deer in southeastern British Columbia. Northwest Science 77:178–181.

DEYOUNG, C. A. 1988. Comparison of net-gun and drive-net capture for white-tailed deer. Wildlife Society Bulletin 16:318–320.

DHONDT, A. A., AND E. J. VAN OUTRYVE. 1971. A simple method for trapping breeding adults in nesting boxes. Bird-Banding 42:119–121.

DIETZ, N. J., P. J. BERGMANN, AND L. D. FLAKE. 1994. A walk-in trap for nesting ducks. Wildlife Society Bulletin 22:19–22.

DILL, H. H., AND W. H. THORNSBERRY. 1950. A cannon-projected net trap for capturing waterfowl. Journal of Wildlife Management 14:132–137.

DOAN, T. M. 1997. A new trap for the live capture of large lizards. Herpetological Review 28:79.

DODD, JR., C. K. 1991. Drift fence-associated sampling bias of amphibians at a Florida sandhills temporary pond. Journal of Herpetology 25:296–301.

DODD, N. L., J. S. STATES, AND S. S. ROSENSTOCK. 2003. Tassel-eared squirrel population, habitat condition, and dietary relationships in north-central Arizona. Journal of Wildlife Management 67:622–633.

DOERR, E. D., V. A. J. DOERR, AND P. B. STACEY. 1998. Two capture methods for black-billed magpies. Western Birds 29:55–58.

DOTY, H. A., AND F. B. LEE. 1974. Homing to nest baskets by wild female mallards. Journal of Wildlife Management 38:714–719.

DOUGLASS, R. J., A. J. KUENZI, T. WILSON, AND R. C. VAN HORNE. 2000. Effects of bleeding nonanesthetized wild rodents on handling mortality and subsequent recapture. Journal of Wildlife Diseases 36:700–704.

DOWNES, S., AND P. BORGES. 1998. Sticky traps: an effective way to capture small terrestrial lizards. Herpetological Review 29:94–95.

DREWIEN, R. C., AND K. R. CLEGG. 1991. Capturing whooping cranes and sandhill cranes by night-lighting. Proceedings of the North American Crane Workshop 6:43–49.

———, AND R. E. SHEA. 1999. Capturing trumpeter swans by night-lighting. Wildlife Society Bulletin 27:209–215.

———, H. M. REEVES, P. F. SPRINGER, AND T. L. KUCK. 1967. Backpack unit for capturing waterfowl and upland game by night-lighting.

Journal of Wildlife Management 31:778–783.

———, R. J. VERNIMEN, S. W. HARRIS, AND C. F. YOCOM. 1966. Spring weights of band-tailed pigeons. Journal of Wildlife Management 30:190–192.

DUBOIS, S. D., AND A. W. PALMISANO. 1974. An evaluation of traps and baits for capturing waterfowl in coastal Louisiana. Proceedings of the Annual Conference of the Southeastern Association of Game and Fish Commissioners 28:474–482.

DUNK, J. E. 1991. A selective pole trap for raptors. Wildlife Society Bulletin 19:208–210.

DUNN, E. H., D. J. T. HUSSELL, AND R. J. ADAMS. 1997. Monitoring songbird population change with autumn mist netting. Journal of Wildlife Management 61:389–396.

DURDEN, L. A., E. M. DOTSON, AND G. N. VOGEL. 1995. Two efficient techniques for catching skinks. Herpetological Review 26:137.

DURTSCHE, R. D. 1996. A capture technique for small smooth-scaled lizards. Herpetological Review 27:12–13.

DYKSTRA, J. N. 1968. A decoy and net for capturing nesting robins. Bird-Banding 39:189–192.

EARLÉ, E. A. 1988. A cast-net for trapping nightjars (and others). Safring News 17:25–28.

EARLE, R. D., D. M. LUNNING, AND V. R. TUOVILA. 1996. Assessing injuries to Michigan bobcats held by #3 Soft Catch® traps. Pages 34–35 in R. D. Earle, editor, Proceedings of the Fourteenth Midwest Furbearer Workshop, Michigan Department of Natural Resources, Lansing, USA.

EDGAR, R. L. 1968. Catching colonial seabirds for banding. Bird-Banding 39:41–43.

ELLIS, D. H., D. HJERTAAS, B. W. JOHNS, AND R. P. URBANEK. 1998. Use of a helicopter to capture flighted cranes. Wildlife Society Bulletin 26:103–107.

ELODY, B. I., AND N. F. SLOAN. 1984. A mist net technique useful for capturing barred owls. North American Bird Bander 9(4):13–14.

ENGE, K. M. 1997. Use of silt fencing and funnel traps for drift fences. Herpetological Review 28:30–31.

———. 2001. The pitfalls of pitfall traps. Journal of Herpetology 35:467–478.

ENGEMAN, R. M. 1998. An easy capture method for brown tree snakes (*Boiga irregularis*). The Snake 28:101–102.

———, AND M. A. LINNELL. 1998. Trapping strategies for deterring the spread of brown tree snakes from Guam. Pacific Conservation Biology 4:348–353.

———, AND D. S. VICE. 2001. A direct comparison of trapping and spotlight searches for capturing brown tree snakes on Guam. Pacific Conservation Biology 7:4–8.

———, H. W. KRUPA, AND J. KERN. 1997. On the use of injury scores for judging the acceptability of restraining traps. Journal of Wildlife Research 2:124–127.

———, M. A. LINNELL, P. AGUON, A. MANIBUSON, S. SAYAMA, AND A. TECHAIRA. 1999. Implications of brown tree snake captures from fences. Wildlife Research 26:111–116.

ENGLUND, J. 1982. A comparison of injuries to leg-hold trapped and foot-snared red foxes. Journal of Wildlife Management 46:1113–1117.

ERICKSON, A. W. 1957. Techniques for live-trapping and handling black bears. Transactions of the North American Wildlife Conference 22:520–543.

ERIKSEN, B., J. CARDOZA, J. PACK, AND H. KILPATRICK. 1995. Procedures and guidelines for rocket-netting wild turkeys. Technical Bulletin 1. National Wild Turkey Federation, Edgefield, South Carolina, USA.

EVANS, J., J. O. ELLIS, R. D. NASS, AND A. L. WARD. 1971. Techniques for capturing and marking nutria. Proceedings of the Annual Conference of the Southeastern Association of Game and Fish Commissioners 25:295–315.

EVRARD, J. O., AND B. R. BACON. 1998. Duck trapping success and mortality using four trap designs. North American Bird Bander 23:110–114.

EWINS, P. J., AND M. J. R. MILLER. 1993. Noose dome trap for ospreys. North American Bird Bander 18:40.

FAIR, W. S., AND S. E. HENKE. 1997. Efficacy of capture methods for a low density population of *Phrynosoma cornutum*. Herpetological Review 28:135–137.

FERGUSON, H. L., AND P. D. JORGENSEN. 1981. An efficient trapping technique for burrowing owls. North American Bird Bander 6:149–150.

FEUER, R. C. 1980. Underwater traps for aquatic turtles. Herpetological Review 11:107–108.

FIRCHOW, K. M., M. R. VAUGHAN, AND W. R. MYTTON. 1986. Evaluation of the hand-held net gun for capturing pronghorns. Journal of Wildlife Management 50: 320–322.

FITCH, H. S. 1992. Methods of sampling snake populations and their relative success. Herpetological Review 23: 17–19.

FITZGERALD, C. S., P. R. KRAUSMAN, AND M. L. MORRISON. 1999. Use of buried and non-buried traps to sample desert rodents. California Fish and Game 85: 140–143.

FLEMING, P. J. S., L. R. ALLEN, M. J. BERGHOUT, P. D. MEEK, P. M. PAVLOV, P. STEVENS, K. STRONG, J. A. THOMPSON, AND P. C. THOMSON. 1998. The performance of wild-canid traps in Australia: efficiency, selectivity and trap-related injuries. Wildlife Research 25: 327–338.

FLOCK, B. E., AND R. D. APPLEGATE. 2002. Comparison of trapping methods for ring-necked pheasants in north-central Kansas. North American Bird Bander 27: 4–8.

FLORES, R. E., AND W. R. EDDLEMAN. 1993. Nesting biology of the California black rail in southwestern Arizona. Western Birds 24: 81–88.

FOLK, M. J., J. A. SCHMIDT, AND S. A. NESBITT. 1999. A trough-blind for capturing cranes. Journal of Field Ornithology 70: 251–256.

FOREYT, W. J., AND W. C. GLAZENER. 1979. A modified box trap for capturing feral hogs and white-tailed deer. Southwestern Naturalist 24: 377–380.

———, AND A. RUBENSER. 1980. A live trap for multiple capture of coyote pups from dens. Journal of Wildlife Management 44: 487–488.

FOSTER, M. S., AND L. A. FITZGERALD. 1982. A technique for live-trapping cormorants. Journal of Field Ornithology 53: 422–423

FOWLER, M. E. 1995. Restraint and handling of wild and domestic animals. Second edition. Iowa State University Press, Ames, USA.

FRANCIS, C. M. 1989. A comparison of mist nets and two designs of harp traps for capturing bats. Journal of Mammalogy 70: 865–870.

FRANK, L., D. SIMPSON, AND R. WOODROFFE. 2003. Foot snares: an effective method for capturing African lions. Wildlife Society Bulletin 31: 309–314.

FRANKLIN, C. J., AND R. W. HARTDEGEN. 1997. A safer capture technique for larger reptiles. Herpetological Review 28: 197.

FRANKLIN, W. L., AND W. E. JOHNSON. 1994. Hand capture of newborn open-habitat ungulates: the South American guanaco. Wildlife Society Bulletin 22: 253–259.

FREDERICK, P. C. 1986. A self-tripping trap for use with colonial nesting birds. North American Bird Bander 11: 94–95.

FRENZEL, R. W., AND R. G. ANTHONY. 1982. Method for live-capturing bald eagles and osprey over open water. U.S. Department of the Interior, Fish and Wildlife Service, Research Information Bulletin 82–13.

FRITTS, T. H., N. J. SCOTT, JR., AND B. E. SMITH. 1989. Trapping *Boiga irregularis* on Guam using bird odors. Journal of Herpetology 23: 189–192.

FRONZUTO, J., AND P. VERRELL. 2000. Sampling aquatic salamanders: tests of the efficiency of two funnel traps. Journal of Herpetology 34: 146–147.

FROST, H. C., AND W. B. KROHN. 1994. Capture, care and handling of fishers (*Martes pennanti*). Technical Bulletin 157. Maine Agriculture and Forest Experiment Station, University of Maine, Orono, USA.

FUERTES, B., J. GARÄIA, AND J. M. COLINO. 2002. Use of fish nets as a method to capture small rails. Journal of Field Ornithology 73: 220–223.

FULLER, A. F. 1984. Drop net capture of bighorn sheep in Arizona. Transactions of the Desert Bighorn Council 28: 39–40.

FUNK, H. D., AND J. R. GRIEB. 1965. Baited cannon-net sampling as an indicator of Canada goose population characteristics. Journal of Wildlife Management 29: 253–260.

GARD, N. W., D. M. BIRD, R. DENSMORE, AND M. HAMEL. 1989. Responses of breeding American kestrels to live and mounted great horned owls. Journal of Raptor Research 23: 99–102.

GARRETTSON, P. R. 1998. Response of breeding season blue-winged teal to decoy trapping. Prairie Naturalist 30: 235–241.

GARTSHORE, M. E. 1978. A noose trap for catching nesting birds. North American Bird-Bander 3: 1–2.

GAUNT, A. S., L. W. ORING, K. P. ABLE, D. W. ANDERSON, L. F. BAPTISTA, J. C. BARLOW, AND J. C. WINGFIELD. 1997. Guidelines to the use of wild birds in research. The Ornithological Council. Washington, D.C., USA.

GEERING, D. J. 1998. Playback tapes as an aid for mist-netting regent honeyeaters. Corella 22: 61–63.

GEHRT, S. D., AND E. K. FRITZELL. 1996. Sex-biased response of raccoons (*Procyon lotor*) to live traps. American Midland Naturalist 135: 23–32.

GENTILE, J. R. 1987. The evolution of anti-trapping sentiment in the United States: a review and commentary. Wildlife Society Bulletin 15: 490–503.

GESE, E. M., O. J. RONGSTAD, AND W. R. MYTTON. 1987. Manual and net-gun capture of coyotes from helicopters. Wildlife Society Bulletin 15: 444–445.

GETTINGER, R. D. 1990. Effects of chemical insect repellents on small mammal trapping yield. American Midland Naturalist 124: 181–184.

GIESEN, K. M., T. J. SCHOENBERG, AND C. E. BRAUN. 1982. Methods for trapping sage grouse in Colorado. Wildlife Society Bulletin 10: 224–231.

GILBERT, F. F. 1976. Impact energy thresholds for anesthetized raccoons, mink, muskrats, and beavers. Journal of Wildlife Management 40: 669–676.

———. 1981a. Assessment of furbearer response to trapping devices. Proceedings of the Worldwide Furbearer Conference 3: 1599–1611.

———. 1981b. Maximizing the humane potential of traps—the Vital and the Conibear 120. Proceedings of the Worldwide Furbearer Conference 3: 1630–1646.

———. 1992. Aquatic trap testing—Washington State University. Pages 20–21 in Wild fur and the international market place. Fur Institute of Canada, Ottawa, Ontario, Canada.

———, AND N. GOFTON. 1982. Terminal dives in mink, muskrat and beaver. Physiology and Behavior 28: 835–840.

GLASGOW, L. L. 1957. The night driving of coots for banding on the wintering ground of Louisiana. Bird-Banding 28: 153–155.

GLAZENER, W. C. 1949. Operation deer trap. Texas Game and Fish 7(10): 6–7, 17, 19.

———, A. S. JACKSON, AND M. L. COX. 1964. The Texas drop-net turkey trap. Journal of Wildlife Management 28: 280–287.

GLENNON, M. J., W. F. PORTER, AND C. L. DEMERS. 2002. An alternative field technique for estimating diversity of small-mammal populations. Journal of Mammalogy 83: 734–742.

GLUESENKAMP, A. G. 1995. The snake rake: a new tool for collecting reptiles and amphibians. Herpetological Review 26: 19.

GODFREY, C. L., K. NEEDHAM, M. R. VAUGHAN, J. HIGGINS VASHON, D. D. MARTIN, AND G. T. BLANK, JR. 2000. A technique for and risks associated with entering tree dens used by black bears. Wildlife Society Bulletin 28: 131–140.

GOODRICH, J. M., L. L. KERLEY, B. O. SCHLEYER, D. G. MIQUELLE, K. S. QUIGLEY, T. N. SMIRNOV, H. B. QUIGLEY, AND M. G. HORNOCKER. 2001. Capture and chemical anesthesia of Amur (Siberian) tigers. Wildlife Society Bulletin 29: 533–542.

GRAHAM, T., AND A. GEORGES. 1996. Struts for collapsible funnel traps. Herpetological Review 27: 189–190.

GRAND, J. B., AND T. F. FONDELL. 1994. Decoy trapping and rocket-netting for northern pintails in spring. Journal of Field Ornithology 65: 402–405.

GRANT, B. W., A. D. TUCKER, J. E. LOVICH, A. M. MILLS, P. M. DIXON, AND J. W. GIBBONS. 1992. The use of coverboards in estimating patterns of reptile and amphibian biodiversity. Pages 379–403 in D. R. McCullough and R. H. Barrett, editors. Wildlife 2001: populations. Elsevier Science Publishing, London, United Kingdom.

GRATTO-TREVOR, C. L., L. W. ORING, AND A. J. FIVIZZANI. 1991. Effects of blood sampling stress on hormone levels in the semipalmated sandpiper. Journal of Field Ornithology 62: 19–27.

GRAUL, W. D. 1979. An evaluation of selected techniques for nesting shorebirds. North American Bird Bander 4: 19–21.

GREENBERG, C. H., D. G. NEARY, AND L. D. HARRIS. 1994. A comparison of herpetofaunal sampling effectiveness of pitfall, single-ended and double-ended funnel traps used with drift fences. Journal of Herpetology 28: 319–324.

GREGORY, P. T., G. J. DAVIES, AND J. M. MACCARTNEY. 1989. A portable device for restraining rattlesnakes in the field. Herpetological Review 20: 43–44.

GRIESEMER, S. J., M. O. HALE, U. ROZE, AND T. FULLER. 1999. Capturing and marking adult North American porcupines. Wildlife Society Bulletin 27: 310–313.

GRIFFITH, R. E., AND J. EVANS. 1970. Capturing jackrabbits by nightlighting. Journal of Wildlife Management 34: 637–639.

GRUBB, T. G. 1988. A portable rocket-net system for capturing wildlife. U.S. Department of Agriculture, Forest Service, Research Note RM-484.

———. 1991. Modifications of the portable rocket-net capture system to improve performance. U.S. Department of Agriculture, Forest Service, Research Note RM-502.

GRUVER, K. S., R. PHILLIPS, AND E. S. WILLIAMS. 1996. Leg injuries to coyotes captured in standard and modified Soft Catch™ traps. Proceedings of the Vertebrate Pest Conference 17:91–93.

GURNELL, J., AND J. LITTLE. 1992. The influence of trap residual odor on catching woodland rodents. Animal Behaviour 43:623–632.

GUTHERY, F. S., AND S. L. BEASOM. 1978. Effectiveness and selectivity of neck snares in predator control. Journal of Wildlife Management 42:457–459.

GUYN, K. L., AND R. G. CLARK. 1999. Decoy trap bias and effects of marks on reproduction of northern pintails. Journal of Field Ornithology 70:504–513.

HAKIM, S., W. J. MCSHEA, AND J. R. MASON. 1996. The attractiveness of a liquid bait to white-tailed deer in the central Appalachian Mountains, Virginia, USA. Journal of Wildlife Diseases 32:395–398.

HAMERSTROM, F. 1963. The use of great horned owls in catching marsh hawks. Proceedings of the International Ornithological Congress 13:866–869.

HAMERSTROM, JR., F. N., AND M. TRUAX. 1938. Traps for pinnated and sharp-tailed grouse. Bird-Banding 9:177–183.

HANDLEY, JR., C. O., AND M. VARN. 1994. The trapline concept applied to pitfall arrays. Pages 285–287 *in* J. F. Merritt, G. L. Kirkland, Jr., and R. K. Rose, editors. Advances in the biology of shrews. Special Publication 18. Carnegie Museum of Natural History, Pittsburgh, Pennsylvania, USA.

HARAMIS, G. M., E. L. DERLETH, AND D. G. MCAULEY. 1987. A quick-catch corral trap for wintering canvasbacks. Journal of Field Ornithology 58:198–200.

HARRIS, S. W. 1952. A throw net for capturing waterfowl on the nest. Journal of Wildlife Management 16:515.

———, AND M. A. MORSE. 1958. The use of mist nets for capturing nesting mourning doves. Journal of Wildlife Management 22:306–309.

HARRISON, SR., M. K., G. M. HARAMIS, D. G. JORDE, AND D. B. STOTTS. 2000. Capturing American black ducks in tidal waters. Journal of Field Ornithology 71:153–158.

HARRISON, R. L. 1997. Chemical attractants for Central American felids. Wildlife Society Bulletin 25:93–97.

HAUKOS, D. A., L. M. SMITH, AND G. S. BRODA. 1990. Spring trapping of lesser prairie-chickens. Journal of Field Ornithology 61:20–25.

HAULTON, S. M., W. F. PORTER, AND B. A. RUDOLPH. 2001. Evaluating 4 methods to capture white-tailed deer. Wildlife Society Bulletin 29:255–264.

HAWKINS, R. E., D. C. AUTRY, AND W. D. KLIMSTRA. 1967. Comparison of methods used to capture white-tailed deer. Journal of Wildlife Management 31:460–464.

———, L. D. MARTOGLIO, AND G. G. MONTGOMERY. 1968. Cannon-netting deer. Journal of Wildlife Management 32:191–195.

HAYES, J. P., E. G. HORVATH, AND P. HOUNIHAN. 1994. Securing live traps to small-diameter trees for studies of arboreal mammals. Northwestern Naturalist 75:31–33.

HAYS, W. S. T. 1998. A new method for live-trapping shrews. Acta Theriologica 43:333–335.

HEATH, J. A., AND P. C. FREDERICK. 2003. Trapping white ibises with rocket nets and mist nets in the Florida Everglades. Journal of Field Ornithology 74:187–192.

HEIMER, W. E., S. D. DUBOIS, AND D. G. KELLYHOUSE. 1980. The usefulness of rocket nets for Dall sheep capture compared with other capture methods. Proceedings of the Biennial Symposium of the Northern Wild Sheep and Goat Council 2:601–613.

HENKE, S. E., AND S. DEMARAIS. 1990. Capturing jackrabbits by drive corral on grasslands in west Texas. Wildlife Society Bulletin 18:31–33.

HERNANDEZ, F., D. ROLLINS, AND R. CANTU. 1997. An evaluation of Trailmaster® camera systems for identifying ground-nest predators. Wildlife Society Bulletin 25:848–853.

HESKE, E. J. 1987. Responses of a population of California voles, *Microtus californicus*, to odor-baited traps. Journal of Mammalogy 68:64–72.

HESS, C. A., P. P. KELLY, R. COSTA, AND J. H. CARTER, III. 2001. Reconsideration of Richardson et al's red-cockaded woodpecker nestling removal technique. Wildlife Society Bulletin 29:372–374.

HEYDON, C., M. NOVAK, AND H. ROWSELL. 1993. Humane attributes of three types of legholding traps. Report. Ontario Ministry of Natural Resources, Toronto, Canada.

HEYER, W. R., M. A. DONNELLY, R. W. MCDIARMID, L. C. HAYEK, AND M. S. FOSTER, editors. 1994. Measuring and monitoring biological diversity. Standard methods for amphibians. Smithsonian Institution Press, Washington, D.C., USA.

HEYLAND, J. D. 1970. Aircraft-supported Canada goose banding operations in arctic Quebec. Transactions of the Northeast Section of The Wildlife Society 27:187–198.

HICKS, L. E., AND D. L. LEEDY. 1939. Techniques for pheasant trapping and population control. Transactions of the North American Wildlife Conference 4:449–461.

HILL, E. P. 1981. Evaluation of improved traps and trapping techniques. Job Progress Report, Federal Aid Project W-44-6, Job IV-B. Alabama Department of Conservation and Natural Resources, Montgomery, USA.

HILTON, JR., B. 1989. Two methods for capturing tree-nesting birds at nests. North American Bird Bander 14:47–48.

HINES, R. K., AND T. W. CUSTER. 1995. Evaluation of an extendable pole-net to collect heron eggs in the canopy of tall trees. Colonial Waterbirds. 18:120–122.

HOBBS, R. J., AND C. D. JAMES. 1999. Influence of shade covers on pitfall trap temperatures and capture success of reptiles and small mammals in arid Australia. Wildlife Research 26:341–349.

———, S. R. MORTON, P. MASTERS, AND K. R. JONES. 1994. Influence of pit-trap design on sampling of reptiles in arid spinifex grassland. Wildlife Research 21:483–490.

HODGDON, K. W., AND J. H. HUNT. 1953. Beaver management in Maine. Game Division Bulletin 3. Maine Department of Inland Fisheries and Game, Augusta, USA.

HOGAN, G. G. 1985. Noosing adult cormorants for banding. North American Bird Bander 10:76–77.

HOGLUND, N. H. 1968. A method of trapping and marking willow grouse in winter. Viltrevy 5:95–101.

HORN, E. E., AND H. S. FITCH. 1946. Trapping the California ground squirrel. Journal of Mammalogy 27:220–224.

HOUBEN, J. M., M. HOLLAND, S. W. JACK, AND C. R. BOYLE. 1993. An evaluation of laminated offset jawed traps for reducing injuries to coyotes. Proceedings of the Great Plains Wildlife Damage Control Workshop 11:148–155.

HOUZE, JR., C. M., AND C. R. CHANDLER. 2002. Evaluation of coverboards for sampling terrestrial salamanders in south Georgia. Journal of Herpetology 36:75–81

HOWARD, W. E. 1952. A live trap for pocket gophers. Journal of Mammalogy 33:61–65.

HUBERT, JR., G. F., R. D. BLUETT, AND G. A. DUMONCEAUX. 1991. Field evaluation of two footholding devices for capturing raccoons in non-drowning water sets. Pages 23–24 *in* L. Fredrickson and B. Coonrod, editors. Proceedings of the Ninth Midwest Furbearer Workshop. South Dakota Department of Game, Fish and Parks, Pierre, USA.

———, L. L. HUNGERFORD, AND R. D. BLUETT. 1997. Injuries to coyotes captured in modified foothold traps. Wildlife Society Bulletin 25:858–863.

———, G. K. WOLLENBERG, L. L. HUNGERFORD, AND R. D. BLUETT. 1999. Evaluation of injuries to Virginia opossums captured in the EGG™ trap. Wildlife Society Bulletin 27:301–305.

———, L. L. HUNGERFORD, G. PROULX, R. D. BLUETT, AND L. BOWMAN. 1996. Evaluation of two restraining traps to capture raccoons. Wildlife Society Bulletin 24:699–708.

HUEMPFNER, R. A., S. J. MAXSON, G. J. ERICKSON, AND R. J. SHUSTER. 1975. Recapturing radio-tagged ruffed grouse by nightlighting and snow-burrow netting. Journal of Wildlife Management 39:821–823.

HUGGINS, J. G. 1999. Gray and fox squirrel trapping: a review. Pages 117–129 *in* G. Proulx, editor. Mammal trapping. Alpha Wildlife Research and Management Ltd., Sherwood Park, Alberta, Canada.

———, AND K. L. GEE. 1995. Efficiency and selectivity of cage trap sets for gray and fox squirrels. Wildlife Society Bulletin 23:204–207.

HUNT, G. S., AND K. J. DAHLKA. 1953. Live trapping of diving ducks. Journal of Wildlife Management 17:92–95.

HYDE, E. J., AND T. R. SIMONS. 2001. Sampling plethodontid salamanders: sources of variability. Journal of Wildlife Management 65:624–632.

INTERNATIONAL ASSOCIATION OF FISH AND WILDLIFE AGENCIES. 1992. Ownership and use of traps by trappers in the United States in 1992. The Fur Resources Committee of The International Association of Fish and Wildlife Agencies, and The Gallup Organization, Inc., Washington, D.C., USA.

———. 1997. Improving animal welfare in U.S. trapping programs: process recommendations and summaries of existing data. Fur Resources Technical Subcommittee, International Association of Fish and Wildlife Agencies, Washington, D.C., USA.

———. 2000. Testing restraining traps for the development of best management practices for trapping in the United States. Furbearer

Resources Technical Work Group, International Association of Fish and Wildlife Agencies, Washington, D.C., USA.

———. 2003. Best management practices for trapping coyotes in the eastern United States. International Association of Fish and Wildlife Agencies, Washington, D.C., USA.

INTERNATIONAL ORGANIZATION FOR STANDARDIZATION. 1999*a*. Animal (mammal) traps—Part 4. Methods for testing killing-trap systems used on land or underwater. International Standard ISO 10990–4. International Organization for Standardization, Geneva, Switzerland.

———. 1999*b*. Animal (mammal) traps—Part 5. Methods for testing restraining traps. International Standard ISO 10990–5. International Organization for Standardization, Geneva, Switzerland.

IVERSON, J. B. 1979. Another inexpensive turtle trap. Herpetological Review 10:55.

JACKMAN, R. E., W. G. HUNT, D. E. DRISCOLL, AND J. M. JENKINS. 1993. A modified floating-fish snare for capture of inland bald eagles. North American Bird Bander 18:98–101.

———, ———, ———, AND F. J. LAPSANSKY. 1994. Refinements to selective trapping techniques: a radio-controlled bow net and power snare for bald and golden eagles. Journal of Raptor Research 28:268–273.

JACKSON, J. A., AND S. D. PARRIS. 1991. A simple, effective net for capturing cavity roosting birds. North American Bird Bander 16:30–31.

JACKSON, R., G. AHLBORN, AND K. B. SHAH. 1990. Capture and immobilization of wild snow leopards. International Pedigree Book of Snow Leopards 6:93–102.

JACOBS, E. A. 1996. A mechanical owl as a trapping lure for raptors. Journal of Raptor Research 30:31–32.

———, AND G. A. PROUDFOOT. 2002. An elevated net assembly to capture nesting raptors. Journal of Raptor Research 36:320–323.

JACOBS, K. F. 1958. A drop-net trapping technique for greater prairie chickens. Proceedings of the Oklahoma Academy of Science 38:154–157.

JAMISON, B. 2002. Wild hog trapping. Wildlife Control Technology 9:26–27, 37.

JANOVSKY, M., T. RUF, AND W. ZENKER. 2002. Oral administration of tiletamine/zolazepam for immobilization of the common buzzard (*Buteo buteo*). Journal of Raptor Research 36:188–193.

JEFFERSON, JR., R. T., AND W. L. FRANKLIN. 1986. Behavioral considerations in the live capture of guanacos with spring-activated foot snares. Proceedings of the Iowa Academy of Science 93:48–50.

JENKINS, C. L., K. MCGARIGAL, AND L. R. GAMBLE. 2002. A comparison of aquatic surveying techniques used to sample *Ambystoma opacum* larvae. Herpetological Review 33:33–35.

JENKINS, M. A. 1979. Tips on constructing monofilament nylon nooses for raptor traps. North American Bird Bander 4:108–109.

JENNI, L., M. LEUNBERGER, AND F. RAMPAZZI. 1996. Capture efficiency of mist nets with comments on their role in the assessment of passerine habitat use. Journal of Field Ornithology 67:263–274.

JESSUP, D. A., W. E. CLARK, AND R. C. MOHR. 1984. Capture of bighorn sheep: management recommendations. Wildlife Management Branch, Administrative Report 24–1. California Department of Fish and Game, Sacramento, USA.

———, R. K. CLARK, R. A. WEAVER, AND M. D. KOCK. 1988. The safety and cost-effectiveness of net-gun capture of desert bighorn sheep (*Ovis canadensis nelsoni*). Journal of Zoo Animal Medicine 19:208–213.

JEWELL, S. D., AND J. T. BANCROFT. 1991. Effects of nest trapping on nesting success of *Egretta* herons. Journal of Field Ornithology 62:78–82.

JOHNSON, C. L., AND R. T. REYNOLDS. 1998. A new trap design for capturing spotted owls. Journal of Raptor Research 32:181–182.

JOHNSON, K. G., AND M. R. PELTON. 1980. Prebaiting and snaring techniques for black bears. Wildlife Society Bulletin 8:46–54.

JONES, C., W. J. MCSHEA, M. J. CONROY, AND T. H. KUNZ. 1996. Capturing mammals. Pages 115–155 *in* D. E. Wilson, F. R. Cole, J. D. Nichols, R. Rudran, and M. S. Foster, editors. Measuring and monitoring biological diversity. Standard methods for mammals. Smithsonian Institution Press, Washington, D.C., USA.

JONES, D., AND L. HAYES-ODUM. 1994. A method for the restraint and transport of crocodilians. Herpetological Review 25:14–15.

JORGENSEN, E. E., S. DEMARAIS, AND W. R. WHITWORTH. 1994. The effect of box-trap design on rodent captures. Southwestern Naturalist 39:291–294.

KAGARISE, C. M. 1978. A simple trap for capturing nesting Wilson's phalaropes. Bird-Banding 49:281–282.

KAHN, R. H., AND B. A. MILLSAP. 1978. An inexpensive method for cap-

turing short-eared owls. North American Bird Bander 3:54.

KAISER, G. W., A. E. DEROCHER, S. CRAWFORD, M. J. GILL, AND I. A. MANLEY. 1995. A capture technique for marbled murrelets in coastal inlets. Journal of Field Ornithology 66:321–333.

KAMLER, J. F., W. B. BALLARD, R. L. GILLILAND, AND K. MOTE. 2002. Improved trapping methods for swift foxes and sympatric coyotes. Wildlife Society Bulletin 30:1262–1266.

KARANTH, K. U. 1995. Estimating tiger *Panthera tigris* populations from camera-trap data using capture-recapture models. Biological Conservation 71:333–338.

KARRAKER, N. E. 2001. String theory: reducing mortality of mammals in pitfall traps. Wildlife Society Bulletin 29:1158–1162.

KATTELL, B., AND A. W. ALLDREDGE. 1991. Capturing and handling of the Himalayan musk deer. Wildlife Society Bulletin 19:397–399.

KAUTZ, J. E., AND T. W. SEAMANS. 1992. Techniques for feral pigeon trapping, tagging, and nest monitoring. North American Bird Bander 17:53–59.

KAYS, R. W. 1999. A hoistable arboreal mammal trap. Wildlife Society Bulletin 27:298–300.

KEARNS, G. D., N. B. KWARTIN, D. F. BRINKER, AND G. M. HARAMIS. 1998. Digital playback and improved trap design enhances capture of migrant soras and Virginia rails. Journal of Field Ornithology 69:466–473.

KEITH, L. B. 1965. A live snare and a tagging snare for rabbits. Journal of Wildlife Management 29:877–880.

———, E. C. MESLOW, AND O. J. RONGSTAD. 1968. Techniques for snowshoe hare population studies. Journal of Wildlife Management 32:801–811.

KELLY, B. P. 1996. Live capture of ringed seals in ice-covered waters. Journal of Wildlife Management 60:678–684.

KERN, J. W., L. L. MCDONALD, M. D. STRICKLAND, AND E. WILLIAMS. 1994. Field evaluation and comparison of four foothold traps for terrestrial furbearers in Wyoming. Western Ecosystems Technology, Cheyenne, Wyoming, USA.

KEYES, B. E., AND C. E. GRUE. 1982. Capturing birds with mist nets: a review. North American Bird Bander 7:2–14.

KIBLER, L. F. 1969. The establishment and maintenance of a bluebird nest-box project. Bird-Banding 40:114–129.

KIMBALL, B. A., J. R. MASON, F. S. BLOM, J. J. JOHNSTON, AND D. E. ZEMLICKA. 2000. Development and testing of seven new synthetic coyote attractants. Journal of Agricultural and Food Chemistry 48:1892–1897.

KING, C. M. 1981. The effects of two types of steel traps upon captured stoats (*Mustela erminea*). Journal of Zoology (London) 195:553–554.

KING, D. T., M. E. TOBIN, AND M. BUR. 2000. Capture and telemetry techniques for double-crested cormorants (*Phalacrocorax auritus*). Proceedings of the Vertebrate Pest Conference 19:54–57.

———, J. D. PAULSON, D. J. LEBLANC, AND K. BRUCE. 1998. Two capture techniques for American white pelicans and great blue herons. Colonial Waterbirds 21:258–260.

———, K. J. ANDREWS, J. O. KING, R. D. FLYNT, J. F. GLAHN, AND J. L. CUMMINGS. 1994. A night-lighting technique for capturing cormorants. Journal of Field Ornithology 65:254–257.

KIRKLAND, JR., G. L., AND R. K. SHEPPARD. 1994. Proposed standard protocol for sampling small mammal communities. Pages 277–283 *in* J. F. Merritt, G. L. Kirkland, Jr., and R. K. Rose, editors. Advances in the biology of shrews. Special Publication 18. Carnegie Museum of Natural History, Pittsburgh, Pennsylvania, USA.

KJOSS, V. A., AND J. A. LITVAITIS. 2001. Comparison of 2 methods to sample snake communities in early successional habitats. Wildlife Society Bulletin 29:153–157.

KNIGHT, J. E. 1994. Mountain lion. Pages C93–C99 *in* S. E. Hynstrom, R. M. Timm, and G. E. Larson, editors. Prevention and control of wildlife damage. University of Nebraska Cooperative Extension Service, Lincoln, USA.

KNITTLE, C. E., AND M. A. PAVELKA. 1994. Hook and loop tabs for attaching a dho-gaza. Journal of Raptor Research 28:197–198.

KOCK, M. D., D. A. JESSUP, R. K. CLARK, C. E. FRANTI, AND R. A. WEAVER. 1987. Capture methods in five subspecies of free-ranging bighorn sheep: an evaluation of drop-net, drive-net, chemical immobilization, and the net-gun. Journal of Wildlife Diseases 23:634–640.

KOPROWSKI, J. L. 2002. Handling tree squirrels with a safe and efficient restraint. Wildlife Society Bulletin 30:101–103.

KRAMER, D. L. 1988. A noose apparatus and its usefulness in capturing nestling bank swallows. North American Bird Bander 13:66–67.

KRAUSMAN, P. R., J. J. HERVERT, AND L. L. ORDWAY. 1985. Capturing deer and mountain sheep with a net-gun. Wildlife Society Bulletin

13:71–73.

KREEGER, T. J., P. J. WHITE, U. S. SEAL, AND J. R. TESTER. 1990. Pathological responses of red foxes to foothold traps. Journal of Wildlife Management 54:147–160.

KRIDELBAUGH, A. 1982. Improved trapping methods for loggerhead shrikes. North American Bird Bander 7:50–51.

KUCERA, T. E., AND R. H. BARRETT. 1993. The Trailmaster^R camera system for detecting wildlife. Wildlife Society Bulletin 21:505–508.

KUEHN, D. W., T. K. FULLER, L. D. MECH, W. J. PAUL, S. H. FRITTS, AND W. E. BERG. 1986. Trap-related injuries to gray wolves in Minnesota. Journal of Wildlife Management 50:90–91.

KUENZI, A. J., AND M. L. MORRISON. 1998. Detection of bats by mistnets and ultrasonic sensors. Wildlife Society Bulletin 26:307–311.

KUNZ, T. H., C. R. TIDEMANN, AND G. R. RICHARDS. 1996. Small volant mammals. Pages 122–143 in D. E. Wilson, F. R. Cole, J. D. Nichols, R. Rudran, and M. S. Foster, editors. Measuring and monitoring biological diversity. Standard methods for mammals. Smithsonian Institution Press, Washington, D.C., USA.

KUTZ, H. L. 1945. An improved game bird trap. Journal of Wildlife Management 9:35–38.

LABISKY, R. F. 1968. Nightlighting: its use in capturing pheasants, prairie chickens, bobwhites, and cottontails. Biological Notes 62. Illinois Natural History Survey, Urbana, USA.

LACHER, J. R., AND D. D. LACHER. 1964. A mobile cannon net trap. Journal of Wildlife Management 28:595–597.

LACKI, M. J., W. T. PENESTON, AND F. D. VOGT. 1990. A comparison of the efficacy of two types of live traps for capturing muskrats, Ondatra zibethicus. Canadian Field-Naturalist 104:594–596.

LANCTOT, R. B. 1994. Blood sampling in juvenile buff-breasted sandpipers: movement, mass change, and survival. Journal of Field Ornithology 65:534–542.

LANNOM, JR., J. R. 1962. A different method of catching the desert lizards, Callisaurus and Uma. Copeia 1962:437–438.

LARKIN, R. P., T. R. VANDEELEN, R. M. SABICK, T. E. GOSSELINK, AND R. E. WARNER. 2003. Electronic signaling for prompt removal of an animal from a trap. Wildlife Society Bulletin 31:391–398.

LARSEN, K. H. 1970. A hoop-net trap for passerine birds. Bird-Banding 41:92–96.

LAUNAY, F., O. COMBREAU, S. J. ASPINALL, R. A. LOUGHLAND, B. GUBIN, AND F. KARPOV. 1999. Trapping of breeding houbara bustard (Chlamydotis undulata). Wildlife Society Bulletin 27:603–608.

LEASURE, S. M., AND D. W. HOLT. 1991. Techniques for locating and capturing nesting short-eared owls (Asio flammeus). North American Bird Bander 16:32–33.

LEE, R. M., J. D. YOAKUM, B. W. O'GARA, T. M. POJAR, AND R. A. OCKENFELS, editors. 1998. Pronghorn management guides. Eighteenth Pronghorn Antelope Workshop, Arizona Game and Fish Department, Phoenix, USA.

LENTLE, P. G., M. A. POTTER, B. P. SPRINGETT, AND K. J. STAFFORD. 1997. A trapping and immobilization technique for small macropods. Wildlife Research 24:373–377.

LERESCHE, R. E., AND G. M. LYNCH. 1973. A trap for free ranging moose. Journal of Wildlife Management 37:87–89.

LESAGE, L., J.-P. L. SAVARD, AND A. REED. 1997. A simple technique to capture breeding adults and broods of surf scoters, Melanitta perspicillata. Canadian Field-Naturalist 111:657–659.

LIBBY, W. L. 1957. A better snowshoe hare live trap. Journal of Wildlife Management 21:452.

LIGHTFOOT, W. C., AND V. MAW. 1963. Trapping and marking mule deer. Proceedings of the Western Association of State Game and Fish Commissioners 43:138–141.

LINDBERG, A. C., J. A. SHIVIK, AND L. CLARK. 2000. Mechanical mouse lure for brown tree snakes. Copeia 2000:886–888.

LINDMEIER, J. P., AND R. L. JESSEN. 1961. Results of capturing waterfowl in Minnesota by spotlighting. Journal of Wildlife Management 25:430–431.

LINHART, S. B., AND G. J. DASCH. 1992. Improved performance of padded jaw traps for capturing coyotes. Wildlife Society Bulletin 20:63–66.

———, AND R. G. LINSCOMBE. 1987. Test methods for steel foothold traps: criteria and performance standards. Pages 148–158 in S. A. Shumake and R. W. Bullard, editors. Vertebrate pest control and management materials. Volume 5. Special Technical Publication 974. American Society for Testing and Materials, Philadelphia, Pennsylvania, USA.

———, G. J. DASCH, AND F. J. TURKOWSKI. 1981. The steel leg-hold trap: techniques for reducing foot injury and increasing selectivity.

Proceedings of the Worldwide Furbearer Conference 3:1560–1578.

———. ———, C. B. MALE, AND R. M. ENGEMAN. 1986. Efficiency of unpadded and padded steel foothold traps for capturing coyotes. Wildlife Society Bulletin 14:212–218.

———, F. S. BLOM, G. J. DASCH, R. M. ENGEMAN, AND G. H. OLSEN. 1988. Field evaluation of padded jaw coyote traps: effectiveness and foot injury. Proceedings of the Vertebrate Pest Conference 13:226–229.

LINSCOMBE, R. G. 1976. An evaluation of the No. 2 Victor and 220 Conibear traps in coastal Louisiana. Proceedings of the Annual Conference of the Southeastern Association of Fish and Wildlife Agencies 30:560–568.

———, AND V. L. WRIGHT. 1988. Efficiency of padded foothold traps for capturing terrestrial furbearers. Wildlife Society Bulletin 16:307–309.

LISCINSKY, S. A., AND W. J. BAILEY, JR. 1955. A modified shorebird trap for capturing woodcock and grouse. Journal of Wildlife Management 19:405–408.

LISHAK, R. S. 1976. A burrow entrance snare for capturing ground squirrels. Journal of Wildlife Management 40:364–365.

LITTELL, R. 1993. Controlled wildlife. Association of Systematic Collections. Second edition. Washington, D.C., USA.

LITVAITIS, J. A., J. A. SHERBURNE, AND J. A. BISSONETTE. 1985. A comparison of methods used to examine snowshoe hare habitat use. Journal of Wildlife Management 49:693–695.

LOCKOWANDT, S. P. E. 1993. An electromagnetic trigger for drop-nets. Wildlife Society Bulletin 21:140–142.

LOGAN, K. A., L. L. SWEANOR, J. F. SMITH, AND M. G. HORNOCKER. 1999. Capturing pumas with foot-hold snares. Wildlife Society Bulletin 27:201–208.

LOGAN, T. J., AND G. CHANDLER. 1987. A walk-in trap for sandhill cranes. Pages 221–223 in J. C. Lewis, editor. Proceedings of the 1985 Crane Workshop.

LOHOEFENER, R., AND J. WOLFE. 1984. A "new" live trap and a comparison with a pit-fall trap. Herpetological Review 15:25–26.

LOMBARDO, M. P., AND E. KEMLY. 1983. A radio-control method for trapping birds in nest boxes. Journal of Field Ornithology 54:194–195.

LOOS, E. H., AND F. C. ROHWER. 2002. Efficiency of nest traps and long-handled nets for capturing upland nesting ducks. Wildlife Society Bulletin 30:1202–1207.

LOPEZ, R. R., N. J. SILVY, J. D. SEBESTA, S. D. HIGGS, AND M. W. SALAZAR. 1998. A portable drop net for capturing urban deer. Proceedings of the Annual Conference of the Southeastern Association of Fish and Wildlife Agencies 52:206–209.

LOW, S. H. 1935. Methods of trapping shorebirds. Bird-Banding 6:16–22.

LUDWIG, J., AND D. E. DAVIS. 1975. An improved woodchuck trap. Journal of Wildlife Management 39:327–329.

LUTTERSCHMIDT, W. I., AND J. F. SCHAEFER. 1996. Mist netting: adapting a technique from ornithology for sampling semi-aquatic snake populations. Herpetological Review 27:131–132.

MACE, R. U. 1971. Trapping and transplanting Roosevelt elk to control damage and establish new populations. Proceedings of the Western Association of State Game and Fish Commissioners 51:464–470.

MAECHTLE, T. L. 1998. The Aba: a device for restraining raptors and other large birds. Journal of Field Ornithology 69:66–70.

MAHAN, B. R., D. R. DUFFORD, N. EMERICK, AND T. J. BEISSEL. 2002. Net and net-box modifications for capturing wild turkeys. Wildlife Society Bulletin 30:960–962.

MALCOLM, J. R. 1991. Comparative abundances of Neotropical small mammals by trap height. Journal of Mammalogy 72:188–192.

MANSFIELD, P., E. G. STRAUSS, AND P. J. AUGER. 1998. Using decoys to capture spotted turtles (Clemmys guttata) in water funnel traps. Herpetological Review 29:157–158.

MARQUARDT, R. E. 1960. Smokeless powder cannon with lightweight netting for trapping geese. Journal of Wildlife Management 24:425–427.

MARTELLA, M. B., AND J. L. NAVARRO. 1992. Capturing and marking greater rheas. Journal of Field Ornithology 63:117–120.

MARTIN, D. J. 1971. A trapping technique for burrowing owls. Bird-Banding 42:46.

MARTIN, F. W., AND E. R. CLARK. 1964. Summer banding of woodcock, 1962–1964. U.S. Department of the Interior, Fish and Wildlife Service, Migratory Bird Populations Station, Administrative Report 43.

MASON, C. E., E. G. GLUESING, AND D. H. ARNER. 1983. Evaluation of snares, leg-hold, and conibear traps for beaver control. Proceedings of the Annual Conference of the Southeastern Association of Fish and Wildlife Agencies 37:201–209.

MASON, J. R., AND S. BLOM. 1998. Coyote lure ingredients—what factors determine success? Wildlife Control Technology 5:26–30.

————, N. J. BEAN, AND L. CLARK. 1993. Development of chemosensory attractants for white-tailed deer (*Odocoileus virginianus*). Crop Protection 12:448–452.

MATSCHKE, G. H. 1962. Trapping and handling European wild hogs. Proceedings of the Annual Conference of the Southeastern Association of Game and Fish Commissioners 16:21–24.

MAULDIN, R. E., AND R. M. ENGEMAN. 1999. A novel snake restraint device. Herpetological Review 30:158.

MAUSER, D. M., AND J. G. MENSIK. 1992. A portable trap for ducks. Wildlife Society Bulletin 20:299–302.

MCBEATH, D. Y. 1941. Whitetail traps and tags. Michigan Conservationist 10(11):6–7.

MCCABE, T. R., AND G. ELISON. 1986. An efficient live-capture technique for muskrats. Wildlife Society Bulletin 14:282–284.

MCCALL, J. D. 1954. Portable live trap for ducks, with improved gathering box. Journal of Wildlife Management 18:405–407.

MCCALLUM, M. L., B. A. WHEELER, AND S. E. TRAUTH. 2002. The "Frog Box": a new bulk holding device for anurans. Herpetological Review 33:107–108.

MCCLOSKEY, J. T., AND S. R. DEWEY. 1999. Improving the success of a mounted great horned owl lure for trapping northern goshawks. Journal of Raptor Research 33:168–169.

MCCOMB, W. C., R. G. ANTHONY, AND K. MCGARIGAL. 1991. Differential vulnerability of small mammals and amphibians to two trap types and two trap baits in Pacific Northwest forests. Northwest Science 65:109–115.

MCCONNELL, P. A., D. M. FERRIGNO, AND D. E. ROSCOE. 1985. An evaluation of muskrat trapping systems and new techniques. Job Progress Report, Federal Aid Project W-59-R-7, Job I-C. New Jersey Division of Fish, Game and Wildlife, Trenton, USA.

MCCULLOUGH, D. R. 1975. Modification of the Clover deer trap. California Fish and Game 61:242–244.

MCDANIEL, G. W., K. S. MCKELVEY, J. R. SQUIRES, AND L. F. RUGGIERO. 2000. Efficacy of lures and hair snares to detect lynx. Wildlife Society Bulletin 28:119–123.

MCGOWAN, K. J., AND C. CAFFREY. 1994. Does drugging crows for capture cause abnormally high mortality? Journal of Field Ornithology 65:453–457.

MCGRADY, M. J., AND J. R. GRANT. 1994. A modified power snare to catch breeding golden eagles (*Aquila chrysaetos*). Journal of Raptor Research 28:61.

————, AND ————. 1996. The use of a power snare to capture breeding golden eagles. Journal of Raptor Research 30:28–31.

MCKINSTRY, M. C., AND S. H. ANDERSON. 1998. Using snares to live-capture beaver, *Castor canadensis*. Canadian Field-Naturalist 112:469–473.

MCNICHOLL, M. K. 1983. Use of a noosing pole to capture common nighthawks. North American Bird Bander 8:104–105.

MECHLIN, L. M., AND C. W. SHAIFFER. 1980. Net-firing gun for capturing breeding waterfowl. Journal of Wildlife Management 44:895–896.

MEEK, P. D., D. J. JENKINS, B. MORRIS, A. J. ARDLER, AND R. J. HAWKSBY. 1995. Use of two humane leg-hold traps for catching pest species. Wildlife Research 22:733–739.

MELQUIST, W. E., AND M. G. HORNOCKER. 1979. Methods and techniques for studying and censusing river otter populations. Technical Report 8. University of Idaho, Forestry, Wildlife and Range Experiment Station, Moscow, USA.

————, AND ————. 1983. Ecology of river otters in west central Idaho. Wildlife Monograph 83.

MENG, H. 1971. The Swedish goshawk trap. Journal of Wildlife Management 35:832–835.

MERENDINO, M. T., AND D. S. LOBPRIES. 1998. Use of rocket netting and airboat nightlighting for capturing mottled ducks in Texas. Proceedings of the Annual Conference of the Southeastern Association of Fish and Wildlife Agencies 52:303–308.

MEYERS, J. M. 1994. Improved capture techniques for psittacines. Wildlife Society Bulletin 22:511–516.

————, AND K. L. PARDIECK. 1993. Evaluation of three elevated mist-net systems for sampling birds. Journal of Field Ornithology 64:270–277.

MILLER, W. R. 1962. Automatic activating mechanism for waterfowl nest trap. Journal of Wildlife Management 26:402–404.

MILLS, T. M., T. L. YATES, J. E. CHILDS, R. R. PARMENTER, T. G. KSIASEK, P. E. ROLLIN, AND C. J. PETERS. 1995. Guidelines for working with rodents potentially infected with hantavirus. Journal of Mammalogy 76:716–722.

MITCHELL, J. C., S. Y. ERDLE, AND J. F. PAGELS. 1993. Evaluation of capture techniques for amphibian, reptile, and small mammal communities in saturated forested wetlands. Wetlands 13:130–136.

MITCHELL, M. S., R. A. LANCIA, AND E. J. JONES. 1996. Use of insecticide to control destructive activity of ants during trapping of small mammals. Journal of Mammalogy 77:1107–1113.

MOCK, D. W., P. L. SCHWAGMEYER, AND J. A. GIEG. 1999. A trap design for capturing individual birds at the nest. Journal of Field Ornithology 70:276–282.

MOLSHER, R. L. 2001. Trapping and demographics of feral cats (*Felis catus*) in central New South Wales. Wildlife Research 28:631–636.

MOORE, D. W., AND M. L. KENNEDY. 1985. Factors affecting response of raccoons to traps and population size estimation. American Midland Naturalist 114:192–197.

MORGAN, J. T., AND G. L. DUSEK. 1992. Trapping white-tailed deer on summer range. Wildlife Society Bulletin 20:39–41.

MORRISON, J. L., AND S. M. MCGEHEE. 1996. Capture methods for crested caracaras. Journal of Field Ornithology 67:630–636.

MORUZZI, T. L., T. K. FULLER, R. M. DEGRAAF, R. T. BROOKS, AND W. LI. 2002. Assessing remotely triggered cameras for surveying carnivore distribution. Wildlife Society Bulletin 30:380–386.

MOSEBY, K. E., AND J. L. READ. 2001. Factors affecting pitfall capture rates of small ground vertebrates in arid South Australia. II. Optimum pitfall trapping effort. Wildlife Research 28:61–71.

MOSES, E. S. 1968. Experimental techniques for capturing American eiders. Transactions of the Northeast Section of The Wildlife Society 25:89–94.

MOWAT, G., AND C. STROBECK. 2000. Estimating population size of grizzly bears using hair capture, DNA profiling and mark-recapture analysis. Journal of Wildlife Management 64:183–193.

————, B. G. SLOUGH, AND R. RIVARD. 1994. A comparison of three live capturing devices for lynx: capture efficiency and injuries. Wildlife Society Bulletin 22:644–650.

MURPHY, C. G. 1993. A modified drift fence for capturing treefrogs. Herpetological Review 24:143–145.

MUSHET, D. M., N. H. EULISS, JR., B. H. HANSON, AND S. G. ZODROW. 1997. A funnel trap for sampling salamanders in wetlands. Herpetological Review 28:132–133.

MUSIANI, M., AND E. VISALBERGHI. 2001. Effectiveness of fladry on wolves in captivity. Wildlife Society Bulletin 29:91–98.

NADOROZNY, N. D., AND E. D. BARR. 1997. Improving trapping success of amphibians using a side-flap pail-trap. Herpetological Review 28:193–194.

NAIDOO, R. 2000. Response of breeding male ruffed grouse, *Bonasa umbellus,* to playbacks of drumming recordings. Canadian Field-Naturalist 114:320–322.

NALL, R. W., L. S. PHILPOT, R. D. SMITH, AND P. W. STURM. 1970. Use of the cannon-net for capturing fallow deer. Proceedings of the Annual Conference of the Southeastern Association of Game and Fish Commissioners 24:282–291.

NASTASE, A. J. 1982. An inexpensive trap for capturing flightless Canada geese. North American Bird Bander 7:46–48.

NAUGLE, D. E., B. J. KERNOHAN, AND J. A. JENKS. 1995. Seasonal capture success and bait use of white-tailed deer in an agricultural-wetland complex. Wildlife Society Bulletin 23:198–200.

NAYLOR, B. J., AND M. NOVAK. 1994. Catch efficiency and selectivity of various traps and sets used for capturing American martens. Wildlife Society Bulletin 22:489–496.

NEAL, B. J. 1959. Techniques of trapping and tagging the collared peccary. Journal of Wildlife Management 23:11–16.

NELLIS, C. H. 1968. Some methods for capturing coyotes alive. Journal of Wildlife Management 32:402–405.

NETTLESHIP, D. N. 1969. Trapping common puffins. Bird-Banding 40:139–144.

NOLAN, JR., V. 1961. A method of netting birds at open nests in trees. Auk 78:643–645.

NORRIS, J. D. 1967. The control of coypus (*Myocastor coypus molina*) by cage trapping. Journal of Applied Ecology 4:167–189.

NORRIS, R. T., J. D. BEULE, AND A. T. STUDHOLME. 1940. Banding woodcocks on Pennsylvania singing grounds. Journal of Wildlife Management 4:8–14.

NORTHCOTT, T. H., AND D. SLADE. 1976. A livetrapping technique for river otters. Journal of Wildlife Management 40:163–164.

NOVAK, M. 1981a. Capture tests with underwater snares, leg-hold, Conibear and Mohawk traps. Canadian Trapper, April:18–23.

———. 1981b. The foot-snare and the leg-hold traps: a comparison. Proceedings of the Worldwide Furbearer Conference 3:1671–1685.

———. 1987. Traps and trap research. Pages 941–969 in M. Novak, J. A. Baker, M. E. Obbard, and B. Malloch, editors. 1987. Wild furbearer management and conservation in North America. Ontario Ministry of Natural Resources, Toronto, Canada.

———. 1990. Evaluation of LDL, Kania and modified Conibear 120 traps in trapping martens. Progress Report. Wildlife Policy Branch, Ontario Ministry of Natural Resources, Queen's Park, Toronto, Canada.

———, J. A. BAKER, M. E. OBBARD, AND B. MALLOCH, editors. 1987. Wild furbearer management and conservation in North America. Ontario Ministry of Natural Resources, Toronto, Canada.

O'FARRELL, M. J., W. A. CLARK, F. H. EMMERSON, S. M. JUAREZ, F. R. KAY, T. M. O'FARRELL, AND T. Y. GOODLETT. 1994. Use of a mesh live trap for small mammals: are results from Sherman live traps deceptive? Journal of Mammalogy 75:692–699.

O'GARA, B. W., AND D. C. GETZ. 1986. Capturing golden eagles using a helicopter and net gun. Wildlife Society Bulletin 14:400–402.

OKARMA, H., AND W. JĄDRZEJEWSKI. 1997. Livetrapping wolves with nets. Wildlife Society Bulletin 25:78–82.

OLSEN, G. H., R. G. LINSCOMBE, V. L. WRIGHT, AND R. A. HOLMES. 1988. Reducing injuries to terrestrial furbearers by using padded foothold traps. Wildlife Society Bulletin 16:303–307.

———, S. B. LINHART, R. A. HOLMES, G. J. DASCH, AND C. B. MALE. 1986. Injuries to coyotes caught in padded and unpadded steel foothold traps. Wildlife Society Bulletin 14:219–223.

OLSON, D. H., W. P. LEONARD, AND R. B. BURY, editors. 1997. Sampling amphibians in lentic habitats: methods and approaches for the Pacific Northwest. Northwest Fauna 4. Society for Northwest Vertebrate Biology, Olympia, Washington, USA.

ONDERKA, D. K. 1999. Pathological examination as an aid for trap selection guidelines: usefulness and limitations. Pages 47–51 in G. Proulx, editor. Mammal trapping. Alpha Wildlife Research & Management Ltd., Sherwood Park, Alberta, Canada.

———, D. L. SKINNER, AND A. W. TODD. 1990. Injuries to coyotes and other species caused by four models of footholding devices. Wildlife Society Bulletin 18:175–182.

OSTROWSKI, S., E. FROMONT, AND B.-U. MEYBURG. 2001. A capture technique for wintering and migrating steppe eagles in southwestern Saudi Arabia. Wildlife Society Bulletin 29:265–268.

OTTO, J. E. 1983. An automatic nest trap for pied-billed grebes. North American Bird Bander 8:52–53.

PACK, J. C., C. I. TAYLOR, D. A. SWANSON, AND S. A. WARNER. 1996. Evaluation of wild turkey trapping techniques in West Virginia. Proceedings of the Annual Conference of the Southeastern Association of Fish and Wildlife Agencies 50:436–441.

PADGETT-FLOHR, G., AND M. R. JENNINGS. 2001. An economical safehouse for small mammals in pitfall traps. California Fish and Game 87:72–74.

PALMEIRIM, J. M., AND L. RODRIGUES. 1993. The 2-minute harp trap for bats. Bat Research News 34:60–64.

PALMER, D. T., D. A. ANDREWS, R. O. WINTERS, AND J. W. FRANCIS. 1980. Removal techniques to control an enclosed deer herd. Wildlife Society Bulletin 8:29–33.

PALMISANO, A. W., AND H. H. DUPUIE. 1975. An evaluation of steel traps for taking fur animals in coastal Louisiana. Proceedings of the Annual Conference of the Southeastern Association of Game and Fish Commissioners 29:342–347.

PARKER, G. R. 1983. An evaluation of trap types for harvesting muskrats in New Brunswick. Wildlife Society Bulletin 11:339–343.

PARMENTER, C. A., T. L. YATES, R. R. PARMENTER, J. N. MILLS, J. E. CHILDS, M. L. CAMPBELL, J. L. DUNNUM, AND J. MILNER. 1998. Small mammal survival and trapability in mark-recapture monitoring programs for hantavirus. Journal of Wildlife Diseases 34:1–12.

PARRIS, K. M., T. W. NORTON, AND R. B. CUNNINGHAM. 1999. A comparison of techniques for sampling amphibians in the forests of southeast Queensland, Australia. Herpetologica 55:271–283.

PATERSON, A. 1998. A new capture technique for arboreal lizards. Herpetological Review 29:159.

PATON, P. W. C., C. J. RALPH, AND J. SEAY. 1991. A mist net design for capturing marbled murrelets. North American Bird Bander 16:123–126.

PATTERSON, K., C. A. HASKELL, AND J. H. SCHULZ. 1993. A modified restraining device for mourning doves. Journal of Field Ornithology 64:413–416.

PATTON, D. R., H. G. HUDAK, AND T. D. RATCLIFF. 1976. Trapping, anesthetizing and marking the Abert squirrel. U.S. Department of Agriculture, Forest Service, Research Note RM-307.

PEARMAN, P. B., A. M. VELASCO, AND A. LOPEZ. 1995. Tropical amphibian monitoring: a comparison of methods for detecting inter-site variation in species' composition. Herpetologica 51:325–337.

PEARSON, D. F., AND L. F. RUGGIERO. 2003. Transects versus grid trapping arrangements for sample-mammal communities. Wildlife Society Bulletin 31:454–459.

PEDERSON, J. C., AND D. H. NISH. 1975. The band-tailed pigeon in Utah. Division of Wildlife Resources, Publication 75–1. Utah Department of Natural Resources, Salt Lake City, USA.

PELREN, E. C., AND J. A. CRAWFORD. 1995. A trap for blue grouse. Great Basin Naturalist 55:284–285.

PENKALA, J. M. 1978. An evaluation of muskrat trapping systems and new techniques. Job Progress Report, Federal Aid Project W-59-R-1, Job I-C. New Jersey Division of Fish, Game and Wildlife, Trenton, USA.

PÉREZ, J. M., J. E. GRANADOS, I. RUIZ-MARTINEZ, AND M. CHIROSA. 1997. Capturing Spanish ibexes with corral traps. Wildlife Society Bulletin 25:89–92.

PERKINS, D. W., AND M. L. HUNTER, JR. 2002. Effects of placing sticks in pitfall traps on amphibian and small mammal capture rates. Herpetological Review 33:282–284.

PETERLE, T. J. 1956. Trapping techniques and banding returns for Michigan sharp-tailed grouse. Journal of Wildlife Management 20:50–55.

PETERSON, L. M., AND J. A. THOMAS. 1998. Performance of Trailmaster® infrared sensors in monitoring captive coyotes. Wildlife Society Bulletin 26:592–596.

PEYTON, L. J., AND G. F. SHIELDS. 1979. A drop net for catching shorebirds. North American Bird Bander 4:97–102.

PHILLIPS, R. L. 1996. Evaluation of 3 types of snares for capturing coyotes. Wildlife Society Bulletin 24:107–110.

———, AND K. S. GRUVER. 1996. Performance of the Paws-I-Trip™ pan tension device on 3 types of traps. Wildlife Society Bulletin 24:119–122.

———, AND C. MULLIS. 1996. Expanded field testing of the No. 3 Victor Soft Catch trap. Wildlife Society Bulletin 24:128–131.

———, F. S. BLOM, AND R. M. ENGEMAN. 1990a. Responses of captive coyotes to chemical attractants. Proceedings of the Vertebrate Pest Conference 14:285–290.

———, ———, AND R. E. JOHNSON. 1990b. An evaluation of breakaway snares for use in coyote control. Proceedings of the Vertebrate Pest Conference 14:255–259.

———, K. S. GRUVER, AND E. S. WILLIAMS. 1996. Leg injuries to coyotes captured in three types of foothold traps. Wildlife Society Bulletin 24:260–263.

———, F. S. BLOM, G. J. DASCH, AND J. W. GUTHRIE. 1992. Field evaluations of three types of coyote traps. Proceedings of the Vertebrate Pest Conference 15:393–395.

PICMAN, J. 1979. A new technique for trapping red-winged blackbirds. North American Bird Bander 4:56–57.

PIMLOTT, D. H., AND W. J. CARBERRY. 1958. North American moose transplantations and handling techniques. Journal of Wildlife Management 22:51–62.

PINKOWSKI, B. C. 1978. Habituation of adult eastern bluebirds to a nest-box trap. Bird-Banding 49:125–129.

PIPAS, M. J., G. H. MATSCHKE, AND G. R. McCANN. 2000. Evaluation of the efficiency of three types of traps for capturing pocket gophers. Proceedings of the Vertebrate Pest Conference 19:385–388.

PITTMAN, M. T., B. P. McKINNEY, AND G. GUZMAN. 1995. Ecology of the mountain lion on Big Bend Ranch State Park in Trans-Pecos, Texas. Proceedings of the Annual Conference of the Southeastern Association of Fish and Wildlife Agencies 49:552–559.

PLICE, L., AND T. G. BALGOOYEN. 1999. A remotely operated trap for American kestrels using nest boxes. Journal of Field Ornithology 70:158–162.

PLUMPTON, D. L., AND R. S. LUTZ. 1992. Multiple-capture techniques for burrowing owls. Wildlife Society Bulletin 20:426–428.

———, D. I. DOWNING, D. E. ANDERSEN, AND J. M. LOCKHART. 1995. A new method of capturing buteonine hawks. Journal of Raptor Research 29:141–143.

POELKER, R. J., AND H. D. HARTWELL. 1973. Black bear of Washington: its biology, natural history and relationship to forest regeneration. Biological Bulletin 14. Washington State Game Department,

Olympia, USA.

POTTS, W. K., AND T. A. SORDAHL. 1979. The gong method for capturing shorebirds and other ground-roosting species. North American Bird Bander 4:106–107.

POTVIN, F., AND L. BRETON. 1988. Use of a net gun for capturing white-tailed deer, *Odocoileus virginianus,* on Anticosti Island, Quebec. Canadian Field-Naturalist 102:697–700.

PREVOST, Y. A., AND J. M. BAKER. 1984. A perch snare for catching ospreys. Journal of Wildlife Management 48:991–993.

PRIBIL, S. 1997. An effective trap for the house wren. North American Bird Bander 22:6–9.

PROUDFOOT, G. A. 2002. Two optic systems assist removal of nestlings from nest cavities. Wildlife Society Bulletin 30:956–959.

———, AND E. A. JACOBS. 2001. Bow net equipped with radio alarm. Wildlife Society Bulletin 29:543–545.

PROULX, G. 1990. Humane trapping program annual report 1989/90. Alberta Research Council, Edmonton, Canada.

———. 1991. Humane trapping program annual report 1990/91. Alberta Research Council, Edmonton, Canada.

———. 1997. A preliminary evaluation of four types of traps to capture northern pocket gophers, *Thomomys talpoides.* Canadian Field-Naturalist 111:640–643.

———. 1999a. A review of current mammal trap technology in North America. Pages 1–46 *in* G. Proulx, editor. Mammal trapping. Alpha Wildlife Research and Management Ltd., Sherwood Park, Alberta, Canada.

———. 1999b. Evaluation of the experimental PG trap to effectively kill northern pocket gophers. Pages 89–93 *in* G. Proulx, editor. Mammal trapping. Alpha Wildlife Research and Management Ltd., Sherwood Park, Alberta, Canada.

———, AND M. W. BARRETT. 1989. Animal welfare concerns and wildlife trapping: ethics, standards and commitments. Transactions of the Western Section of The Wildlife Society 25:1–6.

———, AND ———. 1990. Assessment of power snares to effectively kill red fox. Wildlife Society Bulletin 18:27–30.

———, AND ———. 1991. Evaluation of the Bionic trap to quickly kill mink (*Mustela vison*) in simulated natural environments. Journal of Wildlife Diseases 27:276–280.

———, AND ———. 1993a. Evaluation of mechanically improved Conibear 220 traps to quickly kill fisher (*Martes pennanti*) in simulated natural environments. Journal of Wildlife Diseases 29:317–323.

———, AND ———. 1993b. Evaluation of the Bionic trap to quickly kill fisher (*Martes pennanti*) in simulated natural environments. Journal of Wildlife Diseases 29:310–316.

———, AND ———. 1993c. Field testing the C120 Magnum trap for mink. Wildlife Society Bulletin 21:421–426.

———, AND R. K. DRESCHER. 1994. Assessment of rotating-jaw traps to humanely kill raccoons (*Procyon lotor*). Journal of Wildlife Diseases 30:335–339.

———, M. W. BARRETT, AND S. R. COOK. 1989a. The C120 magnum: an effective quick-kill trap for marten. Wildlife Society Bulletin 17:294–298.

———, ———, AND ———. 1990. The C120 Magnum with pan trigger: a humane trap for mink (*Mustela vison*). Journal of Wildlife Diseases 26:511–517.

———, S. R. COOK, AND M. W. BARRETT. 1989b. Assessment and preliminary development of the rotating-jaw Conibear 120 trap to effectively kill marten (*Martes americana*). Canadian Journal of Zoology 67:1074–1079.

———, A. J. KOLENOSKY, AND P. J. COLE. 1993a. Assessment of the Kania trap to humanely kill red squirrels (*Tamiasciurus hudsonicus*) in enclosures. Journal of Wildlife Diseases 29:324–329.

———, I. M. PAWLINA, AND R. K. WONG. 1993b. Re-evaluation of the C120 Magnum and the Bionic traps to humanely kill mink. Journal of Wildlife Diseases 29:184.

———, A. J. KOLENOSKY, P. J. COLE, AND R. K. DRESCHER. 1995. A humane killing trap for lynx (*Felis lynx*): the Conibear 330 with clamping bars. Journal of Wildlife Diseases 58:57–61.

———, M. J. BADRY, P. J. COLE, AND R. K. DRESCHER. 1993c. Assessment of the Sauvageau 2001–8 trap to effectively kill arctic fox. Wildlife Society Bulletin 21:132–135.

———, ———, ———, ———, AND ———. 1994a. A snowshoe hare snare system to minimize capture of marten. Wildlife Society Bulletin 22:639–643.

———, I. M. PAWLINA, D. K. ONDERKA, M. J. BADRY, AND K. SEIDEL. 1994b. Field evaluation of the number 1 1/2 steel-jawed leghold and the Sauvageau 2001–8 traps to humanely capture arctic fox. Wildlife

Society Bulletin 22:179–183.

———, D. K. ONDERKA, A. J. KOLENOSKY, P. J. COLE, R. K. DRESCHER, AND M. J. BADRY. 1993d. Injuries and behavior of raccoons (*Procyon lotor*) captured in the Soft Catch™ and the EGG™ traps in simulated natural environments. Journal of Wildlife Diseases 29:447–452.

PRUSS, S. D., N. L. COOL, R. J. HUDSON, AND A. R. GABOURY. 2002. Evaluation of a modified neck snare to live-capture coyotes. Wildlife Society Bulletin 30:508–516.

QUINN, H., AND T. PAPPAS. 1997. Restraining and marking method for snapping turtles, *Chelydra serpentina.* Herpetological Review 28:196–197.

RALPH, C. J., G. R. GEUPEL, P. PYLE, T. E. MARTIN, AND D. F. DESANTE. 1993. Handbook of field methods for monitoring landbirds. U.S. Department of Agriculture, Forest Service, General Technical Report PSW-144.

RAMSEY, C. W. 1968. A drop-net deer trap. Journal of Wildlife Management 32:187–190.

RAVELING, D. G. 1966. Factors affecting age ratios of samples of Canada geese caught with cannon-nets. Journal of Wildlife Management 30:682–691.

RECHT, M. A. 1981. A burrow-occluding trap for tortoises. Journal of Wildlife Management 45:557–559.

REDPATH, S. M., AND I. WYLLIE. 1994. Trap for capturing territorial owls, Journal of Raptor Research 28:115–117.

REEVES, H. M., A. E. GEIS, AND F. C. KNIFFIN. 1968. Mourning dove capture and banding. U.S. Department of the Interior, Fish and Wildlife Service, Special Scientific Report, Wildlife 117.

REMPEL, R. D., AND R. C. BERTRAM. 1975. The Stewart modified corral trap. California Fish and Game 61:237–239.

REMSEN, JR., J. V., AND D. A. GOOD. 1996. Misuse of data from mist-net captures to assess relative abundance in bird populations. Auk 113:381–398.

RENDELL, W. R., B. J. STUTCHBURY, AND R. J. ROBERTSON. 1989. A manual trap for capturing hole-nesting birds. North American Bird Bander 14:109–111.

REYNOLDS, R. T., AND B. D. LINKHART. 1984. Methods and materials for capturing and monitoring flammulated owls. Great Basin Naturalist 44:49–51.

RICHARDSON, D. M., J. W. BRADFORD, B. J. GENTRY, AND J. L. HALL. 1998. Evaluation of a pick-up tool for removing red-cockaded woodpecker nestlings from cavities. Wildlife Society Bulletin 26:855–858.

RICHTER, K. O. 1995. A simple aquatic funnel trap and its application to wetland amphibian monitoring. Herpetological Review 26:90–91.

RIEDEL, J. 1988. Snaring as a beaver control technique in South Dakota. U.S. Department of Agriculture, Forest Service, General Technical Report RM-154.

RIEFFENBERGER, J. C., AND F. FERRIGNO. 1970. Woodcock banding on the Cape May Peninsula, New Jersey. Bird Banding 41:1–10.

RIVAS, J. A., M. D. C. MUÑOZ, J. THORBJARNARSON, W. HOLMSTROM, AND P. CALLE. 1995. A safe method for handling large snakes in the field. Herpetological Review 26:138–139.

ROBARDS, F. C. 1960. Construction of a portable goose trap. Journal of Wildlife Management 24:329–331.

ROBERT, M., AND P. LAPORTE. 1997. Field techniques for studying breeding yellow rails. Journal of Field Ornithology 68:56–63.

ROBICHEAUX, B., AND G. LINSCOMBE. 1978. Effectiveness of live-traps for capturing furbearers in a Louisiana coastal marsh. Proceedings of the Annual Conference of the Southeastern Association of Fish and Wildlife Agencies 32:208–212.

ROGERS, J. P. 1964. A decoy trap for male lesser scaups. Journal of Wildlife Management 28:408–410.

RONGSTAD, O. J., AND R. A. MCCABE. 1984. Capture techniques. Pages 655–676 *in* L. K. Halls, editor. White-tailed deer: ecology and management. Stackpole Books, Harrisburg, Pennsylvania, USA.

ROPER, L. A., R. L. SCHMIDT, AND R. B. GILL. 1971. Techniques of trapping and handling mule deer in northern Colorado with notes on using automatic data processing for data analysis. Proceedings of the Western Association of State Game and Fish Commissioners 51:471–477.

ROSELL, F., AND B. HOVDE. 2001. Methods of aquatic and terrestrial netting to capture Eurasian beavers. Wildlife Society Bulletin 29:269–274.

ROSENFIELD, R. N., AND J. BIELEFELDT. 1993. Trapping techniques for breeding Cooper's hawks: two modifications. Journal of Raptor Research 27:171–172.

ROUTE, W. T., AND R. O. PETERSON. 1988. Distribution and abundance of river otters in Voyageurs National Park, Minnesota. U.S. Department of the Interior, National Park Service, Research/Resource Management Report MWR-10. Midwest Regional Office, Omaha, Nebraska, USA.

ROWSELL, H. C., J. RITCEY, AND F. COX. 1981. Assessment of effectiveness of trapping methods in the production of a humane death. Proceedings of the Worldwide Furbearer Conference 3:1647–1670.

RUFF, F. J. 1938. Trapping deer on the Pisgah National Game Preserve, North Carolina. Journal of Wildlife Management 2:151–161.

RUNGE, W. 1972. An efficient winter live-trapping technique for white-tailed deer. Technical Bulletin 1. Saskatchewan Department Natural Resources, Regina, Canada.

SABEAN, B., AND J. MILLS. 1994. Raccoon—6" × 6" body gripping trap study. Report. Nova Scotia Department of Natural Resources, Halifax, Canada.

SACKS, B. N., K. M. BLEJWAS, AND M. M. JAEGER. 1999. Relative vulnerability of coyotes to removal methods on a northern California ranch. Journal of Wildlife Management 63:939–949.

SAHR, D. P., AND F. F. KNOWLTON. 2000. Evaluation of tranquilizer trap devices (TTDs) for foothold traps used to capture gray wolves. Wildlife Society Bulletin 28:597–605.

SALYER, J. W. 1962. A bow-net trap for ducks. Journal of Wildlife Management 26:219–221.

SARGEANT, A. B. 1966. A live trap for pocket gophers. Journal of Mammalogy 47:729–731.

SAUNDERS, B. P., H. C. ROWSELL, AND I. W. HATTER. 1988. A better trap, the search continues. Canadian Trapper, Winter:3, 16.

SAUNDERS, G., AND S. HARRIS. 2000. Evaluation of attractants and bait preferences of captive red foxes (*Vulpes vulpes*). Wildlife Research 27:237–243.

———, B. KAY, AND H. NICOL. 1993. Factors affecting bait uptake and trapping success for feral pigs (*Sus scrofa*) in Kosciusko National Park. Wildlife Research 20:653–665.

SAVARD, J-P. L. 1985. Use of a mirror trap to capture territorial waterfowl. Journal of Field Ornithology 56:177–178.

SAVARIE, P. J., AND J. D. ROBERTS. 1979. Evaluation of oral central nervous system depressants in coyotes. Pages 270–277 *in* J. R. Beck, editor. Vertebrate pest control and management materials. Special Technical Publication 680. American Society for Testing and Materials, Philadelphia, Pennsylvania, USA.

———, K. A. FAGERSTONE, AND E. W. SCHAFER, JR. 1993. Update on the development of a tranquilizer trap device. Proceedings of the Great Plains Wildlife Damage Control Workshop 11:204–208.

SCHARF, C. S. 1985. A technique for trapping territorial magpies. North American Bird Bander 10:34–36.

SCHEMNITZ, S. D. 1961. Ecology of the scaled quail in the Oklahoma panhandle. Wildlife Monograph 8.

———. 1994. Capturing and handling wild animals. Pages 106–124 *in* T. A. Bookhout, editor. Research and management techniques for wildlife and habitats. Fifth edition. The Wildlife Society, Bethesda, Maryland, USA.

SCHIERBAUM, D., AND E. TALMAGE. 1954. A successful diving duck trap. New York Fish and Game Journal 1:116–117.

———, D. BENSON, L. W. DeGRAAF, AND D. D. FOLEY. 1959. Waterfowl banding in New York. New York Fish and Game Journal 6:86–102.

SCHMIDT, R. H., AND J. G. BRUNNER. 1981. A professional attitude toward humaneness. Wildlife Society Bulletin 9:289–291.

SCHROEDER, M. A. 1986. A modified noose pole for capturing grouse. North American Bird Bander 11:42.

———, AND C. E. BRAUN. 1991. Walk-in traps for capturing greater prairie-chickens on leks. Journal of Field Ornithology 62:378–385.

SCHULTZ, R. N., A. P. WYDEVEN, AND R. A. MEGOWN. 1996. Injury levels with five types of leg-hold traps in Wisconsin. Pages 38–39 *in* R. Earle, editor. Proceedings of the Fourteenth Midwest Furbearer Workshop. Michigan Department of Natural Resources, Lansing, USA.

SCHULTZ, V. 1950. A modified Stoddard quail trap. Journal of Wildlife Management 14:243.

SCOTT, N. J., editor. 1982. Herpetological communities. U.S. Department of the Interior, Fish and Wildlife Service, Wildlife Research Report 13.

SCOTTON, B. D., AND D. H. PLETSCHER. 1998. Evaluation of a capture technique for neonatal Dall sheep. Wildlife Society Bulletin 26:578–583.

SEAL, U. S., AND T. J. KREEGER. 1987. Chemical immobilization of furbearers. Pages 191–215 *in* M. Novak, J. A. Baker, M. E. Obbard, and B. Malloch, editors. Wild furbearer management and conservation in North America. Ontario Ministry of Natural Resources, Toronto, Canada.

SEAMANS, T. W., AND J. L. BELANT. 1999. Comparison of DRC-1339 and alpha-chloralose to reduce herring gull populations. Wildlife Society Bulletin 27:729–733.

SERENA, M. 1980. A new technique for capturing *Cnemidophorus*. Journal of Herpetology 14:91–92.

SERFASS, T. L., R. P. BROOKS, T. J. SWIMLEY, L. M. RYMON, AND A. H. HAYDEN. 1996. Considerations for capturing, handling, and translocating river otters. Wildlife Society Bulletin 24:25–31.

SEYMOUR, N. R. 1974. Territorial behavior of wild shovelers at Delta, Manitoba. Wildfowl 25:49–55.

SHAIFFER, C. W., AND G. L. KRAPU. 1978. A remote controlled system for capturing nesting waterfowl. Journal of Wildlife Management 42:668–669.

SHARP, D. E., AND J. T. LOKEMOEN. 1987. A decoy trap for breeding-season mallards in North Dakota. Journal of Wildlife Management 51:711–715.

SHIRLEY, M. G., R. G. LINSCOMBE, AND L. R. SEVIN. 1983. A live trapping and handling technique for river otter. Proceedings of the Annual Conference of the Southeastern Association of Fish and Wildlife Agencies 37:182–189.

SHIVIK, J. A. 1998. Brown tree snake response to visual and olfactory cues. Journal of Wildlife Management 62:105–111.

———, AND L. CLARK. 1997. Carrion seeking in brown tree snakes: importance of olfactory and visual cues. Journal of Experimental Zoology 279:549–553.

———, K. S. GRUVER, AND T. J. DeLIBERTO. 2000. Preliminary evaluation of new cable restraints to capture coyotes. Wildlife Society Bulletin 28:606–613.

SHULER, J. D. 1992. A cage trap for live-trapping mountain lions. Proceedings of the Vertebrate Pest Conference 15:368–370.

SHULER, J. F., D. E. SAMUEL, B. P. SHISSLER, AND M. R. ELLINGWOOD. 1986. A modified nightlighting technique for male American woodcock. Journal of Wildlife Management 50:384–387.

SIEVERT, G. A., P. T. ANDREADIS, AND T. S. CAMPBELL. 1999. A simple device for safely capturing herpetofauna from roads: the "Herp Scoop". Herpetological Review 30:156–157.

SILVY, N. J., AND R. J. ROBEL. 1967. Recordings used to help trap booming greater prairie chickens. Journal of Wildlife Management 31:370–373.

———, AND ———. 1968. Mist nets and cannon nets compared for capturing prairie chickens on booming grounds. Journal of Wildlife Management 32:175–178.

———, J. W. HARDIN, AND W. D. KLIMSTRA. 1975. Use of a portable net to capture free-ranging prairie chickens. Wildlife Society Bulletin 3:27–29.

SIMMONS, J. E. 2002. Herpetological collecting and collections management. Revised edition. Society for the Study of Amphibians and Reptiles. Herpetological Circular 13.

SKINNER, D. L., AND A. W. TODD. 1990. Evaluating efficiency of footholding devices for coyote capture. Wildlife Society Bulletin 18:166–175.

SKINNER, W. R., D. P. SNOW, AND N. F. PAYNE. 1998. A capture technique for juvenile willow ptarmigan. Wildlife Society Bulletin 26:111–112.

SLADE, N. A., M. A. EIFLER, N. M. GRUENHAGEN, AND A. L. DAVELOS. 1993. Differential effectiveness of standard and long Sherman live traps in capturing small mammals. Journal of Mammalogy 74:156–161.

SMITH, D. G., AND D. T. WALSH. 1981. A modified bal-chatri trap for capturing screech owls. North American Bird Bander 6:14–15.

SMITH, G. R., AND J. E. RETTIG. 1996. Effectiveness of aquatic funnel traps for sampling amphibian larvae. Herpetological Review 27:190–191.

SMITH, H. P., F. A. STORMER, AND R. D. GODFREY, JR. 1981. A collapsible quail trap. U.S. Department of Agriculture, Forest Service, Research Note RM-400.

SMITH, W. A. 1968. The band-tailed pigeon in California. California Fish and Game 54:4–16.

SMITH, W. K., K. E. CHURCH, J. S. TAYLOR, D. H. RUSCH, AND P. S. GIPSON. 2001. Modified decoy trapping of male ring-necked pheasant (*Phasianus colchicus*) and northern bobwhite (*Colinus virginianus*). Game and Wildlife Science 18:581–586.

SNEAD, I. E. 1950. A family type live trap, handling cage, and associated techniques for muskrats. Journal of Wildlife Management 14:67–79.

SNOW, W. D., H. L. MENDALL, AND W. B. KROHN. 1990. Capturing common eiders by night-lighting in coastal Maine. Journal of Field Ornithology 61:67–72.

SORDAHL, T. A. 1980. A nest trap for recurvirostrids and other ground-nesting birds. North American Bird Bander 5:1–3.

SOULE, N., AND A. J. LINDBERG. 1994. The use of leverage to facilitate the search for the hellbender. Herpetological Review 25:16.

SOUTHERN, W. E. 1972. Use of cannon-nets in ring-billed gull colonies. Inland Bird Banding News 44:83–93.

SOWLS, L. K. 1955. Prairie ducks: a study of their behavior, ecology, and management. Wildlife Management Institute, Washington, D.C., and The Stackpole Company, Harrisburg, Pennsylvania, USA.

SPARROWE, R. D., AND P. F. SPRINGER. 1970. Seasonal activity patterns of white-tailed deer in eastern South Dakota. Journal of Wildlife Management 34:420–431.

SPILLETT, J. J., AND R. S. ZOBELL. 1967. Innovations in trapping and handling pronghorn antelopes. Journal of Wildlife Management 31:347–351.

STAFFORD, S., C. T. LEE, AND L. E. WILLIAMS, JR. 1966. Drive trapping white-tailed deer. Proceedings of the Annual Conference of the Southeastern Association of Game and Fish Commissioners 20:63–69.

STANBACK, M. T., AND W. D. KOENIG. 1994. Techniques for capturing birds inside natural cavities. Journal of Field Ornithology 65:70–75.

STEENHOF, K., G. P. CARPENTER, AND J. C. BEDNARZ. 1994. Use of mist nets and a live great horned owl to capture breeding American kestrels. Journal of Raptor Research 28:194–196.

STEGER, G. N., AND D. L. NEAL. 1981. Night-lighting: a technique to locate and capture fawns. Transactions of the California-Nevada Chapter of The Wildlife Society Annual Conference 17:155–158.

STEVENS, W. E. 1953. The northwestern muskrat of the Mackenzie delta, Northwest Territories, 1947–48. Wildlife Management Bulletin Series 1, Number 8. Canadian Wildlife Service, Ottawa, Ontario, Canada.

STEWART, P. A. 1954. Combination substratum and automatic trap for nesting mourning doves. Bird-Banding 25:6–8.

———. 1971. An automatic trap for use on bird nesting boxes. Bird-Banding 42:121–122.

STEWART, R. E. 1951. Clapper rail populations of the Middle Atlantic States. Transactions of the North American Wildlife Conference 16:421–430.

STOKES, A. E., B. B. SCHULTZ, R. M. DEGRAAF, AND C. R. GRIFFIN. 2000. Setting mist nets from platforms in the forest canopy. Journal of Field Ornithology 71:57–65.

STOUFFER, P. C., AND D. F. CACCAMISE. 1991. Capturing American crows using alpha-chloralose. Journal of Field Ornithology 62:450–453.

STRONG, D., B. LEATHERMAN, AND B. H. BRATTSTROM. 1993. Two new simple methods for catching small fast lizards. Herpetological Review 24:22–23.

STUTCHBURY, B. J., AND R. J. ROBERTSON. 1986. A simple trap for catching birds in nest boxes. Journal of Field Ornithology 57:64–65.

SULLIVAN, J. B., C. A. DEYOUNG, S. L. BEASOM, J. R. HEFFELFINGER, S. P. COUGHLIN, AND M. W. HELLICKSON. 1991. Drive-netting deer: incidence of mortality. Wildlife Society Bulletin 19:393–396.

SUTTON, P. E., H. R. MUSHINSKY, AND E. D. MCCOY. 1999. Comparing the use of pitfall drift fences and cover boards for sampling the threatened sand skink. (*Neoseps reynoldsi*). Herpetological Review 30:149–151.

SWANK, W. G. 1952. Trapping and marking of adult nesting doves. Journal of Wildlife Management 16:87–90.

SWANN, D. E., A. J. KUENZI, M. L. MORRISON, AND S. DESTEFANO. 1997. Effects of sampling blood on survival of small mammals. Journal of Mammalogy 78:908–913.

SWANSON, D. A., AND J. H. RAPPOLE. 1994. Capturing nesting white-winged doves in subtropical thornforest habitat in south Texas. Wildlife Society Bulletin 22:500–502.

SWEITZER, R. A., B. J. GONZALES, I. A. GARDNER, D. VAN VUREN, J. D. WAITHMAN, AND W. M. BOYCE. 1997. A modified panel trap and immobilization technique for capturing multiple wild pig. Wildlife Society Bulletin 25:699–705.

SWENSON, J. E., AND S. SWENSON. 1977. Nightlighting as a method for capturing nighthawks and other caprimulgids. Bird-Banding 48:279–280.

SYKES, JR., P. W. 1989. A technique to prevent capturing birds in unattended, furled mist nets. North American Bird Bander 14:45–46.

SZARO, R. C., L. H. SIMONS, AND S. C. BELFIT. 1988. Comparative effectiveness of pitfalls and live-traps in measuring small mammal community structure. Pages 282–288 in R. C. Szaro, K. E. Severson, and D. R. Patton, technical coordinators. Management of amphibians, reptiles, and small mammals in North America. U.S. Department of

Agriculture, Forest Service, General Technical Report RM 166.

TAKOS, M. J. 1943. Trapping and banding muskrats. Journal of Wildlife Management 7:400–407.

TANNER, W. D., AND G. L. BOWERS. 1948. A method for trapping ruffed grouse. Journal of Wildlife Management 12:330–331.

TEW, T. E., I. A. TODD, AND D. W. MACDONALD. 1994. The effects of trap spacing on population estimation of small mammals. Journal of Zoology (London) 233:340–344.

THERRIEN, J. E. 1996. Testing three cage traps for house sparrow capture. Sialia 18:105–109.

THIEL, R. P. 1985. A snare for capturing nesting belted kingfishers. North American Bird Bander 10:2–3.

THOMAS, R., AND B. NOVAK. 1991. Helicopter drive-netting techniques for mule deer capture on Great Basin ranges. California Fish and Game 77:194–200.

THOMPSON, J. R., V. C. BLEICH, S. G. TORRES, AND G. P. MULCAHY. 2001. Translocation techniques for mountain sheep: does the method matter? Southwestern Naturalist 46:87–93.

THOMPSON, M. C., AND R. DELONG. 1967. The use of cannon and rocket-projected nets for trapping shorebirds. Bird-Banding 38:214–218.

THOMPSON, M. J., R. E. HENDERSON, T. O. LEMKE, AND B. A. STERLING. 1989. Evaluation of a collapsible Clover trap for elk. Wildlife Society Bulletin 17:287–290.

THORSTROM, R. K. 1996. Methods for capturing tropical forest birds of prey. Wildlife Society Bulletin 24:516–520.

TIDEMANN, C. R., AND R. A. LOUGHLAND. 1993. A harp trap for large megachiropterans. Wildlife Research 20:607–611.

TIMM, D. E., AND R. G. BROMLEY. 1976. Driving Canada geese by helicopter. Wildlife Society Bulletin 4:180–181.

TOEPFER, J. E., J. A. NEWELL, AND J. MONARCH. 1988. A method for trapping prairie grouse hens on display grounds. Pages 21–31 in Prairie chickens on the Sheyenne National Grasslands. U.S. Department of Agriculture, Forest Service, General Technical Report RM-159.

TOLAND, B. 1985. A trapping technique for trap-wary American kestrels. North American Bird Bander 10:11.

TOLLE, D. A., AND T. A. BOOKHOUT. 1974. A comparison of two methods for capturing roosting wood ducks. Wildlife Society Bulletin 2:50–55.

TOMLINSON, R. E. 1963. A method for drive-trapping dusky grouse. Journal of Wildlife Management 27:563–566.

TRAVAINI, A., R. M. PECK, AND S. C. ZAPATA. 2001. Selection of odor attractants and meat delivery methods to control Culpeo foxes (*Pseudalopex culpaeus*) in Patagonia. Wildlife Society Bulletin 29:1089–1096.

TROYER, W. A., R. J. HENSEL, AND K. E. DURLEY. 1962. Live-trapping and handling of brown bears. Journal of Wildlife Management 26:330–331.

TRUMP, R. E., AND G. O. HENDRICKSON. 1943. Methods for trapping and tagging woodchuck. Journal of Wildlife Management 7:420–421.

TUCKER, J. K. 1994. An "easy" method to remove common snapping turtles (*Chelydra serpentina*) from Legler hoop traps. Herpetological Review 25:13.

TULLAR, JR., B. F. 1984. Evaluation of a padded leg-hold trap for capturing foxes and raccoons. New York Fish and Game Journal 31:97–103.

TURKOWSKI, F. J., A. R. ARMISTEAD, AND S. B. LINHART. 1984. Selectivity and effectiveness of pan tension devices for coyote foot-hold traps. Journal of Wildlife Management 48:700–708.

TURNER, L. B. 1956. Improved technique in goose trapping with cannon-type net traps. Journal of Wildlife Management 20:201–203.

VALKENBURG, P., R. D. BOERTJE, AND J. L. DAVIS. 1983. Effects of darting and netting on caribou in Alaska. Journal of Wildlife Management 47:1233–1237.

VAN BALLENBERGHE, V. 1984. Injuries to wolves sustained during live-capture. Journal of Wildlife Management 48:1425–1429.

VAN HORN, R. C., AND R. J. DOUGLASS. 2000. Disinfectant effects on capture rates of deer mice (*Peromyscus maniculatus*). American Midland Naturalist 143:257–260.

VARGAS, G. A., K. L. KRAKAUER, J. L. EGREMY-HERNANDEZ, AND M. J. MCCOID. 2000. Sticky trapping and lizard survivorship. Herpetological Review 31:23.

VERCAUTEREN, K. C., J. BERINGER, AND S. E. HYGNSTROM. 1999. Use of netted cage traps for capturing white-tailed deer. Pages 155–164 in G. Proulx, editor. Mammal trapping. Alpha Wildlife Research and Management Ltd., Sherwood Park, Alberta, Canada.

VERME, L. J. 1962. An automatic tagging device for deer. Journal of Wildlife Management 26:387–392.

VERNES, K. 1993. A drive fence for capturing small forest-dwelling macropods. Wildlife Research 20:189–191.

VIEIRA, E. M. 1998. A technique for trapping small mammals in the forest canopy. Mammalia 62:306–310.

VIRCHOW, D. R., AND D. HOGELAND. 1994. Bobcat. Pages C35-C43 in S. E. Hynstrom, R. M. Timm, and G. E. Larson, editors. Prevention and control of wildlife damage. University of Nebraska Cooperative Extension Service, Lincoln, USA.

VOGT, R. C. 1980. New methods for trapping aquatic turtles. Copeia 1980:368–371.

———, AND R. L. HINE. 1982. Evaluation of techniques for assessment of amphibian and reptile populations in Wisconsin. Pages 201–217 in N. J. Scott, Jr., editor. Herpetological communities. Symposium of the Society for the Study of Amphibians and Reptiles. U.S. Department of the Interior, Fish and Wildlife Service, Wildlife Research Report 13.

WAKKINEN, W. L., K. P. REESE, J. W. CONNELLY, AND R. A. FISCHER. 1992. An improved spotlighting technique for capturing sage grouse. Wildlife Society Bulletin 20:425–426.

WALCZAK, J. T. 1991. A technique for the safe restraint of venomous snakes. Herpetological Review 22:17–18.

WALDIEN, D. L., AND J. P. HAYES. 1999. A technique to capture bats using hand-held mist nets. Wildlife Society Bulletin 27:197–200.

WANG, X.-H., AND C. H. TROST. 2000. Trapping territorial black-billed magpies. Journal of Field Ornithology 71:730–735.

WANG, Y., AND D. M. FINCH. 2002. Consistency of mist netting and point counts in assessing landbird species richness and relative abundance during migration. Condor 104:59–72.

WARBURTON, B. 1982. Evaluation of seven trap models as humane and catch-efficient possum traps. New Zealand Journal of Zoology 9:409–418

———. 1992. Victor foot-hold traps for catching Australian brushtail possums in New Zealand: capture efficiency and injuries. Wildlife Society Bulletin 20:67–73.

WARD, F. P., AND D. P. MARTIN. 1968. An improved cage trap for birds of prey. Bird-Banding 39:18–26.

WATSON, J. W. 1985. Trapping, marking and radio-monitoring rough-legged hawks. North American Bird Bander 10:9–10.

WAY, J. G., I. M. ORTEGA, P. J. AUGER, AND E. G. STRAUSS. 2002. Box-trapping eastern coyotes in southeastern Massachusetts. Wildlife Society Bulletin 30:695–702.

WEAVER, D. K., AND J. A. KADLEC. 1970. A method for trapping breeding adult gulls. Bird-Banding 41:28–31.

WEAVER, K. M., D. H. ARNER, C. MASON, AND J. J. HARTLEY. 1985. A guide to using snares for beaver capture. Southern Journal of Applied Forestry 9:141–146.

WEBB, W. L. 1943. Trapping and marking white-tailed deer. Journal of Wildlife Management 7:346–348.

WEGNER, W. A. 1981. A carrion baited noose trap for American kestrels. Journal of Wildlife Management 45:248–250.

WELLER, M. W. 1957. An automatic nest-trap for waterfowl. Journal of Wildlife Management 21:456–458.

WELSH, JR., H. H., AND A. J. LIND. 2002. Multiscale habitat relationships of stream amphibians in the Klamath-Siskiyou region of California and Oregon. Journal of Wildlife Management 66:581–602.

WHALEN, D. M., AND B. D. WATTS. 1999. The influence of audio-lures on capture patterns of migrant northern saw-whet owls. Journal of Field Ornithology 70:163–168.

WHITAKER, A. H. 1967. Baiting pitfall traps for small lizards. Herpetologica 23:309–310.

WHITE, G. C., AND R. M. BARTMANN. 1994. Drop nets versus helicopter net guns for capturing mule deer fawns. Wildlife Society Bulletin 22:248–252.

WHITING, M. J. 1998. Increasing lizard capture success using baited glue traps. Herpetological Review 29:34.

WHITTAKER, J. C., G. A. FELDHAMER, AND E. M. CHARLES. 1998. Capture of mice, *Peromyscus,* in two sizes of Sherman live traps. Canadian Field-Naturalist 112:527–529.

WILLIAMS, R. D., J. E. GATES, AND C. H. HOCUTT. 1981. An evaluation of known and potential sampling techniques for hellbender, *Cryptobranchus alleganiensis.* Journal of Herpetology 15:23–27.

WILLIAMSON, M. J., AND M. R. PELTON. 1971. New design for a large portable mammal trap. Proceedings of the Annual Conference of the Southeastern Association of Game and Fish Commissioners 25:315–322.

WILSON, D. E., F. R. COLE, J. D. NICHOLS, R. RUDRAN, AND M. S. FOSTER. 1996. Measuring and monitoring biological diversity. Standard methods for mammals. Smithsonian Institution Press, Washington, D.C., USA.

WILSON, J. J., AND T. J. MARET. 2002. A comparison of two methods for estimating the abundance of amphibians in aquatic habitats.

Herpetological Review 33:108–110.

WILSON, R. R., AND R. S. ALLAN. 1996. Mist netting from a boat in forested wetlands. Journal of Field Ornithology 67:82–85.

WINCHELL, C. S. 1999. An efficient technique to capture complete broods of burrowing owls. Wildlife Society Bulletin 27:193–196.

———, AND J. W. TURMAN. 1992. A new trapping technique for burrowing owls-the noose rod. Journal of Field Ornithology 63:66–70.

WITMER, G. W., R. E. MARSH, AND G. H. MATSCHKE. 1999. Trapping considerations for the fossorial pocket gopher. Pages 131–139 in G. Proulx, editor. Mammal trapping. Alpha Wildlife Research and Management Ltd., Sherwood Park, Alberta, Canada.

WITZ, B. W. 1996. A new device for capturing small and medium-sized lizards by hand: the lizard grabber. Herpetological Review 27:130–131.

WOLF, M., AND G. O. BATZLI. 2002. Relationship of previous trap occupancy to capture of white-footed mice (*Peromyscus leucopus*). Journal of Mammalogy 83:728–733.

WOLINSKI, R. A., AND E. A. PIKE. 1985. Hoop-net for the capture of barn and cliff swallows. North American Bird Bander 10:4–5.

WOODS, J. G., D. PAETKAU, D. LEWIS, B. N. MCLELLAN, M. PROCTOR, AND C. STROBECK. 1999. Genetic tagging of free-ranging black and brown bears. Wildlife Society Bulletin 27:616–627.

WOOLF, A., AND C. NIELSEN. 2002. The bobcat in Illinois. Southern Illinois University, Carbondale, USA.

WOOTEN, W. A. 1955. A trapping technique for band-tailed pigeons. Journal of Wildlife Management 19:411–412.

WORONECKI, P. P., AND W. L. THOMAS. 1995. Status of alpha-chloralose and other immobilizing/euthanizing chemicals within the animal damage control program. Proceedings of the Eastern Wildlife Damage Control Conference 6:123–127.

———, R. A. DOLBEER, T. W. SEAMANS, AND W. R. LANCE. 1992. Alpha-choralose efficacy in capturing nuisance waterfowl and pigeons and current status of FDA registration. Proceedings of the Vertebrate Pest Conference 15:72–78.

WUNZ, G. A. 1984. Rocket net innovations for capturing wild turkeys and waterfowl. Transactions of the Northeast Section of The Wildlife Society 41:219.

———. 1987. Rocket-net innovations for capturing wild turkeys. Turkitat 6(2):2–4.

YAHNER, R. H., AND C. G. MAHAN. 1992. Use of a laboratory restraining device on wild red squirrels. Wildlife Society Bulletin 20:399–401.

YERKES, T. 1997. A trap for ducks using artificial nesting structures. Journal of Field Ornithology 68:147–149.

YORK, D. L., J. E. DAVIS, JR., J. L. CUMMINGS, AND E. A. WILSON. 1998. Pileated woodpecker capture using a mist net and taped call. North American Bird Bander 23:81–82.

YOSEF, R., AND F. E. LOHRER. 1992. A composite treadle/bal-chatri trap for loggerhead shrikes. Wildlife Society Bulletin 20:116–118.

YOUNG, J. G., AND S. E. HENKE. 1999. Effects of domestic rabbit urine on trap response in cottontail rabbits. Wildlife Society Bulletin 27:306–309.

YUNGER, J. A., AND L. A. RANDA. 1999. Trap decontamination using hypochlorite: effects on trappability of small mammals. Journal of Mammalogy 80:1336–1340.

———, R. BREWER, AND R. SNOOK. 1992. A method for decreasing trap mortality of *Sorex.* Canadian Field-Naturalist 106:249–251.

YUNICK, R. P. 1990. Some banding suggestions at nest boxes. North American Bird Bander 15:146–147.

ZAHM, G., E. S. JEMISOM, AND R. E. KIRBY. 1987. Behavior and capture of wood ducks in pecan orchards. Journal of Field Ornithology 58:474–479.

ZANI, P. A., AND L. J. VITT. 1995. Techniques for capturing arboreal lizards. Herpetological Review 26:136–137.

ZELIN, S., J. C. JOFRIET, K. PERCIVAL, AND D. J. ABDINOOR. 1983. Evaluation of humane traps: momentum thresholds for four furbearers. Journal of Wildlife Management 47:863–868.

ZEMLICKA, D. E., D. P. SAHR, P. J. SAVARIE, F. F. KNOWLTON, F. S. BLOM, AND J. L. BELANT. 1997. Development and registration of a practical tranquilizer trap device (TTD) for foot-hold traps. Proceedings of the Great Plains Wildlife Damage Control Workshop 13:42–45.

ZICUS, M. C. 1975. Capturing nesting Canada geese with mist nets. Bird-Banding 46:168–169.

———. 1989. Automatic trap for waterfowl using nest boxes. Journal of Field Ornithology 60:109–111.

ZOELLICK, B. W., AND N. S. SMITH. 1986. Capturing desert kit foxes at dens with box traps. Wildlife Society Bulletin 14:284–286.

ZWICKEL, F. C., AND J. F. BENDELL. 1967. A snare for capturing blue grouse. Journal of Wildlife Management 31:202–204.

11

CHEMICAL IMMOBILIZATION OF NORTH AMERICAN MAMMALS

Thomas J. Roffe, Steven J. Sweeney, and Keith E. Aune

INTRODUCTION

Chemical immobilization of wildlife is use of a pharmacologically active substance (drug) to decrease or eliminate an animal's ability to move so that it can be captured and handled for sampling, measurement, instrumentation, or translocation. It differs from physical restraint in types of equipment and conditions under which it is used. Each method has unique advantages and disadvantages. In many instances, physical restraint using devices such as nets, traps, snares and corrals has been effective for capturing wild animals (Schemnitz 2005). In some situations, a more targeted approach using chemical restraint is preferred. Examples include selecting specific animals or cohorts for study, minimizing chasing and disruption of non-target herd animals, lessening public attention to capture operations in parks and reserves, and conducting research and management actions on a limited budget. Frequently, a combination of physical and chemical restraint is used to secure wild animals for handling.

The importance of planning and preparation cannot be overstated when chemically immobilizing wildlife. The success or failure of the entire project may depend on the ability to successfully capture animals; capture costs will likely consume the majority of project resources. The amount of effort devoted to preparatory tasks will affect the quality of the capture operation and effectiveness of associated research or management activity. Clear lines of communication are essential and a competent team leader must be identified. This person is responsible for ensuring safety and health of team members and captured animals, emergency medical management, assigning and communicating roles and expectations of team members, and assuring that records of all activities and data relevant to capture are maintained.

The capture team leader is frequently responsible for sampling, data collection, and/or marking of the animal. At times, these roles may be split between a capture team leader and principle investigator or wildlife manager. However, it must be clear that during field operations the capture team leader has the final responsibility and authority for all procedures to safeguard human and animal health and safety.

Equipment and supplies must be checked for condition and completeness, and everyone must know and execute their respective duties for the operation to be effective. During and/or after capture operations, the team should meet to discuss any needed improvements that will minimize adverse outcomes and maximize future successes.

Regulations

Two federal agencies and several laws affect use of drugs to immobilize wildlife. The intent of these agencies and laws is to ensure the safety of human food, require expertise in drug application, and prevent abuse of drugs.

Human food safety and drug expertise requirements are the purview of the Food and Drug Administration (FDA), which regulates specific conditions for use of drugs in animals and people. In general, a drug must be FDA approved before use in an animal, and it can only be used under the conditions specified on the label, including species, intended use, dosage, and withdrawal time. "Extra-label use" is any use of a drug (species, gender, age, dose, route of administration, etc.) that is outside the conditions specifically identified on the label. Extra-label use is allowed by licensed veterinarians in accordance with established guidelines but does not exempt them from regulations applying to drug residues in meat or milk. All approved drugs used for wildlife species are prescription drugs, which requires use only by, or on the order of, a licensed veterinarian. Most drug uses for wildlife are extra-label applications that have not been formally tested and licensed for the particular species of interest.

The Food and Drug Administration has approved only 4 drugs for use in wildlife. Carfentanil, xylazine, and yohimbine are labeled for use in certain members of Cervidae while ketamine is only approved for use in primates. The Animal Medicinal Drug Use Clarification Act of 1996 allows extra-label use of approved animal and human drugs under certain conditions. In non-food-producing animals, extra-label use is permitted if the drug is approved by FDA, is used by or on order of a licensed veterinarian, and there is a valid veterinarian/client/patient relationship. In food-producing animals (including game species of wildlife), extra-label use is allowed under specific conditions: (1) there is no approved alternative drug labeled for such use (or the approved drug is clinically ineffective), (2) the veterinarian has established a substantially extended withdrawal time, (3) treated animals can be individually identified (e.g., by ear tags and/or collars), and (4) assigned withdrawal times can be assured so there are no illegal residues. The Food Animal Residue Avoidance Database recommends that carfentanil, xylazine, and yohimbine not be used in free-ranging cervids within 30 days of any hunting season. Actual safe withdrawal times are unknown and, frequently, even more conservative times are used.

Many immobilizing drugs are also controlled substances regulated by the Drug Enforcement Administration under the Controlled Substances Act. This Act places substances into 1 of 5 schedules (Box 1). Scheduling of a drug is based on the substance's medicinal value, harmfulness, and potential for abuse or addiction. The Controlled Substances Act requires an individual to have a special registration number to possess a controlled substance. Some specific drugs, such as carfentanil, have additional registration requirements. All registered individuals must maintain complete and accurate inventories, and records of all transactions and use of controlled substances as well as secured storage of controlled substances.

Many biologists have obtained a Drug Enforcement Administration registration number and can purchase scheduled drugs through veterinary product distributors. By law, they cannot use these drugs without veterinary approval. The FDA requires that a valid veterinarian/client/patient relationship be established for prescription drug use. In this context, the biologist is the client and the wild animal is the patient. Although the veterinarian does not have to be present when the drug is used, they must provide general supervision and instruction on the appropriate dose and application to insure the drug is used properly.

GENERAL PRINCIPLES

Terms

The terminology of chemical immobilization can be confusing. Anesthesia is the loss of sensation, which can be local or general. An example of local anesthesia is injection of lidocaine for suturing a wound, or procaine for dental work. General anesthesia is defined as the loss of consciousness. Most drugs used for immobilizing wildlife produce a state of general anesthesia in the animal. Other relevant terms include induction (the process of becoming anesthetized), analgesia (decrease in pain sensation), sedation (calming effect due to mild depression of the central nervous system), tranquilization (muscle relaxation and calmness without drowsiness), agonist (a drug that causes the desired effect relative to chemically restraining an animal), and antagonist (a drug that counters the effect of an agonist).

Although there is no perfect animal capture drug, characteristics of the ideal injectable anesthetic can be used to evaluate available drugs for specific wildlife applications (Kreeger et al. 2002). The ideal immobilizing drug should possess the following characteristics: (1) it should be safe, so that a range of effective doses is well tolerated, and not endanger the animal; (2) it should be potent so that small volumes will effectively immobilize the animal; (3) it should take effect rapidly and produce good muscle relaxation with a minimum of excitement or pain; (4) it should maintain reflexes and minimally depress cardiac and respiratory functions; (5) it should be short acting or fully reversible so the animal quickly recovers and regains all abilities; and (6) it should allow smooth induction and recovery from anesthesia with minimal adverse side effects. Additional desirable properties of an immobilizing drug include safety to people, low potential for abuse, and long shelf life.

Calculating Drug Doses

Three variables must be known or estimated to calculate a drug dose: the animal's weight (kg), the desired dosage (mg/kg), and the concentration of the drug (mg/ml). "Dose" is the quantity (mg) of drug delivered to the animal whereas "dosage" is the quantity per unit weight for the

Box 1. Schedules of controlled substances.

Information on controlled substances can be found under 21 Code of Federal Regulations, Parts 1300-1316, and 21 U.S. Code Service Section 812. Controlled substances (including drugs) are assigned a schedule number (I-V) based on their potential for abuse and medical use.

Schedule I
High potential for abuse.
No currently accepted medical use in the United States.
Accepted safety for use under medical supervision is lacking.
Includes all opiates and opiate derivatives (e.g., heroin and morphine methyl bromide) unless specifically excepted or listed in another schedule, certain hallucinogens (e.g., mescaline, marijuana, and lysergic acid diethylamide [LSD]), depressants (e.g., gamma-hydroybuterate [GHB]), and stimulants (e.g., norephadrone).

Schedule II
High potential for abuse.
Currently accepted medical use in the United States.
Abuse may lead to severe psychological or physical dependence.
Includes other opiates (e.g., codeine, morphine, and most opiate capture drugs like carfentanil, etorphine hydrochloride, and fentanyl), stimulants (e.g., amphetamines), depressants (e.g., pentobarbital, the primary ingredient in most euthanasia drugs), and stimulants (nabilone).

Schedule III
Potential for abuse is less than drugs in Schedule I and II.
Currently accepted for medical use in the United States.
Abuse may lead to moderate or low physical dependence or high psychological dependence.
Includes certain stimulants (e.g., lesser concentration, medicinal mixtures of Schedule II stimulants), depressants (e.g., most of the barbiturates including medicinal mixtures of pentobarbital, ketamine, and tiletamine-zolazepam [Telazol®]), specified small quantities of certain narcotics (e.g., codeine and dihydrocodeine), anabolic steroids, and hallucinogens (e.g., dronabinol, the synthesized active ingredient in marijuana).

Schedule IV
Lower potential for abuse relative to drugs in Schedule III.
Currently accepted for medical use in the United States.
Abuse may lead to limited physical or psychological dependence relative to those in Schedule III.
Specific small quantities of 2 lesser known narcotics, depressants (e.g., most of the benzodiazepines like diazepam [Valium®] and midazolam [Versed®], and butorphenol.

Schedule V
Lower potential for abuse relative to Schedule IV.
Currently accepted for medical use in the United States.
Abuse may lead to limited physical or psychological dependence relative to Schedule IV.
Includes low concentrations of some medicinal narcotics such as codeine and a lesser-known stimulant.

particular species and gender/age class. The animal's weight is usually unknown and must be estimated based on the biologist's experience, advice of others, or published information. Desired dosage is also based on experience or the scientific literature. Most published work on drug use in wildlife reports an estimated dosage. Rarely are exact dosages known because wildlife species are infrequently weighed. The concentration of the drug is labeled on the container or, in cases where the drug is lyophilized (freeze-dried), the concentration is calculated when the drug is reconstituted with liquid solvent.

Without experience as guidance, the scientific literature or discussion with others experienced in capture of the intended species will be the starting point for calculating how much drug is needed for a capture operation. This published dosage may prove inappropriate (too high or too low) for the given circumstances. Experience will allow adjustment to a dose

more appropriate for specific circumstances. With dosage from the literature, an estimated weight of the animal, and the known concentration of drug, the volume of drug needed is calculated (Box 2). One of the most frequent errors in drug dose calculation is concern about using too much drug. Although some drugs have narrow margins of safety, the cyclohexamines and narcotics are safe if properly used in the species for which they were intended. In particular, narcotic anesthesia can be rapidly reversed if an animal progresses too deeply into anesthesia. Death due to cyclohexamine anesthesia is rare. In practice, too little drug is a greater concern where a partially drugged animal becomes a danger to itself, people, and other animals, or escapes and later becomes immobilized unattended. It is best to estimate weight then round "up," particularly with large-bodied animals.

One of the most important aspects of anesthetizing an animal is to ensure using the proper amount of the proper

Box 2. Drug dose calculation.

The goal is to estimate the volume of drug to deliver to an animal for chemical immobilization. Three things must be known or estimated:

- dosage of intended drug for the species (mg drug/kg body weight = mg/kg),
- body weight of the animal (kg body weight = kg [weight in lbs divided by 2.2 = kg]), and
- concentration of drug (mg drug/ml solution of drug = mg/ml).

Numeric calculations should be done including the units of measure. The correct calculation can be checked by mathematically reviewing the units and ending with a unit of volume (milliliters or ml).

Step 1. Select species and drugs. Example, black bear—ketamine and xylazine.

Step 2. Use reference to ascertain dosages for this species.

Ketamine: 4.4 mg/kg.
Xylazine: 2.0 mg/kg.

Step 3. Estimate the bear's weight, e.g., 60 kg (~135 lbs).

Step 4. Calculate drug 1 (ketamine).

Generally sold as 100 mg/ml concentration, but can be more concentrated.

- Set up math: dosage (mg/kg) × weight (kg) = amount of drug (mg).

$$\frac{\text{Amount of drug (mg)}}{\text{Concentration of drug (mg/ml)}} = \text{Volume of drug. (ml)}$$

Substitute numbers: 4.4 mg/kg ketamine × 60 kg bear = 264 mg ketamine.

$$\frac{264 \text{ mg}}{100 \text{ mg/ml}} = 2.64 \text{ ml, rounded to 2.7 ml ketamine.}$$

Step 5. Repeat step 4 with drug 2. In this example, the answer will be 1.2 ml xylazine, assuming a drug concentration of 100 mg/ml xylazine is used.

Step 6. Add the volumes of drugs to be used: 2.7 ml ketamine + 1.2 ml xylazine = 3.9 ml total volume. The dart size needed would be 4 ml, a large dart.

This example demonstrates the advantage in using higher concentration drugs. Simply changing the concentration of ketamine and xylazine to 200 mg/ml decreases the volume to 1.92 ml, which will fit into a "2 ml" dart.

dose of 5.1 mg carfentanil, combined with 30 mg xylazine, works effectively for rapid and safe immobilization of adult female free-ranging bison (*Bison bison*) (Roffe and Sweeney 2002). Using drugs that have a high therapeutic index and are fully reversible provides latitude for situations in which an immobilized animal weighs considerably less than the average used to calculate the dose in the field. A drug with a high therapeutic index is one that is effective at a dose considerably lower than its lethal or dangerous dose. Conversely, a drug with a low therapeutic index is one in which the effective dose is relatively close to a lethal or dangerous dose.

Maintaining quality records is important to retrospectively analyze and improve immobilization techniques. This permits biologists to modify drug dose based on the animals, handling, and circumstances specific to their situation. Drug doses should be part of the record and allow easy recall for other capture events.

CLASSES OF DRUGS
General Anesthetics

Narcotics

Opioids (narcotics) are the most potent drugs available for large mammal immobilization. They are related to opium and interact with specific receptor cells in the central nervous system to induce anesthesia. The 2 most commonly used for wildlife immobilization are carfentanil (Wildnil®) and etorphine (M-99®). Etorphine has only recently become licensed and sold in the United States, but is widely used for large mammal immobilization in Africa and Europe. Carfentanil is licensed in the United States for immobilization of cervids, and has been used for bison, moose (*Alces alces*), elk (*Cervus elaphus*), and other species. More recently, a new synthetic opioid, thiafentanil (A-3080), has been introduced as an investigational drug but is not yet licensed by the FDA. Thiafentanil produces relatively rapid induction in pronghorn (*Antilocapra americana*), which is readily reversible (Kreeger 2000a). We have used thiafentanil in elk and pronghorn because of its shorter duration of activity than carfentanil.

Opioids have several advantages over other drugs. They are potent, allowing use of small quantities. This enhances dart delivery because smaller darts have better ballistic capabilities at longer distances. They are also fully and rapidly reversible with antagonizing drugs such as naltrexone or naloxone. Opioids take effect quickly (2–8 minutes) and, when used with tranquilizers, produce a smooth anesthesia with good recovery. The potency of opioids is also their chief disadvantage. Carfentanil and etorphine are far more potent than morphine and pose a human health hazard. Both drugs are classified as Schedule II (Box 1), and care should be used when handling them. Gloves and protective eyewear must be used, and an antagonist should be readily available. Working alone with these drugs is not recommended.

Another potential problem with opioids is renarcotization. After the antagonist drug has been administered, the animal appears to recover normally only to again come under the influence of the opioid (or related metabolite) after the antagonist has worn off. In severe cases, renarcotization may lead to an animal's death due to predation, failure to avoid environmental hazards, respiratory arrest, or impairment from recumbency. Renarcotization is the

drug. A good practice is to check the drug bottle for drug name and concentration 3 times: once when taken off the shelf, once as the syringe is filled, and again when the drug is replaced on the shelf. The costs of a failed immobilization (or a dead animal) far outweigh any savings gained by using old or improperly labeled drugs.

Although dose calculation is important for all personnel, experienced people often use a single dose for all animals of a particular species, gender, and age class. For example, we have found through experimentation, that a consequence of narcotic presence without antagonist. This can occur in several ways: (1) long-acting narcotics are combined with short-acting antagonists, (2) inadequate amounts of antagonist are used, (3) narcotic injected into fat or other poorly vascularized tissue that is slowly released after the antagonist has disappeared, or (4) re-uptake of narcotic from the gastrointestinal tract after the narcotic has been excreted by the liver. Risk of renarcoti-zation can be reduced by administering a large dose of high potency long-acting antagonist in a manner that provides immediate and sustained release (intramuscularly or intravenous, and subcutaneous) and/or by using narcotics with shorter half-lives.

Cyclohexamines

The cyclohexamine anesthetics, ketamine and tiletamine, are widely used for wildlife immobilization. Although their mode of action is incompletely understood, these drugs appear to work by electrochemically disassociating different parts of the brain from each another. The result is a malleable anesthetic state, in which the animal is unconscious, but the limbs are somewhat rigid and the eyes remain open with intact corneal and light reflexes (Kreeger et al. 2002). Cyclohexamine anesthetics are more often used in carnivores, particularly bears (Ursidae), canids (Canidae), and cats (Felidae). When used alone they may produce violent anesthetic inductions and recoveries, sometimes accompanied by seizures. To mitigate these effects, cyclohexamines are usually administered in conjunction with tranquilizers or sedatives, such as xylazine or diazepam. Some tranquilizers can exacerbate the tendency to produce seizures (e.g., phenothiazine derivatives) and must be avoided when using cyclohexamines. Tiletamine is unavailable as a sole product and is combined in equal parts with zolazepam (sold as Telazol®). Although tiletamine-zolazepam is currently approved only for cats and dogs, it has been used in more than 200 non-domestic species. Likewise, ketamine, although approved only for use in primates, is one of the most widely used anesthetics in wildlife because of its efficacy and high therapeutic index. There are no known antagonists for these drugs, although partial antagonistic properties have been attributed to some drugs that antagonize other drug classes, such as yohimbine and naltrexone (Kreeger et al. 2002).

Barbiturates

Barbiturates have been used to immobilize a variety of wild animals, but are little used now that there are safer and more effective drugs. The barbiturate, pentobarbital, is a major component of euthanasia drugs, while thiopental and thiamylal are ultra-short acting anesthetics used in veterinary surgery. Barbiturates are classified as sedative-hypnotic drugs and act on a variety of tissues in the brain and spinal area (Short 1983). To be effective, they should be delivered by intravenous injection. Intramuscular injection can result in significant tissue necrosis. These drugs have strong respiratory depressant properties and produce relatively little analgesia. In addition, there are no available antagonists.

Neuromuscular Blocking Drugs

Neuromuscular blocking drugs have a relatively long history of use for wildlife immobilization because they are cheap, easy to use, and effective. These drugs function by either blocking or depolarizing receptors in skeletal muscle, resulting in paralysis and immobilization of the animal. This effect generally occurs within 3–5 minutes and lasts for <30 minutes. The most popular drug in this class, succinylcholine, is a depolarizing agent and has no antagonist. In contrast, competitive blocking drugs such as gallamine can be antagonized with cholinesterase-inhibiting drugs.

Despite their effectiveness, these drugs are inferior to modern drugs for most wildlife applications. Their low therapeutic index means the difference between an effective dose and one that causes death is small. Additionally, since neuromuscular blocking drugs have no effect on the central nervous system, immobilized animals are fully aware of their surroundings and can feel pain and distress. In most cases use of these drugs alone would be considered inhumane. Because of these properties, use of neuromuscular blocking drugs should be limited to specific applications, such as captive environments where problems can be quickly addressed, or as part of a chemical euthanasia regimen.

Tranquilizers and Sedatives

The principal use of tranquilizers and sedatives for wildlife capture is to enhance the effectiveness of the primary immobilants—such as opioids and cyclohexamines. Adding these drugs to the anesthetic regimen results in smoother induction and recovery with reduced dosage requirement for the primary agent. We discuss only 3 categories, the alpha-2 adrenergic agonists, and the major and minor tranquilizers. Long-acting tranquilizers are not used for wildlife immobilization, but are used to manage animals for holding or transport.

Alpha-2 Adrenergic Agonists

These drugs are potent sedatives, reducing the activity of the adrenergic neurotransmitter, norepinephrine. Xylazine, which is labeled for use in cervids, is the most widely used alpha-2 agonist for wildlife immobilization. It has been used as an adjunct to carfentanil for immobilizing bison, moose, elk, mountain sheep (*Ovis canadensis*), mule deer (*Odocoileus hemionus*), and white-tailed deer (*O. virginianus*), and with both ketamine and tiletamine/zolazepam in bears. Numerous carnivore anesthetic protocols include the use of xylazine. A more potent alpha-2 agonist, medetomidine, is labeled for use in dogs and is finding increased application in wildlife but is considerably more expensive. Alpha-2 agonists can be fully reversible with yohimbine, tolazoline, and atipamezole. Although yohimbine has been reported to reverse xylazine effects in ungulates (Wallingford et al. 1996), we have found it ineffective. Tolazoline and atipamezole are superior drugs in this group of animals. Atipamezole is a potent, receptor-specific antagonist, but has no advantage for sedation reversal in moose or bison over tolazoline. Using atipamezole, we have observed the same adverse effects in bison generally associated with tolazoline (Roffe and Sweeney 2002). Alpha-2 agonists, used alone, are capable of sedating and sometimes immobilizing animals, but risk of sudden arousal is high and poor immobilization occurs frequently, especially in excited or free-ranging wildlife (Hastings et al. 1989). Alpha-2 agonists have potent respiratory depressant properties which can be additive to the effects of primary capture drugs like opioids. Respiration must be carefully monitored in anesthetized animals.

Other Tranquilizers

In veterinary applications, acepromazine is used to calm animals prior to general anesthesia and to enhance analgesic and anesthetic properties of other drugs. Acepromazine has a high therapeutic index, but can potentiate respiratory and cardiovascular depression of opioids. The chief disadvantage of phenothiazine-derived tranquilizers used in conjunction with dissociative drugs is their ability to decrease the seizure threshold thereby creating a greater potential for seizures to occur. Its principal use in wildlife immobilization has been as an adjunct to the opioid, etorphine.

The diazepinone tranquilizers are Schedule IV drugs (Box 1) used in wildlife anesthesia for their anticonvulsant and calming properties. Most often, the diazepinones are combined with dissociative anesthetics or used independently to halt seizures in immobilized animals. The principal representative of this group is diazepam. Others include zolazepam (a component of Telazol®) and midazolam (Versed®), a water-soluble drug that is better absorbed intramuscularly than diazepam. These drugs are safe if used properly. Diazepam must be injected slowly if given intravascularly; its propylene glycol carrier is irritating to the myocardium and can cause dysrhythmias and cardiac arrest if given too quickly. Diazepinone tranquilizers can be fully antagonized with flumazenil, although this is seldom done in wildlife because dosages are small, tranquilizing effects minimal, and the drugs are rapidly metabolized.

Drug Combinations

We have provided several examples in which drugs are combined to achieve more effective wildlife immobilization. This practice is common when working with wild animals. Advantages of combining drugs include drug synergy, which reduces overall dosage and volume compared to single drugs, mitigating adverse side effects such as muscular rigidity and seizures, and improving anesthetic induction and recovery. Established drug combinations have proven to be safe and effective for specific wildlife applications. Tiletamine-zolazepam, for example, is a highly useful combination for working with carnivores,

and is even combined with other drugs for bears. Xylazine and medetomidine are regularly used to enhance the quality of opioid and cyclohexamine anesthesia, and acepromazine, combined with etorphine (as Immobilon®), is used for both small and large mammal immobilizations.

The downside of drug combinations is that adverse effects can be compounded. For example, if both drugs cause respiratory depression that effect can be enhanced. When immobilization is poor (too deep, slow induction or inadequate immobilization), deciding which drug to increase or decrease and how to mitigate the adverse effects can be difficult.

Antagonists

The development of specific antagonist drugs for reversing large animal anesthesia has created major breakthroughs for wildlife immobilization. Regardless of how well the procedure is performed, general anesthesia affects the normal physiologic processes of the animal. Central nervous system depression, cardiovascular and respiratory depression, impairment of breathing and circulation, environmental hazards, and thermoregulatory disruption are examples of risks posed by anesthesia. The faster an animal can be returned to "normal," the better for the animal and, perhaps, for other members of the social group.

The synthetic opioid antagonist, naltrexone (Trexonil®), is highly effective for reversing narcotic immobilization. Naltrexone is a competitive antagonist with high affinity for the morphine receptor sites. Dose, route of delivery, and pharmacological half-life are the primary factors that influence the effectiveness of narcotic antagonism. For optimum effect, the antagonist should have no agonistic activity, compete so successfully for receptor sites that no agonistic molecules remain at receptor sites, and have a considerably longer half-life than the agonist. To minimize risk of renarcotization, we use naltrexone at a ratio of 125:1 relative to the carfentanil dose. This is higher than the recommended dose of 100:1, but naltrexone has been used as high as 500:1 without adverse effects in elk (Miller et al. 1996). To prolong naltrexone effect, we deliver about two-thirds of the dose subcutaneously. We use naltrexone at a ratio of 100:1 relative to the thiafentanil dose to antagonize thiafentanil (a slightly less potent opioid) in pronghorn although considerably lower ratios have been successfully used with this narcotic.

The introduction of newer, more selective and more potent alpha-2 adrenergic antagonists is rapidly making alpha-2 sedation and immobilization as reversible as that induced by narcotics. The primary alpha-2 antagonists available in the United States are yohimbine (Antagonil®, Yobine®), tolazoline (Tolazine®), and atipamezole (Antisedan®). In our experience, yohimbine has been relatively ineffective as a reversal agent in ungulates. In contrast, both tolazoline and atipamezole have proven to be effective.

HUMAN SAFETY

The working environment for chemical immobilization of wildlife is hazardous. These hazards come from animals (kicking, scratching, biting, goring) and the potentially lethal drugs used to immobilize them. The key to safety is prevention first, and preparation in case of an accident.

Accident prevention is more effective than treatment (Box 3). Both training and experience are useful preventive actions that will reduce the frequency and severity of acci-

---

Box 3. Preventive safety measures.

- Work with and seek advice from an experienced person.
- Know the behavior and expected responses of the species to be captured.
- Obtain formal training in drugs, capture equipment, and first aid.
- Develop a capture plan.
- Clearly delineate task responsibilities, including a capture team leader.
- With opioids work in pairs and use protective gloves and eyewear.
- With opioids have antagonists readily available at all times.
- Avoid using pressurized darts with dangerous drugs.
- Make contingency arrangements for potential emergency needs.

dents. Formal training in chemical immobilization should be a minimum requirement. This training should address drugs (type, pharmacology, action, dangers, treatment) and animals (behavior, approaches, appropriate drugs, dangers, proper handling, basic anatomy).

Drug Exposure

When handling potentially lethal drugs such as opioids, we recommend working with at least one other person and to have the antagonist drawn into a syringe, labeled, and readily available. The primary drug handler and at least one assistant should know the proper dose and route of delivery for opioid antagonists. Gloves and protective eyewear should be worn when handling drugs, whether working with loaded or spent darts. Loaded darts should be stored upright in a stable, hard-sided container. Spent darts, as well as needles and syringes used to load drugs into the darts, must be disposed in a dedicated biohazard container that will be incinerated.

Those working with potentially lethal drugs must assume the drug vial may be pressurized. Poor drug handling technique, increased temperature, or decreased atmospheric pressure can result in a pressurized vial. Pointing the vial in a safe direction and introducing a needle into the air space above the drug using gloved hands should relieve pressure; withdrawing drugs should continue without injecting air. These measures will minimize drug leakage and accidental exposure to anyone touching the vial.

Pressurized darts are commonly used for all forms of drugs. However, nonpressurized darts that inject by internal charge designed to go off on impact are considerably safer. We recommend narcotics be loaded only in nonpressurized darts.

Emergency Response

In case of emergencies, one should remain calm and note the approximate time of exposure and quantity of drug that may have been involved. If there is doubt that a significant amount of drug has been absorbed, the best course of action is to carefully monitor the exposed individual and be prepared to initiate appropriate response if warranted. If it is known that a person received a significant drug exposure, work quickly. Several minutes may elapse before the drug takes full effect. This should be more than adequate to treat the wound and administer the antagonist, if necessary. Irrigate the exposed site with a large volume of water to reduce further drug absorption. Ice or snow can decrease circulation to the site minimizing distribution of the drug in the body.

For exposure to one of the potent opioids, such as carfentanil or etorphine, the most important treatment will be administering the appropriate antagonist. Signs of opioid intoxication include dizziness, lack of coordination, sedation, nausea or vomiting, pinpoint pupils, slow shallow breathing, unconsciousness, and respiratory arrest. Each container of drug will contain a sheet (called a "package insert") with this information. Death is due to hypoxia. Naloxone is the recommended drug for opioid overdose in people, but naltrexone is probably more effective because of its potency and longer half-life. Naltrexone is safe in people and currently used to treat human narcotic and alcohol abuse with varying success (Modesto-Lowe and Van Kirk 2002). Several vials of naltrexone should be kept in the antagonist kit with drug drawn into a labeled syringe ready for use. Use of 50 mg (1.0 ml) naltrexone will usually reverse the effects of opioids on humans. If signs of opioid intoxication persist, the dose can be repeated at 1-minute intervals until central nervous system depression is successfully reversed. Artificial respiration or CPR should be administered as needed. Staying with the patient is important, even after apparent recovery from opioid intoxication, as is transport to an emergency medical center.

These same principles apply to treating accidental exposures to other immobilizing drugs. Readers seeking information on treatments for specific drug exposures should consult Kreeger et al. (2002).

DRUG DELIVERY SYSTEMS

Syringes and Needles

Syringes and needles are the most basic, easy to use tools for delivering drugs. Even in situations where remote dart delivery is the primary mechanism for capture, additional drug administered while the animal is in hand is done using needles and syringes. These tools are also essential to loading drugs into darts. They are sterile and disposable, and should be discarded after a single use. The syringe sizes most useful for working with large ungulates and grizzly bears (*Ursus arctos*) are 1 and 3 ml for loading darts, and 20, 35, and 60 ml for collecting blood. Twenty gauge needles should be used for withdrawing drugs from vials, and 16 to 20 gauge needles should be used for venipuncture. Vacutainers, which allow blood to be drawn directly into centrifuge tubes, are also handy. Needle lengths of 2.5 or 4.0 cm (1 or 1½ inch) are desirable, depending on application and personal preference.

Pole Syringes

A pole syringe, also known as a jabstick, consists of a syringe mounted on the end of a long plunger or pole. This device allows the operator to inject a drug into an animal that is confined in a trap or cage, or an animal that is incompletely immobilized but approachable. Pole syringes are generally limited to delivering relatively small volumes of drug (≤5 ml) and should be used with large gauge needles (16–18-gauge) in the shortest effective length to allow the drug to be injected rapidly into a muscle. "Jabstick" is really a misnomer because the drug is ineffectively injected with a jab action, which rapidly removes the embedded needle. To perform an injection with a pole syringe, place the end of the needle near the injection site and smoothly yet forcefully thrust the needle in and continue to push to ensure the drug is dispensed. Continued pressure is needed to inject the full dose without breaking the needle.

Blowpipes

A blowpipe consists of a hollow tube through which a drug-filled dart is propelled, either by lungpower or by a compressed gas (air or CO_2). This device is most useful for confined animals or those that can be approached closely, for example from a vehicle. The effective range of conventional blowpipes is generally ≤10 m, depending on the skill of the operator; practice is the key to success. Blowpipes are quiet and usually cause little tissue trauma because the dart strikes the subject with low velocity. Because pressurized darts are generally used, reliability of injections can be inconsistent. Conventional blowpipes can be purchased or con-

Table 1. Characteristics of dart rifles used for wildlife immobilization (organized as in Kreeger et al. [2002] for comparison).

Propulsion system	.22-caliber blank	Carbon dioxide	Compressed air
Maximum effective range	70–80 m	30–40 m	15–20 m
Volume of drug delivered	1–20 ml	1–8 ml	1–5 ml
Propellant availability	High	High	Low
Temperature sensitivity	None	High	Low
Impact injury	High	Medium	Low
Maintenance requirement	High	Low	Low
Performance reliability	High	High	Medium
Ease of use	High	Medium	Medium
Overall versatility	High	Medium	Low

structed from aluminum tubing or other lightweight metal, and are usually 1–2 m long. A mouthpiece made of rubber tubing or other material is optional. Use of narcotic drugs with blowpipes is discouraged. Powered blowpipes, which have a metal tube connected to a pistol grip with a pressure-regulating device, can be used for longer distance applications and with non-pressurized darts (Kreeger et al. 2002).

Dart Guns

Dart rifles and pistols are the most versatile and widely used equipment for delivering drugs to wildlife. Darts are propelled from these firearms by expansion of gases from .22-caliber blank cartridges, compressed CO_2 gas, or air. Effective shooting ranges can be as far as 70–80 m for cartridge-powered rifles using small darts (1–2 ml). Larger darts are ballistically inferior and have shorter ranges. For most wildlife applications, dart rifles are equipped with magnifying scopes, although rifles with open sights are preferred for helicopter work.

The features of the different dart gun propulsion systems vary (Table 1). No single system is best for all applications. For free-ranging animals, we prefer a variable port cartridge-powered rifle. This system has the longest range and the greatest versatility for a variety of species and environments, and uses easy-to-obtain .22 caliber blank cartridges. These cartridges are available at most hardware stores since they are widely used in construction tools. Shooting range can be adjusted through a variable porting system that vents propulsion gases depending on the desired range. The charge for providing propulsion to the dart can also be changed for greater or less power. The system is effective over a wide range of distances for virtually all species, and is relatively immune to environmental conditions. The principal weakness of this system is the occasional variability in the .22 cartridge that can provide too much or little power. This system also requires maintenance to remove powder residue. Several companies manufacture and sell dart guns. Regardless of the system used, it is vital to practice with the darts at distances expected in the field.

Darts

Darts used for wildlife immobilization differ in construction and the manner in which the plunger is pushed forward to expel their contents. Some darts use an explosive charge to operate the plunger and discharge the drug, whereas others rely on compressed air or gas, chemical reaction, or loaded spring. These features are activated when the dart suddenly decelerates upon impacting the animal. Darts using explosive charges can expel their contents in less than 1/1,000 second and require large diameter needles to accomplish this task. Dart needles come in a variety of lengths from 1.3 to 4.0 cm (½ to 1½ inches) and have openings on the front or side. Some needles have barbs or collars to secure the dart while the drug is discharged. Barbed darts have to be removed manually, but if the proper dart barb length is used on the appropriate species these slender aluminum projections rarely cause a problem. Dart wounds are usually minimal and seldom need treatment. If a biologist is using older style darts with heavy inflexible barbs, these darts should be removed using a scalpel and the wound treated with a topical antiseptic. If a dart hits bone, fibrous tissue, or fat the needle may become plugged and the drug will not be discharged. If this happens the contents will be pressurized and the dart should be immediately disposed in a safe container.

Some companies make darts that contain a small radio transmitter, enabling researchers to locate an animal that has departed after being darted with immobilizing drugs (e.g., Pneu-dart, Inc., Williamsport, Pennsylvania, USA). We have had 2 problems with these types of darts. First, their size make them ballistically inferior (shorter range, more parabolic trajectory) than smaller conventional darts that hold the same amount of drug. Second, these darts have a midpiece that separates the drug chamber from the transmitter chamber. Since the radio transmitter is not activated until used, the tailpiece must be removable. In front of the midpiece is a detonating charge that propels the plunger, injecting the drug upon contact. Not infrequently we have had pressures build that push the midpiece and, thus, the radio transmitter, out the back end. The result is a darted animal, often with partial injection because of the loss of injection propulsion, which has departed without the radio transmitter. These darts may be useful where there is a high probability of missed shot, and finding the dart is essential. As technology improves, radio transmitter darts could become more practical.

ANCILLARY EQUIPMENT

There are several pieces of equipment helpful or necessary for capturing and monitoring free-ranging wildlife. A laser range finder is useful for estimating distance and shot placement, especially when working with a new species. As the shooter becomes more experienced, the range finder can be used periodically to confirm distance estimates.

Monitoring an animal's body temperature with a rectal thermometer is a simple, but important, practice for wildlife immobilization. In addition to the physical exertion of running after being darted, an animal may have its thermoregulatory ability altered by immobilizing drugs. This can result in hyperthermia, which can kill the animal directly or contribute to capture myopathy. A digital thermometer, with a probe connected to a flexible cord, is durable, relatively inexpensive, and useful for monitoring body temperatures. Inexpensive rectal thermometers (digital or mercury) are available in retail stores. In smaller ani-

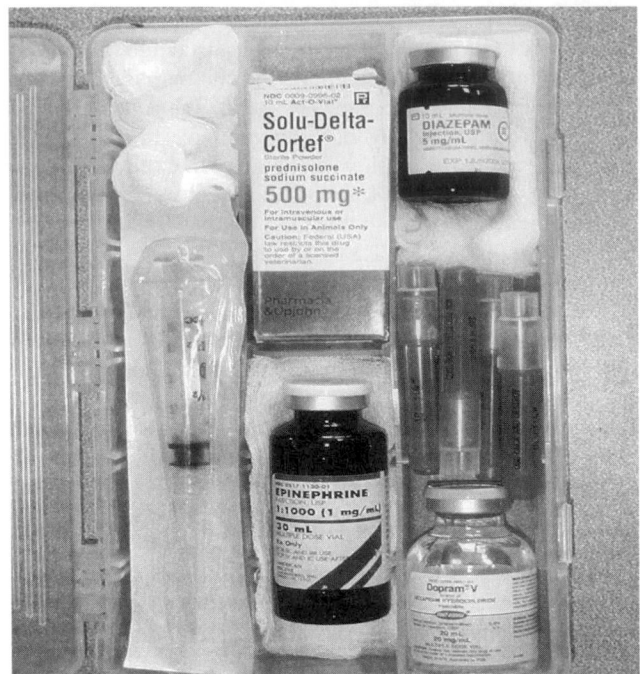

Fig. 1. "Crash kit" for chemical immobilizations allowing rapid access to the drugs most commonly used for emergency response during anesthesia (photograph courtesy of T. J. Roffe).

mals or with drugs designed to "wear off" (taking hours), hypothermia is a significant issue to address.

Pulse oximeters are electronic devices that provide an index of how well the patient is oxygenated. Small, battery-powered oximeters are available for field use and are inexpensive. However, they require use of non-pigmented tissues, and only provide a point of reference for detecting trends rather than a true representation of oxygen saturation. Pulse oximetry should not be used to overrule clinical evidence of hypoxia.

OPERATIONAL PROCEDURES

Planning and Preparation

Planning cannot be overemphasized for field operations, particularly for relative newcomers to the art and science of chemical immobilization. Appropriate materials, drugs, and supplies to accomplish specific tasks need to be readily available (Fig. 1). All possibilities that can go wrong with wildlife capture should be considered. Common to all capture operations is consideration for human and animal safety, and the need to maintain records. Records of each and every capture should be kept for drug accountability. A capture form should be developed (Table 2).

If aircraft (helicopters) are used in the capture event, specific training in aircraft safety is needed for all crew members. The number of people involved with such captures should be kept to a minimum to maximize maneuverability and provide increased space for the dart gun operator. The person responsible for dart delivery must be experienced in free flight shooting and must work closely with the pilot. The pilot is a critical part of the capture team and makes all decisions relative to aircraft safety and performance. An experienced wildlife-capture pilot will know how to position the aircraft for improved darting accuracy.

The dart gun operator and pilot must be able to communicate rapidly and efficiently.

Preparation should involve the entire capture team. All team members should understand safety considerations, specific tasks, capture procedures, and likely hazards associated with the species for capture. The team leader is critical to success and usually is responsible for administration of the drug to the animal. This person manages the operation and defines the team's ability to get the job done. All capture operations should use an experienced person and have the assistance of a wildlife veterinarian for drug-related work.

All equipment should be inspected and in good working order (Fig. 2). Those involved with its use should be familiar with its operation. Remote delivery equipment should be test fired and adjusted, if necessary, for accuracy. Dart-delivery tools should be treated as a "loaded gun" around all people and objects. Considerations that go into planning of a capture event include: species, social structure, age, size, weather, environmental hazards, season, emotional state, nutrition, and body condition.

Species

Drug choice is largely affected by species to be captured. Secondarily, the tasks to be accomplished during the immobilization, and in what time frame, will affect drug choice and immobilization protocol.

Social Structure

Consideration should be given to how the targeted species is socially organized at the time of planned capture. Some species are solitary (e.g., some carnivores, moose) others occur in large gregarious groups (most ungulates). Males and females may be segregated or together. The capture team needs to assess whether conspecifics or other species (for example predators) may interfere with capture operations or pose a hazard to people or immobilized animals. Maternal bonds are especially strong and it is difficult in many species (e.g., bears, moose) to capture maternally dependent young without also immobilizing the mother. Contingencies need to be considered on how to handle interference from other animals during the capture event, especially from predators to animals immobilized with disassociative anesthetics.

Age and Gender

Age and gender may affect an animal's response to drugs. Generally this applies to young or old animals that might be at higher risk for complications or trauma. Large males of many species frequently require lower dosage (drug per unit weight) than lighter conspecifics. Gender can affect the general attitude and, thus, the ability to be affected by drugs. If radio or instrument collars are going to be applied, proper fitting becomes a critical element for young animals or those likely to alter their physical stature during the time the collar is in place. Planning should accommodate growing animals either through recapture or degradable links in the collar material. The effects of capture procedures and consequences (e.g., collars, vaginal radio implants) on reproduction or other social behavior should be assessed.

Weather

Weather may affect the operation directly, for example, by controlling aircraft flights or access to animals. Weather may also affect thermoregulation.

Table 2. Sample chemical immobilization data sheet.

Wildlife Health Immobilization Record

Name_____ Date_____ ID#_____
Species_____ Location _____
Injection Time (= Time 0)_____ Behavior_____
                    Age_____ Gender____ Est. WT_____

	Drug	Dose	Route	Site	Time
Immobilizing					
1.					
2.					
3.					
4.					
Antagonist					
1.					
2.					

Data
   Induction Time _____(min: sec)
   Reversal Time _____(min: sec)
   Recovery Time _____(min: sec)
Treatments or other drug use: _____
Palpation?   Y or N   Pregnant?   Y or N
Palpation comments:

_____
_____

Plane of anesthesia: 1 (Light)   2   3   4   5 (Deep)
Comments:_____

***See back of page for samples collected
Induction Time = Injection of agonist to recumbency
Reversal Time = Injection of agonist to completed injection of antagonist
Recovery Time = Injection of agonist to standing recovery

- -

[*back of datasheet*]
Samples collected:
Description of samples: Handled by:

_____
_____
_____

Environmental Hazards

Capture crews should be familiar with the landscape so that hazards such as cliffs, water, thermal features, fences, roads, human habitation, etc. are known. The approach should be designed to minimize the potential for animal interaction with these hazards. Of particular concern is the risk partially immobilized animals pose to people in the area, particularly in urban/suburban settings with traffic.

Season

Capture operations can be affected by season primarily through weather, social behavior, and physical condition. We have found fall captures to require more immobilizing drug than winter or early spring when animals are in poorer body condition. Physiologic states, such as rut or estrus, can also alter the amount of drug needed for effective immobilization. Season can also affect tracking and locating darted animals; for example, the density of vegetation can affect visibility.

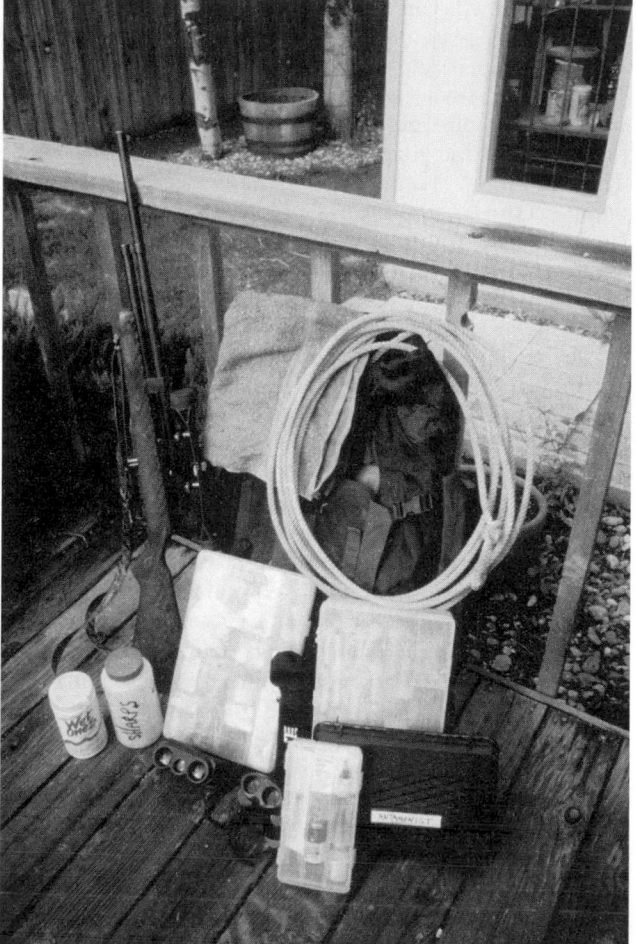

Fig. 2. Capture equipment for remote ground capture of wildlife (photograph courtesy of T. J. Roffe).

Emotional State

Some techniques increase animal apprehension, for example, chases, presence of vehicles or people. Approach can stimulate fight responses in aggressive animals. Handling may induce further struggle and negate the drug effect. Some species may become catatonic during handling. Emotional state not only influences the response from an animal about to be captured, but can also influence their response to drugs.

Nutrition and Body Condition

Poor body condition can commonly lead to adverse effects requiring medical intervention. Less amount of drug is generally needed on compromised individuals. Large-bodied and fatter animals may require longer needles for sufficient penetration and drug delivery.

Immobilizing the Animal

Regardless of preferred approach to the targeted animal (ground, air or water) the best method should stimulate the least amount of response in the target. Generally this means a quiet, calm approach with as few people as possible. In a helicopter, the aircraft should move in for darting and immediately pull back for observation. Pursuit of individual animals from the air should be limited to no more than 5 minutes. Parameters such as body temperature of captured animals can be used to gauge when capture operations should cease on the same group of animals.

Ground approach, including over snow vehicles, foot, snowshoe or 4-wheeled vehicles has worked successfully with a variety of ungulate species. It can be helpful to place personnel in strategic places to haze animals from hazards. The minimum number of people necessary should approach the target animal. Generally, this is just the person responsible for administering the drug and perhaps a single support person if radio telemetry guidance or protection is needed. The remainder of the crew should stay out of sight, hearing, and smell of the target.

The large muscle masses of the animal are the target for darting with the muscles of the shoulder and upper rear leg the preferred sites. The neck is not a particularly good site because of the small usable area and the abundance of critical structures (nerves, large blood vessels, vertebral column, trachea). Darts must impact with sufficient force to penetrate the skin and muscle, and set off the discharge of the dart (or open the port for a pressurized dart) while not causing significant trauma-related damage. Once the dart is delivered, personnel should quietly withdraw and unobtrusively observe the animal for induction. Stimulation of the animal should be kept to the absolute minimum. Missed darts should be recovered if possible.

Numerous adverse consequences can occur after darting, such as the animal departing from sight. If immobilization is incomplete or not at all apparent, an additional dose of drug should be administered. The amount and method (hand inject or remote) depends on the individual species, drug, and effects from the first dose. For narcotics, if the animal is still on its feet and ambulatory, a full second dose is administered. If the animal is down but intractable, partial doses may be administered. With disassociative drugs, partial doses are more commonly delivered because an additional full immobilizing dose significantly delays recovery time.

Once the animal is on the ground the crew leader should approach it quietly from a safe direction (generally from the back and rear of the animal, away from any potential kicking leg or thrashing head). The remainder of the crew should approach quietly. The first step is to properly position the animal to enhance respiration and minimize inhalation of foreign substances (feed, water, saliva, etc.). Because of their massive rumens, ruminants are best placed in sternal recumbency with head uphill when possible (Fig. 3). Gas accumulates in the rumen, and sternal recumbency allows gas to escape through the esophagus while usually preventing regurgitation. If lateral recumbency must be used, place the head uphill, assess bloat and periodically roll the animal sternally to displace accumulated gas. In carnivores, the general position can either be lateral or sternal with head level or slightly down (Fig. 4). The eyes should be covered and, with drugs that maintain open eyes (e.g., cyclohexamines), eye ointment is essential. Once this is accomplished, each crew member completes their assigned task while the person responsible for anesthesia monitors the animal. Minimal monitoring includes temperature, respiration (character and frequency), bloat (most important for ruminants), capillary color and refill, and response to stimuli. In short immobilizations (e.g., simple collar removal or placement) (Fig. 5) involving reversible anesthesia, monitoring temperature and bloat is not necessary. Large animals in lateral recumben-

Fig. 3. Bison in proper sternal recumbency during anesthesia just prior to arousal and recovery (photograph courtesy of T. J. Roffe).

Fig. 4. Grizzly bear in proper position (i.e., sternal recumency with all 4 legs placed out and flat to prevent circulatory impairment) during anesthesia (photograph courtesy of K. E. Aune).

cy should have the downside foreleg pulled forward as much as possible to minimize the chance of radial nerve paralysis. If a wound requires treatment, appropriate therapy should be dispensed. We do not routinely administer antibiotics during captures unless there are contaminated wounds or suspicion of gastric content inhalation. Complications requiring the need for medical intervention should be considered (Table 3). Pond and O'Gara (1994) further discuss medical problems.

EUTHANASIA

Most wildlife biologists and managers have been required to euthanize an animal that was severely injured or part of a terminal study. Several methods are available for euthanasia of large mammals, including gunshot, stunning and bleeding, or lethal chemical injection. The chosen method often depends on the perceptions of the person performing the euthanasia and others who may be present. Chemical euthanasia is generally safe and effective but, depending on drugs used, can leave residues lethal to scavengers. The American Veterinary Medical Association (AVMA) periodically publishes a report from the Panel on Euthanasia (2001). Many of the techniques are not appropriate for wildlife; however, they are the consensus for humane euthanasia techniques in North America.

Fig. 5. Researchers placing radio collar and removing dart from immobilized pronghorn (photograph courtesy of T. J. Roffe).

Table 3. Medical problems during immobilization.

Condition	Signs	Treatment
Respiratory distress	Rapid breathing Cyanosis Depressed breathing Slow capillary refill	Cease all anesthetics Establish patent airway Administer antagonists Artificial respiration Administer doxapram
Bloat	Abdominal distension Labored breathing Excessive salivation	Adjust position to sternal Reduce pressure— stomach tube Trocar Administer antagonists
Hyperthermia	Elevated rectal temp Extremities feel warm Rapid, shallow breathing Rapid, irregular pulse	Cease anesthetics Cool animal - remove from sunlight - water/alcohol bath - cold water enema - ice packs Administer antagonists
Hypothermia	Decreased rectal temp Shivering Extremities feel cold Decreased heart rate	Cease anesthetics Warm animal - blankets, jackets - warm water containers Administer antagonists
Shock	Rapid, "thready" pulse Pale mucous membranes Slow capillary refill	Cease anesthetics Give antagonists **NOW** Provide supportive therapy
Vomiting/ Aspiration	Gurgling when breathing Choking, gasping Cyanosis Respiratory arrest	Clear airway Begin AR if needed Administer antagonists Administer long acting antibiotics

Gunshot is often the most practical method of euthanasia. Shots to the head or neck are preferred to heart or lung shots, and placement is more critical than caliber of the bullet. Only head shots, properly done, are considered humane under AVMA guidelines. The best location for a lethal head shot is at the juncture of an imaginary × connecting the eyes with the opposite ears, or for a lateral shot one placed at the base of the ear. If the animal has a heavy skull, such as a bison or bear, one should aim slightly off center. The muzzle of the gun should be placed near the head and the shot should be perpendicular to the skull to ensure penetration. Any observers should be behind the shooter.

Stunning with a penetrating captive bolt can be used on large animals including bison and elk. This method may not kill the animal and it is necessary to confirm that it has expired by monitoring pulse, respiration, and palpebral reflex. Exsanguination (bleeding the animal to death) frequently accompanies stunning and is done by cutting the jugular vein and carotid artery at the neck. Alternatively, the femoral artery can be severed.

Large mammals can be chemically euthanized with several products formulated for this purpose. Euthanasia drugs sold in the United States contain barbiturates and local anesthetic agents and are classified as Schedule III (Box 1) controlled substances. T61®, a combination of 4 drugs free of drug schedule restrictions, is no longer sold the United States but is available in Canada. Euthanasia drugs should be injected intravenously, e.g., into the jugular vein, although intraperitoneal or intra-cardiac injections will also work. Most of these drugs are quite viscous and must be injected slowly, using a large-gauge needle and firm pressure on the syringe plunger.

An alternative chemical for euthanasia is potassium chloride (KCl), which can be purchased at any grocery store. Also known as a salt alternative such as "No Salt," KCl is benign when ingested orally and presents no hazards for handling. However, when injected intravenously at sufficient concentration, it increases the level of circulating potassium and disrupts the heart's electrical activity and rhythm, leading to cardiac arrest and death. Only pure KCl (not KCl mixed with sodium chloride [NaCl]) should be used. Potassium chloride should only be given to an animal that has first been anesthetized. Mix any fluid (this will be injected into an anesthetized animal to kill it, so sterility is not important) with the KCl, shake, and withdraw about 30–60 ml of saturated salt solution for a large mammal and inject directly into a vein. Cardiac arrest usually takes <30 seconds and should be verified by feeling for a pulse or listening for a heartbeat. Muscle spasms may occur in response to electrolyte changes in muscle.

SPECIES-SPECIFIC CHEMICAL IMMOBILIZATION STRATEGIES

Kreeger et al. (2002) published a handbook containing a synthesis of published data on drugs and drug doses for a variety of species. We avoided duplication and refer the reader to that resource for a listing of the variety of drugs and doses. We present the most common drug-dosing regimen, or discuss alternatives where there is debate or controversy on which is best.

Ungulates

Ungulates occupy a wide variety of habitats in North America each having its own hazards. As prey species, ungulates are prone to flight and escape is their primary defense mechanism. In particular, environmental hazards such as cliffs, water, obstacles, roads, and traffic that are some distance from the capture site should be considered. Failure to locate an immobilized animal will generally lead to its death. In addition, large animals can quickly build up heat from running or aerial chases compromising their ability to tolerate anesthesia. The ungulates we cover are all ruminants and have a large chamber of fermenting foodstuffs that can predispose them to bloat or aspiration during immobilization. Recovering animals can be susceptible to predation and environmental hazards after anesthesia. Many ungulates live in social structures that can increase hazards to capture crews, the immobilized animal, or other members of the social group. Some social hierarchies involve dominance/aggressive behavior by males at certain times of the year. Immobilization can change the dynamics of such situations and predispose an animal to conspecific attack and trauma. Neonates depend heavily on mothers and capture operations may affect maternal bonds resulting in mother-offspring rejection or separation.

Elk

Of all North American ungulates, elk perhaps best embody the traits of a well-adapted prey species. Wary and nervous, these highly social animals have keen senses of smell, hearing, and vision, coupled with the size and speed to avoid or escape predators. Thus, there are only a few situations, such as refuges or feed grounds where elk are habituated to human activities, or captive/trapped animals, where it is feasible to chemically immobilize them. In special circumstances, elk inhabiting remote areas can be successfully darted from a helicopter.

We recommend using 2–2.5 mg carfentanil combined with 20 mg xylazine for adult cows, and 3–3.5 mg carfentanil with 30 mg xylazine for bulls. This corresponds closely to the published doses (Kreeger et al. 2002). Carfentanil is antagonized with naltrexone at 125 times the carfentanil dose and xylazine is antagonized with tolazoline (1–2 mg/kg).

Deer

Mule deer and white-tailed deer are common throughout much of their respective ranges in North America. Neither species is as gregarious as elk, although both may form small groups during the breeding season or larger groups when feeding. Like elk, deer can be difficult to approach; thus, the use of chemical immobilization is limited to situations where the animals are confined (as in traps or corrals), moderately habituated to people, or stalked if only a few animals are needed. Because deer can quickly travel long distances and hide in cover, they can be especially challenging to find once darted.

Many different drug combinations have been used to immobilize deer, none of which has consistently been satisfactory. We have captured deer using carfentanil and xylazine at the same dosages (mg/kg) as used for elk. Because of mortalities associated with chemical immobilization of deer, the California Department of Fish and Game (1995) routinely uses other capture methods such as trapping, drive netting or helicopter net gunning.

Moose

The dietary preferences of moose make them likely to be in areas with water, which presents a drowning hazard. Unlike elk and deer, they are usually solitary and tend to be more tolerant of intruders. Moose can be approached and darted on foot or, if in remote areas, from a helicopter. Roffe et al. (2001) immobilized 48 free-ranging moose in the Greater Yellowstone Area by darting with a combination of xylazine and carfentanil. Immobilized moose were sternally recumbent and generally held their heads in an upright position while researchers collected blood and performed other sampling and diagnostic procedures. The recommended drug dose for an adult cow moose was 50–60 mg xylazine and 3.3–3.6 mg carfentanil. Moose calves (8–12 months old) were effectively immobilized with 40–60 mg xylazine and 2.7–3.6 mg carfentanil. Immobilant drugs were antagonized with tolazoline and naltrexone (400–500 mg and ≥125 times the carfentanil dose, respectively). Tolazoline is well tolerated by moose and higher doses do not apparently cause adverse responses. However, we have since found that 500–600 mg by intravenous or intramuscular routes to be satisfactory. The authors attributed their success with moose immobilization to use of low-stress techniques (slowly stalking by one individual for darting, quietly processing blindfolded animals), and using effective immobilization and antagonist doses. Kreeger (2000b) had significant mortality (9 of 11) with a carfentanil/ xylazine combination in a small number of captive moose and suggested the cause was related to xylazine.

Moose are defensive of their young and are the most aggressive cervid. Thus, we immobilize the pair starting with the mother. We have immobilized calf moose without immobilizing the mother only in situations with adequate personnel for continued vigilance and hazing, and only for a short procedure.

Caribou

Caribou (*Rangifer tarandus*) are conspecific with reindeer. They are highly gregarious, particularly in open tundra where they form migratory herds. Caribou are extremely wary and cannot be approached for chemical immobilization unless captive or darted from a helicopter. Caribou mothers may readily abandon neonates if care is not taken to minimize foreign scent transfer. Ketamine has been a recommended immobilization regimen for caribou and reindeer, but we have used carfentanil/xylazine successfully in a limited number of aerial captures.

Mountain Sheep

Mountain sheep occupy mountainous regions of the western United States, Canada, and Mexico. They are excellent climbers and prefer steep, broken terrain, which is difficult to access. The preferred capture method for mountain sheep is usually by helicopter net gunning with corral traps, drop nets, and drive nets secondary options (California Department of Fish and Game 1995). Chemical immobilization has been associated with higher mortality rates than other capture methods (California Department of Fish and Game 1995). Sheep are susceptible to hyperthermia and capture myopathy. Once properly restrained, mountain sheep become quite docile and can be handled safely without drugs. We have immobilized a small num-

Fig. 6. Researcher preparing to fire an immobilizing dart at a snared blond-colored black bear (photograph courtesy of K. E. Aune).

ber of mountain sheep with carfentanil/xylazine (2.75 mg carfentanil plus 10 mg xylazine for adult ewes and young rams) in captive situations and where habituation to people made them accessible.

Bison

Bison form loose aggregations that move and change composition seasonally. Outside of the breeding season, bulls generally associate together as do cows, particularly during the calving period. During the rut, smaller bands coalesce to form larger herds. Bison react variably to human intrusion depending on time of year, level of habituation to people, type and location of activity, recent experience with predators and humans, and other factors. At times they can be approached quite closely on foot, or from a vehicle; at other times they may flee at the sight of a person more than 1 km away. Generally, bison tolerate approach to within darting range (30–50 m) or they can be pressured to move past an ambush site for darting.

We developed a satisfactory immobilization regimen for bison using carfentanil (~0.01 mg/kg) and xylazine (~0.06 mg/kg) (Roffe and Sweeney 2002). Our current (2003) standard dose for adult cows is 5.1 mg carfentanil plus 30 mg xylazine. Yearlings receive 4.5 mg carfentanil plus 20 mg xylazine, while calves (≥6 months old) receive 3.6 mg carfentanil plus 15 mg xylazine. The adult bull dose is approximately 5.7 mg carfentanil plus 30 mg xylazine. This regimen produces consistently good immobilizations and smooth recoveries, with no residual signs of sedation, agitation or renarcotization. We reverse the anesthesia with naltrexone at ≥125 times the carfentanil dose as do others (Haigh and Gates 1995), and do not antagonize the xylazine. We found the alpha-2 antagonists tolazoline and atipamezole both effectively reversed higher doses of xylazine but produced adverse side effects (agitation, aggression, and non-directed pacing) for up to 2 days. Yohimbine was ineffective in reversing the higher doses of xylazine. Caulkett et al. (2000) reported on bison immobilization using combinations of tiletamine/zolazepam plus medetomidine or xylazine.

Pronghorn

Pronghorn occupy grassland and desert habitats of the western United States, southern Canada, and northern Mexico. The sensory, emotional, and physiological capabilities of pronghorns are unexcelled for detecting, avoiding, and escaping predators. Thus, they are notoriously difficult to handle and are prone to dying from capture myopathy and capture-related trauma. Kreeger (2000a) used thiafentanil (4.0–5.0 mg) with and without xylazine (25 mg) to immobilize 31 pronghorn in Wyoming. He considered thiafentanil more effective than other anesthetic regimens in this species.

We used thiafentanil (6.0–7.5 mg) to immobilize 50 pronghorn in Montana. Following violent recoveries in the first group, we delivered 5 mg diazepam by hand injection to 16 of these animals. Violent recoveries of these animals appeared to be caused by a flight response to large, bulky global position satellite collars placed on them rather than caused by drugs. These problems were not observed in pronghorn captured for collar removal using thiafentanil alone. The diazepam was delivered intravenously immediately after the animal was in hand. The 7.0-mg dose of thiafentanil with 5 mg diazepam produced consistently short inductions and excellent anesthesia with good handling characteristics. During initial captures, some pronghorn still had unacceptably harsh recoveries. During one capture episode, several animals died or were killed by predators as a result of post-reversal trauma and/or myopathy. Subsequent review of techniques suggested the diazepam might have been injected too rapidly. In late 2003, we followed with an additional 10 captures for placement of radio collars by using thiafentanil with diazepam. All immobilizations and recoveries were characterized as "excellent" and no mortalities occurred up to 2 months later.

Carnivores

Bears

Three species of bears—black bear (*Ursus americanus*), grizzly bear, and polar bear (*U. maritimus*)—inhabit parts of North American occupying a wide range of environments. They are smart, powerful, occasionally aggressive, and must be treated with utmost caution and respect. Immobilization must be tailored to the distinctive characteristics of each species, social setting, season, and environment.

Most capture programs for bears initially use some type of physical restraint, such as snares or culvert traps, followed by chemical restraint for handling (Fig. 6). Captured bears often are agitated, overheated, dehydrated, and may be injured. Under these conditions, it can be risky to chemically immobilize a bear.

At times it is necessary to chemically immobilize unrestrained bears. These situations present unique challenges and hazards, both to bears and people. In the arctic, for example, bears are routinely darted from helicopters, and can be exposed to water and other hazards during the induction period. Tracking a recently darted bear requires extreme caution, as the anesthesia may be incomplete. Bears in trees present unique hazards because anatomical target zones are small and darts that miss their mark can endanger the public. Anesthetized bears can fall from or become lodged in trees and capture protocols must consider methods to prevent injuries from falls and ensure that an immobilized bear can be retrieved.

Drugging in dens is routinely used with black bears but not with denned grizzly bears due to their aggressive nature. Induction times are generally delayed in denned bears, due to depressed cardiovascular function, and respiratory arrest can occur with some drugs.

Bear researchers and managers often must immobilize female bears with cubs. Cubs and mothers should be handled at the same location but placed in separate containers for immobilization. Separation eliminates risks to cubs from displaced aggression of the sow during induction or recovery. Immobilizations should be planned to minimize the duration of mother-cub separation.

Two major classes of drugs, cyclohexamines and opioids, augmented with diazepinone tranquilizers and/or alpha-2 adrenergic agonists, are routinely used to immobilize bears. Cyclohexamines have been more popular because they are effective and less risky to handle. Opioid combinations are also effective and have the additional advantage of being fully reversible. This feature may make narcotics a more appropriate drug in certain situations. Depending on location and capture method (physical restraint), immobilants can be administered to bears using dart rifles, dart pistols, blowpipes or syringe poles.

A tiletamine-zolazepam combination is the most frequently used drug for bears. A variety of concentrations can be made by changing the amount of sterile water diluents because the drug comes as a freeze-dried (lyophilized) powder. This makes the drug useful for large bears such as adult grizzly and polar bears. Tiletamine-zolazepam has a wide safety margin, produces a slow and predictable recovery (especially useful for large, dangerous animals in field settings), and has minimal cardiopulmonary and thermoregulatory side effects in bears. This type of recovery may be a disadvantage in situations where bears must recover more quickly to avoid injuries, threats from other bears, or to attend cubs. In addition, tiletamine-zolazepam, by itself, is unsuitable for surgical procedures in bears due to poor analgesic qualities (Caulkett et al. 1999).

The bear research program at Washington State University uses the following drug regimen to immobilize captive grizzly and black bears (C. T. Robbins, unpublished data). For hibernating bears, a combination of ketamine (3.7 mg/kg) and xylazine (0.7 mg/kg) is used. For non-hibernating bears, a combination of tiletamine-zolazepam (2 mg/kg), ketamine (0.9 mg/kg), and xylazine (0.9 mg/kg) is used. Tiletamine-zolazepam alone is reserved for clinical procedures where cardiopulmonary function must be fully maintained. Bears are allowed to recover spontaneously without antagonists.

Premature, explosive recoveries have occurred in bears anesthetized with combinations of ketamine and the alpha-2 agonists, xylazine or medetomidine. It is hypothesized that ketamine is metabolized more quickly than the alpha-2 agonists producing a deep sedation due solely to the alpha-2 drug toward the end of immobilization. During this period, a sudden stimulus can cause a rapid awakening, similar to that reported for bears and other species sedated with xylazine or medetomidine alone. To reduce this risk, when using ketamine-alpha-2 combinations, it is critically important to monitor depth of anesthesia throughout the handling session, particularly in a field setting. We recommend, particularly with dangerous species, that a snare be used to anchor the bear to a fixed structure to permit retreat and minimize danger from a rapidly awakening bear. Needless stimuli should be reduced, particularly exposure of adult females to vocalizations from their cubs.

Wolves

Populations of gray wolves (*Canis lupus*) have recently expanded in the United States as a result of multiple reintroductions and dispersal from new or existing populations. Wolves are pack animals and behave in a manner generally to the advantage of the pack. Thus, it is rare to have other members of the pack present danger to crews when a wolf is captured. Wolves can be chemically immobilized by darting from small aircraft, or by injecting trapped animals using a pole syringe or blowpipe. Leg-hold traps containing sedatives have been used to keep the animal calm and minimize self-mutilation. Cyclohexamine-sedative combinations are the most commonly used drugs for wolf immobilization, although narcotics are also effective. A combination of 10-mg/kg ketamine and 2-mg/kg xylazine is a recommended dose for wolves (Kreeger et al. 2002). To prevent rough recoveries from cyclohexamine anesthetics, one should wait at least 45 minutes after the last ketamine or tiletamine-zolazepam injection before administering yohimbine for xylazine reversal. Our experience with narcotic immobilization of wolves is that hyperthermia is common.

Coyotes

Coyotes (*Canis latrans*) are highly adaptable animals, inhabiting most regions of the United States. Coyotes are usually trapped before chemical immobilization, which is required for prolonged handling. Recommended drug combinations include tiletamine-zolazepam (10 mg/kg), ketamine (10 mg/kg) plus xylazine (2 mg/kg), and ketamine (10 mg/kg) plus acepromazine (0.1 mg/kg) (Kreeger et al. 2002).

Foxes

Five species of foxes are found in North America. They occur in diverse environments from boreal regions of northern Canada and Alaska to dry chaparral and deserts of the southwestern United States and Mexico. Tiletamine-zolazepam is the drug of choice for immobilizing 4 of the species, including kit fox (*Vulpes macrotis*), red fox (*V. vulpes*), swift fox (*V. velox*) (all at 10 mg/kg), and gray fox (*Urocyon cinereoargenteus*) (8.8 mg/kg). Arctic foxes (*Alopex lagopus*) have also been successfully immobilized with tiletamine-zolazepam (10 mg/kg), although Kreeger et al. (2002) recommended ketamine (2.5 mg/kg) plus medetomidine (0.05 mg/kg) antagonized with atipamezole (0.125 mg/kg). An alternative drug combination listed for all 5 species is ketamine (20 mg/kg) plus acepromazine (0.2 mg/kg) (Kreeger et al. 2002).

Mountain Lion

Mountain lions (*Puma concolor*) occupy temperate, subtropical, and tropical regions from British Columbia to Argentina. They prefer areas sparsely inhabited by people and are seldom seen even where relatively common. Mountain lions have come into increasing conflict with humans using and occupying peripheral habitats for lions. Mountain lions are normally solitary and secretive. The most consistent and successful method for capturing them is pursuit with hunting dogs and darting them with drugs once they seek refuge in a tree or rock shelter. Once a mountain lion has been darted, it should be allowed to climb down to prevent injury. The lion can then be followed at a distance until the drug takes effect (California Department of Fish and Game 1995). However, many lions do not leave the tree and equipment for removing the lion (climbing spurs, safety harnesses, and ropes) should be available. The recommended immobilization regimen for mountain lions is ketamine (2 mg/kg) plus medetomidine (0.075 mg/kg) reversed with atipamezole (0.3 mg/kg). Alternative combinations include tiletamine/zolazepam (8 mg/kg), or ketamine (10 mg/kg) plus xylazine (2 mg/kg) antagonized with yohimbine (0.125 mg/kg) (Kreeger et al. 2002).

Bobcat and Canada Lynx

Bobcats (*Lynx rufus*) are common throughout most of North America and occur in forests and shrublands from southern Mexico to southern Canada. Lynx (*L. canadensis*) are closely related to bobcats, but occupy higher elevation forests and boreal regions of the northern United States and Canada. Both species are highly secretive and, generally, can be chemically immobilized only in captivity or after being caught in traps. The drug of choice for both species is tiletamine-zolazepam (10 mg/kg for bobcat, 5 mg/kg for lynx). An alternative drug regimen is ketamine (10 mg/kg) plus xylazine (1.5–2.0 mg/kg) (Kreeger et al. 2002). Antagonists are not used and animals must be monitored until they have fully recovered.

Other Mammals

Raccoon

Raccoons (*Procyon lotor*) are nearly ubiquitous near human habitations and in remote areas. They can be captured in box traps or padded leg-hold traps and chemically immobilized with a pole syringe for safe handling. As raccoons can carry rabies, use of gloves is advised for handling. The recommended immobilization protocol for raccoons is ketamine (20 mg/kg) plus xylazine (4 mg/kg) antagonized with yohimbine (0.15 mg/kg). Alternative regimens include tiletamine/zolazepam (12 mg/kg), or ketamine (20 mg/kg) plus acepromazine (0.1 mg/kg) (Kreeger et al. 2002).

Northern River Otter

River otters (*Lontra canadensis*) occur along streams and estuaries throughout the United States and Canada. They can be caught in a variety of traps and must be chemically immobilized to handle safely. Recommended drug combinations for immobilizing river otters are tiletamine-zolazepam (5.5 mg/kg), or ketamine (2.5 mg/kg) plus medetomidine (0.05 mg/kg) antagonized with atipamezole (0.2 mg/kg) (Kreeger et al. 2002).

American Badger

Badgers (*Taxidea taxus*) occupy dry, open habitats throughout North America, ranging from northern Alberta to southern Mexico. They can be captured in steel-jawed traps, box traps, and snares. Badgers are powerful and pugnacious, and chemical immobilization is essential for handling. Drugs are delivered by pole syringe or blowpipe (California Department of Fish and Game 1995) and restraint will be needed as badgers may struggle or bite the syringe. Kreeger et al. (2002) recommended tiletamine/zolazepam (4.4 mg/kg) to immobilize badgers, or ketamine (15 mg/kg) plus xylazine (1 mg/kg). No antagonist is used.

Wolverine

The range of wolverines (*Gulo gulo*) extends from northern Alaska and Canada to the higher mountain ranges of the contiguous United States. Although not normally aggressive, wolverines are noted for their strength and ferociousness when defending a food cache or young. Thus, wolverines cannot be handled without chemical immobilization. The recommended drug protocol for wolverines is ketamine (5 mg/kg) plus medetomidine (0.1 mg/kg) antagonized with atipamezole (0.2 mg/kg; ½ IV, ½ IM), or ketamine (20 mg/kg) plus acepromazine (0.2 mg/kg) (Kreeger et al. 2002).

Fisher

Fisher (*Martes pennanti*) occupy coniferous forest habitats in Canada, the northeastern United States, and Intermountain West. They can be captured in box traps, and must be chemically immobilized before handling. Injections are given by jab stick or hand-held syringe while the animal is confined with a board or comb at one end of the trap (California Department of Fish and Game 1995). Fishers have been immobilized with ketamine (25 mg/kg) plus xylazine (5 mg/kg), or with ketamine (20 mg/kg) plus acepromazine (0.1 mg/kg) (Kreeger et al. 2002). Antagonist use has not been reported.

SUMMARY

The days of untrained individuals using drugs to capture animals are past. Most wildlife capture work is conducted by government conservation agencies, as a public trust responsibility. Accountability to the public is high and poor performance is not acceptable. Successful, humane, and safe chemical immobilization requires a great deal of skill and knowledge. Those conducting these operations must understand the effects of drugs on animals and humans, and how to mitigate unwanted or unexpected complications. A comprehensive plan for the immobilization operation is a critical element to success. The primary consideration of the plan is for efficient and effective immobilization while maintaining human and animal safety. A key element in a capture plan is an experienced team leader. Once the plan is developed and personnel assigned tasks, the proper equipment should be checked for function and performance. Several tools are available to remotely deliver drugs to free-ranging wildlife. Whichever tools are selected, they must be able to perform under the variables associated with the chosen season, time, location, and species. Those conducting immobilization of wildlife should understand the behavior and characteristics of the targeted species to minimize danger to humans and animals. A basic knowledge of emergency animal medicine is essential. In the event of situations requiring euthanasia of an animal, those conducting wildlife capture need to understand the humane considerations paramount to choice of method, and how to properly and safely conduct euthanasia. Biologists should work with an experienced veterinarian for chemical immobilization of wildlife.

ACKNOWLEDGMENTS

We appreciate the insight and editorial help provided by C. E. Braun and 2 anonymous reviewers.

LITERATURE CITED

AVMA PANEL ON EUTHANASIA. 2001. 2000 Report of the AVMA panel on euthanasia. Journal of the American Veterinary Medical Association 218:669–696.

CALIFORNIA DEPARTMENT OF FISH AND GAME. 1995. Wildlife restraint handbook. California Department of Fish and Game, Wildlife Investigations Laboratory, Rancho Cordova, California, USA.

CAULKETT, N. A., M. R. L. CATTET, J. M. CAULKETT, AND S. C. POLISCHUK. 1999. Comparative physiological effects of Telazol®, medetomidine-ketamine, and medetomidine-Telazol® in captive polar bears (*Ursus maritimus*). Journal of Zoo and Wildlife Medicine 30:504–509.

———, ———, S. CANTWELL, N. COOL, AND W. OLSEN. 2000. Anesthesia of wood bison with medetomidine-zolazepam/tiletamine and xylazine-zolazepam/tiletamine combinations. Canadian Veterinary Journal 41:49–53.

HAIGH, J. C., AND C. C. GATES. 1995. Capture of wood bison (*Bison bison athabascae*) using carfentanil-based mixtures. Journal of Wildlife Diseases 31:37–42.

HASTINGS, B. E., S. G. STADLER, AND R. A. KOCK. 1989. Reversible immobilization of Chinese water deer (*Hydropotes inermis*) with ketamine and xylazine. Journal of Zoo and Wildlife Medicine 20:427–430.

KREEGER, T. J. 2000a. Anesthesia of pronghorn using A-3080 or A-3080 plus xylazine. Annual Conference of the Wildlife Disease Association 49:Abstract.

———. 2000b. Xylazine-induced aspiration pneumonia in Shiras moose. Wildlife Society Bulletin 28:751–753.

———, J. M. ARNEMO, AND J. P. RAATH. 2002. Handbook of wildlife chemical immobilization. Wildlife Pharmaceuticals, Inc., Fort Collins, Colorado, USA.

MILLER, M. W., M. A. WILD, AND W. R. LANCE. 1996. Efficacy and safety of naltrexone hydrochloride for antagonizing carfentanil citrate immobilization in captive Rocky Mountain elk (*Cervus elaphus nelsoni*). Journal of Wildlife Diseases 32:234–239.

MODESTO-LOWE, V., AND J. VAN KIRK. 2002. Clinical uses of naltrexone: a review of the evidence. Experimental Clinical Psychopharmacology 10:213–237.

POND, D. B., AND B. W. O'GARA. 1994. Chemical immobilization of large mammals. Pages 125–139 *in* T. A. Bookhout, editor. Research and management techniques for wildlife and habitats. Fifth edition. The Wildlife Society, Bethesda, Maryland, USA.

ROFFE, T. J., AND S. J. SWEENEY. 2002. Tolazoline reversal of xylazine in bison (*Bison bison*): mitigation of adverse effects. Annual Conference of the Wildlife Disease Association 51:Abstract.

———, K. COFFIN, AND J. BERGER. 2001. Survival and immobilizing moose with carfentanil and xylazine. Wildlife Society Bulletin 29:1140–1146.

SCHEMNITZ, S. D. 2005. Capturing and handling wild animals. Pages 239–285 *in* C. E. Braun, editor. Techniques for wildlife investigations and management. Sixth edition. The Wildlife Society, Bethesda, Maryland, USA.

SHORT, C. E. 1983. Practical use of ultra short-acting barbiturates. Bio-Ceutic Laboratories, Veterinary Learning Systems Company, Inc., Princeton, New Jersey, USA.

WALLINGFORD, B. D., R. A. LANCIA, AND E. C. SOUTIERE. 1996. Antagonism of xylazine in white-tailed deer with intramuscular injection of yohimbine. Journal of Wildlife Diseases 32:399–402.

12

CRITERIA FOR GENDER AND AGE

Michael A. Schroeder and Leslie A. Robb

INTRODUCTION

Accurate classification of an animal's gender and age is fundamental to wildlife research and management (Leopold 1933). Gender and age information is often used to establish harvest regulations and strategies, monitor a population's demographic structure, health, and viability, and provide an understanding of behavioral ecology.

In many situations identifying an animal's gender and age is relatively simple, especially for sexually dimorphic species and those with distinct age-specific patterns of appearance. However, accurate classification of an individual's gender and/or age may be more complicated for species that are monomorphic. Additionally, for many species, young-of-the-year are identifiable, but differentiation among older age classes is difficult. Moreover, in many situations only partial information and/or material, such as a wing, jaw, or tooth, is available for evaluating an individual's gender and/or age. This limitation can be exacerbated by the relatively short and/or sub-optimal time during which many samples are collected, such as during a hunting season.

One objective of this review is to describe basic techniques used to classify gender and age of birds, mammals, reptiles, and amphibians that occur in North America. Techniques that have reduced subjectivity, improved accuracy, a wide range of applicability among numerous species, and a long history of standardized use are emphasized. The second objective is to identify techniques and resources used to examine particular species or groups of species. An exhaustive description of techniques used for evaluating gender and age for all species of interest cannot be achieved in this brief chapter. Consequently, we introduce some of the current techniques used and provide appropriate references for initiating detailed work.

TECHNIQUES FOR CLASSIFICATION OF GENDER AND AGE

The best techniques are those that are versatile and can be used throughout the year with live or dead animals, different body parts, and numerous age categories. In reality,

development of particular techniques has often been affected by time of harvest and/or sampling methodology. For instance, widespread collection of waterfowl and gallinaceous bird wings following harvest has resulted in concentration on subtle differences in wing plumage as a key identifier of species, gender, and age, even though overall differences in plumage patterns among the species may be substantial. Although simple techniques are currently available to ascertain gender and basic age categories for most species, especially game animals, efforts to improve and expand the techniques will undoubtedly continue. These will likely include increased efforts to evaluate species that are endangered, threatened, and/or declining, and species that are indicators of habitat condition.

Behavior

Behavior for most species varies substantially among gender and age classes. Consequently, behavior can be important for identifying outwardly monomorphic species. Behavioral differences can include calls, songs (Fig. 1), visual displays, nest building, clutch incubation, nursing, and urination posture (Fig. 2). However, due to the complicated and species-specific nature of behavioral displays

Fig. 1. Many species of animals, including the sage sparrow (*Amphispiza belli*), exhibit gender-specific behavior. Male sage sparrows have a characteristic song that is not performed by females (photograph by W. M. Vander Haegen).

Fig. 2. Behavior is species-specific. Males of some species may stand and stretch while urinating and females may squat. Exceptions are common, as illustrated by male mule deer (*Odocoileus hemionus*) (Geist 1981) (photograph by V. Geist).

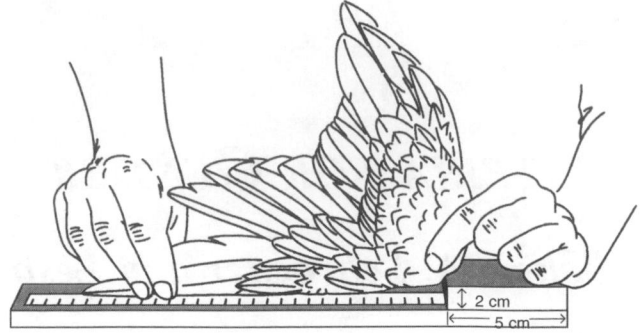

Fig. 4. Technique for measuring wing notch-length (modified from Carney 1992, original drawing from A. J. Godin). The measurement is taken from the notch in the wrist to the tip of the flattened primaries.

(Young 2005), with few exceptions, this chapter will focus on use of morphological characteristics for assessing an individual's gender and/or age.

General Morphology and Appearance

Body Size.—Gender and age categories for many species often differ substantially, thus making classification relatively straight forward with general field guides. For animals in hand, numerous physical characteristics can be measured, but body mass in all animals, forearm length in bats (Fig. 3), snout-vent length in lizards, frogs, and salamanders, and wing chord or wing notch-length in birds, are commonly used. Regardless of technique, care needs to be taken to ensure that measurements are standard and that results can be replicated (Nisbet et al. 1970). For example, in birds wing chord length is measured from, and including, the wrist to the tip of the longest primary. However wing chord can be measured in different ways: (1)

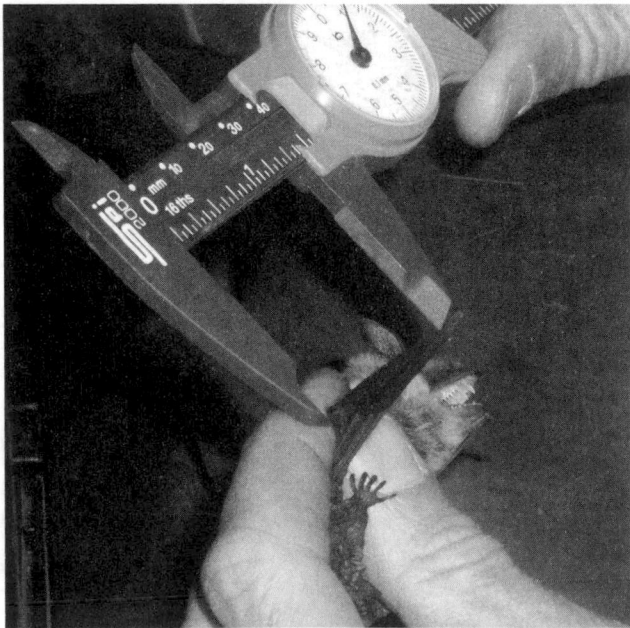

Fig. 3. The length of the forearm of bats is the most common measurement taken, in addition to mass. The slightly curved forearm of this fringed myotis (*Myotis thysanodes*) is measured as the straight-line distance from the end of the ulna to the base of the thumb, preferably using calipers (photograph by M. A. Schroeder).

unflattened, (2) flattened—normal camber of wing reduced with gentle pressure, or (3) maximally flattened—normal camber reduced and feathers gently straightened. Wing flattening and feather straightening can add 0.5–5% to the unflattened length; wing drying can reduce the length (Pyle 1997). Wing notch-length is measured from the notch in the wrist bend to the tip of the longest primary (Fig. 4); this measurement is not synonymous with wing chord. For standardization, waterfowl wings are measured with wing notch-lengths (Carney 1992). Because waterfowl wings are usually dry when measured, the primaries are straightened, but the normal camber of the wing is not altered. Measurements of wing chord or wing notch-length will not be valid if the longest primary (or primaries) is missing, broken, or growing.

Many species display extensive variation in body size/mass associated with subspecies or race, region, and season. This variation often means there may be substantial overlap in the measurements of specific features. For example, even though the average male of many species may be heavier than the average female, there is a range in body mass where the gender could be either. This problem may be exacerbated in monomorphic species when the size of young males is similar to that of adult females.

Appearance.—Features of the head, body, tail, and/or shell of reptiles and amphibians can be used to assess gender and age. For example, the plastron (lower shell) of male turtles tends to be concave while in females the plastron is flat or slightly convex (Powell et al. 1998). The carapace (upper shell) tends to be more rounded with a pronounced median ridge in young turtles (Conant and Collins 1998, Stebbins 2003). Many amphibians have a distinct larval stage that is clearly distinguishable from either the juvenile or adult stages (Powell et al. 1998).

Birds typically have a natal plumage followed by a juvenile (or immature) plumage, and then an adult plumage. Although downy natal plumage is easily identifiable (e.g., chukar, *Alectoris chukar*) (Fig. 5), juvenile plumage can resemble adult plumage in basic appearance while differing in subtle ways such as notched tail feathers (Fig. 6), buffy or worn edges of wing coverts, and variation in color patterns. Most passerines can be separated into 2 age classes based on slight difference in the shape of outer tail feathers (Fig. 7) (Pyle 1997). Knowledge of feather type (Fig. 8) and molt patterns is extremely important for understanding which feathers offer the best clues to an individual's age and gen-

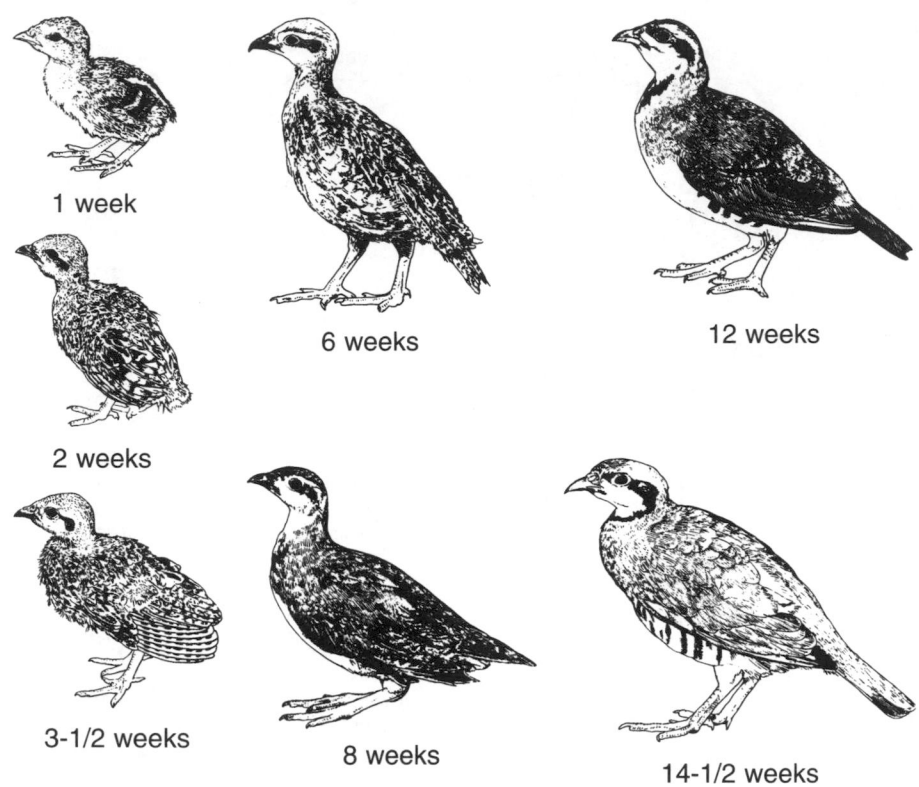

Fig. 5. Changes in appearance of juvenile chukars by age (Alkon 1982).

der. For example, the last juvenile feathers retained on many duck wings are some of the tertial coverts (Carney 1992). The first juvenile feathers to be replaced by adult feathers in spruce grouse (*Falcipennis canadensis*) are on the upper sides of the breast at about 30 days of age, thus permitting identification of gender (Boag and Schroeder 1992).

Males of many bird species have a distinct breeding plumage that can be used to identify gender. For example, male and female white-tailed ptarmigan (*Lagopus leucura*) can be distinguished by plumage during spring, but not during winter (Braun et al. 1993). Females of most bird species develop a brood patch during the breeding season, a bare patch of skin on the abdomen that is critical during incubation; the presence or absence of a brood patch can be useful for assessing gender (Pyle 1997).

Most gallinaceous birds retain juvenile primaries 9 and 10 (numbered from P1 [inner] to P10 [outer]) through the first year and these primaries often differ in appearance from P9 and P10 of adults. Consequently, some gallinaceous birds can be reliably placed into 3 age classes (depending on time of year). These classes include HY (hatch year or juvenile), SY (second year or yearling, usually through the prebasic molt in late summer and early autumn), and ASY (after second year or adult). Later in the hunting season and/or following completion of the prebasic molt, SY birds are usually indistinguishable from ASY birds and, hence, both are referred to as AHY (after hatch year) birds. In this latter case, only 2 age classes are distinguishable (HY and AHY) (Fig. 9). Many other species of birds (except for a few species with intermediate plumage patterns) can only be differentiated into HY and AHY age classes, or in some cases, no differentiation at all (for example after the prebasic molt of mourning doves [*Zenaida macroura*]). Care should be

taken when basing interpretations on the timing of molt. Zwickel and Dake (1977) found that reproductively successful female blue grouse (*Dendragapus obscurus*) tend to have a delayed molt when compared with unsuccessful females.

There can be substantial variation in plumage characteristics associated with region and subspecies. For example, ruffed grouse (*Bonasa umbellus*) in southern populations typically have longer tails than those in northern populations (Uhlig 1953, Davis 1969, Servello and Kirkpatrick 1986). Wild turkeys (*Meleagris gallopavo*) also show regional and subspecific variation (Healy and Nenno 1980). Many juvenile wild turkeys in Florida molt P9, and in some cases P10, in their first autumn (Williams and Austin 1970), in contrast to the normal pattern of gallinaceous

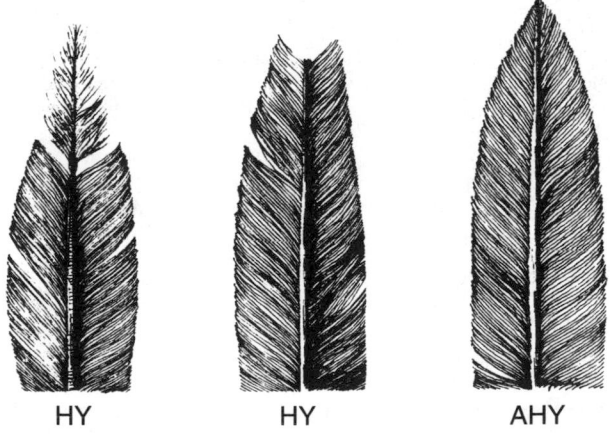

Fig. 6. Tail feathers of HY waterfowl may be notched or have a downy plume attached to the tip, while tail feathers of AHY birds are rounded or pointed (Godin 1960).

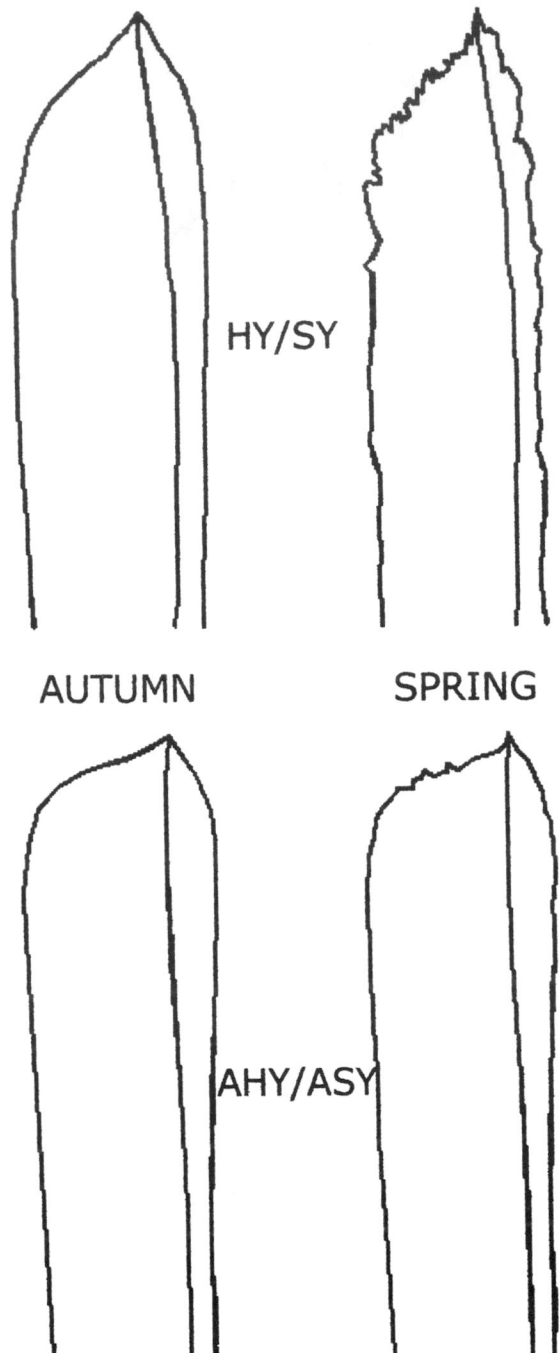

Fig. 7. Shape of outer rectrices of typical passerine during autumn and following spring for 2 age categories. Although feathers for each age category display wear in spring, feathers for HY/SY birds display considerably more (modified from Pyle 1997).

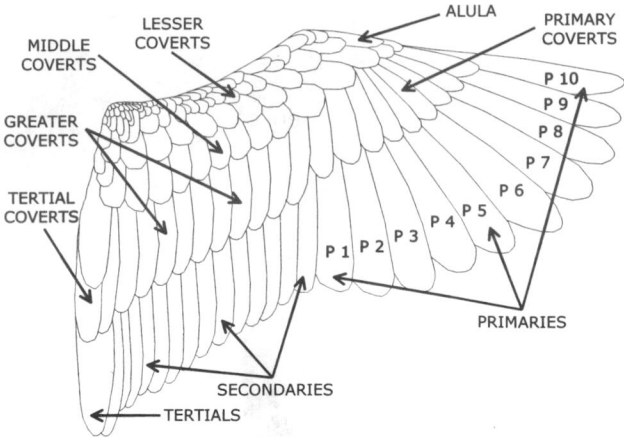

Fig. 8. Basic feather types on a typical wing. Primaries are numbered from proximal to distal (P1 through P10), and secondaries are numbered from distal to proximal (not individually labeled on figure).

birds. The potential variation in appearance and pattern of molt associated with ecological region is not clearly understood, yet this factor may be a problem when samples are drawn from a broad geographic area and/or include multiple subspecies.

Mammals display much greater variation in size, longevity, productivity, and breeding cycles than birds. Many small mammals enter the breeding population in the same year they are born while large mammals can take many years to mature; for example, the house mouse (*Mus musculus*) is sexually mature 5–7 weeks after birth (Bronson 1979) while the gray whale (*Eschrichtius gibbosus*) reaches sexual maturity after at least 8 years (Burt and Grossenheider 1998). These differences add to the complications of assessing mammals, particularly with regard to age.

Ungulate fawns and calves tend to have relatively short head profiles when compared with yearlings and adults (Fig. 10). Other examples of variation include the vulval patches of female moose (*Alces alces*) (Roussel 1975) and caribou (*Rangifer tarandus*) (Bergerud 1978) and the black face patch of male pronghorn (*Antilocapra americana*) (Einarsen 1948). In an unusual example, the patterns on the undersurface of pelts are used to classify the age of muskrats (*Ondatra zibethicus*); juveniles have a symmetrical pattern whereas adults are blotchy (Moses and Boutin 1986) (Fig. 11). The fur on the tail of eastern gray squirrels (*Sciurus carolinensis*) also changes with age (Fig. 12).

Differences in physical features can often be used to assess gender and general age classes. For instance, male ungulates often have antlers while females do not and, in situations where females have antlers or horns, they are usually smaller. In addition, horns and antlers are usually larger for older animals (Fig. 13). Nevertheless, there is substantial variability and often too much overlap in the outward appearance of antlers and horns for this technique to be useful for several age categories (especially from a distance), and horns of females can sometimes resemble those of young males (Lawson and Johnson 1982).

Cloaca and Sex Organs.—In birds, the depth of the bursa of Fabricius (Fig. 14) decreases with age (Gower 1939). Hence, measurement of the bursa with a probe can be used to estimate age class (Wight 1956). However, because most birds display some age-specific variation in plumage, measurement of the bursa is not necessary. During the breeding season, the cloacal protuberance can be used to identify males in many species (particularly passerines), but the lack of a protuberance may not necessarily verify a female (Pyle 1997). Examination of the cloaca is usually not needed because most birds are dimorphic in appearance.

Examination of genitals is often important for classifying gender of mammals due to their monomorphic appearance. With large mammals, genitals often can be observed from a distance. However, careful palpation of many smaller species is needed to identify the testes and/or baculum.

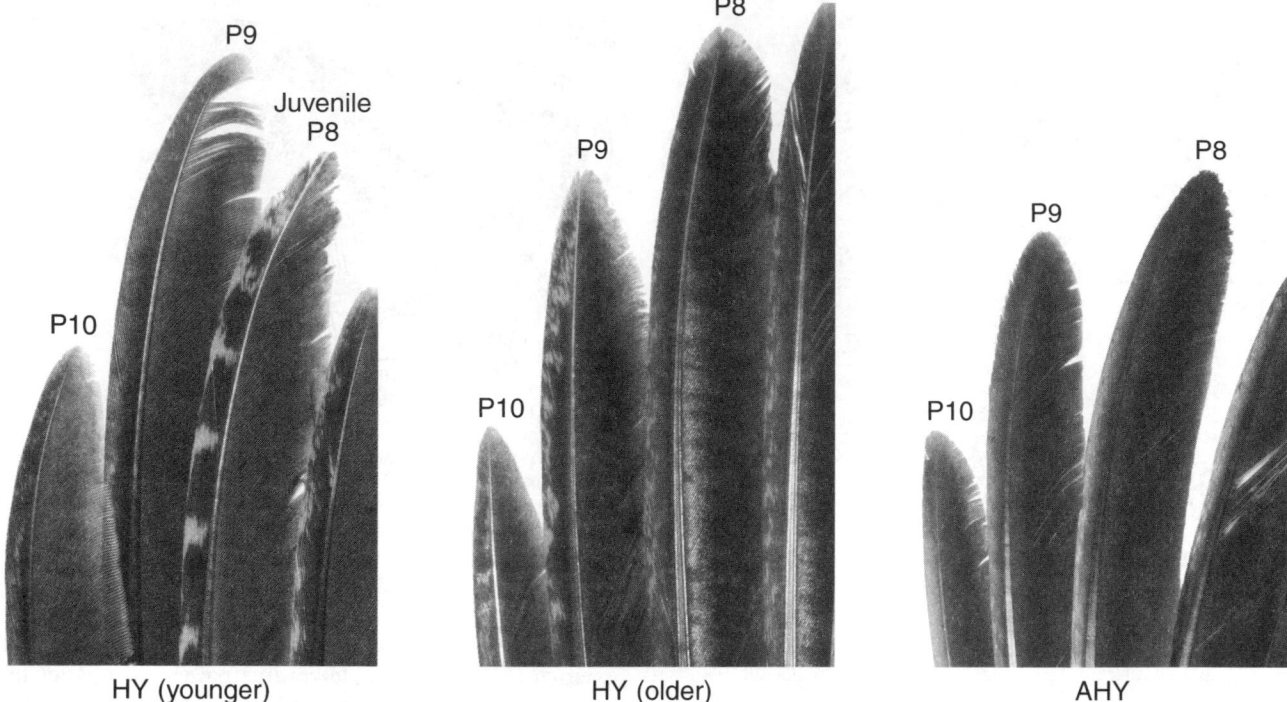

Fig. 9. Comparison of HY (hatch year or juvenile) and AHY (after hatch year) female blue grouse wings collected during the autumn harvest. In the wing on the left, the relatively short juvenile P8 has not yet molted and P9 and P10 are relatively pointed; the wing is clearly definable as HY. In the middle wing, juvenile P8 has been replaced, and P9 and P10 are both relatively pointed; the wing is from an HY bird. On the right wing P9 and P10 are relatively rounded indicating the bird is AHY; because the bird has completed its molt, there is no possibility of differentiating between SY (second year) and ASY (after second year).

Fig. 10. Profile and frontal view of calf, yearling female, and adult female elk (*Cervus elaphus*) during late autumn–winter (Smith and McDonald 2002).

Changes in the appearance of the baculum are used as a technique for classifying age in many species including muskrat (Elder and Shanks 1962) (Fig. 15), mink (*Mustela vison*) (Lechleitner 1954), long-tailed weasel (*M. frenata*) (Wright 1947), striped skunk (*Mephitis mephitis*) (Petrides 1950b), American badger (*Taxidea taxus*) (Petrides 1950b), American marten (*Martes americana*) (Marshall 1951), and wolverine (*Gulo gulo*) (Wright and Rausch 1955). Schulte et al. (1995) also found that male American beaver (*Castor canadensis*) had a viscous anal gland secretion that was brown to sepia while the secretion of females tended to be paler and less viscous.

Reptiles exhibit internal fertilization via double-grooved hemipenes in lizards and snakes, and via a single-grooved

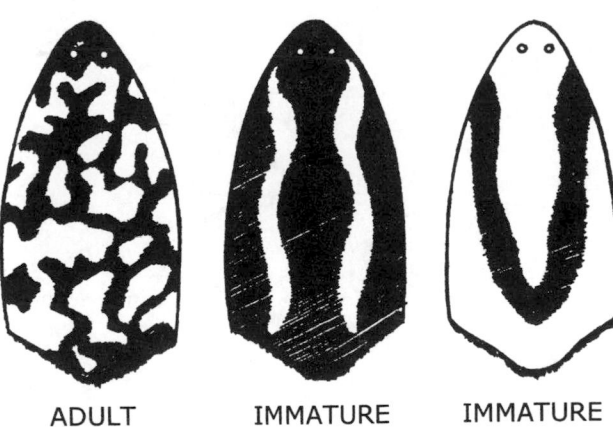

Fig. 11. The undersides of muskrat pelts have different patterns of light (prime) and dark (unprimed) fur that correspond with general age categories (Godin 1960).

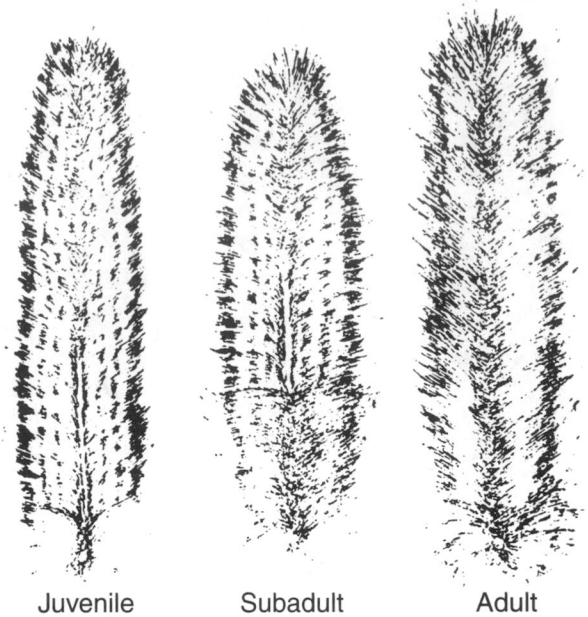

Juvenile   Subadult   Adult

Fig. 12. Increased prevalence of short appressed hairs on the ventral surface of a gray squirrel's tail alters its age-related appearance (Godin 1960).

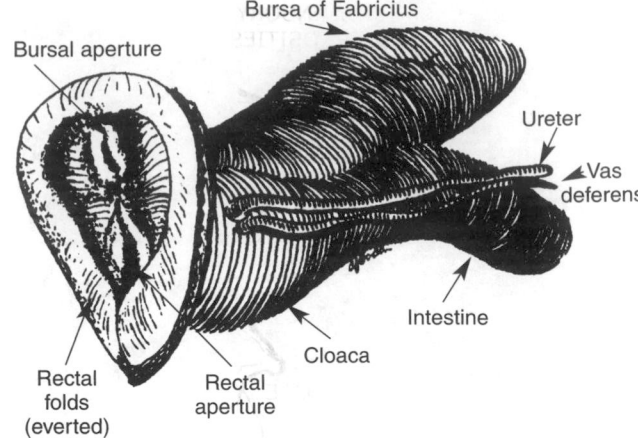

Fig. 14. Bursa of Fabricius in relation to other cloacal structures (from Godin 1960).

penis in turtles. The hemipenes of male lizards and snakes makes the base of their tail appear broader or swollen when compared with females (Gregory 1983). Gentle pressure may be used to evert the hemipenes. Some have recommended careful insertion of a blunt probe caudally at the lateral margins of the vent to confirm the presence or absence of the hemipenes (Schaefer 1934); Harlow (1996) used this technique effectively to ascertain gender of hatchling lizards. However, proper training for this technique is essential and its use is not recommended to avoid damaging reproductive organs (Gregory 1983). In turtles, the cloacal vent is positioned at or beyond the shell margin in males and inside the shell margin for females (Powell et al. 1998). Among amphibians, some salamanders exhibit internal fertilization while others, along with most anurans, fertilize egg masses externally. Male salamanders have a swollen cloaca, or vent, that is visibly lined with tubercles and conceals their copulatory organ (phallodeum); the female's vent does not have tubercles and is not swollen (Petranka 1998).

Internal examination of gonadal material, such as the ovaries in a female, is clearly useful for ascertaining gender and is often used to verify other techniques that are based on external characteristics. Other internal characteristics that are unique to a particular gender may be associated with secondary gender characteristics or directly with reproductive organs such as with suspensory tuberosities in white-tailed deer (*Odocoileus virginianus*) and mule deer (Taber 1956) (Fig. 16). Although suspensory tuberosities are observable in deer ≥2-1/2 years old, they are not obvious in deer as young as 1-1/2. In these cases, the ilio-pectineal

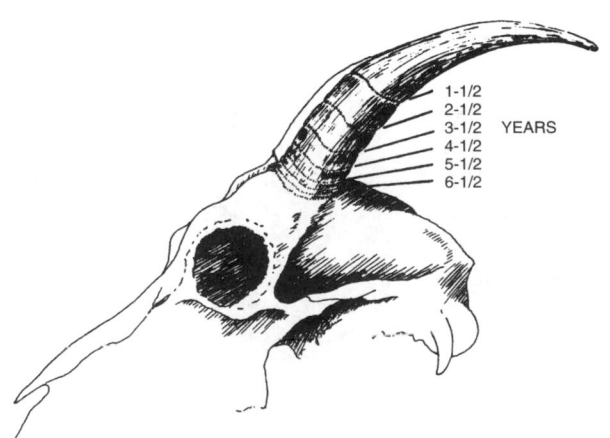

Fig. 13. The horns of mountain goats (*Oreamnos americanus*) may have rings that correspond to year class (Brandborg 1955).

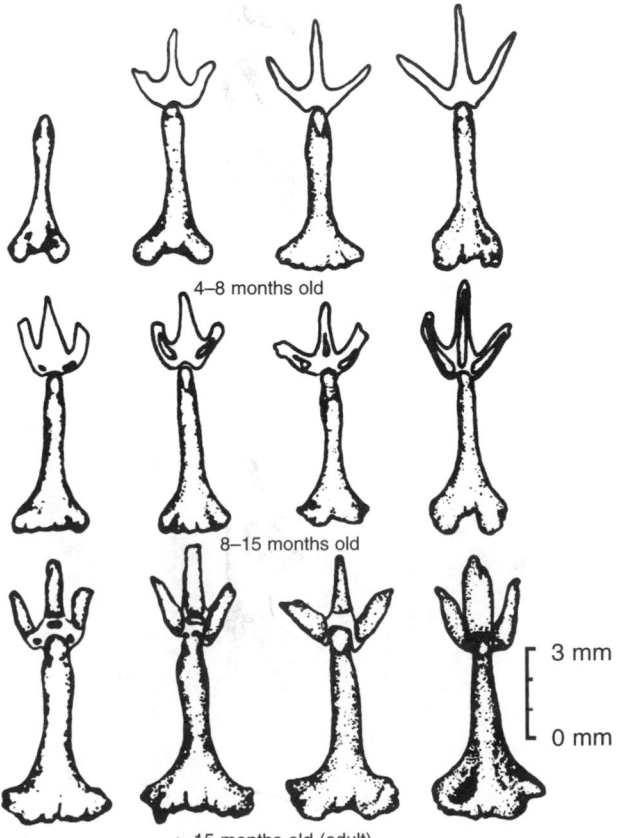

Fig. 15. Variation in baculum appearance of muskrats in relation to age (Elder and Shanks 1962).

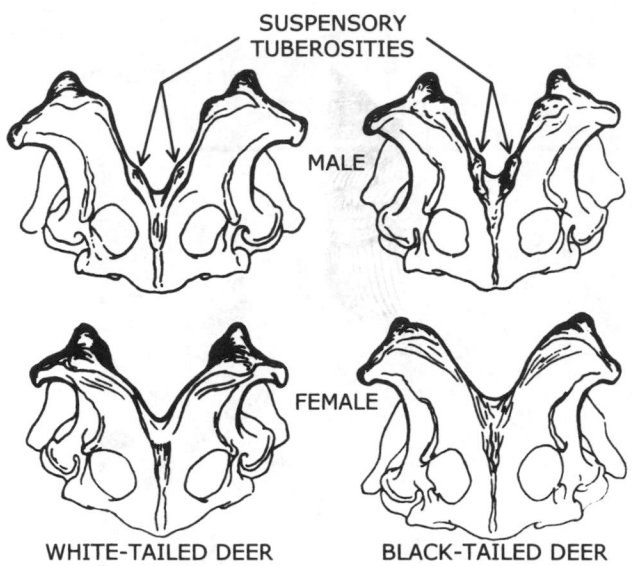

SUSPENSORY
TUBEROSITIES

MALE

FEMALE

WHITE-TAILED DEER   BLACK-TAILED DEER

Fig. 16. Diagram of pelvic girdle of white-tailed deer (A) and black-tailed deer (*O. h. hemionus*) (B) ≥2-1/2 years of age showing suspensory tuberosities for the attachment of the penis ligaments (Taber 1956).

eminences can be used to ascertain gender (Edwards et al. 1982) (Fig. 17). Although internal characteristics are useful, they usually cannot be examined in live animals.

Dentition.—The structure and growth patterns of teeth are commonly used to classify age and gender of mammals

(Fig. 18). General age classes of mammals can be identified by dental characteristics such as thin root walls, wide-open root tips, ratio of pulp width to tooth width, ratio of dentine to enamel, tooth shape, and the timing of tooth emergence (Severinghaus 1949; Jenks et al. 1984; Dix and Strickland 1986a,b; Johnston et al. 1987; Helldin 1997). Examination of teeth may also provide insight into gender for several species. For example, male elk grow an upper canine tooth whereas females do not (Greer and Yeager 1967). The lower canines in male black bear (*Ursus americanus*) (Sauer 1966), marten (Dix and Strickland 1986b), fisher (*Martes pennanti*) (Parsons et al. 1978, Jenks et al. 1984, Dix and Strickland 1986a), and bobcat (*Lynx rufus*) (Friedrich et al. 1983) tend to be larger than the lower canines of females.

In the maturing process of mammals, there is often a consistent pattern of tooth emergence and replacement. For example, in the lower jaw of ungulates there usually are 3 incisors (numbered from center to side, 1–3), 1 canine (incisorform), 3 premolars (numbered from front to back, 2–4), and 3 molars (numbered from front to back, 1–3); the first incisors, canine, and premolars are deciduous and are replaced by permanent teeth (Fig. 18). This evaluation of teeth is further enhanced by differences in appearance between the relatively small, deciduous teeth and their larger, permanent replacements. Three cusps characterize deciduous premolar 4 (third premolar from the front) in many North American ungulates, whereas permanent premolar 4 has only 2 cusps. The timing of these replacements and emergence of permanent molars can be used to estimate age (Table 1).

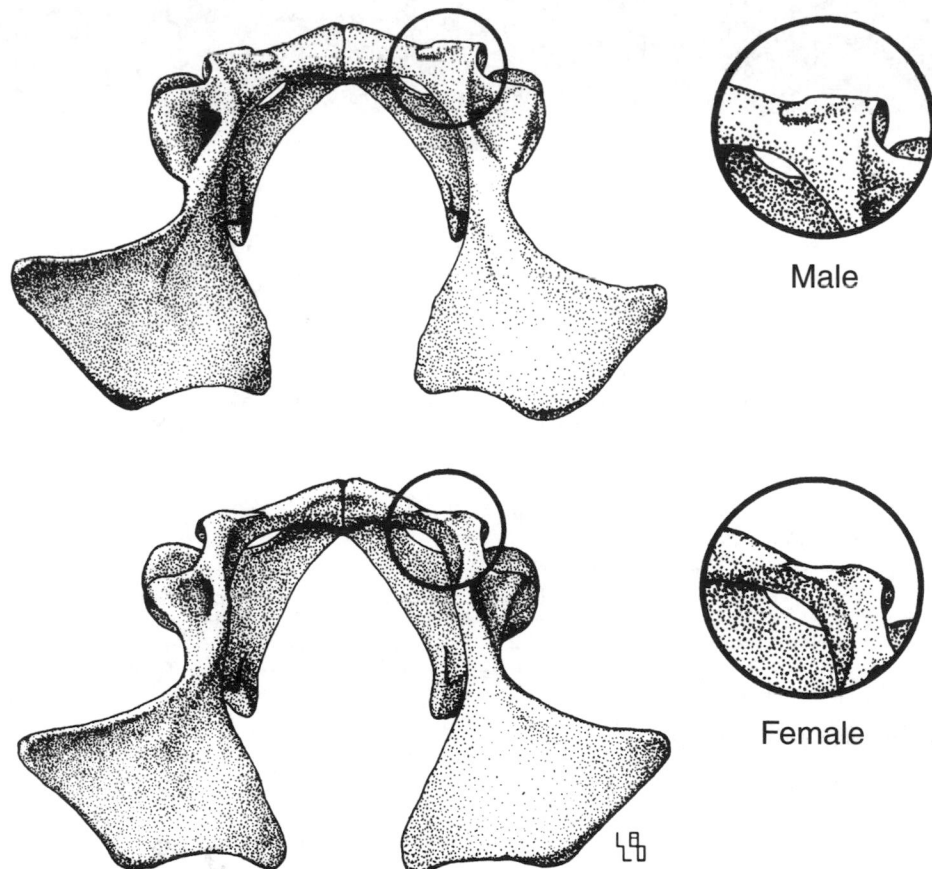

Male

Female

Fig. 17. Pelvic girdles of 1 ½ year-old white-tailed deer can be classified by gender based on the position of the ilio-pectineal eminences (IPE). The IPE is flattened and on the edge of the acetabular branch of the pubis in females, and rounded and above the edge of the acetabular branch of the pubis in males (Edwards et al. 1982).

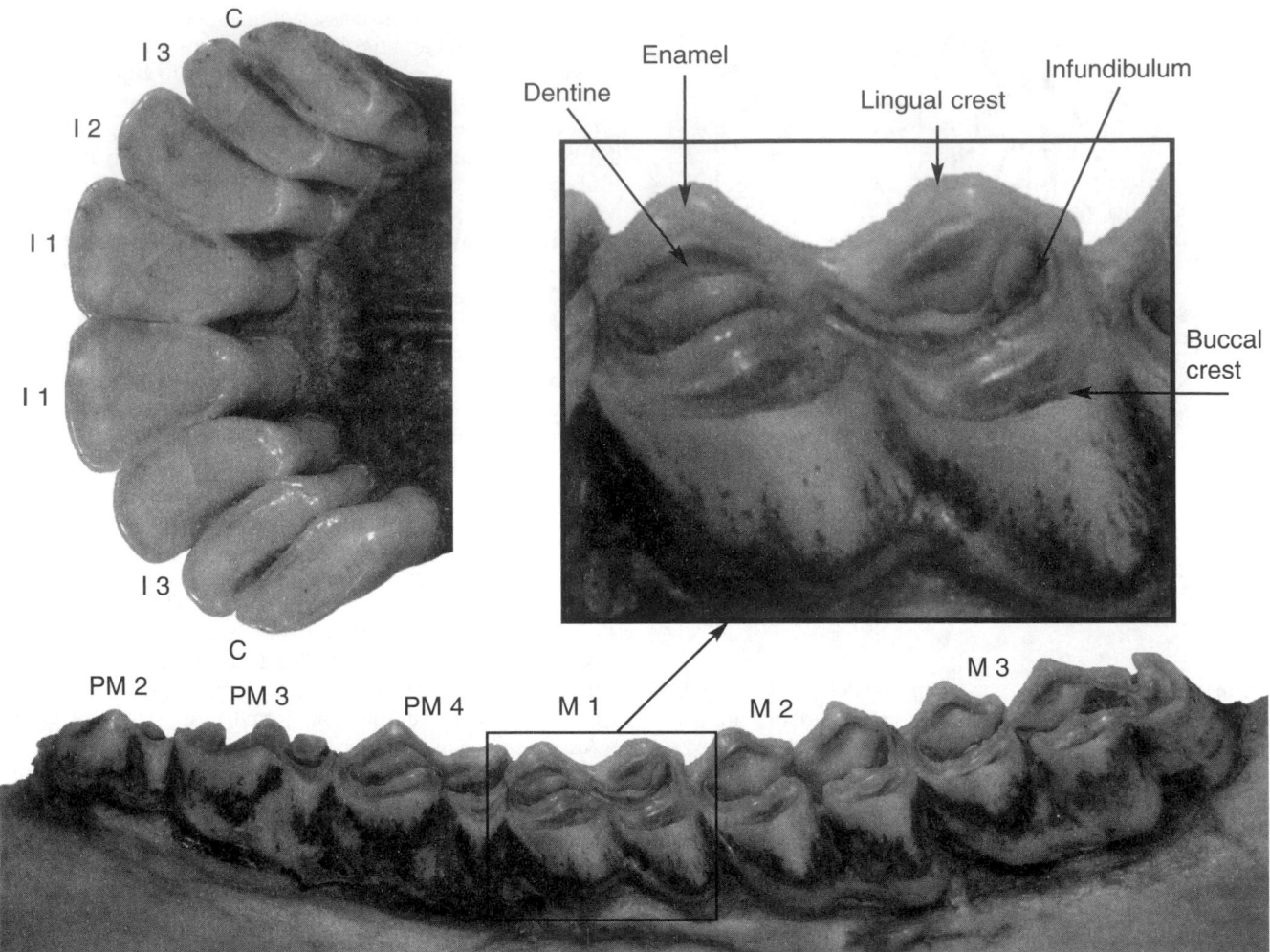

Fig. 18. Lateral view of lower left jaw of mule deer, facing the buccal crest (cheek side). The front of the lower jaw is also shown as well as an enlarged area illustrating the first molar. Teeth are labeled as I (incisor), C (canine), PM (premolar), and M (molar).

There has been substantial effort to use patterns of tooth wear, in addition to emergence and replacement of teeth, to classify older age categories of white-tailed deer (Severinghaus 1949) (Fig. 19) and gray wolf (*Canis lupus*) (Gipson et al. 2000) (Fig. 20). This effort has been accompanied by development of field techniques such as dental impressions (Flyger 1958, Barnes and Longhurst 1960,

Clawson and Causey 1995) and reference sets of gender-specific mandibles (Thomas and Bandy 1975). However, research has often shown that tooth size and wear can vary by individual, subspecies, region, habitat, diet, and gender (Hesselton and Hesselton 1982, Erb et al. 1999, Van Deelen et al. 2000, Gee et al. 2002). Estimation of age of known-age deer with tooth emergence and wear tech-

Table 1. Approximate age in months when permanent molars emerge or incisors, canines, and premolars replace deciduous teeth in the lower jaws of selected North American ungulates.

Species	References	Incisors			Canines	Premolars[a]				Molars		
		1	2	3	1	2	3	4	1	2	3
White-tailed deer	Severinghaus 1949	<6	<12	<12	<12	<18	~18	~12	2–6	~12	<18
Mule deer	Taber and Dasmann 1958	~12	~12	<18	<24	~24	~24	~24	2–6	6–12	18–24
Elk	Quimby and Gaab 1957	<18	~18	<30	<30	~30	~30	~30	~6	<18	<30
Caribou	Miller 1974*b*	10–13	12–15	12–15	12–17	22–29	22–29	22–29	<3	10–15	15–24
Pronghorn	Dow and Wright 1962	<15	<27	<39	39–41	<27	<27	<27	<2	<15	<15
Wild sheep (*Ovis canadensis, O. dalli*)	Lawson and Johnson 1982	12–16	24–28	33–36	45–48	24–32	24–30	24–30	1–6	8–16	22–40
Mountain goat	Brandborg 1955	15–16	26–29	38–40	~48	26–29	26–29	26–29	6–10	10–16	15–29

a   Premolars are numbered from 2 through 4 due to the presumed evolutionary loss of premolar 1.

½ YEARS

PM 4 has 3 cusps.

M 1 unstained.

M 2 may be erupting.

M 3 absent.

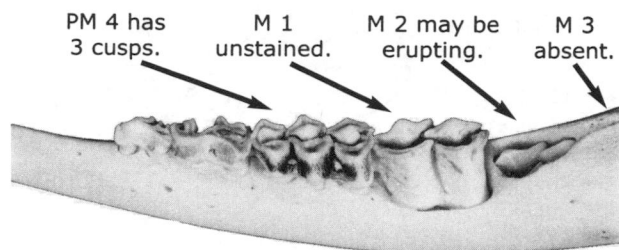

1 ½ YEARS

PM 4 may have 3 cusps (old tooth) or 2 cusps (unstained new tooth).

M 3 unstained and/or not fully erupted.

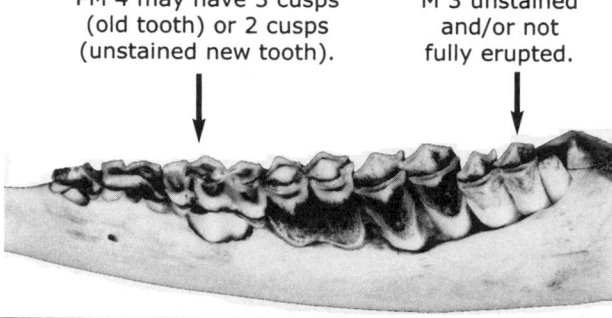

2 ½ YEARS

Dentine width on lingual crests of M 1 is equal to or narrower than strip of surrounding enamel.

PM 4 has 2 cusps.

M 3 fully erupted with little or no dentine showing on lingual side of 2nd crest; back cusp may be worn, but no outward slant.

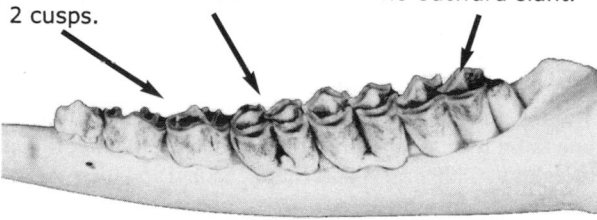

3 ½ YEARS

Dentine width on lingual crests of M 1 wider than surrounding enamel.

Dentine width on M 2 equal to or narrower than surrounding enamel.

Dentine showing slightly on 2nd lingual crest of M 3; back cusp beginning to show wear and an outside slant.

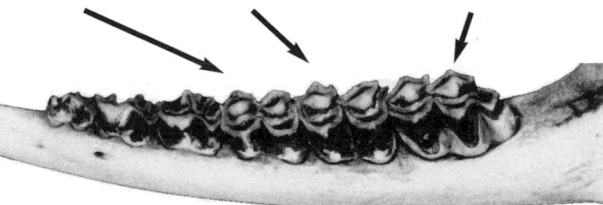

4 ½ YEARS

P 1, P 2, and P 3 showing distinct wear; lingual crests of P 3 starting to erode away.

Dentine on M 1 and M 2 wider than strip of surrounding enamel.

Dentine on M 3 equal to or narrower than surrounding enamel; back cusp beginning to cup and/or slant sharply to outside.

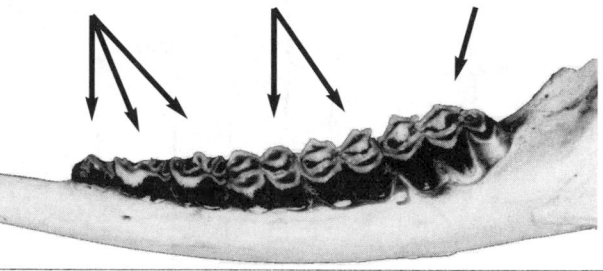

5 ½ YEARS

P 1, P 2, and P 3 heavily worn; lingual crests of P 2 and P 3 often worn nearly flat.

Dentine wider than enamel on M 1 and M 2; infundibulum remains intact.

Dentine on M 3 wider than surrounding enamel; noticeable cup often evident in back cusp with sharp slant to outside.

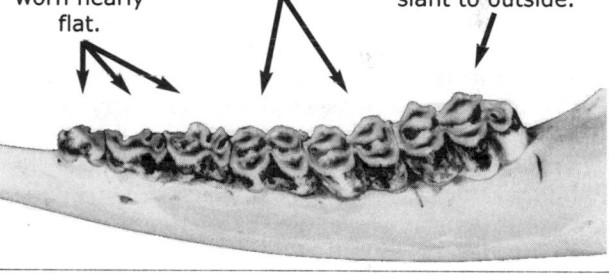

6 ½ YEARS

P 1, P 2, and P 3 heavily worn; lingual crests of P 2 and P 3 worn nearly flat.

Dentine wider than enamel on M 1 and M 2; infundibulum beginning to wear away on M 1.

Dentine on M 3 wider than surrounding enamel; back cusp heavily worn and deeply cupped.

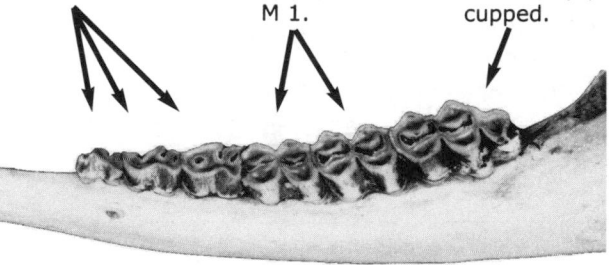

Older than 6 ½ years

More wear than described for previous jaw.

Fig. 19. Progressive age-related wear on premolars and molars (PM 2–4 and M 1–3 left-to-right) of lower left jaw (facing the cheek side) of white-tailed deer (Severinghaus 1949, Godin 1960, Dimmick and Pelton 1994).

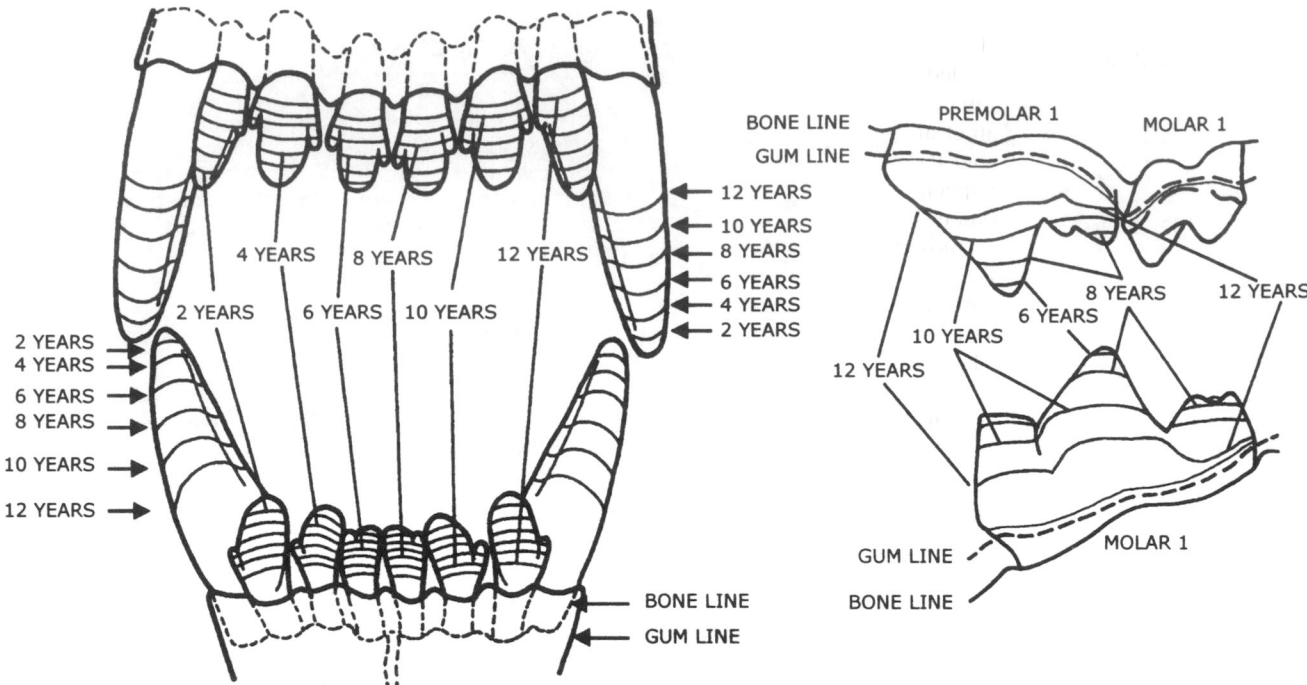

Fig. 20. Progressive wear on incisors and canines in 2-year increments for gray wolves. The lines represent averages for a study of known-age wolves; errors of 1–3 years were observed using this technique (Gipson et al. 2000).

niques has been inaccurate, especially for older age categories (Hamlin et al. 2000, Gee et al. 2002).

Normal variation in tooth wear has been exacerbated by confusion in wear characteristics of teeth necessary to discriminate between age categories (Marchinton et al. 2003). For example, the relative width of dentine (dark-colored region) in relation to enamel (light-colored region) on the lingual crests (tongue side) of molars 1, 2, and 3 (Fig. 18) has been used to classify 2-1/2, 3-1/2, and older white-tailed deer. Severinghaus (1949) suggested that 2-1/2-year-old deer should have dentine narrower than enamel on molar 1, 3-1/2 year-old deer should have dentine wider than enamel on molar 1 and roughly equal to enamel on molars 2 and 3, and older deer should have dentine layers wider than enamel on all molars. Misinterpretation of these characteristics (3-1/2 year-old deer incorrectly

described in Dimmick and Pelton 1994:193) (Fig. 19) can result in deer being misclassified (Marchinton et al. 2003).

For most species, collection of a tooth for cementum annuli analysis is the most accurate method used to estimate age among older age categories (Hamlin et al. 2000). Cementum is deposited annually on the roots of teeth so the layer closest to the dentine is from the earliest year and the layer of the current year lies closest to the root. Because gender, physiology, ecological region, and annual variation in weather appear to minimally influence the layers (Allen and Kohn 1976), the cementum of permanent teeth can indicate the number of years following tooth emergence (Klevezal' and Mina 1973) (Fig. 21).

In teeth with distinct layers (e.g., beaver), grinding and polishing a section of the tooth is sufficient for evaluation of age (Van Nostrand and Stephenson 1964). In most sit-

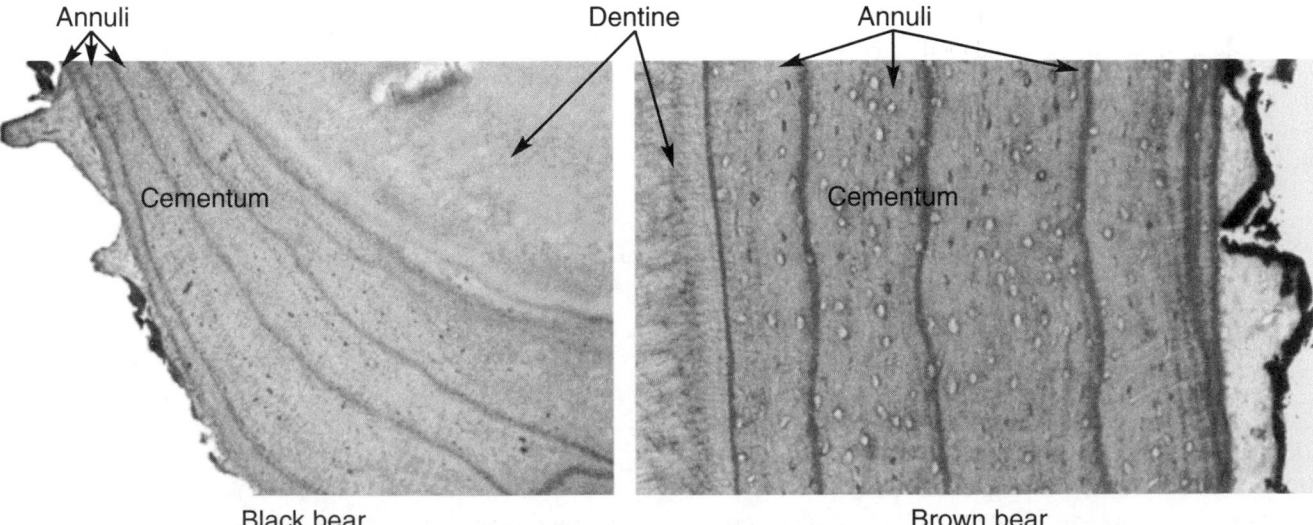

Fig. 21. Cementum annuli analysis of 4-year-old black and brown bears (*Ursus arctos*) (photographs by G. M. Matson).

uations, however, the tooth must be decalcified, cut into thin histological sections, and stained before evaluation. Techniques are also being expanded and developed to deal with other situations and tooth materials, including archaeological specimens (Lieberman et al. 1990, Beasley et al. 1992). All teeth have layers, but the tooth used to assess an animal's age varies among species and collecting conditions. Some teeth, such as incisors and premolars, are easier to extract and may be removed from live animals without obvious adverse effects (Nelson 2001, Bleich et al. 2003). Nevertheless, there is some debate about the ethics of tooth removal from live animals including arguments for (Nelson 2002) and against (Festa-Bianchet et al. 2002).

There are standard teeth and sections of teeth used for evaluation of cementum annuli. The standard tooth is the first incisor (central) for all ungulates, a lower canine or premolar 1 for most carnivores, and premolar 2 for cougar (*Puma concolor*) (Dimmick and Pelton 1994). Premolar 3 or 4 has also been used for marten, the lateral incisor for Canada lynx (*Lynx canadensis*) and bobcat, and an upper canine for bull elk. Standardization minimizes problems associated with differences in eruption time and interpretations of growth layers (Landon et al. 1998). If a nonstandard tooth type is selected for cementum age classification, the tooth must be identified, because differences in eruption time require different interpretations of growth layers. Errors of at least 1 year can result when an unidentified, nonstandard tooth is substituted for the standard. Techniques for tooth removal, mailing, storage, and processing should be selected before initiating research (Bergerud and Russell 1966, Erickson and Seliger 1969, Fancy 1980, Dimmick and Pelton 1994, Harshyne et al. 1998, Nelson 2001).

Use of cementum annuli for age classification appears to be more accurate than tooth wear for older mammals. In an experiment involving 120 known-age samples from 12 species, exact agreement occurred between known and cementum age in 94 individuals; within 1 year for 21 individuals, and >1 year for 5 individuals (Dimmick and Pelton 1994). One reason for incorrect age classification using cementum annuli is the presence of double or uneven layers of cementum (Kolenosky 1987). This problem can result in errors, particularly the overestimation of age in younger animals and underestimation of age in older animals, such as with polar bears (*Ursus maritimus*) (Hensel and Sorensen 1980) and wolves (Landon et al. 1998, Gipson et al. 2000). It is likely that pulp cavities, and tooth eruption and replacement are more accurate for ascertaining younger age classes than cementum annuli; in these cases, use of cementum annuli is unnecessary (Johnston et al. 1987, Jacobson and Reiner 1989, Landon et al. 1998). These characteristics can be examined visually or with radiography (Kuehn and Berg 1981, 1983; Dix and Strickland 1986*a,b*; Nagorsen et al. 1988; Helldin 1997; Knowlton and Whittemore 2001).

Skeletochronology.—Skeletochronology is similar to cementum annuli analysis, but potentially has a wider array of applications. Adhesion lines or annual growth layers in bones can be examined to estimate age. Several studies have addressed this possibility in femur bones of sea turtles with substantial success (Zug et al.1986, Bjorndal et al. 1988, Klinger and Musick 1992, Klinger et al. 1997, Zug and Glor 1999, Zug et al. 2002). Examination of a known age interval following injection with oxytetracycline supported the accuracy of this technique (Coles 1999). Adhesion lines in the sectioned femurs of yellow-pine chipmunks (*Tamias amoenus*) also appear to accurately indicate age categories (Barker et al. 2003). The technique has been expanded to include toe-clipped samples of amphibians (Parham et al. 1996); a transverse histological section through the midpoint of the toe phalanx appears to be best (avoiding cartilaginous areas near the epiphyses).

Eye-lens Weight.—The crystalline eye lens of vertebrates is an indicator of age in mammal species because it grows without shedding cells (Lord 1959, Sanderson 1961*b*, Bloemendal 1977). In addition, an insoluble protein, tyrosine, accumulates in the eye lens and may also be useful (Dapson and Irland 1972, Birney et al. 1975, Ludwig and Dapson 1977). If properly preserved lens specimens are available, analysis of eye-lens weights can be accurate for younger age classes (Friend 1967, Hearn and Mercer 1988, Koubek 1993, Bruns Stockrahm et al. 1996). However, this technique is probably not as accurate as cementum annuli analysis for older age classes.

Development

Embryonic.—In birds altricial young are sparsely feathered and blind at hatching while precocial young are covered with down and have open eyes. Doves, pigeons, raptors, and most songbirds are altricial. Gallinaceous birds, waterfowl, shorebirds, and cranes are precocial. The incubation period is typically shorter for altricial young, but precocial young are able to leave the nest shortly after hatching. The morphological differences between the 2 types of development strategies can be observed using the developmental stages in the 14-day incubation period of the altricial mourning dove (Muller et al. 1984), the 23-day incubation period of the precocial northern bobwhite (*Colinus virginianus*) (Roseberry and Klimstra 1965), and the 26-day incubation period of the precocial wild turkey (Stoll and Clay 1975). When precocial embryos are approximately two-thirds of the way through their normal incubation period, they are similar to newly hatched altricial birds. Development of embryos can be examined in eggs with flotation techniques (Westerskov 1950, Barth 1953, Hays and LeCroy 1971, Dunn et al. 1979, Nol and Blokpoel 1983, Van Paassen et al. 1984, Alberico 1995) and candling (Westerskov 1950, Weller 1956, Young 1988) techniques. Some evidence suggests the age of early stage clutches may be overestimated while the age of late stage clutches may be underestimated with flotation (Walter and Rusch 1997).

Fetal development in mammals can be used to estimate age in days, conception date, and/or parturition date (Bookhout 1964). Prenatal development in white-tailed deer and mule deer are well described (Armstrong 1950, Hudson and Browman 1959, Salwasser and Holl 1979, Larson and Taber 1980, Hamilton et al. 1985) and may be examined using a portable radiography unit (Ozoga and Verme 1985).

Postnatal.—Altricial young remain in the nest until fledging; mourning dove chicks remain in the nest until about 14 days after hatch (Hanson and Kossack 1963). Age of precocial young can be classified in the field with pattern of down replacement or with measurements of primaries and/or their pattern of replacement, as illustrated with spruce grouse (McCourt and Keppie 1975, Towers 1988), blue grouse (Zwickel and Lance 1966, Schladweiler et al. 1970, Redfield and Zwickel 1976), greater sage-grouse (*Centrocercus urophasianus*) (Pyrah 1963), greater

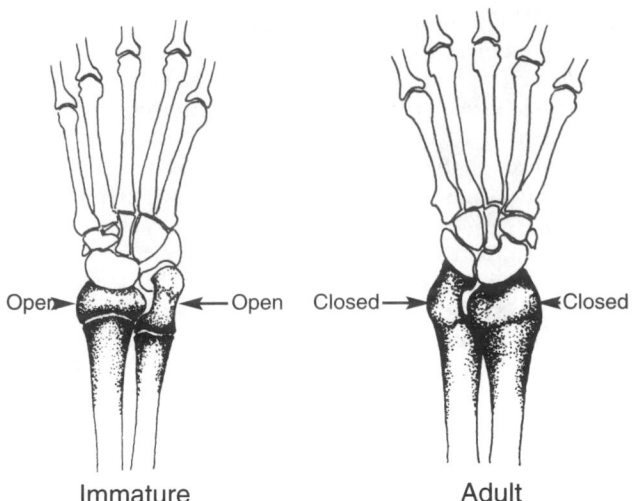

Fig. 22. Diagram of closure of epiphyses in raccoons (*Procyon lotor*) according to age (Sanderson 1961*a*).

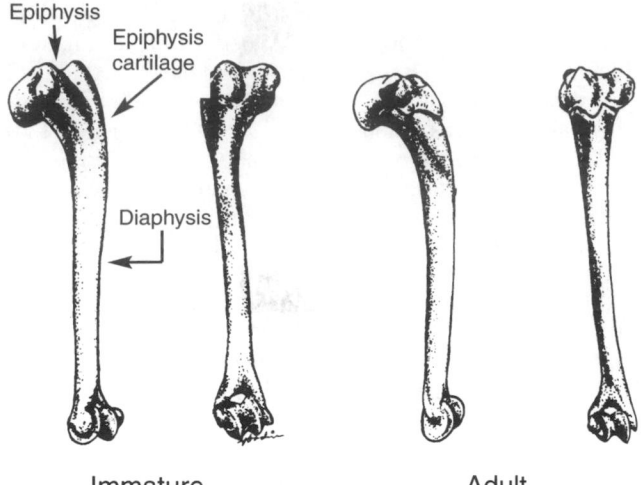

Fig. 24. Illustration of the epiphyseal cartilage of the humerus in an immature and adult cottontail (*Sylvilagus* spp.) (Godin 1960).

prairie-chickens (*Tympanuchus cupido*) (Etter 1963), and northern bobwhite (Petrides and Nestler 1952).

Young mammals differ from adults in numerous ways such as body size, pelt appearance (Fig. 11), baculum shape (Fig. 15), closure of epiphyses (Fig. 22), ossification of sutures (Fig. 23), and the presence of epiphyseal cartilage (Fig. 24). There are also distinct patterns of tooth replacement that have been described for many species including white-tailed deer (Severinghaus 1949), mule deer (Rees et al. 1966), elk (Quimby and Gaab 1957), caribou (Bergerud 1970, Miller 1974*b*), muskox (*Ovibos moschatus*) (Tener 1965), bison (*Bison bison*) (Frison and Reher 1970), and pronghorn (Dow and Wright 1962) (Table 1).

Genetic Characteristics

Gender can be accurately ascertained from a variety of tissue samples using genetic techniques (Mittwoch 1963, Moore 1966, Schmid 1967, DeGraaf and Larson 1972, Amstrup et al. 1993, Oyler-McCance and Leberg 2005). These techniques may be especially important for species that are strongly monomorphic, in situations that require a noninvasive approach, and/or where only small amounts of tissue are available.

Gender can be ascertained with genetic material in a number of ways with new techniques being developed at a rapid pace (Oyler-McCance and Leberg 2005). Examination of general characteristics of the sex chromosomes (X and Y in mammals and W and Z in birds) was used in the past to evaluate gender in many species including whooping cranes

(*Grus americana*) (Van Tuinen and Valentine 1987), white-tailed deer (Segelquist 1966, Crispens and Doutt 1970), and beaver (Larson and Knapp 1971). Techniques currently used are far superior in both their versatility and practicality. These newer techniques can test for the presence of specific genes (e.g., amelogenin) or gene sequences that are novel to a particular gender (Oyler-McCance and Leberg 2005). They can also be used on a variety of tissue samples including small amounts of blood (Hanaoka and Minaguchi 1996, Stacks and Witte 1996, Strom and Rechitsky 1998), teeth (Hanaoka and Minaguchi 1996, Murakami et al. 2000), dried tissue (Faerman et al. 1995, Lin et al. 1995), and fecal material (Reed et al. 1997, Yamauchi et al. 2000, Huber et al. 2002). Some of these techniques are successful with materials (such as teeth) stored at room temperature for more than 20 years (Hanaoka and Minaguchi 1996).

GENDER AND AGE CHARACTERISTICS
Reptiles and Amphibians

The presence of the hemipenes and/or swollen base of the tail can be used to confirm a male lizard or snake (Gregory 1983). A pair of enlarged post-anal scales can be used to identify males in the genus *Sceloporous* (Fig. 25) and a

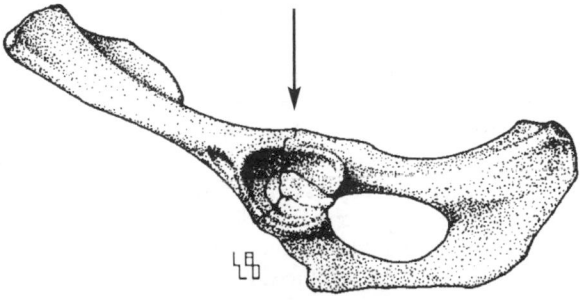

Fig. 23. Innominate bone of <1 year-old white-tailed deer. The arrow points at the area of incomplete ossification (Edwards et al. 1982).

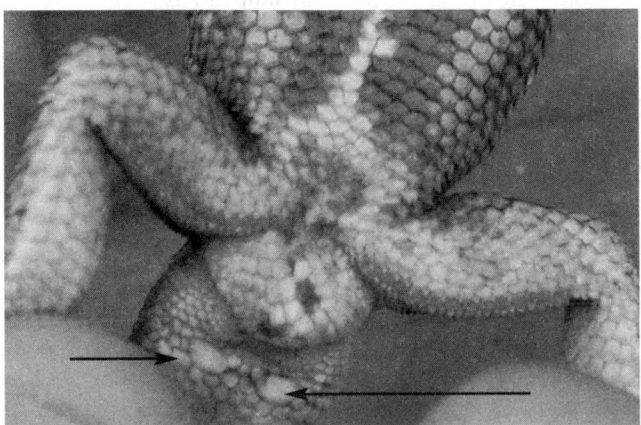

Fig. 25. Male sagebrush lizard (*Sceloporus graciosus*) illustrating the pair of enlarged post-anal scales that are characteristic of a male (photograph by S. S. Germaine).

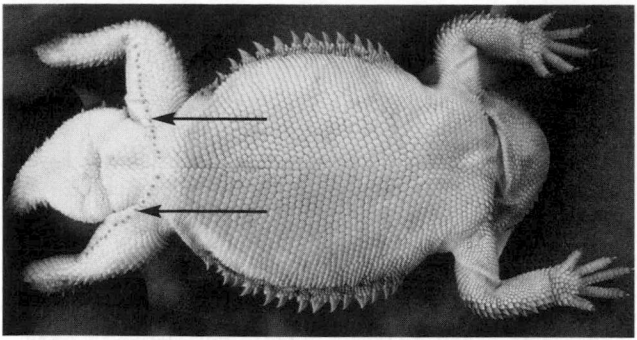

Fig. 26. Short-horned lizard (*Phrynosoma douglassii*) illustrating the femoral pores that extend down the inner thighs that are characteristic of a male (photograph by S. S. Germaine).

Fig. 27. Juvenile and adult short-horned lizards. Size is often a key characteristic in age classification of reptiles and amphibians (photograph by S. S. Germaine).

row of femoral pores on the ventral side of the thighs can be used to identify males in the genus *Phrynosoma* (Fig. 26). Breeding males of many lizard species can be identified by relatively bright coloration on the throat, armpits, belly, thighs, or tail (Stebbins 2003). The shape of the plastron and location of the vent can be used to ascertain gender in turtles. Gender in salamanders can be evaluated by the presence of the phallodeum and/or the appearance of the cloaca (Petranka 1998). Females also appear larger and plumper than males, and generally have shorter tails. Male frogs and toads generally are smaller than females, occasionally of different color, and have well-developed vocal sacs that appear as dark, loose skin along the throat when deflated. Breeding males also develop rough nuptial pads on the inner fingers of the forelimbs during the breeding season; the innermost digit may become enlarged (Fellers and Freel 1995). Male frogs and toads also chorus during the breeding season, while females generally are silent.

Young reptiles and amphibians are distinguishable from adults by size (Fig. 27) and or differences in their body appearance (Halliday and Verrel 1988). Neonate reptiles and terrestrial salamanders resemble adults in general body form, but are smaller and generally have relatively large eyes, head, and limbs (Stebbins 2003). The eggs of aquatic amphibians hatch into larvae bearing gills and tails, which are resorbed during metamorphosis into the juvenile stage, which is similar to adults but smaller (Powell et al. 1998). Some salamanders may be neotenous and attain sexual maturity while in the larval stage.

Growth in most reptile and amphibian species varies regionally, and can be influenced by temperature, food, water quality, population density, predation, and other environmental stressors (MaCartney et al. 1990, Rowe et al. 1992, Adolph and Porter 1996, Cogalniceanu and Miaud 2003). Turtles grow fastest during early years with sexual maturity correlated more with body size than age (Conant and Collins 1998, Stebbins 2003). Many freshwater turtles can live for over 50 years and some in the genus *Terrapene* may live considerably longer (Brown et al. 1995). In many lizard species, differences in size accurately represent distinct age classes until juveniles mature (Tinkle et al. 1993). Some lizards mature in the first year after hatch. In some species, size may continue to accurately indicate age after sexual maturation. In skinks, tails of young are often bright blue, but become duller or change color as they mature. Young snakes grow rapidly and often reach sexual maturity in 2–3 years. Skeletochronology or mark–recapture studies are reliable ways to assess age in reptiles and amphibians.

Birds

Variation in the molt patterns of birds, the material available for examination, and measurement techniques, have resulted in specific procedures for evaluating gender and age among species of birds. Timing of the observation (such as harvest) can be critical. It is easier to confirm a juvenile than an adult (lack of juvenile feathers may be a result of the timing of material collection rather than age). With few exceptions, there are no established techniques for reliably estimating age classes of older birds (≥ 2 years of age). Plumage characteristics (molt, plumage coloration, and feather wear and shape) of gallinaceous birds usually can be used to identify 3 classes (HY, SY, ASY) (Table 2). In swans and geese, gender is distinguishable

(Continued on page 318)

Table 2. Age and gender characteristics for gallinaceous birds. The number of potential age classes is largely dependent on timing of examination relative to completion of prebasic molt. Primaries (P) are numbered from proximal to distal.

Species	Age	Gender
Spruce grouse	Chick age estimated by replacement and growth of primaries (McCourt and Keppie 1975, Quinn and Keppie 1981, Towers 1988). Bursa of Fabricius used (Ellison 1968), but rarely needed as a technique; pointed P9/P10 in HY/SY birds is reliable and easier (Zwickel and Martinsen 1967). P9 (McKinnon 1983) and P1 (Szuba et al. 1987) tend to have smaller shaft diameters in HY/SY birds.	Breast feathers solid black or black tipped with white in males and horizontally barred in females (Ellison 1968, Boag and Schroeder 1992). Rectrices mostly black in males or tipped with light brown and/or white depending on subspecies and age. Rectrices of females mottled black and brown and 1–2 cm shorter for given age category (Zwickel and Martinsen 1967, Boag and Schroeder 1992).

(Continued on next page)

Table 2 (*continued*).

Species	Age	Gender
Ruffed grouse	Bursa of Fabricius length may be useful for ascertaining age, but not after January following hatch (Kalla 1991). HY birds tend to have pointed tips and less sheathing on P9/P10 than on P8, but this is less clear with aging (Hale et al. 1954, Dorney and Holzer 1957, Kalla 1991). HY/SY birds have a smaller P9 diameter or ratio of P9:P8 (Davis 1969, Rodgers 1979).	Males have longer "ruff" feathers on side of neck and 2–3 whitish dots on terminal ends of rump feathers while females have 1 whitish dot on terminal ends of rump feathers (Bump et al. 1947, Hale et al. 1954, Dorney 1966, Davis 1969, Roussel and Ouellet 1975). Starting at about 8 weeks of age, males can usually be distinguished from females by color of the bare patch above the eye; moderate to vivid reddish-orange in males and slight or no pigmentation in females (Palmer 1959). Males have distinct subterminal band on center 2 rectrices while females have indistinct subterminal band; female's tail is about 1 cm shorter for a given age category (Hale et al. 1954, Davis 1969, Rusch et al. 2000).
Blue grouse	Chick age estimated by replacement and growth of primaries (Zwickel and Lance 1966, Schladweiler et al. 1970, Redfield and Zwickel 1976, Zwickel 1992). P9 and P10 are pointed on HY/SY birds and rounded on ASY birds (Van Rossem 1925, Bendell 1955, Smith and Buss 1963, Braun 1971, Hoffman 1985).	Males have cervical apteria edged with white feathers and are 15–25% heavier than females (Caswell 1954, Boag 1965, Bunnell et al. 1977, Zwickel 1992). Males have primaries and rectrices 1–2 cm longer than females (Bendell 1955, Mussehl and Leik 1963, Boag 1965, Braun 1971, Hoffman 1983, Zwickel et al. 1991, Zwickel 1992). Rectrices of males mostly black or black with terminal band of gray, depending on subspecies. Sexual variation appears as early as 6 weeks (Nietfield and Zwickel 1983).
Sharp-tailed grouse (*Tympanuchus phasianellus*)	P9 and P10 tend to be more pointed and worn in HY/SY than ASY birds (Hillman and Jackson 1973).	Male crown feathers are dark with buff-colored edge while female crown feathers are barred (Henderson et al. 1967, Connelly et al. 1998). Central 2 rectrices of male are longitudinally striped and comparable feathers in female are horizontally barred (Henderson et al. 1967).
Lesser (*T. pallidicinctus*) and greater prairie-chicken	Chick age estimated by replacement and growth of primaries (Etter 1963), and from descriptive photographs (Baker 1953). P9 and P10 in HY/SY birds tend to be more pointed and worn, and have more spotting on their anterior portions (Campbell 1972).	Male undertail coverts are solid with a terminal round spot; crown feathers are dark with a buff-colored edge. Female undertail coverts and crown feathers are barred (Copelin 1963, Henderson et al. 1967, Schroeder and Robb 1993, Giesen 1998). Tails of males are solid or lightly barred while those of females are entirely or partially barred (Copelin 1963).
Gunnison (*Centrocercus minimus*) and greater sage-grouse	Chick age estimated based on replacement and growth of primaries (Pyrah 1963). The pointedness of P9 and P10 in juveniles is distinct; examination of the bursa of Fabricius (Eng 1955) provides little additional information. Primaries tend to be longer in ASY than in HY/SY birds, especially P1 which can differ by about 1.5 cm (Crunden 1963, Schroeder et al. 1999).	Males have black chin, white breast, filoplumes, and white tipped undertail coverts. Females have mottled grayish brown breast and undertail coverts, and are 35–50% smaller for a given age category (Dalke et al. 1963, Schroeder et al.1999). Male primaries are 1.5–3.5 cm longer and rectrices are 7–10 cm longer for a given age category than for females (Crunden 1963, Schroeder et al. 1999).
White-tailed ptarmigan	Chick age estimated by replacement and growth of primaries (Giesen and Braun 1979). HY/SY birds have dusky brown flecking on P9/P10; this pigmentation is absent in ASY birds (Braun et al. 1993).	Male has prominent eye combs during the breeding season; upper breast, neck, and head feathers are buff and tipped with blackish gray to dark brown. Female breast feathers are coarsely barred. Gender difficult to distinguish from plumage during autumn and winter (Braun and Rogers 1967, Braun et al. 1993).
Rock ptarmigan (*Lagopus muta*)	HY/SY birds have more dark pigmentation and less gloss on P9 than on P8; pigmentation tends to be equal or greater on P8 and gloss tends to be equal on ASY birds (Weeden and Watson 1967).	Male has distinct red eye combs and blackish brown breast during breeding season; female has mostly brown breast. Gender difficult to distinguish based on plumage during autumn and winter (Holder and Montgomerie 1993).

(*Continued on next page*)

Table 2 (*continued*).

Species	Age	Gender
Willow ptarmigan (*L. lagopus*)	Chick age estimated by replacement and growth of primaries (Bergerud et al. 1963, Parr 1975). HY/SY birds have more dark pigmentation and less gloss on P9 than on P8; in ASY birds pigmentation tends to be equal or greater on P8 and gloss tends to be equal (Bergerud et al. 1963, Weeden and Watson 1967).	Feathers on the neck and breast of male are distinctly rufous to chestnut and eye combs are red during the breeding season. Gender difficult to distinguish during autumn and winter (Hannon et al. 1998). Male has long, black rectrices and black central upper tail coverts. Female has shorter and dark brown rectrices and central upper tail coverts (Bergerud et al. 1963).
Wild turkey	In HY/SY birds the central 3 pairs of rectrices are longer than the outer rectrices, P9/P10 tend to be pointed with no bars in distal portions, and the upper secondary covert patch is narrower and duller (Petrides 1942, Williams 1961, Williams and Austin 1970). Spur and beard length increase with age (Kelly 1975), but overlap is large (Steffen et al. 1990). Tarsometatarsus length used with about 75% accuracy (Wakeling et al. 1997).	Skin on side of neck bare and pink-reddish in male; beard present in older males. Skin on side of neck lightly feathered and grayish-blue in female; shorter beards are occasionally present (Edminster 1954). Tarsometatarsus measurements larger in males and have been used to predict gender with about 96% accuracy (Wakeling et al. 1997). Primaries and rectrices longer in males than females for a given age category (Wallin 1982).
Montezuma quail (*Cyrtonyx montezumae*)	Greater upper primary coverts edged with buff or buffy bars near base in HY birds, or spotted or barred with white in AHY birds (Johnsgard 1973).	Face and throat of male marked with bold black and white pattern; face and throat of female mottled with brown, buff, and white (Leopold 1959).
Northern bobwhite	Chick age estimated based on growth of primaries (Petrides and Nestler 1952). Upper greater primary coverts buffy and tapered in HY birds, and gray-brown and rounded in AHY birds. P9/P10 pointed and dull brown in HY/SY birds, and rounded and grayish in ASY birds (Stoddard 1931, Dimmick 1992).	Male has white chin and eyestripe, except masked bobwhite that is mostly rufous with black head; female has buffy chin and eyestripe (Dimmick 1992). Base of lower mandible black in males and yellow in females. Middle wing coverts have fine, black, sharply pointed undulations in males whereas those in females are wide and dull gray (Thomas 1969, Brennan 1999).
Scaled quail (*Callipepla squamata*)	Primary coverts tipped, edged, or mottled with white in HY/SY birds and uniformly gray in ASY birds (Wallmo 1956).	Side of male's face is uniform gray with a brownish ear patch. Side of female's face is dirty gray streaked with black (Wallmo 1956).
Gambel's and California quail (*C. gambelii, C. californica*)	Greater upper primary coverts are mostly buff-tipped and pointed in HY birds, and uniformly gray and rounded in AHY birds. P9/P10 also more pointed and frayed in HY/SY birds (Calkins et al. 1999).	Male has black throat and crest; female has pale or buffy throat and small, brown crest (Calkins et al. 1999).
Mountain quail (*Oreortyx pictus*)	HY birds have buff-tipped primary coverts and AHY birds have uniform gray coverts. HY/SY birds also have pointed/frayed P9/P10 (Gutiérrez and Delehanty 1999).	Back of neck is gray and plume generally long and black in males. Back of neck is brown and plume shorter and browner in females (Johnsgard 1975, Brennan and Block 1985, Gutiérrez and Delehanty 1999).
Ring-necked pheasant (*Phasianus colchicus*)	Length of P10 may be useful for estimating age of chicks (Etter et al. 1970). Depth of bursa of Fabricius ≤8 or ≤6 mm for AHY males and females, respectively (Johnsgard 1975, Larson and Taber 1980). P1 of ASY birds tend to be longer and thicker than HY/SY birds (Wishart 1969, Greenberg et al. 1972). Spur length and eye-lens weight have not been useful (Stokes 1957, Dahlgren et al. 1965, Gates 1966, Koubek 1993).	Males large and brightly colored throughout with distinct leg spur and longer tail; females mottled brown with no spur and shorter tail (Oats et al. 1985, Rodgers 1985). Day-old males distinguishable from females due to an infantile wattle just below eye (Woehler and Gates 1970). Field-dressed males distinct due to their larger sternum (Oates et al. 1985). Bars on male primaries meet rachi at sharp angles except on unbarred tips. Bars on female primaries meet rachi at right angles (Linder et al. 1971).

(*Continued on next page*)

Table 2 (*continued*).

Species	Age	Gender
Chukar	Growth of juveniles described and illustrated in detail (Alkon 1982, Fig. 5). Primary covert 9 <29 mm in HY and ≥29 mm in AHY birds. P9/P10 pointed in HY/SY and rounded in ASY birds (Weaver and Haskell 1968).	Primary measurements generally greater for males than females (Weaver and Haskell 1968, Cramp and Simmons 1980), but gender difficult to distinguish (Christensen 1996).
Gray partridge (*Perdix perdix*)	P9 covert pointed in HY and rounded in AHY birds. P9/P10 pointed in HY/SY and rounded in ASY birds (Petrides 1942).	Throat and eye stripe buffy-orange for males and buffy for females. Scapulars and median wing coverts lack crossbars in males and have 2–4 crossbars in females (Carroll 1993).

(continued from page 315)

with cloacal examination (Hanson 1962). General patterns of plumage in swans and geese usually can be used for age only (Table 3). Wing characteristics of ducks are particularly important, because wings from many species are collected simultaneously during the harvest; most provide an adequate indication of species (Carney 1992), gender, and age (Table 4). There also is substantial information on classification of gender and age in many other species including shorebirds, pigeons and doves, cranes, rails, and raptors (Table 5). In addition to numerous field guides of birds (e.g., Peterson 1998, 2002; Sibley 2000), there are detailed guides for identifying the gender, age, and subspecies of birds (Pyle et al. 1987, Pyle 1997). Pyle (1997) provides particularly useful information for evaluating birds in the hand. Additionally, each species in North America has been extensively reviewed in individual species accounts produced by the American Ornithologists' Union, 716 accounts in total (Poole and Gill, 1992–2003).

Mammals

Many species of mammals are outwardly monomorphic. Consequently, examination of genitals, patterns of dentition, and cementum annuli in teeth may be essential for classification of gender and age. Such procedures usually require collection or capture of the animal and/or collection of tissue samples. Because field guides (e.g., Hall 1981) are necessarily general in nature, species accounts for individual mammal species produced by the American Society of Mammalogists (first account produced in 1969) may be an essential resource for detailed information (e.g., dentition). These accounts are particularly useful for species receiving little research and management attention. Despite the difficulty of capture and/or collection, current techniques for estimating age of mammals, particularly older mammals, are more effective than comparable techniques for estimating age in birds (Table 6).

(Continued on page 321)

Table 3. Age characteristics for swans and geese (abbreviated and summarized from Bellrose 1980 and other references noted below). Birds are classified as HY (before completion of the prebasic molt) and AHY (after completion of the prebasic molt). All HY swans and geese may have notched tail feathers early in hunting season. Plumage is similar in both genders for all species, with small differences in measurements. Only the male AHY mute swan (*Cygnus olor*) has a fleshy knob on its forehead.

Species	Age
Swans	HY birds usually dull with light gray patches whereas AHY birds are solid white.
Greater white-fronted goose (*Anser albifrons*)	HY birds have grayish body plumage, yellow legs and bill, and lack a white face patch. AHY birds have white face patch, orange legs, and pink bill (Ely and Dzubin 1994).
Snow goose (*Chen caerulescens*)	HY blue phase birds may have brownish-gray patches on head, body, legs, and bills. AHY blue phase birds have slate gray body plumage with white head. HY white phase birds may have patches of sooty gray on otherwise white plumage and grayish brown legs and bill. AHY white phase birds white with black wing tips, red legs, and a pink bill (Mowbray et al. 2000).
Ross' goose (*C. rossii*)	HY birds may have patches of pale gray on otherwise white plumage and AHY birds are white with black wing tips (Ryder and Alisauskas 1995).
Emperor goose (*C. canagica*)	HY birds may have patches of black-brown on head and neck; their legs and bill are black. AHY birds have a white head and upper neck, yellow legs, and a pink bill (Petersen et al. 1994).
Canada goose (*Branta canadensis*)	Tail feathers may be notched, breast feathers relatively narrow, and outer primaries more pointed in HY than AHY birds (Caithamer et al. 1993, Mowbray et al. 2002).
Brant (*B. bernicla*)	HY birds (Atlantic subspecies) have no white on necks until mid-winter; greater and middle wing coverts may be tipped with white. AHY birds have a white crescent on side of neck and the greater and middle coverts are dark brown. HY birds of the "black form" may have dark plumage with white undertail coverts and light gray edging of wing coverts. AHY birds have barred gray and white flanks with dark wing coverts (Reed et al. 1998).

Table 4. Age and gender characteristics of duck wings collected during the autumn hunting season (information abbreviated and summarized from Carney 1992). The number of potential age classes is largely dependent on timing of harvest in relation to completion of the prebasic molt. Other than common (*Somateria mollissima*) and king eider (*S. spectabilis*) with 3 age classes in males (HY, SY, ASY), only 2 age classes are identifiable for most species (HY, AHY). Primaries (P) are numbered from proximal to distal.

Species	Age	Gender
Mallard (*Anas platyrhynchos*)	Tertials frayed or faded, middle coverts narrow and trapezoidal, and inner edge of outer primary coverts relatively light in HY birds; tertials not frayed, middle coverts rounded, and inner edge of outer primary coverts lightly edged or not edged in AHY birds.	White bar on leading edge of speculum extends onto tertials in females, but not males. Males more likely to have vermiculated scapulars.
Am. black duck (*A. rubripes*)	Tertials frayed or faded, middle coverts anterior to tertials more trapezoidal in shape, and inner edge of outer primary coverts relatively light in HY birds; tertials not frayed, middle coverts rounded, and inner edge of outer primary coverts not edged in AHY birds.	Tertials of HY males >88 mm from tip of longest tertial covert and wing notch-length >273 mm; measurements smaller for AHY females. AHY separation is with tertial-tertial covert measurement of 90 mm and wing notch-length of 281 mm.
Mottled duck (*A. fulvigula*)	Tertials frayed or faded if any HY feathers present; tertials not frayed, middle coverts rounded, and inner edge of outer primary coverts lightly edged or not edged in AHY birds.	Birds with ≥3 non-iridescent secondaries likely female and iridescence on all secondaries likely male. Wing notch-length usually ≥251 mm for HY males and ≥255 mm for AHY males; length usually shorter for females.
Am. wigeon (*A. americana*)	Tertials and tertial coverts small and brownish in HY birds. Teritals have black outerwebs in AHY males and sharp white edging in AHY females.	HY males have mottled upperwing patch of mostly white, while HY female may have little white. AHY males have large white upperwing patch whereas patch is small and/or less distinct in AHY females.
Gadwall (*A. strepera*)	Tertials and tertial coverts may be pointed, frayed, and faded in HY birds; same feathers rounded and not frayed or faded in AHY birds.	Coverts mostly either black or cinnamon in AHY males; black and cinnamon restricted to ≤4 rows of coverts in females. Black or cinnamon occurs in ≥3 rows of coverts in HY males; females have little cinnamon in 2 rows. Wing notch-length usually ≥262 mm for AHY males, ≥255 mm for HY males; shorter in females.
Green-winged teal (*A. crecca*)	HY tertials small, narrow, and frayed; AHY tertials rounded and not frayed.	Vermiculated scapulars only occur on males. The outer black or dark brown strip on the most distal tertial sharply divided from the remaining portion of the feather in males and blended somewhat on females. Wing notch-length ≥183 mm characterizes males and ≤175 mm females.
Blue-winged and cinnamon teal (*A. discors*, A. *cyanoptera*)	Tertials and tertial coverts may be pointed, frayed, or faded in HY birds; same feathers rounded and not frayed or faded in AHY birds (see also Hohman et al. 1995).	Green on speculum iridescent in males and rarely iridescent in females. Greater secondary coverts mostly white in males and heavily spotted with dark brown in females.
Northern shoveler (*A. clypeata*)	Tertials and tertial coverts may be pointed, frayed, or faded, often with light edging in HY birds; same feathers rounded and not frayed or faded in AHY birds (Hohman et al. 1995).	All males and a few females have iridescent green speculum. Females typically have cream edging on lesser and middle coverts.
Northern pintail (*A. acuta*)	Tertials coverts may be pointed, frayed, or faded, often with light edging in HY birds; these feathers rounded and not frayed or faded in AHY birds (see also Esler and Grand 1994).	Speculum at least partly iridescent green in males; when green is occasionally present in females, it is not iridescent.
Wood duck (*Aix sponsa*)	HY tertials pale bronze with pointed, frayed tips and tertial coverts narrow, yellow-green; same feathers in AHY birds dark blue (male) or purplish red (female) and not frayed (Harvey et al. 1989).	White trailing edge of the secondaries is wider on the outer webs for females and approximately equal for males.

(Continued on next page)

Table 4 (*continued*).

Species	Age	Gender
Harlequin duck (*Histrionicus histrionicus*)	HY tertials, greater coverts, middle coverts, and lesser coverts dark brown and often frayed at their tips; colors vary in AHY birds depending on gender and feather type, but feathers not frayed.	Males have 3 distal tertials with white on outer webs and secondaries have dark iridescent blue.
Steller's eider (*Polysticta stelleri*)	HY tertials slightly curved, tertials and tertial coverts dark brown, frayed and faded; secondaries with 0.5 cm white band on trailing edge. AHY birds have strongly curved tertials and 1 cm white band on trailing edge of secondaries.	Greater secondary coverts completely white on AHY males and brown with 1 cm wide tip on AHY females.
Redhead (*Aythya americana*)	HY tertials and tertial coverts narrow and frayed; same feathers rounded and not frayed in AHY birds (Sayler 1995).	Vermiculation on tertials, greater tertial coverts, and middle and lesser coverts only present on male.
Canvasback (*A. valisineria*)	HY tertials and coverts narrow and frayed, middle and lesser secondary coverts have trapezoidal shape; same feathers rounded and not frayed in AHY birds.	Heavy vermiculation on tertials, greater tertial coverts, and middle and lesser secondary coverts of males.
Greater and lesser scaup (*A. marila, A. affinis*)	HY tertials and coverts pointed, frayed, and faded; same feathers rounded and not frayed or faded in AHY birds.	AHY males have scapulars, and middle and lesser coverts heavily vermiculated and tertials flecked with white near the tips. HY males have white flecking on middle coverts recessed 0.3 cm from edge. AHY females have flecking near edge of covert; flecking mostly absent from HY females.
Ring-necked duck (*A. collaris*)	HY tertials, tertial coverts, and middle and lesser coverts narrow and frayed; same feathers in AHY birds rounded and not frayed.	Wing notch-length usually >193 mm for AHY males and >189 mm for HY males; length usually shorter for females, but with overlap in 185–195 mm range, depending on age. AHY males have slightly shinier tertials than AHY females and occasional flecking on underwing.
Common goldeneye (*Bucephala clangula*)	Coverts of HY birds are a mixture of white, black, and gray-white, and often frayed; coverts of AHY birds solid white or terminally banded with black, and not frayed.	Wing notch-length separation point for males vs. females 218 mm for AHY and 210 mm for HY birds (males longer). AHY females have black band on tips of greater secondary coverts whereas coverts are solid white in AHY males.
Barrow's goldeneye (*B. islandica*)	Coverts of HY birds are a mixture of white, black, and gray-white, and often frayed; coverts of AHY birds solid white or terminally banded with black, and not frayed.	Wing notch-length separation point for males vs. females 222 mm for AHY birds and 217 mm for HY birds (males longer). AHY females have black band on tips of greater secondary coverts whereas coverts are distally white with occasional black tips for AHY males.
Bufflehead (*B. albeola*)	Tertials and greater coverts often frayed and pointed in HY birds; same feathers rounded and not frayed in AHY birds.	AHY males have entirely white greater, middle, and lesser coverts; same feathers dark brown or black in other age and gender categories. HY males usually have wing notch-length >160 mm; length shorter in HY females.
Hooded merganser (*Lophodytes cucullatus*)	Tertials and middle and greater coverts often frayed, faded, and pointed in HY birds; same feathers rounded and not frayed or faded in AHY birds.	AHY males have longitudinal white stripes on tertials and light gray middle and lesser coverts; white stripes absent in AHY females and middle and lesser coverts are dark brown. HY birds difficult to differentiate until AHY feathers appear.
Red-breasted merganser (*Mergus serrator*)	Greater tertial coverts dark gray-black, pointed, and frayed in HY birds; same feathers not frayed, rounded, and white in AHY males or shiny black in AHY females.	Distal tertials in AHY males mostly white with black margin on outer web; greater tertial coverts and middle and lesser secondary coverts mostly white. HY birds difficult to differentiate until AHY feathers appear.

(Continued on next page)

Table 4 (*continued*).

Species	Age	Gender
Common merganser (*M. merganser*)	Tertials and coverts dark gray with pointed and frayed tips in HY birds; same feathers rounded and not frayed in AHY birds.	Distal tertials in AHY males mostly white with black margin on outer web and greater tertial coverts; middle and lesser secondary coverts mostly white. Wing notch-length separation point 260 mm for AHY males vs. females and 254 mm for HY males vs. females (males longer).
Long-tailed duck (*Clangula hyemalis*)	Tertials and coverts dark gray-brown, frayed, and faded at tips in HY birds; same feathers not frayed or faded in AHY birds and black (males) or dark brown with traces of tan (females).	AHY male tertials, tertial coverts, greater secondary coverts, and middle and lesser coverts black; same feathers in AHY females dark brown with some tan on the tips. HY birds difficult to differentiate until AHY feathers appear.
Black scoter (*Melanitta nigra*)	Tertials and coverts dark brown, pointed, frayed, and faded in HY birds; same feathers rounded, not frayed or faded, and shiny black (males) or dark brown (females) in AHY birds.	AHY males have P10 deeply attenuated for 55–60 mm from the tip and coverts usually shiny black; P10 not attenuated in other age and gender categories. HY birds difficult to differentiate until AHY feathers appear.
Surf scoter (*M. perspicillata*)	Tertials and coverts dark brown, pointed, frayed, and faded in HY birds; same feathers rounded, not frayed or faded, and shiny black (males) or blackish brown (females) in AHY birds.	Outer webs of primaries black and tertials and coverts are shiny black in AHY males and dark blackish brown in other categories. HY birds difficult to differentiate until AHY feathers appear.
White-winged scoter (*M. fusca*)	Tertials and coverts dark brown, faded and frayed at tips in HY birds; same feathers rounded, not frayed or faded, and shiny black (males) or dark brown (females) in AHY birds.	Overall wing is black in AHY males and dark brown in females; black-white interface has a "saw-toothed" appearance in males. HY birds difficult to differentiate until AHY feathers appear.
Common eider	Tertials and coverts faded and frayed in HY birds; same feathers not faded and frayed in AHY birds. SY males distinguishable from ASY and HY males by presence of white mottled tertials and coverts.	HY birds difficult to differentiate until AHY feathers appear (usually white). SY and ASY males distinguishable from females by presence of substantial white on tertials and coverts.
King eider	Tertials and coverts faded and frayed at tips in HY birds; same feathers not faded or frayed in AHY birds. SY males distinguishable from ASY and HY males by presence of mottled white on middle and lesser coverts.	HY birds difficult to differentiate. SY and ASY males distinguishable from females by presence of white on middle and lesser coverts, and blacker coloration of wing.
Ruddy duck (*Oxyura jamaicensis*)	Tertials, tertial coverts, and middle coverts somewhat frayed and slightly trapezoidal in HY birds; same feathers rounded and not frayed in AHY birds.	Gender not distinguishable from wings.
Fulvous whistling duck (*Dendrocygna bicolor*)	Tertials, greater coverts, and lesser coverts somewhat frayed and faded at tips in HY birds; same feathers not frayed or faded in AHY birds.	Gender not distinguishable from wings.
Black-bellied whistling duck (*D. autumnalis*)	Greater coverts slightly mottled near pointed tips in HY birds and entirely white with rounded tips in AHY birds.	Gender not distinguishable from wings.

(*continued from page 318*)

SUMMARY

Effective wildlife research and management depends on accurate assessment of gender and age in amphibians, reptiles, birds, and mammals. These assessments often can be conducted using long-established techniques that are relatively simple to perform including visual examinations of general appearance and/or sex organs. Information also can be gathered through examinations of dentition and/or partial samples such as wings or teeth. Although some species may appear monomorphic, the vast majority readily can be classified to gender and basic age categories. However, newer techniques are constantly being developed and evaluated because there often is a need to obtain better estimates of age or to make assessments using limited material, These techniques include improved cementum annuli analysis, skeletochronol-

(*Continued on page 328*)

Table 5. Age and gender characteristics for miscellaneous species of birds. The number of potential age classes is largely dependent on timing of examination in relation to completion of the prebasic molt. Primaries (P) are numbered from proximal to distal and secondaries (S) from distal to proximal.

Species	Age	Gender
American woodcock (*Scolopax minor*)	Depending on time of year, 3 age classes can be recognized (because of retention of juvenal secondaries during second year, (Sheldon et al. 1958, Martin 1964). Juvenal secondaries have light tips and distinct dark subterminal bars; adult secondaries lack a distinct bar (Petrides 1950*a*, Martin 1964, Roberts 1988). Coloration of neck, foot, and bill also useful (Shissler et al. 1981).	Females heavier than males with overlap in the 160–190 g range (Owen et al. 1977). Bill length >72 mm, combined width of outer 3 primaries ≥12.6 mm, and wing chord (to tip of P 6 or P 7) ≥134 mm characterizes female. Measurements <64 mm, ≤12.4 mm, and ≤133 mm, respectively, characterize males (Artmann and Schroeder 1976, Keppie and Whiting 1994). The combination of characteristics minimizes overlap.
Wilson's snipe (*Gallinago delicata*)	Juveniles may have a faint black tip on some lesser and median secondary coverts; adults have wide dark terminal shaft line (Dwyer and Dobell 1979). Multivariate analysis with feathers useful, but 20% overlap (McCloskey and Thompson 2000).	Not easily distinguishable by plumage or cloacal characteristics (Fogarty et al. 1977, U.S. Department of Interior and Canadian Wildlife Service 1977). Females have shorter outer rectrices and longer bills than males (Mueller 1999); 10% unclassifiable with multivariate analysis of skeletal and feather measurements (McCloskey and Thompson 2000).
White-winged dove (*Zenaida asiatica*)	Primary coverts of juveniles have pale tips and primaries may be edged with white or buff (Cottam and Trefethen 1968); juveniles lack black cheek-patch of adults (Schwertner et al. 2002).	Males larger than females with brighter plumage on crown, nape, and hind neck (Cottam and Trefethen 1968)
Mourning dove	Juveniles have white or buffy tipped primary coverts, or buffy edge on P9/P10 (Petrides 1950*a*, Swank 1955, Wight et al. 1967, Haas and Amend 1976, Cannell 1984). Long breeding season can complicate age classification (Schultz et al. 1995).	Females have tan breast and throat with a brown or brownish-gray crown; males blue or blue-gray with a slightly pink crown (Petrides 1950*a*, Cannell 1984, Mirarchi and Baskett 1994). Accuracy not perfect (Menasco and Perry 1978, Schultz et al. 1995).
Band-tailed pigeon (*Patagioenas fasciata*)	Juvenile growth has been described in detail (White and Braun 1990). Juveniles have buffy edged primaries, worn outer tips of P9/P10, and no wear on tips of S6 and S7. They retain secondary coverts up to 340 days of age (Silovsky et al. 1968, White and Braun 1978).	Breast and crown dull brown-gray in females and purplish to vinaceous in males (White and Braun 1978, Keppie and Braun 2000). This technique is useful as early as 45 days post hatch.
Sandhill crane (*Grus canadensis*)	Juvenal plumage brownish; the same plumage of adults grayish (Walkinshaw 1949). Rusty staining can make separation difficult. Forehead of juveniles may be tawny; adults may be pale gray with a red crown (Lewis 1979).	Plumage differences insignificant; males usually heavier than females (Tacha et al. 1992). Cloacal examination only 66% accurate (Tacha and Lewis 1978).
Whooping crane	Juveniles have brownish patches or buff-tipped feathers; adults are white with black wing tips and a red crown (Lewis 1995).	Gender not distinguishable based on plumage (Walkinshaw 1973), but males tend to be heavier (Lewis 1995).
Rails	Presence of bursa of Fabricius used to classify age of clapper rails (*Rallus longirostris*) (Adams and Quay 1958); juveniles also have paler bill (Eddleman and Conway 1998). The black throat patch of adult soras (*Porzana carolina*) absent in immatures (Melvin and Gibbs 1996). Juvenile black rails (*Laterallus jamaicensis*) slightly duller in plumage than adults (Eddleman et al. 1994).	Male clapper rail brighter on sides and base of bill (Eddleman and Conway 1998), male sora has lighter-colored bill (Melvin and Gibbs 1996), male king rail (*R. elegans*) slightly brighter in coloration (Odom 1977), male black rail has darker throat (Eddleman et al. 1994), and male yellow rail (*Coturnicops noveboracensis*) has distinct yellow bill during the breeding season (Bookhout 1995). Males generally heavier than females, although differences can be small.

(Continued on next page)

Table 5 (*continued*).

Species	Age	Gender
Purple gallinule (*Porphyrula marinica*) and common moorhen (*Gallinula chloropus*)	Juveniles brownish or grayish with white feathers in throat region; bills and/or frontal shields lack red and yellow of adults (Bannor and Kiviat 2002, West and Hess 2002). Evidence of juvenile age class may persist until spring (Holliman 1977).	Gender not distinguishable based on plumage, but males slightly heavier than females in purple gallinule (West and Hess 2002) and up to 100 g heavier in common moorhen (Bannor and Kiviat 2002).
American coot (*Fulica americana*)	Juveniles paler than adults with lighter tipped feathers (Brisbin and Mowbray 2002).	Females smaller than males but overlap large (Fredrickson 1968, Eddleman and Knopf 1985).
Raptors	Most raptors have distinct juvenal plumage that is only slightly worn in first autumn (Dunne 1987). Eye color changes with age in accipiters from yellow (juveniles) to red, orange, or brown (adults) (Dunne 1987). Bald eagles (*Haliaeetus leucocephalus*) can be differentiated into multiple age categories based on increasing whiteness of the tail and head (McCollough 1989).	Wing chord often larger for females than males (U.S. Department of Interior and Canadian Wildlife Service 1977, Dunne 1987, Pyle 1997). Some raptors clearly dimorphic in appearance; male northern harrier (*Circus cyaneus*) is gray while the female is brown (MacWhirter and Bildstein 1996), and the male American kestrel (*Falco sparverius*) has blue-gray wings while the female's are rusty (Smallwood and Bird 2002). Bald eagles do not differ in plumage coloration (Bortolotti 1984), but females tend to be larger (Buehler 2000).

Table 6. Age and gender characteristics for selected mammals. Appearance of external genitalia is sufficient for classification of gender for most species and, in the case of large ungulates, from a distance.

Species	Age	Gender
White-tailed deer	Fawns spotted in summer and smaller with relatively short nose in winter with innominate bone incompletely ossified (Edwards et al. 1982, Fig. 23). Tooth eruption and wear (Severinghaus 1949, Fig. 19) used to estimate age, but results mixed for older deer (Gilbert and Stolt 1970, DeYoung 1989, Jacobson and Reiner 1989, Gee et al. 2002). Examination of tooth replacement and wear should be used for 3 age classes (fawn, yearling, and adult) (Gee et al. 2002), unless reduced accuracy is acceptable. Cementum annuli analysis effective for older animals (Gilbert 1966, Ransom 1966, Lockard 1972, McCullough and Beier 1986).	With rare exceptions, only males have antlers. First year antlers usually small and referred to as "buttons." Presence of tuberosities on the pelvic girdle distinguishes adult males ($\geq$2-1/2 years-of-age) from females (Taber 1956, Fig. 16). Specific differences in the ilio-pectineal eminence of the pelvic girdle can be used to identify gender in animals about 1-1/2 years old (Edwards et al. 1982, Fig. 17).
Mule and black-tailed deer	Fawns spotted in summer and smaller with a relatively short nose in winter. A general analysis of morphology is complicated by habitat type and/or region (Strickland and Demarais 2000). Pattern of tooth eruption used to estimate age of fawns and yearlings (Rees et al. 1966). For deer >2 years old, tooth-wear, eye-lens weight, and molar tooth-ratio techniques are imprecise (Robinette et al. 1957, Connolly et al. 1969a, Erickson et al. 1970, Van Deelen et al. 2000). Counts of cementum annuli from incisors accurate for older ages (Low and Cowan 1963; Thomas and Bandy 1973, 1975; Hamlin et al. 2000).	With rare exceptions, only males have antlers. Tracks of adult and larger yearling males distinguishable from females by their larger arc width (McCullough 1965). Presence of tuberosities on pelvic girdle distinguishes adult males ($\geq$2-1/2 years-of-age) from females (Taber 1956, Fig. 16).

(*Continued on next page*)

Table 6 (*continued*).

Species	Age	Gender
Elk	Head profile and presence/shape of antlers used to identify calves, yearlings, and adults ($\geq$2 years old) (Taber et al. 1982, Smith and McDonald 2002, Fig. 10). Head profile quantifiable with significant variation in rostral length, interorbital width, and ear length for female age classes; yearlings larger than calves and adults larger than yearlings (Smith and McDonald 2002). Yearling males lack brow tines on antlers whereas antlers of adult males have brow tines and are branched (Taber et al. 1982). Pattern of tooth eruption used to estimate age through about 3 years (Quimby and Gaab 1957, Peek 1982); accurate estimation of older animals with cementum annuli analysis (Keiss 1969, Hamlin et al. 2000).	Only males have antlers and upper canines (Greer and Yeager 1967). Antler scars may also be visible following antler drop.
Moose	Calves identifiable by size. Tooth wear considered for aging (Passmore et al. 1955), but cementum annuli analysis of incisors or molars valid indication of year class (Sergeant and Pimlott 1959, Wolfe 1969, Gasaway et al. 1978, Haagenrud 1978).	Only males have antlers and only females have a white vulval patch (Roussel 1975). Differences in gender detectable with dimensions of fecal pellets (MacCracken and Van Ballenberghe 1987).
Caribou	Calves identifiable by small size and relatively short head profile (Bergerud 1978). Antlers usually larger for adults than yearlings. Tooth eruption pattern useful to classify age to about 2 years (Bergerud 1970; Miller 1974a,b; 1982). Cementum annuli analysis best technique for older animals (McEwan 1963, Bergerud and Russell 1966).	Antlers of males larger than those of females (Miller 1982). Presence of dark vulval patch in females most consistent characteristic (Bergerud 1978). Mandible lengths larger for males than females for a given age category (Bergerud 1964, Miller and McClure 1973).
Muskox	Calves are small, yearling males small with straight horn projections of ~ 100 mm, yearling females small with horns ~ 66 mm, and adults larger. Tooth emergence useful for animals to 6 years old; cementum annuli analysis more accurate for older animals. Basal depressions of horns in 4-year-old females maximally developed; bulls maximally developed by year 6 when horns completely cover their forehead (Tener 1965).	Horns of yearlings longer in males than in females (100 vs. 66 mm). In 2-year-olds, horns of males tend to be whiter and project straighter from the head (Tener 1965).
Bison	Cranial fusion used for 2 age classes (Duffield 1973, Shackleton et al. 1975), horn development used for 4 female and 5 male age classes (Fuller 1959, Reynolds et al. 1982), and tooth replacement and wear used for 5–7 age classes (Skinner and Kaisen 1947, Fuller 1959, Frison and Reher 1970). Cementum annuli analysis most reliable for estimating older age classes (Novakowski 1965, Moffitt 1998).	Horns of females more slender and inwardly curved than those of males (Reynolds et al. 1982). Numerous differences in horn cores, burrs, and skeletal measurements (Skinner and Kaisen 1947, Duffield 1973).
Wild sheep	Lambs distinguishable by small size. Because horn size increases with age, yearling rams can be classified based on size of curl (Jones et al. 1954). Horns segments used for older age classes (Geist 1966). Tooth eruption and replacement used to estimate age to 4 years (Hemming 1969, Lawson and Johnson 1982). Cementum annuli analysis reliable for older ages (Turner 1977).	Gender difficult to evaluate for lambs, but males of other age classes have larger horns (Lawson and Johnson 1982). Yearling rams difficult to differentiate from adult ewes unless scrotum is detected.
Mountain goat	Kids distinguishable by size of body and horns (<1/2 ear length in autumn), yearlings have horns about ear length, and adults have longer horns. Replacement of teeth used to estimate ages through ~ 3 and rings on the horn used for all ages (Brandborg 1955, Fig. 13). Cementum annuli analysis presumably would work, but success of horn rings usually makes it unnecessary.	Males stand or stretch while urinating and females squat. Yearling males may have visible scrotum and yearling females may have visible vulval patch under tail. Horns of males generally thicker than those of females but field interpretation difficult (Wigal and Coggins 1982).

(Continued on next page)

Table 6 (*continued*).

Species	Age	Gender
Pronghorn	Animals with horns longer than the ears usually adult males; maximum horn measurements from 2- and 3-year-old males (Mitchell and Maher 2001). Sequence of tooth eruption, replacement, and wear used to estimate age (Dow and Wright 1962, Jensen 1998), but cementum annuli analysis of first permanent incisor used for older age classes (McCutchen 1969, Kerwin and Mitchell 1971).	Horns of females average 42 mm in length and have unsubstantial prongs; horns of yearling males larger (O'Gara 1969). Adult males have black face to horns and black cheek patch; females have black nose area only (Einarsen 1948, Yoakum 1978).
Collared peccary (*Pecari tajacu*)	Tooth emergence and replacement used to estimate age to 21.5 months (Kirkpatrick and Sowls 1962). Eye-lens weights of limited value (Richardson 1966).	External dimorphism limited to genitals. Suspensory tuberosities on pelvic girdle prominent in males (Lochmiller et al. 1984).
Gray wolf	Pups identifiable by small size to 8 months (Carbyn 1987). Tooth eruption, replacement, and size useful to 26 weeks (Schonberner 1965, Van Ballenberghe and Mech 1975). Fusion of epiphyses of radius and ulna occurs at 12–14 months (Rausch 1967); fully grown at 18 months (Young and Goldman 1944). Cementum annuli analysis of teeth useful for estimating age of older animals (Goodwin and Ballard 1985, Landon et al. 1998, Gipson et al. 2000); tooth wear (Landon et al. 1998, Gipson et al. 2000, Fig. 20), cranial sutures, and pulp cavity measurements (Landon et al. 1998) have been considered, but are less versatile.	Urination posture used to identify gender (Carbyn 1987). Examination of nipples, penal scar/opening, and testicles used to identify gender in live wolves or pelts.
Coyote (*Canis latrans*)	Pups classified by size (Barnum et al. 1979, Bekoff 1982). Permanent canines emerge at 4–5 months and complete at 8–12 months (Voigt and Berg 1987); width of canine pulp cavity may be useful for estimating age (Root and Payne 1984, Tumlison and McDaniel 1984, Knowlton and Whittemore 2001). Cementum annuli useful for estimating age >20 months (Linhart and Knowlton 1967, Allen and Kohn 1976, Nellis et al. 1978, Bowen 1982, Root and Payne 1984), particularly for canine teeth (Roberts 1978).	Examination of nipples, penal scar/opening, and testicles used to identify gender in live coyotes or pelts (Voigt and Berg 1987). Sagittal crest of males more developed than females (Gier 1968, Bekoff 1982).
Fox	Canine teeth replacement complete at ~1 year (Geiger et al. 1977); roots (Voigt 1987) and pulp cavities (Bradley et al. 1981, Tumlison and McDaniel 1984) used to estimate age. Cementum annuli analysis also used (Grue and Jensen 1973, Allen 1974, Grue and Jensen 1976, Johnston et al. 1987), but accuracy decreases with number of annuli (Geiger et al. 1977). Eye-lens weight, baculum, body and skull measurements, and cranial sutures used but reliability not high (Sullivan and Haugen 1956, Wood 1958, Lord 1961, Geiger et al. 1977, Harris 1978).	Examination of nipples, penal scar/opening, and testicles used to identify gender in live foxes or pelts (Fritzell 1987). The baculum in males can be detected by palpating.
Black, brown, and polar bear	Eruption of canines used to estimate age to 3–4 years in black bears (Marks and Erickson 1966, Kolenosky and Strathearn 1987) and 2 years in brown bears (Rausch 1969). Cementum annuli analysis (Fig. 21) is preferred method for estimating age in black bears (Stoneberg and Jonkel 1966, Willey 1974, Carrel 1994, Keay 1995), brown bears (Craighead et al. 1970), and polar bears (Hensel and Sorensen 1980, Calvert and Ramsay 1998), but there are occasional errors (Hensel and Sorensen 1980, Kolenosky 1987, Harshyne et al. 1998). Baculum weight also used in brown bears (Pearson 1975). A multivariate approach has been used for black bear cubs including hair length, total length, skull width, and ear length (Bridges et al. 2002).	Males larger than females but substantial overlap in size (Pearson 1975, Craighead and Mitchell 1982). Lower canines of black bears used for gender identification (Sauer 1966). Length of the mandibular canine alveolus and width of the second mandibular molar also used (Gordon and Morejohn 1975).

(Continued on next page)

Table 6 (*continued*).

Species	Age	Gender
Raccoon	Bacula of juvenile males porous at base with cartilaginous tip, <1.2 g in mass and <90 mm in length (Sanderson 1961*a*, Kaufmann 1982). Uterine horns of juvenile females translucent and 1–3 mm in diameter with no placental scars (Sanderson 1950); opaque and 4–7 mm with placental scars in adults. Tooth eruption useful to 110 days (Montgomery 1964), disappearance of cranial sutures and closure of epiphyses at ~12 months (Sanderson 1961*a*, Junge and Hoffmeister 1980, Fig. 22), and cementum annuli analysis for 4 age classes, including older animals (Grau et al. 1970, Johnson 1970).	Males slightly larger than females, but overlap makes characteristic difficult to use. Palpation used to detect baculum and testes in males (Stuewer 1943, Sanderson 1950, Kramer et al. 1999). Penal scars or nipples can be located on pelts.
American marten	Tooth replacement useful for estimating age to 18 weeks (Brassard and Bernard 1939). Radiographs of canine pulp cavities permit separation of juveniles from adults (Dix and Strickland 1986*b*). Cementum annuli analysis used to estimate age for older animals (Strickland et al. 1982, Archibald and Jessup 1984). Suprafabellar tubercle on femur used to separate juveniles from adults (Leach et al. 1982), but fusion of the distal femoral epiphysis not reliable (Dagg et al. 1975). Juvenile males have bacula weighing <0.1 g (Marshall 1951, Brown 1983).	Presence of baculum, preputial orifice on pelt, and larger size of head confirm male and vulva confirms female (Strickland and Douglas 1987). Characteristics of teeth and skull used to identify gender (Strickland et al. 1982, Brown 1983), but regional variation is large (Nagorsen et al. 1988). Tracks may be useful, although there is overlap (Zalewski 1999).
Northern river and sea otters (*Lontra canadensis, Enhydra lutris*)	Radiographs of teeth (Kuehn and Berg 1983, Melquist and Dronkert 1987) and closure of long bone epiphyses (Hamilton and Eadie 1964) useful to classify general ages. Cementum annuli analysis most reliable (Stephenson 1977, Bodkin et al. 1997). Eye-lens weight, baculum and skull characteristics, development of testes, and body size used with less success (Toweill and Tabor 1982, Melquist and Hornocker 1983).	Relative position of anus and urogenital openings used to ascertain gender; baculum detectable with palpation (Thompson 1958).
Wolverine	Genitalia and bone fusion used to separate young-of-the-year from adults (Wright and Rausch 1955, Rausch and Pearson 1972). Body weight, tooth wear, and physiological condition used to estimate age (Whitman et al. 1986). Best assessment for animals >1 year-of-age based on cementum annuli analysis (Rausch and Pearson 1972).	Nipples and genitalia (also scars and holes) used for classifying gender of live animals and pelts (Hash 1987). Females weigh 30% less than males (Hall 1981) with smaller skull condylobasal length (Magoun 1985).
Fisher	Suprafabellar tubercle present only on adult femur (Leach et al. 1982). Adults have prominent sagittal crest (Douglas and Strickland 1987) while young can be identified with bone epiphyses and pulp cavities (Dagg et al. 1975; Kuehn and Berg 1981; Jenks et al. 1984, 1986; Dix and Strickland 1986*a*). Tooth emergence useful through 7 months. Cementum annuli analysis of the first premolar used for estimating age of adults (Douglas and Strickland 1987, Arthur et al. 1992).	Males twice as large as females with larger bones (Leach 1977, Leach and de Kleer 1978). External genitalia or nipples readily apparent on live animals or pelts. Lower canines of males have root widths >5.64 mm (Parsons et al. 1978) and are longer (Kuehn and Berg 1981, Jenks et al. 1984, Dix and Strickland 1986*a*).
Mink and other mustelids	Tooth eruption useful for estimating age to 3 months in mink (Aulerich and Swindler 1968). Cementum annuli analysis useful for older animals (Klevezal' and Kleinenberg 1967, Birney and Fleharty 1968). Baculum mass in mink averages 172 mg in juveniles and 398 mg in adults (Lechleitner 1954, Greer 1957, Godin 1960). Head of baculum is distinctly ridged in adult mink (Lechleitner 1954) or expanded in long-tailed weasel (Wright 1947).	Testes or penis scar identifies male and nipples female (Birney and Fleharty 1966, Eagle and Whitman 1987).
American badger	Techniques used include bone sutures, sagittal crest (Messick 1987), and baculum characteristics (Messick and Hornocker 1981). Cementum annuli analysis best indicator of adult year classes (Crowe and Strickland 1975, Messick and Hornocker 1981).	Body and skull measurements useful, but are overlapping (Messick and Hornocker 1981, Messick 1987). Testes, penis, or penis scar used to classify males and vulva or nipples used to classify females (Petrides 1950*b*).

(Continued on next page)

Table 6 (*continued*).

Species	Age	Gender
Skunks	Cementum annuli analysis good estimator of adult year classes (Nicholson and Hill 1981). Other less effective techniques include bone ossification, tooth wear, and eye-lens weight (Allen 1939, Petrides 1950*b*, Mead 1967, Verts 1967, Bailey 1971, Leach et al. 1982).	Testes, penis, or penis scar used to identify males and vulva or nipples used to identify females. Lower canines may also be indicative of gender (Fuller et al. 1984).
Felids	Tooth emergence and replacement useful for estimating age to 240 days (Crowe 1975, McCord and Cardoza 1982, Lindzey 1987). Cementum annuli analysis useful for estimating age in older animals (Crowe 1972, Nellis et al. 1972); technique less successful with cougar. The foramen of the canine tooth closes at 13–18 months in lynx and bobcat (Saunders 1964, Crowe 1972, Johnson et al. 1981). Gum line recession used to estimate age in older cougar (Laundré et al. 2000), mass, body length, and tail length used to estimate age in younger cougar (Laundré and Hernández 2002); growth rate may vary by population (Maehr and Moore 1992).	Male genitalia detectable but less obvious than in other carnivores (McCord and Cardoza 1982, Lindzey 1987, Rolley 1987). Lower canine size useful to identify gender in bobcat (Friedrich et al. 1983). Body mass differs between male and female cougars, but there is overlap (Lindzey 1987, Laundré and Hernández 2002).
Pinnipedia	Patterns of tooth eruption and body size useful for estimating age (Spalding 1966), but cementum annuli analysis of canines best technique for older animals (Scheffer 1950, Laws 1962, Kenyon and Fiscus 1963, Anas 1970). Eye-lens weights useful in limited situations (Bauer et al. 1964).	Northern fur seal (*Callorhinus ursinus*), Steller sea lion (*Eumetopias jubatus*), California sea lion (*Zalophus californianus*), northern elephant seal (*Mirounga angustirostris*), walrus (*Odobenus rosmarus*), and gray seal (*Halichoerus grypus*) males substantially larger than females (King 1983, Riedman 1990). Harp seal (*Phoca groenlandica*) males only slightly larger than females, but black markings tend to be larger and more distinct. Harbor seal (*P. vitulina*) is exception as it is outwardly monomorphic. Canine teeth larger for males than females in every age category in northern fur seals (Huber 1994) and for animals >5 months in California sea lions (Lowry and Folk 1990).
Lagomorphs	Epiphyseal grooves on bones used to classify age to 14 months (Hale 1949, Godin 1960, Tiemeier and Plenert 1964, Bothma et al. 1972, Kauhala and Soveri 2001, Fig. 24); periosteal layers in mandibles may also be useful (Sullins et al. 1976). Skull length useful for estimating days after birth (Bray et al. 2002). Eye lens weights used to separate juveniles and adults (Lord 1959, Tiemeier and Plenert 1964, Rongstad 1966, Connolly et al. 1969*b*, Pelton 1970, Keith and Cary 1979, Hearn and Mercer 1988, Kauhala and Soveri 2001).	Careful examination can reveal the penis (cylindrical organ) or clitoris (flattened posteriorly); young rabbits and hares difficult to evaluate (Fox and Crary 1972).
Muskrat	Pelt primeness varies substantially between adults and juveniles; the underside of the pelt tends to be mottled in adults and broadly patterned in juveniles (Dozier 1942, Kellogg 1946, Applegate and Predmore 1947, Shanks 1948, Godin 1960, Doude Van Trootswijk 1976, Fig. 11). Adults have less fluting on first upper molar than juveniles (Olsen 1959, Proulx and Gilbert 1988) but pelt primeness appears more useful for classifying age (Moses and Boutin 1986). Adults have lower ratio of crown length to total length of first upper molar than juveniles, but regional variation should be considered (Pankakoski 1980, Erb et al. 1999). Additional characteristics include ossification of the baculum (Elder and Shanks 1962) (Fig. 15), and zygomatic breadth (Alexander 1951, 1960).	Careful examination can reveal the penis or nipples (Dozier 1942, Baumgartner and Bellrose 1943, Schofield 1955, Godin 1960). Sexual dimorphism in teeth not detectable (Lewis et al. 2002).

(*Continued on next page*)

Table 6 (*continued*).

Species	Age	Gender
American beaver	Acceptable accuracy with a small number of age classes can be achieved with radiography of jaws of live or dead animals (Hartman 1992); cementum annuli analysis useful for additional age classes (Van Nostrand and Stephenson 1964, Larson and Van Nostrand 1968). Evaluation of anal-urogenital opening in females useful for classifying adults and juveniles (Thompson 1958). Skull characteristics (Buckley and Libby 1955) and tooth-root closure (Van Nostrand and Stephenson 1964) useful for classifying juveniles and adults of both genders.	Males generally larger and heavier than females (Payne 1979). Careful palpation can identify the testes and baculum (Osborn 1955). Color and viscosity of anal gland secretion is reliable indicator (Schulte et al. 1995).
Tree squirrels	Development of fox (*Sciurus niger*) and eastern gray squirrels can be estimated with basic morphology up to 6 weeks (Uhlig 1955). The fur on the lateral rump of adult eastern gray squirrels has a distinct yellowish streak near the base that is absent in juveniles (Barrier and Barkalow 1967); age-specific patterns in tail pelage also noted (Sharp 1958, Fig. 12). Teats are inconspicuous and hidden by hair in juvenile females and large and noticeable in adults. Cementum annuli analysis useful to estimate age class (Lemnell 1974, Fogl and Mosby 1978). Other techniques include epiphyseal lines in long bones (Petrides 1951, Carson 1961, Nellis 1969), epiphyseal lines in the foot (McCloskey 1977), and eye-lens weight (Beale 1962, Fisher and Perry 1970).	Gender classified by examination of external genitalia, but skulls also useful (Nellis 1969).
Woodchuck (*Marmota monax*)	Juveniles weigh 300–450 g by ~15 May and have eye-lens weights that average 12.3 mg, yearlings have narrow and pointed incisors and eye-lens weights that average 21.8 mg, adults have broad incisors and eye-lens weights that average 28.53 mg (Davis 1964).	Careful examination used to reveal the os penis; testes are often regressed (Kwiecinski 1998).
Virginia opossum (*Didelphis virginiana*)	The pouch is white, shallow, or insignificant in size in juvenile females; it is flabby, fatty, and dark in adults (Petrides 1949). Tooth eruption and emergence is useful characteristic (Lowrance 1949, Petrides 1949, McManus 1974, Tyndale-Biscoe and Mackenzie 1976).	Canines of males longer and heavier than those of females (Gardner 1982). Males have scrotum and females have pouch (McManus 1974, Gardner 1982).
Bats	Cartilaginous epiphyseal plates in the finger bones of juveniles makes joints look "tapered" and less 'knobby' than joints of adults (Anthony 1988).	External genitalia are visible in males; testes are relatively large when male is in breeding condition (Racey 1988).
Small mammals (insectivores, other rodents)	Eye-lens weights are used (Birney et al. 1975, Gourley and Jannett 1975) with mixed success (Dapson and Irland 1972, Barker et al. 2003); tyrosine content in lens may be more accurate (Dapson and Irland 1972). Tooth eruption (Mitchell and Carsen 1967, Beg and Hoffmann 1977), tail collagen strength (Sherman et al. 1985), adhesion lines in the lower jaw (Millar and Zwickel 1972) and femur (Barker et al. 2003), and cementum annuli analysis (Adams and Watkins 1967, Montgomery et al. 1971) also have been used.	Careful examination of genitals in live animals can be useful with most species. Shape of pelvic girdle can be used when only bones are available (Dunmire 1955).

(*continued from page 321*)
ogy, and genetic analysis of small tissue samples. It is likely these techniques will provide a foundation for evaluation of population demography, establishment of harvest regulations and strategies, and development of protocols to monitor population and ecosystem health.

ACKNOWLEDGMENTS

We thank S. S. Germaine, R. L. Marchinton, and 3 anonymous reviewers for providing helpful comments and guidance on previous drafts of the manuscript. We also received suggestions from many others including G. L. Brady, S. H. Fitkin, W. M. Vander Haegen, and N. A. Hedges. Financial support was provided by the Washington Department of Fish and Wildlife.

LITERATURE CITED

ADAMS, D. A., AND T. L. QUAY. 1958. Ecology of the clapper rail in southeastern North Carolina. Journal of Wildlife Management 22:149–156.

ADAMS, L., AND S. G. WATKINS. 1967. Annuli in tooth cementum indicate age in California ground squirrels. Journal of Wildlife Management 31:836–839.

ADOLPH, S. C., AND W. P. PORTER. 1996. Growth, seasonality, and lizard life histories:age and size at maturity. Oikos 77:267–278.

ALBERICO, J. A. R. 1995. Floating eggs to estimate incubation stage does not affect hatchability. Wildlife Society Bulletin 23:212–216.

ALEXANDER, M. M. 1951. The aging of muskrats on the Montezuma National Wildlife Refuge. Journal of Wildlife Management 15:175–186.

———. 1960. Shrinkage of muskrat skulls in relation to aging. Journal of Wildlife Management 24:326–329.

ALKON, P. U. 1982. Estimating the age of juvenile chukars. Journal of Wildlife Management 46:777–781.

ALLEN, D. L. 1939. Winter habits of Michigan skunks. Journal of Wildlife Management 3:212–228.

ALLEN, S. H. 1974. Modified techniques for aging red fox using canine teeth. Journal of Wildlife Management 38:152–154.

———, AND S. C. KOHN. 1976. Assignment of age-classes in coyotes from canine cementum annuli. Journal of Wildlife Management 40:796–797.

AMSTRUP, S. C., G. W. GARNER, M. A. CRONIN, AND J. C. PATTON. 1993. Sex identification of polar bears from blood and tissue samples. Canadian Journal of Zoology 71:2174–2177.

ANAS, R. E. 1970. Accuracy in assigning ages to fur seals. Journal of Wildlife Management 34:844–852.

ANTHONY, E. L. P. 1988. Age determination in bats. Pages 47–57 *in* T. H. Kunz, editor. Ecological and behavioral methods for the study of bats. Smithsonian Institution Press, Washington, D.C., USA.

APPLEGATE, V. C., AND H. G. PREDMORE, JR. 1947. Age classes and patterns of primeness in a fall collection of muskrat pelts. Journal of Wildlife Management 11:324–330.

ARCHIBALD, W. R., AND R. H. JESSUP. 1984. Population dynamics of the pine marten (*Martes americana*) in the Yukon Territory. Pages 81–97 *in* R. Olsen, R. Hastings, and F. Geddes, editors. Northern ecology and resource management:memorial essays honoring Don Gill. University of Alberta, Edmonton, Canada.

ARMSTRONG, R. A. 1950. Fetal development of the northern white-tailed deer (*Odocoileus virginianus borealis* Miller). American Midland Naturalist 43:650–666.

ARTHUR, S. M., R. A. CROSS, T. F. PARAGI, AND W. B. KROHN. 1992. Precision and utility of cementum annuli for estimating ages of fishers. Wildlife Society Bulletin 20:402–405.

ARTMANN, J. W., AND L. D. SCHROEDER. 1976. A technique for sexing woodcock by wing measurement. Journal of Wildlife Management 40:572–574.

AULERICH, R. J., AND D. R. SWINDLER. 1968. The dentition of mink (*Mustela vison*). Journal of Mammalogy 49:488–494.

BAILEY, T. N. 1971. Biology of striped skunks on a southwestern Lake Erie marsh. American Midland Naturalist 85:196–207.

BAKER, M. F. 1953. Prairie chickens of Kansas. Miscellaneous Publication 5. Museum of Natural History, University of Kansas, Lawrence, USA.

BANNOR, B. K., AND E. KIVIAT. 2002. Common moorhen. Number 685 *in* A. Poole and F. Gill, editors. The birds of North America. The Birds of North America, Inc., Philadelphia, Pennsylvania, USA.

BARKER, J. M., R. BOONSTRA, AND A. I. SCHULT-HOSTEDDE. 2003. Age determination in yellow-pine chipmunks (*Tamias amoenus*):a comparison of eye lens masses and bone sections. Canadian Journal of Zoology 81:1774–1779.

BARNES, R. D., AND W. M. LONGHURST. 1960. Techniques for dental impressions, restraining and embedding markers in live-trapped deer. Journal of Wildlife Management 24:224–226.

BARNUM, D. A., J. S. GREEN, J. T. FLINDERS, AND N. L. GATES. 1979. Nutritional levels and growth rates of hand-reared coyote pups. Journal of Mammalogy 60:820–823.

BARRIER, M. J., AND F. S. BARKALOW, JR. 1967. A rapid technique for aging gray squirrels in winter pelage. Journal of Wildlife Management 31:715–719.

BARTH, E. K. 1953. Calculation of egg volume based on loss of weight during incubation. Auk 70:151–159.

BAUER, R. D., A. M. JOHNSON, AND V. B. SCHEFFER. 1964. Eye lens weight and age in the fur seal. Journal of Wildlife Management 28:374–376.

BAUMGARTNER, L. L., AND F. C. BELLROSE, JR. 1943. Determination of sex and age in muskrats. Journal of Wildlife Management 7:77–81.

BEALE, D. M. 1962. Growth of the eye lens in relation to age in fox squirrels. Journal of Wildlife Management 26:208–211.

BEASLEY, M. J., W. A. B. BROWN, AND A. J. LEGGE. 1992. Incremental banding in dental cementum: methods of preparation of teeth from archaeological sites and for modern comparative specimens. International Journal of Osteoarchaeology 2:37–50.

BEG, M. A., AND R. S. HOFFMANN. 1977. Age determination and variation in the red-tailed chipmunk, *Eutamias ruficaudus*. Murrelet 58:26–36.

BEKOFF, M. 1982. Coyote. Pages 447–459 *in* J. A. Chapman and G. A. Feldhamer, editors. Wild mammals of North America. Johns Hopkins University, Baltimore, Maryland, USA.

BELLROSE, F. C. 1980. Ducks, geese and swans of North America. Stackpole Books, Harrisburg, Pennsylvania, USA.

BENDELL, J. F. 1955. Age, molt and weight characteristics of blue grouse. Condor 57:354–361.

BERGERUD, A. T. 1964. Relationship of mandible length to sex in Newfoundland caribou. Journal of Wildlife Management 28:54–56.

———. 1970. Eruption of permanent premolars and molars for Newfoundland caribou. Journal of Wildlife Management 34:962–963.

———. 1978. Caribou. Pages 83–101 *in* J. L. Schmidt and D. L. Gilbert, editors. Big game of North America. Stackpole Books, Harrisburg, Pennsylvania, USA.

———, AND H. L. RUSSELL. 1966. Extraction of incisors of Newfoundland caribou. Journal of Wildlife Management 30:842–843.

———, S. S. PETERS, AND R. McGRATH. 1963. Determining sex and age of willow ptarmigan in Newfoundland. Journal of Wildlife Management 27:700–711.

BIRNEY, E. C., AND E. D. FLEHARTY. 1966. Age and sex comparisons of wild mink. Transactions of the Kansas Academy of Science 69:139–145.

———, AND ———. 1968. Comparative success in the application of aging techniques to a population of winter-trapped mink. Southwestern Naturalist 13:275–282.

———, R. JENNESS, AND D. D. BAIRD. 1975. Eye lens proteins as criteria of age in cotton rats. Journal of Wildlife Management 39:718–728.

BJORNDAL, K. A., A. B. BOLTEN, R. A. BENNETT, E. R. JACOBSON, T. J. WRONSKI, J. J. VALESKI, AND P. J. ELIAZAR. 1988. Age and growth in sea turtles: limitations of skeletochronology for demographic studies. Copeia 1:23–30.

BLEICH, V. C., T. R. STEPHENSON, N. J. HOLSTE, I. C. SNYDER, J. P. MARSHAL, P. W. McGRATH, AND B. M. PIERCE. 2003. Effects of tooth extraction on body condition and reproduction of mule deer. Wildlife Society Bulletin 31:233–236.

BLOEMENDAL, H. 1977. The vertebrate eye lens. Science 197:127–138.

BOAG, D. A. 1965. Indicators of sex, age, and breeding phenology in blue grouse. Journal of Wildlife Management 29:103–108.

———, AND M. A. SCHROEDER. 1992. Spruce grouse. Number 5 *in* A. Poole, P. Stettenheim, and F. Gill, editors. The birds of North America. The Birds of North America, Inc., Philadelphia, Pennsylvania, USA.

BODKIN, J. L., J. A. AMES, R. J. JAMESON, A. M. JOHNSON, AND G. M. MATSON. 1997. Estimating age of sea otters with cementum layers in the first premolar. Journal of Wildlife Management 61:967–973.

BOOKHOUT, T. A. 1964. Prenatal development of snowshoe hares. Journal of Wildlife Management 28:338–345.

———. 1995. Yellow rail. Number 139 *in* A. Poole, P. Stettenheim, and F. Gill, editors. The birds of North America. The Birds of North America, Inc., Philadelphia, Pennsylvania, USA.

BORTOLOTTI, G. R. 1984. Sexual size dimorphism and age-related size variation in bald eagles. Journal of Wildlife Management 48:72–81.

BOTHMA, J. DU. P., J. G. TEER, AND C. E. GATES. 1972. Growth and age determination of the cottontail in south Texas. Journal of Wildlife Management 36:1209–1221.

BOWEN, W. O. 1982. Determining the age of coyotes, *Canis latrans*, by tooth sections and tooth wear patterns. Canadian Field-Naturalist 96:339–341.

BRADLEY, J. A., D. SECORD, AND L. PRINS. 1981. Age determination in the arctic fox (*Alopex lagopus*). Canadian Journal of Zoology 59:1976–1979.

BRANDBORG, S. M. 1955. Life history and management of the mountain goat in Idaho. Wildlife Bulletin 2. Idaho Department of Fish and Game, Boise, USA.

BRASSARD, J. S., AND R. BERNARD. 1939. Observations on breeding and development of martens, *Martes a. americana* (Ken). Canadian Field-Naturalist 53:15–21.

BRAUN, C. E. 1971. Determination of blue grouse sex and age from wing characteristics. Game Information Leaflet 86. Colorado Division of Game, Fish and Parks, Fort Collins, USA.

———, AND G. E. ROGERS. 1967. Determination of age and sex of the southern white-tailed ptarmigan. Game Information Leaflet 54. Colorado Division of Game, Fish and Parks, Fort Collins, USA.

———, K. MARTIN, AND L. A. ROBB. 1993. White-tailed ptarmigan. Number 68 *in* A. Poole and F. Gill, editors. The birds of North America. The Birds of North America, Inc., Philadelphia, Pennsylvania, USA.

BRAY, Y., S. CHAMPELY, AND D. SOYEZ. 2002. Age determination in leverets of European hare *Lepus europaeus* based on body measurements. Wildlife Biology 8:31–39.

BRENNAN, L. A. 1999. Northern bobwhite. Number 397 *in* A. Poole and F. Gill, editors. The birds of North America. The Birds of North America, Inc., Philadelphia, Pennsylvania, USA.

———, AND W. M. BLOCK. 1985. Sex determination of mountain quail reconsidered. Journal of Wildlife Management 49:475–476.

BRIDGES, A. S., C. OLFENBUTTEL, AND M. R. VAUGHAN. 2002. A mixed regression model to estimate neonatal black bear cub age. Wildlife Society Bulletin 30:1253–1258.

BRISBIN, JR., I. L., AND T. B. MOWBRAY. 2002. American coot. Number 697 *in* A. Poole and F. Gill, editors. The birds of North America. The Birds of North America, Inc., Philadelphia, Pennsylvania, USA.

BRONSON, F. H. 1979. The reproductive ecology of the house mouse. Quarterly Review of Biology 54:265–299.

BROWN, H. A., R. B. BURY, D. M. DARLA, L. V. DILLER, C. R. PETERSON, AND R. M. STORM. 1995. Reptiles of Washington and Oregon. Seattle Audubon Society, Seattle, Washington, USA.

BROWN, M. W. 1983. A morphometric analysis of sexual and age variation in the American marten (*Martes americana*). Thesis. University of Toronto, Ontario, Canada.

BRUNS STOCKRAHM, D. M., B. J. DICKERSON, S. L. ADOLF, AND R. W. SEABLOOM. 1996. Aging black-tailed prairie dogs by weight of eye lenses. Journal of Mammalogy 77:874–881.

BUCKLEY, J. L., AND W. L. LIBBY. 1955. Growth rates and age determination in Alaskan beaver. Transactions of the North American Wildlife Conference 20:495–507.

BUEHLER, D. A. 2000. Bald eagle. Number 425 *in* A. Poole and F. Gill, editors. The birds of North America. The Birds of North America, Inc., Philadelphia, Pennsylvania, USA.

BUMP, G., R. W. DARROW, F. C. EDMINSTER, AND W. F. CRISSEY. 1947. The ruffed grouse: life history, propagation, and management. New York State Conservation Department, Albany, USA.

BUNNELL, S. D., J. A. RENSEL, J. F. KIMBALL, JR., AND M. L. WOLFE. 1977. Determination of sex and age of dusky blue grouse. Journal of Wildlife Management 41:662–666.

BURT, W. H., AND R. P. GROSSENHEIDER. 1998. A field guide to the mammals: North America north of Mexico. Houghton Mifflin Company, Boston, Massachusetts, USA.

CAITHAMER, D. F., R. J. GATES, J. D. HARDY, AND T. C. TACHA. 1993. Field identification of age and sex of interior Canada geese. Wildlife Society Bulletin 21:480–487.

CALKINS, J. D., J. C. HAGELIN, AND D. F. LOTT. 1999. California quail. Number 473 *in* A. Poole and F. Gill, editors. The birds of North America. The Birds of North America, Inc., Philadelphia, Pennsylvania, USA.

CALVERT, W., AND M. A. RAMSAY. 1998. Evaluation of age determination of polar bears by counts of cementum growth layer groups. Ursus 10:449–453.

CAMPBELL, H. 1972. A population study of lesser prairie chickens in New Mexico. Journal of Wildlife Management 36:689–699.

CANNELL, P. F. 1984. A revised age/sex key for mourning doves, with comments on the definition of molt. Journal of Field Ornithology 55:112–114.

CARBYN, L. N. 1987. Gray wolf and red wolf. Pages 358–376 *in* M. Novak, J. A. Baker, M. E. Obbard, and B. Malloch, editors. Wild furbearer management and conservation in North America. Ontario Ministry of Natural Resources, Toronto, Canada.

CARNEY, S. M. 1992. Species, age and sex identification of ducks using wing plumage. U.S. Department of the Interior, Fish and Wildlife Service, Washington, D.C., USA.

CARREL, W. K. 1994. Reproductive history of female black bears from dental cementum. International Conference on Bear Research and Management 9:205–212.

CARROLL, J. P. 1993. Gray partridge. Number 58 *in* A. Poole and F. Gill, editors. The birds of North America. The Birds of North America, Inc., Philadelphia, Pennsylvania, USA.

CARSON, J. D. 1961. Epiphyseal cartilage as an age indicator in fox and gray squirrels. Journal of Wildlife Management 25:90–93.

CASWELL, E. B. 1954. A method for sexing blue grouse. Journal of Wildlife Management 18:139.

CHRISTENSEN, G. C. 1996. Chukar. Number 258 *in* A. Poole and F. Gill, editors. The birds of North America. The Birds of North America, Inc., Philadelphia, Pennsylvania, USA.

CLAWSON, R. G., AND M. K. CAUSEY. 1995. Dental casts for white-tailed deer age estimation. Wildlife Society Bulletin 23:92–94.

COGALNICEANU, D., AND C. MIAUD. 2003. Population age structure and growth in four syntopic amphibian species inhabiting a large river floodplain. Canadian Journal of Zoology 81:1096–1106.

COLES, W. C. 1999. Aspects of the biology of sea turtles in the mid-Atlantic Bight. Thesis. College of William and Mary, Williamsburg, Virginia, USA.

CONANT, R., AND J. T. COLLINS. 1998. Peterson field guide to reptiles and amphibians of eastern and central North America. Third edition, expanded. Houghton Mifflin Company, New York, USA.

CONNELLY, J. W., M. W. GRATSON, AND K. P. REESE. 1998. Sharp-tailed grouse. Number 354 *in* A. Poole and F. Gill, editors. The birds of North America. The Birds of North America, Inc., Philadelphia, Pennsylvania, USA.

CONNOLLY, G. E., M. L. DUDZIŃSKI, AND W. M. LONGHURST. 1969a. An improved age-lens weight regression for black-tailed deer and mule deer. Journal of Wildlife Management 33:701–704.

———, ———, AND ———. 1969b. The eye lens as an indicator of age in the black-tailed jack rabbit. Journal of Wildlife Management 33:159–164.

COPELIN, F. F. 1963. The lesser prairie chicken in Oklahoma. Technical Bulletin 6. Oklahoma Wildlife Conservation Department, Oklahoma City, USA.

COTTAM, C., AND J. B. TREFETHEN, editors. 1968. Whitewings:the life history, status and management of the white-winged dove. D. Van Nostrand, Princeton, New Jersey, USA.

CRAIGHEAD, J. J., AND J. A. MITCHELL. 1982. Grizzly bear. Pages 515–556 *in* J. A. Chapman and G. A. Feldhamer, editors. Wild mammals of North America. Johns Hopkins University, Baltimore, Maryland, USA.

———, F. C. CRAIGHEAD, JR., AND H. E. McCUTCHEN. 1970. Age determination of grizzly bears from fourth premolar tooth sections. Journal of Wildlife Management 34:353–363.

CRAMP, S., AND K. E. L. SIMMONS, editors. 1980. The birds of the western Palearctic. Volume 2. Hawks to bustards. Oxford University Press, Oxford, United Kingdom.

CRISPENS, JR., C. G., AND J. K. DOUTT. 1970. Studies of the sex chromatin in the white-tailed deer. Journal of Wildlife Management 34:642–644.

CROWE, D. M. 1972. The presence of annuli in bobcat tooth cementum layers. Journal of Wildlife Management 36:1330–1332.

———. 1975. Aspects of aging, growth, and reproduction of bobcats from Wyoming. Journal of Mammalogy 56:177–198.

———, and M. D. Strickland. 1975. Population structures of some mammalian predators in southeastern Wyoming. Journal of Wildlife Management 39:449–450.

CRUNDEN, C. W. 1963. Age and sex of sage grouse from wings. Journal of Wildlife Management 27:846–849.

DAGG, A. I., D. LEACH, AND G. SUMNER-SMITH. 1975. Fusion of the distal femoral epiphysis in male and female marten and fisher. Canadian Journal of Zoology 53:1514–1518.

DAHLGREN, R. B., C. M. TWEDT, AND C. G. TRAUTMAN. 1965. Lens weights of ring-necked pheasants. Journal of Wildlife Management 29:212–214.

DALKE, P. D., D. B. PYRAH, D. C. STANTON, J. E. CRAWFORD, AND E. F. SCHLATTERER. 1963. Ecology, productivity, and management of sage grouse in Idaho. Journal of Wildlife Management 27:811–841.

DAPSON, R. W., AND J. M. IRLAND. 1972. An accurate method of determining age in small mammals. Journal of Mammalogy 53:100–106.

DAVIS, D. E. 1964. Evaluation of characters for determining age of woodchucks. Journal of Wildlife Management 28:9–15.

DAVIS, J. A. 1969. Aging and sexing criteria for Ohio ruffed grouse. Journal of Wildlife Management 33:628–636.

DeGRAFF, R. M., AND J. S. LARSON. 1972. A technique for the observation of sex chromatin in hair roots. Journal of Mammalogy 53:368–371.

DeYOUNG, C. A. 1989. Aging live white-tailed deer on southern ranges. Journal of Wildlife Management 53:519–523.

DIMMICK, R. W. 1992. Northern bobwhite (*Colinus virginianus*). U.S. Department of Army, Corps of Engineers, Wildlife Resources Management Manual, Technical Report EL-92-18, Section 4.1.3. Waterways Experiment Station, Vicksburg, Mississippi, USA.

———, AND M. R. PELTON. 1994. Criteria of sex and age. Pages 169–214 *in* T. A. Bookhout, editor. Fifth edition. Research and management techniques for wildlife and habitats. The Wildlife Society, Bethesda, Maryland, USA.

DIX, L. M., AND M. A. STRICKLAND. 1986a. Sex and age determination for fisher using radiographs of canine teeth:a critique. Journal of Wildlife Management 50:275–276.

————, AND ————. 1986b. Use of tooth radiographs to classify martens by sex and age. Wildlife Society Bulletin 14:275–279.

DORNEY, R. S. 1966. A new method for sexing ruffed grouse in late summer. Journal of Wildlife Management 30: 623–625.

————, AND F. V. HOLZER. 1957. Spring aging methods for ruffed grouse cocks. Journal of Wildlife Management 21:268–274.

DOUDE VAN TROOSTWIJK, W. J. 1976. Age determination in muskrats, *Ondatra zibethicus* (L.) in the Netherlands. Lutra 18:33–43.

DOUGLAS, C. W., AND M. A. STRICKLAND. 1987. Fisher. Pages 511–529 *in* M. Novak, J. A. Baker, M. E. Obbard, and B. Malloch, editors. Wild furbearer management and conservation in North America. Ontario Ministry of Natural Resources, Toronto, Canada.

DOW, JR., S. A., AND P. L. WRIGHT. 1962. Changes in mandibular dentition associated with age in pronghorn antelope. Journal of Wildlife Management 26:1–18.

DOZIER, H. L. 1942. Identification of sex in live muskrats. Journal of Wildlife Management 6:292–293.

DUFFIELD, L. F. 1973. Aging and sexing the post-cranial skeleton of bison. Plains Anthropologist 18:132–139.

DUNMIRE, W. W. 1955. Sex dimorphism in the pelvis of rodents. Journal of Mammalogy 36:356–361.

DUNN, E. H., D. J. T. HUSSELL, AND R. E. RICKLEFS. 1979. The determination of incubation stage in starling eggs. Bird-banding 50:114–120.

DUNNE, P. 1987. Introduction to raptor identification, aging and sexing techniques. Pages 13–21 *in* B. A. Giron Pendleton, B. A. Millsap, K. W. Cline, and D. M. Bird, editors. Raptor management techniques manual. National Wildlife Federation, Washington, D.C., USA.

DWYER, T. J., AND J. V. DOBELL. 1979. External determination of age of common snipe. Journal of Wildlife Management 43:754–756.

EAGLE, T. C., AND J. S. WHITMAN. 1987. Mink. Pages 615–624 *in* M. Novak, J. A. Baker, M. E. Obbard, and B. Malloch, editors. Wild furbearer management and conservation in North America. Ontario Ministry of Natural Resources, Toronto, Canada.

EDDLEMAN, W. R., AND C. J. CONWAY. 1998. Clapper rail. Number 340 *in* A. Poole, P. Stettenheim, and F. Gill, editors. The birds of North America. The Birds of North America, Inc., Philadelphia, Pennsylvania, USA.

————, AND F. L. KNOPF. 1985. Determining age and sex of American coots. Journal of Field Ornithology 56:41–55.

————, R. E. FLORES, AND M. L. LEGARE. 1994. Black rail. Number 123 *in* A. Poole, P. Stettenheim, and F. Gill, editors. The birds of North America. The Birds of North America, Inc., Philadelphia, Pennsylvania, USA.

EDMINSTER, F. C. 1954. American game birds of field and forest. Charles Scribner's Sons, New York, USA.

EDWARDS, J. K., R. L. MARCHINTON, AND G. F. SMITH. 1982. Pelvic girdle criteria for sex determination of white-tailed deer. Journal of Wildlife Management 46:544–547.

EINARSEN, A. S. 1948. The pronghorn antelope and its management. Wildlife Management Institute, Washington, D.C., USA.

ELDER, W. H., AND C. E. SHANKS. 1962. Age changes in tooth wear and morphology of the baculum in muskrats. Journal of Mammalogy 43:144–150.

ELLISON, L. N. 1968. Sexing and aging Alaskan spruce grouse by plumage. Journal of Wildlife Management 32:12–16.

ELY, C. R., AND A. X. DZUBIN. 1994. Greater white-fronted goose. Number 131 *in* A. Poole and F. Gill, editors. The birds of North America. The Birds of North America, Inc., Philadelphia, Pennsylvania, USA.

ENG, R. L. 1955. A method for obtaining sage grouse age and sex ratios from wings. Journal of Wildlife Management 19:267–272.

ERB, J. D., R. D. BLUETT, E. K. FRITZELL, AND N. F. PAYNE. 1999. Aging muskrats using molar indices: a regional comparison. Wildlife Society Bulletin 27:628–635.

ERICKSON, J. A., AND W. G. SELIGER. 1969. Efficient sectioning of incisors for estimating ages of mule deer. Journal of Wildlife Management 33:384–388.

————, A. E. ANDERSON, D. E. MEDIN, AND D. C. BOWDEN. 1970. Estimating ages of mule deer—an evaluation of technique accuracy. Journal of Wildlife Management 34:523–531.

ESLER, D., AND J. B. GRAND. 1994. Comparison of age determination techniques for female northern pintails and American wigeon in spring. Wildlife Society Bulletin 22:260–264.

ETTER, S. L. 1963. Age determination and growth in juvenile greater prairie chickens. Thesis. University of Illinois, Urbana, USA.

————, J. E. WARNOCK, AND G. B. JOSELYN. 1970. Modified wing molt criteria for estimating the ages of wild juvenile pheasants. Journal of Wildlife Management 34:620–626.

FAERMAN, M., D. FILON, G. KAHILA, C. L. GREENBLATT, P. SMITH, AND A. OPPENHEIM. 1995. Sex identification of archaeological human remains based on amplification of the X and Y amelogenin alleles. Gene 167:327–332.

FANCY, S. G. 1980. Preparation of mammalian teeth for age determination by cementum layers: a review. Wildlife Society Bulletin 8:242–248.

FELLERS, G. M., AND K. L. FREEL. 1995. A standardized protocol for surveying aquatic amphibians. Technical Report NPS/WRUC/NRTR-95-01. U.S. Department of the Interior, University of California, Davis, USA.

FESTA-BIANCHET, M., P. BLANCHARD, J. M. GAILLARD, AND A. J. M. HEWISON. 2002. Tooth extraction is not an acceptable technique to age live ungulates. Wildlife Society Bulletin 30:282–288.

FISHER, E. W., AND A. E. PERRY. 1970. Estimating ages of gray squirrels by lens-weights. Journal of Wildlife Management 34:825–828.

FLYGER, V. F. 1958. Tooth impressions as an aid in the determination of age in deer. Journal of Wildlife Management 22:442–443.

FOGARTY, M. J., K. A. ARNOLD, L. MCKIBBEN, L. B. POSPICHAL, AND R. J. TULLY. 1977. Common snipe. Pages 189–209 *in* G. C. Sanderson, editor. Management of migratory shore and upland game birds in North America. International Association of Fish and Wildlife Agencies, Washington, D.C., USA.

FOGL, J. G., AND H. S. MOSBY. 1978. Aging gray squirrels by cementum annuli in razor-sectioned teeth. Journal of Wildlife Management 42:444–448.

FOX, R. R., AND D. D. CRARY. 1972. A simple technique for the sexing of newborn rabbits. Laboratory Animal Science 22:556–558.

FREDRICKSON, L. H. 1968. Measurements of coots related to sex and age. Journal of Wildlife Management 32:409–411.

FRIEDRICH, P. D., G. E. BURGOYNE, T. M. COOLEY, AND S. M. SCHMIDT. 1983. Use of lower canine tooth for determining the sex of bobcats in Michigan. Wildlife Division Report 2960. Michigan Department of Natural Resources, Lansing, USA.

FRIEND, M. 1967. A review of research concerning eye-lens weight as a criterion of age in animals. New York Fish and Game Journal 14:152–165.

FRISON, G. C., AND C. A. REHER. 1970. Age determination of buffalo by teeth eruption and wear. Plains Anthropologist 15:46–50.

FRITZELL, E. K. 1987. Gray fox and island gray fox. Pages 408–421 *in* M. Novak, J. A. Baker, M. E. Obbard, and B. Malloch, editors. Wild furbearer management and conservation in North America. Ontario Ministry of Natural Resources, Toronto, Canada.

FULLER, T. K., D. P. HOBSON, J. R. GUNSON, D. B. SCHOWALTER, AND D. HEISEY. 1984. Sexual dimorphism in mandibular canines of striped skunks. Journal of Wildlife Management 48:1444–1446.

FULLER, W. A. 1959. The horns and teeth as indicators of age in bison. Journal of Wildlife Management 23:342–344.

GARDNER, A. L. 1982. Virginia opossum. Pages 3–36 *in* J. A. Chapman and G. A. Feldhamer, editors. Wild mammals of North America. Johns Hopkins University, Baltimore, Maryland, USA.

GASAWAY, W. C., D. B. HARKNESS, AND R. A. RAUSCH. 1978. Accuracy of moose age determinations from incisor cementum layers. Journal of Wildlife Management 42:558–563.

GATES, J. M. 1966. Validity of spur appearance as an age criterion in the pheasant. Journal of Wildlife Management 30:81–85.

GEE, K. L., J. H. HOLMAN, M. K. CAUSEY, A. N. ROSSI, AND J. B. ARMSTRONG. 2002. Aging white-tailed deer by tooth replacement and wear:a critical evaluation of a time-honored technique. Wildlife Society Bulletin 30:387–393.

GEIGER, G., J. BROMEL, AND K. H. HABERMEHL. 1977. Concordance of various methods of determining the age of the red fox (*Vulpes vulpes* L. 1758). Zeitschrift fuer Jagdwissenshaft 23:57–64.

GEIST, V. 1966. Validity of horn segment counts in aging bighorn sheep. Journal of Wildlife Management 30:634–635.

————. 1981. Behavior:adaptive strategies in mule deer. Pages 157–223 *in* O. C. Wallmo, editor. Mule and black-tailed deer of North America. University of Nebraska Press, Lincoln, USA.

GIER, H. T. 1968. Coyotes in Kansas. Agricultural Experiment Station Bulletin 393. Kansas State University, Manhattan, USA.

GIESEN, K. M. 1998. Lesser prairie-chicken. Number 364 *in* A. Poole and F. Gill, editors. The birds of North America. The Birds of North America, Inc., Philadelphia, Pennsylvania, USA.

————, AND C. E. BRAUN. 1979. A technique for age determination of juvenile white-tailed ptarmigan. Journal of Wildlife Management 43:508–511.

GILBERT, F. F. 1966. Aging white-tailed deer by annuli in the cementum of the first incisor. Journal of Wildlife Management 30:200–202.

————, AND S. L. STOLT. 1970. Variability in aging Maine white-tailed deer by tooth-wear characteristics. Journal of Wildlife Management

34:532–535.

GIPSON, P. S., W. B. BALLARD, R. M. NOWAK, AND L. D. MECH. 2000. Accuracy and precision of estimating age of gray wolves by tooth wear. Journal of Wildlife Management 64:752–758.

GODIN, A. J. 1960. A compilation of diagnostic characteristics used in aging and sexing game birds and mammals. Thesis. University of Massachusetts, Amherst, USA.

GOODWIN, E. A., AND W. B. BALLARD. 1985. Use of tooth cementum for age determination of gray wolves. Journal of Wildlife Management 49:313–316.

GORDON, K. R., AND G. V. MOREJOHN. 1975. Sexing black bear skulls using lower canine and lower molar measurement. Journal of Wildlife Management 39:40–44.

GOURLEY, R. S., AND F. J. JANNETT, JR. 1975. Pine and montane vole age estimates from eye lens weights. Journal of Wildlife Management 39:550–556.

GOWER, W. C. 1939. The use of the bursa of Fabricius as an indication of age in game birds. Transactions of the North American Wildlife Conference 4:426–430.

GRAU, G. A., G. C. SANDERSON, AND J. P. ROGERS. 1970. Age determination of raccoons. Journal of Wildlife Management 34:364–372.

GREENBERG, R. E., S. L. ETTER, AND W. L. ANDERSON. 1972. Evaluation of proximal primary feather criteria for aging wild pheasants. Journal of Wildlife Management 36:700–705.

GREER, K. R. 1957. Some osteological characters of known-age ranch minks. Journal of Mammalogy 38:319–330.

———, AND H. W. YEAGER. 1967. Sex and age indications from upper canine teeth of elk (wapiti). Journal of Wildlife Management 31:408–417.

GREGORY, P. T. 1983. Identification of sex of small snakes in the field. Herpetological Review 14:42–43.

GRUE, H., AND B. JENSEN. 1973. Annular structures in canine tooth cementum in red foxes (*Vulpes fulva* L.) of known age. Danish Review of Game Biology 8(7):1–12.

———, AND ———. 1976. Annular cementum structures in canine tooth in arctic foxes (*Alopex lagopus* L.) from Greenland and Denmark. Danish Review of Game Biology 10(3):1–12.

GUTIÉRREZ, R. J., AND D. J. DELEHANTY. 1999. Mountain quail. Number 457 *in* A. Poole and F. Gill, editors. The birds of North America. The Birds of North America, Inc., Philadelphia, Pennsylvania, USA.

HAAGENRUD, H. 1978. Layers in secondary dentine of incisors as age criteria in moose (*Alces alces*). Journal of Mammalogy 59:857–858.

HAAS, G. H., AND S. R. AMEND. 1976. Aging immature mourning doves by primary feather molt. Journal of Wildlife Management 40:575–578.

HALE, J. B. 1949. Aging cottontail rabbits by bone growth. Journal of Wildlife Management 13:216–225.

———, R. F. WENDT, AND G. C. HALAZON. 1954. Sex and age criteria for Wisconsin ruffed grouse. Technical Wildlife Bulletin 9. Wisconsin Conservation Department, Madison, USA.

HALL, E. R. 1981. The mammals of North America. Second edition. Volume II. John Wiley and Sons, New York, USA.

HALLIDAY, T. R., AND P. A. VERRELL. 1988. Body size and age in amphibians and reptiles. Journal of Herpetology 22:253–265.

HAMILTON, R. J., M. L. TOBIN, AND W. G. MOORE. 1985. Aging fetal white-tailed deer. Proceedings of the Annual Conference of the Southeastern Association of Fish and Wildlife Agencies 39:389–395.

HAMILTON, JR., W. J., AND W. R. EADIE. 1964. Reproduction in the river otter, *Lutra canadensis*. Journal of Mammalogy 45:242–252.

HAMLIN, K. L., D. F. PAC, C. A. SIME, R. M. DESIMONE, AND G. L. DUSEK. 2000. Evaluating the accuracy of ages obtained by two methods for Montana ungulates. Journal of Wildlife Management 64:441–449.

HANAOKA, Y., AND K. MINAGUCHI. 1996. Sex determination from blood and teeth by PCR amplification of the alphoid satellite family. Journal of Forensic Science 41:855–858.

HANNON, S. J., P. K. EASON, AND K. MARTIN. 1998. Willow ptarmigan. Number 369 *in* A. Poole and F. Gill, editors. The birds of North America. The Birds of North America, Inc., Philadelphia, Pennsylvania, USA.

HANSON, H. C. 1962. Characters of age, sex, and sexual maturity in Canada geese. Biological Notes 49. Illinois Natural History Survey, Urbana, USA.

———, AND C. W. KOSSACK. 1963. The mourning dove in Illinois. Technical Bulletin 2. Illinois Department of Conservation and the Illinois Natural History Survey, Southern Illinois University Press, Carbondale, USA.

HARLOW, P. S. 1996. A harmless technique for sexing hatchling lizards. Herpetological Review 27:71–72.

HARRIS, S. 1978. Age determination in the red fox (*Vulpes vulpes*): an

evaluation of technique efficiency as applied to a sample of suburban foxes. Journal of the Zoological Society 184:94–117.

HARSHYNE, W. A., D. R. DIEFENBACH, G. L. ALT, AND G. M. MATSON. 1998. Analysis of error from cementum-annuli age estimates of known-age Pennsylvania black bears. Journal of Wildlife Management 62:1281–1291.

HARTMAN, G. 1992. Age determination of live beaver by dental x-ray. Wildlife Society Bulletin 20:216–220.

HARVEY, IV, W. F., G. R. HEPP, AND R. A. KENNAMER. 1989. Age determination of female wood ducks during the breeding season. Wildlife Society Bulletin 17:254–258.

HASH, H. S. 1987. Wolverine. Pages 575–585 *in* M. Novak, J. A. Bament, M. E. Obbard, and B. Malloch, editors. Wild furbearer management and conservation in North America. Ontario Ministry of Natural Resources, Toronto, Canada.

HAUGEN, A. O., AND D. W. SPEAKE. 1958. Determining age of young fawn white-tailed deer. Journal of Wildlife Management 22:319–321

HAYS, H., AND M. LECROY. 1971. Field criteria for determining incubation stage in eggs of the common tern. Wilson Bulletin 83:425–429.

HEALY, W. M., AND E. S. NENNO. 1980. Growth parameters and sex and age criteria for juvenile eastern wild turkeys. Proceedings of the National Wild Turkey Symposium 4:168–185.

HEARN, B. J., AND W. E. MERCER. 1988. Eye-lens weight as an indicator of age in Newfoundland arctic hares. Wildlife Society Bulletin 16:426–429.

HELLDIN, J.-O. 1997. Age determination of Eurasian pine martens by radiographs of teeth in situ. Wildlife Society Bulletin 25:83–88.

HEMMING, J. E. 1969. Cemental deposition, tooth succession, and horn development as criteria of age in Dall sheep. Journal of Wildlife Management 33:552–558.

HENDERSON, F. R., F. W. BROOKS, R. E. WOOD, AND R. B. DAHLGREN. 1967. Sexing of prairie grouse by crown feather patterns. Journal of Wildlife Management 31:764–769.

HENSEL, R. J., AND F. E. SORENSEN, JR. 1980. Age determination of live polar bears. International Conference on Bear Resource Management 4:93–100.

HESSELTON, W. T., AND R. M. HESSELTON. 1982. White-tailed deer. Pages 878–901 *in* J. A. Chapman and G. A. Feldhamer, editors. Wild mammals of North America. Johns Hopkins University, Baltimore, Maryland, USA.

HILLMAN, C. N., AND W. W. JACKSON. 1973. The sharp-tailed grouse in South Dakota. Technical Bulletin 3. South Dakota Department of Game, Fish and Parks, Pierre, USA.

HOFFMAN, R. W. 1983. Sex classification of juvenile blue grouse from wing characteristics. Journal of Wildlife Management 47:1143–1147.

———. 1985. Blue grouse wing analysis: methodology and population inferences. Special Report 60. Colorado Division of Wildlife, Fort Collins, USA.

HOHMAN, W. L., J. L. MOORE, D. J. TWEDT, J. G. MENSIK, AND E. LOGERWELL. 1995. Age-class separation of blue-winged ducks. Journal of Wildlife Management 59:727–735.

HOLDER, K., AND R. MONTGOMERIE. 1993. Rock ptarmigan. Number 51 *in* A. Poole and F. Gill, editors. The birds of North America. The Birds of North America, Inc., Philadelphia, Pennsylvania, USA.

HOLLIMAN, D. C. 1977. Purple gallinule. Pages 105–109 *in* G. C. Sanderson, editor. Management of migratory shore and upland game birds in North America. International Association of Fish and Wildlife Agencies, Washington, D.C., USA.

HUBER, H. R. 1994. A technique for determining sex of northern fur seal pup carcasses. Wildlife Society Bulletin 22:479–483.

HUBER, S, U. BRUNS, AND W. ARNOLD. 2002. Sex determination of red deer using polymerase chain reaction of DNA from feces. Wildlife Society Bulletin 30:208–212.

HUDSON, P., AND L. G. BROWMAN. 1959. Embryonic and fetal development of the mule deer. Journal of Wildlife Management 23:295–304.

JACOBSON, H. A., AND R. J. REINER. 1989. Estimating age of white-tailed deer: tooth wear versus cementum annuli. Proceedings of the Annual Conference of the Southeastern Association of Fish and Wildlife Agencies 43:286–291.

JENKS, J. A., R. T. BOWYER, AND A. G. CLARK. 1984. Sex and age-class determination for fisher using radiographs of canine teeth. Journal of Wildlife Management 48:626–628.

———, ———, AND ———. 1986. Sex and age determination for fisher using radiographs of canine teeth: a response. Journal of Wildlife Management 50:277–278.

JENSEN, W. 1998. Aging antelope—it's all in the teeth. North Dakota Outdoors 61(2):16–20.

JOHNSGARD, P. A. 1973. Grouse and quails of North America. University of Nebraska Press, Lincoln, USA.

———. 1975. North American game birds of upland and shoreline. University of Nebraska Press, Lincoln, USA.

JOHNSON, A. S. 1970. Biology of the raccoon (*Procyon lotor varius* Nelson and Goldman) in Alabama. Agricultural Experiment Station Bulletin 402. Auburn University, Auburn, Alabama, USA.

JOHNSON, N. F., B. A. BROWN, AND J. C. BOSOMWORTH. 1981. Age and sex characteristics of bobcat canines and their use in population assessment. Wildlife Society Bulletin 9:203–206.

JOHNSTON, D. H., D. G. JOACHIM, P. BACHMANN, K. V. KARDONG, R. A. STEWART, L. M. DIX, M. A. STRICKLAND, AND I. D. WATT. 1987. Aging furbearers using tooth structure and biomarkers. Pages 228–243 *in* M. Novak, J. A. Baker, M. E. Obbard, and B. Malloch, editors. Wild furbearer management and conservation in North America. Ontario Ministry of Natural Resources, Toronto, Canada.

JONES, F. L., G. FLITTNER, AND R. GARD. 1954. Report on a survey of bighorn sheep and other game in the Santa Rosa Mountains, Riverside County (California). California Department of Fish and Game, Sacramento, USA.

JUNGE, R., AND D. F. HOFFMEISTER. 1980. Age determination in raccoons from cranial suture obliteration. Journal of Wildlife Management 44:725–729.

KALLA, P. I. 1991. Studies on the biology of ruffed grouse in the southern Appalachian Mountains. Thesis. University of Tennessee, Knoxville, USA.

KAUFMANN, J. H. 1982. Raccoon and allies. Pages 567–585 *in* J. A. Chapman and G. A. Feldhamer, editors. Wild mammals of North America. Johns Hopkins University, Baltimore, Maryland, USA.

KAUHALA, K., AND T. SOVERI. 2001. An evaluation of methods for distinguishing between juvenile and adult mountain hares *Lepus timidus*. Wildlife Biology 7:295–300.

KEAY, J. A. 1995. Accuracy of cementum age assignments for black bears. California Fish and Game 81:113–121.

KEISS, R. E. 1969. Comparison of eruption-wear patterns and cementum annuli as age criteria in elk. Journal of Wildlife Management 33:175–180.

KEITH, L. B., AND J. R. CARY. 1979. Eye lens weights from free-living adult snowshoe hares of known age. Journal of Wildlife Management 43:965–969.

KELLOGG, C. E. 1946. Variation in pattern of primeness of muskrat skins. Journal of Wildlife Management 10:38–42.

KELLY, G. 1975. Indices for aging eastern wild turkeys. Proceedings of the National Wild Turkey Symposium 3:205–209.

KENYON, K. W., AND C. H. FISCUS. 1963. Age determination in the Hawaiian monk seal. Journal of Mammalogy 44:280–282.

KEPPIE, D. M., AND C. E. BRAUN. 2000. Band-tailed pigeon. Number 530 *in* A. Poole and F. Gill, editors. The birds of North America. The Birds of North America, Inc., Philadelphia, Pennsylvania, USA.

———, AND R. M. WHITING, JR. 1994. American woodcock. Number 100 *in* A. Poole and F. Gill, editors. The birds of North America. The Birds of North America, Inc., Philadelphia, Pennsylvania, USA.

KERWIN, M. L., AND G. J. MITCHELL. 1971. The validity of the wear-age technique for Alberta pronghorns. Journal of Wildlife Management 35:743–747.

KING, J. E. 1983. Seals of the world. British Museum, London, United Kingdom.

KIRKPATRICK, R. D., AND L. K. SOWLS. 1962. Age determination of the collared peccary by the tooth-replacement pattern. Journal of Wildlife Management 26:214–217.

KLEVEZAL', G. A., AND S. E. KLEINENBERG. 1967. Age determination of mammals from annual layers in teeth and bones. USSR Academy of Science, Moscow, Russia.

———, AND M. V. MINA. 1973. Factors determining the pattern of annual layers in dental tissue and bones of mammals. Zhurnal Obshchei Biologii 34:594–604.

KLINGER, R. C., J. A. MUSICK. 1992. Annular growth layers in juvenile loggerhead sea turtles (*Caretta caretta*). Bulletin of Marine Science 51:224–230.

———, R. H. GEORGE, AND J. A. MUSICK. 1997. A bone biopsy technique for determining age and growth in sea turtles. Herpetological Review 28:31–32.

Knowlton, F. F., and S. L. Whittemore. 2001. Pulp cavity-tooth width ratios from known-age and wild-caught coyotes determined by radiography. Wildlife Society Bulletin 29:239–244.

KOLENOSKY, G. B. 1987. Polar bear. Pages 474–485 *in* M. Novak, J. A. Baker, M. E. Obbard, and B. Malloch, editors. Wild furbearer management and conservation in North America. Ontario Ministry of Natural Resources, Toronto, Canada.

———, AND S. M. STRATHEARN. 1987. Black bear. Pages 443–454 *in* M. Novak, J. A. Baker, M. E. Obbard, and B. Malloch, editors. Wild furbearer management and conservation in North America. Ontario Ministry of Natural Resources, Toronto, Canada.

KOUBEK, P. 1993. Eye-lens weight as an indicator of age in captive pheasant chicks (*Phasianus colchicus*). Folia Zoologica 42:237–242.

KRAMER, M. T., R. J. WARREN, M. J. RATNASWAMY, AND B. T. BOND. 1999. Determining sexual maturity of raccoons by external versus internal aging criteria. Wildlife Society Bulletin 27:231–234.

KUEHN, D. W., AND W. E. BERG. 1981. Use of radiographs to identify age-classes of fisher. Journal of Wildlife Management 45:1009–1010.

———, AND ———. 1983. Use of radiographs to age otters. Wildlife Society Bulletin 11:68–70.

KWIECINSKI, G. G. 1998. *Marmota monax*. Number 591 *in* C. E. Rebar, A. V. Lindzey, K. F. Koopman, E. Anderson, and V. Hayssen, editors. Mammalian species. American Society of Mammalogists, Lawrence, Kansas, USA.

LANDON, D. B., C. A. WAITE, R. O. PETERSON, AND L. D. MECH. 1998. Evaluation of age determination techniques for gray wolves. Journal of Wildlife Management 62:674–682.

LARSON, J. S., AND S. J. KNAPP. 1971. Sexual dimorphism in beaver neutrophils. Journal of Mammalogy 52:212–215.

———, AND R. D. TABER. 1980. Criteria of sex and age. Pages 143–202 *in* S. D. Schemnitz, editor. Wildlife techniques manual. Fourth edition. The Wildlife Society, Washington, D. C., USA.

———, AND F. C. VAN NOSTRAND. 1968. An evaluation of beaver aging techniques. Journal of Wildlife Management 32:99–103.

LAUNDRÉ, J. W., AND L. HERNÁNDEZ. 2002. Growth curve models and age estimation of young cougars in the northern Great Basin. Journal of Wildlife Management 66:849–858.

———, ———, D. STREUBEL, K. ALTENDORF, AND C. LÓPEZ GONZÁLEZ. 2000. Aging mountain lions using gum line recession. Wildlife Society Bulletin 28:963–966.

LAWS, R. M. 1962. Age determination of pinnipeds with special reference to growth layers in the teeth. Zeitschrift fur Saugetierkunde 27:129–146.

LAWSON, B., AND R. JOHNSON. 1982. Mountain sheep. Pages 1036–1055 *in* J. A. Chapman and G. A. Feldhamer, editors. Wild mammals of North America. Johns Hopkins University, Baltimore, Maryland.

LEACH, D. 1977. The descriptive and comparative postcranial osteology of marten (*Martes americana* Turton) and fisher (*Martes pennanti* Erxleben): the appendicular skeleton. Canadian Journal of Zoology 55:199–214.

———, AND V. S. DE KLEER. 1978. The descriptive and comparative postcranial osteology of marten (*Martes americana* Turton) and fisher (*Martes pennanti* Erxleben): the axial skeleton. Canadian Journal of Zoology 56:1180–1191.

———, B. K. HALL, AND A. I. DAGG. 1982. Aging marten and fisher by development of the suprafabellar tubercle. Journal of Wildlife Management 46:246–247.

LECHLEITNER, R. R. 1954. Age criteria in mink (*Mustela vison*). Journal of Mammalogy 35:496–503.

LEMNELL, P. A. 1974. Age determination in red squirrels, (*Sciurus vulgaris* [L.]). International Congress of Game Biologists 11:573–580.

LEOPOLD, A. 1933. Game management. Charles Scribner's Sons, New York, USA.

LEOPOLD, A. S. 1959. Wildlife of Mexico:the game birds and mammals. University of California Press, Berkeley, USA.

LEWIS, J. C. 1979. Field identification of juvenile sandhill cranes. Journal of Wildlife Management 43:211–214.

———. 1995. Whooping crane. Number 153 *in* A. Poole, P. Stettenheim, and F. Gill, editors. The birds of North America. The Birds of North America, Inc., Philadelphia, Pennsylvania, USA.

LEWIS, P. J., R. STRAUSS, E. JOHNSON, AND W. C. CONWAY. 2002. Absence of sexual dimorphism in molar morphology of muskrats. Journal of Wildlife Management 66:1189–1196.

LIEBERMAN, D. E., T. W. DEACON, AND R. H. MEADOW. 1990. Computer image enhancement and analysis of cementum increments as applied to teeth of *Gazella gazella*. Journal of Archaeological Science. 17:519–533.

LIN, Z., T. KONDO, T. MINAMINO, M. OHTSUJI, J. NISHIGAMI, T. TAKAYASU, R. SUN, AND T. OHSHIMA. 1995. Sex determination by polymerase chain reaction on mummies discovered at Taklamakan desert in 1912. Forensic Science International 75:197–205.

LINDER, R. L., R. B. DAHLGREN, AND C. R. ELLIOTT. 1971. Primary feather pattern as a sex criterion in the pheasant. Journal of Wildlife Management 35:840–843.

LINDZEY, F. G. 1987. Mountain lion. Pages 658–668 *in* M. Novak, J. A. Baker, M. E. Obbard, and B. Malloch, editors. Wild furbearer management and conservation in North America. Ontario Ministry of Natural Resources, Toronto, Canada.

LINHART, S. B., AND F. F. KNOWLTON. 1967. Determining age of coyotes by tooth cementum layers. Journal of Wildlife Management 31:362–365.

LOCHMILLER, R. L., E. C. HELLGREN, AND W. E. GRANT. 1984. Sex and age characteristics of the pelvic girdle in the collared peccary. Journal of Wildlife Management 48:639–641.

LOCKARD, G. R. 1972. Further studies of dental annuli for aging white-tailed deer. Journal of Wildlife Management 36:46–55.

LORD, JR., R. D. 1959. The lens as an indicator of age in cottontail rabbits. Journal of Wildlife Management 23:358–360.

———. 1961. The lens as an indicator of age in the gray fox. Journal of Mammalogy 42:109–111.

LOW, W. A., AND I. M. COWAN. 1963. Age determination of deer by annular structure of dental cementum. Journal of Wildlife Management 27:466–471.

LOWRANCE, E. W. 1949. Variability and growth of the opossum skeleton. Journal of Morphology 85:569–593.

LOWRY, M. S., AND R. L. FOLK. 1990. Sex determination of the California sea lion (*Zalophus californianus californianus*) from canine teeth. Marine Mammal Science 6:25–31.

LUDWIG, J. R., AND R. W. DAPSON. 1977. Use of insoluble lens proteins to estimate age in white-tailed deer. Journal of Wildlife Management 41:327–329.

MACCARTNEY, J. M., P. T. GREGORY, AND M. B. CHARLAND. 1990. Growth and sexual maturity of the western rattlesnake *Crotalus viridis* in British Columbia, Canada. Copeia 1990:528–542.

MACCRACKEN, J. G., AND V. VAN BALLENBERGHE. 1987. Age- and sex-related differences in fecal pellet dimensions of moose. Journal of Wildlife Management 51:360–364.

MACWHIRTER, R. B., AND K. L. BILDSTEIN. 1996. Northern harrier. Number 210 *in* A. Poole and F. Gill, editors. The birds of North America. The Birds of North America, Inc., Philadelphia, Pennsylvania, USA.

MAEHR, D. S., AND C. T. MOORE. 1992. Models of mass growth for 3 North American cougar populations. Journal of Wildlife Management 56:700–707.

MAGOUN, A. J. 1985. Population characteristics, ecology, and management of wolverines in northwestern Alaska. Dissertation. University of Alaska, Fairbanks, USA.

MARCHINTON, R. L, K. KAMMERMEYER, AND B. MURPHY. 2003. Aging white-tailed deer by tooth replacement and wear. Quality Whitetails 10(2):22–26.

MARKS, S. A., AND A. W. ERICKSON. 1966. Age determination in the black bear. Journal of Wildlife Management 30:389–410.

MARSHALL, W. H. 1951. An age determination method for the pine marten. Journal of Wildlife Management 15:276–283.

MARTIN, F. W. 1964. Woodcock age and sex determination from wings. Journal of Wildlife Management 28:287–293.

MCCLOSKEY, J. T., AND J. E. THOMPSON. 2000. Aging and sexing common snipe using discriminant analysis. Journal of Wildlife Management 64:960–969.

MCCLOSKEY, R. J. 1977. Accuracy of criteria used to determine age of fox squirrels. Proceedings of the Iowa Academy of Science 84:32–34.

MCCOLLOUGH, M. A. 1989. Molting sequence and aging of bald eagles. Wilson Bulletin 101:1–10.

MCCORD, C. M., AND J. E. CARDOZA. 1982. Bobcat and lynx. Pages 728–766 *in* J. A. Chapman and G. A. Feldhamer, editors. Wild mammals of North America. Johns Hopkins University, Baltimore, Maryland, USA.

MCCOURT, K. H., AND D. M. KEPPIE. 1975. Age determination of juvenile spruce grouse. Journal of Wildlife Management 39:790–794.

MCCULLOUGH, D. R. 1965. Sex characteristics of black-tailed deer hooves. Journal of Wildlife Management 29:210–212.

———, AND P. BEIER. 1986. Upper vs. lower molars for cementum annuli age determination of deer. Journal of Wildlife Management 50:705–706.

MCCUTCHEN, H. E. 1969. Age determination of pronghorns by the incisor cementum. Journal of Wildlife Management 33:172–175.

MCEWAN, E. H. 1963. Seasonal annuli in the cementum of the teeth of barren ground caribou. Canadian Journal of Zoology 41:111–113.

MCKINNON, D. T. 1983. Age separation of yearling and adult Franklin's spruce grouse. Journal of Wildlife Management 47:533–535.

MCMANUS, J. J. 1974. *Didelphis virginiana*. Number 40 *in* S. Anderson,

editor. Mammalian species. American Society of Mammalogists, Lawrence, Kansas, USA.

MEAD, R. A. 1967. Age determination in the spotted skunk. Journal of Mammalogy 48:606–616.

MELQUIST, W. E., AND A. E. DRONKERT. 1987. River otter. Pages 627–641 *in* M. Novak, J. A. Baker, M. E. Obbard, and B. Malloch, editors. Wild furbearer management and conservation in North America. Ontario Ministry of Natural Resources, Toronto, Canada.

———, AND M. G. HORNOCKER. 1983. Ecology of river otters in west central Idaho. Wildlife Monographs 83.

MELVIN, S. M., AND J. P. GIBBS. 1996. Sora. Number 250 *in* A. Poole, P. Stettenheim, and F. Gill, editors. The birds of North America. The Birds of North America, Inc., Philadelphia, Pennsylvania, USA.

MENASCO, K. A., AND H. R. PERRY, JR. 1978. Errors from determining sex of mourning doves by plumage characteristics. Proceedings of the Annual Conference of the Southeastern Association of Fish and Wildlife Agencies 32:224–227.

MESSICK, J. P. 1987. North American badger. Pages 587–597 *in* M. Novak, J. A. Baker, M. E. Obbard, and B. Malloch, editors. Wild furbearer management and conservation in North America. Ontario Ministry of Natural Resources, Toronto, Canada.

———, AND M. G. HORNOCKER. 1981. Ecology of the badger in southwestern Idaho. Wildlife Monographs 76.

MILLAR, J. S., AND F. C. ZWICKEL. 1972. Determination of age, age structure, and mortality of the pika, *Ochotona princeps* (Richardson). Canadian Journal of Zoology 50:229–232.

MILLER, F. L. 1974*a*. Age determination of caribou by annulations in dental cementum. Journal of Wildlife Management 38:47–53.

———. 1974*b*. Biology of the Kaminuriak population of barren ground caribou. Part II. Dentition as an indicator of sex and age; composition and socialization of the population. Report Series 31. Canadian Wildlife Service, Ottawa, Ontario, Canada.

———. 1982. Caribou. Pages 923–959 *in* J. A. Chapman and G. A. Feldhamer, editors. Wild mammals of North America. Johns Hopkins University, Baltimore, Maryland.

———, AND R. L. MCCLURE. 1973. Determining age and sex of barren ground caribou from dental variables. Transactions of the Northeastern Section, The Wildlife Society 30:79–100.

MIRARCHI, R. E. AND T. S. BASKETT. 1994. Mourning dove. Number 117 *in* A. Poole and F. Gill, editors. The birds of North America. The Birds of North America, Inc., Philadelphia, Pennsylvania, USA.

MITCHELL, C. D., AND C. R. MAHER. 2001. Are horn characteristics related to age in male pronghorns? Wildlife Society Bulletin 29:908–916.

MITCHELL, O. G., AND R. A. CARSEN. 1967. Tooth eruption in the arctic ground squirrel. Journal of Mammalogy 48:472–474.

MITTWOCH, V. 1963. Sex differences in cells. Scientific American 209:54–62.

MOFFITT, S. A. 1998. Aging bison by the incremental cementum growth layers in teeth. Journal of Wildlife Management 62:1276–1280.

MONTGOMERY, G. G. 1964. Tooth eruption in preweaned raccoons. Journal of Wildlife Management 28:582–584.

MONTGOMERY, S. J., D. F. BALPH, AND D. M. BALPH. 1971. Age determination of Uinta ground squirrels by teeth annuli. Southwestern Naturalist 15:400–402.

MOORE, K. L., editor. 1966. The sex chromatin. W. B. Saunders, Philadelphia, Pennsylvania, USA.

MOSES, R. A., AND S. BOUTIN. 1986. Molar fluting and pelt primeness techniques for distinguishing age classes of muskrats:a reevaluation. Wildlife Society Bulletin 14:403–406.

MOWBRAY, T. B., F. COOKE, AND B. GANTER. Snow goose. Number 514 *in* A. Poole and F. Gill, editors. The birds of North America. The Birds of North America, Inc., Philadelphia, Pennsylvania, USA.

———, C. R. ELY, J. S. SEDINGER, AND R. E. TROST. 2002. Canada goose. Number 682 *in* A. Poole and F. Gill, editors. The birds of North America. The Birds of North America, Inc., Philadelphia, Pennsylvania, USA.

MUELLER, H. 1999. Common snipe. Number 417 *in* A. Poole and F. Gill, editors. The birds of North America. The Birds of North America, Inc., Philadelphia, Pennsylvania, USA.

MULLER, L. I., T. T. BUERGER, AND R. E. MIRARCHI. 1984. Guide for age determination of mourning dove embryos. Alabama Agricultural Experiment Station Circular 272. Auburn University, Auburn, USA.

MURAKAMI, H., Y. YAMAMOTO, K. YOSHITOME, T. ONO, O. OKAMOTO, Y. SHIGETA, Y. DOI, S. MIYAISHI, AND H. ISHIZU. 2000. Forensic study of sex determination using PCR on teeth samples. Acta Medica Okayama 54:21–32.

MUSSEHL, T. W., AND T. H. LEIK. 1963. Sexing wings of adult blue grouse. Journal of Wildlife Management 27:102–106.

NAGORSEN, D. W., J. FORSBERG, AND G. R. GIANNICO. 1988. An evaluation of canine radiographs for sexing and aging Pacific Coast martens. Wildlife Society Bulletin 16:421–426.

NELLIS, C. H. 1969. Sex and age variation in red squirrel skulls from Missoula County, Montana. Canadian Field-Naturalist 83:324–330.

———, S. P. WETMORE, AND L. B. KEITH. 1972. Lynx–prey interactions in central Alberta. Journal of Wildlife Management 36:320–329.

———, ———, AND ———. 1978. Age-related characteristics of coyote canines. Journal of Wildlife Management 42:680–683.

NELSON, M. E. 2001. Tooth extractions from live-captured white-tailed deer. Wildlife Society Bulletin 29:245–247.

———. 2002. The science, ethics, and philosophy of tooth extractions from live-captured white-tailed deer:a response to Festa-Bianchet et al. Wildlife Society Bulletin 30:284–288.

NICHOLSON, W. S., AND E. P. HILL. 1981. A comparison of tooth wear, lens weight, and cementum annuli as indices of age in the gray fox. Pages 355–367 *in* J. A. Chapman and D. Pursely, editors. Worldwide Furbearer Conference, Frostburg, Maryland, USA.

NIETFIELD, M. T., AND F. C. ZWICKEL. 1983. Classification of sex in young blue grouse. Journal of Wildlife Management 47:1147–1151.

NISBET, I. C. T., J. BAIRD, D. V. HOWARD, AND K. S. ANDERSON. 1970. Statistical comparison on wing lengths measured by four observers. Bird-Banding 41:307–308.

NOL, E., AND H. BLOKPOEL. 1983. Incubation period of ring-billed gulls and the egg immersion technique. Wilson Bulletin 95:283–286.

NOVAKOWSKI, N. S. 1965. Cemental deposition as an age criterion in bison, and the relation of incisor wear, eye lens weight, and dressed bison carcass weight to age. Canadian Journal of Zoology 43:173–178.

OATES, D. W., G. I. HOILIEN, AND R. M. LAWLER. 1985. Sex identification of field-dressed ring-necked pheasants. Wildlife Society Bulletin 13:64–67.

ODOM, R. R. 1977. Sora. Pages 57–65 *in* G. C. Sanderson, editor. Management of migratory shore and upland game birds in North America. International Association of Fish and Wildlife Agencies, Washington, D.C., USA.

O'GARA, B. W. 1969. Horn casting by female pronghorns. Journal of Mammalogy 50:373–375.

OLSEN, P. F. 1959. Dental patterns as age indicators in muskrats. Journal of Wildlife Management 23:228–231.

OSBORN, D. J. 1955. Techniques of sexing beaver, *Castor canadensis*. Journal of Mammalogy 36:141–142.

OWEN, JR., R. B., J. M. ANDERSON, J. W. ARTMANN, E. R. CLARK, T. G. DILWORTH, L. E. GREGG, F. W. MARTIN, J. D. NEWSOM, AND S. R. PURSGLOVE. 1977. American woodcock. Pages 149–186 *in* G. C. Sanderson, editor. Management of migratory shore and upland game birds in North America. International Association of Fish and Wildlife Agencies, Washington, D.C., USA.

OYLER-McCANCE, S. J., AND P. L. LEBERG. 2005. Conservation genetics in wildlife biology. Pages 632–657 *in* C. E. Braun, editor. Techniques for wildlife investigations and management. Sixth edition. The Wildlife Society, Bethesda, Maryland, USA.

OZOGA, J. J., AND L. J. VERME. 1985. Determining fetus age in live white-tailed does by x-ray. Journal of Wildlife Management 49:372–374.

PALMER, W. L. 1959. Sexing live-trapped juvenile ruffed grouse. Journal of Wildlife Management 23:111–112.

PANKAKOSKI, E. 1980. An improved method for age determination in the muskrat, *Ondatra zibethicus* (L.). Annales Zoologici Fennici 17:113–121.

PARHAM, J. P., C. K. DODD, JR., AND G. R. ZUG. 1996. Age estimates (skeletochronology) of the Red Hills salamander, *Phaeognathus hubrichti*. Journal of Herpetology 30:401–404.

PARR, R. 1975. Aging red grouse chicks by primary molt and development. Journal of Wildlife Management 39:188–190.

PARSONS, G. R., M. K. BROWN, AND G. B. WILL. 1978. Determining the sex of fisher from the lower canine teeth. New York Fish and Game Journal 25:42–44.

PASSMORE, R. C., R. L. PETERSON, AND A. T. CRINGAN. 1955. A study of mandibular tooth-wear as an index to age of moose. Appendix A. Pages 223–238 *in* R. L. Peterson, editor. North American moose. University of Toronto Press, Ontario, Canada.

PAYNE, N. F. 1979. Relationship of pelt size, weight, and age for beaver. Journal of Wildlife Management 43:804–806.

PEARSON, A. M. 1975. The northern interior grizzly bear *Ursus arctos* L. Report Series 34. Canadian Wildlife Service, Ottawa, Ontario, Canada.

PEEK, J. M. 1982. Elk. Pages 851–861 *in* J. A. Chapman and G. A. Feldhamer, editors. Wild mammals of North America. Johns Hopkins University, Baltimore, Maryland, USA.

PELTON, M. R. 1970. Effects of freezing on weights of cottontail lenses. Journal of Wildlife Management 34:205–207.

PETERSEN, M. R., J. A. SCHMUTZ, AND R. F. ROCKWELL. 1994. Emperor goose. Number 97 *in* A. Poole and F. Gill, editors. The birds of North America. The Birds of North America, Inc., Philadelphia, Pennsylvania, USA.

PETERSON, R. T. 1998. A field guide to western birds: a completely new guide to field marks of all species found in North America west of the 100th meridian and north of Mexico. Houghton Mifflin, Boston, Massachusetts, USA.

———. 2002. A field guide to the birds of eastern and central North America. Houghton Mifflin, Boston, Massachusetts, USA.

PETRANKA, J. W. 1998. Salamanders of the United States and Canada. Smithsonian Institution Press, Washington D.C., USA.

PETRIDES, G. A. 1942. Age determination in American gallinaceous game birds. Transactions of the North American Wildlife Conference 7:308–328.

———. 1949. Sex and age determination in the opossum. Journal of Mammalogy 30:364–378.

———. 1950*a*. Notes on determination of sex and age in the woodcock and mourning dove. Auk 67:357–360.

———. 1950*b*. The determination of sex and age ratios in fur animals. American Midland Naturalist 43:355–382.

———. 1951. Notes on age determination in squirrels. Journal of Mammalogy 32:111–112.

———, AND R. B. NESTLER. 1952. Further notes on age determination in juvenile bobwhite quails. Journal of Wildlife Management 16:109–110.

POOLE, A., AND F. GILL, editors. 1992–2003. The birds of North America. Numbers 1–716. The Birds of North America, Inc., Philadelphia, Pennsylvania, USA.

POWELL, R., J. T. COLLINS, AND E. D. HOOPER, JR. 1998. A key to amphibians and reptiles of the continental United States and Canada. University of Kansas Press, Lawrence, USA.

PROULX, G., AND F. F. GILBERT. 1988. The molar fluting technique for aging muskrats:a critique. Wildlife Society Bulletin 16:88–89.

PYLE, P. 1997. Identification guide to North American birds. Slate Creek Press, Bolinas, California, USA.

———, S. N. G. HOWELL, R. P. YUNICK, AND D. F. DESANTE. 1987. Identification guide to North American passerines. Slate Creek Press, Bolinas, California, USA.

PYRAH, D. B. 1963. Sage grouse investigations. Federal Aid Project W-125-R-2, P-R Progress Report. Idaho Fish and Game Department, Boise, USA.

QUIMBY, D. C., AND J. E. GAAB. 1957. Mandibular dentition as an age indicator in Rocky Mountain elk. Journal of Wildlife Management 21:435–451.

QUINN, N. W. S., AND D. M. KEPPIE. 1981. Factors influencing growth of juvenile spruce grouse. Canadian Journal of Zoology 59:1790–1795.

RACEY, P. A. 1988. Reproductive assessment in bats. Pages 31–43 *in* T. H. Kunz, editor. Ecological and behavioral methods for the study of bats. Smithsonian Institution Press, Washington, D.C., USA.

RANSOM, A. B. 1966. Determining age of white-tailed deer from layers in cementum of molars. Journal of Wildlife Management 30:197–199.

RAUSCH, R. A. 1967. Some aspects of the population ecology of wolves, Alaska. American Zoologist 7:253–265.

———. 1969. Morphogenesis and age-related structure of permanent canine teeth in the brown bear, *Ursus arctos* L., in arctic Alaska. Zeitschrift fur Morphologie der Tiere 66:167–188.

———, AND A. M. PEARSON. 1972. Notes on the wolverine in Alaska and the Yukon Territory. Journal of Wildlife Management 36:249–268.

REDFIELD, J. A., AND F. C. ZWICKEL. 1976. Determining the age of young blue grouse: a correction for bias. Journal of Wildlife Management 40:349–351.

REED, A., D. H. WARD, D. V. DERKSEN, AND J. S. SEDINGER. 1998. Brant. Number 337 *in* A. Poole and F. Gill, editors. The birds of North America. The Birds of North America, Inc., Philadelphia, Pennsylvania, USA.

REED, J. Z., D. J. TOLIT, P. M. THOMPSON, AND W. AMOS. 1997. Molecular scatology: the use of molecular genetic analysis to assign species, sex and individual identity to seal faeces. Molecular Ecology 6:225–234.

REES, J. W., R. A. KAINER, AND R. W. DAVIS. 1966. Chronology of mineralization and eruption of mandibular teeth in mule deer. Journal of Wildlife Management 30:629–631.

REYNOLDS, H. W., R. D. GLAHOLT, AND A. W. L. HAWLEY. 1982. Bison. Pages 972–1007 *in* J. A. Chapman and G. A. Feldhamer, editors. Wild mammals of North America. Johns Hopkins University, Baltimore, Maryland, USA.

RICHARDSON, G. L. 1966. Eye lens weight as an indicator of age in the collared peccary (*Pecari tajacu*). Thesis. University of Arizona, Tucson, USA.

RIEDMAN, M. 1990. The pinnipeds: seals, sea lions, and walruses. University of California Press, Berkeley, USA.

ROBERTS, J. D. 1978. Variation in coyote age determination from annuli in different teeth. Journal of Wildlife Management 42:454–456.

ROBERTS, T. H. 1988. American woodcock (*Scolopax minor*). U.S. Department of Army, Corps of Engineers, Wildlife Resource Management Manual, Technical Report EL-88. Vicksburg, Mississippi, USA.

ROBINETTE, W. L., D. A. JONES, G. E. ROGERS, AND J. S. GASHWILER. 1957. Notes on tooth development and wear for Rocky Mountain mule deer. Journal of Wildlife Management 21:134–153.

RODGERS, R. D. 1979. Ratios of primary calamus diameters for determining age of ruffed grouse. Wildlife Society Bulletin 7:125–127.

———. 1985. A field technique for identifying the sex of dressed pheasants. Wildlife Society Bulletin 13:528–533.

ROLLEY, R. E. 1987. Bobcat. Pages 671–681 in M. Novak, J. A. Baker, M. E. Obbard, and B. Malloch, editors. Wild furbearer management and conservation in North America. Ontario Ministry of Natural Resources, Toronto, Canada.

RONGSTAD, O. J. 1966. A cottontail rabbit lens-growth curve from southern Wisconsin. Journal of Wildlife Management 30:114–121.

ROOT, D. A., AND N. F. PAYNE. 1984. Evaluation of techniques for aging gray fox. Journal of Wildlife Management 48:926–933.

ROSEBERRY, J. L., AND W. D. KLIMSTRA. 1965. A guide to age determination of bobwhite quail embryos. Biological Notes 55. Illinois Natural History Survey, Springfield, USA.

ROUSSEL, Y. E. 1975. Aerial sexing of antlerless moose by white vulval patch. Journal of Wildlife Management 39:450–451.

———, AND R. OUELLET. 1975. A new criterion for sexing Quebec ruffed grouse. Journal of Wildlife Management 39:443–445.

ROWE, C. L., W. J. SADINSKI, AND W. A. DUNSON. 1992. Effects of acute and chronic acidification on three larval amphibians that breed in temporary ponds. Archives of Environmental Contamination and Toxicology 23:339–350.

RUSCH, D. H., S. DESTEFANO, M. C. REYNOLDS, AND D. LAUTEN. 2000. Ruffed grouse. Number 515 in A. Poole, and F. Gill, editors. The birds of North America. The Birds of North America, Inc., Philadelphia, Pennsylvania, USA.

RYDER, J. P., AND R. T. ALISAUSKAS. 1995. Ross' goose. Number 162 in A. Poole and F. Gill, editors. The birds of North America. The Birds of North America, Inc., Philadelphia, Pennsylvania, USA.

SALWASSER, H., AND S. A. HOLL. 1979. Estimating fetus age and breeding and fawning periods in the North Kings River deer herd. California Fish and Game 65:159–165.

SANDERSON, G. C. 1950. Methods of measuring productivity in raccoons. Journal of Wildlife Management 14:389–402.

———. 1961a. Techniques for determining age of raccoons. Biological Notes 45. Illinois Natural History Survey, Urbana, USA.

———. 1961b. The lens as an indicator of age in the raccoon. American Midland Naturalist 65:481–485.

SAUER, P. R. 1966. Determining sex of black bears from the size of the lower canine tooth. New York Fish and Game Journal 13:140–145.

SAUNDERS, J. K. 1964. Physical characteristics of the Newfoundland lynx. Journal of Mammalogy 45:36–47.

SAYLER, R. D. 1995. Multivariate age assessments of redheads in spring. Journal of Wildlife Management 59:506–515.

SCHAEFER, W. H. 1934. Diagnosis of sex in snakes. Copeia 1934:181.

SCHEFFER, V. B. 1950. Growth layers on the teeth of pinnipedia as an indication of age. Science 112:309–311.

SCHLADWEILER, P., T. W. MUSSEHL, AND R. J. GREENE. 1970. Age determination of juvenile blue grouse by primary development. Journal of Wildlife Management 34:649–652.

SCHMID, W. 1967. Sex chromatin in hair roots. Cytogenetics 6:342–349.

SCHOFIELD, R. D. 1955. Analysis of muskrat age determination methods and their application in Michigan. Journal of Wildlife Management 19:463–466.

SCHONBERNER, V. D. 1965. Beobachtungen zur fortpflanzungsbiologie de wolfes, *Canis lupus*. Zeitschrift fur Saugetierkunde 30:171–178.

SCHROEDER, M. A., AND L. A. ROBB. 1993. Greater prairie-chicken. Number 36 in A. Poole, P. Stettenheim, and F. Gill, editors. The birds of North America. The Birds of North America, Inc., Philadelphia, Pennsylvania, USA.

———, J. R. YOUNG, AND C. E. BRAUN. 1999. Sage grouse. Number

425 in A. Poole and F. Gill, editors. The birds of North America. The Birds of North America, Inc., Philadelphia, Pennsylvania, USA.

SCHULTE, B. A., D. MÜLLER-SCHWARZE, AND L. SUN. 1995. Using anal gland secretion to determine sex in beaver. Journal of Wildlife Management 59:614–618.

SCHULTZ, J. H., S. L. SHERIFF, Z. HE, C. E. BRAUN, R. D. DROBNEY, R. E. TOMLINSON, D. D. DOLTON, AND R. A. MONTGOMERY. 1995. Accuracy of techniques used to assign mourning dove age and gender. Journal of Wildlife Management 59:759–765.

SCHWERTNER, T. W., H. A. MATHEWSON, J. A. ROBERSON, M. SMALL, AND G. L. WAGGERMAN. 2002. White-winged dove. Number 710 in A. Poole and F. Gill, editors. The birds of North America. The Birds of North America, Inc., Philadelphia, Pennsylvania, USA.

SEGELQUIST, C. A. 1966. Sexing white-tailed deer embryos by chromatin. Journal of Wildlife Management 30:414–417.

SERGEANT, D. E., AND D. H. PIMLOTT. 1959. Age determination in moose from sectioned incisor teeth. Journal of Wildlife Management 23:315–321.

SERVELLO, F. A., AND R. L. KIRKPATRICK. 1986. Sexing ruffed grouse in the Southeast using feather criteria. Wildlife Society Bulletin 14:280–282.

SEVERINGHAUS, C. W. 1949. Tooth development and wear as criteria of age in white-tailed deer. Journal of Wildlife Management 13:195–216.

SHACKLETON, D. M., L. V. HILLS, AND D. A. HUTTON. 1975. Aspects of variation in cranial characters of Plains bison (*Bison bison bison* Linnaeus) from Elk Island National Park, Alberta. Journal of Mammalogy 56:871–887.

SHANKS, C. E. 1948. The pelt-primeness method of aging muskrats. American Midland Naturalist 39:179–187.

SHARP, W. M. 1958. Aging gray squirrels by use of tail-pelage characteristics. Journal of Wildlife Management 22:29–34.

SHELDON, W. G., F. GREELEY, AND J. KUPA. 1958. Aging fall-shot American woodcocks by primary wear. Journal of Wildlife Management 22:310–312.

SHERMAN, P. W., M. L. MORTON, L. M. HOOPES, J. BOCHANTIN, AND J. M. WATT. 1985. The use of tail collagen strength to estimate age in Belding's ground squirrels. Journal of Wildlife Management 49:874–879.

SHISSLER, B. P., D. E. SAMUEL, AND D. L. BURKHART. 1981. An aging technique for American woodcock on summer fields. Wildlife Society Bulletin 9:302–305.

SIBLEY, D. A. 2000. The Sibley guide to birds. Alfred A. Knopf, New York, USA.

SILOVSKY, G. D., H. M. WIGHT, L. H. SISSON, T. L. FOX, AND S. W. HARRIS. 1968. Methods for determining age of band-tailed pigeons. Journal of Wildlife Management 32:421–424.

SKINNER, M. F., AND O. C. KAISEN. 1947. The fossil bison of Alaska and preliminary revision of the genus. American Museum of Natural History Bulletin 89:131–256.

SMALLWOOD, J. A., AND D. M. BIRD. 2002. American kestrel. Number 602 in A. Poole and F. Gill, editors. The birds of North America. The Birds of North America, Inc., Philadelphia, Pennsylvania, USA.

SMITH, B. L., AND T. L. MCDONALD. 2002. Criteria to improve age classification of antlerless elk. Wildlife Society Bulletin 30:200–207.

SMITH, N. D., AND I. O. BUSS. 1963. Age determination and plumage observations of blue grouse. Journal of Wildlife Management 27:566–578.

SPALDING, D. J. 1966. Eruption of permanent canine teeth in the northern sea lion. Journal of Mammalogy 47:157–158.

STACKS, B., AND M. M. WITTE. 1996. Sex determination of dried blood stains using the polymerase chain reaction (PCR) with homologous X-Y primers of the zinc finger protein gene. Journal of Forensic Science 41:287–290.

STEBBINS, R. C. 2003. Peterson field guide to western reptiles and amphibians. Third edition. Houghton Mifflin Company, New York, USA.

STEFFEN, D. E., C. E. COUVILLION, AND G. A. HURST. 1990. Age determination of eastern wild turkey gobblers. Wildlife Society Bulletin 18:119–124.

STEPHENSON, A. B. 1977. Age determination and morphological variation of Ontario otters. Canadian Journal of Zoology 55:1577–1583.

STODDARD, H. L. 1931. The bobwhite quail: its habits, preservation and increase. Charles Scribner's Sons, New York, USA.

STOKES, A. W. 1957. Validity of spur length as an age criterion in pheasants. Journal of Wildlife Management 21:248–250.

STOLL, JR., R. J., AND D. CLAY. 1975. Guide to aging wild turkey embryos. Ohio Fish and Wildlife Report 4. Ohio Department of Natural Resources, Division of Wildlife, Columbus, USA.

STONEBERG, R. P., AND C. J. JONKEL. 1966. Age determination of black bears by cementum layers. Journal of Wildlife Management 30:411–414.

STRICKLAND, B. K., AND S. DEMARAIS. 2000. Age and regional differences in antlers and mass of white-tailed deer. Journal of Wildlife Management 64:903–911.

STRICKLAND, M. A., AND C. W. DOUGLAS. 1987. Marten. Pages 531–546 *in* M. Novak, J. A. Baker, M. E. Obbard, and B. Malloch, editors. Wild furbearer management and conservation in North America. Ontario Ministry of Natural Resources, Toronto, Canada.

———, ———, M. NOVAK, AND N. P. HUNZIGER. 1982. Marten. Pages 599–612 *in* J. A. Chapman and G. A. Feldhamer, editors. Wild mammals of North America. Johns Hopkins University, Baltimore, Maryland, USA.

STROM, C. M., AND S. RECHITSKY. 1998. Use of nested PCR to identify charred human remains and minute amounts of blood. Journal of Forensic Science 43:696–700.

STUEWER, F. W. 1943. Reproduction of raccoons in Michigan. Journal of Wildlife Management 7:60–73.

SULLINS, G. L., D. O. MCKAY, AND B. J. VERTS. 1976. Estimating ages of cottontails by periosteal zonations. Northwest Science 50:17–22.

SULLIVAN, E. G., AND A. O. HAUGEN. 1956. Age determination of foxes by x-ray of forefeet. Journal of Wildlife Management 20:210–212.

SWANK, W. G. 1955. Feather molt as an aging technique for mourning doves. Journal of Wildlife Management 19:412–414.

SZUBA, K. J., J. F. BENDELL, AND B. J. NAYLOR. 1987. Age determination of Hudsonian spruce grouse using primary feathers. Wildlife Society Bulletin 15:539–543.

TABER, R. D. 1956. Characteristics of the pelvic girdle in relation to sex in black-tailed and white-tailed deer. California Fish and Game 42:15–21.

———, AND R. F. DASMANN. 1958. The black-tailed deer of the chaparral:its life history and management in the North Coast Range of California. Game Bulletin 8. California Department of Fish and Game, Sacramento, USA.

———, K. RAEDEKE, AND D. A. MCCAUGHRAN. 1982. Population characteristics. Pages 279–300 *in* J. W. Thomas and D. E. Toweill, editors. Elk of North America: ecology and management. Stackpole Books, Harrisburg, Pennsylvania, USA.

TACHA, T. C., AND J. C. LEWIS. 1978. Sex determination of sandhill cranes by cloacal examination. Pages 81–83 *in* J. C. Lewis, editor. Proceedings of the 2nd North American Crane Workshop, International Crane Foundation, Baraboo, Wisconsin, USA.

———, S. A. NESBITT, AND P. A. VOHS. 1992. Sandhill crane. Number 31 *in* A. Poole, P. Stettenheim, and F. Gill, editors. The birds of North America. The Birds of North America, Inc., Philadelphia, Pennsylvania, USA.

TENER, J. S. 1965. Musk-oxen in Canada: a biological and taxonomic review. Monograph 2. Canadian Wildlife Service, Ottawa, Ontario, Canada.

THOMAS, D. C., AND P. J. BANDY. 1973. Age determination of wild black-tailed deer from dental annulations. Journal of Wildlife Management 37:232–235.

———, AND ———. 1975. Accuracy of dental-wear age estimates of black-tailed deer. Journal of Wildlife Management 39:674–678.

THOMAS, K. P. 1969. Sex determination of bobwhites by wing criteria. Journal of Wildlife Management 33:215–216.

THOMPSON, D. R. 1958. Field techniques for sexing and aging game animals. Special Wildlife Report 1. Wisconsin Conservation Department, Madison, USA.

TIEMEIER, O. W., AND M. L. PLENERT. 1964. A comparison of three methods for determining the age of black-tailed jackrabbits. Journal of Mammalogy 45:409–416.

TINKLE, D. W., A. E. DUNHAM, AND J. D. CONGDON. 1993. Life history and demographic variation in the lizard *Sceloporus graciosus*: a long-term study. Ecology 74:2413–2429.

TOWEILL, D. E., AND J. E. TABOR. 1982. River otter. Pages 688–703 *in* J. A. Chapman and G. A. Feldhamer, editors. Wild mammals of North America. Johns Hopkins University, Baltimore, Maryland, USA.

TOWERS, J. 1988. Age determination of juvenile spruce grouse in eastern Canada. Journal of Wildlife Management 52:113–115.

TUMLISON, R., AND V. R. MCDANIEL. 1984. Gray fox age classification by canine tooth pulp cavity radiographs. Journal of Wildlife Management 48:228–230.

TURNER, J. C. 1977. Cemental annulations as an age criterion in North American sheep. Journal of Wildlife Management 41:211–217.

TYNDALE-BISCOE, C. H., AND R. B. MACKENZIE. 1976. Reproduction in *Didelphis marsupialis* and *D. albiventris* in Columbia. Journal of Mammalogy 57:249–265.

UHLIG, H. G. 1953. Weights of ruffed grouse in West Virginia. Journal of Wildlife Management 17:391–392.

———. 1955. The determination of age of nestling and sub-adult gray squirrels in West Virginia. Journal of Wildlife Management 19:479–483.

U.S. DEPARTMENT OF INTERIOR AND CANADIAN WILDLIFE SERVICE. 1977. North American bird banding manual. Volume II. U.S. Department of the Interior, Fish and Wildlife Service, Washington, D.C., USA.

VAN BALLENBERGHE, V., AND L. D. MECH. 1975. Weights, growth, and survival of timber wolf pups in Minnesota. Journal of Mammalogy 56:44–63.

VAN DEELEN, T. R., K. M. HOLLIS, C. ANCHOR, AND D. R. ETTER. 2000. Sex affects age determination and wear of molariform teeth in white-tailed deer. Journal of Wildlife Management 64:1076–1083.

VAN NOSTRAND, F. C., AND A. B. STEPHENSON. 1964. Age determination for beavers by tooth development. Journal of Wildlife Management 28:430–434.

VAN PAASSEN, A. G., D. H. VELDMAN, AND A. J. BEINTEMA. 1984. A simple device for determination of incubation stages in eggs. Wildfowl 35:173–178.

VAN ROSSEM, A. J. 1925. Flight feathers as indicators of age in *Dendragapus*. Ibis (Series 12) 1:417–422.

VAN TUINEN, P., AND M. VALENTINE. 1987. Cytological sex determination in cranes. Pages 571–574 *in* G. Archibald and R. F. Pasquier, editors. Proceedings of the 1983 international crane workshop. International Crane Foundation, Baraboo, Wisconsin, USA.

VERTS, B. J. 1967. The biology of the striped skunk. University of Illinois Press, Urbana, USA.

VOIGT, D. R. 1987. Red fox. Pages 379–392 *in* M. Novak, J. A. Baker, M. E. Obbard, and B. Malloch, editors. Wild furbearers management and conservation in North America. Ontario Ministry of Natural Resources, Toronto, Canada.

———, AND W. E. BERG. 1987. Coyote. Pages 344–357 *in* M. Novak, J. A. Baker, M. E. Obbard, and B. Malloch, editors. Wild furbearer management and conservation in North America. Ontario Ministry of Natural Resources, Toronto, Canada.

WAKELING, B. F., F. E. PHILLIPS, AND R. ENGEL-WILSON. 1997. Age and gender differences in Merriam's turkey tarsometatarsus measurements. Wildlife Society Bulletin 25:706–708.

WALKINSHAW, L. H. 1949. The sandhill cranes. Cranbrook Institute for Science, Bloomfield Hills, Michigan, USA.

———. 1973. Cranes of the world. Winchester Press, New York, USA.

WALLIN, J. A. 1982. Sex determination of Vermont fall-harvested juvenile wild turkeys by the 10th primary. Wildlife Society Bulletin 10:40–43.

WALLMO, O. C. 1956. Determination of sex and age of scaled quail. Journal of Wildlife Management 20:154–158.

WALTER, S. E., AND D. H. RUSCH. 1997. Accuracy of egg flotation in determining age of Canada goose nests. Wildlife Society Bulletin 25:854–857.

WEAVER, H. R., AND W. L. HASKELL. 1968. Age and sex determination of the chukar partridge. Journal of Wildlife Management 32:46–50.

WEEDEN, R. B., AND A. WATSON. 1967. Determining the age of rock ptarmigan in Alaska and Scotland. Journal of Wildlife Management 31:825–826.

WELLER, M. W. 1956. A simple field candler for waterfowl eggs. Journal of Wildlife Management 20:111–113.

WEST, R. L., AND G. K. HESS. 2002. Purple gallinule. Number 626 *in* A. Poole and F. Gill, editors. The birds of North America. The Birds of North America, Inc., Philadelphia, Pennsylvania, USA.

WESTERSKOV, K. 1950. Methods for determining the age of game bird eggs. Journal of Wildlife Management 14:56–67.

WHITE, J. A., AND C. E. BRAUN. 1978. Age and sex determination of juvenile band-tailed pigeons. Journal of Wildlife Management 42:564–569.

———, AND ———. 1990. Growth of young band-tailed pigeons in captivity. Southwestern Naturalist 35:82–84.

WHITMAN, J. S., W. B. BALLARD, AND C. L. GARDNER. 1986. Home range and habitat use by wolverines in southcentral Alaska. Journal of Wildlife Management 50:460–463.

WIGAL, R. A., AND V. L. COGGINS. 1982. Mountain goat. Pages 1008–1020 *in* J. A. Chapman and G. A. Feldhamer, editors. Wild mammals of North America. Johns Hopkins University, Baltimore, Maryland, USA.

WIGHT, H. M. 1956. A field technique for bursal inspection of mourning doves. Journal of Wildlife Management 20:94–95.

———, L. H. BLANKENSHIP, AND R. E. TOMLINSON. 1967. Aging mourning doves by outer primary wear. Journal of Wildlife Management 31:832–835.

WILLEY, C. H. 1974. Aging black bears from first premolar tooth sections. Journal of Wildlife Management 38:97–100.

WILLIAMS, JR., L. E. 1961. Notes on wing molt in the yearling wild turkey. Journal of Wildlife Management 25:439–440.

———, AND D. H. AUSTIN. 1970. Complete post-juvenal (pre-basic) primary molt in Florida turkeys. Journal of Wildlife Management 34:231–233.

WISHART, W. 1969. Age determination of pheasants by measurement of proximal primaries. Journal of Wildlife Management 33:714–717.

WOEHLER, E. E., AND J. M. GATES. 1970. An improved method of sexing ring-necked pheasant chicks. Journal of Wildlife Management 34:228–231.

WOLFE, M. L. 1969. Age determination in moose from cemental layers of molar teeth. Journal of Wildlife Management 33:428–431.

WOOD, J. E. 1958. Age structure and productivity of a gray fox population. Journal of Mammalogy 39:74–86.

WRIGHT, P. L. 1947. The sexual cycle of the male long-tailed weasel (*Mustela frenata*). Journal of Mammalogy 28:343–352.

———, AND R. RAUSCH. 1955. Reproduction in the wolverine (*Gulo gulo*). Journal of Mammalogy 36:346–355.

YAMAUCHI, K., S. HAMASAKI, K. MIYAZAKI, T. KIKUSUI, Y. TAKEUCHI, AND Y. MORI. 2000. Sex determination based on fecal DNA analysis of the amelogenin gene in Sika deer (*Cervus nippon*). Journal of Veterinary Medical Science 62:669–671.

YOAKUM, J. D. 1978. Pronghorn. Pages 103–121 *in* J. L. Schmidt and D. L. Gilbert, editors. Big game of North America. Stackpole Books, Harrisburg, Pennsylvania, USA.

YOUNG, A. D. 1988. A portable candler for birds' eggs. Journal of Field Ornithology 59:266–268.

YOUNG, J. R. 2005. Animal behavior: its role in wildlife biology. Pages 616–631 *in* C. E. Braun, editor. Techniques for wildlife investigations and management. Sixth edition. The Wildlife Society, Bethesda, Maryland, USA.

YOUNG, S. P., AND E. A. GOLDMAN. 1944. The wolves of North America. Part I. Their history, life habits, economic status, and control. American Wildlife Institute, Washington, D.C., USA.

ZALEWSKI, A. 1999. Identifying sex and individuals of pine marten using snow track measurements. Wildlife Society Bulletin 27:28–31.

ZUG, G. R., AND R. F. GLOR. 1999. Estimates of age and growth in a population of green sea turtles (*Chelonia mydas*) from the Indian River Lagoon system, Florida: a skeletochronological analysis. Canadian Journal of Zoology 76:1497–1506.

———, A. H. WYNN, AND C. RUCKDESCHEL. 1986. Age determination of loggerhead sea turtles, *Caretta caretta*, by incremental growth marks in the skeleton. Smithsonian Contributions to Zoology Number 427. Smithsonian Institution, Washington D.C., USA.

———, G. H. BALAZS, J. A. WETHERALL, D. M. PARKER, AND S. K. K. MURAKAWA. 2002. Age and growth in Hawaiian green sea turtles (*Chelonia mydas*): skeletochronology. Fishery Bulletin 100:117–127.

ZWICKEL, F. C. 1992. Blue grouse. Number 15 *in* A. Poole, P. Stettenheim, and F. Gill, editors. The birds of North America. The Birds of North America, Inc., Philadelphia, Pennsylvania, USA.

———, AND J. A. DAKE. 1977. Primary molt of blue grouse (*Dendragapus obscurus*) and its relation to reproductive activity and migration. Canadian Journal of Zoology 55:1782–1787.

———, AND A. N. LANCE. 1966. Determining the age of young blue grouse. Journal of Wildlife Management 30:712–717.

———, AND C. F. MARTINSEN. 1967. Determining age and sex of Franklin spruce grouse by tails alone. Journal of Wildlife Management 31:760–763.

———, M. A. DEGNER, D. T. MCKINNON, AND D. A. BOAG. 1991. Sexual and subspecific variation in the numbers of rectrices of blue grouse. Canadian Journal of Zoology 69:134–140.

13

WILDLIFE MARKING TECHNIQUES

Nova J. Silvy, Roel R. Lopez, and Markus J. Peterson

INTRODUCTION

All captive-animal and many field studies involving wildlife require individuals be marked for future identification. Marked individuals can provide detailed information on population dynamics, movement, behavior, and density estimates. We provide an overview of factors that should be considered before deciding to mark vertebrates (excluding fish), and address factors relevant to the selection of appropriate procedures. Others have addressed these issues previously. Stonehouse (1978) described general marking techniques for animals, and Murry and Fuller (2000) reviewed effects of marking on vertebrates. Marking methods for amphibians, reptiles, birds, and mammals were reviewed by Nietfeld et al. (1994). Methods for marking amphibians and reptiles have been reviewed by Woodbury (1956), Thomas (1977), and Swingland (1978) while Ferner (1979) and Donnelly et al. (1994) reviewed marking methods specifically for reptiles

and amphibians, respectively. Spellerberg and Prestt (1978) and Fitch (1987) reviewed methods for marking snakes. Marion and Shamis (1977), the American Ornithologists' Union (1988), and Calvo and Furness (1992) reviewed marking methods for birds. The American Society of Mammalogists (1998) provided general guidelines for marking mammals. Barclay and Bell (1988) gave detailed information for marking bats. Although not covered in this chapter, overviews for marking fish were provided by Wydowsky and Emery (1983) and Parker et al. (1990). Hagler and Jackson (2001) provided an excellent overview of current techniques for marking insects.

Because of the wide diversity among vertebrate species, no single list of approved methods for marking is practical or desirable. The ultimate responsibility for the ethical and scientific validity of methods used rests with the investigator. In general, natural marks have the least adverse effect on individual animals and should be used whenever possible, whereas invasive techniques have the greatest potential for adverse effects. Moreover, many techniques require capture, recapture, and handling of animals that also might affect their behavior and survival. Separation of these effects from those caused directly by the marking method has yet to be evaluated in most cases.

CONSIDERATIONS PRIOR TO MARKING

Questions to Consider

Before attempting to mark free-ranging wildlife, the following checklist of species and situation-dependent questions should be considered.

1. Do the animals need to be marked or can natural markings be used instead?
2. Do the animals need to be marked as individuals or can they be marked as a group?
3. Do the animals need to be physically captured prior to marking or can they be marked without capture?
4. How visible do the marks need to be and do the animals need to be "recaptured" for the mark to be observed?
5. Will the marking method cause pain and/or decrease survival of the animal?
6. Will the proposed mark affect the animal's health, reproduction, movement patterns, and/or behavior?
7. How long will the mark be required to last to complete the study and how durable is the proposed marking method?
8. Will the proposed marking method interfere with other studies?
9. Will the marks promote public concern about the study and will the marks have to be removed after study completion?
10. Have the appropriate approvals (animal welfare and state and/or federal permits) to mark the animals been obtained?

Considerable thought should be given to these questions before the decision to mark wildlife is made. Techniques for marking wildlife fall into 3 main categories: natural, noninvasive, and invasive marks. If natural marks cannot be used, noninvasive marks are preferable over invasive marks. Although some marking techniques may be unique to a single species, most apply to a wide variety of species. Therefore, unlike previous chapters on this subject in The Wildlife Society's "Techniques Manual," we present marking information by methods. This has eliminated most repetition inherent in presenting this information by animal classes (i.e., amphibians, birds, mammals, and reptiles; Nietfeld et al. 1994). We consolidated general information on proper application of the technique, its retention time and visibility, and any adverse effects of the technique on marked animals (where this information is available). This allows the reader to more easily evaluate and compare individual methods. Additionally, we present these methods in sequence of what we consider most to least preferred. More detailed information, such as species or group, comments, and citations (in chronological order), is presented in tables. This allows readers to select an animal class, identify which methods have been used for the species or group of species of interest, and pursue the cita-

tions for more detailed information on the method's appropriateness for the specific application.

Marking Permits

Before an animal can be captured and marked, the appropriate local (e.g., animal welfare permits), federal, and/or state/provincial permits must be obtained. Wildlife species are regulated within state/provincial borders by the appropriate wildlife agency. The federal government regulates capture and marking of migratory birds and threatened and endangered species. Authorization to mark migratory birds and threatened and endangered species must be approved by the Bird Banding Laboratory, U.S. Geological Survey, Biological Resources Division, Laurel, Maryland 20708-9619, USA, or the Canadian Bird Banding Office, Canadian Wildlife Service, Ottawa, Ontario, Canada KIA OH3.

Natural Marks

The first questions to be considered when contemplating marking animals are: (1) is marking necessary, (2) can the study be conducted without recognition of individuals or a specific group of animals, and (3) if not, can animals be identified without use of applied marks? Perhaps the ideal method of recognizing individuals is to use their own "naturally" occurring unique traits, much as we identify other people by their physiognomic traits. Humans may be unable to differentiate individuals within some wildlife species, but there are others whose physical characteristics allow for individual identification using natural markings or distinct morphological characteristics. Many animals exhibit unique coat patterns (Table 1) or can be identified by unique color patterns (Fig. 1), scarring, fin or fluke notches, antler configuration, and/or other traits. Natural markings are most efficiently used on individuals with complex patterns, and analysis must be confined within a local population or region (Pennycuick 1978).

Natural markings have been used to identify individual mammals, reptiles, and amphibians more commonly than birds (Table 1). Unique plumage or bill patterns can be used as distinguishing features for birds, but such features are rare in avian populations and may change with molt and/or age. Thus, the potential for natural marking systems in birds is limited, but may have short-term application in conjunction with other markers for some species.

Marking as Individuals or Groups

If a study requires the use of applied marks, do the animals have to be marked as individuals or can they be marked as groups? Many herd/flock movement and dispersal studies only require that large numbers of individuals be marked in a given area and relocated later. For example, large numbers of white geese could be marked by placing dye in roost ponds and followed by searching for colored geese. Similarly, many mark-recapture or mark-resight studies conducted only to estimate population density do not require that marked individuals be differentiated from another.

Marking Without Capture

Capture may stress animals and marking without capture is preferred where practical. Remote marking of animals as individuals or groups has a long history (Table 2).

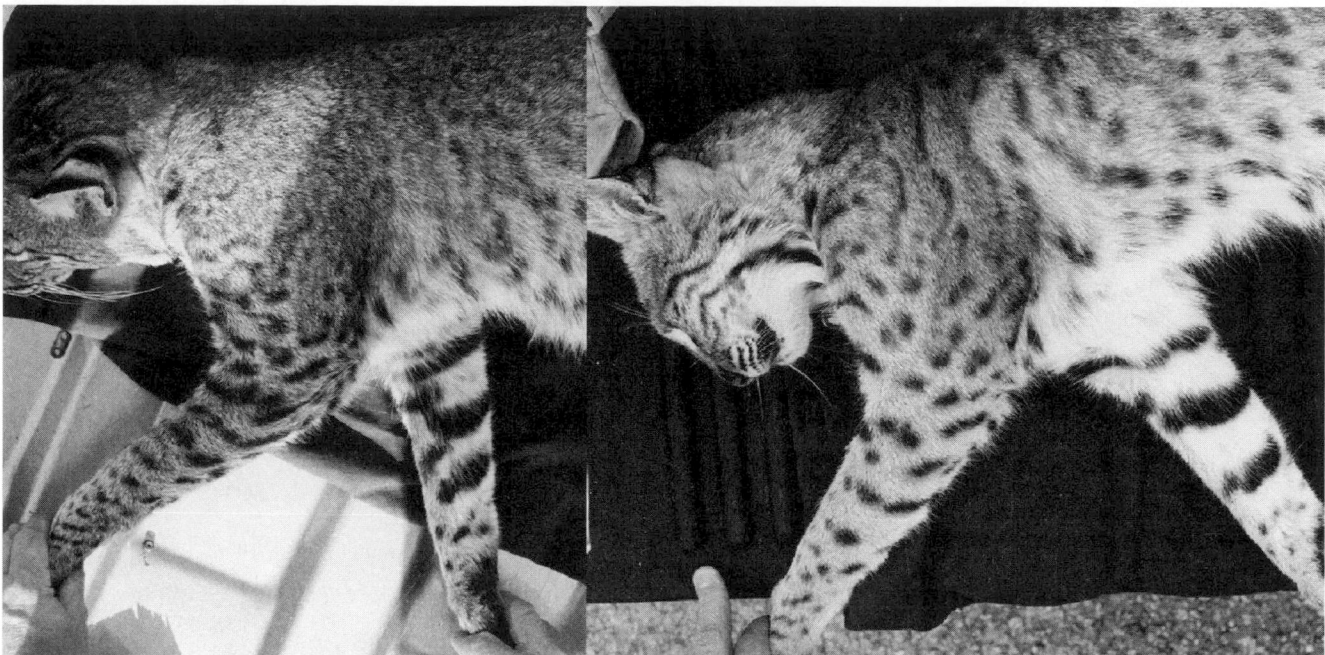

Fig. 1. Unique spots and stripes on 2 bobcats.

Table 1. Natural markings used to identify individual animals [a].

Group/Species	Method for identification	Citations
Amphibians & Reptiles		
Grass snakes	Ventral patterns	Carlstrom and Edelstam 1946
Viviparous lizard	Dorsal patterns	Carlstrom and Edelstam 1946
Slow-worm lizard	Throat patterns	Carlstrom and Edelstam 1946
Smooth newt	Belly patterns	Hagstrom 1973
Anoles	Distinctive patterns and tail regenerations	Stamps 1973
Warty newt	Belly patterns	Hagstrom 1973
Eastern newt	Dorsal spot pattern	Healy 1975
Dusky salamander	Dorsal color patterns	Forester 1977; Tilley 1977, 1980
Snakes	Distinctive characteristic on exuvia	Henley 1981
Snakes	Characteristic of subcaudal scales	Shine et al. 1988
Spotted salamander	Spot pattern	Loafman 1991
Patterned amphibians	Spot and stripe pattern	Doody 1995
Birds		
Bewick's swan	Bill patterns and body features	Scott 1978
Osprey	Using head marking patterns	Bretagnolle et al. 1994
Mammals		
Giraffe	Unique coat patterns	Foster 1966
Tiger	Unique coat patterns	Schaller 1967, Karanth 1995, Karanth and Nichols 1998
African lion	Identified by whisker patterns	Pennycuick and Rudnai 1970
Black rhinoceros	Unique ear markings, horn shape and wrinkle patterns	Mukinya 1976
Cetaceans/manatees	Unique color, scars, and fin or fluke notches	Würsig and Würsig 1977, Irvine et al. 1982, Irvine and Scott 1984
Urban dogs	Unique coat patterns	Heussner et al. 1978
African bushbuck	Unique coat patterns	Seydack 1984
Leopard	Pelt characteristics	Seydack 1984
Bobcat	Spot variation	Rolley 1987, Heilbrun et al. 2003
Cheetah	Pelt characteristics	Caro 1994, Kelly 2001
White-tailed deer	Antler, pelt, and body characteristics	Jacobson et al. 1997

[a] Scientific names are in the Appendix.

Table 2. Remote marking methods used to mark animals[a] as individuals and in groups.

Group/Species	Remote marking method	Citations
Birds		
Sage-grouse	Aniline dyes in tank buried on lek attached to spray head	Moffitt 1942
Ruffed grouse	Aluminum and bronze dust in nests found later on shed feathers	Bendell and Fowle 1950
Glaucous-winged gull	Thief detection powder on eggs and nests	Mossman 1960
Nesting terns	Blow dye from bottle using rubber tubing	Moseley and Mueller 1975
Nesting wood ducks	Rubber band with color marker in nest box hole	Heusmann et al. 1978
Cattle egret and gull eggs	Rhodamine B dye in oil-based silica gel placed on eggs; adults marked 2-6 months	Paton and Pank 1986, Cavanagh et al. 1992
Roosting blackbirds	Aerial application of liquid fluorescent pigmented material, visible under UV light in subsequent collections of marked birds	Otis et al. 1986
Wood stork	Pressurized canister with nozzle on pole with control lever	Rodgers 1986
Waterfowl	Fluorescent particles applied to lakes marked waterfowl for 8 weeks	Godfrey et al. 1993
Common tern	Device using refillable bottles filled with dye, remotely controlled	Wendelin et al. 1996
Mammals		
Deer	Treadle-type spray devices	Clover 1954
White-tailed deer	Self-affixing collar	Verme 1962, Siglin 1966, Taylor 1969
Mountain sheep	Manually-triggered dye-spraying device and modified Cap-Chur darts	Hansen 1964, Simmons and Phillips 1966
Moose	Manually-triggered dye spraying devices	Taber et al. 1956
Pronghorn	Collar-holder frame over water	Beale 1966
Hares and rabbits	Self-affixing collar	Keith et al. 1968
Dall's sheep	Spraying devices used from aircraft	Simmons 1971
Muskox	Paint-pellet pistols	Jonkel et al. 1975
Mountain sheep	Modified Cap-Chur darts	Turner 1982
Elk	Paint-ball guns	Herriges et al. 1989, Herriges et al. 1991
Red squirrel	Remotely applied collars	Mahan et al. 1994

[a] Scientific names are in the Appendix.

Mammals have been marked with paint-tipped arrows (N. J. Silvy, unpublished data) and paint balls (Table 2). Animals also have been marked using a manually triggered dye-spraying device, and dyes can be introduced into the animal's food to produce dyed fat, teeth, pelage, and droppings. Self-affixing collars have been developed for several species (Table 2). Dye-spraying devices affixed to aircraft have been used to mark large mammals and could be used for marking large numbers of white-colored birds (e.g., white geese, egrets). Dyes also can be placed on eggs and nests, marking the adults as they incubate their eggs (Table 2). Subsequent collection or observation of marked animals provides data on dispersal and population dynamics.

Marking After Capture

If animals must be captured, there are numerous marking techniques available. Although the most suitable marking techniques will depend on the needs of the investigator, Barclay and Bell (1988) suggested considering the following factors: duration of study, ability to relocate marked animals, number of animals to be individually identified, and the effect of the mark on the animal. According to Marion and Shamis (1977) and Ferner (1979), an ideal marking technique would: (1) involve minimal pain or stress, (2) produce no adverse effects on survival and behavior, (3) permanently mark individuals, (4) be easy to recognize at a distance, (5) be easy to apply, (6) be easy to obtain and/or assemble, and (7) be relatively inexpensive. Additionally, the selected marking technique should not conflict with other studies in the area and permission to use the techniques should be readily obtainable from the appropriate authorities. Most marking techniques do not satisfy all of these criteria and investigators must prioritize prior to mark selection.

Nietfeld et al. (1994) grouped markers into 3 categories relative to retention time: temporary, semi-permanent, and permanent. We prefer 2 groups: permanent and non-permanent. We define permanent marks as those lasting the life of the animal and non-permanent marks as all others. Permanent marks include branding, tattoos, ear notching, toe clipping, and other invasive techniques although scarring, tearing, and aging may reduce their effectiveness. Non-permanent marks generally are more visible and can be used with permanent marks to increase visibility of the animal, yet still have the animal marked for life. For example, a white-tailed deer (all scientific names are in the chapter Appendix) could be given a unique ear tattoo (permanent) as well as a numbered, brightly colored cattle-ear tag (visible). Animal size, however, limits the size of marks that can be applied, but color-coded marks still can enhance recognition. A point to remember when using

Table 3. Neck collars used on wildlife[a].

Group/Species	Materials and comments	Citations
Amphibians & Reptiles		
American alligator	Vinyl-plastic tape	Chabreck 1965
Birds		
Geese, brant, swans, ducks, and cranes	Plastic collars of flexible vinylite, flexible plastic, rigid acrylic resin, and aluminum with or without letters and numbers with retention up to 11 years on adult geese, but should not be used on goslings because few are retained; icing not a problem with aluminum neckbands, but collared birds may move from breeding areas	Aldrich and Steenis 1955, Helm 1955, Craighead and Stockstad 1956, Idstrom and Lindmeier 1956, Ballou and Martin 1964, Huey 1965, Sherwood 1966, Lensink 1968, MacInnes et al. 1969, Fjetland 1973, Greenwood and Bair 1974, Koerner et al. 1974, Ankney 1975, Chabreck and Schroer 1975, Raveling 1976, Maltby 1977, Craven 1979, Abraham et al. 1983, Zicus et al. 1983, Pirkola and Kalinainen 1984, Hawkins and Simpson 1985, Zicus and Pace 1986, MacInnes and Dunn 1988, Ely 1990, Samuel et al. 1990, Campbell and Becker 1991, Johnson et al. 1995, Castelli and Trost 1996, Menu et al. 2000, Schmutz and Morse 2000
Game birds	Colored plastic neckbands	Taber and Cowan 1963, Marcstrom et al. 1989
Mammals		
Foxes	Metal collar slit for expansion	Sheldon 1949
Ungulates	Plastic, aluminum, nylon fabrics, polyethylene rope with flags, rubberized machine belting, and self-adjusting plastic collars for young	Ealey and Dunnet 1956, Progulske 1957, Fashingbauer 1962, Lightfoot and Maw 1963, Harper and Lightfoot 1966, Knight 1966, Hawkins et al. 1967, Craighead et al. 1969, Hanks 1969, Phillips and Nicholls 1970, Beale and Smith 1973, Brooks 1981, Keister et al. 1988, Hölzenbein 1992
Hares	Leather collar	Hewson 1961
Polar bear	Nylon webbing	Lentfer 1968
African elephant	Rubberized machine belting	Hanks 1969
Feral goats	Galvanized steel chain	Rudge and Joblin 1976
Cetaceans and manatees	Rubberized belts	White et al. 1981
Bats	Spiral bird rings and keychain collars	Moran 1985, Wilkinson 1985
Coyote	Vinyl plastic collars	Gionfriddo and Stoddart 1988

[a] Scientific names are in the Appendix.

color-coded marks is that many people are red/green color-blind. Therefore, selection of contrasting colors that can be recognized at a distance by all individuals involved with the project is important.

The use of marks can influence behavior, particularly color marks used on birds, and can increase predation (Kessler 1964, Burley et al. 1982). The combination of stress and mortality associated with capture and the affect of the mark itself could decrease survival more than either capture or marking alone. Thus, it is important to examine whether necessary data can be obtained without use of marks. If not, researchers must ascertain whether marking animals is likely to result in reliable knowledge that can be used to better manage the population. Further, they should realistically weigh the benefits of this knowledge against the discomfort or harm done to the individual animals. There is no simple checklist that will delineate the most appropriate marking technique(s) for all potential research projects.

NONINVASIVE MARKING TECHNIQUES
Neck Collars

Many different neck collars have been designed for field identification of free-ranging animals (Table 3). Properly fitted collars (Fig. 2) should not restrict feeding, circulation or breathing, or cause entanglement. Collars may be fixed in size or expandable to allow for growth. Many neck collars are placed too loosely on animals (Fig. 2). A loose collar (especially if the collar has the added weight of a radio transmitter) will slip up and down an animal's neck when it lowers and raises its head. This can cause abrasions and possible open sores that can lead to infection and possibly death. If a collar is extremely loose, the animal may get a foot caught in the collar as it extends its front feet to stand from a bedding position. If a collar is placed too tightly around an animal's neck, the collar may cut off blood circulation that can lead to tissue sloughing, infection, and death. During the rut, necks of many

Fig. 2. Oversized neck collar (right) that could allow animal to place leg through collar. Collar should fit snug around neck just below head (left).

male ungulates swell and collars must expand to allow for this swelling. Collars made with nylon elastic will allow expansion of the collar. Collars for fawns may be made entirely of folded nylon elastic with folds stitched together with thread that breaks with pressure of neck growth and allows the collar to expand with the growing animal (Fig 3).

Silvy (1975) developed Boltaron (thermal plastic) expandable collars (Fig. 4) for male white-tailed deer that were 7.4 cm wide and made to fit the neck contours of deer of each gender in each age class. The open ends of the "U"-shaped collars for female deer were riveted (brass split rivets) and no elastic straps were used (Fig. 5). Collars for male deer had elastic straps on the inside that were attached by rivets at the bottom of the "U". Straps passed through brass welding rod guides embedded in the open ends of the plastic collar permitted expansion and contraction. Because the weight of a radio package was on the elastic straps in the "U"-shaped collars, the rubber in the elastic straps degraded over time and the collars sagged. This problem was solved by design of a "C"-shaped collar with ends overlapping at the side of the neck with elastic bands to resist expansion that completely opened the "C". This allowed the weight of the collar and radio to be supported by the Boltaron and not by the elas-

tic. Once a male's neck returned to normal size after the rut, the Boltaron collar returned to its normal shape and reduced tension on the elastic straps. Collars were of 2 thicknesses (0.2 or 0.3 cm Boltaron) and of 2 colors (black or white). Various colors of scotch-lite reflective tape in the form of numbers, letters, or other symbols were attached to collars for ready identification of deer during both day and night. Radios were mounted (using dental acrylic) on, and antennas were either stainless-steel whips or copper wire embedded in the Boltaron collar. Stainless-steel whips tended to break due to salt-water etching; this was not a problem with embedded copper wire antennas.

Typically, collars are highly visible, but their longevity depends on the material used, climate, and behavior and gender of the animal involved. Most studies report either no or insignificant adverse effects of neck collars on breeding-related activities, social behavior, and physical damage beyond minor hair or feather wear and irritation. Neck collars on birds (Fig. 6), however, have been observed to disrupt pair bonds, lower success in agonistic encounters, contribute to starvation, and increase mortality through severe icing. Icing is not a problem with aluminum neck-collars, probably due to their conductive properties.

Fig. 3. Elastic (expandable) radio collar on white-tailed deer fawn.

Fig. 4. Expandable neck collars for male ungulates.

Fig. 5. Non-expandable female ungulate neck collar with holes for brass-split rivets.

Fig. 7. Standard butt-end bands used on the legs of birds.

Bands

Metal bands (Fig. 7) bearing an identification number and return address are the oldest and most common method of marking wild birds (Table 4). Although states and provinces are required to use their own bands for resident game birds, the U.S. Fish and Wildlife Service and the Canadian Wildlife Service issue bands for migratory birds. Aluminum bands are sufficient for marking many species, but are easily damaged by abrasion and corrosion. As a result, monel, incoloy, stainless steel, and titanium bands sometimes are used for long-lived and marine birds.

Colored bands made from plastic or other materials have been used alone or in conjunction with metal bands (Fig. 8) to mark individuals of a variety of species (Table 4). Colored bands are primarily intended to permit rapid identification of individuals without requiring recapture. Color bands deteriorate relatively quickly and are best for short-term studies. Soft plastic, wrap-around bands have the lowest durability and color retention (Anderson 1981), which is somewhat greater in laminated wrap-around bands (Lumsden et al. 1977, Anderson 1981). Retention is higher in wide versus narrow plastic bands. Painted bands are of limited use because abrasion or paint removal by birds results in rapid marker loss (Childs 1952).

Arm and Wing Bands

The attachment of bands to the forearms has been the most widely used technique for marking bats and penguins (Table 4). Flipper bands, made initially of aluminum and more recently from monel metal and stainless steel, have been used on penguins. Several markers are available for bats, including serially-numbered metal bands, color-anodized aluminum bands, numbered and unnumbered colored plastic bands, and celluloid rings. In bats, injuries caused by bands often result due to motion of the forearms during flight. Celluloid rings produce fewer injuries. Bands attached to the bat's back legs are not effective markers due to band loss.

Leg Bands

The butt-end or split ring metal band is widely used for most avian species (Table 4). Lock-on bands are used on raptors and other birds capable of removing butt-end bands. Rivet bands are used for eagles, which are capable of removing both butt-end and lock-on bands. Close-ring bands often are used to mark birds raised in captivity.

Bands should fit properly, allowing movement, and young birds may be ringed with the aid of wax or other materials that yield with growth. Morrow et al. (1987) developed equipment to return nestlings to their tree nest following flushing and banding. Birds can mutilate and

Fig. 6. Plastic neck collar on tundra swan.

Fig. 8. Butt-end aluminum band (right leg) and colored plastic band (left leg) placed on greater prairie-chicken.

Table 4. Bands used on arms, wings, tails, and legs to mark wildlife[a].

Group/Species	Materials and comments	Citations
Amphibians & Reptiles		
Frogs	Butt-end bird bands on toes	Kaplan 1958
Bullfrog	Plastic waist bands	Emlen 1968
Lizards	Colored metal rings around thigh	Subba Rao and Rajabai 1972
Racerunners	Colored plastic bands glued to tails	Paulissen 1986
Anurans	Waist bands	Rice and Taylor 1993
Birds		
Passerines, terns, doves, pheasants, grouse, vultures, parakeets, geese, parrots, and swallows	Butt-end metal bands	Young 1941; Wandell 1943, 1945; Elmes 1955; Dunbar 1959; MacDonald 1961; Kaczynski and Kiel 1963; Hamerstrom and Mattson 1964; Henckel 1976; Burtt and Tuttle 1983; Hatch and Nisbet 1983a, b; Nisbet and Hatch 1983, 1985; Bailey et al. 1987; Marcstrom et al. 1989; Meyers 1994; Powell et al. 2000; Menu et al. 2001
Penguins	Flipper bands of aluminum, Teflon, monel metal, and stainless steel	Sladen 1952, Penny and Sladen 1966, Cooper and Morant 1981, Sallaberry and Valencia 1985
Waterfowl	Plexiglass, butt-end leg bands	Balham and Elder 1953
Doves and waterfowl	Reward bands give higher reporting rates	Bellrose 1955, Tomlinson 1968, Henny and Burnham 1976, Nichols et al. 1991, Reinecke et al. 1992
Raptors	Butt-end and lock-on (can only be removed by eagles) leg bands	Berger and Mueller 1960, Environment Canada 1984, Robson 1986, Young and Kochert 1987
House sparrows	Colored tape around metal leg bands	Gullion 1965a
Finches and grouse	Colored anodized and aluminum butt-end leg bands	Gullion 1965b, Cohen 1969, Godfrey 1975, Stedman 1990
Small birds	Nylon wing tag fastened with a strap around the humerus	Hewitt and Austin-Smith 1966
Captive birds	Close-ring leg bands put on nestlings	Cohen 1969, Godfrey 1975
Finches, geese, oyster-catchers, loons, cranes, woodpeckers, juncos, owls, blackbirds, magpies, & goldfinches	Colored leg bands can affect mate selection, sex ratio of surviving offspring, and longevity	Marin 1963; Ogilvie 1972; Wheeler and Lewis 1972; Reese 1980; Burley 1982; Burley et al. 1982; Goss-Custard et al. 1982; Forsman 1983; Seguin and Cooke 1983; Burley 1985; Hoffman 1985; Burley 1986a, b; Ratcliffe and Boag 1987; Strong et al. 1987; Burley 1988; Hagan and Reed 1988; Cristol et al. 1992; Metz and Weatherhead 1993; Forsman et al. 1996; Watt 2001
Gulls	Butt-end, color leg bands, and rings	Mills 1972, Kadlec 1975, Spear 1980, Ottaway et al. 1984, Shedden et al. 1985
Raptors, ravens, and woodcock	Color fabric wrapped around wing	Kochert 1973, Morgenweck and Marshall 1977, Kochert et al. 1983
Ducklings	Florist's wax or plasticine filled leg bands	Spencer 1978; Blums et al. 1994, 1999
Seabirds and sandpipers	Butt-end and color leg bands; banding tibia rather than tarsus increases longevity and legibility	Anderson 1980, Perdeck and Wassenaar 1981, Zmud 1985, Colclough and Ross 1987, Reed and Oring 1993, Bart et al. 2001
Mammals		
Bats	Bands cause injuries and neonates need room to grow; best attached to forearm as bands are ineffective if attached to hind leg or pollex; do not band during hibernation as populations decline	Davis 1963b, Perry and Beckett 1966, Cockrum 1969, Bonaccorso and Smythe 1972, Bateman and Vaughan 1974, Bonaccorso et al. 1976, Bradbury 1977, LaVal et al. 1977, Morrison 1978, Stebbings 1978, Keen and Hitchcock 1980, Hooper 1983, Moran 1985, Phillips 1985, Racey and Swift 1985, Bell et al. 1986, Barclay and Bell 1988
Small rodents	Leg rings	Fullagar and Jewell 1965
Elephants	Plastic tail collar	Viljoen 1986

[a] Scientific names are in the Appendix.

remove bands, and loss of bands has occurred from nestlings. The main causes of loss of leg bands, however, are abrasion and corrosion from saltwater and feces. Vultures, which excrete down their legs, should not be leg banded as excrement loading of the band can lead to loss of the leg or foot. Ice build-up on banded passerines in

Box 1. **Shrinkage of spiral plastic leg bands result in leg damage to mourning doves.**

Recaptures of mourning doves banded with spiral plastic leg bands revealed these bands were constricting and resulting in loss or severe damage to the legs (Atherton et al. 1982). Band color and temperature affected band shrinkage. Dark colored bands experienced greater shrinkage than light colored bands. Higher temperatures caused bands to shrink more than bands kept at low temperatures. Acetone-treated bands fused coils of the band together to help prevent shrinkage. Birds with "fleshy" legs such as doves and pigeons should have spiral plastic leg bands treated with acetone prior to the birds being released.

Fig. 9. Nasal saddle on the bill of a female mallard.

cold climates also may cause impairment of leg movement or leg loss. Colored plastic bands have caused severe leg abrasions (Reed 1953), band constriction has amputated legs (Atherton et al. 1982) (Box 1), and band displacement can cause crippling in web-footed species. Leg-band loss can lead to inflated mortality estimates and errors in estimations of population size, especially for long-lived species (Nelson et al. 1980).

Nasal Discs and Saddles

Nasal discs and saddles (Fig. 9) have been used extensively to mark waterfowl (Table 5). Nasal tags are generally made from rigid or flexible plastic or nylon, marked with patterns or numbers, and attached by a short nylon or stainless steel pin through the nares. Discs may snag on vegetation and tangle in nets during trapping and probably increase mortality of diving ducks (Table 5). Nasal saddles that properly fit the size and shape of the bill of particular waterfowl species reduce such hazards. Entanglement in fences and traps has resulted in tag loss and icing on nasal saddles may increase mortality.

Backpacks, Harnesses, and Ponchos

Markers designed to lie on the back have been used frequently to mark upland game birds, waterfowl, and other birds (Table 6). Backpacks (Fig. 10) generally are made from flexible plastics or plastic-coated nylon fabric and are attached by a leather or nylon cord harness that passes around each wing base. Nylon straps last longer than those

of leather. Backpack markers also have been modified into ponchos. Back tagging typically is considered too cumbersome for small birds, but a backpack marker that protruded from the bird's back, making it more visible, has been used to mark starling-sized birds. Numbered plastic circles glued to the back of birds as small as hummingbirds have been used, but are lost during molt. Rope harnesses have been used to individually mark large mammals (Table 6).

Trailing Devices

Trailing devices have been used to study movements of amphibians and reptiles with limited movement (Table 7). These devices usually consist of a freewheeling bobbin or spool holding thread or light string attached to an animal's body. In some aquatic situations, lines with floats are attached directly to the animal. Bobbins have been glued to an elastic band secured around the animal, or in the case of turtles, attached to the carapace with waterproof tape. To study movements, one end of the line is secured to a stake at the point of capture and, as the animal moves, the trailing thread is released along the route of movement. Usefulness of the device depends on the amount of thread the bobbin or spool can hold and the speed and distance moved by the animal. The bulkiness of these devices can interfere with normal movement patterns and the waistband attachment can cause skin irritation. These devices have been used to study movement patterns both in terrestrial and aquatic systems, and to locate belowground depth of animals at night.

Table 5. Nasal discs and saddles used to mark waterfowl.

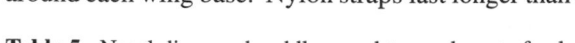

Tag type/Group	Comments	Citations
Nasal discs		
Waterfowl	Snagged on vegetation and tangled in nets used to trap ducks; tag loss high on geese	Bartonek and Dane 1964, Sherwood 1966
Nasal saddles		
Waterfowl	Less tangling than nasal discs, but icing may increase mortality; fewer lost when saddles are sized to shape of bill; problems with small ducks due to large size of saddles and shape of duck bill and nares	Sugden and Poston 1968, Doty and Greenwood 1974, Greenwood and Bair 1974, Joyner 1975, Greenwood 1977, Koob 1981, Davey and Fullagar 1985, Lokemoen and Sharp 1985, Evrard 1986, Byers 1987

Table 6. Backpacks, harnesses, and ponchos used to mark birds and mammals[a].

Group/Mark type/Species	Comments	Citations
Birds		
Backpacks with straps		
Gray partridge, grouse, and pheasant	Leather retained up to 1 year	Blank and Ash 1956, Gullion et al. 1962, Labisky and Mann 1962, Boag et al. 1973
American coot	Leather retained 1 year	Anderson 1963
Small birds	Cumbersome for small birds	Hester 1963, Furrer 1979
Bald eagles, falcons	Could be seen from long distance	Southern 1964, Kenward et al. 2001
Backpacks glued on back		
Gull chicks	Circular numbered tag to synsacrum	Cuthbert and Southern 1975
Hummingbirds	Glued back tags	Baltosser 1978
Ponchos		
Grouse, partridges, and pheasant	Back tag modified into ponchos	Pyrah 1970, Marcstrom et al. 1989
Mammals		
Harnesses		
Peccaries and deer	Braided rope harness	Bigler 1966

[a] Scientific names are in the Appendix.

Nocturnal Tracking Lights

Light sources attached to animals allow them to be visually tracked at night, providing information on movements and foraging behavior. Chemical and radioactive lights can be used alone or in conjunction with radio telemetry (Table 8). Evidence suggests that use of optical light sources does not increase predation of marked individuals or adversely affect their behavior, although this potential exists. Conversely, marked predators might have less success capturing prey and a constant light source may cause undue stress in bats.

Cyalume, a chemical light source, has been used to monitor the activity of wildlife (Table 8). The light was obtained by mixing dibutyl phthalate and dimethyl phthalate liquids and sealing the mixture in small, clear spheres that were glued to animals. Varying the proportions of this mixture controls the brightness and duration of light emission. Battery-operated "pin lights" and neon lights have been used for nocturnal observations of mammals (Table 8). Light intensity or blinking sequence can be varied on neon lights for individual-animal identification.

A light-emitting diode (LED) and flasher have been used to track wildlife at night (Table 8). The device produced consistently timed flashes that could be used for individual identification. A similar system with individually programmable flashes, a light-sensitive flasher, and optional attachment of a radio transmitter to the same circuit was later developed. Battery size and light source intensity influenced the lifespan and visibility of the marker. Use of binoculars or night vision scopes greatly increased the distance at which these markers could be seen.

Betalights are a radioactive light source consisting of phosphor excited by tritium gas in glass capsules. The capsules can be produced in any shape and size with different colors. The useful range varies from about 50 m to 1 km depending on shape, size, and viewing method. The lifespan of Betalights is about 15–20 years. Acceptable radiation levels should be considered when these light sources are used. Colors at different intensities can be used to increase the number of individuals identifiable. Betalights have been used on crabs (Wolcott 1977), birds, and mammals (Table 8). For birds, the most effective location for the Betalight was on a radio antenna away from the bird's body. Betalights did not increase mortality of radio-marked boreal owls, although hunting success could be affected.

Tapes, Streamers, and Bells

Tapes, streamers, and bells have been applied to animals to make them more readily detectable within the natural environment. Fluorescent tapes and bells also allow the animal to be detected and located more easily at night. The effect of these methods on animal survival requires further study.

Fig. 10. Northern goshawk with backpack tag.

Table 7. Trailing devices applied to amphibians and reptiles[a] to follow movements.

Group/Species	Materials	Comments	Citations
Box turtle	Wooden spool and thread with housing	Attached to carapace with waterproof adhesive tape	Stickel 1950
Northern leopard frogs >60 mm	Glued bobbin to elastic band around waist with stake to mark point of capture with sewing thread tied to it	50 m of thread lasted from 1 hr to 7 days; weighed 8.5 g; shortened jumping ability and had difficulty swimming and entering crevices, waistband caused skin irritation	Dole 1965, Grubb 1970
Tiger salamander	Sutured numbered plastic float through tail with monofilament line	Line sufficiently long to allow individual to move through the deepest part of lake	Whitford and Massey 1970
Box turtle	Thread trailer and radio transmitter	Attached to carapace	Lemkau 1970
Box turtle	35-mm film canisters to hold wooden spool and thread	Attached to caudal end of carapace, avoided interference with mating	Reagan 1974
Green sea turtles	Fiberglass-coated floats attached to 24-m lines; 3-v flashlight bulb powered by batteries attached to float; fiberglass mast topped by orange pennant	No adverse effects reported	Carr et al. 1974
Lizards	Small piece of foil attached to 30-cm light string around lower abdomen	Allowed measurements of subterranean depth of lizards at night, located buried lizards for body temperature readings	Deavers 1972, Judd 1975
Turtles	Low-friction thread-release mechanism	Similar to spincast fishing reels	Scott and Dobie 1980

[a] Scientific names are in the Appendix.

Tapes

Colored tapes have been used to improve band retention and field recognition of birds (Table 9). Colored fabric, ripstop nylon, and reflective tape with or without coded numbers have been used to mark other animals. Highly reflective plastic tape strips and plastic-covered tape with coded numbers were glued to the head of bats as temporary individual markers. Colored plastic adhesive tape was used as a durable visual marker on the horns of mountain sheep and as a short-term marker on the quills of porcupines. Labels on colored plastic tape have been used to mark individual eggs in bird nests. The tape label was firmly applied to the egg near the apex, and a different color or color combination was used for each egg laid within a clutch. These markers were not lost prior to hatching.

Streamers

Many types of streamers (Fig. 11) and flags made from materials such as fluorescent plastic, polypropylene, polyurethane, hypalon, orthoplast, nylon-coated vinyl, and vinyl tubing have been used to visibly mark wild animals (Table 9). Nylon-coated fabric streamers were retained for several months to years. Different lengths and color codes provided a means of individual identification at a distance. Streamers often are attached to plastic or metal tags or collars to increase animal visibility.

Table 8. Nocturnal light sources for tracking wildlife[a].

Group/Species	Light source	Comments	Citations
Birds			
Black skimmer	Cyalume or light-emitting diodes	Sealed plastic bulb on back	Clayton et al. 1978
Long-eared owl	Light-emitting diodes	Studied nest behavior	DeLong 1982
Boreal owl	Betalights	On radio antennas	Hayward 1987
Mammals			
Bats	Pin light with battery	Glued to fur	Barbour and Davis 1969
Bats	Cyalume	Glass spheres glued to fur	Buchler 1976, LaVal et al. 1977
Mule deer	Neon light with battery	Neck collars	Carpenter et al. 1977
E. Badger	Betalights	On radio transmitters	Kruuk 1978
Am. Beaver	Light-emitting diodes	Neck collars	Brooks and Dodge 1978
Rabbits	Betalights	Attached to ear tags	Davey et al. 1980
Wallabies	Light-emitting diodes	Neck collars	Batchelor and McMillan 1980
Rodents	Betalights	Glued on head	Thompson 1982
Bats	Cyalume in gelatin capsule tag and lightsticks tag	Miniature lightsticks provided equal or superior results	Hovorka et al. 1996

[a] Scientific names are in the Appendix.

Bells

Bells have been used in conjunction with other individual marking methods (e.g., color-coded ear tags and collars) to facilitate locating and monitoring movements of deer, collared peccaries (Fig. 12), and green iguanas (Table 9). Periods of auditory observation of peccaries provided movement data comparable to those gained from telemetry and allowed activity patterns and habitat use of the animal to be identified. Bells, however, could attract predators.

External Color Marks

Dyes, fluorescent pigments, bleaching, inks, and paints

have been used as short-term external markers to identify wildlife at a distance (Table 10). No adverse physiological effects have been reported for these markers when properly applied on mammals. For birds, no obvious behavioral changes were noted other than temporarily increased preening. Certain markings could disrupt pair bonding, however, and altered intraspecific recognition mechanisms in birds may severely alter social interactions (Rohwer 1977).

Dyes

Waterproof dyes should yield an easily recognizable

Table 9. Tapes, streamers, and bells applied to wildlife[a] for individual or group identification.

Group/Species	Materials	Comments	Citations
Amphibians & Reptiles			
Am. alligator	Flexible chain or plastic strip attached to anchor tag	Beneath skin on side of tail, slow healing	Chabreck 1965
Bullfrog	Nylon waistbands painted with black numerals	Recognizable up to 8-12 months with binoculars	Emlen 1968
Iguanas/lizards	Colored Mystik cloth tape	Around neck	Minnich and Shoemaker 1970
Green iguana	Bells on fishing line	Around neck	Henderson 1974
Spotted turtle	Adhesive with numbers	On carapace	Ward et al. 1976
Amphibians & lizards	Colored beads	Around neck	Nace and Manders 1982, Fisher and Muth 1989
Skink	Pressure sensitive tape	Around neck	Zwickel and Allison 1983
Bullfrog	Reflective tape	Cemented to head	Robertson 1984
Birds			
Pheasants	Plastic streamers, tags	Attached to tail feathers, neck	Trippensee 1941, Taber 1949
Stilt, grackle, gull, and heron nestlings	Plasticized PVC tape	Attached to leg	Downing and Marshall 1959, Carrick and Murray 1970, Willsteed and Fetterolf 1986
Wild turkey, blackbirds, gulls, waterfowl, and raptors	Leg streamers	Attached on leg through slits in the marker or to bands	Campbell 1960, Fankhauser 1964, Thomas and Marburger 1964, Guarino 1968, Arnold and Coon 1971, Royall et al. 1974, Frentress 1976, Platt 1980, Cline and Clark 1981
Gull eggs	Colored plastic tape	Attached to apex of egg	Hayward 1982
Mammals			
Deer and collared peccary	Bells	Used to observe behavior	Jordan 1958, Gruell and Papez 1963, Ellisor and Harwell 1969, Schneegas and Franklin 1972
Gray squirrel	Plasticized PVC tape	Attached around neck with slot and notch system	Downing and Marshall 1959
Ungulates	Colored streamers of plastic, nylon, and nylon-coated fabrics (Herculite, Saflag, or Annortite), and plastic ear pennants	Attached to ears, horns, Achilles tendons, or to other marking devices; some reluctance of does to accept tagged fawns, but survival similar to nontagged fawns	Knowlton et al. 1964, Harper and Lightfoot 1966, Miller and Robertson 1967, Queal and Hlavachick 1968, Downing and McGinnes 1969, Jonkel et al. 1975, Ozoga and Clute 1988, Panagis and Stander 1989
Bats	Reflective plastic tape strips with numbers	Glued to head fur, temporary markers	Williams et al. 1966, Daan 1969
Polar bear	Colored flagging tape	Ear marker	Lentfer 1968
Cetaceans	Streamers and flags	Secured with steel barbs, nylon darts, umbrella anchors, and anchor rivets	Evans et al. 1972, Mitchell and Kozicki 1975, White et al. 1981
Mountain sheep	Colored adhesive tape	On horns	Day 1973
Porcupine	Colored tape or flags	On the quills or radios	Pigozzi 1988, Griesemer et al. 1999

[a] Scientific names are in the Appendix.

Fig. 11. Neck collar and ear streamer on white-tailed deer.

Fig. 13. Colored dye being applied with brush to the white portion of a white-winged dove wing.

color, resist fading, and be nontoxic, harmless to plumage, capable of use with a wetting agent or solvent to ensure quick penetration and coverage, and fast acting in a cool solution (Patterson 1978). Picric acid, Rhodamine B Extra, and Malachite Green yield strong color and exhibit good penetration and retention (Handel and Gill 1983). Avian species with light plumage are most effectively marked with dyes. Dipping, brushing (Fig. 13), and spraying have been used to apply dyes. To avoid hypothermia in cool weather, dye-marked birds should be thoroughly dried before release.

Bleaching

Bird feathers and mammal furs have been bleached and colored using human hair dyes or lighteners mixed with hydrogen peroxide (Table 10). Skin and feather damage can occur if tissues are bleached at too high a temperature or for too long a period. Animals also may be susceptible to hypo- and hyperthermia during the bleaching process.

Fluorescent Pigments

Trapped animals have been dusted with fluorescent pigments so that a fluorescent trail can be traced using ultraviolet (UV) lamps the following night (Table 10). The amount of vegetation cover, precipitation, and ambient

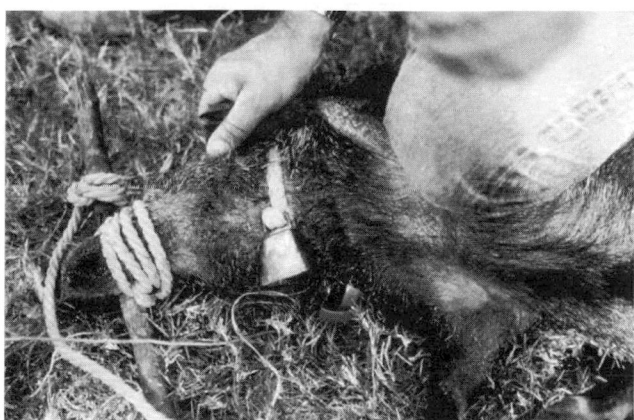

Fig. 12. Bell attached to collared peccary that allows investigators to follow herd movements.

light influenced trail detection. This technique enables collection of detailed information on home range, movement patterns, and habitat within a few days. To increase the duration of this marker beyond the second night, capsules containing pigments can be attached. A promising marker for aquatic mammals is a paste made from fluorescent pigments, vehicle binder, and solvent. It has visibly marked aquatic mammals for up to 2 years with no adverse behavioral effects or tissue abnormalities. Codit white reflective liquid also has been used to mark fresh-water animals.

Inks

Ink has been used to mark salamanders, terrapins, turtle eggs, iguanas, lizards, bird eggs, and deer (R. R. Lopez, unpublished data; Table 10). On deer, ink proved superior to paint for duration and visibility. Marking pens have been used to number eggs within clutches. No harmful effects were observed, but marking pens should be used with discretion until possible embryo toxic effects are evaluated.

Paints

Liquid and spray paints usually are applied to the skin, pelage, horns, or feathers (Table 10) and persist for a few weeks to several months. Individuals must be repainted, as paint is lost due to shedding, molting, and grooming. How these marks influence the behavior of species for which colors have seasonal social significance is unknown. Paints should be dry before animals are released.

INVASIVE MARKING TECHNIQUES
Internal Markers

Chemical, particle, and radioactive markers have been injected or fed animals to either physical mark individual animals or groups of animals (some chemical markers) or to detect byproducts from marked individuals (fecal markers). These methods require animals to be captured prior to marking.

Table 10. Dyes, paints, stains, pigments, ink, and bleaches used to externally mark wildlife [a].

Group/Species	Materials	Comments	Citations
Amphibians & Reptiles			
Tortoises, turtles, and snakes	Colored paints	On carapace of tortoises and on rattles or head of snakes	Woodbury and Hardy 1948, Pough 1966, Bennett et al. 1970, Bayless 1975, Medica et al. 1975, Bennion and Parker 1976, Parker 1976, Brown et al. 1984
Terrapins	Ink	Injected into skin	Burger and Montevecchi 1975, Burger 1976
Frogs and tadpoles	Neutral red, whole-body dye	Some immediate deaths and affected growth	Herreid and Kinney 1966, Guttman and Creasey 1973, Travis 1981
Lizards	Paints/indelible pencil/felt-tipped pen	Lost with shedding; survival same as toe clipping	Tinkle 1967, Jenssen 1970, Stebbins and Cohen 1973, Tinkle 1973, Henderson 1974, Vinegar 1975, Fox 1978, Jones and Ferguson 1980, Simon and Bissinger 1983
Salamanders	Fluorescent pigments	Good for short-term studies	Taylor and Deegan 1982, Nishikawa and Service 1988, Ireland 1991
Frogs and toads	Panjet dye	Lasted up to 2 years	Brown 1997
Juvenile frogs	Tetracycline bath	Failed as marker	Hatfield et al. 2001
Birds			
Small birds, ducks, gulls, pheasants, eagles, swifts, terns, geese, swans, and blackbirds	Dyes	Visibility up to 2 km	Butts 1930, Price 1931, Wadkins 1948, Jones 1950, Winston 1955, Kozlik et al. 1959, Ellis and Ellis 1975, White et al. 1980, Malacarne and Griffa 1987, Underhill and Hofmeyer 1987, Paullin and Kridler 1988, Belant and Seamans 1993
Ruffed grouse, cattle egrets, and bird eggs	Printer's ink	Lasted up to 12 months for cattle egrets with no harmful effects to eggs	Bendell and Fowle 1950, Boss 1963, Siegfried 1971, Olsen et al. 1982
Mourning dove and northern cardinals	Model airplane paint and spray paints	Preening resulted in feather loss; pair-bond disturbance	Swank 1952, Frankel and Baskett 1963, Goforth and Baskett 1965, Dickson et al. 1982
Mammals			
Squirrels, deer, terrestrial mammals, and pinnipeds	Dyes (Gentian violet, Biebrich scarlet, picric acid, Nyanzol A, Rhodamine B, Woollite, clothing and aniline, and human hair dyes with peroxide or hair bleach)	Ear tags and toe clipping best for long-term marking	Baumgartner 1940, Fitzwater 1943, Webb 1943, Hansen 1964, Simmons 1971, Day 1973, Brady and Pelton 1976, Bradbury 1977, Gentry 1979, Pitcher 1979, Johnson et al. 1981, Gentry and Holt 1982, Henderson and Johanos 1988, Hurst 1988
African elephant, bovids, bats, antelopes, and aquatic mammals	Paints, paint-sticks, and spray paints	Applied to hide, horns, or pelage; must remain dry for 15-30 minutes	Pienaar et al. 1966, Hanks 1969, Watkins and Schevill 1976, Gentry and Holt 1982, Clausen et al. 1984, Irvine and Scott 1984, McCracken 1984
Seals and small mammals	Fluorescent pigments	Adequate for <2 years for seals and small mammals dusted after trapping; trail followed with UV lamps	Griben et al. 1984, Lemen and Freeman 1985, Boonstra and Craine 1986, Dickman 1988, Mullican 1988, Mikesic and Drickhamer 1992, Stapp et al. 1994
Woodrat, rats, and pangolin	Capsule containing fluorescent dust	Long-term tracking and trail deposition	Goodyear 1989

[a] Scientific names are in the Appendix.

Chemical Markers

Organic stains placed in the tail-fin cavity or caudal region with a hypodermic needle have been developed as a reasonably permanent marker for amphibians (Table 11). During metamorphosis, the mark was reabsorbed with the tail with no ill effects.

Table 11. Internal particle and chemical markers used to study wildlife [a].

Group/Species	Materials	Comments	Citations
Amphibians & Reptiles			
Salamanders	2:1 Liquitex acrylic polymer to distilled water	Injected into the lateral, proximal, caudal region	Woolley 1973
Salamander larvae	Fine grained fluorescent pigments mixed as paste	Administered with heated probe; short-term tag	Ireland 1973
Frog and salamander larvae	21:20 ratio of mineral oil to petroleum jelly and stains (Oil Red A and Oil Blue M)	Tail fin cavity with a 22-gauge hypodermic needle, no effect on animals	Seale and Boraas 1974
Birds			
Duck and passerine eggs	Food dyes	Injected into egg; hatched young marked for few days	Evans 1951, Rotterman and Monnett 1984
Bait-consuming birds, raptors	Microtaggants (small, color-coded plastic particles)	Fed in baits	Johns and Thompson 1979, Nietfeld et al. 1994
Bait-consumers	Iophenoxic acid and Mirex	Iophenoxic acid ineffective	Larson et al. 1981
Waterfowl	Tetracycline	Injected; detected in eggs; egg-laying rate decreased	Haramis et al. 1983, Eadie et al. 1987
Mammals			
Small mammals	Dyes in food	To mark fat, teeth, pelage, and feces Observed in urine on snow	New 1958, 1959; Kindel 1960; Nass and Hood 1969
Cottontail rabbits	Dye pellets placed under skin	Fed in baits; more intense in mandible and teeth and in young animals	Brown 1961
Coyote, rodents, skunks, raccoon, seals, dolphins, whales, bears, and white-tailed deer	Tetracycline group	Force-fed beads	Owen 1961, Yagi et al. 1963, Linhart and Kennelly 1967, Crier 1970, Nelson and Linder 1972, Best 1976, Geraci et al. 1986, Garshelis and Visser 1997, Taylor and Lee 1994, Van Brackle et al. 1994
Collared peccary	Glass beads	Accuracy with field ID	Sowls and Minnamon 1963
Ground squirrels	Nyanzol A and D fur dyes	Picric acid worked best	Melchior and Iwen 1965
Snowshoe hares	Picric acid and Rhodamine B	Fecal tracer; for <30 days	Keith et al. 1968
Nutria	Codit white reflective liquid	Fecal tracer	Evans et al. 1971
Nutria	Powered aluminum pigment	Stained fat deposits	Evans et al. 1971
Rats and rabbits	Sudan black, orally	Fecal tracer	Taylor and Quy 1973, Cowan et al. 1984
Rabbits and Virginia opossum	Rhodamine B	Fed in baits	Evans and Griffith 1973; Morgan 1981; Cowan et al. 1984, 1987
Bait consuming mammals	Fluorescent acetate floss fibers	Systemic marker, produces fluorescent banding of claws and hair	Randolph 1973, Johns and Thompson 1979, Cowan et al. 1984
Coyote, gophers, and mountain beaver	Rhodamine B	Fluorescent in blood	Ellenton and Johnston 1975, Johns and Pan 1981, Lindsey 1983
Rats	Quinacrine dehydrochloride	Fed in baits	Johns and Pan 1981
Bait-consumers	Microtaggants	Fed with bait	Johns and Thompson 1979
Dogs and foxes	Iophenoxic acid	Fed with bait	Baer et al. 1985, Follmann et al. 1987
Coyote	Chlorinated benzenes		Johnson et al. 1998

[a] Scientific names are in the Appendix.

Rhodamine B taken orally acts as an internal marker, coloring the gall bladder, gut, feces, urine, and oral and urogenital openings producing fluorescent banding of feathers in birds (Table 11). These bands were most evident in primary and secondary feathers. Rhodamine B may become visible within 24 hours of dosing and persist for several weeks. Scanning for fluorescence using portable UV lamps allows trapped animals to be examined and released immediately, thus, reducing stress. Use of Rhodamine B as a systemic marker may be limited to certain periods of the year in birds, because banding probably occurs only in actively growing tissue. Rhodamine B has been used to detect bait consumption, density estimation, and examination of movements. Fisher (1999) summarized the literature on Rhodamine B and concluded the long-term effects of a single dose and the short succession of low dose on live animals should be investigated. She recommended Rhodamine WT as an alternative systemic bait marker.

Certain members of the tetracycline family of antibiotics, given orally or intravenously, combine with calcium in bones and teeth of mammals and eggshells of birds to produce a characteristic yellow fluorescence under UV light (Table 11). Tetracyclines are persistent, quantitative markers that can cross the placental barrier. They have been used to obtain mark-recapture population estimates and to identify the percentage of predators that consumed baits.

Quinacrine dehydrochloride, a fluorescent chemical marker, can be detected in blood with fluorometric and chromatographic analytical techniques (Table 11). Iophenoxic acid, an iodine-containing compound, and mirex, an organochlorine pesticide, have been used as blood and tissue markers for bait-consuming birds and mammals. Codit white-reflective liquid and Sudan black also are satisfactory fecal tracers for most mammals.

Particle Markers

Microtaggants, small plastic particles that are coded by colored layers, do not cause bait aversion, remain intact and, due to their fluorescent and magnetic properties, can be readily recovered from gut or fecal samples (Table 11). Fibers of fluorescent acetate floss also have been tested for measuring bait consumption by birds and mammals and individual movements in small mammals. As with micro-taggants, floss fibers are quantitative, nonpersistent markers. Floss fibers do not affect bait palatability and are more economic than microtaggants. Powdered aluminum placed in baits also has been used as a fecal tracer.

Radioactive Markers

Radioactive tracers have been used to identify and acquire information on behavior of amphibians, reptiles, and mammals but have received little attention for birds. The 3 primary methods of marking animals with radioisotopes are inert implants, external attachments, and metabolizable radio nucleotides (Table 12). Inert implants are suitable for monitoring specific movements, such as nest visits by birds and small mammals, using a manual or automated detector (Griffin 1952, Bailey et al. 1973, Linn 1978). Radioactive wires, pins, and capsules containing isotopes have been inserted subcutaneously in small rodents and bats as inert implants. Radioactive material can be attached to external leg bands and forearm tags, or the bands/tags can be made radioactive. Radioactive material also can be fed, injected, or implanted into the animal in a metabolizable form. These materials may be incorporated into the tissues of the animal, passed on to offspring, or voided in feces and urine; thus, they can be used for many purposes besides tracking (Linn 1978). This approach has been used to estimate population abundance of a number of species.

Table 12. Radioisotopes used for marking wildlife [a].

Group/Species	Radioactive materials	Comments	Citations
Amphibians & Reptiles			
Toads, salamanders, and snakes	Cobalt	Injected	Karlstrom 1957; Breckenridge and Tester 1961; Barbour et al. 1969a, b; Ashton 1975
Northern fence lizard	Gold	In tubing around waist	O'Brien et al. 1965
Salamanders, turtles, skinks, lizards, and snakes	Tantalum	Injected, local ulceration in salamanders	Bennett et al. 1970, Madison and Shoop 1970, Ward et al. 1976, Ferner 1979
Salamander larvae	Sodium	Injected	Shoop 1971
Birds			
Semipalmated plover	Tantalum	Radioactive-leg bands	Griffin 1952
Ring-necked pheasant	Calcium	ID chicks from fed hens	McCabe and LePage 1958
Mammals			
Voles	Phosphorus	Injected	Miller 1957
Bats & small mammals	Iodine	Injected, capsules on rings, implanted, or fed	Gifford and Griffin 1960, Johanningsmeier and Goodnight 1962
Harvest mice	Gold	Implanted	Kaye 1960
Small mammals	Cobalt	Implanted or in capsule on rings	Linn and Shillito 1960, Barbour 1963, Schnell 1968
Small mammals	Tantalum	Implanted	Graham and Ambrose 1967, Schnell 1968
Small mammals, opossum, rabbits, foxes, E. badger, bobcat, black bear	Zinc	Injected, fed	Nellis et al. 1967, Schnell 1968, Gentry et al. 1971, Pelton and Marcum 1975, Kruuk et al. 1980, Conner 1982
Black bear	Magnesium	Injected	Pelton and Marcum 1975
Small mammals	Sulphur	Passed through mother's milk	Dickman et al. 1983
Rodents	Radionuclides	Mother-offspring relatedness and male reproductive success	Tamarin et al. 1983, Scott and Tan 1985
Raccoon	Cadmium	Injected	Conner and Labisky 1985
Coyotes	Several tested	Implanted	Crabtree et al. 1989

[a] Scientific names are in the Appendix.

Table 13. Passive integrated transponders (PIT) used to mark wildlife [a].

Group/Species	Comments	Citations
Amphibians & Reptiles		
Frogs, toads, alligators, snakes, lizards, turtles, sea turtles	Only 1of 118 PIT tags failed, lasted up to 2 years	Camper and Dixon 1988, Brown 1997
Blunt-nosed leopard lizard	250 of 273 scanned successfully	Germano and Williams 1993
Pine snake	92% retained PIT tags	Elbin and Burger 1994
Neonatal snakes	No effect on growth and movement	Keck 1994
Rattlesnakes	No effect on growth and movement	Jemison et al. 1995
Desert tortoises	Detected as they entered culverts	Boarman et al.1998
Great-crested newt larval stage	Up to 2 years	Cummins and Swan 2000
Birds		
Captive birds	Success varied with species and year	Elbin and Burger 1994
Northern bobwhite chicks	5% lost PIT tags	Carver et al. 1999
Mammals		
Black-footed ferret	6 of 48 failed	Fagerstone and Johns 1987
Sea otter	6 of 6 successfully scanned	Thomas et al. 1987
Big brown bat	17 of 17 successfully scanned	Barnard 1989
Mice	4 of 4 successfully scanned	Rao and Edmondson 1990
Norway rat	10 of 10 successfully scanned	Ball et al. 1991
Ground squirrels	No effect on squirrels	Schooley et al. 1993
Captive mammals	Success varied with species and year	Elbin and Burger 1994
Voles	Used to monitor runways	Harper and Batzili 1996
Naked mole rat	Survival not different from toe-clipped	Braude and Ciszek 1998

[a] Scientific names are in the Appendix.

A major disadvantage of using radioactive markers is the restrictions imposed by state or federal regulations. These tags also can cause illness or death of marked animals, be lost, and constitute a hazard to other animals including humans. When selecting a radioactive marker, one should consider availability, type of radiation, energy levels emitted, physical and biological half-life, toxicity, and metabolic characteristics (Pendleton 1956).

Transponders

Passive integrated transponder (PIT) tags have been developed as permanent markers and tested on amphibians, reptiles, birds, and mammals (Table 13). The tags consist of an electromagnetic coil and a custom-designed transponder chip that emits a uniquely programmed alphanumeric ana-

log signal when excited by a scanning wand that discharges electromagnetic energy. The PIT-tag reader displays the code and can store this information for later retrieval. PIT tags are implanted subcutaneously (Fig. 14) with a special syringe and canula (needle).

No adverse effects of transponders have been observed in animals, but PIT tags are not as permanent as first thought; they can fail and be lost (Box 2). The major dis-

> **Box 2. Passive integrated transponders (PIT) should not be used as sole device to mark wildlife.**
>
> Recent research using PIT tags to mark fox squirrels provided a 17% unsuccessful scan rate after a 3-month period since implantation. Recaptured squirrels also were marked with radio collars. In a separate study on pocket gophers where PIT tags were the only mark used, only 1 of the original 13 pocket gophers marked was ever recaptured in 1 year of trapping. Loss of tags, tag breakage, or trap avoidance by previously trapped gophers were possible explanations for the low recapture rate. However, because both the fox squirrels and pocket gophers were tagged in the nape of the neck and both species used areas (holes is trees or burrows in the ground) that rubbed the nape of the neck, this may have caused PIT tags to be lost or crushed. We recommend that PIT tags not be the sole marking device used to mark wildlife.

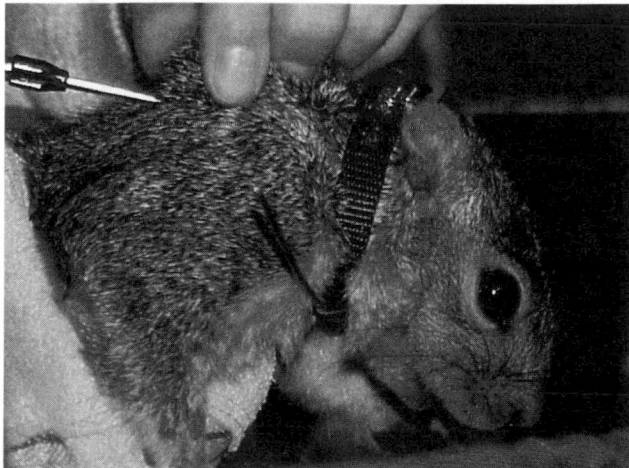

Fig. 14. Implanting a PIT tag into a radio-marked fox squirrel.

Table 14. Wildlife[a] marked using tattoo techniques.

Group/Species	Tattoo location	Comments	Citations
Amphibians & Reptiles			
Snakes	Skin	Method was permanent	Woodbury 1956
Frogs	Skin of the venter	Etched grooves with ink	Kaplan 1958
American alligator	Light skin under tail	Legible for several months	Chabreck 1965
Salamander	Subcutaneous	Fluorescent-elastomer	Davis and Ovaska 2001
Birds			
Nestling starlings	Abdomen	India ink dots using syringe	Ricklefs 1973
Birds of prey	Underside of wing	Captive birds, long lasting	Havelka 1983
Mammals			
Bats	Wing membranes	Slow process	Griffin 1934
Hares and rabbits	Ear	Used Franklin Rotary Tattoo	Thompson and Armour 1954, Keith et al. 1968
Bears	Upper lip, axilla, or groin	Permanent mark	Lentfer 1968, Johnson and Pelton 1980
Deer fawns	Ear	Permanent mark	Downing and McGinnes 1969
Cottontail rabbit	Ear	Permanent mark	Brady and Pelton 1976
Dolphinids	Fin	Proposed only	White et al. 1981
European Badger	Inguinal area	Electrically-powered pen	Cheeseman and Harris 1982
Pere David's deer	Ear	Permanent mark	Carnio and Killmar 1983
Beluga whale	Skin	Unsatisfactory	Geraci et al. 1986
Rats and mice	Ear	Permanent mark	Honma et al. 1986
Marsupial young	Pinnae	Fluorescent pigments	Soderquist and Dickman 1988
Porcupines	Ear	Not necessary with collars	Griesemer et al. 1999
Rodents	Subcutaneous	Chinese ink	Leclercq and Rozenfeld 2001

[a] Scientific names are in the Appendix.

advantage of this system, however, is the reader must be close (few cm) to the animal to record the code, which may necessitate recapturing the animal. Remote readings can be made (Table 13); a reader tube can be inserted into burrows or nesting cavities, or along travel routes, reading the transponder number each time the marked animal passes.

Tattoos

Tattoos provide an efficient means of permanently marking a wide range of species (Table 14). Best results are achieved by tattooing lightly pigmented areas free of hair (inside of ear [Fig. 15], inside legs or arms, lips) or feathers (under wings). Standard or rotary pliers, electric tattooing pencils, and syringes filled with ink have been used to inject contrasting dye (e.g., green or black) (Table 14). Small quantities of fluorescent pigments also have been used to make tattoos that are visible only under UV light. Although tattoos generally cause fewer problems (no added weight, inconspicuous to predators) than other marking techniques, they have the disadvantage of requiring animal recapture for identification. Tattoos often are used with more visible, but less permanent marking methods.

Tags

Tags, as used here, differ from bands in they penetrate some part of the animal's body and generally inflect pain, at least during insertion. With amphibians and reptiles, tags are usually placed through the shell, scutes, fore flipper, scales, tail fin, rattles, or tail (Table 15). In birds, tags generally are placed within the patagium of the wing or the webbing of the foot. Tags typically are placed within the ear, webbing of foot, flipper, or dorsal fin of mammals. Tag loss increases with time since tagging and may result from infection, wear, grooming, or fighting. Bilateral placement of tags and using them in conjunction with more permanent markers (e.g., tattoos) minimizes the chance of losing the identity of an animal over a long period. Study duration and required tag visibility are factors that influence tag choice. Many types of tags require recapturing the animal for identification.

Ear

Tags, manufactured from metals and plastics (Fig. 16) in a variety of shapes, sizes, and colors with identifying numbers stamped into the surface, are commonly used for marking mammals (Table 15). Tag-closing mechanisms can be interlocking, self-locking, or a rivet design that can-

Fig. 15. Numeric characters tattooed on the inside of an ear of a white-tailed deer.

Table 15. Tags used to mark wildlife [a].

Group/Species	Tag type	Citations
Amphibians & Reptiles		
Frogs, toads and snakes	Metal jaw tags	Raney 1940, Stille 1950, Hirth 1966
Frogs and turtles	Bands, rings, and plates fastened through holes in shell	Kaplan 1958, Lonke and Obbard 1977, Graham 1986, Layfield et al. 1988
Am. Alligators	Monel tag to dorsal tail scute	Chabreck 1965
Snakes and turtles	Buttons to caudal musculature	Pough 1970, Froese and Burghardt 1975
Sea turtles	Monel metal and plastic tags in fore flipper	LeBuff and Beatty 1971, Bacon 1973, Pritchard 1976, Bjorndal 1980, Pritchard 1980, Frazer 1983, Balazs 1985, Eckert and Eckert 1989
Rattlesnakes	Colored discs through rattle	Pendlebury 1972, Stark 1984
Turtles	Titanium disks held by adhesive	Gaymer 1973
Hellbender	Floy T-tags	Nickerson and Mays 1973
Turtles	Wooden dowel in scute	Davis and Sartor 1975
Snakes	Colored beads on line	Hudnall 1982
Birds		
Waterfowl	Streamers pinned to head	Gullion 1951
Penguins	Flipper bands made of aluminum, Teflon, monel metal, and stainless steel	Sladen 1952, Penny and Sladen 1966, Cooper and Morant 1981, Sallaberry and Valencia 1985
Am. Woodcock	Plastic neck tag attached with surgical clip	Westfall and Weeden 1956
Waterfowl, turkey, gulls, cranes, coot, willet, vultures, blackbirds, large passerines, wood-peckers, and pigeons	Patagial tag using various materials to attach tag through patagium	Anderson 1963; Knowlton et al. 1964; Mudge and Ferns 1978; Tacha 1979; Bartelt and Rusch 1980; Howe 1980; Wallace et al. 1980; Jackson 1982; Seel et al. 1982; Baker 1983; Curtis et al. 1983; Southern and Southern 1983, 1985; Sweeney et al 1985; Szymczak and Ringelman 1986; Cummings 1987; Hart and Hart 1987
Wood ducks, gull chicks, geese, and ducklings in eggs	Fingerling fish tags attached to foot web through hole in egg	Grice and Rogers 1965; Alliston 1975; Haramis and Nice 1980; Ryder and Ryder 1981; Seguin and Cooke 1985; Blums et al. 1994, 1999
Mammals		
Bats	Fingerling ear tags	Mohr 1934, Stebbings 1978
Rabbits, squirrels, sea lions, deer, caribou, fox, goats, seals, bears, mice, coyote, beaver, elk, porcupine, and moose calves	Plastic or metal ear tag with and without streamers	Trippensee 1941, Scheffer 1950, Tyndale-Briscoe 1953, Labisky and Lord 1959, Craighead and Stockstad 1960, Knowlton et al. 1964, Miller 1964, Harper and Lightfoot 1966, Miller and Robertson 1967, Downing and McGinnes 1969, Larsen 1971, Day 1973, Hubert et al. 1976, Rudge and Joblin 1976, Hobbs and Russell 1979, Stirling 1979, Warneke 1979, Johnson and Pelton 1980, Beasom and Burd 1983, Alt et al. 1985, LeBoulenge-Nguyen and LeBoulenge 1986, Gionfriddo and Stoddart 1988, Ostfeld et al. 1993, Griesemer et al. 1999, Swenson et al. 1999
Fox squirrel	Fingerling toe tags, bands on toes	Linduska 1942, Cooley 1948
Big game	Plastic streamer through slit in ear	Craighead and Stockstad 1960
Hares, nutria, sea otter, and seal pups	Tags placed on hind-foot web or rear flipper	Keith et al. 1968, Evans et al. 1971, Johnson 1979, Miller 1979, Ames et al. 1983, Henderson and Johanos 1988
Cetaceans	Plastic and bolt tags to dorsal fin	Norris and Pryor 1970, Irvine et al. 1982, Tomilin et al. 1983
Whales	Discovery marks and spaghetti tags (stainless steel projectiles) shot from shotgun	Clarke 1971, Evans et al. 1972, Mitchell and Kozicki 1975, Leatherwood et al. 1976, Brown 1978, Irvine and Scott 1984, De La Mare 1985, Miyashita and Rowlett 1985, Kasamatsu et al. 1986

[a] Scientific names are in the Appendix.

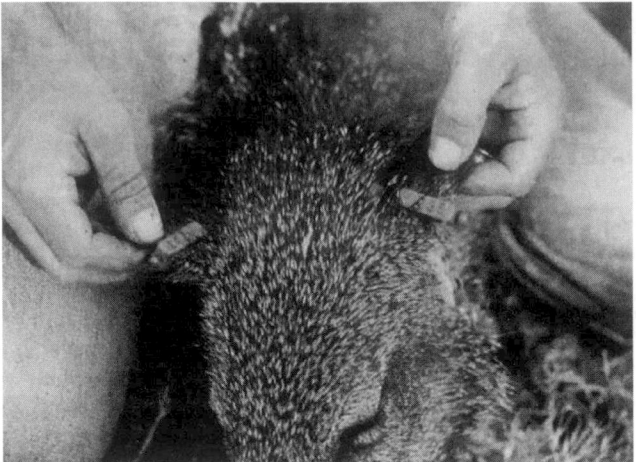

Fig. 16. Plastic numeric numbered tags attached to both ears of a collared peccary.

Fig. 17. Plastic domestic livestock ear tag used on white-tailed deer.

not be easily pried apart once the rivet is flattened. Tags may be self-piercing (Box 3) or inserted through a hole pierced with a knife or punch provided with the tagging kit. Ear tags usually are placed on the lower, inner region of the ear characterized by heavier cartilage and where the tag is best protected from being torn out. Tags should be loose enough to not interfere with blood circulation; puncture marks should be treated appropriately to prevent infection and ensure healing.

Aluminum, monel metal, and plastic tags available for domestic livestock (Fig. 17) work well on ungulates. Fingerling fish tags have been used in the ears of bats since the 1930s. These tags may not be suitable for large-eared bats or species that exhibit rapid ear movement synchronized with their echolocation emissions, or for medium- to large-sized bats due to poor retention. Delrin button tags are satisfactory for marking several species.

Wing

Wing tags commonly are used on birds (Table 15). They generally are made from flexible plastic-coated nylon fabric (Fig. 18), and rigid or upholstery plastic and attached through the patagium using a stainless steel or nylon pin, pop-rivet, or the marker itself. Durability and

colorfastness are functions of material composition and manufacturing (Nesbitt 1979, Young and Kochert 1987) with some materials lasting ≤ 10 years. Tag loss generally is low the first year (Patterson 1978, Stiehl 1983), but gradually increases in subsequent years (Patterson 1978). Double pinning tags reduced marker loss. Streamers often are used with wing tags to make them visible at a distance. If used, they should be sufficiently large for observational purposes, yet not so large as to hinder flight.

Wing markers often have no consistent effect on birds, although the initial adjustment period ranges from a few days to 2 weeks. Light feather wear and patagium callusing commonly have been noted. Severe abrasion has been observed occasionally with some species, and consistently with falcons. Abnormal replacement of feathers may occur and flight can be affected. Double pinning greatly reduces feather abrasion and callusing. Reported effects of wing markers on reproductive and social behavior also are variable. For many species, no significant influence on fledging success was found when ≥1 adult was marked (Young and Kochert 1987). However, reduced brood size, lengthened mean renesting interval, decreased social status, interference with migration, altered habitat selection, increased mortality, and effects on parental behavior (Brubeck et al. 1981) have been documented. Saunders

---

Box 3. Placement of self-piercing metal ear tags is important to retaining tags.

It has been our experience when using self-piercing metal ear tags on white-tailed deer, that placement is important for retention of tags. Tags should be placed near the base of the ear and the metal tag should be flush with the edge of the ear. If space is left between the tag and the edge of the ear, there is greater probability that brush or other foreign objects will become entangled in the tag and rip it from the ear. The tag should not be so tight as to roll the edge of the ear, but should be flush with the edge of the ear. Care also should be taken not to puncture any veins in the ear when applying the tag.

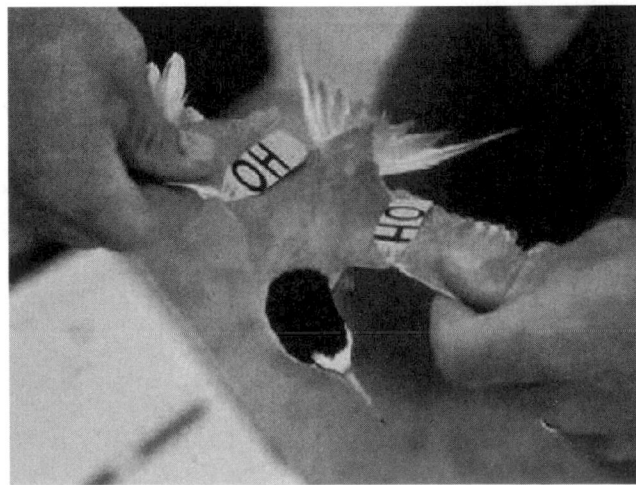

Fig. 18. Patagial-wing markers on a least tern.

Table 16. Wildlife[a] marked using hot-iron, freeze, chemical, and laser branding techniques.

Group/Species	Brand type	Comments	Citations
Amphibians &			
Reptiles	Hot iron	Tortoises and turtles branded on carapace	Woodbury and Hardy 1948, Weary 1969, Clark 1971, Taber et al. 1975
Tortoises, snakes, toads, frogs, turtles, anoles, lizards, and hellbender	Freeze	Tailed frogs branded on ventral surface	Lewke and Stroud 1974, Daugherty 1976, Ferner 1979, Bull et al. 1983
Snakes, sea turtles, frogs, iguanas, and salamanders	Chemical	Silver nitrate	Thomas 1975
Anurans	Laser	Ruby laser	Ferner 1979
Turtles and snakes	Freeze	Tail and rear foot pad	Jennings et al. 1991
American alligator			
Birds	Freeze	Branded feather tracts and premaxillae	Greenwood 1975
Mallard duckling			
Mammals	Hot iron	Branded horns and/or body	Aldous and Craighead 1958, Hanks 1969, Ashton 1978, Summers and Witthames 1978
Mountain sheep, African ungulates, seals, and bovids	Freeze	Branded body	Newsom and Sullivan 1968, Farrell et al. 1969, Hadow 1972, Farrell and Johnston 1973, Lazarus and Rowe 1975, Hobbs and Russell 1979, Rood and Nellis 1980, Russell 1981, Irvine et al. 1982, Miller et al. 1983, Pfeifer et al. 1984, Sherwin et al. 2002
Livestock, lab animals, pets, white-tailed deer, rodents, squirrels, mongoose, seals, dolphins, beaver, bats			
Seals	Explosive hot-iron device	Branded body	Homestead et al. 1972
Dolphins	Pressure stencil on dorsal fin	Lasted for at least 2 years	Tomilin et al. 1983

[a] Scientific names are in the Appendix.

(1988) contended that patagial tags should not be used on rare, vulnerable, or endangered species unless no other marking technique would work.

Other Appendages

Tags designed for marking ears also have been used to mark foot webs (birds, mammals), interdigital webbing of the hind foot (aquatic mammals, birds), flippers (sea turtles, aquatic mammals, sea birds), wings (birds, bats), and dorsal fins (cetaceans) (Table 15). Migration of the tags, injury to the dorsal fin, and covering of the tag with algae were problems associated with dorsal fin tags. For marking fore flippers, monel metal tags are more durable than plastic tags, although they may be less visible on marked animals and exhibit significant rates of loss. Aluminum tags, which wear and corrode easily, are regarded as inferior to stainless steel or monel metal tags for species inhabiting saltwater.

Self-piercing fingerling fish tags, monel metal tags, plastic and metal ear tags, and Delrin button tags also have been used to mark the hind foot webs of mammals and birds with good retention. Web tagging has been used to mark ducklings in pipped eggs—part of the shell and membrane of an egg were removed, a foot extracted, tagged, and replaced, and the hole covered with masking tape. Web tagging did not affect hatching success or survival after nest departure.

Body

Metal and plastic tags have been used to tag the shells of turtles, rattles of snakes, scutes of turtles and alligators, tails of amphibians, and snakes (Table 15). With the exception of turtles, other marking methods typically are recommended over body tags.

Jaw

Jaw tags have been used for amphibians and reptiles, but often were lost and caused irritation (Table 15). Numbered monel metal tags had to be clamped into the corner of the mouth, a technique that has not been widely used and is not recommended.

Branding

Branding provides an inexpensive, permanent, and visible means of marking animals. Hot iron, freeze, chemical, and laser branding all have been used to mark wildlife (Table 16). In addition, brand-like marks have been produced using a special clamp to hold a stencil on either side of the dorsal fin of cetaceans, causing the epithelium under the pressurized area to be exfoliated and replaced by demelanized skin that remained distinct for at least 2 years. This procedure, however, required 4 days for the depigmented tissue to be produced limiting its value as a field marker.

Fig. 19. Freeze branding mark on hip of Thomson's gazelle.

Fig. 20. During the imping process, a feather of a captured bird (left) is clipped and a feather of contrasting color (right) is attached to it by means of a double-pointed needle.

Hot-iron Branding

Historically, hot-iron branding was used to permanently mark domestic livestock. Hot branding has almost no role in modern wildlife management and is not recommended because it causes extreme pain and can produce open wounds that become infected. Currently, the only commonly used application of this technique in wildlife involves marking the horns of bovids.

Freeze Branding

Freeze branding, a technique originally developed for livestock, is a more humane marking method. Highly conductive branding irons are super cooled, most commonly in a mixture of dry ice and methanol or liquid nitrogen, and placed on a shaved and washed area of the skin. The epidermis is temporarily frozen, destroying the pigment-producing melanocytes in the hair follicles and causing regrowth of white (Fig. 19) as opposed to pigmented hair. Freeze branding has been used successfully to mark a variety of wildlife (Table 16). Freeze branding, if properly applied, rarely results in infection. However, freezing the skin for too long can cause scab formation or tissue necrosis, resulting in formation of new cells with intact melanocytes, which creates an indistinct mark. On lightly pigmented animals, however, these can produce a dark mark that can be read at a distance. A disadvantage of freeze branding is that the brand cannot be read until after the animal molts its pelage.

Chemical Branding

Anurans have been branded using silver nitrate or a silver nitrate- potassium nitrate mixture. The silver nitrate caused a brown mark to form immediately with the dark mark fading into a light mark within about 2 weeks. The method was recommended for dark-colored amphibians.

Laser Marking

Ruby lasers have been used to mark snakes, but were unsuccessful in marking a turtle (Table 16).

Tissue Removal

The effect of most tissue-removal marking methods on survival and fitness is not adequately known and is a topic that should be rigorously investigated (Society for the Study of Amphibians and Reptiles 1987). Alternative marking techniques should be used if excessive pain, behavioral changes, or decreased survival is expected.

Feather Imping

Imping (insertion of a colored feather into the clipped shaft of a bird's rectrices or remiges) (Fig. 20) using a double-ended needle, cement or "super glue," and a toothpick has been used to mark birds until molting (Table 17). Rectrices typically are used, although remiges are suitable if the replacement feather closely matches the one cut off. Imping is probably less effective than painting feathers.

Feather Clipping

Portions of vanes are clipped in different sizes and shapes from the shaft of several adjacent feathers, creating unique holes in the wings or tail that are used to identify birds (Table 17). Clipping should be performed to not impair flight. This technique is most suitable for gliding species and is of limited value for sedentary species because the marks cannot be observed on perching birds. Moreover, the number of combinations producing effective marks is limited. Dyed feathers or colored tape attached to natural feathers, attached with wire to the rachis of natural feathers whose vanes have been clipped off, or glued to plumage in unnatural, conspicuous patterns also have been used on birds. All of these marks are lost during molt.

Fur Removal

The removal of fur in a unique pattern is a non-permanent, humane means of marking mammals (Table 17). The marked animal generally is identifiable until the next molt. Hair may be removed with mechanical clippers, chemicals, or heat, allowing recognition of individuals at a distance. Depilatory pastes have been used to mark numbers on mammals, but can be extremely irritating to the skin of seals. Hair burning ("hair branding") produces a sharp, highly visible mark on fur seals and does not damage the skin; however, a fire source and a series of irons are required

Shell Notching

The most commonly used marking technique for turtles is notching the shell (Table 17). Marks on turtles may not be permanent. To avoid weakening the shell, marginals at the bridge or junction of the plastron and carapace should not be notched.

Scale Clipping

Scale clipping with scissors or clippers is the most com-

Table 17. Tissue removal methods used to mark wildlife[a].

Group/Species	Type	Comments	Citations
Amphibians & Reptiles			
Snakes	Subcaudal scale clipping	Permanent mark (regeneration 4-5 years) scars; marks not lost by tail breakage and marks persisted 4 years; 92% of the time shed skin from clipped racers could be precisely identified.	Blanchard and Finster 1933, Carlstrom and Edelstam 1946, Conant 1948, Woodbury 1956, Weary 1969, Pough 1970, Brown and Parker 1976, Ferner 1979
Turtles	Toe clipping and shell notching	Notches on young turtles may not be permanent	Cagle 1939, Ernst 1971
Frogs, toads, newts, iguanas, hellbenders, and other lizards	Toe clipping	Depending on species, some toe regeneration; should avoid clipping thumbs of toads due to use in amplexus	Martof 1953, Jameson 1957, Efford and Mathias 1969, Briggs and Storm 1970, Brown and Alcala 1970, Minnich and Shoemaker 1970, Hillis and Bellis 1971, Clarke 1972, Dole and Durant 1974, Richards et al. 1975, Daugherty 1976, Jones and Ferguson 1980, Hero 1989, Huey et al. 1990, Dodd 1993, Golay and Durrer 1994
Salamanders	Toe clipping	Only successful marking method	Hendrickson 1954, Woodbury 1956, Heatwole 1961, Twitty 1966, Hall and Stafford 1972, Wells and Wells 1976, Davis and Ovaska 2001
Amphibian tadpoles and salamanders	Tail-fin notching	Tadpoles had higher mortality than staining, salamanders regenerated tail in 1 month	Turner 1960, Orser and Shure 1972, Guttman and Creasey 1973, Ferner 1979
American alligators	Toe clip, tail-scute notch, and web punch	Permanent marks	Chabreck 1965, Jennings et al. 1991
Eastern newt	Amputating 1 limb	Not recommended	Healy 1974
Alpine newt	Skin transplantation	95% retention rate after 3 years	Rafinski 1977
Birds			
Large to medium size	Dyed and painted feathers or colored tape attached to cut feathers	These marking techniques are temporary	Edminster 1938, Kozicky and Weston 1952, Neal 1964, Dickson et al. 1982, Ritchison 1984
Medium and large	Imping	Used double-ended needle or cement	Wright 1939, Hamerstrom 1942, Sowls 1950
Penguins and zoo birds	Web punching	More practical than using leg bands, fighting destroyed marks	Richdale 1951, Reuther 1968
Pheasants, raptors, and frigate birds	Feather vane clipping leaving holes in wings or tail	Most suitable for gliding species; reduced breeding success of pheasants	Geis and Elbert 1956, Enderson 1964, Snelling 1970, Gargett 1973, Garnett 1987
Nestling gulls	Grafting the pollex to the skin of the head	Resulted in alula feathers growing from the head region	Coppinger and Wentworth 1966
Mallard	Alula clipping	Did not affect growth rate, behavior, or flight capability	Burger et al. 1970
Nestlings	Toenail and toe clipping	Toenail clipping remained for at least 18 days	Murphy 1981, St. Louis et al. 1989
Mammals			
Bats, beaver, nutria, and seals	Web punching or slits	Distinct after 2 years in fur seals	Aldous 1940, Scheffer 1950, Davis 1963*a*
Small mammals, hares, coyotes, and seal pups	Toe clipping	Best to take only 1 toe per foot	Baumgartner 1940, Dell 1957, Sanderson 1961, Melchior and Iwen 1965, Ambrose 1972, Andelt and Gipson 1980, Riley and William 1981, Fairley 1982, Gentry and Holt 1982, Pavone and Boonstra 1985, Korn 1987, Wood and Slade 1990
Small mammals	Ear punching or clipping	Some effect on movement and behavior	Blair 1941, Honma et al. 1986, Wood and Slade 1990

(*Continued*)

---

[a] Scientific names are in the Appendix.

Table 17 (*continued*). Tissue removal methods used to mark wildlife[a].

Group/Species	Type	Comments	Citations
Mammals (*continued*)			
Rats and seals	Depilatory paste	Caused extreme skin irritation in seals	Chitty and Shorten 1946, Gentry 1979
Bats	Wing hole punching	White scar lasted 1-5 months	Bonaccorso and Smythe 1972, Bonacoorso et al. 1976, Stebbings 1978
Juvenile bats	Claw clipping	Lasted only a few weeks	Stebbings 1978
Seals	Hair burning	Does not burn skin	Gentry 1979
Seals, European badger, and mice	Fur removal	Lasted until next molt	Gentry 1979, Stewart and MacDonald 1997, Johnson 2001

[a] Scientific names are in the Appendix.

monly used method of marking snakes (Table 17). Pieces should be cut from the subcaudals, which leaves "permanent" scars. Subcaudal cuts can be numbered on each side beginning at the proximal end of the tail. No adverse effects have been reported for snakes, but regeneration could be a problem and clipping is difficult on small or young snakes. Ventral scales are larger and are easier to clip than subcaudal scales, and scars in this area cannot be lost by tail breakage.

Toenail Clipping

Clipping the toenail rather than toes (Fig. 21) is preferable for short-term studies of small mammals and nestling birds (Table 17). Clipped toenails remained sufficiently blunt at the tip to be distinguished throughout the nestling period when birds are too young to be banded, although the nails eventually grow back. This method also has been used in bat nursery roosts, but the marks lasted only a few weeks.

Toe Clipping

Toe clipping is widely used to individually mark anurans, small mammals, small turtles, and lizards (Table 17). The nail and first joint of the toe are removed with sterile dissecting scissors. The technique is inexpensive, rapid, and permanent but, at times, clipped toes cannot be distinguished from other causes of toe loss. Kumar (1979) developed a toe-clipping code for identification of up to 9,999 animals using no more than 2 digits clipped per foot. No direct adverse effects of toe clipping were reported for small mammals, and none of the extensive studies documented harmful effects caused by clipping toes of lizards. Toe clipping, however, caused a temporary reduction in capture rates. Toe clipping is not advised for bats because the toes are essential for roosting and grooming. This technique also has been used for identifying tracks of marked individuals. Suitable conditions (e.g., snow) are required for track identification. Ecologists generally avoid toe clipping tree frogs and salamanders for long-term studies because of their regenerative capabilities. Although toe-clipping amphibians and reptiles has disadvantages, it is still the most common marking technique used for anurans.

Ear Punching and Notching

The ears of many small mammals can be marked by punching or clipping them in a variety of coded systems (Table 17). Large-eared ungulates, carnivores, and primates have been marked by cutting 1 or 2 notches at preselected coded sites on the margin of the ear allowing for a number of combinations. Ear notching or punching (using a leather punch) for large mammal species permits identification of marked animals at a distance. Notches usually last longer than tags, although they can be distorted by infection, growth, or injury (Ashton 1978). Ear notching is not advisable for mammals that use their ears for orientation and prey location or have valve-like ears that function during deep-sea dives. The ethical implications of these techniques should be considered.

Web Punching

Slits or holes punched into foot webs, flippers, or wing membranes have been used to mark many birds and mammals (Table 17). The marks are permanent, but unclean cutting may produce a small scar rather than a hole. Leather punches usually produce clean holes. Although some marks on web-footed birds are altered by injury or healing, most marks are identifiable. Some authors reported this method was more practical than leg bands. The major disadvantage of web punching is that birds must be recaptured for the web holes to be read. There are some questions of the ethics of this technique.

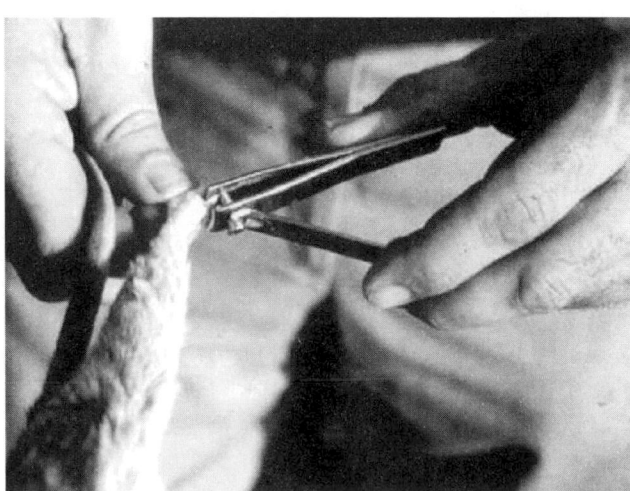

Fig. 21. Clipping the toenail rather than the toe is preferred for short-term marking studies of small mammals.

Tail Clipping

Notches clipped from a tail fin is a traditional method

for marking amphibian tadpoles and some salamanders (Table 17). Fin clipping, however, produced higher mortality than did staining techniques. Scutes clipped on the tails of crocodilians have proved useful in long-term studies.

Skin Transplantation

This method involves removal of skin from one part of the body and transplanting it to another. Although this method has been successful in amphibians and some birds (Table 17), we do not recommend it.

Amputation

Healy (1974) marked post-larval metamorphs of the eastern newt by amputating one limb at the middle of the zeugopodium, but few individuals were recaptured (Table 17). Newts regenerated the limb, usually within a month. Amputation is not recommended.

SUMMARY

If there is a need to recognize individual animals, use of natural markings is the preferred alternative. If this is not feasible, marking animals without capture is the next best option. These methods eliminate stress associated with capture. For animals that must be captured prior to marking, noninvasive techniques are preferred, but are not without problems. They can interfere with reproductive behavior (color marks), increase predation risks (color marks), and cause injury or increased mortality (band constriction, icing, entanglement of marks). Noninvasive methods generally are preferred because application of many invasive marks causes pain. The advantage of some invasive techniques is that many are "permanent." For example, tattoos probably are the most permanent marking method available for many species, but have the disadvantage of requiring the animal to be in hand (recaptured, found dead) to be identified. Use of PIT tags also offers a relatively permanent marking method (some are lost or become inoperable), but have the same primary disadvantage as tattoos—animals usually must be recaptured for identification. If animals only need to be marked for a limited time, then permanency of the mark is not a factor. There are both noninvasive (e.g., dyes) and invasive (e.g., toe-nail clipping) marking methods that can be used for sort-term studies yet have little affect on the animal. The ultimate responsibility regarding which method should be used to mark wildlife for a particular study depends on the ethical and scientific validity of method, and rests with the investigator.

ACKNOWLEDGMENTS

We acknowledge M. T. Nietfeld and M. W. Barrett for compiling much of the literature on mammal and bird marking techniques (Nietfeld et al. 1994). We have expanded and updated this information and provided a different format for its presentation. We also acknowledge A. L. Hensley, A. D. Lopez, E. K. Lyons, J. S. Wagner, R. E. Walser, and S. W. Whisenant for literature searches and copying of relevant papers, T. M. Johnson for scanning papers and photographs, and M. E. Griffin for proofing the manuscript. To these people and R. E. Bennetts for reviewing an earlier draft of the manuscript and an anonymous reviewer, we are deeply grateful. Photographs used in this chapter are from the collection within the Department of Wildlife and Fisheries Sciences, Texas A&M University. Lastly, we appreciate and respect C. E. Braun, editor, for his help, prodding, and patience.

LITERATURE CITED

ABRAHAM, K. F., C. D. ANKNEY, AND H. BOYD. 1983. Assortative mating by brant. Auk 100:201–203.

ALDOUS, M. C., AND F. C. CRAIGHEAD, JR. 1958. A marking technique for bighorn sheep. Journal of Wildlife Management 22:445–446.

ALDOUS, S. E. 1940. A method of marking beavers. Journal of Wildlife Management 4:145–148.

ALDRICH, J. W., AND J. H. STEENIS. 1955. Neck-banding and other color marking of waterfowl; its merits and shortcomings. Journal of Wildlife Management 19:317–318.

ALLISTON, W. G. 1975. Web-tagging ducklings in pipped eggs. Journal of Wildlife Management 39:625–628.

ALT, G. L., C. R. MCLAUGHLIN, AND K. H. POLLOCK. 1985. Ear tag loss by black bears in Pennsylvania. Journal of Wildlife Management 49:316–320.

AMBROSE, III, H. W. 1972. Effect of habitat familiarity and toe clipping on rate of owl predation in *Microtus pennsylvanicus*. Journal of Mammalogy 53:909–912.

AMERICAN ORNITHOLOGISTS' UNION. 1988. Report of committee on use of wild birds in research. Auk 105 (Supplement):1A-41A.

AMERICAN SOCIETY OF MAMMALOGISTS. 1998. Guidelines for the capture, handling, and care of mammals as approved by the American Society of Mammalogists. Journal of Mammalogy 79:1416–1431.

AMES, J. A., R. A. HARDY, AND F. E. WENDELL. 1983. Tagging materials and methods for sea otters, *Enhydra lutris*. California Fish and Game 69:243–252.

ANDELT, W. F., AND P. S. GIPSON. 1980. Toe-clipping coyotes for individual identification. Journal of Wildlife Management 44:293–294.

ANDERSON, A. 1963. Patagial tags for waterfowl. Journal of Wildlife Management 27:284–288.

———. 1980. The effects of age and wear on color bands. Journal of Field Ornithology 51:213–219.

———. 1981. Making polyvinyl chloride (PVC) colored legbands. Journal of Wildlife Management 45:1067–1068.

ANKNEY, C. D. 1975. Neckbands contribute to starvation in female lesser snow geese. Journal of Wildlife Management 39:825–826.

ARNOLD, K. A., AND D. W. COON. 1971. A technique modification for color-marking birds. Bird-Banding 42:49–50.

ASHTON, D. G. 1978. Marking zoo animals for identification. Pages 24–34 in B. Stonehouse, editor. Animal marking: recognition marking of animals in research. University Park Press, Baltimore, Maryland, USA.

ASHTON, JR., R. E. 1975. A study of movement, home range, and winter behavior of *Desmognathus fuscus* (Rafinesque). Journal of Herpetology 9:85-91.

ATHERTON, N. W., M. E. MORROW, A. E. BIVINGS, IV, AND N. J. SILVY. 1982. Shrinkage of spiral plastic leg bands with resulting leg damage to mourning doves. Proceedings of the Annual Conference of the Southeastern Association of Fish and Wildlife Agencies 36:666–670.

BACON, P. R. 1973. The orientation circle in the beach ascent crawl of the leatherback turtle, *Dermochelys coriacea*, in Trinidad. Herpetologica 29:343–348.

BAER, G. M., J. H. SHADDOCK, D. J. HAYES, AND P. SAVARIE. 1985. Iophenoxic acid as a serum marker in carnivores. Journal of Wildlife Management 49:49–51.

BAILEY, E. E., G. E. WOOLFENDEN, AND W. B. ROBERTSON, JR. 1987. Abrasion and loss of bands from Dry Tortugas sooty terns. Journal of Field Ornithology 58:413–424.

BAILEY, G. N. A., I. J. LINN, AND P. J. WALKER. 1973. Radioactive marking of small mammals. Mammal Review 3:11–23.

BAKER, W. W. 1983. A non-clamp patagial tag for use on red-cockaded woodpeckers. Pages 110–111 *in* D. A. Wood, editor. Proceedings of the Red-Cockaded Woodpecker Symposium. Florida Game and Freshwater Fish Commission, Tallahasee, USA.

BALAZS, G. H. 1985. Retention of flipper tags on hatchling sea turtles. Herpetological Review 16:43–45.

BALHAM, R. W., AND W. H. ELDER. 1953. Colored leg bands for waterfowl. Journal of Wildlife Management 17:446–449.

BALL, D. J., G. ARGENTIERI, R. KRAUSE, M. LIPINSKI, R. L. ROBINSON, R. E. STOLL, AND G. E. VISSCHER. 1991. Evaluation of a microchip implant system used for animal identification in rats. Laboratory Animal Science 41:185–186.

BALLOU, R. M., AND F. W. MARTIN. 1964. Rigid plastic collars for marking geese. Journal of Wildlife Management 28:846–847.

BALTOSSER, W. H. 1978. New and modified methods for color-marking hummingbirds. Bird-Banding 49:47–49.

BANKS, R. C., R. M. MCDIARMID, AND A. L. GARDNER. 1987. Checklist of vertebrates of the United States, the U.S. Territories, and Canada. U.S. Department of the Interior, Fish and Wildlife Service, Resource Publication 166.

BARBOUR, R. W. 1963. *Microtus:* a simple method of recording time spent in the nest. Science 141:41.

———, AND W. H. DAVIS. 1969. Bats of America. University Press of Kentucky, Lexington, USA.

———, M. J. HARVEY, AND J. W. HARDIN. 1969*a*. Home ranges, movements and activity of the eastern worm snake. *Carphophis amoenus amoenus.* Ecology 50:470–476.

———, J. W. HARDIN, J. P. SHAFER, AND M. J. HARVEY. 1969*b*. Home range, movements, and activity of the dusky salamander, *Desmognathus fuscus.* Copeia 1969:293–297.

BARCLAY, R. M. R., AND G. P. BELL. 1988. Marking and observational techniques. Pages 59–76 *in* T. H. Kunz, editor. Ecological and behavioral methods for the study of bats. Smithsonian Institute Press, Washington, D.C., USA.

BARNARD, S. M. 1989. The use of microchip implants for identifying big brown bats (*Eptesicus fuscus*). Animal Keepers' Forum 16:50–52.

BART, J., D. BATTAGLIA, AND N. SENNER. 2001. Effects of color bands on semipalmated sandpipers banded at hatch. Journal of Field Ornithology 72:521–526.

BARTELT, G. A., AND D. H. RUSCH. 1980. Comparison of neck bands and patagial tags for marking American coots. Journal of Wildlife Management 44:236–241.

BARTONEK, J. C., AND C. W. DANE. 1964. Numbered nasal discs for waterfowl. Journal of Wildlife Management 28:688–692.

BATCHELOR, T. A., AND J. R. MCMILLAN. 1980. A visual marking system for nocturnal animals. Journal of Wildlife Management 44:497–499.

BATEMAN, G. C., AND T. A. VAUGHAN. 1974. Nightly activities of mormoopid bats. Journal of Mammalogy 55:45–65.

BAUMGARTNER, L. L. 1940. Trapping, handling, and marking fox squirrels. Journal of Wildlife Management 4:444–450.

BAYLESS, L. E. 1975. Population parameters for *Chrysemys picta* in a New York pond. American Midland Naturalist 93:168–176.

BEALE, D. M. 1966. A self-collaring device for pronghorn antelope. Journal of Wildlife Management 30:209–211.

———, AND A. D. SMITH. 1973. Mortality of pronghorn antelope fawns in western Utah. Journal of Wildlife Management 37:343–352.

BEASOM, S. L., AND J. D. BURD. 1983. Retention and visibility of plastic ear tags on deer. Journal of Wildlife Management 47:1201–1203.

BELANT, J. L., AND T. W. SEAMANS. 1993. Evaluation of dyes and techniques to color-mark incubating herring gulls. Journal of Field Ornithology 64:440–451.

BELL, G. P., G. A. BARTHOLOMEW, AND K. A. NAGY. 1986. The roles of energetics, water economy, foraging behavior, and geothermal refugia in the distribution of the bat, *Macrotus californicus.* Journal of Comparative Physiology B 156:441–450.

BELLROSE, F. C. 1955. A comparison of recoveries from reward and standard bands. Journal of Wildlife Management 19:71–75.

BENDELL, J. F. S., AND C. D. FOWLE. 1950. Some methods for trapping and marking ruffed grouse. Journal of Wildlife Management 14: 480–482.

BENNETT, D. H., J. W. GIBBONS, AND J. C. FRANSON. 1970. Terrestrial activity in aquatic turtles. Ecology 51:738–740.

BENNION, R. S., AND W. S. PARKER. 1976. Field observations on courtship and aggressive behavior in desert striped whipsnakes, *Masticophis t. taeniatus.* Herpetologica 32:30–35.

BERGER, D. D., AND H. C. MUELLER. 1960. Band retention. Bird-Banding 31:90–91.

BEST, P. B. 1976. Tetracycline marking and the rate of growth layer formation in the teeth of a dolphin *(Lagenorhynchus obscurus).* South African Journal of Science 72:216–218.

BIGLER, W. J. 1966. A marking harness for the collared peccary. Journal of Wildlife Management 30:213–214.

BJORNDAL, K. A. 1980. Demography of the breeding population of the green turtle, *Chelonia mydas,* at Tortuguero, Costa Rica. Copeia 1980:525–530.

BLAIR, W. F. 1941. Techniques for the study of mammal populations. Journal of Mammalogy 22:148–157.

BLANCHARD, F. N., AND E. B. FINSTER. 1933. A method of marking living snakes for future recognition, with a discussion of some problems and results. Ecology 14:334–347.

BLANK, T. H., AND J. S. ASH. 1956. Marker for game birds. Journal of Wildlife Management 20:328–330.

BLUMS, P., A. MEDNIS, AND J. D. NICHOLS. 1994. Retention of web tags and plasticine-filled leg bands applied to day-old ducklings. Journal of Wildlife Management 58:76–81.

———, J. B. DAVIS, S. E. STEPHENS, A. MEDNIS, AND D. M. RICHARDSON. 1999. Evaluation of a plasticine-filled leg band for day-old ducklings. Journal of Wildlife Management 63:656–663.

BOAG, D. A., A. WATSON, AND R. PARR. 1973. Radio-marking versus back-tabbing red grouse. Journal of Wildlife Management 37: 410–412.

BOARMAN, W. I., M. L. BEIGEL, G. C. GOODLETT, AND M. SAZAKI. 1998. A passive integrated transponder system for tracking animal movements. Wildlife Society Bulletin 26:886–891.

BONACCORSO, F. J., AND N. SMYTHE. 1972. Punch-marking bats: an alternative to banding. Journal of Mammalogy 53:389–390.

———, ———, AND S. R. HUMPHREY. 1976. Improved techniques for marking bats. Journal of Mammalogy 57:181–182.

BOONSTRA, R., AND I. T. M. CRAINE. 1986. Natal nest location and small mammal tracking with a spool and line technique. Canadian Journal of Zoology 64:1034–1036.

BOSS, A. S. 1963. Aging the nests and young of the American coot. Thesis. University of Minnesota, St. Paul, USA.

BRADBURY, J. W. 1977. Lek mating behavior in the hammer-headed bat. Zeitscrift fur Tierpsychologie 45:225–255.

BRADY, J. R., AND M. R. PELTON. 1976. An evaluation of some cottontail rabbit marking techniques. Journal of Tennessee Academy of Science 51:89–90.

BRAUDE, S., AND D. CISZEK. 1998. Survival of naked mole-rats marked by implantable transponders and toe clipping. Journal of Mammalogy 79:360–363.

BRECKENRIDGE, W. J., AND J. R. TESTER. 1961. Growth, local movements and hibernation of the Manitoba toad, *Bufo hemiophrys.* Ecology 42: 637–646.

BRETAGNOLLE, V., J. C. THIBAULT, AND J. M. DOMINICI. 1994. Field identification of individual ospreys using head marking pattern. Journal of Wildlife Management 58:175–178.

BRIGGS, J. L., AND R. M. STORM. 1970. Growth and population structure of the cascade frog, *Rana cascadae* Slater. Herpetologica 26: 283–300.

BROOKS, P. M. 1981. Comparative longevity of a plastic and a new machine-belting collar on large African ungulates. South African Journal of Wildlife Research 11:143–145.

BROOKS, R. P., AND W. E. DODGE. 1978. A night identification collar for beavers. Journal of Wildlife Management 42:448–452.

BROWN, L. J. 1997. An evaluation of some marking and trapping techniques currently used in the study of anuran population dynamics. Journal of Herpetology 31:410–419.

BROWN, L. N. 1961. Excreted dyes used to determine movements of cottontail rabbits. Journal of Wildlife Management 25:199–202.

BROWN, S. G. 1978. Whale marking techniques. Pages 71–80 *in* B. Stonehouse, editor. Animal marking: recognition marking of animals in research. MacMillan, London, United Kingdom.

BROWN, W. C., AND A. C. ALCALA. 1970. Population ecology of the frog, *Rana erythraea*, in southern Negros, Philippines. Copeia 1970: 611–622.

BROWN, W. S., AND W. S. PARKER. 1976. A ventral scale clipping system for permanently marking snakes (Reptilia, Serpentes). Journal of Herpetology 10:247–249.

———, V. P. J. GANNON, AND D. M. SECOY. 1984. Paint-marking the rattle of rattlesnakes. Herpetological Review 15:75–76.

BRUBECK, M. V., B. C. THOMPSON, AND R. D. SLACK. 1981. The effects of trapping, banding, and patagial tagging on the parental behavior of least terns in Texas. Colonial Waterbirds 4:54–60.

BUCHLER, E. R. 1976. A chemiluminescent tag for tracking bats and other small nocturnal animals. Journal of Mammalogy 57:173–176.

BULL, E. L., R. WALLACE, AND D. H. BENNETT. 1983. Freeze-branding: a long-term marking technique on long-toed salamanders. Herpetological Review 14:81–82.

BURGER, G. V., R. J. GREENWOOD, AND R. C. OLDENBURG. 1970. Alula removal technique for identifying wings of released waterfowl. Journal of Wildlife Management 34:137–140.

BURGER, J. 1976. Temperature relationships in nests of the northern diamondback terrapin, *Malaclemys terrapin terrapin*. Herpetologica 32: 412–418.

———, AND W. A. MONTEVECCHI. 1975. Nests site selection in the terrapin, *Malaclemys terrapin*. Copeia 1975:113–119.

BURLEY, N. 1985. Leg-band color and mortality patterns in captive breeding populations of zebra finches. Auk 102:647–651.

———. 1986a. Comparison of the band-color preferences of two species of estrildid finches. Animal Behaviour 34:1732–1741.

———. 1986b. Sex-ratio manipulation in color-banded populations of zebra finches. Evolution 40:1191–1206.

———. 1988. Wild zebra finches have band-colour preferences. Animal Behaviour 36:1235–1237.

———, G. KRANTZBERG, AND P. RADMAN. 1982. Influence of colour-banding on the conspecific preferences of zebra finches. Animal Behaviour 30:444–455.

BURTT, JR., E. J., AND R. M. TUTTLE. 1983. Effect of timing of banding on reproductive success of tree swallows. Journal of Field Ornithology 54:319–323.

BUTTS, W. K. 1930. A study of the chickadee and white-breasted nuthatch by means of marked individuals. Part I. Methods of marking birds. Bird-Banding 1:149–168.

BYERS, S. M. 1987. Extent and severity of nasal saddle icing on mallards. Journal of Field Ornithology 58:499–504.

CAGLE, F. R. 1939. A system of marking turtles for future identification. Copeia 1939:170–173.

CALVO, B., AND R. W. FURNESS. 1992. A review of the use and the effects of marks and devices on birds. Journal of Ringing and Migration 13:129–151.

CAMPBELL, B. H., AND E. F. BECKER. 1991. Neck collar retention in dusky Canada geese. Journal of Field Ornithology 62:521–527.

CAMPBELL, D. L. 1960. A colored leg strip for marking birds. Journal of Wildlife Management 24:431.

CAMPER, J. D., AND J. R. DIXON. 1988. Evaluation of a microchip marking system for amphibians and reptiles. Research Publication 7100–159. Texas Parks and Wildlife Department, Austin, USA.

CARLSTRÖM, D., AND C. EDELSTAM. 1946. Methods of marking reptiles for identification after recapture. Nature 158:748–749.

CARNIO, J., AND L. KILLMAR. 1983. Identification techniques. Pages 39–52 *in* B. B. Beck and C. Wemmer, editors. The biology and management of an extinct species-Pere David's deer. Noyes Publications, Park Ridge, New Jersey, USA.

CARO, T. M. 1994. Cheetahs of the Serengeti Plains: group living in an asocial species. The University of Chicago Press, Chicago, Illinois, USA.

CARPENTER, L. H., D. W. REICHERT, AND F. WOLFE, JR. 1977. Lighted collars to aid night observations of mule deer. U.S. Department of Agriculture, Forest Service, Research Notes RN-338.

CARR, A., P. ROSS, AND S. CARR. 1974. Interesting behavior of the green turtle, *Chelonida mydas*, at a mid-ocean island breeding ground. Copeia 1974:703–706.

CARRICK, R., AND D. MURRAY. 1970. Readable band numbers and "Scotchlite" colour bands for the silver gull. Australian Bird Bander 8:51- 56.

CARVER, A. V., L. W. BURGER, JR., AND L. A. BRENNAN. 1999. Passive integrated transponders and patagial tag markers for northern bobwhite chicks. Journal of Wildlife Management 63:162–166.

CASTELLI, P. M., AND R. E. TROST. 1996. Neck bands reduce survival of Canada geese in New Jersey. Journal of Wildlife Management 60: 891–898.

CAVANAGH, P. M., C. R. GRIFFIN, AND E. M. HOOPES. 1992. A technique to color-mark incubating gulls. Journal of Field Ornithology 63: 264–267.

CHABRECK, R. H. 1965. Methods of capturing, marking and sexing alligators. Proceedings of the Annual Conference of the Southeastern Association of Game and Fish Commissioners 17:47–50.

———, AND J. D. SCHROER. 1975. Effects of neck-collars on reproduction of snow geese. Bird-Banding 46:346–347.

CHEESEMAN, C. L., AND S. HARRIS. 1982. Methods of marking badgers (*Meles meles*). Journal of Zoology 197:289–292.

CHILDS, JR., H. E. 1952. Color bands. Western Bird Banding Association News 27:4.

CHITTY, D., AND M. SHORTEN. 1946. Techniques for the study of the Norway rat *Rattus norvegicus*. Journal of Mammalogy 27:63–78.

CLARK, JR., D. R. 1971. Branding as a marking technique for amphibians and reptiles. Copeia 1971:148–151.

CLARKE, R. 1971. The possibility of injuring small whales with the standard discovery whale mark. International Whaling Commission Report 21:106–108.

CLARKE, R. D. 1972. The effect of toe clipping on survival in Fowler's toad (*Bufo woodhousei fowleri*). Copeia 1972:182–185.

CLAUSEN, B., P. HJORT, H. STRANDGAARD, AND P. L. SOERENSEN. 1984. Immobilization and tagging of muskoxen (*Ovibos moschatus*) in Jameson Land, northeastern Greenland. Journal of Wildlife Disease 20:141–145.

CLAYTON, D. H., C. L. HARTLEY, AND M. GOCHFELD. 1978. Two optical tracking devices for nocturnal field studies of birds. Proceedings of the Colonial Waterbird Group 1978:79–83.

CLINE, K. W., AND W. S. CLARK. 1981. Chesapeake Bay bald eagle banding project: 1981 report and five-year summary. National Wildlife Federation, Raptor Information Center, Washington, D.C., USA.

CLOVER, M. R. 1954. A portable deer trap and catch-net. California Fish and Game 40:367–373.

COCKRUM, E. L. 1969. Migration of the guano bat, *Tadarida brasiliensis*. University of Kansas Museum of Natural History, Miscellaneous Publications 51:303–336.

COHEN, R. 1969. Color-banded house finches. Eastern Bird Banding Association News 32:81–82.

COLCLOUGH, J. H., AND G. J. B. ROSS. 1987. Colour band loss in cape gannets. Safring News 16:35–37.

CONANT, R. 1948. Regeneration of clipped subcaudal scales in a pilot black snake. Natural History Miscellaneous 13:1–2.

CONNER, M. C. 1982. Determination of bobcat (*Lynx rufus*) and raccoon (*Procyon lotor*) population abundance by radioisotope tagging. Thesis. University of Florida, Gainesville, USA.

———, AND R. F. LABISKY. 1985. Evaluation of radioisotope tagging for estimating abundance of raccoon populations. Journal of Wildlife Management 49:326–332.

COOLEY, M. E. 1948. Improved toe-tag for marking fox squirrels. Journal of Wildlife Management 12:213.

COOPER, J., AND P. D. MORANT. 1981. The design of stainless steel flipper bands for penguins. The Ostrich 52:119–123.

COPPINGER, R. P., AND B. C. WENTWORTH. 1966. Identification of experimental birds with the aid of feather autografts. Bird-Banding 37:

203–205.

COWAN, D. P., J. A. VAUGHAN, AND W. G. CHRISTER. 1987. Bait consumption by the European rabbit in southern England. Journal of Wildlife Management 51:386–392.

———, ———, K. J. PROUT, AND W. G. CHRISTER. 1984. Markers for measuring bait consumption by the European wild rabbit. Journal of Wildlife Management 48:1403–1409.

CRABTREE, R. L., F. G. BURTON, T. R. GARLAND, D. A. CATALDO, AND W. H. RICKARD. 1989. Slow-release radioisotope implants as individual markers for carnivores. Journal of Wildlife Management 53:949–954.

CRAIGHEAD, J. J., AND D. S. STOCKSTAD. 1956. A colored neckband for marking birds. Journal of Wildlife Management 20:331–332.

———, AND ———. 1960. Color marker for big game. Journal of Wildlife Management 24:435–438.

———, M. G. HORNOCKER, M. W. SHOESMITH, AND R. I. ELLIS. 1969. A marking technique for elk. Journal of Wildlife Management 33:906–909.

CRAVEN, S. R. 1979. Some problems with Canada goose neckbands. Wildlife Society Bulletin 7:268–273.

CRIER, J. K. 1970. Tetracyclines as a fluorescent marker in bones and teeth of rodents. Journal of Wildlife Management 34:829–834.

CRISTOL, D. A., C. S. CHIU, S. M. PECKHAM, AND J. F. STOLL. 1992. Color bands do not affect dominance status in captive flocks of wintering dark-eyed juncos. Condor 94:537–539.

CUMMINGS, J. L. 1987. Nylon fasteners for attaching leg and wing tags to blackbirds. Journal of Field Ornithology 58:265–269.

CUMMINS, C. P., AND M. J. S. SWAN. 2000. Long-term survival and growth of free-living great crested newts (*Triturus cristatus*) pit-tagged at metamorphosis. Herpetological Journal 10:177–182.

CURTIS, P. D., C. E. BRAUN, AND R. A. RYDER. 1983. Wing markers: visibility, wear, and effects on survival of band-tailed pigeons. Journal of Field Ornithology 54:381–386.

CUTHBERT, F. J., AND W. E. SOUTHERN. 1975. A method for marking young gulls for individual identification. Bird-Banding 46:252–253.

DAAN, S. 1969. Frequency of displacements as a measure of activity of hibernating bats. Lynx 10:13–18.

DAUGHERTY, C. H. 1976. Freeze-branding as a technique for marking anurans. Copeia 1976:836–838.

DAVEY, C. C., AND P. J. FULLAGAR. 1985. Nasal saddles for Pacific black duck *Anas superciliosa* and austral teal. Corella 9:123–124.

———, ———, AND C. KOGON. 1980. Marking rabbits for individual identification and a use for betalights. Journal of Wildlife Management 44:494–497.

DAVIS, R. A. 1963a. Feral coypus in Britain. Proceedings of the Association of Applied Biologists, Great Britain 51:345–348.

DAVIS, T. M., AND K. OVASKA. 2001. Individual recognition of amphibians: effects of toe clipping and fluorescent tagging on the salamander *Plethodon vehiculum*. Journal of Herpetology 35:217–225.

DAVIS, JR., W., AND G. SARTOR. 1975. A method of observing movements of aquatic turtles. Herpetological Review 6:13–14.

DAVIS, W. H. 1963b. Anodizing bat bands. Bat Banding News 4:12–13.

DAY, G. I. 1973. Marking devices for big game animals. Arizona Game and Fish Department Research Abstracts 8:1–7.

DEAVERS, D. R. 1972. Water and electrolyte metabolism in the arenicolous lizard *Uma notata notata*. Copeia 1972:109–122.

DE LA MARE, W. K. 1985. Some evidence for mark shedding with discovery whale marks. International Whaling Commission Report 35:477–486.

DELL, J. 1957. Toe clipping varying hares for track identification. New York Fish and Game Journal 4:61–68.

DELONG, T. R. 1982. Effect of ambient conditions on nocturnal nest behavior in long-eared owls. Thesis. Brigham Young University, Provo, Utah, USA.

DICKMAN, C. R. 1988. Detection of physical contact interactions among free-living mammals. Journal of Mammalogy 69:865–868.

———, D. H. KING, D. C. D. HAPPOLD, AND M. J. HOWELL. 1983. Identification of the filial relationships of free-living small mammals by [35]sulfur. Australian Journal of Zoology 31:467–474.

DICKSON, J. G., R. N. CONNER, AND J. H. WILLIAMSON. 1982. An evaluation of techniques for marking cardinals. Journal of Field Ornithology 53:420–421.

DODD, JR., C. K. 1993. The effects of toe clipping on sprint performance of the lizard *Cnemidophorus sexlineatus*. Journal of Herpetology 27:209–213.

DOLE, J. W. 1965. Summer movements of adult leopard frogs, *Rana pipiens* Schreber, in northern Michigan. Ecology 46:236–255.

———, AND P. DURANT. 1974. Movements and seasonal activity of *Atelopus oxyrhynchus* (Anura: Atelopodidae) in a Venezuelan cloud forest. Copeia 1974:230–235.

DONNELLY, M. A., C. GUYER, J. E. JUTERBOCK, AND R. A. ALFORD. 1994. Techniques for marking amphibians. Pages 277–284 in W. R. Heyer, M. A. Donnelly, R. W. McDiarmid, L. C. Hayek, and M. S. Foster, editors. Measuring and monitoring biological diversity. Standard methods for amphibians. Smithsonian Insitution Press, Washington, D.C., USA.

DOODY, J. S. 1995. A photographic mark recapture method for patterned amphibians. Herpetological Review 26:1920.

DOTY, H. A., AND R. J. GREENWOOD. 1974. Improved nasal-saddle marker for mallards. Journal of Wildlife Management 38:938–939.

DOWNING, R. L., AND C. M. MARSHALL. 1959. A new plastic tape marker for birds and mammals. Journal of Wildlife Management 23:223–224.

———, AND B. S. MCGINNES. 1969. Capturing and marking white-tailed deer fawns. Journal of Wildlife Management 33:711–714.

DUNBAR, I. K. 1959. Leg bands in cold climates. Eastern Bird Banding News 22:37.

EADIE, J. M., K. M. CHENG, AND C. R. NICHOLS. 1987. Limitations of tetracycline in tracing multiple maternity. Auk 104:330–333.

EALEY, E. H. M., AND G. M. DUNNET. 1956. Plastic collars with patterns of reflective tape for marking nocturnal mammals. Australia's Commonwealth Scientific and Industrial Research Organization, Wildlife Research 1:59–62.

ECKERT, K. L., AND S. A. ECKERT. 1989. The application of plastic tags to leatherback sea turtles, *Dermochelys eumochelys corfacea*. Herpetological Review 20:90–91.

EDMINSTER, F. C. 1938. The marking of ruffed grouse for field identification. Journal of Wildlife Management 2:55–57.

EFFORD, I. E., AND J. A. MATHIAS. 1969. A comparison of two salamander populations in Marion Lake, British Columbia. Copeia 1969:723–736.

ELBIN, S. B., AND J. BURGER. 1994. Implantable microchips for individual identification in wild and captive populations. Wildlife Society Bulletin 22:677–683.

ELLENTON, J. A., AND O. H. JOHNSTON. 1975. Oral biomarkers of calciferous tissues in carnivores. Pages 60–67 in R. E. Chambers, editor. Transactions of Eastern Coyote Workshop. Northeastern Fish and Wildlife Conference, New Haven, Connecticut, USA.

ELLIS, D. H., AND C. H. ELLIS. 1975. Color marking golden eagles with human hair dyes. Journal of Wildlife Management 39:445–447.

ELLISOR, J. E., AND W. F. HARWELL. 1969. Mobility and home range of collared peccary in southern Texas. Journal of Wildlife Management 33:425–427.

ELMES, R. 1955. Loss of rings. Bird Study 2:153.

ELY, C. R. 1990. Effects of neck bands on the behavior of wintering greater white-fronted geese. Journal of Field Ornithology 61:249–253.

EMLEN, S. T. 1968. A technique for marking anuran amphibians for behavioral studies. Herpetologica 24:172–173.

ENDERSON, J. H. 1964. A study of the prairie falcon in the central Rocky Mountain region. Auk 81:332–352.

ENVIRONMENT CANADA. 1984. North American bird banding. Environmental Conservation Service 1:1–3.

ERNST, C. H. 1971. Population dynamics and activity cycles of *Chrysemys picta* in southeastern Pennsylvania. Journal of Herpetology 5:151–160.

EVANS, C. D. 1951. A method of color marking young waterfowl. Journal of Wildlife Management 15:101–103.

EVANS, J., AND R. E. GRIFFITH, JR. 1973. A fluorescent tracer and marker for animal studies. Journal of Wildlife Management 37:73–81.

———, J. O. ELLIS, R. D. NASS, AND A. L. WARD. 1971. Techniques for capturing, handling, and marking nutria. Proceedings of the Annual Conference of the Southeastern Association of Game and Fish Commissioners 25:295–315.

EVANS, W. E., J. D. HALL, A. B. IRVINE, AND J. S. LEATHERWOOD. 1972. Methods for tagging small cetaceans. Fisheries Bulletin 70:61–65.

EVRARD, J. O. 1986. Loss of nasal saddle on mallard. Journal of Field Ornithology 57:170–171.

FAGERSTONE, K. A., AND B. E. JOHNS. 1987. Transponders as permanent identification markers for domestic ferrets, black-footed ferrets, and other wildlife. Journal of Wildlife Management 51:294–297.

FAIRLEY, J. S. 1982. Short-term effects of ringing and toe-clipping on the recapture of wood mice (*Apodemus sylvaticus*). Journal of Zoology 197:295–297.

FANKHAUSER, D. 1964. Plastic adhesive tape for color-marking birds. Journal of Wildlife Management 28:594.

FARRELL, R. K., AND S. D. JOHNSTON. 1973. Identification of laboratory animals: freeze marking. Laboratory Animal Science 23:107–110.

———, G. A. LAISNER, AND T. S. RUSSELL. 1969. An international freeze-mark animal identification system. Journal of the American Veterinary Medical Association 154:1561–1572.

FASHINGBAUER, B. A. 1962. Expanding plastic collar and aluminum collar for deer. Journal of Wildlife Management 26:211–213.

FERNER, J. W. 1979. A review of marking techniques for amphibians and reptiles. Herpetological Circular Number 9. Society for the Study of Amphibian and Reptiles, Marceline, Missouri, USA.

FISHER, M., AND A. MUTH. 1989. A technique for permanently marking lizards. Herpetological Review 20:45–46.

FISHER, P. 1999. Review of using Rhodamine B as a marker for wildlife studies. Wildlife Society Bulletin 27:318–329.

FITCH, H. S. 1987. Collecting and life-history techniques. Pages 143–164 in R. A. Seigel, J. T. Collins, and S. S. Novak, editors. Snakes: ecology and evolutionary biology. Macmillan, New York, USA.

FITZWATER, JR., W. D. 1943. Color marking of mammals, with special reference to squirrels. Journal of Wildlife Management 7:190–192.

FJETLAND, C. A. 1973. Long-term retention of plastic collars on Canada geese. Journal of Wildlife Management 37:176–178.

FOLLMANN, E. H., P. J. SAVARIE, D. G. RITTER, AND G. M. BAER. 1987. Plasma marking of arctic foxes with iophenoxic acid. Journal of Wildlife Disease 23:709–712.

FORESTER, D. C. 1977. Comments on the female reproductive cycle and philopatry by *Demognathus ochrophaeus* (Amphibia, Urodela, Plethodontidae). Journal of Herpetology 11:311–316.

FORSMAN, E. D. 1983. Methods and materials for locating and studying spotted owls. U.S. Department of Agriculture, Forest Service, General Technical Report PNW-162.

———, A. B. FRANKLIN, F. M. OLIVER, AND J. P. WARD. 1996. A color band for spotted owls. Journal of Field Ornithology 67:507–510.

FOSTER, J. B. 1966. The giraffe of Nairobi National Park: home range, sex ratios, the herd, and food. East African Wildlife Journal 4:139–148.

FOX, S. F. 1978. Natural selection on behavioral phenotypes of the lizard *Uta stansburiana*. Ecology 59:834–847.

FRANKEL, A. I., AND T. S. BASKETT. 1963. Color marking disrupts pair bonds of captive mourning doves. Journal of Wildlife Management 27:124–127.

FRAZER, N. B. 1983. Survivorship of adult female loggerhead sea turtles, *Caretta caretta*, nesting on Little Cumberland Island, Georgia, USA. Herpetologica 39:436–447.

FRENTRESS, C. 1976. "Pop" rivet fasteners for color markers. Inland Bird Banding Association News 47:3–9.

FROESE, A. D., AND G. M. BURGHARDT. 1975. A dense natural population of the common snapping turtle (*Chelydra s. serpentina*). Herpetologica 31:204–208.

FULLAGAR, P. J., AND P. A. JEWELL. 1965. Marking small rodents and the difficulties of using leg rings. Journal of Zoology 147:224–228.

FURRER, R. K. 1979. Experiences with a new back-tag for open-nesting passerines. Journal of Wildlife Management 43:245–249.

GARGETT, V. 1973. Marking black eagles in the Matopos. Honeyguide 76:26–31.

GARNETT, S. 1987. Feather-clipping: a natural technique for short-term recognition of individual birds. Corella 11:30–31.

GARSHELIS, D. L., AND L. G. VISSER. 1997. Enumerating metapopulations of wild bears with an ingested biomarker. Journal of Wildlife Management 61:466–480.

GAYMER, R. 1973. A marking method for giant tortoises and field trials in Aldabra. Journal of Zoology 169:393–401.

GEIS, A. D., AND L. H. ELBERT. 1956. Relation of the tail length of cock ring-necked pheasants to harem size. Auk 73:289.

GENTRY, R. L. 1979. Adventitious and temporary marks in pinniped studies. Pages 39–43 in L. Hobbs and P. Russell, editors. Report on the pinniped tagging workshop. Seattle, Washington, USA.

———, AND J. R. HOLT. 1982. Equipment and techniques for handling northern fur seals. U.S. Department of Commerce, National Oceanic and Atmospheric Administration, Technical Report, Special Scientific Report Fisheries 758.

———, M. H. SMITH, AND R. J. BEYERS. 1971. Use of radioactively tagged bait to study movement patterns in small mammals. Annales Zoologici Fennici. 8:17–21.

GERACI, J. R., G. J. D. SMITH, AND T. G. FRIESEN. 1986. Assessment of marking techniques for beluga whale: final report to World Wildlife Fund Canada. Department of Pathology, University of Guelph, Guelph, Ontario, Canada.

GERMANO, D. J., AND D. F. WILLIAMS. 1993. Field evaluation of using passive integrated transponders (PIT) tags to permanently mark lizards. Herpetological Review 24:54–56.

GIFFORD, C. E., AND D. R. GRIFFIN. 1960. Notes on homing and migratory behavior of bats. Ecology 41:378–381.

GIONFRIDDO, J. P., AND L. C. STODDART. 1988. Comparative recovery rates of marked coyotes. Wildlife Society Bulletin 16:310–311.

GODFREY, G. A. 1975. Home range characteristics of ruffed grouse broods in Minnesota. Journal of Wildlife Management 39:287–298.

GODFREY, JR., R. D., A. M. FEDYNICH, AND E. G. BOLEN. 1993. Fluorescent particles for marking waterfowl without capture. Wildlife Society Bulletin 21:283–288.

GOFORTH, W. R., AND T. S. BASKETT. 1965. Effects of experimental color marking on pairing of captive mourning doves. Journal of Wildlife Management 29:543–553.

GOLAY, N., AND H. DURRER. 1994. Inflammation due to toe clipping in natterjack toads (*Bufo calamita*). Amphibia-Reptilia 15:81–83.

GOODYEAR, N. C. 1989. Studying fine-scale habitat use in small mammals. Journal of Wildlife Management 53:941–946.

GOSS-CUSTARD, J. D., S. E. A. LE V. DIT DURELL, H. P. SITTERS, AND R. SWINFEN. 1982. Age-structure and survival of a wintering population of oystercatchers. Bird Study 29:83–98.

GRAHAM, T. E. 1986. A warning against the use of Petersen disc tags in turtle studies. Herpetological Review 17:42–43.

GRAHAM, W. J., AND H. W. AMBROSE, III. 1967. A technique for continuously locating small mammals in field enclosures. Journal of Mammalogy 48:639–642.

GREENWOOD, R. J. 1975. An attempt to freeze-brand mallard ducklings. Bird-Banding 46:204–206.

———. 1977. Evaluation of a nasal marker for ducks. Journal of Wildlife Management 41:582–585.

———, AND W. C. BAIR. 1974. Ice on waterfowl markers. Wildlife Society Bulletin 2:130–134.

GRIBEN, M. R., H. R. JOHNSON, B. B. GALLUCCI, AND V. F. GALLUCCI. 1984. A new method to mark pinnipeds as applied to the northern fur seal. Journal of Wildlife Management 48:945–949.

GRICE, D., AND J. P. ROGERS. 1965. The wood duck in Massachusetts. Final Report, Federal Aid Project W-19-R. Massachusetts Division of Fish and Game, Amherst, USA.

GRIESEMER, S. J., M. O. HALE, U. ROZE, AND T. K. FULLER. 1999. Capturing and marking adult North American porcupines. Wildlife Society Bulletin 27:310–313.

GRIFFIN, D. R. 1934. Marking bats. Journal of Mammalogy 15:

202–207.

———. 1952. Radioactive tagging of animals under natural conditions. Ecology 33:329–335.

GRIZIMEK, B. 1990. Grzimek's encyclopedia of mammals. McGraw-Hill, New York, USA.

GRUBB, J. C. 1970. Orientation in post-reproductive Mexican toads, *Bufo valliceps*. Copeia 1970:674–680.

GRUELL, G. E., AND N. J. PAPEZ. 1963. Movements of mule deer in northeastern Nevada. Journal of Wildlife Management 27:414–422.

GUARINO, J. L. 1968. Evaluation of a colored leg tag for starlings and blackbirds. Bird-Banding 39:6–13.

GULLION, G. W. 1951. A marker for waterfowl. Journal of Wildlife Management 15:222–223.

———. 1965a. Another comment on the color-banding of birds. Journal of Wildlife Management 29:401.

———. 1965b. Improvements in methods for trapping and marking ruffed grouse. Journal of Wildlife Management 29:109–116.

———, R. L. ENG, AND J. J. KUPA. 1962. Three methods for individually marking ruffed grouse. Journal of Wildlife Management 26:404–407.

GUTTMAN, S. I., AND W. CREASEY. 1973. Staining as a technique for marking tadpoles. Journal of Herpetology 7:388.

HADOW, H. H. 1972. Freeze-branding: a permanent marking technique for pigmented mammals. Journal of Wildlife Management 36:645–649.

HAGAN, J. M., AND J. M. REED. 1988. Red color bands reduce fledging success in red-cockaded woodpeckers. Auk 105:498–503.

HAGLER, J. R., AND C. G. JACKSON. 2001. Methods for marking insects: current techniques and future prospects. Annual Review of Entomology 46:511–543.

HAGSTRÖM, T. 1973. Identification of newt specimens (*Urodela, Triturus*) by recording the belly pattern and a description of photographic equipment for such registration. British Journal of Herpetology 4:321–326.

HALL, R. J., AND D. P. STAFFORD. 1972. Studies in the life history of Wehrle's salamander, *Plethondon wehrlei*. Herpetologica 28:300–309.

HAMERSTROM, F. 1942. Dominance in winter flocks of chickadees. Wilson Bulletin 54:32–42.

HAMERSTROM, JR., F. N., AND O. E. MATTSON. 1964. A numbered, metal color-band for game birds. Journal of Wildlife Management 28:850–852.

HANDEL, C. M., AND R. E. GILL, JR. 1983. Yellow birds stand out in a crowd. North American Bird Bander 8:6–9.

HANKS, J. 1969. Techniques for marking large African mammals. Puku 5:65–86.

HANSEN, C. G. 1964. A dye-spraying device for marking desert bighorn sheep. Journal of Wildlife Management 28:584–587.

HARAMIS, G. M., AND A. D. NICE. 1980. An improved web-tagging technique for waterfowl. Journal of Wildlife Management 44:898–899.

———, W. G. ALLISTON, AND M. E. RICHMOND. 1983. Dump nesting in the wood duck traced by tetracycline. Auk 100:729–730.

HARPER, J. A., AND W. C. LIGHTFOOT. 1966. Tagging devices for Roosevelt elk and mule deer. Journal of Wildlife Management 30:461–466.

HARPER, S. J., AND G. O. BATZLI. 1996. Monitoring use of runways by voles with passive integrated transponders. Journal of Mammalogy 77:364–369.

HART, A., AND A. D. M. HART. 1987. Patagial tags for herring gulls: improved durability. Journal of Ringing and Migration 8:19–26.

HATCH, J. J., AND I. C. T. NISBET. 1983a. Band wear and band loss in common terns. Journal of Field Ornithology 54:1–16.

———, AND ———. 1983b. Band wear in Arctic terns. Journal of Field Ornithology, 54:91.

HATFIELD, J. S., P. F. R. HENRY, G. H. OLSEN, M. M. PAUL, AND R. S. HAMMERSCHLAG. 2001. Failure of tetracycline as a biomarker in batch-marking juvenile frogs. Journal of Wildlife Diseases 37:318–323.

HAVELKA, P. 1983. Registration and marking of captive birds of prey.

International Zoological Yearbook 23:125–132.

HAWKINS, L. L., AND S. G. SIMPSON. 1985. Neckband – a handicap in an aggressive encounter between tundra swans. Journal of Field Ornithology 56:182–184.

HAWKINS, R. E., W. D. KLIMSTRA, G. FOOKS, AND J. DAVIS. 1967. Improved collar for white-tailed deer. Journal of Wildlife Management 31:356-359.

HAYWARD, G. D. 1987. Betalights: an aid in the nocturnal study of owl foraging habitat and behavior. Journal of Raptor Research 21:98–102.

HAYWARD, JR., J. L. 1982. A simple egg-marking technique. Journal of Field Ornithology 53:173.

HEALY, W. R. 1974. Population consequences of alternative life histories in *Notophthalmus v. viridescens*. Copeia 1974:221–229.

———. 1975. Terrestrial activity and home range in efts of *Notophthalmus viridescens*. American Midland Naturalist 93:131–138.

HEATWOLE, H. 1961. Inhibition of digital regeneration in salamanders and its use in marking individuals for field studies. Ecology 42:593–594.

HEILBRUN, R. D., N. J. SILVY, M. E. TEWES, AND M. J. PETERSON. 2003. Using automatically triggered cameras to individually identify bobcats. Wildlife Society Bulletin 31:748–755.

HELM, L. G. 1955. Plastic collars for marking geese. Journal of Wildlife Management 19:316–317.

HENCKEL, R. E. 1976. Turkey vulture banding problem. North American Bird Bander 1:126.

HENDERSON, J. R., AND T. C. JOHANOS. 1988. Effects of tagging on weaned Hawaiian monk seal pups. Wildlife Society Bulletin 16:312–217.

HENDERSON, R. W. 1974. Aspects of the ecology of the juvenile common iguana (*Iguana iguana*). Herpetologica 30:327–332.

HENDRICKSON, J. R. 1954. Ecology and systematics of salamanders of the genus *Batrochoseps*. University of California Publications in Zoology 54:1–46.

HENLEY, G. B. 1981. A new technique for recognition of snakes. Herpetological Review 12:56.

HENNY, C. J., AND K. P. BURNHAM. 1976. A reward band study of mallards to estimate band reporting rates. Journal of Wildlife Management 40:1–14.

HERO, J. 1989. A simple code for toe clipping anurans. Herpetological Review 20:66–67.

HERREID, II, C. F., AND S. KINNEY. 1966. Survival of Alaskan wood frog (*Rana sylvatica*) larvae. Ecology 47:1039–1041.

HERRIGES, JR., J. D., E. T. THORNE, AND S. L. ANDERSON. 1991. Vaccination to control brucellosis in free-ranging elk on western Wyoming feed grounds. Pages 107–112 *in* R. D. Brown, editor. The biology of deer. Springer-Verlag, Inc., New York, USA.

———, ———, AND H. A. DAWSON. 1989. Vaccination of elk in Wyoming with reduced dose of strain 19 *Brucella*: controlled studies and ballistic implant field trials. Proceedings of the Annual Meeting of the United States Animal Health Association 93:640–655.

HESTER, A. E. 1963. A plastic wing tag for individual identification of passerine birds. Bird-Banding 34:213–217.

HEUSMANN, H. W., R. G. BURRELL, AND R. BELLVILLE. 1978. Automatic short-term color marker for nesting wood ducks. Journal of Wildlife Management 42:429–432.

HEUSSNER, J. C., A. I. FLOWERS, J. D. WILLIAMS, AND N. J. SILVY. 1978. Estimating dog and cat populations in an urban area. Animal Regulation Studies 1:203–212.

HEWITT, O. H., AND P. J. AUSTIN-SMITH. 1966. A simple wing tag for field-marking birds. Journal of Wildlife Management 30:625–627.

HEWSON, R. 1961. Collars for marking mountain hares. Journal of Wildlife Management 25:329–331.

HILLIS, R. E., AND E. D. BELLIS. 1971. Some aspects of the ecology of the hellbender, *Cryptobranchus alleganiensis alleganiensis*. Journal of Herpetology 5:121–126.

HIRTH, H. F. 1966. Weight changes and mortality of three species of snakes during hibernation. Herpetologica 22:8–12.

HOBBS, L., AND P. RUSSELL. 1979. Report on the pinniped tagging workshop. Seattle, Washington, USA.

HOFFMAN, R. H. 1985. An evaluation of banding sandhill cranes with colored leg bands. North American Bird Bander 10:46–49.

HÖLZENBEIN, S. 1992. Expandable PVC collar for marking and transmitter support. Journal of Wildlife Management 56:473–476.

HOMESTEAD, R., B. BECK, AND D. E. SERGEANT. 1972. A portable, instantaneous branding device for permanent identification of wildlife. Journal of Wildlife Management 36:947–949.

HONMA, M., S. IWAKI, A. KAST, AND H. KREUZER. 1986. Experiences with the identification of small rodents. Experimental Animal 35: 347–352.

HOOPER, J. H. D. 1983. The study of horseshoe bats in Devon caves: a review of progress 1947–1982. Studies in Speleology 4:59–70.

HOVORKA, M. D., C. S. MARKS, AND E. MULLER. 1996. An improved chemiluminescent tag for bats. Wildlife Society Bulletin 24: 709–712.

HOWE, M. A. 1980. Problems with wing tags: evidence of harm to willets. Journal of Field Ornithology 51:72–73.

HUBERT, JR., G. F., G. L. STORM, R. L. PHILLIPS, AND R. D. ANDREWS. 1976. Ear tag loss in red foxes. Journal of Wildlife Management 40: 164–167.

HUDNALL, J. A. 1982. New methods for measuring and tagging snakes. Herpetological Review 13:97–98.

HUEY, R. B., A. E. DUNHAM, K. L. OVERALL, AND R. A. NEWMAN. 1990. Variation in locomotor performance in demographically known populations of the lizard *Scleoporus merriami*. Physiological Zoology 63:845–872.

HUEY, W. S. 1965. Sight records of color-marked sandhill cranes. Auk 82:640–643.

HURST, J. L. 1988. A system for the individual recognition of small rodents at a distance, used in free-living and enclosed populations of house mice. Journal of Zoology 215:363–367.

IDSTROM, J. M., AND J. P. LINDMEIER. 1956. Some tests of the rubber styrene neck bands for marking waterfowl. Minnesota Department of Conservation, Quarterly Program Report of Wildlife Research 16: 134–137.

IMMELMANN, K., J. P. HAILMAN, J. R. BAYLIS, D. THISSEN, E. MARTIN, AND N. BURLEY. 1982. Reputed band attractiveness and sex manipulation in zebra finches. Science 215:422–424.

IRELAND, P. H. 1973. Marking larval salamanders with fluorescent pigments. Southwestern Naturalist 18:252–253.

———. 1991. A simplified fluorescent marking technique for identification of terrestrial salamanders. Herpetological Review 22:21–22.

IRVINE, A. B., AND M. D. SCOTT. 1984. Development and use of marking techniques to study manatees in Florida. Florida Scientist 47:12–26.

———, R. S. WELLS, AND M. D. SCOTT. 1982. An evaluation of techniques for tagging small odontocete cetaceans. Fisheries Bulletin 80: 135–143.

JACKSON, J. J. 1982. Effect of wing tags on renesting interval in red-winged blackbirds. Journal of Wildlife Management 46:1077–1079.

JACOBSON, H. A., J. C. KROLL, R. W. BROWNING, B. H. KOERTH, AND M. H. CONWAY. 1997. Infrared-triggered cameras for censusing white-tailed deer. Wildlife Society Bulletin 25:547–556.

JAMESON, D. L. 1957. Population structure and homing responses in the Pacific tree frog. Copeia 1957:221–228.

JEMISON, S. C., L. A. BISHOP, P. G. MAY, AND T. M. FARRELL. 1995. The impact of PIT-tags on growth and movement of the rattlesnake, *Sistrurus miliarius*. Journal of Herpetology 29:129–132.

JENNINGS, M. L., D. N. DAVID, AND K. M. PORTIER. 1991. Effect of marking techniques on growth and survivorship of hatchling alligators. Wildlife Society Bulletin 19:204–207.

JENSSEN, T. A. 1970. The ethoecology of *Anolis nebulosus* (Sauria, Iguanidae). Journal of Herpetology 4:1–38.

JOHANNINGSMEIER, A. G., AND C. J. GOODNIGHT. 1962. Use of iodine-131 to measure movements of small animals. Science 138:147–148.

JOHNS, B. E., AND H. P. PAN. 1981. Analytical techniques for fluorescent chemicals used as systemic or external wildlife markers. American Society for Testing Materials, Vertebrate Pest Control Management Materials 3:86–93.

———, AND R. D. THOMPSON. 1979. Acute toxicant identification in whole bodies and baits without chemical analysis. Pages 80–88 *in* E. E. Kenaga, editor. Avian and mammalian wildlife toxicology. American Society for Testing Materials, Special Technical Publication 693.

JOHNSON, A. M. 1979. Factors contributing to difficulties in the analysis of mark-recapture data. Pages 27–29 *in* L. Hobbs and P. Russell, editors. Report on the pinniped tagging workshop. Seattle, Washington, USA.

JOHNSON, J. J., L. A. WINDBERG, C. A. FURCOLOW, R. M. ENGEMAN, AND M. ROETTO. 1998. Chlorinated benzenes as physiological markers for coyotes. Journal of Wildlife Management 62:410–421.

JOHNSON, K. G., AND M. R. PELTON. 1980. Marking techniques for black bears. Proceedings of the Annual Conference of the Southeastern Association of Fish and Wildlife Agencies 34:557–562.

JOHNSON, P. A., B. W. JOHNSON, AND L. T. TAYLOR. 1981. Interisland movement of a young Hawaiian monk seal between Laysan Island and Maro Reef. Elepaio 41:113–114.

JOHNSON, S. R., J. O. SCHIECK, AND G. F. SEARING. 1995. Neck band loss rates for lesser snow geese. Journal of Wildlife Management 59: 747–752.

JOHNSON, W. C. 2001. A new individual marking technique: positional hair clipping. Southwestern Naturalist 46:126–129.

JONES, G. F. 1950. Observations of color-dyed pheasants. Journal of Wildlife Management 14:81–82

JONES, S. M., AND G. W. FERGUSON. 1980. The effect of paint marking on mortality in a Texas population of *Sceloporus undulates*. Copeia 1980:850–854.

JONKEL, C. J., D. R. GRAY, AND B. HUBERT. 1975. Immobilizing and marking wild muskoxen in Arctic Canada. Journal of Wildlife Management 39:112–117.

JORDAN, P. A. 1958. Marking deer with bells. California Fish and Game 44:183–189.

JOYNER, D. E. 1975. Nest parasitism and brood-related behavior of the ruddy duck *(Oxyura jamaicensis rubida)*. Thesis. University of Nebraska, Lincoln, USA.

JUDD, F. W. 1975. Activity and thermal ecology of the keeled earless lizard, *Holbrookia propinqua*. Herpetologica 31:137–150.

KACZYNSKI, C. F., AND W. H. KIEL, JR. 1963. Band loss by nestling mourning doves. Journal of Wildlife Management 27:271–279.

KADLEC, J. A. 1975. Recovery rates and loss of aluminum, titanium, and incoloy bands on herring gulls. Bird-Banding 46:230–235.

KAPLAN, H. M. 1958. Marking and banding frogs and turtles. Herpetologica 14:131–132.

KARANTH, K. U. 1995. Estimating tiger populations from camera-trap data using capture-recapture models. Biological Conservation 71: 333–338.

———, AND J. D. NICHOLS. 1998. Estimation of tiger densities in India using photographic captures and recaptures. Ecology 79:2852–2862.

KARLSTROM, E. L. 1957. The use of Co (60) as a tag for recovering amphibians in the field. Ecology 38:187–195.

KASAMATSU, F., S. NISHIWAKI, AND M. SATO. 1986. Results of the test firing of improved .410 streamer marks, February 1985. International Whaling Commission Report 36:201–204.

KAYE, S. V. 1960. Gold-198 wires used to study movements of small mammals. Science 131:824.

KECK, M. B. 1994. Test for detrimental effects of pit tags on neonatal snakes. Copeia 1994:226–228.

KEEN, R., AND H. B. HITCHCOCK. 1980. Survival and longevity of the little brown bat *(Myotis lucifugus)* in southeastern Ontario. Journal of Mammalogy 61:1–7.

KEISTER, JR., G. P., C. E. TRAINER, AND M. J. WILLIS. 1988. A self-adjusting collar for young ungulates. Wildlife Society Bulletin 16: 321–323.

KEITH, L. B., E. C. MESLOW, AND O. J. RONGSTAD. 1968. Techniques for snowshoe hare population studies. Journal of Wildlife Management 32:801–812.

KELLY, M. J. 2001. Computer-aided photograph matching in studies using individual identification: an example from Serengeti cheetahs. Journal of Mammalogy 82:440–449.

KENWARD, R. E., R. H. PFEFFER, M. A. AL-BOWARDI, N. C. FOX, K. E. RIDDLE, E. A. BRAGIN, A. LEVIN, S. S. WALLS, AND K. H. HODDER. 2001. Setting harness sizes and other marking techniques for a falcon with strong sexual dimorphism. Journal of Field Ornithology 72:244–257.

KESSLER, F. W. 1964. Avian predation on pheasants wearing differently colored plastic markers. Ohio Journal of Science 64:401–402.

KINDEL, F. 1960. Use of dyes to mark ruminant feces. Journal of Wildlife Management 24:429.

KNIGHT, R. R. 1966. Effectiveness of neckbands for marking elk. Journal of Wildlife Management 30:845–846.

KNOWLTON, F. F., E. D. MICHAEL, AND W. C. GLAZENER. 1964. A marking technique for field recognition of individual turkeys and deer. Journal of Wildlife Management 28:167–170.

KOCHERT, M. N. 1973. Evaluation of a vinyl wing-marker for raptors. Raptor Research News 7:117–118.

———, K. STEENHOF, AND M. Q. MORITSCH. 1983. Evaluation of patagial markers for raptors and ravens. Wildlife Society Bulletin 11:271–281.

KOERNER, J. W., T. A. BOOKHOUT, AND K. E. BEDNARIK. 1974. Movements of Canada geese color-marked near southwestern Lake Erie. Journal of Wildlife Management 38:275–289.

KOOB, M. D. 1981. Detrimental effects of nasal saddles on male ruddy ducks. Journal of Field Ornithology 52:140–143.

KORN, H. 1987. Effects of live-trapping and toe-clipping on body weight of European and African rodent species. Oecologia 71:597–600.

KOZICKY, E. L., AND H. G. WESTON, JR. 1952. A marking technique for ring-necked pheasants. Journal of Wildlife Management 16:223.

KOZLIK, F. M., A. W. MILLER, AND W. C. RIENECKER. 1959. Color-marking white geese for determining migration routes. California Fish and Game 45:69–82.

KRUUK, H. 1978. Spatial organization and territorial behavior of the European badger *Meles meles*. Journal of Zoology 184:1–19.

———, M. GORMAN, AND T. PARRISH. 1980. The use of 65Zn for estimating populations of carnivores. Oikos 34:206–208.

KUMAR, R. K. 1979. Toe-clipping procedure for individual identification of rodents. Laboratory Animal Science 29:679–680.

LABISKY, R. F., AND R. D. LORD, JR. 1959. A flexible, plastic eartag for rabbits. Journal of Wildlife Management 23:363–365.

———, AND S. H. MANN. 1962. Backtag markers for pheasants. Journal of Wildlife Management 26:393–399.

LARSEN, T. 1971. Capturing, handling, and marking polar bears in Svalbard. Journal of Wildlife Management 35:27–36.

LARSON, G. E., P. J. SAVARIE, AND I. OKUNO. 1981. Iophenoxic acid and mirex for marking wild, bait-consuming animals. Journal of Wildlife Management 45:1073–1077.

LAVAL, R. K., R. L. CLAWSON, M. L. LAVAL, AND W. CAIRE. 1977. Foraging behavior and nocturnal activity patterns of Missouri bats, with emphasis on the endangered species *Myotis grisescens* and *Myotis sodalis*. Journal of Mammalogy 58:592–599.

LAYFIELD, J. A., D. A. GALBRAITH, AND R. J. BROOKS. 1988. A simple method to mark hatchling turtles. Herpetological Review 19:78–79.

LAZARUS, A. B., AND F. P. ROWE. 1975. Freeze-marking rodents with a pressurized refrigerant. Mammal Review 5:31–34.

LEATHERWOOD, S., D. K. CALDWELL, AND H. E. WINN. 1976. Whales, dolphins, and porpoises of the western North Atlantic-a guide to their identification. U.S. Department of Commerce, National Oceanic and Atmospheric Administration Technical Report, NMFS Special Scientific Report Fisheries 396.

LEBOULENGE-NGUYEN, P. Y., AND E. LEBOULENGE. 1986. New ear-tag for small mammals. Journal of Zoology 209:302–304.

LEBUFF, C. R., AND R. W. BEATTY. 1971. Some aspects of nesting of the loggerhead turtle, *Caretta caretta caretta* (Linne), on the Gulf Coast of Florida. Herpetologica 27:153–156.

LECLERCQ G. C., AND F. M. ROZENFELD. 2001. A permanent marking method to identify individual small rodents from birth to sexual maturity. Journal of Zoology (London) 254:203–206.

LEMEN, C. A., AND P. W. FREEMAN. 1985. Tracking mammals with fluorescent pigments: a new technique. Journal of Mammalogy 66:134–136.

LEMKAU, P. J. 1970. Movements of the box turtle, *Terrapene c. carolina* (Linnaeus), in unfamiliar territory. Copeia 1970:781–783.

LENSINK, C. J. 1968. Neckbands as an inhibitor of reproduction in black brant. Journal of Wildlife Management 32:418–420.

LENTFER, J. W. 1968. A technique for immobilizing and marking polar bears. Journal of Wildlife Management 32:317–321.

LEWKE, R. E., AND R. K. STROUD. 1974. Freeze branding as a method of marking snakes. Copeia 1974:997–1000.

LIGHTFOOT, W. C., AND V. MAW. 1963. Trapping and marking mule deer. Proceedings of the Western Association of State Game and Fish Commissioners 43:138–142.

LINDSEY, G. D. 1983. Rhodamine B: a systemic fluorescent marker for studying mountain beavers (*Aplodontia rufa*) and other animals. Northwest Scientist 57:16–21.

LINDUSKA, J. P. 1942. A new technique for marking fox squirrels. Journal of Wildlife Management 6:93–94.

LINHART, S. B., AND J. J. KENNELLY. 1967. Fluorescent bone labeling of coyotes with demethylchlortetracycline. Journal of Wildlife Management 31:317–321.

LINN, I. J. 1978. Radioactive techniques for small mammal marking. Pages 177–191 *in* B. Stonehouse, editor. Animal marking: recognition marking of animals in research. MacMillan, London, United Kingdom.

———, AND J. SHILLITO. 1960. Rings for marking very small mammals. Proceedings of the Zoological Society of London 134:489–495.

LOAFMAN, P. 1991. Identifying individual spotted salamanders by spot pattern. Herpetologcal Review 22:91–92.

LOKEMOEN, J. T., AND D. E. SHARP. 1985. Assessment of nasal marker materials and designs used on dabbling ducks. Wildlife Society Bulletin 13:53–56.

LONCKE, D. J., AND M. E. OBBARD. 1977. Tag success, dimensions, clutch size and nesting site fidelity for the snapping turtle, *Chelydra serpentina* (Reptilia, Testudines, Chelydridae) in Algonquin Park, Ontario, Canada. Journal of Herpetology 11:243–244.

LUMSDEN, H. G., V. W. MCMULLEN, AND C. L. HOPKINSON. 1977. An improvement in fabrication of large plastic leg bands. Journal of Wildlife Management 41:148–149.

MACDONALD, R. N. 1961. Injury to birds by ice-coated bands. Bird-Banding 32:59.

MACINNES, C. D., AND E. H. DUNN. 1988. Effects of neck bands on Canada geese nesting at the McConnell River. Journal of Field Ornithology 59:239–246.

———, J. P. PREVETT, AND H. A. EDNEY. 1969. A versatile collar for individual identification of geese. Journal of Wildlife Management 33:330–335.

MADISON, D. M., AND C. R. SHOOP. 1970. Homing behavior, orientation, and home range of salamanders tagged with Tantalum-182. Science 168:1484–1487.

MAHAN, C. G., R. H. YAHNER, AND L. R. STOVER. 1994. Development of remote-collaring techniques for red squirrels. Wildlife Society Bulletin 22:270–273.

MALACARNE, G., AND M. GRIFFA. 1987. A refinement of Lack's method for swift studies. Sitta 1:175–177.

MALTBY, L. S. 1977. Techniques used for the capture, handling and marking of brant in the Canadian high arctic. Canadian Wildlife Service Program Notes 72.

MARCSTROM, V., R. E. KENWARD, AND M. KARLBOM. 1989. Survival of ring-necked pheasants with backpacks, necklaces, and leg bands. Journal of Wildlife Management 53:808–810.

MARION, W. R., AND J. D. SHAMIS. 1977. An annotated bibliography of bird marking techniques. Bird-Banding 48:42–61.

MARTIN, F. R. 1963. Colored vinylite bands for waterfowl. Journal of Wildlife Management 27:288–290.

MARTOF, B. S. 1953. Territoriality in the green frog, *Rana clamitans*. Ecology 34:165–174.

MCCABE, R. A., AND G. A. LEPAGE. 1958. Identifying progeny from pheasant hens given radioactive calcium (Ca45). Journal of Wildlife

Management 22:134–141.

McCracken, G. F. 1984. Communal nursing in Mexican free-tailed bat maternity colonies. Science 223:1090–1091.

Medica, P. A., R. B. Bury, and F. B. Turner. 1975. Growth of the desert tortoise (*Gopherus agassizi*) in Nevada. Copeia 1975:639- 643.

Melchior, H. R., and F. A. Iwen. 1965. Trapping, restraining, and marking arctic ground squirrels for behavioral observations. Journal of Wildlife Management 29:671–678.

Menu, S., G. Gauthier, and A. Reed. 2001. Survival of juvenile greater snow geese immediately after banding. Journal of Field Ornithology 72:282–290.

———, J. B. Hestbeck, G. Gauthier, and A. Reed. 2000. Effects of neck bands on survival of greater snow geese. Journal of Wildlife Management 64:544–552.

Metz, K. J., and P. J. Weatherhead. 1993. An experimental test of the contrasting-color hypothesis of red-band effects in red-winged blackbirds. Condor 95:395–400.

Meyers, J. M. 1994. Leg bands cause injuries to parakeets and parrots. North American Bird Bander 19:133–136.

Mikesic, D. G., and L. C. Drickamer. 1992. Effects of radiotransmitters and fluorescent powers on activity of wild house mice (*Mus musculus*). Journal of Mammalogy 73:663–667.

Miller, D. J. 1979. Sea otter capture and tagging in California. Pages 11–12 in L. Hobbs and P. Russell, editors. Report on the pinniped tagging workshop. Seattle, Washington, USA.

Miller, D. R. 1964. Colored plastic ear markers for beavers. Journal of Wildlife Management 28: 859–861.

———, and J. D. Robertson. 1967. Results of tagging caribou at Little Duck Lake, Manitoba. Journal of Wildlife Management 31:150–159.

Miller, D. S., J. Berglund, and M. Jay. 1983. Freeze-mark techniques applied to mammals at the Santa Barbara Zoo. Zoo Biology 2: 143–148.

Miller, L. S. 1957. Tracing vole movements by radioactive excretory products. Ecology 38:132–136.

Mills, J. A. 1972. A difference in band loss from male and female red-billed gulls, *Larus novaehollandiae scopulinus*. Ibis 114:252–255.

Minnich, J. E., and V. H. Shoemaker. 1970. Diet, behavior and water turnover in the desert iguana, *Dipsosaurus dorsalis*. American Midland Naturalist 84:496–509.

Mitchell, E., and V. M. Kozicki. 1975. Prototype visual mark for large whales modified from "Discovery" tag. International Whaling Commission Report 25:236–239.

Miyashita, T., and R. A. Rowlett. 1985. Test-firing of .410 streamer marks. International Whaling Commission Report 35:305–308.

Moffitt, J. 1942. Apparatus for marking wild animals with colored dyes. Journal of Wildlife Management 6:312–318.

Mohr, C. E. 1934. Marking bats for later recognition. Proceedings of the Pennsylvania Academy of Sciences 8:26–30.

Moran, S. 1985. Banding fruit bats. Israel Journal of Zoology 33: 91–93.

Morgan, D. R. 1981. Monitoring bait acceptance in brush-tailed possum populations: development of a tracer technique. New Zealand Journal of Forestry Science 11:271–277.

Morgenweck, R. O., and W. H. Marshall. 1977. Wing marker for American woodcock. Bird-Banding 48:224–227.

Morrison, D. W. 1978. Foraging ecology and energetics of the frugivorous bat *Artibeus jamaicensis*. Ecology 59:716–723.

Morrow, M. E., N. W. Atherton, and N. J. Silvy. 1987. A device for returning nestling birds to their nests. Journal of Wildlife Management 51:202–204.

Moseley, L. J., and H. C. Mueller. 1975. A device for color-marking nesting birds. Bird-Banding 46:341–342.

Mossman, A. S. 1960. A color marking technique. Journal of Wildlife Management 24:104.

Mudge, G. P., and P. N. Ferns. 1978. Durability of patagial tags on herring gulls. Journal of Ringing and Migration 2:42–45.

Mukinya, J. G. 1976. An identification method for black rhinoceros (*Diceros bicomis* Linn. 1758). East African Wildlife Journal 14: 335–338.

Mullican, T. R. 1988. Radio telemetry and fluorescent pigments: a comparison of techniques. Journal of Wildlife Management 52: 627–631.

Murphy, M. T. 1981. Growth and aging of nestling eastern kingbirds and eastern phoebes. Journal of Field Ornithology 52:309–316.

Murray, D. L., and M. R. Fuller. 2000. A critical review of the effects of marking on the biology of vertebrates. Pages 15–64 in L. Boitani and T. K. Fuller, editors. Research techniques in animal ecology. Columbia University, New York, USA.

Nace, G. W., and E. K. Manders. 1982. Marking individual amphibians. Journal of Herpetology 16:309–311.

Nass, R. D., and G. A. Hood. 1969. Time-specific tracer to indicate bait acceptance by small mammals. Journal of Wildlife Management 33: 584–588.

Neal, W. 1964. Extra white feather makes bird important. Inland Bird Banding Association News 36:69–71.

Nellis, D. W., J. H. Jenkins, and A. D. Marshall. 1967. Radioactive zinc as a feces tag in rabbits, foxes, and bobcats. Proceedings of the Annual Conference of the Southeastern Association of Game and Fish Commissioners 21:205–207.

Nelson, L. J., D. R. Anderson, and K. P. Burnham. 1980. The effect of band loss on estimates of annual survival. Journal of Field Ornithology 51:30–38.

Nelson, R. L., and R. L. Linder. 1972. Percentage of raccoons and skunks reached by egg baits. Journal of Wildlife Management 36: 1327–1329.

Nesbitt, S. A. 1979. An evaluation of four wildlife marking materials. Bird-Banding 50:159.

New, J. G. 1958. Dyes for studying the movements of small mammals. Journal of Mammalogy 39: 416–429.

———. 1959. Additional uses of dyes for studying the movements of small mammals. Journal of Wildlife Management 23:348–351.

Newsom, J. D., and J. S. Sullivan, Jr. 1968. Cryo-branding-a marking technique for white-tailed deer. Proceedings of the Annual Conference of the Southeastern Association of Game and Fish Commissioners 22:128–133.

Nichols, J. D., R. J. Blohn, R. E. Reynolds, R. E. Trost, J. E. Hines, and J. P. Bladen. 1991. Band reporting rates for mallards with reward bands of different dollar values. Journal of Wildlife Management 55:119–126.

Nickerson, M. A., and C. E. Mays. 1973. A study of the Ozark hellbender, *Cryptobranchus alleganiensis bishopi*. Ecology 54:1164–1165.

Nietfeld, M. T., M. W. Barrett, and N. Silvy. 1994. Wildlife marking techniques. Pages 140–168 in T. A. Bookhout, editor. Research and management techniques for wildlife and habitats. Fifth edition. The Wildlife Society, Bethesda, Maryland, USA.

Nisbet, I. C. T., and J. J. Hatch. 1983. Band wear and band loss in roseate terns. Journal of Field Ornithology 54:90.

———, and ———. 1985. Influence of band size on rates of band loss by common terns. Journal of Field Ornithology 56:178–181.

Nishikawa, K. C., and P. M. Service. 1988. A fluorescent marking technique for individual recognition of terrestrial salamanders. Journal of Herpetology 22:351–353.

Norris, K. S., and K. W. Pryor. 1970. A tagging method for small cetaceans. Journal of Mammalogy 51:609–610.

O'Brien, G. P., H. K. Smith, and J. R. Meyer. 1965. An activity study of a radioisotope-tagged lizard, *Sceloporus undulates hyacinthinus* (Sauria, Iguanidae). Southwestern Naturalist 10:179–187.

Ogilvie, M. A. 1972. Large numbered leg bands for individual identification of swans. Journal of Wildlife Management 36:1261–1265.

Olsen, J., T. Billett, and P. Olsen. 1982. A method for reducing illegal removal of eggs from raptor nests. The Emu 82:225.

Orser, P. N., and D. J. Shure. 1972. Effects of urbanization on the salamander *Desmognathus fuscus fuscus*. Ecology 53:1148–1154.

Ostfeld, R. S., M. C. Miller, and J. Schnurr. 1993. Ear tagging increases tick (*Ixodes dammini*) infestation rates of white-footed mice (*Peromyscus leucopus*). Journal of Mammalogy 74:651–655.

Otis, D. L., C. E. Knittle, and G. M. Linz. 1986. A method for estimating turnover in spring blackbird roosts. Journal of Wildlife

Management 50:567–571.

OTTAWAY, J. R., R. CARRICK, AND M. D. MURRAY. 1984. Evaluation of leg bands for visual identification of free-living silver gulls. Journal of Field Ornithology 55:287–308.

OWEN, L. N. 1961. Fluorescence of tetracyclines in bone tumors, normal bone and teeth. Nature 190:500–502.

OZOGA, J. J., AND R. K. CLUTE. 1988. Mortality rates of marked and unmarked fawns. Journal of Wildlife Management 52:549–551.

PANAGIS, K., AND P. E. STANDER. 1989. Marking and subsequent movement patterns of springbok lambs in the Etosha National Park, South West Africa/Namibia. Madoqua 16:71–73.

PARKER, N. C., A. E. GIORGI, R. C. HEIDINGER, D. B. JESTER, JR., E. D. PRINCE, AND G. A. WINANS. 1990. Fish-marking techniques. Symposium 7. American Fisheries Society, Bethesda, Maryland, USA.

PARKER, W. S. 1976. Population estimates, age structure, and denning habits of whipsnakes, *Masticophis t. taeniatus* in a northern Utah *Atriplex-Sarcobatus* community. Herpetologica 32:53–57.

PATON, P. W. C., AND L. PANK. 1986. A technique to mark incubating birds. Journal of Field Ornithology 57:232–233.

PATTERSON, I. J. 1978. Tags and other distant-recognition markers for birds. Pages 54–62 *in* B. Stonehouse, editor. Animal marking: recognition marking of animals in research. MacMillan, London, United Kingdom.

PAULISSEN, M. A. 1986. A technique for marking teiid lizards in the field. Herpetological Review 17:16–17.

PAULLIN, D. G., AND E. KRIDLER. 1988. Spring and fall migration of tundra swans dyed at Malheur National Wildlife Refuge, Oregon. Murrelet 69:1–9.

PAVONE, L. V., AND R. BOONSTRA. 1985. The effects of toe clipping on the survival of the meadow vole *(Microtus pennsylvanicus)*. Canadian Journal of Zoology 63:499–501.

PELTON, M. R., AND L. C. MARCUM. 1975. The potential use of radioisotopes for determining densities of black bears and other carnivores. Pages 221–236 *in* R. L. Phillips and C. Jonkel, editors. Proceedings of the 1975 Predator Symposium. Montana Forest and Conservation Experiment Station, University of Montana, Missoula, USA.

PENDLEBURY, G. B. 1972. Tagging and remote identification of rattlesnakes. Herpetologica 28:349–350.

PENDLETON, R. C. 1956. Uses of marking animals in ecological studies: labeling animals with radioisotopes. Ecology 37:686–689.

PENNY, R. L., AND W. J. L. SLADEN. 1966. The use of Teflon for banding penguins. Journal of Wildlife Management 30:847–850.

PENNYCUICK, C. J. 1978. Identification using natural markings. Pages 147–159 *in* B. Stonehouse, editor. Animal marking: recognition marking of animals in research. MacMillan, London, United Kingdom.

———, AND J. RUDNAI. 1970. A method of identifying individual lions, *Panthera leo,* with an analysis of the reliability of the identification. Journal of the Zoological Society of London 160:497–508.

PERDECK, A. C., AND R. D. WASSENAAR. 1981. Tarsus or tibia: where should a bird be ringed? Journal of Ringing and Migration 3:149–157.

PERRY, A. E., AND G. BECKETT. 1966. Skeletal damage as a result of band injury in bats. Journal of Mammalogy 47:131–132.

PFEIFER, S., F. H. WRIGHT, AND M. DONCARLOS. 1984. Freeze-branding beaver tails. Zoo Biology 3:159–162.

PHILLIPS, R. L., AND T. H. NICHOLLS. 1970. A collar for marking big game animals. U.S. Department of Agriculture, Forest Service, Research Notes NC-I03.

PHILLIPS, W. R. 1985. The use of bird bands for marking tree-dwelling bats—a preliminary appraisal. Macroderma 1:17–21.

PIENAAR, U. D., J. W. VAN NIEKERK, E. YOUNG, P. VAN WYK, AND N. FAIRALL. 1966. The use of oripavine hydrochlorine (M 99) in the drug immobilization and marking of the wild African elephant *(Loxodonta africana* Blumenbach) in the Kruger National Park. Koedoe 9:108–124.

PIGOZZI, G. 1988. Quill-marking, a method to identify crested porcupines individually. Acta Theriologica 33:138–142.

PIRKOLA, M. K., AND P. KALINAINEN. 1984. Use of neckbands in studying the movements and ecology of the bean goose *Anser fabalis.* Annales Zoologici Fennici 21:259–263.

PITCHER, K. 1979. Pinniped tagging in Alaska. Pages 3–4 *in* L. Hobbs and P. Russell, editors. Report on the pinniped tagging workshop. Seattle, Washington, USA.

PLATT, S. W. 1980. Longevity of herculite leg jess color markers on the prairie falcon *(Falco mexicanus).* Journal of Field Ornithology 51:281–282.

POUGH, H. 1966. Ecological relationships of rattlesnakes in southeastern Arizona with notes on other species. Copeia 1966:676–683.

———. 1970. A quick method for permanently marking snakes and turtles. Herpetologica 26:428–430.

POWELL, L. A., M. J. CONROY, J. E. HINES, J. D. NICHOLS, AND D. G. KREMENTZ. 2000. Simultaneous use of mark–recapture and radiotelemetry to estimate survival, movement, and capture rates. Journal of Wildlife Management 64:302–313.

PRICE, J. B. 1931. An experiment on staining California gulls. Condor 33:123.

PRITCHARD, P. C. H. 1976. Post-nesting movements of marine turtles (Cheloniidae and Dermochelyidae) tagged in the Guianas. Copeia 1976:749–754.

———. 1980. The conservation of sea turtles: practices and problems. American Zoologist 20:609–617.

PROGULSKE, D. R. 1957. A collar for identification of big game. Journal of Wildlife Management 21:251–252.

PYRAH, D. 1970. Poncho markers for game birds. Journal of Wildlife Management 34:466–467.

QUEAL, L. M., AND B. D. HLAVACHICK. 1968. A modified marking technique for young ungulates. Journal of Wildlife Management 32:628–629.

RACEY, P. A., AND S. M. SWIFT. 1985. Feeding ecology of *Pipistrellus pipistrellus* (Chiroptera: Vespertilionidae) during pregnancy and lactation. I. Foraging behavior. Journal of Animal Ecology 54:205–215.

RAFINSKI, J. N. 1977. Autotransplantation as a method for permanent marking of urodele amphibians (Amphibia, Urodela). Journal of Herpetology 11:241–242.

RANDOLPH, S. E. 1973. A tracking technique for comparing individual home ranges of small mammals. Journal of Zoology 170:509–520.

RANEY, E. C. 1940. Summer movements of the bullfrog, *Rana catesbeiana* Shaw, as determined by the jaw-tag method. American Midland Naturalist 23:733–745.

RAO, G. N., AND J. EDMONDSON. 1990. Tissue reaction to an implantable identification device in mice. Toxicological Pathology 18:412–416.

RATCLIFFE, L. M., AND P. T. BOAG. 1987. Effects of colour bands on male competition and sexual attractiveness in zebra finches, *Poephila guttata.* Canadian Journal of Zoology 65:333–338.

RAVELING, D. G. 1976. Status of giant Canada geese nesting in southeast Manitoba. Journal of Wildlife Management 40:214–226.

REAGAN, D. P. 1974. Habitat selection in the three-toed box turtle, *Terrapene carolina triunguis.* Copeia 1974:512–527.

REED, J. M., AND L. W. ORING. 1993. Banding is infrequently associated with foot loss in spotted sandpipers. Journal of Field Ornithology 64:145–148.

REED, P. C. 1953. Danger of leg mutilation from the use of metal color bands. Bird-Banding 24:65–67.

REESE, K. P. 1980. The retention of colored plastic leg bands by black-billed magpies. North American Bird Bander 5:136–137.

REINECKE, K. J., C. W. SHAIFFER, AND D. DELNICKI. 1992. Band reporting rates of mallards in the Mississippi Alluvial Valley. Journal of Wildlife Management 56:526–531.

REUTHER, R. T. 1968. Marking animals in zoos. International Zoo Yearbook 8:388–390.

RICE, T. M., AND D. H. TAYLOR. 1993. A new method for making waistbands to mark anurans. Herpetological Review 24:141–142.

RICHARDS, C. M., B. M. CARLSON, AND S. L. ROGERS. 1975. Regeneration of digits and forelimbs in the Kenyan reed frog, *Hyperolius viridiflavus ferniquei.* Journal of Morphology 146:431–446.

RICHDALE, L. E. 1951. Banding and marking penguins. Bird-Banding

22:47–54.

RICKLEFS, R. E. 1973. Tattooing nestlings for individual recognition. Bird-Banding 44:63.

RILEY, J., AND R. G. WILLIAM. 1981. A new ear-punch for small rodents. Journal of Institutional Animal Technicians 32:53–55.

RITCHISON, G. 1984. A new marking technique for birds. North American Bird Bander 9(3):8.

ROBERTSON, J. G. M. 1984. A technique for individually marking frogs in behavioral studies. Herpetological Review 15:56–57.

ROBSON, J. E. 1986. Ring "fit" on blackbreasted snake eagle. Safring News 15:56.

RODGERS, JR., J. A. 1986. A field technique for color-dyeing nestling wading birds without capture. Wildlife Society Bulletin 14:399–400.

ROHWER, S. 1977. Status signaling in Harris sparrows: some experiments in deception. Behaviour 61:107–129.

ROLLEY, R. E. 1987. Bobcat. Pages 670–681 in M. Novak, J. A. Baker, M. E. Obbard, and B. Malloch, editors. Wild furbearer management and conservation in North America. Ontario Ministry of Natural Resources, Ottawa, Canada.

ROOD, J. P., AND D. W. NELLIS. 1980. Freeze marking mongooses. Journal of Wildlife Management 44:500–502.

ROTTERMAN, L. M., AND C. MONNETT. 1984. An embryo-dyeing technique for identification through hatching. Condor 86:79–80.

ROYALL, W. C., J. L. GUARINO, AND O. E. BRAY. 1974. Effects of color on retention of leg streamers by red-winged blackbirds. Western Bird-Bander 49:64–65.

RUDGE, M. R., AND R. J. JOBLIN. 1976. Comparison of some methods of capturing and marking feral goats (Capra hircus). New Zealand Journal of Zoology 3:51–55.

RUSSELL, J. K. 1981. Patterned freeze-brands with canned freon. Journal of Wildlife Management 45:1078.

RYDER, P. L., AND J. P. RYDER. 1981. Reproductive performance of ring-billed gulls in relation to nest location. Condor 83:57–60.

SALLABERRY, A. M., AND D. J. VALENCIA. 1985. Wounds due to flipper bands on penguins. Journal of Field Ornithology 56:275–277.

SAMUEL, M. D., N. T. WEISS, D. H. RUSCH, S. R. CRAVEN, R. E. TROST, AND F. D. CASWELL. 1990. Neck-band retention for Canada geese in the Mississippi Flyway. Journal of Wildlife Management 54:612–621.

SANDERSON, G. C. 1961. Estimating opossum populations by marking young. Journal of Wildlife Management 25:20–27.

SAUNDERS, D. A. 1988. Patagial tags: do benefits outweigh the risks to the animal? Australian Wildlife Research 15:565–569.

SCHALLER, G. B. 1967. Deer and the tiger. University of Chicago, Chicago, Illinois, USA.

SCHEFFER, V. B. 1950. Experiments in the marking of seals and sea lions. U.S. Department of the Interior, Fish and Wildlife Service, Scientific Report Wildlife 4.

SCHMUTZ, J. A., AND J. A. MORSE. 2000. Effects of neck collars and radiotransmitters on survival and reproduction of emperor geese. Journal of Wildlife Management 64:231–237.

SCHNEEGAS, E. R., AND G. W. FRANKLIN. 1972. The Mineral King deer herd. California Fish and Game 58:133–140.

SCHNELL, J. H. 1968. The limiting effects of natural predation on experimental cotton rat populations. Journal of Wildlife Management 32:698–711.

SCHOOLEY, R. L., B. VAN HORNE, AND K. P. BURNHAM. 1993. Passive integrated transponders for marking free-ranging Townsend's ground squirrels. Journal of Mammalogy 74:480–484.

SCOTT, A. F., AND J. L. DOBIE. 1980. An improved design for a thread-trailing device used to study terrestrial movements of turtles. Herpetological Review 11:106–107.

SCOTT, D. K. 1978. Identification of individual Bewick's swans by bill patterns. Pages 160–168 in B. Stonehouse, editor. Animal marking: recognition marking of animals in research. MacMillan, London, United Kingdom.

SCOTT, M. P., AND T. N. TAN. 1985. A radiotracer technique for the determination of male mating success in natural populations. Behavioral Ecology and Sociobiology 17:29–33.

SEALE, D., AND M. BORAAS. 1974. A permanent mark for amphibian larvae. Herpetologica 30:160–162.

SEEL, D. C., A. G. THOMPSON, AND G. H. OWEN. 1982. A wing-tagging system for marking larger passerine birds. Bangor Occasional Papers 14:1–6.

SEGUIN, R. J., AND F. COOKE. 1983. Band loss from lesser snow geese. Journal of Wildlife Management 47:1109–1114.

———, AND ———. 1985. Web tag loss from lesser snow goose. Journal of Wildlife Management 49:420–422.

SEYDACK, A. H. W. 1984. Application of a photo-recording device in the census of larger rain-forest mammals. South African Journal of Wildlife Research 14:10–14.

SHEDDEN, C. B., P. MONAGHAN, K. ENSOR, AND N. B. METCALFE. 1985. The influence of colour-rings on recovery rates of herring and lesser black-backed gulls. Journal of Ringing and Migration 6:52–54.

SHELDON, W. G. 1949. A trapping and tagging technique for wild foxes. Journal of Wildlife Management 13:309–311.

SHERWIN, R. E., S. HAYMOND, D. STRICKLAN, AND R. OLSEN. 2002. Freeze-branding to permanently mark bats. Wildlife Society Bulletin 30:97–100.

SHERWOOD, G. A. 1966. Flexible plastic collars compared to nasal discs for marking geese. Journal of Wildlife Management 30:853–855.

SHINE, C., N. SHINE, R. SHINE, AND D. SLIP. 1988. Use of subcaudal scale anomalies as an aid in recognizing individual snakes. Herpetological Review 19:79.

SHOOP, C. R. 1971. A method for short-term marking of amphibians with 24-sodium. Herpetologica 30:160–162.

SIBLEY, C. G., AND B. L. MONROE, JR. 1990. Distribution and taxonomy of birds of the world. Yale University, New Haven, Connecticut, USA.

SIEGFRIED, W. R. 1971. Communal roosting of the cattle egret. Transactions of the Royal Society of South Africa 39:419–443.

SIGLIN, R. J. 1966. Marking mule deer with an automatic tagging device. Journal of Wildlife Management 30:631–633.

SILVY, N. J. 1975. Population density, movements, and habitat utilization of Key deer (Odocoileus virginianus clavium). Dissertation. Southern Illinois University, Carbondale, USA.

SIMMONS, N. M. 1971. An inexpensive method of marking large numbers of Dall sheep for movement studies. Transactions of the North American Wild Sheep Conference 1:116–126.

———, AND J. L. PHILLIPS. 1966. Modifications of a dye-spraying device for marking desert bighorn sheep. Journal of Wildlife Management 30:208–209.

SIMON, C. A., AND B. E. BISSINGER. 1983. Paint-marking lizards: does the color affect survivorship? Journal of Herpetology 17:184–186.

SLADEN, W. J. L. 1952. Notes on methods of marking penguins. Ibis 94:541–543.

SNELLING, J. C. 1970. Some information obtained from marking large raptors in the Kruger National Park, Republic of South Africa. Ostrich (Supplement) 8:415–427.

SOCIETY FOR THE STUDY OF AMPHIBIANS AND REPTILES. 1987. Guidelines for use of live amphibians and reptiles in field research. Journal of Herpetology (Supplement) 4.

SODERQUIST, T. R., AND C. R. DICKMAN. 1988. A technique for marking marsupial pouch young with fluorescent pigment tattoos. Australian Wildlife Research 15:561–563.

SOKOLOV, V. E. 1988. Dictionary of animal names: amphibians and reptiles. Russky Yazyk, Moscow, Russia.

SOUTHERN, L. K., AND W. E. SOUTHERN. 1983. Responses of ring-billed gulls to cannon-netting and wing-tagging. Journal of Wildlife Management 47:234–237.

———, AND ———. 1985. Some effects of wing tags on breeding ring-billed gulls. Auk 102:38–42.

SOUTHERN, W. E. 1964. Additional observations on winter bald eagle populations: including remarks on biotelemetry techniques and immature plumages. Wilson Bulletin 76:121–137.

SOWLS, L. K. 1950. Techniques for waterfowl-nesting studies. Transactions of the North American Wildlife Conference 15:478–487.

———, AND P. S. MINNAMON. 1963. Glass beads for marking home ranges of mammals. Journal of Wildlife Management 27:299–302.

SPEAR, L. 1980. Band loss from the western gull on southeast Farallon Island. Journal of Field Ornithology 51:319–328.

SPELLERBERG, I. P., AND I. PRESTT. 1978. Marking snakes. Pages 133–141 *in* B. Stonehouse, editor. Animal marking: recognition marking of animals in research. University Park Press, Baltimore, Maryland, USA.

SPENCER, R. 1978. Ringing and related durable methods of marking birds. Pages 45–53 *in* B. Stonehouse, editor. Animal marking: recognition marking of animals in research. University Park Press, Baltimore, Maryland, USA.

ST. LOUIS, V. L., J. C. BARLOW, AND J. P. SWEERTS. 1989. Toenail-clipping: a simple technique for marking individual nidicolous chicks. Journal of Field Ornithology 60:211–215.

STAMPS, J. A. 1973. Displays and social organization in female *Anolis aeneus.* Copeia 1973:264–272.

STAPP, P., J. K. YOUNG, S. VANDE WOUDE, AND B. VAN HORNE. 1994. An evaluation of the pathological effects of fluorescent power on deer mice (*Peromyscus maniculatus*). Journal of Mammalogy 75: 704–709.

STARK, M. A. 1984. A quick, easy and permanent tagging technique for rattlesnakes. Herpetological Review 15:110.

STEBBINGS, R. E. 1978. Marking bats. Pages 81–94 *in* B. Stonehouse, editor. Animal marking: recognition marking of animals in research. University Park Press, Baltimore, Maryland, USA.

STEBBINS, R. C., AND N. W. COHEN. 1973. The effect of parietalectomy on the thyroid and gonads in free-living western fence lizards, *Sceloporus occidentalis.* Copeia 1973:662–672.

STEDMAN, S. J. 1990. Band opening and removal by house finches. North American Bird Bander 15:136–138.

STEWART, P. D., AND D. W. MACDONALD. 1997. Age, sex, and condition as predictors of moult and the efficacy of a novel fur clip technique for individual marking of the European badger (*Meles meles*). Journal of Zoology (London) 241:543–550.

STICKEL, L. F. 1950. Populations and home range relationships of the box turtle, *Terrapene c. carolina* (Linnaeus). Ecological Monographs 20:351–378.

STIEHL, R. B. 1983. A new attachment method for patagial tags. Journal of Field Ornithology 54:326–328.

STILLE, W. T. 1950. The loss of jaw tags by toads. Natural History Miscellaneous Publications 74, Chicago Natural History Museum, Chicago, Illinois, USA.

STIRLING, I. 1979. Tagging Weddell and fur seals and some general comments on long-term marking studies. Pages 13–14 *in* L. Hobbs and P. Russell, editors. Report on the pinniped tagging workshop. Seattle, Washington, USA.

STONEHOUSE, B. 1978. Animal marking: recognition marking of animals in research. University Park Press, Baltimore, Maryland, USA.

STRONG, P. I. V., S. A. LAVALLEY, AND R. C. BURKE, II. 1987. A colored plastic leg band for common loons. Journal of Field Ornithology 58: 218–221.

SUBBA RAO, M. V., AND B. S. RAJABAI. 1972. Ecological aspects of the agamid lizards *Sitana ponticeriana* and *Calotes nemoricola* in India. Herpetologica 28: 285–289. Sugden, L. G., and H. J. Poston. 1968. A nasal marker for ducks. Journal of Wildlife Management 32: 984–986.

SUMMERS, C. F., AND S. R. WITTHAMES. 1978. The value of tagging as a marking technique for seals. Pages 63–70 *in* B. Stonehouse, editor. Animal marking: recognition marking of animals in research. University Park Press, Baltimore, Maryland, USA.

SWANK, W. G. 1952. Trapping and marking of adult nesting doves. Journal of Wildlife Management 16: 87–90.

SWEENEY, T. M., J. D. FRASER, AND J. S. COLEMAN. 1985. Further evaluation of marking methods for black and turkey vultures. Journal of Field Ornithology 56:251–257.

SWENSON, J. E., K. WALLIN, G. ERICSSON, G. CEDERLUND, AND F. SANDEGREN. 1999. Effects of ear-tagging with radiotransmitters on survival of moose calves. Journal of Wildlife Management 63:354–358.

SWINGLAND, I. R. 1978. Marking reptiles. Pages 119–132 *in* B. Stonehouse, editor. Animal marking. University Park Press, Baltimore, Maryland, USA.

SZYMCZAK, M. R., AND J. K. RINGELMAN. 1986. Differential habitat use of patagial-tagged female mallards. Journal of Field Ornithology 57: 230–232.

TABER, C. A., R. F. WILKINSON, JR., AND M. S. TOPPING. 1975. Age and growth of hellbenders in the Niangua River, Missouri. Copeia 1975: 633–639.

TABER, R. D. 1949. A new marker for game birds. Journal of Wildlife Management 13:228–231.

———, AND I. M. COWAN. 1963. Capturing and marking wild animals. Pages 250–283 *in* H. S. Mosby, editor. Wildlife investigational techniques. Second edition. Edwards Brothers, Ann Arbor, Michigan, USA.

———, A. DEVOS, AND M. ALTMANN. 1956. Two marking devices for large land mammals. Journal of Wildlife Management 20:464–465.

TACHA, T. C. 1979. Effects of capture and color markers on behavior of sandhill cranes. Pages 177–179 *in* J. C. Lewis, editor. Proceedings of the 1978 Crane Workshop. Colorado State University, Fort Collins, USA.

TAMARIN, R. H., M. SHERIDAN, AND C. K. LEVY. 1983. Determining matrilineal kinship in natural populations of rodents using radionuclides. Canadian Journal of Zoology 61:271–274.

TAYLOR, J., AND L. DEEGAN. 1982. A rapid method for mass marking of amphibians. Journal of Herpetology 16:172–173.

TAYLOR, K. D., AND R. J. QUY. 1973. Marking systems for the study of rat movements. Mammal Review 3:30–34.

TAYLOR, M., AND J. LEE. 1994. Tetracycline as a biomarker for polar bears. Wildlife Society Bulletin 22:83–89

TAYLOR, R. H. 1969. Self-attaching collars for marking red deer in New Zealand. Deer 1:404–407.

THOMAS, A. E. 1975. Marking anurans with silver nitrate. Herpetological Review 6:12.

THOMAS, J. A., L. H. CORNELL, B. E. JOSEPH, T. D. WILLIAMS, AND S. DREISCHMAN. 1987. An implanted transponder chip used as a tag for sea otters (*Enhydra lutris*). Marine Mammal Science 3:271–274.

THOMAS, J. W., AND R. G. MARBURGER. 1964. Colored leg markers for wild turkeys. Journal of Wildlife Management 28:552–555.

THOMAS, R. A. 1977. Selected bibliography of certain vertebrate techniques. U.S. Department of the Interior, Bureau of Land Management Technical Note 306. Denver, Colorado, USA.

THOMPSON, H. V., AND C. J. ARMOUR. 1954. Methods of marking wild rabbits. Journal of Wildlife Management 18:411–414.

THOMPSON, S. D. 1982. Microhabitat utilization and foraging behavior of bipedal and quadrupedal heteromyid rodents. Ecology 63: 1303–1312.

TILLEY, S. G. 1977. Studies of life histories and reproduction in North American plethodontid salamanders. Pages 1–41 *in* D. H. Taylor and S. I. Guttman, editors. The reproductive biology of amphibians. Plenum Press, New York, USA.

———. 1980. Life histories and comparative demography of two salamander populations. Copeia 1980:806–821.

TINKLE, D. W. 1967. The life and demography of the side-blotched lizard, *Uta stansburiana.* Museum Zoological Publication 132. University of Michigan, Ann Arbor, USA.

———. 1973. A population analysis of the sagebrush lizard, *Sceloporus graciosus* in southern Utah. Copeia 1973:284–296.

TOMILIN, A. G., Y. I. BLIZNYUK, AND A. V. ZANIN. 1983. A new method for marking small cetaceans. International Whaling Commission Report 33:643–645.

TOMLINSON, R. E. 1968. Reward banding to determine reporting rate of recovered mourning dove bands. Journal of Wildlife Management 32: 6–11.

TRAVIS, J. 1981. The effect of staining on the growth of *Hyla gratiosa* tadpoles. Copeia 1981:193–196.

TRIPPENSEE, R. E. 1941. A new type of bird and mammal marker. Journal of Wildlife Management 5:120–124.

TURNER, F. B. 1960. Population structure and dynamics of the western spotted frog, *Rana p. pretiosa* Baird and Girard, in Yellowstone Park, Wyoming. Ecological Monographs 30:251–278.

TURNER, J. C. 1982. A modified Cap-Chur dart and dye evaluation for marking desert sheep. Journal of Wildlife Management 46:553–557.

TWITTY, V. C. 1966. Of scientists and salamanders. W. H. Freeman, San Francisco, California, USA.

TYNDALE-BISCOE, C. H. 1953. A method of marking rabbits for field studies. Journal of Wildlife Management 17: 42–45.

UNDERHILL, L., AND J. HOFMEYER. 1987. Experience with colour-dyed common terns. Safring News 16:29–30.

VAN BRACKLE, M. D., S. B. LINHART, T. E. CREEKMORE, V. F. NETTLES, AND R. L. MARCHINTON. 1994. Oral biomarking of white-tailed deer with tetracycline. Wildlife Society Bulletin 22:483–488.

VERME, L. J. 1962. An automatic tagging device for deer. Journal of Wildlife Management 26:387–392.

VILJOEN, P. J. 1986. A plastic tail collar for marking wild elephants. South African Journal Wildlife Research 16:158–159.

VINEGAR, M. B. 1975. Life history phenomena in two populations of the lizard *Sceloporous undulatus* in southwestern New Mexico. American Midland Naturalist 93:388–402.

WADKINS, L. A. 1948. Dyeing birds for identification. Journal of Wildlife Management 12:388–391.

WALLACE, M. P., P. G. PARKER, AND S. A. TEMPLE. 1980. An evaluation of patagial markers for cathartid vultures. Journal of Field Ornithology 51:309–314.

WANDELL, W. N. 1943. A multi-marking system for ring-necked pheasants. Journal of Wildlife Management 7:378–382.

———. 1945. Rapid method for opening and arranging pheasant bands. Journal of Wildlife Management 9:325.

WARD, F. P., C. J. HOHMANN, J. F. ULRICH, AND S. E. HILL. 1976. Seasonal microhabitat selections of spotted turtles *(Clemmys guttata)* in Maryland elucidated by radioisotope tracking. Herpetologica 32:60–64.

WARNEKE, B. M. 1979. Marking of Australian fur seals, 1966–1977. Pages 7–8 in L. Hobbs and P. Russell, editors. Report on the pinniped tagging workshop. Seattle, Washington, USA.

WATKINS, W. A., AND W. E. SCHEVILL. 1976. Underwater paint marking of porpoises. Fisheries Bulletin 74:687–689.

WATT, D. J. 2001. Recapture rate and breeding frequencies of American goldfinches wearing different colored leg bands. Journal of Field Ornithology 72:236–243.

WEARY, G. C. 1969. An improved method of marking snakes. Copeia 1969:854–855.

WEBB, W. L. 1943. Trapping and marking white-tailed deer. Journal of Wildlife Management 7:346–348.

WELLS, K. D., AND R. A. WELLS. 1976. Patterns of movement in a population of the slimy salamander, *Plethodon glutinosus,* with observations on aggregations. Herpetologica 32:156–162.

WENDELIN H., R. NAGEL, AND P. H. BECKER. 1996. A technique to spray dyes on birds. Journal of Field Ornithology 67:442–446.

WESTFALL, C. Z., AND R. B. WEEDEN. 1956. Plastic neck markers for woodcock. Journal of Wildlife Management 20:218–219.

WHEELER, R. H., AND J. C. LEWIS. 1972. Trapping techniques for sandhill crane studies in the Platte River Valley. U.S. Department of the Interior, Fish and Wildlife Service, Resource Publication 107.

WHITE, JR., M. J., J. G. JENNINGS, W. F. GANDY, AND L. H. CORNELL. 1981. An evaluation of tagging, marking, and tattooing techniques for small dolphinids. U.S. Department of Commerce, National Oceanic and Atmospheric Administration, Technical Memorandum NMFS 16:1–142.

WHITE, S. B., T. A. BOOKHOUT, AND E. K. BOLLINGER. 1980. Use of human hair bleach to mark blackbirds and starlings. Journal of Field Ornithology 51:6–9.

WHITFORD, W. G., AND M. MASSEY. 1970. Responses of a population of *Ambystoma tigrinum* to thermal and oxygen gradients. Herpetologica 26:372–376.

WILKINSON, G. S. 1985. The social organization of the common vampire bat. I. Pattern and cause of association. Behavioral Ecology and Sociobiology 17:111–121.

WILLIAMS, T. C., J. M. WILLIAMS, AND D. R. GRIFFIN. 1966. The homing ability of the neotropical bat, *Phyllostomus hastatus,* with evidence for visual orientation. Animal Behavior 14:473–486.

WILLSTEEN, P. M., AND P. M. FETTEROLF. 1986. A new technique for individually marking gull chicks. Journal of Field Ornithology 57:310–313.

WINSTON, F. A. 1955. Color marking of waterfowl. Journal of Wildlife Management 19:319.

WOLCOTT, T. G. 1977. Optical tracking and telemetry for nocturnal field studies. Journal of Wildlife Management 41:309–312.

WOOD, M. D., AND N. A. SLADE. 1990. Comparison of ear-tagging and toe clipping in prairie voles, *Microtus ochrogaster.* Journal of Mammalogy 71:252–255.

WOODBURY, A. M. 1956. Uses of marking animals in ecological studies: marking amphibians and reptiles. Ecology 37:670–674.

———, AND R. HARDY. 1948. Studies of the desert tortoise, *Gopherus agassizii.* Ecological Monographs 18:145–200.

WOOLLEY, H. P. 1973. Subcutaneous acrylic polymer injections as a marking technique for amphibians. Copeia 1973:340–341.

WRIGHT, E. G. 1939. Marking birds by imping feathers. Journal of Wildlife Management 3:238–239.

WÜRSIG, B., AND M. WÜRSIG. 1977. The photographic determination of group size, composition, and stability of coastal porpoises *(Tursiops truncatus).* Science 198:755–756.

WYDOWSKI, R., AND L. EMERY. 1983. Tagging and marking. Pages 215–237 in L. A. Nielsen, D. L. Johnson, and S. S. Lampton, editors. Fisheries techniques. American Fisheries Society, Bethesda, Maryland, USA.

YAGI, T., M. NISHIWAKI, AND M. NAKAJIMA. 1963. A preliminary study on the method of time marking with lead salt and tetracycline on the teeth of fur seals. Whales Research Institute, Science Report. 7:191–195.

YOUNG, J. B. 1941. Unusual behavior of a banded cardinal. Wilson Bulletin 53:197–198.

YOUNG, L. S., AND M. N. KOCHERT. 1987. Marking techniques. National Wildlife Federation, Scientific Technical Series 10:125–156.

ZICUS, M. C., AND R. M. PACE, III. 1986. Neckband retention in Canada geese. Wildlife Society Bulletin 14:388–391.

———, D. F. SCHULTZ, AND J. A. COOPER. 1983. Canada goose mortality from neckband icing. Wildlife Society Bulletin 11:286–290.

ZMUD, M. E. 1985. Marking of the redshank *Tringa totanus* in the northwestern Pricernomorije. The Ring 11:7–15.

ZWICKEL, F. C., AND A. ALLISON. 1983. A back marker for individual identification of small lizards. Herpetological Review 14:82.

See Appendix next page.

APPENDIX

Common names and scientific names of animals mentioned in the text and tables. Authority for scientific names of North American amphibians, birds, mammals, and reptiles is Banks et al. (1987). Authority for non-North American amphibians and reptiles is Sokolov (1988). Authority for non-North American birds is Sibley and Monroe (1990). Authority for scientific names of non-North American mammals is Grizimek (1990).

Common name	Scientific name
Amphibians and Reptiles	
Alligator, American	*Alligator mississippiensis*
Bullfrog	*Rana catesbeiana*
Frog, northern leopard	*Rana pipiens*
Hellbender	*Cryptobranchus alleganiensis*
Iguana, green	*Iguana iguana*
Lizard, blunt-nosed	*Gambelia silus*
northern fence	*Sceloporus undulatus*
slow-worm	*Anguis fragilis*
viviparous	*Lacerta vivipara*
Newt, alpine	*Trituris alpestris*
eastern	*Notophthalmus viridescens*
great-crested	*Triturus cristatus*
smooth	*Trituris vulgaris*
warty	*Trituris cristatus*
Salamander, dusky	*Desmognathus fuscus*
spotted	*Ambystoma maculatum*
tiger	*Ambystoma tigrinum*
Snake, pine	*Pituophis melanoleucus*
Terrapin	*Malaclemys terrapin*
Tortoise, desert	*Gopherus agassizii*
Turtle, box	*Terrapene* spp.
green sea	*Chelonia mydas*
spotted	*Clemmys guttata*
Birds	
Cardinal, northern	*Cardinalis cardinalis*
Coot, American	*Fulica americana*
Dove, mourning	*Zenaida macroura*
white-winged	*Zenaida asiatica*
Duck, wood	*Aix sponsa*
Eagle, bald	*Haliaeetus leucocephalus*
Egret, cattle	*Bubulcus ibis*
Frigatebird	*Fregata* spp.
Grouse, ruffed	*Bonasa umbellus*
greater sage-	*Centrocercus urophasianus*
Gull, Glaucous-winged	*Larus glaucescens*
Goshawk, northern	*Accipiter gentilis*
Mallard	*Anas platyrhynchos*
Osprey	*Pandion haliaetus*
Owl, boreal	*Aegolius funereus*
long-eared	*Asio otus*
Partridge, gray	*Perdix perdix*
Pheasant, ring-necked	*Phasianus colchicus*
Plover, semipalmated	*Charadrius semipalmatus*
Prairie-chicken, greater	*Tympanuchus cupido*
Quail, northern bobwhite	*Colinus virginianus*
Skimmer, black	*Rynchops niger*
Sparrow, house	*Passer domesticus*
Starling. European	*Sturnus vulgaris*
Stork, wood	*Mycteria americana*
Swan, Bewick's	*Cygnus bewickii*
Tundra	*Cygnus columbianus*
Tern, common	*Sterna hirundo*
least	*Sterna antillarum*
Turkey, wild	*Meleagris gallopavo*
Willet	*Catoptrophorus semipalmatus*
Woodcock, American	*Scolopax minor*
Mammals	
Badger, European	*Meles meles*
Beaver, American	*Castor canadensis*
Bobcat	*Lynx rufus*
Bat, big brown	*Eptesicus fuscus*
Bear, black	*Ursus americanus*
polar	*Ursus maritimus*
Bushbuck, African	*Tragelaphus scriptus*
Caribou	*Rangifer tarandus*
Cheetah	*Acinonyx jubatus*
Coyote	*Canis latrans*
Deer, mule	*Odocoileus hemionus*
Pere David's	*Elaphurus davidanus*
white-tailed	*Odocoileus virginianus*
Elephant, African	*Loxodonta africanus*
Elk	*Cervus elaphus*
Ferret, black-footed	*Mustela nigripes*
Gazelle, Thomson's	*Gazella thomsonii*
Giraffe	*Giraffa camelopardalis*
Gopher, pocket	*Geomys breviceps*
Hare, snowshoe	*Lepus americanus*
Leopard	*Panthera pardus*
Lion, African	*Panthera leo*
Manatee	*Trichechus manatus*
Mouse, harvest	*Reithrodontomys* spp.
Mongoose	*Herpestes* spp.
Moose	*Alces alces*
Mountain beaver	*Aplodontia rufa*
Muskox	*Ovibos moschatus*
Nutria	*Myocastor coypus*
Opossum, Virginia	*Didelphis virginiana*
Otter, sea	*Enhydra lutris*
Pangolin	*Manis* spp.
Peccary, collared	*Tayassu tajacu*
Porcupine	*Erethizon dorsatum*
Pronghorn	*Antilocapra americana*
Rabbit, cottontail	*Sylvilagus* spp.
Raccoon	*Procyon lotor*
Rat, naked mole	*Heterocephalus glaber*
Norway	*Rattus norvegicus*
Rhinoceros, black	*Diceros bicomis*
Seal, northern fur	*Collorhinus ursinus*
Sheep, mountain	*Ovis canadensis*
Dall's	*Ovis dalli*
Squirrel, fox	*Sciurus niger*
gray	*Sciurus carolinensis*
red	*Tamiasciurus hudsonicus*
Tiger	*Panthera tigria*
Wallaby	*Petrogale* spp.
Whale, Beluga	*Delphinapterus leucas*
Woodrat	*Neotoma* spp.

14

WILDLIFE RADIOTELEMETRY

Mark R. Fuller, Joshua J. Millspaugh, Kevin E. Church, and Robert E. Kenward

INTRODUCTION

Radiotelemetry is a technique commonly used to study wildlife behavior, population biology, and ecology. Use of this technique can provide insight into animal ecology and applications to wildlife management. Individual animals that have been radiomarked often can be observed or relocated more consistently and more frequently than animals marked with other methods (Silvy et al. 2005). Use of radiotelemetry provides opportunities to gather information that is neither practical nor possible with other methods. Effective use of radiotelemetry requires knowledge about the technique and advantages and disadvantages of its application. If radiotelemetry is appropriate for the study, successful completion of a project requires careful study design, including data analyses, appropriate equipment, and effective field methods.

This chapter provides basic considerations for designing telemetry studies, examples of analysis methods for telemetry data to address a diversity of objectives, background for selection of equipment, and an introduction to basic use of equipment in field conditions. Use of radiotelemetry has increased in the last decade as witnessed by many journal publications and new books about the technique (Kenward 2001, Millspaugh and Marzluff 2001). The basic advantages of using wildlife telemetry and underlying electronics technology continue to apply,

and considerable new development has occurred in methods for analyzing data from radiotelemetry.

Development continues in technology, analytical procedures, and evaluation of the effects of radiomarking on animals. Consequently, biologists should investigate the latest literature, the Internet (e.g., http://fwie.fw.vt.edu/tws-gis), and correspond with colleagues and providers of equipment and software to remain current in this rapidly expanding area of wildlife biology.

STUDY DESIGN
Objectives

The first steps in developing an appropriate study design are to identify specific objectives and to ask if radiotelemetry is the best method to address the objectives. It is also important to clarify the scope of the inferences to be made from the results. For what age, gender, and other categories of individual (e.g., social status), time of day or season of year, and what geographic area are the results to be representative? The inferences to be made will affect the number of individuals that must be radiomarked and the spatial scale over which they must be sampled. These factors affect the cost of using radiotelemetry and feasibility of using the technique for a particular study.

Radiotelemetry has been used commonly to find animals for subsequent observation; track local movements,

> **Box 1. Recommendations for minimizing effects of radiomarking.**
>
> (1)   Assume there will be an effect(s).
> (2)   Study relevant literature about the species, attachment methods, and documented effects.
> (3)   Correspond about radiomarking same or similar species.
> (4)   Use smallest possible radio transmitter or package.
> (5)   Use most inconspicuous radio package and attachment possible.
> (6)   Test attachment methods.
> (7)   Test attachment method if first attachment type for the species.
> (8)   Practice attachment on species or surrogate.
> (9)   Ensure fit to individual.
> (10) Consider periods of stress (e.g., severe temperature, reproductive season), condition, etc.
> (11) Observe post-attachment behavior.
> (12) Allow post-attachment habituation to capture, handling and to the radio package.
> (13) Publish positive and negative aspects of radiomarking.

dispersal, or migration; estimate space use (e.g., home range); study resource use and selection; estimate population abundance; study intra-specific (e.g., social behavior) or inter-specific (predator–prey) relationships; and estimate survival or fecundity. Guidance about study design is available in White and Garrott (1990), Samuel and Fuller (1994), Kenward (2001), and Garton et al. (2001, 2005).

A disadvantage of most applications of telemetry is that it replaces direct observation of animals and, thus, deprives the investigator of knowing the animals' behavior. Interpretation of animal behavior from radiotelemetry should be based on observation and experimentation, because tallies from activity sensors or measurements from location estimates can be misleading (Rouys et al. 2001). Thus, biologists should consider observing the animals (Drennan and Beier 2003).

Radio transmitters can be used with other markers. Schmid et al. (2003) used radio transmitters and sonic transmitters to study sea turtles. A large sample of individuals might be marked with an alphanumeric color tag and a subset radiomarked. The radiomarked animals can serve as sentinels, permitting biologists to find the larger sample of animals marked with the less expensive technique.

Effects on Animals

Radiomarking affects animals and its use must be justified (Clutton-Brock 2003, Morton et al. 2003). Minimizing the effects of radiomarking animals is important for humanitarian reasons, good science, economy, and to meet legal requirements in many countries (Morton et al. 2003). There are numerous ways that radiomarking can affect an animal (Murray and Fuller 2000, Withey et al. 2001). Use of the appropriate transmitter design, including attachment, is one of the most important aspects of any telemetry project. A study can fail or produce biased results if radiomarking causes aberrant behavior or physiological stress, increased mortality, or reduced reproduction. Con-

sequently, the desired electronic performance must be balanced with transmitter and attachment methods that minimize possible effects.

Animals require restraint, sedation, or anesthesia (Morton et al. 2003, Roffe et al. 2005, Schemnitz 2005) while being radiomarked, which might affect them (Côté et al. 1998), compounding the effects of the transmitter package. Thus, care of animals during capture, handling, and radiomarking is important (Morton et al. 2003). Biologists must be knowledgeable about animal capture, handling, and marking regulations specific to the country where they will be working. In many countries there is oversight (e.g., Canada-Canadian Council of Animal Care; South Africa-Animal Ethics Screening Committee; USA-Institutional Animal Care and Use Committee) and review of study plans to ensure compliance with regulations (Morton et al. 2003, Dein et al. 2005).

The many effects of radiomarking can be short or long term, overt or subtle (Kenward 2001). Effects differ among species, time of year, and ages of animals. Flight and swimming (e.g., long distance migration, fast bursts, slow speed maneuvering) can be affected by transmitter mass and drag. There may be different responses by animals to variation in transmitter size and attachment (Reynolds et al. 2004) and even to how the transmitter is "fitted" to animals by different biologists (Paton et al. 1991). Several publications in the last decade have reviewed effects of radiomarking, including Samuel and Fuller (1994), Murray and Fuller (2000), Kenward (2001), and Withey et al. (2001).

Models have been used to predict effects of radiomarking; for example, the biomechanics basis of flight permits estimating effects of transmitter mass and drag on birds (Pennycuick 1989, Pennycuick et al. 1989). There also are recommendations for minimizing effects of radiomarking (Box 1) (White and Garrott 1990, Withey et al. 2001). However, there is still much to be learned and conveyed about the effects of marking animals. Biologists are encouraged to compare attachment techniques (Schulz et al. 2001) and radiomarked versus animals not radiomarked. These studies can be with captive animals and specific to study objectives and field conditions (Murray and Fuller 2000, Kenward 2001, Withey et al. 2001).

Expense

Costs associated with radiotelemetry include purchase of equipment (transmitters, antennas, and receivers), salaries and expenses for field personnel, and transportation (e.g., vehicles, aircraft). Personnel training and pilot studies also should be considered. Pilot studies may be necessary to test the usefulness of methods, and to learn about variability for planning sample size and sampling. Costs and personnel associated with data management and analysis, report preparation, and publication also must be considered. Typically, the best studies are a result of careful design, compromise between competing objectives, a realistic assessment of the technical capabilities (Sargeant 1980), and available support.

During the planning process, biologists should continually consider alternative, inexpensive methods such as other types of markers including natural markings, visual markers (e.g., neck collars, ear tags, leg bands) (McCann et al. 2001), passive integrated transponders (PIT tags) (Kerth and Reckardt 2003), data loggers with sensors (Tuck et al. 1999), or genetic markers (Oyler-McCance and Leberg 2005).

Box 2. Description and measurement of radio signals.

Radio frequencies are measured in cycles per second, a Hertz (Hz); thus, 100 Hz = 100 cycles per second. Radio signals occur in a range from thousands to billions of cycles per second with quantities abbreviated by the conventional metric prefixes:

G = giga = 1 billion (10^9),   U = micro = 1 millionth (10^{-6}),
M = mega = 1 million (10^6),   N = nano = 1 billionth (10^{-9}), and
K = milo = 1 thousand (10^3),   P = pico = 1 trillionth (10^{-12}).
M = milli = 1 thousandth (10^{-3}),

Therefore, 164.000 megaHertz (MHz) is 164,000,000 cycles/second.

Radio signals travel in the form of sine waves and a cycle is a wavelength. A high-frequency radio signal has a short wavelength and has more cycles per second (e.g., 216 MHz) than a low-frequency signal (e.g., 40 MHz).

Wavelength (λ) usually is expressed in meters and can be calculated by the formula:

$$\lambda = \frac{300}{\text{frequency (MHz)}}.$$

The value 300 is the speed ($\sim 300 \times 10^6$ M s^{-1}) at which electromagnetic waves (e.g., radio, radar, microwaves, infrared, x-ray) travel. The wavelength of a radio frequency is an important characteristic because it affects antenna size.

Radio waves are categorized into spectral bands such as long waves, short waves, Very High Frequency (VHF), and Ultra High Frequency (UHF), each containing a range of radio frequencies (VHF = 30–300 MHz). However, the term band or bandwidth also is used to describe a specific range of frequencies (e.g., a 2-MHz band of 164–166 MHz).

TELEMETRY EQUIPMENT

Biologists have options for obtaining animal location and sensor data. Most frequently they have used Very High Frequency (VHF) transmitters (Box 2). Wildlife telemetry with VHF requires the receiving system to be relatively close to the radiomarked animal. Since the 1970s, studies of many species have been conducted using satellite telemetry, which allows collecting data from animals anywhere around the world.

Proceedings of telemetry conferences and workshops contain papers describing new developments, innovations, and techniques (e.g., Rodgers 2001, International Society on Biotelemetry, http://www.biotelemetry.org/), and occasionally journals provide similar information (Cochran and Pater 2001, Cox et al. 2002, Mourao and Medri 2002). Cochran (1980) noted that biologists should work with equipment manufacturers to explore and exploit the variety of equipment and software options that might fulfill their research needs.

Acquisition of Equipment

Numerous companies specialize in equipment for wildlife telemetry (Appendix). The telemetry business is competitive and equipment should be purchased from the perspective of an informed consumer. We suggest that biologists correspond with the companies after identifying study objective(s) and reviewing relevant literature. Literature about the study species' habits, topography and vegetation in which it occurs, and previous radiomarking projects on similar species, will provide useful information for selecting equipment. Those purchasing equipment should be specific about the needs for their study. For example, basic information when ordering VHF radio transmitters includes: range of potential operating frequencies, separation between frequencies, allowable frequency drift, pulse rate, pulse width, minimum acceptable radiated power, allowable transmitter antenna length, operating temperature range, required operation life, allowable mass, and method of attachment. Most conventional transmitters cost from $100 to $300 and receivers $800 to $4,000 (U.S. dollars). Radio transmitters for use with satellites can cost from $1,500 to more than $4,500. We do not recommend that biologists build transmitter or receiver electronics. Kenward (2001) describes construction of tag attachments for basic transmitters.

Scheduling equipment acquisition to include time for assembly and testing is extremely important (Hulbert and French 2001, D'Eon et al. 2002). Occasionally, the manufacturer must acquire components, modify a circuit or design, and test new equipment. Upon receipt of equipment, biologists should test functions of their radiotelemetry "system" (transmitters, receivers, antennas, coaxial cables, data loggers). This should include field-testing in all topographic and vegetative conditions on the study area. Plans should be devised for backup equipment (e.g., receiver) or parts (e.g., antenna elements) to avoid "downtime" while waiting for repairs or replacement. When unfamiliar with the radio transmitter or its source, ample time should be allowed to request a prototype from several manufacturers that can be compared by field-testing before placing an order. In addition, inquiries should be made as to whether the manufacturer will "refurbish" used transmitters (e.g., replace the battery or damaged antenna), which usually will result in a significant saving (~50%) from the cost of a new radio but may reduce reliability.

VHF Systems
Radio Frequency Selection

Wildlife telemetry is considered a secondary radio service and afforded no protection by government regulations from interference by other authorized use, most of which transmit higher power signals than wildlife radiotracking. Radio frequencies for use on wildlife are regulated in most countries and usually restricted to a small range at a low power of transmission (e.g., <10 milliwatts). Adherence to frequency allocations is necessary for legal use and to avoid interference from other radiotelemetry users such as telephone, and ship-to-shore or citizens band radio. Biologists can consider UHF frequencies for better performance under some circumstances (Cochran and Pater 2001). In the United States, frequency allocations and technical standards are regulated by the Federal Communications Commission for persons who operate under state or local governments or in the private sector, and by the National Telecommunications and Information Administration for federal government projects. All users in the United States must obtain a license to use wildlife telemetry frequencies.

Coordination of frequency use with other biologists is necessary for safety and for avoiding misinterpretation of data. Land managers and state wildlife agencies should be able to provide names of investigators working in their areas, and the Canadian Wildlife Service and U.S. Department of Interior, Geological Survey, bird banding labs can provide names of investigators authorized to use transmitters on migratory birds. Coordination among projects may enable equipment or monitoring tasks to be shared.

Transmitters

The transmitter is often the first piece of equipment biologists consider. Major characteristics to be considered when selecting transmitters are the radio frequency signal repeat ("beep") rate, signal strength (radiated power), configuration and mass of the entire package, method of attachment, duration of operation, and cost. Complete transmitter packages comprise electrical circuitry, a power source, transmitting antenna, encapsulation, and material for attachment to an animal (Figs. 1, 2).

Basic VHF Circuits.—Radio transmitters are designed to minimize spurious emissions that waste power and clutter the frequency spectrum. Emitted signals usually are discontinuous (i.e., pulsed) to conserve battery energy and facilitate coded data transmission. Components of high quality and careful construction are required to precisely control the length (width) of transmissions and time (interval) between them. Limitations in receiver technology and human perception require that pulse duration is usually >12 milliseconds (typically 15–25) and the rate >35 pulses/minute (typically 50–65). Longer pulses are more easily distinguished from ambient noise, and more frequent pulses facilitate discerning the signal origin when using a directional receiving antenna.

Individual animals are typically marked with radio transmitters that emit a signal on a unique radio frequency that varies only about ±1–2 KHz in a temperature range of +30 to –20 C. On this basis, a spacing of about 10 KHz can be used between transmitters in the same study area. Transmitters may be activated at time of attachment by removing a small magnet taped to the outside of the package. Some transmitters use microprocessors and low power quartz crystal clocks to conserve power by turning transmissions on or off at prescribed times (duty cycle).

Wildlife radio transmitters are usually classified as 1- or 2-stage. A 1-stage radio transmitter can use a single cell battery of 1.35–1.55 V to minimize mass but have low signal power. Two-stage transmitters require increased battery voltage (2.70–6.00 V) and, thus, greater package mass and design complexity. The power of the transmitted signal and operational life of the transmitter are often the major concerns of the biologist. Unfortunately, signal power and operational life are almost direct trade-offs because batteries add bulk and mass to transmitter packages. New technology has resulted in additional improvements and options for transmitter construction (Kenward 2001).

Transmitting Antennas.—Transmitting antennas often are the most worrisome component of a radio transmitter because they are inherently inefficient and structurally weak. The point at which the antenna exits the encapsulation of the other transmitter components frequently is a place where moisture might enter the circuitry and where whip antennas might break and destroy the performance of the transmitter.

Whip antennas are the most efficient signal radiators. Quarter wavelengths are recommended and can be calculated by: 7,500 cm/f where f = frequency in MHz. One-quarter wavelength can be too long to be carried by birds and small mammals. Therefore, alternatives are $\lambda/8$ or $\lambda/16$. However, antenna efficiency is greatly reduced (Fig. 3). Short whip antennas are most efficient with a ground wire two thirds as long and perpendicular or opposite in direction to the main whip. However, this antenna configuration is not always practical for small birds and mammals.

Whip antennas often are positioned against or near the animal's body to reduce the likelihood of the animal directing its behavior toward the wire and to reduce aerodynamic drag and snagging on objects. For mammals that easily can break antennas, the antenna is placed between 2 layers of material that comprise the collar. Cochran (1980) noted this position can result in a 20 dB (decibel) loss and, if the antenna is $< \lambda/2$ from the ground (~1 m at 150 MHz), there will be additional loss. Consequently, type, length, and position of the transmitting antenna are important factors affecting signal transmission.

Whip antenna materials should be strong but flexible such as multiple strands of nickel stainless steel cable or guitar string, or other new alloys. Often the wires are covered with tough plastic coating or shrink tubing, which is heated to mold tightly to the surface. A metal spring, layers of shrink tubing, or cone of silicon sealant at the antenna base can distribute the stress from bending and reduce breakage. Shrink tubing and sealant also help retard moisture penetration of the package. The distal end of the tubing over multi-stranded wire should be sealed to retard the wicking of moisture along the antenna. Moisture in the circuitry or antenna damage often causes transmitter failure before the battery is depleted.

Loop antennas are made of a brass or copper band or wire, and incorporated into a collar or necklace attachment. Loops can be tuned for their components and radio frequency to enhance their performance. When a tuned loop antenna is placed on an animal, the size and shape of the loop must not be changed from that delivered by the manufacturer. Larger animals are equipped with collars of heavy belting into which a whip antenna is incorporated.

Power Sources.—In the context of wildlife telemetry, "power" refers to signal strength, measured as decibels in milliwatts (dBm), or to the energy sources (batteries or solar cells) for transmitters. Many battery types and solar cell circuits are available to meet the requirements for signal strength and operational life in conjunction with size, mass, and attachment methods. Lithium and silver oxide are the most common chemical reactants used to create electrical current in

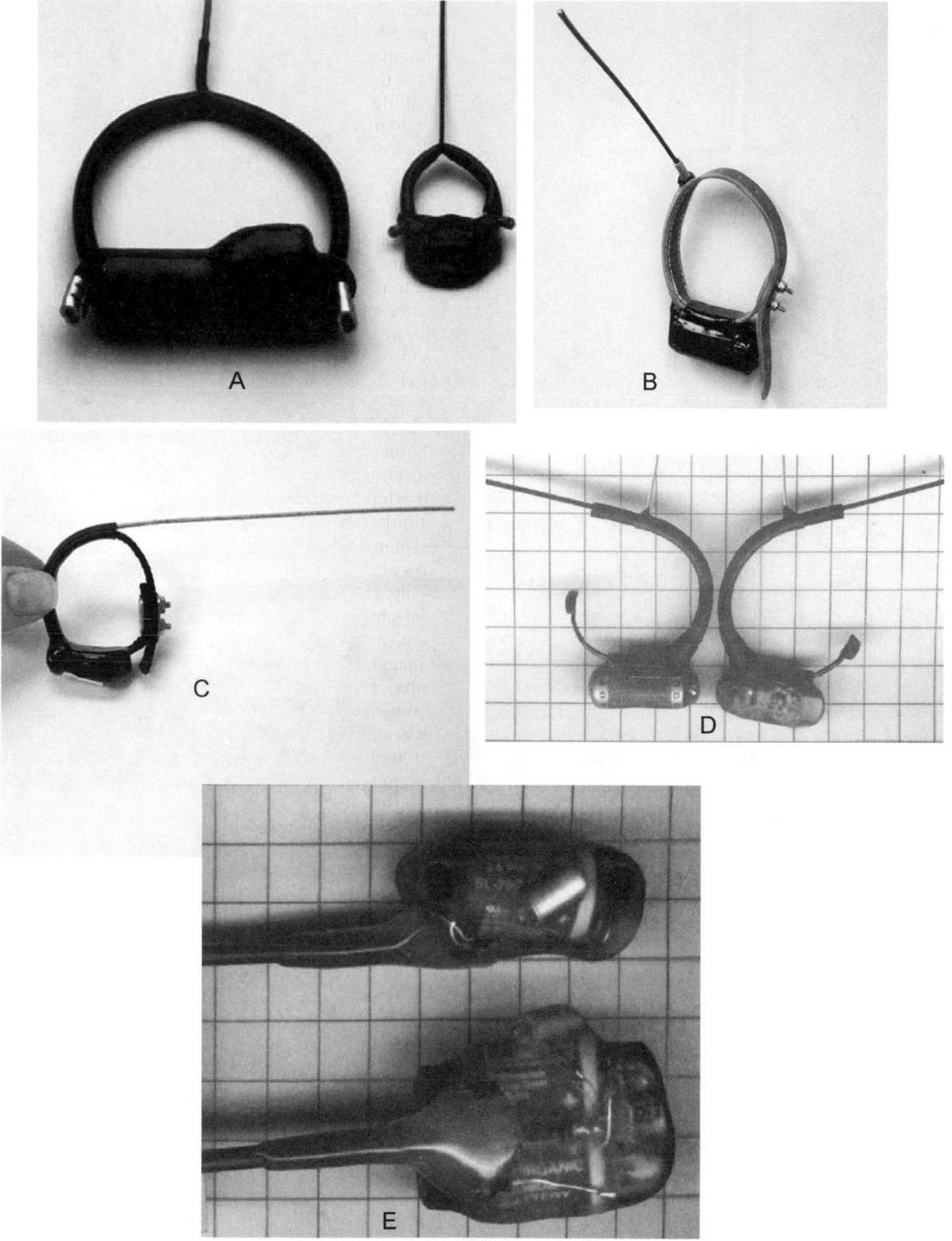

Fig. 1. Wildlife radio transmitters. A, small mammal collars (7–16 g); B, medium size mammal collar (390–435 g depending on battery size); C, small mammal collar; D, small mammal cable-tie collars (18 g); E, avian backpack (35 g).

batteries for radios. The loss of energy (current drain) from a battery is measured in Amperes (A), whereas the energy capacity of a battery is given in milliAmpere-hours (mA-hr). The operation life of a transmitter can be estimated by dividing the battery capacity (mA-hr) by the current drain. This provides a reasonable estimate for lithium batteries, but at least 25% of the estimated life should be subtracted for silver oxide batteries. The power available remains steady until the battery is nearly depleted. A few days before the battery expires the pulse rate often changes rate. Low temperatures also reduce the available battery capacity, terminal voltage, and ability to deliver current.

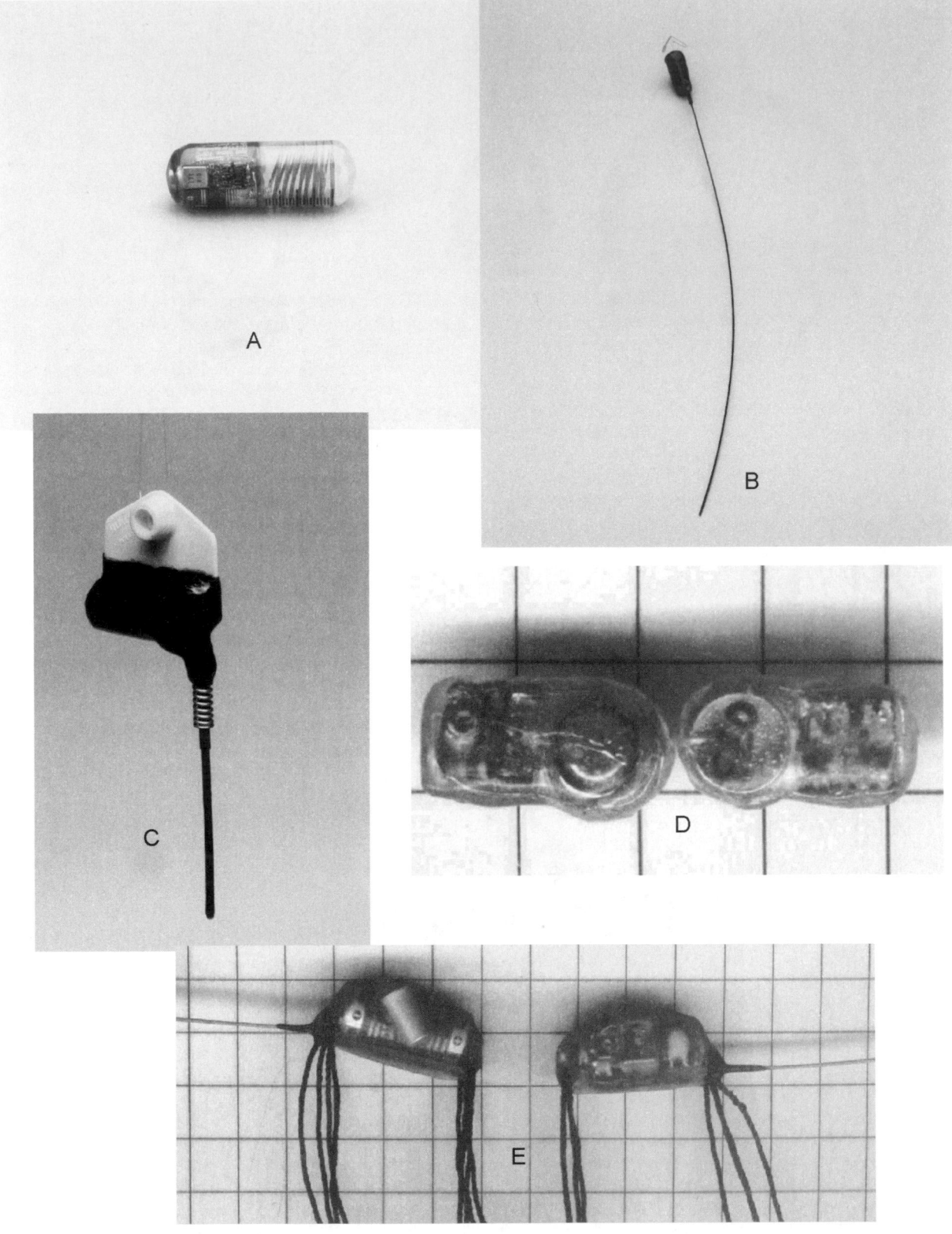

Fig. 2. Wildlife radio transmitters. A, small implant (9–40 g); B, prong and suture (1.3–2.9 g); C, ear tag (22–28 g); D, implant or ingest transmitters (1.6 g); E, tail mount (10 g).

Lithium batteries (2.90–3.90 V) are preferred for transmitters weighing >4 g. Their relatively high voltage makes them suitable for energy demanding programmable options such as duty cycles. Stored lithium cells lose only about 10% of their capacity over 5 years at room temperature. Silver oxide (1.55 V) batteries are used primarily for radio transmitters weighing <4 g. They have relatively short shelf lives and their power is negatively affected by cold temperature (<0 C).

Photovoltaic solar cells are an alternative energy source when restrictions on transmitter mass prevent use of con-

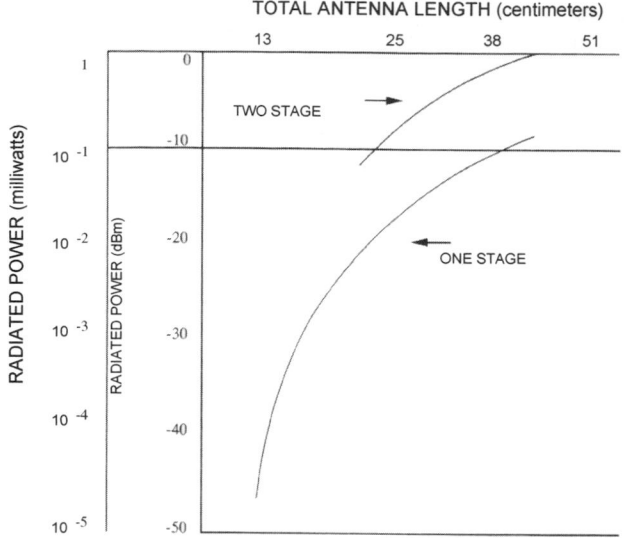

Fig. 3. Relationships between transmitter antenna length and effective radiated power (modified from graph prepared by A. L. Kolz, U.S. Department of Agriculture, Wildlife Services, National Wildlife Research Center, Fort Collins, CO, USA).

ventional batteries. Solar cells can be used with a capacitor to operate powerful transmitters, even in low light conditions, but not in the dark. Special mounts might be required to keep the solar cells clear of obstructions (e.g., Snyder et al. 1989). A 2-stage transmitter, with solar cells and capacitor, can weigh about 8 g and will operate until the transmitter or cells are damaged. Solar cells can be combined with rechargeable nickel-cadmium batteries (1.35 V) for some high-powered transmitters. Generally, daily sunlight of 4–5 hours is needed to charge the nickel-cadmium batteries and charging is limited in hot or cold temperatures. Irregular or incomplete discharge and recharge can cause reduced capacity and ultimately failure of nickel-cadmium batteries. Use of solar cells has become less common due to recent improvements in transmitter efficiency, including management of transmission duty cycles by microcontrollers, to reliably provide relatively long operation life (Kenward 2001).

Encapsulation.—Encapsulating, or potting the transmitter circuitry protects it against shock and moisture, and keeps animals from damaging components. Hermetic sealing in metal canisters maximizes protection of transmitters, but weighs and costs more than the same design potted in other material. Most radio transmitters are therefore potted in acrylics or epoxy resins, none of which is totally waterproof. Large, long-lived transmitters like those in collars for larger mammals usually are cast in a form filled with potting. Biologists should inspect radios for cracks in the potting and for "gaps," especially where the antenna or leads (e.g., to be soldered to turn on the unit) enter the potting.

Most potting methods should protect transmitters in terrestrial applications for at least a year. Transmitters to be implanted require special treatment to prevent rapid penetration by body fluids and preclude adverse reaction from tissues. For implants, beeswax might be adequate, but special formulations, such as Elvax®, have better properties relative to melting point, flexibility, and physiological response. It is important to note that sterilization procedures can melt some waxes. Encasement in tubing or use of new biocompatible polymers is now more common.

Sensors and Options.—In addition to locating animals, transmitters with special circuitry and sensors can provide data. Activity, temperature, and pressure data are typically conveyed with pulse interval modulation coding (i.e., a change in pulse is calibrated to a change in the sensor) (Anderka 1980). Any option that increases pulse rate and power consumption will reduce the operational life of the transmitter. Options that measure activity and temperature are commonly used and readily available from commercial vendors. Depending upon the sensors, it is possible to have more than one type of data (e.g., mortality and temperature) sent from a single transmitter (Lotimer 1980). Special custom circuitry or package design can increase the cost per unit and production time. A pilot study should be conducted to field test special designs.

The temperature of either ambient conditions or the animal's body can be measured and the information conveyed by the pulse rate of the transmitter. Accuracy of the measurement is dependent on the range of the temperature measurement and calibration, and is typically ±1.0 C with a resolution of 0.2 C. The pulse interval can be interpreted with a data logger or manually using a standard receiver and a stopwatch.

An activity sensor can indicate whether an animal is moving, or not, by transmitting an extra pulse each time a tilt switch is closed. The number of pulses varies depending upon animal movement, switch orientation, and transmitter attachment. Experimentation with transmitter positions and observations of marked animals should be conducted to learn which postures and activities affect sensor signals.

A common option is for a sensor(s) to indicate possible mortality of the marked animal with an activity sensor. If there has been no transmitter motion for a programmed period, the pulse rate changes (e.g., twice the base pulse rate, 90 pulses/minute). The transmitter will reset to the base pulse rate (e.g., 45 pulses/minute) if the transmitter is moved or the animal resumes activity. This option can be programmed to "lock" in mortality (e.g., for 21 days) to prevent scavengers or other sources of movement from resetting the mortality signal. If the transmitter is not recovered, after 21 days it will reset to the base pulse rate and resume normal operation.

Mortality also can be identified with a sensor that measures the body temperature of homeotherms, and changes the pulse rate when the marked animal dies and body temperature decreases below a prescribed level. The temperature sensing thermistor must be implanted or in contact with the animal's body (e.g., backpack). Using temperature and motion sensor data together can provide further evidence of mortality or that the transmitter has become detached from the animal (Bates et al. 2003).

A position sensing option reports whether an animal's body is in a particular posture by transmitting either a slow or fast pulse depending on the position of a tilt switch (Bonaccorso et al. 2002). Switch orientation and transmitter attachment are important considerations when using this option (Kenward 2001). Direct observation of the behavior of animals and associated activity sensor data can be used to interpret some behavior based on only the radio signal (Kenward et al. 1982).

A pressure sensor measures the atmospheric pressure (Shannon et al. 2000, 2002a,b; Weimerskirch et al. 2003) and pulse rate of the transmitter varies proportionally to pressure. However, the pulse rate relationship to barometric pressure can vary at the extremes of the pressure sensor range (Shannon et al. 2002*b*). Thus, accuracy is dependent on the researcher's ability to make the appropriate corrections for local temperature and atmospheric pressure, such as when a weather front passes. Typically, depth transmitters measure from 0 to 15 m (0 to 20 psi) to an accuracy of ±0.5 m. Sensors designed for study of diving behavior are also available.

A radio transmitter commonly is set to transmit about once per second for the operational life of the transmitter. However, some transmitters can be programmed to transmit for a given period and then turn off in a duty cycle that conserves battery power and extends operating life. Transmitters can be programmed to transmit for a specified number of hours per day, or days per week, month, or year. This option is particularly useful when biologists wish to minimize transmitter size and conserve battery power by only transmitting during periods of interest. An example of a simple duty cycle is a radio programmed to emit a signal between 0600 and 1800 hours each day. A more complex program would be to transmit between 0900 and 1700 hours for 120 days, no signal for 90 days, and then transmit between 0600 and 1500 hours for 155 days, followed by a repeat of the duty cycle. However, complexity tends to reduce reliability.

Archival, or data storage options allow data to be logged in the transmitter for later downloading from a retrieved transmitter. Temperature, activity, or pressure data can be time stamped and logged for retrieval. This option is most applicable when the radio signal is limited by environmental factors such as saltwater or signal attenuation, or when biologists cannot continuously receive and record the sensor data. Alternatively, data can be transmitted at programmed intervals to a receiver system.

A double pulse option emits 2 pulses (as opposed to one) at a prescribed interval (e.g., every 5th pulse) during a normal transmission cycle. This option reduces the likelihood of confusing the radiomarked animal with another animal with a similar frequency and pulse rate. Double pulses are especially useful where more than one radio-tracking study occurs and frequency allocations are limited or have not been coordinated.

The pulse code option uses unique pulse patterns to identify individual animals transmitting on the same frequency (Howey et al. 1989, Rodgers 2001). A data logger or receiver with code identifying capability is needed for this option. The receiver searches sequentially and quickly for multiple individuals (e.g., 15) on the same frequency. This reduces the time required to scan for signals among all potentially marked animals and the possibility of a radiomarked individual going undetected. It is particularly useful in studies with a large number of transmitters or when aerial searching for many individuals at one time.

There is an option to record when an event occurred. The time of change associated with a selected environmental threshold (e.g., ambient temperature or solar radiation), physiological condition (e.g., body temperature), or animal behavior (e.g., foraging or hibernation) can be conveyed by a 10-second binary pulse code emitted during normal transmission. The precision with which this option can report an event or parameter is 1 in 256. Thus, events ranging from 15 minutes during a 64-hour period to 1 day during a 256-day period can be resolved. An example of

the application of this option is identifying the precise dates of hibernation by taking only one data sample after the event has occurred, rather than monitoring continuously.

Specialized Transmitters.—Data on temperature, relative humidity, incubation, and relative egg position in the nest have been transmitted from sensors built into artificial bird eggs (Howey et al. 1977, 1987; Schwartz et al. 1977). Artificial eggs have also been equipped with a circular mercury switch (Boone and Mesecar 1989).

Radiotelemetry can be used to trigger a release device on traps and to monitor the status of a trap (Hayes 1982, Nolan et al. 1984). Transmitters can be attached to prey that might be taken to a den, nest, or nest site. Transmitters are available for use with anesthetic darts, enabling biologists to track animals until the drugs take effect (Lovett and Hill 1977). Radiotelemetry also can be used to activate an anesthetic dart placed at a bird's nest (Wilson and Wilson 1989) or incorporated in the radio transmitter collar of large mammals (Mech et al. 1990).

Transmitter Attachment

The effects of radiomarking on animals depend on the transmitter attachment design and how it is attached. Kenward (2001) provides a useful initial guide for considering attachment methods. Biologists should rely on the relevant literature, correspond with others who have used specific methods on interest, and gain experience by visiting a field project or practice on captive animals. Special shapes and encapsulation required for implants, harness material, bolts, material, and collar shapes are important components of a wildlife radio transmitter. In addition to selecting an appropriate attachment design, obtaining a good fit to the animal is sometimes critical for the success of a study (Kenward 2001). Proper fitting of radio packages requires practice and patience.

Collars and Necklaces.—Suspending a transmitter from an animal's neck is a common attachment method for mammals and some birds. The transmitter package should be shaped carefully to fit the animal's neck contours, and sufficiently wide and smooth to evenly distribute the transmitter mass to avoid cutting or severe chafing. The fit must accommodate swallowing and seasonal changes in neck circumference. The material must be durable, yet sufficiently flexible to respond to neck, shoulder, or chest movement. The mass of the transmitter and material should be positioned to keep it from interfering with the animal's natural movements and to preclude swaying or flapping of the unit as the animal moves.

A variety of materials can be used for the collar depending on the size of the animal, desired mass, configuration, durability, and attachment method. For small mammals (Fenton et al. 2002) and birds, biologists often use a neck loop made of steel cable, elastic, or braided fishing line covered by flexible, hollow plastic tubing. Each package can be adjusted to fit the individual and secured with a clamp or knot. Ponchos (Amstrup 1980) and necklaces (Marcström et al. 1989, Kenward 2001, Warren and Baines 2002) have been useful for long-term attachment to galliform birds.

When attached to medium or large mammals (Loveridge and Macdonald 2002) the collar is typically constructed of leather, plastic or machine belting, braided nylon, or synthetic dog collar material and secured with bolts, rivets, or buckles. Some mammal collars have been designed to accommodate growth of young animals or a temporary neck expansion in rutting animals (Hölzenbein 1992). Foam rubber inserts and sewn pleats, which tear apart with expansion, have been used (Beale and Smith 1973, Garcelon 1977, Strathearn et al. 1984, Jackson et al. 1985).

Harnesses.—Radio transmitters can be secured on the backs of animals using a harness design. Usually, the transmitter and battery are encapsulated in one package on the center of the back with the antenna at a 45-degree angle from the back or trailing down the back. When using a harness to attach a backpack, biologists must allow for growth and other changes in body size and shape that occur. Harnesses have been used on a variety of mammals (Broekhuizen et al. 1980, Cheeseman and Mallinson 1980, Jennings and Gandy 1980, Kolz et al. 1980). However, because a harness encompasses the animal's body, there can be unacceptable effects (Murray and Fuller 2000, Withey et al. 2001). Therefore, use of harnesses must be carefully considered and application should be undertaken only after training by experienced colleagues and with practice (e.g., with captive animals or surrogate species).

A single body loop of harness material extending around the body, behind the wings, but in front of the legs has been used for short-term marking of birds (Dunstan 1972, Coon et al. 1976, Perry et al. 1981), usually with adhesive between the transmitter and feathers. Double loop harnesses are used to attach large transmitters to birds. Flexible harness materials such as woven Teflon ribbon (Dunstan 1972), elastic (Green 1985), neoprene rubber (Britten et al. 1999), or plastic tubing (Nesbitt et al. 1982) can be fit to each bird's body size while adjusting to the bird's various postures. The loops must be positioned to avoid impinging on the leading or trailing edges of the wings where they join the body. Melvin and Temple (1987) and Buehler et al. (1995) linked neck and body loops by a strand along the sternum in some configurations. Details for fitting and securing Teflon ribbon double loop harness are given in Snyder et al. (1989) and Kenward (2001).

Wing loops also have been used to attach backpack transmitters (Godfrey 1970, Nesbitt et al. 1982, Hill et al. 1999). Care in fitting is required to avoid interfering with wing movement (Nesbitt et al. 1982). Loops around the abdomen and legs, or legs only, have worked in some cases for passerines (Rappole and Tipton 1991) and rails (Rallidae) (Haramis and Kerns 2000).

Materials such as cotton thread have been designed as a weak link into a harness to permit the harness to break and detach (Boshoff et al. 1984, Karl and Clout 1987, Hill et al. 1999). The weak link should break if the harness or transmitter becomes snagged on an object or decompose with time. Elastic harness material loosens with time permitting the transmitter to detach (e.g., 3–15 months) (Godfrey 1970, Amlaner et al. 1978, Hirons and Owen 1982). As with expandable and breakaway collars, weathering of the elastic harness and decomposition of the weak links can be quite variable.

Adhesives.—Backpacks also have been attached with glue (e.g., cyanoacrylic "super glue"), fiberglass resin, tape (e.g., Tesa tape or Velcro fabric), and suturing. Gluing or taping a transmitter to an animal provides an alternative to encumbering it with the mass and potential physical interference of a collar or harness. Adhesives work best with comparatively small, light transmitters for relatively short durations. A variety of adhesives have been tried, but success varies with species and environment. Caution is required because some adhesives are irritants to tissues.

Transmitters have been glued to bats (Chiroptera) (Kerth et al. 2001, Bontadina et al. 2002, Kurta and Murray 2002), bears (Ursidae) (Anderka 1987), and marine mammals (Hammond et al. 1992). Adhesives are commonly used on birds (Bowman et al. 2002, Green et al. 2002, Spears et al. 2002). Alexander and Cresswell (1990) removed dirt and oils from the attachment area with acetone, and used cyanoacrylic glue to hold transmitters on birds. Wanless et al. (1988), used fiberglass resin to hold transmitters on seabirds. Using nylon mesh and 5-minute epoxy, Harrison and Stoneburner (1981) glued transmitters to seabirds. Heath (1987) used a contact cement to affix a Velcro fabric base on the backs of penguins (Spheniscidae) and Velcro fabric on the transmitter to provide a fast means of replacing transmitters. Wilson and Wilson (1989), Culik (2001), and others have wrapped feathers and a transmitter in Tesa tape to hold transmitters on penguins. Suturing has been used to attach small transmitters to the backs of young precocial birds (Burkepile et al. 2002). A combination of suture and a subcutaneous wire prong or anchor (Newman et al. 1999), glue and anchor (Lougheed et al. 2002), and suture with glue and anchor (Guyn and Clark 2000) have been used to attach backpacks to birds.

Implants.—Radio transmitters can be surgically implanted either abdominally in the body cavity, or subcutaneously. Abdominal implants often are used in mammals whose body configuration precludes collar attachment (Melquist and Hornocker 1979, Eagle et al. 1984, Ralls et al. 1989, Van Vuren 1989), or to obtain physiological data (Giacometti et al. 2001, Eloranta et al. 2002, Fuglei et al. 2002). Abdominal implants have been used in birds that do not tolerate externally attached transmitters (Korschgen et al. 1984, Petersen et al. 1995), or to monitor heart rates (Hawkins et al. 2000). Abdominally implanted transmitters are often used in waterfowl because they may have fewer adverse effects on behavior, survival, and nesting than externally attached transmitters (Garrettson et al. 2000). Abdominally implanted transmitters have been used to track reptiles (Barbour et al. 1969, Reinart and Cundall 1982, Weatherhead and Anderka 1984) and amphibians (Stouffer et al. 1983, Smits 1984). Implantation of the entire radio transmitter and antenna in the abdominal cavity can reduce reception range of VHF radios by >50% (Melquist and Hornocker 1979) and precludes use of transmitters for tracking by satellite. However, a percutaneous antenna from an implanted transmitter that exits the body (Korschgen et al. 1996a, Hupp et al. 2003) can improve VHF reception range or allow biologists to implant transmitters for satellite reception.

Subcutaneous implants can be used to attach transmitters to animals too small to accommodate a harness or undergo surgery for abdominal implants. They are typically placed beneath loose skin on the animal's back and have been used in juvenile waterfowl (Korschgen et al. 1996b) and galliforms (Riley et al. 1998), or where biologists wish to monitor heart rates. Schulz et al. (2001) tested subcutaneous implants in mourning doves (*Zenaida macroura*) and found fewer adverse physiological effects than abdominal implants or transmitters attached by harness, and longer retention than transmitters that were glued to the body. Although typically used on small animals, subcutaneous implants have also been used to radiotrack polar bears (*Ursus maritimus*) (Mulcahy and Garner 1999).

Mauser and Jarvis (1991) attached transmitters to one-day-old mallards (*Anas platyrhnchos*) by inserting beneath the skin a metal prong attached to a 2-g transmitter. The transmitter was further secured to the back of the duckling with sutures. A combination of subcutaneous wire and glue or sutures was also used by Newman et al. (1999), Guyn and Clark (2000), and Lougheed et al. (2002) to attach transmitters to the backs of birds.

Only experienced veterinarians and trained biologists should implant radio transmitters. Biologists should check with appropriate regulatory agencies to learn if special permits or licensing is required. Implanted transmitters should be sterilized using zephirran chloride, chlorhexidine diacetate, ethylene oxide gas, or hydrogen peroxide gas plasma. The transmitter manufacturer should be contacted to ensure the planned sterilization procedure would not harm the transmitter coating. When placing radio implants, veterinarians and biologists must be careful to maintain a sterile field around the incision and avoid contamination of surgical equipment and transmitter. An anesthetist should monitor respiration, body temperature, and heart rate when general anesthesia is applied. Animals should be monitored for at least 1 hour after they recover from anesthesia to ensure they are alert, breathing freely, and not bleeding or otherwise injured before they are released. When properly conducted, abdominal implantation of radio transmitters should result in few mortalities (Mulcahy and Esler 1999).

Although implanted transmitters have had negligible effect on reproduction or survival (Esler et al. 2000) in some waterfowl species, impaired reproduction and lowered survival (Hatch et al. 2000) have been observed in some marine birds following abdominal implantation of radios. If implants have not been used previously in a study species, procedure development and a pilot study of transmitter effects may be needed (e.g., Hupp et al. 2003).

Neck- and Leg-bands.—Neck- and leg-band attachment methods have been used to avoid encumbering birds with a harness, and because feather growth on nestlings or fledglings can preclude use of harnesses or tail mounts. Melvin et al. (1983) used a plastic band as the base for battery or solar-powered transmitters. Kenward (1985) described an anklet transmitter for use on raptors. Transmitters have also been affixed to standard plastic neck collars traditionally used as visual markers on waterfowl. Transmitter antennas can be problematic when attached to bands because the antennas are usually shorter than those on comparable backpack transmitters. Further, on leg-band transmitters, antennas are close to the ground, thus reducing reception range. Neck collars should be used cautiously on geese because they have been associated with reduced survival.

Tail Mounts.—Small transmitters, generally ≤2% of body mass, can be mounted at the base of birds' tail feathers. When attached on the ventral side, the package is out of sight, and kept warm and dry among the under tail converts. When attaching the transmitter, biologists must be careful not to bend or mash shafts of the rectrices, or manipulate them with too much pulling or side movement. Excessive transmitter mass or manipulation causes the follicle to "release" the rectrix. Radio transmitters have been attached

to tail feathers by a variety of methods including fiber-packing tape (Fuller and Tester 1973), plastic cable ties (Wanless et al. 1989), threads and contact cement (Kenward 1978), or hot melt glue (Fitzner and Fitzner 1977). Bray and Corner (1972) molded a plastic base and metal clip that can be attached to rectrices in about 1 minute. Tail-mounted transmitters detach when the bird molts.

Ear Tags.—Radio transmitters affixed to ear tags typically used for marking livestock have been attached to some mammals (Servheen et al. 1981), particularly when changes in the diameter of the neck preclude use of conventional collars (Garrott et al. 1985). Ear tags are relatively easy to attach and can be marked for visual identification in the field. However, these units are small, with limited operational life and their short antennas restrict signal range. Rothmeyer et al. (2002) used ear-tag mounted transmitters attached to the tail for tracking American beaver (*Castor canadensis*).

Miscellaneous Attachment Methods.—Many other attachment methods have received incidental use. Swanson et al. (1976) mounted transmitters with activity sensors on the nasal saddle to monitor the feeding behavior of ducks. Perry (1981) used cyanoacrylic glue to hold a transmitter on the top of the bill of diving ducks. Kooyman et al. (1982) used hose clamps to bind the transmitter and feathers together on penguins. Transmitters have been attached successfully to the patagium of large birds that commonly use soaring and gliding flight (Wallace et al. 1994). Nonsurgical techniques have been used to implant transmitters in the vaginal canal (Bowman and Jacobson 1998, Cartensen et al. 2003) and rumen of ungulates. Kenward (2001) references additional attachment sites, such as horns, flippers, blubber, and scutes.

Detachment, Drop-off Options.—Increasingly, researchers want radio transmitters to become detached at the end of a study or according to a predetermined schedule, but early designs were not reliable (Kenward 2001). For example, when the release is a degradable component, varying environmental factors can result in unpredictable retention times. Alternatively, electronic mechanisms with timers or remote controls can be designed to pull a pin, release a clasp, or sever the collar. However, concerns about mechanical problems such as freezing, dirt, or jamming still exist. Radio triggering requires an animal to wear a receiver. This increases the current drain on the power supply, increases size and mass of the radio transmitter, and decreases overall reliability of the system.

Receiving Systems

Receiving systems for VHF wildlife telemetry comprise radio receivers, antennas, cables to connect the antenna to the receiver, accessories (e.g., head phones, chargers), counters and decoders, and recording devices. Receiving systems are electronically complex, but compared to selecting transmitters there are fewer choices of components and options.

Receivers.—Biologists can purchase radio receivers designed specifically for wildlife radiotelemetry (Fig. 4). The receiver must amplify the relatively weak radio signals from wildlife transmitters and reject the stronger signals from other sources on slightly different frequencies (image rejection) (Smith and Amlaner 1989). A tuned radio frequency amplifier, oscillator, and other receiver compo-

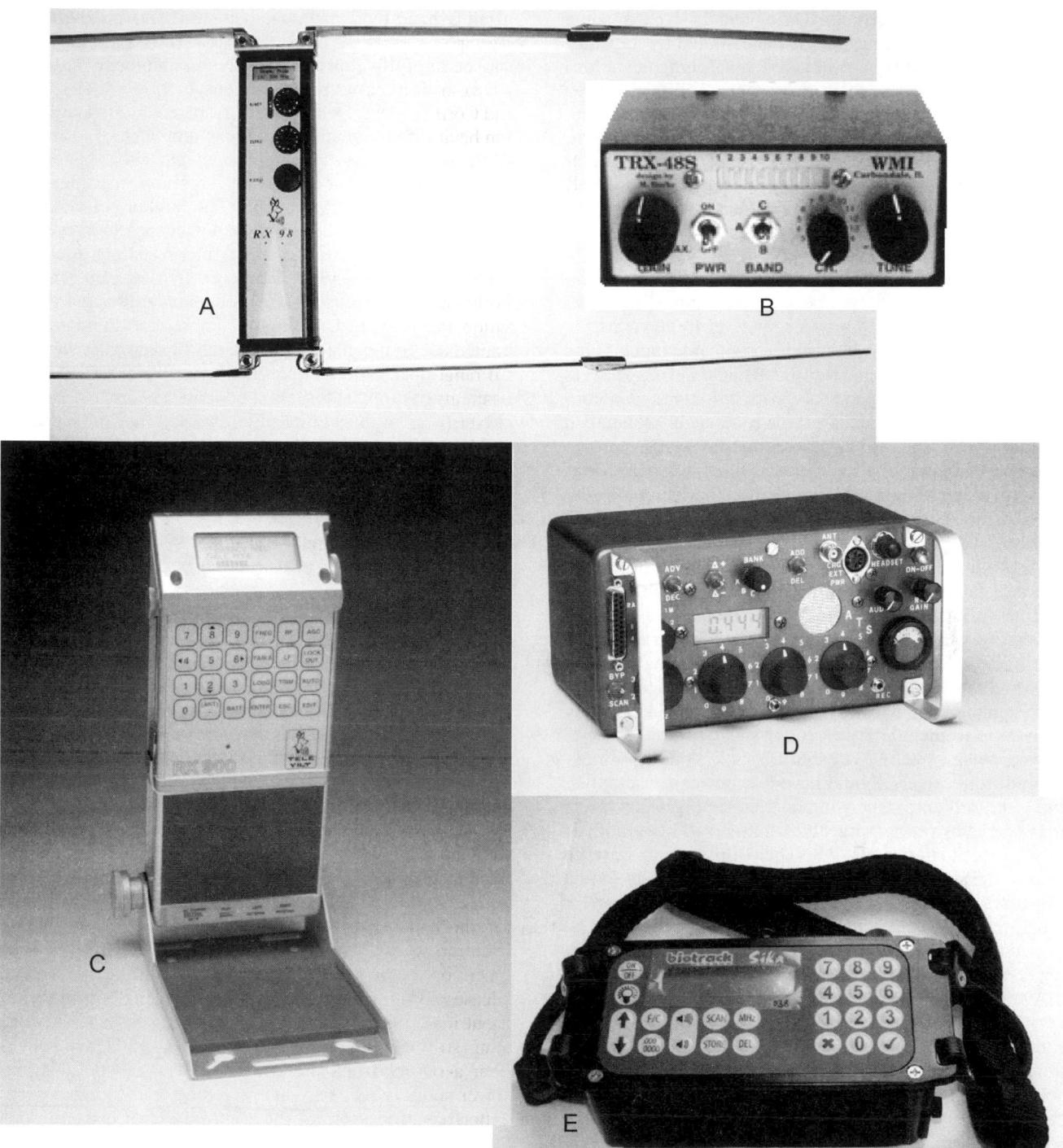

Fig. 4. Wildlife radio receivers. A, compact dial frequency with built-in antenna (24 × 7 × 3.2 cm, 630 g); B, compact dial frequency (17 × 7.5 × 4 cm, 800 g); C, programmable scanning (25.5 × 11.5 × 5.5 cm, 1.65 kg); D, programmable scanning (11 × 21 × 18 cm, 2.3 kg); E, programmable scanning (15 × 8.5 × 5.5 cm, 800 g).

nents are necessary to process the transmitter signal on each frequency, convert the processed signal to an audio tone, and produce other signals for further processing by demodulators, decoders, or pulse counters. Most wildlife receivers are crystal controlled or "crystal referenced."

The minimum discernable level of most wildlife telemetry receivers is –140 to –150 dBm. The human ear can distinguish a signal of about –150 dBm from the "noise" typical of wildlife receivers and most tracking environments, but for automatic recording the signal must

be about –125 dBm. Usually, a "noise blocker" is incorporated into the receiver circuitry to reduce interference from common sources, such as auto or aircraft engines. The smaller, simpler receivers operate within bandwidths of about 50 to 200 KHz, and most can be tuned to a single KHz channel (frequency). These receivers can be used with about 5 to 20 transmitter frequencies. Transmitter frequency stability should be < ±0.1 KHz and frequency drift over the temperature operating range (–40 to +70 C for manual receivers, –10 to +50 C for programmable receivers) should be < ±0.5 KHz. The 10 KHz spacing among transmitter frequencies is necessitated by transmitter drift, transmitter crystal variation, and tuning deviations (e.g., nominal 164.000 MHz, received at 164.005) not by variability within a receiver. More complex (and more expensive) receivers cover from 1 to 45 MHz bandwidths. Usually there is a manual switch for selecting the particular band to be received (e.g., 164 MHz or 165 MHz). Dials or buttons are typically used to select the frequency (channel) for the specific transmitter to be received. Some receivers include a "sweep" option that automatically searches a range (5 KHz) around the selected frequency. Cochran and Pater (2001) discuss use of scanning receivers that operate over a much broader range of frequencies.

Wildlife radio receivers include a control to increase the gain (the power to receive the signal), and some receivers have an automatic gain control. With automatic gain control, the amplitude of the incoming signal is maintained within a range (e.g., 40 dB), even as the signal strength increases or decreases due to transmitter antenna movement, variation in animal body position, and animal proximity to the receiving antenna. Commonly, the relative amplitude of the signal is indicated by a visual display. The volume control does not affect the gain but simply increases the audio signal (including background noise). Receivers should have a built-in speaker and a jack for connecting earphones. Earphones are useful in a noisy environment and for identifying clutter to a signal because the listener can adjust gain and volume to more easily hear weak signals and discern their peak amplitude. Many receivers also include a jack for connecting a recorder or computer (e.g., via RS232 cable).

Wildlife receivers should have low power consumption (e.g., ~40 milliamp depending on gain setting). Receivers are powered by nonrechargeable (8–26 hrs of operation) or rechargeable batteries (5–24 hrs), and most have a meter to indicate the status of the supply voltage. Biologists should have extra batteries or battery packs, or a transformer for recharging NiCad batteries. Most wildlife receivers can be operated or charged with a converter for use with a car battery (12 V).

A programmable, automatic frequency scanning capability is built into some receivers, or can be added to other models as a separate unit (Fig. 4). The duration each frequency can be sampled ("listened" for) varies from 0.5 second to 10 minutes. Most automatic scanning receivers search in an ascending frequency order, but some can be programmed to scan a specified order or a range of frequencies. The scanning function can be interrupted when a radio signal is detected. Programmable receivers are useful when many transmitters are in the area of reception, covering a large area in which many signals might be received, searching an area quickly, such as from aircraft, or when the receiver can be left unattended and signals recorded automatically.

Programmable receivers are larger, more complex, and potentially more delicate than manual models but all receiving equipment is vulnerable to dirt, moisture, or shock. Manufacturers should advise investigators about the vulnerability of the equipment and need for protection with plastic bags, umbrellas, or special carrying cases. Portability of receivers is important in thick vegetation, or at the end of a long monitoring session when one is juggling a hand-held antenna, compass, and notebook and pen. Some receivers weigh as little as 300 g. Biologists should carefully consider the size of equipment and accessories such as protective cases and carrying straps. Kenward (2001) describes the array of receiver types available from wildlife telemetry equipment suppliers.

Recorders, Counters, Decoders, and Data Loggers.—Humans are by far the most common recorders and decoders of telemetry signals. The human ear and brain are more sensitive listeners than mechanical processors and are capable of more complex programming, including feedback and response. However, humans are prone to fatigue and notoriously difficult to standardize and expensive to employ and maintain. Therefore, attempts have been made to mechanize processing of radiotelemetry signals and data. Most equipment available from manufacturers measures intervals between pulses or records changes in signal amplitude, marks the presence or absence of a signal, or decodes a signal and records analog data. Additional processing capabilities are possible using custom-made systems, often developed in university or public research laboratories.

The simplest automatic recording system involves connecting a paper chart (often thermosensitive) recorder to a receiver and recording the presence or absence of a radio signal (Licht et al. 1989). One- and 2-channel chart recorders can be combined with a scanning receiver, but are limited in the number of frequencies that can be monitored (e.g., Kenward 1987). Chart speed can vary with voltage, which is important if the chart recorder is used to time presence-absence or activity events reflected by amplitude changes in the radio signal (Cederlund and Lemnell 1980, Widen 1982). A timing device can be added to strip-chart recorders. Deep-cycle batteries designed to be discharged and recharged many times are important equipment for use in the field to power recording and decoding devices. Signals also can be tape recorded (Kenward 1987) continuously, or sampled periodically (Macdonald and Amlaner 1980) for long durations (Schober et al. 1989, Stanner and Farhi 1989). Tape recorders can be used as the primary recording mechanism (Diehl and Helb 1986, Smith and Aitken 1989), as an alternative to a chart recorder (Stohr 1989), or as permanent storage after some processing (Schober and Oehry 1987).

Computers, from microprocessors to personal computers, commonly serve as data recording and storage devices as well as processors of the received signal (Janeau et al. 1987, Kuechle et al. 1989). Schober et al. (1989) described computer software for extensive processing of incoming radio signals for decoding and storage. All data (except presence/absence) recorded on charts, tapes, and computers require some decoding. Decoders can count pulses or measure pulse intervals and pulse widths, and convert them to voltage using a digital counter with a digital-to-analog option (Kuechle et al. 1987). Data logging (archival) tags often are used with PTTs and GPS receivers in satellite telemetry (Weimerskirch et al. 2002).

Receiving Antennas.—The receiving antenna has radio signal gathering capacity (gain) that lends power to the receiving process. The gain, or power, of a receiving antenna is measured in decibels. Each receiving antenna has a 3-dimensional pattern of power oriented in relation to the element(s) of the antenna (Figs. 5, 6). Making the antenna more

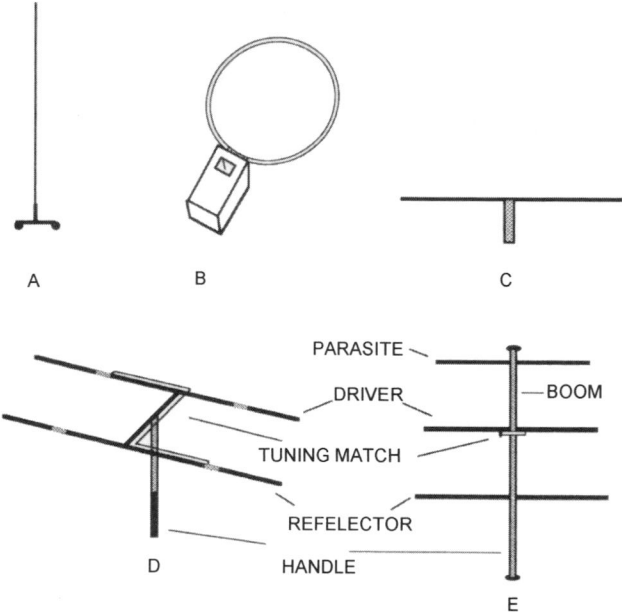

Fig. 5. Receiving antennas: A = omnidirectional whip, B = loop (attached to hand-held receiver), C = dipole, D = Adcock, (H-type), and E = 3-element Yagi.

directional can generally increase gain. A receiving antenna will detect the strongest radio signal when the lobe(s) of the pattern with the greatest gain is directed toward the signal. In addition to this "peak" signal, there will be a "null" with comparatively weak or no reception, between the reception pattern lobes (Fig. 6). The actual pattern of reception most resembles the theoretical pattern when the antenna is > 1/2 λ from anything that affects its properties. Conductors, such as wires, a vehicle's roof, or a person's body can distort patterns, reduce directionality, and lower gain. If these factors are not eliminated, or corrected, variability is introduced into the accuracy of the receiving process. Preamplifiers are sometimes used to overcome power loss.

Receiving antennas are generally hand-held because biologists move about to stay within reception range of a radiomarked animal and to maximize signal strength and clarity by positioning themselves relative to the transmitter. Usually it is best to hold the antenna above one's head to maximize reception, and standing on an elevated place in the terrain also is useful. Antennas should not be held by the elements or by the boom between elements because a person's body, hand, and arms can alter the reception pattern. Large and specialized antenna systems might need to be mounted on a vehicle or mast. Other innovations to facilitate radiotracking in special circumstances include a V aerial for improved reception of vertically polarized signals and a 2-element directional antenna for close-range reception in heavy vegetation (Burchard 1989*a,b*).

Most receiving antennas consist of a boom, metal elements, a tuning device, and connector for a lead to the receiver. The basic factor affecting antenna design is the transmitter frequency. The lower the frequency, the longer the wavelength and the longer the antenna element(s) required. The diameter of the element wire (or rod) also is a factor affecting element length and spacing in multi-element designs. Longer elements or more elements provide directionality and gain, but at the expense of portability.

Portability is an important consideration when moving to remain within reception range of the radiomarked animal. Portability also can be important to accommodate changes in polarization of the radio signals.

The connection from the antenna to the receiver is coaxial cable, which minimizes loss of power. Breaks, nicks, abrasions, or kinks in the coaxial cable can reduce its insulating capacity, causing a loss of power between the antenna and the receiver. Coaxial cable is attached to the antenna and receiver by special connectors of either of 2 types, screw-together UHF connectors or bayonet-mount connectors. Breakage commonly occurs where the cable and connector come together. Biologists should be able to replace cables and broken connectors in the field. Maximum performance of the receiving antenna is obtained when the receiver is matched to the impedance (resistance value) of the antenna. Equipment manufacturers can provide the best combinations of components and tune them for matching impedance.

Dipole antennas (Fig. 5) are simple and the standard to which the gain of other antennas is compared. The dipole provides bearing accuracy of about 5–10° with nulls in opposite directions. Tilting the dipole element about 15° from horizontal provides a narrower null thereby indicating direction to the signal (Parish 1980). Omni-directional antennas also are called "whip" antennas (Fig. 5). Their reception pattern is uniform through 360°. Omni-directional antennas are used commonly to detect presence of signals in relatively confined areas. They are easily adapted for magnetic or bolt-on attachment to vehicles and aircraft. The element of a loop antenna is configured in a circle or diamond (Fig. 5). The main advantage is that the dimensions can be relatively small compared to other directional antennas for the same frequency. A loop antenna for frequencies in the 30–40 MHz range can be hand held. Loops have bearing accuracy of about 5° with nulls in 2 directions. Portable loop antennas for higher frequencies (e.g., 150 mHz) are useful for short-range reception (Kenward 2001).

An Adcock or H antenna (Fig. 5) has only 2 elements and, for any given frequency, smaller dimensions than a Yagi antenna. Some manufacturers use flexible elements or those that fold or screw together so the H antenna can be disassembled quickly and transported compactly. Livezey (1988) described polyvinylchloride element covers to protect the antenna during use without affecting its performance. The maximum gain of an H antenna is slightly less than that for a 3-element Yagi antenna. The reception pattern of an H antenna has a narrow null, allowing the signal location to be estimated within about 2–3° (compared to 5° for a 3-element Yagi antenna). However, 2 nulls occur at 180° from each other, and the actual direction of the signal often must be ascertained by triangulation or prior knowledge of the animal's general location.

The Yagi antenna (Fig. 5) provides the most gain and directionality of the popular wildlife receiving antennas. It comprises 3 or more elements including a driver (from which power is supplied), a parasite element(s) in front of the driver, and a reflector element behind the driver, all of which are mounted on a boom (Fig. 5). The dimensions of a Yagi antenna are critical; lengths of the elements and their spacing depend on the radio frequency to be received. A 4-element Yagi antenna for 164 MHz will be about 100 × 113 cm, while a 5-element Yagi antenna for 216 MHz would be 68 × 120 cm.

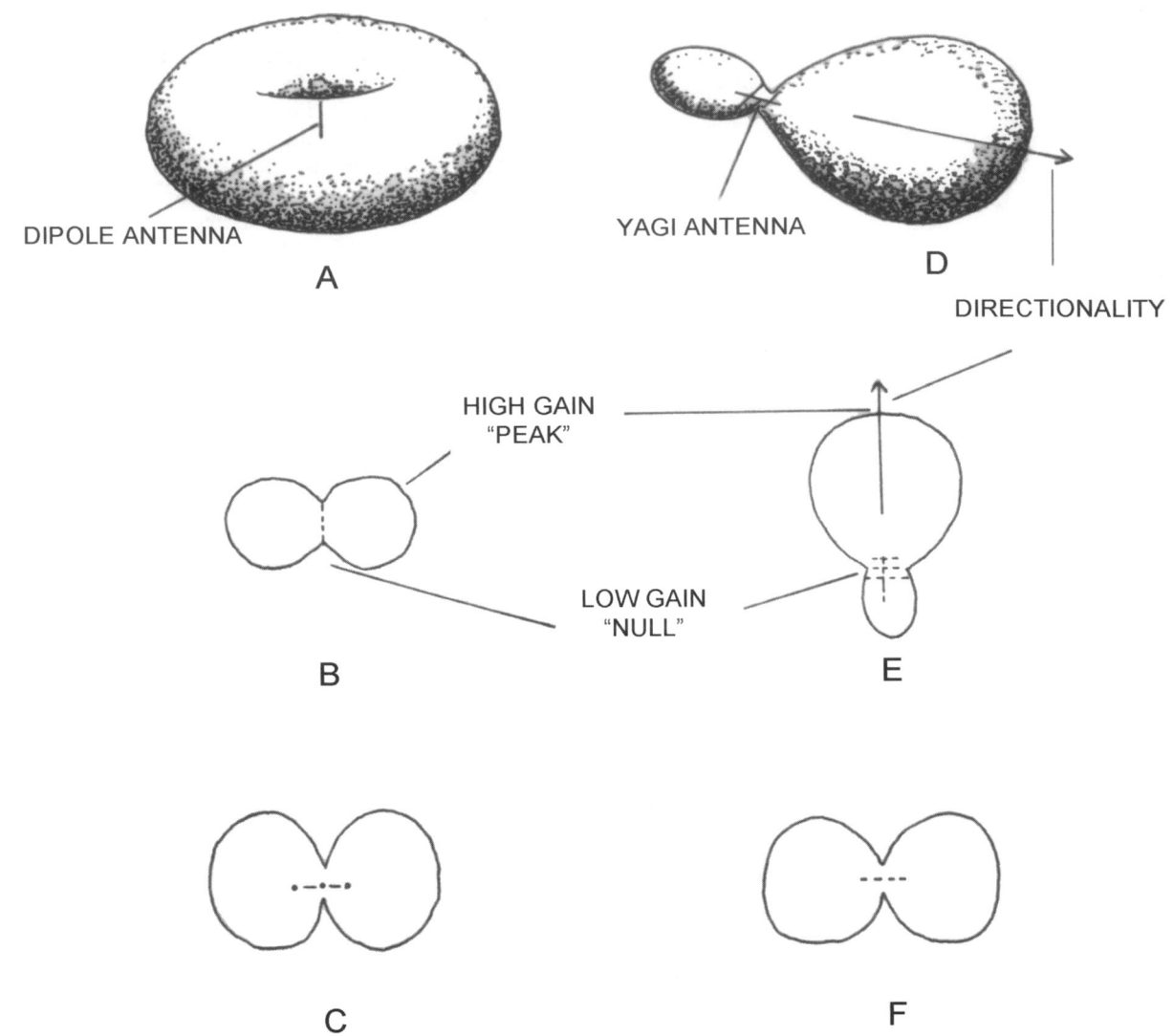

Fig. 6. Reception patterns of receiving antennas: (A) 3-dimensional pattern of a vertical whip dipole, (B) cross section of a vertical whip dipole, (C) cross section of an Adcock ("H") antenna, (D) 3-dimensional pattern of a 3-element Yagi antenna, (E) the horizontal cross section pattern of a 3-element Yagi, and (F) the horizontal cross section pattern of a loop antenna. Direction from the Yagi to the source of the radio signal is most readily detected when the area of high gain is pointing toward the transmitter (modified from Kenward 1987 and used with permission from Academic Press).

The manufacturer typically tunes yagi attennas, but tuning in the field is possible by changing the length of the slide until maximum signal strength is obtained from a source greater than 20 λ from the antenna (Amlaner 1980). A well-tuned Yagi antenna has more gain in front of the antenna than from behind, creating a reception pattern that facilitates identifying the direction of the peak signal (Fig. 6). A 3-element Yagi antenna provides about a ±5.0° bearing accuracy. Increasing the number of elements provides more gain and directionality (Fig. 7), but additional elements increase the boom length, making it more difficult to maneuver the antenna. A 9-element Yagi antenna for 150 MHz will have a beam length of about 4 m. Yagi antennas with more than 5 elements are generally restricted to use on a fixed mast, or on a vehicle. Portable, highly directional Yagi antennas can be constructed to receive UHF frequencies that are the harmonics of common wildlife VHF frequencies; these antennas can be useful in wooded habitat (Cochran and Pater 2001).

Two Yagi antennas can be mounted about 1 λ or λ/4 apart (Voight and Lotimer 1981) and electrically connect-ed by joining their coaxial cables in a switch box between the antennas and receiver to form a null-peak system. This system increases gain and gives a directional error of about ±1° or when switched to create a narrow "beam width" null toward the signal, can reduce error to ±0.5° (Amlaner 1980, Anderka 1987). Accurate and precise performance of a null-peak system requires careful tuning and alignment of all the parts.

Several designs have been devised to mount antennas on vehicles including aircraft. However, the antenna must be elevated to avoid interference caused by the metal on the vehicle. Bray et al. (1975) and Kolz and Johnson (1975) described mounts for car-top carriers while Hegdal and Gatz (1987) placed the mast through a hole in the roof so the antenna could be rotated and elevated from inside the vehicle. Cederlund and Lemnell (1980) and Cox et al. (2002) described a vehicle-mounted null system with an electronic compass, and Medina and Smith (1986) described sturdy mast systems, which can telescope with air pumps (Kenward 2001).

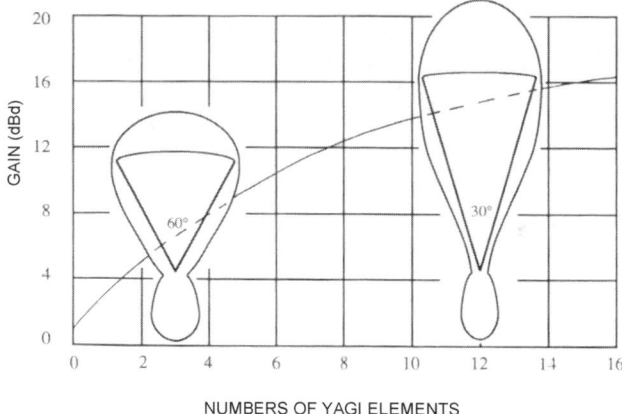

Fig. 7. The gain and directionality of a Yagi antenna in relation to the number of "parasite" elements. Reception range is doubled for each increase of 6 dBd. The reception patterns of 3- and 12-element Yagi antennas illustrate how the increase in gain is accompanied by a narrower (30° vs. 60°) field of reception (modified from Kenward 1987 and used with permission from Academic Press).

Mounting antennas on aircraft requires adaptation for different types and models of aircraft (e.g., high wing, low wing, helicopter). Options include temporary mounting with cuffs for wing struts and helicopter skids (Gilmer et al. 1981, Inglis 1981, Voight and Lotimer 1981), and permanent mounts (Whitehouse and Steven 1977). Multiple element antennas have been mounted on a mast that extends through a hole in the belly of aircraft (e.g., Judd and Knight 1977). Whip antennas are commonly used for communication systems in aircraft and omnidirectional antennas for wildlife can be placed on planes and helicopters. In most countries, addition of any object to the outside of aircraft must be approved. Approval is not universal and usually is dependent on the ownership of the aircraft (e.g., government, private, commercial) or the concerns of individual mechanics and inspectors from one area to another within a country. The International Association of Natural Resources Pilots (http://www.ianrp.org/) can be contacted for information about successful attachment methods for use on aircraft.

Receiving antennas can also be mounted on masts or towers to increase their height and enhance radio signal reception. Many types of poles, including telescoping masts, can be secured by guy wires, tripods, or placed in a hole or cement foundation, depending on the height and strength required to support the antenna(s) (ARRL 1988). Many mounting devices can be obtained from suppliers of radio communications equipment. O'Connor et al. (1987) described a typical fixed-site mount, 5.5 m in height that can be rotated. Smith and Trevor-Deutsch (1980) developed a system where motorized rotors (operated by remote control) turned a null-peak Yagi antenna array on top of masts (also described by Linn and Willcox 1982, Spencer et al. 1987).

Automated Receiving Systems.—Automation of reception and recording has been achieved in a variety of ways, but these systems are largely "custom" designed and constructed. Cochran et al. (1965), Deat et al. (1980), and Bogel (1994) described triangulation by continuously rotating antennas on top of fixed towers with reception coverage ranges from ~10–30 km. Howey et al. (1989)

placed 2 Yagi antennas, facing north and south, on towers about 40 km apart and used a scanning receiver and recorder (laptop computer) to study movements of migrants. Green et al. (2002) placed automatic recording systems comprising antenna, scanning receiver, and recorder (palmtop computer) along a migration route to record passage of shorebirds. Burchard (1989a), Spencer and Savaglio (1995), Larkin et al. (1996), Schober et al. (1992), and Bogel (1994) developed systems for automatic receiving and recording.

Yerbury (1980) and Lemnell et al. (1983) estimated locations within an automatic tracking system that use times of signal arrival at different receiving sites. One automatic system still functioning, based on the Loran-C navigation system, has been used to track large mammals (Findholt et al. 1996, 2002).

Satellite Tracking Systems
The Argos Satellite System

Wildlife radiotelemetry based on the Argos satellite system (http://www.cls.fr/manuel/) is routinely used with remotely occurring or wide ranging (e.g., migrants) species that can carry the specialized transmitters, called Platform Transmitter Terminals (PTTs) (Fig. 8), which weigh >12g. This system provides location estimates and sensor data from PTTs anywhere around the world (Strikwerda et al. 1986, Fancy et al. 1988). Ultra high frequency (UHF) transmissions (401.65 MHz) from PTTs are received on polar orbiting satellites and are relayed to processing centers in France and the United States. Records of processed data can be distributed to users in a variety of formats, including Internet access to data received about 4 hours previously. The cost of data acquisition from Argos ranges from about $12 to $24 per PTT per day in which a transmission(s) is received. Software for managing the data from the files received from Argos is available from equipment suppliers and users. Some applications require receivers to obtain transmissions directly from PTTs or from the satellites.

Platform transmitter terminals work only with the Argos-Tiros satellite system (http://www.argosine.com/) transmitting coded identification and data from up to 8 sensors. The signals are digitally encoded on a pulse width of ~0.33 seconds and a pulse interval usually between 50 and 90 seconds. The transmitting schedule (i.e., the duty cycle) can be programmed for more transmissions during different periods (e.g., seasons), which can prolong the operational life. Some PTTs can be programmed to transmit only during predicted satellite passes. The transmitted radio frequency must be stable (<2 Hz drift), and the radiated power must be relatively high (~0.3–2.0 W) compared to conventional VHF wildlife telemetry. Consequently, the circuitry is more complex than conventional VHF transmitters, and the lightest PTT is about 12 g, limiting their use to comparatively large animals. The radiated power can be adjusted to conserve battery power, but this can lead to fewer location estimates obtained per duty cycle (Walton et al. 2001).

Finding PTTs (Bates et al. 2003) can provide valuable information about the status of the marked animal and facilitate retrieval of PTTs for refurbishing and re-use. Platform transmitter terminals and VHF transmitters can be attached to the same animals for some applications that require finding the animal (Gonzales-Solis et al. 2000,

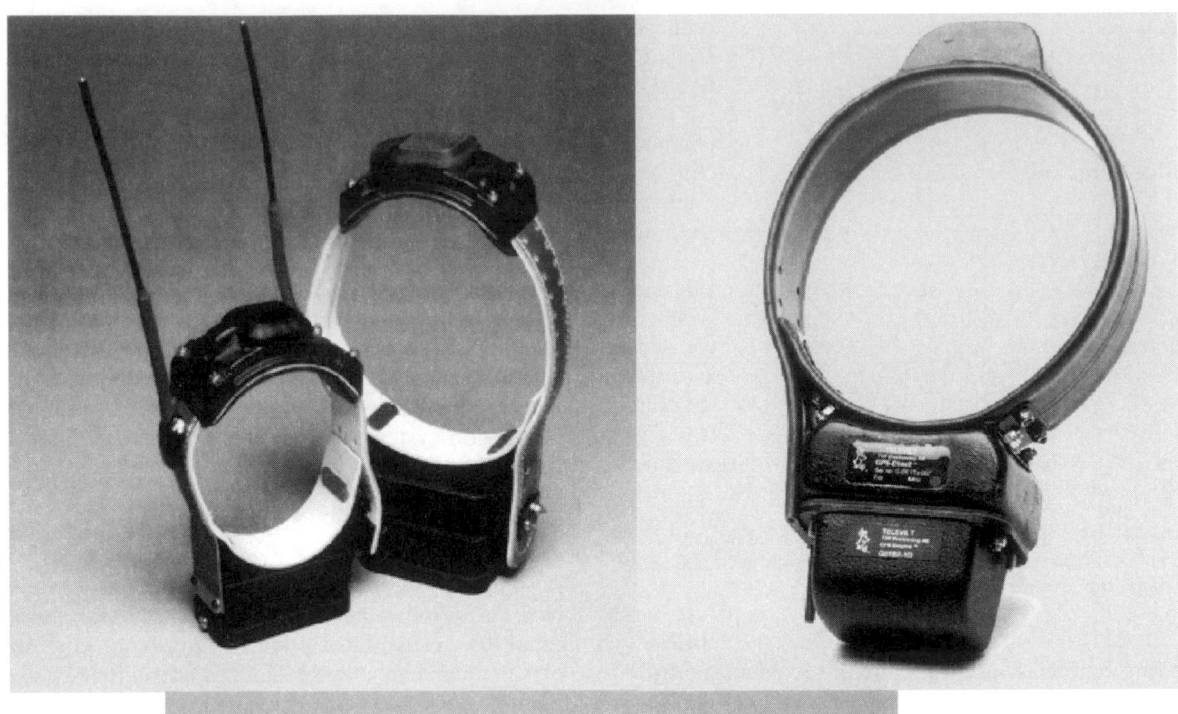

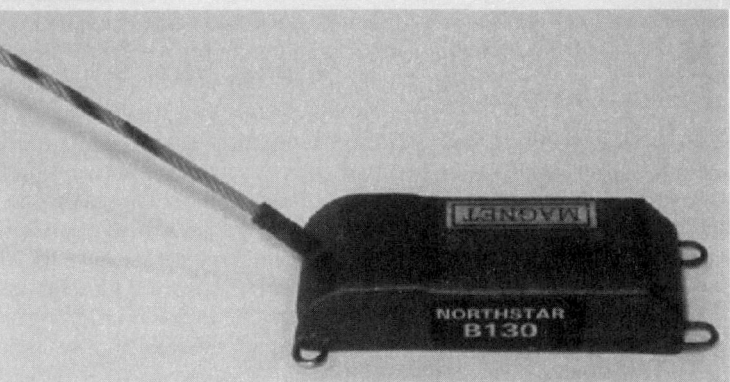

Fig. 8. Satellite telemetry equipment. Upper left, GPS receivers with VHF transmitter and remote release mechanism (1.1 kg). Upper right, GPS receiver and satellite link transmitter (1–8 kg). Center, avian Platform Transmitter Terminal (30 g). Bottom, time and temperature archive and satellite link for marine application (82.5 g).

Amstrup et al. 2001, McLoughlin et al. 2002). PTTs can be used to sample a few animals while others are tracked with VHF telemetry (Ballard et al. 2000). Temperature, activity, and pressure sensors as well as sensor data loggers have been integrated with PTTs (Hedd et al. 2001, Fedak et al. 2002, Harcourt et al. 2002, Shannon et al. 2002*b*). PTTs also can transmit data about the battery to alert biologists of impending loss of reception. PTTs also have been inte-

grated with Global Positioning Satellite (GPS) receivers to convey location estimates to users via the Argos system.

Location estimates based on PTT transmissions are assigned to location classes of which 3 of 7 are associated with nominal location accuracy. However, the location class assigned by Argos underestimates the error associated with most wildlife applications, in part because many PTTs do not transmit 1 Watt of radiated power, on which the Argos system was designed. Radiated power is reduced to about 0.25 W or less for many wildlife applications to conserve energy for prolonged PTT operation. Reduced radiated power can result in fewer location estimates (Walton et al. 2001) and consequently fewer data with which to estimate locations most accurately. Because of the limited accuracy, biologists should examine if the Argos system is appropriate for their objectives, especially if they require regular location accuracy of <1 km of linear error.

There has been little consistency of testing methods and great variability among applications of the Argos system. Furthermore, after animals are PTT tagged and released, the fate of all individual animals or the performance of the equipment might not be known with certainty. When considering satellite telemetry, as with VHF wildlife telemetry, biologists should become familiar with the literature, recent developments, and colleagues' experiences. A pilot study can be useful to assess how satellite telemetry performs under the conditions of a particular project.

Global Positioning Satellite System

Another automatic tracking system based on satellites is the U.S. Department of Defense Global Positioning Satellite (GPS) array that has transmitters on satellites (O'Neil et al. 2005) and receivers on the animal (Fig. 8). Location estimates can be acquired as often as 1 per second (Weimerskirsch et al. 2002) and stored in memory in the receiver tag. The estimates can be obtained by (1) recovering the tag [recapture or retrieved from a drop-off attachment mechanism] and downloading the data to a microprocessor, (2) by receiving the data through a transmitted signal from the tag, or (3) by integration with a PTT to relay the GPS data through the Argos system. The GPS system requires considerable power, which limits operational life or receiver tag size. The advantages of GPS include possibility of more frequent locations and accuracy better than 50 m (O'Neil et al. 2005).

RADIOTRACKING FIELD PROCEDURES

Each receiver should be tuned to the setting that provides a clear signal from a transmitter. Often a specified transmitter frequency, such as 216.123 MHz, will be received most strongly at a different setting on the frequency scale on each receiver, such as 216.120 and 216.129 MHz. It is convenient to record the reception point of each transmitter and tape the list to the receiver or carrying case. The performance of equipment can be altered dramatically by factors such as animal species, topography, vegetation, or climate. Biologists should conduct tests to evaluate equipment performance in the field environment and, when possible, trials with transmitters on the study species or a surrogate. Some transmitters will fail to function before the predicted operation life is achieved. When a minimum sample is critical, it is useful to estimate average operational life and failure rates from a sample of transmitters acquired for the study.

Radio Wave Propagation and Reception Range

The term "line-of-sight," which is often used when discussing wildlife telemetry, is not the same as vision. Radio waves can go through some objects that block our vision and they can be affected by unseen factors (Cochran 1980).

Radio waves tend to remain vertical over flat terrain and water, but dense vegetation often causes horizontal polarization. Above 100 MHz many types of obstructions cause horizontal polarization (ARRL 1988). Polarization is not highly predictable in environments with many obstructions. Thus, biologists need to turn the antenna to orient the elements through horizontal and vertical planes to obtain the maximum gain and directionality of the receiving antenna (Cochran 1980).

Signal strength usually weakens with distance as signal propagation is affected immediately by the animal's body (a conductor) and other factors such as the earth (i.e., soil, rocks). Further, Cochran (1980) noted that if radio waves pass through a dense forest, a 1,000X increase in power might be required to achieve a 4-fold range increase. Elevation of the transmitting and receiving antennas is the most important factor affecting reception range (Anderka 1987). If antennas are 2 λ (~4 m at 150 MHz) above obstructions, ranges of 15 km can be achieved, but as the transmitter approaches the earth, range is reduced to 1–3 km. This can be partially offset by raising the receiving antenna.

Location Error

Identification of animal locations is affected not only by variability in radio-wave propagation, but by animal movement and variability in equipment performance and operation. Consequently, radiotracking usually provides only an estimate of the animal's actual location. Radiotracking results should include estimates of error that can be used to interpret the results. White and Garrott (1990) presented comprehensive discussions about methods for analyzing errors and their effects on radiotracking.

Error can result from misjudging the receiver site location, inaccurate and inappropriate maps, or from plotting mistakes. The width of a pencil mark used to plot a location on a 1:24,000 scale map (i.e., U.S. Geological Survey 7.5' topographic map) can cover 5–10 m. This error adds to that inherent in most direction finding. A 1° error in the compass bearing to a true location causes 17.5 m of linear error/km of distance from the receiving site. Use of surveyed points and small-scale maps can reduce the component of error associated with receiver locations. However, consistent accuracy of ±1° requires better mapping accuracy and more electrical and physical stability of equipment than commonly used in wildlife telemetry Cochran (1980).

Radiotracking equipment and equipment operators also contribute to error. Receiving antenna systems provide from ±0.5 to ~7° accuracy depending on design (Macdonald and Amlaner 1980). Pace (1988) observed that incorrect orientation of vehicle-mounted mobile antenna systems contributed as much or more to location error as the process of signal detection. The use of beacon transmitters at known locations (Kufeld et al. 1987) and careful vehicle orientation procedures can reduce this problem. Springer (1979), Lee et al. (1985), and Kufeld et al. (1987) reported no differences among operator's ability to ascertain signal direction with mast-supported Yagi antennas, but Hoskinson (1976) detected differences among pilots during aerial tracking. Mills and Knowlton (1989) reported significant increases in accuracy when 4 operators knew they were being tested.

Field conditions can influence radio-wave propagation and increase errors associated with direction finding. Kufeld et al. (1987) judged signal quality and accuracy to be diminished with increasing height of surrounding terrain. Garrott et al. (1986) reported excessive error in 52% of the bearings taken when ridges blocked the path toward the transmitter. Hupp and Ratti (1983) recorded greater error in rugged terrain and in rolling forested areas than across flat, open country. Chu et al. (1989) observed that forest vegetation significantly affected error and recommended not using bearings when their intersection angles were <20° or >160°, or when the summed distance between the 2 receivers and the transmitter was >2 km. Other environmental factors such as wind blowing tree limbs (Hupp and Ratti 1983), animal movement (Kenward 1987, White and Garrott 1990), and movement of the transmitter antenna (causing a modulated signal) can contribute to unpredictable error (Lee et al. 1985) and are difficult to detect or quantify during radiotracking.

Direction Finding

Mech (1983), Samuel and Fuller (1994), and Kenward (2001) presented detailed field procedures for direction finding and tracking, including suggestions for numerous special situations (e.g., short range and 3-dimensional). For recording coordinates, we suggest using the Universal Transverse Mercator (UTM) system, as described by White and Garrott (1990). Dodge and Steiner (1986) prepared a program to use UTM for radiotracking, and Dodge et al. (1986) wrote a program to convert latitude-longitude coordinates (e.g., from LORAN or GPS navigations) to UTM's. The methods, examples, and programs in White and Garrott (1990) are based on UTM coordinates.

Homing to a Transmitter

Homing is a method by which the operator uses antenna directionality and signal strength information to move toward the transmitter, ultimately to make visual contact with the animal or to find the transmitter (Mech 1983, Samuel and Fuller 1994). Biologists move toward the signal source while listening to the signal and moving the antenna back and forth in an arc toward the signal. Periodically they reduce the gain and confirm signal direction because the signal should become stronger as the transmitter is approached. If the signal is lost or the direction is ambiguous, the investigator should return to the last position where a directional signal was heard or walk a few meters in 4 directions 90° apart. Moving from the original path can help detect signal reflection and provide another bearing.

If a signal is detected when gain control is at the minimum setting, the transmitter should be relatively close and the operator might have to move only a few meters to lose the signal, indicating it has been passed. A relatively strong signal at close range can "swamp" the receiver's gain control. It might be necessary to use a loop antenna (Cochran 1980, Hegdal and Colvin 1986), or the receiver with the antenna detached.

Aerial Tracking

Radiotracking from aircraft usually is a special case of homing, often used to cover large areas with many transmitters. Gilmer et al. (1981), Mech (1983), Samuel and Fuller (1994), and Kenward (1987, 2001) have described methods for aerial radiotracking in detail. Each flight plan, tracking strategy, and objective should be discussed with the pilot (Gilmer et al. 1981). Transmitters with a reception range of 3–4 km to receiving antennas near the ground can be received from 35 km (Hegdal and Colvin 1986) to 100 km (Anderka 1987) with antenna on aircraft flying up to 3 km above ground level (AGL). The number of animals that can be monitored during searches for presence–absence documentation is limited by the aircraft speed, minimum reception range, transmitter pulse rate and width, and dwell time on a given frequency (Gilmer et al. 1981, Kenward 2001). Signal reception usually is accomplished with 2 directional antennas mounted under the wings (or on helicopter struts) and facing to the side and downward. Coaxial cable, through a window or port, to a switch box allows the operator to select between the left or right antennas, or to listen to both.

Biologists should test equipment function with a beacon transmitter during departure from the airport. They can then, fly to the point of last known location and listen for signals at each antenna as the plane approaches and circle the area from about 300 to 3,000 m AGL until a signal is heard. If no signal is detected where it is expected, the operators should begin a large area search by flying transects spaced at ≤2 times the minimum reception range (at a given AGL) (Samuel and Fuller 1994). The receiver operator can switch reception between antennas to identify direction to the strongest signal. When the plane is flying toward the signal, there will often be a null or weak signal. As the plane approaches the transmitter, the signal will become stronger, often slightly to one side or the other.

The pilot can circle (~3 km diameter) to the strong signal side, and if the stronger signal is outside the circle, turn toward the signal and circle again. If the plane passes the transmitter, a dramatic change from a strong to a weak signal should be detected. If the plane passes over the transmitter, the pilot can turn 180°, pass over it and circle again. If the strongest signal remains in the circle, the transmitter is within the smallest diameter circle the plane can safely circumscribe.

Few data are available from tests of the precision and accuracy of aerial radiotracking, but ±100–200 m can be achieved. Hoskinson (1976) flew unusually low (15–30 m AGL) and slowly (95–115 km/hr) and circled for 5 minutes to obtain minimum errors from 7 to 40 m and maximum errors from 40 to 70 m with different pilots. The antenna-mounting method (Gilmer et al. 1981) and antenna symmetry (Cochran 1980) also can influence accuracy. Using a 4-element Yagi antenna configuration, Fuller et al. (1989) were able to circle radio-marked seabirds within a 1-km diameter area and locate the aircraft with ±1–3 km accuracy using distance measuring equipment (DME) and VHF Omni Range (VOR) aeronautical navigation. Use of GPS and tracking software allows plotting aircraft and animal locations to within 100 m and provides a precise track through the area flown.

Triangulation

The location of a radio-marked animal can be estimated by using direction-finding methods to take bearings from 2 or more receiving sites. The point at which the bearings cross provides a simple estimate of the animal's location. An error area, or polygon, associated with the estimate is based on the standard deviation(s) of the bearings (Heezen and Tester 1967, Springer 1979, Hupp and Ratti 1983). White and Garrott (1990) presented steps needed to convert bearings to an x–y coordinate system (e.g., UTM) and methods to calculate the confidence area of the error polygon. This approach to estimating animal location and triangulation error is probably adequate for small study areas (in relation to signal strength and distances between radiomarked animals and receivers) with environmental conditions that do not contribute to large variability of radio wave propagation.

Many wildlife radiotracking studies involve relatively wide-ranging, fast-moving animals in heterogeneous environments. A relatively small sample of receiving sites and potential animal locations is unlikely to represent the diversity of radiotracking conditions, such as animal behavior, weather, seasons, or differences in terrain. We recommend obtaining at least 3 bearings for each location estimate so that, from the calculations of Lenth (1981), each animal location can have an associated error ellipse (Chu et al. 1989). White and Garrott (1984) provided a computer program for using Lenth's (1981) method. If at least 4 bearings are taken, "bad" signals (outliers) can be discarded and a location estimate still can be obtained. White and Garrott (1990) presented a method (including SAS programs) for estimating the number of useful bearings as a function of the probability of obtaining a bad signal and the number of receiving sites.

APPLICATION OF RADIOTRACKING DATA

Movements and Migration

Since its inception, radiomarking has been used to study movement patterns of wild animals. These studies have evolved from descriptive investigations of movement distances and rates to research directed at specific aspects of animal space-use, resource-selection patterns, survival, and behavior. The usefulness of location estimates depends on the research objectives, biological questions (Kenward 1992), and assumptions for the particular study. The most insightful use of location data is achieved when movement data are combined with information about animal behavior, such as foraging, courtship, reproduction, resting, dispersal, or migration. Many animal movement patterns are of ecological interest, including the presence or absence of animals at a particular site (Plissner et al. 2000), daily movement of individuals (Amstrup et al. 2000, Goguen and Mathews 2001), seasonal movements between winter and summer areas (Nelson and Mech 1999), and dispersal and other movements (Sanderson 1966, Kenward et al. 2001a, King and Belthoff 2001). Analysis of movement data depends on the research objectives, frequency of recording animal locations, and geographic scale of the movement pattern. A first step in any analysis is to plot locations of individual animals. White and Garrott (1990) discussed several approaches to display movement data by plotting all points, sequential movements, and 3-dimensional animation of movement.

Analysis of data about distance and direction of movement (Batschelet 1981, Zar 1996) must consider that the data are circular (i.e., compass bearing), with no absolute zero and arbitrary high and low values (Zar 1996). Several procedures for descriptive statistics and hypothesis tests from circular distributions have been described (Zar 1996). White and Garrott (1990) provided several examples of the analysis of circular data. A variety of software packages exist for analysis of general circular statistics. There are also packages specifically developed to analyze animal location data (e.g., Hooge and Eichenlaub 1997, Kenward et al. 2003).

Perhaps the most common use of movement data from a biotelemetry study is calculation of a movement rate. This rate usually is calculated as the distance moved between 2 consecutive points divided by the elapsed time between locations. The resulting rates are used as a relative index to compare with other factors such as age, gender, or season (Laundré et al. 1987). However, because movements are influenced by a variety of factors (Sanderson 1966), choice of how often to measure rate of movement will be important to the outcome. For example, Laundré et al. (1987) illustrated some of the difficulties by comparing 24-hour movement rates to movement calculated from more frequent observations. They observed little consistent correlation between rates calculated from daily locations and movement rates calculated from more frequent locations of 4 different species. Small and Rusch (1989) concluded that movements between daily locations were so variable that "smoothing" the rate of movement over a 5-day period was necessary to identify the underlying pattern. Because animals seldom travel in a straight line for a long time, the frequency of locations used to examine movement is critical.

It has long been recognized that locations recorded at short intervals are not independent (e.g., Swihart and Slade 1985b). More recently, however, it has been recognized that individual animals have favored locations, such as dens, feeding sites, and routes between them. Thus, analysis should be based on an estimate for each animals' set of data; for example, as an average rate of movement or a proportion of locations in each habitat (Kenward 1992, Aebischer et al. 1993b, Otis and White 1999). Rates and use of area can still be compared between time periods stratified as individuals. The implication of this approach is the need to gain data from many individuals to permit adequate tests of differences between age, gender, or condition categories.

Migratory movement patterns of many bird species and some mammals occur over extensive distances and are difficult to document even by radiotracking. Recent application of satellite telemetry methods has facilitated tracking of animals during long–distance migrations (e.g., Fuller et al. 1998, Mate et al. 1998, Blouin et al. 1999, Nichols et al. 2000, Kjellén et al. 2001). These studies can be a valuable supplement to information obtained from band recoveries, because the actual route followed by individual animals and the length of time at each stopover area can be documented. In many instances, analysis of these data will be a display of the geographic locations of each animal location and time of observation (Strikwerda et al. 1986, Brodeur et al. 1996). These types of studies are becoming more sophisticated (Green et al. 2002, Weimerskirch et al. 2002, Thorup et al. 2003) with continuing advancements in radiotracking equipment (Rodgers 2001).

Movement Path Analysis

Advanced technology has allowed researchers to collect almost continuous data on animal space-use patterns (Rodgers 2001), which can contribute to understanding of animal space-use dynamics. Several analytical procedures, including random walks/diffusion approximation models, have been used to analyze movement data (Turchin 1998) largely from small animals that could be tracked easily (e.g., by sight) (Kareiva and Shigesada 1983, Stapp and Van Horne 1997). Kernohan et al. (2001) categorized these movement approaches into 3 nonexclusive categories: descriptive approaches that estimate or describe movement patterns without reference to an underlying model, general movement models, and *a priori* mechanistic models based on specific biological attributes of the species under investigation. Readers are referred to Kareiva and Shigesada (1983), McCulloch and Cain (1989), Johnson et al. (1992), Turchin (1991, 1996, 1998), Boone and Hunter (1996), Focardi et al. (1996), and Moorcroft et al. (1999) for examples of biological and mechanistic models of animal space use.

Animal Interaction Analysis

Animal interaction analyses have been used in studies of gender segregation (Mace and Waller 1997), wildlife and human interactions (Millspaugh et al. 2000), familial associations (Bull and Baghurst 1998, Walls and Kenward 2001), site fidelity (Van Deelen et al. 1998), and general spatial organization (Ribble and Stanley 1998, Nielsen and Woolf 2001). Techniques available to summarize animal interactions are commonly categorized as either static or dynamic (Macdonald et al. 1980, Doncaster 1990, Kenward 2001). Static analyses measure overall animal association throughout a period without respect to whether the animals were actually close to one another at any time. The most common static interaction analysis involves estimating overlap of home-range areas among adjacent animals or populations (e.g., Mizutani and Jewell 1998). Seidel (1992) advanced home-range overlap analyses by considering the distribution of use within the range (e.g., Millspaugh et al. 2000). Dynamic interaction analyses consider whether animals were proximal at sampling times. Thus, dynamic interaction analyses require simultaneous or near simultaneous locations for each animal (Minta 1992). For this reason, an investigator may observe little dynamic interaction between 2 animals, yet record great static interaction; the opposite is not possible (Doncaster 1990, Minta 1992). Dynamic interactions range from simple meaures of association between 2 animals (e.g., Cole 1949) to the comparison of simultaneously taken distances between 2 individuals with all possible distances between their locations (Kenward et al. 1993).

Home-range Analysis

The description of an animal's space-use pattern traditionally has been called its home range, which is believed to contain many of the essential requirements such as food, cover, and water. Kernohan et al. (2001:126) defined home range as "the extent of area with a defined probability of occurrence of an animal during a specified time period." If a seasonal home range is being measured (e.g., during summer for an annual migrant), the definition can be extended (and readily computed) with the "repeated traverse" criterion of Kenward (2001) to eliminate one-time-travel routes (including dispersals). The definition becomes "an area repeatedly traversed by an animal during a specified time period, with a boundary defined by proportion of occurrence" (Kenward 2001:208).

Several methods have been developed to estimate an animal's home range from telemetry locations. The primary estimates have been identification of home-range boundary, corresponding area, structure, and shape. Methods also have been proposed to identify internal aspects (Adams and Davis 1967) of home-range use. Several techniques, especially

location density estimation (e.g., kernel–based) (Worton 1987, 1989) and cluster techniques (Kenward et al. 2001*b*) offer useful insight into differential-use patterns within the home-range boundary. Core areas containing the principal use sites, refuges, and most dependable food sources (Kaufmann 1962) have been proposed to identify these critical areas within a home range (Samuel et al. 1985, Samuel and Green 1988, Harris et al. 1990, Kenward et al. 2001*b*). Other aspects of internal home-range use such as behavioral patterns (Braun 1985, Samuel and Garton 1987, Marzluff et al. 2001), activity areas (Don and Rennolls 1983, Morrison and Caccamise 1985, Caccamise and Morrison 1986), and overlap with conspecifics have been studied (Harris et al. 1990).

Many animals exhibit differential use of space within their home range. These differential-use patterns may be exaggerated in some species and result in atypical space-use patterns. Melquist and Hornocker (1983) reported that northern river otters (*Lontra canadensis*) traveled water drainages and shorelines in Idaho, and shape and size of otter home ranges were strongly dictated by drainage patterns. Taylor (1978) reported that Norway rats (*Rattus novegicus*) exhibited a linear home-range pattern along hedgerows and agricultural habitats. Animals that follow linear use patterns are difficult to analyze with many of the currently available home-range methods, although extensions of current techniques may be helpful. For example, univariate kernel estimators (Silverman 1986), which are virtually unused in the ecological literature, may help discern use patterns of animals that move in a linear fashion. Thus, a researcher must identify whether an animal's space-use pattern can be adequately analyzed by the available methods.

Researchers must resolve how to handle infrequent or unusual movements outside of the "normal" home range of some animals. These excursions usually are not considered to be part of the animal's home range (Burt 1943). However, these movements may have important biological consequences related to the animal's life history, although often there is little information to explain the reason for the observed movement. Regardless, these movements can have a substantial effect on the estimated home-range area (Schoener 1981, Samuel and Garton 1985).

Four approaches have been developed to reduce the effects of excursions on home-range estimates. Subjective evaluation by researchers may include personal biases and might preclude a repeatable home-range estimate among different researchers. A second method is to include only a portion (e.g., 95%) of the animal's location or distribution of use (Van Winkle 1975). A third method (Koeppl and Hoffmann 1985, Samuel and Garton 1985) reduces the influence of locations that are a considerable distance from the arithmetic center, but assumes an underlying bivariate normal distribution of the animal's locations. This procedure can be helpful in identifying extremely inaccurate location estimates and some recording errors (Samuel and Garton 1985). The fourth method defines an "excursion-exclusive" area by applying statistical techniques, such as outlier-identification, to the distribution of nearest neighbor distances (Kenward et al. 2001*b*).

Delineation of a home range that includes a portion of the animal locations or of the distribution of use should not be arbitrary. Previous studies commonly have used 95% (Jennrich and Turner 1969, Van Winkle 1975) of the distribution for the bivariate normal method as the home-range boundary. However, these and other criteria can result in dramatic changes in home-range estimates (Schoener 1981) and precision of these estimates (Anderson 1982). The principal difficulty is to obtain a home-range estimate that has a sound biological basis (White and Garrott 1990, Kernohan et al. 2001). This estimate will depend on the research objectives and biological questions of the particular study (Kenward 1992).

Researchers should be aware of the time-sampling nature of collecting telemetry data. The sampling scheme should correspond with the assumptions required by the method used to calculate home-range size and objectives of the study. When study objectives are to estimate the animal's space-use patterns, particular attention should be given to sampling schemes that capture the actual activity patterns. Consideration should be given to the diurnal and seasonal aspects of the animal's activity patterns. Casement displays (Geissler and Fuller 1985) can be helpful in identifying diurnal shifts in use patterns or changes in activity patterns in large data sets. These methods assume stability of an encompassing range (Worton 1987) and efforts should be made to reduce chances that range shifts will occur during the period of interest. Comparison of home ranges among different animals and studies should ensure that estimates are comparable in timing and intensity of telemetry data in relation to biological activities and changes in use patterns.

The biological and methodological assumptions appropriate for each estimation technique should be considered and tested, if possible, prior to collection and analysis of radiotracking data. Few tests are available to validate methods, and many tests typically indicate that assumptions of the methods are violated. The principal statistical tests available enable (1) testing the temporal independence of animal locations (Swihart and Slade 1985a,b; 1997); (2) testing for a bivariate normal distribution (Smith 1983, Samuel and Garton 1985); (3) testing for a uniform distribution (Samuel and Garton 1985); and (4) evaluation of sample-size requirements and variance (Kernohan et al. 2001).

Sampling Considerations

Several data sampling issues affect the accuracy of home-range estimates. The amount of time that elapses between consecutive locations (Swihart and Slade 1985a,b; 1997) and number of locations obtained (Stickel 1954, Jennrich and Turner 1969, Bekoff and Mech 1984, Seaman et al. 1999) are 2 important considerations. One must consider the inevitable trade-off between collecting sufficient observations and the time between observations that achieves temporal independence, and whether more locations should be collected from fewer animals or fewer locations should be collected from more animals (Kenward 1992, Otis and White 1999). These decisions should be based on the study objectives and the implications of any decisions.

Many researchers have considered the effects of temporal autocorrelation (i.e., consecutive locations from an animal taken too closely in time) on home-range estimates (Kernohan et al. 2001). For most home-range estimators, the location data are assumed to be independent (Dunn and Gipson 1977). That is, it is assumed that enough time has passed that location at time t is independent of the animal's location at time $t − 1$ (Swihart and Slade 1985a). Estimators, such as the minimum convex polygon (Mohr 1947), are biased when autocorrelated data are used (Cresswell

and Smith 1992, Swihart and Slade 1997). Assuming a fixed time between relocations, Hansteen et al. (1997) reported 3 situations where autocorrelated data sets are created: (1) the animal is not given sufficient time to move away, (2) the animal does not move between consecutive observations, or (3) the animal returns to the previously used portion of its range. Autocorrelated data yield less information than the same number of independent observations (Swihart and Slade 1985a,b) and, thus, underestimate movements and home-range size.

Swihart and Slade (1985a) first presented a formal framework to test for temporal autocorrelation in radiotelemetry data. They proposed use of Schoener's (1981) ratio statistic to identify the time interval necessary to achieve statistical independence between successive observations, called the time to independence. Several researchers have criticized use of Schoener's (1981) ratio. Time to independence was extremely long for migratory species (McNay et al. 1994) because the animal's movements are not centered around one focal use area. Also, home ranges are assumed to be stationary (Swihart et al. 1988). Therefore, before Schoener's (1981) ratio is used, constancy in the activity center should be tested. If this assumption is violated, the independence test presented by Swihart and Slade (1985a) has little value (Kernohan et al. 2001). Others (Andersen and Rongstad 1989, Gese et al. 1990, Reynolds and Laundré 1990) have reported either no difference in home-range estimates from autocorrelated locations, or that autocorrelated data provided a more accurate estimate of home-range size.

An appropriate time interval between consecutive locations should be based on the study objectives. If study objectives warrant an investigation into daily distances moved, then achieving statistical independence may preclude one from meeting study objects (Reynolds and Laundré 1990). Strict adherence to the time to independence concept in all movement studies is not advised (Kernohan et al. 2001). If the primary research focus is on home-range estimates, a systematic sampling scheme that accurately estimates the animal's spatial distributions is more important than achieving location independence (Kenward 1987:145–146, 2001; White and Garrott 1990; McNay et al. 1994; Otis and White 1999; Garton et al. 2001; Kernohan et al. 2001; Millspaugh and Marzluff 2001). For example, this requires that researchers obtain locations day and night if the study objective is to characterize 24-hour home-range characteristics (Smith et al. 1981, Beyer and Haufler 1994). Swihart and Slade (1997:60–61) indicated that "selection of a sampling interval < time to independence (i.e., an interval yielding autocorrelated observations) generally will not invalidate several common estimates and indexes of home-range size provided that the time frame of the study is adequate." Kenward (2001) suggested that autocorrelation analysis might still help indicate optimal sampling intervals, by using a fractional value of the time to independence, provided a fraction could be found that generally minimizes the total time to record range estimates.

Sample Size Requirements

Generally, the more detail of range structure required from the estimator, the more locations required for stability. Thus, few locations are required for ellipse estimates, more are needed for the sharp edges of minimum convex polygons than for smoothed kernel outlines, and most are

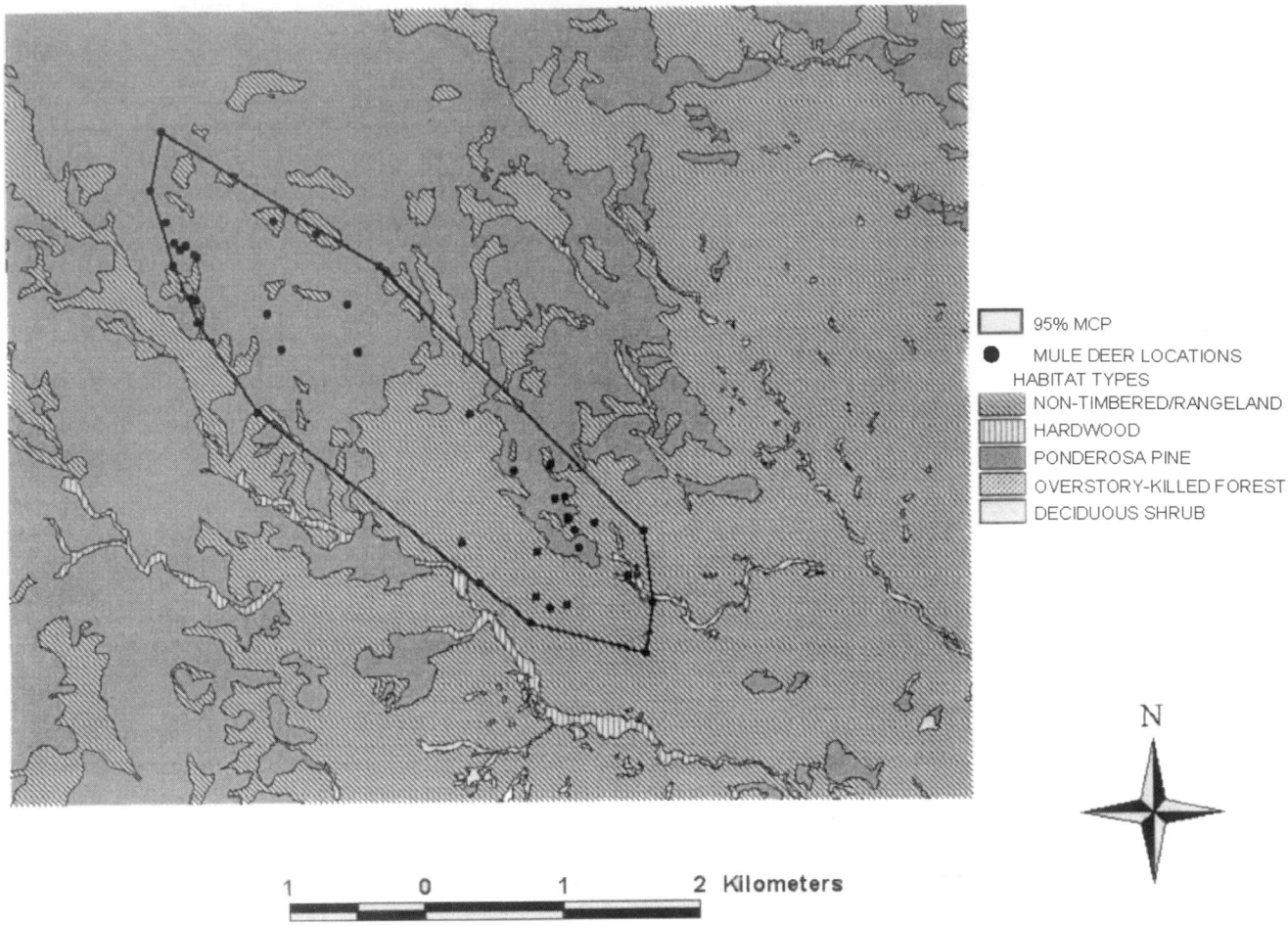

1 0 1 2 **Kilometers**

Fig. 9. Estimated 95% minimum convex polygon home range of an adult female mule deer (*Odocoileus hemionus*) during summer in Custer State Park, South Dakota as computed in the Animal Movements Extension (Hooge and Eichenlaub 1997) (data from Woeck 2003).

needed for cluster polygons (Robertson et al. 1998). Risk of bias from range size variation can be avoided either by standardized collection of the same number of locations in each case or by treating number of locations as a covariate in all analyses (Kenward 1987, 2001). For nonparametric estimators, no explicit variance formula is available (White and Garrott 1990), which prevents standard *a priori* sample size calculations. Several authors have used field data and computer simulations to examine how home-range estimators perform under varying sample sizes (Boulanger and White 1990, Worton 1995*a*, Seaman and Powell 1996, Robertson et al. 1998, Seaman et al. 1999, Gitzen and Millspaugh 2003). Also, bootstrap or jack-knife variance estimates can in principle be calculated for any method of estimating home-range area (Worton 1995*a*, Hansteen et al. 1997, Robertson et al. 1998, Kernohan et al. 2001).

Methods

Minimum Convex Polygon.—The simplest and most common method to estimate home-range area is the minimum area polygon (Mohr 1947, Mohr and Stumpf 1966, Seaman et al. 1999). A convex polygon is constructed by drawing the line with minimum sum of linkage distances connecting the outermost locations (Fig. 9). Unlike some home-range estimators (e.g., bivariate normal), there is no underlying assumption about point distributions, which allows general application of the minimum area estimate.

Although commonly used and intuitive, minimum convex polygon estimates have substantial biological and statistical disadvantages. First, home-range area continues to increase beyond the number of animal locations required for stable ellipses and kernel contour estimates (Anderson 1982, Bekoff and Mech 1984, Harris et al. 1990). Thus, animals with home ranges based on different numbers of data points might not be directly comparable if sufficient locations have not been obtained. Because the technique only considers the outer locations in estimating home range, area estimates may include sites unused by the animal (Boulanger and White 1990, White and Garrott 1990). Concave polygons (Harvey and Barbour 1965) may help overcome this problem, but if sampling was insufficient to obtain truly representative locations at the periphery of the range, home-range size may be underestimated. When only the outermost locations are considered in the home-range estimate, the internal distribution of animal locations is ignored and equal weighting is given to areas with few or many points. The convex polygon should not be used to calculate the interaction between animals based on home-range overlap if animal locations do not follow a normal pattern (Kernohan et al. 2001). The technique might be appropriate for territorial species (Shivik and Gese 2000), provided sample size requirements are met.

Peeled Polygons.—To avoid the large influence of outlying locations, the areas associated with them can be peeled away. One approach is to rank linkage distances of

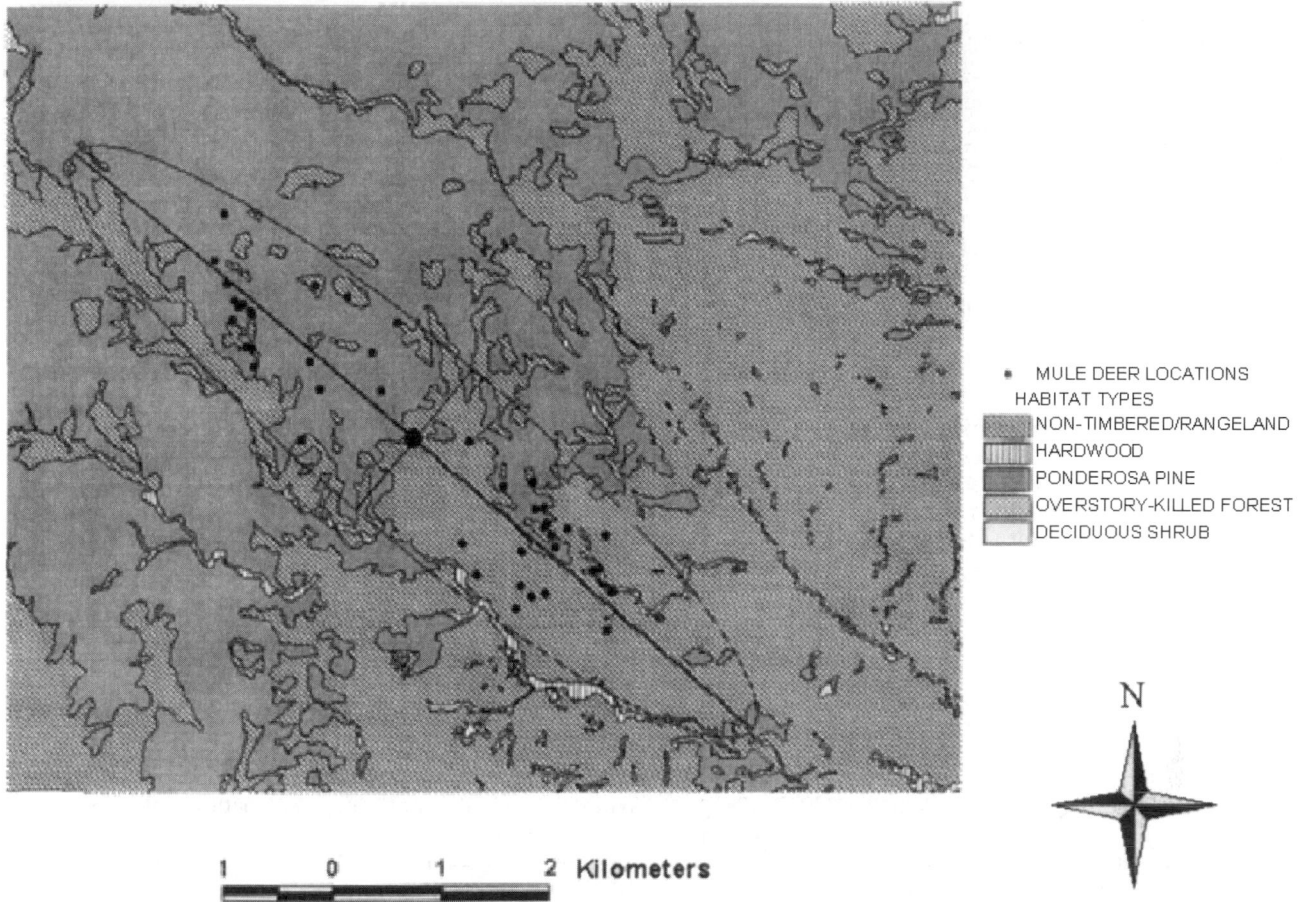

Fig. 10. Estimated 95% bivariate normal ellipse home range of an adult female mule deer during summer in Custer State Park, South Dakota as computed in the Animal Movements Extension (Hooge and Eichenlaub 1997) (data from Woeck 2003).

all locations from a center of activity (e.g., the point at which a distance function to all others is minimal), and then exclude a pre-selected proportion of most distant locations when estimating the convex polygon (Kenward 1987). Alternatively, the exclusion of locations can be based on peeling away the largest areas (Hartigan 1987) or other convex hull criteria (Worton 1995a). Although this approach is appropriate for estimating single territorial boundaries, the convex outline is not appropriate for ranges that curve around habitat features (White and Garrott 1990) or for ranges in which activities are strongly multinuclear.

Cluster Analysis Polygons.—These use nearest-neighbor linkages to estimate ranges as separate polygons around multiple activity nuclei. With incremental hierarchical clustering (Everett 1980), locations link in clusters that give a minimal sum of nearest-neighbor distances. Clusters fuse if the next minimal distance is between 2 clusters and polygons are drawn around clusters when pre-selected proportions of the locations are included (Kenward 1987). A normalized distribution can also be used to define a distance beyond which locations are excluded as outliers (Kenward et al. 2001b), because their separation distance is either beyond 95% of the total nearest-neighbor distance distribution or beyond 1% (or less) of the distribution estimated without each outlier. A single polygon around all the clusters can give better results than a peeled polygon when analyzing territorial issues.

Concave Polygons.—Concave polygons can be drawn with a subsidiary rule that permits no edge linkage to be greater than half the span (maximum distance) across the set of locations (Harvey and Barbour 1965). This concave polygon approach can omit areas of unused habitat, especially if span fractions of less than half are used.

Grid Cells.—If polygons are drawn with a boundary strip and linkage permitted only to locations at the same coordinates, the range is estimated as grid cells. This minimal use of linkage provides precise depiction of animal presence, but typically requires several hundred locations for the use area to asymptote (Macdonald et al. 1980, Harris et al. 1990).

Bivariate Normal.—The bivariate normal home-range model was proposed by Calhoun and Casby (1958) and extended by Jennrich and Turner (1969). Calculation of home-range size using the bivariate normal method assumes an animal's activity is concentrated in the center of the home range. The technique further assumes the probability of finding an animal away from this center decreases according to a normal distribution (Metzgar 1973). The home-range shape is elliptical (Fig. 10) and has only one single center of activity that occurs at the arithmetic center of the distribution. Thus, there is little resolution in the outer boundary (Robertson et al. 1998).

The bivariate normal method of home-range estimation offers advantages. First, home-range size is not influenced greatly by number of locations (Robertson et al. 1998, Garton et al. 2001). Consequently, comparisons among home-range studies may be more comparable if sample sizes differ. Second, this method is useful in identifying the number of "independent" locations required to achieve a specified level of reliability for each home-range estimate (White and Garrott 1990, Garton et al. 2001). Third, it is a probabilistic model of home-range space use, based on the bivariate normal, which has utility (White and Garrott 1990, Kernohan et al. 2001).

There are also disadvantages of using the bivariate normal estimate of home-range size. The assumption that an animal has one concentrated use area at the center of its home range is unrealistic in most wildlife populations (Blundell et al. 2001). Smith (1983) and Samuel and Garton (1985) proposed goodness-of-fit tests to verify that location data meet the bivariate normal assumption. Furthermore, the calculated center of activity may not be within the area most intensively used by the animal (Dixon and Chapman 1980). Schoener (1981) concluded the bivariate normal estimator might be appropriate for some animals (e.g., central place foragers; Rosenberg and McKelvey 1999) where use declines from the center of activity to peripheral portions of its range. Also, extreme locations in the data set can pose significant problems in estimating home-range size because the distance between each location and the arithmetic center is squared in the bivariate normal calculation (Dixon and Chapman 1980). Thus, outliers artificially expand the home-range boundary on the opposite side of the range to maintain a normal distribution (White and Garrott 1990). Finally, because of its elliptical shape, it generally does not conform well to the pattern of animal locations (Macdonald et al. 1980). Important extensions to the Jennrich and Turner (1969) technique have been proposed to help overcome some of these problems (Don and Rennolls 1983, Koeppl and Hoffman 1985, Samuel and Garton 1985). Despite these modifications, contouring techniques, including harmonic mean and kernel-based estimates, have become more popular (Seaman et al. 1999).

Harmonic Mean.—Dixon and Chapman (1980) first proposed the harmonic mean as an alternative home-range method based on the distance between a lattice (grid) of map coordinates and animal locations. These distances are used to estimate activity contours that describe the animal's use pattern within the home range. In this way, the harmonic mean is sensitive to irregular patterns of animal space use and makes no assumption about the internal configuration of the home range. In contrast to the bivariate normal method, the harmonic mean may have multiple activity centers (Samuel et al. 1985), varying distances from one another, and the home-range shape may be irregular. The harmonic mean method relies on the distances between all animal locations and all intersections of a grid lattice to estimate home-range area. After a grid is placed over a set of location points, harmonic means are calculated for each grid node and contours (e.g., 95%) are calculated from the grid.

There are several drawbacks to the harmonic mean estimator. This method implicitly assumes that distance between the grid nodes and each location is an indicator of potential biological activity. Thus, the method can provide poor estimates of home range for animals with linear use patterns or traditional travel corridors. Dixon and Chapman (1980) avoided this problem by setting distances to the minimum interval between coordinates of the locations (the tracking resolution) if locations were close to lattice nodes. Samuel et al. (1985) reported the centering procedure makes harmonic mean estimates dependent on lattice cell size. They proposed an *ad hoc* algorithm to adjust lattice cell size depending upon the number of animal locations and their density within the home-range boundary. Kenward (2001) noted that scale and lattice-size problems are avoided if distances between lattice nodes are no more than half the tracking resolution.

The harmonic mean has demonstrated mixed results from computer simulations. Boulanger and White (1990) reported the harmonic mean, while imprecise, was less biased than 4 other (Fourier series, MCP, and 2 95%-ellipse estimates) home-range estimators. Worton (1995*b*) observed the harmonic mean estimate included unused portions of the range, a result corroborated by several field studies (Spencer and Barrett 1984, Naef-Daenzer 1993). The reason for these results may lie on the importance given to central observations, which largely influence the outer contours (Worton 1995*b*). Despite these issues, the harmonic mean continues to be a popular choice for depicting home range (Seaman et al. 1999).

Fourier Method.—The Fourier transform method was proposed by Anderson (1982) to estimate an animal's distribution of use. This nonparametric method smooths the observed histogram of animal locations by including the appropriate number of high and low–frequency sine and cosine components in the Fourier transform series. Inclusion or exclusion of components is based on the objective criterion established by Tarter and Kronmal (1970). In addition, objective rules have been developed for identifying the best grid cell size to use in calculating Fourier smoothing functions. However, calculation of the appropriate frequency components and grid cell size requires that animal locations be independent. As with other distribution of use techniques (e.g., kernel-based estimators), home-range contours are calculated as the smallest area enclosing a specified percentage (e.g., 50, 75, 95%, etc.) of the volume under the 3-dimensional surface (White and Garrott 1990).

Anderson (1982) observed the Fourier method had difficulty in estimating areas at the edge of the home range, primarily because few locations are usually available for these areas. Worton (1987) also noted the method could produce regions near the home-range boundary where the estimated distribution of use was negative, and was hard to implement robustly for general use. Thus, the Fourier method provided highly variable estimates for large contours (90–95%) of the home range. Fourier home-range estimates near the activity centers (e.g., 50% of the distribution of use) produced unbiased results (Anderson 1982).

The Fourier transformation method provides an objective generalization of grid cell methods (Siniff and Tester 1965, Voigt and Tinline 1980). These methods required an arbitrary specification of the cell influence on contiguous cells. The Fourier method overcomes the greatest problem with grid cell methods of identification of the appropriate grid cell size.

Fixed and Adaptive Kernels.—Worton (1987, 1989) was the first to apply robust kernel methods to estimate an animal's distribution of use (Fig. 11). However, kernel den-

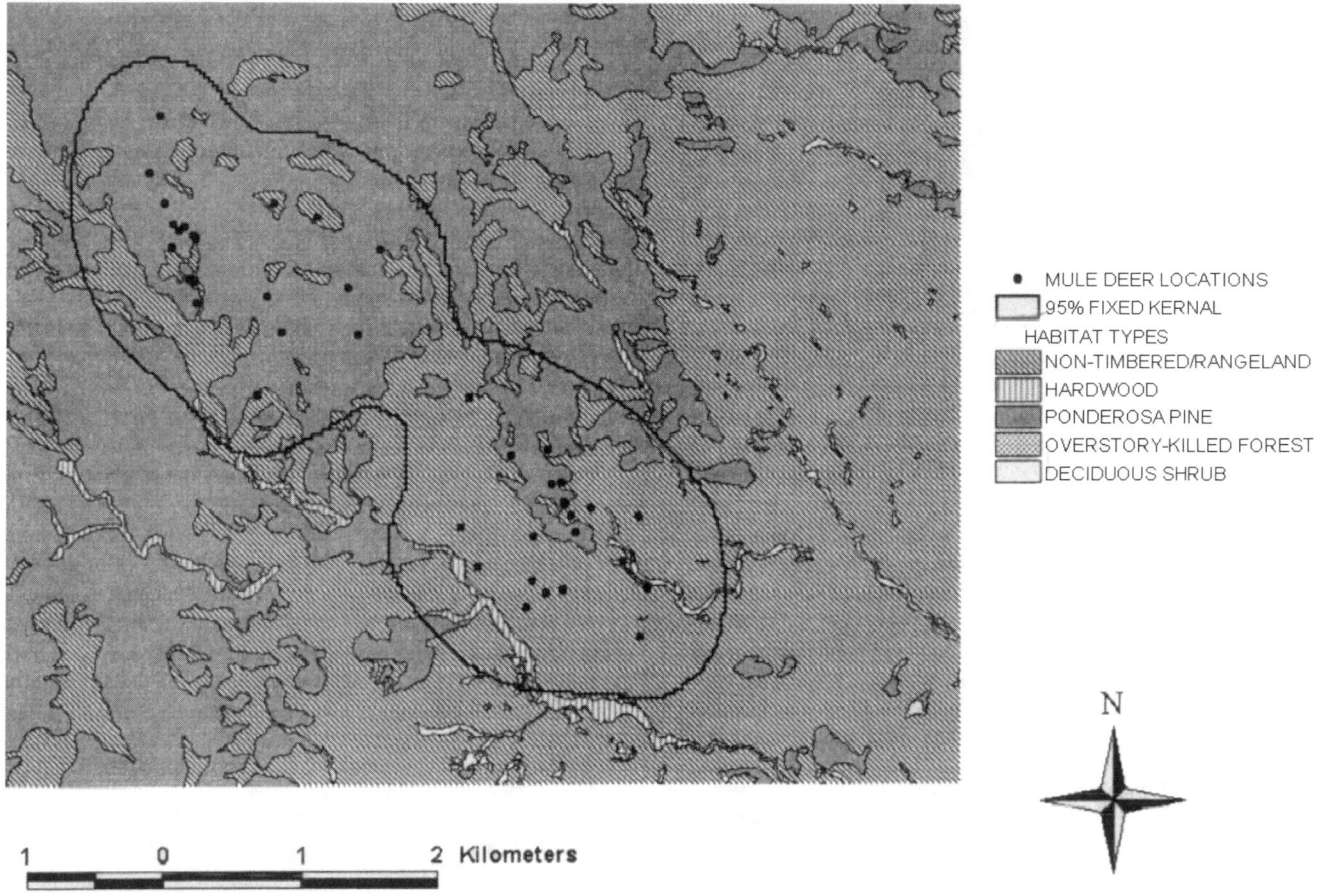

Fig. 11. Estimated 95% fixed kernel home range of an adult female mule deer during summer in Custer State Park, South Dakota as computed in the Animal Movements Extension (Hooge and Eichenlaub 1997) using least–squares cross validation, data from Woeck (2003).

sity estimation has a longer history in the general statistical literature (Silverman 1986, Scott 1992) and the harmonic mean estimator is one type of kernel (Worton 1989). The kernel density function represents the sum of separate kernel functions, each centered at an observed location (Silverman 1986). As with the harmonic mean estimator, generic kernel density functions are evaluated over a lattice to delineate the distribution of use. In contrast to the harmonic mean method, corrections for locations close to lattice nodes are not required by generic kernel functions, as lattice size and spacing does not influence the distribution of use estimate (Worton 1989). Most often, the kernel home-range estimate is reported as the minimum area that includes a fixed percentage (e.g., 50, 75, 95%, etc.) of the volume in the distribution of use (Kernohan et al. 2001).

The bandwidth (a.k.a. smoothing parameter) value dramatically influences kernel density estimation (Silverman 1986, Worton 1995a, Seaman et al. 1999) and is viewed as the major disadvantage in kernel home-range analyses (Kernohan et al. 2001). The bandwidth is important because it controls the width of the individual kernels, which in turn affects the amount of smoothing applied to the data. Kernohan et al. (2001) graphically demonstrated bandwidth effects (Fig. 12). At small bandwidths (i.e., small kernels), the kernel density function partially divides into the individual kernels (Fig. 12C). In contrast, large bandwidths over smooth the data into a single surface (Fig.

12D). Thus, researchers should carefully choose an appropriate bandwidth for their data.

Many bandwidth options exist in the general statistical literature (Wand and Jones 1995) and objective methods that help the user choose the appropriate amount of smoothing are useful for comparing home-range estimates within and between studies (Kernohan et al. 2001). Two bandwidth selection methods, the reference or optimum bandwidth (h_{ref}), and least squares cross validation (h_{lscv}) have been used and evaluated in wildlife home-range studies (Worton 1995a, Seaman and Powell 1996, Seaman et al. 1999, Gitzen and Millspaugh 2003).

Two major subdivisions of the general kernel technique are the fixed and adaptive kernel methods (Worton 1989). With the fixed kernel method, the same bandwidth is used over the entire evaluation area. With the adaptive kernel method, a local bandwidth is selected for each observation. The local bandwidth is relatively larger in areas with fewer observations than in areas with many observations. As a result, the tails of the distribution are smoothed more than the peaks, resulting in generally larger home-range estimates. Despite the close relationship between fixed and adaptive kernel methods, these techniques may produce dramatically different estimates (Seaman and Powell 1996, Seaman et al. 1999). Contrary to initial expectations (Worton 1989), the fixed kernel method generally appears to have lower bias and better surface fit than the adaptive ker-

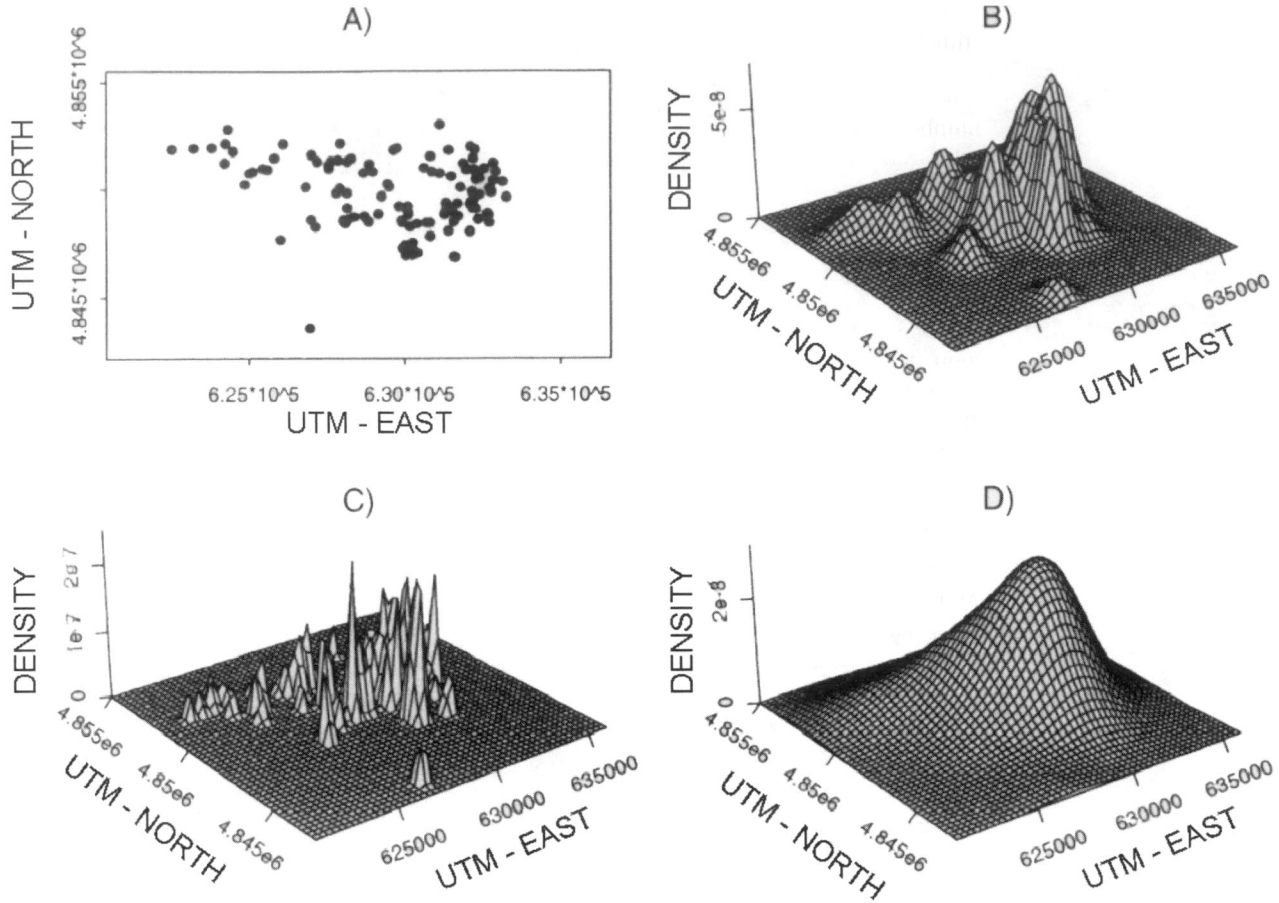

Fig. 12. Effect of different bandwidth values on kernel utilization distribution estimates for a single data set. A) 146 elk (*Cervus elaphus*) locations (from Millspaugh 1999). The fixed kernel distributions for these locations plotted in A, based on 3 bandwidth values (h) are: B, when h = 500, C, when h = 150, and D, when h = 1500 (kernel plotting routines from Bowman and Azzalini 1997) (adapted from Kernohan et al. 2001).

nel for a given bandwidth selection method (Seaman and Powell 1996, Seaman et al. 1999).

Kernel home-range methods share many advantages of other density-based techniques, such as flexibility in conforming to irregular location distributions (Worton 1995*a*, Seaman et al. 1999). Kernel methods, compared to other techniques, perform well in simulation studies (Worton 1995*b*, Seaman and Powell 1996), provided certain bandwidth options (Seaman and Powell 1996) and sample sizes are met (Seaman et al. 1999). Currently, kernel methods set the standard for probabilistic estimation of distribution of use (e.g., estimation based on simple descriptive, statistical models).

Comparison of Space-use Estimators

Several researchers have compared performance of home-range estimators using simulated data where distributional properties and number of locations are controlled. Boulanger and White (1990) compared home-range estimators from 4 relatively distinct distribution patterns over 2 sample sizes (50 and 150) and reported that all estimators showed some bias. With the exception of the bivariate normal estimate from a normal distribution, bias was influenced by sample size. The bivariate normal was substantially biased for all other simulated distributions. The MCP and Fourier method performed poorly for all distri-

bution patterns. Boulanger and White (1990) concluded the harmonic mean was least biased; however, this method also had the lowest precision. Worton (1995*b*) compared the performance of fixed kernel estimators using the same 4 hypothetical distributions. He found that kernel estimates compared favorably to other techniques and recommended their use in home-range analyses (Worton 1995*b*). More recently, Seaman et al. (1999) investigated the influence of sample size on home-range estimates. Their simulated home ranges varied from simple to complex by mixing bivariate distributions (Fig. 13). They also considered fixed and adaptive kernels and varied the number of points from 10 to 200. Kernel estimates were highly influenced by sample size and >50 observations were necessary to reduce average bias. Of significance, they observed that kernel home-range area was overestimated at small sample sizes. The fixed kernel provided the least biased estimates of the 95% home-range area (Seaman et al. 1999). We offer several observations for appropriate application of the available methods.

(1) Methods should be selected that contribute to addressing the project's research objectives (Kenward 1992). Research studies designed to investigate the ecological aspects of an animal's space-use pattern should avoid methods that can only identify an outer boundary for a home range.

(2) Locations of an individual animal are not truly independent. This may influence estimates of home-range size and structure.

(3) Assumptions pertaining to sampling design, frequency of locations, and total number of locations for the method should be considered.

(4) One approach to estimating the number of required locations is to plot the home-range area versus sequentially collected locations until the home-range size reaches an asymptote for most ranges and then standardize on that number of locations.

(5) More locations will be required if sampling intervals are short. Researchers must report the sampling intervals and number of locations used to estimate home ranges, which will facilitate comparisons to other studies.

(6) Investigators should consider whether home-range methods are appropriate for testing the research hypothesis. In some instances, research hypotheses can be tested without relying on home-range methods (White and Garrott 1990).

(7) Numerous helpful software packages exist for analyzing radiotracking data (Larson 2001). However, the user should be aware of differences and hidden assumptions in their chosen software as Lawson and Rodgers (1997) noted that home-range estimates for the same data set differed greatly among software packages.

(8) A method should not be selected only because it is easy to compute or used by others studying that species.

Resource Use and Selection

One of the principal applications of radiotracking has been to evaluate the spatial relationships of animals to features or resources in their environment. Resource selection focuses on choices made by wild animals. Most research on resource selection using radiotelemetry has focused on habitat selection or habitat use (Anderson and Gutzwiller 2005, McDonald et al. 2005). We use a broad definition of the term habitat: habitat provides food, cover, water, and other resources essential for survival. Analyses of animal–habitat relationships have been an important component of wildlife management because, ideally, study of resource selection provides information about the relative importance of habitats.

Wildlife radiotelemetry allows researchers to locate animals as frequently as they like (or nearly so) during different periods, while minimizing disturbances that can affect their use pattern. Many species are elusive and visual observations of their resource use would be impractical or impossible. Additionally, some animals use a variety of vegetation types that causes differential visibility. When visual estimates are influenced by vegetation type, biased estimates of resource use will result. Application of radiotelemetry to habitat studies requires that telemetry locations are sufficiently accurate to correctly distinguish which habitat the animal was using. Assessment of habitat use or selection will depend on study objectives, accuracy of the telemetry locations, patchiness of the habitat, and the resolution of habitat data (e.g., a map of cover types or vegetation) with which the locations are to be associated.

Study Design

The concept of selection order must be considered carefully because of the hierarchical nature of resource selection (Johnson 1980). Research objectives should clearly

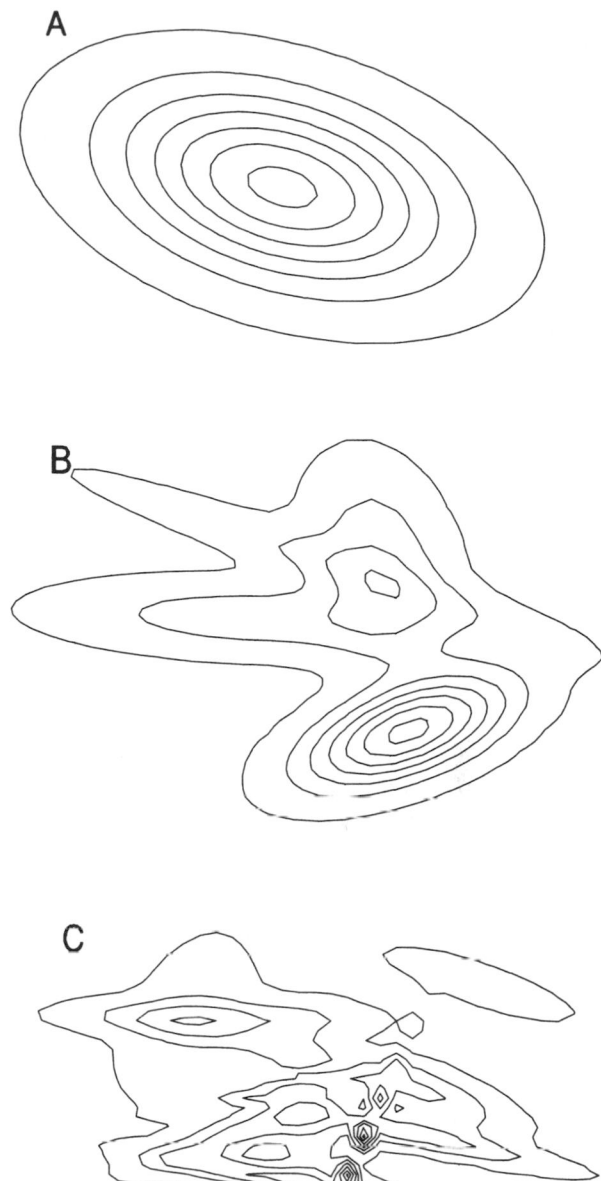

Fig. 13. Example of shapes of simulated home ranges composed of (A) 1, (B) 4, and (C) 16 bivariate normal distributions (from Seaman et al. 1999).

state the order of selection under investigation. First-order selection occurs at the spatial scale of the physical or geographical ranges of a species (Johnson 1980). Second-order resource selection evaluates the selection of a home range within the study area or geographical range of the species (Johnson 1980, Thomas and Taylor 1990). Third-order selection evaluates the importance of resource components within the animal's home range, which does not address the question of why a home range was selected (Thomas and Taylor 1990). The importance of hierarchical selection has conceptually been recognized but should be explicitly examined as part of the research design, because the selection order implicitly identifies the population of interest, experimental units, and level of management interpretation (Thomas and Taylor 1990).

A second critical element is how use and availability data will be collected. There are many proposed approaches that primarily reflect data reliability, quantity of data recorded at each animal location, and the assumption about data independence among animals and animal locations. These approaches have an important role in affecting how often location data are gathered, how many animals will be radiomarked, and which methods can be used to analyze the data. Thomas and Taylor (1990) described 3 study designs for resource selection research depending on whether use or availability information is collected by individual or for the entire population. Study design I allows use and availability data to be collected and summarized at the population level. Study design II records use by individual animals, but defines availability for the entire population. In contrast, study design III estimates use and availability for each animal. Erickson et al. (2001) added a fourth design (IV) that considers recent developments in resource selection studies (Arthur et al. 1996; Cooper and Millspaugh 1999, 2001). What differentiates design IV from the others is the ability to define availability per location. Alldredge et al. (1998) provide a useful discussion on the assumptions of each technique across different designs.

Comparing Use to Availability

Analysis of resource-selection data most often compares resources used by the animal to resources considered available to the animal or population. From these analyses, researchers infer whether resources were "selected" (used more than expected) or used less than expected. Terms such as "use," "selection," and "preference" are not synonyms, although often used as such (Marzluff et al. 2001). Resource use is the quantity of a resource used by the consumer in a fixed period (Johnson 1980). If resources are "selected," resources are used disproportionately more than expected based on their availability (Johnson 1980). Preference for a resource reflects the likelihood of that resource being chosen if offered on an equal basis with others (Johnson 1980). The term "avoided" has been used to refer to resources used disproportionately less than expected based on availability of that resource (Johnson 1980). However, "avoided" is misleading and we discourage its use, because a radiotelemetry location estimate or observation at the location of the resource reveals the resource is used, not avoided.

Assessing Resource Availability.—Resource availability represents the amount of area of each resource type (e.g., meadow, forest) that is accessible for use by the population or individual animal. Unfortunately, it is one of the most troubling aspects of resource selection studies (Cooper and Millspaugh 1999). The biologist's definition of availability might not correspond with what is available to the animal (Marzluff et al. 2001). For example, various factors that are immeasurable to the biologist might influence what is actually available to an animal (e.g., social hierarchies, predation, geographic constraints) (Otis 1997, 1998; Mysterud and Ims 1998). Biologists should base decisions on their knowledge of animal behavior and ecology, and explain why they included and excluded certain resources or areas.

The simplest method for measuring occurrence, or assumed availability, is to measure the areas of each resource type present. Often this measurement can be accomplished within a Geographic Information System (GIS). When habitat availability cannot be measured easily within a GIS, it can be estimated by several different approaches. One method is to estimate the ranks of relative availability of different habitat types (Johnson 1980). This method may be especially advantageous when a detailed account of availability is required. A second method is to draw a random sample of locations to obtain an estimate of proportional occurrence of each habitat (Marcum and Loftsgaarden 1980). This method allows the simple estimation of habitat availability from a habitat map. The area in each habitat type can be estimated from its proportional distribution relative to the size of the study area. Because the random points provide an estimate of the proportional distribution (rather than an exact distribution), this method has sampling error that must be treated in the statistical analysis of resource selection.

Assessing Resource Use.—Methods to estimate animal use patterns usually parallel those applied to availability data and often consider time as the currency of use in telemetry studies (Buskirk and Millspaugh 2004). Animal locations are a sample of use that can be used to estimate proportional use by habitat type or to collect multivariate vectors of use data that can be compared to availability. The number of locations associated with habitat types, or plots (Manly et al. 2002), or stands (North and Reynolds 1996) can be calculated by adding location points into a GIS layer of the resource(s) of interest. If analytical methods based on ranks are used (Johnson 1980), the data for proportional use can be converted to rank scores. In addition to the proportional occurrence of telemetry relocations within habitat types, the amount of time spent in those areas can be quantified using an animal's distribution of use (Marzluff et al. 2001).

Many methods for analyzing habitat-use data assume that animal locations are random and independent, both temporally and spatially. Some investigators have used *ad hoc* procedures to select the appropriate sampling time between sequential locations (Swihart and Slade 1985*a*,*b*; 1997). Decisions about sampling rate can be based on biological knowledge of movement rates (Carey et al. 1989) or actual observations of the distance moved between locations (Porter and Church 1987). Nonrandom sampling would occur if an animal was more easily located in any one habitat. Resource use by one animal is frequently assumed to not influence another animal. This assumption would be violated if animals aggregate or avoid other individuals (Alldredge and Ratti 1986, 1992; Millspaugh et al. 1998). One important and often overlooked aspect of resource selection relates to the animals' behavior at relocation points. Marzluff et al. (2001) argued that knowing what an animal is doing within a particular resource increases understanding of why the animal is there. They developed behavioral specific use distributions based on kernel density estimates to evaluate whether resources were used differently for 4 behaviors (foraging, locomotion, perching, parental care).

Population Estimation

Radiotracking can provide useful information for research on animal population density because the location of radio-marked animals is known. It also provides useful methods of validating assumptions or developing correction factors for other population procedures (Kenward 1987, 2001; White and Shenk 2001). For example, knowledge of whether a marked animal was on a study area at the time of a survey is useful in correcting density estimates (Kenward et al. 2000, White and Shenk 2001). Some techniques to estimate density from radiotracking are straightforward. For example, Fuller and Snow (1988) described an approach for estimating density of gray wolves (*Canis lupus*) over a large area by repeatedly locating radiomarked individuals in winter to identify packs, delineate territories, and count pack members (Mech 1982). Their method requires that all packs are identified and all individuals within packs are counted. Even under these ideal circumstances the number of wolves will be underestimated if lone wolves are not considered.

Detection Models

Aerial survey methods for estimating populations have benefited substantially from radiomarking to assess the importance of visibility bias (e.g., Cogan and Diefenbach 1998, Bleich et al. 2001). Floyd et al. (1979) used radio transmitters to identify the proportion of white-tailed deer (*Odocoileus virginianus*) seen in different habitats during aerial surveys. Biggins and Jackson (1984) used a similar method to evaluate the importance of habitat, snow conditions, and other environmental factors on deer visibility. Gasaway et al. (1985) showed how moose (*Alces alces*) visibility was influenced by behavior (bedded vs. standing). Several authors (Samuel et al. 1987, Unsworth et al. 1990, Smith et al. 1995, Bleich et al. 2001) used radiotracking to develop visibility models to help correct bias resulting from differential visibility of animals during surveys.

Correction for Density Estimation

Radiotelemetry also can be used in 3 ways to correct for bias in density estimates from a trapping grid or other bounded study area (Kenward 1987, 2001; White and Shenk 2001). The simplest method to correct for bias in grid trapping estimates, where habitat is continuous across grid boundaries, is to consider the area trapped extends at these grid boundaries by half the diameter of a circle with average home-range area in comparable habitat (Kenward 1987, 2001). Thus, for squirrels (Sciuridae) trapped in part of a wood lot, a boundary strip is added to the "open" edge where woodland continues beyond the grid, but not to the "closed" edges where the grid abuts a change to unused (unwooded) habitat. The assumptions are: (1) habitat is the same on either side of the open edge, (2) home ranges are relatively compact (not elongated), (3) animals are not attracted from their usual ranges by trapping, and (4) home-range areas are much smaller than the grid.

A second method can be used for any bounded area where animals are radiotracked to identify how likely they are to be located in the area. For example, density estimates may be corrected using home-range data to estimates time spent in and out of a study area from the proportion of locations in the area (Kenward et al. 1981).

Mark–Resight

Radio transmitters have been used with mark–resight techniques to estimate population size of northern goshawks (*Accipiter gentilis*) (Kenward 1977), white-tailed deer (Rice and Harder 1977), mountain sheep (*Ovis canadensis*) (Neal et al. 1993), grizzly bears (*Ursus arctos*) (Miller et al. 1997), and caribou (*Rangifer tarandus*)

(Rivest et al. 1998). Bartmann et al. (1987) tested 3 procedures for combining repeated Lincoln-Petersen estimates with mark–resight approaches with known populations of mule deer in 4 58–70 ha pastures. They concluded that with all 3 procedures, a large portion (>45%) of the population should be marked for reliable estimates and confidence interval calculation. Techniques to collect mark–resight data for population estimation are diverse (Lancia et al. 2005).

Radiotracking also can improve capture–recapture estimates of population size (Seber 1986, White and Garrott 1990, White and Shenk 2001). Most importantly, radiomarking animals allows researchers to calculate the number of marked animals available for capture during surveys. Thus, researchers can investigate important assumptions regarding geographic closure (White et al. 1982). If marked animals are found away from the study site during resighting surveys, the assumption of geographic closure is violated.

Population estimation studies involving radiotracking are frequently constrained by funds and personnel. In the case of mark–resight surveys involving radio transmitters, researchers must consider the costs associated with animal marking and resighting (White and Shenk 2001). White (1996) provided techniques in program NOREMARK to assist researchers in designing efficient population estimation studies involving radio marks.

Survival

Estimation of survival rates has become an important component in the assessment of natural factors regulating animal populations (Fowler 1981, Gavin et al. 1984, Keith et al. 1984, Naef-Daenzer et al. 2001, Thirgood et al. 2002) and management (Anderson and Burnham 1976, Burnham and Anderson 1984, Nichols et al. 1984, McCorquodale 1999, Pack et al. 1999). Studies of radio-marked animals can be extremely useful in identifying causes of mortality, rates of survival, and factors that influence survival. Radiotracking also can be used to locate animals soon after death to identify the cause of mortality. In this context, radiomarking has been used to study the influence of habitat on mortality rates of game birds (Aebischer et al. 1993a, Taylor et al. 1999, Thirgood et al. 2002), to examine the influence of predators on young ungulates (Schlegal 1976, Franzmann et al. 1980, Barrett 1984), and investigate how human activities influence wildlife populations (McCorquodale 1999, Petersburg et al. 2000). Perhaps the more common use of radiomarking in survival analysis has been to calculate survival and to examine which factors (e.g., age and gender) might account for differences in survival rates (e.g., Chamberlain and Leopold 2001, Norman et al. 2001).

Choice of the most appropriate method for telemetry survival depends on specific research objectives, when animals are radiomarked, whether animals lose their radios or leave the study area, and whether mortality rates are constant during the study period. Methods have been well reviewed by White and Garrott (1990), Samuel and Fuller (1994), and Kenward (2001).

Regardless of method, a number of conditions (Bunck 1987, Tsai et al. 1999) should be met to assure correct survival estimates.

(1) The radio-marked sample must be representative of the population to be studied.

(2) Radiomarked animals represent independent samples. Animals that are closely associated (e.g., nestlings) may be subjected to similar mortality factors and, thus, provide less information about mortality rates than data obtained from truly independent individuals.

(3) Radiomarking should not influence survival. Animals with transmitters should provide an unbiased estimate of the survival rate for the population. These first 3 conditions also are required of survival estimates from band recovery and mark–recapture studies (Jolly 1965, Seber 1965, Pollock 1981, Brownie et al. 1985).

(4) When the fate of an animal is unknown (censored), the known survival time is often assumed to be independent of the animal's actual fate. Censoring can occur because of transmitter failure, movement from the study area, or termination of the study before all radiomarked animals die.

(5) The exact time of death is known. This assumption can be relaxed, however, without substantially affecting survival estimates (Johnson 1979, Bart and Robson 1982, Heisey and Fuller 1985)

(6) Newly marked animals have the same survival function as previously marked animals.

SUMMARY

Radiotracking data are often applied to questions about animal space use (e.g., home range, resource selection) and demographics (e.g., survival). Wildlife telemetry technology advances continuously and biologists must consult the literature, colleagues, and equipment suppliers and manufacturers about equipment capabilities and limitations.

Researchers should identify their objectives and carefully consider if radiotelemetry is an appropriate method. The analysis and application of telemetry data has benefited greatly from recent advances in computing software and other technologies (e.g., GPS). These advancements have sparked the development of several new analytical techniques to address long-standing questions. Moreover, the performance of many other techniques has been evaluated and compared. We outlined many general advantages and disadvantages of analytical procedures. However, the biological and methodological assumptions appropriate for each analytical technique must be considered and tested prior to collection and analysis of radiotracking data.

ACKNOWLEDGMENTS

J. R. Tester, V. B. Kuechle, R. A. Reichle, R. J. Schuster, and R. Huempfner introduced M. R. Fuller to wildlife telemetry. He also appreciates the many instructive discussions he has had with A. L. Kolz, P. W. Howey, T. K. Fuller, R. E. Kenward, C. J. Amlaner, Jr., N. Levanon, M. D. Samuel, L. S. Schueck, K. K. Bates, M. A.Yates, and many staff members at the Applied Physics Laboratory, Johns Hopkins University. W. S. Seegar stimulated, encouraged, and provided many opportunities for development and application of telemetry techniques. J. J. Millspaugh appreciates the guidance, advice, and stimulating conversation about the design and analysis of wildlife telemetry studies with G. C. Brundige, A. B. Cooper, R. A. Gitzen, B. J. Kernohan, J. M. Marzluff, C. D. Rittenhouse, J. R. Skalski, and B. N. Woeck. K. E. Church thanks C. O. Kochanny for assistance. R. E. Kenward thanks those in wildlife telemetry who have given him practical advice and insights, of which the first was M. R. Fuller. K. G. McDonald provided line drawings. K. K. Bates, J. W. Hupp, and G. A. Sargeant provided many useful comments about the draft manuscript, and we thank our editor, C. E. Braun. M. S. Tracy, L. L. Sherrill, D. C. Treat, H. A. Jordan, and E. B. Micone helped prepare the manuscript.

LITERATURE CITED

ADAMS, L., AND S. D. DAVIS. 1967. The internal anatomy of home range. Journal of Mammalogy 48:529–536.

AEBISCHER, A. E., V. MARCSTRÖM, R. E. KENWARD, AND M. KARLBOM. 1993a. Survival and habitat utilisation: a case for compositional analysis. Pages 343–353 in J. -D. Lebreton and P. M. North, editors. Marked individuals in the study of bird populations. Birkhauser Verlag, Basel, Switzerland.

AEBISCHER, N. J., P. A. ROBERTSON, AND R. E. KENWARD. 1993b. Compositional analysis of habitat use from animal radio-tracking data. Ecology 74:1313–1325.

ALEXANDER, I. H., AND B. H. CRESSWELL. 1990. Foraging by nightjars *Caprimulgus europaeus* away from their nesting areas. Ibis 132:568–574.

ALLDREDGE, J. R., AND J. T. RATTI. 1986. Comparison of some statistical techniques for analysis of resource selection. Journal of Wildlife Management 50:157–165.

———, AND ———. 1992. Further comparison of some statistical techniques for analysis of resource selection. Journal of Wildlife Management 56:1–9.

———, D. L. THOMAS, AND L. L. MCDONALD. 1998. Survey and comparison of methods for study of resource selection. Journal of Agricultural, Biological, and Environmental Statistics 3:237–253.

AMLANER, JR., C. J. 1980. The design of antennas for use in radiotelemetry. Pages 251–261 in C. J. Amlaner, Jr. and D. W. Macdonald, editors. A handbook on biotelemetry and radio tracking. Pergamon Press, Oxford, United Kingdom.

———, R. M. SIBLEY, AND R. H. MCCLEERY. 1978. The effects of telemetry transmitter weight on breeding success in herring gulls. Biotelemetry Patient Monitor 5:154–163.

AMSTRUP, S. C. 1980. A radio-collar for game birds. Journal of Wildlife Management 44:214–217.

———, G. M. DURNER, I. STIRLING, N. J. LUNN, AND F. MESSIER. 2000. Movements and distribution of polar bears in the Beaufort Sea. Canadian Journal of Zoology 78:948–966.

———, ———, T. L. MCDONALD, D. M. MULCAHY, AND G. W. GARNER. 2001. Comparing movement patterns of satellite-tagged male and female polar bears. Canadian Journal of Zoology 79:2147–2158.

ANDERKA, F. W. 1980. Modulators for miniature tracking transmitters. Pages 181–184 in C. J. Amlaner, Jr. and D. W. Macdonald, editors. A handbook on biotelemetry and radio tracking. Pergamon Press, Oxford, United Kingdom.

———. 1987. Radiotelemetry techniques for furbearers. Pages 216–227 in M. Novak, J. A. Baker, M. E. Obbard, and B. Malloch, editors. Wild furbearer management and conservation in North America. Ontario Ministry of Natural Resources, Toronto, Canada.

ANDERSEN, D. E., AND O. J. RONGSTAD. 1989. Home-range estimates of red-tailed hawks based on random and systematic relocations. Journal of Wildlife Management 53:802–807.

ANDERSON, D. J. 1982. The home range: a new nonparametric estimation technique. Ecology 63:103–112.

ANDERSON, D. R., AND K. P. BURNHAM. 1976. Population ecology of the mallard. VI. The effect of exploitation on survival. U.S. Department of the Interior, Fish and Wildlife Service, Resource Publication 128.

ANDERSON, S. H., AND K. J. GUTZWILLER. 2005. Wildlife habitat evaluation. Pages 489–502 in C. E. Braun, editor. Techniques for wildlife investigations and management. Sixth edition. The Wildlife Society, Bethesda, Maryland, USA.

AMERICAN RADIO RELAY LEAGUE (ARRL). 1988. The ARRL antenna handbook. American Radio Relay League, Newington, Connecticut, USA.

ARTHUR, S. M., B. F. J. MANLY, L. L. MCDONALD, AND G. W. GARNER. 1996. Assessing habitat selection when availability changes. Ecology 77:215–227.

BALLARD, W. B., P. R. KRAUSMAN, S. BOE, S. CUNINGHAM, AND H. A. WHITLAW. 2000. Short-term response of gray wolves, *Canis lupus*, to wildfire in northwestern Alaska. Canadian Field-Naturalist 114:241–247.

BARBOUR, R. W., M. J. HARVEY, AND J. W. HARDIN. 1969. Home-range, movements, and activity of the eastern worm snake, (*Carphophis amoenus*). Ecology 50:470–476.

BARRETT, M. W. 1984. Movements, habitat use, and predation on pronghorn fawns in Alberta. Journal of Wildlife Management 48:542–550.

BART, J., AND D. S. ROBSON. 1982. Estimating survivorship when subjects are visited periodically. Ecology 63:1078–1090.

BARTMANN, R. M., G. C. WHITE, L. H. CARPENTER, AND R. A. GARROTT. 1987. Aerial mark–recapture estimates of confined mule deer in pinyon–juniper woodland. Journal of Wildlife Management 51:41–46.

BATES, K. K., K. STEENHOF, AND M. R. FULLER. 2003. Recommendations for finding PTTs on the ground without VHF telemetry. Proceedings of the Argos Animal Tracking Symposium, Annapolis, Maryland, USA.

BATSCHELET, E. 1981. Circular statistics in biology. Academic Press, New York, USA.

BEALE, D. M., AND A. D. SMITH. 1973. Mortality of pronghorn antelope fawns in western Utah. Journal of Wildlife Management 37:343–352.

BEKOFF, M., AND L. D. MECH. 1984. Simulation analyses of space use: home range estimates, variability, and sample size. Behavior Research Methods, Instruments, and Computers 16:32–37.

BEYER, JR., D. E., AND J. B. HAUFLER. 1994. Diurnal versus 24-hour sampling of habitat use. Journal of Wildlife Management 58:178–180.

BIGGINS, D. E., AND M. R. JACKSON. 1984. Biases in aerial surveys of mule deer. Thorne Ecological Institute Technical Publication 14:60–65.

BLEICH, V. C., C. S. Y. CHUN, R. W. ANTHES, T. E. EVANS, AND J. K. FISCHER. 2001. Visibility bias and development of a sightability model for tule elk. Alces 37:315–327.

BLOUIN F., J. F. GIROUX, J. FERRON, G. GAUTHIER, AND G. J. DOUCET. 1999. The use of satellite telemetry to track greater snow geese. Journal of Field Ornithology 70:187–199.

BLUNDELL, G. M., J. A. K. MAIER, AND E. M. DEBEVEC. 2001. Linear home ranges: effects of smoothing, sample size, and autocorrelation on kernel estimates. Ecological Monographs 71:469–489.

BOGEL, R. 1994. Measuring locations and flight altitudes of griffon vultures *Gyps fulvus* by an automatic telemetry system. Pages 325–334 *in* Raptor Conservation Today: Proceedings of the IV World Conference of Birds of Prey and Owls, Berlin, Germany.

BONACCORSO, F. J., J. R. WINKELMANN, E. R. DUMONT, AND K. THIBAULT. 2002. Home range of *Dobsonia minor* (Pteropodidae): a solitary, foliage-roosting fruit bat in Papua New Guinea. Biotropica 34:127–135.

BONTADINA, F., H. SCHOFIELD, AND B. NAEF-DAENZER. 2002. Radio tracking reveals that lesser horseshoe bats (*Rhinolophus hipposideros*) forage in woodland. Journal of Zoology 258:281–290.

BOONE, R. B., AND M. L. HUNTER, JR. 1996. Using diffusion models to simulate the effects of land use on grizzly bear dispersal in the Rocky Mountains. Landscape Ecology 11:51–64.

———, AND R. S. MESECAR III. 1989. Telemetric egg for use in egg-turning studies. Journal of Field Ornithology 60:315–322.

BOSHOFF, A. F., A. S. ROBERTSON, AND P. M. NORTON. 1984. A radio-tracking study of an adult Cape griffon vulture *Gyps coprotheres* in the southwestern Cape Province. South African Journal of Wildlife Research 14:73–78.

BOULANGER, J. G., AND G. C. WHITE. 1990. A comparison of home-range estimators using Monte Carlo simulation. Journal of Wildlife Management 54:310–315.

BOWMAN, A. W., AND A. AZZALINI. 1997. Applied smoothing techniques for data analysis: the kernal approach with S-PLUS illustrations. Oxford University Press, New York, USA.

BOWMAN, J. L., AND H. A. JACOBSON. 1998. An improved vaginal-implant transmitter for locating white-tailed deer birth sites and fawns. Wildlife Society Bulletin 26:295–298.

———, M. C. WALLACE, W. B. BALLARD, J. H. BRUNJES, M. S. MILLER, AND J. M. HELLMAN. 2002. Evaluation of two techniques for attaching radio transmitters to turkey poults. Journal of Field Ornithology 73:276–280.

BRAUN, S. E. 1985. Home range and activity patterns of the giant kangaroo rat, *Dipodomys ingens*. Journal of Mammalogy 66:1–12.

BRAY, O. E., AND G. W. CORNER. 1972. A tail clip for attaching transmitters to birds. Journal of Wildlife Management 36:640–642.

———, K. H. LARSEN, AND D. F. MOTT. 1975. Winter movements and activities of radio-equipped starlings. Journal of Wildlife Management 39:795–801.

BRITTEN, M. W., P. L. KENNEDY, AND S. AMBROSE. 1999. Performance and accuracy evaluation of small satellite transmitters. Journal of Wildlife Management 63:1349–1358.

BRODEUR, S., R. DECARRIE, D. M. BIRD, AND M. FULLER. 1996. Complete migration cycle of golden eagles breeding in northern Quebec. Condor 98:293–299.

BROEKHUIZEN, S., C. A. VAN'T HOFF, M. B. JANSEN, AND F. J. J. NIEWOLD. 1980. Application of radio tracking in wildlife research in the Netherlands. Pages 65–84 *in* C. J. Amlaner, Jr. and D. W. Macdonald, editors. A handbook on biotelemetry and radio tracking. Pergamon Press, Oxford, United Kingdom.

BROWNIE, C., D. R. ANDERSON, K. P. BURNHAM, AND D. S. ROBSON. 1985. Statistical inference from band recovery data-a handbook. Second edition. U.S. Department of the Interior, Fish and Wildlife Service, Resource Publication 156.

BUEHLER, D. A, J. D. FRASER, M. R. FULLER, L. S. MCALLISTER, AND J. K. D. SEEGAR. 1995. Captive and field-tested radio transmitter attachments for bald eagles. Journal of Field Ornithology 66:173–180.

BULL, C. M., AND B. C. BAGHURST. 1998. Home range overlap of mothers and their offspring in the sleepy lizard, *Tiliqua rugosa*. Behavioral Ecology and Sociobiology 42:357–362.

BUNCK, C. M. 1987. Analysis of survival data from telemetry projects. Journal of Raptor Research 21:132–134.

BURCHARD, D. 1989*a*. Direction finding in wildlife research by Doppler effect. Pages 169–177 *in* C. J. Amlaner, Jr., editor. Biotelemetry X. University of Arkansas Press, Fayetteville, USA.

———. 1989*b*. Towards higher frequencies in outdoor applications. Pages 57–65 *in* C. J. Amlaner, Jr., editor. Biotelemetry X. University of Arkansas Press, Fayetteville, USA.

BURKEPILE, N. A., J. W. CONNELLY, D. W. STANLEY, AND K. P. REESE. 2002. Attachment of radiotransmitters to one-day-old sage grouse chicks. Wildlife Society Bulletin 30:93–96.

BURNHAM, K. P., AND D. R. ANDERSON. 1984. Tests of compensatory vs. additive hypotheses of mortality in mallards. Ecology 65:105–112.

BURT, W. H. 1943. Territoriality and home range concepts as applied to mammals. Journal of Mammalogy 24:346–352.

BUSKIRK, S. W., AND J. J. MILLSPAUGH. 2004. Availability and use: key concepts in modeling resource selection. Pages 1–11 *in* S. Huzzabazar, editor. Resource selection methods and applications. Omnipress, Madison, Wisconsin, USA.

CACCAMISE, D. F., AND D. W. MORRISON. 1986. Avian communal roosting: implications of diurnal activity centers. American Naturalist 128:191–198.

CALHOUN, J. B., AND J. V. CASBY. 1958. Calculation of home range and density of small mammals. U.S. Department of Health and Human Services, Public Health Service, Public Health Monograph 55.

CAREY, A. B., S. P. HORTON, AND J. A. REID. 1989. Optimal sampling for radiotelemetry studies of spotted owl habitat and home range. U.S. Department of Agriculture, Forest Service, Resource Paper PNW-RP-416.

CARSTENSEN, M., G. D. DELGIUDICE, AND B. A. SAMPSON. 2003. Using doe behavior and vaginal-implant transmitters to capture neonate white-tailed deer in north-central Minnesota. Wildlife Society Bulletin 31:634–641.

CEDERLUND, G., AND P. A. LEMNELL. 1980. A simplified technique for mobile radio tracking. Pages 319–322 *in* C. J. Amlaner, Jr. and D. W. Macdonald, editors. A handbook on biotelemetry and radio tracking. Pergamon Press, Oxford, United Kingdom.

CHAMBERLAIN, M. J., AND B. D. LEOPOLD. 2001. Survival and cause-specific mortality of adult coyotes (*Canis latrans*) in central Mississippi. American Midland Naturalist 145:414–418.

CHEESEMAN, C. L., AND P. J. MALLINSON. 1980. Radio tracking in the study of bovine tuberculosis in badgers. Pages 649–656 *in* C. J. Amlaner, Jr. and D. W. Macdonald, editors. A handbook on biotelemetry and radio tracking. Pergamon Press, Oxford, United Kingdom.

CHU, D. S., B. A. HOOVER, M. R. FULLER, AND P. H. GEISSLER. 1989. Telemetry location error in forested habitat. Pages 188–194 *in* C. J. Amlaner, Jr., editor. Biotelemetry X. University of Arkansas Press, Fayetteville, USA.

CLUTTON-BROCK, J. 2003. Risk assessment for animals: should the routine assessment of negative effects of intervention in wild animals be built into research projects? Journal of Zoology 260:117–118.

COCHRAN, W. W. 1980. Wildlife telemetry. Pages 507–520 *in* S. D. Schemnitz, editor. Wildlife management techniques manual. Fourth edition, revised. The Wildlife Society, Washington, D.C., USA.

———, AND L. L. PATER. 2001. Direction finding at ultra high frequencies

(UHF): improved accuracy. Wildlife Society Bulletin 29:594–599.

———, D. W. WARNER, J. R. TESTER, AND V. B. KUECHLE. 1965. Automatic radio tracking system for monitoring animal movements. BioScience 15:98–100.

COGAN, R. D., AND D. R. DIEFENBACH. 1998. Effect of undercounting and model selection on a sightability-adjustment estimator for elk. Journal of Wildlife Management 62:269–279.

COLE, L. C. 1949. The measurement of interspecific association. Ecology 30:411–424.

COON, R. A., P. D. CALDWELL, AND G. L. STORM. 1976. Some characteristics of fall migration of female woodcock. Journal of Wildlife Management 40:91–95.

COOPER, A. B., AND J. J. MILLSPAUGH. 1999. The application of discrete choice models to wildlife resource selection studies. Ecology 80:566–575.

———, AND ———. 2001. Accounting for variation in resource availability and animal behavior in resource selection studies. Pages 243–274 *in* J. J. Millspaugh and J. M. Marzluff, editors. Radio tracking and animal populations. Academic Press, San Diego, California, USA.

CÔTÉ, S. D., M. FESTA-BIANCHET, AND F. FOURNIER. 1998. Life-history effects of chemical immobilization and radiocollars on mountain goats. Journal of Wildlife Management 62:745–752.

COX, JR., R. R., J. D. SCALF, B. E. JAMISON, AND R. S. LUTZ. 2002. Using an electronic compass to determine telemetry azimuths. Wildlife Society Bulletin 30:1039–1043.

CRESSWELL, W. J. AND G. C. SMITH. 1992. The effects of temporally autocorrelated data on methods of home range analysis. Pages 272–284 *in* I. G. Priede and S. M. Swift, editors. Wildlife telemetry: remote monitoring and tracking of animals. Ellis Horwood, West Sussex, United Kingdom.

CULIK, B. 2001. Finding food in the open ocean: foraging strategies in Humboldt penguins. Zoology 104:327–338.

DEAT, A. R., C. MAUGET, R. MAUGET, D. MAUREL, AND A. J. S. SEMPÉRÉ. 1980. The automatic, continuous and fixed radio tracking system of the Chize Forest: theoretical and practical analysis. Pages 439–451 *in* C. J. Amlaner, Jr. and D. W. Macdonald, editors. A handbook on biotelemetry and radio tracking. Pergamon Press, Oxford, United Kingdom.

DEIN, F. J., D. E. TOWEILL, AND K. P. KENOW. 2005. Care and use of wildlife in field research. Pages 185–196 *in* C. E. Braun, editor. Techniques for wildlife investigations and management. Sixth edition. The Wildlife Society, Bethesda, Maryland, USA.

D'EON, R. G., R. SERROUYA, G. SMITH, AND C. O. KOCHANNY. 2002. GPS radiotelemetry error and bias in mountainous terrain. Wildlife Society Bulletin 30:430–439.

DIEHL, P., AND H. W. HELB. 1986. Radiotelemetric monitoring of heart-rate responses to song playback in blackbirds (*Turdus merula*). Behavioral Ecology and Sociobiology 18:213–219.

DIXON, K. R., AND J. A. CHAPMAN. 1980. Harmonic mean measure of animal activity areas. Ecology 61:1040–1044.

DODGE, W. E., AND A. J. STEINER. 1986. XYLOG: a computer program for field processing locations of radio-tagged wildlife. U.S. Department of the Interior, Fish and Wildlife Service, Technical Report 4.

———, D. S. WILKIE, AND A. J. STEINER. 1986. UTMEL: a laptop computer program for location of telemetry "finds" using LORAN C. U.S. Department of the Interior, Geological Survey, Massachusetts Cooperative Fish and Wildlife Research Unit, University of Massachusetts, Amherst, USA.

DON, B. A. C., AND K. RENNOLLS. 1983. A home range model incorporating biological attraction points. Journal of Animal Ecology 52:69–81.

DONCASTER, C. P. 1990. Non-parametric estimates of interaction from radio-tracking data. Journal of Theoretical Biology 143:431–443.

DRENNAN, J. E., AND P. BEIER. 2003. Forest structure and prey abundance in winter habitat of northern goshawks. Journal of Wildlife Management 67:177–185.

DUNN, J. E., AND P. S. GIPSON. 1977. Analysis of radio telemetry data in studies of home range. Biometrics 33:85–101.

DUNSTAN, T. C. 1972. A harness for radio-tagging raptorial birds. Inland Bird Banding News 44:4–8.

EAGLE, T. C., J. CHOROMANSKI-NORRIS, AND V. B. KUECHLE. 1984. Implanting radio transmitters in mink and Franklin's ground squirrels. Wildlife Society Bulletin 12:180–184.

ELORANTA, E., H. NORBERG, A. NILSSON, T. PUDAS, AND H. SAKKINEN. 2002. Individually coded telemetry: a tool for studying heart rate and behavior in reindeer calves. Acta Veterinaria Scandinavica 43:135–144.

ERICKSON, W. P., T. L. MCDONALD, K. G. GEROW, S. HOWLIN, AND J. W. KERN. 2001. Statistical issues in resource selection studies with radio-marked animals. Pages 209–242 *in* J. J. Millspaugh and J. M. Marzluff, editors. Radio tracking and animal populations. Academic Press, San Diego, California, USA.

ESLER, D., D. M. MULCAHY, AND R. L. JARVIS. 2000. Testing assumptions for unbiased estimation of survival of radiomarked harlequin ducks. Journal of Wildlife Management 64:591–598.

EVERETT, B. 1980. Cluster analysis. Second edition. Heinemann, London, United Kingdom.

FANCY, S. G., L. F. PANK, D. C. DOUGLAS, C. H. CURBY, G. W. GARNER, S. C. AMSTRUP, AND W. L. REGELIN. 1988. Satellite telemetry: a new tool for wildlife research and management. U.S. Department of the Interior, Fish and Wildlife Service, Resource Publication 172.

FEDAK, M., P. LOVELL, B. MCCONNELL, AND C. HUNTER. 2002. Overcoming the constraints of long range radio telemetry from animals: getting more useful data from smaller packages. Integrative and Comparative Biology 42:3–10.

FENTON, M. B., P. J. TAYLOR, D. S. JACOBS, E. J. RICHARDSON, E. BERNARD, S. BOUCHARD, K. R. DEBAEREMAEKER, H. TERHOFSTEDE, L. HOLLIS, C. L. LAUSEN, J. S. LISTER, D. RAMBALDINI, J. M. RATCLIFFE, AND E. REDDY. 2002. Researching little known species: the African bat *Otomops martiensseni* (Chiroptera: Molossidae). Biodiversity and Conservation 11:1583–1606.

FINDHOLT, S. L., B. K. JOHNSON, L. D. BRYANT, AND J. W. THOMAS. 1996. Corrections for position bias of a Loran-C radio telemetry system using DGPS. Northwest Science 70:273–280.

———, ———, L. L. MCDONALD, J. W. KERN, A. AGER, R. J. STUSSY, AND L. D. BRYANT. 2002. Adjusting for radiotelemetry error to improve estimates of habitat use. U.S. Department of Agriculture, Forest Service, General Technical Report PNW-GTR-555.

FITZNER, R. E., AND J. N. FITZNER. 1977. A hot melt glue technique for attaching radiotransmitter tail packages to raptorial birds. North American Bird Bander 2:56–57.

FLOYD, T. J., L. D. MECH, AND M. E. NELSON. 1979. An improved method of censusing deer in deciduous–coniferous forests. Journal of Wildlife Management 43:258–261.

FOCARDI, S., P. MARCELLINI, AND P. MONTANARO. 1996. Do ungulates exhibit a food density threshold? A field study of optimal foraging and movement patterns. Journal of Animal Ecology 65:606–620.

FOWLER, C. W. 1981. Density dependence as related to life history strategy. Ecology 62:602–610.

FRANZMANN, A. W., C. C. SCHWARTZ, AND R. O. PETERSON. 1980. Moose calf mortality in summer on the Kenai Peninsula, Alaska. Journal of Wildlife Management 44:764–768.

FUGLEI, E., J. B. MERCER, AND J. M. ARNEMO. 2002. Surgical implantation of radio transmitters in arctic foxes (*Alopex lagopus*) on Svalbard, Norway. Journal of Zoo and Wildlife Medicine 33:342–349.

FULLER, M. R. AND J. R. TESTER. 1973. An automatic radio tracking system for biotelemetry. Raptor Research 7:105–106.

———, W. S. SEEGAR, AND L. S. SCHUECK. 1998. Routes and travel rates of migrating peregrine falcons *Falco peregrinus* and Swainson's hawks *Buteo swainsoni* in the Western Hemisphere. Journal of Avian Biology 29:433–440.

———, H. H. OBRECHT III, C. J. PENNYCUICK, AND F. C. SCHAFFNER. 1989. Aerial tracking of radio-marked white-tailed tropicbirds over the Caribbean Sea. Pages 133–138 *in* C. J. Amlaner, Jr., editor. Biotelemetry X. University of Arkansas Press, Fayetteville, USA.

FULLER, T. K., AND W. J. SNOW. 1988. Estimating winter wolf densities using radiotelemetry data. Wildlife Society Bulletin 16:367–370.

GARCELON, D. K. 1977. An expandable drop-off transmitter collar for young mountain lions. California Fish and Game 63:185–189.

GARRETTSON, P. R., F. C. ROHWER, AND E. B. MOSER. 2000. Effects of backpack and implanted radio transmitters on captive blue-winged teal. Journal of Wildlife Management 64:216–222.

GARROTT, R. A., R. M. BARTMANN, AND G. C. WHITE. 1985. Comparison of radio-transmitter packages relative to deer fawn mortality. Journal of Wildlife Management 49:758–759.

———, G. C. WHITE, R. M. BARTMANN, AND D. L. WEYBRIGHT. 1986. Reflected signal bias in biotelemetry triangulation systems. Journal of Wildlife Management 50:747–752.

GARTON, E. O., J. T. RATTI, AND J. H. GIUDICE. 2005. Research and experimental design. Pages 43–71 *in* C. E. Braun, editor. Techniques for wildlife investigations and management. Sixth edition. The Wildlife Society, Bethesda, Maryland, USA.

———, M. J. WISDOM, F. A. LEBAN, AND B. K. JOHNSON. 2001. Experimental design for radiotelemetry studies. Pages 15–42 *in* J. J. Millspaugh and J. M. Marzluff, editors. Radio tracking and animal populations. Academic Press, San Diego, California, USA.

GASAWAY, W. C., S. D. DUBOIS, AND S. J. HARBO. 1985. Biases in aerial transect surveys for moose during May and June. Journal of Wildlife Management 49:777–784.

GAVIN, T. A., L. H. SURING, P. A. VOHS, JR., AND E. C. MESLOW. 1984. Population characteristics, spatial organization, and natural mortality in the Columbian white-tailed deer. Wildlife Monographs 91.

GEISSLER, P. H., AND M. R. FULLER. 1985. Detecting and displaying the structure of an animal's home range. American Statistical Association Statistical Computing Section Proceedings 1985:378–383.

GESE, E. M., D. E. ANDERSEN, AND O. J. RONGSTAD. 1990. Determining home range size of resident coyotes from point and sequential locations. Journal of Wildlife Management 54:501–506.

GIACOMETTI, M., M. JANOVSKY, G. FLUCH, W. ARNOLD, AND F. SCHOBER. 2001. A technique to implant heart-rate transmitters in red deer. Wildlife Society Bulletin 29:586–593.

GILMER, D. S., L. M. COWARDIN, R. L. DUVAL, L. M. MECHLIN, C. W. SCHAIFFER, AND V. B. KUECHLE. 1981. Procedures for the use of aircraft in wildlife biotelemetry studies. U.S. Department of the Interior, Fish and Wildlife Service, Resource Publication 140.

GITZEN, R. A., AND J. J. MILLSPAUGH. 2003. Evaluation of least squares cross validation bandwidth options for kernel home range estimation. Wildlife Society Bulletin 31:823–831.

GODFREY, G. A. 1970. A transmitter harness for small birds. Inland Bird Banding 42:3–5.

GOGUEN, C. B., AND N. E. MATHEWS. 2001. Brown-headed cowbird behavior and movements in relation to livestock grazing. Ecological Applications 11:1533–1544.

GONZALES-SOLIS, J., J. P. COXALL, AND A. G. WOOD. 2000. Foraging partitioning between giant petrels Macronectes spp. and its relationship with breeding population changes at Bird Island, South Georgia. Marine Ecology Progress Series 204:279–288.

GREEN, M., T. PIERSMA, J. JUKEMA, P. DE GOEIJ, B. SPAANS, AND J. VAN GILS. 2002. Radio-telemetry observations of the first 650 km of the migration of bar-tailed godwits Limosa lapponica from the Wadden Sea to the Russian arctic. Ardea 90:71–80

GREEN, P. 1985. Some results from the use of a long life radio transmitter package on corvids. Ringing and Migration 6:45–51.

GUYN, K. L., AND R. G. CLARK. 2000. Nesting effort of northern pintails in Alberta. Condor 102:619–628.

HAMMOND, P. S., B. J. MCCONNELL, M. A. FEDAK, AND K. S. NICHOLAS. 1992. Grey seal activity patterns around the Farne Islands. Pages 677–686 in I. G. Priede and S. M. Smith, editors. Wildlife telemetry-remote monitoring and tracking of animals. Ellis Horwood, Chichester, United Kingdom.

HANSTEEN, T. L., H. P. ANDREASSEN, AND R. A. IMS. 1997. Effects of spatiotemporal scale on autocorrelation and home range estimators. Journal of Wildlife Management 61:280–290.

HARAMIS, G. M., AND G. D. KEARNS. 2000. A radio transmitter attachment technique for soras. Journal of Field Ornithology 71:135–139.

HARCOURT, R. G., C. J. A. BRADSHAW, K. DICKSON, AND L. S. DAVIS. 2002. Foraging ecology of a generalist predator, the female New Zealand fur seal. Marine Ecology Progress Series 227:11–24.

HARRIS, S., W. J. CRESSWELL, P. G. FORDE, W. J. TREWHELLA, T. WOOLARD, AND S. WRAY. 1990. Home-range analysis using radio-tracking data—a review of problems and techniques particularly as applied to the study of mammals. Mammal Review 20:97–123.

HARRISON, C. S., AND D. STONEBURNER. 1981. Radiotelemetry of the brown noddy (Anous stolidus) of Manana Island (Oahu), Hawaii. Pacific Seabird Group Bulletin 6:45.

HARTIGAN, J. A. 1987. Estimation of a convex density contour in two dimensions. Journal of the American Statistical Association 82:267–270.

HARVEY, M. J., AND R. W. BARBOUR. 1965. Home range of Microtus ochrogaster as determined by a modified minimum area method. Journal of Mammalogy 46:398–402.

HATCH, S. A., P. M. MEYERS, D. M. MULCAHY, AND D. C. DOUGLAS. 2000. Performance of implantable satellite transmitters in diving seabirds. Waterbirds 23:84–94.

HAWKINS, P. A., P. J. BUTLER, A. J. WOAKES, AND J. R. SPEAKMAN. 2000. Estimation of the rate of oxygen consumption of the common eider duck (Somateria mollissima), with some measurements of heart rate during voluntary dives. Journal of Experimental Biology 203:2819–2832.

HAYES, R. W. 1982. A telemetry device to monitor big game traps. Journal of Wildlife Management 46:551–553.

HEATH, R. G. M. 1987. A method for attaching transmitters to penguins. Journal of Wildlife Management 51:399–401.

HEDD, A., R. GALES, AND N. BROTHERS. 2001. Foraging strategies of shy albatross Thalassarche cauta breeding at Albatross Island, Tasmania, Australia. Marine Ecology Progress Series 224:267–282.

HEEZEN, K. L., AND J. R. TESTER. 1967. Evaluation of radio-tracking by triangulation with special reference to deer movements. Journal of Wildlife Management 31:124–141.

HEGDAL, P. L., AND B. A. COLVIN. 1986. Radiotelemetry. Pages 679–698 in A. Y. Cooperrider, R. J. Boyd, and H. R. Stuart, editors. Inventory and monitoring of wildlife habitat. U.S. Department of the Interior, Bureau of Land Management, Service Center, Denver, Colorado, USA.

————, AND T. A. GATZ. 1987. Technology of radiotracking for various birds and mammals. Pages 204–206 in PECORA IV: a symposium on application of remote sensing data to wildlife management. National Wildlife Federation Science and Technical Series 3.

HEISEY, D. M., AND T. K. FULLER. 1985. Evaluation of survival and cause-specific mortality rates using telemetry data. Journal of Wildlife Management 49:668–674.

HILL, I. F., B. H. CRESSWELL, AND R. E. KENWARD. 1999. Field testing the suitability of a new back pack harness for radio-tagging passerines. Journal of Avian Biology 30:135–142.

HIRONS, G. J. M., AND R. B. OWEN, JR. 1982. Radio tagging as an aid to the study of woodcock. Pages 139–152 in C. L. Cheeseman and R. B. Mitson, editors. Telemetric studies of vertebrates. Academic Press, London, United Kingdom.

HÖLZENBEIN, S. 1992. Expandable PVC collar for marking and transmitter support. Journal of Wildlife Management 56:473–476.

HOOGE, P. N., AND B. EICHENLAUB. 1997. Animal movement extension to Arcview: version 1.1. U.S. Department of the Interior, Geological Survey, Alaska Biological Science Center, Anchorage, Alaska, USA.

HOSKINSON, R. L. 1976. The effect of different pilots on aerial telemetry error. Journal of Wildlife Management 40:137–139.

HOWEY, P. W., R. G. BOARD, AND J. KEAR. 1977. A pulse-position-modulated multichannel radio telemetry system for the study of avian nest microclimate. Biotelemetry 4:169–180.

————, W. S. SEEGAR, M. R. FULLER, AND K. TITUS. 1989. A coded tracking telemetry system. Pages 103–107 in C. J. Amlaner, Jr., editor. Biotelemetry X. University of Arkansas Press, Fayetteville, USA.

————, T. E. STRIKWERDA, S. MANTEL, M. R. FULLER, G. F. GEE, S. S. KLUGMAN, W. S. SEEGAR, AND F. P. WARD. 1987. A system for acquiring physiological and environmental telemetry data. Pages 347–350 in H. P. Kimmich and M. R. Neuman, editors. Biotelemetry IX. Doring-Druck, Braunschweig, Germany.

HULBERT, I. A. R., AND J. FRENCH. 2001. The accuracy of GPS for wildlife telemetry and habitat mapping. Journal of Applied Ecology 38:869–878.

HUPP, J. W., AND J. T. RATTI. 1983. A test of radiotelemetry triangulation accuracy in heterogeneous environments. Proceedings of the International Wildlife Biotelemetry Conference 4:31–46.

————, G. A. RUHL, J. M. PEARCE, D. M. MULCAHY, AND M. A. TOMEO. 2003. Effects of implanted transmitters with percutaneous antennas on the behavior of Canada geese. Journal of Field Ornithology 74:250–256.

INGLIS, J. M. 1981. The forward-null twin-Yagi antenna array for aerial radiotracking. Wildlife Society Bulletin 9:222–225.

JACKSON, D. H., L. S. JACKSON, AND W. K. SEITZ. 1985. An expandable drop-off transmitter harness for young bobcats. Journal of Wildlife Management 49:46–49.

JANEAU, G., F. SPITZ, E. LECRIVAIN, M. DARDAILLON, AND C. KOWALSKI. 1987. An automatic biotelemetry system for free ranging animals. Acta Oecologia Applications 8:333–341.

JENNINGS, J. G., AND W. F. GANDY. 1980. Tracking pelagic dolphins by satellite. Pages 753–755 in C. J. Amlaner, Jr. and D. W. Macdonald, editors. A handbook on biotelemetry and radio tracking. Pergamon Press, Oxford, United Kingdom.

JENNRICH, R. I., AND F. B. TURNER. 1969. Measurements of non-circular home range. Journal of Theoretical Biology 22:227–237.

JOHNSON, A. R., B. T. MILNE, AND J. A. WIENS. 1992. Diffusion in fractal landscapes: simulations and experimental studies of tenebrionid beetle movements. Ecology 73:1968–1983.

JOHNSON, D. H. 1979. Estimating nest success: the Mayfield method and an alternative. Auk 96:651–661.

————. 1980. The comparison of usage and availability measurements for evaluating resource preferences. Ecology 61:65–71.

JOLLY, G. M. 1965. Explicit estimates from capture–recapture data with both death and immigration–stochastic models. Biometrika 52:225–247.

JUDD, S. L., AND R. R. KNIGHT. 1977. Determination of grizzly bear movement patterns using biotelemetry. Proceedings of the International Wildlife Biotelemetry Conference 1:93–100.

KAREIVA, P. M., AND N. SHIGESADA. 1983. Analyzing insect movement as a correlated random walk. Oecologia 56:234–238.

KARL, B. J., AND M. N. CLOUT. 1987. An improved radio transmitter harness with a weak link to prevent snagging. Journal of Field Ornithology 58:73–77.

KAUFMANN, J. H. 1962. Ecology and social behavior of the coati, *Nasua nirica* on Barro Colorado Island Panama. University of California Publications in Zoology 60:95–222.

KEITH, L. B., J. R. CARY, O. J. RONGSTAD, AND M. C. BRITTINGHAM. 1984. Demography and ecology of a declining snowshoe hare population. Wildlife Monographs 90.

KENWARD, R. E. 1977. Predation on released pheasants (*Phasianus colchicus*) by goshawks (*Accipiter gentilis*) in central Sweden. Swedish Game Research 10:79–112.

———. 1978. Radio transmitters tail-mounted on hawks. Ornis Scandinavica 9:220–223.

———. 1985. Raptor radio tracking and radio telemetry. International Council for Bird Preservation Technical Bulletin 5:409–420.

———. 1987. Wildlife radio tagging: equipment, field techniques and data analysis. Academic Press, London, United Kingdom.

———. 1992. Quantity versus quality: programmed collection and analysis of radio-tracking data. Pages 231–246 *in* Wildlife telemetry: remote monitoring and tracking of animals. Ellis Horwood, West Sussex, United Kingdom.

———. 2001. A manual of wildlife radio tagging. Academic Press, London, United Kingdom.

———, G. J. M. HIRONS, AND F. ZIESEMER. 1982. Devices for telemetering the behaviour of the free-living birds. Pages 129-137 *in* C. L. Cheeseman and R. G. Mitson, editors. Telemetric studies of vertebrates. Academic Press, London, United Kingdom.

———, V. MARCSTRÖM, AND M. KARLBOM. 1981. Goshawk winter ecology in Swedish pheasant habitats. Journal of Wildlife Management 45:397–408.

———, ———, AND ———. 1993. Post-nestling behaviour in goshawks, *Accipiter gentilis*: II. Sex differences in sociality and nest switching. Animal Behaviour 46:371–378.

———, A. B. SOUTH, AND S. S. WALLS. 2003. Ranges 6 v 1.2: for the analysis of tracking and location data. Anatrack Ltd., Wareham, United Kingdom.

———, S. S. WALLS, AND K. H. HODDER. 2001a. Life path analysis: scaling indicates priming effects of social and habitat factors on dispersal distances. Journal of Animal Ecology 70:1–13.

———, R. T. CLARKE, K. H. HODDER, AND S. S. WALLS. 2001b. Density and linkage estimators of home range: nearest-neighbor clustering defines multinuclear cores. Ecology 82:1905–1920.

———, ———, ———, M. PAHKALA, S. N. FREEMAN, AND V. R. SIMPSON. 2000. The prevalence of non-breeders in raptor populations: evidence from rings, radio-tags, and transect surveys. Oikos 91:271–279.

KERNOHAN, B. J., R. A. GITZEN, AND J. J. MILLSPAUGH. 2001. Analysis of animal space use and movements. Pages 125–166 *in* J. J. Millspaugh and J. M. Marzluff, editors. Radio tracking and animal populations. Academic Press, San Diego, California, USA.

KERTH, G., AND K. RECHARDT. 2003. Information transfer about roosts in female Bechstein's bats: an experimental field study. Proceedings of the Royal Society of London Series B 270:511–515.

———, M. WAGNER, AND B. KÖNIG. 2001. Roosting together, foraging apart: information transfer about food is unlikely to explain sociality in female Bechstein's bats (*Myotis bechsteini*). Behavioral Ecology and Sociobiology 50:283–291.

KING, R. A., AND J. R. BELTHOFF. 2001. Post-fledging dispersal of burrowing owls in southwestern Idaho: characterization of movements and use of satellite burrows. Condor 103:118–126.

KJELLÉN, N., M. HAKE, AND T. ALERSTAM. 2001. Timing and speed of migration in male, female and juvenile ospreys *Pandion haliaetus* between Sweden and Africa as revealed by field observations, radar and satellite tracking. Journal of Avian Biology 32:57–67.

KOEPPL, J. W., AND R. S. HOFFMANN. 1985. Robust statistics for spatial analysis:the bivariate normal home range model applied to syntopic populations of two species of ground squirrels. University of Kansas, Museum of Natural History, Occassional Paper 116.

KOLZ, A. L., AND R. E. JOHNSON. 1975. An elevating mechanism for mobile receiving antennas. Journal of Wildlife Management 39:819–820.

———, J. W. LENTFER, AND H. G. FALLEK. 1980. Satellite radio tracking of polar bears instrumented in Alaska. Pages 743–752 *in* C. J. Amlaner, Jr. and D. W. Macdonald, editors. A handbook on biotelemetry and radio tracking. Pergamon Press, Oxford, United Kingdom.

KOOYMAN, G. L., R. W. DAVIS, J. P. CROXALL, AND D. P. COSTA. 1982. Diving depths and energy requirements of king penguins. Science 217:726–727.

KORSCHGEN, C. E., S. J. MAXSON, AND V. B. KUECHLE. 1984. Evaluation of implanted radio transmitters in ducks. Journal of Wildlife Management 48:982–987.

———, K. P. KENOW, W. L. GREEN, M. D. SAMUEL, AND L. SILEO. 1996a. Technique for implanting radiotransmitters subcutaneously in day-old ducklings. Journal of Field Ornithology 67:392–397.

———, ———, D. H. JOHNSON, M. D. SAMUEL, AND L. SILEO. 1996b. Survival of radio-marked canvasback ducklings in Northwest Minnesota. Journal of Wildlife Management 60:120–132.

KUECHLE, V. B., J. M. HAYNES, AND R. A. REICHLE. 1989. Use of small computers as telemetry data collectors. Pages 695–699 *in* C. J. Amlaner, Jr., editor. Biotelemetry X. University of Arkansas Press, Fayetteville, USA.

———, M. R. FULLER, R. A. REICHLE, R. J. SCHUSTER, AND G. E. DUKE. 1987. Telemetry of gastric motility data from owls. Pages 363–366 *in* H. P. Kimmich and M. R. Neuman, editors. Biotelemetry IX. Doring-Druck, Braunschweig, Germany.

KUFELD, R. C., D. C. BOWDEN, AND J. M. SIPEREK, JR. 1987. Evaluation of a telemetry system for measuring habitat usage in mountainous terrain. Northwest Science 61:249–256.

KURTA, A., AND S.W. MURRAY. 2002. Philopatry and migration of banded Indiana bats (*Myotis sodalis*) and effects of radio transmitters. Journal of Mammalogy 83:585–589.

LANCIA, R. A., W. L. KENDALL, K. H. POLLOCK, AND J. D. NICHOLS. 2005. Estimating the number of animals in wildlife populations. Pages 106–153 *in* C. E. Braun, editor. Techniques for wildlife investigations and management. Sixth edition. The Wildlife Society, Bethesda, Maryland, USA.

LARKIN, R. P., A. RAIM, AND R. H. DIEHL. 1996. Performance of a nonrotating direction finder for automatic radio tracking. Journal of Field Ornithology 67:59–71.

LARSON, M. A. 2001. A catalog of software to analyze radiotelemetry data. Pages 397–421 *in* J. J. Millspaugh and J. M. Marzluff, editors. Radio tracking and animal populations. Academic Press, San Diego, California, USA.

LAUNDRÉ, J. W., T. D. REYNOLDS, S. T. KNICK, AND I. J. BALL. 1987. Accuracy of daily point relocations in assessing real movement of radio-marked animals. Journal of Wildlife Management 51:937–940.

LAWSON, E. J. G., AND A. R. RODGERS. 1997. Differences in home-range size computed in commonly used software programs. Wildlife Society Bulletin 25:721–729.

LEE, J. E., G. C. WHITE, R. A. GARROTT, R. M. BARTMANN, AND A. W. ALLDREDGE. 1985. Accessing accuracy of a radiotelemetry system for estimating animal locations. Journal of Wildlife Management 49:658–663.

LEMNELL, P. A., G. JOHNSSON, H. HELMERSSON, O. HOLMSTRAND, AND L. NORLING. 1983. An automatic radio-telemetry system for position determination and data acquisition. Proceedings of the International Conference on Wildlife Biotelemetry 4:76–93.

LENTH, R. V. 1981. On finding the source of a signal. Technometrics 23:149–154.

LICHT, D. S., D. G. MCAULEY, J. R. LONGCORE, AND G. F. SEPIK. 1989. An improved method to monitor nest attentiveness using radiotelemetry. Journal of Field Ornithology 60:251–258.

LINN, I. J., AND P. WILCOX. 1982. A semi-automated system for collecting data on the movements of radio tagged voles. Pages 197–205 *in* C. L. Chessman and R. B. Mitson, editors. Telemetric studies of vertebrates. Academic Press, London, United Kingdom.

LIVEZEY, K. B. 1988. Protective frame for a 2-element hand-held Yagi antenna. Journal of Wildlife Management 52:565–567.

LOTIMER, J. S. 1980. A versatile coded wildlife transmitter. Pages 185–191 *in* C. J. Amlaner, Jr. and D. W. Macdonald, editors. A handbook on biotelemetry and radio tracking. Pergamon Press, Oxford, United Kingdom.

LOUGHEED, C., B. A. VAN DERKIST, L. W. LOUGHEED, AND F. COOKE. 2002. Techniques for investigating breeding chronology in marbled murrelets, Desolation Sound, British Columbia. Condor 104:319–330.

LOVERIDGE, A. J., AND D. W. MACDONALD. 2002. Habitat ecology of two sympatric species of jackals in Zimbabwe. Journal of Mammalogy 83:599–607.

LOVETT, J. W., AND E. P. HILL. 1977. A transmitter syringe for recovery of immobilized deer. Journal of Wildlife Management 41:313–315.

MACE, R. D., AND J. S. WALLER. 1997. Spatial and temporal interaction of male and female grizzly bears in northwestern Montana. Journal of Wildlife Management 61:39–52.

MACDONALD, D. W., AND C. J. AMLANER, JR. 1980. A practical guide to radio tracking. Pages 143–159 *in* C. J. Amlaner, Jr. and D. W. Macdonald, editors. A handbook on biotelemetry and radio tracking. Pergamon Press, Oxford, United Kingdom.

———, F. G. BALL, AND N. G. HOUGH. 1980. The evaluation of home range size and configuration using radio tracking data. Pages 405–424 *in* C. J. Amlander, Jr. and D. W. Macdonald, editors. A handbook on biotelemetry and radio tracking. Pergamon Press, Oxford, United Kingdom.

MANLY, B. F., L. L. McDONALD, D. L. THOMAS, T. L. McDONALD, AND W. P. ERICKSON. 2002. Resource selection by animals: statistical design and analysis for field studies. Second edition. Kluwer Academic Publishers, Dordrecht, The Netherlands.

MARCSTRÖM, V., R. E. KENWARD, AND M. KARLBOM. 1989. Survival of ring-necked pheasants with backpacks, necklaces, and leg bands. Journal of Wildlife Management 53:808–810.

MARCUM, C. L., AND D. O. LOFTSGAARDEN. 1980. A non-mapping technique for studying habitat preferences. Journal of Wildlife Management 44:963–968.

MARZLUFF, J. M., S. KNICK, AND J. J. MILLSPAUGH. 2001. High-tech behavioral ecology: modeling the distribution of animal activities to better understand wildlife space use and resource selection. Pages 309–328 *in* J. J. Millspaugh and J. M. Marzluff, editors. Radio tracking and animal populations. Academic Press, San Diego, California, USA.

MATE, B. R., R. GISINER, AND J. MOBLEY. 1998. Local and migratory movements of Hawaiian humpback whales tracked by satellite telemetry. Canadian Journal of Zoology 76:863–868.

MAUSER, D. M., AND R. L. JARVIS. 1991. Attaching radio transmitters to 1-day-old mallard ducklings. Journal of Wildlife Management 55:488–491.

McCANN, K. L., K. SHAW, M. D. ANDERSON, AND K. MORRISON. 2001. Techniques for determining movement patterns of blue and wattled cranes in South Africa—colour ringing versus satellite telemetry. Ostrich (Supplement) 15:104–108.

McCORQUODALE, S. M. 1999. Movements, survival, and mortality of black-tailed deer in the Klickitat Basin of Washington. Journal of Wildlife Management 63:861–871.

McCULLOCH, C. E., AND M. L. CAIN. 1989. Analyzing discrete movement data as a correlated random walk. Ecology 70:383–388.

McDONALD, L. L., J. R. ALLDREDGE, M. S. BOYCE, AND W. P. ERICKSON. 2005. Measuring availability and vertebrate use of terrestrial habitats and foods. Pages 465–488 *in* C. E. Braun, editor. Techniques for wildlife investigations and management. Sixth edition. The Wildlife Society, Bethesda, Maryland, USA.

McLOUGHLIN, P. D., H. D. CLUFF, R. J. GAU, R. MULDERS, R. L. CASE, AND F. MESSIER. 2002. Population delineation of barren-ground grizzly bears in the central Canadian arctic. Wildlife Society Bulletin, 30:728–737.

McNAY, R. S., J. A MORGAN, AND F. L. BUNNELL. 1994. Characterizing independence of observations in movements of Columbian black-tailed deer. Journal of Wildlife Management 58:422–429.

MECH, L. D. 1982. Wolves (radio-telemetry). Pages 227–228 *in* D. E. Davis, editor. Handbook of census methods for terrestrial vertebrates. CRC Press, Boca Raton, Florida, USA.

———. 1983. Handbook of animal radio-tracking. University of Minnesota Press, Minneapolis, USA.

———, K. E. KUNKEL, R. C. CHAPMAN, AND T. J. KREEGER. 1990. Field testing of commercially manufactured capture collars on white-tailed deer. Journal of Wildlife Management 54:297–299.

MEDINA, A. L., AND H. D. SMITH. 1986. Designs for an antenna boom and masts for telemetry applications. Wildlife Society Bulletin 14:291–297.

MELQUIST, W. E., AND M. G. HORNOCKER. 1979. Development and use of a telemetry technique for studying river otter. Proceedings of the International Conference on Wildlife Biotelemetry 2:104–114.

———, AND ———. 1983. Ecology of river otters in west central Idaho. Wildlife Monographs 83.

MELVIN, S. M., AND S. A. TEMPLE. 1987. Radio telemetry techniques for international crane studies. Pages 481–492 *in* G. W. Archibald and R. F. Pasquier, editors. Proceedings of the 1983 International Crane Workshop. International Crane Foundation, Baraboo, Wisconsin, USA.

———, R. C. DREWIEN, S. A. TEMPLE, AND E. G. BIZEAU. 1983. Leg-band attachment of radio transmitters for large birds. Wildlife Society Bulletin 11:282–285.

METZGAR, L. H. 1973. Home range shape and activity in *Peromyscus leucopus*. Journal of Mammalogy 54:383–390.

MILLER, S. D., G. C. WHITE, R. A. SELLERS, H. V. REYNOLDS, J. W. SCHOEN, K. TITUS, V. G. BARNES, JR., R. B. SMITH, R. R. NELSON, W. B. BALLARD, AND C. C. SCHWARTZ. 1997. Brown and black bear density estimation in Alaska using radiotelemetry and replicated mark–resight techniques. Wildlife Monographs 133.

MILLS, L. S., AND F. F. KNOWLTON. 1989. Observer performance in known and blind radio-telemetry accuracy tests. Journal Wildlife Management 53:340–342.

MILLSPAUGH, J. J. 1999. Behavioral and physiological responses of elk to human disturbances in the southern Black Hills, South Dakota. Dissertation, University of Washington, Seattle, USA.

———, AND J. M. MARZLUFF, editors. 2001. Radio tracking and animal populations. Academic Press, San Diego, California, USA.

———, G. C. BRUNDIGE, R. A. GITZEN AND K. J. RAEDEKE. 2000. Elk and hunter space-use sharing in South Dakota. Journal of Wildlife Management 64:994–1003.

———, J. R. SKALSKI, B. J. KERNOHAN, K. J. RAEDEKE, G. C. BRUNDIGE, AND A. B. COOPER. 1998. Some comments on spatial independence in studies of resource selection. Wildlife Society Bulletin 26:232–236.

MINTA, S. C. 1992. Tests of spatial and temporal interaction among animals. Ecological Applications 2:178–188.

MIZUTANI, F., AND P. A. JEWELL. 1998. Home-range and movements of leopards (*Panthera pardus*) on a livestock ranch in Kenya. Journal of Zoology (London) 244:269–286.

MOHR, C. O. 1947. Table of equivalent populations of North American small mammals. American Midland Naturalist 37:223–449.

———, AND W. A. STUMPF. 1966. Comparison of methods for calculating areas of animal activity. Journal of Wildlife Management 30:293–304.

MOORCROFT, P. R., M. A. LEWIS, AND R. L. CRABTREE. 1999. Home range analysis using a mechanistic home range model. Ecology 80:1656–1665.

MORRISON, D. W., AND D. F. CACCAMISE. 1985. Ephemeral roosts and stable patches? A radiotelemetry study of communally roosting starlings. Auk 102:793–804.

MORTON, D. B., P. HAWKINS, R. BEVAN, K. HEATH, J. KIRKWOOD, P. PEARCE, L. SCOTT, G. WHELAN, AND A. WEBB. 2003. Refinements in telemetry procedures. Laboratory Animals 37:261–299.

MOURAO, G., AND I. M. MEDRI. 2002. A new way of using inexpensive large-scale assembled GPS to monitor giant anteaters in short time intervals. Wildlife Society Bulletin 30:1029–1032.

MULCAHY, D. M., AND D. ESLER. 1999. Surgical and immediate post-release mortality of harlequin ducks (*Histrionicus histrionicus*) implanted with abdominal radio transmitters with percutaneous antennas. Journal of Zoo and Wildlife Medicine 30:397–409.

———, AND G. GARNER. 1999. Subcutaneous implantation of satellite transmitters with percutaneous antennae into male polar bears (*Ursus maritimus*). Journal of Zoo and Wildlife Medicine 30:510–515.

MURRAY, D. L., AND M. R. FULLER. 2000. Effects of marking on the life history patterns of vertebrates. Pages 15–64 *in* L. Boitani and T. Fuller, editors. Research techniques in ethology and animal ecology. Columbia University Press, New York, USA.

MYSTERUD, A., AND R. A. IMS. 1998. Functional responses in habitat use: availability influences relative use in trade-off situations. Ecology 79:1435–1441.

NAEF-DAENZER, B. 1993. A new transmitter for small animals and enhanced methods of home-range analysis. Journal of Wildlife Management 57:680–689.

———, F. WIDMER, AND M. NUBER. 2001. Differential post-fledging survival of great and coal tits in relation to their condition and fledging date. Journal of Animal Ecology 70:730–738.

NEAL, A. K., G. C. WHITE, R. B. GILL, D. F. REED, AND J. H. OLTERMAN. 1993. Evaluation of mark–resight model assumptions for estimating mountain sheep numbers. Journal of Wildlife Management 57:436–450.

NELSON, M. E., AND L. D. MECH. 1999. Twenty-year home-range dynamics of a white-tailed deer matriline. Canadian Journal of Zoology 77:1128–1135.

NESBITT, S. A., B. A. HARRIS, R. W. REPENNING, AND C. B. BROWNSMITH. 1982. Notes on red-cockaded woodpecker study techniques. Wildlife Society Bulletin 10:160–163.

NEWMAN, S. H., J. Y. TAKEKAWA, D. L. WHITWORTH, AND E. E. BURKETT. 1999. Subcutaneous anchor and attachment increases retention of radio transmitters on Xantus' and marbled murrelets. Journal of Field Ornithology 70:520–534.

NICHOLS, J. D., M. J. CONROY, D. R. ANDERSON, AND K. P. BURNHAM. 1984. Compensatory mortality in waterfowl populations: a review of the evidence and implications for research and management. Transactions of the North American Wildlife and Natural Resources Conference 49:535–554.

NICHOLS, W. J., A. RESENDIZ, J. A. SEMINOFF, AND B. RESENDIZ. 2000. Transpacific migration of a loggerhead turtle monitored by satellite telemetry. Bulletin of Marine Science 67:937–947.

NIELSEN, C. K., AND A. WOOLF. 2001. Spatial organization of bobcats (*Lynx rufus*) in southern Illinois. American Midland Naturalist 146:43–52.

NOLAN, J. W., R. H. RUSSELL, AND F. ANDERKA. 1984. Transmitters for monitoring Aldrich snares set for grizzly bears. Journal of Wildlife Management 48:942–945.

NORMAN, G. W., P. C. PACK, C. I. TAYLOR, D. E. STEFFEN, AND K. H. POLLOCK. 2001. Reproduction of eastern wild turkeys in Virginia and West Virginia. Journal of Wildlife Management 65:1–9.

NORTH, M. P., AND J. H. REYNOLDS. 1996. Microhabitat analysis using radiotelemetry locations and polytomous logistic regression. Journal of Wildlife Management 60:639–653.

O'CONNOR, P. J., G. H. PYKE, AND H. SPENCER. 1987. Radio-tracking honeyeater movements. Emu 87:249–252.

O'NEIL, T. A., P. BETTINGER, B. G. MARCOT, B. W. LUSCOMBE, G. T. KOELN, H. J. BRUNER, C. BARRETT, J. A. POLLOCK, AND S. BERNATUS. 2005. Application of spatial technologies in wildlife biology. Pages 418–447 *in* C. E. Braun, editor. Techniques for wildlife investigations and management. Sixth edition. The Wildlife Society, Bethesda, Maryland, USA.

OTIS, D. L. 1997. Analysis of habitat selection studies with multiple patches within cover types. Journal of Wildlife Management 61:1016–1022.

———. 1998. Analysis of the influence of spatial pattern in habitat selection studies. Journal of Agricultural, Biological, and Environmental Statistics 3:254–267.

———, AND G. C. WHITE. 1999. Autocorrelation of location estimates and the analysis of radiotracking data. Journal of Wildlife Management 63:1039–1044.

OYLER-McCANCE, S. J., AND P. L. LEBERG. 2005. Conservation genetics in wildlife biology. Pages 632–657 *in* C. E. Braun, editor. Techniques for wildlife investigations and management. Sixth edition. The Wildlife Society, Bethesda, Maryland, USA.

PACE, R. M. 1988. Measurement error models for common wildlife radio-tracking systems. Report 5. Minnesota Department of Natural Resources, Saint Paul, USA.

PACK, J. C., G. W. NORMAN, C. I. TAYLOR, D. E. STEFFEN, D. A. SWANSON, K. H. POLLOCK, AND R. ALPIZAR-JARA. 1999. Effects of fall hunting on wild turkey populations in Virginia and West Virginia. Journal of Wildlife Management 63:964–975.

PARISH, T. A. 1980. A collapsible dipole antenna for radio tracking on 102 MHz. Pages 263–268 *in* C. J. Amlaner, Jr. and D. W. Macdonald, editors. A handbook on biotelemetry and radio tracking. Pergamon Press, Oxford, United Kingdom.

PATON, P. W. C., C. J. ZABEL, D. L. NEAL, G. N. STEGER, N. G. TILGHMAN, AND B. R. NOON. 1991. Effects of radio tags on spotted owls. Journal of Wildlife Management 55:617–622.

PENNYCUICK, C. J. 1989. Bird flight performance:a practical calculation manual. Oxford University Press, Oxford, United Kingdom.

———, M. R. FULLER, AND L. McALLISTER. 1989. Climbing performance of Harris' hawks (*Parabuteo unicinctus*) with added load:implications for muscle mechanics and for radiotracking. Journal of Experimental Biology 142:17–29.

PERRY, M. C. 1981. Abnormal behavior of canvasbacks equipped with radio transmitters. Journal of Wildlife Management 45:786–789.

———, G. H. HAAS, AND J. W. CARPENTER. 1981. Radio transmitters for mourning doves: a comparison of attachment techniques. Journal of Wildlife Management 45:524–527.

PETERSBURG, M. L., A. W. ALLDREDGE, AND W. J. DE VERGIE. 2000. Emigration and survival of 2-year-old male elk in northwestern Colorado. Wildlife Society Bulletin 28:708–716.

PETERSEN, M. R., D. C. DOUGLAS, AND D. M. MULCAHY. 1995. Use of implanted satellite transmitters to locate spectacled eiders at sea. Condor 97:276–278.

PLISSNER, J. H., S. M. HAIG, AND L. W. ORING. 2000. Postbreeding movements of American avocets and implications for wetland connectivity in the western Great Basin. Auk 117:290–298.

POLLOCK, K. H. 1981. Capture–recapture models allowing for age-dependent survival and capture rates. Biometrics 37:521–529.

PORTER, W. F., AND K. E. CHURCH. 1987. Effects of environmental pattern on habitat preference analysis. Journal of Wildlife Management 51:681–685.

RALLS, K., D. B. SINIFF, T. D. WILLIAMS, AND V. B. KUECHLE. 1989. An intraperitoneal radio transmitter for sea otters. Marine Mammal Science 5:376–381.

RAPPOLE, J. H., AND A. R. TIPTON. 1991. New harness design for attachment of radio transmitters to small passerines. Journal of Field Ornithology 62:335–337.

REINART, H. K., AND D. CUNDALL. 1982. An improved surgical implantation method for radio-tracking snakes. Copeia 1982:702–705.

REYNOLDS, R. T., G. C. WHITE, S. M. JOY, AND R. W. MANNAN. 2004. Effects of radiotransmitters on northern goshawks: do tailmounts lower survival of breeding males? Journal of Wildlife Management 68:25–32.

REYNOLDS, T. D., AND J. W. LAUNDRÉ. 1990. Time intervals for estimating pronghorn and coyote home ranges and daily movements. Journal of Wildlife Management 54:316–322.

RIBBLE, D. O., AND S. STANLEY. 1998. Home ranges and social organization of syntopic *Peromyscus boylii* and *P. truei*. Journal of Mammalogy 79:932–941.

RICE, W. R., AND J. D. HARDER. 1977. Application of multiple aerial sampling to a mark–recapture census of white-tailed deer. Journal of Wildlife Management 41:197–206.

RILEY, T. Z., W. R. CLARK, D. E. EWING, AND P. A. VOHS. 1998. Survival of ring-necked pheasant chicks during brood rearing. Journal of Wildlife Management 62:36–44.

RIVEST, L. P., S. COUTURIER, AND H. CRÉPEAU. 1998. Statistical methods for estimating caribou abundance using postcalving aggregations detected by radio telemetry. Biometrics 54:865–876.

ROBERTSON, P. A., N. J. AEBISCHER, R. E. KENWARD, I. K. HANSKI, AND N. P. WILLIAMS. 1998. Simulation and jack-knifing assessment of home-range indices based on underlying trajectories. Journal of Applied Ecology 35:928–940.

RODGERS, A. R. 2001. Recent telemetry technology. Pages 79–121 *in* J. J. Millspaugh and J. M. Marzluff, editors. Radio tracking and animal populations. Academic Press, San Diego, California, USA.

ROFFE, T. J., S. J. SWEENEY, AND K. E. AUNE. 2005. Chemical immobilization of North American mammals. Pages 286–302 *in* C. E. Braun, editor. Techniques for wildlife investigations and management. Sixth edition. The Wildlife Society, Bethesda, Maryland, USA.

ROSENBERG, D. K., AND K. S. McKELVEY. 1999. Estimation of habitat selection for central-place foraging animals. Journal of Wildlife Management 63:1028–1038.

ROTHMEYER, S. M., M. C. McKINSTRY, AND S. H. ANDERSON. 2002. Tail attachment of modified ear-tag radio transmitters on beavers. Wildlife Society Bulletin 30:425–429.

ROUYS, S., J. THEUERKAUF, AND M. KRASINSKA. 2001. Accuracy of radiotracking to estimate activity and distances walked by European bison in the Bialowieza Forest, Poland. Acta Theriologica 46:319–326.

SAMUEL, M.D., AND M. R. FULLER. 1994. Wildlife radiotelemetry. Pages 370–418 *in* T. A. Bookout, editor. Research and management techniques for wildlife and habitats. Fifth edition. The Wildlife Society, Bethesda, Maryland, USA.

———, AND E. O. GARTON. 1985. Home range: a weighted normal estimate and tests of underlying assumptions. Journal of Wildlife Management 49:513–519.

———, ———. 1987. Incorporating activity time in harmonic home range analysis. Journal of Wildlife Management 51:254–257.

———, AND R. E. GREEN. 1988. A revised test procedure for identifying core areas within the home range. Journal of Animal Ecology 57:1067–1068.

———, E. O. GARTON, M. W. SCHLEGEL, AND R. G. CARSON. 1987. Visibility bias during aerial surveys of elk in northcentral Idaho. Journal of Wildlife Management 51:622–630.

———, D. J. PIERCE, E. O. GARTON, L. J. NELSON, AND K. R. DIXON. 1985. User's manual for program Home Range. First edition. Forestry, Wildlife, and Range Experiment Station, University of Idaho, Moscow, USA.

SANDERSON, G. C. 1966. The study of mammal movements—a review. Journal of Wildlife Management 30:215–235.

SARGEANT, A. B. 1980. Approaches, field considerations and problems associated with radio tracking carnivores. Pages 57–63 *in* C. J. Amlaner, Jr. and D. W. Macdonald, editors. A handbook on biotelemetry and radio tracking. Pergamon Press, Oxford, United Kingdom.

SCHEMNITZ, S. D. 2005. Capturing and handling wild animals. Pages 239–285 *in* C. E. Braun, editor. Techniques for wildlife investigations and management. Sixth edition. The Wildlife Society, Bethesda, Maryland, USA.

SCHLEGAL, M. W. 1976. Factors affecting calf elk survival in north central Idaho: a progress report. Proceedings of the Western Association of State Game and Fish Commissioners 56:342–355.

SCHMID, J. R., A. B. BOLTEN, K. A. BJORNDAL, W. J. LINDBERG, H. F. PER-

CIVAL, AND P. D. ZWICK. 2003. Home range and habitat use by Kemp's ridley turtles in west-central Florida. Journal of Wildlife Management 67:196–206.

SCHOBER, F., AND B. OEHRY. 1987. Automatic RF receiving system for carrier frequency pulses. Pages 351–354 *in* H. P. Kimmich and M. R. Neuman, editors. Biotelemetry IX. Doring-Druck, Braunschweig, Germany.

———, W. M. BUGNAR, AND J. WAGNER. 1989. A software package for acquisition and evaluation of biotelemetric data from domestic and wildlife animals. Pages 700–708 *in* C. J. Amlaner, Jr., editor. Biotelemetry X. University of Arkansas Press, Fayetteville, USA.

———, R. BOGEL, W. M. BUGNAR, D. BUCHARD, G. FLUCH, AND N. ROHDE. 1992. Automatic direction finding and location system based on Doppler effect. Pages 327–336 *in* P. Mancini, S. Fiorctti, and R. Bedini, editors. Biotelemetry XII. Editricc Univeritaria, Litografen Felici, Pisa, Italy.

SCHOENER, T. W. 1981. An empirically based estimate of home range. Theoretical Population Biology 20:281–325.

SCHULZ, J. H., A. J. BERMUDEZ, J. L. TOMLINSON, J. D. FIRMAN, AND Z. Q. HE. 2001. Comparison of radiotransmitter attachment techniques using captive mourning doves. Wildlife Society Bulletin 29:771–782.

SCHWARTZ, A., J. D. WEAVER, N. R. SCOTT, AND T. J. CADE. 1977. Measuring the temperature of eggs during incubation under captive falcons. Journal of Wildlife Management 41:12–17.

SCOTT, D. W. 1992. Multivariate density estimation: theory, practice, and visualization. John Wiley and Sons, New York, USA.

SEAMAN, D. E., AND R. A. POWELL. 1996. An evaluation of the accuracy of kernel density estimators for home range analysis. Ecology 77:2075–2085.

———, J. J. MILLSPAUGH, B. J. KERNOHAN, G. C. BRUNDIGE, K. J. RAEDEKE, AND R. A. GITZEN. 1999. Effects of sample size on kernel home range estimates. Journal of Wildlife Management 63:739–747.

SEBER, G. A. F. 1965. A note on the multiple–recapture census. Biometrika 52:249–259.

———. 1986. A review of estimating animal abundance. Biometrics 42:267–292.

SEIDEL, K. D. 1992. Statistical properties and applications of a new measure of joint space use for wildlife. Thesis. University of Washington, Seattle, USA.

SERVHEEN, C., T. T. THIER, C. J. JONKEL, AND D. BEATY. 1981. An ear-mounted transmitter for bears. Wildlife Society Bulletin 9:56–57.

SHANNON, H. D., G. S. YOUNG, M. A. YATES, M. R. FULLER, AND W. S. SEEGAR. 2002a. American white pelican soaring flight times and altitudes relative to changes in thermal depth and intensity. Condor 104:679–683.

———, ———, ———, ———, AND ———. 2002b. Measurement of thermal updraft intensity over complex terrain using American white pelicans and a simple boundary-layer forecast model. Boundary-layer Meteorology 104:167–199.

———, G. S. YOUNG, W. S. SEEGAR, M. B. HENKE. S. L. STRUTHERS, AND V. B. KUECHLE. 2000. Bird altitude radio telemetry. Proceeding of the International Symposium on Biotelemetry 15:35–42.

SHIVIK, J. A., AND E. M. GESE. 2000. Territorial significance of home range estimators for coyotes. Wildlife Society Bulletin 28:940–946.

SILVERMAN, B. W. 1986. Density estimation for statistics and data analysis. Chapman and Hall, London, United Kingdom.

SILVY, N. J., R. R. LOPEZ, AND M. J. PETERSON. 2005. Wildlife marking techniques. Pages 339–376 *in* C. E. Braun, editor. Techniques for wildlife investigations and management. Sixth edition. The Wildlife Society, Bethesda, Maryland, USA.

SINIFF, D. B., AND J. R. TESTER. 1965. Computer analysis of animal movement data obtained by telemetry. Bioscience 15:104–108.

SMALL, R. J., AND D. H. RUSCH. 1989. The natal dispersal of ruffed grouse. Auk 106:72–79.

SMITH, D. R., K. J. REINECKE, M. J. CONROY, M. W. BROWN, AND J. R. NASSAR. 1995. Factors affecting visibility rate of waterfowl surveys in the Mississippi Alluvial Valley. Journal of Wildlife Management 59:515–527.

SMITH, E. N., AND E. G. AITKEN. 1989. Low power skin and muscle blood flow photo plethysmography biotelemetry system. Pages 325–331 *in* C. J. Amlaner, Jr., editor. Biotelemetry X. University of Arkansas Press, Fayetteville, USA.

———, AND C. J. AMLANER. 1989. Biotelemetry workshop: an intensive training session. Pages 269–273 *in* C. J. Amlaner, Jr., editor. Biotelemetry X. University of Arkansas Press, Fayetteville, USA.

SMITH, G. J., J. R. CARY, AND O. J. RONGSTAD. 1981. Sampling strategies for radio-tracking coyotes. Wildlife Society Bulletin 9:88–93.

SMITH, R. M., AND B. TREVOR-DEUTSCH. 1980. A practical, remotely-controlled, portable radio telemetry receiving apparatus. Pages 269–273 *in* C. J. Amlaner, Jr. and D. W. Macdonald, editors. A handbook on biotelemetry and radio tracking. Pergamon Press, Oxford, United Kingdom.

SMITH, W. P. 1983. A bivariate normal test of elliptical home-range models: biological implications and recommendations. Journal of Wildlife Management 47:613–619.

SMITS, A. W. 1984. Activity patterns and thermal biology of the toad *Bufo boreas halophilus*. Copeia 1984:689–696.

SNYDER, N. F. R., S. R. BEISSINGER, AND M. R. FULLER. 1989. Solar radio-transmitters on snail kites in Florida. Journal of Field Ornithology 60:171–177.

SPEARS, B. L., W. B. BALLARD, M. C. WALLACE, R. S. PHILLIPS, D. H. HOLDSTOCK, J. H. BRUNJES, R. APPLEGATE, P. S. GIPSON, M. S. MILLER, AND T. BARNETT. 2002. Retention times of miniature radio-transmitters glued to wild turkey poults. Wildlife Society Bulletin 30:861–867.

SPENCER, H. J., AND F. P. SAVAGLIO. 1995. An automatic small-animal radio-tracking system employing spread-spectrum concepts. Proceedings of the International Symposium on Biotelemetry 13:185–191.

———, G. LUCAS, AND P. O'CONNOR. 1987. A remotely switched passive null-peak network for animal tracking and radio direction finding. Australian Wildlife Research 14:311–317.

SPENCER, W. D., AND R. H. BARRETT. 1984. An evaluation of the harmonic mean measure for defining carnivore activity areas. Acta Zoologica Fennica 171:255–259.

SPRINGER, J. T. 1979. Some sources of bias and sampling error in radio triangulation. Journal of Wildlife Management 43:926–935.

STAPP, P., AND B. VAN HORNE. 1997. Response of deer mice (*Peromyscus maniculatus*) to shrubs in shortgrass prairie: linking small-scale movements and the spatial distribution of individuals. Functional Ecology 11:644–651.

STANNER, M., AND E. FARHI. 1989. Computerized radio-telemetric system for monitoring free ranging snakes. Israel Journal of Zoology 35:177–186.

STICKEL, L. F. 1954. A comparison of certain methods of measuring ranges of small mammals. Journal of Mammalogy 35:1–15.

STOHR, W. 1989. Long term heart rate telemetry in small mammals. Pages 352–375 *in* C. J. Amlaner, Jr., editor. Biotelemetry X. University of Arkansas Press, Fayetteville, USA

STOUFFER, JR., R. H., J. E. GATES, C. H. HOCUTT, AND J. R. STAUFFER, JR. 1983. Surgical implantation of a transmitter package for radio-tracking endangered hellbenders. Wildlife Society Bulletin 11:384–386.

STRATHEARN, S. M., J. S. LOTIMER, G. B. KOLENOSKY, AND W. M. LINTACK. 1984. An expanding break-away radio collar for black bear. Journal of Wildlife Management 48:939–942.

STRIKWERDA, T. E., M. R. FULLER, W. S. SEEGAR, P. W. HOWEY, AND H. D. BLACK. 1986. Bird-borne satellite transmitter and location program. Johns Hopkins Applied Physics Laboratory Technical Digest 7:203–208.

SWANSON, G. A., V. B. KUECHLE, AND A. B. SARGEANT. 1976. A telemetry technique for monitoring diel waterfowl activity. Journal of Wildlife Management 40:187–190.

SWIHART, R. K., AND N. A. SLADE. 1985a. Influence of sampling interval on estimates of home range size. Journal of Wildlife Management 49:1019–1025.

———, AND ———. 1985b. Testing for independence of observations in animal movements. Ecology 66:1176–1184.

———, AND ———. 1997. On testing for independence of animal movements. Journal of Agricultural, Biological, and Ecological Statistics 2:48–63.

———, ———, AND B. J. BERGSTROM. 1988. Relating body size to the rate of home range use in mammals. Ecology 69:393–399.

TARTER, M. E., AND R. A. KRONMAL. 1970. On multivariate density estimates based on orthogonal expansions. Annual Mathematics and Statistics 41:718–722.

TAYLOR, J. S., K. E. CHURCH, D. H. RUSCH, AND J. R. CARY. 1999. Macrohabitat effects on summer survival, movements, and clutch success of northern bobwhite in Kansas. Journal of Wildlife Management 63:675–685.

TAYLOR, K. D. 1978. Range of movement and activity of common rats (*Rattus norvegicus*) on agricultural land. Journal of Applied Ecology 15:663–677.

THIRGOOD, S. J., S. M. REDPATH, S. CAMPBELL, AND A. SMITH. 2002. Do habitat characteristics influence predation on red grouse? Journal of Applied Ecology 39:217–225.

THOMAS, D. L., AND E. J. TAYLOR. 1990. Study designs and tests for comparing resource use and availability. Journal of Wildlife Management 54:322–330.

THORUP, K., T. ALERSTAM, M. HAKE, AND N. KJELLEN. 2003. Bird orientation: compensation for wind drift in migrating raptors is age dependent. Proceedings of the Royal Society of London Series B 270:8–11.

TSAI, K., K. H. POLLOCK, AND C. BROWNIE. 1999. Effects of violation of assumptions for survival analysis methods in radiotelemetry studies. Journal of Wildlife Management 63:1369–1375.

TUCK, G. N., T. POLACHEK, J. P. CROXALL, H. WEIMERSKIRCH, P. A. PRINCE, AND S. WOTHERSPOON. 1999. The potential of archival tags to provide long-term movement and behaviour data for seabirds: first results from wandering albatross *Diomedea exulans* of South Georgia and the Crozet Islands. Emu 99:60–68.

TURCHIN, P. 1991. Translating foraging movements in heterogeneous environments into the spatial distribution of foragers. Ecology 72:1253–1266.

———. 1996. Fractal analyses of animal movement: a critique. Ecology 77:2086–2090.

———. 1998. Quantitative analysis of animal movement: measuring and modeling population redistribution in animals and plants. Sinauer Associates, Inc., Sunderland, Massachusetts, USA.

UNSWORTH, J. W., L. KUCK, AND E. O. GARTON. 1990. Elk sightability model validation at the National Bison Range, Montana. Wildlife Society Bulletin 18:113–115.

VAN DEELEN, T. R., H. CAMPA, III, M. HAMADY, AND J. B. HAUFLER. 1998. Migration and seasonal range dynamics of deer using adjacent deeryards in northern Michigan. Journal of Wildlife Management 62:205–213.

VAN VUREN, D. 1989. Effects of intraperitoneal transmitter implants on yellow-bellied marmots. Journal of Wildlife Management 53:320–323.

VAN WINKLE, W. 1975. Comparison of several probabilistic home-range models. Journal of Wildlife Management 39:118–123.

VOIGT, D. R., AND J. S. LOTIMER. 1981. Radio tracking terrestrial furbearers: system design, procedures, and data collection. Pages 1151–1188 *in* J.A. Chapman and D. Pursley, editors. Worldwide Furbearer Conference. Frostburg, Maryland, USA.

———, AND R. R. TINLINE. 1980. Strategies for analyzing radio tracking data. Pages 387–404 *in* C. J. Amlaner, Jr. and D. W. Macdonald, editors. A handbook on biotelemetry and radio tracking. Pergamon Press, Oxford, United Kingdom.

WALLACE, M. P., M. R. FULLER, AND J. WILEY. 1994. Patagial transmitters for large vultures and condors. Pages 381–387 *in* B. U. Meyerburg and R. D. Chancellor, editors. Raptor conservation today. Pica Press, East Sussex, United Kingdom.

WALLS, S .S., AND R. E. KENWARD. 2001. Spatial consequences of relatedness and age in buzzards. Animal Behaviour 61:1069–1078.

WALTON, L. R., H. D. CLUFF, P. C. PAQUET, AND M. A. RAMSAY. 2001. Performance of 2 models of satellite collars for wolves. Wildlife Society Bulletin 29:180–186.

WAND, M. P., AND M. C. JONES. 1995. Kernel smoothing. Chapman and Hall, London, United Kingdom.

WANLESS, S., M. P. HARRIS, AND J. A. MORRIS. 1988. The effect of radio transmitters on the behavior of common murres and razorbills during chick rearing. Condor 90:816–823.

———, ———, AND ———. 1989. Behavior of alcids with tail-mounted radio transmitters. Colonial Waterbirds 12:158–163.

WARREN, P. K., AND D. BAINES. 2002. Dispersal, survival and causes of mortality in black grouse *Tetrao tetrix* in northern England. Wildlife Biology 8:91–97.

WEATHERHEAD, P. J., AND F. W. ANDERKA. 1984. An improved radio transmitter and implantation technique for snakes. Journal of Herpetology 18:264–269.

WEIMERSKIRCH, H., O. CHASTEL, C. BARBRAUD, AND O. TOSTAIN. 2003. Flight performance: frigatebirds ride high on thermals. Nature 421:333–334.

———, F. BONADONNA, F. BAILLEUL, G. MABILLE, G. DELL'OMO, AND H. P. LIPP. 2002. GPS tracking of foraging albatrosses. Science 295:1259.

WHITE, G. C. 1996. NOREMARK: population estimation from mark–resighting surveys. Wildlife Society Bulletin 24:50–52.

———, AND R. A. GARROTT. 1984. Portable computer system for field processing biotelemetry triangulation data. Colorado Division of Wildlife, Game Information Leaflet 110.

———, AND ———. 1990. Analysis of wildlife radio-tracking data. Academic Press, San Diego, California, USA.

———, AND T. M. SHENK. 2001. Population estimation with radio-marked animals. Pages 329–350 *in* J. J. Millspaugh and J. M. Marzluff, editors. Radio tracking and animal populations. Academic Press, San Diego, California, USA.

———, D. R. ANDERSON, K. P. BURNHAM, AND D. L. OTIS. 1982. Capture–recapture and removal methods for sampling closed populations. LA-8787-NERP. Los Alamos National Laboratory, Los Alamos, New Mexico, USA.

WHITEHOUSE, S., AND D. STEVEN. 1977. A technique for aerial radio tracking. Journal of Wildlife Management 41:771–775.

WIDÉN, P. 1982. Radio monitoring the activity of goshawks. Pages 153–160 *in* C. L. Cheeseman and R. L. Mitson, editors. Telemetric studies of vertebrates. Academic Press, London, United Kingdom.

WILSON, R. P., AND M. T. J. WILSON. 1989. Tape: a package-attachment technique for penguins. Wildlife Society Bulletin 17:77–79.

WITHEY, J. C., T. D. BLOXTON, AND J. M. MARZLUFF. 2001. Effects of tagging and location error in wildlife radiotelemetry studies. Pages 43–75 *in* J. J. Millspaugh and J. M. Marzluff, editors. Radio tracking and animal populations. Academic Press, San Diego, California, USA.

WOECK, B. N. 2003. Demographics and space use of mule deer and white-tailed deer in Custer State Park, South Dakota. Thesis. University of Missouri, Columbia, USA.

WORTON, B. J. 1987. A review of models of home range for animal movement. Ecological Modelling 38:277–298.

———. 1989. Kernel methods for estimating the utilization distribution in home-range studies. Ecology 70:164–168.

———. 1995a. A convex hull-based estimator of home-range size. Biometrics 51:1206–1215.

———. 1995b. Using Monte Carlo simulation to evaluate kernel-based home range estimators. Journal of Wildlife Management 59:794–800.

YERBURY, M. J. 1980. Long range tracking of *Crocodylus porosus* in Arnhem Land, northern Australia. Pages 765–776 *in* C. J. Amlaner, Jr. and D. W. Macdonald, editors. A handbook on biotelemetry and radio tracking. Pergamon Press, Oxford, United Kingdom.

ZAR, J. H. 1996. Biostatistical analysis. Third Edition. Prentice-Hall, Englewood Cliffs, New Jersey, USA.

See Appendix next page.

APPENDIX
Telemetry equipment suppliers and manufacturers

Advanced Telemetry Systems, Inc.
470 First Avenue North
P.O. Box 398
Isanti, MN 55040, USA
Phone: 763-444-9267
FAX: 763-444-9384
E-mail: ihume@atstrack.com
http://www.atstrack.com/
(VHF telemetry equipment)

AF Electronics, Inc.
Rural Route 1, Box 82
White Heath, IL 61844, USA
Phone: 217-687-2786
(VHF antennas)

American Wildlife Enterprises
Route 2, Box 32N
Monticello, FL 32344, USA
Phone: 850-997-3551
FAX: 850-997-3552
http://www.fl-dof.com/Pubs/consulting/NWest.pdf
E-mail: BradAWE@cs.com
(VHF telemetry equipment)

Anatrack Ltd.
52 Furzebrook Road
Wareham
Dorset BH20 5AX, United Kingdom
Phone: +44-1929-555432
E-mail: info@anatrack.com
http://www.anatrack.com
(software)

Austec Electronics, Ltd.
1006, 11025-82 Avenue
Edmonton, AB KT6G 0T1, Canada
Phone: 403-432-1878
FAX: 415-449-3980

AVM Instrument Company, Ltd.
P.O. Box 1898
1213 South Auburn Street
Colfax, CA 95713, USA
FAX: 530-346-6306
Phone: 530-346-6300
E-mail: bckermeen@avminstrument.com
http://www.avminstrument.com/
(VHF equipment)

Bally Ribbon Mills
23 North 7th Street
Bally, PA 19503, USA
Phone: 215-845-2211
(Teflon ribbon harness material)

Biosonics, Inc.
4027 Leary Way Northwest
Seattle, WA 98107, USA
Phone: 206-782-2211
FAX: 206-782-2244
E-mail: bio@biosonicsinc.com
http://www.biosonics.com
(Sonic tags)

Biotelemetrics, Inc.
6520 Contempo Lane
Boca Raton, FL 33433, USA
Phone: 561-394-0315
FAX: 561-394-0315
E-mail: biotran@ix.netcom.com
www.biotelemetrics.com/
(Implant telemetry equipment)

Bio Telemetry, Inc./Bio Telemetry Tracking
18 Magill Road
Norwood, SA 5067, Australia
FAX: +61-8-8362-7955
Phone: +61-8-8362-6666
http://www.npwrc.usgs.gov/resource/2002/radiotrk/appendA.htm
(VHF receivers)

Biotrack Ltd.
52 Furzebrook Road
Wareham
Dorset BH20 5AX, United Kingdom
Phone: +441-929-552-992
FAX: +441-929-554-948
http://www.biotrack.co.uk
E-mail: brian@biotrack.co.uk
(VHF telemetry equipment and analytical software)

BlueSky Telemetry Ltd.
P.O. Box 7500
Aberfeldy, Scotland PH15 2YG, United Kingdom
Phone: +44 (0)-1887-820816
FAX: +44 (0)-1887-820979
E-mail: tracking@blueskytelemetry.com
http://www.blueskytelemetry.com
(GPS telemetry equipment)

Clearinghouse for Ecology Software
Illinois Natural History Survey
607 East Peabody Drive
Champaign, IL 61820, USA
Phone: 217-244-0371
FAX: 217-333-6294
E-mail: rdiehl@uiuc.edu
http://nhsbig.inhs.uiuc.edu
(software)

Custom Electronics of Urbana, Inc.
2009 Silver Court West
Urbana, IL 61801, USA
Phone: 217-344-3460
FAX: 217-344-3460
E-mail: CUSTOMEL@aol.com
(VHF telemetry equipment)

Custom Telemetry Company
1050 Industrial Drive
Watkinsville, GA 30677, USA
Phone: 706-769-4024
FAX: 706-769-4026

Global Tracking Systems, Inc.
17 Forest Drive
Sylvan Lake, AB T4S 1H4, Canada
Phone: 403-887-8866 or 403-563-5063
FAX: 403-887-8866
E-mail: gts-rjc@telusplanet.net
www.gtstrack.com
(VHF telemetry equipment)

H.A.B.I.T. Research Ltd.
692 Sumas Street
Victoria, BC V8T 4S6, Canada
Phone: 250-381-9425
FAX: 250-381-9426
E-mail: info@habitresearch.com
http://habitresearch.com
(VHF and satellite telemetry equipment)

Hi-Tech Services
9 Devon Place
Camillus, NY 13031, USA
Phone: 315-487-2484
E-mail: jkenty@aol.com
(VHF telemetry equipment)

Holohil Systems Ltd.
112 John Cavanagh Road
Carp, ON K0A 1L0, Canada
Phone: 613-839-0676
FAX: 613-839-0675
E-mail: info@holohil.com
http://www.holohil.com
(VHF telemetry equipment)

Johnson's Telemetry
3355 Southwest 376 Road
El Dorado Springs, MO 65203, USA
Phone: 417-876-5083
FAX: 417-876-6844

L.L. Electronics
P.O. Box 420
103 North Prairieview Road
Mahomet, IL 61853, USA
Phone: 800-553-5328
FAX: 217-586-5733
E-mail: lle@pdnt.com

Lotek Engineering, Inc.
115 Pony Drive
Newmarket, ON L3Y 7B5, Canada
Phone: 905-836-6680
FAX: 905-836-6455
E-mail: telemetry@lotek.com
http://www.lotek.com
(VHF and sonic equipment)

Lotek Marine Technologies, Inc.
114 Cabot Street
St. John's, NF A1C 1Z8, Canada
Phone: 709-726-3899
FAX: 709-726-5324
E-mail: marine.telemetry@lotek.com
http://www.lotek.com
(VHF and sonic equipment)

Merlin Systems, Inc.
P.O. Box 190257
Boise, ID 83719, USA
Phone: 208-362-2254
FAX: 208-362-2140
E-mail: merlin@cyberhighway.net
http://www.merlin-systems.com/
(VHF equipment emphasizing falconry)

Microwave Telemetry, Inc.
8835 Columbia 100 Parkway, Suites K & L
Columbia, MD 21045, USA
Phone: 410-715-5292
FAX: 410-715-5295
www.microwavetelemetry.com/
(satellite telemetry equipment)

Mini-mitter Company, Inc.
P.O. Box 3385
Sunriver, OR 97707, USA
Phone: 503-593-8639
FAX: 503-593-5604
E-mail: rrushmmtr@aol.com
http://minimitter.com
(physiological telemetry)

North Star Science and Technology, LLC
Technology Center Building
1450 South Rolling Road, Room 4036
Baltimore, MD 21227, USA
Phone: 410-961-6692
FAX: 603-462-5144
http://www.northstarst.com
(satellite telemetry equipment)

SERPE IESM
Z1 des 5 Chemins
56520 Guidel, France
Phone: (33)-2-97-02-49-49
Fax: (33)-2-97-65-00-20
E-mail: pbrault@serpe-iesm.com
http://www.serpe-iesm.com/eng.htm
(satellite telemetry equipment)

Service Argos
18, Avenue Edouard Belin
31055 Toulouse Cedex, France or
1801 McCormick Drive, Suite 10
Landover, MD 20785, USA
Phone: 301-925-4411
FAX: 301-925-8995
E-mail: jw@argosinc.com
http://www.argosinc.com
(satellite telemetry systems)

Sirtrack Limited
Private Bag 1403
Goddard Lane
Havelock North 4201, New Zealand
E-mail: wardd@landcare.cri.nz
Phone: (06)-877-7736
FAX: (06)-877-5422
http://www.landcare.cri.nz
(VHF satellite telemetry equipment)

Smith-Root, Inc.
14014 Northeast Salmon Creek Avenue
Vancouver, WA 98686, USA
Phone: 206-573-0202
FAX: 503-286-1931
E-mail: info@smith-root.com
www.smith-root.com/
(Sonic tags)

Sonotronics
1130 East Pennsylvania Street, Suite 505
Tucson, AZ 85714, USA
Phone: 520-746-3322
FAX: 520-294-2040
E-mail: sales@sonotronics.com
http://www.sonotronics.com/index.html
(Sonic tags)

Telemetry Solutions
1130 Burnett Avenue, Suite J
Concord, CA 94520, USA
Phone:925-798-2373
FAX:925-798-2375
E-mail:qkermeen@telemetrysolutions.com
http://www.telemetrysolutions.com
(VHF telemetry equipment)

Telemetry Systems, Inc.
P.O. Box 187
11005 North Lakeview Road
Mequon, WI 53092-5868, USA
Phone: 262-241-8335
FAX: 262-241-8905
(VHF telemetry equipment)

Televilt International AB
Box 53
S-711 22 Lindesberg, Sweden
Phone: +46-581-17195
FAX: +46-581-17196
E-mail: per-arne.lemnell@televilt.se
http://www.televilt.se
(VHF and satellite telemetry equipment)

Telonics, Inc.
932 Impala Avenue
Mesa, AZ 85204, USA
Phone: 480-892-4444
FAX: 480-892-9139
E-mail: info@telonics.com
http://www.teloncis.com
(VHF and satellite telemetry equipment)

Titley Electronics Pty. Ltd.
P.O. Box 19
Ballina, NSW 2478, Australia
Phone/FAX: 61-(2)-66-866617
E-mail: titley@nor.com.au
http://www.titley.com.au
(VHF telemetry equipment)

Vemco
3895 Shad Bay
Rural Route 4
Armdale, NS B3L 4J4, Canada
Phone: 902-852-3047
FAX: 902-852-4000
E-mail: vemco@fox.nstn.ca
(Sonic equipment)

Wildlife Computers
16150 Northeast 85th Street, #226
Redmond, WA 98052, USA
Phone: 425-881-3048
FAX: 425-881-3405
E-mail: tags@wildlifecomputers.com
http://www.wildlifecomputers.com
(satellite telemetry equipment)

Wildlife Materials, Inc.
Route 1, Box 427A
Carbondale, IL 62901, USA
Phone: 618-549-6330, 618-549-2242
FAX: 618-457-3340
E-mail: wmi@midwest.net
http://www.wildlifematerials.com
(VHF telemetry equipment)

15

APPLICATION OF SPATIAL TECHNOLOGIES IN WILDLIFE BIOLOGY

Thomas A. O'Neil, Pete Bettinger, Bruce G. Marcot, B. Wayne Luscombe, Gregory T. Koeln, Howard J. Bruner, Charley Barrett, Jennifer A. Pollock, and Susan Bernatas

INTRODUCTION

The Information Age is here, and technology has a large and important role in gathering, compiling, and synthesizing data. The old adage of analyzing wildlife data over "time and space" today entails using technologies to help gather, compile, and synthesize remotely sensed information, and to integrate results into research, monitoring and evaluation. Thus, resource managers must understand how to use these technologies, especially for evaluating and assessing land and resource conditions at different scales, such as site, watershed, sub-basin, and basin levels. This chapter explores spatial technologies useful to wildlife managers for acquiring, compiling, and interpreting data. These technologies include: geographic information systems (GIS), global positioning systems (GPS), and using remotely sensed data, including Landsat Imagery and Forward-looking Infrared (FLIR). This chapter also highlights the need to understand data accuracy and Internet applications.

Today's issues and their complexities have a tendency to overwhelm resource managers in a sea of data. Most resource agencies are awash in data, but managers still find themselves with a lack of information. Spatial technolo-

gies provide tools to incorporate and analyze large data sets in a meaningful manner with production of useful information. Data can be converted or displayed by locations or across a landscape and displayed as charts, drawings, or as maps. These technologies provide a way to assess and depict complex relationships among variables, which is useful for incorporating scale and hierarchy concepts into ecosystem-based management assessments (O'Neill 1996) and to help examine environmental impact significance (Antunes et al. 2001). Additionally, they allow spatial depictions of theoretical concepts, such as change in total redundancy of ecosystem functions (Fig. 1). The technologies presented here also allow others to see how decisions are made, thus leaving a foot print(s) in the decision making process to follow. However, as with any analysis and modeling tools, uses of spatial technologies are only as accurate and reliable as the underlying data. Spatial tools on their own cannot improve accuracy, precision, and bias of information.

Spatial technologies should be considered as tools to assist resource managers with mapping. Maps are as important to the manager as calculators and vehicles. Using spatial technologies can provide timely information in usable formats for aiding decision-making, but these

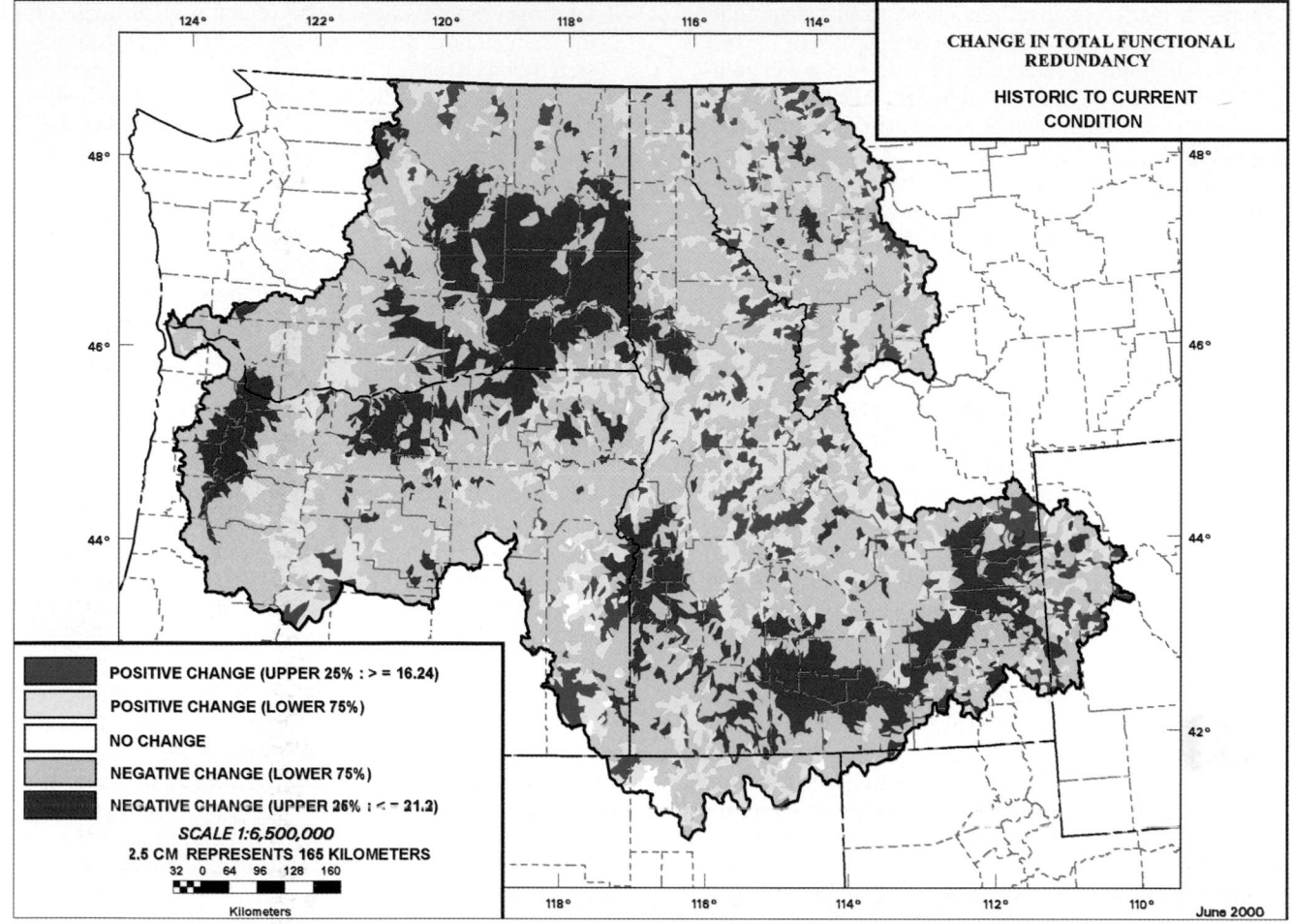

CHANGE IN TOTAL FUNCTIONAL REDUNDANCY

HISTORIC TO CURRENT CONDITION

POSITIVE CHANGE (UPPER 25% : > = 16.24)

POSITIVE CHANGE (LOWER 75%)

NO CHANGE

NEGATIVE CHANGE (LOWER 75%)

NEGATIVE CHANGE (UPPER 25% : < – 21.2)

SCALE 1:6,500,000
2.5 CM REPRESENTS 165 KILOMETERS
32 0 64 96 128 160
Kilometers

June 2000

Fig. 1. Using GIS, Marcot et al. (2002*b*) depicted the concept of Total Functional Redundancy for the Columbia River Basin.

tools should not be viewed as making the final decisions *per se.* Spatial technologies, like GIS, are frequently described in terms of hardware (computers and work stations) and software (computer programs). Typically, more computing power (speed and memory) in combination with large computing storage (disk space) is preferred. Workstations do most of the heavy lifting in handling large and/or complex data sets. Peripherals such as tape storage and retrieval systems, and CD-ROM and DVD-RAM devices are required to effectively transcribe data in and out of systems.

Building and Using a GIS

Many factors should be considered when designing and developing a major GIS application or its' implementation to ensure success and sustainability. These include, but are not limited to those identified.

- *Establish clear objectives*—The purpose and function of the system must be clearly defined so that managers, system developers and operators, and product users know the system's capabilities and limitations. Establishing clear objectives will lead to building a system to deliver answers to management resource questions.
- *Design the system to be driven by demand*—Long-term sustainability and funding for a system can only

be assured if the system meets user's needs for information (Falloux 1989). Demand for system services and support should keep the development and subsequent modification and upkeep of the system focused on its objectives and will promote its use in the decision-making process.

- *Coordinate initiatives and avoid duplication of efforts*—GIS systems are most efficiently developed and effectively used when there is strong coordination between relevant agencies and organizations. Scarce resources can be stretched furthest when there is little overlap or duplication in data development activities. A common problem occurs when different agencies develop similar databases, which inevitably are inconsistent because of possible different data sources, scales, classification systems, or simply different interpretations of facts, patterns, and trends.
- *Develop the system from data, not interpretation*—Much unnecessary duplication of effort has occurred because GIS databases have been developed based on interpretation of data instead of base data from which different interpretations can arise. An example is the multiple GIS maps developed in the Pacific Northwest of the United States to map old-growth forests. Instead of mapping base attributes of forests such as age, mean tree diameter, canopy structure, etc., from which various definitions of old-growth could then be

applied, many organizations chose to just map "old-growth forests" and skip the base data layers. When their definitions differed, the maps were not comparable, and when definitions changed, much GIS work had to be redone or abandoned, wasting time, money, and effort.

- *Develop a data strategy*—Databases providing the GIS foundation must be credible and reliable. Decisions must be made whether or not to use existing databases from other sources or to develop the information from primary sources. Standards should be established for including data in the databases. This helps ensure that information from different sources is technically and thematically compatible. Interoperability, or the ability to use databases directly from one system to another or from one application to another without major conversions or recompilations, is an important factor to consider in the strategy (Prévost and Gilruth 1997). An essential step in the data strategy is development of a data catalog that defines and describes the elements. This metadata, or supra level data about the data, enables a user to decide on the quality and fitness of the information to be used in an analysis. Decisions must also be made about geographic scale of analysis, thematic classification systems, and the relevancy of the current information.

- *Develop a realistic cost estimate*—Building a GIS is more than buying the necessary computer hardware and software (World Bank 1995). Significant efforts and resources are required to build an institutional framework, develop and acquire data, and develop human resources to manage, operate, and use the system. A guideline for estimating relative costs for a GIS initiative is the 20-80 rule. This suggests that 20% of the total cost is for system hardware and software and 80% is for data development activities, institutional costs, and other operating expenses.

- *Build institutional support for the initiative*—Having institutional support and management "buy-in" to the initiative is the single most critical factor for successful planning and development. Enthusiastic acceptance for the initiative from those in an organization responsible for making decisions and allocating resources helps ensure that adequate support is available and that GIS becomes integrated into mainstream decision-making processes. Integrating GIS services with other aspects of an organization's functions, rather than developing them as a stand-alone sideline activity, not only increases their general utility, but also makes them less vulnerable to disruption during times of organizational or management changes. Having the GIS operation prominently located in an organizational structure gives it more recognition as a valuable asset and raises its standing in times of competition for scarce institutional resources. GIS systems are not luxuries but necessities for doing spatial-based land and resource planning, and they should be viewed as tightly woven into assessment, decision-making, and monitoring activities.

- *Establish management and technical steering committees*—Involving a broad base of management and technical expertise in early design stages as well as later operational stages helps obtain a wide range of ideas about how best to accomplish the organization's stated objectives for the system. Involving expertise as advisory groups helps build commitment and support from a more diverse community of interested stakeholders who then share the responsibility of making the initiative a success. Such advisory groups foster better collaboration and cooperation among agencies and departments and help ensure that common data strategies and standards are implemented.

- *Use appropriate technology*—It may seem obvious, but selecting inappropriate technology is still a major cause of failure and cost overruns for well-intentioned GIS initiatives. GIS hardware and software must be appropriately selected to match not only kinds of information to be handled, but also kinds of analysis to be performed, and volume of the information in the databases. For example, it would be inappropriate to select a vector-based system if most information to be processed was raster-based satellite imagery. It would also be inappropriate to select a small, single-user desktop computer system to manage terabytes of information in a national database.

Factors Needed to Sustain a GIS

An often-overlooked aspect of establishing GIS capabilities is a plan or strategy for ensuring that an initiative can be sustained once it has been implemented. Many systems have failed because they have not accounted for the essential factors necessary to sustain a GIS system after its initial development. These factors include but are not limited to those identified.

- *Education and training*—For many managers and decision-makers, integrating spatial information and analysis into decisions and plans is not a familiar process. Many decision-makers need to be informed about how GIS tools and services can assist them in their work (van Genderen 1991). The GIS initiative should include a strategy for ensuring that senior managers and decision-makers have an intimate understanding of and direct experience with how these tools can support their activities. Also, there should be provisions for training those directly responsible for managing and operating the GIS capabilities and for training users on how to access and use the information and analysis functions.

- *Provision of interim products*—During early stages of developing a GIS capability within an agency or a program, it is important that interim products are provided to managers (i.e., those providing the authorization and resources for the initiative) to spark and sustain their interest, enthusiasm, and commitment. A long development period with nothing visible to show for the effort frequently causes managers to lose focus on the initiative and to shift emphasis and resources to other initiatives with more immediate paybacks.

- *Responsiveness to the needs of users and decision-makers*—The support provided by the system must continue to be valuable and vital for decision-making processes (Prévost and Gilruth 1997). If decision-makers and other users of the system are able to perform their functions more effectively and efficiently with information and services provided by the system, they are more apt to ensure the support needed to sustain its operations. Benefits gained from services of an established system, in terms of time saved, cost avoidance of ill-informed decisions, and economic, social, and political benefits achieved from well-informed decisions, should be expressly demonstrated and documented.

- *Integration of scientific information into policy dialog*—GIS analysis can provide information in a structure and manner to directly and positively affect policy discussions. To be useful to decision-makers, spatial information should be more than simple lists or maps of "facts," and should be digested in a way to suggest impacts, consequences, and trade-offs. With environmental issues in general, and wildlife management issues in particular, the chasm that exists between science and policy can frequently be narrowed by skillfully using spatial analysis tools and techniques to bring scientific information into the realm of policy discussions. To illustrate, decision-makers deciding on the fate of a wildlife species, such as the spotted owl (*Strix occidentalis*), need to know more than how the species is spatially distributed. They need to know how this spatial distribution is related to environmental, social, and economic factors and the impacts and benefits of alternative management scenarios. However, the complexity of integrating scientific information into policy dialog and decision-making processes is not simple and should not be underestimated.
- *Ensure adequate resources*—Once established, recurrent resources are required to sustain the on-going operation, management, data development, and data documentation activities. Regular provisions in budgets would be needed for costs associated with hardware and software maintenance and upgrades, updates to databases, and maintaining staffs. Without adequate resources, systems become antiquated and outdated, and no longer effectively support their intended functions.

The first spatial technology addressed in this chapter is GIS, which is a general-purpose technology for handling geographic data in a digital form. GIS has the capability to: (1) pre-process large amounts of data into a form suitable for analysis and evaluation; (2) support models that perform analysis, calibration, forecasting, and prediction of spatial relations of many variables; and (3) post-process results to produce tables, reports, and maps (Goodchild 1993, Peuquet et al. 1993, Franklin 1995, Theobald 2001). Koeln et al. (1996), Korte (2000), Longley et al. (2001), and Rigaux et al. (2001) presented technical descriptions of GIS. Bettinger (1999) presented the challenges and opportunities associated with GIS implementation in field offices.

USING GIS IN THE WILDLIFE PROFESSION

Prior to 1950, vegetation maps were tediously drawn by hand and wildlife biologists interpreted the maps in terms of habitat for wildlife, typically game animals. The availability of aerial photography and then satellite imagery

Box 1. What is a spatial relationship?

Spatial relationships may be important in understanding the resources of concern when developing habitat management strategies (Schroeder et al. 1998). Spatial relationships describe the association among landscape features and may be characterized in both topological and directional aspects. Topology uses methods that develop and remember associations among landscape features. The work of mathematicians, cognitive scientists, and designers of software has driven research into spatial relationships for GIS. In GIS it may not be sufficient to know just the position of a landscape feature, but also to know how the landscape feature relates to other features in the same (or other) databases. For example, it may not be sufficient to just be able to locate a patch of optimal habitat; it may also be important to locate other patches of good or optimal habitat nearby.

Some examples of spatial relationships include:

- polygons that share a common boundary (e.g., adjacent polygons),
- polygons of a certain type (e.g., optimal habitat) nearest to other specific polygons (e.g. proposed harvests),
- polygons that overlap other polygons (e.g., the intersection of soils and timber stands),
- lines that cross one another (e.g., roads that cross streams),
- lines that logically flow into one another (e.g., stream networks),
- lines that are within a certain distance of other landscape features (e.g., roads within a certain distance of streams),
- points contained within polygons (e.g., bird point sample locations within timber stands), and
- points that can be seen from certain other points (e.g., as in defining viewsheds).

later gave biologists a way to more accurately and consistently analyze habitats across broader landscapes. For example, in the early 1970s, Schuerholz (1974) quantified forest edge habitat from aerial photographs and Cowardin and Myers (1974) identified and classified wetland habitats from remotely sensed images. In the later 1970s and 1980s, as computers became more available and capable, vegetation maps were transcribed into digital images and habitat analyses became highly automated (e.g., Marcot et al. 1981, Mead et al. 1981, Mayer 1984, Burroughs 1986, Brekke 1988). Today, GIS is an indispensable tool for analyzing historic, current, and potential future habitat conditions for wildlife (Fig. 2), and for assessing the spatial relationships among landscape features. GIS is widely used for evaluating cumulative effects of management actions and potential effects of alternative management decisions on wildlife habitats, populations, and communities.

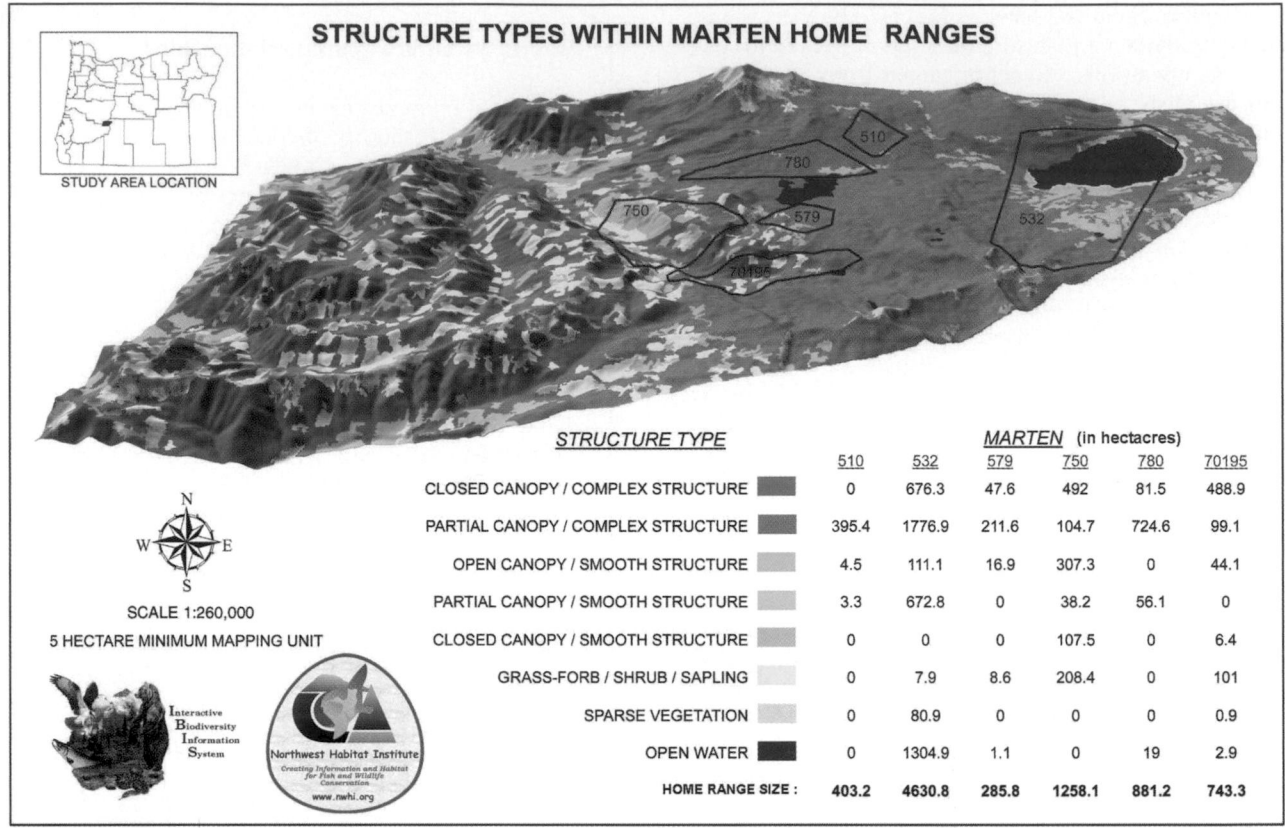

Fig. 2. GIS allows integration of data; American marten (*Martes americana*) home ranges are overlaid on structural habitat conditions and topography (Northwest Habitat Institute, Corvallis, Oregon, USA).

GIS and Modeling Wildlife-habitat Relationships

One of the most common uses of GIS in wildlife management is in analysis of amounts, patterns, and trends of habitat changes for individual wildlife species. For example, McComb et al. (2002) used GIS to model potential habitat of northern spotted owls (*S. o. caurina*) at landscape scales in the Pacific Northwest of the United States. Dettmers and Bart (1999) applied GIS to predict forest songbird habitat in southern Ohio. Carroll et al. (1999) used presence data to construct and validate spatial habitat models of fisher (*Martes pennanti*) in central Oregon. Knick and Dyer (1997) used GIS to analyze black-tailed jackrabbit (*Lepus californicus*) habitat in southwestern Idaho. O'Neil et al. (1995) depicted and mapped all of Oregon's wildlife-habitat types using GIS. Following procedures used by O'Neil et al. (1995), Kiilsgaard and Barrett (2000) created the first wildlife-habitat types map of the entire Pacific Northwest in the United States. Many other examples occur in the literature.

GIS-based wildlife–habitat relationships models use variables such as slope, aspect, and vegetation structure to depict habitat categories and habitat quality for individual species. Variables used are based on factors shown or expected to influence quality of habitat selected by particular species. These models are usually based on professional judgment and experience, or on empirical research. Bettinger (2001) outlined many of the challenges facing integration of wildlife models with remotely sensed imagery and data related to forest structural conditions. Dussault et al. (2001) cautioned that existing forest cover maps might not be adequate for evaluating wildlife habitat suitability without an examination of the correlation between mapped forest features and structural conditions used by specific wildlife species or species groups.

Other types of models for evaluating habitat quality also have been integrated with GIS. For example, Clevenger et al. (2002) integrated expert-based models to help identify and plan for wildlife habitat corridors, Raphael et al. (2001) integrated Bayesian belief network models of species habitat suitability into GIS analyses, Guisse and Gimblett (1997) evaluated state park recreation conflicts by integrating a neural network model with GIS, and Rickel et al. (1998) used a fuzzy logic model in conjunction with GIS to evaluate wildlife habitat quality. The main objective of these approaches has been to develop useful tools for resource managers charged with identifying locations of important areas for wildlife when empirical information is lacking. GIS helps facilitate this process by providing a representation of the spatial features of a landscape into the habitat quality evaluation.

Statistical analyses have also been integrated with GIS processes to evaluate quality of wildlife habitat. For example, Clark et al. (1993) integrated a multivariate analysis of female black bear (*Ursus americanus*) habitat into a GIS model whereas Pereira and Itami (1991) used results of a logistic multiple-regression study of the Mt. Graham red squirrel (*Tamiasciurus hudsonicus grahamensis*) in their GIS model of habitat for the subspecies. Software developed by a variety of organizations is increasingly becoming open to integration. As a result, almost any wildlife habitat quality model that can be described in terms of mappable habitat features can be developed with GIS.

Some researchers have taken integrated GIS-based wildlife-habitat relationships models into National Forest planning processes. This represented a distinct change in forest planning by complementing existing economic or commodity-production objectives with wildlife habitat objectives. Bunnell (1974), Mead et al. (1981), and others pioneered early applications of this type. Later, Hof and Joyce (1992, 1993) and Hof et al. (1994) integrated wildlife habitat concerns in mathematical forest planning models. Models integrating wildlife habitat relationships with forest planning processes have focused on elk (*Cervus elaphus*) in Oregon (Bettinger et al. 1997, 1999), birds in the northwest (Bettinger et al. 2002), birds in the Midwest (Nevo and Garcia 1996), ruffed grouse (*Bonasa umbellus*) habitat in the Midwest (Arthaud and Rose 1996), red-cockaded woodpecker (*Picoides borealis*) habitat in the southeast (Boston and Bettinger 2001), northern flying squirrel (*Glaucomys sabrinus*) in western Oregon (Calkin et al. 2002), spotted owls in Washington state (Hof and Raphael 1997), and late-successional habitat in Oregon (Sessions et al. 2000). Measures of biodiversity also have been integrated into forest planning efforts (Kangas and Pukkala 1996). Other habitat-related concerns can also be included in forest planning processes, such as the desire to develop and maintain contiguous core areas of older forest (Öhman and Eriksson 1998, Öhman 2000), and development of connected habitat corridors (Sessions 1991, Williams 1998).

GIS and Modeling Populations

Spatially explicit wildlife population models consider 2 factors of importance to the estimation of populations: species-habitat relationships, and habitat arrangement over space and time. These population models usually are developed for one (or only a few) species; simultaneously modeling habitats and populations of multiple species across a landscape remains a significant challenge (Turner et al. 1995). Liu et al. (1995) provided an example of the use of a spatially explicit population model in GIS to examine the impact on a nontarget species, Bachman's Sparrow (*Aimophila aestivalis*), of a forest plan developed for other goals. The model results helped managers examine how sparrow population density and distribution might react to planned management activities, such as whether resulting sparrow populations are of a size that meets the minimum management goal for the species, or whether the populations are sensitive to certain projected landscape characteristics. Another example is the work by Mladenoff and Sickley (1998) who used GIS to assess potential population sizes of gray wolf (*Canis lupis*) in the northeastern United States.

GIS has been used as an integral part of population viability analysis (PVA) (Akçakaya 2000). Kingston (1995) reviewed the use of population viability models within a GIS environment. Using GIS for PVA typically entails modeling vital rates (survival, reproduction) and population parameters (e.g., dispersal) of individuals of a species to calculate population size and distribution over time, and rates of population change. To model PVA spatially, data are required on spatial structure (location, size, and quality) of habitat patches that a particular species might use. This allows land managers and planners to evaluate how management practices may affect the probability of species distribution, trends, and extinction. Brook et al. (1999) compared 4 PVA analysis processes, including ones

---

Box 2. Integrating habitat relationships into a forest planning process.

We illustrate with an example provided in Bettinger et al. (2001) to demonstrate the process of integrating habitat relationships into a forest planning process. Wildlife habitat goals can be either qualitatively or quantitatively defined. Quantitative goals can also reference spatial information provided by GIS databases, allowing spatial goals to be developed. Spatial goals may include configurations such as requiring minimum patch sizes, or complementary habitat types and, thus, may indicate that, for optimal benefit to a particular species, one type of habitat should be placed next to another. Great gray owls (*Strix nebulosa*), for example, prefer early seral stage forests (clear cuts) for foraging, yet these areas should be adjacent to single-story open-canopy forests containing snags or large trees with broken tops.

Within a forest-planning environment, one can use a complementary patch goal (one where a patch of one type [e.g., nesting habitat] must be next to a complement—a patch of another type [e.g., foraging habitat]) to guide development of a forest plan that seeks to provide the greatest amount of habitat over time, while also achieving other economic or commodity production goals. The criteria used to measure whether the objective was achieved consist of measuring the percentage of land in each planning period that meets habitat requirements of great gray owls. A further quantification of the habitat goal is required and Bettinger et al. (2001) assumed that maximization of the percentage of land in patches ≥ 20 ha and ≥ 90 years old adjacent to patches ≥ 10 ha and ≤ 10 years old would suffice. In addition, a few practical constraints were added to the forest planning problem: clear cuts were limited to ≤ 48.6 ha, minimum clear-cut harvest ages were 40 years, a minimum volume of about 19,000 m³ per 5-year period was required from the landscape, and only one regeneration harvest was allowed during the planning horizon.

A heuristic planning technique (i.e., one that locates good, feasible solutions to problems, yet not necessarily the best solution to problems), *tabu* search (a deterministic search process based on remembering choices that have been made), was used to develop the forest plan using a spatial arrangement of great gray owl habitat (Fig. 3). The amount of timber volume produced per 5-year planning period averaged 9.5 million board feet (60,000 m³) (Fig. 4). Harvest volume was relatively high in the last few time periods because some cutting was required to create early seral patches to complement the older forest patches.

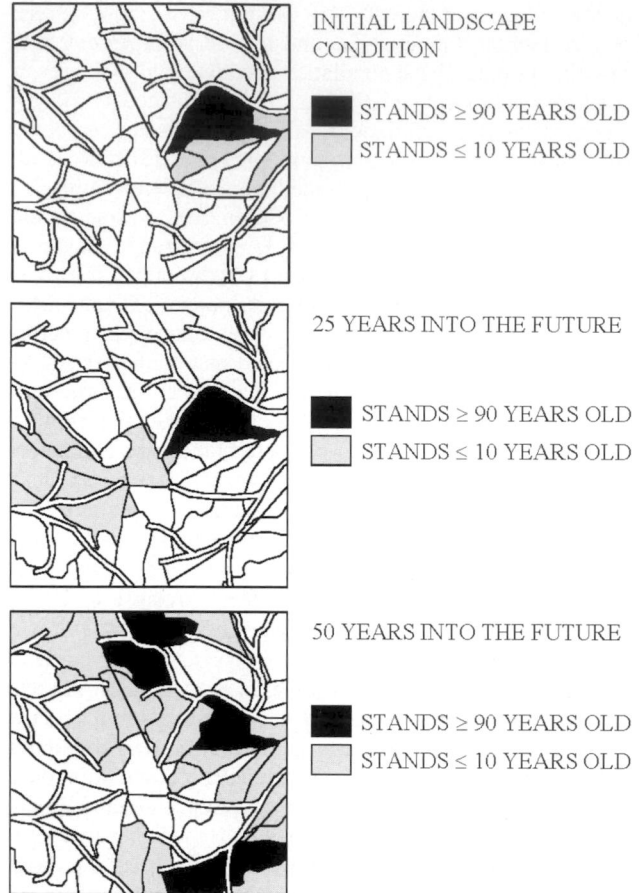

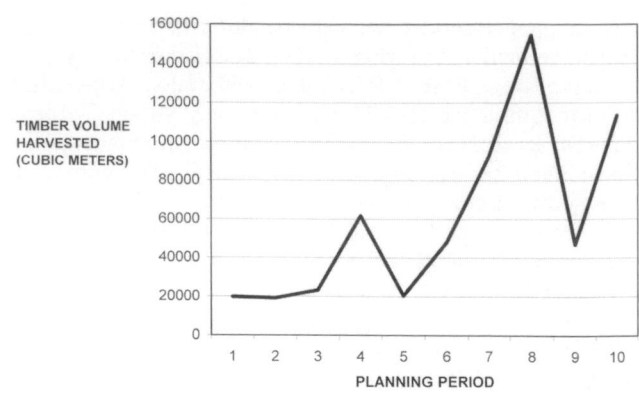

Fig. 4. Timber volume harvested over 50 years at 5-year planning increments.

Fig. 3. Spatial arrangement of great gray owl habitat consisting of early successional stands and stands ≥90 years old over a 50-year planning period.

that use spatial or mapped representations of populations, and concluded that subtle differences among models can affect results. Thus, the modeler should understand the mechanisms of the models used, and coach decision-makers on appropriate interpretation of the results.

Beyond assessing populations and viability, Allen et al. (2001) used GIS gap analysis to model viable populations of mammal species and concluded that defining minimum critical areas for mammals was a useful way to produce maps of critical unprotected sites. Hof and Raphael (1997) developed a geographic model to optimize allocation of northern spotted owl habitat in Washington State. Optimization model parameters included adult survival, fecundity, and occupancy of sites. Some authors have even integrated assessments of population genetics with GIS. For example, Ji and Leberg (2002) evaluated genetic diversity from a regional perspective using GIS. Also, since intensive ground surveys cannot keep pace with the rate of land use change in some areas of the world, presence-absence models are being developed for use in GIS, in conjunction with remote sensing and other technologies, to allow one to map the potential distribution of species at large spatial extents (Osborne et al. 2001, Kilgo et al. 2002).

GIS and Conservation of Wildlife Communities

Another use of GIS in wildlife management is delin-

eation and conservation of wildlife and ecological communities. Delineation of "hot spots" (areas of high species richness or centers of species endemism or rarity) (Dobson et al. 1997, Ceballos et al. 1998, Griffin 1999) has become popular for specifying areas with wildlife and plant assemblages and communities potentially needing protection. Mapping species-rich hot spots has been used to delineate potential protected areas or reserves (e.g., Bójorquez-Tapia et al. 1995). Some spatial algorithms or processes used to delineate hot spots have been rigorously evaluated. For example, Araújo and Williams (2001) discovered bias toward marginal populations when delineating complementary hot spots, and NCASI (1996) reported that results of richness hot spots could be highly sensitive to the accuracy of the underlying distribution maps of individual species.

The "National Gap Analysis" Program (GAP) took delineation of conservation hot spots further by intersecting areas of high species richness with a set of land use allocations under the goal of identifying areas of high richness that may lack protection (Scott et al. 1993). GAP provides an assessment of the extent of representation of native species' habitats and communities across a landscape. Those species or communities not adequately represented in protected status on public lands can be viewed as "gaps" in conservation networks (Pearlstine et al. 2002). The process of identifying "gaps" has been aided by dividing analysis areas into segments to account for geographic variation and to help cover broad geographic areas (Scott et al. 2001). For example, the Florida GAP project is a geographically extensive analysis. One of the objectives of this project is to provide interested stakeholders with GIS databases related to the status of terrestrial vertebrate species and their habitats. Landsat Thematic Mapper satellite imagery is used, as are the National Wetlands Inventory GIS databases, other available databases (e.g., soils), aerial photography, and on-the ground surveys (Pearlstine et al. 2002) to accomplish this objective.

GIS also has been used to design potential reserves or protected areas. One of the fundamental issues for biologists and managers is selection or proposal of areas that should be conserved. Several techniques have been developed to select optimal reserve designs, each using GIS databases to guide selection of reserve areas. Wildlife habitat relationships can be used to delineate areas of special concern, such as the "corridor suitability" GIS database created for Maryland's Green Infrastructure Assessment (Weber and Wolf 2000). Here, GIS databases representing land cover, stream networks, roads, slope classes, aquatic community conditions, and other variables were used to create a database that described the suitability of areas to potentially serve as corridors for wildlife movement. This database was then used in a model that delineated the least-cost pathway between core wildlife management areas.

Other researchers (e.g., McDonnell et al. 2002, Nalle et al. 2002) devised mathematical algorithms to most efficiently design nature reserve systems to meet biodiversity objectives. In addition, reserve area redundancy (ReVelle et al. 2002), complimentarity (Williams et al. 2000), and representativeness (e.g., Mackey et al. 1988, Powell et al. 2000, MacNally et al. 2002) have been discussed in the literature and demonstrated through use of GIS processes. Dobson et al. (2001) advocated integrating strategies and objectives to simultaneously meet multiple needs for people and species.

Efficient identification of potential reserve areas with GIS processes has allowed policy makers to quantitatively address a number of reserve management issues. For example, should reserve areas represent an array of community, productivity, or ecosystem classes as Stokland (1997) suggested for bird and insect conservation in boreal forest reserves of Norway? Should reserve areas be established mainly for species richness, species rarity, or for other objectives such as balancing requirements of rare species conservation by establishing corridors with a broader biodiversity conservation perspective (Fig. 5)? Williams et al. (2000) suggested that more biodiversity could be protected if the few species that attract the most popular support (flagship species) had distributions that covered the broader diversity of organisms across a landscape. Should some level of redundancy be built into reserve areas to guard against potential losses from major disturbance events? Finally, should reserve areas be complementary to one another to efficiently and cost-effectively set aside the least amount of land area with highest biological opportunity cost? Each of these questions can be addressed with the appropriate GIS databases and reserve selection processes.

GIS and Risk Analysis

Another major trend is use of GIS to conduct risk analysis and management. GIS tools provide ways to pose "what if" questions to examine predicted results of potential actions. An example is work by Wright and Tanimoto (1998) who used GIS to set priorities for land conservation by integrating analyses of habitat diversity, ownership, and development into an overall risk analysis. Managers of both public lands and conservation organizations often are interested in purchasing land or acquiring conservation easements. Budgets are usually limited, which presents a need to efficiently spend time and money. Wright and Tanimoto (1998) developed a system for evaluating habitat diversity within a specified proximity of each delineated land unit. The units of privately owned and undeveloped land with highest habitat diversity were considered priority candidates for acquisition.

Llewellyn et al. (1996) used GIS in a decision support model to prioritize wetland sites for restoration along the Mississippi River floodplain. One of the most important phases of the project was to develop a set of GIS databases for the entire ecosystem. In addition, a set of high-resolution GIS databases was developed for a single watershed to generate more detailed land-use conversion statistics and to demonstrate the feasibility of a landscape restoration planning process. Included in the planning process was a method for prioritizing wetland forest patches and other areas suitable for reforestation and connection via corridors.

Other decision-support GIS models have been designed to integrate processes, such as expert systems (Fedra 1995), into evaluation of management alternatives. The main goal of these efforts may be to facilitate examination

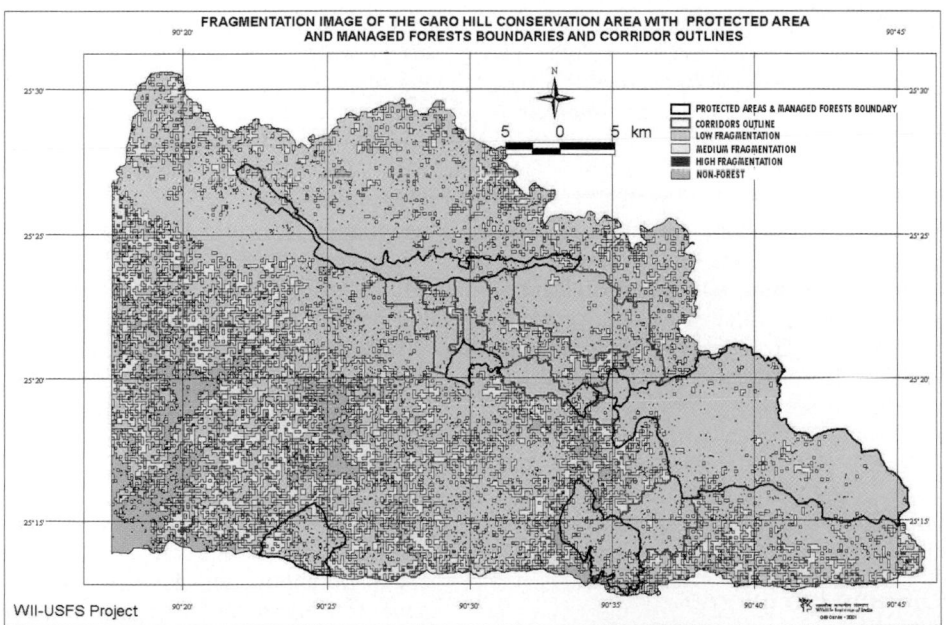

Fig. 5. Use of GIS analysis of fragmentation of elephant (*Elephas maximus*) habitat in Meghalaya, northeastern India, to help delineate habitat corridors (Marcot et al. 2002*a*).

of one of the side effects of the decision-making process that many managers have when overwhelmed with data and analysis; the need to describe the uncertainty and risk associated with potential decisions.

GIS in the International Community

GIS is becoming a commonly used tool to study, understand, and manage environmental issues at local, regional, national, and international levels. Initiatives, which are of particular interest at the international level, are the spatially related information programs of the United Nations Environmental Programme (UNEP). The first is UNEP's Global and Regional Integrated Data (GRID) program. From its conception at UNEP headquarters in Nairobi, Kenya, GRID has evolved into a still expanding network of environmental data centers around the world, each with a particular regional focus but coordinated in their efforts at a larger global scale. The centers facilitate and promote the development, documentation, archiving, and dissemination of environmental GIS and statistical information. With a concentration on environment, conservation, and natural resource issues, the centers' databases and analytical capabilities are designed to assist researchers and analysts in making reliable environmental assessments in support of public policy dialog (UNEP-GRID Europe 2003).

UNEP-GRID centers typically have data sets and information on environmental issues such as biodiversity, ecology, climate, soils, land cover, hydrology, and human impacts, as well as general information concerning geology, atmosphere, oceans and political boundaries. Partly because of its association with prominent information sources such as NASA, NOAA, and USGS, the North American node of UNEP-GRID, at Sioux Falls, South Dakota, has a prominent role in the larger network of centers, providing a number of data sets on a global scale (UNEP-GRID North America 2003). Much of the information is available online through the Internet and can be downloaded to individual GIS workstations.

The other prominent UNEP hosted initiative, relating to spatially referenced environmental information and analysis, is the World Conservation Monitoring Centre (WCMC). In 1988, IUCN (International Union for Conservation of Nature and Natural Resources), WWF (World Wildlife Fund for Nature), and UNEP founded a nonprofit organization, the World Conservation Monitoring Centre to monitor endangered species. This was an outgrowth of an earlier program by IUCN established at Cambridge, United Kingdom. In 2000, WCMC became a formal program of UNEP and has become its primary resource center for providing biodiversity information and assessments on conservation and sustainable use issues that have national, regional, and global impacts (UNEP-WCMC 2003). Its programs focus on species diversity: forests, protected areas, marine, mountain, and freshwater habitats as well as habitats affected by climate change (UNEP-WCMC 2003). Extensive use of GIS and spatial analysis helps recognize global trends, warn of potential sustainability problems, and identify priorities for conservation action in all of the earth's major ecosystems.

GIS and the Internet

With widespread development of data clearinghouses, the Internet has become a key medium for GIS data and metadata exchange. Specialized GIS user groups and organizations such as the Society for Conservation Geographic Information Systems (http://www.scgis.org) are invaluable tools. In addition to using these resources to develop their GIS, most conservation organizations develop their own Internet sites to deliver information to targeted users. This section outlines how conservation GIS users may incorporate Internet technologies into GIS programs and projects. It concludes with a look at the future direction of conservation GIS and the Internet.

One of the most important roles of the Internet in conservation GIS is to find currently available GIS data for one's area of interest. Internet search engines, such as Google (http://www.google.com) or Yahoo (http://www.yahoo.com) (mention of specific products or services in this chapter is for illustration and information only and does not reflect specific recommendations by the affiliations of the authors), can be easily used to search for desired data by keywords. This method may yield some useful results, but better success is often achieved by searching a data clearinghouse or portal (a web site that serves as a gateway to the Internet featuring a suite of services and web links for a niche topic) specifically focused on GIS data, conservation, and/or a desired region. Many GIS data clearinghouse sites exist. For example, the Geography Network (http://www.geographynetwork.com/) provides international search capabilities for GIS data sets, clearinghouses, and web applications. The National Biological Information Infrastructure (http://www.nbii.gov/) provides similar capabilities, including its own metadata clearinghouse, with a specific focus on biologic data and analysis tools. These are just 2 examples of the ever-increasing number and variety of Internet resources for finding existing GIS data.

Another major focus of using the Internet is to acquire and deliver GIS data. GIS projects typically include development of a web site to promote their project and to deliver results and data. These web sites often direct users to where the actual GIS data can be obtained, either by direct download or ordering the data. Some sites have made a business of collecting and delivering, for a fee, GIS data from a wide variety of sources. Sites that actually produce and maintain their own data often provide free GIS data. Government and nonprofit groups typically operate these free data sites. In addition to delivering GIS data, many of these sites include online mapping applications that integrate their GIS data with other data sets (visit the Geography Network for numerous links to examples). These increasingly powerful tools allow users without GIS software to perform spatial queries and produce maps in real time via the Internet.

GIS and Internet programming technologies are rapidly changing and constantly improving. Currently, GIS web applications can be divided into 2 basic types: static and dynamic. Static applications are those that provide premade maps, GIS data files, and statistical summaries. These applications are typically programmed with hypertext markup language (HTML or its variants) to serve maps and statistics previously created by a GIS analyst. The static application delivers data fast because the web server (the computer hosting the web application) does not have to analyze data or create the maps and statistics; it just directs the user to pre-made files. The downside is that static applications work well only for data that does not change often. Each time the GIS data changes, a GIS technician must recreate new maps and statistics, and the Internet application must be updated. The other limitations of static applications are that end-users cannot customize maps or modify data queries. They only get to view the information in the predefined formats created by the GIS technician, which may or may not be what the user needs.

To address these limitations, dynamic Internet mapping applications have become increasingly popular. A dynamic mapping application processes end-user submitted queries in real time using the GIS data sets to produce maps, statistics, and even subsets of the GIS data. A dynamic Internet mapping application can be considered as a customized online GIS, typically for non-GIS experts. This method is superior to static applications for GIS data that are continuously changing since GIS data changes are immediately reflected in the Internet application with no additional programming. The other key benefits are that users have much more flexibility in how they query the GIS data and can customize maps to better suit their needs. Users are, however, still limited to the capabilities designed into the application.

Advanced applications are beginning to focus more on spatial data analysis and manipulation instead of just data presentation. Negative aspects of dynamic mapping applications are that they are more complex and costly to implement. Programming dynamic applications typically requires more robust server programming technologies such as Active Server Pages (ASP), Common Gateway Interface (CGI), Cold Fusion, and/or Java in addition to HTML. To reduce the cost and time of application development, many organizations combine these technologies with third-party software solutions. One example is Environmental Systems Research Institute's (ESRI) ArcIMS (Internet Map Server: http://www.esri.com) that provides pre-developed, modifiable tools and templates to serve and query GIS data over the Internet (or within private intranets). Dynamic mapping applications also require higher-end servers than do static applications. Depending on an Internet site's usage and amount of data being served, multiple servers may be required for optimal performance.

Creating GIS web services is also becoming popular and should become more common in conservation organizations in the near future thanks to recent developments in programming technologies such as ASP.Net and eXtensible Markup Language (XML). Web services are applications that allow approved remote computers to query an organization's web server in predetermined ways for certain data sets. This effectively allows multiple organizations to work together and serve each other's data in different dynamic mapping applications while allowing each group to maintain its own data. Microsoft's TerraService (http://terraserver.homeadvisor.msn.com/terraservice.htm) is an excellent example of a GIS-based web service where remote programmers can incorporate U.S. Geological Survey (USGS) imagery and quadrangle maps into their Internet mapping applications without having to store these immense data sets. The Geography Network (http://www.geographynetwork.com/geoservices/) provides links to several other web services.

Another rapidly evolving technology with implications for the future of conservation GIS is mobile wireless computing. It is becoming more affordable and common to connect to the Internet via wireless phones and computers. Combining these technologies with web services allows field researchers to easily exchange data with their organization and others while in the field. For example, researchers recording bird nesting site activity could upload their findings to their organization's GIS while in the field, or they could download GIS data layers such as USGS quadrangle maps to their computer for integration with a GPS-integrated field-mapping program.

The Internet has become an invaluable resource to conservation GIS users for everything from data development to data delivery. Providing the details of implementing these technologies is impractical in this format as there are many competing technologies, each with pros and cons, and new technologies are constantly appearing that quickly supersede existing technologies. Rapid advancements in Internet server and programming technologies combined with steadily declining hardware costs are causing many conservation groups to focus efforts on dynamic mapping applications over static applications. Web services have also recently surfaced in conservation GIS and are quickly becoming widespread. These technologies, combined with those of wireless mobile computing and GPS, present new opportunities for wildlife professionals. However, through all recent changes and advances, it remains true that developing, maintaining, and delivering GIS systems, locally or via the Internet, demands high computer skill levels, knowledge of arcane macro languages, and advanced skills in computer hardware, software, and communication. More than ever, organizations can expect the need will grow to support personnel with specialized knowledge in GIS and computer hardware and software.

DATA DOCUMENTATION

Documenting information about spatial data provides developers and users with key descriptions about collection techniques, sources, process steps, and geographic details used in creating the data set. Often called metadata, this information comprises a core component of any type of spatial or attribute data. The importance of metadata lies in its ability to reduce the loss of time looking for how information was created, prevent loss of critical information, and as a safety net in case people move to other positions. As a professional, metadata provides you with the tools to record your processes and sources to use the data efficiently and effectively.

Metadata should be recorded throughout the database development process and organizations should develop operational procedures that institutionalize metadata production and maintenance. This retains valuable information about data for internal organizational or external client use, and provides a key component in sustaining a GIS program in the long term.

History of Metadata

The metadata concept was formalized at the federal level in 1994 with release of Executive Order 12906 and the Office of Management and Budget's Circular A-16 as part of a government-wide effort to reduce duplication of effort to collect information and to provide a way for other agencies and taxpayers to access data created with federal funding (Federal Register 1994). The Office of Management and Budget (2002) released a revised circular A-16 to reflect technology changes, but kept the core component of establishing a coordinated approach to electronically develop the National Spatial Data Infrastructure (NSDI). As part of the NSDI, release of the *Content Standard for Digital Geospatial Metadata* provided a common set of terms and definitions needed to document data. All types of spatial and nonspatial data can be documented using this standard. In fact, several profiles of the standard provide users with elements for biological, shoreline, or remote sensing data. Any data set created with federal funding needs documentation using this standard. Many state and local governments and other organizations that receive federal dollars have adopted the standard. Other standards exist, but many GIS professionals either use or work on data created with federal funds and need a working knowledge for their jobs.

In the next few years, the International Organization for Standardization plans to release an international geospatial metadata standard as part of an effort by a network of national standards institutes from 145 countries working in partnership with international organizations, governments, industry, and business and consumer representatives. The United States, through the Federal Geographic Data Committee, participates in this process and plans to adopt the international standard when available. Although some aspects of the standard might change, the content should remain similar and might offer some additional elements.

Overview of Content

The Federal Geographic Data Committee (FGDC) metadata standard is organized into 10 sections (7 main sections and 3 supporting sections) that provide elements to answer a series of questions (Federal Geographic Data Committee 1998, 1999, 2000).

- *Who* collected and *who* distributes the data?
- *What* is the subject, processing, projection of the data?
- *When* were the data collected?
- *Where* were the data collected?
- *Why* were the data collected (*what* is the purpose)?
- *How* were the data collected? *How* should it be used?
- *How* much does it cost?

Although the standard includes many elements, only a few require data entry while users select from a series of other elements that directly apply to their data. Many definitions provide clear descriptions about the type of information to include about the data set. However, 2 sections (2 and 5) of the standard require additional explanation to help in creation of a metadata record.

Section 2 (Data Quality) of the standard provides a general assessment of the quality of the data set.

- *Attribute accuracy report*—Assessments about the attribute values may refer to field checks, cross-referencing, statistical analyses, and parallel independent measures, etc. This does not refer to the positional accuracy of the value.
- *Logical consistency report*—These assessments relate to the fidelity of the line work, attributes and/or rela-

---

> **Box 3. Federal Geographic Data Committee metadata standard.**
>
> *Sections of the Standard*
>
> 1. Identification*
> 2. Data Quality
> 3. Spatial Data Organization
> 4. Spatial Reference
> 5. Entity and Attribute
> 6. Distribution
> 7. Metadata Reference*
>
> *Supporting Sections (reusable)*
>
> 8. Citation
> 9. Time Period
> 10. Contact
>
> * Denotes a mandatory section.

---

tionships including topological checks, arc/node structures that do not easily translate, and database QA/QC routines, such as:
  — are the values in column X always between "0" and "100,"
  — are only text values provided in column Y, and
  — for any given record, does the value in column R equal the difference between the values provided in columns R and S?

- *Completeness report*—This report identifies the data omitted from the databases that might normally be expected, as well as the reason for the exclusion including:
  — geographic exclusions (data were not available for Smith County),
  — categorical exclusions (municipalities with populations under 2,500 were not included in the study), and
  — definitions used (floating marsh was mapped as land).

- *Positional accuracy*—This is an assessment of horizontal and/or vertical positional (coordinate) values including information about digitizing (RMS error), surveying techniques, GPS triangulations, and image processing or photogrammetric methods.

Section 5 (Entity and Attribute) of the standard illustrates data content and should be a product of the data design effort. This section often might include the data dictionary, catalog of terms or some description of fields contained within nonspatial attributes.

- *Relational database format*—This is used as a *guide to record terms:*
  * entity label–table title,
  * attribute label–column titles, and
  * attribute domain values–recorded values within each column.

- *Domain types*—This includes a set of possible data values of an attribute including:
  * enumerated domain
    — a defined pick list of values,
    — categorical, such as road types, departments, tree types, etc.,
  * range domain
    — a continuum of values with a fixed minimum and maximum value, and
    — a numeric measure or count, may be alphabetic (A–ZZZ),
  * codeset domain
    — a defined set of representational values,
    — coding schemes, such as county codes or course number (GEOG 1101),
  * unrepresentable domain
    — an undefined list of values or values that cannot be prescribed, and
    — text fields, such as individual and place names.
- *Entity attribute overview*—This element provides a summary overview of the entities/attributes as outlined in either the detailed description or an existing detailed description cited in the Entity Attribute section. This field should not be used as a stand-alone general description.

Software tools provide a way to enter this information and, in many cases, automatically enter values into elements as users create their data. The FGDC provides a review of tools available for creating metadata at their website http://www.fgdc.gov.

Distributing and Accessing Metadata

A completed metadata record should be posted on the Federal Geographic Data Committee clearinghouse at www.fgdc.gov/clearinghouse/clearinghouse.html. This clearinghouse provides a single point of entry to hundreds of existing servers. Directions for organizations that want to establish a node within the clearinghouse are provided on the above web site. The clearinghouse offers access to a wealth of metadata to help discover potential data sets of interest as well as examples to use when creating records.

The website www.fgdc.gov offers a wide range of tools, training, and information about creating and serving metadata and provides links to a variety of agencies and organizations that specialize in metadata.

> **Box 4. Recommendations for writing metadata (Federal Geographic Data Committee 2000).**
>
> - Use Clear, Familiar Words
> - Use an Informative Title
> - Select Keywords Wisely
> - Write Complete Sentences
> - Use Bulleted Lists
> - Ask Someone to Review Metadata
> - Define and Describe Acronyms, Jargon or Technical Terms

USING GLOBAL POSITIONING SYSTEMS

In recording wildlife information, a fundamental component is location. Thus, it is important to understand the Global Positioning System (GPS) and how it can be used. There are several self-help guides (Letham 1998, Anderson 2002) if one desires a more in-depth understanding. This system helps land, sea, and airborne users locate where they are on earth 24 hours a day by triangulation of earth orbiting satellites; typically 3 satellites are needed to obtain a triangulation. The GPS unit is actually a receiver that measures distance using travel time of radio signals; this signal must be corrected for any delays that it experiences as it travels through the atmosphere.

So how does GPS work? It all relates to the *velocity* that a satellite signal travels versus the *time* it takes the signal to travel; in GPS the velocity is equal to the speed of light or roughly 299,338 km (186,000 miles) per second. The principal problem comes from measuring the travel time. That is, GPS uses Pseudo Random Code, which is a digital code that contains a complicated sequence of "on" and "off" pulses. The signal appears to be random electric noise, however, in actuality the noise is a series of complex patterns to help ensure that receivers do not synchronize to another signal. Because each satellite has its own unique codes, the complexity also assures the receiver will not pick up a signal from another satellite. Thus, all satellites can use the same frequency without jamming one another.

Distance to a satellite is calculated by measuring how long a radio signal takes to reach a receiver. To make this measurement, we assume that both the satellite and our receiver are generating the same random codes at exactly the same time. By comparing the time of the satellite versus our receiver, we can calculate how long it took for the signal to reach us. The travel time is then multiplied by the speed of light to get the distance. However, identifying the exact time is the crucial element in making this calculation.

Satellites used for GPS have atomic clocks, but GPS receivers do not. So how are the clocks synchronized so the calculation can be made? Although 3 satellites can locate a point in 3-dimensional space, a fourth satellite is needed to identify the time (Fig. 6). The premise is to have all 4 satellite signals intersect a single point. Because the

> **Box 5. GPS satellites.**
>
> Navstar GPS was developed by the Department of Defense and manufactured by Rockwell International. These 24 satellites are placed in 6 orbital planes at 10,900 nautical miles or 20,200 km above the earth. Each plane is inclined 55 degrees relative to the equator. Satellites weigh about 710 kg and are 5.2 m wide with solar panels extended. Their orbital period is about 12 hours and they pass over one of the ground stations twice a day. The lifespan of these satellites is planned at 7.5 years. Using 4 or more satellites can yield 3-dimensional estimates while using 3 satellites can only generate 2-diminsional observations.

Fig. 6. Three satellites are used for triangulation while a fourth satellite takes another measurement to check the other 3.

receiver's clock is not as accurate as the satellite's, the fourth signal would not intersect the first 3 satellite's triangulation, so a discrepancy in the fourth measurement occurs. Since any offset of time can affect all of the measurements, the receiver corrects the discrepancy by calculating a factor that can be subtracted from all measurements of time so that all measurements would intersect at one point. Once it has the correction factor, it is applied to all measurements. Thus, any GPS receiver where a precise position is desired will require 4 channels so that it can make 4 measurements simultaneously. But for triangulation to work, one also needs to know where the satellites are in space. The Department of Defense has placed each satellite in a precise orbit in accordance to their GPS Master Plan. Because of their precise orbits, each satellite passes over a ground station twice a day, which affords an opportunity to measure its altitude, position, and speed. Any corrections, called *ephemeris errors*, are sent back to the satellite. The satellite then transmits corrections with its timing information. Thus, each GPS receiver is relayed exact orbital information. To further enhance the location of the satellite, each GPS receiver can obtain an "almanac" from any one of the satellites, which tells where in the sky it should be at any given time. The GPS receiver uses the almanac and transmission corrections to precisely establish each satellite's location.

Because satellite signals are transmitted through space, they are susceptible to degradation and delays. The atmosphere causes some delays while others can come from multi-path effects resulting from the transmitted signal bouncing off another object before getting to the receiver. A quick way to handle atmosphere-induced errors is to compare the relative speeds of 2 different signals. This is called, dual frequency measurement; it is complex and can only be found as a feature on advanced GPS receivers. The ultimate accuracy of GPS is calculated from multiple sources of error, and the process to correct most of the

source errors from a satellite clock, orbit, ionosphere, or troposphere is known as *Differential Correction.*

The military maintains the most precise system (dedicated for military operations) and began in March 1990 to degrade the performance accuracy for commercial or non-military applications by an approach called selective availability. Selective availability essentially involved modifying the clock frequency to randomly degrade the accuracy of commercial performance to about 100 m. In May 2002, the Clinton Administration had the Defense Department stop using selective availability so that a greater accuracy (1–10 m) could be obtained for commercial or nonmilitary uses.

Differential Correction for GPS

Differential GPS involves 2 receivers that are in relatively close proximity (typically within ~200 km); one is stationary and the other is roving and recording data. Because of this close proximity, in comparison to the distance of satellite transmission travel, signals that reach both receivers will have traveled through virtually the same atmospheric conditions and will have the same errors. To correct these errors, the receiver that has a fixed known location brings all satellite information into a local point of reference. This information is compared to the data transmitted from the satellite(s) and corrected. The corrected information is then used in conjunction with data collected by the roving field receiver(s). Because one of the receivers has a known surveyed location, it uses this information to compare what the GPS signals should be versus what they recorded. The difference is the error correction factor provided to the other roving receivers. Since the fixed receiver has no way of knowing which satellites the roving receivers are using, the reference receiver computes error correction factors for each satellite signal it can distinguish. When correcting errors associated with GPS, it can be done while the points are being collected, a process known as real-time *Differential Correction* or, after collection of points, known as *Post-Processing.*

In the early days of GPS, reference stations were established and maintained by private companies. One would then have to buy data from a reference receiver and establish a communication link to a field receiver. Because of the demand by public agencies to use GPS, this reference information is now accessible at no cost. For example, the U.S. Coast Guard has navigation beacon placements throughout the United States; this information can be found at the Coast Guard's web site at www.navcen.uscg.gov/dgps/coverage/Default.htm. More can be learned about Differential GPS from the Starlink website, www.starlinkdgps.com/dgpsexp.htm.

Wide Area Augmentation System

Because of the ability of GPS to fix an airplane's location in real-time, the Federal Aviation Agency (FAA) has developed the Wide Area Augmentation System (WAAS) that extends coverage for differential GPS to the entire United States. WAAS is a critical component of the FAA's strategic objective of a seamless satellite navigation system for civil aviation. This system improves the accuracy, availability, and integrity of GPS, thus, improving its' capacity and safety. Ultimately, WAAS allows GPS to be used as a primary means of navigation from takeoff through Category 1 precision approach (i.e., close to the runway but not zero visibility; Category 3 landings are zero visibility). The ramifications of the FAA maintaining this system go well beyond aviation; because of its design the system helps ensure that differential GPS corrections will be accessible to all who need them. The Garmin website at www.garmin.com/aboutGPS/waas.html further discusses WAAS.

Using GPS

There are 2 main questions to be answered in using GPS to help identify your needs: what is your main purpose—do you need a GPS receiver of mapping or survey grade, and what level of accuracy is required—do you need to use differential GPS techniques for accuracy of 1m or less? Thus, to help set up the GPS unit, you need to be familiar with some data capturing and processing terms (Boxes 7, 8, 9).

GPS Uses in Wildlife

What are the practical applications for using GPS in the field for wildlife biologists and managers? Presently, there are 2 common areas of use: 1) tracking and recording wildlife movements, and 2) inventorying, mapping, and/or surveying wildlife habitats or specific wildlife use areas. Using a GPS tracking collar can aid in recording wildlife movements (Fig. 7) and provide more accuracy than other tracking systems (Rempel and Rodgers 1997). Since 1994 a number of GPS collars have been developed using the Navstar Global Positioning System. GPS collars have been used to successfully track large mammals such as moose (*Alces alces*) (Rodgers et al. 1997), grizzly bears (*Ursus arctos*) (Waller and Servheen 1999), caribou (*Rangifer tarandus*) (Dyer 1999), mountain lions (*Puma concolor*) (Bleich et al. 2000) and gray wolves (Merrill and Mech 2000).

These collars now come in different sizes and can be used on small, midsize, or large mammals. Collar weight varies from 100 to 2,100 g (depending on collar size), and can store up to 10,000 locations (nondifferentially corrected or 5,000 locations differentially corrected) depending on recording frequency and battery configuration. They operate in temperatures ranging from –30 to +50 C, and the data can be retained in the collar at temperatures ranging from –50 to +75 C. Collars can be configured to allow periodic data downloads, or all the data can be transferred

---

Box 8.   Definitions of terms for data capturing standards.

- Static Mode—These are points collected at 1-second intervals; a general guideline is to collect point positions at one-second intervals. The amount of data collected varies with the type of receiver.
- Kinematic Mode—The time between measurements will vary depending on velocity at which data are collected. Measurement interval will usually not exceed 1 second; these data are stored in the receiver for later downloading and post-processing.
- Signal to Noise Ratio (SNR)—The SNR of a signal is a measure of its quality at the GPS receiver. The higher the value, the stronger the desired signal is compared with associated noise. A low value would indicate a weaker signal, and/or higher levels of noise; for example, a setting of 6 might be used.
- Elevation Mask—This ensures the rover (field) receiver is using the same set of satellites as the base station. For a distance of <500 km to the base station, 15° should be used while 20° should be used for a distance of <1,000 km.
- Satellite Vehicles—This is the minimum number of satellites required to record a position, usually 4 or more.
- Datum—This is a smooth mathematical surface that closely fits the mean sea-level surface, for example NAD83.
- Spheroid—This is a spheroid of 'best fit' over the surface of the earth, for example GRS1980.
- Positional Dilution of Precision (PDOP)—This is an indication of the quality of the results that can be expected from a GPS point position. These values should be used as an indication of when GPS is likely not to produce good positioning results and, equally, should not be used as a measure that describes the quality of positioning that has actually taken place; a typical setting would be less than 6.0.
- Base Station—This is a stationary receiver at a known location that provides the data used in the differential corrections of GPS data acquired by a moving receiver; a rover (field) receiver should be within <500 km of the base station when using differential corrections.

Box 7.   Receivers.

GPS receivers can be carried by hand or installed in airplanes, boats, cars, or trucks. These receivers detect, decode, and process GPS satellite signals. The typical hand-held receiver is about the size of a cellular phone or palm computer, and they are getting smaller all the time.

Box 9. Differential processing standards.

- Data Format—The user must acquire the base station data in a format compatible with the software they will use for differential correction, for example, ArcView® shapefile or ArcInfo® coverage.
- Unit of Measurement—One foot equals 0.3048 m exactly.
- Coordinate System—Data are typically collected in longitude and latitude coordinates, however, these can be converted to State Plane, Universal Transverse Mercators (UTM) or others.
- Elevation Mode—NGVD 29 (47).
- An approved Base Station—An example for western Oregon is Corvallis, CORS ARP.

---

to a computer when the collar is retrieved. A source of concern, however, in using GPS collars lies with locating an animal such as elk in a forest of varying density and topography. Rumble and Lindzey (1997) found that nearly 50% of attempted GPS locations failed in stands with >70% overstory canopy cover; in stands with less canopy failure of GPS location attempts was lower. Attempts to model the effects suggested a positive linear relationship ($P \leq 0.01$) between failure of GPS location attempts and tree density, tree basal area, and an index of diameter at breast-height times tree density. Gamo et al. (2000) noted that vegetation could block signals from satellites to GPS radio collars while Dussault et al. (1999) cited vegetation as well as steep terrain and weather as affecting receipt of GPS signals. However, B. K. Johnson of the Oregon Department of Fish and Wildlife (personal communication) indicated that because of recent technology advancements, their recent evaluation of GPS collars demonstrated much better than 60% signal receipt in stands with >70% overstory canopy closure.

GPS technology can also be used to inventory, map, and monitor marine, fish, and wildlife habitats. For instance, GPS has been used to delineate coral reefs (Field et al. 2000), terrestrial wildlife habitats (Kiilsgaard 1999, O'Neil and Barrett 2001), and fish habitats (Martischange 1993, Threloff 1993, Waddle et al. 1997). GPS is also a navigation tool (Anderson 2002) that allows researchers to accurately track their movements and guide themselves to an exact location, such as a coral reef, and then record the delineation of the reefs. Development of wildlife habitat maps requires interfacing GPS with a map database that allows one to store information on the map. This requires the ability to create a moving map, which occurs when the GPS receiver takes the information and displays its current position on the map and, as one moves, the map also moves. Thus, one can be assured of their locations and the location of what they are classifying. Currently, GPS can be directly linked to laptop computers. GPS typically communicates to the computer by using a standard linking mode, NMEAD 183 GGA GSV. Magellan and Trimble have their own standards in which they communicate with a laptop and some are proprietary to a specific GPS model. Also, there are several software programs that interface with GPS to allow on screen recording of information, such as Fieldnotes 32 GPS by Penmetrics (Corvallis, Oregon), SOLO CE by Tripod Data Systems (Portland, Oregon), and ArcPad by ESRI (Redlands, California). In each program, the primary function is to collect positions, attribute these data, as well as locate existing points in the field.

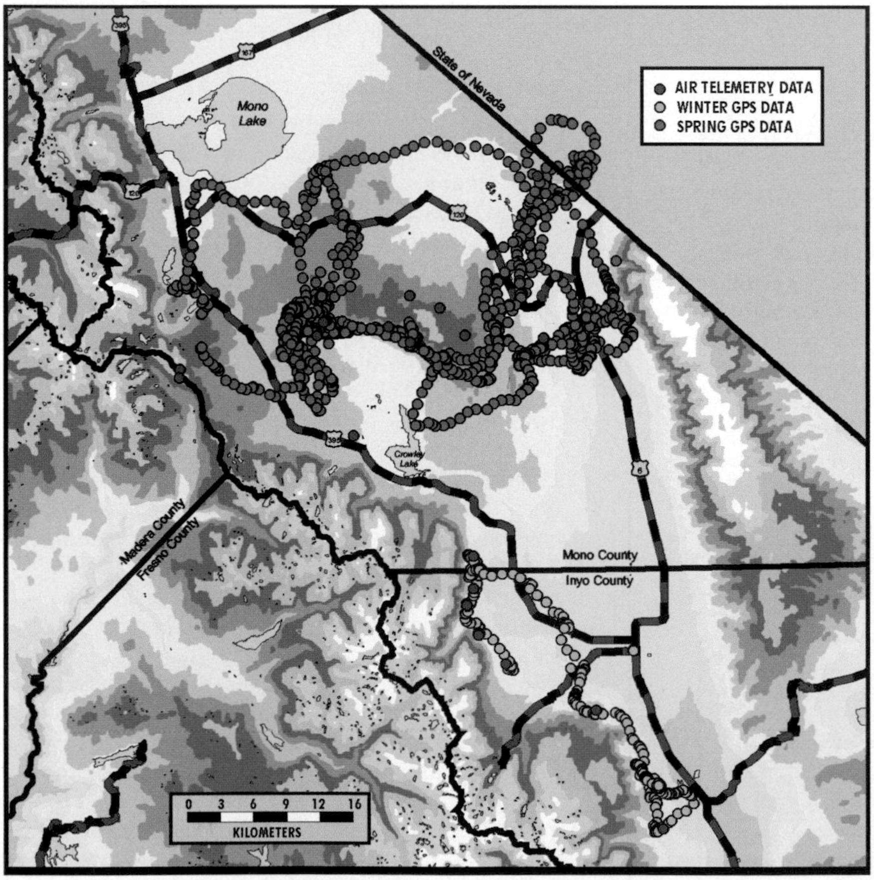

In the future, GPS units will become smaller and the technology will become more wide spread for non-commercial uses. We can also expect GPS to work more effectively with satellites like ARGOS where GPS data is periodically linked to a satellite and then downloaded at a later time by the user. The main factors critical to continuing the development of this tool for wildlife work are: size, power consumption, and reliability. Advances in these areas will help assure that GPS may someday be used on small animals. *GPS World Magazine* (www.gpsworld.com), *Telonics Quarterly* (www.telonics.com), or

Fig. 7. Mountain lion locations during winter and spring as recorded from a GPS collar (Bleich et al. 2000).

GeoCommunity (www.geocomm.com) bring together a great amount of information about the current state of GPS and GeoSpatial technology issues and their applications. Navtech's site, www.navtechgps.com/glossary.asp, presents a link to a GPS Glossary of Terms. Finally, with more and more people using GPS, resource managers will face new problems. One challenge will come with linking GPS to fish echo sounders that will allow people to find and exploit a resource faster than previous methods (Fisheries Western Australia 2000). Thus, technology can help us learn more about a resource or species, as well as cause its accelerated decline, if we do not use it wisely.

USING REMOTELY SENSED DATA
Digital Image Processing

To be effective in management decisions, maps and GISs require timely and accurate information. Remote sensing and digital image processing have the potential to meet these needs as well. In the near future, there will be an unprecedented availability of digital data from satellite sensors in response to concerns about human impacts on the earth, habitat monitoring, and global climate change (Ormsby and Soffen 1989, Justice et al. 2002). However, Graetz (1990) believed that currently available remote sensing technology far exceeds the scientific capability of interpreting and applying it. If remote sensing data are to be used to their fullest potential, the challenge will be to develop realistic spectral, spatial, and temporal processes for extracting information from the images. Several excellent books describe remote sensing and digital image processing (Swain and Davis 1978, Estes et al. 1983, Schowengerdt 1983, Curran 1985, Richards 1986, Campbell 2002).

Digital image processing, the numerical manipulation of digital images, includes procedures for pre-processing, enhancement, and information extraction. Pre-processing involves procedures applied to the original data before enhancement or information extraction. Calibration of image radiometry for atmospheric conditions, illumination and view geometry, correction of geometric distortions, georegistration of the image, and noise suppression are examples of image pre-processing procedures (Schowengerdt 1983).

Image enhancement involves application of procedures designed to facilitate the interpretation of images. These procedures include contrast and color manipulations and spatial-filtering methods (Schowengerdt 1983). The "Tasseled Cap" is a well-known spectral transformation, which derives new variables that allow vegetation and soils information to be extracted, displayed, and understood more easily (Crist et al. 1986). Hodgson et al. (1988) used this transformation with Landsat TM (Thematic Mapper) data to study wood stork (*Mycteria americana*) foraging habitat. Jackson (1983) provided a general procedure to develop spectral indices for user-defined features in a scene.

Development of processes for extracting information from remotely sensed data requires an understanding of the image-forming process. Strahler et al. (1986) provided a framework for identifying appropriate procedures given characteristics of the image and the scene. The most common information-extraction methods used with remote sensing data are spectral classifiers in which each pixel is processed independently of its neighbors or location in the image. This process is appropriate when scene objects are larger than the spatial resolution of the sensor.

The process to automate extraction of information from the imagery, spectral classification, can be generalized as being supervised or unsupervised (Swain and Davis 1978, Schowengerdt 1983). In supervised classification, a sample of image elements for each land cover class is used to estimate parameters, typically a mean vector and covariance matrix, to derive land cover for the entire scene. In unsupervised training, a clustering algorithm is used to partition a sample of the data into populations of pixels with similar reflectance. These are referred to as spectral classes for which parameters can be estimated (Richards and Kelly 1984). In unsupervised training, the analyst attempts to establish correspondence among the spectral classes and land cover classes. A statistics file consisting of a mean vector and covariance matrix for each land cover class is used in a classification algorithm to derive land cover for the entire scene. The product from a maximum likelihood classification, a common method that produces results having the minimum probability of error over the entire set of data classified, is an image in which each pixel is assigned the label of the land cover class for which the *a posteriori* probability was the maximum (Fig. 8).

Digital image processing techniques can also be used when the scene objects are smaller than the resolution element of the sensor. A relationship between the reflectance and a property of a scene, such as canopy cover, is established and used to estimate the property in each pixel in a continuous fashion (Fig. 9). Mixture models are used when the objective is to estimate the proportions of scene objects in each pixel. Mixture models have been used for a variety of resource inventories, including waterfowl habitat (Work and Gilmer 1976), rangeland vegetation and soil cover (Pech et al. 1986), and wintering geese (Strong et al. 1991).

Spectral-spatial scene models exploit the spatial structure of images as well as their spectral characteristics to infer properties and processes at the land surface. Several spectral-spatial models are available. Some scene models segment the image into contiguous groups of pixels that meet a spectral similarity criterion and perform the classification using all pixels of the feature (Strahler et al. 1986) (Fig. 10). Other spectral-spatial models exploit a measure of image texture or the spatial autocorrelation function as an additional feature in the classification process (Shih and Schowengerdt 1983, Pickup and Chewings 1988).

Spectral-temporal models use the change in the spectral properties of images acquired at different times to infer properties or processes at the land surface. The "Tasseled Cap" is an example of a spectral-temporal model of phenological development of agricultural crops that can be used to identify crops and forecast yields (Kauth and Thomas 1976, Wiegand et al. 1986). Time series of the normalized difference vegetation index, calculated from the red and infrared spectral reflectance measurements of the Advanced Very High Resolution Radiometer sensor, have been used to describe and map intra- and inter-year phenological dynamics of biomes at regional, continental, and global scales (Justice et al. 1985), infer net primary productivity (Goward et al. 1985), and measure dynamics of vegetation at transition zones between biomes (Tucker et

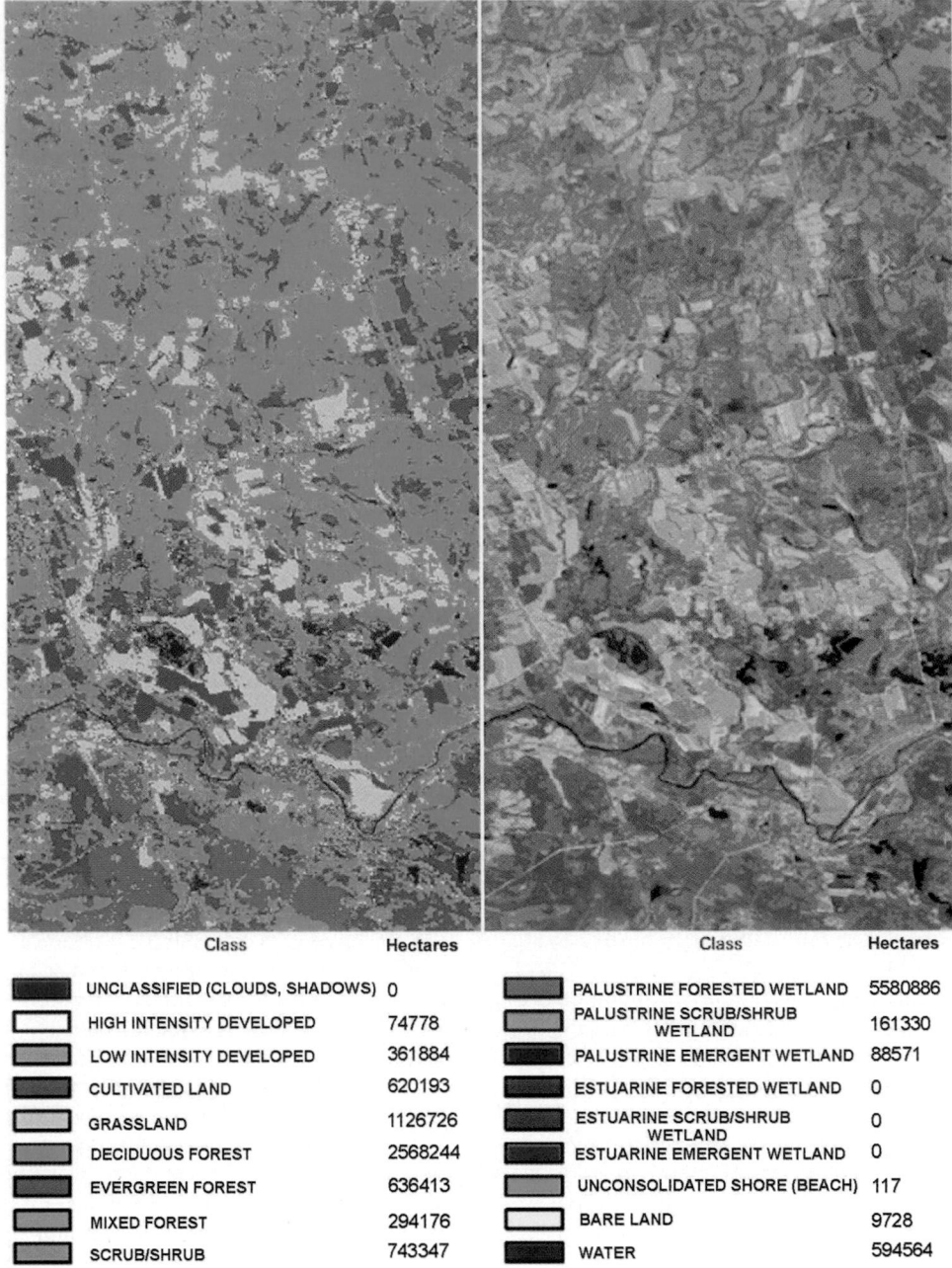

Class	Hectares		Class	Hectares
UNCLASSIFIED (CLOUDS, SHADOWS)	0		PALUSTRINE FORESTED WETLAND	5580886
HIGH INTENSITY DEVELOPED	74778		PALUSTRINE SCRUB/SHRUB WETLAND	161330
LOW INTENSITY DEVELOPED	361884		PALUSTRINE EMERGENT WETLAND	88571
CULTIVATED LAND	620193		ESTUARINE FORESTED WETLAND	0
GRASSLAND	1126726		ESTUARINE SCRUB/SHRUB WETLAND	0
DECIDUOUS FOREST	2568244		ESTUARINE EMERGENT WETLAND	0
EVERGREEN FOREST	636413		UNCONSOLIDATED SHORE (BEACH)	117
MIXED FOREST	294176		BARE LAND	9728
SCRUB/SHRUB	743347		WATER	594564

Fig. 8. Land cover information derived using an unsupervised classification approach from a Landsat image. Land cover is shown on the left and the Landsat image; bands 4, 5, and 3 displayed in red, green, and blue; is shown on the right.

al. 1991). Techniques for detecting change (Singh 1989) use images acquired at different times to infer changes in land cover. Koeln and Bissonette (2000) used "Cross Correlation Analysis" to delineate areas of wetland changes as derived from Landsat imagery (Fig. 11).

The flow of information between remote sensing and GIS should not be one-way. Accuracy of information derived from remote sensing can benefit from access to accurate spatial data within a GIS. Integration of the parallel technologies of GIS and remote sensing will be important to full maturation of both areas.

Remote Sensing of Habitat: Landsat Imagery

Remote sensing has been used in wildlife biology for many years. Historically, small format aerial photographs were the most commonly used method of remote sensing used for mapping habitats. As habitat mapping requirements expanded, use of large format photography from 9 × 9 "inch" metric mapping cameras became more common. The cost of acquiring large format photography and manual interpretation of aerial photographs was high and often prohibitive. Satellite imagery was frequently used to replace or augment use of aerial photography for habitat mapping, primarily to reduce cost. Since the 1970s satellite imagery (primarily Landsat imagery) has been used to map wildlife habitat (Work and Gilmer 1976). In the 1970s the cost of computer systems required to process digital imagery limited using Landsat imagery for habitat mapping. With improvements in software and hardware, and reduction in costs, remote sensing is a frequently used

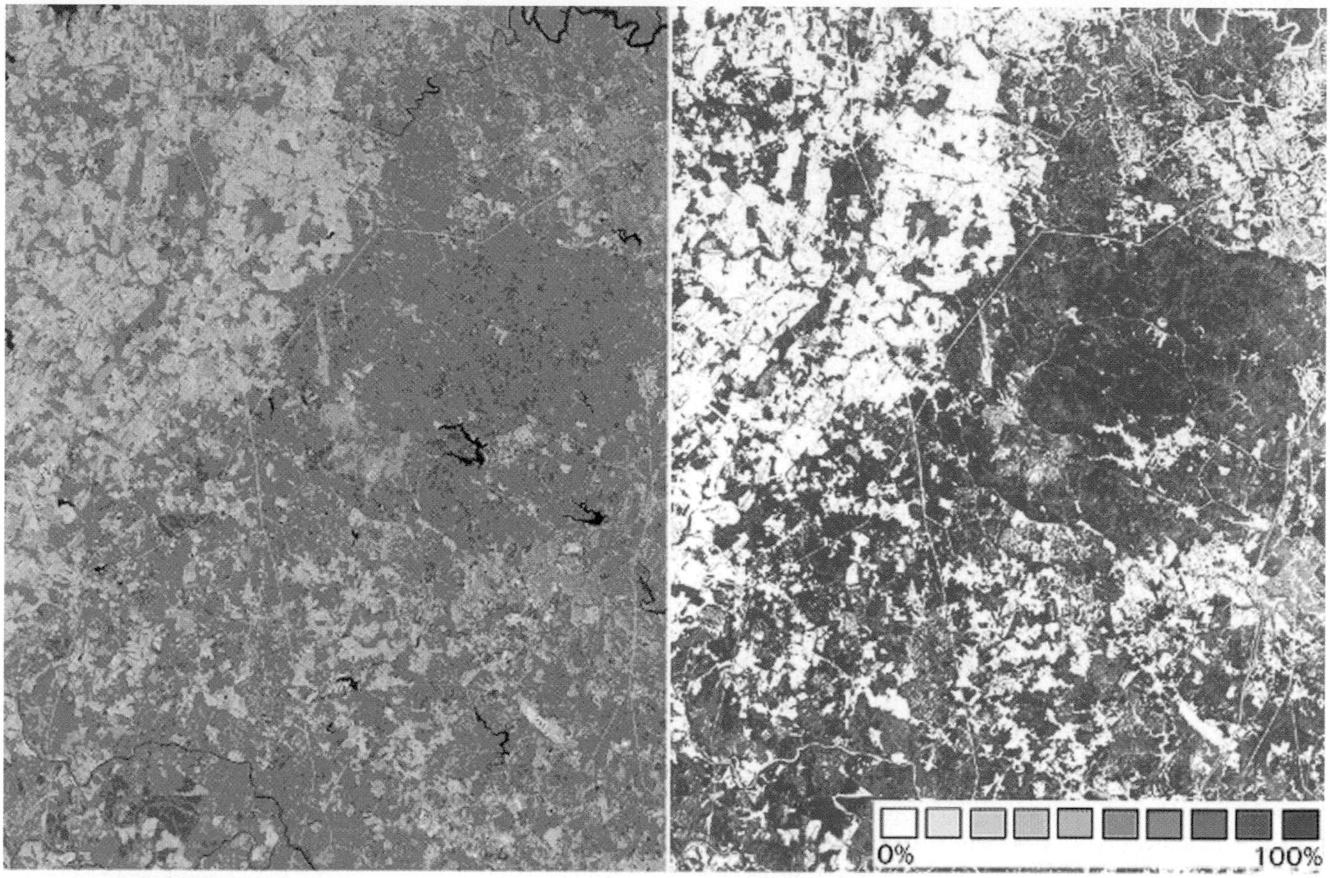

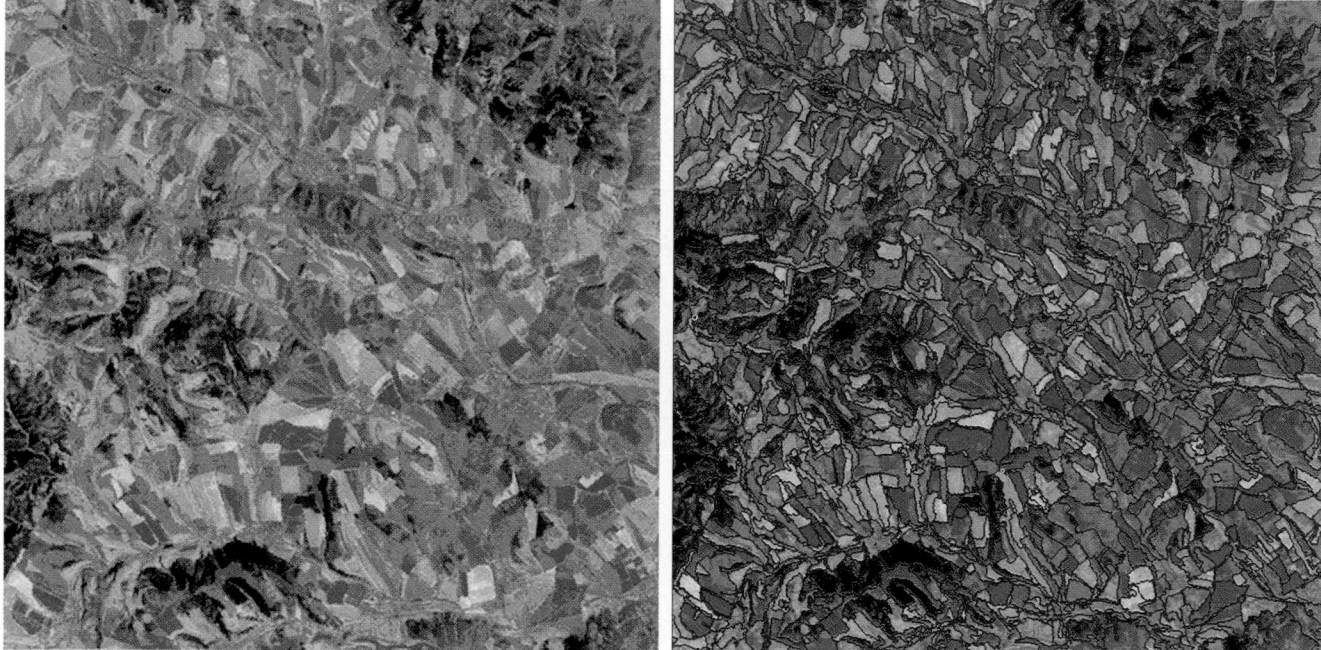

Fig. 9. Percent tree canopy cover (right), ranging from 0 in white to 100% in dark green, calculated using CART technology: samples of high-resolution imagery, and the Landsat image (left).

Fig. 10. Digital image processing algorithms are available for image segmentation and may improve the process of mapping wildlife habitats from digital imagery. A portion of a Landsat image is displayed at the left while the image segments (red polygons) that were delineated in a fully automated process are displayed at right.

tool for mapping habitats, particularly over large regions (watersheds and states). Ducks Unlimited, working with the National Aeronautics and Space Administration (NASA) in the early 1980s was an early pioneer in use of Landsat imagery to map waterfowl habitat (Koeln et al. 1988). Today, many conservation organizations, state wildlife agencies, and resource management organizations such as the U.S. Fish and Wildlife Service, U.S. Forest Service, and the Bureau of Land Management use Landsat imagery for mapping and monitoring habitat. Since the early 1980s, Landsat imagery has been used in the management of many species of wildlife. Palmeirim (1985) used Landsat imagery to identify potential release sites for reintroduction of ruffed grouse in Kansas. Hepinstall and Sader (1997) used Landsat imagery and breeding bird survey data to model the probability of bird species occurring within areas of Maine. Landsat imagery is widely used in the National Biodiversity GAP Analysis Project (Scott et al. 1993, Lillesand et al. 1998, Kiilsgaard 1999, Kiilsgaard and Barrett 2000).

History of Landsat

On 23 July 1972, NASA launched the first in a series of satellites designed to provide repetitive global coverage of the earth's landmasses. It was designated initially as the Earth Resources Technology Satellite-A (ERTS-A). The second in this series of earth resources satellites (designated ERTS-B) was launched 22 January 1975. It was renamed Landsat 2 by NASA, which also renamed ERTS-1 to Landsat 1. Additional Landsat satellites were launched in 1978, 1982, 1984, and 1999 (Landsats 3, 4, 5, and 7, respectively). Landsat 6 was launched on 5 October 1993, but failed to achieve orbit. Each successive satellite system had improved sensor and communications capabilities.

Landsat 1, 2, and 3 had 2 earth-imaging systems, the return beam vidicon (RBV) and the multispectral scanner (MSS). The RBV system generated high-resolution television-like images of the earth's surface. RBV cameras in Landsat 1, 2, and 3 were designed to be the primary imaging systems on Landsat. However, technical problems on all 3 systems precluded routine acquisition of high-quality images from the RBV cameras. The MSS systems were much more successful and became the primary sensors on Landsat.

The RBV cameras were not continued on Landsat 4. In addition to the MSS system, Landsat 4 and 5 also contained the Thematic Mapper (TM) sensor, which provided significant improvement to remote sensing. The TM sensor records 7 bands of information for each pixel in blue-green, green, red, near infrared, 2 wavelengths of mid-infrared, and far infrared spectral regions. Routine collection of MSS data by Landsat 5 was terminated in late 1992.

The Enhanced Thematic Mapper Plus (ETM+) sensor on Landsat 7 (launched on 15 April 1999) is the most advanced of the Landsat sensors. ETM+ replicates the capabilities of the TM instruments on Landsats 4 and 5. It includes new features that make it a more versatile and efficient instrument for global change studies, land cover monitoring, and large area mapping than previous sensors in the Landsat series. These features include:

- a panchromatic band with 15 m spatial resolution,
- a thermal infrared band with 60 m spatial resolution,

- improved radiometric calibration,
- on-board, solid state recording device, and
- improved spatial geometry (improved positional accuracy).

Landsat Characterization

Landsat satellites orbit in a polar (north to south path), sun-synchronous orbit at a nominal altitude of 920 km above earth for Landsats 1-3 and 705 km above earth for Landsats 4, 5, and 7. A sun-synchronous orbit ensures the satellite passes over the earth at the same local sun time so that sun illumination conditions are consistent. Although sun elevation, relative position, and intensity still vary with seasons, each Landsat scene has the illumination of the same time of day. The Landsat 4, 5, and 7 orbit has an equatorial crossing time of 0945 hours and a return period of 16 days (i.e., every 16 days the orbit path would repeat itself). Landsats 1-3 had a return period of 18 days. Each image collects data for an area approximately 185 km east-west and 170 km north-south (for example Fig. 12 presents a full Landsat scene centered over Washington, D.C., USA). Scene locations are identified by path and row; Landsats 4, 5, and 7, require 233 paths to cover the entire earth and each path is divided into 119 rows.

The characteristics of the MSS bands were selected to maximize their capabilities for detecting and monitoring different types of earth's resources. For example, MSS band 1 can be used to detect green reflectance from healthy vegetation, and band 2 was designed for detecting chlorophyll absorption in vegetation. MSS bands 3 and 4 were ideal for recording near-infrared reflectance peaks in healthy green vegetation and for detecting water-land interfaces.

The thematic mapper (TM) is an advanced, multispectral scanning, earth resources sensor designed to achieve higher image resolution, sharper spectral separation, improved geometric fidelity, and greater radiometric accuracy and resolution than the MSS sensor. TM band 1 can penetrate water for bathymetric (water depth) mapping along coastal areas, and is useful for soil-vegetation differentiation and for distinguishing forest types. TM band 2 can detect green reflectance from healthy vegetation, and band 3 is designed for detecting chlorophyll absorption in vegetation. TM band 4 is ideal for near-infrared reflectance peaks in healthy green vegetation and for detecting water-land interfaces. The 2 mid-infrared bands on TM are useful for vegetation and soil moisture studies, and are capable of discriminating between rock and mineral types. The far-infrared band on TM is designed to assist in thermal mapping, and for soil moisture and vegetation studies. All 9 bands (8 spectral ranges) of the ETM+ sensor for a portion of a Landsat scene have specialized uses (Fig 13).

The MSS data have a pixel resolution of 79×57 m. For bands 1-5 and 7 of Landsats 4 and 5, the TM data have a pixel resolution of 30 m and for band 6 (the thermal band), the pixel resolution is 120 m. For the ETM+ sensor on Landsat 7, bands 1-5 and 7 have a pixel resolution of 30 m; band 6 (the thermal band) has a pixel resolution of 60 m, and band 8, the panchromatic band, has a pixel resolution of 15 m.

Obtaining Landsat Imagery

The Landsat Program is a joint initiative of the U.S. Geological Survey (USGS) and NASA. NASA has been

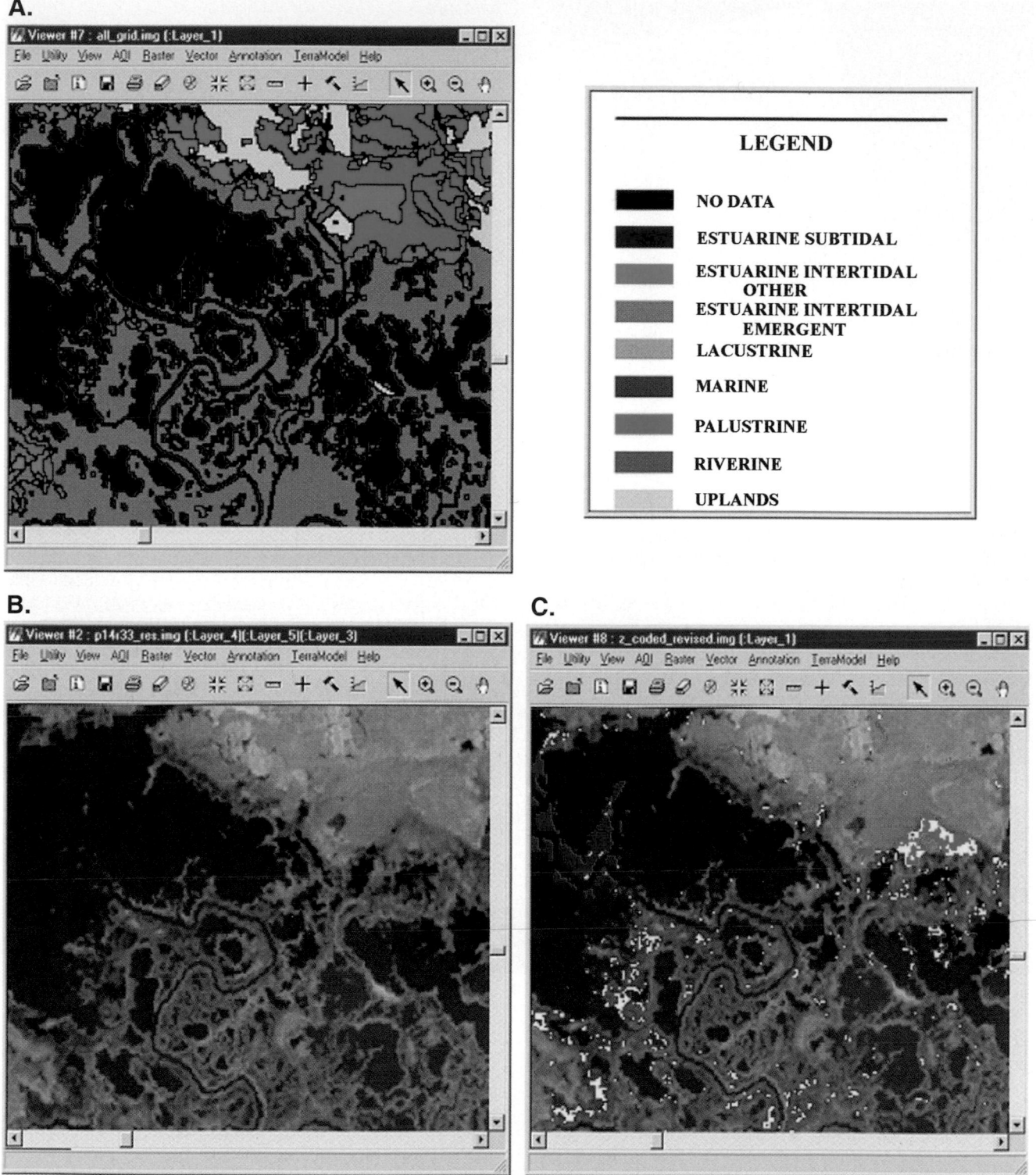

Fig. 11. Cross Correlation Analysis (CCA) can be used to detect changes between 2 images of different dates or an existing map and an image. A, illustrates a portion of a National Wetlands Inventory map with the associated legend. B, illustrates a small portion of a Landsat image used to identify changes in wetlands. The areas shown in red, green, and yellow (C) are the results from CCA and show areas of wetland losses.

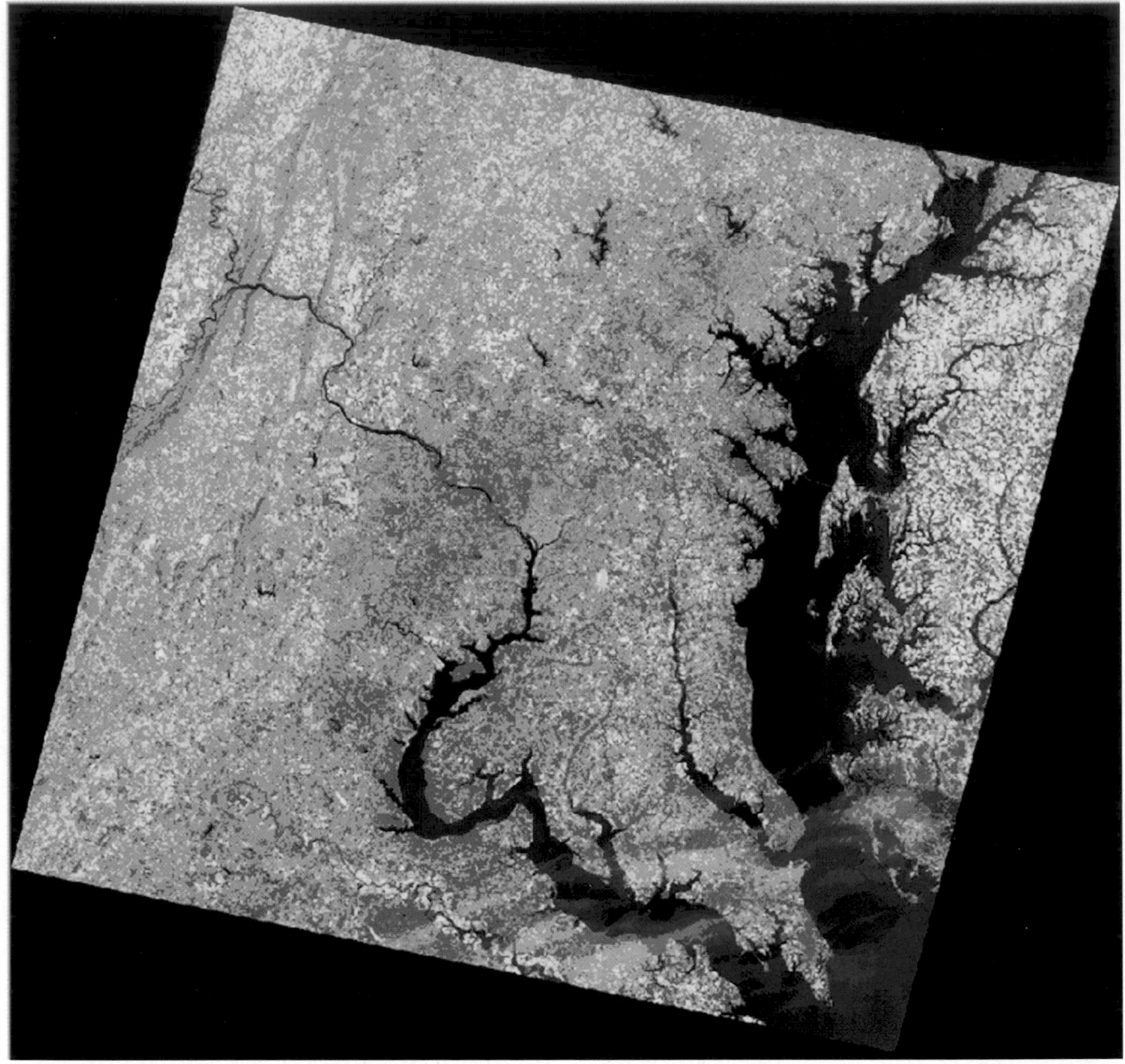

Fig. 12. A Landsat 7 Enhanced Thematic Mapper Plus scene.

responsible for developing and launching spacecraft, while the USGS is responsible for flight operations, maintenance, and management of all ground data reception, processing, archiving, product generation, and distribution. The primary receiving station is the EROS Data Center (EDC) in Sioux Falls, South Dakota. Daily, over 250 Landsat 7 scenes are downloaded to EDC. Some of these scenes covering parts of North America are acquired by direct real-time downlink. Scenes taken in other parts of the world are recorded using the on-board, solid-state, recording device and then downloaded to EDC as Landsat 7 orbits overhead. In addition, there are international ground stations receiving Landsat images in Argentina, Australia, Brazil, Canada, China, Europe, Indonesia, Japan, South Africa, and Thailand.

Users of Landsat imagery can obtain the imagery from EDC or from any of the international ground stations. EDC offers an efficient browse tool to preview and order Landsat imagery (http://edcsns17.cr.usgs.gov/EarthExplorer/). Through this interactive tool, one can select the type of image, spatial coverage required (by geographic coordinates, place name, or path/row), acquisition date, and other requirements. The results of the search are immediately provided and the user can preview any of the scenes and order those that best meet their requirements. Each Landsat scene ordered costs $600.00 ($480.00 per scene when ordering 25 or more scenes) (year 2003 costs) and can be placed on the file transfer protocol (FTP) site for downloading by the purchaser or can be shipped to the purchaser on CD-ROM.

BAND

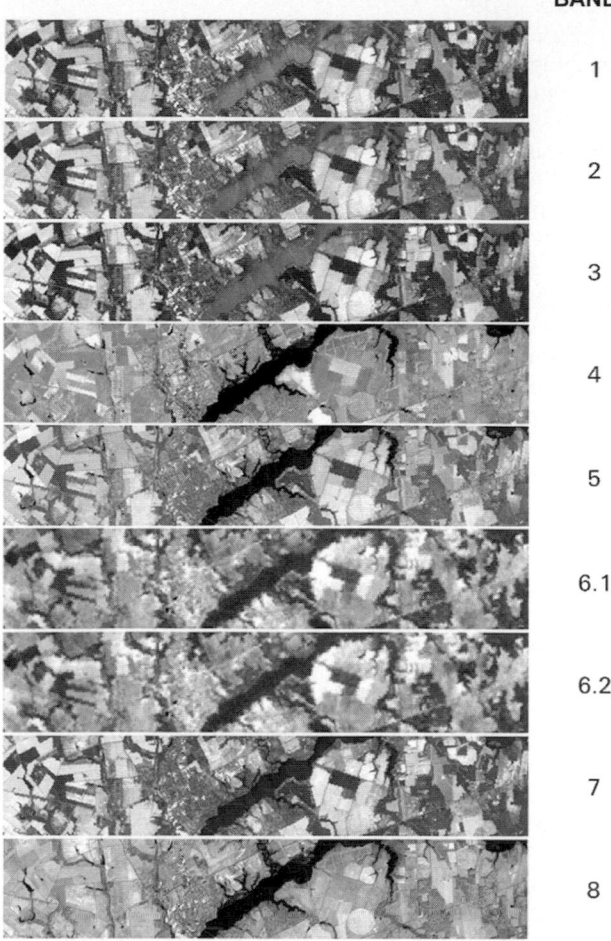

1

2

3

4

5

6.1

6.2

7

8

Fig. 13. The Enhanced Thematic Mapper Plus sensor on Landsat 7 collects imagery in 8 spectral ranges.

Other Sources of Landsat Imagery

Scenes obtained from EROS Data Center are typically not registered precisely to a map base. The process of registering an image to a map base is referred to as orthorectification. Most applications of Landsat imagery require orthorectification to allow the user to obtain precise coordinates of the features extracted from the image. Sponsored under NASA's Scientific Data Buy program, the GeoCover™-Ortho program has created a geodetically accurate digital database of Landsat TM and MSS multispectral imagery covering the earth's land mass and is in

COVER CLASS	A	B	C	D	E	
A	2		1			
B	7	10	3		2	
C	1		6	1		
D				9		
E					8	
						DIAGONAL TOTAL = 35

Fig. 14. Error matrix for hypothetical accuracy assessment data. Data are presented for 5 cover classifications (A, B, C, D, E) sampled 10 times each with possible classification errors. The diagonal total is the number of correctly classified covers: overall accuracy is diagonal total divided by total sampled points, 35/50 = 0.7 or 70% accuracy. Individual cover class accuracies can be calculated via diagonal total divided by column total (producer's accuracy) (e.g., cover class A has a producer's accuracy = 2/10 = 0.2 or 20% producer's accuracy). User's accuracy is diagonal total divided by row total (cover class A has a user's accuracy = 2/3 = 0.66 or 66% user's accuracy).

the process of creating a global digital database of Landsat ETM+ imagery. Earth Satellite Corporation (EarthSat) of Rockville, Maryland was contracted by NASA to obtain the best available Landsat images from the 1980's, 1990's, and 2000's and to orthorectify and spatially co-register these images. These images are available from USGS and can readily be used for habitat mapping and mapping habitat change over time.

The GeoCover™-Ortho coverage is comprised of over 21,000 Landsat images that have been photogrammetrically adjusted and digitally orthorectified to create a seamless global coverage of multispectral digital imagery with 50-m root mean square error (RMSE, a measure of the geodetic positional accuracy of the imagery). The Landsat source images have been hand picked from the Landsat archives of the EROS Data Center and international ground stations, and represent the highest image quality and lowest cloud cover available for the specified time period. GeoCover™-Ortho provides readily available, affordable, and accurate Landsat MSS imagery from the early 1980's, Landsat TM imagery from the early 1990's, and Landsat ETM+ imagery from the early 2000's. This imagery can be used as a geodetically accurate base map and also provides an excellent digital source for multispectral image processing and analysis. These images provide an excellent source of data to monitor habitat changes in 10-year increments over 20 years. These images can be obtained from EDC for $65.00 per scene (year 2003 costs). Working initially with NASA and currently with the National Imagery and Mapping Agency (NIMA), EarthSat has developed a set of procedures and processes to produce a land cover analysis for all land areas of the world using Landsat TM and ETM+ data rectified under the GeoCover™-Ortho program.

Landsat imagery provides an excellent tool for mapping and analyzing changes that have occurred in the landscape. It provides an economical tool (<$0.02/km^2) that has historically been underused by natural resources managers. With reduction in the cost of imagery, and improvements and reduction in costs of computers and image processing software, Landsat imagery will be used more frequently in the future. Landsat imagery has historically been used more than any other source of satellite imagery for habitat mapping. However, Landsat imagery is not the only available source satellite imagery for habitat mapping. Other sensors, AVHRR, MODIS, SPOT, HYPERION, RADARSAT, ASTER, ALI, IKONOS, and QuickBird provide imagery ranging in spatial resolution from 0.6 to 1,000 m, and are readily available for mapping and monitoring natural resources.

Remote Sensing of Animals: Forward-looking Infrared (FLIR)

Aerial census is often the only practical way to estimate wildlife numbers (Remington and Welsh 1989) because of access, response of the animals to ground observers, or size of the study area. An infrared (IR) sensor mounted on an aircraft can increase detection rates of animals at a lower cost than using human observers.

Visibility is the most important factor affecting population estimates (Pollack and Kendall 1987, Samuel et al. 1992, Bodie et al. 1995). A human observer may be able to differentiate perhaps 20 shades of gray (Wyatt et al. 1985), while an 8-bit computer processor can provide 256 shades of gray allowing additional detection capabilities. Infrared is emitted energy while human vision uses reflected energy. Thus, infrared does not require movement, large groups, or contrast (e.g., animals on snow). Aerial surveys using human observers have limitations because biases may occur as a result of observers (Simmons and Hansen 1980), technical problem (Caughley 1974), or more commonly, visibility (Remington and Welsh 1989, Bodie et al. 1995). Little emphasis has been placed on the training process observers must undergo before they become competent (Dirschl et al. 1981). What we see is what is known, but what is missed is unknown. Weather, lighting conditions, season, heterogeneity of terrain, vegetative cover, observer fatigue, search speed, altitude, and distribution of the subject species all affect what is seen (Simmons and Hansen 1980, Remington and Welsh 1989, Bodie et al. 1995).

Airborne IR has been used to survey a range of species and habitats (Table 1). Two advancements in IR sensors have made them useful for wildlife surveys: the decrease in minimum detectable thermal resolution to less than 1 C, and the increase in the number of pixels. These 2 characteristics allow detecting the animal against a wide range of environmental conditions and allow easy identification by body shape. For example, a portion of a deer may be detected under a tree and, by orbiting to provide a better visibility angle, the deer's ear can be identified. IR provides higher detection rates for a given swath width than an aerial survey with human observers with few exceptions.

An IR system mounted on an airplane will cost less than human observers in a helicopter. Further, IR allows for higher flight altitude above ground level. Flight altitudes (e.g., 160 m) used by human observers provide little room to recover from mechanical failures or pilot error.

Using airborne IR for wildlife surveys requires: 1) knowledge of animal behavior and wildlife surveys, 2) an understanding of thermography and sensor capabilities, and 3) selecting the correct airplane or helicopter. Infrared can be used during day and night and year round depending on the survey objective and animal behavior. Knowledge of sampling as well as habitat use and behavior of the subject animal is required for an airborne survey.

Sensor Technology

An infrared sensor captures the emitted IR energy and converts it to a visual image. Infrared energy is transmitted through 2 atmospheric windows, the short (2–5.5 μ) and long wave (8–14 μ) with the middle band (6–7 μ) largely absorbed by the atmosphere. Detectors are designed to transform incident infrared radiation to an analogue signal. This signal is displayed on a screen and the level of infrared energy emitted by objects can be viewed. Typically, sensor detectors are designed to detect either short or long waves. Short wave sensors are better than long wave sensors in warmer more humid environments but fail in extremely cold environments. Long wave sensors have more solar immunity and are less likely to add solar reflectance from water surface or other reflective surfaces such as some rock types. IR sensors cannot detect infrared energy through windowpanes unless the sensors are designed to detect energy below 2 μ.

Sensor Type

There are 2 general types of sensors: radiometer and imaging infrared (also referred to as an IR viewer). Radiometers provide the ability to measure the temperature by calibrating across the image and by measuring variables such as distance, emissivity, and ambient temperature. Some radiometers allow use of isotherms and have an array of palettes to enhance features of interest. Infrared viewers provide a general reference of which objects in the scenes are warmer and colder but there is no way to measure actual temperature. Infrared viewers provide relative temperature using several reference points (low and high temperatures) of known temperature in the scene. However, this approach incorrectly assumes the sensor responds linearly to increases or decreases in temperature. For example, if white is set to represent the hottest points in the scene, a white object on the north side of a canyon may be cooler than a white object on the south side.

Scanning vs. Focal Plane Array

In the past, scanning technology was used to collect emitted energy. One detector moved across the entire image using a rotating mirror to measure emitted energy. It had to collect data at a quarter of a million points within a thirtieth of a second to form an image. Increasing the number of detectors scanning across an image allows more time at each point. The one detector system had substantial distortion and detecting animals was difficult; these systems often required further computer enhancement. Newer systems provide an image with sufficient detail to appear to be a black and white photograph rather than an IR image. Scanning systems allow for capturing a low reference temperature point prior to scanning the images and a high reference temperature point after capturing the image. This provides an opportunity for thermal calibration.

Focal plane array is similar to film in a camera, but the film is replaced with sensor cells. In an infrared system, there is an array of individual detectors (i.e., 340 × 220). A focal plane array doesn't capture a reference point but has a "flag" or a plate with a well-known temperature that covers the array for a second. This calibration can be set for some interval, typically 10–20 minutes, or the operator can push a button to initiate the flag.

Currently, focal plane array systems allow for a smaller minimum detectable thermal resolution than scanning systems (0.07 vs. 0.1 C). A minimum detectable thermal resolution of 0.1 C, however, is sufficient for wildlife applications. To date, scanning systems can provide a larger number of pixels than currently available in a focal plane array. The advantage of more pixels in an infrared system is that they allow more detail.

Hand-held Fixed Position and Gimbal Systems

A hand-held infrared system used from the door or window of an airplane or helicopter can result in significant blur resulting in distorted temperature readings. More troubling are issues of operation safety, fatigue, and wear and tear on equipment. Hand-held systems are relatively inexpensive but require slow airspeeds for good image quality. Looking through a viewfinder while in the air is a poor option for large areas. Fixed position and gimbal systems are mounted (with FAA approval) on an airplane or

Table 1. Wildlife species that have been surveyed using an infrared sensor.

Species	Habitats	Reference
Sandhill cranes (*Grus canadensis*)	Population counts, Platte River, Nebraska	Sidel et al. 1993
Malleefowl (*Leipoa ocellata*)	Incubator-nest mounds, Northwestern Victoria, Australia	Benshemesh and Emison 1996
Canada geese (*Branta canadensis*)	South Dakota	Best et al. 1982.
Birds: Canada geese, Great horned owl (*Bubo virginianus*), Pileated Woodpecker (*Dryocopus pileatus*), Northern Flicker (*Colaptes auratus*), Barrow goldeneye (*Bucephala islandica*), Bufflehead (*B. albeola*), Mallard (*Anas platyrhynchos*), Green-winged teal (*A. crecca*), Lapland longspur (*Calcarius lapponicus*), Pectoral sandpiper (*Calidris melanotos*)	Nests and individuals, Arctic tundra	Boonstra et al. 1995
Whales: minke (*Balaenoptera acutorostrata*), humpback (*Megaptera novaeangliae*), fin (*B. physalus*), blue (*B. musculus*), sperm (*Physeter macrocephalus*)	Northern coast, Norway	Cuyler et al. 1992
Walrus (*Odobenus rosmarus*)	Northwest Territories, Canada	Barber et al. 1991
Moose	Deciduous and mixed coniferous forests, New Hampshire	Adams 1995
Red squirrels, Arctic ground squirrel (*Spermophilus parryii*), snowshow hare (*Lepus americanus*), meadow jumping mice (*Zapus hudsonius*)	Individuals, nests, and burrows; Arctic tundra	Boonstra et al. 1994
Gray Bat (*Myotis grisescens*)	Caves, northern Alabama	Sabol and Hudson 1995
White-tailed deer (*Odocoileus virginianus*)	Deciduous forests, United States	Wiggers and Beckerman 1993, Garner et al. 1995, Naugle et al. 1996, Havens and Sharp 1998
Roe deer (*Capreolus capreolus*), muntjac (*Muntiacus reevesi*), red deer, fallow deer (*Dama dama*), sika deer (*Cervus nippon*)	Deciduous and coniferous woodlands, United Kingdom	Gill et al. 1997
Moose, wild turkeys (*Meleagris gallopavo*)	Deciduous forests, Eastern United States	Garner et al. 1995
Elk	Coniferous forests, southwestern United States	Dunn et al. 2002

helicopter. These systems allow GPS data to be recorded directly on the video. Fixed position sensors are mounted so their orientation is pointing straight down or nadir. These systems are good for mapping purposes but differentiating between species can be difficult because only one angle is provided. Housing a sensor in a gimbal that has 4 stabilized axis helps decrease image blur. The operator controls the system using a "joy stick" and monitor from inside the airplane providing a wide range of visibility angles. Natural color video cameras can also be housed in the gimbal to provide video referencing.

These fixed or FLIR systems have 1 to 3 fields of view (FOV), which are similar to camera lenses. The FOV and altitude above ground level (AGL) are used to calculate the area on the ground viewed by the sensor. The slant range or the hypotenuse of the triangle should be used if the sensor is oriented other than straight down. If the sensor is pointing to an oblique angle, the calculated width (convert degrees to "mils" where 1 degree = 18 mils) is for the image center. A 3-degree field of view spans 3×18 or 54 mils. For example (English units are used in aviation):

where
  AGL = 2,500 ft., the down look angle = 35 degrees,
  SIN of 35 degrees = 0.5735, and with a 10 degree FOV
        = 180 mils.
Thus:
  slant range = 4,357.5 (2,500 AGL / 0.5735), and
  width of view = 784 ft. (180 mil FOV $\times$ 4,358 ft. slant range).

Airborne Platforms

Infrared systems have been mounted (requiring a specially-designed mount) on helicopters and airplanes. Helicopters have the advantage of being able to operate at slow speeds and at low altitudes but along with higher costs, can have greater vibration, which can degrade the image. Fixed-wing aircraft provide less vibration and cost less. Power for the sensor, GPS and video equipment is an issue, as most systems require 24–28 volts.

Most light airplanes and helicopters follow visual flight rules (VFR). Both day and night operations are possible using VFR depending on the lights available in the survey area. However, night flights in mountainous terrain or in areas with little light sources require instrument flight rules (IFR) that could require a twin-engine airplane for safety.

Accuracy Assessment of Remotely Sensed Data

A variety of devices and techniques, such as Landsat Imagery and FLIR, can be used to record characteristics of the earth's surface from remote positions. However, interpretation of remotely sensed data can introduce error (Janssen and van der Wel 1994). Error in mapping can be generated in several ways, error in thematic classification, both by omission and by misclassification (commission) (Story and Congalton 1986), as well as error in cartographic delineation (location error).

Accuracy assessment of landscape maps generated from remotely sensed data is generally accomplished through field verification of a select subset (samples) of thematic or areal map units. The investigator must identify accuracy assessment objectives as well as the level of error acceptable for accuracy estimates (based on planned uses of the map). To keep the sampling design simple, easy to analyze, and statistically robust, it is important to define the sampling unit and to use a basic probability sampling design (inclusion probabilities are equal and non-zero for all members of the population). Design–based statistical inference can be applied when sampling is of characteristics of a real, explicitly defined population (Stehman 2000). Probability sampling designs can be interpreted as accuracy estimates for the entire population via established statistical estimators that vary according to the particular sampling design (Stehman 1999). Limitations of resources for field verification or site access can constrain a sampling design. Sampling designs that meet the requirements of equal probability sampling are: simple random sampling, systematic sampling, stratified systematic unaligned sampling, and one-stage cluster sampling (Stehman and Czaplewski 1998, Stehman 1999).

Investigators initially developed the confusion or error matrix, which permitted calculation of simple test sample ratios (the number of land use classes incorrectly depicted on the map divided by the number of correctly depicted land use classes confirmed by field verification) (van Genderen et al. 1978, Fitzpatrick-Lins 1981). Since those efforts, a great variety of error matrix interpretations and new error metrics have been presented in the literature. The most important contributions of recent work for accuracy findings have been the increase in statistical rigor and decrease in confidence intervals (Richards 1996, Stehman 2001).

Identification of the classification error in maps is accomplished using an *a priori* target level for thematic map accuracy and designing the assessment procedure (number of sampling points, etc.) based on statistical parameters (Fitzpatrick-Lins 1981). There are a variety of methods for setting the number of sample points from the stratified systematic unaligned sampling technique (Rosenfield et al. 1982) to statistically derived sampling levels based on the assumption that samples have normal distributions (Hord and Brooner 1976). Other options include decision-rules processes that can incorporate cover type stratification, cover type abundance weighting, and differential sampling effort.

An estimation of sampling intensity can be based on tables with sample data represented as $x = 1$ for a correct interpretation, and $x = 0$ where the map interpretation is incorrect. Consequently, x has the probability density function for a single observation (Rosenfield et al. 1982):

$$f(x) = p^x (1 - p)^{1-x}, 0 \le p \le 1, x = 0,1.$$

With prior probability estimates, sampling levels could be established based on the cumulative binomial probability that is bracketed with confidence intervals:

$$P_B = {}^{n - k(n) - 1} \Sigma_{s = 0} C_s^n p_o^{n - s} (1 - p_o)^s,$$

where n = sample size, $k(n)$ = largest integer less than or equal to $n(p_o + E)$, E = the error of the estimate (the maximum error we can tolerate), and p_o = the *a priori* value based on experiential knowledge.

Variation in size and frequency of thematic cover types necessitates adjustments in sampling intensity that reflect their relative importance. Thus, a cover type with limited occurrence can be sampled with greater frequency, while those most common and abundant will be sampled according to statistical parameters. Stehman (2001) reported that sample size required to achieve a standard error of 0.05 for a population estimate reaches a maximum of 100, when population size is $\ge 10,000$ [for populations of <10,000, the sample size required to achieve SE = 0.05 is a function of $n = N/(0.01N + 1)$ where n = sample size and N = population size].

The error matrix is composed of orthogonal axis with cover types (Fig. 14) and allows analysis of accuracy and error rate for each cover type. Cover type accuracy is measured by dividing the number of correctly classified sample points for each cover type by total points sampled. Map accuracy can also be presented as user's (diagonal values divided by row totals for each matrix) and producer's (diagonal values divided by column totals for each matrix) values for each cover type, which are the converse of commission and omission error, respectively.

Map accuracy assessment can be handicapped by limitations in field verification procedures (i.e., limited access to sample points can introduce error into the assessment), and there is a chance that interpretation of cover type will not be equivalent between the map producer and those performing the map accuracy assessment. Linguistic variables can be used to quantify field verification confidence values that can then be used to calculate a new set of values for map accuracy (Gopal and Woodcock 1994, Woodcock et al. 1996). Confidence values are factored into the proportion that each contributed to the total individual cover type sample (Woodcock et al. 1996). An example could be labeled Derived Accuracy Assessment Values (DAAV), a new metric that uses confidence values for each sample point factored into the overall accuracy value calculated for each cover type. For example, let the field confidence ratings range from 0 to 5:

where

0 = no access to sample point (value = 0.0);
1 = low confidence, limited access to sample point or map class, a poor match to field-verified class (value = 0.2);
2 = low confidence, access incomplete or map class a poor match to field-verified class (value = 0.40);
3 = location of sample point not easily ascertained, field verification of class based on proximate class or problems with class match to map class (value = 0.6);
4 = confidence high in field-verification of sample point location and class match (value = 0.8); and
5 = sample point is acquired and matches map class designation (value = 1.0).

If a specific cover type had 109 sample points visited of which 92 were correctly classified and 89 had a confidence value of 5; the proportion of confidence value 5 of the correct points is 89/92 = 0.97. The confidence value for a rating of 5 is 1.0 (the multiplier = 1.0) or 0.97 (1.0) = 0.97 and the class accuracy is the percentage of correctly classified sample points in the cover type (92/109 × 100 = 84%). Thus, 0.97 (84%) = 81.5% is the DAAV for confidence value 5. The DAAV for the confidence value of 5 is then combined into an overall value based on the sum of all confidence values for samples of the class; the DAAV for each confidence level recorded for the class sample = overall class accuracy.

The assessment of map accuracy by field verification could benefit from methods that increase the accuracy of sample point capture (Woodcock 1996). This could be accomplished by tagging the sample points with location information (UTMs, Latitude and Longitude), which could be targets for field verification. GPS units could help in quantifying variability encountered in accessing sample points. Further, proximity to each sample point could be quantified and used in the assessment of map accuracy.

The overall objective of performing an accuracy assessment of a map is to provide a quantified measure of how well the map represents reality. If proper procedures are followed in the design, performance, and analysis of sampling, the accuracy assessment results can be used as an integral part of the map.

SUMMARY

All projects, whether habitat or animal related, occur spatially in wildlife biology and management. Thus, spatial technologies can be used to evaluate research and management efforts. This chapter provides a brief look into using 3 spatial technologies: GIS, GPS, and remotely sensed data (Landsat Imagery and FLIR) along with highlighting the need to understand data documentation, data accuracy, and Internet applications. Spatial technologies should be considered as tools to assist resource managers with mapping, and as a way to merge or incorporate data sets from a variety of sources into one format. Maps can focus discussion by presenting what is known or thought to be known about an area or issue. Additionally, most people readily accept maps because they are easier to understand at first glance than some tables or figures, and because many people use them to navigate across town or across a country. Spatial technologies rely on computer technologies and currently are expensive to develop and maintain. However, their value outweighs their costs when information is incorporated into products, which help managers make wise decisions about natural resources.

ACKNOWLEDGMENTS

We thank Matt Lehman from Tripod Data Systems (a Trimble Company) for answering questions about the latest technology for GPS. We are also indebted to Sharon Shin, FGDC, Denver, Colorado; L. D. Wayne, GeoMaxim, Ashville, North Carolina; A. O. Ball and M. E. Moeller, NOAA Coastal Services Center, Charleston, South Carolina; and N. L. Savar, Northeastern Illinois Planning Commission, Chicago, for their contributions to this chapter, and Erin Rose O'Neil for initial editing. Finally, we thank 2 reviewers, Scott D. Klopfer and Larry L. Strong for comments and suggestions on our earlier draft.

LITERATURE CITED

ADAMS, K. P. 1995. Evaluation of moose population monitoring techniques and harvest data in New Hampshire. Thesis. University of New Hampshire, Durham, USA.

AKÇAKAYA, H. R. 2000. Population viability analyses with demographically and spatially structured models. Ecological Bulletin 48:23–38.

ALLEN, C. R., L. G. PEARLSTINE, AND W. M. KITCHENS. 2001. Modeling viable mammal populations in gap analysis. Biological Conservation 99:135–144.

ANDERSON, B. 2002. GPS afloat—gps navigation made simple. Fernhurst Books, West Sussex, United Kingdom.

ANTUNES, P., R. SANTOS, AND L. JORDAO. 2001. The application of geographic information systems to determine environmental impact significance. Environmental Impact Assessment Review 21:511–535.

ARAÚJO, M. B., AND P. H. WILLIAMS. 2001. The bias of complementarity hotspots toward marginal populations. Conservation Biology 15:1710–1720.

ARTHAUD, G. J., AND D. W. ROSE. 1996. A methodology for estimating production possibility frontiers for wildlife habitat and timber value at the landscape level. Canadian Journal of Forest Research 26:2191–2200.

BARBER, D. G., P. R. RICHARD, K. P. HOCHHEIM, AND J. ORR. 1991. Calibration of aerial thermal infrared imagery for walrus population assessment. Arctic 44:58–65.

BENSHEMESH, J. S., AND W. B. EMISION. 1996. Surveying breeding densities of malleefowl using an airborne thermal scanner. Wildlife Research 23:121–42.

BEST, R. G., R. FOWLER, D. HAUSE, AND M. WEHDE. 1982. Aerial thermal infrared census of Canada geese in South Dakota. Photogrammetric Engineering and Remote Sensing 48:1869–1877.

BETTINGER, P. 1999. Distributing geographic information systems capabilities to field offices: benefits and challenges. Journal of Forestry 97(6):22–26.

———. 2001. Challenges and opportunities for linking the modeling of forest vegetation dynamics with landscape planning models. Landscape and Urban Planning 56:107–124.

———, K. BOSTON, AND J. SESSIONS. 1999. Combinatorial optimization of elk habitat effectiveness and timber harvest volume. Environmental Modeling and Assessment 4:143–153.

———, J. SESSIONS, AND K. BOSTON. 1997. Using Tabu search to schedule timber harvests subject to spatial wildlife goals for big game. Ecological Modelling 94:111–123.

————, K. BOSTON, J. SESSIONS, AND W. C. MCCOMB. 2001. Integrating wildlife species habitat goals in quantitative land management planning processes. Pages 567–579 *in* D. H. Johnson and T. A. O'Neil, editors. Wildlife-habitat relationships in Oregon and Washington. Oregon State University Press, Corvallis, USA.

————, D. GRAETZ, K. BOSTON, J. SESSIONS, AND W. CHUNG. 2002. Eight heuristic planning techniques applied to three increasingly difficult wildlife-planning problems. Silva Fennica 36:561–584.

BLEICH, V. C., B. M. PIERCE, S. G. TORRES, AND T. LUPO. 2000. Using space age technology to study mountain lion ecology. Outdoor California 3(3):24–25.

BODIE, W. L., E. O. GARTON, E. R TAYLOR, AND M. MCCOY. 1995. A sightability model for bighorn sheep in canyon habitats. Journal of Wildlife Management 59:832–840.

BOJÓRQUEZ-TAPIA, L. A., I. AZUARA, P. BALVANERA, A. D. CUÁRON, L. A. PEÑA, A. RAMÍREZ, C. ALVEREZ, AND M. L. ALQUICIRA. 1995. Predicting and mapping species-rich areas for environmental assessments with limited data. Pages 546–550 *in* J. A. Bissonette and P. R. Krausman, editors. Integrating people and wildlife for a sustainable future. The Wildlife Society, Bethesda, Maryland, USA.

BOONSTRA, R., J. M. EADIE, C. J. KREBS, AND S. BOUTIN. 1994. Finding mammals using far-infrared thermal imaging. Journal of Mammalogy 75:1063–1068.

————, ————, ————, AND ————. 1995. Limitations of far thermal infrared imaging in locating birds. Journal of Field Ornithology 66:192–198.

BOSTON, K., AND P. BETTINGER. 2001. Development of spatially feasible forest plans: a comparison of two modeling approaches. Silva Fennica 35:425–435.

BREKKE, E. B. 1988. Using GIS to determine the effects of CO_2 development on elk calving in south-central Colorado. U.S. Department of the Interior, Bureau of Land Management Technical Note 381. Service Center, Denver, Colorado, USA.

BROOK, B. W., J. R. CANNON, R. C. LACY, C. MIRANDE, AND R. FRANKHAM. 1999. Comparison of the population viability analysis packages GAPPS, INMAT, RAMAS, and VORTEX for the whooping crane (*Grus americana*). Animal Conservation 2:23–31.

BUNNELL, F. L. 1974. Computer simulation of forest wildlife relations. Pages 39–50 *in* H. C. Black, editor. Wildlife and forest management in the Pacific Northwest. School of Forestry, Oregon State University, Corvallis, USA.

BURROUGHS, P. A. 1986. Principles for geographic information systems for land resource assessment. Oxford University Press, New York, USA.

CALKIN, D. E., C. A. MONTGOMERY, N. H. SCHUMAKER, S. POLASKY, J. L. ARTHUR, AND D. J. NALLE. 2002. Developing a production possibility set of wildlife species persistence and timber harvest value. Canadian Journal of Forest Research 32:1329–1342.

CAMPBELL, J. B. 2002. Introduction to remote sensing. Third edition. The Guilford Press, New Bedford, Massachusetts, USA.

CARROLL, C., W. J. ZIELINSKI, AND R. F. NOSS. 1999. Using presence-absence data to build and test spatial habitat models for the fisher in the Klamath Region, U.S.A. Conservation Biology 13:1344–1359.

CAUGHLEY, G. 1974. Bias in aerial survey. Journal of Wildlife Management 38:921–933.

CEBALLOS, G., P. RODRÍGUEZ, AND R. A. MEDELLIN. 1998. Assessing conservation priorities in megadiverse Mexico: mammalian diversity, endemicity, and endangerment. Ecological Applications 8:8–17.

CLARK, J. D., J. E. DUNN, AND K. G. SMITH. 1993. A multivariate model of female black bear habitat use for a geographic information system. Journal of Wildlife Management 57:519–526.

CLEVENGER, A. P., J. WIERZCHOWSKI, B. CHRUSZCZ, AND K. GUNSON. 2002. GIS-generated, expert-based models for identifying wildlife habitat linkages and planning mitigation passages. Conservation Biology 16:503–514.

COWARDIN, L. M., AND V. I. MYERS. 1974. Remote sensing for identification and classification of wetland vegetation. Journal of Wildlife Management 38:308–314.

CRIST, E. P., R. LAURIN, AND R. C. CICONE. 1986. Vegetation and soils information contained in transformed thematic mapper data. Pages 1465–1470 *in* Proceedings of the International Geoscience and Remote Sensing Symposium. ESA SP-254. ESA Publication Division, Zurich, Switzerland.

CURRAN, P. J. 1985. Principles of remote sensing. Longman Group Limited, London, United Kingdom.

CUYLER, L. C., R. WIULSROD, N. A. ORITSLAND. 1992. Thermal infrared radiation from free living whales. Marine Mammal Science 8:120–134.

DETTMERS, R., AND J. BART. 1999. A GIS modeling method applied to predicting forest songbird habitat. Ecological Applications 9:152–163.

DIRSCHL, H. J., M. NORTON-GRIFFITHS, AND S. P. WETMORE. 1981. Training observers for aerial surveys of herbivores. Wildlife Society Bulletin 9:108–117.

DOBSON, A. P., J. P. RODRÍGUEZ, AND W. M. ROBERTS. 2001. Synoptic tinkering: integrating strategies for large-scale conservation. Ecological Applications 11:1019–1026.

————, ————, ————, AND D. S. WILCOVE. 1997. Geographic distribution of endangered species in the United States. Science 275:550–553.

DUNN, W. C., J. P. DONNELLY, AND W. J. KRAUSMANN. 2002. Using thermal infrared sensing to count elk in the southwestern United States. Wildlife Society Bulletin 30:963–967.

DUSSAULT, C., R. COURTOIS, J. HUOT, AND J. -P. OUELLET. 1999. Evaluation of GPS telemetry collar performance for habitat studies in the boreal forest. Wildlife Society Bulletin 27:965–972.

————, ————, ————, AND ————. 2001. The use of forest maps for the description of wildlife habitats: limits and recommendations. Canadian Journal of Forest Research 31:1227–1234.

DYER, S. J. 1999. Movement and distribution of woodland caribou (*Rangifer tarandus caribou*) in response to industrial development in northeastern Alberta. Thesis. University of Alberta, Edmonton, Canada.

ESTES, J. A., E. J. HAJIC, AND L. R. TINNEY, editors. 1983. Fundamentals of image analysis: analysis of visible and thermal infrared data. Pages 987–1124 *in* R. N. Colwell, editor. Manual of remote sensing. Second edition. Vol. 1. American Society for Photogrammetry and Remote Sensing, Falls Church, Virginia, USA.

FALLOUX, F. 1989. Land information and remote sensing for renewable resource management in sub-Saharan Africa: a demand-driven approach. Technical Paper 108. The World Bank, Washington, D.C., USA.

FEDRA, K. 1995. Decision support for natural resources management: models, GIS, and expert systems. AI Applications 9(3):3–19.

FEDERAL GEOGRAPHIC DATA COMMITTEE. 1998. Content standard for digital geospatial metadata (version 2.0), FGDC-STD-001–1998. Available online at http://www.fgdc.gov/metadata/contstan.html (accessed 4 November 2004).

————. 1999. Content standard for digital geospatial metadata (version 2.0), FGDC-STD-001–1998, Part 1: biological data profile. U.S. Department of the Interior, Geological Survey, Biological Resources Division, Biological Data Working Group, Washington, D.C., USA.

————. 2000. A guide to writing clearly. Metadata Education Program and the National Metadata Cadre. Federal Geographic Data Committee, Reston, Virginia, USA.

FEDERAL REGISTER. 1994. Coordinating geographic data acquisition and access: The National Spatial Data Infrastructure Executive Order 12906. Federal Register 59 (71):17671–17674.

FIELD, M., P. CHAVEZ, AND P. JOKIEL. 2000. Interpreting remotely sensed data on coral reefs. PACON 2000 Conference, Honolulu, Hawaii, USA.

FISHERIES WESTERN AUSTRALIA. 2000. Management directions for western Australia's recreational fisheries. Fisheries Management Paper 136. Fisheries Western Australia, Perth, Australia.

FITZPATRICK-LINS, K. 1981. Comparison of sampling procedures and data analysis for a land-use and land-cover map. Photogrammetric Engineering and Remote Sensing 47:343–351.

FRANKLIN, J. 1995. Predictive vegetation mapping: geographic modeling of biospatial patterns in relation to environmental gradients. Progress in Physical Geography 19:474–499.

GAMO, R. S., M. A. RUMBLE, F. LINDZEY, AND M. STEFANICH. 2000. GPS radio collar 3D performance as influenced by forest structure and topography. Proceedings of the International Symposium on Biotelemetry 15:464–473.

GARNER, D. L., H. B. UNDERWOOD, AND W. F. PORTER. 1995. The use of modern infrared thermography for wildlife population surveys. Environmental Management 19:233–238.

GILL, R. M. A., M. L. THOMAS, AND D. STOCKER. 1997. The use of portable thermal imaging for estimating deer population density in forest habitats. Journal of Applied Ecology 34:1273–1286.

GOODCHILD, M. F. 1993. The state of GIS for environmental problem solving. Pages 8–15 in M. F. Goodchild, B. O. Parks, and L. T. Steyaert, editors. Environmental modeling with GIS. Oxford University Press, New York, USA.

GOPAL, S., AND C. WOODCOCK. 1994. Theory and methods for accuracy assessment of thematic maps using fuzzy sets. Photogrammetric Engineering and Remote Sensing 60:181–188.

GOWARD, S. N., C. J. TUCKER, AND D. G. DYE. 1985. North American vegetation patterns observed with the NOAA-7 advanced very high-resolution radiometer. Vegetation 64:3–14.

GRAETZ, R. D. 1990. Remote sensing of terrestrial ecosystem structure: an ecologist's pragmatic view. Pages 5–30 in R. J. Hobbs and H. A. Mooney, editors. Remote sensing of biospheric functioning. Springer-Verlag, Inc., New York, USA.

GRIFFIN, P. C. 1999. Endangered species diversity "hot spots" in Russia and centers of endemism. Biodiversity and Conservation 8:497–511.

GUISSE, A. W., AND H. R. GIMBLETT. 1997. Assessing and mapping conflicting recreation values in state park settings using neural networks. AI Applications 11:79–89.

HAVENS, K. J., AND E. J. SHARP. 1998. Using thermal imagery in the aerial survey of animals. Wildlife Society Bulletin 26:17–23.

HEPINSTALL, J. A., AND S. A. SADER. 1997. Using Bayesian statistics, thematic mapper satellite imagery, and breeding bird survey data to model bird species probability of occurrence in Maine. Photogrammetric Engineering and Remote Sensing 63:1231–1237.

HODGSON, M. E., J. R. JENSEN, H. E. MACKEY, JR., AND M. C. COULTER. 1988. Monitoring wood stork foraging habitat using remote sensing and geographic information systems. Photogrammetric Engineering and Remote Sensing 54:1601–1607.

HOF, J. G., AND L. A. JOYCE. 1992. Spatial optimization for wildlife and timber in managed forest ecosystems. Forest Science 38:489–508.

———, AND ———. 1993. A mixed integer linear programming approach for spatially optimizing wildlife and timber in managed forest ecosystems. Forest Science 39:816–834.

———, AND M. G. RAPHAEL. 1997. Optimization of habitat placement: a case study of the northern spotted owl in the Olympic Peninsula. Ecological Applications 7:1160–1169.

———, M. BEVERS, L. JOYCE, AND B. KENT. 1994. An integer programming approach for spatially and temporally optimizing wildlife populations. Forest Science 40:177–191.

HORD, R. M., AND W. BROONER. 1976. Land-use map accuracy criteria. Photogrammetric Engineering and Remote Sensing 42:671–677.

JACKSON, R. D. 1983. Spectral indices in n-space. Remote Sensing of Environment 13:409–421.

JANSSEN, L. L. F., AND F. J. M. VAN DER WEL. 1994. Accuracy assessment of satellite derived land-cover data: a review. Photogrammetric Engineering and Remote Sensing 60:419–426.

JI, W., AND P. LEBERG. 2002. A GIS-based approach for assessing the regional conservation status of genetic diversity: an example from the southern Appalachians. Environmental Management 29:531–544.

JUSTICE, C. O., J. R. G. TOWNSHEND, B. N. HOLBEN, AND C. J. TUCKER. 1985. Analysis of the phenology of global vegetation using meteorological satellite data. International Journal of Remote Sensing 6:1271–1318.

———, ———, E. F. VERMOTE, E. MASUOKA, R. E. WOLFE, N. EL SALEOUS, D. P. ROY, AND J. T. MORISETTE. 2002. An overview of MODIS land data processing and product status. Remote Sensing of Environment 83:1–2, 3–15.

KANGAS, J., AND T. PUKKALA. 1996. Operationalization of biological diversity as a decision objective in tactical forest planning. Canadian Journal of Forest Research 26:103–111.

KAUTH, R. J., AND G. S. THOMAS. 1976. The tasseled cap—a graphic description of the spectral-temporal development of agricultural crops as seen by Landsat. Pages 4B41–4B51 in Proceedings: Symposium on Machine Processing of Remotely Sensed Data. Purdue University, West Lafayette, Indiana, USA.

KIILSGAARD, C. 1999. Oregon vegetation: mapping and classification of landscape-level cover types. Final Report. U.S. Department of the Interior, Geological Survey, Biological Resources Division, GAP Analysis Program, Moscow, Idaho, USA.

———, AND C. BARRETT. 2000. Map—Wildlife habitat types of the Pacific Northwest. Northwest Habitat Institute, Corvallis, Oregon, USA.

KILGO, J. C., D. L. GARTNER, B. R. CHAPMAN, J. B. DUNNING, JR., K. E. FRANZREB, S. A. GAUTHREAUX, C. H. GREENBERG, D. J. LEVEY, K. V. MILLER, AND S. F. PEARSON. 2002. A test of an expert-based bird-habitat relationship model in South Carolina. Wildlife Society Bulletin 30: 783–793.

KINGSTON, T. 1995. RAMAS/GIS: linking landscape data with population viability analysis (software review). Conservation Biology 9: 966–968.

KNICK, S. T., AND D. L. DYER. 1997. Distribution of black-tailed jackrabbit habitat determined by GIS in southwestern Idaho. Journal of Wildlife Management 61:75–85.

KOELN, G. T., AND J. BISSONETTE. 2000. Cross-correlation analysis: mapping land cover changes with a historic land cover database and a recent, single-date, multispectral image. CD-ROM, Proceedings of the American Society of Photogrammetry and Remote Sensing, Washington, D.C., USA.

———, L. M. COWARDIN, AND L. L. STRONG. 1996. Geographic information systems. Pages 540–566 in T. A. Bookhout, editor. Fifth edition. Research and management techniques for wildlife and habitats. The Wildlife Society, Bethesda, Maryland, USA.

———, J. E. JACOBSON, D. E. WESLEY, AND R. S. REMPLE. 1988. Wetland inventories derived from Landsat data for waterfowl management planning. Transactions of the North American Wildlife and Natural Resources Conference 53:303–310.

KORTE, G. 2000. The GIS book. OnWord Press, Florence, Kentucky, USA.

LETHAM, L. 1998. GPS made easy. The Mountaineers. Second edition. Seattle, Washington, USA.

LILLESAND, T., J. CHIPMAN, D. NAGEL, H. REESE, M. BOBO, AND R. GOLDMANN. 1998. Upper Midwest Gap analysis program image processing protocol. U.S. Department of the Interior, Geological Survey, Environmental Management Technical Center, Onalaska, Wisconsin, USA.

LIU, J., J. B. DUNNING, JR., AND H. R. PULLIAM. 1995. Potential effects of a forest management plan on Bachman's sparrows (*Aimophila aestivalis*): linking a spatially explicit model with GIS. Conservation Biology 9:62–75.

LLEWELLYN, D. W., G. P. SHAFFER, N. J. CRAIG, L. CREASMAN, D. PASHLEY, M. SWAN, AND C. BROWN. 1996. A decision-support system for prioritizing restoration sites on the Mississippi River alluvial plain. Conservation Biology 10:1446–1455.

LONGLEY, P., M. F. GOODCHILD, D. J. MAGUIRE, AND D. RHIND. 2001. Geographic information systems and science. John Wiley and Sons, London, England.

MACKEY, B. G., H. A. NIX, M. F. HUTCHINSON, J. P. MACMAHON, AND P. M. FLEMING. 1988. Assessing representativeness of places for conservation reservation and heritage listing. Environmental Management 12:501–514.

MACNALLY, R., A. F. BENNETT, G. W. BROWN, L. F. LUMSDEN, A. YEN, S. HINKLEY, P. LILLYWHITE, AND D. WARD. 2002. How well do ecosystem-based planning units represent different components of biodiversity? Ecological Applications 12:900–912.

MARCOT, B., K. MAYER, L. FOX, AND R. J. GUTIÉRREZ. 1981. Application of remote sensing to wildlife habitat inventory workshop. Wildlife Society Bulletin 9:328.

MARCOT, B. G., A. KUMAR, P. S. ROY, V. B. SAWARKAR, A. GUPTA, AND S. N. SANGAMA. 2002a. Towards a landscape conservation strategy: analysis of jhum landscape and proposed corridors for managing elephants in south Garo Hills District and Nokrek area, Meghalaya. The

Indian Forester February: 207–216.

———, W. McConnaha, P. Whitney, T. O'Neil, P. Paquet, L. Mobrand, G. Blair, L. Lestelle, K. Malone, and K. Jenkins. 2002*b*. A multi-species framework approach to the Columbia River Basin—Integrating fish, wildlife and ecological functions. CD-ROM, Northwest Power Planning Council. Portland, Oregon, USA.

Martischange, M. 1993. A technique for moving existing fish habitat data sets into the spatial environment of a vector geographic information system. U.S. Department of Agriculture, Forest Service, Fish Habitat Relationships Technical Bulletin 11, Riverside, California, USA.

Mayer, K. E. 1984. A review of selected remote sensing and computer technologies applied to wildlife habitat inventories. California Fish and Game 70: 101–112.

McComb, W. C., M. T. McGrath, T. A. Spies, and D. Vesely. 2002. Models for mapping potential habitat at landscape scales: an example using northern spotted owls. Forest Science 48: 203–216.

McDonnell, M. D., H. P. Possingham, I. R. Ball, and E. A. Cousins. 2002. Mathematical methods for spatially cohesive reserve design. Environmental Modeling and Assessment 7: 107–114.

Mead, R. A., T. Sharik, and J. T. Heinen. 1981. A computerized spatial analysis system for assessing wildlife habitat from vegetation maps. Canadian Journal of Remote Sensing 7: 34–40.

Merrill, S. B., and L. D. Mech. 2000. Details of extensive movements by Minnesota wolves (*Canis lupus*). American Midland Naturalist 144: 428–433.

Mladenoff, D. J., and T. A. Sickley. 1998. Assessing potential gray wolf restoration in the northeastern United States: a spatial prediction of favorable habitat and potential population levels. Journal of Wildlife Management 62: 1–10.

Nalle, D. J., J. L. Arthur, and J. Sessions. 2002. Designing compact and contiguous reserve networks with a hybrid heuristic algorithm. Forest Science 48: 59–68.

Naugle, D. E., J. A. Jenks, and B. J. Kernohan. 1996. Use of thermal infrared sensing to estimate density of white-tailed deer. Wildlife Society Bulletin 24: 37–43.

NCASI. 1996. The National Gap Analysis Program: ecological assumptions and sensitivity to uncertainty. Technical Bulletin 720. National Council of the Paper Industry for Air and Stream Improvement, Inc., Research Triangle Park, North Carolina, USA.

Nevo, A., and L. Garcia. 1996. Spatial optimization of wildlife habitat. Ecological Modelling 91: 271–281.

Office of Management and Budget. 2002. Coordination of geographic information and related spatial data activities. Circular A-16, Revised. Available online at http://www.whitehouse.gove/omb/circulars/a016/a016_rev.html (accessed 4 November 2004).

Öhman, K. 2000. Creating continuous area of old forest in long-term forest planning. Canadian Journal of Forest Research 30: 1817–1823.

———, and L. O. Eriksson. 1998. The core area concept in forming contiguous areas for long-term forest planning. Canadian Journal of Forest Research 28: 1032–1039.

O'Neil, T. A., and C. Barrett. 2001. Willamette Valley oak and pine habitat conservation project. Final Report. U.S. Department of the Interior, Bureau of Land Management, Eugene, Oregon, USA.

———, R. J. Steidl, W. D. Edge, and B. Csuti. 1995. Using wildlife communities to improve vegetation classification for conserving biodiversity. Conservation Biology 9: 1482–1491.

O'Neill, R. V. 1996. Recent developments in ecological theory: hierarchy and scale. Gap Analysis—a landscape approach to biodiversity planning. American Society for Photogrammetry and Remote Sensing, Bethesda, Maryland, USA.

Ormsby, J. P., and G. A. Soffen. 1989. Forward: special issue on the Earth Observing System (EOS). Institute of Electrical Electronics Engineers Transactions on Geoscience and Remote Sensing 27: 107–108.

Osborne, P. E., J. C. Alonso, and R. G. Bryant. 2001. Modelling landscape-scale habitat use using GIS and remote sensing: a case study with great bustards. Journal of Applied Ecology 38: 458–471.

Palmeirim, J. M. 1985. Use of Landsat imagery and spatial modeling in wildlife habitat mapping and evaluation. Dissertation. University of Kansas, Lawrence, USA.

Pearlstine, L. G., S. E. Smith, L. A. Brandt, C. R. Allen, W. M. Kitchens, and J. Stenberg. 2002. Assessing statewide biodiversity in the Florida Gap analysis project. Journal of Environmental Management 66: 127–144.

Pech, R. P., R. D. Graetz, and A. W. Davis. 1986. Reflectance modelling and the derivation of vegetation indices for an Australian semi-arid shrubland. International Journal of Remote Sensing 7: 389–403.

Pereira, J. M. C., and R. M. Itami. 1991. GIS-based habitat modeling using logistic multiple regression: a study of the Mt. Graham red squirrel. Photogrammetric Engineering and Remote Sensing 57: 1475–1486.

Peuquet, D., J. R. Davis, and S. Cuddy. 1993. Geographic information systems and environmental modeling. Pages 543–556 in A. J. Jakeman, M. B. Beck, and M. J. McAleer, editors. Modelling change in environmental systems. John Wiley and Sons, Sydney, Australia.

Pickup, G., and V. H. Chewings. 1988. Forecasting patterns of soil erosion in arid lands from Landsat MSS data. International Journal of Remote Sensing 9: 69–84.

Pollack, K. H., and W. L. Kendall. 1987. Visibility bias in aerial surveys: a review of estimation procedures. Journal of Wildlife Management 51: 502–510.

Powell, G. V. N., J. Barborak, and M. Rodriguez-S. 2000. Assessing representativeness of protected natural areas in Costa Rica for conserving biodiversity: a preliminary gap analysis. Biological Conservation 93: 35–41.

Prévost, Y. A., and P. Gilruth. 1997. Environmental information systems in sub-Saharan Africa. Towards environmentally sustainable development in sub-Saharan Africa—building blocks for Africa 2025. UNDP Post-UNCED Series Paper 12. The World Bank, Washington, D.C., USA.

Raphael, M. G., M. J. Wisdom, M. M. Rowland, R. S. Holthausen, B. C. Wales, B. G. Marcot, and T. D. Rich. 2001. Status and trends of habitats of terrestrial vertebrates in relation to land management in the Interior Columbia River Basin. Forest Ecology and Management 153: 63–87.

Remington, R., and G. Welsh. 1989. Surveying bighorn sheep. Pages 63–81 in R. M. Lee, editor. The desert bighorn sheep in Arizona. Arizona Game and Fish Department, Phoenix, USA.

Rempel, R. S., and A. R. Rodgers. 1997. Effects of differential correction on accuracy of a GPS animal location system. Journal of Wildlife Management 61: 525–530.

ReVelle, C. S., J. C. Williams, and J. J. Boland. 2002. Counterpart models in facility location science and reserve selection science. Environmental Modeling and Assessment 7: 71–80.

Richards, J. A. 1986. Remote sensing digital image analysis. Springer-Verlag, Inc., Berlin, Germany.

———. 1996. Classifier performance and map accuracy. Remote Sensing of Environment 57: 161–166.

———, and D. J. Kelly. 1984. On the concept of spectral class. International Journal of Remote Sensing 5: 987–991.

Rickel, B. W., B. Anderson, and R. Pope. 1998. Using fuzzy systems, object-oriented programming, and GIS to evaluate wildlife habitat. AI Applications 12: 31–40.

Rigaux, P., M. Scholl, and A. Voisard. 2001. Spatial databases: with application to GIS. Morgan Kaufmann, San Francisco, California, USA.

Rodgers, A. R., R. S. Rempel, R. Moen, J. Paczkowski, C. C. Schwartz, E. J. Lawson, and M. J. Gluck. 1997. GPS collars for moose telemetry studies: a workshop. Alces 33: 203–209.

Rosenfield, G. H., K. Fitzpatrick-Lins, and H. S. Ling. 1982. Sampling for thematic map accuracy testing. Photogrammetric Engineering and Remote Sensing 48: 131–137.

Rumble, M., and F. Lindzey. 1997. Effects of forest vegetation and topography on global positioning system collars for elk. Pages 492–501 in 1997 American Congress on Surveying and Mapping/ American Society for Photogrammetry and Remote Sensing Annual Convention and Exposition Technical Papers. Volume 4. Resource Technology Institute. Seattle, Washington, USA.

Sabol, B. M., and M. K. Hudson. 1995. Technique using thermal infrared imaging for estimating populations of gray bats. Journal of Mammalogy 76: 1242–1248.

SAMUEL, M. D., R. K. STEINSHORST, E. O. GARTON, AND J. W. UNSWORTH. 1992. Estimation of wildlife population ratios incorporating survey design and visibility bias. Journal of Wildlife Management 56: 718–725.

SCHOWENGERDT, R. A. 1983. Techniques for image processing and classification in remote sensing. Academic Press, Inc., New York, USA.

SCHROEDER, R. L., W. J. KING, AND J. E. CORNELY. 1998. Selecting habitat management strategies on refuges. U.S. Department of the Interior, Geological Survey, Biological Resources Division, Information and Technology Report USGS/BRD/ITR–1998–003. Fort Collins, Colorado, USA.

SCHUERHOLZ, G. 1974. Quantitative evaluation of edge from aerial photographs. Journal of Wildlife Management 38:913–920.

SCOTT, J. M., M. MURRAY, R. G. WRIGHT, B. CSUTI, P. MORGAN, AND R. L. PRESSEY. 2001. Representation of natural vegetation in protected areas: capturing the geographic range. Biodiversity and Conservation 10:1297–1301.

———, F. DAVIS, B. CSUTI, R. NOSS, B. BUTTERFIELD, C. GROVES, H. ANDERSON, S. CAICCO, F. D'ERCHIA, T. C. EDWARDS, JR., J. ULLIMAN, AND R. G. WRIGHT. 1993. GAP analysis: a geographic approach to protection of biological diversity. Wildlife Monographs 123.

SESSIONS, J. 1991. Solving for habitat connections as a Steiner network problem. Forest Science 38:203–207.

———, D. JOHNSON, J. ROSS, AND B. SHARER. 2000. The Blodgett Plan, an active management approach to developing mature forest habitat. Journal of Forestry 98(12):29–33.

SHIH, E. H. H., AND R. A. SCHOWENGERDT. 1983. Classification of arid geomorphic surfaces using Landsat spectral and textural features. Photogrammetric Engineering and Remote Sensing 49:337–347.

SIDEL, J. G., H. G. NAGEL, R. CLARK, C. GILBERT, D. STUART, K. WILLBURN, AND M. ORR. 1993. Aerial thermal infrared imaging of sandhill cranes on the Platte River, Nebraska. Remote Sensing of the Environment 43:333–341.

SIMMONS, N. M., AND C. G. HANSEN. 1980. Population survey methods. Pages 260–272 *in* G. Monson, and L. Sumner, editors. The desert bighorn sheep: its life history, ecology, and management. University of Arizona Press, Tucson, USA.

SINGH, A. 1989. Digital change detection techniques using remotely sensed data. International Journal of Remote Sensing 10:989–1003.

STEHMAN, S. V. 1999. Basic probability sampling designs for thematic map accuracy assessment. International Journal of Remote Sensing 20:2423–2441.

———. 2000. Practical implications of design-based sampling inference for thematic map accuracy assessment. Remote Sensing of Environment 72:35–45.

———. 2001. Statistical rigor and practical utility in thematic map accuracy assessment. Photogrammetric Engineering and Remote Sensing 67:727–734.

———, AND R. L. CZAPLEWSKI. 1998. Design and analysis for thematic map accuracy assessment: fundamental principles. Remote Sensing of Environment 64:331–344.

STOKLAND, J. N. 1997. Representativeness and efficiency of bird and insect conservation in Norwegian boreal forest reserves. Conservation Biology 11:101–111.

STORY, M., AND R. G. CONGALTON. 1986. Accuracy assessment: a user's perspective. Photogrammetric Engineering and Remote Sensing 52: 397–399.

STRAHLER, A. H., C. E. WOODCOCK, AND J. A. SMITH. 1986. On the nature of models in remote sensing. Remote Sensing of Environment 20:121–139.

STRONG, L. L., D. S. GILMER, AND J. A. BRASS. 1991. Inventory of wintering geese with a multispectral scanner. Journal of Wildlife Management 55:250–259.

SWAIN, P. H., AND S. M. DAVIS, editors. 1978. Remote sensing: the quantitative approach. McGraw-Hill Book Co., New York, USA.

THEOBALD, D. M. 2001. Topology revisited: representing spatial relations. International Journal of Geographic Information Science 15: 689–705.

THRELOFF, D. 1993. Using Global Positioning System (GPS) to map the distribution of the Cottonball Marsh pupfish. Pages 19–20 *in* D. A. Hendrickson, editor. Desert Fish Council Proceedings, Volume 25.

Monterrey, Nuevo Leon, Mexico.

TUCKER, C. J., H. E. DREGNE, AND W. N. NEWCOMB. 1991. Expansion and contraction of the Sahara Desert from 1980 to 1990. Science 253: 299–301.

TURNER, M. G., G. J. ARTHAUD, R. T. ENGSTROM, S. J. HEJL, J. LIU, S. LOEB, AND K. MCKELVEY. 1995. Usefulness of spatially explicit population models in land management. Ecological Applications 5: 12–16.

UNEP-GRID EUROPE. 2003. UNEP-GRID Division of Early Warning and Assessment, Europe/GRID Geneva website: http://www.grid .unep.ch/ (accessed 4 November 2004).

UNEP-GRID NORTH AMERICA. 2003. UNEP-GRID Division of Early Warning and Assessment—North America web site: http://grid2 .cr.usgs.gov/ (accessed 4 November 2004).

UNEP-WCMC. 2003. UNEP-WCMC website: http://www.unep-wcmc .org/ (accessed 4 November 2004).

VAN GENDEREN, J. L. 1991. Guidelines for education and training in environmental information systems in sub-Saharan Africa: some key issues. Guidelines Series 2. International Advisory Committee, The World Bank, Washington, D.C., USA.

———, B. F. LOCK, AND P. A. VASS. 1978. Remote sensing: statistical testing of thematic map accuracy. Remote Sensing of Environment 7: 3–14.

WADDLE, T., K. BOVEE, AND Z. BOWEN. 1997. Two-dimensional habitat modeling in the Yellowstone/Upper Missouri River System. North American Lake Management Society Meeting, Houston, Texas, USA. Available online at http://smig.usgs.gov/SMIG/features_0398/ habitat.html (accessed 4 November 2004).

WALLER, J., AND C. SERVHEEN. 1999. Documenting grizzly bear highway crossing patterns using GPS technology. Pages 21–24 *in* Proceedings of Third International Conference on Wildlife Ecology and Transportation. Missoula, Montana, USA.

WEBER, T., AND J. WOLF. 2000. Maryland's green infrastructure—using landscape assessment tools to identify a regional conservation strategy. Environmental Monitoring and Assessment 63:265–277.

WIEGAND, C. L., A. J. RICHARDSON, R. D. JACKSON, P. J. PINTER, JR., J. K. AASE, D. E. SMIKA, L. F. LAUTENSCHLAGER, AND J.E. MCMURTREY, III. 1986. Development of agrometeorological crop model inputs from remotely sensed information. Institute of Electrical Electronics Engineers Transactions on Geoscience and Remote Sensing 24:90–98.

WIGGERS, E. P., AND S. F. BECKERMAN. 1993. Use of thermal infrared sensing to survey white-tailed deer populations. Wildlife Society Bulletin 21:263–268.

WILLIAMS, J. C. 1998. Delineating protected wildlife corridors with multi-objective programming. Environmental Modeling and Assessment 3:77–86.

WILLIAMS, P. H., N. D. BURGESS, AND C. RAHBEK. 2000. Flagship species, ecological complementarity and conserving the diversity of mammals and birds in sub-Saharan Africa. Animal Conservation 3: 249–260.

WOODCOCK, C. E. 1996. On roles and goals for map accuracy assessment: a remote sensing perspective. Pages 535–540 *in* T. H. Mowrer, R. L. Czaplewski, and R. H. Hamre, editors. Spatial accuracy assessment in natural resources and environmental sciences: second international symposium. U.S. Department of Agriculture, Forest Service, General Technical Report RM-GTR-277.

———, S. GOPAL, AND W. ALBERT. 1996. Evaluation of the potential for providing secondary labels in vegetation maps. Photogrammetric Engineering and Remote Sensing 62:393–399.

WORK, JR., E. A., AND D. S. GILMER. 1976. Utilization of satellite data for inventorying prairie ponds and lakes. Photogrammetric Engineering and Remote Sensing 42:685–694.

WORLD BANK. 1995. Implementing geographic information systems in environmental assessment. Environmental Assessment Sourcebook Update 9. The World Bank, Washington, D.C., USA.

WRIGHT, R. G., AND P. D. TANIMOTO. 1998. Using GIS to prioritize land conservation actions: integrating factors of habitat diversity, land ownership, and development risk. Natural Areas Journal 18:38–44.

WYATT, C. L., M. M. TRIVEDI, D. R. ANDERSON, AND M. C. PATE. 1985. Measurement techniques for spectral characterization for remote sensing. Photogrammetric Engineering and Remote Sensing 51:245–251.

16

RADAR TECHNIQUES FOR WILDLIFE BIOLOGY

Ronald P. Larkin

INTRODUCTION

During the Second World War English ornithologists found the new secret weapon known as RADAR (RAdio Detection And Ranging) was receiving echoes from gannets (*Sula* spp.) and other birds while looking for ships and aircraft (Lack and Varley 1945). They noted that birds gave rise to "several [torpedo boat] scares and at least one invasion alarm" and "getting visual confirmation of the source of the echo" was difficult. These pioneers immediately recognized that radar was a powerful tool for monitoring and studying movements of flying animals–providing one could interpret the radar information. These themes will reverberate throughout this introduction to radar as a tool in wildlife conservation and ecology.

Radar is distinct from radiotracking and aerial and satellite remote sensing. Radar operates in a different band of the electromagnetic spectrum and mostly relies on different physical principles. Radiotracking involves placing an active (powered) electronic device on an animal and then locating the signal from that device by direction finding or other means. Remote sensing in wildlife biology usually involves visual or infrared data obtained passively from satellites or high-flying aircraft. Radar directs a high-energy beam that is reflected back from objects, in this case flying animals (Eastwood 1967, Vaughn 1985, Bruderer 1997). Flying animals need no electronics mounted on them as their bodies reflect the radar beam. Further, the subjects almost certainly do not know they are being observed (Bruderer et al. 1999).

Using radar, wildlife biologists can observe birds and bats flying above vegetation but not within or near it, especially vegetation being moved by the wind. However, small tripod-mounted radars are used routinely by the military to detect moving soldiers on the ground. Radar can observe animals on extended flat surfaces such as runways or the surface of calm water (Radford et al. 1994). Most large radars have the power and sensitivity to detect birds at great distances when the birds are in the open and can be reached by the radar beam. However, the largest radars are limited in distance they can observe flying animals, especially those flying at low height above ground level (AGL). Failure to detect low-flying animals usually happens because the earth curves from under the radar beam (Fig. 1) or topography prevents a clear view of the animals.

A radar display does not reveal which animal produces a radar echo and, without specialized research to relate animals to echoes (ground truth), radar does not directly allow a wildlife scientist or manager to know how many animals are responsible for an echo. These limitations can be frustrating. However, radar allows following animals through the blackest night (Fig. 1), inside clouds (Griffin 1973, Larkin and Frase 1988), and occasionally at great distances contributing to knowledge of animal movements (Alerstam 1996). Further, the technology is becoming more available. As of mid-2003, one can download radar images of much of the continental United States from the Internet about every 5 to 10 minutes. Computer storage to do this continuously costs about $200 a year and the data are free or available at negligible cost. The technology has enormous potential for use—and misuse.

Meteorologists, aviation agencies, maritime users, and the military operate radars useful for observing wildlife. Those who want to observe wildlife with radar are encouraged to try it. One should not necessarily believe radar operators who may have been taught that birds or bats cannot be "detected" with their equipment. For instance, some time ago the director of a sophisticated radar installation looked over the shoulder of an ecologist sitting at a console of the installation's best radar. "Oh, yes," he remarked, looking at the radar echoes filling the large screen, "atmospheric inhomogeneities." Several days later, after the ecologists had shown him "atmospheric inhomogeneities" flapping their wings on radar displays and zooming past the radar considerably faster than the wind, the director quietly admitted that yes, they might be birds. Most radar biologists can relate similar stories.

RADAR 101

This discussion assumes the radar uses the same antenna to send (transmit) the radar signal and sense (receive) the returning echo and that the radar works in the microwave region. The reader is referred to standard texts for further details (Eastwood 1967, Woolcock 1985, Levanon 1988, Skolnik 1990).

How much radar echo a bird or bat produces is a ratio in The Radar Equation (Box 1). Knowledge of the Radar Equation is useful to understand radar and to converse with engineers. In considering the Radar Equation, P_r is the loudness of the echo; larger values of P_r give more intense dots or brighter colors on a radar display. In simple radar, P_r below the radar's threshold sensitivity is indistinguishable from noise. Technically, echo or "radar return" is back-scattered radiation. P_t is roughly the loudness of a person's shout and is usually constant for any given radar. G is the gain, a dimensionless ratio usually stated in decibels (dB, a logarithmic measure calculated as $10 \times \log$ [ratio]). When you cup your hand behind your ear to hear a faint sound, you experience an increase in loudness of the sound, or gain. Positive gain occurs only forward (directivity). Large radar antennas can produce gains in excess of 40 dB (10^4 or 10,000 times). The gain of a microwave antenna is proportional to its frontal area. Microwaves, like light, are usually described by wavelength (λ), or distance between successive troughs (or crests) in a traveling wave. Wave length is as important for radar as transmitter frequency is for radiotracking and color for visual observation. Radar wave lengths include X-band (North Atlantic Treaty Organization, [NATO] designation I band, about 3 cm), C-band (NATO designation G and H, about 5 cm) and S-band (NATO designation E and F, about 10 cm). L-band, used in aircraft surveillance, is longer than S-band. K-band (NATO designation J and K) is shorter than X-band and is becoming quite widely used in applications such as automotive radar. Most radar used with wildlife operates at a single wave length. One can tell which band radar uses from the size of its wave guide, the metal tubing or "plumbing" that is used in place of wire for conducting microwave energy (Fig. 2).

Radar wave lengths are in the same size range as body parts of bats, birds, and even large insects. In this size region, microwaves wrap around objects and otherwise interact with them in a complex fashion. Thus, the amount of echo from even a simple object such as a sphere is not proportional to its size (Fig. 3). Unfortunately, except for small animals observed at long wave length and large ones observed at short wave length, birds and bats mostly lie in the non-monotonic middle region (Fig. 3). This implication is profound, as physically larger animals do not necessarily generate stronger echoes. For instance, body parts of size $\lambda/2$ will resonate on radar, producing intense echoes.

Effective target area (σ) on radar differs for different wave lengths (Fig. 3). The left end of the curve represents small insects and becomes linear as it extends down to include rain-

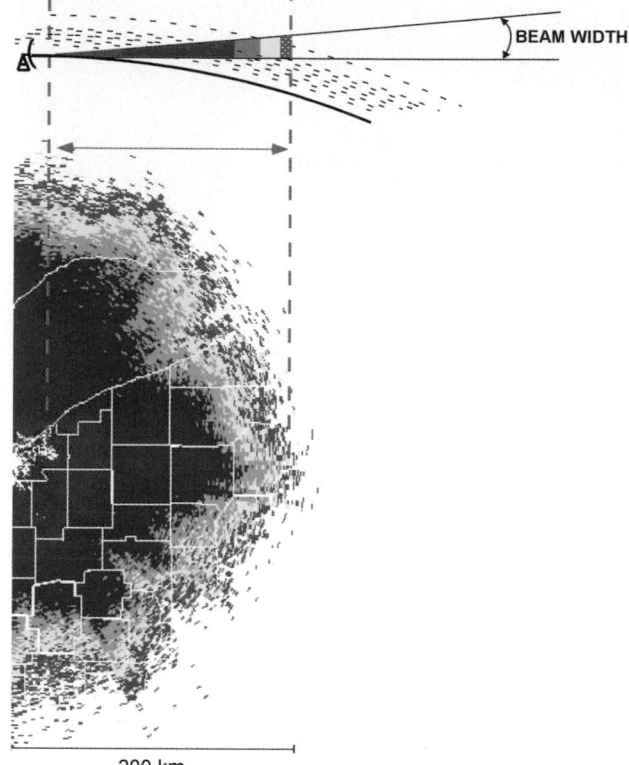

200 km

Fig. 1. Top. The radar beam illuminates migrating birds (and almost certainly some insects and bats), then at greater range it passes completely over the layer of animals. Brighter shades represent stronger echoes. Bottom. East half of a map display of the WSR-88D KCLE radar at 2358 local time. At intermediate ranges an uninterrupted flow of birds passes southward over southern Ontario, Canada, and Lake Erie, northern Ohio, USA. At the periphery the beam encounters only the highest birds and therefore the radar registers weaker echoes.

drops, cloud droplets, and dust. The middle region, where the amount of radar echo is not directly proportional to target size, represents most bats and birds. The right end of the curve lies near the mass of a goose. Wildlife appears on radar like skin-enclosed water, which is 0.56 as reflective as metal (Eastwood 1967). Engineers conclude that poorly conducting tissues such as feathers and chitin are essentially transparent to radar (Edwards and Houghton 1959). Radars can-

---

Box 1. The Radar Equation.

$$P_r = \frac{P_t \times G^2 \times \lambda^2 \times \sigma}{(4 \times \pi)^3 \times R^4},$$

where

P_r (W) = received power from the echo,
P_t (W) = radar transmitted power,
G = antenna gain, or amplification,
λ (m) = wave length of the radar,
σ (m^2) = radar cross section (RCS), and
R (m) = range (straight-line distance) to the target.

Units are: m = meters, W = Watts.

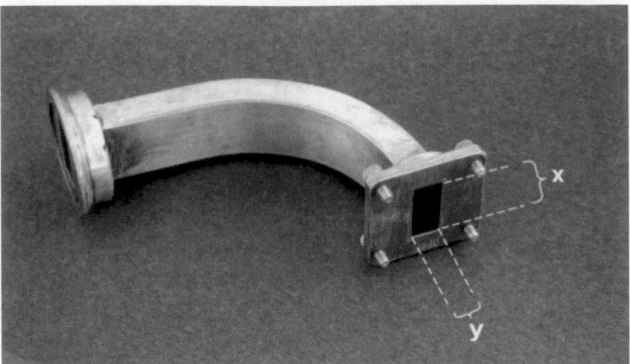

Fig. 2. A piece of rectangular waveguide. Microwave energy travels on the inside surface of the tube, which is machined to tight specifications and must be smooth, clean, and dry. Usually 0.9 wave lengths>X>0.6 wave lengths, and Y=0.5X.

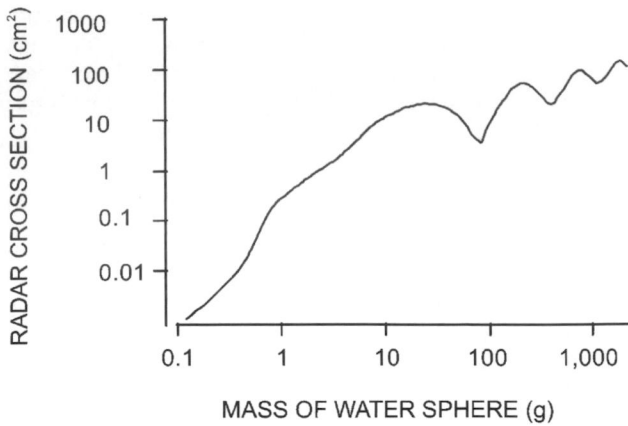

Fig. 3. The nonlinear relationship between apparent size of a target on radar (vertical axis) and actual mass (or volume) of the target, at 10 cm wave length (S-band) (redrawn from Vaughn 1985).

not measure absolute target area of wildlife with great accuracy because even in carefully controlled test facilities, moving targets vary by ~ 2 dB or 60% (Dybdal 1987).

Range (R) is distance to a target and part of the acronym RADAR where an echo arrives after a certain delay. Pulsed radars measure slant range by timing the delay, a constant value near 150 m μs^{-1}. Because energy spreads in 2 dimensions as it travels from the radar to a flying animal and again in 2 dimensions as it travels back from the animal to the radar, the received radar echo is proportional to the inverse 4th power of range. The maximum range at which an animal of a certain size can be detected is:

$$R_{\max} = \left[\frac{P_t G^2 \lambda^2 \sigma}{(4\pi)^3 P_{r,\min}} \right]^{1/4}.$$

This short introduction to the Radar Equation provides a great deal of information. For instance, consider designing radar for observing flying animals over a wide area. Most targets will be at a great distance, R, where the returning echo will be weak. Noting the strong influence of the inverse 4th power of range, we see that several variables have linear effects and, therefore, cannot make much difference. For instance, from the Radar Equation, a more sensitive receiver (able to detect fainter echoes of P_r) will not provide much greater range, nor will size of birds or bats that we want to observe (σ) make much difference. The key is the nonlinear term G^2, antenna gain, in the numerator of the Radar Equation. Antenna gain is itself proportional to (antenna diameter^2); therefore, diameter^4 can compensate for $R^{1/4}$. A large antenna is necessary to work at long ranges. In addition, if the wildlife biologist wishes to be sure to observe subjects through rain or snow or to minimize confusing echoes from clouds of flying insects, it will help to use longer wave lengths to ensure interfering echoes are at the left edge of Fig. 3. A longer wave length will also provide more range directly. A large metal antenna for long wave lengths with motors and apparatus to direct it is expensive, comprising up to 40% of the radar's cost. The expense of large radar may be daunting considering most wildlife budgets. In that case, leasing appropriate radar equipment or using already-existing radar are alternatives to purchase. Working with existing radars, wildlife biologists can learn how to obtain data from local aviation, weather, maritime, or military radar. Thus, they can invest time in understanding the format of available data rather than building radar and designing a format.

ANTENNAS AND SCANNING

A radar antenna's main lobe, or "beam" (Fig. 4) points at targets and its direction, along with range, gives their location. Direction is expressed in polar coordinates familiar to foresters and others (Fig. 5). Returning echoes from birds, bats, and other objects take the reverse path and the antenna concentrates received echoes the same way it concentrates transmitted microwave energy. Large antennas may have beams as narrow as 1°.

Side lobes are weaker concentrations of energy that are, to some extent, symmetrical about the main lobe (Fig. 4). All directional antennas have side lobes and they make a difference. For instance, an X-band radar for field work (Bluestein and Pazmany 2000) has side lobes 22 dB (159 x) weaker than the main lobe. Using the R^4 relationship, $10^{2.2/4}$ is a factor of 3.5 and corresponds to a range difference of 30%. If the antenna is pointing at a bird, another bird of similar size illuminated by a side lobe in a different (deceptive) direction will appear equally prominent on the radar display if it is as close as 0.3 R.

Spillover radiation includes any energy that escapes past the edge of the antenna (Fig. 4). Like side lobes, spillover radiation produces spurious echoes from the ground, structures, and vegetation (ground clutter) in directions different from the main lobe.

Only a few radar beam shapes, such as conical beams to permit spatial precision, are commonly used in wildlife biology (Fig. 6). Many radars used in meteorology (Fig. 1) have a narrow, conical "pencil beam" to provide height information (e.g., on storms). Large radar of this type can operate at great range but its resolution is coarse even though its beam might be narrow (Wurman et al. 1997). For instance, a 1° beam is 1 km across at a range of ~60 km. This type of radar must rotate several times with its antenna at different elevations (a volume scan) to achieve coverage of different heights. Smaller, specialized ornithological research radars use conical beams to obtain

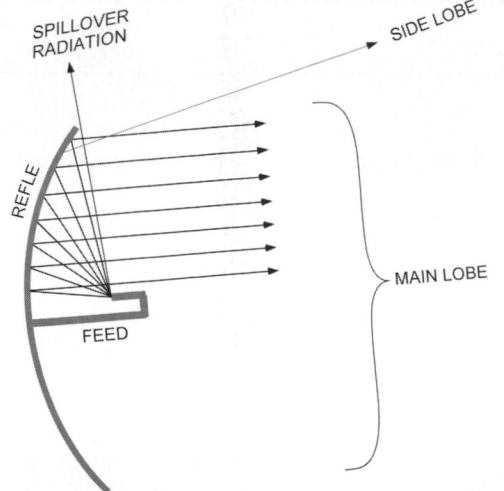

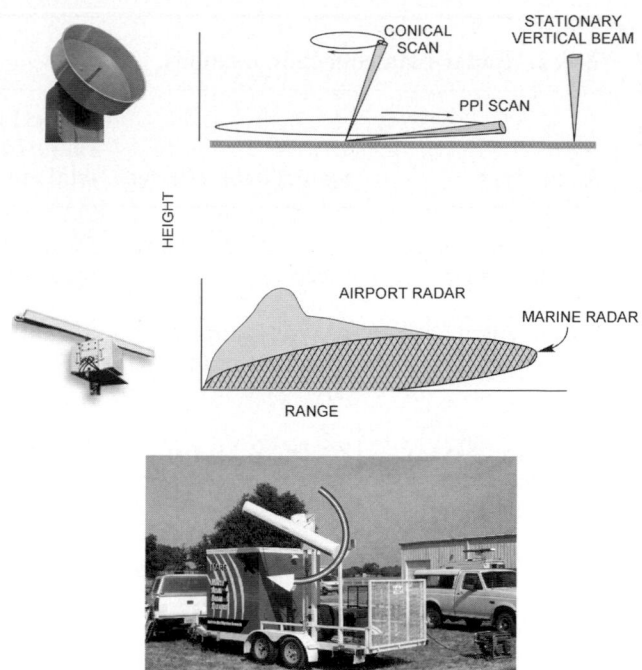

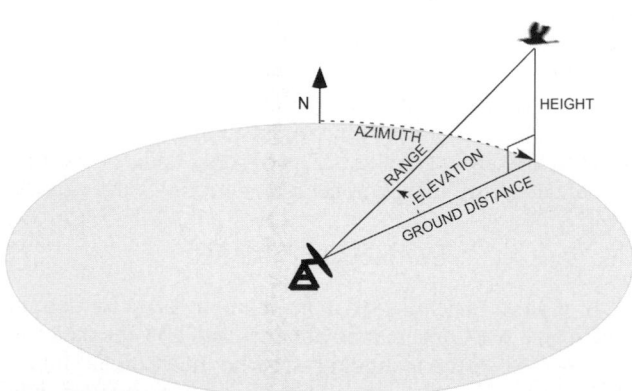

Fig. 4. Top. The 3 principal concentrations of energy in a reflector antenna. Microwave energy emerges from the feed, which directs it toward a solid or mesh reflector, in this case a parabolic reflector. Bottom. A parabolic reflector antenna with a radar fence constructed of 3.04-m (10 ft.) lengths of corrugated sheet metal.

information on animals at specific heights, often even single flocks and individual animals (Larkin 1982, Cooper et al. 1991, Bruderer et al. 1995).

Surveillance radar is any radar designed to scan a wide geographical area repeatedly, usually in the horizontal plane. Some surveillance radars use a beam that is narrow (often 1–2°) in azimuth but broad in elevation (Fig. 6); marine radar beams are shaped this way to detect objects on the surface

Fig. 6. Top. A narrow conical beam ("pencil beam") produced by a small feed evenly illuminating the surface of a paraboloid. The antenna swivels in azimuth and tilts in elevation. A short cylindrical cuff partly shields the paraboloid from ground clutter. Middle. A view of beams narrow in azimuth but wide in elevation. The hatched pattern is produced by a slotted wave-guide antenna typical of marine radars (photo shown) and the additional shaded region at high elevation is typical of airport surveillance radars (not shown). Bottom. A marine radar modified to perform a vertical scan (arrow).

even while the radar platform is pitching and rolling (Williams 1984). These radars provide almost no information on height of flying animals. Animals near the edges of the beam are partially illuminated and the size of the echo they produce depends on their exact position in the beam. Paths of observed targets flying at high elevation on these radars are distorted (Cohen and Williams 1980). The antennas are usually swiveled (rotated in azimuth) through 360° but, in wildlife biology, can be held stationary across the anticipated bird or bat traffic (Fig. 7). Radars designed to find or follow aircraft have even broader beams in elevation to obtain information on fast-moving targets at various heights (Fig. 6).

A conical scanning radar antenna may or may not have a conical beam and rotates in azimuth while elevation is held constant (Fig. 6). A nearly horizontal conical scan generates a Plan Position Indicator (PPI) display that is projected onto the earth as a map (Fig. 1, bottom). This is the

Fig. 5. The polar coordinate system used by radars consists of azimuth (angle from north), elevation (angle up from horizontal), and slant range.

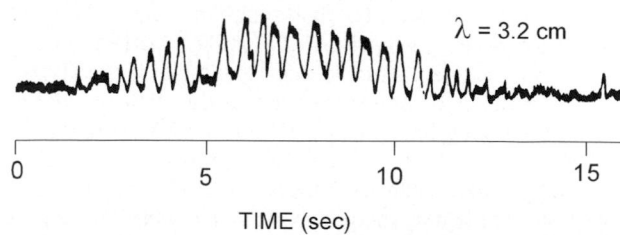

Fig. 7. Echo strength from a single flying animal passing through the beam of a vertically pointed pencil-beam radar. Overall echo strength increases as the target comes into the beam, peaks as it flies through the beam's center, and decreases again as it exits (adapted from Atlas 1965).

Box 2. Radar data collection methods.

Radar type	Spatial data collected	Typical maximum range in a terrestrial environment	Spatial resolution	Normal application
S Band marine surveillance radar	X-Y[a], T[b], M[c], track, speed	30 km @ 30kW peak power	Moderate	Measuring track, behavior, and habitat use
X Band marine surveillance radar	X-Y, T, M, track, speed, estimate of target size	5.5 km @ 25kW peak power	High	Measuring track, behavior, and habitat use
X Band vertical beam modified marine radar	Z[d], D[e], T, M, estimate of target size	2.4 km @ 25kW peak power	High	Measuring height and wing beats at one location
X Band conical scan modified marine radar	Z, D, T, M, heading, speed, estimate of target size	2.4 km @ 25kW peak power	High	Measuring height and track at one location
Vertical scan modified marine radar	X-Y, Z, D, T, M, estimate of target size	2.4 km @ 25kW peak power	High	Measuring height and rate of passage across a line
Tracking radar	X-Y, Z, T, M, accurate estimate of target size, heading derived from x, y, and z	1.5 km @ 40 kW peak power (X-band) to 80 km @ 5 MW (S-band)	High, approaching 1 m precision	Measuring track details, wing beats, rate of climb, and impacts of stimuli
Police or anti-personnel radar	Radial speed and Doppler spectra	<< 1 km	NA	Measuring speed and wing beats
Doppler "weather" radar (e.g., NEXRAD [WSR 88-D])	X-Y, T, M, reflectivity used to estimate aggregate target size, velocity used to derive track	230 km	Low - 1 km	Measuring track and habitat use, measuring heading if uniform

[a] X-Y = Coordinates over the ground.
[b] T = Time observation made.
[c] M = Metadata, additional observations such as location, environmental conditions at the time of the observation.
[d] Z = Height.
[e] D = Density, number of birds in a volume of airspace.

display shown in weather forecasts with stronger targets coded as more intense spots or brighter colors. A PPI scan performed like a windshield wiper (<360°) is called a sector scan. At times, a conical beam is held stationary and animals are counted as they fly through the beam (Crawford 1949, Larkin 1982, Korschgen et al. 1984, Smith and Riley 1996). Specially constructed radar that looks vertically and spins rapidly in azimuth provided useful data on insects with simple wing beat patterns (Riley and Reynolds 1979).

Biologists may use conical-beam radars in conjunction with surveillance radars (Cooper et al. 1991). Some radars have a stacked-beam arrangement in which several stationary narrow beams are arrayed vertically to provide height information as the array is swiveled in azimuth. Vertically scanning radars (Fig. 6, bottom) intercept animals crossing the plane of elevation through which they scan. Radar antennas are designed to scan sufficiently slowly to receive multiple echoes from each target, reducing the effects of many kinds of noise and clutter, yet sufficiently fast to provide information that is timely. Similarly, long pulses give stronger echoes whereas short pulses give greater detail in range. In wildlife biology, advantages of rapid data updates and fine spatial detail may outweigh need for detecting weak echoes.

TYPES OF RADAR

A wildlife scientist or manager new to radar should understand what data can be obtained and how the data can be collected so the technology can be incorporated into a study design. In this section, types of radars, the data they can collect, and their limitations (Box 2) (Richardson 1979, Kelly 2000) are reviewed.

Marine Radar

Marine radars on boats and ocean vessels track other vessels, detect weather and, in the fishing industry, locate birds feeding on large schools of fish. Marine radar can be used to record the horizontal tracks of birds as they move through an area, including their size, speed, track, and position. These radars can precisely register the shape of large flocks of birds (Williams et al. 1976) and can be mounted to point upward to measure height, size, and numbers of flying animals passing overhead.

Marine radar has become the most common type used to detect bird targets. These radars are available from marine suppliers, relatively inexpensive and, most importantly, are reliable and built to operate in the punishing marine environment.

Although marine radars can detect vertebrates straight "out of the box," some may not have the best characteristics for vertebrate data collection. This has led radar ornithologists to modify marine radars to better suit their needs. A factory-made slotted waveguide antenna for marine radars has a horizontally narrow (~1–2°) and vertically wide (20–30°) beam for operation on a vessel that is pitching and rolling (Fig. 6). The 20–30° vertical beam can be undesirable for bird detection. Greater beam width dissipates the power of radar over a larger volume reducing the range at which an object can be detected. This limitation can be partly overcome by using a more powerful transmitter or, more effectively, by replacing the slotted antenna with a parabolic dish antenna having a narrow beam (2–4°). Suitable parabolic antennas with appropriate waveguides can be found as military surplus items.

The other limitation of most marine radar slotted-waveguide antennas, as they come from the manufacturer, is their prominent side lobes. Side lobes are insignificant at sea where the radar gain is usually set low because it is unlikely that another ship will be immediately adjacent to the radar. However, on land, side lobes can detect the ground, trees, buildings, vehicles, and even people. Stationary objects create echoes that do not move from scan to scan, whereas moving targets create echoes that appear and disappear. When side lobes are reflected, the resulting multipath signal can appear on the radar display at an incorrect range, reducing the useful area of the radar display.

Side lobe echoes can be reduced by careful antenna design; however, the cost of a custom built antenna is prohibitive for most wildlife studies. To reduce both side lobes and ground clutter in a terrestrial environment, radar ornithologists elevate the antenna or shield it with radar absorbing or reflecting materials such as aluminum, radar-absorbing foam, radar fences (Fig. 4, bottom), and earth berms.

Level marine radar directs some of its beam below the horizontal to illuminate the horizon when a ship pitches and rolls in high seas. For a land-based radar, this wasted power generates ground clutter, produces multipath echoes, and exacerbates the problems of side lobes. One can rotate the antenna in elevation by attaching a bracket that pushes the front mount of the antenna up by the number of degrees required to place the lower edge of the radar beam parallel to the horizon. However, many marine types of radar are built with rigid metal waveguides that cannot twist. Replacing a portion of the rigid waveguide (Fig. 2) with a compatible length of flexible waveguide solves this problem.

Marine radar is a cost effective, reliable solution that has proven to be adaptable to many survey techniques. Its compactness permits flexibility and allows mounting radar on an extensible boom (Cooper and Blaha 2002). It has been modified to be pencil beam radar, conical scanning radar, or vertical scanning radar. The key is to select a scanning technique that fits the data to be collected.

Doppler "Weather" Radar

Doppler radar usually refers to large weather radars but this name is restrictive because they are also excellent wildlife radars. Older surveillance weather radars that do not use the Doppler principle are being phased out. Doppler weather radars sharply contrast with modified marine radar for use in ornithology (Gauthreaux and Belser 1998, Koistinen 2000). They have lower spatial resolution, significantly higher power, longer range, and highly sensitive receivers at a fixed location but are also expensive. Fortunately data from existing radars can be obtained easily and cheaply.

The real power of a Doppler unit over non-Doppler radar is the additional data it produces from measuring the Doppler shift produced by targets. Current Doppler radars generally produce 3 basic data types: reflectivity, radial velocity, and spectral width. Reflectivity is a measure of the amount of energy returned to the radar by a target (P_r). Brighter colors represent more echo (Figs. 1, 8) while ground clutter produces intense echoes at the center (white and mauve) (Fig. 1).

Radial velocity is a measure of target motion toward or away from the radar and velocity is used synonymously with speed. When a target moves tangential to the radar, the Doppler shift and radial velocity decrease to zero (Fig. 9). Spectral width is a measure of variation in radial velocity during the radar's brief sampling period. Although little used by meteorologists, spectral width is useful for biological targets (Larkin and Diehl 2003). Doppler velocity and spectral width data are available to 230-km range on WSR-88D radars.

Data networks exist to deliver meteorological data, including radar data. The primary source of weather radar data in the United States is the national network of NEXRAD radars (for NEXt generation weather RADar) (Diehl and Larkin in press), but data are also becoming available from Terminal Doppler Weather Radars (TDWR) and privately-owned weather radars. It might also be possible for research and academic institutions to access data from experimental and research radars.

The NEXRAD radar system is composed of WSR-88D radars (Weather Service Radar), which store user data in 2 formats (Crum et al. 1993). The simplest and most commonly available data format is Level III Cartesian, which has 16 data levels. This gives a dynamic range of 56 or 75 dB, much less than that of the radar. To overcome this limitation the data presently are available in clear air mode and precipitation mode. In clear air mode, 16 data levels measure reflectivity on an ascending scale from the lowest detectable signal (–28 dBz, a measure of signal strength used in meteorology). In precipitation mode, the 16 data levels measure from the highest detectable signal (75 dBZ) down. The 2 data modes overlap between 0 and 28 dBZ. The more comprehensive NEXRAD data format is Level II archive data, which fully encodes the data in 0.5 dB increments resulting in much larger files.

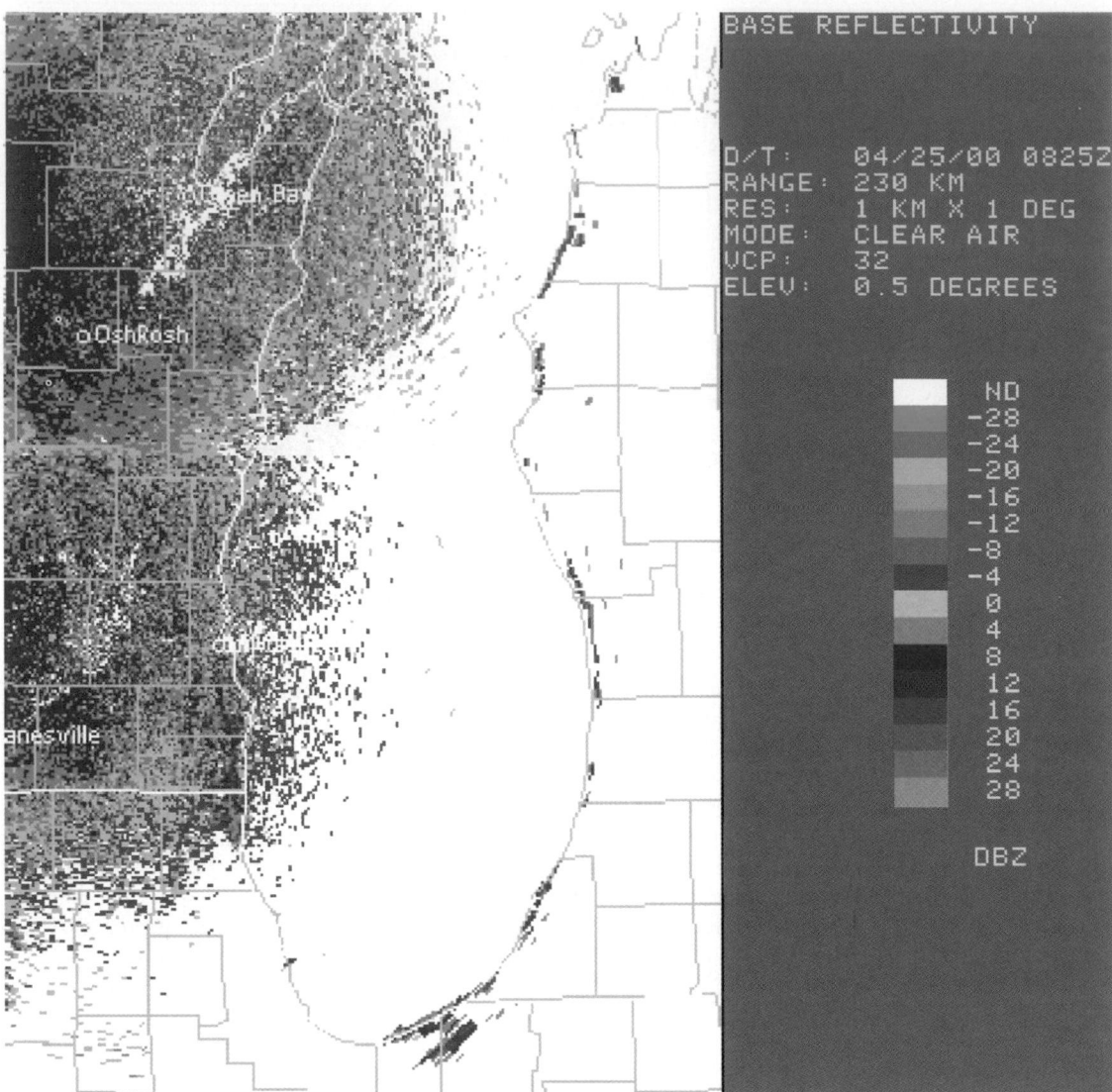

Fig. 8. WSR-88D radars at Green Bay and west of Milwaukee, Wisconsin, USA, present clear images of low cliffs on the east shore of Lake Michigan 200 km away. These have zero Doppler velocity, confirming they are on the ground rather than in the air. In a "normal" atmosphere without ducting, the height of the bottom of the radar beam would exceed 3 km AGL at such ranges.

Several kinds of special artifacts are included with the greater amount of information and wider spatial coverage available from large Doppler radars. The details of Doppler images are beyond the scope of this chapter but users should be familiar with second-trip echoes, false "wrapped" velocities, malfunctioning automated attempts to unwrap velocities, and other situations discussed later in this chapter (see also Rinehart 1991, Doviak and Zrnic 1993, Diehl and Larkin in press). Radars in the NEXRAD system (WSR-88D radars) presently reject point targets such as individual soaring turkey vultures (*Cathartes aura*), a widespread, significant low-level hazard to aviation (Defusco 1995).

Airport Surveillance Radar (ASR)

Aircraft are routinely detected with large, often fast-rotating S- or L-band radars with beams that are broad in elevation (Fig. 6, bottom). Many older but capable and high-power ASRs are still in service and can detect flying animals, especially larger birds (Nisbet 1963, Gauthreaux 1974, Alfiya 1995). Some newer, lower-power ASRs are specialized for following aircraft equipped with transponders that actively transmit microwave pulses; consequently, they may lack the sensitivity to be of use for studying wildlife beyond the immediate airport environs. Airport surveillance radars can be so specialized for large aircraft that they have circuitry to block smaller targets such as small numbers of birds. Lack of height information is also a problem with these radars; one study astutely circumvented that limitation by comparing data from a sea level ASR radar and another nearby ASR radar placed 1,200 m higher (Williams et al. 1986).

Tracking Radar

Military surplus tracking radars can track a single bird target or flock and map its trajectory (Griffin 1973, Able 1977, Larkin 1978, Bruderer 1994, Bruderer et al. 1995, Liechti and Bruderer 1995). These radars can be useful to understand flight dynamics of birds and have been fitted with telephoto cameras. A powerful missile-tracking radar followed single birds at a range of more than 80 km (Williams et al. 1972). Although a continuous signal

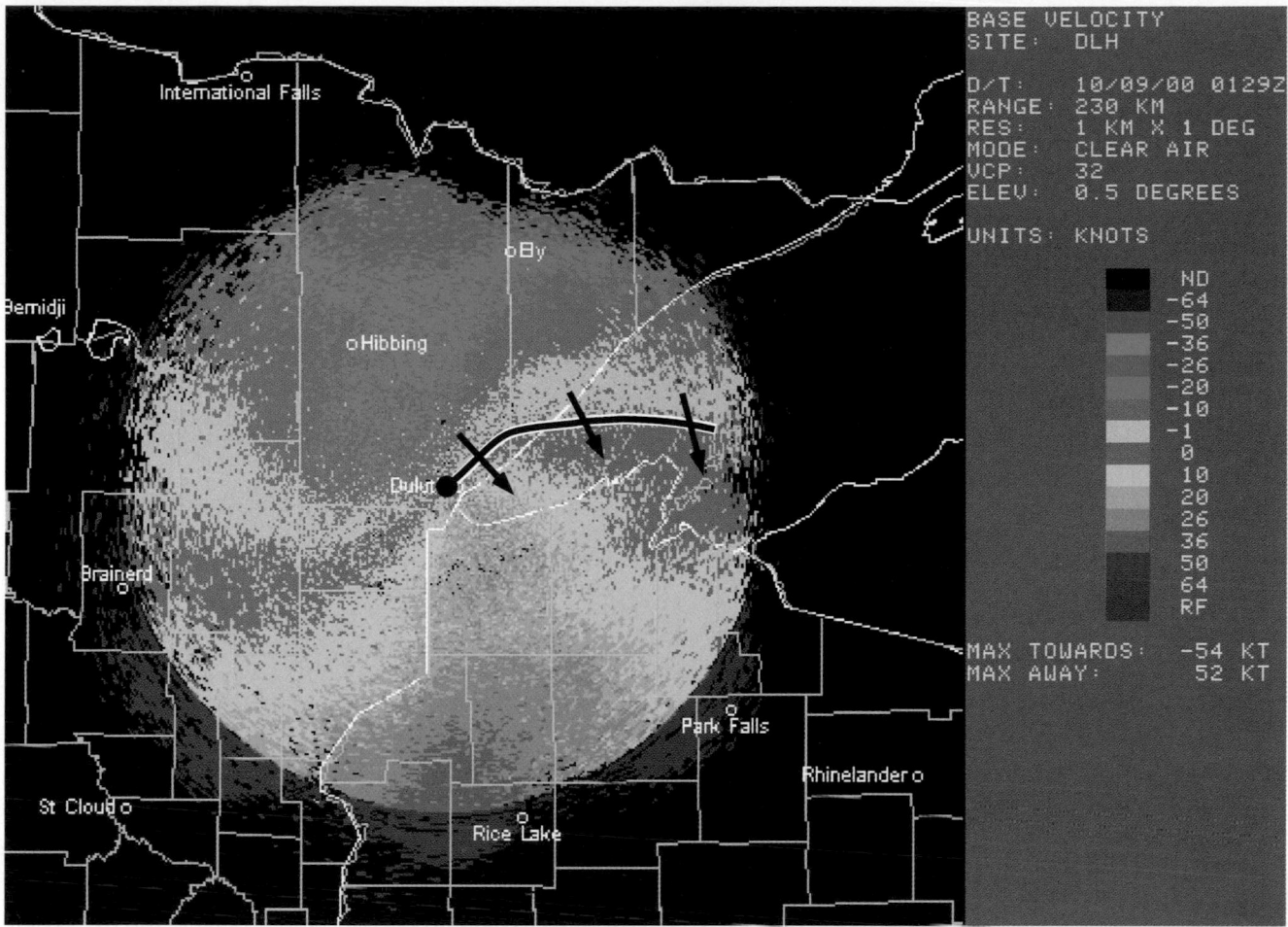

BASE VELOCITY
SITE: DLH

D/T: 10/09/00 0129Z
RANGE: 230 KM
RES: 1 KM X 1 DEG
MODE: CLEAR AIR
VCP: 32
ELEV: 0.5 DEGREES

UNITS: KNOTS

ND
-64
-50
-36
-26
-20
-10
-1
0
10
20
26
36
50
64
RF

MAX TOWARDS: -54 KT
MAX AWAY: 52 KT

Fig. 9. A target moving tangential to the radar has a Doppler shift and radial velocity of zero. In this typical fall night time Doppler image of migrants from the Duluth, Minnesota WSR-88D, echoes with negative velocities (green) approach the radar, positive velocities (red) recede, and a zero velocity line is perpendicular to the direction of travel of migrants at each range on either side of the radar. Birds at farther ranges are higher and flying more clockwise.

showing target size is available from the automatic gain control signal of many tracking radars, that signal is usually poorly suited to quantitative analysis of wildlife wing beats (Schaefer 1968).

Military radars are designed to be robust and some fit into artillery shells. However, they are state-of-the-art designs and often produced in small quantity. Thus, their anticipated reliability might or might not match their actual performance in the field. Capable military radars are expected to appear on the used equipment market in the next decade.

Other Types of Radar

Police (traffic) and military antipersonnel radar use Doppler to detect moving targets in a cluttered environment but provide no information on target range because they send and receive a fixed-frequency continuous rather than a pulsed signal. Provided that wind speed and direction are measured accurately, measurement of speeds of birds with police radars can be converted into flight speeds and energetic estimates (Schnell 1965, Schnell and Hellack 1978, Evans and Drickamer 1994, Brigham et al. 1998). Military antipersonnel radar appears to function similar to traffic radar (Martinson 1973). Small stationary radars are used routinely for monitoring traffic flow and, within a few years, most vehicles sold will include tiny (l shorter than K band) radars mounted on their front surfaces

to serve safety, speed-control, and parking functions (Spectrum Planning Team 2001). Automotive radar will require price structures and production volumes 10^3 times greater than any other existing radar application. Consequently, wildlife biologists might use pinpoint radars as sensors for camera traps and arrays of radars to investigate clutter-plagued problems such as bird kills at tall structures. Airborne radar has been used to monitor insects (Hobbs and Wolf 1996) and can detect birds (Graber and Hassler 1962). Miniature airborne radar might fit into flying "micro vehicles" the size of a bird or insect (Fontana et al. 2002).

Harmonic radar is a specialized research technology using a directional transmitter and receiver at different frequencies combined with miniature tags to convert the transmitted frequency to the received frequency (Mascanzoni and Wallin 1986, Riley et al. 1998). A radar transponder requires a larger, active (powered) circuit (French and Priede 1992). Both have potential for following tagged subjects, even terrestrial wildlife, at useful ranges when line-of-sight visibility is possible.

ACQUIRING RADAR DATA

Wildlife researchers and managers work either with existing radar equipment operated by another agency or with dedicated wildlife radar. Whatever the source of data, obtaining

An A-scope display shows time variation of echoes vs. range (Fig. 14). The radar antenna should be either stationary, with birds and bats flying across the beam, or tracking a bird or bat. On the vertical axis the radar receiver signal produces a positive logarithmic display. The horizontal axis is the delay, or range, corresponding to 150 m μs^{-1}. The outgoing radar pulse ("main bang" in radar terminology) and some ground clutter appears on the left. No biological targets appear beyond a certain range on the right, largely because of the $R^{1/4}$ term in the Radar Equation. Stationary ground targets illuminated by side lobes, slowly-fluctuating vegetation, and narrow peaks from flying animals that wax and wane as they enter and leave the beam may appear in between. If the beam is pointed either along or opposed to the direction of travel of flying targets, the targets will move either right or left on the A-scope, respectively.

One can construct an A-scope using a suitable oscilloscope (less costly on the used electronics market) and 2 high-frequency cables. One cable feeds the radar "video out" or "rectified video" signal into a vertical "signal in" or "voltage in" connection on the oscilloscope, the other feeds the radar "transmitter trigger" or "pulse out" into the oscilloscope's "trigger in" connection.

information useful for statistical analysis, model development, data visualization, and management is the key to radar study of wildlife as a science rather than a curiosity.

One can use existing equipment by borrowing a radar, visiting a radar facility, or by acquiring already archived data on computer media or from the Internet. Using existing equipment often avoids the cost of acquiring, operating, and maintaining equipment. Frequently, someone is available to help instruct and interpret the data. Existing radars can often be directed quickly on a problem, which is an enormous advantage. However existing radars were not placed with wildlife in mind and their managers may not be amenable to modifying them or their operation to help a visiting wildlife scientist.

Purchase of a new or used radar system or assembly of a radar dedicated to biological studies can be productive. Most work with small- to medium-scale radar has involved enterprising biologists who were unafraid of new tools, new skills, and new collaborators. However, overenthusiastic wildlife professionals place themselves in danger of metamorphosing from wildlife managers or field scientists into low skilled, poorly paid engineers. The purchase cost of a radar that is truly suitable for acquiring the needed data can be too expensive and months or years can be wasted trying to make cheaper, unsuitable purchased equipment do a job that is beyond its capability. Furthermore, biologists need good engineering advice before attempting to modify or troubleshoot radio-frequency parts, including the antenna, feed, waveguide, magnetron, receiver front end, or Microwave Integrated Circuit (MIC). Microwave

components need to be clean, dry, and adjusted to tight tolerances to operate well. An untrained biologist may do more harm than good. For a short-duration research project or a feasibility study in a certain management situation, lease or rental of a radar from a dealer, radar manufacturer, or consulting firm should be considered.

The inside of working radar is not safe. Externally, when working near operating marine radars, one should stay away from the motor-driven antenna for both physical safety and general caution about the emitted microwave energy. Most marine radars are not powerful by radar standards (a few tens of kW) and the pulses are so short (about 10^{-7} seconds) that there is no known cause for concern for people in the general vicinity but not close to the antenna. There is seldom need for a user of a large radar to be near the antenna, which may emit up to several MW. If one plans to work near large radar or one with a phased-array antenna, professional advice about safety should be obtained.

The back end of radar that delivers data is at least as important as the front-end antenna and microwave electronics. Recording radar information by videography or time-lapse photography has immediate intuitive appeal and can be handy for obtaining images to accompany oral presentations or proposals. However, for monitoring animals one should avoid photography, preferring direct recording on a computer medium. Signals in the radar exist as voltages (Box 3) and information is lost when the signals are converted into an optical display and subsequently converted back to voltages in a camcorder or camera. More importantly, the deferred labor of quantifying radar data from photographs will quickly become the most expensive part of a radar project and the most tedious. Radars can quickly generate large amounts of data. Infrastructure to clearly label, efficiently quantify, and readily summarize those data is critical and should receive equal importance as the data.

One often has access to radar data in more than one form: as easily-interpreted images such as color PPI images, tracks drawn across a map, or as lower-level numerical data such as angles, decibels, and velocities. Color PPIs and maps are excellent for making decisions, taking notes, and summarizing, but numerical data are superior for quantifying and detecting differences and trends.

If only images are available, one should try to acquire unembellished versions of radar images without thresholds to remove "artifacts" such as biological targets and without non-data such as map overlays. Radar data can be registered to soft-copy maps later. Images are usually stored as computer files that code quantities as colors. Reversing the process, colors can be decoded to yield quantified numerical values. Although image files offer a direct route to quantification, they do not prevent one from becoming inundated with vast amounts of information. For instance, in the United States over 150 NEXRAD (WSR-88D) radars each produce 3 "base products" (fundamental radar images) about every 20 seconds. The resulting archive in North Carolina (Crum et al. 1993) is the second-largest unclassified data base after satellite remote sensing data.

Radar echoes vary 7 orders of magnitude or more in strength. To handle that large dynamic range, radar receivers typically generate logarithmic signals. Consequently, radars often display log (P_r) in decibels, which must be converted into linear units prior to averaging or summing (Black and Donaldson 1999). Older radars with monochromatic PPI

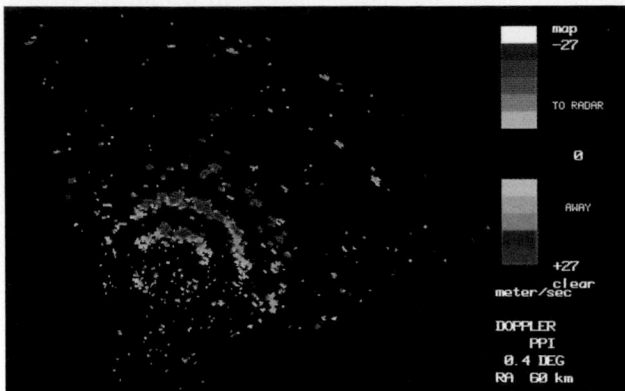

Fig. 10. Doppler velocity image of a dawn exodus from a roost of 1.5 × 10^8 European starlings (*Sturnus vulgaris*) and a few brown-headed cowbirds (*Molothrus ater*). Data were taken with CHILL, then operated by the Illinois State Water Survey.

displays may be incapable of displaying echo strengths over a range greater than about tenfold (Hunt 1973). However, this limitation can be circumvented by clever manipulation of the controls (Gauthreaux 1970, Drake 1981*a,b*). A radar should be calibrated to estimate target size; simple calibration techniques can be used in the field (Atlas 2002).

INTERPRETING RADAR DATA

Enumeration of Flying Animals

Useful data require timely information on antenna position and/or scan pattern. Animal flight takes place in 4 dimensions (north, east, height, time) or frequently reported as direction, speed, height, and time. Enumeration of flying animals can be accomplished in several ways depending on the questions asked (Gauthreaux and Belser 1998, 1999; Black and Donaldson 1999). Using N for animals or biomass, L as a linear measure such as kilometers, and A as area, one can convert a radar signal to meaningful measures. Questions of social behavior or probability of encounter with an animal will require volumetric densities (animals per length³), habitat-related questions will require areal densities (animals per length²) summed over height, and rate-of-passage questions will require rates of crossing a line on the earth summed over height (summed animals per length per time) or rates of passing through a vertical plane (animals per length² per time). Statistical treatments for angular or directional data are available specifically for biology (Batschelet 1981, Zar 1996) and in more depth (Mardia 1972, Fisher 1993).

Echoes from Vertebrates and Other Echoes

Field workers using radiotracking equipment listen for beeps of radio transmitters against an ever-present background of natural and human-generated noise and gradually become sophisticated at that task. Learning to use radar is no different and one should not expect to recognize wildlife immediately. Radar "noise" normally refers to intrinsic noise from the receiver and from external sources such as celestial background radiation. "Clutter" usually refers to spurious received echo from something not regarded as a target.

Close-in ground clutter is ubiquitous and can limit a radar's usefulness for nearby animals and those flying at low height. With long-range radars, a special kind of

ground clutter occurs when air that is cold or moist or both lies close to the ground and bends or refracts the radar beam downward. Radar scientists use the term "Anomalous Propagation" to describe unexpected echoes in conditions of notable refraction. Not uncommonly, layers in the atmosphere can trap part of the radar beam at a certain height above the ground so the beam follows the earth's curvature, allowing low objects and flying animals to be detected from long distances (Fig. 8).

Clutter reduction is accomplished in several ways. Siting a radar in a shallow pit or depression in the ground or behind an earth berm can reduce echoes from the surrounding terrain and still permit an unobstructed view of the air space (Bruderer 1971, 1994). Radar may also benefit from radar-opaque or -absorbing material mounted directly on the antenna to "shape" the radar beam (Freeman 1982, Cooper et al. 1991, Smith and Riley 1996), or a radar fence (Fig. 4) (LaGrone et al. 1964, Priekschat 1964, Becker and Sureau 1966, Freeman 1982). Ideally, a radar fence should be of Radar-Absorbent Material (RAM) to screen the highest point of vegetation, structures, or topography that would otherwise be visible from the tip of the feed of a reflector antenna. A fence of material other than RAM can generate reflections, which also require screening. This normally requires completely encircling the radar antenna. Gaps wider than a small fraction of the wave length should be avoided. Natural vegetation can function as a radar fence in some situations (Seilman et al. 1981, Cooper et al. 1991). Cuffs, shields, and fences do not need to be grounded but should be free of holes and gaps. Most biologists rely on a combination of imitation, trial-and-error, and advice from specialists rather than attempt to understand the theoretical basis of such devices.

RAM (radar-absorbent material) can reduce radiated power by more than 95%. Usually coated to reduce weathering, RAM is somewhat flexible but heavy and expensive. RAM can reduce echoes from unwanted targets when applied in the path of radar side lobes. This technique is used extensively in radar entomology, a field that needs good performance and high radar gain close to the ground (Beerwinkle et al. 1993). One also can install a metal plate extending 20–30 cm forward from the aperture of a marine radar antenna to block the lower part of the radar beam that would otherwise strike the ground or create other unwanted echoes. A similar approach has been used to reduce side lobe echoes in a vertical scanning radar, but the shielding was applied to all 4 sides of the radar aperture to prevent side lobes from reaching the ground (T. A. Kelly, personal observation).

Surveillance radars usually register echoes from stationary ground targets such as structures and terrain. These often use computerized clutter maps of recurring echoes to subtract known ground clutter from a display. Depending on the size of ground targets, echoes from animals near them may be suppressed as well.

Some radar reduce echo with radial velocity near zero by using a Moving Target Indicator (MTI) filter. Most targets flying tangential to the radar will also be suppressed because they too have a radial velocity near zero (Drury and Nisbet 1964). Depending on how MTI circuitry is adjusted echoes from small, slow-moving animals at all azimuths can also be lost. Doppler radars accomplish the same filtering of "stationary" echoes via a filter centered at radial velocity = 0 (Fig. 10) (Keeler et al. 1999). At times notch

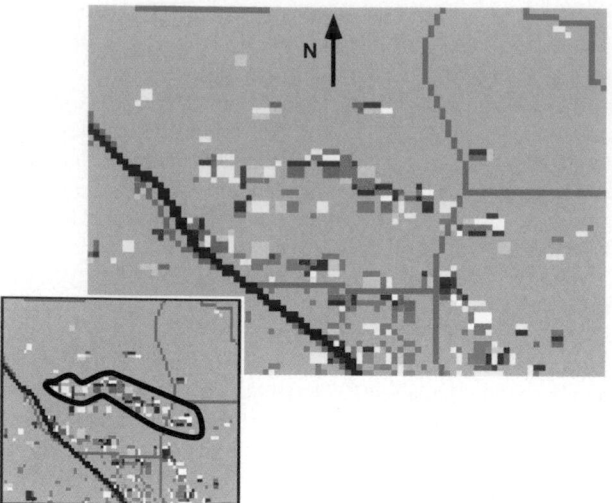

Fig. 11. A spatially extended flock of 6×10^4 snow geese (*Chen caerulescens*) departing from Coffeen Lake in west-central Illinois. The birds were counted during an aerial census by the Illinois Natural History Survey and followed on KLSX (Weldon Springs, Missouri WSR-88D) until after they crossed the Mississippi River (blue) into Missouri. The flock (insert) extends 53 km E-W at 1050 CST at ~100-km range. The green and yellow area at the bottom center is typical ground clutter.

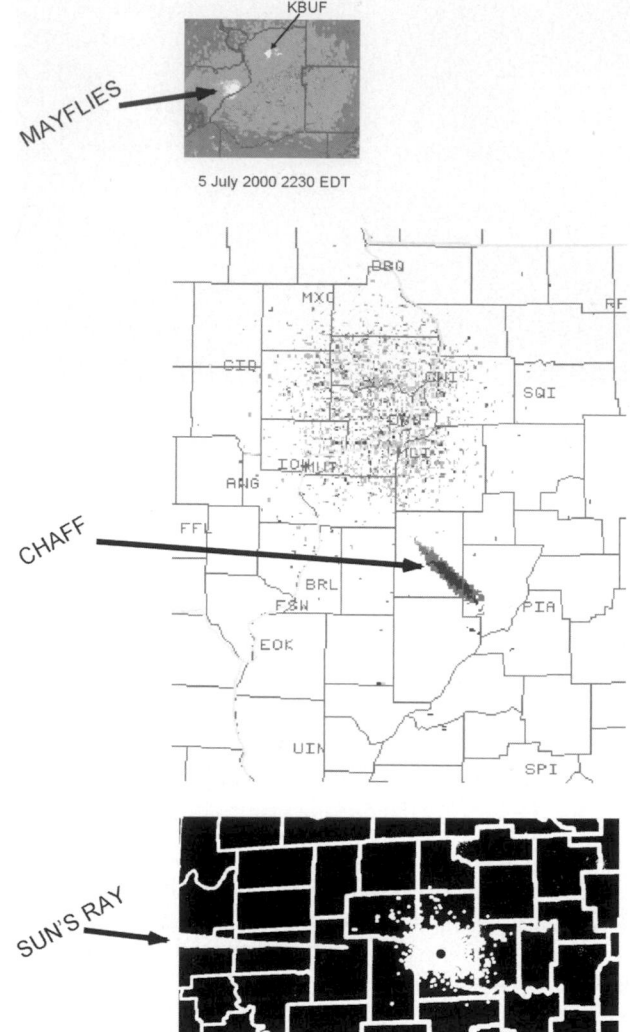

Fig. 12. Insects (mayflies, Plecoptera), military chaff, and a ray from the setting sun, seen on radar images.

filters (filters that pass only a narrow extent of velocities) can be flexibly and creatively programmed to suit the requirements of an individual project. Bats and birds flying over areas with heavy ground clutter are less likely to be detected even though filtering eliminates the ground clutter.

Filters and clutter maps can be applied to alter the signal from the radar receiver, the data sent to specific displays, or both. Filtering displays is accomplished with real-time or published commercial images from Doppler weather radars to diminish or suppress unwanted biological echoes. Displays may be filtered but what the radar records on a computer still contain unfiltered clutter. The wildlife user should prefer unfiltered data and characteristics of filter settings or clutter maps should be identified when publishing radar data.

Sources of clutter (in this context, non-wildlife echoes) vary (Fig. 12) and can include smoke plumes, vehicles on highway overpasses, trees and ocean waves moving in the wind, and railroad trains. Nearby pulsed radars are seldom a source of confusion because they operate at different wave lengths and pulse rates. There is no foolproof way to distinguish birds or bats from other echoes but an experienced observer can usually do so. Generally, careful language should be used in characterizing the many species that may generate radar echoes at any one time. Although ground truth is necessary for radar biology, other indications may also help.

(a) Vertebrates travel at speeds different from the wind. Thus, accurate local wind measurements often permit their identification if one can measure speed and direction of travel from PPI target motion, Doppler radar (Gauthreaux and Belser 2003), or tracking radar.

(b) On many spring and fall evenings when migrating biological targets orient their bodies similarly, their echoes will be more intense from the side than from the front or rear, producing a characteristic butterfly or dumbbell shape on a PPI image (Riley 1980, Buurma 1995).

(c) Weather echoes are characteristically smooth, whereas even dense migrations of birds usually present a somewhat uneven or "stippled" appearance (Fig. 13). Smooth echoes

are particularly characteristic of snow and warm front rain. Widespread echoes over land that extend high into the atmosphere are usually weather, not migrating birds. Insect echoes can be either stippled or smooth in appearance.

(d) Knowledge of the biology of species active at a certain time of year and time of day can provide excellent evidence of the nature of biological echoes. For instance, many animals begin or cease activity at dawn every day, whereas meteorological phenomena are not tightly synchronized to first light. However, without ground truth, one cannot be certain which flying animal is active at dawn or dusk. For example, evening takeoff of migratory birds and emergence from roosts of local bats happen within minutes of each other (Fullard and Napoleone 2001).

(e) Stationary-beam and tracking radars provide an opportunity to identify targets by observing wing beats such as a $2.1 \ s^{-1}$ modulation characteristic of an insect (Fig. 7). Although wing beat frequency by itself does not impart much taxonomic information for vertebrates (Emlen 1974, Vaughn 1974, Williams and Williams 1980, Bruderer 1997, Diehl and Larkin 1998), wing beat signatures can contain fine detail and hold promise for advances in ground truth (Box 3) (Fig. 14). "Signature" properly

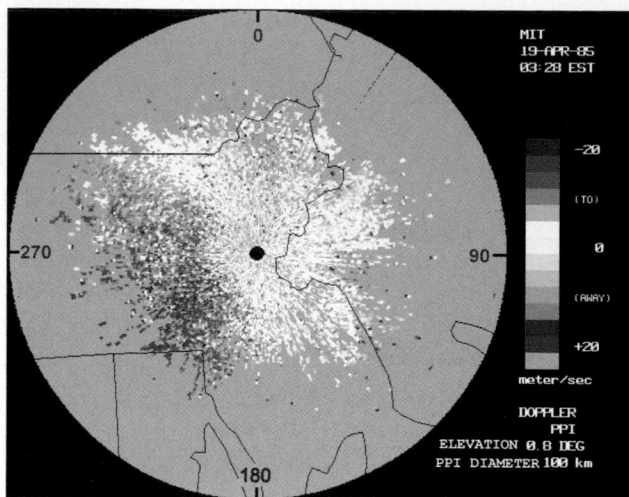

Fig. 13. A Doppler PPI display at low elevation angle from a C-band conical-beam radar in Cambridge, Massachusetts, USA shows nearly complete coverage of birds (and probably some insects and bats) in spring migration toward the northeast except where tall buildings interfere in the southeast quadrant. Some buildings obstruct the radar beam, producing artifactual gaps in the layer of birds. Others reflect it, producing echoes that appear in the southeast but are actually from birds to the northwest. Data courtesy of MIT Weather Radar Lab and Spi Geotis.

applies only to the variation of echo strength over time (Schaefer 1968:53).

Ground Truth

One should acquire sufficient radar data but equal weight should be given to concomitant field observations that establish the identity and numbers of targets (Fig. 15). Ground truth, a term borrowed from radar meteorologists, includes visual observations, infrared, sound, and separate small radars (Williams et al. 1981, Bruderer et al. 1995, Liechti et al. 1995, Gauthreaux and Belser 1998, Larkin et al. 2002). Ground truth should be simultaneous with radar operations, because daily monitoring of migrating birds on the ground is a poor indication of numbers of birds actually migrating overhead (Parslow 1962, Williams et al. 1981). Although the difficulty of discriminating small birds from insects with radar has been appreciated for a long time (Schaefer 1968), failing to do so remains one of the most common mistakes in designing radar studies of wildlife (Larkin 1991a). Magnitudes of radar echoes from insects can be "amazingly high" (Achtemeier 1992:922). Being alert to differences between insect and bird echoes can lead to new insights such as aerial feeding of insectivorous birds (Puhakka et al. 1986, Russell 1999).

The wildlife scientist's inclination is to go into the field to find where flying animals congregate and identify and count them, then look on radar to obtain more information about their movements and spatial patterns. However, with roosting birds, feeding flights of waterfowl, and some other wildlife targets, many wildlife practitioners find it more productive to first use radar to identify places and times where wildlife seems to be aloft and then go into the field with binoculars (Russell and Gauthreaux 1998).

Wildlife as Unwanted Radar Echo

Flying wildlife can be important sources of unwanted echoes for those using radar to observe aircraft and weather. Engineers regard birds as clutter when echoes persist despite

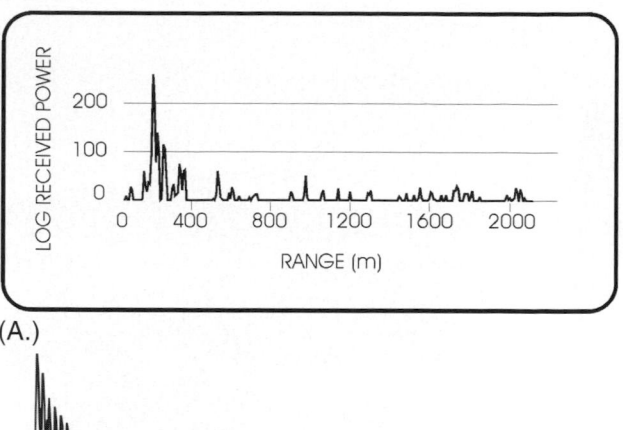

(A.)

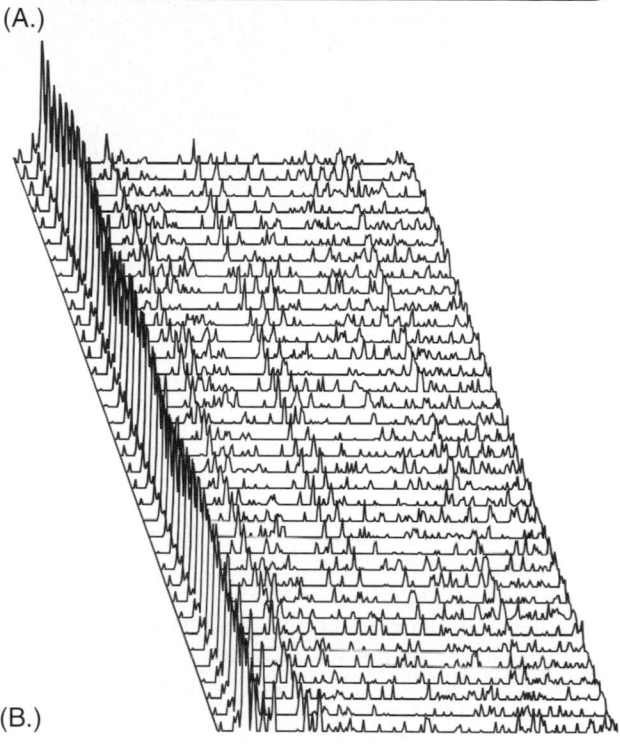

(B.)

Fig. 14. (A). A-scope data from a pencil-beam radar pointed across the path of migrating animals. (B). Behavior of the animals over time revealed in successive traces that descend in 50-ms increments from the top. The outgoing pulse and short-range ground clutter are omitted. Echo strength of the prominent target at slightly over 200-m range varies regularly at 19.4 s^{-1}. Field workers noted, "Bird-like target, range a little less than 2 μs". At greater ranges smaller biological targets wax, then wane over time as they fly through the beam.

use of anti-clutter techniques (Edgar et al. 1973). Doppler weather radars used by meteorologists deliver quantitative information, which is often polluted by echoes from flying animals. Reported wind speeds may actually be ground speeds of flying birds, warm front showers may be spring passerine migrations, and downbursts may be roosts (Larkin 1991b, Jungbluth et al. 1995, Gauthreaux et al. 1998, Serafin and Wilson 2000). Operational meteorologists are partly aware of the problem and should consult local wildlife experts for guidance. In military radar applications, stealth aircraft, remotely piloted vehicles, and tiny autonomous flying robots are intentionally or unintentionally similar to vertebrates.

APPLICATIONS OF RADAR SYSTEMS IN WILDLIFE

Aviation Safety

Radar has long held the promise of being an effective tool for warning of hazardous birds (Blokpoel 1976) and

Fig. 15. Ground truth as supplied by continuous scanning with binoculars and telescopes. Radar observations have shown that some raptors and storks fly higher than visual observers on the ground can detect.

bats (Williams et al. 1973) aloft and is used for this purpose operationally in several countries. Estimated annual losses from collisions of aircraft with wildlife (including "bird strikes") total at least $500M US (summarized in Dolbeer et al. 2000). A small number of these collisions result in serious damage to aircraft and occasionally the loss of the aircraft and occupants. Serious damage is more likely in military aircraft where speeds are higher and aircraft more fragile. The Israeli Air Force estimated that an average of $30M US per year was saved in that small country as a result of bird migration surveys in which radar was used (Leshem 1995).

Impact forces sustained by an aircraft are proportional to the mass of the bird and the square of the closing speed of the bird and aircraft. Because most aircraft operate at specific cruising speeds and because radar studies have shown that birds fly almost every day and night during the year, the key to avoiding collisions with birds is to fly where there are the fewest and smallest birds. Only radar has the potential to monitor birds over long distances by day and night.

Civilian and military aviation have many similarities concerning the dynamics of bird strike risk but also differ in some key areas. Military fighter and attack aircraft often train at low height and high speed (>900 km/hour). Civil aircraft operating at low height, such as to conduct wildlife or pipeline surveys and crop dusting, have much lower speeds. All aircraft, military or civilian, experience similar bird strike hazards when departing or arriving.

A radar system that detects birds over large geographic areas is required to warn military aircraft during low height training (Buurma 1995). Many low level training routes used by the military in the United States pass through the coverage area of several long-range radars, precluding the possibility of using a single radar to warn pilots of bird activity. The U.S. Air Force (USAF) uses the NEXRAD weather radar network to monitor bird activity in its low level airspace under the Avian Hazard Advisory System (AHAS, http://www.ahas.com/). Similar, but smaller, net-

works of radars are used for bird detection systems in Europe. These systems are often integrated with Geographic Information System (GIS) data (O'Neil et al. 2005) to serve the immediate function of providing near-real-time warning of hazardous birds aloft and the more lasting function of monitoring trends in bird activity. Special rapid scan radar systems (2–3 seconds) designed to eventually provide bird track and height information directly to the cockpit will soon supplement the wide area systems to reduce their intrinsic delay in warning. The best bird strike risk reduction methods use more than one strategy. Scheduling to avoid known high-risk periods and seeking to avoid any remaining birds in real time via data gathered by a radar sensor is an example of combining active and passive risk management.

Human Impacts on Wildlife

Because radar can monitor flying vertebrates at night and beyond human vision, it can provide data helpful for assessing and/or reducing wildlife collisions with electrical power distribution lines (Gauthreaux 1985), wind turbines (Cooper 1995, Anderson et al. 1999), and tall structures (Larkin and Frase 1988, Gauthreaux 1996). For impact studies, information on height of flying animals is usually essential; consequently, radars providing poor height information such as marine and other radars with vertically fanned beams are insufficient.

Animal Control in Agriculture

Birds that flock in large numbers can damage crops, impact farmers economically, and even contribute to food shortages. Depredating birds are typically passerines that eat grain (DeGrazio 1989, Elliott 1989), but also include other granivorous species such as cranes (Gruidae) and even fish-eating species such as cormorants (Phalacrocoracidae) that can impact commercial fish farms. Bird species that roost near airports can also pose a danger to aircraft on takeoff and landing (Seubert and Meanly 1974).

Radar offers an opportunity for long- and short-term monitoring of flocking species that cause economic hardship. Data collected with radar can be used to assess effectiveness of management techniques and long-term impacts of the management on the species. In the United States, blackbirds and similar species (Icteridae and Sturnidae) impact crops such as rice and sunflowers. For portions of the year, flights to and from their communal roosts are visible on many radar systems, including NEXRAD. They appear in the morning as rings of echoes that radiate from roost locations (Eastwood et al. 1962). A roost on radar is the center of concentric waves of departing birds (Fig. 10). Birds traveling NNW through ESE are fully visible but echoes of birds traveling NW and SE (tangential to the radar) are suppressed by a Doppler velocity filter (center 3 velocity ranges are black). Birds traveling toward the radar are also less evident because they are flying among urban structures. The velocity of the structures is zero and echoes from them are suppressed along with the birds flying above and among them. As birds fly into surrounding fields to alight and subsequently feed, the red/orange concentric rings disappear from the radar at the radius of the feeding habitat of these birds on that day (Fig. 10).

Monitoring roost echoes as birds disperse provides information on how far and to which areas birds from a single roost go to feed. Following application of a new management program, the effect on the species can be evaluated by comparing roost size, extent, and dispersion before and after treatment. If elimination of the roost habitat itself is considered, the roost location can be easily monitored year round to learn if other species, such as tree swallows (*Tachycineta bicolor*) or purple martins (*Progne subis*) (Russell and Gauthreaux 1998) use the same roosting site at other times of the year than the target birds. Radar provides no information on species but requires less effort than driving to a site on a weekly basis to count birds, especially if they are at distant or remote locations (Brugger et al. 1992).

Population Monitoring

Radar has potential as a conservation tool in population monitoring. Visual surveys are limited by visibility in daytime and can be biased by the observers' skills and persistence. Radar, in contrast, can detect birds in all light conditions and even through light rain with the appropriate signal processing.

A good example of the application of marine radar to population surveys is Burger's (1997) study of marbled murrelets (*Brachyramphus marmoratus*), which demonstrated limitations of audio-visual surveys and strengths of radar (also Cooper et al. 2001). Radar found an influx of murrelets 35–60 minutes before sunrise, which audio-visual surveys failed to detect. Visual surveys indicated a later peak 35 minutes before to 90 minutes after sunrise when radar showed intensive circling and departure. By making careful radar observations of flight speeds and direction and relating them to visual ground-truth observations, it was possible to distinguish seabirds from other groups of radar targets such as bats (Hamer et al. 1995). One of the distinct benefits of radar is that it allows remote observations with minimum disturbance to nesting colonies. Marine radar detected at least 4 times as many marbled murrelets as audio-visual surveys in a later study (Cooper

and Blaha 2002). However, radar was ineffective in detecting low-flying murrelets in or near the forest canopy or in hilly country; flock sizes could not be estimated with confidence on the radar (Burger 1997).

WSR-88D (NEXRAD) and other radar systems can detect waterfowl as birds leave on migration and at stopover and wintering locations when they move from refuges and lakes to feed. For overabundant species such as snow geese, radar offers an enhancement to existing tools for monitoring movements and relative abundance (Fig. 11) (Blokpoel and Richards 1978). Monitoring takeoff, passage, and daily feeding flights of waterfowl with surveillance radar offers a productive alternative to more conventional census and survey techniques. However, detecting arrival of migrating waterfowl on a stopover or wintering area still offers a great challenge. This challenge is worth examination, as fall movements of waterfowl are not easily predicted. "In contrast to spring migration, autumn [waterfowl] migration was not strongly correlated with any of the weather variables examined" (Beason 1980:452).

Waterfowl generally migrate later in fall and earlier in spring than most other bird species; thus, it is easier to recognize waterfowl activity on a large radar system. However, ground truth may be problematic with species such as ducks and geese that may take off near sunset in a sudden and dramatic burst of activity. Identifying the specific species active on a given night may depend on luck that an observer was on the ground at the start of migration to make the observation. An observer along the route who recognizes bird calls may be able to deduce that a particular species was involved in a dramatic overnight rise in numbers at a distant location.

Stopover habitat for migrating birds such as shorebirds (Charadriiformes) and neotropical–temperate migrant passerines is becoming an important conservation issue (Gauthreaux and Belser 2003). Recent large-scale research using intensive observations of populations of marked birds suggests that about 80% of mortality of typical neotropical-temperate passerine migrants is associated with migration rather than in breeding or wintering habitats (Sillett and Holmes 2002). Where large numbers of migrants depend on sparse and patchy habitats for food and cover during migratory stops, radar is a powerful tool. Although radar is not helpful for birds on the ground or in vegetation, fortuitously placed surveillance radars can detect them immediately after takeoff (usually at sunset) and can be helpful in locating areas actually used (Gauthreaux and Belser 1998, Diehl et al. 2003). However, careful ground truth and quantification of radar echoes is needed before different habitats can be evaluated and ranked in terms of their value to migrating birds. Radar observation of departures of migratory birds is feasible only within a certain range from the radar. Radar images have immediate visual impact and can convince the public and land managers more effectively than reports with tables of bird numbers and densities.

THE FUTURE

Sixty years ago, scientists were excited about radar as a new tool for studying animal movements and populations. In the late 1990s this excitement underwent a resurgence fueled by ready accessibility of radar technology. To the extent that wildlife practitioners exercise care with fundamentals such as ground truth, the coming decade will see the fruits of this resurgence. We should see better understanding of the relationship of animal sizes, taxa, flight patterns, speeds, numbers, and density to radar measurements of echo size and its variation as well as Doppler speed and its variation. This will permit new inferences about wildlife and application of the new knowledge to management. Inferences about types of biological targets aloft will primarily be limited by the amount and quality of ground-truth data available from visual observations, small local radars, and acoustic and infrared sensors.

Networks of Doppler weather radars are revolutionizing atmospheric sciences and will revolutionize knowledge of organisms from pollen and insects to the largest birds similar to the way satellites revolutionized geography and earth sciences in the last 20 years of the 20th Century. As data from these powerful instruments are fused with GIS technology, opportunities will emerge to compile data useful for land-use and other decisions in wildlife management and to put displays of this technology to use directly in the classroom and in nature centers. The technology will advance rapidly (National Research Council 2002) and research is underway to improve the NEXRAD system in the United States by adding an additional plane of polarization (Mueller and Larkin 1985, Zrnic and Ryzhkov 1998, Bringi and Chandrasekar 2001) in a future upgrade (Serafin and Wilson 2000). This will augment the data flowing from the NEXRAD system. Presently, individual scientists conduct most research in radar ornithology whereas teams perform research on migrating insect pests. Wildlife scientists may want to change that paradigm to make better use of the new technology.

SUMMARY

Radar has been used for over half a century to observe flying animals. Its application to wildlife research and management is blossoming, primarily because of the availability of capable and reliable small radars and copious data from large networks of Doppler radars designed for monitoring weather. Properly placed radar can observe flying animals at different spatial scales without affecting their behavior. However, radar offers little if any information on species identity. Radar is useful for informing aircraft of flying birds and bats, locating roosts, following birds that depredate crops, and monitoring populations including threatened and overabundant species and waterfowl. Locating areas critical for stopover of migratory birds is an especially useful application. Acquiring radar data necessitates care and accumulation of meaningful numbers. Challenges in using data from radars lie in establishing the identity of radar echoes (ground truth), recognizing different kinds of artifacts, and especially in coping with large amounts of automatically generated data.

ACKNOWLEDGMENTS

I thank F. C. Bellrose, R. H. Diehl, M. M. Horath, and D. B. Quine for radar data and ground-truth; S. J. Franke, D. R. Griffin, E. A. Mueller, and G. W. Swenson, Jr. for insights into radar as a tool; and P. W. Brown for information on waterfowl. T. Adam Kelly contributed substantial expertise and helped with early development of some parts of the chapter. R. H. Diehl, S.A. Gauthreaux, Jr., and an anonymous reviewer gave helpful comments on earlier drafts of the chapter. The U.S. Federal Aviation Administration provided support for preparation of the chapter.

LITERATURE CITED

ABLE, K. P. 1977. The flight behaviour of individual passerine nocturnal migrants: a tracking radar study. Animal Behaviour 25:924–935.

ACHTEMEIER, G. L. 1992. Grasshopper response to rapid vertical displacements within a clear air boundary layer as observed by Doppler radar. Environmental Entomology 21:921–938.

ALERSTAM, T. 1996. The geographical scale factor in orientation of migrating birds. Journal of Experimental Biology 199:9–19.

ALFIYA, H. 1995. Surveillance-radar data on nocturnal bird migration over Israel, 1989–1993. Israel Journal of Zoology 41:517–522.

ANDERSON, R., M. MORRISON, K. SINCLAIR, AND D. STRICKLAND. 1999. Studying wind energy/bird interactions: a guidance document. National Wind Coordinating Committee, Washington, D.C., USA. Available online at http://www.nationalwind.org/pubs/avian99/Avian_booklet.pdf.

ATLAS, D. 1965. Angels in focus. Radio Science Journal of Research NBS/USNC-URSI 69D:871–875.

———. 2002. Radar calibration: some simple approaches. Bulletin of the American Meteorological Society 83:1313–1316.

BATSCHELET, E. 1981. Circular statistics in biology. Academic Press, New York, USA.

BEASON, R. C. 1980. Orientation of waterfowl migration in the southwestern United States. Journal of Wildlife Management 44:447–455.

BECKER, J. E., AND J.-C. SUREAU. 1966. Control of radar site environment by use of fences. IEEE Transactions on Antennas and Propagation 14:768–773.

BEERWINKLE, K. R., J. A. WITZ, AND P. G. SCHLEIDER. 1993. An automated, vertical looking, X-band radar system for continuously monitoring aerial insect activity. Transactions of the American Society of Agricultural Engineers 36:965–970.

BLACK, J. E., AND N. R. DONALDSON. 1999. Comments on "Display of bird movements on the WSR-88D: patterns and quantification." Weather and Forecasting 14:1039–1040.

BLOKPOEL, H. 1976. Bird hazards to aircraft: problems and prevention of bird/aircraft collisions. Clarke, Irwin, and Company, Limited, Ottawa, Ontario, Canada.

———, AND W. J. RICHARDS. 1978. Weather and spring migration of snow geese across southern Manitoba. Oikos 30:350–363.

BLUESTEIN, H. B., AND A. L. PAZMANY. 2000. Observations of tornadoes and other convective phenomena with a mobile, 3-mm wavelength, Doppler radar: the spring 1999 field experiment. Bulletin of the American Meteorological Society 81:2939–2952.

BRIGHAM, R. M., M. B. FENTON, AND H. D. N. J. ALDRIDGE. 1998. Flight speed of foraging common nighthawks (*Chordeiles minor*): does the measurement technique matter? American Midland Naturalist 139:325–330.

BRINGI, V. N., AND V. CHANDRASEKAR. 2001. Polarimetric Doppler weather radar. Cambridge University Press, Cambridge, United Kingdom.

BRUDERER, B. 1971. Radarbeobachtungen über den Frühlingszug im Schweizerischen Mittelland. Der Ornithologische Beobachter 68:89–158.

———. 1994. Nocturnal bird migration in the Negev (Israel)—a tracking radar study. Ostrich 65:204–212.

———. 1997. The study of bird migration by radar. Part 1. The technical basis. Naturwissenschaften 84:1–8.

———, D. PETER, AND T. STEURI. 1999. Behaviour of migrating birds exposed to X-band radar and a bright light beam. Journal of Experimental Biology 202:1015–1022.

———, T. STEURI, AND M. BAUMGARTNER. 1995. Short-range high-precision surveillance of nocturnal migration and tracking of single targets. Israel Journal of Zoology 41:207–220.

BRUGGER, K. E., R. F. LABISKY, AND D. E. DANEKE. 1992. Blackbird roost dynamics at Millers Lake, Louisiana—implications for damage control in rice. Journal of Wildlife Management 56:393–398.

BURGER, A. E. 1997. Behavior and numbers of marbled murrelets measured with radar. Journal of Field Ornithology 68:208–223.

BUURMA, L. S. 1995. Long-range surveillance radars as indicators of bird numbers aloft. Israel Journal of Zoology 41:221–236.

COHEN, B., AND T. C. WILLIAMS. 1980. Short-range corrections for migrant bird tracks on search radars. Journal of Field Ornithology 51:248–253.

COOPER, B. A. 1995. Use of radar for wind power-related avian research. Pages 58–73 in Proceedings of National Avian-Wind Power Planning Meeting II. Avian Subcommitee of the National Wind Coordinating Committee, Palm Springs, California, USA.

———, AND R. J. BLAHA. 2002. Comparisons of radar and audio-visual counts of marbled murrelets during inland forest surveys. Wildlife Society Bulletin 30:1182–1194.

———, M. G. RAPHAEL, AND D. E. MACK. 2001. Radar-based monitoring of marbled murrelets. Condor 103:219–229.

———, R. H. DAY, R. J. RITCHIE, AND C. L. CRANOR. 1991. An improved marine radar system for studies of bird migration. Journal of Field Ornithology 62:367–377.

CRAWFORD, A. B. 1949. Radar reflections in the lower atmosphere. Proceedings of the Institute of Radio Engineers 37:404–405.

CRUM, T. D., R. L. ALBERTY, AND D. W. BURGESS. 1993. Recording, archiving, and using WSR-88D data. Bulletin of the American Meteorological Society 74:645–653.

DEFUSCO, R. P. 1995. Vultures and the U.S. Air Force to share friendly skies. BioScience 45:63.

DEGRAZIO, J. W. 1989. Pest birds—an international perspective. Pages 1–8 in R. L. Bruggers and C. H. Elliott, editors. Quelea quelea—Africa's bird pest. Oxford University Press, Oxford, United Kingdom.

DIEHL, R. H., AND R. P. LARKIN. 1998. Wing beat frequency of Catharus thrushes during nocturnal migration, measured via radio telemetry. Auk 115:591–601.

———, and ———. In press. Introduction to the WSR-88D (Nexrad) for ornithological research. In C. J. Ralph and T. D. Rich, editors. Bird conservation implementation and integration in the Americas: proceedings of the Third International Partners in Flight Conference 2002. U.S. Department of Agriculture, Forest Service, GTR-PSW-191.

———, ———, AND J. E. BLACK. 2003. Bird migration around the Great Lakes on Doppler radar: implications for habitat conservation. Auk 120:278–290.

DOLBEER, R. A., S. E. SRIGHT, AND E. C. CLEARY. 2000. Ranking the hazard level of wildlife species to aviation. Wildlife Society Bulletin 28:372–378.

DOVIAK, R. J., AND D. S. ZRNIC. 1993. Doppler radar and weather observations. Second edition. Academic Press, San Diego, California, USA.

DRAKE, V. A. 1981a. Quantitative observation and analysis procedures for a manually operated entomological radar. CSIRO Australian Division of Entomology Technical Paper 19:1–41.

———. 1981b. Target density estimation in radar biology. Journal of Theoretical Biology 90:545–571.

DRURY, JR., W. H., AND I. C. T. NISBET. 1964. Radar studies of orientation of songbird migrants in southeastern New England. Bird-Banding 35:69–119.

DYBDAL, R. 1987. Radar cross-section measurements. Proceedings of the IEEE 75:498–516.

EASTWOOD, E. 1967. Radar ornithology. Methuen, London, United Kingdom.

———, G. A. ISTED, AND G. C. RIDER. 1962. Radar ring angels and the roosting behavior of starlings. Proceedings of the Royal Society of London B156:242–267.

EDGAR, A. K., E. J. DODSWORTH, AND M. P. WARDEN. 1973. The design of a modern surveillance radar. Pages 8–13 in IEE Conference Publication 105, Radar—present and future. Institute of Electrical Engineers, London, United Kingdom.

EDWARDS, J., AND E. W. HOUGHTON. 1959. Radar echoing area polar diagrams of birds. Nature 184:1059.

ELLIOTT, C. H. 1989. The pest status of the Quelea. Pages 17–34 in R. L. Bruggers and C. H. Elliott, editors. Quelea quelea—Africa's bird pest. Oxford University Press, Oxford, United Kingdom.

EMLEN, S. 1974. Problems in identifying bird species by radar signature analyses: intra-specific variability. Pages 509–524 in Proceedings of a Conference on the Biological Aspects of the Bird/Aircraft Collision Problem. Department of Zoology, Clemson University, Clemson, South Carolina, USA.

EVANS, T. R., AND L. C. DRICKAMER. 1994. Flight speeds of birds determined using Doppler radar. Wilson Bulletin 106:154–156.

FISHER, N. I. 1993. Statistical analysis of circular data. Cambridge University Press, Cambridge, United Kingdom.

FONTANA, R. J., E. A. RICHLEY, ANTHONY J. MARZULLO, L. C. BEARD, R. W. T. MULLOY, AND E. J. KNIGHT. 2002. An ultra wideband radar for micro air vehicle applications. Pages 187–191 in Proceedings IEEE Conference on Ultra Wideband Systems and Technologies, Baltimore, Maryland, USA.

FREEMAN, E. R. 1982. Interference suppression techniques for microwave antennas and transmitters. Artech House, Dedham, Massachusetts, USA.

FRENCH, J., AND I. G. PRIEDE. 1992. A microwave radar transponder for tracking studies. Pages 41–54 in I. G. Priede, editor. Wildlife telemetry. Ellis Horwood, Sussex, United Kingdom.

FULLARD, J. H., AND N. NAPOLEONE. 2001. Diel flight periodicity and the evolution of auditory defences in the Macrolepidoptera. Animal Behaviour 62:349–368.

GAUTHREAUX, JR., S. A. 1970. Weather radar quantification of bird migration. Bioscience 20:17–20.

———. 1974. The detection, quantification, and monitoring of bird movements aloft with airport surveillance radar. Pages 289–307 in Proceedings of a Conference on the Biological Aspects of the Bird/Aircraft Collision Problem. Department of Zoology, Clemson University, Clemson, South Carolina, USA.

———. 1985. An avian mobile research laboratory. Proceedings of the Hawk Migration Conference 4:339–346.

———. 1996. Bird migration: methodologies and major research trajectories (1945–1995). Condor 98:442–453.

———, AND C. G. BELSER. 1998. Displays of bird movements on the WSR-88D: patterns and quantification. Weather and Forecasting 13:453–464.

———, AND ———. 1999. Reply to 'Comments on "Display of bird movements on the WSR-88D: patterns and quantification."' Weather and Forecasting 14: 1041-1042.

———, AND ———. 2003. Radar ornithology and biological conservation. Auk 120:266–277.

———, D. S. MIZRAHI, AND C. G. BELSER. 1998. Bird migration and bias of WSR-88D wind estimates. Weather and Forecasting 13:465–481.

GRABER, R. R., AND S. S. HASSLER. 1962. The effectiveness of aircraft-type (APS) radar in detecting birds. Wilson Bulletin 74:367–380.

GRIFFIN, D. R. 1973. Oriented bird migration in or between opaque cloud layers. Proceedings of the American Philosophical Society 117:117–141.

HAMER, T. E., B. A. COOPER, AND C. J. RALPH. 1995. Use of radar to study the movements of marbled murrelets at inland sites. Northwestern Naturalist 76.73–78.

HOBBS, S. E., AND W. W. WOLF. 1996. Developments in airborne entomological radar. Journal of Atmospheric and Oceanic Technology 13:58–61.

HUNT, F. R. 1973. Bird density and the plan position indicator. Publication 63. Committee on Bird Hazards to Aircraft, National Research Council of Canada, Ottawa.

JUNGBLUTH, K., J. BELLES, M. SCHUMACHER, AND R. ARRITT. 1995. Velocity contamination of WSR-88D and wind profiler data due to migrating birds. International Conference on Radar Meteorology 27:666–668.

KEELER, R. J., D. S. ZRNIC, AND C. L. FRUSH. 1999. Review of range velocity ambiguity mitigation techniques. International Conference on Radar Meteorology 29:158–163.

KELLY, T. A. 2000. Remote sensing and risk management. Pages 152–161 in PNAWPPM-III. Proceedings of National Avian–Wind Power Planning Meeting III. RESOLVE, Inc., Washington D.C., USA.

KOISTINEN, J. 2000. Bird migration patterns on weather radars. Physics and Chemistry of the Earth (B) 25:1185–1193.

KORSCHGEN, C. E., W. L. GREEN, W. L. FLOCK, AND E. A. HIBBARD. 1984. Use of radar with a stationary antenna to estimate birds in a low-level flight corridor. Journal of Field Ornithology 55:369–375.

LACK, D., AND G. C. VARLEY. 1945. Detection of birds by radar. Nature 156:446.

LAGRONE, A. H., A. P. DEAM, AND G. B. WALKER. 1964. Angels, insects, and weather. Radio Science Journal of Research NBS/USNC-URSI 68D:895–901.

LARKIN, R. P. 1978. Radar observations of behavior of migrating birds in response to sounds broadcast from the ground. Pages 209–218 in K. Schmidt-Koenig and W. T. Keeton, editors. Animal migration, navigation, and homing. Springer-Verlag, Inc., New York, USA.

———. 1982. Spatial distribution of migrating birds and small-scale atmospheric motion. Pages 28–37 in F. Papi and H.-G. Wallraff, editors. Avian navigation. Springer-Verlag, Inc., New York, USA.

———. 1991a. Flight speeds observed with radar, a correction: slow "birds" are insects. Behavioral Ecology and Sociobiology 29:221–224.

———. 1991b. Sensitivity of NEXRAD algorithms to echoes from birds and insects. International Conference on Radar Meteorology 25:203–205.

————, AND R. H. DIEHL. 2003. Spectrum width of birds and insects on pulsed Doppler radar. IEEE Transactions on Geoscience and Remote Sensing. In press.

————, AND B. A. FRASE. 1988. Circular paths of birds flying near a broadcasting tower in cloud. Journal of Comparative Psychology 102:90–93.

✓ ————, W. R. EVANS, AND R. H. DIEHL. 2002. Nocturnal flight calls of dickcissels and Doppler radar echoes over south Texas in spring. Journal of Field Ornithology 73:2–8.

LESHEM, Y. 1995. Foreword. Proceedings of the International Conference on Bird Migration of the Society for the Protection of Nature in Israel. Israel Journal of Zoology 41:R7–R8.

LEVANON, N. 1988. Radar principles. John Wiley and Sons, New York, USA.

LIECHTI, F., AND B. BRUDERER. 1995. Direction, speed, and composition of nocturnal bird migration in the south of Israel. Israel Journal of Zoology 41:501–515.

————, ————, AND H. PAPROTH. 1995. Quantification of nocturnal bird migration by moonwatching: comparison with radar and infrared observations. Journal of Field Ornithology 66:457–468.

MARDIA, K. V. 1972. Statistics of directional data. Academic Press, New York, USA.

MARTINSON, L. W. 1973. A preliminary investigation of bird classification by Doppler radar. National Aeronautics and Space Administration, Wallops Island, Virginia, USA.

MASCANZONI, D., AND H. WALLIN. 1986. The harmonic radar: a new method of tracing insects in the field. Ecological Entomology 11:387–390.

MUELLER, E. A., AND R. P. LARKIN. 1985. Insects observed using dual-polarization radar. Journal of Atmospheric and Oceanic Technology 2:49–54.

NATIONAL RESEARCH COUNCIL. 2002. Weather radar technology beyond NEXRAD. Committee on Weather Radar Technology Beyond NEXRAD. National Academies Press, Washington, D.C., USA.

NISBET, I. C. T. 1963. Quantitative study of migration with 23-centimetre radar. Ibis 105:435–460.

O'NEIL, T. A., P. BETTINGER, B. G. MARCOT, B. W. LUSCOMBE, G. T. KOELN, H. BRUNER, C. BARRETT, J. A. POLLOCK, AND S. BERNATUS. 2005. Application of spatial technologies in wildlife biology. Pages 418–447 in C. E. Braun, editor. Techniques for wildlife investigations and management. Sixth edition. The Wildlife Society, Bethesda, Maryland, USA.

PARSLOW, J. L. F. 1962. Immigration of night migrants into southern England in spring 1962. Bird Migration 2:160–175.

PRIEKSCHAT, F. K. 1964. Screening fences for ground reflection reduction. Microwave Journal 7(8):46–50.

PUHAKKA, T., J. KOISTINEN, AND P. L. SMITH. 1986. Doppler radar observation of a sea breeze front. International Conference on Radar Meteorology 23:JP198–JP201.

RADFORD, S. F., R. L. GRAN, AND R. V. MILLER. 1994. Detection of whale wakes with synthetic aperture radar. Marine Technology Society Journal 28:46–52.

RICHARDSON, W. J. 1979. Radar techniques for wildlife studies. National Wildlife Federation, Scientific Technical Series 3:171–179.

RILEY, J. R. 1980. Radar as an aid to the study of insect flight. Pages 131–140 in C. J. Amlaner, Jr. and D. W. Macdonald, editors. A handbook on biotelemetry and radio tracking. Pergamon, New York, USA.

————, AND D. R. REYNOLDS. 1979. Radar-based studies of the migratory flight of grasshoppers in the middle Niger area of Mali. Proceedings of the Royal Society of London B204:67–82.

————, P. VALEUR, A. D. SMITH, D. R. REYNOLDS, G. M. POPPY, AND C. LÖFSTEDT. 1998. Harmonic radar as a means of tracking the pheromone-finding and pheromone-following flight of male moths. Journal of Insect Behavior 11:287–296.

RINEHART, R. E. 1991. Radar for meteorologists. Second edition. Department of Atmospheric Sciences, University of North Dakota, Grand Forks, USA.

RUSSELL, K. R., AND S. A. GAUTHREAUX, JR. 1998. Use of weather radar to characterize movements of roosting purple martins. Wildlife Society Bulletin 26:5–16.

RUSSELL, R. W. 1999. Precipitation scrubbing of aerial plankton: inferences from bird behavior. Oecologia 118:381–387.

SCHAEFER, G. W. 1968. Bird recognition by radar: a study in quantitative radar ornithology. Pages 53–85 in R. K. Murton and E. N. Wright, editors. The problems of birds as pests. Academic Press Inc., London, United Kingdom.

SCHNELL, G. D. 1965. Recording the flight-speed of birds by Doppler radar. The Living Bird 4:79–87.

————, AND J. J. HELLACK. 1978. Flight speeds of brown pelicans, chimney swifts, and other birds. Bird-Banding 49:108–112.

SEILMAN, M. S., L. A. SHERIFF, AND T. C. WILLIAMS. 1981. Nocturnal migration at Hawk Mountain, Pennsylvania. American Birds 35:906–909.

SERAFIN, R. J., AND J. W. WILSON. 2000. Operational weather radar in the United States: progress and opportunity. Bulletin of the American Meteorological Society 81:501–518.

SEUBERT, J. L., AND B. MEANLY. 1974. Relationships of blackbird/starling roosts to bird hazards at airports. Pages 209–219 in Proceedings of a Conference on the Biological Aspects of the Bird/Aircraft Collision Problem. Department of Zoology, Clemson University, Clemson, South Carolina, USA.

SILLETT, T. S., AND R. T. HOLMES. 2002. Variation in survivorship of a migratory songbird throughout its annual cycle. Journal of Animal Ecology 71:296–308.

SKOLNIK, M. I., editor. 1990. Radar handbook. Second edition. McGraw-Hill Book Co., New York, USA.

SMITH, A. D., AND J. R. RILEY. 1996. Signal processing in a novel radar system for monitoring insect migration. Computers and Electronics in Agriculture 15:267–278.

SPECTRUM PLANNING TEAM. 2001. A review of automotive radar systems—devices and regulatory frameworks. http://www.atnf.csiro.au/SKA/intmit/autoradar.doc.

VAUGHN, C. R. 1974. Intraspecific wingbeat rate variability and species identification using tracking radar. Pages 443–476 in A Conference on the Biological Aspects of the Bird/Aircraft Collision Problem. Department of Zoology, Clemson University, Clemson, South Carolina, USA.

————. 1985. Birds and insects as radar targets: a review. Proceedings of the IEEE 73:205–227.

WILLIAMS, T. C. 1984. How to use marine radar for bird watching. American Birds 38:982–983.

————, AND J. M. WILLIAMS. 1980. A Peterson's guide to radar ornithology? American Birds 34:738–741.

————, L. C. IRELAND, AND J. M. WILLIAMS. 1973. High altitude flights of the free-tailed bat, *Tadarida brasiliensis* observed with radar. Journal of Mammalogy 54:807–821.

————, T. J. KLONOWSKI, AND P. BERKELEY. 1976. Angle of Canada goose V flight formation measured by radar. Auk 93:554–559.

————, J. M. WILLIAMS, AND P. D. KLOECKNER. 1986. Airspeed and heading of autumnal migrants over Hawaii. Auk 103:634–635.

————, ————, J. M. TEAL, AND J. W. KANWISHER. 1972. Tracking radar studies of bird migration. Pages 115–128 in S. R. Galler, K. Schmidt-Koenig, G. J. Jacobs, and R. E. Belleville, editors. Animal orientation and navigation. U.S. Government Printing Office, Washington, D.C., USA.

————, J. E. MARSDEN, T. L. LLOYD-EVANS, V. KRAUTHAMER, AND H. KRAUTHAMER. 1981. Spring migration studied by mist netting, ceilometer, and radar. Journal of Field Ornithology 52:177–190.

WOOLCOCK, S. C. 1985. Target characteristics. Pages 2(a)1–18 in J. Clarke, editor. Advances in radar techniques. Peter Pergrinus, Somerset, United Kingdom.

WURMAN, J., J. STRAKA, E. RASMUSSEN, M. RANDALL, AND A. ZAHRAI. 1997. Design and deployment of a portable, pencil-beam, pulsed, 3-cm Doppler radar. Journal of Atmospheric and Oceanic Technology 14:1502–1512.

ZAR, J. H. 1996. Biostatistical analysis. Third edition. Prentice-Hall, Englewood Cliffs, New Jersey, USA.

ZRNIC, D. S., AND A. V. RYZHKOV. 1998. Observations of insects and birds with a polarimetric radar. IEEE Transactions on Geoscience and Remote Sensing 36:661–668.

17

MEASURING AVAILABILITY AND VERTEBRATE USE OF TERRESTRIAL HABITATS AND FOODS

Lyman L. McDonald, J. Richard Alldredge, Mark S. Boyce, and Wallace P. Erickson

INTRODUCTION

Before any management efforts are initiated it is essential that wildlife management studies identify habitats and foods used by animals in comparison to availability of those resources. The availability of the environmental components that are necessary for life impact abundance of animals and distribution of their populations in space and time. Although many studies on these topics have been published for common wildlife species, more knowledge is needed about the life requisites of most terrestrial vertebrates. In addition, information about the habitats and foods used by a particular species may be needed for a specific region or time period. For example, wildlife biologists have become increasingly involved in assessing effects of human activities such as urbanization, highway construction, and power line development on wildlife (Grinder and Krausman 2001). These assessments often require identification of important habitat patches and food resources in the affected area. As a result, a biologist must collect site-specific information on patterns of habitat and food use. But how is such information obtained? What should be considered when a study is designed to identify

habitat or food use? This chapter provides an outline of the major techniques used to study these issues and some problems likely to be encountered.

Methods for design and analysis of wildlife studies have recently been summarized by Morrison et al. (2001) and Williams et al. (2002). Methods for study and modeling of resource selection have been reviewed recently by Alldredge et al. (1998), and a general (mathematical/statistical) theory for analysis of food and habitat selection studies has been updated by Manly et al. (2002).

We have taken different approaches in addressing aspects of habitat and food use to take advantage of other sections of this book. Higgins et al. (2005) outline many of the techniques used to describe wildlife habitats and Servello et al. (2005) provide additional background for understanding food use patterns. Thus, in this chapter we focus on conceptual issues of investigating habitat and food use, availability, and selection.

Before any study of habitat or food use begins, an understanding of how the results will be used is essential (Bart and Notz 2005). Is the objective of the study to describe habitat use patterns or a diet for the entire year or during one season that is considered critical? Is there a need to identify limiting factors or simply to document use? Much of the wildlife research to date has been directed at addressing descriptive questions of how, what, when, and where (Keppie 1990, Gavin 1991). These investigations have provided a detailed foundation on the natural history of many species. However, understanding why an animal occupies a specific habitat (for thermal cover, food abundance, or predator avoidance) or selects a particular forage grass (to maximize energy intake, obtain a specific nutrient, or minimize toxin intake) may reveal much more about the factors that limit a species than simply documenting patterns of use (Gavin 1991, Morrison 2001). Although it may seem obvious, taking the time to "think through a study" and articulate the specific question(s) being addressed is time well spent. One should be able to state concisely to someone else the research question that is being addressed. Results will be only as coherent as the initial conception of the problem (Green 1979, Morrison et al. 2001, Garton et al. 2005). A thorough review of existing literature can help investigators develop an understanding of the variability in resource use patterns and avoid the common pitfall of collecting descriptive information simply because it has not been collected in their specific study areas (Hunter 1989). The final question to consider is the application of results. Are the conclusions of the study to be extrapolated from samples collected at one area during one time period and applied to other regions and time periods? Without consideration of spatial and temporal variations, any extrapolations may mask the effects of spatial and temporal dependencies (Thomas and Taylor 1990).

RESOURCE SELECTION

The words *use, selection,* and *preference* have been applied widely and often interchangeably when information on patterns of resource exploitation is presented. Use indicates an association or consumption when habitats or food resources, respectively, are discussed. Selection, however, implies that an animal is choosing among alternative habitats or foods that are available. Use is selective if components are exploited disproportional to their availability (Johnson 1980). Resource availability, the quantity accessible to the animal or population of animals, is distinguished from abundance, which is defined to be the quantity of the resource in the environment. Preference for resources is defined as selection independent of availability. Studies to examine preference must allow free access to resources that are provided on an equal basis. Information on preference can be obtained only under special conditions, such as enclosure experiments that provide habitat categories in equal abundance, or cafeteria experiments wherein captive animals are presented a variety of foods and allowed to choose among them. Because of the special nature of preference experiments, we focus on developing an understanding of habitat and food selection rather than preference. We use the words "use" and "selection" interchangeably; however, in some technical cases we refer to no selection when use of resources is in proportion to their availabilities.

LEVELS OF SELECTION AND EFFECTS OF SCALE

Elements of a theory of habitat selection have been

developed (e.g., Fretwell 1972, Rosenzweig 1981, Fagen 1988, Hobbs and Hanley 1990), but how to evaluate these theories using field measurements is not always clear. Habitat selection can occur at a variety of levels or scales with animals selecting habitat according to a hierarchical scheme (Johnson 1980). These scales include the biogeographic (e.g., the eastern deciduous forest), home range (e.g., mature hardwood or oak-hickory forest), and the finest scale, that of some activity point, such as a den, nest, or roost site within a home range. Factors that influence selection at each of these scales also vary. For example, climatic extremes may affect the geographic range of a species, whereas habitat structure may influence home range size and shape, and competition with conspecifics may influence territory placement within a home range. The distribution of food and cover is probably most influential in affecting local movements within a home range.

The choice of an appropriate spatial and temporal scale of measurement, and consideration of spatial pattern will directly influence results and their interpretation (Wiens 1981, Otis 1997). Although thinking of scale in discrete levels (e.g., time = daily, seasonal, annual intervals; space = feeding site, home range, geographic range) is convenient, it is important to recognize that scales of measurement and environmental heterogeneity are continuous (Karr 1983). Choosing the wrong scale of measurement may lead to the interpretation that a species is generalized or specialized in its use of available habitats, whereas another scale of measurement might lead to a different interpretation. For example, Wiens (1989) observed the biogeographic range of Brewer's sparrows (*Spizella breweri*) was associated with shrub-dominated habitats. However, at a regional scale (multiple study sites), abundance of sparrows was negatively associated with shrub cover, while at a local scale (single study area), shrub abundance and sparrow abundance were not related.

Habitats can be characterized on several spatial scales, for example from landscape to microenvironment. Wildlife biologists often restrict their studies to a single scale when an examination of several scales may provide great insight to animal-habitat relations (Morris 1984, Sodhi et al. 1999, Apps et al. 2001, Welsh and Lind 2002). For example, the macro (forest-cover type) and microhabitat components (canopy closure and snow depth) of white-tailed deer (*Odocoileus virginianus*) wintering areas (yards) are important management considerations for this species in the northern portion of its range (Verme 1968). Macrohabitats in this example may describe the interspersion of food and cover used by deer. Microhabitat features may have a direct effect on thermoregulation (a factor influenced by variation in canopy closure) and energy costs of travel or ability to escape predators (factors influenced by snow depth).

Many investigators are now using tools such as Geographical Information Systems (GIS) (O'Neil et al. 2005) for discerning land-cover/land-use associations of wildlife species (Periera and Itami 1991, Hepinstall and Sader 1997, Erickson et al. 1998). At this macro scale, habitat data may be acquired remotely, such as from maps (Mosby 1969), aerial photographs (Avery 1968), or satellite images (Short 1982). Unfortunately, associations between animals and habitat attributes at this level of resolution often are general. Care must be taken to ensure that information is gathered at a scale comparable to that at which the research or management question is being observed (Svancara et al. 2002).

Management Implications of Resource Selection

The limits of data should be recognized when applications of research conclusions to manipulations of habitats or populations are considered. Use/availability or related analyses can be helpful in identifying patterns of habitat or food selection. However, biologists should not necessarily conclude biological need from such patterns. For example, suppose that a fictitious species (the blue-nosed yak, *Bos azurostrum*) has demonstrated selective use of forests 40–80 years old; that is, yaks are most abundant or spend a disproportionate amount of time in this habitat. Would we be correct to conclude that if all forests 40–80 years old were eliminated from the range of blue-nosed yaks this species would decline in abundance or go extinct? This conclusion is doubtful. Although we have demonstrated selection, we have not shown how fitness (e.g., survival or reproductive success) of yaks varies with different amounts of the selectively used habitat. We cannot make a "biological leap of faith" and assume that if we increase the amount of the selected habitat (or food) we will have more yaks.

Van Horne (1983) showed that population density and habitat quality (based on animal fitness) can be inversely correlated. Subordinate individuals (especially juveniles) may become locally abundant in less preferred habitats as a result of avoiding contact with dominant individuals that occupy sites that have an abundance of food and cover. As a result, survival and reproductive success in sink habitats are low. Therefore, if our objective is to evaluate the biological importance of a particular habitat, we should consider some type of manipulation experiment in which the amounts of the selected habitat (or food) are varied and fitness is monitored (Van Horne 1983). While these studies are not always practical, they are essential to demonstrate habitat associations. Such studies may be possible when applied to habitat management programs or large-scale habitat manipulations, such as impounding a river with a dam or logging a forest (Macnab 1983, Sinclair 1991, Williams 1997). Management experiments will require considerable planning because biologists rarely have control over the manipulation. Some habitat or food-based questions may allow the researcher to compare a measure of "success" among used and less-used resources and evaluate the features that lead to "success" and, presumably, the basis of selection (e.g., waterfowl nest success and vegetation features that influence concealment).

Sampling Protocols and Study Designs

The researcher must identify the scale of selection to study (Johnson 1980) consisting of resolution (grain) and extent (size). The biology of the animal is important, e.g., if the animal being studied is territorial then selection is commonly studied on a different scale from that used for a nonterritorial animal. For example, an area occupied by one pack of gray wolves (*Canis lupus*) may be unavailable to other packs and the measure of availability of habitat units for a new pack should not include the inhabited areas (Mladenoff and Sickley 1998). If animals tend to forage

from a central location (e.g., a nest site), the resources assumed to be available must be adjusted or predictor variables such as the distance from the nest must be considered in the analysis.

As a general rule, resource selection studies should consider selection at more than one scale. One might study selection of home ranges by a wolf pack and selection of locations for hunting within the home range of a pack. Season, gender, age class, behavioral activity, and daily activity pattern of the animal studied often affect resource selection. For example, if radiolocations are used to assess selection of foraging sites, only locations recorded during certain hours of the day should be analyzed. If resource use and/or availability changes across seasons, the study should focus on habitat selection during relatively short periods of time or fit models that allow for the availability of types to change (Schooley 1994, Arthur et al. 1996, Cooper and Millspaugh 1999). Pooling information across times, subpopulations, age classes, or activities may result in erroneous inferences.

The choice of the study area and its boundaries (extent) essentially defines the habitat or food available to the animals under study. Definition of habitat or food available to the animals is a basic assumption and influences analyses and fitting of models. In many cases, interest will be in examining how habitat selection changes as availability changes. When choosing a study area, one must consider the distribution of resource units, scale of selection studied, what is truly available to the animals, and manpower and budget constraints for collection of data. We use "resource units" to indicate either habitat units, points in the habitat, or food items.

Resource selection may be detected and measured by comparing any 2 of the 3 possible sets of resource units (used units, unused units, or available units). On this basis, the following 3 common sampling protocols (SP-A, SP-B, and SP-C) have been identified depending on the 2 sets measured (Manly et al. 2002). In addition, we define a fourth commonly used sampling design (SP-D) (Box 1).

If all units in a category are sampled, the protocol is a

Box 1. Sampling protocols for resource units.

Sampling protocol (SP)	What is sampled?
SP-A	Available units are randomly sampled and used units are randomly sampled.
SP-B	Available units are randomly sampled and unused units are randomly sampled.
SP-C	Used units are randomly sampled and unused units are randomly sampled.
SP-D	Available units are randomly sampled and classified as used or unused.

"census." The same general analysis is conducted whether a census of all units is taken or not. We consider only the 2 most common sampling protocols that arise in practice: SP-A (available units and used units are independently sampled), and SP-D (available units are randomly sampled and classified as used or unused). Manly et al. (2002) discuss the analysis of data falling under the other cases, e.g., food items available to a population might be sampled before selection and unused food items are sampled after selection.

Three general study designs for evaluating selection have been identified (Thomas and Taylor 1990). These designs differ on whether or not selection of units by individual animals can be identified (e.g., locations of radiomarked animals) and whether or not resource units are defined to be available to the population of animals or to individual animals. Each of the 4 sampling protocols may be implemented for each of the sampling designs. Definition of the 3 study designs follows Thomas and Taylor (1990) and Manly et al. (2002).

Design I. Used, unused, or available resource units are sampled or censused for the study area and use by the population of animals is recorded (but, use by individual animals is not possible to record). Two examples of this design are provided.

1. Aerial or ground surveys are used to locate animals. Variables that potentially influence use by animals are measured at the locations. For example, habitat or forage types, slope, aspect, and density of roads in a plot centered at the locations might be measured at each location and used in a model to predict the relative probability of use of locations by animals in the population. Maps, aerial photographs, or GIS might be used to provide sample or census data on plots (pixels) available to a population of animals. For example, Stinnett and Klebenow (1986) examined cover-type selection by California quail (*Callipepla californica*) by classifying flushes observed during ground surveys into cover types. Maps and aerial photography were partitioned into the respective cover types to measure availability of each cover type. Erickson et al. (1998) studied habitat selection by moose (*Alces alces*) using sampling protocol A on the Innoko National Wildlife Refuge in Alaska. Aerial line-transect surveys were conducted to obtain a sample of locations used by moose during daytime in winter. The assumption was that locations were a random sample of those used by the population of moose. The study area (locations defined to be available to the population of moose) consisted of river corridors on the refuge. Predictor variables were derived from a GIS for circular buffers centered at the moose locations (used units) and for circular buffers centered at the gird intersections of a systematic sample of points in the river corridors (sample of available units). A model called a Resource Selection Function (RSF) was fitted to the data to predict the relative probability of use of a given point (conditional on the specific time period, population density, and sampling protocol).

2. Design I might combine with sampling protocol D if plots are randomly sampled and classified as used or unused on the basis of signs such as pellets or tracks. Variables such as the percentage of vegetation cover, shrub density, and distance to water might be measured at each sampled plot. Traps, nets, camera traps, etc. might be placed in a sample of "available" locations with those locations classified as used if the target species is captured or seen at the point. Predictor variables would be measured at each location and used and unused points compared in the analysis.

Design II. In some cases, the study area (availability) is defined for a population of animals, but individual animals are identifiable and habitat units selected can be recorded for a sample of animals. Four examples of this design are provided.

1. A random sample of animals is obtained from the population of interest and uniquely identified so that a sample of habitat units used by a given animal can be recorded. Also, a sample of units available to the population is selected. Predictor variables are measured on units selected by the *i*th animal, and on the sample of available units. Predictor variables might be measured in the field or from aerial photographs, geographic information systems, or maps.

2. Pendleton et al. (1998) studied habitat use by northern goshawks (*Accipiter gentilis*) in southeast Alaska. Goshawk locations were identified by a variety of sources including systematic surveys, timber sale preparations, and recreational activities. Goshawks were trapped, radiomarked, and their home ranges measured with the assumption that birds captured provided a random sample. A Design II study would involve comparison of proportions of resource types and other variables in home ranges to the same variables measured on similar sized regions randomly sampled from the entire study area.

3. Roy and Dorrance (1985) compared habitat availabilities within coyote (*Canis latrans*) home ranges with the availabilities in the entire study area.

4. Prevett et al. 1985 compared food selected by individual snow (*Chen caerulescens*) and Canada geese (*Branta canadensis*) with random samples of available food from the entire study area.

Design III. In this design, individuals are uniquely identified (usually by radio transmitters) or collected for stomach samples, and either SP-A (sample of available units and sample of used units), or SP-D (sample of available units are classified as used or unused) is applied for each animal. Data from each animal are analyzed to provide a resource selection function for each animal or replication of a more simple analysis. Two examples of this design are provided.

1. The animals in a sample are radiomarked, and the relocations of an animal provide a sample of resource units used by that animal. Available

resource units within an animal's home range are also sampled. Predictor variables are measured on each sampled unit to contrast used units with available units within each home range. This is the type of design used by Pendleton et al. (1998) to study habitat selection by northern goshawks in southeast Alaska. Habitat available to each bird was estimated using a systematic point grid within the minimum convex polygon use area (i.e., estimated home range) of each radio-marked goshawk. A sample of locations used by the birds was obtained from radio-tracking data. Habitat use was evaluated by comparing variables measured at used locations to variables measured on the sample of available points.

2. Individual animals might be collected and stomach analysis performed on each. Predictor variables are measured on prey or food items (e.g., species, color, size). These data are then contrasted to measurements from a sample of prey or food items collected in a certain size buffer surrounding the collection site.

Comparison of Designs

Design I has been the most commonly used in the past; however, it has the least specific information. Inferences can be made to selection (resource use) by the population of animals under study with the assumption that one has obtained a random sample of habitat units used by the population and availability has been correctly identified.

Designs II and III tend to be preferred because data are obtained on individual animals and their habitat or food use. Thus, variation in habitat selection among gender or age classes can be analyzed. However, cost of the resource selection study usually increases when individual animals are captured, marked, and tracked. In Designs II and III, implicit assumptions are made that a random sample of animals is obtained. In practice, when trapping or otherwise capturing animals, this is difficult. However, every effort should be made to "spread the sample of animals over the population." The design then becomes a sequential process: first, selection of a sample of animals and second, selection of samples of used and available resource units for each animal followed by measurement of predictor variables on the selected units.

There are several advantages of Designs II and III. The relocations (used units) of radio-marked animals may be close together in time and space and hence "dependent" as opposed to a random sample of units used by the animals. If data are pooled among animals into a Design I analysis, the mathematical requirements of the analyses may not be satisfied because of the lack of independence of locations of used units. Similarly, in food studies the selection of consecutive prey items may be dependent. When resource selection is analyzed for the individual animals in Designs II and III, all data are typically used regardless of whether they are dependent or not. The next stage, where we consider variation from animal to animal and make inferences to the population of animals, depends only on the assumption that the sample of animals was collected by a random procedure, not on the fact that data on individual animals may have been dependent. Therefore, it is better to estimate sampling variances and test hypotheses using varia-

tion among animals rather than variation among observations on one animal. Thus, inferences rely on random sampling of animals rather than on the assumption the correct statistical model for dependent observations within animals is being used. Estimation techniques applicable at the population level for Design I can be applied to individuals with Designs II and III. The variation due to gender or age differences or to unusual individual animals can be examined.

Models for Resource Selection Functions

Available resource units usually are defined as individual items of food (with food selection) or blocks of land or points on the landscape (with habitat selection). Each resource unit is characterized by the values that it possesses for certain predictor (independent) variables $X_1, X_2, ..., X_p$, representing characteristics such as size and color of food items, or the distance from water and the habitat type of habitat units. Three mathematical functions (i.e., models or curves) (Manly et al. 2002) are involved in studies of resource selection. They can be illustrated with a simple hypothetical example with one X variable (Fig. 1).

The curve labeled "available" represents the probability distribution function (smooth "histogram") of the predictor variable X for the set of units available to an animal. For this hypothetical example it was assumed that X has approximately a normal distribution with mean $\mu = 20$ and variance $\Sigma^2 = 2.5$. The function labeled "used" represents the probability distribution function of the predictor variable X on those units that are selected by the animal. The distribution of X on the used units is approximately a normal distribution with mean $\mu = 22$ and variance $\Sigma^2 = 1.9$.

The third curve (Fig. 1) is the Resource Selection Function (RSF). This is the function that shows how units must be selected from the available units to produce the distribution of the used set. If an animal is selecting from the available units such that the probability of selecting a unit with $X = x$ is proportional to the resource selection function, this will produce the distribution of X that is shown for the used units. For example, the animal must select available units with $X = 25.07$ with about twice the

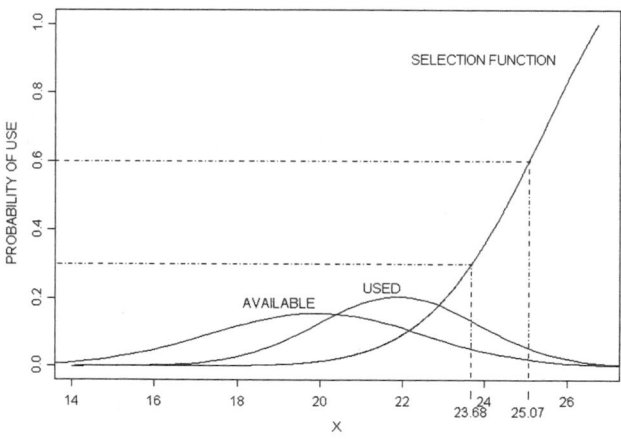

*Fig.*1. A resource selection function for the relative probability of use of resource units with a single variable X (adapted from McDonald and Manly 2001). The "available" curve is approximately a normal distribution with a mean of 20 and variance of 2.5. The "used" curve is approximately a normal distribution with a mean of 22 and variance of 1.9. These 2 distributions define the resource selection function.

probability of units with $X = 23.68$ to produce the distribution of used units. The Resource Selection Function provides a way to rank the relative importance of different units as measured by data for "available" units, data for "used" units, and the resulting relative probability of selection. Values of the relative probability of selection can be computed for all habitat units and mapped using GIS to show areas that are selected with relatively high, medium, or low probability.

Our example (Fig.1) uses approximate normal distributions to illustrate the distributions of X for available and used units and a unique formula from Manly (1985: 61) to calculate the selection function. However, normal distributions rarely fit all predictor variables that may be of interest in resource selection. A general theory allowing multiple predictor variables and based on exponential models, logistic regression, and other special statistical methods was developed by Manly et al. (2002).

Johnson (1980) defined "preference" to be the likelihood that a resource unit will be selected if offered on an equal basis with others. "Preference" can be measured in controlled experimental laboratory or pen studies if, for example, equal abundances of different types of food pellets can be offered to a caged animal with pellets being replaced as they are eaten. Preference functions rarely can be estimated in observational wildlife field studies. For field studies, the resource selection function can provide the relative probability of selection of different habitat units (food types) among those available.

One application of resource selection functions is to produce maps of the relative probability of selection in either 3 dimensions over the study area or as "contour" lines showing the relative probabilities of selection. Erickson et al. (1998) produced this type of map showing areas with relatively high, medium, and low probability of use by moose on the Innoko National Wildlife Refuge, Alaska, in winter 1994 and 1996. Predictor variables included the percentages of different habitat types in buffers surrounding used points (as evidenced by observing a moose group at the point during an aerial survey) and in buffers surrounding a large systematic sample of available points on grid lines. A GIS was used to obtain the predictor variables in the buffers.

Assumptions for Estimation of Resource Selection Functions

There are 5 major assumptions for estimating resource selection functions after defining study area boundaries:

1. Defining what resource units are available to a population or an animal is a critical step in estimation of a resource selection function. For example, if the shape of the distribution of the variable X changes for available units, the resource selection function must change to generate the same distribution for used units (Fig. 1). The set of used units is easier to define in most studies, because evidence of use (tracks, browsing, the presence of animals, etc.) is observed.

2. The second critical assumption is the predictor variables to be measured on sampled units, X_1, X_2, ..., X_p, are correlated with the probability of use and do not change appreciably during the study period. Given samples from the available units and the used units (SP-A) or a sample of available units that are then classified as used or unused (SP-D) and a "good" set of predictor variables, an approximate model can be constructed to predict the relative probability of selection for that specific location, time, and population.

3. Measurement errors for predictor variables, X_1, X_2, ..., X_p, are relatively small in comparison to variation from unit to unit.

4. In Design I and II studies, animals in the population have free and equal access to all available units. If this is not the case, e.g., if animals are territorial, Design III should be used.

5. Available units and used units are randomly sampled. In practice, systematic location of grid lines and selection of units at line intersections, or uniformly spaced units along a linear feature (e.g., a river) can be used to sample available habitat units under the assumption that the systematic sample is random relative to the resource units on the landscape.

A sixth assumption is required for the case that independent samples are obtained for available and for used units. In this case, the particular estimation of the resource selection function requires the proportion of used units is "small" during the study period and as measured by the sampling protocol. Our experience is that if fewer than 20% of the units are "used," the estimation methods illustrated are satisfactory. For example, if radio-marked animals are periodically surveyed to locate pixels used in a GIS, the proportion of used pixels in the data set typically will be small in comparison to the total number of pixels available.

MEASURING HABITAT USE AND AVAILABILITY

We define habitat in its broadest context, including all abiotic and biotic features of the environment. Although other definitions of habitat exist (e.g., Karr 1981, Hall et al. 1997), we consider habitat use as the association of an animal with these features. Selection and use of a particular area or unit of habitat by an animal are the result of proximate and/or ultimate predictor (independent) variables (Partridge 1978). Proximate variables are those features used as cues when an animal evaluates a site (habitat unit). They may include structural features such as understory cover, canopy height, or slope. Other potential structural features are available from GIS such as density of roads in the unit or distance to water. The presence/absence of other animals that may act as competitors or predators also may influence habitat use. Animals may use such features as cues, but they may not be the same as the variables that have resulted in evolutionary associations between animals and habitat. Ultimate variables are those parameters that affect how successful an animal is within a particular habitat. An individual's abilities to reproduce, obtain food, and avoid predators are examples of ultimate variables that influence habitat selection. Studies of habitat use usually involve measure of proximate variables and food availability. However, with adequate data on ultimate variables, for example, measurements of predator abundance and competition, a more complete understanding of habitat selection can be obtained.

The relationship between a habitat feature being measured and its biological link to the animal often is clear. For example, understory stem density frequently is used as an index of escape cover for small or medium-sized mammals, such as snowshoe hares (*Lepus americanus*) (Litvaitis et al. 1985). However, in other instances the animal–habitat relationship may be less obvious, such as using the abundance of snags as an index of insect availability for pileated woodpeckers (*Dryocopus pileatus*). In this situation, a structural feature is correlated with a proximate predictor variable. Because it is much easier to inventory and manage snag abundance than insect abundance, one is tempted to use this association when investigating woodpecker–habitat relations. However, the relationship between snags and insects should be verified to ensure that subsequent research conclusions are reliable.

Techniques for Measuring Habitat Use

Direct and indirect methods have been used to measure wildlife habitat use. Direct methods include observation, capture, and radiotelemetry whereas indirect methods are dependent on some evidence of animal activity within an area or specific site (e.g., bed sites, browsed twigs, feces, nests, or tracks). These measures may be used to sample habitat use along systematic transects, a small-mammal trapping grid, or with other sampling designs appropriate to the animal of interest (Fig. 2). Morrison et al. (2001) provide a good introduction to basic sampling procedures in wildlife study design while Hurlbert (1984) and Williams et al. (2002) provide specific advice on study design.

Direct Methods for Measurement of Habitat Use

Direct observations of animals may allow economical sampling of a large segment of the population and to distinguish activities within habitats (e.g., Biggins and Pitcher 1978, Stinnett and Klebenow 1986, Erickson et al. 1998). Collection of data can be combined with aerial or other survey procedures. Problems to consider are differential visibility among habitats and the difficulty of recording observations during nocturnal periods.

Advantages of animal capture include being able to examine individuals for age/gender and other characteristics (e.g., Parren and Capen 1985). Capture procedures can be combined with mark–recapture methods to estimate abundance. However, differential vulnerability to capture due to age and gender or other factors may bias results and attractants may cause animals to use habitats that are normally not used.

Radiotelemetry also can be used to measure habitat use (Nams 1989, Erickson et al. 2001). Advantages include being able to examine individuals of known age/gender and other characteristics for habitat selection. Animals can be located multiple times throughout the day/night and seasonally. Habitat selection for important components can be studied (e.g., den site selection or roost sites). However, radiotelemetry is relatively expensive resulting in small sample sizes and location accuracy may not be sufficient in patchy environments.

Indirect Methods for Indication of Habitat Use

Detection of tracks (e.g., Litvaitis et al. 1985, Thompson et al 1989) allows one to economically sample

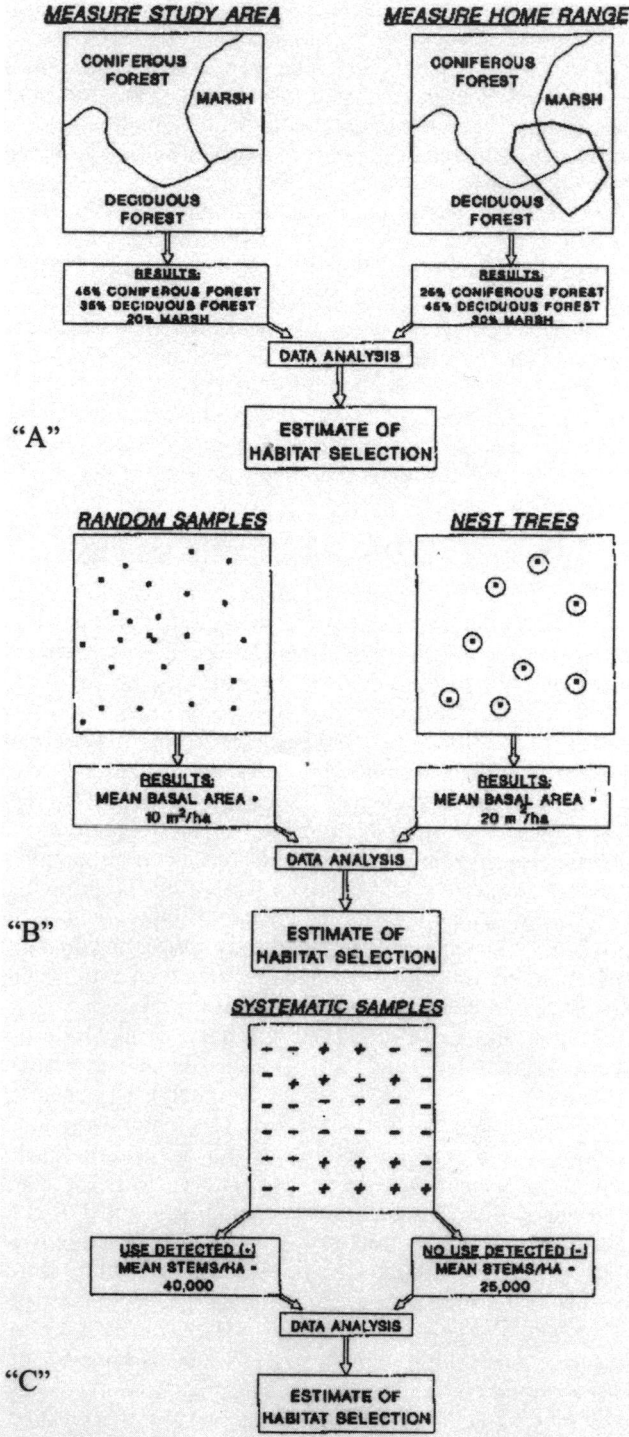

Fig. 2. Representative methods to examine habitat use patterns. "A" illustrates Design II and sampling protocol A: available habitat is inventoried and compared to the composition of an animal's home range. "B" illustrates Design I and sampling protocol A: random samples are compared to characteristics of a sample of sites where use has been detected, such as nests or roost sites. "C" illustrates Design I and sampling protocol D (Box 1): systematic plots (or points) are established and features are compared between sites where use was detected (via captures, tracks, feces, radio relocations, etc.) and sites where use did not occur.

units and evaluate use/no use in a large area in a short time by all segments of the populations. However, the procedure often suffers from lack of good tracking conditions (e.g., uniform snow) and different visibility of tracks in different habitat types.

Detection of pellet groups or scat measures use by all segments of a population (Collins and Urness 1981, Orr and Dodds 1982). With cleared plots, information on seasonal use is obtained, and potentially can be combined with deposition rates to estimate density of animals. However, defecation rates often are unknown or vary with habitat type and activity, and decomposition rates may vary among habitats. Visibility and detection of pellet groups also may vary with habitat type.

Browsing or feeding may provide evidence of use of habitat units by all segments of a population. This technique may provide additional information on food habits and be combined with studies of carrying capacity. Potential biases include competition for the same food by other species and food species must be present before use of a unit can be documented.

Techniques to Measure Habitat Availability

Delineation of available habitat can influence interpretation of habitat selection and subsequent management recommendations. Assessing availability of habitats from the point of view of an animal is not possible; any effort to estimate availability is naturally beset with problems (Chesson 1978, Jaenike 1980, Johnson 1980). In studies of habitat selection, biologists often choose administrative units such as a parks, forests, or refuges to arbitrarily represent the habitat available to study animals because of the obvious management ramifications. This can have significant drawbacks. Habitats considered to be available might be much larger than the area occupied, which could produce biased results. If study animals are not radiomarked, they might use a larger area than anticipated, resulting in a biased interpretation of selection.

Issues with the assumption of habitats available to the study animals are simplified if the scale of selection is clearly delineated. Johnson (1980) defined *first-order selection* as the selection of physical or geographical range of a species. Few if any habitat-use studies are of first-order selection. *Second-order selection* results in the home range of an individual or social group within the physical or geographical range of a species. Second-order selection is of interest in many habitat-selection studies and will typically require radiomarking of individuals or social groups (Design II and III studies). *Third-order selection* is specific use of sites within the home range. This is probably the easiest situation in which to define availability. Typically, the home range of an individual or social group is calculated (e.g., by the minimum convex polygon method, Williams et al. 2002) and all units within the home range are defined to be available. Finally, Johnson (1980) defined *fourth-order selection* as the actual procurement of food items from those available at a feeding site as identified by third-order selection. In this case, paired sample data are typically collected where contents of scat or stomach samples are paired against samples of food items collected from the site. It may be advisable to evaluate habitat availability and selection within several scales—for example, third-order selection of local cover types and second-order selection of regional landscapes (Steventon and Major 1982).

Knowing something about the habitat associations of the animal being studied is essential before study area boundaries are delineated for second-order selection studies or for Design I studies where individuals are not radiomarked or otherwise identifiable. For example, including open fields as available habitat for forest-interior songbirds [e.g., ovenbird (*Seiurus aurocapillus*)] probably would yield 0.0 as the estimated relative probability of use for open fields. Inclusion of open fields in the analysis would not be detrimental, but the results would be trivial because we already know such areas are rarely used by these species. Inclusion of habitat rarely if ever used by members of a population as "available" in a study will not unduly influence the results in an analysis of resource selection by estimation of selection ratios or resource selection functions (Manly et al. 2002). However, delineating study area boundaries or habitat availability should not be so restrictive that potentially available habitats are eliminated.

The distribution and size of cover types within a study area also can influence our ability to detect selection patterns. Porter and Church (1987) illustrated this problem by comparing an area where cover types were regularly distributed within an area where they were clumped. In areas that had regular or random distributions of cover types, the delineation of the study area had little influence on the analysis of habitat use versus availability. However, if cover types were aggregated, delineation of study area boundaries substantially influenced the analysis of selection.

The guidelines presented below may be helpful when study area boundaries are delineated for second-order selection or Design I studies, but each study is unique.

1. Size of the study area should be substantially larger than the home range of the study species.
2. Numbers of study animals, groups, or social units present on the study area should be, as far as possible, adequate for study.
3. An opportunity should exist for independent locations of animals or independent location of home ranges within the study area (i.e., as close as possible to a random sample of sites used by animals or a random sample of home ranges).
4. Study area boundaries should be chosen with consideration of the biology of the animal. Physical barriers such as rivers or mountain ranges might make better boundaries than an arbitrary (geopolitical) straight line on a map.

Availability of cover types and other landscape features within a study area often are measured directly from aerial photographs, maps, satellite images, or data layers in a GIS. In these situations, we are dealing with "known" amounts that, although having measurement error, do not have sampling error associated with them. Biologists often have access to cover type maps or GIS layers produced for multiple-use planning, such as timber type and plant association maps produced for national forests or private forest industry lands. Although the inventory may cover the area of interest, various approximations and measurement errors are part of these products (e.g., smallest forest stand inventoried is often >1 ha), and an understanding of these limitations is required prior to integration with wildlife data. Availabilities of habitat types may also be estimated by procedures to locate random points on maps in which case measurements are subject to sampling error as well as measurement error (Marcum and Loftsgaarden 1980).

Partitioning the available area (e.g., home ranges) into discrete grid cells or pixels (e.g., 100×100 m) provides an approach to use data from maps or GIS. Cells are categorized according to the number of captures, observations, or other index of use by study animals. Habitat features then are sampled within each cell or a subset of cells (or measured on a data layer of a GIS) with comparisons based on intensity of use, a sample of available versus used cells, or used versus unused cells (Porter and Church 1987, Erickson et al. 1998, Manly et al. 2002).

At times the study area may be large and the key issue is to randomly locate samples of available habitat throughout the area studied. If availabilities are estimated with small sample sizes (e.g., using field procedures) and have substantial sampling error, subsequent comparisons with use should be analyzed differently than if the availabilities are known (Thomas and Taylor 1990, White and Garrott 1990, Manly et al. 2002). If available habitat is sampled from a GIS, large sample sizes (i.e., 5,000 or larger) can be easily obtained using computer software. Sampling errors for estimation of availability of resources can essentially be ignored for variables measured at this scale.

Not only are specific attributes of habitat (amount and size) important, but also juxtapositions among habitats, variability between habitats, or spatial pattern may be influential in affecting habitat suitability (Otis 1997, 1998). One of the most important components of habitat structure is the spatial heterogeneity or amount of edge habitat available. Spatial heterogeneity not only integrates the absolute values of the vegetation or physiography, but also their variation in space (Wiens 1976). Many birds and mammals rely on more than one habitat for feeding, mating, nesting, or denning. A specific habitat may have an abundance of one resource, such as food, and not be used by an animal because it lacks or is distant from sites that provide another necessary resource, such as cover. Additionally, distribution of patches and edge habitat may have ramifications on habitat suitability, such as influencing a predator's ability to stalk or ambush prey. Thus, some measure of habitat variation is important. The availability of multiple data layers in a GIS allows easy measurement of some of these important variables (Hepinstall and Sader 1997; Erickson et al. 1998, 2001). For example, the density/length of edge between cover types, density of roads, or number of contour lines crossed by transects radiating from a used site might easily be measured in a buffer surrounding a used site, unused site, or a randomly sampled available site in a GIS. Many formal methods based on measured variables have been developed to access heterogeneity at a variety of scales using ranges, variances, and coefficients of variation (Zar 1998, Morrison et al. 2001, Williams et al. 2002), Wiens' heterogeneity index (Wiens 1974, Rotenberry and Wiens 1980), juxtaposition (Heinen and Cross 1983), spatial diversity indices (Mead et al. 1981, Heinen and Cross 1983, Thomas et al. 1979), interspersion index (Baxter and Wolfe 1972), and land surface ruggedness index (Beasom et al. 1983).

Heterogeneity also can be expressed in vertical and horizontal dimensions. Layering of vegetation in plant communities is a common way to express vertical heterogene-

ity. Techniques such as those that use a vertical density board have been used to describe heterogeneity (De Vos and Mosby 1969, Nudds 1977, Noon 1981, Robbins et al. 1989). Biologists working at the landscape level evaluate such parameters as habitat patch dispersion and corridor development (Forman and Godron 1986, Otis 1997). However, the biological interpretation of these characteristics may be less intuitive than other habitat features and should be addressed before information is collected.

MEASURING FOOD USE AND AVAILABILITY

Abundance and distribution of food resources are among the major environmental features that influence habitat selection. Because food intake relates to energy needs and ultimately to survival and reproduction, understanding food selection is a fundamental component of behavioral ecology.

Techniques to Measure Food Use

Methods most commonly used for investigating wildlife food use include: (1) direct observation of consumption, (2) feeding site investigations where amount of food removed by foraging animals is estimated, and (3) sampling remains of foods in gastrointestinal tracts, feces, or regurgitated pellets. In addition, broad categories of food can be characterized using stable isotopes of carbon and nitrogen. For example, the relative proportions of marine foods and red meat versus vegetation in the diets of bears were successfully identified in a variety of tissues using stable isotope methods (Hilderbrand et al. 1996).

Direct Observations

Individual animals can be observed directly as they are feeding, and recording the number of bites of a particular plant species or feeding minutes in a particular forage type. These values are translated into relative occurrence in the diet by comparing number of bites or minutes in a particular type of food relative to the total during the sampled observation period. Forage intake can be estimated by multiplying bite counts times the average mass per bite for a particular food. Powerful applications of direct observation have been made with tame, hand-raised animals that can be followed closely in the field (Parker et al. 1999). The key to detailed foraging observations is being able to watch the animal from nearby to successfully identify items taken. This can be compromised by the complexity of the plant community and the phenological development of individual plants (Holechek and Gross 1982).

Examination of feeding sites shortly after an herbivore has been observed feeding has been used to estimate food consumption. Recently grazed plants or twigs in the exact location where the animal was observed feeding can be counted and estimates made of the biomass removed. Even under the best of circumstances, this method ignores the "invisible use" problem of entire plants being grazed and leaving no residual indication of their presence (McInnis et al. 1983) as well as the difficulty in ascertaining if all evidence of grazing or browsing was produced by the most recently feeding animal.

Direct observation has been used to document prey taken by large carnivores including prey killed by lions (*Panthera leo*) (Schaller 1972), leopards (*P. pardus*), and wolves (Mech 1966). Detailed monitoring of prey taken also can be facilitated by radiotelemetry. Similarly, observations at raptor nests can provide information on foods brought to the nest for the young (Errington 1932, Marti 1987, Bielefeldt et al. 1992). Remotely triggered photography can be used to document prey returned to the nest by mammals and birds that might be difficult to observe otherwise (Perrins 1979).

Feeding Site/Browse Investigations

Feeding-site investigations were among the earliest approaches used to estimate diets of grazing animals and were developed originally for use with domestic livestock. These methods attempt to estimate the amount of vegetation removed by foraging animals from an area during a unit of time (Edlefson et al. 1960, Smith et al. 1962, Telfer 1969a, Martin 1970, Cooperrider 1986). Compared with other techniques used for wild herbivores, feeding-site investigations provide only general dietary information.

Feeding site methods can be divided into difference and grazed-plant estimates. Difference estimates are obtained by comparing plots before and after grazing or by comparing grazed and ungrazed plots. One method derived from before and after plots is to select 2 similar plots and clip all vegetation from one plot prior to grazing, and clipping the other plot at the end of the growing season. Differences in dry biomass between plots gives an approximation of the amount of forage removed by the grazers (Cook and Subbendieck 1986).

Comparisons of grazed with ungrazed plots are usually done with small wire cages that exclude grazers. Paired plots with similar species composition and production are established prior to the grazing season with one plot randomly caged. At the end of the grazing season, vegetation in both plots is clipped and mass is recorded, or use is estimated by another method. This technique should not be applied to estimates of use during the growing season because protected plants grow at different rates than grazed plants. Woody twig use can be estimated using similar methods. Biomass of twigs clipped in spring in areas subject to ungulate use can be compared with that for plots without browsing (Bobek et al. 1975). Difference methods can be labor intensive and require substantial sample sizes to show differences in use. Generally, one should not use difference methods if use is <50% (Cooperrider 1986).

Grazed-plant methods can be used on herbaceous and browse taxa by relying on estimating frequency of use, height/length conversions, or form-class/ocular estimates. Frequency methods require counting individual plants of each species in an area and calculating the percent grazed. Regression tables or equations, specific to each plant species, can be used to estimate percent use based on the proportion of plants that were grazed or browsed (Cook and Subbendieck 1986). A variation on this method is to estimate the percent cover for browse species within reach of browsers with the ratio of browsed to unbrowsed stems on a subsample of twigs within the plot used to estimate the amount consumed for each species.

Although highly labor intensive, an accurate approach for browse estimation is to tag individual stems which are measured in autumn and again during spring. The length of twig removed by browsers is highly correlated with the amount of forage removed (Smith and Urness 1962).

Post-ingestion Samples

The most common technique for analyzing food habits of terrestrial vertebrates involves sampling during or after digestion. Because mastication and digestion alter the food items, detection of forage may require microscopic examination of vegetation fragments. Similarly, undigested remains such as hair, cuticles, carapaces, or bones give an indication of prey consumed by carnivores.

Sample preservation can be an important consideration, especially in warm humid climates. Stomach or intestinal contents can be frozen. If freezing is not convenient, immersion in 5% formalin for small to mid-sized species and 10% formalin for larger sizes can be effective for preservation. A safer alternative to formalin is a solution of 70% alcohol. Moist feces or regurgitated pellets can be stored by freezing or by oven drying at 80–85 C for several hours to retard microbial and insect degradation. Samples then can be stored in bags with a fumigant (e.g., naphthalene or paradichlorobenzene) to prevent insect infestation. Feces also can be stored in table salt until ready for analysis.

Methods for Identification of Predator Diets

Diets of predators generally are assessed by examining feces (scats), stomach or intestinal contents, and regurgitated pellets. Scats and pellets can be collected noninvasively whereas stomach and intestinal contents usually involve taking specimens from dead animals. Scat identification usually involves size, color, conformation, composition, and odor (Murie 1974) but identification can be difficult, especially in areas with a diverse carnivore fauna. Laboratory methods for identifying species can involve thin-layer chromatography (Major et al. 1980) or DNA methods (Farrell et al. 2000).

Fecal material often is broken apart and separated manually but one should consider autoclaving samples or at least wearing a gauze mask because storage will not destroy tapeworm eggs or other parasites common in carnivore feces. An alternative is to wash feces through a sieve or placing the sample in a nylon bag that can be washed in a household washing machine (gentle cycle) to separate hair, teeth, and other identifiable bits. If hair and feathers are not crucial for identification, samples can be soaked in an 8% solution of NaOH for 12 hours and rinsed over a small (18-mesh) sieve (Schaller 1972, Green et al. 1986). This dissolves non-bony components leaving bone, teeth, insect exoskeletons, and pieces of reptile skin.

The stomach and intestines of animals killed during hunting or trapping can be another useful source of information on food use. Caution must be exercised in the interpretation of data, e.g., less bias is likely if animals are taken by shooting or in snares or kill traps (such as conibears) than in leg-hold traps where animals might consume baits or void contents of their gastrointestinal tract.

Stomach contents from predators should be washed with hot water through a large sieve (12–20 mesh). As for fecal analysis, because some predator parasites may infect humans, care should be taken to avoid direct contact with samples or aerosol. Reference collections are usually necessary to identify items found in the samples. For example, a collection of dorsal guard hairs will be useful as reference for various features of color banding, pigmentation, and morphology of cuticular scales (Moore et al. 1974). For bird feathers and invertebrate prey, reference collections may be invaluable in identification of remains.

Methods for Identification of Herbivore Diets

Fecal pellet analysis is commonly used as a noninvasive method for sampling diets of both mammalian and avian (Eastman and Jenkins 1970, Owen 1975) herbivores. Alimentary tracts can be collected from animals that have been killed by hunting or trapping. Direct access to alimentary contents is possible with esophageal and rumen fistulated animals. Fistulation involves installing a permanent device in the digestive tract of a living animal that allows samples to be taken of food items passing that point in the digestive process (McManus 1981). Fistulation has been used in both domestic (Vavra et al. 1978) and wild ruminants (Rice 1970). Animals must be tame so that they can be approached to collect samples through the fistula; thus, considerable time must be devoted to working with each animal. Emetics, flushing tubes, and manual expression of the gullet also have been used, primarily on birds, to purge the upper portion of the digestive tract without harming the individual (Errington 1932, Vogtman 1945).

Although some plant parts can be identified macroscopically, most food habits studies of herbivores involve microhistological techniques to identify characteristic cells and related structures (cuticle, stomata, aperites, trichomes, crystals, etc.) of the plants. A reference collection of samples from a range of food plants will be necessary to identify plant fragments. The relative proportions of plant species in each sample can be quantified by examining 20 microscope fields at 125X magnification for each of the 5 slides created for each diet sample (Holechek and Vavra 1981). The percent density of each food item can be estimated by dividing the number of plant fragments of a species by the total number of identifiable plant fragments in the sample. Frequency of occurrence can be calculated for each species by reporting the number of microscope fields that contained evidence of the species in a subsample of microscope fields examined per sample. Frequency of occurrence for each species is divided by the total number of observations for all species. This value is then multiplied by 100 to give the relative percentage with which each species occurs in the diet (Holechek and Gross 1982).

Fecal analysis can underrepresent the number of species in the diet, partly because some forbs are highly digestible and may be missing from fecal samples (Anthony and Smith 1974, Vavra et al. 1978, Smith and Shandruk 1979, McInnis et al. 1983). Inaccuracy of the technique, particularly when applied to species with diverse diets, has led some researchers to question the utility of the method for animals other than grazers (Gill et al. 1983). Experience and training of the technician in identifying plant fragments often are cited as the most important sources of error in using microhistological techniques (Holechek et al. 1982). Reference articles and books are available to assist in identifying plant fragments (Howard and Samuel 1979), but becoming proficient with the technique requires considerable experience.

Crop contents of birds are more reliable than scat analysis because little digestion occurs in the crop. The volume of each seed, fruit, or plant fragment can be estimated with a graduated cylinder or burette by displacement of a known quantity of water (Inglis and Barstow 1960). Reference collections for local samples of probable food items are necessary and reference books have been developed to aid in the identification of seeds and fruits (Musil 1963).

Techniques to Measure Food Availability

Wildlife food abundance can be estimated for an area by measuring the annual production of herbaceous plants, woody stems, fruits, and seeds, or by assessing the abundance of potential prey. A complication that requires careful consideration is that food abundance might not be directly related to availability. Availability suggests a food resource is both accessible and usable (Morrison et al. 1992). Access to food resources can vary with weather or by the presence of predators or competitors. Snow can make forage unavailable to herbivores, or alternatively, snow can alter the vulnerability of prey for carnivores (Halpin and Bissonette 1988, Fuller 1991). In resource selection studies, effects that modify food abundance might be modeled using covariates such as snow depth or presence of a predator or competitor.

Grasses and Forbs

Clipping and weighing dried samples of above ground vegetation is the most accurate, but most time-consuming, technique for measuring availability of herbaceous plants. Many techniques have been developed to more rapidly estimate vegetative biomass and to avoid destructive sampling. These include estimating biomass in small quadrats (Shoop and McIlvain 1963), or estimating percent cover by species in small sample plots (Daubenmire 1958). Pin intercept methods have been developed using sampling frames containing rows of pins that are pushed through the vegetation. A coarse method often used in rangelands involves sampling the ground cover below a point on the observer's boot. While walking through an area, at regular intervals, the species of plant beneath the tip of the boot is recorded (Owensby 1973, Cook and Stubbendieck 1986).

Browse

Predictive equations have been developed that relate measures of shrub size to forage production (Lyon 1968, Telfer 1969*b*, Bobek and Bergstrom 1978). Specific equations must be estimated for each species and for individual study sites. The twig-count method estimates available biomass of browse by calculating the average weight of edible material in a single twig and multiplying that value times the number of twigs available (Shafer 1963). A sample of previously browsed twigs is used to estimate the average browsing diameter for each forage species. Mass of browsed twigs is then estimated from a collection of twigs clipped to the size of the average browsed twig. Densities of twigs can be estimated from counts on circular plots (Shafer 1963) or belt transects (Irwin and Peek 1979), and available browse biomass is calculated per unit area. Modifications of this technique include development of equations that use unbrowsed twig length or basal diameter to estimate twig mass (Basile and Hutchings 1966, Telfer 1969*a*).

Fruits and Seeds

Fruits and seeds from low-growing herbs and shrubs can be counted and averaged per plant and summed over an area to estimate biomass per unit area. Similarly, hard mast crops, such as acorns, can be collected in funnel traps that sample an area under the canopy (Gysel 1956). Although traps usually prevent animals from taking mast once it has fallen from the tree, information on production can be biased if seeds are consumed before falling to the ground.

DESIGN CONSIDERATIONS AND ANALYSIS
General Considerations

Sample size considerations are crucial in establishing a study design (Bart and Notz 2005, Garton et al. 2005). A number of papers have outlined sample sizes needed for reliable estimates of diet based on various techniques, e.g., sample sizes for microhistological analysis of vizcacha (*Lagostomus maximus*) diets have been calculated (Bontti and Bóo 2002). These guidelines are variations on power analysis and are difficult to generalize by technique. Primary considerations include the variances of variables of interest and the magnitude of difference needed (i.e., effect size). Standard procedures for power analysis and design of studies have been reviewed by Hurlbert (1984), Williams et al. (2002), Bart and Notz (2005), and Garton et al. (2005).

Frequently, investigators have focused on examining characteristics of a site used by an animal while it is feeding, resting, or rearing young (Stinnett and Klebenow 1986). These sites might then be compared to sites within the study area where use was not detected (sampling protocol SP-D). In this case, a set of predictor variables would be measured on all sampled units with development of logistic regression models (Hosmer and Lemeshow 1989, Neter et al. 1996) to predict probability of use. The other most common study design (SP-A) would involve collection of a sample of "used" units, such as locations of radio-marked animals, to contrast those units with a sample of "available" units. In this case, the models yield estimates of the relative probability of use (i.e., information to the effect that one unit might be selected with twice or 3 times the probability that another unit is selected).

A valid probability sampling procedure (Morrison et al. 2001) is used to sample a variety of features at each used, unused, or available site, cell, or home range (James and Shugart 1970, Dueser and Shugart 1978, Fridell and Litvaitis 1991). The features selected to describe a sampled unit (e.g., litter depth, understory stem density, canopy closure, distance from roads, aspect, slope) are assumed to represent or be highly correlated with the variables used by animals to evaluate a site and often include some measurement of food abundance, cover, and structural characteristics (Fig. 3). With development of GIS, many possibilities exist to measure landscape variables (Erickson et al. 1998, Otis 1998) that may be important for site selection (e.g., density of roads, proportion of habitat types, or density of edge between habitat types in a certain diameter circle centered at the site). Because the actual habitat features influencing selection are not known, measuring several features is appropriate (e.g., Rice et al. 1984). However, as the number of features measured becomes large, the chance of detecting spurious relationships also increases. Therefore, the list of features to be sampled should be limited to those based on biological considerations for the relationships between animals and their habi-

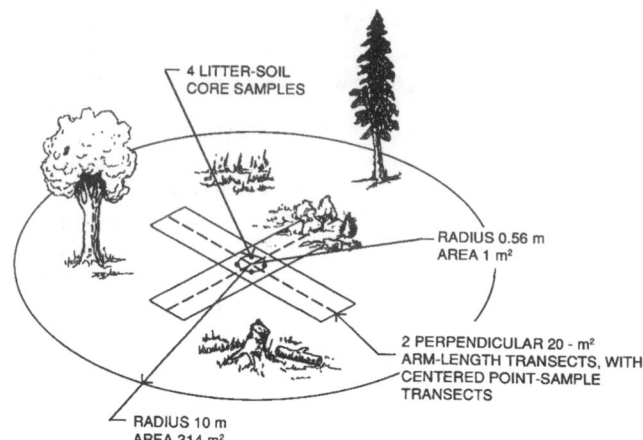

Fig. 3. An example of nested plots used to sample ground litter, understory stem density, and overstory composition (modified from Dueser and Shugart 1978).

tat (Green 1979, Anderson et al. 2001).

Results of fecal or pellet composition analyses are often presented as percent occurrence. Only the presence or absence of a food species in a sample is recorded, regardless of the number of individuals or volume of a given food type. Although this is approach is commonly used, it does not reflect the proportion by volume, weight, or energy that different food items contribute to the diet. Remains of a single mouse in a sample receive the same relative importance as the remains of a deer. The problem is further compounded by differential digestibility of food items. Attempts have been made to estimate biomass of prey consumed based on fecal remains (Lockie 1959, Floyd et al. 1978, Weaver 1993). Correction factors have been developed for converting the weight of identifiable remains in scats to actual weights of foods eaten. This technique has not been used widely, however, despite high correlation between weights of prey consumed and weights of identifiable remains (Floyd et al. 1978). The primary difficulty is identifying the proportion of fecal remains composed of each food type in scat or pellets that contain the remains of more than one food species.

Data from stomach or crop samples often are reported as percent volume or percent dry mass. Results can be aggregated by food type across all stomachs/crops and reported as a percentage of the contents of each sample and averaged across samples. Aggregate percentage is calculated by summing the proportion of sample volume that a particular food item represents in each animal and dividing it by the total number of animals in the sample. Aggregate volume is calculated by summing the volume of a particular food item in all the animals and dividing it by the volume of all foods in all the animals. Aggregate volume gives importance to the absolute volume of food consumed by all animals, whereas aggregate percentage gives equal importance to the percent composition of food items in each animal (Swanson and Bartonek 1970).

Indices based on measures of use have been used to assess resource use with the basic assumption that the index increases with amount of time an animal spends at a site, or that population density increases as the index increases. However, several variables may influence this relationship, including observer bias, or the accumulation rates of indices may vary independent of time spent within a site. Use of indices for measures of habitat importance or population density should be viewed with caution (Anderson 2001). For example, Collins and Urness (1981) observed that defecation rates of mule deer (*Odocoileus hemionus*) varied with activity (feeding vs. traveling). As a result, the distribution of pellet groups gave a biased impression of habitat use. Indices should be calibrated using double sampling procedures (Morrison et al. 2001) to establish empirical relationships between index values and estimates of actual parameter values to help avoid erroneous conclusions.

Standard Statistical Analyses

Analytical methods for resource selection studies usually involve comparison of characteristics of samples or censuses of used, unused, and available resource units. The first step should involve graphical and descriptive comparisons of the distribution of the covariates that describe each unit for the samples being compared (e.g., use vs. available). Patterns described in these analyses also probably will be apparent in any inferential analyses (e.g., hypothesis testing).

Standard statistical procedures (Zar 1998, Morrison 2001) are appropriate for comparison of used and unused sites or making comparisons among other stratifications of the sites or home ranges. Measurements of use might also be partitioned into categories (e.g., not used, occasionally used, frequently used). Comparisons also may be made between portions of home ranges of study animals (activity core vs. outside the core). Univariate statistical tests can be conducted on individual variables with multivariate tests used on several variables simultaneously following standard statistical procedures. In this section, we concentrate on statistical procedures that have been developed specifically for study of resource use by animals.

Several older hypothesis-testing techniques such as chi-square analyses (Neu et al. 1974, Byers et al. 1984), Friedman's test (Friedman 1937, Conover 1999) and the similar Quade (1979) method, and the PREFER method (Johnson 1980) have been extensively reviewed (Alldredge and Ratti 1986, 1992; Alldredge et al. 1998) (Table 1). However, these techniques are becoming less used because of techniques such as compositional analysis (Aebischer et al. 1993), discrete-choice modeling (also known as case control or conditional fixed effects) (Cooper and Millspaugh 2001, Manly et al. 2002), and generalized linear modeling approaches (e.g., log-linear modeling and logistic regression) (Heisey 1985, Hosmer and Lemeshow 1989, Manly et al. 2002). This shift in emphasis is, in part, due to increased use of GIS and because most earlier methods only considered discrete (categorical) resource types (e.g., land-cover types). The latter methods can consider multiple continuous and discrete covariates (e.g., logistic regression and discrete-choice modeling). The GIS technique using the Mahalonobis distance metric has also been used to describe and map habitat use (Knick and

Table 1. Characteristics associated with common statistical analysis methods of resource selection (Y = Yes, N = No) (adapted from Erickson et al. 2001).

Characteristics	Neu et al. (1974)	Johnson (1980)	Friedman (1937)	Compositional Aebischer et al. (1993)	Logistic regression	Log-linear modeling	Discrete choice
Applicable to Design I: individuals not marked, and population level availability.	Y	N	N	N	Y	Y	Y
Applicable to Design II: individuals marked and population level availability.	N[a]	Y	Y	Y	Y	Y	Y
Applicable to Design III: individuals marked, availability defined for each animal.	N[a]	Y	Y	Y	Y	Y	Y
Temporal independence of relocations assumed.	Y	N	N	N	Y/N[b]	Y/N[b]	N
Independence among animals assumed.	Y	Y	Y	Y	Y	Y	Y
Allows for categorical covariates (e.g., gender, subgroups)	N	N	N	Y	Y	Y	Y
Allows for continuous covariates (e.g., distance to roads)	N	N	N	N	Y	N	Y
Assumes the sample of animals is representative of the population, inferences are to average selection of the larger population from which the sample was obtained	Y[c]	Y	Y	Y	Y[d]	Y[d]	Y

[a] Neu et al. (1974) method could be applied by pooling data, but this is not recommended.
[b] Independence important if data are pooled across animals, not important when animals are used as the units of replication.
[c] Assumes the indices of use (e.g., observed tracks) are representative of the population of indices.
[d] Inference is to the larger population if animals are the units of replication (i.e., data are not pooled).

Rotenberry 1998). These techniques have become more readily available in statistical software computer packages. Many of the most common techniques for analyzing resource selection data have been previously reviewed and summarized (Alldredge et al. 1998, Manly et al. 2002). White and Garrott (1990) and Erickson et al. (2001) provide in-depth descriptions of many of the approaches for study of resource selection in radiotelemetry studies.

Specialized methods that have been used for analysis of resource selection data and their assumptions and applications vary (Table 1). We present a summary of the chi-square analysis because of its historical interest and analyze the Neu et al. (1974) data as an example. However, we emphasize use of resource selection functions as the most comprehensive procedure for analysis of resource availability and selection. We show by example that simple selection ratios computed for the Neu et al. (1974) data arise as "odds" or relative probability of use of the habitat types when a resource selection function is specialized to the case of a single categorical variable, e.g., habitat type.

Chi-square Analyses for Categorical Data

For data based on resource categories (e.g., habitats, food types, or categorized continuous predictors), a chi-square test can provide an omnibus answer to the question: is there evidence of selection or not? This test is appropriate when individual observations of selected units are considered independent. Chi-square analyses appear most appropriate in the Design I case and are not appropriate when several animals have multiple (dependent) relocations. This approach was first considered by Neu et al. (1974) and later by Byers et al. (1984). Two statistics that have approximate chi-square distributions are most commonly considered. Suppose there are C resource categories, and that some number of animals (or observations of a single animal) have been observed in each category. Further, suppose the null hypothesis of "no selection" leads to an expected number of observations in each category. The form of test statistic that is most commonly used for this purpose is the Pearson statistic, which takes the form

$$\chi_p^2 = \sum_{i=1}^{c} (O_i - E_i)^2 / E_i,$$

where O_i is an observed sample frequency, E_i is the expected value of O_i according to the hypothesis being considered, and the summation is over all resource categories.

A caution against small observed and/or expected numbers applies (Zar 1998). Tests and confidence intervals on data with one or more categories with low (5 or less) observed or expected numbers may be suspect, since in that case, the standard normal distribution may not be an accurate approximation to the sampling distribution of the statistic.

We provide an example of Design I, Sampling Protocol A, using the popular data set provided by Neu et al. (1974) with the proportions of 4 habitat types available to a population of moose (Table 2). These proportions are contrasted to the proportions of observations of moose tracks in each of the habitat types. The chi-square analysis provides a strong indication that selection is occurring.

Table 2. Chi-square analysis of 117 observations of use by moose (based on tracks) (Neu et al. 1974).

Description	Available	Use	Expected use	Pearson chi-square
Interior of burn	0.340	25	39.78	5.49
Edge of burn	0.101	22	11.82	8.77
Edge of unburned	0.104	30	12.17	26.13
Interior of unburned	0.455	40	53.24	3.29
Totals	1.000	117	chi-square:	43.69
			P-value:	0.00

MODELING RESOURCE SELECTION
Selection Ratios for Categorical Data

The selection ratio for a given resource category is the ratio of the proportion used to the proportion of availability (Manly et al. 2002). If the ratio is close to one, there is evidently no selection. Values smaller than one indicate selection against that category; large values indicate selection for the category.

To differentiate between the 2 proportions of interest (use and availability), we represent the true proportion of availability of habitat i by π_i and the true proportion of use of habitat i by p_i. Let $n_{i,u}$ be the number of animals found in habitat i, with total sample size being n_u. Thus, an estimate of p_i is $n_{i,u}/n_u$. Manly et al. (2002) used the symbol w for the ratio of the proportion used to proportion available. When availability is known, the estimate of the selection ratio is $\hat{w}_i = (n_{i,u}/n_u)/\pi_i$. Estimated availability is n_{ia}/n_a if availability is estimated by random points on a map or in the study area and estimation of availability is based on a total of n_a random points, with n_{ia} being in habitat i. In this case, $\hat{w}_i = (n_{i,u}/n_u)/(n_{ia}/n_a)$. The selection ratios, $\hat{w}_i$, are often standardized between 0 and 1 using the formula $\hat{w}_i = \hat{w}_i/\sum(\hat{w}_i)$. Extensive numerical examples, variance calculations, and modifications to these basic formulae are in Manly et al. (2002: Chapter 4). Estimated variances follow the formula for proportions (known availability) and ratios (estimated availability).

Selection ratios are also applicable to the case of multiple animals with multiple relocations per animal (Erickson et al. 2001, Manly et al. 2002). Making inferences regarding the average selection relationships to a large population of animals can be conducted by averaging individual selection ratios and using the number of animals as the effective sample size, avoiding issues of pseudoreplication (Erickson et al. 2001). This approach assumes the sample of animals is randomly drawn from the population, which may not be the case.

We now revisit the moose track data (Table 2). Selection ratios, and standardized selection ratios are calculated (Table 3) with 95% Bonferroni adjusted confidence limits (e.g., Byers et al. 1984, Manly et al. 2002). Based on these confidence limits, one would conclude there is statistically significant selection against the interior of the burn and the interior of unburned area, with significant selection for the edge of the unburned area. The selection ratio for the edge of the burn, 1.862, indicates selection for this type but the result is not statistically sig-

Table 3. Statistics for moose data (Table 2).

Description	Selection ratio	SE	Confidence interval		Standardized ratio
Interior of burn	0.628	0.111	0.350	0.907	0.110
Edge of burn	1.862	0.358	0.968	2.755	0.326
Edge of unburned	2.465	0.388	1.496	3.435	0.432
Interior of unburned	0.751	0.096	0.511	0.992	0.132

Table 4. Indicator variables for 4 categories with "A" chosen as the baseline category.

Category	X_1	X_2	X_3	Model	Odds ratio (to A)
A	0	0	0	$\exp(\beta_0)$	1
B	1	0	0	$\exp(\beta_0+\beta_1)$	$\exp(\beta_1)$
C	0	1	0	$\exp(\beta_0+\beta_2)$	$\exp(\beta_2)$
D	0	0	1	$\exp(\beta_0+\beta_3)$	$\exp(\beta_3)$

nificant with the conservative Bonferroni procedure because the confidence interval (0.968–2.755) slightly overlaps the number 1.0.

The selection intensity (for or against) of one resource category can be compared to that of another using tests and confidence intervals for differences in pairs of selection ratios. The number of situations that can arise for the analysis of categorical data is quite large and the analyses are tedious. We emphasize the more important case where multiple continuous and discrete variables are considered for their influence on selection of resources. For example, in the moose track data (Table 2), other continuous variables such as density of roads (km of road/km^2) or snow cover might also affect selection of feeding or resting sites. Manly et al. (2002) provide descriptions of further analyses of resource selection when observations of use are assigned to categories.

Resource Selection Function (RSF) for Categorical Data

Logistic regression is a specialized regression tool for working with multiple continuous and discrete variables (Hosmer and Lemeshow 1989, Neter et al. 1996). However, logistic regression also can be used to analyze the effect of a single categorical response variable on resource selection (e.g., the effects of the 4 habitat categories [Tables 2, 3] on selection of locations by moose in Neu et al. [1974]). The technique is presented as a means to analyze selection among categories of a categorical variable and as an introduction to estimation of a resource selection function when there is more than one variable.

Suppose X is an environmental variable thought to be associated with selection of resources by the animal under study. Details for estimation of the coefficients in the model will be deferred, but, for illustration, X could be a simple categorical variable referencing habitat categories. In later examples, the predictor variable X could be a continuous variable such as distance from features (e.g., water) or density of roads in a unit, used alone or in conjunction with other habitat variables, or it could be a categorical variable other than habitats. Manly et al. (2002) provide a detailed discussion of the use of logistic regression for resource selection.

Consider the generic example (Table 4) with 4 categories of habitat type: A, B, C, and D. Suppose category A is chosen as the baseline (the choice is arbitrary), then logistic regression analysis would allow estimation of changes in the odds between categories A and B, A and C, and A and D. "Dummy" (or indicator) variable X_1 (Table 4) indicates a shift from A to B, X_2 from A to C, and X_3 from A to D. There are 4 categories of habitat type, thus,

3 dummy variables are needed, one less than the number of categories. Notice the row for category A has every indicator set to zero. Also, the location of the only "1" in any column identifies for which habitat that predictor is an indicator. These are the 2 key features of indicator variable construction. Mechanically, the use of indicator variables leads to a special form of multiple logistic regression with the following model for the RSF or odds of selection,

$$\text{odds} = \exp(\beta_0 + \beta_1 X_1 + \beta_2 X_2 + \beta_3 X_3),$$

where $\exp(\beta_0 + \beta_1 X_1 + \beta_2 X_2 + \beta_3 X_3)$ denotes the exponential function

$$e^{\beta_0 + \beta_1 X_1 + \beta_2 X_2 + \beta_3 X_3}.$$

That is, the base e of natural logarithms raised to the power $(\beta_0 + \beta_1 X_1 + \beta_2 X_2 + \beta_3 X_3)$. In practice, logistic regression will yield numerical values for the coefficients, the β, in the model. The restricted set of chosen values for the X's (Table 4) lead to the list of possible model expressions and odds ratios. Careful examination of the material (Table 4) will aid understanding in use of indicator variables for logistic regression. For example, the odds for category B is obtained by substitution of $X_1 = 1$, $X_2 = 0$, and $X_3 = 0$ into the above equation and the odds ratio for selection of type B to A is $\exp(\beta_0+\beta_1)/\exp(\beta_0) = \exp(\beta_1)$.

Now assume X is a continuous variable such as distance (km) to water. Logistic regression gives a model for the change in the odds (defined as the ratio of probability of use to probability of "not-use") of habitat use according to the model equation:

$$\text{odds} = \exp(\beta_0 + \beta_1 X).$$

In logistic regression, the impact of changing X to $X + 1$, e.g., to increase the distance to water by 1 km, is in the ratio of the odds for each value of X:

$$\exp(\beta_0 + \beta_1(X + 1))/\exp(\beta_0 + \beta_1(X)) = \exp(\beta_1).$$

For example, if $\beta_1 = -0.41$ the odds ratio would be $\exp(-0.41) = 0.66$ and an increase of 1 km in X, distance to water, is associated with a 33% decrease in the odds of use. If the coefficient were positive for distance to water, and $\beta_1 = +0.2$, the odds ratio would be $\exp(0.2) = 1.22$, and an increase of 1 km in X is associated with a 22% increase in the odds of use.

Estimation of a RSF for Categorical Data Using Logistic Regression

We now reanalyze the moose data (Table 2) using logistic regression. We present this analysis to illustrate the relationship between the selection ratios and odds ratios from logistic regression, although use of logistic regression when considering only one categorical variable is usually not done.

General Theory for Modeling and Estimation of a RSF

We illustrate the general theory for estimation of a RSF for multiple variables by defining 3 "dummy" variables to model the selection among the 4 habitat types (Table 2). Let $w(X_i) = w(X_{i1}, X_{i2}, X_{i3})$ denote the resource selection function, i.e., the odds or relative probability that a unit with covariate vector $X_i = (X_{i1}, X_{i2}, X_{i3})$ is selected where the "dummy variables" are coded (Table 5). Given data from sampling protocol A (i.e., a sample of available points and a sample of used points), we assume the resource selection function can be modeled by the exponential function:

$$w(x_i) = \exp(\beta_1 X_{i1} + \beta_2 X_{i2} + \beta_3 X_{i3}).$$

Then, conditional on the observed sample sizes, probability of use given X_i is

$$\frac{\exp(\beta_0 + \beta_1 X_{i1} + \beta_2 X_{i2} + \beta_3 X_{i3})}{[1 + \exp(\beta_0 + \beta_1 X_{i1} + \beta_2 X_{i2} + \beta_3 X_{i3})]}.$$

This is the form of a logistic regression function and we can now examine a "simulated" sample of available points (coded as $Y = 0$ for the dependent variable) and the sample results for the 117 used points (Table 2) (coded as $Y = 1$ for the dependent variable). Any computer software package for fitting a logistic regression function can be used to obtain estimates of the coefficients and their standard errors. Those estimates can be placed in the exponential function $w(x_i) = \exp(\beta_1 X_{i1} + \beta_2 X_{i2} + \beta_3 X_{i3})$ to obtain the resource selection function, ignoring the constant β_0. Note the coefficient β_0 is not used in the resource selection function for a mathematical technical reason, i.e., the frac-

Table 5. Independent and dependent variables coded for entry into a logistic regression computer software package. The sample of used points is coded $Y = 1$ based on the available sample sizes (Table 2). The "simulated" sample of 20,000 available points was computed to yield the exact proportions of habitats available (Table 2) and are coded $Y = 0$.

Habitat type	Dependent variable Y	Sample size	Independent variables X_{i0}	X_{i1}	X_{i2}	X_{i3}
Interior of burn	1	25	1	1	0	0
Edge of burn	1	22	1	0	1	0
Edge of unburned	1	30	1	0	0	1
Interior of unburned	1	40	1	0	0	0
Interior of burn	0	6,796	1	1	0	0
Edge of burn	0	2,015	1	0	1	0
Edge of unburned	0	2,073	1	0	0	1
Interior of unburned	0	9,114	1	0	0	0

tion of used points in the sample is unknown. It is important to understand the RSF is given by equation $w(x_i) = \exp(\beta_1 X_{i1} + \beta_2 X_{i2} + \beta_3 X_{i3})$ and not by the logistic regression function,

$$\frac{\exp(\beta_0 + \beta_1 X_{i1} + \beta_2 X_{i2} + \beta_3 X_{i3})}{[1 + \exp(\beta_0 + \beta_1 X_{i1} + \beta_2 X_{i2} + \beta_3 X_{i3})]}.$$

Once the logistic regression equation is fitted, values for the coefficients are estimated, and the RSF, $w(x)$ can be evaluated numerically.

Application of the General Theory to Categorical Data

To illustrate the estimation of a RSF for a single categorical variable, we assume the habitat types in Neu et al. (1974) are in a GIS and that a random or systematic sample of 20,000 points was placed across the area. To that end, we assume that 34% (i.e., 6,796) of 20,000 points were in the interior of the burn, 10.1% (i.e., 2,015) were in the edge of the burn, 10.4% (i.e., 2,073) in the edge of the unburned, and 45.5% (i.e., 9,114) in the interior of the unburned habitat to yield a "simulated sample" of the available habitats based on the reported proportions (Table 2). We then coded independent and dependent variables, as they would be placed in a standard logistic regression software program (Table 5). If the available habitat types were actually sampled by visiting points in the field or placing random points on a map, the data would be coded and analyzed in the same manner.

Estimates of the coefficients and their standard errors from a logistic regression software package were then obtained (Table 6). Upper and lower limits of approximate 95% confidence intervals on the coefficients can be computed by the equations, $b_i \pm 1.96(\text{seb}_i)$ or equivalently 95% confidence intervals on the selection ratios can be obtained by $\exp(b_i \pm 1.96(\text{seb}_i))$. We note (Table 6) that 2 of the coefficients are large compared to their standard errors (95% confidence intervals will not contain 0.0). Thus, there is significant selection among the habitat types. We elect to leave all of the habitat types in the RSF for the categorical variable "habitat type."

The RSF evaluated for the type "Interior of burn" is

$$w(x_1) = \exp[-0.179(1) + 0.907(0) + 1.188(0)]$$
$$= \exp(-0.179) = 0.836,$$

where $x_1 = (1,0,0)$ (Table 5) and the constant b_0 is ignored. The values of the RSF were evaluated for the other habitat types and standardized so they sum to 1.0 in the third column (Table 7). Note the fourth habitat type, "interior of unburned," is the reference type with $x_4 = (0,0,0)$.

Table 6. Estimated coefficients and their standard errors for the RSF, $w(x_i) = \exp(\beta_1 X_{i1} + \beta_2 X_{i2} + \beta_3 X_{i3})$, fitted to the moose data from Neu et al. (1974) (Tables 2, 5).

Coefficient	Value	SE
b_0	−5.429	0.1581
b_1	−0.1787	0.2549
b_2	0.9073	0.2655
b_3	1.1882	0.2416

Table 7. Estimated values for the RSF, $w(x_i) = \exp(\beta_1 X_{i1} + \beta_2 X_{i2} + \beta_3 X_{i3})$, for each of the habitat types in the moose example (Table 2). The third column contains the values of the RSF standardized to sum to 1.0.

Habitat type	$w(x_i)$	$w(x_i)/\Sigma w(x_i)$
Interior of burn	0.836	0.110
Edge of burn	2.478	0.326
Edge of unburned	3.281	0.432
Interior of unburned	1.000	0.132
Totals	7.595	1.000

Statistical significance of the other coefficients is judged in comparison to the reference "selection ratio," $w(x_4) = \exp(0) = 1.0$. The coefficient $b_1 = -0.179$ is small compared to its standard error and one could conclude the "interior of burn" does not add a significant contribution to the RSF compared to the reference level, "interior of unburned". In the words of a hypothesis test, there is no significant difference in selection for "interior of burn" and the reference level "interior of unburned." Both coefficients for "edge of burn" and "edge of unburned" are positive and large indicating there is significant selection for those 2 habitat types in comparison to the reference level "interior of unburned" or "interior of the burn."

The interpretation of the results (Tables 3, 7) is that the probability of location of moose tracks in the "edge of burn" by the protocol used in the Neu et al. (1974) study was about 2 1/2 times larger than the probability of location of moose tracks in the "interior of unburned." This interpretation is subject to the specific time, study location, density of the moose population, etc., and specific values for other independent predictor variables such as the depth of snow. Extrapolation of the results to the relative probability of selection or use of the different habitat types by moose depends on the additional assumptions that tracks were equally visible in the different habitat types and that moose selected locations independent of each other (i.e., the animals have free and equal access to all available habitat).

The standardized values (Table 7) are the same as reported based on the simple selection ratios (Table 3). We included the analysis of the Neu et al. (1974) data by use of a computer software package for logistic regression for 2 reasons. First, we wanted to demonstrate the simple selection ratios (Table 3) are equivalent to fitting a more general resource selection function (RSF) that gives the relative probability (odds) of selection among the habitat types based on observed data. The interpretation of the values of the "selection ratios," $w(x)$ (Table 7), or the simple selection ratios (Table 3), are in reference to each other. For example, the probability of selection for the "edge of burn" by moose was about 2.478, or 2 1/2 times larger that the probability of selection of the reference habitat "interior of unburned" by moose.

Second, we also wanted to provide a unified procedure for analysis of categorical data that does not depend on tedious use of formulas for the ratios of random variables Manly et al. (2002: Chapter 4). The above procedure using a standard computer program for logistic regression is one of the easiest ways to analyze habitat selection among categories of a single categorical variable.

Multiple Continuous and Discrete Variables

We illustrate the general theory for estimation of a RSF by analysis of resource selection by alder flycatchers (*Empidonax alnorum*) on the Innoko National Wildlife Refuge in west central Alaska. A complete description of the study is provided in Erickson et al. (2004). Locations of breeding alder flycatchers were gathered by walking transect surveys within the flood plain of the Innoko River during the 2000 and 2001 breeding seasons. Transects were systematically located along the Innoko River perpendicular to the general orientation of the river. Availability of breeding habitat was defined to be the area within the floodplain of the river. This example fits in Design I because breeding areas were sampled for the population of alder flycatchers. Sampling protocol A fits because a separate sample of used locations is contrasted to a sample of available locations in the floodplain.

With ArcInfo GRID, the study area polygon (floodplain) was converted into an image with 30 units (pixel), coincident with Landsat Thematic Mapper (TM) imagery taken on 26 August 1991. Eleven raster layers were co-registered (measured) on each 30-m pixel in the study area and used in subsequent processing. For each pixel the following 11 coverages were considered:

- spectral values of Landsat TM bands 1–5, 7, from 26 August 1991,
- elevation (from USGS 1:63,360 scale quads),
- slope (derived from elevation),
- aspect (derived from elevation),
- distance from unit to river (rivers defined from Landsat TM imagery), and
- distance from unit to closest lake (lakes defined from Landsat TM imagery).

There were 109 observations of breeding birds (109 "used" points) and a systematic sample of 5,094 pixels in the floodplain ("available" pixels of a total of 616,754 pixels). The values of each of the 11 coverages were recorded for each pixel that intersected a 105-m radius of the center of the pixel containing the observed used point. This collection of pixels formed a buffer surrounding each used point. A similar size buffer was defined for each of the pixels in the available sample and for each pixel in the floodplain so the estimated relative probability of use could be mapped for the entire study area. Twenty potential predictor variables were defined for the buffer surrounding each pixel:

- variables 1–6: average of Landsat TM bands 1–5 and 7 for all pixels in the buffer,
- variables 7–12: standard deviation of Landsat TM bands 1–5 and 7 for all pixels in the buffer,
- variable 13: average elevation of all pixels in the buffer,
- variable 14: average slope of all pixels in the buffer,
- variables 15–18: aspects, 4 variables for aspect giving the percentage of pixels in the buffer as north, south, east, and west,
- variable 19: average distance to river for all pixels in the buffer, and
- variable 20: average distance to closest lake for all pixels in the buffer.

Table 8. Importance values and sign of coefficient based on importance value weighting for variables in the models for alder flycatcher, Alaska (Erickson et al. 2004).

Variable	Variable description	Importance value
River	Average distance from river, m	0.7 (−)
Lake	Average distance from lake, m	0
Band 1	Average of band 1 within buffer	0
Band 4	Average of band 4 within buffer	1 (+)
Band 5	Average of band 5 within buffer	0
Std band 1	SD of band 1 within buffer	0.28 (−)
Std band 3	SD of band 3 within buffer	0.89 (+)
Std band 4	SD of band 4 within buffer	0.61 (+)
Std band 7	SD of band 7 within buffer	0.39 (+)
Elevation	Average elevation	1 (−)
Slope	Average slope	0
Aspect	4 categorical variables, % within north, south, east, west aspect	0

Twenty variables are too many to realistically fit and evaluate in a RSF using present computer software. In addition, several of the variables were highly correlated with each other and inclusion of 2 or more highly correlated variables (i.e., multicollinearity) leads to unstable coefficients in the fitted models (Neter et al. 1996). Highly correlated variables were eliminated from consideration resulting in a set of 12 (Table 8).

Because data were collected by sampling protocol A and the proportion of used pixels is "small" in comparison to the total number of available pixels (assumption 6); logistic regression was used to estimate the coefficients in the resource selection function,

$$w(x) = \exp(\beta_1 X_1 + ... + \beta_p X_p).$$

The function $w(x)$ estimates the relative probability of selection of a point in the landscape given the values of variables x_1 through x_p at that point and coefficients, β_1 through β_p, for variables in the model. For each selection of p variables of the 12, the sample of used locations (with the dependent variable $Y = 1$) and the sample of available locations (with $Y = 0$) were fitted to a logistic regression function using a computer software package. The relative probabilities of selection are calculated by taking the coefficients from the product of the logistic regression and placing them into the formula

$$w(x) = \exp(\beta_1 X_1 + ... + \beta_p X_p),$$

rather than using probabilities generated by the computer software.

There were 12 variables available for estimating the resource selection function. All 4,095 ($2^{12} - 1 = 4,095$) possible main effect models were fitted by logistic regression of the dependent variable Y on the independent predictor variables. Quadratic variables and interaction terms were ignored for this study. These 4,095 models were then ranked according to Bayesian Information Criterion (BIC) (Schwarz 1978). The top 5 models (i.e., smallest BICs) from this set were reported as our final "best" models

Table 9. Top 5 models (lowest BIC) for alder flycatcher example, Alaska (Erickson et al. 2004; Fig. 4). Model based on averages and standard deviations of variables in a 105-m radius buffer around each sampled point in the landscape. The available sample was derived from the corridor–wide area.

Model	BIC	Model weight	Variable	Estimate	SE
1	911.36	0.376	river	−0.0008	0.00029
			band 4	0.0412	0.00701
			std band 3	0.2278	0.0347
			std band 4	0.0393	0.0102
			elevation	−0.1191	0.0226
2	912.347	0.229	band 4	0.0471	0.0069
			std band 3	0.2347	0.0342
			std band 4	0.0517	0.00923
			elevation	−0.1228	0.0232
3	912.499	0.213	river	−0.0008	0.00029
			band 4	0.0433	0.00691
			std band1	−0.7367	0.1959
			std band3	0.294	0.0732
			std band7	0.2039	0.0489
			elevation	−0.1231	0.024
4	913.811	0.111	river	−0.0013	0.000295
			band 4	0.0332	0.00525
			std band7	0.1933	0.0268
			elevation	−0.1018	0.0222
5	914.722	0.070	band4	0.0479	0.00687
			std band1	−0.9981	0.1792
			std band 3	0.3839	0.0685
			std band7	0.2149	0.0474
			elevation	−0.1343	0.0247

(Table 9). BIC was defined as, $-2\log(\text{Likelihood}) + p \times \log(n)$, where p was the number of variables in the model, n was number of used bird locations plus number of available locations, Likelihood was the value of the logistic likelihood, and log was the natural logarithm.

Relative probabilities of use were calculated for each pixel in the floodplain based on weights of importance values (Burnham and Anderson 1998) for the top 5 models. For each of the top 5 models the BIC differences were calculated as,

$$\Delta_i + \text{BIC}_i - \min(\text{BIC}),$$

where BIC_i is the BIC for the ith model and $\min(\text{BIC})$ is the minimum BIC value for the 5 models. The BIC weights were calculated as

$$w_i = \exp\left(-\frac{1}{2}\Delta_i\right) \Big/ \exp\left[\sum_{i=1}^{5} \exp\left(-\frac{1}{2}\Delta_i\right)\right].$$

Each model was used to predict the relative probability of selection for a pixel; a weighted average of the 5 predictions was then obtained using the BIC weights (Fig. 4, Table 9). This weighting procedure is similar to the use of Akaike weights by Burnham and Anderson (1998:124). Other model selection criteria such as Akaike's Information Criteria (AIC) (Burnham and Anderson 1998) could have been considered.

model to use is the logistic regression function. The objective was to develop a model to predict relative probability of selection of points by chipping sparrows (*Spizella passerina*) on the Winema National Forest in central Oregon. A complete description of the study is provided in Arnett et al. (2001). Ninety-six points were sampled and surveyed using standard point count methods (Williams et al. 2002). Each of the points was then defined to be "used" or "unused" by a chipping sparrow presence/absence model. Independent (predictor) habitat variables were measured in the field at each point count location. Prior to building habitat relationships models, we screened all habitat variables to eliminate a member of highly correlated pairs (i.e., eliminate multicollinearity) using pairwise Pearson correlations (Zar 1998). A candidate set of variables was then selected based on results of the correlations. One member of a pair of variables was eliminated if $r \geq 0.70$, based on best professional judgment by a qualified ornithologist as to which variables made the most biological sense relative to chipping sparrow life history and breeding and foraging needs.

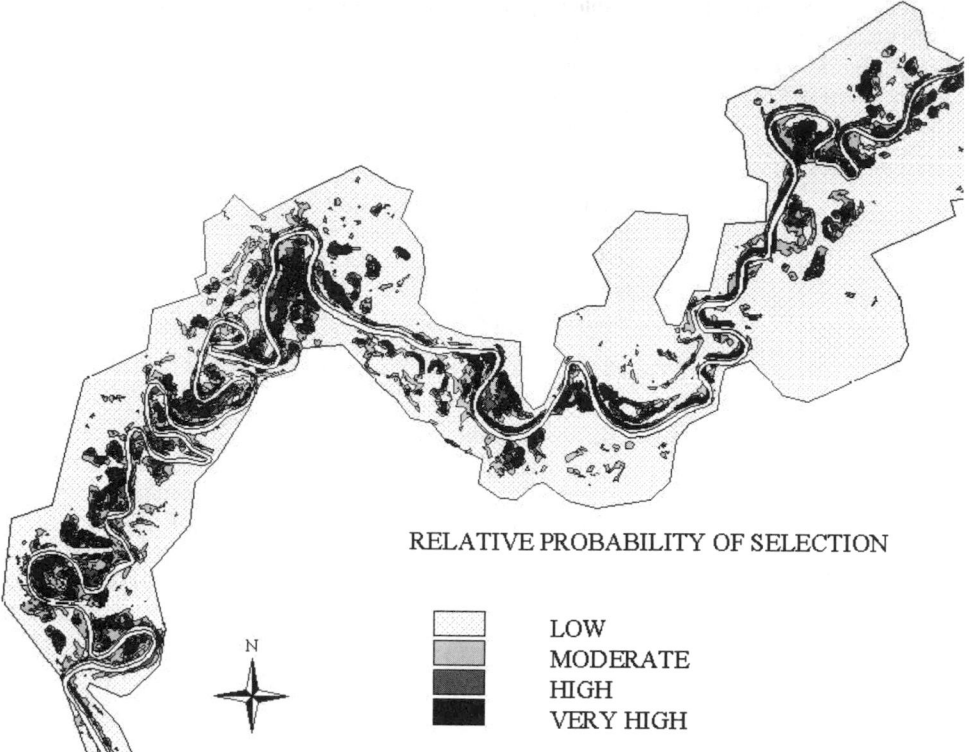

RELATIVE PROBABILITY OF SELECTION

LOW
MODERATE
HIGH
VERY HIGH

Fig. 4. The weighted average of estimated relative probabilities of use by alder flycatchers based on 5 models and weights (Table 9) for the southern section of the floodplain of the Innoko National Wildlife Refuge, Alaska (Erickson et al. 1998). A general pattern of higher probability of use near the river in the southern section of the study area is apparent.

Although not described in this example, model verification and validation techniques are also recommended for further evaluation of the fit and robustness of the selected models. Model verification methods such as Hosmer and Lemeshow's goodness of fit method for logistic regression (Hosmer and Lemeshow 1989) and validation techniques such as those described in Boyce et al. (2002) and Howlin et al. (2004) should be conducted.

The variables elevation and the average of band 4 were included in each of the top 5 models, the standard deviation of band 3 was in 4 of the 5, while distance to river was included in 3 of the top 5. The probability of use tends to decrease as elevation and distance to river increases (negative coefficients in the RSFs). The probability of use tends to increase as the average of band 4 and standard deviation of band 3 increases (positive coefficients in the RSFs). Importance values, following Burnham and Anderson (1998:326–327) for each of the variables considered, varied (Table 8). The variables elevation, band 4, and standard deviation of band 3 had the highest importance values. In this example, interpretation of the mean and standard deviations of the Landsat information is difficult and other variables such as quadratic effects, interactions or ratios of bands might have improved the models. A quality vegetation map was not available that would have allowed for more direct interpretation of importance of different vegetation types.

A second example illustrates the general theory for estimation of a RSF when a single sample of resource units is collected and each unit in the sample is classified as used or unused. This is sampling protocol D and the correct

Because this is a single sample of points classified as used or unused, a logistic regression computer software program was used to estimate the resource selection function (RSF),

$$w(x) = \frac{\exp(\beta_0 + \beta_1 X_{i1} + \beta_2 X_{i2} + \beta_3 X_{i3})}{(1 + \exp(\beta_0 + \beta_1 X_{i1} + \beta_2 X_{i2} + \beta_3 X_{i3}))},$$

where $w(x)$ is the probability of selection of a point in the landscape given the values of the variables x_1 through x_p at that point and the coefficients, β_1 through β_p, for variables in the model.

There were 10 independent variables available for estimating the resource selection function. The dependent variable is defined by stations where chipping sparrow presence was documented (recorded as $Y = 1$) and stations where the species was not documented (recorded as $Y = 0$). All 1,023 ($2^{10} - 1 = 1,023$) possible models, by selecting p variables from the set of 10, were fitted by logistic regression of the dependent variable Y on the independent predictor variables. Quadratic variables and interaction terms were ignored for this study. These 1,023 models then were ranked according to Akaike's Information Criterion (AIC) (Akaike 1973). AIC was defined as

$$\text{AIC} = [-2\log(\text{Likelihood}) + 2p],$$

where p was the number of variables in the model, Likelihood was the value of the logistic likelihood, and log was the natural logarithm. The best (minimum AIC) 25% of the 1,023 models were considered in the remaining analysis. Other model selection criteria such as stepwise or Bayesian Criterion (BIC) (Schwarz 1978) could have been considered.

For each of the models, the AIC differences were calculated as

$$\Delta_i + \text{AIC}_i - \min(\text{AIC}).$$

AIC weights were then calculated for the top 256 models as,

$$w_i = \exp\left(-\frac{1}{2}\Delta_i\right)\bigg/\exp\left[\sum_{i=1}^{256}\exp\left(-\frac{1}{2}\Delta_i\right)\right].$$

The sum of the AIC weights of models containing a variable was calculated as the importance value for that variable (following Burnham and Anderson 1998:326–327). The coefficients of the models for the top 25% of the models were averaged using a weighted linear combination with the AIC weights. The variance of the weighted average estimate was calculated from equation 4.11 in Burnham and Anderson (1998:135) and 95% confidence intervals were computed for parameter estimates. Coefficients and standard errors were computed for the top model and from model averaging, as well as importance values for each of the 10 variables using the top 25% of the models (Table 10).

The most important variable for selection of points by chipping sparrows in the Winema National Forest was estimated to be percent canopy cover, followed closely by percent seedling cover, number of saplings per plot, percent functional ground cover, and number of live trees per plot. These 5 variables formed the best model among those considered, based on the AIC criteria. For sampling protocol D, the probabilities produced by logistic regression programs are correct. In addition, coefficients (Table 10) can be placed into the logistic regression equation

$$\frac{\exp(\beta_0 + \beta_1 X_{i1} + \beta_2 X_{i2} + \beta_3 X_{i3})}{[1 + \exp(\beta_0 + \beta_1 X_{i1} + \beta_2 X_{i2} + \beta_3 X_{i3})]}$$

to compute and map the estimated values of estimated probability of selection throughout the Winema National Forest. Further evaluation of the models using model verification (Hosmer and Lemeshow 1989) and validation techniques (e.g., Boyce et al. 2002, Howlin et al. 2003) would be appropriate.

SUMMARY

This chapter introduces the study of habitat and food use by wildlife in comparison to availability of those resources to help identify important habitat patches and food resources. Selection is defined to exist during a study period if resources are exploited disproportional to their availability (Johnson 1980) at a given scale: geographical range of a species, home range of an individual or social group, use of sites within a home range, or procurement of food items at a feeding site. Generally, resource selection studies should consider selection at more the one scale and should be replicated in time and space.

Common study field sampling protocols are introduced followed by detailed discussion with examples of the 2 most applicable methods: (A) available units are randomly sampled and used units are randomly sampled, and (D) available units are randomly sampled and classified as used or unused. The sampling protocols are considered in association with the most common study designs: (I) available and use of resources are recorded for the study area and for the population under study, and (II and III) use is recorded by individual animals. After presentation of field procedures for recording data on habitat and food availability and use by wildlife, we present the estimation of resource selection functions as a unified theory for study of the relationships between use of habitat or food items and predictor variables measured on those units. These functions allow one to estimate the relative probabilities that habitat units or food items were selected and to rank units according to their value for use by wildlife for the study area, population, and time period.

Modeling of resource selection is introduced for computation of selection ratios among categories of habitat or food types using an often-analyzed set of moose track data (Neu et al. 1974). Logistic regression is the basic tool by which all example sets of data in this chapter are analyzed; it is used to analyze the moose track data and generic data to illustrate the concepts of relative probabilities (odds) of selec-

Table 10. Nest habitat selection model for the chipping sparrow on the Winema National Forest (Arnett et al. 2001). (Variables in best AIC model in **bold**).

Variable	Variable description	I	Model averaging B	Model averaging SE	Variables in top AIC model B′	Variables in top AIC model SE′
INTERCEPT		1.000	–2.139	2.208	–1.110	0.915
CANOPY	**% canopy cover**	**1.000**	**0.081**	**0.020**	**0.088**	**0.020**
SEEDLING	**% seedling cover**	**0.896**	**0.060**	**0.024**	**0.053**	**0.024**
NSAPLING	**# saplings/plot**	**0.871**	**0.016**	**0.008**	**0.019**	**0.008**
GRNDB	**% functional ground cover**	**0.676**	**–0.025**	**0.017**	**–0.036**	**0.014**
LIVETREE	**# live trees/plot**	**0.665**	**–0.035**	**0.022**	**–0.053**	**0.027**
SHRUB	% shrub cover	0.490	0.017	0.018		
DEBR	% ground debris	0.380	0.000	0.014		
DEADTREE	# snags/plot	0.322	–0.021	0.033		
LOGCNT1	# logs/plot	0.284	–0.003	0.013		
GRFO	% grass/forb cover	0.267	0.003	0.018		

Notes: I = importance value, B = model averaged logistic regression coefficient, SE = model averaged standard error, B′ = logistic regression coefficient for top model, and SE' = standard error of coefficient in top model.

tion among habitat types. Estimation of resource selection functions using multiple predictor variables is illustrated for 2 examples: selection of breeding sites by alder flycatchers on the flood plain of the Innoko River in the Innoko National Wildlife Refuge, Alaska; and selection of points by chipping sparrows on the Winema National Forest in central Oregon. Information theory and maximum likelihood procedures are used for selection of appropriate predictor variables for the resource selection functions. Finally, we illustrate mapping of habitat to identify those areas with the highest relative probability of use during the study period by alder flycatchers on the Innoko National Wildlife Refuge.

ACKNOWLEDGMENTS

We thank the authors, John A. Litvaitis, Kimberly Titus, and Eric M. Anderson of this Chapter in the fifth edition as we freely used material from their chapter. We accept responsibility for any errors in the present edition, but could not have completed the writing without their contribution. We thank J. A. Litvaitis, C. E. Braun, and an anonymous reviewer for their suggestions that improved the manuscript.

LITERATURE CITED

AEBISCHER, N. J., P. A. ROBERTSON, AND R. E. KENWARD. 1993. Compositional analysis of habitat use from animal radio-tracking data. Ecology 74:1313–1325.

AKAIKE, H. 1973. Information theory and an extension of the maximum likelihood principle. Pages 267–281 *in* B. Petrov and F. Czakil, editors. Proceedings Second International Symposium on Information Theory. Akademiai Kiado, Budapest, Hungary.

ALLDREDGE, J. R., AND J. T. RATTI. 1986. Comparison of some statistical techniques for analysis of resource selection. Journal of Wildlife Management 50:157–165.

———, AND ———. 1992. Further comparison of some statistical techniques for analysis of resource selection. Journal of Wildlife Management 56:1–9.

———, D. L. THOMAS, AND L. L. McDONALD. 1998. Survey and comparison of methods for study of resource selection. Journal of Agricultural, Biological, and Environmental Statistics 3:237–253.

ANDERSON, D. R. 2001. The need to get the basics right in wildlife field studies. Wildlife Society Bulletin 29:1294–1297.

———, K. P. BURNHAM, W. R. GOULD, AND S. CHERRY. 2001. Concerns about finding effects that are actually spurious. Wildlife Society Bulletin 29:311–316.

ANTHONY, R. G., AND N. S. SMITH. 1974. Comparison of rumen and fecal analysis to describe deer diets. Journal of Wildlife Management 38:535–540.

APPS, C. D., B. N. McLELLAN, T. A. KINLEY, AND J. P. FLAA. 2001. Scale-dependent habitat selection by mountain caribou, Columbia Mountains, British Columbia. Journal of Wildlife Management 65:65–77.

ARNETT, E. B., B. ALTMAN, W. P. ERICKSON, AND K. A. BETTINGER. 2001. Relationships between salvage logging and forest avifauna in lodgepole pine forests of the central Oregon pumice zone. Final report submitted to National Fish and Wildlife Foundation, Oregon Department of Fish and Wildlife, U.S. Fish and Wildlife Service, U.S. Forest Service, U.S. Timberlands, and Weyerhaeuser Company. Weyerhaeuser Company, Springfield, Oregon, USA.

ARTHUR, S. M., B. F. J. MANLY, L. L. McDONALD, AND G. W. GARNER. 1996. Assessing habitat selection when availability changes. Ecology 77:215–227.

AVERY, T. E. 1968. Interpretation of aerial photographs. Second edition.

Burgess Publishers, Minneapolis, Minnesota, USA.

BART, J. R., AND W. I. NOTZ. 2005. Analysis of data in wildlife biology. Pages 72–105 *in* C. E. Braun, editor. Techniques for wildlife investigations and management. Sixth edition. The Wildlife Society, Bethesda, Maryland, USA.

BASILE, J. V., AND S. S. HUTCHINGS. 1966. Twig diameter-length-weight relations of bitterbrush. Journal of Range Management 19:34–38.

BAXTER, W. L., AND C. W. WOLFE. 1972. The interspersion index as a technique for evaluation of bobwhite quail habitat. Proceedings of the National Bobwhite Quail Symposium 1:158–165.

BEASOM, S. L., E. P. WIGGERS, AND J. R. GIARDINO. 1983. A technique for assessing land surface ruggedness. Journal of Wildlife Management 47:1163–1166.

BIELEFELDT, J., R. N. ROSENFIELD, AND J. M. PAPP. 1992. Unfounded assumptions about the diet of the Cooper's hawk. Condor 94:427–436.

BIGGINS, D. E., AND E. J. PITCHER. 1978. Comparative efficiencies of telemetry and visual techniques for studying ungulates, grouse, and raptors on energy development lands in southeastern Montana. National Wildlife Federation Science Technical Series 4:188–193.

BOBEK, B., AND R. BERGSTROM. 1978. A rapid method of browse biomass estimation in a forest habitat. Journal of Range Management 31:456–458.

———, S. BOROWSKI, AND R. DZIECIOLOWSKI. 1975. Browse supply in various forest ecosystems. Polish Ecology Studies 1:17–32.

BONTTI, E. E., AND R. M. BÓO. 2002. Sample numbers for microhistological estimation of fecal vizcacha diets. Journal of Range Management 55:498–501.

BOYCE, M. S., P. R. VERNIER, S. E. NIELSON, AND F. K. A. SCHMIEGELOW. 2002. Evaluating resource selection functions. Ecological Modelling 157:281–300.

BURNHAM, K. P., AND D. R. ANDERSON. 1998. Model selection and inference: a practical information-theoretic approach. Springer-Verlag, Inc., New York, USA.

BYERS, C. R., R. K. STEINHORST, AND P. R. KRAUSMAN. 1984. Clarification of a technique for analysis of utilization-availability data. Journal of Wildlife Management 48:1050–1053.

CHESSON, J. 1978. Measuring preference in selective predation. Ecology 59:211–215.

COLLINS, W. B., AND P. J. URNESS. 1981. Habitat preferences of mule deer as rated by pellet-group distributions. Journal of Wildlife Management 45:969–972.

CONOVER, W. J. 1999. Practical non-parametric statistics. Third edition. John Wiley and Sons, New York, USA.

COOK, C. W., AND J. STUBBENDIECK. 1986. Methods of measuring herbage and browse utilization. Pages 120–132 *in* C. W. Cook and J. Stubbendieck, editors. Range research: basic problems and techniques. Society of Range Management, Denver, Colorado, USA.

COOPER, A. B., AND J. J. MILLSPAUGH. 1999. The application of discrete choice models to wildlife resource selection studies. Ecology 80:566–575.

———, AND ———. 2001. Accounting for variation in resource availability and animal behavior in resource selection studies. Pages 243–273 *in* J. J. Millspaugh and J. M. Marzluff, editors. Radio tracking and animal populations. Academic Press, San Diego, California, USA.

COOPERRIDER, A. Y. 1986. Food habits. Pages 699–710 *in* A. Y. Cooperrider, R. J. Boyd, and H. R. Stuart, editors. Inventory and monitoring of wildlife habitat. U.S. Department of the Interior, Bureau of Land Management, Service Center, Denver, Colorado, USA.

DAUBENMIRE, R. 1958. A canopy-coverage method of vegetational analysis. Northwest Science 33:43–64.

DE VOS, A., AND H. S. MOSBY. 1969. Habitat analysis and evaluation. Pages 135–172 *in* R. H. Giles, Jr., editor. Wildlife management techniques. Third edition. The Wildlife Society, Washington, D.C., USA.

DUESER, R. D., AND H. H. SHUGART, JR. 1978. Microhabitats in a forest-floor small-mammal fauna. Ecology 59:89–98.

EASTMAN, D. S., AND D. JENKINS. 1970. Comparative food habits of red grouse in northeast Scotland, using fecal analysis. Journal of Wildlife

Management 34:612–620.

EDLEFSON, J. L., C. W. COOK, AND J. T. BLAKE. 1960. Nutrient content of the diet as determined by handplucked and esophageal fistula samples. Journal of Animal Science 19:560–563.

ERICKSON, W. P., T. L. MCDONALD, AND R. SKINNER. 1998. Habitat selection using GIS data: a case study. Journal of Agricultural, Biological, and Environmental Statistics 3:296–310.

———, ———, K. G. GEROW, S. HOWLIN, AND J. W. KERN. 2001. Statistical issues in resource selection studies with radio-marked animals. Pages 209–242 in J. J. Millspaugh and J. M. Marzluff, editors. Radio tracking and animal populations. Academic Press, San Diego, California, USA

———, R. NIELSON, R. SKINNER, B. SKINNER, AND J. JOHNSON. 2004. Applications of resource selection modeling using unclassified Landsat Thematic Mapper imagery. Pages 130–140 in S. V. Huzurbazar, editor. Resource selection methods and applications. Omnipress, Madison, Wisconsin, USA.

ERRINGTON, P. L. 1932. Techniques of raptor food habits study. Condor 34:75–86.

FAGEN, R. 1988. Population effects of habitat change: a quantitative assessment. Journal of Wildlife Management 52:41–46.

FARRELL, L. E., J. ROMAN, AND M. E. SUNQUIST. 2000. Dietary separation of sympatric carnivores identified by molecular analysis of scats. Molecular Ecology 9:1583–1590.

FLOYD, T. J., L. D. MECH, AND P. A. JORDAN. 1978. Relating wolf scat content to prey consumed. Journal of Wildlife Management 42:528–532.

FORMAN, R. T. T., AND M. GODRON. 1986. Landscape ecology. John Wiley and Sons, New York, USA.

FRETWELL, S. D. 1972. Populations in a seasonal environment. Princeton University Press, Princeton, New Jersey, USA.

FRIDELL, R. A., AND J. A. LITVAITIS. 1991. Influence of resource distribution and abundance on home-range characteristics of southern flying squirrels. Canadian Journal of Zoology 69:2589–2593.

FRIEDMAN, M. 1937. The use of ranks to avoid the assumption of normality implicit in the analysis of variance. Journal of the American Statistical Association 32:675–701.

FULLER, T. K. 1991. Effect of snow depth on wolf activity and prey selection in north central Minnesota. Canadian Journal of Zoology 69:283–287.

GARTON, E. O., J. T. RATTI, AND J. H. GIUDICE. 2005. Research and experimental design. Pages 43–71 in C. E. Braun, editor. Techniques for wildlife investigations and management. Sixth edition. The Wildlife Society, Bethesda, Maryland, USA.

GAVIN, T. A. 1991. Why ask "why": the importance of evolutionary biology in wildlife science. Journal of Wildlife Management 55:760–766.

GILL, R. B., L. H. CARPENTER, R. M. BARTMANN, D. L. BAKER, AND G. G. SCHOONVELD. 1983. Fecal analysis to estimate mule deer diets. Journal of Wildlife Management 47:902–915.

GREEN. G. A., G. W. WITMER, AND D. S. DECALESTA. 1986. NaOH preparation of mammalian predator scats for dietary analysis. Journal of Mammalogy 67:742.

GREEN, R. H. 1979. Sampling design and statistical methods for environmental biologists. John Wiley and Sons, New York, USA.

GRINDER, M. I., AND P. R. KRAUSMAN. 2001. Home range, habitat use, and nocturnal activity of coyotes in an urban environment. Journal of Wildlife Management 65:887–898.

GYSEL, L. W. 1956. Measurement of acorn crops. Forest Science 2:305–313.

HALL, L. S., P. R. KRAUSMAN, AND M. L. MORRISON. 1997. The habitat concept and a plea for standard terminology. Wildlife Society Bulletin 25:173–182.

HALPIN, M. A., AND J. A. BISSONETTE. 1988. Influence of snow depth on prey availability and habitat use by red fox. Canadian Journal of Zoology 66:587–592.

HEINEN, J., AND G. H. CROSS. 1983. An approach to measure interspersion, juxtaposition, and spatial diversity from cover-type maps. Wildlife Society Bulletin 11:232–237.

HEISEY, D. M. 1985. Analyzing selection experiments with log-linear models. Ecology 66:1744–1748.

HEPINSTALL, J. A., AND S. A. SADER. 1997. Using Bayesian statistics, thematic mapper, and breeding bird survey data to model bird species probability of occurrence in Maine. Photogrammetric Engineering and Remote Sensing. 63:1231–1237.

HIGGINS, K. F., K. J. JENKINS, G. K. CLAMBEY, D. W. URESK, D. E. NAUGLE, J. E. NORLAND, AND W. T. BARKER. 2005. Vegetation sampling and measurement. Pages 524–553 in C. E. Braun, editor. Techniques for wildlife investigations and management. Sixth edition. The Wildlife Society, Bethesda, Maryland, USA.

HILDERBRAND, G. V., S. D. FARLEY, C. T. ROBBINS, T. A. HANLEY, K. TITUS, AND C. SERVHEEN. 1996. Use of stable isotopes to determine diets of living and extinct bears. Canadian Journal of Zoology 74:2080–2088.

HOBBS, N. T., AND T. A. HANLEY. 1990. Habitat evaluation: do use/availability data reflect carrying capacity? Journal of Wildlife Management 54:515–522.

HOLECHEK, J. L., AND B. D. GROSS. 1982. Evaluation of different calculation procedures for microhistological analysis. Journal of Range Management 35:721–723.

———, AND M. VAVRA. 1981. The effect of slide and frequency observation numbers on the precision of microhistological analysis. Journal of Range Management 34:337–338.

———, B. GROSS, S. M. DABO, AND T. STEPHENSON. 1982. Effects of sample preparation, growth stage, and observer on microhistological analysis of herbivore diets. Journal of Wildlife Management 46:502–505.

HOSMER, JR., D. W., AND S. LEMESHOW. 1989. Applied logistic regression. John Wiley and Sons, New York, USA.

HOWARD, G. S., AND M. J. SAMUEL. 1979. Atlas of epidermal plant species fragments ingested by grazing animals. U.S. Department of Agriculture Technical Bulletin 1582. Washington, D.C., USA.

HOWLIN, S., W. P. ERICKSON, AND R. M. NIELSON. 2004. A proposed validation technique for assessing predictive abilities of resource selection functions. Pages 40–51 in S. V. Huzurbazar, editor. Resource selection methods and applications, Omnipress, Madison, Wisconsin, USA.

HUNTER, JR., M. L. 1989. Aardvarks and Arcadia: two principles of wildlife research. Wildlife Society Bulletin 17:350–351.

HURLBERT, S. H. 1984. Pseudoreplication and the design of ecological field experiments. Ecological Monographs 54:187–211.

INGLIS, J. M., AND C. J. BARSTOW. 1960. A device for measuring the volume of seeds. Journal of Wildlife Management 24:221–222.

IRWIN, L. L., AND J. M. PEEK. 1979. Shrub production and biomass trends following five logging treatments within the cedar-hemlock zone of northern Idaho. Forest Science 25:415–426.

JAENIKE, J. 1980. A relativistic measure of variation in preference. Ecology 61:990-991.

JAMES, F. C., AND H. H. SHUGART, JR. 1970. A quantitative method of habitat description. Audubon Field Notes 24:727–736.

JOHNSON, D. H. 1980. The comparison of usage and availability measurements for evaluating resource preference. Ecology 61:65–71.

KARR, J. R. 1981. Rationale and techniques for sampling avian habitats: introduction. Pages 26–28 in D. E. Capen, editor. The use of muitivariate statistics in studies of wildlife habitat. U.S. Department of Agriculture, Forest Service, General Technical Report RM-87.

———. 1983. Commentary. Pages 403–410 in A. H. Brush and G. A. Clark, Jr., editors. Perspectives in ornithology. Cambridge University Press, Cambridge, United Kingdom.

KEPPIE, D. M. 1990. To improve graduate student research in wildlife education. Wildlife Society Bulletin 18:453–458.

KNICK, S. T., AND J. T. ROTENBERRY. 1998. Limitations to mapping habitat use areas in changing landscapes using Mahalanobis distance statistic. Journal of Agricultural, Biological, and Ecological Statistics 3:311–322.

LITVAITIS, J. A., J. A. SHERBURNE, AND J. A. BISSONETTE. 1985. A comparison of methods used to examine snowshoe hare habitat use. Journal of Wildlife Management 49:693–695.

LOCKIE, J. D. 1959. The estimation of the food of foxes. Journal of

Wildlife Management 23:224–227.

LYON, L. J. 1968. Estimating twig production of serviceberry from crown volumes. Journal of Wildlife Management 32:115–119.

MACNAB, J. 1983. Wildlife management as scientific experimentation. Wildlife Society Bulletin 11:397–401.

MAJOR, M., M. K. JOHNSON, W. S. DAVIS, AND T. F. KELLOGG. 1980. Identifying scats by recovery of bile acids. Journal of Wildlife Management 44:290–293.

MANLY, B. F. J. 1985. The statistics of natural selection on animal populations. Chapman and Hall, London, United Kingdom.

———, L. L. MCDONALD, D. L. THOMAS, T. L. MCDONALD, AND W. P. ERICKSON. 2002. Resource selection by animals: statistical design and analysis for field studies. Second edition. Kluwer Academic Publishers, Dordrecht, The Netherlands.

MARCUM, C. L., AND D. O. LOFTSGAARDEN. 1980. A nonmapping technique for studying habitat preferences. Journal of Wildlife Management 44:963–968.

MARTI, C. D. 1987. Raptor food habits studies. Pages 67–80 in B. A. Giron Pendleton, B. A. Milsap, K. W. Cline, and D. M. Bird, editors. Raptor management techniques manual. National Wildlife Federation, Institute for Wildlife Research, Scientific and Technical Series 10, Washington, D.C., USA.

MARTIN, S. C. 1970. Determining animal consumption: relating vegetation measures to forage consumed by animals. Pages 93–100 in Range and wildlife habitat evaluation-a research symposium. U.S. Department of Agriculture, Forest Service, Miscellaneous Publication 1147.

MCDONALD, L. L., AND B. F. J. MANLY. 2001. Modeling wildlife resource selection: can we do better? Pages 137–145 in T. M. Shenk and A. B. Franklin, editors. Modeling in natural resource management: development, interpretation, and application. Island Press, Washington, D.C., USA.

MCINNIS, M. L., M. VAVRA, AND W. C. KRUEGER. 1983. A comparison of four methods used to determine the diets of large herbivores. Journal of Range Management 36:302–306.

MCMANUS, W. R. 1981. Oesophageal fistulation technique as an aid to diet evaluation of the grazing ruminant. Pages 249–260 in J. L. Wheeler and R. D. Mochrie, editors. Forage evaluation: concepts and techniques. American Forage Grassland Council, Lexington, Kentucky, USA.

MEAD. R. A., T. L. SHARIK, S. P. PRISELY, AND J. T. HEINEN. 1981. A computerized spatial analysis system for assessing wildlife habitat from vegetation maps. Canadian Journal of Remote Sensing 7:34–40.

MECH, L. D. 1966. The wolves of Isle Royale. U.S. Department of the Interior, National Park Service Fauna Series 7. Washington, D.C., USA.

MLADENOFF, D. J., AND T. A. SICKLEY. 1998. Assessing potential gray wolf restoration in the northeastern United States: a spatial prediction of favorable habitat and potential population levels. Journal of Wildlife Management 62:1–10.

MOORE, T. D., L. E. SPENCE, AND C. E. DUGNOLLE. 1974. Identification of the dorsal guard hairs of some mammals of Wyoming. Wyoming Game and Fish Department Bulletin 14. Cheyenne, USA.

MORRIS, D. W. 1984. Patterns and scale of habitat use in two temperate-zone, small mammal faunas. Canadian Journal of Zoology 62:1540–1547.

MORRISON, M. L. 2001. A proposed research emphasis to overcome the limits of wildlife-habitat relationship studies. Journal of Wildlife Management 65:613–623.

———, B. G. MARCOT, AND R. W. MANNAN. 1992. Wildlife-habitat relationships: concepts and applications. University of Wisconsin Press, Madison, USA.

———, W. M. BLOCK, M. D. STRICKLAND, AND W. L. KENDALL. 2001. Wildlife study design. Springer-Verlag, Inc., New York, USA.

MOSBY, H. S. 1969. Reconnaissance mapping and map use. Pages 119–134 in R. H. Giles, Jr., editor. Wildlife management techniques. Third edition. The Wildlife Society, Washington, D.C., USA.

MURIE, O. J. 1974. A field guide to animal tracks. Houghton Mifflin, Boston, Massachusetts, USA.

MUSIL, A. F. 1963. Identification of crop and weed seeds. U.S. Department of Agriculture Handbook 219. Washington, D.C., USA.

NAMS, V. O. 1989. Effects of radiotelemetry error on sample size and bias when testing for habitat selection. Canadian Journal of Zoology 67:1631–1636.

NETER, J., M. H. KUTNER, C. J. NACHTSHEIM, AND W. WASSERMAN. 1996. Applied linear models. Fourth edition. McGraw-Hill Book Co., Boston, Massachusetts, USA.

NEU, C. W., C. R. BYERS, AND J. M. PEEK. 1974. A technique for analysis of utilization-availability data. Journal of Wildlife Management 38:541–545.

NOON, B. R. 1981. Techniques for sampling avian habitats. Pages 42–52 in D. E. Capen, editor. The use of multivariate statistics in studies of wildlife habitat. U.S. Department of Agriculture, Forest Service, General Technical Report RM-87.

NUDDS, T. D. 1977. Quantifying the vegetative structure of wildlife cover. Wildlife Society Bulletin 5:113–117.

O'NEIL, T. A., P. BETTINGER, B. G. MARCOT, B. W. LUSCOMBE, G. T. KOELN, H. J. BRUNER, C. BARRETT, J. A. POLLOCK, AND S. BERNATAS. 2005. Application of spatial technologies in wildlife biology. Pages 418–447 in C. E. Braun, editor. Techniques for wildlife investigations and management. Sixth edition. The Wildlife Society, Bethesda, Maryland, USA.

ORR, C. D., AND D. G. DODDS. 1982. Snowshoe hare habitat preferences in Nova Scotia spruce-fir forests. Wildlife Society Bulletin 10:147–150.

OTIS, D. L. 1997. Analysis of habitat selection studies with multiple patches within cover types. Journal of Wildlife Management 61:1016–1022.

———. 1998. Analysis of the influence of spatial pattern in habitat selection studies. Journal of Agricultural, Biological, and Environmental Statistics 3:254-67.

OWEN, M. 1975. An assessment of fecal analysis technique in waterfowl feeding studies. Journal of Wildlife Management 39:271–279.

OWENSBY, C. E. 1973. Modified step-point system for botanical composition and basal cover estimates. Journal of Range Management 26:302–303.

PARKER, K. L., M. P. GILLINGHAM, T. A. HANLEY, AND C. T. ROBBINS. 1999. Energy and protein balance of free-ranging black-tailed deer in a natural forest environment. Wildlife Monographs 143.

PARREN, S. G., AND D. E. CAPEN. 1985. Local distribution and coexistence of two species of Peromyscus in Vermont. Journal of Mammalogy 66:36–44.

PARTRIDGE, L. 1978. Habitat selection. Pages 351–376 in J. R. Kreb and N. B. Davies, editors. Behavioural ecology: an evolutionary approach. Blackwell Scientific Publishers, Oxford, United Kingdom.

PENDLETON, G. W., K. TITUS, R. E. LOWELL, E. DEGAYNER, AND C. J. FLATTEN. 1998. Compositional analysis and GIS for study of habitat selection by goshawks in southeast Alaska. Journal of Agricultural, Biological, and Ecological Statistics 3:280–295.

PERIERA, J. M. C., AND R. M. ITAMI. 1991. GIS-based habitat modeling using logistic multiple regression. A study of the Mt. Graham red squirrel. Photogrammetric Engineering and Remote Sensing. 57:1475–1486.

PERRINS, C. M. 1979. British tits. William Collins Sons and Co., London, United Kingdom.

PORTER, W. F., AND K. E. CHURCH. 1987. Effects of environmental pattern on habitat preference analysis. Journal of Wildlife Management 51:681-685.

PREVETT, J. P., I. F. MARSHALL, AND V. G. THOMAS. 1985. Spring foods of snow and Canada geese at James Bay. Journal of Wildlife Management 49:558-563.

QUADE, D. 1979. Using weighted rankings in the analysis of complete blocks with additive block effects. Journal of the American Statistical Association 74:680–683.

RICE, J., B. W. ANDERSON, AND R. D. OHMART. 1984. Comparison of the importance of different habitat attributes to avian community organization. Journal of Wildlife Management 48:895–911.

RICE, R. W. 1970. Stomach content analyses: a comparison of the rumen vs. esophageal techniques. Pages 127–132 *in* Range and wildlife habitat evaluation-a research symposium. U.S. Department of Agriculture, Forest Service, Miscellaneous Publication 1147, Washington, D.C., USA.

ROBBINS, C. S., D. K. DAWSON, AND B. A. DOWELL. 1989. Habitat area requirements of breeding forest birds of the Middle Atlantic states. Wildlife Monographs 103.

ROSENZWEIG, M. L. 1981. A theory of habitat selection. Ecology 62: 327–335.

ROTENBERRY, J. T., AND J. A. WIENS. 1980. Habitat structure, patchiness, and avian communities in North American steppe vegetation: a multivariate analysis. Ecology 61: 1228–1250.

ROY, L. D., AND M. J. DORRANCE. 1985. Coyote movements, habitat use, and vulnerability in central Alberta. Journal of Wildlife Management 49: 307-313.

SCHALLER, G. B. 1972. The Serengeti lion: a study of predator-prey relations. University of Chicago Press. Chicago, Illinois, USA.

SCHOOLEY, R. L. 1994. Annual variation in habitat selection: patterns concealed by pooled data. Journal of Wildlife Management 58: 367–374.

SCHWARZ, G. 1978. Estimating the dimension of a model. Annals of Statistics 6: 461–464.

SERVELLO, F. A., E. C. HELLGREN, AND S. R. McWILLIAMS. 2005. Techniques for wildlife nutritional ecology. Pages 554–590 *in* C. E. Braun, editor. Techniques for wildlife investigations and management. Sixth edition. The Wildlife Society, Bethesda, Maryland, USA.

SHAFER, JR., E. L. 1963. The twig-count method for measuring hardwood deer browse. Journal of Wildlife Management 27: 428–437.

SHOOP, M. C., AND E. H. McILVAIN. 1963. The micro-unit forage inventory method. Journal of Range Management 16: 172–179.

SHORT, N. M. 1982. The Landsat tutorial workbook: basics of satellite remote sensing. U.S. Department of Commerce, National Aeronautics and Space Administration Reference Publication 1078. Washington, D.C., USA.

SINCLAIR, A. R. E. 1991. Science and the practice of wildlife management. Journal of Wildlife Management 55: 767–773.

SMITH, A. D., AND L. J. SHANDRUK. 1979. Comparison of fecal, rumen, and utilization methods for ascertaining pronghorn diets. Journal of Range Management 32: 275–279.

———, AND P. J. URNESS. 1962. Analysis of the twig-length method of determining utilization of browse. Utah Department of Fish and Game Publication 62–69. Salt Lake City, USA.

SMITH, D. R., P. O. CURRIE, J. V. BASILE, AND N. C. FRISCHKNECHT. 1962. Methods for measuring forage utilization and differentiating use by different classes of animals. Pages 93–102 *in* Range research methods: a symposium. U.S. Department of Agriculture, Forest Service, Miscellaneous Publication 940.

SODHI, N. S., C. A. PASZKOWSKI, AND S. KEEHN. 1999. Scale-dependent habitat selection by American redstarts in aspen dominated forest fragments. Wilson Bulletin 111: 70–75.

STEVENTON, J. D., AND J. T. MAJOR. 1982. Marten use of habitat in a commercially clear-cut forest. Journal of Wildlife Management 46: 175–182.

STINNETT, D. P., AND D. A. KLEBENOW. 1986. Habitat use of irrigated lands by California quail in Nevada. Journal of Wildlife Management 50: 368–372.

SVANCARA, L. K., E. O. GARTON, K.-T. CHANGE, J. M. SCOTT, P. ZAGER, AND M. GRATSON. 2002. The inherent aggravation of aggregation: an example with elk aerial survey data. Journal of Wildlife Management 66: 776–787.

SWANSON, G. A., AND J. C. BARTONEK. 1970. Bias associated with food analysis in gizzards of blue-winged teal. Journal of Wildlife Management 34: 739–746.

TELFER, E. S. 1969*a*. Twig weight-diameter relationships for browse species. Journal of Wildlife Management 33: 917–921.

———. 1969*b*. Weight-diameter relationships for 22 woody plant species. Canadian Journal of Botany 47: 1851–1855.

THOMAS, D. L., AND E. J. TAYLOR. 1990. Study designs and tests for comparing resource use and availability. Journal of Wildlife Management 54: 322–330.

THOMAS. J. W., C. MASER, AND J. E. RODEIK. 1979. Edges. Pages 48–59 *in* J. W. Thomas, editor. Wildlife habitat in managed forests-the Blue Mountains of Oregon and Washington. U.S. Department of Agriculture, Forest Service, Agriculture Handbook 533, Washington, D.C., USA.

THOMPSON, I. D., I. J. DAVIDSON, S. O'DONNELL, AND F. BRAZEAU. 1989. Use of track transects to measure the relative occurrence of some boreal mammals in uncut forest and regeneration stands. Canadian Journal of Zoology 67: 1816–1823.

VAN HORNE, B. 1983. Density as a misleading indicator of habitat quality. Journal of Wildlife Management 47: 893–901.

VAVRA, M., R. W. RICE, AND R. M. HANSEN. 1978. A comparison of esophageal fistula and fecal material to determine steer diets. Journal of Range Management 31: 11–13.

VERME, L. J. 1968. An index of winter weather severity for northern deer. Journal of Wildlife Management 32: 566–574.

VOGTMAN, D. B. 1945. Flushing tube for determining food of game birds. Journal of Wildlife Management 9: 255–257.

WEAVER, J. L. 1993. Refining the equation for interpreting prey occurrence in gray wolf scats. Journal of Wildlife Management 57: 534–538.

WELSH, JR., H. H., AND A. J. LIND. 2002. Multiscale habitat relationships of stream amphibians in the Klamath-Siskiyou region of California and Oregon. Journal of Wildlife Management 66: 581–602.

WHITE, G. C., AND R. A. GARROTT. 1990. Analysis of wildlife radio-tracking data. Academic Press. San Diego, California, USA.

WIENS, J. A. 1974. Habitat heterogeneity and avian community structure in North American grasslands. American Midland Naturalist 91: 195–213.

———. 1976. Population responses to patchy environments. Annual Review of Ecology and Systematics 7: 81–120.

———. 1981. Scale problems in avian censusing. Studies in Avian Biology 6: 513–521.

———. 1989. The ecology of bird communities. Volume 2. Cambridge University Press, New York, USA.

WILLIAMS, B. K. 1997. Logic and science in wildlife biology. Journal of Wildlife Management 61: 1007–1015.

———, J. D. NICHOLS, AND M. J. CONROY. 2002. Analysis and management of animal populations. Academic Press, San Diego, California, USA.

ZAR, J. H. 1998. Biostatistical analysis. Fourth edition. Prentice-Hall, Englewood Cliffs, New Jersey, USA.

18

WILDLIFE HABITAT EVALUATION

Stanley H. Anderson and Kevin J. Gutzwiller

INTRODUCTION

Animals normally occur in areas where their needs for food and shelter are met (Cody 1985). These areas, called habitats, generally are not the same for each species. Some species, such as the tree swallow (*Iridoprocne bicolor*), are found over a large geographic area, yet specific features (tree cavities for this species) are needed within this area for nesting. Other species, such as the striped skunk (*Mephitis mephitis*), use a wide variety of areas and may be limited only by climatic conditions and interactions with other animals. Lyre snakes (*Trimorphodon biscutatus*) occur only in the southwestern United States where rock slabs are parted enough to provide protection from the heat of the day. Some animals have different seasonal or annual habitat needs, whereas others require different habitats for feeding and nesting during the same season. Typically, wildlife managers have considered wildlife, but not wildlife's habitat, to be the primary resource. However, habitat is what enables wildlife to exist (Block and Brennan 1993).

Wildlife managers must evaluate habitat for many reasons. At times, management practices need to be instituted for forests, refuges, national parks, or private lands. In such instances, goals are set to increase or decrease numbers of wildlife or to manipulate wildlife diversity. Wildlife managers also are consulted about land-use planning and need to be able to predict how proposed habitat changes may affect wildlife communities, species (all populations), and populations.

Because managers may want to examine the quantity and quality of available habitat for a particular species, they must be able to measure features of the habitat that relate specifi-

cally to the presence and number of animals. Wildlife managers monitor trends in habitat quality to learn whether a habitat has improved, declined, or remained unchanged and whether hunting quotas for game species should be changed. For example, the quality of mule deer (*Odocoileus hemionus*) winter range influences winter survival. Thus, hunting seasons might be lengthened or shortened depending on habitat quality and the number of deer present.

When environmental assessments are made, it may be desirable to know which species are present. Some forms of habitat evaluation are used to estimate the relative abundance of a species. For example, the size of a marsh will limit the number of pairs of breeding birds. By knowing their approximate territory size, we can predict how many pairs could possibly exist. In addition, habitat assessment procedures can be used along with population monitoring to evaluate habitat improvement efforts. Creating water impoundments or rock piles or leaving timber all are quantified and compared with changes in populations of targeted species (Hoover and Wills 1984).

This chapter discusses how and why wildlife fitness, density, and diversity are related to habitat features. It explains the significance of using natural-history data, autecological relations, and knowledge of the temporal and spatial scales of habitat use to assess animal-habitat associations. We provide examples of habitat variables that are related to wildlife species and describe how such variables can be measured in aquatic and terrestrial habitats. Standardized and nonstandardized techniques to evaluate habitats are presented. Finally, we examine the value, interpretation, and application of wildlife-habitat correlations in the context of evaluating habitat quality and quantity.

RELATING ANIMAL FITNESS, DENSITY, AND DIVERSITY TO HABITAT FEATURES

The ability of an organism to survive and reproduce depends in part on the resources available to it. An animal's habitat supplies critical resources; otherwise the animal could not persist there. For example, cavity-nesting birds require natural tree cavities, nest boxes, or other similar man-made structures to reproduce. In the absence of this resource, cavity nesters will not breed. In such an environment, the fitness of an individual—the extent to which its genes are passed on and represented in subsequent generations—would be low. Biologists often are able to demonstrate positive or negative relationships between number of individuals and productivity of a species and specific habitat features of the area (e.g., Burger 1987, Zwank et al. 1988). Biologists are also interested in the relationship between number of species (species richness) and habitat characteristics (Knopf et al. 1988, Soulé et al. 1988). Such wildlife-habitat associations exist because species depend on habitats for resources.

Once the habitat where the animal may be found is identified, the underlying mechanisms that enable the animal to survive (e.g., food and shelter) should be considered. The suitability of the habitat for the animal must be evaluated by examining these features (Morrison 2001). If resources to survive and reproduce are not in the habitat, animals might still survive but not be able to reproduce.

Density, the number of individuals per unit area, is a widely used indicator of habitat quality. If the density of a species is high, something about the habitat is beneficial to reproduction, survival, or continued high occupation. Van Horne (1983) emphasized that density may not accurately reflect the influences of habitat quality for 3 reasons. First, in northern climates, density-habitat associations based on summer studies may be meaningless if winter conditions ultimately dictate survival. Second, densities are subject to fluctuations in many biotic (e.g., food, predators) and abiotic (e.g., water, soil) resources. Consequently, current densities may mirror recent, short-term changes in environmental conditions, instead of long-term environmental quality. For example, some birds may temporarily use forested areas because of insect outbreaks, not because of present habitat quality. Third, higher-quality habitats may be occupied by dominant individuals, forcing subdominants into lower-quality habitat. Thus, higher densities may be present in poorer, not better, habitats. If interactions among individuals are competitive, high densities may reflect low fitness, whereas if Allee effects (higher reproduction at higher population densities) or conspecific attraction are operating, high densities may reflect high fitness (see Danchin et al. 1998, Greene and Stamps 2001). Misenhelter and Rotenberry (2000) found that sage sparrows (*Amphispiza belli*) preferred areas in which their reproductive performance was low, indicating a negative relationship between habitat attractiveness and habitat suitability. Areas that sage sparrows preferred were actually ecological traps because of high predation (Misenhelter and Rotenberry 2000). Thus, several types of limitations and ecological processes must be considered when density data are used to evaluate habitat quality (Anderson 2002).

Correlations between numbers of individuals or species and habitat features are useful to managers for understanding habitat needs of a species or community. However caution must be exercised in interpreting animal-habitat relations (Anderson 1981), as correlation does not imply causation. Many environmental factors typically influence an individual's fitness, a species' abundance, or the diversity of a community. Although researchers measure what they hope are relevant features, there is the possibility that factors actually responsible for a particular relationship will not be measured, or that the feature associated with a species is correlated with the causal factor but is not the causal agent itself (Box 1).

For example, suppose one is interested in identifying which habitat features influence number of bird species breeding in separate stands of timber. For each stand, the number of breeding bird species and several habitat parameters are estimated and a positive correlation is found between bird species richness and average tree age. But because the species being studied do not require mature trees, this correlation does not make sense. In fact, each species in the stands is capable of using young, intermediate, and late successional stages. A positive correlation is found in the relationship between bird species richness and stand size. The larger the stand, the more species. If stand size, but not tree age, is the factor to which birds are actually responding, the correlation between tree age and number of species is spurious and it does not reflect an actual biological phenomenon. Spurious associations are common and, at times, difficult to unravel in wildlife-habitat studies.

Habitat use and habitat selection are frequently confused in the literature (Hall et al. 1997, Jones 2001). Habitat use, the subject of most habitat studies, refers to the way the animal or population uses the habitat and how the habitat meets life-history needs (Block and Brennan 1993). Habitat selection refers to a complex behavioral response that is hierarchical in nature that may result in disproportional use of habitat by the species (Hutto 1985, Block and Brennan 1993, Jones 2001). Habitat selection implies a choice.

WHICH HABITAT FEATURES SHOULD BE MEASURED?

Time and funding constraints must be considered when objectives are established. Thus, investigators should carefully consider these constraints in their study design. Before fieldwork begins, the investigator must decide which habitat features to measure. Questions to consider include: (1) why is the study being conducted, (2) what is the focus of the study (a population, a species, or a community), (3) what is the autecology of this species or group of species, (4) during what time of day or during which season do animals use different parts of the habitat, and (5) how do habitat features on different spatial scales influence wildlife? The hypothesis(es) to be tested and objective(s) of the study should be clearly stated. Once the goals are clear, a literature search should be conducted to identify habitat factors that may be important to the species. These factors must relate to the animal's ability to survive and reproduce (Morrison 2001). Investigators also should consult experts on the species and spend time in the field to explore potential habitat correlates.

Identifying the Focus

Often a management or research question arises from a problem observed in the field. The questions to be answered then delineate the population to be studied or if other species should be included in an evaluation. If the proposed

Box 1. Seasonal habitat selection.

A researcher wanted to assess whether salamanders selected summer habitat on the basis of several habitat features. She collected the following data and computed a correlation matrix for all of the variables.

Site	Mean fern cover (%)	Mean distance to water (m)	Mean midday temp. (C)	Mean litter depth (cm)	Mean salamander density (#/ha)
1	80	10	20	4	72
2	83	9	18	4	68
3	81	9	19	4	67
4	79	12	21	4	67
5	40	25	26	2	38
6	22	50	31	1	17
7	90	8	17	5	83
8	54	41	22	3	42
9	67	15	23	3	50
10	38	23	29	2	36

Correlation matrix (significance level)

	Fern cover	Distance to water	Midday temp.	Litter depth
Distance to water	−0.861 (0.0014)			
Midday temp.	−0.964 (0.0001)	0.755 (0.0115)		
Litter depth	0.982 (0.0001)	−0.813 (0.0042)	−0.966 (0.0001)	
Salamander density	0.978 (0.0001)	−0.883 (0.0007)	−0.939 (0.0001)	0.984 (0.0001)

Salamander density was significantly correlated with a number of the habitat features measured, but these same habitat variables were also intercorrelated with one another. Were salamanders selecting habitat on the basis of fern cover, distance to water, or some unmeasured feature that was correlated with these variables? The researcher realized it was impossible to infer casual relations between salamander density and habitat features with this data set. An experiment with controls and replicates would be necessary to avoid interpretation problems associated with correlations.

work involves managing for a variety of species, the features of the habitat that support the most diverse wildlife community could be identified. Physiographic (land features such as slope and elevation) and vegetation features of the community must be capable of supporting prey species as well as cover and "habitat" for the species of concern.

Autecology of the Species

Whenever an investigator is considering habitat evaluation, it is important to understand the autecology, or interrelation, of a species with its environment throughout the annual cycle. For example, migratory waterfowl use a number of different areas: winter habitat must provide adequate food and cover for protection from predators; good migration habitat contains lush food supplies; and breeding habitat must include food, nest and brood cover, and pro-

tection from predators. Concerns also exist over loss of forest habitat for migratory birds wintering in Central and South America. Although ideal migratory and breeding habitat for these birds may exist in some areas of North America, populations may decline because of habitat losses on the winter range. We know that some migratory birds nesting in the eastern deciduous forest require habitat patches of specific sizes, often larger than those used by nesting resident birds. Thus, a decrease in size of contiguous habitats may be important and, even though specific features within the habitat are correlated with a species, a decline in patch size may be far more influential. Some animals require several different habitats for biannual movement patterns. Others must have feeding, breeding, and winter habitats available in close proximity. In both situations, movement corridors must be considered.

Sage-grouse (*Centrocerus* spp.) in the western United States are associated with sagebrush (*Artemisia* spp.) and the range-wide population has declined. As researchers investigate habitat requirements of the birds, they find that not only must traditional lekking areas be managed but also habitats for nesting, early brood rearing, late brood rearing, and wintering, as they are all equally important. Disturbance of any one of these habitats may disrupt the birds or affect seasonal movements.

Natural-history Data

The early literature on wildlife and its habitat is dominated by naturalists' accounts obtained subjectively through observation and without standard techniques. Early naturalists made little effort to quantitatively characterize specific habitat features that influenced individuals, species, and communities.

Natural-history data are still essential for habitat management. Managing vegetation for a species without knowing when, where, and how that species uses the habitat to survive and reproduce would be difficult. Detailed natural-history observations help identify which habitat characteristics may be important. Since the late 1960s, there has been a definite shift to objective, quantitative analyses of wildlife-habitat relations. There is now a tremendous array of vegetation-, soil-, and water-sampling techniques to quantitatively describe the environments of target organisms. The goal is to identify more accurately which habitat features are most closely associated with the organism of interest.

Temporal and Spatial Scales

In evaluating habitat for wildlife, one must consider temporal and spatial factors that may affect assessments. Some species use particular habitats during specific periods of the year. For example, 2 subspecies of sandhill crane (*Grus canadensis*) winter in the southern United States and Mexico. They move to the Platte River in southern Nebraska for 6–8 weeks each year between February and April before flying to northern Canada and Alaska to breed. Habitat measurements taken at wintering sites when the birds are absent may not reflect conditions that existed when the birds actually used the winter habitat, particularly if the measured conditions change from winter to spring. Evaluations of winter habitat should be made immediately after the cranes leave for Nebraska, or preferably while the birds are still on the wintering grounds, if such activity is unobtrusive.

If several months are spent measuring habitat features at a series of ruffed grouse (*Bonasa umbellus*) nest sites, canopy cover or herbaceous vegetation height may change. Because of vegetative growth and development, sites described early in the season will not be comparable to those evaluated later. Thus, many biases can be introduced in habitat studies because of the timing of fieldwork, and length of evaluation periods should be minimized. Those features that do not change over time can be measured at the investigator's convenience.

Wildlife managers often use published information about wildlife-habitat relations to predict consequences of habitat alteration or to justify habitat-management decisions. One assumption frequently made is that a relationship on one scale (e.g., habitat immediately around nest sites) can be extrapolated to a larger spatial scale (e.g., entire forests). Such extrapolations may or may not be warranted, and it is not unusual to find that habitat characteristics at several spatial scales, not just one, influence wildlife (Pearson 1993, Saab 1999, Karl et al. 2000). This is not surprising because habitat selection probably involves a series of responses by wildlife to characteristics of the environment related to different spatial scales. A more complete understanding of the habitat attributes important to species and communities can be obtained by analyzing habitat components related to a variety of spatial scales (see Gutzwiller and Anderson 1987b). Patch size, corridors, and isolation may influence population size, the presence or absence of species, and community structure (Forman 1995). Thus, the entire landscape, not just site-specific characteristics of vegetation, may be influential (Rodiek and Bolen 1991).

Which Habitat Features Should be Used to Assess Animal-habitat Relationships?

A literature search at the beginning of a study should identify which habitat features may be important. Further discussions with experts can help define and narrow the focus of the effort. If disagreement arises about which variables are important for a species, or about what should be measured, confounding variables might need further study. Careful observation of species in their natural habitats is also valuable. Both biotic and abiotic conditions (e.g., Wilson 1998, Dettmers and Bart 1999, Martin 2001) should be considered. Review of time and money constraints should continue during the planning phase. These constraints may require one to simplify the project or sample fewer habitat features.

Approaches in which many habitat features are examined are inefficient for developing species-habitat relations and can be justified only for general exploratory analyses. A study in which general habitat characteristics (e.g., grassland, shrubland) are measured can help identify which broad animal taxa might be present. Frequently, general habitat studies are not helpful in identifying habitat features associated with a particular species.

It is valuable to examine the recent literature to learn whether there have been advances in sampling relevant to a particular technique or specific vegetation type. A traditional sampling technique may have been improved or found to be inadequate; the most recent information about the method should be considered. Examples of technique evaluations and advances are provided by Etchberger and Krausman (1997), who compared 5 common methods for measuring desert vegetation; Nuttle (1997), who addressed inherent differences in angular and vertical methods for estimating canopy cover; and Wilson et al. (1998), who described an approach that incorporates spatially explicit information into estimates of habitat availability. It also is important to remember that traditional sampling techniques allow comparisons with previous work.

Examples of Habitat Variables Related to Wildlife

Animals can be classified broadly as generalized and opportunistic, or specialized and competitive. We think of house sparrows (*Passer domesticus*), raccoons (*Procyon lotor*), and coyotes (*Canis latrans*) as being generalists because they can live in a variety of environments. California condors (*Gymnogyps californianus*), lyre snakes, and gray wolves (*Canis lupus*), which are more specialized, are more vulnerable to habitat destruction than are less specialized species.

Some important habitat features are vertical and horizontal structure, moisture, sunlight, and temperature. If only one of these conditions is not present, a species may not be able to survive. Vegetation patchiness, a component of horizontal structure, can be important to a variety of species and should be examined within different spatial extents (see Gutzwiller and Barrow 2002). Evolution has had an important role in how animals adapt to habitat structure. Among Darwin's finches, bills evolved for collecting insects, cracking seeds, and even picking up sticks for use as insect probes. Open-nesting birds begin incubating earlier than do cavity-nesting species, and the nestling period for open-nesting birds is shorter. Thus, young fledge before they are affected by summer temperatures or detected by predators. Cavity-nesting birds avoid these problems and survive even though they have slow growth rates.

The effects of sunlight are most noticeable on vegetation and, in turn, animals are affected by structure and type of vegetation. Temperature is extremely important to reptiles because they are ectothermic. Without sufficient air temperatures, they remain inactive. Cooperrider et al. (1986) provided extensive details and examples of habitat variables important in a variety of major habitats, and they covered all vertebrate groups.

MEASUREMENT OF HABITAT VARIABLES

Once the habitat data to be collected are identified, different collection methods can be considered. Generally, variables are placed in 1 of 2 classes. First, the major or macro features of the habitat, such as size, distance to roadways or water, vegetation cover, and percentage of an area burned, can be measured without actually being in the field (assuming such information is found in a geographic information system or other sources). Often these variables are of landscape scale. Second, measurement of micro variables, such as plant species composition, water chemistry, type of snags, and tree or shrub density usually requires work on site. Most of these variables are specific to the point where the animal was observed.

Investigators should consider the scales at which habitat features may influence a given species. Because influence of vegetation features at different scales is likely to be associated with species' body size, mobility, and life-history requirements, macro and micro scales are relative terms. Scales cannot be defined equally for all species. That is, a macro feature for wide-ranging species may be characterized on a much broader geographic scale than a macro feature for a sedentary animal.

Measuring Macro Features

Remote sensing is an alternative method of collecting wildlife habitat data. It includes satellite imagery (Landsat), infrared aerial photos (Platts et al. 1983), and videography (O'Neil et al. 2004). Habitat size and shape can best be estimated from satellite digital analyses or interpretation of aerial photographs. Generally, large-scale (1:1,000–1:4,800)

aerial photographs are needed to interpret detailed information on streams and vegetation.

Color-infrared photographs are especially valuable for estimating broad vegetation type. The color tones, along with size, shape, pattern, shadow, and texture, are useful for identifying individual species of trees and shrubs. Color-infrared film can be overexposed by ½ f-stop to penetrate clear water in lakes and streams (Cuplin 1978). When a fire burns through an area, the degree of burn and levels of recovery can be evaluated from color-infrared photographs.

Many forms of maps also exist. U.S. Geological Survey topographic maps provide valuable data on location of physical habitat features such as streams, roads, and power lines. On recent maps, information on slopes, elevations, aspects, and general habitat shape also can be obtained. Frequently, county maps provide details such as rock quarries, local roads, and buildings. County land-ownership maps, available in the county courthouse, are often helpful before fieldwork begins.

The U.S. Forest Service provides maps that show elevation, landforms, and trail information. Several different maps with varying details are available from some forest supervisors' offices. U.S. Bureau of Land Management maps, which are available for some western states, provide detail on land ownership and are helpful for locating gross habitat features such as cliffs, ponds, and streams, as are U.S. Geological Survey maps. Other state, provincial, and federal agencies have maps that can be obtained from university libraries or government document repositories. In addition, highway departments of most states and provinces provide generalized maps that assist in locating study sites and topographic features such as lakes, streams, and mountain ranges. Most, if not all of the information on paper maps has recently been digitized and made available in electronic form. O'Neil et al. (2004) describe sources of electronic data and how to use a geographic information system (GIS) to measure macro scale wildlife habitat variables.

Topographic ruggedness may influence the use of areas by certain wildlife species (Box 2). Beasom et al. (1983) demonstrated how to estimate land-surface ruggedness from topographic maps. With a GIS, digital elevation data can be used to estimate landscape ruggedness by computing measures such as topographic relief, and the coefficients of variation of elevation, percent slope, or aspect for an area.

For some species, roads cause wildlife displacement due to traffic noise, act as barriers or filters to movement, and serve as sources of mortality, food, non-native species invasion, habitat fragmentation, pollution, and human disturbance; for other species, roadside vegetation may form corridors that aid movement or serve as habitat (Forman and Alexander 1998, Trombulak and Frissell 2000, Wilkie et al. 2000, Forman et al. 2003). Road density (total length of roads per unit area) has been shown to affect the quality of habitat for some species (Forman 1995). Broad-scale digital data for roads can be obtained as digital line graph files from the Environmental Systems Research Institute (http://www.esri.com), and a GIS can be used to measure road density, distances to roads, or other road attributes.

Measuring Micro Features

Describing the water column, which is the medium of support and movement for fish and aquatic organisms, is

Box 2. Importance of cliffs to wildlife.

In south-central Wyoming, occasional cliffs break the semi-arid grasslands. Biologists evaluating cliff sites found they created an array of vegetative characteristics that appeared to increase wildlife diversity. To evaluate the influence of cliffs on wildlife, they set up 13 cliff study sites and 7 control sites (no cliffs) (Ward and Anderson 1988).

On each study site, birds were sampled within 6 400-m transects, and small mammals were sampled within 3 210-m^2 square grids. Physical features, including cliff exposure, angle, light, height, surface roughness, talus length, and amount of exposed rock, were measured. Distances to water, roads, and fences were measured from maps. Vegetation was sampled with a 1-m^2 sampling frame placed at each small-mammal trapping station.

Analysis of variance was used to compare abundance (total no. individuals of each species) and species richness (no. of species) on cliff sites to control sites. Using an all-subsets regression (Dixon 1981), biologists examined which study-site features were correlated with each measured parameter.

Small-mammal abundance was greater on cliff sites (mean = 97 + 5.94 [SE], n = 13) than on control sites (mean = 59 + 11.03 [SE], n = 7). Abundance of mammals was correlated with talus and topographic roughness. Small-mammal richness was greater on cliff sites (mean = 6.0 ± 0.35 [SE], n = 13) than on control sites (mean = 4.0 ± 0.50 [SE], n = 7). Abundance of male birds was correlated with angle of cliff and distance to water.

Thus, biologists were able to show which features appeared to be associated with wildlife. Their results can be used to improve wildlife habitat in semi-arid, rocky grasslands.

often important. Different life stages of fish use water with different flow rates, and wading birds do not stand or feed in fast-flowing or deep water. Stream width is measured as a horizontal transect line from shore to shore along the existing water surface. Depth is the vertical height of the water column from the existing water surface level to the channel bottom. It is measured at the same place during the same time of day each month to provide reliable results for comparisons (Platts et al. 1983). Shore depth is critical for shorebirds and is measured at the shoreline or at the edge of a bank overhanging the shoreline. Measurements made on streams and pools include width, depth, distance to riffle, and length of riffles.

Light can be measured with a light meter or with light-intensity scales established by the use of shading devices (Platts et al. 1987) to estimate canopy shading at the stream. The vegetation along a stream can vary from providing almost complete shading to providing none at all. This factor influences water temperature and productivity. Heavy use of stream edges by livestock can reduce shade and increase erosion if the vegetation is trampled and killed.

Water turbidity can influence wildlife use of wetlands. Turbidity influences species of invertebrates present, which in turn can influence waterfowl production. Turbidity in lakes often is measured with a Secchi disc (Platts et al. 1987). Water chemistry is an important correlate of invertebrate productivity and species composition.

Physical Characteristics

Physical features of the terrestrial environment often are correlated with wildlife abundance, diversity, or productivity. Elevation gradients are associated with changes in vegetation and climate, thereby causing changes in wildlife. For example, Finch (1989) reported a change in bird species composition along an elevation gradient in Wyoming. Generally, elevation data can be taken from maps or digital elevation data bases (O'Neil et al. 2004) and correlated with species present.

Types of Human Disturbance

Rock piles and impoundments attract wildlife (Dealy et al. 1981). Fence posts and buildings are habitat variables related to disturbances that can change species composition. Some birds use fence posts for perching and roosting, and buildings are used for roosting and nesting. These human disturbance factors should be measured or recorded as present or absent. House density, area of pavement, and distance to areas disturbed by humans also can be influential (Germaine et al. 1998).

Physiographic Features

Two forms of physiographic features generally are described, geomorphic and edaphic (Maser et al. 1979). Geomorphic features are products of the geologic process. They include cliffs, caves, tables, lava flows, sand dunes, and playas. Measurement of geomorphic features generally includes diameter of the feature, height of cliffs above ground, surface ruggedness, presence of caves, and the depth, width, and parent rock of the feature. Edaphic features are local, distinctive soil characteristics that, along with their vegetation, contrast markedly with the surroundings. These edaphic areas often provide specific habitat for animal activities such as reproduction or seclusion (Maser et al. 1979).

Talus is an edaphic feature of accumulated rocks on cliffs or at the base of cliffs. Components of interest include length, depth, width, and rock type of the deposit. Talus can provide protection for some animals, such as pika (*Ochotona princeps*), during reproduction and hibernation periods. Other species of wildlife living near talus use the areas for hunting. Lizards, snakes, birds, and mammals are attracted to talus because they find shelter or food among the rocks.

STANDARDIZED TECHNIQUES OF HABITAT EVALUATION

Spatial Diversity

Spatial diversity is a measure of the horizontal diversity of habitat present. A technique that combines interspersion (intermixing of units of different habitat types) and juxtaposition (a measure of the proximity of year-round habitat) (Giles 1978) can be used (Heinen and Cross 1983).

Cover types that are critical habitat components for the species under study must be identified. Data then must be collected for these critical cover types. Aerial photos or field sampling can be used and it is best to place these data on a photo or map upon which a grid system can be superimposed. The choice of cell size will depend on home-range size or the area an animal defends for its use, and landscape patchiness (density of patches of land-cover types in a landscape [Forman and Godron 1986:207]).

Interspersion is calculated for a given cell by counting the number of surrounding cells that contain different cover types. In the example below, 8 cells surround a centroid cell; thus, the number of cells that differ from the cell of interest is divided by 8. The resultant index value lies between 0 and 1.

An example calculation of interspersion (I_x) is:

A	B	B
B	A	A
A	C	C

where A, B, and C represent different cover-type categories, 5 = total number of cells whose cover-type differs from that of the center cell, and 8 = total possible number of cover-type differences. Thus, $I_x = 5/8 = 0.625$.

Juxtaposition is calculated by first identifying all combinations of edge types around the center cell. A numerical rating is given to each edge type by assigning a value of 1 to diagonal edges and 2 to vertical or horizontal edges. Relative weighting factors ranging from 0 to 1 are assigned to each edge type and represent the quality of different community junctions. The weighting factor is multiplied by the numerical rating of each edge type to give a total value. All values are then totaled and divided by 12 (the maximum total for edge-type ratings) to calculate the juxtaposition index for a given cell.

The calculation of juxtaposition (J_x) for the center cell in our example is:

Edge-type	Numerical rating	Quality	Total
A/A	4	0.2	0.8
A/B	5	0.5	2.5
A/C	3	0.6	1.8
			5.1

In this example $J_x = 5.1/12 = 0.425$.

Although 2 cells of the same cover type being side by side does not represent a true edge, it may be given a weighting factor for the juxtaposition index if large stands of that type are important to the species being considered.

The spatial diversity (Sd) index described by Mead et al. (1981) is:

$$Sd_A = ([\sigma_A I_S] + [\alpha_A J_X](1_A)(2_A)(3_A),$$

where A indicates a particular species, σ_A indicates importance of interspersion relative to juxtaposition, α_A indicates importance of juxtaposition relative to interspersion (σ_A and α_A range between 0 and 1 each but must sum to 1), and 1_A, 2_A, and 3_A indicate exclusion factors, which also range between 0 and 1. An exclusion factor is any habitat com-

ponent with a positive or negative impact on a particular species. For the previous example, the Sd_A index is:

$$Sd_A = (0.5 \times 0.625) + (0.5 \times 0.425) = 0.525.$$

In this example, juxtaposition and interspersion were considered equally important and no exclusion factors were identified. However, any number of exclusion factors may be used depending on the area and species under consideration. An example of an exclusion factor with a positive impact may be the presence of water within 1.6 km. If it is present, 1_A may be given a value of 1 and, thus, does not affect the index. If it is absent, a value of 0 may be assigned, driving the Sd_A index for that parcel of land to 0. An exclusion factor with a negative impact may be the presence of anything that decreases the habitat suitability of an area for the species in question. An example may be the presence of an oil derrick. If it is present, 1_A may be assigned a value of 0 driving the index to 0. The numbers assigned for exclusion factors may range between 0 and 1 giving the Sd_A index more sensitivity to fine differences in spatial diversity.

Broad-scale indices of interspersion, juxtaposition, and other spatial attributes of habitat (Gustafson 1998) can be obtained by applying a GIS to digital land-cover databases. Examples of GIS software designed specifically for measuring such metrics include FRAGSTATS (McGarigal and Marks 1995) (http://www.umass.edu/landeco/research/fragstats/fragstats.html) and the r.le programs in GRASS (Baker and Cai 1992) (http://grass.baylor.edu//index.html).

Habitat Models

Wildlife habitat models attempt to describe relationships of change, often through mathematical equations. It is possible to vary the data on one side of the equation and predict the outcome symbolized by the other side. Thus, this process can be descriptive and predictive. Prior to 1970, wildlife managers rarely used modeling. Use of this approach has increased, and models are now commonly used.

In model building, the natural system must be examined. The different components must be identified and selected so they can be related to one another. A model can be used to predict how timber cutting might affect forest-bird communities. In this situation, it would be necessary to know something about the communities and species' feeding and nesting requirements with respect to vegetation; the relationship between the selected components must be understood. Modelers often write the information they want to evaluate in the model including a general description of the problem and a list of variables with their interrelations. The modeler usually develops a box diagram to show how all variables interact. At times modelers go no further than the descriptive phase; at other times depending on complexity, they develop mathematical relationships (Steury et al. 2002). Once a model has been developed, it should be evaluated to examine its function by manipulating different variables. This process can identify factors associated with the model and how it can be used in the field.

Sensitivity analyses of simulation models (Hannon and Ruth 1997:32–38, Odum and Odum 2000:377) are performed by systematically varying the levels of source variables and assessing the extent of the effects of the changes on response variables. When a simulation model produces approximately the same response values over a range of source parameter values, the model is considered robust (i.e., not highly dependent on assumptions about parameter magnitudes) (Ford 1999:176–178). Sensitivity analysis enables the modeler to examine how dependent the model is on slight differences in the variables altered. Model sensitivity is valuable for judging how much the response information may change if the assumptions about source variables (e.g., their particular magnitudes or variability) do not hold exactly.

Models are used for many different reasons. First, predictions of events can be made. In the western United States, models are used to predict the number of deer each spring based on population size the preceding autumn, known harvest, winter weather conditions, etc. Some models have regional value. For example, knowledge of water flow might be used to predict the general impact on wildlife populations throughout a large region. Other models are useful only in localized areas, at times as small as 0.5 ha or less. Thus, geographic scale should be considered when models are developed and applied.

Because habitat use and selection can vary among years, pooling data across years may conceal interannual variation and result in misleading inferences (Schooley 1994). Unless wildlife-habitat relations can be shown to be the same among seasons or years, separate models that reflect the variation should be developed, and data for habitat use and selection should be presented by year or season (Schooley 1994).

Another important consideration in model development is ease of measuring habitat variables in the field. Models that use subjective terms such as "more," "less," "little," and "big," do not have objective descriptors that are measurable. It is important to select variables, such as the number of trees per hectare or the number of kilometers of riparian habitat, which can be measured and entered into the model. The factors measured should have some probable influence on the species of interest. Thus, those who develop models must carefully examine how they use the model and which factors they will consider. Models with variables too difficult or expensive to measure will not be used. Simple, meaningful models are most desirable. Wakeley (1988) described a way to simplify the application of habitat suitability index models that will enhance their use.

A variety of models have been developed to standardize habitat evaluation techniques. We caution that some models are oversold and expectations are too high. For example, models at times are used to evaluate habitat without examining the presence of other species that influence the species under consideration. Many other models, including statistical models, are subject to the same problems. Models, therefore, should be used with caution and may be useful at a local level, but not applicable on a regional basis (e.g., Storch 2002).

Berry (1986) identified 3 forms of modeling: single species to multiple species, community models, and habitat analysis models. In this context Berry (1986) described habitat suitability index models (HSI), habitat-capacity models, and pattern-recognition models as correlations between species and different habitat components.

Habitat Suitability Index Models

Habitat suitability index models have been developed by the U.S. Fish and Wildlife Service and have generated a great deal of discussion among wildlife scientists. These models use physical and biological attributes of a particular habitat to yield an index of habitat suitability assumed to be proportional to the habitat's carrying capacity for a species (e.g., marsh wren [*Cistothorus palustris*]) (Box 3). These are generally linear models involving a series of habitat variables associated with different species.

The technique for identifying habitat suitability index values must be clearly described in a Habitat Evaluation Procedure to establish credibility, optimize the usefulness of the analysis in decision-making, provide a permanent record of the basis for a decision, and make future improvements in habitat suitability index models. Ellis et al. (1979) confirmed that such descriptions increase the repeatability in calculating an index. Although repeatability does not confirm that values are accurate, it is a prerequisite to improved accuracy.

The recommended method of describing habitat suitability index values is through use of habitat suitability index models. A model may be in word or mathematical format but it must clearly describe the rules and assumptions used to calculate a model. The process of calculating an index involves (1) establishing model requirements, (2) developing a model, and (3) calculating indices for available habitat.

Establishing HSI Model Requirements

Habitat models used in habitat evaluation procedures must be in index form. Inhaber (1976) defined an index as a ratio between some value of interest and a standard of comparison. For model purposes, the value of interest is an estimate of habitat conditions in the study area and the standard of comparison is the optimal habitat condition for the species being evaluated. Therefore,

$$\text{Index Value} = \frac{\text{Value of Interest}}{\text{Standard of Comparison}},$$

or

$$\text{HSI} = \frac{\text{Study Area Habitat Conditions}}{\text{Optimal Habitat Conditions}},$$

where the numerator and denominator have the same units of measure. The HSI ranges between 0 and 1.0 and, like any index, is dimensionless.

Developing an HSI Model

Habitat suitability index models have been developed for more than 100 species (Wakeley 1988), but only a few have been tested or evaluated in the field (e.g., Lancia and Adams 1985). The ideal goal of a model is to produce an index with a proven, quantified relationship to carrying capacity (i.e., units of biomass per unit area or units of biomass production per unit area). This goal is often unobtainable; consequently, a more easily obtainable but acceptable goal must be defined. The minimum acceptable goal for a model might be, for example, an index that a recognized expert, knowledgeable about the habitat requirements of a species, believes is related to long-term carrying capacity.

The accuracy and application of habitat suitability index models may be improved through increased peer review during model development, calibration, verification, and valida-

Box 3. Marsh wren HSI.

The habitat suitability index model for marsh wrens (Gutzwiller and Anderson 1987*a*) produces a habitat suitability index (HSI) from 0 (unsuitable habitat) to 1.0 (optional habitat). The proposed relation between the suitability of wetlands for marsh wrens and wetland features is:

$$HSI = (SIV1 \times SIV2 \times SIV3)^{1/3} \times SIV4,$$

where

SIV1 = suitability index (SI) for growth form of emergent hydrophytes,
SIV2 = suitability index for percent canopy cover of emergent herbaceous vegetation,
SIV3 = suitability index for mean water depth, and
SIV4 = suitability index for percent canopy cover of woody vegetation.

The overall suitability index (HSI) is estimated from the geometric mean and product of individual suitability indices for 4 habitat variables (V1 – V4). This model was developed to estimate the value of wetlands for providing cover and reproductive resources for marsh wrens.

In this example, a biologist wanted to assess the spatial consistency of the value of a wetland's vegetation and water for breeding marsh wrens. He collected data for the above 4 habitat variables at randomly selected points. Using the assumed relations (available in model documentation) between the suitability index for each habitat variable and the actual habitat measurement, he converted his field measurements to suitability indices (SIs). The HSI values were then obtained by applying the above formula.

| | Habitat measurements | | | | Suitability indices (SIs) | | | | Overall |
Sample	V1[a]	V2 (%)	V3 (cm)	V4 (%)	SIV1	SIV2	SIV3	SIV4	HSI
1	1	72	5	10	1.0	0.63	0.37	0.90	0.55
2	2	83	0	12	0.5	0.90	0.00	0.88	0.00
3	1	77	15	53	1.0	0.79	1.00	0.47	0.43
4	3	64	20	62	0.1	0.43	1.00	0.38	0.13
5	1	81	25	11	1.0	0.89	1.00	0.89	0.86
6	1	92	27	20	1.0	1.00	1.00	0.78	0.78
7	2	91	31	36	0.5	1.00	1.00	0.65	0.52
8	4	80	39	29	0.0	0.88	1.00	0.71	0.00
9	1	40	9	75	1.0	0.08	0.55	0.25	0.09
10	1	52	19	5	1.0	0.13	1.00	0.95	0.48

[a] 1 = cattails (*Typha* spp.), cordgrasses (*Spartina* spp.), bulrushes (*Scirpus* spp.); 2 = reedgrass (*Calamagrostis* spp.), canarygrass (*Phalaris* spp.), sedges (*Carex* spp.); 3 = buttonbrush (*Cephalanthus* sp.), mangrove (*Rhizophora* sp.); 4 = other growth forms.

From these calculations, the biologist concluded the value of the habitat was quite heterogeneous because, among the 10 sampling locations, HSIs varied from 0.00 to 0.86, with several values near the midpoint of this range.

tion (Brooks 1997). Roloff and Kernohan (1999) demonstrated use of several criteria to evaluate the completeness of habitat suitability index model validations. When they applied their evaluation framework to 17 validation studies involving 58 models, they found that none of the studies was adequate. Typical deficiencies were "inadequate consideration of input parameter variability, application of the models to inappropriate spatial scales, sampling too narrow a range of HSI values, and population data that were collected over too short a time frame" (Roloff and Kernohan 1999:973). Thus, considerable effort is required to develop a valid model.

Habitat-capacity Models

The habitat-capacity model was developed by the U.S. Forest Service and has been used to describe conditions associated with or necessary to maintain different compositions of wildlife species. It uses weighted values based on habitat capacity ratings at each successional stage of

vegetation for reproduction, resting, and feeding by a particular species (Hurley et al. 1982).

A data system in 3 formats—narratives, habitat-relationship matrices, and status matrices—is generally the beginning of a habitat capacity model. Narratives contain life-history data, status (legal and management), distribution by habitat, reproduction data, special habitat requirements, food habits, territory/home-range sizes, references, and other management information.

Habitat-relationship matrices differ for terrestrial and aquatic species. Matrices for terrestrial species provide information on use of vegetation types and special habitat needs (e.g., snags and talus slopes). Importance to a terrestrial species of each vegetation type and structural stage is related to the biological functions of reproduction, feeding, and resting. Season of use also is included.

Within each cell of a matrix, a value is assigned for the species association with the particular vegetation type and structural stage for each biological function. This value, referred to as habitat-capability rating, is based on current literature and professional knowledge. The values, in whole numbers, range from 1 to 3. A habitat-capability rating of 1 indicates the habitat is optimal (it contains all of the required elements and none is limiting) for that biological function. A habitat-capability rating of 2 signifies acceptable habitat for a particular biological function, but some elements might be preventing the population from reaching its optimal density. A habitat-capability rating of 3 indicates poor habitat. The habitat might be used by the species, but some required elements are missing or limited.

A final value, the habitat-capability coefficient is calculated for each vegetation type and structural stage. The value is an aggregated, weighted value based on habitat capability-ratings for reproduction, feeding, and resting. These values can range from 0.00 to 1.00.

Habitat-relationships matrices for aquatic species do not contain habitat-capability ratings or coefficients, nor do they denote season of use. These matrices have a variety of aquatic habitat and microhabitat elements, and use of an element is shown as "required for survival," "not required for survival," or "unknown."

The final data format is status matrices. These matrices contain information on life form, federal classification as threatened or endangered, state status as threatened or endangered, protected or unprotected nongame, and hunted or trapped (Sheppard et al. 1982).

Pattern-recognition Models

Pattern-recognition models are those that use a series of conditional probabilities to assess whether habitat is suitable for a species. To use this approach one must know what constitutes suitable and unsuitable habitat for a species (Williams et al. 1978).

Usually a series of habitat attributes (such as habitat size, number of dead trees, water availability, etc.) must be considered. How population density is associated with each habitat factor also must be known. Habitat assessment is made from data collected in the field or from aerial photos if appropriate. An "expected habitat suitability" (EHS) can be calculated as:

$$\text{EHS} = \frac{P(H) \times P(I/H)}{P(H) \times P(I/H) + P(L) \times P(I/L)},$$

where P(H) = proportion of high-density habitat, P(I/H) = the probability the area has a high population potential, P(L) = proportion of low-density habitat, and P(I/L) = the probability the area has a low population potential. Low and high population potentials are identified from survey data.

Life-form Models

Life-form models try to include all species in a community. They create a series of life-form categories for the community based on feeding, reproduction, and other necessary life-history activities. All species are placed in one of the life-form categories, reducing the number of species that a manager must consider in an area. For example, in developing the life-form concept for the Blue Mountains of Oregon and Washington, Thomas (1979) combined 327 species into 16 life forms. The habitat is the basis for grouping animals, thus, habitat data must be available to develop the model. Within each life form, more detailed data may be present for individual species. Thus, managers can examine the impact of brush removal or tree harvest and list the life forms affected. How habitat features influence number of species can be viewed by examining the detailed needs of each life form. The effects of plant-community succession also can be examined from the details of change that affect a life form.

Thomas (1979) advanced the life-form concept by preparing a summary of information on each species' seasonal use of habitat. He showed when the animal used an area for breeding and feeding on a monthly basis and used these data to calculate how susceptible each species was to habitat manipulations. The most versatile species are the least sensitive to habitat manipulation, and the least versatile are the most sensitive.

The versatility (V) score for each species is derived from the total number of plant communities and total number of successional stages to which the species show primary association for feeding and reproduction:

$$V = (C_r + S_r) + (C_f + S_f),$$

where C_r is the number of communities used by the species for reproduction, S_r is the number of successional stages used for reproduction, C_f is the number of communities used for feeding, and S_f is the number of successional stages used for feeding.

Guild Models

The guild concept involves a group of species that exploit the same class of environmental resources in a similar way. The investigator defines each guild. However, statistical procedures such as cluster analysis and principal components analysis also have been used to define guilds.

Verner (1984) used this concept to define a management guild. Thus, using birds as an example, he believed that all bird species using a tree canopy for foraging should be one management guild. Removal of timber would affect all birds that forage there. The guild concept can be extended further to include all animals that forage on the ground of a deciduous forest, or all animals that use snags. This establishes a matrix of units within a plant community, and biologists can indicate which animals would be affected by natural or human changes in habitats.

Model Verification

Many wildlife-habitat models have not been verified. Thus, the danger is that a given relationship may hold for one set of conditions but not another. If the results for one area are incorrectly assumed to apply to another, then habitat management efforts will be misguided and ineffective. Experimental testing of wildlife habitat relations is the ideal means of verification. But this approach is often expensive.

Often, wildlife-habitat models perform poorly when they are tested outside the specific conditions for which they were developed (Maurer 1986, O'Neil et al. 1988, Fielding and Haworth 1995). When this happens, implicit model assumptions regarding ecological principles may not be entirely justified. Flather and Hoekstra (1985) demonstrated how ecological theory could be used as a first step to improve population-habitat models. If the model's assumptions are unreasonable based on accepted ecological theory, alteration is needed. A model also may perform poorly because it applies only to local conditions. In this situation, data from other areas can be combined with the original data to generate a new model or to broaden an existing model's applicability (Maurer 1986, O'Neil et al. 1988). Numerous environmental factors not associated with specific habitat features affect wildlife populations and communities directly, indirectly, or both. Thus, models that incorporate only habitat features are sometimes inadequate (O'Neil and Carey 1986). If more accurate models and improved assessments of habitat quantity and quality are to be obtained, more careful analyses of the many influences (including weather, disease, predators, competitors, pollutants, etc.) on wildlife are often necessary (Danchin et al. 1998, Franklin et al. 2000, Davidson et al. 2001, Martin 2001).

Models based on wildlife habitat correlations are often used to evaluate habitat suitability, but these models have uncertainty associated with them that should be understood before they are applied. Gutzwiller and Barrow (2001) discuss 4 sources of uncertainty in predictive models (interannual variation, environmental variation, structural uncertainty, partial observability) that generate dilemmas about which model(s) to use for prediction or decision-making; they also present approaches for coping with these uncertainties. The context of their discussion is predictive models of bird-landscape relations, but the principles and coping strategies they consider apply to wildlife habitat models in general. One can reduce uncertainty associated with interannual variation by using predictions from annual models to develop knowledge about the probable range of variation in the dependent variable in time and space. Model uncertainty associated with random environmental variation (e.g., weather, food availability) can be incorporated into predictions of wildlife variables through stochastic simulation models that link wildlife-habitat relations and randomly varying environmental factors. Structural uncertainty—the limited understanding of the appropriate form of the model based on biological mechanisms—can be reduced by meeting important statistical assumptions, ensuring high statistical power, testing a model's predictive performance, and increasing a model's accuracy via ongoing data collection and model refitting. Using sample sizes that produce precise estimates of wildlife and habitat parameters can control model uncertainty arising from sampling variation (i.e., partial observability). Biologists may be able to decrease structural uncertainty by reducing partial observability.

Wildlife-habitat Correlations

We know that correlations cannot be interpreted as cause-and-effect relationships. Nevertheless, correlations are valuable to managers because they can help direct management of habitats for populations, a species, or a community even though the exact causal mechanism is poorly understood. For example, one may find a negative correlation between number of roads and number of deer in a series of areas but not be able to demonstrate the underlying cause for the relationship. Road-killed animals and hunter success might be expected to increase with increasing numbers of roads, but the real cause might be stress induced by traffic and the presence of people. Knowing the cause would be valuable to managers, but not absolute-

ly necessary. In this example, managers might use the correlation to close roads in areas with small deer populations. Alternatively, if populations are too large, opening or building roads may decrease deer populations and minimize habitat degradation that otherwise would result from overpopulation.

Identifying features that affect whether a habitat is usable or unusable is a central issue in habitat evaluation. What habitat conditions affect whether a species will be present or absent? The researcher first must define "use" and "nonuse" for a specific gender, age class, place, time, and life-history activity (e.g., nesting, feeding, loafing). Johnson (1981) noted that many factors influence whether a habitat is occupied by a species. For example, even if a habitat is usable, it may be vacant when population levels are low and, thus, appear to be unusable. If a habitat is being used but the sampling scheme for assessing use is poor, the presence of a species may not be detected. Spending more time confirming the species' presence or absence can minimize these errors. One then compares habitat characteristics between the 2 types of areas, assuming that statistically significant differences indicate which habitat conditions make an area usable or unusable (Hobbs and Hanley 1990). This assumption is not warranted if sites cannot be correctly identified by the researcher as used or unused.

Regression involving a binary dependent (Y) variable (logistic regression) (Neter et al. 1989, Hair et al. 1998) is especially valuable in these analyses. The dependent variable is coded as 1 or 0 to reflect whether the species was present or absent, respectively. The explanatory variables (Xs) are habitat characteristics at each site. Habitat features may have linear or nonlinear effects and additive or multiplicative effects on the presence or absence of wildlife. Multiple logistic regression enables the researcher to assess such possibilities simultaneously and include many habitat features in the analysis. Techniques that enable us to examine complex associations are desirable because actual wildlife-habitat relations often have these attributes. In contrast, methods that assume simple linear relationships are often inadequate because they are less realistic.

Wildlife scientists spend a great deal of effort identifying which habitat features may affect whether a habitat will be poor, mediocre, or good for an individual, a species, or a community. Van Horne (1983) and Maurer (1986) observed that animal density may be a poor indicator of habitat quality. Instead, it would be better to consider measuring variables that unequivocally reflect the health, reproduction, or survival of wildlife (e.g., Breininger et al. 1998). For example, suppose one decides to identify which habitat features in an arid environment define habitat quality for an endangered lizard. Lizard variables to measure could include body weight, growth rate, fat levels, brood size, brood and adult survival rates, maximum longevity, or other physiological measures. Habitat features associated with food, water, loafing, shelter from predators and temperature extremes, or the abundance of competitors or predators, should be examined.

Habitat quality also may be assessed by identifying which characteristics are most closely related to the frequency of habitat use for a specific purpose (e.g., Gutzwiller and Wakeley 1982) (Box 4). We assume there is something important about the habitat that repeatedly

Box 4. Shorebird use of wetlands.

A biologist wanted to identify which of several habitat features was most closely related to frequency of wetland use by migrant shorebirds. The goal was to find a characteristic that could be managed for and that could be measured on aerial photographs to assess habitat quality and quantity. The investigator collected the following data.

Wetland	Open water area (ha)	Mean bank slope (%)	Mud-flat area (ha)	Frequency of wetland use (% of 30 visits that migrants were present)
1	4	38	3	15
2	7	45	6	30
3	9	25	7	30
4	11	20	10	45
5	3	17	12	55
6	1	7	16	75
7	1	3	15	75
8	8	9	9	43
9	6	14	4	12
10	2	5	5	15

The following correlation coefficients (significance levels) were computed.

	Open water	Bank slope	Mud-flat area
Wetland use	−0.347	−0.451	0.989
	(0.3252)	(0.1905)	(0.0001)

The frequency of wetland use was most closely related to mud-flat area. The relation was positive, suggesting that larger areas of mud flat improved the quality of wetlands for migrant shorebirds, perhaps by supplying more areas for feeding.

---

attracts the species. For example, wintering birds require sources of energy to maintain body heat and weight. Because survival will depend, in part, on caloric intake, sites with food are of higher quality for wintering birds. Thus, areas with available seeds, insects, or other food sources will be used more frequently (other factors being equal) than those without food. Examination of the frequency with which habitats are used, relative to specific habitat characteristics, is applicable for many different wildlife activities.

The concept of preference also can be used to evaluate habitat (e.g., Spencer et al. 1983, Straw et al. 1986). If a particular habitat type constitutes 20% of the available habitat in an area, but a species uses this type more than 20% of the time, one assumes the habitat type is preferred. Because more than 20% of the species' locations are in this type, it is used more often than would be expected by chance alone. If the species uses it 20% of the time, the species is not associated with the habitat any differently than a random association would indicate, and one assumes there is no preference. If a species uses the habitat less than 20% of the time, one assumes there is habitat avoidance. A safer conclusion in the latter situation may be that there is no preference.

Chi-square tests and log-likelihood ratio tests (Zar 1999) typically are used to assess differences between

observed and expected frequencies (see also Thomas and Taylor 1990, Alldredge and Ratti 1992). This approach relies on a large random sample of the habitat in an area to identify availability of resources. One also must make extensive observations of the resource levels actually used. Inaccurate representation of either of these categories will lead to inaccurate preference assessments (see Porter and Church 1987). For example, for frogs in marshes, the available resource is a particular marsh habitat type. The general procedure described can be applied to many other variables. Any variable with a range of values that can be categorized into different groups or levels can be subjected to preference analysis. This includes virtually all variables that one might measure for wildlife, such as soil type, tree density, canopy cover, water temperature, oxygen content, pH, and food levels.

SUMMARY

Appropriate use of habitat evaluation methods requires knowledge of the habitat and life history of the animals and plants present, as well as information about associated populations and communities. It is important to understand how and why animal fitness, density, and diversity are related to habitat features. Habitat features can be measured in a variety of ways depending on the habitat being studied.

Habitat use often correlates with features of the environment and animals present in a particular area. However, this does not necessarily demonstrate causation. Habitat selection involves complex behavioral mechanisms that influence the distribution of animals. Many habitat models are now in use to help describe habitat and habitat use. Models must be used cautiously until biologists know they meet the goals for the questions asked about a specific area.

ACKNOWLEDGMENTS

We thank C. E. Braun, T. C. Edwards, Jr., and an anonymous reviewer for constructive review of the manuscript.

LITERATURE CITED

ALLDREDGE, J. R., AND J. T. RATTI. 1992. Further comparison of some statistical techniques for analysis of resource selection. Journal of Wildlife Management 56:1–9.

ANDERSON, S. H. 1981. Correlating habitat variables and birds. Pages 538–542 in C. J. Ralph and J. M. Scott, editors. Estimating numbers of terrestrial birds. Studies in Avian Biology 6.

———. 2002. Managing our wildlife resources. Prentice-Hall, Englewood Cliffs, New Jersey, USA.

BAKER, W. L., AND Y. CAI. 1992. The r.le programs for multiscale analysis of landscape structure using the GRASS geographical information system. Landscape Ecology 7:291–302.

BEASOM, S. L., E. P. WIGGERS, AND J. R. GIARDINO. 1983. A technique for assessing land surface ruggedness. Journal of Wildlife Management 47:1163–1166.

BERRY, K. H. 1986. Introduction: development, testing, and application of wildlife-habitat models. Pages 3–4 in J. Verner, M. L. Morrison, and C. J. Ralph, editors. Wildlife 2000: modeling habitat relationships of terrestrial vertebrates. University of Wisconsin Press, Madison, USA.

BLOCK, W. M., AND L. A. BRENNAN. 1993. The habitat concept in ornithology: theory and applications. Current Ornithology 11:35–91.

BREININGER, D. R., V. L. LARSON, B. W. DUNCAN, AND R. B. SMITH. 1998. Linking habitat suitability to demographic success in Florida Scrub-jays. Wildlife Society Bulletin 26:118–128.

BROOKS, R. P. 1997. Improving habitat suitability index models. Wildlife Society Bulletin 25:163–167.

BURGER, J. 1987. Physical and social determinants of nest-site selection in piping plover in New Jersey. Condor 89:811–818.

CODY, M. L., editor. 1985. Habitat selection in birds. Academic Press, New York, USA.

COOPERRIDER, A., R. J. BOYD, H. R. STUART, AND S. L. McCULLOCH, editors. 1986. Inventory and monitoring of wildlife habitat. U.S. Department of the Interior, Bureau of Land Management, Denver, Colorado, USA.

CUPLIN, P. 1978. Remote sensing streams. Proceedings of the International Symposium on Remote Sensing of Observation and Inventory of Earth Resources and the Endangered Environment. International Archiwum Photogram, II. Freiburg, Germany.

DANCHIN, E., T. BOULINIER, AND M. MASSOT. 1998. Conspecific reproductive success and breeding habitat selection: implications for the study of coloniality. Ecology 79:2415–2428.

DAVIDSON, C., H. B. SHAFFER, AND M. R. JENNINGS. 2001. Declines of the California red-legged frog: climate, UV-B, habitat, and pesticide hypotheses. Ecological Applications 11:464–479.

DEALY, J. E., D. A. LECKENBY, AND D. M. CONCANNON. 1981. Wildlife habitats in managed rangelands—the Great Basin of southeastern Oregon. Plant communities and their importance to wildlife. U.S. Department of Agriculture, Forest Service, General Technical Report PNW-120.

DETTMERS, R., AND, J. BART. 1999. A GIS modeling method applied to predicting forest songbird habitat. Ecological Applications 9:152–163.

DIXON, W. J., editor. 1981. BMDP statistical software 1981. University California Press, Berkeley, USA.

ELLIS, J. A., J. N. BURROUGHS, M. J. ARMBRUSTER, D. L. HALLET, P. A. KORTE, AND T. S. BASKETT. 1979. Appraising four field methods of terrestrial habitat evaluation. Transactions of the North American Wildlife and Natural Resources Conference 44:369–379.

ETCHBERGER, R. C., AND P. R. KRAUSMAN. 1997. Evaluation of five methods for measuring desert vegetation. Wildlife Society Bulletin 25:604–609.

FIELDING, A. H., AND P. F. HAWORTH. 1995. Testing the generality of bird-habitat models. Conservation Biology 9:1466–1481.

FINCH, D. 1989. Species abundances, guild dominance patterns and community structure of breeding riparian birds. Pages 629–645 in R. Sharitz and J. Gibbons, editors. Freshwater wetlands and wildlife. U.S. Department of Energy Symposium Series 61.

FLATHER, C. H., AND T. W. HOEKSTRA. 1985. Evaluating population-habitat models using ecological theory. Wildlife Society Bulletin 13:121–130.

FORD, A. F. 1999. Modeling the environment: an introduction to system dynamics modeling of environmental systems. Island Press, Washington, D.C., USA.

FORMAN, R. T. T. 1995. Land mosaics: the ecology of landscapes and regions. Cambridge University Press, Cambridge, United Kingdom.

———, AND L. E. ALEXANDER. 1998. Roads and their major ecological effects. Annual Review of Ecology and Systematics 29:207–231.

———, AND M. GODRON. 1986. Landscape ecology. John Wiley and Sons, New York, USA.

———, D. SPERLING, J. A. BISSONETTE, A. P. CLEVENGER, C. D. CUTSHALL, V. H. DALE, L. FAHRIG, R. FRANCE, C. R. GOLDMAN, K. HEANUE, J. A. JONES, F. J. SWANSON, T. TURRENTINE, AND T. C. WINTER. 2003. Road ecology: science and solutions. Island Press, Washington, D.C., USA.

FRANKLIN, A. B., D. R. ANDERSON, R. J. GUTIERREZ, AND K. P. BURNHAM. 2000. Climate, habitat quality, and fitness in northern spotted owl populations in northwestern California. Ecological Monographs 70:539–590.

GERMAINE, S. S., S. S. ROSENSTOCK, R. E. SCHWEINSBURG, AND W. S. RICHARDSON. 1998. Relationships among breeding birds, habitat, and residential development in greater Tucson, Arizona. Ecological Applications 8:680–691.

GILES, R. H. 1978. Wildlife management. W. H. Freeman, San Francisco, California, USA.

GREEN, C. M., AND J. A. STAMPS. 2001. Habitat selection at low population densities. Ecology 82:2091–2100.

GUSTAFSON, E. J. 1998. Quantifying landscape spatial pattern: what is the state of the art? Ecosystems 1:143–156.

GUTZWILLER, K. J., AND S. H. ANDERSON. 1987a. Habitat suitability index models: marsh wren. U.S. Department of the Interior, Fish and Wildlife Service, Biological Report 82(10.139).

———, AND S. H. ANDERSON. 1987b. Multiscale associations between cavity-nesting birds and features of Wyoming streamside woodlands. Condor 89:534–548.

———, AND W. C. BARROW, JR. 2001. Bird-landscape relations in the Chihuahuan Desert: coping with uncertainties about predictive models. Ecological Applications 11:1517–1532.

———, AND ———. 2002. Does bird community structure vary with landscape patchiness? A Chihuahuan Desert perspective. Oikos 98:284–298.

———, AND J. S. WAKELEY. 1982. Differential use of woodcock singing grounds in relation to habitat characteristics. Pages 51–54 in T. J. Dwyer and G. L. Storm, technical coordinators. Woodcock ecology and management. U.S. Department of the Interior, Fish and Wildlife Service Research Report 14.

HAIR, JR., J. F., R. E. ANDERSON, R. L. TATHAM, AND W. C. BLACK. 1998. Multivariate data analysis. Fifth edition. Prentice-Hall, Upper Saddle River, New Jersey, USA.

HALL, L. L., P. R. KRAUSMAN, AND M. L. MORRISON. 1997. The habitat concept and a plea for standard terminology. Wildlife Society Bulletin 25:173–182.

HANNON, B., AND M. RUTH. 1997. Modeling dynamic biological systems. Springer-Verlag, Inc., New York, USA.

HEINEN, J., AND G. H. CROSS. 1983. An approach to measure interspersion, juxtaposition, and spatial diversity from cover-type maps. Wildlife Society Bulletin 11:232–237.

HOBBS, N. T., AND T. A. HANLEY. 1990. Habitat evaluation: do use/availability data reflect carrying capacity? Journal of Wildlife Management 54:515–522.

HOOVER, R. L., AND D. L. WILLS, editors. 1984. Managing forested lands for wildlife. Colorado Division of Wildlife, Denver, USA.

HURLEY, J. F., H. SALWASSER, AND K. SHIMMOTO. 1982. Fish and wildlife habitat capacity models and special habitat criteria. Nevada Wildlife Transactions 40:48.

HUTTO, R. L. 1985. Habitat selection by nonbreeding migratory land birds. Pages 455–476 in M. J. Cody, editor. Habitat selection in birds. Academic Press, New York, USA.

INHABER, H. 1976. Environmental indices. John Wiley and Sons, New York, USA.

JOHNSON, D. H. 1981. The use and misuse of statistics in wildlife habitat studies. Pages 11–19 *in* D. E. Capen, editor. The use of multivariate statistics in studies of wildlife habitat. U.S. Department of Agriculture, Forest Service, General Technical Report RM-87.

JONES, J. 2001. Habitat selection studies in avian ecology: a critical review. Auk 118: 557–562.

KARL, J. W., P. J. HEGLUND, E. O. GARTON, J. M. SCOTT, N. M. WRIGHT, AND R. L. HUTTO. 2000. Sensitivity of species habitat-relationship model performance to factors of scale. Ecological Applications 10:1690–1705.

KNOPF, F. L., J. A. SEDGWICK, AND R. W. CANNON. 1988. Guild structure of a riparian avifauna relative to seasonal cattle grazing. Journal of Wildlife Management 52:280–290.

LANCIA, R. A., AND D. A. ADAMS. 1985. A test of habitat suitability index models for five bird species. Proceedings of the Annual Conference of the Southeastern Association of Fish and Wildlife Agencies 39:412–419.

MARTIN, T. E. 2001. Abiotic vs. biotic influences on habitat selection of coexisting species: climate change impacts? Ecology 82:175–188.

MASER, C., J. M. GEIST, D. M. CONCANNON, R. ANDERSON, AND B. LOVELL. 1979. Wildlife habitats in managed rangelands—the Great Basin of southeastern Oregon. Manmade habitats. U.S. Department of Agriculture, Forest Service, General Technical Report PNW-86.

MAURER, B. A. 1986. Predicting habitat quality for grassland birds using density-dependent correlations. Journal of Wildlife Management 50:556–566.

MCGARIGAL, K., AND B. J. MARKS. 1995. FRAGSTATS: spatial pattern analysis program for quantifying landscape structure. U.S. Department of Agriculture, Forest Service, General Technical Report PNW-GTR-351.

MEAD, R. A., T. L. SHARIK, S. P. PRESLEY, AND J. T. HEINEN. 1981. A computerized spatial analysis system for assessing wildlife habitat from vegetation maps. Canadian Journal of Remote Sensing 7:34–40.

MISENHELTER, M. D., AND J. T. ROTENBERRY. 2000. Choices and consequences of habitat occupancy and nest site selection in sage sparrows. Ecology 81:2892–2901.

MORRISON, M. L. 2001. A proposed research emphasis to overcome the limits of wildlife habitat relationships. Journal of Wildlife Management 65:613–623.

NETER, J., W. WASSERMAN, AND M. H. KUTNER. 1989. Applied linear regression models. Second edition. Richard D. Irwin, Burr Ridge, Illinois, USA.

NUTTLE, T. 1997. Densiometer bias? Are we measuring the forest or the trees? Wildlife Society Bulletin 25:610–611.

ODUM, H. T., AND E. C. ODUM. 2000. Modeling for all scales: an introduction to system simulation. Academic Press, San Diego, California, USA.

O'NEIL, L. J., AND A. B. CAREY. 1986. Introduction: when habitats fail as predictors. Pages 207–208 *in* J. Verner, M. L. Morrison, and C. J. Ralph, editors. Wildlife 2000: modeling habitat relationships of terrestrial vertebrates. University of Wisconsin Press, Madison, USA.

———, T. H. ROBERTS, J. S. WAKELEY, AND J. W. TEAFORD. 1988. A procedure to modify habitat suitability index models. Wildlife Society Bulletin 16:33–36.

O'NEIL, T. A., P. BETTINGER, B. G. MARCOT, B. W. LUSCOMBE, G. T. KOELN, H. J. BRUNER, C. BARRETT, J. A. POLLOCK, AND S. BERNATUS. 2005. Application of spatial technologies in wildlife biology. Pages 418–447 *in* C. E. Braun, editor. Techniques for wildlife investigations and management. Sixth edition. The Wildlife Society, Bethesda, Maryland, USA.

PEARSON, S. M. 1993. The spatial extent and relative influence of landscape-level factors on wintering bird populations. Landscape Ecology 8:3–18.

PLATTS, W. S., W. F. MEGAHAN, AND G.W. MINSHALL. 1983. Methods for evaluating streams, riparian and biotic conditions. U.S. Department of Agriculture, Forest Service, General Technical Report INT-138.

———, C. ARMOUR, G. BOOTH, M. BRYANT, J. BUFFORD, P. CUPLIN, S. JENSEN, G. LIENKAEMPER, G. MARSHALL, S. MINSHALL, S. MONSEN, F. NELSON, J. SEDELL, AND J. TUHY. 1987. Methods for evaluating riparian habitats with applications to management. U.S. Department of Agriculture, Forest Service, General Technical Report INT-221.

PORTER, W. F., AND K. E. CHURCH. 1987. Effects of environmental patterns on habitat preference analysis. Journal of Wildlife Management 51:681–685.

RODIEK, J. E., AND E. G. BOLEN, editors. 1991. Wildlife and habitats in managed landscapes. Island Press, Washington, D.C., USA.

ROLOFF, G. J., AND B. J. KERNOHAN. 1999. Evaluating reliability of habitat suitability index models. Wildlife Society Bulletin 27:973–985.

SAAB, V. 1999. Importance of spatial scale to habitat use by breeding birds in riparian forests: a hierarchical analysis. Ecological Applications 9:135–151.

SCHOOLEY, R. L. 1994. Annual variation in habitat selection: patterns concealed by pooled data. Journal of Wildlife Management 58:367–374.

SHEPPARD, J. L., D. L. WILLS, AND J. L. SIMONSON. 1982. Project applications of the Forest Service Rocky Mountain Region wildlife and fish habitat relationships system. Transactions of the North American Wildlife and Natural Resources Conference 47:128–141.

SOULÉ, M. E., D. T. BOLGER, A. C. ALBERTS, J. WRIGHT, M. SORICE, AND S. HILL. 1988. Reconstructed dynamics of rapid extinctions of chaparral-requiring birds in urban habitat islands. Conservation Biology 2:75–92.

SPENCER, W. D., R. H. BARRETT, AND W. H. ZIELINSKI. 1983. Marten habitat preferences in the northern Sierra Nevada. Journal of Wildlife Management 47:1181–1186.

STEURY, T. D., A. J. WIRSING, AND D. L. MURRAY. 2002. Using multiple treatment levels as a means of improving inference in wildlife research. Journal of Wildlife Management 66:292–296.

STORCH, I. 2002. On spatial resolution in habitat models: can small-scale forest structure explain capercaillie numbers? Conservation Ecology 6(1):6 [serial online]. URL: http://www.consecol.org/vol6/iss1/art6/.

STRAW, JR., J. A., J. S. WAKELEY, AND J. E. HUDGINS. 1986. A model for management of diurnal habitat for American woodcock in Pennsylvania. Journal of Wildlife Management 50:378–383.

THOMAS, D. L., AND E. J. TAYLOR. 1990. Study designs and tests for comparing resource use and availability. Journal of Wildlife Management 54:322–330.

THOMAS, J. W., editor. 1979. Wildlife habitat in managed forests, the Blue Mountains of Oregon and Washington. U.S. Department of Agriculture, Forest Service, Agriculture Handbook 553.

TROMBULAK, S. C., AND C. A. FRISSELL. 2000. Review of ecological effects of roads on terrestrial and aquatic communities. Conservation Biology 14:18–30.

VAN HORNE, B. 1983. Density as a misleading indicator of habitat quality. Journal of Wildlife Management 47:893–901.

VERNER, J. 1984. The guild concept applied to management of bird populations. Environmental Management 8:1–14.

WAKELEY, J. S. 1988. A method to create simplified versions of existing habitat suitability index (HSI) models. Environmental Management 12:79–83.

WARD, J. P., AND S. H. ANDERSON. 1988. Influences of cliffs on wildlife communities in southcentral Wyoming. Journal of Wildlife Management 52:673–678.

WILKIE, D., E. SHAW, F. ROTBERG, G. MORELLI, AND P. AUZEL. 2000. Roads, development, and conservation in the Congo Basin. Conservation Biology 14:1614–1622.

WILLIAMS, G. L., K. R. RUSSELL, AND W. K. SEITZ. 1978. Pattern recognition as a tool in the ecological analysis of habitat. Pages 521–531 *in* A. Marmelstein, editor. Classification, inventory, and analysis of fish and wildlife habitat: proceedings of a national symposium. U.S. Department of the Interior, Fish and Wildlife Service, FWS/OBS-78/76.

WILSON, D. S. 1998. Nest-site selection: microhabitat variation and its effects on the survival of turtle embryos. Ecology 79:1884–1892.

WILSON, S. F., D. M. SHACKLETON, AND K. L. CAMPBELL. 1998. Making habitat-availability estimates spatially explicit. Wildlife Society Bulletin 26:626–631.

ZAR, J. H. 1999. Biostatistical analysis. Fourth edition. Prentice-Hall, Upper Saddle River, New Jersey, USA.

ZWANK, P. J., T. H. WHITE, JR., AND F. G. KIMMEL. 1988. Female turkey habitat use in Mississippi River batture. Journal of Wildlife Management 52:253–260.

19

ECOLOGICAL IMPACT ASSESSMENTS AND HABITAT CONSERVATION PLANS

Joe C. Truett, Marilet A. Zablan, and Kyran Kunkel

INTRODUCTION

Federal laws gave rise to use of ecological impact assessments (EIAs) and habitat conservation plans (HCPs) in wildlife conservation. The concept of ecological impact assessment originated with the National Environmental Policy Act (NEPA) of 1969 and its requirement for environmental impact analysis of major federal actions. The term "ecological impact assessment" commonly refers to that part of a NEPA document that describes impacts to biota, but it also can mean the process of analyzing such impacts. Development of HCPs evolved from requirements of the Endangered Species Act (ESA) of 1973 (as amended in 1982) to alleviate impacts to animals or plants listed as threatened or endangered and candidates for such listing. Major HCPs may require NEPA analysis.

Ecological impact assessments differ from HCPs in policy focus and number of species commonly addressed. An EIA usually attempts to predict (disclose) impacts of a proposed legislative or development action on numerous species potentially affected. A HCP as originally conceived prescribed habitat management or protection for species listed as federally threatened or endangered. More recently HCPs cover some non-listed species as well and may encompass numerous development actions. We include EIAs and HCPs in a single chapter because they share important overriding qualities—a common ecological basis, the need for agency oversight, and involvement of multiple interest groups (Truett et al. 1994, Hemker and Braun 2001).

The need to involve multiple interest groups and follow prescribed protocols complicates the difficulty of preparing effective documents. Different interest groups come with different perspectives and levels of understanding that can frustrate the process (Holling 1978, Hemker and Braun 2001). The common inability of policy makers to understand ecology and appreciate the inadequacy of information often results in misguided directives (Reid 1996, Wilhere 2002). To successfully meet these and related problems requires "people" skills as well as a clear understanding of ecological principles, species–habitat relationships, and limits of knowledge.

We treat EIAs and HCPs somewhat differently. Given the relatively long history of the EIA process, we review its effectiveness rather than repeating what numerous others (e.g., Truett et al. 1994, Traweek 1995) have reported about techniques. Because HCPs are relatively new, we elaborate on the process. Case-history examples of each build on these respective approaches.

HISTORICAL DEVELOPMENT

Implicit in the preparation of EIAs and HCPs is the assumption that presence and abundance of wildlife species are governed by environmental factors that can be measured and managed. From an ecological perspective these endeavors differ little from traditional management of wildlife populations. Biologists who understand the basics of habitat management will have little trouble understanding the ecological underpinnings of impact assessments and conservation plans.

Aldo Leopold (1933) first described the principles of wildlife management in the context of habitat. Successful managers since that time have built upon his insight, often elaborating with new terminology and techniques. Good habitat managers are familiar with the roles of limiting factors, habitat structure, habitat alteration, and population measurement and monitoring.

Ecological impact assessment as a practice separate from wildlife management began in the United States with passage of the National Environmental Policy Act (NEPA). It posed a more complex problem than traditional single-species wildlife management because analysts had to consider many species and managers had little direct control over actions that affected wildlife. Analysts wrestling with these new dimensions progressed through about 4 sequential approaches over the next 3 decades (Truett et al. 1994): (1) an initial preoccupation with species inventories generally intended to be used as baselines against which to measure change, (2) an early shift of focus by some to analyses of ecosystem processes (functions) for helping to predict impacts, (3) an ultimate realization that the complexity introduced by trying to assess impacts to numerous species and complex processes created a measurement dilemma, and (4) a consequent search for responsible integrative measures.

Habitat conservation planning evolved from Endangered Species Act amendments passed in 1982 that were designed to ease the burden of the ESA on private landowners. Simply put, after 1982 landowners could develop, if they chose, a HCP that described how they would alleviate ("mitigate") impacts their actions might have on species listed, or being considered for listing, under the ESA. Impact mitigation could come through such mechanisms as improving habitat for the species or providing them a protected reserve. The process became popular only after 1990, and novel ways of mitigating adverse impacts of land use continue to evolve.

ECOLOGICAL BASIS

Ecological impact assessments and HCPs strive to manage or protect habitat in the context of human actions. The former attempt to ameliorate habitat changes adverse to wildlife by helping decision-makers select among, or mitigate impacts of, human actions (Truett et al. 1994). The latter propose to manage or set aside specific areas to benefit species actually or potentially imperiled (Hemker and Braun 2001). Responsible EIAs and HCPs, whether they

involve habitat modification or habitat preservation, should (1) focus on a limited number of species, (2) base assessments and plans on population limiting factors for these species, (3) develop and apply integrative measures that consider additional species, (4) conduct follow-up monitoring, and (5) iteratively adjust plans and predictions with feedback from monitoring.

Limiting the Number of Species Addressed

Reliably assessing responses of most species to human actions is not only impractical but also usually impossible given constraints of funding, time, and state of knowledge (Diamond 1987, Franklin 1993, Moir and Block 2001). Preparing defensible EIAs and HCPs requires focusing on a few species from among the many potentially affected. How does one make these selections?

Proposed strategies for reducing the number of species addressed in impact assessment have proliferated since the passage of NEPA. Early on, some practitioners focused on species directly valuable to people, e.g., "featured species" (Gould 1977) or "valued ecosystem components" (Beanlands and Duinker 1983). Others proposed using "ecological-indicator" species (Graul et al. 1976) or "management-indicator" species (Graul and Miller 1984) that, in theory, represented the needs of other species with similar habitat relationships. Some analysts proposed that one or a few species could represent entire "guilds" of species with similar habitat needs (Landres 1983). Others suggested using "indicator" species to assay change in habitat quality (Landres et al. 1988), "keystone" species that disproportionately affected other species (Mills et al. 1993), "focal" and "umbrella" species whose requirements encompassed the needs of others (Lambeck 1997), and "flagship" species that rallied support for protection of associated species (Miller et al. 1999).

Habitat conservation plans, unlike EIAs, initially focused on only a few species—those listed under the ESA. But, the process evolved so that many HCPs now include numerous additional species. Similarly to EIAs addressing multiple species, this can complicate the preparation of reliable documents.

Some recommended approaches for limiting the number of species addressed could usefully simplify impact assessment and conservation planning. Some approaches overlap with others in concept. More problematically, some are based on faulty assumptions. Straightforward approaches hampered little by untested or invalid assumptions include focus on listed species (HCPs), featured species, valued ecosystem components, keystone species, and flagship species. We urge caution in using selected species as indicators of needs of other species or to represent species guilds (see Landres et al. 1988).

Focusing on Limiting Factors

Numerous environmental factors affect any given wildlife population but only a few exert major influences. Leopold (1933) called the important ones "limiting factors" and focus on these remains a cornerstone of habitat evaluation and management (Dasmann 1981:71–73, Anderson and Gutzwiller 2005). Application of this principle is important in preparing EIAs and HCPs—like limiting the number of species addressed, it helps reduce complexity to a manageable level.

Limiting factors may range from food scarcity to weather to predation, but commonly impose themselves through the medium of habitat structure (Willson 1974, Short and Williamson 1986, Risser 1995, Wiens 1995). Biologists preparing EIAs and HCPs can increase their effectiveness by focusing on habitat structure and viewing themselves as habitat "architects." Several advantages come with this approach: (1) alteration of habitat structure usually is the most important way in which development affects wildlife habitat (Kautz 1984, Franklin 1993); (2) wildlife responses to structural change frequently are predictable in a general way given existing or easily gathered information (Willson 1974, Short 1988); (3) vegetation communities and microscale "coverts", which provide much of the structure important to wildlife (MacArthur and MacArthur 1961, Maser et al. 1979, Verner 1986), usually are amenable to manipulation; and (4) structure is readily mapped and displayed. A wide range of participants can accept habitat structure as "currency" for measuring habitat quality.

Using Integrative Measures

Focus on some species may encompass the needs of others but invariably many species and the community as a whole remain unaccounted. Ecologists have struggled to develop integrative measures that reflect the "health" of entire wildlife communities and not just the well-being of selected species. Some have used the early-historic (i.e., pre-industrial) state of ecosystems as the explicit or implicit template for good health, and departures therefrom as degrees of "illness." But the assumption of co-evolution of species on which this concept rests may be invalid.

Paleoecological and historical evidence assembled in recent decades makes it increasingly clear that most plants and animals did not co-evolve as members of the same communities they now occupy. Modern communities assembled largely by chance, each species having evolved in association with an ever-changing milieu of other species (Graham 1988, Hunter et al. 1988, Reid 1996, Lockwood et al. 1997). A few interspecific dependencies, such as the black-footed ferret's (*Mustela nigripes*) need for prairie dogs (*Cynomys* spp.), and some host–parasite relationships, do not invalidate the general pattern.

That communities are continually changing assemblages of species rather than co-evolved units raises questions about how to measure community-level impacts. It hints that the concept of "natural" or "pristine" as a template for healthy ecosystems may have arisen from a short view of history (Dickinson 1995) and a poor appreciation for impacts of pre-industrial humans (Sprugel 1991, Wagner and Kay 1993). It suggests that what is healthy in ecosystems depends largely on human judgment (Reid 1996), which varies in time and space. This underscores the need for review by multiple interest groups during the EIA process.

Measures of biodiversity constitute a commonly used integrative index of community value, with greater diversity commonly indicating greater value. Measures of landscape diversity (Westman 1985), smaller-scale structural diversity (Noss and Harris 1986, Noss 1990), and species diversity (richness and equability) (Westman 1990) have been proposed to measure value of habitats or the wildlife community itself. In practice, indices to species richness

(Weller 1978, Scott et al. 1987) appeal to many analysts because they are easy to understand and acquire. None of these methods offers the perfect solution (e.g., Harris 1988, Knopf 1992) and which works best often depends on money available and context of the problem.

Numerous other measures have been proposed as surrogates for community health (Rapport 1989). Many ecologists note the importance of habitat structural measures at landscape (Hansson 1979, Westman 1985, Urban et al. 1987) and other scales (Noss and Harris 1986). Others propose measures of community functional processes such as productivity, nutrient cycling, or energy flow (Truett 1979, Rapport 1989, Vitousek 1990). Yet others plead for retaining species redundancy (2 or more species having similar functions) to hedge against ecosystem instability or collapse if some species disappear (Walker 1995, Naeem 1998). No measures are perfect or even uniformly applicable and some that have been proposed seem ill advised. Beginning analysts would do well to keep current with this rapidly changing field of thought and apply their knowledge of basic ecology and wildlife management to winnow the best ideas from the trivial, the impractical, and (Diamond 1987) the fictitious.

Monitoring

Improving the effectiveness of EIAs and HCPs depends on follow-up monitoring to assess the reliability of impact predictions, habitat plans, and models on which these are based. A major weakness of most EIA protocols is that they do not require monitoring (Duinker 1989). Viewing impact predictions as hypotheses for testing helps focus monitoring in EIAs (Traweek 1995).

A good monitoring program will allow biologists to sort project impacts from effects caused by other human actions or by natural phenomena such as weather. A common design involves comparing post-development wildlife populations at "test" (developed or managed) sites with those at "control" sites similar to test sites in all respects except the development or management action. The best monitoring designs also include pre-development or "baseline" measurements at test and control sites. Unfortunately, conventional baseline studies often lack the measurement focus and inclusion of control areas needed for rigorous post-development monitoring (Truett et al. 1994). Duinker (1989), Walters and Holling (1990), and Murphy and Noon (1991) discuss design of reliable monitoring programs.

What good is monitoring given that meaningful results usually accrue only after development has commenced or a conservation plan prepared? First, results often are applicable to similar future projects. Second, development of EIAs and implementation of HCPs often occur in phases, and results of early monitoring can lead to better decision-making. This iterative process is crucial to improving the utility of EIAs and HCPs.

Adaptive Management

The Achilles heel of EIAs and HCPs is uncertainty. Biologists usually have inadequate knowledge to accurately forecast in detail any of the following: (1) human actions that will occur, (2) responses of wildlife populations to any of the potential actions, and (3) the responses of human social and regulatory institutions to issues surrounding

EIAs and HCPs. Consequently, what actually happens invariably is at odds with the predicted or the expected (Treshow and Allan 1985, Walters and Holling 1990, Moir and Block 2001, Wilhere 2002). One problem with procedural protocols, and especially those associated with NEPA, arises from their failure to acknowledge uncertainty.

An approach commonly used for coping with uncertainty has come to be called adaptive management (Holling 1978, Thomas and Burchfield 2000, Moir and Block 2001). Those applying adaptive management use results of monitoring and experimentation to incrementally improve performance. Information feedback from results of properly designed monitoring programs or experiments (Walters and Holling 1990, Lancia et al. 1996) is key.

Adaptive management can be productively applied to most EIA and HCP situations. Holling (1978) and Walters and Holling (1990) provide a good overview of adaptive management principles and the tools for application in large-scale EIA problems—models, workshops, and experimental design. Murphy and Noon (1991) and Lancia et al. (1996) describe the importance of the hypothetico-deductive process at all scales of effort. Moir and Block (2001) discuss what they consider adaptive management's weakest link—the information feedback system. Walters and Holling (1990) and Lancia et al. (1996) explore "learning by doing" and other shortcuts to conventional experimentation. As the name implies, adaptive management is a creative process for applying science rather than a rigid protocol for action.

ECOLOGICAL IMPACT ASSESSMENT UNDER NEPA: A CRITIQUE

The National Environmental Policy Act requires preparation of environmental impact statements (EISs) that disclose and compare impacts of several alternatives for each major proposed action (Truett et al. 1994). The process of ecological impact assessment (EIA) can take place inside or outside the NEPA context and, indeed, independent research commonly forms the basis for NEPA analyses. But because NEPA documents constitute the formal procedure for disclosing environmental impacts, analysts often think of EIAs in this context.

In the more than 30 years since the passage of NEPA, biologists assessing ecological impacts often have been frustrated by their inability to protect natural resources through the NEPA process. In this section we provide a brief overview of the weaknesses and strengths of this process to inform and empower biologists embarking on a career in impact assessment. We have been inspired by the intent of those who framed NEPA, and hope reviewing its past effectiveness will focus future creativity in using the law to more effectively protect dwindling resources.

Truett et al. (1994) and Traweek (1995) described the formal EIA process in detail. They reviewed legal and procedural requirements, ecological analysis, synthesis of information, impact predictions, and mitigation. They emphasized the purpose of EIA under NEPA—to disclose impacts of development alternatives. Deciding whether a development project should or should not proceed falls upon the shoulders of agency decision-makers and the public.

Box 1.   Applying Science to EIAs and HCPs.

Ecological impact assessments (EIAs) and habitat conservation plans (HCPs) make use of 2 kinds of science, analysis of parts and integration of parts (Walters and Holling 1990). The analysis of parts commonly takes the form of hypothetico-deductive experiments (Romesburg 1981) focused on small parts of ecosystems. Researchers using this methodology have assembled over time reliable sets of data that form the basis of ecological knowledge. The integration of parts requires synthesizing from accumulated knowledge the information applicable to a particular question or problem.

Project-specific experiments (analysis of parts) usually will provide the most reliable and defensible data for a particular EIA or HCP. They can be conducted by project biologists, university researchers, or others trained in experimental design and data collection. But on-site experiments alone rarely suffice to adequately assess impacts because the ecosystems involved prove too complex and the money and time available too limited. Those developing EIAs and HCPs usually will find it necessary to depend on synthesis of relevant information from other times, places, and contexts.

Information synthesis is both the savior and nemesis of reliable EIAs and HCPs. It adds reinforcement to the usually sparse sets of data from project-specific investigations. It requires the knowledge and interpretive skills that come only with in-depth training and experience. Edward O. Wilson (1998:71) characterized predictive synthesis as "formidably difficult." Thomas and Burchfield (2000) lamented the currently popular "raids" on agency and university research staff for expertise to meet the increasing demand for cross-disciplinary synthesis.

Those who aspire to develop defensible and useful impact assessments and conservation plans need to be aware of the level of expertise needed, especially for synthesis and interpretation. They should prepare themselves to meet the doctoral-level or "uptraining" standards recommended by Thomas and Burchfield (2000). Only then can they expect to adequately address the complexities and uncertainties involved in these important arenas of wildlife conservation (Duinker 1989, Stanley 1995, Wilhere 2002).

Our intent is to emphasize lessons that have been learned over time and discuss improvements that could be made, but not to repeat descriptions of procedure. We identify provisions in the law that EIA practitioners might use to enhance resource protection. We identify practices inconsistent with the intent of the law and discuss the potential need for a paradigm shift in the way ecological impact assessments have been developed.

We agree with Lindstrom and Smith (2001) that NEPA offers the ethical framework and administrative tools for moving our society toward ecological sustainability. It identifies a broad set of ecological goals and legislates a rational procedure for arriving at federal decisions and actions regarding the environment. It provides a clear and logical way for moving this country and the world into an ecologically conscious twenty-first century.

Policy provisions of NEPA Section 101, supported by Section 102 and its action-forcing procedure, "authorizes and directs that, to the *fullest extent possible*, the policies and regulations and laws of the United States shall be interpreted and administered in accordance with the policies…in this Act." The courts have left interpretation largely to the discretion of agencies and their respective expertise. This provides great opportunity for biologists to apply science in the disclosure and amelioration of adverse ecological impacts.

Historical Problems

Systemic and Political

Ortolano and Shepherd (1995) argued that several problems associated with NEPA documents since the 1970s were systemic and will persist. Most importantly, many project proponents viewed EIAs only as hurdles to be jumped on the way to project implementation. The hurdles posed risks to project proponents because the NEPA process forced public disclosure of impacts.

The framers of NEPA intended it to "fulfill the responsibilities of each generation as a trustee of the environment for succeeding generations" and to "assure for all Americans safe, healthful, productive, and aesthetically and culturally pleasing surroundings." An EIA that meets only procedural requirements contradicts the act's intent. Investigations of the immediate and cumulative effects of an agency's preferred action and alternatives (Truett et al. 1994) need to reflect NEPA's broad environmental policy vision of sustainability (Lindstrom and Smith 2001).

Some analysts believe ecological impact assessment as practiced under NEPA needs to be restructured. Despite 3 decades of evolution and myriad techniques, the present practice appears unable to prevent environmental disasters such as the Exxon-Valdez oil spill or reduce population declines of many imperiled species. Smith (1993) argued that most environmental problems have occurred not because human activities were unplanned nor their impacts unforeseen but because impact analysts have a flawed view of how impact assessment should function in environmental planning and resource management. Environmental protection has been viewed as a desirable but distinctly secondary objective to development and exploitation of the resource base. Economic gain takes precedence over long-term environmental protection.

Because NEPA is such a broadly worded statute, decision-makers have considerable discretion as to how they address its mandates. As a result, NEPA's apparent intentions, the environmental decisions of federal agencies, and court rulings on implementation often seem at odds with each other (Lindstrom and Smith 2001). Dinah Bear (cited in Lindstrom and Smith 2001) noted the tendency for analysts to focus on process and disregard common sense and substance. Unless presidents, members of congress, administrators, and the courts begin to see NEPA as a tool for environmental protection, it will simply ratify irresponsible actions by agencies unchallenged by the public (Lindstrom and Smith 2001). Over the years some federal managers have learned to comply with the letter of NEPA by preparing EISs that pass the muster of courts and little more (Kennedy 1988).

The history and culture of state and federal agencies influence their preparation of NEPA documents (see Sellars [1997] and Corps of Engineers review below). Because several agencies with different purviews, objectives, and histories collaborate on some EISs, an objective, even-handed assessment becomes difficult. Findings by each agency tend to reflect its own particular ends and priorities.

Agencies may avoid addressing important impacts by pushing for a narrow EIS scope or by presenting alternatives with only superficial differences. Bureaucratic interpretations of "reasonable" alternatives in EIS preparation often conflict with other groups' wishes for choices that are truly different in terms of impact. Smith (1993) found that most impact assessments evaluated only proximate alternatives and not fundamental choices. According to the Council on Environmental Quality's 1997 Effectiveness Study (cited in Lindstrom and Smith 2001), NEPA's ability to protect resources depends on agencies systematically soliciting comments from those affected and using the information to adjust development actions.

Many environmental impact statements are lengthy, technical, and difficult to read despite Council on Environmental Quality regulations that the language be accessible to the general public. Given that most of the public is not trained in law, ecology, or public administration it behooves agencies to be more innovative in their public outreach. Creating a true partnership with the community involves more than holding public meetings and making documents available.

Formal EISs are being replaced by weaker procedures such as "environmental assessments," "findings of no significant impact," and "categorical exclusions" (Clark and Canter 1997). An environmental assessment is in essence a short version of an EIS. It addresses alternatives and must be made available for public inspection but, unlike an EIS, need not be circulated widely for comment. On the basis of an environmental assessment alone, agencies may issue a finding of no significant impact, and permit a project. Categorical exclusions may exempt from the NEPA process entire categories of actions judged not to have significant adverse effects. These procedures streamline the process but circumvent the original purpose of NEPA; cursory treatment may result in impacts being overlooked and the study of alternatives minimized.

The number of findings of no significant impact has skyrocketed as the number of EISs has decreased, and some believe agencies may be adopting this approach specifically to minimize public involvement (Ortolano and Shepherd 1995). Moreover, an environmental assessment can find significant impacts and proponents still can avoid a full EIS by proposing mitigations and issuing a "mitigated finding of no significant impact". Such proposed mitigation measures often are subsequently ignored.

Scientific

Early inadequacies of impact assessment under NEPA

resulted in attempts to improve the science of the process by making impact statements more analytical and informative. But given the inability of ecologists to accurately measure ecosystems and forecast impacts, results of ecological analyses often took second place to hard data from engineering design and economic feasibility studies (Smith 1993).

By the late 1970s it became apparent EISs had fallen short of their promise. The science to that point had not been good (Boothroyd and Rees 1984). A transition stage ensued in which the scientific efficacy of EISs claimed the focus of attention. The ability of impact assessments to protect the environment was brought into question by a paralyzing amount of NEPA-related litigation that reflected the perceived failure of the science.

This period of change resulted in an expansion of the concept of EISs. In the 1980s, social impact assessment, community impact assessment, risk analysis, technology assessment, and adaptive environmental assessment and management became part of the NEPA process based on the assumption that the procedure had not reached its full potential (Smith 1993). Some believed that attempts to resolve the problem through refinements in technical design elements were misguided. Clark and Herington (1988) noted the excessive interest in methodologies and techniques that, in their view, directed attention from the primary purpose of impact assessment. Caldwell (1989) lamented the overshadowing of purpose by technique.

Although some (e.g., Beanlands and Duinker 1983) proposed that a paucity of science was the problem, others placed the blame on the institutional framework. Smith (1993) argued that improving the science of environmental impact assessment per se did nothing to reform the political process that governed the use of information, and that foundations of the assessment process itself needed to be re-examined.

Storey (1986) proposed that impact assessment had placed too much reliance on professional judgment in lieu of procedure that could be tested, replicated, and refuted. One solution, he believed, was to place more emphasis on the *management* of project outcomes than on their estimation. Like Smith (1993), he proposed that impact assessment should be an adaptive, integrative, and interactive means of decision making in environmental planning.

Successive federal administrations chose to leave interpretation and enforcement of NEPA largely to the courts. This resulted in an emphasis on the judicially enforceable aspects of the act to the neglect of its substantive provisions. The science of ecological impact assessment might have been improved but the basic problem remained political (Smith 1993).

Attempts to Resolve Problems

Systemic and Political Problems

Many agree that ecological impact assessment as currently practiced has good technique but inadequate substance. Smith (1993) proposed that it must become a bridge to integrate the science of environmental analysis with the politics of resource management. Taylor (1984) evaluated the statutory framework for environmental analysis in light of what a science-based approach would require. In his view, a system of formal analysis must: (1) focus on important issues, (2) specify how much detail

must be provided, (3) prevent the manipulation of alternatives to obscure real choices, (4) facilitate helpful criticism by outsiders, (5) provide forums for resolving technical disputes, (6) adjust the burden-of-proof rules or distribution of analytical resources to make the system workable if the resources of outsiders and insiders are greatly out of balance, (7) provide incentives for the analysis to be used in decision making, and (8) encourage improvement of analytical methodology. He believed impact assessment as currently practiced under the NEPA framework met few of these requirements. He suggested that environmentally better decisions were likely to result when "inside analysts" were able to explore possible environmental trade-offs and that all projects could benefit from relatively inexpensive environmental mitigation.

Fromby (1990) contended the purpose of EIA was not simply to assess impacts but to improve the quality of decisions. He maintained the "technocratic view" blinded analysts to political realities, resulting in documents that increasingly had little influence on decisions. He urged practitioners to use results of scientific studies to influence the political process.

The U.S. Army Corps of Engineers (Corps) has demonstrated how NEPA can positively influence a bureaucracy dominated by engineers with a tradition of building (Mazmanian and Clarke 1979, Taylor 1984, Ortolano and Shepherd 1995). In the 1970s following the passage of NEPA, the Corps hired several hundred environmental professionals and incorporated them into their planning process. Some were hired specifically to write EISs and some learned how to influence the engineers responsible for projects. Some were able to stop or modify environmentally risky proposals, changes that were extraordinary given the Corps' Congressional allies who wanted new projects constructed in their home districts. Changes in the Corps' mode of operation demonstrate how NEPA programs, coupled with substantial societal pressures, can positively affect organizational structure and behavior of project proponents (Taylor 1984, Smith 1993).

Scientific Problems

The U.S. Council on Environmental Quality in its 1997 NEPA Effectiveness Study advised the use of "adaptive environmental management" in the NEPA process (Lindstrom and Smith 2001). The council recommended ecological predictions be tested by monitoring to assess the validity of the predictions and the mitigation measures designed to counter adverse effects. The council also proposed adaptive management when the environment was not expected to be permanently damaged, when the project could be modified once started, and when there were opportunities to repair past environmental damage.

The lack of formal requirements by NEPA for monitoring project impacts has been and remains one of the main barriers to the development of a sound predictive base for impact assessment (Eberhardt 1976, Traweek 1995). Post-project monitoring could serve at least 2 purposes: to enhance forecasting abilities (Culhane 1993) and to provide a basis for more effective mitigation.

Two emerging procedures for improving the NEPA process are strategic environmental assessment and cumulative effects assessment (Roe et al. 1995). These techniques purport to assess cumulative impacts of multiple programs, policies, and plans. However, they seldom have been put into practice by the federal government (but see Orions et al. 2003). Some states recently have begun to recommend these approaches, and the World Wildlife Fund published a conceptual framework for cumulative effects assessment (Irwin and Rodes 1992). This framework provides general guidance for identifying multiple stresses, understanding how effects may accumulate, and bounding assessments spatially and temporally.

NEPA requires assessment of impacts on biodiversity where it is "possible to both anticipate and evaluate" such effects. Some agencies increasingly use ecological impact assessment within the NEPA process to try to counter losses of biodiversity (Hirsch 1993, Pritchard 1993).

Conclusions

Goodland and Daly (1995) identified the real test of ecological impact assessment: ensuring that possibly 10 billion people could be decently housed and fed without damaging the environment. Environmental sustainability in the face of burgeoning human numbers constitutes the ultimate goal. This desperate situation underscores the importance of NEPA and similar laws in individual states and other countries. Natural capital is the limiting factor for population sustainability. Actions that could deplete this capital must be anticipated and mitigated.

The National Environmental Policy Act has been the most imitated law in United States history, and its effectiveness could form the basis for global sustainability. Lindstrom and Smith (2001) emphasized the need for the environmental assessment process to build on the value paradigm of NEPA and harmonize human actions with ecological processes. The National Environmental Policy Act provides a philosophical and practical context for effective environmental policy (Lindstrom and Smith 2001); the challenge for wildlife biologists is to bring science to policy decisions and fulfill the promise of NEPA as envisioned by those who fashioned it.

EIA CASE STUDY: ARCTIC ALASKA OIL DEVELOPMENT

One of the largest ecological assessment efforts ever undertaken in terms of expense and duration of study focused on the impacts of oil development in arctic Alaska (Maki 1992). We discuss this program because it illustrates the optimum in assessment opportunity—a lot of money spent to study impacts of a major development in a simple ecosystem occupied by few people. Its approaches, successes, and shortcomings offer insight into the options and limitations that may be expected in other projects. Most of the research took place largely outside the formal NEPA context, but results of the studies have been widely used in EISs, environmental assessments, and other NEPA documents.

In June 1968 Atlantic Richfield Company announced a major oil strike near Prudhoe Bay (Truett 2000*a*). The passage of the National Environmental Policy Act shortly thereafter set the stage for escalation of impact-oriented studies, which already had commenced in nearby areas suspected to contain oil (Shaver 1996). The value of the oil accumulation, coupled with the high expectations of NEPA, would during the next few decades attract millions

of dollars and many well-qualified scientists to this massive assessment program.

Low temperatures impose major constraints on the region's ecosystems (Truett 2000*a*). Surface soils and water remain frozen for 9–10 months each year, and subsurface soils are permanently frozen. The low temperatures and frozen terrain in winter lead to specialized adaptations or, more commonly, migratory habits in the common vertebrates. Because of the extreme environment, terrestrial, freshwater, and marine ecosystems exhibit lower biodiversity and simpler food-web structure than temperate ecosystems in similar settings.

Historically low population densities of humans in arctic Alaska resulted in fewer predevelopment impacts than one usually encounters in temperate climates. Still, the subsistence lifestyles of the native peoples had for generations affected populations of fishes, mammals, and birds (Jamison 1978). Europeans exerted increasingly intensive harvest pressures beginning in the late 1800s (Brower 1942). In addition, oil exploration during the 20 years prior to the 1968 strike had conspicuously and extensively scarred the tundra surface (McKendrick 2000).

The low-growing vegetation and nearly flat coastal environments gave striking relief to the oilfield infrastructure that gradually took shape in the decades following

Fig. 1. Pipes carrying oil in arctic Alaska stand ≥1.5 m above the ground to allow caribou (*Rangifer tarandus*) passage. Oestrid flies (*Hypoderma tarandi, Cephenemyia trompe*) harass caribou in late summer, sometimes driving them to seek shelter beside or under facilities as illustrated by this trail caribou made after pipe installation (photograph by M. E. Miller).

1968 (Gilders and Cronin 2000, Truett 2000*a*). Currently, pipelines cross the tundra on stanchions ≥1.5 m above the ground (Fig. 1). Pads of gravel ≤1.5 m thick support drilling operations, production infrastructure, and roads. Gravel fill occupies about 2–4% of the surface of the older oil fields but substantially less of the newer ones. Surface runoff from early summer thaw creates impoundments upslope of gravel roads and pads. Plumes of dust follow trucks on primary roads; the dust settles thickly on the adjacent tundra. In the vicinity of Prudhoe Bay itself, 2 jetties, or causeways, extend from the coastline several km into marine near-shore waters. Artificial islands support wellheads and other facilities in near-shore waters.

Early on, most analysts recognized the impossibility of adequately addressing all or even most species, notwithstanding the large budgets and simple ecosystems involved (Truett 1979). Thereafter, the great majority of impact assessment effort focused on a short list of vertebrates considered most important to people (Truett 1981, Maki 1992, Truett and Johnson 2000). Researchers addressed the habitats, food chains, and processes supporting these "valued ecosystem components" (Duinker 1989). Impacts analysts assessed the potential effects of development on the species and their habitats and food chains.

Most species addressed were abundant and widespread in the oil fields only in summer (Truett 2000*b*). In winter most migrated to other regions, although some assembled in or near the oil fields in restricted areas suitable for their overwinter survival. The fishes that foraged in streams, lakes, and coastal lagoons in summer retreated in winter to the few freshwater and estuarine localities where water was >2 m deep and low in salinity. Nearly all summer-nesting birds migrated south, as did caribou and grizzly bears (*Ursus arctos*). Most arctic foxes (*Alopex lagopus*) moved north onto the sea ice. Polar bears (*Ursus maritimus*) constituted the anomaly—they came into the oil fields in winter but seldom in summer.

The involvement of numerous agencies, public interest groups, scientists, and developers in the EIA studies required special efforts to expedite communication. Periodic workshops, often sponsored by agencies and managed by facilitators, commonly hosted 100 or more attendees and provided the basis for information exchange among the interest groups. Smaller workshops, often conducted by specialists using model-building to structure research (Holling 1978), built rapport among scientific disciplines. Interdisciplinary teams of scientists worked as units on field projects and often lived and ate together in oil-field enclaves; this expedited interdisciplinary communication at the grass-roots level.

Unlike the case with many EIA efforts, the federal government and the petroleum industry provided generous funding for on-site research. The Outer Continental Shelf Environmental Assessment Program (OCSEAP) of the U.S. Department of Commerce was created in 1975 specifically to assess the impacts of the burgeoning Alaska oil industry (Engelmann 1976). This program, and later the U.S. Bureau of Land Management and the U.S. Minerals Management Service, set general research goals and awarded contracts for study. As federal money declined in the 1980s, the oil industry began to pay for larger proportions of the research; their support continues. Universities, federal and Alaska agencies, and private consulting organizations conducted the preponderance of the investigations.

In some research programs (e.g., Truett 1977) adaptive management, introduced by workshop facilitators involved in its development (e.g., Walters 1986), encouraged scientists to adjust their research focus when feedback from initial efforts indicated the need. Interdisciplinary workshops following annual data-collecting forays used models, "looking-outward" matrices, and other adaptive management tools (Holling 1978). Because much research often proceeded independently of NEPA oversight, changes in direction were not constrained by inflexible protocols.

The decades-long succession of research programs and new oil developments offered an ideal setting for adaptive management. Findings of initial studies, often coupled with improvements in engineering design stimulated by the studies, led to new research directions. For example, early studies of caribou responses to above-ground pipelines led to the elevation of pipelines ≥1.5 m and refocusing of subsequent studies to identify which horizontal configurations of elevated pipes least hindered caribou passage (Murphy and Lawhead 2000). Consolidation of oil wellheads on fewer gravel pads with smaller total coverage resulted from early concerns that gravel placement reduced breeding bird populations proportional to the area covered; studies of the fate of birds displaced by the larger pads followed (Troy 2000). Temporal as well as spatial controls proved possible, particularly in some of the later studies.

What happened to wildlife populations in arctic Alaska oil fields in the 3 decades after development commenced? Most oil-field vertebrates intensively studied increased in abundance: several shorebird species (Troy 2000), black brant (*Branta bernicla*) (Sedinger and Stickney 2000), snow goose (*Chen caerulescens*) (Johnson 2000*a*), tundra swan (*Cygnus columbianus*) (Ritchie and King 2000), caribou (Ballard et al. 2000), grizzly bear (Shideler and Hechtel 2000), polar bear (Amstrup 2000), and probably arctic fox (Burgess 2000). Some fishes (Gallaway and Fechhelm 2000) and shorebirds (Troy 2000) have fluctuated annually in abundance with no long-term trend. A few birds, dunlin (*Calidris alpina*) for example (Troy 2000), declined in abundance.

None of these changes except increases in abundances of grizzly bears and arctic foxes can be attributed with any certainty to oil development (Truett 2000*b*). Most changes appear to have resulted from climatic fluctuations or from factors operative in migratory species' ranges outside the oil fields. Causes of many of the population changes remain uncertain.

Some studies disclosed localized impacts within the oil fields (Truett et al. 1994, Truett 2000*b*). Most birds avoided gravel-covered or intensively developed sites (Troy 2000); some mammals appear to have been attracted to them (Ballard et al. 2000, Burgess 2000, Shideler and Hechtel 2000) (Fig. 2). Impoundments displaced some birds and attracted others (Kertell 1996, Troy 2000). Coastal causeways attracted common eiders (*Somateria mollissima*) (Johnson 2000*b*) and altered the distributions and movement patterns of estuarine fishes (Gallaway and Fechhelm 2000). Busy roadways altered caribou distribution when calves were young (Murphy and Lawhead 2000). However, investigators generally could not link

Fig. 2. Caribou cow (in molt) and calf walk along a gravel roadway in an arctic Alaska oil field. Cows with young calves may avoid roads with heavy traffic but, in summer, caribou may assemble on elevated roads and drilling pads to escape intense mosquito harassment (photograph by M. E. Miller).

local changes to increases or decreases in oil-field populations of animals, except that populations of arctic foxes (Burgess 2000) and grizzly bears (Shideler and Hechtel 2000) apparently increased at least seasonally as a consequence of human-related food sources in the oil fields.

Adaptive feedback from research findings prompted mitigative actions (Truett 2000*b*). Consolidation of facilities in newer developments reduced infrastructure density and habitat coverage by gravel. Breeches built in coastal causeways expedited fish passage and reduced arctic fox access to waterfowl nesting on the causeways. Changes in placement and design of pipelines and roadways reduced their barrier effects on caribou. Removal of human refuse alleviated, to some extent, the increases in arctic fox populations. It also reduced habituation by grizzly bears to humans, which apparently had elevated their vulnerability to hunting outside the oil fields.

The inability of well-funded and long-term research to disclose population-level impacts of such a visually impressive development offers lessons for ecological impact assessment. First, even if development-caused impacts occur, factors unrelated to development have a disturbing way of masking them. Although in theory experimental controls can sort development-related causes from others, firm establishment of cause-and-effect remains rare (Lancia et al. 1996). The liberally funded Alaskan oil-field assessment effort illustrates the main assumption underlying NEPA—that impacts can be reliably forecast—is seriously flawed (Walters and Holling 1990).

Experience in the oil fields underscores the need for adaptive approaches in both the political and ecological dimensions of impact assessment. The framework for impact assessment and for mitigation planning must allow feedback and consequent adjustment in direction (Moir and Block 2001). Unfortunately, adaptive management often proves difficult in agency-managed programs because the system of planning and decision-making can be inflexible (Thomas and Burchfield 2000). This emphasizes the need for well-trained and highly experienced analysts—professional judgment often must make up for deficiencies in funding, procedure, and knowledge.

In March 2003 the National Academy of Science released the report *Cumulative Environmental Effects of Oil and Gas Activities on Alaska's North Slope* (Orians et al. 2003). Few among the 19 members of the committee that prepared the report had conducted impact assessment research in the oil fields, but all visited Alaska during report preparation. The committee's report and the National Research Council's summary of the report (National Research Council 2003) implied, with some ambiguity, that development had caused adverse population impacts to several wildlife species, in apparent contradiction to conclusions of some of the researchers referenced above. *The New York Times Magazine* (10 March 2003) referenced the report to present an even more adverse (and less reliable) scenario of impacts to wildlife.

Such is the nature of impact assessment. Science seldom "proves" anything, and people, even scientists, interpret data with their own views and biases (Ludwig et al. 1993). During the past decade many have selectively used findings of research in the Prudhoe Bay area to support their own views for or against development of the nearby Arctic National Wildlife Refuge. Major disagreements about impacts after 30 years illustrate the continuing inadequacy of knowledge and the influence of judgment in the impact assessment process. The challenge for all ecologists is to remain objective despite their own views and pressures from interest groups.

HABITAT CONSERVATION PLANS
Legislative Background

The Endangered Species Act of 1973 affords protections to federally listed endangered and threatened species (hereafter "listed" species). One protection found in Section 9 of the ESA prohibits "taking" of animals, with take defined as "…to harass, harm, pursue, hunt, shoot, wound, kill, trap, capture, or collect, or to attempt to engage in any such conduct". Endangered plants are protected from removal from federal lands and from certain activities on private lands, but the broad "taking" prohibition that applies to listed animals does not apply to plants. Listed species also receive protection through review of the actions of federal agencies.

Section 7(a)(2) of the ESA requires every agency to ensure that any action it authorizes, funds, or carries out will not jeopardize the continued existence of any listed species or adversely modify or destroy its critical habitat. Federal agencies consult with the U.S. Fish and Wildlife Service (USFWS) or National Marine Fisheries Service (NMFS), depending on the species involved, about each of their actions that may affect any listed animal. A formal consultation results in USFWS or NMFS issuing a "biological opinion" about whether the proposed action satisfies the requirements of Section 7(a)(2). The biological opinion typically includes an "incidental take" statement that provides the federal action agency with protective coverage from violation of the Section 9 "taking" prohibition, provided the agency follows the terms and conditions of the "incidental take" statement.

After passage of the ESA, some landowners objected to the stringent "take" prohibitions of Section 7, believing they interfered with legitimate use of private land. In response, Congress in 1982 amended the ESA to authorize "incidental take" permits based on an acceptable conserva-

Box 2.   Environmental Assessment, Sheep Basin Restoration Project.

On 1 August 2001 the Reserve Ranger District of the Gila National Forest in New Mexico released an environmental assessment for its proposed Sheep Basin Restoration Project. This project would "restore" the forest in the 6,000-ha Sheep Basin area to conditions less conducive to high-intensity wildfires and more beneficial to wildlife. The 5 alternatives presented in the assessment differed from each other primarily in whether trees would be cut in groups or singly, to what extent large trees would be cut, how forest thinning and harvesting would be applied, whether and how herbicides would be used, and to what extent forest roads would be decommissioned. Previous public review, resulting from letters to interested parties, a notice in a local newspaper, and guided field trips to the project area, influenced the content of the assessment.

On 24 April 2002 the Gila Forest supervisor issued a "Decision of Notice and Finding of No Significant Impact" that announced her intent to proceed with a modified Alternative 2. The decision notice summarized comments from about a dozen parties. Some of the comments objected to the proposed removal of large, old ponderosa pine trees (*Pinus ponderosa*).

In summer 2002 the Reserve Ranger District marked trees for cutting. Public objection intensified, primarily because many of the marked trees were large and old pines. The Catron County (New Mexico) Citizens Group commissioned an information review of the importance of large, old pines to wildlife. Three environmental groups submitted separate appeals against the decision notice. In response, the U.S. Forest Service Regional Office remanded the original environmental assessment back to the Reserve Ranger District for revision.

On 15 November 2002 the Reserve Ranger District released a revised environmental assessment. A sixth alternative had been added; it resembled the originally preferred Alternative 2 except that no "yellow pines" would be cut. (Bark of ponderosa pine trees turns from dark to yellow as they age; pines in the project area turn yellow usually when they reach 100-120 years old [R. C. Moore, Catron County Citizens Group, personal communication]).

On 29 January 2003 the Gila Forest supervisor issued another "Decision Notice and Finding of No Significant Impact" that identified Alternative 6 of the revised assessment as the preferred action. The decision notice specified: "There will be no size limitation for trees that will be cut but all yellow-barked ponderosa pine will be retained". Two of the 3 environmental groups submitted appeals to this second decision notice. As of this writing, the Forest Service Regional Office has not responded to these appeals.

This project illustrates the importance of public involvement in the NEPA process. Even should environmental assessments (or impact statements) identify adverse impacts of proposed projects to wildlife, the projects still can legally proceed. The purpose of NEPA is to disclose impacts, not stop projects. Public objection often is necessary to alter or prevent projects that threaten wildlife or wildlife habitat. Appeals and environmental litigation in recent years have become popular mechanisms to this end.

Fig. 3. Large trees, the snags and logs resulting from them, and forest openings elevate wildlife diversity and abundance in southwestern ponderosa pine forests conventionally managed as young, even-aged stands (photograph by J. C. Truett).

tion plan, commonly referred to as a "habitat conservation plan" (HCP). Specifically, through creation of ESA section 10(a)(1)(B), Congress authorized otherwise prohibited "taking" of federally listed threatened and endangered animals "if such taking is incidental to, and not the purpose of, the carrying out of an otherwise lawful activity." Congress used as a model for HCP development an effort to reconcile land development on San Bruno Mountain near San Francisco with conservation of the endangered mission blue butterfly (*Icaricia icarioides missionensis*) and the callippe fritillary butterfly (*Speyeria callippee callippee*) (Bean et al. 1991). Spurred by proposed designation of critical habitat for one of the butterfly species, the county, state and federal wildlife agencies, developers, and a local environmental organization negotiated a conservation agreement. The main participants in the San Bruno process were the primary proponents of the 1982 ESA amendments.

Unlike Section 7 and other legal requirements of the ESA, the Section 10(a)(1)(B) "incidental-take" permitting process is applicant-driven. An applicant seeks a permit to ensure his or her activities are not in violation of the "take" prohibitions of ESA Section 9. This permit provides non-federal landowners relief from the strict "taking" prohibition of the ESA parallel to the relief available for federal actions under Section 7. Congress amended the ESA in 1982 under the assumption that every action that might result in incidental "taking" of listed species could be classified as either a federal agency action that would follow the Section 7 process or a non-federal action that could follow the Section 10 (HCP) process. But sometimes non-federal developers perceive that Section 7 results in a quicker solution for incidental "taking" than Section 10. In such cases they may search for a way to "federalize" their projects to bring them under the umbrella of Section 7 (Bean et al. 1991).

The HCP process has evolved into an ambitious program. Proponents now use it to integrate development activities with listed species conservation, provide a framework for broad-based conservation planning, and foster a climate of cooperation between the public and private sectors. After a slow start—only 3 HCPs were approved between 1983 and 1989—the procedure gained favor. As of 17 April 2002, 379 HCPs had been approved, addressing approximately 12 million ha and protecting more than 200 endangered or threatened species. Nationwide, HCPs are now seen as one of the fundamental approaches to resolving listed species issues on non-federal lands.

"Incidental Take" Permitting

Depending on the species involved, either the USFWS or the NMFS issues "incidental take" permits. The permitting process consists of 3 phases: (1) HCP development phase, (2) formal permitting phase, and (3) HCP and permit implementation phase.

In Phase 1, the applicant (often through a consultant) prepares a HCP with technical assistance from a USFWS or NMFS field office that outlines the requirements. The application package includes the permit application form, application fee (if applicable), the proposed HCP, the Implementing Agreement (if required by the USFWS or NMFS regional director or requested by the applicant), a draft document outlining compliance with NEPA (an environmental action memorandum, environmental assessment, or environmental impact statement), and certification by the USFWS or NMFS field office that it has reviewed these documents and finds them statutorily complete (U.S. Department of Interior 1996). The applicant may choose to combine the HCP and required NEPA analysis in a single document.

During Phase 2, the appropriate USFWS regional office or the NMFS office in Washington, D.C., reviews the application for compliance with legal standards. The USFWS or NMFS announces in the *Federal Register* the receipt of the permit application and availability of the NEPA analysis for public review and comment. Issuance of an "incidental take" permit and approval of a HCP requires the USFWS or NMFS conduct a formal internal ESA Section 7 consultation and draft a "biological opinion" that assesses the permit's impact on all listed species, candidate species, and critical habitat for those species.

The ESA requires 5 criteria be met to the satisfaction of the USFWS or the NMFS before an "incidental take" permit can be issued.

1. The "taking" will be incidental, that is, unanticipated and not purposeful.
2. The applicant will, to the maximum extent practicable, minimize and mitigate the impacts of such "taking."
3. The applicant will ensure that adequate funding for the HCP and procedures to deal with unforeseen circumstances will be provided.
4. The "taking" will not appreciably reduce the likelihood of survival and recovery of the species in the wild.
5. The applicant satisfactorily ensures other requirements will be met and the HCP will be implemented.

During Phase 3, a *Federal Register* notice announces the issuance of the permit, and the permittee and other responsible parties prepare the HCP. The USFWS or the NMFS tracks a permittee's compliance with the HCP, "incidental take" permit, the implementing agreement, and monitors the HCP's progress and success.

Because the HCP is at the core of the permitting process, our focus is on the HCP itself. Comprehensive guides to the "incidental take" permitting process include the *Habitat Conservation Planning Handbook* (U.S. Department of Interior 1996) and federal regulations governing permits for the USFWS (Code of Federal Regulations 50:13) and NMFS (Code of Federal Regulations 50:217, 220, and 222). Thorough explanations of the requirements for an ESA section 10(a)(1)(B) permit are provided by U.S. Department of Interior (1985, 1988), Webster (1987), Arnold (1991), Houck (1993), and U.S. Department of Interior (1996).

HCP Requirements and Scope

Regardless of project size, all HCPs must specify (1) the impact of the "taking," (2) steps to be taken and funding available to "minimize and mitigate" such impacts, (3) alternative actions considered and reasons for their rejection, and (4) other measures deemed necessary or appropriate by the Secretary of Interior. Habitat conservation plans not consistent with species' recovery plan objectives are discouraged (U.S. Department of Interior 1996).

Habitat conservation plans vary enormously in geographic area covered, number of species addressed, and time frame. Geographic boundaries of HCPs should encompass the applicant's project or land-use area, or the jurisdiction within which " incidental take" could occur. The size of the area must be appropriate to the planning effort. For endemic species with restricted ranges (e.g., some invertebrates or fish), the plan should ideally cover the entire range of the species. More widely distributed species need larger areas, the exact size depending on HCP objectives.

"Covered species" is a term often used to refer to all species specifically addressed in a HCP. Covered species include listed species specified in the HCP's associated "incidental take" permit. They also may include species that are federal candidates for listing, and even "sensitive species" or "species of concern" without current federal or state listing or candidate listing status. Thus, non-listed species may benefit from HCPs designed primarily for listed species.

Until the mid 1990s, most HCPs were for relatively small projects including single-family housing lots, but some HCPs now encompass hundreds of thousand of hectares and even entire states. A Massachusetts Division of Wildlife single-species HCP for the piping plover (*Charadrius melodus*) addresses 325 km of Massachusetts's coastline. A 100-year HCP with a timber company in Washington State affects nearly 70,000 ha and, directly or indirectly, nearly 200 listed and unlisted species.

Quantifying and Mitigating "Incidental Take"

To quantify "incidental take" requires estimating the number of individuals or amount of habitat in the project area and, on this basis, (1) the number of animals to be "killed, harmed, or harassed" or (2) habitat units (e.g., area of land, volume of water) to be affected. The latter is typically expressed as all individuals occupying a given area or volume of habitat (U.S. Department of Interior 1996). Geographic information systems (GIS) can be invaluable for displaying the projected level of "take" by proposed activities.

After expected "take" has been estimated, the USFWS or the NMFS examines whether estimates are consistent with the ESA Section 10 permit issuance criteria. Authorized "take" cannot "appreciably reduce the likelihood of the survival and recovery of the species in the wild", and a mitigation program must minimize and mitigate "incidental take" to the "maximum extent practicable." A population viability assessment may help explore whether these criteria can be met. If the USFWS or the NMFS finds that initially anticipated "take" levels exceed what can be permitted, additional "take avoidance" and other mitigation measures must be developed. Identifying level of "take" and mitigation needed may be easy or difficult depending on species status; type, location, and urgency of the project; and local politics.

The U.S. Department of Interior (1996) noted that mitigation in HCPs usually takes one of the following forms: (1) avoiding the impact to the extent practicable, (2) minimizing the impact, (3) rectifying the impact, (4) reducing or eliminating the impact over time, or (5) compensating for the impact. For example, project effects can be (1) avoided by relocating project facilities within the project area; (2) minimized through timing restrictions and buffer zones; (3) rectified by restoration and revegetation of disturbed project areas; (4) reduced or eliminated over time by proper management, monitoring, and adaptive management; and (5) compensated by habitat restoration or protection at an onsite or offsite reserve. In practice, HCPs often use more than one of these strategies simultaneously or consecutively. Mitigation measures for species conservation and reserve design should follow what has been learned from experience as well as theoretical considerations (MacArthur and Wilson 1967, Diamond 1975, Noss et al. 1997).

Establishing a reserve as the primary mitigation measure presents many challenges. Scott and Sullivan (2000) observed that constraints to reserve configuration (e.g., land costs, fragmentation, pre-existing amounts of edge, lack of connectivity) cause problems requiring long-term, post facto management. It may be productive to set goals for the persistence of species (states) and ecosystems (processes) within reserves, and accept that reserve configuration will be defined by the landscape and politics of the area and that long-term management will be needed.

The views of independent scientists are important. These individuals may help design mitigation measures or prepare listing documents, recovery plans, and conservation agreements used by applicants to develop HCPs. Their reviews and suggestions also can occur during the public comment period.

The best source of information can be the species' recovery plans (http://endangered.fws.gov), especially if the plans were published or recently revised. Recovery plans may identify the utility of HCPs and the management actions needed for a species' conservation. Bean et al. (1991) discussed the desired coordination between recovery plan measures and habitat conservation planning.

An "incidental take" permit, and often the HCP itself, requires monitoring to track "take" levels and ensure the conservation program is being properly implemented. Both the permittee and the USFWS or NMFS are responsible for monitoring the success of the HCP; the USFWS has the added responsibility of ascertaining whether the permittee is complying with its regulatory requirements. Bean et al. (1991) recommended that HCPs include specifically stated, measurable indicators of plan success or failure to increase objectivity in monitoring.

"No Surprises"

"No Surprises" assurances are provided by the USFWS and NMFS to non-federal landowners through the ESA Section 10(a)(1)(B) process and as codified in federal regulations. Private landowners are assured that, if "unforeseen circumstances" arise, the USFWS or the NMFS will not subject them to additional commitments or restrictions on land and resource use (U.S. Department of Interior 1998). The government will honor these assurances as long as a permittee implements in good faith the terms and conditions of the HCP, permit, and other associated documents. The assurances apply only to those species that are "adequately covered" in a HCP.

For a species to be "covered" under a HCP it must be listed on the Section 10(a)(1)(B) permit. "Adequately covered" listed species in the HCP must have satisfied the permit issuance criteria. "Adequately covered" non-listed species are addressed in the HCP as if actually listed.

Adaptive Management

Significant data gaps often appear in a HCP's operating conservation program. In such cases, adaptive management (Walters 1986, Walters and Holling 1990) becomes an integral component of the HCP. Adaptive management encourages consideration of alternative strategies for research or monitoring, and iteratively adjusts actions based on what is learned. Biologists can use adaptive management effectively if they identify uncertainties in the HCP, incorporate alternatives for addressing those uncertainties, monitor success of the alternatives, and adjust management strategies as monitoring indicates the need. In June 2000 the USFWS and the NMFS amended their HCP Handbook (U.S. Department of Interior 2000) to address the "No Surprises" rule and to further enhance the HCP process through improvements in 5 areas: permit duration, public participation, monitoring provisions, establishment of clear biological goals, and adaptive management (Nelson 2000).

Fig. 4. The desert tortoise is listed under the Endangered Species Act as "threatened." Human development activities have reduced its populations in many areas (photograph by R. A. Fridell).

HCP CASE STUDY: DESERT TORTOISE IN WASHINGTON COUNTY, UTAH

Background

This case involved the establishment of a reserve in Utah as the core mitigation measure for impacts to desert tortoise (*Gopherus agassizii*), a federally listed threatened species (Fig. 4). The species' range in the southwestern United States extends northeast to the vicinity of St. George, Washington County, in extreme southwestern Utah. The Upper Virgin River Recovery Unit (Recovery Unit) in this area is classified as a distinct unit for management and recovery of the tortoise (U.S. Department of Interior 1994). It covers 180–230 km^2 and can support an estimated 7,000–9,000 adult tortoises.

Washington County, Utah, has been one of the fastest growing counties in the country, with an 83% increase in human population from 1980 (26,125) to 1990 (48,560) (Washington County Habitat Conservation Plan Steering Committee 1995). Growth projections for 2010 range from 80,500 to 139,000. The preferred habitat for desert tortoise—sandstone outcrops and dunes—comprise the most valuable remaining real estate because of its scenic beauty, water availability, and proximity to St. George.

Box 3. Successful Habitat Conservation Planning.

Habitat conservation planning becomes more effective as more plans are written, "incidental take" permits issued, and outcomes of plans monitored. Beatley (1994) suggested multiple guidelines for improving habitat conservation plans.

- Include representatives of all affected stakeholder groups in the process.
- Compile the best possible base of biological and scientific information.
- Integrate the habitat conservation plan into local and regional long-range planning.
- Develop an equitable, long-term funding program that spreads the financial burden of habitat conservation over groups that will benefit (e.g., developers, property owners, and conservation organizations).
- Protect multiple species and broader patterns of diversity rather than focusing only on listed species.
- Seek ways of combining habitat conservation with other community goals such as establishment of public recreation lands and open space and protection of water quality.

Noss et al. (1997) also offered recommendations for judgment and negotiation.
- Set aside preconceived notions of what constitutes scientifically defensible conservation planning—there usually will be far less reliable information than you would like to have available.
- Use science as the foundation for conservation planning, but don't expect planners to follow all of your suggestions.
- Be as honest, objective, and unbiased as possible.
- Do not let your science be corrupted or used improperly by any parties in the negotiations.

A sound plan does not guarantee adequate conservation. The best-designed, most scientifically credible plan is worth little if not implemented as intended (Noss et al. 1997). The habitat conservation planning process is inherently political. Estimating the level of "take" and the mitigation measures needed result from often-grueling negotiations under extreme political pressures. Science-based judgments by biologists can make the difference between plans that promote species recovery and those that allow species decline.

The distribution of existing and proposed development in the late 1980s and early 1990s overlapped tortoise distribution, and loss of tortoise habitat to development outpaced protection of habitat at an accelerating rate.

On 1 October 1990 the Washington County Commission established the Washington County Desert Tortoise Habitat Scoping Committee to conduct a feasibility study on habitat conservation planning. This 9-member group identified potential funding, organized the plan development phase, and recommended the county proceed with the HCP process by creating a 15-member Washington County HCP Steering Committee. The Steering Committee held its first official meeting on 29 January 1991 and its last on 24 February 1994.

The project required much effort. Forty-four formal daylong meetings of the Steering Committee went into plan development. These meetings constituted only a small fraction of the effort of the Scoping Committee, 14 subcommittees, individual advocates and negotiators, and contractors who prepared maps, plan components, and other technical products.

HCP Development

Scope

The HCP covers a 20-year permit period and all of Washington County. The proposed "take" areas are all within the Recovery Unit. The permit applied to "incidental take" of desert tortoises only, but the reserve was designed to encompass a large portion of the Recovery Unit and benefit numerous other species. By future amendment, the permit can address the "take" of additional listed and unlisted species.

Duration

The USFWS issued an "incidental take" permit to Washington County in February 1996. Including permit review and processing, the development phase of the Washington County HCP lasted 6 years and 4 months. This protracted length resulted largely from the effort required to form the reserve. This required, in addition to resolving complex reserve location and boundary issues, the Steering Committee confirm that all private landowners within the area were willing sellers or traders. Consensus building among disparate groups proved difficult, reflecting the common pattern for development of region-wide HCPs to take several years. During one period of several months the Steering Committee reached an impasse on reserve design that most thought would terminate development of the HCP. Only when the county named a new Steering Committee chair did discussions resume.

During the HCP development period, an individual HCP was issued by the USFWS for one developer. This individual HCP and other measures were part of a settlement agreement for illegal "take" of desert tortoises resulting from the developer's bulldozing of a road through occupied desert tortoise habitat during the countywide HCP negotiations.

Funding

The State of Utah provided start-up funds for plan development. In addition, local governments, private developers, and ESA Section 7 funds generated as compensation for an earlier pipeline project contributed to the budget. This broad-based funding, totaling $760,622, garnered commitment by the parties to complete the plan.

Leadership

Local government and interest groups provided leadership. A Washington County commissioner chaired the first Steering Committee and a local attorney with experience in arbitrating environmental controversies chaired the second. Involvement of local officials in this process resulted in development of a new county department, now headed by the administrator of the HCP.

Organization

The plan development team included the Steering Committee, specialized subcommittees, and an environmental consulting firm that prepared documents and maps. Voting members of the Steering Committee represented land developers, landowners, Southern Utah Wilderness Alliance, The Nature Conservancy, U.S. Bureau of Land Management (BLM), Utah Division of Wildlife Resources, Utah Division of State Lands and Forestry, Washington County Commission, Washington County Water Conservancy District, Washington County Mayors' Association, and Washington County Cattlemen's Association. Non-voting members included U.S. Representative James V. Hansen, U.S. senators Robert F. Bennett and Orrin G. Hatch, and USFWS representatives. Initially, 3 subcommittees and a majority vote determined action; later decisions were consensus-based. Eleven subcommittees provided specific technical products that were approved or modified at Steering Committee meetings and incorporated into the HCP by the consultant.

Public Relations

Messages for and against the project reached the public through a variety of channels. During the first 18 months, a 20-minute video and an educational pamphlet explaining the natural history of the area and the benefits of habitat conservation planning were produced and made available to local schools and community groups. The project spawned numerous radio talk shows on natural history topics. During the last 2 years of the process, strong anti-conservation stories led the media coverage. A television series, for example, criticized efforts to conserve desert tortoises and desert habitat. The Steering Committee issued few formal news releases itself, although some Steering Committee members provided their individual perspectives to the media. Steering Committee meetings were well attended by the public, especially landowners, and media representatives.

Scientific Support

One of the first subcommittees formed by the Steering Committee was the Technical Advisory Committee. This committee collected and evaluated scientific information, and its members reviewed and analyzed proposed plan elements as they became available. It consisted of federal, state, and private biologists with experience studying desert tortoises and their habitat.

Project participants censused tortoises and mapped habitat. From 1988 through 1990, BLM and the Utah Division of Wildlife Resources conducted 288 1.6-km desert tortoise transects in Utah, and a consultant for the

Steering Committee surveyed 709 transects in the Recovery Unit. The BLM mapped the soils and vegetation of the Recovery Unit and delineated desert tortoise habitat. The Technical Advisory Committee combined transect data and maps to portray desert tortoise distribution and relative abundance across the areas. Mapping became an important tool for designing the HCP and reserve.

The Utah Division of Wildlife Resources periodically surveyed 2 standard 2.6-km^2 study plots for tortoises. Their biologists surveyed the City Creek Plot in the Recovery Unit in 1988 and 1994 and the Woodbury-Hardy Plot in the Northeast Mojave Recovery Unit in 1992. These surveys continue as the basis for estimating tortoise population numbers and trend.

Biological research provided important technical information throughout the process. One member of the Technical Advisory Committee studied radio–marked desert tortoises in the Recovery Unit beginning in 1989 and provided information on habitat use and home range size. These data were incorporated into the reserve design. Contacts with the desert tortoise recovery team and with desert tortoise biologists from other states ensured the HCP process benefited from current information on reserve design theory, disease, genetics, and other relevant topics.

Law Enforcement

During early stages of HCP development, some members of the Steering Committee opposed strong law enforcement, believing it would jeopardize progress of the program. The resulting weak enforcement allowed development to continue in many parts of the county. Consequently, some developers saw no incentive to proceed with the HCP and withdrew from the process.

In response, resource management agencies coordinated an enforcement effort in early April 1992 to provide a higher profile presence, make contacts, and gather information. From 15 April to 15 June 1992, over 40 contacts were made, including 18 with developers and property owners, and 5 of those resulted in major law enforcement investigations. After the initial contacts, USFWS took the lead in 3 cases involving desert tortoise habitat destruction. The Utah Division of Wildlife Resources pursued 2 cases involving "take" of individual desert tortoises, one of which led to a felony conviction.

Minimization and Mitigation of "Take"

The HCP outlined a 7-pronged approach for habitat conservation in Washington County.

1. Place under federal and state ownership and management a reserve including 15,700 ha of desert tortoise habitat and an additional 9,000 ha as buffer and "other species" habitat. Currently, less than two-thirds of this area is under federal management.
2. Remove, by fencing and other means, competing and other consumptive uses within the reserve that may adversely impact the desert tortoise and other Mojave Desert species.
3. Develop controls for minimizing "take" through county-wide ordinances, fees, environmental education, and enforcement, and develop a translocation program to attempt to preserve individuals that oth-

erwise would be killed.
4. Seek Congressional support for establishment of a National Conservation Area.
5. Assist the BLM and the Utah Division of Wildlife Resources in reserve management until a National Conservation Area can be established.
6. Monitor desert tortoise population trends in the reserve.
7. Fund surveys and other actions to gather information, and identify and implement actions to help other listed or candidate species.

These actions serve as the primary mitigation for an estimated level of "incidental take" on 4,965 ha of primarily low-density desert tortoise habitat in the county. Estimated maximum "take" was calculated based on areas likely to be developed within the next 20 years and areas that could be developed without significantly affecting the tortoise.

Numerous conservation measures were instituted to ensure the reserve's effectiveness. The HCP included measures to reduce or eliminate threats (U.S. Department of Interior 1994) and prescribed management for 5 zones within the reserve. A budget covered HCP administrative staff, land management planning, fencing, purchase of grazing permits, tortoise population monitoring, environmental education, law enforcement, tortoise translocation, and conservation of other threatened and endangered species. Strict guidelines governed utility development in the reserve.

Development eventually will reduce the total amount of tortoise habitat in the Recovery Unit. However, the mitigation specified should more than compensate for this loss. Biologists expect implementation of the HCP will improve the quality of habitat in the reserve and chances for the tortoise's long-term survival.

Reserve Design

The Technical Advisory Committee collaborated with a Boundary Subcommittee established in March 1993 to negotiate reserve boundaries. The Boundary Subcommittee included 2 attorneys, 2 realtors, a developer, and several landowners. The advisory committee used reserve design criteria summarized in the draft Desert Tortoise Recovery Plan to evaluate numerous configuration options. Once a controversial segment was agreed to and mapped, surveyors often marked it with stakes to avoid later confusion.

The Technical Advisory Committee reviewed several reserve design plans in succession. In February 1992 it criticized the county's first proposal for the large amount of habitat included. This resulted in a revised version in December 1992. A third reserve, proposed by a small group of landowners in May 1993, was judged too small and fragmented. The advisory committee criticized the initial proposals primarily because they largely ignored design criteria used by the Desert Tortoise Recovery Team and advocated small, fragmented reserves with unmanageable inholdings.

In April 1994 the Steering Committee incorporated most recommendations of the Technical Advisory Committee and Boundary Subcommittee into a final reserve design. The final plan proved more responsive to needs of the tortoise population than did initial proposals, partly because it built on the draft recovery plan. This design accompanied the county's HCP and application to the USFWS for an "incidental take" permit.

HCP Implementation

The Habitat Conservation Advisory Committee advises the county on implementation of the HCP. It draws representation from state and federal agencies, an environmental organization, local government, local development, and the public at large. It meets monthly about important issues such as proposals for the installation and maintenance of utility lines, minor reserve boundary changes, administrative budgets, and quarterly reports prepared by the county.

The Technical Advisory Committee, with help from outside experts, evaluates biological impacts of new issues or proposals (e.g., construction of a utility line). On this basis it advises the Habitat Conservation Advisory Committee, which reviews this advice to consult with the USFWS and make decisions. This "adaptive management" strategy helps address new questions or issues. Technical Advisory Committee biologists also monitor flora and fauna within the reserve.

The Dixie (Utah) Field Office of the BLM quickly exchanged and acquired land and, as of June 2002, had incorporated 2,910 ha into the "Red Cliffs Desert [Tortoise] Reserve" to be managed by the BLM or the state of Utah. Most acquisitions came through exchanges, some were bought with funds from the USFWS and the Land and Water Conservation Fund, and some were donated. Land purchases and exchanges are far from complete.

The county and its conservation partners have taken additional actions. Because cattle compete with tortoises for forage, all grazing permits within the reserve's tortoise habitat have been retired by Washington County. A coun-

ty-funded law enforcement officer's sole responsibility is protection of the reserve. The BLM also has prohibited off-road vehicle use except on a few designated roads and trails. The BLM has withdrawn the entire reserve from new mining claims. Washing-ton County employs a full-time HCP administrator, a biologist, and a technician who coordinates and conducts day-to-day conservation measures. The county annually funds seasonal technicians for the Utah Division of Wildlife Resources to monitor tortoise populations within the reserve. Several entities have built more than 48 km of fencing to exclude tortoises from roads or other hazards, and to control illegal dumping, vandalism, and off-road vehicle use.

Education and research programs support tortoise conservation. Washington County provides information on tortoises and other wildlife to thousands of its residents. It helped fund a multi-species plan for other wildlife in the reserve. A translocation experiment is providing valuable information about which habitats tortoises prefer, how far they travel, and whether successful translocation is possible. Development of a nature education center focusing on sensitive reserve species is forthcoming.

Areas of disagreement remain. Many local residents would like the reserve open to unlimited recreational use. The USFWS, BLM, and the Utah Division of Wildlife Resources, concerned that unrestrained recreation could harm tortoises and their habitat, developed a public use plan to address these issues. Discussions continue about new utility development proposals within the reserve and about costs of acquiring the remaining private property. Reserve properties still to be acquired are currently worth over $100 million (Owens 2000).

Implications

Washington County's Habitat Conservation Plan addressed complex conflicts between conservation needs

Fig. 5. A habitat conservation plan developed in southern Utah used the threatened desert tortoise as the cornerstone for a reserve that offers protection for an entire ecosystem (photograph by T. C. Esque).

Box 4. Habitat Conservation Plan, Plum Creek Native Fishes.

The Plum Creek Native Fish Habitat Conservation Plan (http://www.plumcreek.com) was developed by Plum Creek Timber Company, Inc., in cooperation with the U.S. Fish and Wildlife Service and the National Marine Fisheries Service. It was designed to conserve 17 native salmonids in the context of practicable long-term forest management. It encompassed about 650,000 ha, primarily in Montana but partly in Idaho and Washington.

The Plum Creek plan proposed an "incidental take" permit period of 30 years for the species covered. Seven conservation categories included 56 commitments intended to meet the biological goals for the 17 species of fish.

The working relationship between the Plum Creek Timber Company and the federal agencies began in June 1997. The draft Plum Creek plan and a Draft Environmental Impact Statement on the plan were released 17 December 1999, followed by a 90-day public comment period. The Final Environmental Impact Statement was issued on 21 September 2000.

After reviewing and developing responses to 83 public letters and other comments, the Plum Creek Timber Company and the 2 agencies identified issues that needed to be resolved prior to release of the final impact statement. These issues provided the framework for revisions to the habitat conservation plan.

Adaptive Management

The greatest number of issues leading to changes in the plan related to adaptive management.
- Expanding the description of the monitoring studies to be conducted.
- Clarifying that adaptive management decisions were based on an equal partnership, i.e., making sure the Plum Creek Timber Company could not unilaterally veto changes.
- Adding a commitment to establish a process for adding selected watersheds to the plan.
- Adding a commitment to monitor landslides.

Riparian Areas

The next greatest number of issues related to riparian management.
- Improving 8 of 9 commitments with more specific language.
- Adding more fish habitat protection for intermittent streams.
- Extending perennial stream measures to intermittent streams that flowed through unstable landscape features.
- Adding measures to mitigate impacts of streamside roads.
- Incorporating a clearcut limitation into "Interface Caution Areas."

Roads

Several changes related to road management.
- Improving 5 of 8 commitments with more specific language.
- Identifying specific watersheds for high priority treatment and for "Road Sediment Delivery Analyses."
- Incorporating a requirement to avoid building new roads on steep slopes.
- Developing a new, site-specific commitment to address landslide risk at Papoose Creek in the Lochsa River Planning Area basin.

Administration and Implementation

A few changes related to administration and implementation of the plan; the greatest concern was whether the 2 agencies would have sufficient resources to continue a creative partnership once the "incidental take" permit was issued.
- Improving 2 of 6 commitments with more specific language to help ensure long-term viability of the plan.
- Developing a specific protocol for third-party audits (financed by Plum Creek Timber Company) that would verify compliance and streamline the agencies' involvement.

---

and local development demands. It began to shift HCP and land-management efforts beyond a single species to accommodate an entire ecosystem (Fig. 5) that transcended traditional land management boundaries.

This project exemplified the potential of the HCP approach for species conservation. Conservation plan areas may be defined in terms of ecosystems rather than a species' distribution and thereby can produce an efficiency of scale in conservation funding and management. HCP efforts also may fund ecological research, inventories, and habitat monitoring. But despite the potential benefits, application of habitat conservation plans cannot always prevent regional declines in populations of listed species.

SUMMARY

Ecological impact assessments and habitat conservation plans evolved as conservation tools from provisions of the National Environmental Policy Act and the Endangered Species Act, respectively. They use legal protocols and public involvement to protect wildlife and habitats from impacts of human development. Analysts involved in their preparation need in-depth understanding of wildlife-habitat relationships and skills in working with people. The complexity of ecosystems, institutional agendas, and human motivations commonly involved offer challenges far beyond those ordinarily experienced by most wildlife biologists.

Three decades of application of NEPA have revealed shortcomings in the ability of the EIA process to halt or reverse ecosystem decline. A primary assumption of NEPA—that impacts could be reliably predicted—often has proved invalid. Monitoring to ascertain accuracy of predictions and usefulness of mitigation usually has not been required. Agencies have become good at meeting the letter of the law but often disregard its intention to protect natural resources. Potential improvements to the EIA process could come through monitoring and adaptive management, but even when applied these often have been offset by administrative shortcuts to the process that avoid in-depth analyses and public involvement. Some analysts have proposed ways to restructure the EIA process but change has been slow.

A large and long-term EIA program surrounding oil development in arctic Alaska exemplified some of the strengths and weaknesses of the process. Although well funded and often well designed, research to measure impacts on a number of species usually could not clearly identify whether population changes resulted from development or from other factors. Adaptive approaches characterized both research and management, and adjustments in both over time reduced the likelihood that adverse impacts occurred. Application of NEPA concepts coupled with generous research funding greatly increased scientific understanding of the arctic ecosystem. Major disagreements about oil-field impacts persist for at least 2 reasons: inadequate data sets and differing interpretations of existing data.

Habitat conservation plans have been in common usage only since 1990. Their initial focus on one or a few imperiled species simplified the task of predicting impacts, but the concept has broadened to include numerous species. Their emphasis on monitoring and adaptive management allows for flexibility to meet uncertainties. This voluntary way for developers to participate in conservation lends itself to positive collaboration and creative compromise for resource protection. For sedentary species at least, the option of establishing reserves to mitigate impacts may prove to be a better way than the ecological impact assessment process for protecting whole ecosystems against the chronic "nibbling" away of wildlife and habitats by successions of development projects.

Development of a habitat conservation plan to protect the threatened desert tortoise in southwestern Utah brought together proponents and opponents of development and resulted in creation of a tortoise reserve as mitigation. Positive aspects of this program included research on and monitoring of tortoises, productive collaboration among interest groups, distribution of conservation information to the public, and consolidation of land ownership into a reserve for tortoises that protected other species as well. The increasing use of HCPs suggests such a strategy can provide long-term ecosystem protection in many areas.

ACKNOWLEDGMENTS

The Turner Endangered Species Fund and the U.S. Fish and Wildlife Service supported us in preparation of this paper. C. J. Walters, R. Hilborn, and their colleagues at the University of British Columbia and ESSA Limited taught JCT the importance of uncertainty and the limitations and strengths of models. R. D. Williams, R. A. Fridell, S. C. Belfit, M. R. Topham, A. P. McLuckie, E. W. Owens, and E. A. Boeke contributed importantly to the development and/or continuing implementation of the Washington County HCP. M. K. Phillips encouraged 2 of us to pursue this project. M. W. Rowland contributed through provision of childcare. J. A. Truett and J. C. Marston helped with organization and word processing skills. W. M. Block and T. E. Olson provided excellent reviews, and C. E. Braun encouraged us and helped in the editorial process.

LITERATURE CITED

AMSTRUP, S.C. 2000. Polar bear. Pages 133–157 *in* J. C. Truett and S. R. Johnson, editors. The natural history of an arctic oil field: development and the biota. Academic Press, San Diego, California, USA.

ANDERSON, S. H., AND K. J. GUTZWILLER. 2005. Wildlife habitat evaluation. Pages 489–502 *in* C. E. Braun, editor. Techniques for wildlife investigations and management. Sixth edition. The Wildlife Society, Bethesda, Maryland, USA.

ARNOLD, C. A. 1991. Conserving habitats and building habitats: the emerging impact of the Endangered Species Act on land use development. Stanford Environmental Law Journal 10(1):1–43.

BALLARD, W. B., M. A. CRONIN, AND H. A. WHITLAW. 2000. Caribou and oil fields. Pages 85–104 *in* J. C. Truett and S. R. Johnson, editors. The natural history of an arctic oil field: development and the biota. Academic Press, San Diego, California, USA.

BEAN, M. J., S. G. FITZGERALD, AND M. A. O'CONNELL. 1991. Reconciling conflicts under the Endangered Species Act: the habitat conservation planning experience. World Wildlife Fund, Washington, D.C., USA.

BEANLANDS, G. E., AND P. N. DUINKER. 1983. An ecological framework for environmental impact assessment in Canada. Institute for Resource and Environmental Studies, Dalhousie University, Halifax, Nova Scotia, and Federal Environmental Assessment Review Office, Ottawa, Ontario, Canada.

BEATLEY, T. 1994. Habitat conservation planning: endangered species and urban growth. University of Texas Press, Austin, USA.

BOOTHROYD, P., AND W. E. REES. 1984. Impact assessment: from pseudo-science to planning process. School of Community and Regional Planning, University of British Columbia, UBC Planning Papers, DP 3, Vancouver, Canada.

BROWER, D.C. 1942. Fifty years below zero: a lifetime of adventure in the far north. Dodd, Mead, New York, USA.

BUCKLEY, R. C. 1991. How accurate are environmental impact predictions? Ambio 20:161–162.

BURGESS, R. M. 2000. Arctic fox. Pages 159–178 *in* J. C. Truett and S. R. Johnson, editors. The natural history of an arctic oil field: development and the biota. Academic Press, San Diego, California, USA.

CALDWELL, L. K. 1989. Understanding impact analysis: technical process, administrative reform, policy principle. Pages 7–16 *in* R. V. Bartlett, editor. Policy through impact assessment. Greenwood Press, Westport, Connecticut, USA.

CLARK, M., AND J. HERINGTON. 1988. The role of environmental impact assessment in the planning process. Mansell Publications, London, United Kingdom.

CLARK, R., AND L. W. CANTER. 1997. Environmental policy and NEPA: past, present and future. St. Lucie Press, Boca Raton, Florida, USA.

CULHANE, P. J. 1993. Post-EIS environmental auditing: a first step to make rational environmental assessment a reality. Environmental Professional 15:66–75.

DASMANN, R .F. 1981. Wildlife biology. Second edition. John Wiley and Sons, New York, USA.

DIAMOND, J. M. 1975. The island dilemma: lessons of modern biogeographic studies for the design of natural preserves. Biological Conservation 7:129–146.

———. 1987. Reflections on goals and on the relationship between theory and practice. Pages 329–335 *in* W. R. Jordan, III, M. E. Gilpin, and J. D. Aber, editors. Restoration ecology: a synthetic approach to ecological research. Cambridge University Press, New York, USA.

DICKINSON, W. R. 1995. The times are always changing: the Holocene saga. Geological Society of America Bulletin 107:1–7.

DUINKER, P. N. 1989. Ecological effects monitoring in environmental impact assessment: what can it accomplish? Environmental Management 13:797–805.

EBERHARDT, L. L. 1976. Quantitative ecology and impact assessment. Journal of Environmental Management 4:27–70.

ENGELMANN, R. J. 1976. Environmental assessment research in Alaska – an overview. Science in Alaska 27:83–108.

FRANKLIN, J. F. 1993. Preserving biodiversity: species, ecosystems, or landscapes? Ecological Applications 3:202–205.

FROMBY, J. 1990. The politics of environmental impact assessment. Impact Assessment Bulletin 8:191–196.

GALLAWAY, B .J., AND R. G. FECHHELM. 2000. Anadromous and amphidromous fishes. Pages 349–369 *in* J. C. Truett and S. R. Johnson, editors. The natural history of an arctic oil field: development and the biota. Academic Press, San Diego, California, USA.

GILDERS, M. A., AND M. A. CRONIN. 2000. North Slope oil field development. Pages 15–33 *in* J. C. Truett and S. R. Johnson, editors. The natural history of an arctic oil field: development and the biota. Academic Press, San Diego, California, USA.

GOODLAND, R., AND H. DALY. 1995. Environmental sustainability. Pages 303–322 *in* F. Vanclay and D. A. Bronstein, editors. Environmental and social impact assessment. John Wiley and Sons, West Sussex, United Kingdom.

GOULD, N. E. 1977. Featured species planning for wildlife on southern national forests. Transactions of the North American Wildlife and Natural Resources Conference 42:435–437.

GRAHAM, R. W. 1988. The role of climatic change in the design of biological reserves: the paleoecological perspective for conservation biology. Conservation Biology 2:391–394.

GRAUL, W. D., AND G. C. MILLER. 1984. Strengthening ecosystem management approaches. Wildlife Society Bulletin 12:282–289.

———, J. TORRES, AND R. DENNEY. 1976. A species-ecosystem approach for nongame programs. Wildlife Society Bulletin 4:79–80.

HANSSON, L. 1979. On the importance of landscape heterogeneity in northern regions for the breeding population densities of homeotherms: a general hypothesis. Oikos 33:182–189.

HARRIS, L. D. 1988. Edge effects and conservation of biotic diversity. Conservation Biology 2:330–332.

HEMKER, T. P., AND C. E. BRAUN. 2001. Innovative approaches for development of conservation plans for sage grouse: examples from Idaho and Colorado. Transactions of the North American Wildlife and Natural Resources Conference 66:456–463.

HIRSCH, A. 1993. Improving consideration of biodiversity in NEPA assessments. Environmental Professional 15:103–115.

HOLLING, C. S., editor. 1978. Adaptive environmental assessment and management. John Wiley and Sons, New York, USA.

HOUCK, O. A. 1993. The Endangered Species Act and its implementation by the U.S. Departments of Interior and Commerce. Colorado Law Review 64:277–370.

HUNTER, JR., M. L., G. L. JACOBSON, JR., AND T. WEBB, III. 1988. Paleoecology and the coarse-filter approach to maintaining biological diversity. Conservation Biology 2:375–385.

IRWIN, F., AND B. RODES. 1992. Making decisions on cumulative environmental impacts. World Wildlife Fund Publications, Baltimore, Maryland, USA.

JAMISON, P. L. 1978. Ethnohistory of research populations. Pages 31–39 *in* P. L. Jamison, S. L. Zegura, and F. A. Milan, editors. Eskimos of northwestern Alaska: a biological perspective. Dowden, Hutchinson and Ross, Stroudsburg, Pennsylvania, USA.

JOHNSON, S. R. 2000a. Lesser snow goose. Pages 233–257 *in* J. C. Truett and S. R. Johnson, editors. The natural history of an arctic oil field: development and the biota. Academic Press, San Diego, California, USA.

———. 2000b. Pacific eider. Pages 259–275 *in* J. C. Truett and S. R. Johnson, editors. The natural history of an arctic oil field: develop-

ment and the biota. Academic Press, San Diego, California, USA.

KAUTZ, R. S. 1984. Criteria for evaluating impacts of development on wildlife habitats. Proceedings of the Annual Conference of the Southeastern Association of Fish and Wildlife Agencies 38:121–136.

KENNEDY, W. V. 1988. Environmental impact assessment in North America, western Europe: what has worked where, how, and why. International Environmental Reporter II:262.

KERTELL, K. 1996. Response of Pacific loons (*Gavia pacifica*) to impoundments at Prudhoe Bay, Alaska. Arctic 49:356–366.

KNOPF, F. L. 1992. Faunal mixing, faunal integrity, and the biopolitical template for diversity conservation. Transactions of the North American Wildlife and Natural Resources Conference 57:330–342.

LAMBECK, R. J. 1997. Focal species: a multi-species umbrella for nature conservation. Conservation Biology 11:849–856.

LANCIA, R. A., C. E. BRAUN, M. W. COLLOPY, R. D. DUESER, J. G. KIE, C. J. MARTINKA, J. D. NICHOLS, T. D. NUDDS, W. R. PORATH, AND N. G. TILGHMAN. 1996. ARM! For the future: adaptive resource management in the wildlife profession. Wildlife Society Bulletin 24:436–442.

LANDRES, P. B. 1983. Use of the guild concept in environmental impact assessment. Environmental Management 7:393–398.

———, J. VERNER, AND J. W. THOMAS. 1988. Ecological uses of vertebrate indicator species: a critique. Conservation Biology 2:316–328.

LEOPOLD, A. 1933. Game management. Charles Scribner's Sons, New York, USA.

LINDSTROM, M. J., AND Z. A. SMITH. 2001. The National Environmental Policy Act: judicial misconstruction, legislative indifference, and executive neglect. Texas A&M University Press, College Station, USA.

LOCKWOOD, J. L., R. D. POWELL, M. P. NOTT, AND S. L. PIMM. 1997. Assembling ecological communities in time and space. Oikos 80:549–553.

LUDWIG, D., R. HILBORN, AND C. WALTERS. 1993. Uncertainty, resource exploitation, and conservation: lessons from history. Science 120:17, 36.

MACARTHUR, R. H., AND J. W. MACARTHUR. 1961. On bird species diversity. Ecology 42:594–598.

———, AND E. O. WILSON. 1967. The theory of island biogeography. Princeton University Press, Princeton, New Jersey, USA.

MAKI, A. W. 1992. Of measured risks: the environmental impacts of the Prudhoe Bay, Alaska, oil field. Environmental Toxicology and Chemistry 11:1691–1707.

MASER, C., J. W. THOMAS, I. D. LUMAN, AND R. ANDERSON. 1979. Wildlife habitats in managed rangelands — the Great Basin of southeastern Oregon. Manmade habitats. U.S. Department of Agriculture, Forest Service, General Technical Report PNW-86.

MAZMANIAN, D., AND J. N. CLARKE. 1979. Can organizations change? Environmental protection, citizen participation, and the Army Corps of Engineers. Brookings Institution, Washington D.C., USA.

MCKENDRICK, J. D. 2000. Vegetation responses to disturbance. Pages 35–56 *in* J. C. Truett and S. R. Johnson, editors. The natural history of an arctic oil field: development and the biota. Academic Press, San Diego, California, USA.

MILLER, B., R. READING, J. STRITTHOLT, C. CARROLL, R. NOSS, M. SOULÉ, O. SANCHEZ, J. TERBROUGH, D. BRIGHTSMITH, T. CHEESEMAN, AND D. FOREMAN. 1999. Using focal species in the design of nature reserve networks. Wild Earth, Winter 1998/1999:81–92.

MILLS, L. C., M. E. SOULÉ, AND D. F. DOAK. 1993. The keystone-species concept in ecology and conservation. BioScience 43:219–224.

MOIR, W. H., AND W. M. BLOCK. 2001. Adaptive management on public lands in the United States: commitment or rhetoric? Environmental Management 28:141–148.

MURPHY, D. D., AND B. D. NOON. 1991. Coping with uncertainty in wildlife biology. Journal of Wildlife Management 55:773–782.

MURPHY, S. M., AND B. E. LAWHEAD. 2000. Caribou. Pages 59–84 *in* J. C. Truett and S. R. Johnson, editors. The natural history of an arctic oil field: development and the biota. Academic Press, San Diego, California, USA.

NAEEM, S. 1998. Species redundancy and ecosystem reliability. Conservation Biology 12:39–45.

NATIONAL RESEARCH COUNCIL. 2003. Cumulative environmental effects of oil and gas activities on Alaska's North Slope. Summary of committee's report. Available online at http://www.nap.edu (accessed 20 April 2003).

NELSON, M. 2000. The changing face of HCPs. Endangered Species Bulletin. 25(4): 4–7. U.S. Department of the Interior, Fish and Wildlife Service. Washington, D.C., USA.

NOSS, R. F. 1990. Indicators for monitoring biodiversity: a hierarchical approach. Conservation Biology 4:355–364.

———, AND L. D. HARRIS. 1986. Nodes, networks, and MUMs: preserving diversity at all scales. Environmental Management 10:299–309.

———, M. A. O'CONNELL, AND D. D. MURPHY. 1997. The science of conservation planning: habitat conservation under the Endangered Species Act. Island Press, Washington, D.C., USA.

ORIANS, G., T. ALBERT, G. BROWN, R. CAMERON, P. COCHRAN, S. R. GEHLBACH, R. GRAMLING, G. GRYC, D. HITE, M. KENNICUTT II, A. LACHENBRUCH, L. LOWRY, L. MOULTON, C. PIELOU, J. SEDINGER, K. J. LINDSTEDT-SIVA, L. SPEER, D. WALKER, AND D. POLICANSKY. 2003. Cumulative environmental effects of oil and gas activities on Alaska's North Slope. National Academies Press, Washington, D.C., USA.

ORTOLANO, L., AND A. SHEPHERD. 1995. Environmental impact assessment. Pages 1–32 in F. Vanclay and D. A. Bronstein, editors. Environmental and social impact assessment. John Wiley and Sons, New York, USA.

OWENS, E. W. 2000. Washington County's HCP: four years later. Endangered Species Bulletin 25(4): 16–17. U.S. Department of the Interior, Fish and Wildlife Service, Washington, D.C., USA.

PRITCHARD, D. 1993. Towards sustainability in the planning process: the role of EIA. Ecos 14:10–15.

RAPPORT, D. J. 1989. What constitutes ecosystem health? Perspectives in Biology and Medicine 33:120–132.

REID, W. V. 1996. Beyond protected areas: changing perceptions of ecological management objectives. Pages 442–453 in R. C. Szaro and D. W. Johnston, editors. Biodiversity in managed landscapes: theory and practice. Oxford University Press, New York, USA.

RISSER, P. G. 1995. Biodiversity and ecosystem function. Conservation Biology 9:742–746.

RITCHIE, R. J., AND J. G. KING. 2000. Tundra swans. Pages 197–220 in J. C. Truett and S. R. Johnson, editors. The natural history of an arctic oil field: development and the biota. Academic Press, San Diego, California, USA.

ROE, D., B. DALAL-CLAYTON, AND R. W. HUGHES. 1995. A directory of impact assessment guidelines. Sixth edition. IIED, London, United Kingdom.

ROMESBURG, H. C. 1981. Wildlife science: gaining reliable knowledge. Journal of Wildlife Management 45:293–313.

SCOTT, J. M., B. CSUTI, J. D. JACOBI, AND J. E. ESTES. 1987. Species richness: a geographic approach to protecting future biological diversity. BioScience 37:782–788.

SCOTT, T. A., AND J. E. SULLIVAN. 2000. The selection and design of multiple-species habitat preserves. Environmental Management 26:37–53.

SEDINGER, J. S., AND A. A. STICKNEY. 2000. Black brant. Pages 221–232 in J. C. Truett and S. R. Johnson, editors. The natural history of an arctic oil field: development and the biota. Academic Press, San Diego, California, USA.

SELLERS, R. W. 1997. Preserving nature in the national parks: a history. Yale University Press, New Haven, Connecticut, USA.

SHAVER, G. R. 1996. Integrated ecosystem research in northern Alaska, 1947–1994. Pages 19–34 in J. F. Reynolds and J. D. Tenhunen, editors. Landscape function and disturbance in arctic tundra. Springer-Verlag, Inc., New York, USA.

SHIDELER, R., AND J. HECHTEL. 2000. Grizzly bear. Pages 105–132 in J. C. Truett and S. R. Johnson, editors. The natural history of an arctic oil field: development and the biota. Academic Press, San Diego, California, USA.

SHORT, H. L. 1988. A habitat structure model for natural resource management. Journal of Environmental Management 27:289–305.

———, AND S. C. WILLIAMSON. 1986. Evaluating the structure of habitat for wildlife. Pages 97–104 in J. Verner, M. L. Morrison, and C. J. Ralph, editors. Wildlife 2000: modeling habitat relationships of terrestrial vertebrates. University of Wisconsin Press, Madison, USA.

SMITH, G. L. 1993. Impact assessment and sustainable resource management. Burnt Mill, Harlow, Essex, United Kingdom.

SPRUGEL, D. G. 1991. Disturbance, equilibrium, and environmental variability: what is 'natural' vegetation in a changing environment? Biological Conservation 58:1–18.

STANLEY, JR., T. R. 1995. Ecosystem management and the arrogance of humanism. Conservation Biology 9:255–262.

STOREY, K. 1986. From prediction to management: increasing the effectiveness of EIA. Pages 539–551 in H. A. Becker and A. L. Porter, editors. Impact assessment today. Volume 2. Jan Van Arkel Press, Utrecht, The Netherlands.

TAYLOR, S. 1984. Making bureaucracies think: the environmental impact statement strategy of administrative reform. Stanford University Press, Stanford, California, USA.

THOMAS, J. W., AND J. BURCHFIELD. 2000. Science, politics, and land management. Rangelands 22(4): 45–48.

TRAWEEK, J. 1995. Ecological impact assessment. Pages 171–191 in F. VanClay and D. A. Bronstein, editors. Environmental and social impact assessment. John Wiley and Sons, New York, USA.

TRESHOW, M., AND J. ALLAN. 1985. Uncertainties associated with the assessment of vegetation. Environmental Management 9:471–478.

TROY, D. M. 2000. Shorebirds. Pages 277–303 in J. C. Truett and S. R. Johnson, editors. The natural history of an arctic oil field: development and the biota. Academic Press, San Diego, California, USA.

TRUETT, J. C. 1977. Research plan of the Beaufort Sea barrier island-lagoon ecological process studies. U.S. Department of Commerce, National Oceanic and Atmospheric Administration, Outer Continental Shelf Environmental Assessment Program Annual Report. Washington, D.C., USA.

———. 1979. Pre-impact process analysis: design for mitigation. Pages 355–360 in G. A. Swanson, technical coordinator. The mitigation symposium: a national workshop on mitigating losses of fish and wildlife habitats. U.S. Department of Agriculture, Forest Service, General Technical Report RM-65.

———. 1981. Synthesis, impact analysis, and a monitoring strategy. Pages 259–359 in Beaufort Sea barrier island-lagoon ecological process studies: Simpson Lagoon. U.S. Department of Commerce, National Oceanic and Atmospheric Administration, Outer Continental Shelf Environmental Assessment Program. Final Report 7. Washington, D.C., USA.

———. 2000a. Introduction. Pages 3–13 in J. C. Truett and S. R. Johnson, editors. The natural history of an arctic oil field: development and the biota. Academic Press, San Diego, California, USA.

———. 2000b. Synthesis. Pages 401–408 in J. C. Truett and S. R. Johnson, editors. The natural history of an arctic oil field: development and the biota. Academic Press, San Diego, California, USA.

———, AND S. R. JOHNSON, editors. 2000. The natural history of an arctic oil field: development and the biota. Academic Press, San Diego, California, USA.

———, H. L. SHORT, AND S. C. WILLIAMSON. 1994. Ecological impact assessment. Pages 607–622 in T. A. Bookhout, editor. Research and management techniques for wildlife and habitats. The Wildlife Society, Bethesda, Maryland, USA.

U.S. DEPARTMENT OF INTERIOR. 1985. 50 CFR Parts 13 and 17, Endangered and threatened wildlife and plants; permits and prohibitions, final rule. Federal Register 50(189): 39681–39691.

———. 1988. Endangered Species Act of 1973 as amended through the 100th Congress. U.S. Department of the Interior, Fish and Wildlife Service, Washington, D.C., USA.

———. 1994. Desert Tortoise (Mojave Population) Recovery Plan. U.S. Department of the Interior, Fish and Wildlife Service, Portland, Oregon, USA.

———. 1996. Endangered species habitat conservation planning handbook. U.S. Department of the Interior, Fish and Wildlife Service, Washington, D.C., USA.

———. 1998. Habitat conservation plan assurances ("no surprises") rule, final rule. Federal Register 63(35): 8859–8873.

———. 2000. Notice of availability of a final addendum to the handbook for habitat conservation planning and incidental take permitting process, notice of final policy. Federal Register 65(106): 35242–35257.

URBAN, D. L., R. V. O'NEILL, AND H. H. SHUGART, JR. 1987. Landscape ecology: a hierarchical perspective can help scientists understand spatial patterns. BioScience 37: 119–127.

VERNER, J. 1986. Summary: predicting effects of habitat patchiness and fragmentation — the researcher's viewpoint. Pages 327–329 *in* J. Verner, M. L. Morrison, and C. J. Ralph, editors. Wildlife 2000: modeling habitat relationships of terrestrial vertebrates. University of Wisconsin Press, Madison, USA.

VITOUSEK, P. M. 1990. Biological invasions and ecosystem processes: towards an integration of population biology and ecosystem studies. Oikos 57:7–13.

WAGNER, F. H., AND C. E. KAY. 1993. "Natural" or "healthy" ecosystems: are U.S. National Parks providing them? Pages 257–270 *in* M. J. McDonnell and S. T. A. Pickett, editors. Humans as components of ecosystems: the ecology of subtle human effects and populated areas. Springer-Verlag, Inc., New York, USA.

WALKER, B. 1995. Conserving biological diversity through ecosystem resilience. Conservation Biology 9:747–752.

WALTERS, C. J. 1986. Adaptive management of renewable resources. McGraw-Hill Book Co., New York, USA.

———, AND C. S. HOLLING. 1990. Large-scale management experiments and learning by doing. Ecology 71:2060–2068.

WASHINGTON COUNTY HABITAT CONSERVATION PLAN STEERING COMMITTEE. 1995. Habitat conservation plan, Washington County, Utah. SWCA, Inc., Environmental Consultants, Flagstaff, Arizona, USA.

WEBSTER, R. E. 1987. Habitat conservation plans under the Endangered Species Act. San Diego Law Review 24:243–271.

WELLER, M. W. 1978. Management of freshwater marshes for wildlife. Pages 267–284 *in* R. E. Good, D. F. Whigham, R. L. Simpson, and C. G. Jackson, Jr., editors. Freshwater wetlands: ecological processes and management potential. Academic Press, New York, USA.

WESTMAN, W. E. 1985. Species and landscape diversity. Pages 444–479 *in* W. E. Westman. Ecology, impact assessment, and environmental planning. John Wiley and Sons, New York, USA.

———. 1990. Managing for biodiversity: unresolved science and policy questions. BioScience 40:26–33.

WIENS, J. A. 1995. Landscape mosaics and ecological theory. Pages 1–25 *in* L. Hansson, L. Fahrig, and G. Merriam, editors. Mosaic landscapes and ecological processes. Chapman and Hall, London, United Kingdom.

WILHERE, G. F. 2002. Adaptive management in habitat conservation plans. Conservation Biology 16:20–29.

WILLSON, M. F. 1974. Avian community organization and habitat structure. Ecology 55:1017–1029.

WILSON, E. O. 1998. Consilience: the unity of knowledge. Alfred A. Knopf, New York, USA.

20

VEGETATION SAMPLING AND MEASUREMENT

Kenneth F. Higgins, Kurt J. Jenkins, Gary K. Clambey, Daniel W. Uresk, David E. Naugle, Jack E. Norland, and William T. Barker

INTRODUCTION

What is the utility of vegetation measurements for wildlife managers? In the prairie, savanna, tundra, forest, steppe, and wetland regions of the world, mixtures of plant species provide wildlife with food, cover and, in some circumstances, water, the 3 essential habitat elements necessary to sustain viable wildlife populations. In strict definition, the variety of wildlife using plants ranges from snails and voles to bison (*Bison bison*) and elephants (*Loxodonta* spp.) in uplands and from mosquitoes and ducks to muskrats (*Ondatra zibethicus*) and manatees (*Trichechus manatus*) in wetlands. Through evolutionary processes, some wildlife species are totally dependent on vegetation for all annual life requirements, whereas other species use vegetation only for cover or food. Regardless of the role of vegetation in the sustenance of wildlife, any management or research project that requires evaluation of wildlife and habitat relationships on a unit of land will necessitate some form of vegetation measurement.

The term vegetation can refer to a single plant or species on a specific site or a community in the landscape. Vegetation may occur naturally or be introduced, and may be live or dead. Uses of vegetation measurements are many: (1) evaluation of vegetation response to management, (2) estimation of carrying capacity, (3) characterization of cover and habitat components for an endangered species, or (4) long-term monitoring of the general trend of plant vigor or habitat condition.

Surveying and measuring *quantity* and *quality* of vegetation within habitats are basic to wildlife research and management. Grassland, shrubland, and woodland habitats are comprised of populations in which individual plants are usually too numerous to inventory completely. Consequently, wildlife biologists usually use sampling techniques to make inferences about the total plant population within a given habitat.

Vegetation sampling methodologies have evolved within several ecological disciplines (e.g., plant ecology, forestry, range science) and for a variety of management or research objectives (e.g., estimating forage for ungulates, describing habitat use by passerine birds). Description of every method that has been used to sample vegetation is beyond the scope of this chapter. We describe how to measure vegetation structure, which Dansereau (1957) defined as the spatial organization (distribution) of individuals that form a stand. We have organized this chapter into a description of basic methods of vegetation sampling with examples of how those methods have been applied or modified in wildlife research and management. We assume the investigator has adequate knowledge of the concepts of wildlife ecology, primary habitat requirements of wildlife species under study, and ability to systematically identify the species of wildlife and vascular plants within the geographical area of the investigation.

INITIAL STEPS TO SAMPLING VEGETATION
Development of Objectives

The critical element of any project, whether management or research, is to define objectives. Data should not be collected if a project has neither an objective for vegetative measurements nor a defined use for each type of measurement. Collecting vegetation data is time-consuming and often difficult, and that time should be used to meet well-defined objectives. It is important to review management or research plans to assure the information being collected fulfills the objectives and that critical information is not neglected.

Objectives must be specific. They should include what will be sampled, when it will be sampled, and where it will be sampled. Although these factors often are taken for granted, their identification requires the investigator to make a thorough analysis of the biology of the wildlife

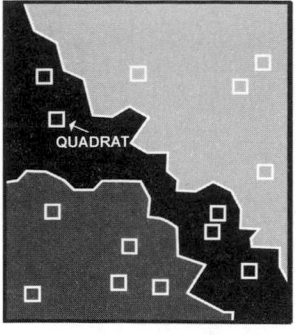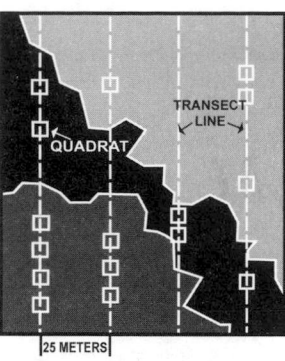

Fig. 1. Random (left) and systematic (right) distribution of quadrats with and without use of transect lines on a site with 3 different vegetative cover types.

species to be studied, factors that relate to the study, and management or research needs. Elzinga et al. (1998) elaborate on components of vegetation sampling objectives and provide examples of effective measurement objectives.

General Aspects of Vegetation

After listing the objectives of the study and primary habitat requirements of the wildlife species under study, one then may identify which aspects of the vegetation to sample. Some or all of the following may be important in describing primary wildlife habitat requirements:

(1) species composition,
(2) vertical and/or horizontal spatial distribution,
(3) temporal variation in structure,
(4) biomass,
(5) overall stand structure, and
(6) surrounding environment (landscape structure).

A reconnaissance survey of an area is usually sufficient to provide the investigator with an overview of vegetation structure. Reconnaissance can be done on the ground or with aerial photography. In either instance, the objective of a preliminary survey is to decide *whether* to sample, identify *what* to sample, and which environmental factors will influence *how* and *when* to sample.

Consider the following example. Suppose the goal of a study is to inventory potential, natural nesting sites for wood ducks (*Aix sponsa*). The wood duck nests only in cavities in trees. Because nesting cavities within a reasonable distance of water are a primary habitat requirement of wood ducks, 3 objectives are to:

(1) quantify the number of wood duck nesting cavities,
(2) identify the species of trees containing the cavities, and
(3) calculate the age-distribution of trees with cavities.

Assume a reconnaissance survey has revealed the study area is a riparian system with a permanent stream, riparian vegetation bordering the stream, and farmland bordering the riparian vegetation. Because wood ducks nest in trees, one would not sample the area with crops, but would sample the riparian vegetation. A sample would be designed to randomly select a number of trees for examination. The objectives require identifying the species of trees in which wood duck cavities occur. Because we are interested in estimating the number of potential nest cavities, our sample will need to provide an estimate of tree density, one aspect of horizontal spatial distribution. We are not, however, interested in heights of cavities, thus vertical distribu-

tion will not be of interest. Cavities often are present in older and larger trees and in dead trees, and the age distribution of trees is important. In addition, dead trees are likely to be blown over in windstorms, and we may decide to mark cavity trees and follow them over time to measure the rate of loss. Biomass of trees is not of interest; however, if a mast crop is produced by the trees, we would be interested in biomass of mast, a food item of wood ducks.

Study Site Selection

Study site selection is a critical phase of any vegetation study and is directly related to the objectives. If the objective is to describe vegetation conditions in relation to patterns of animal distribution or abundance, location of vegetation plots may be influenced by locations of animal observations or influenced by wildlife population sampling objectives. If the objective is to describe vegetation conditions of selected habitats, the first issue is to define the targeted sample population and develop an appropriate sampling frame following sampling principles described by Garton et al. (2005). Elzinga et al. (1998) provide a thorough overview of the step-by-step procedures for vegetation surveys.

A variety of factors influence selection of study sites (e.g., topography, elevation, slope, aspect, soil type, management history, distance to human-caused disturbances, vegetation, etc.). Generally, one is interested in selecting sites that are similar to one another and, care must be taken to select sites so that the inter-site variation is natural and not affected by some factor not accounted for in the objectives and design of the study. This may require mapping of the project area so that all habitat types, their location, and their size are enumerated. The objectives may require that samples be taken in all or in only several sites containing a certain habitat type.

The size of the study site must be sufficiently large so that vegetation characteristics being measured are not influenced by adjacent habitat types (often called edge effect). Edge effect may increase the variation in the sample. Unless such variation is explained by the sampling design (Garton et al. 2005), the results of the sample will be biased with regard to the objectives of the study. For example, if one were to sample browse production in a 100 ha stand of upland willow (*Salix* spp.), one would avoid sampling adjacent to the edge of a habitat type that offered resting cover for moose (*Alces alces*), because those plants measured within close proximity of resting cover likely would have higher use (and perhaps lower levels of production) than plants measured in the middle of the willow stand.

Visualizing how vegetation sampling plots, or plots along a transect, will appear in field applications can be difficult. Many layout designs are possible (Figs. 1–3), and the final choice of a design also will depend on the objectives and requirements of the statistical analysis. For those not familiar with statistical principles of sampling, it is important to consult a biometrician before committing project resources to vegetation sampling.

PREPARATIONS AND GETTING STARTED

Leadership

Vegetation sampling is time consuming and demanding (Table 1). Good leadership is essential to maintaining enthusiasm and quality of data collection. The principal investigator can demonstrate leadership by (1) being

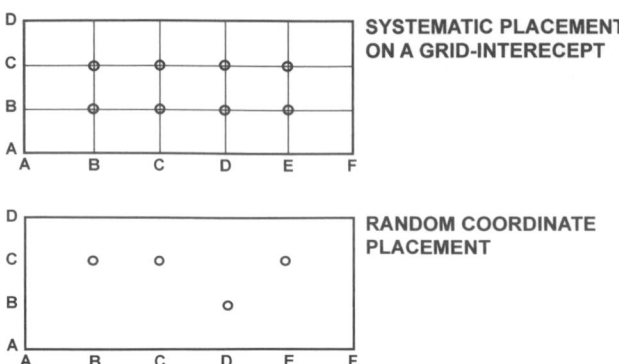

Fig. 2. Systematic and random placement of quadrats with grid coordinates.

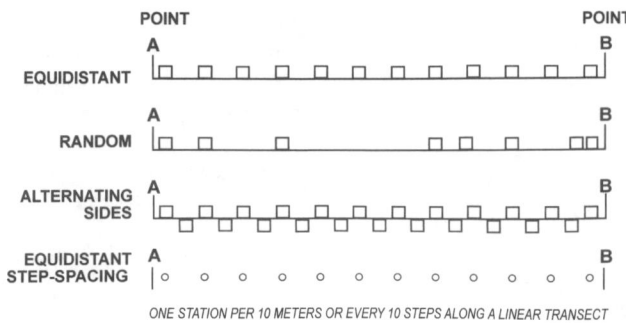

ONE STATION PER 10 METERS OR EVERY 10 STEPS ALONG A LINEAR TRANSECT

Fig. 3. Examples of patterns of quadrat placement along permanent transect lines.

enthusiastic and knowledgeable about the study area, research design, equipment, plant identification, and data collection, (2) being organized and efficient during all aspects of vegetation sampling, (3) explaining to other team members how the data will be used to make decisions on resource management, and (4) doing their share of the data collection. The principal investigator also should listen to suggestions from team members. They often have ideas that make data collection more efficient. Explaining the entire project, answering questions, and incorporating appropriate suggestions will make team members feel they are an integral part of the project (and they are!).

Initial Planning and Preparation

Considerable office preparation is required before the team goes into the field to conduct a vegetation study. The development of a list of supplies and equipment necessary to complete the task (Table 2) is an important first step. Equipment lists will vary, depending on sampling objectives and whether sampling is in grasslands, wetlands, shrublands, or woodlands. These lists should be all-inclusive and should include everything from the number of pencils, color of data sheets and plot markers, and size and shape of the sampling frame, to calipers, photometers, seed traps, and field vehicles.

Data Forms.—Develop forms for recording the field data. Even though major advances have been made with entry of field data directly into laptop computers at the time of sampling, most data still are recorded on paper forms. Field data forms can be developed to facilitate simple mathematical analysis with conventional calculators or to facilitate entry onto a personal computer for detailed and complex analysis. In either situation, a set of instruction codes defining what is represented by each number or letter entry should accompany each field data form. Team members must understand the meaning of zeros and blank spaces. Although a blank space usually means no value was available to measure or no attempt was made to make a measurement, we have found that a hash mark rather than a blank space reduces confusion about whether the blanks were accidental or intentional. We suggest use of different color forms for different sampling tasks to aid organization and recording efficiency. For example, one color might be used for sampling shrub density and another for herbaceous cover when both were measured at a site and required use of 2 different sampling techniques. White paper reflects direct sunlight, and the investigator may want to use colored paper to reduce eyestrain. Waterproof or water-legible paper is more convenient and reliable than regular bond in regions with frequent rainfall or snow.

Preliminary Field Test.—It is important and useful to conduct a small-scale preliminary field test of a site before initiating full-scale sampling with the entire team. This field test provides the investigator with an opportunity to identify and collect plants for field mounts (Burleson 1975) for technician use, evaluate and test equipment and sampling methods, evaluate and adjust experimental design, and make final estimates of the time required to complete the work. Many research projects and surveys that were designed in the office have been completely abandoned after the first day of fieldwork because the investigator failed to test the procedures and equipment under field conditions.

Training The Field Crew.—An important step to maximize field efficiency is to properly train field assistants. Field assistants should have a thorough understanding of the safe and proper use of equipment, be familiar with the plants and study area, understand the correct methods for collecting and recording the data, and thoroughly understand the rationale of the study so that, in the principal investigator's absence, they can make an intelligent and informed decision when an unforeseen situation arises. We have found that several questions and concerns arise during the first week of data collection even when the crew is adequately trained. We suggest that each day end with a short meeting of the entire field crew to answer questions, inspect data forms for completeness and legibility, and discuss problems encountered in collecting data. We suggest that experienced members be teamed with those less experienced and that membership rotate daily if the field crew is divided into smaller teams for collecting data. Daily rotation of field teams increases the number of questions that arise early in the project, and the prompt settlement of problems results in more uniform collection of data and builds better rapport among crew members.

The principal investigator or field team leader is responsible for quality control of the project. We recommend the principal investigator spend at least one day working with each crew member early in the field season. This provides the opportunity to discuss the project more fully, provide assistance and guidance in field methodologies, demonstrate enthusiasm about the project, and learn more about the background and interests of the individual crew members. These all contribute to building a quality field team and improving the quality of data collected. An important

Table 1. Representative times to complete a transect or a number of plots for different vegetative sampling techniques in various habitats or for different purposes. The numbers are relative, so they may not meet any specific project; however, they should help the investigator during initial planning. The times were derived from published literature, personal communication, and personal experience.

Sampling technique	Habitat type or vegetative component or unit site	Estimated time necessary to complete a plot, a practicable number of sample plots, or a transect by 1 to 3 persons	Minimum and range of plots usually necessary to characterize the community vegetative structure	References
Grassland				
30.5-m transect, line-intercept method for basal area		1.8–2.5 hr/transect[a]		Johnson 1957
30.5-m transect, point quadrat for basal area		0.5–0.8 hr/transect[a]		Johnson 1957
30.5-m transect, loop method for basal area		0.3–0.4 hr/transect[a]		Johnson 1957
0.30-m² clipped plots	California annual grasses	7 min/plot		Reppert et al. 1962
2.9-m² circular plots, clipped all species	Southeastern U.S.	32 min/plot, one person		Hilmon 1959
Single-point basal-hit Sampling	Tallgrass prairie	7 hr/3,000–4,000 points/ 3 persons	~ 25 ha	Owensby 1973
Foliage density readings (Robel et al. 1970)	Any grassland	8 hr/1,000 readings/ 2 persons	10 sites	J. M. Callow, personal communication
Nudds-board foliage density readings (Nudds 1977)	Any grassland	8 hr/100–200 readings/ 2 persons		L. D. Flake, personal communication
10-pin point frame (Smith 1959)	Mixed and tallgrass prairie	8 hr/4,000–6,000 points/ 2 persons		L. L. Manske, personal communication
10-pin point frame (Smith 1959)	Wet meadow wetland	8 hr/2,000–3,000 points/ 2 persons		L. L. Manske, personal communication
Shrubs				
Shrub dimension/ Production estimates	Boreal forest	2 hr/25 plants/2 persons		Peek 1970
3- × 5-m clipped plots	Boreal forest	24.7 hr/17 plots[a]		Bobek and Bergstrom 1978
Height × diameter measurements in 3- × 5-m plots	Boreal forest	2.3 hr/21 plots[a]		Bobek and Bergstrom 1978
Clipped plots	Southern forests	10–50 plots/2 person-days	28–158/site	Harlow 1977
Twig-length method to measure browse use	Montane shrub	50 min/50 plants/2 persons	50/site	Jensen and Scotter 1977
30.5-m² plot, weight-estimation method for twig production	Eastern deciduous forest	1.5 hr/41 plots/2 persons		Shafer 1963
30.5-m² plot, twig-count method for twig production	Eastern deciduous forest	1.5 hr/39 plots/2 persons		Shafer 1963
30.5-m² plot, clip and weigh for twig production	Eastern deciduous forest	6.5 hr/37 plots/2 persons		Shafer 1963
30.5-m line-point transect, sample every 0.30 m for shrub cover	Chaparral	7 min/transect[a]	4–26 transects/site	Heady et al. 1959
30.5-m line-intercept for shrub cover	Chaparral	16 min/transect[a]	9–13 transects/site	Heady et al. 1959
0.1- × 0.5-m quadrats for shrub cover	Shrub steppe	15–30 min/80 quadrats/ 2 persons		Hanley 1978
1.2- × 7.6-m plot for shrub cover mapping	Shrub steppe	12 plots/day/2 persons		Pickford and Stewart 1935

(continued on next page)

Table 1 (*continued*).

Sampling technique	Habitat type or vegetative component or unit site	Estimated time necessary to complete a plot, a practicable number of sample plots, or a transect by 1 to 3 persons	Minimum and range of plots usually necessary to characterize the community vegetative structure	References
1- × 5-m quadrats for shrub density	Boreal forest (postburn)	50 quadrats/day[a]		Oldemeyer and Regelin 1980, K. J. Jenkins, personal communication
Trees				
0.1-ha circular plots	Upland forest	10–15/day[a]	5–20 needed/site	Lindsey et al. 1958, James and Shugart 1970
Point-centered quarter method	Upland forest	20–50/day	10–50 needed/site	Lindsey et al. 1958, James and Shugart 1970
Bitterlich variable radius sampling	Upland forest	40–75/day[a]	10–50 needed/site	Lindsey et al. 1958, James and Shugart 1970
Camera on a stick	Grassland	36 images of scanned 35-mm slides could be analyzed for total cover in 2.5 hours		Bennett et al. 2000
Visual obstruction readings	Grassland	20 stations/transect in 25 minutes		Benkobi et al. 2000
Clip	Grassland	6 0.25-m² circular quadrats in 45 minutes		Benkobi et al. 2000

[a] One to 2 persons were used to collect data in specified time.

point is to make sure all crew members have a personal stake in the quality of data collected. Emphasize creating a sense of "ownership" in the outcome of the project.

TECHNIQUES FOR SAMPLING VEGETATION
Frequency of Occurrence

Frequency is the proportion of sample units in which a species occurs (Bonham 1989). If, for example, 50 small plots were examined in a study site and bitterbrush (*Purshia tridentata*) occurred in 20 of those plots, the frequency of bitterbrush would be 20/50 × 100, or 40%. Frequency is an easy attribute to estimate because the plant either occurs in the sample unit or it does not (Fig. 4). Frequency is a useful characteristic for describing distribution of plants within a community and it is a measure that is related to plant density (Mueller-Dombois and Ellenberg 1974). It is also useful for monitoring changes in the plant

community over time or comparing different communities (Bonham 1989). If frequency is low (<15%), plants have an aggregated distribution (occur in clumps) within the community. When frequency is high (>90%), plants are uniformly distributed. Most statistical procedures rely on plants being randomly distributed, i.e., having a frequency of 63–86% (Bonham 1989:92). Wild plants generally have an aggregated distribution that is related to the morphological characteristics of the species in the community, the extent and nature of competitive interaction among individuals and species, and environmental patterns (e.g., differences in soil characteristics, fire history, herbivory, etc.) (West 1989). Thus, each species may have its own distributional pattern and the pattern of the plant community may be different from those of component species. Sampling methods to deal with complex plant distribution patterns are not adequately developed (West 1989). In an attempt to identify a best method of sampling complex

Table 2. Supplies and equipment needed in the field for vegetation sampling.

Data forms and notebooks	Metal tags and wire
Camera and film	Quadrat frame
Pencils and ink pens	Sunscreen lotion
Hammer and hatchet	Cover board
Rulers and tape measures	Insect repellent
Transect markers	Point frame
Plant identification guides	Hand gloves
Shovel and hand trowel	Hand magnifying lens
Plant press	Backpack on frame
Knife	Maps and aerial photos
Tags and plastic bags	Compass

Fig. 4. Color demarcation and subplot frame attachments (bottom) are also used to provide quick representation of percentage of frame coverage of vegetation.

Fig. 5. An inclined 10-pin frame for frequency estimates.

communities, Etchberger and Krausman (1997) evaluated 5 methods of measuring plant species occurrence in complex desert vegetation communities where they had a complete census of the vegetation. They found that using a line-intercept method whereby the plants that intercept the line are counted as hits rather than measuring the length of vegetation canopy intercepting the line most closely estimated the true vegetation census.

Frequency varies with size and shape of the sample unit when compared over time or among communities. Consequently, sample unit size and shape must remain constant because it is difficult, if not impossible, to compare frequency data among sampling sites when different sizes and shapes of quadrats have been used. The size and shape of the sample unit is a function of whether one is sampling herbaceous vegetation, shrubs, or trees. Cain and Castro (1959:146) presented sample unit sizes for different forms of vegetation.

Herbaceous vegetation	1–2 m^2
Tall herbs and low shrubs	4 m^2
Tall shrubs and low trees	10 m^2
Trees	100 m^2

When the total vegetation of a community is sampled, one size of sample unit will not adequately sample frequency for each form of vegetation. The mean frequency of the several species within a given vegetation form should not be <5% or >95% (Hyder et al. 1965). Nesting plots of different sizes within each other can solve this problem. Preliminary surveys of vegetation may be made using the size recommendations of Cain and Castro (1959). Further refinements of sample unit size may then be made by use of the relationship between density and frequency suggested by Hyder et al. (1965).

Plots may be square, rectangular, or round. Ordinarily, plot boundaries are either marked or measured to size with a ruler or tape measure or they are defined by the inside dimensions of a frame (Fig. 4). Frames may be of permanent shape and made of welded steel rod or some other rigid material, or they may be collapsible and made with hinged wood products or jointed PVC pipe. Collapsible frames are useful when they enhance efficiency of placement on the ground or travel to remote areas that are inaccessible to vehicle use. We have found that frames with

one open end are useful for placing the plot around shrubs or other obstructions in shrubby terrain.

Frequency also may be measured with points. A pin (knitting needle or pointed, small-diameter steel rod) is lowered to the ground over herbaceous cover and will either hit or miss a plant part (Fig. 5). The percentage of hits gives an estimate of the frequency of a species. A single pin may be used to measure frequency (or cover) (Owensby 1973), or, commonly, a frame containing several (usually 10) pins is used and pins may be positioned vertically or at an inclined angle. Spacing of the pins within the frame is dependent on the vegetative type, but it is commonly 4–15 cm (Hays et al. 1981). Although the point frame can be placed in random locations, pins are usually spaced systematically. Single point sampling is self-descriptive. Cook and Stubbendieck (1986) provided useful suggestions for making a 10-pin frame. Along a 10-pin frame (Fig. 5), the same plant may be intercepted more than once in communities with large-sized or clumped plants. This can result in overestimates of cover for those species (Bonham 1989).

Sample size is a consideration when frequency is estimated. Frequency data have a binomial distribution, and confidence limits are wide for small samples. Grieg-Smith (1964:39) recommended that no fewer than 100 sample units be read to obtain estimates that provide reliable comparisons from one community to another or over time. With a 10-point frame, data from 1,000 (100 frames) points (hits) are usually sufficient to describe grassland vegetation at one location, whereas fewer points (200–500) (20–50 frames) usually will provide data similar to those from a single-point method (Goodall 1952).

Density

Density is the total number of objects (e.g., individual plants, seeds) per unit area. One advantage of the density parameter is that count data are straightforward to obtain and interpret, and results obtained from different methods are directly comparable (Gysel and Lyon 1980). A disadvantage of measuring shrub density is that data are tedious to obtain and often are excessively variable. Such variability requires an often prohibitively large sample size for statistical reliability. Density is a useful and often important measurement for evaluation of wildlife habitat for bunchgrasses, annual grasses and forbs, some shrubs, and trees.

However, by itself, density is not an adequate descriptor of a plant community because it does not provide information about how plants are distributed within the community. With frequency, density provides a good description of a plant community. With biomass of individual plants, density may provide estimates of total biomass within a plant community.

The definition of an individual plant poses a problem when density is sampled. For perennial grasses and forbs, and shrubs that produce several stems from below ground, definition of an individual plant may be impossible or not sufficiently important to warrant the effort or the potential error. However, individual plant identity may be necessary in studies of plant succession whereas counting the number of stems, etc., may be sufficient when the objective is to quantify cover or food availability. In these situations, frequency combined with some other measurement, such as cover, may provide more useful descriptions of the plant community. For shrubs, the problem is best resolved either by counting stems at ground level, thereby eliminating the need to define an individual shrub, or by establishing a distance criterion to define individuals arbitrarily. For example, Lyon (1968a) considered stems rooted within 15 cm of each other to represent a single shrub, whereas those sprouting more than 15 cm apart were counted as separate individuals.

Quadrat Methods.—Density can be measured with either quadrats or plotless methods. Quadrats are made of materials with fixed boundaries whereas plotless methods are estimated occularly. If quadrats are used, the investigator must distribute quadrats of uniform size representatively throughout each experimental unit and then count each individual within each quadrat. Quadrats require that 3 characteristics be considered (Bonham 1989): (1) distribution of the plants, (2) size and shape of the quadrat, and (3) number of observations needed to obtain adequate estimates of frequency and density.

Sample frames typically are rectangular, square, or circular. Rectangular plots have the largest perimeter per unit area and the most edge where decisions must be made about including or excluding the plant. Circular quadrats often are more efficient to use than square or rectangular quadrats. Sampling in circular quadrats also is effective for characterizing the vicinity around a point of interest, such as a nest, a den location, or a feeding or resting site. A review of recent wildlife habitat studies reveals frequent use of circular quadrats, which are typically in the range of 0.01-0.1 ha (e.g., Hirst 1975, Pierce and Peek 1984, Ratti et al. 1984, Wiggers and Beasom 1986, Degraaf and Chadwick 1987, Edge et al. 1987, Bentz and Woodard 1988). For these areas, the radius of a quadrat would range from 5.6 to 17.8 m. Increasing the size of a quadrat generally results in lower variance and reduces the perimeter:area ratio (Bonham 1989). Numerous studies have evaluated quadrat size, and no consistent recommendation has been made about the size to use for herbaceous vegetation, shrubs, or trees.

For herbaceous vegetation, 1×1-m quadrats frequently are used (Bonham 1989). However, in dense vegetation, smaller quadrats such as 20×50 cm may be appropriate. Eddleman et al. (1964) compared quadrats of 4 sizes and several shapes in alpine vegetation. They recommended against using 100-cm^2 plots because of high standard devi-

ations and highest frequencies of <50%. Even though plot sizes >400-cm^2 provided similar estimates of density, they favored 400-cm^2 rectangular plots because the chance for counting error was reduced and fewer rectangular plots were required (over square plots of the same size) to obtain a 10% standard error of the mean.

Quadrats sufficiently large to contain an average of 4 individuals have been recommended in shrub communities (Curtis and McIntosh 1950, Cottam and Curtis 1956). Although quadrats as small as 1 m^2 have been used to measure shrub density (Alaback 1982), 4 to 10-m^2 plots are more commonly selected (Irwin and Peek 1979). Oldemeyer and Regelin (1980) recommended a 1×5-m quadrat over a 2×5-m quadrat in an Alaskan shrub community because the smaller quadrat provided nearly the same precision and required only one-half the sampling time as the larger quadrat. Rectangular plots have advantages over square and circular plots in aggregated shrub communities because they have the greatest chance of overlapping individual clusters of shrubs. A rectangular quadrat 1 m wide of any length may be delineated easily by marking one long side of the rectangle with 2 chaining pins and a chain, and using a meter stick to define the remaining boundaries while one counts shrubs along the strip as the meter stick passes over them.

Quadrats must be quite large when trees are sampled, typically in the range of 0.01–0.1 ha. Curtis (1959) used square quadrats 10 m on a side (0.01 ha) in deciduous and coniferous forests of Wisconsin. Mueller-Dombois and Ellenberg (1974) concluded that forest quadrats typically should be squares of 10 or 20 m on a side (0.01 or 0.04 ha). Quadrats can be positioned with tape measures or other measuring devices and surveyor's pins after sampling points are located. This might require considerable time and effort in dense vegetation or in some types of terrain. To reduce that time, Penfound and Rice (1957) proposed using an elongated 0.0004-ha quadrat established by measuring the width of one's outstretched arms and then, knowing the average pace length, walking the appropriate number of paces along a compass line and recording the trees within reach. It is important to realize that, although this method is faster to implement under natural forest conditions, the area sampled is approximate, and accuracy is sacrificed without careful attention. Further, the advent of laser rangefinders now favors use of circular plots as an alternative, relatively quick method of estimating tree density. From any established plot center, the field biologist using a laser rangefinder may quickly estimate distances of trees from plot center. Thus, the biologist may quickly count all trees present within a predetermined fixed radius. The method has the added advantage of minimizing the perimeter:area ratio of the sample plot, but care must be exercised to ensure the laser rangefinder being used is both accurate and precise.

The number of samples measured varies from community to community and among the different vegetation forms within a community. Because many species are not randomly distributed, variation normally is quite high and number of samples required is quite large. To calculate sample size, one can use results from the preliminary field test to obtain an estimate of the variance for use in the sample size equation (Garton et al. 2005). Frequently, less common species require a larger number of samples than

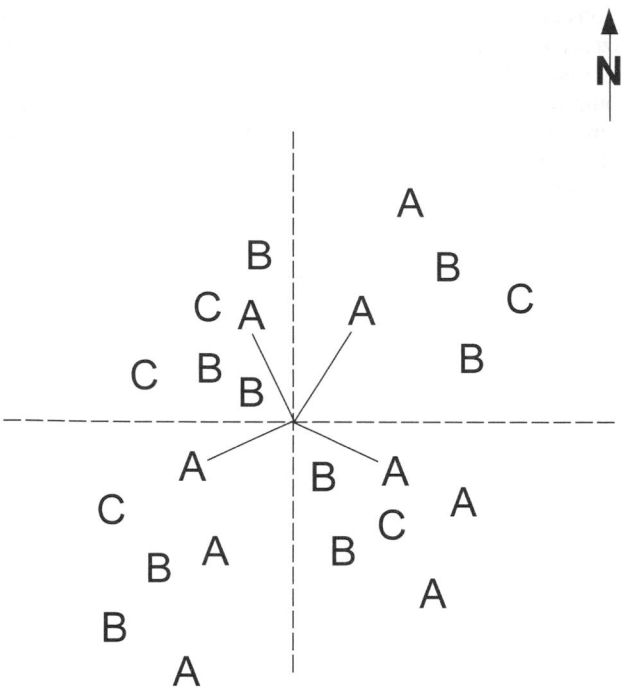

Fig. 6. Point-centered quadrat sampling wherein the point-to-plant distance is measured for the individual of each species nearest the point in each of the 90° quadrants around the point.

do the more common species. For example, to obtain a 10% standard error of the mean in a 10 × 40-cm plot, Eddleman et al. (1964) concluded that 816 plots would be required for a species with a density of 0.13 (no area units given), whereas 69 plots would be required for a species with a density of 5.6. Oldemeyer and Regelin (1980) reported that 50 1 × 5-m quadrats produced estimates of shrub density within 2 standard errors of actual (counted) shrub densities. Lyon (1968*a*), however, reported that >400 1.5 × 6.1-m quadrat samples would be necessary to obtain an estimate of shrub density within 10% of the true mean 95% of the time. Sample sizes in the hundreds are not an uncommon result. As an alternative, one may plot the running mean density against the number of samples taken (Kershaw 1964). One may stop sampling when the density of the target, or more abundant, species does not significantly change with additional quadrats. Mueller-Dombois and Ellenberg (1974:77) suggested that sampling stop when the running mean of a sample is within 5–10% of a "maximum" sample. Clearly, one must critically evaluate the objectives of a project and the end product of the data when designing a study of plant density. It may not be necessary to have the density (or frequency or cover) estimate be within 5% of the true value; however, it is a waste of time and effort to undersample a community and obtain totally unreliable estimates.

Plotless Methods.—Plotless methods of sampling density have been in use since the 1950s. These methods do not use boundaries and are based on the premise that density may be estimated from the mean area occupied per tree; i.e., density (trees/m²) = 1/mean area (m²/tree). The challenge then becomes estimating the area occupied per tree from distance measurements that can be obtained in the field.

Cottam and associates (Cottam and Curtis 1949, Cottam et al. 1953, Cottam and Curtis 1956) pioneered research on plotless methods. These included the closest individual method, nearest-neighbor method, random-pairs method, and point-centered-quarter method. Of these, the point-centered-quarter method has been widely used in many vegetation types throughout North America. Using this method, one randomly or systematically selects a number of points within a community and measures the distance to the nearest plant within each of 4 quadrants around the point (Fig. 6). Mean area is calculated by squaring the mean distance between points and individual stems:

$$\text{density} = 1/d^2.$$

This method may be used to calculate density of all species collectively. Or, density of individual species can be estimated by measuring distances to each species in every quadrant around each point. A reliable estimate of an individual species' density cannot be obtained by using only those distances for an individual of the species that was the closest plant in a sample and the distance was measured to the nearest plant regardless of species. That is, if 25 points were sampled, and distances to 100 plants of several species were measured, the density of all plants can be estimated based on the 100 distances. The density of one of the several species from the sample cannot be estimated reliably, because the distance measured to the plant when it was the closest plant in a particular quadrant may not be the least distance when all plants of that species within the entire circle around the point are considered (e.g., species A in Fig. 6).

The point-centered-quarter method has been criticized because it provides reliable estimates of density only when plants are distributed randomly and not when plants are clumped or uniformly distributed. Studying stands of known density, Oldemeyer and Regelin (1980) concluded this method accurately estimated density of white spruce (*Picea glauca*) saplings, which were more randomly distributed, but underestimated density of paper birch (*Betula papyrifera*) and aspen (*Populus tremuloides*) saplings, which had clumped distributions. The point-centered-quarter method overestimates density in communities with regularly distributed plants (Mueller-Dombois and Ellenberg 1974). This method likely provides reliable estimates of density when total plant density within a community is the only concern. However, Laycock and Batcheler (1975) reported that evaluating composition from the proportion of times each species occurred in the total measurements resulted in biased composition estimates.

Methods have been developed to correct for density estimates in nonrandom plant populations (Morisita 1957, Batcheler 1973). The angle-order method (Morisita 1957) measures the distance from the point to the center of the third nearest plant in each quadrant around the point. This method is based on the assumption that the area may be divided into several smaller units in which the plants will be distributed randomly or uniformly even though they are distributed nonrandomly over the larger area. The method was tested on known populations of grasses, forbs, and shrubs (Laycock and Batcheler 1975, Oldemeyer and Regelin 1980) and provided estimates of density that were more accurate than those of the point-centered-quarter method. Oldemeyer and Regelin (1980) reported the method provided density estimates closest to the true density in shrub stands and that it's coefficient of variation was lower than other accurate estimators. However, because of the time required, Laycock (1965) recommended against using the angle-order method when density is measured for each species within a community. Bonham (1989) provided a detailed description of the procedures for calculating density and the variance when the angle-order method is used.

The corrected-point-distance (Batcheler 1973) is a modification of the point-centered-quarter that uses measurements to the second and third nearest plants to correct for nonrandomness. That is, from a sample point, one measures the distance to the nearest plant, the distance from that plant to its nearest neighbor, and the distance from the nearest neighbor to its nearest neighbor, exclusive of the first plant measured. In aggregated populations, the distance between the nearest plant and its nearest neighbor is generally less than the distance from the point to the nearest plant. Density is calculated by the equation:

$$ m = \frac{a}{\pi \, [\sum r_i^2 + (N-1)R^2]} $$

where m = density, R = the maximum distance over which a search is made for a plant at any point, a = number of points at which a plant is found at a distance $\leq R$, and r_i = the ith distance measured. As R decreases, m approaches the true density; however, variance generally will increase because fewer measurements are included (Bonham 1989). Although this equation is designed for random and nonrandom distributions, densities will be biased in nonrandom populations (Bonham 1989). This problem may be corrected by using a factor based on distances from the nearest plant to its nearest neighbor. Laycock and Batcheler (1975) recommended use of the corrected-point-distance method over other distance methods because the density estimate was within 12% of the true density and because the method is relatively fast and easy to use.

Recently, Engeman et al. (1994) reviewed 24 plotless density estimators and compared the relative biases among methods in relation to simulated differences in plant aggregation patterns. These simulated results verified field results described above, indicating that when plant distributions are clumped, the point-centered-quarter method produces biased results compared to angle-order methods. The authors observe, however, that the added effort of measuring several plants per quarter complicates the method and results in fewer sample points. Generally, for any fixed amount of effort it is better to sample more independent points than to invest more effort at individual points. Based on this practical consideration and the evaluation of bias under simulated conditions, Engeman et al. (1994) recommend using ordered-distance (Morisita 1957, Pollard 1971) or variable area transect (Parker 1979) sampling methods for estimating density. The ordered-distance estimator involves measuring distance to the third closest tree to sampling points. The variable area transect involves measuring the distance along a fixed-width strip transect (generally 1–2 m in most field applications) until the gth individual tree is encountered (generally g = 3). The review paper by Engeman et al. (1994) or the original authors should be consulted for the analytical formulae.

The choice of using a plotless method over a quadrat method will depend on the objectives of the study. If the density of 1 or 2 species is required, plotless methods appear to be faster than quadrat methods. If the density of all species in the community is desired, the quadrat method is recommended.

Cover

Cover is defined as the vertical projection of the crown or stem of a plant onto the ground surface. Canopy cover serves as a criterion for relative dominance within a community and is of practical importance because of its influence on interception of light or precipitation and on soil temperature (Hanley 1978). It may be used by plant ecologists to describe total vegetation cover, by range managers to define cover of forage for livestock, or by foresters to describe basal area of merchantable timber. Cover can be an estimator of biomass when height structure of a community is known. Daubenmire (1959) suggested that canopy cover is the surface area over which a plant has influence, thus, cover provided by seedlings and seed stalks might not be measured because they have little influence in the ecosystem. Although canopy or crown cover may vary within a season or among years, basal cover is relatively stable. Basal cover is a reliable measurement for bunchgrasses, tussocks, and trees. Cover is frequently measured at a height of about 2 cm on bunchgrasses and tussocks (Bonham 1989:98), whereas on single-stemmed trees it is measured at 1.5 m above ground (Mueller-Dombois and Ellenberg 1974:88). This latter measurement is referred to as diameter at breast height or DBH. Basal cover is measured at the ground surface on trees with multiple stems or on trees with buttressed trunks. Cover often is expressed in percent and, in a dense or multilayered community, total vegetation cover may exceed 100%. Cover can be measured directly with quadrat-charting (Gibbens and Beck 1988) or pantographic methods (Mueller-Dombois and Ellenberg 1974, Fehmi and Bartolome 2001), an ocular-estimation technique (Daubenmire 1959, Mueller-Dombois and Ellenberg 1974), or line-intercept (Canfield 1941), and point-intercept methods (Levy and Madden 1933, Owensby 1973).

Quadrat-charting Method.—This method has its greatest utility in low, herbaceous vegetation where one can stand and look over the vegetation. Cover is mapped to scale on graph paper from a small quadrat (e.g., 1 m²). The idea is to map the crown area or the basal area onto the graph paper. This may be facilitated by subdividing the larger quadrats into smaller quadrats. Quadrat charting is useful generally only in long-term studies when quadrats are permanently marked at each corner and can be exactly relocated for each measurement (Gibbens and Beck 1988). Rather than charting indirectly from what the observer sees on the ground, the observer may use a pantograph (Mueller-Dombois and Ellenberg 1974) or take photographs (Wimbush et al. 1967).

Ocular Estimates.—Ocular estimates of basal and canopy cover can be obtained with relative ease in grasslands because of their low profile and height. However, the task becomes more difficult in wetland vegetation because of the combination of water depth and plant height, often requiring use of SCUBA equipment or a ladder.

Cover can be estimated to the nearest percentage point, or to the nearest 5th or 10th percentile; however, most commonly it is estimated according to some form of cover class (Brown 1954, Daubenmire 1959, Braun-Blanquet et al. 1965, Mueller-Dombois and Ellenberg 1974, Floyd and Anderson 1987).

A cover-class scale (below) often has been used in grasslands (Daubenmire 1959). Division of class range (%) is facilitated by painting lengths on the frame in different colors. Zero has been used separately as a data integer by some users.

Scale of Cover Classes for a 2- × 5-dm Quadrat

Data integer	Class range (%)	Midpoint (%)
1	0–5	2.5
2	5–25	15.0
3	25–50	37.5
4	50–75	62.5
5	75–95	85.0
6	95–100	97.5

A variety of plot sizes has been used to estimate vegetation cover (Brummer et al. 1994). Daubenmire (1959) recommended using 20 × 50 cm quadrats for both shrubs and herbaceous vegetation because cover is more easily estimated in small quadrats. However, data from a transect, generally having 20–30 quadrats, are summed into one mean for each variable. The transect is the basic unit of sampling. Meter-square frames also have been commonly used to estimate shrub cover. Cook and Bonham (1977) suggested dividing 1-m^2 frames into 5 × 5-cm cells, each corresponding to 0.25% cover. One may estimate cover with a gridded quadrat by counting the number of grid cells covered by shrubs and adding the number of obstructed cells to calculate the total percentage. Although ocular estimation is a rapid method of estimating data on basal or canopy cover, there are drawbacks. Ocular estimates are subject to personal bias, thus estimation error among investigators may add unnecessary variability to the data. Hence, these methods require consistent training and calibration among investigators. Dimensions of plant cover, even on permanently marked plots, also are subject to the influences of precipitation, heat, and sunlight on plant growth. Consequently, care must be exercised in data interpretation, because a reduction in the cover of a species on the same plot in different years may be a result of drought as much as of interspecies competition for the same site.

Line-intercept.—The line-intercept method is particularly suited for measuring basal area of bunchgrasses or tussocks and canopy cover of shrubs, particularly in arid or semiarid lands (e.g., sagebrush [*Artemisia* spp.]; see Connelly et al. 2003). The identification of intercept can be quite difficult and prone to error in less clumped forms of vegetation. In this technique, a line or tape measure is placed between 2 stakes, and basal width or canopy width of all plants touching the line or tape is measured, even if only a small part of the plant is in contact with the tape. Cover is expressed as a percent of the total length of tape intercepted by vertical projections of the canopy. Keeping a tape line taut and straight may be difficult in tall, dense vegetation. Canfield (1941) reported that a minimum of 16 15–30-m transects was necessary to adequately describe

shrub vegetation in Arizona rangelands. A 15.2-m transect was adequate in shrub fields with 5–15% shrub cover, whereas a 30.4-m transect was necessary on sites with <5% cover.

The principal advantages of the line-intercept method are the high level of accuracy and precision that are attributed to direct measurement of vegetation rather than estimation (Cook and Stubbendieck 1986, Connelly et al. 2003). The main limitation of the method is the time required to measure intercepts compared to estimating cover within quadrats. Hanley (1978) reported that line-intercept and quadrat sampling methods produced comparable estimates of shrub cover in a semiarid shrubland. Of the 2 methods, the line-intercept method was more precise, whereas the quadrat method was quicker. Hanley (1978) concluded the line-interception method is preferable to 0.1-m^2 quadrats in scientific research when precision of the cover estimate may be more important than cost efficiency. The 0.1-m^2 quadrat method may be preferable when lower levels of statistical confidence are acceptable. Based on comparisons of several techniques, Floyd and Anderson (1987) and Etchberger and Krausman (1997) found the line-intercept method was equal to or better than alternative methods.

Point-intercept.—Basal and canopy cover also may be measured as the percentage of points whose vertical or angled projections intercept vegetation. The point intercept method is best suited for estimating cover of herbaceous and low shrub vegetation, but also has been used to estimate leaf-area index in sagebrush steppe communities (Clark and Seyfried 2001). For relatively large-scale surveys of plant cover, points may be defined by putting a v-shaped notch or line in the tip of a boot and using the notch or line as a single point (Evans and Love 1957, Etchberger and Krausman 1997) while walking over a tract of grassland. This method offers rapid assessment or survey of cover, but it may be prone to observer bias and less repeatable than other point-sampling methods. When more precision is required, generally at a smaller scale of study, points may be defined with a multiple point frame (Levy and Madden 1933, Cook and Stubbendieck 1986) or a single point frame (Owensby 1973). With either method, a single pin is lowered towards the ground. The first strike of any part of the vegetation canopy becomes a canopy cover hit; if it strikes the basal area of a plant it is a basal hit. Often a pin will miss all vegetation in its line of travel. Percent canopy or basal cover is calculated as the total number of hits divided by the total number of pin placements times 100. The diameter of the pin and the point affect the accuracy of cover estimates. Because a point does not have a diameter, and the pin point does have a diameter, cover is generally somewhat overestimated (Winkworth 1955). The point-intercept method is frequently used along transect lines. The user should be aware the line is the sample unit and that it is better to have fewer points per line and more lines than vice versa (Bonham 1989).

Heady et al. (1959) reported that line-transect and point-intercept procedures produced comparable estimates of shrub cover when ground cover was >3%; however, the point-intercept procedure was quicker and thus preferable. Species with ≤3% cover required extremely large samples with the point-intercept method. Thus, the line-interception procedure should be used in sparse shrub communities.

Sampling and Measuring

Bitterlich Variable Radius Method.—The Bitterlich variable radius method is a modified point-sampling method developed for use in forestry (Bitterlich 1948, Grosenbaugh 1952) to measure basal area of trees. The method was subsequently modified for use in range habitats to measure canopy cover of shrubs (Cooper 1957). Hyder and Sneva (1960) recommended the method for sampling basal cover of bunchgrasses. Shrubs or trees are viewed with one of several types of sighting devices (angle gauges) that delimit a certain sighting angle from randomly located sampling points (Cooper 1957, Mueller-Dombois and Ellenberg 1974:102). The sighting device must be held as nearly horizontal as possible. Shrubs with widths or trees with trunks larger in diameter than a specified angle when seen through the sighting device are reported. To be included in the count, small shrubs or trees must be relatively close to the observer, but larger ones can be farther away and yet exceed the viewing angle. The probabilities of species being sampled are proportional to their size, and the correction factor needed to calculate cover depends on size of the viewing angle. Percentage cover is defined as:

$$P = [(n \times W^2)/L^2] \times 25,$$

where P = percent cover, W = the width of the crosspiece of the sighting device, L = the distance of the crosspiece from the observer's eye, and n = the number of plants counted. Using a sighting device with a width:length ratio of 1:50 gives a viewing angle of 1 degree, 10 minutes, and the count of trees within that angle is numerically equal to the tree basal area in square meters per hectare (Mueller-Dombois and Ellenberg 1974). Generally, a ratio of 1:7.07 is most acceptable for shrub communities (Fisser 1961, Cooper 1963), and the average count per plot is divided by the correction factor 2. Correction factors for different width crosspieces used for sampling shrubs were given by Cooper (1957).

Clear-glass prisms have largely replaced wooden sighting sticks as a means of measuring basal areas of trees (Dilworth 1989). The prism is a wedge-shaped piece of glass that refracts light rays to establish the critical angle used to estimate basal area of tree stems. In using the prism, the observer holds the prism immediately over the sample point while viewing tree stems both through the glass and over the top of the prism. Distance of the prism from the viewer's eyes is not a factor as long as tree stems appear clearly when viewed through the glass. Viewed through the prism, tree trunks appear displaced to one side due to refraction of light passing through the glass. Basal area is calculated by recording the number of trees whose trunks, when viewed through the prism, appear displaced within the trunkline of the actual tree. The tree is not recorded if the trunk viewed through the prism is completely displaced beyond the trunkline. Trees whose displaced trunklines are even with the actual trunk are counted as a half tree. Prisms are readily available through most forestry equipment suppliers and come in a variety of metric and English "Basal Area Factors" that are used to convert stem counts to basal area per hectare or acre, respectively. The stem count per sample point multiplied by the Basal Area Factor gives the total basal area of stems (m² or ft²) per unit of area (ha or ac). Generally, a Basal Area Factor should be chosen that gives a tree count of 4–8 trees per point (Dilworth 1989).

The utility of the variable-plot method for sampling shrub stands is influenced by several factors. The method assumes the plant is round. Thus, the estimate of cover will be overestimated for species or stands with shrub crowns, particularly of irregular shape. Individual shrubs or trees that should be counted, but are shielded from view by another plant may be missed in dense stands. Cooper (1957) reported the method could be used in desert shrub stands when cover was <35%, and Fisser (1961) observed that shorter investigators underestimated cover compared to taller investigators. The chief advantage of the variable-plot method is that it is quick and requires counts rather than measurements in the field. Several studies have shown the variable-plot method produced estimates of cover comparable to those of the line-intercept method in shrub fields with <30% shrub cover (Cooper 1957, Kinsinger et al. 1960, Fisser 1961). Kinsinger et al. (1960) reported that readings from only 3 to 6 variable plots were required to produce the same precision as estimates obtained from 20 30-m long line transects, which required considerably more time to measure. Cooper (1963) reasoned this precision, and the lower coefficients of variation, from the variable-radius method was because of the larger area covered than that with point or line-transect methods. Kinsinger et al. (1960) concluded that within the stated constraints, the variable-plot method was faster and more precise than the line-intercept method, but it could not be used as effectively to study subtle changes in shrub cover.

Tree Canopy Cover.—At times, tree canopy cover is an adequate, perhaps even preferred, measure of overstory structure and composition. In this situation, line or point sampling or ocular estimates within plots can be used to estimate canopy cover. Many workers prefer to use a spherical densiometer (Lemmon 1957) (Fig. 7) for making these estimates. The spherical densiometer uses a curved, gridded mirror that reflects the overstory at a point and provides estimates of relative amounts of the area covered. Although there are variations (Cook et al. 1995), the observer levels the densiometer at about chest height and counts the proportion of quarter cells (etched in the mirror) obscured by the reflected vegetation. Because the mirror is curved, the spherical densiometer measures canopy within a 30-60° angle of view projected upward through the canopy (Cook et al. 1995). Lemmon (1957) concluded: (1) there was no difference in overstory estimates between the spherical densiometer and other instruments used to estimate overstory, (2) variation among replicated measurements increased as overstory cover declined, and (3) reliability was greater when the actual grid count was used rather than broader overstory classes obtained from grouping the counts. Alternative ocular methods of estimating forest overstory cover include sighting tubes (Ganey and Block 1994), moosehorn (Cook et al. 1995), and photographic fisheye lenses (Chan et al. 1986). The moosehorn (Fig. 8) is a sighting tube with a 25-point grid etched in glass on one end. The observer sights through the tube and counts the proportion of dots obscured by overhead vegetation. Because the moosehorn samples a narrower (10°) angle of view than the densiometer, it produces a truer estimate of the vertical projection of canopy on the ground (Bunnel and Vales 1990, Cook et al. 1995).

Fig. 7. A spherical densiometer used to estimate percent overstory cover in woodlands.

Although the moosehorn provides the most accurate assessment of vertical projection of overstory canopy, spherical densiometers also may measure biologically relevant influences of tree canopies on an area (i.e., light interception or angular canopy cover) (Nuttle 1997). The appropriate measurement tool depends upon study objectives and consideration of how tree canopy influences the environmental properties of interest (Nuttle 1997).

Biomass or Standing Crop

One of the best indicators of species importance within a plant community is composition based on dry weight (Daubenmire 1968). Wildlife and land managers frequently require data on biomass or standing crop rather than density or cover because biomass is closely related to forage availability and habitat carrying capacity (Bonham 1989). Herein we use the term biomass to include both live and dead vegetation and synonymously with the term standing crop. Woody biomass and size structure are required to estimate fuel loading, a necessity for formulating fire prescriptions and predicting fire behavior in wildlands. Wildlife managers often are interested in measuring biomass of edible components of browse such as current annual growth, foliage, or twigs. Total biomass and biomass of edible components may be estimated directly by clipping and weighing or indirectly by dimension analyses or through the use of capacitance meters (Gonzalez et al. 1990).

Clipping Techniques.—Plant biomass can be measured directly by removing all of the vegetation in a sample plot to ground level and measuring its mass immediately

(wet mass) or after air- or oven-drying the sample (dry mass). Clipping, drying, and weighing plant material directly is accomplished with minimal variation in results among investigators; however, proper implementation of methods necessary to obtain good data is both labor and time intensive. For consistency, herbage should be clipped at a specific height or location on the plant and may be separated into edible and inedible portions, depending on the objectives. Mean biomass per unit area then may be estimated as the product of mean biomass per plant (e.g., g/plant) and mean density of plants (e.g., plants/m^2). Sample variance may be computed as the variance of a product (Goodman 1960). Data from a site or transect are pooled into a mean. Variances are calculated from across sites or transects from which harvesting was conducted in each quadrat. Because clipping is a destructive sampling method, new plots must be selected in subsequent sampling periods to avoid the effects of previous sampling activities.

In wetlands, biomass samples of macrophytes may be obtained by harvesting all vegetation within a quadrat frame placed above the sediment level (Whigham et al. 1978). Harvesting consists of clipping plants within floating (Tanner and Drummond 1985) or submerged metal rod frames or within an open-ended cylinder or box enclosures (Sefton 1977, Anderson 1978). Water depth also should be measured near the center of each quadrat and recorded. Clipping can be done easily in conventional waders in shallow (<1 m) wetlands. However, deeper wetlands (>1 m) may require sampling with specialty gear such as swimmer's goggles, wetsuits, or even SCUBA equipment. Vegetation samples should be dried to a constant weight. Drying temperature is dependent on the purpose of the plant materials; if one is interested only in dry weight, then 80 °C for 48 hours may be used. If the plants are to be analyzed for nutritional analysis, lower temperatures (e.g., 60 °C for 48 hours) are required to avoid volatilizing nutritional components. If drying and weighing cannot be done onsite, vegetation samples should be frozen or kept at 4 °C to stop further respiration activity.

The "clip-and-weigh" method may also be used to estimate twig biomass within plots. Clipping all twigs within plots is a highly accurate yet laborious means of measuring browse biomass (Shafer 1963). Several investigations have reported that total browse collection may require 10 to 120 times as long as estimating browse biomass from

Fig. 8. A "moosehorn" densiometer used to estimate percent overstory cover in woodlands.

dimension analysis or twig count methods (Shafer 1963, Uresk et al. 1977, Bobek and Bergstrom 1978). This is an important consideration given high sampling variation inherent in browse estimation.

Ocular Estimations.—Herbage biomass also may be ascertained by ocular estimation techniques (Pechanec and Pickford 1937, Ahmed and Bonham 1982, Ahmed et al. 1983, Stohlgren et al. 1998). Requirements of biomass estimation techniques include intensive training of investigators. This may be facilitated by incorporating double sampling procedures into the activity. Double sampling requires that ocular biomass estimates be made in each quadrat or for each plant and that a subset of quadrats or plants be clipped and weighed after the estimates are made. Weighing the plants helps the observer develop more accurate ocular estimates. Regression of the estimates and actual weights provides an estimator for the plots or plants for which only estimates were made. Procedures to calculate an adequate ratio of clipped to estimated samples were provided by Ahmed and Bonham (1982), Ahmed et al. (1983), and Reich et al. (1993).

Dimension Analyses.—Dimension analysis has been used in forestry for timber attributes and in wildlife and range management for estimating shrub biomass. The technique assumes that plant attributes are related and that one attribute can be predicted from another that is more easily measured (Whittaker 1965). Because clipping, drying, and weighing require so much time, and yet biomass frequently is a critical attribute of a plant community, numerous investigators have developed regression equations of biomass and some more easily measured attribute. Biomass of individual grass plants has been estimated from volume as measured by height and basal diameter (Johnson et al. 1988). Biomass estimates of individual shrubs have been obtained with, as independent variables, measures of basal stem diameter (Telfer 1969b, Brown 1976), maximum plant height (Ohmann et al. 1976), and various crown dimensions including diameter, area, volume, and height $\times$ circumference (Lyon 1968b, Rittenhouse and Sneva 1977, Uresk et al. 1977, Murray and Jacobson 1982). Common forms of the predictive equations include linear ($Y = a + bX$) and power ($Y = a\ b^x$) curves. Traditionally, researchers have linearized the power curve with logarithmic transformations (ln $Y =$ ln $a + b \cdot$ ln x), but such transformations may introduce bias (Baskerville 1972). There is little reason to transform the nonlinear relationships with nonlinear regression procedures commonly available in statistical software packages. Several independent variables may provide satisfactory estimates of shrub biomass (Oldemeyer 1982), but care must be taken to select those variables that provide the best predictive accuracy and that are not correlated.

Generally, one measures stem and crown dimensions from a sample of individual shrubs in the field. The plant material then is clipped, taken to the laboratory, oven-dried, and weighed. A sample of 25 plants per species is usually adequate for calculating predictive equations for total shrub weight (Peek 1970). Care must be taken in the field to adequately sample the full range of plant sizes present, because one may not estimate biomass of plants that fall outside the size-range of plants used to develop the regression. We believe more reliable regression equations may be developed if one stratifies the plants within the

community into size classes, measures the variance of biomass within each size class, and calculates the number of plants to measure within each size class on the basis of the variance. For example, if the relative variance of the largest size class was 20% and if 25 plants were to be measured for the regression analysis, then 5 plants (0.2 $\times$ 25) would be measured from the largest size class.

Weight-dimension relationships of shrubs vary among sites and years (Oldemeyer 1982), making it necessary to test the influence of site factors on the regression parameters if predictive relationships are to be applied to a broad area. Developing separate predictive equations for each shrub species in each vegetation community of the study area is often necessary. Once satisfactory predictive equations have been developed, biomass can be estimated from data on shrub density and shrub biomass estimates without destroying shrubs. Dimension analysis represents a substantial savings in time and expenditure over traditional clip-and-weigh methods when only one, or at most a few, predictive relationships need to be developed for use for a variety of site conditions. Because the method is nondestructive, plants can be measured annually in the permanent plots.

Dimension analysis has been used to estimate twig and foliage production of individual shrubs in the same manner as described above for total aboveground standing-crop biomass. Production estimates for individual shrubs are obtained by measuring a sample of shrubs in the field; the shrubs then are harvested, and all current annual growth of twigs and foliage is clipped, sorted, and dried. Sampling and analytical considerations are the same as for estimating total shrub biomass.

Lyon (1968b) and Peek (1970) reported that total twig production was related linearly to crown volume and crown area with the resulting equation explaining more than 80% of the variation in twig production. Oldemeyer (1982) used multiple regression procedures to estimate twig production as a function of shrub circumference, shrub height, crown length, and number of current annual growth twigs. Despite the high predictive accuracy of the equations, Lyon (1968b) and Peek (1970) warned that production-dimension relationships of shrubs were influenced strongly by site factors and they varied among species, which necessitated developing unique predictive equations for each shrub species on each distinctive "site type." Dimension analysis is a convenient, nondestructive alternative to the traditional clip-and-weigh methods once predictive equations are developed for a particular "site type."

The "twig-count" method (Shafer 1963) for measuring browse biomass is based on the simple conversion of twig counts to browse weight by using an average weight per individual twig. In its basic form, an average browsing diameter of a particular shrub species is calculated from a random sample of 100 browsed twigs. An average weight per twig then is calculated by weighing 50 unbrowsed twigs clipped at the average browsing diameter. Shafer (1963) suggested counting twigs in 9.3-m^2 circular plots. Twig densities then were converted to biomass estimates from a mean twig weight. Irwin and Peek (1979) observed it was faster and easier to count twigs in 1 $\times$ 1-m or 1 $\times$ 4-m belt transects. Shafer (1963) reported the twig-count method was nearly as accurate as the clip-and-weigh method. The twig-count method is also nondestructive, making it suitable for repeated measurement of permanent

Fig. 9. Cover boards used to index or quantify cover or provide visual record to changes in cover when photographed from the same reference point.

plots. Additionally, individual twigs are easily counted and recorded in different height categories, permitting easy assessment of the influence of snow depth and browsing heights on available browse (Potvin and Huot 1983).

A commonly used modification of Shafer's (1963) twig-count method involves development of weight-diameter or weight-length equations to estimate mean twig weights (Basile and Hutchings 1966, Telfer 1969a, Halls and Harlow 1971). This method is based on the principle that average twig weights may be estimated by regressions of twig diameters or twig lengths. Predictive equations relating twig weight to twig diameter or length may be developed by clipping a number of unbrowsed twigs (50 are recommended), measuring twig length and basal diameter, oven-drying, and weighing to the nearest 0.01g. Care must be taken to collect the full range of twig sizes from several shrubs and to stratify the sample among lower and upper portions of each shrub (Basile and Hutchings 1966). Because twigs are often elliptical in cross section, it may be necessary to estimate twig basal diameter as the average of 2 perpendicular measurements. Linear regression produces acceptable predictive equations if the range of twig diameters or lengths is not great (Basile and Hutchings 1966, Halls and Harlow 1971); however, curvilinear regression may be required if twig sizes vary widely (Telfer 1969a). Peek et al. (1971) reported there might be considerable site variation in length-weight and diameter-weight relationships of twigs, which would require developing a separate regression equation for each shrub species and each "site type" under investigation.

Other Attributes

Visual Obstruction.—Visual obstruction caused by vegetation may be functionally important to wildlife both as hiding cover (i.e., cover necessary to escape a sense of danger) and as thermal cover (i.e., cover that creates a beneficial thermal environment). The measurement of horizontal cover of vegetation has been used extensively by wildlife managers and researchers in assessing wildlife habitat suitability, habitat preference, and impacts of land use practices on wildlife habitats (Griffith and Youtie 1988, Reece et al. 2001, Vermeire and Gillen 2001). Some measure of horizontal obstruction also has been used by researchers to

examine the relative influence of visibility biases associated with wildlife surveys in different vegetation classes. Further, measures of horizontal obstruction have been used reliably in many instances as a relatively rapid surrogate measure to estimate standing crop biomass of grassland vegetation (Harmoney et al. 1997, Volesky et al. 1999, Benkobi et al. 2000, Vermeire and Gillen 2001).

A variety of devices has been used to measure horizontal visual obstruction caused by vegetation. Wight (1939) first proposed use of a "density board," a 1.83-m tall board, each 30.48-cm mark labeled 1 to 6 (Fig. 9). Horizontal cover is assessed by placing the board in cover, viewing the board from a distance of 20 m, and adding the numbers unobstructed by vegetation. The method produces an index of horizontal cover that ranges from 0 (no obstruction) to 21 (complete obstruction), but provides no means of describing the vertical distribution of the obstructing vegetation.

Nudds (1977) devised a "vegetation profile board" that enables the investigator to assess visual obstruction of shrub vegetation in 5 0.5-m vertical intervals above ground. The board is 2.5-m high and 30.48-cm wide and is marked in alternate black and white colors at 0.5-m intervals. Horizontal cover is assessed in each interval by viewing the board from 15 m in a randomly chosen direction. The percentage of each interval concealed by vegetation is recorded as a single-digit score, ranging from 1 to 5, corresponding to 0–20, 21–40, 41–60, 61–80, and 81–100% estimated concealment. Although the vegetation profile board has been widely used, its size, weight, and inconvenience associated with use in remote areas are drawbacks of the technique. The board may, however, be reproduced on thin vinyl or nylon material that is easily rolled and transported in the field; it can be held in place conveniently by a single pole or by a field assistant. Griffith and Youtie (1988) modified the Nudds-type checkerboard into standing- and bedded-deer silhouettes. Values of the height and percentage of the silhouette blocks covered by vegetation were estimated ocularly from the 4 cardinal directions and at 4 0.5-m levels. Haukos et al. (1998) reported sample size, power, and other analytical considerations when using profile boards in wetland plant cover. Naugle et al. (2000) used a profile board to investigate black tern (*Chlidonias niger*) nest site selection in wetland vegetation.

Robel et al. (1970) used a pole-shaped cover board (3 × 150 cm) that could be read from a standard distance (4 m) and height (1 m) in any direction (Fig. 10). The pole was marked in decimeters and the height of total visual obstruction was recorded. For example, if the pole was not visible until the fifth decimeter, the reading was 4. Additionally, all vegetation was clipped, dried, and weighed from a 2 × 5-dm quadrat next to the pole and regressions were developed from the average obstruction reading and biomass of 30 transects. The $R^2 = 0.95$ indicated the obstruction reading could be used as a method of estimating biomass in tall grasses to assess prairie-chicken (*Tympanuchus* spp.) habitat. Benkobi et al. (2000) modified the Robel pole with alternating gray and white 2.5-cm rings with vegetation clipping around the pole. This modification makes the pole useful and accurate in short vegetation. Their modified pole greatly improved the precision and accuracy for mid- and short-grass prairie. Sample size for number of pole stations and transects are presented as are monitoring or sampling protocols for small areas (section

Fig. 10. Visual obstruction estimates from a specific height and distance.

Fig. 11. Estimating horizontal cover using the staff-ball method of Collins and Becker (2001).

or less) to large landscape areas of 1,215 to 46,560 ha (3,000 to 115,000 ac). This modified pole provides an assessment of standing crop on grasslands, can be used to monitor livestock grazing, and provides status of vegetation structure for wildlife habitat.

Alternatively, Griffith and Youtie (1988) reported that a 2.5 × 200-cm "cover pole," which is easily transported in the field, produced measures of horizontal shrub cover indistinguishable from those produced by the vegetation profile board. The cover pole was painted with alternating 0.1-m black and white bands, and 3 red bands divided the board into 0.5-m zones. Visual obstruction in each zone is recorded as the number (1–5) of 0.1-m bands that are ≥25% concealed by vegetation in each 0.5-m level.

Collins and Becker (2001) developed a new point sampling method, the staff-ball method (Fig. 11), to characterize horizontal cover and compared time and precision of use among observers and with 3 other methods (cover pole, profile tube, checker board). Their results indicate the staff-ball method provided estimates of horizontal cover from 5.1 to 14.3 times faster than other methods and with greater precision because observers only needed to make yes/no decisions rather than subjective estimates and/or counts. The staff-ball method also can be used in a variety of habitat types. Staff-ball point cover readings are taken at the point where the ball meets the pole (one side only) and this point is or is not obscured. The ball or balls are positioned at set heights on the pole depending on vegetation type.

Marlow and Clary (1996) and Dudley et al. (1998) used photography in combination with cover boards to assess vegetation differences. Although the technique enables visual assessment of cover changes through time, it does not provide measurable differences. To ensure comparisons from year to year, photographs must be annually taken from the same point (height, distance, and direction) with similar film, date, and time of day. At times, the date is adjusted to phenological characters of specific plant species.

Users of visual estimation techniques to characterize vegetation structure should be aware of potential amounts of interobserver judgments and associated biases (Schultz et al. 1961). In studies comparing visual estimation data sets to data sets obtained using instrument measurements, Gotfryd and Hansell (1985) and Block et al. (1987), using univariate and multivariate analyses, found significant dif-

ferences between observer estimates and measurements for many habitat variables. Thus, studies that rely solely on visual (ocular) estimation techniques may forfeit accuracy to save on labor and sampling costs.

Herbaceous Height.—Height of herbage is probably the easiest attribute of vegetation to measure in grasslands, but has received little attention in published literature. Plant height can be estimated with high precision in many grasslands. Plant height correlates well with other structural attributes of herbage important to the management of grasslands. For example, Higgins and Barker (1982) reported that herbaceous height explained 63% of the foliage density values that were taken concurrently with the use of a modified visual obstruction pole (Robel et al. 1970). Herbage height in grassland habitats has an important role in predator deterrence and prey security. Average plant (stubble) height can also be used to evaluate the impact of livestock grazing on a pasture (reviewed by Clary and Leininger 2000, Turner and Clary 2001).

Herbage height can refer to the tallest portion of a plant or the effective cover height (generally the upper limit of vegetation leafiness), or the area-height of herbage below a specific area such as under a 30 cm diameter plastic disk. Maximum plant height can be measured readily with a calibrated ruler or tape placed next to a plant. Multiple measurements (≥10) usually are expressed as an average height.

Effective plant height usually is measured as the maximum height of leafy cover for grasses and forbs; however, effective plant height of a forb (e.g., alfalfa [*Medicago sativa*]) also may be equivalent to its maximum height. Effective herbage height also may be measured by holding a pole or meter stick parallel to the ground and reading the

Fig. 12. Calipers used to measure tree diameter at breast height.

effective height at the point where leafy plant parts touch the horizontal pole in a minimum of 3 places along its length. Bakker et al. (2002) found that effective plant height was associated with savannah sparrow (*Passerculus sandwichensis*) use of grassland habitats in eastern South Dakota.

The height of herbage per unit area can be measured with a disk or plate in combination with a ruler (Higgins and Barker 1982, Gonzalez et al. 1990). Clear or lightly colored plastic allows plant parts to be seen beneath the disk. Maximum area-height measurements are made at the point where the plastic disk is first touched by a plant part. If a weighted disk is used, measurements are made at the lowest point where the disk settles on the vegetation (Bransby et al. 1977, Gonzalez et al. 1990).

Rangeland canopy height also can be measured by counting the number of laser measurements by 1.3-cm (0.5-in.) height categories and dividing by the total number of laser measurements for a line transect (Ritchie et al. 1992). The laser transmits and receives reflected wavelength signals and, at 4,000 pulses per second with an aircraft altitude of about 150 m and a speed of 60 m per second, a vertical measurement is taken at 1.5-cm intervals along the flight line. These data can be obtained with a laser profiler mounted in a fixed-wing aircraft that measures the distance between the aircraft and the defined surface material to be sampled (e.g., vegetation) with this method.

Tree Dimensions.—The size and dimensions of individual trees affect the physiognomic structure of forested wildlife habitats. In many forested habitats, large trees provide critical structures necessary for nesting, reproduction, or survival. For example, studies of nesting sites of northern (*Strix occidentalis caurina*) and California spotted owls (*S. o. occidentalis*) indicate that presence of large old-growth trees or snags is a key characteristic of nesting habitat in western forests (Mills et al. 1993, North et al. 2000). In other situations, a variety of tree sizes, age classes, and structures contribute to habitat complexity and overall diversity of wildlife species inhabiting the forest. Choosing which characteristics of trees to measure depends on study objectives and biological characteristics of the species under study. Morrison et al. (1998:139–167) provide a complete discussion of measuring forest habitat structure. Here we describe a few of the most common measurements.

Three common, interrelated measures of tree size are height, crown volume, and trunk diameter. Height of tall trees may be measured using a trigonometric function of horizontal distance of an observer to the trunk of a tree and the angle measured between the horizontal distance and a sighting to the treetop. Crown volume may be measured from similar measurements of minimum and maximum canopy height and canopy diameters measured horizontally (Sturman 1968, reviewed in Morrison et al. 1998).

Trunk diameter and cross-sectional area are the most common measurements of tree size because of ease of measurement and high correlation with height and volume. Diameter can be measured with a diameter tape that measures diameter directly when placed around the circumference of a tree trunk or with calipers (Fig. 12). By convention, the measurement (DBH) is made 1.4 m above ground level (Spurr 1964) and above the enlarged base of some trees; DBH also is a representative height where measurements can be made consistently and rapidly. Such data often are summarized as numbers of individuals of species per size class per unit of land area. If exact diameter measurements are not needed, a forester's Biltmore stick (Avery 1959) can be used to estimate diameters within size classes.

Trunk cross-sectional area, calculated as ($A = \pi\, r^2$), also is measured at breast height, and the results (commonly identified by the misnomer "basal area") are given as area units of trunk per unit land area. Individual tree areas can be computed from diameter measurements or measured directly with a tape scaled with area equivalent units. Data can be presented as the value just described or as a relative value (percent of the total contributed by a single species).

Tree Age.—For many wildlife studies it is sufficient to get one or more expressions of tree size, without age, although at times the latter also has value. Age data are beneficial in forest history and dynamics, including predictions of future status. For instance, knowledge of the approximate life span of a tree species aids in assessment of the current tree population age structure and of regeneration success. Past events influencing the forest and its wildlife inhabitants can be revealed by the presence of fire scars or periods of reduced growth.

Some wildlife species have tree-size and age-specific requirements. For example, in longleaf pine (*Pinus palustris*) forests of the southeastern United States, trees >95 years old have been judged important for red-cockaded woodpeckers (*Picoides borealis*) (Hooper 1988). Ruffed grouse (*Bonasa umbellus*) in northern forests do best in a mosaic of aspen stands of various ages (Sharp 1963, Dessecker and McAuley 2001).

Age classification of trees is possible because trunk lateral growth occurs in annular increments related to the seasonality of temperate zone climates (Raven et al. 1986). The increments are especially evident in so-called "ring-porous" species. Large-pored vascular tissue is formed early in the growing season, followed by small-pored tissue later, and then termination of growth that year, followed by the onset of obvious spring growth as another growing season begins. Examples of these species include oaks (*Quercus*), ashes (*Fraxinus*), and elms (*Ulmus*). "Diffuse-porous" angiosperm species, e.g., maples (*Acer*), aspens, and birches, have less apparent growth rings. Conifers, unlike angiosperms, have a somewhat different anatomical structure, yet they too typically have easily recognized growth rings. Extra treatments of the wood, such as applying light oil, certain stains, or water, or sanding or shaving with a razor blade can help make growth rings more evident.

Growth rings can be seen on trunk or stump cross-sections. Vegetation sampling in concert with timber harvest or removal of damaged/dead trees is an easy way to collect such data. Where destructive sampling is not in order, small cylindrical cores can be collected with a wood increment borer. Cores can be analyzed onsite or stored, for example in soda straws, until they are viewed in the laboratory. They also can be affixed to a grooved board and kept for future reference. Together with classifying age, tree ring analysis can be used to measure growth rate and to date discernable past events, such as fire resulting in scarred tissue or varied climatic or competitive regimes revealed by varied growth ring widths.

Plant Use.—Quantification of plant use and its effect on the ecosystem are important for estimating the number of herbivores that can use the land without deterioration of the soil base and plant community (Bonham 1989, Clary and Leininger 2000, Turner and Clary 2001). Maintenance of adequate plant and litter cover retards water runoff and reduces erosion. Early methods to evaluate use of range grasses were developed during 1930–1950 (Stoddart 1935, Pechanec 1936, Lommasson and Jensen 1938, Canfield 1944, Roach 1950) and, with some modification, they are still used today. Many of the methods of estimating shrub use are modifications of those used for grasses, and we discuss methods for each in the following paragraphs. To avoid confusion, we use stems to refer to stems of grasses and twigs for shrubs and saplings.

As with estimation of biomass, plant use may be estimated with ocular methods. These require training with ungrazed plants that are clipped to simulate different intensities of grazing. Such estimates vary by individual investigator and may be inconsistent from year to year. Commonly accepted methods of measuring use vary from simply counting used or unused stems, to obtaining "before and after" measures of stem lengths, to regression methods.

The stem-count method (Stoddart 1935, Cole 1956) is a minor modification of the range survey method described above, in which used and unused stems are counted rather than estimated. Stems may be counted in plots or along transect lines. Pechanec (1936) observed the stem count did not compare favorably with other methods for estimating grass use. Stickney (1966) and Jensen and Scotter (1977) reported that proportion of shrub stems used correlated well with proportions of lengths removed, but the method was insensitive under heavy use. Stickney (1966) observed that virtually all shrub stems received at least minor browsing at use levels above 55% of length for black chokecherry (*Prunus virginiana*) and 60% of length for Saskatoon serviceberry (*Amelanchier alnifolia*). Those wishing to compare among sites that receive >50% use will need to select a method that remains sensitive under a wider range of use.

Use may be estimated by measuring height of grass stems or length of shrub stems before and after use by herbivores. Relationships are calculated for height/length removed and biomass used (Lommasson and Jensen 1938, Stickney 1966, Jensen and Scotter 1977). For both grasses and shrubs, the relationship is not linear, so curvilinear relationships must be developed. Jensen and Scotter (1977) reported the stem-length method provided a sensitive measure of shrub use across a range of use levels (0 to 100%). A primary disadvantage of the method is that it requires 2 trips to the field, one prior to and one following the brows-

ing season, yet it provides no estimate of production. Curves must be developed individually for each species, site, and year to accurately estimate use (Bonham 1989).

Browse use also may be estimated with dimension analyses of twigs by predicting the prebrowsing lengths or weights of twigs from diameter-weight or diameter-length relationships (Basile and Hutchings 1966; Telfer 1969*a,b*; Lyon 1970). Once the diameter-weight or diameter-length equations have been developed, the technique requires 3 additional types of data:

(1) an estimate of the percentage of twigs browsed,
(2) mean diameters at the point of browsing of a stratified sample of browsed twigs, and
(3) mean lengths or weights of the twig parts remaining after browsing.

Prebrowsing weights or lengths of browsed twigs can be estimated from regression equations. Postbrowsing weights of browsed twigs can be measured by clipping and weighing the residual twigs. Alternatively, postbrowsing lengths of browsed twigs can be measured directly. The percent use can be computed from the formula:

$$U = B \times [(P - A)/P] \times 100,$$

where B = percentage of browsed twigs, P = predicted prebrowsing mean length or weight of browsed twigs, and A = postbrowsing mean length or weight of browsed twigs (Lyon 1970).

As an alternative to the above procedure, several workers have estimated weights of consumed twigs directly using the diameter at point of browsing in weight-diameter equations (Oldemeyer 1982, Rumble 1987). In that instance, use may be computed as:

$$U = [(B \times C)/P] \times 100,$$

where B = proportion of browsed twigs, P = predicted prebrowsing mean weight of browsed twigs (based on diameter of current annual growth), and C = predicted mean weight of consumed portions of twigs (based on browsing diameter).

Several authors (Jensen and Urness 1981, Provenza and Urness 1981) demonstrated that use estimates obtained from twig-diameter measurements are rapid and compare favorably with twig-length measurements. Once weight-diameter or length equations have been developed for a site, the method represents a considerable savings in time over the twig-length method because all measurements of use can be obtained during a single trip to the field after use has occurred.

Percentage of plants or stems used by herbivores often is used as an estimator of plant use. This method requires a combination of techniques. For grasses, one measures the percentage of biomass removed, using height-weight relationships, and regresses percentage of plants used on biomass removed from a sample of several sites (Roach 1950). Similar regressions can be developed for shrubs with percentage of plants used and results of dimension analysis (Oldemeyer 1982).

Another evaluation technique commonly used to assess levels of plant use at the landscape scale is classification of key browse species into form and age-classes (Dasmann 1951, Cole 1959, Patton and Hall 1966). In this procedure, a minimum of 25 plants of a key browse species is marked along permanently established survey courses in selected key winter range areas. For each plant in the survey, the observer records:

    (1) hedging—classified as light, moderate, or severe based on the length and appearance of the previous year's growth below the current leaders;

    (2) availability—classified as available or unavailable based on shrub height and maximum browsing reach of the principal browsing species; and

    (3) age/decadence—classified as seedling, young, mature, or decadent based on stem diameter classes (any living plant with 25% or more of the crown dead is classified as decadent).

Hedging, availability, and age class are summarized as percentages of shrubs in each class. The method has the advantage of being quite rapid allowing for completion of extensive surveys. However, like all subjective ratings, there is considerable variation among individual examiners in the assignment of form classes.

Keigley (1997) recently proposed a new method of evaluating browse growth form based on explicit definitions of browsing intensity and plant architecture. In this procedure, browsing intensity of individual shrub stems is rated as "light-to-moderate" or "intense" depending on whether the current annual production consistently develops from the previous years growth ("light-to-moderate" browsing) or from stem segments >1 year old because the previous year's growth was killed by browsing ("intense" browsing). At the whole-plant level (including multiple stems that comprise the plant), plant architecture is classified as "uninterrupted-growth-type" (reflecting light-to-moderate browsing), "arrested-type" (reflecting intense browsing), "retrogressed-type" (reflecting light-to-moderate changing to intense browsing), or "released-type" (reflecting intense changing to light-to-moderate browsing). Explicit definitions are given for each architecture type. Additional details and applications of the method are provided by Keigley et al. (2002*a,b*).

TECHNIQUES FOR SAMPLING FRUITS

Data on fruit abundance can be quite important when certain species of wildlife are dependent on annual fruit production (DeGange et al. 1989, McShea and Schwede 1993, Wolff 1996, McShea 2000, Suthers et al. 2000). However, few habitat analyses include an inventory of fruit production. An enumeration of the number and size of fruiting plants is often as far as managers go to describe fruit-bearing potential and its value to wildlife. The inconsistent and seasonal fruiting tendencies of plants, coupled with their often-sporadic distribution, minimize the usefulness of simple enumeration of plants.

In studies of wildlife food habits, fruits generally are referred to as mast and are divided into 2 categories, "hard" and "soft." Consequently, mast can be defined as the fruits and seeds of all plants, both woody and herbaceous, used as food by animals. The importance of fruit as wildlife food is well known; for example, oak mast alone is used by 185 wildlife species and is available for up to 8 months (Van Dersal 1940). Mast is high in food energy, especially carbohydrates and fats (Goodrum et al. 1971).

Soft mast includes fruits with fleshy exteriors such as berries, drupes, and pomes. Hard mast, in contrast, includes fruits with dry or hard exteriors such as achenes, nuts, samaras, cones, pods, seeds, and capsules. Numerous factors affect fruit production, including age of plant, size of plant, genetics of the individual plant, climate, soil, competition for resources, and previous use by animals (Schupp 1990). Annual variation in yield of wild food plants makes it difficult to estimate fruit production over large land units (Koenig and Knops 1995). Consequently, management practices that provide for the greatest variety of food-producing plants will assure favorable conditions for the greatest variety of wild animals.

Large or Heavy Fruits of Trees

The sampling design necessary for species with large or heavy fruits depends on whether total mast production or an index of annual mast abundance is desired. Choosing a large number of random points for trap locations may be necessary if the objective is to characterize mast production at the landscape scale. Although this design is costly, it avoids intentional bias and allows statistical inference from the sample to the larger area. Depending on the objectives of the project, one may want to sample only under the canopies of mast-producing trees. This would be appropriate if one is measuring the production per unit area of mast-producing canopy within the forest or obtaining an annual index of mast production.

Sampling may be random in forests with well-defined stands of trees (Thompson 1962) or stratified by vegetation type, stand age classes, or stand location (edge or interior). Sampling methods have been devised to estimate production by small versus large trees (Minckler and McDermott 1960), to compare production of 2 or more species of oaks (Tryon and Carvell 1962, Koenig and Knops 1995), and to estimate production in mixed oak stands from 63 to 82 years of age (Beck and Olson 1968).

Mast production can be estimated by counts of mast in ground plots (Goodrum et al. 1971), counts of mast on trees (Gysel 1956, Koenig et al. 1994, Koenig and Knops 1995), or use of seed traps (Schupp 1990, Sork et al. 1993, Ostfeld et al. 1996). Counts of mast in plots on the forest floor are generally unreliable estimators of mast production because mast frequently is taken by wildlife before counts are made; however, such counts, when used with seed traps, may be a good estimator of wildlife use of fallen mast. Total counts of mast on trees may be quite accurate for small trees, but difficult and time consuming for large trees. Consequently, many researchers and managers have opted to use relatively rapid indices of mast production rather than more labor-intensive methods. Indices based on visual counts have the advantage of being quick, permitting rapid assessment of acorn production. In the most general index, acorn production may be rated on a visual scale from 0 to 4: 0 (no acorns), 1 (a few acorns seen after close scrutiny), 2 (a fair number), 3 (a good crop), and 4 (a bumper crop) (Koenig et al. 1994). The obvious disadvantage of such a rating system is its subjectivity. As an example of a more quantitative index, Koenig et al. (1994) and Koenig and Knops (1995) counted as many acorns as they were able on a single tree during a 30-second interval. Although such an index may be limited by the maximum rate at which an observer may count under high acorn abundances, Koenig et al. (1994) found the index was highly correlated with values obtained from acorn traps. Alternatively, Wolff (1996) used visual counts of acorns on 10 randomly selected branches as an index of mast production in oak woodlands of California.

Many kinds of mast traps have been used to measure mast fall. Downs and McQuilkin (1944) developed square traps made of hardware cloth on a wood frame. These traps were about 1 m² in size and 2 were placed under each tree. Since that time, several trap designs have been developed, ranging from makeshift types such as large oil drums to large fruit baskets to those made from wood, cardboard, or polyethylene film and particularly designed for catching acorns. Because rodents and other wildlife will eat mast in the traps, early traps used predator guards; however, these deflected mast from the trap, and guards are not recommended. A study of 8 types of traps comparing catching efficiency, durability, and cost (Thompson and McGinnes 1963) revealed 3 types to be most suitable: polyethylene film traps; square, wire cage traps; and paperboard seed traps. The polyethylene, conical-shaped, seed trap sampled an area of 0.00004 ha (0.4 m²) and had an acorn-retention efficiency of 99%. Fifty of these traps can be carried by one person a considerable distance without discomfort. The wire cage trap (Moody et al. 1954) sampled 0.0001 ha (1.0 m²). With a wire cover, it had an acorn-catching efficiency of 87% and a durability of 10 years. The design was similar to traps used by Downs and McQuilkin (1944). Of the 8 traps compared, the wire cage model was the most expensive to construct. The paperboard seed trap (Klawitter and Stubbs 1961) was a modified version of the pine seed trap (Easley and Chaiken 1951), which has a sampling area of 0.0003 ha (3.2 m²). The paperboard trap had 96% acorn-retention efficiency and was durable for 2–3 years.

Christisen and Kearby (1984) constructed acorn traps of 8-gauge steel wire formed into a circle 0.73 m in diameter. They attached clear, 4-mil plastic, cut into a semi-circle to the wire, forming a cone (Fig. 13). Holes punched in the bottom of the cone allowed water to drain. The trap was attached to wooden stakes to hold it off the ground. They concluded the plastic cone was superior to baskets and wire mesh traps, because the soft plastic prevented acorns from bouncing out of the trap, acorn predation was eliminated, and traps were inexpensive and portable. The primary disadvantage was that the plastic lasted only 1 year. Sork et al. (1993) and Schroeder and Vangilder (1997) used a similar seed-collecting trap made of 6-mil plastic and a trap area of 0.5 m². Schupp (1990) studied seedfall from the understory trees in Panama using 1.0-m² traps constructed of 1.5-mm mesh plastic window screening on 1 × 1-m frames of 1.25-cm PVC tubing.

Mast production varies considerably among tree species (Sork et al. 1993), among trees of the same species, and among years (Christisen and Kearby 1984, Koenig et al. 1994). Thus, one must design a mast-production study with great care. Traps have been placed under trees at a distance of two-thirds the crown radius from the trunk; however, we are not aware that a consistent distance from the trunk is required. Christisen and Kearby (1984) randomly placed 3 traps under each sample tree with the stipulations that no 2 traps were in the same direction and that no traps be placed under a side of a tree that lacked canopy. Further, they imagined the canopy as consisting of 2 concentric circles and either placed 2 traps in the inner circle and one in the

Fig. 13. Trap for estimation of fruit production.

outer, or vice versa. Traps should be examined at 1–2 week intervals from the time large fruits (e.g., acorns) begin to drop until all have fallen. Fruits removed from traps should be counted and may be placed into categories such as: (1) well developed and sound, (2) well developed but damaged by birds or squirrels, (3) well developed but showing insect emergence holes, and (4) imperfectly developed, deformed, or aborted (Downs and McQuilkin 1944, McQuilkin and Musbach 1977, McShea and Schwede 1993).

Gysel (1957) estimated acorn production by multiplying the number of acorns collected per trap and species by 1.1 to compensate for losses by deflection. He then multiplied that value (acorns per unit area of trap) by the average weight of sound acorns and total crown area of the stand to derive an estimate of weight of acorn production per unit area.

Small or Light Fruits of Trees

Like large mast, smaller seeds and fruits are important wildlife foods used by many small rodents, tree and ground squirrels, and game and nongame birds (Trousdell 1954, Hooven 1958, Yeatman 1960, Abbott 1961, Abbott and Dodge 1961, Asher 1963, Powell 1965, Landers and Johnson 1976, McShea and Schwede 1993, Schroeder and Vangilder 1997, McCracken et al. 1999). Abundance of small or light mast (e.g., pine seeds) varies from year to year like all fruiting species. For example, loblolly pine (*Pinus taeda*) seed varied from nearly 0 to as high as 243,000 seeds/ha (Allen and Trousdell 1961). The 2 principal techniques of sampling small or light seed production of trees are placing seed traps in a stand (Lotti and LeGrande 1959, Allen and Trousdell 1961, Graber 1970, McCracken et al. 1999) or counting the number of ripening cones on a tree with binoculars (Wenger 1953). The latter method may be simplified by counting only a portion of the tree (Wenger 1953) or by categorizing the relative abundance of cones on the tree as none, few (1–25 cones), medium (29–90), and heavy (100+).

Fruits of Shrubs

Soft and hard mast of shrubs often is within reach of a biologist and may be counted (Suthers et al. 2000) or harvested directly from the shrub (Perry et al. 1999). In Georgia, Johnson and Landers (1978) collected all fruits, by species, in 4-m^2 plots on a monthly basis from April through October. Their small sample of 5 plots per line had such high sampling error that they were not able to compare production among the months sampled. Harlow et al. (1980) counted mast on scrub oaks (*Quercus ilicifolia*) in Florida in a series of 0.004-ha circular plots to estimate mast abundance. Total counts of mast were made for each species within each of 20–40 plots in each stand. Stransky and Halls (1980) counted fruits of shrubs and woody vines in 20 1-m^2 quadrats within 0.6-ha plots in eastern Texas. They dried fresh fruits of each species to obtain an average weight of each fruit and projected the yield per quadrat based on the quadrat counts. Stransky and Halls (1980) further developed regressions between fruit yield and plant height and density to simplify the sampling effort, similar to regressions of browse production. Perry et al. (1999) conducted soft mast surveys for 31 taxa in Arkansas and Oklahoma by counting berries present within 3-m^2 plots during mid-June, mid-July, and mid-August to coincide with ripening phenology of the major fruit-producing species. To estimate dry mass production they counted and weighed samples of each fruit type and developed wet to dry-mass conversion factors. They developed species-specific regressions relating seed-head volume with dry mass for species with large seed heads containing abundant fruits so that dry mass was estimated from counts and measurements of seed heads rather than individual berries. Like most total enumeration methods, estimating total production of berries may be quite time consuming. Consequently, soft mast production may be characterized for extensive surveys on a scale of relative abundance ranging from 0 to 4, in much the same manner as for hard mast (Clark et al. 1994). Further, double sampling methods have been used to "calibrate" relative abundance indices to actual production by measuring fruit production on a sample of plots on which relative abundance is measured (Noyce and Coy 1989). Biologists must remain aware of the potentially serious variation in relative abundance estimates made by different observers, or among different regions or years.

Fruits of Herbaceous Vegetation

Herbaceous vegetation provides an abundant supply of seeds for wildlife. Sampling seeds of herbaceous species has not been as well developed as for trees because more plant species are involved, and wildlife that use those seeds generally are less obvious. Sampling for seeds of herbaceous species is a miniature of sampling for large mast from trees; samples may be taken from the ground,

from traps, or directly from the plant. Ripley and Perkins (1965) sampled ground seed supplies (primarily legumes) for northern bobwhite (*Colinus virginianus*) from soil samples. They removed soil cores (7.6 cm diameter × 2.5 cm deep), screened the cores of litter and soil, and counted number of seeds within each core. Eight soil cores were taken at each of 3 points along a transect line, and the 8 samples were combined to project an estimated seed density and weight. Variation among lines was not greater than variation among points; thus, Ripley and Perkins (1965) suggested that random sampling may be as efficient as using lines. They also reported decreased numbers of seeds in the soil cores from autumn to spring, suggesting removal by wildlife. Larger plots and different sampling depths have been used by others. Haugen and Fitch (1955) used 15 30.5 × 30.5-cm plots but took material only to the soil surface when sampling for lespedeza (*Lespedeza* spp.) and partridgepea senna (*Cassia marilandica*) seeds. Young et al. (1983) used 32 × 32-cm open-bottom metal boxes driven into soil 15 cm to estimate abundance of Indian ricegrass (*Oryzopsis hymenoides*) seed in Nevada. They further removed the soil in 2.5-cm depth increments to identify where seed reserves occurred.

Seed traps for herbaceous plant seeds are smaller than those used for tree mast. Traps with fine-screen wire for the bottom and 0.64-cm hardware screen for the top have been used for estimating seed yield for game birds (Davison et al. 1955). Traps of this type eliminate seed predation by wildlife. Others have used traps with adhesives to hold the seeds. A Petri dish containing filter paper sprayed with Tanglefoot® or other nondrying sticky substance was used by Werner (1975), Rabinowitz and Rapp (1980), and Potvin (1988) to sample seed deposition in prairie grasslands. Rabinowitz and Rapp (1980) believed that seed production was underestimated in tallgrass prairie because leaves closed over the trap and seeds were intercepted by overhanging leaves. When temperatures dropped below freezing or when traps became covered with snow, they were not effective for catching seed. Huenneke and Graham (1987) used house-construction insulation hangers coated with a smooth surface of adhesive to sample seed rain in grasslands. They observed that height of seedfall affected the proportion of seeds adhering to the trap surface; at 60 cm, only about 3% of the seeds adhered, whereas at 10 cm, 65% adhered to the trap surface. Exposure to light, high temperatures, and dust had little effect on capture rates, but shape and form of seed did affect capture rates.

Seed traps also can be used over water to sample seed production and availability in wetlands. Olinde et al. (1985) constructed 12 × 30-cm traps and floated the traps on styrofoam blocks. These blocks were held in place with ropes and stakes driven into the soil, and the blocks could rise and fall with changing water levels.

Laubhan and Fredrickson (1992) and Gray et al. (1999) describe techniques to sample and estimate seed yields in wetland and moist-soil environments. Laubhan and Fredrickson (1992) collected inflorescence measurements and all seeds from inflorescences of 13 common moist-soil plant species within a 25 × 25-cm sample frame. Sample stations were randomly placed within distinct vegetation zones or patches per wetland area. They found that seed yield varied widely among plant species. Gray et al. (1999) developed models to predict seed yield per wetland plant species that also required an estimate of plant stem density per species. They used regression calculations of the mean stem density multiplied by mean seed yield per 60 plants per species to provide extrapolated species-specific seed yield data. Metabolizable energy values per seed yields per species can be used to estimate waterfowl carrying capacities per unit area of moist-soil or wetland habitat.

MULTIPLE-SCALE VEGETATION SURVEYS

Vegetation measurement on the ground can be facilitated with several technologies. Ground-based digital imaging systems such as digital cameras, with and without infra-red viewing, have been shown to measure vegetation cover, amount of green vegetation and Leaf Area Index in grass and shrub dominated ecosystems (White et al. 2000, Rundquist 2002). Dycam ADC and Decagon First Cover systems are specifically made for vegetation measurement. Measurement of green vegetation cover is accomplished through automated procedures by classifying pixels in the digital image as green vegetation, bare ground, litter, woody material or other non-green material. Software classifies the image as a percentage of each specified material. Species and plant form coverages are developed by sampling digital images for each component with trained observers and viewer software, after field image acquisition. Digital cameras provide rapid field collection with minimally trained personnel and provide an extensive record of field conditions that is easily moved to computers where further and more detailed analyses can occur.

Wildlife personnel have long desired to have methods to estimate live herbaceous biomass or structure and use at a fine scale over large areas (Olenicki 2001). Ground-based passive sensors or radiometers that measure electromagnetic reflectance from vegetation have been used to measure biomass, amount of green cover, and biochemical constituents along with classifying vegetation in grass, shrub, and forest-dominated systems (Van der Meer and de Jong 2001). These sensors measure several areas of the electromagnetic spectrum (multispectral) and some can measure continuously from the visible to well into the thermal portion (hyperspectral). Calibration via ground truthing is often required to accurately relate reflectance to traditional vegetation measurements. Ratios of the amount of energy reflected in different regions or bands of the electromagnetic spectrum are used to develop the relationship between reflectance and traditional vegetation measures. Radiometer readings need to be taken during midday on sunny days so incoming electromagnetic radiation is similar for all readings. Differences between ecosystems, plant forms, soils, and changes in vegetation during the year prevent universal calibrations from being developed for ground-based radiometers (Asner 1998). Calibrations using local conditions are needed to ensure the best fit (Moulin et al. 1998). Calibration of radiometers with vegetation measurement techniques that have poor repeatability such as ocular estimation of cover will result in poor relationships to vegetation reflectance because of the inherent variability of ocular estimations (Bonham 1989).

Ground-based systems have become lighter, more mobile, and easier to use in the field which has enabled operators to take more samples in less time than with traditional field methods. Resolution is in the centimeter to meter range, so large numbers of samples are needed to adequately characterize diverse vegetation types over large areas. These systems also can be automated so that field personnel do not need to be extensively trained in instrument operation.

Olenicki (2001) proposed that real-time GPS receivers or military precision lightweight GPS receivers (PLGR's) can aid relocation of points within 1 m accuracy, making the combination of ground-based radiometers and real-time GPS units ideal for monitoring temporal and spatial change in vegetation over large areas. As an example, Merrill and Boyce (1991) successfully linked field sampling of herbaceous phytomass in Yellowstone National Park with spectral values taken from Landsat Multi-Spectral Scanners for the same field sites to describe trends in phytomass availability on the northern Yellowstone elk (*Cervus elaphus*) range.

Aerial or satellite based technologies have been used extensively to measure regional vegetation patterns at the largest scale of sampling (Avery and Berlin 1992, Van der Meer and de Jong 2001). Passive sensors ranging from panchromatic (aerial photographs) to multispectral to hyperspectral have potential applications to vegetation measurement for wildlife managers. Passive sensors have been used to develop digital land use coverages that are available from government sources (O'Neil et al. 2005). Most current land use and habitat coverages are derived from either aerial photography or Landsat thematic mapper multispectral imagery (30-m resolution). Aerial photography provides detailed images with resolutions ranging from 1 to 100 m. Aerial photography is limited to expert visual interpretation that requires extensive training and results in many hours to interpret small numbers of images. In contrast, Landsat thematic mapper multispectral imagery can be processed with an automated classification that increases efficiency. However, the 30-m resolution is not at the scale that is useful for wildlife managers. Smaller resolution multispectral sensors are available, such as Ikonos, Quickbird, Orbview, as well as special aerial-based sensors, but efforts at vegetation measurement are project-specific and full coverage is not available for large-scale areas. Wildlife managers who want vegetation measurements at smaller resolutions will have to initiate and fund projects to acquire such information at increased effort and cost.

Satellite- and some aerial-based sensors have been used for vegetation measurements that are time-limited such as green vegetation coverage, Leaf Area Index, and biomass (National Oceanic and Atmospheric Administration Advanced Very High Resolution Radiometer products, and National Aeronautics and Space Administration Distributed Active Archive Center for Modis products). These sensors need to be calibrated with traditional on-the-ground vegetation measurements. Band ratios are commonly used to develop reflectance relationships. The biggest problems with satellite and aerial sensors are atmospheric interference and inter-sensor differences, thus, images are not directly related to each other, preventing direct comparisons.

Although much of the use of aerial or remote sensing methods relates to mapping, recent improvements in spatial accuracy of Geographic Information Systems tools have helped bridge the science to vegetation measurement and sampling or the lack of vegetation such as in forest canopy gaps. The importance of forest canopy gaps to location of songbird nests (Fox et al. 2000) was evaluated with data obtained from color-infrared photos scanned at

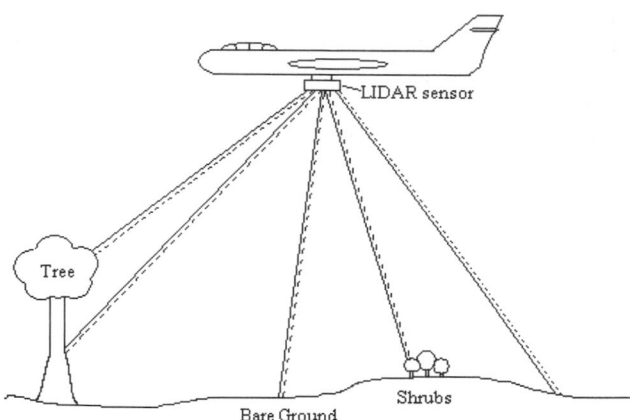

Fig. 14. Schematic illustration of a laser altimetry or lidar (light detection and ranging) remote sensing device. The basic measurement is the distance between the sensor and the target surface and is 1/2 the elapsed time between the emission of a short-duration laser pulse (----) and the arrival of the reflection (- - -) of that pulse at the sensor's receiver.

high resolution, spatially rectified to ground control points. With use of stereo air photos and scopes, Fox et al. (2000) created 3-dimensional images of canopy gaps which could be used in ARC info computer GIS files to aid digital software analyses. Tanaka and Nakashizuka (1997) used similar methodology to analyze long-term (15 years) canopy dynamics of a 25.25-ha mixed deciduous forest in Japan.

Several other methods have been used to detect temporal changes in habitat structure at 5 scales of resolution that could be transformed to digital data sets including: cameras on sticks (Bennett et al. 2000), tethered balloons or blimps (Mims 1990, Pitt and Glover 1993, Murden and Risenhoover 2000), tower crane with a horizontal jib (Parker et al. 1992), ultralight aircraft (Cohen et al. 1990), fixed-wing aircraft (Everitt and Nixon 1985, Everitt et al. 1991, Ritchie et al. 1992, Blackburn and Milton 1996), and high altitude remote sensing [Satellite Probatoire d'Observation de la Terre High Resolution Visible Imaging System panchromatic and Landsat thematic mapper data] (Cohen et al. 1990, Bradshaw and Spies 1992). Reviews of these methods are provided by Everitt et al. (1991), Ritchie et al. (1992), Pitt and Glover (1993), and Blackburn and Milton (1996).

Active sensors are finding more application in vegetation measurement and will have an increasing role in this area. Radar applications are being developed to measure forest canopy and stand characteristics (Waring et al. 1995, Ranson et al. 2001). Lidar or laser altimetry is currently being used in canopy measurement for forests and shrubs (Lefsky et al. 2002). The basic measurement by a lidar device is the distance between the aircraft sensor and a target surface that is expressed as the elapsed time between the laser pulse and the time it took to reflect back to the sensor divided by 2 (Fig. 14). Lidar's capability to characterize 3-dimensional canopies at small resolutions holds much promise for wildlife managers. Lidar technology is being quickly implemented compared to radar and there are many providers available. Lidar is still limited in that clouds can interfere with its functions whereas radar is an all-weather technology.

Lefsky et al. (2002) discussed the state-of-the-art of applications of lidar remote sensing relative to natural resources. They noted that numerous applications are fea-

sible but have not yet been explored, making it difficult to predict which applications will be dominant in the future.

According to their review, current applications of lidar remote sensing in vegetation and ecological measurements fall into 3 general categories: remote sensing of ground topography, measurement of the 3-dimensional structure of vegetation canopies, and prediction of forest stand attributes such as above ground biomass. They also identify efforts of bathymetric lidar systems to measure elevations in shallow water bodies. According to Lefsky et al. (2002), mapping of topographic features is the largest and fastest growing area of application for lidar remote sensing, mainly for commercial land surveys (Flood and Gutelis 1997) and mainly because airborne laser altimetry is more accurate and cost effective than other methods.

Measurements of vegetation canopy and function are of primary interest to wildlifers who study forest animal-vegetation relationships. Alimetric canopy heights (maximum and mean) and cover or lack of cover (gaps in the canopy) have been computed for temperate (Maclean and Krabill 1986), tropical (Nelson et al. 1997), boreal (Magnussen et al. 1999), and temperate deciduous forests (Ritchie et al. 1995). Caution must be made if considerable understory vegetation is present under the tree canopy because it can interrupt exact elevation measures to the ground surface.

Relative to forest stand structure attributes when species composition was noted, Maclean and Krabill (1986) were able to account for 92% of the variation in timber volume in stands of oak and loblolly pine. Nelson et al. (1997) successfully estimated basal area, volume and biomass in tropical wet forests. The availability of information and results from lidar devices will increase as technology and analytical skills improve including satellite lidar devices. Applications of lidar measurements will have application to estimating levels of taxa biodiversity ranging from guilds and communities to specific species. One example would be old-growth forest with natural cavities that are natural nesting sites for wood ducks.

APPLICATIONS OF VEGETATION MEASUREMENT

To this point, we have presented methods for measuring plants or plant attributes of different life forms of vegetation. We now discuss how some of these methods have been applied to studies of wildlife habitat.

Loft et al. (1987:656) evaluated mule deer (*Odocoileus hemionus*) habitat during 3 growing seasons in California. Their objectives were to "determine the effects of cattle stocking rate on hiding cover structure during the summer grazing season" and to measure levels of herbivory on willows and herbaceous meadow vegetation. Estimates of herbaceous forage production, deer hiding cover, and browse use were made in 0.1-ha cattle exclosures and adjacent sites subjected to moderate and heavy levels of cattle grazing. Herbaceous forage was clipped from 0.1-m² plots, oven-dried, and weighed 2 to 5 times each growing season. Hiding cover in aspen and meadow habitats was estimated at 8 locations around circular plots of 5.65-m radius with a 1-m² grid subdivided into 100 cells. A narrower 1.0 × 0.4-m grid, similar to that described by Nudds (1977), was placed at 2-m intervals along 2 20-m transects and the grids were read from a distance of 5.65 m in patchy willow habitat, where structure of the shrubs precluded use of the larger grid. The grids were read at 3 0.5-m increments to 1.5 m; the percentage obscured by vegetation from ground level to 1 m was considered hiding cover for fawns and the percentage obscured from 0.5 to 1.5 m was considered cover for adult deer. To evaluate the browsing level of willows, Loft et al. (1987) tagged willow branches with ≤24 new shoots and measured the percentage of shoots browsed after cattle were removed from the site.

Litvaitis et al. (1985:866) studied understory characteristics of snowshoe hare (*Lepus americanus*) habitat in Maine. Their objectives were to "examine hare habitat use and density in 2 areas of Maine with differing forest composition, and determine how those variables were influenced by forest understory characteristics." Snowshoe hare pellets were counted within 105 circular plots of 1-m radius on 7 700-m transects at each of 2 sites at each study area. Habitat features were measured at each pellet plot. Percent ground (canopy) cover of softwood, hardwood, herbaceous plants, and moss was estimated in each circular plot by projecting the plant crown to the ground surface. Understory stem density was estimated by counting the number of hardwood and softwood stems ≤7.5 cm DBH and ≥0.5 m tall in 2 15 × 0.5-m quadrats beginning at each pellet plot and running perpendicular to the transect. Visual obscurity at each pellet plot was estimated from a distance of 15 m for 3 0.5-m strata 0.50–2.0 m above the plot with profile boards (Nudds 1977). Overstory canopy closure was estimated with a spherical densiometer (Lemmon 1957) at each pellet plot. Correlation coefficients were calculated between each of the habitat variables and the associated snowshoe hare pellet counts to identify which variables influenced pellet density.

Sedgwick and Knopf (1990:112) studied habitat relationships of cavity-nesting birds in plains cottonwood (*Populus sargentii*) along the South Platte River, Colorado. One of their objectives was to "compare nest sites of cavity-nesting birds with available (random) nesting habitat." Each nest tree was characterized by its species, DBH, height (measured with a clinometer), and the estimated length of dead limbs ≥10 cm diameter. Habitat was characterized in a 0.04-ha circle centered at each nest tree and at 31 random points within the cottonwood-dominated riparian habitat. Numbers of snags, trees <23 cm DBH, trees 23–69 cm DBH, and trees >69 cm DBH were counted within each circle to estimate density of the 4 classes. Overstory canopy cover was estimated at 4 points on the perimeter of each circle with a spherical densiometer. Tree basal area was measured in a circle around each tree and random point with a 10 Basal Area Factors prism. These data were compared among the species of cavity-nesters using the cavity to characterize habitat use.

Kirsch et al. (1978) studied habitat characteristics of upland nesting birds, particularly of ducks in North Dakota. One of their objectives was to evaluate the height-density (obstruction) of residual grassland vegetation structure in relationship to success and density of duck nests. Height-density of grassland was measured with a modified version of a visual obstruction pole (Robel et al. 1970) in which readings of 100% obstruction were taken from a distance of 4 m and an eye-level height of 1 m. Results of their study indicated that higher nest density and success for ducks occurred in residual grassland cover with the highest average height-density readings at 100% obstruction.

Gilbert and Allwine (1991) studied relationships between small mammals and habitat characteristics of unmanaged Douglas-fir (*Pseudotsuga menziesii*) forests in Oregon. One of their objectives was to identify which environmental factors might be responsible for differences in small mammal communities among young, mature, and old growth Douglas-fir stands. They sampled small mammal abundance and vegetation in 56 young, mature, or old growth stands in 3 locations. At each stand, mammals were sampled in a 6 × 6 pitfall grid or 12 × 12 snap trap grid. In the pitfall grids, 9 points were sampled for vegetation; 16 points were sampled in the snap trap grid. Measurements were made in nested circular plots of 5.6 and 15-m radius. Within the 5.6-m radius plot, cover of logs by decay class, and cover on the ground of bare rock, exposed bare mineral soil, organic litter, moss, and lichen were estimated visually. Cover of foliage to 2-m height and by life form was estimated visually. Number and species of small and medium live trees, snags, and stumps were counted to obtain density. Within the larger circular plot, cover of shrubs and trees >2-m height was estimated in 3 canopy layers—midstory, main canopy, and super canopy. Number and species of large live trees and snags were counted. Within the larger circle, the presence and type of water and occurrence of rock outcrop and exposed talus were recorded. The number of recent tree-fall mounds with exposed roots and mineral soil was counted. Vegetation components and small mammal numbers were summarized by stand, and data from the 56 stands were analyzed by detrended correspondence analysis (Hill and Gauch 1980) to explore relationships between species abundance and environmental variables.

Hobbs et al. (1982:12) studied carrying capacity of elk in Colorado. Their objectives were to "demonstrate that estimates of nutritional carrying capacity are viable habitat-evaluation procedures and to identify sensitive parameters in the range supply-animal demand algorithm." Estimates of biomass of plants comprising >2% of the elk's diet were necessary to develop the carrying capacity model. They obtained biomass estimates from 32 1-ha stands stratified by habitat. In each stand, forbs and grasses were clipped at ground level in 30 0.25-m^2 plots. Ten 2-m^2 plots were sampled for shrubs, and current stem growth was collected between ground level and 2.5-m high. Species were individually separated, dried, and weighed. These data were used to develop biomass estimates for habitat types within the winter range of elk and combined with nitrogen concentrations and in vitro dry-matter digestibility to estimate range supply of energy and nitrogen.

Schupp (1990:504) studied seedfall and seedling recruitment of a fruit-producing tree in Panama. Fruits of this tree are eaten by monkeys and birds, and the seeds are eaten by a variety of rodents. Seedlings are eaten by deer and other large browsers. One of the objectives of the study was to examine if there were "extensive year-to-year differences in viable seedfall, postdispersal seed predation, seedling emergence, early seedling mortality, and seedling recruitment." Seedfall was monitored with 84 1.0-m^2 traps constructed of 1.5-mm mesh plastic window screening in 1 × 1-m frames. Two traps were placed randomly in each of 42 adjacent 20 × 20-m plots. Traps were not intentionally placed either under or outside the canopy of individual trees, although no traps occurred in large openings. Seeds were counted and

Fig. 15. Electronic data logger with bar codes referenced to specific attributes of plants or animals.

point-centered-quarters) to wildlife habitat use. In contrast, comparatively little research has been conducted to assess the importance of vegetation characteristics at larger scales to habitat use. As a result, resource managers confronted with conserving ecosystems extrapolate local recommendations to regional levels because landscape studies are lacking.

Advancements in the capabilities of electronic equipment (e.g., computers, video cameras, GPS units) and increased availability of landscape scale data or mapping units for soils, aquatics, vegetation, weather, climate, and land use effects have allowed natural resource researchers and managers to scale-up measurements of vegetation made within individual quadrat plots to the landscape level and to combine multiple coverages of other environmental attributes with vegetation data. These advancements include digital imaging systems, radiometers, laser altimetry or lidar, and satellite/aerial systems that use active sensors (radar) or passive sensors (panchromatic to hyperspectral imagers). These technologies can be used to measure vegetation at different scales from small resolution studies in small site-specific areas (cm^2, m^2) to regional or global assessments. Selection of the correct technology is a function of factors such as cost, time, smallest resolution of vegetation to be measured, scale, and availability of technology. In addition, field data can be electronically entered on site in palm or lap top computers or data loggers (Fig. 15) and can be identified to specific transects, quadrats or points using GPS locator UTM coordinates.

Researchers have used remotely sensed land cover data to incorporate regional variation in climate and land use into vegetation sampling schemes (Meentemeyer 1989, Bakker et al. 2002). Sampling designs that account for regional variability provide more reliable information to land managers that must deliver habitat programs across large geographic regions. Results from this type of work are being used to direct conservation planning efforts and design nature reserves (Askins et al. 1987, Hansson and Angelstam 1991, Pearson 1993).

Scale issues also are now widely recognized in wildlife science as a critical concept that influences the way that organisms relate to landscape habitat patterns. Turner et al. (2001) formally defined scale as the spatial or temporal dimension of an object or process. Scale is important because individual species often perceive the same spatial arrangement of habitats quite differently (Wiens 1989, Levin 1992). For example, a highly mobile species like a northern harrier (*Circus cyaneus*) that forages widely may be less sensitive to fine-scale changes in grassland vegetation than a sedentary meadow vole (*Microtus pennsylvanicus*) that uses dense grasslands to escape predation. Although it is easy to acknowledge that scale is an important study component, identifying the "right" scale at which to work remains a challenging issue. A key to selecting appropriate scales at which to work is to replace our own human perceptions of scale with a view of how individual wildlife species view the landscape in space and time (Wiens 1976, Pearson et al. 1996). The concept of ecological neighborhoods (Addicott et al. 1987) provides a useful framework for thinking about how space and time components of an organisms' behavior may be used to define an appropriate scale for study. However, studies of wildlife habitat at different spatial scales has confirmed there is no

removed from traps on a weekly basis. Seedling emergence was studied by scattering a known number of seeds and fruits directly under traps and counting the number of seedlings that emerged. Seedling recruitment was estimated in 3 × 3-m plots that centered at the seed trap. Newly emerged seedlings were counted twice a year and marked with numbered colored plastic bird bands. The number of seedlings marked in a year was an estimate of that year's seedling emergence. From 58 to 74% of the seedlings marked in the first count of the year were present in the second, indicating moderate mortality of newly emerged seedlings. The total number present at the second count represented the year's seedling recruitment. Predation of individual seeds was measured by gluing a 30-cm piece of nylon fishing line to 576 seeds each year, attaching that line to wire-stake flags, and measuring unnatural changes in position of the seed or loss of the seed. Schupp's (1990) experiments showed that removal generally indicated loss to vertebrate seed predators. Among-year variation in viable seedfall, seedling emergence, seedling recruitment, and seedling survival was analyzed with parametric and nonparametric analysis of variance methods. An actuarial life-table method was used to analyze seed predation.

Wildlife ecologists have spent considerable time linking fine-grain vegetation measurements (e.g., quadrats and single "correct" scale at which to work, but that ecologists should identify a suite of appropriate scales at which to analyze their data (Pearson 1993, Sisk et al. 1997, Woodward et al. 2001). Relatively new information–theoretical approaches (Burnham and Anderson 1998) provide statistical methodology for conducting multiscale habitat analyses.

Specific software is needed for display and data analysis to use the new technologies. At the most basic level, workers need to view the imagery. Providers of free viewer products include ESRI, Erdas, PCI, ER Mapper, Leica Geosystems, UC Berkeley, ENVI, and Global Mapper. Full-featured programs that can view and analyze data range from modestly priced packages, such as Idrisi, to expensive packages such as Erdas, ENVI, ER Mapper, PCI, and those from ESRI. Other software such as Adobe Photoshop has some use for applications using digital cameras.

Although some techniques are fairly recent in application, by combining a knowledge of the spatial characteristics of tree canopy and canopy gaps with principles of plant ecology, wildlife ecology, and landscape ecology, several inferences can be made regarding the distribution and diversity of wildlife and plant species within habitats across and at edges of geographic ecosystems and gradients of extensive scale.

SUMMARY

Vegetation structure, arrangement, and location are considered the primary components of wildlife conservation and management. Natural resource managers and research biologists use a variety of equipment and techniques to sample and measure vegetation in a multitude of different aquatic and terrestrial plant communities and habitat types.

Aquatic vegetation assessment is more difficult to accomplish than for terrestrial vegetation because it involves floating, submergent, and emergent plant species. In most years, aquatic vegetation assessment is conducted while wading, from a boat or from aerial photography. Due to circumstances, equipment such as quadrat frames, etc., must be constructed of materials that will float to facilitate aquatic vegetation sampling and measurement in wetlands.

Terrestrial vegetation assessment is fairly straightforward but sampling and measurement techniques vary considerably among grassland, shrubland, and woodland habitat types. For example, rulers and tape measures can be used to measure plant height or canopy cover (e.g., line intercept) for grass and forb species whereas prisms, angle gauges, and spherical densiometers are needed to obtain the same measurements for trees. Relative to vegetative food items, the amount of fruit or mast production may be estimated by ocular counts on sample limbs or by collecting falling mast in various traps.

Vegetation sampling and measurement are generally conducted within vegetation patches or field-size units of a local nature. In contrast, landscale-level assessments of vegetation are usually conducted using satellite, aerial, or video photography coupled with geographic information system techniques. Recent advances in computer capabilities have enabled managers and researchers to work with larger and more complex data sets to assess vegetation characteristics. These capabilities also enable the integration of other data sets such as animal population demographics, weather, topography, and soils with the vegetation data for greater in-depth analytical and modeling exercises (Anderson and Gutzwiller 2005).

To comprehensively address all of the possible ways to sample and measure vegetation would require volumes of text and figures. As authors, we have tried to introduce the reader to as wide array of vegetation sampling and measuring techniques as possible within the limits of this Chapter. We encourage others to explore the literature we have presented and any new literature that will enhance their ability to assess vegetation in a manner that best fits their research or management objectives.

ACKNOWLEDGMENTS

We thank J. L. Oldemeyer (retired) and R. F. Harlow (deceased) for their authorship help with the 1994 version of this Chapter on vegetation sampling and measurement. M. A. Rumble, P. J. Happe, A. R. Lewis, R. D. Schilowsky, E. D. Salo, K. A. Sager, F. R. Quamen, R. W. Klaver, D. M. Gardner, and S. J. Bandas assisted with obtaining photographs or literature references and/or proofreading of text and tables. T. L. Symens was responsible for all typing and word processing. We thank C. E. Braun and an anonymous reviewer for editorial corrections and suggestions that enhanced the manuscript.

LITERATURE CITED

ABBOTT, H. G. 1961. White pine seed consumption by small mammals. Journal of Forestry 59:197–201.

———, AND W. E. DODGE. 1961. Photographic observations of white pine seed destruction by birds and mammals. Journal of Forestry 59:292–294.

ADDICOTT, J. F., J. M. AHO, M. F. ANTOLIN, D. K. PADILLA, J. S. RICHARDSON, AND D. A. SOLUK. 1987. Ecological neighborhoods: scaling environmental patterns. Oikos 49:340–346.

AHMED, J., AND C. D. BONHAM. 1982. Optimum allocation in multivariate double sampling for biomass estimation. Journal of Range Management 35:777–779.

———, AND W. A. LAYCOCK. 1983. Comparison of techniques used for adjusting biomass estimates by double sampling. Journal of Range Management 36:217–221.

ALABACK, P. B. 1982. Dynamics of understory biomass in Sitka spruce-western hemlock forests of southeast Alaska. Ecology 63:1932–1948.

ALLEN, P. H., AND K. B. TROUSDELL. 1961. Loblolly pine seed production in the Virginia–North Carolina Coastal Plain. Journal of Forestry 59:187–190.

ANDERSON, M. G. 1978. Distribution and production of sago pondweed (*Potamogeton pectinatus* L.) on a northern prairie marsh. Ecology 59:154–160.

ANDERSON, S. H., AND K. J. GUTZWILLER. 2005. Wildlife habitat evaluation. Pages 489–502 *in* C. E. Braun, editor. Sixth edition. Techniques for wildlife investigations and management. The Wildlife Society, Bethesda, Maryland, USA.

ASHER, W. C. 1963. Squirrels prefer cones from fertilized trees. U.S. Department of Agriculture, Forest Service Research Note SE-3.

ASKINS, R. A., M. J. PHILBRICK, AND D. S. SUGENO. 1987. Relationship between the regional abundance of forest and the composition of forest bird communities. Biological Conservation 39:129–152.

ASNER, G. P. 1998. Biophysical and biochemical sources of variability in canopy reflectance. Remote Sensing of Environment 64:234-253.

AVERY, T. E. 1959. An all-purpose cruiser stick. Journal of Forestry 57:924–925.

———, AND G. L. BERLIN. 1992. Fundamentals of remote sensing and airphoto interpretation. Fifth edition. Prentice-Hall, Inc., Upper Saddle River, New Jersey, USA.

BAKKER, K. K., D. E. NAUGLE, AND K. F. HIGGINS. 2002. Incorporating landscape attributes into models for migratory grassland bird conservation. Conservation Biology 16:1638–1646.

BASILE, J. V., AND S. S. HUTCHINGS. 1966. Twig diameter-length-weight relations of bitterbrush. Journal of Range Management 19:34–38.

BASKERVILLE, G. L. 1972. Use of logarithmic regression in the estimation of plant biomass. Canadian Journal of Forest Research 2:49–53.

BATCHELER, C. L. 1973. Estimating density and dispersion from truncated or unrestricted joint point-distance nearest-neighbor distances. Proceedings of the New Zealand Ecological Society 20:131–147.

BECK, D. E., AND D. F. OLSON, JR. 1968. Seed production in southern Appalachian oak stands. U.S. Department of Agriculture, Forest Service Research Note SE-91.

BENKOBI, L., D. W. URESK, G. SCHENBECK, AND R. M. KING. 2000. Protocol for monitoring standing crop in grasslands using visual obstruction. Journal of Range Management 53:627–633.

BENNETT, L.T., T. S. JUDD, AND M. A. ADAMS. 2000. Close-range vertical photography for measuring cover changes in perennial grasslands. Journal of Range Management 53:634–641.

BENTZ, J. A., AND P. M. WOODARD. 1988. Vegetation characteristics and bighorn sheep use on burned and unburned areas in Alberta. Wildlife Society Bulletin 16:186–193.

BITTERLICH, W. 1948. Die winkelzahlprobe. Allgemeine Forst-und Holzwirtschaftlich Zeitung 59:4–5.

BLACKBURN, G. A., AND E. J. MILTON. 1996. Filling the gaps: remote sensing meets woodland ecology. Global Ecology and Biogeography Letters 5:175–191.

BLOCK, W. M., K. A. WITH, AND M. L. MORRISON. 1987. On measuring bird habitat: influence of observer variability and sample size. Condor 89:241–251.

BOBEK, B., AND R. BERGSTROM. 1978. A rapid method of browse biomass estimation in a forest habitat. Journal of Range Management 31:456–458.

BONHAM, C. D. 1989. Measurements for terrestrial vegetation. John Wiley and Sons, New York, USA.

BRADSHAW, G. A., AND T. A. SPIES. 1992. Characterizing canopy gap structure in forests using wavelet analysis. Journal of Ecology 80:205–215.

BRANSBY, D. I., A. G. MATCHES, AND G. F. KRAUSE. 1977. Disk meter for rapid estimation of herbage yield in grazing trials. Agronomy Journal 69:393–396.

BRAUN-BLANQUET, J., G. D. FULLER, AND H. S. CONARD. 1965. Plant sociology: the study of plant communities. Second edition. Hafner, London, United Kingdom.

BROWN, D. M. 1954. Methods of surveying and measuring vegetation. Commonwealth Agriculture Bureau, Farnham Royal, Bucks, United Kingdom.

BROWN, J. K. 1976. Estimating shrub biomass from basal stem diameters. Canadian Journal of Forest Research 6:153–158.

BRUMMER, J. E., J. T. NICHOLS, R. K. ENGEL, AND K. M. ESKRIDGE. 1994. Efficiency of different quadrat sizes and shapes for sampling standing crop. Journal of Range Management 47:84–89.

BUNNELL, F. L., AND D. J. VALES. 1990. Comparison of methods for estimating forest overstory cover: differences among techniques. Canadian Journal of Forest Research 20:101–107.

BURLESON, W. H. 1975. A method of mounting plant specimens in the field. Journal of Range Management 28:240–241.

BURNHAM, K. P., AND D. R. ANDERSON. 1998. Model selection and inference: a practical information–theoretic approach. Springer-Verlag, Inc., New York, USA.

CAIN, S. A., AND G. M. DE O. CASTRO. 1959. Manual of vegetation analysis. Harper & Brothers Publication, New York, USA.

CANFIELD, R. H. 1941. Application of the line interception method in sampling range vegetation. Journal of Forestry 39:388–394.

———. 1944. Measurement of grazing use by the line interception method. Journal of Forestry 42:192–194.

CHAN, S. S., R. W. McCREIGHT, J. D. WALSTAD, AND T. A. SPIES. 1986. Evaluating forest vegetative cover with computerized analysis of fisheye photographs. Forest Science 32:1085–1091.

CHRISTISEN, D. M., AND W. H. KEARBY. 1984. Mast measurement and production in Missouri (with special reference to acorns). Missouri Department of Conservation Terrestrial Series 13. Columbia, USA.

CLARK, J. D., D. L. CLAPP, K. L. SMITH, AND B. EDERINGTON. 1994. Black bear habitat use relation to food availability in the interior highlands of Arkansas. International Conference on Bear Research and Management 9:309–318.

CLARK, P. E., AND M. S. SEYFRIED. 2001. Point sampling for leaf area index in sagebrush steppe communities. Journal of Range Management 54:589–594.

CLARY, W. P. AND W. C. LEININGER. 2000. Stubble height as a tool for management of riparian areas. Journal of Range Management 53:562–573.

COHEN, W. B., T. A. SPIES, AND G. A. BRADSHAW. 1990. Semivariograms of digital imagery for analysis of conifer canopy structure. Remote Sensing of Environment 34:167–178.

COLE, G. F. 1956. Pronghorn antelope, its range use and food habits in central Montana with special reference to alfalfa. Montana State College Agricultural Experiment Station Technical Bulletin 516, Bozeman, USA.

———. 1959. Key browse survey method. Proceedings of the Western Association of State Fish and Game Commissioners 39:181–185.

COLLINS, W. B., AND E. F. BECKER. 2001. Estimation of horizontal cover. Journal of Range Management 54:67–70.

CONNELLY, J. W., K. P. REESE, AND M. A. SCHROEDER. 2003. Monitoring of greater sage-grouse habitats and populations. Idaho Forest, Wildlife and Range Experiment Station, Moscow, USA.

COOK, C. W., AND C. D. BONHAM. 1977. Techniques for vegetation measurements and analysis for a pre- and post-mining inventory. Colorado State University Range Science Series 28, Fort Collins, USA.

———, AND J. STUBBENDIECK. 1986. Range research: basic problems and techniques. Society of Range Management, Denver, Colorado, USA.

COOK, J. G., T. W. STUTZMAN, C. W. BOWERS, K. A. BRENNER, AND L. L. IRWIN. 1995. Spherical densiometers produce biased estimates of forest canopy cover. Wildlife Society Bulletin 23:711–717.

COOPER, C. F. 1957. The variable plot method for estimating shrub density. Journal of Range Management 10:111–115.

———. 1963. An evaluation of variable plot sampling in shrub and herbaceous vegetation. Ecology 44:565–569.

COTTAM, G., AND J. T. CURTIS. 1949. A method for making rapid surveys of woodlands by means of randomly selected trees. Ecology 30:101–104.

———, AND ———. 1956. The use of distance measures in phytosociological sampling. Ecology 37:451–460.

———, ———, AND B. W. HALE. 1953. Some sampling characteristics of a population of randomly dispersed individuals. Ecology 34:741–757.

CURTIS, J. T. 1959. The vegetation of Wisconsin; an ordination of plant communities. University of Wisconsin Press, Madison, USA.

———, AND R. P. McINTOSH. 1950. The interrelations of certain analytic and synthetic phytosociological characters. Ecology 31:434–455.

DANSEREAU, P. M. 1957. Biogeography: an ecological perspective. Ronald Press Co., New York, USA.

DASMANN, W. P. 1951. Some deer range survey methods. California Fish and Game 37:43–52.

DAUBENMIRE, R. F. 1959. A canopy-coverage method of vegetational analysis. Northwest Science 33:43–64.

———. 1968. Plant communities: a textbook of plant synecology. Harper & Row Publishers, Inc., New York, USA.

DAVISON, V. E., L. M. DICKERSON, K. GRAETZ, W. W. NEELEY, AND L. ROOF. 1955. Measuring the yield and availability of game bird foods. Journal of Wildlife Management 19:302–308.

DeGANGE, A. R., J. W. FITZPATRICK, J. N. LAYNE, AND G. E. WOOLFENDEN. 1989. Acorn harvesting by Florida scrub jays. Ecology 70:348–356.

DeGRAAF, R. M., AND N. L. CHADWICK. 1987. Forest type, timber size class, and New England breeding birds. Journal of Wildlife Management 51:212–217.

DESSECKER, D. R., AND D. G. McAULEY. 2001. Importance of early successional habitat to ruffed grouse and American woodcock. Wildlife Society Bulletin 29:456–465.

DILWORTH, J. R. 1989. Log scaling and timber cruising. Oregon State University Book Stores, Inc., Corvallis, USA.

DOWNS, A. A., AND W. E. McQUILKIN. 1944. Seed production of southern Appalachian oaks. Journal of Forestry 42:913–920.

DUDLEY, S. J., C. D. BONHAM, S. R. ABT, AND J. C. FISCHENICH. 1998. Comparison of methods for measuring woody riparian vegetation density. Journal of Arid Environments 38:77–86.

Easley, L. T., and L. E. Chaiken. 1951. An expendable seed trap. Journal of Forestry 49:652–653.

EDDLEMAN, L. E., E. E. REMMENGA, AND R. T. WARD. 1964. An evaluation of plot methods for alpine vegetation. Bulletin of the Torrey Botanical Club 91:439–450.

EDGE, W. D., C. L. MARCUM, AND S. L. OLSON-EDGE. 1987. Summer habitat selection by elk in western Montana: a multivariate approach. Journal of Wildlife Management 51:844–851.

ELZINGA, C. L., D. W. SALZER, AND J. W. WILLOUGHBY. 1998. Measuring and monitoring plant populations. BLM Technical Reference 1730-1. U.S. Department of the Interior, Denver, Colorado, USA.

ENGEMAN, R. M., R. T. SUGIHARA, L. F. PANK, AND W. E. DUSENBERRY. 1994. A comparison of plotless density estimators using monte carlo simulation. Ecology 75:1769–1779.

ETCHBERGER, R. C., AND P. R. KRAUSMAN. 1997. Evaluation of five methods for measuring desert vegetation. Wildlife Society Bulletin 25:604–609.

EVANS, R. A., AND R. M. LOVE. 1957. The step-point method of sampling—a practical tool in range research. Journal of Range Management 10:208–212.

EVERITT, J. H., AND P. R. NIXON. 1985. Video imagery: a new remote sensing tool for range management. Journal of Range Management 38:421–424.

———, D. E. ESCOBAR, R. VILLARREAL, J. R. NORIEGA, AND M. R. DAVIS. 1991. Airborne video systems for agricultural assessments. Remote Sensing of Environment 35:231–242.

FEHMI, J. S., AND J. W. BARTOLOME. 2001. A grid-based method for sampling and analyzing spatially ambiguous plants. Journal of Vegetation Science 12:467–472.

FISSER, H. G. 1961. Variable plot, square foot plot, and visual estimate for shrub crown cover measurements. Journal of Range Management 14:202–207.

FLOOD, M., AND B. GUTELIS. 1997. Commercial implications of topographic terrain mapping using scanning airborne laser radar. Photogrammetric Engineering and Remote Sensing 63:327–366.

FLOYD, D. A., AND J. E. ANDERSON. 1987. A comparison of three methods for estimating plant cover. Journal of Ecology 75:221–228.

FOX, T. J., M. G. KNUTSON, AND R. K. HINES. 2000. Mapping forest canopy gaps using air-photo interpretation and ground surveys. Wildlife Society Bulletin 28:882–889.

GANEY, J. L., AND W. M. BLOCK. 1994. A comparison of two techniques for measuring canopy closure. Western Journal of Applied Forestry 9:21–23.

GARTON, E. O., J. T. RATTI, AND J. H. GIUDICE. 2005. Research and experimental design. Pages 43–71 in C. E. Braun, editor. Techniques for wildlife investigations and management. Sixth edition. The Wildlife Society, Bethesda, Maryland, USA.

GIBBENS, R. P., AND R. F. BECK. 1988. Changes in grass basal area and forb densities over a 64-year period on grassland types of the Jornada Experimental Range. Journal of Range Management 41:186–192.

GILBERT, F. F., AND R. ALLWINE. 1991. Small mammal communities in the Oregon Cascade Range. Pages 257–267 in L. F. Ruggiero, K. B. Aubry, A. B. Carey, and M. H. Huff, technical coordinators. Wildlife and vegetation of unmanaged Douglas-fir forests. U.S. Department of Agriculture, Forest Service General Technical Report PNW-GTR-285.

GONZALEZ, M. A., M. A. HUSSEY, AND B. E. CONRAD. 1990. Plant height, disk, and capacitance meters used to estimate bermudagrass herbage mass. Agronomy Journal 82:861–864.

GOODALL, D. W. 1952. Some considerations in the use of point quadrats for the analysis of vegetation. Australian Journal of Scientific Research, Series Biological Sciences 5:1–41.

GOODMAN, L. A. 1960. On the exact variance of products. Journal of the American Statistical Association 55:708–713.

GOODRUM, P. D., V. H. REID, AND C. E. BOYD. 1971. Acorn yields, characteristics, and management criteria of oaks for wildlife. Journal of Wildlife Management 35:520–532.

GOTFRYD, A., AND R. I. C. HANSELL. 1985. The impact of observer bias on multivariate analysis of vegetation structure. Oikos 45:223–234.

GRABER, R. E. 1970. Natural seed fall in white pine (*Pinus strobus* L.) stands of varying density. U.S. Department of Agriculture, Forest Service Research Note NE-119.

GRAY, M. J., R. M. KAMINSKI, AND G. WEERAKKODY. 1999. Predicting seed yield of moist-soil plants. Journal of Wildlife Management 63:1261–1268.

GRIEG-SMITH, P. 1964. Quantitative plant ecology. First edition. Plenum Press, New York, USA.

GRIFFITH, B., AND B. A. YOUTIE. 1988. Two devices for estimating foliage density and deer hiding cover. Wildlife Society Bulletin 16:206–210.

GROSENBAUGH, L. R. 1952. Plotless timber estimates, new, fast, easy. Journal of Forestry 50:32–37.

GYSEL, L. W. 1956. Measurement of acorn crops. Forest Science 2:305–313.

———. 1957. Acorn production on good, medium, and poor oak sites in southern Michigan. Journal of Forestry 55:570–574.

———, AND L. J. LYON. 1980. Habitat analysis and evaluation. Pages 305–327 in S. D. Schemnitz, editor. Wildlife management techniques manual. Fourth edition. The Wildlife Society, Washington, D.C., USA.

HALLS, L. K., AND R. F. HARLOW. 1971. Weight-length relations in flowering dogwood twigs. Journal of Range Management 24:236–237.

HANLEY, T. A. 1978. A comparison of the line-interception and quadrat estimation methods of determining shrub canopy coverage. Journal of Range Management 31:60–62.

HANSSON, L., AND P. ANGELSTAM. 1991. Landscape ecology as a theoretical basis for nature conservation. Landscape Ecology 5:191–201.

HARLOW, R. F. 1977. A technique for surveying deer forage in the South-

east. Wildlife Society Bulletin 5:185–191.

———, B. A. SANDERS, J. B. WHELAN, AND L. C. CHAPPEL. 1980. Deer habitat on the Ocala National Forest: improvement through forage management. Southern Journal of Applied Forestry 4:98–102.

HARMONEY, K. R., K. J. MOORE, J. R. GEORGE, E. C. BRUMMER, AND J. R. RUSSELL. 1997. Determination of pasture biomass using four indirect methods. Agronomy Journal 89:665–672.

HAUGEN, A. O., AND F. W. FITCH, JR. 1955. Seasonal availability of certain bush lespedeza and partridge pea seed as determined from ground samples. Journal of Wildlife Management 19:297–301.

HAUKOS, D. A., H. Z. SUN, D. B. WEBSTER, AND L. M. SMITH. 1998. Sample size, power, and analytical considerations for vertical structure data from profile boards in wetland vegetation. Wetlands 18:203–215.

HAYS, R. L., C. SUMMERS, AND W. L. SEITZ. 1981. Estimating wildlife habitat variables. U.S. Department of the Interior, Fish and Wildlife Service, FWS/OBS-81/47.

HEADY, H. F., R. P. GIBBENS, AND R. W. POWELL. 1959. A comparison of the charting, line intercept, and line point methods of sampling shrub types of vegetation. Journal of Range Management 12:180–188.

HIGGINS, K. F., AND W. T. BARKER. 1982. Changes in vegetation structure in seeded nesting cover in the prairie pothole region. U.S. Department of the Interior, Fish and Wildlife Service Special Scientific Report 242.

HILL, M. O., AND H. G. GAUCH. 1980. Detrended correspondence analysis: an improved ordination technique. Vegetation 42:47–58.

HILMON, J. B. 1959. Determination of herbage weight by double-sampling: weight estimate and actual weight. Pages 20–25 in Technique and methods of measuring understory vegetation. U.S. Department of Agriculture, Forest Service, Southern and Southeast Forest Experiment Stations, New Orleans, Louisiana, USA.

HIRST, S. M. 1975. Ungulate-habitat relationships in a South African woodland/savanna ecosystem. Wildlife Monographs 44.

HOBBS, N. T., D. L. BAKER, J. E. ELLIS, D. M. SWIFT, AND R. A. GREEN. 1982. Energy-and nitrogen-based estimates of elk winter-range carrying capacity. Journal of Wildlife Management 46:12–21.

HOOPER, R. G. 1988. Longleaf pines used for cavities by red-cockaded woodpeckers. Journal of Wildlife Management 52:392–398.

HOOVEN, E. 1958. Deer mouse and reforestation in the Tillamook burn. Oregon Forest Lands Research Center Research Note 37, Corvallis, USA.

HUENNEKE, L. F., AND C. GRAHAM. 1987. A new sticky trap for monitoring seed rain in grasslands. Journal of Range Management 40:370–372.

HYDER, D. N., AND F. A. SNEVA. 1960. Bitterlich's plotless method for sampling basal ground cover of bunchgrasses. Journal of Range Management 13:6–9.

———, R. E. BEMENT, E. E. REMMENGA, AND C. TERWILLIGER, JR. 1965. Frequency sampling of blue grama range. Journal of Range Management 18:90–94.

IRWIN, L. L., AND J. M. PEEK. 1979. Shrub production and biomass trends following five logging treatments within the cedar-hemlock zone of northern Idaho. Forest Science 25:415–426.

JAMES, F. C., AND H. H. SHUGART, JR. 1970. A quantitative method of habitat description. Audubon Field Notes 24:727–736.

JENSEN, C. H., AND G. W. SCOTTER. 1977. A comparison of twig-length and browsed-twig methods of determining browse utilization. Journal of Range Management 30:64–67.

———, AND P. J. URNESS. 1981. Establishing browse utilization from twig diameters. Journal of Range Management 34:113–116.

JOHNSON, A. S., AND J. L. LANDERS. 1978. Fruit production in slash pine plantations in Georgia. Journal of Wildlife Management 42:606–613.

JOHNSON, P. S., C. L. JOHNSON, AND N. E. WEST. 1988. Estimation of phytomass for ungrazed crested wheatgrass plants using allometric equations. Journal of Range Management 41:421–425.

JOHNSTON, A. 1957. A comparison of the line interception, vertical point quadrat, and loop methods as used in measuring basal area of grassland vegetation. Canadian Journal of Plant Science 37:34–42.

KEIGLEY, R. B. 1997. A growth form method for describing browse condition. Rangelands 19(3):26–29.

———, M. R. FRISINA, AND C. W. FAGER. 2002a. Assessing browse trend at the landscape level. Part I. Preliminary steps and field survey. Rangelands 24(3):28–33.

———, ———, AND ———. 2002b. Assessing browse trend at the landscape level. Part II. Monitoring. Rangelands 24(3):34–38.

KERSHAW, K. A. 1964. Quantitative and dynamic ecology. Edward Arnold Publishing Company Ltd., London, United Kingdom.

KINSINGER, F. E., R. E. ECKERT, AND P. O. CURRIE. 1960. A comparison of the line-interception, variable-plot, and loop methods as used to measure shrub-crown cover. Journal of Range Management 13:17–21.

KIRSCH, L. M., H. F. DUEBBERT, AND A. D. KRUSE. 1978. Grazing and haying effects on habitats of upland nesting birds. Transactions of the North American Wildlife and Natural Resources Conference 43:486–497.

KLAWITTER, R. A., AND J. STUBBS. 1961. A reliable oak seed trap. Journal of Forestry 59:291–292.

KOENIG, W. D., AND J. KNOPS. 1995. Why do oaks produce boom-and-bust seed crops? California Agriculture 49(5):7–12.

———, R. L. MUMME, W. J. CARMEN, AND M. T. STANBACK. 1994. Acorn production by oaks in central coastal California: variation within and among years. Ecology 75:99–109.

LANDERS, J. L., AND A. S. JOHNSON. 1976. Bobwhite quail food habits. Tall Timbers Research Station Miscellaneous Publication 4, Tallahassee, Florida, USA.

LAUBHAN, M. K., AND L. H. FREDRICKSON. 1992. Estimating seed production of common plants in seasonally flooded wetlands. Journal of Wildlife Management 56:329–337.

LAYCOCK, W. A. 1965. Adaptation of distance measurements for range sampling. Journal of Range Management 18:205–211.

———, AND C. L. BATCHELER. 1975. Comparison of distance-measurement techniques for sampling tussock grassland species in New Zealand. Journal of Range Management 28:235–239.

LEFSKY, M. A., W. B. COHEN, G. G. PARKER, AND D. J. HARDING. 2002. Lidar remote sensing for ecosystem studies. BioScience 52:19–30.

LEMMON, P. E. 1957. A new instrument for measuring forest overstory density. Journal of Forestry 55:667–669.

LEVIN, S. A. 1992. The problem of pattern and scale in ecology. Ecology 73:1943-1967.

LEVY, E. E., AND E. A. MADDEN. 1933. The point method of pasture analysis. New Zealand Agricultural Journal 46:267–279.

LINDSEY, A. A., J. D. BARTON, JR., AND S. R. MILES. 1958. Field efficiencies of forest sampling methods. Ecology 39:428–444.

LITVAITIS, J. A., J. A. SHERBURNE, AND J. A. BISSONETTE. 1985. Influence of understory characteristics on snowshoe hare habitat use and density. Journal of Wildlife Management 49:866–873.

LOFT, E. R., J. W. MENKE, J. G. KIE, AND R. C. BERTRAM. 1987. Influence of cattle stocking rate on the structural profile of deer hiding cover. Journal of Wildlife Management 51:655–664.

LOMMASSON, T., AND C. JENSEN. 1938. Grass volume tables for determining range utilization. Science 87:444.

LOTTI, T., AND W. P. LEGRANDE. 1959. Loblolly pine seed production and seedling crops in the lower Coastal Plain of South Carolina. Journal of Forestry 57:580–581.

LYON, L. J. 1968a. An evaluation of density sampling methods in a shrub community. Journal of Range Management 21:16–20.

———. 1968b. Estimating twig production of serviceberry from crown volumes. Journal of Wildlife Management 32:115–119.

———. 1970. Length- and weight-diameter relations of serviceberry twigs. Journal of Wildlife Management 34:456–460.

MACLEAN, G. A., AND W. B. KRABILL. 1986. Gross-merchantable timber volume estimation using an airborne LIDAR system. Canadian Journal of Remote Sensing 12:7–18.

MAGNUSSEN S., P. EGGERMONT, AND V. N. LARICCIA. 1999. Recovering tree heights from airborne laser scanner data. Forest Science 45:407–422.

MARLOW, C. B., AND W. P. CLARY. 1996. Natural resource monitoring for the Daubenmire disadvantaged. Pages 13–18 in K. E. Evans, compiler. Sharing common ground on western rangelands: proceedings of a livestock/big game symposium. U.S. Department of Agriculture, Forest Service General Technical Report INT-GTR-343.

MCCRACKEN, K. E., J. W. WITHAM, AND M. L. HUNTER, JR. 1999. Relationships between seed fall of three tree species and *Peromyscus leucopus* and *Clethrionomys gapperi* during 10 years in an oak–pine forest. Journal of Mammalogy 80:1288–1296.

MCQUILKIN, R. A., AND R. A. MUSBACH. 1977. Pin oak acorn production on green tree reservoirs in southeastern Missouri. Journal of Wildlife Management 41:218–225.

MCSHEA, W. J. 2000. The influence of acorn crops on annual variation in rodent and bird populations. Ecology 81:228–238.

———, AND G. SCHWEDE. 1993. Variable acorn crops: responses of white-tailed deer and other mast consumers. Journal of Mammalogy 74:999–1006.

MEENTEMEYER, V. 1989. Geographical perspectives of space, time, and scale. Landscape Ecology 3:163–173.

MERRILL, E. H., AND M. S. BOYCE. 1991. Summer range and elk population dynamics in Yellowstone National Park. Pages 263–273 in R. B. Keiter and M. S. Boyce, editors. The greater Yellowstone eco-

system: redefining America's wilderness heritage. Yale University Press, New Haven, Connecticut, USA.

MILLS, L. S., R. J. FREDRICKSON, AND B. B. MOORHEAD. 1993. Characteristics of old-growth forests associated with northern spotted owls in Olympic National Park. Journal of Wildlife Management 57:315–321.

MIMS, III, F. M. 1990. The amateur scientist: a remote-control camera that catches the wind and captures the landscape. Scientific American 263(October):126–129.

MINCKLER, L. S., AND R. E. MCDERMOTT. 1960. Pin oak acorn production and regeneration as affected by stand density, structure and flooding. University of Missouri Agricultural Experiment Station Research Bulletin 750, Columbia, USA.

MOODY, R. D., J. O. COLLINS, AND V. H. REID. 1954. Oak production study underway. Louisiana Conservationist 6(9):6–8.

MORISITA, M. 1957. A new method for the estimation of density by the spacing method applicable to non-randomly distributed populations. Physiological Ecology 7:134–144.

MORRISON, M. L., B. G. MARCOT, AND R. W. MANNAN. 1998. Wildlife-habitat relationships: concepts and applications. Second edition. University of Wisconsin Press, Madison, USA.

MOULIN, S., A. DONDEAU, AND R. DELECOLLE. 1998. Combining agricultural crop models and satellite observations from field to regional scales. International Journal of Remote Sensing 19:1021–1036.

MUELLER-DOMBOIS, D., AND H. ELLENBERG. 1974. Aims and methods of vegetation ecology. John Wiley and Sons, New York, USA.

MURDEN, S. B., AND K. L. RISENHOOVER. 2000. A blimp system to obtain high-resolution, low-altitude aerial photography and videography. Wildlife Society Bulletin 28:958–962.

MURRAY, R. B., AND M. Q. JACOBSON. 1982. An evaluation of dimension analysis for predicting shrub biomass. Journal of Range Management 35:451–454.

NAUGLE, D. E., K. F. HIGGINS, M. E. ESTEY, R. R. JOHNSON, AND S. M. NUSSER. 2000. Local and landscape-level factors influencing black tern habitat suitability. Journal of Wildlife Management 64:253–260.

NELSON, R., R. ODERWALD, AND T. G. GREGOIRE. 1997. Separating the ground and airborne laser sampling phases to estimate tropical forest basal area, volume, and biomass. Remote Sensing of Environment 60:311–326.

NORTH, M., G. STEGER, R. DENTON, G. EBERLEIN, T. MUNTON, AND K. JOHNSON. 2000. Association of weather and nest-site structure with reproductive success in California spotted owls. Journal of Wildlife Management 64:797–807.

NOYCE, K. V., AND P. L. COY. 1989. Abundance and productivity of bear food species in different forest types of northcentral Minnesota. International Conference on Bear Research and Management 8:169–181.

NUDDS, T. D. 1977. Quantifying the vegetative structure of wildlife cover. Wildlife Society Bulletin 5:113–117.

NUTTLE, T. 1997. Densiometer bias? Are we measuring the forest or the trees? Wildlife Society Bulletin 25:610–611.

OHMANN, L. F., D. F. GRIGAL, AND R. B. BRANDER. 1976. Biomass estimation for five shrubs from northeastern Minnesota. U.S. Department of Agriculture, Forest Service Research Paper NC-133.

OLDEMEYER, J. L. 1982. Estimating production of paper birch and utilization by browsers. Canadian Journal of Forest Research 12:52–57.

———, AND W. L. REGELIN. 1980. Comparison of 9 methods for estimating density of shrubs and saplings in Alaska. Journal of Wildlife Management 44:662–666.

OLENICKI, T. 2001. Ground-based radiometers, real-time GPS receivers, and laser rangefinders—new techniques for estimating vegetation parameters and animal use sites. Intermountain Journal of Sciences 6:384–385.

OLINDE, M. W., L. S. PERRIN, F. MONTALBANO, III, L. L. ROWSE, AND M. J. ALLEN. 1985. Smartweed seed production and availability in southcentral Florida wetlands. Proceedings of the Annual Conference of the Southeastern Association of Fish and Wildlife Agencies 39:459–464.

O'NEIL, T. A., P. BETTINGER, B. G. MARCOT, B. W. LUSCOMBE, G. T. KOELN, H. J. BRUNER, C. BARRETT, J. A. POLLOCK, AND S. BERNATUS. 2005. Application of spatial technologies in wildlife biology. Pages 418–447 in C. E. Braun, editor. Sixth edition. Techniques for wildlife investigations and management. The Wildlife Society, Bethesda, Maryland, USA.

OSTFELD, R. S., C. G. JONES, AND J. O. WOLFF. 1996. Of mice and mast: ecological connections in eastern deciduous forests. BioScience 46:323–330.

OWENSBY, C. E. 1973. Modified step-point system for botanical composition and basal cover estimates. Journal of Range Management 26:302–303.

PARKER, G. G., A. P. SMITH, AND K. P. HOGAN. 1992. Access to the upper forest canopy with a large tower crane: sampling the treetops in three dimensions. BioScience 42:664–670.

PARKER, K. R. 1979. Density estimation by variable area transect. Journal of Wildlife Management 43:484–492.

PATTON, D. R., AND J. M. HALL. 1966. Evaluating key browse by age and form class. Journal of Wildlife Management 30:476–480.

PEARSON, S. M. 1993. The spatial extent and relative influence of landscape-level factors on wintering bird populations. Landscape Ecology 8:3–18.

———, M. G. TURNER, R. H. GARDNER, AND R. V. O'NEILL. 1996. An organism based perspective of habitat fragmentation. Pages 77–95 in R. C. Szaro, editor. Biodiversity in managed landscapes: theory and practice. Oxford University Press, Covelo, California, USA.

PECHANEC, J. F. 1936. Comments on the stem-count method of determining the percentage utilization of range. Ecology 17:329–331.

———, AND G. D. PICKFORD. 1937. A weight estimate method for the determination of range or pasture production. Journal of the American Society of Agronomy 29:894–904.

PEEK, J. M. 1970. Relation of canopy area and volume to production of three woody species. Ecology 51:1098–1101.

———, L. W. KREFTING, AND J. C. TAPPEINER. 1971. Variation in twig diameter–weight relationships in northern Minnesota. Journal of Wildlife Management 35:501–507.

PENFOUND, W. T., AND E. L. RICE. 1957. An evaluation of the arms-length rectangle method in forest sampling. Ecology 38:660–661.

PERRY, R. W., R. E. THILL, D. G. PEITZ, AND P. A. TAPPE. 1999. Effects of different silvicultural systems on initial soft mast production. Wildlife Society Bulletin 27:915–923.

PICKFORD, G. D., AND G. STEWART. 1935. Coordinate method of mapping low shrubs. Ecology 16:257–261.

PIERCE, D. J., AND J. M. PEEK. 1984. Moose habitat use and selection patterns in north-central Idaho. Journal of Wildlife Management 48:1335–1343.

PITT, D. G., AND G. R. GLOVER. 1993. Large-scale 35-mm aerial photographs for assessment of vegetation-management research plots in eastern Canada. Canadian Journal of Forest Research 23:2159–2169.

POLLARD, J. H. 1971. On distance estimators of density in randomly distributed forests. Biometrics 27:991-1002.

POTVIN, F., AND J. HUOT. 1983. Estimating carrying capacity of a white-tailed deer wintering area in Quebec. Journal of Wildlife Management 47:463–475.

POTVIN, M. A. 1988. Seed rain on a Nebraska sandhills prairie. Prairie Naturalist 20:81–89.

POWELL, J. A. 1965. The Florida wild turkey. Florida Game and Fresh Water Fish Commission Technical Bulletin 8, Tallahassee, USA.

PROVENZA, F. D., AND P. J. URNESS. 1981. Diameter-length-weight, weight relations for blackbrush (*Coleogyne ramosissima*) branches. Journal of Range Management 34:215–217.

RABINOWITZ, D., AND J. K. RAPP. 1980. Seed rain in a North American tall grass prairie. Journal of Applied Ecology 17:793–802.

RANSON, K. J., G. SUN, R. G. KNOX, E. R. LEVINE, J. F. WEISHAMPEL, AND S. T. FIFER. 2001. Northern forest ecosystem dynamics using coupled models and remote sensing. Remote Sensing of Environment 75:291–302.

RATTI, J. T., D. L. MACKEY, AND J. R. ALLDREDGE. 1984. Analysis of spruce grouse habitat in north-central Washington. Journal of Wildlife Management 48:1188–1196.

RAVEN, P. H., R. F. EVERT, AND S. E. EICHHORN. 1986. Biology of plants. Fourth edition. Worth Publishers, Inc., New York, USA.

REECE, P. E., J. D. VOLESKY, AND W. H. SCHACHT. 2001. Cover for wildlife after summer grazing on sandhills rangeland. Journal of Range Management 54:126–131.

REICH, R. M., C. D. BONHAM, AND K. K. REMINGTON. 1993. Double sampling revisited. Journal of Range Management 46:88–90.

REPPERT, J. N., R. H. HUGHES, AND D. DUNCAN. 1962. Herbage yield and its correlation with other plant measurements. Pages 115–121 in Range research methods. U.S. Department of Agriculture, Forest Service Miscellaneous Publication 940.

RIPLEY, T. H., AND C. J. PERKINS. 1965. Estimating ground supplies of seed available to bobwhites. Journal of Wildlife Management 29:117–121.

RITCHIE, J. C., K. S. HUMES, AND M. A. WELTZ. 1995. Laser altimeter measurements at Walnut Gulch watershed, Arizona. Journal of Soil and Water Conservation 50:440–442.

———, J. H. EVERITT, D. E. ESCOBAR, T. J. JACKSON, AND M. R. DAVIS. 1992. Airborne laser measurements of rangeland canopy cover and distribution. Journal of Range Management 45:189–193.

RITTENHOUSE, L. R., AND F. A. SNEVA. 1977. A technique for estimating big sagebrush production. Journal of Range Management 30:68–70.

ROACH, M. E. 1950. Estimating perennial grass utilization on semidesert cattle ranges by percentage of ungrazed plants. Journal of Range Management 3:182–185.

ROBEL, R. J., J. N. BRIGGS, A. D. DAYTON, AND L. C. HULBERT. 1970. Relationships between visual obstruction measurements and weight of grassland vegetation. Journal of Range Management 23:295–297.

RUMBLE, M. A. 1987. Using twig diameters to estimate browse utilization on three shrub species in southeastern Montana. Pages 172–175 in F. D. Provenza, J. T. Flinders, and E. D. McArthur, editors. Proceedings: symposium on plant–herbivore interactions. U.S. Department of Agriculture, Forest Service General Technical Report INT-222.

RUNDQUIST, B. C. 2002. The influence of canopy green vegetation fraction on spectral measurements over native tallgrass prairie. Remote Sensing of Environment 81:129–135.

SCHROEDER, R. L., AND L. D. VANGILDER. 1997. Tests of wildlife habitat models to evaluate oak-mast production. Wildlife Society Bulletin 25:639–646.

SCHULTZ, A. M., R. P. GIBBENS, AND L. DEBANO. 1961. Artificial populations for teaching and testing range techniques. Journal of Range Management 14:236–242.

SCHUPP, E. W. 1990. Annual variation in seedfall, postdispersal predation, and recruitment of a Neotropical tree. Ecology 71:504–515.

SEDGWICK, J. A., AND F. L. KNOPF. 1990. Habitat relationships and nest site characteristics of cavity-nesting birds in cottonwood floodplains. Journal of Wildlife Management 54:112–124.

SEFTON, D. F. 1977. Productivity and biomass of vascular hydrophytes on the Upper Mississippi. Pages 53–61 in C. B. Dewitt and E. Soloway, editors. Wetlands ecology, values and impacts. Proceedings Waubesa conference on wetlands. University of Wisconsin, Institute of Environmental Studies, Madison, USA.

SHAFER, JR., E. L. 1963. The twig-count method for measuring hardwood deer browse. Journal of Wildlife Management 27:428–437.

SHARP, W. M. 1963. The effects of habitat manipulation and forest succession on ruffed grouse. Journal of Wildlife Management 27:664–671.

SISK, T. D., N. M. HADDAD, AND P. R. EHRLICH. 1997. Bird assemblages in patchy woodlands: modeling the effects of edge and matrix habitats. Ecological Applications 7:1170–1180.

SMITH, J. G. 1959. Additional modifications of the point frame. Journal of Range Management 12:204–205.

SORK, V. L, J. BRAMBLE, AND O. SEXTON. 1993. Ecology of mast-fruiting in three species of North American deciduous oaks. Ecology 74:528–541.

SPURR, S. H. 1964. Forest ecology. Ronald Press Company, New York, USA.

STICKNEY, P. F. 1966. Browse utilization based on percentage of twig numbers browsed. Journal of Wildlife Management 30:204–206.

STODDART, L. A. 1935. Range capacity determination. Ecology 16:531–533.

STOHLGREN, T. J., K. A. BULL, AND Y. OTSUKI. 1998. Comparison of rangeland vegetation sampling techniques in the central grasslands. Journal of Range Management 51:164–172.

STRANSKY, J. J., AND L. K. HALLS. 1980. Fruiting of woody plants affected by site preparation and prior land use. Journal of Wildlife Management 44:258–263.

STURMAN, W. A. 1968. Description and analysis of breeding habitats of the chickadees, *Parus atricapillus* and *P. rufescens*. Ecology 49:418–431.

SUTHERS, H. B., J. M. BICKAL, AND P. G. RODEWALD. 2000. Use of successional habitat and fruit resources by songbirds during autumn migration in central New Jersey. Wilson Bulletin 112:249–260.

TANAKA, H., AND T. NAKASHIZUKA. 1997. Fifteen years of canopy dynamics analyzed by aerial photographs in a temperate deciduous forest. Japanese Ecology 78:612–620.

TANNER, G. W., AND M. E. DRUMMOND. 1985. A floating quadrat. Journal of Range Management 38:287.

TELFER, E. S. 1969a. Twig weight-diameter relationships for browse species. Journal of Wildlife Management 33:917–921.

———. 1969b. Weight-diameter relationships for 22 woody plant species. Canadian Journal of Botany 47:1851–1855.

THOMPSON, R. L. 1962. An investigation of some techniques for measuring availability of oak mast and deer browse. Thesis, Virginia Polytechnic Institute and State University, Blacksburg, USA.

———, AND B. S. MCGINNES. 1963. A comparison of eight types of mast traps. Journal of Forestry 61:679–680.

TROUSDELL, K. B. 1954. Peak population of seed-eating rodents and shrews occurs 1 year after loblolly stands are cut. U.S. Department of Agriculture, Forest Service Research Note 68.

TRYON, E. H., AND K. L. CARVELL. 1962. Acorn production and damage. West Virginia University Agricultural Experiment Station Bulletin

466-T, Morgantown, USA.

TURNER, D. L., AND W. P. CLARY. 2001. Sequential sampling protocol for monitoring pasture utilization using stubble height criteria. Journal of Range Management 54:132–137.

TURNER, M. G., R. H. GARDNER, AND R. V. O'NEILL. 2001. Landscape ecology in theory and practice: pattern and process. Springer-Verlag, Inc., New York, USA.

URESK, D. W., R. O. GILBERT, AND W. H. RICKARD. 1977. Sampling big sagebrush for phytomass. Journal of Range Management 30:311–314.

VAN DER MEER, F. D., AND S. M. DE JONG. 2001. Imaging spectrometry: basic principles and prospective applications. Kluwer Academic Publishers, The Netherlands.

VAN DERSAL, W. R. 1940. Utilization of oaks by birds and mammals. Journal of Wildlife Management 4:404–428.

VERMEIRE, L. T., AND R. L. GILLEN. 2001. Estimating herbage standing crop with visual obstruction in tallgrass prairie. Journal of Range Management 54:57–60.

VOLESKY, J. D., W. D. SCHACHT, AND P. E. REECE. 1999. Leaf area, visual obstruction, and standing crop relationships on Sandhills rangeland. Journal of Range Management 52:494–499.

WARING, R. H., J. B. WAY, R. HUNT, JR., L. MORRISEY, K. J. RANSON, J. F. WEISHAMPEL, R. OREN, AND S. E. FRANKLIN. 1995. Imaging radar for ecosystem studies. BioScience 45:715–723.

WENGER, K. F. 1953. The effect of fertilization and injury on the cone and seed production of loblolly pine seed trees. Journal of Forestry 51:570–573.

WERNER, P. A. 1975. A seed trap for determining patterns of seed deposition in terrestrial plants. Canadian Journal of Botany 53:810–813.

WEST, N. E. 1989. Spatial pattern—functional interactions in shrub-dominated plant communities. Pages 283–305 in C. M. McKell, editor. The biology and utilization of shrubs. Academic Press, San Diego, California, USA.

WHIGHAM, D. F., J. MCCORMICK, R. E. GOOD, AND R. L. SIMPSON. 1978. Biomass and primary production in freshwater tidal wetlands of the Middle Atlantic Coast. Pages 3–20 in R. E. Good, D. F. Whigham, and R. L. Simpson, editors. Freshwater wetland ecological processes and management potential. Academic Press, New York, USA.

WHITE, M. A., G. P. ASNER, R. R. NEMANI, J. L. PRIVETTE, AND S. W. RUNNING. 2000. Measuring fractional cover and leaf area index in arid ecosystems: digital camera, radiation transmittance, and laser altimetry methods. Remote Sensing of Environment 74:45–57.

WHITTAKER, R. H. 1965. Branch dimensions and estimation of branch production. Ecology 46:365–370.

WIENS, J. A. 1976. Population responses to patchy environments. Annual Review of Ecology and Systematics 7:81–120.

———. 1989. Spatial scaling in ecology. Functional Ecology 3:385–397.

WIGGERS, E. P., AND S. L. BEASOM. 1986. Characterization of sympatric or adjacent habitats of 2 deer species in west Texas. Journal of Wildlife Management 50:129–134.

WIGHT, H. M. 1939. Field and laboratory technic in wildlife management. University of Michigan Press, Ann Arbor, USA.

WIMBUSH, D. J., M. D. BARROW, AND A. B. COSTIN. 1967. Color stereophotography for the measurement of vegetation. Ecology 48:150–152.

WINKWORTH, R. E. 1955. The use of point quadrats for the analysis of heathland. Australian Journal of Botany 3:68–81.

WOLFF, J. O. 1996. Population fluctuations of mast-eating rodents are correlated with production of acorns. Journal of Mammalogy 77:850–856.

WOODWARD, A. J. W., S. D. FUHLENDORF, D. M. LESLIE, JR., AND J. SHACKFORD. 2001. Influence of landscape composition and change on lesser prairie-chicken (*Tympanuchus pallidicinctus*) populations. American Midland Naturalist 145:261–274.

YEATMAN, H. C. 1960. Population studies of seed-eating mammals. Journal of the Tennessee Academy of Science 35:32–48.

YOUNG, J. A., R. A. EVANS, AND B. A. ROUNDY. 1983. Quantity and germinability of *Oryzopsis hymenoides* in seed in Lahontan sands. Journal of Range Management 36:82–86.

21

TECHNIQUES FOR WILDLIFE NUTRITIONAL ECOLOGY

Frederick A. Servello, Eric C. Hellgren, and Scott R. McWilliams

INTRODUCTION

Like other aspects of wildlife science, the scope and sophistication of nutritional analyses have expanded significantly in recent years. For example, our expanding knowledge of the role of plant secondary metabolites as defenses against herbivory has greatly changed the concept of food quality for wild herbivores. Also, indirect assessments of diet and nutrition parameters using stable isotopes, urine metabolites, and fatty acid analyses are now relatively common. Further, there have been refinements or new applications of techniques to assess the ecological energetics and nutritional condition of animals in wild populations. Overall, our more comprehensive understanding of wildlife nutritional ecology has contributed greatly to efforts to understand foraging strategies of wildlife species and assess management and ecological questions via modeling.

Nutritional ecology is the study of the inter-relationships between food resources in the environment and consumptive use of these food resources by wild animals. Consumptive use includes how wild animals procure, digest, absorb, and metabolize available foods to satisfy their requirements for health, growth, reproduction, and activity. In this chapter, we review techniques for understanding the nutritional ecology of wildlife and assessing wildlife habitats and populations from a nutritional perspective. While the basic principles of nutritional ecology are applicable to all species, approaches and techniques used may vary greatly among taxonomic groups because of the nature of the foods eaten, species' behavior, or the feasibility of collecting data in particular environments. We have strived to include a wide range of vertebrate wildlife in our examples and literature sources, and to note the applicability of individual techniques for different taxa. This chapter also covers techniques for both captive wildlife studies and assessments of wild populations.

To understand the nutrition of wild species, a biologist must integrate information on an animal's consumptive use of foods with its requirements for maintenance and production. Interactions among nutritional variables are common with food consumption and nutrient requirements influenced by environmental and social factors. This increases the potential for a complex web of interactions. Therefore, interpreting nutritional data involves evaluating it in the larger context of a species' ecology. This higher level of synthesis, which often involves modeling, has the potential to reveal new insights about a species' nutritional ecology or change perspectives on the importance of individual nutritional factors. Thus, we have briefly reviewed goals and approaches for studying feeding strategies and simulation modeling of nutritional ecology.

NUTRITIONAL AND ENERGETIC REQUIREMENTS

Factors Affecting Energy and Nutrient Requirements

An important but complex endeavor in wildlife nutrition research is the estimation of energy and nutrient requirements of animals. Requirements vary with life functions (maintenance, growth, reproduction), season, and temperature, and also may be influenced significantly by physiological adaptations. For example, white-tailed deer (*Odocoileus virginianus*) reduce food and energy intake in winter as the result of seasonal fluctuations in hormone production (Silver et al. 1969, Thompson et al. 1973). In addition, nutrient or energy requirements for diets are sometimes interactive. For example, the protein: energy ratio is as important as the protein content of the diet in affecting performance in poultry (Scott et al. 1982), and may be the case for wild monogastric species. Rode and Robbins (2000) showed that maintenance energy requirements in 2 species of bears (Ursidae) decreased with increasing protein content (2.3 to 35%) of the diet. Increasing dietary fiber content also can reduce energy and protein digestibility and lead to decreased basal metabolism (Veloso and Bozinovic 1993).

Energy expended and nutrients used by an animal can be for different purposes. The maintenance energy requirement is the chemical energy required to meet the costs of basal metabolism, thermoregulation (in homeotherms), and activity (Robbins 1993). Basal metabolism, which is measured under conditions of rest, thermoneutrality, and a post-absorptive state, is the energy required to maintain basic life processes and cellular activity of an animal. Homeotherms have additional energy demands to thermoregulate or maintain their body temperature. Other activities necessary for survival of the animal, such as feeding, predator avoidance, social interactions, and migration also require energy expenditure simply for maintenance. Nutrient (e.g., N, minerals) requirements for maintenance are adequate amounts of nutrient intake to balance nutrient use in a nonreproductive, adult animal. Energetic and nutrient requirements for growth and reproduction are above and beyond maintenance requirements because extra energy and nutrients are required to produce new body tissue (growth) or to produce biomass in offspring (reproduction).

Techniques Used with Captive Wildlife

Energy requirements of captive animals can be estimated by measuring energy expenditure or by using feeding trials. Nutrient requirements usually are calculated through feeding trials. Nutrient or energy requirements have been quantified for relatively few wild species, and even less is known about suboptimal tolerances. Because diets of suboptimal quality are probably common in wild populations, understanding the effects of nutrient intake over a range of suboptimal levels is important.

Feeding Trials and Energy Requirements

A feeding trial approach involves placing an animal on diets of differing levels of digestible or metabolizable energy intake and measuring the energy level necessary to maintain body weight. The most common approach is to vary the amount of food offered to captive animals and to plot weight change versus energy intake. Regression analysis is used and the point on the regression line where body weight change equals 0 is taken as the energy requirement for maintenance (Ullrey et al. 1970). Variations on this method include altering the amount of food given to each animal until weight stabilizes (Keiver et al. 1984) or, taking as an estimate, the energy intake level for a time period when weight change was stable (<1–2%) (Case and Robel 1974, Williams and Kendeigh 1982). Maintenance requirements estimated in this way are greater than basal metabolic rate because the animal is thermoregulating and conducting some activities, but will generally be less than the maintenance requirements of a free-ranging animal (Robbins 1993). Caution is necessary if body mass is used as the only criterion for energy or nutrient balance because, as the composition of body tissue changes, the energy density of additional lost body mass changes. For example, the energy density of lipid tissue is about 8–9 times that of muscle.

Feeding Trials and Nutrient Requirements

Nutrient requirements, especially nitrogen (or protein), are measured primarily through feeding trials. The nitrogen requirement for maintenance is digestible nitrogen intake that produces tissue nitrogen balance (TNB) equal to 0. Tissue nitrogen balance (also called nitrogen retention) equals 0 when nitrogen intake is equal to excretion of endogenous and indigestible or nonmetabolizable nitrogen plus assimilated nitrogen for normal tissue replacement (e.g., hair replacement). Nitrogen is lost from the body as either endogenous urinary nitrogen (EUN) or metabolic fecal nitrogen (MFN). Endogenous urinary nitrogen is the excreted nitrogen resulting from normal metabolism and is a constant proportion of metabolic body mass (Mould and Robbins 1981*b*). It is normally expressed as a rate (mg/day or mg/kg$^{0.75}$/day). Metabolic body mass is body mass (in kg) raised to the 0.75 power. This conversion is based on the scaling relationship between body mass and metabolic rate in mammals. Metabolic fecal nitrogen consists of microbes, digestive enzymes, mucus, and gastrointestinal epithelial cells accumulated during digestion and is proportional to feed intake (Mould and Robbins 1981*b*). Except during periods of substantial adult tissue growth (e.g., molt), nitrogen costs for adult growth are small and generally ignored (Maynard et al. 1979). Metabolic fecal nitrogen and EUN can be measured in mammals, and their sum is a minimal estimate of maintenance nitrogen requirements (Mould and Robbins 1981*b*). Separate estimates of MFN and EUN cannot be readily obtained for birds because fecal matter and uric acid mix in the cloaca and are excreted together.

A commonly used alternative approach for estimating nutrient requirements is to relate nutrient intake to nutrient balance using a balance trial. Experimental diets containing varying levels of a particular nutrient (N, Na, Ca, K, P) are fed to captive animals to produce varying levels of nutrient intake. For nitrogen balance trials, experimental diets must contain sufficient energy to maintain energy balance; otherwise part of urinary nitrogen may result from tissue catabolism and inflate estimated nitrogen requirements (Maynard et al. 1979, Carl and Brown 1985). Food intake and feces and urine production are measured during a collection period. After the nutrient of interest in the food, feces, and urine is measured, balance is calculated as nutrient ingested (intake) – nutrient excreted (used) expressed in units of g or mg/metabolic body mass/day. Minimal nutrient requirements can be estimated as the *x*-intercept of the regression of nutrient balance versus nutrient intake (Felicetti et al. [2000] provide an example with nitrogen requirements in porcupines [*Erethizon dorsatum*]), much the same as it is with energy requirements.

The balance method to quantify nutritional intake and use is not new as it was initially used in animal science prior to 1860 (Schneider and Flatt 1975). Limitations of balance trials have been discussed by several authors (Hegsted 1976, Jeejeebhoy 1986, Young 1986). The major criticism is that balance studies typically produce high estimates of retention because of the difficulty in quantifying all excretory materials and, thus, requirements are underestimated (Hegsted 1976, Young 1986). For zero balance (intake = excretion) to represent a valid estimate of maintenance requirements, all dietary intake and excretory outgo must be measured. Another assumption for zero balance to accurately estimate the maintenance requirement is for zero balance to be associated with good health (Jeejeebhoy 1986). Those who have critically appraised the balance technique conclude that nutritional balance studies provide useful and important data on nutrient requirements and changes in nutrient metabolism under varying physiological states (Young 1986). The limitations of the technique should be recognized and further investigation into its utility is suggested (Young 1986, Murphy 1993). Once requirements are estimated, additional feeding trials should be conducted to test their validity.

A variant of the balance technique to measure nutrient requirements is to examine the relationship between nutrient intake and use and to identify the point at which the slope changes in this relationship. Raubenheimer and Simpson (1994) provided a general approach to the study of nutritional processes that involved discriminating the various compartments to which ingested nutrients are allocated. The most basic form of a nutrient budget for nutrient *n* over time *t* is

$$I_n = (R + D)_n ,$$

where I is nutrient intake, R is nutrient retained, and D is nutrient dissociated, or not retained, during the defined

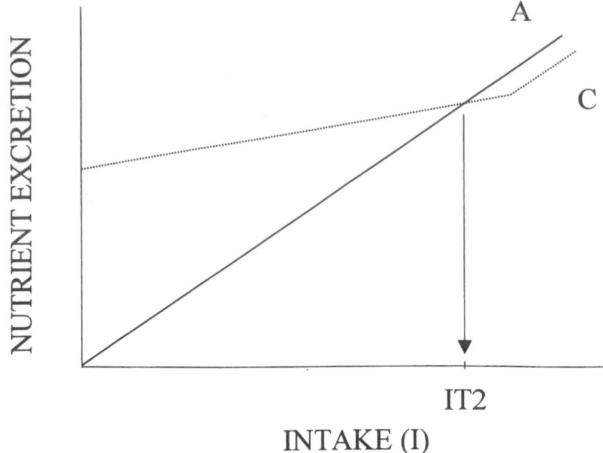

Fig. 1. Plot of nutrient intake vs. nutrient excretion, where line A is where intake = excretion, and line C represents a decrease in nutrient use efficiency with increases in intake (adapted from Raubenheimer and Simpson 1994).

time period. Plots of these components, especially of intake on the *x* axis and use (D) on the *y* axis allow exploration of nutritional efficiencies (Fig. 1, line A represents intake = use). A key element of the model of Raubenheimer and Simpson (1994) is their expectation that efficiency of use of a nutrient should be maximal when intake is below requirements and that it should decrease thereafter (Fig. 1). The level of intake at which this change in slope occurs has been termed the nutrient target (Raubenheimer and Simpson 1994) or, alternatively, the requirement. Because of obligatory endogenous losses necessarily added to nutrients dissociated, line C (Fig. 1) is a closer representation of a mineral budget, with the point where intake equals use (IT2) being the predicted requirement. This model has strong deductive support because the notion of a physiological requirement implies that nutrient dissociation will increase once the intake requirement has been reached (Raubenheimer and Simpson 1994). It is axiomatic that nutrient intake and use remain in long-term balance at varying rates of intake (Guyton and Hall 1996) in adult, nonreproductive mammals. For example, net retention or depletion of sodium could result in severe physiological alterations, such as extracellular expansion or reduction, acid-base imbalance, and electrochemical abnormalities.

Grasman and Hellgren (1993) estimated phosphorus requirements in white-tailed deer by modeling phosphorus excretion (*y*) as a function of phosphorus intake (*x*) using an exponential model ($y = ae^{bx}$). Requirements were assumed to be where intake equalled excretion, and these estimates were supported by data collected concomitantly on endocrine, physiologic, and performance (body mass, feed intake) responses to varying phosphorus intake. Estimates of nitrogen (Murphy 1993, Asleson et al. 1996) and sodium (Hellgren and Pitts 1997) requirements for maintenance were measured by similar approaches.

Calorimetry

Energy expenditure can be measured directly through heat production by an animal, a technique termed direct calorimetry. Although this method is technologically feasible, it has not been widely used for wildlife species

Fig. 2. Energy expenditure measured for American woodcock (*Scolopax minor*) walking on a treadmill in a respiration chamber (photograph by W. M. Vander Haegan).

because indirect measures are easier and more economical (Mautz 1978). Indirect calorimetry measures energy metabolism from estimates of O_2 consumption or CO_2 production. Sampling the volume and composition of expired air is required to estimate energy expenditure by this technique, which requires animals be confined to sealed chambers through which atmospheric air is pumped (Fig. 2), placing face masks on experimental animals that route expired air into sensors of sampling bags, or using tracheal fistulas (Mautz 1978, Robbins 1993). Chambers are usually used for small species (<1 kg) with masks primarily restricted to large mammals (Robbins 1993). The method is indirect because O_2 consumption/CO_2 production is equivalent to a given amount of energy expenditure depending on which substrate (fat, protein, or carbohydrate) is being metabolized. The energy equivalent of consumed O_2 is less variable than respired CO_2; therefore, measurement of O_2 consumption is preferred (Robbins 1993).

The difficulty of collecting gases expelled from an animal in a free-ranging state restricts measurement of energetic expenditure by indirect calorimetry to captive animals. However, in small vertebrates confined to sealed chambers that are sufficiently large to allow activity, indirect calorimetry may provide a reasonable estimate of free-ranging expenditures. In addition, energy expenditure involved in individual activities (e.g., standing, swimming, locomotion) can be estimated using indirect calorimetry in captive animals by measuring gas production/consumption during the target activity. These estimates can be combined with field data to create time-energy budgets.

Estimates of energetic expenditures are not equivalent to energetic requirements, at least if requirements are defined as maintaining body mass, maintaining a given body composition, or producing some level of performance (e.g., growth, reproductive rate). These estimates simply measure metabolism by animals during the time of measurement.

We have focused on explaining techniques for measuring energy requirements and metabolic rate of a focal species. A fundamental concept that has emerged from comparative studies of metabolic rate of a wide diversity of animals is that metabolic rate increases with body size in a predictable, quantitative manner (Kleiber 1932, Schmidt-Nielsen 1984). This allows researchers to predict the metabolic rate of any animal, even a species for which no empirical measurements of metabolic rate have been made, given only measurements of body size and published quantitative relationships. The study of how aspects of an animal's biology such as metabolic rate change with body size of the animal is known as allometrics (Schmidt-Nielsen 1984).

NUTRITIONAL CONDITION

A primary focus of wildlife management is to ensure that wildlife in a given area have the requisite food, water, and cover for adequate survival and reproduction. Evaluating whether habitat is satisfying the requirements of wildlife at some point in time often involves assessing the "condition" of wildlife. Because an animal's nutritional condition can affect its survival and reproduction, understanding how animal condition changes over time and in different habitats provides insights into population dynamics, competitive interactions, and other important aspects of wildlife ecology.

Quantifying the nutritional condition of a wild animal is unlike the task of most medical doctors and veterinarians assessing the health of people or pets, although some methods used to assess condition of wildlife are borrowed from the medical and veterinary sciences. When wildlife biologists measure the nutritional condition of an animal, they typically measure or indirectly estimate one or more of the following 5 major body components: water, fat, protein, carbohydrates, and minerals. In contrast, a medical doctor or veterinarian would rarely be interested in an analysis of body composition in part because most humans or pets are usually not deficient in body fat, protein, or minerals. In this section, we describe techniques used to estimate the 5 major body components of an animal, although we primarily focus on techniques used to estimate body fat because of its central importance in metabolism and energetics, and hence nutritional status, of wildlife. We also briefly discuss other techniques (e.g., blood and urine metabolites) used to assess the health and condition of wildlife.

Methods used for evaluating condition of wildlife can be categorized into 2 main groups based on whether the animal's condition is assessed while alive (nondestructive techniques) or after death (destructive techniques). Many traditional techniques used to evaluate nutritional condition of wildlife were based on analysis of hunter-killed animals. The literature on condition of game species based on carcass analysis has a long history and forms the foundation upon which many contemporary approaches for assessing nutritional condition of wildlife have been developed. Nondestructive techniques by definition provide an indirect estimate of body condition in that fat, protein, or some other body components are not directly measured in total as can be done with destructive techniques. "Condition indices" are an important subset of both nondestructive and destructive techniques. Such indices provide a measure that is correlated with some body component (e.g., a fat score of 1 on a 7-point scale) as opposed to providing a direct measure or estimate of the quantitative amount of the body component.

We discuss each major technique used to assess the nutritional condition of wildlife. For each technique, we describe the method and discuss its applicability for a diversity of wild vertebrates. We begin with a description of whole-animal body composition because it allows us to define the 5 major body components and describe how they are measured. Whole-animal body composition is the primary destructive technique used to assess body condition of wild animals. It is also necessary for assessing the accuracy and precision of any of the nondestructive techniques used to estimate or index body condition of live animals. Ideally, a measure, estimate or index of body condition is accurate and precise, but also relatively easy to obtain, objective, and able to detect changes in body con-

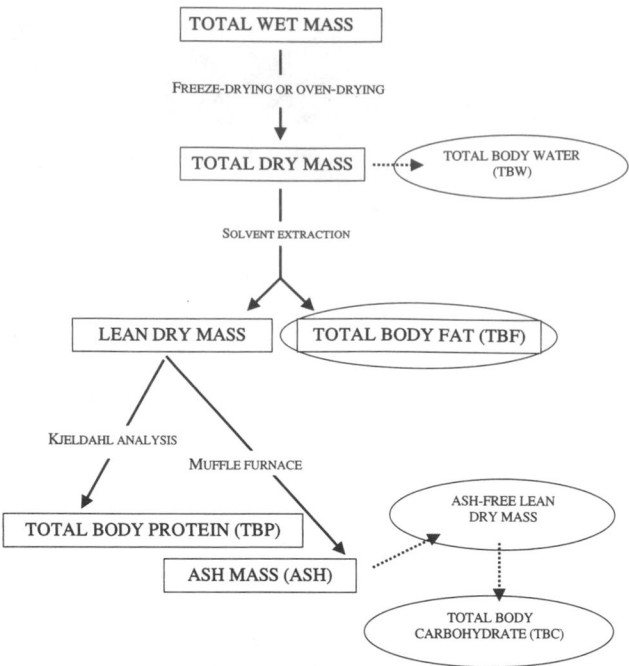

Fig. 3. Flow diagram of the stepwise procedure for conducting whole-body analysis to estimate the 5 major body components of an animal: water, fat, protein, carbohydrates, and minerals (or ash). Body components in boxes are directly measured whereas those in circles are calculated as the difference between 2 measured body components. For example, total body water (TBW) is estimated as the difference between total wet mass and total dry mass of the carcass. Note that total body fat (TBF) is measured directly when using a Goldfisch apparatus, but must be estimated by subtraction of lean dry mass from total dry mass if fat is extracted using the Soxhlet apparatus. Ash-free lean dry mass has been used as an index of TBP and is calculated as the difference between lean dry mass and ash mass. Total body carbohydrates (TBC) are commonly estimated as the difference between ash-free lean dry mass and total body protein. All measurements are typically expressed as dry mass (g dry) except for total wet mass (g wet).

dition of individuals of different age and gender, and at different seasons and locations (Harder and Kirkpatrick 1994).

Whole-animal Body Composition

In the discussion that follows, we assume the body composition analysis is conducted using the whole carcass, although subsampling or dividing the carcass may be necessary or more convenient for some studies. Methods of storage and preparation of the carcass prior to whole-body analysis are beyond the scope of this chapter and vary depending on the objectives of the study (Alisauskas and Ankney 1992, Reynolds and Kunz 2001).

The first step in whole-body analysis is drying the carcass by either freeze-drying or oven drying using a convection or vacuum oven (Fig. 3). The difference between total wet body mass and total dry body mass provides a direct measure of total water mass (or total body water, TBW). We recommend freeze-drying because it does not change tissue composition, although change in tissue composition associated with oven drying may be minimal for fat (Kerr et al. 1982). If oven drying is used, we recommend a drying temperature of 60–90 C. Overheating of tissue in ovens can cause volatilization and loss of organic matter (especially proteins), whereas slow drying of tissue at warm temperatures may allow decomposition of tissue.

After drying, the carcass is ground using a meat grinder or electric mill to homogenize the sample and to ensure complete extraction of nutrients. Total body fat is then measured by solvent extraction of lipids from the dried, ground carcass using a Soxhlet apparatus (Sawicka-Kapusta 1975), Goldfisch apparatus (Anonymous 1990), or ANKOM fat extractor. Petroleum ether or diethyl ether is the preferred solvent for most wildlife studies because these solvents extract neutral lipids, which are the primary form of storage energy in animals (Blem 1980, 1990). Chloroform and methanol extract other lipids (e.g., phospholipids which are primarily structural fats in animals) as well as non-lipids (Dobush et al. 1985), which results in an overestimate of total body fat. The difference between total dry body mass and the dried, extracted (fat-free dry or lean dry) mass provides a direct measure of total body fat (Fig. 3). Total body fat can also be expressed on a mass-dependent basis by dividing total body fat by body mass (either wet or dry) or by lean dry mass. Total body fat has been used as an index of general nutritional condition in small mammals (Fleharty et al. 1973), in a few studies of ungulates (Torbit et al. 1985), and commonly in studies of birds (Brown 1996).

For many wildlife studies, the whole-animal body composition analysis ends after fat extraction with estimates of total body water (TBW), total body fat (TBF), and lean dry mass (LDM) (Fig. 3). Lean dry mass has been used as an index for body protein in birds (e.g., Raveling 1979, Alisauskas and Ankney 1985) and mammals (e.g., Kiell and Millar 1980, Atkinson et al. 1996, Reynolds and Kunz 2000), although this can be inaccurate because lean dry mass is composed of 3 components: proteins, ash, and carbohydrates. However, carbohydrates are typically only a small proportion of an animal's mass. A more complete analysis of LDM is necessary if proteins and minerals in animals are dynamic such as in growing animals, reproducing females, or in migratory wildlife.

Ash content is measured by combusting lean dry samples in an ash-oven or muffle furnace at 500–550 C for at least 5 hours (Pierson and Stack 1988). After combustion, the remaining ash is composed of inorganic minerals. The difference between lean dry mass and ash mass is appropriately called ash-free lean dry mass (AFLDM) (Fig. 3) and is primarily composed of protein (91–94%, Reynolds and Kunz 2001) and carbohydrates. Generally, AFLDM provides a better estimate of body protein than LDM, although an accurate direct estimate of body protein requires separate analysis of either the lean dry mass or a subsample of the whole dry carcass. Total body protein (TBP) is usually estimated by directly measuring nitrogen content of the sample by the Kjeldhal procedure.

Body Mass and Structural Measures

Body Mass

Changes in body mass over time may indicate changes in nutritional condition of the animal. For example, state wildlife agencies often use dressed carcass weights of 1.5-year-old male deer taken during the autumn hunting season as a measure of deer condition and habitat quality. In this instance, body mass is a function of fat content and structural size of the animal, so that changes in body mass over several years indicate changes in condition of the deer herd. A younger age-class of male deer is used in part because body mass of older male deer changes dramatically during the rut period (Warren et al. 1981). Anderson et al. (1972) concluded that eviscerated carcass weight (whole body weight minus all fat within the body cavity and all viscera except the esophagus and trachea) was a good index of condition in female mule deer (*Odocoileus hemionus*) but not in males.

Biologists should be cautious about general use of body mass as a condition index. Body mass dynamics can be influenced by age, reproductive status, and other physiological factors that may complicate inferences about food resources or habitat (e.g., Servello and Kirkpatrick 1988). Although changes in body mass over time are often thought to indicate changes in fat content of wildlife, the relationship between body mass and actual fat mass is often weak ($r^2 = 0.4$–0.6; Bailey 1979, Whyte and Bolen 1984, Johnson et al. 1985). The use of body mass as an index of fat assumes there are no simultaneous changes in body components other than fat. This assumption is clearly violated for many species of birds and mammals because they change both their lean and fat components over time (van der Meer and Piersma 1994, Reynolds and Kunz 2000).

Structural Measures as Indices of Body Condition

Various structural measures have been used as indices of body condition and nutritional status of wildlife. For example, Klein (1964) used a ratio of femur length to hind foot length to compare long-term nutritional status of 2 populations of Sitka black-tailed deer (*O. h. sitkensis*). The index is based on the fact that growth of the bones in the hind foot is relatively more complete at birth than is the femur. Thus, this ratio in an adult deer can indicate the amount of skeletal growth occurring over the lifetime of an animal and, hence, the relative long-term nutritional regime.

Antler beam diameters have long been used as indices of nutritional status in cervids (e.g., Severinghaus et al. 1950, Riney 1955). Rasmussen (1985) suggested that antler beam diameter of yearling males was the most practical method for monitoring the health and vitality of deer populations. However, antler size of deer may be primarily influenced by nutritional status just prior to antler development and not necessarily of range conditions and nutritional status throughout the year (Ullrey 1982).

Condition Indices Based on Ratios of Body Mass to Size

A primary difficulty with using only changes in body mass or structural measures to indicate nutritional condition is that individual animals often differ in body size. Thus, bigger, heavier animals in one location may be in no better condition than smaller, lighter animals in another location. This has led many researchers to calculate a condition index that divides the body mass of an animal by some estimate of its size (usually a linear measure such as arm/wing, leg, or body length, but lean mass and fat-free body mass have also been used [Harder and Kirkpatrick 1994, Hayes and Shonkwiler 2001]). Such body condition indices are believed to be correlated with animal quality such as nutritional condition, fat content, or even

Darwinian fitness (Krebs and Singleton 1993, Brown 1996, Viggers et al. 1998). Unfortunately, few studies test the validity of a condition index and demonstrate the index actually indicates what the biologist thinks it indicates (e.g., fat mass, production of offspring, survival).

Although condition indices that use a ratio of body mass to body size are easy to compute and commonly used in wildlife studies, they may have serious flaws. Most importantly, they are dimensionless variables that are often difficult to interpret biologically (Alisauskas and Ankney 1992, Hayes and Shonkwiler 2001) and, in most cases, the relationship between body mass and size is not isometric as assumed (Packard and Boardman 1987, Packard and Boardman 1999). The common problem with such indices is they work only if body mass increases linearly with body size (slope = 1, intercept = 0) so that deviations of an individual from this overall pattern indicates differences in animal condition (Hayes and Shonkwiler 2001). If this assumption is true, the ratio of body mass: body size will not be correlated with body size. Typically, however, the condition index is correlated with body size, so that animals with different condition index values may have different nutritional condition or they may simply differ in size. In addition, ratio variables are plagued with numerous statistical and inferential problems (Jacob et al. 1996, Hayes and Shonkwiler 2001).

Unfortunately, more sophisticated statistical approaches for estimating body size (e.g., Principal Components Analysis of many structural measures) or the condition index (e.g., using residuals from a regression of body mass on body size) do not solve the problems of biological interpretation and allometry (Green 2001, Hayes and Shonkwiler 2001). Instead, the best approach is direct analysis of the data used to generate the condition indices combined with well-designed validation studies, rather than the continued use and faith in simple ratios of body mass and body size (Packard and Boardman 1999, Hayes and Shonkwiler 2001).

Growth Rate

One special case where body mass and structural size are often accurately used to indicate nutritional status of animals is when used for growing animals. Whereas differences in growth patterns between species can reveal evolutionary adaptations to ecological conditions (Derrickson 1992, Ricklefs and Starck 1998), variation in growth between individuals of the same species reflects in part variation in the nutritional environment during growth (Ricklefs et al. 1998, Schew and Ricklefs 1998). Thus, variation in growth rate of immature animals has been used to assess the adequacy of the nutritional environment for a wide range of wildlife including colonial nesting waterbirds (Nisbet et al. 1998, Golet et al. 2000), waterfowl (Sedinger 1992), landbirds (Schew and Ricklefs 1998), as well as many mammals (Crête and Huot 1993, Wigginton and Dobson 1999, Lesage et al. 2001).

Ideally, a complete growth curve (i.e., animal size as a function of time) for many individuals is measured so that the nonlinear pattern of growth can be statistically modeled and a few interpretable parameters of growth rate can then be estimated [e.g., asymptotic mass or size, growth rate(s) for specified time periods]. Ricklefs (1968, 1973) and Starck and Ricklefs (1998) presented a detailed discus-

sion of the types of mathematical analysis, curve fitting, and statistical models used in describing animal growth. However, estimating growth rate of young animals in wild populations is complicated because it is often difficult to regularly capture and measure body mass and structural size of many individuals throughout growth without negatively affecting growth rate. More often, measurements of body mass or structural size are made a few times and growth rates are estimated for roughly the middle portion of the growth period when growth is linear (e.g., Emms and Verbeek 1991, Golet et al. 2000).

Fat Indices

Discrete Fat Depots

Subcutaneous, visible fat depots are commonly used as an index of fat reserves in live migratory birds. A qualitative index called a "fat score" is used to rank the amount of visible fat in the furcular region (claviculocoracoid area; Fig. 4) of songbirds (Helms and Drury 1960). Fat scoring can provide a reliable index of subcutaneous fat, although accurate use of this technique requires extensive training of observers (Krementz and Pendelton 1990). Similarly, the shape of the abdominal profile of geese (Anserinae) has been categorized into 4 fat-reserve classes (Owen 1981) and used to document changes in goose condition in relation to age, gender, and habitats used.

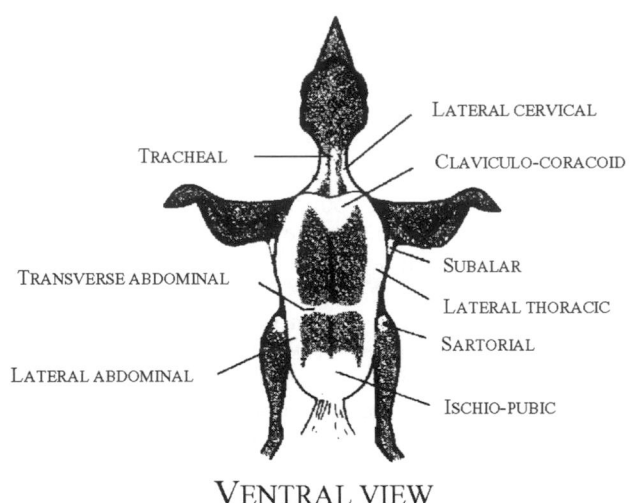

VENTRAL VIEW

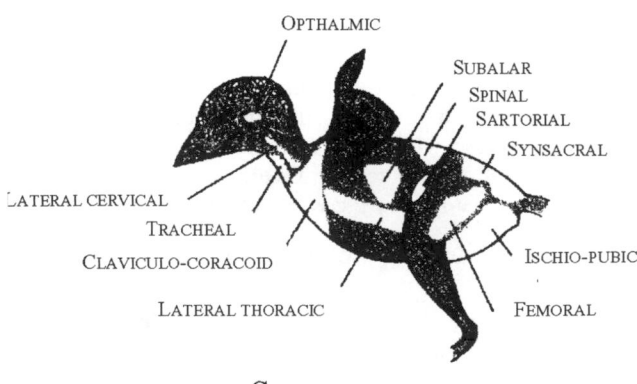

SIDE VIEW

Fig. 4. Distribution of subcutaneous fat in the white-crowned sparrow (*Zonotrichia leucophrys*) (copied with permission from King and Farner 1965).

Discrete fat depots within dead birds and mammals have been used as an index of total body fat, specifically, and body condition, in general. Fat depots in certain locations within the animal may provide better indices of total body fat in part because the use and deposition of fat may occur in a relatively prescribed order. The following pattern of fat catabolism has been described for mammals (Riney 1955): subcutaneous fat over the rump and saddle is used first, then fat in the abdominal cavity, and finally bone marrow fat is used. The opposite sequence is followed during replenishment of fat stores. Although these patterns of use and deposition of certain fat stores appear to be generally true, there is considerable overlap in the timing of this mobilization and storage for a given fat depot (Ransom 1965). The pattern of fat use and deposition in birds is less clear and shows more interspecific variation than in mammals. For example, fat catabolism in Canada geese (*Branta canadensis*) initially involved the simultaneous use of both abdominal and subcutaneous fat, although the subcutaneous fat depots were the last to be used (Raveling 1979). Blem (1976) reported that birds deposit subcutaneous fat first followed by abdominal fat, whereas King (1967) observed the opposite pattern. Even if a certain pattern of fat catabolism and storage is evident in a given species, distinguishing between abdominal and subcutaneous is often difficult, especially in relatively fat animals. Thus, it is not surprising that the best predictors of total body fat in wild animals used the combined weight or a ranked index of all these fat depots (Ankney and MacInnes 1978, Cook et al. 2001).

Fat associated with specific internal organs has also been used as an index of body fat in birds and mammals. For example, gizzard fat has been reported to be a suitable index of body fat in ring-necked pheasants (*Phasianus colchicus*) (Dowell and Warren 1982), ruffed grouse (*Bonasa umbellus*) (Servello and Kirkpatrick 1987*a*), and northern bobwhite (*Colinus virginianus*) (Koerth and Guthery 1988). Similarly, kidney fat has been used as an indicator of whole body fat in white-tailed deer (Finger et al. 1981) and fisher (*Martes pennanti*) (Garant and Crête 1999), but it is more commonly used as a good indicator of abdominal fat reserves in many mammals, particularly ungulates (Smith 1970) and lagomorphs (Flux 1971, Jacobson et al. 1978) although not brush-tailed possum (*Trichosurus vulpecula*) (Bamford 1970). Riney (1955) described the standard method for measuring the kidney fat index (KFI; ratio of fat on kidney: kidney mass) in mammals (Fig. 5). Because kidney weight of ungulates changes seasonally (Batcheler and Clarke 1970, Dauphiné 1975), some control for effect of season and perhaps age is required if KFI is to be used to indicate seasonal changes in fat reserves (Van Vuren and Coblentz 1985).

Bone Marrow Fat

The amount of fat within certain bones of freshly killed wildlife has been commonly used as a condition index for larger mammals, especially Cervidae (Cheatum 1949, but see Cook et al. 2001). Bone marrow fat has also been effectively used as a condition index for smaller mammals [e.g., cottontails (*Sylvilagus* spp.) (Jacobson et al. 1978, Warren and Kirkpatrick 1978), brush-tailed possum (Bamford 1970)], and waterfowl (Raveling et al. 1978, Hutchinson and Owen 1984). In general, less bone mar-

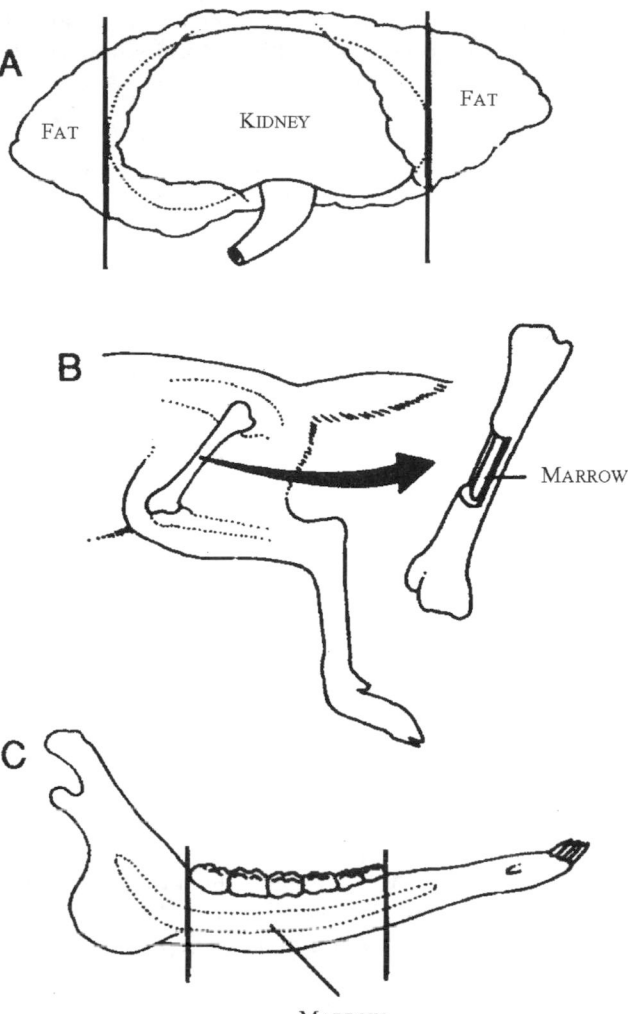

Fig. 5. The amount of fat surrounding the kidney (A) provides an index to visceral fat (adapted from Riney 1955). The amount of fat in the marrow of mammalian long bones such as the femur (B) (adapted from Cheatum 1949) or the mandible (C) (adapted from Nichols and Pelton 1974) provides a measure of energy in this depot of last resort. Fat (in A) or bone (in C) lateral to the vertical lines is trimmed and discarded.

row fat indicates poor condition and malnutrition of individuals because animals in good or excellent condition have similar, maximum amounts of marrow fat (Mech and DelGiudice 1985, Cook et al. 2001). Bone marrow fat in combination with the kidney fat index may provide an estimate of nutritional status of mammals over a wider range of conditions than either technique alone (Ransom 1965, Kie et al. 1983). We caution that analyzing these data using mean fat or index values is problematic because relationships to total body fat are not linear.

Measuring bone marrow fat involves choosing a specific bone(s) and then quantitatively measuring the amount of fat (Fig. 5). Traditionally, fat is measured in a bone marrow sample from the femur of birds and mammals or the mandibular (jaw) cavity of cervids (Harder and Kirkpatrick 1994). The amount of fat in the bone marrow sample is measured by oven drying (Neiland 1970) or solvent extraction (Verme and Holland 1973), and then expressed as the percentage of fat in the wet or dry mass of bone. Fat levels in bone marrow should be expressed on a dry-matter basis to avoid problems associated with dehydration of samples after collection and before oven drying (Harder and Kirkpatrick 1994).

Isotope Dilution of Body Water

Water within an animal is not evenly distributed among its tissues. For example, a gram of body fat in an animal contains almost no water whereas a gram of body protein contains on average about 70% water (Speakman et al. 2001). This uneven distribution of body water among body tissues means the fatter an animal becomes the lower the water content as a percentage of it's body mass. Thus, in principle, body fat can be estimated by measuring body mass and water content of any animal. Empirical studies of a variety of wild animals have demonstrated that total body water is positively related to fat-free body mass ($r^2 >$ 0.95; Child and Marshall 1970, Campbell and Leatherland 1980) and negatively related to body fat ($r^2 > 0.95$; Bailey 1979, Johnson et al. 1985). Direct measurements of body water in dead individuals generally provide a reliable method for estimating total lean or fat mass of the animal (Gessaman 1998).

Recent advances in use and measurement of stable isotopes of water provide great promise for estimating body composition of live wild animals by nondestructively measuring their body mass and total body water (Speakman et al. 2001). Radioactive isotopes of water (most often tritium, ^3H_2O) have also been successfully used to estimate total lean and fat mass of wildlife species (Crum et al. 1985, Hildebrand et al. 1998). However, using radioactive compounds in the field requires additional safety precautions and permits that are often difficult to obtain. Stable isotopes of water (most often deuterium, ^2H_2O) require no such permits and can be used to conveniently and accurately estimate total body water of live wild animals.

The isotope-dilution technique involves injecting a known amount of deuterium (or other isotopically-labeled water) into the animal, allowing the isotope time to equilibrate with normal body water (ca. 30 min for small songbirds and mammals, as long as 3 hrs for bears), taking a blood sample, and then measuring the concentration of deuterium in the sample (Speakman et al. 2001) (Box 1). The accuracy and precision of this technique can be ascertained by conducting a calibration study in which estimates of body water using isotope dilution are directly related to measured lean and fat mass of individuals (e.g., Oftedal et al. 1996, Karasov and Pinshow 1998). The isotope dilu-

---

Box 1.   Isotope-dilution method for estimating body composition of a live animal.

A known amount of isotopically labeled water (usually deuterium, ^2H, or tritium, ^3H, although ^{17}O and ^{18}O can be used) is administered orally or by injection into the animal. Administration of the labeled water is normally performed by intraperitoneal or intramuscular injection. Immediately after administration, the labeled water is localized near the site of injection and needs time to equilibrate with the entire body water pool of the animal. For animals provided no food or water, this equilibration period is only 15–30 minutes for small (<30 g) animals, between 30–60 minutes for larger animals such as quail and geese, and as long as 3–7 hours for bears and horses (Speakman et al. 2001). Provision of water and food during the equilibration period directly dilutes the body water pool, affects the isotope enrichment, and complicates estimation of body water pool size (Speakman et al. 2001). We suggest no food or water be provided to the animal during the relatively short equilibration period.

After the equilibration period, the body water pool is sampled most commonly by taking a blood sample, although urine, saliva, feces, and breath have also been used (Speakman et al. 2001). Blood samples (10–100 µL) from animals are typically collected in glass, flame-sealed capillary tubes and stored in the refrigerator. For studies that use deuterium or tritium-labeled water, blood samples are microdistilled under vacuum (Wood et al. 1975) prior to analysis. Tritium is analyzed by scintillation counting. Deuterium can be analyzed by infrared spectroscopy (Karasov et al. 1988) or isotope ratio mass spectrometry (Speakman et al. 2001). Estimates of body water using isotope dilution are used to predict body composition of the living animal as shown below for predicting fat mass of 2 species of bear (A) (from Hildebrand et al. 1998) and black-capped warblers (*Sylvia atricapilla*) (B) (from Karasov and Pinshow 1998).

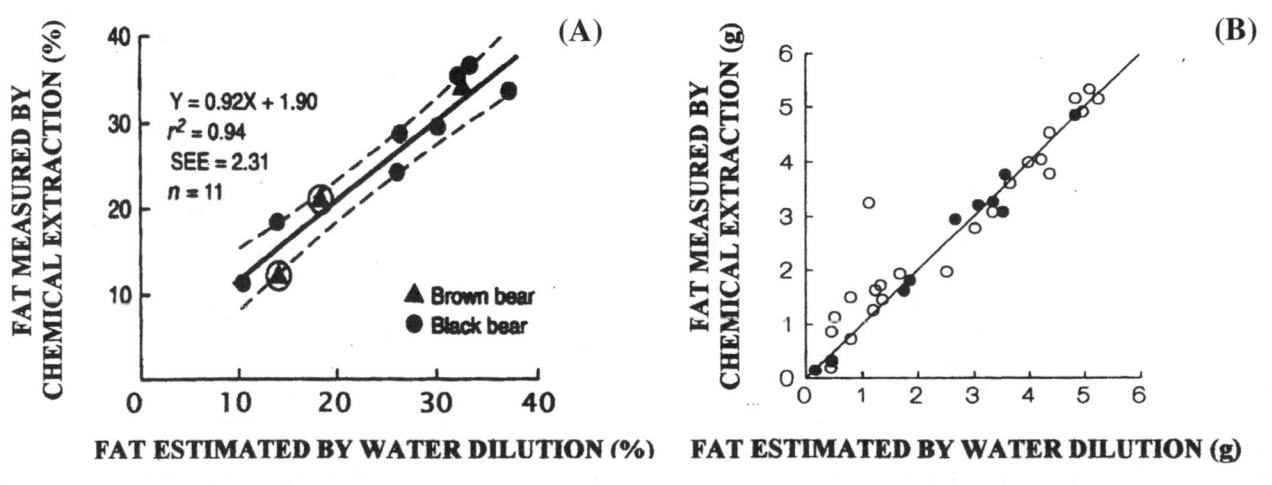

tion technique has been used to predict lean and fat mass within 5 and 15%, respectively, of actual lean and fat mass in wildlife including bears, seals (Pinnipeda), and songbirds (Gessaman 1998, Speakman et al. 2001).

The primary advantage of isotope dilution for estimating lean and fat mass of wildlife is that it can be performed on a live animal that can then be released. Also, estimates of body composition are relatively accurate and precise, and can be used, in principle, on wildlife of any size and type. The primary disadvantages of this technique are that it is invasive (requiring blood sampling), requires some expertise to administer a quantitative amount of isotope in the field, and the laboratory analysis of the blood samples requires sophisticated equipment (e.g., infrared spectroscopy or isotope ratio mass spectrometry) although commercial laboratories conduct such analyses for a fee.

Electrical Conductivity and Bioelectrical Impedance

The conductivity of a live animal is directly related to the amount of dissolved electrolytes (primarily potassium, sodium, and chloride ions) in its tissues, with lean tissue containing the majority of body water and, thus, dissolved electrolytes. This means, in principle, that a measure of an animal's conductivity can be used to estimate amount of lean mass in the animal, as well as its' fat mass usually by subtraction of lean mass from total body mass.

Electrical conductivity can be measured between 2 discrete points on the surface of the animal [a technique known as bioelectrical impedance analysis (BIA)] or by placing the animal within a chamber and recording conductivity of the whole animal using a technique known as total body electrical conductivity (TOBEC®). Bioelectrical impedance analysis has been used primarily on humans (van Marken Lichtenbelt 2001) although it has been used for estimating body condition of large mammals such as elk (*Cervus elaphus*) (Cook et al. 2001) and bears (Farley and Robbins 1994, Hildebrand et al. 1998). Total body electrical conductivity has been used to estimate body composition of a diversity of wild animals including reptiles (Angilletta 1999), and many birds and mammals (e.g., Walsberg 1988, Zuercher et al. 1997, Scott et al. 2001).

Total body electrical conductivity instruments directly measure the energy absorbed by the animal while it is within the detection chamber. The instrument provides the user with a relative measure of the energy absorbed (an "E value") by the animal, which is proportional to the total body electrical conductivity of the animal. Estimation of lean or fat mass from the E value requires a calibration study. This involves recording the E value of a subset of live animals and directly measuring the body composition of these same animals using destructive methods. Regression models are then developed that relates TOBEC® E value to measured lean (or fat) mass for this subsample of animals. These models are used to predict lean (or fat) mass of individuals that were not used in the calibration study given their measured E value.

A number of factors will introduce substantial error in the TOBEC® measurement if they are not carefully controlled including size of the measurement chamber relative to size of the animal, positioning of the animal within the detection chamber, hydration state and body temperature of the animal, and fullness of the animal's digestive tract (Scott et al. 2001). With appropriate procedural controls,

TOBEC® has been used to accurately predict lean mass (within 1–5% of actual lean mass) but not fat mass in a variety of wildlife species (Scott et al. 2001). Poor accuracy and precision of fat mass estimates occurs primarily because the absolute error (in grams of tissue) is the same for predicted lean and fat mass, and fat mass is a relatively small portion of whole body mass in animals.

Typically, species-specific calibrations have been used to estimate body composition using TOBEC® primarily because species often differ in size and shape which can greatly affect the accuracy and precision of the estimates (Scott et al. 1991, Asch and Roby 1995). Unfortunately, this limits use of TOBEC® to species for which a calibration study is feasible or has been done. Recent work with small migratory songbirds (10–30 g body mass) demonstrated that interspecific predictive models could be as accurate as intraspecific models (Whitman 2002), which may prove especially advantageous for studies of body composition of rare and endangered wildlife.

The primary advantages of TOBEC® for estimating lean mass of wildlife are that it is entirely noninvasive, measurements can be quickly made (<3 min), and the instrument is portable and easy to use in the field. In addition, TOBEC® is one of the few nondestructive techniques that can be used to measure short-term changes in body composition of the same individual(s) (e.g., Karasov and Pinshow 1998). The primary disadvantages of the technique are that it can only be used on certain wildlife (i.e., those that can fit into the detection chamber), separate validation studies must be conducted for each species or perhaps groups of species with similar body geometry, and it can reliably estimate only lean mass (not fat mass) of animals. Bioelectrical impedance analysis provides a potentially useful electrical conductivity technique for estimating body condition of wildlife that are too large to fit within TOBEC® detection chambers, although more validation studies are needed that evaluate accuracy and precision of BIA in field situations (e.g., Farley and Robbins 1994).

Ultrasound and DXA

Ultrasound is primarily used to estimate size of certain internal organs and fat depots rather than whole-animal body composition (Starck et al. 2001). Rump fat thickness measured using ultrasonography has been used to predict total body fat in ungulates (e.g., Stephenson et al. 2002), although such measurements become meaningless if animals have depleted these reserves (Cook et al. 2001). Baldassare et al. (1980) estimated fat depots in mallards (*Anas platyrhynchos*) using ultrasound, but could explain only 58, 65, and 59% of the variation in total body fat, subcutaneous fat, and omental fat, respectively, using this technique. Recent field-portable ultrasound models have been used to accurately measure the dynamics of pectoral muscle and stomach size in medium-sized shorebirds in relation to diet switching and migration chronology (Dietz et al. 1999). Starck et al. (2001) provide a discussion of the advantages and disadvantages of the technique and possible applications of ultrasound for studies of free-living wildlife.

Dual-energy X-ray absorptiometry (DXA) is a new technique (~10 years old) that is widely used for measuring bone density in humans. It has recently been adapted for measuring fat and bone-free lean mass in small (mouse- or sparrow-sized) animals using a "portable" 27 kg model and for dog-sized animals using larger models (Nagy 2001). The basic principle of the technique is that fat, bone-free lean tissue, and bone tissue attenuate photons produced by the instrument by different amounts; sophisticated software integrates this attenuation information from the scanned animal into an estimate of fat mass, bone-free lean mass, and bone mineral mass (and density). At present, scanning requires the animal be motionless (anaesthetized or dead); a scan requires 5–30+ minutes depending on resolution, and the instruments are relatively expensive (>$30,000 U.S.) (Nagy 2001). Recent validation studies have shown that DXA estimates of fat and lean mass were closely correlated ($r > 0.90$) with actual fat and lean mass measured by chemical extraction, and measurement precision was <10% (Nagy and Clair 2000). However, fat mass was consistently overestimated while lean mass was consistently underestimated (Nagy 2001). Application of this technique to most wildlife species awaits further technological innovations.

Blood and Urine Indices

Blood Indices

Blood characteristics have been used for decades as indicators of the nutritional status of wild animals. Reviews of their utility have been prepared by LeResche et al. (1974), Hanks (1981), and Franzmann (1985). LeResche et al. (1974) outlined steps required to identify relationships between nutritional status and blood characteristics. First, baseline values and ranges within boundary conditions need to be established for the species of interest. Next, major sources of variation (e.g., age, gender, season, time of day, handling procedures) that affect concentration of blood characteristics need to be identified. Finally, changes in blood values need to be tied to shifts in diet quality and animal condition when controlled for other sources of variation. Most research in this field has been conducted with large herbivores (Franzmann 1985) and carnivores (Franzmann and Schwartz 1988, Hellgren et al. 1989) in attempts to find indicators of the energetic and protein status of target species.

Blood urea nitrogen (BUN) is a key indicator of protein status in mammals. Urea, a nitrogenous compound, is a byproduct of protein metabolism and concentrations of BUN are positively related to protein intake when energy intake is above maintenance (reviewed by Harder and Kirkpatrick 1994). Blood urea nitrogen is relatively unaffected by stress of handling or by drug anesthesia. However, low-energy intake often leads to an increase in BUN concentrations as a result of protein catabolism to meet energetic requirements, and high-energy intake can lead to a depression of BUN concentrations due to more efficient use of protein (Harder and Kirkpatrick 1994). Hematological profiles (red blood cells, hemoglobin, hematocrit) also show promise as indicators of long-term protein and overall nutritional status (Franzmann 1985), although controlled experimental work tied to useful field applications are necessary to verify this promise.

Assessment of energy status or recent energy intake has been problematic. Several indices, including cholesterol, non-esterified fatty acids, and ketone bodies have been studied, but not found to be consistent or reliable indices across a range of energy intake levels (Franzmann 1985,

Harder and Kirkpatrick 1994). Glucose concentrations are extremely sensitive to acute stress and virtually useless as a nutritional indicator. Triiodothyronine (T_3) was a consistent indicator of energy status in white-tailed deer in 60-day and 6-month feeding trials (Brown et al. 1995). Other researchers have reported similar findings with T_3 and thyroxine (T_4) (Bahnak et. al. 1981, DelGiudice et al. 1990, Watkins et al. 1991).

We reiterate the caution of Harder and Kirkpatrick (1994) regarding use of blood chemistries in nutritional research. All blood samples should be collected and handled as uniformly as possible. They should be taken at approximately the same time of day (due to diurnal rhythms in several physiological characteristics) and refrigerated as soon as possible after the sample is collected. If serum or plasma is collected for later analysis, samples should be centrifuged as soon as possible and frozen to prevent changes in blood values. Serum or plasma can be analyzed for individual characteristics with commercially available assay kits and basic laboratory equipment (e.g., spectrophotometry) or by commercial laboratories that use autoanalyzers to simultaneously analyze sample chemistries.

Managers considering use of blood variables to assess nutritional status should attempt to examine relationships between these variables and an independent measure of body composition, such as percent body fat. Gau and Case (1999) reported that individual parameters in blood were poorly related to percent body fat (estimated by bioelectrical impedance analysis) in grizzly bears (*Ursus arctos*) and advised against use of blood variables as indicators of nutritional condition. However, use of multivariate analyses, such as discriminant analysis, can be used to classify animals into broad nutritional groups. Hawley (1987) used blood variables to separate bison (*Bison bison*) into ration groups, and Brown et al. (1995) could discriminate among white-tailed deer on high- and low-protein or high- and low-energy diets. Blood chemistries are well suited for multivariate analyses because samples from individual animals are often analyzed for many variables.

Urine Indices

Nutritional indices based on analyses of urine collected in snow have been an expanding field of research in wildlife science. Urine indices have been tested and used primarily for ungulates in northern ecosystems, but there are some applications for carnivores. The primary advantage of urine indices is that large numbers of animals and multiple populations can be repeatedly sampled over the course of a winter in marked contrast to other techniques that typically are limited by the necessity to capture animals. Several urine metabolites have been evaluated as indicators of overall nutritional restriction, mobilization of energy reserves, digestible energy intake, food intake, or plant secondary compounds in diets. In all cases, metabolite concentrations are expressed as ratios with creatinine (C) to eliminate errors from dilution by snow. Creatinine is excreted at a relatively constant proportion to muscle mass (DelGiudice et al. 1995) and satisfactorily standardizes snow-diluted samples for all indices examined (DelGiudice et al. 1988, Saltz and Cook 1993, White et al. 1995).

Urea nitrogen (UN) has received the most in-depth evaluation. The UN:C ratio has a complex interpretation and is thought to be an index of overall nutritional restriction (DelGiudice 1995). The theoretical basis of the UN:C index for ungulates is that N content of diets is normally low in winter and N conservation by these species also keeps UN excretion low except when a combination of low food intake and reduced fat reserves causes substantial body protein catabolism and consequently elevated UN:C levels (DelGiudice 1995). DelGiudice et al. (1994) found a close relationship with the UN:C ratio and mass loss in captive deer, but relationships with fat reserves are less clear for wild deer apparently because the UN:C ratio is influenced by short-term food intake patterns (Parker et al. 1993*a*). Consequently, the UN:C ratio is interpreted as a generalized nutritional restriction index (DelGiudice 1995). Deer with ratios above 3.5 are considered in a state of serious nutritional restriction, and ratios of approximately 23 or more are indicative of animals approaching death from starvation (DelGiudice and Seal 1988, DelGiudice 1995). Controlled experiments with related species are limited, but similar relationships would be expected. It is recommended that data be reported as proportions of animals with ratios above 3.5 because proportions are simpler to interpret than mean values given the nonlinear relationship between nutritional restriction and UN:C (Ditchkoff and Servello 1999). Sample sizes of 20–35 per sampling period or unit are adequate for most applications, but sampling requirements are dependent on statistical approaches to be used (Ditchkoff and Servello 1999). Urea nitrogen:C in urine collected from snow also can be used as an index of fasting and recent feeding by gray wolves (*Canis lupus*). Wolves that had recently fed after fasting have sharply elevated UN:C ratios as a result of excretion of excess N from meat intake (DelGiudice et al. 1987*a*, Mech et al. 1987), but these authors caution that high UN:C also could result from wolves nearing death from starvation. Urea nitrogen:C likely is applicable to other carnivores in northern ecosystems and has been used to study the nutritional ecology of coyotes (*Canis latrans*) (Patterson et al. 2000); however, species-specific testing is recommended.

Allantoin (A) has good potential as a nutritional index for ungulates. Allantoin concentration in urine is associated with microbial biomass in the rumen and, with much of the energy and N absorption in ungulates a product of microbial fermentation, allantoin concentrations exhibit a positive relationship with intake of digestible energy (Vagnoni et al. 1996). Garrott et al. (1996) described A:C as an index of metabolizable energy intake. Field data from elk are consistent with expected winter patterns in food intake lending support to the value of this index (Garrott et al. 1996). A potential bias is that allantoin also may originate from endogenous sources as a result of loss of body mass (DelGiudice et al. 2000).

Cortisol:C has been evaluated as another general index of energetic status with ungulates (Saltz and White 1991, Saltz et al. 1992). Elevated cortisol:C indicates that energy reserves are being mobilized in response to an energy deficit, and Saltz et al. (1992) described the index as the rate of deterioration of animal condition. However, controlled studies on this index are limited and interpretation of field results may be complex (White et al. 1997).

Potassium:C is a potential index of food intake for ungulates (DelGiudice et al. 1987*b*). Potassium excretion is directly related to dietary intake, and K concentration in winter browses is relatively high (DelGiudice et al. 1987*b*, DelGiudice 1995). However, recent work has found that K:C may have a poor relationship with intake for deer eating mixed diets of browse (Servello and Schneider 2000), a potential problem for comparisons among populations. A second caution is that moribund deer may exhibit high excretion of K, another potential bias for this indicator (DelGiudice 1995). Nevertheless, K:C ratios in wild populations of deer have exhibited expected declining trends in winter (DelGiudice et al. 1989, Ditchkoff and Servello 2002). Potassium:C is recommended as supportive information to broader indexes of nutritional restriction (DelGiudice 1995).

Glucuronic acid (GA), a urine metabolite associated with excretion of secondary plant metabolites (McArthur et al. 1991), has been proposed as an indicator of diet quality for herbivores, i.e., dietary intake of anti-nutritional compounds (Servello and Schneider 2000). A problem with interpreting a GA:C index is that it also is affected by daily food intake because GA:C reflects total secondary plant metabolite intake. High GA:C values would indicate high intake of secondary metabolites, but low values could represent 1) low intake of food regardless of quality or 2) high intake of foods with low concentrations of secondary metabolites. A conservative approach of reporting the proportion of animals with high GA:C ratios (>6) is recommended (Servello and Schneider 2000).

A number of general recommendations have been made that apply to most or all urinary indices (Box 2). Finally,

---

Box 2. General recommendations for use of urine-based indices of nutritional status with ungulates.

1. Samples can be collected within 4 days after snowfall as long as ambient temperature remains below freezing (DelGiudice et al. 1988).
2. Sample sizes of 20–35 per sampling period are generally adequate, but the actual number required will depend on planned statistical approaches (Ditchkoff and Servello 1999, Pils et al. 1999).
3. Sampling schemes should be designed to avoid collecting >1 sample from an animal during a collection period.
4. There may be gender and age differences in urinary index data that may introduce biases in population-level results when examining temporal trends within or differences among populations (White et al. 1995, Pils et al. 1999).
5. Examine temporal trends in indices rather than rely on measurements for a single point in time (DelGiudice 1995).
6. Ancillary information on environmental factors or populations may be important for interpreting urinary index data (e.g., DelGiudice et al. 1989).
7. Use of multiple indices may strengthen conclusions because each measures a different aspect of nutritional status. Several indices can be measured in a single sample.

there has been a healthy discussion of the pros and cons of various urinary indices in the literature (e.g., Saltz et al. 1995) that is recommended reading for new users of these techniques.

Ptilochronology

Ptilochronology is a technique in which width of sequential dark and light bands on a bird's feather(s), called growth bars, are used to quantify daily growth rate of the feather. Feather growth rate is assumed to relate to nutritional status of the bird during feather growth (Grubb 1989). A standard protocol has been developed for measuring feather growth rate using growth bars of tail feathers (Grubb 1989). Because birds will replace tail feathers that are pulled out by predators or researchers, growth bars on an induced tail feather can be used to assess nutritional status of a bird during feather regrowth (~6 weeks) (Grubb 1995).

An early criticism of the technique was that feather growth rate seemed relatively insensitive to nutritional condition of the bird except when the bird was severely nutrient-limited (Murphy and King 1991, Murphy 1992). Recent studies have demonstrated that, at least in some songbird species, relatively mild nutrient-limitation can cause measurable declines in feather growth rate as estimated using growth bars (Grubb 1995, Jenkins et al. 2001). What remains to be demonstrated is whether the extent of under-nutrition consistently and quantitatively influences growth rates of feathers. Another difficulty with the technique is that growth bars are not sufficiently obvious in corresponding feathers of all individuals, for reasons yet unknown (Murphy 1992). In addition, feather growth bars are influenced by factors other than nutritional condition including gender and age of the bird, and season (e.g., Carrascal et al. 1998). Comparisons of feather growth bars in the original and induced feather on the same individual can help control for these factors, but requires assumptions about the nutritional status of the bird when the original feather was produced (Grubb 1992).

Ptilochronology appears to be a promising technique for nondestructively estimating nutritional status of birds during feather regrowth. However, widespread acceptance of the technique requires that we learn more about factors that influence feather growth rate and conditions that influence growth bars.

NUTRITIONAL ANALYSES OF FOODS

A common starting point for evaluating habitat from a nutritional perspective is to chemically or physically analyze available foods to assess their nutritional quality or value. The food constituents that might be measured include those that supply useful nutrients or energy, such as protein, fat, or soluble carbohydrates, and those that have negative effects on nutritional value, such as plant secondary metabolites. The number of nutritional variables that might be measured has increased greatly as we have learned more about the requirements of wildlife and factors that influence the nutritional value of foods. Broadly speaking, foods can be divided into 2 major fractions, or classes of chemically similar compounds. One is the easy to digest components such as protein, fats, sugars, and starches. These are sometimes categorized as soluble food components and are available to the animal via verte-brate enzyme and acid digestion. The complementary fraction is the variably digested and usually insoluble components, the fiber fraction in plants and bones, hair, feathers, etc. in carnivore prey. Some components of plants complicate the soluble versus insoluble (i.e., fiber) dichotomy. For example, some fiber compounds are soluble, and plant secondary metabolites, which may constitute significant proportions of plant biomass, may be misclassified as highly digestible fractions by some analyses. Although it is convenient to discuss food composition in terms of broad chemical fractions or classes of compound, more intensive analyses for individual nutrients or compounds may be desired.

Interpreting data on nutritional quality of foods can be complex.

1. *The importance of a particular nutrient or fraction differs among wildlife species.* For example, soluble fiber is undigestible for some species (e.g., bears, Pritchard and Robbins 1990), but is highly digestible by ruminant species. Or, 2 wildlife species may have different capabilities for reducing negative effects of plant secondary metabolites (McArthur et al. 1991), thereby mitigating the relative significance of that fraction. Unfortunately, despite improvements in techniques for measuring nutritional quality, there is still limited information on species-specific requirements and adaptations. Therefore, one must recognize that interpretation of nutritional quality of a given food is based on generally accepted relationships that have not been evaluated for all species or even all major species groups.

2. *The composition of a nutritional fraction is typically treated as if it is uniform even though it is not.* For example, 2 foods may have the same total fiber level suggesting equal nutritional value, but types of fiber and therefore digestibility, may differ substantially. Analogous problems occur with plant secondary metabolites because measured fractions have different arrays of compounds, each with unique nutritional effects.

3. *Analysis methods may not accurately measure a particular nutritional fraction in all foods.* Analysis methods theoretically divide food samples into fractions that have uniform chemical structure and nutritional characteristics. However, some analysis methods may fail in this regard, particularly when applied to plants with more complex chemistries than those used to develop the technique. For example, the sticky resins of conifer needles are not fats, but will be extracted as part of a fat analysis that uses organic solvents. One should be particularly careful when applying techniques to forages with unusual structure (e.g., ground lichens) that were not included in technique testing. Even given the above cautions, chemical analysis techniques provide a standardized and efficient approach for studying large numbers of foods. Methods for analyzing and quantifying nutritional value of wildlife foods have evolved greatly and, in the process, some methods have been discarded or changed as errors or problems were identified. While there is much useful information on nutritional value of wildlife foods from the 1940s to the present, data from early analyses should be re-evaluated based on our current knowledge of nutrition and method biases. For

example, the Proximate Analysis System (Scott et al. 1982), which was developed for agricultural crops, was used extensively in published reports on wildlife foods into the 1970–80s. Parts of this analysis system are valid and still used but some analyses have serious flaws.

Sample Collection and Preparation

Food samples collected for nutritional analyses need to be representative of those eaten by the wildlife species of interest. This can be a challenge because chemical composition of foods can be significantly affected by season, environmental conditions, plant size or growth form, and plant or animal part. For example, snowshoe hares (*Lepus americanus*) tend to avoid feeding on juvenile plants of paper birch (*Betula papyrifera*) because of higher secondary metabolite concentrations than in more mature stems (Reichardt et al. 1984). Similarly, decisions on plant parts to sample will be dependent on the wildlife species studied because the average bite size of herbivores may vary. For example, moose (*Alces alces*) browse twigs to a greater diameter-at-point-of-browsing than deer and, therefore, will eat twigs with lower average protein content because protein content of woody twigs increases from twig bases to tips (Moen 1985). For small species, like voles (*Microtus* spp.) that feed primarily on herbaceous vegetation, there may be even finer-scale selection for plant parts that may not be apparent to humans. Therefore, gross sampling of the above-ground vegetative parts of plants may not be representative of the foods actually eaten by small herbivores (Servello et al. 1984). Larger-scale sampling issues include seasonal and site-specific influences (e.g., shade vs. sun-lit areas) on the chemical composition of plants (Van Horne et al. 1988, Happe et al. 1990). For analyses of the prey of carnivores, decisions must be made about whether it is appropriate to include hair or feathers in samples. Overall, sampling designs for collecting foods for analyses must be based on knowledge of habitat selection, species of foods eaten, and foraging behavior of the wildlife species of interest. Study designs in Regelin et al. (1974), Schwartz et al. (1977), and Hobbs et al. (1983) are examples of intensive efforts to obtain representative samples. They attempted to duplicate food selection by observing tame animals as they fed and by simultaneously handpicking plants and plant parts at foraging sites.

The methods used to store and prepare samples for analyses can be critical for obtaining accurate results. Typically plant or prey samples need to be stored, dried, and ground or pulverized for analysis, although there are important exceptions with potential problems more common for plant tissue. Physical damage to leaves may affect measured concentrations of secondary plant metabolites and nutrients because compounds sequestered in vacuoles in leaves (Harborne 1991*b*) may interact with plant compounds when leaves are crushed (McLeod 1974, Swain 1979). Damaged leaves containing high concentrations of phenolics, a class of secondary plant metabolites, sometimes will develop a brown or black coloration indicating that oxidation of compounds has occurred (Ribereau-Gayon 1972). Crushing leaves also can cause release of volatile compounds (Mabry and Gill 1979).

Generally, collected plant samples should be kept cool after collection and processed as soon as possible. Even after plant leaves are picked, losses of sugars from respiration and enzymatic conversions of sugars to starches can occur (Smith 1973). These losses and changes can be reduced by cold storage. For accurate measurements of some nutritional variables, freezing is a necessity. For example, volatile terpene loss is reduced in collected samples by freezing immediately with dry ice or liquid nitrogen (Schwartz et al. 1980, Welch and McArthur 1981). Freezing fresh plant tissue is a common and useful method of long-term storage, but we caution that frozen-storage and subsequent thawing may cause changes in composition. It is more likely the freezing or thawing processes rather than storage causes the problems. For example, during the thawing process leaves with high concentrations of some secondary plant metabolites may develop a black coloration. The resulting new complexes of compounds may be mis-classified by some analyses (Mould and Robbins 1981*a*). Even dried plant samples will discolor over time at room temperature indicating that changes are occurring. Drying samples prior to freezing for storage should minimize problems. If samples will be dried by lypholization (i.e., freeze-drying) after frozen storage, the samples should be transferred to the lypholizer in a frozen state and not allowed to thaw.

Typically samples are dried for processing and analyses, but there are exceptions. Terpenoid fractions are extracted from fresh or fresh-frozen plant tissue because some terpene compounds are highly volatile (Mabry and Gill 1979, Personius et al. 1987). Extracts of fresh material can be used for analyses of plants that are highly affected by drying or storage methods but are awkward for analyzing large numbers of samples. If sample drying is required, it should be completed as soon as possible because chemical changes are less likely at low moisture levels. After drying, samples should be kept in individual airtight containers or a dessicator to prevent re-absorption of moisture from the air.

The choice of drying method may be critical. Oven drying can substantially alter measurements of chemical composition. Smith (1973) reported that oven-drying leaves below 50 C provides time for dry matter losses of nonstructural carbohydrates by respiration and enzymatic conversion of compounds. Drying above 80 C can result in thermochemical degradation, and drying above 50 C can cause nonenzymatic reactions among proteins and carbohydrates known as the browning or Maillard reaction. The latter causes analytical errors in fiber analyses (Van Soest 1965). Even at relatively low temperatures (40–60 C), oven drying can substantially decrease measured phenolic levels, a secondary plant metabolite, in plant tissue (Julkumen-Tiitto 1985, Servello et al. 1987, Nastis and Malechek 1988). Frozen storage and thawing before oven drying reduces phenolic concentrations more than oven-drying fresh material (Servello et al. 1987). Lyophilizing (freeze-drying) may be the mildest drying treatment because samples are held frozen during the drying process. It results in greater and likely more accurate values for some phenolic and fiber measurements (Servello et al. 1987, Nastis and Malechek 1988).

There is not one best drying method for plant samples. If extractions or analyses do not need to be done with fresh material, we recommend lyophilizing whenever possible, particularly when samples have been stored fresh-frozen.

If oven drying is the only practical option, we suggest drying at 40 C to minimize chemical changes. Most importantly, we suggest that researchers carefully review the potential effects of sample preparation on analytical methods used and foods being studied. We recommend lyophilizing for drying all animal tissue.

Most samples must be ground to a small particle size for analyses and for uniform sub-sampling. Generally, samples should be ground to pass a 0.5- or 1.0-mm screen, but larger tissues sizes may be acceptable for some analyses.

Food Quality Variables and Analytical Techniques

Water

Water content (%) is measured by weighing samples before and after oven drying at 100 C for 24 hours. We typically have little interest in the water content of foods *per se* although preformed water in food may be important for desert animals in meeting their water requirements. More commonly this procedure is used to measure the percent dry matter in samples that have been dried and ground for analysis. Percent dry matter is then used to express the data for other nutritional fractions on a dry-matter basis. Expressing all data on a dry matter basis allows comparisons among samples, nutritional fractions, and other studies.

Fat

Fats are the energy-rich tryglycerides and related compounds indicative of higher nutritional value. Crude fat content is measured by extracting a food sample with petroleum ether or diethyl ether, most commonly in a Soxhlet extraction device, which repeatedly washes the sample with ether (Maynard et al. 1979). The crude fat content is measured as percentage loss in dry weight of the sample after extraction. The estimate is referred to as crude fat because it measures all nonpolar compounds. It is also frequently referred to in the literature as the ether extract fraction, the name from the proximate analysis system. This method is generally satisfactory for measuring fat content in animal tissue. With plants, however, the crude fat estimate will include resins, waxes, and volatile oils and related compounds that have little or negative nutritional value. Seeds may be an exception in that they may contain significant concentrations of digestible oils. Fat data for plant foods should be interpreted with caution.

Protein

Protein provides building blocks in the form of amino acids and can be used for energy. Protein is generally highly digestible (>90%) by vertebrates (Robbins 1993). The crude protein content (%) of a food is estimated by measuring its nitrogen content and converting that to a crude estimate of protein based on the average proportion of nitrogen in protein. The commonly used Kjeldahl procedure for measuring nitrogen involves digesting the sample in H_2SO_4, neutralizing with NaOH, distilling the resulting ammonium, and titrating with acid (Church and Pond 1988). The estimated nitrogen content (%) expressed on a dry matter basis is then multiplied by 6.25 to calculate the crude protein content because, on average, protein contains 16% nitrogen (100/16 = 6.25). This fraction is referred to as crude protein because nitrogen occurs in compounds other than proteins. Crude protein may over-

estimate true protein content by as much as 22-52% in some plants (Sedinger 1984, Levey et al. 2000), but generally the nonprotein nitrogen fraction is considered small and ignored. Another caution in interpreting crude protein data is that some secondary plant metabolites may bind with plant proteins in an animal's digestive system, making a portion of the measured crude protein unavailable (Robbins et al. 1987*b*). The Kjeldahl procedure can be used with animal tissue (Fisher et al. 1992), but the protein content of animal tissue also can be measured indirectly using body composition analyses.

Fiber

In broad terms, the carbohydrate fraction of foods is comprised of soluble carbohydrates and fiber. Soluble carbohydrates are the completely digestible sugars and starches, whereas fiber is a complex of carbohydrates and other compounds that vary in digestibility. However, there is a soluble fiber fraction. Therefore, to measure fiber levels in wildlife foods and interpret this information, it is often important to know both the total fiber content and the relative amount of major fiber fractions. The detergent analysis system (Goering and Van Soest 1970) of measuring fiber fractions is recommended for herbivores capable of microbial digestion of fiber, whereas the total dietary fiber method (Prosky et al. 1984) is recommended for other species (Robbins 1993). Detergent analysis does not measure soluble fiber components, which is not a significant analytical error for species with microbial digestion, but may be important for other species especially if soluble fiber is a significant component of foods. In the detergent analysis system, a series of treatments is used to divide a food sample into various fractions. The principal division is to identify the proportions of highly digestible cell contents and variably digestible cell wall (i.e., fiber) fractions in a food sample using a detergent solution at neutral pH (Fig. 6). The division between cell contents and walls is not perfect; therefore, these fractions are more accurately referred to as neutral detergent solubles (NDS) and neutral

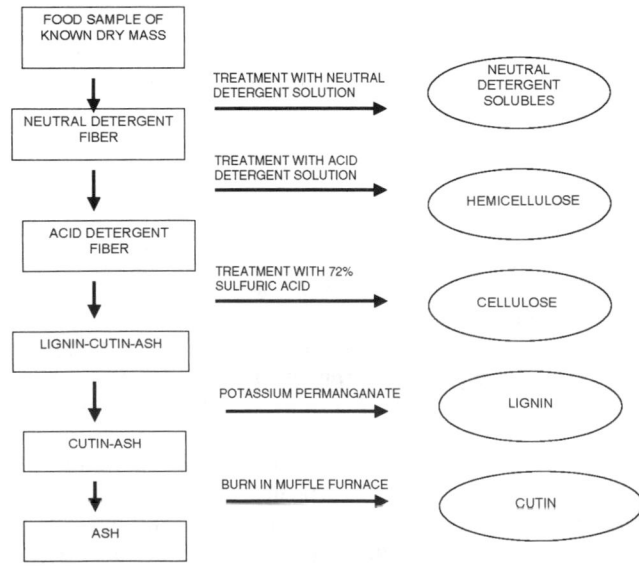

Fig. 6. Treatment steps and products from sequential detergent analysis of plant foods. Drying and weighing after each treatment gives the mass of each fraction remaining or removed. Rectangles are fractions remaining after analytical steps and ellipses are fractions removed.

detergent fiber (NDF) (Mould and Robbins 1981*a*). Theoretically, the magnitude of the soluble fraction is an indication of the proportion of readily digestible material in the food for both animals with simple stomachs and those that ferment foods. Additional steps are used to identify the composition of the insoluble fiber fraction. Treatment of the neutral detergent fiber with acid detergent theoretically removes hemicellulose and other minor compounds, which leaves a fraction called acid detergent fiber. It should be noted the hemicellulose fraction that is removed and measured by difference is poorly defined because it varies in composition and can be greatly influenced by relatively small analytical errors in the measurement of the larger NDF and ADF fractions. Acid detergent fiber is comprised of the major structural components of plants, cellulose and lignin, and is an important measure of forage quality. Subsequent treatment steps with either strong acids or oxidizers, depending on the method used, followed by burning in a furnace to measure ash content quantifies the proportions of cellulose and lignin in the food sample and ADF. Cutin, typically a small fraction, may be measured as part of the lignin fraction or may be measured separately. For mammalian herbivores, the amount of lignin-cutin in the ADF is the major factor affecting the digestibility of the total fiber fraction; digestibility of the ADF or total fiber fraction increases with a decreasing lignin content in the ADF (Mould and Robbins 1982).

Users should be aware of a number of modifications to the original system of detergent analyses and some potential biases. The original method used separate samples of foods for measurement of NDF and ADF. Currently, sequential measurement of NDF and ADF on the same sample is recommended (Mould and Robbins 1981*a*). It is also generally recommended that sodium sulfite not be used in the neutral detergent because it dissolved some lignin (Mould and Robbins (1981*a*), unless the forages contain tannins (Hanley et al. 1992). Also, treatment with amylase during neutral detergent extraction is recommended for foods with high soluble carbohydrate content to avoid overestimates of fiber concentrations (Robertson and Van Soest 1977).

The detergent analysis system was initially developed for analysis of agricultural crop species and analytical errors may occur when it is applied to the diverse array of plants eaten by wildlife. A common problem is that plant secondary metabolites will usually be extracted as part of the NDS. Therefore, the NDS fraction cannot be assumed to be highly digestible (or valuable) when plant secondary metabolites compose a substantial fraction of the dry matter in foods. Also, plants that do not primarily use a cellulose-lignin structure for physical support (e.g., ground lichens) may produce flawed detergent analysis data because relatively unique chemical components may be mis-classified.

The total dietary fiber method (Prosky et al. 1984) accounts for both insoluble and soluble fiber, such as pectins and gums, which may be undigestible by monogastric species (Robbins 1993). In this method, the food sample is first treated with an enzyme, and total dietary fiber is the percentage of the sample weight remaining after filtering and applying corrections for percent protein and percent ash in the sample. If the food has more than 5% fat, a preliminary fat extraction step is used.

Finally, there is a large body of published data on crude fiber concentrations in wildlife foods reported prior to 1980. Crude fiber is the fiber measurement from the outdated proximate analysis system (Scott et al. 1982), and is not appropriate for wildlife foods. Therefore, wildlife researchers should be cautious interpreting earlier published results.

Soluble Carbohydrates

It is not common to measure concentrations of sugars and starches in studies of wildlife foods for habitat evaluation. More typical is the measurement of neutral detergent solubles, which is the total fraction of highly digestible components (i.e., soluble carbohydrates, protein, fat). However, there are techniques for measuring soluble carbohydrates if desired (Smith 1973).

Ash

Ash is the mineral matter remaining after all water and organic matter are removed. Ash is measured by burning a sample in a muffle furnace at 500-600°C for at least 5 hours and weighing the residue. The ash content is expressed as a percentage of original dry matter. More detailed studies of specific minerals require further analysis of the ash content, usually by atomic absorption spectrophotometry.

Plant Secondary Metabolites

A number of types of plant secondary metabolites (PSM), also called allelochemicals, serve a role in defense against herbivory. Therefore, the concentrations of PSMs in wildlife foods are indicators of food quality. These metabolites are referred to as secondary because they do not have a primary role in plant growth or development (Gershenzon and Croteau 1991). Routine surveys of PSMs in wildlife foods are not commonly done as part of habitat assessments because laboratory analyses are complex. However, there is considerable effort to understand the significance of PSMs in foraging ecology of wild herbivores. This new information is greatly improving our understanding of habitat from a nutritional perspective. But, the widespread occurrence of PSMs greatly increases the complexity of habitat evaluation because 1) there are a large number of types of PSMs and specific compounds (Rosenthal and Berenbaum 1991), and the magnitude and types of negative effects on wildlife nutrition differ greatly among PSMs (Harborne 1991*a*); 2) herbivore species have varying adaptations, strategies, and capabilities for coping with intake of PSMs (Cork and Foley 1991, McArthur et al. 1991, Hagerman and Robbins 1993); and 3) PSM concentrations may be influenced by local environments (Bryant et al. 1991), plant growth stage (Connolly et al. 1980), browsing by herbivores (Bryant et al. 1992), and other factors (Jakubas et al. 1994). A comprehensive review of PSMs is beyond the scope of this chapter as is a review of analytical techniques because of the wide array of compounds and analyses. We recommend Palo and Robbins (1991) and Rosenthal and Berenbaum (1991) as excellent reviews on PSMs for wildlife biologists and suggest that anyone beginning work in this area undertake a detailed review of analytical techniques.

Phenolics are broadly categorized functionally and structurally as tannins or non-tannins. Tannins are large compounds (>500 molecular weight) that complex with and precipitate proteins in solution (Hagerman and Butler 1991). The smaller non-tannin phenolics include the common flavonoid pigments and other simple phenols (Harborne 1991b). Actual effects on herbivores may differ substantially among specific compounds within the above classes. Phenolic concentrations in plants vary seasonally, by stage of growth, and by plant part (Bryant 1981, Palo et al. 1985, Van Horne et al. 1988), and there is evidence that production of phenolic compounds by plants may be influenced by environmental conditions at a particular site and by browsing by herbivores (Bryant et al. 1991). Browsing damage also may influence plant growth rates and subsequent production of phenolic metabolites (Bryant et al. 1992). There are many studies of induction of PSM production, primarily by insects but also with vertebrate herbivores (Tallamy and Raupp 1991). All of these factors should be considered when designing field studies of PSM-wildlife interactions.

Tannin phenolics may reduce food intake, decrease protein digestibility, increase metabolic rates, alter digestive functions, alter acid-base balance with resulting effects on metabolic processes, or be toxic to wild herbivores (Buchsbaum et al. 1984, Lindroth and Batzli 1984, Smallwood and Peters 1986, Thomas et al. 1988, McArthur and Sanson 1993, Foley et al. 1995, Hewitt and Kirkpatrick 1997, Hewitt et al. 1999). Non-tannin phenolics, which may occur in relatively high concentrations in plants, also can reduce food intake (Lindroth and Batzli 1984) or can require significant energy expenditure for simply processing and eliminating these compounds after absorption (Lindroth and Batzli 1984). Actual effects on wildlife will depend not only on the nature of the specific tannin compounds, but also on adaptations of individual species for coping with phenolic ingestion. For example, some mammals have proline-rich saliva that reduces effects of tannin compounds by interfering with protein complexing (Foley and McArthur 1994). However, there is wide variation among species in capability to bind specific types of tannins, and these capabilities appear to be related to diet breadth (Hagerman and Robbins 1993). In addition, there is substantial variation among species in physiological strategies for detoxifying and excreting absorbed PSMs (McArthur et al. 1991, Robbins et al. 1991, Guglielmo et al. 1996). The metabolic oxidative system in animals includes several pathways for modifying or conjugating PSMs with other compounds to excrete them (McArthur et al. 1991). These physiological strategies may vary among species (Foley and McArthur 1994). Not only may these metabolic processes increase energy requirements (Guglielmo et al. 1996, Iason and Murray 1996), but also conjugation of large quantities of phenolics to other compounds for excretion may reduce pools of nutritionally valuable substrates (Illius and Jessop 1995). While there are general responses of herbivores to ingestion of phenolic compounds, the variety of compounds, effects, and adaptations suggest caution when evaluating the nutritional significance of PSM data for foods unless the ecology of the plant-herbivore interaction is well understood.

Phenolics are usually extracted from fresh or dried plant material with a polar solvent, usually methanol, acetone, ethanol, or ethyl acetate in an aqueous mixture (Martin and Martin 1982). Total phenolics are commonly assayed colorimetrically in plant extracts by the Folin-Ciocalteu procedure (Singleton and Rossi 1965). Total phenolic content provides a measure of a fraction of dry matter and gross energy in plants that is eaten, potentially absorbed and processed, and excreted without energetic gain (Foley 1992). However, total phenolic content has a poor relationship with protein-precipitating capability because it is a mixture of tannin and nontannin phenolics (Martin and Martin 1982). The total tannin fraction in plants is difficult to measure directly, and indirect measures that assay protein-binding capability appear to provide the most biologically meaningful indices of tannin effects because these methods mimic the reduction in protein digestion generally expected from tannins (Martin and Martin 1982, Mole and Waterman 1987). Precipitation of the protein, bovine serum albumin (BSA) (Hagerman and Butler 1978), has been used to quantify tannins in wildlife foods (e.g., McArthur et al. 1993). Hagerman (1987) also developed a relatively simple and inexpensive BSA precipitation method based on diffusion of tannin in a BSA-impregnated agar slab that is recommended for studies that require analyses of large numbers of samples (Hagerman and Butler 1991). These authors provide a good review of quantitative analyses for tannins. One should recognize that different protein-precipitating assays might not produce identical results (Martin and Martin 1982, Mole and Waterman 1987). In physiological studies of tannin fates in animals, different assays are used for measuring tannin concentrations or activity in biological samples such as saliva and urine (e.g., Austin et al. 1989, Hewitt and Kirkpatrick 1997).

Terpenoids are a large and abundant class of organic compounds in plants that are characterized by nonpolar carbon skeletons (Gershenszon and Croteau 1991). The major classes include the monoterpenoids, sesquiterpenoids, diterpenoids, and triterpenoids (Gershenszon and Croteau 1991) and are based on the number of 5-carbon units present (Harborne 1991a). Plant substances commonly referred to as essential oils, volatile oils, and resins contain terpenoid components (Nagy et al. 1964, Schwartz et al. 1980). Terpenes often function as feeding deterrents and the volatile nature of many makes them detectable by olfaction by mammalian herbivores (Epple et al. 1996). Therefore, food selection issues have been the focus of many wildlife studies on terpenes (Schwartz et al. 1980, Cluff et al. 1982, Personius et al. 1987, Duncan et al. 1994). Ingestion of terpenes also may decrease microbial digestion rates in herbivores (Schwartz et al. 1980, Cluff et al. 1982), alter acid-base homeostasis (Foley et al. 1995), can be toxic (Harborne 1991a), or increase water requirements (Dearing et al. 2002). The latter may be critical for species in arid environments (Dearing et al. 2002). As with phenolic compounds, absorbed terpenes may have to be metabolically modified for excretion (Dash 1988, McLean et al. 1993, Boyle et al. 2000) with a potential metabolic cost to the animal. These unusable compounds can represent a significant fraction of the gross energy in high-terpene forages (Foley and McArthur 1994). Detoxification of ingested terpenes by herbivores and its implications on feeding strategies is currently a major area of research in plant-herbivore interactions (e.g., Dearing et al. 2002). Because chromatography allows identification of many individual terpene compounds, these data are available in the literature for many plant species (e.g.,

Kamdem and Hanover 1993). However, interpretation of this detailed terpenoid information is difficult because of the paucity of parallel information on effects of individual compounds on wild herbivores. Analytical procedures are varied for this complex chemical class, but in wildlife studies terpenes are typically extracted by steam-distillation from fresh or fresh-frozen plant material because some compounds are highly volatile (Foley 1992, Personius et al. 1987) and quantification is done chromatographically (Gershenzon and Croteau 1991)

Gross Energy

The gross energy in a food is the total amount of energy released by complete oxidation and is expressed on a density basis as calories, kilocalories or joules per gram of food. The gross energy content of foods ranges from approximately 4 kcal/g for foods high in carbohydrates to about 9 kcal/g for foods high in fats (Church and Pond 1988:144). The proportion of useful energy for animals will vary among foods because some food constituents are more difficult to digest, and digestive capability varies among animal species. The gross energy content of food samples is routinely measured using adiabatic bomb calorimetry. Food samples are combusted in a high-pressure oxygen-filled chamber and released heat is measured in a surrounding water bath. Gessaman (1987) provided a good description of bomb calorimetry and sampling considerations.

MEASURING DIGESTION AND METABOLISM OF FOODS

Chemical or physical analyses of foods provide information on energy, nutrients, and anti-nutritional factors. Generally, one needs to measure digestion to understand the actual availability of nutrients and energy in a given food. Feeding trials of several types are widely used to measure amounts or proportions of nutrients and energy in foods that can be extracted by wildlife species. The general approach involves quantitatively measuring intake and excretion of dry matter, nutrients, or energy for a number of individual animals over several days. Feeding trials cannot be routinely done to survey food quality in habitats because this requires maintenance of experimental animals and laborious collections of test foods. A widely used alternative to feeding trials, particularly with ruminant species, is in-vitro digestion where food samples are subjected to a laboratory process that mimics the fermentation and digestive environment in the animal. This approach allows evaluation of a relatively large number of food samples, but has limitations. Considerable effort in the wildlife nutrition field has focused on understanding relationships between proportions of usable energy and nutrients measured in feeding trials, and food quality variables that can be measured via chemical analyses. These relationships allow indirect assessments of digestible energy and nutrients in foods, and provide a more time- and cost-efficient approach when large numbers of food samples must be measured for habitat evaluations.

The terminology used to describe digestion and metabolism of foods by animals is complex and not consistent. We use the term digestibility to refer to the proportion of dry matter or energy (kilocalories or joules) in the food eaten that is absorbed across the gut wall of the animal (i.e., not excreted in feces). Metabolizability refers to the proportion of dry matter or energy eaten that is retained for metabolic use by the animal (i.e., not excreted in feces, urine or as a gas). These variables are usually expressed more specifically as digestible dry matter (DDM), digestible energy (DE), or metabolizable energy (ME). When these variables are used to describe digestive or metabolic efficiency of an animal, it is more appropriate to express them on a proportion or percentage basis. In contrast, when these variables are used to describe quality of a food it is usually more appropriate to express them as a density function such as DE (kcal or joules) per gram of food dry matter. This accounts for foods that have varying gross energy or nutrient content. For example, 2 plant species eaten by a desert tortoise (*Gopherus agassizii*) may have the same proportions of digestible energy extracted, but one may have a considerably greater gross energy content. The food with the greater amount of gross energy will contribute more DE per gram eaten than that with a lower value.

The term, assimilation, is frequently used in the ecological literature, e.g., assimilated energy. Whether authors are using assimilation as a substitute for digestibility or metabolizability may not be clear, and one has to examine the methods and measurement units to identify the specific variable being reported. Also, only metabolizability is reported for birds because feces and urine cannot be easily separated for measurement, precluding calculations of digestibility. Digestion and metabolism values will sometimes be labeled as apparent or true values. Standard measurements from feeding trials produce "apparent" values because some fecal and urinary dry matter originates from the animal's tissues and not the test food. These endogenous losses include digestive enzymes, gastrointestinal epithelial cells, microbes, and excreted end products of metabolism (Maynard et al. 1979). True digestibility or metabolism values are calculated from the amounts of endogenous dry matter, energy, or nutrients in the excreta and then correcting the apparent values. However, when food intake is sufficiently high to maintain body mass, apparent and true values for waterfowl vary only by an average of 3 percentage units (Miller and Reinecke 1984).

Metabolizable energy values for foods are sometimes calculated as "nitrogen-corrected" because individual animals losing or gaining weight during a feeding trial will vary in the amount of endogenous urinary nitrogen in their excreta. Making this correction provides a more accurate measure of the rate of metabolism of the food. In practice though, nitrogen-corrected ME values usually differ little from uncorrected values (e.g., Beckerton and Middleton 1982, Sibbald and Morse 1982).

Feeding Trial Methods

The total collection feeding trial is the most common method for measuring digestive capability of animals, and digestibility and metabolizability of energy and nutrients in foods. The method for measuring true metabolizable energy in birds and techniques that use indigestible markers are variations of the total collection method, but unique enough for separate treatment.

Total Collection Method

The basic approach is to feed known amounts of a test

Fig. 7. Ten-week old snow goose (*Chen caerulescens*) in a total collection digestibility trial. Food intake and fecal production are quantitatively measured on a daily basis. Digestibility of the diet or components of the diet (e.g., fiber) are then estimated given measured intake and excretion rates.

food to a number of individual animals over a number of days. The food eaten is measured and the excreta produced is collected and weighed (Fig. 7). Hydrochloric acid or H_2SO_4 is added to urine collection bottles to prevent ammonia loss. Concentrations of energy or other nutrients in food consumed and excreta produced are used in calculations of digestibility or metabolizability. Typically an animal is fed a single food or diet, but there are techniques for measuring digestibility of single foods fed in mixed diets. Feeding trials are typically conducted in cages designed for separation and collection of food, feces, and urine. For species not using foregut fermentation, 3–6-day acclimation periods to test diets and 3–6-day collection periods are commonly used (e.g., Robel et al. 1979, Campbell and MacAuthur 1996), but longer periods may be more appropriate for some species. For ruminants and other foregut fomenters, 7–10-day acclimation periods and 7-day collection periods are commonly used. Mothershead et al. (1972) reported that a 10-day collection period was most accurate for white-tailed deer, but 7 days was not much of a disadvantage.

Total collection trials have been conducted with a wide array of wildlife species, and descriptions of digestion cages or crates, procedures, and additional helpful information for many species are available in methods and materials sections in published reports. Significant modifications of the basic approach are common with reptiles. It is a common practice to force-feed lizards and turtles when there is difficulty achieving satisfactory intake (Troyer 1984, Karasov et al. 1986*a*, Nagy and Medica 1986). Because of long food transit times in turtles, indigestible plastic markers have been used to demark a period of food intake and the resulting pulse of feces for measuring digestibility (Meienberger et al. 1993, Nagy et al. 1998). Reptiles must be allowed to bask or cage temperature must be regulated (Bjorndal 1991) because body temperature can influence digestive functions as well as metabolic rate and, therefore, food intake. For carnivores, it may be necessary to allow time for gut volume changes that may occur naturally in response to prey scarcity or abundance. For example, Harlow (1981) found that American badgers (*Taxidea taxus*) that had been fasted before the collection period had a slower food passage rate and metabolized 11% more of the energy in food than animals fed on a daily basis prior to the trial. Welch et al. (1997) used a long acclimation period with bears to ensure their digestive tracts had expanded to maximum capacity. Providing long acclimation periods or appropriate maintenance diets also may be important with herbivorous birds, such as grouse (Tetraoninae) and waterfowl (Anseriformes) as well as migratory landbirds, because their gizzards, intestines, or ceca change in size in response to diet (Moss 1973, McWilliams and Karasov 2001). The total collection method may be impractical for some species or situations, such as aquatic turtles (Bjorndal and Bolten 1993) and some seals (Goodman-Lowe et al. 1999).

Experimental animals must be acclimated or trained for handling and confinement in metabolism cages. In some cases, particularly with small species, wild-captured animals can be used if individuals will adapt to confinement. Experimental animals are frequently reared in captivity; however, even captive-raised animals must be acclimated to metabolic cages. For example, Mautz (1971) observed that food intake decreased with some captive-raised deer after confinement, and it required 9–12 days to return to pre-confinement levels. Training animals to accept confinement also lowers the risk of accidental injury to the animal and researchers. The number of animals used for an individual measurement of digestion or metabolism rates is variable, but 4–6 animals per trial is common. Mothershead et al. (1972) suggested that 5 deer per test diet were adequate for most digestion trials. If the animals are healthy and eating normally, standard errors for DDM, DE, and ME estimates are usually within acceptable limits with these sample sizes.

Maintaining regular and adequate food intake is important for accurate results. Low and variable food intake may increase data variability because relatively constant endogenous excretion increases error as food intake decreases (Miller and Reinecke 1984). Animals should be fed at the same time each day. Test diets are often fed *ad libitum,* but constant intake can be assured and selective feeding can be reduced by feeding at a slight reduction (e.g., 90% *ad libitum*). Chopping or pelleting plant material or homogenizing animal tissue often is used to prevent selective feeding; however, these treatments may influence digestion or feeding behavior in other ways (Petrie et al. 1997). In unusual circumstances, food might be force-fed to circumvent problems with low or variable intake and food selection such as with turtles (Meienberger et al. 1993). Access to grit may be necessary for herbivorous birds in metabolism trials, but studies have produced mixed conclusions (Robel and Bisset 1979, Petrie et al. 1997).

Digestion and metabolism rates are easily calculated (Box 3). Apparent dry matter digestibility is the proportion or percentage of food eaten on a dry basis that was not excreted in feces. The apparent digestibility of a specific food component (e.g., fiber, N) is calculated as the proportion of the nutrient consumed in the food that was digested. Similarly, apparent digestible energy (%) is calculated by measuring the gross energy in the food and feces and converting dry-matter mass to energy equivalents. To transform percent digestible energy values into energy densities (DE/g dry matter) for a food, the proportion of digestible energy is multiplied by the gross energy (kcal or joules/g) of the food. Apparent metabolizable energy is calculated by subtracting urinary and gaseous energy losses. The loss of gross energy as gas (primarily methane) production is sufficiently low that it is often ignored. Nitrogen-corrected metabolizable energy is calculated as: deviations from nitrogen balance (gains or losses of nitrogen) are corrected by adding to or subtracting from the excreta energy value the energy content of urinary nitrogen. Equivalents for these calculations are 8.22 kcal/g of nitrogen for birds (Scott et al. 1982:537) and 7.45 kcal/g (Maynard et al. 1979:196) for each gram of nitrogen retained or lost.

Some forages are too unpalatable or too low or high in nutritional quality to be fed singly in a total collection trial. An alternative approach is to mix test forages with a more palatable basal diet (often a commercial feed) and to measure the digestibility of both mixed and basal diets in total collection trials. The digestible dry matter of the test food can be calculated by difference from these data with the formula:

$$DDM_f = \frac{DDM_m - (DDM_b \times Proportion_b)}{Proportion_f},$$

where

DDM = digestible dry matter of foods or diets in percent,

Proportion = proportion of test food or basal diet in the mixed diet, and

$$f = \text{test food,}$$

$$b = \text{basal diet, and}$$

$$m = \text{mixed diet.}$$

It is assumed the basal diet has no effect on the digestibility of the test food, but associative effects can occur (Bjorndal 1991).

True Metabolizable Energy Method for Birds

Sibbald (1976, 1979) developed a method for measuring the true metabolizable energy (TME) in foods for poultry, which has been applied to wild avian species, primarily waterfowl (e.g., Petrie et al. 1998). The TME method is relatively fast and requires less of the test food than a conventional feeding trial. Birds are first fasted for 24–48 hours and then force-fed a small amount of food in a period of several minutes. Feces and urine are then collected in metabolism cages over the next 24-48 hours. Control birds are treated similarly except they are not fed; experimental birds can serve as their own controls in sequential trials. The excreta of control birds is collected and

---

Box 3. Equations for calculating dry matter digestibility (DDM), digestible energy (DE), digestibility of a specific nutrient, and metabolizable energy (ME) using data from digestion or metabolism trials. All equations calculate apparent values.

$$DDM\ (\%) = \frac{\text{Food intake}^a - \text{Fecal dry matter}^a}{\text{Food intake}} \times 100$$

$$DE\ (\%) = \frac{(\text{Food intake} \times \text{GE food}^a) - (\text{Fecal dry matter} \times \text{GE feces})}{(\text{Food intake} \times \text{GE food})} \times 100$$

Digestibility (%) of nutrient A

$$= \frac{(\text{Food intake} \times \%\ A\ \text{in food}) - (\text{Fecal dry matter} \times \%\ A\ \text{in feces})}{(\text{Food intake} \times \%\ A\ \text{in food})} \times 100$$

$$ME\ (\%) = \frac{\text{GE intake} - (\text{Fecal GE} + \text{Urinary GE} + \text{Gaseous GE})^c}{\text{GE intake}} \times 100$$

[a] Food intake and fecal dry matter measured in grams or kilograms.

[b] Gross energy in kilocalories or kilojoules per gram dry matter.

[c] GE intake, fecal GE, etc. are calculated by multiplying dry matter eaten or excreted by the respective GE concentration. Gaseous GE loss is usually ignored.

weighed to estimate metabolic and endogenous dry matter and energy losses. The TME of the test food is calculated by subtracting the endogenous and metabolic energy losses of the control birds (C) from the fecal and urinary energy of the force-fed birds (F) as: TME (kcal or joules/g) = ([GE intake$_f$ – (EE$_f$ – EE$_c$)]/GE intake$_f$) × GE of test food, where GE intake$_f$ is the gross energy (kcal or joules) of the test food that was force-fed, EE$_f$ is the energy in the excreta from the fed bird (kcal or joules/g), and EE$_c$ is the energy in the excreta of the control bird (Guglielmo and Karasov 1993). This TME method has not been extensively tested against standard total collection trials with a variety of wild avian species.

Guglielmo and Karasov (1993) provide an alternative approach for estimating endogenous mass and energy losses in wild birds that does not require fasting (which is known to affect gut structure and function in birds, McWilliams and Karasov 2001). The method involves conducting a series of 3-day total collection feeding trials while feeding animals the food of interest over a range of fairly natural levels of food intake. Nitrogen-corrected endogenous mass and energy losses are then estimated using regression techniques.

Indicator Methods

For some wildlife species, measuring food intake and collecting all excreta for several days in conventional feeding trials may be impractical. This is the case for seals and turtles that periodically need to be in water. Indicator methods offer an alternative approach for measuring digestibility. An indigestible indicator is added to the test food and is measured in samples of food and feces during a subsequent feeding period. An accounting of total intake and excretion is not required. Percent digestible dry matter is calculated as:

$$\text{Digestible dry matter} = 1 - \frac{\%\text{ indicator in food}}{\%\text{ indicator in feces}} \times 100\%.$$

This method assumes the indicator is indigestible or is not changed in the digestive tract and that it mixes and moves uniformly with food. Chromic oxide has been used frequently (e.g., Goodman-Lowe et al. 1999), but other indicators have been used including uniquely-labeled radioactive or stable isotopes (Gasaway et al. 1976, Karasov et al. 1986b, McWilliams et al. 1999). Goodman-Lowe et al. (1999) provide a good example of the application of this technique with seals and describe calculations in detail.

In Vitro Methods

In vitro methods measure food digestibility by mimicking fermentation and digestive processes of ruminants and other foregut-fermenting species. In vitro digestion only requires small amounts of the test food samples and, therefore, is a more efficient method for evaluating large numbers of foods. The disadvantages of this technique are that animals must be available for the collection of rumen fluid, and a number of potential biases may influence results. The basic approach was developed by Tilley and Terry (1963) and involves inoculating a sample of food with rumen fluid and a buffer solution designed to simulate saliva. The fermenting sample is first maintained in a hot water bath for 48 hours. In a second stage, the fermented sample is treated with pepsin and mild acid. Modifications of this method include addition of a phosphate-carbonate buffer to reduce foaming and a reduced ratio of rumen fluid to buffer solution (Campa et al. 1984) or substituting the second stage of pepsin and mild acid with a neutral detergent extraction (Van Soest 1982).

Although the in vitro method is an efficient method for measuring digestibility, there are a number of potential sources of bias. There are conflicting reports on whether source of rumen fluid (e.g., donor species, wild vs. captive animals) can significantly influence digestibility estimates (Palmer et al. 1976, Welch et al. 1983, Campa et al. 1984, Jenks and Leslie 1988), but it seems clear the source can have an effect in some instances. Nastis and Malechek (1988) also found the donor animal's diet can have a substantial effect on estimates and that other additional bias may interact to produce highly variable results. Therefore, with wild herbivores, in vitro techniques are more appropriate for ranking food quality than predicting actual digestibility (Campa et al. 1984).

ASSESSING DIETS, DIET QUALITY, FOOD INTAKE, AND CARRYING CAPACITY

Ultimately the goal of wildlife nutrition research is to evaluate and understand the biochemical and biophysical relationships between animals and their environment, and how these relationships affect survival and reproduction of individuals and populations (Robbins 1993). We have largely discussed nutritional techniques and methods that occur in the laboratory or captive animal facilities in a reductionist, compartmentalized fashion (Parker et al. 1999). Several methods have been used to study the nutritional ecology of free-ranging animals and populations. These methods generally have been used to avoid assumptions, inadequacies, or difficulties of captive animal methods. For example, feeding trial data have limited value for estimating energy requirements of free-ranging animals. Also, analyzing or experimenting with all combinations of individual foods in the varied diets of some species can be impractical. Therefore, techniques that can provide information on natural diets selected by the animal are of value.

Indicators of Diet Composition
Stable Isotope Methods

The analysis of stable isotopes of carbon (^{13}C/^{12}C) and nitrogen (^{15}N/^{14}N) has been applied to a number of questions in ecology (Tieszen and Boutton 1989, Kelly 2000). In the area of nutritional ecology of wildlife, applications include using stable isotope ratios to reconstruct diets, assess physiological condition, and learn the fate of assimilated nutrients in individual animals (Gannes et al. 1997). Although stable isotope data cannot replace the detail provided by traditional dietary analyses, they have other advantages relative to understanding the trophic ecology of wild species.

Carbon, nitrogen, oxygen, and hydrogen, as well as other elements, have more than one naturally occurring isotope (Peterson and Fry 1987). Stable isotope data are expressed in the notation:

$$\delta = ([R_{\text{sample}}/R_{\text{standard}}] - 1) * 1{,}000,$$

where R is the ratio of heavy to light isotopes (e.g., $^{13}C/^{12}C$) and δ is the isotope ratio of a sample relative to a standard in units of parts per thousand or per mil (‰) (Kelly 2000). Standards for carbon and nitrogen are Peedee Belemite limestone and atmospheric nitrogen, respectively. Most plant and animal tissues have a negative value of $\delta^{13}C$ and a positive value of $\delta^{15}N$, meaning a lower $^{13}C/^{12}C$ ratio and a higher $^{15}N/^{14}N$ ratio than the standards. Samples are analyzed after combustion using mass spectrometry. Several types of tissue can be used for isotopic analysis, including whole blood, plasma, liver, muscle, bone collagen, hair, and feathers.

The value of stable isotopes of carbon in animal ecology arises from the different isotope ratios of carbon fixed by terrestrial C_3, terrestrial C_4, and marine (C_3) plants. The photosynthetic pathways of the former 2 types of plants use different CO_2-fixing enzymes and lead to different $\delta^{13}C$ values (range of –10 to –14 ‰ vs. a range of –25 to –30 ‰). Marine plants have intermediate $\delta^{13}C$ values (–22 ‰) (Kelly 2000). Experimental studies in birds and mammals have demonstrated the carbon isotope ratio of animal tissues is a direct reflection of the carbon isotope ratio of plant tissues assimilated (not merely eaten) by that animal (DeNiro and Epstein 1978; Hobson and Clark 1992a, b). Therefore, animal tissue samples can be used to assess the relative importance of different groups of plants in dietary assimilation. For example, because warm-season grasses are typically C_4 plants, and forbs, shrubs, and cool-season grasses are C_3 plants, browsing and grazing herbivores can be distinguished in regions where C_4 grasslands dominate (Kelly 2000). In turn, carbon isotope values of tissues of carnivores are reflective of the carbon isotope ratios of their prey. Carbon-isotopic turnover also varies by tissue type, ranging from 2.6 days in liver to 173 days in bone collagen in Japanese quail (*Coturnix japonica*) (Hobson and Clark 1992a), allowing researchers to monitor temporal changes in the assimilated diet by measuring stable-isotope values in different tissues (Tieszen et al. 1983).

Nitrogen-isotope ratios of animal tissues are particularly important for supplementing food web and dietary studies. The review of Kelly (2000) summarized 3 conclusions about nitrogen-isotope studies: a 3–4 ‰ enrichment in $\delta^{15}N$ occurs with each trophic level; nitrogen-isotope ratios are useful for distinguishing among diets based on marine, terrestrial or nitrogen-fixing plants; and nutritional and water stress can cause variation in $\delta^{15}N$ levels.

Gannes et al. (1997) discussed several assumptions of the technique upon which inferences are based and recommended additional controlled experiments to understand the behavior of stable-isotope ratios. For example, using isotope data to identify the relative contribution of different food items to an animal's diet depends on the assumption that isotopic composition of the animal's tissues equals the weighted average of the isotopic components of the diet. However, this assumption usually fails because animals assimilate diet components with different efficiencies, animal tissues fractionate or change the isotope ratios from the ratios in the diet, and animals allocate diet nutrients differentially to specific tissues (Gannes et al. 1997). For example, Hobson and Clark (1992b) found that tissues in several bird species were enriched in $\delta^{13}C$ and $\delta^{15}N$ relative to their diet but this fractionation varied by species, diet, and tissue type. We recommend that researchers interested in using stable-isotope techniques consult with those already active in the field, refer to reviews of the subject to recognize the varied applications of these data to ecological questions (Peterson and Fry 1987, Tieszen and Boutton 1989, Kelly 2000), and realize the limitations and assumptions involved (Gannes et al. 1997).

Fatty Acid Analysis Methods

Fatty acid profiles of animal tissues provide an alternative, powerful approach for studying important aspects of the nutritional ecology of wildlife. These techniques take advantage of unique patterns of fatty acid composition in prey that reflect those of their local food webs and which are retained as they are transferred up the food chain by predation (Iverson 1993, Kelly 2000). For example, lipids in milk and storage tissue of marine mammals are characterized by an unusual array of fatty acids that are largely of ecological origin (Ratnayake et al. 1989, Smith et al. 1996) and which have been used to detect shifts in diet during breeding and nonbreeding periods (Iverson et al. 1997). Fatty acid profiles in milk of black bear (*Ursus americanus*) were derived mostly from endogenous fat stores, which presumably reflected the diet of the animals before the period of winter dormancy (Iverson and Oftedal 1992).

Assessing Diet Quality of Free-ranging Wildlife
Combining Food Habits and Diet Quality Data

A commonly used method for estimating quality of natural diets is to mathematically combine food habits data (percentages of foods in diets) with digestibility or nutrient data from nutritional analyses and feeding trials (e.g., Schwartz et al. 1977, Hobbs et al. 1982, Leslie and Starkey 1985). Composite diet quality for a given nutrient is calculated as:

$$\sum_i^n x_i y_i,$$

where x_i is the proportion of food item i in the diet and y_i represents the nutrient value of food item i. This method assumes hand-collected forages for analyses are representative of forages selected by the animal and food habits analyses are unbiased.

Equations for predicting digestible or metabolizable energy content and digestible protein of forages from chemical composition (Table 1) are available for white-tailed deer and elk (Mould and Robbins 1982; Robbins et al. 1987a, b), ruffed grouse (Servello et al. 1987a, b), black bear (Pritchard and Robbins 1989) and voles (*Microtus pinetorum, M. pennsylvanicus*) (Servello et al. 1983, MacPherson et al. 1985). With only a small amount of forage needed for chemical analyses (compared to that needed for feeding trials), estimates of DE and ME values can be obtained for a large number of forages and for specific plant parts in all seasons or under specific environmental conditions.

We caution that tests of these equations are necessary to validate their generality. Hanley et al. (1992) validated equations for predicting digestible protein and dry matter developed from feeding trials using white-tailed and mule deer by conducting digestion trials with an independent set of forages and black-tailed deer. Conversely, Guglielmo and Karasov (1995) found that equations predicting metabolizable energy from leaf and fruit foods of ruffed grouse

(Servello et al. 1987*b*) consistently overestimated metabolizability of winter grouse browse. The value of predictive regressions to refine evaluations of diet and habitat quality is unquestioned. However, the approach requires further assessment.

Analyses of Gastrointestinal Tract Contents

Analysis of gut contents from free-ranging animals is one step closer than forage analysis to measuring actual nutrient intake because foods and food parts actually selected by the animal can be analyzed. For example, Servello et al. (1984) and MacPherson et al. (1988) measured digestible energy in diets of wild voles using equations to predict digestible energy from a chemical analysis of stomach contents. Dietary ME for ruffed grouse can be predicted similarly from chemical analyses of crop contents (Servello and Kirkpatrick 1987*b*). Similar efforts were made to measure nutrient content in deer rumen contents (Kirkpatrick et al. 1969). These methods eliminate the bias between hand-picked samples and those selected by the animal. However, there is an assumption that the plant material is not substantially altered in the animal before collection by chemical or enzymatic reactions. This assumption does not appear to be a significant problem with voles (Servello et al. 1983), which are monogastric, or ruffed grouse (Servello and Kirkpatrick 1987*b*), which

store food in the crop, but is likely a problem with ruminants. Another limitation is that destructive sampling is required to obtain the sample.

Indicator Techniques

Variations of the indicator techniques described for feeding trials have been applied to wild populations to measure digestibility of natural diets. Indicators must be naturally present in the food or prey, must not be digested or absorbed, and it must be possible to collect feces from wild individuals for analyses. For example, magnesium has been used with grouse (Moss 1973) and manganese has potential for use with northern fur seals (*Callorhinus ursinus*) (Fadely et al. 1990).

Fecal Indices of Diet Quality

Fecal nitrogen concentration has been proposed as an index of diet quality (Kie and Burton 1984, Leslie and Starkey 1985); however, there is considerable disagreement on its usefulness (Hobbs 1987, Leslie and Starkey 1987). Robbins et al. (1987*a*) reported high dietary tannin levels increased fecal nitrogen, which can lead to inaccurate conclusions. Recently, Barten et al. (2001) used fecal nitrogen as an index of dietary quality to test hypotheses about habitat-use tradeoffs by female caribou (*Rangifer tarandus*). Another proposed fecal index is DAPA, 2,6

Table 1. Equations for predicting the percent apparent digestible dry matter (DDM), digestible protein (DP; g/100g dry food), digestible energy (DE), metabolizable energy (ME), in diets from chemical analyses of foods.

Species	Foods	Equations[a]	Source
Elk	Forages, diets[b]	$DDM = 1.11\ NDS - 21.88 + NDF\ \dfrac{(176.92 - 40.50\ \mathrm{Log}\ e^x)}{100}$	Mould and Robbins 1982
White-tailed and mule deer[c]	Forages, diets	$DDM = [0.923e^{-0.0451x} - 0.03z](NDF) + [(-16.03 + 1.02\ NDS) - 2.8\ P]$ where: $P = -0.01 + (11.82\ \mathrm{BSA\ precipitation})$	Robbins et al. 1987*a*
		$DP = -3.87 + 0.928\ (\%\ \mathrm{crude\ protein}) - 11.82\ \mathrm{BSA\ precipitation}$	Robbins et al. 1987*b*
Ruffed grouse	Diets, foods, or crop[d]	$ME = 0.87\ (NDS - \mathrm{total\ phenolics}) - 5.76$	Servello et al. 1987*b*
Black bear	Diets (plant foods) Diets (whole animals) Diets (meat and fish) Diets	$DP = -3.46 + 0.881\ (\%\ \mathrm{crude\ protein})$ $DP = -9.77 + 1.01\ (\%\ \mathrm{crude\ protein})$ $DP = -3.82 + 1.01\ (\%\ \mathrm{crude\ protein})$ $DDM = 101.3 - 1.39\ (TDF)$	Pritchard and Robbins 1990
Pine vole	Diets, foods	$DDM = 1.18\ NDS - 19.42$ $DE = 1.12\ NDS - 14.31$	Servello et al. 1983
	Stomach contents	$DDM = 1.14\ AFNDS - 14.89$ $DE = 1.07\ AFNDS - 8.50$	
Meadow vole	Diets, foods	$DDM = 1.09\ NDS - 11.12$ $DE = 1.09\ NDS - 11.84$	MacPherson et al. 1985
	Stomach contents	$DDM = 1.08\ AFNDS - 1.30$ $DE = 1.07\ AFNDS - 1.60$	

[a] Chemical composition abbreviations: NDS = neutral detergent solubles; NDF = neutral detergent fiber; AFNDS = acid-insoluble, ash-free neutral detergent solubles; x = lignin and cutin content as a percent of the NDF; z = biogenic silica content of grasses; P = reduction in protein digestion; BSA = bovine serum albumin; TDF = total dietary fiber.

[b] Forages or diets low in tannin phenolic content.

[c] Also validated with black-tailed deer by Hanley et al. (1992).

[d] A modification of this equation is required for diets containing acorns.

diaminopinelic acid, which is found in cell walls of rumen bacteria. It is hypothesized that diet quality changes that alter rumen bacterial numbers will result in correlated changes in DAPA concentrations in ruminant feces (Kie and Burton 1984). Research has shown positive relationships among forage production, forage quality, other indices, and fecal DAPA (Kie and Burton 1984, Leslie et al. 1989, McCown et al. 1991). Under controlled, captive conditions, fecal DAPA was positively related to dietary energy, but negatively related to dietary protein in white-tailed deer (Brown et al. 1995).

Estimating Food Intake and Energetics of Free-ranging Wildlife

Field Techniques to Measure Energetics

Time–energy budget (TEB) and doubly-labeled water (DLW) methods are the 2 most commonly used techniques for estimating total daily energy expenditures of free-ranging animals. The TEB method has 2 parts: time spent in major activities or behaviors (e.g., foraging, resting) by the animal is quantified, and the activity data are converted to energetic equivalents from estimates of energy costs for each activity as measured in laboratory or controlled studies (Goldstein 1988, Karasov 1992, Speakman 1997). In some cases, estimates of the energy costs of activities are made using allometric models based on taxonomic groups (Weathers et al. 1984, Karasov 1992, Robbins 1993). Energy expenditure is calculated as:

$$E = \sum_{i=1}^{n} b_i \times t_i,$$

where E is energy expenditure (kilojoules/d), t_i is time (h/d) spent in activity i, and b_i is the energy equivalency (kilojoules/h) of activity i (McNab 2002). This method is most commonly used with birds because of the relative ease of collecting activity data (e.g., Ashkenazie and Safriel 1979, Stalmaster and Gessaman 1984, Morton et al. 1989). Problems include measuring energy equivalents of each activity, incorporating cost of thermoregulation into the equation (McKinney and McWilliams 2005), and large variances (because the variance is the sum of a series of terms; Travis 1982). Validation studies that compare estimates of daily energy expenditure (DEE) based on time-energy budgets with direct measures of DEE have shown that relatively minor errors in estimates of time and energy budgets can significantly affect estimates of DEE (Weathers et al. 1984).

Doubly-labeled water involves injection (labeling) of oxygen (oxygen-18) and hydrogen (tritium or deuterium) isotopes into an animal before its release and calculating the rate of CO_2 production (Fig. 8), which can be equated to metabolic rate, from the relative turnover rates of the isotopes measured upon recapture of the animal (Nagy 1980, Williams and Nagy 1984, Kam et al. 1987, Speakman 1997). Carbon dioxide production can be estimated from the difference in decay rates of the oxygen and hydrogen isotopes from the body over time because oxygen is lost as CO_2 and H_2O whereas hydrogen is only lost as H_2O (Fig. 9). Animals are usually sampled at least twice—once to obtain background measurements, inject the isotope, and obtain an initial equilibrated sample, and at least one other time to take the final sample to measure

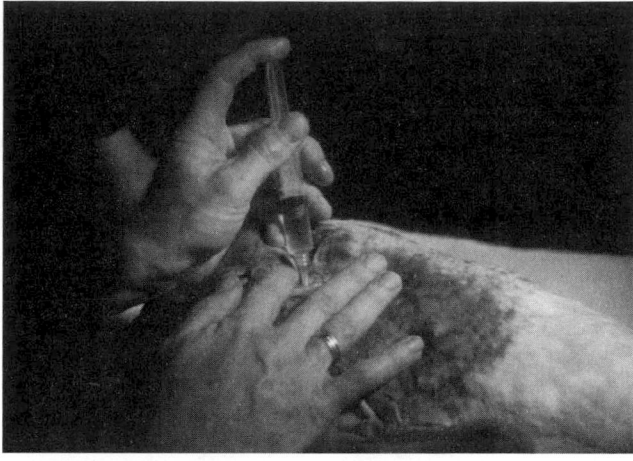

Fig. 8. Injection of deuterated water, a stable isotope of water, into the pectoral muscle of a Canada goose. After injection, individuals are allowed to rest undisturbed until the deuterated water has equilibrated with the animal's body water (ca. 60–90 min for a Canada goose).

decay rates of the isotopes (Fig. 10). Webster and Weathers (1989) validated a single-sample DLW method for use with small or stress-sensitive species. Any biological sample containing body water can be used (Robbins 1993). Accuracy of the method was reported originally to be within 8-11% of validation methods (e.g., actual measurements of O_2 consumption or CO_2 production) (Nagy 1989), but with more recent refinements of the method, accuracy is within 2–4% (Nagy et al. 1999).

Energy expenditure using the DLW method in free-ranging species is called field metabolic rate (Nagy 1987), which incorporates all metabolic costs incurred by the animal—basal metabolism, thermoregulation, activity, growth, etc. It does not, however, include the potential energy incorporated into new tissue produced during growth or reproduction. Its use has been limited in the past to smaller wildlife (Bryant et al. 1985, Tatner and Bryant 1986, Williams and Prints 1986, Gabrielsen et al. 1987) because of high costs of working with isotopes (Nagy 1989). However, better analytical methods now make possible its use on larger species (Nagy and Knight 1994,

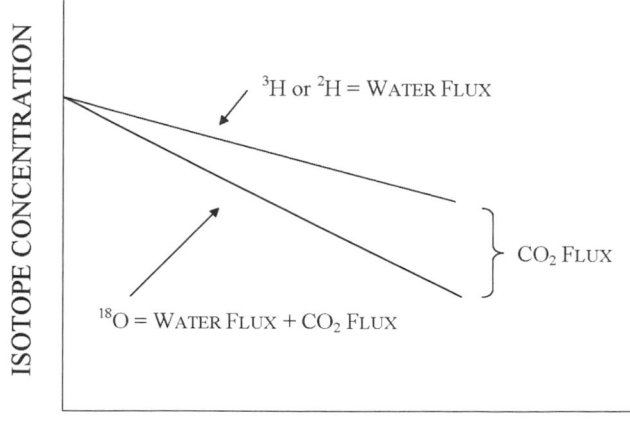

Fig. 9. The basis for use of doubly labeled water to measure CO_2 production and energy expenditure of wild animals (adapted from Robbins 1993).

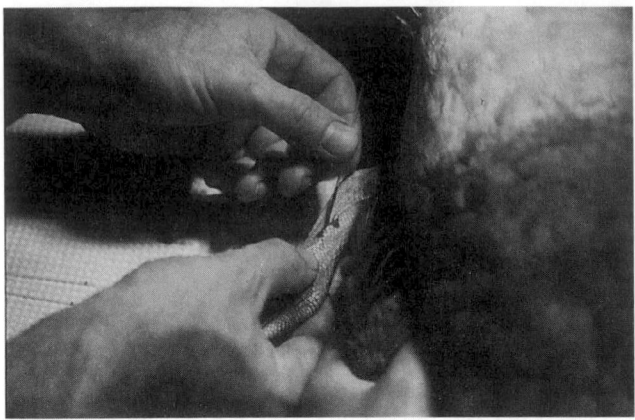

Fig. 10. Blood sample (50–100 µL) of a Canada goose is drawn into a capillary tube after puncture of a leg vein with a 27-gauge needle. Blood is also commonly collected from the brachial vein on the wing of birds (not shown). Capillary tubes with blood samples can be temporarily sealed with clay (e.g., Critoseal) and permanently sealed and stored by flame sealing. Capillary tubes with blood should be refrigerated until laboratory analysis.

Williams et al. 2001). Nagy et al. (1999) provide the most complete review of field metabolic rates in mammals, birds, and reptiles.

Attempts have been made to examine energy expenditure by measuring heart rate (Holter et al. 1976, Wooley and Owen 1978, Mautz and Fair 1980, Kautz et al. 1981, Freddy 1984, Fancy and White 1985). Gessaman (1980) reported that heart rate satisfactorily measured energy expenditure of some American kestrels (*Falco sparverius*) he examined, but not of others. Seasonal variations also were a problem. Holter et al. (1976) observed that heart rate accounted for 78% of the variation observed in metabolic rates, whereas Mautz and Fair (1980) reported it ccounted for only 36% of the variance in energy expenditures. Thus, heart rate can be monitored remotely in free-ranging animals through telemetry, but variability in results restricts its application. A final method of examining energy requirements of animals is through use of stuffed mounts of a species with implanted heaters. The amount of heat required to maintain the mount at a certain temperature can be measured in different environmental settings or in different types of thermal cover. The heat required can be calibrated to the energy expenditure of a live animal in a laboratory thermal chamber by respiratory exchange. Estimation of incremental costs of thermoregulation under different conditions also can be made with this method. This method has been used for several wildlife species (Heller 1972, Thorkelson and Maxwell 1974, Bakken et al. 1983, Thompson and Fritzell 1988).

Techniques to Estimate Food Intake

In measuring energetic constraints on animal populations, food (or nutrient) intake may be the most useful parameter to measure because it represents the actual resource demand of animals on the environment (Nagy 1989). However, food intake is difficult to measure in the field. Most direct estimates of food intake have been made using tame, tractable animals. For example, esophageal fistulation has been used to measure food intake for grazing ungulates (Holleman et al. 1979, Wickstrom et al. 1984). A more complex method used by Renecker and

Hudson (1985) involved clipping plant samples to simulate the diet of moose observed in an enclosure and measuring diet digestibility by the nylon-bag technique using fistulated animals. After total fecal collections from individual moose feeding in the enclosure were made for 24 hours, daily food intake was back-calculated. The bite-count method has been used frequently with captive ungulates to estimate food intake (Collins et al. 1978; Bengtson 1983; Wickstrom et al. 1984; Parker et al. 1993*b*, 1999). For this method, estimates are obtained for bite rate, simulated or actual bite weight, and total foraging time to calculate intake.

Isotope methods have also been used to estimate food intake. For example, sodium flux has been estimated by means of ^{22}Na turnover (Green 1978, Staaland et al. 1982, Gallagher et al. 1983, Green et al. 1984). If the sodium content of food items is known, food intake can be directly correlated with sodium turnover. Most of this work has been conducted with carnivores (DelGiudice et al. 1991) or nursing mammals (Green et al. 1997), which consume diets with fairly constant sodium content. DelGiudice et al. (1991) discussed several potential sources of discrepancies between sodium intake and turnover that could lead to under- or overestimation of sodium and overall food intake. For example, the exchangeable sodium pool may have a steadily increasing component from slow exchange of body fluid sodium with bone sodium. This would lead to overestimation of Na intake by ^{22}Na turnover (DelGiudice et al. 1991) until equilibrium is reached between these 2 pools (8 days in wolves). Bone sodium was believed to be a significant source of nonradioactive sodium diluting the exchangeable pool of sodium and leading to overestimates of sodium turnover in reindeer (Staaland et al. 1982). Gender differences in sodium metabolism associated with reproduction also affect the relationship between ^{22}Na turnover and sodium intake (DelGiudice et al. 1991). Finally, Alldredge et al. (1974) and Holleman et al. (1979) reported on use of natural fallout of radiocesium (cesium 137) to estimate intake for ungulates.

Food Availability and Nutritional Carrying Capacity

Food availability is often considered the most common limiting factor for wild animal populations. Boutin (1990) concluded from a review of population responses to food supplementation that in temperate environments, vertebrate populations are limited by food. However, it has proven difficult to integrate nutrient requirements of animals with available nutrient quality and quantity to estimate carrying capacity, and therefore assess the relationship of animal density to food availability. Data requirements for nutritional carrying capacity models are daunting. Necessary model parameters include individual animal requirements (e.g., daily energy expenditure or nitrogen requirements) and endogenous nutrient reserves, and biomass availability, production, and nutrient content of all food items consumed by the species in question. Because each of these parameters varies in space and time, it is easy to understand the difficulty in estimating nutritional carrying capacity.

Early models of nutritional carrying capacity assumed that food resources represented a single homogeneous quantity partitioned among animals according to their needs, with no or little adjustment for diet quality (Wallmo et al. 1977, Hobbs et al. 1982). The latter authors recognized that carrying-capacity estimates must account for biomass distribution of foods of different nutrient quality to properly reflect individual animal condition and population density. Hobbs and Swift (1985) subsequently developed a model that could predict the maximum number of animals that could obtain diets of a specified diet quality level (e.g., dietary protein, dietary digestible energy) or the maximum quality of diets obtained by a specified number of animals (Box 4). Hanley and Rogers (1989) provided an adjustment to the model that allowed for simultaneous consideration of digestible dry matter (a surrogate for digestible energy) and digestible protein. This model allowed managers to meet goals for individual animal condition and population density.

Use of the Hobbs and Swift (1985) model has been rare due to the large labor requirements to collect the data

involved, and because the model is limited to ungulates (Ditchkoff and Servello 1998, DeYoung et al. 2000). However, nutritionally based carrying capacity models can be used for any species given that necessary data are collected (e.g., northern bobwhites; Guthery 1999). Changes in carrying capacity can be detected by sampling over time. For example, with the proper sampling design, managers can estimate changes in food supplies associated with management strategies and convert those to changes in estimated animal carrying capacity (Guthery 1999).

SYNTHESIS OF NUTRITIONAL INFORMATION

We have presented methods and techniques for measuring individual elements of the nutritional ecology of wildlife. Accurately interpreting data from analyses can be a challenge because individual nutritional factors are part

---

Box 4. Nutritionally based carrying capacity models that incorporate diet quality requirements: which data are needed and how can I use the model?

The model of Hobbs and Swift (1985) posed and attempted to answer the question "How much food is present in the environment that will allow a population of animals to obtain diets averaging a specific level of some nutrient?" Behind this question lay 2 other questions: 1) which nutrient, and 2) what is the nutrient level of interest? These latter 2 questions are specific to the objectives of the researcher or manager. In most cases, the nutrient would be the presumed limiting nutrient in the system or energy (e.g., digestible or metabolizable energy, nitrogen, phosphorus) and the specific level would be the concentration required for a particular nutritional state (e.g., maintenance, reproduction, growth). We refer the reader to Hobbs and Swift (1985) for a full description of the carrying capacity model that incorporates explicit nutritional constraints.

The model assumes a nutrient distribution relating forage quality to forage biomass (Fig. 11). Field data necessary to parameterize a discrete version (Fig. 11) of the continuous model are provided below.

1. A catalog of items in the diet of the study species. This list may include plant parts (leaves vs. stems) if animals distinguish these in their diet.
2. Biomass of each food item on the study area.
3. Nutrient content of each food item.

Hobbs and Swift (1985) provide an algorithm that allows one to calculate the amount of biomass available that has an average nutrient concentration equivalent to the management or research objective, given the data listed above. Once this biomass has been calculated, nutritional carrying capacity (animal-days/ha) is estimated by dividing this biomass (kg/ha) by average daily animal requirements (obtained from the literature or from separate experiments designed to measure daily nutrient requirements).

The model has been used in 2 recent papers to study the relative value of litterfall to white-tailed deer wintering in Maine (Ditchkoff and Servello 1998) and to estimate seasonal changes in nitrogen-related carrying capacity for desert mountain sheep (*Ovis canadensis nelsoni*) in Texas (DeYoung et al. 2000). The original paper (Hobbs and Swift 1985) illustrated how burned areas could support more mule deer and mountain sheep at a high nutritional plane than unburned areas. Prescribed fire produced greater amounts of higher-quality forage relative to controls. However, overall forage biomass decreased on burned sites, and traditional models estimating carrying capacity based on range forage supply would have concluded that burning was not an effective practice for habitat improvement.

Carrying capacity is a dynamic state and the model of Hobbs and Swift (1985) has the flexibility to track changes in carrying capacity, if the correct data can be collected. In addition, the model provides alternative estimates of carrying capacity based on the biology of the species under study. For example, estimates provided by DeYoung et al. (2000) showed how seasonal changes in forage availability and quality alter carrying capacity, especially at higher diet-quality levels. In spring, DeYoung et al. (2000) estimated that carrying capacity at a diet level of 1.5% nitrogen (approximately 9.4% crude protein and adequate for meeting lactation requirements) averaged 3.2 animals/km² across 3 mountain ranges. By winter, the ability of the habitat to support desert mountain sheep at this level averaged 0.1 animals/km² because of a decreasing supply of nutritious forage and a local drought. However, carrying capacity increased to 5.5 animals/km² in winter because lactational needs decreased after lambs weaned and the required dietary level of nitrogen was only 0.89% (approximately 5.6% crude protein) (DeYoung et al. 2000).

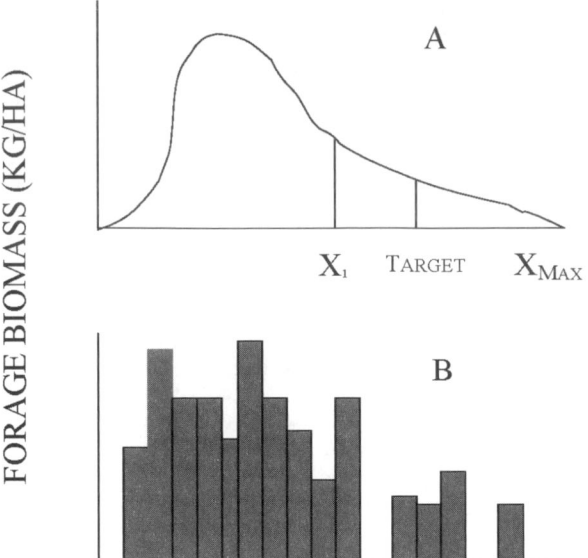

FORAGE NUTRIENT CONCENTRATION

Fig. 11. Hypothetical continuous nutrient distribution (A) relating forage nutrient quality to forage biomass. "Target" represents the management objective for average nutrient level in the diet of the animal population, X_{MAX} represents the maximum concentration of nutrient found in any forage item, and X_1 represents the point at which the mean concentration of the biomass to the right of this point equals the target concentration (adapted from Hobbs and Swift 1985). Hypothetical discrete nutrient distribution (B) relating forage nutrient quality to forage biomass obtained from field data collection.

of larger physiological and behavioral processes. Some factors may have more or less importance when considered in this larger context, and some new insights may only be revealed from a more comprehensive analysis of overall ecology.

Foraging Strategies

The terms "foraging strategy" or "feeding strategy" are shorthand for the suite of behavioral, morphological, and physiological adaptations that allow an animal to consume and metabolize available energy and nutrients in its natural habitat. Study of wildlife feeding strategies shifts the focus from purely descriptive studies of diet and animal requirements to an analysis of how the selected diet of a certain species is influenced by, for example, distribution and abundance of potential foods, or costs of foraging including risk of predation and increased energy expenditure associated with chasing, handling, and digesting different prey (Schoener 1971, Stephens and Krebs 1986, Robbins 1993, Belovsky 1997). By placing the process of feeding and nutrition in an evolutionary context, study of feeding strategies relates the process of diet selection ultimately to an animal's fitness (Hughes 1990, Belovsky et al. 1999).

Feeding strategies have been studied in a wide range of wild animals including carnivores (MacCracken and Hansen 1987), primates (Chivers et al. 1984), rodents (Jenkins 1975), songbirds (Zach and Falls 1979, Krebs and Kacelnik 1991), waterfowl (Wood and Hand 1985, Tome 1988), and in many species of mammalian herbivores (Hanley and Hanley 1982, Hobbs et al. 1983, Krueger

1986, Belovsky and Schmitz 1994, Laca and Demment 1996). These studies used optimization models of food and habitat selection to compare predicted with actual preferences of wild animals (Pulliam 1989), relate diet selection to numerical and functional responses of prey and predator (Krebs et al. 1999, 2001), and incorporate survival probability and reproductive success into dynamic programming models of diet and habitat selection (Belovsky 1986, Mangel and Clark 1988). Studies of foraging strategies of wildlife have also focused on behavioral, morphological, and physiological characteristics that constrain diet and habitat selection (Demment and Van Soest 1985, Spalinger and Hobbs 1992, Illius and Gordon 1999, Dearing et al. 2000, Rode et al. 2001, Karasov and McWilliams 2004).

Despite many important studies, considerably more work is needed on feeding strategies of most wild species given their central importance in the ecology and management of wildlife. For example, wildlife biologists too often assume that an adequate quantity of food in the environment is sufficient for a given population regardless of the food's distribution and abundance. But, as observed by Robbins (1993) for elk in Yellowstone National Park, the quality of the food resource, its spatial distribution, and social interactions between and within wildlife species can reduce the density of usable food to below required levels. A more complete understanding of the feeding strategies of wildlife would greatly improve our assessments of the nutritional adequacy of natural habitats.

Modeling

Simulation modeling is used to identify the relative importance of nutrition variables and to gain new insights into interactions among factors that potentially affect nutritional ecology of a species. Models may address specific nutritional and physiological processes, such as the dynamics of a urinary index (Moen and DelGiudice 1997). We concentrate on more comprehensive modeling of nutritional ecology done for the purpose of evaluating habitats, populations, or management (e.g., Stalmaster 1983). A primary advantage of a modeling approach is that it may produce unforeseen information or hypotheses that are the product of the entire system in contrast to conclusions drawn from data on a few variables in field studies. Modeling also allows examination of questions that would otherwise be difficult using traditional experimental approaches. The common approach for evaluating relative importance of individual factors with a modeling study is with sensitivity analyses. In a sensitivity analysis, a single variable is changed a standard amount to identify effects on response variables in the model when all other variables are held constant. The relative sensitivity of model products to changes in each variable can be compared to gauge the relative importance of nutritional and related factors. Parallel fieldwork on variables can greatly strengthen modeling results and conclusions, and can be used to test *a priori* predictions from model simulations (e.g., Farmer and Wiens 1999).

Energetic models based on species autecology are the typical approach for linking nutrition with habitat or populations. This is because of the primary importance of energy acquisition for animals and that most nutrition and environmental parameters can be translated into energy

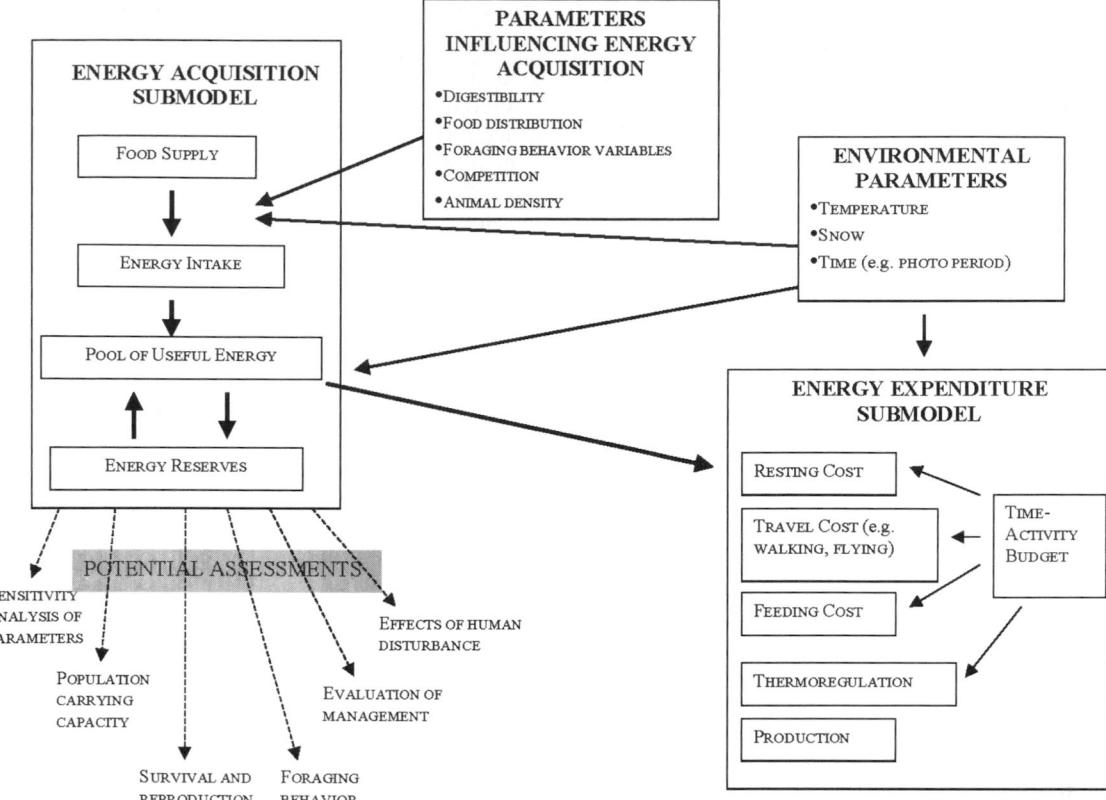

Fig. 12. Simplified diagram of an energetic simulation model for evaluating nutritional ecology of wildlife (adapted from Stalmaster [1983] and Hobbs [1989]). Small rectangles represent energy pools or expenditures. Thick solid arrows represent energy flows. Thin solid arrows represent variables that influence the system. Dashed arrows are indicators of potential applications of energetic modeling.

units. Most energetic simulation models have 2 basic elements (Fig. 12), calculation of energy acquisition and storage by individual animals from an available food supply, and calculation of energy expenditure by animals in response to basic metabolic requirements as well as activity patterns (e.g., Stalmaster 1983, Hobbs 1989). Classification of time spent in common activities (e.g., flying, walking, running, roosting) used in concert with average costs of activities allows evaluation of natural and human influences on energetic status (e.g., Stalmaster 1983). A variety of environmental and behavior parameters also may be incorporated into acquisition and expenditure submodels. Positive or negative energy balances of individual animals or populations are the basic metric for evaluating simulation results, but information generated on dynamics of other parameters may be just as valuable. For example, simulations of severe winter conditions may be examined to study the importance of traveling or thermoregulatory costs on energetics. There are a number of example conclusions possible from energetic modeling studies.

1. Use of stopover sites along migration routes for pectoral sandpipers (*Calidris melanotos*) is a function of the spacing and quality (for foraging) of the sites (Farmer and Wiens 1999).
2. Factors that influence energy acquisition by mule deer were generally more important than factors that influence energy expenditure (Hobbs 1989).
3. Browse digestibility affects body mass of moose more

than other nutritional factors, including some forage distribution variables (Moen et al. 1997).
4. Salmon (*Oncorhynchus* spp.) carcass availability (including accessibility in river habitat) is as influential as salmon escapement past dams for predicting population sizes of wintering bald eagles (*Haliaeetus leucocephalus*) (Stalmaster 1983).

These examples represent information that would be difficult to generate from reductionist field studies. Thus, insights gained via nutritional ecology modeling add significantly to our knowledge of wildlife ecology and management.

SUMMARY

The wide array and improved techniques available today for nutritional ecology will help advance our understanding of wildlife-habitat relationships and improve investigations of habitat management issues. There is not a simple formula for nutritional ecology investigations with wild species because the nature of the foods eaten, species behavior, physiological adaptations to nutritional stress, life history strategies, and feasibility of collecting data in specific environments may vary greatly among species. Before undertaking nutritional ecology investigations, biologists should carefully consider the importance of nutrition and foraging variables in the ecology of the focal species, as well as practical issues for adequate data collection.

Nutritional ecology research frequently involves laboratory analyses of foods and studies with captive animals. While contributing important baseline information, we encourage biologists to also use parallel field studies to examine animal responses in natural settings or in wild populations. For complex questions, modeling may be required to better understand interactions of multiple variables including influences of behavioral and environmental factors.

ACKNOWLEDGMENTS

We thank 2 anonymous reviewers, David Podlesak, and R. A. McKinney who provided excellent criticism and helpful suggestions on the manuscript.

LITERATURE CITED

ALISAUSKAS, R. T., AND C. D. ANKNEY. 1985. Nutrient reserves and the energetics of reproduction in American coots. Auk 102:133–144.

———, AND ———. 1992. The cost of egg laying and its relationship to nutrient reserves in waterfowl. Pages 30–61 *in* B. D. J. Batt, A. D. Afton, M. G. Anderson, C. D. Ankney, D. H. Johnson, J. A. Kadlec, and G. L. Krapu, editors. Ecology and management of breeding waterfowl. University of Minnesota Press, Minneapolis, USA.

ALLDREDGE, A. W., J. F. LIPSCOMB, AND F. W. WHICKER. 1974. Forage intake rates of mule deer estimated with fallout cesium-137. Journal of Wildlife Management 38:508–516.

ANDERSON, A. E., D. E. MEDIN, AND D. C. BOWDEN. 1972. Indices of carcass fat in a Colorado mule deer population. Journal of Wildlife Management 36:579–594.

ANGILLETTA, JR., M. J. 1999. Estimating body composition of lizards from total body electrical conductivity and total body water. Copeia 1999:587–595.

ANKNEY, C. D., AND C. D. MACINNES. 1978. Nutrient reserves and reproductive performance of female lesser snow geese. Auk 95:459–471.

ANONYMOUS. 1990. Fat (crude) or ether extract in animal feed. Pages 920–929 *in* K. Helrich, editor. Official methods of analysis. Fifteenth edition. Association of Official Analytical Chemists, Arlington, Virginia, USA.

ASCH, A., AND D. D. ROBY. 1995. Some factors affecting precision of the total body electrical conductivity technique for measuring body composition in live birds. Wilson Bulletin 107:306–316.

ASHKENAZIE, S., AND U. N. SAFRIEL. 1979. Time–energy budget of the semipalmated sandpiper *Calidris pusilla* at Barrow, Alaska. Ecology 60:783–799.

ASLESON, M. A., E. C. HELLGREN, AND L. W. VARNER. 1996. Nitrogen requirements for antler growth and maintenance in white-tailed deer. Journal of Wildlife Management 60:744–752.

ATKINSON, S. N., R. A. NELSON, AND M. A. RAMSAY. 1996. Changes in body composition of fasting polar bears (*Ursus maritimus*): the effects of relative fitness in protein conservation. Physiological Zoology 69:304–316.

AUSTIN, P. J., L. A. SUCHAR, C. T. ROBBINS, AND A. E. HAGERMAN. 1989. Tannin-binding proteins in saliva of deer and their absence in saliva of sheep and cattle. Journal of Chemical Ecology 15:1335–1347.

BAHNAK, B. R., J. C. HOLLAND, L. J. VERME, AND J. J. OZOGA. 1981. Seasonal and nutritional influences on growth hormone and thyroid activity in white-tailed deer. Journal of Wildlife Management 45:140–147.

BAILEY, R. O. 1979. Methods of estimating total lipid content in the redhead duck (*Aythya americana*) and an evaluation of condition indices. Canadian Journal of Zoology 57:1830–1833.

BAKKEN, G. S., D. I. ERSKINE, AND W. R. SANTEE. 1983. Construction and operation of heated taxidermic mounts used to measure standard operative temperature. Ecology 64:1658–1662.

BALDASSARRE, G. A., R. J. WHYTE, AND E. G. BOLEN. 1980. Use of ultra-sonic sound to estimate body fat depots in the mallard. Prairie Naturalist 12:79–86.

BAMFORD, J. 1970. Estimating fat reserves in the brush-tailed possum, *Trichosurus vulpecula* Kerr (Marsupialia: Phalangeridae). Australian Journal of Zoology 18:415–425.

BARTEN, N. L., R. T. BOWYER, AND K. J. JENKINS. 2001. Habitat use by female caribou: tradeoffs associated with parturition. Journal of Wildlife Management 65:77–92.

BATCHELER, C. L., AND C. M. H. CLARKE. 1970. Note on kidney weights and the kidney fat index. New Zealand Journal of Science 13:663–668.

BECKERTON, P. R., AND A. L. A. MIDDLETON. 1982. Effects of dietary protein levels on body weight, food consumption, and nitrogen balance in ruffed grouse. Condor 85:53–60.

BELOVSKY, G. E. 1986. Optimal foraging and community structure: implications for a guild of generalist grassland herbivores. Oecologia 70:35–52.

———. 1997. Optimal foraging and community structure: the allometry of herbivore food selection and competition. Evolutionary Ecology 11:641–672.

———, AND O. J. SCHMITZ. 1994. Plant defenses and optimal foraging by mammalian herbivores. Journal of Mammalogy 75:816–832.

———, J. FRYXELL, AND O. J. SCHMITZ. 1999. Natural selection and herbivore nutrition: optimal foraging theory and what it tells us about the structure of ecological communities. Pages 1–70 *in* H. J. G. Jung and G. C. Fahey, editors. Nutritional ecology of herbivores. Proceedings of the Fifth International Symposium on the Nutrition of Herbivores. American Society of Animal Science, Savoy, Illinois, USA.

BENGTSON, J. L. 1983. Estimating food consumption of free-ranging manatees in Florida. Journal of Wildlife Management 47:1186–1192.

BJORNDAL, K. A. 1991. Diet mixing: nonadditive interactions of diet items in an omnivorous freshwater turtle. Ecology 72:1234–1241.

———, AND A. B. BOLTEN. 1993. Digestive efficiencies in herbivorous and omnivorous freshwater turtles on plant diets: do herbivores have a nutritional advantage? Physiological Zoology 66:384–395.

BLEM, C. R. 1976. Patterns of lipid storage and utilization in birds. American Zoologist 16:671–684.

———. 1980. The energetics of migration. Pages 175–224 *in* S. A. Gauthreaux, Jr., editor. Animal migration, orientation, and navigation. Academic Press. New York, USA.

———. 1990. Avian energy storage. Current Ornithology 7:59–113.

BOUTIN, S. 1990. Food supplementation experiments with terrestrial vertebrates: patterns, problems, and the future. Canadian Journal of Zoology 68:203–220.

BOYLE, R., S. MCLEAN, W. J. FOLEY, B. D. MOORE, N. W. DAVIES, AND S. BRANDON. 2000. Fate of the dietary terpene, p-cymene, in the male koala. Journal of Chemical Ecology 26:1095–1111.

BROWN, M. E. 1996. Assessing body condition in birds. Current Ornithology 13:67–135.

BROWN, R. D., E. C. HELLGREN, M. ABBOTT, D. C. RUTHVEN, III, AND R. L. BINGHAM. 1995. Effects of dietary energy and protein restriction on nutritional indices of female white-tailed deer. Journal of Wildlife Management 59:595–609.

BRYANT, D. M., C. J. HAILS, AND R. PRYS-IONES. 1985. Energy expenditure by free-living dippers (*Cinclus cinclus*) in winter. Condor 87:177–186.

BRYANT, J. P. 1981. Phytochemical deterrence of snowshoe hare browsing by adventitious shoots of four Alaskan trees. Science 213:889–890.

———, P. B. REICHARDT, AND T. P. CLAUSEN. 1992. Chemically mediated interactions between woody plants and browsing mammals. Journal of Range Management 45:18–24.

———, P. J. KUROPAT, P. B. REICHARDT, AND T. P. CLAUSEN. 1991. Controls over the allocation of resources by woody plants to chemical antiherbivore defense. Pages 83–102 *in* R. T. Palo and C. T. Robbins, editors. Plant defenses against mammalian herbivory. CRC Press, Boston, Massachusetts, USA.

BUCHSBAUM, R., I. VALIELA, AND T. SWAIN. 1984. The role of phenolic compounds and other plant constituents in feeding by Canada geese in a coastal marsh. Oecologia 63:343–349.

CAMPA, III, H., D. K. WOODYARD, AND J. B. HAUFLER. 1984. Reliability of captive deer and cow in vitro digestion values in predicting wild deer digestion levels. Journal of Range Management 37:468–470.

CAMPBELL, K. L., AND R. A. MACARTHUR. 1996. Digestibility of animal tissue by muskrats. Journal of Mammalogy 77:755–760.

CAMPBELL, R. R., AND J. F. LEATHERLAND. 1980. Estimating body protein and fat from water content in lesser snow geese. Journal of Wildlife Management 44:438–446.

CARL, G. R., AND R. D. BROWN. 1985. Protein requirement of adult collared peccaries. Journal of Wildlife Management 49:351–355.

CARRASCAL, L. M., J. C. SENAR, I. MOZETICH, F. URIBE, AND J. DOMENECH. 1998. Interactions among environmental stress, body condition, nutritional status, and dominance in great tits. Auk 115:727–738.

CASE, R. M., AND R. J. ROBEL. 1974. Bioenergetics of the bobwhite. Journal of Wildlife Management 38:638–652.

CHEATUM, E. L. 1949. Bone marrow as an index of malnutrition in deer. New York State Conservation 3:19–22.

CHILD, G. I., AND S. G. MARSHALL. 1970. A method of estimating carcass fat and fat-free weights in migrant birds from water content of specimens. Condor 72:116–119.

CHIVERS, D. J., B. A. WOOD, AND A. BILSBOROUGH, editors. 1984. Food acquisition and processing in primates. Plenum Press, New York, USA.

CHURCH, D. C., AND W. G. POND. 1988. Basic animal nutrition and feeding. Third Edition. John Wiley and Sons, New York, USA.

CLUFF, L. K., B. L. WELCH, J. C. PEDERSON, AND J. D. BROTHERSON. 1982. Concentration of monoterpenoids in the rumen ingesta of wild mule deer. Journal of Range Management 35:192–194.

COLLINS, W. B., P. J. URNESS, AND D. D. AUSTIN. 1978. Elk diets and activities on different lodgepole pine habitat segments. Journal of Wildlife Management 42:799–810.

CONNOLLY, G. E., B. O. ELLISON, J. W. FLEMING, S. GENG, R. E. KEPNER, W. M. LONGHURST, J. H. OH, AND G. F. RUSSELL. 1980. Deer browsing of Douglas-fir trees in relation to volatile terpene composition and in vitro fermentability. Forest Science 26:179–193.

COOK, R. C., J. G. COOK, D. L. MURRAY, P. ZAGER, B. K. JOHNSON, AND M. W. GRATSON. 2001. Development of predictive models of nutritional condition for Rocky Mountain elk. Journal of Wildlife Management 65:973–987.

CORK, S. J., AND W. J. FOLEY. 1991. Digestive and metabolic strategies of arboreal mammalian folivores in relation to chemical defenses in temperate and tropical forests. Pages 133–166 in R. T. Palo and C. T. Robbins, editors. Plant defenses against mammalian herbivory. CRC Press, Boca Raton, Florida, USA.

CRÊTE, M., AND J. HUOT. 1993. Regulation of a large herd of migratory caribou: summer nutrition affects calf growth and body reserves of dams. Canadian Journal of Zoology 71:2291–2296.

CRUM, B. G., J. B. WILLIAMS, AND K. A. NAGY. 1985. Can tritiated water-dilution space accurately predict total body water in chukar partridges? Journal of Applied Physiology 59:1383–1388.

DASH, J. A. 1988. Effect of dietary terpenes on glucuronic acid excretion and ascorbic acid turnover in the brushtail possum (*Trichosurus vulpecula*). Comparative Biochemistry and Physiology 89B: 221–226.

DAUPHINÉ, JR., T. C. 1975. Kidney weight fluctuations affecting the kidney fat index in caribou. Journal of Wildlife Management 39:379–386.

DEARING, M. D., A. M. MANGIONE, AND W. H. KARASOV. 2000. Diet breadth of mammalian herbivores: nutrient versus detoxification constraints. Oecologia 123:397–405.

———, ———, AND ———. 2002. Ingestion of plant secondary compounds causes diuresis in desert herbivores. Oecologia 130:576–584.

DELGIUDICE, G. D. 1995. Assessing winter nutritional restriction of northern deer with urine in snow: considerations, potential, and limitations. Wildlife Society Bulletin 23:687–693.

———, AND U. S. SEAL. 1988. Classifying winter undernutrition in deer via serum and urinary urea nitrogen. Wildlife Society Bulletin 16:27–32.

———, L. D. MECH, AND U. S. SEAL. 1988. Chemical analyses of deer bladder urine and urine collected from snow. Wildlife Society Bulletin 16:324–326.

———, ———, AND ———. 1989. Physiological assessment of deer populations by analysis of urine in snow. Journal of Wildlife Management 53:284–291.

———, ———, AND ———. 1990. Effects of winter undernutrition on body composition and physiological profiles of white-tailed deer. Journal of Wildlife Management 54:539–550.

———, ———, AND ———. 1994. Undernutrition and serum and urinary urea nitrogen of white-tailed deer during winter. Journal of Wildlife Management 58:430–436.

———, U. S. SEAL, AND L. D. MECH. 1987a. Effects of feeding and fasting on wolf blood and urine characteristics. Journal of Wildlife Management 51:1–10.

———, M. A. ASLESON, L. W. VARNER, AND E. C. HELLGREN. 1995. Twenty-four-hour urinary creatinine and urea nitrogen excretion in male white-tailed deer. Canadian Journal of Zoology 73:493–501.

———, L. S. DUQUETTE, U. S. SEAL, AND L. D. MECH. 1991. Validation of estimating food intake in gray wolves by ²²Na turnover. Journal of Wildlife Management 55:59–71.

———, K. D. KERR, L. D. MECH, AND U. S. SEAL. 2000. Prolonged winter undernutrition and the interpretation of urinary allantoin: creatinine ratios in white-tailed deer. Canadian Journal of Zoology 78: 2147–2155.

———, L. D. MECH, U. S. SEAL, AND P. D. KARNS. 1987b. Winter fasting and refeeding effects on urine characteristics in white-tailed deer. Journal of Wildlife Management 51:860–864.

DEMMENT, M. W., AND P. J. VAN SOEST. 1985. A nutritional explanation for body-size patterns of ruminant and nonruminant herbivores. American Naturalist 125:641–672.

DENIRO, M. J., AND S. EPSTEIN. 1978. Influence of diet on the distribution of nitrogen isotopes in animals. Geochimica et Cosmochimica Acta 45:341–351.

DERRICKSON, E. M. 1992. Comparative reproductive strategies of altricial and precocial eutherian mammals. Functional Ecology 6:57–65.

DEYOUNG, R. W., E. C. HELLGREN, T. E. FULBRIGHT, W. F. ROBBINS, JR., AND I. D. HUMPHREYS. 2000. Modeling nutritional carrying capacity for translocated desert bighorn sheep in western Texas. Restoration Ecology 8(supplement):57–65.

DIETZ, M. W., A. DEKINGA, T. PIERSMA, AND S. VERHULST. 1999. Estimating organ size in small migrating shorebirds with ultrasonography: an intercalibration exercise. Physiology, Biochemistry and Zoology 72:28–37.

DITCHKOFF, S. S., AND F. A. SERVELLO. 1998. Litterfall: an overlooked food source for wintering white-tailed deer. Journal of Wildlife Management 62:250–255

———, AND ———. 1999. Sampling recommendations to assess nutritional restriction in deer. Wildlife Society Bulletin 27:1004–1009.

———, AND ———. 2002. Patterns in winter nutritional status of white-tailed deer *Odocoileus virginianus* populations in Maine, USA. Wildlife Biology 8:137–143.

DOBUSH, G.R., C. D. ANKNEY, AND D. G. KREMENTZ. 1985. The effect of apparatus, extraction time, and solvent type on lipid extractions of snow geese. Canadian Journal of Zoology 63:1917–1920.

DOWELL, J. H., AND R. J. WARREN. 1982. Variations in nutritional indices of Texas ring-necked pheasants. Proceedings of the Annual Conference of the Southeastern Association of Fish and Wildlife Agencies 36:586–593.

DUNCAN, A. J., S. E. HARTLEY, AND G. R. IASON. 1994. The effect of monoterpene concentrations in Sitka spruce (*Picea sitchensis*) on browsing behaviour of red deer (*Cervus elaphus*). Canadian Journal of Zoology 72:1715–1720.

EMMS, S. K., AND N. A. M. VERBEEK. 1991. Brood size, food provisioning and chick growth in the pigeon guillemot *Cepphus columba*. Condor 93:943–951.

EPPLE, G., H. NIBLICK, S. LEWIS, D. L. NOLTE, D. L. CAMPBELL, AND J. R. MASON. 1996. Pine needle oil causes avoidance behaviors in pocket gophers *Geomys bursarius.* Journal of Chemical Ecology 22: 1013–1025.

FADELY, B. S., G. A. J. WORTHY, AND D. P. COSTA. 1990. Assimilation efficiency of northern fur seals determined using dietary manganese. Journal of Wildlife Management 54:246–251.

FANCY, S. G., AND R. G. WHITE. 1985. Energy expenditures by caribou while cratering in snow. Journal of Wildlife Management 49:987–993.

FARLEY, S. D., AND C. T. ROBBINS. 1994. Development of two methods to estimate body composition of bears. Canadian Journal of Zoology 72:220–226.

FARMER, A. H., AND J. A. WIENS. 1999. Models and reality: time–energy trade-offs in pectoral sandpiper (*Calidris melanotos*) migration. Ecology 80:2566–2580.

FELICETTI, L. A., L. A. SHIPLEY, G. W. WITMER, AND C. T. ROBBINS. 2000. Digestibility, nitrogen excretion, and mean retention time by North American porcupines (*Erethizon dorsatum*) consuming natural forages. Physiological and Biochemical Zoology 73:772–780.

FINGER, S. E., I. L. J. BRISBIN, JR., M. H. SMITH, AND D. F. URBSTON. 1981. Kidney fat as a predictor of body condition in white-tailed deer. Journal of Wildlife Management 45:964–968.

FISHER, K. I., R. E. A. STEWART, R. A. KASTELEIN, AND L. D. CAMPBELL. 1992. Apparent digestive efficiency in walruses (*Odobenus rosmarus*) fed herring (*Clupea harengus*) and clams (*Spisula* sp.). Canadian Journal of Zoology 70:30–36.

FLEHARTY, E. D., M. E. KRAUSE, AND D. P. STINNETT. 1973. Body composition, energy content and lipid cycles of four species of rodents. Journal of Mammalogy 54:426–438.

FLUX, J. E. C. 1971. Validity of the kidney fat index for estimating the condition of hares: a discussion. New Zealand Journal of Science 14:238–244.

FOLEY, W. J. 1992. Nitrogen and energy retention and acid–base status in the common ringtail possum (*Pseudocheirus peregrinus*): evidence of the effects of absorbed allelochemicals. Physiological Zoology 65:403–421.

———, AND C. MCARTHUR. 1994. The effects and costs of allelochemicals for mammalian herbivores: an ecological perspective. Pages 370–391 in D. J. Chivers and P. Langer, editors. The digestive system in mammals: food, form and function. Cambridge University Press, Cambridge, United Kingdom.

———, S. MCLEAN, AND S. J. CORK. 1995. Consequences of biotransformation of plant secondary metabolites on acid–base metabolism in mammals—a final common pathway? Journal of Chemical Ecology 21:721–743.

FRANZMANN, A. W. 1985. Assessment of nutritional status. Pages 239–260 in R. J. Hudson and R. G. White, editors. Bioenergetics of wild herbivores. CRC Press, Boca Raton, Florida, USA.

———, AND C. C. SCHWARTZ. 1988. Evaluating condition of Alaskan black bears with blood profiles. Journal of Wildlife Management 52:63–70.

FREDDY, D. J. 1984. Heart rates for activities of mule deer at pasture. Journal of Wildlife Management 48:962–969.

GABRIELSEN, G. W., F. MEHLUM, AND K. A. NAGY. 1987. Daily energy expenditure and energy utilization of free-ranging black-legged kittiwakes. Condor 89:126–132.

GALLAGHER, K. J., D. A. MORRISON, R. SHINE, AND G. C. GRIGG. 1983. Validation and use of ^{22}Na turnover to measure food intake in free-ranging lizards. Oecologia 60:76–82.

GANNES, L. Z., D. M. O'BRIEN, AND C. MARTINEZ DEL RIO. 1997. Stable isotopes in animal ecology: assumptions, caveats, and a call for more laboratory experiments. Ecology 78:1271–1276.

GARANT, Y., AND M. CRÊTE. 1999. Prediction of water, fat, and protein content of fisher carcasses. Wildlife Society Bulletin 27:403–408.

GARROTT, R. A., P. J. WHITE, D. B. VAGNONI, AND D. M. HEISEY. 1996. Purine derivatives in snow-urine as a dietary index for free-ranging elk. Journal of Wildlife Management 60:735–743.

GASAWAY, W. C., R. G. WHITE, AND D. F. HOLLEMAN. 1976. Digestion of dry matter and absorption of water in the intestine and cecum of rock ptarmigan. Condor 78:77–84.

GAU, R. J., AND R. CASE. 1999. Evaluating nutritional condition of grizzly bears via select blood parameters. Journal of Wildlife Management 63:286–291.

GERSHENZON, J., AND R. CROTEAU. 1991. Terpenoids. Pages 165–219 in G. A. Rosenthal and M. Berenbaum, editors. Herbivores: their interactions with secondary plant metabolites. Second edition. Academic Press, London, United Kingdom.

GESSAMAN, J. A. 1980. An evaluation of heart rate as an indirect measure of daily energy metabolism of the American kestrel. Comparative Biochemistry and Physiology 65(A):273–289.

———. 1987. Energetics. Pages 289–320 in B. A. Giron Pendleton, B. A. Millsap, K. W. Clire, and D. M. Bird, editors. Raptor management techniques manual. Scientific and Technical Series 10. National Wildlife Federation, Washington, D.C., USA.

———. 1998. Evaluation of some nonlethal methods of estimating avian body fat and lean mass. Pages 2–16 in N. Adams and R. Slotow, editors. Proceedings of the 22nd International Ornithological Congress. Durban, South Africa.

GOERING, H. K., AND P. I. VAN SOEST. 1970. Forage fiber analyses (apparatus, reagents, procedures, and some applications). U.S. Department of Agriculture Handbook 379.

GOLDSTEIN, D. L. 1988. Estimates of daily energy expenditure in birds: the time–energy budget as an integrator of laboratory and field studies. American Zoologist 28:829–844.

GOLET, G. H., K. J. KULETZ, D. D. ROBY, AND D. B. IRONS. 2000. Adult prey choice affects chick growth and reproductive success in pigeon guillemots. Auk 117:82–91.

GOODMAN-LOWE, G. D., J. R. CARPENTER, AND S. ATKINSON. 1999. Assimilation efficiency of prey in the Hawaiian monk seal (*Monachus schauinslandi*). Canadian Journal of Zoology 77:653–660.

GRASMAN, B. T., AND E. C. HELLGREN. 1993. Phosphorus nutrition in male white-tailed deer: nutrient balance, physiological responses, and antler growth. Ecology 74:2279–2296.

GREEN, A. J. 2001. Mass/length residuals: measures of body condition or generators of spurious results? Ecology 82:1473–1483.

GREEN, B. 1978. Estimation of food consumption in the dingo, *Canis familiaris dingo*, by means of ^{22}Na turnover. Ecology 59:207–210.

———, J. ANDERSON, AND T. WHATELEY. 1984. Water and sodium turnover and estimated food consumption in free-living lions (*Panthera leo*) and spotted hyaenas (*Crocuta crocuta*). Journal of Mammalogy 65:593–599.

———, J. MERCHANT, AND K. NEWGRAIN. 1997. Lactational energetics of a marsupial carnivore, the eastern quoll (*Dasyurus viverrinus*). Australian Journal of Zoology 45:295–306.

GRUBB, JR., T. C. 1989. Ptilochronology: feather growth bars as indicators of nutritional status. Auk 106:314–320.

———. 1992. Ptilochronology: a consideration of some empirical results and "assumptions." Auk 109:673–676.

———. 1995. Ptilochronology: a review and prospectus. Current Ornithology 12:89–114.

GUGLIELMO, C. G., AND W. H. KARASOV. 1993. Endogenous mass and energy losses in ruffed grouse. Auk 110:386–390.

———, AND ———. 1995. Nutritional quality of winter browse for ruffed grouse. Journal of Wildlife Management 59:427–436.

———, ———, AND W. J. JAKUBAS. 1996. Nutritional costs of a plant secondary metabolite explain selective foraging by ruffed grouse. Ecology 77:1103–1115.

GUTHERY, F. S. 1999. Energy-based carrying capacity for quails. Journal of Wildlife Management 63:664–674.

GUYTON, A. C., AND J. E. HALL. 1996. Textbook of medical physiology. Ninth edition. W. B. Saunders Co., Philadelphia, Pennsylvania, USA.

HAGERMAN, A. E. 1987. Radial diffusion method for determining tannin in plant extracts. Journal of Chemical Ecology 13:437–449.

———, AND L. G. BUTLER. 1978. Protein precipitation method for the quantitative determination of tannins. Journal of Agricultural and Food Chemistry 26:809–812.

———, AND ———. 1991. Terpenoids. Pages 355–388 in G. A. Rosenthal and M. Berenbaum, editors. Herbivores: their interactions with secondary plant metabolites. Second edition. Academic Press,

London, United Kingdom.

———, AND C. T. ROBBINS. 1993. Specificity of tannin-binding salivary proteins relative to diet selection by mammals. Canadian Journal of Zoology 71:628–633.

HANKS, J. 1981. Characterization of population condition. Pages 47–73 *in* C. W. Fowler and T. D. Smith, editors. Dynamics of large mammal populations. John Wiley and Sons, New York, USA.

HANLEY, T. A., AND K. A. HANLEY. 1982. Food resource partitioning by sympatric ungulates on Great Basin rangeland. Journal of Range Management 35:152–158.

———, AND J. J. ROGERS. 1989. Estimating carrying capacity with simultaneous nutritional constraints. U.S. Department of Agriculture, Forest Service, Research Note PNW-RN-485.

———, C. T. ROBBINS, A. E. HAGERMAN, AND C. MCARTHUR. 1992. Predicting digestible protein and digestible dry matter in tannin-containing forages consumed by ruminants. Ecology 73:537–541.

HAPPE, P. J., K. J. JENKINS, E. E. STARKEY, AND S. H. SHARROW. 1990. Nutritional quality and tannin astringency of browse in clear-cuts and old-growth forests. Journal of Wildlife Management 54:557–566.

HARBORNE, J. B. 1991*a*. The chemical basis of plant defense. Pages 45–59 *in* R. T. Palo and C. T. Robbins, editors. Plant defenses against mammalian herbivory. CRC Press, Boston, Massachusetts, USA.

———. 1991*b*. Flavonoid pigments. Pages 389–426 *in* G. A. Rosenthal and M. Berenbaum, editors. Herbivores: their interaction with secondary plant metabolites. Second edition. Volume I. The chemical participants. Academic Press, New York, USA.

HARDER, J. D., AND R. L. KIRKPATRICK. 1994. Physiological indices in wildlife research. Pages 275–306 *in* T. A. Bookhout, editor. Research and management techniques for wildlife and habitats. Fifth edition. The Wildlife Society, Bethesda, Maryland, USA.

HARLOW, H. J. 1981. Effect of fasting on rate of food passage and assimilation efficiency in badgers. Journal of Mammalogy 62:173–177.

HAWLEY, A. W. L. 1987. Identifying bison ration groups by multivariate analysis of blood composition. Journal of Wildlife Management 51:893–900.

HAYES, J. P., AND J. S. SHONKWILER. 2001. Morphometric indicators of body condition: worthwhile or wishful thinking? Pages 8–38 *in* J. R. Speakman, editor. Body composition analysis of animals: a handbook of non-destructive methods. Cambridge University Press, New York, USA.

HEGSTED, D. M. 1976. Balance studies. Journal of Nutrition 106:307–311.

HELLER, H. C. 1972. Measurements of convective and radiative heat transfer in small mammals. Journal of Mammalogy 53:289–295.

HELLGREN, E. C., AND W. J. PITTS. 1997. Sodium economy in white-tailed deer (*Odocoileus virginianus*). Physiological Zoology 70:547–555.

———, M. R. VAUGHAN, AND R. L. KIRKPATRICK. 1989. Seasonal patterns in physiology and nutrition of black bears in Great Dismal Swamp, Virginia-North Carolina. Canadian Journal of Zoology 67:1837–1850.

HELMS, C. W., AND W. H. DRURY, JR. 1960. Winter and migratory weight and fat field studies on some North American buntings. Bird-Banding 31:1–40.

HEWITT, D. G., AND R. L. KIRKPATRICK. 1997. Ruffed grouse consumption and detoxification of evergreen leaves. Journal of Wildlife Management 61:129–139.

———, N. W. LAFON, AND R. L. KIRKPATRICK. 1999. Effect of tannins on Galliform cecal partitioning. Physiological Zoology 70:175–180.

HILDEBRAND, G. V., S. D. FARLEY, AND C. T. ROBBINS. 1998. Predicting body condition of bears via two field methods. Journal of Wildlife Management 62:406–409.

HOBBS, N. T. 1987. Fecal indices to dietary quality: a critique. Journal of Wildlife Management 51:317–320.

———. 1989. Linking energy balance to survival in mule deer: development and test of a simulation model. Wildlife Monographs 101.

———, AND D. M. SWIFT. 1985. Estimates of habitat carrying capacity incorporating explicit nutritional constraints. Journal of Wildlife Management 49:814–822.

———, D. L. BAKER, AND R. B. GILL. 1983. Comparative nutritional ecology of montane ungulates during winter. Journal of Wildlife Management 47:1–16.

———, ———, J. E. ELLIS, D. M. SWIFT, AND R. A. GREEN. 1982. Energy- and nitrogen-based estimates of elk winter-range carrying capacity. Journal of Wildlife Management 46:12–21.

HOBSON, K. A., AND R. G. CLARK. 1992*a*. Assessing avian diets using stable isotopes I: turnover of ^{13}C in tissues. Condor 94:181–188.

———, AND ———. 1992*b*. Assessing avian diets using stable isotopes II: factors influencing diet-tissue fractionation. Condor 94:189–197.

HOLLEMAN, D. F., J. R. LUICK, AND R. G. WHITE. 1979. Lichen intake estimates for reindeer and caribou during winter. Journal of Wildlife Management 43:192–201.

HOLTER, J. B, W. E. URBAN, JR., H. H. HAYES, AND H. SILVER. 1976. Predicting metabolic rate from telemetered heart rate in white-tailed deer. Journal of Wildlife Management 40:62–29.

HUGHES, R. N., editor. 1990. Behavioural mechanisms of food selection. Springer-Verlag, Inc., New York, USA.

HUTCHINSON, A. E., AND R. B. OWEN. 1984. Bone marrow fat in waterfowl. Journal of Wildlife Management 48:585–591.

IASON, G. R., AND A. H. MURRAY. 1996. The energy costs of ingestion of naturally occurring nontannin plant phenolics by sheep. Physiological Zoology 69:532–546.

ILLIUS, A. W., AND I. J. GORDON. 1999. Scaling up from functional response to numerical response in vertebrates. Pages 397–425 *in* H. Olff, V. K. Brown, and R. H. Drent, editors. Herbivores: between plants and predators. Blackwell Science Publications, Oxford, United Kingdom.

———, AND N. S. JESSOP. 1995. Modeling metabolic costs of allelochemical ingestion by foraging herbivores. Journal of Chemical Ecology 21:693–719.

IVERSON, S. J. 1993. Milk secretion in marine mammals in relation to foraging: can milk fatty acids predict diet? Symposia of the Zoological Society of London 66:263–291.

———, AND O. T. OFTEDAL. 1992. Fatty acid composition of black bear (*Ursus americanus*) milk during and after the period of winter dormancy. Lipids 27:940–943.

———, J. P. Y. ARNOULD, AND I. L. BOYD. 1997. Milk fatty acid signatures indicate both major and minor shifts in the diet of lactating Antarctic fur seals. Canadian Journal of Zoology 75:188–197.

JACOB, E. M., S. D. MARSHALL, AND G. W. UETZ. 1996. Estimating fitness: a comparison of body condition indices. Oikos 77:61–67.

JACOBSON, H. A., R. L. KIRKPATRICK, AND B. S. MCGINNES. 1978. Disease and physiologic characteristics of two cottontail populations in Virginia. Wildlife Monographs 60.

JAKUBAS, W. J., R. A. GARROTT, P. J. WHITE, AND D. R. MERTENS. 1994. Fire-induced changes in the nutritional quality of lodgepole pine bark. Journal of Wildlife Management 58:35–46.

JEEJEEBHOY, K. N. 1986. Nutritional balance studies: indicators of human requirements or adaptive mechanisms? Journal of Nutrition 116:2061–2063.

JENKINS, K. D., D. M. HAWLEY, C. S. FARABAUGH, AND D. A. CRISTOL. 2001. Ptilochronology reveals differences in condition of captive white-throated sparrows. Condor 103:579–586.

JENKINS, S. H. 1975. Food selection by beavers: a multidimensional contingency table analysis. Oecologia 21:157–173.

JENKS, J. A., AND D. M. LESLIE, JR. 1988. Effects of lichen and in vitro methodology on digestibility of winter deer diets in Maine. Canadian Field-Naturalist 102:216–220.

JOHNSON, D. H., G. L. KRAPU, K. J. REINECKE, AND D. G. JORDE. 1985. An evaluation of condition indices for birds. Journal of Wildlife Management 49:569–575.

JULKUNEN-TIITTO, R. 1985. Phenolic constituents in the leaves of northern willows: methods for the analysis of certain phenolics. Journal of Agricultural Food Chemistry 33:213–217.

KAM, M., A. A. DEGEN, AND K. A. NAGY. 1987. Seasonal energy, water, and food consumption of Negev chukars and sand partridges. Ecology 68:1029–1037.

KAMDEM, P. D., AND J. W. HANOVER. 1993. Inter-tree variation of essential oil composition of *Thuja occidentalis* L. Journal of Essential Oil Research 5:279–282.

KARASOV, W. H. 1992. Daily energy expenditure and the cost of activity in mammals. American Zoologist 32:238–248.

———, AND S. R. McWILLIAMS. 2004. Digestive constraint in mammalian and avian ecology. Pages 87–112 *in* M. Starck and T. Wang, editors. Consequences of feeding in vertebrates. Science Publishers Inc., Enfield, New Hampshire, USA.

———, AND B. PINSHOW. 1998. Changes in lean mass and in organs of nutrient assimilation in a long-distance passerine migrant at a spring-time stopover site. Physiological Zoology 71:435–448.

———, L. R. HAN, AND J. C. MUNGER. 1988. Measurement of ^2H_2O by IR absorbance in doubly labeled H_2O studies of energy expenditure. American Journal of Physiology 255:R174–R177.

———, E. PETROSSIAN, L. ROSENBERG, AND J. M. DIAMOND. 1986*a*. How do food passage rate and assimilation differ between herbivorous lizards and nonruminant mammals? Journal of Comparative Physiology B156:599–609.

———, D. PHAN, J. M. DIAMOND, AND F. L. CARPENTER. 1986*b*. Food passage and intestinal nutrient absorption in hummingbirds. Auk 103:453–464.

KAUTZ, M. A., W. W. MAUTZ, AND L. H. CARPENTER. 1981. Heart rate as a predictor of energy expenditure of mule deer. Journal of Wildlife Management 45:715–720.

KEIVER, K. M., K. RONALD, AND F. W. H. BEAMISH. 1984. Metabolizable energy requirements for maintenance and faecal and urinary losses of juvenile harp seals (*Phoca groenlandica*). Canadian Journal of Zoology 62:769–776.

KELLY, J. F. 2000. Stable isotopes of carbon and nitrogen in the study of avian and mammalian trophic ecology. Canadian Journal of Zoology 78:1–27.

KERR, D. C., C. D. ANKNEY, AND J. S. MILLAR. 1982. The effect of drying temperature on extraction of petroleum ether soluble fats of small birds and mammals. Canadian Journal of Zoology 60:470–472.

KIE, J. G., AND T. S. BURTON. 1984. Dietary qualities, fecal nitrogen, and 2,6-diaminopimelic acid in black-tailed deer in northern California. U.S. Department of Agriculture, Forest Service, Research Note PSW-364.

———, M. WHITE, AND D. L. DRAWE. 1983. Condition parameters of white-tailed deer in Texas. Journal of Wildlife Management 47:583–594.

KIELL, D. J., AND J. S. MILLAR. 1980. Reproduction and nutrient reserves of arctic ground squirrels. Canadian Journal of Zoology 58:416–421.

KING, J. R. 1967. Adipose tissue composition in experimentally induced fat deposition in the white-crowned sparrow. Comparative Biochemistry and Physiology 21:393–403.

———, AND D. S. FARNER. 1965. Fat deposition in migratory birds. New York Academy of Sciences 131:422–445.

KIRKPATRICK, R. L., J. P. FONTENOT, AND R. F. HARLOW. 1969. Seasonal changes in rumen chemical components as related to forages consumed by white-tailed deer of the Southeast. Transactions of the North American Wildlife and Natural Resources Conference 34:229–238.

KLEIBER, M. 1932. Body size and metabolism. Hilgardia 6:315–353.

KLEIN, D. R. 1964. Range-related differences in growth of deer reflected in skeletal ratios. Journal of Mammalogy 45:226–235.

KOERTH, N. E., AND F. S. GUTHERY. 1988. Reliability of body fat indices for northern bobwhite populations. Journal of Wildlife Management 52:150–152.

KREBS, C. J., AND G. R. SINGLETON. 1993. Indices of condition in small mammals. Australian Journal of Zoology 41:317–323.

———, S. A. BOUTIN, AND R. BOONSTRA. 2001. Ecosystem dynamics of the boreal forest: the Kluane project. Oxford University Press, New York, USA.

———, A. R. E. SINCLAIR, R. BOONSTRA, S. BOUTIN, K. MARTIN, AND J. N. M. SMITH. 1999. Community dynamics of vertebrate herbivores: how can we untangle the web? Pages 447–473 *in* H. Olff, V. K. Brown, and R. H. Drent, editors. Herbivores: between plants and predators. Blackwell Science Publications, Oxford, United Kingdom.

KREBS, J. R., AND A. KACELNIK. 1991. Decision-making. Pages 105–136 *in* J. R. Krebs and N. B. Davies, editors. Behavioural ecology: an evolutionary approach. Third edition. Blackwell Scientific Publications, Oxford, United Kingdom.

KREMENTZ, D. G., AND G. W. PENDELTON. 1990. Fat scoring: sources of variability. Condor 92:500–507.

KRUEGER, K. 1986. Feeding relationships among bison, pronghorn, and prairie dogs: an experimental analysis. Ecology 67:760–770.

LACA, E. A., AND M. W. DEMMENT. 1996. Foraging strategies of grazing animals. Pages 137–158 *in* J. Hodgson and A. W. Illius, editors. The ecology and management of grazing systems. CAB International. Wallingford, United Kingdom.

LERESCHE, R. E., U. S. SEAL, P. D. KARNS, AND A. W. FRANZMANN. 1974. A review of blood chemistry of moose and other Cervidae with emphasis on nutritional assessment. Naturaliste Canadiene 101:263–290.

LESAGE, L., M. CRÊTE, J. HUOT, AND J. P. OUELLET. 2001. Evidence for a trade-off between growth and body reserves in northern white-tailed deer. Oecologia 126:30–41.

LESLIE, JR., D. M, AND E. E. STARKEY. 1985. Fecal indices to dietary quality of cervids in old-growth forests. Journal of Wildlife Management 49:142–146.

———, AND ———. 1987. Fecal indices to dietary quality: a reply. Journal of Wildlife Management 51:321–325.

———, J. A. JENKS, M. CHILELLI, AND G. R. LAVIGNE. 1989. Nitrogen and diaminopimelic acid in deer and moose feces. Journal of Wildlife Management 53:216–218.

LEVEY, D. J., H. A. BISSELL, AND S. F. O'KEEFE. 2000. Conversion of nitrogen to protein and amino acids in wild fruit. Journal of Chemical Ecology 26:1749–1763.

LINDROTH, R. L., AND G. O. BATZLI. 1984. Plant phenolics as chemical defenses: effects of natural phenolics on survival and growth of prairie voles (*Microtus ochrogaster*). Journal of Chemical Ecology 10:229–244.

MABRY, T. J., AND J. E. GILL. 1979. Sesquiterpene lactones and other terpenoids. Pages 502–537 *in* G. A. Rosenthal and D. H. Janzen, editors. Herbivores: their interaction with secondary plant metabolites. Academic Press, New York, USA.

MacCRACKEN, J. G., AND R. M. HANSEN. 1987. Coyote feeding strategies in southeastern Idaho: optimal foraging by an opportunistic predator? Journal of Wildlife Management 51:278–285.

MacPHERSON, S. L., F. A. SERVELLO, AND R. L. KIRKPATRICK. 1985. A method of estimating diet digestibility in wild meadow voles. Canadian Journal of Zoology 63:1020–1022.

———, ———, AND ———. 1988. Seasonal variation in diet digestibility of pine voles. Canadian Journal of Zoology 66:1484–1487.

MANGEL, M., AND C. W. CLARK. 1988. Dynamic modeling in behavioral ecology. Princeton University Press, Princeton, New Jersey, USA.

MARTIN, J. S., AND M. M. MARTIN. 1982. Tannin assays in ecological studies: lack of correlation between phenolics, proanthocyanidins and protein-precipitating constituents in mature foliage of six oak species. Oecologia 54:205–211.

MAUTZ, W. W. 1971. Confinement effects on dry-matter digestibility coefficients displayed by deer. Journal of Wildlife Management 35:366–368.

———. 1978. Nutrition and carrying capacity. Pages 321–348 *in* J. L. Schmidt and D. L. Gilbert, editors. Big game of North America: ecology and management. Stackpole Books, Harrisburg, Pennsylvania, USA.

———, AND J. FAIR. 1980. Energy expenditure and heart rate for activities of white-tailed deer. Journal of Wildlife Management 44:333–342.

MAYNARD, L. A., J. K. LOOSLI, H. F. HIRTZ, AND R. G. WARNER. 1979. Animal nutrition. Seventh edition. McGraw-Hill Book Co., New York, USA.

McARTHUR, C., AND G. D. SANSON. 1993. Nutritional effects and costs of a tannin in a grazing and a browsing macropodid marsupial herbivore. Functional Ecology 7:690–696.

————, A. E. HAGERMAN, AND C. T. ROBBINS. 1991. Physiological strategies of mammalian herbivores against plant defenses. Pages 103–114 *in* R. T. Palo and C. T. Robbins, editors. Plant defenses against mammalian herbivory. CRC Press, Boston, Massachusetts, USA.

————, C. T. ROBBINS, A. E. HAGERMAN, AND T. A. HANLEY. 1993. Diet selection by a ruminant generalist browser in relation to plant chemistry. Canadian Journal of Zoology 71:2236–2243.

McCOWN, J. W., M. E. ROELKE, D. J. FORRESTER, C. T. MOORE, AND J. C. ROBOSKI. 1991. Physiological evaluation of 2 white-tailed deer herds in southern Florida. Proceedings of the Annual Conference of the Southeastern Association of Fish and Wildlife Agencies 45:81–90.

McKINNEY, R. A., AND S. R. McWILLIAMS. 2005. A new model to estimate daily energy expenditure for wintering waterfowl. Wilson Bulletin 117:44-55.

McLEAN, S., W. J. FOLEY, N. W. DAVIES, S. BRANDON, L. DUO, AND A. J. BLACKMAN. 1993. Metabolic fate of dietary terpenes from *Eucalyptus radiata* in common ringtail possum (*Pseudocheirus peregrinus*). Journal of Chemical Ecology 19:1625–1643.

McLEOD, M. N. 1974. Plant tannins—their role in forage quality. Nutrition Abstract Review 11:803–815.

McNAB, B. K. 2002. The physiological ecology of vertebrates: a view from energetics. Cornell University Press, Ithaca, New York, USA.

McWILLIAMS, S. R., AND W. H. KARASOV. 2001. Phenotypic flexibility in digestive system structure and function in migratory birds and its ecological significance. Comparative Biochemistry and Physiology 129A:579–593.

————, E. CAVIEDAS-VIDAL, AND W. H. KARASOV. 1999. Digestive adjustments in cedar waxwings to high feeding rates. Journal of Experimental Zoology 283:394–407.

MECH, L. D., AND G. D. DELGIUDICE. 1985. Limitations of the marrow-fat technique as an indicator of body condition. Wildlife Society Bulletin 13:204–206.

————, U. S. SEAL, AND G. D. DELGIUDICE. 1987. Use of urine in snow to indicate condition of wolves. Journal of Wildlife Management 51:10–13.

MEIENBERGER, C., I. R. WALLIS, AND K. A. NAGY. 1993. Food intake rate and body mass influence transit time and digestibility in the desert tortoise (*Xerobates agassizii*). Physiological Zoology 66:847–862.

MILLER, M. R., AND K. J. REINECKE. 1984. Proper expression of metabolizable energy in avian energetics. Condor 86:396–400.

MOEN, A. N. 1985. Season and twig-length effects on cell composition of red maple. Journal of Wildlife Management 49:521–524.

MOEN, R., AND G. D. DELGIUDICE. 1997. Simulating nitrogen metabolism and urinary urea nitrogen: creatinine ratios in ruminants. Journal of Wildlife Management, 61:881–894.

————, J. PASTOR, AND Y. COHEN. 1997. A spatially explicit model of moose foraging and energetics. Ecology 78:505–521.

MOLE, S., AND P. G. WATERMAN. 1987. A critical analysis of techniques for measuring tannins in ecological studies. I. Techniques for chemically defining tannins. Oecologia 72:137–147.

MORTON, J. M., A. C. FOWLER, AND R. L. KIRKPATRICK. 1989. Time and energy budgets of American black ducks in winter. Journal of Wildlife Management 53:401–410.

MOSS, R. 1973. The digestion and intake of winter foods by wild ptarmigan in Alaska. Condor 75:293–300.

MOTHERSHEAD, C. L., R. L. COWAN, AND A. P. AMMANN. 1972. Variations in determinations of digestive capacity of the white-tailed deer. Journal of Wildlife Management 36:1052–1060.

MOULD, E. D., AND C. T. ROBBINS. 1981*a*. Evaluation of detergent analysis in estimating nutritional value of browse. Journal of Wildlife Management 45:937–947.

————, AND ————. 1981*b*. Nitrogen metabolism in elk. Journal of Wildlife Management 45:323–334.

————, AND ————. 1982. Digestive capabilities in elk compared to white-tailed deer. Journal of Wildlife Management 46:22–29.

MURPHY, M. E. 1992. Ptilochronology: accuracy and reliability of the technique. Auk 109:676–680.

————. 1993. The protein requirement for maintenance in the white-

crowned sparrow *Zonotrichia leucophrys gambelii*. Canadian Journal of Zoology 71:2111–2120.

————, AND J. R. KING. 1991. Ptilochronology: a critical evaluation of assumptions and utility. Auk 108:695–704.

NAGY, J. G., H. W. STEINHOFF, AND G. M. WARD. 1964. Effects of essential oils of sagebrush on deer rumen microbial function. Journal of Wildlife Management 28:785–790.

NAGY, K. A. 1980. CO_2 production in animals: analysis of potential errors in the doubly labeled water method. American Journal of Physiology 238:R466–R473.

————. 1987. Field metabolic rate and food requirement scaling in mammals and birds. Ecological Monographs 57:111–128.

————. 1989. Field bioenergetics: accuracy of models and methods. Physiological Zoology 62:237–252.

————, AND M. H. KNIGHT. 1994. Energy, water, and food use by Springbok antelope (*Antidorcas marsupialis*) in the Kalahari Desert. Journal of Mammalogy 75:860–872.

————, AND P. A. MEDICA. 1986. Physiological ecology of desert tortoises in southern Nevada. Herpetologica 42:73–92.

————, I. A. GIRARD, AND T. K. BROWN. 1999. Energetics of free-ranging mammals, reptiles, and birds. Annual Review of Nutrition 19:247–277.

————, B. T. HENEN, AND D. B. VYAS. 1998. Nutritional quality of native and introduced food plants of wild desert tortoises. Journal of Herpetology 32:260–267.

NAGY, T. R. 2001. The use of dual-energy X-ray absorptiometry for the measurement of body composition. Pages 211–229 *in* J. R. Speakman, editor. Body composition analysis of animals: a handbook of non-destructive methods. Cambridge University Press, Cambridge, United Kingdom.

————, AND A. L. CLAIR. 2000. Precision and accuracy of dual-energy X-ray absorptiometry for determining in vivo body composition of mice. Obesity Research 8:392–398.

NASTIS, A. S., AND J. C. MALECHEK. 1988. Estimating digestibility of oak browse diets for goats by in vitro techniques. Journal of Range Management 41:255–258.

NEILAND, K. A. 1970. Weight of dried marrow as indicator of fat in caribou femurs. Journal of Wildlife Management 34:904–907.

NICHOLS, R. G., AND M. R. PELTON. 1974. Fat in the mandibular cavity as an indicator of condition in deer. Proceedings of the Annual Conference of the Southeastern Association of Game and Fish Commissioners. 28:540–548.

NISBET, I. C. T., J. A. SPENDELOW, J. S. HATFIELD, J. M. ZINGO, AND G. A. GOUGH. 1998. Variations in growth of roseate tern chicks. II. Early growth as an index of parental quality. Condor 100:305–315.

OFTEDAL, O. T., W. D. BOWEN, AND D. J. BONESS. 1996. Lactation performance and nutrient deposition in pups of the harp seal, *Phoca groenlandica*, on ice floes off southeast Labrador. Physiological Zoology 69:635–657.

OWEN, M. 1981. Abdominal profile—a condition index for wild geese in the field. Journal of Wildlife Management 45:227–230.

PACKARD, G. C., AND T. J. BOARDMAN. 1987. The misuse of ratios to scale physiological data that vary allometrically with body size. Pages 216–236 *in* M. E. Feder, A. F. Bennett, W. W. Burggren, and R. B. Huey, editors. New directions in ecological physiology. Cambridge University Press, Cambridge, United Kingdom.

————, AND ————. 1999. The use of percentages and size-specific indices to normalize physiological data for variation in body size: wasted time, wasted effort? Comparative Biochemistry and Physiology 122A:37–44.

PALMER, W. L., R. L. COWAN, AND A. P. AMMANN. 1976. Effect of inoculum source on in vitro digestion of deer foods. Journal of Wildlife Management 40:301–307.

PALO, R. T., AND C. T. ROBBINS, editors. 1991. Plant defenses against mammalian herbivory. CRC Press, Boston, Massachusetts, USA.

————, K. SUNNERHEIM, AND O. THEANDER. 1985. Seasonal variation of phenols, crude protein and cell wall content of birch (*Betula pendula* Roth.) in relation to ruminant in vitro digestibility. Oecologia 65:314–318.

PARKER, K. L., G. D. DELGIUDICE, AND M. P. GILLINGHAM. 1993*a*. Do urinary urea nitrogen and cortisol ratios of creatinine reflect body-fat reserves in black-tailed deer? Canadian Journal of Zoology 71:1841–1848.

———, M. P. GILLINGHAM, AND T. A. HANLEY. 1993*b*. An accurate technique for estimating forage intake of tractable animals. Canadian Journal of Zoology 71:1462–1465.

———, ———, ———, AND C. T. ROBBINS. 1999. Energy and protein balance of free-ranging black-tailed deer in a natural forest environment. Wildlife Monographs 143.

PATTERSON, B. R., L. K. BENJAMIN, AND F. MESSIER. 2000. Winter nutritional condition of eastern coyotes in relation to prey density. Canadian Journal of Zoology 78:420–427.

PERSONIUS, T. L., C. L. WAMBOLT, J. R. STEPHENS, AND R. G. KELSEY. 1987. Crude terpenoid influence on mule deer preference for sagebrush. Journal of Range Management 40:84–88.

PETERSON, B. J., AND B. FRY. 1987. Stable isotopes in ecosystem studies. Annual Review of Ecology and Systematics 18:293–320.

PETRIE, M. J., R. D. DROBNEY, AND D. A. GRABER. 1997. Evaluation of true metabolizable energy for waterfowl. Journal of Wildlife Management 61:420–425.

PIERSON, E. D., AND M. H. STACK. 1988. Methods of body composition analysis. Pages 387–403 *in* T. H. Kunz, editor. Ecological and behavioral methods in the study of bats. Smithsonian Institution Press, Washington, D.C., USA.

PILS, A. C., R. A. GARROTT, AND J. J. BORKOWSKI. 1999. Sampling and statistical analysis of snow-urine allantoin: creatinine ratios. Journal of Wildlife Management 63:1118–1132.

PRITCHARD, G. T., AND C. T. ROBBINS. 1990. Digestive and metabolic efficiencies of grizzly and black bears. Canadian Journal of Zoology 68:1645–1651.

PROSKY, L., N. ASP, I. FURDA, J. W. DEVRIES, T. F. SCHWIEZER, AND B. F. HARLAND. 1984. Determination of total dietary fiber in foods, food products, and total diets: interlaboratory study. Journal of the Association of Official Agricultural Chemists 67:1044–1052.

PULLIAM, H. R. 1989. Individual behavior and the procurement of essential resources. Pages 25–38 *in* J. Roughgarden, R. M. May, and S. A. Levin, editors. Perspectives in ecological theory. Princeton University Press, Princeton, New Jersey, USA.

RANSOM, A. B. 1965. Kidney and marrow fat as indicators of white-tailed deer condition. Journal of Wildlife Management 29:397–398.

RASMUSSEN, G. P. 1985. Antler measurements as an index to physical condition and range quality with respect to white-tailed deer. New York Fish and Game Journal 32:97–113.

RATNAYAKE, W. M. N., B. OLSSON, AND R. G. ACKMAN. 1989. Novel branched-chain fatty acids in certain fish oils. Lipids 24:630–637.

RAUBENHEIMER D., AND S. J. SIMPSON. 1994. The analysis of nutrient budgets. Functional Ecology 8:783–791.

RAVELING, D. G. 1979. The annual cycle of body composition of Canada geese with special reference to control of reproduction. Auk 96:234–252.

———, M. SIFRI, AND R. B. KNUDSEN. 1978. Seasonal variation of femur and tibiotarsus constituents in Canada geese. Condor 80:246–248.

REGELIN, W. L., O. C. WALLMO, J. NAGY, AND D. R. DIETZ. 1974. Effect of logging on forage values for deer in Colorado. Journal of Forestry 72:282–285.

REICHARDT, P. B., J. P. BRYANT, T. P. CLAUSEN, AND G. D. WIELAND. 1984. Defense of winter-dormant Alaska paper birch against snowshoe hares. Oecologia 65:58–69.

RENECKER, L. A., AND R. J. HUDSON. 1985. Estimation of dry matter intake of free-ranging moose. Journal of Wildlife Management 49:785–792.

REYNOLDS, D. S., AND T. H. KUNZ. 2000. Changes in body composition during reproduction and postnatal growth in the little brown bat, *Myotis lucifugus* (Chiroptera: Verspertilionidae). Ecoscience 7:10–17.

———, AND ———. 2001. Standard methods for destructive body composition analysis. Pages 39–55 *in* J. R. Speakman, editor. Body composition analysis of animals: a handbook of non-destructive methods.

Cambridge University Press, Cambridge, United Kingdom.

RIBEREAU-GAYON, P. 1972. Plant phenolics. Oliver and Boyd, Ltd., Edinburgh, Scotland.

RICKLEFS, R. E. 1968. Patterns of growth in birds. Ibis 110:419–451.

———. 1973. Patterns of growth in birds. II. Growth rate and mode of development. Ibis 115:177–201.

———, AND J. M. STARCK. 1998. The evolution of the developmental mode in birds. Pages 366–380 *in* J. M. Starck and R. E. Ricklefs, editors. Avian growth and development: evolution within the altricial-precocial spectrum. Oxford University Press, New York, USA.

———, ———, and M. Konarzewski 1998. Internal constraints on growth in birds. Pages 266–287 *in* J. M. Starck and R. E. Ricklefs, editors. Avian growth and development: evolution within the altricial-precocial spectrum. Oxford University Press, New York, USA.

RINEY, T. 1955. Evaluating condition of free ranging red deer (*Cervus elaphus*), with special reference to New Zealand. New Zealand Journal of Science and Technology 36B:429–463.

ROBBINS, C. T. 1993. Wildlife feeding and nutrition. Second edition. Academic Press, San Diego, California, USA.

———, S. MOLE, A. E. HAGERMAN, AND T. A. HANLEY. 1987*a*. Role of tannins in defending plants against ruminants: reduction in dry matter digestion? Ecology 68:1606–1615.

———, A. E. HAGERMAN, P. J. AUSTIN, C. MCARTHUR, AND T. A. HANLEY. 1991. Variation in mammalian physiological responses to a condensed tannin and its ecological implications. Journal of Mammalogy 72:480–486.

———, T. A. Hanley, A. E. Hagerman, O. Hjeljord, D. L. Baker, C. C. Schwartz, and W. W. Mautz. 1987*b*. Role of tannins in defending plants against ruminants: reduction in protein availability. Ecology 68:98–107.

ROBEL, R. J., AND A. R. BISSET. 1979. Effects of supplemental grit on metabolic efficiency of bobwhites. Wildlife Society Bulletin 7:178–181.

———, ———, T. M. CLEMENT, JR., A. D. DAYTON, AND K. L. MORGAN. 1979. Metabolizable energy of important foods of bobwhites in Kansas. Journal of Wildlife Management 43:982–987.

ROBERTSON, J. B., AND P. J. VAN SOEST. 1977. Dietary fiber estimation in concentrate foodstuffs. Annual meeting of the American Society of Animal Science. 69:Abstract. University of Wisconsin, Madison, USA.

RODE, K. D., AND C. T. ROBBINS. 2000. Why bears consume mixed diets during fruit abundance. Canadian Journal of Zoology 78:1640–1645.

———, AND L. A. SHIPLEY. 2001. Constraints on herbivory by grizzly bears. Oecologia 128:62–71.

ROSENTHAL, G. A., AND M. BERENBAUM. 1991. Herbivores: their interactions with secondary plant metabolites. Second edition. Volume 1. The chemical participants. Academic Press, New York, USA.

SALTZ, D., AND D. E. COOK. 1993. Effect of time and snow dilution on cortisol: creatinine rations in mule deer urine. Journal of Wildlife Management 57:397–399.

———, AND G. C. WHITE. 1991. Urinary cortisol and urea nitrogen responses to winter stress in male deer. Journal of Wildlife Management 55:1–16.

———, ———, AND R. M. BARTMANN. 1992. Urinary cortisol, urea nitrogen excretion, and winter survival in mule deer fawns. Journal of Wildlife Management 56:640–644.

———, ———, ———, G. D. DELGIUDICE, M. R. RIGGS, L. D. MECH, AND U. S. SEAL. 1995. Assessing animal condition, nutrition, and stress from urine in snow: a critical review and response. Wildlife Society Bulletin 23:694–704.

SAWICKA-KAPUSTA, K. 1975. Fat extraction in the Soxhlet apparatus. Pages 228–292 *in* W. Grodzinski, R. Z. Klekowski, and A. Duncan, editors. Methods for ecological bioenergetics. Blackwell Scientific Publications, Oxford, United Kingdom.

SCHEW, W. A., AND R. E. RICKLEFS. 1998. Developmental plasticity. Pages 288–304 *in* J. M. Starck and R. E. Ricklefs, editors. Avian growth and development: evolution within the altricial-precocial spectrum. Oxford University Press, New York, USA.

SCHMIDT-NIELSEN, K. 1984. Scaling: why is animal size so important?

Cambridge University Press, New York, USA.

SCHNEIDER, B. H., AND W. P. FLATT. 1975. The evaluation of feeds through digestibility experiments. University of Georgia Press, Athens, USA.

SCHOENER, T. W. 1971. Theory of feeding strategies. Annual Review of Ecology and Systematics 2:369–404.

SCOTT, I., M. GRANT, AND P. R. EVANS. 1991. Estimation of fat-free mass of live birds: use of total body electrical conductivity (TOBEC) measurements in studies of single species in the field. Functional Ecology 5:314–320.

———, C. SELMAN, P. I. MITCHELL, AND P. R. EVANS. 2001. The use of total body electrical conductivity (TOBEC) to determine body composition in vertebrates. Pages 127–160 in J. R. Speakman, editor. Body composition analysis of animals: a handbook of non-destructive methods. Cambridge University Press, Cambridge, United Kingdom.

SCOTT, M. L., M. C. NESHEIM, AND R. J. YOUNG. 1982. Nutrition of the chicken. Third edition. M. L. Scott and Associates, Ithaca, New York, USA.

SCHWARTZ, C. C., J. G. NAGY, AND W. L. REGELIN. 1980. Juniper oil yield, terpenoid concentration, and antimicrobial effects on deer. Journal of Wildlife Management 44:107–113.

———, ———, AND R. W. RICE. 1977. Pronghorn dietary quality relative to forage availability and other ruminants in Colorado. Journal of Wildlife Management 41:161–168.

———, W. L. REGELIN, AND J. G. NAGY. 1980. Deer preference for juniper forage and volatile oil treated foods. Journal of Wildlife Management 44:114–120.

SEDINGER, J. S. 1984. Protein and amino acid composition of tundra vegetation in relation to nutritional requirements of geese. Journal of Wildlife Management 48:1128–1136.

———. 1992. Ecology of prefledging waterfowl. Pages 109–127 in B. D. J. Batt, A. D. Afton, M. G. Anderson, C. D. Ankney, D. H. Johnson, J. A. Kadlec, and G. L. Krapu, editors. Ecology and management of breeding waterfowl. University of Minnesota Press, Minneapolis, USA.

SERVELLO, F. A., AND R. L. KIRKPATRICK. 1987a. Fat indices for ruffed grouse. Journal of Wildlife Management 51:173–177.

———, AND ———. 1987b. Regional variation in the nutritional ecology of ruffed grouse. Journal of Wildlife Management 51:749–770.

———, AND ———. 1988. Nutrition and condition of ruffed grouse during the breeding season in southwestern Virginia. Condor 90:836–842.

———, AND J. W. SCHNEIDER. 2000. Evaluation of urinary indices of nutritional status for white-tailed deer: tests with winter browse diets. Journal of Wildlife Management 64:137–145.

———, R. L. KIRKPATRICK, AND K. E. WEBB, JR. 1987. Predicting metabolizable energy in the diet of ruffed grouse. Journal of Wildlife Management 51:560–567.

———, K. E. WEBB, JR., AND R. L. KIRKPATRICK. 1983. Estimation of the digestibility of diets of small mammals in natural habitats. Journal of Mammalogy 64:603–609.

———, R. L. KIRKPATRICK, K. E. WEBB, JR., AND A. R. TIPTON. 1984. Pine vole diet quality in relation to apple tree root damage. Journal of Wildlife Management 48:450–455.

SEVERINGHAUS, C. W., H. F. MAGUIRE, R. A. COOKINGHAM, AND J. E. TANCK. 1950. Variations by age class in the antler beam diameters of white-tailed deer related to range conditions. Transactions of the North American Wildlife Conference 15:551–570.

SIBBALD, I. R. 1976. A bioassay for true metabolizable energy in feeding stuffs. Poultry Science 55:303–308.

———. 1979. A bioassay for available amino acids and true metabolizable energy in feeding stuffs. Poultry Science 58:668–673.

———, AND P. M. MORSE. 1982. Effects of the nitrogen correction and of feed intake on true metabolizable energy values. Poultry Science 62:138–142.

SILVER, H., N. F. COLOVOS, AND H. H. HAYES. 1969. Fasting metabolism of white-tailed deer. Journal of Wildlife Management 33:490–498.

SINGLETON, V. L., AND J. A. ROSSI, JR. 1965. Colorimetry of total phenolics with phosphomolybdic-phosphotungstic acid reagents. American Journal of Enology and Viticulture. 16:144–158.

SMALLWOOD, P. D., AND W. D. PETERS. 1986. Grey squirrel food preferences: the effects of tannin and fat concentration. Ecology 67:168–174.

SMITH, D. 1973. Influence of drying and storage conditions on nonstructural carbohydrate analysis of herbage tissue—a review. Journal of the British Grassland Society 28:129–134.

SMITH, N. S. 1970. Appraisal of condition estimation methods for East African ungulates. East African Wildlife Journal 8:123–129.

SMITH, R. J., K. A. HOBSON, H. N. KOOPMAN, AND D. M. LAVIGNE. 1996. Distinguishing between populations of fresh and saltwater harbour seals (*Phoca vitulina*) using stable-isotope ratios and fatty acid profiles. Canadian Journal of Fisheries and Aquatic Sciences 53:272–279.

SPALINGER, D. E., AND N. T. HOBBS. 1992. Mechanisms of foraging in mammalian herbivores: new models of functional response. American Naturalist 140:325–348.

SPEAKMAN, J. R. 1997. Doubly labeled water: theory and practice. Chapman and Hall, London, United Kingdom.

———, G. H. VISSER, S. WARD, AND E. KROL. 2001. The isotope dilution method for the evaluation of body composition. Pages 56–98 in J. R. Speakman, editor. Body composition analysis of animals: a handbook of non-destructive methods. Cambridge University Press, Cambridge, United Kingdom.

STAALAND, H., D. F. HOLLEMAN, J. R. LUICK, AND R. G. WHITE. 1982. Exchangable sodium pool size and turnover in relation to diet in reindeer. Canadian Journal of Zoology 60:603–610.

STALMASTER, M. V. 1983. An energetics simulation model for managing wintering bald eagles. Journal of Wildlife Management 47:349–359.

———, AND J. A. GESSAMAN. 1984. Ecological energetics and foraging behavior of overwintering bald eagles. Ecological Energetics 54:407–428.

STARCK, J. M., AND R. E. RICKLEFS. 1998. Avian growth rate data set. Pages 381–423 in J. M. Starck and R. E. Ricklefs, editors. Avian growth and development: evolution within the altricial-precocial spectrum. Oxford University Press, New York, USA.

———, M. W. DIETZ, AND T. PIERSMA. 2001. The assessment of body composition and other parameters by ultrasound scanning. Pages 188–210 in J. R. Speakman, editor. Body composition analysis of animals: a handbook of non-destructive methods. Cambridge University Press, Cambridge, United Kingdom.

STEPHENS, D. W., AND J. R. KREBS. 1986. Foraging theory. Princeton University Press, Princeton, New Jersey, USA.

STEPHENSON, T. R., V. C. BLEICH, B. M. PIERCE, AND G. P. MULCAHY. 2002. Validation of mule deer body composition using in vivo and post-mortem indices of nutritional condition. Wildlife Society Bulletin 30:557–564.

SWAIN, T. 1979. Tannins and lignins. Pages 657–682 in G. A. Rosenthal and D. H. Janzen, editors. Herbivores: their interaction with secondary plant metabolites. Academic Press, New York, USA.

TALLAMY, D. W., AND M. J. RAUPP, editors. 1991. Phytochemical induction by herbivores. John Wiley and Sons, New York, USA.

TATNER, P., AND D. M. BRYANT. 1986. Flight cost of a small passerine measured using doubly labeled water: implications for energetics studies. Auk 103:169–180.

THOMAS, D. W., C. SAMSON, AND J. M. BERGERON. 1988. Metabolic costs associated with ingestion of plant phenolics by *Microtus pennsylvanicus*. Journal of Mammalogy 69:512–515.

THOMPSON, C. B., J. B. HOLTER, H. H. HAYES, H. SILVER, AND W. E. URBAN, JR. 1973. Nutrition of white-tailed deer. I. Energy requirements of fawns. Journal of Wildlife Management 37:301–311.

THOMPSON, III, F. R., AND E. K. FRITZELL. 1988. Ruffed grouse winter roost site preference and influence on energy demands. Journal of Wildlife Management 52:454–460.

THORKELSON, J., AND R. K. MAXWELL. 1974. Design and testing of a heat transfer model of a raccoon (*Procyon lotor*) in a closed tree den. Ecology 55:29–39.

TIESZEN, L. L., AND T. W. BOUTTON. 1989. Stable carbon isotopes in terrestrial ecosystem research. Pages 167–195 in P. W. Rundel, J. R.

Ehleringer, and K. A. Nagy, editors. Stable isotopes in ecological research. Springer-Verlag, Inc., New York, USA.

———, ———, K. G. Tesdahl, and N. A. Slade. 1983. Fractionation and turnover of stable carbon isotopes in animal tissues: implications of δ13C analysis of diet. Oecologia 57:32–37.

Tilley, J. M. A., and R. A. Terry. 1963. A two-stage technique for the in vitro digestion of forage crops. Journal of the British Grassland Society 18:104–111.

Tome, M. W. 1988. Optimal foraging: food patch depletion by ruddy ducks. Oecologia 76:27–36.

Torbit, S. C., L. H. Carpenter, A. W. Alldredge, and D. M. Swift. 1985. Mule deer body composition—a comparison of methods. Journal of Wildlife Management 49:86–91.

Travis, J. 1982. A method for the statistical analysis of time–energy budgets. Ecology 63:19–25.

Troyer, K. 1984. Diet selection and digestion in *Iguana iguana*: the importance of age and nutrient requirements. Oecologia 61:201–207.

Ullrey, D. E., W. G. Youatt, H. E. Johnson, L. D. Fay, B. L. Schoepke, and W. T. Magee. 1970. Digestible and metabolizable energy requirements for winter maintenance of Michigan white-tailed does. Journal of Wildlife Management 34:863–869.

Vagnoni, D. B., R. A. Garrott, J. G. Cook, P. J. White, and M. K. Clayton. 1996. Urinary allantoin: creatinine ratios as a dietary index for elk. Journal of Wildlife Management 60:728–734.

van der Meer, J., and T. Piersma. 1994. Physiologically inspired regression models for estimating and predicting nutrient stores and their composition in birds. Physiological Zoology 67:305–329.

Van Horne, B., T. A. Hanley, R. G. Cates, J. D. McKendrick, and J. D. Horner. 1988. Influence of seral stage and season on leaf chemistry of southeastern Alaska deer forage. Canadian Journal of Forest Research 18:90–99.

van Marken Lichtenbelt, W. D. 2001. The use of bioelectrical impedance analysis (BIA) for estimation of body composition. Pages 161–187 *in* J. R. Speakman, editor. Body composition analysis of animals: a handbook of non-destructive methods. Cambridge University Press, Cambridge, United Kingdom.

Van Soest, P. J. 1965. Use of detergents in analysis of fibrous feeds. III. Study of effects of heating and drying on yield in fiber and lignin in forages. Journal of the Association of Official Agricultural Chemists 48:785–790.

———. 1982. Nutritional ecology of the ruminant. O and B Books, Inc., Corvallis, Oregon, USA.

Van Vuren, D., and B. E. Coblentz. 1985. Kidney weight variation and the kidney fat index: an evaluation. Journal of Wildlife Management 49:177–179.

Veloso, C., and F. Bozinovic. 1993. Dietary and digestive constraints on basal energy metabolism in a small herbivorous rodent. Ecology 74:2003–2010.

Verme, L. J., and J. C. Holland. 1973. Reagent-dry assay of marrow fat in white-tailed deer. Journal of Wildlife Management 37:103–105.

Viggers, K. L., D. B. Lindenmayer, R. B. Cunningham, and C. F. Donnelly. 1998. Estimating body condition in the mountain brush-tail possum, *Trichosurus caninus*. Wildlife Research 25:499–509.

Wallmo, O. C., L. H. Carpenter, W. L. Regelin, R. B. Gill, and D. L. Baker. 1977. Evaluation of deer habitat on a nutritional basis. Journal of Range Management 30:122–127.

Walsberg, G. E. 1988. Evaluation of a nondestructive method for determining fat stores in small birds and mammals. Physiological Zoology 61:153–159.

Warren, R. J., and R. L. Kirkpatrick. 1978. Indices of nutritional status in cottontail rabbits fed controlled diets. Journal of Wildlife Management 42:154–158.

———, ———, A. Oelschlaeger, P. F. Scanlon, and F. C. Gwazdauskas. 1981. Dietary and seasonal influences on nutritional indices of adult male white-tailed deer. Journal of Wildlife Management 45:926–936.

Watkins, B. E., J. H. Witham, D. E. Ullrey, D. J. Watkins, and J. M. Jones. 1991. Body composition and condition evaluation of white-tailed deer fawns. Journal of Wildlife Management 55:39–51.

Weathers, W. W., W. A. Buttemer, A. M. Hayworth, and K. A. Nagy. 1984. An evaluation of time-budget estimates of daily energy expenditure in birds. Auk 101:459–472.

Webster, M. D., and W. W. Weathers. 1989. Validation of single-sample doubly labeled water method. American Journal of Physiology 256:R572–R576.

Welch, B. L., and E. D. McArthur. 1981. Variation of monoterpenoid content among subspecies and accessions of *Artemisia tridentata* grown in a uniform garden. Journal of Range Management 34:380–384.

———, J. C. Pederson, and W. P. Clary. 1983. Ability of different rumen inocula to digest range forages. Journal of Wildlife Management 47:873–877.

Welch, C. A., J. Keay, K. C. Kendall, and C. T. Robbins. 1997. Constraints on frugivory by bears. Ecology 78:1105–1119.

White, P. J., R. A. Garrott, and D. M. Heisey. 1995. Variability in snow-urine assays. Canadian Journal of Zoology 73:427–432.

———, ———, and ———. 1997. An evaluation of snow-urine ratios as indices of ungulate nutritional status. Canadian Journal of Zoology 75:1687–1694.

———, ———, C. A. V. White, and G. A. Sargeant. 1995. Interpreting mean chemical ratios from simple random collections of snow-urine samples. Wildlife Society Bulletin 23:705–710.

Whitman, M. 2002. Quantifying body condition of songbirds at a coastal New England stopover site during their migration. Thesis. University of Rhode Island, Kingston, USA.

Whyte, R. J., and E. G. Bolen. 1984. Variation in winter fat depots and condition indices of mallards. Journal of Wildlife Management 48:1370–1373.

Wickstrom, M. L., C. T. Robbins, T. A. Hanley, D. E. Spalinger, and S. M. Parish. 1984. Food intake and foraging energetics of elk and mule deer. Journal of Wildlife Management 48:1285–1301.

Wigginton, J. D., and F. S. Dobson. 1999. Environmental influences on geographic variation in body size of western bobcats. Canadian Journal of Zoology 77:802–813.

Williams, J. B., and K. A. Nagy. 1984. Daily energy expenditure of savannah sparrows: comparison of time-energy budget and doubly-labeled water estimates. Auk 101:221–229.

———, and A. Prints. 1986. Energetics of growth in nestling savannah sparrows: a comparison of doubly labeled water and laboratory estimates. Condor 88:74–83.

———, S. Ostrowski, E. Bedin, and K. Ismail. 2001. Seasonal variation in energy expenditure, water flux, and food consumption of Arabian oryx, *Oryx leucoryx*. Journal of Experimental Biology 204:2301–2311.

Williams, J. E., and S. C. Kendeigh. 1982. Energetics of the Canada goose. Journal of Wildlife Management 46:588–600.

Wood, C. C., and C. M. Hand. 1985. Food-searching behaviour of the common merganser, (*Mergus merganser*). I: functional responses to prey and predator density. Canadian Journal of Zoology 63:1260–1270.

Wood, R. A., K. A. Nagy, N. S. MacDondald, S. T. Wakakuwa, R. J. Beckman, and H. Kaaz. 1975. Determination of oxygen-18 in water contained in biological samples by charged particle activation. Analytical Chemistry 47:646–650.

Wooley, Jr., J. B., and R. B. Owen, Jr. 1978. Energy costs of activity and daily energy expenditure in the black duck. Journal of Wildlife Management 42:739–745.

Young, V. R. 1986. Nutritional balance studies: indicators of human requirements or adaptive mechanisms? Journal of Nutrition 116:700–703.

Zach, R., and J. B. Falls. 1979. Foraging and territoriality of male ovenbirds (Aves: Parulidae) in a heterogeneous habitat. Journal of Animal Ecology 48:33–52.

Zuercher, G. L., D. D. Roby, and E. A. Rexstad. 1997. Validation of two new total body electrical conductivity (TOBEC) instruments for estimating body composition of live northern red-backed voles *Clethrionomys rutilus*. Acta Theriologica 42:387–397.

22

REPRODUCTION AND HORMONES

John D. Harder

INTRODUCTION

Measures of reproductive rate and natality are central to understanding the biology of populations and, in many cases, they are more readily obtained than other components such as population size. Estimates of diverse parameters from ovulation rate to neonatal survival provide a basis for calculation of natality and recruitment for a variety of wildlife species. Moreover, during the last 2–3 decades, hormonal regulation of reproductive cycles of both domestic and wild species has been clarified, so that it is now possible to assess reproductive status and performance from blood levels of certain hormones. Promising new developments in contraceptive technology provide methods that are safe, effective, and sufficiently practical to offer an alternative, under some conditions, to traditional methods of population control.

Stress is an important issue in wildlife research, first as a potential factor in natural regulation of population size and, second, as a consideration in the welfare of animals held captive for research and conservation. An expanding knowledge of the biology and endocrinology of stress provides measures and standards for meaningful evaluation of this factor in both wild and captive animals.

This chapter is organized to meet 3 objectives: (1) review reproductive cycles of amphibians, reptiles, birds, and mammals and describe procedures to assess reproductive rates in each of these groups; (2) review basic endocrinology relative to measures of reproduction and stress; and (3) review recent developments in reproductive technology, particularly as they relate to contraception and control of recruitment in wild mammals. These objectives represent a departure from those of a related chapter in the Fifth Edition (Harder and Kirkpatrick 1996) in which emphasis was placed on the well-established relationship between nutritional condition and reproductive performance of mammals and birds (Verme 1969, Beckerton and Middleton 1982). Measures of nutritional status are now covered by Servello et al. (2005).

The precipitous, worldwide decline in populations of amphibians (Semlitsch 2000) and reptiles, particularly exploited species (Fitzgerald and Painter 2000), increasingly demands the attention of wildlife biologists, and background information and techniques relevant to these groups have been added. In this chapter, "vertebrate" refers only to terrestrial vertebrates and does not include fishes. Detailed instructions for some of the most commonly used methods are provided; for others the reader is referred to primary sources and authoritative reviews (e.g., Zug et al. 2001). The goal of this chapter is to increase awareness of and appreciation for a full spectrum of reproductive techniques and their potential application to the study and conservation of wild terrestrial vertebrates.

REPRODUCTIVE CYCLES AND MEASURES OF REPRODUCTION

Estimation of natality (i.e., number of young produced per unit of population per unit of time) is a fundamental requirement for understanding dynamics of a wild population. In some instances, this information can be obtained indirectly through mark–recapture procedures. However, this estimation is often difficult because mortality of newborn young is high and younger age groups may be difficult to trap for marking. Consequently, it is necessary to measure clutch sizes or examine ovaries and reproductive tracts to measure a reproductive parameter, such as average number of preovulatory follicles or corpora lutea (for ovulation rate) or fetuses per female collected during the breeding season. Information on gender and age structure of the population, and estimates of reproductive rate can be used to calculate the number of young born per unit of population (i.e., gross natality).

Reproductive rates can be estimated at several points in the reproductive cycle, beginning with courtship and ending with fledging or weaning and dispersal of offspring. The value of estimates made at different points varies with the species or taxon and with the goals of the investigation.

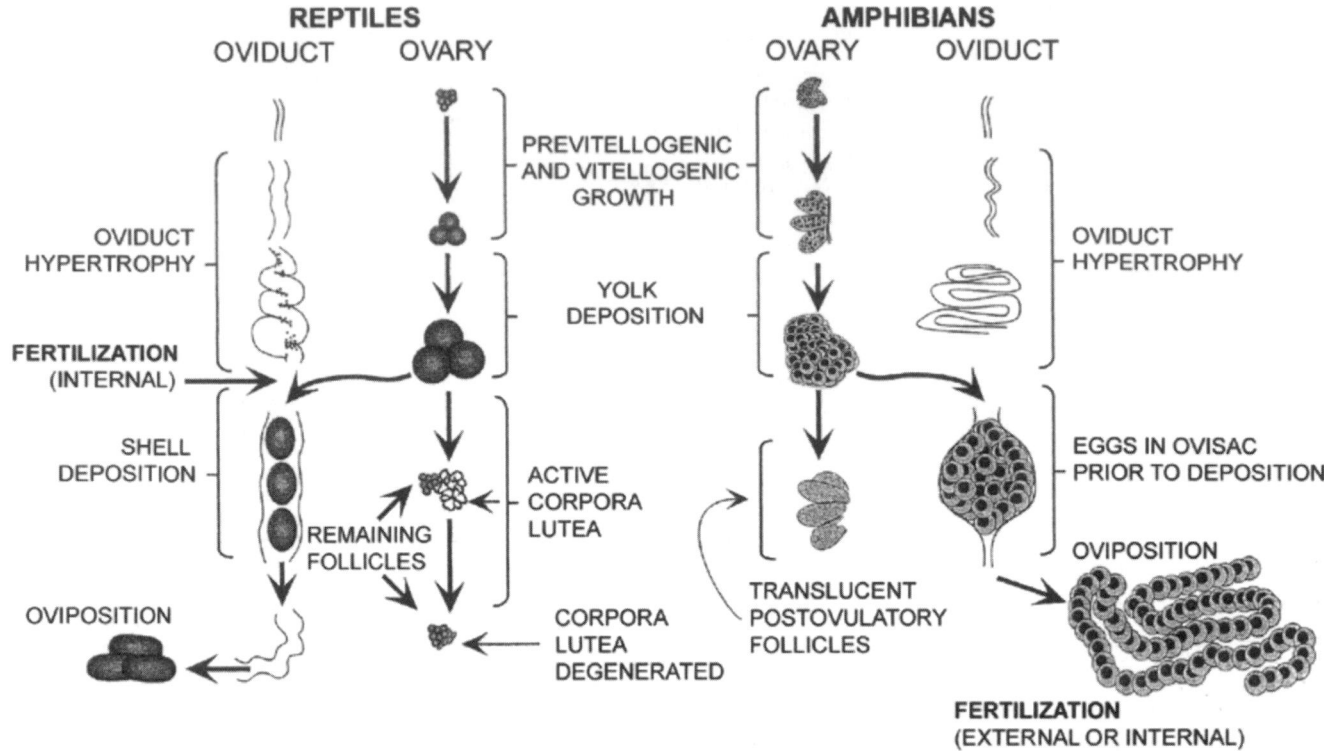

Fig. 1. Modes of reproduction in amphibians and reptiles. Fertilization is internal in reptiles and external in amphibians. Postovulatory follicles develop into corpora lutea (CL) in most reptiles but remain empty in most amphibians. In viviparous reptiles, embryos are retained within the uterus without a shell and are nourished via a placenta (copied from Zug et al. [2001] with permission from Academic Press).

For example, observations of singing males or nests in a given area will establish density of reproductive pairs, whereas counts of placental scars in mammals at necropsy provide only a size estimate of previous litters.

Knowledge of the measurements of reproductive performance that can be made throughout the reproductive cycle of a given species provides the investigator with more options for meeting specific study objectives. This knowledge also allows the investigator to consider techniques that might be used at different times of the year to achieve more efficient use of fiscal resources and biological material. Accordingly, the sequential events in the reproductive cycle, from gametogenesis and breeding to fledging or weaning, form an outline for this review of techniques and measurements used in the study of reproduction.

Reproductive Modes and Performance in Females

Amphibians and reptiles exhibit a fascinating array of reproductive patterns compared to the relatively uniform condition among birds and in mammals and, although similar protocols can be used with these taxa to study male reproduction (spermatogenesis), females are more challenging. Fertilization is external in amphibians (Fig. 1) but internal in amniotes (i.e., reptiles, birds, and mammals). Moreover, all birds and nearly all amphibians are *oviparous* (i.e., eggs are laid and hatch outside the mother), whereas all mammals, except monotremes, are *viviparous* (i.e., embryos develop to term in utero, sustained on nutrients transferred through a placenta). Most reptiles are oviparous, but about one-fifth of all lizards and snakes are viviparous (Blackburn 1993). Even in some oviparous

species, the shelled eggs are retained and hatch within the uterus. Awareness of these diverse modes and patterns of reproduction is important because they pose constraints as well as opportunities in planning research. For example, in field studies of frogs, does one search for egg masses or sample for tadpoles? With viviparous snakes, can ovulation rate be estimated from counts of corpora lutea and can pregnancy be diagnosed from plasma progesterone levels, as in mammals? These and similar questions often can be studied effectively through comparative biology in which knowledge of a process in a well studied taxon (e.g., gestation in mammals) is applied to the same process in a closely related taxon (e.g., viviparous reptiles).

Three major stages of reproduction in females provide a framework for comparative methodology of reproduction in terrestrial vertebrates: (1) ovarian activation and mating, including seasonal and social activation, follicular development, yolking of eggs, and courtship behavior; (2) ovulation, fertilization, and embryonic development (incubation and gestation); and (3) hatching or birth and parental care of neonates and young.

Ovarian Activation and Mating

Follicular Development.—Onset of the breeding season in vertebrates is indicated by an increase in size of the ovary, stemming from an increase in number and size of tertiary follicles (i.e., large, yolk-filled [except in mammals], preovulatory follicles). For example in toads (*Bufo* spp.), a small subset of the 30,000–40,000 oocytes in the ovary is responsive to gonadotropin in any given cycle and begins to accumulate yolk. Vitellogenesis is rapid just prior to ovulation when mature ova reach 10–100 times their original size (Jorgensen 1992). In most oviparous species, the ovary, nearly undetectable in the nonbreeding season, increases to nearly fill the body cavity with yolked eggs, a process wherein ovarian mass increases to represent up to 30% of the total body mass in some taxa. In such species a gonadosomatic index (GSI, i.e., ovarian mass divided by body mass) provides a convenient indication of the onset of the breeding season (Licht et al. 1983, Itoh et al. 1990) and, by extrapolation, the proportion of breeding females in a population.

Tertiary follicle counts have been used as measures of reproductive activity in band-tailed pigeons (*Patagioenas fasciata*) (March and Sadlier 1970) and mourning doves (*Zenaida macroura*) (Guynn and Scanlon 1973). Ankney and MacInnes (1978) were able to distinguish a group of large (>20 mm diameter), highly vascularized preovulatory follicles from smaller (<10 mm) ones (Fig. 2) and thereby estimate potential clutch size in a sample of snow geese (*Chen caerulescens*) shot as they arrived in nesting areas. Because these estimates of ovulation rate are collected at necropsy, they can be analyzed with reference to other data such as carcass weight, nutrient reserves, and blood hormone concentrations.

Courtship and Estrus.—Follicular development and yolking of eggs is accompanied by increased secretion of estrogen from large ovarian follicles and onset of breeding behavior that ultimately brings male and female together to fertilize eggs. Elaborate courtship behaviors are obvious and well known in many species of vertebrates. These include calling of male frogs, toads, and passerine birds and visual displays such as the head-bob/dewlap extension of the male green anole (*Anolis carolinensis*) (Crews 1980). In other groups including salamanders, reptiles, and mammals, social status and readiness to breed may not be communicated in obvious vocal or visual displays but through pheromones and olfactory communication, behavior that is not readily observed by biologists. Pheromones, which are released by specialized glands (e.g., cloacal glands in salamanders and skin glands in many snakes) (Norris 1997), attract and activate reproductive behavior in the opposite gender. In the red-sided garter snake (*Thamnophis sirtalis parietalis*), the loss of attractivity and receptivity after mating is also communicated by a mating pheromone (Mendonca and Crews 2001).

Wildlife biologists have found that captive breeding programs may be required when prospects for natural reproduction are diminished, as with endangered species such as the California condor (*Gymnogyps californianus*) and black-footed ferret (*Mustela nigripes*). Zoos holding threatened or endangered species have begun to use more advanced techniques such as artificial insemination and embryo transfer. Estrus is the behavioral state of sexual receptivity associated with elevated estrogen immediately preceding or coincident with ovulation. Detection of the time of estrus relative to the time of impending ovulation is essential to success of nearly all captive breeding programs. Artificial insemination requires placement of sperm into the vagina within a relatively narrow time period within 6–24 hours of ovulation. This can be accomplished in large species by monitoring follicular development near the time of estrus by laparoscopy or ultrasonography (Ginther 1990).

Hormonal changes that occur throughout the estrous cycle induce changes in the relative proportion of leukocytes and types of epithelial cells in the vaginae of rodents

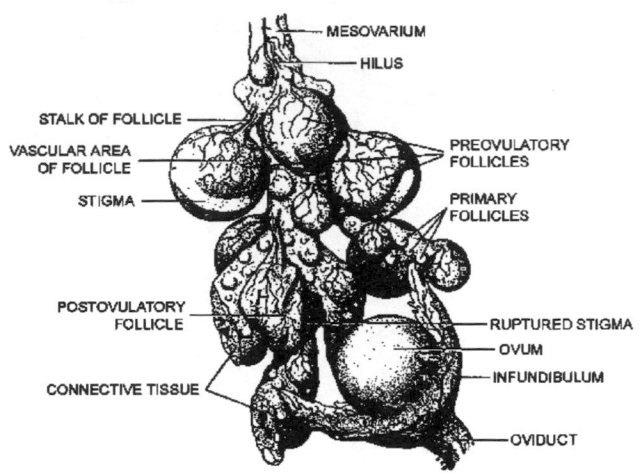

Fig. 2. Avian ovary showing a presumptive clutch (group of preovulatory follicles) within a hierarchy of follicles. Also shown is a postovulatory (collapsed) follicle with a ruptured stigma and an ovum entering the infundibulum of the oviduct (copied with permission from Nelsen 1953).

and certain other mammals (Fig. 3). A rise in circulating estradiol that occurs just prior to estrus stimulates a rapid proliferation and sloughing of keratinized epithelial cells into the lumen of the vagina, a condition indicative of estrus. Because each stage of the cycle is characterized by a particular vaginal cytology, estrous cycles can be monitored, and time of estrus can be predicted (Box 1). The technique, first described for domestic rodents (guinea pigs, rats, and mice, [Zarrow et al. 1964]), has been applied to diverse species including pine voles (*Microtus pinetorum*) (Kirkpatrick and Valentine 1970), American beaver (*Castor canadensis*) (Doboszynska 1976), domestic dogs and cats (Stabenfeldt and Shille 1977), coyotes (*Canis latrans*) (Kennelly and Johns 1976), and Virginia opossums (*Didelphis virginiana*) (Jurgelski and Porter 1974).

Ovulation and Embryonic Development

Perhaps the one reproductive parameter of greatest importance to natality and recruitment in all vertebrates is ovulation rate. Fortunately, it can be measured directly, or indirectly, with accuracy in most species.

Postovulatory Follicles.—After ovulation and release of mature eggs into the oviduct, the collapsed wall of the ovarian follicle in most vertebrates does not form a corpus luteum (CL), as it does in viviparous reptiles and mammals. Instead, postovulatory follicles (POF) regress, the process being completed in many avian species within a month after ovulation (Payne 1973). However, in some species, such as the ring-necked pheasant (*Phasianus colchicus*), POF persist for months as small (1–2 mm), pigmented (reddish brown) structures that can be viewed macroscopically (Fig. 2). Kabat et al. (1948) reported a high correlation between number of eggs laid and number of POF counted in captive pheasants killed up to 100 days after ovulation, thus providing a potential method for estimating clutch sizes in summer from hens harvested the following autumn. However, Hannon (1981) found that POF in blue grouse (*Dendragapus obscurus*) could not be counted macroscopically beyond approximately 25 days of age, although they could be used to distinguish laying from nonlaying hens shot during the hunting season.

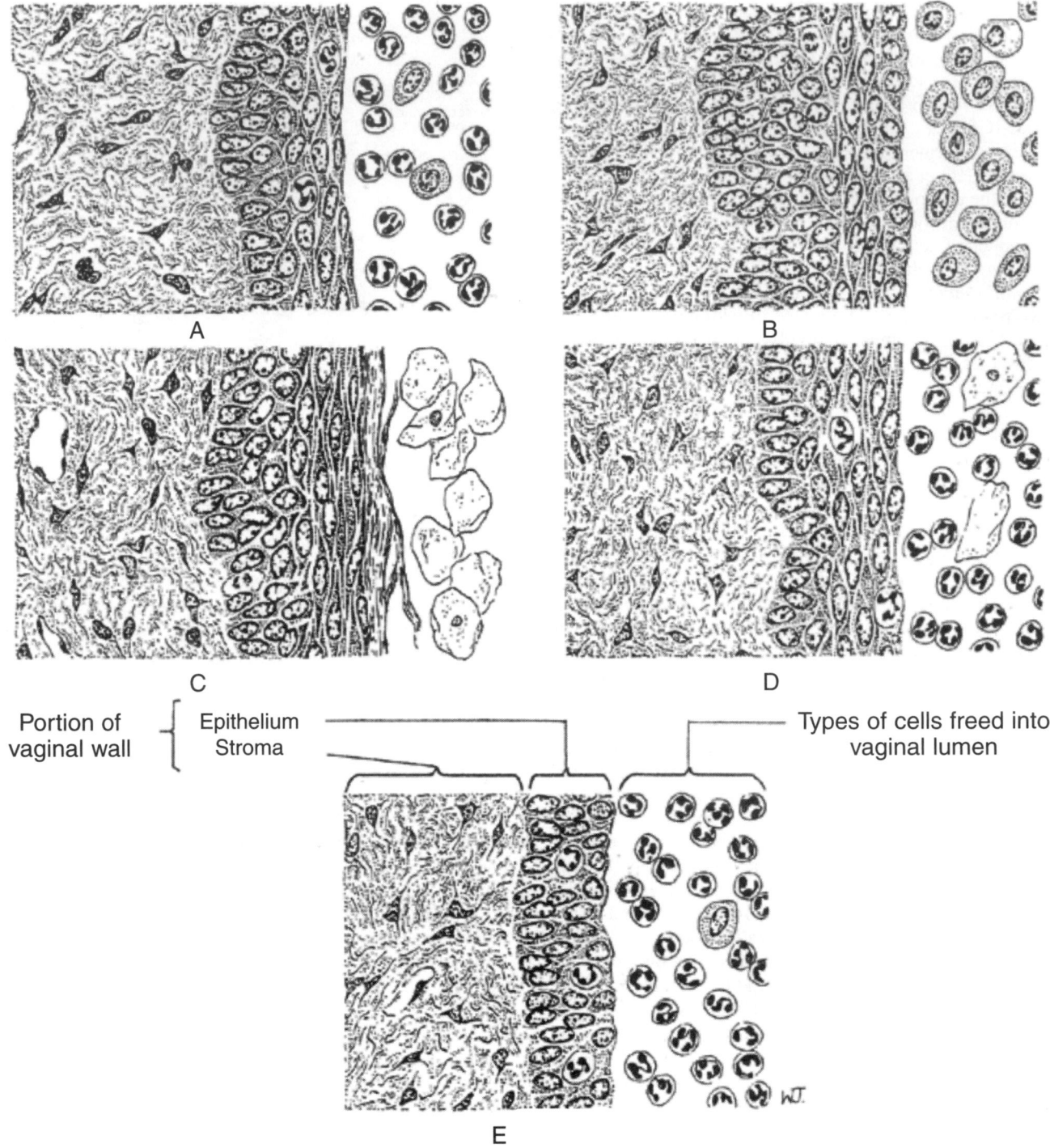

Portion of
vaginal wall
{ Epithelium
Stroma
Types of cells freed into
vaginal lumen

Fig. 3. Sections through the vaginal wall of the rat illustrating changes in the proportions of 2 types of epithelial cells and leucocytes that are released into the lumen of the vagina during each stage of the estrous cycle. (A) diestrus: a predominance of leucocytes; (B) proestrus: primarily nucleated (basal) epithelial cells; (C) estrus: an abundance of keratinized epithelial cells; (D) metestrus; (E) a female that had been ovariectomized for 6 months, i.e., diestrus (copied with permission from Turner and Bagnara 1976).

Observation of the avian ovary need not be limited to necropsies. Laparotomy has been widely used for identifying the sex of monomorphic birds that are captured live in mist nets and other types of traps (Risser 1971). An incision is made on the left side to expose the left testis or ovary, the latter being distinguished by the presence of follicles (Bailey 1953). The incision is small and the procedure can be accomplished in the field providing that appropriate surgical procedures are used (Wingfield and Farner

1976). Although an accurate classification or count of pre-ovulatory follicles is not feasible under such conditions, laparotomy can provide useful information on the stage of follicular development and proportion of birds nearing the egg laying stage. Avian gonads and other internal organs also can be examined through laparoscopy.

Clutch Size.—Estimation of clutch size; i.e., the number of eggs in a clutch, is by far the most popular and practical method of estimating ovulation rate in oviparous verte-

Box 1. Characteristic vaginal cytology for each stage of the estrous cycle and procedures for collection and staining of cells from the vagina.

The estrous cycle is a sequence of changes in ovarian activity and physiology of the reproductive tract punctuated with recurring periods of sexual receptivity (estrus) and ovulation. Although estrous cycles of different species vary considerably in length (from a few days to several weeks) and in the timing of cytological changes around estrus, the following description of the 4 to 5-day estrous cycle of the laboratory rat (adapted from Turner and Bagnara 1976) is reasonably representative of the 4 stages in other species that exhibit cyclic vaginal cytology.

Diestrus – This is a relatively long stage (60–70 hrs) that extends into pregnancy if fertilization occurs or into anestrus during the nonbreeding season of many wild mammals. CL begin to regress and progesterone levels decline late in this stage. Leukocytes migrate through the thin vaginal mucosa and appear as the predominate cell type in vaginal smears (Fig. 3A).

Proestrus – This stage, which precedes estrus and lasts for 17–21 hours, is also known as the follicular phase in species with longer estrous cycles. It is characterized by growth of preovulatory follicles, elevated estrogen levels, and swelling of the uteri. Nucleated epithelial cells dominate the vaginal smears collected at this time (Fig. 3B).

Estrus – This is the period of heat, peak estrogen levels, and ovulation; sexual receptivity is high and limited to this period, which lasts for 9–15 hours. The vaginal epithelium proliferates rapidly, causing the upper layers to exfoliate into the vaginal lumen. Vaginal smears taken at this time are dominated by keratinized (wrinkled) epithelial cells with low numbers of nucleated epithelial cells and leukocytes (Fig. 3C).

Metestrus – This stage, which lasts for 10–14 hours in the rat, begins with formation of CL following ovulation and is characterized by elevated progesterone levels. Metestrus and diestrus are generally known as the luteal phase in species with longer estrous cycles. Large numbers of leukocytes invade the vaginal lumen and often appear clumped around a few keratinized epithelial cells in the vaginal smear (Fig. 3D).

Vaginal Smear Procedure
1. Appropriate restraint for collection of the smear varies with size and behavior of the animal under study, but many species, ranging from mice to opossums in size, can be handled by grasping the tail. The animal is allowed to stand on the top of a bench or a cage while the tail is raised to expose the vaginal orifice. With this approach, the animal's struggling is reduced and focused on escape, which directs the head (and teeth) away from the handler.

2. To collect cells from the vaginal lumen, a cotton swab is moistened with physiological saline and inserted into the vagina, rotated and removed. Cells are transferred by rolling the tip of the swab over the surface of a microscope slide. Alternatively, cells can be collected by vaginal lavage, which is the recommended approach for mouse-sized animals. With this procedure, the tip of a fire-polished Pasteur pipette or medicine dropper containing a drop of physiological saline is inserted a few millimeters into the vagina. The saline solution is aspirated several times to rinse the vaginal lumen and collect cells. A drop of the aspirated cell suspension is then placed on a microscope slide to dry.

3. The dried vaginal smear may be fixed by immersing the slide in methanol and allowing the smear to dry.

4. The smear is then stained by immersion in a methylene blue solution for 10–15 minutes. After the smear is rinsed gently with water and dried, it is ready for microscopic examination.

Reliable monitoring of estrous cycles by vaginal cytology requires that observers be able to recognize 3 types of cells found in the smears (Fig. 3A, B, C).

Polymorphonuclear Leukocyte – A small cell (less than half the size of epithelial cells) with a large, lobed nucleus and little visible cytoplasm. This cell is represented by small, dark-staining, C-shaped nuclei in vaginal smears (Fig. 3A).

Nucleated Epithelial Cell – This large, rounded cell with a prominent nucleus (basal cell) appears in greatest numbers during proestrus but can be found in smears collected during all stages of the cycle (Fig. 3B).

Keratinized Epithelial Cell – This is a large, squamous cell with a wrinkled, "potato chip" appearance. The nucleus is degenerate and often not visible, even in stained preparations. It is present in such large numbers at estrus that a vaginal lavage takes on a milky appearance (Fig. 3C).

brates. However, locating the nest is a challenge, particularly with many species of frogs and salamanders. Even when nests or egg masses are obvious, difficulty may be encountered in developing unbiased sampling procedures that permit projection of estimates to the population level or unit area of habitat. In species where nests and egg masses can be reliably located, number of nests, their distribution, and survival to time of hatching are recorded but seldom the number of eggs per egg mass. Enumeration of the tadpole and larval stage is more commonly recorded and used as an index of reproductive rate and hatching.

Clutch size has been most extensively studied and applied to population ecology in avian species. Most birds lay up to one egg per day immediately prior to incubation. Release of the egg from the ovary (i.e., ovulation), precedes laying or deposition of the egg by approximately 26 hours. Thus, close observation of a laying bird provides immediate, real-time data on ovulation rate and an opportunity to study the temporal relationships among courtship behavior, copulation, ovulation, and associated hormone changes.

Avian nests found early in the incubation period provide not only a good estimate of number of eggs laid but also a basis for estimating egg loss and hatching success. Furthermore, sampling procedures normally provide estimates of nest density, which in turn can be used to calculate size of the breeding population of females in monogamous species. In such cases, estimates of reproductive rate and

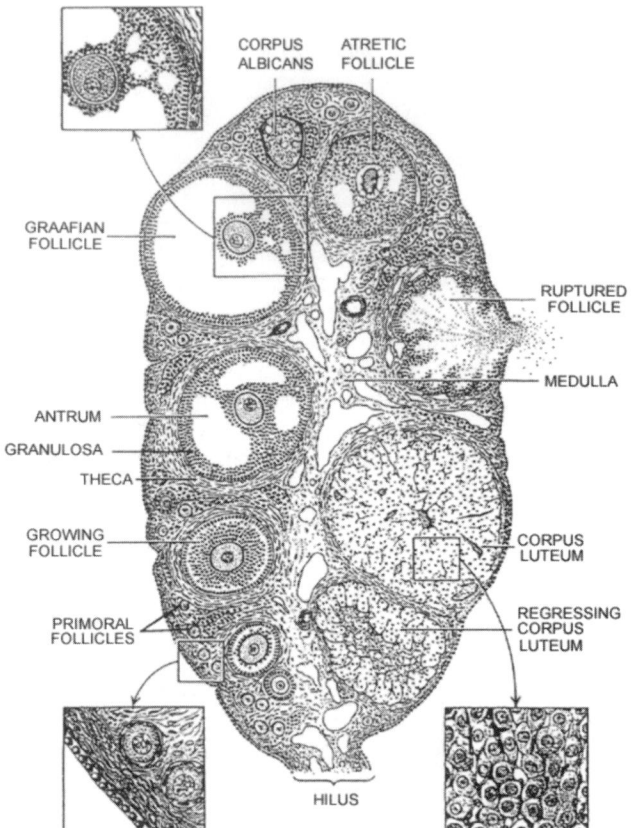

CORPUS ALBICANS   ATRETIC FOLLICLE

GRAAFIAN FOLLICLE

RUPTURED FOLLICLE

MEDULLA

ANTRUM

GRANULOSA

THECA

GROWING FOLLICLE

CORPUS LUTEUM

PRIMORAL FOLLICLES

REGRESSING CORPUS LUTEUM

HILUS

Fig. 4. Drawing of the mammalian ovary illustrating (in clockwise progression) follicular development (from primordial to Graafian follicle), ovulation, development of a corpus luteum (CL), and regression of the CL. The ovum is released with follicular fluid from the ruptured follicle (copied with permission from Turner and Bagnera 1976).

population structure are available allowing valid estimates of gross natality to be calculated.

Clutch size has been estimated in relatively few amphibians. More often numbers of nests or egg masses per area or habitat type are recorded. Crouch and Paton (2000) found these data more useful than estimates of the number of calling males as an index to abundance of wood frogs (*Rana sylvatica*). However, even with frogs that lay obvious egg masses, the number of eggs is most often expressed in 10s or 100s and seldom with estimates of mean and variance.

Follicular development (Leyton and Valencia 1992) and clutch size have been estimated for a large number of reptiles. It is possible to visualize even partially calcified eggs in the oviduct with X-ray photography and, thereby estimate time of ovulation and future clutch size (Gibbons and Green 1979). However, the short and long-term effects of radiation exposure on the young remain largely unknown. Vitt (1992) summarized studies of 26 species of squamate reptiles in the Caatinga of Brazil; clutch sizes across species were primarily in the range of 2–15 (maximum of 31) and positively correlated with body size within some species (Abell 1999, King 2000). Many reptiles, including turtles, lay more than one clutch per season. Congdon and Gibbons (1996) provide clutch size data on nests (>2,500) of 3 species of turtles, part of a long term, multifaceted study of community structure and dynamics in southern Michigan.

Nesting behavior and clutch size have been studied extensively in several species of sea turtles (Cheloniidae).

Their nests are concentrated in traditional nesting beaches and, thus, can be located with relative ease. Nests are the focus of sea turtle biology because all other phases of the life cycle occur in the open ocean and are largely unavailable for study. Most species require more than 20 years to reach maturity and have complex, multiyear reproductive cycles with evidence of delayed fertilization. Females lay from 2–5 clutches during a season. Owens (1995) recommended establishment of colonies of adult turtles held captive in large natural ponds with beaches to study these events in greater detail. This could be particularly valuable in clarifying details of male reproductive biology and temporal relationships between insemination and fertilization in a number of sea turtle species. Clutch size in sea turtles usually exceeds 100 (Miller 1997) and shows a positive correlation with body size of the female, at least in green (*Chelonia mydas*) and loggerhead turtles (*Caretta caretta*) (Ehrhart 1995). Although largely peripheral to the scope of this chapter, it should be noted that Cheloniidae is 1 of 19 families of reptiles with species in which gender determination is temperature-dependent (Zug et al. 2001). For example, if the average incubation temperature in the nest of many species of turtles exceeds approximately 30 C, nearly all young will be female, while the opposite effect is seen in some lizards and alligators (Nelson 2000).

Because the avian egg contains all nutrients and energy required by young from conception through the immediate post-hatching period, egg size and quality are major factors affecting hatching success and survival of avian young as clearly demonstrated in studies of yolk and albumen content of eggs of snow geese (Ankney 1980). Beckerton and Middleton (1982) found that increasing protein content (from 7.6 to 20.1%) in isocaloric diets of ruffed grouse (*Bonasa umbellus*) was associated with linear increases ($P < 0.025$) in a series of 9 reproductive parameters ranging from clutch size and egg weight to chick survival. Vangilder and Peterle (1981) observed a reduction in eggshell thickness and proportion of yolk contained in eggs laid by mallards (*Anas platyrhynchos*) fed either crude oil or DDE.

Ovarian Function and Ovulation in Mammals

Mammalian eggs are microscopic (10–30 μm), retained within the female reproductive tract and, therefore, cannot be easily counted. Direct enumeration of the number of eggs released in a given estrous cycle requires flushing eggs from the oviduct and/or uterus with isotonic medium and examining the resulting fluid microscopically. This approach is impractical for most wildlife investigations and seldom used except for embryological studies, or intensive studies of reproductive physiology such as those involving embryo transfer. Instead, ovaries are examined for follicular development or evidence of ovulation such as the presence of corpora lutea (CL, also the abbreviation for the singular, corpus luteum) and related scar structures.

Ovarian analysis requires a basic understanding of anatomy and physiology with respect to the events preceding and following ovulation. The mammalian ovary contains a life-long supply of primary oocytes (in prophase of meiosis) at birth, contained within small, primary follicles (Fig. 4). During each estrous cycle, a small fraction of these follicles begin growing more rapidly and develop a fluid-filled cavity or antrum (Norris 1997). These growing

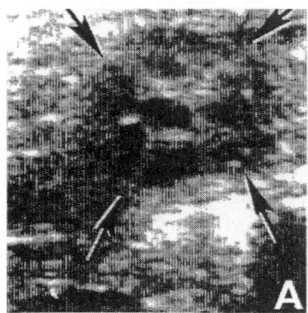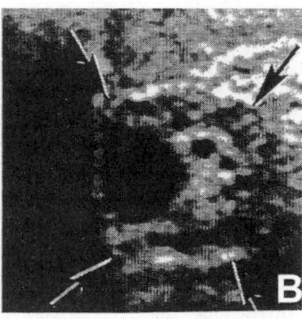

Fig. 5. Ultrasound images of ovaries in cattle; arrows mark the periphery of the ovary. (A) Three medium follicles (5–7 mm in diameter) are visible as dark, round objects. (B) Several small (2–3 mm) follicles are visible to the right of a large (12 mm) follicle on this ovary (copied with permission from Pierson and Ginther 1988).

follicles secrete increasing amounts of estrogen, which stimulates estrus and, indirectly, ovulation in spontaneous ovulators. Some of these antral (Graafian) follicles reach precisely the appropriate stage of preovulatory development to respond to a surge in luteinizing hormone (LH) secretion at estrus and ovulate. Most follicles, however, do not reach the preovulatory state, but instead undergo atresia, a degenerative process leading to disassociation of the granulosa layers of the follicle and death of the oocyte. Thus, a dynamic balance of follicular development and atresia affects the ovulation rate in any given estrous cycle.

Ovulation results in rupture of the follicle that leaves a corpus hemorrhagicum (the ovulation point or blood spot) and initiates immediate luteinization of thecal and granulosa cells of the follicle wall (i.e., they enlarge and sequester lipids). This process results in filling of the cavity and the formation of the CL (Fig. 4), a transient endocrine gland that secretes progesterone, a hormone essential for support of pregnancy.

If fertilization or pregnancy fails, the CL regresses and a new estrous cycle begins with growth of preovulatory follicles. However, if conception occurs and embryos implant in the uterus, CL persist and secrete large amounts of progesterone throughout a substantial portion of the gestation period. CL of pregnancy become large, often occupying much of the volume of the enlarged ovary (Fig. 4). Prior to, or coincident with parturition, CL begin to regress and progesterone secretion declines sharply.

Laparoscopy and Ultrasonography.—Ovarian analysis of wild mammals is usually conducted on material collected during necropsy of carcasses obtained at hunter-check stations or other sources, such as traffic accidents. However, with application of fiber optics to surgical instruments, internal examination of live animals has become safer and more convenient through a technique known as laparoscopy. The abdominal wall is punctured with a large needle canula through which a fiber optic scope (2–10 mm diameter) is inserted. Organs can be manipulated with a probe inserted through a second canula. With this technique, it is possible to observe ovarian follicles and CL as well as uterine swellings. The animal must be anesthetized, but incisions, *per se*, are not made, which minimizes surgical trauma and risk of infection. An extensive review of laparoscope methodology is presented in Harrision and Wildt (1980). Although laparoscopy is widely used in medicine and animal science, applications in wildlife re-

search have been limited. Nelson and Woolf (1983) used a portable generator and laparoscope to observe ovaries of white-tailed deer (*Odocoileus virginianus*) captured or immobilized in the field. No mortalities or complications related to this procedure were observed in 20 radio-collared deer monitored after the operation. Laparotomy and laparoscopy both require special equipment and training and are recommended only in situations where (1) multiple observations on the same animals are required, as in pen-based experiments; (2) the animal under study is rare or endangered; or (3) the animals are valuable and little is known of their basic physiology, e.g., zoo animals.

Echoes of high frequency sound (3–8 mHz), processed by real-time, computerized video displays, can also be used to reveal internal morphology. This technique, known as ultrasound or ultrasonography and widely used in human medicine, is recognized as a practical and reliable approach to monitoring estrous cycles and gestation in livestock and several wild species, such as bottlenose dolphins (*Tursiops truncatus*) (Williamson et al. 1990), red deer (*Cervus elaphus*), rhinoceros (*Diceros bicornis*), giraffe (*Giraffa camelopardalis*), and gaur (*Bos gaurus*) (Adams et al. 1991). It is particularly effective in visualizing antral follicles, because the liquid phase absorbs ultrasound and appears black in contrast to surrounding tissue that emit strong ultrasound echoes. Pierson and Ginther (1987) achieved remarkable success in cattle (Fig. 5). Follicles >2 mm in diameter were measured and counted, and growth of individual follicles (5–15 mm) was monitored in cows (Sirois and Fortune 1988). Ultrasonography with this level of resolution appears to have potential in monitoring ovarian activity in larger carnivores and ungulates without use of invasive surgical procedures. It has also been used extensively to count and measure ovarian follicles in gravid sea turtles (Kuchling 1999).

Enumeration of Corpora Lutea.—Follicle counts will not predict ovulation rate in mammals. However, the ovary develops an unambiguous sign of ovulation, the CL that, in most species, grows to occupy most of the volume of the ovary. In large mammals such as domestic cattle, the CL can be palpated through the rectum with a gloved arm and hand. This procedure, routinely used in the dairy and beef industry, has limited utility in wildlife studies because of size limitations, although it has been used on elk (Greer and Hawkins 1967).

CL can be counted, and ovulation rate estimated, in medium to large mammals through gross (or with the aid of a dissecting microscope) examination of sliced ovaries obtained at necropsy (Box 2) (Fig. 6). This approach has been applied widely to many species, including beaver (Provost 1962), moose (*Alces alces*) (Simkin 1965), red fox (*Vulpes vulpes*) (Oleyar and McGinnes 1974), and eastern cottontail rabbits (*Sylvilagus floridanus*) (Zepp and Kirkpatrick 1976). Accessory CL (i.e., unovulated, luteinized follicles) and other structures unrelated to ovulation can, at times, be distinguished by size and appearance.

Counts of CL provide an accurate measure of ovulation rate, but only an index to number of young in utero. This is because CL form during the normal course of each estrous cycle whether or not conception occurs. Even though most animals collected from the wild with active CL will be pregnant, each ovulated follicle forms a CL whether or not the egg from each follicle is fertilized and

Box 2. Preservation of tissues and gross ovarian analysis.

Preservation of Tissues at Necropsy

Postmortem changes are slowed considerably at low temperatures (e.g., 4 C), and organs may be frozen before subsequent gross examination. However, ice crystals that form in the cytoplasm ruin cells for microscopic study. If histology is planned, organs and tissues must be placed in a fixative solution at necropsy.

Fixatives are used prior to histology to (1) prevent purification, (2) coagulate protein, and (3) protect the tissue against shrinkage and distortion in subsequent procedures. Buffered 10% formalin (1:10 dilution of 40% formaldehyde) is used widely, but it is only one among many options. A histology manual (e.g., Humason 1979) should be consulted for specific recommendations. The volume of fixative should exceed that of the tissue by 5 or 10 times to avoid excessive dilution of the fixative by water diffusing from the tissue.

Gross Examination of Deer Ovaries

1. Ovaries are removed by cutting the mesovarium, the mesentery that suspends the ovary in the body cavity, near the ostium of the oviduct. Ovaries are more easily manipulated if some mesovarium remains with the ovaries, and left and right ovaries can be identified later if extra mesovarium is routinely left on the ovary from one side.

2. After ovaries have been in a fixative such as formalin for 36 hours, they will harden sufficiently to withstand slicing. Each is removed from the fixative and rinsed thoroughly in tap water. Latex gloves should be worn to reduce damage to skin on the hands.

3. An ovary can be secured by grasping the mesovarium close to the ovary with curved forceps or hemostat.

It is then sliced along the long axis with a scalpel or razor blade, cutting toward the mesovarium and forceps (Fig. 6). With practice, horizontal slices of about 2 mm thickness can be cut, stopping just before the mesovarium is reached. In this way, the sliced ovary will stay together like pages of a book, ready for thorough, repeated examination. Hawley et al. (1982) described a razor-blade device used to slice moose ovaries into uniform 1.5-mm sections.

4. Ovaries collected during the breeding season will contain a number of follicles of mixed size and, perhaps, recently ovulated follicles or new CL with ovulation points still evident. New CL of pregnancy grow to near full size (7-mm diameter) within the first 2–3 weeks after ovulation and eventually occupy most of the ovarian volume during pregnancy in deer. Thus, they can be "followed" through several slices from one side of the ovary to the other. The sliced surface is solid, cheesy in texture and creamy white in color. The color varies from yellowish to gray in other species.

5. Far less evident are the small copora albicantia (CA), pigmented scars of the regressing CL of the previous pregnancy (Cheatum 1949). Each slice of ovary must be carefully examined on both sides for these small (1 to 3-mm diameter) rust-colored structures, which are often compressed into triangular or crescent shapes by surrounding follicles and growing CL. Color is the primary distinguishing characteristic, but this can vary from dark yellow to deep brownish orange.

6. If the ovary is to be saved for further macroscopic or microscopic examination, it should be stored in 70% ethanol to prevent excessive hardening.

---

develops. Thus, if the fertilization rate in a given species is low or if embryonic or fetal losses are high, CL counts will overestimate number of young produced. For example, the Virginia opossum has a high ovulation rate (30 CL/ovary/cycle) (Fleming and Harder 1983) but gives birth to only 10–20 young and weans 6–8. Although conception rates in most species are much higher than for opossums, fertilization rates and in utero survival vary considerably among species and must be identified for each separately (Brambell 1948).

Ovarian Analysis of Deer.—All CL leave scar tissue in the ovary as they regress. In most mammals they are visible only in microscopic examination as whitish bodies of connective tissue known as corpora albicantia (CA). However, the large, long-lived CL of pregnancy in cervids regress slowly after parturition and are grossly visible as pigmented CA (sometimes called corpora rubra) (Cheatum 1949) (Box 2). Ovaries of deer are most often collected at hunter-check stations in October–December. This is often before all does in a population have had an opportunity to ovulate and before fetuses are visible in utero. Therefore, considerable attention has focused on CA as a basis for estimating number of fetuses carried to term in the previous pregnancy (preceding spring).

The value of CA counts in estimation of average litter size in previous pregnancies depends on knowledge of the

fertilization rate and longevity of the CA. The fertilization rate (fetuses/CL) in deer is high and remarkably constant (85–90%) (Roseberry and Klimstra 1970, Barron and Harwell 1973, Woolf and Harder 1979). Unfortunately, the longevity of CA is variable, sometimes remaining grossly visible for more than a year. Identifying the age of CA through histological examination (Mansell 1971) would largely eliminate biases in estimation of previous litter sizes, but this is seldom feasible for management surveys.

Potential errors associated with CA data, particularly ambiguities concerning number of reproductive seasons represented, have led to reduction in use of this technique for assessing reproductive rate in deer. This is unfortunate because the method has great utility in estimating the percentage of fawns breeding in a population. With few exceptions, the maximum ovulation rate for fawns that reach puberty and ovulate is one ovum per female. Thus, yearlings that are killed during the hunting season or in traffic accidents during July through February will yield reliable CA data because, for all practical purposes, only 2 possibilities exist: 0 or 1 CA per doe. The proportion of females that conceive in their first year reflects the nutritional status of the herd and varies from zero (Woolf and Harder 1979) to a high of 77–82% (Nixon 1971, Haugen 1975). This is an important demographic parameter because the 6-month age class is the largest in any population and, there-

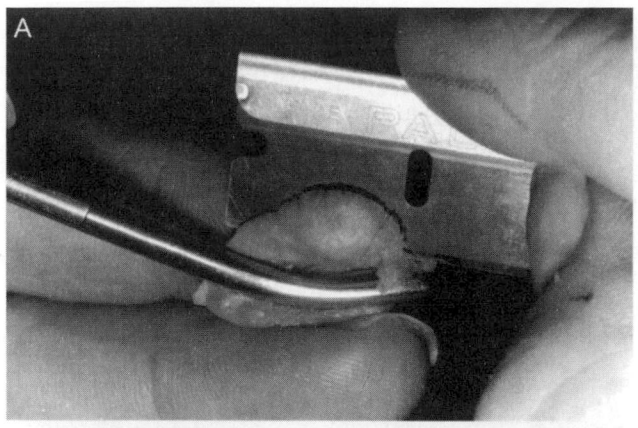

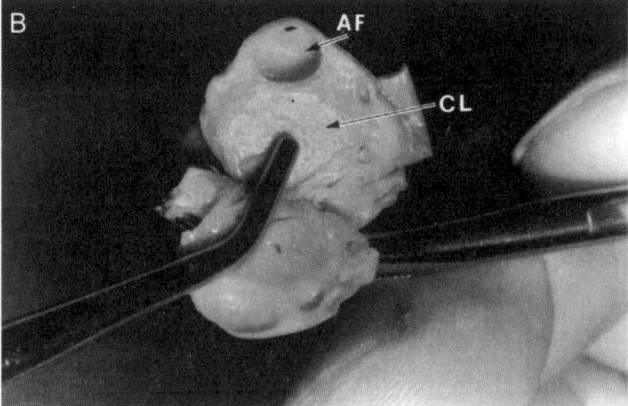

Fig. 6. Procedure for slicing a fixed ovary with a razor blade (A) and a view of the sliced ovary showing an antral follicle and a CL (B) (photographs by Dave Dennis, The Ohio State University).

fore, one that has great potential for impact on natality, population growth, and sustainable yield (Harder 1980).

Uterine Analysis in Reptiles and Mammals

Viviparous reptiles and mammals retain developing young in utero and, thus, present evidence of reproductive performance equivalent to clutch size in oviparous vertebrates. Enumeration of embryos or fetuses in utero has long been a popular and convenient measure of the reproductive performance of a population. Popular, because the number in utero, especially during the third trimester of gestation, is often a reliable indicator of the number of young that will be born, i.e., litter size. Uterine examination for embryos or fetuses is convenient, particularly in later stages of gestation, because fetuses are grossly visible and can be reliably counted by hunters or personnel handling animals killed on highways. The entire uterus with fetuses may be collected and frozen or fixed for later study, or it can be inspected on location. Crown-rump length measurements can be used to estimate age of white-tailed deer (Armstrong 1950) and coyote fetuses (Kennelly et al. 1977) and, by backdating, to estimate breeding dates. The primary sex ratio for a population can be estimated from examination of fetuses, a parameter of practical value in population models and of considerable interest among theoretical and experimental ecologists (Trivers and Willard 1973, Austad and Sunquist 1986, Gosling 1986).

Fetal counts are most often done at necropsy but, in many instances, this information must be obtained from living animals, such as with investigations of rare and endangered species or animals in zoos. Uterine swellings, indicative of fetuses, and CL of pregnancy can be counted in living animals by laparotomy. This approach has been used on cottontails (Murphy et al. 1973), white-tailed and mule deer (*Odocoileus hemionus*) (Zwank 1981), and elk (Follis et al. 1972). Ultrasound readings were used to successfully diagnose pregnancy during the last trimester of gestation in mountain sheep (*Ovis canadensis*) (Harper and Cohen 1985) and pronghorn (*Antilocapra americana*) (Canon et al. 1997). Several non-invasive methods, based on hormonal and biochemical changes in blood, are available for diagnosing pregnancy.

Birth and Parental Care of Young

Nest Success.—The number of young per female is the most ecologically important reproductive parameter that can be measured. It is the basis for calculating gross natality and can be obtained with reasonable accuracy with many avian species and some herptiles. If the location of nests and clutch size are known, the number of live young can be obtained by repeated inspection of the nest. This is the basis for the Mayfield method of estimating nest success of birds (Dinsmore and Johnson 2005). The eggs of most viviparous reptiles are laid in spring and hatch by late summer, but in a number of turtles; e.g., painted turtles (*Chrysemys picta*) (Breitenbach et al. 1984), emergence of young from the nest is delayed until the following spring when foraging conditions are presumably more favorable (Fig. 7).

Amphibians, particularly frogs, exhibit the greatest diversity of modes of parental care among terrestrial vertebrates. What might be viewed as a typical pattern in north temperate regions (i.e., eggs deposited in vernal pools and hatching into free-foraging tadpoles) is just 1 of 27 different modes recognized by Zug et al. (2001). Seemingly every possible pattern has been observed: from tadpoles emerging from eggs laid on tree leaves and dropping into ponds or streams to eggs that are carried in the dorsal pouch of the female, which develop directly into froglets. These diverse patterns represent fascinating natural history and opportunities for expanding knowledge of traditional reproductive ecology of a group that is undergoing an alarming decline in diversity and abundance (Semlitsch 2000). The challenge is to devise search and sampling procedures that produce estimates useful for population models. The most common approach for estimating number of young at birth in amphibian populations involves use of funnel traps for tadpoles and larvae (Adams et al. 1997) or setting of pitfall traps along a drift fence that encircles a breeding pond (Semlitsch et al. 1996).

The nests of many oviparous and viviparous species (some lizards, snakes, and mammals) cannot be located with statistical validity. Thus, the number of young born must be inferred from data collected *in utero* or, for some frogs, other parts of the body. Ovarian and uterine analyses described in some detail for white-tailed deer could be developed for other viviparous species. More studies of mammals and reptiles are needed to establish the relationship between ovarian scars of CL to the number of young carried and born. Thus, ovaries collected from females shortly after they gave birth might provide a measure of litter size. The extent to which uteri of viviparous reptiles might reveal early implantation sites as indicators of potential litter size is largely unknown.

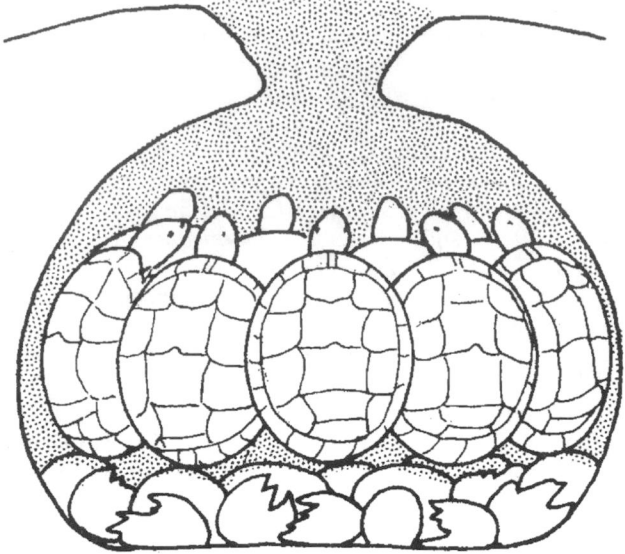

Fig. 7. Arrangement of painted turtle hatchlings in an overwintering nest (copied with permission from Breitenbach et al. 1984).

Crop Glands.—Crop gland development is an index of reproductive activity that can be examined at necropsy. Doves and pigeons of the family Columbidae, feed their young on a curd-like material ("pigeon milk") produced by desquamation of epithelial cells lining the crop (Levi 1969). Development of the crop glands of pigeons and doves is readily apparent in both males and females by macroscopic appearance and increased weight of the crop between the 9th day of incubation and the 14th day post hatching (Levi 1969, Mirarchi and Scanlon 1980) (Fig. 8). March and Sadlier (1970) described macroscopic changes in appearance of the crop glands of band-tailed pigeons classed as inactive, growing, active, and declining. Because mourning doves breed throughout much of the year, crop glands from birds shot in early fall hunting seasons can indicate the proportion of birds that are incubating or rearing young. However, Books-Blenden et al. (1984) cautioned that crop gland regression might be prolonged in late summer, particularly in males, producing an overestimation of the proportion of nesting doves in the autumn harvest.

Placental Scars.—These are pigmented areas of uterine tissue marking sites of previous placental attachment (Fig. 9). Their formation, described by Deno (1937) and Martin et al. (1976), is limited to taxa with deciduous placentae (Wydoski and Davis 1961). Erosion of the uterine endometrium by the embryonic trophoblast and an interdigitation of uterine and chorionic tissue is such that endometrial tissue is torn away when the placenta is expelled at birth (i.e., the placenta is deciduous) (Vaughan et al. 2000). As the new uterine endometrium grows over this wound, stagnant pools of blood become trapped, and the hemoglobin in the red blood cells is degraded to hemosiderin (an iron-containing pigment) by macrophages. The entrapped hemosiderin remains visible as a placental scar for varying lengths of time.

Species known to develop prominent placental scars belong primarily to the mammalian orders Insectivora, Chiroptera, Lagomorpha, Rodentia, and Carnivora. However, scarring has also been described in such divergent taxa as elephants (Elephantidae) (Laws 1967), and it is

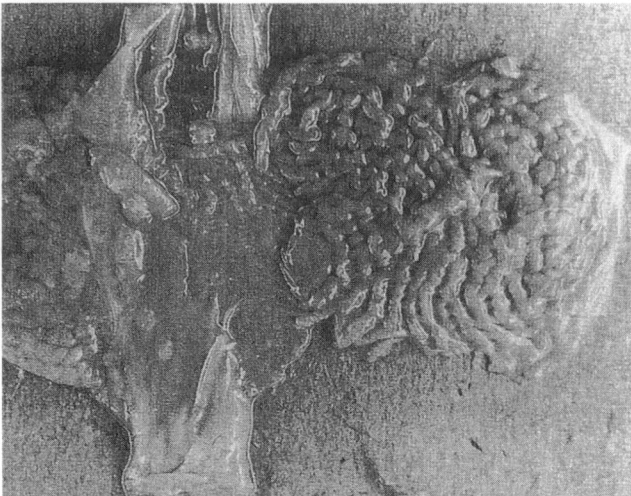

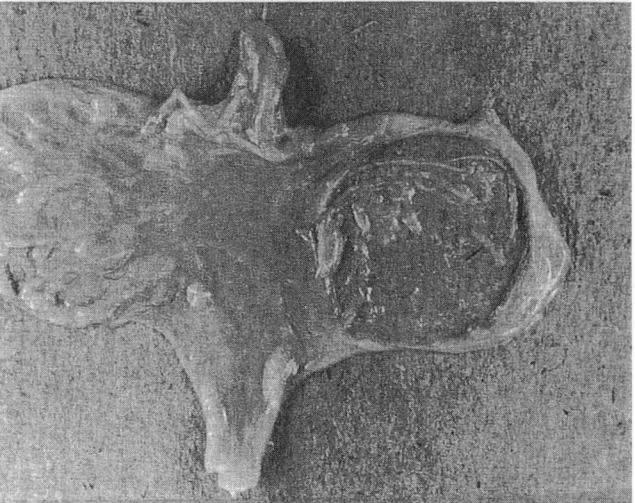

Fig. 8. Active (upper) and inactive (lower) crop glands from the mourning dove (photographs by R. E. Mirarchi).

possible that some squamate reptiles, with mammalian-like chorioallantoic placentae (Blackburn 1993), also develop placental scars. Litter size has been estimated from placental scars in a variety of carnivores including brown bears (*Ursus arctos*) (Hensel et al. 1969), raccoons (*Procyon lotor*) (Sanderson 1950), and gray fox (*Urocyon cinereoargenteus*) (Oleyar and McGinnes 1974). Placental scars are most useful in mammals that have only 1 or 2 litters per year such as beaver (Henry and Bookhout 1969) or gray squirrels (*Sciurus carolinensis*) (Nixon et al. 1975); the reliability of the method has been recently confirmed in the European hare (*Lepus europeus*) (Bray et al. 2003). Observations of smaller rodents, which have several litters in rapid succession, often entail problems in separating scars into "sets" representing different litters or pregnancies (Rolan and Gier 1967, Martin et al. 1976).

In many species, placental scars can be seen easily in fresh, thawed, or preserved tissue without special treatment. They stand out as darkened spots or bands in the uterine horns. If females are collected soon after parturition, the tissue around the old implantation sites will still be swollen. With increasing time after parturition, however, the scars fade and additional steps must be taken to clearly see them. The first step, at least with small mammals, is to compress the uterine horns between 2 microscope slides (or with

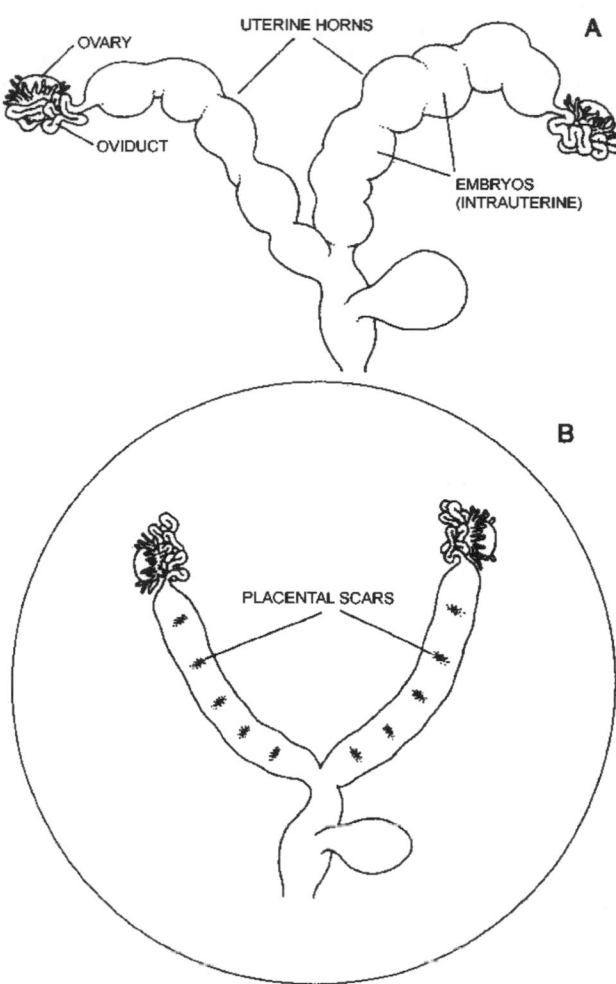

Fig. 9. Uterine swellings of a pregnant white-footed mouse (*Peromyscus leucopus*) (A) and postpartum uterine horns compressed between the lid and the inverted base of a petri dish to reveal placental scars (B) (drawings by Dave Dennis, The Ohio State University).

larger uteri, between the nested lid and base of a petri dish (Fig. 9). The scars can then be viewed on a dissecting scope and, with backlighting, it is possible to distinguish and count scars in sets. With larger species it usually is necessary to expose the endometrium of the uterus by cutting longitudinally along the length of each horn with scissors. The scars then appear as darkened bands or discs in the uterine lumen. In some species, placental scars are indistinct and special clearing or staining procedures are required to make them more visible (Orsini 1962, Henry and Bookhout 1969, Humason 1979, Bray et al. 2003).

Lactation and Nursing.—The transition from late gestation to lactation is a critical period in the reproductive cycle of mammals. Mammary glands of lactating females grow and fill with milk, which can be expressed from the teats of all but the smallest species. If milk cannot be expressed from a female at necropsy, the mammary gland should be sliced open and inspected for pools of milk within the tissue. Nipples of lactating females become swollen and pinkish, and often the fur immediately surrounding the nipple is thin or absent. These and other indications of lactation are only indirect signs that a female is nursing or has recently weaned young. They should be verified, preferably through measurements of females with known reproductive histories,

including those nursing young. Some progress has been made in this regard through studies of teat length of yearling white-tailed deer in autumn. Sauer and Severinghaus (1977) concluded that any yearling with 1 of 4 teats less than 10 mm was without young and those with one teat longer than 15 mm was nursing or had recently weaned a fawn. This index needs additional testing and verification, but it is particularly attractive because data can be collected from field-dressed carcasses brought to hunter check stations. A recent study of wild and captive fisher (*Martes pennanti*) (Frost et al. 1999) critically evaluates both placental scars and teat length as indicators of reproductive success.

Because marsupials lactate and carry young in their pouch for an extended period (50–60 days in the Virginia opossum), they are attractive subjects for study of the effect of nutritional status on near-weaning litter size (Hossler et al. 1994) and other aspects of reproductive ecology (Harder and Fleck 1997). Given the reality of substantial neonatal mortality in many wildlife populations, an estimate of the proportion of females in a population that is lactating is more relevant to reproductive success than parameters measured earlier in the reproductive cycle (e.g., ovulation rate). Coupled with estimates on average litter sizes, lactation indices could substantially improve estimates of net natality (i.e., the number of young weaned per female).

Reproductive Patterns and Performance in Males

Reproductive activity in male vertebrates, within the breeding season, is decidedly noncyclic and less complex than in females, particularly in regard to assessment of reproductive performance. Spermatogenesis begins at puberty and, except for periods of seasonal regression, testes normally remain active in production of sperm and secretion of testosterone throughout the life of the individual. Sperm are produced by the millions, well in excess of the few hundred that might be required to fertilize even the largest mass of frog eggs. In most species, reproductive success of fertile males is ultimately based on the number of females mated or eggs fertilized. This is often a function of courtship behavior or the outcome of interactions with competing males.

Because testes increase in mass with onset of spermatogenesis, testis weight is most often used to monitor the onset of breeding and as an index to the number of breeding males in populations of herptiles, birds, and mammals. Warm spring weather signals the onset of breeding in the Mexican leaf frog (*Pachymedusa dacnicolor*) when active spermatogenesis is coupled with increased testis weight and plasma androgen levels (Bagnara and Rastogi 1992). Testicular enlargement coincides with ovarian activation in some species of salamanders (Semlitsch 1985), but not all (Marvin 1996). Most reptiles have an *associative* reproductive pattern in which breeding is associated with elevated androgen secretion and spermatogenesis. However, some squamates, such as the red-sided garter snake, have a *dissociative* pattern. In this species, sperm produced during summer are stored by the male for use during the following spring breeding season when testes are actually regressed and androgen levels are low (Fig. 10).

Testis Weight and Spermatozoan Counts.—The gonads and reproductive tracts of birds generally remain in a regressed state during the nonbreeding season but increase markedly during the breeding season. For example, the testis of a mature male white-crowned sparrow (*Zonotrichia*

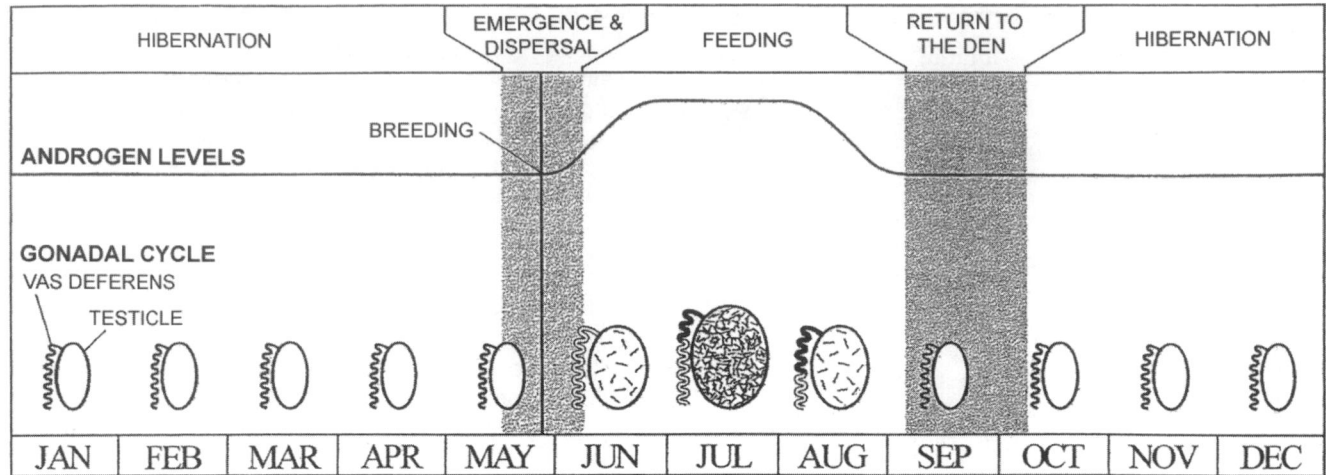

Fig. 10. The annual gonadal-reproductive cycle of the red-sided garter snake illustrates a dissociative reproductive pattern. Males mate with females in spring when testes are small and circulating concentrations of androgens are relatively low. Spermatozoa produced during the summer, when testes enlarge and androgen levels are high, are stored in the epididymis until the following spring (adapted with permission from Crews and Garstka 1982).

leucophrys) will grow from <10 to >600 mg during the breeding season (Wingfield and Farner 1980). Seasonal growth and recrudescence of testes and accessory glands of mammals are much less pronounced and more variable across taxa than in birds. In some, such as tammar walla-by (*Macropus eugenii*) and brush-tailed possum (*Trichosu-rus vulpecula*), testis weight changes little throughout the year, although prostate weight and testosterone levels show marked seasonal variation (Gilmore 1969, Inns 1982). Most seasonally breeding mammals, however, show noticeable to marked increases in testis size as well as androgen levels (Mirarchi et al. 1977*b*). Weight and volume (by water displacement in a graduated cylinder) can be obtained at necropsy, but 2-dimensional measurements of scrotal testes on live males also provide a valid index of testicular volume and reproductive status. For example, the volume of testes of white-tailed deer (measured on both live and dead animals) increased from a low of 50 cc in June to >150 cc in November (breeding season) during the same time that plasma testosterone increased from basal (near zero levels) to >3 ng/ml (McMillan et al. 1974).

The presence of spermatozoa in the testes or epi-didymides provides evidence of reproductive status and is particularly useful for examining age of puberty or onset of seasonal breeding. Spermatozoan counts also have been used to examine seasonal differences in male reproductive activity (Mirarchi et al. 1977*a*), social stress (Sullivan and Scanlon 1976), and exposure to environmental contaminants (Sanders and Kirkpatrick 1975).

An estimate of sperm density or total spermatozoa per testis or epididymis may be obtained by homogenizing a known mass of sliced tissue in a blender or tissue homogenizer with an appropriate culture medium, such as Hank's solution. Triton X-100 (J. T. Baker, Phillipsburg, New Jersey) can be added (0.01 to 0.05% by volume) to prevent foaming in the blender (Amann and Lambiase 1969, Sullivan and Scanlon 1976). Alternatively, testes or sections of epididymides of small species can be thoroughly minced with scissors and rinsed repeatedly with a known volume of culture medium to collect spermatozoa. An aliquot of homogenate or rinse is then removed and added to both chambers of a standard hemocytometer. Sperm density rela-

tive to tissue mass can then be calculated with the appropriate dilution factors (Box 3). A test for the presence of motile spermatozoa involves cutting the tail of the epididymis from a freshly killed specimen and making a smear on a slide for microscopic examination to detect sperm (Kibbe and Kirkpatrick 1971). Morphology and motility are commonly used to assess the quality of sperm in human fertility clinics, livestock management, and zoo studies of endangered species, e.g., cheetahs (*Acinonxy jubatus*) (Wildt et al. 1993). However, these measures are made on sperm in semen that, in wildlife species requires anesthesia and electroejaculation, an approach that is seldom taken in studies of wild animals.

Testicular Biopsy.—Counts of spermatozoa are usually made from tissues or fluid collected at necropsy or in ejaculates. However, needle biopsy procedures offer an opportunity to obtain testicular tissue and spermatogenic cells from living animals. The animal is anesthetized and the surface of the scrotum is thoroughly cleansed and disinfected. A testis is punctured with a 19–22-gauge needle, carefully avoiding the epididymis (Sundqvist et al. 1986). Slight pressure applied to the testis or negative pressure in an attached syringe will ensure aspiration of tissue into the needle. The needle is then withdrawn from the testis and the material contained in the needle is spread onto a microscope slide, dried, and stained prior to examination of the cells. The biopsy smears are scored: low (1–2) when only sertoli cells or spermatogonia are present to high (9–10) when large numbers of mature spermatids are counted. This procedure, used in diagnosing human infertility, has been used with ranch mink (*Mustela vison*), in which up to 20% of the males are infertile. Mink with biopsy scores <7 are considered infertile (Sundqvist et al. 1986). Berndtson (1977) reviewed testis biopsy and other methods for quantifying mammalian spermatogenesis.

ENDOCRINOLGY OF REPRODUCTION AND STRESS
Background

The nervous and endocrine systems act in concert to coordinate physiological processes and behavior. Responses regulated by the endocrine system are generally slower and

Box 3. Procedure for estimating density of spermatozoa and other types of cells with a hemacytometer.

A hemacytometer is a thick, glass microscope slide with 2 identical counting chambers of known volume. It was originally developed to provide standard conditions for human blood cell counts but has found application in a wide variety of cytological work, including estimation of sperm density for assessment of male fertility. The highly polished floor of each counting chamber is gridded with fine lines spaced at exact intervals as shown below.

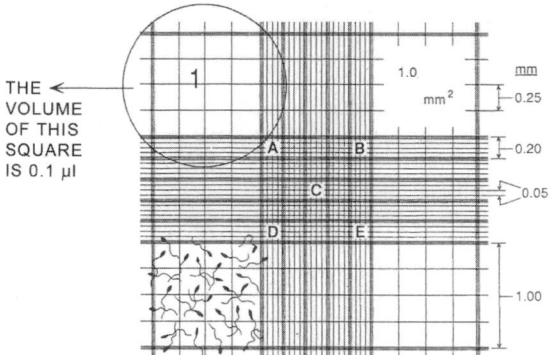

Ridges on the sides of the hemacytometer hold the cover slip exactly 0.1 mm above the floor of the counting chamber. Consequently, cells counted within a given section of the chamber are related to volume, and cell density can be calculated. Counts can be made on fresh, frozen or fixed material, but fresh material provides the option of rating spermatozoa for motility. In reality, a hemacytometer provides a convenient system of grids that can be readily applied to a wide variety of microscopic sampling problems.

Procedure

1. Spermatozoa may be obtained from a homogenized testis, but if mammalian sperm are to be evaluated for motility, they must be obtained from ejaculated semen or flushed from the tail of the epididymis. Semen or other material should be diluted with an appropriate culture medium such as Hank's solution rather than saline, particularly if motility is to be assessed. Medium and the hemacytometer should be held on a slide warmer at normal scrotal temperature, e.g., 35 C.

2. The source material is diluted with a known volume of medium and a drop is added to both chambers of the hemacytometer.

3. After spermatozoa have settled for 5 minutes, count the number of spermatozoa in sections A, B, C, D, and E of the center grid and multiply the total by 5 to obtain an estimate of the total number in the center grid (1 mm on a side or 0.01 cm^2). Alternatively, select 1 of the 4 corner grids (comprised of 16 squares) at random and count all spermatozoa with heads inside the perimeter lines. If sperm density is high (>40 cells/square), count within a randomly chosen row of 4 squares and multiply the total by 4 to obtain an estimate of the total in all 16 squares (0.01cm^2).

4. This procedure should be repeated in a grid in the other counting chamber to permit calculation of mean and standard deviation, and an estimate of counting precision.

5. The cover slip is held 0.1 mm above the floor of the counting chamber which, in this example, creates a chamber volume of $1 \times 10^{-4} \text{ cm}^3$ or $0.1 \text{ } \mu l$.

6. The concentration or density of sperm in the source material is calculated with the appropriate dilution factors. For example, a 150-mg epididymis is minced and rinsed with 600 μl of medium and a sample of the resulting cell suspension is placed in a hemacytometer. If 500 spermatozoa are counted in a 0.01 cm^2 section ($0.1 \text{ } \mu l$) of the hemacytometer; sperm density or concentration (C, i.e., number of spermatozoa per mg of epididymis) would be calculated as: $C = N \times D/0.1 \div S$; where N = number of spermatozoa counted in 0.1 μl of the hemacytometer, D = volume of medium used to rinse or dilute the sample, and S = volume or weight of the original sample. In this case, $C = 500 \times 600/0.1 \div 150 = 20,000$ spermatozoa per mg of epididymis.

of longer duration (hours and days) than those provided by the nervous system, which acts in the realm of seconds and minutes. Glands of the endocrine system respond to both internal signals and to external, environmental cues by secretion of hormones that are carried in the blood stream, usually to other parts of the body, where they have their effect. Environmental stimuli (e.g., photoperiod or social interaction) are relayed through a basal part of the brain, the hypothalamus, which responds by secretion of releasing factors, including gonadotropin releasing hormone (GnRH) that control the secretory activity of the anterior pituitary gland (Norris 1997). The anterior pituitary gland secretes several peptide hormones including follicle stimulating hormone (FSH) and luteinizing hormone (LH), which control gametogenesis and hormone secretion by the gonads. The pituitary also secretes adrenocorticotropic hormone (ACTH), which stimulates secretion of corticosteroids (e.g., cortisol and corticosterone) by the adrenal cortex. Control of circulating levels of hormones is achieved by feedback regulation. For example, when increasing blood levels of testosterone in a male exceed a threshold or set point in the hypothalamus, the release of GnRH is inhibited. Thus, less GnRH reaches the anterior pituitary, less LH is released and reaches the testes and, consequently, secretion of testosterone is reduced to appropriate levels.

Hormonal control of reproduction ultimately functions to coordinate development of the reproductive tract, expression of mating behavior, and gametogenesis so that sperm and eggs are brought together to accomplish fertilization and conception. Each stage in the reproductive cycle is controlled by a sequence of endocrine signals, which can be visualized with hormone profiles, i.e., plots of concentrations in blood (serum or plasma) over time. Although many hormones are involved, much has been learned of the reproductive processes in wildlife through study of a relatively few pituitary hormones and gonadal steroids (Table 1). The extent to which endocrine respons-

Table 1. Hormone data relevant to the assessment of reproductive activity in selected male (M) and female (F) terrestrial vertebrates. Hormone concentrations are pg/ml serum or plasma for estrogens and ng/ml serum or plasma for all others, except steroid conjugates in urine, which are expressed in µg, ng, or pg per mg of creatinine. Two concentrations indicate the approximate lows and highs associated with a given reproductive event.

Species (Gender)	Hormone	Change in concentration	Reproductive event	References[***]
Frog (M)	FSH	2–4	Peaks with spermatogenesis	1
	Estradiol	0–8	Peaks with FSH	
	Androgen[*]	0–10	High in recrudescence and breeding	
Bullfrog (M)	LH		Seasonal, highest at amplexus	2
(*Rana catesbeiana*)	DHT[**]	2–34	Seasonal elevation 2–4 × > T[*]	
(F)	LH	4–32	Surges at time of ovulation	2
Toad (F)	Progesterone	0.1–0.3	Low, highest prior to mating	3
	Estradiol	1000–3900	High, peak early in breeding	
Anole lizard (F)	Estradiol	500–2100	Lower during sexual receptivity	4
Lizard (F)	Progesterone	2–13	Rise from preovulatory to gravid state	5
Tortoise (M)	Testosterone	5–25	Low during mating and elevated during spermatogenesis	6
Sea turtles (F)	Estrogen	200	Highest prior to nesting	7
(general model)	Testosterone	300	Highest during mating	
	Gonadotropin	4	Surge levels at ovulation	
	Progesterone	12	Highest levels at ovulation	
Turkey (F)	Prolactin	90–709	Elevated during incubation, low in laying and brooding hens	8
White-crowned sparrow (F)	Estradiol	35–400	Increase with courtship and egg laying	9
Japanese quail (M) (*Coturnix japonica*)	Testosterone	0–5	Increase with daylength and onset of breeding season	10
Woodchuck (M) (*Marmota monax*)	Testosterone	0–3	Increased during breeding season	11
White-tailed deer (M)	Testosterone	0–3	Increased with hardened antlers and rut	12
Red howler monkey (F) (*Alouatta seniculus*)	Urinary progesterone	77–212	High in luteal phase of estrous cycle and highest during gestation	13
Little brown bat (F) (*Myotis lucifugus*)	Progesterone	7–136	Increased from early to late pregnancy	14
Woodchuck (F)	Progesterone	0–60	Progesterone higher in post-partum than pregnant females	15
White-tailed deer	Progesterone	0–6	Rises with CL formation and in early pregnancy	16, 17
White-tailed deer	Estrogens	11–295	Increase near parturition	18
Indian rhinoceros	Estrone sulfate	47–1	High at estrus and drops rapidly at ovulation	19
Okapi (*Okapi johnstoni*)	Pregnanediol-3-glucuronide	1–24	Rises with luteal phase of cycle (active CL)	20
Killer whale (*Orcinus orca*)	Estrone conjugates	0–35	Increases prior to presumptive ovulation	21
	Pregnanediol-3-glucuronide	0–100	Elevated during pregnancy	

[*] Testosterone (T) and related hormones; e.g., DHT and androstenedione

[**] Dihydrotestosterone (DHT)

[***]1- Polzonetti-Magni et al. (1998), 2- Licht et al. (1983), 3- Itoh et al. (1990), 4- Jones et al. (1983), 5- Norris (1997), 6- Kuchling (1999), 7- Owens (1997), 8- Wentworth et al. (1983), 9- Wingfield and Farner (1980), 10- Follett and Maung (1978), 11- Baldwin et al. (1985), 12- McMillin et al. (1974), 13- Herrick et al. 2000, 14- Buchanan and Younglai (1986), 15- Concannon et al. (1983), 16- Plotka et al. (1977), 17- Harder and Moorhead (1980), 18- Harder and Woolf (1976), 19- Kasman et al. (1986), 20- Loskutoff et al. (1982), 21- Walker et al. (1988).

es to chronic stress (i.e., corticosteroid secretion) affect reproductive processes is a long-standing question in wildlife population ecology. Thus, endocrine measures of stress are also considered in this section.

This introduction provides only a brief outline of the principles and terminology of reproductive endocrinology. Appreciation of information presented in this section will be enhanced with a basic understanding of the anatomic-functional axis consisting of the hypothalamus, pituitary, and gonads (HPG axis) as described in most introductory biology textbooks. More extensive presentations of principles and related primary literature are available in a number of references and textbooks including Van Tienhoven (1983), Austin and Short (1984), Tyndale-Biscoe and Renfree (1987), Bronson (1989), Norris (1997), Knobil and Neill (1998), and Nelson (2000).

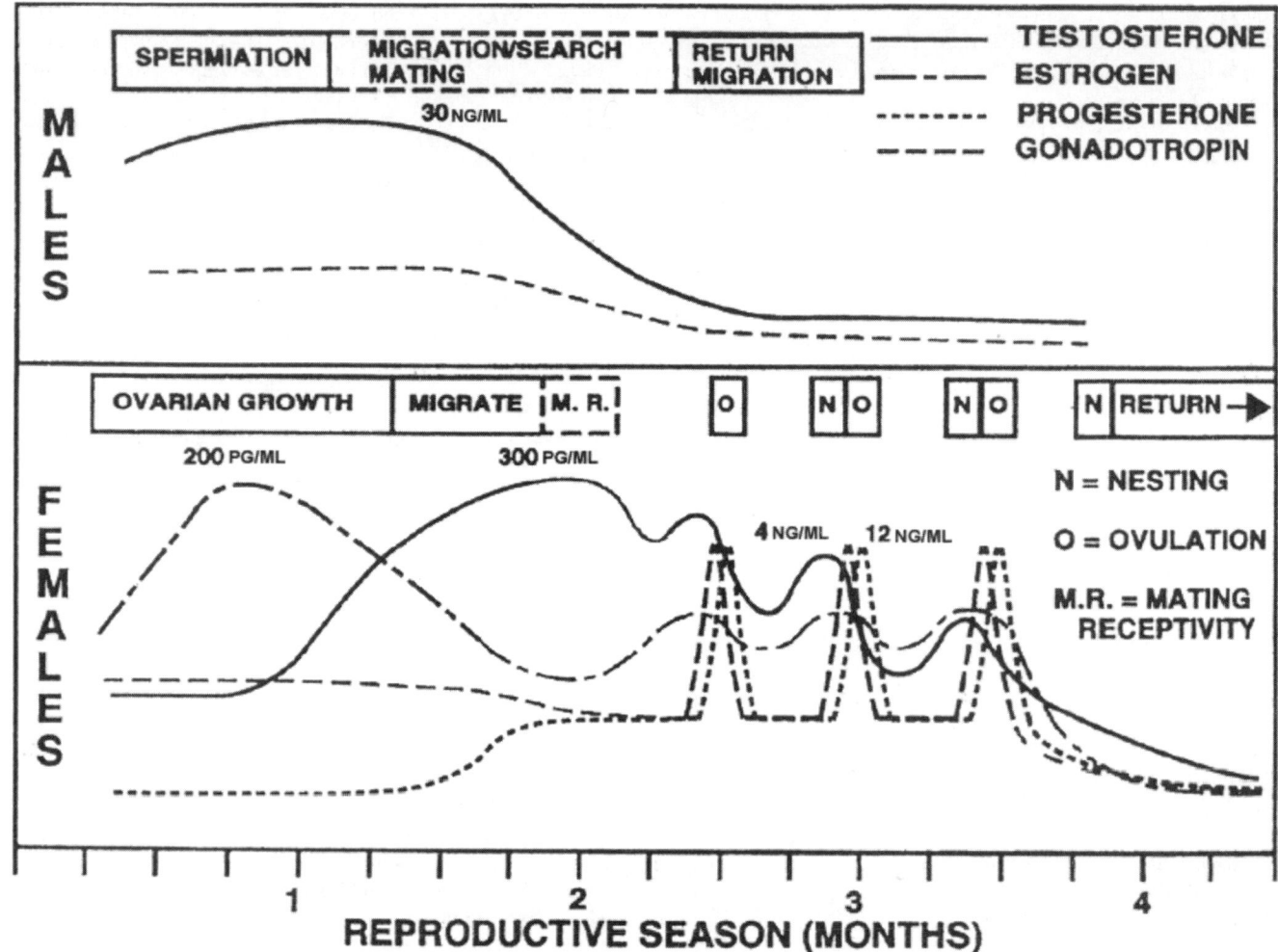

Fig. 11. A graphic model for endocrine control of reproductive events and behavior, generalized for both male and female sea turtles (copied with permission from Owens 1997).

Hormones and Reproduction

Hormones and Reproductive Cycles in Females.—Peak ovarian mass and numbers of yolked eggs in frogs generally coincide with peak levels of ovarian steroids at the time of amplexsus and oviposition, as in the Mexican leaf frog (Bagnara and Rastogi 1992). Similarly, in female reptiles with associated reproductive patterns, increased ovarian mass and elevated gonadal steroids also coincide with breeding behavior. One of the most thoroughly studied lizards in this group is the green anole. Unlike most lizards that ovulate about half of each clutch of eggs from each ovary, the green anole (and other species of *Anolis*) ovulate a single egg, alternately from each ovary, every 14 days. Females are receptive to males during the 7 days preceding ovulation when the estradiol to progesterone ratio is low (Table 1) (Jones et al. 1983).

Less is known about factors controlling breeding behavior in dissociative breeders such as the red-sided garter snake. Activation of courtship behavior in the male of this species does not depend on the presence of gonadal steroids, and for some time there was little evidence that females were different (Whittier and Tokarz 1992). However, Mendonca and Crews (2001) demonstrated that low levels of circulating estradiol must be present during hibernation if females are to be receptive upon emergence in the spring.

Following ovulation, the CL of both oviparous and viviparous lizards secretes progesterone (Norris 1997) (Table 1).

Owens (1997) synthesized much of the sea turtle literature on gonadotropins and gonadal steroids in a graphic model for endocrine control of reproductive events and behavior in both males and females. Estrogen is highest during follicular growth, rising slightly with each oviposition. Testosterone is also high during migration and the nesting period. Both gonadotropin and progesterone surge during ovulation of each clutch (Table 1, Fig. 11).

The sequence of hormonal signals responsible for the circadian cycle of ovulation and egg laying in birds is complex. A major component in the domestic hen is a positive feedback relationship between progesterone from the ovarian follicle and LH release from the anterior pituitary, which stimulates ovulation (Johnson 1986). Prior to ovulation elevated estrogen also induces courtship behavior (Fig. 12, Table 1) and stimulates mobilization of yolk precursors from the liver and their deposition in the egg while it is in the follicle (Van Tienhoven 1983). Incubation behavior and brood patch formation are stimulated by high prolactin levels in association with estradiol and progesterone (Fig. 12). Prolactin from the anterior pituitary also stimulates production of "milk" in crop glands of doves and pigeons.

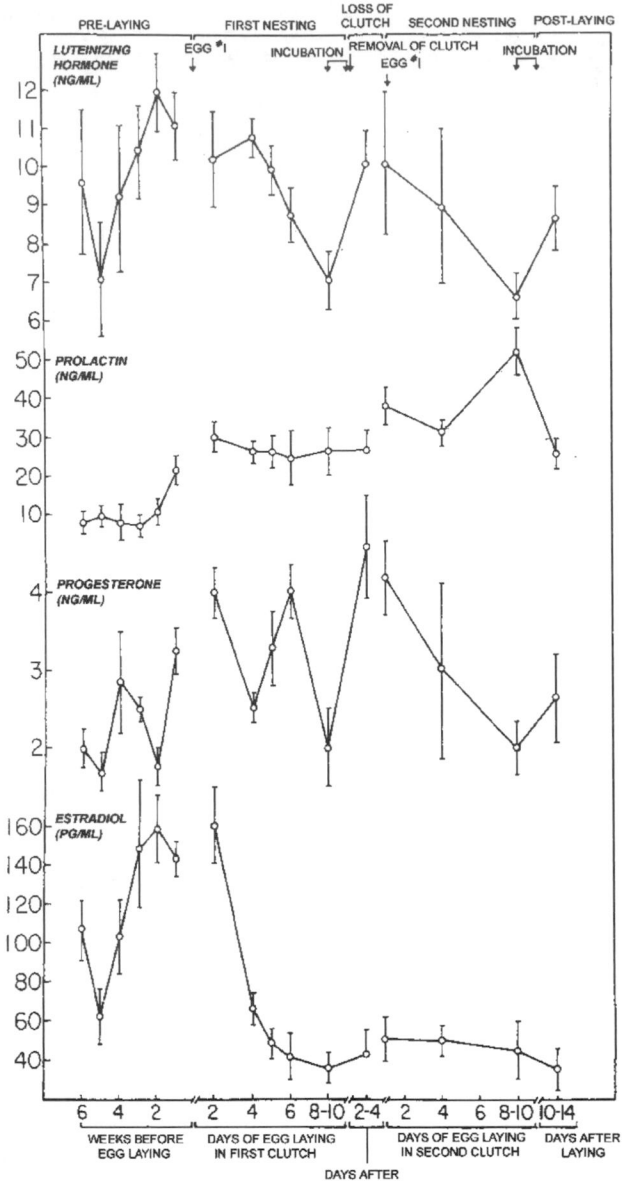

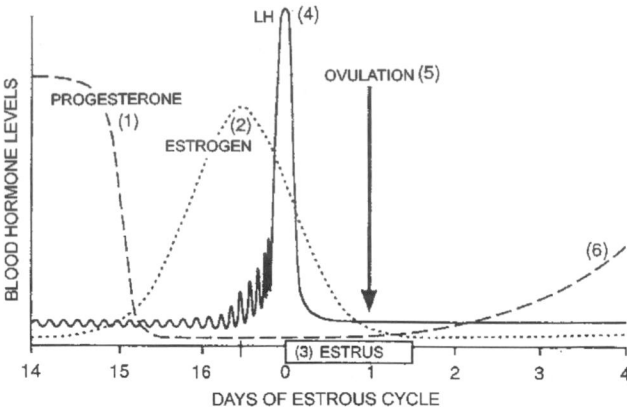

Fig. 13. Temporal relationships of estrus and ovulation to circulating levels of progesterone, estrogen, and LH during the estrous cycle of the ewe, which has preovulatory hormone dynamics similar to many mammalian species with spontaneous ovulation (copied with permission from Short 1972).

Fig. 12. Serum concentrations of luteinizing hormone (LH), prolactin, estradiol, and progesterone during the laying cycle of canvasback (*Aythya valisineria*) ducks (copied with permission from Bluhm et al. 1983).

Measurements of circulating hormones are useful in studies of the effects of toxic substances on reproductive performance of birds. Progesterone levels peaked earlier relative to oviposition in mourning doves treated with dietary polychlorinated biphenyls than in controls (Koval et al. 1987). Nonlaying canvasbacks had lower serum concentrations of prolactin and LH than laying hens. Progesterone levels in laying hens increased during the breeding season, while those in the nonlaying birds declined (Bluhm et al. 1983).

The estrous cycle of mammals is a sequence of interrelated physiological events in the hypothalamus, anterior pituitary, ovary, and reproductive tract marked by a period of sexual receptivity (estrus) and ovulation. Preovulatory follicles secrete large amounts of estradiol that stimulates estrus and a preovulatory surge of LH. The LH surge stim-

ulates ovulation and formation of the CL (Figs. 4, 13). This general pattern appears to hold true for many mammals as evidenced from data from such widely divergent taxa as tammar wallabies (Harder et al. 1985), rats (Nequin et al. 1979), deer (Plotka et al. 1980), and sheep (Hauger et al. 1977). The rise in estrogen around estrus confirms normal ovarian activity and is potentially valuable as a predictor of time of ovulation in mammals that ovulate spontaneously. This knowledge is essential for artificial insemination and embryo transfer, techniques that are being used with increasing frequency by zoos, endangered species programs, and modern game farms. Jacobson et al. (1989) achieved conception in 75% of 53 trials of artificial insemination in white-tailed deer.

Changes in estrogen levels prior to estrus and ovulation are often small, of short duration, and difficult to detect. In contrast, events following ovulation, namely CL formation and the luteal phase of the estrous cycle or gestation, are of relatively long duration (several days to months in larger species) and characterized by elevated levels of circulating progesterone (secreted by the CL and/or placenta) (Fig. 13). Therefore, useful progesterone profiles can be obtained with relatively low blood sampling frequencies that are feasible in many wildlife studies. If breeding is highly synchronized, much can be learned from single samples taken from animals soon after they are shot. In white-tailed deer, this approach revealed a shortened, nonfertile cycle that preceded the first estrus and normal luteal cycle during onset of the breeding season (Harder and Moorhead 1980).

Progesterone profiles are considered the most reliable means of monitoring the 15-week estrous cycles of captive Asian (*Elephus maximus*) and African elephants (*Loxodonta africana*) (Plotka et al. 1988). Until a validated, sensitive, and accurate progesterone radioimmonassay was applied to a long series of serum samples from the same cows (Hess et al. 1983), the now-documented 15-week estrous cycle of the Asian elephant was believed to be only 3 weeks long. More recently, LH and progesterone profiles in African elephants have revealed an anovulatotory luteinizing hormone (LH) peak followed by 3 weeks of low progesterone, ending in a small rise that precedes the next ovulatory LH surge (Kapustin et al. 1996). Thus, daily measurement of progesterone concentrations might be used to detect this small rise and predict the time of the next LH surge, ovulation, and optimal time for artificial insemination.

The practical value of progesterone data for detecting pregnancy in live animals has been widely recognized, particularly for larger species in which the gestation period extends well beyond the breeding season. Blood can be collected in the field from trapped or anesthetized animals and assayed later, whereas other techniques (e.g., laparotomy or ultrasonography) require transport of the animal or equipment. Care must be used in selection of drugs and other methods of restraint because they can affect progesterone levels. Plasma progesterone concentrations in pregnant white-tailed deer are generally above 2 ng/ml, whereas those of nonpregnant deer are <1 ng/ml (Abler et al. 1976). The potential errors associated with this generalization (Plotka et al. 1983) notwithstanding, properly validated progesterone assays have permitted accurate (<2% error) diagnosis of pregnancy in white-tailed and mule deer (Wood et al. 1986). Gadsby et al. (1972) reported higher progesterone levels in domestic ewes carrying 2 fetuses than in ewes with a single fetus.

The uterus and placenta secrete numerous nutritive and regulatory proteins during gestation, some of them unique to gestation and therefore useful in identifying pregnant animals. Wood et al. (1986) used a qualitative test for pregnancy-specific protein B (bovine) to identify (4% error) pregnant mule and white-tailed deer. Similar results were reported for this pregnancy test in mountain goats (*Oreamnos americanus*) (Houston et al. 1986) and elk (Noyes et al. 1997).

Spermatogenesis and Onset of Breeding in Males.—The marked growth of the testis in vertebrates during onset of the breeding season is associated with rapid increases in secretion of follicle stimulating hormone (FSH) and LH from the anterior pituitary gland and testosterone and other androgens from the testes (Fig. 14, Table 1). However, in bullfrogs, androgen levels show greater seasonal variation than testis size. High androgen levels in spring stimulate breeding behavior in frogs, while a peak in FSH and estradiol levels is associated with onset of spermatogenesis (Polzonetti-Magni 1998, Table 1). In most species, reproductive tract activation (increased size, sperm production, and androgen secretion) is closely associated with breeding behavior. However, some reptiles such as tortoise (*Gopherus* spp.) (Kuchling 1999) and red-sided garter snakes exhibit dissociative reproduction in which testosterone is relatively low during the spring mating season and elevated during spermatogenesis in late summer and early autumn.

In temperate regions of the world, photoperiod is the principle environmental cue for reproductive activation. In tropical regions where day length is nearly constant, other factors such as food stimulate reproduction. Gonad size and singing rate increased in male antbirds (*Hylophylax naevioides*) following addition of crickets to their diet, and even the sight (only) of live crickets increased their singing rate (Hau et al. 2000). Modern techniques permit hormone measurements of small blood samples (50–500 µl), volumes that can be obtained from small wild birds. This has facilitated diverse experiments in avian field endocrinology (Wingfield and Moore 1987). For example, circulating levels of testosterone in male song sparrows actively defending territories is elevated compared to those with

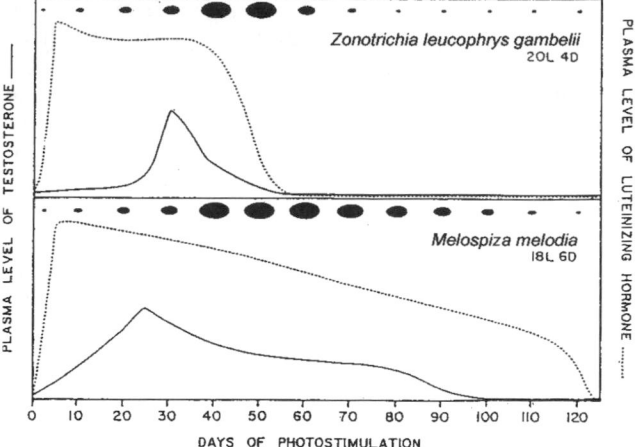

Fig. 14. Plasma levels of luteinizing hormone (LH), testosterone, and testis size (solid ovals) in photostimulated male white-crowned and song sparrows (*Melospiza melodia*) (copied with permission from Wingfield and Farner 1980).

uncontested territorial boundaries (Wingfield 1985). Transitory increases (to 1.6 ng/ml) of testosterone above year-round basal levels were recorded in the tropical male antbird during times of territory intrusions and social instability (Wikelski et al. 1999).

In mammals, circulating levels of testosterone and other androgens also increase substantially during the breeding season (Table 1), a requisite condition for full spermatogenic activity and breeding behavior; e.g., during the rut in white-tailed deer (McMillan et al. 1974) or during musth (an aggressive behavioral state) in Asian elephants (Cooper et al. 1990). In some species, such as the tammar wallaby (Catling and Sutherland 1980) and domestic livestock (Katongole et al. 1971), full seasonal elevation of testosterone appears to be dependent on direct association with females in breeding condition. If this occurs in other polygynous species, it would provide a potential method for identifying the dominant or reproductively active males, even in the absence of detailed behavioral observations.

Hormone Metabolites in Urine and Feces.—For many wild species, even pen-reared individuals, stress associated with restraint and veinupunctures often precludes collection of blood samples, so that even minimal information about normal ovarian activity is unavailable. Fortunately, another approach is available. Steroids (e.g., progesterone) are metabolized in the liver and excreted as conjugates (primarily sulfates and glucuruonides). During the last decade, considerable progress has been made in monitoring gestation and estrous cycles of several zoo species (e.g., rhinoceros, marmosets [*Callithrix* spp.], blackbuck [*Antilope cervicapra*], and pandas [*Ailuropoda melanoleuca*]) through assay of hormone metabolites in their urine and feces (Table 1).

Midstream collection is preferred for urine samples and many species, even killer whales, can be trained for this procedure. It is also possible to collect samples from some arboreal species urinating from tree branches. This approach was used with individually marked, free-ranging, red howler monkeys to monitor urinary progesterone concentrations (Table 1) and to develop progesterone profiles that characterize temporal features of the apparent 28-day estrous cycle and gestation in this species (Herrick et al. 2000). Individualized feces or urine can be collected from the floor of pens, small enclosures, or even open range. Kirkpatrick et al. (1988) described detailed validation experiments and procedures for estimation of estrone sulfate concentrations in soil soaked with urine by free-roaming feral horses with unique marks. Twelve of 15 mares with estrone sulfate >1.0 ug/mg creatinine later produced foals, whereas no mares with lower concentrations foaled. Fecal samples are convenient, because the source animal can be observed from a distance and the sample collected at extended intervals after defecation. Extraction of steroids from fecal samples may be more complex than extraction from urine (Loskutoff et al. 1982, Safar-Hermann et al. 1987), but efficient assay procedures have been developed for use on fecal samples from an array of mammalian and avian species (Wasser et al. 2000).

Control of Reproduction and Wildlife Contraception

The demand for nonlethal control of nuisance wildlife populations has driven research in contraceptive technology for more than 40 years, an effort that has benefited from developments in human medicine and animal science. Contraceptive trials have been conducted on a variety of species, including coyotes, a number of rodent and avian species, and even African elephants, but white-tailed deer and wild horses have been the primary focus of this research in North America. Similar efforts are underway with the eastern gray kangaroo (*Macropus giganateus*) in Australia (Nave et al. 2002). Many options are available for interrupting reproductive processes in wildlife, but most fall into 2 categories: hormonal and immunological intervention in females. Males are seldom the subjects of contraceptive programs, because in polygamous species, control of nearly all males in a population is required to achieve a meaningful reduction in conception by females.

Subcutaneous implants provide slow, prolonged release of hormone into circulation and, thus, have the potential to provide long-term (months to years) contraception. Implants of synthetic, progesterone-like compounds or progestogens, such as melengestrol acetate, are widely used to control reproduction in zoo mammals by suppressing estrus and ovulation. Bell and Peterle (1975) provided early evidence of the effectiveness of this approach in a population of white-tailed deer. More recently, promising results of long-term fertility control in gray kangaroos have been obtained with a related compound, levonorgestrel (Nave et al. 2002). However, even with long-acting implants, practicality is an issue, because animals must be captured for installation of the implants. Remote delivery of contraceptive in a ballistic implant (Jacobsen et al. 1995) might eliminate the need for restraining animals, but other logistical problems remain. Although hormones are released from implants at low, near-physiological levels, they have the potential to accumulate in tissues of treated animals and present an unknown health risk to wild animals and humans that might consume them.

Long-standing questions regarding the practicality of wildlife contraception prompted early research on oral application of contraceptive to a large, enclosed but free-ranging population of deer (Harder and Peterle 1974). However, regardless of efficacy and practicality of an oral

application, low specificity of bait systems entail unknown risks to nontarget species (Grandy and Rutberg 2002). This has discouraged research in this area.

Prostaglandin F_{2a} (PGF$_{2a}$), a hormone secreted by the uterus and other tissues, induces regression of the CL and is an important signal in hormonal control of parturition in mammals. The abortifacient effects of PGF$_{2a}$ have been applied with success in terminating pregnancy in white-tailed deer (Waddell 2001). One important advantage of using PGF$_{2a}$ for wildlife is that it is rapidly metabolized in the lungs and, thus, does not accumulate in tissues or present health risks for nontarget species or humans. The principle disadvantage of PGF$_{2a}$ is that effects are limited to a single reproductive season.

Immunocontraception has received much attention in recent years because it is less intrusive, physiologically, than hormone treatments and does not present a heath risk to nontarget species. Animal welfare groups have supported research in this area (Grandy and Rutberg 2002). Immunological methods can involve antibodies to hormones (e.g., GnRH, and gonadotropins), but most techniques are directed at preventing fertilization by interfering with binding of spermatozoa to the zona pellucida, which surrounds the egg. Stimulating production of antibodies against proteins in the porcine zona pellucida is, by far, the most popular approach. Effective immunocontraceptive technology is currently available for a number of species including wild horses (Kirkpatrick et al. 1997), white-tailed deer (Naugle et al. 2002), and elephants (Fayrer-Hosken et al. 2000). Animals injected with vaccines, often with dye marking darts, become infertile for periods ranging from 1 to 3 years. The problem is one of achieving adequate population control in free-ranging populations. Results of simulation analysis of data from trials on a suburban white-tailed deer population suggest that immunocontraception is useful only on small, localized populations with fewer than 100 breeding females (Rudolph et al. 2000). The literature on wildlife contraception has expanded considerably in recent years; several reviews are available including Miller et al. (1998), Fagerstone et al. (2002), and Kirkpatrick et al. (2002). Fagerstone et al. (2002) concluded that wildlife managers of the future will face 2 challenges: (1) integrating contraceptive methods with traditional approaches to population control, and (2) providing the public with accurate information about the feasibility of fertility control compared to lethal methods for reducing wildlife populations.

Endocrinology of Stress

Background and Effects of Stress on Reproduction.— Decades of research stimulated by Hans Selye's landmark paper on stress and human health (Selye 1936), have provided both the technical foundation and a conceptual framework for understanding the biology of stress. Stress is defined as a significant disturbance of homeostasis caused by marked or unpredictable environmental change (Wingfield and Raminofsky 1999, Nelson 2000). A stressor, in this context, is an environmental change or stimulus such as pain, fear, cold, blood loss, environmental contaminants, pathogenic microbes, and social tension (Selye 1976). Sudden, life-threatening disturbances (e.g., a predator attack) stimulate release of adrenalin from the adrenal medulla and the well-known "fight or flight" response.

Acute or short-term stress also activates the hypothalamic-pituitary-adrenal (HPA) axis wherein release of corticotropin releasing factor (CRF) from the hypothalamus stimulates secretion of adrenocorticotrophic hormone (ACTH) from the anterior pituitary. ACTH, in turn, stimulates secretion of adrenal cortex steroids (corticosteroids), including those that regulate glucose metabolism (i.e., glucocorticoids), primarily cortisol and corticosterone (Asterita 1985). This acute response is adaptive because it allows individuals to maintain essential functions (e.g., by elevation of blood glucose) in the presence of the stressor. However, prolonged, chronic activation of the HPA axis is associated with pathological conditions, such as gastrointestinal ulcers (Moberg 1985) and reduced reproductive performance.

Laboratory studies have clearly demonstrated the deleterious effect of stress on reproduction in a variety of vertebrates (reviewed by Pottinger 1999, Dobson et al. 2003). For example, social stress and subordination can lead to elevated corticosteroids (Sapolsky 1998) and alteration of reproductive function in some primates (Ziegler et al. 1995). Reduction of gonadotropin secretion has been associated with food restriction in some mammals (Bronson 1989), and overwintering stress in white-throated sparrows (*Zonotrichia albicollis*) (Schwabl et al. 1988). Stress of transport and hypoglycemia reduced LH pulse frequency and delayed the LH surge in ewes (Dobson and Smith 2000). Rivier and Rivest (1991) present a model that explains the roles of CRF, ACTH, endorphin, and corticosteroids in modulating the effects of stress on reproductive function.

Christian (1950) and colleagues were quick to recognize the potential relevance of Selye's (1946) observations for population ecology. They postulated that elevated corticosteroid levels interfered with hormonal control of reproduction and induced mortality in high-density populations (Christian 1963, Christian and Davis 1964). Numerous studies have addressed this controversial hypothesis and it now appears that emigration and other factors such as nutrition prevent most natural populations from attaining densities sufficiently high to evoke a pathogenic hormonal response that would be regulatory at the population level. Experiments with high-density snowshoe hare (*Lepus americanus*) (Windberg and Keith 1976, Vaughan and Keith 1981) and deer populations (Seal et al. 1983) support this conclusion. In contrast, studies that focused on segments of a population (e.g., gender or social status) have produced the clearest evidence for endocrine responses to social stress (Carrick 1963, McDonald et al. 1981, Sapolsky 1987), which suggests that more attention should be given to stress as a factor in the natural structure and functioning of populations.

Indicators and Measures of Stress.—Circulating levels of corticosteroids such as cortisol or corsticosterone provide a direct measure of the endocrine response to acute stress and, with radioimmunoassay, it is possible to measure hormone concentrations in relatively small (0.05–0.3 ml) plasma samples. Consequently, such measures are increasingly used to assess stress responses in wild animals; e.g., birds during spring migration (Landys-Ciannelli et al. 2002) or care of hatchlings (O'Reilly and Wingfield 2001), and to evaluate stress and welfare of laboratory animals (Broom and Johnson 1993). The major technical problem with such studies is that blood levels of corticos-

terone can rise rapidly within 2–3 minutes (Gartner et al. 1980), or less (Roy and Woolf 2001) following initial disturbance of the animal. Moreover, some species show clear, diurnal rhythms and even marked hourly fluctuation in plasma corticosteriod levels (Tapp et al. 1984). Corticosteroid responses to stress should be first measured under controlled laboratory conditions (Carruthers and Path 1983) before conducting field trials. In this way it is possible to assess the potential stress effect of acute environmental changes, such as changes in dove hunting regulations (Roy and Woolf 2001).

A wide range of measures is available for assessment of stress in free ranging and captive animals. Some are indicators of acute stress while others indicate chronic stress acting over a period of weeks or months. In planning research, it is useful to recognize stress indicators in 1 of 3 categories: (1) non-invasive—those that require little or no handling of animals, (2) invasive, and (3) and post-mortem. Non-invasive indicators include behavioral observations, food and water consumption, body weight, respiratory rate, and assay of hormones in saliva, urine, or feces.

Corticosteroids and other hormones are secreted into the blood and continuously metabolized in the liver and excreted in urine and feces. Because these metabolites accumulate during the hours between defecations, their concentrations in fecal samples represent an average of more variable corticosteroid concentrations in circulation. Fecal glucocorticoid concentrations show promise for assessment of stress in white-tailed deer (Millspaugh et al. 2002) and, because the subjects are undisturbed, the confounding effects of stress due to handling and blood collection are avoided. However, extraction and assay of hormone metabolites in feces is more complex and interpretation of results is more difficult than for hormones in blood. These and other factors to be considered in measuring stress with fecal glucocorticoids are reviewed by von der Ohe and Servheen (2002). Nearly all endocrine and immune (e.g., lymphocyte mitogenesis) indicators of stress are considered invasive because they require restraint of the animal for blood sampling. However, once installed, an indwelling, intravenous catheter allows for essentially non-invasive collection of blood samples.

Providing that animals are processed immediately after death, post-mortem examinations or necropsies provide a wealth of information, particularly if glands and organs can be examined for abnormalities (e.g., gastric ulceration) and histopathology. All the endocrine and immune parameters available in blood samples are available at this time.

Increased secretory activity of the adrenal cortex in response to stress is accompanied by an increase in size of the gland (Adams and Hane 1972). Methods for analysis of adrenal gland weight and morphology were reviewed in detail by Harder and Kirkpatrick (1996). Manser (1992) presented a comprehensive, yet concise and well organized, guide to assessment of stress in animals. Given the availability of this resource and several authoritative reviews on the biology of stress (Broom and Johnson 1993, Balm 1999, Nelson et al. 2002), it seems wise to conclude this section and emphasize that stress is a complex biological concept. Anyone who hopes to contribute in this field should first read widely and train, or at least consult, with established investigators, and then design their studies and experiments with the greatest of care.

Collection of Samples and Hormone Measurements

Blood Sampling Procedures.—Hormone concentrations can be measured in all tissue types with application of appropriate tissue homogenization and hormone extraction techniques, but blood is by far most commonly assayed. The goal in any sampling procedure should be to collect an adequate volume of blood quickly and efficiently while minimizing stress to the animal. Reaching this goal often requires administration of a sedative or anesthetic, although this step can be omitted for domesticated species or animals that have been conditioned to handling and appear less stressed when restrained.

The effect of restraint or anesthetics on hormone levels should be investigated with each species to be studied, and not just in studies of progesterone or adrenal hormones. For example, hormone concentrations in a series of plasma samples collected from bullfrogs recaptured in the field remained relatively constant, but if the frogs were held in a collecting sack, levels of gonadotropin and gonadal steroids began to decline within 2–4 hours, often to basal levels within 20 hours (Licht et al. 1983). Immobilization with succinylcholine chloride elevated circulating progesterone levels in white-tailed deer (Wesson et al. 1979), and certain anesthetics depressed serum concentrations levels of this steroid (Plotka et al. 1983). Apparently, stress from prolonged (15–45 min) restraint can induce significant release of corticosteroids, including progesterone (Plotka et al. 1983).

Blood samples can be collected from quiet animals fitted with an indwelling catheter to investigate the effects of restraint or anesthesia on blood hormone levels. Periodic samples will reveal the natural diel pattern of circulating levels, including episodic changes, which can be distinguished from those that might be related to stress of handling or anesthesia in the same animal. An alternative (and less desirable) approach is to collect blood samples immediately upon restraint of the animal. The animal can then be anesthetized or restrained with standard procedures for collection of blood samples at intervals over a period that would be in excess of the maximum required for routine collection. If the blood sampling procedure alters secretion of the hormone(s) under study, blood concentrations will change in successive samples relative to that in the initial sample. These experiments will identify the need to standardize timing of blood collection (from time of restraint or anesthesia) in situations where stress to the animal being sampled cannot be avoided.

Peripheral blood (i.e., from the heart or any vein not directly draining the endocrine gland under study) is usually collected from the jugular or a prominent leg or tail vein. The orbital plexus in the corner of the eye may be used to obtain small volumes from mice. The brachial (wing) vein is commonly used in birds, although Arora (1979) concluded the jugular vein was the best source of blood for Japanese quail. Blood collection from living animals should be performed only by trained personnel. This is particularly important when blood is to be obtained by cardiac puncture, in which case the animal should be anesthetized or sedated to alleviate pain and prevent movement of the animal while the needle is in the heart.

If plasma is to be separated from blood, the needle and syringe are rinsed with a sterile heparin solution or other anticoagulant. Syringes or tubes containing blood should be placed in crushed ice to cool before the plasma is separated by centrifugation. Alternatively, if serum instead of blood is desired, blood is allowed to clot for 2–3 hours at room temperature or overnight in the refrigerator. The serum can then be poured carefully from the tube or removed by pipette. Any cellular material remaining with the serum is separated by centrifugation.

Hormone concentrations can be measured in either plasma or serum, but plasma is preferred because blood can be chilled and centrifuged immediately after collection. This is important if the hormone under study is temperature sensitive or subject to degradation when it is in contact with blood cells before separation of serum or plasma as is progesterone in cattle (Vahdat et al. 1984) and muskox (*Ovibos moschatus*) (Rowell and Flood 1987). Blood destined for hormone assays, particularly gonadotropins, should be chilled immediately after collection and centrifuged as quickly as possible with a uniform time interval between collection and centrifugation for all samples (Wiseman et al. 1982). Blood and other biological specimens should be protected from direct sunlight to avoid possible photo-oxidation of compounds under study. Plasma and serum also should be stored frozen at –15 C or lower and assayed as soon as practical to avoid degradation of hormones. However, steroid hormone concentrations do not appear to change in plasma and serum stored frozen over periods of 3–8 years.

Timing of collection of blood and other tissue samples for studies of reproductive physiology is important (Figs. 11–14). In most field studies, the exact stage of egg laying or estrous cycle is not known, and blood samples must be grouped to represent broad categories of reproductive activity (e.g., courtship, incubation, pregnancy, or lactation). The problem of temporal specificity in blood sampling is particularly complex relative to the ovulatory cycle of birds because many changes occur within a 20–30-hour period.

Hormone Assays.—Because radioimmunoassay (RIA) is highly specific and sensitive, reliable measurement of hormone concentrations can be obtained from small plasma samples, typically 0.05–0.5 ml; at times as little as 0.02 ml is adequate. Not surprisingly, RIA has not only revolutionized the study of reproductive physiology since its first wide application in the early 1970s but also has found ready application in wildlife studies and has been a key factor in the development of true field endocrinology (Wingfield and Moore 1987).

RIA uses 2 key reagents: (1) an antiserum that selectively binds the hormone under study, and (2) a radiolabeled form of the hormone (e.g., ^{3}H-progesterone). The antiserum is diluted to where it will bind only about 50% of a fixed amount of labeled hormone so that addition of unlabeled hormone (from standard solutions or a plasma sample) to the same tubes will displace some of the labeled hormone from the antibody in a dose-related manner. Unbound steroid is adsorbed on charcoal and the radiolabeled hormone bound to the antibody is decanted and counted in a liquid scintillation spectrometer. Alternatively, the antibody is coated to assay tubes so that unbound hormone is decanted and the radioactivity adhering to the walls of the tube is counted. The technique is highly sensitive and capable of measuring 2–5-pg/ml plasma (pg [picogram] = 1×10^{-12} g, a ng [nanogram] = 1×10^{-9} g).

Caution is in order regarding use of RIA in wildlife research; underlying seemingly straightforward procedures are complex antigen-antibody interactions that can generate misleading data. Those contemplating use of RIA should train in a laboratory specializing in its routine application. Most importantly, each laboratory must establish and validate procedures for each hormone in each species under study. Results of validation experiments, designed to demonstrate accuracy, precision, and quality control (Jaffe and Berhman 1974, Abraham et al. 1977, Jeffcoate 1981) should be published. These procedures are required in manuscripts submitted to many endocrine journals (i.e., *Endocrinology* 105:112). Reagents and procedures in commercial RIA "kits" most often have been established only for human, rat, or monkey plasma and should not be used for other species unless validated. Improper application of such kits to plasma or serum from other species can lead to highly erroneous and misleading results. Common problems include variable hormone extraction efficiency and nonspecific interference of hormone-antibody binding. For example, high lipid content of blood of laying hens can interfere with steroid extraction as well as binding and charcoal separation phases of RIA. Gonadotropic hormones, such as luteinizing hormone (LH), exhibit species-specific molecular structures that complicate assay validation based on antibodies raised to the gonadotropin of another species. For example, antiserum raised against LH from sheep has been used to measure LH in a wide range of mammalian species. These heterologous assays require rigorous validation and are usually less sensitive than when used to measure LH in sheep.

SUMMARY

The techniques and methodology for study of reproduction are more highly developed for birds and mammals than for amphibians and reptiles, largely because of the historical importance of birds and mammals in medicine, agriculture, and sport hunting. The need for more research on reproduction in amphibians and reptiles is obvious, particularly in terms of conservation. These taxa exhibit fascinating reproductive patterns that offer opportunities for monitoring the health of populations. Reproductive processes in many amphibians are particularly sensitive to environmental change, and there is a critical need to understand the mechanisms by which endocrine disruptors and other environmental contaminants affect recruitment and loss in populations. Methods developed for study of reproduction in birds and mammals (e.g., nest success, corpus luteum counts, ultrasonography) can also be applied to herptiles, but new methodologies are also needed, particularly for sampling designs and tissue collection techniques relevant to their diverse reproductive patterns.

Interpretation of the seemingly abundant data for select species can be compromised by: incomplete knowledge of the normal value for a given parameter in a given season or geographic area and inadequate sample sizes. Physiological parameters are often measured only as components of specific, short-term research projects wherein values from the control group and published literature are used for reference. Much has been learned from such efforts, but limitations in temporal and geographic distribution of samples in a typical 2- to 5-year research project can limit the generality of results and conclusions. Coupling of research projects with follow-up sampling of the same physiological indices over wide geographic areas would enhance the reliability of the conclusions reached and improve their potential application to conservation programs.

ACKNOWLEDGMENTS

I thank Roy Kirkpatrick and Alan Woolf who reviewed the original draft and made insightful and constructive suggestions that significantly improved the content and balance of this chapter. I thank Dave Dennis and Barbara Shardy for their contributions of photography and graphic illustration. I am grateful to Donna Harder for her support and tireless attention to detail and pursuit of clarity in preparation of this chapter.

LITERATURE CITED

ABELL, A. J. 1999. Variation in clutch size and offspring size relative to environmental conditions in the lizard (*Sceloporus virgatus*). Journal of Herpetology 33:173–180.

ABLER, W. A., D. E. BUCKLAND, R. L. KIRKPATRICK, AND P. F. SCANLON. 1976. Plasma progestins and puberty in fawns as influenced by energy and protein. Journal of Wildlife Management 40:442–446.

ABRAHAM, G. E., F. S. MANLIMOS, AND R. GAZARA. 1977. Radioimmunoassay of steroids. Pages 591–656 *in* G. E. Abraham, editor. Handbook of radioimmunoassay. Marcel Dekker, Inc., New York, USA.

ADAMS, G. P., E. D. PLOTKA, C. S. ASA, AND O. J. GINTHER. 1991. Feasibility of characterizing reproductive events in large nondomestic species by transrectal ultrasonic imaging. Zoo Biology 10:247–259.

ADAMS, L., AND S. HANE. 1972. Adrenal gland size as an index of adrenocortical secretion rate in the California ground squirrel. Journal of Wildlife Disease 8:19–23.

ADAMS, M. J., K .O. RICHTER, AND W. P. LEONARD. 1997. Surveying and monitoring amphibians using aquatic funnel traps. Pages 47–54 *in* D. A. Olson, W. P. Leonard, and R. B. Bury, editors. Sampling amphibians in lentic habitats: methods and approaches for the Pacific Northwest. Northwest Fauna 4. Society for Northwest Vertebrate Biology, Olympia, Washington, USA.

AMANN, R. P., AND J. T. LAMBIASE, JR. 1969. The male rabbit. III. Determination of daily sperm production by means of testicular homogenates. Journal of Animal Science 28:369–374.

ANKNEY, C. D. 1980. Egg weight, survival, and growth of lesser snow goose goslings. Journal of Wildlife Management 44:174–182.

———, AND C. D. MACINNES. 1978. Nutrient reserves and reproductive performance of female lesser snow goose. Auk 95:459–471.

ARMSTRONG, R. A. 1950. Fetal development of the northern white-tailed deer (*Odocoileus virginianus borealis* Miller). American Midland Naturalist 43:650–666.

ARORA, K. L. 1979. Blood sampling and intravenous injections in Japanese quail (*Coturnix coturnix japonica*). Labatory Animal Science 29:114–118.

ASTERITA, M. F. 1985. The physiology of stress: with special reference to the neuroendocrine system. Human Sciences Press, New York, USA.

AUSTAD, S. N., AND M. E. SUNQUIST. 1986. Sex-ratio manipulation in the common opossum. Nature 324:58–60.

AUSTIN, C. R., AND R. V. SHORT, editors. 1984. Hormonal control of reproduction. Second edition. Cambridge University Press, New York, USA.

BAGNARA, J. T., AND R. K. RASTOGI. 1992. Reproduction in the Mexican leaf frog, (*Pachymedusa dacnicolor*). Pages 98–111 *in* W. C. Hammett, editor. Reproduction in South American vertebrates. Springer-Verlag, Inc., New York, USA.

BAILEY, R. E. 1953. Surgery for sexing and observing gonad condition in birds. Auk 70:497–499.

BALDWIN, B. H., B. C. TENNANT, T. J. REIMERS, R. G. COWAN, AND P. W. CONCANNON. 1985. Circannual changes in serum testosterone concentrations of adult and yearling woodchucks (*Marmota monax*). Biology of Reproduction 32:804–812.

BALM, P. H. M., editor. 1999. Stress physiology in animals. CRC Press LLC, Boca Raton, Florida, USA.

BARRON, J. C., AND W. F. HARWELL. 1973. Fertilization rates of south Texas deer. Journal of Wildlife Management 37:179–182.

BECKERTON, P. R., AND A. L .A. MIDDLETON. 1982. Effects of dietary protein levels on ruffed grouse reproduction. Journal of Wildlife Management 46:569–579.

BELL, R. L., AND T. J. PETERLE. 1975. Hormone implants control reproduction in white-tailed deer. Wildlife Society Bulletin 3:152–156.

BERNDTSON, W. E. 1977. Methods for quantifying mammalian spermatogenesis: a review. Journal of Animal Science 44:818–833.

BLACKBURN, D. G. 1993. Standardized criteria for the recognition of reproductive modes in squamate reptiles. Herpetologica 49:118–132.

BLUHM, C. K., R. E. PHILLIPS, AND W. H. BURKE. 1983. Serum levels of luteinizing hormone (LH), prolactin, estradiol, and progesterone in laying and nonlaying canvasback ducks (*Aythya valisineria*). General and Comparative Endocrinology 52:1–16.

BOOKS-BLENDEN, P., T. S. BASKETT, AND M. W. SAYRE. 1984. Crop gland activity vs. nesting records for assessing September nesting of mourning doves. Wildlife Society Bulletin 12:376–381.

BRAMBELL, F. W. R. 1948. Prenatal mortality in mammals. Biological Review, Cambridge Philosophical Society 23:370–407.

BRAY, Y., É. MARBOUTIN, R. PÉROUX, AND J. FERRON. 2003. Reliability of stained placental-scar counts in European hares. Wildlife Society Bulletin 31:237–246.

BREITENBACH, G. L., J. D. CONGDON, AND R. C. VAN LOBEN SELS. 1984. Winter temperatures of *Chrysemys picta* nests in Michigan: effects on hatchling survival. Herpetologica 40:76–81.

BROOM, D. M., AND K. G. JOHNSON. 1993. Stress and animal welfare. Chapman and Hall, London, United Kingdom.

BRONSON, F. H. 1989. Mammalian reproductive biology, University of Chicago Press, Chicago, Illinois, USA.

BUCHANAN G. D., AND E. V. YOUNGLAI. 1986. Plasma progesterone levels during pregnancy in the little brown bat *Myotis lucifugus* (Vespertilionidae). Biology of Reproduction 34:878–884.

CANON, S. K., F. C. BRYANT, K. N. BRETSLAFF, AND J. M. HELLMAN. 1997. Pronghorn pregnancy diagnosis using trans-rectal ultrasound. Wildlife Society Bulletin 25:832–834.

CARRICK, R. 1963. Ecological significance of territory in the Australian magpie, *Gymnorhina tibicen*. Thirteenth International Ornithological Congress 1:740–753.

CARRUTHERS, M., AND M. R. C. PATH. 1983. Instrumental stress tests. Pages 331–362 in H. Selye, editor. Selye's guide to stress research. Volume 2. Scientific and Academic Editions, New York, USA.

CATLING, P. C., AND R. L. SUTHERLAND. 1980. Effect of gonadectomy, season, and the presence of female tammar wallabies (*Macropus eugenii*) on concentrations of testosterone, luteinizing hormone and follicle stimulating hormone in the plasma of male tammar wallabies. Journal of Endocrinology 86:25–33.

CHEATUM, E. L. 1949. The use of corpora lutea for determining ovulation incidence and variations in fertility of white-tailed deer. Cornell Veterinarian 39:282–291.

CHRISTIAN, J. J. 1950. The adreno-pituitary system and population cycles in mammals. Journal of Mammalogy 31:247–259.

———. 1963. Endocrine adaptive mechanisms and the physiologic regulation of population growth. Pages 189–353 in W. V. Mayer and R. C. Vangelder, editors. Physiological mammalogy. Volume I. Mammalian populations. Academic Press, New York, USA.

———, AND D. E. DAVIS. 1964. Endocrines, behavior, and population. Social and endocrine factors are integrated in the regulation of growth of mammalian populations. Science 146:1550–1560.

CONCANNON, P., B. BALDWIN, J. LAWLESS, W. HORNBUCKLE, AND B. TENNANT. 1983. Corpora lutea of pregnancy and elevated serum progesterone during pregnancy and postpartum anestrus in woodchucks (*Marmota monax*). Biology of Reproduction 29:1128–1134.

CONGDON, J. D., AND J. W. GIBBONS. 1996. Structure and dynamics of a turtle community over two decades. Pages 137–159 in M. L. Cody and J. A. Smallwood, editors. Long-term studies of vertebrate communities. Academic Press, New York, USA.

COOPER, K. A., J. D. HARDER, D. H. CLAWSON, D. L. FREDRICK, G. A. LODGE, H. C. PEACHEY, T. J. SPELLMIRE, AND D. P. WINSTEL. 1990. Serum testosterone in musth in captive male African and Asian elephants. Zoo Biology 9:297–306.

CREWS, D. 1980. Interrelationships among ecological, behavioral, and neuroendocrine processes in the reproductive cycle of *Anolis carolinensis* and other reptiles. Advances in the Study of Behavior 11:1–74.

———, AND W. R. GARSTKA. 1982. The ecological physiology of a garter snake. Scientific American 247 (November):158–168.

CROUCH, W. B., AND P. W. C. PATON. 2000. Using egg-mass counts to monitor wood frog populations. Wildlife Society Bulletin 28:895–901.

DENO, R. A. 1937. Uterine macrophages in the mouse and their relation to involution. American Journal of Anatomy 60:433–471.

DINSMORE, S. J., AND D. H. JOHNSON. 2005. Population analysis in wildlife biology. Pages 154–184 in C. E. Braun, editor. Techniques

for wildlife investigations and management. Sixth edition. The Wildlife Society, Bethesda, Maryland, USA.

DOBOSZYŃSKA, T. 1976. A method for collecting and staining vaginal smears from the beaver. Acta Theriologica 21:299–306.

DOBSON, H., AND R. F. SMITH. 2000. What is stress, and how does it affect reproduction? Animal Reproduction Science 60–61:743–752.

———, S. GHUMAN, S. PRABHAKAR, AND R. SMITH. 2003. A conceptual model of the influence of stress on female reproduction. Reproduction 125:151–163.

EHRHART, L. M. 1995. A review of sea turtle reproduction. Pages 29–38 in K. A. Bjorndal, editor. Biology and conservation of sea turtles. Smithsonian Institution Press, Washington, D.C., USA.

FAGERSTONE, K. A., M. A. COFFEY, P. D. CURTIS, R. A. DOLBEER, G. J. KILLIAN, L. A. MILLER, AND L. M. WILMONT. 2002. Wildlife fertility control. Technical Review 02-2. The Wildlife Society, Bethesda, Maryland, USA.

FAYRER-HOSKEN, R. A., D. GROBLER, J. J. VAN ALTENA, H. J. BERTSCHINGER, AND J. F. KIRKPATRICK. 2000. Immunocontraception of African elephants. Nature 407:149.

FITZGERALD, L. A., AND C. W. PAINTER. 2000. Rattlesnake commercialization: long-term trends, issues, and implications for conservation. Wildlife Society Bulletin 28:235–253.

FLEMING, M. W., AND J. D. HARDER. 1983. Luteal and follicular populations in the ovary of the opossum (*Didelphis virginiana*) after ovulation. Journal of Reproduction and Fertility 67:29–34.

FOLLETT, B. K., AND S. L. MAUNG. 1978. Rate of testicular maturation, in relation to gonadotrophin and testosterone levels, in quail exposed to various artificial photoperiods and to natural daylengths. Journal of Endocrinology 78:267–280.

FOLLIS, T. B., W. C. FOOTE, AND J. J. SPILLET. 1972. Observation of genitalia in elk by laparotomy. Journal of Wildlife Management 36:171–173.

FROST, H. C., E. C. YORK, W. B. KROHN, K. D. ELOWE, T. A. DECKER, S. M. POWELL, AND T. K. FULLER. 1999. An evaluation of parturition indices in fishers. Wildlife Society Bulletin 27:221–230.

GADSBY, J. E., R. B. HEAP, D. G. POWELL, AND D. E. WALTERS. 1972. Diagnosis of pregnancy and of the number of fetuses in sheep from plasma progesterone concentrations. Veterinary Research 90:339–342.

GARTNER, K., D. BUTTNER, K. DOHLER, R. FRIEDEL, J. LINDENA, AND I. TRAUTSCHOLD. 1980. Stress response of rats to handling and experimental procedures. Laboratory Animal 14:267–274.

GIBBONS, J. W., AND J. L. GREEN. 1979. X-ray photography: a technique to determine reproductive patterns of freshwater turtles. Herpetological 35:86–89.

GILMORE, D. P. 1969. Seasonal reproductive periodicity in the male Australian brush-tailed possum (*Trichosurus volpecula*). Journal of Zoology 157:75–98.

GINTHER, O. J. 1990. Folliculogenesis during the transitional period and early ovulatory season in mares. Journal of Reproduction and Fertility 90:311–320.

GOSLING, L. M. 1986. Biased sex ratios in stressed animals. American Midland Naturalist 127:893–896.

GRANDY, J. W., AND A. T. RUTBERG. 2002. An animal welfare view of wildlife contraception. Pages 1–7 in J. F. Kirkpatrick, B. L. Lasley, W. R. Allen, and C. Doberska, editors. Fertility control in wildlife. Reproduction: Supplement 60.

GREER, K. R., AND W. W. HAWKINS, JR. 1967. Determining pregnancy in elk by rectal palpation. Journal of Wildlife Management 31:145–149.

GUYNN, D. E., AND P. F. SCANLON. 1973. Crop-gland activity in mourning doves during hunting seasons in Virginia. Proceedings of the Annual Conference of the Southeastern Association of Game and Fish Commissioners 27:36–42.

HANNON, S. J. 1981. Postovulatory follicles as indicators of egg production in blue grouse. Journal of Wildlife Management 45:1045–1047.

HARDER, J. D. 1980. Reproduction of white-tailed deer in the north central United States. Pages 23–35 in R. L. Hine, and S. Nehls, editors. White-tailed deer population management in the north central states. North Central Section, The Wildlife Society, Eau Claire, Wisconsin, USA.

———, AND D. W. FLECK. 1997. Reproductive ecology of New World marsupials. Pages 173–201 in L. A. Hinds and N. R. Saunders, editors. Recent advances in marsupial biology. University of New South Wales Press, Sydney, Australia.

———, AND R. L. KIRKPATRICK. 1996. Physiological methods in wildlife research. Pages 275–306 in T. A. Bookhout, editor. Research and management techniques for wildlife and habitats. Fifth edition. The Wildlife Society, Bethesda, Maryland, USA.

———, AND D. L. MOORHEAD. 1980. Development of corpora lutea and plasma progesterone levels associated with the onset of the breeding season in white-tailed deer (*Odocoileus virginianus*). Biology of Reproduction 22:185–191.

———, AND T. J. PETERLE. 1974. Effect of diethylstilbestrol on reproductive performance of white-tailed deer. Journal of Wildlife Management 38:183–196.

———, AND A. WOOLF. 1976. Changes in plasma levels of oestrone and oestradiol during pregnancy and parturition in white-tailed deer. Journal of Reproductive Fertility 47:161–163.

———, L. A. HINDS, C. A. HORN, AND C. H. TYNDALE-BISCOE. 1985. Effects of removal in late pregnancy of the corpus luteum, Graafian follicle or ovaries on plasma progesterone, oestradiol, LH, parturition and post-partum oestrus in the tammar wallaby, *Macropus eugenii*. Journal of Reproduction and Fertility 75:449–459.

HARPER, W. L., AND R. D. H. COHEN. 1985. Accuracy of Doppler ultrasound in diagnosing pregnancy in bighorn sheep. Journal of Wildlife Management 49:793–796.

HARRISON, R. M., AND D. E. WILDT. 1980. Animal laparoscopy. Williams and Wilkins Company, Baltimore, Maryland, USA.

HAU, M., M. WIKELSKI, AND J. C. WINGFIELD. 2000. Visual and nutritional food cues fine-tune timing of reproduction in a neotropical rainforest bird. Journal of Experimental Zoology 286:494–504.

HAUGEN, A. O. 1975. Reproductive performance of white-tailed deer in Iowa. Journal of Mammalogy 56:151–159.

HAUGER, R. L., F. J. KARSCH, AND D. L. FOSTER. 1977. A new concept of the control of the estrous cycle of the ewe based on the temporal relationships between luteinizing hormone, estradiol and progesterone in peripheral serum and evidence that progesterone inhibits tonic LH secretion. Endocrinology 101:807–817.

Hawley, A. W. L. 1982. A simple device for sectioning ovaries. Journal of Wildlife Management 46:247–249.

HENRY, D. B., AND T. A. BOOKHOUT. 1969. Productivity of beavers in northeastern Ohio. Journal of Wildlife Management 33:927–932.

HENSEL, R. J., W. A. TROYER, AND A. W. ERICKSON. 1969. Reproduction in the female brown bear. Journal of Wildlife Management 33:357–365.

HERRICK, J. R., G. AGORAMOORTHY, R. RUDRAN, AND J. D. HARDER. 2000. Urinary progesterone in free-ranging red howler monkeys (*Alouatta seniculus*): preliminary observations of the estrous cycle and gestation. American Journal of Primatology 51:257–263.

HESS, D. L., A. M. SCHMIDT, AND M. J. SCHMIDT. 1983. Reproductive cycle of the Asian elephant (*Elephus maximus*) in captivity. Biology of Reproduction 28:767–773.

HOSSLER, R. J., J. B. MCANINCH, AND J. D. HARDER. 1994. Maternal denning behavior and juvenile survival of opossums in southeastern New York. Journal of Mammalogy 75:60–70.

HOUSTON, D. B., C. T. ROBBINS, C. A. RUDER, AND R. G. SASSER. 1986. Pregnancy detection in mountain goats by assay for pregnancy-specific protein B. Journal of Wildlife Management 50:740–742.

HUMASON, G. L. 1979. Animal tissue techniques. Third edition. W. H. Freeman and Company, San Francisco, California, USA.

INNS, R. W. 1982. Seasonal changes in the accessory reproductive system and plasma testosterone levels of the male tammar wallaby, *Macropus eugenii*, in the wild. Journal of Reproduction and Fertility 66:675–680.

ITOH, M., M. INOUE, AND S. ISHII. 1990. Annual cycle of pituitary and plasma gonadotropins and plasma sex steroids in a wild population of the toad, *Bufo japonicus*. General and Comparative Endocrinology 78:242–253.

JACOBSEN, N. K., D. A. JESSUP, AND D. J. KESLER. 1995. Contraception in captive black-tailed deer by remotely delivered norgestomet ballistic implants. Wildlife Society Bulletin 23:718–722.

JACOBSON, H. A., H. J. BEARDEN, AND D. B. WHITEHOUSE. 1989. Artificial insemination trials with white-tailed deer. Journal of Wildlife Management 54:224–227.

JAFFE, B. M., AND H. R. BEHRMAN. 1974. Methods of hormone radioimmunoassay. Academic Press, New York, USA.

JEFFCOATE, S. L. 1981. Efficiency and effectiveness in the endocrine laboratory. Academic Press, New York, USA.

JOHNSON, A. L. 1986. Reproduction in the female. Pages 403–431 *in* P. D. Sturkie, editor. Avian physiology. Fourth edition. Springer-Verlag, Inc., New York, USA.

JONES, R. E., L. J. GUILLETTE, JR., C. H. SUMMERS, R. R. TOKARZ, AND D. CREWS. 1983. The relationship among ovarian condition, steroid hormones, and estrous behavior in *Anolis carolinensis*. Journal of Experimental Zoology 227:145–154.

JORGENSEN, C. B. 1992. Growth and reproduction. Pages 439–466 *in* M. E. Feder and W. W. Burggren, editors. Environmental physiology of the Amphibia. University of Chicago Press, Chicago, Illinois, USA.

JURGELSKI, JR., W., AND M. E. PORTER. 1974. The opossum (*Didelphis virginiana* Kerr) as a biomedical model. III. Breeding the opossum

in captivity: methods. Laboratory Animal Science 24:412–425.

KABAT, C., I. O. BUSS, AND R. K. MEYER. 1948. The use of ovulated follicles in determining eggs laid by the ring-necked pheasant. Journal of Wildlife Management 12:399–416.

KATONGOLE, C. B., F. NAFTOLIN, AND R. V. SHORT. 1971. Relationship between blood levels of luteinizing hormone and testosterone in bulls, and the effects of sexual stimulation. Journal of Endocrinology 50:456–557.

KAPUSTIN, N., J. K. CRITSER, D. OLSON, AND P. V. MALVEN. 1996. Non-luteal estrous cycles of 3-week duration are initiated by anovulatory luteinizing hormone peaks in African elephants. Biology of Reproduction 55:1147–1154.

KASMAN, L. H., E. C. RAMSAY, AND B. L. LASLEY. 1986. Urinary steroid evaluations to monitor ovarian function in exotic ungulates. III. Estrone sulfate and pregnanediol-3-glucuronide excretion in the Indian rhinoceros (*Rhinoceros unicornis*). Zoo Biology 5:355–361.

KENNELLY, J. J., AND B. E. JOHNS. 1976. The estrous cycle of coyotes. Journal of Wildlife Management 40:272–277.

———, ———, C. P. BREIDENSTEIN, AND J. D. ROBERTS. 1977. Predicting female coyote breeding data from fetal measurements. Journal of Wildlife Management 41:746–750.

KIBBE, D. P., AND R. L. KIRKPATRICK. 1971. Systematic evaluation of late summer breeding in juvenile cottontails, *Sylvilagus floridanus*. Journal of Mammalogy 52:465–467.

KING, R. B. 2000. Analyzing the relationship between clutch size and female body size in reptiles. Journal of Herpetology 34:148–150.

KIRKPATRICK, J. F., L. H. KASMAN, B. L. LASLEY, AND J. W. TURNER, JR. 1988. Pregnancy determination in uncaptured feral horses. Journal of Wildlife Management 52:305–308.

———, ———, W. R. ALLEN, AND C. DOBERSKA, editors. 2002. Fertility control in wildlife. Reproduction, Supplement 60.

———, J. W. TURNER, JR., I. K. M. LIU, R. A. FAYRER-HOSKEN, AND A. T. RUTBERG. 1997. Case studies in wildlife immunocontraception: wild and feral equids and white-tailed deer. Reproduction, Fertility and Development 9.105–110.

KIRKPATRICK, R. L., AND G. L. VALENTINE. 1970. Reproduction in captive pine voles, *Microtus pinetorum*. Journal of Mammalogy 51:779–785.

KNOBIL, E., AND J. D. NEILL, editors. 1998. Encyclopedia of reproduction, 4 volumes. Academic Press, New York, USA.

KOVAL, P. J., T. J. PETERLE, AND J. D. HARDER. 1987. Effects of polychlorinated biphenyls on mourning dove reproduction and circulating progesterone levels. Bulletin of Environmental Contamination and Toxicology 39:663–670.

KUCHLING, G. 1999. The reproductive biology of the Chelonia. Zoophysiology. Volume 38. Springer-Verlag, Inc., New York, USA.

LANDYS-CIANNELLI, M. M., M. RAMENOFSKY, T. PIERSMA, J. JUKEMA, AND J. C. WINGFIELD. 2002. Baseline and stress-induced plasma corticosterone during long-distance migration in the bar-tailed godwit, *Limosa lapponica*. Physiological and Biochemical Zoology 75:101–110.

LAWS, R. M. 1967. Occurrence of placental scars in the uterus of the African elephant (*Loxodonta africana*). Journal of Reproduction and Fertility 14:445–449.

LEVI, W. M. 1969. The pigeon. Levi Publishing Company, Sumter, South Carolina, USA.

LEYTON, V., AND J. VALENCIA. 1992. Follicular population dynamics: its relation to clutch and litter size in Chilean *Liolaemus* lizards. Pages 123–134 *in* W. C. Hammett, editor. Reproduction in South American vertebrates. Springer-Verlag, Inc., New York, USA.

LICHT, P., B. R. MCCREERY, R. BARNES, AND R. PANG. 1983. Seasonal and stress related changes in plasma gonadotropins, sex steroids, and corticosterone in the bullfrog, *Rana catsbeiana*. General and Comparative Endocrinology 50:124–145.

LOSKUTOFF, N. M., J. E. OTT, AND B. L. LASLEY. 1982. Urinary steroid evaluations to monitor ovarian function in exotic ungulates. I. Pregnanediol-3-Glucuronide immunoreactivity in the okapi (*Okapia johnstoni*). Zoo Biology 1:45–53.

MANSELL, W. D. 1971. Accessory corpora lutea in ovaries of white-tailed deer. Journal of Wildlife Management 35:369–374.

MANSER, C. E. 1992. The assessment of stress in laboratory animals. RSPCA, Causeway Horsham, West Sussex, United Kingdom.

MARCH, G. L., AND R. M. F. S. SADLIER. 1970. Studies on the band-tailed pigeon (*Columba fasciata*) in British Columbia. I. Seasonal changes in gonadal development and crop gland activity. Canadian Journal of Zoology 48:1353–1357.

MARTIN, K. H., R. A. STEHN, AND M. E. RICHMOND. 1976. Reliability of placental scar counts in the prairie vole. Journal of Wildlife Management 40:264–271.

MARVIN, G. A. 1996. Life history and population characteristics of the salamander *Plethodon kentucki*, with a review of *Plethodon* life histories. American Midland Naturalist 136:385–400.

McDonald, I. R., A. K. Lee, A. J. Bradley, and K. A. Than. 1981. Endocrine changes in Dasyurid marsupials with differing mortality patterns. General and Comparative Endocrinology 44:292–301.

McMillin, J. M., U. S. Seal, K. D. Keenlyne, A. W. Erickson, and J. E. Jones. 1974. Annual testosterone rhythm in the adult white-tailed deer (*Odocoileus virginianus borealis*). Endocrinology 94:1034–1040.

Mendonca, M. T., and D. Crews. 2001. Control of attractivity and receptivity in female red-sided garter snakes. Hormones and Behavior 40:43–50.

Miller, J. D. 1997. Reproduction in sea turtles. Pages 51–82 *in* P. L. Lutz and J. A. Musick, editors. The biology of sea turtles. CRC Press, New York, USA.

Miller, L. A., B. E. Johns, and D. J. Elias. 1998. Immunocontraception as a wildlife management tool: some perspectives. Wildlife Society Bulletin 26:237–243.

Millspaugh, J. J., B. E. Washburn, M. A. Milanick, J. Beringer, L. P. Hansen, and T. M Meyer. Non-invasive techniques for stress assessment in white-tailed deer. Wildlife Society Bulletin 30:899–907.

Mirarchi, R. E., and P. F. Scanlon. 1980. Duration of mourning dove crop gland activity during the nesting cycle. Journal of Wildlife Management 44:209–213.

———, ———, and R. L. Kirkpatrick. 1977*a*. Annual changes in spermatozoa production and associated organs of white-tailed deer. Journal of Wildlife Management 41:92–99.

———, ———, ———, and C. B. Schreck. 1977*b*. Androgen levels and antler development in captive and wild white-tailed deer. Journal of Wildlife Management 41:178–183.

Moberg, G. P. 1985. Biological response to stress: key to assessment of animal well-being? Pages 27–49 *in* G. P. Moberg, editor. Animal stress. First edition. Waverly Press, Baltimore, Maryland, USA.

Murphy, Jr., W. F., P. F. Scanlon, and R. L. Kirkpatrick. 1973. Examination of ovaries in living cottontail rabbits by laparotomy. Proceedings of the Annual Conference of the Southeastern Association of Game and Fish Commissioners 27:343–344.

Naugle, R. E., A. T. Rutberg, H. B. Underwood, J. W. Turner, Jr., and I. K. M. Liu. 2002. Field testing of immunocontraception on white-tailed deer (*Odocoileus virginianus*) on Fire Island National Seashore, New York, USA. Pages 143–153 *in* J. F. Kirkpatrick, B. L. Lasley, W. R. Allen, and C. Doberska, editors. Fertility control in wildlife. Reproduction, Supplement 60.

Nave, C. D., G. Coulson, A. Poiani, G. Shaw, and M. B. Renfree. 2002. Fertility control in the eastern grey kangaroo using levonorgestrel implants. Journal of Wildlife Management 66:470–477.

Nelsen, O. E. 1953. Comparative embryology of the vertebrates. McGraw-Hill Book Co., New York, USA.

Nelson, R. J. 2000. An introduction to behavioral endocrinology. Second edition. Sinauer Associates, Sunderland, Massachusetts, USA.

———, G. E. Demas, S. L. Klein, and L. J. Kriegsfeld. 2002. Seasonal patterns of stress, immune function, and disease. Cambridge University Press, Cambridge, United Kingdom.

Nelson, T. A., and A. Woolf. 1983. Field laparoscopy of female white-tailed deer. Journal of Wildlife Management 47:1213–1216.

Nequin, L. G., J. Alvarez, and N. B. Schwartz. 1979. Measurement of serum steriod and gonadotropin levels and uterine and ovarian variables throughout 4 day and 5 day estrous cycles in the rat. Biology of Reproduction 20:659–670.

Nixon, C. M. 1971. Productivity of white-tailed deer in Ohio. Ohio Journal of Science 71:217–225.

———, M. W. McClain, and R. W. Donohoe. 1975. Effects of hunting and mast crops on a squirrel population. Journal of Wildlife Management 39:1–25.

Norris, D. O. 1997. Vertebrate endocrinology. Academic Press, New York, USA.

Noyes, J. H., R. G. Sasser, B. K. Johnson, L. D. Bryant, and B. Alexander. 1997. Accuracy of pregnancy detection by serum protein (PSPB) in elk. Wildlife Society Bulletin 25:695–698.

Olfyar, C. M., and B. S. McGinnes. 1974. Field evaluation of diethylstilbestrol for suppressing reproduction in foxes. Journal of Wildlife Management 38:101–106.

O'Reilly, K. M., and J. C. Wingfield. 2001. Ecological factors underlying the adrenocortical response to capture stress in arctic breeding shorebirds. General and Comparative Endocrinology 124:1–11.

Orsini, M. W. 1962. Technique of preparation, study and photography of benzyl-benzoate cleared material for embryological studies. Journal of Reproduction and Fertility 3:283–287.

Owens, D. W. 1995. The role of reproductive physiology in the conservation of sea turtles. Pages 39–44 *in* K.A. Bjorndal, editor. Biology and conservation of sea turtles. Smithsonian Institution Press, Washington, D.C., USA.

———. 1997. Hormones in the life history of sea turtles. Pages 315–341 *in* P. L. Lutz and J. A. Musick, editors. The biology of sea turtles. CRC Press, New York, USA.

Payne, R. B. 1973. Individual laying histories and the clutch size and numbers of eggs of parasitic cuckoos. Condor 75:414–438.

Pierson, R. A., and O. J. Ginther. 1987. Reliability of diagnostic ultrasonography for identification and measurement of follicles and detecting the corpus luteum in heifers. Theriogenology 28:929–936.

———, and ———. 1988. Ultrasound imaging of the ovaries and uterus in cattle. Theriogenology 29:21–27.

Plotka, E. D., and U. S. Seal, L. J. Verme, and J. J. Ozoga. 1980. Reproductive steroids in deer. III. Luteinizing hormone, estradiol and progesterone around estrus. Biology of Reproduction 22:576–581.

———, ———, ———, and ———. 1983. The adrenal gland in white-tailed deer: a significant source of progesterone. Journal of Wildlife Management 47:38–44.

———, ———, G. C. Schmoller, P. D. Karns, and K. D. Keenlyne. 1977. Reproductive steroids in the white-tailed deer (*Odocoileus virginianus borealis*). I. Seasonal changes in the female. Biology of Reproduction 16:340–343.

———, ———, F. R. Zarembka, L. G. Simmons, A. Teare, L. G. Phillips, K. C. Hinshaw, and D. G. Wood. 1988. Ovarian function in the elephant: luteinizing hormone and progesterone cycles in African and Asian elephants. Biology of Reproduction 38:309–314.

Polzonetti-Magni, A. M., G. Mosconi, O. Carnevali, K. Yamamoto, Y. Hanaoka, and S. Kikuyama. 1998. Gonadotropins and reproductive function in the anuran amphibian, *Rana esculenta*. Biology of Reproduction 58:88–93.

Pottinger, T. G. 1999. The impact of stress on animal reproductive activities. Pages 130–163 *in* P. H. M. Balm, editor. Stress physiology in animals. CRC Press LLC, Boca Raton, Florida, USA.

Provost, E. E. 1962. Morphological characteristics of the beaver ovary. Journal of Wildlife Management 26:272–278.

Risser, Jr., A. C. 1971. A technique for performing laparotomy on small birds. Condor 73:376–379.

Rivier, C., and S. Rivest. 1991. Effects of stress on the activity of the hypothalamic-pituitary-gonadal axis: peripheral and central mechanisms. Biology of Reproduction 45:523–532.

Rolan, R. G., and H. T. Gier. 1967. Correlation of embryo and placental scar counts of *Peromyscus maniculatus* and *Microtus ochrogaster*. Journal of Mammalogy 48:317–319.

Roseberry, J. L., and W. D. Klimstra. 1970. Productivity of white-tailed deer on Crab Orchard National Wildlife Refuge. Journal of Wildlife Management 34:23–28.

Rowell, J., and P. F. Flood. 1987. Changes in muskox blood progesterone concentration between collection and centrifugation. Journal of Wildlife Management 51:901–903.

Roy, C., and A. Woolf. 2001. Effects of hunting and hunting-hour extension on mourning dove foraging and physiology. Journal of Wildlife Management 65:808–815.

Rudolph, B. A., W. F. Porter, and H. B. Underwood. 2000. Evaluating immunocontraception for managing suburban white-tailed deer in Irondequoit, New York. Journal of Wildlife Management 64:463–473.

Safar-Hermann, N., M. N. Ismail, H. S. Choi, E. Mostl, and E. Bamberg. 1987. Pregnancy diagnosis in zoo animals by estrogen determination in feces. Zoo Biology 6:189–193.

Sanders, O. T., and R. L. Kirkpatrick. 1975. Effects of a polychlorinated biphenyl (PCB on sleeping times, plasma corticosteroids, and testicular activity of white-footed mice. Environmental Physiology 5:308–313.

Sanderson, G. C. 1950. Methods of measuring productivity in raccoons. Journal of Wildlife Management 14:389–402.

Sapolsky, R. M. 1987. Stress, social status, and reproductive physiology in free-living baboons. Pages 291–322 *in* D. Crews, editor. Psychobiology of reproductive behavior: an evolutionary perspective. First edition. Prentice-Hall, Inc., Englewood Cliffs, New Jersey, USA.

———. 1998. Why zebras don't get ulcers: a guide to stress, stress-related diseases, and coping. W. H. Freeman, New York, USA.

Sauer, P. R., and C. W. Severinghaus. 1977. Determination and application of fawn reproductive rates from yearling teat length. Transactions of the Northeastern Section, The Wildlife Society 33:133–144.

Schwabl, H., M. Ramenofsky, I. Schwabl-Benzinger, D. S. Farner, and J. C. Wingfield. 1988. Social status, circulating levels of hormones, and competition for food in winter flocks of the white-throated sparrow. Behaviour 107:107–121.

SEAL, U. S., L. J. VERME, J. J. OZOGA, AND E. D. PLOTKA. 1983. Metabolic and endocrine responses of white-tailed deer to increasing population density. Journal of Wildlife Management 47:451–462.

SELYE, H. 1936. A syndrome produced by diverse nocuous agents. Nature 138:32.

———. 1946. The general adaptation syndrome and the diseases of adaptation. Journal of Clinical Endocrinology 6:117–230.

———. 1976. Stress in health and disease. Butterworths, Boston, Massachusetts, USA.

SEMLITSCH, R. D. 1985. Reproductive strategy of a facultatively paedomorphic salamander *Ambystoma talpoideum*. Oecologia 65:305–313.

———. 2000. Principles for management of aquatic-breeding amphibians. Journal of Wildlife Management 64:615–631.

———, D. E. SCOTT, J. H. K. PECHMANN, AND J. W. GIBBONS. 1996. Structure and dynamics of an amphibian community, evidence from a 16-year study of a natural pond. Pages 217–248 *in* M. L. Cody and J. A. Smallwood, editors. Long-term studies of vertebrate communities. Academic Press, New York, USA.

SERVELLO, F. A., E. C. HELLGREN, AND S. R. McWILLIAMS. 2005. Techniques for wildlife nutritional ecology. Pages 554–590 *in* C. E. Braun, editor. Techniques for wildlife investigations and management. Sixth edition. The Wildlife Society, Bethesda, Maryland, USA.

SHORT, R. V. 1972. The role of hormones in sex cycles. Pages 43–72 *in* C. R. Austin and R. V. Short, editors. Hormones in reproduction. Cambridge University Press, New York, USA.

SIMKIN, D. W. 1965. Reproduction and productivity of moose in northwestern Ontario. Journal of Wildlife Management 29:740–750.

SIROIS, J., AND J. E. FORTUNE. 1988. Ovarian follicular dynamics during the estrous cycle in heifers monitored by real-time ultrasonography. Biology of Reproduction 39:308–317.

STABENFELDT, G. H., AND V. M. SHILLE. 1977. Reproduction in the dog and cat. Pages 499–527 *in* H. H. Cole and P. T. Cupps, editors. Reproduction in domestic animals. Third edition. Academic Press, New York, USA.

SULLIVAN, J. A., AND P. F. SCANLON. 1976. Effects of grouping and fighting on the reproductive tracts of male white-footed mice (*Peromyscus leucopus*). Research in Population Ecology 17:164–175.

SUNDQVIST, C., A. LUKOLA, AND M. PARVINEN. 1986. Testicular aspiration biopsy in evaluation of fertility of mink (*Mustela vison*). Journal of Reproduction and Fertility 77:531–535.

TAPP, W. N., J. W. HOLADAY, AND B. H. NATELSON. 1984. Ultradian glucocorticoid rhythms in monkeys and rats continue during stress. American Journal of Physiology 247:866–871.

TRIVERS, R. L., AND D. E. WILLARD. 1973. Natural selection of parental ability to vary the sex ratio of offspring. Science 179:90–92.

TURNER, C. D., AND J. T. BAGNARA. 1976. General endocrinology. Sixth edition. W. B. Saunders Company, Philadelphia, Pennsylvania, USA.

TYNDALE-BISCOE, C. H., AND M. B. RENFREE. 1987. Reproductive physiology of marsupials. Cambridge University Press, New York, USA.

VAHDAT, F., B. E. SEGUIN, H. L. WHITMORE, AND S. D. JOHNSTON. 1984. Role of blood cells in degradation of progesterone in bovine blood. American Journal of Veterinary Research 45:240–243.

VAN TIENHOVEN, A. 1983. Reproductive physiology of vertebrates. Second edition. Cornell University Press, Ithaca, New York, USA.

VANGILDER, L. D., AND T. J. PETERLE. 1981. South Louisiana crude oil or DDE in the diet of mallard hens: effects on egg quality. Bulletin of Environmental Contamination and Toxicology 26:328–336.

VAUGHAN, M. R., AND L. B. KEITH. 1981. Demographic response of experimental snowshoe hare populations to overwinter shortage. Journal of Wildlife Management 45:354–380.

VAUGHAN, T. A., J. M. RYAN, AND N. J. CZAPLEWSKI. 2000. Mammalogy. Fourth edition. Saunders College Publishing, New York, USA.

VERME, L. J. 1969. Reproductive patterns of white-tailed deer related to nutritional plane. Journal of Wildlife Management 33:881–887.

VITT, L. J. 1992. Diversity of reproductive strategies among Brazilian lizards and snakes: the significance of lineage and adaptation. Pages 135–149 *in* W. C. Hammett, editor. Reproduction in South American vertebrates. Springer-Verlag, Inc., New York, USA.

VON DER OHE, C. G., AND C. SERVHEEN. 2002. Measuring stress in mammals using fecal glucocorticoids: opportunities and challenges. Wildlife Society Bulletin 30:1215–1225.

WADDELL, R. B., D. A. OSBORN, R. J. WARREN, J. C. GRIFFIN, AND D. J. KESLER. 2001. Prostaglandin F$_{2a}$-mediated fertility control in captive white-tailed deer. Wildlife Society Bulletin 29:1067–1074.

WALKER, L. A., L. CORNELL, K. DAHL, N. CZEKELA, C. DARGEN, B. JOSEPH, A. HSUEH, AND B. LASLEY. 1988. Urinary concentrations of ovarian steroid hormone metabolites and bioactive follicle-stimulating hormone in killer whales (*Orcinus orchus*) during ovarian cycles and pregnancy. Biology of Reproduction 39:1013–1020.

WASSER, S. K., K. E. HUNT, J. L. BROWN, K. COOPER, C. M. CROCKETT, U. BECHERT, J. J. MILLSPAUGH, S. LARSON, AND S. L. MONFORT. 2000. A generalized fecal glucocorticoid assay for use in a diverse array of nondomestic mammalian and avian species. General and Comparative Endocrinology 120:260–275.

WENTWORTH, B. C., J. A. PROUDMAN, H. OPEL, J. J. WINELAND, N. G. ZIMMERMANN, AND A. LAPP. 1983. Endocrine changes in the incubating and brooding turkey hen. Biology of Reproduction 29:87–92.

WESSON, III, J.A., P. F. SCANLON, R. L. KIRKPATRICK, H. S. MOSBY, AND R. L. BUTCHER. 1979. Influence of chemical immobilization and physical restraint on steroid hormone levels in blood of white-tailed deer. Canadian Journal of Zoology 57:768–776.

WHITTIER, J. M., AND R. R. TOKARZ. 1992. Physiological regulation of sexual behavior in female reptiles. Pages 24–69 *in* C. Gans and D. Crews, editors. Biology of the reptilia. Volume 18. Hormones, brain, and behavior. University of Chicago Press, Chicago, Illinois, USA.

WIKELSKI, M., M. HAU, AND J. C. WINGFIELD. 1999. Social instability increases plasma testosterone in a year-round territorial neotropical bird. Proceedings of the Royal Society of Biological Sciences, Series B 266:551–556.

WILDT, D. E., J. L. BROWN, M. BUSH, M. A. BARONE, K. A. COOPER, J. GRISHAM, AND J. G. HOWARD. 1993. Reproductive status of cheetahs (*Acinonyx jubatus*) in North American zoos: the benefits of physiological surveys for strategic planning. Zoo Biology 12:45–80.

WILLIAMSON, P., N. J. GALES, AND S. LISTER. 1990. Use of real-time B-mode ultrasound for pregnancy diagnosis and measurement of fetal growth rate in captive bottlenose dolphins (*Tursiops truncates*). Journal of Reproduction and Fertility 88:543–548.

WINDBERG, L. A., AND L. B. KEITH. 1976. Snowshoe hare population response to artificial high densities. Journal of Mammalogy 57:523–553.

WINGFIELD, J. C. 1985. Short-term changes in plasma levels of hormones during establishment and defense of a breeding territory in male song sparrows, *Melospiza melodia*. Hormone and Behavior 19:174–187.

———, AND D. S. FARNER. 1976. Avian endocrinology—field investigations and methods. Condor 78:570–573.

———, AND ———. 1980. Control of seasonal reproduction in temperate-zone birds. Pages 62–101 *in* R. J. Reiter, and B. K. Follet, editors. Progress in reproductive biology. Volume 5. S. Karger, Basel, Switzerland.

———, AND M. C. MOORE. 1987. Hormonal, social, and environmental factors in the reproductive biology of free-living male birds. Pages 148–175 *in* D. Crews, editor. Psychobiology of reproductive behavior: an evolutionary perspective. First edition. Prentice-Hall, Englewood Cliffs, New Jersey, USA.

———, AND M. RAMINOFSKY. 1999. The impact of stress on animal reproductive activities. Pages 130–163 *in* P. H. Balm, editor. Stress physiology in animals. CRC Press LLC, Boca Raton, Florida, USA.

WISEMAN, B. S., D. L. VINCENT, P. J. THOMFORD, N. S. SCHEFFRAHN, G. F. SARGENT, AND D. J. KESLER. 1982. Changes in porcine, ovine, bovine and equine blood progesterone concentration between collection and centrifugation. Animal Reproductive Science 5:157–165.

WOOD, A. K., R. E. SHORT, A.-E. DARLING, G. L. DUSEK, R. G. SASSER, AND C. A. RUDER. 1986. Serum assays for detecting pregnancy in mule and white-tailed deer. Journal of Wildlife Management 50:684–687.

WOOLF, A., AND J. D. HARDER. 1979. Population dynamics of a captive white-tailed deer herd with emphasis on reproduction and mortality. Wildlife Monographs 67.

WYDOSKI, R. S., AND D. E. DAVIS. 1961. The occurrence of placental scars in mammals. Proceedings of the Pennsylvania Academy of Science 35:197–204.

ZARROW, M. X., J. M. YOCHIM, AND J. L. McCARTHY. 1964. Experimental endocrinology: a sourcebook of basic techniques. Academic Press, New York, USA.

ZEPP, JR., R. L., AND R. L. KIRKPATRICK. 1976. Reproduction in cottontails fed diets containing a PCB. Journal of Wildlife Management 40:491–495.

ZIEGLER, T. E., G. SCHEFFLER, AND C. T. SNOWDON. 1995. The relationship of cortisol levels to social environment and reproductive functioning in female cotton-top tamarins, *Saguinus edipus*. Hormones and Behavior 29:407–424.

ZUG, G. R., L. J. VITT, AND J. P. CALDWELL. 2001. Herpetology—an introductory biology of amphibians and reptiles. Second edition. Academic Press, New York, USA.

ZWANK, P. J. 1981. Effects of field laparotomy on survival and reproduction of mule deer. Journal of Wildlife Management 45:972–975.

23

ANIMAL BEHAVIOR: ITS ROLE IN WILDLIFE BIOLOGY

Jessica R. Young

INTRODUCTION

A species' relationship to its environment cannot be interpreted without understanding factors influencing its social behavior. The study of animal behavior or ethology has been a key component of our abilities to use and conserve wildlife. Skilled hunters or biologists can describe with detail the behaviors of the individual they are tracking. A founder of the field of wildlife biology, Aldo Leopold (1949), used animal behavior to illustrate the need for new management paradigms in *A Sand County Almanac*. Currently, wildlife biologists and managers struggle with understanding animal movements, site fidelity, and social transmission of information in an increasingly fragmented environment. Given the importance of comprehending animal behavior, it is remarkable how few studies combine the fields of wildlife management and animal behavior.

Despite the importance of understanding animal behavior, its study has not been widely used in the field of conservation or management because of differences in training and study emphases. Sutherland (1998*b*), in a 1996 survey of *Animal Behaviour,* reported that of 229 papers, none directly related to conservation or management. Martin (1998) reviewed 8 behavioral texts and found that only one had a chapter on the application of behavior studies to management and conservation. These authors and others have proposed hypotheses about reasons why wildlife biology and animal behavior have not become more integrated. One of the major issues may be the unit of study used. Animal behavioral biologists tend to focus on the individual or behavioral differences among populations created by individual adaptations to local environmental challenges. Wildlife biologists are generally more concerned with study of populations; consequently, as individuals become numbers within demographic models, behavior of individual animals is often lost (Martin 1998).

Traditional boundaries between different academic departments reinforce disconnection of animal behavior from management studies (Martin 1998). Within the United States and Canada, practitioners in their respective fields are generally in different academic departments within colleges and universities. While it is fairly common for a behavioral ecologist in a higher education program to include coursework in community and population ecology, wildlife biology programs rarely (less than 3% in the United States) (J. R. Young, unpublished data), include a required course in animal behavior or behavioral ecology. Many wildlife biologists presently believe that most studies in animal behavior have little direct impact on species management and conservation.

There are notable exceptions in which wildlife studies and conservation biology studies have thoughtfully integrated behavior into management. Increasingly, proceedings from wildlife management and conservation symposia (e.g., Weller 1988), books (Gosling and Sutherland 2000), and book series (Chapman and Hall's [London, United Kingdom SE1 8HN] *Wildlife Ecology and Behaviour*) demonstrate an increasing awareness of the importance of studying animal behavior. While more papers in management journals include aspects of animal behavior, studies generally are focused on basic descriptions of foraging behaviors and habitat use, and fail to integrate modern developments such as game theory, optimal foraging, cultural evolution and the importance of phenotypic plasticity (Sutherland 1998*b*). Frequently, wildlife studies are not conducted in a manner that encourages development of predictive models of population demography, dispersal, or habitat use based on changes in individual behaviors due to anthropogenic activities. Two solutions are needed to correct the disconnect between wildlife biology and animal behavior: researchers and students in each discipline need more exposure to the concepts and ideas of both disciplines, and management teams should include behavioral biologists to incorporate behavioral studies relevant to management or conservation issues.

ANIMAL BEHAVIOR AND WILDLIFE BIOLOGY
Behavior of Whooping Cranes

Wildlife biologists have learned to include insights from animal behavior into management of wildlife populations. For example, the whooping crane (*Grus americana*) has become an international symbol of the challenges of managing and recovering populations of endangered species. This largest of North American cranes was once widely distributed across the north-central United States and southern Canada. During the late 1800s and early 1900s, over-harvesting by settlers and homesteaders led to large-scale population declines (Allen 1952). By 1939, J. J. Lynch (unpublished data) reported the large size and conspicuous plumage of the whooping crane had made it an easy mark for hunters and there were only a few scattered pairs left breeding in the wild. By 1939 only 2 populations remained, a migratory population, which nested in Canada and wintered in Texas, and a nonmigratory group nesting in Louisiana. Wildlife biologists faced a crisis when, by 1941, only 16 birds remained in the migratory population in winter at Aransas National Wildlife Refuge, Texas (Lewis 1995), and less than a dozen in the nonmigratory population. Today, all whooping cranes are genetic descendants of those 16 individuals. The nonmigratory genetic heritage was lost with the death of Josephine in the New Orleans Zoo (R. C. Drewien, personal communication). A major challenge for wildlife biologists was to increase the size of the migratory population since migration routes, nesting locations, and wintering sites were "learned" behaviors. While in many species migration appears to be an "innate" behavior (Box 1), in whooping cranes social interactions appear key to the establishment of migration routes. In 1975, a field experiment was initiated to re-establish a migratory flock through cross-fostering whooping cranes using sandhill cranes (*Grus canadensis*) as foster parents.

Wildlife biologists "cross-fostered" whooping cranes by having them raised by closely related sandhill crane parents. Whooping cranes generally produce 2 eggs but raise only one chick. Wildlife biologists took advantage of this behavior by removing one of the eggs from nests of wild and captive birds and placing it in nests of selected pairs of sandhill cranes at Grays Lake National Wildlife Refuge, Idaho in 1975.

This experiment initially appeared to be successful, as the foster parents raised whooping crane chicks and successfully taught them feeding habits and the 1,350-km migratory pathway to Bosque Del Apache National Wildlife Refuge, New Mexico (Drewien and Bizeau 1978). However, it became apparent that lack of previous behavioral studies on one key aspect of the social behavior of whooping cranes was critical to understanding the underlying failures of the experiment. While migratory behavior was a learned behavior, sexual imprinting influenced choice of mates. This is a special type of imprinting in which choice of sexual partner is determined during early development. Exposure in the initial hours after hatching can permanently influence the choice of mates for many species of birds. Unfortunately, no one had studied the extent to which whooping cranes became sexually imprinted on their parents, as there was little opportunity to do so prior to the cross-fostering experiment. While male whooping cranes raised by foster parents established breeding territories and nests, they did not pair with whooping crane females. However, at least one hybrid was produced by a male whooping crane and a female sandhill crane. The last known whooping crane in the experimental population disappeared in 2002.

Wildlife managers and conservation biologists learned from this experience and recently established a new migratory population of whooping cranes that migrate between Wisconsin and Florida following motorized ultralights. The first fall migration occurred in 2001. In fall 2002, 16 young whooping cranes imprinted to ultralight aircraft migrated over 7 states in a 1,900-km journey lasting 49 days (www.operationmigration.org). In 2002, birds from the previous year migrated north without aid of the ultralight aircraft. The success of this experiment, as measured by successful reproduction with members of their own species, will not be known for several years.

The use of information from behavioral studies has been critical to the initial success of the Wisconsin-Florida experiment (Operation Migration) (as well as releases of over 200 fledged juveniles in the Florida nonmigratory population, R. C. Drewien, personal communication). Care has been taken in these experiments to prevent imprinting young whooping cranes on humans. In the Wisconsin-Florida experiment, cranes hatched from eggs incubated by captive mothers are taken to Necedah National Wildlife Refuge, Wisconsin for acclimation to the wild. Human handlers dress in costumes and teach the young cranes critical survival skills including foraging, predator avoidance and avoidance of humans (Fig. 1).

Box 1.   Learned and innate behaviors.

These are behaviors that are modified by experience and the environment. For example, young whooping cranes learn which types of areas are suitable for foraging by following adults. In contrast, innate behaviors are behaviors that are performed the same way each time after their initial expression. Innate behaviors are usually "hard-wired" in species nervous systems. An example of an innate behavior in cranes is performing highly ritualized mating displays such as head bowing and leaping into the air.

Fig. 1. A costumed pilot works to train young whooping cranes by using a puppet head and a loud speaker playing a soft purring sound that chicks would normally hear from their mother (photograph courtesy of Operation Migration).

Placement of Wood Duck Nest Boxes

Understanding the mechanisms of social interactions among female wood ducks (*Aix sponsa*) has led to recent management changes. Wood ducks are secondary-cavity nesters and inhabit wetlands including swamps and marshes during the breeding season, and seek cavities created by other species such as the pileated woodpecker (*Dryocopus pileatus*) (Bellrose and Holn 1994). In such cavities, wood ducks may lay a clutch of up to 14 eggs (Semel and Sherman 1992). In a natural setting, wood ducks typically nest solitarily in dispersed and cryptic tree cavities. Deforestation and wetland habitat loss led ornithologists to predict that wood ducks would be extinct around the turn of the 20th century (Hepp and Bellrose 1995). Several factors have contributed to the existence of the healthy populations observed today. Approval of the Migratory Bird Treaty Act, conservation and creation of wetlands, and use of nest boxes (Fig. 3) to replace cavities lost from old growth forest harvesting were major factors leading to wood duck recovery.

Undoubtedly, use of artificial nest boxes has led the overall recovery of wood duck populations since the turn of the 20th century (Hepp and Belrose 1995). Ironically, the mechanism for recovery led to an overall reduction of clutch sizes when artificial boxes were compared to natural cavities. While establishment of nest boxes helped provide nest cavities for wood ducks, it also increased intraspecific brood parasitism (Semel et al. 1990, Semel and Sherman 1993). The most common method of placing wood duck nesting boxes by wildlife managers was to cluster the boxes to make them visible. This changed the solitary nesting practices of wood ducks to semicoloniality. Thus, females had a much higher chance of being observed by con-

Eventually, these birds are taught to follow their costumed trainer as the trainer operates a motorized ultralight (Fig. 2). Efforts for the nonmigratory flock in Florida include teaching young cranes to avoid predators by roosting in water as well as other survival skills. The challenge of teaching learned behaviors to long-lived species that depend on social transmission of behavior is difficult with experimental flocks. The lesson learned from whooping cranes is that prior studies of species' behavior within their natural environment are critical for future management and conservation efforts.

Fig. 2. Whooping cranes follow an ultralight craft from Wisconsin to Florida, possibly establishing a new migratory population (photograph courtesy of Operation Migration).

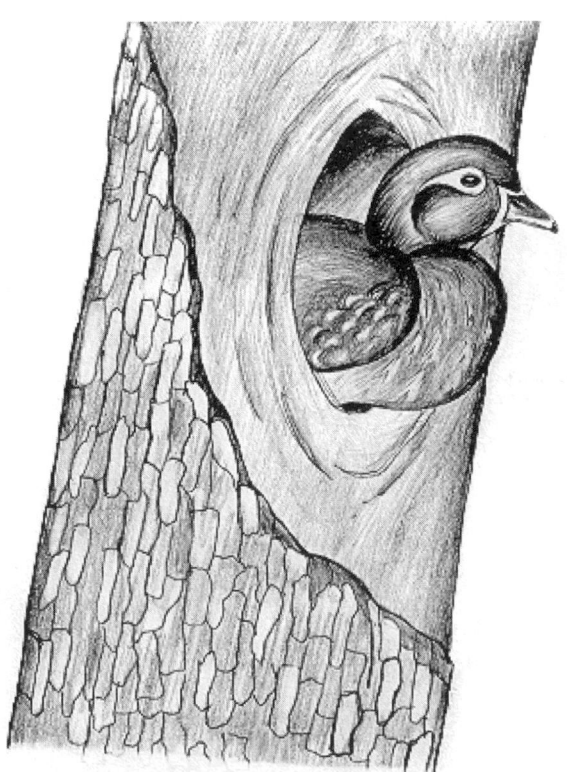

Fig. 3. Wood duck female emerging from nest (drawing courtesy of R. W. Henninger).

specifcs and, therefore, a higher probability of having their nest parasitized (Semel and Sherman 1986).

Intraspecific brood parasitism occurs when a female lays eggs (egg dumping) into the nest of another female. Egg dumping is triggered in wood ducks by females observing members of their own species entering or leaving nest sites (Semel et al. 1988). Waterfowl have relatively high rates of nest parasitism and studies have shown that nest parasitism in wood ducks can exceed 50% (Semel et al.1988). A consequence of intraspecific nest parasitism can be unusually high clutch sizes. While natural cavity nests of wood ducks have an average clutch size of 9–12 eggs, parasitized nests in nest boxes often contain 20 or more eggs and have lower hatching success (Semel et al. 1988). One possible reason could be that larger clutch sizes have a greater hatching asynchrony, or eggs that hatch at different times, causing fewer chicks to be produced per clutch. Hatching success may also be lower because of aggressive interactions between females when nest parasitism is attempted. At Nauvoo Slough, Illinois, 379 eggs of 76 nesting females were crushed due to female intraspecific aggression (Bellrose and Holm 1994).

Animal behavior biologists have teamed with wildlife managers to find solutions to enhance wood duck populations. Understanding female intraspecific nest parasitism behavior has led to placement of nest boxes in dispersed and concealed areas within habitats preferred by wood ducks. While occupation rates may be lower, clutch success should be higher and the dispersed nesting behavior of the species will be preserved.

Ibex Reintroductions

Understanding natural behavioral rhythms is critical as reintroductions and population augmentations often have an initial high failure rate. One reason for lack of success may be absence of integration of animal behavior into study designs. Unfortunately, despite considerable effort to examine habitat suitability and food availability, rarely do wildlife managers seek to understand how the fundamental behavioral ecology of a species might differ among populations, subspecies, or between individuals of different ages and gender.

A classic example of reintroduction efforts not succeeding due to a lack of behavioral knowledge occurred when ibex (*Capra ibex*) from the Tatra Mountains in Czechoslovakia became extirpated during the first half of the 19th century. The Tatra Mountains rise in elevation to 2,600 m and are quite cold in spring with frequent snowstorms and temperatures below 0 C. Local populations of ibex were adapted for the mountainous environment and bred in mid-winter causing young to be born in late spring (Turcek 1951).

During the beginning of the 20th century, ibex from 3 different populations (nearby Austria and warmer climates in Asia) and 3 different species (*Capra ibex, C. hircus,* and *C. nubiana*) were translocated to the Tatra mountains. The 3 species interbred and their hybrids had different physical and behavioral characteristics than the ancestral stock. The breeding season for the hybrids occurred in late summer and offspring were born in early spring. Young born in early spring were unable to survive the cold temperatures and storms so generation after generation failed until they became locally extirpated (Turcek 1951). An under-

standing of the reproductive behavior of the 3 species would probably have helped provide better management solutions to re-establish ibex to the Tatra Mountains.

SENSORY PERCEPTION

The previous examples demonstrate how understanding fundamental aspects of an animal's behavior can lead to better management and conservation decisions. A major challenge for wildlife biologists is to not let their own sensory limitations blind them to the importance of sources of information for other species. This could lead to *anthropomorphism* of the behavior, or interpretation of the behavior in human contexts, motivations, and biases. When wildlife managers are deciding which behavioral information is important, they should consider that one of the fundamental principles of animal behavior is to learn to comprehend the world through the senses of the animal being studied. Jakob von Uexkull (1864–1944) coined the term "Umwelt" to describe how an animal senses its universe (von Uexkull 1921). He recognized that preconceived ideas about how animals should behave often came from ignorance of how animal senses worked. He challenged us to imagine the world from an animal's perspective by learning what senses were available and active during different stages of their lives.

One example von Uexkull (1921) used, which is useful to consider for all who have walked the woods, is how a tick's perception of its universe changes depending on environmental stimulus. Ticks have simple sequential behaviors based on which sensory perceptions of their external environments are functioning. While adult ticks are waiting on the end of a piece of vegetation they are in a form of almost suspended animation until their olfactory senses detect the unique shape of a butyric acid molecule (common in mammalian sweat). Their nervous system reacts by sending signals that allow them to let go of the vegetation. They then quit receiving signals from their butyric acid receptors and can only detect heat. When they detect heat, they burrow toward the sources of greatest heat. Imagine a world from a tick's perspective. One would not see or hear or feel until they encountered butyric acid. The encounter would "turn on" a new sensory perspective of the world centered on heat. Other environmental signals would have little meaning.

Often our lack of understanding of other animals' sensory perception and its importance have led to poor management decisions or unintended consequences. Studies contrasting our sensory perception to that of other animals have shown how differently they view the world from us. Animal senses are the mechanisms through which animals find food, mates, and shelter and affect timing and processes of migration and hibernation. Most senses such as hearing, sight, smell, taste, and touch are familiar to us; however, sensitivity to the stimuli activating the senses varies greatly. Radar, compasses, and infrared detectors are technologies that allow us to mimic other animals' senses that we do not possess.

Understanding the importance of animals' sensory mechanisms has become increasingly important in understanding subtle impacts of human activities on the landscape. For example, some forest birds depend on certain light conditions before performing their mating displays. Further, changes in stream turbidity due to forest management can affect the duration and location of fish mating behaviors (Endler 1997). The major point of understanding sensory perception is that researchers cannot begin to comprehend animal behavior until they let go of their human biases and place themselves in the animal's world.

Hearing

Hearing has a large role in how most mammals interpret their environments. It also has a critical role for many species for individual recognition, mate choice (Howard and Young 1998), locating prey (Ryan et al. 1982), avoiding predators and navigating (Roeder and Treat 1961). We can misunderstand animal behavior because our hearing is often less acute. Because animals use sound for so many purposes, we often underestimate the extent to which our sound pollution interferes with vital functions of wildlife, such as mating activities and foraging behavior (reviewed by Larkin 1996). For example, recent evidence suggests that military use of strong sonar can cause different species of whales (Cetacea) to beach themselves due to brain hemorrhages (Jepson et al. 2003).

Mammals and birds hear sounds by detecting pressure waves with the use of membranes and hair cell sensory receptors (Bradbury and Vehrencamp 1998). The tympanic membrane vibrates in tune to the frequencies of the pressure waves and stimulates sensory cells within the ear that send signals for processing in the brain. Sound waves have no inherent directionality so one challenge for wildlife is to localize sounds. Most mammals have pinnae or external ears to aid in localizing the source of sounds (Bradbury and Vehrencamp 1998). Bats (Chiroptera) and many ungulates such as mule deer (*Odocoileus hemionus*) can rotate their pinnae toward the source of the sound to aid in locating it. Barn owls (*Tyto alba*) have offset ear openings to allow them to localize small running rodents by sound in the complete absence of all light. Their offset ears and facial ruffs allow processing differences in the intensity and timing of the arrival of sound waves of running rodents to help precisely locate them (Proctor and Konishi 1997).

There is significant variation in animal hearing. Elephants (Elephantidae) use low frequency sounds undetectable to humans (less than 20 Hz) for communication across vast expanses of open savannah environments (Heffner and Heffner 1982, Langbauer et al. 1991). Many avian species can hear faint sounds at low frequencies that may warn them of approaching storms or may disrupt their flight when exposed to commercial jet sound shockwaves (Hagstrum 2000). Bats hear high frequency sounds above our detection abilities (greater than 20,000 kHz) and use these sounds to detect prey as small as mosquitoes. Cave swiftlets (*Aerodramus linchi*) and oilbirds (*Steatornis caripensis*) use relatively high frequencies for echolocation to find entrances to caves and relatively large ($\leq$ 20 mm) items in the dark (Griffin and Suthers 1970).

Perhaps one of the most common reasons for animals to produce sounds is for communication. There is a rich body of research examining the different things animals communicate through sound. For example, Gunnison sage-grouse (*Centrocercus minimus*) perform elaborate mating displays (Fig. 4) in which their sounds can be heard for $\geq$ 1 km. Their vocalizations and mechanical sounds are used to communicate their willingness to mate, warn members of the same gender away from potential mates, and attract

Fig. 4. Gunnison sage-grouse perform ritualized displays on their mating grounds. Sounds are produced both by syringeal vocalizations and mechanically releasing air from their yellow air sacs (photograph courtesy of J. D. Sartore).

females to their mating site (Young 1994). Bull elk (*Cervus elaphus*) produce a variety of calls during rut, which serve to defend their territories and attract cows to their location. Common ravens (*Corvus corax*) vocalize loudly when finding a large carcass. This behavior seems counterintuitive (why bring competitors for food to the scene?). Careful testing of alternative hypotheses led to the discovery that young ravens intruding on territories of older pairs vocalized to draw large groups of conspecifics to the scene to avoid being forced from the food bonanza by the territory owners (Heinrich 1988). Begging by young birds is a signal to parents to increase food delivery. This communication between parents and their offspring has been used by species such as brown-headed cowbirds (*Molothrus ater*) in which the young brood parasites produce louder calls than their nest mates.

Vision

While almost all organisms are sensitive to light, vertebrates have developed the ability to capture images from their environment and synthesize information about those images. We can misunderstand the impact of different levels of visual acuity unless we understand that humans have only moderate abilities for detecting electromagnetic energy or light. Most other animals have evolved different levels of light sensitivity for finding food, detecting threats, and orienting themselves in their environments (Bradbury and Vehrencamp 1998).

Light is captured in photoreceptor cells that contain photopigments. In vertebrates, the cells are called rods and cones and are packed densely within the eyes to form the retina. Rods allow for vision in low light conditions and cones are responsible for color vision in high-light-intensity environments. The ability to resolve fine details in the environment depends on the number of receptor cells in a given area, the optical system, and the neurological mechanism for passing the signals to the brain (Bradbury and Vehrencamp 1998).

One of the most obvious ways we alter visual habitats is the extent to which we illuminate the nights. *Photopollution* is the detrimental addition of light into an animal's environment with nocturnal animals being most at risk. For example, most species of sea turtles (Cheloniidae and Dermochelyidae) are listed as threatened or endangered and will not nest on preferred habitat beaches if the beaches are lit (Witherington 1992). If they do nest on beaches with night lighting, their hatchlings are often at risk as they move toward the light rather than toward the relative safety of the sea. Behavioral research is providing wildlife managers with guidelines for safely lighting beaches without impacting sea turtle behavior (Witherington 1997). Another problem with light pollution occurs from *phototaxis* or light attraction by birds towards lighted radio towers at night. When weather conditions bring low cloud ceilings or fog, lights on towers cause refraction creating areas of illumination around the towers. Thousands of migrating birds that have lost their stellar cues are attracted to the lighted area and may die if they collide with the tower or its supports (Avery et al. 1976).

In general, most birds have better distance vision than mammals and can see 2–3 times farther than humans (Gill 1995). One of the greatest variations in vision among species is differing abilities to see color. Many mammals such as hamsters (Cricetinae), Virginia opossum (*Didelphis virginiana*), raccoons (*Procyon lotor*), and some monkeys (Primates) and bats, have little to no color vision while birds can sense portions of the color spectrum such as ultraviolet light. For example, Eurasian kestrels (*Falco tinnunculus*) use ultraviolet trails left by small mammals marking their runs with urine to locate prey corridors (Koivula et al. 1999) and female European starlings (*Sturnus vulgaris*) use ultraviolet cues for mate choice (Bennett et al. 1997). Some snakes, such as rattlesnakes (*Crotalis* spp.) and other pit vipers (Viperidae), use wavelengths of light that allow them to detect infrared waves not visible to us at the other end of the visual spectrum (Hartline et al. 1978). The ability to sense an infrared wavelength is critical for their success in hunting small mammals emitting such frequencies of light. The position of a tail may send subtle signals to subordinate members of a gray wolf (*Canis lupus*) pack. The same wolves may end a chase of white-tailed deer (*Odocoileus virginianus*) that wave their tail (Fig. 5) in a conspicuous flagging behavior, alerting the wolves that they have been seen. Species such as Thomson's gazelles (*Gazella thomsonii*) use vigorous "*stotting*" displays to warn approaching predators they have been seen by their prey (Caro 1986). Stotting occurs when gazelles bound up and down with all four legs held stiffly while displaying their white rump patch (Fig. 5).

Olfaction

Smell is poorly understood and we are only beginning to recognize the extent anthropogenic activities influence the "smellscape." Species such as Pacific salmon (*Oncorhynchus* spp.), an important food item for bears (Ursidae), are significantly impacted by our olfactory pollution of their streams. One mechanism involved in the decline of salmon in the Pacific Northwest appears to be their dependence on olfactory cues for returning to their natal streams (Scholz et al. 1976, Nevitt et al. 1994).

Olfaction is possible through reception of chemicals and was likely one of the first animal senses to evolve. Most, if not all, wildlife possess some sort of olfactory organ that allows them to detect airborne chemical messages. In general, there is some type of inlet (e.g., mouth or nose) that leads to a chamber carpeted in sensory cells that respond differentially to diverse olfactory chemicals (Bradbury and Vehrencamp 1998). Historically, scientists believed that birds had poor or no sense of smell due to the

Fig. 5. Stotting activities of gazelles (left) and tail wagging by white-tailed deer (right) provide visual signals to potential prey and predators. These signals are probably adaptive evolutionary traits as the prey signal the unprofitability of pursuit to the predator. Thus, both prey and predator can save energy by avoiding energetically expensive escape activities and chases (drawing courtesy of R. W. Henninger).

relatively small olfactory bulbs in their brains. Currently, we know that most, if not all, birds possess a sense of smell and can detect odors as accurately as mammals (Clark et al. 1993). Nocturnal birds and carrion eaters such as vultures have better senses of smell than other birds. Turkey vultures (*Cathartes aura*) can detect traces of the chemical ethyl mercaptan that is released from decaying meat (Smith and Paselk 1986). Engineers have taken advantage of the vultures' olfaction abilities by pumping small amounts of ethyl mercaptan into pipelines with breaks and then watching where vultures gather (Gill 1995). Leach's storm-petrels (*Oceanodroma leucorhoa*) can detect odors up to 25 km emitted by krill, small crustacea that occur in groups in the ocean (Clark and Shah 1992). Mammals also have a keen sense of smell, with nocturnal predators having abilities thought to be 10–100 fold as great as our own.

There are many advantages of using chemical communication over auditory cues. For example, pheromones in urine are likely to last days or weeks while songs and howls last only until the singer is finished. *Allomones* are chemical signals passed between species such as between predator and prey. *Pheromones* are chemical messages (organic compounds with a carbon skeleton) passed within the same species. Pheromones are likely used by mammals for mate identification and attraction, territory marking and defense, and as alarms of danger or stress (Bradbury and Vehrencamp 1998).

Sources for pheromones include excretory products such as urine and feces or specialized glands on the outside of the animal's body. Some mammals, such as ground squirrels (*Spermophilus* spp.) and goats (Bovidae), produce pheromones from sebaceous glands associated with their skin and hair follicles. Other mammals, such as mustelids (Mustelidae), have anal glands that produce secretions. Some ungulates, such as pronghorn (*Antilocapra americana*), have preorbital glands by their eyes. Most cervids, such as mule deer, produce pheromones from tarsal and metatarsal glands on their legs and tails. They often rub their leg against their head and then rub their forehead on stems and bark to transfer their scent.

Pheromones can be used for courtship and cervids likely convey information about individual identification, reproductive status as well as social status (Eisenberg and Kleiman 1972, Johnston 1998). Some birds may use pheromones to elicit sexual responses in males. The ability of mallards (*Anas platyrhynchos*) to mate may depend on males detecting pheromones produced by females. Balthazart and Schoffeniels (1979) found that male mallards with their olfactory nerves excised did not exhibit courtship behavior in the presence of females. Animals often also use pheromones for territorial marking. Pheromones in mammalian urine are a common method of territorial marking for large carnivores and other mammals.

Taste/Contact Reception

While smell is sensing airborne chemicals, taste depends on contact reception of chemical molecules. We know little about how changes in animals' environments interfere with their sense of taste. Currently, most management activities studying taste are taste aversion studies. *Conditioned taste aversion* is a learned behavior that occurs when negative consequences (getting ill, hurt,

shocked, etc.) occur following consumption. Cowen et al. (2000) published an excellent review of the use of taste aversion for reducing predation.

Chemical receptor cells in the mouth are specialized nerve cells that react upon contact with different molecules. Taste is shaped by an initial molecule which binds tightly to a specific protein receptor and then undergoes a physical change causing a neurological signal to be passed to the brain. The intensity of a taste is influenced by the number of cells binding to receptors, types of cells, and density of receptors being activated at a given moment in time. Chemical receptor cells are some of the shortest-lived cells in an animal's body, only functioning for a few days until they are replaced (Bradbury and Vehrencamp 1998).

The number and kinds of receptors present likely influence taste. Birds have relatively few taste receptors (usually less than 100) while mammals such as humans have over 10,000 taste buds on their tongues (Gill 1995, Mason and Clark 2000). Both number and types of receptors are important in the sense of taste.

One way that mammals communicate by taste is through use of a chemosensory organ called the *vomeronasal organ* (Jacobson's organ), which is a single opening lying between the nasal cavity and the roof of the mouth (Bradbury and Vehrencamp 1998). Some ungulates perform a behavior called *flehmen* (Fig. 6) after they contact another individual's urine or secretions during which they pull back their upper lip to cover their nostrils and raise their head to close off airflow into their epiglottis (Doty 2001). This behavior enables them to draw air into their vomeronasal organ. The receptors within the organ are more structurally similar to taste receptors than those located in the nose for smell. This form of communication is probably important for assessing information about mating status and territoriality.

Touch

Touch is commonly used by all wildlife but is poorly understood and studied. While we recognize the importance of touch in mating rituals, antagonistic encounters, social grooming, and other social behaviors, its role compared to visual and vocal displays is not well investigated. In addition to using touch for communication, it can be a

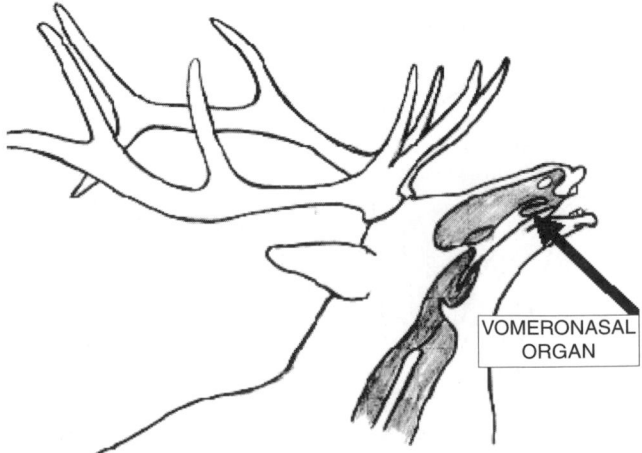

Fig. 6. Elk performing Flehman behavior as it exposes its vomeronasal organ to "taste" the air (drawing courtesy of R. W. Henninger after Bradbury and Vehrencamp [1998]).

critical sense for navigation in the dark in forests or through subterranean or subnivian (below the snow) environments.

Touch occurs when *mechanoreceptors* are directly stimulated. While tactile sensory systems are most developed in burrowing mammals, moles (Talpidae) and elephants have tactile sensors in their lips and snout allowing them to sense their environment through touch. In birds, filoplumes and bristles are specialized feather mechanoreceptors used for sensory functions. Filoplumes associated with flight feathers in the joints of the wings help adjust to minute changes in wind pressures during flight, while those associated with general body feathers may provide information about airspeed (Clark and De Cruz 1989, Gill 1995). Flightless birds, such as penguins (Spheniscidae) and ostriches (Struthionidae), are devoid of filoplumes.

The types of mechanoreceptors can vary as well as their location and numbers. Specialized mechanoreceptors occur in the vibrissae (whiskers) of many mammals and in filoplumes and bristles on birds. Touch receptors in the bristles of birds can be seen in flying insectivores such as common nighthawk (*Chordeiles minor*) and swallows (Hirundinidae) which have bristles around their mouths to sense the lightest touch of a mosquito (Gill 1995). In mammals, vibrissae often occur around the eyes, muzzle, ears or tail and can provide detailed information to the animal about size, shape, and movement in its environment (Ahl 1986). Pressure receptors are often associated with hair in mammals. Social grooming in primates stimulates the receptors and is an important aspect of many primates' social systems. Many small mammals, such as kangaroo rats (*Dipodomys* spp.), use touch for seismic communication in their environment. Kangaroo rats communicate by foot-thumping species-specific and individually recognized patterns (Randall 1997). Blind mole-rats (*Spalax ehrenbergi*) thump their heads against their subterranean tunnel walls to defend territories (Hill 2001).

Other Senses

Barometric Pressure

Many species of birds apparently have some form of mechanical receptors to allow them to assess subtle changes in barometric pressure (Bagg et al. 1950). Many species of songbirds often engage in feeding frenzies prior to low-pressure systems creating winter storms. Birds of the same species are often found in the same altitudes during nocturnal migration, suggesting they can adjust their flights based on pressure differences (Gill 1995).

Magnetic Fields

Another important sense that birds and other species possess is the ability to sense magnetic fields. The exact mechanism behind this sense is still under debate (Walcott et al. 1979, Phillips and Borland 1992); however, there is strong evidence that many avian species can detect weak magnetic fields from the earth (Wiltschko and Wiltschko 2003). While use of magnetic fields for information appears to be common in invertebrates (Boles and Lohmann 2003), bacteria (Blakemore 1975), and sea turtles (Fig. 7) (Lohmann et al. 2001), the extent to which mammalian species can detect magnetic fields is just now being explored. Some evidence suggests that rats are influenced by magnetic fields (Reuss and Oclese 1986).

Fig. 7. Lohmann et al. (2001) outfitted loggerhead sea turtle (*Caretta caretta*) hatchlings with harnesses tethered to an electronic tracking unit that recorded the turtles' position as they responded to manipulated magnetic fields. The hatchlings processed magnetic information to follow innate migration routes, suggesting they possess a "magnetic map" (photograph courtesy of K. J. Lohmann).

FORMING BEHAVIORAL HYPOTHESES

Our activities and efforts can have unintended consequences on management of a species because of ignorance of how those actions will change the animals' social behavior and social organization (e.g., attempts to control animal populations believed to have an economic impact on our activities). Efforts to control the transmission of bovine tuberculosis by killing European badgers (*Meles meles*), which are hosts of the disease, may actually cause higher transmission rates as individuals encounter each other at higher rates because of the changing dynamics of their social organization (Swinton et al. 1997).

Once wildlife biologists have accepted that animals have different senses that are adapted to increase the probability of reproductive success or survival in different environments, they can begin to understand the importance of developing hypotheses about how an animal's behavior can influence its reactions to efforts to manage or conserve its population. Garton et al. (2005) present an excellent review of critical features for hypothesis testing in wildlife biology and management. However, it is important to understand how formation of hypotheses for testing ideas about behavioral ecology may differ from traditional hypothesis testing for wildlife science.

Tingbergen (1963) recognized that all behavioral hypotheses could be examined using 4 categories: evolution, development/ontogeny, function, and causation. One way to develop hypotheses is to distinguish between *ultimate* (those involving evolution and development) and *proximate* (those involving function and causation) questions. Imagine behavioral biologists coming upon a male mule deer rubbing its antlers back and forth across a small aspen (*Populus tremuloides*) tree or a bush. When forming an evolutionary or ultimate hypothesis, they would ask questions such as "Does the rubbing of its antlers increase its survival or reproductive success?" or "When did rubbing behavior evolve in this species?" These questions can turn into testable ultimate hypotheses with specific predictions. Behavioral biologists may form mechanistic or proximate hypotheses about the physiological or neurological mechanisms leading to the rubbing behavior by asking questions such as "Do the male's hormones trigger the rubbing behavior?" or "Are males more likely to rub their antlers during certain seasons?" These questions can be turned into testable hypotheses regarding the mechanisms behind the expression of the behavior.

Both ultimate and proximate hypotheses can lead to important insight into the management and conservation of species. For example, if after careful study it was concluded that males which had more rubs on small diameter trees were more likely to mate, subsequent management of aspen tree age classes could influence the distribution and reproductive success of mule deer in that area. If it was found that males only rubbed their antlers during certain seasons, antler rubs would be an indication of population use of habitat on a seasonal basis promoting management decisions about access and physical disturbance activities during different times of the year. It is important to recognize that while there are 2 major types of behavioral hypotheses, examining one logically leads to examining the other.

DIRECT METHODS FOR OBSERVING BEHAVIOR

Direct observation is generally necessary to gather sufficient independent quantitative data for statistical testing of hypotheses about animal behavior. One of the most important and often overlooked methods for observing and recording behavior is keeping a daily field journal that can lead to formation and testing of hypotheses about animal behavior. A good field journal should always include: dates, times, places, conditions (wind, clouds, etc.), description of the habitat, and description of activities and distributions of animals in the habitat.

During direct observations, the researcher must consider and implement ways to minimize observer effect on animal behavior, yet still understand and acknowledge that observer presence may cause changes in their subject's behavior. While considering how to mask the observer's presence, our sensory biases may lead us astray and we consider only visual masking with blinds or platforms. Olfactory presence is probably of even greater significance for mammals in general and especially critical for carnivores.

Visual masking is important; however, the observer should acknowledge that animals generally know the observer is present in blinds and towers. Often the observer will arrive well before the animal and leave after their study organism has left. While studying Gunnison sage-grouse in Colorado, Young (1994) often arrived by 0300 hours and spent long, cold hours in a blind until the last bird left the display ground after 0900. While the visual presence of the observer was somewhat masked, it is uncertain to what extent olfactory presence influenced the bird's breeding behavior. Even when the study organism appears to be habituated or accustomed to the observer's presence, it is difficult to ascertain the extent to which categories of individuals (genders, age classes, etc.) are differentially affected by other sensory indications that an observer is near. Bekoff (2000) provides a more complete

review of observer effects on study animals.

There are a variety of ways to mark individuals to allow behavioral observation at a distance. The study design may require that marks are observable from a few to hundreds of meters. The common error of overestimating sample sizes in wildlife studies is exacerbated by a tendency for wildlife managers to mark study populations rather than uniquely mark each individual, as is more common in behavioral studies. Behavioral ecologists should carefully consider their needs before embarking on individually marking their study organism. One critical question that should be asked is the extent to which retention of the mark is needed. For example, amphibians may rapidly re-grow clipped toes and bands may discolor or be lost from birds. Other considerations should include minimizing stress or possibility of injury to the study animal. Finally, many marking techniques may have unintended consequences on the behavior of the study animal or the behavior of individuals interacting with the marked individual. For example, Burley (1988) found that color banding zebra finches (*Poephila guttata*) influenced mate choice. Schemnitz (2005) provides a more complete review of marking.

After animals are marked, researchers may assign a name for field recognition. Most researchers advocate use of letters or numbers that have no subjective bias associated with them and avoid using personal names. Bekoff (1997) offers a contrasting view that naming an animal increases researchers' respect for their study organism.

STRATEGIES FOR DEFINING BEHAVIORS
Observations

Observing animals, leading to increased familiarity, is a critical step in defining behaviors for a study organism. Martin and Bateson (1996) suggest it is vital to get to know the organism and to review the literature before defining terms. There are 2 reasons for informal observations preceding quantitative studies. The first is that it is generally through informal observations that hypotheses are formed. The second is that choosing the appropriate methods to address hypotheses is greatly assisted by a period of observation. Young researchers, or those studying an animal for the first time, should also review published literature on how behavioral definitions have been formed and used.

Lehner (1996) distinguished between watching animals and rigorously observing them. Informal observers should understand the difference. A baby sitter may watch children while a psychologist observes them. Both are valuable activities, but the psychologist's observations are far more likely to lead to testable hypotheses. While observations can initially be informal, they should still be able to provide intricate detail about individuals and their social behaviors.

Behavioral Definitions

Behavioral definitions should be sufficiently precise so they can be communicated clearly to other field personnel and researchers; definitions should avoid bias. For example, defining types of movement such as still, walking, running or flying, is generally more objective than suggesting the cause of the movement (resting, boredom, fear, migration, etc.). For each term, the researcher should apply a definition that makes the term mutually exclusive from

Table 1. Types of data obtained and behaviors measured with different sampling methods (modified from Altmann 1974).

Sampling method	State or event sampling	Behavioral measure	Weakness
Ad libitum	Either	Opportunistic measures suitable for field notes or for initial observations prior to hypotheses testing	Over-estimates rare behaviors, cannot use statistics on observations given nonrandomness of sampling
Focal-animal	Either	Provides good information about rates, durations, within animal sequences, and interactions	Difficult to gather data on sequence of interactions among individuals
Scan	State	Provides good estimates of time budgets or the percentage of time individuals spend doing different activities in a group	Does not provide duration data and usually is limited to recording a few types of behavioral acts
Sociometric matrix	Event	May provide information about dominance structure and other group social structures	Obtaining random sequences is challenging and rarely done

other terms. Walking could be defined as taking less than 10 steps in a 5-second interval while running could be defined as taking greater than 5 steps in a 10-second interval. Behaviors can either describe structure (posture, movement, etc.), consequences (escape, compete, etc.), or relative position with inter- or intraspecifics (approach, flee). Two warnings are appropriate. Behavioral definitions based on consequences of the behavior and those based on inter- or intraspecific interactions are often larger categories of activities and can be associated with human bias. Definitions based on structure can often generate excessive detail that does not necessarily test general hypotheses well.

Indirect vs. Direct Measures of Behavior

It is important to consider types of questions that can be addressed with indirect behavioral observations. For many animals, direct observations are challenging at best and indirect observations may provide valuable insight into the social behavior of the species. Indirect observations of behavior include studying tracks, markings, foraging sites, bite marks, frequency of scars, feces, and even chewing of radio-transmitter collars. One exciting method for using indirect behavior has been recording of nocturnal avian migration vocalizations to provide survey measurements (Evans and Mellinger 1999).

TYPES OF SAMPLING

Altmann (1974) provided an excellent paper on sampling methods for behavioral biologists. There are 4 basic sampling methods: *ad libitum* sampling, focal-animal sampling, scan sampling, and social sampling. Each type of sampling method has benefits and costs associated with its use (Table 1).

Ad libitum sampling occurs when the observer notes what they see that seems relevant or interesting. A major problem with this type of sampling is that it lacks randomization for meeting the requirement of independence for statistical tests and it is likely to bias observers to over-estimate conspicuous behaviors. Consider the excitement of watching a coyote (*Canis latrans*) chase a ground squirrel.

While it may be interesting to note the sequence of action and the depredation event, it would not provide a researcher with information on the frequency or duration of predatory events for either species. Ad libitum sampling can be useful when the observer is first observing a species to gather preliminary information for hypothesis formation or to record rare events, but is rarely useful for actually testing hypotheses.

Focal-animal sampling occurs when one individual or group (when several groups are present) is watched continuously for a set period of time and all acts which the animal either initiates or has directed toward it are recorded. Generally, the investigator has formed an *Ethogram* or a catalog of carefully defined, mutually exclusive behaviors to use to categorize the behavioral repertoire of the focal animal (Table 2). The choice of the focal animal is often randomized to prevent observer bias or established for experimental design reasons prior to the initiation of the study. One major challenge of focal-animal sampling is that the targeted individual may move from sight or leave before the period of time for their sampling is finished. Behavioral biologists form explicit rules about how to proceed with this common occurrence. While each rule may differ among studies, the critical aspect is that they are applied equally by different observers and across time within the same study. For example, while watching a herd of pronghorn, the targeted individual may disappear behind a hill. The observer can either record "time out" for the period it is out of sight or switch observations to a new focal animal. One caution about using this type of sampling occurs if the study animal generally performs certain behaviors secretly or with great privacy (e.g., birthing, mating, etc.), which would lead to those behaviors being under-represented. Focal-animal sampling provides good information about rates, durations, sequences, and interactions. It is considered by most biologists to be the type of sampling that will have the highest dividends for testing the original hypothesis, as well as providing information for subsequent studies.

Scan sampling uses a census (total count) of an entire group of animals for a single behavior or a small set of behaviors. For example, while watching a flock of geese

Table 2. An ethogram for bald eagles (*Haliaeetus leucocephalus*) providing mutually exclusive descriptions of behaviors. This ethogram identifies relative amount of time spent by male and female eagles in foraging but does not distinguish between relative frequencies of different types of aggressive behaviors.

Resting (RS)	The eagle is not performing any active behavior, remaining stationary for more than 10 seconds.
Self-preening (SP)	The eagle is manipulating its own feathers with its beak.
Allo-preening (AP)	The eagle is manipulating feathers of a conspecific.
Foraging (FG)	The eagle is actively attacking or consuming food items.
Nest Building (NB)	The eagle is creating a nesting structure or carrying nesting material to a nesting structure.
Nest Incubation (NI)	The eagle is sitting in a nest or manipulating an egg within a nest.
Courtship Flight (CF)	The eagle is performing aerial flight displays with his mate.
Vocalizing (VC)	The eagle is vocalizing.
Flying (FY)	The eagle is in the air and not courting a mate.
Walking (WK)	The eagle is hopping or walking on the ground.
Aggression (AG)	The eagle is demonstrating aggressive behaviors toward a conspecific (pecking, erecting feathers, etc.).

(Anatidae), a researcher would scan the group for 15 seconds every 5 minutes to record how many geese in the group have their heads up in an alert manner. While short sampling periods are important for this methodology, realistically the sampling period will be affected by group size and complexity of behaviors. The important factor is to keep sampling short and constant across samples. The time it takes will be a function of group size, number of behaviors recorded, and general visibility. Scan sampling is a good method of measuring the distribution of behaviors within a group and can also be used to measure the extent behaviors are synchronized within a group. Scan sampling can also help the observer estimate *time budgets* or the percentage of time individuals spend doing different activities. For example, if the researcher wanted to know whether male green-winged teal (*Anas crecca*) spent more time (and therefore energy) on vigilance behavior than their mates prior to the nesting season, scan samples could be quite useful. One problem with this type of sampling is that it does not provide the ability to estimate the duration of behaviors (unless they are performed for long periods of time or the sampling is virtually instantaneous), and it is generally limited in the number of behaviors that can be investigated.

Social structure sampling examines social structure rather than individual behavior. It is an important type of sampling that can be useful for examining social dynamics between pairs of individuals and among groups (McDonald et al. 2000). Social dynamics are the resultant interaction of an individual's ecology and behavior. Understanding the social dynamics of a species is critical to predicting the consequences of actions taken to manage wildlife.

Historical methods for studying social dynamics include sequence sampling, which allows the investigator to follow a chain of behavioral interactions between individuals or successive animals in a group. It can be challenging to identify the beginning or end of a sequence and choosing sequences at random is rarely done.

Pair-wise interactions between individuals or species that can be measured using sociometric matrix sampling can be useful for identifying social dominance (Lehner 1996) or other types of social behaviors. McDonald et al. (2000) provide an excellent review of current methodologies for examining and organizing questions about social structure.

Each sampling method has strengths and weaknesses. Most behavioral biologists combine more than one methodology to test their research hypotheses. The key to selecting the correct methodology is being certain the methods chosen are best to measure the behavior to be quantified to statistically test the hypothesis and the methodology has been carefully defined to allow others to repeat the experiments.

TYPES OF BEHAVIORAL MEASUREMENT

Behaviors can be recorded as either *events* or *states*. Events are behaviors, such as mounting, vocalizing, etc., which occur for a relatively short duration while states are behaviors such as rutting or foraging which indicate prolonged activity.

Frequencies are measurements of how often specific behaviors occur during some unit of time (Fig. 8). Frequency of events, such as fighting, is often used to measure behaviors for social interactions. In general, frequencies are the most common type of behavior measurement. *Durations* are often used to measure states such as rutting or migratory behavior. Durations are important measurements in time budget analyses. *Latency* or the *initiation time* is measuring the time when a behavior begins following another behavior (Fig. 8). For example, a researcher may be interested in the latency to attack after a gray wolf raises the hair on the back of its neck. *Intensity* is an indication of how extreme the behavior expressed is or how loud a vocalization may be. Researchers can associate the presence of certain acts with either high or low intensity to provide more objective measurements. For example, a threat display from a gray wolf may be of higher intensity if it has hair raised, lips curled, and its tail is

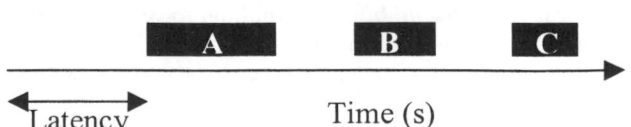

Fig. 8. The black bars measure the occurrences of a behavior such as foraging by mountain sheep (*Ovis canadensis*) over time. The bars represent 3 occurrences of foraging in time (t) and frequency of foraging would be 3/t. Latency is the measure of time until the behavior first occurred. The total duration of foraging during the observation period is (a + b + c). The proportion of time spent foraging is (a + b + c)/t (after Risenhoover and Bailey 1985).

held in an upright posture. *Bouts* are common post-field analyses. Bouts reduce behavioral observations into temporal clusters (courting bouts, foraging bouts, singing bouts, etc.) of behavior. A bout is generally recognized as a period of time in which a behavior occurs regularly but not continuously (Bart et al. 1998). Occasionally, defining bouts is easy because the behavioral activities occur in discrete clumps of time separated by a standard amount of time. When Gunnison sage-grouse perform mating displays, they have a fairly regular pattern of behaviors followed by a few seconds of rest (Young et al. 1994). However, sage-grouse can be quite variable in how long they perform the displays and how long they rest between "bouts" of mating displays. Because bouts of displays can vary by individuals, absolute definitions of time defining a bout often mask individual variation within a species. There are several techniques that allow observers to define bouts mathematically (Slater and Lester 1982, Sibly et al. 1990, Martin and Bateson 1996).

USEFUL NEW CONCEPTS

Improved technology has made aspects of recording animal behavior easier and allowed us to view previously inaccessible types of behavior. Use of computers, specialized software, and improved camera technology has dramatically aided our ability to record and analyze behavioral data.

Software

There are numerous programs available that allow a laptop computer or personal digital assistant (PDAs) to record and analyze behavioral data. For example, Biobserve (http://www.biobserve.com/) provides software for generating ethograms, recording events and social interactions, and creating x/y coordinate systems from videos. They also provide hardware for using infrared sensors and illumination to record observations of behaviors directly onto computers. Many products work on PDAs (Palm Pilot, Pocket PC, etc.) as well as more traditional hardware. Other commercial products include "Forager," a program designed to simulate current foraging concepts, record data, and produce reports and maps. Many academic laboratories produce software for use on both Windows and MacIntosh platforms. The Animal Behavior Society has both a website with current software (http://www.animalbehavior.org/Resources/software.htm) and archives of software. Software has been developed for quantifying animal behaviors, social structure, movements, spatial data, and vocalizations. Colorado State University (Fort Collins) has a large collection of software developed for examining mark–recapture data for population estimates and distributions (http://www.cnr.colostate.edu/~gwhite/software.html).

There are several challenges associated with using computers or hand-held personal digital assistants to record observational data. Many researchers have been confronted with the unfortunate reality that their electronic information has not been recorded or saved through a variety of failures. Another challenge, not unique to this platform, is that watching behavioral interactions while operating recording computers (or pencil and paper!) causes observers to take their eye off of their subjects. The advent

of voice recognition software will likely replace tape recorders as a solution to this enduring problem.

Cameras

Video can be useful for field studies because observations can be viewed multiple times and different sampling methodologies can be used on the same behavioral sample. Videos of field observations can also be used as important training tools to increase inter-observer reliability. Video cameras can help observers see details of rapidly performed behaviors and understand the mechanisms of those behaviors. Longer battery life, (up to 12 hours) has made video cameras more portable for field studies. Along with changes in size and weight have come improvements in technology. Even a relatively inexpensive video camera has superior light gathering ability compared to those commercially available during the last decade, allowing high quality records during dusk and dawn. There are also video cameras and optical devices sensitive to infrared light that have infrared light emitters within them for night viewing. Another technology change has been the advent of fiber optic cameras that can be placed into nests, dens, and burrows to allow glimpses of behaviors previously unavailable for observation.

Digital cameras can be used to take pictures of feathers, pelage, skin, or scar patterns on animals, allowing them to be individually identified. While traditional cameras can also perform this task, the resolution and ability to immediately access and manipulate digital images make them much more useful in the field. Both video and digital cameras can be set to automatically record events in the absence of the investigator. While there is some risk of technology failure with such endeavors, the ability to capture rare events of particularly secretive animals or to record depredation events makes automatic recordings a welcome additional field tool.

Internet Access

The advent of increased access to the Internet has enormous potential for allowing exchange of raw data and observations that can enhance research efforts and collaborations. Most peer-reviewed journals no longer publish general observations or common and rare events that can provide insight into behavioral events. The inability to examine other researchers' data in a form that leads to new analyses increases wasteful efforts of repeating studies and hinders population comparisons. Posting of such data on personal websites would be helpful. A second opportunity provided by the Internet is the ability for researchers to share video examples of tools such as digital ethograms. Stewart et al. (1997) created a multimedia vocal ethogram of European badgers based on digital video. These types of contributions, while not publishable in the traditional sense, enhance communication among scientists and help alleviate disagreements in the published literature from misunderstandings of basic methodology. Sharing of Internet databases and methodologies led to major advances in DNA research and could do the same in the field of behavioral ecology.

MANAGING HUMAN (ANIMAL) BEHAVIOR

Managing human behavior will be one of the most

Fig. 9. The increase in wildlife viewing requires new approaches to managing human behavior to prevent impacts on wildlife (photograph courtesy of J. R. Young).

important wildlife management priorities in the 21st century. Historically, managing human exploitation of resources was the most common form of behavioral management. Currently, human behavior associated with non-consumptive uses of wildlife is of growing concern. Many states and provinces receive greater economic benefits and associated human impacts from recreational activities such as wildlife watching than they do from hunting. Wildlife watchers (Fig. 9) who visited, photographed, and fed wildlife had a reported economic value of 82 billion dollars including paying 13 billion dollars in state and federal taxes in 2001 (La Rouche 2003). While federal land management agencies are beginning to grasp the implications of changing uses of wildlife and their ecosystems, most state and provincial agencies are still focused on hunting and other consumptive uses.

As habitat and wildlife viewing becomes increasingly restricted due to reduced areas of suitable habitat and growing conservation concerns, the impact on animal behavior and fitness will increase due to human disturbance (Hockin et al. 1992, Knight and Gutzwiller 1995, Gill and Sutherland 2000). Animals may avoid areas with high human traffic, noise or light pollution, or structures such as blinds resulting in habitat sinks or areas unsuitable for their reproduction and habitation. Several studies have demonstrated that at least some species will avoid roads (Mattson et al. 1987, Gill 1996) causing the effects of roads to be greater than the actual area of habitat loss. Sutherland (1998a) developed mathematical models to examine the effects of human disturbance at the species level. A critical role for behavioral biologists and ecologists is to provide information to wildlife managers about the consequences of human disturbance on population parameters such as density-dependent breeding and mortality.

Increasingly, wildlife managers will need to take proactive steps toward managing the impacts of human behavior on wildlife. While the formation of "Watchable Wildlife" sites may help consolidate impacts, it is important that such sites are monitored and evaluated as to their population level impacts. In the Gunnison Basin, Colorado, the designation of Gunnison sage-grouse as a new species

(Young et al. 2000) led to enormous increases in visitation at a designated viewing area. As visitor numbers increased, attendance of males and females at that mating ground declined at a rate greater than at mating grounds not designated for public viewing (J. R. Young, unpublished data). Clear criteria for managing human impacts are needed as well as studies providing wildlife managers with data to make informed decisions. Incidents such as bear attacks and other negative interactions with wildlife are increasing at refuges and national parks. Research, management, and education will be important undertakings as increasing numbers of people seek visitation to such sites with concomitant effects on wildlife and human behaviors.

FUTURE DIRECTIONS

The challenge for future biologists in wildlife management and animal behavior is to examine how studies can better integrate the fields. A recent study by Sherri Huwer, a graduate student at Colorado State University, demonstrates the importance of integrating the fields of wildlife biology and animal behavior. Huwer is using human imprinted sage-grouse chicks (Fig. 10) to test ideas about effects of habitat quality on chick development. Her study is helping resolve important management and conservation questions in sage-grouse management that could not be resolved with traditional radiotracking or observational studies. Other areas of investigation that could allow behavioral studies to provide new insight into wildlife

Fig. 10. Sherri Huwer uses a field incubator to collect her human-imprinted greater sage-grouse (*Centrocercus urophasianus*) chicks at the end of the field day (photograph courtesy of J. R. Young).

Table 3. Examples of animal behavior studies that could enhance current efforts to manage and conserve species (Sutherland 1998*b*, Gosling and Sutherland 2000).

Allee effect	The Allee effect is a decline in individual fitness due to low population density. Recent behavioral studies suggest that mechanisms for reduced fitness at low population densities may be behavioral. An important tool for conservation will be to understand the role of individual behavior in increasing risk of extirpation or extinction in small populations.
Communication	Detecting sources of communication among conspecifics can enhance understanding of social structure and increase ability to census animals.
Dispersal	Knowing which gender and at what age animals disperse from family groups, distances they travel, as well as the conditions leading to survival success, will be critical for habitat designation in multiple use areas and for reserve design.
Diversity	Research quantifying behavioral diversity among individuals and populations is an important tool for wildlife management. While many wildlife managers are sensitive to the concept of maintaining morphological and genetic diversity, few consider the importance of managing to maintain variation in behavior. Behavioral diversity is critical for allowing adaptation to different ecological conditions and changing landscapes.
Foraging behavior	Studies showing the effects of habitat quality on distribution of animals and subsequent changes in behavior in sub-optimal habitat patches will be important as increasing human populations intrude into traditional foraging sites of animals.
Learning and cultural transmission of behavior	One of the major causes of failure of reintroductions has been that newly released animals fail to know where to forage and hide from predators. Field studies of species investigating the importance of con specifics roles in the transmission of behavior could be invaluable.
Life history traits	Traits such as fecundity, age class, and survival can change due to behavioral responses to exploitation of species. Understanding population responses to exploitation will require an understanding of individual behavior.
Mating systems	A fundamental understanding of how changes in densities of populations and preferred habitats affect mating systems, could help in understanding population level responses of species of concern as well as hunted species. A second important area of research is to understand how variation in mating systems among populations change effective population sizes.
Migration	Understanding species mechanisms and ultimate causes of migration will be critical during the next century as human population growth leads to greater habitat degradation, fragmentation, and loss. Knowing why an area is critical for migratory success will allow either preservation or replacement to facilitate historical movements.
Sensory studies	We are only beginning to understand the unintended consequences of how odor and light pollution impact migrating species. Basic research into animal senses could provide answers to some of the more intractable wildlife management and conservation challenges. A second area requiring more research is learning how to manipulate the distribution of animals through aversion conditioning based on an understanding of their sensory systems.
Sexual imprinting	Studying the mechanisms behind sexual choice is important to successful captive breeding programs, releases, and re-introductions.
Sexual selection	Studies examining the relationship between mating preferences and trait variation among populations could allow predictions of success for population augmentations.
Stress	Changes due to atypical weather, pollution, and population density can change hormonal secretions leading to adaptable change in behavior. Understanding which factors cause a physiological and behavior change due to an animal's stress levels will be critical for managing sources of noise pollution and human activity patterns in important wildlife habitats.

management include communication, dispersal, diversity, Allee effect, foraging behavior, etc. (Table 3).

SUMMARY

This chapter introduces methods for studying behavior by wildlife biologists and suggests important future areas of study. Given the global biodiversity crisis, integrating knowledge of animal behavior with wildlife management and conservation is critical. A fundamental understanding of animal behavior will be necessary to develop robust metapopulation models, understand true effective population sizes, and understand consequences of anthropomorphic changes on landscapes. While the goal of conservation is often at the ecosystem level and the goal of wildlife management generally deals with populations, all levels of biological inquiry (from genes to communities) are necessary for successful management and recovery of species and their ecosystems. Important first steps to fostering cross-disciplinary approaches include additional understanding of animal behavior in wildlife curriculums, joint regional and national meetings of disciplinary societies, developing chapters and units on applied animal behavior for courses and programs, and willingness to embrace collaboration across traditional disciplinary boundaries.

ACKNOWLEDGMENTS

I acknowledge C. E. Braun for editorial assistance; S. L. Thode and K. L. Brown for support and grammar skills; and J. L. Bacon for technical writing skills. P. A. Magee, R. C. Drewien, and K. M. Martin helped with chapter revisions. P. J. French and P. J. Muckleroy provided invaluable assistance with revision, format, and research. I thank Western State College of Colorado for support while this chapter was being prepared.

LITERATURE CITED

AHL, A. S. 1986. The role of vibrissae in behavior: a status review. Veterinary Research Communications 10:245–68.

ALLEN, R. P. 1952. The whooping crane. Resource Report 3. National Audubon Society, New York, USA.

ALTMANN, J. 1974. Observational study of behavior: sampling methods. Behaviour 49:227–267.

AVERY, M., P. F. SPRINGER, AND J. F. CASSEL. 1976. The effects of a tall tower on nocturnal bird migration: a portable ceilometer study. Auk 93:281–291.

BAGG, A. M., W. W. H. GUNN, D. S. MILLER, J. T. NICHOLS, W. SMITH, AND F. P. WOLFARTH. 1950. Barometric pressure patterns and spring bird migration. Wilson Bulletin 62:5–19.

BALTHAZART, J., AND E. SCHOFFENIELS. 1979. Pheromones are involved in the control of sexual behaviour in birds. Naturwissenschaften 66:55–56.

BART, J., M. A. FLIGNER, AND W. I. NOTZ. 1998. Sampling and statistical methods for behavioral ecologists. Cambridge University Press, Cambridge, United Kingdom.

BEKOFF, M. 1997. Deep ethology. Pages 35–44 in M. Tobias and K. Solisti, editors. Intimate relationships, embracing the natural world. Beyond Worlds Publishing, Hillsboro, Oregon, USA.

———. 2000. Field studies and animal models: the possibility of misleading inferences. Pages 1553–1560 in M. Balls, A.-M. van Zeller, and M. E. Halder, editors. Progress in the reduction, refinement and replacement of animal experimentation. Elsevier Science, Philadelphia, Pennsylvania, USA.

BELLROSE, F. C., AND D. J. HOLM. 1994. The ecology and management of wood ducks. Wildlife Management Institute and Stackpole Books, Harrisburg, Pennsylvania, USA.

BENNETT, A. T. D., I. C. CUTHILL, J. C. PARTRIDGE, AND K. LUNAU. 1997. Ultraviolet plumage colors predict mate preference in starlings. Proceedings of the National Academy of Sciences 94:8618–8621.

BLAKEMORE, R. 1975. Magnetotactic bacteria. Science 190:377–379.

BOLES, L. C., AND K. J. LOHMANN. 2003. True navigation and magnetic maps in spiny lobsters. Nature 421:60–63.

BRADBURY, J. W., AND S. L. VEHRENCAMP. 1998. Principles of animal communication. Sinauer Associates, Sunderland, Massachusetts, USA.

BURLEY, N. T. 1988. Wild zebra finches have band colour preferences. Animal Behaviour 36:1235–1237.

CARO, T. M. 1986. The function of stotting: a review of the hypotheses. Animal Behaviour 34:649–662.

CLARK, JR., A. C., AND J. B. DE CRUZ. 1989. Functional interpretation of protruding filoplumes in oscines. Condor 91:962–965.

CLARK, L., AND P. S. SHAH. 1992. Information content of prey odor plumes: what do foraging Leach's storm petrels know? Pages 421–427 in R. L. Doty and D. Müller-Schwarze, editors. Chemical signals in vertebrates. VI. Plenum Press, New York, USA.

———, K. V. AVILOVA, AND N. J. BEAN. 1993. Odor thresholds in passerines. Comparative Biochemistry and Physiology 104A:305–312.

COWAN, D. P., J. C. REYNOLDS, AND E. L. GILL. 2000. Reducing predation through conditioned taste aversion. Pages 281–291 in L. M. Gosling and W. J. Sutherland, editors. Behaviour and conservation. Cambridge University Press, Cambridge, United Kingdom.

DOTY, R. L. 2001. Olfaction. Annual Review of Psychology 52:423–452.

DREWIEN, R. C., AND E. G. BIZEAU. 1978. Cross-fostering whooping cranes to sandhill crane foster parents. Pages 201–222 in S. A. Temple, editor. Endangered birds: management techniques for preserving threatened species. University of Wisconsin Press, Madison, USA.

EISENBERG, J. F., AND D. G. KLEIMAN. 1972. Olfactory communication in mammals. Annual Review of Ecology and Systematics 3:1–32.

ENDLER, J. A. 1997. Light, behavior, and conservation of forest dwelling organisms. Pages 329–355 in J. R. Clemmons and R. Buchholz, editors. Behavioral approaches to conservation in the wild. Cambridge University Press, Cambridge, United Kingdom.

EVANS, W. R., AND D. K. MELLINGER. 1999. Monitoring grassland birds in nocturnal migration. Studies in Avian Biology 19:219–229

GARTON, E. O., J. T. RATTI, AND J. H. GIUDICE. 2005. Research and experimental design. Pages 43–71 in C. E. Braun, editor. Techniques for wildlife investigations and management. Sixth edition. The Wildlife Society, Bethesda, Maryland, USA.

GILL, F. B. 1995. Ornithology. Second edition. W. H. Freeman and Company, New York, USA.

GILL, J. A. 1996. Habitat choice in pink-footed geese: quantifying the constraints of winter site use. Journal of Applied Ecology 33:884–892.

———, AND W. J. SUTHERLAND. 2000. Predicting the consequences of human behavior disturbance from behavioral decisions. Pages 51–64 in L. M. Gosling and W. J. Sutherland, editors. Behaviour and conservation. Cambridge University Press, Cambridge, United Kingdom.

GOSLING, L. M., AND W. J. SUTHERLAND. 2000. Behaviour and conservation. Cambridge University Press, Cambridge, United Kingdom.

GRIFFIN, D. R., AND R. A. SUTHERS. 1970. Sensitivity of echolocation in cave swiftlets. The Biological Bulletin 139:495–501.

HAGSTRUM, J. T. 2000. Infrasound and the avian navigational map. Journal of Experimental Biology 203:1103–1111.

HARTLINE, P. H., L. KASS, AND M. S. LOOP. 1978. Merging modalities in the optic tectum: infrared and visual interaction in rattlesnakes. Science 199:1225–1229

HEFFNER, R. S., AND H. E. HEFFNER. 1982. Hearing in the elephant: absolute sensitivity frequency discrimination, and sound localization. Journal of Comparative Physiology 96:926–944

HEINRICH, B. 1988. Winter foraging at carcasses by three sympatric corvids, with emphasis on recruitment by the raven, *Corvus corax*. Behavioral Ecology and Sociobiology 23:141–156.

HEPP, G. R., AND F. C. BELLROSE. 1995. Wood duck (*Aix sponsa*). Number 169 in A. Poole and F. Gill, editors. The birds of North America. Academy of Natural Sciences, Philadelphia, and American Ornithologists' Union, Washington, D.C., USA.

HILL, P. S. M. 2001. Vibration and animal communication: a review. American Zoologist 41:1135–1142.

HOCKIN, D., M. OUNSTED, M. GORMAN, D. HILL, V. KELLAR, AND M. A. BARKER. 1992. Examination of the effects of disturbance on birds with reference to its importance in ecological assessments. Journal of Environmental Management 36:253–286.

HOWARD, R. D., AND J. R. YOUNG. 1998. Individual variation in male vocal traits and female mating preferences in *Bufo americanus*. Animal Behaviour 55:1165–1179.

JEPSON, P. D., M. ARBELO, R. DEAVILLE, I. A. P. PATTERSON, P. CASTRO, J. R. BAKER, E. DEGOLLADA, H. M. ROSS, P. HERRÁEZ, A. M. POCKNELL, F. RODRÍGUEZ, F. E. HOWIE, A. ESPINOSA, R. J. REID, J. R. JABER, V. MARTIN, A. A. CUNNINGHAM, AND A. FERNÁNDEZ. 2003. Was sonar responsible for a spate of whale deaths after an Atlantic military exercise? Nature 425:575–576.

JOHNSTON, R. E. 1998. Pheromones, the vomeronasal system, and communication: from hormonal responses to individual recognition. Annals of the New York Academy of Sciences 855:333–348.

KNIGHT, R. L., AND K. J. GUTZWILLER. 1995. Wildlife and recreationists: coexistence through management and research. Island Press, Washington, D.C., USA.

KOIVULA, M., J. VIITALA, AND E. KORPIMÄKI. 1999. Kestrels prefer scent marks according to species and reproductive status of voles. Ecoscience 6:415–420.

LA ROUCHE, G. P. 2003. Birding in the United States: a demographic and economic analysis. 2002. Addendum to the 2001 National Survey of Fishing, Hunting and Wildlife-Associated Recreation. Report 2001-1. U.S. Department of the Interior, Fish and Wildlife Service, Washington, D.C., USA.

LANGBAUER, JR., W. R., K. B. PAYNE, R. A. CHARIF, L. RAPAPORT, AND F. OSBORN. 1991. African elephants respond to distant playbacks of low-frequency conspecific calls. Journal of Experimental Biology 157:35–46.

LARKIN, R. 1996. Effects of military noise on wildlife: a literature review. U.S. Army Corps of Engineers, Construction Engineering Research Laboratory (CREL) Technical Report. Champaign, Illinois, USA.

LEHNER, P. N. 1996. Handbook of ethological methods. Second edition. Cambridge University Press, New York, USA.

LEOPOLD, A. 1949. A Sand County almanac and sketches here and there. Oxford University Press, New York, USA.

LEWIS, J. C. 1995. Whooping crane (*Grus americana*). Number 153 *in* A. Poole and F. Gill, editors. The birds of North America. Academy of Natural Sciences, Philadelphia, Pennsylvania and American Ornithologists' Union, Washington, D.C., USA.

LOHMANN, K. J., S. D. CAIN, S. A. DODGE, AND C. M. LOHMANN. 2001. Regional magnetic fields as navigational markers for sea turtles. Science 12:364–366.

MARTIN, K. 1998. The role of animal behavior studies in wildlife science and management. Wildlife Society Bulletin 26:911–920.

MARTIN, P., AND P. BATESON. 1996. Measuring behaviour: an introductory guide. Third edition. Cambridge University Press, Cambridge, United Kingdom.

MASON, J. R, AND L. CLARK. 2000. The chemical senses of birds. Pages 39–56 *in* Sturkie's avian physiology. Fifth edition. Academic Press, San Diego, California, USA.

MATTSON, D., R. KNIGHT, AND B. BLANCHARD. 1987. The effects of development and primary roads on grizzly bear habitat use in the Yellowstone National Park, Wyoming. International Conference on Bear Research and Management 7:259–273.

MCDONALD, D. W., P. D. STEWART, P. STOPKA, AND N. YAMAGUCHI. 2000. Measuring the dynamics of mammalian societies: an ecologist's guide to ethological methods. Pages 332–380 *in* L. Boitani and T. K. Fuller, editors. Research techniques in animal ecology: controversies and consequences. Columbia University Press, New York, USA.

NEVITT, G. A., A. H. DITTMAN, T. P. QUINN, AND W. J. MOODY. 1994. Evidence for a peripheral olfactory memory in imprinted salmon. Proceedings of the National Academy of Sciences 91:4288–4292.

PHILLIPS, J. B., AND S. C. BORLAND. 1992. Behavioural evidence for use of a light-dependent magnetoreception mechanism by a vertebrate. Nature 359:142–144.

PROCTOR, L., AND L. M. KONISHI. 1997. Representation of sound localization cues in the auditory thalamus of the barn owl Proceedings of the National Academy of Sciences 94:10421–10425.

RANDALL, J. A. 1997. Species-specific foot drumming in kangaroo rats: *Dipodomys ingens, D. deserti, D. spectabilis.* Animal Behaviour 54:1167–1175.

REUSS, S. P., AND J. OCLESE. 1986. Magnetic field effects on the rat pineal gland: role of retinal activation by light. Neuroscience Letter 64:97–101.

RISENHOOVER, K. L., AND J. A. BAILEY. 1985. Foraging ecology of mountain sheep: implications for habitat management. Journal of Wildlife Management 49:797–804.

ROEDER, K. D., AND A. E. TREAT. 1961. The detection and evasion of bats by moths. American Scientist 49:135–148.

RYAN, M. J., M. D. TUTTLE, AND A. S. RAND. 1982. Bat predation and sexual advertisement in a neotropical frog. American Naturalist 119:136–139.

SCHEMNITZ, S. D. 2005. Capturing and handling wild animals. Pages 239–285 *in* C. E. Braun, editor. Techniques for wildlife investigations

and management. Sixth edition. The Wildlife Society, Bethesda, Maryland, USA.

SCHOLZ, A., T. ROSS, M. HORRALL, J. C. COOPER, AND A. D. HASLER. 1976. Imprinting to chemical cues: the basis for home stream selection in salmon. Science 192:1247–1249.

SEMEL, B., AND P. W. SHERMAN. 1986. Dynamics of nest parasitism in wood ducks. Auk 103:813–816.

———, AND ———. 1992. Use of clutch size to infer brood parasitism in wood ducks. Journal of Wildlife Management 56:495–499.

———, AND ———. 1993. Answering basic questions to address management needs: case studies of wood duck nest box programs. Transactions of the North American Wildlife and Natural Resources Conference 58:537–550.

———, ———, AND S. M. BYERS. 1988. Effects of brood parasitism and nest box placement on wood duck breeding ecology. Condor 90:920–930.

———, ———, AND ———. 1990. Nest boxes and brood parasitism in wood ducks: a management dilemma. Pages 163–170 *in* L. H. Fredrickson, G. V. Burger, S. P. Havera, D. A. Graber, R. E. Kirby, and T. S. Taylor, editors. Proceedings 1988 North American Wood Duck Symposium. St. Louis, Missouri, USA.

SIBLY, R. M., H. M. R. NOTT, AND D. J. FLETCHER. 1990. Splitting behaviour into bouts. Animal Behaviour 39:63–69.

SLATER, P. J. B., AND N. P. LESTER. 1982. Minimising errors in splitting behaviour into bouts. Behaviour 79:153–161.

SMITH, S. A., AND R. A. PASELK. 1986. Olfactory sensitivity of the turkey vulture (*Cathartes aura*) to three carrion-associated odorants. Auk 103:586–592.

STEWART, P. D., S. A. ELLWOOD, AND D. W. MACDONALD. 1997. Video surveillance of wildlife: an introduction from experience with the European badger *Meles meles.* Mammal Review 27;185–209.

SUTHERLAND, W. J. 1998a. The effect of local change in habitat quality on populations of migratory species. Journal of Applied Ecology 35:418–421.

———. 1998b. The importance of behavioural studies in conservation biology. Animal Behaviour 56:801–809.

SWINTON, J., F. TUYTTENS, D. W. MACDONALD, D. J. NOKES, C. L. CHEESEMAN, AND R. S. CLIFTON-HADLEY. 1997. A comparison of fertility control and lethal control of bovine tuberculosis in badgers: the impact of perturbation induced transmission. Philosophical Transactions of the Royal Society of London, Series B 352:619–631.

TINBERGEN, N. 1963. On aims and methods of ethology. Zeitschrift für tierpsychologie 20:410–433.

TURCEK, F. J. 1951. Effect of introductions on two game populations in Czechoslovakia. Journal of Wildlife Management 15:113–114.

VON UEXKULL, J. 1921. Umwelt und Innenwelt der Tiere. Springer-Verlag, Inc., Berlin, Germany.

WALCOTT, C., J. L. GOULD, AND J. L. KIRSCHVINK. 1979. Pigeons have magnets. Science 205:1027–1029.

WELLER, M. W. 1988. Waterfowl in winter: selected papers from symposium and workshop. University of Minnesota Press, Minneapolis, USA.

WILTSCHKO, R., AND W. WILTSCHKO. 2003. Avian navigation: from historical to modern concepts. Animal Behaviour 65:257–272.

WITHERINGTON, B. E. 1992. Behavioral responses of nesting sea turtles to artificial lighting. Herpetolgica 48:31–39.

———. 1997. The problem of photopollution for sea turtles and other nocturnal animals. Pages 303–328 *in* J. R. Clemmons and R. Buchholz, editors. Behavioral approaches to conservation in the wild. Cambridge University Press, Cambridge, United Kingdom.

YOUNG, J. R. 1994. The influence of sexual selection on phenotypic and genetic divergence among sage grouse populations. Dissertation. Purdue University, West Lafayette, Indiana, USA.

———, C. E. BRAUN, S. J. OYLER-MCCANCE, J. W. HUPP, AND T. W. QUINN. 2000. A new species of sage-grouse (Phasianidae: *Centrocercus*) from southwestern Colorado. Wilson Bulletin 112:445–453.

24

CONSERVATION GENETICS IN WILDLIFE BIOLOGY

Sara J. Oyler-McCance and Paul L. Leberg

INTRODUCTION

Prior to 1980, genetic techniques were not typically used in wildlife biology. With recent technological advances, straightforward and rather inexpensive genetic techniques have emerged, which can be directly applied to wildlife studies. In this chapter we discuss molecular genetic techniques and how they can be applied in wildlife biology. This material is intended for wildlife biologists and managers. Geneticists and those interested in detailed descriptions of each technique are referred to Avise (1994) and Hillis et al. (1996). Here we present a compilation of ideas, techniques, and applications of use to wildlife students and professionals seeking to use molecular genetic techniques.

Molecular Genetic Techniques

Nuclear vs. Mitochondrial Genomes

All genetic techniques and molecular markers described in this chapter examine portions of DNA at some scale. Two different genomes are used in genetic studies of animals. The nuclear genome is biparentally inherited and is found in the cell nucleus. It is large and not well mapped in most species. The mitochondrial genome is housed in the mitochondrion, an organelle involved in cellular metabolism. It is small compared to the nuclear genome and is a circular, maternally inherited molecule that has been well mapped in many species. Nuclear DNA on average evolves slowly although some portions (e.g.,

microsatellites) evolve quickly. Mitochondrial DNA (mtDNA) on average evolves more quickly than the nuclear genome and some areas (e.g., control region) evolve very rapidly. These features make mtDNA and some regions of nuclear DNA suitable targets for certain genetic studies (Avise 1994).

Investigating Genetic Variation

Some molecular techniques consider gene products (e.g., proteins), and some examine DNA variation at the nucleotide level (e.g., DNA sequencing, fragment analysis). In the past, analysis of certain proteins has been easy and economical; however, quantifying variation at the nucleotide level has become a more powerful molecular tool for population genetics and systematics. Some techniques look for differences in actual nucleotide sequence, while others infer relatedness based on analysis of fragments and restriction sites.

The advent of the Polymerase Chain Reaction (PCR) has revolutionized molecular biology. Essentially, PCR is a reaction in which a region of DNA is targeted and amplified exponentially (Avise 1994, Palumbi 1996). This reaction requires development of unique primers, which flank both sides of the targeted region of DNA. Once amplified to large quantities, the targeted region (usually between 100–2,000 base pairs) is available for study with a wide variety of molecular techniques. We briefly review several techniques that have been and are currently used in wildlife studies (Table 1). More detailed and excellent

Table 1. Applicability of common types of molecular markers for wildlife biologists. The number of X's indicates the relative applicability of each technique to a specific question (modified from Mace et al. 1996).

Type of marker	Taxonomic delineations	Regional/ subspecific population structure	Genetic diversity and sub- population structure	Individual ID and paternity/ maternity analysis
Allozymes	XXX	XXX	XXX	X
MtDNA sequences and RFLP	XXXX	XXXX	XX	X
Microsatellites	XX	XX	XXXX	XXXX
Minisatellites	X	X	XX	XXXX
RAPD	X	XX	X	X
AFLP	X	X	XX	XXX

reviews of these and additional genetic markers available for studying genetic diversity in wildlife populations have been presented elsewhere (Avise 1994, Smith and Wayne 1996, Haig 1998).

Analysis of Gene Products

Protein electrophoresis is a technique that can be used to examine population subdivision or structure. Proteins are a series of amino acids joined by peptide bonds. Each amino acid has a distinctive side chain, some of which are either positively or negatively charged. Thus, when an electric current is present these proteins migrate differentially through a matrix based on their charge and on their size and shape. Proteins can then be visualized through histochemical staining or other methods (Murphy et al. 1996). Mutations cause changes in the DNA sequences of amino acids forming proteins, which in turn cause changes in the shape, net charge, and migration rates of proteins. Such changes can be revealed through electrophoresis and provide information showing variability between individuals, populations, or species. While inexpensive, this technique can examine only a small proportion of the variation present in the DNA that codes for the proteins; differences in proteins are not necessary detected. The subset of proteins typically studied with this approach is called allozymes. These proteins, however, may be under selective pressure and may not represent the diversity and divergence present in other genes. Further, the tissue required for this type of analysis typically requires highly invasive/destructive sampling and is logistically difficult to manage in field situations.

Fragment Analysis

Fragment analysis comprises a group of different genetic techniques that explore nucleotide variation indirectly by comparing the size of DNA fragments electrophoretically. Although fragment analysis offers less resolution than direct DNA sequencing, it is cost effective when examining many individuals and many different loci. Among fragment analysis techniques, some cut (cleave) DNA in certain areas, (i.e., Restriction Fragment Length Polymorphisms [RFLPs] and minisatellite fingerprinting), while others amplify many different loci (Random

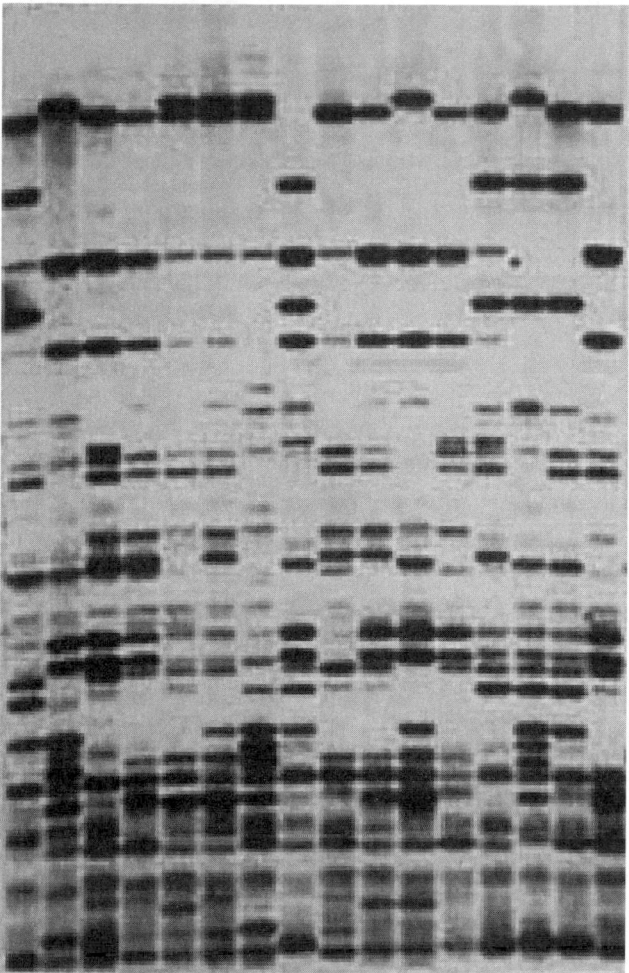

Fig. 1. Example of variation at multiple minisatellite loci. This illustration shows variation within and between families of pukeko (*Porphyrio porphyrio*) detected using markers pV47-2 and 3'HVR (from Lambert et al. 1994).

Amplified Polymorphic DNAs [RAPD], Amplified Fragment Length Polymorphisms [AFLP], and microsatellites). With the exception of microsatellites, these techniques produce multiple fragments (bands) per individual (Fig. 1). In these cases, individuals are compared by the extent of band sharing among individuals. These markers, with the exception of microsatellites, are considered dominant which refers to the fact that they document presence or absence of an allele. Codominant markers are those that reveal both alleles at a given locus (i.e., heterozygotes can be distinguished from homozygotes). Thus, they provide much more information and allow for the documentation of heterozygosity and tests of Hardy-Weinberg Equilibrium and Mendelian inheritance.

For RFLP analysis, the template DNA is typically a small portion of the nuclear or mitochondrial genome that has been amplified using PCR. RFLPs characterize genetic variation using restriction endonucleases, which are enzymes that cleave at specific locations within DNA sequences. Restriction enzymes cleave at a specific recognition sequence, usually 4–6 base pairs long. The enzyme EcoRI, for example, cuts between G and A when it comes across the sequence GAATTC. Thus, every string of GAATTC in the PCR product will be cut in the same location and will produce many fragments of different sizes. Mutations that cause changes in the cleavage site (e.g., GATTC changed to GATAC) prevent the enzyme from cutting at that location thereby producing a different series of fragments (different numbers or sizes of fragments). The series of fragments is then compared to examine the similarity of individuals or populations.

While RFLPs look for variation within a single targeted segment of DNA, other fragment-based methods examine variation throughout the genome. Minisatellites refer to portions of DNA that have variable numbers of tandem repeats (sometimes called VNTRs); the length of each repeat unit is approximately 20 base pairs long. Typically, genomic DNA is digested into many fragments with restriction enzymes. These fragments are then separated by size using electrophoresis. The number of fragments produced by this process precludes visualization of individual bands, so radioactive or fluorescent probes specific for the minisatellite repeat are used to visualize and compare these sequences (Jeffreys et al. 1988). Because such "repeats" are commonly repeated in the genome, it is not unusual for this technique to produce dozens of bands. Although DNA fingerprinting with minisatellites has typically involved analysis with restriction enzymes and labeled probes, PCR-based approaches are becoming more common.

Rapid amplified polymorphic DNAs (RAPD) provide an alternate approach to documenting variation among individuals by generating a set of PCR products (bands) using short, random PCR primers. Variation is presumably due to sequence changes in priming sites or length changes in the PCR products. Analysis involves examining the presence or absence of bands of a particular size. RAPD analysis has the advantage of being a multilocus technique, whereby hundreds of polymorphic loci can be scored with minimal a priori knowledge of the target genome. Two disadvantages with this technique limit its utility: it is a dominant marker system (heterozygotes cannot be distinguished from homozygotes), and its repeatability has been questioned (Ellsworth et al. 1993, Muralidharan and Wakeland 1993).

Amplified fragment length polymorphism (AFLP) analysis is another multilocus technique that involves randomly primed loci and requires no *a priori* knowledge of the target genome (Hill et al. 1996). Analysis of AFLPs involves cutting the genomic DNA with restriction enzymes, and ligating (attaching) short "adapters" of known sequence to the fragment ends. PCR is then used to selectively amplify subsets of these fragments. As with RAPDs, AFLPs produce a series of hundreds of bands on a gel. Scoring is based on the presence or absence of a particular PCR product. AFLP analysis is also a dominant marker system, but has the advantage of being highly repeatable and is being used with increasing frequency (Mueller and Wolfenbarger 1999).

Microsatellite analysis, another PCR-based technique, differs from most other fragment analyses because the attempt is to identify diploid (codominant) genotypes for specific loci. Like minisatellites, microsatellites are VNTRs; however, the repeated sequence is short (2–5 base pairs). Mutation rates of these regions are high and the number of alleles (versions of a particular sequence) per locus in a population is also typically high. Allelic varia-

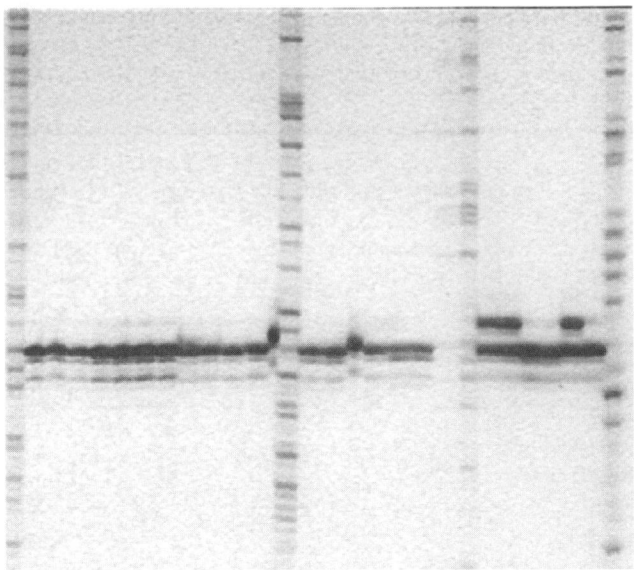

Fig. 2. Example of variation at single microsatellite loci. In this example, the microsatellite locus LST 1 is amplified in 24 individual Gunnison sage-grouse (*Centrocercus minimus*) from 3 different populations. Note that individuals in the first 2 populations are all monomorphic and homozygous for the same allele.

tion is usually in the form of length polymorphism, which can easily be detected on a high-resolution gel. Amplification results in either 1 (homozygote) or 2 (heterozygote) bands per individual (Fig. 2). Microsatellite primers are specific to a single locus and are usually specific to a particular species or group of closely related species. Because of this primer specificity, the development of primers for an individual species can be expensive. The advantages of microsatellite analysis include codominance and high levels of polymorphism. Typically, data from several microsatellite loci are used in a particular study.

DNA Sequence Analysis

Direct DNA sequencing (nuclear or mitochondrial) is one of the most widely used techniques today because it is highly informative and, recently, has become much easier and less expensive to perform. It is also appealing because evolutionary processes can be modeled and integrated into analyses. Further, because the genome is so vast, the amount of information gleaned from sequencing may be quite large. DNA sequencing involves amplifying a target region and then creating a series of labeled (either radioactively or fluorescently) DNA fragments that correspond to each nucleotide in that region (Hillis et al. 1996). The DNA fragments are then separated using eletrophoresis and visualized. Recent technological advances have automated the sequencing process using fluorescently labeled DNA fragments (reviewed by Hillis et al. 1996) that are read by a laser and interpreted by computer software.

Genetic Sampling

For genetic data to be used in a wildlife study, material must be collected from animals in the field. The type of material sampled, sample size, and sampling regime vary according to the questions being asked and the molecular markers being used (reviewed by Baverstock and Moritz 1996). DNA can be extracted from a variety of different tissue including muscle, heart, liver, blood, skin, hair, feathers, saliva, feces, urine, scales, bone, fins, eggshell membranes and, potentially, cervid antlers. DNA extraction techniques for most tissues are well established and involve the isolation of DNA from proteins and lipids using a digestion with the enzyme proteinase K followed by extraction with organic solvents (Sambrook et al. 1989). Modifications to traditional extraction methods, for example, are needed when using hair or feathers when the DNA is encased in the hardened tissue of the shaft and root (reviewed by Morin and Woodruff 1996). DNA has been successfully extracted and used from museum specimens (Mundy et al. 1997) although these techniques can be highly labor intensive and expensive. When considering what type of tissue to sample, several different factors must be addressed. It must first be decided what quantity and quality of DNA is needed to answer the question of interest. Second, the necessity, feasibility, and logistics of trapping and sampling animals must be examined. Finally, field preservation and sample storage issues should be addressed prior to the beginning of a study.

Some molecular techniques require a reasonable quantity of high quality DNA (e.g., sequencing large fragments of mtDNA, DNA-DNA hybridization, protein electrophoresis) while others (most PCR-based techniques) are much more forgiving. Samples of feathers, hair, feces, and urine may contain small amounts of DNA that may be of low quality (sheared into many fragments), whereas, blood, skin, and muscle tissue often yield DNA of high quantity and quality.

The logistics of trapping and sampling wildlife vary greatly depending upon the species of interest. Some species are relatively easy to trap and sample, while others are difficult and/or dangerous. Destructive sampling refers to instances where the organism is killed during the process of sampling such as for collection of muscle, heart, liver, or embryo. If an animal is killed (hunting) or found dead (road kill or disease) samples can easily be taken for genetic analysis. Nondestructive (or noninvasive) sampling occurs when a genetic sample can be obtained without sacrificing the animal. Feathers, blood, shell membranes from hatched eggs, skin, hair, feces, and urine can all be collected nondestructively and provide potential sources of DNA for genetic analysis. Genetic samples can also be gathered without having to handle the animal in question (e.g., feathers, hair, feces, and urine).

In most cases, genetic samples can be stored on ice, refrigerated, desiccated, collected into a preservative buffer, or frozen almost immediately after collection (Table 2). When fieldwork occurs in remote areas, sampling certain tissues (e.g., skin, feathers) may be more feasible than tissues such as blood. All samples should be kept cold or dry or placed in a preservation buffer. When working with blood, only a small amount is needed (5 drops) and should be mixed with a preservative such as EDTA or with a blood buffer storage solution such as Longmire Buffer. Muscle tissue should be either placed in a preservation buffer (e.g., buffer containing Tris/HCL, EDTA, NaCl, N Lauroyl sarcosine) or frozen immediately. Contour or wing feathers provide the best source of DNA but smaller downy feathers can suffice. Feathers from individual birds should be kept in separate bags. Eggshell membranes can also be a good source of DNA as long as

Table 2. Sources of DNA and how samples should be collected.

Tissue type	Amount	Quantity of DNA	Quality of DNA	Preservation method
Blood	5–10 drops	High	Good	EDTA coated tubes, Lysis Buffer (Longmire)
Muscle	Square 2 cm on a side	High	Good	Buffer
Feather	At least 1	Low	Good	Dry
Egg shell membranes	As much as is possible	Depends	Good	Dry
Hair	At least 1	Low	Good	Dry
Scat	Variable	Low	Poor	Ethanol or Dry
Teeth	Variable	Low	Depends	Dry
Bone	Variable	Low	Depends	Dry

there is vascularization of the membrane. Each membrane should be stored dry in separate bags. Hair, bone, and teeth can be used as a DNA source if they are stored dry. For hair, only the follicle is needed. Scat can also be used but the quantity and quality of DNA are often low. Scat should be preserved in either liquid ethanol or with silica beads. Detailed protocols for sample collections and descriptions of buffer are available at http://www.absc.usgs.gov/research/genetics/sampling.doc.

TAXONOMY
Species/Subspecies Identification

Taxonomists have been categorizing organisms into hierarchical groups ranging from kingdom and phylum levels to genus and species for hundreds of years. Classifications have been defined using morphological and behavioral characteristics. Taxonomic delineations derived only from morphological characteristics can be erroneous (Avise 1989) as they can either fail to recognize distant forms (Avise and Nelson 1989) or they can recognize forms that exhibit little evolutionary differentiation (Laerm et al. 1982). While classifications based on morphology and behavior have been acceptable, use of genetics can often resolve discrepancies and refine taxonomic definitions. However, using genetic data alone for taxonomic classifications is not advised.

While most taxonomic definitions are somewhat arbitrary (subspecies, genera, order), classification at the species level is perceived to be based on real, evolutionary units (Dobzhansky 1970). Because the species definition is integral to the Endangered Species Act (ESA) and the protection and management of many species, we briefly mention species definitions. Many definitions of species exist (reviewed by Avise 1994); the 2 most commonly used are the biological species concept (Dobzhansky 1937) and the phylogenetic species concept (Cracraft 1983). The major difference between these 2 species concepts is that the biological species concept emphasizes reproductive isolation and the resultant limitation and/or preclusion of gene flow, while the phylogenetic species concept defines species solely using genetic data.

Genetic data can be used to address the species question regardless of which definition is used. Documenting an absence of gene flow among sympatric populations is one piece of evidence that can be used along with morphological and behavioral data to suggest delineation of a species. Constructing phylogenetic relationships among individuals to examine whether a monophyletic group exists can also be achieved by comparing DNA sequences.

Until recently, genetic information was difficult and expensive to acquire and, at times, could only be used to resolve differences between distantly related species. Protein electrophoresis (allozymes) became a useful genetic tool to distinguish differences between some species but is less useful when delineating the taxonomic relationship among closely related organisms (whether they are species, subspecies, etc.). The advent of PCR and automated sequencing has made it relatively straightforward to collect data at a high resolution in a cost-effective manner from a large number and variety of organisms. Further, sequence data from genes evolving at widely different rates can be gathered, which allows for taxonomic comparisons at immensely different levels (from kingdom/phylum/class to genus/species/subspecies). This allows for re-evaluation of taxonomic status using genetic information or for the addition of supplementary data to unresolved taxonomic questions.

There are several molecular techniques with which to assess taxonomic relationships (e.g., DNA-DNA hybridization, protein electrophoresis). Perhaps the most widely used and most applicable to questions in wildlife biology is analysis of the mtDNA sequence. The mitochondrial genome is small (15,000–20,000 base pairs) and contains approximately 37 genes although the order of these genes is not constant (Avise 1994). It is maternally inherited and does not recombine, as does nuclear DNA. While comparisons of the gene order of mtDNA have been used in investigations of taxa, direct comparison of sequences has proved to be an effective technique in finer level taxonomic questions (among more closely related species) (Avise 1994) which are much more common wildlife management concerns. Mitochondrial DNA is well mapped in many animals (Bibb et al. 1981, Anderson et al. 1982, Roe et al. 1985) and evolves 5–10 times faster than single copy nuclear genes (Brown et al. 1979, 1982). It also contains a noncoding control region in which some areas are even more variable (4–5 times more variable than mtDNA as a whole) that can be used to delineate closely related species and populations (Greenberg et al. 1983). Each mtDNA gene evolves at a different rate allowing for different level comparisons using genes with different mutation rates.

Once an appropriate gene is chosen for the taxonomic issue in question, DNA sequence from that region is obtained and the relationship among individuals is inferred by comparing the DNA sequences. Metrics, such as the percent sequence divergence, provide some measure of how similar or different the DNA sequences may be. Genetic distances or phylogenetic relationships (trees) are then estimated using either algorithms (e.g., unweighted pair group method) or optimality criterion (e. g., parsimony, maximum likelihood). These methods are well established and reviewed extensively by Miyamoto and Cracraft (1991) and Swofford et al. (1996). Nucleotide substitution patterns in the mitochondrial control region are quite elaborate and models that estimate the rate of nucleotide substitutions have been developed (Tamura and Nei 1993, Tamura 1994). Modeling substitution rates circumvents violations of assumptions used by parsimony methods.

Using genetic data to address taxonomic questions becomes important for wildlife management primarily at the species and subspecies level. Wildlife managers are often charged with managing species and subspecies while these definitions are yet unresolved. Further, some subspecies (and even species) are difficult to distinguish in the field without extensive morphological measurements and comparisons with museum type specimens (e.g., Prebles meadow jumping mouse, *Zapus hudsonius preblei*) or detailed analyses of behavior or song (Southwestern willow flycatcher, *Empidonax traillii extimus*).

The ESA and other national and international environmental programs charge managers with protection of species, subspecies, and distinct population segments that are deemed threatened or endangered. At times, little is known about the taxonomic status of species or subspecies that are petitioned to be listed as threatened or endangered. This classification is also important for recovery of the species/subspecies because funding priorities generally are based on taxonomic status (O'Brien and Mayr 1991). Taxonomic delineations are often based only on morphological characteristics and could be refined by adding behavioral and genetic characteristics.

The taxonomic status of many different species has recently been re-evaluated using genetic data. For example, the status of sage-grouse (*Centrocercus* spp.) has recently been examined using behavioral, morphological, and genetic data resulting in the recognition of a new species (Box 1). Other examples include the Kemp's Ridley sea turtle (*Lepidochelys kempii*), which has been recognized as a separate species qualifying for protection under ESA because of data from a recent mtDNA study (Bowen et al. 1991). The taxonomic status of right whales (*Eubalaena* spp.), which has historically been based on a single morphological character in the orbital region of the skull, has been redefined as the result of analysis of mtDNA data (Rosenbaum et al. 2000a).

Hybridization

Defining "hybrid" is as perplexing as is definition of the term species. Classically, "hybridization" and "introgression" are used to describe interbreeding between 2 distinct species. However, because a definitive definition of a species is still nonexistent, "hybridization" is sometimes relaxed to include interbreeding between 2 groups that are genetically different while introgression refers to the movement of genes between 2 genetically differentiated groups (Avise 1994). Hybridization can be positive or negative (Haig 1998). In a positive sense, hybridization events can increase the overall genetic diversity of a taxonomic group; it can produce increased fitness (hybrid vigor) in some cases, and can produce progeny that are more adaptable than either parent. However, in some instances, hybrids can have reduced viability and fertility. Further, the effects of outbreeding depression (decrease in fitness due to a loss of alleles which are locally adaptive) on a species due to a hybridization event can be quite negative. Because true hybrids are generally not protected by the

Box 1.   Using genetics to help define taxonomic definitions for sage-grouse.

Large-scale habitat loss and degradation have resulted in the decline of sage-grouse populations throughout their range (Braun 1998) and have caused an increased concern over their status. Historically, sage-grouse were classified into 2 subspecies: eastern *(Centrocercus urophasianus urophasianus)* and western *(C. u. phaios)* sage-grouse based on plumage and coloration differences in 8 individuals collected from Washington, Oregon, and California (Aldrich 1946). The western sage-grouse presumably occurred in southern British Columbia, central Washington, east-central Oregon, and northeastern California (Aldrich 1946). Populations in other areas of the range were considered to be eastern sage-grouse. The validity of this taxonomic distinction has been questioned (Johnsgard 1983). Recently, sage-grouse from southwestern Colorado and southeastern Utah were found to be morphologically (Hupp and Braun 1991), behaviorally (Young et al. 1994), and genetically (Kahn et al. 1999, Oyler-McCance et al. 1999) different from sage-grouse throughout the rest of the range. This led to description of a new species, the Gunnison sage-grouse (Young et al. 2000).

With the validity of the 2 present subspecies in question, Benedict et al. (2003) sequenced a rapidly evolving portion of the control region of the mtDNA for 16 populations of sage-grouse on both sides of the subspecific boundary. The sequencing results provide no genetic support for the subspecies distinction. The authors suggest that further morphological and behavioral comparisons need to be conducted before overturning the subspecific classifications. This study did, however, identify a population of sage-grouse in the Lyon, Nevada and Mono, California area that was genetically unique from all other sage-grouse populations sampled throughout the species' range (Benedict et al. 2003). This group of sage-grouse is currently being studied morphologically and behaviorally.

Comparison of greater sage-grouse (left) and Gunnison sage-grouse (right) (photographs by R. E. Bennetts [left] and L. F. Swift [right]).

ESA, hybridization provides interesting challenges for those charged with management and protection of species (O'Brien and Mayr 1991).

Molecular techniques provide an increasingly more accurate estimation of taxonomic relationships and history of gene flow (Haig 1998). These techniques are being used to address questions of hybridization, introgression, and taxonomic status. For example, large canids occupying the southeastern United States have long been classified as the red wolf *(Canis rufus)*. Extinction of red wolves in the wild has led to serious conservation efforts to preserve and restore them into the wild. However, mtDNA data and microsatellite data both strongly suggest the red wolf is a hybrid between the gray wolf *(C. lupus)* and coyote *(C. latrans)* (Wayne and Jenks 1991, Roy et al. 1994). The hybrid origin of the red wolf has led to debate over its eligibility for protection under the ESA.

Molecular techniques can also be used to identify the maternity and paternity of hybrids. Aldridge et al. (2001) described 2 sage-grouse × sharp-tailed grouse *(Centrocercus urophasianus × Tympanuchus phasianellus)* hybrids in Alberta. Using analysis of mtDNA control region sequence, they demonstrated the mother of each hybrid was a sage-grouse rather than a sharp-tailed grouse. Similarly, hybrids resulting from crosses in both directions of blue *(Balaenoptera musculus)* and fin whales *(B. physalus)* have been documented using both nuclear and mtDNA (Arnason et al. 1991, Spilliaert et al. 1991).

Evolutionary Significant Units and Management Units

Given that genetic analysis can help refine taxonomic relationships, how else can genetic data be used to address management issues? Recently, there has been debate about how to objectively prioritize conservation or management value below the species level. This discussion began with Ryder (1986:9) who defined the term Evolutionary Significant Unit (ESU) as "a subset of the inclusive entity species, which possess genetic attributes significant for the present and future generations of the species in question." In an attempt to develop an operational definition more useful to managers, Waples (1991) defined ESUs using 2 criteria. A population or groups of populations had to demonstrate substantial reproductive isolation from other populations of the same species and, at nuclear loci, it had to show significant divergence of allele frequencies. Moritz (1994*b*:373) further defined ESUs as "a population (or set of populations) that is reciprocally monophyletic for mtDNA alleles" and " shows significant divergence of allele frequencies at nuclear loci." Moritz (1994*a*) defined a second unit called a Management Unit as a group with less separation than an ESU but deserving of specific management attention. This unit was defined to have significant divergence of nuclear or mtDNA allele frequencies regardless of the phylogenetic differentiation of alleles. While Moritz's ESUs protect distinct units allowing for preservation of their long-term genetic variability, his Management Unit concept allows for shorter-term conservation goals. Several other scientists have put forth alternate ideas on the concept of ESUs (Dizon et al. 1992, Avise 1994, Vogler and DeSalle 1994, Crandall et al. 2000, Fraser and Bernatchez 2001). While definitions of an ESU are as highly debated and diverse (Fraser and Bernatchez 2001) as the species concepts, the ESU is useful if one is aware of the lack of agreement surrounding the best definition. Most genetic studies with applications to management use Moritz's (1994*a*, *b*) definitions because they are well defined when using genetic data. Also, these definitions appear to be among the most well accepted and applied to date. These concepts have been applied to tiger quolls (*Dasyurus maculates*) (Box 2), spotted owls (*Strix occidentalis*), koalas (*Phascolarctos cinereus*), and brown bears (*Ursus arctos*) (Firestone et al. 1999, Houlden et al. 1999, Waits et al. 2000, Haig et al. 2001).

CONSERVATION OF GENETIC DIVERSITY

A focus of conservation genetics has been preservation of genetic diversity within and between populations, especially in rare or endangered taxa. Genetic diversity can be estimated using molecular markers or morphological measurements. While studies have examined the underlying genetic variation and heritability of specific morphological traits in both captive and free-ranging wildlife (Williams et al. 1994, Merilä 1997, Kruuk et al. 2000, Réale and Festa-Bianchet 2000), intensive investigations are difficult to implement for many species. Frankham et al. (2002) reviewed using quantitative genetic approaches in a conservation context to study the effects of multiple genes and environmental variation on complex traits like morphology and behavior. Our primary focus is on what molecular markers tell us about the demography and genetics of a population and how that information can be applied to issues in wildlife conservation.

Genetic diversity and genetic variation are often used interchangeably to refer to a dizzying array of population characteristics. We use genetic diversity to refer to variation in frequencies of alleles at individual genes. It is difficult to quantify total genetic diversity in populations; most studies look at surrogates of this measure based on

> **Box 2. Taxonomic redefinition of tiger quolls in Australia.**
>
> Firestone et al. (1999) defined Evolutionary Significant Units (ESUs) and Management Units (MUs) for tiger quolls that revised taxonomic classification and management plans for these carnivorous marsupials in Australia. Previously, 2 allopatric subspecies of tiger quoll have been recognized. The smaller subspecies, *Dasyurus maculatus gracilis* occurs only in northern Australia in northeastern Queensland. The larger subspecies, *D. m. maculatus* occurs in southeastern Australia and Tasmania. Each subspecies has been placed on the International Union for Conservation of Nature and Natural Resources list as either endangered or as vulnerable to extinction. Firestone et al. (1999) used both mtDNA sequencing and nuclear microsatellites to survey the genetic relatedness of tiger quolls. Their mtDNA sequencing results show reciprocal monophyly and significant differences in nuclear microsatellite allele frequencies between Tasmanian and all mainland tiger quolls. This suggests that, even though Tasmanian tiger quolls are recognized as the same subspecies as those in southeastern Australia, they are a separate ESU and that their taxonomic status should be revisited. The 2 subspecies on the mainland do not constitute different ESUs even though they are considered separate subspecies. Firestone et al. (1999) suggest that morphological differences between the 2 subspecies may reflect adaptation to climatic differences. Differences in microsatellite allele frequencies and mtDNA haplotypes exist between the 2 subspecies on the mainland suggesting they should be considered as distinct MUs. Thus, assessment of genetic data (Firestone et al. 1999) revealed differences between the 2 subspecies at the MU level in Australia, yet the classification in Tasmania should be reconsidered to recognize and preserve the unique genetic makeup and evolutionary path of tiger quolls.

variation at molecular markers. Four processes are generally thought to influence patterns of genetic diversity: mutation, gene flow, drift, and selection.

Mutation

The original source for most genetic differences we observe among individuals is mutation. The mutation rates of markers used by wildlife geneticists affects their information content. For example, if habitat fragmentation results in recent isolation of a number of small populations, there might be insufficient time for mutation to result in detectable levels of interpopulation divergence in mtDNA sequences. However, microsatellites, which have a high mutation rate and many alleles, lose many alleles when populations become small (Spencer et al. 2000). Thus, small populations in fragmented habitats may exhibit measurable differentiation for highly polymorphic markers. Alternately, if the objective of an investigation is to examine phylogenetic relationships between subspecies that may have been isolated for a long period, mtDNA sequences might be preferred over microsatellites, as rapid evolution in microsatellites could obscure phylogenetic relationships. An understanding of the mutational processes associated with different molecular markers can also be used to select the most appropriate statistical models for analyses of demographic bottlenecks and gene flow (Luikart and Cornuet 1998, Balloux and Lugon-Moulin 2002, Neigel 2002).

Normally mutation does not have a major role in management issues. One exception is the case of exposure of populations to environmental mutagens. Animals exposed to radioactive or chemical mutagens might be expected to have more genetic diversity because of an increased number of genetic mutations. This hypothesis was tested using bank voles (*Clethrionomys glareolus*) and barn swallows (*Hirundo rustica)* from the vicinity of the Chernobyl nuclear accident site (Matson et al. 2000). Microsatellite analysis provided evidence of increased mutation rates in the swallows (Ellegren et al. 1997). In the voles, higher levels of mtDNA variation were found near Chernobyl than at reference sites; however, it is difficult to attribute this increased genetic diversity to increased mutation, as immigration from nearby genetically differentiated populations provides another explanation (Baker et al. 2001). Other investigations have failed to detect any evidence of increased mutation in wildlife from contaminated sites (Johnson et al. 1999, Dahl et al. 2001, Stapleton et al. 2001). Given that mutations at specific genetic markers are relatively rare events, it is not surprising that it is difficult to detect increased mutation rates in the face of other powerful genetic forces such as gene flow and drift. Examinations of exposed populations for increased mutation rates will probably expand greatly in coming years as automated analysis has made it possible to screen large numbers of individuals and genes. There is also a growing number of assays for assessing DNA damage in wildlife populations (Matson et al. 2000, Theodorakis 2001).

Gene Flow

When organisms disperse to new populations and reproduce, they contribute genetic material to their new population. This process increases the genetic similarity of populations exchanging individuals. Reductions in gene flow allow populations to diverge through processes of genetic drift, the accumulation and spread of different mutations, and selection for local conditions.

Gene flow differs from dispersal as typically measured by studies of animal movement. Radiotelemetry or tagging studies can often provide insight into the proportion of individuals that depart from their natal areas, but are inadequate for measuring the reproductive contribution of dispersing individuals to their new populations. While molecular tags are providing novel ways to track dispersing individuals, gene flow is typically measured through indirect methods using genetic markers (Slatkin 1985a).

One of most common approaches for estimating gene flow involves use of Wright's F_{ST} (1951). One common definition of F_{ST} is the proportion of the total variance in allele frequencies due to differences among populations. An attractive feature of this measure of genetic differentiation is that F_{ST} can be expressed as a function of the number of migrants per generation (*Nm*). Mills and Allendorf (1996) and Whitlock and McCauley (1999) discuss the assumptions necessary to use F_{ST} to estimate *Nm* and the difficulties of obtaining unbiased estimates of gene flow. Many estimators of F_{ST} have been developed and there is a large literature evaluating their merits and performance (reviewed by Slatkin 1985a and Neigel 1997, 2002). Other approaches to estimating gene flow include estimation of the frequencies of alleles that only occur in one of the populations in a comparison, i.e., the private alleles method (Slatkin 1985b). If alleles occur in one population at high frequencies but are absent from others, gene flow is probably low. A third set of methods involves using phylogenetic information from mtDNA sequences to estimate gene flow and dispersal distance (Slatkin and Maddison 1990, Neigel et al. 1991).

One problem with most indirect estimates of gene flow is that effects of recent gene flow on gene frequencies are often confounded with historical gene flow. If isolation is recent, populations might appear to have high gene flow even if they are completely isolated because molecular differences have not had time to accumulate (Slatkin 1985a; Neigel 1997, 2002). Many estimators of gene flow are based on populations being in an "equilibrium" condition where population size and number of successful migrants have not changed dramatically for many generations. These conditions are not typical of many settings in which resource managers wish to estimate gene flow, such as in fragmented landscapes. Thus, estimates of gene flow, while useful in a relative sense, should be regarded with some caution. One widely used approach to distinguish between the effects of current and historical gene flow, as well as other factors, on patterns of population differentiation is nested clade analysis (Templeton 2001). Nested clade analysis tests a number of hypotheses associated with the spatial distribution of sequence variation. Knowles and Maddison (2002) cautioned that this approach does not estimate error rates and performs poorly in computer simulations.

The greater the exchange of individuals between populations the more that genetic similarity of the populations will increase. However, the relationship between gene flow and genetic similarity is not linear (Fig. 3); a few successful individuals moving between populations each generation is often sufficient to retard the effects of genetic drift on the similarity of gene frequencies. A consequence of the nonlinear relationship of gene flow and genetic differentiation is that once gene flow is sufficiently high to erase most genetic differences between populations, estimates of F_{ST} approach zero and it is difficult to estimate the number of migrants per generation (Waples 1998). However, knowledge that gene flow is high enough to minimize F_{ST} should be sufficient for most management decisions; a precise estimate of *Nm* is not needed.

Dispersal and Population Structure

Among wildlife species, there is considerable variation in the gender of dispersing individuals. Gender of individuals moving between populations, as well as a species' social structure, can have a large effect on partitioning of

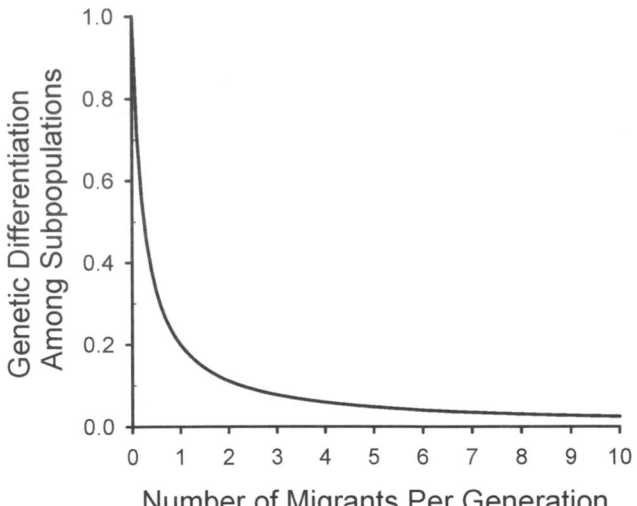

Fig. 3. Equilibrium relationship of genetic differentiation among subpopulations (as measured by the statistic F_{ST}) and number of migrants per generation (modified from Mills and Allendorf 1996).

genetic variation within and among populations (Chesser 1991, Chesser and Baker 1996). Gender of dispersing individuals is typically beyond the control of wildlife biologists; however, it is important to understand that breeding systems and gender-biased dispersal are likely to affect estimates of gene flow. Gender-biased dispersal and social structure within populations can alter effective population size, influencing rates of loss of genetic diversity (Chesser et al. 1993).

Gender-biased dispersal will have large consequences for data generated by maternally inherited markers like mtDNA. There is a large set of literature, reviewed by Avise (1994), documenting differences in spatial distribution of biparental nuclear markers (e.g., allozymes and microsatellites) and mtDNA. For example, frequencies of mtDNA genotypes of green turtle (*Chelonia mydas*) differ dramatically among some nesting beaches (Bowen et al. 1992). However, nuclear DNA in this species exhibits much less spatial subdivision than does mtDNA (Karl et al. 1992). This pattern suggests males may be responsible for most of the gene flow among beaches with females generally returning to a beach near their birthplace. Among the many applications using combinations of nuclear genes and mtDNA to characterize gender-specific gene flow and breeding systems in wildlife are studies of macaques (*Macaca* spp.), African wild dogs (*Lycaon pictus*), snow geese (*Chen caerulescens*), and red grouse (*Lagopus lagopus scoticus*) (Avise et al. 1992, Melnick and Hoelzer 1992, Piertney et al. 2000, Girman et al. 2001).

Given the important contributions of mtDNA studies to understanding of gender-specific gene flow, it is clear that markers tracing gene flow in males would be of great value. In mammals, an obvious choice for a paternally inherited marker would be the Y chromosome, which is only passed from males to their sons. Sequences on the Y, as well as other markers, such as Y-linked microsatellites have contributed to the study of human gene flow and show promise in investigations of free-ranging mammals (Hurles and Jobling 2001). In one of the few wildlife studies published to date, sequences from the Y-chromosome were used to

show there was little male mediated gene flow between a recently colonized population of wolves and more established populations (Sundqvist et al. 2001). Identification of new microsatellite loci as well as other easy-to-assay markers on the Y chromosome would greatly enhance the ability to characterize gene flow by males in many mammals (Hurles and Jobling 2001, Sundqvist et al. 2001).

The process of studying male-specific markers in birds is more complicated because in heterogametic (ZW) gender identification, females are heterogametic. Thus, there are no paternally inherited genetic markers similar to the Y chromosome in mammals. Scribner et al. (2001) provide an example of how information from different types of molecular markers, together with theoretical models, can be used to estimate male and female specific gene flow in birds. In their study of spectacled eider (*Somateria fisheri*), they used mtDNA, a gender-linked Z-specific microsatellite locus, and biparentally inherited microsatellites to document large differences in gender-specific gene flow.

If gene flow is limited for many generations by natural barriers to dispersal, populations on opposite sides of the barrier can exhibit striking levels of differentiation. Fragmentation of habitat should, given sufficient time, also result in genetic differentiation among recently isolated populations, especially if sizes of populations inhabiting the habitat remnants are small. Leberg (1991) found that genetic differentiation among populations of wild turkeys (*Meleagris gallopavo*) stocked onto semi-isolated areas was much higher than in native populations in continuous habitat. Gene flow, assayed with microsatellites, was much lower in populations of Sika deer (*Cervus nippon*) in areas of habitat fragmentation (Goodman et al. 2001). Similar associations between recent habitat fragmentation and low gene flow have been made in the Greater rhea (*Rhea americana*), bank voles, collared lizards (*Crotaphyus collaris*), and moor frogs (*Rana arvalis*) (Gerlach and Musolf 2000, Bouzat 2001, Templeton et al. 2001, Vos et al. 2001). There is one caveat for most studies of the effects of recent habitat fragmentation on genetic differentiation; they lack temporal control. While it might be true that recent fragmentation of continuous habitat reduced gene flow, it is often difficult to eliminate the possibility that observed patterns of genetic differentiation are due to events that occurred long before any human activities affected the populations. Analyses of genetic differentiation before and after a fragmentation event should be possible given the ability to isolate DNA from specimens preserved in museums (Roy et al. 1996, Mundy et al. 1997, Bouzat et al. 1998a, Iudica et al. 2001, Whitehouse and Harley 2001).

Gene Flow Through Translocations

One consequence of translocation programs is gene flow (Leberg 1990a). Sometimes this aspect of translocations is intentional. For example, many authors have explored the possibility of using translocations to restore gene flow between populations isolated by habitat loss (Triggs et al. 1989, Leberg 1990a, Haig et al. 1996, Moritz 1999, Storfer 1999). There has been little direct assessment of the genetic effects of such activities. Based on the relationship between gene flow and F_{ST} (Fig. 3), movement of only a few individuals per generation should be necessary to minimize the tendency of isolated populations to genetically differentiate. Mills and Allendorf (1996) provide an excellent review of factors to be considered when designing programs to restore genetic connectivity of populations. It might be necessary to release more individuals than genetic considerations might suggest, because released individuals often don't survive to reproduce (Leberg 1990*b*).

When translocations are used to establish new or augment existing populations, gene flow is expected to increase the similarity of populations at release sites to that of the population that served as the source of the released individuals. For example, Taylor et al. (1997) found that frequencies of mtDNA genotypes of recipient populations of koala were more similar to those of the source population than to other populations. These observations can be useful, because it is often difficult to know whether individuals released in augmentation efforts successfully contributed genetic material to the recipient population. This approach was used to assess the relative reproductive contributions of different subspecies to populations of northern bobwhite (*Colinus virginianus*) and wild turkey established by translocations from multiple sources (Nedbal et al. 1997, Mock et al. 2001).

The success of a translocation program can also be examined by assessing whether patterns of genetic similarity expected from natural dispersal have been disrupted (Leberg 1999). For example, Leberg et al. (1994) assessed whether genetic structure of wild turkey and white-tailed deer (*Odocoileus virginianus*) populations in the southeastern United States had been influenced by extensive translocations of these species. They found populations connected by translocations to be more genetically similar than populations that had not had individuals transferred between them. With similar data, Ellsworth et al. (1994*a,b*) concluded that releases of white-tailed deer had little effect on the genetics of native populations arguing that most translocated deer had not made genetic contributions to their recipient populations. Additional analysis led Leberg and Ellsworth (1999) to conclude that translocated individuals did contribute to the recovery of recipient populations; however, genetic contributions of the released individuals were restricted to the populations into which they were released. This set of studies illustrates the complexities of understanding the genetic and demographic consequences of translocations when only samples collected after the translocation event are available for analysis. Considerably more information about translocations could be discerned by obtaining genetic profiles of translocated individuals prior to release so information could be used to track post-release reproductive success (Leberg 1999).

Drift and Bottlenecks

The genetic composition of a wildlife population is not constant. As a result of chance differences in reproductive success and survival among individuals with different genotypes, allele frequencies will change from one generation to another. Random change in the frequencies of alleles is referred to as genetic drift. The effect of drift on a population is expected to be small when population sizes are large. In large populations, small random changes in allele frequencies will occasionally cause an allele to be lost; however, this loss is mitigated by formation of new alleles through mutation. However, when populations are

small and isolated from other populations, gene frequencies can drift dramatically. A population that is maintained at a small size for several generations has different genetic characteristics than it had prior to the reduction in size. Because of large random changes in allele frequencies, alleles will be lost in a small population faster than they are replaced through mutation, reducing allelic diversity. The average number of genes at which an individual is heterozygous (mean multi-locus heterozygosity) is also expected to decrease if a population remains small because matings between relatives will become unavoidable. Another consequence of drift associated with small population size is increased genetic differentiation. Genetic differences, based on neutral, molecular markers, between 2 populations will increase rapidly if there is no gene flow among them and at least one is small enough to experience substantial genetic drift.

When a normally large population goes through a constriction in size, it is referred to as a genetic bottleneck. During bottlenecks, drift is greatly accelerated. Bottlenecks can occur in wildlife populations for any reason that might result in a reduction in population size such as overharvest, disease, pollution exposure, or habitat loss (Leberg 1991, Ellegren et al. 1993, Van Hooft et al. 2000, Bouzat 2001, Van der Walt et al. 2001, Whitehouse and Harley 2001). Bottlenecks often occur at the establishment of a new population. This type of bottleneck is referred to as a founder event. Founder events are often severe bottlenecks, as only a few individuals may establish a population; however, they tend to be of short duration.

The duration and size of the bottleneck have large effects on loss of genetic diversity. During severe bottlenecks of short duration, theory (Nei et al. 1975) and experiments (Spencer et al. 2000) indicate many alleles will be lost. However, because most alleles are relatively rare in populations, there is no large loss of heterozygosity (Leberg 1992, Spencer et al. 2000). However, if the bottleneck is of long duration, relatedness of individuals will increase along with associated loss of heterozygosity (Nei et al. 1975). Thus, population growth rate can have a large effect on levels of genetic diversity following a reduction in population size.

Detecting Bottlenecks and Drift

A severe reduction in population size will lead to loss of heterozygosity, reduced allelic diversity, and drift of allele frequencies. Because pre-bottleneck samples are often absent, samples from populations that may have experienced a bottleneck are often compared to populations of the same or related species that are believed to have levels of genetic variation not affected by small population sizes (Leberg 1991, Ellegren et al. 1993, Scribner 1993, Ardern and Lambert 1997, Pertoldi et al. 2000, Williams et al. 2000, Nichols et al. 2001, Whitehouse and Harley 2001). This approach requires the assumption the populations had similar levels of genetic variation prior to the putative bottleneck event (Bouzat 2000). Use of preserved materials would provide a more straightforward way to estimate pre-bottleneck levels of diversity. Matocq and Villablanca (2001) provide examples of the use of museum specimens to show that low genetic variation in endangered species was due to bottlenecks that occurred prior to a known recent reduction in population size. Conversely, museum specimens of greater prairie-chickens (*Tympanuchus cupido*) provided evidence that recent population reductions in Illinois resulted in reduced levels of genetic variation (Bouzat et al. 1998*a*). Unfortunately, sizes of museum collections from localities of interest are often insufficient to make strong statistical comparisons with contemporary populations. For populations that are likely to be of management concern, it would be appropriate to establish baseline genetic characteristics and preserve DNA samples for monitoring future changes in population size.

The commonly used genetic indices of bottlenecks differ in their sensitivity to population contractions. A series of experiments producing known bottlenecks indicate that loss of allelic diversity is much more sensitive to population bottlenecks than is heterozygosity (Leberg 1992, Spencer et al. 2000). This observation is supported by theory and studies of natural bottlenecks (Nei et al. 1975, Stockwell et al. 1996). Not surprisingly, it is easier to detect loss of alleles when using loci with many alleles, such as microsatellites, than with less polymorphic allozyme markers (Spencer et al. 2000). Both simulations and experiments indicate that temporal change in allele frequencies is also a much better index of bottleneck severity when drift is estimated with highly polymorphic loci (Richards and Leberg 1996, Luikart et al. 1999, Spencer et al. 2000). Although allelic richness is strongly influenced by past size of a population, this parameter is also sensitive to sample size. Thus, when comparing allelic richness among samples, estimates should be adjusted to the smallest sample size of any population used in comparison (Leberg 2002).

Several approaches have been developed to alleviate the need to compare a sample of interest to a reference sample to see if a population has experienced a loss of genetic variation. When a population experiences a bottleneck, the proportion of alleles that are present at low frequencies is reduced. Thus, it is possible to compare the distribution of alleles with different frequencies to the null distribution expected in the absence of a bottleneck; deviation from the null distribution is evidence that the population has experienced a contraction in size (Luikart et al. 1998). It is also possible to compare the heterozygosity in a population, based on Hardy-Weinburg expectations and the observed number of alleles, to the heterozygosity obtained from a null distribution (Cornuet and Luikart 1996, Luikart and Cornuet 1998). A similar approach examines the ratio of the number of alleles to the range of allele sizes of microsatellite loci (Garza and Williamson 2001); this ratio decreases when a population is reduced in size. These approaches are dependent on selection of the correct model of mutation used to generate the null distributions. An examination of populations that had experienced known reductions in population size suggests they provide reasonable indices of a population's history of bottlenecks (Luikart and Cornuet 1998, Spencer et al. 2000).

When considering the effects of bottlenecks on genetic variation, it is critical to realize that not all population reductions will result in measurable losses of genetic variation. Population sizes often have to be quite small for several generations to produce a substantial loss of variation. Thus, a 90% reduction in size of a European rabbit population (*Oryctolagus cuniculus*) was insufficient to produce measurable genetic response, because the remnant population was not reduced below approximately 50 individuals and recovered rapidly (Queney et al. 2000). Likewise, experimental populations reduced to 16 individuals for one generation exhibited almost no loss of variation when they rapidly recovered to a large size (Spencer et al. 2000).

Effective vs. Census Population Size

One goal of conservation genetics is to understand how much genetic diversity would be lost from a population reduction or management activity. Genetic diversity is often lost more rapidly than would be predicted from the number of individuals in the population (referred to as the census population size or N_c). At times many individuals in a population are not reproductively active because of age or social constraints. Some individuals are vastly more successful than others in transmitting their genes to the next generation. When individuals differ in their ability to successfully reproduce, genetic diversity will be lost more rapidly than expected on the basis of N_c. One way of understanding these issues is to estimate the effective population size, N_e. N_e is the number of individuals in an ideal population that would lose genetic variation at the same rate as the actual population being studied. An ideal population is a one where all individuals have an equal chance of producing any progeny making up the next generation. The list of possible factors that can could cause $N_e < N_c$ is large (Crow and Kimura 1970, Nunney 1999, Hedrick 2000). We discuss only those factors likely to have a large effect in wildlife populations with emphasis on those that might fall under the control of managers.

Temporal variation in population size can have large effects on loss of genetic variation (Crow and Kimura 1970, Vucetich et al. 1997), and may have strong influence on the effective size of wildlife populations (Frankham 1995*a*). A normally large population that occasionally experiences a large decline in numbers, may lose considerable genetic variation during those periods when it is small; this variation is not immediately recovered when the population returns to a large size. Kalinowski and Waples (2002) provide a framework for examining the relationship between N_e and N_c over multiple generations when population size is not stable.

Unequal sex ratios reduce effective population size (Wright 1931). If one gender is much more common than the other, members of the more rare gender will disproportionately contribute genes to the next generation. If sex ratios are highly skewed and the rare gender is only represented by a few individuals then $N_e \ll N_c$. In species with nonoverlapping generations, highly polygamous mating systems can also result in small estimates of N_e (Nunney 1993).

The age structure of a population can complicate efforts to estimate effective population size in wildlife species. Most wildlife populations have overlapping generations; simple formulations of the effects of sex ratio and temporal variation of effective size assume nonoverlapping generations. In some age-structured populations, fairly large numbers of individuals might be too young or too old to reproduce. To make the issue even more confusing, the influence of sex ratio and mating system on N_e are modified by generation length in complex ways (Nunney 1993). Equations developed for populations with nonoverlapping generations should be applied with caution when attempting to estimate effective size of wildlife populations.

There are several genetic techniques for estimating effective population size. One approach is to quantify genetic changes through time by taking 2 or more temporal samples (Waples 1989, Jorde and Ryman 1995). If insufficient time is available to obtain 2 samples separated by several generations, it might be possible to compare the genetic characteristics of contemporary populations with those of museum specimens (Bouzat et al. 1998*a*, Glenn et al. 1999, Rosenbaum et al. 2000*b*, Whitehouse and Harley 2001). Other approaches include assessing linkage disequilibrium between physically unlinked loci (Hill 1981, Bartley et al. 1992) and the amount of heterozygote excess in progeny (Pudovkin et al. 1996, Luikart and Cornuet 1999). Finally, there is a set of approaches based on expectations of patterns and levels of variation resulting from mutations (Slatkin and Hudson 1991, Hedrick 1996, Jensen-Seaman and Kidd 2001). Such approaches require knowledge of mutational processes and are more appropriate for estimates of effective population size over longer time periods than those that are the focus of management. In addition to genetic approaches, demographic data can be used to estimate N_e (Harris and Allendorf 1989, Nunney 1993). When using any of these approaches, it is important to realize that "effective size" can refer to several population genetic parameters and, thus, measure loss of different components of genetic diversity (see Crow and Kimura 1970, Schwartz et al. 1998).

Drift and Bottlenecks From Human Activities

Reduced levels of genetic variation have been documented in large numbers of threatened species or populations (Ardern and Lambert 1997, Hoelzel et al. 1999, Rossiter et al. 2000). Reductions of genetic diversity are often symptomatic of small populations that have become endangered through loss of habitat and other causes.

Even in abundant species, individual populations can lose genetic variation when they become isolated in fragments of habitat incapable of supporting large populations (Sarre 1995, Haavie et al. 2000, Pertoldi et al. 2000, Bouzat 2001, Goodman et al. 2001, Lee et al. 2001). Creation of corridors between these fragments or the imposition of gene flow through translocations have been suggested as strategies for prevention of loss of diversity within fragmented populations (Hedrick 1995, Mills and Allendorf 1996, Mech and Hallett 2001).

By definition, reintroduction programs create founder events. Populations established through releases will often have less genetic diversity than those that are the source of released individuals; this loss is related to the number of individuals released (Grobler and Van de Bank 1994, Tarr et al. 1998, Le Page et al. 2000, Stockwell and Leberg 2002). For example, Fitzsimmons et al. (1997) found that populations established with translocated mountain sheep (*Ovis canadensis*) often had low levels of genetic diversity compared to the source of the released individuals. These releases were often between 8 and 69 individuals per population. In releases that involved large numbers of eggs, Rowe et al. (1998) found no loss of variation in populations of Natterjack toad (*Bufo calamita*) created through translocations. Scribner and Stuwe (1994) found the amount of genetic drift experienced by populations of

Alpine ibex (*Capra ibex*) was related to the number and sex ratio of individuals used to establish a population as well as by subsequent population growth. Slow population growth following translocation appears to be responsible for a loss of heterozygosity in a population of elk (Williams et al. 2002).

Not surprisingly, allele frequencies of translocated populations often differ from those of their sources (Scribner 1993, Fitzsimmons et al. 1997, Rowe et al. 1998, Tarr et al. 1998). Founder events associated with translocations can also create large differences among translocated populations from the same sources (Leberg 1991, Scribner 1993, Tarr et al. 1998). However, caution should be used when interpreting differences in allele frequencies among translocated populations and their sources. While differences might be the result of the founder event, they could also have occurred through drift after the translocated population became established (Williams et al. 2000).

Reintroduction strategies that may make sense based on the species' ecology might have the unintended consequence of reducing the effective population size of the newly established population (Leberg 1990*b*). The benefits of such strategies, such as faster initial population growth by releasing more females than males, or of reduced dispersal through release of family groups, should be evaluated in light of their genetic consequences. For example, if it makes sense to release family groups to reduce post-release dispersal, it would be best to release as many groups as possible to avoid inbreeding and loss of genetic variation.

Most harvest programs should have little effect on genetic variation because loss of variation due to drift is small when population size is large. However, harvest strategies can reduce effective population size far below the census population size, creating the potential for rates of drift that might be surprising if only the total population size is considered (Laikre and Ryman 1996). Ryman et al. (1981) evaluated a range of harvest strategies for moose (*Alces alces*) and found the largest relative differences between N_e and N_c occurred when harvest mortality was higher for adults than for calves and when harvests skewed sex ratios. Harris et al. (2002) reviewed the possible effects of game harvests on genetic diversity.

Selection

Many of the genetic markers used by conservation geneticists are thought to be selectively neutral. Thus, the specific genotypes associated with these marker systems have little or no effect on the survival or reproduction of individuals. This assumption is most likely violated from time to time but most of the genetic variation examined using many types of markers probably has little consequence for the fitness of individuals (Hedrick 2000). Because marker systems are unlikely to be under direct selection, they are useful for measuring phenomena such as gene flow, inbreeding, and drift that tend to affect variation throughout the genome and, thus, result in genetic signatures that are detectable with molecular markers.

Although the neutrality of molecular markers aids in their usefulness for studying many population processes, it also means the linkage of molecular markers and genetic traits of concern to the well being of individual organisms is at best indirect. The relationship between levels of molecular variation within and among populations with genetic variation affecting traits related to individual fitness may often be weak (Morgan et al. 2001, Reed and Frankham 2001). The lack of direct concordance often observed between patterns of variation at molecular markers and complex traits has led to calls for conservation geneticists to more critically evaluate whether molecular data are sufficient for designating conservation priorities (Pearman 2001, Reed and Frankham 2001).

If a specific trait such as body size, disease resistance, or fecundity was the target of management activities; it is unlikely that assays of genetic variation with molecular markers would be informative. At times the distributions of traits of adaptive importance correspond with patterns of other genetic markers; however, strong selection on a trait can obscure the influences of gene flow and drift measured with neutral markers. One exception to the general disconnect between studies of molecular markers and variation in fitness traits is the recent application of large numbers of markers to identify specific genes, referred to as Quantitative Trait Loci (or QTLs), responsible for variation in complex morphological or behavioral traits. The work of Slate et al. (2002) identifying QTLs for birth weight in red deer (*Cervus elaphus*) may be the first application of this approach in an unmanipulated population of a wildlife species.

In spite of the general assumption that much of the variation characterized by molecular markers is neutral, there is a large body of work attempting to understand the role of natural selection in maintaining variation in molecular markers in wildlife populations. Initial surveys of natural populations detected higher levels of allozyme variation than expected. This generated interest in examining whether individuals that were heterozygous for allozyme loci might have high fitness; such selection would promote high levels of variation (Allendorf and Leary 1986).

Many studies have found that individuals that are heterozygous for one or more allozyme loci have traits that might enhance fitness such as high growth, increased survival and fecundity, or developmental stability (Allendorf and Leary 1986, Reed and Frankham 2003). Examples of fitness-related traits of wildlife associated with specific allozyme genotypes at single or with multiple locus heterozygosity include spur length in wild turkeys (Leberg 1994), horn growth in mountain sheep (Fitzsimmons et al. 1995), developmental stability in the brown hare (*Lepus europaeus*) (Hartl et al. 1995a) and survival in marbled salamanders (*Ambystoma opacum*) and red deer (Pemberton et al. 1988, Chazal et al. 1996). In white-tailed deer, single or multiple locus heterozygosity has been associated with many traits (Smith et al. 2001b) including fetal and adult growth (Cothran et al. 1983), fat accumulation (Cothran et al. 1987), and antler size (Scribner et al. 1989). However, there have also been studies that found no relationship between heterozygosity and traits related to fitness (Britten 1996). In red deer, antler growth was actually lower in heterozygotes for some allozymes (Hartl et al. 1995b). Furthermore, there is little direct evidence that it is the allozyme loci under examination that are producing variation in fitness components. The allozymes might be physically linked, through proximity on chromosomes, to genes producing the effect or, alternatively, high heterozygosity might indicate that an individual's parents were not

closely related (Leberg et al. 1990). Arguments can be found to favor or discredit any explanations of allozyme heterozygosity-fitness correlations.

Understanding relationships between heterozygosity and fitness is being enhanced by examining similar relationships using molecular markers that are probably not under selection. Associations between fitness traits and several indices of heterozygosity or outbreeding, based on microsatellite loci, have been detected for several wildlife species (Coulson et al. 1998, Slate et al. 2000, Hansson et al. 2001, Hoglund et al. 2002, Slate and Pemberton 2002). For example, survival was positively associated with a measure of outbreeding in greater horseshoe bats (*Rhinolophus ferrumequinum*) (Rossiter et al. 2001). Because microsatellites are typically found in regions of the genome that are not transcribed, it seems likely that heterozygosity-fitness correlations are not due to these loci. It is more likely that such associations reflect the relatedness of an individual's parents or the physical proximity of assayed microsatellites to other loci affecting the traits of interest.

Recently there has been considerable interest in examining relationships between individual viability and loci in the major histocompatiblity complex. These genes are involved in immune responses and there is some evidence that selection maintains variation within populations (Hughes 1991, Hughes and Yeager 1998, Richman et al. 2001). For example, Ditchkoff et al. (2001) found that specific genotypes of the major histocompatibility complex were associated with antler development, body mass, and serum testosterone in white-tailed deer. It is possible that such associations are due to variation in pathogen resistance of different major histocompatibility complex genotypes. Studies have also suggested the major histocompatibility complex might influence mate choice in mammals (Potts et al. 1991, Brown 1998, Penn 2002).

Although examination of correlations between genotypes at molecular markers and traits related to individual fitness has been a focus of wildlife genetics, there have been few attempts to apply knowledge in this area directly to management. Any program designed to increase abundance of certain genotypes would be difficult to implement in a natural setting and might be ill advised. While it has been argued that breeding programs in captive populations should emphasize maintenance of allozyme or major histocompatibility complex diversity because these loci may influence individual survival or fecundity (Wayne et al. 1986, Hughes 1991), selective breeding schemes to favor variation at a few molecular markers could result in an increase in the rate of loss of genetic variation at all loci (Hedrick et al. 1986, Vrijenhoek and Leberg 1991, Miller 1995, Lacy 2000). Because there is a poor understanding of how different genes interact to affect individual well being, most captive breeding programs advocate maintenance of overall genetic variation and reduction of relatedness. Models have also shown that selection of individuals, on the basis of marker genotype, to be used in reintroduction programs can result in an overall reduction in genetic variation in newly established populations (Haig et al. 1990).

Genetic Diversity and Population Viability

Observations of inbreeding depression in captive (Lacy et al. 1996) and field populations (Jimenez et al. 1994,

Keller et al. 1994, Keller and Waller 2002), and studies of heterozygosity-fitness relationships (Reed and Frankham 2003) have led to the realization that loss of genetic variation could affect population viability (Gilpin and Soulé 1986, Lacy 1997). Simulation models (Mills and Smouse 1994, Robert et al. 2002) and laboratory studies (Ayala 1968, Spielman and Frankham 1992, Frankham 1999, Reed and Bryant 2000) have demonstrated decreased population growth and increased extinction rates with loss of genetic variation. Furthermore, observations of wildlife populations that have experienced loss of genetic variation due to bottlenecks also support the conclusion that such losses can affect population productivity (Bouzat et al. 1998*b*).

Practices that lead to reduced genetic variation, such as establishing populations with only a few individuals or allowing populations to remain small and fragmented, might have serious consequences for population viability. These concerns about effects of inbreeding on demography occur on a time scale relevant to management activities (e.g., Westemeier et al. 1998). On a longer time scale, managers must be concerned about loss of allelic variation that can affect the ability of populations to adapt to new environmental challenges (Allendorf and Leary 1986, Frankham 1995*b*).

Most conservation geneticists promote maintaining large effective sizes of populations to prevent loss of genetic variation and possible associated reductions in population viability. Recommendations concerning population sizes necessary to prevent adverse genetic consequences vary considerably; there is no general agreement on what appropriate minimum numbers are acceptable for long-term management goals (Gilpin and Soulé 1986, Simberloff 1988, Hedrick and Kalinowski 2000, Reed and Bryant 2000). Most published recommendations of minimum population size are in terms of minimum effective size; the number of breeding age individuals in most populations should be at least twice as large. Maintaining large populations can be especially difficult in captive breeding programs and several strategies have been developed to maintain genetic diversity in captivity.

The relationship between loss of genetic diversity and population viability is not as straightforward as the discussion above might suggest. A population with a history of inbreeding might suffer from future inbreeding less than other populations (Fu et al. 1998), and inbreeding depression may be influenced by environmental conditions (Bijlsma et al. 1999). Furthermore, matings of individuals from genetically differentiated populations, as might occur through translocation, could under some circumstances increase genetic variation in a population while causing a decrease in individual viability (Templeton 1986, Leberg 1993). Additionally, other mechanisms beside inbreeding and the loss of genetic variants, such as slow accumulation of mutations with slight deleterious effects, may affect the long-term consequences for small populations (Lande 1995). Reviews of the mechanisms through which genetic diversity can affect population viability can be found in Soule (1986) and Frankham et al. (2002).

USING DNA AS AN INDIVIDUAL MARKER
Estimating Population Size/Survival

Wildlife biologists are often interested in estimating population size and survival rates of individuals within a population. Traditional wildlife studies typically use some mark and recapture methods to reach these goals. The methodologies behind these techniques have been well established (Jolly 1965, Seber 1965, Otis et al. 1978, Nichols et al. 1981, Pollock 1981, White et al. 1982, Lebreton et al. 1992) and are widely used (Lancia et al. 2004). These techniques involve capturing a sample of the population, giving each animal a unique tag and then releasing the animal into the population. In subsequent time periods, additional samples are taken and the proportion of the population that is marked is estimated and used to estimate population size and survival. Sophisticated modeling of capture probabilities and model selection techniques exist and are widely used.

While traditional mark and recapture techniques work well for many species, there are others for which this type of analysis does not work well. Species that are dangerous and expensive to catch (e.g., grizzly bears, *Ursus arctos horribilis*) and those that are highly elusive do not lend themselves to conventional mark and recapture techniques. Because DNA can be obtained from hair (Foran et al. 1997, Taberlet et al. 1997, Woods et al. 1999, Sloane et al. 2000), feathers (Ellegren 1991), feces (Reed et al. 1997, Flagstad et al. 1999, Ernest et al. 2000), and even frozen urine (Valiere and Taberlet 2000) biologists have non-invasive ways (through hair snags or from collecting feathers, feces, or frozen urine) to sample individuals that have been difficult to sample in the past. Because each individual animal has a unique molecular fingerprint that remains with them throughout their lifetime, it is reasonable to believe this fingerprint (or a portion of it) may be used in an analogous way to the unique "mark" assigned by a biologist in a traditional mark and recapture study. As a result, biologists are beginning to use molecular approaches to estimate population size.

For mark and recapture methods to work using DNA as an unique "mark", molecular biologists need to use a genetic marker (or series of markers) that are variable enough that no 2 individuals will have the same 'molecular tag'. This means that an adequate number of molecular markers that are sufficiently polymorphic need to be used. These markers need to be biparentally inherited, dominant, and highly polymorphic. Microsatellites are currently the best marker for this application; with each individual's "molecular tag" based on its genotype for a number of highly polymorphic microsatellite loci. Once sufficient microsatellite loci are examined to uniquely identify an individual, traditional mark and recapture methods can be used. Using DNA to identify individuals, scientists have been able to estimate population size of humpback whales (*Megaptera novaeangliae*) (Palsbøll et al. 1997), mountain lions (*Puma concolor*) (Ernest et al. 2000), coyotes (Kohn et al. 1999), and Pyrenean brown bears (*U. a. pyrenensis*) (Taberlet et al. 1997) although in most cases more sophisticated mark and recapture methodologies could have been used. Currently, use of DNA as a unique molecular tag is being added to traditional methodologies and is being integrated into the mark and recapture software (K. P. Burnham, personal communication).

This technique has excellent potential for estimating population size (and potentially survival rates) of species that are difficult to trap. However, it has several limitations. The first is the quantity and quality of DNA that is extracted from hair, feathers, feces, and frozen urine. Typically, only small amounts of DNA (often in the range of picograms) can be extracted from such samples (Taberlet et al. 1999). The DNA that is successfully extracted often is degraded and chopped into smaller pieces and may contain PCR inhibitors. With low quantity DNA, contamination becomes a serious issue, as does a phenomenon known as allelic dropout (Taberlet et al. 1999). Allelic dropout occurs when pipetting small amounts of DNA and only 1 of 2 alleles of template DNA gets amplified by PCR. The consequences are that only one allele of a heterozygous genotype is amplified resulting in incorrect assignment of that individual as a homozygote instead of a heterozygote. Low quality DNA (severed into many short fragments) is undesirable because it becomes difficult to amplify a microsatellite allele if the template DNA of a certain microsatellite is severed in that region. Failure to address possible genotyping errors can result in large overestimates of population size (Waits and Leberg 2000). These issues can be handled by using strict extraction protocols to avoid contamination, adopting a multi-tube approach to prevent allelic dropout, and using only short microsatellite loci to avoid problems with degraded DNA (Taberlet et al. 1999).

The second issue deals with the assumption the method used can uniquely identify individuals. For this type of analysis, a sufficient number of highly polymorphic microsatellite loci are needed so that no 2 individuals will share the same molecular tag. The difficulty lies in knowing how many microsatellite loci are sufficient to assure unique molecular tags (Mills et al. 2000*b*, Waits and Leberg 2000). Using simulations, Waits and Leberg (2000) demonstrated that population estimates tended to be biased downward as the probability that 2 or more individuals shared a molecular tag increased. Mills et al. (2000*b*) found similar results using Lincoln-Peterson estimators and multiple-recapture estimators in program CAPTURE. The probability of sampling identical genotypes can be estimated using theoretical equations (Paetkau and Stobeck 1994). However, these estimators assume random associations between alleles within and among loci, which is likely inaccurate for populations with substructure (Waits et al. 2001). Waits et al. (2001) introduced a probability of identity estimator that can be used as a conservative upper bound for the probability of observing identical genotypes for multiple individuals that may be related from the same population. Application of molecular genetics to mark and recapture methodology is relatively new. While methodologies and logistics of this application are still being examined, it is believed that it will become a widely applied and accepted use of molecular genetics in wildlife studies.

Tracking Individual Movements

Because individuals can be identified with highly polymorphic markers and sampled through collections of scat or hair, it is possible to obtain information concerning their movements (Kohn and Wayne 1997). In these studies, movement data are obtained by "recapturing" individuals as a result of multiple collections of their DNA at different locations and times. This method has been applied to a number of mammalian carnivores (Taberlet et al. 1997, Kohn et al. 1999, Ernest et al. 2000, Lucchini et al. 2002).

Information obtained is often limited by sampling protocols; if sampling is confined to roads or paths, an incomplete picture of an individual's use of space will be obtained. Use of specially trained dogs to find scat provides one approach for detecting scat in areas off roads and paths (Smith et al. 2001*a*). Using DNA from skin samples, Palsbøll et al. (1997) studied long distance migration of individual humpback whales.

At times it is not necessary to identify "recaptured" individuals to obtain information on movements. If breeding populations differ in genetic composition it is possible to identify the origin of dispersing or migrating individuals. Genetic stock identification allows estimates of the proportion of a sample of individuals that originated from different source populations (Smouse et al. 1990, Xu et al. 1994, Pearce et al. 2000). Assignment tests estimate the probability that a specific individual was a member of the different source populations in the sample (Cornuet et al. 1999, Manel et al. 2002). Variations on these approaches have been used to gain insight into migratory patterns of Canada geese (*Branta canadensis*) (Pearce et al. 2000), noctule bats (*Nyctalus noctula*) (Petit and Mayer 2000), and shorebirds (Haig 1998, Wennerberg 2001). Stock identification has proven useful in assigning samples of loggerhead turtles (*Caretta caretta*) collected in foraging areas to their nesting beaches (Bowen et al. 1995, Bass and Witzell 2000), and by identifying which populations are most affected by incidental captures associated with commercial fisheries (Laurent et al. 1998). Genetic tests have been have been used to identify which of several populations of wolves and rock wallabies (*Petrogale lateralis*) was the source of dispersing individuals that established new populations (Eldridge et al. 2001, Lucchini et al. 2002). In another example, Blanchong et al. (2002) were able to ascertain whether individual white-tailed deer were likely to have been harvested from a specific management unit. Assignment tests might also improve the ability to detect poaching when populations are governed by different harvest regulations (Manel et al. 2002). Precise estimates from either technique require the genetic composition of possible source populations are well characterized by a large number of genetic markers and individuals; sampling requirements decrease as genetic differences among populations increase. Although stock identification and assignment tests can be powerful, levels of genetic differentiation in many species, such as northern pintails (*Anas acuta*) and double-crested cormorants (*Phalacrocorax auritus*) (Cronin et al. 1996, Waits et al. 2003), is sufficiently small making identification of natal or source populations impractical.

Species Identification

Wildlife biologists often find "signs" of wildlife such as feces, tufts of hair, feathers, blood, and even frozen urine and need to know what species (or individual of a known species) left that sign. This is particularly important for programs monitoring status of regulated or protected species. DNA can be extracted from these materials and either sequenced or used in a fragment analysis (such as microsatellites) to identify which species left the "sign." If a species has uniquely identifiable populations or regions, this technique may also be applied to identify to which population or region a sample belongs.

To perform molecular species identification, one must first find an area in the genome (usually in the mitochondrial genome) that is not polymorphic between members of the same species but is polymorphic among members of different species. Typically, there will be certain areas within the sequence that are diagnostic of particular species. To differentiate American marten (*Martes americana*), fisher (*M. pennanti*), wolverine (*Gulo gulo*), and Canada lynx (*Lynx canadensis*), for example, Foran et al. (1997) compared DNA sequences (approximately 600 base pairs) of the cytochrome b and D-loop region of the mitochondrial genome from the 4 different species. After amplifying the 600 base pair region, they cut that region with a series of restriction enzymes, which resulted in a variable restriction pattern that was diagnostic to each species (Foran et al. 1997). Valiere and Taberlet (2000) were able to distinguish different canid species using frozen urine. Similarly, Ernest et al. (2000) used a panel of 12 microsatellite loci to distinguish mountain lion and bobcat (*Lynx rufus*) DNA from feces. This type of analysis can be done at the population level if there is a diagnostic region that defines different populations. A further application of this approach to a management issue is the National Canada Lynx Survey (Box 3).

Dietary Analysis

Molecular probes can be used to examine food habits in the absence of recognizable remnants of plant and animal parts such as hair or seeds (Symondson 2002). Possible sources of dietary information useful for such analyses include stomach contents, mammalian scat, and bird regurgitant (Symondson 2002). For example, Scribner and Bowman (1998) used microsatellite analysis to distinguish between several species of juvenile waterfowl in stomachs of glaucous gulls (*Larus hyperboreous*). Taberlet and Fumagalli (1996) demonstrated that it was possible to identify the species of bones found in owl pellets. In such an analyses, care must be used to select genetic markers with an appropriate level of resolution. If markers only work on a small number of species, some prey will not be identified. However, using approaches that can identify a wide range of species might also detect non-dietary items. For example, while attempting to identify large felids from scat, Farrell et al. (2000) detected dipterian DNA that could be the result of flies visiting the feces. Molecular approaches allow not only the analysis of contemporary scat samples, but also from prehistoric materials such as coprolites of the extinct ground sloth (*Nothrotheriops*

Box 3. Documenting the presence of lynx using molecular techniques.

When lynx populations declined in the contiguous United States, the federal government implemented a survey based partially on DNA approaches. The survey was designed to learn where lynx did or did not occur. Across the potential range of the species south of Canada, transects were established and hair snares, designed to snag samples of hair, and attractant were used to collect samples (McDaniel et al. 2000). The technique of Foran et al. (1997) could not be used because it required amplification of a long fragment of DNA (~900 bp) that could not be amplified using degraded DNA from hair samples. Instead, a shorter fragment was used and sequences of that fragment from hairs were amplified with PCR. Restriction enzymes were then used to create DNA fragments and hairs of lynx were distinguished from other samples by banding patterns (Mills et al. 2000*a*).

Baiting a hair snare with catnip (photograph by G. W. McDaniel).

shastensis) (Hofreiter et al. 2000). Symondson (2002) reviewed several recent studies of dietary analysis of mammal and bird excrement; considerable effort and expense would be required to apply this approach to a large number of samples.

CAPTIVE BREEDING PROGRAMS
Pedigree Analysis

When populations decline drastically and only a small number of individuals remain, biologists often capture some of the remaining individuals in attempts to establish a captive population. These animals are bred to expand the captive population so individuals can be released into the wild. It has been shown that sound management of the genetic aspects of breeding programs is needed to be successful (Ralls and Ballou 1986, Foose and Ballou 1988, Hedrick and Miller 1992). Because number of individuals brought into captivity is usually small, inbreeding is a serious problem. Thus, it is important to consider the genetic identity of animals bred in captivity so that net genetic variability is maximized and inbreeding is minimized. After several generations are mated, pedigrees are developed to document matings from all previous generations.

The methodology for maximizing genetic diversity and minimizing mean kinship in captively bred populations is well established (Ballou and Lacy 1995). There are other methods of quantifying genetic structure in pedigrees such as founder equivalents (Hedrick and Miller 1994), although minimizing mean kinship appears to be superior (Miller 1995). Some biologists have suggested that instead of maximizing genetic variation at the genome level, selective breeding of individuals with certain alleles at specific loci (e.g., those containing alleles with particular selective benefits) should be implemented (Allendorf 1986, Hughes 1991). It has been advocated (Hughes 1991) that breeding programs maximize diversity at the Major Histocompatibility Complex. Others believe that by selecting for rare alleles at a particular locus, the overall genomic diversity is reduced more quickly (Gilpin and Wills 1991, Miller and Hedrick 1991, Vrijenhoek and Leberg 1991). Miller (1995) used Przewalski's horse (*Equus caballus*) and California condor (*Gymnogyps californianus*) pedigrees to evaluate using "rare kinship" as a management strategy. He found this strategy increased population mean kinship and reduced gene diversity compared to a "no management" control and was inferior to a strategy based on minimizing mean kinship (Miller 1995).

The founding individuals are assumed to be unrelated in most captive breeding programs (Lacy et al. 1995). All subsequent analyses calculate relatedness as a measure of common ancestry relative to the founding population (Lacy 1995). It is important to understand the relatedness of the founding individuals to maximize the remaining genetic diversity and minimize inbreeding in captive breeding programs. Molecular genetic techniques are an effective method to assess relatedness of founders of captive breeding programs. The relatedness of founders of several captively bred species has been examined using multilocus DNA fingerprinting (Brock and White 1992; Geyer et al. 1993; Haig et al. 1994, 1995). More recently, microsatellite analyses have proven to be valuable for inferring relatedness (Queller at al. 1993, Haig 1998) and promise to be useful for examining relatedness of founders. Jones et al. (2002) used microsatellite data to augment wild and captive pedigree information on whooping cranes (*Grus americana*). Microsatellite data revealed unknown shared genotype information for founders and allowed them to develop a pedigree based on DNA that will help in the genetic management of the species.

MATING SYSTEMS

Study of mating systems is not new and has been broadly characterized in many species. Biologists have been interested not only in the type of mating system (monogamy, polygamy, polyandry, etc.) but also in how such systems evolved. This often involves examination of parentage and mating success. Historically, mating systems have been studied through direct behavioral observations (Young 2005). Biologists spend hours observing mating rituals and copulations to characterize different mating behavior. This characterization is particularly difficult where females mate with more than one male outside a socially bonded pair, and where females store sperm for long periods of time making it difficult to discern the true biological father. As a result, true patterns of gametic exchange may differ substantially from the apparent mating systems characterized by behavioral observations. Inaccurate estimation of parentage can be a major obstacle in understanding selection and evolution of mating systems (Mock 1983, Gyllensten et al. 1990). An accurate documentation of reproductive success reduces the possibility of inaccurately equating mating prowess or other reproductive features with actual transfer of genes across generations (Avise 1994). Because effective population size, N_e relies heavily on an accurate depiction of the mating system (Chesser 1991, Nunney 1993), confirmation of mating systems using genetic techniques is crucial.

Maternity and Paternity Analysis

With advent of more advanced molecular genetic techniques, it has become possible to accurately assign parentage. This allows biologists to accurately assess mating success and to re-evaluate characterizations of mating systems. Many different molecular techniques can be used to assess different questions of parentage. Quinn et al. (1987, 1989) used Restriction Fragment Length Polymorphisms to examine whether snow goose goslings in a brood were the offspring of the nest attendants and apparent parents. They documented intraspecific brood parasitism where not all goslings in the brood had the same mother, likely extrapair fertilization where not all goslings had the same father, and where neither nest attendant was the parent. Burke et al. (1989) used multilocus fingerprinting to show that dunnock sparrow (*Prunella modularis*) broods could have multiple fathers. Previously, Kemp's ridley sea turtles were thought to have little or no multiple paternity. Kichler et al. (1999) used microsatellite analysis to show they are polyandrous. Richardson and Burke (1999) used single-locus minisatellite DNA profiling to examine the relationship between the age and instance of extra-pair fertilization in male Bullock's orioles (*Icterus bullockii*). Amplified Fragment Length Polymorphisms were used by Questiau et al. (1999) to document frequency of extra-pair parentage in a population of bluethroat (*Luscinia svecica*).

Mating Success

Molecular genetic techniques simplify studies of mating success of males and social organization. Murphy (1998) used microsatellite analysis to investigate correlations between phenotypic and behavioral traits and reproductive success in mountain lions in the Northern Yellowstone ecosystem (Box 4). Pemberton et al. (1992) were able to assess the mating success of red deer using DNA fingerprinting. They found that behavioral methods used to estimate male reproductive success underestimated true success of successful males and overestimated success of unsuccessful males. Similarly, Semple et al. (2001) showed that sage-grouse broods had multiple fathers suggesting that dominant males may not be as reproductively successful as once thought. The complex social structure of the cooperatively breeding acorn woodpecker (*Melanerpes formicivorus*) has been clarified (Haycock et al. 2001) and, similarly, insight into the social organization of the brown long-eared bat (*Plecotus auritus*) has been established (Burland et al. 2001).

GENDER IDENTIFICATION

Wildlife biologists studying animals in the field typically need to know the gender of individuals to examine differences between males and females. For example, studies of population dynamics often compare survival rates between males and females. In sexually dimorphic wildlife species it is straightforward to differentiate males from females. However, for some species it is difficult to accurately assign gender to an individual without invasive procedures. The same problem arises with gender identification from wildlife "signs" such as feces, urine, feathers, or hair. Molecular genetic techniques can be used on a variety of different species to assign gender to individuals using only a small sample (e.g., blood, feathers, feces, urine, hair). Forensic scientists can use DNA-based identification approaches when gender of a tissue sample or bloodstain might indicate a violation of wildlife harvest regulations (Gilson et al. 1998, Wilson and White 1998).

Mammals

Gender can be identified from DNA samples for many groups of mammals including wombats, rabbits, ungulates, carnivores, seals, primates, and whales (Aasen and Medrano 1990, Griffiths and Tiwari 1993, Reed et al. 1997, Taberlet et al. 1997, Sloane et al. 2000, Wallner et al. 2001, Ensminger and Hoffman 2002, Huber et al. 2002). Most protocols call for detection of genetic markers, such as the SRY locus, that is associated with the Y chromosome to identify males. If the marker is not detected the sample is assumed to be a female. However, because degraded DNA or inhibitory compounds found in some samples can prevent detection of a locus (Kohn and Wayne 1997), it is necessary to have controls with other markers to verify there is nothing about the sample that would prevent correct gender identification (Taberlet et al. 1997, Wilson and White 1998). Generally, genetic methods of gender identification have proven to be quite reliable for mammals. However, an approach that works for one set of species, might not work for others (Ensminger and Hoffman 2002). Thus, the reliability of any protocol should be verified with samples where the gender is

Box 4. Documentation of reproductive success of mountain lions using paternity analysis.

Reproductive success is important in an evolutionary sense because it relates an individual's phenotypic traits to overall fitness. Variation in reproductive success is typically associated with variation in traits such as differences in age, mate access, survival of young, and longevity of adults. Alternatively, reproductive success may be the result of environmental variation or purely by chance. Murphy (1998) examined variation in reproductive success of male and female mountain lions in the Northern Yellowstone Ecosystem and its relation to spacing patterns and mating systems.

Because male mountain lions spend little or no time with young, it is difficult to identify the father of litters without extensive monitoring of male behavior. Therefore, Murphy (1998) used a panel of 18 polymorphic microsatellite loci to identify the paternity of 23 litters. He used the number of young produced by females and the number of litters fathered by males to describe short-term variation in reproductive success for mountain lions. He then tested whether phenotypic and behavioral traits were correlated with reproductive success. Murphy (1998) found that a single male sired each litter and that reproductive success was positively correlated with age of the male and the number of females in his territory. Neither age of the female nor the size of the male territory was correlated with reproductive success. This study confirmed that the mating system of mountain lions is classically polygynous.

Mountain lion (photograph by K. M. Murphy).

known. Care must also be taken when using DNA markers from scat to identify the gender of carnivores. Ernest et al. (2000) found that scat from 3 of 4 female mountain lions contained male genotypes. They hypothesized the male genotype might be the result of DNA from male prey since the SRY marker is not species-specific.

Birds

Gender of birds is typically difficult to assign as the majority of the world's bird species have males that look identical to females (Griffiths et al. 1998). To address this issue, Griffiths et al. (1998) designed primers around homologous regions in the chromo-helicase-DNA-binding (CHD) gene on sex chromosomes W and Z in birds. This technique takes advantage of the fact that chromosomes W and Z evolve at different rates. Homologous regions on sex chromosomes typically are different sizes due to mutations involving insertions and deletions of DNA nucleotides. Their method simultaneously amplifies homologous regions on the W and Z chromosome followed by a restriction digest, which allows for differentiation of males (ZZ–1 band) and females (ZW–2 bands) in many species of birds with the possible exception of Struthioniformes. Ellegren (1996) developed PCR primers for collared flycatchers (*Ficedula albicollis*) within the CHD gene that resulted in gender identification of closely related species without the restriction digest step. Kahn et al. (1998) designed a different set of primers in a more conserved region of the CHD gene that works in most avian species. Bello and Sanchez (1999) further modified this technique to allow for gender identification in ostriches (*Struthio camelus*). This technique has been used to identify gender of many species including mountain plover (*Charadrius montanus*) (Dinsmore et al. 2000) using feathers and kakapo (*Strigops habroptilus*) from feces (Robertson et al. 1999).

SUMMARY

Molecular genetic techniques represent a relatively new and powerful set of tools that can address both research and management issues in wildlife science. These approaches have shown their utility in wildlife management by helping identify species and appropriate units for conservation. Knowledge gained about the factors affecting distribution and loss of genetic variants has led to refinements in population management such as maintaining effective population sizes and connectivity between reserves. More recently, the introduction of PCR has allowed noninvasive collection of genetic material from a variety of sources such as hair, feathers, and feces. Together with the ability to examine highly polymorphic loci and gender-specific markers, noninvasive sampling has allowed genetic assays to contribute to ecological studies of sex ratios, food habits, population size, and mating systems. In this chapter we provide general theory of population genetics and have identified those techniques and applications currently used in wildlife studies. This body of literature is expanding rapidly and readers are referred to more detailed accounts of population genetic theory, techniques, and applications. With rapid development of DNA-based technologies, it is likely that currently unforeseen applications of genetic approaches will soon be available to assist wildlife scientists addressing a wide variety of problems.

ACKNOWLEDGMENTS

We thank L. S. Mills and K. E. Mock for helpful comments on this chapter. We are also appreciative of members of P. L. Leberg's lab and to J. St. John, S. M. Pearson, H.-P. Liu, and A. L. Child for their review of the chapter. The Environmental Protection Agency (R-82942001) and Louisiana Department of Wildlife and Fisheries provided support for P. L. Leberg during manuscript preparation.

LITERATURE CITED

AASEN, E., AND J. F. MEDRANO. 1990. Amplification of the Zfy and Zfx genes for sex identification in humans, cattle, sheep and goats. Bio-Technology 8:1279–1281.

ALDRICH, J. W. 1946. New subspecies of birds from western North America. Proceedings of the Biological Society of Washington 59:129–136.

ALDRIDGE, C. L., S. J. OYLER-MCCANCE, AND R. M. BRIGHAM. 2001. Occurrence of greater sage-grouse × sharp-tailed grouse hybrids in Alberta. Condor 103:657–660.

ALLENDORF, F. W. 1986. Genetic drift and the loss of alleles versus heterozygosity. Zoo Biology 5:181–190.

———, AND R. W. LEARY. 1986. Heterozygosity and fitness in natural populations of animals. Pages 51–65 *in* M. E. Soulé, editor. Conservation biology: the science of scarcity and diversity. Sinauer Associates, Sunderland, Massachusetts, USA.

Anderson, S., H. L. De Bruijn, A. R. Coulson, I. C. Eperon, F. Sanger, and I. G. Young.1982. Complete sequence of bovine mitochondrial DNA. Conserved features of the mammalian mitochondrial genome. Journal of Molecular Biology 156:683–717.

ARDERN, S. L., AND D. M. LAMBERT. 1997. Is the black robin in genetic peril? Molecular Ecology 6:21–28.

ÁRNASON, Ú., R. SPILLIAERT, Á. PÁLSDÓTTIR, AND A. ÁRNASON. 1991. Molecular identification of hybrids between the two largest whale species, the blue whale (*Balaenoptera musculus*) and the fin whale (*B. physalus*). Hereditas 115:183–189.

AVISE, J. C. 1989. A role for molecular genetics in the recognition and conservation of endangered species. Trends in Ecology and Evolution 4:279–281.

———. 1994. Molecular markers, natural history, and evolution. Chapman and Hall, New York, USA.

———, AND W. S. NELSON. 1989. Molecular genetic relationship of the extinct dusky seaside sparrow. Science 243:646–648.

———, R. T. ALISAUKAS, W. S. NELSON, AND C. D. ANKNEY. 1992. Matriarchal population genetic structure in an avian species with female natal philopatry. Evolution 46:1084–1096.

AYALA, F. J. 1968. Genotype, environment, and population numbers. Science 162:1453–1459.

BAKER, R. J., A. M. BICKHAM, M. BONDARKOV, S. P. GASCHAK, C. W. MATSON, B. E. RODGERS, J. K. WICKLIFFE, AND R. K. CHESSER. 2001. Consequences of polluted environments on population structure: the bank vole (*Clethrionomys glareolus*) at Chernobyl. Ecotoxicology 10:211–216.

BALLOU, J. D., AND R. C. LACY. 1995. Identifying genetically important individuals for management of genetic diversity in pedigreed populations. Pages 76–85 *in* J. D. Ballou, M. Gilpin, and T. J. Foose, editors. Population management for survival and recovery. Columbia University Press, New York, USA.

BALLOUX, F., AND N. LUGON-MOULIN. 2002. The estimation of population differentiation with microsatellite markers. Molecular Ecology 11:155–165.

BARTLEY, D., M. BAGLEY, G. GALL, AND B. BENTLEY. 1992. Use of linkage disequilibrium data to estimate effective size of hatchery and natural fish populations. Conservation Biology 6:365–375.

BASS, A. L., AND W. N. WITZELL. 2000. Demographic composition of immature green turtles (*Chelonia mydas*) from the east central Florida coast: evidence from mtDNA markers. Herpetologica 56:357–367.

BAVERSTOCK, P. R., AND C. MORITZ. 1996. Project Design. Pages 17–28 *in* D. M. Hillis, C. Moritz, and B. K. Mable, editors. Molecular systematics. Sinauer Associates, Sunderland, Massachusetts, USA.

BELLO, N., AND A. SÁNCHEZ. 1999. The identification of a sex-specific DNA marker in the ostrich using random amplified polymorphic DNA (RAPD) assay. Molecular Ecology 8:667–669.

BENEDICT, N. G., S. J. OYLER-MCCANCE, S. E. TAYLOR, C. E. BRAUN, AND T. W. QUINN. 2003. Evaluation of the eastern (*Centrocercus urophasianus urophasianus*) and western (*Centrocercus urophasianus phaios*) subspecies of sage-grouse using mitochondrial control-region sequence data. Conservation Genetics 4:301–310.

BIBB, M. J., R. A. VAN ETTEN, C. T. WRIGHT, M. W. WALBERG, AND D. A. CLAYTON. 1981. Sequence and gene organization of mouse mitochondrial DNA. Cell 26:167–180.

BIJLSMA, R., J. BUNDGAARD, AND W. F. VAN PUTTEN. 1999. Environmental dependence of inbreeding depression and purging in *Drosophila melanogaster*. Journal of Evolutionary Biology 12:1125–1137.

BLANCHONG, J. A., K. T. SCRIBNER, AND S. R. WINTERSTEIN. 2002. Assignment of individuals to populations: Bayesian methods and multi-locus genotypes. Journal of Wildlife Management 66:321–329.

BOUZAT, J. L. 2000. The importance of control populations for the identification and management of genetic diversity. Genetica 110:109–115.

———. 2001. The population genetic structure of the greater rhea (*Rhea americana*) in an agricultural landscape. Biological Conservation 99:277–284.

———, H. A. LEWIN, AND K. N. PAIGE. 1998a. The ghost of genetic diversity past: historical DNA analysis of the greater prairie chicken. American Naturalist 152:1–6.

———, H. H. CHENG, H. A. LEWIN, R. L. WESTEMEIER, J. D. BRAWN, AND K. N. PAIGE. 1998b. Genetic evaluation of a demographic bottleneck in the greater prairie chicken. Conservation Biology 12:836–843.

BOWEN, B. W., A. B. MEYLEN, AND J. C. AVISE. 1991. Evolutionary distinctiveness of the endangered Kemp's ridley sea turtle. Nature 352:709–711.

———, ———, J. P. ROSS, C. J. LIMPUS, G. H. BALAZS, AND J. C. AVISE. 1992. Global population structure and natural history of the green turtle (*Chelonia mydas*) in terms of matriarchal phylogeny. Evolution 46:865–881.

———, F. A. ABREU-GROBOIS, G. H. BALAZS, N. KAMEZAKI, C. J. LIMPUS, AND R. J. FERL. 1995. Trans-Pacific migrations of the loggerhead turtle (*Caretta caretta*) demonstrated with mitochondrial-DNA markers. Proceedings of the National Academy of Sciences of the United States of America 92:3731–3734.

BRAUN, C. E. 1998. Sage grouse declines in western North America: what are the problems? Proceedings of the Western Association of State Fish and Wildlife Agencies 78:139–156.

BRITTEN, H. B. 1996. Meta-analyses of the association between multilocus heterozygosity and fitness. Evolution 50:2158–2164.

BROCK, M. K., AND B. N. WHITE. 1992. Application of DNA fingerprinting to the recovery program of the endangered Puerto Rican parrot. Proceedings of the National Academy of Science of the United States of America 89:11121–11125.

BROWN, J. L. 1998. The new heterozygosity theory of mate choice and the MHC. Genetica 104:215–221.

BROWN, W. M., M. GEORGE, JR., AND A. C. WILSON. 1979. Rapid evolution of animal mitochondrial DNA. Proceedings of the National Academy of Sciences of the United States of America 76:1967–1971.

———, E. M. PRAGER, A. WANG, AND A. C. WILSON. 1982. Mitochondrial DNA sequences of primates: tempo and mode of evolution. Journal of Molecular Evolution 18:225–239.

BURKE, T., N. B. DAVIES, M. W. BRUFORD, AND B. J. HATCHWELL. 1989. Parental care and mating behavior of polyandrous dunnocks *Prunella modularis* related to paternity by DNA fingerprinting. Nature 338:249–251.

BURLAND, T. M., E. M. BARRATT, R. A. NICHOLS, AND P. A. RACEY. 2001. Mating patterns, relatedness and the basis of natal philopatry in the brown long-eared bat, *Plecotus auritus*. Molecular Ecology 10:1309–1321.

CHAZAL, A. C., J. D. KRENZ, AND D. E. SCOTT. 1996. Relationship of larval density and heterozygosity to growth and survival of juvenile marbled salamanders (*Ambystoma opacum*). Canadian Journal of Zoology 74:1122–1129.

CHESSER, R. K. 1991. Influence of gene flow and breeding tactics on gene diversity within populations. Genetics 129:573–583.

———, AND R. J. BAKER. 1996. Effective sizes and dynamics of uniparentally and diparentally inherited genes. Genetics 144:1225–1235.

———, O. E. RHODES, JR., D. W. SUGG, AND A. SCHNABEL. 1993. Effective sizes for subdivided populations. Genetics 135:1221–1232.

CORNUET, J.-M., AND G. LUIKART. 1996. Description and power analysis of two tests for detecting recent population bottlenecks from allele frequency data. Genetics 144:2001–2014.

———, S. PIRY, G. LUIKART, A. ESTOUP, AND M. SOLIGNAC. 1999. New methods employing multilocus genotypes to select or exclude populations as origins of individuals. Genetics 153:1989–2000.

COTHRAN, E. G., R. K. CHESSER, M. H. SMITH, AND P. E. JOHNS. 1983. Influences of genetic variability and maternal factors on fetal growth in white-tailed deer. Evolution 37:282–291.

———, ———, ———, AND ———. 1987. Fat levels in female white-tailed deer during the breeding season and pregnancy. Journal of Mammalogy 68:111–118.

COULSON, T. N., J. M. PEMBERTON, S. D. ALBON, M. BEAUMONT, T. C. MARSHALL, J. SLATE, F. E. GUINNESS, AND T. H. CLUTTON-BROCK. 1998. Microsatellites reveal heterosis in red deer. Proceedings of the Royal Society of London, Series B-Biological Sciences 265:489–495.

CRACRAFT, J. 1983. Species concepts and speciation analysis. Pages 159–187 in R. F. Johnston, editor. Current ornithology. Volume 1. Plenum Press, New York, USA.

CRANDALL, K. A., O. R. P. BINIDA-EMONDS, G. M. MACE, AND R. K. WAYNE. 2000. Considering evolutionary processes in conservation biology. Trends in Ecology and Evolution 17:390–395.

CRONIN, M. A., J. B. GRAND, D. ESLER, D. V. DERKSEN, AND K. T. SCRIBNER. 1996. Breeding populations of northern pintails have similar mitochondrial DNA. Canadian Journal of Zoology 74:992–999.

CROW, J. F., AND M. KIMURA. 1970. An introduction to population genetics theory. Harper and Row, New York, USA.

DAHL, C. R., J. W. BICKHAM, J. K. WICKLIFFE, AND T. W. CUSTER. 2001. Cytochrome b sequences in black-crowned night-herons (*Nycticorax nycticorax*) from heronries exposed to genotoxic contaminants. Ecotoxicology 10:291–297.

DINSMORE, S. J., G. C. WHITE, AND F. L. KNOPF. 2002. Advanced techniques for modeling avian nest survival. Ecology 83:3476–3488.

DITCHKOFF, S. S., R. L. LOCHMILLER, R. E. MASTERS, S. R. HOOFER, AND R. A. VAN DEN BUSSCHE. 2001. Major-histocompatibility-complex-associated variation in secondary sexual traits of white-tailed deer (*Odocoileus virginianus*): evidence for good-genes advertisement. Evolution 55:616–625.

DIZON, A. E., C. LOCKYER, W. F. PERRIN, D. P. DEMASTER, AND J. SISSON. 1992. Rethinking the stock concept: a phylogeographic approach. Conservation Biology 6:24–36.

DOBZHANSKY, T. G. 1937. Genetics and the origin of species. Columbia University Press, New York, USA.

———. 1970. Genetics of the evolutionary process. Columbia University Press, New York, USA.

ELDRIDGE, M. D. B., J. E. KINNEAR, AND M. L. ONUS. 2001. Source population of dispersing rock wallabies (*Petrogale lateralis*) identified by assignment tests on multilocus genotypic data. Molecular Ecology 10:2867–2876.

ELLEGREN, H. 1991. DNA typing of museum birds. Nature 354:113.

———. 1996. First gene on the avian W chromosome (CHD) provides a tag for universal sexing of non-ratite birds. Proceedings of the Royal Society of London, Series B 263:1635–1641.

———, G. HARTMAN, M. JOHANSSON, AND L. ANDERSSON. 1993. Major histocompatibility complex monomorphism and low levels of DNA fingerprinting variability in a reintroduced and rapidly expanding population of beavers. Proceedings of the National Academy of Sciences of the United States of America 90:8150–8153.

———, G. LINDGREN, C. R. PRIMMER, AND A. P. MOLLER. 1997. Fitness loss and germline mutations in barn swallows breeding in Chernobyl. Nature 389:593–596.

ELLSWORTH, D. L., K. D. RITTENHOUSE, AND R. L. HONEYCUTT. 1993. Artifactual variation in randomly amplified polymorphic DNA banding patterns. BioTechniques 14:214–217.

———, R. L. HONEYCUTT, N. J. SILVY, J. W. BICKHAM, AND W. D. KLIMSTRA. 1994a. Historical biogeography and contemporary patterns of mitochondrial DNA variation in white-tailed deer from the southeastern United States. Evolution 48:122–136.

———, ———, ———, M. H. SMITH, J. W. BICKHAM, AND W. D. KLIMSTRA. 1994b. White-tailed deer restoration to the southeastern United States: evaluating genetic-variation. Journal of Wildlife Management 58:686–697.

ENSMINGER, A. L., AND S. M. G. HOFFMAN. 2002. Sex identification assay useful in great apes is not diagnostic in a range of other primate species. American Journal of Primatology 56:129–134.

ERNEST, H. B., M. C. T. PENEDO, B. P. MAY, M. SYVANEN, AND W. M. BOYCE. 2000. Molecular tracking of mountain lions in the Yosemite Valley region in California: genetic analysis using microsatellites and faecal DNA. Molecular Ecology 9:433–441.

FARRELL, L. E., J. ROMAN, AND M. E. SUNQUIST. 2000. Dietary separation of sympatric carnivores identified by molecular analysis of scats. Molecular Ecology 9:1583–1590.

FIRESTONE, K. B., M. S. ELPHINSTONE, W. B. SHERWIN, AND B. A. HOULDEN. 1999. Phylogeographical population structure of tiger quolls *Dasyurus maculatus* (Dasyuridae: Marsupialia), an endangered carnivorous marsupial. Molecular Ecology 8:1613–1625.

FITZSIMMONS, N. N., S. W. BUSKIRK, AND M. H. SMITH. 1995. Population history, genetic variability, and horn growth in bighorn sheep. Conservation Biology 9:314–323.

——, ——, AND ——. 1997. Genetic changes in reintroduced Rocky Mountain bighorn sheep populations. Journal of Wildlife Management 61:863–872.

FLAGSTAD, O., K. RØED, J. E. STACEY, AND K. S. JAKOBSEN. 1999. Reliable noninvasive genotyping based on excremental PCR of nuclear DNA purified with a magnetic bead protocol. Molecular Ecology 8:879–883.

FOOSE, T. J., AND J. D. BALLOU. 1988. Population management: theory and practice. International Zoo Yearbook 27:26–41.

FORAN, D. R., S. C. MINTA, AND K. S. HEINEMEYER. 1997. DNA-based analysis of hair to identify species and individuals for population research and monitoring. Wildlife Society Bulletin 25:840–847.

FRANKHAM, R. 1995a. Conservation genetics. Annual Review of Genetics 29:305–327.

——. 1995b. Effective population size/adult population size ratios in wildlife: a review. Genetical Research 66:95–107.

——. 1999. Resolving conceptual issues in conservation genetics: the roles of laboratory species and meta-analyses. Hereditas 130:195–201.

——, J. D. BALLOU, AND D. A. BRISCOE. 2002. Introduction to conservation genetics. Cambridge University Press, New York, USA.

FRASER, D. J., AND L. BERNATCHEZ. 2001. Adaptive evolutionary conservation: towards a unified concept for defining conservation units. Molecular Ecology 10:2741–2752.

FU, Y. B., G. NAMKOONG, AND J. E. CARLSON. 1998. Comparison of breeding strategies for purging inbreeding depression via simulation. Conservation Biology 12:856–864.

GARZA, J. C., AND E. G. WILLIAMSON. 2001. Detection of reduction in population size using data from microsatellite loci. Molecular Ecology 10:305–318.

GERLACH, G., AND K. MUSOLF. 2000. Fragmentation of landscape as a cause for genetic subdivision in bank voles. Conservation Biology 14:1066–1074.

GEYER, C. J., O. A. RYDER, L. G. CHEMNICK, AND E. A. THOMPSON. 1993. Analysis of relatedness in the California condors, from DNA fingerprints. Molecular and Biological Evolution. 10:571–589.

GILPIN, M. E., AND M. E. SOULÉ. 1986. Minimum viable populations: processes of species extinctions. Pages 19–34 in M. E. Soulé, editor. Conservation biology: the science of scarcity and diversity. Sinauer Associates, Sunderland, Massachusetts, USA.

——, AND C. WILLS. 1991. MHC and captive breeding: a rebuttal. Conservation Biology 5:554–555.

GILSON, A., M. SYVANEN, K. LEVINE, AND J. BANKS. 1998. Deer gender determination by polymerase chain reaction: validation study and application to tissues, bloodstains, and hair forensic samples from California. California Fish and Game 84:159–169.

GIRMAN, D. J., C. VILÀ, E. GEFFEN, S. CREEL, M. G. L. MILLS, J. W. MCNUTT, J. GINSBERG, P. W. KAT, K. H. MAMIYA, AND R. K. WAYNE. 2001. Patterns of population subdivision, gene flow and genetic variability in the African wild dog (Lycaon pictus). Molecular Ecology 10:1703–1723.

GLENN, T. C., W. STEPHAN, AND M. J. BRAUN. 1999. Effects of a population bottleneck on whooping crane mitochondrial DNA variation. Conservation Biology 13:1097–1107.

GOODMAN, S. J., H. B. TAMATE, R. A. WILSON, J. NAGATA, S. TATSUZAWA, G. M. SWANSON, J. M. PEMBERTON, AND D. R. MCCULLOUGH. 2001. Bottlenecks, drift and differentiation: the population structure and demographic history of sika deer (Cervus nippon) in the Japanese archipelago. Molecular Ecology 10:1357–1370.

GREENBERG, B. D., J. E. NEWBOLD, AND A. SUGINO. 1983. Intraspecific nucleotide sequence variability surrounding the origin of replication in human mitochondrial DNA. Gene 21:33–49.

GRIFFITHS, R., AND B. TIWARI. 1993. Primers for the differential amplification of the sex-determining region Y-gene in a range of mammal species. Molecular Ecology 2:405–406.

——, M. C. DOUBLE, K. ORR, AND R. J. G. DAWSON. 1998. A DNA test to sex most birds. Molecular Ecology 7:1071–1075.

GROBLER, J. P., AND F. H. VAN DE BANK. 1994. Allozyme variation in South African impala populations under different management regimes. South African Journal of Wildlife Research 24:89–94.

GYLLENSTEN, U. B., S. JAKOBSSON, AND J. TEMRIN. 1990. No evidence for illegitimate young in monogamous and polygynous warblers. Nature 343:168–170.

HAAVIE, J., G.-P. SÆTRE, AND T. MOUM. 2000. Discrepancies in population differentiation at microsatellites, mitochondrial DNA and plumage colour in the pied flycatcher - inferring evolutionary processes. Molecular Ecology 9:1137–1148.

HAIG, S. M. 1998. Molecular contributions to conservation. Ecology 79:413–425.

——, J. D. BALLOU, AND S. R. DERRICKSON. 1990. Management options for preserving genetic diversity: reintroduction of Guam rails to the wild. Conservation Biology 4:290–300.

——, ——, AND N. J. CASNA. 1994. Identification of kin structure among Guam rail founders: a comparison of pedigrees and DNA profiles. Molecular Ecology 3:109–119.

——, ——, AND ——. 1995. Genetic identification of kin in Micronesian kingfishers. Journal of Heredity 86:423–431.

——, R. BOWMAN, AND T. D. MULLINS. 1996. Population structure of red-cockaded woodpeckers in south Florida: RAPDs revisited. Molecular Ecology 5:725–734.

——, R. S. WAGNER, E. D. FORSMAN, AND T. D. MULLINS. 2001. Geographic variation and genetic structure in spotted owls. Conservation Genetics 2:25–40.

HANSSON, B., S. BENSCH, D. HASSELQUIST, AND M. ÅKESSON. 2001. Microsatellite diversity predicts recruitment of sibling great reed warblers. Proceedings of the Royal Society of London, Series B-Biological Sciences 268:1287–1291.

HARRIS, R. B., AND F. W. ALLENDORF. 1989. Genetically effective population size of large mammals: an assessment of estimators. Conservation Biology 3:181–191.

——, W. A. WALL, AND F. W. ALLENDORF. 2002. Genetic consequences of hunting: what do we know and what should we do? Wildlife Society Bulletin. 30:634–643.

HARTL, G. B., F. SUCHENTRUNK, R. WILLING, AND R. PETZNEK. 1995a. Allozyme heterozygosity and fluctuating asymmetry in the brown hare (Lepus europaeus): a test of the developmental homeostasis hypothesis. Philosophical Transactions of the Royal Society of London, Series B-Biological Sciences 350:313–323.

——, F. KLEIN, R. WILLING, M. APOLLONIO, AND G. LANG. 1995b. Allozymes and the genetics of antler development in red deer (Cervus elaphus). Journal of Zoology 237:83–100.

HAYCOCK, J., W. D. KOENIG, AND M. T. STANBACK. 2001. Shared parentage and incest avoidance in the cooperatively breeding acorn woodpecker. Molecular Ecology 10:1515–1525.

HEDRICK, P. W. 1995. Gene flow and genetic restoration: the Florida panther as a case study. Conservation Biology 9:996–1007.

——. 1996. Bottleneck(s) or metapopulation in cheetahs. Conservation Biology 10:897–899.

——. 2000. Genetics of populations. Jones and Bartlett Publishers, Boston, Massachusetts, USA.

——, AND S. T. KALINOWSKI. 2000. Inbreeding depression in conservation biology. Annual Review of Ecology and Systematics 31:139–162.

——, AND P. S. MILLER. 1992. Conservation genetics: techniques and fundamentals. Ecological Applications 2:30–46.

——, AND ——. 1994. Rare alleles, MHC, and captive breeding. Pages 187–204 in V. Loeschke, J. Tomiuk, and S. K. Jain, editors. Conservation genetics. Birkhaeuser Verlag, Basel, Switzerland.

——, P. F. BRUSSARD, F. W. ALLENDORF, J. A. BEARDMORE, AND S. ORZACK. 1986. Protein variation, fitness, and captive propagation. Zoo Biology 5:91–99.

HILL, M., H. WITSENBOER, M. ZABEAU, P. VOS, R. KESSELI, AND R. MICHELMORE. 1996. PCR-based fingerprinting using AFLPs as a tool for studying genetic relationships in Lactuca spp. Theoretical and Applied Genetics 93:1202–1210.

HILL, W. G. 1981. Estimation of effective population size from data on linkage disequilibrium. Genetical Research 38:209–216.

HILLIS, D. M., B. K. MABLE, A. LARSON, S. K. DAVIS, AND E. A. ZIMMER. 1996. Nucleic acids IV: sequencing and cloning. Pages 321–384 in D. M. Hillis, C. Moritz, and B. K. Mable, editors. Molecular systematics. Sinauer Associates, Sunderland, Massachusetts, USA.

HOELZEL, A. R., J. C. STEPHENS, AND S. J. O'BRIEN. 1999. Molecular genetic diversity and evolution at the MHC DQB locus in four species of pinnipeds. Molecular Biology and Evolution 16:611–618.

HOFREITER, M., H. N. POINAR, W. G. SPAULDING, K. BAUER, P. S. MARTIN, G. POSSNERT, and S. PÄÄBO. 2000. A molecular analysis of ground sloth diet through the last glaciation. Molecular Ecology 9:1975–1984.

HÖGLUND, J., S. B. PIERTNEY, R. V. ALATALO, J. LINDELL, A. LUNDBERG, AND P. T. RINTAMÄKI. 2002. Inbreeding depression and male fitness in black grouse. Proceedings of the Royal Society of London, Series

B-Biological Sciences 269:711–715.

HOULDEN, B. A., B. H. COSTELLO, D. SHARKEY, E. V. FOWLER, A. MELZER, W. ELLIS, F. CARRICK, P. R. BAVERSTOCK, AND M. S. ELPHINSTONE. 1999. Phylogeographic differentiation in the mitochondrial control region in the koala Phascolarctos cinereus. Molecular Ecology 8: 999–1011.

HUBER, S., U. BRUNS, AND W. ARNOLD. 2002. Sex determination of red deer using polymerase chain reaction of DNA from feces. Wildlife Society Bulletin 30:208–212.

HUGHES, A. L. 1991. MHC polymorphism and the design of captive breeding programs. Conservation Biology 5:249–251.

———, AND M. YEAGER. 1998. Natural selection at major histocompatibility complex loci of vertebrates. Annual Review of Genetics 32:415–435.

HUPP, J. W., AND C. E. BRAUN. 1991. Geographic variation among sage grouse in Colorado. Wilson Bulletin 103:255–261.

HURLES, M. E., AND M. A. JOBLING. 2001. Haploid chromosomes in molecular ecology: lessons from the human Y. Molecular Ecology 10:1599–1613.

IUDICA, C. A., W. M. WHITTEN, AND N. H. WILLIAMS. 2001. Small bones from dried mammal museum specimens as a reliable source of DNA. Biotechniques 30:732–736.

JEFFREYS, A. J., N. J. ROYLE, V. WILSON, AND Z. WONG. 1988. Spontaneous mutation rates to new length alleles at tandem-repetitive hypervariable loci in human DNA. Nature: 332:278–281.

JENSEN-SEAMAN, M. I., AND K. K. KIDD. 2001. Mitochondrial DNA variation and biogeography of eastern gorillas. Molecular Ecology 10:2241–2247.

JIMÉNEZ, J. A., K. A. HUGHES, G. ALAKS, L. GRAHAM, AND R. C. LACY. 1994. An experimental study of inbreeding depression in a natural habitat. Science 266:271–273.

JOHNSGARD, P. A. 1983. The grouse of the world. University of Nebraska Press, Lincoln, USA.

JOHNSON, K. P., J. STOUT, I. L. BRISBIN, R. M. ZINK, AND J. BURGER. 1999. Lack of demonstrable effects of pollutants on cyt b sequences in wood ducks from a contaminated nuclear reactor cooling pond. Environmental Research 81:146–150.

JOLLY, G. M. 1965. Explicit estimates from capture-recapture data with both death and immigration-stochastic model. Biometrika 52:225–247.

JONES, K. L., T. C. GLENN, R. C. LACY, J. R. PIERCE, N. UNRUH, C. M. MIRANDE, AND F. CHAVEZ-RAMIREZ. 2002. Refining the whooping crane studbook by incorporating microsatellite DNA and leg-banding analysis. Conservation Biology 16:789–799.

JORDE, P. E., AND N. RYMAN. 1995. Temporal allele frequency change and estimation of effective size in populations with overlapping generations. Genetics 139:1077–1090.

KAHN, N. W., J. ST. JOHN, AND T. W. QUINN. 1998. Chromosome-specific intron size differences in the avian CHD gene provide an efficient method for sex identification in birds. Auk 115:1074–1078.

———, C. E. BRAUN, J. R. YOUNG, S. WOOD, D. R. MATA, AND T. W. QUINN. 1999. Molecular analysis of genetic variation among large and small-bodied sage grouse using mitochondrial control-region sequences. Auk 116:819–824.

KALINOWSKI S.T., AND R. S. WAPLES. 2002. Relationship of effective to census size in fluctuating populations. Conservation Biology 16:129–136.

KARL, S. A., B. W. BOWEN, AND J. C. AVISE. 1992. Global population genetic structure and male-mediated gene flow in the green turtle (Chelonia mydas): RFLP analyses of anonymous nuclear loci. Genetics 131:163–173.

KELLER, L. F., AND D. M. WALLER. 2002. Inbreeding effects in wild populations. Trends in Ecology and Evolution 17:230–241.

———, P. ARCESE, J. N. M. SMITH, W. M. HOCHACHKA, AND S. C. STEARNS. 1994. Selection against inbred song sparrows during a natural-population bottleneck. Nature 372:356–357.

KICHLER, K., M. T. HOLDER, S. K. DAVIS, R. MARQUEZ-M, AND D. W. OWENS. 1999. Detection of multiple paternity in the Kemp's ridley sea turtle with limited sampling. Molecular Ecology 8:819–830.

KNOWLES, L. L., AND W. P. MADDISON. 2002. Statistical phylogeography. Molecular Ecology 11:2623–2635.

KOHN, M. H., AND R. K. WAYNE. 1997. Facts from feces revisited. Trends in Ecology and Evolution 12:223–227.

———, E. C. YORK, D. A. KAMRADT, G. HAUGT, R. M. SAUVAJOT, AND R. K. WAYNE. 1999. Estimating population size by genotyping faeces. Proceedings of the Royal Society of London, Series B-Biological Sciences 266:657–663.

KRUUK, L. E. B., T. H. CLUTTON-BROCK, J. SLATE, J. M. PEMBERTON, S. BROTHERSTONE, AND F. E. GUINNESS. 2000. Heritability of fitness in a wild mammal population. Proceedings of the National Academy of Sciences of the United States of America 97:698–703.

LACY, R. C. 1995. Clarification of genetic terms and their use in the management of captive populations. Zoo Biology 14:565–578.

———. 1997. Importance of genetic variation to the viability of mammalian populations. Journal of Mammalogy 78:320–335.

———. 2000. Should we select genetic alleles in our conservation breeding programs? Zoo Biology 19:279–282.

———, G. ALAKS, AND A. WALSH. 1996. Hierarchical analysis of inbreeding depression in Peromyscus polionotus. Evolution 50:2187–2200.

———, J. D. BALLOU, F. PRINCÉE, A. STARFIELD, AND E. A. THOMPSON. 1995. Pedigree analysis for population management. Pages 57–75 in J. D. Ballou, M. Gilpin, and T. J. Foose, editors. Population management for survival and recovery: analytical methods and strategies in small population conservation. Columbia University Press, New York, USA.

LAERM, J., J. C. AVISE, J. C. PATTON, AND R. A. LANSMAN. 1982. Genetic determination of the status of an endangered species of pocket gopher in Georgia. Journal of Wildlife Management 46:513–518.

LAIKRE, L., AND N. RYMAN. 1996. Effects on intraspecific biodiversity from harvesting and enhancing natural populations. Ambio 25:504–509.

LAMBERT, D. M., C. D. MILLAR, K. JACK, S. ANDERSON, AND J. L. CRAIG. 1994. Single- and multilocus DNA fingerprinting of communally breeding pukeko: do copulations or dominance ensure reproductive success? Proceedings of the National Academy of Sciences of the United States of America 91:9641–9645.

LANCIA, R. A., W. L. KENDALL, K. H. POLLOCK, AND J. D. NICHOLS. 2005. Estimating the numbers of animals in wildlife populations. Pages 106–153 in C. E. Braun, editor. Techniques for wildlife investigations and management. Sixth edition. The Wildlife Society, Bethesda, Maryland, USA.

LANDE, R. 1995. Mutation and conservation. Conservation Biology 9: 782–791

LAURENT, L., P. CASALE, M. N. BRADAI, B. J. GODLEY, G. GEROSA, A. C. BRODERICK, W. SCHROTH, B. SCHIERWATER, A. M. LEVY, D. FREGGI, E. M. ABD EL-MAWLA, D. A. HADOUD, H. E. GOMATI, M. DOMINGO, M. HADJICHRISTOPHOROU, L. KORNARAKY, F. DEMIRAYAK, AND C. GAUTIER. 1998. Molecular resolution of marine turtle stock composition in fishery bycatch: a case study in the Mediterranean. Molecular Ecology 7:1529–1542.

LEBERG, P. L. 1990a. Genetic considerations in the design of introduction programs. Transactions of the North American Wildlife and Natural Resources Conference 55:609–619.

———. 1990b. Influence of genetic variability on population growth: implications for conservation. Journal of Fish Biology 37:193–195.

———. 1991. Influence of fragmentation and bottlenecks on genetic divergence of wild turkey populations. Conservation Biology 5:522–530.

———. 1992. Effects of population bottlenecks on genetic diversity as measured by allozyme electrophoresis. Evolution 46:477–494.

———. 1993. Strategies for population reintroduction: effects of genetic variability on population growth and size. Conservation Biology 7:194–199.

———. 1994. Genetic diversity, morphology, and demography of the wild turkey. Pages 126–131 in I. Thompson, editor. Forests and wildlife: towards the 21st century. International Union of Game Biologists, Halifax, Nova Scotia, Canada.

———. 1999. Using genetic markers to assess the success of translocation programs. Transactions of the North American Wildlife and Natural Resources Conference 64:174–190.

———. 2002. Estimating allelic richness: effects of sample size and bottlenecks. Molecular Ecology 11:2445–2449.

———, AND D. L. ELLSWORTH. 1999. Further evaluation of the genetic consequences of translocations on southeastern white-tailed deer populations. Journal of Wildlife Management 63:327–334.

———, M. H. SMITH, AND O. E. RHODES. 1990. The association between heterozygosity and growth of deer fetuses is not explained by effects of the loci examined. Evolution 44:454–458.

———, P. W. STANGEL, H. O. HILLESTAD, R. L. MARCHINTON, AND M. H. SMITH. 1994. Genetic structure of reintroduced wild turkey and white-tailed deer populations. Journal of Wildlife Management 58:698–711.

LEBRETON, J.-D., K. P. BURNHAM, J. CLOBERT, AND D. R. ANDERSON.

1992. Modeling survival and testing biological hypotheses using marked animals: a unified approach with case studies. Ecological Monographs 62:67–118.

LEE, P. L. M., R. B. BRADBURY, J. D. WILSON, N. S. FLANAGAN, L. RICHARDSON, A. J. PERKINS, AND J. R. KREBS. 2001. Microsatellite variation in the yellowhammer *Emberiza citrinella*: population structure of a declining farmland bird. Molecular Ecology 10:1633–1644.

LE PAGE, S. L., R. A. LIVERMORE, D. W. COOPER, AND A. C. TAYLOR. 2000. Genetic analysis of a documented population bottleneck: introduced Bennett's wallabies (*Macropus rufogriseus rufogriseus*) in New Zealand. Molecular Ecology 9:753–763.

LUCCHINI, V., E. FABBRI, F. MARUCCO, S. RICCI, L. BOITANI, AND E. RANDI. 2002. Noninvasive molecular tracking of colonizing wolf (*Canis lupus*) packs in the western Italian Alps. Molecular Ecology 11:857–868.

LUIKART, G., AND J.-M. CORNUET. 1998. Empirical evaluation of a test for identifying recently bottlenecked populations from allele frequency data. Conservation Biology 12:228–237.

———, AND ———. 1999. Estimating the effective number of breeders from heterozygote excess in progeny. Genetics 151:1211–1216.

———, ———, AND F. W. ALLENDORF. 1999. Temporal changes in allele frequencies provide estimates of population bottleneck size. Conservation Biology 13:523–530.

———, F. W. ALLENDORF, J.-M. CORNUET, AND W. B. SHERWIN. 1998. Distortion of allele frequency distributions provides a test for recent population bottlenecks. Journal of Heredity 89:238–247.

MACE, G. M., T. B. SMITH, M. W. BRUFORD, AND R. K. WAYNE. 1996. An overview of the issues. Pages 3–21 *in* T. B. Smith and R. K. Wayne, editors. Molecular genetic approaches in conservation. Oxford University Press, New York, USA.

MANEL, S., P. BERTHIER, AND G. LUIKART. 2002. Detecting wildlife poaching: identifying the origin of individuals with Bayesian assignment tests and multilocus genotypes. Conservation Biology 16:650–659.

MATOCQ, M. D., AND F. X. VILLABLANCA. 2001. Low genetic diversity in an endangered species: recent or historic pattern? Biological Conservation 98:61–68.

MATSON, C. W., B. E. RODGERS, R. K. CHESSER, AND R. J. BAKER. 2000. Genetic diversity of *Clethrionomys glareolus* populations from highly contaminated sites in the Chernobyl Region, Ukraine. Environmental Toxicology and Chemistry 19:2130–2135.

MCDANIEL, G. W., K. S. MCKELVEY, J. R. SQUIRES, AND L. F. RUGGIERO. 2000. Efficacy of lures and hair snares to detect lynx. Wildlife Society Bulletin 28:119–123.

MECH, S. G., AND J. G. HALLETT. 2001. Evaluating the effectiveness of corridors: a genetic approach. Conservation Biology 15:467–474.

MELNICK, D. J., AND G. A. HOELZER. 1992. Differences in male and female macaque dispersal lead to contrasting distributions of nuclear and mitochondrial-DNA variation. International Journal of Primatology 13:379–393.

MERILÄ, J. 1997. Expression of genetic variation in body size of the collared flycatcher under different environmental conditions. Evolution 51:526–536.

MILLER, P. S. 1995. Selective breeding programs for rare alleles: examples from the Przewalski horse and California condor pedigrees. Conservation Biology 9:1262–1273.

———, AND P. W. HEDRICK. 1991. MHC polymorphism and the design of captive breeding programs: simple solutions are not the simple answer. Conservation Biology 5:556–558.

MILLS, L. S., AND F. W. ALLENDORF. 1996. The one-migrant-per-generation rule in conservation and management. Conservation Biology 10:1509–1518.

———, AND P. E. SMOUSE. 1994. Demographic consequences of inbreeding in remnant populations. American Naturalist 144:412–431.

———, K. L. PILGRIM, M. K. SCHWARTZ, AND K. MCKELVEY. 2000a. Identifying lynx and other North American felids based on mtDNA analysis. Conservation Genetics 1:285–288.

———, J. J. CITTA, K. P. LAIR, M. K. SCHWARTZ, AND D. A. TALLMON. 2000b. Estimating animal abundance using noninvasive DNA sampling: promise and pitfalls. Ecological Applications 10:283–294.

MIYAMOTO, M. M., AND J. CRACRAFT. 1991. Phylogenetic analysis of DNA sequences. Oxford University Press, New York, USA.

MOCK, D. W. 1983. On the study of avian mating systems. Pages 55–84 *in* A. H. Brush and G. A. Clark, Jr., editors. Perspectives in ornithology. Cambridge University Press, London, United Kingdom.

MOCK, K. E., T. C. THEIMER, B. F. WAKELING, O.E. RHODES, D.L. GREENBERG, AND P. KEIM. 2001. Verifying the origins of a reintroduced population of Gould's wild turkey. Journal of Wildlife Management 65:871–879.

MORGAN K. K., J. HICKS, K. SPITZE, L. LATTA L, M. E. PFRENDER, C. S. WEAVER, M. OTTONE, AND M. LYNCH. 2001. Patterns of genetic architecture for life-history traits and molecular markers in a subdivided species. Evolution 55:1753–1761.

MORIN, P. A., AND D. S. WOODRUFF. 1996. Noninvasive genotyping for vertebrate conservation. Pages 298–313 *in* T. B. Smith, and R. K. Wayne, editors. Molecular genetic approaches in conservation. Oxford University Press, New York, USA.

MORITZ, C. 1994a. Applications of mitochondrial DNA analysis in conservation: a critical review. Molecular Ecology 3:401–411.

———. 1994b. Defining evolutionarily significant units for conservation. Trends in Ecology and Evolution 9:373–375.

———. 1999. Conservation units and translocations: strategies for conserving evolutionary processes. Hereditas 130:217–228.

MUELLER, U. G., AND L. L. WOLFENBARGER. 1999. AFLP genotyping and fingerprinting. Trends in Ecology and Evolution 14:389–394.

MUNDY, N. I., P. UNITT, AND D. S. WOODRUFF. 1997. Skin from feet of museum specimens as a non-destructive source of DNA for avian genotyping. Auk 114:126–129.

MURALINDHARAN, K., AND K. E. WAKELAND. 1993. Concentration of primer and template qualitatively affects products in random-amplified polymorphic DNA PCR. BioTechniques 14:362–364.

MURPHY, K. M. 1998. The ecology of the cougar (*Puma concolor*) in the Northern Yellowstone Ecosystem: interactions with prey, bears, and humans. Dissertation. University of Idaho, Moscow, USA.

MURPHY, R. W., J. W. STILES, D. G. BUTH, AND C. H. HAUFLER. 1996. Proteins: isozyme electrophoresis. Pages 51–120 *in* D. M. Hillis, C. Moritz, and B. K. Mable, editors. Molecular systematics. Sinauer Associates, Sunderland, Massachusetts USA.

NEDBAL, M. A., R. L. HONEYCUTT, S. G. EVANS, R. M. WHITING, JR., AND D. R. DIETZ. 1997. Northern bobwhite restocking in east Texas: a genetic assessment. Journal of Wildlife Management 61:854–863.

NEI, M., T. MARUYAMA, AND R. CHAKRABORTY. 1975. The bottleneck effect and genetic variability in populations. Evolution 29:1–10.

NEIGEL, J. E. 1997. A comparison of alternative strategies for estimating gene flow from genetic markers. Annual Review of Ecology and Systematics 28:105–128.

———. 2002. Is F_{ST} obsolete? Conservation Genetics 3:167–173.

———, R. M. BALL, JR., AND J. C. AVISE. 1991. Estimation of single generation migration distances from geographic variation in animal mitochondrial DNA. Evolution 45:423–432.

NICHOLS, J. D., B. R. NOON, S. L. STOKES, AND J. E. HINES. 1981. Remarks on the use of mark-recapture methodology in estimating avian population size. Studies in Avian Biology 6:121–136.

NICHOLS, R. A., M. W. BRUFORD, AND J. J. GROOMBRIDGE. 2001. Sustaining genetic variation in a small population: evidence from the Mauritius kestrel. Molecular Ecology 10:593–602.

NUNNEY, L. 1993. The influence of mating system and overlapping generations on effective population size. Evolution 47:1329–1341.

———. 1999. The effective size of a hierarchically structured population. Evolution 53:1–10.

O'BRIEN, S. J., AND E. MAYR. 1991. Bureaucratic mischief: recognizing endangered species and subspecies. Science 251:1187–1188.

OTIS, D. L, K. P. BURNHAM, G. C. WHITE, AND D. R. ANDERSON. 1978. Statistical inference from capture data on closed animal populations. Wildlife Monographs 62.

OYLER-MCCANCE, S. J., N. W. KAHN, K. P. BURNHAM, C. E. BRAUN, AND T. W. QUINN. 1999. A population genetic comparison of large and small-bodied sage grouse in Colorado using microsatellite and mitochondrial DNA markers. Molecular Ecology 8:1457–1465.

PAETKAU, D., AND C. STROBECK. 1994. Microsatellite analysis of genetic variation in black bear populations. Molecular Ecology 3:489–495.

PALSBØLL, P. J., J. ALLEN, M. BÉRUBE, P. J. CLAPHAM, T. P. FEDDERSEN, P. S. HAMMOND, R. R. HUDSON, H. JØRGENSEN, S. KATONA, A. H. LARSEN, F. LARSEN, J. LIEN, D. K. MATTILA, J. SIGURJÓNSSON, R. SEARS, T. SMITH, R. SPONER, P. STEVICK, AND N. ØIEN. 1997. Genetic tagging of humpback whales. Nature 388:767–769.

PALUMBI, S. R. 1996. Nucleic acids II: the polymerase chain reaction. Pages 205–148 *in* D. M. Hillis, C. Moritz, and B. K. Mable, editors. Molecular systematics. Sinauer Associates, Sunderland, Massachusetts, USA.

PEARCE, J. M., B. J. PIERSON, S. L. TALBOT, D. V. DERKSEN, D. KRAEGE, AND K. T. SCRIBNER. 2000. A genetic evaluation of morphology used to identify harvested Canada geese. Journal of Wildlife Management 64:863–874.

PEARMAN, P. B. 2001. Conservation value of independently evolving units: sacred cow or testable hypothesis? Conservation Biology 15:780–783.

PEMBERTON, J. M., S. D. ALBON, F. E. GUINNESS, T. H. CLUTTON-BROCK, AND R. J. BERRY. 1988. Genetic variation and juvenile survival in red deer. Evolution 42:921–934.

———, ———, ———, ———, AND G. A. DOVER. 1992. Behavioral estimates of male mating success tested by DNA fingerprinting in a polygynous mammal. Behavioral Ecology 3:66–75.

PENN, D. J. 2002. The scent of genetic compatibility: sexual selection and the major histocompatibility complex. Ethology 108:1–21.

PERTOLDI, C., V. LOESCHCKE, A. B. MADSEN, AND E. RANDI. 2000. Allozyme variation in the Eurasian badger *Meles meles* in Denmark. Journal of Zoology 252:544–547.

PETIT, E., AND F. MAYER. 2000. A population genetic analysis of migration: the case of the noctule bat (*Nyctalus noctula*). Molecular Ecology 9:683–690.

PIERTNEY, S. B., A. D. C. MACCOLL, P. J. BACON, P. A. RACEY, X. LAMBIN, AND J. F. DALLAS. 2000. Matrilineal genetic structure and female-mediated gene flow in red grouse (*Lagopus lagopus scoticus*): an analysis using mitochondrial DNA. Evolution 54:279–289.

POLLOCK, K. H. 1981. Capture-recapture models: a review of current methods, assumptions and experimental design. Studies in Avian Biology 6:426–435.

POTTS, W. K., C. J. MANNING, AND E. K. WAKELAND. 1991. Mating patterns in seminatural populations of mice influenced by MHC genotype. Nature 352:619–621.

PUDOVKIN, A. I., D. V. ZAYKIN, AND D. HEDGECOCK. 1996. On the potential for estimating the effective number of breeders from heterozygote-excess in progeny. Genetics 144:383–387.

QUELLER, D. C., J. E. STRASSMAN, AND C. R. HUGHES. 1993. Microsatellites and kinship. Trends in Ecology and Evolution. 8:285–288.

QUENEY, G., N. FERRAND, S. MARCHANDEAU, M. AZEVEDO, F. MOUGEL, M. BRANCO, AND M. MONNEROT. 2000. Absence of a genetic bottleneck in a wild rabbit (*Oryctolagus cuniculus*) population exposed to a severe viral epizootic. Molecular Ecology 9:1253–1264.

QUESTIAU, S., M.–C. EYBERT, AND P. TABERLET. 1999. Amplified fragment length polymorphism (AFLP) markers reveal extra-pair parentage in a bird species: the bluethroat (*Luscinia svecica*). Molecular Ecology 8:1331–1339.

QUINN, T. W., J. S. QUINN, F. COOKE, AND B. N. WHITE. 1987. DNA marker analysis detects multiple maternity and paternity in single broods of the lesser snow goose. Nature 326:392–394.

———, J. C. DAVIES, F. COOKE, AND B. N. WHITE. 1989. Genetic analysis of offspring of a female-female pair in the lesser snow goose (*Chen c. caerulescens*). Auk 106:177–184.

RALLS, K., AND J. D. BALLOU. 1986. Proceedings of the workshop on genetic management of captive populations. Zoo Biology 5:81–238.

RÉALE, D., AND M. FESTA-BIANCHET. 2000. Quantitative genetics of life-history traits in a long-lived wild mammal. Heredity 85:593–603.

REED, D. H., AND E. H. BRYANT. 2000. Experimental tests of minimum viable population size. Animal Conservation 3:7–14.

———, AND R. FRANKHAM. 2001. How closely correlated are molecular and quantitative measures of genetic variation? A meta-analysis. Evolution 55:1095–1103.

———, AND ———. 2003. Correlation between fitness and genetic diversity. Conservation Biology 17:230–237.

———, D. J. TOLLIT, P. M. THOMPSON, AND W. AMOS. 1997. Molecular scatology: the use of molecular genetic analysis to assign species, sex and individual identity to seal faeces. Molecular Ecology 6:225–234.

RICHARDS, C., AND P. L. LEBERG. 1996. Temporal changes in allele frequencies and a population's history of severe bottlenecks. Conservation Biology 10:832–839.

RICHARDSON, D. S., AND T. BURKE. 1999. Extra-pair paternity in relation to male age in Bullock's orioles. Molecular Ecology 8:2115–2126.

RICHMAN, A. D., L. G. HERRERA, AND D. NASH. 2001. MHC class II beta sequence diversity in the deer mouse (*Peromyscus maniculatus*): implications for models of balancing selection. Molecular Ecology 10:2765–2773.

ROBERT, A., D. COUVET, AND F. SARRAZIN. 2002. Fitness heterogeneity and viability of restored populations. Animal Conservation 5:153–161.

ROBERTSON, B. C., E. O. MINOT, AND D. M. LAMBERT. 1999. Molecular sexing of individual kakapo, *Strigops haproptilus* Aves, from faeces. Molecular Ecology 8:1349–1350.

ROE, B. A., D.-P. MA, R. K. WILSON, AND J. F.–H. WONG. 1985. The complete nucleotide sequence of the *Xenopus laevis* mitochondrial genome. Journal of Biological Chemistry 260:9759–9774.

ROSENBAUM, H. C., M. G. EGAN, P. J. CLAPHAM, R. L. BROWNELL, JR., S. MALIK, M. W. BROWN, B. N. WHITE, P. WALSH, AND R. DESALLE. 2000*a*. Utility of north Atlantic right whale museum specimens for assessing changes in genetic diversity. Conservation Biology 14:1837–1842.

———, R. L. BROWNELL, JR., M. W. BROWN, C. SCHAEFF, V. PORTWAY, B. N. WHITE, S. MALIK, L. A. PASTENE, N. J. PATENAUDE, C. S. BAKER, M. GOTO, P. B. BEST, P. J. CLAPHAM, P. HAMILTON, M. MOORE, R. PAYNE, V. ROWNTREE, C. T. TYNAN, J. L. BANNISTER, AND R. DESALLE. 2000*b*. World-wide genetic differentiation of *Eubalaena*: questioning the number of right whale species. Molecular Ecology 9:1793–1802.

ROSSITER, S. J., G. JONES, R. D. RANSOME, AND E. M. BARRATT. 2000. Genetic variation and population structure in the endangered greater horseshoe bat *Rhinolophus ferrumequinum*. Molecular Ecology 9:1131–1135.

———, ———, ———, AND ———. 2001. Outbreeding increases offspring survival in wild greater horseshoe bats (*Rhinolophus ferrumequinum*). Proceedings of the Royal Society of London, Series B-Biological Sciences 268:1055–1061.

ROWE, G., T. J. C. BEEBEE, AND T. BURKE. 1998. Phylogeography of the natterjack toad *Bufo calamita* in Britain: genetic differentiation of native and translocated populations. Molecular Ecology 7:751–760.

ROY, M. S., E. GEFFEN, D. SMITH, AND R. K. WAYNE. 1996. Molecular genetics of pre-1940 red wolves. Conservation Biology 10:1413–1424.

———, ———, E. A. OSTRANDER, AND R. K. WAYNE. 1994. Patterns of differentiation and hybridization in North American wolflike canids, revealed by analysis of microsatellite loci. Molecular Biology and Evolution 11:553–570.

RYDER, O. A. 1986. Species conservation and systematics: the dilemma of subspecies. Trends in Ecology and Evolution 1:9–10.

RYMAN, N., R. BACCUS, C. REUTERWALL, AND M. II. SMITH. 1981. Effective population size, generation interval, and potential loss of genetic variability in game species under different hunting regimes. Oikos 36:257–266.

SAMBROOK, E., F. FRITSCH, AND T. MANIATIS. 1989. Molecular cloning: a laboratory manual. Cold Springs Harbor Press, Cold Spring Harbor, New York, USA.

SARRE, S. 1995. Mitochondrial-DNA variation among populations of *Oedura reticulata* (Gekkonidae) in remnant vegetation: implications for metapopulation structure and population decline. Molecular Ecology 4:395–405.

SCHWARTZ, M. K., D. A. TALLMON, AND G. LUIKART. 1998. Review of DNA-based census and effective population size estimators. Animal Conservation 1:293–299.

SCRIBNER, K. T. 1993. Conservation genetics of managed ungulate populations. Acta Theriologica 38, Supplement 2:89–101.

———, AND T. D. BOWMAN. 1998. Microsatellites identify depredated waterfowl remains from glaucous gull stomachs. Molecular Ecology 7:1401–1405.

———, AND M. STUWE. 1994. Genetic relationships among alpine ibex (*Capra ibex*) populations reestablished from a common ancestral source. Biological Conservation 69:137–143.

———, M. H. SMITH, AND P. E. JOHNS. 1989. Environmental and genetic components of antler growth in white-tailed deer. Journal of Mammalogy 70:284–291.

———, M. R. PETERSEN, R. L. FIELDS, S. L. TALBOT, J. M. PEARCE, AND R. K. CHESSER. 2001. Sex-biased gene flow in spectacled eiders (Anatidae): inferences from molecular markers with contrasting modes of inheritance. Evolution 55:2105–2115.

SEBER, G. A. F. 1965. A note on the multiple recapture census. Biometrika 52:249–259.

SEMPLE, K., R. K. WAYNE, AND R. M. GIBSON. 2001. Microsatellite analysis of female mating behavior in lek-breeding sage grouse. Molecular Ecology 10:2043–2048.

SIMBERLOFF, D. 1988. The contribution of population and community biology to conservation science. Annual Review of Ecology and Systematics 19:473–511.

SLATE, J., AND J. M. PEMBERTON. 2002. Comparing molecular measures for detecting inbreeding depression. Journal of Evolutionary Biology 15:20–31.

———, L. E. B. KRUUK, T. C. MARSHALL, J. M. PEMBERTON, AND T. H. CLUTTON-BROCK. 2000. Inbreeding depression influences lifetime breeding success in a wild population of red deer (*Cervus elaphus*). Proceedings of the Royal Society of London, Series B-Biological

Sciences 267:1657–1662.

———, P. M. VISSCHER, S. MacGREGOR, D. STEVENS, M. L. TATE, AND J. M. PEMBERTON. 2002. A genome scan for quantitative trait loci in a wild population of red deer (*Cervus elaphus*). Genetics 162:1863–1873.

SLATKIN, M. 1985*a*. Gene flow in natural populations. Annual Review of Ecology and Systematics 16:393–430.

———. 1985*b*. Rare alleles as indicators of gene flow. Evolution 39:53–65.

———, AND R. R. HUDSON. 1991. Pairwise comparisons of mitochondrial DNA sequences in stable and exponentially growing populations. Genetics 129:555–562.

———, AND W. P. MADDISON. 1990. Detecting isolation by distance using phylogenies of genes. Genetics 126:249–260.

SLOANE, M. A., P. SUNNUCKS, D. ALPERS, L. B. BEHEREGARAY, AND A. C. TAYLOR. 2000. Highly reliable genetic identification of individual northern hairy-nosed wombats from single remotely collected hairs: a feasible censusing method. Molecular Ecology 9:1233–1240.

SMITH, D. A., K. RALLS, B. DAVENPORT, B. ADAMS, AND J. E. MALDONADO. 2001*a*. Canine assistants for conservationists. Science 291:435.

SMITH, M. H., J. M. NOVAK, J. D. PELES, AND J. R. PURDUE. 2001*b*. Genetic heterogeneity of white-tailed deer: management lessons from a long-term study. Mammalian Biology 66:1–12.

SMITH, T. B., AND R. K. WAYNE. 1996. Molecular genetic approaches in conservation. Oxford University Press, New York, USA.

SMOUSE, P. E., R. S. WAPLES, AND J. A. TWOREK. 1990. A genetic mixture analysis for use with incomplete source population data. Canadian Journal of Fisheries and Aquatic Sciences 47:620–634.

SOULÉ, M., E. 1986. Conservation biology: the science of scarcity and diversity. Sinauer Associates, Inc., Sunderland, Massachusetts, USA.

SPENCER, C. C., J. E. NEIGEL, AND P. L. LEBERG. 2000. Experimental evaluation of the usefulness of microsatellite DNA for detecting demographic bottlenecks. Molecular Ecology 9:1517–1528.

SPIELMAN, D., AND R. FRANKHAM. 1992. Modeling problems in conservation genetics using captive *Drosophila* populations: improvement of reproductive fitness due to immigration of one individual into small partially inbred populations. Zoo Biology 11:343–351.

SPILLIAERT, R., G. VIKINGSSON, U. ARNASON, A. PALSDOTTIR, J. SIGURJONSSON, AND A. ARNASON. 1991. Species hybridization between a female blue whale (*Balaenoptera musculus*) and a male fin whale (*B. physalus*): Molecular and morphological documentation. Journal of Heredity 82:269–274.

STAPLETON, M., P. O. DUNN, J. McCARTY, A. SECORD, AND L. A. WHITTINGHAM. 2001. Polychlorinated biphenyl contamination and minisatellite DNA mutation rates of tree swallows. Environmental Toxicology and Chemistry 20:2263–2267.

STOCKWELL, C. A., AND P. L. LEBERG. 2002. Ecological genetics and the translocation of native fishes: emerging experimental approaches. Western North American Naturalist 62:32–38.

———, M. MULVEY, AND G. L. VINYARD. 1996. Translocations and the preservation of allelic diversity. Conservation Biology 10:1133–1141.

STORFER, A. 1999. Gene flow and endangered species translocations: a topic revisited. Biological Conservation 87:173–180.

SUNDQVIST, A.-K., H. ELLEGREN, M. OLIVER, AND C. VILÀ. 2001. Y chromosome haplotyping in Scandinavian wolves (*Canis lupus*) based on microsatellite markers. Molecular Ecology 10:1959–1966.

SWOFFORD, D. L., G. J. OLSEN, P. J. WADDELL, AND D. M. HILLIS. 1996. Phylogeny reconstruction. Pages 407–514 *in* D. M. Hillis, C. Moritz, and B. K. Mable, editors. Molecular systematics. Sinauer Associates, Sunderland, Massachusetts, USA.

SYMONDSON, W. O. C. 2002. Molecular identification of prey in predator diets. Molecular Ecology 11:627–641.

TABERLET, P., AND L. FUMAGALLI. 1996. Owl pellets as a source of DNA for genetic studies of small mammals. Molecular Ecology 5:301–305.

———, L. P. WAITS, AND G. LUIKART. 1999. Noninvasive genetic sampling: look before you leap. Trends in Ecology and Evolution 14:323–327.

———, J. J. CAMARRA, S. GRIFFIN, E. UHRES, O. HANOTTE, L. P. WAITS, C. DUBOISPAGANON, T. BURKE, AND J. BOUVET. 1997. Noninvasive genetic tracking of the endangered Pyrenean brown bear population. Molecular Ecology 6:869–876.

TAMURA, K. 1994. Model selection in the estimation of the number of nucleotide substitutions. Molecular Biology and Evolution 11:154–157.

———, AND M. NEI. 1993. Estimation of the number of nucleotide substitutions in the control region on mitochondrial DNA in humans and chimpanzees. Molecular Biology and Evolution 10:512–526.

TARR, C. L., S. CONANT, AND R. C. FLEISCHER. 1998. Founder events and variation at microsatellite loci in an insular passerine bird, the Laysan finch (*Telespiza cantans*). Molecular Ecology 7:719–731.

TAYLOR, A. C., J. M. GRAVES, N. D. MURRAY, S. J. O'BRIEN, N. YUHKI, AND B. SHERWIN. 1997. Conservation genetics of the koala (*Phascolarctos cinereus*), low mitochondrial DNA variation amongst southern Australian populations. Genetical Research 69:25–33.

TEMPLETON, A. R. 1986. Coadaptation and outbreeding depression. Pages 105–116 *in* M.E. Soulé, editor. Conservation biology: the science of scarcity and diversity. Sinauer Associates, Inc., Sunderland, Massachusetts, USA.

———. 2001. Nested clade analyses of phylogeographic data: testing hypotheses about gene flow and population history. Molecular Ecology 7:381–397.

———, R. J. ROBERTSON, J. BRISSON, AND J. STRASBURG. 2001. Disrupting evolutionary processes: the effect of habitat fragmentation on collared lizards in the Missouri Ozarks. Proceedings of the National Academy of Sciences of the United States of America 98:5426–5432.

THEODORAKIS, C. W. 2001. Integration of genotoxic and population genetic endpoints in biomonitoring and risk assessment. Ecotoxicology 10:245–256.

TRIGGS, S. J., R. G. POWLESLAND, AND C. H. DAUGHERTY. 1989. Genetic-variation and conservation of kakapo (*Strigops habroptilus* - Psittaciformes). Conservation Biology 3:92–96.

VALIERE, N., AND P. TABERLET. 2000. Urine collected in the field as a source of DNA for species and individual identification. Molecular Ecology 9:2150–2152.

VAN DER WALT, J. M., L. H. NEL, AND A. R. HOELZEL. 2001. Characterization of major histocompatibility complex DRB diversity in the endemic South African antelope *Damaliscus pygargus*: a comparison in two subspecies with different demographic histories. Molecular Ecology 10:1679–1688.

VAN HOOFT, W. F., A. F. GROEN, AND H. H. T. PRINS. 2000. Microsatellite analysis of genetic diversity in African buffalo (*Syncerus caffer*) populations throughout Africa. Molecular Ecology 9:2017–2025.

VOGLER, A. P., AND R. DESALLE. 1994. Diagnosing units of conservation management. Conservation Biology 8:354–363.

VOS, C. C., A. G. ANTONISSE-DE JONG, P. W. GOEDHART, AND M. J. M. SMULDERS. 2001. Genetic similarity as a measure for connectivity between fragmented populations of the moor frog (*Rana arvalis*). Heredity 86:598–608.

VRIJENHOEK, R. C., AND P. L. LEBERG. 1991. Let's not throw the baby out with the bathwater: a comment on management for MHC diversity in captive populations. Conservation Biology 5:252–254.

VUCETICH, J. A., T. A. WAITE, AND L. NUNNEY. 1997. Fluctuating population size and the ratio of effective to census population size. Evolution 51:2017–2021.

WAITS, J. L., AND P. L. LEBERG. 2000. Biases associated with population estimation using molecular tagging. Animal Conservation 3:191–199.

———, M. L. AVERY, M. E. TOBIN, AND P. L. LEBERG. 2003. Low mitochondrial DNA variation in double-crested cormorant in eastern North America. Waterbirds. 26:196–200.

WAITS, L. P., G. LUIKART, AND P. TABERLET. 2001. Estimating the probability of identity among genotypes in natural populations: cautions and guidelines. Molecular Ecology 10:249–256.

———, P. TABERLET, J. E. SWENSON, F. SANDEGREN, AND R. FRANZÉN. 2000. Nuclear DNA microsatellite analysis of genetic diversity and gene flow in the Scandinavian brown bear (*Ursus arctos*). Molecular Ecology 9:421–431.

WALLNER, B., S. HUBER, AND R. ACHMANN. 2001. Non-invasive PCR sexing of rabbits (*Oryctolagus cuniculus*) and hares (*Lepus europaeus*). Mammalian Biology 66:190–192.

WAPLES, R.S. 1989. A generalized approach for estimating effective population size from temporal changes in allele frequency. Genetics 121:379–391.

———. 1991. Pacific salmon *Oncorhynchus* spp. and the definition of 'species' under the endangered species act. Marine Fisheries Reviews, 53(3):11–22.

———. 1998. Separating the wheat from the chaff: patterns of genetic differentiation in high gene flow species. Journal of Heredity 89:438–450.

WAYNE, R. K., AND S. M. JENKS. 1991. Mitochondrial DNA analysis implying extensive hybridization of the endangered red wolf *Canis rufus*. Nature 351:565–568.

———, L. FORMAN, A. K. NEWMAN, J. M. SIMONSON, AND S. J. O'BRIEN. 1986. Genetic markers of zoo populations: morphological and electrophoretic assays. Zoo Biology 5:215–232

WENNERBERG, L. 2001. Breeding origin and migration pattern of dunlin (*Calidris alpina*) revealed by mitochondrial DNA analysis. Molecular Ecology 10:1111–1120.

WESTEMEIER R.L., J. D. BRAWN, S. A. SIMPSON, T. L. ESKER, R. W. JANSEN, J. W. WALK, E. L. KERSHNER, J. L. BOUZAT, AND K. N. PAIGE. 1998. Tracking the long-term decline and recovery of an isolated population. Science 282:1695–1698.

WHITE, G. C., D. R. ANDERSON, K. P. BURNHAM, AND D. L. OTIS. 1982. Capture-recapture and removal methods for sampling closed populations. Los Alamos National Laboratory, LA-8787-NERP, Los Alamos, New Mexico, USA.

WHITEHOUSE, A. M., AND E. H. HARLEY. 2001. Post-bottleneck genetic diversity of elephant populations in South Africa, revealed using microsatellite analysis. Molecular Ecology 10:2139–2149.

WHITLOCK, M. C., AND D. E. MCCAULEY. 1999. Indirect measures of gene flow and migration: F-ST not equal 1/(4Nm+1). Heredity 82:117–125.

WILLIAMS C. L., T. L. SERFASS, R. COGAN, AND O.E. RHODES. 2002. Microsatellite variation in the reintroduced Pennsylvania elk herd. Molecular Ecology 11:1299–1310.

WILLIAMS, J. D., W. F. KRUEGER, AND D. H. HARMEL. 1994. Heritabilities for antler characteristics and body weight in yearling white-tailed deer. Heredity 73:78–83.

WILLIAMS, R. N., O. E. RHODES, AND T. L. SERFASS. 2000. Assessment of genetic variance among source and reintroduced fisher populations.

Journal of Mammalogy 81:895–907.

WILSON, P. J., AND B. N. WHITE. 1998. Sex identification of elk (*Cervus elaphus canadensis*), moose (*Alces alces*), and white-tailed deer (*Odocoileus virginianus*) using the polymerase chain reaction. Journal of Forensic Sciences 43:477–482

WOODS, J. G., D. PAETKAU, D. LEWIS, B. N. MCLELLAN, M. PROCTOR, AND C. STROBECK. 1999. Genetic tagging of free-ranging black and brown bears. Wildlife Society Bulletin 27:616–627.

WRIGHT, S. 1931. Isolation by distance. Genetics 28:114–138.

———. 1951. The genetical structure of populations. Annals of Eugenetics. 15:323–353.

XU, S., C. J. KOBAK, AND P. E. SMOUSE. 1994. Constrained least squares estimation of mixed population stock composition from mtDNA haplotype frequency data. Canadian Journal of Fisheries and Aquatic Sciences 51:417–425.

YOUNG, J. R. 2005. Animal behavior: its role in wildlife biology. Pages 616–631 *in* C. E. Braun, editor. Techniques for wildlife investigations and management. Sixth edition. The Wildlife Society, Bethesda, Maryland, USA.

———, J. W. HUPP, J. W. BRADBURY, AND C. E. BRAUN. 1994. Phenotypic divergence of secondary sexual traits among sage grouse, *Centrocercus urophasianus*, populations. Animal Behavior 47:1353–1362.

———, C. E. BRAUN, S. J. OYLER-MCCANCE, J. W. HUPP, AND T. W. QUINN. 2000. A new species of sage-grouse (Phasianidae: *Centrocercus*) from southwestern Colorado. Wilson Bulletin 112:445–453.

25

HARVEST MANAGEMENT

John W. Connelly, James H. Gammonley, and James M. Peek

INTRODUCTION

Interest in managing wildlife harvests has been widespread throughout history. Elements of harvest management can be dated to the 8th century when Charlemagne instituted a detailed set of game laws (Caughley 1985). Caughley (1985) further suggested that current deliberations leading to hunting regulations are little different than those of the hunting subcommittee of the Mongol Supreme Command in 13th Century China. However, concepts of hunting licenses and bag limits are reasonably new, having been introduced only in the second half of the 19th century (Caughley 1985). In 1864, New York became the first state to require a license for hunting and in 1878 the Iowa legislature enacted one of the first bag limits restricting prairie-chicken (*Tympanuchus* spp.) hunters to 25 birds per day (Leopold 1933).

Harvest management in North America dates to colonial times when colonies established closed seasons for white-tailed deer (*Odocoileus virginianus*) (Schmidt 1980). By the early 20th century, thoughts about harvest management and sport hunting were influenced by the doctrine of wise use advanced by Theodore Roosevelt and Gifford Pinchot in 1910 (Strickland et al. 1994). Early management efforts were largely directed at recovering populations and preventing over harvest (Schmidt 1980). As populations of game species (particularly deer) recovered, concerns developed about the impact of wildlife on their habitats and emphasis changed towards population control (Schmidt 1980, Strickland et al. 1994). Prior to establishment of professional state fish and wildlife agencies in the 1930s, harvest management decisions were largely based on anecdotal data and decisions were often politically motivated (Wing 1951, Trefethen 1964). Increased mobility of the American public and a doubling of licensed sport hunters from 3 to 6 million between 1910 and 1920 led to increasing concerns over the welfare of wildlife populations (Trefethen 1975, Autenrieth 1981). Both hunters and nonhunters demanded a greater accountability on the part of the states for managing wildlife resources (Hornaday 1916, Trefethen 1975).

Following publication of the *American Game Policy* (Leopold 1930), *The Bobwhite Quail* (Stoddard 1931), and *Game Management* (Leopold 1933), the profession of wildlife management in North America developed rapidly. Together, these 3 publications stressed the importance of a biological approach to managing wildlife. Moreover, the *American Game Policy* called for training of wildlife professionals and to "find facts" or conduct research. Enactment of the Federal Aid to Wildlife Restoration Act (Pittman-Robertson program) in 1937 provided states with a stable funding source to fund the needed research and monitoring projects to further support harvest management programs (Murray 1938, Williamson 1987). As a result, information on population dynamics of a variety of wildlife species was obtained rather quickly and this new knowledge was applied to harvest management.

Sport hunting of game species is an extremely popular and economically important activity. In 2001, over 13 million hunters in the United States spent over 228 million days hunting on over 200 million trips, and spent over 10 billion dollars in hunting-related expenditures (U.S. Department of Interior and U.S. Department of Commerce 2002) (Box 1). Sport hunting can result in substantial harvests. For example, an estimated 16.1 million ducks and 4.2 million geese were harvested in the United States and Canada during the 2001–02 recreational hunting seasons (Martin and Padding 2002), with unknown additional numbers of waterfowl harvested by subsistence hunters. In some cases, recreational harvest can represent up to 25% of the post-breeding population size (Anderson 1975).

This chapter discusses species that are commonly hunted in North America. Although harvest of furbearers is also important and involves some of the same concepts discussed here, furbearer management is beyond the scope of this chapter. Our purpose is to discuss the rationale and theory underlying harvest management in North America and provide examples of successful harvest management programs. We focus primarily on techniques used to address biological goals for harvest management. However, we also understand that hunter participation and satisfaction are important considerations in formulating hunting regulations, and managers typically are interested in maximizing hunting opportunity to meet these objectives (Smith and Roberts 1976, Babcock and Sparrowe 1989, Johnson and Case 2000).

Some principles that provide a foundation for harvest management strategies have been questioned. Thus, we provide a synopsis of the important literature related to harvest management and attempt to identify and briefly discuss these principles. We recognize there is no "one-size-fits-all" approach to harvest management and focus on differences in harvest management among groups of species.

RATIONALE FOR HARVEST
North American Model

Two relatively early court decisions influenced development of harvest management in the United States. In 1896 a Connecticut court (Greer vs. Connecticut), ruled that states have the right to control the manner in which wildlife is taken (Smith and Coggin 1984). In 1910, a Missouri Court decision (State vs. Heger) found that wildlife species within the boundaries of a state are the sole property of that state and not subject to private ownership on the land they inhabit (Autenrieth 1981). These decisions, combined with passage of the Weeks-McLean Act (1913) and Migratory Bird Treaty Act (1918) that place migratory birds under federal custody (Williamson 1987) largely provided a legal foundation for harvest management in the United States. Canada's system is similar to that in the United States. However, in Canada wildlife is considered government property but the Canadian government's roles are not as clearly defined as they are in the United States (Smith and Coggin 1984). Generally in North America, states and provinces are responsible for harvest regulations pertaining to "resident" wildlife while federal authorities set regulations for migratory game birds. Unlike Europe, these regulations apply regardless of ownership of the land the animals occupy.

A general underpinning of harvest management systems is that a biological surplus exists that can be harvested with little impact on subsequent breeding populations (Denney 1978, McCullough 1979). A major objective of most harvest management programs is to apportion harvest opportunity equitably among hunters. The 3 approaches to harvest management include: harvesting at a low rate to ensure population increase, harvesting to maintain a population, and harvesting to reduce a population (Smith and Coggin 1984). Actual amount and type of harvest are affected by population objectives set by the responsible agency (Denney 1978). The appropriate harvest level may vary among and within species depending on the status of the population (e.g., stable vs. increasing) and whether or not the environment fluctuates annually (Caughley and Sinclair 1994).

Harvest management includes 3 basic components: 1) inventory of populations, 2) identification of population and harvest goals, and 3) development of regulations that allow goals to be met (Strickland et al. 1994). These components are usually part of harvest management programs for some species (e.g., deer, elk [*Cervus elaphus*] but one or more are often lacking for other species (e.g., spruce grouse [*Falcipennis canadensis*], gray partridge [*Perdix perdix*]). Caughley and Sinclair (1994) argued that most harvesting of wildlife for recreational purposes has been largely managed by trial and error but that this strategy often works well because of the conservative approach taken by management agencies.

Box 1. Hunting activity in the United States during 2001 (U.S. Department of Interior and U.S. Department of Commerce 2002).

	Upland game	Migratory birds	Big game
Hunters	5,434,000	2,956,000	10,911,000
Trips	46,450,000	24,155,000	114,445,000
Days of hunting	60,142,000	29,310,000	153,191,000
Expenditures ($)	1,816,199,000	1,388,581,000	10,087,930,000

In recent decades there has been a greater emphasis on making informed management decisions, based on knowledge about the effects of harvest on game populations. There are 4 basic requirements for successful, informed management of game harvests (Nichols and Johnson 1989, Nichols et al. 1995). First, managers must develop and agree upon explicit goals and objectives for harvest management. Second, managers must be able to implement actions designed to achieve harvest management objectives. Third, managers must have some idea of the likely effects of alternative management actions. Fourth, systems must be in place to measure the outcome of actions in relation to management objectives (e.g., population size and harvest).

Principles—Past and Present

Many wildlife management principles and concepts currently applied to harvest management were first developed and then reinforced by research conducted from the 1930s through the 1960s (Wing 1951, Allen 1962, Dasmann 1964, Giles 1978). The writings of Aldo Leopold, Paul Errington, and Durwood Allen, among others, and principles they introduced still influence harvest management decisions (Strickland et al. 1994). We define the most common of these principles below and provide a brief assessment of their usefulness as reflected in recent literature.

Additive Mortality

The premise is that each animal killed by hunters is an additional death that adds to the natural mortality resulting in total mortality being greater than if hunting did not occur (Anderson and Burnham 1976). Mackie et al. (1998) reported that hunting was additive to over winter mortality for white-tailed deer and mule deer (*Odocoileus hemionus*). Bergerud (1988) suggested this applied to many grouse species and Connelly et al. (2000*a*, 2003) provided additional evidence that this was the case for greater sage-grouse (*Centrocercus urophasianus*), a species that has low overwinter mortality.

Compensatory Mortality

This type of mortality occurs when animals have relatively stable annual mortality, regardless of which decimating factors may be acting on the population; that is, removal of hunting will result in increased mortality from predation or disease (Dasmann 1964). Hunting has long been thought to be a compensatory form of mortality for virtually all species of upland game. However, recent work (Roseberry 1979, Smith and Willebrand 1999, Connelly et al. 2003, Williams et al. 2004*b*) suggests that hunting mortality is often not compensatory. Ellison (1991) concluded there is little evidence for density-dependent breeding in tetraonids and that hunting may result in an age structure that lowers a population's productivity. Compensatory survival has been characterized as dogma within the field of wildlife management (Romesburg 1981, Warner 1992).

Diminishing Returns

This concept is often referred to as a "the law of diminishing returns" (Wing 1951, Strickland et al. 1994), a concept indicating that past a certain point, hunting is largely unrewarded (i.e., few successful hunters) resulting in relatively few hunters in the field suggesting that hunting is largely self regulating (Allen 1962). In conjunction with the concept of compensatory mortality, the idea of diminishing returns was used to support the argument that small game seasons could be quite long without any risk of harming the population. Cole (1995) provided some evidence to support this concept but Roseberry (1979) concluded that seasonal declines in hunter success were considerably less than expected considering the progressive loss of birds throughout the hunting season. This concept has generally been applied to upland game hunting and has not been widely accepted among waterfowl and big game managers. This concept also fails to recognize observations that late season hunters may be more experienced and effective hunters (i.e., the "diehards"). The idea of diminishing returns appears to have little value for present day harvest management programs.

Doomed Surplus

This has been considered the number of animals produced that exceed the capacity of the habitat to support and keep secure from predation (Errington 1956, Roseberry 1979, Bailey 1984). Roseberry (1979) argued that for northern bobwhite (*Colinus virginianus*), there is a considerable "carryover" effect from year to year. Thus, birds not harvested in the fall may contribute to the next breeding population and are not necessarily part of a doomed surplus. A number of wildlife species actually have high over winter survival (Keppie 1979, Wood et al. 1989, Mackie et al. 1998, Schroeder et al. 1999) and this concept would seem to have limited usefulness.

Harvestable Surplus

Leopold (1933) formulated this concept indicating that most animals produce more young than necessary to maintain the population; this extra number can be removed by hunting without affecting the population. McCullough (1979:233) challenged this concept by arguing that it fails to include "…the dynamic and compensatory nature of population responses…."

Inversity

It has been believed that an inverse relationship exists between productivity and abundance; when a species is particularly numerous in an area, that population is assumed to have relatively low productivity (Wing 1951, Errington 1956). Roseberry (1979) suggested for bobwhites, the rate of increase is linear or slightly curvilinear, but the amount of recruitment necessary to maintain stability increases exponentially. He concluded the system's ability to compensate for hunting losses progressively deteriorates as harvest increases. Williams et al. (2004*b*) argued the principles of inversity and doomed surplus are mutually exclusive.

Opening Day Phenomenon

This concept suggests most mortality for a given species occurs on the opening day (or opening weekend) of the season because that is when most hunters are afield (Giles 1978). Although this seems intuitively correct, there appears to be few quantitative data available that document hunting pressure and harvest throughout the season. Rusch et al. (1984) reported that >40% of the harvest of ruffed grouse (*Bonasa umbellus*) occurred in the last 3 months of a season that extended from October to January.

Threshold of Security

This is the population size above which some animals are not secure from predation; a carrying capacity concept indicating that habitat ultimately decides population size (Errington 1956, Bailey 1984). Romesburg (1981) indicated this concept passed into the wildlife profession's lore without being critically evaluated or tested. Myrberget (1989) referred to this idea as a "winter bottleneck" hypothesis and provided evidence to refute this concept for willow ptarmigan (*Lagopus lagopus*). The "doomed surplus" and "threshold of security" concepts are related and subject to the same criticism.

Uncertainty in Harvest Management

Increased knowledge of wildlife populations suggests that many of the concepts discussed above have limited application for today's manager. Thus, rather than blindly adhering to principles developed 30–70 years ago under vastly different environmental conditions, today's manager should first ask if any of the concepts currently apply and second under what conditions. Wildlife professionals should follow Roseberry's (1981:1056) advice that "...as professionals, we are obligated to provide more credible

justification for hunting than clichés such as 'they would have all died anyway'. "

Assuming that explicit management objectives can be agreed upon, managers charged with developing harvest regulations are faced with several sources of uncertainty (Box 2). Each of these sources pose challenges, but they also interact to complicate efforts to understand the effects of hunting regulations on game populations and to use this knowledge to make informed harvest management decisions. For example, limits on the ability to precisely monitor harvest and population sizes hamper efforts to understand the structural relationships between these measures. Similarly, lack of control over actual harvest rates resulting from a given set of regulations, due in part to uncontrolled environmental conditions, is further complicated by limitations on the ability to precisely observe harvest rates (Williams et al. 1996).

MANAGEMENT OF UPLAND GAME HARVESTS

Development of Harvest Strategies

Early Years (1900–1945)

In response to public demand and a general lack of biological knowledge, harvest management during the early part of the 20th century was largely characterized by a

---

Box 2. Sources of uncertainty about the relationship between hunting regulations and the status of game populations (Nichols et al. 1995, Williams et al. 1996, Johnson et al. 1997).

Partial Observability. — Although extensive, costly monitoring systems have been developed to track some game populations and their harvests, results of these efforts are imprecise and/or subject to bias (Williams et al. 1996). This inability to perfectly observe the managed system hampers the ability of managers to make informed decisions, (e.g., increased protection or increased harvest) (Nichols et al. 1995, Williams et al. 1996). New or expanded monitoring efforts may provide improved information and at finer spatial resolutions, but this benefit must be weighed against the costs of such programs (Johnson and Case 2000).

Partial Management Control. — Harvest managers attempt to influence harvests through changes in hunting regulations, but harvest levels cannot be precisely controlled through regulations (Nieman et al. 1987, Trost et al. 1987, Johnson et al. 1997). Biologically meaningful changes in harvests or harvest rates may only occur between relatively different, discrete sets of regulations (Nichols and Johnson 1989, Johnson et al. 1997, Nichols 2000).

Structural Uncertainty. — This type of uncertainty refers to our limited understanding of the influence of harvest rate on subsequent population size (Nichols 1991, Williams et al. 1996, Johnson et al. 1997). Uncertainty about the structure of population dynamics is the source of many of the debates over how to manage harvests (Johnson et al. 1993, Nichols et al. 1995). The 2 central components of structural uncertainty involve hunting as additive or compensatory mortality (Burnham and Anderson 1984, Burnham et al. 1984, Nichols et al. 1984), and density dependence of the reproductive process (Nichols 1991, Hilborn et al. 1995). These hypotheses have important implications for harvest management, because if hunting mortality is mostly compensatory and reproductive rate is strongly density-dependent, populations can sustain higher harvest levels than if hunting mortality is primarily additive to other forms of mortality and reproductive rate is largely density-independent (Nichols et al. 1995, Williams et al. 1996). Thus, structural uncertainty may lead managers to make decisions that are too liberal for sustaining populations or overly restrictive of hunting opportunity (Williams et al. 1996).

Environmental variation. —Habitats supporting many game populations in North America are subject to large, uncontrolled spatial and temporal variation, and these changing conditions can have significant impacts on the status of populations (e.g., Pospahala et al. 1974). Managers cannot precisely (or even accurately) predict future conditions when setting current regulations. However, efforts have been made to examine the relationships between habitat status and population size, which can in turn assist managers in assessing the expected harvest under different environmental conditions (Johnson et al. 1997).

reduction in bag limits and season length for many species of upland game. By today's standards, established seasons in the early 20th century tended to vary considerably among years often with liberal bag limits (Tables 1, 2). Leopold (1933) indicated the season for ruffed grouse in the north-central states declined from about 50 days in 1900 to about 10 days in 1930 while daily bag limits changed from 25/day to 7/day over the same period. Similarly, in Idaho the greater sage-grouse season decreased from 137 days with a bag limit of 18 grouse/day in 1903 to being completely closed by 1939 (Table 1). During this same period laws were also enacted to regulate firearms, hunting from boats and vehicles, and to provide refuges (Leopold 1933). Game bird hunting was generally restricted to the use of shotguns no larger than 10 or 12 gauge. Shooting hours were implemented and some states eliminated hunting on Sunday. Use of nets and traps was outlawed (Leopold 1933, Strickland et al. 1994).

Changing Strategies (1946–1980)

The general approach to harvest management of upland game was developed during the 1930s and 1940s. During this period, the concepts of threshold of security, doomed surplus, and compensatory mortality were introduced and subsequently formalized in several early wildlife management textbooks (Wing 1951, Allen 1962, Dasmann 1964). Taken together, these concepts suggested that small game populations produce a large number of young each year, most of which are available for harvest because they would not survive the winter and add to the next season's breeding population. These ideas further suggested that hunting was a compensatory form of mortality and implied that a large portion of a small game population could be harvested each fall because, if not taken by hunters, they would likely die prior to the next breeding season from some other cause. Harvest strategies tended to stabilize and became somewhat more liberal in the 1960s and 1970s compared to the 1940s and 1950s (Table 1).

Early researchers provided evidence to support their ideas from studies of muskrat (*Ondatra zibethicus*), northern bobwhite, ring-necked pheasant (*Phasianus colchicus*), ruffed grouse, and cottontail rabbit (*Sylvilagus* spp.) (Leopold et al. 1943; Errington 1945, 1956; Bump et al. 1947; Allen 1962). There was a strong tendency to believe reproductive characteristics and effects of exploitation were the same for all species of upland game (Allen 1962, Strickland et al. 1994). Allen (1962:43) summarized this situation well when he wrote, "…Our populations of small animals operate under a one-year plan of decimation and replacement; and Nature habitually maintains a wide margin of overproduction. She kills off a huge surplus of animals whether we take our harvest or not." Unfortunately, these early studies provided virtually no empirical evidence to assess the impacts of exploitation. Population characteristics were often documented for relatively discrete areas rather than compared over large portions of the species' range. Moreover, the habitats, landscapes, and general conditions under which these populations existed are markedly different now than in the 1930s, 1940s, and 1950s. For northern bobwhite, many agencies and individuals still rely on management guidelines (Stoddard 1931, Rosene 1969) developed during eras when land-use practices were drastically different than today (Kuvlesky et al. 1993).

Table 1. Representative greater sage-grouse hunting seasons in Idaho from the early 1900s to 2002.

Year	Opening date	Days	Bag/possession limits	Area closures
Early Years				
1903	15 Jul	137	18/18	No
1909	15 Aug	108	12/12	No
1921	15 Aug	31	6/6	Yes
1925	1 Aug	30–32	6/6	Yes
1929	10 Aug	10–12	4/4	Yes
1933	1 Aug	15	4/4	No
1939–42	None	0	0/0	Entire state
1943	29 Aug	5	3/3	Yes
Changing Strategies				
1944–47	None	0	0/0	Entire state
1948	4 Sep	2	2/2	Yes
1956	3rd Sat[a]	1.5	0/0	Yes
1957	3rd Sat	4.5	2/2	Yes
1966–67	3rd Sat	5–16	2/2, 3/6	No
1968	3rd Sat	7–16	2/2, 3/6	No
1971–72	3rd Sat	2–23	2/2, 3/6, 4/8	No
1977–78	3rd Sat	2–14	2/2, 2/4, 3/6	Yes
Current Knowledge				
1980–82	3rd Sat	9–21	2/2, 2/4, 3/6	No
1985	3rd Sat	9–21	2/2, 3/6	Yes
1986–87	3rd Sat	14–21	2/4, 3/6	Yes
1988–89	3rd Sat	16–23	2/4, 3/6	Yes
1990–95	3rd Sat	30	3/6	Yes
1996–02	3rd Sat	7–23	1/2, 2/4	Yes

[a] In September.

Table 2. Pheasant hunting seasons in South Dakota, 1919–1940 (Trautman 1982).

Year	Opening date	Days	Bag/possession limits	Area closures
1919	30 Oct	1	2/2	Yes
1920	4 Nov	2	2/2	Yes
1921	21 Nov	7	2/2	Yes
1922	9 Nov	20	2/2	Yes
1923	19 Nov	6	3/3	Yes
1924	7 Nov	15	3/3	Yes
1925	30 Oct	15	3/15	Yes
1926	15 Oct	20	7/21	Yes
1927	26 Nov	40	4/12	Yes
1928	25 Oct	40	5/15	Yes
1929	29 Oct	16	5/15	Yes
1930	16 Oct	30	5/15	Yes
1931	15 Oct	12	3/6	Yes
1932	20 Oct	30	4/8	Yes
1933	10 Oct	30	5/10	Yes
1934	21 Oct	30	5/10	No
1935	21 Oct	37	6/12	No
1936	10 Oct	20	4/8	Yes
1937	9 Oct	4	3/6	Yes
1938	1 Oct	14	4/8	Yes
1939	14 Oct	29	4/8	Yes
1940	1 Oct	40	5/10	Yes

> ## Box 3. Early modeling effort to assess impacts of hunting.
>
> Roseberry (1979) used real and simulated data to assess the impacts of hunting on northern bobwhite and concluded that harvests >55% of the autumn population would depress the following spring's population.

> ## Box 4. Additive mortality and grouse.
>
> Bergerud (1988) concluded that hunting was additive to over-winter mortality for blue grouse (*Dendragapus obscurus*), white-tailed ptarmigan (*Lagopus leucura*), ruffed grouse, and greater prairie-chickens (*Tympanuchus cupido*).

By the 1970s, new techniques and long-term studies provided wildlife managers with a wealth of new information on many species of upland game. Modeling began to be used to assess the impacts of exploitation on wildlife (Box 3). Upland game populations were being routinely monitored and at least some of these data were considered in harvest management decisions (Braun 1979, Roseberry 1979, Braun and Beck 1985, Hoffman 1985). Despite this increase in knowledge, the general approach to harvest management had not changed from the 1950s or 1960s. As an example, in reporting on sage-grouse management in Montana, Wallestad (1975:27) provided the statements quoted from Allen (1962) above and then wrote: "Gamebird seasons in Montana are largely based on the philosophy that most birds will not survive the winter, hence replacing natural mortality with hunting mortality."

Current Knowledge (1981–2004): A New Paradigm

Although early efforts suggested that response to exploitation was similar for most, if not all, upland game species, Peek (1986:279) argued "...each population responds to exploitation according to its characteristics; to the nature, timing and duration of the exploitation; and to the effect on other organisms that it interacts with." Peek further indicated that it might be inappropriate to apply inferences from data collected on one population to another population of the same species if those populations have different characteristics or are affected by different environmental factors. Similarly, Caughley and Sinclair (1994) observed that a safe sustained yield could only be estimated with knowledge of the population's growth pattern, measured by the relationship between the population and its resources.

Both Peek (1986) and Caughley and Sinclair (1994) were reflecting new information suggesting that earlier views of harvest management were not always correct. In referring to upland game in general and wildlife managers in particular, Brennan (1994:411) leveled relatively harsh criticism of upland game management when he observed "I have a nagging suspicion that wildlife and natural resource professionals have been missing the mark with respect to operating as responsible stewards for these unique vertebrate resources." Gutiérrez (1994) reinforced this idea by also concluding that research and management have not met the challenge of upland game management.

During the 1980s and 1990s, evidence began to accumulate suggesting that, under some circumstances, harvesting may have an additive effect on mortality for a number of species (Gregg 1990, Robinette and Doer 1993, Dixon et al. 1996). Bergerud (1985, 1988) summarized the effect of exploitation on a variety of game bird species (Box 4).

Robertson and Rosenberg (1988) also addressed the issue of compensatory and additive mortality and concluded that in natural populations hunting mortality usually falls between the 2 extremes of being totally additive or totally compensatory. Strickland et al. (1994:463) indicated that through the early 1990s, the trends in harvest management were generally toward liberal seasons based on the idea that "...hunting has so little effect on upland game populations." That trend seems to be changing (Table 1) with a greater recognition that effects of hunting may vary depending on population and habitat characteristics. As examples, Idaho changed their sharp-tailed grouse (*Tympanuchus phasianellus*) season to begin later in the fall to relieve hunting pressure on birds during the fall lekking period and to also reduce hunting pressure on isolated and possibly declining greater sage-grouse populations (the seasons were held concurrently). Additionally, Idaho (Table 1) and Wyoming reduced harvest on sage-grouse and Wyoming changed the opening date for greater sage-grouse from 1 September to mid-September and reported these changes resulted in lower harvest (Heath et al. 1997).

Agencies are beginning to integrate information acquired from the last 20 years of research into their upland game management strategies. There seems to be a growing recognition that a successful harvest management program must integrate knowledge of a species' reproductive characteristics and quality of habitat that a population occupies. This change appears to be accompanied by an increasing awareness that it is no longer acceptable to base management decisions on dogmatic beliefs and findings from early wildlife studies (Williams et al. 2004*b*). More information is needed on the effects of exploitation on a variety of upland species over relatively large areas. The importance of this information for establishing biologically sound harvest management programs will continue to increase as habitats are continually lost to expanding human populations and populations of some species continue to dwindle.

Inventory

A general approach to harvest management would base harvest on abundance of the species, but this is rarely done for upland game. Instead, as Caughley and Sinclair (1994) suggested, most harvest strategies seem to have been developed through trial and error.

Some states conduct routine population surveys just prior to the hunting season. For example, the Iowa Department of Natural Resources uses roadside surveys to assess upland game populations. Pheasants, quail, partridge, cottontail rabbits, and jackrabbits (*Lepus* spp.) are counted along survey routes during August each year.

Trautman (1982) described an inventory program for pheasants in South Dakota that included crowing counts, brood surveys, winter surveys, aerial counts, and storm mortality surveys. Trautman (1982) suggested these data are used in formulating recommendations for hunting seasons but did not explain how this was done. Similarly, Schulz (1990) reported that North Dakota conducts a variety of gray partridge surveys to aid in establishing hunting regulations but did not indicate how these data might be used. Other states have similar programs; the main purpose of these inventories appears to be public information rather than assessing populations to guide decisions on hunting seasons. Kurzejeski and Vangilder (1992) summarized wild turkey (*Meleagris gallopavo*) hunting seasons and regulations. They reported that seasons tend to be either conservative or liberal but gave no indication that population inventory data were used to establish season frameworks. Strickland et al. (1994) also summarized factors considered in turkey hunting seasons and concluded that many of the factors were political rather than biological. One of the few instances of using inventory data to guide harvest management of small game species occurs with greater sage-grouse in Oregon. In that state, the Oregon Department of Fish and Wildlife uses data from lek counts and production surveys to help adjust hunting seasons so that harvest takes $\leq 5\%$ of the estimated fall population.

Seasons for most small game species are kept relatively constant from year to year but may vary considerably among states (Table 3). Strickland et al. (1994:463) reported that many states have de-emphasized collection of population data for upland game species "…because the lack of harvest impact indicates little need for the data." In contrast, Stauffer (1993) argued that biologists should track population trends and demographics to help examine the outcome of management activities.

Harvest Surveys

A recent survey of states with sage-grouse seasons indicated that all monitored harvest, usually with telephone or mail questionnaires (Connelly et al. 2004). At a minimum, all states estimated harvest, number of hunters, and number of days hunting. Similar estimates for hunted species are available from most, if not all, states because states have emphasized collection of harvest data (Strickland et al. 1994). However, many estimates of harvest have wide confidence intervals that make comparisons among areas or years difficult. Moreover, the lack of population data makes it virtually impossible to assess the proportion of the population taken by hunters. Clearly, where concerns have been identified, greater effort must be made by professional biologists to better document harvest and the relationship of harvest to the overall population. Almost 25 years ago, Roseberry (1979) and Lindén (1981) suggested that reliable estimates of harvest rates and knowledge of population characteristics are necessary requirements for sound management, but that information was generally lacking for upland game populations. Although progress has been made, the same observation could be made today.

Developing Regulations

Development of regulations varies among wildlife agencies but initial steps normally include soliciting comments from agency personnel and the public, often through meetings or open houses. Regions or other administrative units then formulate recommendations and pass these on to the chief administrator for the agency's wildlife program. At some point, these recommendations are discussed with the agency director who may ask for modifications. Ultimately, the recommendations are passed on to the Wildlife Commission for approval and possible changes. Seasons are sometimes set 2–3 years in advance, in other cases they may be set just a few weeks before opening day.

Hurst and Rosene (1985) reported that quail harvest regulations developed from numerous factors including tradition, biopolitics, sportsmen's perceptions, and research. A similar assessment was made for wild turkeys (Kurzejeski and Vangilder 1992, Strickland et al. 1994). We suggest the

Table 3. Variation in season lengths and bag and possession limits for small game species among states.

Area	N[a]	Cottontail rabbit	Tree squirrel[b]	Pheasant	Bobwhite
			Species		
Northeast	6				
Season[c]		89–183	92–182	36–92	14–152
Bag/possession		1–6/2–8	4–8/8–12	2/4	2–5/8–10
Southeast	6				
Season		99–177	119–213	57–82	64–107
Bag/possession		4–12/8–20	6–12/8–24	2–none[d]/2–none	3–12/9–12
Central	7				
Season		82–365	114–273	27–86	23–94
Bag/possession		4–none/10–none	4–10/10–20	2–4/4–16	5–10/10–32
West	9				
Season		151–365	75–365	15–80	72–109
Bag/possession		5–none/15–none	4–none/4–none	2–3/4–15	8–10/20–30

  [a] Number of states surveyed per area. Not all species were hunted in every state surveyed.

  [b] Gray (*Sciurus carolinensis*) and fox squirrels (*S. niger*).

  [c] Number of days. Season lengths vary annually in some states because opening days depend on a day of the week rather than a date (e.g., third Saturday of October).

  [d] None indicates no bag or possession limit.

same holds true for harvest regulations for most species of upland game. Thus, seasons vary within and among states even though the species hunted is the same. The Policy Analysis Center for Western Public Lands (Wambolt et al. 2002) reviewed seasons for sage-grouse in the western United States. They reported opening dates ranging from 1 September to 13 October with season lengths of 2 to 62 days. Bag and possession limits also varied considerably. We examined season lengths, and daily bag and possession limits provided by state wildlife agency Internet sites (*n* = 28) for 4 commonly hunted species: cottontail rabbit, tree squirrels, ring-necked pheasant, and bobwhite (Table 3). Regulations varied regionally and among states but tended to be more conservative in the heavily populated northeastern United States. Overall, season lengths for cottontails varied from 82 to 365 days and daily bag limits varied from 1 to 12 rabbits. For squirrels, season lengths similarly varied from 75 to 365 days and bag limits ranged from 4 to 12. Several states had no bag or possession limits for either rabbits or squirrels. Regulations for game birds were equally varied but tended to be more conservative than those for rabbits or squirrels. Pheasant seasons ranged from 15 to 92 days while daily bag limits ranged from 2 to 4 birds. However, one southeastern state reported having no bag or possession limits for pheasants. Season lengths for bobwhite were perhaps the most varied, ranging from 14 to 152 days while daily bag limits varied from 2 to 12 quail (Table 3).

Recently, Burger et al. (1994) argued for broad scale experiments to better understand the effects of exploitation on quail. Thus far, field research to assess the impacts of harvest and guide season setting seems relatively rare. Both Weeden (1972) and Braun et al. (1993) suggested that later hunting seasons were appropriate for reducing impacts of harvest on ptarmigan (*Lagopus* spp.) populations. There is also some evidence that later opening dates are more appropriate for sharp-tailed grouse and sage-grouse (Gregg 1990, Heath et al. 1997). There is apparently much uncertainty associated with the effects of exploitation on game birds (Box 2) but population declines, usually related to habitat deterioration or loss, have been documented for many species. Therefore, Ellison's (1991) strategy of basing seasons on the assumption that hunting is additive to adult mortality but at least partially compensatory mortality in juveniles, may be the most appropriate in many cases.

Population Responses to Hunting

Until the late 1970s, most studies of the effects of exploitation on upland game species suggested there were few adverse impacts of hunting. Within the last 20 years, numerous investigations have documented adverse effects of hunting on a variety of upland game species. In some cases, early researchers may simply have drawn erroneous conclusions, especially when dealing with species that had relatively low reproductive rates and long lives (e.g., sage-grouse). In other cases, more recent findings may reflect the results of changing environments occupied by upland game. Climate and landscape-scale habitat changes have recently been linked to long-term declines of black grouse (*Tetrao tetrix*) in Europe (Loneux and Ruwet 1996, Loneux 2000). It is likely that similar changes in North America have effected the distribution and populations of

many upland game species. The earlier studies concluding that hunting had no effect on a species may have been correct at that time, just as more recent results correctly reflect current conditions.

Strickland et al. (1994:459) reported, "Hunting of upland game, as practiced since the 1950s, has not been shown to have a measurable adverse effect upon upland game populations." The authors did not define the term "measurable adverse effect" but over the last 20 years numerous papers have been published challenging this general assertion. As an example, the Policy Analysis Center for Western Public Lands (Wambolt et al. 2002:20) concluded that in some instances hunting might slow population recovery of sage-grouse or stabilize populations at "lower-than-desirable levels." The Center further concluded that states should not assume that hunting is a totally compensatory form of mortality, nor should they base hunting seasons on the concept that seasons and bag limits can be liberal because of high annual turnover in the population (Allen 1962, Wallestad 1975).

We define "adverse effect" as an action that results in reduction in the size of subsequent breeding populations or a reduction in average survival of a population or a specific age/gender group within a population. Population characteristics such as recruitment and survival may affect the response of a population to exploitation (Peek 1986) and these characteristics vary among species and perhaps even populations within species. Kokko (2001:148) warned that ignoring information on mating systems, age structures, density dependence, and seasonal behaviors will "easily cause hunting to be harmful to an unnecessary extent." Thus, we address effects of harvest by species and groups of species and include a brief description of population characteristics for each species discussed to allow a better understanding of opportunities and potential constraints on harvest management. We also try to avoid gross generalization while seeking common patterns that may help establish biologically meaningful harvest practices among groups of species.

Pheasants, Quail, and Partridge

As a group (Box 5), these species are characterized by relatively short lives and high reproductive rates (Rosene 1969, Farris et al. 1977, Trautman 1982, Carroll 1993, Schemnitz 1994). In North America, these species are often associated with agricultural lands or, at least for part of their life depend on landscapes dominated by early successional stages. The chukar (*Alectoris chukar*) is one of the few exceptions but it depends on habitats dominated by cheatgrass (*Bromus tectorum*), an exotic annual.

George et al. (1980) and Trautman (1982) reported that hunting season length and season closures had no impact on pheasant populations in the upper midwestern United States. Edwards (1988) indicated that hunting seasons should open early in the fall because of high nonhunting mortality in the fall and early winter, and 40–60-day, cocks-only, seasons were reasonable. However, Whiteside and Guthery (1983) reported that a longer hunting season (30 vs.16 days) was associated with decreased survival of pheasants in northwest Texas. They also noted (1983:252) that seasons longer than 30 days "…could result in excessively distorted sex ratios and low productivity." Further, illegal and accidental harvest of hens is often ≥15% of the fall population of hens, thus legal hunting of hens is rarely warranted (Edwards 1988).

Many studies of quail and hunting suggested that harvest had little or no adverse effect on populations, and biologists often argued that harvest would substitute for natural population reductions (Parmalee 1953, Kabat and Thompson 1963, Vance and Ellis 1972, Campbell et al. 1973, Robinette and Doerr 1993). Cole (1995) evaluated effects of hunting on northern bobwhite and concluded that hunting had no effect on spring breeding populations or recruitment. Rosene (1969) indicated that it was "safe" to remove about 45% of a bobwhite population by hunting without adversely affecting the breeding stock.

Stoddard (1931:226) was the first to report that in some cases hunting may result in population declines when he wrote "…the balance between the reproduction of the birds and their natural mortality may be so nearly even that to shoot any considerable number for sport will quickly deplete the supply." Almost 50 years later, Roseberry (1979) reported that compensation for hunting losses is incomplete from fall to spring, resulting in depression of breeding populations for northern bobwhite. Roseberry (1979) further argued that liberalized regulations for bobwhite are inconsistent with the realities of a shrinking resource and contended that hunting seasons should be structured to provide reasonable recreational opportunities while not seriously depleting stocks. Robinette and Doerr (1993) and Dixon et al. (1996) reported that survival of bobwhites in hunted coveys was significantly lower than in nonhunted coveys. Williams et al. (2004a) concluded harvest is additive to natural mortality of northern bobwhites and indicated local movements can mask the true effect of harvest on observed densities. Given evidence supporting both contentions that hunting has little impact on the population and that hunting may adversely impact populations, the recommendations that research be conducted to identify threshold densities and hunting pressures that may result in additive mortality, and that state resource agencies be creative in their approaches to season length and bag limits (Kuvlesky et al. 1993) seem reasonable.

Although gray partridge are a common game bird in many states, they are often shot opportunistically by hunters pursuing other species (e.g., ring-necked pheasants, chukar, sharp-tailed grouse) (Vander Zouwen 1990). Weigand (1980) indicated that about 3% of the gray partridge population was harvested in his Montana study area and suggested that doubling the bag limit (i.e., from 6 to 12

birds/day) was biologically acceptable. Similarly, Carroll (1990) suggested that hunting was not a problem for most populations in North America because of low hunting pressure and interest. Christensen (1958) reached the same conclusions for chukar in Nevada. However, Bro et al (2003) recommended that a prudent approach to managing gray partridge populations in France was to consider hunting mortality as additive.

Grouse and Ptarmigan

Species within this general group can be classified as forest grouse (blue, spruce, ruffed grouse), prairie grouse (greater and lesser prairie-chicken [*Tympanuchus pallidicinctus*], sharp-tailed grouse, greater and Gunnison sage-grouse [*Centrocercus minimus*]) and ptarmigan (white-tailed, willow, rock [*Lagopus muta*]). Compared to pheasants, quail, and partridge, many grouse and ptarmigan species (Box 6) tend to be longer lived with lower reproductive rates (Johnsgard 1973, Arnold 1988, Zwickel 1992, Braun et al. 1993, Connelly et al. 1993, Schroeder et al. 1999). Many of these species depend on habitats dominated by late seral or climax vegetation and some have large annual ranges (Zwickel et al. 1968, Connelly et al. 1988, Schroeder and Robb 1993, Connelly et al. 2000a, Leonard et al. 2000).

Forest Grouse.—Mussehl (1960) concluded that hunting had only a minor influence on yearly population turnover of blue grouse. Similarly, Hoffman (1985) indicated that spring densities of blue grouse were not affected by the preceding fall's harvest. Zwickel (1982) argued that adult female blue grouse in British Columbia were more vulnerable to hunting than males, resulting in an age structure shifted towards yearlings, thus reducing productivity of the population. However, Zwickel (1982) indicated that under the existing hunting pressure, reduction in productivity appeared to have no effect on subsequent breeding densities. Zwickel (1992) also suggested that autumn migration into rugged areas reduced hunting impacts.

Early studies of the effects of hunting on ruffed grouse suggested exploitation had little adverse impact on grouse populations (Edminster 1947, Dorney and Kabat 1960). Dorney and Kabat (1960) concluded from an 8-year study there was no detectable relationship between hunting and subsequent ruffed grouse populations. Palmer and Bennett (1963) compared ruffed grouse populations on hunted and nonhunted areas in Michigan and concluded that hunting had no effect on population size and a much longer hunting season was justifiable. Fischer and Keith (1974) also concluded that fall hunting had no measurable effect on spring population levels of ruffed grouse in Alberta. Clark (1996, 2000) examined survival of ruffed grouse in hunted and nonhunted areas in Michigan and suggested that hunting may decrease juvenile survival but concluded there was little evidence suggesting that hunting was additive to natural mortality.

Other research has provided evidence that hunting may have adverse effects on some ruffed grouse populations. Kubisiak (1984) compared ruffed grouse populations on hunted and nonhunted areas in Wisconsin and found that exploitation may be a major factor depressing populations in areas subject to relatively heavy harvest. Similarly, Small et al. (1991) suggested that hunting mortality of ruffed grouse was at least partially, if not completely, addi-

---

Box 6. Grouse and ptarmigan productivity and survival characteristics.

Clutch sizes range from 1–12 eggs, 3–24 eggs, and 4–9 eggs, for blue, ruffed, and spruce grouse, respectively and annual survival may exceed 70% for adult blue grouse and 50% for adult spruce grouse (Edminster 1947, Johnsgard 1973, Ellison 1974, Robinson 1980, Zwickel 1992).

Lesser and greater prairie-chickens lay 5–17 eggs per clutch and readily renest (Hamerstrom and Hamerstrom 1949; Johnsgard 1973; Taylor and Guthery 1980a,b; Svedarsky 1988; Schroeder and Robb 1993). Greater prairie-chickens may have relatively high survival during summer, fall and winter (McKee 1995). The average clutch size for sharp-tailed grouse is about 12 eggs and they also readily renest (Hillman and Jackson 1973, Connelly et al. 1999).

In contrast, sage-grouse have low annual turnover, several studies have indicated that not all females nest each year, (Schroeder et al. 1999, Leonard et al. 2000), average clutch size ranges from 7–9 eggs, and renesting is uncommon in some populations (Schroeder et al. 1999). Generally, prairie-chickens and sharp-tailed grouse have greater reproductive rates and lower annual survival rates than sage-grouse.

All ptarmigan species seem to have population characteristics similar to sage-grouse (i.e., relatively low reproductive rates and annual turnover) (Choate 1963, Giesen et al. 1980, Martin et al. 1989, Braun et al. 1993) but reproductive characteristics may vary substantially among years and populations (Myrberget 1988, Martin et al. 1989).

---

tive to natural mortality. They further concluded that ruffed grouse numbers would be substantially reduced in fragmented habitats with high hunting mortality. Clark (2000) suggested that reducing harvest during population lows might benefit ruffed grouse populations. Finally, Bergerud (1988) summarized data from 3 study areas in Minnesota and concluded that populations occupying heavily hunted areas were being depressed by excessive harvest.

Spruce grouse have high overwinter survival (Keppie 1979), but there appears to be little information on the effects of harvest on this species. Ellison (1974) reported about 13% of grouse banded within 3.2 km of roads were killed by hunters on the Kenai Peninsula, Alaska. Bergerud (1988) re-examined Ellison's data and concluded that hunting increased natural mortality by 14% (i.e., hunting was additive to the natural mortality rate).

Prairie Grouse.—Differences in population characteristics (Box 6) and annual home ranges complicate attempts to assess impacts of harvest on prairie grouse. Lesser and greater prairie-chickens have relatively large annual ranges (Hamerstrom and Hamerstrom 1949; Johnsgard 1973; Taylor and Guthery 1980a,b; Svedarsky 1988; Schroeder and Robb 1993). Juveniles of both lesser and greater prairie-chickens make extensive movements in fall (Robel et al. 1970, Taylor and Guthery 1980a, Schroeder and Robb 1993). Sharp-tailed grouse tend to have small annual home ranges (Hillman and Jackson 1973, Connelly et al. 1999). In contrast, sage-grouse have large annual home ranges (Schroeder et al. 1999, Leonard et al. 2000).

Early information on the effects of hunting on prairie grouse follows the same pattern as for other game bird species—a general indication that hunting does not negatively affect populations. Although there is little published information on the effects of hunting on prairie-chickens (Schroeder and Robb 1993), Hamerstrom et al. (1957) suggested that hunting did not pose any problems for greater prairie-chicken populations in Wisconsin during periods of population highs. Hart et al. (1950), Ammann (1963), and Hillman and Jackson (1973) provided evidence that hunting had little effect on sharp-tailed grouse populations. Numerous studies also suggested that hunting had little impact on sage-grouse populations (June 1963, Crawford

1982, Braun and Beck 1985, Braun 1987). Wallestad (1975) reported that despite fluctuating population trends, Montana maintained liberal sage-grouse seasons because of high annual turnover, "law of diminishing returns" and "opening day phenomenon."

Despite the fact that these species differ in life history traits and some information to the contrary, much of the available data suggest hunting may adversely affect many populations of prairie grouse, regardless of species. Hamerstrom and Hamerstrom (1973) reported that hunted cohorts of greater prairie-chickens in Wisconsin had higher average mortality rates than unhunted cohorts. They concluded that hunting increased "normal mortality" by 25%. Copelin (1963) suggested that hunting seasons for lesser prairie-chickens in Oklahoma only open during years when populations were increasing but provided little information on the impacts of harvest on this species. For sharp-tailed grouse in Wisconsin, Grange (1949) considered a 24% harvest of the fall population to be excessive and Gregg (1990) reported that harvest rates ranging from 15 to 56% of the fall population were associated with stable to declining breeding populations. Similarly, Mossop (1994) reported that harvest rates in parts of the Yukon Territory ranged from 4 to 39% and in some years harvest may negatively impact populations. Sage-grouse may be more susceptible to over-harvest than other upland game bird species because they have population characteristics more typical of k-selected species (relatively low reproductive rates, long lives, low annual turnover) (Schroeder et al. 1999). Autenrieth (1981) and Crawford and Lutz (1985) suggested that hunting might have some negative effects on sage-grouse populations. Johnson and Braun (1999) analyzed lek count and hunter harvest data and concluded that, up to some threshold level, hunting mortality was compensatory, but, at or beyond that level, exploitation of sage-grouse may be additive. Connelly et al. (2000a, 2003) concluded that hunting can slow the rate of increase for sage-grouse populations and that harvest losses are likely additive to winter mortality and may result in lower breeding populations.

Ptarmigan.—Bergerud and Huxter (1969) reported that harvest rates removing up to 70% of populations apparently had no effect on trends in breeding populations of willow ptarmigan in Newfoundland. Although Weeden (1972) suggested that spring hunting of rock ptarmigan may affect breeding populations, he generally concluded that harvest of 40% of the fall population had no effect on subsequent breeding populations. Similarly, McGowan (1975) reported that hunting had no effect on rock ptarmigan breeding populations. Bergerud (1970, 1972) indicated that late-hatched willow ptarmigan young are more vulnerable to hunting than early-hatched birds and vulnerability of ptarmigan populations to hunting varied among years.

Braun (1969) was one of the first to suggest that fall hunting could reduce subsequent breeding populations of white-tailed ptarmigan. Bergerud (1988) reviewed data from hunted and nonhunted populations of white-tailed ptarmigan from Colorado and concluded that birds in the hunted populations had mortality rates approximately double those of nonhunted populations. Additionally, Mossop (1994) provided information suggesting that in some years, hunting in the Yukon Territory may remove enough willow ptarmigan to negate any population increases and Steen and Erikstad (1996) produced similar results by modeling a willow ptarmigan population. Other research has provided evidence indicating hunting can remove relatively large portions of the autumn population of willow ptarmigan (Smith and Willebrand 1999, Willebrand and Hörnell 2001). Finally, Smith and Willebrand (1999:722) concluded "... hunting mortality was mostly, if not totally additive to natural mortality..." of willow ptarmigan in Sweden.

Wild Turkey

Hunting for wild turkey differs from that for other game birds because male turkeys are traditionally hunted during spring when females are protected. Some areas support both spring (male only) and fall (either gender) seasons. Markley (1967) indicated that harvest rates vary widely among areas and years but suggested that in good southeastern United States habitat, 40–60% of turkey populations could be harvested without harming the population. He further concluded that hunting is not a serious limiting factor to population increases where suitable habitat exists. Weaver and Mosby (1979) examined the influence of hunting regulations on turkey populations and concluded a population can continue to decline even with restrictive fall harvest regulations (bearded-turkey [males, few females] only) but that a productive population can withstand at least a 20% annual harvest.

Lobdell et al. (1972) indicated that spring hunting of male turkeys was biologically innocuous if reproduction (Box 7) was adequate to ensure a self-sustaining population. However, Kurzejeski and Vangilder (1992) indicated the effects of spring season length and bag limits on turkey populations were not well understood.

Some research has indicated that fall harvest exceeding 10% of the population can result in a population decline (Vangilder and Kurzejeski 1995, Hubbard et al. 1999), but minimal fall harvest with restricted numbers of hunters seems to have little impact (Hubbard et al. 1999). Pack et al. (1999) compared survival of radio-marked turkeys in areas closed and open to fall hunting. They reported that mean annual survival rates were higher in closed areas than in open areas and attributed these differences to legal hunt-

> **Box 7. Wild turkey productivity and survival characteristics.**
>
> Wild turkeys have low to moderate annual survival rates (15–75%) and high reproductive potential (Petersen and Richardson 1975, Vangilder 1992). Thus, they tend to be more like pheasants, quail, and partridge than grouse and ptarmigan.

ing. Kurzejeski and Vangilder (1992) reported that fall seasons have a greater potential than spring seasons to affect populations, especially in years of poor production. Generally, a 15% fall harvest level can result in population declines (Kurzejeski and Vangilder 1992).

Rabbits and Squirrels

Regardless of variation in reproductive rates, given the relatively high reproduction for these small game species, they should have a high likelihood of compensatory responses to hunting mortality (Peek 1986). Most of the published literature for both squirrels and rabbits indicates this is the case (Wight 1959, Mosby 1969, Mosby et al. 1977). However, some instances of inappropriate harvest levels have been documented for both gray and fox squirrels (Peek 1986). Nixon et al. (1974) concluded an adult fox squirrel population was reduced by hunting to a level that could not produce enough young to bring preseason densities up to population levels attained in previous years. These authors also indicated small woodlots on public hunting areas may be difficult to manage for fox squirrels without restraining hunting opportunity. Management of these woodlots should be based on sustained yield rather than hunter success, because hunter demand exceeds the supply of squirrels (Nixon et al. 1974). Nixon et al. (1975) further concluded that harvest and population densities affect subsequent survival of adult female gray squirrels. Additionally, Rose (1977) provided evidence that cottontail rabbits had higher mortality rates as a result of hunting but also argued that greater hunting mortality was compensated for by increased production, increased survival, or immigration.

Future Directions

Stocking

Stocking game birds is seen as a legitimate and often necessary function of harvest management. In part, the release of pen-reared pheasants, northern bobwhite, or other species is likely reinforced among the hunting public because stocking is a common activity of fisheries management. There are 2 different programs that involve game bird stocking, although the differences may not be apparent to some sportsmen. The first is the release of birds before the gun, usually just before or during the hunting season. Krauss et al. (1987) reported that survival of wild male pheasants was considerably higher than that of pheasants from state or commercial hatcheries. Strickland et al. (1994) summarized information on harvests of pen-reared birds and generally indicated survival rates were low. Stocking pen-reared birds also tends to concentrate hunters in relatively small areas and may create lead shot "hot spots" (Strickland et al. 1994). These authors concluded that stocking was not an appropriate harvest management practice.

The second stocking program involves attempts to establish or augment existing game bird populations and, thus, expand hunting opportunity. Although stocking activities now principally involve ring-necked pheasants, chukars, and quail, early efforts included a variety of species including Reeves pheasants (*Syrmaticus reevesii*), francolins (*Francolinus* spp.), Chilean tinamou (*Nothoprocta perdicaria*), red-legged partridge (*Alectoris rufa*), and others (Korschgen and Chambers 1970, Banks 1981). Initial successes in the late 19th and early 20th centuries with ring-necked pheasants, chukar, and gray partridge encouraged agencies to attempt to establish other non-native game bird species. With few exceptions, most releases of other species were unsuccessful (Banks 1981). Additionally, many of the more recent efforts to augment existing populations failed because of relatively low survival and reproduction (Korschgen and Chambers 1970, Krauss et al. 1987, Prince et al. 1988, Leif 1994, Niewoonder et al. 1998). Prince et al. (1988) suggested that a program to release Sichuan pheasants (*P. c. strauchi*) might enhance existing pheasant populations. However, Niewoonder et al. (1998) reported that survival and reproduction of female Sichuan pheasants was low and concluded that survival of released pheasants in their study could not sustain a wild population.

Shooting Preserves

Suburban sprawl and limited amounts of publicly owned areas with adequate game bird habitat, coupled with declining game bird populations have increased the popularity of shooting preserves. These preserves raise and stock their own birds, usually pheasants but sometimes include quail, chukar, and gray partridge. Depending on the organization, guides and dogs may be provided. Generally, preserves operate either as a club, open to members only, or as a business that charges by the bird and day. In both cases, meals, lodging and other activities including fishing and sporting clays may also be offered. Hunting seasons on preserves are usually much longer than those available to the general public and preserve operators set daily bag limits.

Hunting preserves offer additional hunting opportunity as well as a chance for individuals to train dogs prior to a general season. They often provide habitat used by wild game birds and other wildlife. Although somewhat expensive, hunting preserves appear to fill a need for more hunting areas with a better than average chance at being successful.

A somewhat different approach to the hunting preserve concept occurs in some states and is used by clubs that own little or no land. Instead, they lease hunting rights on privately owned land and stock these areas with domestically reared game birds, usually pheasants. These clubs regulate hunting pressure and monitor take by their members through a reservation and mandatory reporting system. They are also responsible for posting the property and establishing safety zones around buildings and livestock. In at least one case in Connecticut, private lands are "leased" by simply offering free membership in the club to landowners.

MANAGEMENT OF MIGRATORY GAME BIRD HARVESTS
Development of Harvest Strategies

Approaches to harvest management of migratory game birds in North America have been shaped primarily by the recognition that these highly mobile birds routinely cross local, state, provincial, and international borders over the course of their life cycles. Consequently, effective monitoring of populations and harvests, and development of appropriate hunting regulations, depends upon cooperation across multiple levels of government. In contrast to management of most other wildlife in North America, primary regulatory responsibility and authority for migratory game birds lies with federal governments.

Prior to the development of reliable information about populations and harvests, management of hunting regulations was subjective. As monitoring data became more available, the information became incorporated into the regulatory process. In the United States, regulations that were often consistent across the country became more complex, as regional or "flyway"-specific differences in bird distribution and harvest pressure were recognized (Nichols et al. 1995). A general approach emerged in which relatively restrictive regulations were routinely imposed when populations appeared to be declining or at low levels. Regulations for many lightly harvested species (e.g., Wilson's snipe [*Gallinago delicata*]) often remained relatively stable over long periods, whereas waterfowl regulations were subject to much annual variation and increasing use of special regulations (Boyd 1983, Ladd et al. 1989).

As information from monitoring programs was accumulated, population models were developed for use in setting duck hunting regulations (Crissey 1957, Geis et al. 1969, Brown et al. 1976). These models assumed that hunting mortality acted in a completely additive manner to increase overall mortality (Nichols 2000). However, Anderson and Burnham (1976) produced new analyses of the relationships between harvest and survival of mallards (*Anas platyrhynchos*) that supported compensatory hunting mortality. This work was a key turning point in harvest management, because it formally introduced structural uncertainty into the management process (Nichols 2000). Subsequent analyses have provided mixed evidence concerning the effects of hunting mortality on annual survival in ducks (Nichols et al. 1984, Smith and Reynolds 1992), whereas hunting mortality appears to be primarily additive for geese (Rexstad 1992, Hestbeck 1994) and cranes (Tacha et al. 1994).

Following the development of alternative hypotheses about the impacts of hunting on population dynamics, there was a greater focus on addressing partial management control and structural uncertainty in harvest management. However, efforts to understand relationships between regulations, harvests, and population sizes of migratory game birds were hampered because under traditional harvest management approaches these variables tended to covary over time and space. In addition, increasing complexity of regulations at smaller spatial scales, particularly for waterfowl, interfered with attempts to understand relationships between regulations and harvests (Nichols 1991, Nichols et al. 1995). Proposals for formal experiments with hunting regulations to directly address uncertainties about the effects of harvest on populations (Nichols et al. 1984, Anderson et al. 1987, Nichols and Johnson 1989) were largely resisted by managers seeking to maintain traditional hunting opportunities and regulatory approaches. However, the United States and Canada stabilized duck hunting regulations during 1979–85 in an attempt to examine the relationships between hunting regulations and harvests (Brace et al. 1987, Sparrowe and Patterson 1987). Results of monitoring information for mallards during stabilized regulations indicated that while regulations were held steady, harvest varied mainly in response to mallard population size and hunter numbers, but harvest rates remained fairly constant over the period (Trost 1987, Trost et al. 1987).

After the period of stabilized regulations, federal authorities in the United States adopted an approach of "risk-aversive conservatism" toward setting hunting regulations, in which relatively restrictive regulations would be adopted for populations at low levels (U.S. Department of Interior 1988). In addition, a policy of controlled use of special regulations (see Annual Regulations Process, below) was adopted (U.S. Department of Interior 1988), based on the idea that the scale of harvest management should be consistent with the availability of monitoring information and the ability to evaluate the impact of regulations on harvests and populations (Babcock and Sparrowe 1989, Nichols and Johnson 1989). This idea emphasized that partial observability (Box 2) and partial management control impose limits on the scale at which informed management can be used. This led to the conclusion that improved harvest opportunities associated with fine-scale regulations may not justify the increased costs of monitoring and evaluation (Nichols and Johnson 1989, Johnson and Case 2000).

Inventory

Federal mandates to consider the current status of migratory game birds when setting hunting regulations motivated the development of extensive monitoring programs in North America (Martin et al. 1979, Hawkins et al. 1984). These monitoring systems support the annual regulatory process and consist of annual collection of data on abundance, production, distribution, harvest levels, and other population parameters, as well as habitat conditions (Martin et al. 1979, Reynolds 1987, Smith et al. 1989).

A variety of operational surveys are conducted annually to obtain estimates or indices of the size of migratory bird populations. Coo-counts for mourning (*Zenaida macroura*) and white-winged doves (*Z. asiatica*) provide indices of population trends for these species (Dolton 1993, George et al. 1994). Singing-ground surveys are conducted to provide estimates of relative abundance of American woodcock (*Scolopax minor*) throughout much of its primary North American breeding range (Sauer and Bortner 1991). Hunted populations of sandhill cranes (*Grus canadensis*) are monitored through annual counts on spring (Mid-continent Population) and fall (Rocky Mountain Population) staging areas, or on breeding and wintering areas (Pacific Coast Population) (Tacha et al. 1994, Sharp et al. 2002). No specific population surveys are conducted for some other migratory game birds, particularly lightly harvested or secretive species such as

Wilson's snipe and rails (Rallidae). For these species, the North American Breeding Bird Survey (Robbins et al. 1986) provides indices to the distribution and relative abundance of breeding populations.

Population monitoring programs for waterfowl have a longer history and are more extensive than surveys developed for most other migratory game birds in North America (Smith et al. 1989). Since 1955, the U.S. Fish and Wildlife Service and the Canadian Wildlife Service have conducted annual aerial transect surveys, coupled with ground counts in some areas to correct for visibility bias, during May to estimate numbers of ducks in more than 3.6 million km^2 of breeding habitat in the north central United States, western and northern Canada, and Alaska (Reynolds 1987, Smith 1995). Each July, a portion of these transects is surveyed to obtain counts of total duck broods, which provide an index of duck production. Breeding Canada geese (*Branta canadensis*) are also recorded in the continental duck survey area, and additional operational surveys have also been established to track breeding populations of geese that occupy other areas (Trost et al. 1990). Winter (January) surveys of waterfowl have been conducted since the 1930s (Martin et al. 1979). Prior to implementation of breeding ground surveys, the winter survey was intended to provide information on the relative abundance and population trends, as well as the winter distribution, of waterfowl species; cranes and American coots (*Fulica americana*) are also counted during winter surveys. This survey is still the primary population index for duck species that occur outside of the May survey area, and provides population indices used to manage many goose populations in North America. Federal and state personnel in the lower 48 states conduct the survey cooperatively, and methods vary from state to state (Smith et al. 1989). Portions of Mexico are periodically included in winter aerial surveys conducted by the U.S. Fish and Wildlife Service (Saunders and Saunders 1981).

Although variation in habitat conditions is considered an important influence on the status of many migratory game bird populations, few large-scale, operational surveys are conducted to assess the status of habitats. One exception is the annual monitoring of wetland numbers and conditions in northern prairie regions to assess habitat for breeding ducks (Smith et al. 1989). During the aerial waterfowl surveys conducted in May and July, observers record the number of ponds containing water along each transect in southern Canada and the north central United States. In addition, the Canadian Wildlife Service monitors wetland habitat conditions on a sample of survey transects each year in southern Canada (Turner et al. 1987).

Harvest Surveys

In the United States, annual waterfowl harvest estimates are obtained using surveys consisting of 2 components. The Hunter Questionnaire Survey, in operation since 1952, traditionally sampled names and addresses of hunters who purchased federal waterfowl stamps from randomly selected post offices (Martin and Carney 1977, Martin et al. 1979). The Hunter Questionnaire Survey is used to obtain information on hunter activity and number of ducks and geese harvested each year. The Parts Collection Survey involves mailing of special envelopes to a sample of hunters who are asked to mail in wings of ducks and tail feathers of geese they shoot during the hunting season. These parts are identified to species, gender, and age by federal, state, and private biologists during annual "wing bees" conducted after each hunting season, to identify the composition of the annual waterfowl harvest in the United States. Parts collection surveys are also conducted for American woodcock and band-tailed pigeons (*Patagioenas fasciata*) to provide indices to annual recruitment.

The traditional sampling frame used for conducting waterfowl harvest surveys did not include hunters who did not purchase a waterfowl stamp, but hunted migratory game birds other than waterfowl (Tautin et al. 1989). The International Association of Fish and Wildlife Agencies and the U.S. Fish and Wildlife Service began working to address this problem in 1989. In 1991, a new Harvest Information Program (HIP) was initiated to provide a reliable, nation-wide sampling frame of all migratory bird hunters to conduct annual harvest surveys for each migratory game bird species (Elden et al. 2002). Under HIP, each state is required to collect the name, address, and date of birth of each person hunting migratory game birds in that state; ask each hunter a series of screening questions about their hunting success the previous year (for the purpose of improving the precision of estimates from subsequent harvest surveys [Moore et al. 2002]); and provide this information to the U.S. Fish and Wildlife Service each year. HIP became fully operational in 49 states (Hawaii is exempted) in 1998, and the traditional sampling procedure used in the federal waterfowl survey was replaced with the HIP sampling frame beginning with the 2002–03 hunting season. Using the 49 sampling frames and hunter responses to screening questions, the U.S. Fish and Wildlife Service conducts separate annual harvest surveys for (1) waterfowl; (2) mourning doves, white-winged doves, and band-tailed pigeons; (3) American coots, gallinules, rails, and Wilson's snipe; (4) American woodcock; and (5) sandhill cranes.

In Canada, harvest surveys have been conducted since 1967, using purchasers of Migratory Game Bird Hunting permits as the sampling frame (Cooch et al. 1978). As in the United States, the survey has 2 components. The National Harvest Survey involves a mail questionnaire sent to a sample of permit purchasers, who provide data on their hunting activity and harvest of species or groups of migratory game birds. In the Species Composition Survey, a sample of permit purchasers supply wings (ducks and woodcock) and tail feathers (geese) from birds that they harvest for use in identifying the species, gender, and age composition of the annual harvest.

Some estimates from operational surveys are adjusted for crippling loss (birds downed but not retrieved by hunters) to obtain estimates of total harvest (Martin and Carney 1977, Martin et al. 1979). No operational surveys have been developed to estimate magnitude or composition of subsistence harvest in Alaska or Canada, where short-term studies indicate this take can represent a significant portion of total annual mortality for some bird populations (Raveling 1984, Finney 1990). In addition, illegal harvest by recreational hunters is not accounted for in harvest estimates, but is usually assumed to be relatively insignificant (U.S. Department of Interior 1988, but see Gray and Kaminski 1999).

The Role of Banding Studies

Mark–recovery methods (Brownie et al. 1985, Williams et al. 2001) enable managers to obtain important information about animal populations. To use these methods, individually numbered leg bands are placed on migratory game birds, usually just prior to the hunting season, and hunters are relied upon to report the band number, date, and location of harvest of banded birds they recover. Banding information is used to identify the distribution of harvest and harvest areas associated with different breeding areas, to estimate harvest rates and relative vulnerabilities to harvest of different gender and age cohorts, and to estimate age- and gender-specific survival rates (Smith et al. 1989).

Banding has been particularly important in the management of waterfowl populations and their harvests. An operational duck-banding program has been in place in Canada and the United States for over 5 decades (Smith et al. 1989). Information from banding has been increasingly incorporated into harvest management, particularly for mallards. Large-scale banding programs also provided much of the information used to manage mourning doves in the United States (Dunks et al. 1982, Tomlinson et al. 1988).

Developing Regulations

Governmental Roles in Regulating Hunting

Primary federal authority and responsibility for migratory birds was established after signing of the Convention for the Protection of Migratory Birds by representatives from the United States and Great Britain (for Canada) in 1916. The Migratory Bird Treaty Act of 1918 implemented the convention in the United States (U.S. Department of Interior 1988). This Act was later amended to incorporate similar treaties with Mexico (1936), Japan (1972), and Russia (1976). In North America, compliance with these treaties is the responsibility of the Minister of Environment in Canada, Secretary of the Interior in the United States, and Director General de Flora y Fauna Silvestre in Mexico.

The migratory bird conventions between the United States and Canada, and the United States and Mexico define migratory game birds as those species belonging to the following families: Anatidae (ducks, geese, and swans), Rallidae (rails, gallinules, and coots), Gruidae (cranes), Charadriidae (plovers and lapwings), Haematopodidae (oystercatchers), Recurvirostridae (stilts and avocets), Scolopacidae (sandpipers, phalaropes, and allies), and Columbidae (pigeons and doves) (U.S. Department of Interior 1988). The treaties allow take of migratory birds only between 1 September and 10 March each year, and constrain hunting to seasons not exceeding 3½ months in any one region. The treaty between the United States and Canada was amended in 1995 to allow for subsistence take of birds, including some species not originally designated as game birds, in Alaska and Canada outside normal hunting seasons; the amended treaty was formally implemented in the United States in 1999.

Under the Migratory Bird Treaty Act, the Secretary of the Interior authorizes when hunting and other "take" of migratory game birds is permitted, and adoption of regulations for this purpose, or imposes closed seasons if hunting

Fig. 1. Waterfowl flyways and boundaries of the 4 waterfowl Flyway Councils in the United States.

is incompatible with population status. These regulations must be based on the status and distribution of migratory game birds and must be updated annually. This responsibility has been delegated to the U.S. Fish and Wildlife Service of the Department of the Interior.

Information from monitoring programs about bird distribution and migration pathways and increased state involvement in migratory game bird management efforts led in 1947 to the division of the United States into 4 administrative Flyway Councils (Fig. 1) for establishing annual hunting regulations (Hawkins et al. 1984). Through these Councils, representatives from state and federal agencies in the United States, as well as from Canada and Mexico, have major roles in coordinating management activities and developing annual hunting regulations for migratory game birds (U.S. Department of Interior 1988).

Annual Regulations Process

Extensive and elaborate processes have been developed for setting regulations for migratory game birds to allow involvement by multiple levels of government, follow legal requirements for consultation with the public, and use of annually updated monitoring information (Blohm 1989). In the United States, federal regulations are considered either "basic" or "annual" (U.S. Department of Interior 1988). Basic regulations generally remain the same from year to year, and include constraints such as methods of take and ammunition types that can be used in hunting. Basic regulations are generally tied to safety issues and general views about ethical hunting practices.

Annual regulations are subject to more frequent change and are usually tied more closely to the current status of hunted populations. Annual regulations are further divided into either "framework" or "special" regulations. Framework regulations are the main tools used to adjust harvest levels at flyway or continental scales, and include framework dates (the earliest opening and latest closing dates), season length, and bag limits (U.S. Department of Interior 1988). Special regulations modify framework regulations that are intended to influence harvest or hunter opportunity at finer spatial scales or for individual species. Examples include season splits (dividing the total hunting season length in a state into 2 or 3 nonconsecutive segments), zoning (delineating a state into separate areas in which regulations can be set independently), area closures

(reducing overall harvest of a species by prohibiting hunting in major concentration areas), special seasons (allowing take of particular species outside the regular season), and bonus birds (birds of lightly harvested species added to the regular daily bag limit) (U.S. Department of Interior 1988, Ladd et al. 1989, Nichols 1991). Special regulations usually are not changed annually, but have been controversial because they add complexity to the regulatory process. They also are difficult to evaluate because they are usually implemented at spatial scales too fine for existing monitoring programs to track.

The regulatory process in the United States involves a series of meetings and consultations beginning in January and ending in late September each year (Box 8). The director of the U.S. Fish and Wildlife Service appoints a Migratory Bird Regulations Committee, which is responsible for recommendations on regulations. This committee meets in January to review current regulations and identify important issues. Each of the 4 flyway Councils meet in late March and again in July to formulate recommendations for regulations. The Migratory Bird Regulations Committee meets in June to recommend regulations for "early" seasons, which begin in September and include most "webless" (non-waterfowl) species, and again in late July or early August to develop recommendations for

---

Box 8. **Schedule for the annual process of setting migratory game bird hunting regulations in the United States, and associated population and harvest monitoring programs.**

Regulations process	Month	Monitoring
U.S. Fish and Wildlife Service Regulations	Jan	Mid-winter waterfowl and crane surveys
Committee (SRC) meets to identify issues	Feb	Parts Collection Survey wing bees
Flyway Councils develop recommendations	Mar	Hunter Questionnaire Surveys; banding analyses for duck harvest/survival rates
	Apr	
	May	Breeding waterfowl and habitat, dove coo-count, and woodcock singing-ground surveys
SRC meets to recommend "early" season regulations	Jun	Harvest survey results available
Flyway Councils develop recommendations	Jul	Waterfowl production surveys
SRC recommend "late" season regulations	Aug	Pre-season duck banding
"Early" hunting seasons begin	Sep	Fall surveys for sandhill cranes, greater white-fronted geese (*Anser albifrons*)
"Late" hunting seasons begin	Oct	

"late" season regulations, which begin near 1 October and include most waterfowl. Representatives from each flyway Council participate in these deliberations. Throughout this series of meetings, results of population and harvest monitoring programs are reviewed as they become available to help clarify the decision-making process. Early season recommendations are published for public comment in July so that final federal guidelines and state regulations can be selected before 1 September. Final federal frameworks for late seasons are published in mid-September, following a public comment period, and are adopted as law by the end of September.

Final regulations enacted by states may be the same or more restrictive but not more liberal than applicable federal regulation frameworks. Within each flyway, states generally attempt to design hunting seasons that coincide with typical patterns of migration chronology. For example, northern states typically begin seasons as early as federal frameworks allow, whereas southern states attempt to provide hunting opportunity as late as possible.

The annual process for developing migratory game bird regulations in Canada requires that final proposals for any changes be made by early March (Canadian Wildlife Service Waterfowl Committee 2002). Thus, results from annual breeding population, production, and breeding habitat surveys for the current year are not available. The Canadian Wildlife Service of Environment Canada reviews hunting regulations and recent trend data for game bird populations annually, with comments from the provinces, territories, and other stakeholders. During November and December, Canadian Wildlife Service personnel review biological information and develop recommendations for hunting regulations for the following year. In January, the Canadian Wildlife Service issues proposed regulations and solicits public comments. After this consultation period, final regulation proposals are submitted to Parliament, and in June final hunting regulations, adjusted if necessary to account for public comment, are passed into law.

Adaptive Harvest Management

In 1995, the U.S. Fish and Wildlife Service, in cooperation with the 4 flyway Councils, implemented an adaptive harvest management approach for setting duck hunting regulations in the United States (Box 9). In this approach, key sources of uncertainty are explicitly incorporated into the modeling and decision-making processes used to select regulations. Thus, management can be used as a tool to help reduce uncertainty about the managed system (Walters 1986, Lee 1993, Lancia et al. 1996).

The adaptive harvest management process is currently used in setting regulations for 2 populations of mallards. Mid-continent mallards are defined as those mallards breeding in the traditional breeding survey area and the states of Minnesota, Wisconsin, and Michigan; these mallards are harvested primarily in the Mississippi, Central, and Pacific flyways. Eastern mallards breed in Ontario, Quebec, and the northeastern United States and are harvested primarily in the Atlantic Flyway. For each of these populations, sets of alternative population models have been developed that describe competing hypotheses about the effects of harvest on annual survival (i.e., additive vs. compensatory mortality) and the effect of mallard abundance on reproductive rate (i.e., density-dependent reproductive success). Alternative "packages" of framework regulations have been developed for each flyway, with expected mallard harvest rates associated with each pack-

---

Box 9. Features of adaptive harvest management for mallard populations in the United States.

Key components of adaptive harvest management (Johnson et al. 1993, Williams and Johnson 1995, Johnson 2001) include:

1) a set of alternative models describing population responses to harvest and uncontrolled environmental variation;
2) a measure of reliability (probability or "weight") for each model;
3) a limited set of regulatory alternatives (season lengths, bag limits, and framework dates) that differ in their expected harvest rates; and
4) an objective function, or mathematical description of the objective(s) of harvest management.

These components are used in a stochastic optimization procedure to derive an optimal harvest policy, which is used to identify the appropriate regulatory alternative for population levels and probabilities associated with the alternative population models (Johnson et al. 1997). The setting of annual hunting regulations then involves a 4-step process:

1) each year, the optimal regulatory alternative is identified based on duck breeding populations and resource conditions, and on current model weights;
2) once the regulatory decision is made, model-specific predictions for subsequent breeding population size are calculated;
3) when monitoring data are available, model weights are updated based on how well the population size predicted by each alternative model agree with the observed population size; and
4) the new model weights are used to start a new iteration of the process.

Over time, this iterative process of updating model weights and optimizing regulatory choices should identify which model is the best predictor of changes in population size.

age. The harvest management objective for both populations is to maximize cumulative harvest over the long term. For mid-continent mallards, this objective is constrained to avoid regulations that could be expected to result in subsequent population sizes below an established objective.

Approaches such as that used in adaptive harvest management force managers to specify and reach consensus on harvest management objectives and formally acknowledge fundamental disagreements about the influence of different management actions on achieving those objectives. This approach also provides a process for objectively making decisions about regulations in the face of these disagreements (Johnson and Williams 1999, Humburg et al. 2000, Johnson and Case 2000). Although adaptive harvest management is focused on optimal management performance, the approach also allows for learning about the underlying systems involved in and affected by harvest management (Johnson et al. 2002).

Harvest Management of Overabundant Species

A primary goal of harvest management for migratory game birds in North America continues to be prevention of overharvests that result in significant population declines. Within this constraint, hunting has often been used to reduce or control the density of birds on local scales. However, in recent decades several continental populations of geese in North America have grown rapidly (Ankney 1996). In this case, the intent of harvest management is the large-scale reduction of populations to sustainable levels, and to address environmental and economic damage caused by these overabundant birds. Articles of the 1999 amended Migratory Bird Treaty between the United States and Canada address this situation by allowing these governments to "provide for and protect habitat necessary for the conservation of migratory birds" and to "take appropriate measures to preserve and enhance the environment of migratory birds." The amended treaty also authorizes "permitting the take of migratory birds that, under extraordinary conditions, become seriously injurious to agriculture or other interests."

During the last half of the twentieth century, some populations of light geese (snow geese [*Chen caerulescens*] and Ross' geese [*C. rossi*]) in North America grew rapidly and are now causing widespread habitat damage on their arctic and subarctic breeding areas (Batt 1997). In the United States, managers first attempted to reduce this population growth by increasing bag limits and extending the hunting season length for light geese to 107 days, the maximum allowed by the Migratory Bird Treaty Act. However, due to continued increases in light goose numbers and low hunter success, the harvest rate on light geese actually declined. In 1999, the U.S. Fish and Wildlife Service authorized new methods of take for light geese (electronic calls and unplugged shotguns) and established a conservation order that permitted take outside the dates established for hunting seasons by the Migratory Bird Treaty Act. Similar regulatory approaches are being used in Canada. The purpose of these efforts is to reduce light goose populations to sustainable levels and stop the spread of habitat deterioration. If current regulatory approaches are not effective, more aggressive population reduction efforts may be warranted (Batt 1997, U.S. Department of Interior 2001).

Similarly, in recent years populations of Canada geese which nest and reside predominantly in the United States have increased dramatically and conflicts with people, including personal and public property damage, are increasing in many areas (Ankney 1996, U.S. Department of Interior 2002). Expanded hunting opportunities and the use of a conservation order for take of resident Canada geese have been proposed to reduce numbers and influence the distribution of these geese throughout their range.

Future Directions

Management of migratory game bird harvests in the United States and Canada has changed dramatically over the past century. Federal governments have primary authority in regulating harvests, but elaborate systems have been developed to encourage suggestions and interactions with state, provincial, and territorial governments, as well as other stakeholders. Extensive monitoring programs have been developed to assess the status of many populations and their harvests. These systems have led to an annual process where managers work cooperatively to review available data and attempt to establish hunting regulations that result in harvest levels consistent with population management objectives.

A major goal of migratory game bird management has been to predict the influence of hunting regulations, and resulting harvests, on the future size of bird populations. Over time, this goal has led to a greater emphasis on the use of objective biological information in making management decisions. More recently, there has been explicit recognition that managers will need to contend with uncertainties about the status of bird populations and the consequences of harvest management actions. Adaptive management approaches can be used to explicitly account for (and work to reduce) these uncertainties, while trying to achieve management objectives. It seems likely that the pursuit of improved understanding of the impacts of harvest on migratory game bird populations will continue.

Measures of success in harvest management include greater agreement among managers and stakeholders on harvest management goals, and an improved understanding of the effectiveness and limitations of different management actions in achieving these goals. As approaches toward harvest management of migratory game birds continue to evolve in North America (Nichols 2000), we expect that future developments will include:

1) greater focus on and resolution of the priorities and specific objectives (both biological and sociological) of harvest management;
2) continued efforts to expand and refine the accuracy and precision of monitoring programs for priority species and populations (with debates over the spatial, temporal, and ecological scale of harvest management objectives helping drive the scale of monitoring efforts);
3) increased use of mathematical models to objectively drive harvest management decision-making processes (in relation to explicit, agreed-upon objectives);
4) a reduction in the number of regulatory alternatives available for different groups of migratory game birds, with large differences in expected harvests or harvest

rates among the alternatives; and

5) increased emphasis on reducing uncertainty about important biological mechanisms that drive population dynamics, and the influence of harvest on these mechanisms, for key harvested populations.

Meeting these challenges will require greater commitments of resources, communication, and cooperation among managers at all governmental levels. However, the long history of migratory bird management in North America has helped set the stage for success in these efforts.

MANAGEMENT OF BIG GAME HARVESTS
Development of Harvest Strategies

A wide variety of hunting regulations exist for big game species (Table 4). States tend to open hunting seasons that are not limited in participation by permits or other means on the same dates across the state. This is intended to disperse hunters, improve the quality of the hunt, and spread harvest across a broad area. Seasons that are open during the breeding season and a few weeks earlier tend to increase harvest of adult males that are more vulnerable at this time. Late October and later hunting seasons vary in harvest levels depending upon weather and snow conditions. The presence of snow in northern and mountainous areas enhances harvest. Long seasons that may experience different weather patterns are more likely to have high harvest and high hunter satisfaction than shorter seasons. Weekday openings may reduce the number of hunters on opening day compared to weekend openings, but may not decrease harvest. Either-gender seasons and permits for females tend to increase harvests of younger males and are used to manage populations at certain levels. Male-only seasons provide opportunities for more hunters to participate without affecting population levels. Antler and horn size restrictions allow harvest of specific age groups, but may or may not improve survival of males, depending upon the specific restriction and intensity of harvest. Muzzle-loader and archery seasons are intended to increase participation and opportunity and are often held before or after seasons where modern firearms are legal. If primitive weapon seasons are the only seasons allowed, reduced opportunity and participation may occur. Also, wounding loss with primitive weapons may be sufficiently high to warrant consideration.

Exploitation theory relevant to big game is based on principles related to the carrying capacity of the habitat to produce a certain density of animals at steady state (Box 10), the resource-based carrying capacity (McCullough 1979). Assumptions in using this model are that the stock is more or less self-contained, it had attained a steady state at carrying capacity, there were no significant trends in carrying capacity, and implied density dependence and time lags in response by the stock to exploitation will not cause fluctuations of large amplitude (Holt and Talbot 1978). These assumptions are routinely violated in nature. Populations are seldom self-contained and immigration and emigration should be expected to occur. Exceptions are isolated, small, fragmented populations. Fryxell et al. (1991) reported time lags in growth and recruitment rates to changes in density of a population of white-tailed deer in Ontario that caused large oscillations in numbers. In many regions, resource-based carrying capacity will vary extensively as precipitation patterns affect forage production. In practice, resource-based carrying capacity is rarely measured.

Caughley (1985) provided a partial compensation model indicating populations harvested below some threshold are resistant to change from harvesting. Above that threshold, a population will be extinguished. Below that threshold, an exploited population will decline to some level below carry capacity. Maximum sustained yield occurs at some level at about one-half resource-based carrying capacity. The model is a useful means to consider population exploitation and affords opportunities to consider and evaluate the inevitable violations of the assumptions and their effects on predicted patterns.

Inventory

Inventory generally includes delineation of management units or areas and assessment of populations within these areas (Strickland et al. 1994). Management units may be based on terrain, political boundaries or some combination of the 2 factors. These units should be sufficiently large to support a viable population of the species or group of species of interest, be easily recognizable by

Table 4. Components of hunting regulations for big game species and expected effects (modified from Strickland et al. 1994).

Regulation	Characteristics
Unlimited entry "general season"	Maximizes participation, reduces success, control of harvest is low
Limited entry "permit" seasons	Restricts participation, increases success, maximizes control of harvest
Common opening date	Disperses hunters across more area
September season	Rutting males more vulnerable, nonrutting species less vulnerable
Firearms season in October	Deer in rut more vulnerable, animals more vulnerable if concentrated on winter ranges
Long season	Allows more opportunity for harvest especially if weather conditions are favorable
Short season	Concentrates harvest and hunters, reduces differential vulnerability of gender/age in harvest
Weekend openings	More hunters participate on opening day
Weekday openings	May spread participation, decrease vulnerability
Either gender seasons	Increases harvest of younger males, encourages harvest of some females
Male only	Reduces survival of males, allows populations to respond to limiting factors other than hunting.
Antler/horn restrictions	Hunter numbers may decline, reduces survival of targeted males, may increase illegal kill
Legal firearm or bow	Maximizes opportunity
Primitive weapons	Reduces opportunity and participation
Archery	Lowest opportunity, may increase wounding loss

Box 10. Principles involved in behavior of exploited populations (Silliman and Gutsell 1958, Caughley 1976).

1. Any exploitation of an animal population reduces its abundance.
2. Below a certain exploitation level, populations may be resilient and increase their survival and/or production rates and growth rates to compensate for the individuals removed.
3. When populations are regulated through density-dependent processes, exploitation rates up to some level will tend to increase productivity and reduce natural mortality of the remaining individuals.
4. Exploitation rates above the maximum sustained yield level will reach a point at which extinction will occur if continued.
5. Age composition and the number of animals remaining after exploitation are key factors in the dynamics of exploited animal populations.
6. If a population is stable in numbers, it must be reduced below that density to generate a harvestable surplus.
7. For each density to which a population is reduced, there is an appropriate sustained yield.
8. For each sustained yield, there are 2 density levels from which it can be harvested.
9. The maximum sustained yield may be harvested at only one density, about one-half of resource-based carrying capacity (McCullough 1979).

---

hunters, and allow for long-term collection of population data. Strickland et al. (1994) and Stalling et al. (2002) provided a detailed discussion of management units for big game.

Agencies normally track big game populations within management units. Monitoring techniques are diverse. In western states, helicopter surveys are often used to provide ungulate population estimates, as well as data on age and gender. For many years, Oregon used winter counts from fixed-wing aircraft and summer classification surveys (from ground and air) to monitor pronghorn (*Antilocapra americana*) populations. However, the variability and reliability of these data were difficult to assess because of a lack of sampling design and replicate counts (Whittaker et al. 2003). Because of these problems, many agencies have begun using more rigorous techniques for monitoring big game populations including models that estimate observation rates (Unsworth et al. 1990, Samuel et al. 1992) and line transects (White et al. 1989, Whittaker et al. 2003).

Normally surveys are conducted during winter or early spring. The intensity of survey efforts may be influenced by funding and personnel availability. In some cases, inventory efforts are influenced by habitat. For example, Idaho biologists routinely monitor elk, mule deer, and moose (*Alces alces*) populations with aerial surveys. However, less effort is devoted to white-tailed deer because the species normally inhabits heavy cover and animals are difficult to detect using normal aerial survey techniques. States with relatively few species of big game may use a variety of techniques to assess their big game populations (Strickland et al. 1994).

Regardless of an agency's inventory efforts, some individuals or organizations may strongly disagree with inventory data. Freddy et al. (2004) reported that a sportsman's group in Colorado refused to accept survey results for mule deer even though the group was involved in the design, analysis, and interpretation of the inventory. They concluded that use of good science to assess mule deer populations did not change entrenched opinions of individuals who distrusted agency programs.

Harvest Surveys

Methods used to obtain data on big game harvest vary within and among states. Harvest data typically include information on species, gender, and age of the animal, number of days spent hunting, harvest unit or area, date of kill, type of weapon (rifle, archery or muzzleloader), and type of hunt (general, limited entry, depredation, etc.). Additional data will often be collected on size of antlers or horns or size of animal. This information may be collected during field checks of hunters, check stations, mandatory checks at specific locations (e.g., a local wildlife agency office), telephone surveys, or report cards. Check stations are used in many states to obtain gender and age information from given management units.

In some cases, the information is supplied on a voluntary basis. In others, the wildlife agency requires mandatory checks of harvested animals. Mandatory check of the animal is often required for trophy species including mountain sheep (*Ovis canadensis*), mountain goats (*Oreamnos americanus*), and moose. This allows agencies a complete count of the harvest for these species. For other big game species, harvest may be estimated through telephone surveys or hunter report cards (Stalling et al. 2002). Strickland et al. (1994) reported 3 forms of bias in mail (report card) surveys: 1) individuals who do not hunt are less likely to respond than those who do, 2) unsuccessful hunters are less apt to respond than those that are successful, and 3) respondents may inflate their success to enhance their self-image or prestige. Largely for these reasons, random phone surveys are now frequently used to assess harvest (Stalling et al. 2002).

Developing Regulations

Deer

White-tailed deer are the most commonly hunted big game species in the United States. The approach to managing populations has evolved substantially in the past decade as populations have expanded and habitat has been modified. Current management of white-tailed deer may be classified into 3 categories: (1) attempts to reduce populations in areas where hunting is not allowed or severely restricted, (2) attempts to increase survival of bucks and reduce the number of does, and (3) attempts to maximize recreational opportunity consistent with the needs of the resource and societal demands. Most states and provinces allow general, unlimited entry hunting during seasons of varying lengths. Many offer special hunts in areas where agricultural damage or other circumstances require more controlled types of hunting. The tradition of preference for harvesting bucks makes population management through harvest difficult, and often results in reducing survival of adult males to low levels. Traditions in hunting vary by region, and in southeastern states, use of dogs is common while use of dogs is prohibited in northern and western states. Hunting during the rut when mature bucks are most vulnerable to the gun is preferred in many states but avoided in others.

In states with extensive private land holdings by timber companies, livestock producers, and others, an intensive form of deer harvest management may be practiced because access, hunter numbers, and harvest can be regulated. In states where private landholdings are not extensive or hunting traditions preclude intensive control of the harvest, or where public lands are extensive, management will not be as intensively regulated. Like other ungulates, white-tailed deer have the capability of modifying their habitats, especially when at high densities. This capability means that deer grazing and browsing may also affect plants and associated fauna. This is a major reason for management strategies that limit populations to levels that do not affect habitat characteristics.

Quality Deer Management.—Programs intended to reduce the size of deer populations and to increase size and numbers of adult bucks occur in many states. These "Quality Deer Management" programs may serve several objectives and may include management for large-antlered bucks, population reduction, or stabilization of herd numbers. They are most applicable to large private land ownerships where hunter numbers and deer harvests can be directed at accomplishing program objectives. Kroll (1991) and Miller and Marchinton (1995) provide useful guidelines and recommendations for implementation of quality deer management programs. Woods et al. (1996) reported that participants are actively involved in management, have an ability to increase and express their knowledge of deer, and tend to be supportive of these programs. Hunter conduct tends to improve under quality deer management programs, which may have the benefit of improving the image of hunters among those who do not hunt.

The procedure used in Georgia to decide the number and kind of deer to be harvested through quality deer management is recommended by the hunters who participate. This procedure involves calculating the:

1. average beam length of yearling bucks,
2. the percentage of yearling bucks in the harvest of all bucks,
3. the total buck harvest per 1.6 km², and then by
4. comparing these values to information provided in established tables, and then by
5. setting the doe harvest goal by multiplying total buck harvest by a factor provided in the established table.

Elk

Elk hunting is a sport with extensive traditions, including hunting during the rut for bugling bulls. These traditions are strongly institutionalized in hunting culture, and exert a pervasive influence on how elk are managed. For this fundamental reason, reductions in adult bull populations and increased densities of populations predominantly comprised of females are prevalent in many of today's elk populations. Managers have been forced to compromise in efforts to balance the high demand for adult bulls, and the demand for high elk populations, with the conservation needs of populations and habitats. However, there is extensive uncertainty concerning the effects of different harvest management strategies. The quality deer management programs are a prime example of how hunting traditions have to be directly confronted with information and results if change is to be achieved and accepted. These programs also demonstrate that when positive results occur, namely that more mature bucks are produced with lower population densities, hunters will accept the program.

Elk harvest management involves balancing maximum hunting opportunity with numbers taken. Numerous approaches to this issue have been tried, including limiting harvest to spike bulls only, restricting take to brow-tined bulls, to bulls with fewer than 6 points per antler, to numbers of bulls up to a limit after which the season is closed, and to limited entry hunts that restrict hunter participation. Hunting season length and type of weapons allowed also influence the harvest. Biederbeck et al. (2001) reviewed the different seasons and evaluations that are available. The problem involves how many hunters participate and their success. In areas with good access and/or open cover, sheer number of hunters will overwhelm efforts to restrict harvest and limited entry hunting is the only option. Biederbeck et al. (2001) suggest that efforts to improve bull survival in the Oregon Coast Range will require more intensive regulation of take than minimum point antler regulations, implying that some combination of limited entry and reduced access will have to be implemented.

Long term declines in calf:cow ratios observed in northeastern Oregon were thought to be associated with concomitant declines in bull survival (Noyes et al. 1996). Investigations of captive elk demonstrated that when yearling bulls did most of the breeding, conception dates were delayed. In addition, pregnancy rates increased from 89 to 97% of cows when bulls >5 years old were the principal sires. Populations with high calf:cow ratios and high proportions of mature bulls were hunted under limited entry regulations, while populations with lower calf:cow ratios and lower proportions of mature bulls were hunted with unlimited entry regulations for males and light or no hunting of cows and calves.

In contrast, analysis of 465 elk surveys in 39 units from 1960 to 1998 in Colorado did not find a correlation between low sex ratios and calf:cow ratios (White et al. 2001). Investigators concluded that increases in sex ratios would not be an efficient method for increasing productivity in elk populations. Hamlin and Ross (2002) reported no correlation between low sex ratios and calf production/survival in a southwestern Montana elk population as well. These studies included few samples where sex ratios were severely skewed, i.e., <5 bulls:100 cows.

A working hypothesis concerning the circumstances under which severely skewed sex ratios could affect calf production and survival involves a combination of high population density, severe weather conditions, and yearling bulls doing most of the breeding. If severe winter or prolonged summer drought affects growth of calves, as yearlings these individuals may not become sexually mature in time for the initial rut. While the second rut of the year may be successful, calving would occur later and calf size entering winter would be small. If another severe winter follows, reduced survival and delayed sexual maturity of the subsequent calf crop may result. Under these conditions, calf survival may decline abruptly, and numbers of cows that are bred may also be reduced. Studies of red deer demonstrate the relationship between successful breeding by yearling males and nutritional levels during early development (Clutton-Brock et al. 1987). Thus, populations that exist at high densities and contain large numbers of females and few bulls are most likely to exhibit low calf production and survival.

Access Restrictions For Managing Elk Harvest.— Gratson and Whitman (2000a) reported that >60% of elk hunters they surveyed in central Idaho felt road closure was at least a "tolerable" management tool, suggesting that hunters are aware of the problem and attempts to resolve it. The case history nature of this work was recognized and the researchers recommended their results would serve best within an adaptive management approach wherein experimental road closures could be evaluated. The results of road closure investigations in central Idaho were reductions in number of elk hunters, increases in hunter success, and higher elk densities in managed access areas without roads when compared to areas with roads (Gratson and Whitman 2000b). The differences between areas where access was managed, or where roads were closed, and areas without roads were not great when compared with managed areas and areas with open roads. Bjornn and Dalke (1975) reported that approximately 75% of Idaho hunters they surveyed felt that no more roads were needed for big game hunting in Idaho. These investigations suggest that hunters are amenable to road closures and have been aware of the problem for over 2 decades.

Virtually all states have long hunting seasons in at least some management units through the fall. Thus, some elk in the most accessible areas are disturbed sufficiently to cause significant movement to areas where they are less disturbed. These elk most likely move to secure areas upon first being disturbed, a one-time movement each fall. These secure areas are probably known to individual elk in the population and the timing and location of the shift into them is affected by when the animals are first disturbed. While this movement may entail considerable expenditure of energy, once the animals have accomplished it, they are likely to regain lost energy by minimizing movement and engaging in considerable feeding at crepuscular hours and at night. In many areas, hunting seasons are not long, and opportunities for elk to recover energy reserves or at least stabilize weight losses are high. However, early and late-season archery hunts may allow disturbance to persist for longer periods of time. The effect of disturbance from hunting on subsequent production/survival has not been demonstrated but the assumption that archery hunts do not cause sufficient disturbance to affect elk behavior may no longer be tenable.

Bear

Black bear (*Ursus americanus*) harvests are typically managed to emphasize male harvest and reduce the number of females harvested. Harvests should be monitored using a variety of population attributes, including gender and age composition of the harvest, population size and trend, hunter success, forage conditions, and amount of property damage and associated complaints. Gender and age composition of the harvest and hunting success may not be reliable indicators of population status by themselves because of differential vulnerability by gender and age (Pelton 2000).

Females with cubs are commonly protected from hunter harvest. This suggests that over 50% of adult females are not subject to hunting if cubs are produced every 2 years, sows are without cubs for one year only in their reproductive cycle, and sexual maturity occurs at 2–5 years depending upon region. Areas where bears are protected from harvest serve as reservoirs for populations and can maintain harvests of individuals that disperse into hunted areas (Miller 1990, Garshelis 1993). Also, males are likely to be harvested in greater proportions in early spring seasons because they tend to emerge from dens earlier than females.

Controversy over use of dogs and bait has provided information on the effects of these methods on harvest, as well as ethical considerations involving their use. Litvaitis and Kane (1994) reported that hunters using bait and dogs tended to harvest higher proportions of males than did hunters who used still hunting and stalking techniques. Hunters who use dogs and bait may be more selective of the bears they harvest than still hunters and stalkers, who will not often see the bear they harvest as close, nor for as long a time.

Other Big Game Species

Populations of big game species that are small, occur in open habitats, highly vulnerable, or occur in limited habitat, are harvested using limited entry hunts where permits are allocated by lottery. Limited entry hunting provides the ultimate means of regulating harvest because numbers, gender and ages of animals, and number of hunters and their distribution can be controlled. A complete enumeration of the harvest and examination of all animals taken can be obtained. Hunters can be distributed in time and space to maximize and distribute hunting opportunity and quality of the experience. This intensive level of management enables managers to obtain virtually complete and accurate information on harvest characteristics.

Mountain sheep harvest management exemplifies the highly regulated types of hunting that occur. In British Columbia, guide-outfitter quotas for Stone sheep (*Ovis dalli stonei*) specify not only numbers but also age classes of sheep that influence subsequent harvests. When rams harvested remain over 9 years of age, no penalties in quotas occur, but if a certain proportion of rams under 9 is reached, then quotas may be decreased until the age level again increases. Wild sheep hunting in most situations involves limited entry hunts that restrict harvests to rams with 3/4 curl, 7/8 curl, or full curl, the most conservative kind of hunting. Bunnell (1978) estimated that harvest of all males of 3/4 curl or greater from a Dall sheep (*O. dalli*) population in the Yukon would remove 55 to 60% of the male population. Harvests of males at full curl would remove 35 to 40% of the male population. Males reach 3/4 curl horns at 4 years of age or older.

Gender of mountain goats is assumed to not be distinguishable by most hunters in the field, so both males and females are harvested. Regulations are typically quite conservative and harvest levels of between 4 and 7% of populations will maintain population levels (Hebert and Turnbull 1977).

Population Responses to Hunting

White-tailed Deer

Density is one of many interacting ecological factors that influences populations. Density-dependent responses to changes in population size through harvest are most likely to occur in white-tailed deer inhabiting high quality habitat. The extent to which density-dependent responses can be assumed or applied in management models and in affecting harvest strategies can vary in time and space. Quality deer management programs illustrate density-dependent responses in weights, antler development, and body sizes when populations are reduced. In Georgia, sufficient information on yearling buck antler beam length and field dressed weights has been obtained to demonstrate the ranges that can be expected (Georgia Department of Natural Resources, http://georgiawildlife.dnr.state.ga.us) when doe populations are reduced below the resource-based carrying capacity of the habitat. Weights of yearling bucks may range from less than 27 to over 45 kg, and antler lengths may range from >5 to >28 cm, with variation between geographic regions. Recruitment rates in Georgia range from 0.3 to 1.4 fawns per doe, depending upon density and geographic region.

Dusek et al. (1989) reported that density-dependent responses in an eastern Montana white-tailed deer population were primarily evidenced in the recruitment of fawns to autumn and varied inversely with density of adult females. This was related to social interactions among females that relegated younger females to lower quality habitats during summer, with corresponding lower recruitment. Both McCullough (1979) and Dusek et al. (1989) concluded that density-related phenomena were more important in regulating recruitment rate than environmental stochasticity within the range of conditions associated with their studies. However, when severe winters, drought, disease, or hurricanes reduce populations, these conditions may result in density-independent responses (Ransom 1967), and hunting may become additive.

Mule Deer

McCullough (1979) considered deer recruitment to have strong density-dependent effects, with high recruitment rates at low population densities that progressively decline as density increases. McCullough (1990) demonstrated the relationship with a California black-tailed deer (*Odocoileus hemionus hemionus*) population where increased doe kills resulted in subsequent increases in numbers of bucks. The Hopland Field Station black-tailed deer population sustained harvests of 20.5–21.5% of pre-harvest numbers over a 7-year period that included an extended drought. At lower population levels, males increased in the harvest, and more yearlings had branched antlers, but no changes in body mass or antler size were noted (McCullough 2001). He reported this contrasted with white-tailed deer population changes where the largest bucks with the best antlers were present when populations were at low densities. Thus, highest yield and high trophy quality were not correlated in black-tailed deer

populations. Bartmann et al. (1992) reported that reductions in mule deer populations resulted in increased survival of fawns, but not increased productivity.

While populations of white-tailed deer commonly show density-related responses in production, growth, and survival, mule deer may not always respond to changes in density. Connolly (1981) concluded that on the National Bison Range, Montana, there were instances of high mortality from other causes when hunting mortality was also high, suggesting that different mortality factors were not compensatory. Approximately 24% of the population was harvested over a 7-year period without causing a decline in breeding stock. Mackie et al. (1998) concluded that reducing mule deer population density with harvest might not stimulate higher rates of fawn recruitment in some Montana populations, because drought and severe winters may intervene. Also, reductions in population size through female harvest may not be sufficient to enable compensatory responses of a magnitude that can be detected if climatic factors and predation are involved. Further, if populations are already well below resource-based carrying capacity, additional female harvest may not stimulate changes in population attributes.

These investigations suggest the need to examine characteristics of individual populations in relation to habitats used and other mortality factors rather than generalizing from investigations elsewhere. Reductions may be compensated by increased production and/or survival, increased body and antler size, or increased numbers of males, depending upon population. If other limiting factors such as predation or severe winters prevail, population reductions may not result in compensations.

Adaptive management tailored to the characteristics of individual mule deer populations occupying different kinds of habitat is being implemented in Montana (Montana Fish, Wildlife and Parks 2001). Adjustments of hunting regulation strategies will be based on monitoring and modeling of these populations. These kinds of programs will eventually provide more insight into the interaction of hunter harvest with other mortality factors affecting mule deer as well as other big game species.

Elk

The issue of bull survival probably is best considered in terms of natural selection. Antlers are a major means by which adult males signify their rank and by which they obtain access to breeding opportunities (Darwin 1871, Leuthold 1977, Clutton-Brock et al. 1982, Lundrigan 1996, Geist 1998). Antler size is correlated with body weight and animal condition, as well as age (Flook 1970, Wolfe 1983, Freddy 1987, McCorquodale et al.1989, Frisina and Douglass 1993, Smith 1997). Flook (1970) and Haigh et al. (1984) reported that greatest body mass, scrotum circumference, and production of spermatozoa occurred at 7 years of age, suggesting that maximum antler development may be reached later than maximum breeding activity. Mitchell (1973) reported that in an unhunted population of red deer, males seldom held hinds (females) until they were 5 years old, suggesting that body weight may also affect fighting ability. The evidence suggests that presence of bulls between 5 and 10 years of age is needed to ensure that selection processes involving antler and body size, and physiological development occur.

The biology of the mature bull is different from younger bulls and females. Breeding bulls expend enormous amounts of energy and undergo over 15% reduction in body mass through the rut (Mitchell et al. 1976). Geist (1986) reported that males acquire numerous antler wounds during the rut, averaging 20–30 wounds. Clutton-Brock et al. (1979) reported that in two-thirds of a sample of 107 fights they recorded, 1 of the 2 stags was holding hinds. In 22 cases when stags not holding hinds initiated a fight, they increased harem size in 17 cases. Stags holding hinds appear more likely to gain fewer hinds and lose more when initiating a fight. Stags that repel challengers seldom gain from fights and may lose hinds. Reproductive success and fighting success was closely related, peaking in animals 7–10 years of age. Skill in fighting involves taking advantage of ground surface, slope, and opponents' behavior including ability to judge an opponent, persistence, and determination. Size of stag is most closely associated with success in fighting and, subsequently, breeding success. Breeding activities for adult males are obviously the major process involving natural selection and consume extensive amounts of energy and risk of injury.

In elk, antlers are retained into early spring and continue to convey access to forage. Bulls tend to occur in groups comprised of adult males, away from cows and calves and younger bulls (Peek and Lovaas 1968, Franklin et al. 1975). The intensity of interactions through winter among bulls that have lost considerable amounts of energy and weight from rutting activities is expected to be low. Nevertheless, Smith (1998) was able to correlate body and antler mass of the adult bull with its development as a calf and subsequent longevity.

Given the effects of lower age structures in males that may result from harvests, a goal of management should be to maintain older breeding adults, especially males, in each population, and particularly in smaller populations. A harvest regime that targets large, old bulls at high rates is likely to appreciably reduce effective population size. Long-term effects on effective population size, as well as changes in life history characteristics can result from excessive harvest of bulls. In the smaller herds that may be effectively isolated (<1 new immigrant per generation, Mills and Allendorf 1996), demographic benefits from a skewed sex ratio could be cancelled by slower population growth due to inbreeding depression.

Post-season evaluations of production and survival are related to harvest management. Calf:cow or age ratios are obtained through aerial surveys along with sex ratios. Age ratios are equivocal indicators of herd productivity and may not reflect population trend (Caughley 1974). A population may exhibit either rapid growth or rapid decline while the age ratio may not change appreciably, because ratios of numbers in each age class are constant (White et al. 2001). Information from an elk population in the Blue Mountains, Washington (Table 5) indicated an age ratio of 27 calves:100 cows represents a stable population, while a ratio of 34:100 represents a rapidly declining population. A statistical difference in these age ratios would likely not be detectable in field data (Czaplewski et al. 1983). The calf:cow ratio reflects some combination of adult female survival, adult female fecundity, and calf survival. Calf survival is typically the most variable of the 3 parameters (Sauer and Boyce 1983; Coughenour and Singer 1996;

Table 5. Effects of changing female elk harvest rate on finite rate of increase (λ), calf:cow ratios, and population size using a Blue Mountains, Oregon, model (Peek et al. 2002). The population starts at 4,399 individuals and was close to stable at a female harvest rate of 0.01 ($\lambda = 0.998$).

Rate	Female harvest at 20 years (λ)	Calf:cow ratio	Population size at 20 years
0.01	0.998	27:100	4,259
0.03	0.996	28:100	3,780
0.05	0.991	31:100	3,263
0.075	0.981	32:100	2,606
0.10	0.967	33:100	1,999
0.15	0.934	34:100	1,071

Gaillard et al. 1998, 2000), so changes in calf survival should have greatest influence on the calf:cow ratio.

More recently, Taper and Gogan (2002) confirmed previously reported relationships between density and calf production/survival (Houston 1982, Merrill and Boyce 1991). When females and calves are harvested, changes in winter ratios will reflect some bias towards calves that typically will be harvested at a lower rate than cows. "It is commonly the case that the first consequences of increasing population density are a rise in juvenile mortality and that effects on fecundity and adult mortality are initially less pronounced" (Clutton-Brock et al. 1982:275).

Sex ratios are at best rough indicators of bull survival and knowledge of male age structure is more useful. However, ratios are used because they can be more readily obtained from direct observation. Frequency distributions of age typically involve direct examination of hunter harvest, a laborious effort, and are fraught with biases attributable to sample size limitations and differential vulnerability of different ages of bulls to hunters. When possible, aerial surveys classifying bulls by antler size may provide a useful approximation of age structure.

Hurley and Sargeant (1991) reported that 2-year-old bulls were more vulnerable to harvest than were yearling bulls, while Unsworth et al. (1993) found no differences in survival rates for yearling and older bulls. Petersburg et al. (2000) reported high mortality of yearling bulls that dispersed from populations in which they were born, mostly attributable to hunting mortality.

For the northern Yellowstone population, age ratios ranged from 4–57 calves:100 cows during 1982–1991 (Coughenour and Singer 1996). Sex ratios ranged from 14 to 26 bulls:100 cows over the same period, with significant differences across different areas of the winter range. Age ratios on the National Elk Refuge ranged from 15 to 45 calves:100 cows during 1927–1985 (Boyce 1989), while sex ratios ranged from 7 to 46 bulls:100 cows over the same period. These data reflect some combination of differential distribution attributable to winter conditions and the actual composition of the population. Flook (1970) reported a sex ratio of 36 bulls:100 cows among 1,596 elk removed from Jasper, Banff, and Waterton Lakes National parks, Canada, between 1957 and 1966. These elk were removed by shooting and trapping without deliberate selection, and, except for the removal, were not hunted.

This information suggests that elk populations have a density-dependent response to reductions in numbers. While low calf survival is often blamed on predation, elk populations have generally been high over the past decade and low calf survival should be expected regardless of proximate causes of mortality or productivity. Managers should focus on reducing elk numbers in large populations through harvest of adult cows. An adaptive management strategy (Lancia et al. 1996) that incorporates hunter involvement, monitoring, and change in harvest strategy is suggested as an approach to addressing this problem.

Sex ratios, while being relatively easy to obtain through aerial surveys, are actually a surrogate estimate for bull survival. Managers should strive to ensure that bulls in the 6 + age category are present in populations. If sex ratios are the most appropriate measure, then post-season ratios of 15 + bulls:100 cows are suggested as appropriate goals.

Effects of Hunting on Elk Behavior.—Concerns over the effects of continuous hunting pressure over long periods on elk production/survival and condition going into the winter are long-standing. Effects of hunting on public lands that causes elk to shift to private lands and cause depredations to crops or become unavailable to hunters are also a major concern. In areas without much public land, increased elk populations interfere with agriculture and intrude into housing developments. There is substantial literature on the effects of human disturbance on elk during all seasons (Joslin and Youmans 1999). While elk in national parks and other areas where they are unhunted become conditioned to the presence of humans and do not appear to show much response, elk that are hunted respond to human activity at all times of the year. Cassirer et al. (1992) reported that cross-country skiers cause elk to move from 4 to 800 m in Yellowstone National Park. Energy expended moving from skiers was approximately 5.5% of the estimated daily energy expenditure of 6,035 kcal for elk in winter, requiring consumption of an additional 295 g/day of forage to compensate for the disturbance. Joslin and Youmans (1999) reviewed investigations showing that distances elk move from snowmobiles in winter are lower than from skiers.

Responses of elk to disturbance during hunting seasons have been evaluated in several areas. Hurley and Sargeant (1991) reported elk moving up to 6.16 km over a 2-day opening weekend in northwestern Montana in forested, mountainous terrain, with different kinds of access. Hamlin and Ross (2002) described long-distance movements entirely out of hunting units in open terrain of southwestern Montana. Washington biologists report examples of archery hunters continually stalking and disturbing elk over a 6-hour period in coastal forests, using a combination of 4-wheel drive trucks, all terrain vehicles, and foot travel. Such extreme examples of disturbance may promote weight loss, alter habitat use, and predispose affected animals to lower condition and perhaps reduced survival and subsequent productivity, especially if subsequent winter conditions are severe.

Increased levels of disturbance may precipitate changes in habitat use and behavior, including nocturnal feeding and use of areas further from roads and in more forested and rough terrain (Morgantini and Hudson 1979, Cassirer et al. 1982, Edge and Marcum 1985, Joslin and Youmans 1999, Strohmeyer and Peek 1996). Joslin and Youmans

(1999) concluded that while there was little information on the effects of off road vehicles, it might be inferred that these vehicles traveling on trails or closed roads are comparable to conventional vehicles using roads. Off road vehicles traveling in areas without roads are likely comparable to conventional vehicles traveling in unrestricted, high road-density situations. Management of access has become a major problem in elk harvest management and restrictions on vehicle access are an important tool in allowing elk to remain in relatively undisturbed areas.

A recent investigation in Colorado (Conner et al. 2001) suggested that opening the archery season a week early (23 Aug) caused elk to move to private lands 10 days earlier than where seasons were opened 2 weeks later (13 Sep). The difference in timing of movement between areas was attributed to topography and migration differences. These researchers reviewed a number of studies showing responses of elk to hunting that include movement away from hunters and heavily hunted areas, increased movement, movement to denser cover, shifts to nocturnal feeding, alteration of migration patterns, and movement to private land or areas where hunting was excluded. Walsh et al. (1991) demonstrated that bulls harassed during rut by hunters do not bugle as often as when they are not harassed. Conner et al. (2001) concluded that managers need to decide whether archery hunters, and by extension, other hunters, affect elk movements and other behaviors sufficiently to alter management schemes. In situations where elk shift to private lands and cause damage, changes in season dates and lengths, as well as hunter participation will have to be considered to address the issues.

In terms of predicted energy expenditures, fall disturbance would have to be persistent and repeated to have an effect. If there is an effect, it is likely to occur during severe, prolonged winters followed by late summer drought, and would be most likely to affect calves. An analysis of the effects of disturbance on elk populations involves an assessment of energy expenditure for each time an elk is disturbed, and the number of times an individual is disturbed. Work by Parker et al. (1984), Freddy et al. (1986), and Cassirer et al. (1992) has been directed at the costs of energy expenditure from disturbance in winter. Cook et al. (1996) examined energy requirements of elk calves in late summer and fall.

Elk in western rainforests are less likely to experience extensive snow cover than elk further east. However, potential values of forage may be considerably depressed in areas of high rainfall, where leaching of nutrients from the rainfall occurs (Laycock and Price 1970). The abilities of elk to sustain protracted disturbance and still recover energy reserves on low quality forage may be low. This should be examined further, but the conservative approach to management would be to minimize the potential for prolonged disturbance during late-season hunting.

Most authorities recommend restrictions of human activity to reduce displacement and energy loss in elk in winter (Parker et al. 1984, Edge and Marcum 1985, Cassirer et al. 1992, Joslin and Youmans 1999). While the possibility of elk becoming habituated to logging activity and skiers exists, elk cannot be expected to habituate to hunters. Hunting in December should be monitored to examine if hunter activity and behavior is at levels that cause elk to alter activity patterns and seek denser cover with less forage. The presence of snow cover is especially critical in compounding the added energy loss, suggesting that restrictions of hunter activity should be flexible and based on conditions at the time of the hunt.

Bear

The percentage of males in black bear harvests typically declines with increasing age; this is attributed to the higher vulnerability of males to hunting (Fraser et al. 1982). Yearling and 2-year-old males that leave the area where they were raised and wander long distances are most vulnerable to hunting (Beecham and Rohlman 1994). When females comprised over 40% of the harvest in Idaho, populations could be expected to decline (Beecham and Rohlman 1994). Noyce and Garshelis (1997) reported that natural food abundance also influenced harvest. Declines in abundance of forage sources caused increases in the percentage of females in the harvest and the mean age of females harvested. A simple index to forage abundance explained most of the variation in hunter success and gender-age composition in the harvest.

Taylor (1994) concluded that for all 3 bear species, the maximum sustainable yield would occur close to the carrying capacity of the habitat, and that evidence of density-related responses to population change is inconclusive. Bears have low reproductive potential, adults tend to survive for long periods, and populations tend to exist at low densities. The recommendation was for managers to assume no increases in reproduction or declines in rates of natural mortality would result from changes in population size.

Other Big Game Species

Mountain sheep are susceptible to diseases and parasites that can be the proximate cause of substantial mortality in addition to hunting. Since density of mountain sheep relative to forage resources is associated with many die-offs, work in Alberta by Jorgenson et al. (1993, 1997) showed that yearly removals of 12–24% of the total ewe population did not affect ewe mortality due to other causes, lamb production by adult ewes, or lamb survival. Approximately 12% of the population could be removed annually if predation was not significant. While number of trophy rams in the population and number harvested by hunters were independent of ewe numbers, it appeared that ewe harvests did cause increases in size of trophy rams. Reductions in ewe numbers may not cause reduced incidence of diseases because population die-offs were not related to population density. Population growth following die-offs appears slow and density-independent, thus, hunting mortality would likely be additive.

Population reductions of mountain goats may not cause production and survival of young to increase (Kuck 1977, Hebert 1978), provided the adult females harvested are those that occupy the most productive habitats or females using less productive habitat are less vulnerable to hunting. Insufficient data are available to explore response of mountain goats to different levels of harvest.

Sustained Yield Management

McCullough (1979) provided the most comprehensive analysis of yield (the number of individuals taken by humans) for white-tailed deer. On the George Reserve, Michigan, which was surrounded by a deer-proof fence

and which had no predators, a post-hunt population could be stabilized at 120 animals by removing approximately 46 deer or 38% of the population. However, with the stochastic variation attributable to different weather, habitat conditions, and other causes of mortality, harvesting the maximum sustained yield would lead to extinction because random variation would eventually result in lower gain and the subsequent harvest would take more than the maximum sustained yield.

In a southeastern Montana white-tailed deer population, Dusek et al. (1989) concluded that harvesting approximately 26% of yearling and older females would maintain numbers, while 58% of antlered deer could be removed with no effect on population trend. Nixon et al. (1991) reported that harvests of 35–40% of female white-tailed deer were needed to stabilize deer numbers in Illinois. However, these conclusions assume that harvest is uniform or proportional to abundance across populations and habitats, which is rarely the case across large areas or hunting units. Efforts to distribute hunters across areas may mean imposing restrictions on where they can hunt, which may not be acceptable.

Harvest strategies directed at sustained yield must consider crippling losses that can be important causes of added mortality during or following deer hunts. Nixon et al (1991) reported that >20% of the legal firearms kill and 38.6% of the legal archery kill may die from crippling losses. Dusek et al. (1989) reported crippling losses equivalent to 24% of the legal harvest, comparable to rates observed by Roseberry et al. (1969) and Stormer et al. (1979). Thus, crippling losses should be included in evaluations of harvest levels.

Future Directions

Current directions in deer management and the importance of increasing adult males in elk populations suggest trends applicable to future management of harvest of other species. Quality deer management programs are practical applications of the adaptive management program envisioned by Walters (1986). These programs provide insights into management of big game in other situations because they use biological information on deer, integrated with the capability of the habitat, and include the stakeholders as integral to the program. Morphological attributes such as dressed carcass weights, antler lengths and number of points in yearling males, femur lengths, and reproductive materials can be obtained from harvested animals to judge the condition of the population. Most habitat management will be integrated with other land uses such as timber management or agriculture, an especially desirable attribute. Goals for antler sizes, age distributions, and productivity can be established that are keyed to the capability of the habitat, and serve as a guide in harvest management. It is important that hunters can see the results of their efforts and participation. These programs can be adapted to public lands for a variety of big game species. At a time when hunting is under more scrutiny than ever, programs that intend to keep populations productive and healthy serve as a justification for hunter harvest.

Survival of males in many big game populations is a major concern and will have to be effectively addressed. While sex ratios are one way to estimate male survival, age structure information is needed. The proportion of adult breeding males in populations will vary and more information is needed, but the presence of 4-year-old white-tailed deer bucks, and 6-year old elk bulls in populations in some proportion appear to be appropriate goals for these species. However, these are approximations and more experience is needed to clarify the best age structure for males, and variation between areas will likely occur.

Future management of big game may require more intensive regulation of the harvest through limited entry programs. While efforts to restrict harvest by limiting access to habitat may provide short-term benefits, many populations that are now hunted with unlimited entry seasons will likely have to be hunted with more restrictions to improve survival of males. Additionally, harvests of females will have to be managed more closely and can be liberalized in many cases to reduce breeding populations to enhance their productivity, or reduce depredations and property damage. Programs for managing suburban deer in eastern states have application for moose, elk, mule deer, and in some instances, other big game species elsewhere. Big game management will become more complex and require more and better information in the future.

SUMMARY

Harvest management is continually evolving largely because information on species biology is improving and the landscapes occupied by many wildlife species are continually changing. As interest of nonhunters in wildlife populations and management increases, the importance of managing biologically defensible harvests will also increase. Gutiérrez (1994) argued that professionals are at a crossroads in game bird management and the direction taken will affect the future of game bird hunting. This observation most likely applies to all hunted species. Monitoring populations and harvests will become more critical to managers attempting to implement appropriate harvest regulations. Further, changing landscapes will alter at least some and perhaps many wildlife populations. Approaches to harvest management for some of these populations will also likely have to change. Managing the harvest will continue to be a difficult and sometimes frustrating effort for many wildlife professionals. However, management decisions backed by sound science and rigorous data collection will alleviate some of these difficulties.

ACKNOWLEDGMENTS

We appreciate the thoughts and ideas of the many state and federal wildlife biologists that have influenced our thinking on harvest management. Although we did not always agree, we always listened. We also appreciate the discussions and sometimes surprising insight provided by both undergraduate and graduate students over the years. Finally, this chapter was much improved by thorough reviews by R. J. Mackie, R. L. Eng, and an anonymous reviewer.

LITERATURE CITED

ALLEN, D. L. 1962. Our wildlife legacy. Funk and Wagnall's, New York, USA.

AMMANN, G. A. 1963. Status and management of sharp-tailed grouse in Michigan. Journal of Wildlife Management 27:802–809.

ANDERSON, D. R. 1975. Population ecology of the mallard. V. Temporal and geographic estimates of survival, recovery, and harvest rates. U.S. Department of the Interior, Fish and Wildlife Service, Resource Publication 125.

———, AND K. P. BURNHAM. 1976. Population ecology of the mallard. VI. The effect of exploitation on survival. U.S. Department of the Interior, Fish and Wildlife Service, Resource Publication 128.

———, ———, J. D. NICHOLS, AND M. J. CONROY. 1987. The need for experiments to understand population dynamics of American black ducks. Wildlife Society Bulletin 15:282–284.

ANKNEY, C. D. 1996. An embarrassment of riches: too many geese. Journal of Wildlife Management 60:217–223.

ARNOLD, T. W. 1988. Life histories of North American game birds: a reanalysis. Canadian Journal of Zoology 66:1906–1912.

AUTENRIETH, R. E. 1981. Sage grouse management in Idaho. Wildlife Bulletin 9. Idaho Department of Fish and Game, Boise, USA.

BABCOCK, K. M., AND R. D. SPARROWE. 1989. Balancing expectations with reality in duck harvest management. Transactions of the North American Wildlife and Natural Resources Conference 54:594–599.

BAILEY, J. A. 1984. Principles of wildlife management. John Wiley and Sons, New York, USA.

BANKS, R. C. 1981. Summary of foreign game bird liberations, 1969–78. U.S. Department of the Interior, Fish and Wildlife Service, Special Scientific Report Wildlife 239.

BARTMANN, R. M., G. C. WHITE, AND L. H. CARPENTER. 1992. Compensatory mortality in a Colorado mule deer population. Wildlife Monographs 121.

BATT, B. D. J., editor. 1997. Arctic ecosystems in peril: report of the Arctic Goose Habitat Working Group. Arctic Goose Joint Venture Special Publication. U.S. Department of the Interior, Fish and Wildlife Service, Washington, D.C., USA and Canadian Wildlife Service, Ottawa, Ontario, Canada.

BEECHAM, J. J. AND J. ROHLMAN. 1994. A shadow in the forest: Idaho's black bear. University of Idaho Press, Moscow, USA.

BERGERUD, A. T. 1970. Vulnerability of willow ptarmigan to hunting. Journal of Wildlife Management 34:282–285.

———. 1972. Changes in the vulnerability of ptarmigan to hunting in Newfoundland. Journal of Wildlife Management 36:104–109.

———. 1985. The additive effect of hunting mortality on the natural mortality rates of grouse. Pages 345–364 in S. L. Beasom and S. F. Roberson, editors. Game harvest management. Caesar Kleberg Wildlife Research Institute, Kingsville, Texas, USA.

———. 1988. Increasing the numbers of grouse. Pages 686–731 in A. T. Bergerud and M. W. Gratson, editors. Adaptive strategies and population ecology of northern grouse. University of Minnesota Press, Minneapolis, USA.

———, AND D. S. HUXTER. 1969. Effects of hunting on willow ptarmigan in Newfoundland. Journal of Wildlife Management 33:866–870.

BIEDERBECK, H. H., M. C. BOULAY, AND D. H. JACKSON. 2001. Effects of hunting regulations on bull elk survival and age structure. Wildlife Society Bulletin 29:1271–1277.

BJORNN, T. C., AND P. D. DALKE. 1975. A survey of behavior, preferences and opinions of Idaho hunters. Bulletin 7. University of Idaho Forest, Wildlife, and Range Experiment Station, Moscow, USA.

BLOHM, R. J. 1989. Introduction to harvest: understanding surveys and season setting. Pages 118–133 in K. H. Beattie, editor. Proceedings of the Sixth International Waterfowl Symposium. Ducks Unlimited, Memphis, Tennessee, USA.

BOYCE, M. S. 1989. The Jackson elk herd: intensive wildlife management in North America. Cambridge University Press, New York, USA.

BOYD, H. 1983. Intensive regulation of duck hunting in North America: its purpose and achievements. Occasional Paper 50. Canadian Wildlife Service, Ottawa, Ontario, Canada.

BRACE, R. K., R. S. POSPAHALA, AND R. L. JESSEN. 1987. Background and objectives on stabilized duck hunting regulations: Canadian and U.S. perspectives. Transactions of the North American Wildlife and Natural Resources Conference 52:177–185.

BRAUN, C. E. 1969. Population dynamics, habitat, and movements of white-tailed ptarmigan in Colorado. Dissertation. Colorado State University, Fort Collins, USA.

———. 1979. Evaluation of the effects of changes in hunting regulations on sage grouse populations. Federal Aid Project W-37-R-32, Job 9a, Colorado Division of Wildlife, Denver, USA.

———. 1987. Current issues in sage grouse management. Proceedings of the Western Association of State Fish and Wildlife Agencies 67: 134–144.

———, AND T. D. I. BECK. 1985. Effects of changes in hunting regulations on sage grouse harvest and populations. Pages 335–342 in S. L. Beasom and S. F. Roberson, editors. Game harvest management. Caesar Kleberg Wildlife Research Institute, Kingsville, Texas, USA.

———, K. MARTIN, AND L. A. ROBB. 1993. White-tailed ptarmigan. Number 68. In A. Poole, P. Stettenheim, and F. Gill, editors. The birds of North America. Academy of Natural Sciences, Philadelphia, Pennsylvania, USA.

BRENNAN, L. A. 1994. Introductory remarks: do we need a national upland gamebird plan? Transactions of the North American Wildlife and Natural Resources Conference 59: 411–414.

BRO, E., B. DELDALLE, M. MASSOT, F. REITZ, AND S. SELMI. 2003. Density dependence of reproductive success in grey partridge *Perdix perdix* populations in France: management implications. Wildlife Biology 9: 93–102.

BROWN, JR., G. M., J. HAMMACK, AND M. F. TILLMAN. 1976. Mallard population dynamics and management models. Journal of Wildlife Management 40: 542–555.

Brownie, C., D. R. Anderson, K. P, Burnham, and D. S. Robson.1985. Statistical inference from band recovery data-a handbook. U.S. Department of the Interior, Fish and Wildlife Service, Resource Publication 156.

BUMP, G., R. W. DARROW, F. C. EDMINSTER, AND W. F. CRISSEY. 1947. The ruffed grouse: life history, propagation, management. New York State Conservation Department, Albany, USA.

BUNNELL, F. L. 1978. Horn growth and population quality in Dall sheep. Journal of Wildlife Management 42: 764–775.

BURGER, JR., L. W., E. W. KURZEJESKI, L. D. VANGILDER, T. V. DAILEY, AND J. H. SCHULZ. 1994. Effects of harvest on population dynamics of upland gamebirds: are bobwhite the model? Transactions of the North American Wildlife and Natural Resources Conference 59:466–476.

BURNHAM, K. P., AND D. R. ANDERSON. 1984. Tests of compensatory vs. additive hypotheses of mortality in mallards. Ecology 65:105–112.

———, G. C. WHITE, AND D. R. ANDERSON. 1984. Estimating the effect of hunting on annual survival rates of adult mallards. Journal of Wildlife Management 48: 350–361.

CAMPBELL, H., D. K. MARTIN, P. E. FERKOVICH, AND B. K. HARRIS. 1973. Effects of hunting and some other environmental factors on scaled quail in New Mexico. Wildlife Monographs 34.

CANADIAN WILDLIFE SERVICE WATERFOWL COMMITTEE. 2002. Migratory game bird hunting regulations in Canada: July 2002. Migratory Birds Regulatory Report 3, Canadian Wildlife Service, Ottawa, Ontario, Canada.

CARROLL, J. P. 1990. Winter and spring survival of radio-marked gray partridge in North Dakota. Journal of Wildlife Management 54:657–662.

———. 1993. Gray partridge. Number 58. In A. Poole, P. Stettenheim, and F. Gill, editors. The birds of North America. Academy of Natural Sciences, Philadelphia, Pennsylvania, USA.

———, R. D. CRAWFORD, AND J. W. SCHULZ. 1990. Nesting and brood-rearing ecology of gray partridge in North Dakota. Pages 272–294 in K. E. Church, R. E. Warner, and S. J. Brady, editors. Perdix V: gray partridge and ring-necked pheasant workshop. Kansas Department of Wildlife and Parks, Emporia, USA.

CASSIRER, E. F., D. J. FREDDY, AND E. D. ABLES. 1992. Elk responses to disturbance by cross-country skiers in Yellowstone National Park. Wildlife Society Bulletin 20: 375–381.

CAUGHLEY, G. 1974. Interpretation of age ratios. Journal of Wildlife Management 38: 557–562.

———. 1976. Wildlife management and the dynamics of ungulate populations. Applied Biology 1: 183–246.

———. 1985. Harvesting of wildlife: past, present, and future. Pages 3–14 in S. L. Beasom and S. F. Roberson, editors. Game harvest management. Caesar Kleberg Wildlife Research Institute, Kingsville, Texas, USA.

———, AND A. R. E. SINCLAIR. 1994. Wildlife ecology and management. Blackwell Scientific Publications, Cambridge, Massachusetts, USA.

CHOATE, T. S. 1963. Habitat and population dynamics of white-tailed ptarmigan in Montana. Journal of Wildlife Management 27:684–699.

CHRISTENSEN, G. C. 1958. The effects of drought and hunting on the chukar partridge. Transactions of the North American Wildlife Conference 23:329–341.

———. 1970. The chukar partridge. Biological Bulletin 4. Nevada Department of Fish and Game, Reno, USA.

CHURCH, K. E., AND W. F. PORTER. 1990. Population responses by gray partridge to severe winter conditions. Pages 295–303 in K. E. Church, R. E. Warner, and S. J. Brady, editors. Perdix V: gray partridge and ring-necked pheasant workshop. Kansas Department of Wildlife and Parks, Emporia, USA.

CLARK, M. E. 1996. Movements, habitat use, and survival of ruffed grouse (*Bonasa umbellus*) in northern Michigan. Thesis. Michigan State University, East Lansing, USA.

———. 2000. Survival, fall movements, and habitat use of hunted and non-hunted ruffed grouse in northern Michigan. Dissertation. Michigan State University, East Lansing, USA.

CLUTTON-BROCK, T. H., F. E. GUINNESS, AND S. D. ALBON. 1982. Red deer: behavior and ecology of two sexes. University of Chicago Press, Chicago, Illinois, USA.

———, S. D. ALBON, R. M. GIBSON, AND F. E.GUINNESS. 1979. The logical stag: adaptive aspects of fighting in red deer (*Cervus elaphus* L.). Animal Behaviour 27: 211–225.

———, M. MAJOR, S. D ALBON, AND F. E. GUINNESS. 1987. Early development and population dynamics in red deer. I. Density dependent effects on juvenile survival. Journal of Animal Ecology 56: 53–67.

COLE, J. C. 1995. Effects of hunting and non-hunting mortality on seasonal bobwhite densities in Tennessee. Thesis. University of Tennessee, Knoxville, USA.

CONNELLY, J. W., H. W. BROWERS, AND R. J. GATES. 1988. Seasonal movements of sage grouse in southeastern Idaho. Journal of Wildlife Management 52: 116–122.

———, M. W. GRATSON, AND K. P. REESE. 1999. Sharp-tailed grouse. Number 354. In A. Poole, P. Stettenheim, and F. Gill, editors. The birds of North America. Academy of Natural Sciences, Philadelphia, Pennsylvania, USA.

———, A. D. Apa, R. B. Smith, and K. P. Reese 2000a. Effects of predation and hunting on adult sage grouse *Centrocercus urophasianus* in Idaho. Wildlife Biology 6:227–232.

———, S. T. KNICK, M. A. SCHROEDER, AND S. J. STIVER. 2004. Conservation assessment of greater sage-grouse and sagebrush habitats. Western Association of Fish and Wildlife Agencies, Cheyenne, Wyoming, USA.

———, K. P. REESE, E. O. GARTON, AND M. L. COMMONS-KEMNER. 2003. Response of greater sage-grouse *Centrocercus urophasianus* populations to different levels of exploitation in Idaho, USA. Wildlife Biology 9: 255–260.

———, M. A. SCHROEDER, A. R. SANDS, AND C. E. BRAUN. 2000b. Guidelines to manage sage grouse populations and their habitats. Wildlife Society Bulletin 28: 967–985.

———, R. A. FISCHER, A. D. APA, K. P. REESE, AND W. L. WAKKINEN. 1993. Renesting by sage grouse in southeastern Idaho. Condor 95:1041–1043.

CONNER, M. M., G. C. WHITE, AND D. J. FREDDY. 2001. Elk movement in response to early-season hunting in northwest Colorado. Journal of Wildlife Management 65:926–940.

CONNOLLY, G. E. 1981. Limiting factors and population regulation. Pages 245–285 in O. C. Wallmo, editor. Mule and black-tailed deer of North America. University of Nebraska Press, Lincoln, USA.

COOCH, F. G., S. WENDT, G. E. J. SMITH, AND G. BUTLER. 1978. The Canada migratory game bird hunting permit and associated surveys. Pages 8–39 in H. Boyd and G. H. Finney, editors. Migratory game bird hunters and hunting in Canada. Canadian Wildlife Service Report Series 43.

COOK, J. G., L. J. QUINLAN, L. L. IRWIN, L. D. BRYANT, R. A. RIGGS, AND J. W. THOMAS. 1996. Nutrition-growth relations of elk calves during late summer and fall. Journal of Wildlife Management 60:528–541.

COPELIN, F. F. 1963. The lesser prairie chicken in Oklahoma. Technical Bulletin 6. Oklahoma Wildlife Conservation Department, Oklahoma City, USA.

COUGHENOUR, M. B., AND F. J. SINGER. 1996. Elk population processes in Yellowstone National Park under the policy of natural regulation. Ecological Applications 6:573–593.

CRAWFORD, J. A. 1982. Factors affecting sage grouse harvest in Oregon. Wildlife Society Bulletin 10:374–377.

———, AND R. S. LUTZ. 1985. Sage grouse population trends in Oregon, 1941–1983. Murrelet 66:69–74.

CRISSEY, W. F. 1957. Forecasting waterfowl harvest by flyways. Transactions of the North American Wildlife Conference 22:256–268.

CZAPLEWSKI, R. L., M. M. CROWE, AND L. L. MCDONALD. 1983. Sample sizes and confidence intervals for wildlife population ratios. Wildlife Society Bulletin 11:121–128.

DARWIN, C. 1871. The descent of man, and selection in relation to sex. A.L. Burt, New York, USA.

DASMANN, R. F. 1964. Wildlife biology. John Wiley and Sons, New York, USA.

DENNEY, R. N. 1978. Managing the harvest. Pages 95–408 in J. L. Schmidt and D. L. Gilbert, editors. Big game of North America. Stackpole Books, Harrisburg, Pennsylvania, USA.

DIXON, K. R., M. A HORNER, S. R. ANDERSON, W. D. HENRIQUES, D. DURHAM, AND R. J. KENDALL. 1996. Northern bobwhite habitat use and survival on a South Carolina plantation during winter. Wildlife Society Bulletin 24:627–635.

DOLTON, D. D. 1993. The call-count survey: historic development and current procedures. Pages 233–252 in T. S. Baskett, M. W. Sayre, R. E. Tomlinson, AND R. E. Mirarchi, editors. Ecology and management of the mourning dove. Stackpole Books, Harrisburg, Pennsylvania, USA.

DORNEY, R. S., AND C. KABAT. 1960. Relation of weather, parasitic disease and hunting to Wisconsin ruffed grouse populations. Technical Bulletin 20. Wisconsin Conservation Department, Madison, USA.

DUNKS, J. H., R. E. TOMLINSON, H. M. REEVES, D. D. DOLTON, C. E. BRAUN, AND T. P. ZAPATKA. 1982. Migration, harvest, and population dynamics of mourning doves banded in the Central Management Unit, 1967–77. U.S. Department of the Interior, Fish and Wildlife Service, Special Scientific Report—Wildlife 249.

DUSEK, G. L., R. J. MACKIE, J. D. HERRIGES, JR., AND B. B. COMPTON. 1989. Population ecology of white-tailed deer along the lower Yellowstone River. Wildlife Monographs 104.

EDGE, W. D., AND C. L. MARCUM. 1985. Movements of elk in relation to logging disturbances. Journal of Wildlife Management 49:926–930.

EDMINSTER, F. C. 1947. The ruffed grouse: its life story, ecology and management. Macmillan Publishing Company, New York, USA.

EDWARDS, W. R. 1988. Realities of "population regulation" and harvest management. Pages 307–335 in D. L. Hallet, W. R. Edwards, and G. V. Burger, editors. Pheasants: symptoms of wildlife problems on agricultural lands. North Central Section, The Wildlife Society, Bloomington, Indiana, USA.

ELDEN, R. C., W. V. BEVILL, P. I. PADDING, J. E. FRAMPTON, AND D. L. SHROUFE. 2002. A history of the development of the Harvest Information Program. Pages 7–16 in J. M. Ver Steeg and R. C. Elden, compilers. Harvest information program: evaluation and recommendations. Migratory Shore and Upland Game Bird Working Group, Ad Hoc Committee on HIP, International Association of Fish and Wildlife Agencies, Washington, D.C., USA.

ELLISON, L. N. 1974. Population characteristics of Alaskan spruce grouse. Journal of Wildlife Management 38:383–395.

———. 1991. Shooting and compensatory mortality in tetraonids. Ornis Scandinavica 22:229–240.

ERRINGTON, P. L. 1945. Some contributions of a fifteen-year local study of the northern bobwhite to a knowledge of population phenomena.

Ecological Monographs 15:1–34.

———. 1956. Factors limiting higher vertebrate populations. Science 124:304–307.

FARRIS, A. L., E. D. KLONGLAN, AND R. C. NOMSEN. 1977. The ring-necked pheasant in Iowa. Iowa Conservation Commission, Des Moines, USA.

FINNEY, G. H. 1990. Native hunting of waterfowl in Canada. Pages 140–144 in G. V. T. Matthews, editor. Managing waterfowl populations. International Waterfowl and Wetlands Research Bureau, Slimbridge, United Kingdom.

FISCHER, C. A., AND L. B. KEITH. 1974. Population responses of central Alberta ruffed grouse to hunting. Journal of Wildlife Management 38:585–600.

FLOOK, D. R. 1970. Causes and implications of an observed sex differential in the survival of wapiti. Canadian Wildlife Service Report Series-11.

FRANKLIN, W. L., A. S. MOSSMAN, AND M. DOLE. 1975. Social organization and home range of Roosevelt elk. Journal of Mammalogy 56:102–118.

FRASER, D., J. F. GARDNER, G. B. KOLENOSKY, AND S. STRATHEARN. 1982. Estimation of harvest rate of black bears from age and sex data. Wildlife Society Bulletin 10:53–57.

FREDDY, D. J. 1987. The White River elk herd: a perspective, 1960–1985. Technical Publication 37. Colorado Division of Wildlife, Fort Collins, USA.

———, W. M. BRONAUGH, AND M. C. FOWLER. 1986. Responses of mule deer to disturbance by persons afoot and snowmobiles. Wildlife Society Bulletin 14:63–68.

———, G. C. WHITE, M. C. KNEELAND, R. H. KAHN, J. W. UNSWORTH, W. J. DEVERGIE, V. K. GRAHAM, J. H. ELLENBERGER, AND C. H. WAGNER. 2004. How many mule deer are there? Challenges of credibility in Colorado. Wildlife Society Bulletin 32:916–927.

FRISINA, M. R., AND K. DOUGLASS. 1993. Number of antler points and antler main beam length in relation to age of Rocky Mountain elk (*Cervus elaphus*). Proceedings of the Montana Academy of Sciences 53:33–38.

FRYXELL, J. M., D. J. T. HUSSELL, A. B. LAMBERT, AND P. C. SMITH. 1991. Time lags and population fluctuations in white-tailed deer. Journal of Wildlife Management 55:377–385.

GAILLARD, J.-M., M. FESTA-BIANCHET, AND N. G. YOCCOZ. 1998. Population dynamics of large herbivores: variable recruitment with constant adult survival. Trends in Ecology and Evolution 13:58–63.

———, ———, ———, A. LOISON, AND C. TOIGO. 2000. Temporal variation in fitness components and population dynamics of large herbivores. Annual Review of Ecology and Systematics 31:367–393.

GARSHELIS, D. L. 1993. Monitoring black bear populations: pitfalls and recommendations. Proceedings Western Black Bear Workshop on Research and Management 4:123–144.

GEIS, A. D., R. K. MARTINSON, AND D. R. ANDERSON. 1969. Establishing hunting regulations and allowable harvest of mallards in the United States. Journal of Wildlife Management 33:848–859.

GEIST, V. 1986. New evidence of high frequency of antler wounding in cervids. Canadian Journal of Zoology 64:380–384.

———. 1998. Deer of the world: their evolution, behavior, and ecology. Stackpole Books, Mechanicsburg, Pennsylvania, USA.

GEORGE, R. R., R. E. TOMLINSON, R. W. ENGEL-WILSON, G. L. WAGGERMAN, AND A. G. SPRATT. 1994. White-winged dove. Pages 29–50 in T. C. Tacha and C. E. Braun, editors. Migratory shore and upland game bird management in North America. International Association of Fish and Wildlife Agencies, Washington, D.C., USA.

———, J. B. WOOLEY, JR., J. M. KIENZLER, A. L. FARRIS, AND A. H. BERNER. 1980. Effect of hunting season length on ring-necked pheasant populations. Wildlife Society Bulletin 8:279–283.

GIESEN, K. M., C. E. BRAUN, AND T. A. MAY. 1980. Reproduction and nest site selection by white-tailed ptarmigan in Colorado. Wilson Bulletin 92:188–199.

GILES, JR., R. H. 1978. Wildlife management. W. H. Freeman and Company, San Francisco, California, USA.

GRANGE, W. B. 1949. The way to game abundance, with an explanation of game cycles. Charles Scribner's Sons, New York, USA.

GRATSON, M. W., AND C. WHITMAN. 2000*a*. Characteristics of Idaho elk hunters relative to road access on public lands. Wildlife Society Bulletin 28:1016–1022.

———, AND ———. 2000*b*. Road closures and density and success of elk hunters in Idaho. Wildlife Society Bulletin 28:302–310.

GRAY, B. T., AND R. M. KAMINSKI. 1989. Illegal harvest of waterfowl: what do we know? Transactions of the North American Wildlife and Natural Resources Conference 54:333–340.

GREGG, L. E. 1990. Harvest rates of sharp-tailed grouse on managed areas in Wisconsin. Research Report 152. Wisconsin Department of Natural Resources, Park Falls, USA.

GUTIERRÉZ, R. J. 1994. North American upland gamebird management at crossroads: which road will we take? Transactions of the North American Wildlife and Natural Resources Conference 59:494–497.

HAIGH, J. C., W. F. CATES, G. I. GLOVER, AND N. C. RAWLINGS. 1984. Relationships between seasonal changes in serum testosterone concentrations, scrotal circumference and sperm morphology of male wapiti, *Cervus elaphus*. Journal of Reproductive Fertility 70:413–418.

HAMERSTROM, JR., F. N., AND F. HAMERSTROM. 1949. Daily and seasonal movements of Wisconsin prairie chickens. Auk 66:313–337.

———, AND ———. 1973. The prairie chicken in Wisconsin: highlights of a 22-year study of counts, behavior, movements, turnover, and habitat. Technical Bulletin 64. Wisconsin Department of Natural Resources, Madison, USA.

———, O. E. MATTSON, AND F. HAMERSTROM. 1957. A guide to prairie chicken management. Technical Wildlife Bulletin 15. Wisconsin Conservation Department, Madison, USA

HAMLIN, K. L., AND M. S. ROSS. 2002. Effects of hunting regulation changes on elk and hunters in the Gravelly-Snowcrest Mountains, Montana. Montana Fish, Wildlife and Parks, Helena, USA.

HART, C. M., O. S. LEE, AND J. B. LOW. 1950. The sharp-tailed grouse in Utah: its life history, status, and management. Publication 3. Utah Department of Fish and Game, Salt Lake City, USA.

HAWKINS, A. S., R. C. HANSON, H. K. NELSON, AND H. M. REEVES, editors. 1984. Flyways: pioneering waterfowl management in North America. U.S. Government Printing Office, Washington, D.C., USA.

HEATH, B. J., R. STRAW, S. H. ANDERSON, AND J. LAWSON. 1997. Sage grouse productivity, survival, and seasonal habitat use near Farson, Wyoming. Project Completion Report. Wyoming Game and Fish Commission, Laramie, USA.

HEBERT, D. M. 1978. A systems approach to mountain goat management. Proceedings of the Biennial Symposium of the Northern Wild Sheep and Goat Council 2:227–243.

———, AND W. G. TURNBULL. 1977. A description of southern interior and coastal mountain goat ecotypes in British Columbia. Proceedings of the International Mountain Goat Symposium 1:126–146.

HESTBECK, J. B. 1994. Survival of Canada geese banded in winter in the Atlantic Flyway. Journal of Wildlife Management 58:748–756.

HILBORN, R., C. J. WALTERS, AND D. LUDWIG. 1995. Sustainable exploitation of renewable resources. Annual Review of Ecology and Systematics 26:45–67.

HILLMAN, C. N., AND W. W. JACKSON. 1973. The sharp-tailed grouse in South Dakota. Technical Bulletin 3. South Dakota Department of Game, Fish and Parks, Pierre, USA.

HOFFMAN, R. W. 1985. Effects of changes in hunting regulations on blue grouse populations. Pages 327–334 *in* S. L. Beasom and S. F. Roberson, editors. Game harvest management. Caesar Kleberg Wildlife Research Institute, Kingsville, Texas, USA.

HOLT, S. J., AND L. M. TALBOT. 1978. New principles for the conservation of wild living resources. Wildlife Monographs 59.

HORNADAY, W. T. 1916. Save the sage grouse from extinction, a demand from civilization to the western states. New York Zoological Park Bulletin 5:179–219.

HOUSTON, D. B. 1982. The northern Yellowstone elk: ecology and management. MacMillan Publishing Company, New York, USA.

HUBBARD, M. W., D. L. GARNER, AND E. E. KLAAS. 1999. Factors influencing wild turkey hen survival in southcentral Iowa. Journal of Wildlife Management 63:731–738.

HUMBURG, D. D., T. W. ALDRICH, S. BAKER, G. COSTANZO, J. H. GAMMONLEY, M. A. JOHNSON, B. SWIFT, AND D. YPARRAGUIRRE. 2000. Adaptive harvest management: has anything really changed? Transactions of the North American Wildlife and Natural Resources Conference 65:78–93.

HURLEY, M. A., AND G. A. SARGEANT. 1991. Effects of hunting and land management on elk habitat use, movement patterns, and mortality in western Montana. Pages 94–98 *in* A. G. Christiansen, L. J. Lyon, and T. N. Lonner, compilers. Proceedings of Elk Vulnerability Symposium. Montana State University, Bozeman, USA.

HURST, G. A., AND W. ROSENE. 1985. Regulations and restrictions pertaining to bobwhite quail harvests in the southeast. Pages 301–308 *in* S. L. Beasom and S. F. Roberson, editors. Game harvest management. Caesar Kleberg Wildlife Research Institute, Kingsville, Texas, USA.

JOHNSGARD, P. A. 1973. Grouse and quails of North America. University of Nebraska Press, Lincoln, USA.

JOHNSON, F. A. 2001. Adaptive regulation of waterfowl hunting in the U.S. Pages 113–131 *in* R. G. Stahl, Jr., R. A. Bachman, A. L. Barton, J. R. Clark, P. L. deFur, S. J. Ellis, C. A. Pittinger, M. W. Slimak, and R. S. Wentsel, editors. Risk management: ecological risk-based decision-making. SETAC Press, Pensacola, Florida, USA.

———, AND D. J. CASE. 2000. Adaptive regulation of waterfowl harvests: lessons learned and prospects for the future. Transactions of the North American Wildlife and Natural Resources Conference 65:94–108.

———, AND B. K. WILLIAMS. 1999. Protocol and practice in the adaptive management of waterfowl harvests. Conservation Ecology 3:8. [serial online]. Available at http://www.consecol.org/vol3/iss1/art8 (accessed December 2002).

———, W. L. KENDALL, AND J. A. DUBOVSKY. 2002. Conditions and limitations on learning in the adaptive management of mallard harvests. Wildlife Society Bulletin 30:176–185.

———, C. T. MOORE, W. L. KENDALL, J. A. DUBOVSKY, D. F. CAITHAMER, J. R. KELLEY, JR., AND B. K. WILLIAMS. 1997. Uncertainty and the management of mallard harvests. Journal of Wildlife Management 61:203–216.

———, B. K. WILLIAMS, J. D. NICHOLS, J. E. HINES, W. L. KENDALL, G. W. SMITH, AND D. F. CAITHAMER. 1993. Developing an adaptive management strategy for harvesting waterfowl in North America. Transactions of the North American Wildlife and Natural Resources Conference 58:565–583.

JOHNSON, K. H., AND C. E. BRAUN. 1999. Viability and conservation of an exploited sage grouse population. Conservation Biology 13:77–84.

JORGENSON, J. T., M. FESTA-BIANCHET, AND W. D. WISHART. 1993. Harvesting bighorn ewes: consequences for population size and ram production. Journal of Wildlife Management 57:429–435.

———, ———, J.-M. GAILLARD, AND W. D. WISHART. 1997. Effects of age, sex, disease, and density on survival of bighorn sheep. Ecology 78:1019–1032.

JOSLIN, G., AND H. YOUMANS, COORDINATORS. 1999. Effects of recreation on Rocky Mountain wildlife: a review for Montana. Montana Chapter, The Wildlife Society. Montana Fish, Wildlife and Parks, Helena, USA.

JUNE, J. W. 1963. Wyoming sage grouse population measurement. Proceedings of the Western Association of State Game and Fish Commissioners 43:206–211.

KABAT, C., AND D. R. THOMPSON. 1963. Wisconsin quail, 1834–1962: population dynamics and habitat management. Technical Bulletin 30. Wisconsin Conservation Department, Madison, USA.

KEPPIE, D. M. 1979. Dispersal, overwinter mortality, and recruitment of spruce grouse. Journal of Wildlife Management 43:717–727.

KOKKO, H. 2001. Optimal and suboptimal use of compensatory responses to harvesting: timing of hunting as an example. Wildlife Biology 7:141–150.

KORSCHGEN, L. J., AND G. D. CHAMBERS. 1970. Propagation, stocking, and food habits of Reeves pheasants in Missouri. Journal of Wildlife Management 34:274–282.

KRAUSS, G. D., H. B. GRAVES, AND S. M ZERVANOS. 1987. Survival of wild and game-farm cock pheasants released in Pennsylvania. Journal of Wildlife Management 51:555–559.

KROLL, J. C. 1991. A practical guide to producing and harvesting white-tailed deer. Stephen F. Austin State University Press, Nacogdoches, Texas, USA.

KUCK, L. 1977. The impacts of hunting on Idaho's Pahsimeroi mountain goat herd. Proceedings of the International Mountain Goat Symposium 1:114–125.

KUBISIAK, J. F. 1984. The impact of hunting on ruffed grouse populations in the Sandhill Wildlife Area. Pages 151–168 *in* W. L. Robinson, editor. Ruffed grouse management: state of the art in the early 1980's. North Central Section, The Wildlife Society, St. Louis, Missouri, USA.

KURZEJESKI, E. W., AND L. D. VANGILDER. 1992. Population management. Pages 165–184 *in* J. G. Dickson, editor. The wild turkey: biology and management. Stackpole Books, Harrisburg, Pennsylvania, USA.

KUVLESKY, JR., W. P., B. D. LEOPOLD, P. D. CURTIS, J. L. ROSEBERRY, AND T. HUTTON. 1993. Strategic plan for quail management and research in the United States: issues and strategies—Population dynamics and effects of hunting. Pages 180–181 *in* K. E. Church and T. V. Dailey, editors. Quail III: national quail symposium. Kansas Department of Wildlife and Parks, Pratt, USA.

LADD, JR., W. N., J. C. BARTONEK, K. E. GAMBLE, AND J. R. SERIE. 1989. Experiences with special harvest management strategies for ducks. Transactions of the North American Wildlife and Natural Resources Conference 54:552–565.

LANCIA, R.A., C. E. BRAUN, M. W. COLLOPY, R. D. DUESER, J. G. KIE, C. J. MARTINKA, J. D. NICHOLS, T. D. NUDDS, W. R. PORATH, AND N. G. TILGHMAN. 1996. ARM! For the future: adaptive resource management in the wildlife profession. Wildlife Society Bulletin 24:436–442

LAYCOCK, W. A., AND D. A. PRICE. 1970. Environmental influences on nutritional value of forage plants. Pages 37–47 *in* H. A. Paulson and E. H. Reid, editors. Range and wildlife habitat evaluation. U.S. Department of Agriculture, Forest Service, Miscellaneous Publication 1147.

LEE, K. N. 1993. Compass and gyroscope: integrating science and politics for the environment. Island Press, Washington, D.C., USA.

LEIF, A. P. 1994. Survival and reproduction of wild and pen-reared ring-necked pheasant hens. Journal of Wildlife Management 58:501–506.

LEONARD, K. M., K. P. REESE, AND J. W. CONNELLY. 2000. Distribution, movements, and habitats of sage-grouse *Centrocercus urophasianus* on the upper Snake River Plain of Idaho: changes from the 1950s to the 1990s. Wildlife Biology 6:265–270.

LEOPOLD, A. 1930. Report to the American Game Conference on an American game policy. Transactions of the American Game Conference 17:284–309.

———. 1933. Game management. Charles Scribner's Sons, New York, USA.

———, T. M. SPERRY, W. S. FEENEY, AND J. A. CATENHUSEN. 1943. Population turnover on a Wisconsin pheasant refuge. Journal of Wildlife Management 7:383–394.

LEUTHOLD, W. 1977. African ungulates: a comparative review of their ethology and behavioral ecology. Springer-Verlag, Inc., New York, USA.

LINDÉN, H. 1981. Hunting and tetraonid populations in Finland. Finnish Game Research 39:69–78.

LITVAITIS, J. A., AND D. M. KANE. 1994. Relationships of hunting technique and hunter selectivity to composition of black bear harvest. Wildlife Society Bulletin 22:604–606.

LOBDELL, C. H., K. E. CASE, AND H. S. MOSBY. 1972. Evaluation of harvest strategies for a simulated wild turkey population. Journal of Wildlife Management 36:493–497.

LONEUX, M. 2000. Modelisation de l'influence du climat sur les fluctuations de population du tetras lyre *tetrao tetrix* en Europe. Cahiers d'Ethologie 20:191–216.

———, AND J. C. RUWET. 1996. Evolution des populations du tetras lyre *Tetrao tetrix* en Europe: un essai de synthése. Cahiers d'Ethologie 17:287–343.

LUNDRIGAN, B. 1996. Morphology of horns and fighting behavior in the family Bovidae. Journal of Mammalogy 77:462–475.

MACKIE, R. J., D. F. PAC, K. L. HAMLIN, AND G. L. DUSEK. 1998. Ecology and management of mule deer and white-tailed deer in Montana. Federal Aid Project W-120-R. Montana Fish, Wildlife and Parks, Helena, USA.

MARKLEY, M. H. 1967. Limiting factors. Pages 199–244 *in* O. H. Hewitt, editor. The wild turkey and its management. The Wildlife Society, Washington, D.C., USA.

MARTIN, E. M., AND S. M. CARNEY. 1977. Population ecology of the mallard. IV. A review of duck hunting regulations, activity and success, with special reference to the mallard. U.S. Department of the Interior, Fish and Wildlife Service, Resource Publication 130.

———, AND P. I. PADDING. 2002. Preliminary estimates of waterfowl harvest and hunter activity in the United States during the 2001 hunting season. U.S. Department of the Interior, Fish and Wildlife Service, Washington, D.C., USA.

———, R. S. POSPAHALA, AND J. D. NICHOLS. 1979. Assessment and population management of North American migratory birds. Pages 187–239 *in* J. Cairns, Jr., G. P. Patil, and W. E. Water, editors. Environmental and biomonitoring, assessment, prediction, and managent—certain case studies and related quantitative issues. Statistical Ecology. Volume 11. International Cooperative Publishing House, Fairland, Maryland, USA.

MARTIN, K., S. J. HANNON, AND R. F. ROCKWELL. 1989. Clutch size variation and patterns of attrition in fecundity of willow ptarmigan. Ecology 70:1788–1799.

MCCORQUODALE, S. M., L. E. EBERHARDT, AND G. A. SARGEANT. 1989. Antler characteristics in a colonizing elk population. Journal of Wildlife Management 53:618–621.

MCCULLOUGH, D. R. 1979. The George Reserve Deer Herd: population ecology of a k-selected species. University of Michigan Press, Ann Arbor, USA.

———. 1990. Detecting density dependence: filtering the baby from the bathwater. Transactions of the North American Wildlife sand Natural Resources Conference 55:534–543.

———. 2001. Population manipulations of North American deer, *Odocoileus* spp.: balancing high yield with sustainability. Wildlife Biology 7:161–170.

MCGOWAN, J. D. 1975. Effect of autumn and spring hunting on ptarmigan population trends. Journal of Wildlife Management. 39:491–495.

MCKEE, G. 1995. Ecology of greater prairie-chickens in relation to habitat characteristics in southwestern Missouri. Thesis. University of Missouri, Columbia, USA.

MERRILL, E. H., AND M. S. BOYCE. 1991. Summer range and elk population dynamics in Yellowstone National Park. Pages 263–273 *in* R. B. Keiter and M. S. Boyce, editors. The Greater Yellowstone Ecosystem: redefining America's wilderness heritage. Yale University Press, New Haven, Connecticut, USA.

MILLER, K. V., AND R. L. MARCHINTON, editors. 1995. Quality whitetails. Stackpole Books, Mechanicsburg, Pennsylvania, USA.

MILLER, S. D. 1990. Population management of bears in North America. International Conference on Bear Research and Management 8:357–373.

MILLS, L. S., AND F. W. ALLENDORF. 1996. The one-migrant-per-generation rule in conservation and management. Conservation Biology 10:1509–1518.

MITCHELL, B. 1973. The reproductive performance of wild Scottish red deer *Cervus elaphus*. Journal of Reproductive Fertility, supplement, 19:271–285.

———, D. MCCOWAN, AND I. A. NICHOLSON. 1976. Annual cycles of body weight and condition in Scottish red deer, *Cervus elaphus*. Journal of Zoology, London 180:107–127.

MONTANA FISH, WILDLIFE AND PARKS. 2001. Mule deer adaptive harvest management. Montana Department of Fish, Wildlife and Parks, Helena, USA. Available online at http://www.fwp.state.mt.us/default.aspx (accessed August 2003).

MOORE, M. T., S. L. SHERIFF, AND D. T. COBB. 2002. Do the HIP screening questions provide the information necessary to stratify the survey as envisioned? Pages 17–29 *in* J. M. Ver Steeg and R. C. Elden, compilers. Harvest information program: evaluation and recommendations. Migratory Shore and Upland Game Bird Working Group, Ad Hoc Committee on HIP, International Association of Fish and Wildlife Agencies, Washington, D.C., USA.

MORGANTINI, L. E., AND R. J. HUDSON. 1979. Human disturbance and habitat selection in elk. Pages 132–139 *in* M. S. Boyce and L. D. Hayden-Wing, editors. North American elk: ecology, behavior and management. University of Wyoming, Laramie, USA.

MOSBY, H. S. 1969. The influence of hunting on the population dynamics of a woodlot gray squirrel population. Journal of Wildlife Management 33:59–73.

———, R. L. KIRKPATRICK, AND J. O. NEWELL. 1977. Seasonal vulnerability of gray squirrels to hunting. Journal of Wildlife Management 41:284–289.

MOSSOP, D. H. 1994. Trends in Yukon upland gamebird populations from long-term harvest analysis. Transactions of the North American Wildlife and Natural Resources Conference 59:449–456.

MURRAY, T. B. 1938. Upland gamebirds in Idaho and their future. Pages 55–60 *in* A. B. Hatch, editor. First and Second Idaho Game Management Conferences. University of Idaho, Moscow, USA.

MUSSEHL, T. W. 1960. Blue grouse production, movements, and populations in the Bridger Mountains, Montana. Journal of Wildlife Management 24:60–68.

MYRBERGET, S. 1988. Demography of an island population of willow ptarmigan in northern Norway. Pages 379–419 *in* A. T. Bergerud and M. W. Gratson, editors. Adaptive strategies and population ecology of northern grouse. University of Minnesota Press, Minneapolis, USA.

———. 1989. Norwegian research on willow grouse: implications for management. Finnish Game Research 46:17–25.

NICHOLS, J. D. 1991. Responses of North American duck populations to exploitation. Pages 498–525 *in* C. M. Perrins, J. -D. Lebreton, and G. J. M. Hirons, editors. Bird population studies: their relevance to conservation and management. Oxford University Press, Oxford, United Kingdom.

———. 2000. Evolution of harvest management for North American waterfowl: selective pressures and preadaptations for adaptive harvest management. Transactions of the North American Wildlife and Natural Resources Conference 65:65–77.

———, AND F. A. JOHNSON. 1989. Evaluation and experimentation with duck management strategies. Transactions of the North American Wildlife and Natural Resources Conference 54:566–593.

———, ———, AND B. K. WILLIAMS. 1995. Managing North American waterfowl in the face of uncertainty. Annual Review of Ecology and Systematics 26:177–199.

———, M. J. CONROY, D. R. ANDERSON, AND K. P. BURNHAM. 1984. Compensatory mortality in waterfowl populations: a review of the evidence and implications for research and management. Transactions of the North American Wildlife and Natural Resources Conference 49:535–554.

NIEMAN, D. J., G. S. HOCHBAUM, F. D. CASWELL, AND B. C. TURNER. 1987. Monitoring hunter performance in prairie Canada. Transactions of the North American Wildlife and Natural Resources Conference 52:233–245.

NIEWOONDER, J. A., H. H. PRINCE, AND D. R. LUUKKONEN. 1998. Survival and reproduction of female Sichuan, ring-necked, and F_1 hybrid pheasants. Journal of Wildlife Management 62:933–938.

NIXON, C. M., R. W. DONOHOE, AND T. NASH. 1974. Overharvest of fox squirrels from two woodlots in western Ohio. Journal of Wildlife Management 38:67–80.

———, M. W. MCCLAIN, AND R. W. DONOHOE. 1975. Effects of hunting and mast crops on a squirrel population. Journal of Wildlife Management 39:1–25.

———, L. P. HANSEN, P. A. BREWER, AND J. E. CHELSVIG. 1991. Ecology of white-tailed deer in an intensively farmed region of Illinois. Wildlife Monographs 118.

NOYCE, K. V., AND D. L. GARSHELIS. 1997. Influence of natural food abundance on black bear harvests in Minnesota. Journal of Wildlife Management 61:1067–1074.

NOYES, J. H., B. K. JOHNSON, L. D. BRYANT, S. L. FINDHOLT, AND J. W. THOMAS. 1996. Effects of bull age on conception dates and pregnancy rates of cow elk. Journal of Wildlife Management 60:508–517.

PACK, J. C., G. W. NORMAN, C. I. TAYLOR, D. E. STEFFEN, D. A. SWANSON, K. H. POLLOCK, AND R. ALPIZAR-JARA. 1999. Effects of fall hunting on wild turkey populations in Virginia and West Virginia. Journal of Wildlife Management 63:964–975.

PALMER, W. L., AND C. L. BENNETT, JR. 1963. Relation of season length to hunting harvest of ruffed grouse. Journal of Wildlife Management 27:634–639.

PARKER, K. L., C. T. ROBBINS, AND T. A. HANLEY. 1984. Energy expenditures for locomotion by mule deer and elk. Journal of Wildlife Management 48:474–488.

PARMALEE, P. W. 1953. Hunting pressure and its effect on bobwhite quail populations in east-central Texas. Journal of Wildlife Management 17:341–345.

PEEK, J. M. 1986. A review of wildlife management. Prentice-Hall, Englewood Cliffs, New Jersey, USA.

———, AND A. L. LOVAAS. 1968. Differential distribution of elk by sex and age, Gallatin winter range, Montana. Journal of Wildlife Management 32:553–557.

———, M. S. BOYCE, E. O. GARTON, J. J. HARD, AND L. S. MILLS. 2002. Risks involved in current management of elk in Washington. Washington Department of Fish and Wildlife, Olympia, USA.

PELTON, M. R. 2000. Black bear. Pages 389–408 *in* S. Demarais and P. R. Krausman, editors. Ecology and management of large mammals in North America. Prentice-Hall, Inc. Upper Saddle River, New Jersey, USA.

PETERSBURG, M. L., A. W. ALLDREDGE, AND W. J. deVERGIE. 2000. Emigration and survival of 2-year-old male elk in northwestern Colorado. Wildlife Society Bulletin 28:708–716.

PETERSEN, L. E., AND A. H. RICHARDSON. 1975. The wild turkey in the Black Hills. Bulletin 6. South Dakota Department of Game, Fish and Parks, Pierre, USA.

POSPAHALA, R. S., D. R. ANDERSON, AND C. J. HENNY. 1974. Population ecology of the mallard. II. Breeding habitat conditions, size of the breeding populations, and production indices. U.S. Department of the Interior, Fish and Wildlife Service, Resource Publication 115.

PRINCE, H. H., P. SQUIBB, AND G. Y. BELYEA. 1988. Sichuans, pheasants of the future?—learning from past release programs. Pages 291–305 *in* D. L. Hallet, W. R. Edwards, and G. V. Burger, editors. Pheasants: symptoms of wildlife problems on agricultural lands. North Central Section, The Wildlife Society, Bloomington, Indiana, USA.

RANSOM, A. B. 1967. Reproductive biology of white-tailed deer in Manitoba. Journal of Wildlife Management 31:114–123.

RAVELING, D. G. 1984. Geese and hunters of Alaska's Yukon Delta: management problems and political dilemmas. Transactions of the North American Wildlife and Natural Resources Conference 49:555–575.

REXSTAD, E. A. 1992. Effect of hunting on annual survival of Canada geese in Utah. Journal of Wildlife Management 56:297–305.

REYNOLDS, R. E. 1987. Breeding duck population, production and habitat surveys, 1979–85. Transactions of the North American Wildlife and Natural Resources Conference 52:186–205.

ROBBINS, C. S., D. BYSTRAK, AND P. H. GEISSLER. 1986. The breeding bird survey: its first fifteen years, 1965–1979. U.S. Department of the Interior, Fish and Wildlife Service, Resource Publication 157.

ROBEL, R. J., J. N. BRIGGS, J. J. CEBULA, N. J. SILVY, C. E. VIERS, AND P. G. WATT. 1970. Greater prairie chicken ranges, movements, and habitat usage in Kansas. Journal of Wildlife Management 34:286–306.

ROBERTSON, P. A., AND A. A. ROSENBERG. 1988. Harvesting gamebirds. Pages 177–201 *in* P. J. Hudson and M. R. W. Rands, editors. Ecology and management of gamebirds. BSP Professional Books, Oxford, United Kingdom.

ROBINETTE, C. F., AND P. D. DOER. 1993. Survival of northern bobwhite on hunted and nonhunted study areas in the North Carolina sandhills. Pages 74–78 *in* K. E. Church and T. V. Dailey, editors. Quail III: national quail symposium. Kansas Department of Wildlife and Parks, Pratt, USA.

ROBINSON, W. L. 1980. Fool hen: the spruce grouse on the Yellow Dog

Plains. University of Wisconsin Press, Madison, USA.

ROMESBURG, H. C. 1981. Wildlife science: gaining reliable knowledge. Journal of Wildlife Management 45:293–313.

ROSE, G. B. 1977. Mortality rates of tagged adult cottontail rabbits. Journal of Wildlife Management 41:511–514.

ROSEBERRY, J. L. 1979. Bobwhite population responses to exploitation: real and simulated. Journal of Wildlife Management 43:285–305.

———. 1981. Bobwhite population responses: a reply. Journal of Wildlife Management 45:1054–1056.

———, D.C. AUTRY, W. D. KLIMSTRA, AND L. A. MEHRHOFF, JR. 1969. A controlled deer hunt on Crab Orchard National Wildlife Refuge. Journal of Wildlife Management 33:791–795.

ROSENE, W. 1969. The bobwhite quail, its life and management. Rutgers University Press, New Brunswick, New Jersey, USA.

RUSCH, D. H., S. DESTEFANO, AND R. J. SMALL. 1984. Seasonal harvest and mortality of ruffed grouse in Wisconsin. Pages 137–150 in W. L. Robinson, editor. Ruffed grouse management: state of the art in the early 1980's. North Central Section, The Wildlife Society, St. Louis, Missouri, USA.

SAMUEL, M. D., K. R. STEINHORST, E. O. GARTON, AND J. W. UNSWORTH. 1992. Estimation of wildlife population ratios incorporating survey design and visibility bias. Journal of Wildlife Management 56:718–725.

SAUER, J. R., AND J. B. BORTNER. 1991. Population trends from the American woodcock singing ground survey, 1970–88. Journal of Wildlife Management 55:300–312.

———, AND M. S. BOYCE. 1983. Density dependence and survival of elk in northwestern Wyoming. Journal of Wildlife Management 47:31–37.

SAUNDERS, G. B., AND D. C. SAUNDERS. 1981. Waterfowl and their wintering grounds in Mexico, 1937–64. U.S. Department of the Interior, Fish and Wildlife Service, Resource Publication 138.

SCHEMNITZ, S. D. 1994. Scaled quail. Number 106. In A. Poole, P. Stettenheim, and F. Gill, editors. The birds of North America. Academy of Natural Sciences, Philadelphia, Pennsylvania, USA.

SCHMIDT, J. L. 1980. Early management: intentional and otherwise. Pages 257–270 in J. L. Schmidt and D. L. Gilbert, editors. Big game of North America, ecology and management. Stackpole Books, Harrisburg, Pennsylvania, USA.

SCHROEDER, M. A. AND L. A. ROBB. 1993. Greater prairie chicken. Number 36. In A. Poole, P. Stettenheim, and F. Gill, editors. The birds of North America. Academy of Natural Sciences, Philadelphia, Pennsylvania, USA.

———, J. R. YOUNG, AND C. E. BRAUN. 1999. Sage grouse. Number 425. In A. Poole, P. Stettenheim, and F. Gill, editors. The birds of North America. Academy of Natural Sciences, Philadelphia, Pennsylvania, USA.

SCHULZ, J. W. 1990. Population surveys and gray partridge during winter in North Dakota: a comparison. Pages 131–143 in K. E. Church, R. E. Warner, and S. J. Brady, editors. Perdix V: gray partridge and ring-necked pheasant workshop. Kansas Department of Wildlife and Parks, Emporia, USA.

SHARP, D. E., J. A. DUBOVSKY, AND K. L. KRUSE. 2002. Population status and harvests of Mid-continent and Rocky Mountain sandhill cranes, 2002. U.S. Department of the Interior, Fish and Wildlife Service, Denver, Colorado, USA.

SILLIMAN, R. P., AND J. S. GUTSELL. 1958. Experimental exploitation of fish populations. U.S. Department of the Interior, Fish and Wildlife Service, Fish Bulletin 58(133):214–252.

SMALL, R. J., J. C. HOLZWART, AND D. H. RUSCH. 1991. Predation and hunting mortality of ruffed grouse in central Wisconsin. Journal of Wildlife Management 55:512–520.

SMITH, A., AND T. WILLEBRAND. 1999. Mortality causes and survival rates of hunted and unhunted willow grouse. Journal of Wildlife Management 63:722–730.

SMITH, G. W. 1995. A critical review of the aerial and ground surveys of breeding waterfowl in North America. U.S. Department of the Interior, National Biological Service, Biological Science Report 5.

———, AND R. E. REYNOLDS. 1992. Hunting and mallard survival,

1979–88. Journal of Wildlife Management 56:306–316.

SMITH, R. I., R. J. BLOHM, S. T. KELLY, R. E. REYNOLDS, AND F. D. CASWELL. 1989. Review of databases for managing duck harvests. Transactions of the North American Wildlife and Natural Resources Conference 54:537–544.

———, AND R. J. ROBERTS. 1976. The waterfowl hunter's perceptions of the waterfowl resource. Transactions of the North American Wildlife and Natural Resources Conference 41:188–193.

SMITH, R. L., AND J. L. COGGIN. 1984. Basis and role of management. Pages 571–600 in L. K. Halls, editor. White-tailed deer ecology and management. Stackpole Books, Harrisburg, Pennsylvania, USA.

SPARROWE, R. D., AND J. H. PATTERSON. 1987. Conclusions and recommendations from studies under stabilized duck hunting regulations: management implications and future directions. Transactions of the North American Wildlife and Natural Resources Conference 52:320–326.

STALLING, D. H., G. J. WOLF, AND D. K. CROCKETT. 2002. Regulating the hunt. Pages 749–791 in D. E. Toweill and J. W. Thomas, editors. North American elk: ecology and management. Smithsonian Institution Press, Washington, D.C., USA.

STAUFFER, D. 1993. Quail methodology: where are we and where do we need to be? Pages 21–33 in K. E. Church and T. V. Dailey, editors. Quail III: national quail symposium. Kansas Department of Wildlife and Parks, Pratt, USA.

STEEN, H., AND K. E. ERIKSTAD. 1996. Sensitivity of willow grouse *Lagopus lagopus* population dynamics to variations in demographic parameters. Wildlife Biology 2:27–35.

STODDARD, H. L. 1931. The bobwhite quail: its habits, preservation and increase. Charles Scribner's Sons, New York, USA.

STORMER, F. A., C. M. KIRKPATRICK, AND T. W. HOEKSTRA. 1979. Hunter-inflicted wounding of white-tailed deer. Wildlife Society Bulletin 7:10–16.

STRICKLAND, M. D., H. J. HARJU, K. R. MCCAFFERY, H. W. MILLER, L. M. SMITH, AND R. J. STOLL. 1994. Harvest management. Pages 445–473 in T. A. Bookhout, editor. Research and management techniques for wildlife and habitats. The Wildlife Society, Bethesda, Maryland, USA.

STROHMEYER, D. C., AND J. M. PEEK. 1996. Wapiti home range and movement patterns in a sagebrush desert. Northwest Science 70:79–87.

SVEDARSKY, W. D. 1988. Reproductive ecology of female greater prairie chickens in Minnesota. Pages 193–239 in A. T. Bergerud and M. W. Gratson, editors. Adaptive strategies and population ecology of northern grouse. University of Minnesota Press, Minneapolis, USA.

TACHA, T. C., S. A. NESBITT, AND P. A. VOHS. 1994. Sandhill crane. Pages 77–94 in T. C. Tacha and C. E. Braun, editors. Migratory shore and upland game bird management in North America. International Association of Fish and Wildlife Agencies, Washington, D.C., USA.

TAPER, M. L., AND P. J. P. GOGAN. 2002. The northern Yellowstone elk: density dependence and climatic conditions. Journal of Wildlife Management 66:106–122.

TAUTIN, J., S. M. CARNEY, AND J. B. BORTNER. 1989. A national migratory gamebird harvest survey: a continuing need. Transactions of the North American Wildlife and Natural Resources Conference 54:545–551.

TAYLOR, M., editor. 1994. Density-dependent population regulation in black, brown, and polar bears. Ninth International Conference on Bear Research and Management Monograph Series 3.

TAYLOR, M. A., AND F. S. GUTHERY. 1980a. Fall-winter movements, ranges, and habitat use of lesser prairie chickens. Journal of Wildlife Management 44:521–524.

———, AND ———. 1980b. Status, ecology, and management of the lesser prairie chicken. U.S. Department of Agriculture, Forest Service, General Technical Report RM-77.

TOMLINSON, R. E., D. D. DOLTON, H. M. REEVES, J. D. NICHOLS, AND L. A. MCKIBBEN. 1988. Migration, harvest, and population characteristics of mourning doves banded in the Western Management Unit, 1964–1977. U.S. Department of the Interior, Fish and Wildlife Service, Fish and Wildlife Technical Report 13.

TRAUTMAN, C. G. 1982. History, ecology and management of the ring-necked pheasant in South Dakota. Wildlife Research Bulletin 7. South Dakota Department of Game, Fish, and Parks, Pierre, USA.

TREFETHEN, J. B. 1964. Wildlife management and conservation. D. C. Heath and Company, Boston, Massachusetts, USA.

———. 1975. An American crusade for wildlife. Winchester Press, New York, USA.

TROST, R. E. 1987. Mallard survival and harvest rates: a reexamination of relationships. Transactions of the North American Wildlife and Natural Resources Conference 52:264–284.

———, K. E. GAMBLE, AND D. J. NIEMAN. 1990. Goose surveys in North America: current procedures and suggested improvements. Transactions of the North American Wildlife and Natural Resources Conference 55:338–349.

———, D. E. SHARP, S. T. KELLY AND F. D. CASWELL. 1987. Duck harvests and proximate factors influencing hunting activity and success during the period of stabilized regulations. Transactions of the North American Wildlife and Natural Resources Conference 52:216–232.

TURNER, B. C., G. S. HOCHBAUM, F. D. CASWELL, AND D. J. NIEMAN. 1987. Agricultural impacts on wetland habitats on the Canadian prairies, 1981–85. Transactions of the North American Wildlife and Natural Resources Conference 52:206–215.

UNSWORTH, J. W., L. KUCK, AND E. O. GARTON. 1990. Elk sightability model validation at the National Bison Range, Montana. Wildlife Society Bulletin 18:113–115.

———, ———, M. D. SCOTT, AND E. O. GARTON. 1993. Elk mortality in the Clearwater drainage of northcentral Idaho. Journal of Wildlife Management 57:495–502.

U.S. DEPARTMENT OF INTERIOR. 1988. Final supplemental environmental impact statement: issuance of annual regulations permitting the sport hunting of migratory birds. U.S. Department of the Interior, Fish and Wildlife Service, Washington, D.C., USA.

———. 2001. Draft environmental impact statement: light goose management. U.S. Department of the Interior, Fish and Wildlife Service, Washington, D.C., USA.

———. 2002. Draft environmental impact statement on resident Canada goose management. U.S. Department of the Interior, Fish and Wildlife Service, Washington, D.C., USA.

———, AND U.S. DEPARTMENT OF COMMERCE. 2002. National survey of fishing, hunting, and wildlife associated recreation: reference aid. U.S. Department of the Interior, Fish and Wildlife Service and U.S. Department of Commerce, Washington, D.C., USA.

VANCE, D. R., AND J. A. ELLIS. 1972. Bobwhite populations and hunting on Illinois public hunting areas. Proceedings of the National Bobwhite Quail Symposium 1:165–174.

VANDER ZOUWAN, W. J. 1990. Recent status of gray partridge in North America. Pages 21–31 in K. E. Church, R. E. Warner, and S. J. Brady, editors. Perdix V: gray partridge and ring-necked pheasant workshop. Kansas Department of Wildlife and Parks, Emporia, USA.

VANGILDER, L. D. 1992. Population dynamics. Pages 144–164 in J. G. Dickson, editor. The wild turkey: biology and management. Stackpole Books, Harrisburg, Pennsylvania, USA.

VANGILDER, L. D., AND E. W. KURZEJESKI. 1995. Population ecology of the eastern wild turkey in northern Missouri. Wildlife Monographs 130.

WALLESTAD, R. O. 1975. Life history and habitat requirements of sage grouse in central Montana. Montana Department of Fish, Game and Parks, Helena, USA.

WALSH, N. E., G. C. WHITE, AND D. J. FREDDY. 1991. Responses of bull elk to simulated elk vocalizations during rut. Journal of Wildlife Management 55:396–400.

WALTERS, C. J. 1986. Adaptive management of renewable resources. MacMillan Publishing Company, New York, USA.

WAMBOLT, C. L., A. J. HARP, B. L. WELCH, N. SHAW, J. W. CONNELLY, K. P. REESE, C. E. BRAUN, D. A. KLEBENOW, E. D. MACARTHUR, J. G. THOMPSON, L. A. TORRELL, AND J. A. TANAKA. 2002. Conservation of greater sage-grouse on public lands in the western U.S.: implications of recovery and management policies. Policy Analysis Center for Western Public Lands policy paper SG-02–02, Caldwell, Idaho, USA.

WARNER, R. E. 1992. Long-term perspectives of upland game bird research in North America. Pages 709–717 in D. R. McCullough and R. H. Barrett, editors. Wildlife 2001: populations. Elsevier Science Publishers, Ltd., Sussex, United Kingdom.

WEAVER, J. K., AND H. S. MOSBY. 1979. Influence of hunting regulations on Virginia wild turkey populations. Journal of Wildlife Management 43:128–135.

WEEDEN, R. B. 1972. Effects of hunting on rock ptarmigan along the Steese Highway. Wildlife Technical Bulletin 2. Alaska Department of Fish and Game, Anchorage, USA.

WEIGAND, J. P. 1980. Ecology of the Hungarian partridge in north-central Montana. Wildlife Monographs 74.

WHITE, G. C., R. M. BARTMANN, L. H. CARPENTER, AND R. A. GARROTT. 1989. Evaluation of aerial line transect for estimating mule deer densities. Journal of Wildlife Management 53:625–635.

———, D. J. FREDDY, R. B. GILL, AND J. H. ELLENBERGER. 2001. Effect of adult sex ratio on mule deer and elk productivity in Colorado. Journal of Wildlife Management 65:543–551

WHITESIDE, R. W., AND F. S. GUTHERY. 1983. Effects of hunting on ring-necked pheasants in northwest Texas. Wildlife Society Bulletin 11:250–252.

WHITTAKER, D. G., W. A. VAN DYKE, AND S. L. LOVE. 2003. Evaluation of aerial line transect for estimating pronghorn antelope abundance in low-density populations. Wildlife Society Bulletin 31:443–453.

WIGHT, H. 1959. Eleven years of rabbit-population data in Missouri. Journal of Wildlife Management 23:34–39.

WILLEBRAND, T., AND M. HÖRNELL. 2001. Understanding the effects of harvesting willow ptarmigan *Lagopus lagopus* in Sweden. Wildlife Biology 7:205–212.

WILLIAMS, B. K., AND F. A. JOHNSON. 1995. Adaptive management and the regulation of waterfowl harvests. Wildlife Society Bulletin 23:430–436.

———, ———, AND K. WILKINS. 1996. Uncertainty and the adaptive management of waterfowl harvests. Journal of Wildlife Management 60:223–232.

———, J. D. NICHOLS, AND M. J. CONROY. 2001. Analysis and management of animal populations. Academic Press, San Diego, California, USA.

WILLIAMS, C. K., R. S. LUTZ, AND R. D. APPLEGATE. 2004a. Winter survival and additive harvest in northern bobwhite coveys in Kansas. Journal of Wildlife Management 68: 94–100.

———, F. S. GUTHERY, R. D. APPLEGATE, AND M. J. PETERSON. 2004b. The northern bobwhite decline: scaling our management for the twenty-first century. Wildlife Society Bulletin 32: 861–869.

WILLIAMSON, L. L. 1987. Evolution of a landmark law. Pages 1–17 in H. Kallman, editor. Restoring America's wildlife. U.S. Department of the Interior, Fish and Wildlife Service, Washington, D.C., USA

WING, L. W. 1951. Practice of wildlife conservation. John Wiley and Sons, New York, USA

WOOD, A. K., R. J. MACKIE, AND K. L. HAMLIN. 1989. Ecology of sympatric populations of mule deer and white-tailed deer in a prairie environment. Montana Department of Fish, Wildlife and Parks, Helena, USA.

WOODS, G. R., D. C. GUYNN, W. E. HAMMITT, AND M. E. PATTERSON. 1996. Determinants of participant satisfaction with quality deer management. Wildlife Society Bulletin 24:318–324.

WOLFE, G. J. 1983. The relationship between age and antler development in wapiti. Pages 29–36 in R. D. Brown, editor. Antler development in Cervidae. Caesar Kleberg Wildlife Research Institute, Kingsville Texas, USA.

YEATTER, R. E. 1934. The Hungarian partridge in the Great Lakes Region. Bulletin 1. School of Forestry and Conservation, University of Michigan, Ann Arbor, USA.

ZWICKEL, F. C. 1982. Demographic composition of hunter-harvested blue grouse in east central Vancouver Island, British Columbia. Journal of Wildlife Management 46:1057–1061.

———. 1992. Blue grouse. Number 15. In A. Poole, P. Stettenheim, and F. Gill, editors. The birds of North America. Academy of Natural Sciences, Philadelphia, Pennsylvania, USA.

———, I. O. BUSS, AND J. H. BRIGHAM. 1968. Autumn movements of blue grouse and their relevance to populations and management. Journal of Wildlife Management 32:456–468.

26

ECOLOGY AND MANAGEMENT OF SMALL POPULATIONS

L. Scott Mills, J. Michael Scott, Katherine M. Strickler, and Stanley A. Temple

INTRODUCTION

Human-caused changes to natural landscapes are fragmenting wildlife habitats and causing many species to decline, often creating small, isolated populations. Consequently, understanding the dynamics of small populations is becoming increasingly important, not only for endangered species biologists, but also for those working with nonendangered populations as well.

Management concerns for small populations are frequently unlike those for large or thriving populations. When the small population of concern is a threatened or endangered species, management is a high-profile process, occurring in a regulatory environment and typically involving intensive management practices (Temple 1978, Scott et al. 1994). In many cases, the issues faced by managers of small populations are intensified versions of tasks important for managing any wildlife population: regulating rates of birth, dispersal, and mortality; maintaining habitat quantity and quality; and managing disease, predators, competitors, and other extrinsic factors. These issues often become critically important in management of small populations with limited time and few second chances for management to succeed. In addition, managers must cope with a number of questions more specific to small popula-

tions, such as avoiding genetic problems, doing viability analyses, and stimulating population growth.

In this chapter, we address a number of issues of special interest in management of small populations. First, we summarize biological and legal criteria for identifying small populations, and review the range of population sizes that have been considered to be "small." We then discuss factors that affect whether small populations will persist or become extirpated. Finally, we provide management guidelines for small populations, including a detailed description of viability assessment in general and population viability analysis in particular as practical, powerful tools for planning the management of small populations.

WHAT IS A SMALL POPULATION?

There are few precise definitions of a "small population." The reluctance to assign specific criteria is no doubt because so many variables are involved when considering population size across a wide range of species and conditions.

The Oxford English Dictionary (1989, XV:767) defines "small" as: "of limited size; of comparatively restricted dimensions; not large in comparison with other things, esp. of the same kind." This definition highlights the comparative nature of any criteria; except in extreme cases (what

Box 1. The "50–500 rule."

As a historical footnote while considering the meaning of a small population, it is worth reviewing the famous "50–500 rule." This rule of thumb emerged from a meeting on the application of conservation genetics to wild species (Franklin 1980, Soulé 1980, Frankel and Soulé 1981), and over the next decade was accepted into a number of management plans and biological opinions (e.g., U.S. Department of Interior 1987, 1998), including the Puerto Rican parrot (*Amazona vittata*) recovery plan. In essence, the "rule" provides a minimum genetic effective size for short-term and long-term protection, respectively.

An effective size of 50 was proposed as a minimum to protect against short-term loss of fitness due to inbreeding, based on empirical observations of the decrease in fitness-related traits with incremental inbreeding in a variety of animal species. Several caveats implicit in the original rule were lost as management was applied (Soulé 1987, Soulé and Mills 1992). For example, 50 is the *genetic effective size (Ne)*, which is only about 1/5 to 1/3 that of the total population size (Frankham et al. 2002); thus a Ne of 50 would translate to 150 to 250 or so actual animals. Second, the rule was proposed as a short-term guideline for captive breeding and similar "holding operations", not to long-term survival of wild populations, which would have many other factors affecting their persistence. Third, this was a rule based on genetic factors, not incorporating other factors that would increase the minimum necessary size for persistence. Based on these considerations, it is untenable to argue that an actual population size of 50 is sufficient as a rule to support any wildlife population into the foreseeable future.

The 500 number was proposed as the minimum size necessary to ensure long-term maintenance of genetic variation, thereby preserving evolutionary options for future adaptation. In more formal terms, the number was the estimated minimum genetic effective size where the loss of additive genetic variation of a quantitative character due to genetic drift would be balanced by new variation due to mutations. This number has received serious scrutiny by population geneticists, with arguments ranging from as large as 5,000 or more (Frankham et al. 2002). This debate will likely continue (Allendorf and Ryman 2002), but there is little doubt that the *actual* (as opposed to genetic effective) population size necessary to maintain evolutionary potential for the long term should be thousands of individuals and not hundreds.

Scott et al. [2001] called "vanishingly small populations"), small size is a relative concept. Whether or not a population is considered small is dependent on a series of comparisons with populations of conspecifics, similar species, historical population sizes, and even arbitrary management standards. For an exploited species such as the canvasback (*Aythya valisineria*), conservation plans may call for corrective management to be implemented when population sizes decrease to the tens of thousands. In contrast, conservation efforts for threatened species may be delayed until the population falls below 100 or is putatively extinct (e.g., 'ō 'ū [*Psittirostra psittacea*]). Thus, an attempt to define a universal criterion for small based on numbers may be useful as a heuristic exercise, but should not be interpreted too strictly (Box 1).

The definition of a small population may also be influenced by a species' life history characteristics. In general, extinction probability increases as population size decreases, an idea deeply rooted in wildlife biology and ecology (e.g., Leopold 1933, MacArthur and Wilson 1967). In some (but not all) cases, restricted geographic range or local endemism can serve as proxies for small population size (Channell and Lomolino 2000, Purvis et al. 2000).

Populations with higher variance in population growth rate relative to mean population growth rate will have to be larger in size to avoid extinctions (Lande 1993; Fagan et al. 1999, 2001). Species attributes such as litter or clutch size, age at first reproduction, and intervals between births may be useful for predicting population growth rate or variation in growth rate and, therefore, vulnerability of a population (Purvis et al. 2000, Fagan et al. 2001). By contrast, the use of secondary surrogates such as home range size, group size, or body size as general indicators of extinction vulnerability has been largely unsuccessful because correlations are weak and inconsistent (e.g., large-bodied animals tend to show lower variation in numbers but also

lower population growth rates) (Lawton 1995). Some animals may be more vulnerable because of their sensitivity to anthropogenic threats, limited dispersal capability, narrow habitat requirements, and the extent to which a species is harvested or persecuted by humans rather than because of body size or home range size *per se*. Vulnerability may also derive in part from particular behavioral attributes (Reed 1999); for example, species might be more vulnerable if they show Allee effects (reduced survival or reproduction at small numbers), naiveness toward predators (e.g., dodo [*Raphus cucullatus*]), or aggregated dispersion (e.g., passenger pigeon [*Ectopistes migratorius*]).

The final utility of these ecological and life history characteristics as predictors of extinction depends on the specific context of the environment and the species in question (Tracy and George 1992, Belovsky et al. 1994, Channell and Lomolino 2000). For example, vulnerabilities of primates and carnivores were underestimated by a model based on species characteristics in cases where the species had lost habitat, been commercially overexploited, or where problems had been created by exotic species (Purvis et al. 2000).

Finally, a proposal has been made that criteria for small be scaled according to the population size necessary to retain 95% of the heterozygosity of the population for 100 years (Allendorf and Ryman 2002). What this size will be depends on mating system and other characteristics affecting the genetic effective population size (Oyler-McCance and Leberg 2005), as well as generation time.

Guidelines to "Small" from Categorization Systems

Guidelines to what is considered "small" have been established by agencies. For example, the International Union for the Conservation of Nature (IUCN, or World Conservation Union) has developed a categorical system for assigning risk

Table 1. IUCN Red List (IUCN 2001).

Red list category	Very small population	Small population and declining
Critically endangered	< 50 mature individuals	< 250 mature individuals, population declining
Endangered	< 250 mature individuals	< 2,500 mature individuals, population declining
Vulnerable	< 1,000 mature individuals	< 10,000 mature individuals, population declining

based in part on small population size ("Rule of Thumb" approach discussed later in chapter). Species with small, stable populations are considered "critically endangered" if their populations fall below 50 mature individuals, "endangered" if their populations have fewer than 250 mature individuals, and "vulnerable" if they consist of 1,000 or fewer mature individuals. Small, declining populations have higher threshold values for each category (Table 1).

In the United States, a comprehensive system of assessing the conservation status and extinction risk for species has been developed by the Natural Heritage Network and The Nature Conservancy (Master et al. 2000). The heritage ranking system is based on the perceived vulnerability of a species to extinction, taking into consideration both intrinsic risks and external threats. A species is considered to be "critically imperiled" if fewer than 1,000 individuals exist across its range; at the other end of the spectrum are "apparently secure" species with 10,000 or more individuals (Table 2). Although these categories are not based on scientific criteria, they provide insights into what may be considered a "small population" for management purposes.

Finally, a measure of a "small population" might be extracted from listings under the Endangered Species Act (ESA). Between 1985 and 1991 the median population size for threatened and endangered species at time of listing was 1,075 individuals for vertebrates, 999 for invertebrates, and 120 for plants (Wilcove et al. 1993).

Types of Rarity

It is important to note that "rare" and "small" are not necessarily synonymous with reference to wild populations. Although we tend to associate both terms with an increased risk of extinction (Rabinowitz et al. 1986), rare species do not necessarily have small populations. This point was developed by Rabinowitz et al. (1986), who defined 7 forms of rarity based on population size, geographic distribution, and habitat specificity. Species with large populations may be considered rare in 3 permutations of these characteristics: species that are narrow in both habitat specificity and geographic range; species that are restricted to limited habitats that are widely distributed; and species that have broad habitat requirements within a narrow distribution. For example, elk (*Cervus elaphus*) have broad habitat tolerance, large population sizes locally, and are widely distributed, whereas gray wolves (*Canis lupus*) were

formerly widely distributed, with broad habitat tolerance and locally small population sizes. In contrast are species with restricted habitat requirements and narrow geographic range such as the American dipper (*Cinclus mexicanus*) and tri-colored blackbird (*Agelaius tricolor*), both of which may be locally abundant. These examples underscore the distinction between rarity and small population size. In general, small populations of narrowly distributed species are most vulnerable to extinction (Rabinowitz et al. 1986).

Naturally Small vs. Declining Populations

Not all small populations have declined. There are many examples of populations that are naturally small, persisting for many generations at levels that would be vulnerable to stochastic factors in declining populations (Brown 1995). Naturally small populations are often found on true islands, or island-like continental environments (Walter [1990] provided an example with the Socorro Island hawk [*Buteo jamaicensis socorroensis*]). Other wildlife species that typically occur in naturally small populations include top carnivores such as wolverines (*Gulo gulo*); large animals such as mountain sheep (*Ovis canadensis*); and species restricted to small areas of habitat (e.g., big-eared kangaroo rat, *Dipodomys elephantinus*). These populations may share some risk factors with declining populations, but more likely have distinctive life-history features that allow them to persist (Angermeier 1995, Fagan et al. 2001). Management of naturally small populations may focus primarily on maintaining the status quo: supporting natural disturbance regimes, avoiding habitat loss or degradation, and preventing the introduction of competitors, predators, parasites, or diseases.

In contrast to naturally small populations are species that were once common or widely distributed but are now restricted to small, isolated populations following a reduction in population size. A population's decline may be due to habitat fragmentation or loss, competition with introduced species, disease, overharvest, or a combination of factors, but the end result is a population that is usually at increased risk of extinction due to both deterministic and stochastic factors (Clark et al. 1990). For example, greater prairie-chickens (*Tympanuchus cupido*) were once abundant over the North American grasslands, but they have declined to small, isolated, endangered populations because of habitat loss and fragmentation (Bouzat et al. 1998*a,b*; Soulé and Mills 1998). Native birds of the Hawaiian Islands and Guam (Scott et al. 1986, Savidge

Table 2. Natural Heritage Program conservation status rank definitions (Master et al. 2000).

G1	Critically imperiled. Typically 5 or fewer occurrences or 1,000 or fewer individuals
G2	Imperiled. Typically 6 to 20 occurrences or 1,000 to 3,000 individuals
G3	Vulnerable. Rare; typically 21 to 100 occurrences or 3,000 to 10,000 individuals
G4	Apparently secure. Uncommon but not rare; some cause for long-term concern; usually more than 100 occurrences and 10,000 individuals
G5	Secure. Common; widespread and abundant

1987) are examples of situations where entire avifaunas have been placed at risk because of a combination of factors. The first challenge for managers of these "small through decline" populations is to identify the ultimate and proximate causes of population reductions. Because small populations are more vulnerable to extinction (Lima et al. 1996), additional management activities may be required.

LEGAL MANDATES FOR MANAGEMENT OF SMALL POPULATIONS

In the United States there are 15 federal statutes that conserve species through restrictions on take and commerce, 18 that provide for conservation of wildlife habitat, and 19 that include both conservation of species and habitat (Table 3). Detailed descriptions of these statutes and treaties can be found in Goble and Freyfogle (2002*a*, *b*). These statutes, while providing the legal framework for protecting species, deal with issues of population size only vaguely; none use the phrase "small population size" or define when population size reaches the point at which management is mandated. In contrast, the Marine Mammal Act (Section 2) states "population stocks should not be permitted to diminish beyond the point at which they cease to be significant functioning elements of the ecosystem of which they are a part and, consistent with this major objective, they should not be permitted to diminish below their optimum sustainable populations." The 1982 federal reg-

Table 3. Federal statutes related to the management of wildlife (from Goble and Freyfogle 2002*a*).

Conserving Species Through Restrictions on Take and Commerce
    Lacey Act, 1900, 1981
    Migratory Bird Treaty Act, 1918
    Tariff Act of 1930
    Bald and Golden Eagle Protection Act, 1940, 1962
    Act Prohibiting the Use of Aircraft and Motor Vehicles to
        Hunt Feral Horses and Burros, 1959
    Airborne Hunting Act, 1971
    Wild Free-Roaming Horses and Burros Act, 1971
    Marine Mammal Protection Act, 1972
    Magnuson-Stevens Fisheries Conservation and Manage-
        ment Act, 1976
    Neotropical Migratory Bird Conservation Act, 1999
    Wild Exotic Bird Conservation Act, 1992
    African Elephant Conservation Act, 1988
    Asian Elephant Conservation Act, 1998
    Rhinoceros and Tiger Conservation Act, 1998
    Great Ape Conservation Act, 2000
Conserving Wildlife Habitat
  Federal Wildlife Refuges
    Refuge Acquisition
        Migratory Bird Conservation Act, 1929
        Migratory Bird Stamp Act, 1934
        Wetlands Loan Act, 1961
Refuge Management
        Refuge Revenue Sharing Act, 1935, 1964
        Refuge Trespass Act, 1948
        Refuge Recreation Act, 1962
        Refuge Administration Act, 1966
        National Marine Sanctuaries Act, 1992
        National Wildlife Refuge System Improvement Act, 1997
Funding State Acquisition of Habitat
        Federal Aid in Wildlife Restoration Act, 1937 (The
            Pittman-Robertson Act)
        Federal Aid in Fish Restoration Act, 1950 (Dingell-Johnson
            Act)
        Land and Water Conservation Fund Act, 1964
        Fish & Wildlife Conservation Act, 1980
Consideration of the Effect of Federal Actions on Wildlife
Habitat
        Fish and Wildlife Coordination Act, 1934, 1946, 1958
        National Environmental Policy Act, 1969

Planning and Coordination
        The Anadromous Fish Act, 1965
        Sikes Act Extension, 1974
Conserving Biodiversity
  Conserving Endangered Species
        Endangered Species Act, 1973
Conservation of Both Species and Habitat – Federal Lands
    National Park Service
        Antiquities Act, 1906
        National Park Service Organic Act, 1916 and General
            Authorities Act, 1970
U.S. Forest Service
        National Forest Service Organic Act, 1897
        Multiple-Use Sustained-Yield Act, 1960
        National Forest Management Act, 1976
Bureau of Land Management
        Federal Land Policy and Management Act, 1976
        Public Rangelands Improvement Act, 1978
Military Lands
        Sikes Act, 1960, 1997
Preservation Land Systems
        Wilderness Act, 1964
        Wild and Scenic Rivers Act, 1968
Federal Waters
        Rivers and Harbors Act, 1899
        Federal Power Act, 1920
        Federal Water Pollution Control Act, 1972
Conservation of Both Species and Habitat – Private Lands
  Wetlands
        Federal Water Pollution Control Act, 1972
        "Swampbuster" Provisions, 1985, 1990, 1996
        Coastal Barrier Resources Act, 1982
Uplands
        Conservation Reserve Program, 1985
        Environmental Easement Program, 1990
        Forest Legacy Program, 1990
Problem Wildlife
        Lacey Act, 1900
        Animal Damage Control, 1931
        Nonindigenous Aquatic Nuisance Prevention and Control
            Act, 1990

ulations implementing the National Forest Management Act of 1976 directed the U.S. Forest Service to maintain habitat to support viable populations of native and desired nonnative vertebrate species (Andelman et al. 2001), with viability measured primarily by population size.

Endangered Species Act

Foremost in the United States among federal wildlife statutes that specifically address the management needs of "small populations" is the Endangered Species Act of 1973 with its subsequent amendments (Goble and Freyfogle 2002*b*). The Act provides for the protection and recovery of species (defined as species, subspecies, and distinct population segments for vertebrates, and as species and subspecies for plants and invertebrates). The Act's objective was to conserve "to the extent practicable the various species of fish and wildlife and plants facing extinction throughout all or a significant part of their range." No numerical criteria for either population size or trends are specified in the ESA as a threshold for listing a species as endangered or threatened. The number of individuals at the time of listing varies by orders of magnitude even within a class of organisms (Wilcove et al. 1993). For example, the Inyo California towhee (*Pipilo crissalis eremophilus*) was listed as threatened when it reached a population size of less than 175 individuals, whereas the coastal California gnatcatcher (*Polioptila californica californica*) still numbered in the thousands when it was listed as endangered. Similarly, there are no demographic criteria for downlisting or delisting species beyond a directive for "objective, measurable criteria which, when met, would result in a determination … that the species should be removed from the list" of threatened and endangered species (Goble and Freyfogle 2002*a*:354).

Species at Risk Act

The recently passed Species at Risk Act (SARA) of Canada (S.C. 2002, c.29) provides for the protection of rare wildlife, which includes species, subspecies, variety or geographically or genetically distinct populations. The criteria for listing or delisting a species in Canada are more similar to IUCN criteria and more specific than those for the ESA. In 1988 the Council of Canadian Wildlife Ministers signed an agreement establishing the Recovery of Nationally Endangered Wildlife (RENEW) program (Scudder 1999). The objectives of RENEW are to prevent the extinction of species, prevent additional species from becoming threatened or endangered, reintroduce extirpated species, establish recovery plans to remove species from the threatened and endangered list, and prepare recovery plans for all threatened and endangered species (Canadian Wildlife Service 2001).

CITES

The Endangered Species Act of 1973 also included provisions for increased protection of endangered and threatened species worldwide (Bean 1983). The Endangered Species Act implemented the Convention on International Trade in Endangered Species of Wild Flora and Fauna (CITES) in the United States and provided a program to encourage foreign governments to establish programs for conservation of species (Bean 1983). Species listed under CITES cannot be transported between countries without special permit. The criteria for listing are only vaguely defined and the decision to list a species depends largely on consensus of the parties. Mexico is also signatory to CITES.

The United States/Mexico Joint Committee on Wildlife Conservation was established in 1974 to help address the question of vulnerable species. This agreement provides the basis for cooperation on conservation efforts for species occurring in both nations, such as sharing survey information and cooperation on recovery efforts for species. However, it is vague about defining a small population.

FACTORS AFFECTING PERSISTENCE IN SMALL POPULATIONS

Deterministic Factors

In managing a small and declining population, the most important factors to consider are what caused the population to become small, and how to reverse the decline. Whether the cause of decline was habitat loss, overharvest, exotic species, change in disturbance regime, or some combination of these or other causes, the perturbations that led to the population becoming small are of paramount importance (Caughley and Gunn 1996) and greatly influence the possibility of recovery (Abbitt et al. 2000, Miller et al. 2002). These factors are "deterministic," indicating the outcome for the population can be expected to follow in a predictable way. We cannot predict the specific ways perturbations (habitat loss, overharvest, etc.) will affect population dynamics. However, deterministic factors that affect population growth in known ways are distinguished from "stochastic" or random factors that also affect small populations.

Stochastic Factors

Unfortunately, when a population becomes small it becomes particularly susceptible to a host of other threats that interact with and exacerbate problems caused by deterministic factors. Thus, for small populations, even if the deterministic problems were reversed so the population achieved a positive average population growth, the population could still be driven toward extinction. Factors are called "stochastic" because they have a large element of randomness in how they affect any particular population.

Two important points emerge from an understanding of stochastic factors: a) with all else equal, small populations are more likely to become extinct than large ones; and b) with all else equal, populations with large variation in vital rates are more likely to become extinct than those with small variation. There are 3 main types of stochasticity that affect population persistence (Shaffer 1987): demographic, environmental, and genetic. Because the operation and effect of stochastic factors on populations are less intuitive than deterministic factors, we explain how they impact small populations.

Demographic Stochasticity

Demographic stochasticity arises from inevitable deviations around mean birth and death rates because these rates are probabilistic. For small populations, demographic stochasticity causes variation in population growth even in a constant environment, with no change in mean birth or death rates. One of the easiest ways to understand demographic stochasticity and its special effects on small populations is by example. If you toss a fair coin, the expected probability of heads is a constant 50%. But if you toss the coin only 3 times, you cannot possibly get 50% heads: either you get 0, or 33%, or 67%, or 100% heads, by chance! Even if you tossed it 4 times, you would not be too surprised to get something other than 50:50. However, if you tossed the coin 100 times you would expect the percentage of heads to be much closer to 50%, and if you tossed it 1,000 times you would be confident of converging on 50%, the expected probability of heads.

Consider how this analogy would apply to sex ratios, which are typically expected to be close to 50:50 at birth if there are many births occurring in the population. If, however, there are few births because of small population size, stochasticity could easily result in a marked deviation from the expected 50:50 ratio; this stochastic change could impair the population's ability to recover. Similarly, survival and birth rates in a small population could deviate widely from the expected mean by chance alone. Thus, demographic stochasticity can affect sex ratio, reproduction, and/or survival causing each to be more or less than the mean expectation. Therefore, even if the environment is relatively constant and birth and death rates are such that average population growth should be positive, demographic stochasticity in a small population could still cause a decline towards extinction. An often-cited example of the effects of demographic stochasticity in sex ratio is the extinction of the dusky seaside sparrow (*Ammospiza maritime nigrescens*) when all of the last 6 survivors happened to be males (James 1980, Avise and Nelson 1989, Post and Greenlaw 1994).

Just as a coin toss converges on 50:50 with many tosses, demographic stochasticity is minimized when abundance exceeds about 100 individuals (Morris and Doak 2002: 25), so only relatively small populations are highly likely to decline from this factor alone. In some cases, individual variation is characterized as stochastic to ease analytical tractability when really there are deterministic drivers—perhaps due to maternal provisioning, genetic makeup, territory quality, or other factors. The extent to which this occurs can affect the influence of demographic stochasticity (McCarthy et al. 1994, Fox and Kendall 2002, Kendall and Fox 2002).

Environmental Stochasticity

In contrast to demographic stochasticity, environmental stochasticity produces random changes in mean vital rates across individuals. Environmental stochasticity results from factors that are extrinsic to the population. Although environmental factors can be either physical or biotic, they occur in unpredictable patterns. The most obvious form of environmental stochasticity is climate, including normal vagaries of temperature and other weather-related phenomena, such as severe storms. Regardless of the underlying (and usually unknown) mechanism, mean vital rates for all animals in the population—and therefore population growth rate—varies over time and space in unpredictable ways. Unlike demographic stochasticity, environmental stochasticity does not disappear in large populations. For example, a change in population growth rate from a 2% increase to a 2% decrease per year translates into changes in population size whether there are 50 or 500 animals in the population.

An important result of environmental stochasticity in small populations is that a population with a positive average growth rate from one year to the next may actually decline over the long term (Morris and Doak 2002). This possibly counter-intuitive result is because population growth is a geometric (or multiplicative) process, not an arithmetic process, so growth is governed by the geometric mean of the yearly population changes and not the arithmetic mean. Consider a population whose annual population growth rate alternates between $\lambda = 1.6$ and $\lambda = 0.6$ ($\lambda = 1.0$ is stationary). The arithmetic mean of the growth rate is 1.1, indicating an increasing population, but the geometric mean is 0.98 ($\lambda = \sqrt{1.6 x 0.6}$); over time this population would be expected to decline. Whenever the variance in the average population growth rate is more than about twice its mean, the long-term population growth of that population will be negative even if its intrinsic growth rate is positive. A related implication is that ignoring environmental variation in population models will lead to predictions of persistence that are overly optimistic (Boyce 1977).

A practical point to remember about environmental stochasticity is that it is estimated from field data, which has an associated sampling error. In essence, sampling variation adds noise to the estimate of environmental variation. Thus, total variance should be partitioned into true process variance (spatial and temporal variation) distinct from the "noise" of sampling variance. The use of total variance for environmental stochasticity, instead of true process variance, will make nature seem more "variable" than it is, which will tend to bias (higher) predictions of extinction in population viability analysis (Ludwig 1999). Methods for partitioning total variance into the component process versus sampling variation are discussed in Thompson et al. (1998) and White (2000).

Finally, we note that populations can be exposed to stochastic events that are extreme beyond the tails of expected environmental stochasticity. These events are called "catastrophes" or "bonanzas," and can have profound effect on persistence of small populations (Shaffer 1987, Morris and Doak 2002). For example, a 1963 hurricane decimated the last Laysan teal (*Anas laysanensis*) population; volcanic eruptions in Japan almost destroyed the last colony of the short-tailed albatross (*Phoebastria albatrus*); and a severe winter coupled with overbrowsing killed all but 50 of the 6,000 reindeer (*Rangifer tarandus*) on St. Matthew Island (Simberloff 1988).

Genetic Stochasticity

The third stochastic factor refers to random loss of alleles (alternative forms of a gene), and the subsequent effects on population dynamics in small populations. Genetic stochasticity arises from genetic drift, the process whereby random inheritance of alleles in a small randomly-mating population leads to the "drifting" of the frequency of alternative alleles towards either 1.0 or 0.0 and an accompanying increase in homozygosity (Oyler-McCance and Leberg 2005). Vertebrates carry enough deleterious alleles—bad genes (called "lethal equivalents per individual")—to kill each individual about 3 times over (reviewed by Keller 1998), but in large populations natural selection holds them at low frequency, and their recessive nature means their effects are masked by a non-harmful allele. However, genetic drift can lead to reduced survival or reproduction via inbreeding depression when these deleterious alleles become expressed as homozygotes.

Loss of heterozygosity and expression of inbreeding depression due to genetic drift in small wildlife populations are well-established processes that can affect both captive and wild populations (Mills and Tallmon 1999). Like any other process (predation, disease, weather events, etc.), the effects of inbreeding depression for any particular population will range from non-existent to a strong driver of persistence. In a comprehensive review of effects of inbreeding depression on wild species measured under natural conditions, Crnokrak and Roff (1999) used 169 estimates of inbreeding depression on fitness traits (e.g., reproduction) or traits indirectly related to fitness (e.g., juvenile body mass) from 35 species. Overall, approximately 55% of the data sets demonstrated inbreeding depression. For the subset of mammal and bird species (63 trait measurements in 15 species), there was a 27% average reduction in fitness for inbred compared to outbred individuals (see also Keller and Waller 2002).

Thinking beyond short-term persistence to long-term prospects of a species, genetic variation is the raw material of evolution, underlying the ability of populations to adapt to changes in climate, habitat, competitors, disease, etc. If it is lost in small populations, the ability to survive future changes can be compromised even if the population subsequently recovers to its former size (Soulé 1980, Frankham et al. 2002). As an example, Botta's pocket gopher (*Thomomys bottae*) populations that have low genetic variation are actually able to accept reciprocal skin grafts from individuals within their population; populations with high variation reject the grafts (Sanjayan et al. 1996). This extreme consequence of loss of variation, resulting in an individual not being able to distinguish self from non-self, implies that ability to recognize and destroy intruder viruses, microbes, and other diseases will be compromised.

PREDICTING THE RISKS OF SMALL POPULATION SIZE

The Extinction Vortex

We have stressed that both deterministic and stochastic factors affect the likelihood of a small population declining, or becoming extinct. The interaction of all of these factors is portrayed by the *extinction vortex* (Fig. 1). This captures the idea that primary drivers of concern for declining and/or small populations are deterministic human-caused perturbations (including habitat loss and degradation, exotics, overharvest, etc.). How the perturbation affects a particular population depends on its structure (life history characteristics, age structure, behavioral interactions, distribution, physiological status, etc.), and on the environment (habitat, weather, competition, predators, food abundance, etc.). These perturbations can decrease vital rates (reproduction and survival), thereby decreasing both population growth rate and population size. Each turn of the feedback cycle increases extinction probability because decreased population size and growth rate can lead to increased effects of inbreeding depression and stochastic events, further decreasing population size and growth. The extinction vortex emphasizes the need to consider the relative importance of these different factors and how they interact in a particular case (Gilpin and Soulé 1986, Lande 1988, Soulé and Mills 1992, Mills and Smouse 1994, Mills 1996).

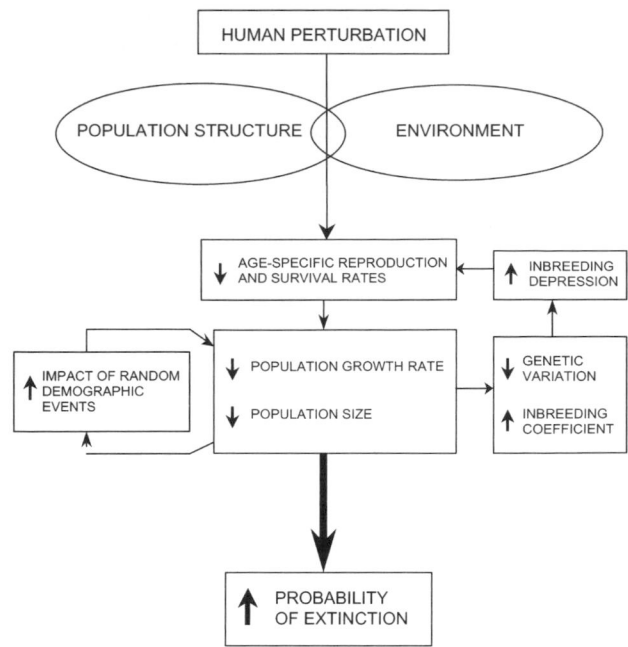

Fig. 1. Simplified representation of the extinction vortex (adapted from Soulé and Mills 1998).

A recent example of the extinction vortex (from Westemeier et al. 1998; Bouzat et al. 1998*a,b*; Soulé and Mills 1998) affecting a small population is instructive. As native grasslands have been increasingly fragmented, the Illinois population of the greater prairie-chicken became isolated from other populations and small, declining from about 2,000 individuals in the early 1960s to less than 50 birds by the early 1990s. Although habitat destruction and degradation, and associated increases in predators clearly caused the decline, stochastic factors became relevant at small population size. The decline continued despite intense and somewhat successful efforts to control predators and increase the quality and quantity of habitat. Genetic stochasticity was identified as a contributor to the decline because genetic variation was lower for prairie-chickens in Illinois when compared to populations in neighboring states (which had remained relatively large and widespread). Genetic variability was also lower for the present Illinois population than for historical samples collected from that population before the demographic contraction. Translocations of prairie-chickens from neighboring states since 1992 have increased egg fertility and hatching success. Thus, inbreeding apparently contributed to depressed hatching success, and gene flow helped to restore it. Continued vigilance in addressing deterministic causes of declines remains necessary for all small populations (Maehr and Lacy 2002).

The Process of Viability Assessment

Wildlife viability assessment (Table 4) formalizes evaluation of the processes of the extinction vortex. It places intuition, field data, and theory into an operational framework to allow assessment of the factors that caused decline and that may cause further decline in the future. Because it is a framework for incorporating multiple, interacting processes, it can reveal non-intuitive and non-obvious out-

Table 4. Components of a population viability risk management process (from Marcot and Murphy 1996).

---

1. *Describe the species.* Identify and screen for species at risk.
2. *Describe pertinent regulations and laws.* Define the range of acceptable conditions that meet policy regulations or law. Identify responsible agencies and institutions and coordinate their planning activities.
3. *Describe species conditions and ecology.* Describe the species' environmental relationships and reasons for viability concern or population decline.
4. *Develop planning alternatives.* Develop a range of planning or management strategies. Describe risk attitudes of publics and responsible agencies and institutions. Describe perceived and expected utilities of planning alternatives. Identify factors and value ranges in decision criteria to be used to select among the alternatives.
5. *Evaluate viability effects of the alternatives.* Conduct a viability risk analysis. Analyze how the alternatives affect population size, distribution, and persistence, resource tradeoffs, and social concerns.
6. *Array the alternatives according to anticipated effects.* Assess the benefits to population viability, indirect costs, opportunity costs, and foregone options for each alternative. Identify and array the range of acceptable alternatives that meet decision criteria.
7. *Select an alternative.* Apply decision criteria to results and select a course of action.
8. *Implement the alternative.* Institutionalize management guidelines of the selected alternative. Develop budgets and track implementation.
9. *Monitor results.* Compile and interpret monitoring information; revisit steps 1–8 as suggested by monitoring information and changing conditions.

---

comes that can help in management decisions. The intellectual roots of assessing viability of wildlife populations date to at least the 1930s (Reed et al. 1998*b*). Leopold (1933:47) noted the importance for wildlife managers to recognize "the minimum number of individuals which may successfully exist as a detached population."

A subset of viability assessment procedures includes Population Viability Analysis (PVA). As the quantitative arm of the body of approaches to assessing viability, PVA can be defined as the application of data and models to predict a series of likelihoods that a population will persist for specified times into the future (and to provide insights into factors that constitute the biggest threats).

We believe PVA embraces the concept of a "Minimum Viable Population (MVP)" and makes this concept somewhat obsolete. MVP is problematic for both philosophic and scientific reasons. Philosophically, it strikes us as risky to manage for the "minimum" number of individuals that could persist on this planet. Scientifically, the problem is that we cannot specify the number of individuals that will insure long-term viability, because of all the uncertainties involved in the persistence of a small population.

Thorough reviews of practical applications of PVA have been published recently (e.g., Boyce 1992, Sjögren-Gulve and Ebenhard 2000, Young and Clarke 2000, Beissinger and McCullough 2002, Morris and Doak 2002, Reed et al.

2002). We highlight these applications for management of small populations, focusing both on the quantitative framework of PVA as well as on other methods that constitute the assessment of viability.

Three Characteristics of Population Viability Analysis

Quantitative viability assessment using PVA has 3 central concepts: persistence, time, and likelihood. Persistence is usually in the sense of "not extinct," implying that a population remains above zero individuals (or 1 mating pair). This is an important threshold, but there are often thresholds other than zero that are useful to track for biological or management reasons. These "quasi-extinction" thresholds might include, for example, biological thresholds below which Allee effects occur or where strongly interacting species become unable to perform critical ecosystem functions (Conner 1988, Soulé et al. 2003). Quasi-extinction thresholds may also include management thresholds such as the triggering number to bring a wild population into captivity, or the abundance below which a threatened species would be reclassified as endangered (Ginzburg et al. 1990, Burgman et al. 1993, Scott et al. 1995). Therefore, when we refer to "extinction" we include both true extinction and quasi-extinction thresholds.

A second important component of our PVA definition is time (Frankel and Soulé 1981). As with any other prediction (e.g., weather, stock market), the assumptions used in PVA will be less and less reliable further into the future. Scott et al. (1995) proposed that when PVA is used in endangered species recovery plans it should incorporate short-term projections that are evaluated over time against a long-term goal (see also Goodman 2002). The long-term viability assessment should include goals that are biologically based. The short-term projections should explicitly incorporate political/legal/social constraints; monitoring and the iterative application of short-term PVAs can be used to evaluate how well long-term goals are being achieved. Thus, public review (and political tradeoffs) can be incorporated in choosing short-term management strategies, but ultimate success is judged against the yardstick of the long-term, biologically based goal.

The final component of the definition of PVA is "likelihood." Obviously, a higher probability of persistence over a given time will require a larger initial population size. Likelihoods are captured in quantitative PVAs with "quasi-extinction curves" (Burgman et al. 1993, Groom and Pascual 1998, Akçakaya 2000). There are many ways these likelihoods can be portrayed; they are usually presented as the probability of reaching a quasi-extinction threshold over a range of time, or the probability of reaching different population sizes at some point over a fixed time, or the risk of decline by a given amount.

Consideration of these PVA components—viability threshold, persistence time, and likelihood of persistence—argue for PVA being conducted as an examination of alternatives, with a range of data and products, instead of performing just one PVA for a species with "X" data for "Y" probability of persistence over "Z" years.

Many key aspects of PVA have a strong biological basis but the selection of goals requires the addition of a social component. Issues such as "For how long do we want to evaluate persistence?" and "How secure should that persistence be?" require social, cultural, economic, and political considerations (Shaffer 1987, Ludwig and Walters 2002).

APPROACHES TO ASSESS VIABILITY

We describe several approaches to assessing viability. The first 3 methods are quantitative approaches of Population Viability Analysis. The second 2 are alternate methods for assessing viability when data are sparser.

Population Viability Analysis Methods

Time Series

If a series of abundance estimates is available for a small population, those data can be used to estimate the probability of reaching quasi-extinction thresholds. The mathematical approaches can become complicated as they attempt to accommodate real-world biological and sampling issues such as density dependence, the ability to sample only one stage of a population (e.g., egg counts, breeding adults), sampling variation, and missing data. Morris and Doak (2002) provide a readable overview of this considerable literature.

Underlying all approaches is the idea that a series of abundance estimates can be characterized by an average trend and variance in that trend; if past trends and variability are assumed to be reflective of the future, one can calculate the probability that the population might reach some quasi-extinction threshold in the future. The math captures the non-intuitive but important fact discussed earlier that variance in population growth rate means that even populations that tend to increase, on average, may be most likely to decrease to extinction. From a practical viewpoint, this implies that effects of management on variability in population growth can be as important as effects on the growth rate itself (Burgman et al. 1993).

How long must a time series be to estimate extinction risk for a single population? At the least, 10–15 years of data are needed to be able to characterize population growth and correlation structure (Swanson 1998, Holmes 2001, Morris and Doak 2002). Considerably longer time series may be necessary to capture properly the variance in growth rates (Goodman 2002).

Demographically Explicit Models

This class of PVA models uses estimates of vital rates, including age- (or stage-) specific survival and reproduction rates, their variances and covariances, and other information such as age structure and sex ratio of the population, density dependence, and effects of inbreeding depression. Although this method requires difficult-to-obtain information, it has the advantage of assembling biological information in a way that suggests specific actions that might reduce the chance of extinction (Beissinger and Westphal 1998). Demographically explicit methods transcend prediction of viability and permit diagnosis and potential treatment of factors that most threaten a population.

Because of the multiple interacting factors in a demographically explicit PVA, computer simulations are typically used. Demographic stochasticity in survival is usually applied in 1 of 2 ways. The first approach draws the number of survivors in a cohort from a binomial distribution with the specified mean survival rate for that time step

and number of individuals in the cohort. The second way that demographic stochasticity is incorporated is to pick, for each individual, a random number from a uniform distribution; if the chosen number is greater than the mean survival rate of that time step the individual dies, if it is less, the animal lives.

Mean survival (and reproduction) rates change in each time step due to environmental stochasticity. Operation of environmental stochasticity is mimicked in a PVA by choosing mean vital rates for each time step from a distribution of random numbers with a specified mean and variance (the variance is the process variance, separated from sampling variance). An alternate approach may randomly pick one of several vital rates measured in the field (or even entire matrices of vital rates from field data, Akçakaya 2000). When modeling environmental stochasticity, it is also important to specify correlation among vital rates and through time for particular rates because it affects both variance in population growth and probability of extinction (Ferson and Burgman 1995, Groom and Pascual 1998). If necessary, PVAs can include catastrophes—the extreme events outside the normal range of environmental stochasticity—by specifying the magnitude and average timing for their occurrence.

Genetic stochasticity, or the consequences of inbreeding due to genetic drift in a small population, is incorporated into demographically explicit PVAs by decreasing vital rates at different levels of inbreeding. It is difficult to measure both inbreeding level and fitness for most wildlife species (Oyler-McCance and Leberg 2005). Thus, in many PVAs a range of values from other species are used to bracket possible effects; measurements of inbreeding depression have recently emerged for many wildlife populations (Crnokrak and Roff 1999, Keller and Waller 2002). The shape of the curve relating inbreeding to fitness is complex and includes the extent to which cost of inbreeding is or is not "purged" over time (Mills and Smouse 1994, Ballou 1997, Lacy 1997, Frankham et al. 2002). The range of inbreeding costs expected for any species, as well as uncertainty in the shape of the curve relating inbreeding to fitness, implies that incorporating genetic stochasticity is the same as with any other uncertain parameter in PVA (for example, dispersal rates, density dependence, breeding structure, etc.); the user should include a range of plausible possibilities, including "worst" and "best case" scenarios.

Density dependence can and should be incorporated into demographically explicit PVAs if field data are sufficient. Relating vital rates to density and specifying the extent to which vital rates are modified at particular densities can be used to create density dependence models. Unfortunately, density dependence is one of the hardest parameters to estimate in field populations, yet subtle differences in how it is included in PVA models can drastically affect predictions (Mills et al. 1996). Burgman et al. (1993:163) argue, "It is probably silly to pretend there exists a perfect density-dependence curve in a scattergram of data and tortuously thread some guess at its form." They present an alternate strategy using field data to describe density dependence in a "density vague" manner. The uncertainty of parameterizing density dependence, and its effect on PVA projections, has led to the recommendation that PVA models should include at least one set of runs without density dependence, to provide a baseline under-

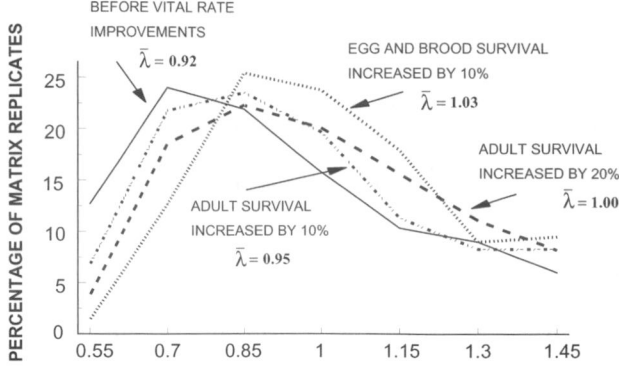

FINITE RATE OF INCREASE (INTERVAL MIDPOINTS)

Fig. 2. An example of sensitivity analysis for greater prairie-chickens (from Wisdom et al. 2000). Simulations indicate that different potential management actions will vary in how successful they are in modifying the population growth rate.

standing of extinction risks (Ginzburg et al. 1990, Mills et al. 1996). The real existence of density dependence will affect the interpretation of the products of the model for a particular management scenario (Boyce 1992, Groom and Pascual 1998).

The framework for incorporating factors into a demographically explicit PVA varies widely. In some cases, it is possible to use "canned" PVA programs. Two of the most popular are the matrix-based RAMAS (Ferson and Akçakaya 1990, Akçakaya 2002) and the individual-based VORTEX (Lacy 2000). Examples of species with published PVAs using these 2 programs include Chinese Hainan Eld's deer (*Cervus eldi hainanus* or *C. e. siamensis*) (Song 1996), Hawaiian black-necked stilt (*Himantopus mexicanus*) (Reed et al. 1998*a*), Florida manatee (*Trichechus manatus latirostris*) (Marmontel et al. 1997), and Florida scrub jay (*Aphelocoma coerulescens*) (Root 1998). In other cases, particular aspects of proposed management options or of the animal's life history lead to development of PVA programs that are more species-specific such as for African wild dogs (*Lycaon pictus*) (Vucetich and Creel 1999), cheetah (*Acinonyx jubatus*) (Kelly and Durant 2000), greater sage-grouse (*Centrocercus urophasianus*) (Johnson and Braun 1999), and red-cockaded woodpeckers (*Picoides borealis*) (Daniels et al. 2000).

Demographically explicit PVAs also allow the user to perform a *sensitivity analysis* to evaluate which life history components and/or management actions will have the largest effect on population recovery (Fig. 2). Sensitivity analysis in the broad sense (reviewed by Mills and Lindberg 2002) includes a variety of approaches including direct perturbation of vital rates in a model, analytical sensitivity and elasticity calculations, and simulation-based approaches such as life-stage simulation analysis. Regardless of the approach, sensitivity analysis can guide both research and management. For example, field research into causes of global amphibian declines would be more efficient if coupled with sensitivity analysis that indicated whether changes in certain vital rates would lead to decreased population growth (Biek et al. 2002). Citta and Mills (1999) showed that sensitivity analysis could be used to explore how to decrease pest population growth by examining management options that would cause brown-headed cowbird (*Molothrus ater*) populations to decline. Similarly,

sensitivity analysis can be used to explicitly incorporate human demographic, economic, and social systems with PVA of wildlife species (Lacy and Miller 2002).

The main obstacle to using demographically explicit PVA approaches is that they require substantial data. If data are not available, biologists should resist the temptation to guess and, instead, should focus on collecting the relevant information or choose a different approach. However, where the match between model needs and data availability are reasonable, a useful approach is to "embrace uncertainty" about processes or parameters by acknowledging the uncertainty explicitly, and considering scenarios across a range of plausible values.

PVA with Multiple Populations

Any PVA approach for a single population can be scaled up from single population analysis to consider multiple populations across the landscape. With sufficient data, multiple population PVA models can be spatially explicit, incorporating exact spatial locations of populations or individuals or other features (Reed et al. 2002). Two additional concepts that enter into PVA evaluation of multiple small populations are the extent of connectivity and correlation in dynamics among the populations. Connectivity is important because it can lead to gene flow, which affects genetic structure (Mills and Allendorf 1996). It can also facilitate colonization or recolonization of unoccupied patches (Singer et al. 2000) and decrease local extinction probability via a "rescue effect" (Brown and Kodric-Brown 1977). Connectivity can, at times, have negative ramifications for small populations across a landscape, as when diseases are transmitted (Cunningham 1996) or maladaptive learned traits are transferred socially (Laland and Williams 1998). Connectivity involves complex behavioral processes such as dispersal (Reed et al. 2002) that have traditionally been difficult to measure accurately. However, measurement of connectivity for wildlife populations is becoming easier with development of field and analytical tools based on telemetry, mark–recapture analysis, and genetic sampling (Mills et al. 2003).

The other important component of multiple population models is the extent of correlation in dynamics of different populations. If there is *decoupling* of environmental stochasticity among small populations, it becomes much less likely that a single bad year or series of years would cause all populations to be lost (Harrison and Quinn 1989). For example, consider 3 populations of 50 animals each. If all 3 populations had probabilities of extinction of 0.2 per year, but their probabilities were independent (because of decoupling of environmental stochasticity), the probability of total extinction for all 3 populations in a given year would be $(0.2^3) = 0.008$. In contrast, if the fates of the populations were completely coupled (for example, the populations were adjacent to each other), the probability of total extinction would be 0.2 per year, the same as for one population.

The extent of correlation, or coupling, in environmental stochasticity can be largely affected by distance among populations, because similar climatic events or other perturbations (invasions by exotics, deaths caused by predators or disease, etc.) are more likely to occur simultaneously to populations that are close together. Movement of individuals (connectivity) also facilitates correlations among population. For example, Canada lynx (*Lynx canadensis*) populations across western North America are connected by dispersal, which may facilitate the relatively synchronous dynamics of lynx populations at the continent-wide scale (Schwartz et al. 2002).

In addition to application of time series or demographically explicit models across more than one population, data for species with multiple populations facilitates another type of PVA. These are broadly called "patch occupancy models," or "incidence function models" (Hanski and Ovaskainen 2000, Hanski 2002). They are conceptually similar to logistic regression modeling of colonization and extinction events (e.g., Sjögren-Gulve and Ray 1996, Sjögren-Gulve and Hanski 2000). Focusing on the widely used incidence function models, the key data are patch occupancies (whether or not a patch is occupied). The other parameters are distance between patches (metrics of connectivity other than distance can be used if available) and size of the patches ("size" can be scaled to account for habitat quality, but population size is ignored, and patches are assumed to be distinct). Patch areas and connectivities are surrogates for population size and dispersal rates, both of which are important drivers of local extinction and establishment of new populations. An important assumption of incidence function models is there is no increasing or decreasing trend in patch occupancy, for example due to recent severe habitat loss (Moilanen 1999, 2000). Incidence function models are best suited for short-term predictions of consequences of management scenarios rather than predicting long-term extinction risk. They are most appropriately used for relatively common species with rapid turnover of local populations in fragmented landscapes (Hanski 2002). If populations are relatively large or long-lived, so that local (within-population) dynamics are important, then other approaches are more appropriate (e.g., Lindenmayer et al. 1995).

Other Approaches to Assess Viability

From a biological perspective, the worst-case scenario is conducting an assessment of viability when time is short and data are scarce to non-existent. Yet, this is normal for many biologists around the world; quantitative PVA using time series analysis, demographic rates, or multiple population models is not possible. For example, in 1993, the President of the United States appointed a Forest Ecosystem Management Assessment Team (FEMAT) to evaluate the effects of large-scale timber harvest options on wildlife species in western Washington, Oregon, and northern California (Forest Ecosystem Management Assessment Team 1993, Meslow et al. 1994, Thomas 1994). More than 1,000 plant and animal species were to be included in the assessment, including many species that were (and are) little known. The team had 3 months to complete the job. Difficult, if not impossible, tasks such as this are given to biologists far too often, and the problem is exacerbated on the global scale where data are often even sparser.

In the case of the 1,000 species assessed as part of FEMAT, the best that could be done was to implement a subjective "expert panel" approach to assess viability. This method had evolved from earlier use in analyses in the Pacific Northwest of the United States (e.g., Thomas et al. 1993), and continued to evolve after the FEMAT process (Marcot et al. 1997). Unfortunately, whenever expert opinion or other subjective approaches are all that are available to assess viability, the results will be somewhat suspect.

Humans are inherently bad at guessing risks (even when they are informed guesses), in part because we are led astray by factors such as how visible or controllable the risk appears, or the consequences of the risks (Burgman et al. 1993). Thus, we overestimate many low level risks (e.g., death by tornado) and underestimate high-level risks (e.g., death by heart disease). Second, and perhaps more importantly, the subjective decision-making process is based on the experience of the "expert" making the decision; "severe risk" will mean different things to different people. It is difficult to make transparent or testable the logic, mechanisms, predictor variables, sources of uncertainty, or other processes that go into the outcome of an expert judgment. Expert opinion assessments of viability will remain an uncomfortable and insufficient last resort.

In closing the discussion of PVA, it is important to consider less data-intensive methods that are not part of PVA per se, but which can be used to assess viability when detailed population data are not available. Two approaches are described.

Rules of Thumb

Rule of thumb approaches assign qualitative ranks of risk using specified, operational criteria (reviewed by O'Grady 2002). Common rule of thumb approaches include those developed by The Nature Conservancy (Master 1991, Master et al. 2000, Samson 2002) and the World Conservation Union (IUCN) Red List Categorization System (Mace 1995, IUCN 2001).

As an example of a rule of thumb approach, we focus on the IUCN Red List Categorization System (Mace and Lande 1991; Mace 1994, 1995; Gärdenfors 2000; IUCN 2001), which forms the basis for "Red Lists" that assess the conservation status of more than 18,000 plant and animal species worldwide.

Specifically, the IUCN approach assigns species to 1 of 9 categories. To be placed in 1 of the 3 categories at risk of extinction (i.e., critically endangered, endangered, and vulnerable) (Table 1, Fig. 3), at least one operational rule of thumb criteria must apply. These criteria are: (a) deep declines in population size, (b) reduction in geographic range or populations, (c) small population size coupled with decline or fluctuations, (d) very small or restricted population, or (e) quantitative analysis (Fig. 3). The fifth criteria for assigning species—quantitative analysis—includes a direct quantitative estimate of extinction probability within specified time frames using a PVA. However, data limitations mean that, in practice, the IUCN system usually consists of criteria A through D (Mace and Lande 1991, Gärdenfors 2000). Sophisticated methods for making uncertainty explicit in the risk assessment procedure have been proposed for IUCN categorization (Todd and Burgman 1998, Akçakaya et al. 2000, Taylor et al. 2002).

A key philosophy behind the IUCN approach underscores an important general point about small population management; a distinction is made between assessing the severity of threat and setting conservation priorities (Mace 1994, 1995; Gärdenfors et al. 2001). Categories of threat established by the rules of thumb are just one piece of information used to set conservation priorities. At least as important are additional criteria, which might include likelihood of success in restoring the species, number of other threatened species occupying the same habitat, taxonomic

A) Categories.

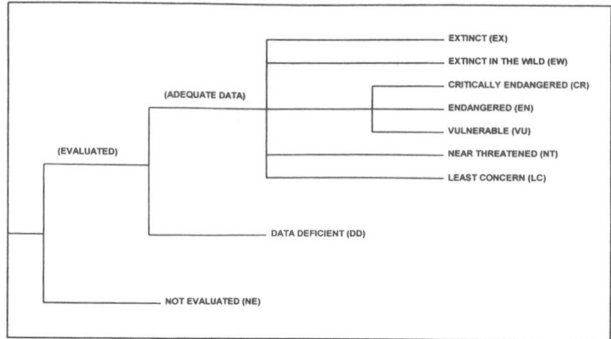

B) "Rule of thumb" criteria.

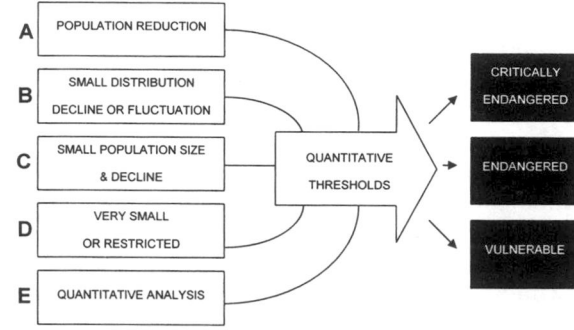

Fig. 3. The IUCN population assessment procedures (Gärdenfors et al. 2001, IUCN 2001).

uniqueness, availability of funds, and the legal and political framework for conserving a particular species.

There are obvious limitations to any rule-of-thumb approach. For example, a single set of rules will not fit all species and situations (O'Grady 2002). Despite the limitations, biologists must turn to these methods at times, because they may be the best available. Mace and Hudson (1999:244) report that "Although the IUCN system may be efficient at picking up different species facing diverse threats, it is not designed to be an accurate tool for measuring extinction risk, for projecting population status, or for designing population management plans. Its role is to highlight species exhibiting one of several symptoms of pending extinction and to classify species according to the relative severity of the apparent threat. The Red List is a useful conservation tool only when listing leads to measures to assess the causes of threat and to develop, where necessary, appropriate management responses and species recovery plans. In short, the IUCN red list criteria are designed to be robust and precautionary across a wide range of circumstances, to operate when data are scarce, and to pinpoint species in need of attention."

In contrast to the IUCN guidelines, the Endangered Species Act of the United States does not offer specific rules of thumb criteria for identifying species at risk of extinction. The ESA uses qualitative assessments to classify species as endangered ("...in danger of extinction throughout all or a significant portion of its range") or threatened ("likely to become an endangered species within the foreseeable future throughout all or a significant portion of its range"). Classification, or listing, is based "solely on the basis of the best scientific and commercial data available...after conducting a review of the status of the species." In the

absence of robust criteria for listing and recovery, listing determinations and recovery goals have often been inconsistently applied (Scott et al. 1995, Tear et al. 1995).

Approaches Based on Habitat and Other Information

At times, more information is available about habitat relations than demographic variables for a species of concern. Although we believe the relevant population data should be collected for a proper viability assessment, there are cases where habitat information alone can contribute useful information (Boyce 1992). Recently, researchers in federal land management agencies in the United States have developed a "Bayesian Belief Network" approach that combines habitat associations with other information for region-wide or species-wide assessments (Lee 2000, Marcot et al. 2001, Raphael et al. 2001). Information in the Bayesian Belief Network includes associations with habitat and other variables, as well as expert opinion and ancillary models (including true PVA models). When expert opinion is included, it is incorporated so it can be easily scrutinized. Using a Bayesian statistical framework, input variable values are combined with conditional probability tables to estimate the probability of a response relevant to population status. Risks associated with alternative courses of actions can be explored. As an example of this approach, 28 species have recently been assessed as part of land planning for the 58-million-ha Interior Columbia River Basin (for example, Wisdom et al. [2002] for assessment of greater sage-grouse and Rowland et al. [2003] for wolverine).

Marcot et al. (2001:29–30) described the utility and limitations of these approaches, noting that when scant scientific data are available but a decision-making process is moving forward: "the experts must provide their best professional evaluation or step aside and let activities proceed... Our ... models of wildlife population response, however, do not substitute for empirically based, quantitative, stochastic analyses of population demography, genetics, and persistence such as those used in population viability analysis...[our approach is] most useful when empirical data on population trends, demography, and genetics are unavailable."

PRACTICAL THOUGHTS ABOUT WILDLIFE RISK ASSESSMENT

The largest benefit to assessing viability for a small population is that it forces us to be explicit about the threats to a population. It places assumptions on the table where they can be discussed. For example, if one person believes that genetic isolation is the largest threat for a particular species, they may argue that connectivity enhances viability; alternatively, someone else concerned about disease risk for that species might argue that connectivity decreases viability. The assumptions are explicit.

From published works and our own experience, we offer 3 important messages regarding assessing viability as part of the management of small populations. First, be aware of the quality of data available and match those data with the most appropriate approach. Currently there is interest in the effects of data quality and sampling error on model performance. Sampling error will tend to make nature seem more "variable," which tends to bias upward the predicted probability of extinction. The extent to which sampling error compromises PVA has been discussed intensely (Lud-

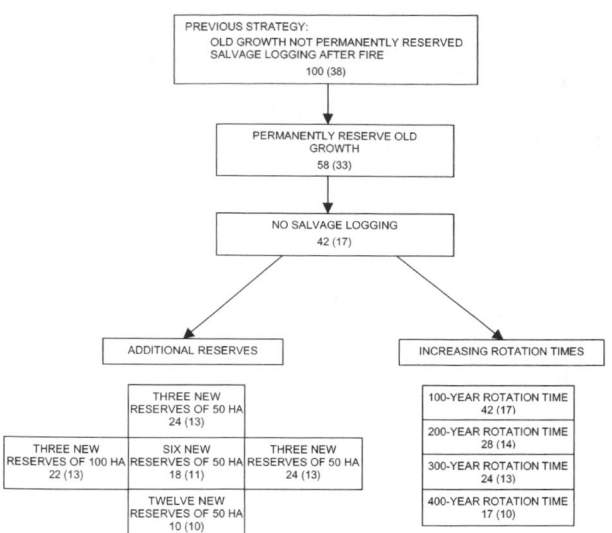

Fig. 4. Population viability analysis for decision analysis in the case of Leadbeater's possum (from Possingham et al. 2002). For each option, the number gives the probability of extinction over the next 150 years (in parentheses) and over a typical 150-year period in the future when the forest has reached an equilibrium with the management actions (think of this as the period 500–650 years from now, assuming constant conditions).

wig 1999, Fieberg and Ellner 2000, Meir and Fagan 2000, Holmes 2001, Sæther and Engen 2002). In any case, wildlife biologists should heed suggestions on how parameters of viability models can be estimated so that sampling error can be quantified (White 2000, White et al. 2002).

Second, viability assessment is more useful as a comparative tool for ranking management options than it is for making precise predictions of viability. While there can be heartening matches between PVA predictions and actual population trajectories (Brook et al. 2000), instances where this is true are likely limited (Lindenmayer et al. 2000, Coulson et al. 2001).

Using PVA to evaluate relative merits of different management options allows it to be incorporated into the decision-making process that guides management action and policy (Maguire 1991, Noon and McKelvey 1996). For example, consider a case of how PVA was used to improve the decision-making process (Fig. 4). Management of the Australian marsupial, Leadbeater's possum (*Gymnobelideus leadbeateri*), is one of the most contentious forestry issues in Australia. The primary threat to this species is its requirement for nest sites in trees over 150 years old. Early this century, fires burned more than 60% of the forest within the range of the species, and clear-cut logging has more recently occurred over 75% of its known distribution. The species now occupies an area 60 × 50 km in the central highlands of the state of Victoria in southeastern Australia. Current management is to avoid cutting in certain areas (including old growth patches) while clear cutting continues in other areas; areas that burn in the future may be salvage logged.

Possingham et al. (2002) examined the viability of Leadbeater's possum subject to current and potential future management options (Fig. 4). Under current management, possums would be likely to persist for the next 150 years (only 38% chance of extinction), but not into the future (100% chance of extinction). If existing old-growth forest was not salvage logged, trees damaged but alive after a fire

would not be removed; this would increase possum viability so that extinction probability would decrease to 33% and 58% over the next 150 years and expected long term, respectively. If there were further limitations to salvage logging, so that it was prohibited both in old growth and in other areas that could grow into old growth, extinction probability drops even more. Two popular suggestions for further aiding this species are to increase the rotation time and to make more reserves, so these possibilities were considered next. Although increasing rotation time decreases extinction probabilities, it requires an almost complete halt of logging for the next 150 years, hardly a politically realistic possibility! In contrast, setting aside reserves improves viability even more but reduces logging little; for example, setting aside just 6 50-ha reserves (5% of the forest block) decreases extinction probability to 18% over the long term but reduces logging by only 5% at most. With identification of additional permanent reserves as a viable approach, a number of scenarios was considered, trading size and number of reserves. The authors assessed the sensitivity of conclusions by modeling a range of possibilities for processes about which they were uncertain. The recommendations emerging from this work are currently being implemented (Possingham et al. 2002).

A third message is to consider a range of possibilities for every step of a PVA for which there is doubt about a process, functional relationship, or measured parameter. The worst PVAs are those that take one set of data and provide one estimate of extinction probabilities, while the best are those that consider a variety of biological and management information to produce a range of predictions (Taylor 1995, Ellner et al. 2002). For example, Armbruster et al. (1999) showed that although an Asian elephant (*Elaphus maximus*) population had a low probability of extinction over 100 years, extending the time frame a few additional elephant generations, to 200 years or more, substantially increased the probability of extinction. Ideally, a PVA would be performed with multiple methods (Mills et al. 1996, Gärdenfors 2000, Kindvall 2000). Sensitivity analysis in the broad sense, evaluating how information affects products, is an essential part of PVA (Reed et al. 1998b, Mills and Lindberg 2002). Also, Bayesian approaches directly incorporate parameter uncertainty into analysis (Taylor et al. 1996, 2002; Goodman 2002; Wade 2002).

Burgman and Possingham (2000:104) recall the comment that "All models are wrong but some are useful" (from Box 1979) to emphasize their point that "The only correct model is an entire reconstruction of the actual system—whereupon it ceases to be a model. The utility of a PVA is affected by several things, including the care taken to include all ecological intuition faithfully, the care taken to represent all views (hypotheses) as structural alternatives, the detail and transparency of statements about assumptions, and the role of the model within the decision-making framework. One of the most important steps in establishing the credibility of a PVA is to communicate the uncertainties embedded in the model and its assumptions."

MANAGEMENT OF SMALL POPULATIONS

The results of a viability assessment can provide managers with specific insights into how to most effectively increase size of a small population and reduce risk of extinction. A variety of techniques can be used; some are identical to those used with more abundant species, but many others are specially adapted to the needs of populations with small numbers of individuals.

Effective management of small populations must address both ultimate and proximate causes of population declines. The ultimate cause of a species' decline is usually some change in the environment resulting from human activities. These changes might be novel events the species has not experienced (e.g., introduction of synthetic toxic chemicals, like DDT, into a species' food chain) or somewhat normal events that suddenly occur in temporal or spatial patterns that are unprecedented (e.g., disturbing a forest through logging more frequently and on a different spatial scale than would occur under natural disturbance regimes, thus eliminating old-growth conditions). Regardless of the ultimate cause, the population fails to cope, resulting in proximate causes of decline such as reduced survival and reproduction.

The distinction between ultimate and proximate causes of species declines can lead to a dichotomy in management approaches (Temple 1978). Clearly, management must correct the ultimate causes of decline by addressing the specific environmental changes that threatened the species. These causes include such widespread problems as habitat loss or deterioration, impacts of exotic organisms, toxic chemicals, and mortality directly related to human activities. Frequently, ultimate problems are difficult to remedy; typically a long time is required for corrective measures to improve a species' environment. Time is a factor working against the persistence of most small populations.

To hasten recovery of a perilously small population, managers often must address proximate factors in a manner that is somewhat unrelated to the ultimate cause of a population's decline. Typically, the approach is to increase survival and reproductive rates by whatever means possible to stimulate population growth. Ultimate problems are then addressed somewhat independently of these activities, which are similar to the treatment of a critical ill patient in a hospital's emergency room: treat the life-threatening symptoms and then remedy underlying problems (Zimmerman 1975).

Two birds, osprey (*Pandion haliaetus*) and peregrine falcon (*Falco peregrinus*), illustrate the benefits of addressing proximate problems (Spitzer 1978, Cade et al. 1988). Both species were threatened by the ultimate problem of contamination of their food chains with chlorinated hydrocarbons, especially DDT. In each situation populations declined precipitously after reproduction was impaired when eggs with DDT-thinned shells failed to hatch. Although measures were taken during the late 1960s and early 1970s to address the ultimate problem, by curtailing use of the offending toxic chemicals, both species continued to decline and remained at risk because of the persistence of the chemicals already in the environment.

To offset the proximate problem of inadequate recruitment, managers successfully augmented reproduction in wild ospreys and released captive-reared individuals into wild populations of peregrine falcons. Reproduction of ospreys was enhanced by reducing nest-site limitations through erecting artificial nest platforms in areas that lacked natural nesting sites (Postupalsky 1978), and by replacing thin-shelled eggs with thick-shelled eggs (Spitzer 1978). Captive breeding and subsequent reintroduction of peregrine falcons provided an important boost

to recruitment to populations that were producing too few young (Cade et al. 1988). In both situations, regional populations were doomed to eventual extinction unless attention to proximate causes improved the status of the species while ultimate problems were being addressed (Kauffman et al. 2003). In the post-DDT era, both ospreys and peregrine falcons recovered impressively after chlorinated hydrocarbon pesticides eventually were purged from the food chain (Spitzer et al. 1983, Cade et al. 1988).

The efficacy of specific management actions affecting particular vital rates can be assessed using sensitivity analysis. Next we describe some specific management actions used to improve prospects for small populations.

Improving Recruitment

Increasing the rate at which new individuals are added to a small population through reproduction or immigration can stimulate rapid population growth. For many species, manipulating aspects of reproduction can result in (1) an increase in natality (i.e., litter size or clutch size), (2) an increase in the frequency of reproduction, (3) an increase in the proportion of individuals in a population that breed, or (4) an increase in the success rate of breeders. For other species, translocations of animals from one population to another and reintroductions of individuals produced in captivity can duplicate the positive contributions of natural immigration toward recruitment in a declining population.

Increasing natality has been a particularly attractive strategy for birds, because many species can be stimulated to lay more eggs than typical when managers remove eggs from the nest. Viability can be multiplied impressively by artificially incubating the extra eggs or placing them in nests of foster parents (Cade 1978).

A few species present the opportunity to increase frequency of reproduction. Animals that have long periods of parental care of offspring are inhibited from reproducing while caring for dependent young. Shortening the time to independence can reduce the intervals between breeding. For example, California condors (*Gymnogyps californianus*) can be induced to breed annually in contrast to the normal biennial rate, thus effectively doubling fecundity (Snyder and Hamber 1985).

In some populations, only a proportion of the reproductively competent individuals have the opportunity to breed. Shortages of specific resources essential for breeding typically are responsible for limiting the number of breeders in a population. If these limitations to breeding can be removed, previously excluded individuals can breed. Nesting sites frequently limit the number of breeders and provision of artificial nesting sites such as nest boxes, cavities, and burrows can result in improved fecundity (Snyder 1978).

Reproductive failures normally reduce recruitment below the potential rate suggested by a species' natality. Losses of young before recruitment into the population can be substantial. Preventing those losses effectively increases recruitment. Many techniques have been used, including the quality of breeding sites, reducing risks (e.g., predation) to young animals, or implementing "head starting" approaches that give young animals improved prospects for survival to breeding age (Temple 1978).

Improving Survival

All else being equal, improved survival of individuals should stimulate population growth. Reducing impacts of predators, pathogens, competitors, and accidents can be effective (Jackson 1978). These manipulations may reduce losses below normally expected levels and enhance survival in a population, even if poor survival is not an important factor in the population's decline. For example, protecting an endangered species from human exploitation can improve survival, even if overexploitation is not an identified cause of endangerment. Improving the quality of a species' habitat also can improve survival; however, habitat improvement is rarely a short-term solution.

Population Augmentation

Translocations can be used for augmenting small populations to increase population size, enhance genetic diversity, diversify age or gender composition or create new populations through reintroduction to a previously occupied area. Examples include amphibians (Arano et al. 1995, Marsh and Trenham 2001, Rathbun and Schneider 2001, but see Seigel and Dodd [2002] and Trenham and Marsh [2002]), adders (*Vipera berus*) (Madsen et al. 1996, 1999), greater prairie-chickens (Soulé and Mills 1998), red-cockaded woodpeckers (Allen et al. 1993, Haig et al. 1993, Carrie et al. 1999), Florida scrub jays (Mumme and Below 1999), New Zealand robins (*Petroica australis*) (Armstrong and Ewen 2002), sea otters (*Enhydra lutris*) (Bodkin et al. 1999), cougars (*Puma concolor*) (Ruth et al. 1998), black bears (*Ursus americanus*) (Eastridge and Clark 2001), and woodland caribou (Compton et al. 1995). Guidelines for integrating biological and sociological considerations (Maguire and Servheen 1992) have been developed for population augmentation but success is not guaranteed. Griffith et al. (1989) and Wolf et al. (1996) found that only about two-thirds of translocations in the United States, Canada, Australia, and New Zealand were considered successful with success rates varying among taxonomic groups.

Translocations of individuals can have positive and negative implications both to individuals released and the ecological community into which they are introduced. Potential detrimental effects to translocated animals include death during transportation to release sites and premature death after release because of starvation, predation, or disease. Further information is available through the electronic *Annotated Bibliography of Animal Translocations* (Griffith et al. 1998) maintained by the Alaska Cooperative Fish and Wildlife Research Unit.

Differences in survival among captive-reared and wild-caught individuals have been documented, with captive-reared animals having lower survival rates after translocation (Griffith et al.1989, Snyder et al. 1994). Training of captive-reared animals to increase their post-release survival includes teaching them how to forage and avoid predators as well as other survival skills (Griffin et al. 2000, but see Wolf et al. 1996). In the past many translocation efforts have been incompletely documented with few guidelines for selecting, screening, or monitoring of released individuals or for evaluating habitat suitability.

Today, there are formal guidelines for translocation programs (IUCN 1987, 1995). These guidelines should be used to evaluate proposals to move animals from wild or captive populations into extant populations (i.e., augmentation, supplementation, or re-enforcement). Any effort to augment a population should have a designated team leader responsible for coordination among the groups involved, funding, publicity, and informing the public about the project (Kleiman 1989, Clark et al. 1994). The latter is particularly important prior to reintroductions of species that may be controversial, such as large carnivores, endangered or threatened species, or any species that is considered a threat to human health and welfare. Notable examples include grizzly bear (*Ursus arctos*), red wolf (*Canis rufus*), gray wolf, Mexican gray wolf (*C. lupus baileyi*), and sea otter. The IUCN guidelines include pre-project activities such as a feasibility study and background research (e.g., genetic studies of the host population and translocated animals, detailed studies of the status and biology of wild populations, review of strengths and weaknesses of previous reintroductions of the same or similar species). Knowledge of the natural history of the species is crucial to the success of the program and evaluation of proposed reintroduction sites is essential. For example, have ultimate factors thought responsible for the decline of the species been eliminated or reduced, and is enough suitable habitat available? Release stock will preferably be drawn from wild populations, but removal of individuals for release must not endanger the source population (captive or wild).

Funding and staffing sufficient to complete any translocation project should be guaranteed prior to initiation. Social and economic costs, and benefits to local human populations should also be considered, as the attitudes of those living in the release area are vital to program success. Programs have failed or been delayed because of lack of local or political support (U.S. Department of the Interior 2001). It is important that those in the release area understand and support the reasons for the release. If the reintroduced animal threatens human life or property, steps should be made to minimize these effects and compensate affected individuals when appropriate. The program for compensating ranchers for cattle lost to wolf depredations in the Greater Yellowstone area is an excellent example of such efforts (Defenders of Wildlife 2003).

Habitat Protection

When populations are small because of the ultimate problem of habitat loss or fragmentation, protection or restoration of habitat is a necessary step in preventing further declines and increasing population size. Although Belovsky et al. (1994) properly cautioned against regarding habitat protection as a panacea against extinction, the isolation of small populations in habitat fragments could lead to stochastic extinction (Hunter 2002). Recovery of populations to sizes that are robust to stochastic factors will not occur unless larger habitat patches are available to support a viable population size. A PVA can provide managers with an estimate of the habitat requirements (quantitatively and qualitatively) for a viable population and goals for habitat protection and restoration. For example, spatially explicit PVA models examined how proposed habitat management actions in a U.S. Forest Service District would affect Bachman's sparrows (*Aimophila aestivalis*), a species endemic to pine woodlands of the southeastern United States (Liu et al. 1995).

Because we live in an increasingly fragmented world, nearly all protected areas (e.g., National Wildlife Refuges, National Parks, wilderness areas, private nature reserves, wildlife management areas) are small and increasingly embedded in substrates that prevent distant movements of many of the species for which protected areas were established. Newmark (1987, 1995) found that in western North American parks, extinctions have exceeded colonizations since park establishment and that rate of extinction was inversely related to park area.

DellaSala et al. (2001) found 97% of all protected areas in North America to be less than 10,000 ha in size with 76% of all reserves less than 200 ha. These areas are too small to support viable populations of even small animals and far short of the area needed to support larger carnivores or ungulates (Schonewald–Cox 1983). When reserve sizes were compared to minimum area requirements for terrestrial mammals in eastern North America (Gurd et al. 2001), only 14 of 2,355 existing reserves (0.06%) were sufficiently large to meet the lower confidence limit of the area required to prevent loss of terrestrial mammal species. This analysis may be optimistic for species conservation, as use of the upper confidence limit rather than the lower would mandate even larger reserves for maintaining viable populations of mammals.

When areas are set aside to protect habitat for small populations, managers should consider the potential impact of major habitat perturbations that occur as infrequently as every 100 years. Protected areas must be sufficiently large or a large number of smaller areas must be set aside and distributed in a manner that all habitats are not vulnerable to the same perturbation. A spatially explicit PVA may help identify what number, size, and distribution of habitat reserves will be adequate.

It is uncommon for most rare species to have their habitat requirements defined specifically to guide habitat protection efforts (Murphy and Noon 1991). Usually, important habitat is characterized through a detailed analysis of potential limiting factors. A variety of approaches that work well for nonendangered species may be used (e.g., Habitat Suitability Index models or multivariate habitat analyses). Regardless of the specific approach used, careful definition of important habitat areas is important, because protection and restoration of habitat are often key components of the recovery of small populations to more viable sizes.

Even after important habitat areas are identified for protection, it is frequently necessary to plan for ecological restoration (a long-term process) to create habitat in areas not presently suitable for the species (Howell 1988). In addition to occurring in but a fraction of the species' historical range, many small declining populations occur at the extremes of former range in habitats that may be suboptimal. The whooping crane (*Grus americana*) provides an example (Lewis 1986), as do many of the upland forest birds of Hawaii (Scott et al. 1986, Channel and Lomolino 2000). Habitat restoration may be essential to allow a small population to expand its size to the point that it can be considered to be no longer in danger of extirpation.

Monitoring

Establishing monitoring programs for small populations presents special challenges for the manager. At the most fundamental level, the range of a rare species and its specific habitat requirements may not be known. Surveys may thus be conducted in unused or unsuitable habitat, unnecessarily increasing the cost of monitoring efforts. Also, observers may be unfamiliar with identification of a rare species and, after failing to find it, conclude incorrectly the population has been extirpated (Scott et al. 1986, Diamond 1987, Reed

1996). Finally, small populations will inherently have statistical limitations of insufficient power to detect trends.

Ideally, a monitoring program should address these issues by incorporating as much information as possible about the species' putative range and its habitat associations within that range. It should include a species-specific program to train observers in survey techniques and accurate identification of the species of interest, including exposure to the full range of variation (e.g., plumage, pelage, vocalizations, or sign) for the species (Kepler and Scott 1981, Scott et al. 1986). To infer the presence or absence of the species, an important component of the monitoring program will be estimation of the probability of detecting the species at a particular point (Reed 1996, MacKenzie et al. 2002). Detection is dependent on a variety of factors including density of individuals, sampling effort, species behavioral characteristics, observer bias, weather conditions, time of day, season, and ambient noise (e.g., wind, water, or anthropogenic noise) (Kepler and Scott 1981, Scott et al. 1986, Reed 1996). Non-invasive genetic sampling (Box 2) has particular promise (although not without pitfalls) for both identifying distribution and monitoring abundance of hard-to-sample and rare populations (Mills et al. 2000*a*,*b*; Oyler-McCance and Leberg 2005).

Even when monitoring an area where a small population is known to exist, low densities can lead to a low capture or detection probability, which increases sample variance and decreases the likelihood of detecting real declines. The problem of low power in monitoring is relevant to all wildlife biology studies (Steidl et al. 1997, Gibbs 2000). It takes on amplified importance in small populations where failure to detect a decline (Type II error) can lead to extinction (Taylor and Gerrodette 1993, Reed and Blaustein 1997). The concern over inherently low power to reject the null hypothesis of "no decline" for small populations has led to consideration of how to reverse the "burden of proof" for detecting a decline (Mapstone 1995).

In the absence of reliable, precise monitoring data, an additional risk lies in overestimating population size. An overestimated population size can lead to management decisions (e.g., setting recovery goals, harvest levels, or listing under the ESA) that offer inadequate protection for small populations. An approach to avoiding this problem has been implemented by the National Marine Fisheries Service. In guidelines developed under the Marine Mammal Protection Act, stock assessments are based in part on an estimate of minimum population size (U.S. Department of Commerce 1995). The estimated minimum population size (N_{min}) is defined as the lower 60% confidence limit of a distribution resulting from a point estimate of abundance and its coefficient of variation. This method increases the probability that population size is equal to or greater than the estimate, and provides a margin of error for the variability of an estimate.

SPECIAL CONSIDERATIONS FOR MANAGING ENDANGERED SPECIES

Permit Requirements for Endangered Species Programs

When a species is listed as endangered or threatened in the United States, permits are required to undertake all types of "hands-on" management or any activity, including research, which may disturb the species. Permits can be granted for scientific research or management activities that enhance the welfare of the species.

Applications for permits to manipulate a listed species must be submitted to the U.S. Fish and Wildlife Service or the National Marine Fisheries Service. Once a permit application has been received and accepted as providing the necessary information, a notice is published in the *Federal Register* to allow for public review and comment on the application. Once the review is completed, a permit is issued if the activity is not likely to jeopardize the continued existence of the species.

Scientific permits generally are issued for research and management that will benefit the recovery effort for the species, or for research related to the assessment of threats to the species. In general, permits are not likely to be granted for research that can be accomplished on closely related or surrogate species.

Public Scrutiny of Endangered Species Management

All wildlife management activities are subject to public review. However, endangered species conservation and management programs can be especially contentious. Endan-

---

Box 2. The National Lynx Survey.

For many small populations, the first step in monitoring requires an inventory to identify where the species exists. In the United States, Canada lynx became a species of special concern to land managers in the late 1990s, and was listed in March 2000 as a Federally threatened species across its range. However, it was not known precisely where the species occurred in the United States. The National Lynx Survey was conceived to bring the properties of consistency, standardization, and reliability to the process of identifying current range for lynx, thereby providing a basis for subsequent monitoring.

The National Lynx Survey sampled lynx distribution at an unprecedented scale: 16 states across the United States. Collection of samples required the efforts of hundreds of field personnel. The sampling device for this elusive and low-density species was non-invasive, based on 10×10 cm carpet pads with nails sticking out and smothered in a beaver castoreum and catnip oil scent lure. Lynx (and other species) willingly rub against it and leave hairs behind (McDaniel et al. 2000) which can be analyzed for species identification using DNA markers. At each sampling site, 125 rub pads were placed in a systematic grid: 25 transects 3.2 km apart, with each transect consisting of 5 rub pads 100 m apart. Pads were checked after 2 weeks. The survey was conducted for 3 years, with an additional pilot year.

Before the survey was initiated, the principal investigators at the University of Montana and U.S. Forest Service, Rocky Mountain Research Station developed reliable DNA-based tests to distinguish lynx from other species based on the degraded and low-quantity samples obtained from single hairs (Mills et al. 2000a). Importantly for identification of species of political concern, exhaustive tests to validate the species-identification protocol were conducted prior to initiating the survey (Mills et al. 2000a, Mills 2002).

The survey has recently completed its third year of sampling, and can claim considerable success (McKelvey et al. 2002). More than 21,000 pads were placed, and approximately 4,000 samples were processed. About 80% of the hair samples—including single hairs or fragments of hairs—were identified to species. Many other species were detected even though the sampling method was designed to target lynx.

Examples by species (including numbers of times detected in 1999 and 2000 samples) were black bear (647), bobcat (*Lynx rufus*) (166), coyote (*Canis latrans*) (160), lynx (42), cougar (39), domestic cat (12), grizzly bear (6), wolf/dog (5), and wolverine (1). Despite its success in verifying and establishing lynx presence on a nationwide scale, the implementation of the National Lynx Survey identified a challenge that is broadly relevant to sampling small populations at large scales. Because integrity of the data stream was particularly crucial in a study of such enormous scope and scale, the protocol sent to the field was explicit, with comprehensive written instructions for all aspects of gathering, labeling, and submitting samples. However, a handful of field personnel labeled hair from elsewhere as if it were a field-collected sample and sent it in without informing the principal investigators they were taking this action, thereby threatening the integrity of the data stream in the nationwide study. A nationwide political and media furor erupted (Mills 2002, Thomas and Pletscher 2002). Fortunately, firewalls were in place in terms of field and lab protocols to protect the scientific integrity of the study to contribute to land-management decision-making. Of these firewalls, the most important was that hair collection in the National Lynx Survey was only the first step in evaluating lynx presence. Follow-up snow tracking and trapping efforts were built into the study to separate actual lynx populations from transient individuals, fur farm escapees, or mislabeled samples (McKelvey et al. 2002).

A lesson learned was the particular need for communication between field workers and principal investigators in charge of the large-scale study and, that if questions arise in implementing the field protocol, the principal investigators should be contacted (Thomas and Pletscher 2002).

In identifying the distribution of lynx via the National Lynx Survey, agencies plan to begin monitoring surveys in several areas across the United States. A suite of tools will be used, including snow tracking, trapping, telemetry, and additional genetic sampling. With non-invasive genetic sampling of hairs (or feces), there are technical challenges in moving from the species identification level to individual identification necessary for monitoring, but it can be done (e.g., Woods et al. [1999] and Mowat and Strobeck [2000] for grizzly bears, Kohn et al. [1999] for coyotes, and Sloane et al. [2000] for highly endangered northern hairy-nosed wombats [*Lasiorhinus krefftii*]).

gered species managers must be prepared for the biological, social, economic, and political controversies that seem inevitably to surround most activities (e.g., Snyder and Snyder 1989, Liverman 1990) (Box 2).

Although the recovery process prescribed by the Endangered Species Act specifically avoids issues that are not biologically based, endangered species managers frequently are asked to defend their biological proposals in arenas where the challenges are nonbiological (Tilt 1989). Designations of critical habitat and the attendant need to protect or restore specific areas for the benefit of endangered species often have social and economic impacts that precipitate acrimonious debates, e.g., conflicts between northern spotted owl (*Strix occidentalis caurina*) recovery programs and the logging industry in the Pacific Northwest (Doak 1989, Thomas et al. 1990).

SUMMARY

This chapter addresses a range of considerations and tools for managing small populations. It should be clear there is no cookbook approach. The recovery of small populations will be most effective when "adaptive management" strategies (e.g., Walters 1986) are used. Because of uncertainties that can affect the persistence and recovery of a small population, managers must be prepared for unexpected problems and adjust their management plans accordingly. Each species and situation presents a unique set of challenges for the manager; the same species may present different management issues in different time periods and different ecological settings. Thus, a modeling framework can be exceptionally helpful to choose among potential management scenarios, and to account for uncertainty in what is known about the species and what the management will accomplish. Population Viability Analysis is a well-grounded framework for considering dynamics of small and declining wildlife populations. We know that vital rates (e.g., reproduction and survival) are not "created equal" in their effect on population growth or persistence, and that different management alternatives are not equal in the extent that population characteristics can be changed. Thus, sensitivity analyses in the broad sense are a vital component to decide which specific management actions are most likely to aid a small or declining population. As a precautionary and general rule, however, management of small populations should begin early rather than late, because with diminishing population size, a population's vulnerability to extinction increases as management options become more and more constrained.

ACKNOWLEDGMENTS

A small portion of this chapter is based in part on Chapter 20 in the 5th edition (*Research and management techniques for wildlife and habitats*) and we thank D. L. Harlow and M. L. Shaffer for their contribution to that effort. Some material in this chapter was adapted from L. S. Mills (In Prep). We thank J. R. Gilbert, C. C. Schwartz, and wildlife students at the University of Idaho for valuable reviews of the manuscript. LSM was on sabbatical leave at Virginia Polytechnic and State University during preparation of this manuscript and thanks the University of Montana and the Wildlife and Fisheries Sciences Department at Virginia Tech for supporting his sabbatical leave. Funding for LSM was also provided by the National Science Foundation (DEB-9870654). KMS was supported by a Budweiser Conservation Scholarship from the National Fish and Wildlife Foundation during her work on this chapter.

LITERATURE CITED

ABBITT, R. J. F., J. M. SCOTT, AND D. S. WILCOVE. 2000. The geography of vulnerability: incorporating species geography and human development patterns into conservation planning. Biological Conservation 96:169–175.

AKÇAKAYA, H. R. 2000. Population viability analyses with demographically and spatially structured models. Ecological Bulletins 48:23–38.

———. 2002. RAMAS GIS: linking landscape data with population viability analysis. Version 4.0. Applied Biomathematics, Setauket, New York, USA.

———, S. FERSON, M. A. BURGMAN, D. A. KEITH, G. M. MACE, AND C. R. TODD. 2000. Making consistent IUCN classifications under uncertainty. Conservation Biology 14:1001–1013.

ALLEN, D. H., K. E. FRANZREB, AND R. E. F. ESCANO. 1993. Efficacy of translocation strategies for red-cockaded woodpeckers. Wildlife Society Bulletin 21:155–159.

ALLENDORF, F. W., AND N. RYMAN. 2002. The role of genetics in population viability analysis. Pages 50-85 in S. R. Beissinger and D. R. McCullough, editors. Population viability analysis. University of Chicago Press, Chicago, Illinois, USA.

ANDELMAN, S. J., S. R. BEISSINGER, J. F. COCHRANE, L. GERBER, P. GOMEZ-PRIÉGO, C. GROVES, J. HAUFLER, R. S. HOLTHAUSEN, D. LEE, L. MAGUIRE, B. NOON, K. RALLS, AND H. REGAN. 2001. Scientific standards for conducting viability assessment under the National Forest Management Act: report and recommendations of the NCEAS working group. National Center for Ecological Analysis and Synthesis, Santa Barbara, California, USA.

ANGERMEIER, P. L. 1995. Ecological attributes of extinction-prone species: loss of freshwater fishes of Virginia. Conservation Biology 9:143-158.

ARANO, B., G. LLORENTE, M. GARCÍA-PARIS, AND P. HERRERO. 1995. Species translocation menaces Iberian waterfrogs. Conservation Biology 9:196–198.

ARMBRUSTER, P., P. FERNANDO, AND R. LANDE. 1999. Timeframes for population viability analysis of species with long generations: an example with Asian elephants. Animal Conservation 2:69–73.

ARMSTRONG, D. P., AND J. G. EWEN. 2002. Dynamics and viability of a New Zealand robin population reintroduced to regenerating fragmented habitat. Conservation Biology 16:1074–1085.

AVISE, J. C., AND W. S. NELSON. 1989. Molecular genetic relationships of the extinct dusky seaside sparrow. Science 243:646–648.

BALLOU, J. D. 1997. Ancestral inbreeding only minimally affects inbreeding depression in mammalian populations. Journal of Heredity 88:169–178.

BEAN, M. J. 1983. The evolution of national wildlife law. Second edition. Praeger Publishers, New York, USA.

BEISSINGER, S. R., AND D. R. MCCULLOUGH, editors. 2002. Population viability analysis. University of Chicago Press, Chicago, Illinois, USA.

———, AND M. I. WESTPHAL. 1998. On the use of demographic models of population viability in endangered species management. Journal of Wildlife Management 62:821–841.

BELOVSKY, G. E., C. MELLISON, C. LARSON, AND P. A. VAN ZANDT. 2002. How good are PVA models? Testing their practices with experimental data on the brine shrimp. Pages 257–283 in S. R. Beissinger and D. R. McCullough, editors. Population viability analysis. University of Chicago Press, Chicago, Illinois, USA.

———, J. A. BISSONETTE, R. D. DUESER, T. C. EDWARDS, JR., C. M. LUECKE, M. E. RITCHIE, J. B. SLADE, AND F. H. WAGNER. 1994. Management of small populations: concepts affecting the recovery of endangered species. Wildlife Society Bulletin 22:307–316.

BIEK, R., W. C. FUNK, B. A. MAXELL, AND L. S. MILLS. 2002. What is missing in amphibian decline research: insights from ecological sensitivity analysis. Conservation Biology 16:728–734.

BODKIN, J. L., B. E. BALLACHEY, M. A. CRONIN, AND K. T. SCRIBNER. 1999. Population demographics and genetic diversity in remnant and translocated populations of sea otters. Conservation Biology 13:1378–1385.

BOUZAT, J. L., H. A. LEWIN, AND K. N. PAIGE. 1998a. The ghost of genetic diversity past: historical DNA analysis of the greater prairie chicken. American Naturalist 152:1–6.

————, H. H. CHENG, H. A. LEWIN, R. L. WESTEMEIER, J. D. BRAWN, AND K. N. PAIGE. 1998*b*. Genetic evaluation of a demographic bottleneck in the greater prairie chicken. Conservation Biology 12:836–843.

BOX, G. E. P. 1979. Robustness in the strategy of scientific model building. Pages 201–236 *in* R. L. Launer and G. N. Wilkinson, editors. Robustness in statistics. Academic Press, New York, USA.

BOYCE, M. S. 1977. Population growth with stochastic fluctuations in the life table. Theoretical Population Biology 12:366–373.

————. 1992. Population viability analysis. Annual Review of Ecology and Systematics 23:481–506.

BROOK, B. W., J. J. O'GRADY, A. P. CHAPMAN, M. A. BURGMAN, H. R. AKÇAKAYA, AND R. FRANKHAM. 2000. Predictive accuracy of population viability analysis in conservation biology. Nature 404:385–387.

BROWN, J. H. 1995. Macroecology. University of Chicago Press, Chicago, Illinois, USA.

————, AND A. KODRIC-BROWN. 1977. Turnover rates in insular biogeography: effect of immigration and extinction. Ecology 58:445–449.

BURGMAN, M. A., AND H. P. POSSINGHAM. 2000. Population viability analysis for conservation: the good, the bad and the undescribed. Pages 97–112 *in* A. G. Young and G. M. Clarke, editors. Genetics, demography and viability of fragmented populations. Cambridge University Press, Cambridge, United Kingdom.

————, S. FERSON, AND H. R. AKÇAKAYA. 1993. Risk assessment in conservation biology. Chapman and Hall, London, United Kingdom.

CADE, T. J. 1978. Manipulating the nesting biology of endangered birds: a review. Pages 167–170 *in* S. A. Temple, editor. Endangered birds: management techniques for preserving threatened species. University of Wisconsin Press, Madison, USA.

————, J. H. ENDERSON, C. G. THELANDER, AND C. M. WHITE, editors. 1988. Peregrine falcon populations: their management and recovery. The Peregrine Fund, Boise, Idaho, USA.

CANADIAN WILDLIFE SERVICE. 2001. 2001–02 annual report: recovery of nationally endangered wildlife. Annual Report 12. Canadian Wildlife Service, Ottawa, Ontario, Canada.

CARRIE, N. R., R. N. CONNER, D. C. RUDOLPH, AND D. K. CARRIE. 1999. Reintroduction and postrelease movements of red-cockaded woodpecker groups in eastern Texas. Journal of Wildlife Management 63:824–832.

CAUGHLEY, G., AND A. GUNN. 1996. Conservation biology in theory and practice. Blackwell Science Publishers, Cambridge, Massachusetts, USA.

CHANNEL, R., AND M. V. LOMOLINO. 2000. Dynamic biogeography and conservation of endangered species. Nature 403:84–86.

CITTA, J. J., AND L. S. MILLS. 1999. What do demographic sensitivity analyses tell us about controlling brown-headed cowbirds? Studies in Avian Biology 18:121–134.

CLARK, T. W., R. P. READING, AND A. L. CLARKE, editors. 1994. Endangered species recovery: finding lessons, improving the process. Island Press, Washington, D.C., USA.

————, R. M. WARNEKE, AND G. G. GEORGE. 1990. Management and conservation of small populations. Pages 1–18 *in* T. W. Clark and J. H. Seebeck, editors. Management and conservation of small populations. Chicago Zoological Society, Chicago, Illinois, USA.

COMPTON, B. B., P. ZAGER, AND G. SERVHEEN. 1995. Survival and mortality of translocated woodland caribou. Wildlife Society Bulletin 23:490–496.

CONNER, R. N. 1988. Wildlife populations: minimally viable or ecologically functional? Wildlife Society Bulletin 16:80–84.

COULSON, T., G. M. MACE, E. HUDSON, AND H. P. POSSINGHAM. 2001. The use and abuse of population viability analysis. Trends in Ecology and Evolution 16:219–221.

CRNOKRAK, P., AND D. A. ROFF. 1999. Inbreeding depression in the wild. Heredity 83:260–270.

CUNNINGHAM, A. A. 1996. Disease risks of wildlife translocations. Conservation Biology 10:349–353.

DANIELS, S. J., J. A. PRIDDY, AND J. R. WALTERS. 2000. Inbreeding in small populations of red-cockaded woodpeckers: insights from a spatially explicit individual-based model. Pages 127–148 *in* A. G. Young and G. M. Clarke, editors. Genetics, demography and viability of fragmented populations. Cambridge University Press, London, United Kingdom.

DEFENDERS OF WILDLIFE. 2003. The Bailey Wildlife Foundation wolf compensation trust. Available online at http://www.defenders.org/wolfcomp.html.

DELLASALA, D. A., N. L. STAUS, J. R. STRITTHOLT, A. HACKMAN, AND A. IACOBELLI. 2001. An updated protected areas database for the United States and Canada. Natural Areas Journal 21:124–135.

DIAMOND, J. M. 1987. Extant unless proven extinct? Or, extinct unless proven extant? Conservation Biology 1:77–79.

DOAK, D. 1989. Spotted owls and old-growth logging in the Pacific Northwest. Conservation Biology 3:389–396.

EASTRIDGE, R., AND J. D. CLARK. 2001. Evaluation of 2 soft-release techniques to reintroduce black bears. Wildlife Society Bulletin 29:1163–1174.

ELLNER, S. P., J. FIEBERG, D. LUDWIG, AND C. WILCOX. 2002. Precision of population viability analysis. Conservation Biology 16:258–261.

FAGAN, W. F., E. MEIR, AND J. L. MOORE. 1999. Variation thresholds for extinction and their implications for conservation strategies. American Naturalist 154:510–520.

————, ————, J. PRENDERGAST, A. FOLARIN, AND P. KAREIVA. 2001. Characterizing population vulnerability for 758 species. Ecology Letters 4:132–138.

FOREST ECOSYSTEM MANAGEMENT ASSESSMENT TEAM. 1993. Forest ecosystem management: an ecological, economic, and social assessment. U.S. Department of Agriculture, Forest Service; U.S. Department of Commerce, National Oceanic and Atmospheric Administration; U.S. Department of the Interior, Bureau of Land Management, Fish and Wildlife Service, National Park Service; and U.S. Environmental Protection Agency. U.S. Government Printing Office, Washington, D.C., USA.

FERSON, S., AND H. R. AKÇAKAYA. 1990. RAMAS/age: modeling fluctuations in age-structured populations. Applied Biomathematics, Setauket, New York, USA.

————, AND M. A. BURGMAN. 1995. Correlations, dependency bounds and extinction risks. Biological Conservation 73:101–105.

FIEBERG, J., AND S. P. ELLNER. 2000. When is it meaningful to estimate an extinction probability? Ecology 81: 2040–2047.

FOX, G. A., AND B. E. KENDALL. 2002. Demographic stochasticity and the variance reduction effect. Ecology 83:1928–1934.

FRANKEL, O. H., AND M. E. SOULÉ. 1981. Conservation and evolution. Cambridge University Press, Cambridge, Massachusetts, USA.

FRANKHAM, R., J. D. BALLOU, AND D. A. BRISCOE. 2002. Introduction to conservation genetics. Cambridge University Press, Cambridge, United Kingdom.

FRANKLIN, I. R. 1980. Evolutionary change in small populations. Pages 135–149 *in* M. E. Soulé and B. A. Wilcox, editors. Conservation biology: an evolutionary-ecological perspective. Sinauer Associates, Sunderland, Massachusetts, USA.

GÄRDENFORS, U. 2000. Population viability analysis in the classification of threatened species: problems and potentials. Ecological Bulletins 48:181–190.

————, C. HILTON-TAYLOR, G. M. MACE, AND J. P. RODRÍGUEZ. 2001. The application of IUCN Red List criteria at regional levels. Conservation Biology 15:1206–1212.

GIBBS, J. P. 2000. Monitoring populations. Pages 213–252 *in* L. Boitani and T. K. Fuller, editors. Research techniques in animal ecology: controversies and consequences. Columbia University Press, New York, USA.

GILPIN, M. E., AND M. E. SOULÉ. 1986. Minimum viable populations: processes of species extinction. Pages 19–34 *in* M. E. Soulé, editor. Conservation biology: the science of scarcity and diversity. Sinauer Associates, Sunderland, Massachusetts, USA.

GINZBURG, L. R., S. FERSON, AND H. R. AKÇAKAYA. 1990. Reconstructability of density dependence and the conservative assessment of extinction risks. Conservation Biology 4:63–70.

GOBLE, D. D., AND E. T. FREYFOGLE. 2002*a*. Federal wildlife statutes: texts and contexts. Foundation Press, New York, USA.

————, AND ————. 2002*b*. Wildlife law: cases and materials. Foundation Press, New York, USA.

GOODMAN, D. 2002. Predictive Bayesian population viability analysis: a logic for listing criteria, delisting criteria, and recovery plans. Pages 447–469 *in* S. R. Beissinger and D. R. McCullough, editors. Population viability analysis. University of Chicago Press, Chicago, Illinois, USA.

GRIFFIN, A. S., D. T. BLUMSTEIN, AND C. S. EVANS. 2000. Training captive-bred or translocated animals to avoid predators. Conservation Biology 14:1317–1326.

GRIFFITH, B., J. M. SCOTT, J. W. CARPENTER, AND C. REED. 1989. Translocation as a species conservation tool: status and strategy. Science 245:477–480.

————, L. M. COMLY, M. CHILELLI, K. R. ROCK, J. M. SCOTT, T. H. TEAR, AND J. W. CARPENTER. 1998. Annotated bibliography of wildlife translocations. Available online at http://mercury.bio.uaf.edu/~brad_griffith/translocation.shtml.

GROOM, M. J., AND M. A. PASCUAL. 1998. The analysis of population persistence: an outlook on the practice of population viability analysis. Pages 4–27 *in* P. L. Fielder and P. M. Kareiva, editors. Conservation biology for the coming decade. Second edition. Chapman and Hall, New York, USA.

GURD, D. B., T. D. NUDDS, AND D. H. RIVARD. 2001. Conservation of mammals in eastern North American wildlife reserves: how small is too small? Conservation Biology 15:1355–1363.

HAIG, S. M., J. R. BELTHOFF, AND D. H. ALLEN. 1993. Population viability analysis for a small population of red-cockaded woodpeckers and an evaluation of enhancement strategies. Conservation Biology 7:289–301.

HANSKI, I. 2002. Metapopulations of animals in highly fragmented landscapes and population viability analysis. 2002. Pages 86–108 *in* S. R. Beissinger and D. R. McCullough, editors. Population viability analysis. University of Chicago Press, Chicago, Illinois, USA.

———, AND O. OVASKAINEN. 2000. The metapopulation capacity of a fragmented landscape. Nature 404:755–758.

HARRISON, S., AND J. F. QUINN. 1989. Correlated environments and the persistence of metapopulations. Oikos 56:293–298.

HOLMES, E. E. 2001. Estimating risks in declining populations with poor data. Proceedings of the National Academy of Sciences 98:5072–5077.

HOWELL, E. 1988. The role of restoration in conservation biology. Endangered Species Update 5:1–4.

HUNTER, M. L. 2002. Fundamentals of conservation biology. Blackwell Science Publishers, Malden, Massachusetts, USA.

INTERNATIONAL UNION FOR THE CONSERVATION OF NATURE. 1987. IUCN position paper on translocation of living organisms. International Union for the Conservation of Nature, Gland, Switzerland.

———. 1995. Guidelines for reintroductions. International Union for the Conservation of Nature, Gland, Switzerland.

———. 2001. IUCN Red List categories and criteria: Version 3.1. Species Survival Commission, International Union for the Conservation of Nature, Gland, Switzerland and Cambridge, United Kingdom.

JACKSON, J. A. 1978. Alleviating problems of competition, predation, parasitism, and disease, in endangered species. Pages 75–84 *in* S. A. Temple, editor. Endangered birds: management techniques for preserving threatened species. University of Wisconsin Press, Madison, USA.

JAMES, F. C. 1980. Miscegenation in the dusky seaside sparrow? BioScience 30:800–801.

JOHNSON, K. H., AND C. E. BRAUN. 1999. Viability and conservation of an exploited sage grouse population. Conservation Biology 13:77–84.

KAUFFMAN, M. J., W. F. FRICK, AND J. LINTHICUM. 2003. Estimation of habitat-specific demography and population growth for peregrine falcons in California. Ecological Applications 13:1802–1816.

KELLER, L. F. 1998. Inbreeding and its fitness effects in an insular population of song sparrows (*Melospiza melodia*). Evolution 52:240–250.

———, AND D. M. WALLER. 2002. Inbreeding effects in wild populations. Trends in Ecology and Evolution 17:230–241.

KELLY, M. J., AND S. M. DURANT. 2000. Viability of the Serengeti cheetah population. Conservation Biology 14:786–797.

KENDALL, B. E., AND G. A. FOX. 2002. Variation among individuals and reduced demographic stochasticity. Conservation Biology 16:109–116.

KEPLER, C. B., AND J. M. SCOTT. 1981. Reducing count variability by training observers. Studies in Avian Biology 6:366–371.

KINDVALL, O. 2000. Comparative precision of three spatially realistic simulation models of metapopulation dynamics. Ecological Bulletins 48:101–110.

KLEIMAN, D. G. 1989. Reintroduction of captive mammals for conservation: guidelines for reintroducing endangered species into the wild. BioScience 39:152–161.

KOHN, M. H., E. C. YORK, D. A. KAMRADT, G. HAUGHT, R. M. SAUVAJOT, AND R. K. WAYNE. 1999. Estimating population size by genotyping faeces. Proceedings of the Royal Society of London Series B 266:657–663.

LACY, R. C. 1997. Importance of genetic variation to the viability of mammalian populations. Journal of Mammalogy 78:320–335.

———. 2000. Structure of the VORTEX simulation model for population viability analysis. Ecological Bulletins 48:191–203.

———, AND P. S. MILLER. 2002. Incorporating human populations and activities into population viability analysis. Pages 490–510 *in* S. R. Beissinger and D. R. McCullough, editors. Population viability analysis. University of Chicago Press, Chicago, Illinois, USA.

LALAND, K. N., AND K. WILLIAMS. 1998. Social transmission of maladaptive information in the guppy. Behavioural Ecology 9:493–499.

LANDE, R. 1988. Genetics and demography in biological conservation. Science 241:1455–1460.

———. 1993. Risks of population extinction from demographic and environmental stochasticity and random catastrophes. American Naturalist 142:911–927.

LAWTON, J. H. 1995. Population dynamic principles. Pages 147–163 *in* J. H. Lawton and R. M. May, editors. Extinction rates. Oxford University Press, Oxford, United Kingdom.

LEE, D. C. 2000. Assessing land-use impacts on bull trout using Bayesian belief networks. Pages 127–147 *in* S. Ferson and M. Burgman, editors. Quantitative methods in biology. Springer-Verlag, New York, USA.

LEOPOLD, A. 1933. Game management. Charles Scribner's Sons, New York, USA.

LEWIS, J. C. 1986. The whooping crane. Pages 659–676 *in* R. L. DiSilvestro, editor. Audubon wildlife report 1986. National Audubon Society, New York, USA.

LIMA, M., P. A. MARQUET, AND F. M. JAKSIC. 1996. Extinction and colonization processes in subpopulations of five neotropical small mammal species. Oecologia 107:197–203.

LINDENMAYER, D. B., R. C. LACY, AND M. L. POPE. 2000. Testing a simulation model for population viability analysis. Ecological Applications 10:580–597.

———, M. A. BURGMAN, H. R. AKÇAKAYA, R. C. LACY, AND H. P. POSSINGHAM. 1995. A review of the generic computer programs ALEX, RAMAS/Space, and VORTEX for modeling the viability of wildlife metapopulations. Ecological Modelling 82:161–174.

LIU, J., J. B. DUNNING, AND H. R. PULLIAM. 1995. Potential effects of a forest management plan on Bachman's sparrows (*Aimophila aestivalis*): linking a spatially explicit model with GIS. Conservation Biology 9:62–75.

LIVERMAN, M. C. 1990. The (endangered) Endangered Species Act: political economy of the northern spotted owl. Endangered Species Update 7:1–4.

LUDWIG, D. 1999. Is it meaningful to estimate a probability of extinction? Ecology 80:298–310.

———, AND C. J. WALTERS. 2002. Fitting population viability analysis into adaptive management. Pages 511–520 *in* S. R. Beissinger and D. R. McCullough, editors. Population viability analysis. University of Chicago Press, Chicago, Illinois, USA.

MACARTHUR, R. H., AND E. O. WILSON. 1967. The theory of island biogeography. Princeton University Press, Princeton, New Jersey, USA.

MACE, G. M. 1994. An investigation into methods for categorizing the conservation status of species. Pages 293–312 *in* P. J. Edwards, R. M. May, and N. R. Webb, editors. Large-scale ecology and conservation biology. Blackwell Scientific Publishers, Oxford, United Kingdom.

———. 1995. Classification of threatened species and its role in conservation planning. Pages 197–213 *in* J. H. Lawton and R. M. May, editors. Extinction rates. Oxford University Press, New York, USA.

———, AND E. J. HUDSON. 1999. Attitudes toward sustainability and extinction. Conservation Biology 13:242–246.

———, AND R. LANDE. 1991. Assessing extinction threats: towards a reevaluation of IUCN threatened species categories. Conservation Biology 5:148–157.

MACKENZIE, D. I., J. D. NICHOLS, G. B. LACHMAN, S. DROEGE, J. A. ROYLE, AND C. A. LANGTIMM. 2002. Estimating site occupancy rates when detection probabilities are less than one. Ecology 83:2248–2255.

MADSEN, T., B. STILLE, AND R. SHINE. 1996. Inbreeding depression in an isolated population of adders *Vipera berus*. Biological Conservation 75:113–118.

———, R. SHINE, M. OLSSON, AND H. WITTZELL. 1999. Restoration of an inbred adder population. Nature 402:34–35.

MAEHR, D. S., AND R. C. LACY. 2002. Avoiding the lurking pitfalls in Florida panther recovery. Wildlife Society Bulletin 30:971–978.

MAGUIRE, L. A. 1991. Risk analysis for conservation biologists. Conservation Biology 5:123–125.

———, and C. SERVHEEN. 1992. Integrating biological and sociological concerns in endangered species management: augmentation of grizzly bear populations. Conservation Biology 6:426–434.

MAPSTONE, B. D. 1995. Scalable decision rules for environmental impact studies: effect size, Type I, and Type II errors. Ecological Applications 5:401–410.

MARCOT, B. G., AND D. D. MURPHY. 1996. On population viability analysis and management. Pages 58–76 *in* R. C. Szaro and D. W. Johnston, editors. Biodiversity in managed landscapes: theory and practice. Oxford University Press, New York, USA.

———, R. S. HOLTHAUSEN, M. G. RAPHAEL, M. M. ROWLAND, AND M. J. WISDOM. 2001. Using Bayesian belief networks to evaluate fish and wildlife population viability under land management alternatives from an environmental impact statement. Forest Ecology and Management 153:29–42.

———, M. A. CASTELLANO, J. A. CHRISTY, L. K. CROFT, J. F. LEHMKUHL, R. H. NANEY, R. E. ROSENTRETER, R. E. SANDQUIST, AND E. ZIEROTH. 1997. Terrestrial ecology assessment. Pages 1497–1713 *in* T. M.

Quigley and S. J. Arbelbide, editors. An assessment of ecosystem components in the Interior Columbia Basin and portions of the Klamath and Great Basins. Volume III. U.S. Department of Agriculture, Forest Service, General Technical Report PNW-GTR-405.

MARMONTEL, M., S. R. HUMPHREY, AND T. J. O'SHEA. 1997. Population viability analysis of the Florida manatee (*Trichechus manatus latirostris*), 1976–1991. Conservation Biology 11:467–481.

MARSH, D. M., AND P. C. TRENHAM. 2001. Metapopulation dynamics and amphibian conservation. Conservation Biology 15:40–49.

MASTER, L. L. 1991. Assessing threats and setting priorities for conservation. Conservation Biology 5:559–563.

———, B. A. STEIN, L. S. KUTNER, AND G. A. HAMMERSON. 2000. Vanishing assets: conservation status of U.S. species. Pages 93–118 *in* B. A. Stein, L. S. Kutner, and J. S. Adams, editors. Precious heritage: the status of biodiversity in the United States. Oxford University Press, New York, USA.

MCCARTHY, M. A., D. C. FRANKLIN, AND M. A. BURGMAN. 1994. The importance of demographic uncertainty: an example from the helmeted honeyeater *Lichenostomus melanops cassidix*. Biological Conservation 67:135–142.

MCDANIEL, G. W., K. S. MCKELVEY, J. R. SQUIRES, AND L. F. RUGGIERO. 2000. Efficacy of lures and hair snares to detect lynx. Wildlife Society Bulletin 28:119–123.

MCKELVEY, K. S., J. J. CLAAR, L. S. MILLS, K. L. PILGRIM, G. HANVEY, J. R. SQUIRES, L. F. RUGGIERO, AND J. MALLOY. 2002. National Lynx Survey. U.S. Department of Agriculture, Forest Service, Rocky Mountain Research Station, Missoula, Montana, USA.

MEIR, E., AND W. F. FAGAN. 2000. Will observation error and biases ruin the use of simple extinction models? Conservation Biology 14:148–154.

MESLOW, E. C., R. S. HOLTHAUSEN, AND D. A. CLEAVES. 1994. Assessment of terrestrial species and ecosystems. Journal of Forestry 92:24–27.

MILLER, J. K., J. M. SCOTT, C. R. MILLER, AND L. P. WAITS. 2002. The Endangered Species Act: dollars and sense? BioScience 52:163–168.

MILLS, L. S. 1996. Cheetah extinction: genetics or extrinsic factors? Conservation Biology 10:315.

———. 2002. False samples are not the same as blind controls. Nature 415:471.

———, AND F. W. ALLENDORF. 1996. The one-migrant-per-generation rule in conservation and management. Conservation Biology 10:1509–1518.

———, AND M. S. LINDBERG. 2002. Sensitivity analysis to evaluate the consequences of conservation actions. Pages 338–366 *in* S. R. Beissinger and D. R. McCullough, editors. Population viability analysis. University of Chicago Press, Chicago, Illinois, USA.

———, AND P. E. SMOUSE. 1994. Demographic consequences of inbreeding in remnant populations. American Naturalist 144:412–431.

———, AND D. TALLMON. 1999. Genetic issues in forest fragmentation. Pages 171–184 *in* J. A. Rochelle, L. A. Lehmann, and J. Wisniewski, editors. Forest fragmentation: wildlife and management implications. Brill Publishers, Leiden, The Netherlands.

———, K. L. PILGRIM, M. K. SCHWARTZ, AND K. S. MCKELVEY. 2000a. Identifying lynx and other North American felids based on mtDNA analysis. Conservation Genetics 1:285–288.

———, M. K. SCHWARTZ, D. A. TALLMON, AND K. P. LAIR. 2003. Measuring and interpreting changes in connectivity for mammals in coniferous forests. Pages 587–613 *in* C. J. Zabel and R. G. Anthony, editors. Mammal community dynamics: management and conservation in the coniferous forests of western North America. Cambridge University Press, New York, USA.

———, J. J. CITTA, K. P. LAIR, M. K. SCHWARTZ, AND D. A. TALLMON. 2000b. Estimating animal abundance using noninvasive DNA sampling: promise and pitfalls. Ecological Applications 10:283–294.

———, S. G. HAYES, C. BALDWIN, M. J. WISDOM, J. CITTA, D. J. MATTSON, AND K. MURPHY. 1996. Factors leading to different viability predictions for a grizzly bear data set. Conservation Biology 10:863–873.

MOILANEN, A. 1999. Patch occupancy models of metapopulation dynamics: efficient parameter estimation using implicit statistical inference. Ecology 80:1031–1043.

———. 2000. The equilibrium assumption in estimating the parameters of metapopulation models. Journal of Animal Ecology 69:143–153.

MORRIS, W. F., AND D. F. DOAK. 2002. Quantitative conservation biology: theory and practice of population viability analysis. Sinauer Associates, Sunderland, Massachusetts, USA.

MOWAT, G., AND C. STROBECK. 2000. Estimating population size of grizzly bears using hair capture, DNA profiling, and mark–recapture analysis. Journal of Wildlife Management 64:183–193.

MUMME, R. L., AND T. H. BELOW. 1999. Evaluation of translocation for the threatened Florida scrub jay. Journal of Wildlife Management 63:833–842.

MURPHY, D., AND B. NOON. 1991. Exorcising ambiguity from the Endangered Species Act: critical habitat as an example. Endangered Species Updates 8:6.

NEWMARK, W. D. 1987. A land–bridge island perspective on mammalian extinctions in western North American parks. Nature 325:430–432.

———. 1995. Extinction of mammal populations in western North American national parks. Conservation Biology 9:512–526.

NOON, B. R., AND K. S. MCKELVEY. 1996. Management of the spotted owl: a case history in conservation biology. Annual Review of Ecology and Systematics 27:135–162.

O'GRADY, J. J. 2002. Evaluating the accuracy of species assessment systems using population viability analysis. Dissertation. Macquarie University, New South Wales, Australia.

OYLER-MCCANCE, S. J., AND P. L. LEBERG. 2005. Conservation genetics in wildlife biology. Pages 632–657 *in* C. E. Braun, editor. Techniques for wildlife investigations and management. Sixth edition. The Wildlife Society, Bethesda, Maryland, USA.

POSSINGHAM, H. P., D. B. LINDENMAYER, AND G. N. TUCK. 2002. Decision theory for population viability analysis. Pages 470–489 *in* S. R. Beissinger and D. R. McCullough, editors. Population viability analysis. University of Chicago Press, Chicago, Illinois, USA.

POST, W., AND J. S. GREENLAW. 1994. Seaside sparrow (*Ammodramus maritimus*). Number 127 *in* A. Poole and F. Gill, editors. The birds of North America. The Academy of Natural Sciences, Philadelphia, Pennsylvania, and The American Ornithologists' Union, Washington, D.C., USA.

POSTUPALSKY, S. 1978. Artificial nesting platforms for ospreys and bald eagles. Pages 35–45 *in* S. A. Temple, editor. Endangered birds: management techniques for preserving threatened species. University of Wisconsin Press, Madison, USA.

PURVIS, A., J. L. GITTLEMAN, G. COWLISHAW, AND G. M. MACE. 2000. Predicting extinction risk in declining species. Proceedings of the Royal Society of London Series B 267:1947–1952.

RABINOWITZ, D., S. CAIRNS, AND T. DILLON. 1986. Seven forms of rarity and their frequency in the flora of the British Isles. Pages 182–204 *in* M. E. Soulé, editor. Conservation biology: the science of scarcity and diversity. Sinauer Associates, Sunderland, Massachusetts, USA.

RAPHAEL, M. G., M. J. WISDOM, M. M. ROWLAND, R. S. HOLTHAUSEN, B. C. WALES, B. G. MARCOT, AND T. D. RICH. 2001. Status and trends of habitats of terrestrial vertebrates in relation to land management in the Interior Columbia River Basin. Forest Ecology and Management 153:63–87.

RATHBUN, G. B., AND J. SCHNEIDER. 2001. Translocation of California red-legged frogs (*Rana aurora draytonii*). Wildlife Society Bulletin 29:1300–1303.

REED, J. M. 1996. Using statistical probability to increase confidence of inferring species extinction. Conservation Biology 10:1283–1285.

———. 1999. The role of behavior in recent avian extinctions and endangerments. Conservation Biology 13:232–241.

———, AND A. R. BLAUSTEIN. 1997. Biologically significant population declines and statistical power. Conservation Biology 11:281–282.

———, C. S. ELPHICK, AND L. W. ORING. 1998a. Life history and viability analysis of the endangered Hawaiian stilt. Biological Conservation 84:35–45.

———, D. D. MURPHY, AND P. F. BRUSSARD. 1998b. Efficacy of population viability analysis. Wildlife Society Bulletin 26:244–251.

———, L. S. MILLS, J. B. DUNNING, JR., E. S. MENGES, K. S. MCKELVEY, R. FRYE, S. R. BEISSINGER, M.-C. ANSTETT, AND P. MILLER. 2002. Emerging issues in population viability analysis. Conservation Biology 16:7–19.

ROOT, K. V. 1998. Evaluating the effects of habitat quality, connectivity, and catastrophes on a threatened species. Ecological Applications 8:854–865.

ROWLAND, M. M., M. J. WISDOM, D. H. JOHNSON, B. C. WALES, J. P. COPELAND, AND F. B. EDELMANN. 2003. Evaluation of landscape models for wolverines in the Interior Northwest, USA. Journal of Mammalogy 84:92–105.

RUTH, T., K. A. LOGAN, L. L. SWEANOR, M. G. HORNOCKER, AND L. J. TEMPLE. 1998. Evaluating cougar translocation in New Mexico. Journal of Wildlife Management 62:1264–1275.

SÆTHER, B.-E., AND S. ENGEN. 2002. Including uncertainties in population viability analysis using population prediction intervals. Pages 191–212 *in* S. R. Beissinger and D. R. McCullough, editors. Population viability analysis. University of Chicago Press, Chicago, Illinois, USA.

SAMSON, F. B. 2002. Population viability analysis, management, and conservation planning at large scales. Pages 425–446 *in* S. R.

Beissinger and D. R. McCullough, editors. Population viability analysis. University of Chicago Press, Chicago, Illinois, USA.

SANJAYAN, M. A., K. CROOKS, G. ZEGERS, AND D. FORAN. 1996. Genetic variation and the immune response in natural populations of pocket gophers. Conservation Biology 10:1519–1527.

SAVIDGE, J. A. 1987. Extinction of an island forest avifauna by an introduced snake. Ecology 68:660–668.

SCHONEWALD-COX, C. M. 1983. Guidelines to management: a beginning attempt. Pages 414–445 in C. M. Schonewald-Cox, editor. Genetics and conservation: a reference for managing wild animal and plant populations. Benjamin Cummings, Menlo Park, California, USA.

SCHWARTZ, M. K., L. S. MILLS, K. S. MCKELVEY, L. F. RUGGIERO, AND F. W. ALLENDORF. 2002. DNA reveals high dispersal synchronizing the population dynamics of Canada lynx. Nature 415:520–522.

SCOTT, J. M., S. CONANT, AND C. VAN RIPER, III. 2001. Evolution, ecology, conservation, and management of Hawaiian birds: a vanishing avifauna. Studies in Avian Biology 22:1–428.

———, T. H. TEAR, AND L. S. MILLS. 1995. Socioeconomics and the recovery of endangered species: biological assessment in a political world. Conservation Biology 9:214–216.

———, S. MOUNTAINSPRING, F. L. RAMSEY, AND C. B. KEPLER. 1986. Forest bird communities of the Hawaiian Islands: their dynamics, ecology, and conservation. Studies in Avian Biology 9:1–143.

———, S. A. TEMPLE, D. L. HARLOW, AND M. L. SHAFFER. 1994. Restoration and management of endangered species. Pages 531–539 in T. A. Bookhout, editor. Research and management techniques for wildlife and habitats. Fifth edition. The Wildlife Society, Bethesda, Maryland, USA.

SCUDDER, G. G. E. 1999. Endangered species protection in Canada. Conservation Biology 13:963–965.

SEIGEL, R. A., AND C. K. DODD, JR. 2002. Translocations of amphibians: proven management method or experimental technique? Conservation Biology 16:552–554.

SHAFFER, M. L. 1987. Minimum viable populations: coping with uncertainty. Pages 69–86 in M. E. Soulé, editor. Viable populations for conservation. Cambridge University Press, Cambridge, United Kingdom.

SIMBERLOFF, D. 1988. The contribution of population and community biology to conservation science. Annual Review of Ecology and Systematics 19:473–511.

SINGER, F. J., M. E. MOSES, S. BELLEW, AND W. SLOAN. 2000. Correlates to colonizations of new patches by translocated populations of bighorn sheep. Restoration Ecology 8:66–74.

SJÖGREN-GULVE, P., AND C. RAY. 1996. Using logistic regression to model metapopulation dynamics: large-scale forestry extirpates the pool frog. Pages 111–137 in D. R. McCullough, editor. Metapopulations and wildlife conservation. Island Press, Washington, D.C., USA.

———, AND T. EBENHARD, editors. 2000. The use of population viability analyses in conservation planning. Ecological Bulletins 48.

———, AND I. HANSKI. 2000. Metapopulation viability analysis using occupancy models. Ecological Bulletins 48:53–71.

SLOANE, M. A., P. SUNNUCKS, D. ALPERS, L. B. BEHEREGARAY, AND A. C. TAYLOR. 2000. Highly reliable genetic identification of individual northern hairy-nosed wombats from single remotely collected hairs: a feasible censusing method. Molecular Ecology 9:1233–1240.

SNYDER, N. F. R. 1978. Increasing reproductive effort and success by reducing nest-site limitations. Pages 27–35 in S. A. Temple, editor. Endangered birds: management techniques for preserving threatened species. University of Wisconsin Press, Madison, USA.

———, AND J. A. HAMBER. 1985. Replacement-clutching and annual nesting of California condors. Condor 87:374–378.

———, AND H. A. SNYDER. 1989. Biology and conservation of the California condor. Current Ornithology 6:175–267.

———, S. E. KOENIG, J. KOSCHMANN, H. A. SNYDER, AND T. B. JOHNSON. 1994. Thick-billed parrot releases in Arizona. Condor 96:845–862.

SONG, Y-L. 1996. Population viability analysis for two isolated populations of Haianan eld's deer. Conservation Biology 10:1467–1472.

SOULÉ, M. E. 1980. Thresholds for survival: maintaining fitness and evolutionary potential. Pages 151–169 in M. E. Soulé and B. A. Wilcox, editors. Conservation biology: an evolutionary-ecological perspective. Sinauer Associates, Sunderland, Massachusetts, USA.

———, editor. 1987. Viable populations for conservation. Cambridge University Press, New York, USA.

———, AND L. S. MILLS. 1992. Conservation genetics and conservation biology: a troubled marriage. Pages 55–69 in O. T. Sandlund, K. Hindar, and A. H. D. Brown, editors. Conservation of biodiversity for sustainable development. Scandinavian University Press, Oslo, Norway.

———, AND ———. 1998. No need to isolate genetics. Science 282:1658–1659.

———, J. A. ESTES, J. BERGER, AND C. M. DEL RIO. 2003. Ecological effectiveness: conservation goals for interactive species. Conservation Biology 17:1–13.

SPITZER, P. R. 1978. Osprey egg and nestling transfers: their value as ecological experiments and as management procedures. Pages 171–182 in S. A. Temple, editor. Endangered birds: management techniques for preserving threatened species. University of Wisconsin Press, Madison, USA.

———, A. POOLE, AND M. SCHEIBEL. 1983. Initial population recovery of breeding ospreys in the region between New York City and Boston. Pages 231–241 in D. Bird, editor. Biology and management of bald eagles and ospreys. Harpell Press, St. Anne de Bellevue, Quebec, Canada.

STEIDL, R. J., J. P. HAYES, AND E. SCHABER. 1997. Statistical power analysis in wildlife research. Journal of Wildlife Management 61:270–279.

SWANSON, B. J. 1998. Autocorrelated rates of change in animal populations and their relationship to precipitation. Conservation Biology 12:801–808.

TAYLOR, B. L. 1995. The reliability of using population viability analysis for risk classification of species. Conservation Biology 9:551–558.

———, AND T. GERRODETTE. 1993. The uses of statistical power in conservation biology: the vaquita and northern spotted owl. Conservation Biology 7:489–500.

———, P. R. WADE, R. A. STEHN, AND J. F. COCHRANE. 1996. A Bayesian approach to classification criteria for spectacled eiders. Ecological Applications 6:1077–1089.

———, ———, U. RAMAKRISHNAN, M. GILPIN, AND H. R. AKÇAKAYA. 2002. Incorporating uncertainty in population viability analyses for the purpose of classifying species by risk. Pages 239–256 in S. R. Beissinger and D. R. McCullough, editors. Population viability analysis. University of Chicago Press, Chicago, Illinois, USA.

TEAR, T. H., J. M. SCOTT, P. H. HAYWARD, AND B. GRIFFITH. 1995. Recovery plans and the Endangered Species Act: are criticisms supported by data? Conservation Biology 9:182–195.

TEMPLE, S. A. 1978. The concept of managing endangered birds. Pages 3–8 in S. A. Temple, editor. Endangered birds: management techniques for preserving threatened species. University of Wisconsin Press, Madison, USA.

THOMAS, J. W. 1994. Forest Ecosystem Management Assessment Team: objectives, process and options. Journal of Forestry 92:12–19.

———, AND D. H. PLETSCHER. 2002. The "lynx affair"—professional credibility on the line. Wildlife Society Bulletin 30:1281–1286.

———, E. D. FORSMAN, J. B. LINT, E. C. MESLOW, B. R. NOON, AND J. VERNER. 1990. A conservation strategy for the northern spotted owl: a report to the Interagency Scientific Committee to address the conservation of the northern spotted owl. U.S. Department of Agriculture, Forest Service; U.S. Department of the Interior, Fish and Wildlife Service, and National Park Service, Washington, D.C., USA.

———, M. G. RAPHAEL, R. G. ANTHONY, E. D. FORSMAN, A. G. GUNDERSON, R. S. HOLTHAUSEN, B. G. MARCOT, G. H. REEVES, J. R. SEDELL, AND D. M. SOLIS. 1993. Viability assessments and management considerations for species associated with late-successional and old-growth forests of the Pacific Northwest. U.S. Department of Agriculture, Forest Service, U.S. Government Printing Office, Washington, D.C., USA.

THOMPSON, W. L., G. C. WHITE, AND C. GOWAN. 1998. Monitoring vertebrate populations. Academic Press, New York, USA.

TILT, W. 1989. The biopolitics of endangered species. Endangered Species Update 6:35–40.

TODD, C. R., AND M. A. BURGMAN. 1998. Assessment of threat and conservation priorities under realistic levels of uncertainty and reliability. Conservation Biology 12:966–974.

TRACY, C. R., AND T. L. GEORGE. 1992. On the determinants of extinction. American Naturalist 139:102–122.

TRENHAM, P. C., AND D. M. MARSH. 2002. Amphibian translocation programs: reply to Seigel and Dodd. Conservation Biology 16:555–556.

U.S. DEPARTMENT OF COMMERCE. 1995. Notice of completion of final marine mammal stock assessment reports and guidelines. Federal Register 60:44308–44314.

U.S. DEPARTMENT OF INTERIOR. 1987. Recovery plan for the Puerto Rican parrot, *Amazona vittata*. U.S. Department of the Interior, Fish and Wildlife Service, Atlanta, Georgia, USA.

———. 1998. Conference opinion of the proposed Shadowrock Ventures project and its effects on the proposed endangered Peninsular bighorn sheep (*Ovis canadensis*). U.S. Department of the Interior, Fish and Wildlife Service, Portland, Oregon, USA.

———. 2001. Reevaluation of the record of decision for the final environmental impact statement and selection of alternative for grizzly bear recovery in the Bitterroot Ecosystem. Federal Register 66:33623–33624.

VUCETICH, J. A., AND S. CREEL. 1999. Ecological interactions, social organization, and extinction risk in African wild dogs. Conservation Biology 13:1172–1182.

WADE, P. R. 2002. Bayesian population viability analysis. Pages 213–238 *in* S. R. Beissinger and D. R. McCullough, editors. Population viability analysis. University of Chicago Press, Chicago, Illinois, USA.

WALTER, H. S. 1990. Small viable population: the red-tailed hawk of Socorro Island. Conservation Biology 4:441–443.

WALTERS, C. J. 1986. Adaptive management of renewable resources. McMillan Publishing Company, New York, USA.

WESTEMEIER, R. L., J. D. BRAWN, S. A. SIMPSON, T. L. ESKER, R. W. JANSEN, J. W. WALK, E. L. KERSHNER, J. L. BOUZAT, AND K. N. PAIGE. 1998. Tracking the long-term decline and recovery of an isolated population. Science 282:1695–1698.

WHITE, G. C. 2000. Population viability analysis: data requirements and essential analyses. Pages 288–331 *in* L. Boitani and K. Fuller, editors. Research techniques in animal ecology: controversies and consequences. Columbia University Press, New York, USA.

——, A. B. FRANKLIN, AND T. M. SHENK. 2002. Estimating parameters of PVA models from data on marked animals. Pages 169–190 *in* S. R. Beissinger and D. R. McCullough, editors. Population viability analysis. University of Chicago Press, Chicago, Illinois, USA.

WILCOVE, D. S., M. McMILLAN, AND K. C. WINSTON. 1993. What exactly is an endangered species? An analysis of the U.S. endangered species list: 1985-1991. Conservation Biology 7:87–93.

WISDOM, M. J., L. S. MILLS, AND D. F. DOAK. 2000. Life-stage simulation analysis: estimating vital rate effects on population growth for conservation. Ecology 81:628–641.

——, B. C. WALES, M. M. ROWLAND, M. G. RAPHAEL, R. S. HOLTHAUSEN, T. D. RICH, AND V. A. SAAB. 2002. Performance of greater sage-grouse models for conservation assessment in the Interior Columbia Basin, USA. Conservation Biology 16:1232–1242.

WOLF, C. M., B. GRIFFITH, C. REED, AND S. A. TEMPLE. 1996. Avian and mammalian translocations: update and reanalysis of 1987 survey data. Conservation Biology 10:1142–1154.

WOODS, J. G., D. PAETKAU, D. LEWIS, B. N. McLELLAN, M. PROCTOR, AND C. STROBECK. 1999. Genetic tagging of free-ranging black and brown bears. Wildlife Society Bulletin 27:616–627.

YOUNG, A. G., AND G. M. CLARKE. 2000. Genetics, demography and viability of fragmented populations. Cambridge University Press, Cambridge, United Kingdom.

ZIMMERMAN, D. R. 1975. To save a bird in peril. Coward, McCann, and Geoghegan, New York, USA.

27

MANAGING URBAN HABITATS AND WILDLIFE

Lowell W. Adams, Larry W. VanDruff, and Maciej Luniak

INTRODUCTION

This chapter introduces the occurrence and attributes of wildlife and ecosystems across a landscape dominated by intensive human settlement. Wildlife biologists working in the urban environment, and students planning to become urban biologists, should be knowledgeable of techniques in wildlife field research and monitoring, habitat restoration and management, habitat conservation planning, human dimensions research and management, and management of nuisance situations and problem animals, relative to the metropolitan environment. These attributes are introduced after a description of the urban landscape and factors that affect urban wildlife.

Urban Wildlife—The Resource

The human-dominated landscape of urban and urbanizing areas supports varied biotic communities. Recognition of the opportunity and need to manage the urban ecosystem to benefit wildlife and people has been a conspicuous trend in natural resources management during the past few decades. A growing awareness exists that humans and global cultures are enhanced through maintaining sustainable landscape mosaics, including viable wildlife communities, from cities to wilderness areas. Contemporary sci-

entific knowledge and practical experiences offer many possibilities for managing for coexistence of people and wildlife in cities. The urban environment is a frontier for understanding and applying ecological, conservation biology, and resource management principles.

Urbanization

Human settlements began in Mesopotamia (Van De Mieroop 1997). Modern urbanization began about 250 years ago during the Industrial Revolution. The world's urban population multiplied tenfold during the last century. In 1950, 29% of the world's human population lived in cities; in 2010, 50% will be doing so (United Nations data). In several countries (e.g., Belgium, UK, Kuwait) over 90% of the population already lives in cities. Civilization has become increasingly urban, and all forecasts are for the process to continue, along with its impacts on ecosystems (Marzluff 2001, Pickett et al. 2001).

Urbanization alters wildlife habitats. For populations of some species it causes local extirpation, other species tolerate some changes, while a few species have increased success. Urbanization is the second most frequently cited cause of species endangerment in the United States (Czech and Krausman 1997). There is also a global tendency for certain types of animal species to settle in this new environment.

Thus, biologists involved with local, regional, or statewide urban wildlife programs will spend appreciable time, effort, and budget not only on enhancement programs for desirable wildlife, but also on managing nuisance wildlife.

The Urban Landscape

Structure and function of cities are dominated by anthropogenic factors. Four main features characterize urban ecosystems.

(1) A low proportion of energy and organic matter is acquired from local primary production in urban systems, and a huge volume of energy and materials is imported.
(2) Limited recycling of materials by natural processes of decomposition occurs in urban systems. Large volumes of waste materials are discarded locally. Conversely, large volumes of waste are also exported or destroyed, which requires extra use of energy.
(3) Import of energy and materials and export of industrial products, waste materials, and pollutants to and from urban systems, and direct impacts of activities of urban dwellers such as recreation and transportation outside cities, cause strong and long-distance external impacts beyond urban areas.
(4) High saturation with abiotic artificial structures and materials (including pollutants and toxins) and a dense human population in the city have direct local effects.

These artificial factors do not usually occur in nonurban ecosystems. Urban conditions limit and disturb structures and functions of subsystems in the city. However, urban environments and biota should be considered a system showing structure and functional patterns of "normal" ecosystems. This is expressed by impoverishment of the natural components of habitats, vegetation, and animal life of urban ecosystems—particularly in terms of biodiversity. Also, the main functions of urban ecosystems are limited and disturbed. Use of local insolation energy for primary production is low because of the small biomass of green plants. Flow of matter rarely forms complete circles and self-regulation functions are disturbed. Consequently, urban ecosystems are less predictable because they are dependent on external anthropogenic factors.

Urban areas are not ecologically homogenous. Intensity and mode of impact of urban-anthropogenic factors on the city's ecosystems vary within the wide range of urban habitats. Ecosystems of peripheral forest parks or those of large city parks with old tree stands are more natural than in densely built areas in the central city. Extreme cases of artificial habitats within urban ecosystems are building interiors and sanitary installations such as ventilation, drainage, and sewage systems. Parcel size is small, unusual juxtaposition often exists, and connectivity is reduced among biotic units in the city.

Cities—New Habitats for Wildlife

Urbanization has created, on a global scale, an entirely new type of landscape, which is novel for wildlife in terms of biological evolution. The ecology of contemporary plant and animal species was formed during many thousands of years, whereas urban ecosystems, at the landscape scale, appeared during the last 2 centuries. Expanding urbanization creates new sites for wild animals with obstacles and opportunities that were not available during thousands of generations of their existence. The most distinctive features of the city as a complex of habitats for wild animals, in comparison to nonurban habitats, are those described by Luniak (1996).

(1) Changes in mesoclimatic and hydrological conditions: higher temperatures, reduced humidity, lower groundwater levels, reduced wind speed and insolation, and artificial lights at night. The urban mesoclimate is usually milder and drier. Furthermore, microclimates inside buildings, pipes, tunnels, and other human-made structures where animals can live are often highly independent of outdoor atmospheric conditions. In cold and temperate zones this creates favorable conditions for wintering animals and for existence of exotic species from warmer and drier regions.
(2) Rapid and radical degradation of habitats as a result of urban development and management. Human effects disturb or completely destroy historical continuity and survival of animal communities. This also influences speed at which environmental changes occur inside a city due to abiotic factors, habitat structure, and land use. These elements eliminate many aspects of wildlife habitat and disrupt population dynamics and interspecific relationships.
(3) Distribution and concentration of physical structures and traffic increases fragmentation and isolation of animal habitats and reduces favorable space for wildlife. This factor strongly restrains distribution of fauna and also causes direct destruction of animals from collisions with vehicles, windows, and electrical wires. Additionally, new artificial sites are created that are often occupied predominantly by local and alien generalist species.
(4) High levels of pollution in air, water, and soil and abundance of chemicals, dust, and garbage. These factors affect animals directly by poisoning or indirectly by changes in vegetation, interspecific competition, or reduced survivorship. These conditions influence particularly soil and aquatic fauna.
(5) Large amounts of human food accessible for wild animals in storage, rubbish, and sewage as well as given directly to wildlife by people. This creates favorable feeding conditions for some species, which may become concentrated and less dependent on natural resources.
(6) Intensive gardening, management of vegetation strata (e.g., herbaceous lawns), and other human impacts on soil and vegetation such as trampling, fertilization, and pesticide application. These cause impoverishment of the urban environment's natural components and increase the proportion of cultivated and exotic plants. Horticultural practices remove leaf litter and old trees, and reduce the understory. These factors change the habitats of animals causing ecological degradation, loss of cover, and decreased food resources. They also enable colonization and local settling by exotic species.
(7) Permanent human presence and domestic animals have direct impacts on wildlife. Humans may frighten, kill, or even protect wild animals. Dogs and cats, as predators, do not depend for food on their prey, con-

trary to the essential principle of predator–prey relations. These subsidized predators, and commensals such as rock pigeon (*Columba livia*), and habitat associates such as raccoon (*Procyon lotor*), strongly influence the success of native wildlife populations.

An exciting aspect of understanding and managing wildlife resources in an urbanized area is addressing the social and cultural systems that directly influence ecological conditions as well as appropriateness and success of management programs. Understanding and incorporating social, political, and human dimensions factors into resource assessment, planning, and management is a major challenge. Comprehensive management of urban nature and wildlife resources necessitates work with urban planners, landscape architects, and leaders of nongovernment organizations, elected officials, environmental activists, and educators. Those planning careers in urban wildlife management should include introductory coursework in several of these other areas, including public relations and environmental law and policy. Practicing biologists, resource managers, and responsible agency administrators should establish coalitions of professionals and stakeholders having broad environmental expertise and enthusiasm for human aspects of the urban ecological setting.

Current Issues in Urban Wildlife Management

Current issues in urban wildlife management fall into 6 broad areas.

(1) Habitat and ecosystem destruction, alteration, fragmentation, and isolation.
(2) Isolation of humans from the components and functions of the natural world.
(3) Lack of public information and education, and lack of awareness by the public of the agencies responsible for management of the resource.
(4) Inappropriate responses by humans and stakeholders to wildlife.
(5) Lack of visionary thinking, multidisciplinary efforts, and multi-agency commitments to manage wildlife in the complex ecological, social, and political environment of the urbanized landscape.
(6) The need for comprehensive and integrated plans, continuing action, and adaptive management.

Future Trends and Challenges

Urban wildlife programs must work with the cumulative effect of human population growth, urbanization, and land use changes on the natural landscape and with the human dimensions impacts of societal priorities and programs. Anticipated trends include continuing urbanization of the world's population, continued isolation of humans from natural processes and biotic events, and increased public adoration and preservation of nature. A broadening coalition of stakeholders demanding husbandry and veterinarian services for individual wild animals in local populations also is predicted. A new millennium and prospects for new wildlife funding provide the impetus for more attention to urban wildlife conservation in developed countries. Students of urban ecology identify numerous challenges for multidisciplinary efforts involving regional and city planners, natural resource managers, and urban conserva-

tionists. The scale of needs and opportunities ranges from the backyard sanctuary to the regional landscape level.

We suggest the following areas and priorities for heightened attention to urban wildlife conservation.

(1) An accelerated need for understanding and programs addressing wildlife damage management.
(2) Planning and mitigation of the impact of urbanization on wildlife, valued ecosystems, and human-wildlife interactions such as artificial feeding.
(3) Restoration and management of urban green spaces.
(4) Research and education programs directed at social need for wildlife and nature, the role of wildlife in outdoor recreation, and maintaining naturalness of the wildlife resource under sustainable development and continued urbanization.

Well-rounded urban wildlife programs, whether they are federal, state, regional, or municipal in sponsorship, should include strong efforts in: inventory, research, and monitoring; planning and management; public and multi-agency information, education, and extension services; and urban habitat acquisition, development, preservation, restoration, and conservation (Tylka et al. 1987).

LANDSCAPE ECOLOGY AND BIOLOGICAL DIVERSITY IN THE URBAN ENVIRONMENT

Landscape ecology is the subdiscipline that includes both natural and cultural systems (Vink 1983). At least 2 approaches may be taken in landscape ecology. The biocentric approach emphasizes the significance of landscape phenomena, and processes are assessed with reference to plant and animal communities. Conversely, the anthropocentric approach places emphasis on human relationships within landscapes. In the latter, short-term as well as long-term needs of humans are emphasized, along with the responsibilities of humans for the landscape and its wildlife. According to Vink (1983:7), "Towns and cities ought to be viewed as cultural ecosystems and urban ecology may be able to make important contributions to providing man with a better urban environment in the future." The importance of urban areas to maintaining biological diversity also was observed by Murphy (1988:76) who stated "Our urban centers can be viewed as bellwethers of our global environmental fate. Our success at meeting the challenges of protecting biological diversity in urban areas is a good measure of our commitment to protect functioning ecosystems worldwide. If we cannot act as responsible stewards in our own backyards, the long-term prospects for biological diversity in the rest of this planet are grim indeed." We review landscape ecology and biological diversity in relation to the urban environment.

Characteristics of Urban Plant Communities

Natural plant communities typically are highly modified by urbanization. Much vegetation is eradicated and replaced with pavement and buildings, leaving less growing space for plants. Composition and structure of the remaining vegetation are also altered. As urbanization intensifies, native vegetation is replaced by exotic species (Table 1). In former West Berlin, Germany, some 41% of

Table 1. Loss of native plant species with increasing urbanization in Poland (adapted from Kowarik 1990).

Type of settlement	Native species (%)
Forest	70–80
Small towns	60–65
Medium towns	50–60
Cities	30–50

1,432 plant species that persisted were not native (Kowarik 1990). The proportion of non-native species was at least twice as high in urban areas as in nonurban areas.

Vegetation structure usually is simplified by urbanization. Often, the ground leaf layer in wooded areas is removed and replaced with shade-tolerant grass. This practice disrupts decay of the leaf litter into rich organic matter that helps to build soils. The shrub layer often is removed or heavily modified, creating a savanna-type community (Dorney et al. 1984). Such actions are devastating to birds and other animals that depend on the forest floor and shrub layers for food and nest sites.

Urbanization results in 3 broadly recognizable plant community categories. First, there usually are some remnants of natural communities that remain after development. These make up a small component of the urban vegetation complex. Second, colonizing communities are found on vacant lots and waste or derelict lands. Little study of the plant ecology of such sites has occurred in North America but more work has been done in England and Europe. Vegetation of such sites is dominated by alien species that typically have wide geographical and ecological ranges. These plants tend to be pioneer species of early successional stages, with rapid growth and dispersal rates. Such species usually are common or abundant on recently disturbed urban sites (Hodgson 1986). The term "recombinant" community has been used to describe these plant assemblages (Barker 2000). A third recognizable category of urban plant communities is termed "planted communities." This component includes public and private open spaces of parks, institutional grounds, and businesses, as well as street rights-of-way and residential yards. Planted communities are characterized by active human effort to plant trees, shrubs, and other vegetation. Such landscaping is mostly practiced in high-use public areas, near buildings, along streets, and in individual yards, although business parks and campus settings may have rather extensive landscaping. Some original trees and shrubs may be retained during development but this category consists mostly of new plantings, many of which are non-native species.

Characteristics of Urban Animal Communities

Although our knowledge of animal communities in urban areas is incomplete, some patterns are emerging. We know that urban development fragments the natural landscape. It destroys habitat required for many species, modifies habitat of others, and creates new habitat for some species. Natural vegetation destroyed in the process generally impacts habitat specialists most severely. This pattern seems to hold for birds (Aldrich and Coffin 1980), mammals (VanDruff and Rowse 1986), amphibians and reptiles (Cochran 1989), and invertebrates (Arnold and Goins 1987). Habitat specialists

have co-evolved with specific assemblages of natural vegetation and are dependent on them for survival.

Modified habitat and newly created habitat in the wake of urbanization are most attractive to habitat generalists. Opportunists with regard to food and habitat needs, these species are capable of using a wide range of food resources and habitat types. Among birds, granivores and omnivores predominate over insectivores and carnivores (Tomialojc and Profus 1977). This pattern probably holds for other taxa as well.

Often, a few species become superdominant in the city. With birds in Syracuse, New York, rock pigeon, house sparrow (*Passer domesticus*), and European starling (*Sturnus vulgaris*) comprised 80% of the city bird community during summer and 95% of the community during winter (Johnsen and VanDruff 1987). In inner Warsaw, Poland, rock pigeon and house sparrow accounted for 73% of the total breeding bird population (Nowicki 2001). A similar pattern has been noted for invertebrate communities in Warsaw (Czechowski and Pisarski 1986–1987). Proportions between species in natural communities are much more balanced, with dominants rarely exceeding 10% (Tomialojc and Profus 1977, Klausnitzer 1993, Tomialojc 1998).

Urban animal communities are generally characterized by lower species diversity when compared to animal communities in nonurban areas (Tables 2, 3). The proportion of exotic species increases with urbanization. The most common birds typically found associated with metropolitan centers in the United States are house sparrow, rock pigeon, and European starling. All 3 species are exotics, having been introduced to North America in the early 1600s (rock pigeon), 1851 (house sparrow), and 1890 (starling) (Levine 1998). In Berlin, Germany, 4 alien bird species settled in the city during the last 3 decades (Witt 2000) and 4 of the mammal species breeding in Berlin are of alien origin (Sukopp 1990). Humans have introduced most alien species in cities, intentionally or unintentionally.

Although numbers of species are reduced in urban areas, animal biomass and density typically are higher. Nourteva (1971) found that in the city center of Helsinki, the number of bird species was reduced to one half or one third in comparison to surrounding areas, but total biomass of the bird community in the city was as much as 20–30 times higher. Other comparisons from the European ornithological literature (Sasvari 1990, Tomialojc 1998) indicate that bird communities in urban parks have higher breeding densities than those in outlying forests. A similar pattern has been noted in North America. Researchers in Ohio found the biomass of birds in a residential area of Oxford was over 2.7 times the biomass and 1.3 times the density of birds in a nearby natural forest (Beissinger and Osborne 1982). In Arizona, one study reported both biomass and density were 26 times greater in Tucson than in the surrounding desert (Emlen 1974).

Species favoring warmer and dryer conditions may take advantage of the altered urban mesoclimate. Examples from cities in central Europe show that higher proportions of Mediterranean species are present in urban animal communities than in those in other habitats of the region (Klausnitzer 1993).

Poor diversity of urban areas leads to simplified regulation processes of animal communities in these areas. In species-poor communities, intrapopulation processes of autoregulation, including microbiological, genetic, demo-

Table 2. Species richness of invertebrates in and around the city of Warsaw, Poland (from Czechowski et al. 1981–1982, Czechowski and Pisarski 1986–1987, and Pisarski 1990).

Animal taxa	Region[a]	Warsaw[b]	Urban parks	City center[c]
Earthworms (Lumbricidae)	12	15	8	8
Spiders (Araneae)	424	254	134	43
Carabids (Carabidae)	323	276	96	44
Coccinellids (Coccinellidae)	58	51	28	14
Flies (Diptera–Tabanomorpha)	131	95	29	10
Ants (Formicidae)	43	37	21	11
Wasps (Vespidae)	42	14	10	8
Leafhoppers (Auchenorrhyncha)	270	171	97	43
Noctuid moths (Noctuidae)	309	270	49	90
Mosquitoes (Culicidae)	35	26	13	7
Springtails (Collembola)	141	44	32	27
Total species (%)	1788 (100)	1253 (70)	517 (29)	305 (17)
All species studied	3534 (100)	2005 (57)	1109 (31)	489 (14)

[a] Semi-natural habitats of Mazowsze, Central Poland.

[b] Including green areas in suburbs.

[c] Green sites of courtyards and lawns with trees on street sides in the city center.

graphical, and behavioral factors, have a larger role than do interspecific processes such as predation and competition (Andrzejewski 1982). Because of intensive changes in land use, technical structure, and management of urban areas, new animal communities are organized from colonization or stabilization into new ecological niches. Transformations of animal communities of other ecosystems are relatively more stabilized; they "adjust" their organization to changes of environment, but rarely create entirely new communities.

Factors That Shape Urban Animal Communities
Direct Impact of Urbanization

The effect of long-term, gradual development on an urban bird community was shown by Batten (1972) who analyzed changes of avifauna in a locality near London, England. During 140 years, urbanization gradually increased from < 1 to 65% of the land area and number of regularly breeding species decreased from about 70 to 43. The prediction for 100% urbanization was 20 species. Another long-term study of the effect of gradual urbaniza-

Table 3. Differences in bird communities of urban vs. natural habitats (adapted from Adams 1994).

	Habitat	
Community attribute	Urban	Natural
Abundance of exotic species	Higher	Lower
Abundance of native species	Lower	Higher
Number of species	Lower	Higher
Biomass	Higher	Lower
Density	Higher	Lower
Method of feeding	Generalists—many are seed eaters or feed on a variety of plants and animals.	Specialists—many are primarily insect eaters.

tion on vegetation, birds, and small mammals was in a suburban area of Warsaw, where, from 1800 to 1975, the proportion of built up area increased from 4 to 28%, causing gradual impoverishment of floral diversity. During the last 2 decades, more than a dozen bird species have declined in number or disappeared, replaced by increasing numbers of a few species such as rook (*Corvus frugilegus*) (Mackin-Rogalska et al. 1988).

The effect of rapid urbanization on bird communities was studied in Warsaw (Luniak 1994) and Olsztyn (Dulisz 2001), Poland. In both cities, avian communities of suburban habitats (forest, cultivated field, extensive built up settlement, allotment garden) were compared with communities of housing developments in the initial stage of construction and from 1 to 35–50 years. In both studies, changes of original habitat by construction for a new housing development were catastrophic for the bird community, reducing number of breeding species in 3 of 4 suburban habitats studied to 15–30% of the original species and number of breeding pairs to 7–21%. After 3–5 years, bird abundance in new housing areas was higher than that of 3 bird-rich suburban habitats. However, species diversity increased slowly. In developments 20 years or older, species diversity was about half that in suburban habitats but density was much higher. Even in the oldest (50 years) housing developments studied in both cities, number of breeding species was lower than in suburban green settlements (Table 4).

Similar "succession" in a new bird community after rapid development has been observed in other European (Plath 1985, Idzelis 1992) and American (Geis 1974) studies. The slow increase in diversity is limited by growth of newly managed vegetation. The rapid, intensive increase in abundance and density results from the rapid settling of a few species that nest on buildings and use anthropogenic food resources.

Landscape Patterns Resulting from Urbanization

Many factors contribute to the value of habitats for particular species of wildlife. Habitat types, such as forest, wetland, or grassland, influence the kind of species that will be present. Plant species composition and the age and structure of the plant community also are important. In addition, size and configuration of any given habitat are significant as is the nature of surrounding land use (Adams 1994).

In the urban complex particularly, where natural habitats are fragmented and isolated, scattered habitat reserves and interconnecting corridors are especially valuable. Broadly viewed, wildlife reserves consist of designated areas such as wildlife refuges, sanctuaries, and preserves, as well as undesignated areas of differing sizes that meet the basic needs of wildlife. The latter category includes parks, cemeteries, and community open space. Corridors are linear strips of habitat that serve as travel lanes for movements of wildlife and as interconnecting links between or among habitat reserves. These may be natural, such as ridge tops and riparian strips along rivers, or constructed, such as railroad rights-of-way, irrigation channels, fencerows, or hedgerows.

The size, configuration, and spatial arrangement of habitat reserves, and the effectiveness of corridor linkages of urban habitat patches with rural surroundings, affect wildlife use. Studies in urban areas show that larger habitat patches support more species than do smaller patches (Table 5). Species composition also changes with habitat patch size. For example, in forested areas of eastern North America, woodland species such as worm-eating (*Helmitheros vermivorus*), Kentucky (*Oporornis formosus*), and hooded (*Wilsonia citrina*) warblers are replaced by edge species such as gray catbird (*Dumetella carolinensis*), brown thrasher (*Toxostoma rufum*), and indigo bunting (*Passerina cyanea*) as habitat island size decreases (Whitcomb et al. 1981). Corridors connecting habitat reserves may increase the value of those reserves for wildlife (Adams and Dove 1989). By knowing how different species and groups of species may respond to different habitat sizes and patterns, we are better able to manage for them.

Synurbization

The term "synurbization" was introduced by Andrzejewski et al. (1978) and has been used in recent literature (Klausnitzer 1988, Gliwicz et al. 1994, Jedlicke 2000, Jerzak 2001). Synurbization is defined as an adjustment of population of the given animal species to specific conditions of the urban environment, in connection with regular existence (often breeding) there in the wild (Luniak 1996). The term is applied to existence of urban populations of the species, not to individual animals that may happen to reside in the city. In Warsaw, Poland, about 20 bird species have colonized or significantly increased their distribution in highly urbanized areas of the city during the last 3 decades (Luniak et al. 2001). A similar number of new bird species settled recently in Berlin (Witt 2000), Moscow (Ilyichev et al. 1987), and St. Petersburg (Khrabriy 1991). Studies in 27 cities in central and Eastern Europe confirmed this tendency in all cities investigated (Luniak 1990). This process is also observed in mammals and has global and progressive character. It does not change the fact that many other animal species show declines caused by growing urbanization.

Synurbization is a response of wildlife to the global expansion of urbanization. Urban development destroys original natural habitats and associated fauna. The process also creates new, empty ecological niches. This expanding "ecological vacuum" attracts species that adapt successfully to specific conditions offered by the new niche. In the Palearctic fauna, the best studied species in this respect are Eurasian blackbird (*Turdus merula*) (Kovshar and Suyko 1984, Luniak et al. 1990), wood pigeon (*Columba palumbus*) (Tomialojc 1980), mallard (*Anas platyrhynchos*) (Avilova et al. 1994), black-billed magpie (*Pica pica*) (Jerzak 2001), striped field mouse (*Apodemus agrarius*) (Andrzejewski et al. 1978, Babinska-Werka et al. 1979), and red fox (*Vulpes vulpes*) (MacDonald and Newdick 1982). In North America, among the best-studied examples of synurbization are peregrine falcon (*Falco peregrinus*) (Cade and Bird 1990), and American robin (*Turdus migratorius*) (Morneau et al. 1995). The behavior and ecology of species that adapt to urban habitats differ from behavior and ecology of those species in nonurban habitats (Fig. 1).

Adaptable omnivorous mammals such as Virginia opossum (*Didelphis virginiana*), raccoon, and coyote (*Canis latrans*) have higher population densities, smaller home ranges, and less movement in urban than in rural areas; they also may be larger bodied and exhibit a higher reproductive rate (reviewed by Adams 1994). Reduced home range size also has been recorded for white-tailed deer (*Odocoileus virginianus*) in urban settings (Kilpatrick and Spohr 2000*b*, Etter et al. 2002, Grund et al. 2002). The scale of differences

Table 4. Effect of housing development on bird community structure, Warsaw, Poland (from Luniak 1994).

Parameter	SS[a]	Years after development				
		0	1	2–5	5–23	17–50
Breeding species	23	7	9	10	10	16
Wintering species	17	7	8	11	15	15
Breeding density[b]	98	21	54	128	167	190
Wintering density[c]	270	25	105	174	424	502
Biomass, kg/10 ha						
Breeding pairs	18	3	8	35	54	69
Winter population	29	7	19	39	122	143

[a] Suburban village-like green settlement.
[b] Pairs/10 ha.
[c] Birds/10 ha.

Fig. 1. Mallards, such as these in downtown Warsaw, Poland, have adapted to urban living conditions around the world. Urban populations typically have higher densities, longer breeding seasons, altered migratory and feeding behaviors, and other differences from nonurban populations (photograph by Teresa Bogucka).

Table 5. Predicted numbers of species for urban terrestrial "habitat islands" of different sizes (from Adams and Dove 1989.)

Island size (ha)	Woodland birds[a]	Woodland birds[b]	Woodland birds[c]	Chaparral birds[d]	Land vertebrates[c]	Urban parks[e]	
						Flies	Beetles
1			6.4	1.6	8.7		
2		24.0	13.8	2.5	13.5		
4	13.0	27.0	21.2	3.4	21.0	25.2	6.6
8	21.0	31.0	28.6	4.3	32.8	29.7	7.7
12	27.0	33.0	32.9	4.8	42.5	32.6	8.5
16	29.0	36.0	36.0	5.2	51.1	34.9	9.0
20	31.0	37.0	38.3	5.5	58.9	36.8	9.5
24	31.5	39.0	40.3	5.7	66.2	38.4	9.9
30	32.5	40.0	42.7	6.0	76.4	40.5	10.4
36	33.0	42.0	44.6	6.2	85.8	42.2	10.8
42	33.5	43.0	46.2	6.4	94.7	43.8	11.2
65		48.0		7.0		48.5	12.3
100				7.5		53.7	13.6
200						63.2	15.8
300						69.5	17.3

[a] Estimated from Fig. 2 of Luniak (1983).
[b] Estimated from Fig. 2 of Tilghman (1987).
[c] From Vizyová (1986).
[d] From Soulé et al. (1988).
[e] From Faeth and Kane (1978).

recorded in densities between urban versus nonurban populations is impressive (Table 6). An abundance of food and den or nest sites, and perhaps warmer urban temperatures, probably are important influences. Also, the lower interspecific pressure of predation and competition in species-poor urban animal communities, and limitations of suitable green islands in built up areas may be contributing factors. High densities may have ecosystem impacts. For example, high white-tailed deer densities impact forest plant communities (Augustine and Frelich 1998, Augustine and Jordan 1998) and consequently forest birds (McShea and Rappole 2000).

Migratory behavior is typically reduced in urban birds. This behavior is connected with space and ecological barriers posed by the city, and also with better possibilities for wintering caused by milder urban mesoclimate, snow-free spaces and ice-free waters, and rich resources of anthropogenic food. In central Europe, a high proportion of urban populations of Eurasian blackbird, mallard, Eurasian coot

(*Fulica atra*), mute swan (*Cygnus olor*), and rook winter in breeding areas, whereas rural populations of these species migrate long distances to winter.

In urban areas, a prolonged breeding season is allowed by a sedentary life and favorable microclimatic conditions. More time in the phenological cycle is left for breeding, physical condition of individuals after winter is better, and some breeding sites such as in buildings are warmed or well sheltered against the cold. Urban hooded crows (*Corvus corone cornix*) in Moscow begin breeding 4–5 weeks earlier than their rural counterparts (Ilyichev et al. 1987). Eurasian blackbirds in urban areas begin breeding 1–4 weeks earlier than those in rural areas, and their last fledglings leave the nest about one month later in the summer (Luniak et al. 1990). In cities, Eurasian blackbirds usually have 2–3 broods, whereas those in forests have 1–2 (Luniak et al. 1990). Winter broods of some species have been recorded in central European cities (Luniak 1996). Urban magpies

Table 6. Recorded densities of some birds and mammals in urban and nonurban habitats.

Species, locality	Density		Source
	nonurban	Urban[a]	
Eurasian blackbird, Poland	0.5–3 pairs/10 ha	> 20x	Luniak et al. 1990
Wood pigeon, Poland	0.1–7 pairs/10 ha	10–30x	Tomialojc 1980
Black-billed magpie, Poland	0.2–0.6 pairs/10 ha	20–50x	Jerzak 2001
Hooded crow, Moscow	3–10 individuals/km^2	20–60x	Ilyichev et al. 1987
Eurasian coot, Poland	4–5 pairs/km of shore	2x	Jedraszko-Dabrowska 1990
Eastern screech-owl, USA	0.7–2.2 pairs/km^2	> 3x	Gehlbach 1994
Striped field mouse, Poland	4–8 individuals/ha	5–10x	Gliwicz et al. 1994
Red fox, England	< 0.1 family/km^2	> 10x	MacDonald and Newdick 1982
White-tailed deer, USA	7–10 individuals/km^2	2–6x	Adams 1994
Gray squirrel, USA	2–5 individuals/ha	2.5–6x	Adams 1994

[a] Increase over nonurban density.

in western Poland build nests 3–4 weeks earlier than those in rural areas, occasionally even in winter (Jerzak 2001). Earlier nesting in mallards (Errington 1934) and eastern screech-owls (*Megascops asio*) (Gehlbach 1994) have been recorded in the United States. In Warsaw, Poland, the striped field mouse shows sexual behavior in October, and even in winter, a phenomenon observed rarely in rural populations of the species (Gliwicz et al. 1994).

Improved longevity in urban areas results from higher winter survival because of favorable food and climatic conditions in cities, and a reduction in migrations that are more dangerous and more exhausting than sedentary life. A further important factor is lower predator pressure, as many raptor species avoid cities. The result is weaker individual selection in urban populations. Thus, albinos and impaired individuals are commonly observed in urban populations, whereas they are largely absent from natural habitats. Investigation of the striped field mouse in Warsaw, Poland, revealed altered blood parameters and higher infestation by parasites in an urban population compared to one in a rural area. Eurasian blackbirds in urban areas live 1–1.8 years longer than those in rural areas (Luniak et al. 1990). Birds and mammals in the urban landscape are more often victims of collisions with objects such as vehicles, glass panes, and wires in the air space. Studies of Eurasian blackbirds in Vienna, Austria, indicated a substantial percentage of individuals with healed wounds (Lidauer 1983).

Prolonged circadian activity may be connected with artificial lighting or with the tendency of wildlife to spend the hours of most intensive human activity in shelters. Urban birds begin singing earlier in the morning and finish later in the evening. Eurasian blackbird, black redstart (*Phoenicurus ochruros*), European redstart (*P. phoenicurus*), European robin (*Erithacus rubecula*), and peregrine falcon in urban areas show nocturnal activity (singing, feeding), something rarely observed in their rural populations. Rock pigeons active at night are commonly observed in cities. Equally, the striped field mouse, which is nocturnal in natural habitats, is active in open spaces in urban parks during the day, and gray squirrels (*Sciurus carolinensis*) may remain active into the night in well-lighted city parks.

The use of a variety of anthropogenic objects as shelters, nesting places, and material for nests is common in the urban environment. In inner Warsaw, Poland, 81% of the overall bird community nests in constructed objects, mainly buildings (Nowicki 2001). Urban populations of birds show a tendency to place their nests higher than those in rural areas. In Eurasian blackbirds, the mean difference is about 1 m (Luniak et al. 1990). Mallards in the inner area of Warsaw, Poland, nest only in tree cavities and in other elevated sites (e.g., on buildings) (Luniak et al. 2001). Mallards in rural areas commonly nest on the ground.

A city offers rich resources of anthropogenic food (refuse, feeding by people) that attracts many bird and mammal species. For some, e.g., rock pigeon, house sparrow, Eurasian collared-dove (*Streptopelia decaocto*), mallard, corvids, and gulls, this food is substantial, particularly in the winter season (Luniak et al. 2001). The feeding behavior of these birds, as well as of some mammals such as squirrels, mice, and red fox is adjusted to human customs and is directed at finding or receiving food from people.

Wildlife living in cities shows tameness toward people not seen in outlying areas. Coexistence with humans is a condition for successfully inhabiting the city. Almost all bird and mammal species living there reduce their escape distance in comparison to that maintained in rural areas. They often follow people begging for food, or even sit or perch on people. Many examples show that species, which in natural circumstances are particularly shy towards people, become tame in cities. Jedraszko-Dabrowska (1990) described aggressive reactions to humans by Eurasian coots in urban areas. Such behavior is not observed in rural populations of this species.

Increased intraspecific aggression is observed in urban populations, probably caused by the high density of individual territories and spatial limitations. Such behavior is commonly observed in Eurasian blackbirds in urban areas (Luniak et al. 1990), and it was also described in the Eurasian coot (Jedraszko-Dabrowska 1990).

Genetic distinctness of urban populations from those in rural areas has not been clearly tested. Differences in ecological and behavioral parameters can be explained by the direct effect of urban conditions and seem to be within the range of the species' natural plasticity. Morphological, anatomical, and physiological differences between urban and rural populations of the striped field mouse have been found, and have been interpreted as being genetically related (Gliwicz et al. 1994). Such differentiation was also found in tests of the behavior of Eurasian blackbirds of urban and forest origin reared in the laboratory (Walasz 1990). In midwestern North America, 90% of peregrine falcons of identified urban origin nested in cities, whereas 83% of peregrines reared in nonurban habitats on cliffs nested on cliffs (Septon et al. 1995). Thus, imprinting may have an important role in adjustments that make urban populations different.

Introduction of Species

The urban ecosystem, as an "ecological vacuum" with favorable conditions for some species, is visited by wintering birds from nonurban populations or colonized by alien species that follow humans. Examples include rock pigeon, house sparrow, and Norway rat (*Rattus norvegicus*). In many cases, humans introduce animals intentionally or unintentionally. They could be feral populations originating from individuals escaped or released. Among the exotic examples that have created stabilized wild populations in many European cities are Canada goose (*Branta canadensis*), Mandarin duck (*Aix galericulata*), rose-ringed parakeet (*Psittacula krameri*), and common myna (*Acridotheres tristis*), and mammals such as raccoon (Hohmann et al. 2001). In Cologne, Germany, the population of rose-ringed parakeet numbers about 1,000 birds (Kahl-Dunkel and Werner 2002). In Tokyo, Japan, and its vicinity, the wild existence of 71 feral bird species was reported during 1961 to 1981, 20 of which were breeding (Narasue and Obara 1982). Thirty-five of these species were from distant continents (Africa and America). The significance of this factor to urban fauna (particularly avifauna) is expected to increase. In American cities, the best examples of successful colonization are European birds such as house sparrow, European starling, and rock pigeon.

Managed reintroduction of species into urban areas also has been done. The peregrine falcon has been successfully reintroduced into cities in North America (Cade and Bird 1990), Germany (Brauneis 1994), and into Prague, Czech

Republic (Peske 1997) and Warsaw, Poland (Luniak et al. 2001), enhancing the natural recovery of the overall population of this species.

FIELD RESEARCH AND MONITORING TECHNIQUES
Techniques for Studying Diversity, Distribution, Density, and Abundance

Birds

Three techniques have been most commonly used to study the distribution, abundance, and composition of bird communities: belt transects, point counts, and territorial mapping (Bibby et al. 2000). For belt transects, the observer generally walks slowly along the centerline of the transect counting all birds seen or heard on either side to a given distance. Belt transects about 50 m wide were used to study the distribution and density of birds over a 1-year period in 3 residential communities of Edmonton, Alberta (Edgar and Kershaw 1994). Transects followed streets and an observer slowly walked the center of the transect counting birds to the roofline of the nearest dwelling (typically about 25 m away). Pell and Tidemann (1997a,b) studied the ecology of the common myna and the European starling in suburban Canberra, Australia. Density estimates were obtained from strip transects 100 to 150 m wide and of variable length. Strip transects 50 m wide of variable lengths were used to study species composition of breeding birds in relation to size of urban woodlands in Seoul, Korea (Park and Lee 2000), and 50 × 100-m belt transects were used to study breeding bird use of large parks in Madrid, Spain (Fernández-Juricic 2000).

Point counts differ from belt transects in that the observer remains stationary at a point and counts birds seen or heard, generally within a specified distance from the point (Bibby et al. 1992). Blair (1996) used point counts to study breeding birds in an urban-suburban matrix near Palo Alto, California. He estimated bird densities within a variable circular plot around the sample point. Five minutes were spent at each sample point and distance from the point to a bird was recorded in 5-m wide increments up to 30 m and in 2, 10-m wide increments between 30 and 50 m from the point. Bolger et al. (1997) used 8-minute point counts within circular plots with a 100-m radius to study breeding bird abundance in an urbanizing landscape in the city and county of San Diego, California. The researchers justified such a large radius because the shrub habitat surveyed allowed for fairly easy detection of birds. Point counts also have been used to study effects of development on area-sensitive breeding birds near Washington, D.C. (Darr et al. 1998).

Territorial mapping (Dowd 1992) was used to study effects of urbanization on species composition of breeding birds in forested wetlands of Staten Island, New York. Dowd (1992) calculated the number of territorial males or breeding pairs for all species within 2 7-ha study plots. A modified territorial mapping method was used to study breeding bird diversity in the city of Olsztyn, Poland (Dulisz and Nowakowski 1996).

Other techniques may be used to study the distribution, abundance, and composition of bird communities. Jokimäki and Suhonen (1998) used a study plot method to investigate distribution and habitat selection of wintering birds in small and large settlements in Finland. Each study plot was

30 ha and observers made a zigzag walk through the plot at a rate of 10 ha per 20 minutes. A bird feeder survey was used in Iowa to document broad population trends of the state's winter birds (Jackson and Hollis 1991), and mist netting has been studied and recommended for population monitoring of migratory songbirds during autumn (Dunn et al. 1997). Population data from large-scale monitoring projects such as the Breeding Bird Survey (Sauer et al. 2001), Christmas Bird Count (LeBaron 2001), and bird atlases (Lewis and Pomeroy 1989, Robbins 1996, Shirihai 1996, Hagemeijer and Blair 1997) might be available and useful to urban wildlife biologists. Atlases compiled specifically for metropolitan areas (Montier 1977, Luniak et al. 2001, Mitschke and Baumung 2001) also might be helpful. Luniak et al. (1990) discussed the advantages and disadvantages of the 2 systems on which data are collected and referenced. A grid system, usually 1 km^2 or 0.25 km^2 is most often used, but data collection based on habitat types seems to be more useful for urban planning and nature conservation.

Predation impacts distribution, abundance, and composition of bird populations and artificial nests can be used to study nest predation in the urban environment. For example, Major et al. (1996) used artificial nests containing 2 plasticine eggs (colored modeling clay) to study nest predation by pied currawong (*Strepera graculina*) in urban habitats in Australia. Nests were halved tennis balls covered with coconut fiber and wool manufactured to resemble nests of willie wagtails (*Rhipidura leucophrys*). Also in Australia, Matthews et al. (1999) used artificial nests to study effects of habitat fragmentation and edge on rate of nest predation in Sydney. Similarly constructed nests were lined with *Casuarina* needles to imitate nests of the eastern yellow robin (*Eopsaltria australis*) and plasticine eggs were placed in the nests. In the United States, artificial nests have been used to study nest predation in relation to rural and suburban forest edges in western Massachusetts (Danielson et al. 1997) and to study the influence of urbanization on predation in southwestern Ohio (Gering and Blair 1999).

Mammals

Live trapping is frequently used for studying mammal diversity, distribution, density, and abundance in metropolitan environments (Matthiae and Stearns 1981, Nilon 1986, VanDruff and Rowse 1986, Nilon and VanDruff 1987). Live trapping mammals in urban environments presents challenges to the field crew. Because urban lands are parceled into small units, much time must be spent seeking permission to work on private lots. Such efforts frequently require visits, often in the evening, with homeowners in the study area. Another challenge is the potential for vandalism and theft of live traps and other field equipment. Some biologists avoid this problem by concealing collapsible traps in the daytime and setting traps at dusk (VanDruff and Rowse 1986). Larger traps such as box or clover traps for deer should be labeled and risks to humans and pets minimized by bait selection, trap placement, and time of operation. Encounters with curious people—and sometimes investigating police—also require additional time when urban wildlife studies are conducted.

Bat detector devices have been used to study bat use in urban habitats. Everette et al. (2001) used such a device on an urban wildlife refuge 16 km northeast of Denver. These investigators measured echolocation calls beginning 30 minutes after sunset to examine bat use of the refuge. They also captured bats with mist nets (sunset to midnight) and radiomarked lactating female big brown bats (*Eptesicus fuscus*) to locate maternity roosts. Legakis et al. (2000) used a bat detector device to survey bats along transects in the Athens, Greece metropolitan area. These investigators recorded the number of calls per km of transect to obtain an indicator of foraging activity. Examples of other field techniques reported in urban studies of mammals include time-area counts of eastern gray squirrels (Williamson 1983), hair-sampling tubes for small mammals (Dickman 1987), and use of visual marking devices, such as colored neck collars (Vogel 1989).

Other Vertebrates and Invertebrates

Pitfall traps were used to study amphibian occurrence in relation to wetland characteristics in the Puget Sound Basin of Washington (Richter and Azous 1995), and nighttime tape playback calling surveys for frogs and toads were conducted statewide in Iowa and Wisconsin to measure relative abundance and species richness relative to land use (Knutson et al. 1999). Distribution and habitat use of lizards were studied using 30 × 200-m transects with the aid of binoculars in the Tucson, Arizona metropolitan area (Germaine and Wakeling 2001). Invertebrates studied in the urban environment have included dragonflies (Anisoptera) in South Africa (Samways and Steytler 1996), damselflies (Zygoptera) in Italy (Solimini et al. 1997), and butterflies in the United States (Blair and Launer 1997) and Japan (Natuhara et al. 1999). Methods applied in complex studies on terrestrial invertebrate fauna of Warsaw, Poland were described by Czechowski et al. (1981–1982).

Radiotelemetry for Studying Survival, Home Range, and Movement Patterns

Radiotelemetry is an important technique in wildlife management and research (Fuller et al. 2005). The technique has application in urban areas just as it does in rural areas for examining habitat use, home range size, survival, and movement patterns of a wide variety of species. Most recent work in urban areas has focused on birds and mammals. The technique has been used to study bald eagle (*Haliaeetus leucocephalus*) use of open space in the Chesapeake Bay watershed (Chandler et al. 1995), and movements and home range of Cooper's hawks (*Accipiter cooperii*) during the breeding season in Tucson, Arizona (Mannan and Boal 2000). Raccoon population density and survival in relation to rabies were studied in Rock Creek Park, in the Washington, D.C. metropolitan area (Riley et al. 1998) as was survival and movements of translocated raccoons in north central Illinois (Mosillo et al. 1999). Habitat use and preference of red foxes have been studied in the city of Bristol, England (Saunders et al. 1997) and home range and activity of gray foxes (*Urocyon cinereoargenteus*) were studied in residential and undeveloped areas in New Mexico (Harrison 1997). Urban coyotes are of growing interest in many communities and radiotelemetry has been used to study their home range and movement patterns in the metropolitan area of Tucson, Arizona (Bounds and Shaw 1997), habitat use in the greater Seattle, Washington metropolitan area (Quinn 1997*b*), and

habitat preference in the vicinity of Banff, Alberta (Gibeau 1998). Other investigators have used the technique to study diurnal bed-site selection of urban-dwelling collared peccary (*Pecari tajacu*) in Prescott, Arizona (Ticer et al. 2001), and movements and habits of brush-tailed possums (*Trichosurus vulpecula*) in an urban area of Launceston, Tasmania (Statham and Statham 1997). As more radiotelemetry units become equipped with internal GPS devices, radiotelemetry will become even more applicable in urban areas.

Habitat Gradients for Studying Impact of Urbanization

Research on birds and other species along development gradients has increased in recent years. From such studies, predictions can be made about the effects of development on wildlife. For example, Blair and Launer (1997) studied the distribution and abundance of butterflies across an urban gradient near Palo Alto, California. The gradient ranged from relatively undisturbed land (nature preserve) to highly developed land (business district). Germaine and Wakeling (2001) studied lizard distribution and habitat use along a gradient ranging from undisturbed land to highly developed land in Tucson, Arizona. Bird distribution, abundance, and community structure have been studied in California (Blair 1996, Bolger et al. 1997), Florida (Millsap and Bear 2000), Finland (Jokimäki and Suhonen 1993), Italy (Rolando et al. 1997), and Japan (Natuhara and Imai 1996). Gering and Blair (1999) studied predation on artificial bird nests along an urban gradient ranging from a mature beech-maple (*Fagus-Acer*) forest to a business district in the small city of Oxford, Ohio. An urban-rural gradient was used to compare bird abundance and diversity between the cities of Québec, Canada, and Rennes, France (Clergeau et al. 1998).

Other Techniques

Other techniques have been used to study urban wildlife. Hõrak and Lebreton (1998) used nest boxes during the breeding season to capture and leg band great tits (*Parus major*) for studying survival of urban and rural populations in southeast Estonia. Stout et al. (1998) located red-tailed hawk (*Buteo jamaicensis*) nests from a vehicle, or by foot if woodlots were not visible from a road, in late winter-early spring. Nests were later visited during the nesting season to estimate productivity. In Poland, pellets were collected to study the diet of urban and suburban tawny owls (*Strix aluco*) in Torun during the breeding season (Zalewski 1994) and infrared video cameras were used to study diet and feeding activity of urban peregrine falcons and Eurasian kestrels (*Falco tinnunculus*) in Warsaw (Rejt et al. 2000, Rejt 2001). Food habits of urban coyotes and gray foxes have been studied by collecting and analyzing scats (Harrison 1997, Quinn 1997*a*). Galeotti (1994) used playback recordings of owl calls from fixed positions along roads to study territory size and defense in rural and urban populations of tawny owls in northern Italy. Mail questionnaire surveys have been used to ascertain presence of coyotes and to document problems associated with human–coyote interactions in national parks in the United States (Bounds and Shaw 1994), and to study characteristics of sightings and attitudes of homeowners toward bobcats (*Lynx rufus*) in residential areas in central New Mexico (Harrison 1998).

HABITAT MANAGEMENT TECHNIQUES

Considerable opportunity exists in the metropolitan environment to restore and manage disturbed sites. Parks and recreation departments throughout the United States are becoming more involved with restoration and management programs. One example is the Natural Resources Group of New York City's Parks and Recreation Department, which focuses on restoration and management programs in that city (Matsil and Feller 1996).

Techniques that have been used historically to restore and manage wildlife generally include: passage of laws and regulations, establishment of refuges, control of predators, reintroduction, feeding, erection of nesting structures, and habitat restoration and management. All have application to the urban environment (Adams 1994).

Restoration and management of habitats are particularly important for maintaining wildlife populations and discussion of techniques for doing so follows.

No Active Management

At times, the habitat management goal may be to "let nature take its course." Strictly hands-off management, however, may not protect a site. Too many deer may impact the area by heavily overbrowsing it, inhibiting plant regeneration. If the management objective is to maintain and perpetuate the plant community, deer may have to be controlled through active management. Ignoring invasive exotic plant species encroachment may be harmful. Insect or disease outbreaks may also need to be controlled through active management or the habitat of interest may be lost or seriously degraded.

Advancing Succession

Wide expanses of open lawn are typical in post development landscapes, severely restricting wildlife diversity. To enhance the habitat value of such areas, more advanced successional stages are needed. Simply not mowing would allow the process to evolve but this approach is slow and the vegetation that grows may not be what the manager desires (Hodge and Harmer 1996). As an alternative, one could speed up succession by planting trees, shrubs, vines, and herbaceous vegetation (Holloran 1996). It might be possible to take advantage of the seed dispersal actions of birds in this regard. For example, Robinson and Handel (2000) sparsely planted a degraded urban reclamation site in the Hackensack Meadowlands of New Jersey and found that plots with planted trees and shrubs had higher recruitment of new woody plants than did unplanted plots, due primarily to differences in avian-dispersed seedlings.

In a landscape-planting scheme for wildlife, it is important to consider vegetation structure, arrangement (pattern), and species composition. With regard to vegetation structure and arrangement, both vertical layering and horizontal pattern are critical factors. Creating vertical layers of vegetation, from ground covers to low and tall shrubs to trees, is essential to sustain species diversity (MacArthur and MacArthur 1961, Karr and Roth 1971). For horizontal pattern considerations, clumping of vegetation to maximize patch size, rather than planting in rows, is best for birds (DeGraaf 1987) and probably other species as well. Connecting patches with corridors also is important (Haas 1995, Fernández-Juricic 2000). With regard to species composition, it is desirable to plant trees, shrubs, and other vegetation of known food and cover value to wildlife, and consideration should be given to wildlife use through different seasons. Giving preference to native species in the landscape-planting scheme will help ensure survival of native plants and associated wildlife communities (Aldrich and Coffin 1980). Unfortunately, most urban landscaping has incorporated exotic plants and these still dominate local nurseries, although interest in native plants is growing. Recognizing limitations posed by development, succession can be advanced even on a small scale in metropolitan centers. Plant community advancement also can be practiced on urban and suburban residential lots.

Setting Back Succession

"Arresting" succession generally involves mechanical means of grass or tree and shrub cutting, with use of herbicides also quite common. Controlled fires (prescribed burns) are used frequently in rural areas, but fire has limited use in the urban environment. Opportunities may exist to restore natural savanna landscapes in metropolitan environments because savannas have structural characteristics that are appealing to people. Mature, even-aged trees that provide high overstory canopy rate high as "openness" of the landscape. Natural oak (*Quercus* spp.) savannas of the Midwest region of the United States have been largely destroyed by humans and replaced with agriculture and urban development. Effective techniques for restoring and managing these habitats include spring and fall burning, thinning of overstory oaks, and removal of non-oaks and understory brush (Abella et al. 2001). Although many people favor structural qualities of oak savanna, some may react negatively to management techniques like tree cutting, burning, or use of herbicides needed to maintain these habitats (Boxes 1, 2).

Managing Edges

Urban areas have many edge habitats. Edges demark private property boundaries; occur along streams, power lines and transportation corridors; and in cemeteries, on golf courses, and in community and neighborhood parks where they separate active from passive use areas. Edges can provide connectivity between habitat islands.

Edges can serve multiple purposes. For people who find fences along property boundaries unsightly, "living fences" of trees or shrubs with wildlife value can be substituted that are aesthetically pleasing as well as functional for screening and privacy. A dense planting of hawthorn (*Crataegus* spp.) will be impenetrable to people, but will provide food and cover for wildlife. Combining taller trees and shrubs with shorter ones in the foreground also is aesthetically more pleasing and provides better habitat for wildlife. Such a design creates soft edge rather than hard edge.

The open nature and numerous edges of urban areas offer opportunities to manage habitat for butterflies, mammals such as meadow voles (*Microtus pennsylvanicus*) and cottontails (*Sylvilagus* spp.), and birds such as meadowlarks (*Sturnella* spp.), field sparrows (*Spizella pusilla*), and eastern bluebirds (*Sialia sialis*). Designing and planting edges following a curvilinear pattern presents a more natural appearance that generally is more aesthetically pleasing than straight edges.

Box 1. Restoring oak openings in Ohio and Michigan.

Prior to European settlement, the Oak Openings ecological region of northwestern Ohio and southeastern Michigan encompassed over 40,000 ha of oak savanna, oak woodland, and wet prairie. Savanna and woodland were dominated by sparse overstories of white (*Quercus alba*) and black oak (*Q. velutina*), and fire was important in maintaining all 3 communities. In the late 1800s, land clearing for agriculture, logging of oaks, draining of wet prairies, and fire suppression altered much of the area.

Toledo Metroparks now manages the 1,495-ha Oak Openings Preserve Metropark. Abella et al. (2001) tested several restoration practices at study sites in the 3 plant community types within the preserve. In 1998, spring and fall burning regimes were initiated. No other treatment was applied to the woodland site. At the savanna site, overstory oaks were partially thinned and non-oaks were removed along with understory brush. At the wet prairie site, overstory red maples (*Acer rubrum*), sassafras (*Sassafras albidum*), and other non-oak species were removed along with understory brush. Sites were inventoried twice in 1998 before restoration practices were applied and twice each year in 1999 and 2000.

Response to the treatments varied among the 3 community types, but a pattern emerged. Within the oak woodland, plant species composition remained about the same, but percent cover of native species increased due to an increase in tree seedlings of black cherry (*Prunus serotina*) and white oak and increases in shrubs such as witchhazel (*Hamamelis virginiana*) and blueberry (*Vaccinium* spp.). Thinning the overstory to 100–125 trees per ha to decrease annual litter and implementation of a long-term periodic burn regime (every 2–5 years) to thin the surface organic litter layer were recommended. This should result in increased light penetration leading to greater ground layer diversity more characteristic of historic levels while continuing to support native understory dominated by shrubs and sedges.

A shift in species composition was noted at the wet prairie site following restoration efforts. Goldenrod (*Solidago* spp.) increased but several characteristic oak opening wet prairie species were lacking, including big bluestem (*Andropogon gerardii*), swamp milkweed (*Asclepias incarnata*), wild bergamot (*Monarda fistulosa*), dense blazing star (*Liatris spicata*), cardinal flower (*Lobelia cardinalis*), and Virginia mountain-mint (*Pycnanthemum virginianum*). This vegetation response may be influenced by the altered hydrology. An attempt may be made to restore the original hydrology by blocking ditches.

At the savanna site, native species richness increased following restoration treatments. With continued burning, selective brush removal, and interseeding of absent and underrepresented species it is expected that ground layer diversity and grass cover will continue to increase. The authors believe that an irregular burning regime (varying the time of year and frequency) will increase the percent cover of wild lupine (*Lupinus perennis*), which is the larval food source for several rare savanna butterflies. The authors conclude (page 159), "Our results demonstrate that within three years controlled burning, overstory thinning, and other restoration treatments began to increase native species diversity and restore historic structure in three degraded Oak Openings communities…Restoration, combined with key land purchases, has a central role in the future ecological health of the northwest Ohio Oak Openings region in an increasingly urbanizing landscape."

Restoring and Managing Streams and Wetlands

Streams and wetlands often are altered or eliminated in the development process. The high percentage of impervious surfaces such as rooftops, and concrete and asphalt parking lots, streets, and sidewalks in the urban environment restricts water infiltration through the soil. In addition, soils are often severely compacted during construction or due to heavy use, which also restricts infiltration. Reduced infiltration leads to lower underground water tables and increased surface water runoff (Fig. 2). Surface water runoff (storm water runoff) may contain polluting sediment and toxic materials in addition to nutrients such as nitrogen and phosphorus washed from lawns, golf courses, and similar areas (U.S. Environmental Protection Agency 1983). In the past, streams typically were channelized to quickly remove urban storm water runoff. This involved removing riparian vegetation, removing tree branches and logs from the streambed, and straightening the stream channel. At the extreme, channelized urban streams have been modified to flow in concrete channels or in underground pipes. Such practices devastated natural plant communities (Auble et al. 1997) and associated wildlife populations, and added to downstream flooding. Greater effort is needed to restore the natural functions of streams and to manage them in the urban environment.

Soil bioengineering techniques are recommended to help restore degraded urban streams (Riley 1998). These techniques use both live and dead plant material to provide an immediate structural component to stabilize the stream bank as well as long-term bank protection. Brush deflectors, tree revetments, and root wads, along with live cuttings, can be used for this purpose (Riley 1998). Brush deflectors are brush piles staked to the stream bank and tree revetments are whole trees cabled against the stream bank with the top of the tree facing downstream. Root wads are uprooted trees from which the tree crowns have been removed. The trunk and attached root mass are placed perpendicular to the flow of water and earth is placed over the trunk, with the root mass providing support to the stream bank. Several root wads may be placed together along a stream. As a last resort for difficult situations where these techniques will not work, carefully constructed rock walls, gabions, or log crib walls might be considered (Riley 1998). Structures such as small check dams, boulder clusters, and logs can be placed in the stream to reduce water velocity. These structures create riffles and pools that help

Fig. 2. Streams often are heavily impacted by urbanization. A common scene in the metropolitan environment is stream bank erosion. Following rains, excess water from rooftops, parking lots, and streets is diverted to nearby stream channels. Thus, even small rainstorms can create flood conditions, and the high volume and velocity of water can erode the stream bank (photograph by L. W. Adams).

oxygenate the water and provide habitat for fish. They also help trap organic material such as leaves and wood, which contributes to the stream's nutrient level and benthic and macro-invertebrate communities. Care must be taken in the design and construction of such structures to ensure that migratory fish can continue to use the stream unimpeded. Culverts should be replaced or modified to allow fish passage where migratory species exist. In addition, removing accumulated sediment (from the development process) and replacement with gravel beds will enhance fish habitat by providing spawning sites. The goal should be to restore the correct physical dimensions of the stream and create a well-vegetated, stable stream bank environment (Riley 1998). Restoring degraded streams is expensive. It is far better to protect such habitat as development expands than to institute corrective measures at a later date.

Degraded wetlands also can be restored and new ones created (Adams et al. 1986, Demgen 1988, Morrison and Williams 1988, Zentner 1988). A comparative study in the Portland, Oregon metropolitan area revealed that constructed mitigation wetlands contained a greater percentage of native plant species and greater plant species richness than did naturally occurring wetlands (Magee et al. 1999).

Box 2. Restoring pine forests in Colorado.

The city of Boulder, Colorado owns and manages about 14,600 ha of open space and mountain parklands, some 3,240 ha of which are montane forests dominated by ponderosa pine (*Pinus ponderosa*). The forests consist mostly of young, small-diameter trees in dense stands because of fire suppression and logging over the last 100 years.

Historically, surface fires were common in ponderosa pine forests of the area. These generally were low-intensity fires that burned through grasses, herbaceous plants, and tree seedlings and saplings. Beginning in the late 1800s, fire suppression became a major management goal and this activity, along with logging, resulted in the current dense stands of small trees. In addition, livestock grazing has caused woody plant encroachment at the forest-grassland boundary because selective grazing pressures favor unpalatable woody species. These stands pose high potential for devastating crown fires, which are more hazardous to humans and alter ecological processes. For example, less sunlight reaches the forest floor in dense pine forests resulting in lower diversity and productivity of ground vegetation. Dense pine stands also result in reduced nutrient cycling and stream flows, and there is evidence that increased homogeneity of the forests leads to more extensive outbreaks of insect infestations.

The city of Boulder has developed a forest management plan designed to restore variability in forest structure and disturbance processes that mimics historical processes to the extent possible and practical (Brown et al. 2001). The plan calls for thinning many of the current stands but leaving, in most cases, trees greater than 30 cm DBH (diameter at breast height). This practice will promote development of old-growth forest conditions and allow regeneration of pine at lower densities. Douglas-fir (*Pseudotsuga menziesii*) will be removed from some stands in preference to ponderosa pine.

Once pine stands are thinned, prescribed fire will be used to maintain conditions in a more historically natural state. These low-intensity surface fires will promote greater diversity in the vegetation, enhance nutrient cycling, and reduce tree encroachment on the forest-grassland boundary. The plan calls for monitoring responses to management actions so that future treatments can be altered if needed.

This plan applies to low-elevation forest stands. At higher elevations and on steep slopes of the mountains west of the city, natural lightning fires will be allowed to burn under prescribed weather conditions.

The city recognizes that successful implementation of the plan depends on support by local residents and adherence to air quality standards in the area. A recent survey showed that 72% of Boulder residents support use of prescribed fire as a management tool to enhance ecological values and to reduce fire hazards.

Fig. 3. Ponds in the metropolitan landscape provide aesthetic and recreational values to people and habitat to wildlife. Such structures also can help to better manage water resources in the urban environment (photograph by L. W. Adams).

Shallow water wetlands developed in association with construction of storm water control impoundments, gravel quarries, and sewage treatment lagoons can provide wildlife habitat (Fig. 3). Helfield and Diamond (1997) reported that constructed wetlands are better suited for removing suspended solids, dissolved nutrients, and bacteria than for removing heavy metals and organic compounds. The latter materials should be controlled at the source to reduce the potential for toxicity to wetland fish and wildlife.

Impoundments should be constructed with irregular shorelines, gently sloping sides, and islands if the impoundment is larger than about 2 ha (Adams et al. 1986). Irregular shorelines increase the amount of edge habitat and provide numerous sites for waterfowl and other species. This reduces the sight line of breeding ducks and decreases territorial fights among males. Irregular shorelines also help reduce wave action at the shore-water boundary, reducing erosion and retardation of vegetation establishment.

Gently sloping sides of 10:1 will provide a littoral shelf, or bench, of shallow water habitat around the impoundment. About 25 to 50% of the water surface area should be 0.6 m deep or less (Adams et al. 1986). This will encourage wetland plant growth and improve resting and feeding habitat for ducks and a variety of marsh birds and shorebirds. If mosquitoes are of concern, fish that feed on mosquito larvae and pupae, such as bluegill (*Lepomis macrochirus*) or mosquito fish (*Gambusia affinis*), could be introduced. Both species are native to North America and have been introduced widely elsewhere. Careful evaluation should precede introduction of any animal to avoid negative impacts on native species.

Islands with gently sloping sides and appropriate vegetation in larger impoundments provide nesting and resting sites for waterfowl and other wildlife. They also reduce nest predation by mammalian predators.

The kind, amount, and distribution of plants are important considerations. Species of pondweed (*Potamogeton* spp.), bulrush (*Scirpus* spp.), and smartweed (*Polygonum* spp.) provide excellent food and cover for waterfowl and other species. Solid stands of cattail (*Typha* spp.) or common reed (*Phragmites australis*) are of lesser value. Maintaining an interspersion of open water and emergent vege-

tation in a ratio of about 50:50 is most ideal (Weller 1987). Also, emergent vegetation around the edge of the impoundment should not exceed 50% of the shoreline. Ducks, geese, and other species prefer such interspersion patterns (Weller 1987).

Seeding or planting is generally not necessary for vegetation establishment along streams and wetlands. Natural seed banks are usually adequate if water levels can be manipulated to induce germination (Weller 1987). If rapid plant establishment is required, transplants or sprouts can be used or the area can be seeded. On larger areas, wave action may inhibit natural vegetation establishment (Demgen 1988). In urban areas where soils have been highly disturbed, it may be necessary to import marsh soil to ensure a source of seeds and rootstocks for vegetation establishment (Zentner 1988).

The capability of regulating water levels is a valuable tool for managing vegetation. The amount of standing water and soil moisture greatly influence plant species establishment and successional trends. Thus, water level regulation can assist in controlling succession and maintaining interspersion of vegetation and plant species composition.

Drawdown refers to periodic removal of water from a wetland or water impoundment. It may be partial or complete. Maintaining a series of wetland sites in stages of drawdown is best. Moist-soil vegetation management benefits a diversity of waterfowl, songbirds, shorebirds, marsh birds, mammals, amphibians, and reptiles (Laubhan et al. 2005).

Constructed impoundments should be near existing wetlands whenever possible. This will enhance their wetland wildlife value and ensure a seed source for vegetation establishment. Richter (1997) presented guidelines for restoring and creating wetland habitats for amphibians in mitigation projects in the Seattle, Washington metropolitan area.

Better water management requires public support. Information programs can remind local citizens to not dispose of used motor oil, antifreeze, household cleaners, paints, solvents, pesticides, or other chemicals into household or storm drains. These programs also are helpful for presenting guidelines for lawn and garden maintenance. Fertilizer should be applied after spring rains with a nonfertilized buffer along the water's edge to reduce nutrient flow into waterways. Nutrients like nitrogen and phosphorus stimulate rampant algae growth (Odum 1971). This is often aesthetically unappealing to residents and can negatively impact the aquatic community.

Managing Human Activity

An important element of managing urban wildlife habitats is human activity in those habitats. This is particularly true for public open space areas and urban parks. Unlike rural areas, hunting generally is not allowed in the metropolitan environment, but other factors must be considered and evaluated. One such factor is theft of vegetation. In a small nature reserve in Florida, 6 of 17 orchid species were extirpated due to human theft (Dawson 1991).

Another factor is significant disruption of behavior and activity of animals. Intense human recreational use of forested areas may reduce density and diversity of breeding birds (van der Zande et al. 1984), especially ground and low shrub nesters. Disturbance of breeding activity may result from presence of large numbers of people in an area, or it may be more direct such as destruction of bird nests by children (Burr and Jones 1968).

Other potential impacts of humans should be considered. Heavy human use of an area may trample vegetation and compact the soil, leading to loss of plants and soil erosion. During dry conditions, potential for accidental fire is increased from discarded cigarettes and children playing with matches. People also may introduce undesirable exotic plants and animals to an area.

Several techniques may minimize detrimental impacts to wildlife while providing human use and enjoyment of a site. An on-site naturalist has proven effective in reducing vandalism and other misuse by people. If a full-time position is not possible, a volunteer host program or regular inspection will help. Maintaining use by the public also will help to reduce misuse by a few individuals. During the breeding season, restrictions on human access may be necessary in certain areas. Finally, continual education is important. This can be through on-site signs and brochures, and through the print, radio, and TV media as well as formally through local school systems (Baines and Smart 1991).

Although humans affect urban wildlife habitats, urban parks and open space areas are designed primarily for people. The public should be encouraged to use and enjoy such areas. This does not mean, however, that wildlife should be neglected. Part of urban open space's attraction to people is the wildlife it supports. The real issue is how to balance human use of such areas with the needs of wildlife. An appropriate balance can only be achieved through effective management.

HABITAT CONSERVATION PLANNING TECHNIQUES

Habitat conservation strategies should strive to maintain regional species diversity and meet human needs and desires. Grounded in island biogeography theory (MacArthur and Wilson 1967), the concept of multiple-use modules was introduced by Noss and Harris (1986). It calls for identifying core areas of high conservation value, surrounded by multiple-use buffer zones, and interconnected with habitat corridors. The overall strategy is to integrate conservation and development planning for long-term maintenance of environmental quality (Adams and Dove 1989). Wildlife biologists should be trained to identify areas of high conservation value and work with planners and landscape architects in implementing the overall conservation strategy. Harrison and Martinez (1995) observed that "bird atlas" data sets, which are being completed worldwide, may be useful in helping to identify areas of high conservation value. They presented data from the Southern African Bird Atlas Project and suggested an 8-step process for using the information for conservation purposes that should prove useful in other geographical areas where data consist of checklists. A focus on habitats supporting "area-sensitive" species is another approach for helping to identify areas of high conservation value (Darr et al. 1998). Greater use also might be made of biodiversity data available from state Natural Heritage Programs (Cort 1996).

Geographic Information Systems (GIS) can be used to graphically display areas of high conservation value. For example, Hadidian et al. (1997*b*) used GIS to associate distribution of breeding birds in Washington, D.C. with land use patterns. These authors observed that such work could provide city planners, urban ecologists, conservation groups, and others with information on bird distribution and abundance in association with land use classes over large areas. Shaw et al. (1998) also studied wildlife habitat on a city-wide scale using GIS in Tucson, Arizona. The technique has application in conservation planning for future development (Darr et al. 1998).

The concept of multiple-use modules is receiving serious consideration by planners and landscape architects as developing a landscape scale plan is an essential first step in planning for urban wildlife (Johnson 1995). It is often difficult to preserve or restore urban open space solely as habitat for wildlife and it is better if other uses can also be accommodated. Other uses might include air and water pollution control, erosion and flood control, and watershed stabilization. Forested areas not only provide habitat for wildlife but also shade and cool the urban environment. Naturalizing some areas can reduce mowing and pruning costs to cities. Parks and other open spaces have social and aesthetic values, providing areas for neighborhood socialization and offering stress-releasing areas for harried urbanites. These concepts have been incorporated into a *Wildlife Conservation Manual for Urbanizing Areas in Utah* (Johnson 1993). This manual serves to inform planners, developers, and landscape architects as well as the general public about the value of wildlife in urban environments. It provides guidance for incorporating wildlife conservation into master planning procedures, a valuable aid to county and community planning authorities. Rookwood (1995) also incorporated the concept of multiple-use modules in recommendations for biodiversity plans at regional and local levels. Collinge (1996) called for better collaboration among planners, landscape architects, biologists, and ecologists. She reviewed the ecological literature on effects of habitat fragmentation on plants and animals and argued that landscape architects and planners can lessen the detrimental impact of development through creative design and planning that make use of ecological knowledge.

In the United States, state governments are becoming more involved with land use planning. For example, the Maryland Economic Growth, Resource Protection, and Planning Act of 1992 more directly involves that state in such issues (Maryland Office of Planning 1992). Local governments are responsible under the Act for ensuring that growth is directed to existing population centers, development is concentrated in suitable areas, and sensitive resource areas are protected. At least 8 other states have active growth management acts (Ryder 1995).

Durban, South Africa has been progressive in implementing the concept of multiple-use modules in its land-use planning efforts. The Durban program's purpose is to improve the long-term quality of life for residents and preserve viable and representative examples of the region's indigenous plant and animal communities within the city (Roberts 1994). The Durban system incorporates 3 basic principles in an attempt to maximize ecological viability: (1) maximized reserve areas, (2) maximized landscape continuity, and (3) minimized system linearity. Core areas are indigenous community types where conservation is the primary function and are linked by dispersal corridors. Buffer areas are other open spaces, such as sports fields, golf courses, parks, cemeteries,

Box 3. Using cluster development to conserve wildlife habitat.

Extensive planning was devoted to design of the 'new town' of Columbia, Maryland. Development of Columbia has been largely completed on 5,670 ha of former forest and farmland about halfway between Baltimore, Maryland and Washington, D.C. The original new town zoning, approved in May 1965, called for a minimum of 20% open space, 15% low-density residential properties, and attached housing not to exceed 10%. Over the years, several modifications were made in zoning, with the overall tendency being to cluster housing more tightly while providing larger patches of open space. For example, 405 ha of valuable riparian habitat were slated for single-family detached housing (Geis 1986). Local citizens, including knowledgeable biologists, formed the Middle Patuxent Valley Association and convinced the developer and local authorities the area should be preserved. As a result, the development plan was modified, slightly increasing planned housing density elsewhere in Columbia to preserve this natural area. The site now not only will retain its wildlife value, but also will be of exceptional value to people. It will be used as an environmental study area for school children, and adults will have access to the nature trails and other facilities and programs.

industrial parks, private gardens, and road and rail rights-of-way. Researchers studying threatened wildlife in Chiba, Japan recently recommended the concept be incorporated into land-use policies to help maintain biodiversity in that country (Nakamura and Short 2001).

Cluster-type development offers greater flexibility than traditional-type development for maintaining some natural land features and habitats. Lot sizes, setback requirements, and road rights-of-way are typically reduced, and development is placed away from high conservation value areas that are preserved as open space. Compared to traditional lot development, clustering generally allows the same overall building density on a site and is recommended to better conserve wildlife habitat (Blair 1996, Theobald et al. 1997) (Box 3).

A variety of approaches may be available for acquiring/protecting lands in the urban environment for conservation purposes. Two approaches are land purchase and protection by law. Land purchase is expensive but generally secure. Protection by law could be at the federal, state, or local level. Examples include laws protecting wetlands and endangered species, local zoning regulations, and required open space set-asides (Adams and Dove 1989).

A third approach to acquiring/protecting conservation lands is through government incentive programs such as property donation, trade agreements, and conservation easements (Adams and Dove 1989). To encourage donation of lands for conservation purposes, federal or state law may allow the value of donated property to be deducted from the donor's tax liability. Gifts must be made to a nonprofit

organization as defined in the tax code or to a government agency. Trade agreements should be made with the donor's knowledge and concurrence. Such agreements may include tax-deductible gifts of property of low ecological value sold at fair-market value to purchase more desirable areas. An easement conveys a limited interest in real property from the property owner to another party who becomes the easement owner or grantee. In a conservation easement, the landowner gives up the right to develop the land under the easement but may retain other rights to the property. In practice, development rights are transferred so that those rights will not be exercised. The landowner may claim some value of conservation easements for tax deduction (Adams and Dove 1989).

Voluntary protection represents a fourth approach that may be effective. A variety of programs is available for landowners including those of The Nature Conservancy, National Wildlife Federation, The Humane Society of the United States, and state agencies.

Towne (1998) described factors that contributed to conservation of open space in Thousand Oaks, California. Perhaps most important was a common vision among residents, elected officials, and agency staff that open space conservation was essential to maintaining a high quality of life for people in the area. Resident attitudes were monitored by a city survey conducted about every 5 years starting in 1968. Community support led to effective open space conservation policies. Techniques used for securing open space lands included zoning regulations, land donations, land trades, and outright purchase (Towne 1998).

TECHNIQUES FOR HUMAN DIMENSIONS RESEARCH AND MANAGEMENT

Working with people, both individually and collectively, is critical for successful wildlife research projects and management actions in urban environments. Biologists should understand public knowledge and attitudes regarding wildlife. Both quantitative and qualitative social science methods may be used to gain such information (Knuth et al. 2001a,b; Siemer et al. 2001). Qualitative methods include in-depth interviews, facilitated small-group processes, direct observation, and analysis of written documents. Quantitative methods make use of face-to-face interviews, telephone interviews, mail surveys, behavioral observations, content analysis (making inferences from text), and secondary data analysis (using pre-existing data). A telephone survey was used to identify public preferences of central Missouri residents regarding management alternatives for Canada geese (Coluccy et al. 2001) whereas a mail survey was used to ascertain suburban resident attitudes toward management alternatives for white-tailed deer, American beaver (*Castor canadensis*), and Canada geese in the state of New York (Loker et al. 1999).

Several guidelines have been recommended for gaining public support in planning and implementing savanna restoration projects (Gobster 1994). One should be sensitive to location and size of the restoration relative to where people live. In high human use areas, restoration projects that are small and garden-like will be more acceptable than large projects with little management. Small projects will serve more as symbols rather than working ecosystems and have education value as well as aesthetic appeal. An attractive rail fence or a mowed strip can be used as design cues to separate the restoration area from higher human use areas. Gobster (1994) further recommends use of on-site signs, newsletters, and other outlets to interpret the management practices needed to maintain a restored savanna. Finally, restorationists should involve the public in an active way with a project (Gobster 1994). Judicious use of nature trails can help inform interested citizens with regard to the restoration effort. Sponsored tours can be conducted for the same purpose. Involving the public actively in restoration management practices will also help communicate management needs to maintain a savanna landscape.

Conflict resolution is becoming increasingly important in urban areas and use of a citizen task force is one of several approaches involving stakeholders in the management decision-making process (Decker and Chase 2001). For urban areas, a local governing authority such as a county, municipality, or community or homeowners' association typically establishes a citizen task force. This body includes comprehensive representation of interest groups and is charged with identifying a problem, reviewing management options, and recommending a management solution by consensus, if possible. An impartial facilitator is used to keep meetings on track and one or more technical resource advisors provide information when asked. Recommended management solutions are implemented by the local authority in conjunction with the state wildlife agency (McAninch and Parker 1991, Curtis et al. 1993).

Wildlife biologists working in urban environments also must be skilled in multi-agency coordination. Working with local elected officials, building managers, police and fire departments, and other agencies is necessary to gain support for research and management activities.

TECHNIQUES FOR MANAGING NUISANCE SITUATIONS AND PROBLEM ANIMALS

In this section, we highlight the different types of problems wildlife sometimes causes in urban areas and outline a general approach to management, with specific examples. Emphasis is placed on understanding and manipulating habitat components. Problems with nuisance wildlife usually are because of overabundance of one or more components—food, cover, water, or space—that creates a pest problem (VerCauteren et al. 2005).

Animals That Enter Houses

Most terrestrial wildlife species seek shelter for protection from the weather and predators, and in which to raise their young. In doing so, they may enter houses and other buildings designed for human use. This occupancy may result in general annoyance or nuisance, or it may involve more serious property damage or threat to human health and safety.

Raccoons and squirrels are among the most common nuisance mammals in North America (de Almeida 1987). Bats, mice, and birds such as house sparrows, starlings, and rock pigeons may also become pests by entering people's homes and other buildings. Animals commonly occupy attics, chimneys, garages, and basements. In addition, starlings and house sparrows may enter houses through unboxed eaves and unscreened louvered vents of clothes dryers or kitchen exhaust fans.

Human dwellings should be inspected periodically for evidence of wildlife intrusion. Attic, clothes dryer, and kitchen exhaust fan vents should be intact and screened. Animals gaining access to a building generally will discolor the paint or other finish around the entrance hole, leaving a dull or well-worn appearance; entry points are common at the juncture of the roof and sides. The inside of attics occasionally should be inspected for signs of wildlife use. Mice, rat, bat, or bird droppings, nest sites, or chewed wires or wood are evidence of such use. If not capped or screened, the inside of chimneys should be inspected with a flashlight for possible use by raccoons or other animals (Adams 1994).

If bats or birds have been roosting in an attic, expert advice should be sought before attempting to clear accumulated droppings. Wild animals that seem tame or perhaps injured should not be handled, as they may be diseased. The public health department or other experts should be contacted for assistance with both situations.

Homeowners with wildlife intruders generally want the offending animal removed unharmed and released at some distance so it will not return. Consequently, many animals are live-trapped and transported to more secluded habitats outside the city. This approach, however, may not be sound. Mortality of transposed wildlife is frequently high (Rosatte and MacInnes 1989, Bryant and Ishmael 1991, Reeve 1998, Adams et al. 2004), particularly if the new habitat already contains the species. Released animals tend to travel more in search of unoccupied territory (Mosillo et al. 1999). Road crossings are more frequent and many animals are killed from collisions with vehicles. Diseases can be spread to new areas by transported animals (Cunningham 1996, Craven et al. 1998) and, in much of the eastern United States, it is illegal to live-capture and translocate raccoons. Rabies is now endemic in the raccoon population and movement would increase the potential for spread of the disease. Finally, removal of live-trapped animals from a given locality creates a vacuum that is filled by animals moving in from the surrounding area.

To avoid problems associated with live-capture and translocation of wildlife, many biologists now recommend excluding the offending animal from a house or other building and repairing the access hole or capping the chimney so that reentry is prevented. Trained specialists use one-way doors that allow animals in the dwelling to leave but not to reenter (Greenhall 1982, Hadidian et al. 1997a). Once animals are excluded, entry holes should be repaired and cracks and crevices boarded, caulked, or otherwise weather proofed. Clothes dryers and kitchen exhaust fan vents should be covered with heavy screen or hardware cloth if necessary and chimneys should be capped or screened. These efforts will not only prevent reentry by offending animals but will improve the energy efficiency of the house as well. The use of one-way doors should be used only when it is certain that young are not present in the building. Most animals have additional den sites in their territory and will continue to use them.

Burrowing Animals

Skunks (Mustelidae), opossums, woodchucks (*Marmota monax*), and armadillos (Dasypodidae) may create problems by denning under porches, decks, or concrete patios. Routine inspection of building foundations, avoiding outdoor food dishes for pets, and keeping garbage tightly contained will do much to reduce problems from skunks, opossums, and raccoons. Other fossorial species such as moles (Talpidae), prairie dogs (*Cynomys* spp.), pocket gophers (Geomyidae), and ground squirrels (*Spermophilus* spp.) may become a nuisance in lawns and gardens. These animals are attracted to habitat components in the metropolitan environment. Hygnstrom et al. (1994) and Hadidian et al. (1997a) provided recent reviews of control methods for these mammals.

Mammals in the Yard and Garden

Deer generally are the largest animals that cause widespread trouble by feeding in gardens and on landscape plantings around the home. It is difficult to find plants they do not eat, although white-tailed deer have shown preference among common ornamental species (Conover and Kania 1988). Deer generally prefer broad-leafed evergreens to deciduous species, except for resinous evergreens such as pines (*Pinus* spp.), spruces (*Picea* spp.), and firs (*Abies* spp.). Highly preferred winter foods are yews (*Taxus* spp.), whereas low browsing pressure has been shown for American holly (*Ilex opaca*), shadbush (*Amelanchier* spp.), and flowering dogwood (*Cornus florida*).

Controlling deer numbers in urban areas is not easy, although techniques are available to do so. Techniques for population control may be classified as direct or indirect (Brush and Ehrenfeld 1991). Direct methods include live capture and transfer, hunting and regulated shooting, and fertility control. Indirect methods include repellents, fencing, and manipulation of succession and habitat interspersion.

Deer live captured and translocated often have difficulty establishing new home ranges and their mortality is higher than for resident deer (Jones and Witham 1990, Bryant and Ishmael 1991, Cromwell et al. 1999). Newly translocated deer travel more than resident deer and frequently are killed on highways. Some animals die from capture-related stress. In addition, they sometimes become pests in the new area. Finally, live capture and translocation are expensive, with costs ranging from $273.00 to $400.00 per deer (Bryant and Ishmael 1991). Unless suitable habitat is available that is devoid of deer, this technique is not a good option for handling nuisance urban deer.

Hunting and regulated shooting are the most effective direct techniques for controlling deer numbers (Robertson 1994, Kilpatrick and Walter 1999, Kilpatrick and Spohr 2000a, Doerr et al. 2001). An excessive deer population might be reduced through a "welfare harvest" where professionals harvest animals and the meat is sent to a processing plant for later distribution to qualifying institutions and welfare agencies (Oetting 1987). Illinois has a Good Samaritan Food Donor Act, which makes possible processing of wildlife for welfare. The meat must be handled in a licensed facility and arrive packaged at the welfare agency. Maryland also has an active donation program and other states are initiating similar approaches.

Work continues in fertility control (Fagerstone et al. 2002). Four decades of contraceptive research has not yet led to development of effective programs for controlling wildlife populations (Miller et al. 1998). Early research in the 1960s and 1970s focused on use of synthetic steroids, estrogens, and progestins (i.e., chemosterilants) in a variety of animals. More recent research has focused on immunocontraception, which involves preparation and delivery of a vaccine that stimulates production of antibodies (Fagerstone et al. 2002).

There is considerable current interest in the research community on use of porcine zona pellucida vaccine, particularly for white-tailed deer. The vaccine appears to inhibit fertilization through blockage of sperm-binding sites on the ovum and is free of many of the disadvantages of steroids. The vaccine was remotely delivered by dart gun to captive, unrestrained white-tailed deer and found to be effective and its effects reversible (Turner et al. 1996). It was effective in reducing fawn production in white-tailed deer under experimental conditions (McShea et al. 1997) and is beginning to be evaluated under field conditions (Rudolph et al. 2000). Miller et al. (2001) concluded the vaccine had no major physiological effects on health of deer in a managed, penned setting. Some concerns remain as young may be produced later in the year and the breeding season may be extended in treated populations (McShea et al. 1997).

Of the indirect methods for controlling deer, fencing is the most effective, and several types have proven useful. Animals rarely jump over standard wire mesh fence that extends 2.4 m above the ground. However, wire mesh fencing is expensive. Electric fencing is cheaper, but requires more maintenance. Several designs of slanted or angled fence have been tested and found to be effective (Craven and Hygnstrom 1994, Hadidian et al. 1997a).

Repellents have been proposed for controlling deer damage and some are commercially available. Commercial products along with human hairballs and products containing thiram have shown variable effectiveness (Conover 1984). A dog tied to a long run or trained to remain in a designated area can effectively repel deer.

Manipulation of plant succession and habitat interspersion may help provide a long-term solution to excess deer. For white-tailed deer in the East, reduction of habitat diversity and maintenance of late succession mature forest will lower an area's carrying capacity. Habitat manipulation, however, will most likely have to be combined with other methods.

Of the smaller animals, rabbits and woodchucks are among the most common species that can become pests in the garden. Hygnstrom et al. (1994) and Hadidian et al. (1997a) provided recent reviews of control methods for these mammals.

Other Mammals

Beaver may cause problems in some metropolitan areas by cutting down trees and flooding areas through their dam-building activities (Fig. 4). Fencing can be used to keep these mammals from small ponds, lakes, and valuable trees and shrubs. Individual trees and shrubs can be wrapped in hardware cloth, wire mesh, or tree wrap to a height of 1.1–1.2 m from the ground. In addition, several devices can be used to either lower pond water level or keep it from rising. This may cause the animals to move elsewhere. Hygnstrom et al. (1994) and Hadidian et al. (1997a) provided recent reviews of control methods for these mammals.

In some regions, localized wildlife problems may occur. In Arizona, collared peccary can become pests. Ticer et al. (2001) observed that, in Prescott, collared peccary preferred areas with dense cover, varied habitat structure, and aspects that optimized solar warming in cold months for diurnal bed sites. Vegetation modification at bed sites may be the most feasible option for reducing these populations.

Fig. 4. Beaver populations are thriving throughout much of North America, including many urban areas. In low numbers, they usually can be accommodated in cities, towns, and villages and are appreciated by residents. Too many animals, however, may prompt complaints from citizens upset at the loss of backyard trees and shrubs, which are used as beaver food and construction material for dams and lodges (photograph by L. W. Adams).

In Florida and other southern states, armadillos may cause problems by uprooting plants in search for insects and earthworms. Both species generally can be excluded from small areas by using specialized fencing. Coyotes present problems in some towns and cities. Baker and Timm (1998) provided recommendations for reducing coyote-human conflicts in the metropolitan environment (Box 4).

Roosting Birds

Many species of birds form flocks in winter but disperse to individual breeding and nesting sites in spring. In the southeastern United States where large winter bird roosts are common, blackbird flocks generally consist of several species, with red-winged blackbirds (*Agelaius phoeniceus*), starlings, common grackles (*Quiscalus quiscula*), and brown-headed cowbirds (*Molothrus ater*) being most typical. American crows (*Corvus brachyrhynchos*) also roost in flocks (Gorenzel and Salmon 1995). Winter flocks of blackbirds roost in large concentrations and typically reuse roosting sites nightly. Some roosts are in metropolitan areas. Large roosts can cause damage or create nuisance problems and the shear weight of birds may break tree branches. However, noise, foul odor, and accumulated bird droppings on sidewalks, cars, and buildings are most annoying to urban residents. The droppings are corrosive and can deface homes, buildings, and automobiles if not removed regularly. Accumulated droppings from roosts that are used repeatedly over several years create an environment for growth of the fungus that causes histoplasmosis in humans, a disease of the respiratory system. Histoplasmosis generally is not a problem unless the accumulated deposits of bird droppings are disturbed. In addition to large blackbird roosts, urban residents at times have problems with smaller numbers of roosting or congregating house sparrows, starlings, and rock pigeons.

Scaring tactics are used most often to reduce bird use of an area. Tape recorded alarm and distress calls of birds can be played through loud speakers at roost sites, discouraging incoming birds from landing (Gorenzel and Salmon 1993). Moving the playback calls throughout the roosting area enhances effectiveness of this method. So-called "shell crack-

Box 4. Techniques for reducing coyote–human conflicts.

Coyotes have become established in many metropolitan areas of North America and are continuing to expand their distribution. Several techniques exist for reducing coyote–human conflicts in the metropolitan environment. A qualified wildlife biologist should be consulted to evaluate a given situation. Public education materials should be prepared that discuss how to reduce habitat attractiveness to coyotes and how to maintain fear of people in the animals. Information should be included on fencing, proper sanitation, scaring techniques, and proper human behavior when approached or attacked by a coyote. With regard to sanitation, composting sites and trash-garbage cans should be "animal proofed"; tree fruit should be cleared from the ground; pets should not be allowed to run loose; and rodent–rabbit populations should be limited. Avoiding ornamental plants that produce fruit or that attract rabbits or rats can reduce habitat attractiveness. Ground covers should be maintained low and thin. Shrubs and trees near wild land areas or near children's play areas should be pruned several feet off the ground. A community ordinance against feeding wildlife may be needed. Scaring devices that have been successfully used include starter pistols, .22-caliber blanks, slingshots, rocks, portable air horns, auto horns, propane cannons, and halogen spotlights (Baker and Timm 1998). If the above techniques do not work, coyotes at a problem site should be trapped and euthanized, or shot. Leghold traps with padded jaws are effective in this regard. These traps can be used with pan tension devices to avoid capture of smaller animals. Cage traps are ineffective except for capturing young or sick coyotes. The goal at a given site should not be to eradicate coyotes but to re-instill fear of humans in the local population. Trapped coyotes should be euthanized according to American Veterinarian Medical Association standards.

ers" also can be effective. These typically are 12-gauge exploding shells fired from a shotgun. Explosions in the air near birds are more effective than those near the ground. Automatic gas exploders also should be elevated above ground for best results, and effectiveness of these devices is enhanced by mobility. Generally, no technique is effective when used alone. Experience has shown that it is better to integrate a combination of techniques into a scaring program (Johnson et al. 1985). Typically, a scaring program should be started in the evening on arrival of the birds at the roost and continue until dark. The procedure is repeated for 4–5 nights, which is usually adequate to move the birds elsewhere. Hygnstrom et al. (1994) and Hadidian et al. (1997*a*) provided recent reviews of control methods for these birds.

Waterfowl

Live capture and translocation are publicly acceptable techniques for dealing with excess ducks and geese (Adams et al. 1987; Cooper 1987, 1991). However, the procedures are labor intensive and expensive, and become self-limiting as other areas establish populations. Geese are most effectively captured during an approximate 3-week period in summer when they are growing new primary feathers and are thus flightless. During this period, the birds are easily herded into walk-in corral-type traps. Ducks are most effectively captured on cold winter days in walk-in bait traps.

Another approach to controlling waterfowl is to use scare tactics. Objects that move in the wind, such as scarecrows, tethered balloons, flags, and aluminum pie plates at times can be effective. Black plastic flags may be the most useful and least expensive technique in this category (Hygnstrom et al. 1994, Hadidian et al. 1997a). The effectiveness of such tactics may be short-lived because birds usually learn quickly that no real danger is present.

Explosive scare devices also may move birds to other locations (Aguilera et al. 1991). Such devices include automatic propane exploders as well as "screamer" shells, "shell crackers," and other manually operated noisemakers. Propane exploders should be set to fire about every 10–20 minutes and should be elevated. They should be moved every 2–3 days so that birds do not become habituated to them. Manually operated explosive devices are most effective if directed through the air over birds.

A third approach to nuisance waterfowl situations is to create a barrier or otherwise modify the habitat in a manner to make it less attractive. Unfortunately, features that make a lake or pond attractive to waterfowl also are often those attractive to people. At the extreme, impoundments can be de-watered, but this drastic measure is not likely to be publicly acceptable. Geese, particularly, like to walk from the water's edge to surrounding lawns and other open spaces for grazing. In doing so, they seek an unobstructed view to remain vigilant toward predators. Birds may be discouraged from using a water area by cessation of mowing to the water's edge in conjunction with planting of a shrub hedge or erection of a fence. Removal of islands and floating nest sites also can be effective in discouraging use.

Hunting or otherwise humanely reducing a population is a fourth approach to a nuisance waterfowl problem. Hunting is not generally feasible in most urban situations. However, a goose or duck population might be reduced through a "welfare harvest" whereby birds are trapped and humanely killed, with the meat sent to a processing plant for distribution to qualifying institutions and welfare agencies.

Other approaches to dealing with nuisance waterfowl include egg oiling, and use of herding dogs and alpha-chloralose. Christens et al. (1995) found that oiling eggs with white mineral oil was effective in preventing their hatching. Vegetable oil also works in this regard. One practical difficulty may be locating sufficient nests to effectively curtail reproduction. Herding dogs have been used in recent years to help control nuisance Canada geese (Castelli and Sleggs 2000). Well-trained dogs herd geese from lawn areas into a nearby pond or lake, from which the birds eventually fly to feed elsewhere. The technique may provide a site-specific solution to a nuisance goose problem but does not address the problem of goose overabundance on a regional scale. Alpha-chloralose (an anesthetic) has been used in field settings to capture Canada geese and other species (Belant et al. 1999). These investigators believe the drug was an effective tool in removing nuisance water-

fowl from locations where other techniques were either less efficient or impractical.

If a problem situation exists and people feed birds, such feeding should cease as other control measures are implemented. Supplemental feeding may be the primary reason for concentration of birds, leading to the nuisance situation. Some research has been conducted to examine whether or not waterfowl can be taught to avoid food handouts through conditioned food aversions. Methiocarb and dimethyl anthranilate, 2 chemicals that, on ingestion, cause some short-term discomfort for birds but do not kill them, were tested by Conover (1999). He concluded that further research was needed before conditioned food aversions can be adopted as a management technique.

Other Birds

Nesting populations of herring gulls (*Larus argentatus*) and ring-billed gulls (*L. delawarensis*) have increased in the Great Lakes region of the United States during the past 30 years. Along with this trend has been increased use of urban habitats such as roofs of buildings and mowed grass fields of airports where gulls may cause damage or create safety or nuisance situations. Ickes et al. (1998) recommended egg removal as an inexpensive, long-term technique for reducing roof-nesting colonies. Nest-and-egg destruction or egg destruction alone were recommended for controlling ground-nesting colonies.

Laughing gulls (*L. atricilla*) have recolonized Long Island, New York and pose concern to nearby John F. Kennedy International Airport. Buckley and McCarthy (1994) recommended an airport-wide program encouraging taller grasses, draining of standing water, and control of beetles on which the birds feed.

Australian magpies (*Gymnorhina tibicen*) create problems in some Australian towns and cities. One particular characteristic of magpie behavior that creates conflict with humans is the bird's aggressive defense of its territory, which is particularly strong during the breeding season. The birds, usually males, which presumably regard people as threats to nests and young, may attack anyone walking, running, or cycling near nests. Several management approaches have been suggested to deal with aggressive magpies (Jones and Thomas 1999). Research should be conducted to examine effectiveness of the various proposed management actions and perhaps discover better solutions to the problem.

SUMMARY

Wildlife biologists working in the urban environment, and students planning to become urban biologists, should be knowledgeable of techniques in wildlife field research and monitoring, habitat restoration and management, habitat conservation planning, human dimensions research and management, and management of nuisance situations and problem animals, relative to the metropolitan environment. Civilization has become increasingly urban, and the process of urbanization continues worldwide. Urban wildlife biologists must work with the cumulative effect of human population growth, urbanization, and land use changes on the natural landscape and with the human dimensions impacts of societal priorities and programs.

Plant and animal communities are modified by urbanization. A pattern of change in such communities is emerging. Urbanization results in a loss of native and increase of exotic species with lower overall species richness compared with predevelopment conditions. Many animal communities in urban areas, however, show higher biomass and density because of mass occurrence of a few highly successful species that tend to be generalists with broad ecological tolerance as opposed to specialists with more narrow tolerance. For effective management, biologists must understand the factors that shape urban plant and animal communities.

Urban biologists generally use field research and monitoring techniques that nonurban biologists use. For birds, belt transects, point counts, and territorial mapping of breeding pairs are used to study diversity, distribution, density, and abundance. Live trapping is frequently used for studying these factors in urban mammals. Radiotelemetry is used for examining habitat use, home range size, survival, and movement patterns of a wide variety of species. Habitat gradients can be used to study impact of urbanization and artificial nests to study nest predation in the urban environment. Other techniques include use of playback recordings of owl calls to study habitat use and mail questionnaire surveys to ascertain presence of coyotes and bobcats in metropolitan areas.

Techniques that have been used historically to restore and manage wildlife generally include: passage of laws and regulations, establishment of refuges, control of predators, reintroduction, feeding, erection of nesting structures, and habitat restoration and management. All have application to the urban environment. With regard to habitat restoration and management, techniques generally include: no active management, advancing succession, setting back succession, managing edges, restoring and managing streams and wetlands, and managing human activity.

Habitat conservation planning techniques should strive to maintain regional species diversity and meet human needs and desires. The overall strategy is to integrate conservation and development planning for long-term maintenance of environmental quality. Based on island biogeography theory, urban biologists identify core areas of high conservation value, surrounded by multiple-use buffer zones, and interconnected with habitat corridors. Biologists must work with planners and landscape architects in implementing a conservation strategy. Cluster-type development often is helpful in this regard as it offers greater flexibility than does traditional-type development for maintaining some natural land features and habitats.

Both qualitative and quantitative techniques are used in human dimensions work to gain understanding of public knowledge and attitudes regarding wildlife. Qualitative methods include in-depth interviews, facilitated small-group processes, direct observation, and analysis of written documents. Quantitative methods make use of face-to-face interviews, telephone interviews, mail surveys, behavioral observations, content analysis (making inferences from text), and secondary data analysis (using pre-existing data). Citizen task forces, which involve stakeholders in the management decision-making process, are used to resolve conflicts in some situations.

Urban biologists must be knowledgeable of techniques for managing nuisance situations and problem animals. One-way doors, which allow animals in a house or other building to leave but not to reenter, may be used for many situations. Scaring tactics are often used to reduce bird use of an area. Tape-recorded alarm and distress calls of birds can be played through loud speakers at roost sites, and "shell crackers" and automatic gas exploders also can be effective. Generally, it is better to integrate a combination of techniques into a scaring program, as no single technique is effective when used alone. Problems with nuisance wildlife usually are because of overabundance of one or more habitat components—food, cover, water, or space. Biologists attempt to manipulate these components to reduce or eliminate the nuisance situation or problem animal.

ACKNOWLEDGMENTS

We greatly appreciate the helpful comments of 2 anonymous reviewers.

LITERATURE CITED

ABELLA, S. R., J. F. JAEGER, D. H. GEHRING, R. G. JACKSY, K .S. MENARD, AND K .A. HIGH. 2001. Restoring historic plant communities in the Oak Openings region of northwest Ohio. Ecological Restoration 19:155–160.

ADAMS, L. W. 1994. Urban wildlife habitats: a landscape perspective. University of Minnesota Press, Minneapolis, USA.

———, AND L. E. DOVE. 1989. Wildlife reserves and corridors in the urban environment: a guide to ecological landscape planning and resource conservation. National Institute for Urban Wildlife, Columbia, Maryland, USA.

———, J. HADIDIAN, AND V. FLYGER. 2004. Movement and mortality of translocated urban–suburban grey squirrels. Animal Welfare 13:45–50.

———, C. D. RHODEHAMEL, AND J. S. MCKEGG. 1987. A strategy for managing urban waterfowl populations. Page 235 *in* L. W. Adams and D. L. Leedy, editors. Integrating man and nature in the metropolitan environment. National Institute for Urban Wildlife, Columbia, Maryland, USA.

———, T. M. FRANKLIN, L. E. DOVE, AND J. M. DUFFIELD. 1986. Design considerations for wildlife in urban stormwater management. Transactions of the North American Wildlife and Natural Resources Conference 51:249–259.

AGUILERA, E., R. L. KNIGHT, AND J. L. CUMMINGS. 1991. An evaluation of two hazing methods for urban Canada geese. Wildlife Society Bulletin 19:32–35.

ALDRICH, J. W., AND R. W. COFFIN. 1980. Breeding bird populations from forest to suburbia after thirty-seven years. American Birds 34:3–7.

ANDRZEJEWSKI, R. 1982. Problems and prospects of faunistical investigations in towns. Pages 9–15 *in* M. Luniak and B. Pisarski, editors. Animals in urban environment. Ossolineum, Wroclaw, Poland.

———, J. BABINSKA-WERKA, J. GLIWICZ, AND J. GOSZCZYNSKI. 1978. Synurbization processes in a population of *Apodemus agrarius*. 1. Characteristics of populations in an urbanization gradient. Acta Theriologica 23:341–358.

ARNOLD, R. A., AND A. E. GOINS. 1987. Habitat enhancement techniques for the El Segundo blue butterfly: an urban endangered species. Pages 173–181 *in* L. W. Adams and D. L. Leedy, editors. Integrating man and nature in the metropolitan environment. National Institute for Urban Wildlife, Columbia, Maryland, USA.

AUBLE, G. T., M. L. SCOTT, J. M. FRIEDMAN, J. BACK, AND V. J. LEE. 1997. Constraints on establishment of plains cottonwood in an urban riparian preserve. Wetlands 17:138–148.

AUGUSTINE, D. J., AND L. E. FRELICH. 1998. Effects of white-tailed deer on populations of an understory forb in fragmented deciduous forests. Conservation Biology 12:995–1004.

———, AND P. A. JORDAN. 1998. Predictors of white-tailed deer grazing intensity in fragmented deciduous forests. Journal of Wildlife Management 62:1076–1085.

AVILOVA, K. V., V. V. KORBUT, AND S. FOKIN, JR. 1994. Urban population of waterfowl (*Anas platyrhynchos*) of the Moscow city. Moscow State University of M. V. Lomonosov, Moskva, Russia.

BABINSKA-WERKA, J., J. GLIWICZ, AND J. GOSZCZYNSKI. 1979. Synurbization processes in a population of *Apodemus agrarius*. 2. Habitats of the striped field mouse in town. Acta Theriologica 24:405–415.

BAINES, C., AND J. SMART. 1991. A guide to habitat creation. Packard Publishing Limited, Chichester, United Kingdom.

BAKER, R. O., AND R. M. TIMM. 1998. Management of conflicts between urban coyotes and humans in southern California. Proceedings of the Vertebrate Pest Conference 18:299–312.

BARKER, G., editor. 2000. Ecological recombination in urban areas: implications for nature conservation. Centre for Ecology and Hydrology, Monks Wood, United Kingdom.

BATTEN, L. A. 1972. Breeding bird species diversity in relation to increasing urbanization. Bird Study 19:157–166.

BEISSINGER, S. R., AND D. R. OSBORNE. 1982. Effects of urbanization on avian community organization. Condor 84:75–83.

BELANT, J. L., L. A. TYSON, AND T. W. SEAMANS. 1999. Use of alpha-chloralose by the Wildlife Services program to capture nuisance birds. Wildlife Society Bulletin 27:938–942.

BIBBY, C. J., N. D. BURGESS, D. A. HILL, AND S. MUSTOE. 2000. Bird census techniques. Second edition. Academic Press, London, United Kingdom.

BLAIR, R. B. 1996. Land use and avian species diversity along an urban gradient. Ecological Applications 6:506–519.

———, AND A. E. LAUNER. 1997. Butterfly diversity and human land use: species assemblages along an urban gradient. Biological Conservation 80:113–125.

BOLGER, D. T., T. A. SCOTT, AND J. T. ROTENBERRY. 1997. Breeding bird abundance in an urbanizing landscape in coastal southern California. Conservation Biology 11:406–421.

BOUNDS, D. L., AND W. W. SHAW. 1994. Managing coyotes in U.S. national parks: human–coyote interactions. Natural Areas Journal 14:280–284.

———, AND ———. 1997. Movements of suburban and rural coyotes at Saguaro National Park, Arizona. Southwestern Naturalist 42:94–121.

BRAUNEIS, W. 1994. The new population of peregrine falcons in central Germany—the results of a conservation project. Falke 41:78–89.

BROWN, P. M., D. R. D'AMICO, A. T. CARPENTER, AND D. ANDREWS. 2001. Restoration of montane ponderosa pine forests in the Colorado Front Range: a forest ecosystem management plan for the city of Boulder. Ecological Restoration 19:19–26.

BRUSH, C. C., AND D. W. EHRENFELD. 1991. Control of white-tailed deer in non-hunted reserves and urban fringe areas. Pages 59–66 in L. W. Adams and D. L. Leedy, editors. Wildlife conservation in metropolitan environments. National Institute for Urban Wildlife, Columbia, Maryland, USA.

BRYANT, B. K., AND W. ISHMAEL. 1991. Movement and mortality patterns of resident and translocated suburban white-tailed deer. Pages 53–58 in L. W. Adams and D. L. Leedy, editors. Wildlife conservation in metropolitan environments. National Institute for Urban Wildlife, Columbia, Maryland, USA.

BUCKLEY, P. A., AND M. G. MCCARTHY. 1994. Insects, vegetation, and the control of laughing gulls (*Larus atricilla*) at Kennedy International Airport, New York City. Journal of Applied Ecology 31:291–302.

BURR, R. M., AND R. E. JONES. 1968. The influence of parkland habitat management on birds in Delaware. Transactions of the North American Wildlife and Natural Resources Conference 33:299–306.

CADE, T. J., AND D. M. BIRD. 1990. Peregrine falcons, *Falco peregrinus,* nesting in an urban environment: a review. Canadian Field-Naturalist 104:209–218.

CASTELLI, P. M., AND S. E. SLEGGS. 2000. Efficacy of border collies to control nuisance Canada geese. Wildlife Society Bulletin 28:385–392.

CHANDLER, S. K., J. D. FRASER, D. A. BUEHLER, AND J. K. D. SEEGAR. 1995. Perch trees and shoreline development as predictors of bald eagle distribution on Chesapeake Bay. Journal of Wildlife Management 59:325–332.

CHRISTENS, E., H. BLOKPOEL, G. RASON, AND S. W. D. JARVIE. 1995. Spraying white mineral oil on Canada goose eggs to prevent hatching. Wildlife Society Bulletin 23:228–230.

CLERGEAU, P., J.-P. L. SAVARD, G. MENNECHEZ, AND G. FALARDEAU. 1998. Bird abundance and diversity along an urban-rural gradient: a comparative study between two cities on different continents. Condor 100:413–425.

COCHRAN, P. A. 1989. Historical changes in a suburban herpetofauna in DuPage County, Illinois. Bulletin of the Chicago Herpetological Society 24:1–7.

COLLINGE, S. K. 1996. Ecological consequences of habitat fragmentation: implications for landscape architecture and planning. Landscape and Urban Planning 36:59–77.

COLUCCY, J. M., R. D. DROBNEY, D. A. GRABER, S. L. SHERIFF, AND D. J. WITTER. 2001. Attitudes of central Missouri residents toward local giant Canada geese and management alternatives. Wildlife Society Bulletin 29:116–123.

CONOVER, M. R. 1984. Effectiveness of repellents in reducing deer damage in nurseries. Wildlife Society Bulletin 12:399–404.

———. 1999. Can waterfowl be taught to avoid food handouts through conditioned food aversions? Wildlife Society Bulletin 27:160–166.

———, AND G. S. KANIA. 1988. Browsing preference of white-tailed deer for different ornamental species. Wildlife Society Bulletin 16:175–179.

COOPER, J. A. 1987. The effectiveness of translocation control of Minneapolis-St. Paul Canada goose populations. Pages 169–171 in L. W. Adams and D. L. Leedy, editors. Integrating man and nature in the metropolitan environment. National Institute for Urban Wildlife, Columbia, Maryland, USA.

———. 1991. Canada goose management at the Minneapolis-St. Paul international airport. Pages 175–183 in L. W. Adams and D. L. Leedy, editors. Wildlife conservation in metropolitan environments. National Institute for Urban Wildlife, Columbia, Maryland, USA.

CORT, C. A. 1996. A survey of the use of natural heritage data in local land-use planning. Conservation Biology 10:632–637.

CRAVEN, S. R., AND S. E. HYGNSTROM. 1994. Deer. Pages D25–40 in S. E. Hygnstrom, R. M. Timm, and G. E. Larson, editors. Prevention and control of wildlife damage. University of Nebraska Cooperative Extension Service, Lincoln, USA.

———, T. BARNES, AND G. KANIA. 1998. Toward a professional position on the translocation of problem wildlife. Wildlife Society Bulletin 26:171–177.

CROMWELL, J. A., R. J. WARREN, AND D. W. HENDERSON. 1999. Live-capture and small-scale relocation of urban deer on Hilton Head Island, South Carolina. Wildlife Society Bulletin 27:1025–1031.

CUNNINGHAM, A. A. 1996. Disease risks of wildlife translocations. Conservation Biology 10:349–353.

CURTIS, P. D., R. J. STOUT, B. A. KNUTH, L. A. MYERS, AND T. M. ROCKWELL. 1993. Selecting deer management options in a suburban environment: a case study from Rochester, New York. Transactions of the North American Wildlife and Natural Resources Conference 58:102–116.

CZECH, B., AND P. R. KRAUSMAN. 1997. Distribution and causation of species endangerment in the United States. Science 277:1116–1117.

CZECHOWSKI, W., AND B. PISARSKI, editors. 1986–1987. Structure of the fauna of Warsaw; effects of the urban pressure on animal communities. Parts 1–2. Memorabilia Zoologica Volumes 41–42.

———, H. GARBARCZYK, B. PISARSKI, AND J. SAWONIEWICZ, editors. 1981–1982. Species composition and origin of the fauna of Warsaw. Parts 1–3. Memorabilia Zoologica Volumes 34–36.

DANIELSON, W. R., R. M. DEGRAAF, AND T. K. FULLER. 1997. Rural and suburban forest edges: effect on egg predators and nest predation rates. Landscape and Urban Planning 38:25–36.

DARR, L. J., D. K. DAWSON, AND C. S. ROBBINS. 1998. Land-use planning to conserve habitat for area-sensitive forest birds. Urban Ecosystems 2:75–84.

DAWSON, K. J. 1991. Human predation on isolated nature reserves. Pages 83–88 in L. W. Adams and D. L. Leedy, editors. Wildlife conservation in metropolitan environments. National Institute for Urban Wildlife, Columbia, Maryland, USA.

DE ALMEIDA, M. H. 1987. Nuisance furbearer damage control in urban and suburban areas. Pages 996–1006 in M. Novak, J. A. Baker, M. E. Obbard, and B. Malloch, editors. Wild furbearer management and conservation in North America. Ontario Trappers Association, North Bay, Canada.

DECKER, D. J., AND L. C. CHASE. 2001. Stakeholder involvement: seeking solutions in changing times. Pages 133–152 in D. J. Decker, T. L. Brown, and W. F. Siemer, editors. Human dimensions of wildlife management in North America. The Wildlife Society, Bethesda, Maryland, USA.

DEGRAAF, R. M. 1987. Urban wildlife habitat research—application to landscape design. Pages 107–111 in L. W. Adams and D. L. Leedy, editors. Integrating man and nature in the metropolitan environment. National Institute for Urban Wildlife, Columbia, Maryland, USA.

DEMGEN, F. C. 1988. A review of eighteen wetland mitigation sites in the San Francisco Bay region. Pages 318–322 in J. A. Kusler, S. Daly, and G. Brooks, editors. Urban wetlands: proceedings of the national wetland symposium. Association of Wetland Managers, Berne, New York, USA.

DICKMAN, C. R. 1987. Habitat fragmentation and vertebrate species richness in an urban environment. Journal of Applied Ecology 24:337–351.

DOERR, M. L., J. B. MCANINCH, AND E. P. WIGGERS. 2001. Comparison of 4 methods to reduce white-tailed deer abundance in an urban community. Wildlife Society Bulletin 29:1105–1113.

DORNEY, J. R., G. R. GUNTENSPERGEN, J. R. KEOUGH, AND F. STEARNS. 1984. Composition and structure of an urban woody plant community. Urban Ecology 8:69–90.

DOWD, C. 1992. Effect of development on bird species composition of two urban forested wetlands in Staten Island, New York. Journal of Field Ornithology 63:455–461.

DULISZ, B. 2001. Changes in species composition, quantitative structure and ecological characteristics of breeding bird communities in relation to urbanization. Pages 164–173 in P. Indykiewicz, T. Barczak, and G. Kaczorowski, editors. Biodiversity and ecology of animal populations in urban environments. Wyd. NICE, Bydgoszcz, Poland.

———, AND J. J. NOWAKOWSKI. 1996. The species diversity of the avifauna in built-up areas of the city of Olsztyn (NE Poland). Acta Ornithologica 31:33–38.

DUNN, E. H., D. J. T. HUSSELL, AND R. J. ADAMS. 1997. Monitoring songbird population change with autumn mist netting. Journal of Wildlife Management 61:389–396.

EDGAR, D. R., AND G. P. KERSHAW. 1994. The density and diversity of the bird populations in three residential communities in Edmonton, Alberta. Canadian Field-Naturalist 108:156–161.

EMLEN, J. T. 1974. An urban bird community in Tucson, Arizona: derivation, structure, and regulation. Condor 76:184–197.

ERRINGTON, P. L. 1934. Second broods in the mallard duck. Auk 51:78–80.

ETTER, D. R., K. M. HOLLIS, T. R. VAN DEELEN, D. R. LUDWIG, J. E. CHELSVIG, C. L. ANCHOR, AND R. E. WARNER. 2002. Survival and movements of white-tailed deer in suburban Chicago, Illinois. Journal of Wildlife Management 66:500–510.

EVERETTE, A. L., T. J. O'SHEA, L. E. ELLISON, L. A. STONE, AND J. L. McCANCE. 2001. Bat use of a high-plains urban wildlife refuge. Wildlife Society Bulletin 29:967–973.

FAETH, S. H., AND T. C. KANE. 1978. Urban biogeography: city parks as islands for Diptera and Coleoptera. Oecologia 32:127–133.

FAGERSTONE, K. A., M. A. COFFEY, P. D. CURTIS, R. A. DOLBEER, G. J. KILLIAN, L. A. MILLER, AND L. M. WILMONT. 2002. Wildlife fertility control. Technical Review 02–2. The Wildlife Society, Bethesda, Maryland, USA.

FERNÁNDEZ-JURICIC, E. 2000. Avifaunal use of wooded streets in an urban landscape. Conservation Biology 14:513–521.

FULLER, M. R., J. J. MILLSPAUGH, K. E. CHURCH, AND R. E. KENWARD. 2005. Wildlife radiotelemetry. Pages 377–417 in C. E. Braun, editor. Techniques for wildlife investigations and management. Sixth edition. The Wildlife Society, Bethesda, Maryland, USA.

GALEOTTI, P. 1994. Patterns of territory size and defence level in rural and urban tawny owl (*Strix aluco*) populations. Journal of Zoology, London 234:641–658.

GEHLBACH, F. R. 1994. The eastern screech owl: life history, ecology, and behavior in the suburbs and countryside. Texas A&M University Press, College Station, USA.

GEIS, A. D. 1974. Effects of urbanization and types of urban development on bird populations. Pages 97–105 in J. H. Noyes and D. R. Progulske, editors. Wildife in an urbanizing environment. University of Massachusetts, Amherst, USA.

———. 1986. Planning and design for wildlife conservation in new residential developments—Columbia, Maryland. Pages 67–70 in K. Stenberg and W. W. Shaw, editors. Wildlife conservation and new residential developments. School of Renewable Natural Resources, University of Arizona, Tucson, USA.

GERING, J. C., AND R. B. BLAIR. 1999. Predation on artificial bird nests along an urban gradient: predatory risk or relaxation in urban environments? Ecography 22:532–541.

GERMAINE, S. S., AND B. F. WAKELING. 2001. Lizard species distributions and habitat occupation along an urban gradient in Tucson, Arizona, USA. Biological Conservation 97:229–237.

GIBEAU, M. L. 1998. Use of urban habitats by coyotes in the vicinity of Banff, Alberta. Urban Ecosystems 2:129–139.

GLIWICZ, J., J. GOSZCZYNSKI, AND M. LUNIAK. 1994. Characteristic features of animal populations under synurbization—the case of the blackbird and of the striped field mouse. Memorabilia Zoologica 49:237–244.

GOBSTER, P. H. 1994. The urban savanna: reuniting ecological preference and function. Restoration and Management Notes 12:64–71.

GORENZEL, W. P., AND T. P. SALMON. 1993. Tape-recorded calls disperse American crows from urban roosts. Wildlife Society Bulletin 21:334–338.

———, AND ———. 1995. Characteristics of American crow urban roosts in California. Journal of Wildlife Management 59:638–645.

GREENHALL, A. M. 1982. House bat management. U.S. Department of the Interior, Fish and Wildlife Service, Resource Publication 143.

GRUND, M. D., J. B. McANINCH, AND E. P. WIGGERS. 2002. Seasonal movements and habitat use of female white-tailed deer associated with an urban park. Journal of Wildlife Management 66:123–130.

HAAS, C. A. 1995. Dispersal and use of corridors by birds in wooded patches on an agricultural landscape. Conservation Biology 9:845–854.

HADIDIAN, J., G. R. HODGE, AND J. W. GRANDY, editors. 1997a. Wild neighbors: the humane approach to living with wildlife. The Humane Society of the United States, Washington, D.C., USA.

———, J. SAUER, C. SWARTH, P. HANDLY, S. DROEGE, C. WILLIAMS, J. HUFF, AND G. DIDDEN. 1997b. A citywide breeding bird survey for Washington, D.C. Urban Ecosystems 1:87–102.

HAGEMEIJER, W. J. M., AND M. J. BLAIR, editors. 1997. The EBCC atlas of European breeding birds: their distribution and abundance. T & A D Poyser, London, United Kingdom.

HARRISON, J. A., AND P. MARTINEZ. 1995. Measurement and mapping of avian diversity in southern Africa: implications for conservation planning. Ibis 137:410–417.

HARRISON, R. L. 1997. A comparison of gray fox ecology between residential and undeveloped rural landscapes. Journal of Wildlife Management 61:112–122.

———. 1998. Bobcats in residential areas: distribution and homeowner attitudes. Southwestern Naturalist 43:469–475.

HELFIELD, J. M., AND M. L. DIAMOND. 1997. Use of constructed wetlands for urban stream restoration: a critical analysis. Environmental Management 21:329–341.

HODGE, S. J., AND R. HARMER. 1996. Woody colonization on unmanaged urban and ex-industrial sites. Forestry 69:245–261.

HODGSON, J. G. 1986. Commonness and rarity in plants with special reference to the Sheffield flora. Part I. The identity, distribution and habitat characteristics of the common and rare species. Biological Conservation 36:199–252.

HOHMANN, U., S. VOIGT, AND U. ANDREAS. 2001. Quo vadis raccoon? New visitors in our backyards—on the urbanization of an allochthone carnivore in Germany. Pages 143–148 in E. Gottschalk, A. Barkow, M. Muehlenberg, and J. Settele. Naturschutz und Verhalten UFZ Bericht 2/2001. Leipzig, Germany.

HOLLORAN, P. 1996. The greening of the golden gate: community-based restoration at the Presidio of San Francisco. Restoration & Management Notes 14:112–123.

HÕRAK, P., AND J.-D. LEBRETON. 1998. Survival of adult great tits *Parus major* in relation to sex and habitat; a comparison of urban and rural populations. Ibis 140:205–209.

HYGNSTROM, S. E., R. M. TIMM, AND G. E. LARSON, editors. 1994. Prevention and control of wildlife damage. University of Nebraska Cooperative Extension Service, Lincoln, USA.

ICKES, S. K., J. L. BELANT, AND R. A. DOLBEER. 1998. Nest disturbance techniques to control nesting by gulls. Wildlife Society Bulletin 26:269–273.

IDZELIS, R. 1992. On the development of the avifauna in a new residential district of Vilnius. Acta Ornithologica Lituanica 5–6:72–77.

ILYICHEV, V. D., V. T. BUTIEV, AND V. M. KONSTANTINOV. 1987. Birds of Moscow and vicinity. Nauka, Moskva, Russia.

JACKSON, L. S., AND R. J. HOLLIS. 1991. Iowa bird feeder survey. Pages 248–249 in L. W. Adams and D. L. Leedy, editors. Wildlife conservation in metropolitan environments. National Institute for Urban Wildlife, Columbia, Maryland, USA.

JEDLICKE, E. 2000. Urban and village ecosystems: environmental factors, bird communities, habitat requirements, urbanzation and conservation. Vogelwelt 121:67–86.

JEDRASZKO-DABROWSKA, D. 1990. Specific features of an urban lake bird community (case of the Czerniakowskie Lake in Warsaw). Pages 167–181 in M. Luniak, editor. Urban ecological studies in central and eastern Europe. Ossolineum, Wroclaw, Poland.

JERZAK, L. 2001. Synurbization of the magpie in the Palearctic. Pages 403–425 in J. M. Marzluff, R. Bowman, and R. Donnelly, editors. Avian ecology and conservation in an urbanizing world. Kluwer Academic Publishers, Norwell, Massachusetts, USA.

JOHNSEN, A. M., AND L. W. VANDRUFF. 1987. Summer and winter distribution of introduced bird species and native bird species richness within a complex urban environment. Pages 123–127 in L. W. Adams and D. L. Leedy, editors. Integrating man and nature in the metropolitan environment. National Institute for Urban Wildlife, Columbia, Maryland, USA.

JOHNSON, C. W. 1993. A wildlife conservation manual for urbanizing areas in Utah. Utah State University Extension Service Publications, Logan, USA.

———. 1995. Planning and designing for the multiple use role of habitats in urban/suburban landscapes in the Great Basin. Landscape and Urban Planning 32:219–225.

JOHNSON, R. J., P. H. COLE, AND W. W. STROUP. 1985. Starling response to three auditory stimuli. Journal of Wildlife Management 49:620–625.

JOKIMÄKI, J., AND J. SUHONEN. 1993. Effects of urbanization on the breeding bird species richness in Finland: a biogeographical comparison. Ornis Fennica 70:71–77.

———, AND ———. 1998. Distribution and habitat selection of wintering birds in urban environments. Landscape and Urban Planning 39:253–263.

JONES, D. N., AND L. K. THOMAS. 1999. Attacks on humans by Australian magpies: management of an extreme suburban human–wildlife conflict. Wildlife Society Bulletin 27:473–478.

JONES, J. M., AND J. H. WITHAM. 1990. Post-translocation survival and movements of metropolitan white-tailed deer. Wildlife Society Bulletin 18:434–441.

KAHL-DUNKEL, A., AND R. WERNER. 2002. Winter distribution of ring-necked parakeet *Psittacula krameri* in Cologne. Vogelwelt 123:17–20.

KARR, J. R., AND R. R. ROTH. 1971. Vegetation structure and avian diversity in several new world areas. American Naturalist 105:423–435.

KHRABRIY, V. M. 1991. Birds of Sankt Petersburg—fauna, distribution, conservation. Zoological Institute, USSR Academy of Sciences, St. Petersburg, Russia.

KILPATRICK, H. J., AND S. M. SPOHR. 2000a. Movements of female white-tailed deer in a suburban landscape: a management perspective. Wildlife Society Bulletin 28:1038–1045.

———, AND ———. 2000b. Spatial and temporal use of a suburban landscape by female white-tailed deer. Wildlife Society Bulletin 28:1023–1029.

———, AND W. D. WALTER. 1999. A controlled archery deer hunt in a residential community: cost, effectiveness, and deer recovery rates. Wildlife Society Bulletin 27:115–123.

KLAUSNITZER, B. 1988. Urbanization of animals. A. Ziemsen Verlag, Wittenberg Lutherstadt, Germany.

———. 1993. Ecology of the big city fauna. G. Fischer Verlag, Stuttgart, Germany.

KNUTH, B. A., W. F. SIEMER, M. D. DUDA, S. J. BISSELL, AND D. J. DECKER. 2001a. Wildlife management in suburban environments. Pages 219–242 in D. J. Decker, T. L. Brown, and W. F. Siemer, editors. Human dimensions of wildlife management in North America. The Wildlife Society, Bethesda, Maryland, USA.

———, ———, ———, ———, AND ———. 2001b. Wildlife management in urban environments. Pages 195–217 in D. J. Decker, T. L. Brown, and W. F. Siemer, editors. Human dimensions of wildlife management in North America. The Wildlife Society, Bethesda, Maryland, USA.

KNUTSON, M. G., J. R. SAUER, D. A. OLSEN, M. J. MOSSMAN, L. M. HEMESATH, AND M. J. LANNOO. 1999. Effects of landscape composition and wetland fragmentation on frog and toad abundance and species richness in Iowa and Wisconsin, U.S.A. Conservation Biology 13:1437–1446.

KOVSHAR, A. F., AND B. P. SUYKO. 1984. Biologische daten zur verstaedterung der amsel (*Turdus merula*) in Alma-Ata, Kazakhstan, USSR. Mitteilungen aus dem Zoologischen Museum Berlin 8:97–105.

KOWARIK, I. 1990. Some responses of flora and vegetation to urbanization in central Europe. Pages 45–74 in H. Sukopp, S. Hejny, and I. Kowarik, editors. Urban ecology: plants and plant communities in urban environments. SPB Academic Publishing, Hague, The Netherlands.

LAUBHAN, M. K., S. L. KING, AND L. H. FREDRICKSON. 2005. Managing inland wetlands for wildlife. Pages 797–838 in C. E. Braun, editor. Techniques for wildlife investigations and management. Sixth edition. The Wildlife Society, Bethesda, Maryland, USA.

LEBARON, G. S. 2001. The one-hundred-first Christmas Bird Count. Pages 6–12 in G. S. LeBaron, editor. American birds. National Audubon Society, New York, USA.

LEGAKIS, A., C. PAPADIMITRIOU, M. GAETHLICH, AND D. LAZARIS. 2000. Survey of the bats of the Athens metropolitan area. Myotis 38:41–46.

LEVINE, E., editor. 1998. Bull's birds of New York state. Cornell University Press, Ithaca, New York, USA.

LEWIS, A., AND D. POMEROY. 1989. A bird atlas of Kenya. A. A. Balkema Publishers, Brookfield, Vermont, USA.

LIDAUER, R. M. 1983. Knochenfrakturen bei stadtamseln (*Turdus merula*). Oekologie Voegel 5:111–126.

LOKER, C. A., D. J. DECKER, AND S. J. SCHWAGER. 1999. Social acceptability of wildlife management actions in suburban areas: 3 cases from New York. Wildlife Society Bulletin 27:152–159.

LUNIAK, M. 1983. The avifauna of urban green areas in Poland and possibilities of managing it. Acta Ornithologica 19:3–61.

———. 1990. Avifauna of cities in central and eastern Europe—results of the international inquiry. Pages 131–149 in M. Luniak, editor. Urban ecological studies in central and eastern Europe. Ossolineum, Wroclaw, Poland.

———. 1994. The development of bird communities in new housing estates in Warsaw. Memorabilia Zoologica 49:257–267.

———. 1996. Synurbization of animals as a factor increasing diversity of urban fauna. Pages 566–575 in F. Di Castri and T. Younès, editors. Biodiversity, science and development: towards a new partnership. CAB International, Paris, France.

———, R. MULSOW, AND K. WALASZ. 1990. Urbanization of the European blackbird—expansion and adaptations of urban population. Pages 186–200 in M. Luniak, editor. Urban ecological studies in central and eastern Europe. Ossolineum, Wroclaw, Poland.

———, P. KOZLOWSKI, W. NOWICKI, AND J. PLIT. 2001. Birds of Warsaw 1962–2000. Instytut Geografii PAN, Warszawa, Poland.

MACARTHUR, R. H., AND J. W. MACARTHUR. 1961. On bird species diversity. Ecology 42:594–598.

———, AND E. O. WILSON. 1967. The theory of island biogeography. Princeton University Press, Princeton, New Jersey, USA.

MACDONALD, D. W., AND M. T. NEWDICK. 1982. The distribution and ecology of foxes, *Vulpes vulpes* (L.) in urban areas. Pages 123–135 in R. J. Bornkamm, J. A. Lee, and M. R. D. Seaward, editors. Urban ecology. Blackwell Scientific Publications, Oxford, United Kingdom.

MACKIN-ROGALSKA, R., J. PINOWSKI, J. SOLON, AND Z. WÓCIK. 1988. Changes in vegetation, avifauna, and small mammals in a suburban habitat. Polish Ecological Studies 14:293–330.

MAGEE, T. K., T. L. ERNST, M. E. KENTULA, AND K. A. DWIRE. 1999. Floristic comparison of freshwater wetlands in an urbanizing environment. Wetlands 19:517–534.

MAJOR, R. E., G. GOWING, AND C. E. KENDAL. 1996. Nest predation in Australian urban environments and the role of the pied currawong, *Strepera graculina*. Australian Journal of Ecology 21:399–409.

MANNAN, R. W., AND C. W. BOAL. 2000. Home range characteristics of male Cooper's hawks in an urban environment. Wilson Bulletin 112:21–27.

MARYLAND OFFICE OF PLANNING. 1992. Managing Maryland's growth: what you need to know about the planning act of 1992. Maryland Office of Planning Publication 92–7. Baltimore, USA.

MARZLUFF, J. 2001. Worldwide urbanization and its effects on birds. Pages 19–47 in J. M. Marzluff, R. Bowman, and R. Donnelly, editors. Avian ecology and conservation in an urbanizing world. Kluwer Academic Publishers, Norwell, Massachusetts, USA.

MATSIL, M. A., AND M. J. FELLER. 1996. Natural areas restoration in New York City: a bite of the apple. Restoration & Management Notes 14:5–14.

MATTHEWS, A., C. R. DICKMAN, AND R. E. MAJOR. 1999. The influence of fragment size and edge on nest predation in urban bushland. Ecography 22:349–356.

MATTHIAE, P. E., AND F. STEARNS. 1981. Mammals in forest islands in southeastern Wisconsin. Pages 55–66 in R. L. Burgess and D. M. Sharpe, editors. Forest island dynamics in man-dominated landscapes. Springer-Verlag, New York, USA.

MCANINCH, J. B., AND J. M. PARKER. 1991. Urban deer management programs: a facilitated approach. Transactions of the North American Wildlife and Natural Resources Conference 56:428–436.

MCSHEA, W. J., AND J. H. RAPPOLE. 2000. Managing the abundance and diversity of breeding bird populations through manipulation of deer populations. Conservation Biology 14:1161–1170.

———, S. L. MONFORT, S. HAKIM, J. KIRKPATRICK, I. LIU, J. W. TURNER, JR., L. CHASSY, AND L. MUNSON. 1997. The effect of immunocontraception on the behavior and reproduction of white-tailed deer. Journal of Wildlife Management 61:560–569.

MILLER, L. A., B. E. JOHNS, AND D. J. ELIAS. 1998. Immunocontraception as a wildlife management tool: some perspectives. Wildlife Society Bulletin 26:237–243.

———, K. CRANE, S. GADDIS, AND G. J. KILLIAN. 2001. Porcine zona pellucida immunocontraception: long-term health effects on white-tailed deer. Journal of Wildlife Management 65:941–945.

MILLSAP, B. A., AND C. BEAR. 2000. Density and reproduction of burrowing owls along an urban development gradient. Journal of Wildlife Management 64:33–41.

MITSCHKE, A., AND S. BAUMUNG. 2001. Atlas of breeding birds of Hamburg. Arbeitskreis an der Staatlichen Vogelschutzwarte Hamburg. Hamburg, Germany.

MONTIER, D. J., editor. 1977. Atlas of breeding birds of the London area. B. T. Batsford, London, United Kingdom.

MORNEAU, F., C. LÉPINE, R. DÉCARIE, M.-A. VILLARD, AND J.-L. DESGRANGES. 1995. Reproduction of American robin (*Turdus migratorius*) in a suburban environment. Landscape and Urban Planning 32:55–62.

MORRISON, J., AND P. WILLIAMS. 1988. Warm Springs marsh restoration. Pages 340–349 *in* J. A. Kusler, S. Daly, and G. Brooks, editors. Urban wetlands: Proceedings of the National Wetland Symposium. Association of Wetland Managers, Berne, New York, USA.

MOSILLO, M., E. J. HESKE, AND J. D. THOMPSON. 1999. Survival and movements of translocated raccoons in northcentral Illinois. Journal of Wildlife Management 63:278–286.

MURPHY, D. D. 1988. Challenges to biological diversity in urban areas. Pages 71–76 *in* E. O. Wilson, editor. Biodiversity. National Academy Press, Washington, D.C., USA.

NAKAMURA, T., AND K. SHORT. 2001. Land-use planning and distribution of threatened wildlife in a city of Japan. Landscape and Urban Planning 53:1–15.

NARASUE, M., AND H. OBARA. 1982. Feralization of cage birds, in and around Tokyo. Pages 82–86 *in* M. Numata, editor. Chiba Bay-Coast Project, IV, Tokyo, Japan.

NATUHARA, Y., AND C. IMAI. 1996. Spatial structure of avifauna along urban-rural gradients. Ecological Research 11:1–9.

———, ———, AND M. TAKAHASHI. 1999. Pattern of land mosaics affecting butterfly assemblage at Mount Ikoma, Osaka, Japan. Ecological Research 14:105–118.

NILON, C. H. 1986. Quantifying small mammal habitats along a gradient of urbanization. Dissertation. SUNY College of Environmental Science and Forestry, Syracuse, New York, USA.

———, AND L. W. VANDRUFF. 1987. Analysis of small mammal community data and applications to management of urban greenspaces. Pages 53–59 *in* L. W. Adams and D. L. Leedy, editors. Integrating man and nature in the metropolitan environment. National Institute for Urban Wildlife, Columbia, Maryland, USA.

NOSS, R. F., AND L. D. HARRIS. 1986. Nodes, networks, and MUMs: preserving diversity at all scales. Environmental Management 10:299–309.

NOURTEVA, P. 1971. The synanthropy of birds as an expression of the ecological cycle disorder caused by urbanization. Annales Zoologici Fennici 8:547–553.

NOWICKI, W. 2001. Birds of inner Warsaw. Muzeum i Instytut Zoologii PAN, Warszawa, Poland.

ODUM, E. P. 1971. Fundamentals of ecology. Third edition. W. B. Saunders Company, Philadelphia, Pennsylvania, USA.

OETTING, R. B. 1987. Some management strategies for resident Canada geese. Annual Meeting of the Association of Midwest Fish and Wildlife Agencies 54:Abstract.

PARK, C.-R., AND W.-S. LEE. 2000. Relationship between species composition and area in breeding birds of urban woods in Seoul, Korea. Landscape and Urban Planning 51:29–36.

PELL, A. S., AND C. R. TIDEMANN. 1997a. The ecology of the common myna in urban nature reserves in the Australian Capital Territory. Emu 97:141–149.

———, AND ———. 1997b. The impact of two exotic hollow-nesting birds on two native parrots in savannah and woodland in eastern Australia. Biological Conservation 79:145–153.

PESKE, L. 1997. Successful breeding of peregrine falcon (*Falco peregrinus*) within Prague. Buteo 9:109–114.

PICKETT, S. T. A., M. L. CADENASSO, J. M. GROVE, C. H. NILON, R. V. POUYAT, W. C. ZIPPERER, AND R. COSTANZA. 2001. Urban ecological systems: linking terrestrial, ecological, physical, and socioeconomic components of metropolitan areas. Annual Review of Ecology and Systematics 32:127–157.

PISARSKI, B. 1990. The invertebrate fauna of urbanized areas of Warsaw. Pages 98–111 *in* M. Luniak, editor. Urban ecological studies in central and eastern Europe. Ossolineum, Wroclaw, Poland.

PLATH, L. 1985. Colonization of the new housing district by birds—results of 13-year inventory. Falke 32:335–342.

QUINN, T. 1997a. Coyote (*Canis latrans*) food habits in three urban habitat types of western Washington. Northwest Science 71:1–5.

———. 1997b. Coyote (*Canis latrans*) habitat selection in urban areas

of western Washington via analysis of routine movements. Northwest Science 71:289–297.

REEVE, N. J. 1998. The survival and welfare of hedgehogs (*Erinaceus europaeus*) after release back into the wild. Animal Welfare 7:189–202.

REJT, L. 2001. Feeding activity and seasonal changes in diet of urban peregrine falcons *Falco peregrinus*. Acta Ornithologica 36:165–169.

———, K. BRONCHE, AND A. M. TOPCZEWSKI. 2000. Can food caching increase frequency of chick's feeding in urban kestrels *Falco tinnunculus*? Acta Ornithologica 35:217–221.

RICHTER, K. O. 1997. Criteria for the restoration and creation of wetland habitats of lentic-breeding amphibians of the Pacific Northwest. Pages 72–94 *in* K. B. Macdonald and F. Weinmann, editors. Wetland and riparian restoration: taking a broader view. Publication EPA 910-R-97–007. U.S. Environmental Protection Agency, Seattle, Washington, USA.

———, AND A. L. AZOUS. 1995. Amphibian occurrence and wetland characteristics in the Puget Sound Basin. Wetlands 15:305–312.

RILEY, A. L. 1998. Restoring streams in cities: a guide for planners, policymakers, and citizens. Island Press, Washington, D.C., USA.

RILEY, S. P. D., J. HADIDIAN, AND D. A. MANSKI. 1998. Population density, survival, and rabies in raccoons in an urban national park. Canadian Journal of Zoology 76:1153–1164.

ROBBINS, C. S., editor. 1996. Atlas of the breeding birds of Maryland and the District of Columbia. University of Pittsburgh Press, Pittsburgh, Pennsylvania, USA.

ROBERTS, D. C. 1994. The design of an urban open-space network for the city of Durban (South Africa). Environmental Conservation 21:11–17.

ROBERTSON, D. J. 1994. White-tailed deer management in the Pennypack Wilderness Preserve (Pennsylvania). Restoration and Management Notes 12:206–207.

ROBINSON, G. R., AND S. N. HANDEL. 2000. Directing spatial patterns of recruitment during an experimental urban woodland reclamation. Ecological Applications 10:174–188.

ROLANDO, A., G. MAFFEI, C. PULCHER, AND A. GIUSO. 1997. Avian community structure along an urbanization gradient. Italian Journal of Zoology 64:341–349.

ROOKWOOD, P. 1995. Landscape planning for biodiversity. Landscape and Urban Planning 31:379–385.

ROSATTE, R. C, AND C. D. MACINNES. 1989. Relocation of city raccoons. Proceedings of the Great Plains Wildlife Damage Control Workshop 9:87–92.

RUDOLPH, B. A., W. F. PORTER, AND H. B. UNDERWOOD. 2000. Evaluating immunocontraception for managing suburban white-tailed deer in Irondequoit, New York. Journal of Wildlife Management 64:463–473.

RYDER, B. A. 1995. Greenway planning and growth management: partners in conservation? Landscape and Urban Planning 33:417–432.

SAMWAYS, M. J., AND N. S. STEYTLER. 1996. Dragonfly (Odonata) distribution patterns in urban and forest landscapes, and recommendations for riparian management. Biological Conservation 78:279–288.

SASVARI, L. 1990. Structure of bird communities in urban and suburban habitats. Pages 155–166 *in* M. Luniak, editor. Urban ecological studies in central and Eastern Europe. Ossolineum, Wroclaw, Poland.

SAUER, J. R., J. E. HINES, AND J. FALLON. 2001. The North American breeding bird survey, results and analysis 1966–2000. U.S. Department of the Interior, Geological Survey. Version 2001.2. Patuxent Wildlife Research Center, Laurel, Maryland, USA. Available at http://www.mbr-pwrc.usgs.gov/bbs/.

SAUNDERS, G., P. C. L. WHITE, AND S. HARRIS. 1997. Habitat utilization by urban foxes (*Vulpes vulpes*) and the implications for rabies control. Mammalia 61:497–510.

SEPTON, G., J. B. MARKS, AND T. ELLESTAD. 1995. A preliminary assessment of peregrine falcon *Falco peregrinus* recovery in midwestern North America. Acta Ornithologica 30:65–68.

SHAW, W. W., L. K. HARRIS, AND M. LIVINGSTON. 1998. Vegetative characteristics of urban land covers in metropolitan Tucson. Urban Ecosystems 2:65–73.

SHIRIHAI, H. 1996. The birds of Israel. Academic Press, San Diego, California, USA.

SIEMER, W. F., N. A. CONNELLY, T. L. BROWN, AND D. J. DECKER. 2001. Methods of inquiry: some basics for the manager. Pages 375–400 *in* D. J. Decker, T. L. Brown, and W. F. Siemer, editors. Human dimensions of wildlife management in North America. The Wildlife Society, Bethesda, Maryland, USA.

SOLIMINI, A. G., G. A. TARALLO, AND G. CARCHINI. 1997. Life history and species composition of the damselfly assemblage along the urban tract of a river in central Italy. Hydrobiologia 356:21–32.

SOULÉ, M. E., D. T. BOLGER, A. C. ALBERTS, J. WRIGHT, M. SORICE, AND S. HILL. 1988. Reconstructed dynamics of rapid extinctions of chaparral-requiring birds in urban habitat islands. Conservation Biology 2:75–92.

STATHAM, M., AND H. L. STATHAM. 1997. Movements and habits of brushtail possums (*Trichosurus vulpecula* Kerr) in an urban area. Wildlife Research 24:715–726.

STOUT, W. E., R. K. ANDERSON, AND J. M. PAPP. 1998. Urban, suburban and rural red-tailed hawk nesting habitat and populations in southeast Wisconsin. Journal of Raptor Research 32:221–228.

SUKOPP, H. 1990. Urban ecology—the case of Berlin. D. Reimer Verlag, Berlin, Germany.

THEOBALD, D. M., J. R. MILLER, AND N. T. HOBBS. 1997. Estimating the cumulative effects of development on wildlife habitat. Landscape and Urban Planning 39:25–36.

TICER, C. L., T. E. MORRELL, AND J. C. DeVOS, JR. 2001. Diurnal bedsite selection of urban-dwelling javelina in Prescott, Arizona. Journal of Wildlife Management 65:136–140.

TILGHMAN, N. G. 1987. Characteristics of urban woodlands affecting breeding bird diversity and abundance. Landscape and Urban Planning 14:481–495.

TOMIALOJC, L. 1980. The impact of predation on urban and rural woodpigeon (*Columba palumbus*) populations. Polish Ecological Studies 5:141–220.

———. 1998. Breeding densities in some urban versus non-urban habitats: the Dijon case. Acta Ornithologica 33:159–171.

———, AND P. PROFUS. 1977. Comparative analysis of breeding bird communities in two parks of Wroclaw and in an adjacent *Querco-Carpinetum* forest. Acta Ornithologica 16:117–177.

TOWNE, M. A. 1998. Open space conservation in urban environments: lessons from Thousand Oaks, California. Urban Ecosystems 2:85–101.

TURNER, JR., J. W., J. F. KIRKPATRICK, AND I. K. M. LIU. 1996. Effectiveness, reversibility, and serum antibody titers associated with immunocontraception in captive white-tailed deer. Journal of Wildlife Management 60:45–51.

TYLKA, D. L., J. M. SCHAEFER, AND L. W. ADAMS. 1987. Guidelines for implementing urban wildlife programs under state conservation agency administration. Pages 199–205 in L. W. Adams and D. L. Leedy, editors. Integrating man and nature in the metropolitan environment. National Institute for Urban Wildlife, Columbia, Maryland, USA.

U.S. ENVIRONMENTAL PROTECTION AGENCY. 1983. Results of the nationwide urban runoff program. Volume 1—final report. U.S. Environmental Protection Agency, Washington, D.C., USA.

VAN DE MIEROOP, M. 1997. The ancient Mesopotamian city. Oxford University Press, New York, USA.

VAN DER ZANDE, A. N., J. C. BERKHVIZEN, H. C. VAN LATESTEIJN, W. J. TER KEURS, AND A. J. POPPELAARS. 1984. Impact of outdoor recreation on the density of a number of breeding bird species in woods adjacent to urban residential areas. Biological Conservation 30:1–39.

VANDRUFF, L. W., AND R. N. ROWSE. 1986. Habitat association of mammals in Syracuse, New York. Urban Ecology 9:413–434.

VERCAUTEREN, K. C., R. A. DOLBEER, AND E. M. GESE. 2005. Identification and management of wildlife damage. Pages 740–778 in C. E. Braun, editor. Techniques for wildlife investigations and management. Sixth edition. The Wildlife Society, Bethesda, Maryland, USA.

VINK, A. P. A. 1983. Landscape ecology and land use. Longman Inc., New York, USA.

VIZYOVÁ, A. 1986. Urban woodlots as islands for land vertebrates: a preliminary attempt on estimating the barrier effects of urban structural units. Ecology (CSSR) 5:407–419.

VOGEL, W. O. 1989. Response of deer to density and distribution of housing in Montana. Wildlife Society Bulletin 17:406–413.

WALASZ, K. 1990. Experimental investigations on the behavioural differences between urban and forest blackbirds. Acta Zoologica Cracoviensia 33:235–271.

WELLER, M. W. 1987. Freshwater marshes: ecology and wildlife management. Second edition. University of Minnesota Press, Minneapolis, USA.

WHITCOMB, R. F., C. S. ROBBINS, J. F. LYNCH, B. L. WHITCOMB, M. K. KLIMKIEWICZ, AND D. BYSTRAK. 1981. Effects of forest fragmentation on avifauna of the eastern deciduous forest. Pages 125–205 in R. L. Burgess and D. M. Sharpe, editors. Forest island dynamics in man-dominated landscapes. Springer-Verlag, New York, USA.

WILLIAMSON, R. D. 1983. Identification of urban habitat components, which affect eastern gray squirrel abundance. Urban Ecology 7:345–356.

WITT, K. 2000. Changes in birdlife of Berlin since 1970 with historical references. Berliner Ornithologische Berichte 10:140–152.

ZALEWSKI, A. 1994. Diet of urban and suburban tawny owls (*Strix aluco*) in the breeding season. Journal of Raptor Research 28:246–252.

ZENTNER, J. 1988. Wetland restoration in urbanized areas: examples from coastal California. Pages 310–312 in J. A. Kusler, S. Daly, and G. Brooks, editors. Urban wetlands: Proceedings of the National Wetland Symposium. Association of Wetland Managers, Berne, New York, USA.

28

IDENTIFICATION AND MANAGEMENT OF WILDLIFE DAMAGE

Kurt C. VerCauteren, Richard A. Dolbeer, and Eric M. Gese

INTRODUCTION

Wildlife management is usually considered as the protection, enhancement, and nurturing of wildlife populations and the habitats needed for their well-being. However, many species at one time or another require management actions to reduce conflicts with people, other

Fig. 1. Examples of wildlife damage: A. elk (*Cervus elaphus*) consuming stored feed, B. aircraft collisions with birds, C. deer damage to habitat, D. wildlife-damaged corn, E. woodchuck damage in vineyards, and F. blackbird damage to sorghum.

wildlife species, or other resources. Examples include an airport manager modifying habitats to reduce gull activity near runways, a forester controlling pocket gophers to increase tree seedling survival in a reforestation setting, or a biologist trapping an abundant predator or competing species to enhance survival of an endangered species (Fig. 1).

Wildlife damage management is an increasingly important component of the wildlife profession because of expanding human populations and intensified land-use practices. Wildlife damage in the United States approaches $22 billion annually (Conover 2002). Concurrent with this growing need to reduce wildlife–people conflicts, public attitudes and environmental regulations are restricting use of some traditional tools of control, such as toxicants and traps. Agencies and individuals conducting control programs are being scrutinized more carefully to ensure their actions are justified, environmentally safe, humane, and in the best public interest. Thus, wildlife damage management activities must be based on sound economic, ecological, and sociological principles and conducted as positive, necessary components of overall wildlife management programs.

Wildlife damage management programs have 4 parts: (1) problem definition, (2) ecology of the problem species, (3) management methods application, and (4) evaluation of management effort. Problem definition refers to identification of the species and numbers of animals causing the problem, amount of loss or nature of the conflict, and other biological and social factors related to the problem. Ecology of problem species refers to understanding the life history of the species, especially in relation to the conflict. Management methods application refers to taking informa-

tion gained from parts 1 and 2 to develop an appropriate management program to alleviate or reduce the conflict. Evaluation of management effort permits an assessment of the reduction in damage in relation to costs and impact of the management effort on target and nontarget populations. Emphasis is often placed on integrated wildlife damage management whereby several damage management methods are used in combination and coordinated with other management practices being used at that time.

We focus on techniques related to parts 1 (problem definition) and 3 (management methods application). Each major section on groups of wildlife species (birds, ungulates, etc.) has 3 parts: damage assessment, identification of damage by species, and control techniques; the last of these is an elaboration of those techniques listed under each species write-up.

LEGAL REQUIREMENTS FOR MANAGEMENT

Capturing or Killing Wildlife Species

Before action is taken to control or manage wildlife damage, it is important to understand the laws regarding both target and nontarget wildlife species. Management of most wild mammals, reptiles, and amphibians in the United States and Canada is the responsibility of the individual state or province. State or provincial laws regulate capture, possession, or killing of these vertebrates to control damage or nuisance situations. The main exception for mammals, reptiles, and amphibians in the United States relates to endangered and threatened species that are regulated federally by the Endangered Species Act of 1973, as amended.

Migratory birds, in contrast to other vertebrates, are managed in North America at the federal level under the Migratory Bird Treaty Act of 1918. The treaty has been amended several times and includes formal agreements with Canada, Mexico, Japan, and the former Soviet Union. Federal regulations in the United States and Canada require that a depredation permit be obtained from the U.S. Fish and Wildlife Service and Canadian Wildlife Service, respectively, before any person may capture, kill, possess, or transport most migratory birds to control depredations. No federal permit is required merely to frighten or herd depredating birds other than endangered or threatened species, and bald eagles (*Haliaeetus leucocephalus*) or golden eagles (*Aquila chrysaetos*).

Birds introduced to the United States, such as house sparrows (*Passer domesticus*), rock pigeons (*Columba livia*), European starlings (*Sturnus vulgaris*), and monk parakeets (*Myiopsitta monachus*) have no federal protection. Furthermore, a federal permit is not required to control yellow-headed (*Xanthocephalus xanthocephalus*), red-winged (*Agelaius phoeniceus*), tri-colored (*A. tricolor*), rusty (*Euphagus carolinus*), and Brewer's (*E. cyanocephalus*) blackbirds, brown-headed cowbirds (*Molothrus ater*), all grackles (*Quiscalus* spp.), crows (*Corvus* spp.), and magpies (*Pica hudsonica* and *P. nuttalli*) when they are committing or about to commit depredations upon ornamental or shade trees, agricultural crops, livestock, or wildlife or when they are concentrated in such numbers and manner as to constitute a health hazard. However, federal provisions do not circumvent any state laws or regulations which may be more, but not less, restrictive.

Anyone contemplating capture of or killing a vertebrate species for damage management must first review state or provincial regulations for that species. For birds and endangered or threatened species, federal regulations must also be followed. In addition to reviewing the legal aspects of species take, one must comply with state or local laws or ordinances regulating or restricting control methods. For example, use of foothold traps is banned in many states, and cities and townships often have noise ordinances which restrict or prohibit use of firearms, propane cannons, and other noise-generating devices commonly used to kill or haze animals and birds.

EPA Registration of Chemicals

The Federal Insecticide, Fungicide, and Rodenticide Act (FIFRA), as amended, requires all pesticides and other chemicals used in controlling or repelling organisms in the United States to be approved and registered by the Environmental Protection Agency (EPA). The registration process is complex and costly, not only for new products but also for previously registered products being reviewed and re-evaluated (Goldman 1988). Products federally registered under Section 3 of FIFRA may not be available for use everywhere, because many states have their own registration requirements that might be more restrictive. Some products have Section 24c registrations that are valid only for specific states that have localized problems. Occasionally, products are available temporarily in specific localities for emergency use under Section 18 provisions of FIFRA. Finally, many of the registered compounds, such as vertebrate toxicants, are classified as "Restricted Use" pesticides. These products can only be used by, or

under the direct supervision of, a certified pesticide applicator. Each state has its own certification requirements. Thus, anyone contemplating use of chemicals in wildlife damage management must review the status of and requirements for use of those chemicals in their particular locality. Jacobs (1994) provided a comprehensive list of registered chemicals for wildlife damage management.

BIRDS
Damage Assessment

Birds annually destroy many millions of dollars worth of agricultural crops in North America. The greatest loss appears to be from blackbirds feeding on ripening corn; a survey in 1993 conservatively estimated a loss of 285,000 metric tons, worth $30 million in the United States (Wywialowski 1996). Blackbird damage to sunflowers in the upper Great Plains states was estimated at $5 million in 1979 and $8 million in 1980 (Hothem et al. 1988). Damage by bird species to fruit crops such as cherries, grapes, and blueberries also can be severe in localized areas (Dolbeer et al. 1994*a*). Fish-eating birds can cause major losses at fish-rearing facilities (Glahn and Brugger 1995). Economic losses from bird strikes to aircraft in the United States are even more substantial than those in agriculture—at least $490 million annually for civil aviation (Clare et al. 2003) and $100 million for military aircraft (Conover et al. 1995).

Unlike most mammals, which are secretive when causing damage, birds are often highly visible and their damage is usually conspicuous. For these reasons, subjective estimates often overestimate losses as much as 10-fold (Weatherhead et al. 1982). Thus, objective estimates of bird damage to agricultural crops are important to accurately define the magnitude of the problem and to plan appropriate, cost-effective control actions (Dolbeer 1981).

To estimate losses to birds in agricultural crops, one must devise a sampling scheme to select fields to be examined and plants or areas to be measured in the selected fields (Stickley et al. 1979). For example, to objectively estimate the amount of blackbird damage in a ripening corn or sunflower field, the estimator should examine at least 10 locations widely spaced in the field. If a field has 100 rows and is 300 m long, the estimator might walk staggered distances of 30 m along 10 randomly selected rows (e.g., 0–30 m in row 9, 31–60 m in row 20, and so on). In each 30-m length, the estimator should randomly select 10 plants and estimate the damage on each plant's ear(s) or seed head. Bird damage to corn can be estimated by measuring the length of damage on the ear (DeGrazio et al. 1969) or by visually estimating the percent loss of kernels (Woronecki et al. 1980) and converting to yield loss per hectare. Fruit loss can be estimated by counting numbers of undamaged, pecked, and removed fruits per sampled branch (Tobin and Dolbeer 1987). Sprouting rice removed by birds can be estimated by comparing plant density in exposed plots with that in adjacent plots protected by wire bird exclosures (Otis et al. 1983). The seeded surface area of sunflower heads destroyed by birds can be estimated with the aid of a clear plastic template (Dolbeer 1975) (Fig. 2).

Losses of agricultural crops to birds can be estimated indirectly through avian bioenergetics. By estimating the number of birds of the depredating species feeding in an

Fig. 2. Clear plastic template used to estimate damage to sunflower heads.

area, percentage of the agricultural crop in the birds' diet, caloric value of the crop, and daily caloric requirements of the birds, one can project the total biomass of crop removed by birds on a daily or seasonal basis (Weatherhead et al. 1982, White et al. 1985, Glahn and Brugger 1995).

Species Damage Identification

Most bird damage occurs during daylight hours, and the best way to identify the species causing damage is by observation. Presence of a bird species in a crop receiving damage does not automatically demonstrate the species is guilty, however. As one example, large, conspicuous flocks of common grackles (*Quiscalus quiscula*) in sprouting winter wheat fields were found, after careful observation and examination of stomach contents, to be eating corn residue from the previous crop. Smaller numbers of starlings were removing the germinating wheat seeds (Dolbeer et al. 1979). In another example, detailed research showed that great blue herons (*Ardea herodias*) at catfish farms primarily fed on diseased, dying fish (Glahn et al. 2002). The characteristics of damage for groups of birds are described in the sections below.

Gulls

Several gull species have adapted to existing in proximity to people, taking advantage of landfills and open trash containers for food. For example, a survey in 1994 revealed at least 15,000 nesting ring-billed (*Larus delawarensis*) and herring (*L. argentatus*) gulls in over 30 colonies on roofs in cities in the United States on the Great Lakes (Dwyer et al. 1996). Besides causing structural damage to roofs, gulls increasingly cause problems in urban areas by begging for food, defacing property, and contaminating municipal water supplies (Belant 1997). Gulls are a serious threat to flight safety at airports, representing 25% of the birds reported struck by civil aircraft during 1990–2002 (Cleary et al. 2003). In rural areas, gulls sometimes feed on fruit crops and farm-reared fish

and ducklings, and compete with threatened bird species for nest sites. Damage management techniques to control gulls include habitat modification, netting and screening, frightening devices, toxicants, and shooting.

Blackbirds and Starlings

The term "blackbird" loosely refers to a group of about 10 species of North American birds, the most common of which are red-winged blackbirds, common grackles, and brown-headed cowbirds. The European starling, introduced to North America in the late 1800s, superficially resembles native blackbirds and often associates with them. Together, blackbirds and starlings constitute the most abundant group of birds in North America, comprising a combined population of more than 500 million (Dolbeer 1990).

Blackbird damage to ripening corn, sunflowers, and rice can be serious (Dolbeer 1999). Much of this damage occurs in late summer during the "milk" or "dough" stage of seed development. The seed contents of corn are removed, leaving the pericarp or outer coat on the cob. Blackbird damage to sprouting rice in the spring can be serious in localized areas.

Starling depredations at feedlots in winter can cause substantial losses (Glahn et al. 1983). Although contamination of livestock feed by starling feces is often a concern of farmers, research indicated this contamination did not interfere with food consumption or weight gain of cattle and pigs (Glahn and Stone 1984) (Fig. 3). Starlings can also seriously damage fruit crops such as cherries and grapes (Dolbeer et al. 1994*a*).

Perhaps the greatest problem caused by blackbirds and starlings is their propensity to gather in large, nocturnal roosting congregations, especially in winter (Dolbeer et al. 1995a). The noise, fecal accumulation, and general nuisance caused by millions of birds roosting together near human habitations can be significant (White et al. 1985). Roosting birds near airports can create a safety hazard for aircraft and roost sites, if used for several years, can become focal points for the fungus that causes histoplasmosis, a respiratory disease in humans. Damage management techniques to control this group of birds include habitat modification, cultural practices (e.g., planting resistant crop varieties), netting and screening, frightening devices, repellents, toxicants, traps, and shooting.

Fig. 3. Starlings congregate at feedlots where they consume and contaminate livestock feed.

Rock Pigeons and House Sparrows

Rock pigeons and house sparrows are urban and farmyard birds whose droppings deface and deteriorate buildings. Around storage facilities they consume and contaminate grain. Pigeons and sparrows may carry and spread diseases to people, primarily via their droppings (Weber 1979). Of particular concern, droppings that are allowed to accumulate over several years may harbor spores of the fungus that cause histoplasmosis. Sparrows build bulky grass nests in buildings, drain spouts, and other sites where they can cause fire hazards or other problems. Flocks of pigeons at airports pose a hazard to departing and arriving aircraft (Dolbeer et al. 2000). Damage management techniques for rock pigeons and house sparrows include netting and screening (such as networks of overhead wires), toxicants and capture agents (alpha-chloralose), trapping, and shooting.

Crows, Ravens, and Magpies

Crows, ravens, and magpies are demonstrated predators of eggs and nestlings of other birds. In certain situations, these species cause death of newborn lambs or other livestock by pecking their eyes. Magpies at times peck scabs on freshly branded cattle.

Crows occasionally damage agricultural crops such as corn, apples, and pecans. Most of this loss is localized and minor. Crow damage to apples can be distinguished from damage by smaller birds by the deep (up to 5 cm), triangular peck holes (Tobin et al. 1989). Roosting congregations of crows in trees in parks and cemeteries may cause nuisance problems because of noise and feces. Damage management techniques for corvids include frightening devices, toxicants, traps, and shooting.

Herons, Egrets, and Cormorants

These species can concentrate at fish-rearing facilities and cause substantial losses. Salmon smolts released in rivers in the northeastern United States have suffered heavy depredation by double-crested cormorants (*Phalcrocorax auritus*). In recent years, cormorants have caused serious losses at commercial fish ponds in the southern United States (Glahn and Brugger 1995). They are also implicated in impacting fisheries in the Great Lakes. Observations at night may be necessary to identify the depredating species, because some species are nocturnal. Damage management techniques for this group include habitat modification, netting and screening, frightening devices, and shooting.

Raptors

Raptors most often implicated in predation problems with livestock (primarily poultry) are red-tailed hawks (*Buteo jamaicensis*), great horned owls (*Bubo virginianus*), and northern goshawks (*Accipiter gentilis*) (Hygnstrom and Craven 1994). Unlike mammalian predators, raptors usually kill only a single bird a day. Raptor kills usually have bloody puncture wounds in the back and breast. Owls often remove the head of their prey. Raptors generally pluck birds, leaving piles of feathers. Plucked feathers that have small amounts of tissue clinging to their bases were pulled from a cold bird that probably died from other causes and was scavenged by the raptor. If the base of a plucked feather is smooth and clean, the bird was plucked soon after being killed. Because raptors have large territories and are not numerous in any one area, removal of 1–2 individuals will generally solve a problem, although damage areas along migration routes can be problematic.

Golden eagles occasionally kill livestock, primarily lambs and goat kids on open range. Livestock predation can be locally severe in sheep-producing areas from New Mexico through Montana (Phillips and Blom 1988). Close examination is needed to identify an eagle kill. Eagles have 3 front toes opposing the hind toe, or hallux, on each foot. The front talons normally leave punctures about 2.5–5.0 cm apart in a straight line or small "V", and the wound from the hallux will be 10–15 cm from the middle toe. In contrast, mammalian predators usually leave 4 punctures or bruises from their canine teeth. Talon punctures are usually deeper than tooth punctures, and there is seldom any crushing of tissue between the talon punctures. If a puncture cannot be seen from the outside, the carcass should be skinned to identify the pattern of talon or tooth marks. Often a young lamb is killed with a single puncture from the hallux in the top of the skull and punctures from the 3 opposing talons in the base of the skull or top of the neck (O'Gara 1978*b*, 1994).

Raptors, especially red-tailed hawks and American kestrels (*Falco sparverius*), are frequently attracted to grassland areas at airports to hunt for rodents and large insects. These birds can cause serious damage to aircraft when drawn into engines (Dolbeer et al. 2000). Damage management techniques include habitat modification, netting and screening, frightening devices, traps (accompanied by translocation), and shooting.

Woodpeckers

Woodpeckers may cause damage to buildings with wood siding, especially cedar and redwood (Evans et al. 1983, Belant et al. 1997). The birds peck holes to locate insects, store acorns, or establish nest sites. They also damage utility poles. Sapsuckers attack trees to feed on sap, bark tissue, and insects attracted to the sap. Their feeding can sometimes kill the tree or degrade the quality of wood for commercial purposes. Woodpeckers occasionally annoy homeowners by hammering on metal rain gutters and stovepipes to advertise their territories. Damage management techniques for this group include cultural practices (exclusion), frightening devices, repellents (sticky tactile compounds to prevent birds from landing on structures), traps (snap and live traps), and shooting.

Ducks, Geese, and Sandhill Cranes

Damage by ducks and cranes to swathed or maturing small-grain crops during the autumn harvest is a serious, localized problem in the northern Great Plains (Knittle and Porter 1988). Damage occurs from direct consumption of grain and from trampling, which dislodges kernels from heads.

Canada (*Branta canadensis*) and snow geese (*Chen caerulescens*) grazing on winter wheat and rye crops can reduce subsequent grain and vegetative yields (Kahl and Samson 1984, Conover 1988). Canada geese also can be a serious problem to sprouting soybeans in spring and in fields of standing corn in autumn. Canada geese have adapted to suburban environments in the past 30 years, creating nuisance problems through grazing, defecation, and nest defense (Smith et al. 1999). Canada geese are the most serious bird threat to aircraft (Dolbeer et al. 2000). Damage management techniques for ducks, geese, and cranes include habitat modification (planting lure crops), netting and screening (such as networks of overhead wires), frightening devices, capture agents (alpha-chloralose), traps (accompanied by translocation), and shooting (hunting).

Control Techniques

Habitat Modification and Cultural Practices

Habitat modification and cultural practices can be implemented in many situations to make roosting, loafing, or feeding sites less attractive to birds. Although the initial investment of time and money may be high, modifications often provide long-lasting relief. Thinning or pruning vegetation can cause roosting birds such as blackbirds and starlings to move, often increasing the commercial or aesthetic value of the trees or marsh at the same time (Micacchion and Townsend 1983, Leitch et al. 1997). Eliminating standing water and prohibiting nearby landfills can reduce gull activity at airports. The U.S. Federal Aviation Administration's policy is that solid-waste disposal sites should not be located within 3 km of any runway used by turbojet aircraft (Cleary and Dolbeer 1999).

Use of lure crops, where waterfowl or blackbirds are encouraged to feed, may be cost-effective in reducing damage to nearby commercial fields of grain and sunflowers where bird-frightening programs are in place (Cummings et al. 1987). Bird-resistant cultivars of corn, sunflower, and sorghum have proven effective in reducing damage. For example, varieties of sweet and field corn with ears having long, thick husks difficult for blackbirds to penetrate experience less damage than varieties with ears having short, thin husks (Dolbeer et al. 1988*b*, 1995*b*). Certain varieties of cherries are more vulnerable to bird damage than others (Tobin et al. 1991). Planting crops so they do not mature unusually early or late also can reduce damage by blackbirds (Bridgeland and Caslick 1983). Control of insects in cornfields can make those fields less attractive to blackbirds and reduce subsequent damage to corn (Dolbeer 1990).

Netting and Screening

Plastic netting is cost effective for excluding birds from individual fruit trees or high value crops such as blueberries or grapes (Fuller-Perrine and Tobin 1993). Netting or wire screening can be used to exclude birds from rafter areas of airport hangars, undersides of bridges, fish hatcheries, and vent openings of buildings. Ledges on buildings designed at, or modified to, a 45° angle will prevent perching or nesting by birds. Electrically charged wires or arrays of wire (porcupine wire) or plastic spikes installed on ledges and other sites can prevent birds from perching.

Parallel strands of monofilament lines or wires placed at 2.5- to 12-m intervals over ponds, landfills, and other structures can reduce gull activity (Blokpoel and Tessier 1984, Belant and Ickes 1996). Monofilament lines at 30- to 60-cm intervals repelled house sparrows from feeding sites (Agüero et al. 1991). Gulls and house sparrows are reluctant to fly through these strands even though the spacing is larger than their wingspans. Overhead lines have also excluded birds from fish hatcheries. Heavy plastic (PVC) strips hung from open doorways will help exclude starlings and other birds from buildings (Johnson and Glahn 1994).

Frightening Devices

Many sonic and visual devices, homemade and marketed commercially, are available to frighten birds. Birds usually habituate to such devices, no matter how effective they may be initially. Thus, 2 important rules are: (1) do not rely solely on one type of device for frightening, and (2) vary the timing of deployment and location of devices. More succinctly, frightening devices are only as effective as the person deploying them.

Probably the most widely used frightening device is the propane cannon, which produces a loud explosion at timed intervals. Several models are marketed, including ones with automatic timers, remote activation, and rotating barrels. To be effective in frightening birds from crops, at least one cannon should be used for each 2 ha and cannons should be moved every few days. An occasional shotgun patrol to reinforce the cannons is important (Dolbeer 1980), using either live ammunition or shell crackers. Shell crackers, fired from a 12-gauge shotgun, shoot a projectile that explodes 50–75 m away. Other pyrotechnic devices for frightening birds include rockets and whistle bombs (Cleary and Dolbeer 1999).

Recorded alarm and distress calls of birds broadcast over a speaker system may work well to frighten birds (Bomford and O'Brien 1990). Some airports have speakers mounted on vehicles from which personnel broadcast amplified calls for bird species frequently encountered during runway patrols. Shooting at birds with a shotgun is often used to reinforce the distress calls. These calls are commercially available.

Ultrasonic devices emitting sounds with frequencies above the level of human hearing (20,000 Hz) are marketed for bird control in and around buildings. However, objective field tests have not demonstrated effectiveness of ultrasonic devices (Woronecki 1988). Most birds detect sounds in about the same range of frequencies as do humans.

Flags, helium-filled balloons with and without eyespots, and hawk kites suspended from balloons or bamboo poles have been used with some success to repel birds (Conover 1984, Seamans 2002). Mylar flags, 15 cm × 1.5 m in size, have been used to exclude geese from agricultural crops and gulls from loafing sites (Heinrich and Craven 1990, Belant and Ickes 1997). Ten flags per 4 ha are recommended. Reflecting tape made of mylar, placed in parallel lines at 3- to 7-m intervals, reduced blackbird numbers in agricultural fields (Dolbeer et al. 1986). Dead vulture effigies suspended from structures have caused abandonment of vulture roosts (Tillman et al. 2002). Inflatable human effigies have been used to disperse cormorants from aquaculture facilities (Stickley et al. 1995). Lasers have been effective in dispersing Canada geese, cormorants, crows, and other species from night roosts (Blackwell et al. 2002).

Blackbird roosts containing up to several million birds can be moved by use of a combination of devices, particularly recorded distress calls, shell crackers, rockets, and propane cannons (Mott 1980). Strobe lights placed in the roost are also helpful. The operation should begin before sunset, when the first birds arrive, and end at dark. People with shotguns and shell crackers should be stationed on the perimeter of the roost to intercept flight lines as they enter the roost. Three to 5 nights of harassment may be required to achieve complete dispersal. If not modified as a part of the dispersal program, the habitat of the roost should be altered (e.g., tree thinning) after birds have been hazed from the site to discourage the roost from reforming.

Repellents

Most birds have poor senses of smell and taste in general; hence, repellents targeting these senses are usually not effective (Rogers 1974, Belant et al. 1998*b*). For example, naphthalene crystals, although registered as an odor repellent for starlings, rock pigeons, and house sparrows in indoor roosts, have not been effective in field trials (Dolbeer et al. 1988*a*). Taste repellents used as seed treatments to prevent consumption of germinating seeds are also of questionable value (Heisterberg 1983).

In contrast, chemicals that produce illness or adverse physiological response upon ingestion (i.e., conditioned aversion) appear to work well as bird repellents (Rogers 1974). Methiocarb, a carbamate insecticide, is a condition-aversive repellent that has been used as a seed treatment for corn (applied as a powder to the seed at planting) and as a spray treatment for ripening cherries and blueberries (Dolbeer et al. 1994*a*). Another conditioned aversion repellent, anthraquinone, has shown effectiveness in repelling geese from feeding on turf (Dolbeer et al. 1998). Formulations containing methyl anthranilate, a chemical that irritates the trigeminal nerve in birds, have shown some success as a repellent (Belant et al. 1995).

Toxicants and Capture Agents

The use of toxic baits to control pest birds without harming nontarget organisms requires patience and a thorough understanding of the habits and food preferences of target species. Prebaiting for several days with untreated bait is critical, not only to enhance bait acceptance but to assess the amount of toxic bait to be used and possible nontarget hazards. Nearby sources of preferred food should be restricted as much as possible during the prebaiting period. Strict control must be maintained over the toxic bait. Dead birds should be collected at least daily and buried.

DRC-1339 is an EPA-registered toxicant incorporated into poultry pellets and marketed as Starlicide Complete® for control of starlings at feedlots and poultry yards. DRC-1339, incorporated into bread baits, also is registered for control of certain gull species that compete with threatened bird species for nest sites (Seamans and Belant 1999). DRC-1339 affects the renal and circulatory systems, killing the bird 24–72 hours after ingestion.

Avitrol® is an EPA-registered frightening agent. The active ingredient, 4-aminopyridine, when ingested in small doses, causes the affected bird to emit distress calls while flying in erratic circles. The affected bird usually dies within 0.5 hour, but its initial behavior can act to frighten other birds away. Avitrol is registered for use on rock pigeons, gulls, house sparrows, starlings, and blackbirds around structures and nesting and roosting sites, starlings at feedlots, gulls at airports, and blackbirds in corn and sunflower fields. Avitrol-treated bait is usually diluted 1:10 or 1:99 with untreated bait so that only a portion of the birds feeding is affected (Woronecki et al. 1979).

Alpha-chloralose is a drug that can be mixed with corn or bread baits to immobilize and capture nuisance waterfowl, American coots (*Fulica americana*), and rock pigeons. Birds typically become immobilized 30 minutes after ingesting bait and fully recover 4–24 hours later (Woronecki et al. 1992). Alpha-chloralose is restricted by the U.S. Food and Drug Administration for use by U.S. Department of Agriculture biologists in the Wildlife Services Program (Belant et al. 1999).

Traps

Starlings and certain blackbird species often can be captured in decoy traps. A decoy trap is a large (e.g., 6 × 6 × 1.8 m) poultry wire or net enclosure containing 5–20 live decoy birds, food, water, and perches. Birds enter the trap by folding their wings and dropping through an opening (0.6 × 1.2 m) in the cage top covered with 5- × 10-cm welded wire to reach the food (cracked corn, millet) below. Decoy traps have been used to reduce local populations of starlings, to remove cowbirds from the nesting area of the endangered Kirtland's warbler (*Dendroica kirtlandii*) (Kelly and DeCapita 1982), and vireos (*Vireo* spp.) in Oklahoma and to capture blackbirds for banding and research purposes. Rock pigeons and house sparrows can be captured in walk-in or funnel traps (Corrigan 1989) (Fig. 4). Mist nets can be used to remove house sparrows around barns and small farms (Plesser et al. 1983).

Various trapping techniques are used to capture raptors, including bal-chatri traps, harnessed rock pigeons, Swedish goshawk traps, bow-nets, and padded foothold traps (Bloom 1987). Raptors often become wary to one trapping technique, requiring use of 2 or 3 different techniques before successfully capturing some birds. Golden eagles preying on livestock can be captured for translocation with a net gun fired from a helicopter (O'Gara and Getz 1986).

Shooting

Shooting can be effective for reducing local populations of depredating or hazardous birds (Dolbeer et al. 1993). For example, a skilled shooter with an air rifle (pellet gun) can efficiently remove rock pigeons roosting and nesting inside buildings. For large populations of flocking birds, shooting may have little impact on the overall population (Dolbeer 1998) but can enhance efforts to repel birds from

Fig. 4. Walk-in traps set on a grain elevator to catch rock pigeons.

areas needing protection (Murton et al. 1974). This concept has been promoted in Wisconsin through a hunter referral program in which farmers allow goose hunters to shoot in agricultural fields experiencing chronic damage (Heinrich and Craven 1987).

UNGULATES

Damage Assessment

In North America, ungulates associated with resource damage are typically members of the deer (Cervidae) and swine (Tayassuidae and Suidae) families. They include native (e.g., white-tailed deer [*Odocoileus virginianus*], elk, collared peccary [*Pecari tajacu*]) and introduced species (e.g., fallow deer [*Dama dama*], red deer [*Cervus elaphus barbarus*], feral swine, feral goats). Populations of some species of ungulates, primarily white-tailed deer, elk, and feral swine, have been increasing steadily in recent decades (Gipson et al. 1998). Feral swine include domestic swine that have reverted to living in the wild, exotic wild boar (*Sus scrofa scrofa*) that were introduced, and hybrids

(Mungall 2000). Overabundant populations of ungulates can cause a variety of types of damage at landscape, regional, and local scales. Ungulates damage plants in agricultural, forestry, natural, and urban settings resulting in losses in the hundreds of millions of dollars each year (Fig. 5). They can also transmit diseases to livestock and humans and threaten human safety when involved in collisions with vehicles—including airplanes. Repair costs associated with deer–vehicle collisions exceed $1.6 billion annually. Conover (2002) discussed the economics associated with types of damage caused by deer and other wildlife.

Ungulates feed on various agricultural crops, especially soybeans, corn, and alfalfa. Yield reductions in soybean fields are most severe when feeding occurs during the first week of sprouting (DeCalesta and Schwendeman 1978), and corn yield is impacted most when feeding occurs during the silking-tasseling stage (Hygnstrom et al. 1991). Ungulates, especially when food stressed, can also cause damage to stored crops (VerCauteren et al. 2003c).

Ungulates cause damage to trees, primarily from browsing and antler rubbing. Deer browsing in late winter on

Fig. 5. Urban and rural damage caused by deer includes: A. deformation of individual trees by browsing, B. stripping of branches and bark through antler rubbing, C. creation of a browse line, and D. crop damage.

buds of fruit trees can reduce yields. Similar browsing on nursery plants and in Christmas-tree plantations can negatively impact market values (Scott and Townsend 1985). Browsing of hardwood saplings and young Douglas-fir (*Pseudotsuga menziesii*) trees in regenerating forests can reduce growth rates, mis-shape trees, and even cause plantation failures (Crouch 1976, Tilghman 1989). Antler rubbing, to remove velvet and hone sparring skills for the mating season (rut), can also damage or kill trees. On larger spatial scales, overabundant populations of ungulates have had deleterious impacts on entire biotic communities, impacting flora and fauna (Miller et al. 1992, DeCalesta 1994, Waller and Alverson 1997).

Unlike other ungulates that are strictly herbivorous, feral swine are omnivorous. Besides being destructive to vegetation, they can be predatory and have had deleterious impacts on fauna (Roythe 1995).

Species Damage Identification

Identification of ungulate damage is not difficult, as the culprits are often observed causing damage. Also, their tracks are readily identifiable. Cervids lack upper incisors and, therefore, leave a rough, shredded break on the twigs and stems they browse. Vegetation fed upon by rodents and lagomorphs, however, shows a neat, sharp-cut edge. Evidence of browsing damage higher than rodents or lagomorphs can reach is indicative of ungulate damage (realizing these smaller animals can cause damage higher on vegetation when standing on snow). Mule (*O. hemionus*) and white-tailed deer damage typically occurs from ground level to 1.8 m and they seldom browse on branches >2.5 cm in diameter. Moose (*Alces alces*) and elk damage can reach 3 m in height and they will use their incisors to scrape the bark of aspen (*Populus tremuloides*) trees. In the fall, male cervids rub the velvet from their antlers, often removing tree bark in the process. Scarring is generally confined to the trunk up to 1 m high for mule and white-tailed deer and up to 2 m for elk. Rooting of feral swine is readily visible as, through their omnivorous feeding, they turn over soil and in the process cause damage to pastureland, crops, and native plants.

Control Techniques

The public generally approves of nonlethal management techniques, especially in urban settings, where traditional hunting may not be safe, yet damage levels are high. While population reduction through lethal means is often necessary to reduce ungulate damage to tolerable levels, there are many nonlethal strategies that may have a role in a comprehensive ungulate management program. However, the limited effectiveness and high cost of nonlethal strategies frequently make them economically impractical, even when used in conjunction with lethal strategies.

Habitat and Food Modifications

Reduction of permanent cover in a local area could reduce ungulate carrying capacity, but would also destroy habitat that is important for other wildlife. Selecting plants that are less preferred foods or are resistant to ungulate damage can minimize ungulate damage in urban areas and to human-made plantings. Craven and Hygnstrom (1994) present a list of common plants and their susceptibility to damage. Crops should be harvested as early as possible to minimize the time they are susceptible to damage. Researchers are beginning to develop genetic strains of plants that are less palatable to ungulates; advancements in this area may greatly improve our ability to reduce damage through habitat modification. Lure crops have been used to draw ungulates from more valuable crops, but providing additional forage for ungulates could lead to higher densities, resulting in increased damage. Similarly, feeding and baiting ungulates ultimately leads to increased damage. Baiting can result in higher reproductive and survival rates and lead to congregated (Doenier et al. 1997) and tame populations. It also makes the ungulate population more susceptible to diseases (Davidson and Nettles 1997), some of which can be spread to other species of wildlife and livestock.

Fencing and Barriers

Frequently the only effective nonlethal method to minimize ungulate damage is fencing. Several fence designs are available (Fig. 6), although an effective yet low-cost fence

Fig. 6. Examples of fence types: A. electrified poly-wire, B. slanted high-tensile wire, C. high, woven wire, D. plastic "snow fence", E. peanut butter-baited electric fence, and F. low, woven wire with electrified wire.

design has yet to be perfected. Fencing typically acts in 1 of 2 ways to exclude ungulates: as a physical barrier or as a psychological barrier. The standard deer fence, a woven-wire fence 2.4-m high, is a physical barrier and greatly reduces the possibility of an animal passing through, over, or under. Conversely, a single- or double-strand electric poly-tape fence acts as a psychological barrier through aversive conditioning. The training occurs when an animal attempts to breach the fence and receives a powerful electric shock. Some fences incorporate both concepts, such as a 2.4-m high, 11-strand high-tensile electric fence with the goal of increasing the efficacy of the barrier. Broad classes of fence designs include: wire mesh, modified woven-wire mesh, high-tensile electric, barbed wire, slanted, and temporary electric poly tape, wire, or rope (Table 1). Variables to be considered when deciding on fence design include: level of protection desired from the fence, seasonal presence of the resource being protected, the animal's ability to breach different fence designs, motivation to breach, behavioral characteristics and physical abilities of the species being excluded, costs associated with constructing and maintaining the fence, longevity of the fence, and possible negative effects of erecting a fence (VerCauteren and Lavelle 2005). While fencing may have the potential to greatly reduce damage, its expense may not make it economical, especially in situations where the value of the resource being protected is low and the area to be protected is large. In addition, size, shape, and perimeter of the area to be protected influence the amount of fencing required and, thus, the cost (Conover 2002).

Alternatives to fencing include tree cylinders, tree wraps, and bud caps, all of which provide protection for individual trees or tree parts (DeCalesta and Witmer 1994). These devices reduce damage by minimizing access to the roots, stems, vegetation, and growing points until plants are no longer highly vulnerable to serious damage. Because these damage reduction methods do not completely exclude animals from large portions of their habitat, they may be a preferred option over fencing. One must consider number of plants (usually tree seedlings) and size of the area being protected, because at slightly <$1.00 to >$3.00/seedling protected, individual plant protection expenses may

approach the expense of fencing. Chicken-wire cylinders, photodegradable polypropylene cylinders, and a variety of flexible mesh sleeves can effectively protect seedlings. Because use of a protective cylinder provides protection only until the terminal bud protrudes from the top of the cylinder and then becomes accessible to ungulates, it may be advantageous to apply bud caps at this time.

Dogs as a Deterrent

Dogs within the perimeter of invisible fencing systems that surround agricultural crops have been shown to reduce damage by deer (Beringer et al. 1994) and several producers are actively using dogs to protect orchards and annual crops. Dog selection, training, and care are important components to the success of this strategy. Use of dogs also has the potential to reduce transmission of disease in wild ungulates to livestock. Dogs also serve to control damage from other wildlife species, such as raccoons (*Procyon lotor*).

Repellents

Several repellents have been evaluated to assess their ability to reduce ungulate damage (El Hani and Conover 1997, Nolte and Wagner 2000). There are 3 general categories of repellents: odor, contact, and systemic. Odor repellents are designed to repel animals from an area and either mimic predator odors (e.g., human or coyote [*Canis latrans*] hair) or are repugnant (e.g., moth balls, bone tar). Contact repellents are applied directly to the resource to be protected, and are therefore ingested by the offending animal. They function by creating a gustatory aversion or causing illness (aversive conditioning). Systemic repellents are incorporated into plants, either naturally (e.g., tannins) or through genetic manipulation.

Currently, use of repellents is best suited to settings with high-value plants (e.g., orchards, nurseries, gardens, ornamentals) because costs, application restrictions, and variable effectiveness make them impractical for use on low-value resources (i.e., row crops, pasture) (DeNicola et al. 2000). Repellents cannot be expected to totally eliminate damage (Craven and Hygnstrom 1994) and are at best a short-term protection measure. Repellents are

Table 1. Fence types including cost, height, efficacy level, longevity (years), and level of required maintenance.

Fence type	Cost/m ($)	Height (m)	Efficacy	Longevity	Maintenance
Woven wire or v-mesh	>6.00	3.64	High	30 to 40	Low
Chain link	>6.00	2.4	High	30 to 40	Low
Polypropylene mesh	>6.00	2.4	Moderate-high	10 to 20	Medium
New poly-rope (9-strand)	4.00–6.00	1.82	Moderate	20 to 30	Medium
Welded-wire mesh	4.00–6.00	3.64	High	20 to 30	Low
Plastic snow fence	4.00–6.01	2.12	Moderate-high	5 to 10	Medium
Modified woven wire with 2-strand barbed wire	4.00–6.02	2.4	Moderate-high	20 to 30	Medium
Modified woven wire with 5-strand high tensile	4.00–6.03	2.4	Moderate-high	20 to 30	Medium
Barbed-wire (18-strand)	2.00–4.00	2.4	Moderate	20 to 30	Medium
Non-electrified 15-strand high tensile	0.50–2.00	2.4	Moderate	20 to 30	Medium
New Hampshire (onset 3-strand)	0.50–2.01	1.05	Low	20 to 30	High
Slanted 7-strand high tensile	0.50–2.02	1.5	Moderate	20 to 30	High
Penn State 5 (5-strand electrified high tensile)	0.50–2.03	1.12	Moderate	20 to 30	High
Two-strand polytape	0.50–2.04	0.9	Low	5 to 10	High
Non-electrified 8-strand high tensile	0.50–2.05	1.82	Low	20 to 30	High
Peanut butter-baited electric	<0.50	1.12	Low	10 to 20	High

most effective on vegetation during the dormant season, but results are inconsistent. Even under optimal conditions, some damage usually occurs. Factors such as ungulate population density, availability of alternate foods, target plant species, weather, repellent concentration, and duration of the problem can influence repellent effectiveness.

The history of pesticide regulations has compromised the effectiveness and marketing of repellents. In 1978, amendments to the Federal Insecticide Fungicide and Rodenticide Act (FIFRA) gave the Environmental Protection Agency (EPA) the option to waive data submission requirements for efficacy of pesticides. The EPA took advantage of this provision except for certain public-health uses (Jacobs 2002). In 1982, the waiver was extended to all vertebrate pesticide products but, within 2 years, data submission requirements for public-health uses were fully reinstated with the added proviso that the waiver applied only to the submission of data and that EPA could request efficacy data for any product at any time. Armed with this option, the agency began to require submission of efficacy data for reregistration of products claimed to repel vertebrate pests; the efficacy of many such products had been in question for several years. The Office of Pesticide Programs reversed this policy in 1995, except for products making claims to repel pests of public health significance (Jacobs 2002). The result of these legislative actions is that efficacy data are not required for most products making claims to repel vertebrate pests, because these products are not typically labeled for public health uses (Jacobs 2002). As a result, there are many repellents currently on the market and many are not effective.

Frightening and Hazing

Propane cannons, flashing lights, shell crackers, and other sonic devices used near a resource can provide temporary relief from ungulate damage. The proper deployment of these frightening devices to maximize effectiveness was discussed earlier. Ungulates adjust or habituate to frightening devices rather quickly, and these devices are generally not effective for an entire growing season. Recent research has evaluated the efficacy of animal-activated frightening devices, with mixed results (Belant et al. 1998a, Beringer et al. 2003, Gilsdorf et al. 2004a,b). Infrared beams or passive infrared sensors activate these new devices in the presence of ungulate-sized animals (Fig. 7). Beringer et al. (2003) significantly reduced soybean damage with a deer-activated system that played a randomly selected recording of sounds chosen to frighten ungulates (i.e., aggressive dogs, gunshot barrages, ungulate distress calls) and included an illuminated human effigy. Lasers, which are effective in dispersing some bird species, are ineffective on deer (VerCauteren et al. 2003b).

Fertility Control

Considerable effort has been expended to develop fertility control agents for, and methods of delivery to, ungulates. However, safe, practical, and cost-effective fertility control methods are not yet available (Fagerstone et al. 2002). It is unlikely that fertility control will become a viable ungulate management strategy in the near future (DeNicola et al. 2000).

Fig. 7. Animal-activated frightening devices being developed to reduce deer damage include: A. motion- and heat-activated alarms positioned over bait, B. an infrared beam-triggered acoustic system that plays frightening sounds, and C. same as B with the addition of a pop-up effigy and strobe light.

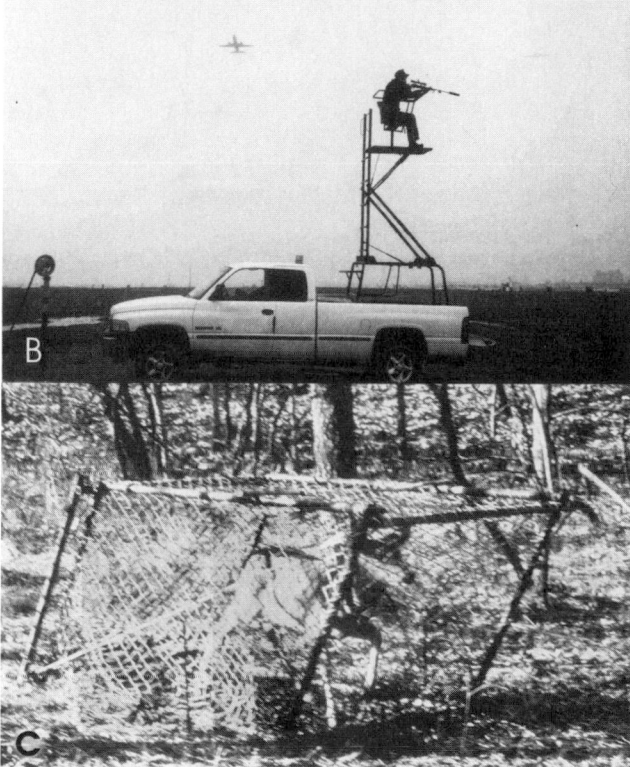

Fig. 8. Population control methods for deer include: A. well-managed hunting, B. sharp-shooting, and C. trapping (for euthanasia or translocation).

Hunting, Shooting, and Trapping

Regulated, managed hunting in rural settings is the most practical and effective method of managing overabundant deer populations and controlling damage (Fig. 8A). It is also the most ecologically, socially, and fiscally responsible method. Some states have special depredation permits that can be issued to a landowner to remove a specific number of deer at a problem site outside the normal hunting season, if sufficient control cannot be achieved during the hunting season. Well-managed hunting can also be effective for reducing burgeoning deer numbers in urban settings. Several case studies have outlined strategies to ensure the success of deer hunts in areas that are also populated with humans (McAninch 1995, VerCauteren and Hygnstrom 2002, Warren 2002). Professional sharpshooters have also been employed effectively to reduce deer numbers in areas where hunting was not considered safe (DeNicola et al. 2000) (Fig. 8B).

Deer can be captured with drop-door traps (Fig. 8C), rocket nets, drop nets, or tranquilizer guns, and then relocated or euthanized. However, these methods of deer removal are usually at least twice as expensive as shooting. In addition, there are problems with holding deer humanely in captivity until they can be transported somewhere for release, and with finding suitable release sites. In areas such as arboretums, where shooting is normally prohibited, the use of a skilled marksman under permit is probably preferable to live capture (Ishmael and Rongstad 1984). Live capture/transplanting is generally the control option of last resort, mandated by safety considerations or sensitive public relations issues.

RODENTS AND OTHER SMALL MAMMALS
Damage Assessment

Rodents and other small mammals are often not readily observed causing damage, and their damage is frequently difficult to measure and quantify. Likewise, accurate estimates of monetary losses of much of this damage are difficult to ascertain. Damage assessments indicate rodents and nonpredatory small mammals cause tremendous annual losses of food and fiber. Conover (2002) estimated the value of rodent damage to agriculture in the United States could be as high as $7 billion annually. In the timber industry, American beaver (*Castor canadensis*) and pocket gophers (Family Geomyidae) cause the most damage. Miller (1987) surveyed forest managers and natural resource agencies in 16 southeastern states and estimated annual wildlife-caused losses, primarily attributed to beaver, to be $11.2 million on 28.4 million ha. Comparatively, in 1998 Louisiana expended $2 million to control nutria (*Myocastor coypus*) (Bounds and Carowan 2000). Other types of damage include losses of sugarcane to rats (*Rattus* spp.), orchard damage by voles (*Microtus* spp.), and decreased forage quantity on rangelands caused by rodents, rabbits, and hares (Fig. 9). In households, house mice (*Mus musculus*) are the primary species conflicting with humans.

Quantifying losses to evaluate efficacy of techniques can be challenging. Most research compares plots where the resource was protected to those with no protection, or production in areas with no rodents to areas with rodents. However, loss estimates must be converted to accurate assessments of dollar losses to compare cost/benefit evaluation of control programs (VerCauteren et al. 2002*b*). Conversion to dollars is often difficult, given the vast areas involved and variability in rodent populations. Given these considerations and the complexity of damage situations, it is easy to realize the need for better monitoring techniques, damage assessment methods, and control effort evaluation.

Species Damage Identification

Most wild mammals are secretive and not easily observed; many are nocturnal. Often the investigator must rely on sign, such as tracks, trails, tooth marks, feces, or burrows to identify the species responsible for damage. Trapping may be necessary to make a positive identification of damage-causing small rodents; frequently, more than one species is involved.

Characteristics of the damage may provide clues to the species involved. In orchards, for example, major strip-

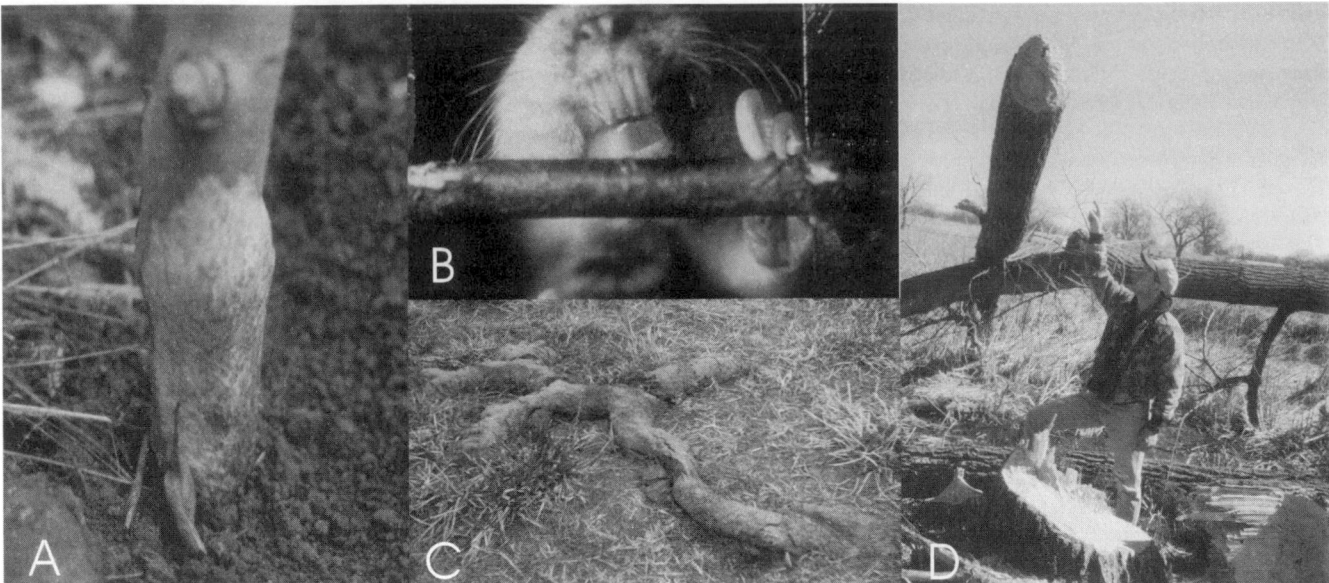

Fig. 9. Examples of rodent damage: A. tree damage in orchards by voles, B. damage to underground cables by pocket gophers, C. soil cast left by pocket gophers, and D. beaver damage to trees.

ping of roots is usually caused by pine voles (*Microtus pinetorum*), whereas damage at the root collar or on the trunk up to the extent of snow depth is most often caused by meadow voles (*Microtus pennsylvanicus*). Rats gnaw stalks of sugarcane until they are hollowed out between the internodes but usually not completely severed. Rabbits, in contrast, usually gnaw through the stalks, leaving only the ring-shaped nodes. Damage to plants can generally be grouped as: 1) root damage—pocket gophers and pine voles; 2) trunk debarking—meadow voles, squirrels (Family Sciuridae), porcupines (*Erethizon dorsatum*), woodrats (*Neotoma* spp.), rabbits, and mountain beavers (*Aplodontia rufa*); 3) stem and branch cutting—beavers, rabbits, meadow voles, mountain beavers, pocket gophers, woodrats, squirrels, and porcupines; 4) needle clipping— mice, squirrels, mountain beavers, porcupines, and rabbits; debudding—red squirrels (*Tamiasciurus hudsonicus* and *T. douglasii*) and chipmunks (*Tamias striatus* and *Eutamias* spp.). These characteristics can aid in identification of the species responsible, but positive identification should be made either by species-specific sign (e.g., tracks, feces) or by capture of individuals.

Bats

Bats, the only mammals capable of true flight, eat vast quantities of insects. Only a few of the 190 species of bats in North America cause problems; primarily when they form roosts or maternity colonies in human dwellings or structures. Bats are susceptible to many pesticides (Fitzgerald et al. 1994). Those most commonly encountered in pest situations are: little brown bat (*Myotis lucifugus*), big brown bat (*Eptesicus fuscus*), Mexican free-tailed bat (*Tadarida brasiliensis*), pallid bat (*Antrozous pallidus*) in the Southwest, and the Yuma myotis (*Myotis yumanensis*) in the West (Greenhall 1982, Frantz 1986). Species identification may be difficult, but is important because several bat species are threatened or endangered and protected by state and federal laws.

The presence of bats in a building is usually evidenced

by noise (squeaking, scratching) and by presence and distinctive pungent odor of accumulated feces and urine. Bat feces are readily identified from those of rodents by odor, insect content, and ease with which they are crushed. Many people are fearful of bats and panic in their presence. Bats can carry and transmit rabies, although <0.05% of bats are thought to be rabid (Fitzgerald et al. 1994). However, because infected bats may exhibit weakness or paralysis, they are often unable to fly or roost and therefore pose a greater risk of contact with humans and domestic animals. Where bat colonies are allowed to persist, fecal deposits accumulate, and the fungus that causes histoplasmosis can develop. Damage management techniques involve education to overcome phobias, habitat modifications (one-way valve devices on structures after young reach flight stage and construction of artificial roosts), repellents (naphthalene), and traps.

Beaver, Muskrat, and Nutria

Burrowing aquatic rodents, as agents of disturbance, can alter habitats in positive and negative ways. American beaver, muskrat (*Ondatra zibethicus*), and nutria are aquatic rodents that can cause damage in and around natural and human-created wetlands. Due to their burrowing habits, they cause damage to man-made dams, levees, and irrigation canals. The presence of these species is evidenced by the damage they cause and by their tracks, droppings, and trails. Beaver and muskrat are native to North America and nutria were introduced from South America. The regulations regarding control of these species vary from state to state.

Beaver damage is easily identified by the distinctive, cone-shaped tree stumps that result from their gnawing (Fig. 9D). Other beaver sign includes dams, lodges, bank burrows, and green sticks with the bark freshly peeled off. Muskrat and nutria are smaller than beaver and do not build dams or plug culverts. Nutria scat has distinctive parallel lines running along its length (LeBlanc 1994).

Beaver eat a wide variety of plant species, but are usually locally selective, which can result in overexploitation of preferred species (Fitzgerald et al. 1994). Damage caused by beaver results from feeding behavior (tree cutting) and their efforts to control water levels (dam building) (Miller and Yarrow 1994). Beaver also fell and girdle large-diameter trees to access the branches, contributing to losses in timber value (Fitzgerald et al. 1994). They also cause flooding of roads, dwellings, and other human property.

The most serious damage caused by muskrats is washouts and cave-ins of pond dams, levees, and irrigation canals. They can also cause severe damage to grain, such as rice, and to garden crops growing near water. Their cone-shaped huts of aquatic material projecting 0.5–1 m above the water surface, feeding platforms of aquatic vegetation, and burrow entrances indicate muskrat presence. Their burrow entrances, 13–17 cm in diameter, are much smaller than those of nutria.

Nutria can cause significant damage to rice and sugarcane, especially in fields adjacent to Gulf Coast marshes (LeBlanc 1994). They may severely impede cypress (*Taxodium distichum*) regeneration (Conner and Toliver 1987) and damage wooden structures and floating marinas. Nutria have been implicated as a threat to the persistence of coastal marshes (Ford and Grace 1998).

Beaver, muskrat, and nutria can be infected with several pathogens, and internal and external parasites that can be transmitted to humans (Perry 1982, Thorne et al. 1982, Davidson and Nettles 1997). Proper water treatment measures should be taken before drinking water in regions where these species occur. Damage management techniques include habitat modification (explosives for dams, drain devices in dams or culverts), exclusion, traps (live traps accompanied by translocation, Conibears, footholds), snares, and shooting.

Deer and White-footed Mice

Deer and white-footed mice (*Peromyscus maniculatus* and *P. leucopus*) are common and widely distributed throughout North America (Timm and Howard 1994). Species of *Peromyscus* are the primary reservoirs of the Sin Nombre hantavirus (Corrigan 2001), which was recently found to be the cause of an often-fatal pulmonary syndrome in humans. These mice are nocturnal, active year round, and their populations may show large fluctuations. Their cheek pouches give them the capacity to carry 3–5 times more food than other species of mice and may increase their efficiency in exploiting small, particulate food items that are patchily distributed (Vander Wall and Longland 1999). *Peromyscus* can be significant seed predators (Sullivan 1978), and in some areas direct seeding for reforestation has failed as a result of their foraging activities. Their effects on reforestation have caused a shift to the use of hand-planted seedlings in many areas. *Peromyscus* also can cause significant losses to corn seedlings in conservation tillage systems, but this damage may be offset by their consumption of harmful insects and weed seeds (Clark and Young 1986, Johnson 1986). *Peromyscus* invade homes where they eat stored food and damage upholstered furniture or other materials shredded for use in nest building. Trapping with snap or live traps is the best method to identify the species present. Damage management techniques for *Peromyscus* include habitat

and food modifications, exclusion, traps (snap traps and live traps), repellents, and toxicants.

Ground Squirrels

Ground squirrels, genus *Spermophilus*, are important pest species in north-central and western North America, causing serious economic losses to agricultural and range resources. Belding's (*S. beldingi*), California (*S. beechyi*), and rock (*S. variegatus*) ground squirrels are all considered pests in at least part of their range (Marsh 1994a). They can inflict serious damage to pastures, rangelands, vegetable gardens, and grain, fruit, or nut crops. A careful search of an area showing damage will reveal opened seed hulls and caches. They often live in colonies or concentrate in localized areas (Marsh 1994b). As a group, ground squirrels are widely recognized for their ability to achieve high population levels in suitable habitats (Giusti et al. 1996). Ground squirrel burrows can collapse irrigation levees, increase erosion, damage farm machinery, and cause injury to livestock and humans. Ground squirrels also predate nests of ground-nesting birds, including those of waterfowl (Sargeant and Arnold 1984, Marsh 1994a).

Ground squirrels are diurnal and easily observed (Marsh 1985a). They hibernate and estivate and show major dietary shifts during the year (Marsh 1985a, 1986). Effective control strategies must consider these factors. Ground squirrels are extremely adaptable, so indirect control through habitat modification, exclusion, or use of chemical and visual repellents has limited, if any, benefit in most situations (Whisson et al. 2000). Ground squirrels carry several zoonotic diseases, including plague; in plague-endemic areas, ground squirrel control should be combined with ectoparasite control (Marsh and Howard 1982). Damage management techniques include habitat modification (exclusion, burrow ripping, and flooding), toxicants, fumigants, traps (live traps, size #0–1½ foothold traps, snap traps), and shooting.

Marmots

Marmots (*Marmota* spp.), also known as woodchucks, can cause damage to a variety of crops; forage production may be markedly reduced by marmot feeding and trampling (Marsh 1985a). Damage to crops such as alfalfa, soybeans, beans, squash, and peas can be costly and extensive. They damage fruit trees and ornamental shrubs by gnawing or scratching woody vegetation. Damage often occurs on farms, in home gardens, orchards, nurseries, around buildings, and occasionally on dikes (Bollengier 1994). Their burrows, often positioned along field edges, can cause damage to farm machinery and injure livestock; burrows can compromise the structural integrity of irrigation ditches, resulting in loss of water. In suburban areas, burrows under buildings or in landscaped areas cause problems (Marsh and Howard 1982). The presence of marmots is easily ascertained by direct observation of animals and burrows. During periods of forage growth, vegetation around burrows is noticeably shorter than in surrounding areas. Occupied burrows can be identified in spring by the presence of dirt pellets ranging from marble to fist size. Damage management techniques include frightening devices, fumigants, traps (Conibear traps, foothold traps, live traps) and shooting.

Voles

Voles, also called meadow mice, field mice, and pine mice, cause extensive damage to forests, orchards, and ornamentals by gnawing bark and roots (Sullivan et al. 1987, O'Brien 1994). In North America, there are 19 species of voles, 4 of which are of pest significance. They are the most prolific of all rodent species and probably the most important item in the food chain among secondary consumers (Corrigan 2001). Tree or shrub damage usually occurs under snow or dense vegetation; the bark is gnawed from small trees near the root collar and up the trunk to the snow surface (Fig. 9A). Voles gnaw through small trees or shoots up to about 6 mm in diameter. Some species also cause extensive damage to root systems; this damage may not be detected until spring when it is reflected in condition of new foliage. Voles can damage field and garden crops as well; when vole populations are high, losses can be severe (Clark 1984, Marsh 1985*a*). They are also carriers of bubonic plague and tularemia.

Vole populations are characterized by 3 levels: low, high, and irruptive (Johnson and Johnson 1982). In North America, population peaks occur about every 4 years, although not in explosive numbers and not predictably (Johnson and Johnson 1982). Voles are active throughout the year. Their presence is most easily ascertained by searching for their runways and burrow systems. In orchards, these can be found by pulling the grass and other debris from the bases of trees. Gnawing on trunks and roots of trees is usually less uniform than that of other rodents. Tooth marks can be at all angles, even on small branches, and may vary from light scratches to channels 3 mm wide, 2 mm deep, and 10 mm long. In hay crops, runways with numerous burrow openings, clipped vegetation, and feces can be detected in dense vegetation. Damage management techniques for voles include habitat modification (provision of alternative foods), exclusion, toxicants, and traps (snap traps).

Moles

There are 7 species of moles (representing 5 genera) in North America; 4 of these species have distributions restricted to the Pacific Northwest and West Coast of the United States (Yates and Pedersen 1982). Moles feed primarily on soil invertebrates, especially earthworms and grubs (insect larvae). Vegetation can comprise up to 20% of the diet of some species of moles; although they cause some damage to crops and ornamentals, they are most detrimental to turf areas (Marsh 1996). They are active year round. Voles and mice also use burrows of moles and can be responsible for some damage attributed to moles (Henderson 1994*a*).

The presence of moles usually can be detected by the mounds of soil brought up from extensive tunnels dug in search of food and by the raised soil of surface burrows. Shallow tunnels of moles can be confused with those of pocket gophers but moles typically leave volcano-shaped mounds composed of clods of soil and their burrow plugs are at the peaks of the hills; gophers leave fan-shaped mounds, with the burrow plug near the base of the mound (Henderson 1994*a*). Generally, gophers produce larger mounds than moles, but the Townsend's mole (*Scapanus townsendii*) can produce up to 4 mounds per day (Yates and Pedersen 1982).

The burrowing activity of moles may reduce production of forage crops by undermining and smothering vegetation and by exposing root systems to drying. Forage production in pastures can be reduced by 10–50% by burrowing activity (Yates and Pedersen 1982). Their surface burrows can also plug harvesting machinery and contaminate hay and silage. The burrowing activity of moles can extensively damage lawns and golf greens. Damage management techniques include habitat modification (soil compaction, flooding), exclusion, chemical repellents, insecticides (to reduce the mole's primary food source), fumigants, toxicants, and traps.

Pocket Gophers

Thirteen species of pocket gophers (*Geomys* spp., *Pappogeomys castanops*, *Thomomys* spp.) occur in the United States. They can cause substantial damage to agricultural crops, lawns, rangeland, and tree plantings. Gophers feed primarily on underground portions of plants and trees. Root crops such as potatoes, sweet potatoes, beets, parsnips, turnips, and carrots are favorite foods, as are field crops such as alfalfa and clover (Marsh 1998). Damage is often undetected until a tree shows aboveground signs of stress, by which time the damage may be lethal. Pocket gophers may also damage plastic irrigation lines in agricultural settings as well as underground pipes and cables (Fig. 9B). In rangeland, soil disturbance and mound building by pocket gophers results in increased plant diversity, favoring annual and invasive species. They can also reduce the carrying capacity of rangeland for livestock. Gopher mounds can cause equipment breakage and increase wear of haying machinery. Furthermore, their burrows can cause substantial losses of irrigation water, especially in flood-irrigated crops (Marsh 1998).

Pocket gophers are a major impediment to reforestation in the western United States (Crouch 1986). They damage trees by stem girdling and cutting, root clipping, and exposing roots to drying (Case and Jasch 1994). In winter, pocket gophers often forage above ground by tunneling through snow. Extensive aboveground girdling is fairly easy to detect. Damage to roots, however, may go unnoticed until seedlings become discolored and tip over (Nolte et al. 2000).

Fan-shaped soil mounds in contrast to the conical mounds of moles easily identify pocket gopher presence. Burrow entrances are typically plugged. Above ground debarking damage caused by pocket gophers shows small tooth marks, differing from the distinct broader grooves left by porcupines and the finely gnawed surface caused by meadow voles. Gophers sometimes pull saplings and vegetation into their burrows. Gophers also fill some of their snow tunnels with soil, forming long, tubular "soil snakes" that remain after the snow melts (Fig. 9C). Damage management techniques include habitat modification (flood irrigation, crop rotation), cultural practices (plastic mesh cylinders to protect seedlings, protective coverings for pipes and cables), fumigants, toxicants, and traps.

Prairie Dogs

There are 5 species of prairie dogs (*Cynomys* spp.) in North America; the Mexican (*C. mexicanus*) (endangered) and Utah (*C. utahensis*) (threatened) prairie dogs are federally listed. Prairie dogs live in colonies that are easily identified by conical mounds around burrow entrances and by the presence of these highly visible rodents. Populations were reduced greatly by intensive control and conversion of habitat to agriculture in the early- to mid-1900s. In recent years populations have been expanding, commensurate with reduced control efforts.

Prairie dogs damage rangelands and pastures by clipping vegetation for food and nesting material and by clearing cover from the vicinity of burrows (Hygnstrom and Virchow 1994). Their activity not only reduces available forage but also can alter species composition of vegetative communities in favor of forbs. Competition with cattle is minimal and, in some situations, beneficial effects of prairie dogs may offset competition. Thus, each conflict situation should be evaluated individually (Fagerstone 1981). Crops planted near prairie dog colonies can receive serious damage from feeding and trampling. Also, damage to irrigation systems is common, and American badgers (*Taxidea taxus*) digging for these rodents cause even greater damage. The burrows and mounds created by prairie dogs can increase soil erosion and drainage of irrigation water, and cause damage to farm machinery. Prairie dogs also serve as a reservoir for bubonic plague (Hygnstrom and Virchow 1994).

In recent years, prairie dogs have thrived in urban areas that were historically prairie dog habitat. Damage in these environments includes degradation of community open space, clipping of landscape vegetation, and encroachment into residential yards. Populations in urban areas can increase the probability of bubonic plague transmission to pets.

Prairie dog colonies provide habitat for other species such as the endangered black-footed ferret (*Mustela nigripes*). It is a violation of federal law to poison a prairie dog town where ferrets are present (Hygnstrom and Virchow 1994). Damage management techniques include habitat modification (e.g., deferred grazing), exclusion, fumigants, toxicants, traps (foothold and Conibear), and shooting.

Rabbits and Hares

Rabbits (*Sylvilagus* spp.) and hares (*Lepus* spp.) (Family Leporidae) can damage or completely destroy landscape plantings, gardens, agricultural crops, and rehabilitated rangeland. In winter, leporids may strip bark from and debud fruit trees, conifers, and other trees and shrubs (Craven 1994). Populations of hares show large fluctuations and, during peak densities, hares can severely damage vegetation and compete with livestock for forage (Fig. 10).

Stems clipped by rabbits and hares have a clean, oblique, knife-like cut. Rabbits and hares usually clip stems 6 mm in diameter or less at a height not more than 50 cm above the ground. Repeated clipping will deform seedlings. Leporids can often be observed at damage sites along with their tracks, trails, and droppings.

Rabbits are known vectors of tularemia, a zoonotic disease, and they may carry larvae of several ascarid roundworms that can produce disease if uncooked, infected meat is ingested by humans (Davidson and Nettles 1997). Damage management techniques include rabbit "drives" or "roundups," use of ferrets, habitat modification, exclusion, chemical repellents, traps, snares, and shooting.

Fig. 10. High jackrabbit densities negatively impact vegetation.

Tree Squirrels

Tree squirrels can be grouped into 3 categories: large tree squirrels (gray [*Sciurus carolinensis*], fox [*S. niger*], and tassel-eared [*S. aberti*]), pine squirrels (red and Douglas), and flying squirrels (northern [*Glaucomys sabrinus*] and southern [*G. volans*]) (Jackson 1994*b*). Squirrels eat plants and fruits, dig up newly planted bulbs and seeds, strip bark and leaves from trees and shrubs, invade homes, and consume bird eggs (Hadidian et al. 1987, Jackson 1994*b*). Squirrels can also cause problems by traversing power lines, gnawing on them, and shorting out transformers.

Squirrels often can be observed at the damage site. Damage to conifers is indicated by green, unopened cones scattered on the ground under mature trees and by accumulated cone scales and "cores" at feeding stations. Bark stripping can be observed in trees, and bark fragments are often found on the ground, as are the tips of twigs and small branches. These activities may interfere with natural reseeding of trees that are important to forestry, particularly in ponderosa pine (*Pinus ponderosa*) forests where pine squirrels may remove 60–80% of the cones in poor to fair seed years (Jackson 1994*b*). Damage management techniques include cultural practices (trimming limbs near buildings and transformers), exclusion, frightening devices, chemical repellents, toxicants, traps (Conibear, foothold, and live traps), and shooting.

Woodrats

Woodrats, also called pack rats, brush rats, or trade rats, are attracted to human food supplies in buildings and will remove small objects such as utensils and other items, sometimes leaving sticks or other objects "in trade." There are 9 species of woodrats in the United States; several have become significant pests in suburban and semi-rural developments in the Southwest (Corrigan 2001). They often construct conspicuous stick houses in cabins, unused vehicles, rocky outcroppings, or in the upper branches of trees (Marsh and Howard 1982, Salmon and Gorenzel 1994). They will shred mattresses and upholstery for nesting material.

Woodrats are agile climbers and consume fruits, seeds, and green foliage of herbaceous and woody plants. They clip small branches and strip and finely shred patches of bark for their nests. Their damage may be confused with that of tree squirrels and porcupines; however, woodrats leave a relatively smooth surface with a few scattered tooth marks and tend to litter the ground beneath the tree less than tree squirrels. Woodrats have been involved in epizootics of plague and have been infected with tularemia. At least 6 species of woodrats have been identified as reservoirs of trypanosomes (parasitic blood-infesting protozoans) that cause Chagas disease (Corrigan 2001). Because some subspecies of woodrats are endangered, one should check local regulations before undertaking control efforts. Damage management techniques include exclusion, chemical repellents, toxicants, traps (snap and live traps), and shooting.

Commensal Rodents

The 3 species of commensal rodents (those that live primarily around human habitation) are Norway rats (*Rattus norvegicus*), roof or black rats (*R. rattus*), and house mice.

These omnivorous rodents consume millions of bushels of grain each year: in the field, on the farm, in the elevator, mill, store, home, and in transit. They also waste many more millions of bushels by contamination. One rat can eat approximately 9–18 kg of feed per year and probably contaminates 10 times that amount with its urine and droppings (Timm 1994*a,b*).

Besides consuming plant products, commensal rodents will feed on poultry chicks and occasionally will attack adult poultry, wild birds, newborn pigs, lambs, and calves. In buildings and vehicles, rodents gnaw electrical wires, creating a serious risk to human safety (Corrigan 2001) and sometimes starting fires. Their gnawing also causes considerable property damage. Extensive damage to foundations and concrete slabs sometimes results when rats burrow under buildings; and burrowing into dikes and outdoor embankments causes erosion. Health departments annually report hundreds of human babies bitten by rats. Many viral and bacterial diseases are transmitted to humans by rodent feces and urine-contaminated food and water. Among the diseases rats may transmit to humans or livestock are plague, murine typhus, leptospirosis, trichinosis, salmonellosis, and ratbite fever.

Signs of commensal rodents include gnawing, droppings, tracks, burrows, and darkened or smeared areas along walls where they travel. Reviews of problems caused by these species and methods of control are provided by Timm (1994*a,b*), Hygnstrom and VerCauteren (1995), and Corrigan (2001). Damage management techniques include tracking powder, habitat modification, cultural practices (sanitation), exclusion, fumigants, toxicants, and traps (snap and multiple-catch traps).

Control Techniques

There are 2 general categories of control related to rodents and other small mammals: nonlethal and lethal. Many traditional methods of wildlife damage management are lethal; however, these methods are increasingly being questioned by society on the basis of humaneness and target specificity. Presently, we lack ability to alleviate many wildlife damage problems in effective and economical ways using only nonlethal techniques (Conover 2002). Wildlife researchers specializing in wildlife damage management are expending considerable effort to develop nonlethal means to reduce damage. The following section briefly reviews control techniques commonly used to manage populations of rodents and small mammals. An Integrated Pest Management (IPM) approach is recommended for the control of rodents and other small mammals. The IPM concept favors timely and strategic incorporation of a combination of cost-effective control techniques to reduce the impact of species on valuable resources.

Habitat Modification and Cultural Practices

All animals are dependent on food and shelter; therefore, elimination of one or both of these requirements will force them to move from the immediate area. This method of control, where practical, is the most desirable and usually has the most permanent effect in reducing small mammal damage. However, other species often are dependent upon the same habitat. Modifications of the habitat can result in greater adverse impacts to desirable nontarget species and natural communities than careful use of a registered toxicant or other control tool. Modifications can also create situations that contribute to other species becoming pests.

Many rodents and small mammal pests can be discouraged from using areas by removal of brush and woodpiles, weeds, and other debris. Commensal rodent control can be greatly facilitated by removal of harborage, garbage, and refuse. Squirrel interference with power transformers may be reduced if vegetation near power poles is managed (Hamilton et al. 1987). Mountain beaver populations in silvicultural areas may be decreased by removing surface shelter such as stumps, logs, and brush piles (Cafferata 1992). High populations of muskrats in sugarcane are associated with debris remaining in fields after harvest (Steffen et al. 1981).

Control of pine voles with anticoagulant baits was enhanced in apple orchards cultivated 2 or 3 times a year (Byers 1976). Davis (1976) reported that pine vole damage in an apple orchard was reduced by mowing 3 times a year, clearing vegetation from under the trees, removing pruned branches, restricting distribution of fertilizer and, after harvest, inspecting and cleaning vulnerable parts of the orchard. Byers (1984), however, found that cultural controls (combinations of mowing, cultivation, and herbicide application) were much more expensive than application of toxic baits and offered no advantages in vole control.

Water levels behind beaver dams can be manipulated by installing a perforated pipe or a 3-log drain (Miller and Yarrow 1994) through the dam. Various mechanical methods have been developed to prevent beaver from stopping water flow through culverts (Roblee 1987). Muskrat damage to farm pond dams can be reduced by maintaining a 3:1 slope on the water side of the dam, a 2:1 slope on the outer face, and a top width of 2.4 m (Miller 1994).

Provision of alternative foods can reduce conifer seed loss to mice in forest regeneration projects (Sullivan and Sullivan 1982) and may be useful in reducing loss of agricultural crop seedlings in no-tillage fields (Hygnstrom et al. 2000) and orchards (Sullivan and Sullivan 1988). Pocket gopher infestations in logged areas can be reduced by prompt regeneration and minimal site preparation. Selective cutting, when feasible, can be used in areas with high potential for gopher infestations (Crouch 1986). Use of insecticides to reduce numbers of soil invertebrates can protect turf from nine-banded armadillos (*Dasypus novemcinctus*) and moles, but damage may initially increase due to increased food searching by animals already present (Henderson 1994*a*).

Exclusion

Exclusion involves installation of barriers that prevent access by pest species into structures or areas, or elimination of their physical contact with specific objects. Rodent proofing of structures is achieved most economically if incorporated into construction plans. Corrigan (2001) provides detailed suggestions on how to accomplish rodent-proof construction. Basically, all openings or sites where rodents might create openings are protected with wire mesh, sheet metal, or concrete, providing long-term protection.

Exclusion is a necessary part of an effective program to remove bats from structures. Final closure of entrances to the structure should not be made until all young have reached the flight stage. At that time these openings can be closed with a one-way door that permits bats to leave the structure but prohibits re-entry.

In small orchards, rodent and rabbit damage can be eliminated by wrapping trees with hardware cloth or burlap that is buried about 5 cm deep around the tree base. Fences made of 1.2- to 2.5-cm mesh net wire 0.7–1 m high can protect small areas against nonclimbing rodents and small mammals. Lower edges of fences should be buried with an "L" shape on the outside of the fence to prohibit burrowing under the fence.

A 0.6-m-wide expandable metal band placed around tree trunks 2 m above the ground will keep squirrels out of individual trees. Branches should be trimmed within 2 m of the ground or buildings.

Steel-sheathed wire may be used on underground power and telephone lines to prevent pocket gopher gnawing. Plastic seedling protectors will protect conifer seedlings from rodents and rabbits. These plastic net-tubes are placed over seedlings at planting. Some allow branches to grow through the netting and provide protection for the terminal bud for 3–5 years as the terminal leader grows through the tube.

Frightening Devices

Frightening devices may deter rodents and small mammals from localized areas for short periods of time. These devices are designed to frighten animals by targeting their visual or auditory senses. Visual repellents (e.g., eye spots, predator effigies, mylar) were designed to repel birds, although some of these visual devices may also affect mammals (Mason 1998). Sonic devices include distress calls, pyrotechnics (e.g., live ammunition, shell crackers, fire crackers), propane cannons, and sirens. Ultrasonic devices are no more effective at frightening animals than sonic devices. Although readily available and commonly used, most frightening devices are ineffective. Limited research with frightening devices has been conducted on rodents and small mammals.

Chemical Repellents

Several compounds have been registered for use as small-mammal repellents (Jacobs 1994); however, definitive efficacy data for most are lacking (Mason 1998), as is information on why some chemicals repel offending animals. Repellents are most effective when applied directly to foods with the intent of reducing consumption (Mason 1998). Chemical repellents are grouped into 3 categories: sensory irritants, semiochemical odors (e.g., predator urines), and those that produce conditioned taste avoidance behavior (Clark 1998, Mason 1998). They function by producing smell or taste aversions, or gastrointestinal malaise. Sensory irritants are usually more effective than semiochemicals. Use of some area repellents, such as naphthalene or para-dichlorobenzene, in structures is often limited because the vapors cannot be prevented from permeating areas occupied by people. The efficacy of repellents applied to plants or seeds is affected by availability of natural foods and ability to withstand weathering. "Bitter" chemicals (e.g., thiram, denatonium benzoate, denatonium saccharide, sucrose octaacetate), are not necessarily perceived by animals as such, and are not inherently repellent to herbivores. Repellents claiming to work because they are perceived as bitter by humans probably are either ineffective or are paired with some other compounds that cause illness or distress (Mason 1998, Nolte 1999). Some repellents create a burning sensation (e.g., capsaicin). Various taste sensations (bitter, sour, sweet, etc.) affect animals differently, or may have no effects. Thiram, the most widely used taste repellent, can be applied to trees, tree seeds, seedlings, bulbs, and shrubs to protect them from rodents and moles. Thiram should not be used on plant parts eaten by humans or domestic animals. Fruit trees must be sprayed only in the dormant season.

Fumigants

Fumigants registered for rodent control include smoke-producing gas cartridges, aluminum phosphide, chloropicrin, and methyl bromide (Corrigan 2001). Fumigants are lethal when inhaled and are used to kill burrowing mammals. When fumigants are used, all burrow openings should be closed after introduction of the pesticide. The active ingredients in gas cartridges are a combination of sulfur, nitrate, charcoals, or phosphorous compounds which, when ignited, produce carbon monoxide and other gases; these gases asphyxiate rodents in their burrows (Corrigan 2001).

Aluminum phosphide is a fumigant available in tablets or pellets that produces toxic phosphine gas when exposed to atmospheric moisture; this gas is flammable or explosive at some concentrations. Chloropicrin is typically used as an additive to fumigants to provide an exposure warning (like sulfur is added to natural gas). Its only other registered rodent uses are in empty grain and potato storage bins to control rats and mice. Methyl bromide, because it has been documented to deplete atmospheric ozone, will not have its registration renewed. Hygnstrom and VerCauteren (2000) evaluated effectiveness of 5 fumigants (aluminum phosphide, gas cartridge, methyl bromide, chloropicrin, and a methyl bromide–chloropicrin mixture) for managing prairie dogs; all reduced burrow activity by 95–98%. Jacobs (1994) provides information on specific fumigants.

Toxicants

Toxicants are the most common method used to control damage-causing populations of rodents and other small mammals. Toxicants require little labor and can be used to kill large numbers of animals, even in remote areas. Damage reduction is the goal of any control program, and must be the final measure of efficacy. Efficacy of a control program may be increased by using several toxicants in combination or by periodically alternating those used; this strategy aids in avoiding development of resistance to the primary toxicant (Marsh 1988).

One disadvantage of toxicants is that they usually are not species specific (Conover 2002). Potential hazards to nontarget species must be considered when toxicants are used. Hazards associated with use of a toxicant are not necessarily related to toxicity of the compound, but are more often associated with how they are applied. Hazards to nontarget wildlife can be reduced by properly selecting toxicants, bait composition and formulation techniques (including bait color, size, shape, texture, and hardness), and bait delivery systems (Marsh 1985b). Some toxicants

may be absorbed by plants and pose a risk to herbivores (Conover 2002). To reduce environmental hazards, the U.S. EPA closely regulates registration of toxicants, approving only those that decompose rapidly and do not pose a significant threat to other species. Above- and below-ground carcass searches can be conducted to evaluate efficacy and nontarget mortalities of the management effort (Witmer et al. 1995, VerCauteren et al. 2002a).

Toxicants are classed as either anticoagulants or non-anticoagulants. Historically, anticoagulants were considered multidose or chronic toxicants and non-anticoagulants as single-dose or acute toxicants. New-generation anticoagulants, however, can be effective in a single feeding and some new non-anticoagulants need to be ingested by individuals of the target species over a period of several days (Marsh 1988). Baits come in a variety of forms including food, block, pellets, loose meal, seeds, packets, liquids, tracking powder, and nontoxic monitoring blocks.

Numerous toxicant formulations are registered for use in commensal rodent control, around farm buildings, and in noncrop areas; fewer are available for use in crops. Development of registrations for in-crop use of toxicants, particularly anticoagulants, is a high priority research area. However, use of toxicants is expected to decline as alternative methods of reducing damage are developed (Fagerstone and Schafer 1998).

Anticoagulants are chemicals that disrupt the normal clotting process of blood. Death in poisoned rodents results from internal hemorrhaging and damage to capillaries (Corrigan 2001). There are 2 classes of anticoagulants, first-generation (multiple-dose) and second generation (single-dose). First-generation anticoagulants typically require several consecutive doses to kill, while second-generation anticoagulants cause death after a single dose. First-generation anticoagulants generally require ingestion for 3–14 consecutive days to be effective. Bait shyness is generally not a problem because animals do not associate ill effects with bait consumption. However, bait delivery procedures must consider the need for making toxicants available over several consecutive days. Warfarin was the first, most widely used, of the "rat poisons" for many years (Corrigan 2001). Despite a popular misconception that warfarin is no longer used because mice and rats have developed a physiological resistance to it, in actuality, its patent has expired and newer pesticides more profitable for manufacturers have displaced the older pesticides. Physiological resistance to warfarin and other first-generation anticoagulants is actually a minor problem; such resistance usually only occurs after continuous use at the same site for several years, and can be overridden by switching temporarily to another rodenticide, such as zinc phosphide. Nevertheless, manufacturers and marketers of the second-generation anticoagulants, which are effective against rodents resistant to the first-generation compounds, have touted this effectiveness against resistant rodents in their sales pitch. Chlorophacinone and diphacinone are other first-generation anticoagulants still widely used, but neither is effective against rats resistant to warfarin. Vitamin K is an antidote for first-generation anticoagulants.

The active ingredients brodifacoum, bromadiolone, and difethialone comprise the most popular second-generation anticoagulants used in the United States (Corrigan 2001).

These anticoagulants are highly toxic to rodents and a single feeding on baits with an active ingredient concentration as low as 0.005% can produce death (Marsh 1988). Currently, all second-generation anticoagulants are effective against warfarin-resistant rodents.

Anticoagulants can be obtained in prepared baits or purchased as concentrates for mixing with fresh bait. Baits should be placed where rodents feed, drink, or travel. For anticoagulants that require multiple ingestions, bait stations, purchased from pesticide supply houses or constructed from wood or metal, are particularly useful in protecting the bait from weather and nontarget species (Fig. 11). Some baits come in packets that are gnawed open by rodents, others are available in moisture-resistant paraffin blocks. Several anticoagulants are registered for use in tracking powders, which are dusted into burrows and along runways where house mice or Norway rats travel. Rodents ingest the anticoagulant by licking the toxic dust from their feet and fur.

Toxicants with different modes of action provide an obvious answer to anticoagulant resistance. The 3 most common non-anticoagulant baits used in the structural pest management industry are zinc phosphide, cholecalciferol, and bromethalin. Zinc phosphide is an effective, acute toxicant that has been in use for over 50 years with minimal nontarget hazards (to humans and other nontarget species). A key to success with zinc phosphide is prebaiting to establish a feeding routine. For some species of field rodents, such as prairie dogs, it is the only pesticide currently registered for use (Fagerstone and Schafer 1998). Hygnstrom et al. (2000) found that zinc phosphide pellets applied in-furrow at planting reduced corn yield loss; zinc phosphide has since been registered for this use. Hygnstrom et al. (1994) provide species-specific baiting strategies using zinc phosphide. Cholecalciferol (vitamin D₃) is both a single- and multiple-feeding toxicant effective on commensal rodents (Marshall 1984). No second-

Fig. 11. Bait station and packet of anticoagulant bait used for rodent control.

ary hazards have been associated with its use (Marsh 1988). Bromethalin is also effective on rats, including those resistant to warfarin.

Strychnine is another non-anticoagulant acute rodenticide used to control pocket gophers and some species of ground squirrels to reduce damage to forest seedlings, agricultural crops, and home landscaping (Fagerstone and Schafer 1998). As a result of regulatory and court actions, its former widespread use has now been restricted to underground applications (in pocket gopher and ground squirrel burrows).

Traps

Live traps are often used to capture mammals of all sizes without harming them (Fig. 12). They are an excel-

Fig. 12. Live traps come in a variety of sizes and styles for almost any mammalian species.

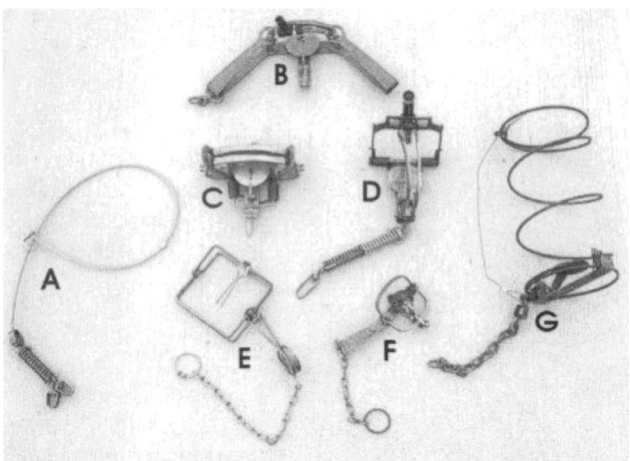

Fig. 13. Examples of several types of traps including: foothold (B, C, D, and F), snares (A and G), and body-gripping trap (E).

lent option for use in residential areas or in situations where rodents and other small mammals causing damage are to be relocated. Various homemade designs can be constructed of wire mesh or wood, or wire mesh and plastic models can be purchased commercially. Certain models can be used to capture a variety of species while others are species specific. Some designs have doors at both ends, permitting visibility through the trap, thereby reducing trap shyness. Suggested baits, which depend on the species being trapped, include apple slices, sunflower seeds, peanut butter, and rolled oats.

Foothold traps are manufactured in several sizes and designs. Traditional foothold traps are commonly used for beaver, muskrat, and nutria control, while smaller sizes are used to capture tree and ground squirrels, rats, and marmots. Use of foothold traps, body-gripping traps, and snares is controversial; however, properly used they are effective and valuable wildlife management tools. Some states prohibit their use, whereas others sanction only traps with padded or offset jaws. Like other types of traps, there is potential to capture nontarget species; this danger can be lessened by using proper trap sizes, pan tension devices, break-away mechanisms, species-specific baits, and selecting trap locations that target the habits of the species being trapped (Conover 2002).

Body-gripping traps, primarily Conibears® (Fig. 13E), are used in water sets for beaver, muskrat, and nutria. Manufactured in a variety of sizes, they have the humane feature of killing quickly. These traps have a pair of opposing, heavy-gauge rectangular rods that close like scissors when triggered, killing the animal with a quick body blow. Conibear® traps are lightweight and easy to use. They can be placed at entrances of burrows and lodges and in dams, runs, and slides. Care should be taken when large Conibear® traps are used due to the potential hazard to pets, children, and nontarget species. Some states prohibit the use of dry-land sets.

Somewhat similar body-gripping traps are available for moles and pocket gophers. For moles, the trap is placed over a section of the burrow that has been intentionally collapsed or compressed by the broad trap pan. The trap is activated when the mole traveling the runway pushes up on the compressed roof, trips the trigger pan, and is caught by the loops or scissor action of the jaws. The harpoon trap is set in a similar fashion, but a spring-loaded harpoon spears the mole. For gophers, traps are placed into the exposed laterals or main tunnels of the burrow system. The openings can then either be left exposed or covered.

Snap traps are most commonly used for controlling rats and mice, and are used regularly in houses and other buildings. Advantages to using snap traps include: reduced danger to children or pets compared to some chemicals, easy recovery of killed animals, and no contaminants. Obstacles such as boxes or boards can be used to direct rodents to traps. Preferred baits include a mix of peanut butter and rolled oats, a small piece of bacon or apple, or a raisin. Snap traps can be used outdoors to capture small field rodents when only a few animals are involved or to capture animals for identification or population ecology studies.

Snares

Beaver can be captured as effectively with snares as with Conibear® or foothold traps (Weaver et al. 1985). Snares cost and weigh less than traps. Depending on whether the snare has a stop lock device to restrict tightening, the behavior of the captured animal and the length of time it's been held, as well as the part of the anatomy that is being held, the animal may or may not die before it can be found and released. Snares are also effective in controlling small populations of rabbits. Animals must be traveling a well defined trail or using a specific entrance such as a hole in a fence. Snares are made of a loop of lightweight wire or cable incorporating a locking device to prevent the animal from backing off the tension in the cable. Snares can be set to kill the captured animal or to hold it by the leg or neck. Research is being conducted to make snares more species selective. State wildlife regulations should be checked to ascertain legality of usage.

Shooting

Shooting can be a selective method of eliminating individual pest mammals. Small-bore shotguns, rifles, and air guns are effective firearms. Some animals can be shot most effectively at night by using a spotlight with a red lens or night-vision equipment. Shooting is especially useful in controlling animals with low reproductive rates, such as porcupines. Local wildlife codes must be reviewed before shooting is used. Shooting at night, in particular with a spotlight, is not legal in some states.

CARNIVORES AND OTHER MAMMALIAN PREDATORS
Damage Assessment

Depredations of livestock by mammalian predators have been a concern to livestock producers for many centuries and continue to be an economic burden to some individuals. In the United States, 273,000 sheep and lambs were estimated to have been lost to predators in 1999 (U.S. Department of Agriculture 2000). Losses to predators represented 36.7% of total losses to all causes and were valued at $16.5 million to farmers and ranchers. The loss of goats to all predators was valued at $3.4 million. In 1999, depredations of sheep and lambs were principally caused by coyotes (60.7%), dogs (15.1%), mountain lions (*Puma concolor*) [5.7%], and bobcats (*Lynx rufus*) [4.7%]. Cattle and calf losses to predators in the United States totaled

147,000 head during 2000 with an estimated value of $51.6 million (U.S. Department of Agriculture 2001). Coyotes caused 64.6% of the losses to cattle and calves, followed by dogs (17.7%), and felids (mountain lions and bobcats) (7.5%). Losses of poultry to predators, although not well documented, are also believed to be substantial.

Predation by coyotes, wolves (*Canis lupus*), bears (*Ursus americanus* and *U. arctos*), and mountain lions can be a significant mortality factor for many ungulate species, mainly white-tailed deer, mule deer, black-tailed deer (*O. h. columbianus* and *O. h. sitkensis*), moose, caribou (*Rangifer tarandus*), and elk (Ballard et al. 2001). Predation on neonatal ungulates with losses exceeding 50% of the fawn cohort is commonly documented, especially in areas with coyotes (Barrett 1984, Hamlin et al. 1984, Whittaker and Lindzey 1999). Whether predation is a significant factor regulating ungulate populations and whether predator control can enhance ungulate populations continues to be a matter of debate among the scientific community and remains controversial within the general public (Connolly 1978, Messier 1991, Sinclair 1991, Boutin 1992, Ballard et al. 2001).

Predation by mammalian predators (generally smaller carnivores, such as red foxes [*Vulpes vulpes*], skunks [genera *Conepatus*, *Mephitis*, and *Spilogale*], raccoons, and mink [*Mustela vison*]) can be a major source of mortality to waterfowl (Sovada et al. 2001), grouse (subfamily Tetraoninae) (Hewitt et al. 2001, Schroeder and Baydack 2001), ring-necked pheasant (*Phasianus colchicus*) (Riley and Schulz 2001), quail (subfamily Odontophorinae) (Rollins and Carroll 2001), Neotropical migrant songbirds (Heske et al. 2001), and vulnerable ground-nesting species such as sea turtles (Family Cheloniidae) (Ratnaswamy et al. 1997) and rare birds (e.g., ancient murrelets [*Synthliboramphus antiquus*]) (Hartman et al. 1997). Predation may affect nest success, juvenile survival, and adult survival. The red fox is possibly the most serious predator of waterfowl because it is capable of killing nesting hens as well as destroying eggs (Sargeant et al. 1984). Nest predation by raccoons and skunks can also impact nesting waterfowl, as well as threatened and endangered species.

Actually witnessing a predator killing a prey item is rare. Therefore, an accurate assessment of a predation event requires careful observational skills (O'Gara 1978a, Wade and Bowns 1984) (Fig. 14). O'Gara (1978a), Wade and Bowns (1984), and Acorn and Dorrance (1998) provide a thorough review of examination and identification of predators involved in depredation events. In general, upon arrival at a depredation site, personnel should approach the site carefully, and be sure not to trample tracks, feces, blood, vegetation, or other evidence that may assist in identifying the cause of death and the predator involved (if it is a predation event). Signs of predation and the possible predator involved should be searched for on the prey item and around the kill site. Extensive hemorrhaging usually is characteristic of predation. If predation is suspected, skinning the carcass (particularly around the neck, throat, and head) may provide clues to the predator involved by examination for subcutaneous hemorrhage, tissue damage, and the size, spacing, and location of tooth marks (O'Gara 1978a, Wade and Bowns 1984). Hemorrhaging occurs only if the skin and tissue damage occurred while the animal was still alive. Animals that die

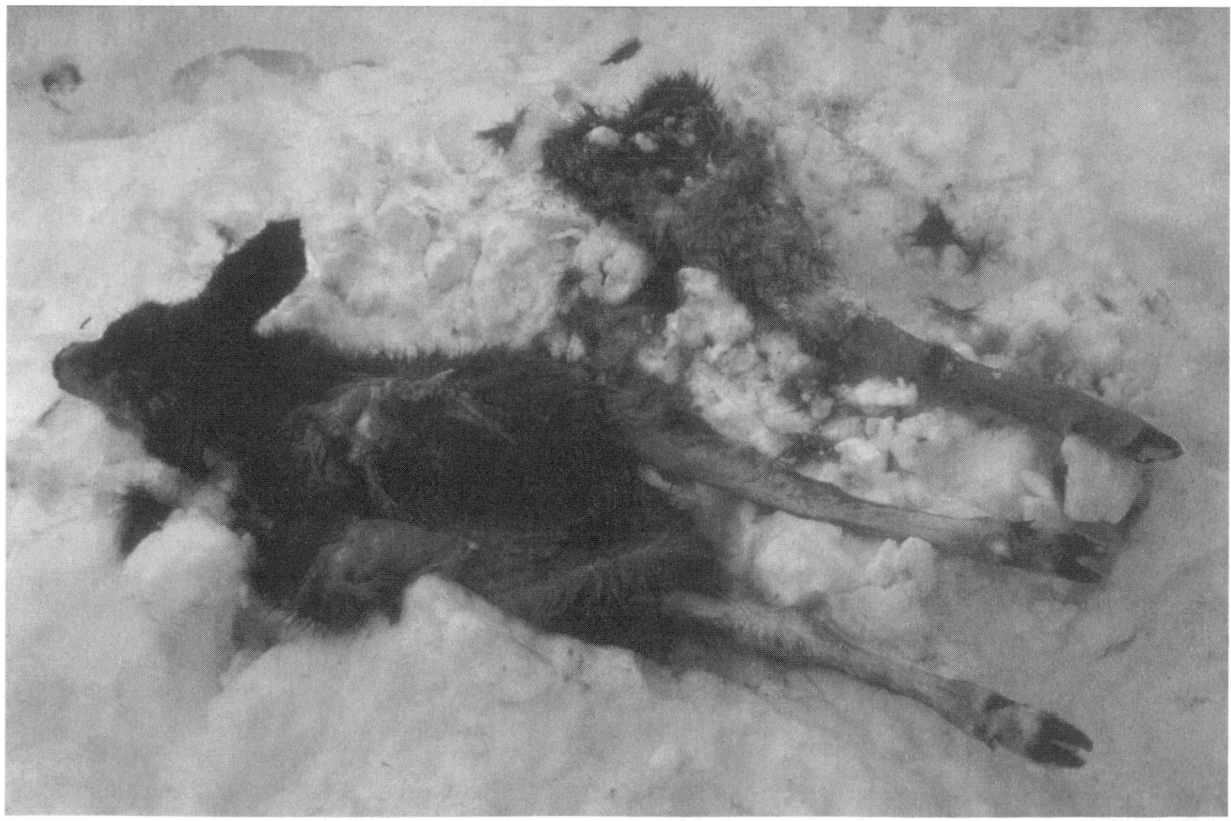

Fig. 14. Bobcat tracks surround a deer carcass with evidence that the bobcat fed. More investigation is required to ascertain if the bobcat killed the deer or scavenged it.

from causes other than predation normally do not show external or subcutaneous bleeding, although bloody fluids may be lost from body openings (O'Gara 1978a, Wade and Bowns 1984). The cause of death is best evaluated if the carcass is examined when fresh (Wade and Bowns 1984). Tracks and scats alone are not proof of depredation or of the species responsible, only that a particular predator is in the area. Other signs associated with a depredation event include nervous or alert livestock, injured livestock, or females calling or searching for young (Acorn and Dorrance 1998). Thus, all evidence must be considered to ascertain if the death was due to a predator and the predatory species responsible. Many predators will scavenge carcasses; hence, scavenging should not be confused with predation.

Species Damage Identification

Badgers

American badgers are opportunistic feeders, but prey mostly on mice, prairie dogs, marmots, pocket gophers, and ground squirrels, and occasionally on rabbits, especially young (Messick 1987, Lindzey 1994). Badgers destroy nests of ground-nesting birds and occasionally kill small lambs and poultry. Their burrows in a field may slow harvesting or cause damage to machinery, and their digging can damage earthen dams or dikes (Dolbeer et al. 1994b, Lindzey 1994). Badger tracks are similar to those of coyotes but, on closer examination, badger tracks appear to be pigeon-toed and impressions from the long toenails are apparent under most conditions (Dolbeer et al. 1994b). Signs of digging near prey remains may be the best evidence of badger activity. Damage management techniques include fencing, frightening devices, traps (foothold), snares, and shooting.

Bears

Conflicts with black and brown bears occur when they prey on livestock, feed on field crops, destroy beehives, or become a general nuisance around campgrounds, cabins, landfills, and garbage dumps (Hygnstrom 1994, Jonkel 1994). Bears usually kill by biting the neck or by slapping the victim, leaving a characteristic mauled and mutilated carcass (O'Gara 1978a, Dolbeer et al. 1994b). The neck may be broken as well (Acorn and Dorrance 1998). Bears will trample the vegetation and often vomit or defecate near the carcass. Large prey items are usually opened ventrally and the heart and liver consumed (Bowns and Wade 1980); the udder of lactating females may be consumed. The intestines often are spread around the kill site, and the animal may be partially skinned where the carcass is fed upon (Dolbeer et al. 1994b). Smaller livestock such as sheep and goats may be consumed almost entirely, with only the rumen, skin, and large bones remaining (Acorn and Dorrance 1998). Bears use their feet while feeding and do not slide the prey around as do coyotes (O'Gara 1978a). However, if the prey is brought down in the open, the carcass may be dragged to a more secluded spot before or after initial consumption (Acorn and Dorrance 1998).

Brown bears have a feeding and killing pattern similar to that of black bears (Jonkel 1994), but they usually cover their prey after the initial feeding, whereas black bears rarely cover the prey item (Acorn and Dorrance 1998). Cattle are usually killed by a bite through the back of the neck and large prey often has claw marks on the flanks or hams (Dolbeer et al. 1994b). The back of an ungulate is often broken in front of the hips where the bear pushes the animal down. Young calves are sometimes bitten through the forehead. Sheep may readily stampede at the onset of a bear attack and injure or kill themselves by tripping on downed timber or running over cliffs (Jonkel 1994). Jonkel (1994:20) states, "most bear depredations are easily identified, especially if there is wet or soft ground in the area. Bears are not sneaky—they march right in and take what they consider is theirs."

Black bears can cause significant damage to trees, especially in second-growth forests (Noble and Meslow 1998, Partridge et al. 2001). Damage can be recognized by the large, vertical incisor and claw marks on the sapwood and ragged strips of hanging bark, or branches broken to feed on fruit (Dolbeer et al. 1994b, Hyngstrom 1994). Most bark damage occurs from May to July (Packham 1970). Damage to field crops can also be substantial, with corn and oats being preferred crops (Hygnstrom 1994). Damage management techniques include supplemental feeding, aversive conditioning, fencing, frightening devices, repellents, traps (foothold and live traps), foot snares, and hunting with dogs.

Coyotes, Wolves, and Dogs

These canids prey on animals ranging in size from big game and livestock to rodents, native birds, and poultry (Carbyn 1987, Voigt and Berg 1987). Coyotes are the most common and most serious predator of livestock in the western United States (U.S. Department of Agriculture 2000, 2001) and are becoming more of a problem throughout the eastern United States. Coyotes normally kill livestock with bites to the neck and throat, but may pull the animal down by attacking the side and hindquarters (O'Gara 1978a, Wade and Bowns 1984, Green et al. 1994, Acorn and Dorrance 1998). The rumen and intestines are not eaten, but often removed and dragged away from the carcass. When canids kill small lambs, their upper canine teeth can penetrate the top of the neck or the skull (Wade and Bowns 1984). Calf predation by coyotes is most common when calves are young. Calves attacked, but not killed, exhibit wounds to the flank, hindquarter, or front shoulder (Wade and Bowns 1984). Deer that are killed are completely dismembered and eaten (Dolbeer et al. 1994b). With increased urbanization, complaints of pets being killed by coyotes have increased and attacks on humans (mainly children) are an increasing concern in urban areas (e.g., Howell 1982, Baker and Timm 1998). Agricultural producers using drip irrigation systems report that coyotes chew holes in plastic pipe and disrupt irrigation (Werner et al. 1997). Fruit crops, particularly watermelons, can also be consumed or damaged by coyotes (Green et al. 1994).

Wolves prey mainly on larger ungulates such as deer, caribou, moose, elk, and cattle. Cattle, especially calves, are most vulnerable to wolf predation (Paul and Gipson 1994, Acorn and Dorrance 1998). However, predation on livestock is rare (Fritts et al. 1992). Wolves usually kill ungulates by attacking the hindquarters or by seizing the flanks (Paul and Gipson 1994). Slash marks made by the canine teeth may be found on the rear legs and flanks (Dolbeer et al. 1994b). When the victim is badly wounded and collapses, wolves will often disembowel the animal (Paul and Gipson 1994). Wolves usually eat the viscera and hindquarters first. Most of the carcass is consumed and large bones may be chewed or cracked open (Acorn and Dorrance 1998). Wolves may carry parts of the carcass to dens or rendezvous sites for pups to consume.

Domestic dogs can be a serious problem to livestock, especially to sheep pastured near cities and suburbs (Green and Gipson 1994). Dogs may be indiscriminate as to how and where they attack, but often attack the hindquarters, flanks, and head, and rarely kill as effectively as coyotes (Dolbeer et al. 1994*b*, Green and Gipson 1994). O'Gara (1978*a*) considered dogs to be "sloppy" killers, often slashing and tearing victims and leaving many cripples (Acorn and Dorrance 1998). If dogs eat sheep or big game, they normally eat the hams and often vomit near the site (O'Gara 1978*a*). Normally little flesh is consumed (Green and Gipson 1994, Acorn and Dorrance 1998). Dogs generally wound the animal in the neck and front shoulders; the ears often are badly torn (Dolbeer et al. 1994*b*). Attacking dogs often severely mutilate the prey (Acorn and Dorrance 1998); skinning the animal will often reveal 80% of the body bruised by bites that did not penetrate the skin (O'Gara 1978*a*).

Coyote and dog tracks are similar but distinguishable (Dolbeer et al. 1994*b*). The larger size of wolf tracks often separates them from coyotes and dogs. Coyote tracks are more oval in shape and compact than dogs (Green et al. 1994, Acorn and Dorrance 1998). Dog tracks are round with the toes spread apart and toenail marks usually are visible on all toes (Dorsett 1987). Coyote tracks tend to follow a straight line more closely than dogs (Green et al. 1994). Damage management techniques include good livestock husbandry practices, livestock protection collars, guard animals (dogs, llamas, and donkeys), electronic training collars, fencing, frightening devices, reproductive interference, M-44s, aerial hunting, calling and shooting, denning, traps (foothold), and snares.

Felids

Felids that cause damage are primarily mountain lions, bobcats, and Canada lynx (*Lynx canadensis*). Mountain lions are almost exclusively carnivorous and prey on native ungulates, mainly deer and elk, and domestic stock, particularly horses, sheep, goats, and cattle (Lindzey 1987). They will also eat rodents and other small mammals when available (Dolbeer et al. 1994*b*). Livestock depredations are often random and unpredictable; it is not uncommon for several animals to be killed in a short period of time (Knight 1994*a*). A lion killing 5–10 sheep in a single night has been documented (Shaw 1983).

Lions typically kill sheep, goats, calves, and deer with bites to the top of the neck or head (Knight 1994*a*, Acorn and Dorrance 1998). Lions may also sever the vertebral column and break the neck of its prey. Lions kill in a similar manner as bobcats, but the tooth punctures of a lion kill will be larger (0.63–0.79 cm) and more round than bobcat punctures (O'Gara 1978*a*). Strips of skin will also be present at the kill site from the lacerations caused by the lion's claws. Lions usually feed first upon the shoulders of their prey (O'Gara 1978*a*). The stomach generally is untouched (Acorn and Dorrance 1998). The large leg bones of prey may be crushed and ribs may be broken (Dolbeer et al.

1994*b*). Often a lion will cover its kill with soil, leaves, grass, and other debris (Knight 1994*a*) and may return to feed on a kill for 3–4 nights. They normally uncover the kill at each feeding and move it 10–25 m before covering the carcass again. After the last feeding the remains may be left uncovered (Shaw 1983).

Lion tracks may be difficult to observe except in snow or sandy or wet soil. Adult lion tracks are approximately 10 cm across and have a distinguishable 3-lobed heel pad (Knight 1994*a*). Lions have retractable claws; therefore, no claw marks will be evident. Large dog tracks could be confused with lion tracks. However, dog tracks normally show distinctive claw marks, are less round than lion tracks, and have different heel pad marks (Dolbeer et al. 1994*b*).

Bobcats are opportunistic predators, feeding mainly on rabbits, rodents, and birds (Rolley 1987). Occasionally they will kill and consume poultry, sheep, goats, small dogs, house cats, and, rarely, calves (Virchow and Hogeland 1994). Bobcats usually kill their prey by biting the back of the neck or base of the skull (O'Gara 1978*a*). Bobcats often may be carried a short distance by an adult deer before the cat can complete the kill. Prey usually die of suffocation and shock, or from dislocated neck vertebrae. Hair and strips of hide may be found at the site where the cat first attacked. Scratches are usually evident on the shoulders, back, or sides of the prey (Virchow and Hogeland 1994). Bobcats often attack and kill lambs by holding the animal with its claws while biting the neck or head. Skulls may be fractured, but not crushed like those bitten by coyotes (O'Gara 1978*a*). The hindquarters of deer or sheep usually are eaten first by bobcats, although the shoulder, neck, or flank also may be consumed first (Dolbeer et al. 1994*b*). The rumen is often untouched. Carcasses are usually covered before being left and may be buried under leaves, snow, or soil, or the remains may be carried and cached under shrubs (O'Gara 1978*a*, Virchow and Hogeland 1994). Bobcats reach out 30–35 cm when covering their kill, whereas mountain lions reach out to 90 cm (Young 1958). Poultry usually are killed by biting the head and neck (Young 1958); the heads usually are eaten. Tooth punctures from a bobcat are similar to those of a coyote, but tend to slash more than those of canids (O'Gara 1978*a*). The distance between the canine teeth marks will also help distinguish a mountain lion kill from a bobcat kill: 3.8 cm versus 1.9–2.5 cm, respectively (Wade and Bowns 1984). Lynx rarely kill livestock and are mainly a specialist on snowshoe hares (*Lepus americanus*) (Quinn and Parker 1987). Bobcat and lynx feces are similar in size and shape. In areas inhabited by both species, careful examination of the tracks will help identify the species responsible for a depredation event. The lynx has larger feet with much more hair, and the toes tend to spread more than those of bobcats (Dolbeer et al. 1994*b*). Small Neotropical felids in the United States, such as the ocelot (*Felis pardalis*), margay (*F. wiedii*), and jaguarundi (*Herpailurus yagouaroundi*), pose little threat to livestock, but may occasionally kill a chicken. They mostly consume native birds, small mammals, and reptiles (Tewes and Schmidly 1987). Damage management techniques include fencing, frightening devices, traps (foothold), snares, and hunting (by calling and shooting, and with dogs).

Foxes

Gray (*Urocyon cinereoargenteus*) and red foxes feed primarily on rabbits, hares, small rodents, poultry, birds, fruit, and insects (Voigt 1987). Although poultry is the most common domestic prey, red foxes (and to a lesser extent gray foxes) may prey on livestock, mainly lambs and kids (Phillips and Schmidt 1994). Predation of poultry by swift (*V. velox*) and kit (*V. macrotis*) foxes is almost nonexistent (O'Farrell 1987, Scott-Brown et al. 1987). Arctic foxes (*Alopex lagopus*) in Iceland may prey on livestock (Garrott and Eberhardt 1987). Foxes usually attack the throat of lambs and kids, but kill some prey by multiple bites to the neck and back (Wade and Bowns 1984, Dolbeer et al. 1994*b*). Foxes do not have the body or jaw power of larger canids; thus, they are unable to seize and immobilize large prey and multiple bites may be evident (Wade and Bowns 1984). Foxes generally eat the viscera first and may begin feeding through the ribs (Wade and Bowns 1984). Foxes killing fowl usually leave behind only a few drops of blood and feathers and carry the prey from the kill location (Phillips and Schmidt 1994). Eggs usually are opened enough to allow the contents to be licked out and are often left beside the nest (Dolbeer et al. 1994*b*).

When attempting to identify the predator of a depredated animal, note the canine teeth are smaller and the spacing is narrower in foxes compared to coyotes (Wade and Bowns 1984). Red fox tracks may resemble coyote tracks, but fox tracks are generally smaller than coyote tracks and have a shorter stride. Gray fox tracks are slightly smaller than those of red foxes. Damage management techniques include guard dogs, fencing, frightening devices, M-44s, aerial hunting, traps (foothold), snares, calling and shooting, and hunting dogs.

Opossums

Virginia opossums (*Didelphis virginiana*) are primarily insectivorous and omnivorous and prefer eating fish, crustaceans, insects, mushrooms, fruits, vegetables, eggs, and carrion (Seidensticker et al. 1987). Opossums will occasionally raid poultry houses and generally kill one chicken at a time, often mauling the victim (Dolbeer et al. 1994*b*). Eggs will be mashed and messy; the shells often are chewed into small pieces and left in the nest (Dolbeer et al. 1994*b*). Young poultry or game birds are consumed entirely. Opossums in urban areas may be a nuisance where they get into garbage cans, compost piles, bird feeders, and pet food (Jackson 1994*a*). Damage management techniques include fencing, traps (foothold and live traps), shooting, and hunting dogs.

Raccoons

Raccoons are one of the most omnivorous predators, eating mice, small birds, snakes, frogs, insects, crawfish, grass, berries, acorns, corn, melons, turtle eggs, and a variety of grain crops (Sanderson 1987). They are notorious for raiding fields of sweet corn and tearing ears off the plants. In watermelon fields, raccoons will dig into the melon and scoop out the contents with their front paws (Boggess 1994). In urban areas, raccoons readily raid garbage cans and dumps. They can cause damage to houses and buildings when trying to gain access to attics and chimneys. Agricultural fields and gardens near wooded areas may experience severe damage from raccoons (Dolbeer et al. 1994*b*). Raccoons may prey on eggs and young of ground- and cavity-nesting birds, or raid artificial nesting structures (Boggess 1994). Predation by raccoons on nests of sea turtles (Ratnaswamy et al. 1997), ancient murrelets (Hartman et al. 1997), and other threatened and endangered species is a growing concern for conservation efforts.

Raccoons rarely kill small lambs. When they do, they usually grab their prey with their paws and bite the neck (O'Gara 1978*a*). Similar to the bites of a fox, bites from a raccoon attack usually encircle the whole neck (O'Gara 1978*a*). Skinning the carcass will reveal bruises where the prey was grabbed, but not deep scratches like bobcats. Raccoons often feed on a carcass at the loins or by making a small hole in the side of the carcass and pulling the viscera from the body cavity to consume it (O'Gara 1978*a*).

Raccoons occasionally raid poultry houses and may kill many birds in a night (Dolbeer et al. 1994*b*). The heads of adult birds are usually bitten off and left (Boggess 1994). The breast and crop may be torn and chewed, and the entrails may be consumed (Boggess 1994). Young birds in pens or cages may be killed or injured when the raccoon grabs a bird through the wire mesh and tries to pull it from the cage. Eggs may be removed and eaten away from the nest, or consumed on the spot with only shell fragments remaining.

Raccoons leave a distinctive 5-toed track resembling a small human hand print (Boggess 1994). Tracks usually are paired, and the left hind foot is placed beside the right forefoot. Raccoon and opossum tracks can be difficult to distinguish in soft sand where toe prints are not distinctive. Damage management techniques include fencing, traps (foothold and live traps), shooting, and hunting dogs.

Skunks

Skunks are opportunistic omnivorous predators consuming insects (particularly grasshoppers, beetles, and crickets), bird eggs, mice, and occasionally rats and cottontail rabbits (Rosatte 1987, Knight 1994*b*). Skunks become a nuisance when they dig small (7–10 cm), cone-shaped holes, or turn over patches of earth in lawns, gardens, and golf courses in search of insect grubs (Dolbeer et al. 1994*b*). They may burrow under porches and buildings. Their odor is a common complaint when they take up residence under human dwellings. Skunks may damage beehives when attempting to eat the bees.

Skunks are major predators of waterfowl nests. Nonlethal techniques to reduce skunk predation on waterfowl nests have had limited success (Greenwood and Sovada 1996, Greenwood et al. 1998). Skunks occasionally kill domestic poultry and eat eggs, but usually will not climb fences to raid poultry houses (Knight 1994*b*). When skunks kill poultry, they generally kill only 1–2 birds and often maul them (Dolbeer et al. 1994*b*). Eggs usually are opened at one end with the edges crushed inward as the skunk punches its nose into the hole to lick out the contents (Knight 1994*b*). When in a more advanced stage of incubation, eggs are likely to be chewed in small pieces. Eggs may be removed from the nest, but are rarely moved far (Dolbeer et al. 1994*b*).

Inhabited dens can be recognized by fresh droppings containing undigested insect parts near the mound or hole

(Dolbeer et al. 1994*b*). Dens usually have a characteristic skunk odor, although the odor may not be strong. Tracks are relatively distinctive with both front and rear feet having 5 toes with claw marks often visible (Knight 1994*b*). The heel of the fore feet may not be visible and in some cases the fifth toe may not be obvious (Knight 1994*b*). Damage management techniques for skunks include fencing, repellents and fumigants, traps (foothold and live traps), and shooting.

Weasels and Mink

Weasels (*Mustela erminea, M. frenata, M. nivalis*) feed primarily on insects and small rodents, and occasionally prey on birds, fish, amphibians, reptiles, eggs of ground-nesting birds, and berries (Fagerstone 1987). Mink are generalists and feed on a variety of mammalian prey, mainly small rodents, muskrats, and lagomorphs. Mink will also prey upon fish, birds, and invertebrates (Eagle and Whitman 1987). Weasels and mink have a similar killing pattern in which they bite the prey item through the skull and upper neck. When feeding on muskrats, mink will often make an opening at the back or side of the neck. As the mink consumes the flesh, ribs, and pieces of the adjacent hide, the head and hindquarters are pulled through the same hole, skinning the animal (Dolbeer et al. 1994*b*). McCracken and Van Cleve (1947) noted a similar feeding pattern by weasels when consuming small rodents.

Weasels and mink will raid poultry houses at night and kill or injure domestic fowl (Henderson 1994*b*). They often kill many birds by biting them in the head and often eat only the heads of the victims, but will consume the body as well. Rat predation usually differs from weasel predation in that portions of the chicken are eaten and carcasses are dragged into holes or concealed places (Henderson 1994*b*). Waterfowl eggs destroyed by weasels tend to be broken at the ends with openings 15–20 mm in diameter (Teer 1964). Close examination of shell fragments will often disclose finely chewed edges and tiny tooth marks left by a weasel (Rearden 1951).

Weasels den in burrows in the ground, under rocks or brush piles, in barns, or in piles of stored hay (Dolbeer et al. 1994*b*). The den itself is an enlarged chamber (3.5–5.0 cm) lined with dry grass and the fur of previous kills (Fagerstone 1987). Mink may use cavities in roots of trees, rocks, brush piles, logjams, and beaver lodges (Eagle and Whitman 1987). Mink will also use abandoned burrows of other animals as den sites, especially those of muskrats. Damage management techniques include fencing and trapping (Conibear®, foothold, and live traps).

Feral Cats

Feral cats are house cats living in the wild, although even house cats can cause damage by killing native small mammals and songbirds. Feral cats are opportunistic predators that prey on songbirds, ducks, pheasants, rabbits, quail, rodents, insects, reptiles, amphibians, and fish (Fitzwater 1994). Similar to feral dogs, feral cats are often described as "sloppy" killers, with parts of their prey strewn about when feeding. Cats generally consume the meaty portions of large birds, leaving loose skin with feathers attached (Dolbeer et al. 1994*b*). Small birds generally are consumed and only the wings and scattered feathers remain. Cats usually leave tooth marks on every exposed bone of their prey. Nesting birds particularly are vulnerable to cat predation and cats can exact a heavy toll on bird populations (Churcher and Lawton 1987, Jurek 1994, Coleman et al. 1997). Unlike domestic house cats, feral cats often are extremely wary of humans. Damage management techniques include fencing, frightening devices (dogs), traps (foothold and live traps), snares, and shooting.

Control Techniques

Protecting livestock and poultry from predators is a complex endeavor, with each case requiring an assessment of the legal, social, economic, biological, and technical aspects with no one technique solving the problem in all circumstances (Knowlton et al. 1999). Successful resolution of conflicts with predators involves an analysis of the efficacy, selectivity, and efficiency of management scenarios. Control techniques may be considered either corrective (after a depredation event) or preventive (before the event). Selectivity of the technique is extremely important when attempting to actually solve the depredation problem. General population reduction may not solve the depredation problem (e.g., Conner 1995), but techniques (e.g., livestock protection collars, calling and shooting) that selectively remove the offending individual (Sacks et al. 1999*a,b*; Blejwas et al. 2002) are preferred over nonselective techniques (e.g., traps or snares) that the predators may avoid (Sacks et al. 1999*a*). Identifying the "problem" animal can be difficult (Linnell et al. 1999). Methods that are more benign in their effects on other species are preferred to those creating greater perturbations (Knowlton et al. 1999).

A diverse array of techniques (nonlethal and lethal) has been used to prevent or deter depredations on livestock and poultry (Fall 1990, Green et al. 1994, Knowlton et al. 1999). Regrettably, these techniques do not often carry over to protecting wildlife resources. Some techniques (e.g., fencing, lethal removal) developed for protection of domestic commodities may reduce depredations on natural resources (Ratnaswamy et al. 1997, Garrettson and Rohwer 2001), but are generally limited to small-scale applications. Most nonlethal procedures are within the operational purview of the agricultural producer. While there are reports of success with some methods, failures are common, few have been subjected to critical evaluation or testing, and none has proven a panacea (Knowlton et al. 1999).

Livestock Husbandry Practices

Numerous livestock management practices have been suggested as a means of reducing depredation losses (Robel et al. 1981, Wagner 1988, Acorn and Dorrance 1998). Some of the most common practices include: (1) confining or concentrating flocks during periods of vulnerability (e.g., at night or during lambing), (2) using herders, (3) shed lambing, (4) removing livestock carrion from pastures, (5) synchronizing birthing, and (6) keeping young animals in areas with little cover and in proximity to human activity (Knowlton et al. 1999). These procedures generally require additional resources and effort, and frequently only delay onset of predation, or may have undesirable side effects (Knowlton et al. 1999). For these methods to be effective, producers must develop strategies for their own situations. Producers must also realize that economic advantages of modifying their husbandry practices may be difficult to demonstrate (Knowlton et al. 1999), but can assist in herd management and production. Surveys indicate that producers use herding (11%), night penning (47%), and shed lambing (51%) in their livestock management operations (U.S. Department of Agriculture 2000).

Guard Dogs

Use of guard dogs to deter coyotes from livestock has been a traditional method of damage control used by many sheep producers, particularly in fenced pastures (Acorn and Dorrance 1998) (Fig. 15). In several western states, about 32% of producers surveyed used guard dogs to protect their flocks (U.S. Department of Agriculture 2000). In Colorado, Andelt (1992) reported that 11 sheep producers estimated their guard dogs saved an average of $3,216 of sheep annually and reduced their need for other predator control techniques. Dog breeds most commonly used as livestock guardians include Great Pyrenees, Komondor, Akbash, Anatolian, and Maremma. While there does not appear to be one breed of dog that is most effective, livestock producers rated the Akbash breed as most effective at deterring predation because it is more aggressive, active, intelligent, and faster (Andelt 1999). The Great Pyrenees is the most common guard dog breed in Alberta (Acorn and Dorrance 1998). Studies investigating efficacy of guard dogs have shown the dogs to be effective in some situations and ineffective in others (Linhart et al. 1979, Coppinger et al. 1983, Green et al. 1984, Green and Woodruff 1987, Conner 1995, Andelt and Hopper 2000).

This disparity may be due to inherent difficulty of guard dogs to effectively protect large flocks dispersed over rough terrain and in areas where thick cover conceals approaching predators. Training and close supervision of the dogs seem to be important steps contributing to the success of this technique (Acorn and Dorrance 1998). Some poorly trained or minimally supervised guard dogs have killed sheep and lambs, harassed or killed wildlife, and threatened people that intrude upon their territory. However, not all guard dog failures or undesired behaviors stem from poor training or supervision. There is considerable behavioral diversity within even a particular litter of guard dog pups; some turn into valuable and effective guard animals, while others do not, despite similar training and effort. Use of guard dogs precludes use of other control devices (e.g., traps, snares, M-44's) and techniques (e.g., calling and shooting) (Knowlton et al. 1999). Dogs can be killed or injured by poisons, snares, and traps used for predator control (Acorn and Dorrance 1998).

Guard Llamas

Use of llamas for protecting livestock from predators takes advantage of their evolution with predators and defensive capabilities. Using llamas as guard animals is growing in popularity (Markham et al. 1993) with about 22% of western producers surveyed using them (U.S. Department of Agriculture 2000). Studies have found llamas to be a practical and effective tool to deter predators, mainly coyotes and dogs, from depredating livestock (Franklin and Powell 1994, Meadows and Knowlton 2000). Llamas can be kept in fenced pastures with sheep

Fig. 15. A Great Pyrenees guard dog protecting sheep.

or goats, do not require any special feeding program, are relatively easy to handle, and live longer than guard dogs (Knowlton et al. 1999). Although guard animals may not deter coyotes from habiting the immediate area of livestock, they may change the behavior and activity patterns of predators when in those areas (Knowlton et al. 1999). Traits that may be useful in selecting a llama for use as a livestock guardian include leadership, alertness, and body weight (Cavalcanti and Knowlton 1998).

Guard Donkeys

Donkeys have also been used as livestock guardians (Green 1989, Acorn and Dorrance 1998), with about 6% of producers in the western United States using donkeys as a management tool (U.S. Department of Agriculture 2000). The protective behavior of donkeys apparently stems from their dislike of dogs. A donkey will bray, bare its teeth, chase, and try to kick and bite coyotes and dogs (Acorn and Dorrance 1998). Recommendations on selection of donkeys as livestock guardians include using only a jenny or gelded jack (intact jacks are too aggressive towards livestock), placing one donkey per flock or group and keeping other donkeys or horses away to prevent the guard donkey from bonding with any animal but those to be protected. Furthermore, donkeys should be introduced to the livestock about 4–6 weeks prior to the onset of anticipated predation events to properly bond with the group (Acorn and Dorrance 1998). Donkeys are most effective in small, fenced pastures.

Supplemental Feeding

Supplemental feeding as a nonlethal technique to divert a predatory species from a vulnerable commodity for a period of time has received some attention. Many predators will readily consume food provisioned by humans. Greenwood et al. (1998) found that while skunks and other predators responded to supplemental feeding, depredations on waterfowl nests remained unchanged. They concluded that food provisioning had limited value for managing depredations on waterfowl nests in the Prairie Pothole region of North America because the predator community was large and complex. In the Pacific Northwest, black bears damage coniferous trees by feeding on sapwood during spring (Noble and Meslow 1998, Partridge et al. 2001). Collins (1999) reported that damage to trees by black bears was highest in areas where bears did not receive supplemental feeding (i.e., pellet feeders). Supplemental feeding of bears reduced damage to the trees with apparently no long-lasting effect on bear condition or productivity (Partridge et al. 2001).

Fencing and Barriers

Livestock, poultry, crops, and waterfowl and sea turtle eggs may be protected from predators with a properly constructed and located barrier. About 36% of livestock producers surveyed reported they used fencing to reduce predator losses (U.S. Department of Agriculture 2000). Barriers may take the form of an exclosure, electric fence, nest screen, or even a moat (e.g., DeCalesta and Cropsey 1978, Linhart et al. 1982, Shelton 1984, Nass and Theade 1988, Melvin et al. 1992, Lokemoen and Woodward 1993, Ratnaswamy et al. 1997). Standard fencing will not keep most predators from entering gardens or poultry ranges because they learn to jump over or dig under such fences. Many large predators (coyotes, foxes) may be deterred or excluded by adding an electrified single-wire strand charged by a commercial fence charger along a wire mesh fence. The electrified wire should be placed 20 cm outside of the main fence line and 20 cm above the ground (Dolbeer et al. 1994*b*). A fence 1.5 m high with 9 to 12 alternating ground and charged wires spaced 10–15 cm apart is an effective barrier against coyotes (Gates et al. 1978, Acorn and Dorrance 1998). A woven-wire fence that is more versatile, longer lasting, and can be tightened more than conventional wire mesh can also be used (Acorn and Dorrance 1998).

Skunks may be deterred from entering a poultry area with a 0.9-m high wire mesh fence extending 0.6 m above ground and 0.3 m below the surface; a 15-cm length of the portion below ground should be bent outward at right angles and buried 15 cm deep (Dolbeer et al. 1994*b*). Mink and weasels may be excluded from barns or coops by covering all openings larger than 2.5 cm with metal or hardware cloth. Asiatic black bears (*Ursus thibetanus*) in Japan were successfully deterred from entering crop fields and apiaries with an electric fence (Huygens and Hayashi 1999). Installation costs usually preclude use of fences for protecting livestock in large pastures or under range conditions. For wildlife resources, fencing may be best suited to protecting waterfowl nests or high-value commodities in small areas (e.g., sea turtle nests, Ratnaswamy et al. 1997). If electric fencing is used, the behavior of the wildlife resource being protected should also be considered (Trottier et al. 1994) and modifications to the design may assist in protection efforts without deleterious impacts on the species being protected (Pietz and Krapu 1994).

Frightening Devices

Devices such as lights, distress calls, loud noises, scarecrows, plastic streamers, propane cannons, aluminum pie pans, and lanterns have been used to frighten predators (Acorn and Dorrance 1998). Most testing has focused on devices which periodically emit bursts of light or sound to deter coyotes from sheep in fenced pastures and open-range situations (Linhart 1984, Linhart et al. 1984, 1992), but the benefits are often short-lived (Bomford and O'Brien 1990, Koehler et al. 1990). All of these devices can provide temporary relief from damage or in deterring predators, but habituation is common (Acorn and Dorrance 1998). Changing the location of devices, the pattern of the stimuli, or combining several techniques can prolong the frightening effect (Linhart et al. 1992). Linhart (1984) reported that a combination of warbling-type sirens and strobe lights reduced coyote predation on lambs by 44%. These battery-operated devices were activated in the evening by a photocell set on a schedule of 10-second bursts at 7- to 13-minute intervals. Pfeifer and Goos (1982) found use of propane exploders delayed or prevented lamb losses to coyotes for a period of time. Similarly, VerCauteren et al. (2003*a*) reported no kills during the lambing period when flocks were bedded near predator-activated frightening devices. A recent development used to deter wolf predation is the Radio Activated Guard (RAG). The RAG is activated only when a radiocollared wolf is in the vicinity, preventing habituation of the animal to the lights and siren. The RAG has application only in areas with radio-marked animals, but can deter endangered predators from causing problems to livestock producers. In general, use of frightening devices is not widespread, with only about 6% of producers using frightening devices (U.S. Department of Agriculture 2000). The use of sirens and strobe lights at night near people is generally not acceptable (Knowlton et al. 1999).

Repellents and Aversive Conditioning

Presently, there are no commercially available repellents that effectively deter predation (Knowlton et al. 1999). A variety of noxious gustatory, olfactory, and irritating compounds have been tested with a few (e.g., thiabendazole, pulegone, cinnamaldehyde, allyl sulfide) reducing food consumption among predators (Hoover and Conover 1998, 2000; Ternent and Garshelis 1999). While quinine hydrochloride and capsaicin may discourage coyotes from chewing on irrigation hoses (Werner et al. 1997), there is little information demonstrating these repellents deter predation (Lehner 1987, Burns and Mason 1997). Polson (1983) used thiabendazole to condition black bears to avoid beehives. Ternent and Garshelis (1999) reported that black bears could be discouraged from consuming meals-ready-to-eat (MREs) on a military reservation by treating the MREs with thiabendazole. Skunks may be repelled from areas with ammonia-soaked cloths or moth balls (Knight 1994b).

Conditioned taste aversion, using lithium chloride, to reduce coyote predation on sheep has received much attention. Results of studies were mixed, with some reporting success (Gustavson et al. 1974, Ellins and Martin 1981, Gustavson et al. 1982, Forthman-Quick et al. 1985a,b), while others were either unable to replicate those findings or found lithium chloride to be ineffective in field situations (Conover et al. 1977, Burns 1980, Bourne and Dorrance 1982, Burns 1983, Burns and Connolly 1985). While lithium chloride reduces prey consumption, it apparently does not deter the act of predation. Ten years after extensive field trials using lithium chloride (Gustavson et al. 1982, Jelinski et al. 1983), a survey of the same sheep producers revealed that only one producer still used it (Conover and Kessler 1994). Available evidence suggests that conditioned taste aversions are either ineffective or unreliable for deterring predation (Knowlton et al. 1999), but may limit food consumption (Polson 1983, Ternent and Garshelis 1999). Predation on sea turtle nests by raccoons in Florida was unaffected using conditioned taste aversion (Ratnaswamy et al. 1997).

Aversive conditioning may be effective in "teaching" brown bears to fear and avoid humans. Jonkel (1994:22) relates, "problem bears were captured and brought into holding facilities where they were repeatedly confronted by humans and repelled by chemical sprays. The captive process, called 'bear school', lasts only 4–6 days." For valuable endangered species, such as subspecies of brown bear, the expense of such a method (about $6,000 per animal), may be necessary considering the alternative for problem bears is usually destruction of the animal (Jonkel 1994).

Electronic Training Collar

A relatively new device receiving attention as a nonlethal method to deter predation on livestock is an electronic training (shock) collar usually used for training domestic dogs (Andelt et al. 1999). Using captive coyotes, Andelt et al. (1999) reported the training sequence with the electronic collar stopped all attempted attacks on lambs, decreased the probability of an attempted attack, eliminated successive chases, and even caused avoidance of lambs. Application may be limited under field conditions because the predator must be captured and the training collar attached, but does suggest avenues of future research on response-contingent aversive stimuli that change the behavior of the predator during the attack phase of a predatory sequence (Andelt et al. 1999). Lending support to this concept, Nolte et al. (2003) used these collars on deer and successfully eliminated feeding in protected plots.

Reproductive Interference

An interest in influencing the reproductive rate of coyotes with chemical sterilants dating to the 1960s assumed that reduced reproduction would reduce population levels and that fewer coyotes would result in fewer depredations (Balser 1964, Knowlton et al. 1999). Trials with diethylstilbesterol indicated reproduction among coyotes could be curtailed (Balser 1964, Linhart et al. 1968), but timing was critical and the approach was impractical without effective delivery systems; given these limitations, research on this substance was eventually curtailed (Knowlton et al. 1999). Currently there is renewed interest in reproductive inhibition using immunocontraceptive agents (DeLiberto et al. 1998), mainly as a means of changing the predatory behavior of coyotes (Till and Knowlton 1983). Surgical sterilization (tubal ligation and vasectomy) of coyotes was effective in reducing predation rates on domestic lambs without affecting social behavior and territory maintenance (Bromley and Gese 2001a,b). Vasectomy of males has been proposed as a method of population control among wolves (Haight and Mech 1997). However, at present there are no substances available for predator fertility control that are species specific. Species specificity will have to be achieved through appropriately designed delivery systems.

Livestock Protection Collar

The livestock protection collar (LPC) is a collar with an attached rubber pouch or bladder filled with Compound 1080. The device is placed around the neck of lambs and kid goats (Acorn and Dorrance 1998). Compound 1080 is an acute toxicant formerly used as a predacide and rodenticide. Most predacide uses were cancelled in 1972 because of nontarget hazards, and rodenticide uses were canceled in 1990 because technical registrants did not submit adequate data in support of Compound 1080 to the EPA (Fagerstone and Schafer 1998). The LPC is designed to kill coyotes when they puncture the bladders during an attack on a lamb or kid. The major advantage of LPCs is they selectively remove the problem animal and frequently kill individual predators that have evaded other control techniques (Connolly 1980, Connolly and Burns 1990, Blejwas et al. 2002). The LPC comes in 2 sizes (large and small), with the larger LPC working effectively on larger lambs (Burns et al. 1996). The major disadvantages of LPCs are initial purchase costs and labor required for application and maintenance (collars must be adjusted as animals grow), incidental puncturing of the collar (by thorns, wire, or other snags), anticipating which lambs or kids are most likely to be attacked, and record keeping (accounting for the Compound 1080 in the collars) (Wade 1985, Acorn and Dorrance 1998, Knowlton et al. 1999).

M-44

The M-44 is a mechanical device that ejects sodium cyanide into the mouth of an animal after it pulls on the device (Connolly 1988, Acorn and Dorrance 1998). The unit consists of a case holder wrapped with cloth, fur, wool, or steel wool; a plastic capsule or case that holds the cyanide; and a 7-cm ejector unit (Dolbeer et al. 1994b). The M-44 case is loaded with 0.78 g of sodium cyanide and an additive to reduce caking. A spring-loaded plunger ejects the cyanide. When assembled, the components are encased in a tube driven into the ground. The cocked ejector with the case in the holder is screwed on top, placed into the tube, and baited with fetid meat, a lure, or tallow. When an animal is attracted to the bait and tries to pick up the baited case holder with its teeth, the cyanide is ejected into its mouth. Canids, skunks, raccoons, bears, and opossums sometimes are attracted to the bait used on M-44s; however, species specificity can be enhanced by proper site and lure selection (Acorn and Dorrance 1998). A study of coyotes in California found the M-44 was not a selective technique in targeting or removing the breeding animals involved in sheep depredations (Sacks et al. 1999a). The M-44 is registered and authorized by different agencies depending upon the country of use (e.g., Pest Control Products Act of Canada, U.S. Environmental Protection Agency) for control of coyotes, foxes, and feral dogs, and has numerous restrictions.

Aerial Hunting

Aerial hunting is a commonly used method for reducing predator numbers (e.g., Wagner and Conover 1999). Various kinds of fixed- and rotary-wing aircraft have been used in control programs for wolves, coyotes, bobcats, and foxes (Wade 1976). Hunting is most effective with snow cover because the target animals can be more readily observed and tracked. When the specific animal is found, the pilot approaches at approximately 20 m of altitude, preferably into the wind. The ground speed of the aircraft is around 60–85 km/h, but the airspeed should not approach the stall speed of the aircraft. A 12-gauge semi-automatic shotgun is the most common weapon used, with number 4 buckshot, BB, and number 2 shot preferred.

Several modifications have been made to fixed-wing airplanes to increase safety and effectiveness, including a larger propeller and drooped wingtips to provide added power, lift, stability, and maneuverability (Dolbeer et al. 1994b). Larger balloon-type tires have been added to provide clearance for the longer propeller and to better use primitive runways for landings. Rotary-wing aircraft (helicopters) are also used in predator control. The helicopter, with its ability to hover, can be more effective in rough, brushy terrain. Visibility and tracking ability are improved in models with a Plexiglas bubble cockpit.

Fixed-wing aircraft and helicopters can be used cooperatively. The helicopter is used for tracking and dispatching the animal, while the fixed-wing aircraft flies above the helicopter and maintains surveillance. This combination works well in areas with thick vegetation or where animals have been hunted heavily with helicopters. Aerial hunting can be more efficient if a ground crew works with the aircraft (Wade 1976). The ground crew induces coyotes to howl by using a horn, siren, voice, or recorded howl. When animals respond, the aircraft is directed to the area by 2-way radio communication. Early morning and late afternoon tend to be the most productive times for aerial hunting. Federal law requires each state where aerial hunting is allowed to issue aerial hunting permits. Some states also require low-level flying waivers.

Denning

Increased depredations of livestock (mainly sheep) and poultry during spring and summer by coyotes and foxes usually indicate that a pair of coyotes or foxes has a litter of pups nearby. During spring and summer, adults will increase their predation rates for provisioning pups (Till and Knowlton 1983). In a study in Wyoming, sheep losses to coyotes were greatly reduced after removal of only the pups, and were similar to reduction in predation rate when both pups and adults were removed (Till and Knowlton 1983). Direct removal by digging or use of a chemical smoke cartridge is often used to destroy the pups (Acorn and Dorrance 1998). An alternative to denning is surgical sterilization of adult breeding coyotes, which worked as effectively as denning, with a long-term (several year) efficacy but without the requirement of finding the den (Bromley and Gese 2001a,b).

Dens are usually located by tracking or observing the adults, or use of simulated howling to get the pups to respond. Den hunting is often based upon the assumption that adults that kill livestock will return to the den via the most direct route possible. An active den is evidenced by hairs around the entrance, fresh tracks, and, if the pups are large enough to have emerged from the den, matted and worn vegetation around the entrance and small scats. Dens may also have prey remains lying about the den area.

Den hunting is difficult and time-consuming, particularly on hard ground and in heavy cover (Acorn and Dorrance 1998). Some people use a dog to aid in locating the den. A call imitating a frightened or injured pup sometimes will bring adult coyotes within range near a den site. Caution should be taken while digging out dens because of the possibility of cave-ins and ectoparasites. These hazards can be eliminated if a gas cartridge is used to kill the pups in the den. At times an aircraft is used to locate coyote and fox dens. From the air, signs of an active den include cleaned-out holes and trampled vegetation.

Traps

Live traps of variable construction are available from several companies in a variety of sizes and configurations to capture small, medium, and even large predators such as bears. Problem bears can be caught in a live trap made from steel culverts equipped with a trap door and trigger device, and mounted on a trailer permitting personnel to easily relocate the bear (Dolbeer et al. 1994b). Generally, coyotes, foxes, and bobcats are difficult to live trap because of their cautious nature and reluctance to enter confined areas.

Canned dog or cat foods are effective baits to entice raccoons, opossums, skunks, and cats into live traps. As described by Dolbeer et al. (1994b), traps for skunks can be covered with a canvas or heavy cloth and provided with a flap for the door. When a skunk is captured, the trapper can approach the trap on the covered side and carefully drop the flap over the door, allowing the skunk to be transported to the release site. To release it, the trapper should stand beside the trap and ease the flap and door open; the door may need to be propped open to allow the animal to leave when it is ready.

Foothold or steel traps are manufactured in a variety of sizes (Fig. 13B, C, D, F). Modification of traps (e.g., padded jaws) and attachment of a trap tranquilizer device can greatly diminish injuries to the animal (Sahr and Knowlton 2000). Tension devices should also be considered to minimize captures of nontarget species (Phillips and Gruver 1996). Selectively removing the offending animal causing the depredations with a trap can be difficult (Sacks et al. 1999*a*). The following trap sizes are recommended:

- #0 and 1: weasels and ground squirrels;
- #1 and 1½: skunks, opossums, mink, feral cats, and muskrats;
- #2 and 3: foxes, raccoons, small feral dogs, nutria, marmots, and mountain beavers;
- #3 and 4: bobcats, coyotes, large feral dogs, badgers, and beavers;
- #4 and 4½: wolves; and
- #4½ and 114: mountain lions.

Success in trapping depends on placing the trap along travel ways, such as along dirt roads and trails. As described by Dolbeer et al. (1994*b*) a trap usually is set in the ground by digging a shallow trench the size of the trap and deep enough to allow the stake (or drag) and chain to be placed in the bottom of the hole and covered with soil. The trap is set firmly on top of the buried chain and should be about 11 mm below the soil surface. A piece of canvas, cloth, mesh screen, or a plastic sandwich bag is placed over the pan to prevent soil from getting beneath the pan and preventing its depression. The trap is then covered with soil and other material natural to the area in the vicinity of the trap. The trap can be set unbaited in a trail; this is called a "blind" or trail set. Traps also may be set off the trail and baited with a lure, bait, or natural substance, such as scat or urine (a dirt-hole set). The latter is effective for raccoons, foxes, and mink. The trap is set in the same manner as the blind set, but instead of placing the scent on the ground, the lure is placed in a small hole (about 15 cm deep) dug behind the trap. Lure selectivity for the target species is important. The location of a set also influences its selectivity. When placed beside a carcass, a trap can catch nontarget animals such as vultures (*Cathartes aura, Coragyps atratus*), eagles, badgers, and other nontarget predators. Many states no longer allow trapping in the vicinity of a carcass. Weather also can impact operation of traps, with frozen or wet ground preventing a trap from springing.

Foothold traps must be checked often to minimize time captured animals are restrained. Most states have regulations on types of traps, baits, sets, and trap visitation schedules. Some states no longer allow use of foothold traps; state and local regulations should be consulted prior to conducting any trapping activity.

Calling and Shooting

Calling and shooting can be a selective means to control coyotes, bobcats, and foxes. Calling and shooting, with or without help of lure dogs, can be a selective means of removing offending coyotes that kill livestock, particularly during denning and pup-rearing seasons (Coolahan 1990, Sacks et al. 1999*a*). Several commercial calls and recorded calls are available from a variety of manufacturers or outlets. The call is blown to imitate the sound of a rabbit in distress. This sound either arouses the predator's curiosity or indicates an easy meal. However, some predators become wise to calling. Conversely, the call may be an effective method to remove a trap-wise animal. Calls imitating a pup in distress can also attract the adults. Generally, 3 factors should be considered to successfully call in a predator: (1) ensure the caller is downwind from the area being called to prevent the predator from detecting the caller's scent before the animal comes into shooting range (2) within limits imposed by terrain and vegetation, acquire a full view of the area so the predator will be unable to approach unseen, and (3) avoid being seen by wearing camouflage clothing and hiding in vegetation (Acorn and Dorrance 1998). The most effective times to call predators are early morning and late afternoon. The hunter can gain an added advantage by locating an animal before beginning to call by inducing howls. Calling at night and using a spotlight (where legal) can also be effective.

Hunting Dogs

Two types of dogs can be used for lethal predator control. Dogs that hunt by sight, such as greyhounds, can be kept in a box or cage until the predator is seen, then released to catch and kill the animal. This type of dog is effective only in relatively open terrain. The other type of dog is the trail hound, which follows an animal by its scent. Trail hounds hunt on bare ground; however, snow or heavy dew makes trailing easier. Hot, dry weather makes trailing difficult; therefore, early morning is the most effective time to hunt with trail hounds. Several breeds, such as bluetick, black and tan, Walker, and redbone, in packs of 2–5 dogs are most commonly used. Trained trail hounds are used to catch and "tree" raccoons, opossums, bobcats, bears, and mountain lions. Often these dogs are able to track a depredating predator from a kill, making this control method highly selective. State and local regulations should be consulted prior to hunting with dogs.

Snares

Snares are made of varying lengths and sizes of wire or cable looped through a locking device that allows the snare to tighten. There are generally 2 types of snares: body and foot (Fig. 13A, G). As described by Dolbeer et al. (1994*b*), the body snare is used primarily on coyotes and foxes. This snare is set where an animal crawls under a fence, at a den entrance, or in some other narrow passageway. The snare is placed so that the animal must put its head through the noose as it passes through the restricted area. When the snare is felt around the neck, the animal normally will thrust forward and tighten the noose.

The spring-activated foot snare has been used to capture large predators (Bacus 1968, Logan et al. 1999). As described by Dolbeer et al. (1994*b*), when the animal steps on the trigger the spring is released, propelling the noose around the foot. The animal instinctively recoils, tightening the snare cable around the foot. The foot snare can be used in a bear pen or cubby set. A bear pen is just large enough to accommodate the bait, which usually is the carcass remains of an animal killed earlier by the predator. The pen can be built of brush or poles and has an open end where the snare is set. The pen and guide sticks force the bear to step into the snare while trying to reach the bait. Bears also can be caught with a foot snare in a trail set.

The foot snare also can be used to capture mountain lions (Logan et al. 1999). The snare should be set in a narrow trail known to be traveled by the target animal. Deer and livestock can be prevented from interfering with the snare with a pole or branch placed across the trail, directly over the set about 0.9 m above the ground.

Selectivity of the foot snare may be improved by placing sticks under the trigger that break only under the weight of heavier animals (Dolbeer et al. 1994b). Open-cell foam pads can be placed under trigger pans to prevent unintentional triggering of snares by small mammals (Logan et al. 1999). Foot snares have advantages over large bear traps in that they are lighter, easier to carry, and less dangerous to humans and nontarget animals.

SUMMARY

Wildlife damage management is one of the fastest growing segments of the wildlife profession. Wildlife damage can no longer be viewed as only an agricultural problem. As human and wildlife populations grow, the number of conflicts and their severity also increase. Continual human expansion into rural and remote areas and the ability of some wildlife species to continually adapt and thrive in proximity to human society assures that the number and magnitude of conflicts will keep increasing. Many wildlife conservation issues are related to wildlife damage, particularly the impact of some predators on certain threatened and endangered species (e.g., coyotes killing endangered kit foxes), or mediating the impact of an endangered species on a human resource (e.g., reintroduced wolves killing livestock). As observed by Conover (2002), when humans and wildlife conflict, both are losers. The goal of this chapter has been to examine the current state of wildlife damage management, addressing the main issues and means of mediating damage between wildlife and human interests. New issues will continually come to the forefront and additional means to manage them will be required. Research to add more tools to the wildlife damage management "toolbox" is required. Development and evaluation of socially acceptable, primarily nonlethal, means to reduce damage are needed, especially in the wake of the banning of traditional tools in some areas. The challenges facing wildlife damage management professionals are not only biological and ecological. Sociological changes in values related to wildlife damage management are occurring. Some suggest this is due to the public's ignorance and disconnect with the natural world, while others may view it as an ethical responsibility to care for the occupants of our natural world. Professionals in this field must continue to be as versed in human dimensions (social, political, legal, and economic) aspects of human–wildlife conflict as they are with the biological and ecological aspects. Thus, it is important that university curriculums offer classes on wildlife damage management, so that we properly prepare and educate future wildlife professionals to face the challenges they will experience.

ACKNOWLEDGMENTS

We thank M. J. Pipas, M. J. Lavelle, and S. M. Jojola for assisting with the preparation of this chapter. The comments of C. E. Braun, M. R. Conover, and an anonymous reviewer were much appreciated and served to improve the chapter. We thank the authors of the wildlife damage chapter in the previous edition of this volume (Dolbeer et al. 1994b); their work served as our template and, where applicable, its contents were incorporated. We also thank the many colleagues who captured the images used in the chapter. The USDA/APHIS/Wildlife Services/National Wildlife Research Center supported this effort.

LITERATURE CITED

ACORN, R. C., AND M. J. DORRANCE. 1998. Coyote predation on livestock. AGDEX 684–19. Alberta Agriculture, Food, and Rural Development, Edmonton, Canada.

AGÜERO, D. A., R. J. JOHNSON, AND K. M. ESKRIDGE. 1991. Monofilament lines repel house sparrows from feeding sites. Wildlife Society Bulletin 19:416–422.

ANDELT, W. F. 1992. Effectiveness of livestock guarding dogs for reducing predation on domestic sheep. Wildlife Society Bulletin 20:55–62.

———. 1999. Relative effectiveness of guarding-dog breeds to deter predation on domestic sheep in Colorado. Wildlife Society Bulletin 27:706–714.

———, AND S. N. HOPPER. 2000. Livestock guard dogs reduce predation on domestic sheep in Colorado. Journal of Range Management 53:259–267.

———, R. L. PHILLIPS, K. S. GRUVER, AND J. W. GUTHRIE. 1999. Coyote predation on domestic sheep deterred with electronic dog-training collar. Wildlife Society Bulletin 27:12–18.

BACUS, L. C. 1968. The bear foot snare. U.S. Department of the Interior, Fish and Wildlife Service, Field Training Aid 2.

BAKER, R. O., AND R. M. TIMM. 1998. Management of conflicts between urban coyotes and humans in southern California. Proceedings of the Vertebrate Pest Conference 18:299–312.

BALLARD, W. B., D. LUTZ, T. W. KEEGAN, L. H. CARPENTER, AND J. C. deVOS, JR. 2001. Deer-predator relationships: a review of recent North American studies with emphasis on mule and black-tailed deer. Wildlife Society Bulletin 29:99–115.

BALSER, D. S. 1964. Management of predator populations with antifertility agents. Journal of Wildlife Management 28:352–358.

BARRETT, M. W. 1984. Movements, habitat use, and predation on pronghorn fawns in Alberta. Journal of Wildlife Management 48:542–550.

BELANT, J. L. 1997. Gulls in urban environments: landscape level management to reduce conflict. Landscape Urban Planning 38:245–258.

———, AND S. K. ICKES. 1996. Overhead wires reduce roof-nesting by ring-billed gulls and herring gulls. Proceedings of the Vertebrate Pest Conference. 17:108–112.

———, AND ———. 1997. Mylar flags as gull deterrents. Proceedings of the Great Plains Wildlife Damage Control Workshop 13:73–80.

———, T. W. SEAMANS, AND L. A. TYSON. 1998a. Evaluation of electronic frightening devices as white-tailed deer deterrents. Proceedings of the Vertebrate Pest Conference 18:107–110.

———, L. A. TYSON, AND T. W. SEAMANS. 1999. Use of alpha-chloralose by the Wildlife Services program to capture nuisance birds. Wildlife Society Bulletin 27:938–942.

———, S. W. GABREY, R. A. DOLBEER, AND T. W. SEAMANS. 1995. Methyl anthranilate formulations repel gulls and mallards from water. Crop Protection 14:171–175.

———, T. W. SEAMANS, R. A. DOLBEER, AND P. P. WORONECKI. 1997.

Evaluation of methyl anthranilate as a woodpecker repellent. International Journal of Pest Management 43:59–62.

———, P. P. WORONECKI, R. A. DOLBEER, AND T. W. SEAMANS. 1998*b*. Ineffectiveness of five commercial deterrents for nesting starlings. Wildlife Society Bulletin 26:264–268.

BERINGER, J., K. C. VERCAUTEREN, AND J. J. MILSPAUGH. 2003. Evaluation of an animal-activated scarecrow and a monofilament fence for reducing deer use of soybean fields. Wildlife Society Bulletin 31:492–498.

———, L. P. HANSEN, R. A. HEINEN, AND N. F. GIESSMAN. 1994. Use of dogs to reduce damage by deer to a white pine plantation. Wildlife Society Bulletin 22:627–632.

BLACKWELL, B. F., G. E. BERNHARDT, AND R. A. DOLBEER. 2002. Lasers as nonlethal avian repellents. Journal of Wildlife Management 66:250–258.

BLEJWAS, K. M., B. N. SACKS, M. M. JAEGER, AND D. R. MCCULLOUGH. 2002. The effectiveness of selective removal of breeding coyotes in reducing sheep predation. Journal of Wildlife Management 66:451–462.

BLOKPOEL, H., AND G. D. TESSIER. 1984. Overhead wires and monofilament lines exclude ring-billed gulls from public places. Wildlife Society Bulletin 12:55–58.

BLOOM, P. H. 1987. Capture and handling raptors. Pages 99–123 *in* B. A. G. Pendleton, B. A. Millsap, K. W. Cline, and D. M. Bird, editors. Raptor management techniques manual. National Wildlife Federation, Washington, D.C., USA.

BOGGESS, E. K. 1994. Raccoons. Pages C101–C107 *in* S. E. Hygnstrom, R. M. Timm, and G. E. Larson, editors. Prevention and control of wildlife damage. University of Nebraska Cooperative Extension Service, Lincoln, USA.

BOLLENGIER, JR., R. M. 1994. Woodchucks. Pages B183–B187 *in* S. E. Hygnstrom, R. M. Timm, and G. E. Larson, editors. Prevention and control of wildlife damage. University of Nebraska Cooperative Extension Service, Lincoln, USA.

BOMFORD, M., AND P. H. O'BRIEN. 1990. Sonic deterrents in animal damage control: a review of device tests and effectiveness. Wildlife Society Bulletin 18:411–422.

BOUNDS, D., AND G. A. CAROWAN, JR. 2000. Nutria: a nonnative nemesis. Transactions of the North American Wildlife and Natural Resources Conference 65:405–413.

BOURNE, J., AND M. J. DORRANCE. 1982. A field test of lithium chloride aversion to reduce coyote predation on domestic sheep. Journal of Wildlife Management 46:235–239.

BOUTIN, S. 1992. Predation and moose population dynamics: critique. Journal of Wildlife Management 56:116–127.

BOWNS, J. E., AND D. A. WADE. 1980. Physical evidence of carnivore depredation. 35-mm slide series and script. Texas Agricultural Extension Service, College Station, USA.

BRIDGELAND, W. T., AND J. W. CASLICK. 1983. Relationships between cornfield characteristics and blackbird damage. Journal of Wildlife Management 47:824–829.

BROMLEY, C., AND E. M. GESE. 2001*a*. Effects of sterilization on territory fidelity and maintenance, pair bonds, and survival rates of free-ranging coyotes. Canadian Journal of Zoology 79:386–392.

———, AND ———. 2001*b*. Surgical sterilization as a method of reducing coyote predation on domestic sheep. Journal of Wildlife Management 65:510–519.

BURNS, R. J. 1980. Evaluation of conditioned predation aversion for controlling coyote predation. Journal of Wildlife Management 44:938–942.

———. 1983. Microencapsulated lithium chloride bait aversion did not stop coyote predation on sheep. Journal of Wildlife Management 47:1010–1017.

———, AND G. E. CONNOLLY. 1985. A comment on "coyote control and taste aversion". Appetite 6:276–281.

———, AND J. R. MASON. 1997. Effectiveness of Vichos non-lethal collars in deterring coyote attacks on sheep. Proceedings of the Vertebrate Pest Conference 17:204–206.

———, D. E. ZEMLICKA, AND P. J. SAVARIE. 1996. Effectiveness of large livestock protection collars against depredating coyotes. Wildlife Society Bulletin 24:123–127.

BYERS, R. E. 1976. Review of cultural and other control methods for reducing pine vole populations in apple orchards. Proceedings of the Vertebrate Pest Conference 7:242–243.

———. 1984. Economics of *Microtus* control in eastern U.S. orchards. Pages 297–302 *in* A. C. Dubock, editor. Organization and practice of vertebrate pest control. Imperial Chemical Industries PLC, Surrey, United Kingdom.

CAFFERATA, S. L. 1992. Mountain beaver. Pages 231–251 *in* H. C. Black, editor. Silvicultural approaches to animal damage management in Pacific Northwest forests. U.S. Department of Agriculture, Forest Service, General Technical Report PNW-GTR-287.

CARBYN, L. N. 1987. Gray wolf and red wolf. Pages 359–376 *in* M. Novak, J. A. Baker, M. E. Obbard, and B. Malloch, editors. Wild furbearer management and conservation in North America. Ontario Ministry of Natural Resources, Toronto, Canada.

CASE, R. M., AND B. A. JASCH. 1994. Pocket gophers. Pages B17–B29 *in* S. E. Hygnstrom, R. M. Timm, and G. E. Larson, editors. Prevention and control of wildlife damage. University of Nebraska Cooperative Extension Service, Lincoln, USA.

CAVALCANTI, S. M. C., AND F. F. KNOWLTON. 1998. Evaluation of physical and behavioral traits of llamas associated with aggressiveness toward sheep-threatening canids. Applied Animal Behaviour Science 61:143–158.

CHURCHER, P. B., AND J. H. LAWTON. 1987. Predation by domestic cats in an English village. Journal of Zoology 212:439–455.

CLARK, J. P. 1984. Vole control in field crops. Proceedings of the Vertebrate Pest Conference 11:5–6.

CLARK, L. 1998. Review of bird repellents. Proceedings of the Vertebrate Pest Conference 18:330–337.

CLARK, W. R., AND R. E. YOUNG. 1986. Crop damage by small mammals in no-till cornfields. Journal of Soil and Water Conservation 41:338–341.

CLEARY, E. C., AND R. A. DOLBEER. 1999. Wildlife hazard management at airports, a manual for airport personnel. U.S. Department of Transportation, Federal Aviation Administration, Office of Airport Safety and Standards, Washington, D.C., USA.

———, ———, AND S. E. WRIGHT. 2003. Wildlife strikes to civil aircraft in the United States, 1990–2002. U.S. Department of Transportation, Federal Aviation Administration Serial Report 9 DOT/FAA/AS/00–8(AAS-310). Washington, D.C., USA.

COLEMAN, J. S., S. A. TEMPLE, AND S. R. CRAVEN. 1997. Cats and wildlife: a conservation dilemma. University of Wisconsin Cooperative Extension Service, Madison, USA.

COLLINS, G. H. 1999. Behavioral ecology of black bear damage to conifer stands. Thesis. Washington State University, Pullman, USA.

CONNER, M. M. 1995. Identifying patterns of coyote predation on sheep on a northern California ranch. Thesis. University of California, Berkeley, USA.

CONNER, W. H., AND J. R. TOLIVER. 1987. The problem of planting Louisiana swamplands when nutria (*Myocastor copus*) are present. Proceedings of the Eastern Wildlife Damage Control Conference 3:42–49.

CONNOLLY, G. E. 1978. Predators and predator control. Pages 369–394 *in* J. L. Schmidt and D. L. Gilbert, editors. Big game of North America: ecology and management. Stackpole Books, Harrisburg, Pennsylvania, USA.

———. 1980. Use of compound 1080 in livestock neck collars to kill depredating coyotes: a report on field and laboratory research. U.S. Department of the Interior, Fish and Wildlife Service, Denver Wildlife Research Center, Colorado, USA.

———. 1988. M-44 sodium cyanide ejectors in the animal damage control program, 1976–1986. Proceedings of the Vertebrate Pest Conference 13:220–225.

———, AND R. J. BURNS. 1990. Efficacy of compound 1080 livestock protection collars for killing coyotes that attack sheep. Proceedings of the Vertebrate Pest Conference 14:269–276.

CONOVER, M. R. 1984. Comparative effectiveness of Avitrol, exploders, and hawk-kites in reducing blackbird damage to corn. Journal of Wildlife Management 48:109–116.

———. 1988. Effect of grazing by Canada geese on the winter growth of rye. Journal of Wildlife Management 52:76–80.

———. 2002. Resolving human-wildlife conflicts: the science of wildlife damage management. Lewis Publishers, Boca Raton, Florida, USA.

———, AND K. K. KESSLER. 1994. Diminished producer participation in an aversive conditioning program to reduce coyote depredation on sheep. Wildlife Society Bulletin 22:229–233.

———, J. G. FRANCIK, AND D. E. MILLER. 1977. An experimental evaluation of aversive conditioning for controlling coyote predation. Journal of Wildlife Management 41:775–779.

———, W. C. PITT, K. K. KESSLER, T. J. DuBOW, AND W. A. SANBORN. 1995. Review of human injuries, illnesses, and economic losses caused by wildlife in the United States. Wildlife Society Bulletin 23:407–414.

COOLAHAN, C. 1990. The use of dogs and calls to take coyotes around dens and resting areas. Proceedings of the Vertebrate Pest Conference 14:260–262.

COPPINGER, R., J. LORENZ, AND L. COPPINGER. 1983. Introducing livestock guarding dogs to sheep and goat producers. Proceedings of the Eastern Wildlife Damage Control Conference 1:129–132.

CORRIGAN, R. M. 1989. A guide to managing pigeons and house sparrows. Pest Control Technology 17:38–50.

———. 2001. Rodent control: a practical guide for pest management professionals. GIE Media, Cleveland, Ohio, USA.

CRAVEN, S. R. 1994. Cottontail rabbits. Pages D75–D80 in S. E. Hygnstrom, R. M. Timm, and G. E. Larson, editors. Prevention and control of wildlife damage. University of Nebraska Cooperative Extension Service, Lincoln, USA.

———, AND S. E. HYGNSTROM. 1994. Deer. Pages D25–D40 in S. E. Hygnstrom, R. M. Timm, and G. E. Larson, editors. Prevention and control of wildlife damage. University of Nebraska Cooperative Extension Service, Lincoln, USA.

CROUCH, G. L. 1976. Deer and reforestation in the Pacific Northwest. Proceedings of the Vertebrate Pest Conference 7:298–301.

———. 1986. Pocket gopher damage to conifers in western forests: a historical and current perspective on the problem and its control. Proceedings of the Vertebrate Pest Conference 12:196–198.

CUMMINGS, J. L., J. L. GUARINO, C. E. KNITTLE, AND W. C. ROYALL, JR. 1987. Decoy plantings for reducing blackbird damage to nearby commercial sunflower fields. Crop Protection 6:56–60.

DAVIDSON, W. R., AND V. F. NETTLES. 1997. Field manual of wildlife diseases in the southeastern United States. Second edition. Southeastern Cooperative Wildlife Disease Study, University of Georgia, Athens, USA.

DAVIS, D. E. 1976. Management of pine voles. Proceedings of the Vertebrate Pest Conference 7:270–275.

DeCALESTA, D. S. 1994. Effect of white-tailed deer on songbirds within managed forests in Pennsylvania. Journal of Wildlife Management 58:711–717.

———, AND M. G. CROPSEY. 1978. Field test of a coyote-proof fence. Wildlife Society Bulletin 6:256–259.

———, AND D. B. SCHWENDEMAN. 1978. Characteristics of deer damage to soybean plants. Wildlife Society Bulletin 6:250–253.

———, AND G. W. WITMER. 1994. Elk. Pages D41–D50 in S. E. Hygnstrom, R. M. Timm, and G. E. Larson, editors. Prevention and control of wildlife damage. University of Nebraska Cooperative Extension Service, Lincoln, USA.

DeGRAZIO, J. W., J. F. BESSER, J. L. GUARINO, C. M. LOVELESS, AND J. L. OLDEMEYER. 1969. A method for appraising blackbird damage to corn. Journal of Wildlife Management 33:988–994.

DeLIBERTO, T. J., E. M. GESE, F. F. KNOWLTON, R. J. MASON, M. R. CONOVER, L. MILLER, R. H. SCHMIDT, AND M. HOLLAND. 1998. Fertility control in coyotes: is it a potential management tool? Proceedings of the Vertebrate Pest Conference 18:144–149.

DeNICOLA, A. J., K. C. VerCAUTEREN, P. D. CURTIS, AND S. E. HYGNSTROM. 2000. Managing white-tailed deer in suburban environments. Cornell University Cooperative Extension Service, Ithaca, New York, USA.

DOENIER, P. B., G. D. DelGIUDICE, AND M. R. RIGGS. 1997. Effects of winter supplemental feeding on browse consumption of white-tailed deer. Wildlife Society Bulletin 25:235–243.

DOLBEER, R. A. 1975. A comparison of two methods for estimating bird damage to sunflowers. Journal of Wildlife Management 39:802–806.

———. 1980. Blackbirds and corn in Ohio. U.S. Department of the Interior, Fish and Wildlife Service, Resource Publication 136.

———. 1981. Cost-benefit determination of blackbird damage control for cornfields. Wildlife Society Bulletin 9:44–51.

———. 1990. Ornithology and integrated pest management: red-winged blackbirds *Agelaius phoeniceus* and corn. Ibis 132:309–322.

———. 1998. Population dynamics: the foundation of wildlife damage control for the 21st century. Proceedings of the Vertebrate Pest Conference 18:2–11.

———. 1999. Overview and management of vertebrate pests. Pages 663–691 in J. R. Ruberson, editor. Handbook of pest management. Marcel Dekker Inc., New York, USA.

———, M. L. AVERY, and M. E. TOBIN 1994a. Assessment of field hazards to birds from methiocarb applications to fruit crops. Pesticide Science 40:147–161.

———, J. L. BELANT, AND J. L. SILLINGS. 1993. Shooting gulls reduces strikes with aircraft at John F. Kennedy International Airport. Wildlife Society Bulletin 21:442–450.

———, N. R. HOLLER, AND D. W. HAWTHORNE. 1994b. Identification and control of wildlife damage. Pages 474–506 in T. A. Bookhout, editor. Research and management techniques for wildlife and habitats. Fifth edition. The Wildlife Society, Bethesda, Maryland, USA.

———, M. A. LINK, AND P. P. WORONECKI. 1988a. Naphthalene shows no repellency for starlings. Wildlife Society Bulletin 16:62–64.

———, D. F. MOTT, AND J. L. BELANT. 1995a. Blackbirds and starlings killed at winter roosts from PA-14 applications, 1974–1992: implications for regional population management. Proceedings of the Eastern Wildlife Damage Control Conference 7:77–86.

———, A. R. STICKLEY, JR., AND P. P. WORONECKI. 1979. Starling (*Sturnus vulgaris*) damage to sprouting wheat in Tennessee and Kentucky, U.S.A. Protection Ecology 1:159–169.

———, P. P. WORONECKI, AND R. L. BRUGGERS. 1986. Reflecting tapes repel blackbirds from millet, sunflowers, and sweet corn. Wildlife Society Bulletin 14:418–425.

———, ———, AND J. R. MASON. 1988b. Aviary and field evaluations of sweet corn resistance to damage by blackbirds. Journal of the American Society of Horticultural Science 113:460–464.

———, ———, AND T. W. SEAMANS. 1995b. Ranking and evaluation of field corn hybrids for resistance to blackbird damage. Crop Protection 14:399–403.

———, S. E. WRIGHT, AND E. C. CLEARY. 2000. Ranking the hazard level of wildlife species to aviation. Wildlife Society Bulletin 28:372–378.

———, T. W. SEAMANS, B. F. BLACKWELL, AND J. L. BELANT. 1998. Anthraquinone formulation (Flight Control) shows promise as avian feeding repellent. Journal of Wildlife Management 62:1558–1564.

DORSETT, J. 1987. Trapping coyotes. Leaflet L-1908. Texas Animal Damage Control Service, San Antonio, USA.

DWYER, C. P., J. L. BELANT, AND R. A. DOLBEER. 1996. Distribution and abundance of roof-nesting gulls in the Great Lakes region of the United States. Ohio Journal of Science 96:9–12.

EAGLE, T. C., AND J. S. WHITMAN. 1987. Mink. Pages 615–624 in M. Novak, J. A. Baker, M. E. Obbard, and B. Malloch, editors. Wild furbearer management and conservation in North America. Ontario Ministry of Natural Resources, Toronto, Canada.

EL HANI, A., AND M. R. CONOVER. 1997. Comparative analysis of deer repellents. Pages 147–155 in J. R. Mason, editor. Repellents in wildlife management. U.S. Department of Agriculture, National Wildlife Research Center, Fort Collins, Colorado, USA.

ELLINS, S. R., AND G. C. MARTIN. 1981. Olfactory discrimination of lithium chloride by the coyote (*Canis latrans*). Behavioral and Neural Biology 31:214–224.

EVANS, D., J. L. BYFORD, AND R. H. WAINBERG. 1983. A characterization of woodpecker damage to houses in east Tennessee. Proceedings of the Eastern Wildlife Damage Control Conference 1:325–330.

FAGERSTONE, K. A. 1981. A review of prairie dog diet and its variability among animals and colonies. Proceedings of the Great Plains Wildlife Damage Control Workshop 5:178–184.

———. 1987. Black-footed ferret, long-tailed weasel, short-tailed weasel, and least weasel. Pages 549–573 in M. Novak, J. A. Baker, M. E. Obbard, and B. Malloch, editors. Wild furbearer management and conservation in North America. Ontario Ministry of Natural Resources, Toronto, Canada.

———, AND E. W. SCHAFER, JR. 1998. Status of APHIS vertebrate pesticides and drugs. Proceedings of the Vertebrate Pest Conference 18:319–324.

———, M. A. COFFEY, P. D. CURTIS, R. A. DOLBEER, G. J. KILLIAN, L. A. MILLER, AND L. M. WILMOT. 2002. Wildlife fertility control.

Technical Review 02-2. The Wildlife Society, Bethesda, Maryland, USA.

FALL, M. W. 1990. Control of coyote depredation on livestock - progress in research and development. Proceedings of the Vertebrate Pest Conference 14:245–251.

FITZGERALD, J. P., C. A. MEANEY, AND D. M. ARMSTRONG. 1994. Mammals of Colorado. Denver Museum of Natural History, University Press of Colorado, Niwot, USA.

FITZWATER, W. D. 1994. House cats (feral). Pages C45–C49 *in* S. E. Hygnstrom, R. M. Timm, and G. E. Larson, editors. Prevention and control of wildlife damage. University of Nebraska Cooperative Extension Service, Lincoln, USA.

FORD, M. A., AND J. B. GRACE. 1998. Effects of vertebrate herbivores on soil processes, plant biomass, litter accumulation, and soil elevation changes in a coastal marsh. Journal of Ecology 86:974–982.

FORTHMAN-QUICK, D. L., C. R. GUSTAVSON, AND K. W. RUSINIAK. 1985*a*. Coyotes and taste aversion: the authors' reply. Appetite 6:284–290.

——, ——, AND ——. 1985*b*. Coyote control and taste aversion. Appetite 6:253–264.

FRANKLIN, W. L., AND K. J. POWELL. 1994. Guard llamas. Extension Publication PM-1527. Iowa State University, Ames, USA.

FRANTZ, S. C. 1986. Batproofing structures with birdnetting check-valves. Proceedings of the Vertebrate Pest Conference 12:260–268.

FRITTS, S. H., W. J. PAUL, L. D. MECH, AND D. P. SCOTT. 1992. Trends and management of wolf-livestock conflicts in Minnesota. U.S. Department of the Interior, Fish and Wildlife Service, Resource Publication 181.

FULLER-PERRINE, L. D., AND M. E. TOBIN. 1993. A method for applying and removing bird-exclusion netting in commercial vineyards. Wildlife Society Bulletin 21:47–51.

GARRETTSON, P. R., AND F. C. ROHWER. 2001. Effects of mammalian predator removal on production of upland-nesting ducks in North Dakota. Journal of Wildlife Management 65:398–405.

GARROTT, R. A., AND L. E. EBERHARDT. 1987. Arctic fox. Pages 395–406 *in* M. Novak, J. A. Baker, M. E. Obbard, and B. Malloch, editors. Wild furbearer management and conservation in North America. Ontario Ministry of Natural Resources, Toronto, Canada.

GATES, N. L., J. E. RICH, D. D. GODTEL, AND C. V. HULET. 1978. Development and evaluation of anti-coyote electric fencing. Journal of Range Management 31:151–153.

GILSDORF, J. M., S. E. HYGNSTROM, K. C. VERCAUTEREN, E. E. BLANKENSHIP, AND R. M. ENGEMAN. 2004*a*. Propane exploders and Electronic Guards were ineffective at reducing deer damage in corn-fields. Wildlife Society Bulletin 32: 524-531.

——, ——, ——, G. M. CLEMENTS, E. E. BLANKENSHIP, AND R. M. ENGEMAN. 2004*b*. Evaluation of a deer-activated bio-acoustic device for reducing deer damage in cornfields. Wildlife Society Bulletin 32: 515-523.

GIPSON, P. S., B. HLAVACHICK, AND T. BERGER. 1998. Range expansion by wild hogs across the central United States. Wildlife Society Bulletin 26:279–286.

GIUSTI, G. A., D. A. WHISSON, AND W. P. GORENZEL. 1996. Rodents and cover crops—a review. Proceedings of the Vertebrate Pest Conference 17:59–61.

GLAHN, J. F., AND K. E. BRUGGER. 1995. The impact of double-crested cormorants on the Mississippi delta catfish industry: a bioenergetics model. Colonial Waterbirds 18:168–175.

——, AND W. STONE. 1984. Effects of starling excrement in the food of cattle and pigs. Animal Production 38:439–446.

——, D. J. TWEDT, AND D. L. OTIS. 1983. Estimating feed loss from starling use of livestock feed troughs. Wildlife Society Bulletin 11:366–372.

——, B. DORR, J. B. HARREL, AND L. KHOO. 2002. Foraging ecology and depredation management of great blue herons at Mississippi cat-fish farms. Journal of Wildlife Management 66:194–201.

GOLDMAN, D. S. 1988. Current and future EPA requirements concerning good laboratory practices relative to vertebrate pesticides. Proceedings of the Vertebrate Pest Conference 13:22–25.

GREEN, J. S. 1989. Donkeys for predation control. Proceedings of the Eastern Wildlife Damage Control Conference 4:83–86.

——, AND P. S. GIPSON. 1994. Dogs (feral). Pages C77–C81 *in* S. E. Hygnstrom, R. M. Timm, and G. E. Larson, editors. Prevention and control of wildlife damage. University of Nebraska Cooperative

Extension Service, Lincoln, USA.

——, AND R. A. WOODRUFF. 1987. Livestock-guarding dogs for pred-ator control. Pages 62–68 *in* J. S. Green, editor. Protecting livestock from coyotes. U.S. Department of Agriculture, Agricultural Research Service, Sheep Experiment Station, Dubois, Idaho, USA.

——, F. R. HENDERSON, AND M. D. COLLINGE. 1994. Coyotes. Pages C51–C76 *in* S. E. Hygnstrom, R. M. Timm, and G. E. Larson, editors. Prevention and control of wildlife damage. University of Nebraska Cooperative Extension Service, Lincoln, USA.

——, R. A. WOODRUFF, AND T. T. TUELLER. 1984. Livestock-guarding dogs for predator control: costs, benefits and practicality. Wildlife Society Bulletin 12:44–50.

GREENHALL, A. M. 1982. House bat management. U.S. Department of the Interior, Fish and Wildlife Service, Resource Publication 143.

GREENWOOD, R. J., AND M. A. SOVADA. 1996. Prairie duck populations and predation management. Transactions of the North American Wildlife and Natural Resources Conference 61:31–42.

——, D. G. PIETRUSZEWSKI, AND R. D. CRAWFORD. 1998. Effects of food supplementation on depredation of duck nests in upland habitat. Wildlife Society Bulletin 26:219–226.

GUSTAVSON, C. R., J. R. JOWSEY, AND D. N. MILLIGAN. 1982. A 3-year evaluation of taste aversion coyote control in Saskatchewan. Journal of Range Management 35:57–59.

——, J. GARCIA, W. G. HANKINS, AND K. W. RUSINIAK. 1974. Coyote predation control by aversive conditioning. Science 184:581–583.

HADIDIAN, J., D. MANSKI, V. FLYGER, C. COX, AND G. HODGE. 1987. Urban gray squirrel damage and population management: a case his-tory. Proceedings of the Eastern Wildlife Damage Control Conference 3:219–227.

HAIGHT, R. G., AND L. D. MECH. 1997. Computer simulation of vasecto-my for wolf control. Journal of Wildlife Management 61:1023–1031.

HAMILTON, J. C., R. J. JOHNSON, R. M. CASE, M. W. RILEY, AND W. W. STROUP. 1987. Fox squirrels cause power outages: an urban wildlife problem. Proceedings of the Eastern Wildlife Damage Control Conference 3:228.

HAMLIN, K. L., S. J. RILEY, D. PYRAH, A. R. DOOD, AND R. J. MACKIE. 1984. Relationships among mule deer fawn mortality, coyotes, and alternate prey species during summer. Journal of Wildlife Management 48:489–499.

HARTMAN, L. H., A. J. GASTON, AND D. S. EASTMAN. 1997. Raccoon pre-dation on ancient murrelets on East Limestone Island, British Columbia. Journal of Wildlife Management 61:377–388.

HEINRICH, J. W., AND S. R. CRAVEN. 1987. Distribution and impact of Canada goose crop damage in east-central Wisconsin. Proceedings of the Eastern Wildlife Damage Control Conference 3:18–19.

——, AND ——. 1990. Evaluation of three damage abatement tech-niques for Canada geese. Wildlife Society Bulletin 18:405–410.

HEISTERBERG, J. F. 1983. Bird repellent seed corn treatment: efficacy evaluations and current registration status. Proceedings of the Eastern Wildlife Damage Control Conference 1:255–258.

HENDERSON, F. R. 1994*a*. Moles. Pages D51–D58 *in* S. E. Hygnstrom, R. M. Timm, and G. E. Larson, editors. Prevention and control of wildlife damage. University of Nebraska Cooperative Extension Service, Lincoln, USA.

——. 1994*b*. Weasels. Pages C119-C122 *in* S. E. Hygnstrom, R. M. Timm, and G. E. Larson, editors. Prevention and control of wildlife damage. University of Nebraska Cooperative Extension Service, Lincoln, USA.

HESKE, E. J., S. K. ROBINSON, AND J. D. BRAWN. 2001. Nest predation and neotropical migrant songbirds: piecing together the fragments. Wildlife Society Bulletin 29:52–61.

HEWITT, D. G., D. M. KEPPIE, AND D. F. STAUFFER. 2001. Predation effects on forest grouse recruitment. Wildlife Society Bulletin 29:16–23.

HOOVER, S. E., AND M. R. CONOVER. 1998. Effectiveness of volatile irri-tants at reducing consumption of eggs by captive coyotes. Journal of Wildlife Management 62:399–405.

——, AND ——. 2000. Using eggs containing an irritating odor to teach mammalian predators to stop depredating eggs. Wildlife Society Bulletin 28:84–89.

HOTHEM, R. L., R. W. DEHAVEN, AND S. D. FAIRAIZL. 1988. Bird dam-age to sunflower in North Dakota, South Dakota, and Minnesota, 1979–1981. U.S. Department of the Interior, Fish and Wildlife

Service, Technical Report 15.

HOWELL, R. G. 1982. The urban coyote problem in Los Angeles County. Proceedings of the Vertebrate Pest Conference 10:21–23.

HUYGENS, O. C., AND H. HAYASHI. 1999. Using electric fences to reduce Asiatic black bear depredation in Nagano prefecture, central Japan. Wildlife Society Bulletin 27:959–964.

HYGNSTROM, S. E. 1994. Black bears. Pages C5–C15 *in* S. E. Hygnstrom, R. M. Timm, and G. E. Larson, editors. Prevention and control of wildlife damage. University of Nebraska Cooperative Extension Service, Lincoln, USA.

———, AND S. R. CRAVEN. 1994. Hawks and owls. Pages E53–E61 *in* S. E. Hygnstrom, R. M. Timm, and G. E. Larson, editors. Prevention and control of wildlife damage. University of Nebraska Cooperative Extension Service, Lincoln, USA.

———, AND K. C. VERCAUTEREN. 1995. Vertebrate pest management in grain storage facilities. Stored Product Management. Oklahoma State University Cooperative Extension Service, Stillwater, USA.

———, AND ———. 2000. Cost-effectiveness of five burrow fumigants for managing black-tailed prairie dogs. International Biodeterioration and Biodegradation 45:159–168.

———, AND D. R. VIRCHOW. 1994. Prairie dogs. Pages B85–B96 *in* S. E. Hygnstrom, R. M. Timm, and G. E. Larson, editors. Prevention and control of wildlife damage. University of Nebraska Cooperative Extension Service, Lincoln, USA.

———, R. M. TIMM, AND G. E. LARSON, editors. 1994. Prevention and control of wildlife damage. University of Nebraska Cooperative Extension Service, Lincoln, USA.

———, K. C. VERCAUTEREN, R. A. HINES, AND C. W. MANSFIELD. 2000. Efficacy of in-furrow zinc phosphide pellets for controlling rodent damage in no-till corn. International Biodeterioration and Biodegradation 45:215–222.

———, J. R. HYGNSTROM, K. C. VERCAUTEREN, N. S. FOSTER, S. B. LEMBEZEDER, AND D. J. HAFER. 1991. Effects of chronological deer damage on corn yields. Proceedings of the Eastern Wildlife Damage Control Conference 5:65.

ISHMAEL, W. E., AND O. J. RONGSTAD. 1984. Economics of an urban deer-removal program. Wildlife Society Bulletin 12:394–398.

JACKSON, J. J. 1994*a*. Opossums. Pages D59–D63 *in* S. E. Hygnstrom, R. M. Timm, and G. E. Larson, editors. Prevention and control of wildlife damage. University of Nebraska Cooperative Extension Service, Lincoln, USA.

———. 1994*b*. Tree squirrels. Pages B171–B175 *in* S. E. Hygnstrom, R. M. Timm, and G. E. Larson, editors. Prevention and control of wildlife damage. University of Nebraska Cooperative Extension Service, Lincoln, USA.

JACOBS, W. W. 1994. Pesticides federally registered for control of terrestrial vertebrate pests. Pages G1–G22 *in* S. E. Hygnstrom, R. M. Timm, and G. E. Larson, editors. Prevention and control of wildlife damage. University of Nebraska Cooperative Extension Service, Lincoln, USA.

———. 2002. Current issues with vertebrate pesticides—from a regulator's perspective. Proceedings of the Vertebrate Pest Conference 20:261–266.

JELINSKI, D. E., R. C. ROUNDS, AND J. R. JOWSEY. 1983. Coyote predation on sheep, and control by aversive conditioning in Saskatchewan. Journal of Range Management 36:16–19.

JOHNSON, M. L., AND S. JOHNSON. 1982. Voles. Pages 326–354 in J. A. Chapman and G. A. Feldhamer, editors. Wild mammals of North America: biology, management, and economics. Johns Hopkins University Press, Baltimore, Maryland, USA.

JOHNSON, R. J. 1986. Wildlife damage in conservation tillage agriculture: a new challenge. Proceedings of the Vertebrate Pest Conference 12:127–132.

———, AND J. F. GLAHN. 1994. European starlings. Pages E109–E120 *in* S. E. Hygnstrom, R. M. Timm, and G. E. Larson, editors. Prevention and control of wildlife damage. University of Nebraska Cooperative Extension Service, Lincoln, USA.

JONKEL, C. J. 1994. Grizzly/brown bears. Pages C17–C23 *in* S. E. Hygnstrom, R. M. Timm, and G. E. Larson, editors. Prevention and control of wildlife damage. University of Nebraska Cooperative Extension Service, Lincoln, USA.

JUREK, R. M. 1994. A bibliography of feral, stray and free-ranging domestic cats in relation to wildlife conservation. California Department of Fish and Game, Wildlife Management Division, Sacramento, USA.

KAHL, R. B., AND F. B. SAMSON. 1984. Factors affecting yield of winter wheat grazed by geese. Wildlife Society Bulletin 12:256–262.

KELLY, S. T., AND M. E. DECAPITA. 1982. Cowbird control and its effect on Kirtland's warbler reproductive success. Wilson Bulletin 94:363–365.

KNIGHT, J. E. 1994*a*. Mountain lions. Pages C93–C99 *in* S. E. Hygnstrom, R. M. Timm, and G. E. Larson, editors. Prevention and control of wildlife damage. University of Nebraska Cooperative Extension Service, Lincoln, USA.

———. 1994*b*. Skunks. Pages C113–C118 *in* S. E. Hygnstrom, R. M. Timm, and G. E. Larson, editors. Prevention and control of wildlife damage. University of Nebraska Cooperative Extension Service, Lincoln, USA.

KNITTLE, C. E., AND R. D. PORTER. 1988. Waterfowl damage and control methods in ripening grain: an overview. U.S. Department of the Interior, Fish and Wildlife Service, Technical Report 14.

KNOWLTON, F. F., E. M. GESE, AND M. M. JAEGER. 1999. Coyote depredation control: an interface between biology and management. Journal of Range Management 52:398–412.

KOEHLER, A. E., R. E. MARSH, AND T. P. SALMON. 1990. Frightening methods and devices/stimuli to prevent animal damage - a review. Proceedings of the Vertebrate Pest Conference 14:168–173.

LEBLANC, D. J. 1994. Nutria. Pages B71–B80 *in* S. E. Hygnstrom, R. M. Timm, and G. E. Larson, editors. Prevention and control of wildlife damage. University of Nebraska Cooperative Extension Service, Lincoln, USA.

LEHNER, P. N. 1987. Repellents and conditioned avoidance. Pages 56–61 *in* J. S. Green, editor. Protecting livestock from coyotes. U.S. Department of Agriculture, Agricultural Research Service, Sheep Experiment Station, Dubois, Idaho, USA.

LEITCH, J. A., G. M. LINZ, AND J. F. BALTEZORE. 1997. Economics of cattail (*Typha* spp.) control to reduce blackbird damage to sunflower. Agricultural Ecosystems and the Environment 65:141–149.

LINDZEY, F. C. 1987. Mountain lion. Pages 657–668 *in* M. Novak, J. A. Baker, M. E. Obbard, and B. Malloch, editors. Wild furbearer management and conservation in North America. Ontario Ministry of Natural Resources, Toronto, Canada.

———. 1994. Badgers. Pages C1–C3 *in* S. E. Hygnstrom, R. M. Timm, and G. E. Larson, editors. Prevention and control of wildlife damage. University of Nebraska Cooperative Extension Service, Lincoln, USA.

LINHART, S. B. 1984. Strobe light and siren devices for protecting fenced-pasture and range sheep from coyote predation. Proceedings of the Vertebrate Pest Conference 11:154–156.

———, H. H. BRUSMAN, AND D. S. BALSER. 1968. Field evaluation of an antifertility agent, stilbesterol, for inhibiting coyote reproduction. Transactions of the North American Wildlife and Natural Resources Conference 33:316–326.

———, J. D. ROBERTS, AND G. J. DASCH. 1982. Electric fencing reduces coyote predation on pastured sheep. Journal of Range Management 35:276–281.

———, R. T. STERNER, T. C. CARRIGAN, AND D. R. HENNE. 1979. Komondor guard dogs reduce sheep losses to coyotes: a preliminary evaluation. Journal of Range Management 32:238–241.

———, ———, G. J. DASCH, AND J. W. THEADE. 1984. Efficacy of light and sound stimuli for reducing coyote predation upon pastured sheep. Protection Ecology 6:75–84.

———, G. J. DASCH, R. R. JOHNSON, J. D. ROBERTS, AND C. J. PACKHAM. 1992. Electronic frightening devices for reducing coyote depredation on domestic sheep: efficacy under range conditions and operational use. Proceedings of the Vertebrate Pest Conference 15:386–392.

LINNELL, J. D. C., J. ODDEN, M. E. SMITH, R. AANES, AND J. E. SWENSON. 1999. Large carnivores that kill livestock: do "problem individuals" really exist? Wildlife Society Bulletin 27:698–705.

LOGAN, K. A., L. L. SWEANOR, J. F. SMITH, AND M. G. HORNOCKER. 1999. Capturing pumas with foot-hold snares. Wildlife Society Bulletin 27:201–208.

LOKEMOEN, J. T., AND R. O. WOODWARD. 1993. An assessment of predator barriers and predator control to enhance duck nest success on peninsulas. Wildlife Society Bulletin 21:275–282.

MARKHAM, D., P. HILTON, J. TOMPKINS, D. HOCHSPRUNG, D. SCHREINER,

AND G. YOHE. 1993. Guard llamas—an alternative for effective predator management. Educational Brochure 2. International Llama Association, Kalispell, Montana, USA.

MARSH, R. E. 1985*a*. Competition of rodents and other small mammals with livestock in the United States. Pages 485–508 *in* S. M. Gaafar, W. E. Howard, and R. E. Marsh, editors. Parasites, pests, and predators, Elsevier Science Publishers, Amsterdam, The Netherlands.

———. 1985*b*. Techniques used in rodent control to safeguard non-target wildlife. Pages 47–55 *in* W. F. Laudenslayer, Jr., editor. Transactions of the Western Section, The Wildlife Society, Monterey, California.

———. 1986. Ground squirrel control strategies in Californian agriculture. Pages 261–276 *in* C. G. J. Richards and T. Y. Ku, editors. Control of mammal pests. Taylor and Francis, Inc., Philadelphia, Pennsylvania, USA.

———. 1988. Current (1987) and future rodenticides for commensal rodent control. Bulletin of the Society of Vector Ecology 13:102–107.

———. 1994*a*. Belding's, California, and Rock ground squirrels. Pages B151–B158 *in* S. E. Hygnstrom, R. M. Timm, and G. E. Larson, editors. Prevention and control of wildlife damage. University of Nebraska Cooperative Extension Service, Lincoln, USA.

———. 1994*b*. Current (1994) ground squirrel control practices in California. Proceedings of the Vertebrate Pest Conference 16:61–65.

———. 1996. Mole control- a historical perspective. Proceedings of the Vertebrate Pest Conference 17:34–39.

———. 1998. One hundred years of pocket gopher traps and trapping. Proceedings of the Vertebrate Pest Conference 18:221–226.

———, AND W. E. HOWARD. 1982. Vertebrate pests. Pages 791–861 *in* A. Mallis, editor. Handbook of pest control. Sixth edition. Franzak and Foster Company, Cleveland, Ohio, USA.

MARSHALL, E. F. 1984. Cholecalciferol: a unique toxicant for rodent control. Proceedings of the Vertebrate Pest Conference 11:95–98.

MASON, J. R. 1998. Mammal repellents: options and considerations for development. Proceedings of the Vertebrate Pest Conference 18:325–329.

MCANINCH, J. B., editor. 1995. Urban deer: a manageable resource? 1993 Symposium of the North Central Section, The Wildlife Society, St. Louis, Missouri, USA.

MCCRACKEN, H., AND H. VAN CLEVE. 1947. Trapping: the craft and science of catching fur-bearing animals. Barnes Company, New York, USA.

MEADOWS, L. E., AND F. F. KNOWLTON. 2000. Efficacy of guard llamas to reduce canine predation on domestic sheep. Wildlife Society Bulletin 28:614–622.

MELVIN, S. M., L. H. MACIVOR, AND C. R. GRIFFIN. 1992. Predator exclosures: a technique to reduce predation at piping plover nests. Wildlife Society Bulletin 20:143–148.

MESSICK, J. P. 1987. North American badger. Pages 587–597 *in* M. Novak, J. A. Baker, M. E. Obbard, and B. Malloch, editors. Wild furbearer management and conservation in North America. Ontario Ministry of Natural Resources, Toronto, Canada.

MESSIER, F. 1991. The significance of limiting and regulating factors on the demography of moose and white-tailed deer. Journal of Animal Ecology 60:377–393.

MICACCHION, M., AND T. W. TOWNSEND. 1983. Botanical characteristics of autumnal blackbird roosts in central Ohio. Ohio Journal of Science 83:131–135.

MILLER, J. E. 1987. Assessment of wildlife damage on southern forests. Pages 48–52 *in* J. G. Dickinson and D. E. Maughan, editors. Proceedings of the Conference on Management of Southern Forests for Wildlife and Fish. U.S. Department of Agriculture, Forest Service, General Technical Report SO-65.

———. 1994. Muskrats. Pages B61–B69 *in* S. E. Hygnstrom, R. M. Timm, and G. E. Larson, editors. Prevention and control of wildlife damage. University of Nebraska Cooperative Extension Service, Lincoln, USA.

———, AND G. K. YARROW. 1994. Beaver. Pages B1-B11 *in* S. E. Hygnstrom, R. M. Timm, and G. E. Larson, editors. Prevention and control of wildlife damage. University of Nebraska Cooperative Extension Service, Lincoln, USA.

MILLER, S. G., S. P. BRATTON, AND J. HADIDIAN. 1992. Impacts of white-tailed deer on endangered plants. Natural Areas Journal 12:67–74.

MOTT, D. F. 1980. Dispersing blackbirds and starlings from objectionable roost sites. Proceedings of the Vertebrate Pest Conference 9:38–42.

MUNGALL, E. C. 2000. Exotics. Pages 736–764 *in* S. Demarais and P. R. Krausman, editors. Ecology and management of large mammals in North America. Prentice Hall, Inc., Upper Saddle River, New Jersey, USA.

MURTON, R. K., N. J. WESTWOOD, AND A. J. ISAACSON. 1974. A study of wood-pigeon shooting: the exploitation of a natural animal population. Journal of Applied Ecology 11:61–81.

NASS, R. D., AND J. THEADE. 1988. Electric fences for reducing sheep losses to predators. Journal of Range Management 41:251–252.

NOBLE, W. O., AND E. C. MESLOW. 1998. Spring foraging and forest damage by black bears in the central coast ranges of Oregon. Ursus 10:293–298.

NOLTE, D. L. 1999. Behavioral approaches for limiting depredation by wild ungulates. Bulletin 70. Idaho Forest, Wildlife, and Range Experiment Station, University of Idaho, Moscow, USA.

———, AND K. K. WAGNER. 2000. Comparing the efficacy of delivery systems and active ingredients of deer repellents. Proceedings of the Vertebrate Pest Conference 19:93–100.

———, K. R. PERRY, AND K. C. VERCAUTEREN. 2003. Training deer to avoid sites through negative reinforcement. Proceedings of the Wildlife Damage Management Conference. 10:95–104.

———, K. K. WAGNER, A. TRENT, AND S. BULKIN. 2000. Fumigant dispersal in pocket gopher burrows and benefits of a blow system. Proceedings of the Vertebrate Pest Conference 19:377–384.

O'BRIEN, J. M. 1994. Voles. Pages B177–B182 *in* S. E. Hygnstrom, R. M. Timm, and G. E. Larson, editors. Prevention and control of wildlife damage. University of Nebraska Cooperative Extension Service, Lincoln, USA.

O'FARRELL, T. P. 1987. Kit fox. Pages 423–431 *in* M. Novak, J. A. Baker, M. E. Obbard, and B. Malloch, editors. Wild furbearer management and conservation in North America. Ontario Ministry of Natural Resources, Toronto, Canada.

O'GARA, B. W. 1978*a*. Differential characteristics of predator kills. Proceedings of the Biennial Pronghorn Antelope Workshop 8:380–393.

———. 1978*b*. Sheep depredation by golden eagles in Montana. Proceedings of the Vertebrate Pest Conference 8:206–213.

———. 1994. Eagles. Pages E41–E48 *in* S. E. Hygnstrom, R. M. Timm, and G. E. Larson, editors. Prevention and control of wildlife damage. University of Nebraska Cooperative Extension Service, Lincoln, USA.

———, AND D. C. GETZ. 1986. Capturing golden eagles using a helicopter and net gun. Wildlife Society Bulletin 14:400–402.

OTIS, D. L., N. R. HOLLER, P. W. LEFEBVRE, AND D. F. MOTT. 1983. Estimating bird damage to sprouting rice. Pages 76–89 *in* D. E. Kaukeinen, editor. Vertebrate pest control and management materials. Special Technical Report 817. American Society for Testing Materials, West Conshohocken, Pennsylvania, USA.

PACKHAM, C. J. 1970. Forest animal damage in California. U.S. Department of Interior, Fish and Wildlife Service, Sacramento, California, USA.

PARTRIDGE, S. T., D. L. NOLTE, G. J. ZIEGLTRUM, AND C. T. ROBBINS. 2001. Impacts of supplemental feeding on the nutritional ecology of black bears. Journal of Wildlife Management 65:191–199.

PAUL, W. J., AND P. S. GIPSON. 1994. Wolves. Pages C123–C129 *in* S. E. Hygnstrom, R. M. Timm, and G. E. Larson, editors. Prevention and control of wildlife damage. University of Nebraska Cooperative Extension Service, Lincoln, USA.

PERRY, JR., H. R. 1982. Muskrat (*Ondatra zibethicus* and *Neofiber alleni*). Pages 282–325 *in* J. A. Chapman and G. A. Feldhamer, editors. Wild mammals of North America: biology, management, and economics. Johns Hopkins University Press, Baltimore, Maryland, USA.

PFEIFER, W. K., AND M. W. GOOS. 1982. Guard dogs and gas exploders as coyote control tools in North Dakota. Proceedings of the Vertebrate Pest Conference 10:55–61.

PHILLIPS, R. L., AND F. S. BLOM. 1988. Distribution and magnitude of eagle/livestock conflicts in the western United States. Proceedings of the Vertebrate Pest Conference 13:241–244.

———, AND K. S. GRUVER. 1996. Performance of the Paws-I-Trip pan tension device on 3 types of traps. Wildlife Society Bulletin

24:119–122.

———, AND R. H. SCHMIDT. 1994. Foxes. Pages C83–C88 *in* S. E. Hygnstrom, R. M. Timm, and G. E. Larson, editors. Prevention and control of wildlife damage. University of Nebraska Cooperative Extension Service, Lincoln, USA.

PIETZ, P. J., AND G. L. KRAPU. 1994. Effects of predator exclosure design on duck brood movements. Wildlife Society Bulletin 22:26–33.

PLESSER, H., S. OMASI, AND Y. YOM-TOV. 1983. Mist nets as a means of eliminating bird damage to vineyards. Crop Protection 2:503–506.

POLSON, J. E. 1983. Application of aversion techniques for the reduction of losses to beehives by black bears in northeastern Saskatchewan. SRC Publication C-805–13-E-83. Department of Supply and Service, Ottawa, Ontario, Canada.

QUINN, N. W. S., AND G. PARKER. 1987. Lynx. Pages 683–694 *in* M. Novak, J. A. Baker, M. E. Obbard, and B. Malloch, editors. Wild furbearer management and conservation in North America. Ontario Ministry of Natural Resources, Toronto, Canada.

RATNASWAMY, M. J., R. J. WARREN, M. T. KRAMER, AND M. D. ADAM. 1997. Comparisons of lethal and nonlethal techniques to reduce raccoon depredation of sea turtle nests. Journal of Wildlife Management 61:368–376.

REARDEN, J. D. 1951. Identification of waterfowl nest predators. Journal of Wildlife Management 15:386–395.

RILEY, T. Z., AND J. H. SCHULZ. 2001. Predation and ring-necked pheasant population dynamics. Wildlife Society Bulletin 29:33–38.

ROBEL, R. J., A. D. DAYTON, F. R. HENDERSON, R. L. MEDUNA, AND C. W. SPAETH. 1981. Relationships between husbandry methods and sheep losses to canine predators. Journal of Wildlife Management 45:894–911.

ROBLEE, K. J. 1987. The use of the T-culvert guard to protect road culverts from plugging damage by beavers. Proceedings of the Eastern Wildlife Damage Control Conference 3:25–33.

ROGERS, JR., J. G. 1974. Responses of caged red-winged blackbirds to two types of repellents. Journal of Wildlife Management 38.418–423.

ROLLEY, R. E. 1987. Bobcat. Pages 671–681 *in* M. Novak, J. A. Baker, M. E. Obbard, and B. Malloch, editors. Wild furbearer management and conservation in North America. Ontario Ministry of Natural Resources, Toronto, Canada.

ROLLINS, D., AND J. P. CARROLL. 2001. Impacts of predation on northern bobwhite and scaled quail. Wildlife Society Bulletin 29:39–51.

ROSATTE, R. C. 1987. Striped, spotted, hooded, and hog-nosed skunk. Pages 599–613 *in* M. Novak, J. A. Baker, M. E. Obbard, and B. Malloch, editors. Wild furbearer management and conservation in North America. Ontario Ministry of Natural Resources, Toronto, Canada.

ROYTHE, E. 1995. On the brink: Hawaii's vanishing species. National Geographic 188:2–37.

SACKS, B. N., K. M. BLEJWAS, AND M. M. JAEGER. 1999a. Relative vulnerability of coyotes to removal methods on a northern California ranch. Journal of Wildlife Management 63:939–949.

———, M. M. JAEGER, J. C. C. NEALE, AND D. R. MCCULLOUGH. 1999b. Territoriality and breeding status of coyotes relative to sheep predation. Journal of Wildlife Management 63:593–605.

SAHR, D. P., AND F. F. KNOWLTON. 2000. Evaluation of tranquilizer trap devices (TTDs) for foothold traps used to capture gray wolves. Wildlife Society Bulletin 28:597–605.

SALMON, T. P., AND W.P. GORENZEL. 1994. Woodrats. Pages B133–B136 *in* S. E. Hygnstrom, R. M. Timm, and G. E. Larson, editors. Prevention and control of wildlife damage. University of Nebraska Cooperative Extension Service, Lincoln, USA.

SANDERSON, G. C. 1987. Raccoon. Pages 487–499 *in* M. Novak, J. A. Baker, M. E. Obbard, and B. Malloch, editors. Wild furbearer management and conservation in North America. Ontario Ministry of Natural Resources, Toronto, Canada.

SARGEANT, A. B., AND P. M. ARNOLD. 1984. Predator management for ducks on waterfowl production areas in the northern plains. Proceedings of the Vertebrate Pest Conference 11:161–167.

———, S. H. ALLEN, AND R. T. EBERHARDT. 1984. Red fox predation on breeding ducks in midcontinent North America. Wildlife Monographs 89.

SCHROEDER, M. A., AND R. K. BAYDACK. 2001. Predation and the management of prairie grouse. Wildlife Society Bulletin 29:24–32.

SCOTT, J. D., AND T. W. TOWNSEND. 1985. Characteristics of deer dam-

age to commercial tree industries of Ohio. Wildlife Society Bulletin 13:135–143.

SCOTT-BROWN, J. M., S. HERRERO, AND J. REYNOLDS. 1987. Swift fox. Pages 433–441 *in* M. Novak, J. A. Baker, M. E. Obbard, and B. Malloch, editors. Wild furbearer management and conservation in North America. Ontario Ministry of Natural Resources, Toronto, Canada.

SEAMANS, T. W. 2002. Evaluation of the Allsop Helikite as a bird scaring device. Proceedings of the Vertebrate Pest Conference 20:129–134.

———, AND J. L. BELANT. 1999. Comparison of DRC-1339 and alpha-chloralose to reduce herring gull populations. Wildlife Society Bulletin 27:729–733.

SEIDENSTICKER, J., M. A. O'CONNELL, AND A. J. T. JOHNSINGH. 1987. Virginia opossum. Pages 247–263 *in* M. Novak, J. A. Baker, M. E. Obbard, and B. Malloch, editors. Wild furbearer management and conservation in North America. Ontario Ministry of Natural Resources, Toronto, Canada.

SHAW, H. G. 1983. Mountain lion field guide. Special Report 9. Arizona Game and Fish Department, Phoenix, USA.

SHELTON, M. 1984. The use of conventional and electric fencing to reduce coyote predation on sheep and goats. MP 1556. Texas Agricultural Experiment Station, College Station, USA.

SINCLAIR, A. R. E. 1991. Science and the practice of wildlife management. Journal of Wildlife Management 55:767–773.

SMITH, A. E., S. R. CRAVEN, AND P. D. CURTIS. 1999. Managing Canada geese in urban environments. Jack Berryman Institute Publication 16, and Cornell Cooperative Extension Service, Ithaca, New York, USA.

SOVADA, M. A., R. M. ANTHONY, AND B. D. J. BATT. 2001. Predation on waterfowl in arctic tundra and prairie breeding areas: a review. Wildlife Society Bulletin 29:6–15.

STEFFEN, D. E., N. R. HOLLER, L. W. LEFEBVRE, AND P. F. SCANLON. 1981. Factors affecting the occurrence and distribution of Florida water rats in sugarcane fields. Proceedings of the American Society of Sugar Cane Technology 9:27–32.

STICKLEY, JR., A. R., D. F. MOTT, AND J. O. KING. 1995. Short-term effects of an inflatable effigy on cormorants at catfish farms. Wildlife Society Bulletin 23:73–77.

———, D. L. OTIS, AND D. T. PALMER. 1979. Evaluation and results of a survey of blackbird and mammal damage to mature field corn over a large (three-state) area. Pages 169–177 *in* J. R. Beck, editor. Vertebrate pest control and management materials. Special Technical Publication 680. American Society for Testing Materials, West Conshohocken, Pennsylvania, USA.

SULLIVAN, T. P. 1978. Biological control of conifer seed damage by the deer mouse (*Peromyscus maniculatus*). Proceedings of the Vertebrate Pest Conference 8:237–250.

———, AND D. S. SULLIVAN. 1982. The use of alternative foods to reduce lodgepole pine seed predation by small mammals. Journal of Applied Ecology 19:33–45.

———, AND ———. 1988. Influence of alternative foods on vole populations and damage in apple orchards. Wildlife Society Bulletin 16:170–175.

———, J. A. KREBS, AND H. A. KLUGE. 1987. Survey of mammal damage to tree fruit orchards in the Okanagan Valley of British Columbia. Northwest Science 61:23–31.

TEER, J. G. 1964. Predation by long-tailed weasels on eggs of blue-winged teal. Journal of Wildlife Management 28:404–406.

TERNENT, M. A., AND D. L. GARSHELIS. 1999. Taste-aversion conditioning to reduce nuisance activity by black bears in a Minnesota military reservation. Wildlife Society Bulletin 27:720–728.

TEWES, M. E., AND D. J. SCHMIDLY. 1987. The neotropical felids: jaguar, ocelot, margay, and jaguarundi. Pages 697–712 *in* M. Novak, J. A. Baker, M. E. Obbard, and B. Malloch, editors. Wild furbearer management and conservation in North America. Ontario Ministry of Natural Resources, Toronto, Canada.

THORNE, E. T., N. KINGSTON, W. R. JOLLEY, AND R. C. BERGSTROM. 1982. Diseases of wildlife in Wyoming. Second edition. Wyoming Game and Fish Department, Cheyenne, USA.

TILGHMAN, N. G. 1989. Impacts of white-tailed deer on forest regeneration in northwestern Pennsylvania. Journal of Wildlife Management 53:524–532.

TILL, J. A., AND F. F. KNOWLTON. 1983. Efficacy of denning in alleviating coyote depredations upon domestic sheep. Journal of Wildlife Management 47:1018–1025.

TILLMAN, E. A., J. S. HUMPHREY, AND M. L. AVERY. 2002. Use of effigies and decoys to reduce vulture damage to property and agriculture. Proceedings of the Vertebrate Pest Conference 20:123–128.

TIMM, R. M. 1994a. House mice. Pages B31–B46 in S. E. Hygnstrom, R. M. Timm, and G. E. Larson, editors. Prevention and control of wildlife damage. University of Nebraska Cooperative Extension Service, Lincoln, USA.

——. 1994b. Norway rats. Pages B105–B120 in S. E. Hygnstrom, R. M. Timm, and G. E. Larson, editors. Prevention and control of wildlife damage. University of Nebraska Cooperative Extension Service, Lincoln, USA.

——, AND W. E. HOWARD. 1994. White-footed and deer mice. Pages B47–B51 in S. E. Hygnstrom, R. M. Timm, and G. E. Larson, editors. Prevention and control of wildlife damage. University of Nebraska Cooperative Extension Service, Lincoln, USA.

——, AND R. E. MARSH. 1997. Vertebrate pests. Pages 954–1019 in D. Moreland, editor. Handbook of pest control: the behavior, life history, and control of household pests. Eighth edition. Mallis Handbook and Technical Training Company, Cleveland, Ohio, USA.

TOBIN, M. E., AND R. A. DOLBEER. 1987. Status of Mesurol® as a bird repellent for cherries and other fruit crops. Proceedings of the Eastern Wildlife Damage Control Conference 3:149–158.

——, ——, AND P. P. WORONECKI. 1989. Bird damage to apples in the Mid-Hudson Valley of New York. Horticultural Science 24:859.

——, ——, C. M. WEBSTER, AND T. W. SEAMANS. 1991. Cultivar differences in bird damage to cherries. Wildlife Society Bulletin 19:190–194.

TROTTIER, G. C., D. C. DUNCAN, AND S. C. LEE. 1994. Electric predator fences delay mallard brood movements to water. Wildlife Society Bulletin 22:22–26.

U.S. DEPARTMENT OF AGRICULTURE. 2000. Sheep and goats predator loss. National Agricultural Statistics Service, Agricultural Statistics Board, Washington, D.C., USA.

——. 2001. Cattle predator loss. National Agricultural Statistics Service, Agricultural Statistics Board, Washington, D.C., USA.

VANDER WALL, S. B., AND W. S. LONGLAND. 1999. Cheek pouch capacities and loading rates of deer mice (*Peromyscus maniculatus*). Great Basin Naturalist 59:278–280.

VERCAUTEREN, K. C., AND S. E. HYGNSTROM. 2002. Efficacy of hunting for managing a suburban deer population in eastern Nebraska. Pages 51–58 in R. J. Warren, editor. First National Bowhunting Conference Proceedings. Archery Manufacturers and Merchants Organization, Comfrey, Minnesota, USA.

——, AND M. J. LAVELLE. 2005. Fencing and barriers. in D. Nolte, editor. Reducing wildlife damage to forest resources. In press.

——, ——, AND S. MOYLES. 2003a. Efficacy of coyote-activated frightening devices for reducing sheep predation. Proceedings of the Wildlife Damage Management Conference. 10:146–151.

——, M. J. PIPAS, AND J. BOURASSA. 2002a. A camera and hook system for viewing and retrieving rodent carcasses from burrows. Wildlife Society Bulletin 30:1057–1061.

——, ——, P. PETERSON, AND S. BECKERMAN. 2003c. Stored-crop loss due to deer consumption. Wildlife Society Bulletin 31:578–582.

——, S. E. HYGNSTROM, M. J. PIPAS, P. B. FIORANELLI, S. J. WERNER, AND B. F. BLACKWELL. 2003b. Red lasers are ineffective for dispersing deer at night. Wildlife Society Bulletin 31:247–252.

——, R. M. TIMM, R. M. CORRIGAN, J. G. BELLER, L. L. BITNEY, M. C. BRUMM, D. MEYER, D. R. VIRCHOW, AND R. W. WILLS. 2002b. Development of a model to assess rodent control in swine facilities. Pages 59–64 in L. Clark, J. Hone, J. A. Shivik, R. A. Watkins, K. C. VerCauteren, and J. K. Yoder, editors. Human conflicts with wildlife: economic considerations. U.S. Department of Agriculture, Wildlife Services, Fort Collins, Colorado, USA.

VIRCHOW, D. R., AND D. HOGELAND. 1994. Bobcats. Pages C35–C43 in S. E. Hygnstrom, R. M. Timm, and G. E. Larson, editors. Prevention and control of wildlife damage. University of Nebraska Cooperative Extension Service, Lincoln, USA.

VOIGT, D. R. 1987. Red fox. Pages 379–392 in M. Novak, J. A. Baker,

M. E. Obbard, and B. Malloch, editors. Wild furbearer management and conservation in North America. Ontario Ministry of Natural Resources, Toronto, Canada.

——, AND W. E. BERG. 1987. Coyote. Pages 345–357 in M. Novak, J. A. Baker, M. E. Obbard, and B. Malloch, editors. Wild furbearer management and conservation in North America. Ontario Ministry of Natural Resources, Toronto, Canada.

WADE, D. A. 1976. The use of aircraft in predator control. Proceedings of the Vertebrate Pest Conference 7:154–160.

——. 1985. Applicator manual for compound 1080. Bulletin B-1509. Texas Agricultural Extension Service, San Antonio, USA.

——, AND J. E. BOWNS. 1984. Procedures for evaluating predation on livestock and wildlife. Bulletin B-1429. Texas Agricultural Extension Service, San Angelo, USA.

WAGNER, F. H. 1988. Predator control and the sheep industry: the role of science in policy formation. Regina Books, Claremont, California, USA.

WAGNER, K. K., AND M. R. CONOVER. 1999. Effect of preventive coyote hunting on sheep losses to coyote predation. Journal of Wildlife Management 63:606–612.

WALLER, D. M., AND W. S. ALVERSON. 1997. The white-tailed deer: a keystone herbivore. Wildlife Society Bulletin 25:217–226.

WARREN, R. J., editor. 2002. First National Bowhunting Conference Proceedings. Archery Manufacturers and Merchants Organization, Comfrey, Minnesota, USA.

WEATHERHEAD, P. J., S. TINKER, AND H. GREENWOOD. 1982. Indirect assessment of avian damage to agriculture. Journal of Applied Ecology 19:773–782.

WEAVER, K. M., D. H. ARNER, C. MASON, AND J. J. HARTLEY. 1985. A guide to using snares for beaver capture. Southern Journal of Applied Forestry 9:141–146.

WEBER, W. J. 1979. Health hazards from pigeons, starlings and English sparrows. Thompson Publications, Fresno, California, USA.

WERNER, S. J., A. EL HANI, AND J. R. MASON. 1997. Repellent coatings for irrigation hose: effectiveness against coyotes. Journal of Wildlife Research 2:146–148.

WHISSON, D. A., T. P. SALMON, AND W. P. GORENZEL. 2000. Reduced risk anticoagulant baiting strategies for California ground squirrels. Proceedings of the Vertebrate Pest Conference 19:362–364.

WHITE, S. B., R. A. DOLBEER, AND T. A. BOOKHOUT. 1985. Ecology, bioenergetics, and agricultural impacts of a winter-roosting population of blackbirds and starlings. Wildlife Monographs 93.

WHITTAKER, D. G., AND F. G. LINDZEY. 1999. Effect of coyote predation on early fawn survival in sympatric deer species. Wildlife Society Bulletin 27:256–262.

WITMER, G. W., M. J. PIPAS, AND D. L. CAMPBELL. 1995. Effectiveness of search patterns for recovery of animal carcasses in relation to pocket gopher infestation control. International Biodeterioration and Biodegradation 36:177–187.

WORONECKI, P. P. 1988. Effect of ultrasonic, visual, and sonic devices on pigeon numbers in a vacant building. Proceedings of the Vertebrate Pest Conference 13:266–272.

——, R. A. STEHN, AND R. A. DOLBEER. 1980. Compensatory response of maturing corn kernels following simulated damage by birds. Journal of Applied Ecology 17:737–746.

——, R. A. DOLBEER, C. R. INGRAM, AND A. R. STICKLEY, JR. 1979. 4-aminopyridine effectiveness reevaluated for reducing blackbird damage to corn. Journal of Wildlife Management 43:184–191.

——, T. W. SEAMANS, AND W. R. LANCE. 1992. Alpha-chloralose efficacy in capturing nuisance waterfowl and pigeons and current status of FDA registration. Proceedings of the Vertebrate Pest Conference 15:72–78.

WYWIALOWSKI, A. P. 1996. Wildlife damage to field corn in 1993. Wildlife Society Bulletin 24:264–271.

YATES, T. L., AND R. J. PEDERSEN. 1982. Moles. Pages 37–51 in J. A. Chapman and G. A. Feldhamer, editors. Wild mammals of North America: biology, management, and economics. Johns Hopkins University Press, Baltimore, Maryland, USA.

YOUNG, S. P. 1958. The bobcat of North America. Stackpole Company, Harrisburg, Pennsylvania, and Wildlife Management Institute, Washington, D.C., USA.

29

ASSESSMENT AND MANAGEMENT OF WILDLAND RECREATIONAL DISTURBANCE

Kevin J. Gutzwiller and David N. Cole

INTRODUCTION

Disturbance from wildland recreation is widespread, extending even to many remote and protected areas, and its effects have important ramifications for wildlife. Yet, many wildlife scientists and managers do not receive training to assess and manage this disturbance. Unlike many topics in this book, wildland recreation has not been a traditional subject of analysis or concern in wildlife curricula. Recreational activity and disturbance occurs in many natural areas near suburbs and cities, but wildlands typically are larger and more complex, provide more living space for wildlife, and are more likely to be managed by trained wildlife professionals. Thus, defining and characterizing wildland recreation, based on earlier literature (Flather and Cordell 1995, HaySmith and Hunt 1995, Hammitt and Cole 1998:3–5) and our experience, is where we begin.

Wildland recreation refers to nonwork outdoor activities that are conducted in natural environments. In contrast to activities in developed recreation areas (e.g., amusement parks, swimming pools, sports complexes), wildland recreation depends significantly on one or more of the natural resources (e.g., forests, water, wildlife) that occurs in a wild or undeveloped environment. Stated differently, in wildland recreation, a primary focus and source of motivation for activities is the natural setting itself or components thereof.

Although not all wildlands are wilderness, wildland recreation occurs in places where management seeks to sustain natural conditions. Consequently, facilities are usually few in number, small in size, and designed primarily to improve visitor safety or to protect resources, not to entertain or comfort recreationists. Recreation occurs in undeveloped lands that are small and close to urban areas, but lands used for wildland recreation are typically isolated from dense human populations; roads, when present, are often of lower quality, and trails may not exist. In this chapter, we focus on recreational activities that occur in large remote wildlands. Within such areas, recreational use tends to occur in many different places. Most wildland recreation occurs on public lands, such as federal and state parks, refuges, forests, and grasslands, but some occurs on private lands.

Many wildland recreational activities depend directly on wildlife. *Wildlife-dependent activities* are pursued with the goal of encountering wildlife for some purpose (e.g., harvest, watch, photograph); wildlife is the primary motivator for participation. Other recreational activities are not contingent on wildlife. For these activities, wildlife may add enjoyment (e.g., watching wildlife), present risk and challenge (e.g., grizzly bears [*Ursus arctos*] near camping areas in Glacier National Park), or may be a nuisance (e.g., bears and rodents pilfering packs in Yosemite National Park), but participation does not depend primarily on wildlife occurrence because encounters with wildlife are incidental. Some wildlife-dependent activities (e.g., big-game and upland-game hunting) involve harvest and have been referred to as *consumptive*, whereas recreational activities that do not involve harvest have been referred to as *nonconsumptive*. The latter term can be misleading, however, because significant disturbance from some non-hunting activities, including some that are not wildlife-dependent, can decrease wildlife reproduction and survival, causing these activities to be consumptive in their effects. This chapter emphasizes nonharvest activities. The chapter on harvest management in this volume (Connelly et al. 2005) addresses the effects of hunting on wildlife. Fishing can be consumptive, but fish are not typically considered wildlife. Consequently, we do not consider the extractive effects of angling on fisheries, but we do discuss wildland disturbance from fishing because the presence and movements of anglers may affect terrestrial and aquatic wildlife.

Recent analyses (Flather and Cordell 1995, Cordell and Super 2000), from which we derived the brief discussion that follows, trace the history of outdoor recreation development in the United States and forecast the wildland recreational activity we can expect in this country in the coming years. Outdoor recreation demand has grown since the late 1940s, when the post-World-War-II economy expanded and general affluence increased. During some or many of the last 5 decades, number of participants and days of participation increased for consumptive pursuits (fishing and big-game hunting) and nonconsumptive activities such as camping, backpacking, hiking, off-road vehicle driving, horseback riding, swimming in natural waters, boating, waterskiing, downhill and cross-country skiing, and snowmobiling. In recent years, some of the most dramatic increases in participation have occurred for nonconsumptive, wildlife-dependent activities, such as wildlife watching. In addition, relatively new activities, such as mountain biking, mountain climbing, rock climbing, caving, orienteering, rafting and tubing, and jet skiing have become increasingly popular.

Most wildland recreational activities are not wildlife-dependent, and participation (number of trips) in many of these activities is projected to increase substantially (Fig. 1). Wildlife managers should anticipate growth in wilderness use, rock climbing, white-water activities, caving, cross-country snow travel, and ice climbing. Participation (number of participants) in fishing and in wildlife-dependent activities that do not involve harvest (e.g., wildlife observation and photography) is expected to rise 63–142% during 1985–2040. For this same period, big-game hunting participation is predicted to change little, whereas small-game hunting participation is projected to decrease. Although disturbance from consumptive activities may stabilize or decline, nonconsumptive activities, which are frequently detrimental to wildlife (e.g., Boyle and Samson 1985), are on the rise. Thus, wildland managers should expect recreational disturbance of wildlife to continue to increase in intensity and geographic scope as demand for experiences in natural environments expands.

Disturbance from direct contact with recreationists has been linked to such effects as declines in reproduction, survival, and vigor; higher predation rates; increased vigilance at the expense of activities such as brooding of young and foraging; displacement from habitats that are needed for important life-history activities; and alteration of food habits (Boyle and Samson 1985, Burger 1995, Knight and Gutzwiller 1995, Joslin and Youmans 1999). Indirect effects are defined as those that arise through habitat (soil, vegetation, water) degradation by recreationists. They can

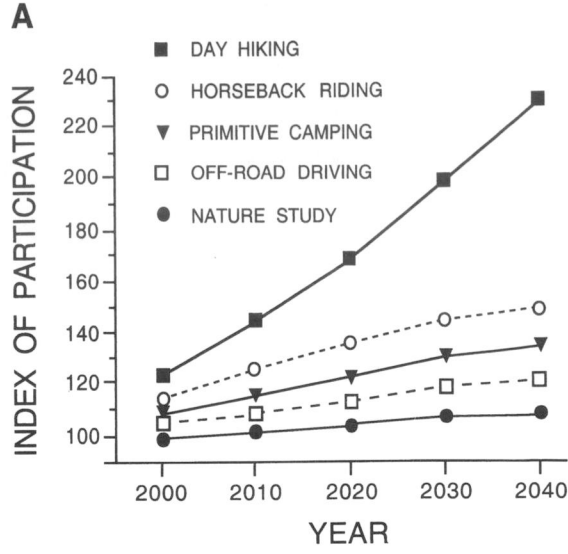

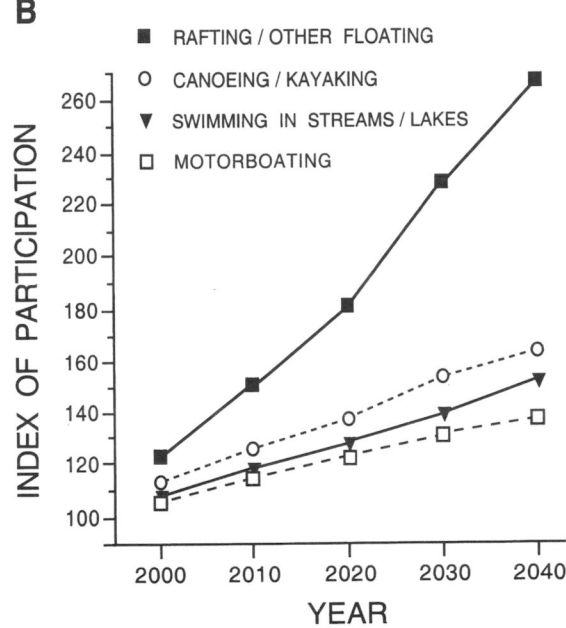

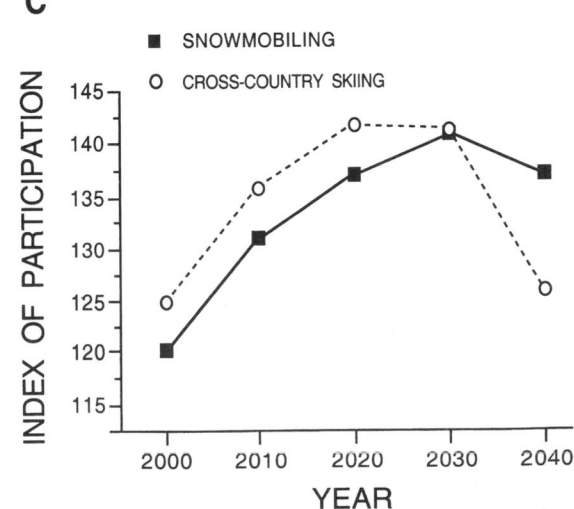

Fig. 1. Projected participation indices (growth in wildland recreation trips, 1987 = 100) for land- (A), water- (B), and snow-based (C) activities in the United States, 2000–40. Data are from Flather and Cordell (1995).

be just as problematic for wildlife as are direct effects (Cole and Landres 1995, Joslin and Youmans 1999). The effects of human disturbance in wildlands can vary among species, populations, and individuals (Knight and Temple 1995*a*) and with such factors as time of year (Hamr 1988, Götmark 1992), prior experience with humans (Knight and Fitzner 1985, Marzluff 1988), noise levels (Bowles 1995), speed of recreationist movement (Richens and Lavigne 1978, Burger 1981), location of recreationists (Herbert and Herbert 1965, Hicks and Elder 1979, MacArthur et al. 1982), and type of recreation (Burger 1995, Knight and Cole 1995*a*). Cumulative and synergistic effects of these influences also are possible (Bell and Austin 1985, Gutzwiller 1995). Clearly, the effects of recreation can depend on the specific set of circumstances involved; the consequences that develop for one set of conditions may or may not develop for others. Accordingly, assessment and management of recreational disturbance typically does not entail simply applying approaches used previously; instead, efforts must be tailored to a particular disturbance situation.

Land-management agencies operate under multiple mandates, including some that require provision of recreation opportunities; therefore, minimizing recreational disturbance to wildlife must usually be balanced with other goals. For example, the public derives substantial benefits from viewing wildlife, so management actions that drastically limit such activities may not be appropriate. Recreational disturbance of wildlife may not be severe enough to require restriction of recreation. In some situations, recreational activities have minimal negative effects on wildlife (Knight and Gutzwiller 1995). Many groups of wildland recreationists are among the strongest advocates for wildlife or the environment, and it is important that wildlife professionals not alienate these groups by acting on preconceived notions about the effects of their recreation. Thus, during assessment and management efforts, it is crucial that wildlife scientists remain objective about potential influences, and that wildlife managers carefully consider both the costs (wildlife disturbance) and benefits (public enjoyment and support) of providing recreational opportunities. We recommend that techniques described in this chapter be used to develop and implement a policy of coexistence—one that seeks a balance between wildlife protection and the provision of opportunities for recreation.

The need to assess and manage recreational disturbance is pressing because it is occurring on public and private wildlands, which are the most natural areas that remain for support of wildlife. This chapter discusses methods for assessing the nature and magnitude of recreational disturbance and for avoiding or reducing such disturbance. Specifically, we (1) describe how existing information can be used to evaluate the potential for harmful effects; (2) indicate how to conduct field studies to obtain new information; (3) present a framework for disturbance management based on objectives, monitoring, and effects of previous management actions; (4) provide options for managing recreationists, including approaches for informing visitors and regulating aspects of their activities; and (5) explain how to reduce recreational disturbance through wildland planning and management, with emphasis on facilities and infrastructure placement, and regulation of their use.

ASSESSING EFFECTS OF RECREATIONAL DISTURBANCE ON WILDLIFE

Because some recreational disturbance of wildlife occurs on all wildlands, the potential severity of impacts should be assessed routinely. The nature of assessments will vary greatly, however, with such variables as management goals, available information, perceived threats, and available funding. All areas should assess impact potential. Most should conduct routine monitoring, and some should initiate field studies. As uncertainty about wildlife impacts mounts and the importance of wildlife conservation grows, managers increasingly face 2 choices—either conduct field studies of wildlife impact or err on the side of unnecessary restriction when managing recreational activity. Although field studies can be costly in the short-term, long-term costs are inevitably greater if wildlife is disturbed severely or recreationists are restricted needlessly.

EVALUATION OF IMPACT POTENTIAL

The purpose of an evaluation is to use existing information (data, expert knowledge, and logical thinking) to identify wildlife species that may require unusual management emphasis. These may be species with special status (e.g., threatened and endangered species), game species, or species that are major attractions for recreationists. In addition, they may be species that are judged to be most vulnerable to substantial recreational disturbance in particular places and at certain times. Definitions of what constitutes high vulnerability and substantial disturbance are not absolute; they will vary from place to place. An assessment of the relative vulnerability of different species, places, and times is a means of prioritizing monitoring efforts and management techniques. If there is sufficient uncertainty about impacts, field studies are warranted.

The initial step in any evaluation of impact potential is to compile an inventory of species either known or likely to be in the area. The next step is to gather existing literature and expert opinion about likely impacts on these species. Joslin and Youmans (1999) provide an excellent example of the wealth of insight that can be gained by compiling existing information for Rocky Mountain wildlife in Montana. Their report highlights information about recreational effects on groups of animals, such as amphibians and reptiles, as well as on important individual species, such as wolverine (*Gulo gulo*) and Canada lynx (*Lynx canadensis*).

Species with special status should be identified first. The most obvious are species listed as endangered or threatened under the Endangered Species Act, those proposed for listing, or those identified as sensitive by the U. S. Forest Service, U. S. Bureau of Land Management, or state organizations. In most cases, recreation should be managed so that recreational disturbance of these species is negligible. These species will probably be the focus of most monitoring, most field studies, and much of the recreation management program. However, other species should not be ignored, particularly if their populations are vulnerable to significant recreational disturbance, they are important game species, or they attract the wildlife-viewing public.

Populations of rare species that have large home ranges or territories are often vulnerable simply because so few individuals exist. Loss of just a few individuals can have a substantial impact on the entire population. Field studies or monitoring of such species should be a priority. Many of these should already be on lists of species of special concern.

The species most vulnerable to recreational disturbance are those for which a substantial portion of the population is impacted by recreation and for which individual animals are profoundly affected by recreational disturbance. Particularly in large wildlands, the vast majority of species will probably not be impacted substantially by recreation because their populations are widespread, home ranges or territories are small, and recreational disturbance is often localized around the recreation site. For example, recreation will alter the behavior and food habits of individual chipmunks (*Tamias* spp.) that live close to trails or campsites. As undesirable as this is for these individuals, recreation may not substantially threaten chipmunk populations if only a small portion of a healthy and abundant population will be impacted. Most chipmunks will not come in contact with humans and will remain completely undisturbed by recreation. Many invertebrates, fish, amphibians, reptiles, birds, and small mammals may be in this category. If there is little potential for widespread impact, little effort needs to be expended on monitoring recreation impacts on these species unless the situation changes (e.g., increasing habitat fragmentation or development of adjacent lands). This does not mean there is no impact on these species. Nor does it mean that educational programs should not be developed to reduce impacts as much as possible.

Of the species with small home ranges or territories, the most vulnerable are those that are highly selective in the habitats they occupy. Even these species may not be highly vulnerable if there is little spatial overlap between wildlife habitat and recreational activities. Suitable habitat for selective species can be mapped, either on the basis of direct observation or from predictive models, and the information can be overlaid on maps of recreational use to identify potential areas of conflict or to suggest where trails and facilities should and should not be constructed. Given the attraction of recreationists to riparian strips (Blakesley and Reese 1988), species that occupy riparian zones are of particular concern in many places. Some species, such as invertebrates, reptiles, and amphibians, are concentrated and therefore more vulnerable at certain times of the year. Management of the timing of recreational activity can effectively limit impact on these species.

It is more difficult to generalize about impacts on species that are populous but that have large home ranges or territories. For these species, a substantial proportion of individuals in the population may come into conflict with recreationists even when recreational use is localized. These individuals have the capacity to learn from encounters with recreationists. Field studies or at least monitoring of such species is desirable. Severity of impact to such species is influenced by the nature of the learned response, along with the spatial pattern of recreational use and critical habitat. Populations in which most individuals learn strong avoidance behavior may be substantially impacted if recreational use is widely dispersed and/or occurs within much of the preferred habitat for feeding, breeding, or birthing. Populations in which most individuals exhibit strong attraction responses also can be impacted significantly if the outcomes of encounters are often lethal, as is the case with black bears (*Ursus americanus*) (Singer and Bratton 1980).

MONITORING

Routine monitoring should be a part of any management program. Both recreational use and wildlife populations of concern should be monitored. It is important to monitor recreational activity because most techniques for mitigating wildlife impact involve managing visitor use. The amount and type of recreational use, including how use is distributed in space and time, should be monitored. It would be efficient to focus monitoring of visitor use in places where wildlife species are highly concentrated or particularly vulnerable. Techniques for monitoring visitor use are varied and highly developed. Numerous devices are commercially available for measuring car traffic and flow through developed facilities. Monitoring dispersed travel, particularly foot travel in remote wildlands, is more challenging. Watson et al. (2000) provide a handbook on alternative techniques for estimating magnitude, type, and location of recreational use in wildlands; it includes practical information about establishing objectives, deciding what variables to monitor, designing and implementing a sampling plan, and calculating statistics that can be used to affect management decisions.

Techniques for monitoring wildlife populations also are diverse and well-developed. The high cost of monitoring populations makes it important to focus monitoring efforts carefully. The primary species on which to focus monitoring are threatened and endangered species, species of special concern, or species that are locally concentrated in space or at particular times of the year. Techniques for monitoring wildlife populations are covered at length in other chapters of this manual. Monitoring the effects of recreation on wildlife can be problematic because it is seldom possible to separate the effects of recreation from other influences on wildlife populations. Consequently, it is often necessary to conduct field studies to establish cause-and-effect relationships between recreation and wildlife and then to monitor recreation use carefully. Even if field studies have been conducted, it is still important to monitor wildlife populations. Moreover, if dramatic changes in management are undertaken, monitoring of wildlife populations can provide crucial information about the effectiveness of these actions.

CONDUCTING FIELD STUDIES

When potential exists for significant recreational disturbance to wildlife, and when available information does not provide an adequate scientific basis for evaluating the actual effects of this disturbance, field studies should be conducted. These studies should attempt to evaluate factors that influence the nature and magnitude of impact and whether the activity is detrimental. This work is needed to verify suspected recreational impacts so that decisions about how to manage these activities are consistent with their real impact. If careful studies confirm that an activity with significant disturbance potential actually has negligible effects, restrictive management would not be necessary; indeed, regulation of recreation in this case would be indefensible and detrimental to relationships between recreationists and wildland managers. If field studies indicate that a recreational activity is substantially detrimental to wildlife, decisions must then be made about how to manage the activity so that wildlife impacts are not significant. Because of the context-specific nature of recreational impacts on wildlife, it is not wise to apply blindly a management technique that has been used previously for a similar problem. Differences between one's local situation and the situation in which the management technique was applied previously (e.g., the species, frequency of recreation, habitat conditions, historical context of human disturbance) may reduce or eliminate the method's effectiveness. Thus, in many cases, field studies may be needed not only to reveal actual impacts, but also to evaluate the success of a management approach.

Field Study Type and Design

Experimental and non-experimental (observational or correlational) studies can shed light on recreational disturbance and how to manage it. Each of these 2 study types has advantages and disadvantages, and the decision about which type of study to conduct will be affected largely by the specific type of recreational disturbance in question, available resources (e.g., funding, personnel, time), and the need for information about cause-and-effect relations. An additional consideration is how the results of a study will be used to dictate management actions. For example, simple initial studies can be used to identify the factors on which more expensive, in-depth research should focus, but such pilot studies would not by themselves be rigorous enough to formulate management policy. Research approaches must be scientifically valid if one intends to use the results to direct management because inaccurate information may lead to mismanagement of wildlife or recreational activity, and because user groups may challenge management actions. Regardless of study type, the usual principles of sampling, replication, statistical power, study design, and data analysis must be applied. We do not discuss these principles because they are described in detail elsewhere (e.g., Green 1979, Hurlbert 1984, Cohen 1988, Hairston 1989, Hair et al. 1998, Zar 1999, and chapters in this volume).

Experimental Studies

Lack of understanding about cause-and-effect relations is a significant impediment to managing recreational disturbance. The most credible, defensible, and efficient way to surmount this problem is to conduct properly designed experiments. In contrast to many other aspects of wildlife science, assessment of recreational disturbance lends itself quite well to experiments (Gutzwiller 1991). The reason is that human activity is the primary factor of interest, and we can often experimentally manipulate such activity (Yarmoloy et al. 1988, Skagen et al. 1991, Knight and Cole 1995a). In a recreational disturbance experiment, one manipulates the activity of concern to test a hypothesis about the effect of that activity on wildlife. Control units, for which no disturbance occurs, must be included so that one can separate the effects of other factors that vary

through space or time from the effects of changes in the activity of interest. Without controls in space and time, cause-and-effect relations cannot be established. Examples of units in recreational studies include sites (Gutzwiller et al. 1997), nests (Knight and Fitzner 1985), individual animals (Stalmaster and Newman 1978), and family groups (Keller 1991).

One experimental approach is to mimic recreational disturbance through use of investigators who conduct the recreational activity in question. The key advantage of this technique is that factors associated with recreationists, such as movements in time and space, noise levels, vehicle type, frequency of occurrence, and party size, can be controlled. The result can be a more precisely controlled and, hence, more interpretable experiment. However, such studies must ensure the simulated activity matches the actual recreational activity as closely as possible so the results are applicable to real-world situations (Gutzwiller 1991). In addition, if investigators are implementing recreation treatments as well as evaluating their effects, investigators must be blind to the hypotheses being tested (e.g., Gutzwiller et al. 2002) so preconceived notions about the influence of the disturbance do not bias their observations of effects. Using investigators to simulate recreational disturbance also requires funding for personnel, transportation, housing, and equipment needed to mimic the recreation, as well as development of specific treatment (disturbance) protocols (e.g., Gutzwiller and Anderson 1999). Depending on the activity and the spatial and temporal scales involved, costs of mimicking recreational disturbance can be high.

Another experimental approach is to assess recreational disturbance through serial management experiments (Macnab 1983, Gutzwiller 1993), an adaptive approach in which activities of actual recreationists are manipulated in time, space, or both through management actions. After each experiment, new knowledge can be gained about the effect of the disturbance on wildlife. No funding for personnel and other resources to simulate recreational disturbance is needed because these management experiments make use of actual recreational activities. Realism of the disturbances is ensured because actual recreationists and their activities are involved. With cooperation among natural resource agencies, management experiments can be devised to address recreational disturbances that span spatial and temporal scales.

Management experiments are not often used to assess recreational disturbance on wildlife, but they should be used whenever feasible (Gutzwiller 1993). A single experiment may not reveal the specific facet or level of recreational disturbance that underlies a problem, so researchers should be prepared to conduct a series of experiments. Initial management experiments should consider broad ranges of one or more suspected disturbance factors (e.g., location, duration, frequency, intensity, spatial scale, or seasonal timing), and follow-up experiments should focus increasingly on recreation aspects that previous experiments in the series indicated were most influential (Gutzwiller 1993). User groups may object to manipulation or curtailment of their activities during such experiments, but wildlife scientists should explain that these experiments are in the best long-term interests of wildlife *and* recreationists. These experiments are the best way to identify the actual cause of a problem; this knowledge may prevent unnecessary closure of areas to recreationists, or it may preclude the need to even regulate a recreational activity.

Non-experimental Studies

When constraints on logistics, funding, time, or other resources preclude experimental assessment, non-experimental studies can often be used to identify associations between recreational disturbance and wildlife responses. Compared to experimental studies, non-experimental studies may be more realistic to implement because they can be quicker, easier, and less expensive to conduct (Gutzwiller 1991). These characteristics may be especially advantageous when influence of a recreational activity must be discerned quickly, as might be the case when species of special concern are involved. A non-experimental study also can be valuable as a way to gain general insight about recreational impacts because such a study can be broader and more holistic than can most field experiments. Wildlife scientists can use non-experimental studies to help identify the most relevant factors and hypotheses to address in subsequent experiments.

Through measurement of wildlife responses for disturbed and undisturbed study units, both before and after recreational activity, the study design of non-experimental studies can be used to avoid many biases. Control of the effects of extraneous variables on inferences also can be accomplished analytically with such techniques as regression or analysis of covariance (Huitema 1980). Non-experimental studies are based not on experimental manipulation of a recreational activity but on observed associations. These studies are therefore subject to spurious interpretations that can originate from confounded effects. For example, it would be difficult to separate the effects of recreational disturbance and food availability on habitat use by a species if the recreational activity coincided (was confounded) in space or time with weather-induced changes in food density. Thus, other factors being equal, inferences about cause-and-effect relations cannot be made with as much confidence from non-experimental studies as they can from experimental studies.

Complex Effects

Although complex influences—including interaction, cumulative, ripple, threshold, and lag effects—may often reflect reality better than do simple main effects, wildlife scientists have not typically assessed complex effects of recreational disturbance on wildlife. Main effects occur when levels of an independent variable differ in their influence on a response variable; interaction effects occur when the effect of one independent variable changes with the levels of another independent variable (Fig. 2). Wildlife scientists should consider whether there are interaction effects between different aspects of the same recreational activity (e.g., number of visitors and seasonal timing for wildlife viewing) or between different types of recreation (e.g., hiking and angling). Interaction effects of recreational activities and environmental conditions (e.g., habitat quality, food availability) also should be considered because impacts of recreationists may vary with ecological states and natural disturbances. Two-way interaction effects on a wildlife response variable are the simplest to study (Box 1).

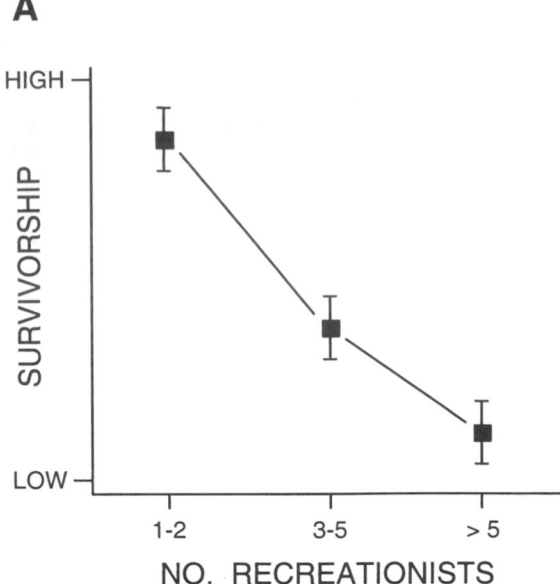

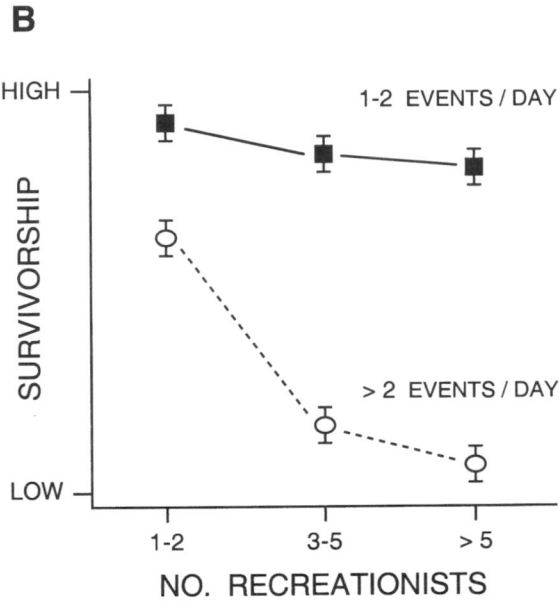

Fig. 2. Illustration of a main effect (A), in which a wildlife response variable (e.g., mean survivorship ± 2 SD) differs among levels of one independent variable (e.g., number of recreationists); and an interaction effect (B), in which the influence of one independent variable (number of recreationists) on the response variable differs between levels of another independent variable (e.g., frequency of recreational activity).

Cumulative effects occur when impacts add up through time or space (Riffell et al. 1996). For a given type of recreation, a single disturbance may not generate a serious problem for wildlife, but recurring disturbances may lead to substantial problems through temporal or spatial summation of impacts. Consequently, some activities that have no obvious individual effects may result in cumulative impacts. It also is possible that recreational disturbances that have significant short-term or local effects may not result in temporally or spatially cumulative effects. The reason these outcomes are possible is that development of cumulative effects is affected in part by whether wildlife

Box 1. Assessing interaction effects.

Two-way interaction effects are usually easier to assess than are 3-way or higher-order interaction effects because they are easier to gather data for and interpret. To study 2-way interaction effects, one collects data on the dependent variable (wildlife response variable) for all combinations of the levels of 2 independent variables (also known as factors). Here we focus on the interaction effect of a recreational activity and an environmental condition.

Suppose that a biologist wants to know whether the number of fledglings for a species is influenced by an interaction involving the number of wildlife viewers and food abundance. For each nest (unit of analysis), the biologist would collect data on number of fledglings (dependent variable) for nests that were in areas with different numbers of viewers and different levels of food abundance. For breeding birds, one might estimate food levels by measuring arthropod abundance. The matrix below illustrates the basic design needed to assess 2-way interaction effects.

Arthropod abundance (g/m^3)	Number of wildlife viewers/day		
	0–2	3–5	6–8
0–30	3, 3, 3, 4 (3.3)	2, 2, 1, 2 (1.8)	0, 0, 1, 0 (0.3)
31–60	2, 4, 4, 5 (3.8)	4, 3, 2, 4 (3.3)	2, 2, 2, 3 (2.3)
61–90	4, 3, 5, 4 (4.0)	3, 3, 5, 5 (4.0)	3, 3, 4, 4 (3.5)

We have 3 levels of each of the 2 factors, and we have number of fledglings for 4 nests (mean number of fledglings in parentheses) for each of the 9 factor-level combinations ($n = 36$). It is reasonable to study from 2 to approximately 4 levels of each factor, but higher numbers of levels make it difficult to obtain adequate replication for each factor-level combination. The number of replicates shown here is for illustrative purposes only. Analysis of required sample sizes (see other chapters in this volume) should be used to calculate the number of replicates needed for each factor-level combination. Analysis of variance can be used to assess whether the effect of number of wildlife viewers on number of fledglings is statistically influenced by arthropod abundance.

Wildlife viewers may disturb adults and reduce the number of feeding visits to the nest. Number of feeding visits to the nest, and hence number of fledglings, also may be influenced by food abundance. In this example, mean number of fledglings generally decreases with increasing number of viewers, and the decreases are more severe (rates of decline are higher) with decreasing levels of arthropod abundance. Because the effect of number of wildlife viewers on number of fledglings differs between levels of arthropod abundance, we conclude the 2 factors interact to affect number of fledglings. A biological interpretation of this interaction effect is that the impact of wildlife viewers on number of fledglings gets progressively larger as food becomes less plentiful.

recovers from a disturbance before the next disturbance in time or space is encountered. If recovery to an undisturbed state occurs before wildlife experiences the next disturbance, cumulative effects are less likely to develop than if wildlife does not recover before the onset of the next disturbance (see Sousa 1984, Rapport et al. 1985, Petraitis et al. 1989, Spaling and Smit 1993, Riffell et al. 1996). Cumulative effects do not develop when the initial disturbance causes the maximum amount of impact possible. The study by Riffell et al. (1996) demonstrates how to assess whether a repeated recreational activity has temporally cumulative impacts on bird communities.

Ripple effects occur when the wildlife response to a disturbance leads to changes at other levels of biological organization, at other trophic levels, or at other places. Two examples illustrate these effects. If off-road-vehicle activities displaced numerous individuals from a carnivore population, predation by that species would decrease in the disturbed area. With reduced predation, the richness and evenness of the carnivore's prey community may change. Thus, disturbance at a population level may cause changes at a community level, and disturbance to one component of a food chain (predator) may affect other food-chain components (prey). When recreational disturbances have effects beyond their site of origin, the influence of the original disturbance has rippled through space. For example,

boating activity may displace foraging waterfowl from a lake and force them to feed at undisturbed but overcrowded wetlands. Waterfowl may experience lower food availability or higher risks for diseases at such locations. In this instance, an influence at one place (displacement from lake) had an effect elsewhere (increased overcrowding and associated problems). Holistic thinking is needed to assess ripple effects (Box 2).

Wildlife responses to disturbances may exhibit thresholds (Fig. 3) or lags (Fig. 4), which can complicate detection of recreational effects. For example, a recreational disturbance may have little or no effect until it reaches a critical level (threshold), and this level will not be detected if it lies outside of the range of the disturbance variable considered. Similarly, a recreational disturbance may not induce a problem until well after the initial disturbance, and assessments that measure wildlife responses only immediately after the disturbance will fail to detect such impacts. To avoid these problems, researchers should conduct studies that involve a wide range of conditions for the disturbance variable and continue to monitor wildlife responses for some time after recreational activities cease. Decisions about how wide the assessed range of a disturbance variable should be can be based on the range of recreational disturbance that is possible or probable in a given area. Decisions about how long assessments should last

Box 2.   Assessing ripple effects.

The design of studies to assess ripple effects should center on probable connections between different levels of biological organization (e.g., individuals, populations, communities, ecosystems), between trophic levels (e.g., carnivores, herbivores), and between events at different places. To identify possible ripple effects of recreational disturbance, biologists need to think holistically about the biology of the species involved, especially about such issues as behavior, food habits, habitat requirements, natural-history characteristics, home range and territory sizes, relationships with other organisms (e.g., competitive, predator-prey, mutualistic), and the spatial connectivity of the landscape. Knowledge about the effect on wildlife from the disturbance that is presumed to initiate the ripple effect, obtained from the literature or field studies, also is important to consider.

The fundamental question is whether a recreational effect at one level of biological organization, trophic level, or place has an effect on wildlife at, respectively, another level of biological organization, trophic level, or place. Once the biologist identifies possible ways in which recreational disturbance may cause ripple effects, standard field research approaches can be used to assess whether hypothesized or suspected impacts are real. The following hypothetical scenario illustrates these ideas.

A biologist suspected that off-road-vehicle (ORV) activity was affecting use of streams by northern river otters (*Lontra canadensis*). The situation was perplexing, however, because observations indicated abundance of otters was not affected by ORV noise or the presence of the off-road enthusiasts themselves. A closer examination of the situation revealed that uplands and floodplains damaged by ORV tires were depositing sediment into nearby streams during heavy rains and spring thaws. The biologist hypothesized there may be a connection between this sediment, density of fish and aquatic invertebrates in the stream (river otter prey), and abundance of otters in the streams. She decided to assess whether there was a ripple effect of the ORVs that affected stream use by otters through sediment impacts on their prey.

The biologist obtained estimates of otter, fish, and invertebrate numbers for both stream groups (adjacent ORV activity, no adjacent ORV activity) at paired sites (i.e., 2 sites per location). Each pair involved 2 streams that were in close proximity to one another and that occurred in comparable landscape contexts; however, at each location, one stream had nearby ORV activity and the other did not. The paired design helped to control for variation in otter, fish, and invertebrate numbers associated with among-location differences in bank slope, rainfall, snowmelt, stream temperature, and stream depth, which can affect soil erosion or fish and invertebrate numbers. This design reduced the chance these factors would be confounded with (inseparable from) or obscure (through added variance) the effects of the ORVs on otters.

She found that fish and invertebrate numbers were lower in streams that experienced sedimentation from nearby ORV activity than in streams without nearby ORV activity. Otter numbers exhibited the same pattern. The biologist concluded that her study supported the hypothesis that ORV activity had a ripple effect on otters that was transmitted through a food-chain connection.

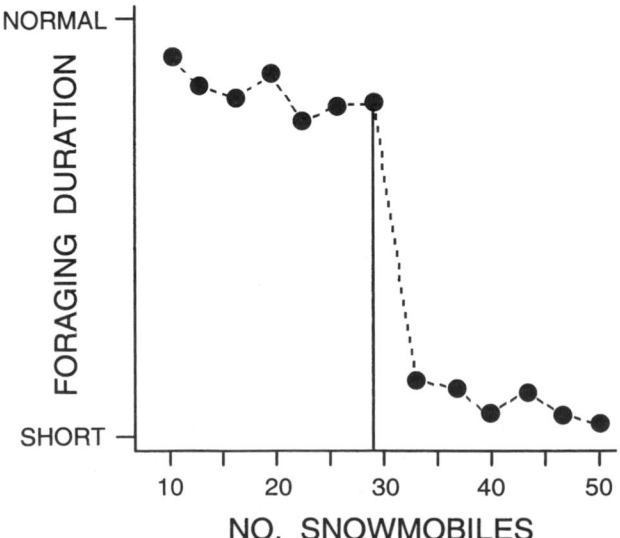

Fig. 3. Illustration of how to identify a recreational disturbance threshold. A plot of a wildlife response variable (e.g., foraging duration) versus a disturbance variable (e.g., number of snowmobiles) can be used to assess whether there is a disturbance level beyond which there is an abrupt change in the response variable—the threshold level of the recreational activity (vertical line).

following disturbances can be based on the length of time that the disturbance may appreciably affect the biology of the species (e.g., reproduction, survivorship) or the integrity of its habitat (e.g., availability of food and shelter).

Variables that represent complex effects are incorporated into studies in the design phase and assessed for their importance in the data-analysis phase. Complex effects cannot be revealed through an analysis of main effects alone. If complex effects were influential in a system, management based on information from a main-effects study would be misleading and may result in inappropriate management of wildlife or recreational activities. Thus, knowledge about complex effects is crucial for effective management, and assessments of disturbance should consider these effects.

Deciding Which Response and Disturbance Variables to Measure

Management objectives, the potential for direct and indirect (habitat) effects, and the importance of addressing wildlife fitness (reproduction, survivorship, lifespan) should be used to decide which response and disturbance variables to measure. Variables that specifically address management objectives for wildlife and wildland recre-

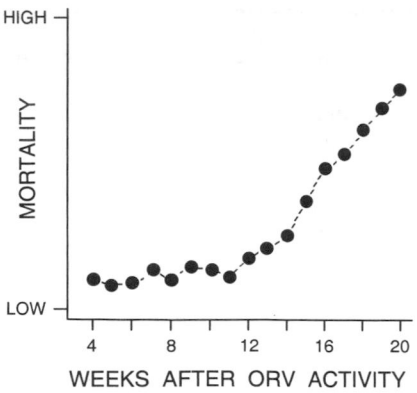

Fig. 4. Example of a lag in the effects of a recreational disturbance. If off-road-vehicle (ORV) activities during early fall damage winter-range vegetation such that winter forage quantity and quality are seriously reduced, effects of the disturbance may not become apparent until months later. Ungulate mortality is not influenced appreciably soon after ORV activities because most animals have not yet moved to winter range and energy demands are not yet high. But by mid or late winter, when high-quality forage is extremely limited and ungulates are struggling to maintain a positive energy balance, ORV damage to winter forage becomes apparent as animals succumb to reduced nutrition and harsh winter conditions.

ation must be studied, and the resulting data must be directly applicable to management situations. Managers should not have to extrapolate the results of a study to their particular situation. For example, if a management objective relates to wildlife reproduction, the response variable should be number of individuals produced, percent of young that survived to a certain date, or some other variable that directly reflects reproduction, not a variable that may only be a weak correlate, such as number of calling males. To be maximally useful, response and disturbance variables must directly reflect the spatial scale, time frame, and level of biological organization (e.g., population, community, ecosystem) that a management objective addresses (Box 3).

Studies that consider direct effects will require variables that measure actual wildlife responses at the level of individuals (e.g., behavior, physiology, productivity, and mortality), populations (abundance, distribution, and demographics), or communities (species composition and interactions) (Gabrielsen and Smith 1995, Knight and Cole 1995b). Studies of indirect effects will require variables that measure effects of recreational activity on soil, vege-

---

Box 3.   Measuring response and disturbance variables that directly address management objectives.

If biologists gather data about variables that are directly pertinent to a management objective, managers do not have to extrapolate or guess how to apply the study's results to their situation. This approach can help managers avoid inappropriate application of results and improve conservation effectiveness. The example that follows illustrates how one should match response and disturbance variables to the spatial scale, time frame, and level of biological organization that a management objective addresses.

Suppose the management objective is to regulate mountain biking activity (if necessary) so that reproductive activities of an elk (*Cervus elaphus*) population on the calving grounds are not impacted. Data for several response and disturbance variables are needed to assess whether there is need for concern about mountain biking and, if so, what aspect of this disturbance is problematic.

The spatial scale to be considered includes areas used by reproducing cows and their calves. The time frame includes the period just prior to, during, and immediately after calving. Outside of this time interval, mountain biking in the study area occurs either rarely or in areas not used by reproducing elk. If pregnant females were displaced from wintering areas and their nutritional status was compromised as a result, they may reproduce less successfully. But in the area for which the management objective was developed, this was not an issue because mountain biking did not occur on the wintering grounds. However, mountain bikers use areas that pregnant females use for feeding just prior to calving, so impacts on the health of cows at this time and in this part of their range are a concern. The population is the level of biological organization of interest here. Data for individual cows and their calves are needed to characterize reproductive activities for the population.

The biologist identifies several response variables that relate to reproductive performance so he can assess whether mountain biking disturbed reproductive activity. He considers measuring the percentage of time that cow elk spend in alert behavior or fleeing from mountain bikers, and whether females fitted with radio collars (including heart rate and movement sensors) are displaced from birthing areas or exhibit stress in the form of abnormal heart rates and daily movements. Because of limited time and resources, however, the biologist decides to focus on birth rate and calf mortality—fitness-related response variables. He also reasons that, compared to the behavioral and physiological variables he considered, these fitness variables would provide information that is more directly relevant to the population's reproductive performance.

Using the literature on elk responses to human activity during the breeding season, as well as his understanding of general ungulate behavior, the biologist identifies disturbance variables that have high potential for being problematic. He knows that important activities such as feeding and resting occur at specific times of day and decides to measure the daily timing of mountain biking activity throughout the identified time frame. For each day, the average size and number of mountain-biker groups also are estimated because the intensity of disturbance may be an issue. Ungulates may react more strongly to bikers that leave established trails (either on foot or with their bikes) than they may to bikers who remain on trails. Thus, the biologist decides to measure the daily frequency with which off-trail activity occurs and distances involved. If necessary, these disturbance variables can be manipulated by management, through restrictions on the daily timing of activity or number of mountain bikers, and through education about and enforcement of trail-use regulations.

tation, and water components of wildlife habitat. Examples of variables for assessment of indirect effects are soil compaction, erosion, rutting, productivity, chemistry, moisture, temperature, and microbiota; vegetation density, cover, species composition (including invasive exotic species), vertical structure, and spatial pattern; and water chemistry, turbidity, organic matter content, and flow (Cole and Landres 1995, Douglass et al. 1999). Response variables that measure wildlife fitness should be studied so that effects of recreation on processes that underlie long-term conservation (e.g., population dynamics, survivorship) can be better understood.

Response Variables

Examples of response variables that relate directly to fitness include number of clutches or litters, clutch or litter size, average mass of young, percent survivorship of young and adults, recruitment into the breeding population, lifetime reproduction, mortality rate, and lifespan. Hatching efficiency, nest success, fledging efficiency, and potential replacement rate are additional fitness metrics that can be used to assess effects of recreational disturbance (Box 4).

Although fitness variables may be most important to consider, it is sometimes difficult to obtain adequate fitness data because of logistical constraints, limits to funding and other resources, inability to find reproduction sites, or the difficulty of capturing animals or studying individuals for extended periods. Variables that relate less directly to fitness can be valuable and are sometimes easier to measure. Examples of such variables include time spent brooding, foraging, being vigilant, and fleeing from recreationists; wildlife occurrence and abundance; and the distance from recreationists at which physiological, behavioral, reproductive, or distributional effects are induced (e.g., Burger 1991, Knight et al. 1991, Staine and Burger 1994, Klein et al. 1995).

Disturbance Variables

Biologists should measure disturbance variables that can be directly regulated or manipulated through management actions. Examples of disturbance variables that may affect wildlife and that managers can alter include: mode of travel (e.g., vehicle, foot, stock, skis); type, frequency, predictability, spatial extent, location, daily and seasonal timing, duration, and speed of recreational activity; impacts to soil, vegetation, and water; noise properties and sources; and the total length or density of trails or roads that increase human access (e.g., Bowles 1995; Cole and Landres 1995; Knight and Cole 1995*a,b*; Claar et al. 1999; Gutzwiller and Anderson 1999).

Prior recreational activities should be considered in studies of present situations because the current status of wildlife at a site may reflect effects of previous recreational disturbances. For instance, large carnivores may have been displaced by previous disturbances, resulting in communities that now are depauperate in top predators despite an otherwise natural environment. Or a present lack of response to a recreational activity may reflect habituation to recurring disturbances that took place over several years, and the initial effects of disturbances on the individuals or populations involved are no longer apparent.

Historical data for disturbance variables can be used to assess impacts of prior activities on present conditions.

Box 4.   Additional examples of fitness variables.

Gehlbach and Gehlbach (2000) reported results of studies that assessed whether recreationists impacted the reproductive success of whiskered screech-owls (*Megascops trichopsis*) in the Chiricahua and Huachuca mountains, Arizona during 1995–99. Most of the recreationists were birdwatchers (individuals and guided groups), but a few were campers and hikers. Recreationists visited whiskered screech-owl nests in camping areas and near trails, sometimes repeatedly. Disturbances included "Repeated use of tape recordings and imitations to call whiskered screech-owls into view, use of strong lights to see them at night, flash photography, and pounding or rubbing on nest trees to induce appearance..." (Gehlbach and Gehlbach 2000:18). The effect of the investigators' research protocol on the owls was negligible.

Although first clutch hatching efficiency (hatchlings/eggs) was 84% for undisturbed clutches and 62% for disturbed clutches, the difference was not statistically significant. Undisturbed nests were 87% successful ($\geq$1 chick fledged), whereas disturbed nests were 70% successful, but these rates did not differ statistically. Undisturbed nests had an average of 2.8 nestlings and 2.7 fledglings, and these values were statistically higher than were those for disturbed nests (2.0 nestlings, 1.5 fledglings). Statistically significant differences also emerged for average fledging efficiency (fledglings/hatchlings) (87% for undisturbed, 65% for disturbed); productivity (fledglings/eggs) (84% for undisturbed, 57% for disturbed); and potential replacement rate (fledglings/breeding pair) (2.9 for undisturbed, 1.4 for disturbed).

For example, analyses could assess whether the present distribution of a rare species is correlated with seasonal timing, daily frequency, and spatial extent of ecotourist disturbance during previous years. Or one could examine whether the current abundance of a species that is popular with photographers is correlated with the amount of time that has elapsed since trails or roads were established. Present and historical data for disturbance variables also can be combined in a study to test for interaction effects of current and previous recreational disturbances (Box 5). Historical variables, which can provide insights about the long-term effects of recreational impacts, can be used to help develop management approaches and policies that foster the perpetual coexistence of wildlife and recreationists.

MANAGING RECREATIONAL DISTURBANCE OF WILDLIFE

In terms of time, personnel, funding, disturbance to wildlife, and inconvenience to recreationists, it usually is less costly to preclude a recreational problem than it is to correct one. Although not all situations lend themselves to pre-emptive strategies, we recommend that managers

Box 5.   Assessing interaction effects of present and historical recreational disturbances.

An interaction effect involving present and historical disturbances would imply the effect of present disturbance on wildlife depends on levels of the historical disturbance. Such an interaction would indicate a temporal connection between current and previous disturbances. Note that current and previous disturbances can be of the same type (e.g., present and historical boating activity) or of different types (e.g., present ecotourist numbers, historical backpacker use). A hypothetical example illustrates how one might assess these interaction effects.

A biologist is concerned that caving (recreational cave exploration) may affect the reproductive performance of bat populations. Because bats often breed in the same caves each year, and because caves in her study areas were visited by ecotourists during previous years, the biologist suspects the effect of current caving activity may be exacerbating impacts of prior ecotourist activity on bat reproductive performance. She decides to assess whether past ecotourist activity and current caving activity interact to affect present bat reproduction. The following matrix contains the data for the study.

Previous ecotourist activity (years)	Current caving activity (spelunker groups/week)		
	0	1–2	3–4
0	1.2, 0.9, 1.0, 0.8, 0.8	1.0, 0.9, 0.8, 0.6, 0.7	0.8, 0.9, 0.6, 0.4, 0.5
1–3	1.1, 0.8, 1.0, 0.7, 0.9	0.9, 0.7, 1.0, 0.7, 0.8	1.0, 0.9, 0.7, 0.3, 0.6
4–6	1.3, 0.7, 0.9, 0.8, 0.9	1.2, 0.9, 0.8, 0.7, 0.5	0.9, 0.8, 0.5, 0.4, 0.7

Reliable data on the number of bat breeding seasons (years) during which ecotourists visited each of 45 caves were available for 6 prior consecutive years. Data for number of weeks during which spelunker groups visited each cave during the present breeding season were recorded. The mean number of young produced per female (table entries) was estimated for each of 5 caves for each of the 9 factor-level combinations. The biologist measured the size of areas within each cave that were suitable for bat breeding. This variable was used as a covariate in the analysis to control analytically for the effect of area of suitable breeding substrate on number of young produced per female. In the analysis, the covariate adjusts for differences among caves in breeding area so that interaction effects can be assessed without concern they are confounded with (indistinguishable from) effects of suitable breeding area.

The biologist used analysis of covariance to control for suitable breeding area and to test for an interaction effect of past ecotourism activity and current caving activity on present bat reproductive performance. She found there was no significant interaction effect, that previous ecotourism activity did not affect present reproduction, but that current caving activity decreased reproductive performance. The lack of an interaction effect indicated the effect of current caving activity did not depend on or vary with past ecotourist activity.

apply proactive (rather than reactive) approaches to manage recreational impacts whenever feasible.

Framework for Management

Managing recreational disturbance of wildlife is both art and science. It involves value judgments as well as scientific information. Contemporary management frameworks attempt to bring values and science together (while making the distinctions clear) in processes that lead to effective management solutions to problems that are explicitly defined and based on societal values. The *Limits of Acceptable Change* process is the original and best known of these processes (Stankey et al. 1985). Another closely related process is *Visitor Impact Management* (Vaske et al. 1995). Managers need not use these processes as formal or rigid procedures. They are equally useful as informal ways to structure thinking and decision-making.

Each of these processes involves (1) identifying problems—situations where monitoring data (scientific information) show that management objectives (value judgments) are not being met, (2) implementing management solutions to problems based on insight into causal factors, and (3) obtaining feedback from periodic monitoring to assess both the effectiveness of management solutions and

whether new problems have developed (Fig. 5). Although these steps are conceptually simple, their implementation is often hindered by reluctance on the part of managers to make their value judgments as transparent and explicit as they are in this process. Implementation also is stymied by the challenge of making monitoring an integral, ongoing part of management. The alternatives—management in the absence of science or based on personal biases of mid-level managers—are no longer acceptable to a pluralistic and democratic society.

The initial steps in these frameworks involve collecting information, assessing values, and then codifying value judgments into quantifiable management objectives. Individual steps each result in a greater level of specificity for management objectives. The first step generally involves compiling legislative and policy mandates, earlier planning documents and planning constraints, and existing data. Some natural areas may have been established largely for protection of one or several species, whereas other areas may have been established to preserve natural landscapes and processes. Some areas may emphasize ecosystem preservation, whereas others might emphasize recreational opportunities. Particular attention should be given to describing the purpose of the area and its significance (or niche) at larger spatial scales. If the area is the primary

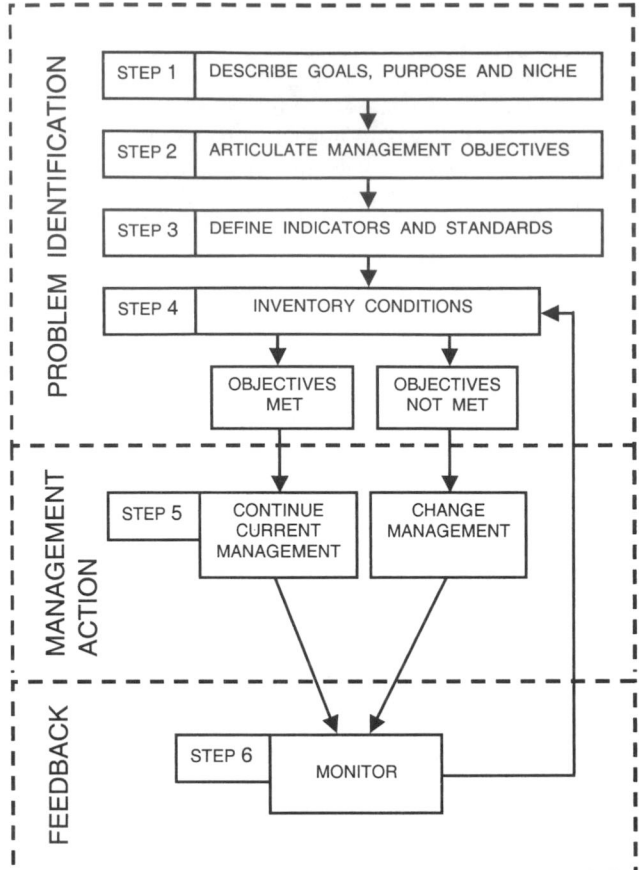

Fig. 5. A framework for managing recreational impacts on wildlife.

life forms and the desires of a wider spectrum of recreationists.

The third step, defining indicators and standards, amounts to stating objectives in quantifiable terms. Indicators are measurable variables that are either important components of desired conditions or that are related to (or proxies for) those conditions. For example, given the objective of minimal disturbance of nesting birds, an indicator might be number of abandoned nests, and a proxy indicator might be the number of vehicles/day observed within the nesting area. Standards are the limits—generally the minimum acceptable conditions—assigned to each indicator. In our nesting bird example, the standard might be no more than 2% of nests abandoned, or no more than one vehicle/day. If there are multiple zones, each zone may have the same indicator but a different standard.

The fourth step involves inventorying conditions, with most attention given to monitoring selected indicators. In this way, existing conditions can be compared to standards. By definition, where conditions are out of compliance with standards, a problem exists that requires management attention. Through this process, problems have been identified in a more objective and comprehensive manner than has been the norm. Problem definition, in theory, flows from agreed-upon value judgments (objectives and standards) and scientific data (inventoried conditions).

The fifth step is to develop or fine-tune management programs to reflect where problems do and do not occur. Where conditions are in compliance with standards, little change in management is needed. However, where they are not in compliance, managers need to search for causes of problems and implement management actions with the potential to alleviate problems.

The final, often-neglected step in the process is monitoring. Periodically, conditions need to be monitored both within an adaptive management framework (to assess the effectiveness of management programs and how they might be fine-tuned), as well as to reassess whether management objectives are being met. Too often, planners, managers, and researchers perceive monitoring as something that should be someone else's responsibility. Also, monitoring is frequently perceived as an end rather than a means, and as a task rather than a tool. Monitoring is a tool for (1) developing the understanding needed to build an effective management program, and (2) obtaining the scientific evidence for defending your management program if necessary.

Management Strategies

There are many potentially effective approaches for managing recreational disturbance of wildlife. Working through a management framework should narrow the array of alternatives by (1) specifying problems in terms of what, where, and when, and (2) suggesting the relative social acceptability of different approaches. However, it is important to consider all possible management avenues, and it is often most effective to combine approaches and attack a problem from several different perspectives. It is particularly helpful to consider the strategic purpose of alternative management actions.

Fundamentally, the magnitude of wildlife disturbance is a function of the magnitude of recreational disturbance and the vulnerability of wildlife to that disturbance. This sug-

refuge for a particular wildlife species, management objectives are likely to be different than if the area is simply one of many refugia in the region. Broad statements of goals, purpose, and significance or niche are the products of this step.

The second step is to develop narrative descriptions of management objectives or what are frequently referred to as *desired future conditions.* This is a prescriptive step as it is a statement of what should be rather than a description of what is present. Generally, objectives address ecological, social, and managerial conditions. They describe appropriate compromises between competing objectives. For example, area goals might be to provide not only recreational access to beaches, but also to ensure the preservation of beach-nesting birds. Objectives might state there will be minimal disturbance of nesting birds, with recreational use allowed only to the extent that birds are not disturbed on nests. This compromise will result in different management and different conditions than will one in which recreational access is given a higher priority than is protection of birds.

This can be an uncomfortable step for many managers because it involves making value-laden decisions that have serious consequences. Decisions will promote certain life forms and landscapes and be detrimental to others. They will be favorable to some people and unfavorable to others. Particularly in large areas, several different zones may be established, each with unique objectives. This provides one means of favoring the needs of a broader diversity of

Table 1. Strategies for managing recreational impacts on wildlife.

Manage People
- Reduce amount of recreational use.
- Reduce per capita impact of use.
    Manipulate type of use.
    Manipulate visitor behavior.
    Concentrate recreational use.
    Manipulate location of use.
    Manipulate timing of use.

Manage Wildlife
- Reduce vulnerability to disturbance.
    Increase habituation to recreational use.
    Decrease attraction to humans.
    Increase avoidance behavior.

Manage Wildlife Habitat
- Reduce vulnerability to disturbance.
    Attract wildlife to locations far from users.
    Screen wildlife from recreationists.
- Compensate for disturbance.
    Create new habitat.
    Improve habitat quality.

gests 3 basic strategies for management: (1) manipulate visitor characteristics to reduce recreational disturbance, (2) manipulate wildlife to reduce vulnerability to disturbance, and (3) manipulate habitat either to reduce wildlife vulnerability or to compensate for recreational disturbance. Each of these 3 primary strategies consists of several substrategies (Table 1).

Manipulation of Visitor Characteristics

Amount of recreational use is one obvious factor that influences the magnitude of disturbance. Some have suggested that carrying capacities for people should be developed, much as they have been for wildlife. Consequently, one strategy is to reduce or limit amount of use. There are many ways to limit use, ranging from requiring entry permits to more subtle approaches such as limiting parking spaces, making access more difficult, and even manipulating the type of information provided to visitors. Somewhat counterintuitively, reducing amount of use by itself is often not an effective management approach. The relationship between amount of use and amount of impact is often highly curvilinear. As use levels increase, additional use has less and less additional effect (e.g., Ferguson and Keith 1982). Consequently, use limitation may be most worthwhile in places where use levels are currently low and regulations are effective in keeping disturbance levels below thresholds (Hammitt and Cole 1998:256–257).

Other strategies try to reduce the per capita impact of recreationists (Table 1). The type of recreational activity can have a large effect on disturbance. Consider the difference in impact between a hunter and a photographer, or the difference in the extent of the area potentially impacted in a sand-dune ecosystem by a pedestrian versus someone driving an off-road vehicle. Although there are exceptions, motorized uses will generally cause more disturbance than nonmotorized uses, groups with stock and/or dogs will cause more impact than groups without animals, and overnight users cause more disturbance than day users

(Knight and Cole 1995b, Hammitt and Cole 1998: 182–198).

The behavior of recreationists may have an even greater influence on the magnitude of disturbance than type of activity. Disturbance depends on decisions about whether or not to approach wildlife and, if they are approached, how close to get to them. Studies have shown that fast-moving snowmobiles cause more disturbance of white-tailed deer (*Odocoileus virginianus*) than do slow-moving snowmobiles, but the greatest disturbance occurs when the snowmobile stops (Richens and Lavigne 1978). Noisy behavior also can be particularly problematic (Bowles 1995). Although some of the worst cases of disturbance are caused by malicious acts, well-intentioned but uninformed people likely cause most impact.

The spatial distribution of use affects both the overall amount and distribution of impact. In most situations, impact on wildlife should be less when use is concentrated as opposed to widely dispersed. Indirect impacts on wildlife from destruction of habitat are least when use is concentrated, as are direct impacts such as feeding or harassment. Concentration also increases the predictability of human activity. Many animals habituate to (and therefore are not highly disturbed by) human activities that are predictable and nonthreatening (Knight and Cole 1995a). Miller et al. (2001) found, for example, that the alert distance, flush distance, and distance moved by deer and birds increased when hikers were off-trail compared to when hikers were on-trail. They attributed these results to trail-use habituation by wildlife and to the unpredictability of off-trail activity.

The location where recreation occurs also influences the magnitude of disturbance. When recreational activities occur near or even within the view of nest sites, nests can be abandoned or more frequently subject to predation (Miller et al. 1998). However, Miller and Hobbs (2000) showed that relationships are far from simplistic. They found that birds that were able to nest close to trails actually suffered less nest predation, presumably because predators avoided trails. Activities close to preferred feeding sites can result in reduced feeding, increased energy expenditure, and even displacement of birds to less-productive habitat (e.g., Stalmaster and Kaiser 1998).

Finally, timing of recreational use has a pronounced effect on the likelihood of serious impact because animals are most susceptible to disturbance at certain critical times of the year, most notably during the nesting season for birds and the post-natal period for mammals. This may be an oversimplification, however. There is substantial evidence that disturbance while feeding can be cause for concern as well (Hobbs 1989, Skagen et al. 1991). Moreover, some species are particularly vulnerable at certain times because they become highly concentrated. Examples include migrating birds concentrated on stopover sites, and amphibians that are migrating during the breeding season.

Manipulation of Wildlife

There may be some potential to manipulate wildlife so they are not severely impacted by ongoing recreational disturbance. The most obvious examples are aversive conditioning of animals that are attracted to humans, and attempting to habituate animals to recreational activities. For example, black bears that have learned to associate backpackers with food may destroy equipment and endanger human lives. Ultimately, bears that are attracted to human food are likely to be destroyed. In Glacier National Park, managers have used cracker shells, rubber bullets, and specially trained Karelian dogs in attempts to teach bears to stay away from human food (Joslin and Youmans 1999). It is not clear how successful such attempts have been. Bears also have been the subjects of successful attempts to habituate animals to human activities. In Alaska there are places such as McNeil River Falls where people come to watch brown bears fish in salmon streams. The bears' feeding habits are not disrupted by this activity because viewer number, location, timing, and behavior remain constant, and the bears habituate to the viewers (Aumiller and Matt 1994). Whittaker and Knight (1998) observe, however, that there can be unintended consequences of such efforts. Habituated bears, for example, may become easier targets for hunters and poachers outside of protected areas.

Manipulation of wildlife behavior may be particularly important for captive-raised animals. For example, one of the barriers to success of programs to re-establish the California condor (*Gymnogyps californianus*) in the wild is the reduction in avoidance behavior exhibited by released condors. As a result, condors spend more time in developed environments where they are more subject to a host of problems (e.g., flying into power lines) than they are when they remain in remote wildlands.

Manipulation of Habitat

Habitat modification can serve both to reduce disturbance and to compensate for recreational disturbance. Hockin et al. (1992) provide examples of manipulations that reduce disturbance, such as creating attractive nesting sites away from areas of recreational activity or visually screening recreationists from nesting sites. They also discuss examples of compensation, such as creating new habitat to replace habitat altered by recreational use (e.g., in wetlands) and improving the productivity or nutritional quality of feeding areas to which recreation displaces wildlife.

Burger (1995) reports on the positive effect of creating sandy shoals and inlet islands for colonially nesting birds in New Jersey. Signs had to be posted to keep boaters from using the islands for picnicking. However, even posting just half of an island as closed, with the other half available for recreation, increased breeding success. Habitat manipulations, such as feeding or fertilization of grass to attract wildlife to places where they come in contact with frequent, predictable, and nonthreatening activities, can increase wildlife habituation, reducing their vulnerability to disturbance.

Synergistic Effects

It is important to consider the effects of multiple management strategies working in combination. Limiting amount of use, by itself, is seldom an effective management strategy. However, it can be a highly effective supplement to actions that concentrate and control location of use. The most effective management programs generally apply a variety of management techniques, particularly visitor education, activity restrictions and zoning, and thoughtful design of roads, trails, and facilities.

Visitor Education

Education is one of the keys to reducing recreational impacts on wildlife. The public needs to be informed about the values of wildlife, wildlife behavior, and the need to respect wild animals, as well as practical techniques for minimizing disturbance. By changing human behavior (Klein 1993), education can be an effective means of reducing per capita impact. Without education, impact management will be primarily reactive. Through education, management can become more proactive and preventive in nature. But there are limits to what education can accomplish. Education is not a panacea; instead, it is a foundation on which to build a comprehensive management program. Development of an effective low-impact educational program requires considerable thought. It requires attention to both content of educational messages and communication media that will be used to disseminate messages.

Message Content

Knowledge about appropriate low-impact techniques has developed slowly during the past few decades with accumulation of personal experience and recreation ecology research. But low-impact techniques related to wildlife continue to be poorly developed, in part because of site-specific, species-specific, and even individual-specific characteristics of wildlife disturbance. Progress in developing consistent educational messages for wildland users, in general, has been profound. Over the past 2 decades, numerous books have been written about low-impact use of wildlands (e.g., Hampton and Cole 1995), and a national *Leave No Trace* low-impact education program was developed (Swain 1996). Leave No Trace is a partnership between federal land-managing agencies, nonprofit educational organizations, and the recreation industry, with a mission to develop a nationally recognized minimum-impact education system to educate federal land managers and the general public through training, publications, videos, and electronic webs (www.LNT.org). With the Leave No Trace program, consistency in low-impact education has emerged, even among different land-managing agencies. This consistency is most apparent in the 7 low-impact principles that are the crux of the program (Table 2).

Although "Respect Wildlife" is 1 of 7 Leave No Trace principles, recommended behaviors are poorly developed. General recommendations include: (1) travel quietly and give animals the space they need to feel secure; (2) avoid approaching animals too closely, feeding them, or touching them; (3) learn about locations and times of the year when disturbance of animals is particularly problematic; and (4) leave pets at home or keep them under control. Individual managers must craft recommendations that are specific to

Table 2. Leave no trace principles.

- Plan ahead and prepare.
- Travel and camp on durable surfaces.
- Dispose of waste properly.
- Leave what you find.
- Minimize campfire impacts.
- Respect wildlife.
- Be considerate of other visitors.

the situation that exists in the place they manage. The Leave No Trace program recognizes that education needs to be tailored to individual places and user groups. Behavior that may be appropriate in one place may be disastrous in another. Ultimately, visitors must accumulate the knowledge and wisdom to consider the many variables that delineate the most appropriate behavior for any given situation. Then they must use their own judgment.

Effective Communication

There are many different ways to try to persuade recreation visitors to adopt recommended low-impact practices. Some of the most common educational media include brochures, personnel at agency offices, maps and signs, personnel in the field, and displays at visitor centers or in parking areas. Research by social psychologists, who have been studying persuasive communication for years (e.g., Eagly and Chaiken 1993), suggests that low-impact education is a difficult task. Informing people is relatively easy; gaining their commitment to change their behaviors is more difficult. Principles of low-impact education that have been compiled from experience and research are varied (Table 3) (Roggenbuck 1992).

Activity Restrictions and Zoning

A common means of limiting disturbance is to restrict or prohibit activities that are particularly disturbing. Motorized use is perhaps the most common activity that is restricted, both because motorized use can be particularly destructive and motor vehicles can reach and disturb remote places. In some situations, however, motorized use is less disturbing to wildlife than is slow-moving, less-predictable pedestrian use (e.g., MacArthur et al. 1982). Activity restrictions commonly placed on hunters include limits on the number of shells they can carry and the type of shot they can use (Purdy et al. 1987). Anglers often must use certain types of bait and release the fish they catch. Off-trail travel and overnight camping might be prohibited or only permitted in designated sites.

Zoning is a means of restricting activities while not prohibiting them entirely. It involves dividing a large area into a number of different zones that vary in terms of what recreational activities are allowed. Certain activities are allowed in some zones but not in others. In the context of managing wildlife, the general idea is to provide refuge for wildlife from repetitive disturbance. Depending on the situation, zones that provide refuge might be particularly critical locations for birthing, watering, roosting, or feeding, or they might simply provide some portion of the area to which disturbed animals can escape.

Zones might provide absolute protection from disturbance by prohibiting all recreational use. Alternatively, zones may only provide protection from severe types of disturbance. In these zones, recreational use would be allowed, but it might be restricted in quantity or in terms of the activities and behaviors that are allowed. In some zones, the only option for access might be to join a guided group of limited size. In other zones, recreationists might be required to travel on designated roads or trails. Some zones might only permit day use, whereas others may allow overnight use as well. Some zones might prohibit motorized use, hunting, or walking with dogs, while allowing other types of use.

Because timing can be critical to the overall effect of recreational disturbance, temporal restrictions can be an important component of a management scheme. Although temporal restrictions can be applied to entire areas, particularly if the areas are small, they are more commonly part of a zoning plan. Typically, use would be prohibited in critical locations (e.g., nesting sites) during crucial periods (e.g., nesting season). Knight and Temple (1995*b*) observed that, although most temporal restrictions involve seasonal closures for weeks or months, daily cycles of vulnerability also exist, with wildlife feeding mostly at night or primarily during the morning hours. In these cases, restrictions would be frequent but short-lived.

Wildlife-sensitive Design of Roads, Trails, and Facilities

Wildlife disturbance is affected largely by where and when people and wildlife come in contact; thus, the design of traffic networks and facilities is critically important. Planning and design, to keep wildlife disturbance to acceptable levels, must be done at multiple spatial scales.

Table 3. Principles for effective communication.

- Educational programs should be guided by specific objectives.
    It is important to identify specific problems and users that are the primary cause of the problems.
- Focus the message.
    Address a few critical problems and desired behaviors instead of overwhelming the visitor with information. Clearly state the problem, type of behavior that aggravates the problem, and how a change in behavior will improve the situation.
- Identify the audience.
    Different messages should be targeted to specific users and problems and delivered using different media in different places. For example, hunters should receive a different message than non-hunters and should be contacted in different places and manners (e.g., in hunter-safety classes). Certain behaviors and user groups will be more amenable to change than will others.
- Use a combination of techniques.
    A combination of techniques allows messages to be repeated and makes it more likely that most visitors will be contacted. Personal contact supplemented with written materials can be particularly effective.
- Present messages in a professional manner.
    Productions need not be slick, but they should not be perceived as amateurish. If they are, credibility will suffer. Text and dialogue should be accurate and easy to understand. High-quality equipment and materials should be used for graphics and productions. Personnel who contact the public should be cheerful, polite, outgoing, have a positive attitude, and be trained in communication skills and low-impact techniques.

Particularly in smaller areas, linkages between the management area and surrounding lands must be considered. For example, it is important to consider the possibility of displacing wildlife from public to private lands, where increases in conflicts between humans and wildlife may occur. Impacts of noise and development, as well as the likelihood that nonindigenous species might invade from adjacent lands, should be considered. Regardless of the size of the management area, it is important to develop a broad-scale perspective of the distribution of species, their habitat, and their corridors of movement. Roads, facilities, and the flow of traffic should be designed to minimize vehicle collisions with wildlife, disruption of travel corridors, fragmentation of habitat, and impact to regionally rare species and habitats.

The location of access points or trailheads, beyond which motorized use is not allowed, can influence the spatial distribution of visitor use. If sensitive areas are far from the closest access point, use can often be kept to low levels without having to implement use limits or closures. Use distributions also can be influenced by the placement of facilities such as viewpoints, which attract use from sensitive areas.

Viewpoints can be located and designed to minimize impact. For example, cliff-nesting birds are less tolerant to disturbance when approached from the top of a cliff compared to when they are approached from the bottom (Herbert and Herbert 1965). Therefore, it would be better to place viewpoints at the cliff base. If overlooks are provided, they should be placed away from nest sites so that disturbance is limited (Hooper 1977). Larson (1995) describes a variety of design features built into a system of observation sites at a wildlife-viewing area in Colorado, where there was concern about disturbance of nesting great blue herons (*Ardea herodias*) and double-crested cormorants (*Phalacrocorax auritus*). Trails leading to the viewpoints were constructed such that colonies were approached tangentially instead of directly. In addition, timbers of varying height were placed vertically along trails to disrupt human profiles. Trails were built below ground level and existing vegetation was maintained to minimize visual intrusion.

Campgrounds also should be located and designed to minimize disturbance. Campgrounds are often placed in riparian zones because humans are attracted to water. However, the importance of riparian zones to wildlife means that location and design of riparian campgrounds are particularly critical. In a study of avian use of campgrounds, Blakesley and Reese (1988) found that species that nest on the ground or in shrubs and small trees were under-represented at campsites. To support a diversity of bird species in frequently disturbed places such as campgrounds, active intervention may be necessary to maintain a diverse vertical structure and appropriate spatial pattern of vegetation. Maintenance of shrub and tree patches between individual campsites and between the campground and stream banks is critically important for such species.

One of the keys to controlling wildlife disturbance is appropriate trail system design. Design at broad scales can leave substantial portions of the area without trails, providing refuges for wildlife. If possible, trails should avoid sensitive locations, such as ungulate wintering areas, key foraging areas, areas used for birthing and the immediate post-natal period for mammals, and breeding areas for birds. At finer scales, trail design should seek to avoid fragmenting habitat and to provide adequate buffering between hikers and wildlife. It is often possible to use natural features (topography and vegetation) as visual and acoustic buffers.

Information about flush and flight distances can be helpful in deciding on desirable widths of buffer zones around refuges for wildlife. For example, in deciding where to locate their wildlife viewing facility in relation to nesting wading birds, Colorado Parks and Outdoor Recreation relied on the research of Erwin (1989) and others, which indicated that colonies of nesting wading birds did not respond to human intrusions at distances greater than 150 m (Larson 1995). Unfortunately, there can be considerable variation in flushing responses within the same species as well as over time (Knight and Temple 1995*b*). Fernández-Juricic et al. (2001) propose using alert distance (the distance between an animal and an approaching human at which the animal begins to exhibit alert behaviors to the human) as the most conservative estimate of minimum approach distance.

In addition to considering direct impacts on wildlife, trail system design should consider indirect impacts—impacts of recreation on vegetation, soil, and water, the living space and food source for wildlife. Like animals, vegetation and soil vary spatially and temporally in their vulnerability to disturbance (Hammitt and Cole 1998:155–173). Trails and facilities should be placed in more resistant environments. Careful trail design can reduce the need for spatial and temporal restrictions on use.

SUMMARY

Recreational disturbance, which can detrimentally affect wildlife reproduction, survival, distributions, and behavior, is expected to increase in the coming decades. Wildland recreation occurs on most lands that are valuable for supporting wildlife, so the need to assess and manage recreational disturbances is pressing. To conserve wildlife and maintain support for wildlife from wildland recreationists, we advocate management actions that protect wildlife *and* permit recreational activity as long as it is not significantly harmful. Such approaches must be based on evaluations of existing data and, because recreational impacts are often context-dependent, new field studies. Study design and data analysis must consider not only simple main effects, but also complex influences of recreation (e.g., interaction, cumulative, ripple, threshold, and lag effects) that heretofore have largely been ignored. Field studies must involve wildlife response variables and recreational disturbance variables that are directly relevant to management objectives and that are responsive to management. A variety of techniques are available to manage recreational impacts. Most involve managing the behavior, activities, or distribution of recreationists, managing habitat, or designing facilities and transportation infrastructure that are minimally disruptive to wildlife.

ACKNOWLEDGMENTS

We thank C. E. Braun, J. L. Marion, and S. K. Riffell for suggesting improvements to a draft of this chapter.

LITERATURE CITED

AUMILLER, L., AND C. MATT. 1994. Management of McNeil River State Game Sanctuary for viewing of brown bears. International Conference on Bear Research and Management 9:51–61.

BELL, D. V., AND L. W. AUSTIN. 1985. The game-fishing season and its effects on overwintering wildfowl. Biological Conservation 33:65–80.

BLAKESLEY, J. A., AND K. P. REESE. 1988. Avian use of campground and noncampground sites in riparian zones. Journal of Wildlife Management 52:399–402.

BOWLES, A. E. 1995. Responses of wildlife to noise. Pages 109–156 *in* R. L. Knight and K. J. Gutzwiller, editors. Wildlife and recreationists: coexistence through management and research. Island Press, Washington, D.C., USA.

BOYLE, S. A., AND F. B. SAMSON. 1985. Effects of nonconsumptive recreation on wildlife: a review. Wildlife Society Bulletin 13:110–116.

BURGER, J. 1981. The effect of human activity on birds at a coastal bay. Biological Conservation 21:231–241.

———. 1991. Foraging behavior and the effect of human disturbance on the piping plover (*Charadrius melodus*). Journal of Coastal Research 7:39–52.

———. 1995. Beach recreation and nesting birds. Pages 281–295 *in* R. L. Knight and K. J. Gutzwiller, editors. Wildlife and recreationists: coexistence through management and research. Island Press, Washington, D.C., USA.

CLAAR, J. J., N. ANDERSON, D. BOYD, M. CHERRY, B. CONARD, R. HOMPESCH, S. MILLER, G. OLSON, H. IHSLE PAC, J. WALLER, T. WITTINGER, AND H. YOUMANS. 1999. Carnivores. Pages 7.1–7.63 *in* G. Joslin and H. Youmans, coordinators. Effects of recreation on Rocky Mountain wildlife: a review for Montana. Montana Chapter, The Wildlife Society, Helena, USA.

COHEN, J. 1988. Statistical power analysis for the behavioral sciences. Second edition. Lawrence Erlbaum, Hillsdale, New Jersey, USA.

COLE, D. N., AND P. B. LANDRES. 1995. Indirect effects of recreation on wildlife. Pages 183–202 *in* R. L. Knight and K. J. Gutzwiller, editors. Wildlife and recreationists: coexistence through management and research. Island Press, Washington, D.C., USA.

CONNELLY, J. W., J. H. GAMMONLEY, AND J. M. PEEK. 2005. Harvest management. Pages 658–690 *in* C. E. Braun, editor. Techniques for wildlife investigations and management. Sixth edition. The Wildlife Society, Bethesda, Maryland, USA.

CORDELL, H. K., AND G. R. SUPER. 2000. Trends in Americans' outdoor recreation. Pages 133–144 *in* W. C. Gartner and D. W. Lime, editors. Trends in outdoor recreation, leisure and tourism. CABI International, Wallingford, United Kingdom.

DOUGLASS, K. S., J. HAMANN, AND G. JOSLIN. 1999. Vegetation, soils, and water. Pages 9.1–9.11 *in* G. Joslin and H. Youmans, coordinators. Effects of recreation on Rocky Mountain wildlife: a review for Montana. Montana Chapter, The Wildlife Society, Helena, USA.

EAGLY, A. H., AND S. CHAIKEN. 1993. The psychology of attitudes. Harcourt Brace College Publishers, Fort Worth, Texas, USA.

ERWIN, R. M. 1989. Responses to human intruders by birds nesting in colonies: experimental results and management guidelines. Colonial Waterbirds 12:104–108.

FERGUSON, M. A. D., AND L. B. KEITH. 1982. Influence of Nordic skiing on distribution of moose and elk in Elk Island National Park, Alberta. Canadian Field-Naturalist 96:69–78.

FERNÁNDEZ-JURICIC, E., M. D. JIMENEZ, AND E. LUCAS. 2001. Alert distance as an alternative measure of bird tolerance to human disturbance: implications for park design. Environmental Conservation 28:263–269.

FLATHER, C. H., AND H. K. CORDELL. 1995. Outdoor recreation: historical and anticipated trends. Pages 3–16 *in* R. L. Knight and K. J. Gutzwiller, editors. Wildlife and recreationists: coexistence through management and research. Island Press, Washington, D.C., USA.

GABRIELSEN, G. W., AND E. N. SMITH. 1995. Physiological responses of wildlife to disturbance. Pages 95–107 *in* R. L. Knight and K. J. Gutzwiller, editors. Wildlife and recreationists: coexistence through

management and research. Island Press, Washington, D.C., USA.

GEHLBACH, F. R., AND N. Y. GEHLBACH. 2000. Whiskered screech-owl (*Otus trichopsis*). Number 507. *In* A. Poole and F. Gill, editors. The birds of North America. The Birds of North America, Inc., Philadelphia, Pennsylvania, USA.

GÖTMARK, F. 1992. The effects of investigator disturbance on nesting birds. Pages 63–104 *in* D. M. Power, editor. Current ornithology. Volume 9. Plenum Press, New York, USA.

GREEN, R. H. 1979. Sampling design and statistical methods for environmental biologists. John Wiley and Sons, New York, USA.

GUTZWILLER, K. J. 1991. Assessing recreational impacts on wildlife: the value and design of experiments. Transactions of the North American Wildlife and Natural Resources Conference 56:248–255.

———. 1993. Serial management experiments: an adaptive approach to reduce recreational impacts on wildlife. Transactions of the North American Wildlife and Natural Resources Conference 58:528–536.

———. 1995. Recreational disturbance and wildlife communities. Pages 169–181 *in* R. L. Knight and K. J. Gutzwiller, editors. Wildlife and recreationists: coexistence through management and research. Island Press, Washington, D.C., USA.

———, AND S. H. ANDERSON. 1999. Spatial extent of human-intrusion effects on subalpine bird distributions. Condor 101:378–389.

———, S. K. RIFFELL, AND S. H. ANDERSON. 2002. Repeated human intrusion and the potential for nest predation by gray jays. Journal of Wildlife Management 66:372–380.

———, E. A. KROESE, S. H. ANDERSON, AND C. A. WILKINS. 1997. Does human intrusion alter the seasonal timing of avian song during breeding periods? Auk 114:55–65.

HAIR, JR., J. F., R. E. ANDERSON, R. L. TATHAM, AND W. C. BLACK. 1998. Multivariate data analysis. Fifth edition. Prentice-Hall, Upper Saddle River, New Jersey, USA.

HAIRSTON, N. G. 1989. Ecological experiments: purpose, design and execution. Cambridge University Press, New York, USA.

HAMMITT, W. E., AND D. N. COLE. 1998. Wildland recreation: ecology and management. Second edition. John Wiley and Sons, New York, USA.

HAMPTON, B., AND D. COLE. 1995. Soft paths. Second edition. Stackpole Books, Mechanicsburg, Pennsylvania, USA.

HAMR, J. 1988. Disturbance behaviour of chamois in an alpine tourist area of Austria. Mountain Research and Development 8:65–73.

HAYSMITH, L., AND J. D. HUNT. 1995. Nature tourism: impacts and management. Pages 203–219 *in* R. L. Knight and K. J. Gutzwiller, editors. Wildlife and recreationists: coexistence through management and research. Island Press, Washington, D.C., USA.

HERBERT, R. A., AND K. G. S. HERBERT. 1965. Behavior of peregrine falcons in the New York City Region. Auk 82:62–94.

HICKS, L. L., AND J. M. ELDER. 1979. Human disturbance of Sierra Nevada bighorn sheep. Journal of Wildlife Management 43:909–915.

HOBBS, N. T. 1989. Linking energy balance to survival in mule deer: development and test of a simulation model. Wildlife Monographs 101.

HOCKIN, D., M. OUNSTED, M. GORMAN, D. HILL, V. KELLER, AND M. A. BARKER. 1992. Examination of the effects of disturbance on birds with reference to its importance in ecological assessments. Journal of Environmental Management 36:253–286.

HOOPER, R. G. 1977. Nesting habitat of common ravens in Virginia. Wilson Bulletin 89:233–242.

HUITEMA, B. E. 1980. The analysis of covariance and alternatives. John Wiley and Sons, New York, USA.

HURLBERT, S. H. 1984. Pseudoreplication and the design of ecological field experiments. Ecological Monographs 54:187–211.

JOSLIN, G., AND H. YOUMANS, coordinators. 1999. Effects of recreation on Rocky Mountain wildlife: a review for Montana. Montana Chapter, The Wildlife Society, Helena, USA.

KELLER, V. E. 1991. Effects of human disturbance on eider ducklings *Somateria mollissima* in an estuarine habitat in Scotland. Biological Conservation 58:213–228.

KLEIN, M. L. 1993. Waterbird behavioral responses to human disturbance. Wildlife Society Bulletin 21:31–39.

———, S. R. HUMPHREY, AND H. F. PERCIVAL. 1995. Effects of ecotourism on distribution of waterbirds in a wildlife refuge.

Conservation Biology 9:1454–1465.

KNIGHT, R. L., AND D. N. COLE. 1995a. Factors that influence wildlife responses to recreationists. Pages 71–79 in R. L. Knight and K. J. Gutzwiller, editors. Wildlife and recreationists: coexistence through management and research. Island Press, Washington, D.C., USA.

———, AND ———. 1995b. Wildlife responses to recreationists. Pages 51–69 in R. L. Knight and K. J. Gutzwiller, editors. Wildlife and recreationists: coexistence through management and research. Island Press, Washington, D.C., USA.

———, AND R. E. FITZNER. 1985. Human disturbance and nest site placement in black-billed magpies. Journal of Field Ornithology 56:153–157.

———, AND K. J. GUTZWILLER, editors. 1995. Wildlife and recreationists: coexistence through management and research. Island Press, Washington, D.C., USA.

———, AND S. A. TEMPLE. 1995a. Origin of wildlife responses to recreationists. Pages 81–91 in R. L. Knight and K. J. Gutzwiller, editors. Wildlife and recreationists: coexistence through management and research. Island Press, Washington, D.C., USA.

———, AND ———. 1995b. Wildlife and recreationists: coexistence through management. Pages 327–333 in R. L. Knight and K. J. Gutzwiller, editors. Wildlife and recreationists: coexistence through management and research. Island Press, Washington D.C., USA.

———, D. P. ANDERSON, AND N. V. MARR. 1991. Responses of an avian scavenging guild to anglers. Biological Conservation 56:195–205.

LARSON, R. A. 1995. Balancing wildlife viewing with wildlife impacts: a case study. Pages 257–270 in R. L. Knight and K. J. Gutzwiller, editors. Wildlife and recreationists: coexistence through management and research. Island Press, Washington D.C., USA.

MACARTHUR, R. A., V. GEIST, AND R. H. JOHNSTON. 1982. Cardiac and behavioral responses of mountain sheep to human disturbance. Journal of Wildlife Management 46:351–358.

MACNAB, J. 1983. Wildlife management as scientific experimentation. Wildlife Society Bulletin 11:397–401.

MARZLUFF, J. M. 1988. Do pinyon jays alter nest placement based on prior experience? Animal Behavior 36:1–10.

MILLER, J. R., AND N. T. HOBBS. 2000. Recreational trails, human activity, and nest predation in lowland riparian areas. Landscape and Urban Planning 50:227–236.

MILLER, S. G., R. L. KNIGHT, AND C. K. MILLER. 1998. Influence of recreational trails on breeding bird communities. Ecological Applications 8:162–169.

———, ———, AND ———. 2001. Wildlife responses to pedestrians and dogs. Wildlife Society Bulletin 29:124–132.

PETRAITIS, P. S., R. E. LATHAM, AND R. A. NIESENBAUM. 1989. The maintenance of species diversity by disturbance. Quarterly Review of Biology 64:393–418.

PURDY, K. G., G. R. GOFF, D. J. DECKER, G. A. POMERANTZ, AND N. A. CONNELLY. 1987. A guide to managing human activity on national wildlife refuges. U.S. Department of the Interior, Fish and Wildlife Service, Office of Information Transfer, Fort Collins, Colorado, USA.

RAPPORT, D. J., H. A. REGIER, AND T. C. HUTCHINSON. 1985. Ecosystem behavior under stress. American Naturalist 125:617–640.

RICHENS, V. B., AND G. R. LAVIGNE. 1978. Response of white-tailed deer to snowmobiles and snowmobile trails in Maine. Canadian Field-Naturalist 92:334–344.

RIFFELL, S. K., K. J. GUTZWILLER, AND S. H. ANDERSON. 1996. Does repeated human intrusion cause cumulative declines in avian richness and abundance? Ecological Applications 6:492–505.

ROGGENBUCK, J. W. 1992. Use of persuasion to reduce resource impacts and visitor conflicts. Pages 149–208 in M. J. Manfredo, editor. Influencing human behavior: theory and applications in recreation, tourism, and natural resources management. Sagamore Publishing, Champaign, Illinois, USA.

SINGER, F. J., AND S. P. BRATTON. 1980. Black bear/human conflicts in the Great Smoky Mountains National Park. International Conference on Bear Research and Management 4:137–140.

SKAGEN, S. K., R. L. KNIGHT, AND G. H. ORIANS. 1991. Human disturbance of an avian scavenging guild. Ecological Applications 1:215–225.

SOUSA, W. P. 1984. The role of disturbance in natural communities. Annual Review of Ecology and Systematics 15:353–391.

SPALING, H., AND B. SMIT. 1993. Cumulative environmental change: conceptual frameworks, evaluation approaches, and institutional perspectives. Environmental Management 17:587–600.

STAINE, K. J., AND J. BURGER. 1994. Nocturnal foraging behavior of breeding piping plovers (*Charadrius melodus*) in New Jersey. Auk 111:579–587.

STALMASTER, M. V., AND J. L. KAISER. 1998. Effects of recreational activity on wintering bald eagles. Wildlife Monographs 137.

———, AND J. R. NEWMAN. 1978. Behavioral responses of wintering bald eagles to human activity. Journal of Wildlife Management 42:506–513.

STANKEY, G. H., D. N. COLE, R. C. LUCAS, M. E. PETERSEN, AND S. S. FRISSELL. 1985. The Limits of Acceptable Change (LAC) system for wilderness planning. U.S. Department of Agriculture, Forest Service, General Technical Report INT-176.

SWAIN, R. 1996. Leave No Trace (LNT)—outdoor skills and ethics program. International Journal of Wilderness 2(3):24–26.

VASKE, J. J., D. J. DECKER, AND M. J. MANFREDO. 1995. Human dimensions of wildlife management: an integrated framework for coexistence. Pages 33–49 in R. L. Knight and K. J. Gutzwiller, editors. Wildlife and recreationists: coexistence through management and research. Island Press, Washington D.C., USA.

WATSON, A. E., D. N. COLE, D. L. TURNER, AND P. S. REYNOLDS. 2000. Wilderness recreation use estimation: a handbook of methods and systems. U.S. Department of Agriculture, Forest Service, General Technical Report RMRS-GTR-56.

WHITTAKER, D., AND R. L. KNIGHT. 1998. Understanding wildlife responses to humans. Wildlife Society Bulletin 26:312–317.

YARMOLOY, C., M. BAYER, AND V. GEIST. 1988. Behavior responses and reproduction of mule deer, *Odocoileus hemionus*, does following experimental harassment with an all-terrain vehicle. Canadian Field-Naturalist 102:425–429.

ZAR, J. H. 1999. Biostatistical analysis. Fourth edition. Prentice-Hall, Upper Saddle River, New Jersey, USA.

30

MANAGING INLAND WETLANDS FOR WILDLIFE

Murray K. Laubhan, Sammy L. King, and Leigh H. Fredrickson

INTRODUCTION

The successful management of wetlands is complex and challenging because it requires the correct application of information from multiple disciplines on heterogeneous landscapes. The United States is a leader in the application of wetland management strategies on public and private lands and has willingly invested huge amounts of public and private monies in many different programs. The result has been the protection of millions of hectares of wetlands through establishment of national wildlife refuges and state wildlife management areas, the Wetland Reserve Program, and conservation easements established by non-governmental organizations (e.g., Ducks Unlimited, The Nature Conservancy). In the National Wildlife Refuge System alone, over 500 national wildlife refuges and 203 Waterfowl Production Areas protect over 12 million ha of wetlands (R. L. Fowler, U.S. Fish and Wildlife Service, personal communication).

Undoubtedly, wetland conservation efforts in the United States surpass those of any other country. However, despite the monetary investments in wetlands protection and restoration, the potential benefits of these activities have not been fully realized. Numerous refuges and other public lands are threatened by activities outside their borders that alter ecological processes within protected areas (Pringle 2000). Further, as water becomes more limited, increasing conflicts are expected between human uses and wetland and wildlife conservation (Naiman and Turner 2000, Postel 2000).

Within the conservation arena, most activities involve creation, enhancement, restoration, and manipulation of habitats. However, many programs and projects have led to less than optimum results. In some cases, this has resulted because well defined habitat-based goals and objectives at different spatial and temporal scales have been lacking. As a result, it has been difficult to evaluate past actions because there often is little to measure other than number of projects or size of the area associated with the program or project. Further, funding has focused more on implementation of projects rather than on planning and evaluation. Coupled with increasing societal demands on natural resources, the lack of clearly articulated goals causes confusion and stimulates controversy among entities regarding the need and purpose of acquiring and managing wetlands. Because of increasing interest and investment in wetland protection, restoration, and management, opportunities are increasing for employment as well as the correct and efficient use of human and monetary resources to promote wetland benefits to society.

The goal of this chapter is to describe an approach that leads to an improved process for wetland management and restoration decisions across multiple temporal and spatial scales. Our approach emphasizes a multi-scale decision-making process rather than a comprehensive overview of techniques at the local scale because the decision process has been grossly underemphasized in the wetland-wildlife literature. Failure to develop and follow a well defined decision making process frequently has led to limited project success often at great monetary expense. Individuals interested in wetland conservation and management must have a broad understanding of a variety of topics including hydrology, geomorphology, soils, plant ecology and taxonomy, and wildlife biology. In addition, a basic understanding of policies, societal values, and economics regarding wetlands is becoming increasingly important. This chapter should be viewed as an introduction to management of wetland systems and we encourage biologists to explore the vast amount of literature regarding the ecology and management of these unique and valuable systems.

HISTORY OF WETLAND ATTITUDES

Perception of the values and importance of wetlands in the conterminous United States has changed through time as evidenced by changes in federal regulations governing wetland protection and use. Because regulations largely mirror public attitudes, a brief synopsis of policies and laws provides a convenient and suitable method of illustrating changing perceptions. Further, regulations influence how wetlands are defined, classified, and managed. Thus, understanding current regulatory issues is important for managing wetland resources today.

Prior to the mid-1800s, wetlands were not regulated and local citizenry decided the fate of resources. In general, wetlands were perceived as evil and sinister by early colonists because they provided shelter for their enemies, harbored diseases, and were an obstacle for agriculture (Vileisis 1997). In 1849, the federal government passed the Swamp Lands Act, which granted swamps and overflow lands in Louisiana to the state for reclamation. The state was directed to sell their swamplands and use the proceeds to construct the necessary levees and drains to reclaim these areas. In 1850, this act was applied to 12 other states and, in 1860, to 2 additional states (Shaw and Fredine 1956). The 1850 act resulted in the transfer of nearly 26 million ha of land that was considered wet and unfit for cultivation to the states (National Research Council 1995). This legislation clearly indicated the government promoted wetland drainage and reclamation for settlement and development (Dahl and Allord 1997).

In 1899, the Rivers and Harbors Act was passed which gave the U.S. Army Corps of Engineers authority in regulating dredging, filling, construction, and dumping activities in navigable waters (Vileisis 1997). At this time, wetlands did not receive protection from these activities. In fact, the U.S. Army Corps of Engineers interpreted navigable waters narrowly (Silverberg and Dennison 1993) and the general nature of polices and land-use trends until the 1930s was to facilitate removal of wetlands.

The 1930s through the 1960s represented a period of competing government policies. The federal government enacted legislation that encouraged wetland preservation and restoration as well as provided incentives to continue wetland drainage. For example, the Migratory Bird Hunting Stamp Act was passed in 1934 and represented one of the first legislative acts to initiate acquisition and restoration of wetlands. In contrast, the government actually shared the cost of draining wetlands for agricultural production in the 1940s (Burwell and Sugden 1964), the Water Protection and Flood Prevention Act of 1954 directly and indirectly increased drainage of wetlands near flood-control projects (Erickson et al. 1979), and the fed-

eral government directly subsidized or facilitated wetland losses through many public-works projects and technical practices administered by the U.S. Department of Agriculture (Erickson 1979).

In 1972, amendments to Section 404 of the Federal Water Pollution Control Act (a.k.a., Clean Water Act) were enacted and became a primary protection mechanism for wetlands in the United States that remains important today. Anyone interested in dredging, filling, or impacting "waters of the United States", including the development of wetland management units, must apply for a permit from the U.S. Army Corps of Engineers prior to the activity. Normal farming, ranching, and silvicultural activities are exempt from the Clean Water Act; however, these activities must follow certain guidelines. The Clean Water Act does not specifically mention wetlands and early interpretations by the U.S. Army Corps of Engineers were focused on protecting only navigable waters. This protection was an extension of the 1899 Rivers and Harbors Act, which mandated authority to the U.S. Army Corps of Engineers to regulate dredging the fill in navigable waters. Court decisions in 1975, however, expanded the scope of the Clean Water Act to include protection of wetlands (Mitsch and Gosselink 2000). Originally, only wetlands that were adjacent to navigable waters were protected, but in 1977 the U.S. Army Corps of Engineers adopted a regulation [33 CFR 328.3(a)] that protected intrastate wetlands and other water bodies that could affect interstate commerce. Later rulings by the U.S. Army Corps of Engineers and the U.S. Environmental Protection Agency afforded protection for isolated wetlands (i.e., wetlands with no apparent surface water connection to perennial rivers, streams, estuaries, or the ocean) (Tiner et al. 2002). The basis for this ruling was that migratory birds use these wetlands and, therefore, interstate commerce associated with bird watching and waterfowl hunting would be affected. The interpretation of these rulings became known as the "migratory bird rule." Passage of this new judicial interpretation of the Clean Water Act required the U.S. Army Corps of Engineers and U.S. Environmental Protection Agency to develop a regulatory definition of a wetland.

During the 1980s several additional actions indicated increased recognition of wetland values and functions. The loss of wetlands to agricultural conversion was curtailed by the wetland conservation (Swampbuster) provision in the 1985 Food Security Act. This provision stated that farmers would not be eligible for federal program benefits if natural wetlands were converted to cropland after December 1985 (National Research Council 1995). However, effectiveness of these provisions was compromised by lack of individuals familiar with the dynamic nature of wetlands and processes important for long-term sustainability. Thus, in the years immediately following implementation of the 1985 Food Security Act, the trend was to capture all water moving through a drainage to make deep-water habitat rather than wetland habitat. During this period, additional policies were enacted that eliminated incentives to destroy wetlands and encouraged acquisition and protection of wetlands. For example, the Emergency Wetland Resources Act of 1986 authorized purchase of wetlands with Land and Water Conservation Fund monies and required establishment of a National Wetlands Priority Conservation Plan.

By the mid-1990s, nearly every federal agency that administers public lands had some form of wetland restoration and compensation program in place (Scodari 1997). For example, the U.S. Fish and Wildlife Service and the Natural Resources Conservation Service established wetland restoration programs in the 1990s. In addition, further wetland legislation was enacted, including the Water Resources Development Act of 1990. This act established a new interim goal for the water resources program of "no overall net loss of the Nation's remaining wetland base as defined by acreage and function" and a long-term goal "to increase the quality and quantity of the Nation's wetlands".

Although recent federal legislation clearly advocates the importance of wetlands, there is no federal regulation specifically designed to govern the preservation and use of wetlands (Gaddie and Regens 2000). Consequently, the fate of wetland resources is not secure. This is exemplified in a 2001 court case that has significant implications for regulation of isolated wetlands in the United States. In the case entitled "Solid Waste Agency of Northern Cook County vs. U.S. Army Corps of Engineers", Solid Waste Agency of Northern Cook County, Illinois wanted to develop a waste disposal facility on a site that contained isolated wetlands and supported several dozen species of migratory birds. The Supreme Court ruled the U.S. Army Corps of Engineers did not have authority under Section 404 of the Clean Water Act to regulate isolated wetlands. This ruling prompted the U.S. Fish and Wildlife Service's National Wetlands Inventory Laboratory to conduct a study to estimate the number of isolated wetlands by physiographic region in the United States. They evaluated 72 study sites that encompassed 49,200 km^2 in 44 states. Their results indicated that isolated wetlands composed >50% of wetlands in 8 of the study areas, and >80% in 7 of these 8 areas. Wetlands that may be particularly affected by the ruling are salt flats, channeled scabland wetlands, playas, prairie potholes, Carolina bays, vernal pools, and Rainwater Basin wetlands (Tiner et al. 2002). Some isolated wetlands receive varying amounts of protection under state statutes or the Swampbuster provisions of the Food Security Act of 1985, but provisions are ineffective in many states and non-agricultural areas (Petrie et al. 2001). Debate continues regarding what the Supreme Court actually decided; thus, the impacts of this ruling remain unclear (see *Wetlands* 23:471–684 a special issue dedicated to the isolated wetland issue). However, isolated wetlands provide unique resources and are critical to the long-term sustainability of many species of flora and fauna (Tiner et al. 2002). Therefore, a ruling that results in widespread destruction or modification of isolated wetlands would significantly impact the nation's wetland resources.

DEFINING WETLANDS

The diversity of wetland types makes it difficult to develop a single definition of what constitutes a wetland (National Research Council 1992). Much of the difficulty arises because factors influencing physiognomy of wetlands are numerous and include climate, soils, topography, landscape position, hydrology, and water chemistry among others. These factors vary over a wide range of temporal and spatial scales. Wetlands range from barely perceptible depressions that hold surface water for at most a few weeks each year to large basins that are flooded every year. Wetlands can support plant communities ranging from small carnivorous plants in northern bogs to common baldcypress (*Taxodium distichum*) trees several meters in diameter in southern-forested wetlands. Finally, wetlands occur along river systems with frequent overbank flooding, in regions of permafrost where snowmelt is captured in depressions formed in frozen ground, and in arid regions where ecological conditions are often driven by groundwater.

Historically, wetlands were defined for specific purposes, such as individual research studies or general classification and inventory. However, recognition that wetlands are a critical part of the nation's social, cultural, and economic network resulted in development of federal statutes to protect and govern uses of wetlands. The diverse functions of wetlands have complicated delineation and management because public opinion regarding the fate of a wetland often is based on specific attributes rather than the entire suite of functions. The flood retention benefits associated with a given wetland may be favored more than benefits for wildlife. As a result, modifications or management to increase flood storage may be advocated even though this may decrease wildlife benefits. Consequently, decisions regarding wetlands often occur within a strong political context (Hollis 1998). To help resolve such issues, the federal government has established regulations to identify and protect certain wetland types. Enforcement of these regulations requires a clear and legally defensible definition of wetlands because regulation often is viewed as a form of land use restriction imposed by the federal government on private landowners. Detailed definitions have been developed by federal agencies responsible for wetland identification and delineation from a federal regulatory perspective. Each agency developed its definition based on laws and regulations that protected specific interests (Federal Interagency Committee for Wetland Delineation 1989). Wetlands that meet these requirements are often termed jurisdictional wetlands to separate them from wet areas that may provide similar functions but do not meet legal criteria. With the exception of the U.S. Fish and Wildlife Service definition that incorporates nonvegetated areas (e.g., mudflats, gravel beaches), all 4 definitions are conceptually similar as they include 3 basic attributes for defining a wetland: (1) hydrology that results in surface saturation or inundation, (2) presence of hydric soil, and (3) hydrophytic vegetation. However, even these definitions were too general to be used directly; thus, technical manuals were developed for identifying and delineating wetlands (U.S. Department of Army 1987, U.S. Environmental Protection Agency 1988, U.S. Department of Agriculture 1994). The technical guidance for interpreting the 3 basic wetland attributes differed among manuals (reviewed by National Research Council 1995). This prompted an attempt to consolidate the manuals and adopt a uniform approach for delineating wetland boundaries by all federal agencies (Federal Interagency Committee for Wetland Delineation 1989). This manual was withdrawn due to criticism and each agency reverted to using their original manuals (National Research Council 1995).

Although development of legal definitions to protect wetlands is beneficial, some problems have been identified. First, according to definitions of the U.S. Army

Corps of Engineers and U.S. Environmental Protection Agency, not all wetland types meet established legal criteria and are not considered jurisdictional wetlands. These wetlands are not protected under existing laws. For example, in the arid West, wetlands may be completely dry for several years and the concept of average conditions is difficult to apply (National Research Council 1995). These shallow or intermittently flooded wetlands support a distinct water-dependent biota (Kantrud et al. 1989) and can help maintain water quality (Johnston et al. 1990). Also, many riparian zones are excluded from consideration as wetlands, especially in arid and semi-arid Western states (Johnson et al. 1984, Kusler 1985, Lowe et al. 1986). These areas comprise <1% of the total land base in the western United States, but are used by more species of breeding birds than any other habitat in North America (Knopf et al. 1988). Second, delineating wetland boundaries can be difficult. Analysis of vegetation is often used to identify boundaries (National Research Council 1995), but location of hydrophytic vegetation may change due to variation in short- and long-term hydrology (van der Valk and Davis 1976, Weller 1981, Zedler 1987, Stromberg et al. 1991). Because transitional areas between uplands and wetlands are critical to the flow of energy and nutrients, incorrect boundary identification may jeopardize the long-term health and sustainability of some jurisdictional wetlands. Finally, wetlands within a regulatory context are considered as discrete units independent of the surrounding landscape. However, values of wetlands are often dependent on conditions at larger scales. For example, the long-term sustainability of many vertebrate populations (e.g., amphibians) depends on type and condition of terrestrial communities surrounding wetlands (Gibbs 1993, Burke et al. 1995, Fischer and Fischenich 2000, Semlitsch 2000a, Higgins et al. 2002, Saunders et al. 2002).

In this chapter, we use the definition of wetlands by Cowardin et al. (1979). This definition is not regulatory, but it is significant because it is used to report the status of the nation's wetlands to Congress (National Research Council 1995). Thus, wetlands are transitional areas between terrestrial and aquatic systems where the water table is usually at or near the surface or the land is covered by shallow water (Cowardin et al. 1979). Specifically, wetlands must have 1 or more of the following 3 attributes: (1) at least periodically, the land supports predominantly hydrophytes; (2) the substrate is predominantly undrained hydric soils; and (3) the substrate is nonsoil and is saturated with water or covered by shallow water at some time during the growing season each year. This definition is more inclusive because the temporal nature of some wetlands is acknowledged by stating that hydrophytic vegetation and hydrologic indicators need only be present periodically (National Research Council 1992). In contrast, the U.S. Environmental Protection Agency and U.S. Army Corps of Engineers definitions require evidence of all 3 attributes (hydrophytes, hydric soils, and hydrology). Thus, some areas considered wetlands by the Cowardin et al. (1979) definition might not be considered jurisdictional wetlands according to federal statutes.

The Cowardin et al. (1979) definition captures the dynamic nature of wetlands and identifies the importance of hydrology. Hydrology is a key component because water modifies and affects the substrates in wetlands, which together influence specific responses in water, soils, vegetation, invertebrates, birds, and fish (Mitsch and Gosselink 1993). Another strength of this definition is the reference to "systems", a critical concept that should be considered in defining a wetland (National Research Council 1995). The term "transitional" also correctly implies that wetlands form a continuum connecting terrestrial to aquatic ecotypes and are influenced by the type of terrestrial (e.g., grass, forest) and aquatic (e.g., lake, ocean) environments of which they are a part.

WETLAND CLASSIFICATION

The concept of classifying wetlands has been in existence for over a century. Early attempts at classification largely were motivated by interest in converting wetlands for agriculture (Wright 1907). This system placed wetlands into a few general categories (e.g., river swamps, lake swamps, upland swamps) on the basis of location. Other classification systems were related to the amount of inundation and used terms such as permanent, wet, and periodically swampy (Dachnowski 1920). By the 1950s, the need for classifying wetlands broadened to other purposes, including a need to differentiate wetlands from other land-cover types for regional and national planning purposes (Tiner 1997). However, most methods were developed for use by states. By 1974, more than 50 schemes had been developed, but only one was national in scope (U.S. Department of Interior 1976). However, the need for a nationwide classification scheme became evident with the advent of federal wetland regulations, including passage of the Emergency Wetland Resources Act of 1986 that required the U.S. Fish and Wildlife Service to conduct wetland status and trend studies and report the results to Congress each decade. In addition, new approaches to management and scientific study (e.g., ecosystems) required access to information that was consistent across political boundaries.

Numerous large-scale wetland classification systems were devised to group wetlands into classes to facilitate surveys and inventories for management and conservation purposes (reviewed by Finlayson and van der Valk 1995). Of all the systems devised, that developed by the U.S. Fish and Wildlife Service (Cowardin et al. 1979) is most useful. It has become the national and international standard for identifying and classifying wetlands (Gopal et al. 1982, Mader 1991). This system represents an ecological basis rather than attempting to classify wetlands based on the needs of particular user groups (Cowardin and Golet 1995, Tiner 1997). It designates wetland types on the basis of hydrology, vegetation, soils, geomorphic and chemical factors, and size. The system uses a hierarchal approach to group wetlands into ecologically similar categories at different levels of resolution. There are 5 system types, 8 subsystems, 11 classes, 28 subclasses, and a large number of dominance types based on dominant plants or substrates. Thus, wetlands can be differentiated into 55 ecologically distinct types providing uniformity in wetland terminology. This system has been used by the National Wetland Inventory to map wetlands, special aquatic sites, and deepwater habitats of the United States for 3 decades.

Brinson (1993) developed another classification system, known as the hydrogeomorphic method. This is a scientific method of wetland classification and functional assessment based on a wetland's location in the landscape, and the sources and duration of water flow (Brinson 1995). This approach identifies the wetland classes present in each region, defines the functions that each class of wetlands performs, and establishes reference sites to define the range of functioning of each wetland class. The 3 primary factors used in the hydrogeomorphic method to classify wetlands are geomorphic setting, water source, and hydrodynamics. Geomorphic setting is the landscape position of the wetland, and categories include depressional, slope-flat, peatland, riverine, and fringe. Water source may be precipitation, groundwater discharge, and surface or near-surface inflow. Hydrodynamics are differentiated into 3 qualitative categories: vertical fluctuation of water table, unidirectional flow, and bidirectional flow. Further groupings and classifications occur at regional and local levels.

The hydrogeomorphic method is mentioned because it has been particularly valuable in restoration and mitigation activities. In fact, use of functional assessments has been identified as the preferred option for evaluating performance of wetland mitigation banks (Federal Register 1995). Although numerous issues regarding use of this system have arisen (Magee 1996, Brinson et al. 1997), it represents an improvement compared to using area assessments as the sole attribute in measuring restoration or mitigation success. Users must consider that wetland functions, even among wetlands of similar vegetation structure, vary according to hydrologic characteristics and geomorphic settings. Guidelines have been established using the hydrogeomorphic method to assess wetland functions in the 404 Regulatory Program as well as other regulatory, planning, and management situations (Brinson et al. 1995). Consequently, this approach can be used to standardize the analysis of wetland functions to quantify gains and losses for compensatory mitigation, compare project alternatives, identify the impacts of a proposed project, assess mitigation requirements or success as well as other applications (Smith et al. 1995, Brinson and Rheinhardt 1996). Thus, a wetland being examined based on regulatory statutes can be compared to reference sites that have been extensively studied and functionally evaluated. The amount of wetland area needed to replace the lost functions can be calculated based upon the functional values of the reference wetland. This information can be used to establish ratios or indices to estimate how much mitigation is required. Similarly, comparisons of functional equivalency between reference wetlands and mitigation banks also can be used to identify the amount of credit a mitigation bank should receive.

A final functional assessment method is the Index of Biotic Integrity (IBI) (Karr 1981). Biotic integrity is a measure of a particular wetland or stream to support and maintain a balanced, integrated, adaptive community of organisms having a species composition, diversity, and functional organization comparable to that of a natural wetland habitat in the region (Karr and Dudley 1981). Application of this method requires collections of invertebrates, fish, or other organisms in wetlands that span a gradient of human disturbance from natural to highly disturbed. Species metrics sensitive to this disturbance gradient would be selected for inclusion in the final model. For example, fish vary in their ability to tolerate suspended sediments. Thus, the proportion or total abundance of a particular species may be an effective indicator of human-induced sediment problems and may facilitate classification of the condition within a particular wetland or stream. Although this method has been highly effective for evaluating some aquatic systems (Karr 1981, 1991; Deegan et al. 1997), recent research suggests application of this method in many wetlands is limited (Wilcox et al. 2002, Tangen et al. 2003). Because wetlands are highly variable environments that exhibit dynamic short- and long-term hydroperiods that alter plant and invertebrate communities, the ability to distinguish between anthropogenic effects and natural variability is often difficult. Thus, use of this technique is compromised in wetland environments.

DISTRIBUTION AND STATUS
Wetland Loss

At the time of colonial America (1600s), wetlands constituted 11% of the landscape (National Research Council 1992) and encompassed an estimated 89.5 million ha in the conterminous United States (Dahl 1990). Wetland drainage and modification began with permanent settlement of the colonies and continued as the human population expanded. Between 1600 and about 1970, wetlands were largely considered wastelands that provided little value to society and no economic value to private landowners (National Research Council 1992). Wetlands were drained for a variety of reasons, including disease prevention, agricultural production, development of transportation and communication networks, natural products production, and urban development (Dahl and Allord 1997). Tile and open-ditch drainage caused wetland losses averaging 222,580 ha annually from the mid-1950s to mid-1970s (U.S. Congress 1984).

Consequently, less than 40.1 million ha of wetlands remained by the mid-1970s when federal regulations were enacted that protected some wetlands. However, between the mid-1970s and mid-1980s, wetlands continued to be lost at an annual rate of 117,360 ha (Dahl and Johnson 1991). By the mid-1980s, wetlands constituted only 5% of the landscape and their distribution had been severely altered (National Research Council 1992). For example, wetland losses exceeded 20% in all 48 conterminous states except New Hampshire (9%) by the mid-1980s. Wetland losses exceeded 85% in 6 states and 50% in 22 states (Dahl 1990).

The most recent status and trend report developed by the National Wetland Inventory revealed that freshwater and estuarine wetlands composed 95% (40.67 million ha) and 5% (2.02 million ha), respectively, of the remaining wetland area in the conterminous United States (Dahl 2000). This report estimated wetland losses between 1986 and 1997 decreased about 80% (23,675 ha annual loss; 260,620 ha net loss) compared to the previous decade. However, an additional 404,690 ha (4.6%) of freshwater emergent wetlands and 485,630 ha (2.4%) of forested wetlands were lost during this period. Of the original area, only 40.1 million ha (47.7%) of wetlands remain. For the first time in the nation's history, there are fewer than 20.2 million ha of forested wetlands in the conterminous United States.

Wetland Alteration

Comprehensive data necessary to document trends in wetland alteration are not available. However, there are national reports and studies that indicate the majority of wetlands remaining in the lower 48 states have been altered. One of the most comprehensive reports was developed by the H. John Heinz III Center for Science, Economics and the Environment (2002). According to this report, (1) of 140 large river sites sampled, about 50% had phosphorus concentrations that exceeded Environmental Protection Agency standards (600 ppb) for preventing excess algal growth; (2) 60% of streams sampled (*n* = 867 sites) exhibited major changes in the magnitude of high or low flows, or the timing of these flows; (3) approximately 800 (20%) of 4,000 native animal species that depend on streams, lakes, wetlands, or riparian areas are considered "imperiled" or "critically imperiled"; (4) 213 (60%) of 350 watersheds sampled contained 1–10 non-native species; (5) about 940 (60%) of the 1,560 wetland communities whose status is known are considered to be at risk; and (6) approximately 23% of streams and rivers have farmlands or urban development within 30 m of the water's edge. Although these figures do not provide quantitative estimates of wetland area impacted, they indicate that aquatic environments ranging from rivers to reservoirs have been severely impacted biologically, physically, or chemically as a result of human activities.

Causes of Wetland Loss and Alteration

The causes of wetland losses in the United States have received much attention. From the mid-1950s to the mid-1970s, conversion of wetlands for agricultural purposes was responsible for 87% of wetland losses in the United States (Frayer et al. 1983). Between the mid-1970s and mid-1980s, agriculture remained a primary cause, but losses decreased to 54%. The trend of decreasing losses due to agriculture continued into the 1990s. During 1986–1997, agriculture was responsible for only 26% of wetland losses (Dahl 2000).

Conversely, the proportion of wetland losses to "other" land-use practices increased from 8% (mid-1950s–mid-1970s) to 41% (mid-1970s–mid-1980s). During this period, urban land uses accounted for only 5% of the losses (Tiner 1984), whereas a large component was attributable to drainage and clearing of wetlands for uses that were not specifically identified (Dahl and Johnson 1991). Similar to agricultural losses, the annual rate of loss due to nonagricultural activities decreased from 47,461 ha/year between the mid-1970s and mid-1980s to 17,540 ha/year between 1986 and 1997. However, the proportion of losses attributable to nonagricultural activities increased from 46 to 74% (National Research Council 2001).

The National Resources Inventory is another source of information to document conditions and trends in natural resources on non-federal lands in the United States. The U.S. Department of Agriculture's Natural Resources Conservation Service in cooperation with the Iowa State University Statistical Laboratory conducts the National Resources Inventory. Compiled at 5-year intervals beginning in 1987, this inventory captures data on features such as land cover and use, soil erosion, wetlands, and habitat diversity at more than 800,000 scientifically selected sample sites. In 1997, federal and non-federal land accounted for about 163 million and 607 million ha of land in the conterminous United States, respectively. Further, approximately 59% of wetlands occurred on forestland and 16.5% on agricultural cropland, pasture, and land in the Conservation Reserve Program. On non-federal land, annual average net loss of wetlands was 13,150 ha (U.S. Department of Agriculture 2000). Of the total losses recorded, development was responsible for 49%, followed by agriculture (26%), silviculture (12%), and miscellaneous (13%).

Impact of Federal Regulations

Based on National Wetland Inventory data, wetland losses in the conterminous United States declined each decade (Dahl and Johnson 1991, Dahl 2000) and efforts to create or restore wetlands have increased. Although there is no precise number for total wetland area restored, it is estimated that about 36,422 ha were added to the wetland inventory between 1987 and 1990 (U.S. Department of Interior 1991) and, between 1992 and 1997 annual gains of 27,920 ha were reported (U.S. Department of Agriculture 2000). Also, data from the Section 404 permitting program during the 1990s suggest a net gain in wetland area. The area of permitted impacts was approximately 9,712 ha/year during the 1990s, whereas the compensatory mitigation averaged over 16,997 ha/year (National Research Council 2001). Once completed, this mitigation would result in a net gain of over 7,285 ha/year. However, the literature on compensatory mitigation suggests that required projects often are not undertaken or failed to meet permit conditions (National Research Council 2001).

Loss of some wetland types continues at an alarming rate in certain regions of the United States. For example, forested palustrine wetlands (e.g., swamps, riparian corridors) decreased 6.2% from 22.3 million ha in the mid-1970s to 20.9 million ha in the mid-1980s. Most of this loss occurred in the southeastern United States (Dahl and Johnson 1991). In addition, it is apparent that cumulative impacts of individual actions threaten the integrity of entire wetland landscapes (National Research Council 2001). Although U.S. Army Corps of Engineers and U.S. Environmental Protection Agency regulations require consideration of cumulative impacts, they are seldom evaluated in permit review processes (Gosselink et al. 1990*a*). As a result, continued degradation of some wetlands continues to occur. For example, although the loss of forested palustrine wetlands has been significant, individual permits that allow the incremental conversion of forested palustrine wetlands often occur because such losses are not perceived to have a significant ecological effect (Gosselink et al. 1990*b*).

Impacts of Wetland Loss and Alteration on Wildlife Resources

Impacts of wetland loss on fish and wildlife resources are difficult to assess, but they have been severe. There are numerous reports documenting the decrease in prairie breeding habitats (Tiner 1984, Pederson et al. 1989) and the demise of waterfowl stopover and winter habitats (Korte and Fredrickson 1977, Frayer et al. 1989, Dahl and Johnson 1991). This information is supported by national and regional reports on status and habitat conditions of migratory birds, including wading birds, waterfowl, shorebirds, and Neotropical migrant songbird species. Of the 50 shorebird species considered in the United States Shorebird Conservation Plan, 5 (10%) are considered highly imperiled, 22 (44%) are species of high concern, and 15 (30%) are of moderate concern at a national scale (Brown et al. 2001). Similarly, the North American Waterbird Conservation Plan provides a continental-scale framework for the conservation and management of 210 species, including seabirds, coastal waterbirds, wading birds, and marsh birds in 29 nations (Kushlan et al. 2002). Of the 166 species of colonial waterbirds assessed in the plan, 12 (7%) are highly imperiled, 43 (26%) are of high concern, and 52 (31%) are of moderate concern. Approximately, 33–34% of these species use freshwater wetlands for nesting and foraging.

The U.S. Fish and Wildlife Service recently produced a report that identifies migratory and non-migratory birds of the United States of conservation concern (U.S. Department of Interior 2002). The species considered in this report are nongame birds, gamebirds without hunting seasons, subsistence-hunted nongame birds in Alaska, and species categorized as candidate, proposed, and recently delisted from the Endangered Species Act. Assessment scores used by the 3 major bird conservation plans (U.S. Shorebird Conservation Plan, North American Waterbird Conservation Plan, and Partners In Flight) were used in assessing conservation status at 3 geographic scales: national, U.S. Fish and Wildlife Service regions, and Bird Conservation Regions. At the national level, this report considers 131 bird species (12% of all native species) to be of conservation concern. At the scale of individual U.S. Fish and Wildlife Service regions (n = 7), the number of species listed ranges from 28 to 87 (average = 45). The number of species considered being of conservation concern within the 24 Bird Conservation Regions encompassing the lower 48 states ranges from 10 to 48 (average = 26). The North American Bird Conservation Initiative has endorsed Bird Conservation Regions as the basic ecological unit to be used in planning and evaluation of all-bird conservation efforts (North American Bird Conservation Initiative Committee 2000a, b). Although not all of the species occurring in the lists are considered wetland-dependent, palustrine and riparian wetlands often fill a crucial niche in the annual life cycle of many species on these lists.

A similar scenario is evident for amphibians and reptiles, even though the data are less complete. Natural fluctuations and local extinctions are common in both reptiles and amphibians (Blaustein et al. 1994). Thus, although observed population trends of many species have declined, ascertaining if these trends constitute natural fluctuations or unnatural declines is difficult because most field studies have not been conducted for a sufficient period (Pechmann and Wilbur 1994). However, the number of reported declines and documentation of adverse impacts suggest that amphibian declines represent a serious threat and reptiles appear to be in even greater danger of extinction (Gibbons et al. 2000). For example, 27 and 87 species of herpetofauna are listed as threatened and endangered, respectively, under the Endangered Species Act. This list includes 37 turtles (33 endangered, 4 threatened), 14 frogs and toads (9 endangered, 5 threatened), and 12 salamanders (8 endangered, 4 threatened). On a global scale, the International Union for the Conservation of Nature lists 149 species of herpetofauna as endangered, including 38 frogs and toads, 11 salamanders, and 38 turtles. In addition, 228 species are considered vulnerable to extinction if current trends continue, including 50 frogs and toads, 25 salamanders, and 58 turtles (International Union for the Conservation of Nature 2000). There are many factors known or suspected to be associated with population declines of amphibians and reptiles, including habitat loss, introduced or native invasive species, disease, pollution, and global climate change (Gibbons and Stangel 1999). However, many scientists consider habitat loss and alteration to be the largest single factor contributing to declines of many amphibians and semiaquatic reptiles. Buhlmann (1995), Buhlmann and Gibbons (1997), and Alford and Richards (1999), provide specific examples.

WETLAND FUNCTIONS AND VALUES

Wetland functions are diverse and include the biological, physical, and chemical processes that occur in or are associated with wetlands. The most widely valued wetland function is providing habitat for wildlife and contributing to the maintenance of biodiversity (National Research Council 1992). The U.S. Fish and Wildlife Service estimates that up to 43% of federally threatened and endangered species require wetland habitats during some part of their annual cycle (U.S. Environmental Protection Agency 2000), and more than 50% of protected migratory birds rely on wetlands (Wharton et al. 1982, U.S. Environmental Protection Agency 2001a). In addition, wetlands support 31% of the plant species occurring in the conterminous United States even though they compose only 5% of the land surface (U.S. Environmental Protection Agency 2001a).

Although the importance of wetlands to wildlife is well known, wetlands also perform numerous other functions. Wetlands positioned at low topographic positions relative to uplands aid society by moderating flood events (e.g., floodwater storage, reducing peak flows). These wetlands, if intact, function to store and slowly release floodwaters. In addition, trees and other wetland vegetation slow flow velocity and distribute floodwaters over floodplains. In combination, these functions can decrease the frequency and intensity of floods and reduce downstream erosion. In some cases, wetlands and other water retention facilities often provide a level of flood protection otherwise provided by expensive dredging operations and levees.

Wetlands also help reduce shoreline erosion, as well as maintain (e.g., groundwater recharge) and improve water quality (e.g., sediment accretion, nutrient uptake). As water passes through wetlands, excess nitrogen and phosphorus is processed, organic pollutants decompose, and suspended sediments are trapped. Wetlands may be capable of removing between 70 and 90% of the nitrogen entering a system (Gilliam 1994), whereas the estimated mean retention of phosphorus is 45% (Johnston 1991). However, excessive additions of nitrogen and phosphorus can cause the development of large algal blooms that consume oxygen and result in low oxygen concentrations (i.e., hypoxia) that cannot be tolerated by many aquatic organisms (U.S. Environmental Protection Agency 2001b).

Hypoxia can occur naturally, but human activities have undoubtedly increased the frequency, extent, and severity at which this condition occurs. In the conterminous United States, the largest known area where hypoxia occurs is off the Louisiana coast, but other areas include Long Island

Sound and Chesapeake Bay (Turner and Rabalais 2003). Wetlands also have been reported to remove 20–100% of metals, depending on individual site characteristics and metal type (Taylor et al. 1990, Delfino and Odum 1993, Gambrell 1994). In terms of quantity, sediment is the major pollutant of wetlands, lakes, estuaries, and reservoirs in the United States (Baker 1992). Sediment quality is also an environmental concern because it may act as both a sink and source for water-quality constituents. As with some nutrients, sedimentation naturally occurs in many wetlands. However, excessive sedimentation can negatively impact aquatic plant and animal communities (Rybicki and Carter 1986, Dieter 1991, Jurik et al. 1994, Wang et al. 1994, Gleason and Euliss 1998). In some cases, sediment accrual can actually result in the loss of all basin volume (Luo et al. 1997).

Finally, many wetlands may be important in carbon sequestration and reduction of atmospheric concentrations of greenhouse gases (Mitsch and Gosselink 1993). Although much attention has been focused on bogs, forested wetlands, and tidal marshes, restored prairie wetlands also have been recently identified as carbon sinks (U.S. Environmental Protection Agency 2003). High primary productivity by plants that fix carbon through photosynthesis, high rates of organic matter uptake, and low decomposition rate of organic matter are characteristics that result in the net storage of carbon in wetlands. For example, a study of coastal marshes in Florida indicated that soils in high and low marshes contained 73 and 287% more organic carbon, respectively, than nearby upland forest soils (Choi et al. 2001).

Wetland values, which are based on functions, usually are associated with goods or services that society recognizes as worthy, desirable, or useful to humans. The reasons that wetlands are often legally protected are related to their societal values rather than ecological processes (Mitsch and Gosselink 1993). Thus, the value of a wetland often depends on type and location as well as human perception. One of the most consistently reported wetland values is provision of recreational opportunity. Ninety-seven percent of all Americans over 16 years of age participate in some sort of outdoor recreation, with 33% of Americans reporting they bird-watch (Cordell and Herbert 2002). Based on the National Survey of Fishing, Hunting, and Wildlife-Associated Recreation, more than 82 million residents of the United States spent $108 billion dollars to fish, hunt, or watch wildlife in 2001 (U.S. Departments of Interior and Commerce 2001). Participants spent a total of $70 billion in 2001, including $36 billion on fishing, $21 billion on hunting, and $38 billion on trips, equipment, and other items related to watching wildlife. A comparison of survey results between 1991 and 2001 indicates Americans continue to enjoy wildlife recreation. However, while the number of participants decreased from 40 million in 1991 to 37.8 million in 2001, their expenditures increased from $53 billion (adjusted for inflation and comparability between Surveys) in 1991 to $70 billion in 2001. Similarly, the total number of wildlife watchers decreased by 13% between 1991 and 2001, but expenditures increased by 41% due to equipment purchases. Although the economic benefits reported in these studies encompass all habitats, wetlands obviously contribute to the economic value of outdoor recreation.

The economic value that wetlands provide in relation to water purification and flood protection has been estimated in some regions. In South Carolina, for example, the Congaree Bottomland Hardwood Swamp annually removes pollutants that would require $5 million to remove using a wastewater treatment facility (U.S. Environmental Protection Agency 2000). The U.S. Army Corps of Engineers found that protecting wetlands along the Charles River in Massachusetts saved $17 million in potential flood damage (Thibodeau and Ostro 1981), the Minnesota Department of Natural Resources estimated that replacing the natural floodwater storage function of wetlands is $2,430/ha-m ($300/ac-ft) of water (U.S. Department of Interior 1995), and in western Washington the value of wetlands for flood protection ranged from $14,600 to $20,600/ha (Leschine et al. 1997). In contrast, drainage of wetlands and diversion of the Mississippi and Missouri rivers from their original floodplains were partially responsible for the billions of dollars in damage to businesses, homes, crops, and property that occurred as a result of the 1993 Mississippi River flood (Office Environmental Policy 1993, Parrnett et al. 1993).

Wetlands also are commercially important sites for production of natural products, including fish, shellfish, fur, and timber. Seafood is a $50 billion industry (U.S. Department of Commerce 1995) and species dependent on wetlands for food or habitat comprise more than 75% of the commercial harvest (Feierabend and Zelazny 1987, U.S. Environmental Protection Agency 1994). The U.S. commercial fisheries harvest is valued at more than $2 billion annually and is the basis for a $26.8 billion fishery processing and sales industry (U.S. Environmental Protection Agency 1995). The commercial harvest of fish and shellfish in Louisiana's coastal marshes alone was worth $244 million in 1991 (U.S. Environmental Protection Agency 1995). Many mammals and reptiles harvested for their skins are dependent on wetlands, including muskrat (*Ondatra zibethicus*), American beaver (*Castor canadensis*), mink (*Mustela vison*), northern river otter (*Lontra canadensis*), and American alligator (*Alligator mississippiensis*). The nation's harvest of muskrat pelts alone is worth over $70 million annually, while the alligator industry is valued at more than $16 million (Mitsch and Gosselink 1993, U.S. Congress 1993). Finally, forested wetlands have the potential to provide a substantial amount of wood products. The value of bottomland hardwoods and cypress swamps in the southeastern United States alone has been estimated at about $8 billion (Johnson 1979).

Wetlands have multi-functional resources that supply humans with a number of important products (e.g., fish, timber, wildlife), but they also perform an unusually large number of ecological functions that support economic activity (Barbier et al. 1997). However, not all wetlands perform every function nor do wetlands perform all functions equally well. Factors that influence the kind of functions a wetland performs include type (palustrine, riverine), position in the landscape, type of landscape (e.g., agriculture, forest), size, soils, vegetation composition, residence time of the water, and the nutrient, sediment and chemical concentrations of water (Novitzki et al. 1997). In addition, wetland functions have value at several different spatial scales, including internal, local, regional, and global. For example, water storage functions and provision of migratory bird resources are applicable at regional scales, whereas the effects of wetlands on air quality (e.g., carbon and nitrogen cycles) are most appropriate to consider at a global level. Finally, there are different methods available to measure the value of wetlands, including ecology, sociology, and economics. Some products such as commercial fish and timber harvest can be directly assigned monetary value, but it is difficult to calculate economic return on biodiversity, clean air, and clean water (Barbier et al. 1997). Consequently, there are a great number of uncertainties that must be considered when attempting to assign values to wetlands. Wetlands often represent public goods that are not priced the same as other services and goods; thus, many private individuals and firms make economic choices that affect the status of wetlands on the basis of costs and benefits that neglect or undercount broader social issues (Leschine et al. 1997). It has been suggested that failure to adequately account for nonmarket environmental values in development decisions is a major reason wetlands have been lost and converted to other uses (Barbier et al. 1997). However, there are increasing efforts to conduct total wetland valuation studies that capture both direct and indirect values. A total valuation study of Louisiana's coastal wetlands resulted in an estimate of $983/ha based on an 8% discount rate (Costanza et al. 1989). Using a variety of techniques, the authors calculated that commercial fishing and trapping, recreation, and storm protection services accounted for 19%, 2%, and 79% of the total, respectively.

Wetland management in today's society requires strategic planning and a diverse set of skills because decisions regarding the values of wetlands must be based on many competing interests. Managers must also recognize and address the increasing pressures being placed on wetlands as a result of an increasing human population and economic wealth. Since 1950, there has been a 40% increase in per capita demand for grain, a 100% increase in fish, and 33% increase in timber (Watson 1999). In addition, decisions that were historically made within fish and wildlife agencies are now made with citizen involvement. These pressures often form the basis for decisions regarding the fate of individual wetlands and entire landscapes. In many cases, decisions are often biased in favor of uses that have marketed products that result in conversion and exploitation of environmental resources (Barbier et al. 1997). Uses with marketable products often are advocated because there is a belief that technological advances will allow replacing the wetland functions lost by modifying or destroying the wetland. However, functions and values lost often are not completely replaced, especially with regard to the abiotic and biotic processes necessary to support healthy and sustainable fish and wildlife populations. Therefore, in addition to making decisions regarding how to manage land, managers must also create opportunities to inform public officials and interested individuals on the need to conserve or restore wetlands for a wide variety of reasons, including value as wildlife habitat. This will require development of new and interdisciplinary approaches to problem solving, including use of information from other disciplines (e.g., political, economic, and social) during the decision making process.

WETLAND CHARACTERISTICS

Traditionally, wetlands often have been created,

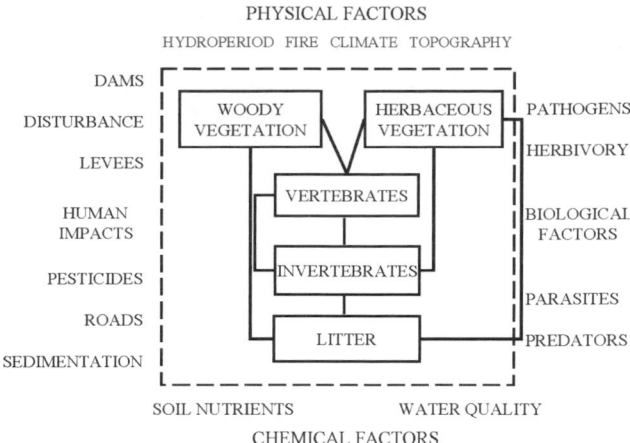

Fig. 1. Factors influencing wetland characteristics, functions, and values.

restored, or managed without accounting for differences in structure and function affected by abiotic and biotic factors. One of the most common approaches has been to acquire a site, select a familiar development or management scenario that has worked elsewhere, and implement it without considering onsite geomorphic and current ecological processes (e.g., nutrient cycling). These natural processes are in a constant state of flux because of dynamic biotic and abiotic factors. Consequently, wetlands often have been described as sieves that are continually modified and influenced by a myriad of factors that affect both short- and long-term productivity and values (Fig. 1). For example, the type and quantity of nutrients that are imported and exported from a wetland varies among locations, seasons, and years (Hammer and Bastian 1989). Examples of abiotic factors that influence wetland processes include hydroperiod, climate, soil, and disturbance (e.g., fire, herbivory) regimes (Fig. 1). Biotic factors include those that are stationary within a wetland basin (e.g., plants) and those that operate at larger scales (e.g., waterbirds, pathogens). Failure to incorporate this information into the decision-making framework prior to site acquisition, development, or management often has resulted in the inability to sustain long-term productivity and, ultimately, the inability to reach desired goals and objectives. In this section we provide information on the primary abiotic and biotic factors, and their interrelationships with wetland structure and function, because this information represents the cornerstone of effective management.

Geomorphic Setting and Soils

Geomorphology is the science of the earth's relief features. A basic understanding of geomorphic processes is critical because structure and function of wetlands varies depending on how wetlands were formed (Klimas et al. 2005). The patterns and rates of sediment transport and deposition are primary factors affecting formation, structure, and function of wetlands (Saucier 1994). The magnitude and types of sediments deposited greatly influence hydrology, water quality and, hence, vegetation structure and wildlife habitat quality (Bornette et al. 1998, Hupp 2000, Johnson 2000b).

Landforms on the earth's surface can be grouped into 4 categories: structural, weathering, erosional, and depositional. Structural landforms include those created by mas-

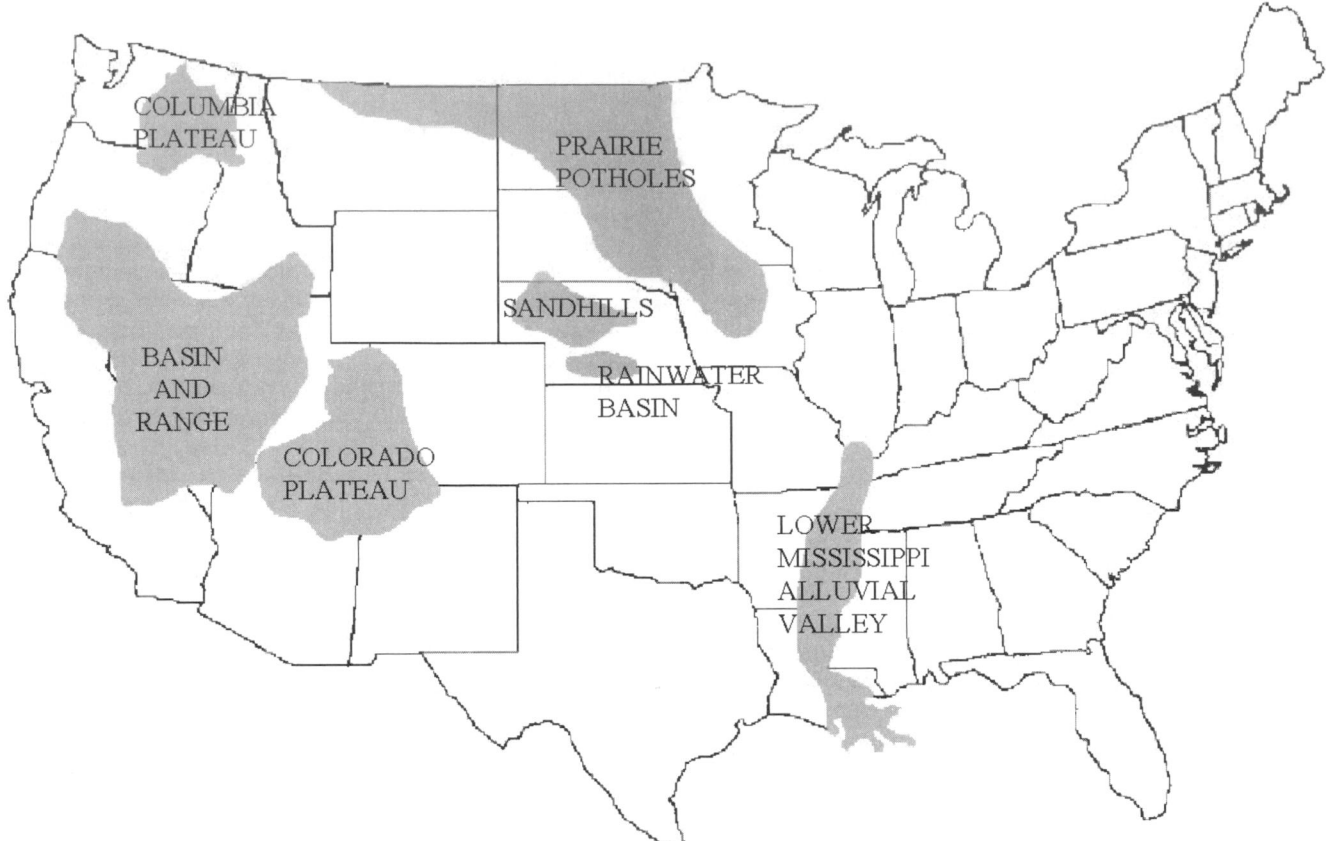

Fig. 2. Landforms in the Intermountain West and Great Plains regions of the United States.

sive earth movements such as mountains, rift valleys, and volcanoes. In contrast, weathering landforms (e.g., karst, patterned ground) are created by the physical or chemical decomposition of rock. Erosional (e.g., river and glacial valleys) and depositional (e.g., deltas, floodplains) landforms are the result of the erosion or deposition, respectively, of surface materials caused by wind, water, glaciers, and gravity. Landforms that have been influenced by more than one of these processes are termed polygenetic, whereas landscapes that have undergone several cycles of development are termed polycyclic.

Wetlands occur in all of the above landforms and many are the result of polygenetic and/or polycyclic processes (Fig. 2). For example, in the Rocky Mountains, wetlands of mountain valleys are often distinguished from those of intermountain basins based on distinctly different geologic origins, weather, and resulting soil types (Windell et al. 1986). Mountain valleys were shaped by erosional forces of water and by glacial movements at higher elevations (Wright 1983). In contrast, intermountain basins were largely formed by ancient tectonic and volcanic events (Windell et al. 1986). Direct or indirect effects of glaciers in mountains have resulted in the formation of many different types of palustrine wetlands, including cirque basins; spring, seep, and snowbed wetlands; tarns; kettles; and terminal or lateral moraine lakes.

Erosional and depositional forces caused by glaciations also were the single most important process involved in the formation of the Lower Mississippi River Alluvial Valley (Saucier 1994). The diversity of wetland types and soil

conditions that characterize many floodplains are the result of varying patterns of sediment deposition (Wharton et al. 1982, Stanturf and Schoenholtz 1998, Richardson 2000). The distribution of different floodplain landforms is especially well described for the Lower Mississippi Alluvial Valley (Saucier 1994). The location of point bars, abandoned channels, natural levees, valley trains, and other features are well mapped from Cairo, Illinois to the Gulf Coast. The complexity of contemporary surface features is still evident from remote imagery despite extensive land surface changes resulting from agriculture.

Glaciation also was the dominant force creating pothole wetlands in the Columbia Basin (Bretz 1923) and Prairie Pothole Region of the northern Great Plains (Sloan 1972). However, south of the Missouri River to about the Nebraska-South Dakota boundary there is greater evidence of erosion (Laubhan and Fredrickson 1997). Further south in the central and southern Great Plains, wetlands exhibit a depositional rather than an erosional surface. In the central Great Plains, multiple hypotheses of wetland genesis have been proposed but all involve weathering or erosion. Wetlands in this region are thought to have formed as a result of deflation, differential compaction of unconsolidated materials, and solution of soluble layers (Shimer 1972). For example, the numerous isolated wetlands in the Rainwater Basin (Fig. 2) of south central Nebraska typically developed in depressions where leaching concentrated clay particles in the subsoil (Erickson and Leslie 1987). In contrast, the Sandhill Region of Nebraska was formed as wind blown sand accumulated against low hills and ridges

(Tiner 1984). In this region, wetland type and distribution are largely affected by the dynamics of a large underground reservoir that is part of the Ogallala Aquifer (Bleed and Flowerday 1990). Playas, the dominant palustrine wetland type in the southern Great Plains, also are thought to have formed by deflation (Reeves 1966).

Wetlands in the Great Basin Region of the Basin and Range Province formed as a result of different processes (Duffy and Al-Hassan 1988). First, alluvial fan deposits of Quarternary age occurred along the margin of depressions and, in many cases, individual fans coalesced to form a piedmont plain or bajada. Second, the depressions filled with deposits of mixed fluvial and lacustrine origin. Third, pluvial lakes inundated the area. As conditions became drier and warmer, pluvial lakes evaporated resulting in saline lakes and playas. Notable water bodies include Walker and Pyramid lakes, which are remnants of Lake Lahontan, and the Great Salt and Utah lakes, which are remnants of Lake Bonneville (Fiero 1986). Additional wetlands were formed as erosional material was transported by streams and deposited at the base of mountains or farther out in depressions (Snyder 1962, Burkham 1988). An alluvial fan from one mountain may extend outward and merge with a fan from an adjacent range (Lamke and Moore 1965), which typically results in a nearly flat area where fine-grained deposits accumulate and surface flooding may occur during wet periods (Mabbutt 1979, Burkham 1988).

Examples of wetlands formed by weathering include tinajas, also called potholes or weathering pits. Tinajas are depressional wetlands eroded from bedrock and are abundant on friable sandstones of the Colorado Plateau where they locally create a distinct dome-and-pit landscape (Spence and Henderson 1993). Most theories regarding formation of tinajas include a combination of physical, chemical, and biological-weathering processes that promote mineral decomposition followed by removal of the decomposed material by wind or water (Twidale and Bourne 1975, Godfrey 1980). The aridity of the region also contributes to wetland development by limiting vegetation cover, which permits wind deflation, and by concentrating salts that facilitate rock disintegration (Goudie 1991).

Wetlands formed by the same processes may differ markedly depending on the type of original material. Depressional wetlands referred to as potholes occur in both the Columbia Basin and the northern Great Plains. Potholes in both regions resulted from glaciation and have many similar attributes, including size (<8 ha in the Great Plains and <1 to >32 ha in the Columbia Basin), location (typically in areas with a high water table), and isolation (Harris 1954, Johnsgard 1956, Sloan 1972, Steward and Kantrud 1972, Laubhan and Fredrickson 1997, Tiner et al. 2002). However, glaciers in the Columbia Basin scoured basalt deposited by lava flows (Bretz 1923, Fenneman 1931), whereas the advance and retreat of glaciers in the Great Plains deposited glacial drift, a general term that includes unsorted rock debris called till, sorted sand and gravel called outwash, and fine-grained sediments deposited in lakes (Sloan 1972). These differences in the composition of material underlying the potholes in each region can influence hydrology, soil and water chemistry (e.g., nutrients, pH), and other factors important in affecting the composition of wetland flora and fauna. Thus, applying standard techniques across sites that appear similar may not be successful due to differences in topographic position, soils, or hydroperiod (Stanturf and Schoenholtz 1998).

The importance of material that becomes the substrate of wetland basins as a result of geomorphic processes also is critical for understanding wetland structure and function. For example, glacial deposits vary in texture and chemical composition, which affects the quantity of wetlands, their hydrologic connectivity, and water quality (Winter 1989). In contrast, different rock types, climate, and geomorphic processes (e.g., glaciation, erosion) have resulted in a complex mosaic of heterogeneous, discontinuous soil types in the Rocky Mountains (Retzer 1962, Price 1981). Relatively undeveloped soils are common in areas dominated by fragmented bedrock, talus, or recent glacial moraine deposits (Rink and Kiladis 1986). In comparison, tinajas in the Colorado Plateau are covered with sandy sediments or alternating layers of materials that vary in organic content (Netoff et al. 1995). The amount of sediment deposited in the basin, in combination with hydrology, largely affects vegetation composition (Netoff et al. 1995).

Floodplain systems also exhibit differential patterns of sediment erosion and deposition that results in a diversity of wetland types and soil conditions (Leopold et al. 1964, Wharton et al. 1982, Stanturf and Schoenholtz 1998, Richardson 2000). Geomorphic features, such as natural levees, point bars, backswamps, abandoned channels, oxbows, sloughs, and swales greatly influence abiotic conditions (e.g., hydroperiod, soil and drainage characteristics). Natural levees adjacent to a river are formed when heavier, coarse-grained sediments (e.g., sand) are deposited as the river overtops its bank during flood events and the water velocity is slowed by vegetation (Hupp 2000). In contrast, water is ponded for much longer periods in backswamps and fine sediments are filtered out forming heavy clay soils. Such differences impact hydrology, which influences the floristic and structural characteristics of vegetation (Kellison et al. 1998, Ward 1998, Heitmeyer et al. 2002). The diversity of these sites is important for providing habitat for a wide range of species, including amphibians, reptiles, waterbirds, and fish (Bellrose et al. 1979, Burbrink et al. 1998, Hoover and Killgore 1998, Wigley and Lancia 1998). However, differences among floodplain wetlands often have been overlooked in many restoration efforts because these features have not been recognized. Hydrologic restoration of sloughs and swales has been under emphasized or ignored in many efforts. Further, improper site selection is a leading cause of failure in bottomland hardwood reforestation (Allen et al. 2001) and management efforts (King and Fredrickson 1998). Development of management units ringed by levees in areas where a natural levee or point bar exists may lead to failure because sandy deposits may make it difficult to maintain water levels, particularly during drought conditions.

Historically, forces that altered surface features and created wetlands were the result of natural events that impacted large areas and occurred thousands of years ago. However, geomorphic processes continue to occur through time and act to alter wetland structure and function. These processes are now largely influenced by anthropomorphic activities, including agriculture, physical structures such as levees, and urban development. For example during the Missouri River flood of 1993, deep scouring often occurred at sites where man had placed barriers (such as roads, railroads, or levees) in the floodplain. Thus, the distribution of scours sites connected to and not connected to the river was largely influenced by human development (Galat et al. 1998). Development of reservoirs in the pothole area of the Columbia Basin has elevated groundwater levels and has increased the hydroperiod and lowered salinities in many wetlands that are not actually submerged (Johnsgard 1956). Repeated agricultural cultivation has reduced the porosity of the upper soil horizons, causing serious erosion of loessal (wind blown) soils (Daubenmire 1942, Busacca 1991). Excessive sedimentation can result in dramatic habitat alterations in a relatively short time (Bellrose et al. 1979, Kleiss 1996, Oswalt 2003). In addition, activities such as stream channelization can alter hydrologic and geomorphic processes throughout an entire watershed, thus influencing vegetation communities and reducing habitat quality for a variety of fish and wildlife (Fredrickson 1979, Shankman and Pugh 1992, Oswalt 2003). These influences must be considered when developing restoration and management plans because areas properly designed based on local site conditions may still fail because of offsite conditions. Thus, restoration plans must often be developed for larger scale landscapes and involve all affected stakeholders (National Research Council 1999).

Hydrology and Climate

Hydrology probably is the single most important factor controlling the establishment and maintenance of specific wetlands and wetland processes (Mitsch and Gosselink 2000). In fact, the hydrological regime separates wetlands systems from true terrestrial and aquatic systems. Hydrology influences chemical and physical properties of wetlands and ultimately affects the biota (Fig. 1).

Components influencing hydroperiod include those that affect the amount of water entering and leaving a wetland (Marble 1992). Precipitation, groundwater, surface water, and tidal fluctuations represent important inflow components. Possible outflow components include evaporation, transpiration, groundwater and surface water discharge, and tidal fluctuations. These components are often placed in an equation, termed a water budget, to express the relationship between inflow and outflow. This equation is based on the premise that the amount of water in a wetland is equal to the water that enters a wetland minus the amount of water discharged from the wetland. A generalized form of this equation is:

water volume = precipitation + surface water inflow
　　　　　+ groundwater inflow − evaporation
　　　　　− transpiration − surface water outflow
　　　　　− groundwater outflow.

The exact form of the equation varies depending on several factors, including geomorphic setting, landscape position, and climate. Tidal fluctuations contribute largely to the hydroperiod of coastal wetlands, whereas changes in surface water are a controlling influence in riparian wetlands. Palustrine wetlands also exhibit wide variability relative to the importance of inflow and outflow components. All Physiographic Provinces composing the Intermountain West (Columbia Plateau, Colorado Plateau, Basin and Range, Rocky Mountains) exhibit either semiarid or arid climates (Bailey 1995) and, with the exception of high elevation wetlands in the Rocky Mountains, experience negative annual precipitation–evapotranspiration ratios (Nelson and Tiernan 1983, Hidy and Klieforth 1990, Bailey 1995). However, local features differ within and among provinces, resulting in different hydrologic cycles. In the Columbia Basin portion of the Columbia Plateau, the hydrologic condition of many remnant natural wetlands is affected by precipitation and evaporation cycles; however, larger lakes and permanently flooded potholes also receive water from springs and have surface outlets to streams (Whittaker and Fairbanks 1958). Precipitation is also of primary importance in affecting timing and frequency of hydroperiods in natural wetlands of the Basin and Range Province, but other factors such as elevation, aspect, slope, climate, and soil properties also are important (Snyder 1962, Beatley 1974, Eakin et al. 1976, Ehleringer 1985, Duffy and Al-Hassan 1988). In general, spring represents the primary, and often the only, soil moisture recharge period (Caldwell 1985, Ehleringer et al. 1991). Because of the general aridity of the region, temporary hydroperiods are widespread, and permanently flooded palustrine wetlands are few (Williams 1985).

In contrast, external drainage is prominent in the Colorado Plateau with about 90% of the region drained by the Colorado River and its tributaries (Thornbury 1965). Surface water availability is further influenced by local climatic conditions that vary considerably depending on elevation, landscape position, and aspect (Comstock and Ehleringer 1992). Consequently, although natural marshes are common in the Basin and Range Province, they are an uncommon feature of the Colorado Plateau (Harper et al. 1994). In Arizona, most natural marshes are largely seasonal, the hydrology being dependent on summer precipitation and snowmelt rather than groundwater (Brown 1985).

Wetland hydrology in the Rockies is complex because the relative contribution of surface (direct and indirect) and groundwater components varies depending on numerous physical and climatic factors. The majority of water inflow to wetlands results from indirect precipitation occurring in the watershed. In contrast, direct precipitation is probably the least significant source of water (Knud-Hansen 1986), except in terrain depressions where snow has accumulated (Willard 1979) and bogs (Cooper 1986). Groundwater hydrology varies greatly depending on geology, watershed topography, soil characteristics, and season (Rink and Kiladis 1986). Peak groundwater flow, although poorly studied, appears to be a comparatively minor source of water with the exception of sites where seeps and springs surface (Leaf 1975). However, snowmelt at higher elevations supplies a large volume of water that can contribute to groundwater dynamics and indirectly impact wetland hydroperiods. The frequency, time, depth, and duration of flooding are affected by several factors, including the renewal rate of water and the timing, regularity, and predictability of daily and seasonal water availability (Gosselink and Turner 1978).

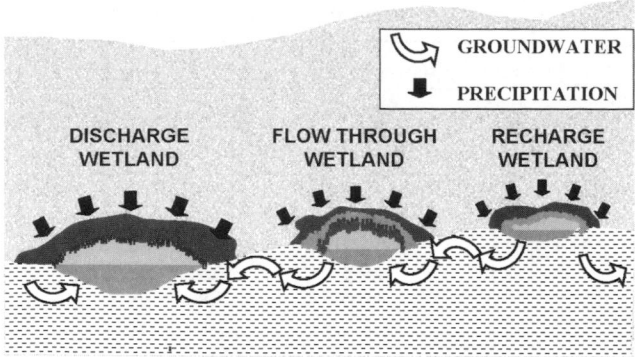

Fig. 3. Influence of groundwater and surface water relative to recharge, flow-through, and discharge wetlands.

Historically, most wetland managers focused solely on surface water and ignored the dynamics of groundwater, including its quality, volume, and seasonality. However, given current and future human demands for water (Postel 2000), understanding groundwater conditions will be increasingly important for successful wetland management. Depletion of aquifers as a result of withdrawal for agricultural irrigation and drinking water is an increasing problem, but the impact on wetlands depends on the connectivity between wetlands and groundwater (Postel 2000). Perched wetlands, which have an impervious layer between the wetland and the groundwater table (Mitsch and Gosselink 2000), are disconnected from the aquifer and groundwater impacts are minimal. However, groundwater is an important hydrologic component of recharge, flow-through, and discharge wetlands (Fig. 3). Flow-through wetlands have both surface and groundwater flow and discharge some water into the ground. Discharge wetlands typically occur at low topographic positions and receive some surface flow, but groundwater discharging into the wetland influences the geochemistry. Although this classification may seem straightforward, a given wetland may change status. For example, if a local aquifer becomes depleted, a discharge wetland may shift to a recharge wetland (Richardson et al. 2001). Thus, water depth and duration may decline in the wetland resulting in ecological and functional changes.

In some systems (Intermountain West, Prairie Potholes of the northern Great Plains), groundwater may be either a critical water source or influence wetland geochemistry (Winter and Rosenberry 1995). The influence of ground water is often more evident in geographic regions that have a negative precipitation/evaporation ratio because groundwater flow often allows plants with low-salinity tolerance

to exist among plants with high-salinity tolerance. The influence of groundwater is more difficult to identify for wetlands in areas where precipitation exceeds evapotranspiration because groundwater constituents are diluted by precipitation. However, in some systems, groundwater may be more important than precipitation or surface flooding at particular times of the year.

Short- and long-term hydrologic conditions affect many abiotic factors. Water fluxes affect nutrient cycling in wetland basins by influencing the type and quantity of nutrients that enter and exit wetlands, and decomposition rates (Livingston and Loucks 1979). Hydroperiod and water source (e.g., groundwater vs. surface water) also affects water quality, nutrient cycling, and soil conditions (Gambrell and Patrick 1978, Wharton et al. 1982, Mitsch and Gosselink 2000). These abiotic conditions in turn influence biotic components of wetlands, including composition, distribution, and productivity of wetland vegetation (Bedinger 1979, van der Valk and Welling 1988, Squires and van der Valk 1992) and invertebrate community composition and structure (Eakin et al. 1976, Kadlec 1982, Duffy and Al-Hassan 1988, Dobrowolski et al. 1990, Williams et al. 1990, Comstock and Ehleringer 1992). Ultimately, vertebrate use of wetlands is indirectly and directly affected by the hydrologic regime (Table 1). Hydroperiod indirectly affects vertebrates by affecting vegetation composition and structure as well as food resources for waterbirds (Weller and Spatcher 1965, Weller and Fredrickson 1974, Kaminski and Prince 1981, Ball and Nudds 1989, Weller 1999).

Similar interactions occur with respect to herpetofauna that often spend only short periods in wetlands. For example, many species of amphibians require vegetation for attachment of egg masses, and both adults and larval forms require invertebrates for food. Therefore, wetland vegetation is extremely important for amphibians because composition affects (1) type, quantity, and nutritive quality of plant foods available (Table 2); (2) distribution, density, and structure that provides cover and egg attachment sites; and (3) quantity and type of substrate for invertebrates. Hydrologic regime also directly influences wildlife use because time of flooding relative to the life-history cycle of the organism, duration of flooding, and water depth affect availability of resources (e.g., foods, cover) for waterbirds (Laubhan and Roelle 2001). For example, many waterbirds (e.g., dabbling ducks, shorebirds) require shallow water depths to forage efficiently (White and James 1978, Reid et al. 1989) (Fig. 4). Foods and cover in wetlands that are flooded too deep are largely unavailable to these species. In addition, successful recruitment of many amphibian species

Table 1. Representative vertebrates that use 7 wetland types (Stewart and Kantrud 1971) classed as palustrine by Cowardin et al. (1979).

Wetland type	Description	Flood duration (months)	Vertebrate use
I	Ephemeral ponds	<1	Dabbling ducks, shorebirds
II	Temporary ponds	<1	Dabbling ducks, shorebirds, waders
III	Seasonal ponds and lakes	2–4	Dabbling ducks, diving ducks, frogs, rails, shorebirds, waders
IV	Semipermanent ponds and lakes	11–12	Dabbling ducks, diving ducks, frogs, grebes, rails, terns, turtles, waders
V	Permanent ponds and lakes	12	Dabbling ducks, diving ducks, fish, turtles,
VI	Alkali ponds and lakes	6–12	Dabbling ducks, diving ducks, shorebirds
VII	Fen ponds	12	Blackbirds, chickadees, frogs, jays, kingbirds, snakes, sparrows

Table 2. Chemical composition of selected annual seeds and row crops.

Common name	Scientific name	Gross energy (kcal/g)	Fat	Protein	NFE[a]	Ash[b]
Barnyardgrass	*Echinochloa crusgalli*	3.9	2.4	8.3	40.5	18.0
Chufa flatsedge	*Cyperus esculentus*	4.3	6.9	6.7	55.4	2.5
Corn	*Zea mays*	4.4	3.8	10.8	79.8	1.5
Fall panicum	*Panicum dichotomiflorum*	4.0	3.1	12.3	50.1	16.1
Milo	*Sorghum vulgare*	4.2	3.1	10.2	72.2	3.5
Rice cutgrass	*Leersia oryzoides*	4.0	2.0	12.0	57.8	9.5
Sticktights	*Bidens frondosa*	5.2	15.0	25.0	27.5	7.2

[a] Nitrogen-free extract: a measure of highly digestible carbohydrates.

[b] Ash: measure of mineral content.

is enhanced in wetlands that dry seasonally because this prevents fish and invertebrate predators from becoming established (Pechmann et al. 1989, Semlitsch 2000*b*).

Algae

Historically, biologists have focused on the structure and biomass of emergent plants in wetland systems but have overlooked the importance of algae. However, algal biomass can equal that of submersed macrophytes (Goldsborough 2001). Further, algae can be important sources of primary production and dissolved oxygen as they transform and retain nutrients, serve as habitat for other organisms, and often form the base of wetland food webs (Murkin 1989, Stevens et al. 1989, Murkin et al. 1992, Browder et al. 1994, MacIntyre et al. 1996, Wetzel 1996, Robinson et al. 2000, Stevenson 2001). In saline systems, the algal biomass within a wetland often exceeds the biomass of macrophytes (Zedler 1980) and is of criti-

cal importance for invertebrate fauna. In freshwater systems, algae are important in the decomposition process and provide important nutrition for invertebrates. Epiphytic algae are an important food for many macroinvertebrate grazers (Allanson 1973). Algae readily respond to available nutrients in the water column and may form massive blooms, particularly when water temperatures are warm. During slow drainage of a wetland, algae are retained within a basin because they tend to attach to vegetation or other substrates, thus preventing the export of important nutrients. However, algae are sensitive to many physical and chemical factors, including human activities (Pan and Stevenson 1996, Stevenson et al. 1999). Fertilizer runoff can result in excessive addition of some nutrients (e.g., phosphorous) that can stimulate extensive algal blooms that deplete dissolved oxygen concentrations and cause fish mortality, or reduce light penetration below thresholds required for growth of some aquatic plant species.

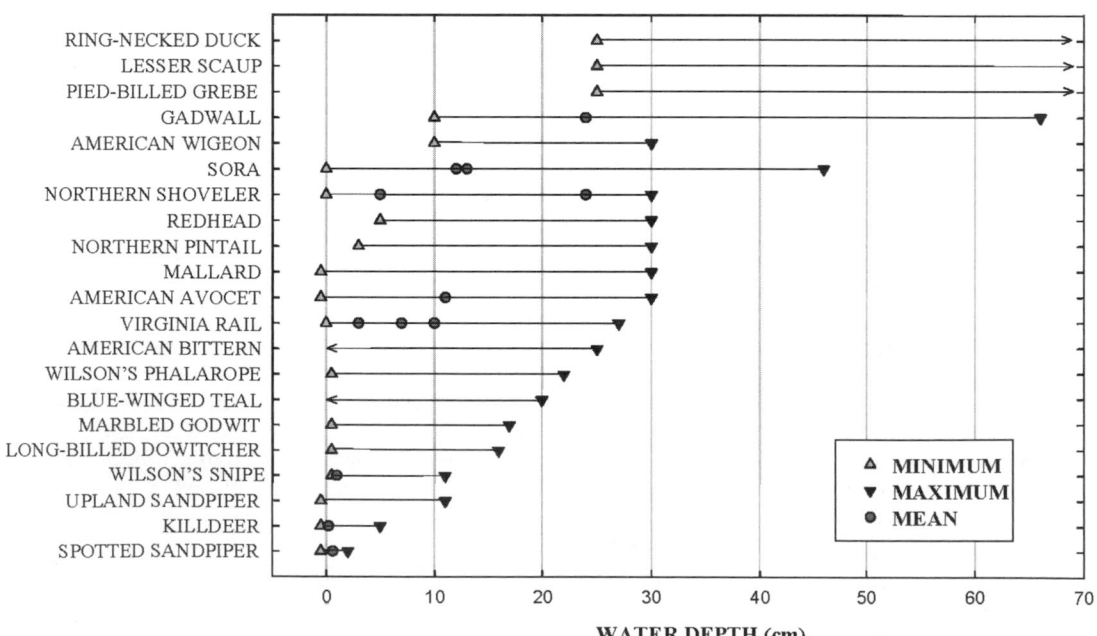

Fig. 4. Foraging depths of some common species using wetland habitats based on review of the scientific literature (ring-necked duck [*Aythya collaris*], lesser scaup [*A. affinis*], pied-billed grebe [*Podilymbus podiceps*], gadwall [*Anas strepera*], American wigeon (*A. americana*), sora [*Porzana carolina*], northern shoveler [*A. clypeata*], redhead [*Aythya americana*], northern pintail [*Anas acuta*], mallard [*A. platyrhynchos*], American avocet [*Recurvirostra americana*], Virginia rail [*Rallus limicola*], American bittern [*Botaurus lentiginosus*], Wilson's phalarope [*Phalaropus tricolor*], blue-winged teal [*A. discors*], marbled godwit [*Limosa fedoa*], long-billed dowitcher [*Limnodromus scolopaceus*], Wilson's snipe [*Gallinago delicata*], upland sandpiper [*Bartramia longicauda*], killdeer [*Charadrius vociferus*], and spotted sandpiper [*Actitis macularia*]).

Vascular Vegetation

Wetland vascular plants can be divided into 4 life forms: (1) submergent, (2) emergent, (3) floating leaf, and (4) floating. Submergent plants are rooted in substrate but the stems and leaves are mostly, if not entirely, in water. Emergent plants grow with their roots in wet soil part or all of their life, but stems and leaves extend through the water column to above the water surface. Floating-leaf plants are rooted in substrate but extend broad, floating leaves to the surface. Floating plants are not rooted and usually remain on the surface of the water.

The composition, distribution, and productivity of vegetation within a wetland are dependent on both biotic and abiotic factors (Whittaker and Niering 1975, Grubb 1977, Bedinger 1979, van der Valk and Welling 1988). Species that potentially occur within a basin are dependent on 2 primary factors. First, colonization can occur via dispersal of reproductive propagules (e.g., seeds, tubers) from outlying areas into the basin. There are many natural dispersal mechanisms that facilitate movement of seeds to new areas. Species such as overcup oak (*Quercus lyrata*) have floating seeds that are easily dispersed by water, whereas willow (*Salix* spp.) and cottonwood (*Populus* spp.) seeds are light and dispersed via both wind and water (Cronk and Fennessy 2001). In contrast, seeds of other species often attach to, or are digested by, mammals or birds and can be transported great distances from the original source (Collon and Velasquez 1989, Vivian-Smith and Stiles 1994, Mueller and van der Valk 2002).

There are also numerous human activities that facilitate spread of plant propagules, including automobiles, boats, and farm machinery (Cronk and Fennessy 2001). Human-facilitated dispersal is often cited as the vector responsible for the spread of many invasive species, including zebra mussels (*Dreissena polymorpha*) (Johnson and Padilla 1996) and purple loosestrife (*Lythrum salicaria*) (Thompson 1989). The other primary source of plant propagules occurs on or beneath the surface of the soil in the wetland basin. Commonly referred to as the seed bank, these propagules include tubers, corms, and other reproductive parts as well as seeds that have either dispersed into or were produced within the wetland basin. The persistence of seeds in the seed bank varies by species in relation to complex physiological requirements involving the interaction of temperature, light, moisture, and the gaseous environment, as well as seed size (Baskin and Baskin 1989, Murdoch and Ellis 1992). The soil seed bank rarely reflects the composition of the standing vegetation (Thompson 1992).

Of the potential suite of plant species, abiotic conditions act as a sieve affecting types and densities of species that germinate and survive to maturity (van der Valk 1981). Recruitment from the seed bank is partially dependent on the depth propagules are buried; only seeds in the upper portion of the soil profile (termed the "active" seed bank) are capable of germination (Simpson et al. 1989). Other abiotic factors influencing recruitment are soil temperature, moisture, and oxygen concentrations; photoperiod; quality and quantity of light; and soil and water chemistry (Simpson et al. 1989, Cronk and Fennessy 2001). Submergent plants germinate under flooded conditions, whereas most emergents germinate during drawdown conditions. In addition, requirements or tolerances exist among different propagules of the same species. Cattail (*Typha* spp.) can reproduce by seed or vegetatively by rhizomes. Optimum seed germination occurs in shallow (<1.25 cm) water or exposed mudflats (van der Valk and Davis 1978, Sojda and Solberg 1993) at soil temperatures ranging from 25 to 35 C (Bonnewell et al. 1983). Following germination, however, cattail establishment may occur when soil moisture conditions range from saturated soil to 15 cm depth (Bedish 1967).

In many cases, factors influencing germination of a species are interrelated. Soil temperatures tend to increase with increasing day-length, whereas soil oxygen content decreases as soil moisture increases. Likewise soil temperatures are higher when the surface color is dark rather than light or when there is no residual vegetation. The relationships between other factors are subtler, yet still important. For example, the amount of light that reaches the basin substrate decreases as turbidity or the amount of residual vegetation increases.

Some common wetland plants are naturalized (Table 3) but their presence has not significantly compromised wetland values. Annuals such as curltop ladysthumb (*Polygonum lapathifolium*), and common barnyardgrass (*Echinochloa crusgalli*) are abundant in seasonal wetlands managed for moist-soil plants and are considered desirable by most managers, yet both species are naturalized. Common millet (*Setaria italica*), another naturalized

Table 3. Common wetland plants naturalized in wetlands of the conterminous states ("+" indicates relative value for invertebrates) with value for ducks and invertebrate structure.

Common name	Scientific name	Origin	Value Seeds for ducks	Value Quality of invertebrate structure
Curly dock	*Rumex crispus*	Europe	+	+
Water pepper	*Polygonun hydropiper*	Eurasia	+	+++
Lady's thumb	*P. persicaria*	Europe	+	+++
Curltop ladysthumb	*P. lapathifolium*	Europe	+++	+++
Jungle rice barnyardgrass	*Echinochloa colonum*	Old World	+++	+
Japanese millet	*E. frumentacea*	Asia	+++	+
Common barnyardgrass	*E. crusgalli*	Old World	+++	+
Common millet	*Setaria italica*	Eurasia	+++	+
Green foxtail	*S. viridus*	Eurasia	+	+

species, is often planted in wetlands managed for wildlife. In contrast, some native plants such as chufa flatsedge (*Cyperus esculentus*) are classed as noxious by agriculturists but are important food for wildlife in wetlands.

Unfortunately, numerous plant species with invasive characteristics have been introduced into wetlands, particularly during the past 50 years (Table 4). For example, in Hawaii about 55% of plants in wetlands are exotics (Stemmermann 1981). In some cases, invasive plants have expanded rapidly into wetlands after a major perturbation such as a flood. This appears to have been the case with the spread of tall whitetop (*Lepidium latifolium*) on Ouray National Wildlife Refuge on the Green River in Utah and reed canarygrass (*Phalaris arundinacea*) in floodplain habitats throughout the Upper Mississippi Drainage Basin following the 1993 flood.

Aggressive exotic plants have compromised management because they alter wetland functions and processes. Managers often do not have information on effective and reliable control of many species or costs associated with known control techniques are prohibitive. For example, the distribution and density of saltcedar (*Tamarisk* spp.) throughout the southwestern United States is so extensive that removal is extremely costly (e.g., nearly $1,480/ha on Bosque del Apache National Wildlife Refuge in New Mexico). In monotypic stands of saltcedar, the conversion to native species can require aerial spraying with a herbicide, burning the treated area, using heavy equipment to root rake and push debris in piles, and re-establishing a more natural hydrologic regime with appropriate manipulations to favor native plants over exotics.

Often, the purpose of implementing management strategies is to manipulate abiotic conditions to favor germination and survival of desirable plant communities or to inhibit exotic and invasive plant species development. In many cases, desirable is defined based on cover and food values for target organisms. Regardless of the definition, understanding plant germination and growth requirements, as well as other processes of plant community dynamics, are critical for successful wetland management. Time and rate of drawdown not only directly affect the presence or

absence of mudflats, but also influence soil temperature and oxygen concentrations. However, many abiotic factors (e.g., time and amount of rainfall, temperature) that directly or indirectly influence propagule establishment vary among years at the same site. Therefore, implementing the same management action among years often will result in the establishment of different plant communities. Thus, the calendar date an activity is implemented is not an appropriate benchmark on which to base management actions. Rather, the time and type of management activity must be based on the specific conditions necessary for plant germination, seedling establishment, and growth as well as existing conditions at the site relative to the organisms of interest (e.g., presence of mudflat during least sandpiper [*Calidris minutilla*] migration).

Several handbooks and models that relate common activities (e.g., drawdown time and date) to germination requirements of plant groups common in seasonally flooded wetlands have been developed to provide managers with general guidelines (Fredrickson and Taylor 1982, Fredrickson 1991). However, guidelines are not available for all wetland types or geographic regions. Also, our understanding of factors that influence the establishment and spread of invasive species is limited. Thus, the best option is to develop a monitoring program to collect site-specific information necessary to construct relationships between management activities and plant response.

Van der Valk (1981) developed a model of wetland plant succession for prairie marshes. The interactions between plant life-history characteristics and abiotic factors are common to virtually all prairie wetlands and similar models could be developed for other wetland types using the same criteria. In this model, wetland plants are divided into groups based on life span (annual, perennial with limited life, perennial with unlimited life), propagule longevity (short, long), and requirements for propagule establishment (drawdown, surface water). Species can further be classified into shade intolerant or shade tolerant.

Annual plants generally have long-lived propagules in the seed bank and, following a drawdown, production of seeds can be large. However, if the wetland remains satu-

Table 4. Examples of invasive plants that may compromise wetland management potential and successful control options.

Common name	Scientific name	Geographic location	Control options		
			Biological	Chemical	Mechanical
Saltcedar	*Tamarisk* spp.	Southwest		X	X
Chinese tallow tree	*Sapium sebifera*	Gulf Coast		X	X
Pepper tree	*Schinus terebintisfolius*	Florida			X
Purple loosestrife	*Lythrum salicaria*	Northeast, North Central	X		
Reed canarygrass	*Phalaris arundinacea*	Northeast, North, Northwest		X	X
Alligator weed	*Altermanthera* spp.	Southeast		X	X
Water chestnut	*Trapa natans*	Northeast, Southeast	X		
Hydrilla	*Hydrilla verticillata*	Southeast		X	
Tall whitetop	*Lepidium latifolium*	West, Northeast		X	X
Eurasian milfoil	*Myriophyllum spicata*	United States		X	
Giant salvinia	*Salvinia* spp.	Southeast, Hawaii		X	
California grass	*Brachiaria mutica*	Hawaii		X	X
Water hemp	*Amaranthus rudis*	Southeast, Southwest		X	
Joint vetch	*Sesbania* spp.	Southeast		X	X
Water hyacinth	*Eichhornia* spp.	Southeast		X	

rated or flooded for more than a year, the abundance of annuals typically decreases because they are incapable of germinating in water. In contrast, abundance of perennial vegetation tends to increase because these species propagate by rhizomes as well as seeds, and they can tolerate deeper water. Through time, particularly under stable water regimes, perennial plants (e.g., cattail, bulrush [*Scirpus* spp.]) capable of reproducing vegetatively begin to dominate the wetland plant community. In many cases, dense, monotypic stands of robust vegetation develop throughout the basin and a decline in biodiversity occurs. In coastal and north temperate wetlands, feeding and house-building activities of herbivores such as muskrats and beaver are extremely important at this stage in the cycle. These activities, in conjunction with water level fluctuations, function to create openings in the marsh and facilitate the production of annuals when the next drawdown occurs.

This model illustrates an important facet of wetlands: abiotic factors controlling germination are dynamic and result in vegetation changes that influence vertebrate use. Plant communities dominated by annuals normally produce abundant seeds that contain important sources of carbohydrates, vitamins, minerals, and essential amino acids for waterbirds (Table 2). In addition, drawdowns often result in fish mortality; thus, amphibian survival should improve the year following a drawdown due to the absence of predators. In comparison, seed production will decrease as vegetation shifts to perennial species, but the stems of perennials provide vertical and horizontal cover for seclusion of waterbird pairs and broods, sites for nest attachment, food for herbivorous mammals, and egg attachment sites for amphibians. In addition, succulent new growth and rhizomes serve as browse for geese. However, continued flooding for long periods would result in the development of dense, monotypic stands of perennial vegetation throughout the basin. This would likely facilitate development of a fish population, but cause a decline in waterbird diversity, and amphibian survival and breeding success

(Weller and Spatcher 1965, Weller and Fredrickson 1974, Werner and McPeek 1994).

Changes in vegetation composition represent an important component of natural wetland function. These changes dramatically influence habitat suitability for different vertebrate species. Attempts to consistently provide the same vegetation distribution and composition during consecutive years require implementing management activities to constrain abiotic factors that are inherently dynamic. For example, consistently promoting the growth of specific annuals requires drawdowns to be conducted at roughly similar times (e.g., early spring) every year (Table 5). Although this hydroperiod occurs naturally in some wetland types in certain regions, it represents an extreme variation from natural hydroperiods of other wetland types in many regions. In these latter wetlands, implementing this strategy over consecutive years often leads to disrupted wetland function, which can be costly and time-consuming to correct. In these cases, short-term habitat objectives to benefit target organisms must be balanced with long-term objectives of sustainable productivity.

Macroinvertebrates and Plant Decomposition

Our understanding of wetland invertebrates has advanced considerably in the past decade (Batzer et al. 1999). Wetlands provide many habitat niches for invertebrates, which are important foods for waterbirds, amphibians, reptiles, and fish (Mott et al. 1972, Swanson and Meyer 1973, Weller 1988, Eldridge 1990). Many invertebrates are extremely small (<1 mm), and their use as food is restricted to a few vertebrates with specialized foraging mechanisms and large invertebrates. Thus, our focus is on macroinvertebrate communities typically associated with different wetland types.

Differences in invertebrate composition and distribution among wetland types are driven by hydrologic regimes and vegetation structure (Murkin et al. 1992). The life-history strategies of wetland macroinvertebrates have been shaped by long-term hydrologic cycles, particularly type of flood-

Table 5. Effect of drawdown date and rate on soil drying and germination of selected moist-soil plants on Mingo National Wildlife Refuge, Missouri.

Drawdown Date[a]	Rate[b]	Ambient temperature[c]	Daylight[d]	Rate of soil drying[e]	Representative plant[f] germination
Early	Slow	Low	Short	Slow	Smartweed, spikerush, barnyardgrass
	Fast	Low	Short	Medium-slow	Barnyardgrass, black willow, chufa
Midseason	Slow	Intermediate	Intermediate	Medium-slow	Rice cutgrass, burhead, barnyardgrass, chufa
	Fast	Intermediate	Intermediate	Medium	Beggarticks, ragweed, panicum
Late	Slow	High	Long	Medium	Redroot flatsedge, toothcup
	Fast	High	Long	Fast	Cocklebur, aster, crabgrass, morningglory

[a] Early: prior to 15 May; Midseason: 16 May–1 Jul; Late: after 1 Jul.
[b] Slow: >14 days; Fast: <7 days.
[c] Low: less then 16 C; Intermediate: between 16 and 27 C; High: greater than 27 C.
[d] Short: 10 hours or less; Intermediate: 10–12 hours; Long: 12 hours or more.
[e] Slow: similar moisture for a week or more; Medium-slow: similar moisture for 5–7 days; Medium: similar moisture for 3–5 days; Fast: similar moisture for <2 days.
[f] Aster (*Aster* spp.), barnyardgrass (*Echinochloa crusgalli*), beggerticks (*Bidens* spp.), black willow (*Salix nigra*), blunt spikerush (*Eleocharis obtusa*), common burhead (*Echinodorus cordifolius*), common cocklebur (*Xanthium strumarium*), common ragweed (*Ambrosia artemisiifolia*), crabgrass (*Digitaria* spp.), morningglory (*Ipomoea* spp.), fall panicum (*Panicum dichotomiflorum*), redroot flatsedge (*Cyperus eythrorhizos*), chufa (*C. esculentus*), rice cutgrass (*Leersia oryzoides*), smartweed (*Polygonum* spp.), and toothcup (*Ammannia* spp.).

ing and dynamic water fluctuations. Among the most important are morphological or behavioral adaptations to tolerate or avoid drought. Adaptations that have evolved as a result of long-term hydrologic cycles include at least one of the following: (1) ability to withstand drought in the egg, pupal, or larval state; (2) rapid growth; (3) ability to produce numerous offspring; (4) ability to complete the life cycle within 1 year; and (5) high mobility (Wiggins et al. 1982). Several invertebrate groups, including flatworms (Order Turbellaria); fairy, clam and seed shrimp (Orders Anostraca, Conchostraca, and Ostracoda); water fleas (Order Cladocera); mayflies (Order Ephemeroptera); and mosquitoes and phantom midges (Order Diptera) have resistant egg stages that help prevent drought-induced mortality. Aquatic earthworms (Order Oligochaeta) may use mucosal secretions to survive drought, whereas bloodworm larvae aestivate in cocoons and fingernail clams (Order Telecytoda) burrow into the wet litter layer and rely on their shell to avoid desiccation. Gastropods develop a seal over the opercal and can survive buried in mud for decades. In contrast, aquatic sowbugs (Order Isopoda) and sideswimmers (Order Amphipoda) have no morphological adaptations to resist drought, but adults aestivate and survive dry seasons by locating suitable conditions in the deeper litter layers. Many macroinvertebrates that exploit wetlands also have adaptations that enable them to thrive in specific habitats or vegetation types (Euliss et al. 2002).

Macroinvertebrate communities can be grouped based on habitat association into those that occur primarily in (1) benthic substrates, (2) submergent vegetation, (3) perennial herbaceous vegetation, (4) annual herbaceous vegetation, and (5) leaf litter. Species that compose each group have life-history strategies that allow them to exploit a particular hydrologic regime (Table 6). For example, a wetland invertebrate fauna often exists in the dry substrates of an ephemeral or intermittently flooded wetland. When such sites are flooded, invertebrates initiate life-cycle responses that may result in large numbers and biomass of invertebrates in the flooded basin (Batema 1987, Severson 1987, Fredrickson and Reid 1988a). Further, habitat requirements of some invertebrates change depending on

life-cycle stage (Pennak 1978). One habitat may be important for egg laying, whereas a different habitat may be required for feeding.

Although long-term hydrologic cycles and habitat type influence adaptive strategies of macroinvertebrates, other factors affect the occurrence, abundance, growth rate, and reproduction of individual species at any given time. Among the most important are the short-term water regime and physical, chemical, and biological factors (Pennak 1978, Wiggins et al. 1982, Pinder 1986). In wetlands that exhibit dynamic, short-term flooding regimes, macroinvertebrates that exhibit rapid growth during periods of adequate water and nutrient availability have an advantage. Furthermore, producing large numbers of young and completing the life cycle in 1 year allow for greater success. When water levels decline, species that cannot tolerate drought must avoid dry conditions. Those most successful often are highly mobile and capable of immigrating to suitable sites. Beetles (Order Coleoptera) and water boatmen (Order Hemiptera, *Sigara* spp.), in particular, respond to drawdowns by aerial dispersal to available wetlands.

Another important factor affecting invertebrate abundance and diversity is litter type and availability. After senescence, plant materials form litter. Forms of herbaceous litter include stems, leaves, and flower structures, whereas leaves are the primary litter from woody vegetation. Nutrients and organic matter rapidly leach from litter upon initial contact with water and concentrate in the water column (Peterson and Cummins 1974, Yates and Day 1983, Wylie 1985). Fungi, bacteria, and microinvertebrates associated with litter accelerate decomposition and release additional energy and nutrients (Fig. 5). Macroinvertebrates also feed on litter conditioned by bacteria and fungi, further assisting in litter decomposition and nutrient cycling. Because they are readily consumed as food, macroinvertebrates are an important functional link in the transfer of nutrients from detritus to waterbirds, herptiles,

Table 6. Invertebrates associated with different flooding regimes in seasonally flooded impoundments.

Flooding regime	Invertebrates
Late drawdown	Mosquitoes
	Pond snail
	Water boatmen
	Chironomids
Early drawdown	Mosquitoes
	Pond snail
	Water boatman
Autumn–winter	Mosquitoes
	Water boatman
	Chironomids
Long vernal flooding	Fairy shrimp
	Mosquitoes
	Water boatman
Short vernal flooding	Fairy shrimp
	Mosquitoes

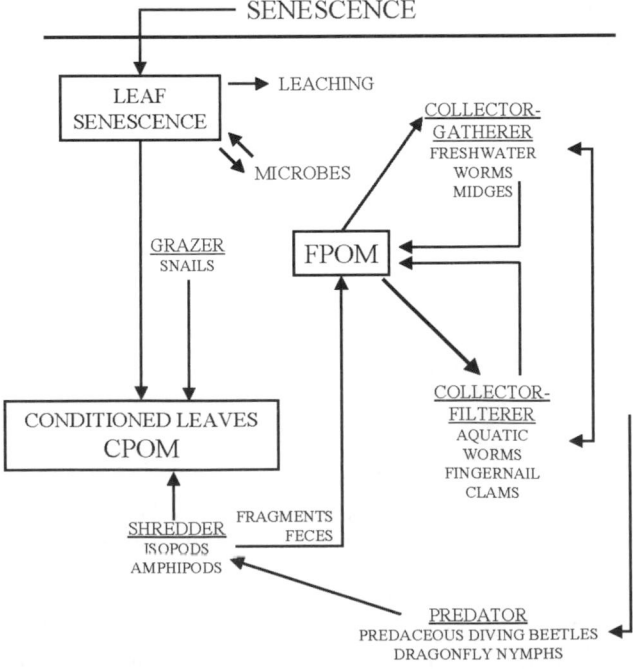

Fig. 5. Litter decomposition pathway in a detrital-based wetland (CPOM = coarse particulate organic matter; FPOM = fine particulate organic matter).

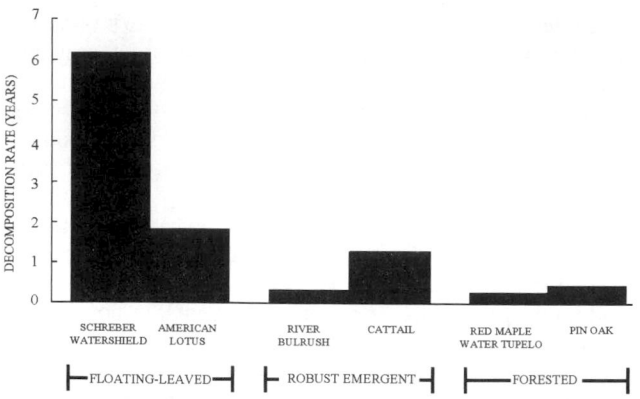

Fig. 6. Decomposition rates of litter types (Schreber watershield [*Brasenia schreberi*], American lotus [*Nelumbo lutea*], river bulrush [*Scirpus fluviatilis*], cattail, red maple [*Acer rubrum*], water tupelo [*Nyssa aquatica*], and pin oak [*Quercus palustris*]) (data from Boyd 1970, Yates and Day 1983, Wylie 1985).

and fish (Batema et al. 2005).

Decomposition rate is governed by several factors including litter type, lignin and nutrient content of the litter, hydrologic condition, and temperature (Webster and Benfield 1986, Middleton et al. 1992). Under a given set of environmental conditions, herbaceous litter generally decomposes faster than woody vegetation (Fig. 6). Robust emergents often decompose slower than submergent plants because they contain greater lignin content. Regardless of litter type, decomposition rates generally increase when litter is shallowly flooded and temperatures increase. Deep flooding may result in anaerobic conditions that restrict the faunal community actively associated with the decomposition process (Suthers and Gee 1986). The decomposition process may cause anaerobic conditions, resulting in subsequent elimination of invertebrate communities. Because factors controlling decomposition are changing constantly, peaks in macroinvertebrate abundance often are dramatic and short-lived. This cycle or "pulsing" of macroinvertebrate populations, although variable among years and habitat types, is typical of invertebrates that exploit nutrient-rich, detrital-based systems that are in a constant state of hydrologic flux.

Vertebrates

Vertebrates have a myriad of life history strategies that reflect adaptations to the dynamic nature of wetlands. Understanding the temporal and spatial scale of vertebrate use is becoming increasingly important because contemporary managers are challenged to provide suitable habitat for an increasing array of wildlife within highly modified landscapes. With this growing responsibility, the need to summarize information related to life-cycle requirements of vertebrates is increasing. Species abundance, chronology and duration of stay, mobility, habitat and nutritional requirements, and sensitivity to disturbance are important aspects to consider when evaluating management options. Unfortunately, detailed scientific information does not exist for many species. Further, there has been little effort to integrate species requirements with general wetland ecology principles (Laubhan and Roelle 2001). Consequently our ability to provide long-term benefits for

multiple vertebrate species is constrained (Fredrickson and Laubhan 1994). However, experimentation and monitoring, personal observations, discussions with local experts, and literature review can often be beneficial.

Our intent in this section is to provide a broad overview of: (1) the complexities of life-history strategies of different groups of species, (2) identify important linkages among life history strategies and wetland habitat dynamics, and (3) emphasize the importance of providing necessary habitat resources at the appropriate time and spatial scale for the target organism. Thus, we do not provide an exhaustive analysis of all species or taxonomic groups. For example, mammals and fish are not considered, but they are important components of wetland ecosystems and should be considered in management decisions.

Waterbirds

Waterbirds are a diverse group that includes waterfowl (swans, geese, and ducks), loons, pelicans, grebes, cranes, rails, shorebirds, and wading birds among others (Weller 1999). Although not considered waterbirds, many songbirds are also dependent upon wetland resources for breeding, wintering, and migration (Greenberg 1988, Grover and Baldassarre 1995, Yong et al. 1998, Weller 1999, Shutler et al. 2000). Some species, such as willow flycatchers (*Empidonax traillii*), are considered facultative wetland birds and spend as much time foraging in uplands as around wetlands (Weller 1999). Others, such as prothonotary warblers (*Protonotaria citrea*) and swamp sparrows (*Melospiza georgiana*), are obligate wetland species that depend upon wetlands for their entire life cycle (Mowbray 1997, Petit 1999). These latter species are not considered further, but information on habitat requirements is available and should be considered in the development and management of wetland habitats.

There are 43 species of waterfowl (Bellrose 1980) and more than 70 species of other waterbirds that breed, migrate, winter, or are resident in North America (Laubhan and Roelle 2001). This group of species is probably the most extensively studied of wetland-dependent vertebrates. Numerous books on waterbird ecology and management are available (e.g., Bellrose 1980, Richards 1988, Baldassarre and Bolen 1994, Weller 1999, Kushlan and Hafner 2000). In addition, the North American Bird Conservation Initiative has compiled regional and national summaries of population status and trends for many waterbird species, as well as identified critical wetland resources for protection. Examples of these initiatives include the United States Shorebird Conservation Plan (Brown et al. 2001) and Waterbird Conservation for the Americas (Kushlan et al. 2002).

Use of wetlands by foraging waterbirds largely is affected by type, quality, distribution, and availability of suitable foods and cover. Considerable research has been conducted on the food habits of waterbirds. This information has been synthesized and published for many taxonomic groups, including breeding waterfowl (Krapu and Reinecke 1992); shorebirds (Skagen and Oman 1996); and herons, rails, and grebes (Laubhan and Roelle 2001). In addition, the *Birds of North America* species accounts provide detailed lists of food items for individual species (Poole et al. 1992–2003). In general, diet varies greatly among species and includes amphibians, reptiles, fish, invertebrates, mammals, and plant foods (e.g., seeds, stems, leaves, tubers).

Waterfowl consume a wide variety of plant and animal foods, including reproductive parts (e.g., tubers, seeds), stems, and leaves of plants, as well as invertebrates and vertebrates, especially fish. However, the proportion of each item consumed varies among species and annual cycle events (Krapu and Reinecke 1992). For example, diets of diving ducks contain a larger proportion of animal foods than diets of dabbling ducks (Sedinger 1992) and mergansers eat mostly fish (Krapu and Reinecke 1992). The diet of other waterbirds is also diverse. Grebes and herons consume mostly fish, but also forage on invertebrates, reptiles, and amphibians (Laubhan and Roelle 2001). Shorebirds consume primarily invertebrates during all phases of the annual cycle (Helmers 1992), but seeds also contribute to the diet (Skagen and Oman 1996). Rails also consume varied amounts of seeds and invertebrates, but seeds generally constitute a greater proportion of the diet during fall and winter (Rundle and Sayre 1983, Meanley 1992). Finally, cranes, geese, and some dabbling ducks often consume foods (e.g., agricultural grains) in terrestrial habitats (Tacha et al. 1994).

Food selection also varies within many species (e.g., waterfowl) during different portions of the annual cycle (Fredrickson and Heitmeyer 1988, Plissner et al. 2000). Dietary shifts largely are correlated with different annual cycle events (e.g., migration, breeding) that require different nutrients to complete. Flight requires large amounts of energy, whereas protein is required for feather molt and egg production. Therefore, nutritional requirements vary among annual life cycle events and many species shift food types to meet these demands (Fig. 7). In most cases, dietary changes occur in the relative proportion of animal and plant foods rather than specific food items. Prefledging waterfowl and females of most species during the pre-breeding and breeding periods increase protein intake by foraging on invertebrates (Krapu and Reinecke 1992, Sedinger 1992). In contrast, seeds and other plant foods high in carbohydrates are consumed during migration (Drobney and Fredrickson 1979, Fredrickson and Heitmeyer 1988). Although some waterbirds tend to consume certain food types during specific annual cycle

events, most species exhibit considerable dietary breadth. For example, over 400 genera of invertebrate prey are consumed by 43 species of shorebirds in the western hemisphere (Skagen and Oman 1996), white-faced ibis (*Plegadis chihi*) consume invertebrates from 13 orders, and Virginia rails consume seeds belonging to 14 different families (Laubhan and Roelle 2001).

Dietary differences among species often can be related to differences in morphology or modes of foraging. Species with large bodies and long necks (e.g., swans) can acquire foods at deeper depths than species with smaller bodies and shorter necks (e.g., dabbling ducks). In comparison, diving ducks have short bodies, legs that are positioned toward the rear of the body, and large, lobed feet that enable these species to acquire foods at deeper depths than dabbling ducks. Bill morphology also is important. Swans and snow geese (*Chen caerulescens*) have powerful mandibles that can be used to dislodge roots and tubers not accessible to ducks. In contrast, ruddy ducks (*Oxyura jamaicensis*) and northern shovelers have mandibles with closely spaced lamellae that enable consumption of plankton and microinvertebrates (Krapu and Reinecke 1992).

Factors influencing availability of foods and foraging efficiency include water depth, vegetation structure, and vegetation distribution (Elphick and Oring 1998, Weller 1999, Bancroft et al. 2002). Many species, including rails, shorebirds, herons, and ibises, forage by standing on a substrate, thus, foraging locations are constrained by water depth (Fig. 4). As a result, leg length (i.e., metatarsus) may affect available foraging habitat for these species. Small waterbirds, such as shorebirds and rails, require shallow flooded habitats, whereas herons are capable of capturing foods in deeper water (Fig. 4). Species capable of swimming also are constrained by water depth. Waterfowl are frequently observed in deep aquatic habitats (e.g., lakes, reservoirs); however, foods must be accessible within the constraints of their body and bill morphology. For example, water depths must be less than the neck length of swans or dabbling ducks for foods (tubers, benthic invertebrates) to be available for these species. In contrast, grebes are capable of foraging at depths to 6 m because they forage while diving (Storer and Nuechterlein 1992).

Foraging requires expenditure of energy because individuals must search and capture food items before they can be consumed. At a minimum, sufficient foods must be obtained to offset these costs. Therefore, factors that hinder the location and capture of food items can influence foraging location. Subtle differences in foraging habitats used exist among species in the same taxonomic group, but some general management rules apply. Optimum foraging habitat for most shorebirds is characterized by <25% cover of short vegetation (notable exceptions include Wilson's snipe and pectoral sandpipers [*Calidris melanotos*] that forage in denser vegetation) (Helmers 1992, Holmes and Pitelka 1998). Cranes, herons, and ibises also forage in these habitats, but herons and ibises are capable of foraging in habitats with taller and denser vegetation (Kushlan and Bildstein 1992). Most waterfowl species are capable of exploiting food resources in a wide range of vegetative conditions. In contrast, bitterns prefer to forage in marshes with densely vegetated habitats that provide concealment (Gibbs et al. 1992a, b) and rails prefer dense emergent cover interspersed with openings (Meanley 1992).

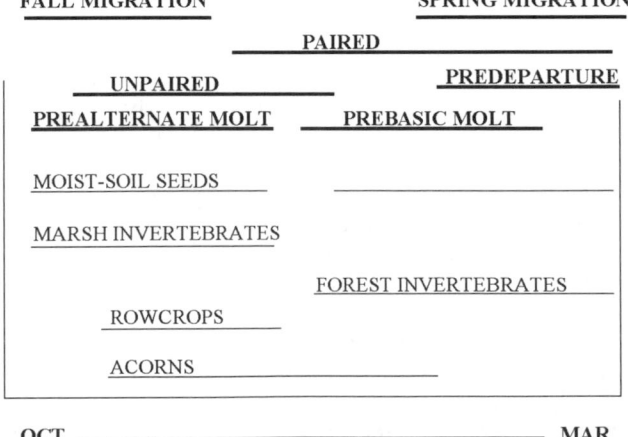

Fig. 7. Dietary changes of female mallards from October to March while undergoing 7 important life history stages in wintering habitats in the southern United States.

Water volume also influences foraging efficiency (items consumed per unit time), particularly when prey is highly mobile. Locating and capturing fish or nektonic invertebrates is more difficult as water volume (depth and surface area) increases. Thus, foraging efficiency of wading birds increases when wetlands are dewatered and food items (fish, macroinvertebrates) become concentrated (Kushlan 2000).

Breeding requirements of waterbirds are complex due to the myriad of activities that occur during this portion of the annual cycle. Suitable nest sites must be located, sufficient foods of adequate quality must be obtained to lay and incubate eggs and, following hatching, suitable foraging habitat must be available for young to survive. Further, many of these activities occur simultaneously. Similar to foraging habitats, hydroperiod and vegetation are important components affecting suitability and quality of breeding habitats (Weller and Spatcher 1965, Weller and Fredrickson 1974, Kaminski and Prince 1981, Ball and Nudds 1989). However, numerous factors directly or indirectly influence selection and use of different habitats by individual species. Examples include weather, predation, food type and availability, and competition. Relationships among these factors often affect success or failure of individual breeding attempts and, ultimately, population size of a species. However, they often are subtle and may change among years. Waterfowl nest success often is dramatically different between wet and drought years. Although nest site selection of individuals may not have changed, other factors important in affecting breeding success of the entire population may be different, including amount of wetland habitat available, abundance of predators, or the ability of predators to find nests (Batt et al. 1992).

The primary requisites of breeding habitat for waterbirds include an appropriate interspersion of suitable nesting, brood rearing, and foraging areas (Laubhan and Roelle 2001). Of the 13 species of shorebirds that breed in the conterminous states, all nest on the ground, typically on elevated areas near water (Helmers 1992). Nest sites are in areas ranging from bare sand and gravel beaches (e.g., piping plover [*Charadrius melodus*]) to vegetation of moderate height and density (Fig. 8). If invertebrates are available, areas suitable for nesting also provide suitable brood habitat (Laubhan and Roelle 2001).

Dabbling ducks also typically nest on the ground. However, these species nest in vegetation that provides concealment. Most studies indicate nest densities and nesting success increase with increasing availability of dense grass, forbs, and shrubs (Duebbert and Lokemoen 1976, Lokemoen et al. 1984, Sugden and Beyersbergen 1987). For example, visual obstruction readings (VOR) of vegetation at nest sites of mallards and gadwalls range from about 20 to 45 cm, whereas blue-winged teal and northern shoveler nests are in vegetation that typically ranges from 10 to 20 cm VOR (Fig. 8). A notable exception is the northern pintail, which tends to nest in sparser cover than other dabbling ducks (Duncan 1987). After eggs hatch, females typically move young to wetlands with

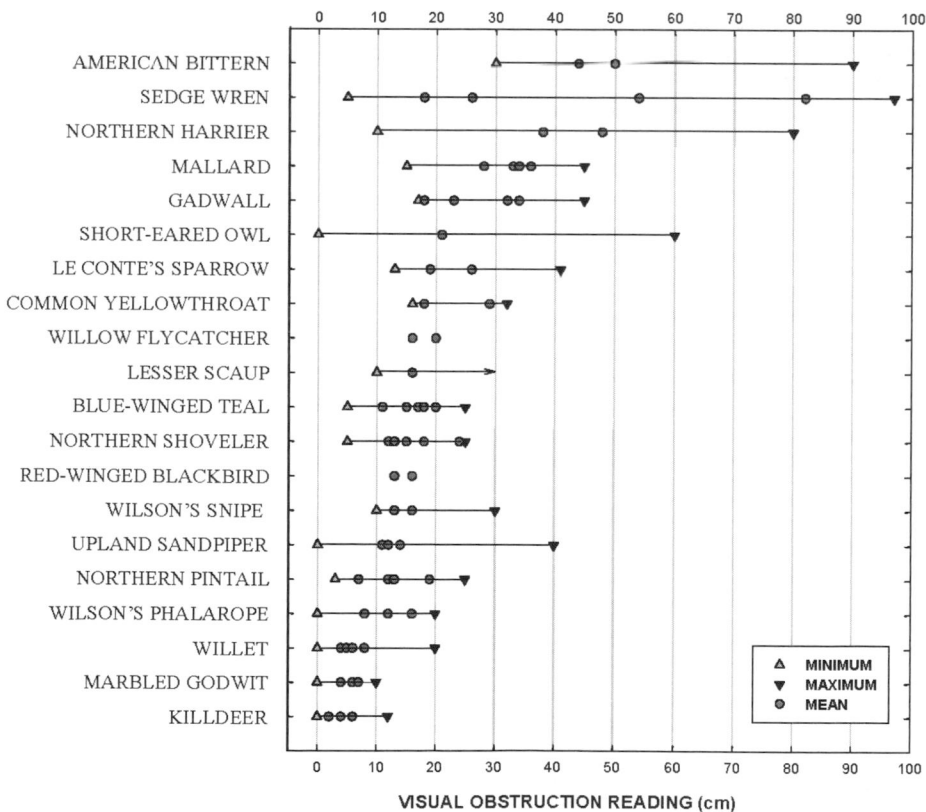

Fig. 8. Range of visual obstruction readings (VOR) at nest sites of breeding birds (American bittern, sedge wren [*Cistothorus platensis*], northern harrier [*Circus cyaneus*], mallard, gadwall, short-eared owl [*Asio flammeus*], LeConte's sparrow [*Ammodramus leconteii*], common yellowthroat [*Geothlypis trichas*], willow flycatcher, lesser scaup, blue-winged teal, northern shoveler, red-winged blackbird [*Agelaius phoeniceus*], Wilson's snipe, upland sandpiper, northern pintail, Wilson's phalarope, willet [*Catoptrophorus semipalmatus*], marbled godwit, and killdeer) that use wetland habitats based on reports in the published literature. Minimum and maximum values may represent mean values and some measurements were obtained from grasslands adjacent to wetland habitats.

abundant invertebrates and emergent vegetation that provides concealment from predators (Courcelles and Bedard 1979, Pehrsson 1979, Monda and Ratti 1988). Thus, juxtaposition between suitable ground vegetation and water is important and most species tend to nest within 100 m of water (Bellrose 1980).

Grebes, American coots (*Fulica americana*), and most diving ducks generally nest over water. Grebes nest in stands of emergent cover or on mats of submerged aquatic vegetation (Terres 1980) surrounded by large expanses of open water (Storer and Nuechterlein 1992). If emergent vegetation is selected, stem densities must be sufficient to support nests. However, there is considerable variability in vegetation characteristics at nest sites within and among species (Glover 1953, Burger 1985). In comparison, nests of diving ducks are restricted to emergent vegetation. Nest site selection and nest success have been shown to correlate positively with amount of vegetative concealment (Hines 1977, Kaminski and Weller 1992). Wetlands used by broods of diving ducks contain a suitable type and abundance of invertebrates (Minot 1980, Talent et al. 1983, Wright and Street 1985). Diving ducks usually move relatively short distances (usually ≤1 km) between nest site and brood habitat (Ringelman and Longcore 1982). Further, broods tend to use deeper water than dabbling ducks and are more likely to forage near submerged aquatic vegetation (Monda and Ratti 1988).

Rails and bitterns also nest in flooded areas characterized by tall, dense, emergent cover interspersed with sparsely vegetated sites (Fig. 8). However, least bitterns (*Ixobrychus exilis*) (Weller 1961) and clapper rails (*Rallus longirostris*) (Eddleman and Conway 1998) also nest in shrubs. Nests are placed in dense vegetation while young use areas that are more open as foraging sites than adults (Johnson and Dinsmore 1985, Davidson 1992, Eddleman and Conway 1998). Water depth at nests range from saturated soil to 46 cm for rails (Bookhout 1995), whereas American and least bitterns nest in areas flooded from 5 to 20 cm and 8 to 96 cm, respectively (Gibbs et al. 1992*a, b*). Most individuals nest in elevated areas with vegetation capable of supporting nests and providing concealment (Laubhan and Roelle 2001).

Other members of the Ardeidae (herons) nest in a variety of habitats, including trees, shrubs, and occasionally emergent vegetation or on the ground. Site selection depends on geographic area and available substrate (Butler 1992, Davis and Kushlan 1994). Nests often occur in single- or mixed-species colonies near or over water; however, specific locations often are influenced by distribution of foraging habitats and predators (Davis and Kushlan 1994). Parents feed young in the nest for a short time following hatching; thus, special habitat requirements for broods are not required.

Most, but not all, members of waterfowl, herons, ibises, cranes, and rails that breed in temperate North America either reside in breeding areas all year or migrate to the southern United States during winter (Ehrlich et al. 1988). In contrast, only a few shorebirds occur in the conterminous United States during winter (Hayman et al. 1986). Many species wintering in the United States exhibit greater flexibility in selection of winter habitats compared to breeding habitat. For example, factors important in habitat selection during the breeding season (e.g., location of

nest sites relative to foraging sites and brood habitat) do not constrain use of winter habitats. However, annual cycle events that impact-breeding success occur during the winter in some species, including courtship, pair formation, and molt. These activities often require specific habitats and food resources. Other important parameters of winter habitats include suitable roosting areas and habitats that provide protection from extremes in climatic conditions (Laubhan and Roelle 2001). These resources are provided by a variety of habitats, including flooded forests, emergent marshes, scrub-shrub, and agricultural fields.

Collectively, waterbirds are highly mobile and many species are migratory. Thus, habitat selection must be considered from a macro- to microhabitat scale (Soulé 1991, Kaminski and Weller 1992) to identify temporal and spatial variability in factors involved (Wiens 1985). Although extensive variability exists among species, a single wetland usually cannot provide all the habitat needs of a single species, nor can a single wetland provide habitat for all species simultaneously (Fredrickson and Laubhan 1994). For example, waterfowl in the Prairie Pothole Region require ephemeral, semipermanent, and permanent wetlands in close proximity to nesting areas to successfully complete brood rearing (Afton and Paulus 1992).

Wetland complexes are generally needed to provide necessary resources within and among seasons (Plissner et al. 2000, Haig et al. 2002). However, even at the scale of a single wetland complex, numerous factors influence avian use, including size, topographic complexity, and dominant vegetation of individual wetlands (Laubhan and Roelle 2001). Reductions in wetland density or size can influence avian richness and abundance (Shutler et al. 2000), and reduce nest density and success of many species (Brown and Dinsmore 1986, Hunter et al. 1993, Grover and Baldassarre 1995). In addition, changes in land use surrounding wetlands also are important. Floodplain forests typically support a diversity of habitats in close juxtaposition, including vernal pools, seasonally flooded forests and scrub-shrub habitats, and permanently flooded oxbows and sloughs. The juxtaposition of forested habitat to wetlands also is important for many amphibian species that breed in wetlands but spend the remainder of their annual cycle in the forest. Colonial waterbirds often nest in scrub-shrub or forested habitats, but may forage in nearby oxbows, sloughs, and flooded swales (Huner et al. 2002). Trees and shrubs also provide seclusion for mated pairs of waterfowl and thermal cover for waterbirds during periods of inclement weather (Magee 1996). Mast (e.g., acorns, samaras) produced in flooded timber also is a source of carbohydrates, and a distinct macroinvertebrate community often develops after leaf-fall (Batema et al. 2005).

Vertebrates requiring tree cavities also rely extensively on forested habitat. Cavities in large trees that occur in or adjacent to wetlands are particularly important as nest sites for wood ducks (*Aix sponsa*) and hooded mergansers (*Lophodytes cucullatus*), and also serve as den sites for raccoons (*Procyon lotor*), squirrels, and other mammals (Soulliére 1990). Cavities in smaller trees are important for a host of smaller birds and mammals such as prothonotary warblers and golden mice (*Ochrotomys nuttalli*).

Issues of scale are complex, but types and interspersion of wetland habitats are extremely relevant to development and management activities. Considering existing wetland features within a landscape context is valuable for identifying missing or degraded wetland types and can assist in prioritizing land acquisitions. This information can be used to identify and develop strategies to correct altered wetland processes caused by past land uses.

Amphibians

Amphibians represent a diverse group of species that have received increased attention during the past decade due to reported population declines (Barinaga 1990). Current evidence suggests many species may be experiencing population declines, range constriction, or extinctions at scales ranging from local to possibly global (Wake 1998, Alford and Richards 1999, Gibbons et al. 2000). Potential factors related to suspected declines include disease, invasive species, chemical contamination, and commercial trade; however, most biologists agree that habitat destruction at local scales is a major factor.

Conservation of amphibians is important not only to preserve biodiversity, but also because they are an integral component affecting wetland functions and processes. Amphibians occupy a variety of positions in the food web and can differentially affect energy flow in wetland systems. During the larval stage, amphibians may regulate primary production through suspension feeding (Dickman 1968, Seale 1980). As adults, they are both predators and a high-quality food source for predators and may heavily influence invertebrate populations, thereby indirectly affecting litter decomposition (Burton and Likens 1975).

Amphibians have complex life cycles (Wilbur 1980). Many species are biphasic, spending most of their adult life in terrestrial habitats and using aquatic environments only for mating, oviposition, and larval development. In addition, population sizes naturally undergo wide fluctuations (Semlitsch et al. 1996, Pechmann et al. 2001). Thus, persistence of a species is dependent on the production of large numbers of metamorphs during favorable years, rather than consistently producing some metamorphs every year (Pechmann et al. 1989, Berven 1990).

Breeding adults of some species (e.g., spadefoot toads [*Scaphiopus holbrooki*], wood frogs [*Rana sylvatica*]) spend only 1 to 2 days in aquatic environments, whereas others (e.g., green frogs [*R. clamitans*], gray treefrogs [*Hyla versicolor*]) spend several weeks or months (Semlitsch 2000*a*). Similarly, the time aquatic larvae spend in wetland habitats also varies, ranging from 21 days for spadefoot toads to 1 to 2 years for bullfrogs (*Rana catesbeiana*) (Semlitsch 2000*a*). Abiotic (e.g., temperature, hydroperiod) and biotic (e.g., vegetation, predation) factors, as well as interactions between these factors, influence the rate and success of larval growth and development (Wilbur and Collins 1973, Carey et al. 1999, Semlitsch 2000*a*). Further, these interactions constantly change due to the dynamic nature of wetlands.

Hydroperiod is often considered among the most critical factors associated with habitat conditions for amphibians because it directly or indirectly affects other factors known to influence amphibian populations. Hydroperiod affects floristic composition and structure, the likelihood of larvae achieving metamorphosis, and influences the distribution and abundance of predators that feed on amphibian eggs and larvae (Schneider and Frost 1996, Wellborn et

al. 1996). If wetlands dry prior to metamorphosis, larvae die. Likewise, increased water permanence can also negatively affect larval amphibians by enhancing survival of predators such as fish and salamanders (Morin 1981, Werner and McPeek 1994, Skelly 1995, Wellborn et al. 1996). Consequently, most amphibians occupy wetlands during only a portion of the entire hydrologic cycle (e.g., temporary to permanent) (Skelly 1997). Some studies indicate that wetlands with hydroperiods <30 days or >1 year are used by fewer species than wetlands with intermediate hydroperiods (Heyer et al. 1975, Wilbur 1980). Consequently, amphibians are sensitive to altered hydroperiod (Semlitsch 2000*a*, Paton and Crouch 2002). Filling or draining wetlands, developments to increase water permanency, and urbanization all can have significant impacts on local populations (Orser and Shure 1972, Semlitsch 2000*a*).

Amphibians are sensitive to changes in temperature and moisture because their skin has a thin epidermal layer. Changes in climatic events (e.g., rain, drought) have been associated with changes in behavior (e.g., Burke et al. 1994, Semlitsch 2000*a*). Water chemistry also is important in regions with acid or oligotrophic waters, which are avoided by many anurans (Strijbosch 1979). While some amphibians are able to successfully breed at low pH levels, acid tolerance varies among species (Dale et al. 1985). Negative correlations also have been reported between amphibian species richness and chloride, conductivity, magnesium, total hardness, and turbidity (Hecnar and McCloskey 1996).

Vegetation characteristics can affect local environmental conditions (e.g., temperature, Tester et al. [1965]) as well as the availability of resources required by amphibians. Wood frogs commonly use wooded wetlands, while northern leopard frogs (*Rana pipiens*) use deeper wetlands with more open surroundings (DeBenedictis 1974). In Minnesota, wood frogs did not use a recently flooded site because it did not provide appropriate vegetation for egg mass attachment (Fishbeck 1968). Stijbosch (1979) reported differences in breeding site selection among anurans based on underwater structure of plants. Finally, the proportion of wetland supporting vegetation cover affected the occurrence of anurans in seasonal and semipermanent wetlands (Fischer 1998).

Vegetation structure of terrestrial habitats also is important. Leopard frogs frequently inhabited short grass (15–30 cm) adjacent to wetlands, but avoided heavily wooded and sandy areas that were either bare or had short, sparse vegetation (Merrell 1977). Anurans that are more terrestrial overwinter beneath leaf litter in moist terrestrial habitats (Schmid 1982).

There have been mixed reports on the effects of habitat size and shape on amphibians. A study evaluating the relationships among isolated wetland size, hydroperiod, and amphibian species richness found no relationship between species richness and wetland size, but hydroperiod was extremely important (Snodgrass et al. 2000). In another study, streamside zones 30–95 m in width contained a higher abundance of species than widths < 25 m (Rudolph and Dickson 1990).

An extremely important consideration in conservation and management of amphibians is metapopulation structure (Marsh and Trenham 2001). A metapopulation is a set of local populations among which gene flow, extinction, and colonization may occur. Two primary factors influence metapopulation dynamics: (1) the number of individuals dispersing among ponds, and (2) the dispersal distances and probability of successfully reaching ponds (Gibbs 1993, Semlitsch 2000a). Most pond-breeding amphibians reside in terrestrial habitats that are usually within 200 m of wetlands during the nonbreeding season (Madison 1997). Most individual amphibians cannot migrate more than 200–300 m due to physiological constraints, such as desiccation (Schmid 1965, Grover 2000, Semlitsch 2000a). Thus, suitable terrestrial and aquatic habitat, including connecting corridors between wetlands, must be provided over relatively small spatial scales to ensure population persistence (Semlitsch 1998). Distance between wetlands is important because it directly affects the probability of recolonization and, therefore, the chance of preventing isolated local populations from extinction (Skelly et al. 1999, Semlitsch 2000a). As wetlands are actively drained or dry naturally in drought years, the required travel distance between suitable habitats may increase so that dispersal to other wetlands becomes impossible. Thus, understanding amphibian life cycle characteristics and needs have important implications for management that differ from those of more mobile avifauna.

Reptiles

Snakes, turtles, crocodilians, and other reptiles are important components of wetland systems, but they have received relatively little attention. Reptiles may be experiencing even greater declines than amphibians worldwide (Gibbons et al. 2000). The U.S. Fish and Wildlife Service listed 70 species of reptiles as endangered and another 18 species as threatened (Gibbons et al. 2000). In contrast, only 17 species of amphibians were listed as endangered and 9 species were listed as threatened. Ernst et al. (1994) suggested that if current trends continue, all turtle species in North America would be threatened with extinction in the 21st century.

Factors involved with declines in reptiles are similar to those for amphibians. Habitat loss and degradation, including loss and degradation of wetlands and adjacent uplands, are considered to be major factors affecting declines of reptiles (Gibbons et al. 2000). Invasive species, global climate change, disease, pollution, and unsustainable use are other factors that have reduced reptile populations (Gibbons et al. 2000). Although most threats can be placed into these categories, a different suite of problems may affect each species depending upon its life history needs. Thus, conservation and management efforts must be developed for individual species (Ernst et al. 1994).

Wetland-dependent reptiles have diverse life-history strategies and habitat needs. Some species complete their entire life cycle in wetlands, sometimes in a single wetland, whereas other species require a diversity of wetland and/or upland environments to complete their annual cycle (Siegel 1986, Ernst et al. 1994, Johnson 2000a, Rowe 2003). Bodie and Semlitsch (2000) found that habitat use of false map turtles (*Graptemys pseudogeographica*) and slider turtles (*Trachemys scripta*) differed among seasons, gender, and age, but a diversity of habitats, including uplands, were heavily used. In Missouri, the endangered eastern massasauga (*Sistrurus c. catenatus*) uses crayfish burrows in prairie areas for hibernation, but is more common in old fields and upland forests later in the growing season (Siegel 1986).

The protection of hibernacula for both snakes and turtles is important for survival of these species. Many species of turtles overwinter in mud of wetlands and snakes often use crayfish or other burrows and stump holes near wetlands to overwinter (Carpenter 1953, Ernst et al. 1994, Kingsbury and Coppola 2000). In northern climates, water near the ground surface in burrows is critical for overwintering snakes because it provides protection from freezing (Maple and Orr 1968). Some snakes overwinter singly (Kingsbury and Coppola 2000), whereas others overwinter in dense aggregations that can include multiple species of snakes as well as other vertebrate taxa (Carpenter 1953). Hibernacula are not necessarily protected by wetland regulations or by wetland management activities. Burke and Gibbons (1995) found that wetland regulations would not protect any of 93 nest sites of mud turtles (*Kinosternon subrubrum*), Florida cooters (*Pseudemys floridana*), and slider turtles. Wetland regulations would also not protect any of the hibernation burrows of 24 mud turtles. Kingsbury and Coppola (2000) noted that clearing of uplands to the edge of wetland hibernacula would have devastating effects on copperbelly water snakes (*Nerodia erythrogaster neglecta*).

Reptiles are particularly susceptible to road kill (Ernst et al. 1994) and new road construction near wetlands or between wetlands and upland habitats should be avoided. Closing roads on refuges during periods of pronounced movements can also reduce impacts to these species (Siegel 1986). As with amphibians, waterbirds, and other wetland-dependent wildlife, effective conservation and management requires an understanding of the life history needs of the organism to provide the necessary habitat resources at the appropriate time and at an acceptable spatial scale.

WETLAND PLANNING

Proper planning is critical to maximizing long-term natural resource production regardless of whether activities involve acquisition, protection, creation, restoration, enhancement, or annual management. Unfortunately, planning often is approached as an obstacle that must be overcome to either secure funds or obtain permission to implement actions, rather than as an integral and necessary component of achieving success. Consequently, planning often is ignored, completed in haste, or used to validate selected decisions based on subjective information or the desires of a few individuals. In cases where an objective approach to planning is used, common mistakes include making decisions prior to acquiring and synthesizing information from all relevant disciplines and failure to consider the overarching reasons for wetland activities at multiple landscape scales.

The lack, or inappropriate use, of planning is a fundamental cause of highly variable results of many wetland projects because factors (e.g., soils, hydrologic condition, social perspectives) that may affect management potential and success are not considered when making decisions. Consequently, projects may fail even after considerable resources in time and money have been invested, or require further development and management costs after completion because original designs were based on incorrect assumptions. This has prompted many agencies to establish policies that require resource management planning based on science. Passage of the 1997 National Wildlife Refuge System Improvement Act mandates that management decisions be consistent with the principles of sound fish and wildlife management and available science. In this section we provide an overview of important considerations that lead to better decisions that are ecologically based and sensitive to wetland processes.

Planning Approaches

There are numerous approaches to planning. A common feature of most approaches is a hierarchical framework that provides an increasing level of detail regarding specific attributes that will be used to measure success (Table 7). Each tier within the framework is usually denoted by a keyword, such as mission, purpose, goals, objectives, and strategies. Agency missions are typically broad statements (e.g., ecosystem integrity), goals are open-ended and provide general management guidance (e.g., wetlands to support waterbirds), and objectives are detailed statements that include specific, quantifiable information (e.g., seasonally flooded wetlands with food resources necessary to support foraging shorebirds). The goal is achieved if all objectives pertaining to the goal are achieved. The term strategy is most often used to denote specific actions that will be implemented to achieve objectives. A primary value of this approach in wetland management is that the intent of a project becomes more refined in each successive tier and, ultimately, development and management approaches selected are less likely to conflict with the ecological potential of the site. Also, both abiotic and biotic factors influencing wetlands can be incorporated at the level of objectives. Interrelationships among and within these factors are important because they form the foundation of effective management.

Use of a hierarchical approach also is important in wetland management because no wetland can maximize all potential functions. A given wetland often provides different functions and has different values depending on scale. Thus, the spatial distribution and types of wetlands necessary to support one taxonomic group or wetland function may not be sufficient to support another taxonomic group or wetland function. Migratory avifauna link individual wetlands within a defined flyway, wetlands within a floodplain are linked with respect to floodwater storage or sediment retention, and pond-breeding amphibians may link isolated wetlands within a watershed. Thus, conservation efforts designed for waterfowl may be insufficient to ensure floodwater storage functions of wetlands or to conserve amphibians and isolated wetlands. Therefore, goals and objectives must be articulated in a manner that avoids confusion regarding the spatial, temporal, and taxonomic scales being considered. Identifying the scale is critical because specific habitat-based objectives must reflect the habitats required and the life history needs of the species associated with those habitats.

Need and Purpose

A primary reason for planning is to establish specific criteria that will be used to: (1) define success, (2) identify activities (e.g., acquisition, restoration, creation) and management procedures (e.g., levees, roads, water-control structures) that are best suited for achieving success, and (3) developing monitoring protocols to evaluate progress toward success. The necessity of defining success in explicit terms may seem obvious, but planning often focuses only on broad statements of value and, consequently, success often is based on wetland area rather than on wetland functions and long-term productivity. Often, this occurs because wetland projects are linked to agency or programmatic missions that encompass large geographic areas. Such statements are valuable for describing and prioritizing resources that use wetlands at scales such as continents, including waterfowl and shorebirds. They also can be valuable for identifying appropriate types and distributions of wetlands necessary to sustain or enhance certain wetland values (e.g., bird populations, floodwater storage along a river).

Statements related to total wetland area or the spatial

Table 7. Tiered framework illustrating increasing level of detail during the planning process. Based on U.S. Fish and Wildlife Service guidance (U.S. Department of Interior 2003).

Framework	General description	Example
Purpose	Specified or derived from law, proclamation, executive order, or other legal document establishing, authorizing, or expanding a refuge.	Migratory Bird Conservation Act… "for use as an inviolate sanctuary, or for any other management purpose, for migratory birds."
Vision	Statement of what the planning unit should be, based primarily on the mission, purpose, or other mandates.	Area is managed to benefit the diversity of plants and wildlife native to the Rocky Mountains.
Goal	Descriptive, open-ended, and often broad statement of desired future conditions that conveys a purpose, but does not define measurable units.	Provide and manage natural and man-made wetlands to provide habitat for migratory waterfowl, shorebirds, wading birds, and associated wetland-dependent wildlife.
Objective	Concise statement that is specific, measurable, achievable, results-oriented, and time-fixed.	Manage 40–70% of available wetland area for dense (> 70% distribution) seed-producing plants flooded <30 cm to maximize seed availability for foraging of fall (Sep–Oct) migrating dabbling ducks (teal, pintail, mallard).
Strategy	A specific action or technique, or combination of actions or techniques, used to meet an objective.	Water level manipulations (e.g., drawdown), fire, herbivory, mechanical actions (e.g., disk)

distribution of wetlands might be appropriate for coarse goals over large spatial scales. However, more specific goals and objectives must be developed at local scales because the biotic and abiotic conditions of individual wetlands and their temporal availability are critical for conservation success. Thus, success at landscape and continental scales is driven by success at local scales and vice versa. Acquisition of large wetland areas may be a critical component of conservation at the flyway scale. However, if these individual sites are in an inappropriate setting, or if they are severely altered or temporally unavailable, large-scale conservation efforts will fail or be severely hampered. At both local and landscape scales, a more appropriate definition of success may be total *functional* area rather than simply the amount of area acquired, managed, or restored.

After success has been defined, activities (e.g., acquisition, restoration, creation) and management strategies that involve development (e.g., levees, water-control structures, roads) or applications (water management, fire, herbivory) must be identified that are best suited for achieving success. This requires gathering a diversity of information from a variety of scientific disciplines and conducting extensive field evaluations. Often, the information necessary to make decisions may vary depending on the intended outcome of the proposed project. Thus, information searches should be conducted for individual projects.

Another important consideration is to document both historic and current abiotic and biotic conditions as thoroughly as possible (Table 8). Comparing historic and current conditions can be helpful in identifying important physical changes to the landscape and how wetland processes have been modified. This information can be used to examine management options most likely to contribute to project success. The definition of historic should be clearly defined, because many ecological communities have been extensively disrupted in the 48 contiguous states. Depending on the extent of disruption, it may not

be possible to emulate conditions that occurred 100 years ago, or even 15 years ago. In these cases, decisions may be based on restoring specific attributes that may or may not be representative of historic conditions, but will contribute to success of the project. Regardless of the definition of success, realistic decisions must be made regarding the ability to use "management" to achieve desired results. Sources of historical data include long-term climate and hydrologic data, explorer notes, general land office records, public land survey notes, historic aerial photographs, digital soil maps, digital elevation models of the project site, and analyses conducted by paleobotantists and anthropologists on plants and activities prior to human settlement, respectively.

Social, cultural, economic, and political factors should be considered when evaluating acquisition, restoration, management, and other activities (Table 8). Given the increasing and diverse demands placed on remaining wetlands by society, this information is becoming necessary to gain public support for proposed project design and implementation. Thus, managers must maintain credibility with the general public by integrating their concerns and priorities into management decisions. Managers must also guard against false or exaggerated benefits of particular management or restoration activities. Justification of a project based on water quality benefits could be misleading and erode support for the program if large tracts of land are restored and no water quality benefits are realized. The benefits of any project must be clearly articulated to ensure that public expectations are reasonable and accurate to ensure long-term support of wetland conservation and management activities.

Use of scientific information to evaluate the ability to meet project criteria and select appropriate activities and strategies will undoubtedly improve success of wetland projects. However, much remains to be known regarding wetland processes and how wildlife responds to changing

Table 8. Factors important to consider in wetland planning.

Category	Factor	Examples
Biological		
Historic	Geomorphology	Formative process, parent material, soils
	Climate	Precipitation, temperature, growing season length, evapotranspiration
	Hydrology	Frequency, time, duration, amount, source (groundwater, surface water), annual and long-term variations
	Plants	Composition and distribution
	Animals	Composition and distribution
Current	Hydrology	Variation from historic conditions (type and extent of modification and related affects on wetland processes)
	Plants	Changes in composition and distribution from historic (e.g., endangered species, nonnatives), life history requirements (e.g., soil moisture and salinity tolerances for germination)
	Animals	Changes in composition and distribution from historic (e.g., endangered species, nonnatives), life history requirements (e.g., vegetation composition and structure needed for breeding and migration)
Social	Public use groups	Impacts of management on hunters, fishermen, hikers, photographers, bird watchers
	Local community	Potential changes in farming and ranching practices, time and amount of water use
Economic	Local and regional	Potential impacts of management relative to number of jobs, access to land, fees and restrictions associated with use of land for economic gain (e.g., ranching, agriculture)
Legal		Hydrology (e.g., water rights or drainage issues), legal mandates related to land unit (e.g., land purchased under Endangered Species Act, Migratory Bird Conservation Act)

conditions caused by natural and anthropogenic agents, both within and outside public land boundaries. Consequently, there is no guarantee that decisions made during planning will result in project success. Thus, monitoring schemes must be developed and implemented to periodically check progress and adjust management approaches to unexpected problems or changing conditions (i.e., adaptive resource management). In addition, proper monitoring permits an objective review of past actions and greatly improves the ability to make better decisions on future projects.

Monitoring often requires considerable time and funds. In the past, these resources often were considered to be better-spent implementing additional projects. This attitude is changing as more interest has been focused on the long-term sustainable productivity of wetlands. However, resources remain limited; therefore, technical guidance should be sought in the design, selection of methods, and implementation of monitoring programs. This will ensure that time and money are used efficiently without sacrificing the types and value of information necessary to implement adaptive resource management (Holling 1978, Walters 1986).

WETLAND MANAGEMENT

Individual wetlands should be evaluated using a hierarchical planning approach to ensure that values at different spatial scales are identified prior to making decisions and initiating management. However, pristine wetlands that have retained their inherent hydrologic characteristics and functions should be protected and passively managed (Errington 1963, Weller 1988, Fredrickson and Reid 1990). Unfortunately, only a small percentage of wetlands in the conterminous United States and Hawaii have remained unaltered by human activity. In contrast, the hydrologic condition of many wetlands in Alaska and northern Canada remains largely unchanged from historic conditions. Developing a better understanding and protecting the natural hydrologic regimes and land use in northern areas should be a primary management goal.

Wetlands that have been modified or impacted often must be actively managed to ensure long-term sustainable productivity, including consistent provision of resources to wetland wildlife (Fredrickson and Reid 1990). Success often depends on implementing activities that can be broadly categorized as restoration, enhancement, or creation. The goals and objectives of these activities often differ. Wetland restoration is defined as "the return of an ecosystem to a close approximation of its condition prior to disturbance" (National Research Council 1992). If the site originally was a wetland and the objective is to specifically enhance a selected wetland function(s) that produced a value that originally existed, the most appropriate term describing wetland activities is enhancement (U.S. Department of Agriculture 1999*b*). According to this definition, some functions may remain unchanged while others may be degraded. In contrast, implementing a wetland project "on a site that historically was not a wetland, or is a wetland but the site will be converted to a wetland with a different hydrologic regime, vegetation type, or function than naturally occurred on the site" is termed a creation (U.S. Department of Agriculture 1999*a*).

Many of the same techniques are used regardless of whether the project meets the definition of restoration, enhancement, or creation. Designs that allow wetlands to become self-regulating and do not require management are often considered ideal (Mitsch and Wilson 1996). However, some type of management will normally be necessary to achieve wildlife habitat objectives. Therefore, design and management considerations are presented collectively in the following section. However, design, location, specifications, and purpose for constructing physical features, as well as management strategies, often differ due to differences in criteria used to define success. We present 2 case studies to illustrate how information in this chapter can be used to make decisions and increase the probability that management will be successful.

Design and Management Considerations

The ability to sustain wetland productivity requires an appropriate design based on emulating wetland processes necessary to promote desirable habitat conditions needed by wetland wildlife to survive and reproduce. A primary challenge often is to emulate important hydrological parameters (Weller et al. 1991). A successfully managed wetland contains foods and cover of a type, quality, and distribution that are the same or functionally similar to those found in natural, unmanaged wetlands. Management should provide resources that meet the physiological and behavioral needs of wildlife while simultaneously ensuring long-term productivity.

Restoring important hydrological parameters often requires construction and/or installation of physical structures (e.g., levees, water control structures, water supply and discharge systems, pumping systems) that facilitate control of water inflow, distribution, and discharge. Water management is necessary to create soil and water conditions suitable for germination and growth of desirable plant communities, control problem vegetation, stimulate invertebrate production, and make resources available for target species (Fredrickson 1991). Water control particularly is critical for providing habitat conditions required by foraging waterbirds (Fig. 4). For example, of 81 species of waterbirds using wetlands in the southwestern United States, only 19 successfully forage in water >25 cm in depth, but 10 of these readily use water <25 cm. Twice as many species (38) forage in water <10 cm deep (Fredrickson and Reid 1986).

Capital investments to achieve hydrologic control can be large. However, costs can be reduced appreciably and wildlife benefits maximized if developments are designed to complement existing topographic and geomorphic features. Highways, dirt roads, ditches, and even fencerows often disrupt sheetflow of water across the landscape into wetlands. Removing a fence, adding culverts in strategic areas, plugging a ditch, or lowering gravel roadbeds can be inexpensive and simple measures to restore surface water movement. For groundwater-fed wetlands, locating and breaking drainage tiles can be a relatively inexpensive and effective technique for restoring hydrologic conditions. In some cases, however, the costs can be large. For example, the U.S. Army Corps of Engineers is currently working to restore the Kissimmee River in Florida, which they channelized several decades ago (Toth et al. 1993, 1995, 1998). Following channelization, two-thirds of the floodplain wetlands were eliminated and waterfowl use of these wetlands decreased by 92% (Perrin et al. 1982). Large-scale restoration projects require involvement by numerous stakeholders, policy makers, and political groups and can be long-term, slow moving efforts (National Research Council 1999). The ability to conduct some activities can be limited by outside considerations, including social and economic constraints. In the Lower Mississippi Alluvial Valley, removal of flood control levees, reconstructing meanders in channelized streams and rivers, eliminating drainage ditches, and reforesting the floodplain would be necessary to achieve hydrologic restoration. These activities are not likely (King and Keeland 1999). First, this system has been degraded to the extent that current technology and engineering tools available are not capable of restoring historic hydrologic regimes. Second, existing levees are necessary to prevent flooding of urban areas and productive farmland. Thus, levee removal is neither economically or socially acceptable.

Wetland Configuration

Flight has allowed waterbirds to exploit a variety of habitats across the continent. In the Lower Mississippi Alluvial Valley, dabbling ducks use wetlands within a 16-km radius to meet daily nutritional and physiological requirements (Delnicki and Reinecke 1986). In other cases, objectives also may require restoring habitats surrounding wetlands. In the Prairie Pothole Region, extensive loss and fragmentation of grassland habitats adjacent to wetlands has resulted in increased concentration of predators and low rates of waterfowl nest success because of high nest predation rates (Greenwood et al. 1987, Sargeant and Raveling 1992). Beauchamp et al. (1996) noted that waterfowl nest success had declined from about 33% in 1935 to 10% in 1992. Nest success of 15–20% is needed to sustain many dabbling duck populations (Cowardin et al. 1985, Klett et al. 1988). Thus, to achieve a goal of improved waterfowl nesting success, restoration projects must address increased predation rates. Trapping of predators is an option, but trapping is costly, difficult to implement over a large scale, and may be ineffective in many landscapes (Sargeant et al. 1995).

One alternative strategy that has been implemented is to integrate grassland and wetland restoration over large-scales, improving landscape structure, and reducing the impacts of predators on nest success (Reynolds et al. 2001). Estimated nest success was 46% higher and recruitment rates were 30% higher for 5 species of dabbling ducks following large-scale grassland restoration (1.9 million ha) associated with the Conservation Reserve Program in the Prairie Pothole Region (Reynolds et al. 2001). Similar consideration must be incorporated when considering habitat suitability for amphibians. Wetland amphibians are not as vagile as waterbirds, but some species move between wetlands in close proximity. Semlitsch (1998) estimated that 6 species of salamanders were capable of moving an average of only 164 m, with some individuals traveling 450–625 m. Thus, the extent and type of use a wetland receives by wildlife is influenced not only by habitat conditions in that wetland but also by the condition of adjacent wetland and terrestrial habitats. Provision for development and management of a complex of different wetland types in a localized area often increases overall

diversity and density of wildlife species (Fredrickson and Reid 1988*b*). Wetlands ranging in size from <1 to 1,400 ha can be important for wildlife if they are managed as a complex.

Before development the area should be assessed to identify potential wildlife use. Food and cover requirements of target species should be considered in relation to existing habitats within the local area to identify habitats that may be limited. If possible within the constraints of existing abiotic and biotic factors, the proposed site should be developed to provide the most limiting habitats that historically were present in a physiographic region. Engineering and biological technology exists for creating or rehabilitating most wetland types, but successful long-term operation and wildlife use of a wetland will occur only if the type is correctly matched with local site conditions. Types of wildlife use desired must match the geographic location of the area. For example, habitat for breeding birds often is the focus of management, but the site may be best suited for migrating or wintering birds.

Levees

Levees are an integral component of many degraded, altered, or created wetlands because they permit control of water levels and affect the maximum managed water depth. They also may enable water transfer to and from designated wetlands. Although levee dimensions vary depending on wetland type and proposed function, levees should be constructed along natural contours to prevent further disrupting surface water flows (Fig. 9). Contour levees also assure the wetland can be completely dewatered if necessary to favor growth of desirable vegetation communities (e.g., annuals adapted to germinate on moist soil), control problem vegetation (e.g., drying, flooding, disking, mowing), reduce the incidence of disease out-

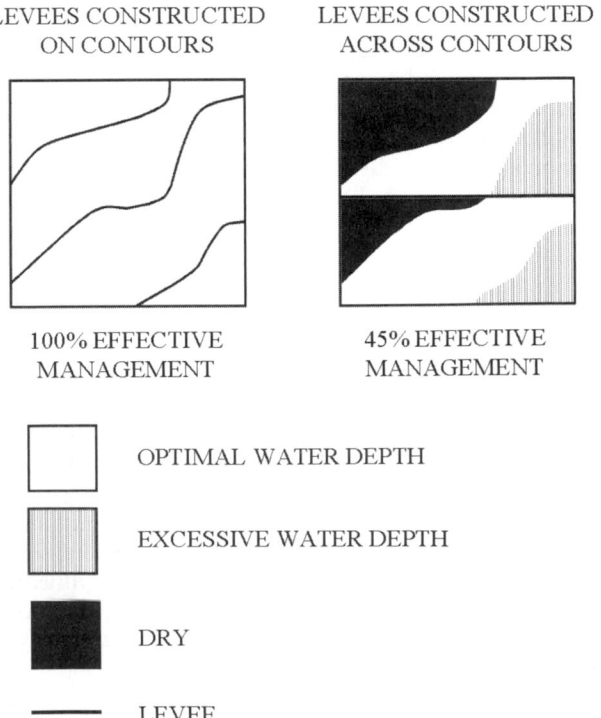

Fig. 9. Schematic depicting the importance of levee placement on contours.

breaks, and conform to legal statutes (e.g., mosquito abatement policies).

In contrast, levees placed perpendicular to natural slopes tend to impede water discharge and may result in surface water that cannot be removed unless lateral ditches are constructed into the interior of the wetland. Although lateral ditches enable complete dewatering of a basin, they increase development costs, require periodic maintenance, and often reduce the area that can be effectively managed. Decisions concerning the contour interval on which to establish levees should be balanced among construction costs, detrimental impacts to existing habitats, and maximizing the area flooded to desired depths. Construction of levees on 30-cm contours to create a greentree reservoir may result in optimum water control, but also may require removal of numerous mast-bearing trees and increase habitat fragmentation. The contour interval selected should maximize the area flooded to desired depths while minimizing removal of valuable bottomland hardwoods (King and Fredrickson 1998).

Levees can be constructed using a variety of methods. The choice often depends on the objective as well as soil type, availability of equipment, and imagination of the technical staff. Commonly used equipment includes bulldozers, motor graders, rice dike plows, and fire plows. Regardless of construction method, dimensions should be based on engineering criteria. Physical and chemical properties (e.g., organic matter content, texture) of soils influence compactibility and shear strength, and ultimately will dictate the required dimensions necessary to assure long-term levee stability. However, within acceptable engineering standards, levees also should permit accomplishment of normal management operations.

Levees should be capable of supporting machinery (e.g., tractor, mower, disk) necessary to maintain them and manage vegetation. Further, levee side slopes should be gradual to deter potential damage by erosion and burrowing mammals (Fig. 10). Constructing levees with 4-m crowns and minimum side slopes of 3:1 normally can satisfy these objectives. Most agencies have recognized the value of constructing levees with slopes of 4:1 or greater for ease of mowing, deterring burrowing animals, and to reduce erosion associated with wave action. In extreme cases, slopes as great as 10:1 have been used for specific purposes. Levees with more gradual side slopes require an increased volume of material and also impact more wetland habitat, but they may be needed to satisfy ecological or engineering requirements.

Levee height depends on the size of the impoundment and expected depth of flooding. Levees in large wetlands (e.g., >32 ha) or wetlands constructed to simulate permanently flooded habitats are susceptible to wave action and erosion. Consequently, large or deeply flooded wetlands require more substantial levees than seasonally flooded wetlands (Fig. 10). Levee height should be a minimum of 1 m above the predicted annual maximum flooding depth. If this is not possible, levee height should be uniform or spillways should be incorporated into the design to permit exchange and equalization of floodwater on both sides of the levee to minimize damage during high water.

Water Control Structures

Permanent water control structures that allow water

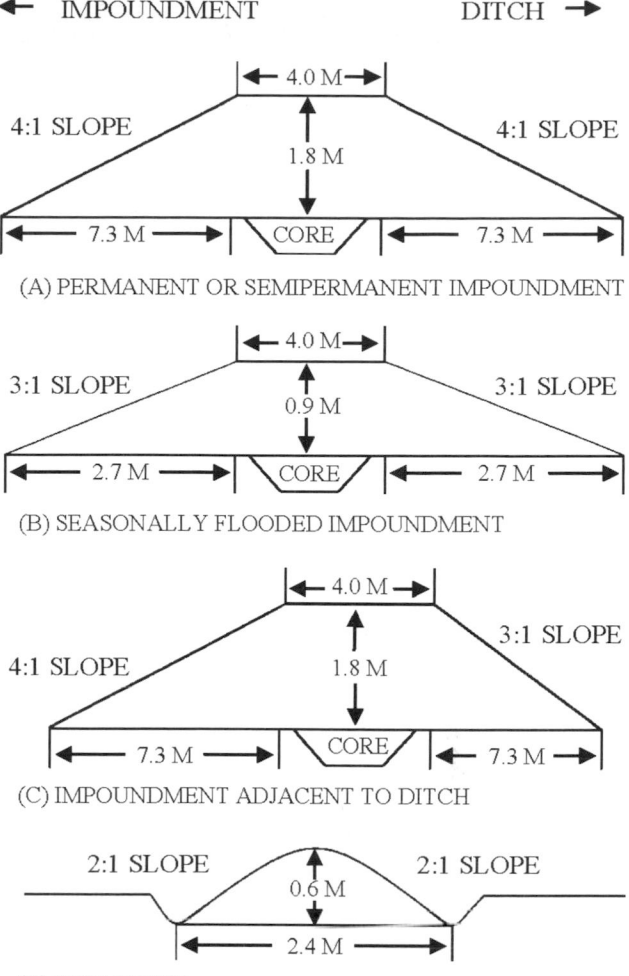

Fig. 10. Base specifications of levee types to facilitate wetland management activities.

level manipulation are essential if natural hydrologic regimes are to be emulated (Fredrickson 1991). Because annual, seasonal, and even daily changes in hydrologic parameters (e.g., depth) are common in most functional wetlands, the ability to alter water levels or completely remove water from a wetland is essential. Therefore, type and location of water control structures are important. In most situations, stoplog water control structures are ideal for controlling water discharge at increments as small as 5 cm (Fig. 11). These structures require less frequent monitoring because stoplogs can be preset at the desired elevation and additional water that enters the wetland is removed from the surface via gravity flow. In contrast, control of water movement with screwgates (i.e., sluice gates) is more difficult because water discharge is accomplished by removing water from the bottom of the wetland (Fig. 11). If screwgates are opened and left unchecked, complete water discharge will occur. Screwgates may be used as intake structures, but not as discharge structures (Fredrickson 1991).

The proper locations of intake and discharge structures are the highest and lowest elevations within the wetland, respectively (King and Fredrickson 1998). The same structure should not be used for intake and discharge (Fredrickson 1991). In areas with high salinities, multiple

STOPLOG WATER CONTROL STRUCTURE

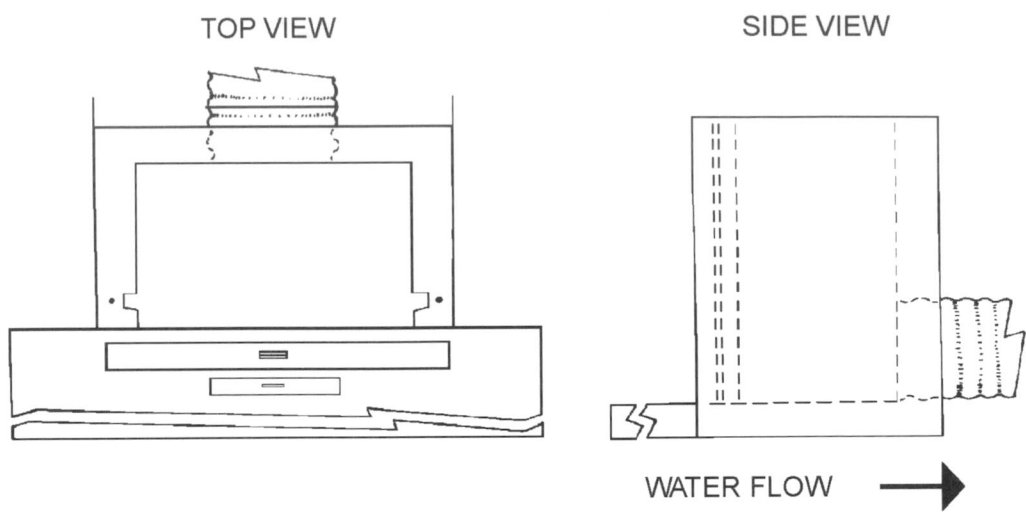

TOP VIEW   SIDE VIEW

WATER FLOW ⟶

SCREWGATE WATER CONTROL STRUCTURE

FRONT VIEW   SIDE VIEW

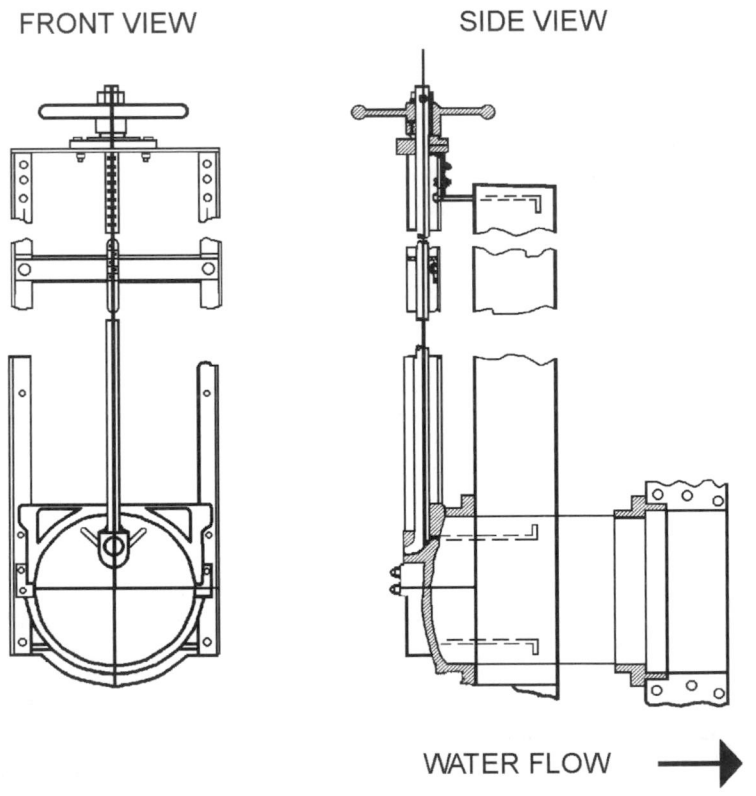

WATER FLOW ⟶

Fig. 11. Stoplog and screwgate water control structures.

inlet structures at the highest elevations and multiple drains at the lowest elevations provide the best management options. This design enables complete water discharge necessary to control plant community establishment and permits optimum flooding necessary to make resources available to waterbirds. Additionally, correct placement of water control structures maximizes water circulation within a wetland, which prevents accumulation of soil salts, reduces the risk of disease outbreaks, and facilitates nutrient cycling.

Water Level Management

Historically, many palustrine wetlands outside of floodplains were flooded as a result of precipitation, groundwater, or a combination of both. Small, localized precipitation events saturated the soil, whereas larger events resulted in surface runoff of water from adjacent uplands that filled wetlands. In arid locations with a deep capillary fringe, rainfall of only 84 mm (0.25 in.) may result in extensive flooding. In these systems, all wetlands types were not necessarily flooded every year, but some habitats were available in most years. Maintaining these conditions is especially important for species with limited mobility because they must survive between wet and dry cycles at the site. This is an increasing challenge because runoff from rainfall in many regions of the United States is diverted for agricultural or urban uses and does not reach wetland sites.

In contrast, off-channel floodplain wetlands were historically inundated during flood events. Channelization and diversion of river flows and associated tributaries has resulted in serious hydrologic alterations in many of these systems. Depending on wetland type and location, the impacts of these modifications may be manifest in either severe flooding (Belt 1975, Galat et al. 1998) or an almost complete lack of floodwater (Reinecke et al. 1988). Channelization in the upper reaches of the Mississippi River and its tributaries has resulted in severe water fluxes in the lower reaches. Too much water inundates wetlands near the river delta, whereas upstream wetlands do not receive sufficient water to cause surface flooding. In either situation, waterbird use often is limited. Sediments or toxicants also degrade water quality in many rivers (Longcore et al. 1987, Grue et al. 1989).

Wetland development and management must often rely on alternative sources of water because hydroperiods have been severely altered across the entire conterminous United States. Common solutions include obtaining water from ditches and rivers, use of wells to transport groundwater to the surface, and construction of reservoirs to capture precipitation and runoff for later use (Reid et al. 1989). Groundwater and reservoirs are more reliable sources of good quality water, but construction of expensive levee or pump systems may be required to accomplish water transport to managed sites. Reservoirs also are disadvantageous because a considerable amount of area often must be converted to deep-water habitats to store sufficient water, and siltation frequently limits reservoir life. Long- and short-term costs associated with using groundwater vary, depending on type of pump and power unit and distance to the water table.

It is also important to recognize that water quality varies among sources. Thus, use of water from sources that differ from those occurring historically can potentially influence some wetland processes. For example, groundwater often contains more salts than rainwater. If salinity of groundwater is sufficiently high, or salts are allowed to accumulate in the basin over many years, a shift in vegetation composition is possible. Thus, types of alternative solutions to obtaining water should be evaluated not only based on costs, but also on the potential to impact project success.

Obtaining water is frequently considered the most important issue in wetland management. However complete discharge of water at appropriate times during the annual cycle is also essential. It may seem counterproductive to enhance drainage in managed wetlands, but creating conditions necessary for annual plant germination and the ability to control problem vegetation using water or mechanical equipment requires timely and complete removal of surface water.

Case Studies

Bottomland Hardwood Forest Management

Bald Knob National Wildlife Refuge, Arkansas and the Mollicy Farms Unit of Upper Quachita National Wildlife Refuge, Louisiana share many similar characteristics. Both refuges were originally bottomland hardwood forests in the Lower Mississippi Alluvial Valley before being converted to rice farms, and both provided critical habitat for wintering waterfowl. In addition, both refuges are in the Mississippi Flyway and occur within the Lower Mississippi River Valley Joint Venture. The Joint Venture, along with other conservation organizations, has developed conservation goals for Neotropical migrant songbirds, shorebirds, and waterfowl that help guide refuge management in the region. Despite these similarities, decisions made in the planning process led to different long-term management plans for each of these areas.

Bald Knob National Wildlife Refuge is in central Arkansas along the Red River near its confluence with the White River. When first acquired, the 6,000-ha refuge consisted of about 4,047 ha of rice cropland and about 1,820 ha of mature forested wetlands. At times, the refuge supported as many as 200,000 northern pintails and over 400,000 total waterfowl. In addition, rice management on the area provided important habitat for migrating and wintering shorebirds and year-round habitat for wading birds. The original farm was ideal for rice agriculture because of the lack of topographic relief, a reliable water supply, and infrequent overbank flooding from the river enabled water to be managed reliably in most years. The area immediately surrounding Bald Knob was largely nonforested, although an extensively forested wildlife management area, Hurricane Lake, was within 16 km of the refuge.

Mollicy Farms, an area of 7,689 ha, is in northeastern Louisiana within the floodplain of the Ouachita River. Mollicy was in an area adjacent to several state and federal wildlife refuges, including the Big Timbers Wildlife Management Area, Upper Ouachita National Wildlife Refuge, and Felsenthal National Wildlife Refuge. These refuges provide about 50,587 ha of contiguous forested habitat. Originally, Mollicy Farms also was forested. However, the area was converted for rice agriculture by constructing an earthen ring levee to isolate land to be farmed from the Ouachita River. In addition, a large pump was installed to remove water from within the area protected by the levee during periods of high rainfall and to pump water from the river into the farm during the summer growing season. The levee construction initially cost several million dollars and repairs were frequent and expensive. After the levee was constructed and the pump installed, the 7,689 ha of bottomland hardwood forest were cleared.

Both areas were high priority acquisitions to help the U.S. Fish and Wildlife Service meet the goals established by the Lower Mississippi River Valley Joint Venture. Both sites were acquired in the 1990s and planning efforts to

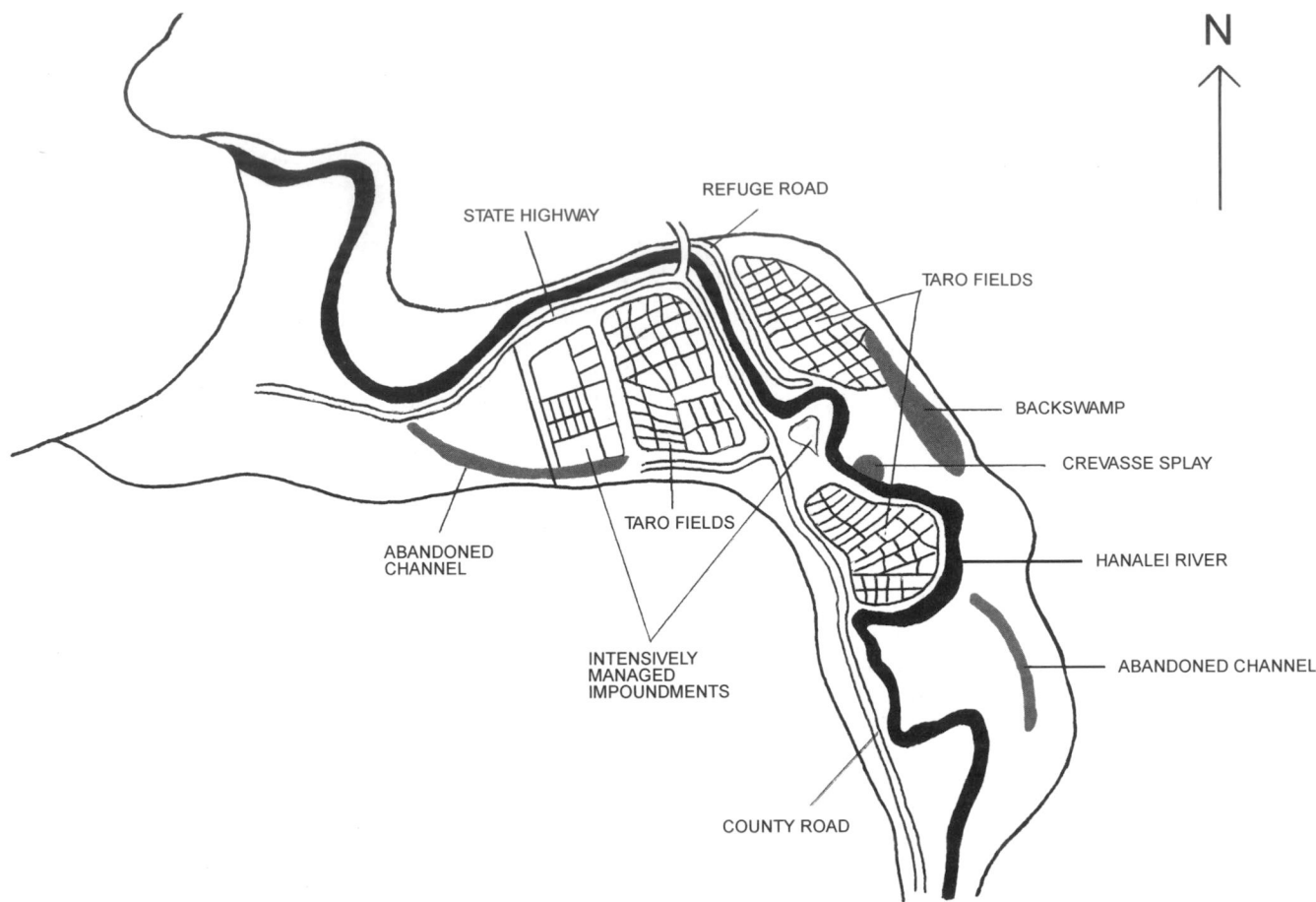

Fig. 12. Wetland development within the Hanalei River floodplain in Kauai in relation to selected geomorphic features.

define long-term goals and objectives for each refuge were initiated. However, decisions regarding development and management of the 2 refuges differed because of the landscape setting, local biotic and abiotic conditions, and the existing infrastructure.

Based on the tradition of Bald Knob National Wildlife Refuge as a wintering ground for large concentrations of waterfowl, coupled with an existing water management infrastructure for rice production that was considered suitable for intensive management of emergent wetlands, it was decided that management of this refuge was best suited to benefit waterfowl. The lack of forested cover on surrounding lands made reforestation a less desirable option because benefits to forest interior nesting songbirds would be minimal without other large-scale acquisitions. Thus, specific objectives regarding the amount of habitat provided and when it would be available were developed first for waterfowl, second for other waterbirds, and finally for Neotropical migrant songbirds.

Mollicy Farms differed dramatically from Bald Knob National Wildlife Refuge. The surrounding watershed was predominately forested and Mollicy Farms fragmented this habitat. The wetland management infrastructure was in disrepair; the levee was collapsing in several areas and would require extensive and expensive repairs. Reforestation was much more attractive at this refuge and restoration of bottomland hardwood forests became the primary goal of the refuge. The secondary objective was

to provide some moist-soil and agricultural habitat for waterfowl but, because of the poor condition of the levee, this objective may be eliminated. A restoration plan was developed where 4,856 ha were designated for reforestation with tree seedlings of appropriate species, an additional 405 ha were designated for natural regeneration, and 1,214 ha were designated as moist soil and agricultural habitat. Ditches were plugged at strategic locations to restore the local hydrologic regime, and the perimeter levee will be removed or allowed to disintegrate over a period of years to restore floodplain connectivity.

Floodplain Wetland Management

The small (371 ha) Hanalei National Wildlife Refuge on Kauai, Hawaii has many of the management challenges common to wetlands on floodplains. The geomorphologic setting of the island is unique; Kauai is of volcanic origin and has distinct, wedge-shaped watersheds that transport surface water from high, mountainous, interior elevations to the ocean. The porous volcanic rock surrounding the valley also transports water below the surface (i.e., groundwater). Drainages are well developed and the Hanalei River (length = 25.7 km) is one of the larger river systems in the state. This river, which drains a 49.5-km^2 area, is on the north shore of Kauai and exhibits features typical of a riverine system (e.g., natural levees, cut banks, point bars, abandoned channels, crevasse splays, and backswamps) as it enters the broad, low valley and begins to meander within the floodplain (Fig. 12). Near the ocean, the river cuts through old beach ridges. The lower 3.2 km of the river flows through the refuge and 2 large private land holdings and past taro (*Colocasia esculenta*) farms, small businesses, and residences before emptying into Hanalei Bay. Backswamps and abandoned channels have fine textured materials while coarse materials dominate natural levees, point bars, crevasse splays, and old beach ridges. A veneer of fine textured material with variable thickness is common within the valley. This veneer thins on the buried beach ridges as one moves closer to the ocean.

Hanalei National Wildlife Refuge is one of the most important sites in Hawaii for 4 endangered Hawaiian waterbirds including the Hawaiian coot (*Fulica alai*), moorhen (*Gallinula chloropus sandvicensis*), stilt (*Himantopus mexicanus knudseni*), and Koloa or Hawaiian duck (*Anas wyvilliana*). In addition, the endangered Hawaiian goose or Nene (*Branta sandvicensis*) currently nests on the refuge, and there may be the potential to reintroduce the Laysan duck (*A. laysanensis*).

Thus, Hanalei National Wildlife Refuge has the typical suite of physical disruptions related to agriculture and flood control including roads, channelized stream, incised stream, levees, ditches (supply and drainage), disruption of surface deposits, and irrigation infrastructure. These physical disruptions also influence natural processes by changing hydrologic conditions, topography, and the amount of river water in the lower floodplain.

Agricultural activities in the Hanalei River Valley have been present for 1,300 years (Schilt 1980). Thus, this site has a long history of agricultural development including the infrastructure required for crops that require flooded conditions. Flooded conditions associated with these agricultural practices also attract waterbirds.

The U.S. Fish and Wildlife Service continued to develop wetlands after the refuge was established, but objectives changed from agricultural to conservation. New levees, drains, and water-control structures provided opportunities for hydrologic manipulations required to produce conditions more conducive to the life history needs of endangered waterbirds. Placement of these new developments was based on availability of sites in relation to the previous infrastructure rather than a comprehensive understanding of geomorphic features or local hydrologic conditions. The suite of conditions at Hanalei National Wildlife Refuge requires managers to address multiple problems.

1. A floodplain with physical disruptions to the natural flow of water.
2. Changes in the river channel that compromise water intake.
3. Alteration of natural processes because of physical disruptions, changes in water use, and presence of exotic plants and animals.
4. A poorly sited infrastructure in relation to geomorphic and hydrologic conditions.
5. An infrastructure with inadequate supply, control, and discharge of water.
6. Poor understanding of water use on taro and wetland impoundments.
7. Cultural issues associated with taro, a food source with nutritional and ceremonial value to native Hawaiians.
8. Endangered species, including 4 wetland-dependent birds for which there is limited knowledge.
9. Inadequate knowledge of native plants and their life history requirements, especially the abiotic conditions that stimulate germination, growth, and seed production.
10. Predation and disease potential.
11. Permits required to change the infrastructure.
12. Funds to implement changes to the infrastructure, management, and research.

On Hanalei National Wildlife Refuge, plans are being formulated to rehabilitate some wetland impoundments and to construct more impoundments for intensive management. Intensive wetland management was preferred over restoration because of the extensive abiotic and biotic disruptions in the landscape. Restoration of a sufficiently large area to support endangered waterbirds was not practical, thus intensive management was a logical choice.

SUMMARY

Wetlands are dynamic habitats that provide many benefits to wetland-dependent wildlife as well as to society. Understanding wetlands and their benefits is complex and requires information on their abiotic and biotic characteristics. Unfortunately, many societal benefits were not well recognized historically and, as a result, vast areas of wetland habitats were lost or modified in the lower 48 states and Hawaii following European settlement. Many wetlands were either converted to other uses such as agriculture or were influenced by anthropomorphic changes that modified the physical condition or disrupted wetland processes. These changes in wetland area and functions resulted in legislation that led to state and federal programs for wetland management and protection that benefit wildlife and society. Some wetland programs are especially important for wildlife because wetlands provide valuable habitat for a wide suite of species, many of which are either endangered or species of regional or national concern. Thus, management or protection of remnant wetlands is critical to maintain viable populations of many wetland-dependent species. Historically wetland management techniques were applied without recognition of the temporal or landscape setting that characterized a site and the focus was on migratory birds, especially waterfowl. We describe an approach that identifies the importance of understanding geomorphic setting, climatic conditions, and life history strategies of plants and animals including birds other than waterfowl, as well as cold-blooded vertebrates as the basis for wetland decision-making. Case histories provide insights into the contemporary challenges of making decisions in highly modified environments.

ACKNOWLEDGMENTS

M. W. Weller, P. L. Errington, F. C. Bellrose, L. R. Jahn, C. C. Cottam, and Glenn Jones stimulated a life-long interest in wetland management by L. H. Fredrickson. The ideas in this paper reflect over 80 years of collective experience with wetlands and their management. Interactions with wetland managers have been of great importance over the past 40 years on hundreds of federal, state, and private wetlands extending across North America as well as those in Hawaii, Europe, and Australia. Exposure to wetlands from low to high elevations, from the tropics to the arctic, and from sites with little to high rainfall has helped us understand wetland dynamics and management challenges. Foremost among the biologists and managers that have been generous in sharing their ideas across a large spatial scale have been Barry Allen, R. K. Baskett, S. S. Berlinger, J. L. Boyles, P. R. Covington, J. M. Davis, M. B. Epstein, Tom Foti, D. A. Graber, D. L. Helmers, D. D. Humburg, Ted Joanen, K. K. Karrow, H. P. Laskowski, W. R. Leonard, J. M. Minnerath, P. W. Norton, J. B. Pagan, Ray Palermo, F. L. Paveglio, Carrel Ryan, D. W. Sharp, M. D. Silbernagle, J. P. Taylor, J. E. Toll, D. J. Widner, and G. R. Zahm. Belinda Ederington, B. W. Schuster, K. K. Kyle, and M. A. Hartman provided assistance with tables and figures. N. H. Euliss, Jr., M. E. Heitmeyer, R. A. Laubhan, Billy Minser, and S. N. Oswalt, provided suggestions to improve the manuscript.

LITERATURE CITED

AFTON, A. D., AND S. L. PAULUS. 1992. Incubation and brood care. Pages 62–108 *in* B. D. J. Batt, A. D. Afton, M. G. Anderson, C. D. Ankney, D. H. Johnson, J. A. Kadlec, and G. L. Krapu, editors. Ecology and management of breeding waterfowl. University of Minnesota Press, Minneapolis. USA.

ALFORD, R. A., AND R. N. RICHARDS. 1999. Global amphibian declines: a problem in applied ecology. Annual Review of Ecology and Systematics 30:133–165.

ALLANSON, B. R. 1973. The fine structure of the periphyton of *Chara* sp. and *Potamogeton natans* from Wytham Pond, Oxford, and its significance to the macrophyte-periphyton metabolic model of R. G. Wetzel and H. L. Allen. Freshwater Biology 3:535–542.

ALLEN, J. A., B. D. KEELAND, J. A. STANTURF, A. F. CLEWELL, AND H. E. KENNEDY, JR. 2001. A guide to bottomland hardwood restoration. U.S. Department of the Interior, Geological Survey, Biological Resources Division, Information and Technology Report USGS/BRD/ITR-2000-0011.

BAILEY, R. G. 1995. Description of the ecoregions of the United States. Second edition. U.S. Department of Agriculture, Forest Service, Washington, D.C., USA.

BAKER, L. A. 1992. Introduction to nonpoint source pollution in the United States and prospects for wetland use. Ecological Engineering 1:1–26.

BALDASSARRE, G. A., AND E. G. BOLEN. 1994. Waterfowl ecology and management. John Wiley and Sons, New York. USA.

BALL, J. P., AND T. D. NUDDS. 1989. Mallard habitat selection: experiments and implications for management. Pages 659–671 *in* R. R. Sharitz and J. W. Gibbons, editors. Freshwater wetlands and wildlife. U.S. Department of Energy Symposium Series 61.

BANCROFT, G. T., D. E. GAWLIK, AND K. RUTCHEY. 2002. Distribution of wading birds relative to vegetation and water depths in the northern Everglades of Florida, USA. Waterbirds 25:265–277.

BARBIER, E. B., M. C. ACREMAN, AND D. KNOWLER. 1997. Economic valuation of wetlands: a guide for policy makers and planners. Ramsar Convention Bureau, Gland, Switzerland.

BARINAGA, M. 1990. Where have all the froggies gone? Science 247:1033–1034.

BASKIN, J. M., AND C. C. BASKIN. 1989. Physiology of dormancy and germination in relation to seed bank ecology. Pages 53–66 *in* M. A. Leck, V. T. Parker, and R. L. Simpson, editors. Ecology of soil seed banks. Academic Press, San Diego, California, USA.

BATEMA, D. L. 1987. Nutrient dynamics in a bottomland hardwood ecosystem. Dissertation. University of Missouri, Columbia, USA.

―――, R. M. KAMINSKI, AND P. A. MAGEE. 2005. Wetland invertebrate communities and management of hardwood bottomlands in the Mississippi Alluvial Valley. Pages 173–190 *in* L. H. Fredrickson, R. M. Kaminski, and S. L. King, editors. Ecology and management of bottomland hardwood systems: the state of our understanding. University of Missouri-Columbia, Gaylord Memorial Laboratory,

Puxico, Missouri, USA.

BATT, B. D. J., A. D. AFTON, M. G. ANDERSON, C. D. ANKNEY, D. H. JOHNSON, J. A. KADLEC, AND G. L. KRAPU, editors. 1992. Ecology and management of breeding waterfowl. University of Minnesota Press, Minneapolis, USA.

BATZER, D. P., R. B. RADER, AND S. A. WISSINGER. 1999. Invertebrates in freshwater wetlands of North America: ecology and management. John Wiley and Sons, New York, USA.

BEATLEY, J. C. 1974. Phenological events and their environmental triggers in Mojave Desert ecosystems. Ecology 55:856–863.

BEAUCHAMP, W. D., R. R. KOFORD, T. D. NUDDS, R. G. CLARK, AND D. H. JOHNSON. 1996. Long-term decline in nest success of prairie ducks. Journal of Wildlife Management 60:247–257.

BEDINGER, M. S. 1979. Relation between forest species and flooding. Pages 427–435 *in* P. C. Greeson, J. R. Clark, and J. E. Clark, editors. Wetland functions and values: the state of our understanding. Technical Publication 79–2. American Water Resources Association, Minneapolis, Minnesota, USA.

BEDISH, J. W. 1967. Cattail moisture requirements and their significance to marsh management. American Midland Naturalist 78:288–300.

BELLROSE, F. C. 1980. Ducks, geese, and swans of North America. Wildlife Management Institute and Stackpole Books, Harrisburg, Pennsylvania, USA.

―――, F. L. PAVEGLIO, JR., AND D. W. STEFFECK. 1979. Waterfowl populations and the changing environment of the Illinois River Valley. Illinois Natural History Survey Bulletin 32:1–53.

BELT, JR., C. B. 1975. The 1973 flood and man's construction of the Mississippi. River Science 189:681–684.

BERVEN, K. A. 1990. Factors affecting population fluctuations in larval and adult stages of the wood frog (*Rana sylvatica*). Ecology 71:1599–1608.

BLAUSTEIN, A. R., D. B. WAKE, AND W. P. SOUSA. 1994. Amphibian declines: judging stability, persistence, and susceptibility of populations to local and global extinctions. Conservation Biology 8:60–71.

BLEED, A., AND C. FLOWERDAY, editors. 1990. An atlas of the Sandhills: resource atlas Number 5a. Institute of Agriculture and Natural Resources, Conservation and Survey Division, University of Nebraska, Lincoln, USA.

BODIE, J. R., AND R. D. SEMLITSCH. 2000. Spatial and temporal use of floodplain habitats by lentic and lotic species of aquatic turtles. Oecologia 122:138–146.

BONNEWELL, V., W. L. KOUKKARI, AND D. C. PRATT. 1983. Light, oxygen, and temperature requirements for *Typha latifolia* seed germination. Canadian Journal of Botany 61:1330–1336.

BOOKHOUT, T. A. 1995. Yellow rail. Number 139 *in* A. Poole and F. Gill, editors. The birds of North America. The Academy of Natural Sciences, Philadelphia, Pennsylvania, and The American Ornithologists' Union, Washington, D.C., USA.

BORNETTE, G., C. AMOROS, H. PIEGAY, J. TACHET, AND T. HEIN. 1998. Ecological complexity of wetlands within a river landscape. Biological Conservation 85:35–45.

BOYD, C. E. 1970. Losses of mineral nutrients during decomposition of *Typha latifolia*. Archives Hydrobiologia 66:511–517.

BRETZ, J. H. 1923. The channeled scablands of the Columbia Plateau. Journal of Geology 31:617–649.

BRINSON, M. M. 1993. Hydrogeomorphic classification for wetlands. U.S. Department of the Army, Corps of Engineers, Waterways Experiment Station, Final Report. WES/TR/WRP-DE-4. Vicksburg, Mississippi, USA.

―――. 1995. The HGM approach explained. National Wetlands Newsletter 17:7–13.

―――, AND R. D. RHEINHARDT. 1996. The role of reference wetlands in functional assessment and mitigation. Ecological Applications 6:69–76.

―――, F. R. HAUER, L. C. LEE, W. L. NUTTER, AND R. D. RHEINHARDT. 1995. Guidebook for application of hydrogeomorphic assessments to riverine wetlands. Draft report. WES/TR/WRP-DE-11. U.S. Department of the Army, Corps of Engineers, Waterways Experiment Station, Vicksburg, Mississippi, USA.

―――, L. C. LEE, W. AINSLIE, R. D. RHEINHARDT, G. G. HOLLANDS, R. D. SMITH, D. F. WHIGHAM, AND W. B. NUTTER. 1997. Clearing up misconceptions about HGM. National Wetlands Newsletter 19:14–18.

BROWDER, J. A., P. J. GLEASON, AND D. R. SWIFT. 1994. Periphyton in the Everglades: spatial variation, environmental correlates, and ecological implications. Pages 379–418 *in* S. M. Davis and J. C. Ogden, editors.

Everglades: the ecosystem and its restoration. St. Lucie Press, Delray Beach, Florida, USA.

BROWN, D. E. 1985. Arizona wetlands and waterfowl. University of Arizona Press, Tucson, USA.

BROWN, M., AND J. J. DINSMORE. 1986. Implications of marsh size and isolation for marsh bird management. Journal of Wildlife Management 50:392–97.

BROWN, S., C. HICKEY, B. HARRINGTON, AND R. G. GILL, editors. 2001. United States shorebird conservation plan. Second edition. Manomet Center for Conservation Sciences, Manomet, Massachusetts, USA.

BUHLMANN, K. A. 1995. Habitat use, terrestrial movements and conservation of the turtle *Dierochelys reticularia* in Virginia. Journal of Herpetology 29:173–181.

———, AND J. W. GIBBONS. 1997. Imperiled aquatic reptiles of the southeastern United States: historical review and current conservation status. Pages 201–232 *in* G. Benz and D. E. Collins, editors. Aquatic fauna in peril: the southeastern perspective. Lenz Design and Communications, Decatur, Georgia, USA.

BURBRINK, F. T., C. A. PHILLIPS, AND E. J. HESKE. 1998. A riparian zone in southern Illinois as a potential dispersal corridor for reptiles and amphibians. Biological Conservation 86:107–115.

BURGER, J. 1985. Habitat selection in temperate marsh-nesting birds. Pages 253–281 *in* M. L. Cody, editor. Habitat selection in birds. Academic Press, Orlando, Florida, USA.

BURKE, V., AND J. W. GIBBONS. 1995. Terrestrial buffer zones and wetland conservation: a case study of freshwater turtles in a Carolina bay. Conservation Biology 9:1365–1369.

———, ———, AND J. L. GREENE. 1994. Prolonged nesting forays by common mud turtles (*Kinosternon subrubrum*). American Midland Naturalist 131:190–195.

———, J. L. GREENE, AND J. W. GIBBONS. 1995. The effect of sample size and study duration on metapopulation estimates for slider turtles (*Trachemys scripta*). Herpetologica 51:451–456.

BURKHAM, D. E. 1988. Methods for delineating flood-prone areas in the Great Basin of Nevada and adjacent sites. U.S. Department of the Interior, Geological Survey, Water Supply Paper 2316.

BURTON, T. M., AND G. E. LIKENS. 1975. Energy flow and nutrient cycling in salamander populations in the Hubbard Brook Experimental Forest, New Hampshire. Ecology 56:1068–1080.

BURWELL, R. W., AND L. G. SUGDEN. 1964. Potholes—going, going.... Pages 369–380 *in* J. P. Linduska, editor. Waterfowl tomorrow. U.S. Department of the Interior, Fish and Wildlife Service, Washington, D.C., USA.

BUSACCA, A. J. 1991. Loess deposits and soils of the Palouse and vicinity. Pages 216–228 *in* R. B. Morrison, editor. Quaternary non-glacial geology of the United States. Geology of North America. Volume K-2. Geological Society of America, Boulder, Colorado, USA.

BUTLER, R. W. 1992. Great blue heron. Number 25 *in* A. Poole, P. Stettenheim, and F. Gill, editors. The birds of North America. The Academy of Natural Sciences, Philadelphia, Pennsylvania, and The American Ornithologists' Union, Washington, D.C., USA.

CALDWELL, M. M. 1985. Cold desert. Pages 198–212 *in* B. F. Chabot and H. Mooney, editors. Physiological ecology of North American plant communities. Chapman and Hall, London, United Kingdom.

CAREY, C. L., N. COHEN, AND L. ROLLINS-SMITH. 1999. Amphibian declines: an immunological perspective. Developmental and Comparative Immunology 23:459–472.

CARPENTER, C. C. 1953. A study of hibernacula and hibernating associations of snakes and amphibians in Michigan. Ecology 34:74–80.

CHOI, Y., Y. WANG, Y. HSIEH, AND L. ROBINSON. 2001. Vegetation succession and carbon sequestration in a coastal wetland in northwest Florida: evidence from carbon isotopes. Global Biogeochemical Cycles 15:311–319.

COLLON, E. G., AND J. VELASQUEZ. 1989. Dispersion, germination and growth of seedlings of *Sagittaria lancifolia* L. Folia Geobotanica et Phytotaxonomica 24:37–49.

COMSTOCK, J. P., AND J. R. EHLERINGER. 1992. Plant adaptation in the Great Basin and Colorado Plateau. Great Basin Naturalist 52:195–215.

COOPER, D. J. 1986. Community structure and classification of Rocky Mountain wetland ecosystems. Pages 66–147 *in* J. T. Windell, B. E. Willard, D. J. Cooper, S. Q. Foster, C. F. Knud-Hansen, L. P. Rink, and G. N. Kiladis, editors. An ecological characterization of Rocky Mountain montane and subalpine wetlands. U.S. Department of the Interior, Fish and Wildlife Service, Biological Report 86.

CORDELL, H. K., AND N. G. HERBERT. 2002. The popularity of birding is still growing. Birding 34:54–61.

COSTANZA, R., S. C. FARBER, AND J. MAXWELL. 1989. Valuation and management of wetland ecosystems. Ecological Economics 1:335–361.

COURCELLES, R., AND J. BEDARD. 1979. Habitat selection by dabbling ducks in the Baie Noire marsh, southwestern Quebec. Canadian Journal of Zoology 57:2230–2238.

COWARDIN, L. M., AND F. C. GOLET. 1995. U.S. Fish and Wildlife Service 1979 wetland classification: a review. Vegetatio 118:139–152.

———, D. S. GILMER, AND C. W. SHAIFFER. 1985. Mallard recruitment in the agricultural environment of North Dakota. Wildlife Monographs 92.

———, V. CARTER, F. C. GOLET, AND E. T. LAROE. 1979. Classification of wetlands and deepwater habitats of the United States. U.S. Department of the Interior, Fish and Wildlife Service, Publication FWS/OBS-79-31.

CRONK, J. K., AND M. S. FENNESSY. 2001. Wetland plants: biology and ecology. Lewis Publishers, New York, USA.

DACHNOWSKI, A. P. 1920. Peat deposits in the United States and their classification. Soil Science 10:453–456.

DAHL, T. E. 1990. Wetlands losses in the United States 1780's to 1980's. U.S. Department of the Interior, Fish and Wildlife Service, Washington, D.C., USA.

———. 2000. Status and trends of wetlands in the conterminous United States 1986 to 1997. U.S. Department of the Interior, Fish and Wildlife Service, Washington, D.C., USA.

———, AND G. J. ALLORD. 1997. Technical aspects of wetlands: history of wetlands in the conterminous United States. National water summary: wetland resources. U.S. Department of the Interior, Geological Survey, Water-Supply Paper 2425.

———, AND C. E. JOHNSON. 1991. Status and trends of wetlands in the conterminous United States, mid-1970's to mid-1980's. U.S. Department of the Interior, Fish and Wildlife Service, Washington, D.C., USA.

DALE, J. M., B. FREEDMAN, AND J. KEREKES. 1985. Acidity and associated water chemistry of amphibian habitats in Nova Scotia. Canadian Journal of Zoology 63:97–105.

DAUBENMIRE, R. F. 1942. An ecological study of the vegetation of southeastern Washington and adjacent Idaho. Ecological Monographs 12:55–79.

DAVIDSON, L. M. 1992. Black rail, *Laterallus jamaicensis*. Pages 119–134 *in* K. J. Schneider and D. M. Pence, editors. Migratory nongame birds of management concern in the Northeast. U.S. Department of the Interior, Fish and Wildlife Service, Newton Corner, Massachusetts, USA.

DAVIS, JR., W. E., AND J. A. KUSHLAN. 1994. Green heron. Number 129 *in* A. Poole and F. Gill, editors. The birds of North America. The Academy of Natural Sciences, Philadelphia, Pennsylvania, and The American Ornithologists' Union, Washington, D.C., USA.

DEBENEDICTIS, P. A. 1974. Interspecific competition between tadpoles of *Rana pipiens* and *Rana sylvatica*: an experimental field study. Ecological Monographs 44:129–151.

DEEGAN, L. A., J. T. FINN, S. G. AYVAZIAN, C. A. RYDER-KIEFFER, AND J. BUONACCORSI. 1997. Development and validation of an estuarine biotic integrity index. Estuaries 20:601–617.

DELFINO, J. J., AND H. T. ODUM. 1993. Wetland retention of lead from a hazardous waste site. Bulletin of Environmental Contaminants and Toxicology 51:430.

DELNICKI, D., AND K. J. REINECKE. 1986. Mid-winter food use and body weights of mallards and wood ducks in Mississippi. Journal of Wildlife Management 50:43–51.

DICKMAN, M. 1968. The effect of grazing by tadpoles on the structure of a periphyton community. Ecology 49:1188–1190.

DIETER, C. D. 1991. Water turbidity in tilled and untilled prairie wetlands. Journal of Freshwater Ecology 6:185–89.

DOBROWOLSKI, J. P., M. M. CALDWELL, AND J. H. RICHARDS. 1990. Basin hydrology and plant root systems. Ecological Studies 80:243–292.

DROBNEY, R. D., AND L. H. FREDRICKSON. 1979. Food selection by wood ducks in relation to breeding status. Journal of Wildlife Management 43:109–120.

DUEBBERT, H. F., AND J. T. LOKEMOEN. 1976. Duck nesting in fields of undisturbed grass-legume cover. Journal of Wildlife Management 40:39–49.

DUFFY, C. J., AND S. AL-HASSAN. 1988. Groundwater circulation in a closed desert basin: topographic scaling and climatic forcing. Water Resources Research 24:1675–1678.

DUNCAN, D. C. 1987. Nest-site distribution and overland brood movements of northern pintails in Alberta. Journal of Wildlife Management 51:716–723.

EAKIN, T. E., D. PRICE, AND J. R. HARRILL. 1976. Summary appraisals of the nation's groundwater resources – Great Basin Region. U.S. Department of the Interior, Geological Survey, Professional Paper 813-G, Washington, D.C., USA.

EDDLEMAN, W. R., AND C. J. CONWAY. 1998. Clapper rail. Number 340 in A. Poole and F. Gill, editors. The birds of North America. The Academy of Natural Sciences, Philadelphia, Pennsylvania, and The American Ornithologists' Union, Washington, D.C., USA.

EHLERINGER, J. 1985. Annuals and perennials of warm deserts. Pages 162–180 in B. F. Chabot and H. A. Mooney, editors. Physiological ecology of North American plant communities. Chapman and Hall, New York, USA.

———, S. L. PHILLIPS, W. S. F. SCHUSTER, AND D. R. SANDQUIST. 1991. Differential utilization of summer rains by desert plants. Oecologia 88:430–434.

EHRLICH, P. R., D. S. DOBKIN, AND D. WHEYE. 1988. The birder's handbook. Simon and Schuster, New York, USA.

ELDRIDGE, J. 1990. Aquatic invertebrates important for waterfowl production. U.S. Department of the Interior, Fish and Wildlife Service, Waterfowl Management Handbook, Leaflet 13.3.3.

ELPHICK, C. S., AND L. W. ORING. 1998. Winter management of California rice fields for waterbirds. Journal of Applied Ecology 35: 95–108.

ERICKSON, N. W., AND D. M. LESLIE. 1987. Soil-vegetation correlations in the Sandhills and Rainwater Basin wetlands of Nebraska. U.S. Department of the Interior, Fish and Wildlife Service, Biological Report 87(11).

ERICKSON, R. E. 1979. Federal programs influencing wetlands. Proceedings of the Seventh Annual Michigan Land Use Policy Conference. Michigan State University, East Lansing, USA.

———, R. L. LINDER, AND K. W. HARMON. 1979. Stream channelization (P.L. 83–566) increased wetland losses in the Dakotas. Wildlife Society Bulletin 7:71–78.

ERNST, C. H., J. E. LOVICH, AND R. W. BARBOUR. 1994. Turtles of the United States and Canada. Smithsonian Institution Press, Washington, D.C., USA.

ERRINGTON, P. L. 1963. The pricelessness of untampered nature. Journal of Wildlife Management 27:313–320.

EULISS, JR., N. H., D. M. MUSHET, AND D. H. JOHNSON. 2002. Use of aquatic invertebrates to delineate seasonal and temporary wetlands in the prairie pothole region of North America. Wetlands 22:256–262.

FEDERAL INTERAGENCY COMMITTEE FOR WETLAND DELINEATION. 1989. Federal manual for identifying and delineating jurisdictional wetlands. Cooperative Technical Publication. U.S. Department of the Army, Corps of Engineers, U.S. Environmental Protection Agency, U.S. Department of the Interior, Fish and Wildlife Service, and U.S. Department of Agriculture, Soil Conservation Service, Washington, D.C., USA.

FEDERAL REGISTER. 1995. Federal guidance for the establishment, use and operation of mitigation banks. Federal Register 60:43.

FEIERABEND, S. J., AND J. M. ZELAZNY. 1987. Status report on our Nation's wetlands. National Wildlife Federation, Washington, D.C., USA.

FENNEMAN, N. M. 1931. Physiography of the western United States. McGraw-Hill Book Co., New York, USA.

FIERO, B. 1986. Geology of the Great Basin. University of Nevada Press, Reno, USA.

FINLAYSON, C. M., AND A. G. VAN DER VALK, editors. 1995. Classification and inventory of the world's wetlands. Kluwer Academic Publishers, Dordrecht, The Netherlands.

FISCHER, R. A., AND J. C. FISCHENICH. 2000. Design recommendations for riparian corridors and vegetated buffer strips. EMRRP Technical Notes Collection (TN EMRRP-SR-24). U.S. Department of the Army, Corps of Engineers, Research and Development Center, Vicksburg, Mississippi, USA.

FISCHER, T. D. 1998. Anura of eastern South Dakota: their distribution and characteristics of their wetland habitats, 1997–1998. Thesis. South Dakota State University, Brookings, USA.

FISHBECK, D. W. 1968. A study of some phases in the ecology of *Rana sylvatica* Le Conte. Dissertation. University of Minnesota, Minneapolis, USA.

FRAYER, W. E., D. D. PETERS, AND H. R. PYWELL. 1989. Wetlands of the California Central Valley: status and trends 1939 to mid-1980's. U.S.

Department of the Interior, Fish and Wildlife Service, Portland, Oregon, USA.

———, T. J. MONAHAN, D. C. BOWDEN, AND F. A. GRAYBILL. 1983. Status and trends of wetlands and deepwater habitats in the conterminous United States:1950's to 1970's. Department of Forest and Wood Science, Colorado State University, Fort Collins, USA.

FREDRICKSON, L. H. 1979. Impact of water management on the resources of lowland hardwood forests. Pages 51–64 in R. A. Chabreck and R. H. Mills, editors. Proceedings of the 29th Annual Forest Symposium. Louisiana State University, Baton Rouge, USA.

———. 1991. Strategies for water level manipulations in moist-soil systems. U.S. Department of the Interior, Fish and Wildlife Service, Waterfowl Management Handbook, Leaflet 13.4.6.

———, AND M. E. HEITMEYER. 1988. Waterfowl use of forested wetlands of the southern United States: an overview. Pages 307–323 in M. W. Weller, editor. Waterfowl in winter. University of Minnesota Press, Minneapolis, USA.

———, AND M. K. LAUBHAN. 1994. Intensive wetland management: a key to biodiversity. Transactions of the North American Wildlife and Natural Resources Conference 59:555–565.

———, AND F. A. REID. 1986. Wetland and riparian habitats: a nongame overview. Pages 58–96 in J. B. Hale, L. B. Best, and R. L. Clawson, editors. Management of nongame wildlife in the Midwest: a developing art. North Central Section, The Wildlife Society, Grand Rapids, Michigan, USA.

———, AND ———. 1988a. Invertebrate response to wetland management. U.S. Department of the Interior, Fish and Wildlife Service, Waterfowl Management Handbook, Leaflet 13.3.1.

———, AND ———. 1988b. Waterfowl use of wetland complexes. U.S. Department of the Interior, Fish and Wildlife Service, Waterfowl Management Handbook, Leaflet 13.2.1.

———, AND ———. 1990. Impacts of hydrologic alteration on management of freshwater wetlands. Pages 72–90 in J. M. Sweeney, editor. Management of dynamic ecosystems. North Central Section, The Wildlife Society, Springfield, Illinois, USA.

———, AND T. S. TAYLOR. 1982. Management of seasonally flooded impoundments for wildlife. U.S. Department of the Interior, Fish and Wildlife Service, Resource Publication 148.

GADDIE, R. K., AND J. L. REGENS. 2000. Regulating wetland protection: environmental federalism and the states. State University of New York Press, Albany, USA.

GALAT, D. L., L. H. FREDRICKSON, D. D. HUMBURG, K. J. BATAILLE, J. R. BODIE, J. DOHRENWEND, G. T. GELWICKS, J. E. HAVEL, D. L. HELMERS, J. B. HOOKER, J. R. JONES, M. S. KNOWLTON, J. KUBISIAK, J. MAZOUREK, A. C. MCCOLPIN, R. B. RENKIN, AND R. D. SEMLITSCH. 1998. Flooding to restore connectivity of regulated, large-river wetlands: natural and controlled flooding as complimentary processes along the lower Missouri River. BioScience 48:721–733

GAMBRELL, R. P. 1994. Trace and toxic metals in wetlands: a review. Journal of Environmental Quality 23:883–892.

———, AND W. H. PATRICK, JR. 1978. Chemical and microbiological properties of anaerobic soils and sediments. Pages 375–423 in D. D. Hook and R. M. M. Crawford, editors. Plant life in anaerobic environments. Scientific Publications, Ann Arbor, Michigan, USA.

GIBBONS, J. W., AND P. W. STANGEL, editors. 1999. Conserving amphibians and reptiles in the new millennium. Proceedings of the Partners in Amphibian and Reptile Conservation (PARC) Conference. Herp Outreach Publication Number 2. Savannah River Ecology Laboratory, Atlanta, Georgia, USA.

———, D. E. SCOTT, T. J. RYAN, K. A. BUHLMANN, T. D. TUBERVILLE, B. S. METTS, J. L. GREENE, T. MILLS, Y. LEIDEN, S. POPPY, AND C. T. WINNE. 2000. The global decline of reptiles, déjà vu amphibians. BioScience 50:653–666.

GIBBS, J. P. 1993. Importance of small wetlands for the persistence of local populations of wetland-associated animals. Wetlands 13:25–31.

———, S. MELVIN, AND F. A. REID. 1992a. American bittern. Number 18 in A. Poole, P. Stettenheim, and F. Gill, editors. The birds of North America. The Academy of Natural Sciences, Philadelphia, Pennsylvania, and The American Ornithologists' Union, Washington, D.C., USA.

———, F. A. REID, AND S. MELVIN. 1992b. Least bittern. Number 17 in A. Poole, P. Stettenheim, and F. Gill, editors. The birds of North America. The Academy of Natural Sciences, Philadelphia, Pennsylvania, and The American Ornithologists' Union, Washington, D.C., USA.

GILLIAM, J. W. 1994. Riparian wetlands and water quality. Journal of

Environmental Quality 23:896–900.

GLEASON, R. A., AND N. H. EULISS, JR. 1998. Sedimentation of prairie wetlands. Great Plains Research 8:97–112.

GLOVER, F. A. 1953. Nesting ecology of the pied-billed grebe in northwestern Iowa. Wilson Bulletin 65:32–39.

GODFREY, A. E. 1980. Porphyry weathering in a desert climate. Pages 189–196 in M. D. Picard, editor. Henry Mountains Symposium. Utah Geological Association, Salt Lake City, USA.

GOLDSBOROUGH, G. 2001. Sampling algae in wetlands. Pages 263–295 in R. B. Rader, D. P. Batzer, and S. Wissinger, editors. Biomonitoring and management of North American freshwater wetlands. John Wiley and Sons, New York, USA.

GOPAL, B. R., R. E. TURNER, R. G. WETZEL, AND D. F. WHIGHAM. 1982. Wetlands: ecology and management. Proceedings of the First International Wetlands Conference, New Delhi, India. National Institute of Ecology and International Scientific Publications, Juipur, India.

GOSSELINK, J. G., AND R. E. TURNER. 1978. The role of hydrology in freshwater wetland ecosystems. Pages 63–78 in R. E. Good, editor. Freshwater wetlands: ecological processes and management potential. Academic Press, New York, USA.

———, L. C. LEE, AND T. A. MUIR. 1990a. Ecological processes and cumulative impacts. Lewis Publishers, Chelsea, Michigan, USA.

———, G. P. SHAFFER, L. C. LEE, D. M. BURDICK, D. L. CHILDERS, N. C. LEIBOWITZ, S. C. HAMILTON, R. BOUMANS, D. CUSHMAN, S. FIELDS, M. KOCH, AND J. M. VISSER. 1990b. Landscape conservation in a forested wetland watershed. BioScience 40:588–600.

GOUDIE, A. S. 1991. Pans. Progress in Physical Geology 15:221–237.

GREENBERG, R. 1988. Water as a habitat cue for breeding swamp and song sparrows. Condor 90:420–427.

GREENWOOD, R. J., A. B. SARGEANT, D. H. JOHNSON, L. COWARDIN. 1987. Mallard nest success and recruitment in prairie Canada. Transactions of the North American Wildlife and Natural Resources Conference 52:298–309.

GROVER, A. M., AND G. A. BALDASSARRE. 1995. Bird species richness within beaver ponds in south-central New York. Wetlands 15:108–118.

GROVER, M. C. 2000. Determinants of salamander distributions along moisture gradients. Copeia 2000:156–168.

GRUBB, P. 1977. The maintenance of species richness in plant communities: the importance of the regeneration niche. Biological Reviews 52:107–145.

GRUE, C. E., M. W. TOME, T. A. MESSMER, D. B. HENRY, G. A. SWANSON, AND L. R. DEWEESE. 1989. Agricultural chemicals and prairie pothole wetlands: meeting the needs of the resource and the farmer – U.S. perspective. Transactions of the North American Wildlife and Natural Resources Conference 54:43–58.

H. JOHN HEINZ III CENTER FOR SCIENCE, ECONOMICS AND THE ENVIRONMENT. 2002. The state of the nation's ecosystems: measuring the lands, waters, and living resources of the United States. Cambridge University Press, New York, USA.

HAIG, S. M., L. W. ORING, P. M. SANZENBACHER, AND O. W. TAFT. 2002. Space use, migratory connectivity, and population segregation among willets breeding in the western Great Basin. Condor 104:620–630.

HAMMER, D. A., AND R. K. BASTIAN. 1989. Wetland ecosystems: natural water purifiers? Pages 5–19 in D. A. Hammer, editor. Constructed wetlands for wastewater treatment: municipal, industrial, and agricultural. Lewis Publishers, Chelsea, Michigan, USA.

HARPER, K. T., L. L. ST. CLAIR, K. H. THORNE, AND W. M. HESS. 1994. Geologic contrasts of the Great Basin and Colorado Plateau. Pages 1–7 in K. T. Harper, L. L. St. Clair, K. H. Thorne, and W. M. Hess, editors. Natural history of the Colorado Plateau and Great Basin. University Press of Colorado, Niwot, USA.

HARRIS, S. W. 1954. An ecological study of the waterfowl of the potholes area, Grant County, Washington. American Midland Naturalist 52:403–432.

HAYMAN, P., J. MARCHANT, AND T. PRATER. 1986. Shorebirds: an identification guide to the waders of the world. Houghton Mifflin Company, Boston, Massachusetts, USA.

HECNAR, S. J., AND R. T. MCCLOSKEY. 1996. Amphibian species richness and distribution in relation to pond water chemistry in southwestern Ontario, Canada. Freshwater Biology 36:7–15.

HEITMEYER, M. E., L. H. FREDRICKSON, B. EDERINGTON, AND S. L. KING. 2002. An evaluation of ecosystem restoration options for the Bayou Meto region of Arkansas. Special Publication Number 5. University of Missouri, Gaylord Memorial Laboratory, Puxico, USA.

HELMERS, D. L. 1992. Shorebird management manual. Western Hemisphere Shorebird Reserve Network, Manomet, Massachusetts, USA.

HEYER, W. R., R. W. MCDIARMID, AND D. L. WEIGMANN. 1975. Tadpoles, predation, and pond habitats in the tropics. Biotropica 7:100–111.

HIDY, G. M., AND H. E. KLIEFORTH. 1990. Atmospheric processes and the climates of the Basin and Range. Ecological Studies 80:17–45.

HIGGINS, K. F, D. E. NAUGLE, AND K. J. FORMAN. 2002. A case study of changing land use practices in the northern Great Plains, U.S.A.: an uncertain future for waterbird conservation. Waterbirds 25:42–50.

HINES, J. E. 1977. Nesting and brood ecology of lesser scaup at waterhen marsh, Saskatchewan. Canadian Field-Naturalist 91:248–255.

HOLLING, C. S., editor. 1978. Adaptive environmental assessment and management. John Wiley and Sons, New York, USA.

HOLLIS, G. E. 1998. Future wetlands in a world short of water. Pages 5–18 in A. J. McComb and J. A. Davis, editors. Wetlands for the future. Gleneagles Publishing, Glen Osmond, Australia.

HOLMES, R. T., AND F. A. PITELKA. 1998. Pectoral sandpiper. Number 348 in A. Poole and F. Gill, editors. The birds of North America. The Academy of Natural Sciences, Philadelphia, Pennsylvania, and The American Ornithologists' Union, Washington, D.C., USA.

HOOVER, J. J., AND K. J. KILLGORE. 1998. Fish communities. Pages 237–260 in M. G. Messina and W. H. Conner, editors. Southern forested wetlands. Lewis Publishers, Boca Raton, Florida, USA.

HUNER, J. V., C. W. JESKE, AND W. NORLING. 2002. Managing agricultural wetlands for waterbirds in the coastal regions of Louisiana, U.S.A. Waterbirds 25:66–78.

HUNTER, W. C., D. N. PASHLEY, AND R. E. ESCANO. 1993. Neotropical migratory landbird species and their habitats of special concern within the southeast region. Pages 159–171 in D. M. Finch and P. W. Stangel, editors. Status and management of neotropical migratory birds. U.S. Department of Agriculture, Forest Service, General Technical Report RM-229.

HUPP, C. R. 2000. Hydrology, geomorphology, and vegetation of Coastal Plain rivers in the southeastern USA. Hydrological Processes 14:2991–3010.

INTERNATIONAL UNION FOR THE CONSERVATION OF NATURE. 2000. Available online at http://www.iucn.org/themes/ssc/96anrl/dtable1.htm (accessed June 2003).

JOHNSGARD, P. A. 1956. Effects of water fluctuation and vegetation change on bird populations, particularly waterfowl. Ecology 37:689–701.

JOHNSON, G. 2000a. Spatial ecology of the eastern massasauga (Sistrurus c. catenatus) in a New York peatland. Journal of Herpetology 34:1 86–192.

JOHNSON, L. E., AND D. K. PADILLA. 1996. Geographic spread of exotic species: ecological lessons and opportunities from the invasion of the zebra mussel Dreissena polymorpha. Biological Conservation 78:23–33.

JOHNSON, R. L. 1979. Timber harvests from wetlands. Pages 598–605 in P. E. Greeson, J. R. Clark, and G. E. Clark, editors. Wetlands functions and values: the state of our understanding. American Water Resource Association, Minneapolis, Minnesota, USA.

———, S. W. CAROTHERS, AND J. M. SIMPSON. 1984. A riparian classification system. Pages 375–382 in R. E. Warner and K. M. Hendrix, editors. Californian riparian systems. University of California Press, Berkeley, USA.

JOHNSON, R. R., AND J. J. DINSMORE. 1985. Brood-rearing and postbreeding habitat use by Virginia rails and soras. Wilson Bulletin 97:551–554.

JOHNSON, W. C. 2000b. Tree recruitment and survival in rivers: influences of hydrological processes. Hydrological Processes 14:3051–3074.

JOHNSTON, C. A. 1991. Sediment and nutrient retention by freshwater wetlands: effects on surface water quality. Critical Reviews in Environmental Control 21:491–565.

———, N. E. DETENBECK, AND G. J. NIEMI. 1990. The cumulative effect of wetlands on stream water quality and quantity: a landscape approach. Biogeochemistry 10:105–141.

JURIK, T. W., S. WANG, AND A. G. VAN DER VALK. 1994. Effects of sediment load on seedling emergence from wetland seed banks. Wetlands 14:159–165.

KADLEC, J. A. 1982. Mechanisms affecting salinity of Great Salt Lake marshes. American Midland Naturalist 107:82–94.

KAMINSKI, R. M., AND H. H. PRINCE. 1981. Dabbling duck activity and foraging responses to aquatic macroinvertebrates. Auk 98:115–126.

——, AND M. W. WELLER. 1992. Breeding habitats of nearctic water-fowl. Pages 568–589 in B. D. J. Batt, A. D. Afton, M. G. Anderson, C. D. Ankney, D. H. Johnson, J. A. Kadlec, and G. L. Krapu, editors. Ecology and management of breeding waterfowl. University of Minnesota Press, Minneapolis, USA.

KANTRUD, H. A., G. L. KRAPU, AND G. A. SWANSON. 1989. Prairie basin wetlands of the Dakotas: a community profile. U.S. Department of the Interior, Fish and Wildlife Service, Biological Report 85.

KARR, J. R. 1981. Assessment of biotic integrity using fish communities. Fisheries 6(6):21–27.

——. 1991. Biological integrity: a long-neglected aspect of water resource management. Ecological Applications 1:66–84.

——, AND D. R. DUDLEY. 1981. Ecological perspective on water quality goals. Environmental Management 5:55–68.

KELLISON, R. C., M. J. YOUNG, R. R. BRAHAM, AND E. J. JONES. 1998. Major alluvial floodplains. Pages 291–323 in M. G. Messina and W. H. Conner, editors. Southern forested wetlands. Lewis Publishers, Boca Raton, USA.

KING, S. L., AND L. H. FREDRICKSON. 1998. Bottomland hardwood guidebook: the decision-making process, design, management, and monitoring of GTRs. U.S. Environmental Protection Agency, Dallas, Texas. USA.

——, AND B. D. KEELAND. 1999. Evaluation of reforestation in the lower Mississippi River Alluvial Valley. Restoration Ecology 7:348–359.

KINGSBURY, B. A., AND C. J. COPPOLA. 2000. Hibernacula of the copper-belly watersnake (*Nerodia erythrogaster neglecta*) in southern Indiana and Kentucky. Journal of Herpetology 34:294–298.

KLEISS, B. A. 1996. Sediment retention in a bottomland hardwood wetland in eastern Arkansas. Wetlands 16:321–333.

KLETT, A. T., T. L. SHAFFER, AND D. H. JOHNSON. 1988. Duck nest success in the Prairie Pothole Region. Journal of Wildlife Management 52:431–440.

KLIMAS, C. V., R. D. SMITH, AND J. RAASCH. 2005. Hydrogeomorphic classification of forested wetlands in the Lower Mississippi Valley. Pages 77–92 in L. H. Fredrickson, R. M. Kaminski, and S. L. King, editors. Ecology and management of bottomland hardwood systems: the state of our understanding. University of Missouri-Columbia, Gaylord Memorial Laboratory, Puxico, Missouri, USA.

KNOPF, F. L., R. R. JOHNSON, T. RICH, F. B. SAMSON, AND R. C. SZARO. 1988. Conservation of riparian ecosystems in the United States. Wilson Bulletin 100:272–284.

KNUD-HANSEN, C. F. 1986. Ecological processes in Rocky Mountain wetlands. Pages 148–176 in J. T. Windell, B. E. Willard, D. J. Cooper, S. Q. Foster, C. F. Knud-Hansen, L. P. Rink, and G. N. Kiladis, editors. An ecological characterization of Rocky Mountain montane and subalpine wetlands. U.S. Department of the Interior, Fish and Wildlife Service, Biological Report 86.

KORTE, P. A., AND L. H. FREDRICKSON. 1977. Loss of Missouri's lowland hardwood ecosystem. Transactions of the North American Wildlife and Natural Resources Conference 42:31–41.

KRAPU, G. L., AND K. J. REINECKE. 1992. Foraging ecology and nutrition. Pages 1–29 in B. D. J. Batt, A. D. Afton, M. G. Anderson, C. D. Ankney, D. H. Johnson, J. A. Kadlec, and G. L. Krapu, editors. Ecology and management of breeding waterfowl. University of Minnesota Press, Minneapolis, USA.

KUSHLAN, J. A. 2000. Heron feeding habitat conservation. Pages 219–235 in J. A. Kushlan and H. Hafner, editors. Heron conservation. Academic Press, London, United Kingdom.

——, AND K. L. BILDSTEIN. 1992. White ibis. Number 9 in A. Poole, P. Stettenheim, and F. Gill, editors. The birds of North America. The Academy of Natural Sciences, Philadelphia, Pennsylvania, and The American Ornithologists' Union, Washington, D.C., USA.

——, AND H. HAFNER. 2000. Heron conservation. Academic Press. London, United Kingdom.

——, M. J. STEINKAMP, K. C. PARSONS, J. CAPP, M. ACOSTA CRUZ, M. COULTER, I. DAVIDSON, L. DICKSON, N. EDELSON, R. ELLIOT, R. M. ERWIN, S. HATCH, S. KRESS, R. MILKO, S. MILLER, K. MILLS, R. PAUL, R. PHILLIPS, J. E. SALIVA, B. SYDEMAN, J. TRAPP, J. WHEELER, AND K. WOHL. 2002. Waterbird conservation for the Americas: the North American waterbird conservation plan. Version 1. Waterbird Conservation for the Americas, Washington, D.C., USA.

KUSLER, J. 1985. A call for action: protection of riparian habitat in the arid and semi-arid West. Pages 6–8 in R. R. Johnson, C. D. Ziebell, D. R. Patton, P. F. Folliott, and R. H. Hamre, technical coordinators. Riparian ecosystems and their management: reconciling conflicting

uses. U.S. Department of Agriculture, Forest Service, General Technical Report RM-120.

LAMKE, R. D., AND D. O. MOORE. 1965. Interim inventory of surface water resources of Nevada. Water Resources Bulletin 30. Nevada Department of Conservation and Natural Resources, Reno, USA.

LAUBHAN, M. K., AND L. H. FREDRICKSON. 1997. Wetlands of the Great Plains: habitat characteristics and vertebrate aggregations. Ecological Studies 125:20–48.

——, AND J. E. ROELLE. 2001. Managing wetlands for waterbirds. Pages 387–411 in R. B. Rader, D. P. Batzer, and S. Wissinger, editors. Biomonitoring and management of North American freshwater wetlands. John Wiley and Sons, New York, USA.

LEAF, C. F. 1975. Watershed management in the central and southern Rocky Mountains: a summary of the status of our knowledge by vegetation types. U.S. Department of Agriculture, Forest Service, Research Paper RM-142.

LEOPOLD, L. B., M. G. WOLMAN, AND J. P. MILLER. 1964. Fluvial processes in geo-morphology. W. H. Freeman and Company, San Francisco, California, USA.

LESCHINE, T. M., K. F. WELLMAN, AND T. H. GREEN. 1997. The economic value of wetlands: wetlands' role in flood protection. Final Report. Ecology Publication Number 97–100. Washington State Department of Ecology, Northwest Regional Office, Bellevue, USA.

LIVINGSTON, R. J., AND O. L. LOUCKS. 1979. Productivity, trophic interactions, and food web relationships in wetlands and associated systems. Pages 101–119 in P. E. Greeson, J. R. Clark, and J. E. Clark, editors. Wetland functions and values: the state of our understanding. American Water Resources Technical Publication 79–2. Minneapolis, Minnesota, USA.

LOKEMOEN, J. T., H. F. DUEBBERT, AND D. E. SHARP. 1984. Nest spacing, habitat selection, and behavior of waterfowl on Miller Lake Island, North Dakota. Journal of Wildlife Management 48:309–321.

LONGCORE, J. R., R. K. ROSS, AND K. L. FISHER. 1987. Wildlife resources at risk through acidification of wetlands. Transactions of the North American Wildlife and Natural Resources Conference 52:608–618.

LOWE, C. H., R. R. JOHNSON, AND P. S. BENNETT. 1986. Riparian lands are wetlands: the problem of applying eastern American concepts and criteria to environments in the North America southwest. Pages 89–100 in Hydrology and water resources in Arizona and the southwest. Proceeding of the American Water Resources Association, Arizona Section, Tucson, USA.

LUO, H., L. M. SMITH, D. A. HAUKOS, AND B. L. ALLEN. 1997. Sources of recently deposited sediments in playa wetlands. Wetlands 19:176–181.

MABBUTT, J. 1979. Desert landforms. Massachusetts Institute of Technology Press, Cambridge, USA.

MACINTYRE, H. L., R. J. GEIDER, AND D. C. MILLER. 1996. Microphytobenthos: the ecological role of the "secret garden" of unvegetated, shallow water marine habitats. I. Distribution, abundance, and primary production. Estuaries 19:186–201.

MADER, S. F. 1991. Forested wetlands classification and mapping: a literature review. Technical Bulletin Number 606. National Council of the Paper Industry for Air and Stream Improvement, Inc., New York, USA.

MADISON, D. M. 1997. The emigration of radio-implanted spotted salamanders, *Ambystoma maculatum*. Journal of Herpetology 31:542–552.

MAGEE, D. W. 1996. The hydrogeomorphic approach: a different perspective. Bulletin of the Society of Wetland Scientists 13:12–14.

MAPLE, W. T, AND L. P. ORR. 1968. Overwinter adaptations of *Sistrurus c. catenatus* in northeastern Ohio. Journal of Herpetology 2:179–180.

MARBLE, A. D. 1992. A guide to wetland functional design. Lewis Publishers, Chelsea, Michigan, USA.

MARSH, D. M., AND P. C. TRENHAM. 2001. Metapopulation dynamics and amphibian conservation. Conservation Biology 15:40–49.

MEANLEY, B. M. 1992. King rail. Number 3 in A. Poole, P. Stettenheim, and F. Gill, editors. The birds of North America. The Academy of Natural Sciences, Philadelphia, Pennsylvania, and The American Ornithologists' Union, Washington, D.C., USA.

MERRELL, D. J. 1977. Life history of the leopard frog, *Rana pipiens*, in Minnesota. Occasional Papers 15. Bell Museum of Natural History, Minneapolis, USA.

MIDDLETON, B. A., A. G. VAN DER VALK, R. L. WILLIAMS, AND D. H. MASON. 1992. Litter decomposition in an Indian monsoonal wetland overgrown with *Paspalum distichum*. Wetlands 12:37–44.

MINOT, E. O. 1980. Tidal, diurnal and habitat influences on common eider rearing activities. Ornis Scandinavia 11:165–172.

MITSCH, W. J., AND J. G. GOSSELINK. 1993. Wetlands. Second edition. Van Nostrand Reinhold, New York, USA.

———, AND ———. 2000. Wetlands. Third edition. John Wiley and Sons, New York, USA.

———, AND R. F. WILSON. 1996. Improving the success of wetland creation and restoration with know-how, time, and self design. Ecological Applications 6:77–83.

MONDA, M. J., AND J. T. RATTI. 1988. Niche overlap and habitat use by sympatric duck broods in eastern Washington. Journal of Wildlife Management 52:95–103.

MORIN, P. J. 1981. Predatory salamanders reverse the outcome of competition among three species of anuran tadpoles. Science 212: 1284–1286.

MOTT, D. F., R. R. WEST, J. W. DE GRAZIO, AND J. L. GUARINO. 1972. Foods of the red-winged blackbird in Brown County, South Dakota. Journal of Wildlife Management 36:983–987.

MOWBRAY, T. B. 1997. Swamp sparrow. Number 279 *in* A. Poole and F. Gill, editors. The birds of North America. The Academy of Natural Sciences, Philadelphia, Pennsylvania, and The American Ornithologists' Union, Washington, D.C., USA.

MUELLER, M. H., AND A. G. VAN DER VALK. 2002. The potential role of ducks in wetland seed dispersal. Wetlands 22:170–178.

MURDOCH, A. J., AND R. H. ELLIS. 1992. Longevity, viability and dormancy. Pages 193–229 *in* M. Fenner, editor. Seeds. The ecology of regeneration in plant communities. Wallingford, Cab International, United Kingdom.

MURKIN, E. J., H. R. MURKIN, AND R. D. TITMAN. 1992. Nektonic invertebrate abundance and distribution at the emergent vegetation-open water interface in the Delta Marsh, Manitoba, Canada. Wetlands 12: 45–52.

MURKIN, H. R. 1989. The basis for food chains in prairie wetlands. Pages 316–338 *in* A. van der Valk, editor. Northern prairie wetlands. Iowa State University Press, Ames, USA.

NAIMAN, R. J., AND M. G. TURNER. 2000. A future perspective on North America's freshwater ecosystems. Ecological Applications 10: 958–970.

NATIONAL RESEARCH COUNCIL. 1992. Restoration of aquatic ecosystems: science, technology, and public policy. National Academy Press, Washington, D.C., USA.

———. 1995. Wetlands: characteristics and boundaries. National Academy Press, Washington, D.C., USA.

———. 1999. New strategies for America's watersheds. National Academy Press, Washington, D.C., USA.

———. 2001. Compensating for wetland losses under the Clean Water Act. National Academy Press, Washington, D.C., USA.

NELSON, D. L., AND C. F. TIERNAN. 1983. Winter injury of sagebrush and other wildland shrubs in the western United States. U.S. Department of Agriculture, Forest Service, Research Paper IMT-314.

NETOFF, D. I., B. J. COOPER, AND R. R. SHROBA. 1995. Giant sandstone weathering pits near Cookie Jar Butte, southeastern Utah. Pages 25–53 *in* Proceedings of the Second Biennial Conference on Research in Colorado Plateau National Parks. U.S. Department of the Interior, National Park Service, Transactions and Proceedings Service, NPS/NRAU/NRTP-95/11.

NORTH AMERICAN BIRD CONSERVATION INITIATIVE COMMITTEE. 2000*a*. North American bird conservation initiative bird conservation regions map. U.S. Department of the Interior, Fish and Wildlife Service, Arlington, Virginia, USA.

———. 2000*b*. North American bird conservation initiative: bringing it all together. U.S. Department of the Interior, Fish and Wildlife Service, Arlington, Virginia, USA.

NOVITZKY, R. P., R. D. SMITH, AND J. D. FRETWELL. 1997. Restoration, creation, and recovery of wetlands; wetland functions, values, and assessment. National water summary: wetland resources. U.S. Department of the Interior, Geological Survey, Water-Supply Paper 2425.

OFFICE OF ENVIRONMENTAL POLICY. 1993. Protecting America's wetlands: a fair, flexible approach. White House Office of Environmental Policy, Washington, D.C., USA.

ORSER, P. N., AND D. J. SHURE. 1972. Effects of urbanization on the salamander *Desmognathus fuscus fuscus*. Ecology 53:1148–1154.

OSWALT, S. N. 2003. Evaluation and description of a floodplain system: the Middle Fork Forked Deer River, west Tennessee. Thesis. University of Tennessee, Knoxville, USA.

PAN, Y., AND R. J. STEPHENSON. 1996. Gradient analysis of diatom assemblages in western Kentucky wetlands. Journal of Phycology 32: 222–232.

PARRNETT, C., N. B. MELCHER, AND R. W. JAMES, JR. 1993. Flood discharges in the Upper Mississippi River basin, 1993. U.S. Department of the Interior, Geological Survey, Circular 1120-A.

PATON, P. W., AND W. B. CROUCH, III. 2002. Using the phenology of pond-breeding amphibians to develop conservation strategies. Conservation Biology 16:194–204.

PECHMANN, J. H. K., AND H. M. WILBUR. 1994. Putting declining amphibian populations in perspective: natural fluctuations and human impacts. Herpetologica 50:65–84.

———, R. A. ESTES, D. E. SCOTT, AND J. W. GIBBONS. 2001. Amphibian colonization and use of ponds created for trial mitigation of wetland loss. Wetlands 21:93–111.

———, D. E. SCOTT, J. W. GIBBONS, AND R. D. SEMLITSCH. 1989. Influence of wetland hydroperiod on diversity and abundance of metamorphosing juvenile amphibians. Wetlands Ecology and Management 1:3–11.

PEDERSON, R. L., D. G. JORDE, AND S. G. SIMPSON. 1989. Northern Great Plains. Pages 281–310 *in* L. M. Smith, R. L. Pederson, and R. M. Kaminski, editors. Habitat management for migrating and wintering waterfowl in North America. Texas Tech University Press, Lubbock, USA.

PEHRSSON, O. 1979. Feeding behaviour, feeding habitat utilization and feeding efficiency of mallard ducklings (*Anas platyrhynchos* L.) as guided by a domestic duck. Viltrevy 10:193–218.

PENNAK, R. W. 1978. Freshwater invertebrates of the United States. Second edition. John Wiley and Sons, New York, USA.

PERRIN, L. S., M. J. ALLEN, L. A. ROWSE, F. MONTALBANO, III, K. J. FOOTE, AND M. W. OLINDE. 1982. A report of fish and wildlife studies in the Kissimmee River basin and recommendations for restoration. Florida Game and Fresh Water Fish Commission, Office of Biological Services, Okeechobee, USA.

PETERSON, D. L., AND K. W. CUMMINS. 1974. Leaf processing in a woodland stream. Freshwater Biology 4:343–368.

PETIT, L. J. 1999. Prothonotary warbler. Number 408 *in* A. Poole and F. Gill, editors. The birds of North America. The Academy of Natural Sciences, Philadelphia, Pennsylvania, and The American Ornithologists' Union, Washington, D.C., USA.

PETRIE, M., J. ROCHON, G. TORI, R. PEDERSON, AND T. MOORMAN. 2001. The SWANCC decision: implications for wetlands and waterfowl. Final Report. Ducks Unlimited, Memphis, Tennessee, USA.

PINDER, L. C. V. 1986. Biology of freshwater Chironomidae. Annual Review of Entomology 31:1–23.

PLISSNER, J. H., S. M. HAIG, AND L. W. ORING. 2000. Postbreeding movements of American avocets and implications for wetlands connectivity in the western Great Basin. Auk 117:290–298.

POOLE, A., P. STETTENHEIM, AND F. GILL, editors. 1992–2003. The birds of North America. The Academy of Natural Sciences, Philadelphia, Pennsylvania, and The American Ornithologists' Union, Washington, D.C., USA.

POSTEL, S. L. 2000. Entering an era of water scarcity: the challenges ahead. Ecological Applications 10:941–948.

PRICE, L. W. 1981. Mountains and man: a study of processes and environment. University of California Press, Los Angeles, USA.

PRINGLE, C. M. 2000. Threats to U.S. public lands from cumulative hydrologic alterations outside of their boundaries. Ecological Applications 10:971–989.

REEVES, JR., C. C. 1966. Pluvial lake basins of west Texas. Journal of Geology 74:269–291.

REID, F. A., J. R. KELLEY, JR., T. S. TAYLOR, AND L. H. FREDRICKSON. 1989. Upper Mississippi Valley wetlands – refuges and moist-soil impoundments. Pages 181–202 *in* L. M. Smith, R. L. Pederson and R. M. Kaminski, editors. Habitat management for migrating and wintering waterfowl in North America. Texas Tech University Press, Lubbock, USA.

REINECKE, K. J., R. C. BARKLEY, AND C. K. BAXTER. 1988. Potential effects of changing water conditions on mallards wintering in the Mississippi Alluvial Valley. Pages 325–337 *in* M. W. Weller, editor. Waterfowl in winter. University of Minnesota Press, Minneapolis, USA.

RETZER, J. L. 1962. Soil survey of the Fraser alpine area, Colorado. U.S. Department of Agriculture, Forest Service and Soil Conservation Service, Service Paper 20.

REYNOLDS, R. R., T. L. SHAFFER, R. W. RENNER, W. E. NEWTON, AND B.

D. J. BATT. 2001. Impact of the Conservation Reserve Program on duck recruitment in the U.S. Prairie Pothole region. Journal of Wildlife Management 65:765–780.

RICHARDS, A. 1988. Shorebirds: a complete guide to their behavior and migration. Gallery Books, New York, USA.

RICHARDSON, C. J. 2000. Freshwater wetlands. Pages 449–499 *in* M. G. Barbour and W. D. Billings, editors. North American terrestrial vegetation. Cambridge University Press, Cambridge, United Kingdom.

RICHARDSON, J. L., J. L. ARNDT, AND J. A. MONTGOMERY. 2001. Hydrology of wetland and related soils. Pages 35–84 *in* J. L. Richardson and M. J. Vepraskas, editors. Wetland soils: genesis, hydrology, landscapes, and classification. Lewis Publishers, Boca Raton, Florida, USA.

RINGELMAN, J. K., AND J. R. LONGCORE. 1982. Movements and wetland selection by brood-rearing black ducks. Journal of Wildlife Management 46:615–621.

RINK, L. P., AND G. N. KILADIS. 1986. Geology, hydrology, climate, and soils of the Rocky Mountains. Pages 42–65 *in* J. T. Windell, B. E. Willard, D. J. Cooper, S. Q. Foster, C. F. Knud-Hansen, L. P. Rink, and G. N. Kiladis, editors. An ecological characterization of Rocky Mountain montane and subalpine wetlands. U.S. Department of the Interior, Fish and Wildlife Service, Biological Report 86.

ROBINSON, G. G. C., S. E. GURNEY, AND L. G. GOLDSBOROUGH. 2000. Algae in prairie wetlands. Pages 163–199 *in* H. R. Murkin, A. G. van der Valk, and W. R. Clark, editors. Prairie wetland ecology: the contribution of the Marsh Ecology Research Program. Iowa State University Press, Ames, USA.

ROWE, J. W. 2003. Activity and movements of midland painted turtles (*Chrysemys picta marginata*) living in a small marsh system on Beaver Island, Michigan. Journal of Herpetology 37:342–353.

RUDOLPH, D. C., AND J. G. DICKSON. 1990. Stream-side zone width and amphibian and reptile abundance. Southwestern Naturalist 35:472–476.

RUNDLE, W. D., AND M. W. SAYRE. 1983. Feeding ecology of migrant soras in southeastern Missouri. Journal of Wildlife Management 47:1153–1159.

RYBICKI, N. B., AND V. CARTER. 1986. Effect of sediment depth and sediment type on the survival of *Vallisneria americana* Mich. grown from tubers. Aquatic Botany 24:233–40.

SARGEANT, A. B., AND D. H. RAVELING. 1992. Mortality during the breeding season. Pages 396–422 *in* B. D. J. Batt, A. D. Afton, M. G. Anderson, C. D. Ankney, D. H. Johnson, J. A. Kadlec, and G. L. Krapu, editors. Ecology and management of breeding waterfowl. University of Minnesota Press, Minneapolis, USA.

———, M. A. SOVADA, AND T. L. SHAFFER. 1995. Seasonal predator removal relative to hatch rate of duck nests in waterfowl production areas. Wildlife Society Bulletin 23:507–513.

SAUCIER. R. T. 1994. Geomorphology and quaternary geological history of the Lower Mississippi Valley. Volumes I and II. U.S. Department of the Army, Corps of Engineers, Waterways Experiment Station, Vicksburg, Mississippi, USA.

SAUNDERS, D. L., J. J. MEEUWIG, AND A. C. J. VINCENT. 2002. Freshwater protected areas: strategies for conservation. Conservation Biology 16:30–41.

SCHILT, A. R. 1980. Archeological investigations in specified areas of the Hanalei National Wildlife Refuge, Hanalei Valley, Kaua'i. Bishop Museum, Honolulu, Hawaii, USA.

SCHMID, W. D. 1965. Some aspects of the water economies of nine species of amphibians. Ecology 46:261–269.

———. 1982. Survival of frogs in low temperature. Science 215:697–698.

SCHNEIDER, D. W., AND T. M. FROST. 1996. Habitat duration and community structure in temporary ponds. Journal of the North American Benthological Society 15:64–86.

SCODARI, P. F. 1997. Measuring the benefits of federal wetland programs. Environmental Law Institute, Washington, D.C., USA.

SEALE, D. B. 1980. Influence of amphibian larvae on primary production, nutrient flux, and competition in a pond ecosystem. Ecology 61:1531–1550.

SEDINGER, J. S. 1992. Ecology of prefledging waterfowl. Pages 109–127 *in* B. D. J. Batt, A. D. Afton, M. G. Anderson, C. D. Ankney, D. H. Johnson, J. A. Kadlec, and G. L. Krapu, editors. Ecology and management of breeding waterfowl. University of Minnesota Press, Minneapolis, USA.

SEMLITSCH, R. D. 1998. Biological delineation of terrestrial buffer zones for pond-breeding salamanders. Conservation Biology 12:1113–1119.

———. 2000a. Principles for management of aquatic breeding amphibians. Journal of Wildlife Management 64:615–631.

———. 2000b. Size does matter: the value of small isolated wetlands. National Wetlands Newsletter 22:5–6 and 13–14.

———, D. E. SCOTT, J. H. K. PECHMANN, AND J. W. GIBBONS. 1996. Structure and dynamics of an amphibian community: evidence from a 16-year study of a natural pond. Pages 217–248 *in* M. L. Cody and J. A. Smallwood, editors. Long-term studies of vertebrate communities. Academic Press, San Diego, California, USA.

SEVERSON, D. J. 1987. Macroinvertebrate populations in seasonally flooded marshes in the northern San Joaquin Valley of California. Thesis. Humbolt State University, Arcata, California, USA.

SHANKMAN, D., AND T. B. PUGH. 1992. Discharge response to channelization of a coastal plain stream. Wetlands 12:157–162.

SHAW, S. P., AND C. G. FREDINE. 1956. Wetlands of the United States: their extent and their value to waterfowl and other wildlife. U.S. Department of the Interior, Fish and Wildlife Service, Circular 39.

SHIMER, J. A. 1972. Field guide to landforms in the United States. Macmillan Publishing, New York, USA.

SHUTLER, D., A. MULLIE, AND R. G. CLARK. 2000. Bird communities of prairie uplands and wetlands in relation to farming practices in Saskatchewan. Conservation Biology 14:1441–1451.

SIEGEL, R. A. 1986. Ecology and conservation of an endangered rattlesnake, *Sistrurus catenatus*, in Missouri. Biological Conservation 35:333–346.

SILVERBERG, S. M., AND M. S. DENNISON. 1993. Wetlands and coastal zone regulation compliance. John Wiley and Sons, Somerset, New Jersey, USA.

SIMPSON, R. L., M. A. LECK, AND V. T. PARKER. 1989. Seed banks: general concepts and methodological issues. Pages 3–21 *in* M. A. Leck, V. T. Parker, and R. L. Simpson, editors. Ecology of soil seed banks. Academic Press, San Diego, California, USA.

SKAGEN, S. K., AND H. D. OMAN. 1996. Dietary flexibility of shorebirds in the Western Hemisphere. Canadian Field-Naturalist 10:419–444.

SKELLY, D. K. 1995. A behavioral trade-off and its consequence for the distribution of *Pseudacris* treefrog larvae. Ecology 76:150–164.

———. 1997. Tadpole communities. American Scientist 85:36–45.

———, E. E. WERNER, AND S. CORTWRIGHT. 1999. Long-term distributional dynamics of a Michigan amphibian assemblage. Ecology 80:2326–2337.

SLOAN, C. E. 1972. Ground-water hydrology of prairie potholes in North Dakota. U.S. Department of the Interior, Geological Survey, Geological Survey Professional Paper 585-C.

SMITH, R. D., A. AMMANN, C. BARTOLDUS, AND M. M. BRINSON. 1995. Approach for assessing wetland functions using hydrogeomorphic classification: reference wetlands, and functional indices. Final Report. WES/TR/WRP-DE-9. U.S. Department of the Army, Corps of Engineers, Waterways Experiment Station, Vicksburg, Mississippi, USA.

SNODGRASS, J. W., M. J. KOMOROSKI, A. L. BRYAN, JR., AND J. BURGER. 2000. Relationships among isolated wetland size, hydroperiod, and amphibian species richness: implications for wetland regulations. Conservation Biology 14:414–419.

SNYDER, C. T. 1962. A hydrologic classification of valleys in the Great Basin, western United States. Bulletin of the International Association of Science and Hydrology 7:53–59.

SOJDA, R. S., AND K. L. SOLBERG. 1993. Management and control of cattails. U.S. Department of the Interior, Fish and Wildlife Service, Waterfowl Management Handbook, Leaflet 13.4.13.

SOULÉ, M. E. 1991. Theory and strategy. Pages 91–104 *in* W. E. Hudson, editor. Landscape linkages and biodiversity. Island Press, Washington, D.C., USA.

SOULLIÉRE, G. J. 1990. Review of wood duck nest-cavity characteristics. Pages 153–162 *in* L. H. Fredrickson, G. V. Burger, S. P. Havera, D. A. Graber, R. E. Kirby and T. S. Taylor, editors. Proceedings of the North American Wood Duck Symposium, St. Louis, Missouri, USA.

SPENCE, J. R., AND N. R. HENDERSON. 1993. Tinaja and hanging garden vegetation of Capitol Reef National Park, southern Utah, U.S.A. Journal of Arid Environments 24:21–36.

SQUIRES, L., AND A. G. VAN DER VALK. 1992. Water-depth tolerances of the dominant emergent macrophytes of the Delta Marsh, Manitoba. Canadian Journal of Botany 70:1860–1867.

STANTURF, J. A., AND S. H. SCHOENHOLTZ. 1998. Soils and landforms. Pages 123–147 *in* M. G. Messina and W. H. Conner, editors. Southern forested wetlands. Lewis Publishers, Boca Raton, Florida, USA.

STEMMERMAN, L. 1981. A guide to Pacific wetland plants. U.S. Department of the Army, Corps of Engineers. Honolulu District, Honolulu, Hawaii, USA.

STEVENS, JR., S. E., K. DIONIS, AND L. R. STARK. 1989. Manganese and iron encrustation on green algae living in acid mine drainage. Pages 765–773 *in* D. A. Hammer, editor. Constructed wetlands for wastewater treatment: municipal, industrial, and agricultural. Lewis Publishers, Chelsea, Michigan, USA.

STEVENSON, R. J. 2001. Using algae to assess wetlands with multivariate statistics, multimetric indices, and an ecological risk assessment framework. Pages 113–140 *in* R. B. Rader, D. P. Batzer, and S. Wissinger, editors. Biomonitoring and management of North American freshwater wetlands. John Wiley and Sons, New York, USA.

———, P. R. SWEETS, Y. PAN, AND R. E. SCHULTZ. 1999. Algal community patterns in wetlands and their use as indicators of ecological conditions. Pages 517–527 *in* A. J. McComb and J. A. Davis, editors. Proceedings of INTECOL's Fifth International Wetland Conference. Gleneagles Press, Adelaide, Australia.

STEWART, R. E., AND H. A. KANTRUD. 1971. Classification of natural ponds and lakes in the glaciated prairie region. U.S. Department of the Interior, Fish and Wildlife Service, Resource Publication 92.

———, AND ———. 1972. Vegetation of prairie potholes, North Dakota, in relation to quality of water and other environmental factors. U.S. Department of the Interior, Geological Survey, Professional Paper 585-D.

STORER, R. W., AND G. L. NUECHTERLEIN. 1992. Western and Clark's grebe. Number 26 *in* A. Poole, P. Stettenheim, and F. Gill, editors. The birds of North America. The Academy of Natural Sciences, Philadelphia, Pennsylvania, and The American Ornithologists' Union, Washington, D.C., USA.

STRIJBOSCH, H. 1979. Habitat selection of amphibians during their aquatic phase. Oikos 33:363–372.

STROMBERG, J. C., D. T. PATTEN, AND B. D. RICHTER. 1991. Flood flows and dynamics of Sonoran riparian forests. Rivers 2:221–235.

SUGDEN, L. G., AND G. W. BEYERSBERGEN. 1987. Effect of nesting cover density on American crow predation of simulated duck nests. Journal of Wildlife Management 51:481–485.

SUTHERS, I. M., AND J. H. GEE. 1986. Role of hypoxia in limiting diel spring and summer distribution of juvenile yellow perch (*Perca flavescens*) in a prairie marsh. Canadian Journal of Fisheries and Aquatic Science 43:1562–1570.

SWANSON, G. A., AND M. I. MEYER. 1973. The role of invertebrates in the feeding ecology of Anatinae during the breeding season. Pages 143–185 *in* Waterfowl habitat management symposium, Moncton, New Brunswick, Canada.

TACHA, T. C., S. A. NESBITT, AND P. A. VOHS, JR. 1994. Sandhill crane. Pages 77–94 *in* T. C. Tacha and C. E. Braun, editors. Migratory shore and upland game bird management in North America. International Association of Fish and Wildlife Agencies, Washington, D.C., USA.

TALENT, L. G., R. L. JARVIS, AND G. L. KRAPU. 1983. Survival of mallard broods in south-central North Dakota. Condor 85:74–78.

TANGEN, B. A., M. G. BUTLER, AND M. J. ELL. 2003. Weak correspondence between macroinvertebrate assemblages and land use in prairie pothole region wetlands, USA. Wetlands 23:104–115.

TAYLOR, J. R., M. A. CARDAMONE, AND W. J. MITSCH. 1990. Bottomland hardwood forests: their functions and values. Pages 13–86 *in* L. C. Lee, J. G. Gosselink, and T. A. Muir, editors. Ecological processes and cumulative impacts illustrated by bottomland hardwood wetland ecosystems. Lewis Publishers, Chelsea, Michigan, USA.

TERRES, J. K. 1980. The Audubon Society encyclopedia of North American birds. Alfred A. Knopf, New York, USA.

TESTER, J. R., A. PARKER, AND D. B. SINIFF. 1965. Experimental studies on habitat preference and thermoregulation of *Bufo americanus*, *B. hemiophrys* and *B. cognatus*. Journal of the Minnesota Academy of Science 33:27–32.

THIBODEAU, F. R., AND B. D. OSTRO. 1981. An economic analysis of wetland preservation. Journal of Environmental Management 12:19–30.

THOMPSON, D. Q. 1989. Control of purple loosestrife. U.S. Department of the Interior, Fish and Wildlife Service, Waterfowl Management Handbook, Leaflet 13.4.11.

THOMPSON, K. 1992. The functional ecology of seed banks. Pages 231–258 *in* M. Fenner, editor. Seeds. The ecology of regeneration in plant communities. Wallingford, Cab International, United Kingdom.

THORNBURY, W. D. 1965. Regional geomorphology of the United States. John Wiley and Sons, New York, USA.

TINER, JR., R. W. 1984. Wetlands of the United States: current status and recent trends. U.S. Department of the Interior, Fish and Wildlife Service, Washington, D.C., USA.

———. 1997. Technical aspects of wetlands: wetland definitions and classifications in the United States. National water summary: wetland resources. U.S. Department of the Interior, Geological Survey, Water-Supply Paper 2425.

———, H. C. BERGQUIST, G. P. DEALESSIO, AND M. J. STARR. 2002. Geographically isolated wetlands: a preliminary assessment of their characteristics and status in selected areas of the United States. U.S. Department of the Interior, Fish and Wildlife Service, Hadley, Massachusetts, USA.

TOTH, L. A., D. A. ARRINGTON, M. A. BRADY, AND D. A. MUSZICK. 1995. Conceptual evaluation of factors potentially affecting restoration of habitat structure within the channelized Kissimmee River ecosystem. Restoration Ecology 3:160–180.

———, S. L. MELVIN, D. A. ARRINGTON, AND J. CHAMBERLAIN. 1998. Hydrologic manipulations of the channelized Kissimmee River. BioScience 48:757–764.

———, J. T. B. OBEYSEKERA, W. A. PERKINS, AND M. K. LOFTIN. 1993. Flow regulation and restoration of Florida's Kissimmee River. Regulated Rivers 8:155–166.

TURNER, R. E., AND N. N. RABALAIS. 2003. Linking landscape and water quality in the Mississippi River Basin for 200 years. BioScience 53:563–572.

TWIDALE, C. R., AND J. A. BOURNE. 1975. Episodic exposure of inselbergs. Geologic Society of America Bulletin 86:1473–1481.

U.S. CONGRESS. 1984. Wetlands: their use and regulation. U.S. Congress, Office of Technology Assessment, OTA-0-206. Washington, D.C., USA.

———. 1993. Preparing for an uncertain climate. U.S. Congress, Office of Technology Assessment. Volume 2. OTA-O-568. U.S. Government Printing Office, Washington D.C., USA.

U.S. DEPARTMENT OF AGRICULTURE. 1994. National Food Security Act Manual. Part 519, 180-V-NFSAM. Third edition. U.S. Department of Agriculture, Soil Conservation Service, Washington, D.C., USA.

———. 1999a. Natural Resources Conservation Service, Conservation Practice Standard: wetland creation. Code 658, Denver, Colorado, USA.

———. 1999b. Natural Resources Conservation Service, Conservation Practice Standard: wetland enhancement. Code 659, Denver, Colorado, USA.

———. 2000. Summary Report 1997, revised December 2000. U.S. Department of Agriculture, Natural Resources Conservation Service, Washington, D.C., USA.

U.S. DEPARTMENT OF ARMY. 1987. Corps of Engineers wetland delineation manual. U.S. Department of the Army, Corps of Engineers, Technical Report Y-87 1. Waterways Experiment Station, Vicksburg, Mississippi, USA.

U.S. DEPARTMENT OF COMMERCE. 1995. A $1.01 million project to restore wetlands in Louisiana to combat severe shoreline erosion. National Oceanic and Atmospheric Administration. Available online at http://www.noaa.gov (accessed June 2003).

U.S. DEPARTMENT OF INTERIOR. 1976. Existing state and local wetland surveys (1965–1975). Volume II. U.S. Department of Interior, Fish and Wildlife Service, Office of Biological Services, Washington, D.C., USA.

———. 1991. United States Department of the Interior budget justification: fiscal year 1992. Washington, D.C., USA.

———. 1995. Economic impacts of protecting rivers, trails and greenway corridors. Rivers and Trails Conservation Assistance. U.S. Department of the Interior, National Park Service, Washington, D.C., USA.

———. 2002. Birds of conservation concern 2002. U.S. Department of the Interior, Division of Migratory Bird Management, Arlington, Virginia, USA.

———. 2003. Writing refuge management goals and objectives: a handbook. U.S. Department of the Interior, Fish and Wildlife Service, National Wildlife Refuge System, Arlington, Virginia, USA.

U.S. DEPARTMENTS OF INTERIOR AND COMMERCE. 2001. National survey of fishing, hunting, and wildlife-associated recreation. Washington, D.C., USA.

U.S. ENVIRONMENTAL PROTECTION AGENCY. 1988. EPA wetland identification and delineation manual. Volumes I and II. W. S. Sipple, editor. U.S. Environmental Protection Agency, Office of Wetlands Protection, Washington, D.C., USA.

———. 1994. National water quality inventory: 1992 report to Congress. U.S. Environmental Protection Agency. EPA 841-R-

94–001. Washington, D.C., USA.

———. 1995. Wetlands fact sheets. U.S. Environmental Protection Agency. EPA843-F-95–001. Office of Water, Wetlands, Oceans and Watersheds, Washington, D.C., USA.

———. 2000. National water quality inventory: 2000 report. U.S. Environmental Protection Agency. EPA 841-R-02–001. Washington, D.C., USA.

———. 2001*a*. Functions and values of wetlands. U.S. Environmental Protection Agency. EPA Number 843-F-01–002c. Office of Water, Wetlands, Oceans and Watersheds. Washington, D.C., USA.

———. 2001*b*. Hypoxia and wetland restoration. U.S. Environmental Protection Agency. EPA Number 843-F-02–002. Office of Water, Wetlands, Oceans and Watersheds. Washington, D.C., USA.

———. 2003. Inventory of U.S. greenhouse gas emissions and sinks: 1990–2001. U.S. Environmental Protection Agency. Washington, D.C., USA.

VAN DER VALK, A. G. 1981. Succession in wetlands: a Gleasonian approach. Ecology 62:688–696.

———, AND C. B. DAVIS. 1976. Changes in composition, structure, and production of plant communities along a perturbed wetland coenocline. Vegetation 32:87–96.

———, AND ———. 1978. The role of seed banks in the vegetation dynamics of prairie glacial marshes. Ecology 59:322–335.

———, AND C. H. WELLING. 1988. The development of zonation in freshwater wetlands: an experimental approach. Pages 145–158 *in* H. During, M. Werger, and J. Willems, editors. Diversity and pattern in plant communities. Academic Publishing, The Hague, The Netherlands.

VILEISIS, A. 1997. Discovering the unknown landscape: a history of America's wetlands. Island Press, Washington, D.C., USA.

VIVIAN-SMITH, G., AND E. W. STILES. 1994. Dispersal of salt marsh seeds on the feet and feathers of waterfowl. Wetlands 14:316–319.

WAKE, D. B. 1998. Action on amphibians. Trends in Ecology and Evolution 13:379–380.

WALTERS, C. J. 1986. Adaptive management of renewable resources. Macmillan Press, New York, USA.

WANG, J. A., T. W. JURIK, AND A. G. VAN DER VALK. 1994. Effects of sediment load on various stages in the life and death of cattail (*Typha x Glauca*). Wetlands 14:66–73.

WARD, J. V. 1998. Riverine landscapes: biodiversity patterns, disturbance regimes, and aquatic conservation. Biological Conservation 83:269–278.

WATSON, R. 1999. Common themes for ecologists in global issues. Journal of Applied Ecology 36:1–10.

WEBSTER, J. R., AND E. F. BENFIELD. 1986. Vascular plant breakdown in freshwater ecosystems. Annual Review of Ecological Systematics 17:567–594.

WELLBORN, G. A., D. K. SKELLY, AND E. E. WERNER. 1996. Mechanisms creating community structure across a freshwater habitat gradient. Annual Review of Ecology and Systematics 27:337–363.

WELLER, M. W. 1961. Breeding biology of the least bittern. Wilson Bulletin 73:11–35.

———. 1981. Freshwater marshes, ecology and wildlife management. University of Minnesota Press, Minneapolis, USA.

———. 1988. Freshwater marshes: ecology and wildlife management. Second edition. University of Minnesota Press, Minneapolis, USA.

———. 1999. Wetland birds: habitat resources and conservation implications. Cambridge University Press, Cambridge, United Kingdom.

———, AND L. H. FREDRICKSON. 1974. Avian ecology of a managed glacial marsh. The Living Bird 12:269–291.

———, AND C. E. SPATCHER. 1965. Role of habitat in the distribution and abundance of marsh birds. Entomology Special Report 43. Department of Zoology, Agriculture and Home Economics Experiment Station, Iowa State University, Ames, USA.

———, G. W. KAUFMAN, AND P. A. VOHS, JR. 1991. Evaluation of wetland development and waterbird response at Elk Creek Wildlife Management Area, Lake Mills, Iowa, 1961–1990. Wetlands 11:245–262.

WERNER, E. E., AND M. A. MCPEEK. 1994. Direct and indirect effects of predators on two anuran species along an environmental gradient. Ecology 75:1368–1382.

WETZEL, R. G. 1996. Benthic algae and nutrient cycling in lentic freshwater ecosystems. Pages 641–667 *in* R. J. Stevenson, M. L. Bothwell, and R. L. Lowe, editors. Algal ecology: freshwater benthic ecosys-

tems. Academic Press, San Diego, California, USA.

WHARTON, C. H., W. M. KITCHENS, E. C. PENDLETON, AND T. W. SIPE. 1982. The ecology of bottomland hardwood swamps of the southeast: a community profile. U.S. Department of the Interior, Fish and Wildlife Service, Biological Services Program, FWS/OBS-81/37.

WHITE, D. H., AND D. JAMES. 1978. Differential use of freshwater environments by wintering waterfowl of coastal Texas. Wilson Bulletin 90:99–111.

WHITTAKER, R. H., AND C. W. FAIRBANKS. 1958. A study of plankton copepod communities in the Columbia Basin, southeastern Washington. Ecology 39:46–65.

———, AND W. NIERING. 1975. Vegetation of the Santa Catalina Mountains, Arizona. V. Biomass, production, and diversity along the elevation gradient. Ecology 56:771–790.

WIENS, J. A. 1985. Habitat selection in variable environments: shrub-steppe birds. Pages 227–251 *in* M. L. Cody, editor. Habitat selection in birds. Academic Press, Orlando, Florida, USA.

WIGGINS, G. B., R. J. MACKAY, AND I. M. SMITH. 1982. Evolutionary and ecological strategies of animals in annual temporary pools. Archives Hydrobiologia 58:97–206.

WIGLEY, T. B., AND R. A. LANCIA. 1998. Wildlife communities. Pages 205–236 *in* M. G. Messina and W. H. Conner, editors. Southern forested wetlands. Lewis Publishers, Boca Raton, Florida, USA.

WILBUR, H. M. 1980. Complex life cycles. Annual Review of Ecology and Systematics 11:67–93.

———, AND J. P. COLLINS. 1973. Ecological aspects of amphibian metamorphosis. Science 182:1305–1314.

WILCOX, D. A., J. E. MEEKER, P. L. HUDSON, B. J. ARMITAGE, M. G. BLACK, AND D. G. UZARSKI. 2002. Hydrologic variability and the application of index of biotic integrity metrics to wetlands: a Great Lakes evaluation. Wetlands 22:588–615.

WILLARD, B. E. 1979. Plant sociology of alpine tundra, Trail Ridge, Rocky Mountain National Park, Colorado. Colorado School of Mines Quarterly 74:1–119.

WILLIAMS, W. D. 1985. Biotic adaptations in temporary lentic waters, with special reference to those in semi-arid and arid regions. Hydrobiologia 125:85–110.

———, A. J. BOULTON, AND R. G. TAAFFE. 1990. Salinity as a determinant of salt lake fauna: a question of scale. Hydrobiologia 197:257–266.

WINDELL, J. T., B. E. WILLARD, AND S. Q. FOSTER. 1986. Introduction to Rocky Mountain wetlands. Pages 1–41 *in* J. T. Windell, B. E. Willard, D. J. Cooper, S. Q. Foster, C. F. Knud-Hansen, L. P. Rink, and G. N. Kiladis, editors. An ecological characterization of Rocky Mountain montane and subalpine wetlands. U.S. Department of the Interior, Fish and Wildlife Service, Biological Report 86.

WINTER, T. C. 1989. Hydrological studies of wetlands in the northern prairie. Pages 16–54 *in* A. G. van der Valk, editor. Northern prairie wetlands. Iowa State University Press, Ames, Iowa.

———, AND D. O. ROSENBERRY. 1995. The interaction of ground water with prairie pothole wetlands in the Cottonwood Lake area, east-central North Dakota. Wetlands 15:193–211.

WRIGHT, JR., H. E. 1983. Late-Quaternary environments of the United States. Volume I. The late Pleistocene. S. C. Porter, editor. University of Minnesota Press, Minneapolis, USA.

WRIGHT, J. O. 1907. Swamp and overflowed lands in the United States. U.S. Department of Agriculture, Circular 76. Office of Experiment Stations, Washington, D.C., USA.

WRIGHT, R., AND M. STREET. 1985. The influence of fish on the survival of wildfowl broods. Game Conservation Annual Review 16:77–80.

WYLIE, G. D. 1985. Limnology of lowland hardwood wetlands in southeast Missouri. Dissertation. University of Missouri, Columbia, USA.

YATES, R. F. K., AND F. P. DAY, JR. 1983. Decay rates and nutrient dynamics in confined and unconfined leaf litter in the Great Dismal Swamp. American Midland Naturalist 110:37–45.

YONG, W., D. M. FINCH, F. R. MOORE, AND J. F. KELLY. 1998. Stopover ecology and habitat use of migratory Wilson's warblers. Auk 115:829–842.

ZEDLER, J. B. 1980. Algae mat productivity: comparisons in a salt marsh. Estuaries 3:122–131.

ZEDLER, P. H. 1987. The ecology of southern California vernal pools: a community profile. U.S. Department of the Interior, Fish and Wildlife Service, Biological Report 85.

31

MANAGING COASTAL WETLANDS FOR WILDLIFE

Robert H. Chabreck and John A. Nyman

DESCRIPTION OF COASTAL MARSHES

Coastal wetlands differ greatly from those inland primarily because of seawater stresses to vegetation and tidal action that makes water levels more dynamic. Most coastal wetlands in the United States are marshes; i.e., dominated by emergent herbaceous vegetation, rather than swamps; i.e., dominated by trees or shrubs, because there are no trees that can tolerate freezing and even moderate salinity. Salt tolerant mangrove trees (*Rhizophora mangle, Avicennia germinans*) occur in Florida and form extensive swamps only in the tropics. Mangrove swamps are not addressed further because they are rarely managed for wildlife. In contrast, coastal marshes have been managed for wildlife, particularly waterfowl, since the early 1900s. Understanding the relationships among coastal marshes, wildlife, and fish has evolved slowly from trial-and-error efforts to attract waterfowl to more sophisticated application of scientific methods and ecological theories to accommodate multiple wildlife and fish species. In this chapter, we summarize the form, function, ecological relationships, wildlife value, and management of coastal marshes of the United States outside of Alaska and Hawaii.

Regional Variation

Physical features of a coastal region influence development of coastal marshes. Regions bordered by a broad, flat coastal plain onshore and a gently sloping continental shelf offshore, such as the southeastern United States, contain the greatest expanse of coastal marshes. Marshes form along the shoreline when sediment deposited by rivers or the sea fill shallow waters and extend seaward as shoals that gradually accrete from the water bottom to elevations suitable for plant growth (Coleman 1988). Coastlines bordered by mountainous terrain, such as the northwestern United States, usually contain deep water near shore and produce conditions unfavorable for marsh development (Seliskar and Gallagher 1983). Near mountainous coasts, the continental shelf is narrow and steep curtailing sediment accumulation and accretion necessary for extensive marsh formation; marshes do develop along the fringes of rivers or shallow embayments.

Coastal marshes comprise ~24,380 km^2 in the United States outside of Alaska, Hawaii, and the Great Lakes (Alexander et al. 1986). For perspective, this area is larger than New Hampshire but smaller than Vermont. Most are along the shoreline of the Gulf of Mexico and the south Atlantic and are associated with extensive coastal plains and drowned river valleys. Much of the New England and Pacific coasts have rocky coastlines and contain marshes only in protected embayments.

Gulf Coast.—The Gulf of Mexico coastal region contains ~14,190 km^2 of marsh, an area which is larger than Connecticut but smaller than Hawaii, or 58% of the total coastal marshes (Alexander et al. 1986). Much of this marsh (~9,840 km^2) occurs in Louisiana and developed as deltaic deposits and Chenier Plain deposits of the Mississippi River (West 1977, Penland and Sutter 1989). Marshes border the entire coastline of Louisiana and extend inland up to 80 km in the eastern half of the state, which contains the Mississippi River Deltaic Plain (Chabreck 1988). Because of the tremendous extent of these marshes, waters range from oceanic to fresh. Also, broad transitional zones of brackish and intermediate marsh occur (O'Neil 1949, Chabreck 1972).

The Texas coastline contains ~1,915 km^2 of marsh in a narrow band (Alexander et al. 1986), with most east of Galveston Bay representing a westward continuation of the Chenier Plain of the Mississippi River. Marshes of the region display the gradual transition from saline to fresh and provide wide habitat diversity (Stutzenbaker and Weller 1989). Westward along the Texas coast to the Rio Grande River, small marshes fringe lagoons of extremely high salinity, up to 55 ppt (Buller 1964, McMahan 1968, West 1977).

Mississippi, Alabama, and the Gulf coast of Florida contain ~2,435 km^2 of coastal marsh (Alexander et al. 1986). Marshes along the west coast of Mississippi are part of the Mississippi River Deltaic Plain but now are nourished by freshwater and sediments from the Pearl River. Elsewhere along the coasts of Mississippi, Alabama, and northern Florida, marshes are limited to alluvial pockets along shorelines of protected bays and rivers. The western coast of Florida contains extensive lowlands and large areas of coastal marsh. South of Tampa Bay, however, mangroves dominate coastal lowlands, and marsh occurs only in isolated openings among stands of these trees.

Along the northwestern (Texas) and northeastern (Alabama and Mississippi) segments of the Gulf coast, land is 1.5–4.5 m above sea level near the shoreline, which limits the areas affected by tidal inundation. Southeastern Texas, Louisiana, and western Florida have broad coastal lowlands near sea level.

Atlantic Coast.—The Atlantic coast contains ~9,815 km^2 of marsh (Alexander et al. 1986), an area which is larger than Delaware but smaller than Connecticut. Three-fourths of the marsh is south of Maryland, mostly in North Carolina, South Carolina, and Georgia (Shaw and Fredine 1954, Reimold 1977). Broad, flat coastal plains slope gently to the shoreline in these states and produce vast lowlands near sea level.

In Virginia and Maryland, coastal marshes are largely associated with Chesapeake Bay and tidal creeks and rivers draining into the bay. Many of these marshes were extensively ditched in the 1930s by mosquito control agencies (Hindman and Stotts 1989). Delaware and New Jersey contain sizable areas of marsh associated with Delaware Bay. Also, scattered marshes occur as fringes along seashores protected by barrier islands. In South Carolina, many coastal marshes were impounded to grow rice in the 1800s but most of those impoundments are now managed for wintering waterfowl (Landers et al. 1976). Marshes in New York lie principally along tidal creeks leading inland into Long Island. Most tidal marshes along the east coast of Florida border large rivers and extend inland for great distances, such as along the St. John's River.

Much of the New England coastline is rugged with rock outcroppings. Marshes along the coast are relatively small (combined they occupy ~555 km^2) and subjected to larger tidal fluctuation (4 m) than most other coastal marshes in the United States (Nixon and Oviatt 1973). They border tidal creeks, bay shores, and other protected waters. Coastal marshes in the northern Atlantic states are threatened by common reed (*Phagmites australis*) as well as purple loosestrife (*Lythrum salicaria*) (Jorde et al. 1989).

Pacific Coast.—The Pacific coast lacks a broad coastal plain; instead, steep mountains parallel the shoreline and slope abruptly to the ocean (Inman and Nordstrom 1971). The continental shelf is narrow and steep restricting formation of barrier islands and spits; consequently, coastal marshes have developed only in protected bays and fringing the borders of rivers that empty into the Pacific Ocean. In many of these marshes, smooth cordgrass (*Spartina alterniflora*) was introduced during the 1970s and threatens native plant communities (Callaway and Josselyn 1992).

The Pacific coast outside of Alaska contains only ~375 km^2 of coastal marsh (Alexander et al. 1986), much of which is associated with San Francisco Bay. Other significant marshes are associated with Puget Sound, Gray's Harbor, and Willapa Bay in Washington and Tillamook and Coos bays in Oregon. Marshes at other locations consist mainly of fringe zones along bay shores or in the mouths of rivers with sandbars that minimize wave action (Sanderson and Bellrose 1969).

Types of Marshes

Coastal marshes can be classified based on water salinity, elevation, flooding, plant species, or a combination of these variables. A classification system based on water salinity by Cowardin et al. (1979) is commonly used nationwide. Cowardin et al. (1979) noted the years of data needed to estimate average salinity are uncommon and suggested that managers instead use plant species or associations to indicate broad salinity classes. Thus, in practice, the Cowardin et al. (1979) system of classifying marshes by average water salinity has been based on emergent vegetation rather than salinity measurements.

Classification systems based on elevation are common within several regions of the United States (Mitsch and Gosselink 2000:261–334). Classifying marshes by elevation has also been based on emergent vegetation rather than elevation measurements. These systems complicate communication among regions because different terms are used for similar habitats. For instance, areas dominated by smooth cordgrass that is stunted by flooding can be classified as high marsh in coastal New England but as low marsh on the Atlantic coast of the southern United States. Classification systems directly based on emergent vegetation are more straightforward but still can complicate communication among regions. For instance, areas dominated by marshhay cordgrass (*Spartina patens*) occur in coastal New England and on the Gulf coast but are known as salt marshes in New England and brackish marshes on the Gulf coast. Managers and researchers must be familiar with all of the differing classification systems. Species of emergent vegetation are the key to converting among classification systems, and to communicating with managers and researchers from other regions. Regardless of the variable used as the basis of classification, the boundaries between classes are arbitrary because water salinity, elevation, and plant species form gradients.

Common plant associations have been identified for many regions (Chabreck 1970, Nixon 1982, Zedler 1982, Josselyn 1983, Seliskar and Gallagher 1983, Odum et al. 1984, Teal 1986, Weigert and Freeman 1990). Recently, statistical analyses have been used to identify common plant associations that are more detailed than earlier classification schemes (Visser et al. 2000). For broad descriptive purposes, marsh types often are known as salt (polyhaline), brackish (mesohaline), intermediate (oligohaline), or fresh, reflecting the amount of contact with seawater. These types generally occur in bands paralleling the shoreline. In small rivers, the bands can be tens of meters wide and some may not occur but, because of the great width of marsh along the Louisiana coast, all marsh types are well represented (salt = 21%, brackish = 31%, intermediate = 11%, fresh = 31%) and the bands exceed 20 km in some areas (Chabreck and Linscombe 1978).

Botanical nomenclature follows ITIS (2003) but nomenclature changes. Recent changes create potential confusion because one of the most important genera to wildlife managers was referred to in many publications as *Scirpus*, following the nomenclature of Radford et al. (1968) and Godfrey and Wooten (1979): recent publications often refer to this genus as *Schoenoplectus*, following ITIS (2003).

Salt Marsh.—Salt marsh has the greatest tidal fluctuation of all marsh types and contains a well-developed drainage system. In Louisiana, water salinity averages 18.0 ppt (range = 8.1–29.4 ppt) and soils have a lower organic content (mean = 17.5%) than types farther inland (Chabreck 1972). On the Gulf coast, vegetation within this type is salt-tolerant and is dominated by smooth cordgrass, seashore saltgrass (*Distichlis spicata*), and needlegrass rush (*Juncus roemerianus*). On the Pacific coast, the most saline marshes contain plants such as Virginia glasswort (*Salicornia virginica*), arrowgrass (*Triglochin maritimum*), and native California cordgrass (*Spartina foliosa*) or the nonnative smooth cordgrass (Seliskar and Gallagher 1983, Callaway and Josselyn 1992, Zedler et al. 1999).

Brackish Marsh.—Brackish marsh lies inland from the salt marsh type farther removed from the influence of saline waters, but is still affected by daily tidal action. Normal water depth exceeds that of salt marsh. In Louisiana, soils contain higher organic content (mean = 31.2%), and water salinity averages 8.2 ppt (range = 1.0–18.4 ppt) (Chabreck 1972).

Brackish marsh contains greater plant diversity than salt marsh and, in Louisiana, is dominated by 2 perennial grasses, marshhay cordgrass and seashore saltgrass. An important wildlife food plant of brackish marsh of the Atlantic and Gulf coasts, Olney bulrush (*Schoenoplectus americanus*), grows best in tidal marsh free from excessive flooding, prolonged drought, and drastic salinity changes. Olney bulrush is, however, crowded out by marshhay cordgrass unless stands (of Olney bulrush) are periodically burned (Chabreck 1981). Widgeongrass (*Ruppia maritima*), the dominant submerged aquatic plant of brackish marsh, is a preferred food of ducks and American coot (*Fulica americana*). On the Pacific coast, brackish marsh contains short and tall forms of Lyngbye's sedge (*Carex lyngbyei*), which appears to be an analog of smooth cordgrass (Seliskar and Gallagher 1983).

Intermediate Marsh.—The intermediate marsh type lies inland from brackish marsh. Intermediate marsh receives some influence from tides. In Louisiana, water salinity averages 3.3 ppt (range = 0.5–8.3 ppt), water levels are slightly higher than in brackish marsh and soil organic content averages 33.9% (Chabreck 1972). Plant species diversity is higher than in brackish or saline marsh, and intermediate marsh contains both halophytes and freshwater species used as food by a wide variety of herbivores. In Louisiana, marshhay cordgrass dominates intermediate marsh as it does brackish marsh, but to a lesser extent. Other common marsh plants in intermediate zones are common reed, bulltongue (*Sagittaria lancifolia*), and coastal waterhyssop (*Bacopa monnieri*). This type also contains an abundance of submerged aquatic plants that are important foods for ducks and American coot (Chabreck 1972). Use of "intermediate marsh" is uncommon outside the Gulf coast perhaps because this type is rare or because it is known as tidal freshwater marsh. Even in Louisiana, intermediate marsh is the smallest type and occupies only ~2,523 km^2, of which ~1,533km^2 are emergent wetlands and the remainder is open water (ponds, lakes, etc.) (Chabreck 1972).

Fresh Marsh.—Fresh marsh occupies the zone between the intermediate marsh and uplands or forested wetlands in the alluvial plain of major river systems. Tidal fresh marsh is normally free from salinity, but periodic periods of salinity prevent conversion to swamps. Water levels can be only slightly affected by tides, as on the Gulf coast where high tide slows river discharge more than it raises water level, or greatly affected by tides as in the northern United States. In Louisiana, water salinity averages only 1.0 ppt (range = 0.1–3.4 ppt), and water depth and soil organic content (mean = 52.0%) are greatest in fresh marsh because of slow drainage (Chabreck 1972). In some Louisiana fresh marshes, soil organic matter content exceeds 80% and the substrate for plant growth is a floating organic mat referred to as "flotant" by Russell (1942).

Fresh marsh supports the greatest diversity of plants and contains many species that are preferred foods of wildlife. Dominant plants include maidencane (*Panicum hemitomon*), spikerushes (*Eleocharis* spp.), and alligator weed (*Alternanthera philoxeroides*) in Louisiana (O'Neil 1949). On the Atlantic coast, Odum et al. (1984) identified 8 communities in tidal fresh water marsh with dominant species such as Virginia peltandra (*Peltandra virginica*), annual wildrice (*Zizania aquatica*), and giant cutgrass (*Zizaniopsis mileacea*). The type also contains submerged and floating-leafed aquatic plants of value as wildlife foods. In many areas, tidal freshwater marsh was converted to agriculture as it was in the delta of the Sacramento and San Joaquin rivers (Herbold and Moyle 1989). As with emergent vegetation, submersed aquatic vegetation is richer and more abundant in fresh marshes than in saline marshes (Chabreck 1971, Yozzo and Smith 1998, Simenstad et al. 2000). Some floating aquatics, such as spatter-dock (*Nuphar luteum*), are sufficiently common that they are the basis of identified communities (Odum et al. 1984) whereas others, such as the exotic water hyacinth (*Eichhornia crassipes*), form dense stands that block waterways and are considered pest plants.

Tides

Water level, in addition to salinity, is a major factor affecting plant and animal communities in coastal marshes; the tidal cycle is the major factor affecting water levels.

The tidal range varies daily, monthly, annually, and regionally. Marshes bordering the Gulf of Mexico are subject to a daily tidal range of less than 0.6 m (Marmer 1954). In some areas along the coasts of New England and the Pacific Northwest, tides may fluctuate 3.6–4.8 m daily (Hedgpeth and Obrebski 1981, Whitlatch 1982). Tides within a locality may also vary; south of Cape Cod the range is 0.9–1.5 m while north of Cape Cod the range is 3.0–4.0 m (Whitlatch 1982).

Highest tide levels occur in coastal marsh during the full and new moons. Factors such as wind direction and intensity, freshwater inflow, and barometric pressure also affect the range and level of individual tides at a locality. The rate of movement and level of tides decreases as water moves inland. The rate of movement decreases because coastal streams become narrower farther inland and carry less water. Moreover, meandering or winding of streams increases the distance that water must travel to move inland. The rate of flow of tidewater moving across the marsh surface also is reduced by dense vegetation.

Channel size and length affect the rate of water exchange; interior marshes connected to the sea by large channels are influenced to a greater extent by tides than marshes with small drainages. Coastal marshes transected by large, straight canals that connect to the sea are exposed to greatest tidal action. In such canals, tidal waters can move farther inland, in greater volume, and at a greater rate than through natural streams. Such canals also accelerate drainage of freshwater from interior marshes during low tides (Gunter 1967).

HABITAT REQUIREMENTS OF SELECTED FISH AND WILDLIFE

Coastal marshes and associated water bodies are among the most productive habitats for fish and wildlife. Some species spend their entire lives in this habitat, whereas others use the habitat only seasonally or during a portion of their life cycles. This review describes habitat requirements of selected groups that are important because of their commercial, sporting, or recreational qualities. Basic information is provided for discussion of the effects of management of coastal marshes on groups of fish and wildlife.

Waterfowl

Coastal wetlands and waters serve as wintering habitat for a large segment of the continental migratory waterfowl population. Major groups include dabbling and diving ducks, and geese. These groups have different habitat requirements that vary considerably even among species within groups (Bellrose 1980).

Dabbling ducks mostly prefer shallow water areas with depths less than 45 cm. These birds feed by tipping to reach the bottom of marsh ponds or the surface of flooded marsh. Small species such as blue-winged (*Anas discors*) and green-winged teal (*A. crecca*) prefer areas with water less than 15 cm deep (Chabreck 1979). Teal, mallard (*A. platyrhynchos*), and pintail (*A. acuta*) feed mainly on seeds that they pick up on the bottom. Other dabblers, such as gadwall (*A. strepera*) and American wigeon (*A. americana*) feed extensively on leaves and stems of aquatic plants; consequently, they are able to use areas with a greater water depth (Gordon et al. 1989). Brant (*Branta bernicla*) feed heavily on seagrass (*Zostera marina*).

Diving ducks may consume plant or animal materials on reservoir bottoms or aquatic plants growing in the water. Diving ducks may be found in association with dabbling ducks; however, they usually occupy open water areas much deeper than those used for feeding by dabbling ducks.

Snow geese (*Chen caerulescens*) commonly winter in coastal marshes and prefer areas containing short grasses and sedges having water levels near or below the marsh surface. Snow geese seldom venture into salt marsh along the Gulf coast, but salt marsh is an important habitat along the Atlantic coast (Smith and Odum 1981). A preferred habitat is recently burned marshhay cordgrass, which often contains dense stands of Olney bulrush.

Most waterfowl depend on coastal marshes only part of the year, the non-breeding season. American black duck (*Anas rubripes*), mottled duck (*A. fulvigula*), and Florida duck (*A. f. fulvigula*) nest as well as winter in coastal marshes and depend on coastal marshes year round. Little is known about population trends of Florida duck and mottled duck, but American black duck populations declined in the latter 1900s; loss of habitat and interbreeding with mallards are believed to be 2 of several factors contributing to the decline of black ducks (Conroy et al. 2002). Black ducks use impounded marsh less than tidal marsh and encounter more mallards in impounded marsh than in tidal marsh (Belanger and Lehoux 1994). Restoration of tidal flow to impounded marshes in the northeastern United States might increase black duck populations.

Coots, Gallinules, and Rails

The American coot is a winter resident of coastal wetlands and concentrates in large flocks on ponds and lakes (Lowery 1974*a*). It is equally at home on shallow ponds with dense growth of aquatic plants for food or deeper lakes with small fishes available as food. The American coot occupies shallow water areas and tolerates widely ranging water salinities, but limits its use of deep-water lakes to freshwater systems.

Gallinules and rails are less gregarious than coots and prefer marshes with readily available, dense escape cover. The common moorhen (*Gallinula chloropus*) is a year-round resident of Gulf coast marshes while the purple gallinule (*Porphyrula martinica*) breeds in the area and migrates during winter. Gallinules occupy freshwater marshes and prefer feeding areas along shorelines of small ponds.

Several species of rails are present in coastal marshes. Clapper rails (*Rallus longirostris*) occupy saline marshes while the king rail (*R. elegans*) occurs in fresh marshes. Rails prefer moist soil conditions and are driven from marshes by prolonged flooding.

Wading Birds and Shorebirds

Shorebirds include sandpipers, dowitchers, etc. Shorebirds do not nest in wetland vegetation, but feed in shallow ponds and tidal channels common in coastal marshes. Most shorebirds use shallower water (<5 cm deep) than waterfowl (>10 cm deep) (Isola et al. 2000). Wading birds include herons, egrets, ibises, and similar birds and are abundant throughout the coastal area but few species nest in wetland vegetation. These birds feed in shallow ponds by slowly walking and capturing fishes and other small animals. They also use shallower water than waterfowl. Their wide ranging foraging and low site fidelity allows them to quickly respond to changing environmental conditions; changes in their abundance are a good measure of habitat condition but not population changes (Melvin et al. 1999). In the Pacific Northwest for instance, wading birds may be losing foraging areas as shallow water areas are replaced by non-native smooth cordgrass; it is not known if wading bird populations have been affected. Shallow water is an essential part of their habitat and birds often concentrate around small pools to capture fishes trapped by receding water (Lowery 1974*a*). A mix of unmanaged ponds that drain naturally and managed ponds that rarely drain provide foraging habitat across a wide range of conditions (Spiller and Chabreck 1975). If ponds with different water depths cannot be provided, as in former agriculture fields, managers should be able to provide feeding habitat for more species with shallower water than deeper water (Safran et al. 1997).

Passerines

Many songbirds use coastal marshes and a few are limited to these marshes during part or all of the year. Some are species of concern such as sedge wren (*Cistothorus platensis*) and seaside sparrow (*Ammodramus maritimus*), whereas one, the Cape Sable seaside sparrow (*A. m. mirabilis*) is endangered. These songbirds forage for spiders and insects and require relatively short, open vegetation such as smooth cordgrass, marshhay cordgrass, and sand cordgrass (*Spartina bakeri*). On the northeast Atlantic coast, restoration of smooth cordgrass to areas invaded by common reed should increase habitat for seaside sparrows and salt marsh sharp-tailed sparrows (*A. caudacutus*) because they are less abundant in marshes dominated by common reed (Benoit and Askins 1999). Even areas dominated by suitable plant species may be unsuitable for dependent songbirds if the vegetation is too thick or too sparse. On the Gulf coast, managed marshes, where marshhay cordgrass is vigorous, support fewer seaside sparrows and Nelson's sharp-tailed sparrows (*A. nelsoni*) than unmanaged marsh where salinity stunts marshhay cordgrass (Gabrey et al. 1999). At the other extreme, marshes that burned the previous winter had too little vegetation and supported fewer marsh wrens (*Cistothorus palustris*), Nelson's sharp-tailed sparrows, seaside sparrows, and sedge wrens than marshes that had burned earlier (Gabrey et al. 1999). In addition to vegetative structure, patch size influences habitat suitability for songbirds that depend on coastal marshes. Density of salt marsh sharp-tailed sparrows, seaside sparrows, and willets (*Catoptrophorus semipalmatus*) is greater in larger patches than in smaller patches of otherwise suitable habitat (Benoit and Askins 2002).

Fire might be a useful tool in managing coastal marshes for some dependent songbirds. On the Atlantic coast of Florida, fire favors the expansion of sand cordgrass, which is critical habitat for the endangered Cape Sable seaside sparrow, at the expense of needlegrass rush (Schmalzer et al. 1991). Even where fire is not a tool, it can be managed to ensure that vegetative stands in different stages of recovery from fire are present simultaneously rather than managing large tracts on the same burning schedule.

Unlike wading birds, many songbirds do not respond quickly to changes in habitat. Jenkins et al. (2003) reported that some Cape Sable seaside sparrows remained in unsuitable habitat that was formerly suitable, and that areas of suitable habitat lacked birds. Thus, the high site fidelity of this endangered species complicates its management.

Fur-bearing Mammals

Fur-bearing mammals are common inhabitants of coastal marshes and waterways and occupy a wide variety of habitat types, ranging from fresh to saline. Major species include muskrat (*Ondatra zibethicus*), nutria (*Myocastor coypus*), raccoon (*Procyon lotor*), mink (*Mustela vison*), and northern river otter (*Lontra canadensis*). Muskrat and nutria are herbivores and feed on a wide assortment of plants; however, certain plant types will support greater population densities than others (O'Neil 1949, Palmisano 1973). Muskrats are more specialized than nutria and prefer marshes where Olney bulrush is abundant (O'Neil 1949), which causes recently burned brackish marsh to support greatest muskrat densities (Palimisano 1972). Nutria eat a wider variety of plants than muskrats and reach greatest density in fresh marshes (Palmisano 1973).

The raccoon is usually omnivorous but coastal marshes often lack plant foods used by raccoons; consequently, they feed largely on animal materials. Mink are carnivores and feed mainly on fishes, crustaceans, small mammals and birds, snakes, and frogs. The river otter also is a carnivore and feeds heavily on fishes and crustaceans (Lowery 1974*b*).

The river otter ranges over an area of several square kilometers and spends a major portion of its time in or near water. Prolonged drought adversely affects the species; however, the impact of drought is less severe if water is available in deeper channels. Nutria, raccoon, and mink also are affected by excessive marsh drying; but excessive flooding may also cause the animals to abandon an area, particularly when protective cover becomes submerged (Lowery 1974*b*).

Alligators

The American alligator (*Alligator mississippiensis*) occurs in the southeastern United States and occupies coastal marshes and water bodies with salinities ranging from fresh to slightly brackish. Alligators are opportunistic feeders consuming both vertebrates and invertebrates; prey size varies with size of the alligator (Wolfe et al. 1987). Marsh water depths are critical in limiting populations and affecting nesting effort, nest flooding, egg desiccation mortality, and predation on alligator eggs and young (Nichols et al. 1976).

Freshwater Fisheries

Ponds, lakes, bayous, and canals in freshwater marshes of coastal areas are highly productive habitats for freshwater fisheries. Major families found in these habitats include sunfishes (Centrarchidae) and catfishes (Ictaluridae), and contain both foraging and predacious species. Important variables regulating productivity of aquatic habitats are suitable water depths, favorable water quality, adequate nutrients to supply primary producers, and low abundance of undesirable plants such as the exotic water hyacinth (Meador 1988).

Estuarine Fisheries

Estuarine fisheries included are those that use a coastal marsh environment as a part of their life cycle, mainly during post larval and juvenile stages. These include important commercial or sporting species such as Gulf menhaden (*Brevoortia patronus*), Atlantic croaker (*Micropogonias undulatus*), white shrimp (*Penaeaus setiferus*), and blue crab (*Callinectes sapidus*). These species breed in offshore waters and young move inland as larval or post larval forms. Young that reach favorable nursery areas, such as tidal marsh ponds and bayous, grow rapidly. Favorable nursery areas are those having suitable water salinity and temperature and an abundance of available food. The major food source is derived from detritus or fragments of marsh plants that have been carried into tidal marsh ponds by tidal currents. The young remain in the marsh systems for several months and then gradually make their way to deeper water, enroute to the sea (Gunter 1967).

Crawfish

Crawfish (*Cambarus* spp., *Procambarus* spp.) are an important component of freshwater marshes but occasionally occur even in marshes dominated by marshhay cordgrass during times of prolonged low salinity (J. A. Nyman, personal observation). Crawfish are important as predators of fish and vegetation, and as prey for many other species of fish and wildlife. Crawfish can be voracious consumers of wetland plants, particularly seedlings (Nystrom and Strand 1996). Some species such as red swamp crawfish (*P. clarkii*) provide a commercial and recreational resource for man. Summer drying of freshwater marshes is essential for completion of certain life stages and to reduce predators, which would otherwise feed on the crawfish once water is returned to the marsh (Perry et al. 1970). The red swamp crawfish is native to the southeastern United States but is threatening native flora and fauna where it was introduced elsewhere in the United States and throughout the world (Lodge et al. 2000, Smart et al. 2002).

COASTAL ALTERATIONS AND WETLAND LOSS

With a better understanding of how wetlands are affected by hydrological processes, coastal wetland managers (1) can better evaluate the effect of changes in water level or salinity and thereby prevent or restrict undesirable wetland changes, and (2) more accurately compare cost and effectiveness of management or restoration options. Small-scale direct alterations, such as those associated with the extensive ditching of Atlantic coast marshes during the early 1900s (Bourn and Cottam 1950, Dale and Hulsman 1990) and accelerating development of most coastal areas in the late 1900s (Culliton et al. 1992), can directly alter hydrological conditions in managed wetlands. An example of human activity that indirectly affects wetlands estuarine-wide is the deepening from 15 to 40 m of the Calcasieu Ship Channel in Louisiana, which probably increased water depths 40 cm (Suhayda et al. 1989) in adjacent wetlands such as in the Sabine National Wildlife Refuge. Another example is the dredging of the Cooper and Santee rivers in North Carolina that lowered salinity in adjacent wetlands.

Global sea-level rise and regional subsidence increases flooding and salinity in many coastal marshes. This combination is called submergence and averages 2.5–3.0 mm/yr along most of the United States coast (Titus 1996). In North America, submergence is slower in the far north because the earth's crust is still rebounding following the last ice age. Submergence also is faster where geologically recent sediments are deeper, such as in channels eroded by rivers during the last ice age that subsequently filled with sediments. These deposits are common in all drowned river valleys but are deepest in the deltaic plain of the Mississippi River, where submergence exceeds 10 mm/yr (Penland and Ramsey 1990). Subsidence and associated wetland loss is also accelerated by groundwater withdrawals (Stevenson et al. 2000). Global sea-level rise has been relatively slow since the end of the last ice age, but the rate may increase because of global warming (Titus 1996). Submergence requires that marshes increase in elevation by vertically accreting new layers of soil over former marsh surfaces, or that marshes migrate inland and upslope over former uplands.

On the Pacific Northwest and the Gulf coasts, faulting causes marsh loss by lowering the elevation of the marsh surface instantly, which causes flooding stresses that even wetland plants cannot tolerate. Faulting is caused by earthquakes in the Pacific Northwest (Kelsey et al. 2002), by the extraction of hydrocarbons in Texas (White and Morton 1997), and by the migration of fluids and gases within ancient and modern deposits of the Mississippi River in Louisiana (Kuecher et al. 2001). Faulting lowers the elevation of the marsh too rapidly to be offset by vertical accretion; thus, managing marsh loss resulting from faulting requires creating new marshes. In the Pacific Northwest, new marshes likely will develop naturally where earthquakes reduce the elevation of uplands. In Louisiana until the early 1900s, new marshes developed naturally as the Mississippi River built new deltas but current management of the river virtually prevents delta building (Coleman 1988). Some delta building occurs in Atchafalaya Bay (Coleman 1988), and delta building has been re-established on a small scale at the mouth of the Mississippi River (Boyer et al. 1997).

Coastal wetland managers must manage at different spatial scales. Small-scale hydrologic management activities can effectively counter undesirable small-scale hydrologic conditions. In Connecticut coastal marshes for example, restoring tidal exchange in the 1970s and 1980s reduced coverage by common reed, which had increased following impoundment that had been initiated to counter excessive drainage caused by ditching (Fell et al. 2000). Effectiveness of small-scale hydrologic management is limited because it can alter hydrological conditions only within the constraints imposed by larger-scale hydrological conditions. Altering larger-scale hydrological processes, such as those resulting from navigation and flood control projects, requires participation with governmental and private organizations in estuarine and watershed-level planning activities. Plans have been developed and initiated for many coastal wetlands in the United States. Those plans were summarized (RAE 2002) but are continually evolving. Managing to accommodate global sea-level rise and faulting likewise requires large scale planning to accommodate creation of new marshes. Even when managing and restoring small wetlands, landscape position can influence success. Landscape position can be critical when coastal wetland restoration or management tools are used in the management of estuarine-dependent fish or migratory shorebirds (Skagen et al. 1999, Simenstad et al. 2000).

VERTICAL ACCRETION

Vertical accretion results from formation of new soil on a marsh surface. Without vertical accretion, global sea-level rise would soon drown vegetation of coastal marshes.

Vertical accretion during gradual submergence can be self-regulating because tidal delivery of mineral sediments slows as flooding increases; soil organic matter also decomposes slower as flooding increases (Mitsch and Gosselink 1986:178). This process prevents vertical accretion from converting wetlands to uplands. Where submergence is rapid and mineral sediment deposition is inadequate, vertical accretion may be unable to maintain the marsh surface in the intertidal zone (DeLaune et al. 1983a, Hatton et al. 1983). Without adequate accretion, flooding stresses vegetation (DeLaune et al. 1983b, Mendelssohn et al. 1988), the vegetation eventually dies and the marsh converts to a shallow pond (DeLaune et al. 1994). The most rapid accretion recorded, 98 mm/yr, was in a portion of the Mississippi River Deltaic Plain that was submerging even faster (Nyman et al. 1993a).

Marsh soil is composed of mineral and organic matter; thus, vertical accretion results from their accumulation. Mineral matter remains after burning, whereas organic matter is consumed (Ball 1964, Davies 1974). Mineral and organic matter accumulation are related because clay sediments can supply plant nutrients (DeLaune et al. 1981) and because vegetation promotes sedimentation by reducing water velocity and biologically trapping sediments too fine to settle from the water column (Stumpf 1983). Thus, plant biomass and soil mineral content are positively correlated in marshes dominated by marshhay cordgrass and smooth cordgrass (DeLaune and Pezeshki 1988, Nyman et al. 1994). It is widely concluded that accretion is inadequate if mineral sedimentation is inadequate and that fate of coastal wetlands primarily depends on mineral sediment accumulation (Hatton et al. 1983, Stevenson et al. 1985, Reed 1989, Nyman et al. 1990b). Accretion in some New England and Louisiana marshes depends on organic matter accumulation via an unexplained vegetative growth mechanism (McCaffrey and Thomson 1980, Hatton et al. 1983, Bricker-Urso et al. 1989, Nyman et al. 1993a, Callaway et al. 1997).

The relative amounts of mineral and organic matter cannot be used to identify which limits accretion anymore than the relative amounts of N and P can be used to identify which, if either, limits plant production. Simple correlations between accretion and mineral sedimentation or between accretion and organic matter accumulation should not be used to infer which limits accretion. Controlled experiments to identify which limits accretion are impractical because it takes decades to accrete several millimeters of soil. Several teams used logic to conclude that sedimentation controlled soil bulk density (g/cm^3) and that organic matter accumulation controlled accretion (mm/yr) (McCaffrey and Thomson 1980, Gosselink et al. 1984). Nyman et al. (1993a) and Turner et al. (2000) used multiple regression to reach the same conclusions.

Mineral Sediments

Mineral sediments originate from either oceanic sources that are carried landward by coastal currents (Meade 1969), river sediments deposited directly by rivers (Frazier 1967), or river sediments discharged into nearshore coastal waters that are subsequently deposited by coastal currents. Sediment quality and quantity varies seasonally and among years. During low discharge years, riverine sediments are greatest shortly before or coincide with maximum river discharge (Mossa and Roberts 1990).

Table 1. Estimates of the amounts of mineral and organic matter required for vertical accretion depending on the submergence rate (x). Requirements vary with marsh type and submergence rate (cm/yr). Estimates are from Nyman et al. (1990b).

Marsh type	Mineral matter (g/m^2 yr^1)	Organic matter (g/m^2 yr^1)
Fresh	424 x	1,700 + 269 x
Brackish	1,052 x	553 + 583 x
Saline	1,798 x	923 + 601 x

During high discharge years, riverine sediment concentrations are greatest well before maximum discharge as the riverbed is scoured to accommodate increased flow (Mossa and Roberts 1990). Tides deliver mineral sediments to southeastern Atlantic coast marshes (Stevenson et al. 1988). Storms, however, deliver more sediments than tides in Louisiana and New England marshes (Stumpf 1983, Reed 1989). Different marsh types apparently require different amounts of mineral matter to accrete (Table 1).

Marsh managers should promote accretion where it varies with mineral sedimentation, plant biomass varies with soil mineral content, or where the role of mineral sediments in accretion and plant growth is unknown. Levees and spoil banks can prohibit sedimentation (Cahoon 1994) and fixed-crest weirs can reduce mineral sedimentation in streamside marsh but not the marsh interior (Reed et al. 1997). In managed marshes with levees and water control structures, managers should open structures when sediment availability is greatest in adjacent water bodies.

Organic Matter

Marsh soils need continual additions of soil organic matter because it continually decays. Even where there is no submergence, marsh surface elevation declines when more soil organic matter decays than is produced by emergent vegetation. The amount of soil organic matter needed varies among marsh types (Table 1) because soils contain different amounts of organic matter, and soil organic matter in different marsh types decomposes at different rates. Field and laboratory studies indicate that soil organic matter decays slower in marshes dominated by marshhay cordgrass than in those dominated by maidencane or smooth cordgrass (Smith et al. 1983, Nyman and DeLaune 1991). In addition to origin of soil organic matter, coastal marsh managers should consider soil aeration and soil temperature. Soil aeration greatly controls soil organic matter decay (Nyman and DeLaune 1991). Permanent wetland drainage accelerates soil organic matter decay and can cause loss of several meters of elevation. Permanently lowered water levels can also cause wetlands to loose elevation. Ditching permanently lowered water levels and reduced marsh elevation up to 10 cm in a Delaware marsh (Bourn and Cottam 1950:5). Tidal restriction permanently lowered water levels and reduced marsh elevation in Long Island Sound marshes (Roman et al. 1984). Unfortunately, the effects of drawdowns, which are 2–3 month-long drainage events used to promote establishment of annual vegetation in drained ponds, on elevation have seldom been studied. Extended low waters in Gulf coast marshes during 1996 lowered marsh surface elevations enough to reduce marsh surface elevation in an unmanaged marsh (Weifenbach and Clark 2000). Elevation loss was greater in a managed marsh that had been managed with a drawdown (Weifenbach and Clark 2000). Temperature greatly controls decomposition with fastest decay occurring during summer. The interaction of temperature and aeration probably causes prolonged low water, such as occur during a managed drawdown or natural drought, and reduces marsh elevation more during late summer than a similar event during spring.

Marsh managers should promote organic matter accumulation where accretion varies with organic matter accumulation, or where the role of organic matter in vertical accretion is unknown. Organic matter accumulation depends on interactions among plant production, soil organic matter decomposition, and litter accumulation. Soil strength also varies with live root content of the soil rather than mineral sediments in some marshes (McGinnis 1997). Thus, marsh managers should maximize live root biomass to reduce erosion around marsh ponds.

VARIABLES AFFECTING PLANT ESTABLISHMENT AND GROWTH

One of the most striking aspects of coastal marsh vegetation is predictable change in vegetation types across elevation and salinity gradients, or for several years following a disturbance. The apparent predictability of vegetation types implies that managers can manipulate disturbance and stresses of flooding and salinity to change vegetation. Common emergent plant species rarely are valuable wildlife food plants. Marsh managers often attempt to increase the carrying capacity for resident wildlife or use-days by migrant wildlife by increasing the abundance of preferred or important food plants. This management involves trade-offs when common plant species are valuable for vertical accretion, soil strength, or wildlife cover. Submerged aquatic vegetation species generally are valuable wildlife food plants. Marsh managers therefore generally seek to promote growth rather than to alter species composition within the submerged aquatic vegetation community. Exotic species are an important exception to this generalization. The potential to increase the abundance of submerged aquatic vegetation and emergent food plants decreases as salinity increases. Stress and disturbance are the primary variables that constrain and create management opportunities. For emergent vegetation, the primary stressors are salinity and flooding; the primary natural disturbances are from fire, ice, storms, and herbivory. Turbidity and the above variables, except fire, also control establishment and growth of submerged aquatic vegetation. Marsh managers cannot control these factors but can influence some of them.

Salinity

Seawater is a complex solution of dissolved salts, dominated by sodium chloride. The salt concentration in seawater is 36 parts per thousand (ppt); thus, 1,000 g of seawater contains 36 g of salt. Salinity in coastal marshes ranges from fresh (1 ppt) to greater than oceanic (36 ppt) with a gradient existing between marine and fresh waters. Annually, salinity in some marshes changes relatively little while other marshes range from fresh to oceanic. During

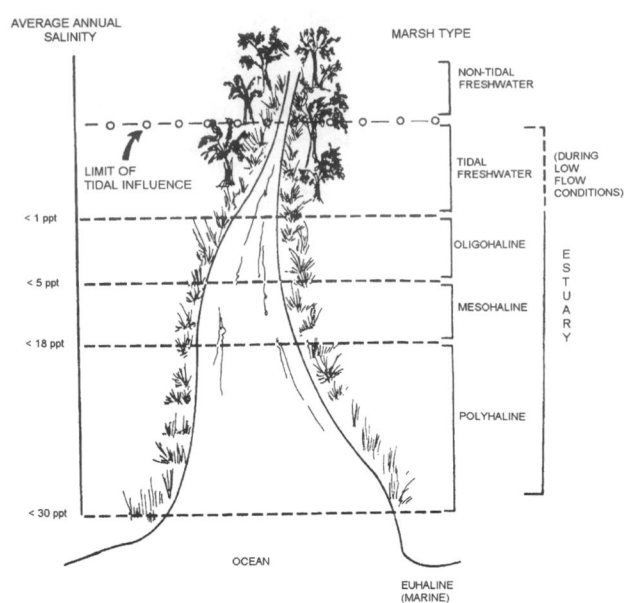

Fig. 1. The relationship between marsh type and average annual salinity (values are approximate only, after Odum et al. 1984). Terminology is based on Cowardin et al. (1979).

high tides, seawater flows inland through channels and is gradually diluted with freshwater. Tides generally intrude into rivers further upstream than salinity, which creates tidal, freshwater marshes. Examples abound from the Atlantic coast (Pasternack et al. 2000), the Gulf coast (Holm and Sasser 2001), and the Pacific coast (Simenstad et al. 2000). Evaporation can concentrate salts until salinity exceeds that of seawater. This is especially true where evaporation exceeds rainfall and marshes flood infrequently. Examples occur on the Gulf coast (Hedgepeth 1947) and Atlantic coast (Weigert and Freeman 1990).

Water salinity strongly controls vegetation composition (Fig. 1) and productivity because salinity stresses vegetation (DeLaune et al. 1987). Emergent vegetation in tidal, non-saline marshes generally is richer and has more complex patterns than in saline marshes (Chabreck 1970, Pasternack et al. 2000). Similarly, submerged aquatic vegetation in tidal non-saline marshes generally is richer and more abundant than in saline marshes (Chabreck 1971, Yozzo and Smith 1998, Simenstad et al. 2000). Richness declines as salinity increases because few species can tolerate salinity. Species that can tolerate saline water actually thrive in freshwater, but the reverse is not true. Salt-tolerant plants rarely occur in freshwater marshes because they are out-competed by salt-intolerant plants for root space, sunlight, or other unknown factors when salinity is low. For example, smooth cordgrass grows best at 0 ppt in the absence of competition (Parrondo et al. 1978) but, in Louisiana, it is restricted to marshes where average salinity exceeds 15 ppt (Chabreck 1970). On the Gulf coast of the Unites States, the terms fresh, intermediate, brackish, and saline (Chabreck 1970) reflect the perception that salinity is the primary cause of species associations.

Average salinity may be less important than salinity peaks in controlling species composition but, more important than salinity maximums in controlling productivity. Salinity in the pore-water of the soil, which is the salinity environment experienced by emergent vegetation, is often different from that in floodwater on the marsh surface or in adjacent ponds, lakes, bayous, and canals. In regularly flooded marshes, pore-water may reflect long-term salinity. In irregularly flooded marshes, pore-water exceeds salinity of floodwater because evaporation from the marsh surface concentrates salts. Seawater trapped in coastal lagoons or slightly elevated marshes, where high evaporation and low freshwater occur, may contain salt levels much greater than sea strength. These waters, such as in the Laguna Madre of Texas and Mexico (Hedgepeth 1947), are described as hypersaline and contain salt concentrations that few plants can tolerate.

Human activity has altered salinity in some coastal marshes sufficiently to change one marsh type to another. Small-scale examples abound on the Atlantic coast of the United States where roadways restrict freshwater drainage and maintain a body of water that dilutes incoming tides (Roman et al. 1984). These changes may be helping the spread of common reed on the Atlantic coast (Chambers et al. 1999). Whereas roads across streams and rivers can freshen coastal marshes, navigation channels within streams and rivers can increase salinity. A large-scale example occurs in southeastern Louisiana where construction of a navigation channel (Mississippi River Gulf Outlet) accelerated drainage of freshwater and replacement by marine waters over thousands of hectares of baldcypress (*Taxodium distichum*) swamp and low-salinity marshes. Even where navigation channels cause only periodic salinity incursions, emergent vegetation has been altered (Holm and Sasser 2001). Coastal marshes also can be affected by the damming of rivers. Dams on rivers flowing to the Texas coast resulted in hypersaline conditions in the Laguna Madre (Stutzenbaker and Weller 1989). Attempts to counter large-scale salinity increases with local restrictions on tidal exchange have been unsuccessful (Chabreck et al. 1979, Bourgeois and Webb 1999). Total impoundment of a marsh where rainfall exceeds evaporation can maintain nonsaline conditions. An example is a 26,000-ha impoundment in Sabine National Wildlife Refuge in southwestern Louisiana, which is the only freshwater marsh remaining between Sabine Lake and Calcasieu Lake (Gosselink et al. 1979).

Flooding

Some coastal marshes flood daily while others rarely flood. Flooding strongly controls vegetation composition and productivity because it deprives plant roots of oxygen. The resulting stress can kill plants (Mendelssohn and McKee 1988). Flooding stress is probably more related to length than to frequency of flooding events. Several classification schemes are used to classify coastal marshes on the basis of flooding. In areas where water levels result primarily from solar/lunar tides, such as the Pacific and northeast Atlantic coasts of the United States, these classification schemes are feasible because flood frequency and duration can be predicted from tide charts and measurements of marsh elevation. Coats et al. (1989) illustrated the usefulness of such data in planning wetland restoration and management in San Francisco Bay. In areas where tides are dominated by winds, such as Chesapeake Bay and the Gulf coast of the United States, these classification schemes are of little use to marsh managers because of a lack of long-

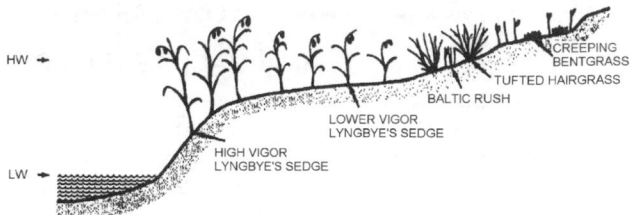

Fig. 2. Possible zonation pattern in a brackish Pacific Northwest tidal marsh (after Seliskar and Gallagher 1983).

term hourly data needed to calculate flood duration. In practice, most coastal marsh managers classify marshes based on species composition of emergent vegetation rather than flooding. On the northeast Atlantic coast of the United States, classifying marshes as regularly or irregularly flooded reflect the perception that flood frequency is the primary cause of differences in species associations. Within most coastal marshes, emergent vegetation is taller and more productive adjacent to creeks and bayous than in the marsh interior because interior soils regularly drain. This generally applies whether the streamside marsh is lower (Fig. 2) or higher than interior marsh (Fig. 3).

Fire

Fire is the primary disturbance factor in many tidal, non-saline marshes but is less common in saline marshes. Plant species richness is generally greatest in the growing season immediately following a fire. After several growing seasons, species richness declines as a few species regain dominance. Fire has been occurring in coastal marshes since before European settlement (Frost 1995). Fires start naturally via lightning and by spontaneous combustion (Viosca 1931). Native Americans and initial European settlers regularly burned coastal marshes but their activity may have been irrelevant in the southeastern United States because fire size and frequency of lightning were great (Frost 1995). On the Pacific coast, however, burning by Native Americans probably was important in governing vegetation structure because size of fires was smaller and lightning was less frequent (Frost 1995). Prescribed burning decreased by the early 1900s, at least on the Gulf coast of the United States, but returned by 1926 (Hoffpauer 1968). By the 1930s, wildlife managers concluded that periodic burning prevented wild fires and increased abundance of important wildlife food plants (Arthur 1931:262–265, Griffith 1940, Lynch 1941, Smith 1942, Uhler 1944, O'Neil 1949:93–107). Many marsh managers on the Gulf and Atlantic coasts burn marshes regularly (Nyman and Chabreck 1995, Stevenson et al. 2000). However, some burning apparently is done because of tradition rather than to achieve clearly stated, measurable goals.

Hurricanes

Hurricanes regularly impact marshes on the Gulf and southeastern Atlantic coasts. Although coastal marshes help reduce inland movement of storm-driven floodwaters, hurricanes may be the most destructive force affecting marshes and wildlife populations. Harris and Chabreck (1958) noted removal of sod that was 0.3 m thick and up to 1.5 m in diameter by a hurricane and a 140% increase in openings in the vegetation. Chabreck and Palmisano

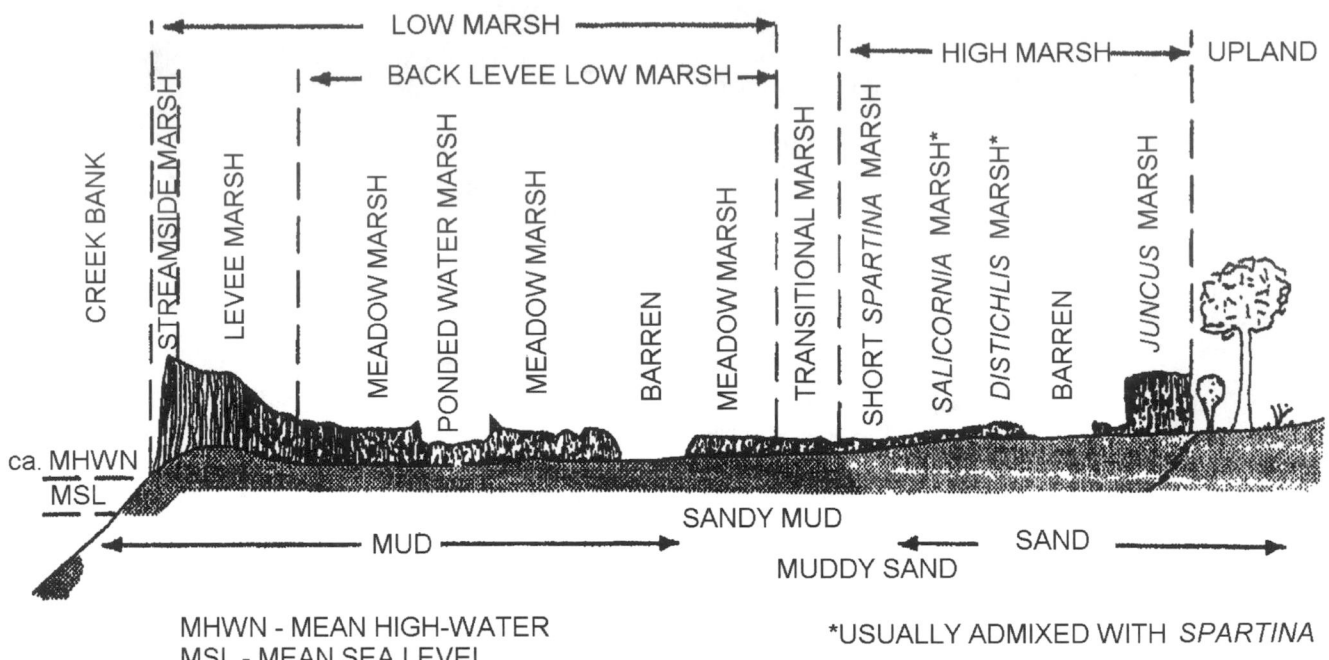

Fig. 3. Possible zonation pattern in a southeastern Atlantic tidal saline marsh showing sedimentary development (after Weigert and Freeman 1990).

(1973) noted a 118% increase in openings in the emergent vegetation following a hurricane. In 2002, tropical storm Isadore and/or hurricane Lilly virtually eliminated submerged aquatic vegetation from over 100 km of coastal Louisiana (J. A. Nyman, personal observation). Hurricanes have reduced white-tailed deer (*Odocoileus virginianus*), muskrat, nutria, rabbit (*Sylvilagus* spp.), and raccoon numbers by 60–70% (Ensminger and Nichols 1957, Harris and Chabreck 1958). Marsh managers can do little to manage such damage.

Hurricanes push high salinity water over normal impediments and into nonsaline marshes where high salinity levels may be maintained for weeks or months. Vegetation may be stressed or killed if the storm surge is much saltier than normal waters and higher salinity is maintained in the marsh. One of the dangers of using levees to manage coastal marshes is the threat of storm tides pushing high salinity water over levees and the resulting long period of flooding. Some managers of marsh impoundments in coastal Louisiana have removed portions of levees following hurricanes to reduce flooding because they have concluded that it is better to lose water control for several years than it is to flood with high salinity water for several weeks.

Herbivory

Wildlife managers face conflicting goals regarding herbivory. A common management goal is to increase availability of food plants for geese, muskrats, nutria, or cattle. Conversely, herbivory by geese, muskrats, and nutria can be sufficient to denude coastal marshes of vegetation and cause emergent marsh to convert to shallow open water (Lynch et al. 1947). In the ideal situation, plant mortality caused by herbivory is compensatory to other forms of mortality. Thus, no need would exist to increase food plant abundance because herbivore populations would be limited by a factor other than food availability.

In situations where food limits herbivore populations, increasing abundance of food plants would increase herbivore populations. This was a common situation and management objective before the 1990s when pelt prices of nutria and muskrat were sufficiently high to support commercial trapping. Currently, populations of nutria and muskrats are adequate to support limited commercial trapping and there is little need to encourage growth of food plants for furbearers.

Herbivores may consume plants faster than plants can replace themselves eliminating vegetation and destroying habitat for many species. This denuding of vegetation has been called "eatouts" and occurs on all North American coasts (e.g., Lynch et al. 1947, Smith and Odum 1981). In these situations, herbivore populations are limited by a variable other than food availability until vegetation is denuded. After vegetation is reduced, animals starve or migrate to adjacent areas. Species causing most "eatouts" are muskrats, nutria, and geese (Lynch et al. 1947, Smith and Odum 1981).

Turbidity

Water clarity, measured as turbidity, is the most important variable limiting submersed aquatic vegetation in coastal marsh ponds because it controls the amount of sunlight available for photosynthesis. Silt, clay, and phytoplankton can cause high turbidity. Fish can indirectly cause high turbidity by constantly disturbing loose bottom sediments. Sedimentation can be sufficiently rapid to bury emergent and submerged aquatic vegetation. Commercial culture of Pacific oysters (*Crassostrea gigas*) can reduce and eliminate submerged aquatic vegetation beds in the Pacific Northwest by increasing sedimentation rates (Everett et al. 1995). Limiting the inflow of surface waters that carry river-borne or marine silt and clays can reduce turbidity. Drawdowns are also used to reduce turbidity by causing bottom material to cement together and removing fish (Chabreck 1960).

Competition and Succession

Much of the variation in vegetation across a marsh results from stress gradients (flooding or salinity) because stresses influence competition among plant species for light and nutrients. Managing stresses generally requires manipulating water exchange between marshes and adjacent water bodies. Restoring tidal exchange to remove common reed is an example of increasing salinity stress to achieve a management goal (Fell et al. 2000).

Variation in vegetation over time results from succession following disturbances (fire, ice, hurricanes and, on the Pacific coast of the United States, vertical land movement). Robust, perennial plants that are unimportant wildlife foods such as cordgrasses, maidencane, or common reed usually dominate a recently undisturbed marsh. Most important wildlife food plants, such as the flatsedges (*Cyperus* spp.), smartweed (*Polygonum* spp.), and barnyard grasses (*Echinochloa* spp.), are annual plants and must have open, exposed soil for germination and growth. Small seedlings are unable to compete with larger plants and, to survive, must take advantage of openings created by disturbances that kill other plants.

The primary tool that marsh managers use to disturb emergent vegetation is fire. Managers also can drain marsh ponds to initiate the establishment of annual vegetation on exposed bottoms. The goal of drainage, or drawdown, is to promote growth of annual species that are abundant seed producers. Drawdowns are harder to achieve in microtidal than in regularly flooded or seasonal wetlands because continuous levees and pumps generally are needed. In regularly flooded wetland, gravity drainage is sufficient to achieve drawdown.

MARSH MANAGEMENT PLANNING

Marsh management is costly and benefits gained depend upon the amount invested and skill with which the program is planned. Unfortunately, management frequently has been initiated to correct problems that were not fully understood or to achieve vague goals. This is a problem on the Atlantic (Perry et al. 2001), Gulf (Chabreck 1988), and Pacific coasts (Williams and Farber 2001). Planning by persons familiar with a problem and the ecological processes operating in the area will reduce the cost of the program and increase its effectiveness.

Ecological processes in coastal marshes are complex and involve the action and interaction of numerous factors. Managers manipulate these processes to produce the desired plant and animal communities. Achieving management goals may require changing conditions; achieving other management goals may require protective measures to maintain existing conditions.

In management of extensive areas of marsh, the only practical tool is manipulation of water levels and water salinities. By manipulating water levels and salinities, the marsh manager can either encourage desirable plants or discourage undesirable plants until favorable conditions are created. Under more intensive management, measures such as sediment trapping may be used to create special habitat conditions.

All plants of a particular area have a range of tolerance for water salinity, quality, and depth, and, generally, plants will grow as long as the conditions are within this range (Penfound and Hathaway 1938, Chabreck 1972). Whenever water conditions go above or below the tolerance range for an extended period of time, plants unable to tolerate the changed conditions will die and other species, whose requirements have been met as a result of the change, will invade the area.

In planning a marsh management project, careful consideration should be given to several factors. There should first be an evaluation of environmental conditions present in the area such as major plant communities, drainage patterns, water quality, water levels, soils, and existing structures. This evaluation should consider the area to be managed as well as the estuary and watershed level. Second, animal communities in the area should be identified and target species selected for management. The objectives should be clearly stated, site specific, measurable, and long-term. Third, habitat conditions including plant communities, water quality and levels, soils, and other factors necessary to produce the target animal communities should be identified. Fourth, the optimal growth requirements to produce the desired and undesired plant communities should be identified. Fifth, management procedures available for producing the habitat conditions required by target animal communities should be evaluated to develop specific management guidelines. Sixth, acquisition of data that can be used to evaluate the management effectiveness must be planned. Management activities implemented without subsequent data collection can be neither defended nor criticized objectively. Regular collection of post-management data is needed to guide management improvement. Objectively evaluating marsh management requires data from either a similar unmanaged area or from a suite of unmanaged areas (Brinson and Rheinhardt 1996). Simply comparing the managed area before and after management is initiated or altered is unlikely to be useful because of annual variability in hydrological conditions, and plant and animal abundance (Neckles et al. 2002, Restore America's Estuaries 2002).

STRUCTURAL MARSH MANAGEMENT
Marsh Creation and Restoration

Marsh Creation.—Created marshes generally have broad habitat goals with some having been created to benefit several fish species (Simenstad et al. 2000) or a single bird species (Zedler 1993). Studies of coastal marsh creation on dredged spoil largely have been conducted by the U.S. Army Corps of Engineers. Early studies were in North Carolina (Woodhouse et al. 1972) while others dealing with dredged material and shoreline stabilization were along Chesapeake Bay (Garbisch et al. 1975), Galveston Bay (Dodd and Webb 1975), and San Francisco Bay (Knutson 1976, Josselyn and Buchholz 1984).

Two types of marsh creation are used in coastal regions. One involves creation of marsh from material taken from navigation channels and deposited in shallow water. The other type involves sedimentation that results from diversion of river water into shallow bays (Chabreck 1989) or restoration of tidal flow to impounded, former wetlands (Chamberlain and Barnhart 1993). Site selection for marsh creation projects requires field investigations and laboratory tests to evaluate location, bottom topography, wave and water energy, and substrate characteristics such as consolidation and sedimentation.

Material dredged from navigation channels can be used to create emergent wetlands if the dredged material is placed to create an intertidal surface. Goals of projects to create marsh on dredged material are to optimize use of the material, expand area of wetlands, and slow erosion. This activity generally has been successful at creating new habitat for emergent vegetation, but success varies with region. In marshes with firm substrates, success is greater than in areas where the substrate is poorly consolidated. Without a firm base for support of deposits, the dredged material rapidly subsides and sinks below the surface of the water (Chabreck 1989). Substrate composed of fine clays and silts may remain in a slurry state for a significant period after placement and require a retaining structure for containment. The final elevation when such substrates dry is much more difficult to predict than when substrates are composed of sandy material that lose water and dry quickly (U.S. Army Corps of Engineers 1986). Many dredged marsh creation projects in coastal Louisiana are more elevated, flood less, and have different vegetation than natural marshes (J. A. Nyman, personal observation).

The hydraulic pipeline dredge is most commonly used for projects involving dredged material. Placement sites should be as near the excavation site as possible to reduce expense. However, material can be moved through the pipeline for several kilometers with intermediate booster pumps at substantially greater costs. Important hydrological factors in marsh design are water salinity, tidal range, flood stages, and wave and wind action. Mining all sediments from a single site minimizes expense. The effects of the resulting deep water on biota are unknown and likely undesirable.

Riverine flow can be used to re-establish wetlands where they have subsided and been replaced by shallow, open water. Cycles of marsh creation, subsidence, and rebuilding are natural to virtually all river and even stream deltas worldwide but are most apparent in the Mississippi River Deltaic Plain (Coleman 1988). Openings in natural or artificial levees permit water confined in river channels to enter adjacent shallow water areas where the unconfined water spreads and slows. This allows sediment to be deposited as river water spreads into shallow waters and velocity decreases, creating deltas (Chabreck 1988). Sediment diversions in the lower Mississippi River have created wetlands at a rate of 4.7 ha/year (Boyer et al. 1997).

Tidal flow can be used to recreate wetlands where they were impounded for other uses, generally agriculture or salt production. Some refer to these projects as restoration (Williams and Farber 2001) perhaps because they are tools in the restoration of larger ecosystems; we refer to them as marsh creation. Some of these efforts have specific goals such as creating wading bird habitat (Fell et al. 2000) or creating fish habitat (Simenstad et al. 2000). Success of these projects depends on sufficient sediments in adjacent waters and tidal energy to carry sediments into the restoration area because impounded, former wetlands are generally lower in elevation than adjacent water levels. Restoring tidal flow to impounded, former wetlands is common on the Atlantic and Pacific coasts (Chamberlain and Barnhart 1993, Able et al. 2000), but not on the Gulf coast because tidal energy and sediment availability are so low that breached impoundments remain shallow open water. On the Atlantic coast, Perry et al. (2001) recommended grading sites to favor low marsh rather than high marsh

prior to re-establishing tidal exchange to reduce coverage by common reed.

Establishment of marsh plants on dredged material can be left to natural invasion or attained with artificial propagation. In freshwater areas, natural invasion by marsh plants will occur within one growing season. In other marsh types, several years may be required for natural invasion of marsh plants and planting desired species is recommended. Planting marshhay cordgrass is recommended for sites in intermediate and brackish marshes along the Gulf of Mexico (Eleuterius 1974). A large seed source makes plantings unnecessary in San Francisco Bay (Williams and Farber 2001). In saltwater areas, smooth cordgrass should be planted below mean high tide, and marshhay cordgrass above mean high tide (Allen et al. 1978, Landin 1986). Plant spacings of 45 and 90 cm were tested (the 45-cm spacing required 4 times more plants). The 45-cm spacing had lower plant survival but produced stands with greater density. Fertilization of plantings did not increase survival (Allen and Webb 1983).

Created marshes generally lack flora and fauna of natural marshes, which can be problematic when the goal is to create habitat for an endangered species (Zedler 1993). Many differences between natural and created marshes arise from lower amounts of soil organic matter in created marshes (Craft et al. 2002). The resulting differences in soil chemical environment cascade up the food web and alter emergent vegetation, soil annelids and insects (Levin and Talley 2002), and fish (Chamberlain and Barnhart 1993). Dredged material wetlands create benthic and avian communities similar to natural wetlands if the created wetlands have water levels and circulation patterns that mimic those in natural wetlands and, if the created wetlands are near natural wetlands (Brusati et al. 2001). There appear to be fewer differences between created and natural wetlands when tidal or riverine energy, rather than dredging equipment, deposits the sediments. This may occur because tidal and riverine waters cannot elevate the sediments higher than found in natural wetlands (J. A. Nyman, personal observation).

Marsh Restoration.—Marsh restoration primarily involves re-establishment of vegetation in a deteriorating marsh. This can be accomplished through diversion of freshwater or sediment into the marsh to offset factors causing the deterioration. In some situations, factors causing deterioration can be regulated or offset by impoundment or by constructing weirs in drainage systems of the marsh. These projects may be classified as marsh enhancement.

Diversion of freshwater into marshes is currently used, to a limited extent, at several locations along the lower Mississippi River to restore deteriorating marshes; it is being considered in other areas where feasible. Weir construction has been widespread in coastal Louisiana, but marsh impoundment construction has been largely restricted to areas where soil conditions permit construction of continuous levee systems.

Restoring a coastal marsh to its original condition is costly and, in most cases, extremely difficult. Coastal marshes are dynamic systems and, if it were possible to completely restore a marsh, it could be restored to only one stage in its frequently changing past. Thus, a goal of restoration is to maximize productivity and enhance the quality and diversity of the environment. Other possible goals include restoration of saline conditions to marshes freshened by tidal constrictions (Atlantic coast) and restoration of fresher conditions to marshes affected by salt-water intrusion caused by navigation channels (Gulf coast).

Freshwater re-introduction from the Mississippi River has been used for marsh restoration to restore extensive portions of the rapidly deteriorating marshes of the Mississippi River Deltaic Plain. These actions are more commonly called river diversions and restore spring floods prevented by flood protection levees on the Mississippi River. Culverts and siphons are used to allow river water to pass through or over levees during flood stages. Water is allowed to flow through the marsh adding sediment and nutrients, and lowering water salinity. The added sediment may raise elevation of the marsh and help offset land loss. Reducing water salinity and adding nutrients promotes plant growth, increases plant species diversity, and improves the marsh and adjacent waters for fish and wildlife. A major handicap of this type of restoration is that it can only be used in marshes in drainage basins adjacent to the freshwater source. Areas on the landward side of flood protection levees are usually developed; diverting river water for marsh nourishment raises not only environmental but also socioeconomic and political issues (Chabreck 1988).

Freshwater re-introduction into an estuarine basin will change salinity regimes and enhance vegetation growth; however, concern has been expressed regarding other impacts associated with water salinity changes. Harvestable resources such as eastern oysters (*Crassostrea virginica*) and brown shrimp become more accessible as salt water encroaches into formerly freshwater or low salinity habitats closer to urban areas. Unfortunately, industrial and domestic pollution also are more severe in these areas and may affect these resources (Chatry and Chew 1985).

Marsh Impoundments

Marsh impoundments have been used to improve waterfowl habitat since the mid-1900s (Griffith 1940, Landers et al. 1976). Improving habitat for wading birds will require providing shallower water than for waterfowl (Isola et al. 2000). Impoundments have been criticized because they reduce tidal exchange which may provide an energy subsidy that can increases plant production (Odum et al. 1983), reduce mineral sedimentation which can be important to vertical accretion (Reed et al. 1997), and reduce access to the marsh by estuarine-dependent fish and crustaceans. However, studies on the Gulf and Pacific coasts found that plant production increases in response to tidal restriction if it reduces salinity or flooding stress (Zedler et al. 1980, Flynn et al. 1999). A problem for marsh managers is that some marsh impoundments can fail to reduce stress as intended (Flynn et al. 1999).

Marsh impoundments can be categorized based on water depths and salinity regimes into 4 types: permanently flooded with freshwater, manipulated freshwater, permanently flooded with brackish water, and manipulated brackish water (Chabreck 1960). The effects of impoundments on fish and wildlife resources vary with the resources involved and means for controlling water levels and salinities to accomplish specific objectives. These objectives include improvement of wildlife habitat, aquaculture, water storage for agricultural irrigation and industrial uses, flooding marshes for mosquito control, and maintaining favorable water depths for navigation.

Many impoundments are drawn down, i.e., drained for several months in spring and summer to establish annual vegetation by converting pond areas to mud flat areas. When reflooded, the ponds provide abundant seeds for waterfowl (Landers et al. 1976). While these efforts are generally successful in fresh marshes, they fail in saline marshes. Even in marshes dominated by marshhay cordgrass where salinity averaged 5 ppt, exposed pond bottoms generally fail to develop stands of annual vegetation (J. A. Nyman, personal observation) even though the drawdowns reduced pond edge erosion (McGinnis 1997). Drawdowns in saline marsh and some brackish marsh can kill living vegetation (Neely 1962). The resulting conditions create pH < 2 and acid-sulfate soils (Moore et al. 1999). Problems with acid-sulfate soils rarely develop in the United Sates but continue to develop where mangrove swamps are drained for rice or shrimp production. Drawdowns in any marsh might reduce marsh elevation by accelerating oxidation of soil organic matter, and increase flooding stress on emergent vegetation when normal water levels return. Many brackish and saline marsh impoundments focus on submerged aquatic vegetation such as widgeongrass rather than emergent, seed-producing species (Landers et al. 1976).

Although impoundments are usually constructed with a primary objective, secondary values often develop that can be incorporated into the management scheme. For example, impoundments were constructed in southwestern Louisiana to improve habitat for migratory ducks (Chabreck 1960). Wetland managers found the water manipulation system used to produce duck foods in freshwater impoundments could be modified slightly to produce crops of red swamp crawfish without affecting growth of duck foods. Consequently, management of this secondary resource was included in operational plans (Perry et al. 1970), and the impoundments were opened to sport fishing for crawfish during spring and summer.

A permanently flooded brackish water impoundment constructed for duck habitat in Louisiana also was managed as a nursery area for shrimp and blue crabs as a secondary objective. Similar multiple-use management was conducted in South Carolina (Strange 1987). In Louisiana, brown shrimp were introduced in February and white shrimp were introduced in July by opening water control structures at high tide when post-larval shrimp were present. Sport fishermen were permitted to harvest shrimp with cast nets and blue crabs with hand lines. The annual harvest from the impoundments was estimated to be 68 kg of shrimp and 15 dozen crabs per hectare over an area of 2000 ha (Davidson and Chabreck 1989).

A permanently flooded freshwater impoundment was constructed and managed for waterfowl in southwestern Louisiana. The impoundment received high use by waterfowl, but also developed large crops of sunfish and was heavily used by fishermen. Sport fishing was included as an important aspect of management plans (Turner 1966).

Engineering and Hydrology of Impoundments.— Impoundments are constructed in coastal marshes by enclosing an area with a continuous levee system or by using levee systems in conjunction with elevated ridges or uplands to form a closed system (Ensminger 1963). Water control structures are an important part of an impoundment. Spillways are used to remove surplus water associated with rainfall or hurricanes, and stop-logs are used to

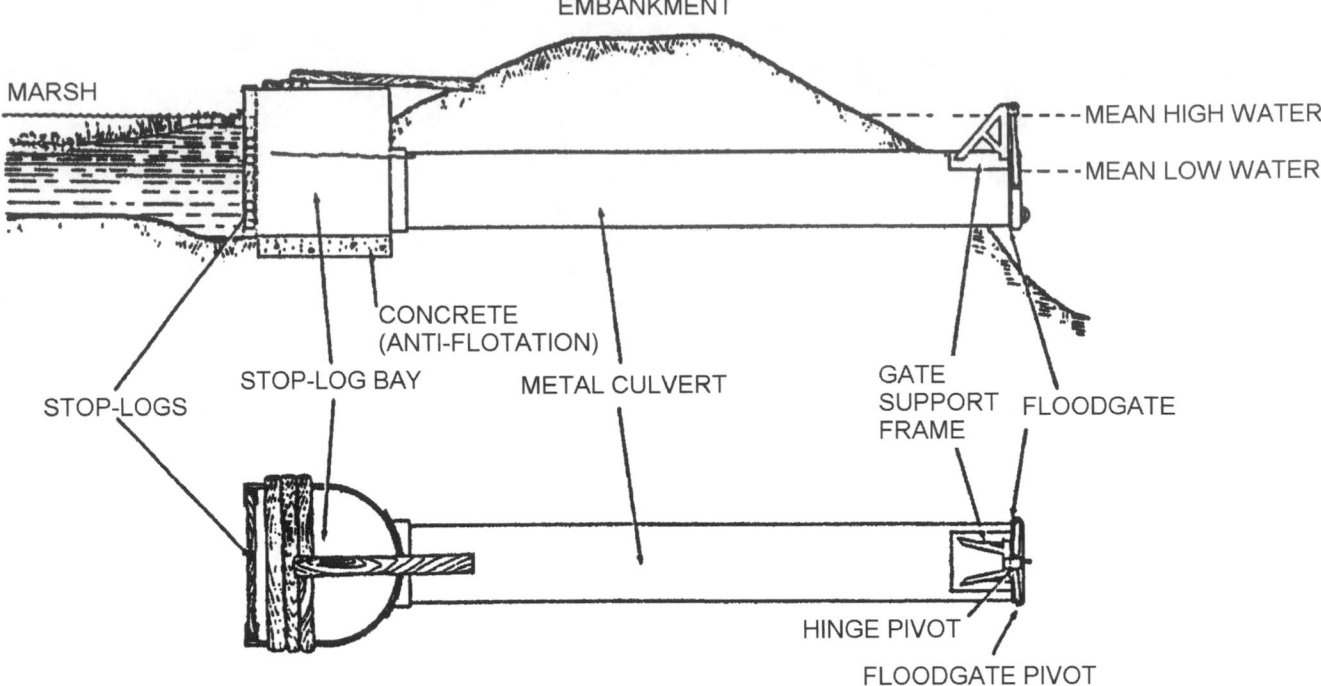

Fig. 4. Side and top views of a flap-gated culvert with stop-logs. The stop-logs are inside the managed marsh and can be removed to allow water to drain in the managed marsh, or stacked to prevent drainage. The flap-gate is outside the managed marsh and can be raised to allow the entry of outside water, or left flapping out. When flapping out, the flap will close when the outside water is higher than inside water, but open when outside water is lower than inside water. Stop-logs are removed and the flap gate is left flapping out to draw down a marsh (after L. J. Broussard, U.S. Department of Agriculture, Soil Conservation Service, Alexandria, Louisiana, USA).

vary minimum water levels. Increasingly, flap-gated culverts are combined with stop-log structures (Fig. 4).

Facilities must also be provided for completely draining and flooding impoundments. Gravity drainage may effectively remove water through gated culverts in areas with extreme tidal fluctuation. However, in many areas gravity drainage is inadequate and marsh managers must use pumping units to remove water.

Rainfall is the primary water source for most marsh impoundments, particularly freshwater systems. If rainfall is not adequate, ample water may be unavailable to meet management requirements and pumps may be needed. Some marsh managers use one pumping system, with appropriate control structures, to either drain or flood an impoundment. Pumping may also be used to flood brackish water impoundments. In some areas, water can be added by opening control gates on high tides and closing them as tides fall. This process can be facilitated with structures having flap gates that are opened and closed by water pressure (Neely 1960, Williams 1987).

The vegetation and hydrologic characteristics of coastal wetlands are primary factors affecting their value to fish and wildlife. Vegetation produced in wetlands serves as a primary food source and influences the number of animals a given area will support. Different species of wildlife have preferences for different species of vegetation; consequently, plant species composition of an area often governs the animal species in the area. Hydrologic characteristics are important factors and water depth affects the ability of many animals to use an area. Hydrologic factors such as water salinity and tidal action may affect species tolerance and access to a particular habitat.

Permanently Flooded Freshwater Impoundments.— Marsh impoundments of this type are usually inland and have minor tidal influence. In non-impounded fresh marsh, drainage is usually slow and water is deeper than in regularly flooded tidal marsh. Marshes permanently flooded by impounding usually have even greater water depths. During periods with unusually abundant rainfall, water may be as much as 1.2 m deep.

Marsh soils typically have low mineral content because of a lack of sediment in floodwater and because decomposition is slower in flooded soils. In permanently flooded freshwater impoundments, organic matter accumulates at a greater rate and marsh elevations increase above that of natural marsh. Scattered floating mats of organic material often develop on the water surface. Water level manipulation in this type of impoundment is minimal and operational costs are greatly reduced.

Typical vegetation consists of perennial plants adapted to growth in deep water. Common plants are spikerushes, California bulrush (*Schoenoplectus californicus*), bulltongue, and many species of aquatic and floating-leaf plants. Floating mats of organic matter that develop are held together by emergent species such as water pennyworts (*Hydrocotyle* spp.) and maidencane (Chabreck 1960).

Manipulated Freshwater Impoundments.—Marsh impoundments of this type are usually inland from the normal influence of tides. A water manipulation system similar to moist soil management is used to affect plant growth. Impoundments managed for ducks are drained during the growing season to encourage germination and growth of annual plants. The major species produced by drying are grasses and sedges, such as coast cockspur (*Echinochloa wal-*

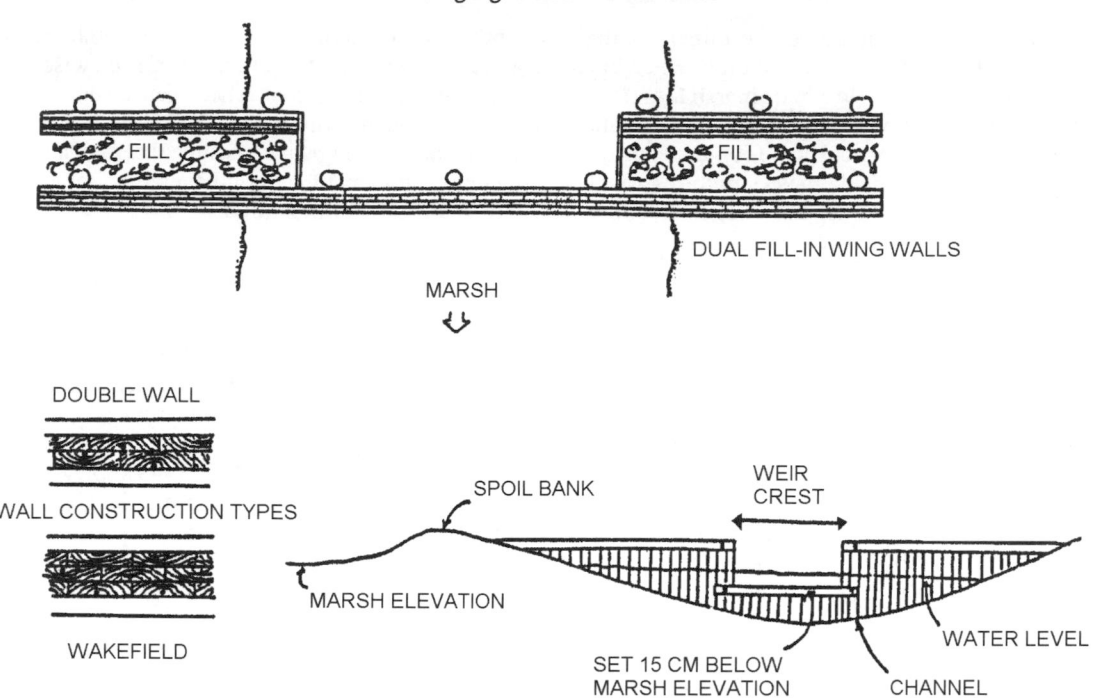

Fig. 5. Side and top views of a fixed-crest weir. Increasingly, stop-logs are used to vary the crest of the weir (after L. J. Broussard, U.S. Department of Agriculture, Soil Conservation Service, Alexandria, Louisiana, USA).

teri), fall panicum (*Panicum dichotomiflorum*), and fragrant flatsedge (*Cyperus odoratus*) (Chabreck 1960, Baldwin 1968). Other plants often found in this type are bulltongue, California bulrush, and spikerushes. Impoundments can be reflooded when seedlings are about 15 cm tall. Water depths are usually maintained at low levels (10–50 cm) during winter to make the areas attractive to dabbling ducks. Crawfish are produced in abundance by this management system and provide food for many forms of wildlife (Perry et al. 1970).

Permanently Flooded Brackish Water Impoundments.— Impoundments of this type are usually managed to produce widgeongrass and dwarf spikerush (*Eleocharis parvula*) to attract ducks (Chabreck 1960, Gordon et al. 1989). A survey of marsh impoundments in South Carolina disclosed that permanently flooded brackish water impoundments were used most often (Morgan et al. 1975). Although these impoundments are described as permanently flooded, temporary drainage at 2- to 3-yr intervals to remove fish, consolidate bottom material, and reduce water turbidity was necessary for best widgeongrass growth (Chabreck 1960, Joanen and Glasgow 1965).

Manipulated Brackish Water Impoundments.—Impoundments are often constructed in tidal marsh and alternately flooded with brackish water to a depth of 15–20 cm and then drained during the growing season to encourage growth of sturdy bulrush (*Schoenoplectus robustus*) and widgeongrass (Neely 1960, Landers et al. 1976). Plant production during drawdown can be 3–4 times greater than in unmanaged marsh but even well designed impoundments can fail to properly drawdown and produce enhanced plant growth (Flynn et al. 1999). Impoundments of this type comprised approximately 10% of the total area of marsh impoundments in South Carolina (Morgan et al. 1975). These areas are flooded to a depth of 25–30 cm during fall and winter to provide habitat for ducks. If water salinity exceeds 15 ppt, growth and seed production

of sturdy bulrush will be adversely affected (Gordon et al. 1989).

Weirs, Sills, and Flashboards

Water control structures in marsh drainage systems are important tools that can be used to counter human-induced increases in tidal exchange and prevent undesirable, natural drainage of marsh ponds. Initially, sod was used to restore waterfowl habitat quality impaired by mosquito ditches (Bradbury 1938) but sheet pilings and rocks are now more commonly used to restore more natural hydrologic conditions (Fig. 5). The term "weir" is common on the Gulf coast while "flashboard" or "sill" is common on the Atlantic coast. These structures resemble low dams that have the top or crest set 15 cm below the elevation of the surrounding marsh to allow water to flow back and forth across the structures. These structures have long been used on the Atlantic and Gulf coasts to counter the effects of ditches and canals (Smith 1942, Chabreck and Hoffpauir 1962). These structures reduce tidal exchange and establish a basin of water behind the structure that cannot recede below the crest; consequently, complete drainage of most ponds at low tides is prevented (Chabreck and Hoffpauer 1962). Constructing weirs and flashboards in unwanted artificial channels is a less costly alternative to filling the channels with sediments. Flashboards are used in Chesapeake Bay marshes to prevent complete drainage of marshes that were ditched to control mosquitoes in the 1930s (Hindman and Stotts 1989). Weirs are used in coastal Louisiana to counter tidal action into natural channels caused by intersecting canals and navigation channels. Weirs also have been constructed in natural channels that completely drain during winter-cold fronts; these weir-managed ponds are preferred by wintering waterfowl (Spiller and Chabreck 1975). Weirs with fixed crests have increased the abundance of submersed aquatic vegetation

(Nyman and Chabreck 1996) and decreased mineral sedimentation (Reed 1992), but have not altered emergent plant communities (Nyman et al.1993b) or marsh loss rates (Nyman et al. 1990a). Weirs, sills, and flashboards might affect marsh loss rates where vertical accretion depends on mineral sedimentation. It is unlikely these structures affect soil water logging where they do not alter marsh flooding (Chabreck and Hoffpauir 1962). They may increase plant stress where they increase flooding duration (Bourgeois and Webb 1999).

SEDIMENT CAPTURE TECHNIQUES

Terracing

Terraces are constructed by dredging shallow open water areas and piling the dredged material in 5–20 m-wide rows to form a linear, intertidal surface. Emergent vegetation, such as cordgrasses, is generally planted on the edges to accelerate the establishment of rooted vegetation, which reduces erosion. Terraces are used in coastal Louisiana and Texas to counter the conversion of emergent wetlands to shallow open water. It is assumed that 1 ha of terrace ($10 \times 1,000$ m) provides more fish and wildlife habitat than 1 ha^2 (100×100 m) of created marsh because of the tremendous ratio of edge to area in terraces. It is also believed that terraces promote sedimentation by slowing wave and wind energy in the ponds (Turner 1999). Unlike spoil banks, which are continuous and rise above normal tides, terraces are discontinuous and flood at high tide. Constructing terraces gained popularity as a restoration and mitigation technique following reports that terraces near the Calcasieu Ship Channel on Sabine National Wildlife Refuge reversed shoreline erosion and created almost 7 ha of salt marsh with an interface of almost 1,525 m (Steyer 1993). Terraces may also increase submersed aquatic vegetation and, hence, waterfowl, fish, and invertebrates. The assumption that terraces promote submersed aquatic vegetation and, hence, waterfowl, fish, and invertebrates, is a factor in the recent popularity of terraces as a restoration and mitigation technique.

Terraces have also been attempted with vegetative plantings. Rows of California bulrush have been planted where wetlands have converted to shallow open water in coastal Louisiana. As with terraces constructed of sediment, rows of bulrush are planted to slow erosion of adjacent shorelines and to promote sediment deposition (Louisiana Department of Natural Resources, unpublished report). Some bulrush plantings have been killed by high salinity associated with drought (Louisiana Department of Natural Resources, unpublished report). Their effectiveness has not been demonstrated.

Wave Dampening Fences

Since 1989, discarded Christmas trees held in place by fence materials have been used in coastal Louisiana to slow wetland erosion and create wetlands. Fike and Wicker (1992) described projects constructed in coastal Louisiana through 1992 and made recommendations to improve planning and construction. Bahlinger (1996) examined 6 Christmas tree projects and documented effects ranging from marsh creation, to increased coverage by submersed aquatic vegetation, to reducing depth of ponds and channels. Nyman (1997) concluded that 8 of 29 Christmas tree projects in coastal Louisiana appeared to slow erosion and/or create emergent wetlands. Boumans et al. (1997) and Scarton et al. (2000) likewise reported that although Christmas tree fences cause sediment accumulation in adjacent ponds, they had little effect on emergent vegetation. It is logical to assume that Christmas tree fences increase submersed aquatic vegetation abundance because they increase sedimentation.

CATTLE GRAZING

Cattle grazing can be used to advantage in marshes managed for wildlife (Chabreck 1968, Neely 1968). Carefully regulated grazing will open dense stands of vegetation and create conditions favorable for certain species. Marshes managed for maximum fur animal production should not be grazed (O'Neil 1949). Grazing will reduce available cover, and cattle trample dens and underground tunnels, and compete with herbivores for food.

Grazing, which can be easily controlled, is usually beneficial to ducks. Not only will grazing remove dense stands of vegetation, but it also sets back plant succession and increases food production (Stutzenbaker and Weller 1989). Certain low value plants, such as marshhay cordgrass, decrease with grazing while some high value plants, such as seashore paspalum (*Paspalum vaginatum*) increase with grazing. To improve grazed marshes for ducks, cattle should be removed from the marsh during July through September to permit annual grasses and sedges to grow and produce seeds. Marshes should be flooded (10–15 cm depth) from October through February to attract ducks and make the seeds available.

Snow geese are attracted to marshes where dense stands of mature vegetation have been removed; consequently, moderate grazing usually benefits this species (Chabreck 1968). Geese will feed on new sprouts, plus roots and rhizomes of marsh grasses and sedges. Wilson's snipe (*Gallinago delicata*) also benefits from cattle grazing. This species prefers areas with exposed mineral soil and no overhead cover; largest concentrations of snipe are usually found on over-grazed marsh range.

FOOD PLANTINGS

One of the first procedures generally considered to improve marshes for wildlife is to plant vegetation in the marsh to produce food. These plantings are usually made without site preparation and almost invariably fail to meet the objective. Usually, the absence of natural food plants in a marsh is a result of unfavorable soil and water conditions or excessive competition from less desirable plants. These conditions will cause failure of plantings in the same marsh area. Plantings in a marsh cannot substitute for regulating water levels and salinities to produce natural foods. Only with application of agronomic techniques have favorable results been achieved with artificial plantings (Neely 1968).

Because Olney bulrush is a choice food plant of muskrats and snow geese in coastal marshes of the southeastern United States, considerable interest has been generated in managing marshes for this species. Procedures for establishing or re-establishing Olney bulrush through planting have been intensively investigated (Ross and Chabreck 1972, Palmisano 1973, Hess 1975). These studies disclosed this species could be established by transplanting rootstock. However, plantings must be made within certain water and salinity levels, and protection must be provided against excessive competition from other plants and animal herbivory.

WEED CONTROL

Chemical control of undesirable plant species in marshes has been used on a limited basis partly because undesirable species generally return within a few years (Rollings and Warden 1964, Wood et al. 1996). Herbicides may gain emphasis in the future as management efforts become more intensive. Also, herbicides are being developed which are more effective and can be applied to marshes at a more economical cost. As with other management techniques, a marsh manager should consult a specialist in this field before attempting widespread applications of herbicides. In special situations, salt water can be introduced into management units to control undesirable freshwater plants. Biological and mechanical control is most effective for some weed species.

PRESCRIBED FIRE

Prescribed as well as natural marsh fires can be classified as cover burns or peat burns (Lynch 1941, Smith 1942, Uhler 1944, O'Neil 1949:93–107). Water levels during the burn control the type of fire that occurs and water levels following the fire control plant regrowth. Much of the following information is summarized from Nyman and Chabreck (1995).

Peat burns are those that actually burn marsh soil; they occur when a marsh with peat soil is drained and the soil is dry. The depth of the burn depends on how deeply the soil is dry. Peat burns lower surface elevation and can convert marsh to ponds and are most common in coastal Louisiana. They are not normally used as a management tool but could if the goal was to increase pond area at the expense of emergent vegetation and if the peat burn could be prevented from spreading to adjacent areas. Peat burns also have been used (unsuccessfully) to reverse the spread of cattails (*Typha* spp.) and common reed (Ward 1942, Uhler 1944). Peat burns are rare and were believed to be growing rarer because of global sea-level rise and widespread channelization and ditching in coastal marshes (Nyman and Chabreck 1995). However, low water levels in Gulf coast marshes, a lack of local rainfall, and lightning resulted in thousands of hectares of peat burns in coastal Louisiana during the drought of 2000 (T. J. Hess, Jr., unpublished data).

Fires that remove standing biomass and litter without killing plant roots are classified as cover burns. They result from fires that occur when there is moist soil to several centimeters of water on the marsh surface. Plant communities can quickly recover from cover burns because living roots and seed banks are not destroyed if the marsh is not flooded after the fire. If the marsh remains flooded following a cover burn, whether prescribed or natural, all vegetation can be killed by flooding stresses (Hoffpauer 1968).

Root burns are a category of fire described by O'Neil (1949) that have not been confirmed. They are probably cover burns in early fall just prior to high vernal equinox tides. Such a tide killed about 500 ha of burned marshhay cordgrass marsh on Rockefeller Wildlife Refuge in Louisiana in the 1950s (R. H. Chabreck, personal observation). After the water receded, it appeared the vegetation was killed by a root burn.

Cover burns are valuable and widely used on Gulf and Atlantic coasts because they increase the abundance of wildlife food plants (Arthur 1931:262–265, Griffith 1940, Lynch 1941, Uhler 1944). Cover burns are used primarily in marshhay cordgrass-dominated marshes when cordgrass forms nearly monotypic stands. In the first or second year following a cover burn, Olney bulrush and other valuable food plants can become more abundant. Within 3–5 years, marshhay cordgrass again creates nearly monotypic stands. Cover burns should be limited to fall and winter because spring and summer burning can destroy nests or kill young wildlife.

Little is known about the effects of fire on organic matter export to adjacent estuaries and vertical accretion. Stevenson et al. (2000) feared that fire management at Blackwater National Wildlife Refuge in Maryland contributed to marsh loss by reducing organic matter accumulation. A prudent plan would be to burn only as frequently as needed to prevent unplanned burns. Ending prescribed burning would not eliminate fire as a disturbance because large accumulations of litter develop, and lightning can still ignite that fuel.

SUMMARY

Coastal marshes vary regionally in the United States because of variation in slope, tidal range, and riverine discharge. Within regions, coastal marshes vary from saline with large tidal ranges to tidal, freshwater marshes where tides cause an ebb and flow of water rather than a rise and fall. Water level, water salinity, and fire often are manipulated in coastal wetlands to improve habitat quality for waterfowl, furbearers, wading birds, or American alligators. Mangrove swamps occur in non-fresh water areas that lack freezing temperatures, such as the south Florida coast. They rarely are managed for wildlife and are not addressed.

Management to improve habitat for waterfowl and furbearers in tidal, non-saline wetlands, particularly those dominated by marshhay cordgrass, began in the mid-1900s and continues to be common on the Gulf and Atlantic coasts. In the mid-1900s, some saline marshes were freshened via impoundments to improve waterfowl habitat; this management is not currently undertaken. Many earlier efforts are being reversed to restore saline habitats for shorebirds and estuarine fish. In the late 1900s, coastal marsh management to improve anadromous fish habitat began on the Pacific coast.

Unlike inland marshes, coastal marshes must gradually increase in elevation; i.e., vertically accrete, to survive global sea-level rise and local subsidence. Accretion depends on accumulation of mineral sediments from tides and storms, organic matter from emergent vegetation, or a combination of both. Where accretion depends on mineral sediments, levees and water control structures used to manipulate hydrological conditions may inadvertently slow accretion and eventually drown emergent vegetation. Where accretion depends on organic matter, drawdowns used to promote annual vegetation may inadvertently reduce marsh elevation and eventually drown emergent vegetation. Evaluating the effects of management on accretion is a recently recognized challenge facing coastal marsh managers.

Management goals should be clearly documented and measurable. Management practices generally must be developed via trial and error to accommodate site-specific hydrologic conditions. Regardless of the locale, one of the most valuable practices is the systematic collection of hydrologic, vegetation, and wildlife data that can be used to evaluate management efficiency and guide changes in management practices.

ACKNOWLEDGMENTS

Preparation of this manuscript was supported by the Louisiana State University Agricultural Center. We thank 3 anonymous reviewers and C. E. Braun for suggestions that helped improve the manuscript.

LITERATURE CITED

ABLE, K. W., D. M. NEMERSON, P. R. LIGHT, AND R. O. BUSH. 2000. Initial response of fishes to marsh restoration at a former salt hay farm bordering Delaware Bay. Pages 749–773 *in* M. P. Weinstein and D. A. Kreeger, editors. Concepts and controversies in tidal marsh ecology. Kluwer Academic Publishers, Boston, Massachusetts, USA.

ALEXANDER, C. E., M. A. BOUTMAN, AND D. W. FIELD. 1986. An inventory of coastal wetlands of the USA. U.S. Department of Commerce, Washington, D.C., USA.

ALLEN, H. A., E. V. CLAIRAIN, JR., R. J. DIAZ, A. W. FORD, H. L. HUNT, AND B. R. WELLS. 1978. Habitat development field investigation, Bolivar Peninsula, marsh and upland habitat development site, Galveston Bay, Texas. U.S. Army Corps of Engineers, Waterways Experiment Station Technical Report D-78-15.

ALLEN, H. H., AND J. W. WEBB. 1983. Erosion control with salt marsh vegetation. Symposium on Coastal and Ocean Management 3:735–748.

ARTHUR, S. C. 1931. The fur animals of Louisiana. Bulletin 18. Louisiana Department of Conservation, New Orleans, USA.

BAHLINGER, K. D. 1996. Effectiveness of Christmas tree projects. PCWRP Information Series 2. Louisiana Department of Natural Resources, Parish Coastal Wetlands Restoration Program, Coastal Restoration Division, Baton Rouge, USA.

BALDWIN, W. P. 1968. Impoundments for waterfowl on south Atlantic and Gulf coastal marshes. Pages 127–133 *in* J. D. Newsom, editor. Proceedings of the Coastal Marsh and Estuary Management Symposium. Louisiana State University, Baton Rouge, USA.

BALL, D. F. 1964. Loss-on-ignition as an estimate of organic matter and organic carbon in non-calcareous soils. Journal of Soil Science 15:84–92.

BELANGER, L., AND D. LEHOUX. 1994. Use of a tidal salt marsh and coastal impoundments by sympatric breeding and staging American black ducks, *Anas rubripes*, and mallards, *A. platyrhynchos*. Canadian Field-Naturalist 108:311–317.

BELLROSE, F. C. 1980. Ducks, geese, and swans of North America. Third edition. Stackpole Books, Harrisburg, Pennsylvania, USA.

BENOIT, L. K., AND R. A. ASKINS. 1999. Impact of the spread of *Phragmites* on the distribution of birds in Connecticut tidal marshes. Wetlands 19:194–208.

———, AND ———. 2002. Relationship between habitat area and the distribution of tidal marsh birds. Wilson Bulletin 114:314–323.

BOUMANS, R. M. J., J. W. DAY, G. P. KEMP, AND K. KILGEN. 1997. The effect of intertidal sediment fences on wetland surface elevation, wave energy and vegetation establishment in two Louisiana coastal marshes. Ecological Engineering 9:37–50.

BOURGEOIS, J. A., AND E. C. WEBB. 1999. Effects of weirs on the depth and duration of flooding in a Louisiana marsh. Pages 241–244 *in* L. P. Rozas, J. A. Nyman, C. E. Proffitt, N. N. Rabalais, D. J. Reed, and R. E. Turner, editors. 1999. Recent research in coastal Louisiana: natural system function and response to human influences. Louisiana Sea Grant College Program, Baton Rouge, USA.

BOURN, W. S., AND C. COTTAM. 1950. Some biological effects of ditching tidewater marshes. U.S. Department of the Interior, Fish and Wildlife Service, Research Report 19.

BOYER, M. E., J. O. HARRIS, AND R. E. TURNER. 1997. Constructed crevasses and land gain in the Mississippi River delta. Restoration Ecology 5:85–92.

BRADBURY, H. M. 1938. Mosquito control operations on tide marshes in Massachusetts and their effect on shore birds and waterfowl. Journal of Wildlife Management 2:49–52.

BRICKER-URSO, S., S. W. NIXON, J. K. COCHRAN, D. J. HIRSCHBERG, AND C. HUNT. 1989. Accretion rates and sediment accumulation in Rhode Island salt marshes. Estuaries 12:300–317.

BRINSON M. M., AND R. RHEINHARDT. 1996. The role of reference wetlands in functional assessment and mitigation. Ecological Applications 6:69–76.

BRUSATI, E. D., P. J. DUBOWY, AND T. E. LACHER, JR. 2001. Comparing ecological functions of natural and created wetlands for shorebirds in Texas. Waterbirds 24:371–380.

BULLER, R. J. 1964. Central Flyway. Pages 209–232 *in* J. P. Linduska, editor. Waterfowl tomorrow. U.S. Department of the Interior, Fish and Wildlife Service, Washington, D.C., USA.

CAHOON, D. R. 1994. Recent accretion in two managed marsh impoundments in coastal Louisiana. Ecological Applications 4:166–176.

CALLAWAY, J. C., AND M. N. JOSSELYN. 1992. The introduction and spread of smooth cordgrass (*Spartina alterniflora*) in San Francisco Bay. Estuaries 15:218–226.

———, R. D. DELAUNE, AND W. H. PATRICK, JR. 1997. Sediment accretion rates from four coastal wetlands along the Gulf of Mexico. Journal of Coastal Research 13:181–191.

CHABRECK, R. H. 1960. Coastal marsh impoundments for ducks in Louisiana. Proceedings of the Annual Conference of the Southeastern Association of Game and Fish Commissioners 14:24–29.

———. 1968. The relation of cattle and cattle grazing to marsh wildlife and plants in Louisiana. Proceedings of the Annual Conference of the Southeastern Association of Game and Fish Commissioners 22:55–58.

———. 1970. Marsh zones and vegetative types of the Louisiana coastal marshes. Dissertation. Louisiana State University, Baton Rouge, USA.

———. 1971. Ponds and lakes of the Louisiana coastal marshes and their value to fish and wildlife. Proceedings of the Annual Conference of the Southeastern Association of Game and Fish Commissioners 25:206–215.

———. 1972. Vegetation, water and soil characteristics of the Louisiana coastal marshes. Bulletin 664. Louisiana Agricultural Experiment Station, Baton Rouge, USA.

———. 1979. Winter habitat of dabbling ducks: physical, chemical, and biological aspects. Pages 133–142 *in* T. A. Bookhout, editor. Waterfowl and wetlands: an integrated review. North Central Section, The Wildlife Society, Madison, Wisconsin, USA.

———. 1981. Effect of burn date on regrowth of *Scirpus olneyi* and *Spartina patens*. Proceedings of the Annual Conference of the Southeastern Association of Fish and Wildlife Agencies 35:201–210.

———. 1988. Coastal marshes: ecology and wildlife management. University of Minnesota Press, Minneapolis, USA.

———. 1989. Creation, restoration and enhancement of northcentral Gulf coast marshes. Pages 127–142 *in* J. A. Kusler and M. E. Kentula, editors. Wetland creation and restoration: the status of the science. Vol. I. Regional Reviews. EPA/600/3-89/038a. Environmental Protection Agency, Research Laboratory, Corvallis, Oregon, USA.

———, AND C. M. HOFFPAUIR. 1962. The use of weirs in coastal marsh management in Louisiana. Proceedings of the Annual Conference of the Southeastern Association of Game and Fish Commissioners 16:102–122.

———, AND G. LINSCOMBE. 1978. Vegetative type map of the Louisiana coastal marshes. Louisiana Department of Wildlife and Fisheries, Baton Rouge, USA.

———, AND A. W. PALMISANO. 1973. The effects of hurricane Camille on the marshes of the Mississippi River delta. Ecology 54:1118–1123.

———, R. J. HOAR, AND W. D. LARRICK, JR. 1979. Soil and water characteristics of coastal marshes influenced by weirs. Pages 127–146 *in* J. W. Day, Jr., D. D. Cully, Jr., R. E. Turner, and A. J. Mumphrey, Jr., editors. Proceedings of the Third Coastal Marsh and Estuary Management Symposium. Louisiana State University, Division of Continuing Education, Baton Rouge, USA.

CHAMBERLAIN, R. H., AND R. A. BARNHART. 1993. Early use by fish of a mitigation salt marsh, Humboldt Bay, California. Estuaries 16:769–783.

CHAMBERS R. M., L. A. MEYERSON, AND K. SALTONSTALL. 1999. Expansion of *Phragmites australis* into tidal wetlands of North America. Aquatic Botany 64:261–273.

CHATRY, M., AND D. CHEW. 1985. Freshwater diversion in coastal Louisiana: recommendations for development of management criteria. Pages 71–84 *in* C. F. Bryan, P. J. Zwank, and R. H. Chabreck, editors. Proceedings of the Fourth Coastal Marsh and Estuary Management Symposium. Louisiana State University, Baton Rouge, USA.

COATS, R., M. SWANSON, AND P. WILLIAMS. 1989. Hydrologic analysis for coastal wetland restoration. Environmental Management 13:715–727.

COLEMAN, J. M. 1988. Dynamic changes and processes in the Mississippi River delta. Geological Society of America Bulletin 100:999–1015.

COLWELL, M. A., AND O. W. TAFT. 2000. Waterbird communities in managed wetlands of varying water depth. Waterbirds 23:45–55.

CONROY, M. J., M. W. MILLER, AND J. E. HINES. 2002. Identification and synthetic modeling of factors affecting American black duck populations. Wildlife Monographs 150.

COWARDIN, L. M., V. CARTER, F. C. GOLET, AND E. T. LaROE. 1979. Classification of wetlands and deepwater habitats of the United States. FWS/OBS-79/31. U.S. Department of the Interior, Fish and Wildlife Service, Washington, D.C., USA.

CRAFT C., S. BROOME, AND C. CAMPBELL. 2002. Fifteen years of vegetation and soil development after brackish-water marsh creation. Restoration Ecology 10:248–258.

CULLITON, T. J., J. J. McDONOUGH, III, D. G. REMER, AND D. M. LOTT. 1992. Building along America's coasts, 20 years of building permits, 1970–1989. U.S. Department of Commerce, National Oceanic and Atmospheric Administration, National Ocean Service, Coastal Trends Series.

CUNNINGHAM, R. 1981. Atchafalaya Delta: subaerial development, environmental implications and resource potential. Pages 349–365 in R. Cross and D. Williams, editors. Proceedings of the Natural Symposium on Freshwater Inflow to Estuaries. FWS/OBS-81/04. U.S. Department of the Interior, Fish and Wildlife Service, Washington, D.C., USA.

DALE, P. E. R., AND K. HULSMAN. 1990. A critical review of salt marsh management methods for mosquito control. Aquatic Sciences 3:281–311.

DAVIDSON, R. B., AND R. H. CHABRECK. 1989. Recreational use of management units in brackish marsh. Pages 212–221 in W. G. Duffy and D. Clark, editors. Marsh management in coastal Louisiana: effects and issues. Biological Report 89(22). U.S. Department of the Interior, Fish and Wildlife Service, Washington, D.C., USA.

DAVIES, B. E. 1974. Loss-on-ignition as an estimate of soil organic matter. Proceedings of the Soil Science Society of America 38:150–151.

DeLAUNE, R. D., AND S. R. PEZESHKI. 1988. Relationship of mineral nutrients to growth of *Spartina alterniflora* in Louisiana salt marshes. Northeast Gulf Science 10:55–60.

———, R. H. BAUMANN, AND J. G. GOSSELINK. 1983a. Relationships among vertical accretion, coastal submergence, and erosion in a Louisiana gulf-coast marsh. Journal of Sedimentary Petrology 53:147–157.

———, J. A. NYMAN, AND W. H. PATRICK, JR. 1994. Peat collapse, ponding, and wetland loss in a rapidly submerging coastal marsh. Journal of Coastal Research 10:1021–1030.

———, S. R. PEZESHKI, AND W. H. PATRICK, JR. 1987. Response of coastal plants to increase in submergence and salinity. Journal of Coastal Research 3:535–546.

———, C. N. REDDY, AND W. H. PATRICK, JR. 1981. Accumulation of plant nutrients and heavy metals through sedimentation processes and accretion in a Louisiana salt marsh. Estuaries 4:328–334.

———, C. J. SMITH, AND W. H. PATRICK, JR. 1983b. Relationship of marsh elevation, redox potential, and sulfide to *Spartina alterniflora* productivity. Soil Science Society of America Journal 47:930–935.

DODD, J. D., AND J. W. WEBB. 1975. Establishment of vegetation for shoreline stabilization in Galveston Bay. U.S. Department of Army, Corps of Engineers, Miscellaneous Paper 75-6. Vicksburg, Mississippi, USA.

ELEUTERIUS, L. N. 1974. A study of plant establishment on dredge spoil in Mississippi Sound and adjacent waters. Gulf Coast Research Laboratory, Ocean Springs, Mississippi, USA.

ENSMINGER, A. B. 1963. Construction of levees for impoundments in Louisiana marshes. Proceedings of the Annual Conference of the Southeastern Association of Game and Fish Commissioners 17:440–445.

———, AND L. G. NICHOLS. 1957. Hurricane damage to Rockefeller Refuge. Proceedings of the Annual Conference of the Southeastern Association of Game and Fish Commissioners 11:52–56.

EVERETT R. A., G. M. RUIZ, AND J. T. CARLTON. 1995. Effect of oyster mariculture on submerged aquatic vegetation—an experimental test in a Pacific Northwest estuary. Marine Ecology Progress Series 125:205–217.

FELL, P. E., R. S. WARREN, AND W. A. NEIRING. 2000. Restoration of salt and brackish tidelands in southern New England: angiosperms, macro invertebrates, fish, and birds. Pages 845–858 in M. P. Weinstein and D. A. Kreeger, editors. Concepts and controversies in tidal marsh ecology. Kluwer Academic Publishers, Boston, Massachusetts, USA.

FIKE, E., AND K. WICKER. 1992. Management and monitoring of Christmas tree brush fence construction (1991–1992). Louisiana Department of Natural Resources, Coastal Restoration Division, Baton Rouge, USA.

FLYNN, K. M., I. A. MENDELSSOHN, AND B. J. WILSEY. 1999. The effect of water level management on the soils and vegetation of two coastal Louisiana marshes. Wetlands Ecology and Management 7:193–218.

FRAZIER, D. E. 1967. Recent deltaic deposits of the Mississippi River: their development and chronology. Transactions of the Gulf Coast Association of Geological Societies 17:287–311.

FROST, C. C. 1995. Presettlement fire regimes in southeastern marshes, peatlands, and swamps. Proceedings Tall Timbers Fire Ecology Conference—Fire in Wetlands: A Management Perspective 19:39–60.

GABREY, S. W., A. D. AFTON, AND B. C. WILSON. 1999. Effects of winter burning and structural marsh management on vegetation and wintering bird abundance in the Gulf Coast Chenier Plain, USA. Wetlands 22:594–606.

GARBISCH, JR., E. W., P. B. WOLLER, AND R. J. McCALLUM. 1975. Salt marsh establishment and development. Technical Memorandum 52. U.S. Department of Army, Corps of Engineers, Fort Belvoir, Virginia, USA.

GODFREY, R. K., AND J. W. WOOTEN. 1979. Aquatic and wetland plants of the southeastern United States, Monocotyledons. University of Georgia Press, Athens, USA.

GORDON, D. H., B. T. GRAY, R. D. PERRY, M. B. PREVOST, T. H. STRANGE, AND R. K. WILLIAMS. 1989. South Atlantic coastal wetlands. Pages 57–92 in L. M. Smith, R. L. Pederson, and R. M. Kaminski, editors. Habitat management for migrating and wintering waterfowl in North America. Texas Tech University Press, Lubbock, USA.

GOSSELINK, J. G., C. L. CORDES, AND J. W. PARSONS. 1979. An ecological characterization study of the Chenier Plain coastal ecosystem of Louisiana and Texas. Volume I. U.S. Department of the Interior, Fish and Wildlife Service, Office of Biological Services, National Coastal Ecosystems Team, Slidell, Louisiana, USA.

———, R. HATTON, AND C. S. HOPKINSON. 1984. Relationship of organic-carbon and mineral-content to bulk-density in Louisiana marsh soils. Soil Science 137:177–180.

GRIFFITH, R. E. 1940. Waterfowl management on Atlantic coast refuges. Transactions of the North American Wildlife Conference 5:373–377.

GUNTER, G. 1967. Some relationships of estuaries to the fisheries of the Gulf of Mexico. Pages 621–638 in G. H. Lauff, editor. Estuaries. Publication 83. American Association for the Advancement of Science, Washington, D.C., USA.

HARRIS, V. T., AND R. H. CHABRECK. 1958. Some effects of hurricane Audrey on the marsh at Marsh Island, Louisiana. Proceedings of the Louisiana Academy of Science 21:47–50.

HATTON, R. S., R. D. DeLAUNE, AND W. H. PATRICK, JR. 1983. Sedimentation, accretion, and subsidence in marshes of Barataria Basin, Louisiana. Limnology and Oceanography 28:494–502.

HEDGEPETH, J. W. 1947. The Laguna Madre of Texas. Transactions of the North American Wildlife Conference 12:364–380.

———, AND S. OBREBSKI. 1981. Willapa Bay: a historical perspective and a rationale for research. FWS/OBS-81/03. U.S. Department of the Interior, Fish and Wildlife Service, Washington D.C., USA.

HERBOLD, B., AND P. B. MOYLE. 1989. The ecology of the Sacramento-San Joaquin Delta: a community profile. U.S. Department of the Interior, Fish and Wildlife Service, Biological Report 85(7.22).

HESS, T. J. 1975. An evaluation of methods for managing stands of *Scirpus olneyi*. Thesis. Louisiana State University, Baton Rouge, USA.

HINDMAN, L. J., AND V. D. STOTTS. 1989. Chesapeake Bay and North Carolina sounds. Pages 27–55 in L. M. Smith, R. L. Pederson, and R. M. Kaminski, editors. Habitat management for migrating and wintering waterfowl in North America. Texas Tech University Press, Lubbock, USA.

HOFFPAUER, C. M. 1968. Burning for coastal marsh management. Pages 134–139 in J. D. Newsom, editor. Proceedings of the Marsh and Estuary Management Symposium. Louisiana State University, Baton Rouge, USA.

HOLM, G. O., AND C. E. SASSER. 2001. Differential salinity response between two Mississippi River subdeltas: implications for changes in plant composition. Estuaries 24:78–89.

INMAN, D. L., AND C. E. NORDSTROM. 1971. On the tectonic and morphologic classification of coasts. Journal of Geology 79:1–21.

ISOLA, C. R., M. A. COLWELL, O. W. TAFT, AND R. J. SAFRAN. 2000. Interspecific differences in habitat use of shorebirds and waterfowl foraging in managed wetlands of California's San Joaquin Valley. Waterbirds 23:196–203.

INTEGRATED TAXONOMIC INFORMATION SYSTEM (ITIS). 2003. Integrated Taxonomic Information System on-line database. U.S. Department of

Agriculture. Available online at http://www.itis.usda.gov.

JENKINS, C. N., R. D. POWELL, O. L. BASS, AND S. L. PIMM. 2003. Why sparrow distributions do not match model predictions. Animal Conservation 6:39–46.

JOANEN, T. AND L. L. GLASGOW. 1965. Factors influencing the establishment of widgeongrass stands in Louisiana. Proceedings of the Annual Conference of the Southeastern Association of Game and Fish Commissioners 19:78–92.

JORDE, D. G., J. R. LONGCORE, AND P. W. BROWN. 1989. Tidal and nontidal wetlands of northern Atlantic states. Pages 1–26 in L. M. Smith, R. L. Pederson, and R. M. Kaminski, editors. Habitat management for migrating and wintering waterfowl in North America. Texas Tech University Press, Lubbock, USA.

JOSSELYN, M. 1983. The ecology of San Francisco Bay tidal marshes: a community profile. FWS/OBS-83-23. U.S. Department of the Interior, Fish and Wildlife Service, Division of Biological Services, Washington, D.C., USA.

———, AND J. BUCHHOLZ. 1984. Marsh restoration in San Francisco Bay: a guide to design and planning. Tiburon Center for Environmental Studies, Technical Report 3. San Francisco State University, California, USA.

KELSEY H. M., R. C. WITTER, AND E. HEMPHILL-HALEY. 2002. Plate-boundary earthquakes and tsunamis of the past 5500 yr, Sixes River estuary, southern Oregon. Geological Society of America Bulletin 114:298–314.

KNUTSON, P. L. 1976. Dredge spoil disposal study: San Francisco Bay and estuary: Appendix K. Marsh development. U.S. Department of Army, Corps of Engineers, San Francisco, California, USA.

KUECHER, G. J., H. H. ROBERTS, M. D. THOMPSON, AND I. MATTHEWS. 2001. Evidence for active growth faulting in the Terrebonne Delta Plain, south Louisiana: implications for wetland loss and the vertical migration of petroleum. Environmental Geosciences 8:77–94.

LANDERS, J. L., A. S. JOHNSON, P. H. MORGAN, AND W. P. BALDWIN. 1976. Duck foods in managed tidal impoundments in South Carolina. Journal of Wildlife Management 40:721–728.

LANDIN, M. C. 1986. Wetland beneficial use applications of dredged material disposal sites. Proceedings of the Annual Conference on Wetlands Restoration and Creation 13:118–129.

LEVIN, L. A., AND T. S. TALLEY. 2002. Natural and manipulated sources of heterogeneity controlling early faunal development of a salt marsh. Ecological Applications 12:1785–1802.

LODGE D. M., C. A. TAYLOR, D. M. HOLDICH, AND J. SKURDAL. 2000. Nonindigenous crayfishes threaten North American freshwater biodiversity: lessons from Europe. Fisheries 25:7-20.

LOVELESS, C. M. 1959. A study of the vegetation in the Florida Everglades. Ecology 40:1–9.

LOWERY, JR., G. H. 1974a. Louisiana birds. Louisiana State University Press, Baton Rouge, USA.

———. 1974b. The wild mammals of Louisiana and adjacent waters. Louisiana State University Press, Baton Rouge, USA.

LUNZ, G. R. 1967. Farming the salt marshes. Pages 172–177 in J. D. Newsom, editor. Coastal marsh and estuary management symposium. Louisiana State University, Baton Rouge, USA.

LYNCH, J. J. 1941. The place of burning in management of Gulf coast wildlife refuges. Journal of Wildlife Management 5:454–457.

———, T. O'NEIL, AND D. W. LAY. 1947. Management significance of damage by geese and muskrats to Gulf Coast marshes. Journal of Wildlife Management 11:50-76.

MARMER, H. A. 1954. Tides and sea level in the Gulf of Mexico. Pages 101–118 in P. S. Galtsoff, editor. Gulf of Mexico: its origin, waters, and marine life. U.S. Department of the Interior, Fish and Wildlife Service, Fishery Bulletin 89.

McCAFFREY, R. J., AND J. THOMSON. 1980. A record of the accumulation of sediment and trace metals in a Connecticut salt marsh. Advances in Geophysics 22:165–236.

McGINNIS, T. E., III. 1997. Factors of soil strength and shoreline movement in a Louisiana coastal marsh. Thesis. University of Southwestern Louisiana, Lafayette, USA.

McMAHAN, C. A. 1968. Biomass and salinity tolerance of shoalgrass and manateegrass in lower Laguna Madre, Texas. Journal of Wildlife Management 32:501–506.

MEADE, R. H. 1969. Landward transport of bottom sediments in estuaries of the Atlantic coastal plain. Journal of Sedimentary Petrology 39:222–234.

MEADOR, M. R. 1988. Behavioral and physiological adaptations of largemouth bass (*Micropterus salmoides*) to low salinity environments. Dissertation. Louisiana State University, Baton Rouge, USA.

MELVIN, S. L., D. E. GAWLIK, AND T. SCHARF. 1999. Long-term movement patterns for seven species of wading birds. Waterbirds 22:411–416.

MENDELSSOHN, I. A., AND K. L. McKEE. 1988. *Spartina alterniflora* dieback in Louisiana: time course investigation of soil waterlogging effects. Journal of Ecology 76:509–521.

MITSCH, W. J., AND J. G. GOSSELINK. 2000. Wetlands. Van Nostrand Reinhold Company, Inc., New York, USA.

MOORE, JR., P. A., N. VAN BREEMEN, AND W. H. PATRICK, JR. 1999. Effects of drainage on the chemistry of acid sulfate soils. Pages 1107–1112 in R. W. Skaggs and J. Van Schilfgaarde, editors. Agricultural drainage. American Society of Agronomy, Crop Science Society of America and Soil Science Society of America, Madison, Wisconsin, USA.

MORGAN, P. H., A. S. JOHNSON, W. P. BALDWIN, AND J. L. LANDERS. 1975. Characteristics and management of tidal impoundments for wildlife in a South Carolina estuary. Proceedings of the Annual Conference of the Southeastern Association of Game and Fish Commissioners 29:526–539.

MOSSA, J., AND H. H. ROBERTS. 1990. Synergism of riverine and winter-storm related sediment transport processes in Louisiana's coastal wetlands. Transactions of the Gulf Coast Association of Geological Societies 40:635–642.

NECKLES, H. A., M. DIONNE, D. M. BURDICK, C. T. ROMAN, R. BUCHSBAUM, AND E. HUTCHINS. 2002. A monitoring protocol to assess tidal restoration of salt marshes on local and regional scales. Restoration Ecology 10:556–563.

NEELY, W. W. 1960. Managing *Scirpus robustus* for ducks. Proceedings of the Annual Conference of the Southeastern Association of Game and Fish Commissioners 14:30–34.

———. 1962. Saline soils and brackish waters in management of wildlife, fish, and shrimp. Transactions of the North American Wildlife and Natural Resources Conference 27:321–335

———. 1968. Planting, disking, mowing, and grazing. Pages 212–221 in J. D. Newsom, editor. Proceedings of the Coastal Marsh and Estuary Management Symposium. Louisiana State University, Baton Rouge, USA.

NICHOLS, J. D., D. L. VIEHMAN, R. H. CHABRECK, AND B. FENDERSON. 1976. Simulations of a commercially harvested alligator population in Louisiana. Bulletin 691. Louisiana Agricultural Experiment Station, Baton Rouge, USA.

NIXON, S. W. 1982. The ecology of New England high salt marshes: a community profile. FWS/OBS-81-55. U.S. Department of the Interior, Fish and Wildlife Service, Office of Biological Services, Washington, D.C., USA.

———, AND C. A. OVIATT. 1973. Ecology of a New England salt marsh. Ecological Monographs 43:463–498.

NYMAN, J. A. 1997. Wetland acres created by or protected from erosion by the parish coastal wetlands restoration program. Louisiana Department of Natural Resources, Coastal Restoration Division, Biological Monitoring Section, Baton Rouge, USA.

———, AND R. H. CHABRECK. 1995. Fire in coastal marshes: history and recent concerns. Proceedings of the Tall Timbers Fire Ecology Conference—Fire in Wetlands: A Management Perspective 19:135–141.

———, AND ———. 1996. Some effects of 30 years of weir management on coastal marsh aquatic vegetation and implications to waterfowl management. Gulf of Mexico Science 14:16–25.

———, AND R. D. DELAUNE. 1991. CO^2 emission and soil Eh responses to different hydrological conditions in fresh, brackish, and saline marsh soils. Limnology and Oceanography 36:1406–1414.

———, R. H. CHABRECK, AND R. G. LINSCOMBE. 1990a. Effects of weir management on marsh loss, Marsh Island, Louisiana USA. Environmental Management 14:809–814.

———, ———, AND N. KINLER. 1993b. Some effects of herbivory and 30 years of weir management on emergent vegetation in a brackish marsh. Wetlands 13:165–175.

———, R. D. DELAUNE, AND W. H. PATRICK, JR. 1990b. Wetland soil formation in the rapidly subsiding Mississippi River Deltaic Plain: mineral and organic matter relationships. Estuarine, Coastal and Shelf Science 31:57–69.

———, M. CARLOSS, R. D. DELAUNE, AND W. H. PATRICK, JR. 1994. Erosion rather than plant dieback as the mechanism of marsh loss in an estuarine marsh. Earth Surface Processes and Landforms 19:69–84.

———, R. D. DELAUNE, H. H. ROBERTS, AND W. H. PATRICK, JR. 1993a. Relationship between vegetation and soil formation in a rapidly submerging coastal marsh. Marine Ecology Progress Series 96:269–279.

NYSTROM, P., AND J. A. STRAND. 1996. Grazing by a native and an exotic crayfish on aquatic macrophytes. Freshwater Biology 36:673–682.

ODUM, E. P., J. B. BIRCH, AND J. L. COOLEY. 1983. Comparison of giant cutgrass productivity in tidal and impounded marshes with special reference to tidal subsidy and waste assimilation. Estuaries 6:88–94.

ODUM, W. E., T. J. SMITH, III, J. K. HOOVER, AND C. C. MCIVOR. 1984. The ecology of tidal freshwater marshes of the United States east coast: a community profile. FWS/OBS-83/17. U.S. Department of the Interior, Fish and Wildlife Service, Washington, D.C., USA.

O'NEIL, T. 1949. The muskrat in the Louisiana coastal marsh. Louisiana Department of Wildlife and Fisheries, New Orleans, USA.

PALMISANO, A. W. 1973. Habitat preferences of waterfowl and fur animals in the northern Gulf coast marshes. Pages 163–190 in R. H. Chabreck, editor. Proceedings of the Second Coastal Marsh and Estuary Management Symposium. Louisiana State University, Baton Rouge, USA.

PARRONDO, R. T., J. G. GOSSELINK, AND C. S. HOPKINSON. 1978. Effects of salinity and drainage on the growth of three salt marsh grasses. Botanical Gazette 139:102–107.

PASTERNACK, G. B., W. B. HILGARTNER, AND G. S. BRUSH. 2000. Biogeomorphology of an upper Chesapeake Bay river-mouth tidal freshwater marsh. Wetlands 20:520–537.

PENFOUND, W. T., AND E. S. HATHAWAY. 1938. Plant communities in the marshlands of southeastern Louisiana. Ecological Monographs 8:1–56.

PENLAND, S., AND K. E. RAMSEY. 1990. Relative sea-level rise in Louisiana and the Gulf of Mexico: 1908–1988. Journal of Coastal Research 6:323–342.

———, AND J. R. SUTTER. 1989. The geomorphology of the Mississippi River Chenier Plain. Marine Geology 90:231–258.

PERRY, J. E., T. A. BARNARD, JR., J. G. BRADSHAW, C. T. FRIEDRICHS, K. J. HAVENS, P. A. MASON, W. I. PRIEST, III, AND G. M. SILBERHORN. 2001. Creating tidal salt marsh in the Chesapeake Bay. Journal of Coastal Research 27:170–191.

PERRY, JR., W. G., T. JOANEN, AND L. MCNEASE. 1970. Crawfish–waterfowl, a multiple use concept for impounded marsh. Proceedings of the Annual Conference of the Southeastern Association of Game and Fish Commissioners 24:506–519.

RADFORD, A. E., H. E. AHLES, AND C. R. BELL. 1968. Manual of the vascular flora of the Carolinas. University of North Carolina Press, Chapel Hill, USA.

REED, D. J. 1989. Patterns of sediment deposition in subsiding coastal salt marshes, Terrebonne Bay, Louisiana: the role of winter storms. Estuaries 12:222–227.

———. 1992. Effect of weirs on sediment deposition in Louisiana coastal marshes. Environmental Management 16:55–65.

———, N. DE LUCA, AND A. L. FOOTE. 1997. Effect of hydrologic management on marsh surface sediment deposition in coastal Louisiana. Estuaries 20:301–311.

REIMOLD, R. J. 1977. Mangals and salt marshes of eastern United States. Pages 157–166 in V. J. Chapman, editor. Ecosystems of the world. I. Wet coastal ecosystems. Elsevier Scientific, New York, USA.

RESTORE AMERICA'S ESTUARIES. 2002. A national strategy to restore coastal and estuarine habitat. Restore America's Estuaries, Arlington, Virginia, USA.

ROLLINGS, C. T., AND R. L. WARDEN. 1964. Weedkillers and waterfowl. Pages 593–598 in J. P. Linduska, editor. Waterfowl tomorrow. U.S. Department of the Interior, Fish and Wildlife Service, Washington, D.C., USA.

ROMAN, C. T., W. A. NIERING, AND R. S. WARREN. 1984. Salt marsh vegetation change in response to tidal restriction. Environmental Management 8:141–150.

ROSS, W. M., AND R. H. CHABRECK. 1972. Factors affecting the growth and survival of natural and planted stands of *Scirpus olneyi*. Proceedings of the Annual Conference of the Southeastern Association of Game and Fish Commissioners 26:178–188.

RUSSELL, R. J. 1942. Flotant. Geographical Review 32:74–98.

SAFRAN, R. J., C. R. ISOLA, M. A. COLWELL, AND O. E. WILLIAMS. 1997. Benthic invertebrates at foraging locations of nine waterbird species in managed wetlands of the northern San Joaquin Valley, California. Wetlands 17:407–415.

SANDERSON, G. C., AND F. C. BELLROSE. 1969. Wildlife habitat management of wetlands. Annals Academia Brasiliera de Ciencios (Suplemento) 41:153–204.

SCARTON, F., J. W. DAY, JR., A. RISMONDO, AND D. ARE. 2000. Effects of an intertidal sediment fence on sediment elevation and vegetation distribution in a Venice (Italy) lagoon salt marsh. Ecological Engineering 16:223–233.

SCHMALZER, P. A., C. R. HINKLE, AND J. L. MAILANDER. 1991. Changes in community composition and biomass in *Juncus romerianus* Scheele and *Spartina bakeri* Merr marshes one year after a fire. Wetlands 11:67–86.

SELISKAR, D. M., AND J. L. GALLAGHER. 1983. The ecology of tidal marshes of the Pacific Northwest coast: a community profile. FWS/OBS-82/32. U.S. Department of the Interior, Fish and Wildlife Service, Washington, D.C., USA.

SHAW, S. P., AND C. G. FREDINE. 1954. Wetlands of the United States. U.S. Department of the Interior, Fish and Wildlife Service, Circular 39.

SIMENSTAD, C. A., W. G. HOOD, R. M. THOM, D. A. LEVY, AND D. L. BOTTOM. 2000. Landscape structure and scale constraints on restoring estuarine wetlands for Pacific coast juvenile fishes. Pages 597–630 in M. P. Weinstein and D. A. Kreeger, editors. Concepts and controversies in tidal marsh ecology. Kluwer Academic Publishers, Boston, Massachusetts, USA.

SKAGEN, S. K., P. B. SHARPE, R. G. WALTERMIRE, AND M. B. DILLON. 1999. Biogeographical profiles of shorebird migration in midcontinental North America. Biological Science Report USGS/BRD/BSR-2000-0003. U.S. Department of the Interior, Geological Survey, Denver, Colorado, USA.

SMART, A. C., D. M. HARPER, F. MALAISEE, F. SCHMITZ, S. COLEY, AND A. C. G. DE BEAUREGARD. 2002. Feeding of the exotic Louisiana red swamp crayfish, *Procambarus clarkii* (Crustacea, Decapoda), in an African tropical lake: Lake Naivasha, Kenya. Hydrobiologia 488:129–142.

SMITH, C. J., R. D. DELAUNE, AND W. H. PATRICK, JR. 1983. Carbon dioxide emission and carbon accumulation in coastal wetlands. Estuarine, Coastal, and Shelf Science 17:21–29.

SMITH, R. H. 1942. Management of salt marshes on the Atlantic coast of the United States. Transactions of the North American Wildlife Conference 7:272–277.

SMITH, III, T. J., AND W. E. ODUM. 1981. The effects of grazing by snow geese on coastal salt marshes. Ecology 62:98–106.

SPILLER, S. F., AND R. H. CHABRECK. 1975. Wildlife populations in coastal marshes influenced by weirs. Proceedings of the Annual Conference of the Southeastern Association of Game and Fish Commissioners 29:518–525.

ST. AMANT, L. S. 1959. Louisiana wildlife inventory and management plan. Fish and Game Division, Louisiana Wildlife and Fisheries Commission, Baton Rouge, USA.

STRANGE, T. H. 1987. Goals and objectives of water level manipulations in impounded wetlands in South Carolina. Pages 130–137 in W. R. Whitman and W. H. Meredith, editors. Waterfowl and wetlands symposium. Department of Natural Resources and Environmental Control, Delaware Coastal Management Program, Dover, USA.

STEVENSON, J. C., M. S. KEARNEY, AND E. C. PENDLETON. 1985. Sedimentation and erosion in a Chesapeake Bay brackish system. Marine Geology 67:213–235.

———, L. G. WARD, AND M. S. KEARNEY. 1988. Sediment transport and trapping in marsh systems—implications of tidal flux studies. Marine Geology 80:37–59.

———, J. E. ROOTH, M. S. KEARNEY, AND K. L. SUNDBERG. 2000. The health and long term stability of natural and restored marshes in Chesapeake Bay. Pages 709–735 in M. P. Weinstein and D. A. Kreeger, editors. Concepts and controversies in tidal marsh ecology. Kluwer Academic Publishers, Boston, Massachusetts, USA.

STEYER, G. D. 1993. Sabine terracing project. Final report. Louisiana Department of Natural Resources, Coastal Restoration Division, Baton Rouge, USA.

STUMPF, R. P. 1983. The process of sedimentation on the surface of a salt marsh. Estuarine, Coastal and Shelf Science 17:495–508.

STUTZENBAKER, C. D., AND M. W. WELLER. 1989. The Texas coast. Pages 385–405 in L. M. Smith, R. L. Pederson, and R. M. Kaminski, editors. Habitat management for migrating and wintering waterfowl in North America. Texas Tech University Press, Lubbock, USA.

SUHAYDA, J., M. YOUNG, AND X. REN. 1989. Simulation study on natural and man-made changes in estuarine systems. Pages 82–85 in M. H. Hamza, editor. Applied simulation and modeling. Acta Press, Anaheim, California, USA.

TEAL, J. M. 1986. The ecology of regularly flooded salt marshes of New England: a community profile. U.S. Department of the Interior, Fish and Wildlife Service, Biological Report 85(7.4).

TITUS, J. G. 1996. The risk of sea level rise. Climate Change 33:151–212.

TURNER, D. D. 1966. Distribution and abundance of fishes in impoundments of Lacassine and Sabine National Wildlife refuges. Thesis. Louisiana State University, Baton Rouge, USA.

TURNER, R. E. 1999. Low-cost wetland restoration and creation projects for coastal Louisiana. Pages 229–240 in L. P. Rozas, J. A. Nyman, C. E. Proffitt, N. N. Rabalais, D. J. Reed, and R.E. Turner, editors.

Recent research in coastal Louisiana: natural system function and responses to human influences. Louisiana Sea Grant College Program, Baton Rouge, USA.

————, E. M. SWENSON, AND C. S. MILAN. 2000. Organic and inorganic contribution to vertical accretion in salt marsh sediments. Pages 583–595 *in* M. P. Weinstein and D. A. Kreeger, editors. Concepts and controversies in tidal marsh ecology. Kluwer Academic Publishers, Boston, Massachusetts, USA.

UHLER, F. M. 1944. Control of undesirable plants in waterfowl habitats. Transactions of the North American Wildlife Conference 9:295–303.

U.S. ARMY CORPS OF ENGINEERS. 1986. Beneficial uses of dredged material. EM1110-2-5026. U.S. Department of Army, Corps of Engineers, Chief of Engineers, Washington, D.C., USA.

VIOSCA, JR., P. 1931. Spontaneous combustion of the marshes in southern Louisiana. Ecology 12:439–442.

VISSER, J. M., C. E. SASSER, R. H. CHABRECK, AND R. G. LINSCOMBE. 2000. Marsh vegetation types of the Chenier Plain, Louisiana, USA. Estuaries 23:318–327.

WARD, E. 1942. *Phragmites* management. Transactions of the North American Wildlife Conference 7:294–298.

WEIFENBACH, D., AND N. CLARK. 2000. Three-year comprehensive monitoring report, Coast 2050 Region 4, East Mud Lake Marsh Management. Monitoring Series CS-20-MSTY-0799-1. Louisiana Department of Natural Resources, Coastal Management Division, Baton Rouge, USA. Available online at http://www.savelawetlands.org/site/projects.html.

WEIGERT, R. G., AND B. J. FREEMAN. 1990. Tidal salt marshes of the southeast Atlantic coast: a community profile. U.S. Department of the Interior, Fish and Wildlife Service, Biological Report 85(7.29).

WEST, R. C. 1977. Tidal salt marsh and mangal formations of Middle and South America. Pages 193–213 *in* V. J. Chapman, editor. Ecosystems of the world. I. Wet coastal ecosystems. Elsevier Scientific Publishing Company, New York, USA.

WHITE, W. A., AND R. A. MORTON. 1997. Wetland losses related to fault movement and hydrocarbon production, southeastern Texas coast. Journal of Coastal Research 13:1305–1320.

WHITLATCH, R. B. 1982. The ecology of New England tidal flats: a community profile. FWS/OBS-81/01. U.S. Department of the Interior, Fish and Wildlife Service, Washington, D.C., USA.

WILLIAMS, P., AND P. FARBER. 2001. Salt marsh restoration experience in San Francisco Bay. Journal of Coastal Research 27:203–211.

WILLIAMS, R. K. 1987. Construction, maintenance and water control structures of tidal impoundments in South Carolina. Pages 138–166 *in* W. R. Whitman and W. H. Meredith, editors. Waterfowl and wetlands symposium. Delaware Coastal Management Program, Department of Natural Resources and Environmental Control, Dover, USA.

WOLFE, J. L., D. K. BRADSHAW, AND R. H. CHABRECK. 1987. Alligator feeding habitats: new data and a review. Northeast Gulf Science 9:1–8.

WOOD, D. W., K. V. MILLER, AND D. L. FORSTER. 1996. Glyphospate and fluridone for control of giant cutgrass (*Zizaniopsis miliaceae*) in waterfowl impoundments. Proceedings of the Annual Conference of the Southeastern Association of Fish and Wildlife Agencies 50:592–598.

WOODHOUSE, JR., W. W., E. D. SENECA, AND S. W. BROOME. 1972. Marsh building with dredge spoil in North Carolina. Bulletin 445. North Carolina State University Agricultural Experiment Station, Raleigh, USA.

YOZZO, D. J., AND D. E. SMITH. 1998. Composition and abundance of resident marsh-surface nekton: comparison between tidal freshwater and salt marshes in Virginia, USA. Hydrobiologia 362:9–19.

ZEDLER, J. B. 1982. The ecology of southern California coastal salt marshes: a community profile. FWS/OBS-81/54. U.S. Department of the Interior, Fish and Wildlife Service, Biological Services Program, Washington, D.C., USA.

————. 1993. Canopy architecture of natural and planted cordgrass marshes—selecting habitat evaluation criteria. Ecological Applications 3:123–138.

————, T. WINFIELD, AND P. WILLIAMS. 1980. Salt marsh productivity with natural and altered tidal circulation. Oecologia 44:236–240.

————, J. C. CALLAWAY, J. S. DESMOND, G. VIVIAN-SMITH, G. D. WILLIAMS, G. SULLIVAN, A. E. BREWSTER, AND B. K. BRADSHAW. 1999. Californian salt-marsh vegetation: an improved model of spatial pattern. Ecosystems 2:19–35.

32

MANAGING FARMLANDS FOR WILDLIFE

Richard E. Warner, Jeffery W. Walk, and Catherine L. Hoffman

INTRODUCTION

Agricultural land use and associated technologies have dramatically changed over the past century, contributing to sweeping alterations of the natural flora and fauna. Natural resource agencies have been challenged to develop habitat programs to counter the negative effects of these changes on wildlife.

Wildlife management programs that succeed in farmlands are generally tied to other resource-conserving initiatives. These initiatives are driven by federal farm legislation that allocates resources and sets the rules framing conservation opportunities. Public support for programs that maintain and enhance wildlife in addition to other natural resource goals is growing. There are hints that public policy will more directly address issues concerning the sustainability of farming and natural resources, and emerging farm policies and programs are likely to specifically integrate wildlife conservation with agriculture. We emphasize a systems approach to addressing farmland habitat needs and opportunities. There are numerous habitat management guides that provide technical information on the development and long-term maintenance of specific habitat types (e.g., Newman et al. 2003).

CHALLENGES TO MANAGING WILDLIFE IN FARMLANDS

1. Goals of wildlife management and agriculture have tended to diverge, especially in recent decades.

Many wildlife species thrived during agricultural settlement in the late 1800s and early 1900s when farm landscapes comprised small, diversified farms that practiced field rotations of grains, forage grasses, and legumes (Leopold 1933:307). Subtle variations in the nature and timing of farming disturbances over time and space largely described trends in the abundance of many upland wildlife species. Modern agricultural systems, by comparison, show reduced diversity in terms of vegetation structure and the spatial arrangement of vegetation types (Fig. 1). Cropping practices now include mechanical and chemical disturbances that occur rapidly and extensively on farmland causing habitat conditions to have deteriorated in many respects.

2. Farm conservation programs, widely promoted for wildlife benefits, often do not accommodate wildlife management priorities.

Since the New Deal era of the 1930s, farm policies and programs have strongly influenced agricultural land use in the United States (Schlebecker 1975, Brady and Hamilton 1988) and have provided incentives for farmers to adopt conservation practices (Langner 1985, Jahn 1988). Conservation-related aspects of farm programs have the potential to affect large-scale changes in habitat conditions and, therefore, are of critical importance to wildlife managers. However, the year-to-year nature of some programs as well as permitted (and sometimes required) disturbances during the growing season have diminished their potential benefits for farmland wildlife.

3. Reliable knowledge about results of wildlife habitat initiatives is lacking.

Although wildlife agencies monitor and predict year-to-year trends in the relative abundance of selected farmland

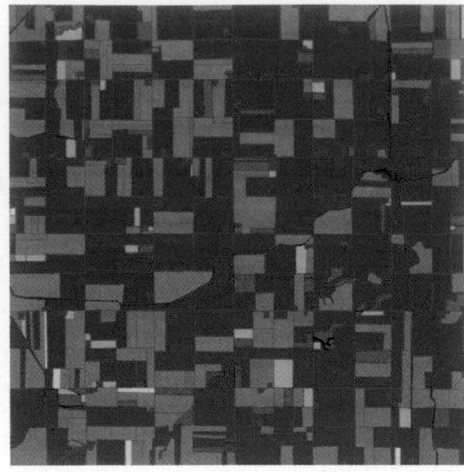

WHEAT
CORN
SOYBEANS
PASTURED HAY
HAY & OATS
CORRIDORS
NON-AGRICULTURAL
GRASS PASTURES
PLOWING

Fig. 1. Expansion of intensive row crop agriculture in the Sibley Study Area in Ford County, Illinois between 1954 (left) and 1965 (right). The transition from small, diversified farms to large-scale row crop enterprises occurred throughout much of the most intensively farmed regions of the United States during this period.

species, especially game animals and other economically important species, mechanisms that cause these trends are often poorly understood. Only rarely have agricultural practices been carefully documented relative to the population ecology of a target species. Land use changes have occurred too fast and with so many confounding factors that reliable knowledge is often lacking, especially given the minimal time and resources directed to these questions (Warner 1992). Moreover, there are many species (e.g., reptiles and amphibians) for which little at all is known about their population ecology or status in farmland settings (Corn and Peterson 1996, Hecnar and M'Closkey 1996, Maisonneuve and Rioux 2001).

4. *Wildlife agencies need to redouble efforts to communicate the importance of wildlife in critical ecosystem functions.*

The ecological and economic values of wildlife in agricultural settings should be better communicated to society (Pimentel et al. 1987, Daily 1997). Indeed, one of the greatest failures of wildlife professionals has been their inability to translate research findings of management practices into ecological and socioeconomic benefits. For example, wildlife management has the potential to be prominent in future biological control strategies (Box 1). These efforts will be important as more attention is paid to sustainability (Goodland 1995) of farming and natural resources.

5. *Wildlife managers must address both the positives and negatives of interactions between humans and wildlife.*

As wildlife issues become more prominent, biologists should expect that landowners and the general public will have varied and often contradictory perceptions of wildlife management initiatives. Wildlife managers are increasingly responding to perceived problems, such as to species that are declining and in need of immediate habitat interventions or to species that cause problems for humans. Given that some species considered as successes of wildlife management interventions [e.g., white-tailed deer (*Odocoileus virginianus*)] are now frequently perceived as

causing problems, maintaining credibility is a challenge. In efforts to promote habitat management, wildlife managers should anticipate responding to the wildlife-related problems espoused by their clients. Biologists have too often downplayed these problems.

6. *Wildlife managers must facilitate access to private lands to meet the public's need for sporting and other recreational wildlife activities.*

Since 1940, individual farm operations in the United States have nearly tripled in size, while the number of farms has decreased by about 70%. Meanwhile, the proportion of Americans living on farms has decreased from 23% to less than 2% (U.S. Department of Agriculture 2001*a*). As a result, gaining access to wildlife resources on private lands has become increasingly difficult to obtain by an urban public with few ties to agricultural communities. Furthermore, perceptions of liability and property damage, decreasing wildlife populations, and increasing demand by outsiders have led many landowners to curb access. Convincing landowners to allow access to wildlife resources on their land requires creative solutions (Box 2).

IMPACTS OF FARMING PRACTICES ON WILDLIFE

Rotation Farming

Prior to the early 1960s, rotation farming characterized the most intensively farmed landscapes of North America. Corn was usually planted the first year, followed by small grains. These small grains served as a nurse crop for hay (typically forage grasses and/or legumes) that typically persisted for 2 years. Hay fields pastured livestock and maintained soil fertility.

The rotation farming system provided a spectrum of habitat needs for upland wildlife (Warner 1994). For instance, grain fields supported abundant and diverse food resources that included an understory of weedy plants during the growing season (in the absence of herbicides) and waste grains during fall and winter (Warner 1984, Warner and Etter 1985). Hay fields provided permanent (year-

---

Box 1. Birds as predators of agricultural insect pests.

A number of historical and anecdotal references to the significance of birds as predators of insect pests exist; however, fewer experimental studies have been reported. Following the development of DDT and other effective pesticides after World War II, "economic ornithology" has been neglected. Kirk et al. (1996) reviewed the evidence for birds as predators of pest insects, evaluated the likelihood that avian species could reliably keep insect populations at or below economic threshold levels, and made a number of recommendations for enhancing bird predation on insects in farmland situations.

Based upon abundance, geographical distributions, and association with crop types, Kirk et al. (1996) identified egrets, plovers and other shorebirds, gulls, woodpeckers, crows, emberizine sparrows, and icterine blackbirds as probably having the greatest economic effects (see also O'Connor et al. 1999). Songbirds are most likely to maintain insect pests at low and moderate densities over broad geographical areas. Using data from a variety of sources, Kirk et al. (1996) estimated that one pair of savannah sparrows (*Passerculus sandwichensis*) that successfully raised 2 broods consumes 3.7 kg of grasshoppers (149,000 individuals) in one breeding season! Larger and flocking species may significantly reduce "outbreak" populations of pests. As an example, one California gull (*Larus californicus*) collected from a feeding flock in Alberta contained 535 large two-striped grasshoppers (*Melanoplus bivittatus*).

Some of the most convincing evidence that birds can effectively control insect populations involves codling moths (*Cydia pomonella*) and other orchard pests. Woodpeckers and bark-gleaning birds have removed over 90% of larvae in some orchards (MacLellan1959, 1971; Stairs 1985). Black et al. (1970) reported birds, particularly northern flickers (*Colaptes auratus*), removed 64 and 81% of overwintering southwestern corn borer larvae (*Diataea grandiosella*) during the 2 years of their study. Near a 90,000-bird roost in southwestern Ontario, Quiring and Timmins (1988) excluded American crows (*Corvus brachyrhynchos*) from corn plants. On average 2.01 European corn borer larvae (*Ostrinia hubilalis*) successfully overwintered in caged plants, compared to 0.93 larvae per unprotected plant. Within 7 km of a red-winged blackbird (*Agelaius phoeniceus*) roost, none of 27 sampled fields had a corn rootworm (*Diabrotica longicornis*) density greater than 8 individuals/plant; however, 20% of cornfields 7–20 km from the roost had a greater density of rootworms (Bollinger and Caslick 1985).

Over much of Europe and North America, farmland bird populations continue to decline. Kirk et al. (1996) identified the need for more habitats: fencerows, shelterbelts, woodlots, grassed waterways, field margins, appropriately managed roadsides, and nest boxes. They advocated reduced pesticide use, reducing the frequency and changing the timing of mechanical operations, and farming organically. Managing grasslands, by considering patch size, juxtaposition, and floral composition and structure, will also increase the abundance and diversity of birds. To improve the efficacy of birds as natural control agents, field size or shape may need to be altered. Sensitive to their own predation risk, many birds will not forage far into fields when crop plants are small or absent. Thus, smaller or more linear crop fields are appropriate.

---

round) cover and prime nesting habitat for many grassland bird species. Due to the relatively small sizes of fields, a variety of cover types occurred in close proximity. Permanent vegetation along field borders were ecotones that allowed wildlife to move freely between patches of cover. In addition, the farmland matrix during this era was interspersed with permanent cover such as wetlands, wood lots, and riparian areas.

Modern Farming Practices

Changes in agricultural practices in recent decades have profoundly affected habitat conditions and altered the nature and juxtaposition of landscape elements (Noss et al. 1995) in farmland settings. Larger farm equipment has led to larger fields and farms, resulting in a dramatic loss of field borders (Best 1983, Baltensperger 1987). Since World War II, increased applications of synthetic fertilizers have reduced the need for crop rotations that include legumes to fix nitrogen in the soil. Production of row crops, especially soybeans, has expanded, and some cattle operations have been phased out further eliminating semi-permanent fields of forage grasses and legumes. These changes have produced a farmland matrix dominated by highly disturbed monocultures, with little connectivity among landscape elements. The collective impact of intensive farming practices has been to decrease the likelihood that farmlands will offer

the complexity of life-sustaining resources wildlife need (van Emden 1965, Auclair 1976, Oldfield and Alcorn 1987, Power and Follett 1987, Turner 1987, Woolhouse and Harmsen 1987). This has led to a general decrease in wildlife traditionally common within farmland settings (National Research Council 1982) (Figs. 2, 3).

The nature and timing of farm disturbances, in particular, are increasingly hazardous to wildlife (Freemark and Boutin 1995, Dailey 2002). Modern agricultural practices have reduced the temporal diversity of farm disturbances by increasing their rapidity and intensity across the landscape. The uniform maturation of modern crop cultivars allows tilling, planting, and harvesting to be increasingly synchronous. These physical disturbances often coincide with critical periods of wildlife reproduction, maturation, and dispersal (Warner and Etter 1989, Bollinger et al. 1990, Frawley and Best 1991, Warner et al. 2000). For example, cutting of hay is becoming earlier and progressing more rapidly during the nesting season (Warner and Etter 1989, Bollinger et al. 1990, Frawley and Best 1991). Likewise, increased autumn tillage in some areas has reduced availability of crop stubble as forage and cover for wildlife during autumn and winter (Warner and Havera 1989) challenging wildlife to disperse in the context of radical landscape changes, often for long distances and at significant mortality risk (Warner et al. 1999, 2000).

Box 2. Public hunting on private lands: the Kansas Walk-In Hunting Access Program.

A common human-dimensions issue faced by natural resource agencies is facilitating access by the sporting public to wildlife on private lands. While a number of states have crafted similar solutions, one successful example has been the Walk-In Hunting Access (WIHA) program in Kansas. The combination of vast lands enrolled in the Conservation Reserve Program, strong populations of upland game, an influx of non-resident hunters, and little public hunting land magnified access needs in Kansas. In this program, landowners submit a request to the Kansas Department of Wildlife and Parks (KDWP) for their property to be included. KDWP biologists inspect the land for hunting potential and, if accepted, post the land. Funding for WIHA is derived from a combination of hunting license fees and Federal Aid to Wildlife Restoration Funds. The pilot project in 1995 enrolled about 4,000 hectares. Feedback from both hunters and landowners was overwhelmingly positive. In 2001, this program had grown to include 342,000 hectares of private land.

This program offers a number of benefits to landowners and hunters, alike. In exchange for seasonal leases of their land for public hunting, landowners receive payments based on area enrolled and duration of the lease. As added incentive, under Kansas state law, landowners that lease their land to KDWP for public hunting are free of liability. Conservation officers periodically patrol WIHA properties, and hunters are actively discouraged from trying to contact cooperating landowners since landowners may have participated to reduce or avoid contact with hunters. Hunters, in turn, gain access to hundreds of thousands of hectares of wildlife habitat. The KDWP provides hunters with detailed atlases and maps illustrating enrolled properties and listing species of game most likely to be encountered at each site. Responsible behavior by hunters is credited with making WIHA an initial success. Ethical treatment of private lands will be key to the future growth and continuance of the program.

Chemical disturbances, much more frequent now due to applications of fertilizers, pesticides, and herbicides, have also negatively impacted wildlife. As pesticides and their metabolites have pervaded terrestrial and aquatic ecosystems, they have reduced target and nontarget plants and insects of value to wildlife (National Research Council 1982). These agricultural pollutants have destroyed many bottomland lakes (Bellrose et al. 1983, Judy et al. 1984), and they have adversely affected the fish community in a substantial portion of the waters of the United States (Flather and Hoekstra 1989).

Source/Sink Paradigm

One way of conceptualizing the impacts of farming on wildlife follows the "source/sink" paradigm, which describes how a species fares in a particular setting (Pulliam 1988). The focus of this paradigm is the net effect of births (b), deaths (d), and movement (immigration i and emigration e) on numbers of a given species in a defined area (Donovan et al. 1995, McCoy et al. 1999). In some settings, production of young exceeds annual mortality; $b + d$ is positive, and the setting is a source. In others, young do not replenish the loss of adults, and $b + d$ is negative indicating a habitat sink. Movement of individuals between populations ($i + e$) is influenced by connectivity of habitats.

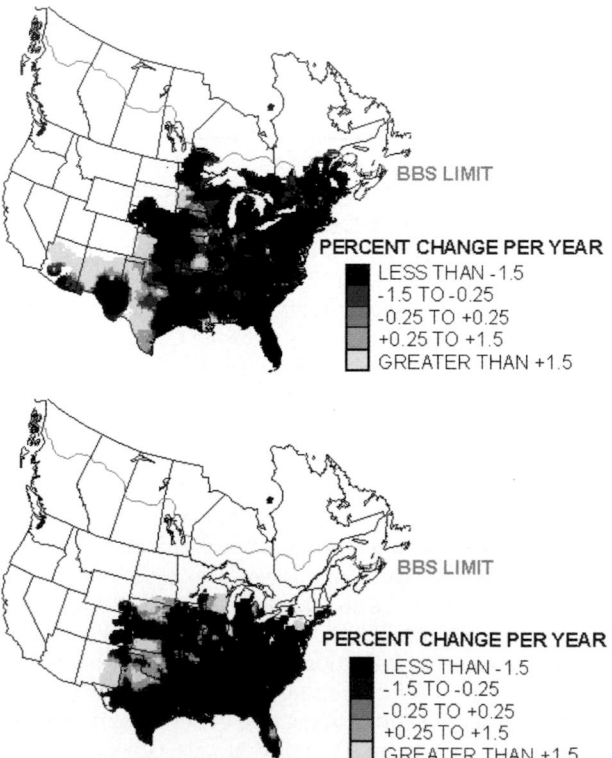

Fig. 3. Population trends from the North American Breeding Bird Survey (1966–2000) for 2 characteristic farmland birds, the eastern meadowlark (*Sturnella magna*) (top) and northern bobwhite (*Colinus virginianus*) (bottom) (from Sauer et al. 2002). Percent changes per year of –1.5 to –2.5%, typical of these and other farmland birds, suggest overall population declines of 40–60% during the 35-year period.

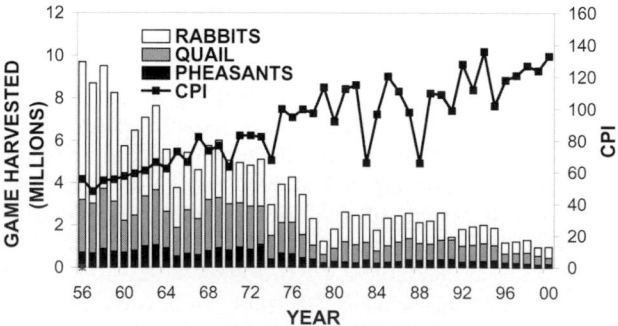

Fig. 2. Changes in the hunter harvest of selected upland game species in Illinois and the Crop Production Index (CPI), Illinois, 1956–2000. The CPI measures the productivity of agriculture by multiplying yearly production by season average prices, then dividing by the same value for 1977 (the year the index was developed). The trends portray that agricultural practices were compatible with habitat needs of upland wildlife until recent decades (data from the Illinois Department of Agriculture and the Illinois Department of Natural Resources).

Over the past century agricultural landscapes have tended toward fewer, smaller, structurally and florally simpler, more isolated and more disturbed habitat patches that are less likely to attract an abundance and diversity of breeding species. This has caused a decrease in the portion of settings that are sources. In addition, attractive areas will be sinks unless wildlife agencies provide guidance or incentives to encourage farmers to minimize field disturbances during critical periods. Even in regions where attractive patches of cover abound, the intensity and timing of disturbances cause most settings inhabited by wildlife to be sinks (Burger 1978, Best 1986, O'Neil and Carey 1986).

MANAGING LANDSCAPES FOR WILDLIFE

In accordance with the source/sink paradigm, habitat management within farmlands should strive to increase the number of settings attractive to targeted wildlife and the portion of settings that foster high rates of reproduction and survival. Managers should be cognizant of improvements that can be made on as many landscape elements as possible, increasing the likelihood that farmland settings inhabited by target species will be sources. In farmlands the major landscape elements are habitat patches, corridors, and the surrounding farmland matrix (Forman and Godron 1981, Forman 1995).

The following guidelines are useful for developing habitat management plans that emphasize the ecological functions of landscapes and spatial relationships between key elements:

- manage for self-sustaining wildlife populations in densities that are suitable and achievable for the setting, given ecological, socioeconomic, and political considerations;
- preserve, enhance, or restore the structure and function of existing patches and corridors;
- create new patches or corridors to replace lost habitat,
- minimize negative impacts and maximize positive habitat attributes of the matrix; and
- restore or mimic natural disturbance regimes (U.S. Department of Agriculture 1999).

Habitat Patches

Habitat patches are areas of natural or restored native vegetation. In farmlands these consist primarily of woodlots, wetlands, and a few scattered prairie remnants (typically on slopes too steep to cultivate). These habitat patches are typically the focus of management efforts to enhance vegetation and other cover for wildlife (Roseberry and Klimstra 1984, Walk and Warner 1999). Biological conservation strategies, in particular, often emphasize management of natural (unfarmed) habitats for rare and endangered plants and animals. However, most habitat patches in farmlands tend to be small and isolated (Herkert 1994), and the extent to which they are connected by permanent field edges and other corridors has been reduced. Furthermore, they are primarily edge. Hence, game and other edge-adapted species are often the primary benefactors of small natural areas, not species that typically require interior habitats (Noss 1983). Nonetheless, attention should be focused on characteristics of the land that can preserve or enhance its biotic integrity.

The following principles provide a useful framework when managing habitat patches for wildlife:

- large patches are better than small patches,
- connected patches are better than separated patches,
- unified patches are better than fragmented patches,
- several patches are better than one patch,
- proximate patches are better than separate patches,
- structurally diverse patches are better than simple patches, and
- patches with native plants are better than patches with introduced plants (U.S. Department of Agriculture 1999).

Corridors

Corridors are linear strips of permanent or semi-permanent vegetation such as field borders, fencerows, roadsides, drainage ditches, and riparian areas. Corridors are important because they help sustain flora and fauna in the region by connecting habitat patches (Stamps et al. 1987, Chapman and Ribic 2002). They deter movement of soil and water. By facilitating dispersal of organisms between habitat patches, corridors tend to dampen population fluctuations within patches, reduce the risk of extinction of subpopulations within patches, and increase the probability of recolonization of unoccupied patches (Noss 1983, Stacey et al. 1997). Even narrow field borders such as hedgerows and fences are important in the daily activities of vertebrates in farmland settings and, therefore, deserve management attention (Arnold 1983, Best 1983).

The following principles provide a useful framework when managing corridors for wildlife:

- continuous corridors are better than fragmented corridors,
- wider corridors are better than narrow corridors,
- natural connectivity should be maintained or restored,
- introduced connectivity should be studied carefully,
- 2 or more corridor connections between patches are better than one,
- structurally diverse corridors are better than simple corridors, and
- corridors with native plants are better than corridors with introduced plants (U.S. Department of Agriculture 1999).

Farmland Matrix

Row crops, small grains, pasture, and hay characterize the farmland matrix. Wildlife may make extensive use of this matrix and are affected, both directly and indirectly, by farming disturbances thereon (Herkert et al. 1996, Kershner 2001, Walk 2001). Therefore, agricultural practices are an important consideration for optimizing habitat conditions for farmland wildlife (Dahlberg 1992). For example, use of pesticides is an important consideration relative to the abundance and diversity of plants and invertebrates (Potts 1986) available to wildlife as food sources.

Management strategies for enhancing the farmland matrix for wildlife can be linked with soil conservation efforts. Soil-conserving measures tend to improve cover in farmlands. For example, conservation tillage leaves some or all of the crop residues (cornstalks, wheat stubble) on the soil surface rather than turning them under. Leaving residue on the surface reduces soil erosion and also provides some useful habitat for wildlife (Basore et al. 1986, Best 1986). Similarly, contour-strip cropping uses interspersed strips of close-grown crops (hay and small grains) on the contour between strips of row crops to control erosion. These alternating strips of corn, oats, and hay can provide the juxtaposition and configuration of cover types important for enhancing landscape diversity and food webs (Brady 1985). Implementation of these techniques not only improves habitat for terrestrial wildlife but also improves water quality for aquatic wildlife by reducing the amount of agricultural pollutants reaching waterways. However, managing for structural diversity and the optimal juxtaposition of cover are of little value if agricultural disturbances continue to occur during critical periods, such as mowing of legumes and agricultural grasses during the nesting season.

FARM PROGRAMS AS A CONTEXT FOR HABITAT MANAGEMENT

Through much of the 1900s, farm programs diverted cropland from production to adjust commodity production and prices, and to promote conservation. These "set-aside" programs have been important because they can potentially establish early successional cover, which is at a premium in farm landscapes. They also reduce the hazards of farming disturbances at critical times for wildlife, e.g., the nesting season.

Most programs diverting land from production have fallen far short of their potential for improving habitat conditions on farmland (Warner et al. 1999). Since these programs affect millions of hectares of cropland in the United States annually (Fig. 4), influence should be brought, where possible, so that farmers will be encouraged to provide quality habitat for wildlife while meeting the guidelines of agricultural programs. Biologists working in farmland settings should be well informed of these programs in their region, and should strive to optimize the management guidelines that govern these programs. Familiarity with conservation programs (which are perpetually changing) will enable biologists to make informed recommendations to landholders, which in turn establishes credibility and facilitates landowner participation (i.e., getting more and better habitat on the land).

Early Set-aside Programs

The Agricultural Conservation Program of the 1930s and 1940s, the Soil Bank Program of the 1950s, and the Set-Aside Acres Program of the early 1960s were important for moderating the negative impacts of increasingly intensive farming on wildlife (Berner 1984, Edwards 1984, Jahn 1988). Most of the land diverted as part of these programs was seeded with forage grasses and legumes, and fields of forage legumes and grasses already in place were often idled. With minimal farm disturbances, these habitats were immediately attractive to upland wildlife. These set-aside programs, in conjunction with rotation farming, produced upland game densities of historic proportions.

Conservation Reserve Program

The Conservation Reserve Program (CRP) emerged in the mid-1980s and has significantly more potential for wildlife management compared to other programs in recent decades (Fig. 5). Through this program environmentally sensitive farmland is idled for 10–15 years to reduce soil erosion, improve water quality, and provide wildlife habitat (Table 1). Specifically, these initiatives protect highly erodable soils and establish permanent grass and/or woody vegetation along land–water interfaces to improve water quality. Landowners receive annual payments based on local land rental values and up to 50% cost-share for establishing permanent vegetation. Additional cost-share arrangements and technical support are often available through state or local agencies and private conservation organizations. The CRP increasingly offers a variety of incentives to manage for critical habitats. However, this program has complex regulations that influence where contracts are likely to be targeted, and it does not necessarily offer the most opportunities where habitat needs are the greatest.

Modern Set-aside Programs

Building on CRP, modern set-aside programs offer considerable promise for addressing habitat needs at farm and regional scales. The Conservation Reserve Enhancement Program (CREP), the Wildlife Habitat Incentive Program (WHIP), and the Environmental Quality Incentives Program (EQIP) all offer important habitat opportunities. These programs are administered by the U.S. Department of Agriculture (USDA) and are optimized at local and regional levels by interagency agreements and on-the-

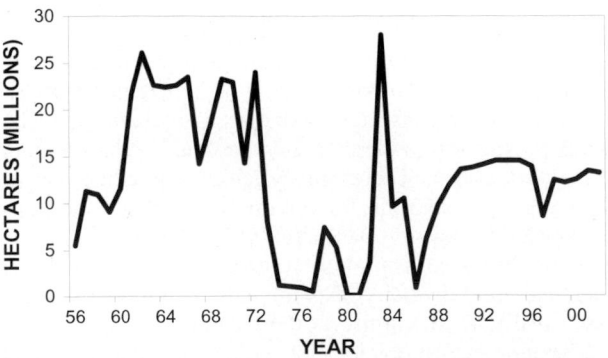

Fig. 4. Farmland diverted from production in the United States, 1956–2002 (Dahlgren 1988, Osborn et al. 1995, U.S. Department of Agriculture 2002). These "set-aside" programs have been important elements of farm conservation initiatives since the New Deal era.

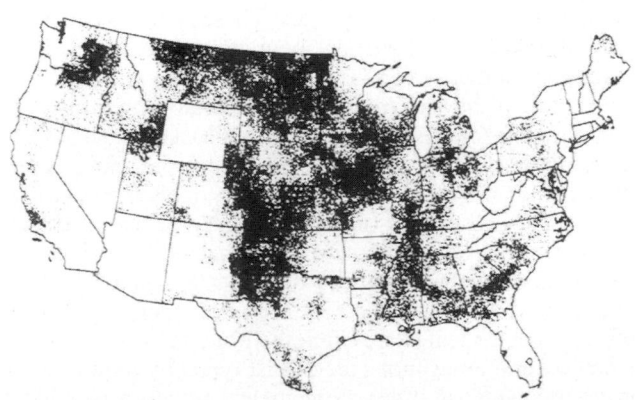

Fig. 5. Distribution of Conservation Reserve Program enrollment in the United States at its peak in 1993 (from Osborn et al. 1995).

Table 1. Wildlife-related conservation practices available under the Conservation Reserve Program (U.S. Department of Agriculture 2001*b*).

Conservation practice	Description	Contract length (years)
CP1	Introduced grasses and legumes	10
CP2	Native grasses	10
CP3	Tree plantings	10
CP3A	Hardwood tree plantings	10–15
CP4B	Permanent wildlife habitat–corridors	10–15
CP4D	Permanent wildlife habitat	10
CP5A	Field windbreaks	10–15
CP8A	Grass waterways	10
CP9	Shallow water areas for wildlife	10
CP10	Previously established grass	10
CP11	Previously established trees	10
CP12	Wildlife food plot	10
CP15A	Permanent contour grass strips	10
CP15B	Permanent contour grass strips on terraces	10
CP16A	Shelterbelts	10–15
CP17A	Living snow fences	10–15
CP21	Filter strips	10–15
CP22	Riparian buffers	10–15
CP23	Wetland restoration	10–15
CP24	Permanent vegetation for cross wind trap strips	10
CP25	Rare and declining habitat	10–15

ground cooperation. Similar to CRP, landholders are offered annual lease payments and other incentives to enroll in these programs, often at rates that offer an attractive financial alternative to producing crops on the land.

CREP is a joint state-federal program that addresses specific, local environmental needs. CREP is similar to CRP in contract length, approved practices and cost sharing, but has more local flexibility and may offer one-time or annual "bonus payments" to encourage participation or adoption of specific practices (e.g., participants receive an additional 20% annual bonus payment for installing filter strips). Similarly, additional financial incentives and cost-share resources may be available though state or local agencies and private conservation organizations. CREP in Maryland is well known for its efforts to improve water quality in the Chesapeake Bay watershed. As part of this cleanup effort, Maryland has committed to restoring up to 40,000 ha of streamside property, including 28,000 ha of riparian forest and 4,000 ha of wetlands (Maryland Department of Agriculture 2002). The CREP in Iowa also provides an example of how these programs can benefit wildlife (Box 3).

The goals of WHIP are to develop upland and wetland habitat for wildlife, fish, and threatened or endangered species. Landowners develop wildlife habitat plans with Natural Resources Conservation Service personnel. WHIP offers technical assistance and 75% federal cost-share, with up to 25% cost-share by state or local agencies and private conservation organizations, for 5–10 year agreements. Sample projects include restoring native grasslands, controlling exotic species, stream bank stabilization,

and cave closures for bat (Chiroptera) habitat.

EQIP offers financial and technical assistance to farmers and ranchers for installing or implementing structural or management practices on agricultural land. Examples include integrated pest management and improved grazing practices. EQIP provides federal support at 75% cost-share (90% in limited cases) and annual payments for up to 3 years.

OPTIMIZING FARM PROGRAMS FOR WILDLIFE: STEPS TOWARD PROGRESS

Historically, wildlife managers have a poor record using farm programs as a platform to improve habitat for wildlife. The success of farmland habitat programs is associated with how well managers are able to accommodate the ecological, political, economic, and social contexts in which these habitat initiatives must occur.

Identifying Target Species and Ecological Communities

Biologists should consider the community (ecosystem) approach to habitat development, a perspective that implies appraisal of the potential impacts of management on the number and relative abundance of wildlife species regionally. A community perspective does not preclude emphasizing one or several species in habitat initiatives at localized scales, but ensures the impact of management at larger spatial scales is at least considered. A management program that focuses on relatively common species, such as upland game, should avoid altering prime habitats of uncommon, rare, or endangered species in larger tracts or remnant patches of native vegetation. Large, permanent tracts of habitat in predominately agricultural settings are now uncommon. Where large tracts are present, managers should beware of maximizing edge, a practice that does not benefit area-sensitive species, and may facilitate penetration of cover by predators and by brood-parasitic birds (Winter and Faaborg 1999, Winter et al. 2000).

Identifying Physiographic Characteristics

Once identified, the target region should be examined to assess significant physiographic features from which to build a habitat management plan (Risser et al. 1984, Swanson et al. 1988). Experienced biologists often perform this assessment informally, but it is important to review this process and document criteria used. What are the natural features that give definition to the region (Noss et al. 1995)? What was the natural vegetation prior to settlement: prairie, savanna, forest? What are the significant habitat features that define the wildlife community, including forests, wetlands, riparian corridors, intensive grain cropping, and livestock grazing? Are there remnant patches of natural vegetation or other significant semi-permanent vegetation (such as trees along a stream) from which to start? What life history needs of target species are being fulfilled in the existing agricultural matrix? What life history requisites are lacking? These are the kinds of questions that generally define the resident fauna and should guide habitat management strategies.

Regional habitat strategies should permit development of corridors connecting important landforms and natural areas (Flather and Sauer 1996). The physical dimensions of corridors and how these corridors are managed will affect the reproduction and survival of wildlife at local and

Box 3. Iowa Conservation Reserve Enhancement Program: helping landowners protect Iowa's natural resources (Iowa Department of Agriculture and Land Stewardship 2002).

The Iowa Conservation Reserve Enhancement Program (CREP) is a major state/federal initiative to develop strategically located wetlands and remove nitrate from tile-drainage water in cropland areas. The program is being implemented in cooperation with the Farm Service Agency and Natural Resources Conservation Service of the U.S. Department of Agriculture to provide $38 million in funding during 2002-04 to construct and restore up to 3,600 hectares of wetlands and buffers. Financial incentives are provided to private landowners to develop and restore wetlands that intercept tile drainage from agricultural watersheds. Landowners receive annual land payments over 15 years and reimbursements for costs of wetland and buffer establishment. Easements to maintain the wetlands and buffers are required for a minimum of 15 years beyond the CREP payments, for a total of 30 years. Additional one-time, up front incentive payments are used to encourage participating landowners to enter into perpetual easements.

Research at Iowa State University has confirmed that strategically located and designed wetlands under the program requirements will remove 40–90% of the nitrate and 90+% of the herbicide in tile drainage water from croplands. The Iowa CREP is available in the 37 counties in the tile-drained region of north central Iowa and will specifically target the North Raccoon River Watershed. This watershed is noted for some of the highest nitrate loads in the Mississippi River Basin. Over the next decade, the Iowa CREP could develop wetlands in the program area with the capacity for removing over 5,000 metric tons of nitrate-nitrogen annually. In addition to reducing nitrate loads to surface waters, the wetlands will provide wildlife habitat and increased recreational opportunities.

regional scales. River and stream corridors, their riparian vegetation, and quality of water that flows through them merit special consideration. In addition to upland erosion control, emphasis should be placed on the land-water interface, including near- and in-channel processes. Vegetative buffers, riparian forests, and wetlands represent opportunities to mitigate nonpoint source pollution from agricultural lands. Further, expanded riparian greenbelts provide additional perennial wildlife cover.

Recognizing Issues of Spatial Scale

Agricultural land use affects wildlife habitat at all spatial scales. Wildlife agencies usually develop habitat at the patch or field scale. These sites are readily affected by ecological phenomena occurring in nearby cover types, e.g., interactions at the farm scale. Likewise, regional phenomena influence responses by wildlife at farm and field scales. Regardless of the extent of control over local conditions brought about by habitat initiatives, the response of wildlife is affected by habitat conditions at larger scales where physiographic and land use factors are similar.

Temporal Factors

The goal of intensive habitat efforts is generally to improve reproduction and survival of target species on a regional basis (Dumke et al. 1981). The resources needed to enhance the demographics of target species often are poorly understood, and habitat programs may require several years of development before responses by wildlife are apparent. For example, successful intensive ring-necked pheasant (*Phasianus colchicus*) management programs typically require efforts for 5–10 years on a high percentage of farms over a region that is a township or larger in size.

Planning and Coordinating Management Plans

Biologists are prone to underestimate and understate the time needed for different facets of a management plan. They need to carefully consider the time needed to plan,

develop support from key agencies and groups, coordinate and implement the initial habitat work, evaluate and refine the approach, and maintain or rejuvenate habitat over the long term.

We recommend resource planning as a method for the comprehensive management of the resource base—soil, water, and related plant and animal resources—within intensively farmed landscapes. Management toward multiple natural resource objectives is a widely supported approach but is difficult to accomplish on private lands (Jahn 1988). It requires considerable "front end" efforts by biologists that may seem counter to getting habitat in the ground. One problem is that it requires multidisciplinary expertise and interagency cooperation. In the absence of interagency cooperation, only the most persistent landholders will contact the agencies responsible for delivering independently derived plans for wildlife management, soil erosion control, woodland management, and commodity marketing.

Effective coordination is a major effort, and one of the most important aspects is to form an advisory group (Phipps 1972). Just as the wildlife biologist evaluates habitat conditions for selected species and provides technical guidelines for management, other professionals provide similar information from their areas of expertise. Members should represent targeted groups (landowners, renters, farm managers), the community, public agencies (e.g., Natural Resources Conservation Service, State Department of Agriculture, and Cooperative Extension Service), farm organizations, and private entities such as sporting and other outdoor groups. An effective advisory group is invaluable in forming realistic goals and benchmarks of success while having a key role in legitimizing and promoting the effort.

Working with Landowners

There is often a direct relationship between effective interactions among biologists and landholders during the planning process and the subsequent success of the program. Biologists must learn what farm operators want accomplished on their land as it is the management goals of the landholder—not those of the managing agency—that are likely to be applied and maintained over the years. Skills in communicating, marketing, and salesmanship are essential to success, but they must be supported with technical knowledge that demonstrates to farmers an understanding of wildlife management, agribusiness, and the complex world in which adequate cash flow and profitability are essential.

Of particular importance is recognition of the time and other resources required for the farm operator to complete the new tasks generated by the habitat plan. An ecologically sound habitat management plan will fail if the varied needs of land users are not met. For example, the interests and options available to a hobby farmer with considerable time and other resources for habitat development would differ from those of a large scale farm operator. The plan should include local contact information for the USDA office, state wildlife agency, conservation organizations, and other groups that might be sources of cost-sharing monies or incentives, equipment, seed or plant materials, and labor.

Little habitat management will be achieved and little demand generated if the contact with a farm operator is represented only by a quick trip over his land and a hastily delivered "plan." Follow-up is important because it gives the biologist opportunity to diagnose and correct unanticipated problems such as what to do about "all of the weeds" in the grass planting, and it provides opportunity to emphasize the need for long term maintenance of vegetation, which is often a shortcoming in habitat plans. Follow-up also facilitates reevaluating and updating the plan as conditions change on the farm (e.g., government farm programs or finances). Further, maintaining a close liaison with program participants creates opportunities for the biologist to make additional contacts allowing for expansion of the habitat program to other farms. If a professional plan is prepared with the landholder's interests in mind, and follow-up assistance is provided as reinforcement and to correct unforeseen problems, wildlife biologists can be assured the demand for their assistance in the farm community will grow.

Being Opportunistic and Flexible

Habitat opportunities on farmland are strongly influenced by policy changes that are shaped by an increasingly global economy, public opinion, resources available to landholders and agencies, and changing priorities in resource conservation. Some of the most creative and effective habitat programs were crafted and have been kept alive by biologists who effectively anticipated these changes and articulated the benefits of aggressive action to society.

EVALUATING AND REFINING PROGRAMS

The success or failure of a program should be documented, cost-effectiveness evaluated, and the appropriateness of program modifications considered. Evaluation can include (1) adherence by agencies to time tables, costs, and objectives; (2) success rates in establishing and maintaining desired vegetative configurations and structures; (3) participation by landholders, initially and over time (including assessments of opinions, attitudes, knowledge, and conservation behavior); and (4) responses by targeted

species to management. The number of farmland habitat programs that have received rigorous evaluation with well-documented costs and benefits is small, and few published accounts are available.

Monitoring Vegetation

The extent to which monitoring of vegetation is warranted depends on how reliable the planting method is assumed to be. The success of vegetation established and maintained by landholders—when planting methods are proven and widely known—is likely to be more variable than if personnel from wildlife agencies had undertaken the task. Monitoring vegetation should minimally include the inspection of a randomly selected sample of treated sites; these should be evaluated with respect to initial and long-term success in achieving desired plant forms. Alternatively, landholders familiar with particular plant forms can provide feedback through questionnaires.

Monitoring Participation by Landholders

Participation by landholders can be evaluated in several ways. Opinion surveys can be taken before promotion of the program is initiated; follow-up surveys can document the effects of participation in the program on attitudes and knowledge. Special recognition of outstanding cooperators can enhance the visibility and importance of wildlife management programs to landholders. Ideally, a rural sociologist or an education specialist should participate in program development and evaluation.

Monitoring Responses by Wildlife

Evaluating responses by target species to habitat programs can be accomplished by direct or indirect means, depending in part on the extent to which species-habitat responses are known. Direct evaluation involves at a minimum the use of proven survey methods to establish trends in relative wildlife abundance. More involved evaluation of demographic responses may require activities such as nest and radiotelemetry studies. In some instances, abundance of wildlife is not necessarily an indicator of a demographically healthy population (Van Horne 1983, Vickery et al. 1992). Although increased visibility and access to wildlife are important components of farmland management programs, biologists must ensure habitat manipulations are creating self-sustaining and expanding "source" wildlife populations rather than "sinks" that drain animals from larger scale metapopulations.

Indirect methods of evaluating habitat programs are gaining wide use by wildlife agencies because they are easy to use and relatively inexpensive. The most widely used method of inferred evaluation is the habitat index in which changes in habitat quality are measured by computing change. Measuring and computing habitat indices are not, however, the same as measuring the responses of target species to management (Flather et al. 1992, Morrison 2001).

Game species are the most common target of management interventions. Hunter success rates and changes in perceptions of the quality of hunting experiences are highly appropriate measures of the success of a program. Indeed, the perception of the success of wildlife management programs by user groups is likely to be more important in many ways than actual responses by wildlife.

Table 2. Typical sources of errors in planning and assessing effects of habitat programs for upland wildlife species in intensively farmed areas (from Warner and Brady 1994).

Animal response	Response detected	Sources of errors	Biological explanation
Yes	No	Evaluation period too short	Lag effects Development of vegetation Demographic responses
Yes/No	Yes/No	Measurement techniques	High variability in animal responses and/or census techniques inappropriate
Yes	No	Limited spatial scale	Dispersal

Evaluating Interactions Between Wildlife and Habitat

If responses by target species to habitat initiatives are a true measure of success, few farmland habitat programs have been evaluated, let alone proven successful over a sustained period. Following the concepts of validity in statistical design, faulty evaluations can be categorized as to type of error (Table 2). For example, invalid procedures can lead the evaluator to conclude that a positive response by target species to habitat interventions occurred, when in fact the response was negative, negligible, or nonexistent. In these instances, important underlying biological phenomena may go undetected, and some of the same factors that limit success of habitat interventions also lead to failure in evaluation.

SUMMARY

Forces that shape agricultural land use and frame the habitat needs and opportunities for wild vertebrates are now global. As the human population continues to increase, pressures to produce more food and fiber per unit of land are increasing on all continents. Concerns about how to address these challenges are now front-and-center in the news media, discussions by policy makers, and opinion polls. The challenges are greater than ever, but so is the will of the public to make steady progress in achieving multiple natural resource goals on farmland. The knowledge and performance of wildlife agencies and professionals will be important in integrating the habitat needs of wild vertebrates in these emerging programs. The spatial and temporal factors requisite for successful farmland habitat interventions are tied to a complex farming system with ecological and socioeconomic dimensions. Wildlife managers need to be aware of—and influence—this system, ranging from regional policies and programs, to the practices that are used on the ground, and to the perceptions of landholders.

ACKNOWLEDGMENTS

We thank C. E. Braun, W. D. Snyder, and an anonymous reviewer for their constructive reviews.

LITERATURE CITED

ARNOLD, G. W. 1983. The influence of ditch and hedgerow structure, length of hedgerows, and area of woodland and garden on bird numbers on farmland. Journal of Applied Ecology 20:731–750.

AUCLAIR, A. N. 1976. Ecological factors in the development of intensive-management ecosystems in the midwestern United States. Ecology 57:431–444.

BALTENSPERGER, B. H. 1987. Hedgerow distribution and removal in non-forested regions of the Midwest. Journal of Soil and Water Conservation 42:60–64.

BASORE, N. S., L. B. BEST, AND J. B. WOOLEY, JR. 1986. Bird nesting in Iowa no-tillage and tilled cropland. Journal of Wildlife Management 50:19–28.

BELLROSE, F. C., S. P. HAVERA, F. L. PAVEGLIO, AND D. W. STEFFECK. 1983. The fate of lakes in the Illinois River valley. Biological Notes 119. Illinois Natural History Survey, Urbana, USA.

BERNER, A. H. 1984. Federal land retirement programs: a land management albatross. Transactions of the North American Wildlife and Natural Resources Conference 49:118–131.

BEST, L. B. 1983. Bird use of fencerows: implications of contemporary fencerow management practices. Wildlife Society Bulletin 11:343–347.

———. 1986. Conservation tillage: ecological trap for nesting birds? Wildlife Society Bulletin 14:308–317.

BLACK, JR., E. R., F. M. DAVIS, C. A. HENDERSON, AND W. A. DOUGLAS. 1970. The role of birds in reducing overwintering populations of the southwestern corn borer, *Diatraea grandiosella* (Lepidoptera: Crambidae), in Mississippi. Annals of the Entomological Society of America 63:701–706.

BOLLINGER, E. K., AND J. W. CASLICK. 1985. Red-winged blackbird predation on northern corn rootworm beetles in field corn. Journal of Applied Ecology 22:39–48.

———, P. B. BOLLINGER, AND T. A. GAVIN. 1990. Effects of hay-cropping on eastern populations of the bobolink. Wildlife Society Bulletin 18:142–150.

BRADY, S. J. 1985. Important soil conservation techniques that benefit wildlife. Pages 55–62 *in* Technologies to benefit agriculture and wildlife: workshop proceedings. U.S. Congress, Office of Technology Assessment OTA-BP-F-34, Washington, D.C., USA.

———, AND R. HAMILTON. 1988. Wildlife opportunities within federal agricultural programs. Pages 95–109 *in* D. L. Hallett, W. R. Edwards, and G. V. Burger, editors. Pheasants: symptoms of wildlife problems on agricultural lands. North Central Section, The Wildlife Society, Bloomington, Indiana, USA.

BURGER, G. V. 1978. Agriculture and wildlife. Pages 89–107 *in* H. P. Brokaw, editor. Wildlife and America. Council on Environmental Quality, U.S. Government Printing Office, Washington, D.C., USA.

CHAPMAN, E. W., AND C. A. RIBIC. 2002. The impact of buffer strips and stream-side grazing on small mammals in southwestern Wisconsin. Agriculture, Ecosystems, and Environment 88:49–59.

CORN, P. S., AND C. R. PETERSON. 1996. Prairie legacies—amphibians and reptiles. Pages 125–134 *in* F. B. Samson and F. L. Knopf, editors. Prairie conservation: preserving North America's most endangered ecosystem. Island Press, Washington, D.C., USA.

DAHLBERG, K. A. 1992. The conservation of biological diversity and U.S. agriculture: goals, institutions, and policies. Agriculture, Ecosystems, and Environment 42:177–193.

DAHLGREN, R. B. 1988. Distribution and abundance of the ring-necked pheasant in North America. Pages 29–43 *in* D. L. Hallett, W. R. Edwards, and G. V. Burger, editors. Pheasants: symptoms of wildlife problems on agricultural lands. North Central Section, The Wildlife Society, Bloomington, Indiana, USA.

DAILEY, T. V. 2002. Emerging trends in Midwest bobwhite culture. Pages 8–19 *in* S. J. DeMaso, W. P. Kuvlesky, Jr., E. Hernandez, and M. E. Berger, editors. Quail V: Proceedings of the Fifth National Quail Symposium. Texas Parks and Wildlife Department, Austin, USA.

DAILY, G. C. 1997. Preface. Pages xv–xvi *in* G. C. Daily, editor. Nature's services: societal dependence on natural ecosystems. Island Press, Washington, D.C., USA.

DONOVAN, T. M., F. R. THOMPSON, III, J. FAABORG, AND J. R. PROBST. 1995. Reproductive success of migratory birds in habitat sources and sinks. Conservation Biology 9:1380–1395.

DUMKE, R. T., G. V. BURGER, AND J. R. MARCH, editors. 1981. Wildlife management on private lands. Wisconsin Chapter, The Wildlife Society, Madison, USA.

EDWARDS, W. R. 1984. Early ACP and pheasant boom and bust! A historic perspective with rationale. Pages 71–83 *in* R. T. Dumke, R. B. Stiehl, and R. B. Kahl, editors. Perdix III: gray partridge and ring-necked pheasant workshop. Wisconsin Department of Natural Resources, Madison, USA.

FLATHER, C. H., AND T. W. HOEKSTRA. 1989. An analysis of the wildlife and fish situation in the United States: 1989–2040. U.S. Department of Agriculture, Forest Service, General Technical Report RM-178.

———, AND J. R. SAUER. 1996. Using landscape ecology to test hypotheses about large-scale abundance patterns in migratory birds. Ecology 77:28–35.

———, S. J. BRADY, AND D. B. INKLEY. 1992. Regional habitat appraisals of wildlife communities: a landscape-level evaluation of a resource planning model using avian distribution data. Landscape Ecology 7:137–147.

FORMAN, R. T. T. 1995. Land mosaics: the ecology of landscapes and regions. Cambridge University Press, New York, USA.

———, AND M. GODRON. 1981. Patches and structural components for a landscape ecology. BioScience 31:733–740.

FRAWLEY, B. J., AND L. B. BEST. 1991. Effects of mowing on breeding bird abundance and species composition in alfalfa fields. Wildlife Society Bulletin 19:135–142.

FREEMARK, K., AND C. BOUTIN. 1995. Impacts of agricultural herbicide use on terrestrial wildlife in temperate landscapes: a review with special reference to North America. Agriculture, Ecosystems, and Environment 52:67–91.

GOODLAND, R. 1995. The concept of environmental sustainability. Annual Review of Ecology and Systematics 26:1–24.

HECNAR, S. J., AND R. T. M'CLOSKEY. 1996. Regional dynamics and the status of amphibians. Ecology 77:2091–2097.

HERKERT, J. R. 1994. The effects of habitat fragmentation on midwestern grassland bird communities. Ecological Applications 4:461–471.

———, D. W. SAMPLE, AND R. E. WARNER. 1996. Management of midwestern grassland landscapes for the conservation of migratory birds. Pages 89-116 *in* F. R. Thompson, III, editor. Management of midwestern landscapes for the conservation of Neotropical migratory birds. U.S. Department of Agriculture, Forest Service, General Technical Report NC-187.

IOWA DEPARTMENT OF AGRICULTURE AND LAND STEWARDSHIP. 2002. Iowa Conservation Reserve Enhancement Program: helping landowner's protect Iowa's natural resources. Available online at http://www.agriculture.state.ia.us/CREP.htm.

JAHN, L. R. 1988. The potential for wildlife habitat improvements. Journal of Soil and Water Conservation 43:67-69.

JUDY, JR., R. D., P. N. SEELEY, T. M. MURRAY, S. C. SVIRSKY, M. R. WHITWORTH, AND L. S. ISCHINGER. 1984. 1982 national fisheries survey. Volume 1. Technical report: initial findings. U.S. Department of the Interior, Fish and Wildlife Service, OBS-84/06.

KERSHNER, E. L. 2001. Conservation of grassland birds in an agricultural landscape: the importance of habitat availability and demography. Dissertation, University of Illinois, Urbana, USA.

KIRK, D. A., M. D. EVENDEN, AND P. MINEAU. 1996. Past and current attempts to evaluate the role of birds as predators of insect pests in temperate agriculture. Current Ornithology 13:175–269.

LANGNER, L. 1985. An economic perspective on the effects of federal conservation policies on wildlife habitat. Transactions of the North American Wildlife and Natural Resources Conference 50:200–209.

LEOPOLD, A. 1933. Game management. Charles Scribner's Sons, New York, USA.

MACLELLAN, C. R. 1959. Woodpeckers as predators of the codling moth in Nova Scotia. Canadian Entomology 42:469–479.

———. 1971. Woodpecker ecology in the apple orchard environment. Proceedings of the Tall Timbers Conference on Ecological Animal Control by Habitat Management 2:273–284.

MAISONNEUVE, C., AND S. RIOUX. 2001. Importance of riparian habitats for small mammal and herpetofaunal communities in agricultural landscapes of southern Quebec. Agriculture, Ecosystems, and Environment 83:165–175.

MARYLAND DEPARTMENT OF AGRICULTURE. 2002. Streamside conservation has never looked so good. Available online at http://www.mda.state.md.us/resource/crep.htm.

MCCOY, T. D., M. R. RYAN, E. W. KURZEJESKI, AND L. W. BURGER, JR. 1999. Conservation Reserve Program: source or sink habitat for grassland birds in Missouri. Journal of Wildlife Management 63:530–538.

MORRISON, M. L. 2001. A proposed research emphasis to overcome the limits of wildlife-habitat relationship studies. Journal of Wildlife Management 65:613–623.

NATIONAL RESEARCH COUNCIL. 1982. Impacts of emerging agricultural trends on fish and wildlife habitat. National Academic Press, Washington, D.C., USA.

NEWMAN, D. S., R. E. WARNER, AND P. C. MANKIN. 2003. Creating habitats and homes for Illinois wildlife. Illinois Department of Natural Resources and University of Illinois, Urbana, USA.

NOSS, R. F. 1983. A regional landscape approach to maintain diversity. BioScience 33:700–706.

———, E. T. LAROE, III, AND J. M. SCOTT. 1995. Endangered ecosystems of the United States: a preliminary assessment of loss and degradation. U.S. Department of the Interior, Biological Report 28. National Biological Survey, Washington, D.C., USA.

O'CONNOR, R. J., M. T. JONES, R. B. BOONE, AND T. B. LAUBER. 1999. Linking continental climate, land use, and land patterns with grassland bird distribution across the conterminous United States. Studies in Avian Biology 19:45–59.

OLDFIELD, M. L., AND J. B. ALCORN. 1987. Conservation of traditional agroecosystems. BioScience 37:199–208.

O'NEIL, L. J., AND A. B. CAREY. 1986. Introduction: when habitats fail as predictors. Pages 207–208 *in* J. Verner, M. L. Morrison, and C. J. Ralph, editors. Wildlife 2000: modeling habitat relationships of terrestrial vertebrates. University of Wisconsin Press, Madison, USA.

OSBORN, C. T., F. LLACUNA, AND M. LINSENBIGLER. 1995. The Conservation Reserve Program: enrollment statistics for signup periods 1-12 and fiscal years 1986–93. U.S. Department of Agriculture, Economic Research Service, Statistical Bulletin 925. Natural Resources and Environment Division, Washington, D.C., USA.

PHIPPS, L. J. 1972. Handbook on agricultural education in public schools. Third edition. Interstate, Danville, Illinois, USA.

PIMENTEL, D., J. ALLEN, A. BEERS, L. GUINAND, R. LINDER, P. McLAUGHLIN, B. MEER, D. MUSONDA, D. PERDUE, S. POISSON, S. SIEBERT, K. STONER, R. SALAZAR, AND A. HAWKINS. 1987. World agriculture and soil erosion. BioScience 37:277–283.

POTTS, G. R. 1986. The partridge: pesticides, predation and conservation. Collins, London, United Kingdom.

POWER, J. F., AND R. F. FOLLETT. 1987. Monoculture. Scientific American 256(3):78–86.

PULLIAM, H. R. 1988. Sources, sinks, and population regulation. American Naturalist 132:652–661.

QUIRING, D. T., AND P. R. TIMMINS. 1988. Predation by American crows reduces overwintering European corn borer populations in southwestern Ontario. Canadian Journal of Zoology 66:2143–2145.

RISSER, P. G., J. R. KARR, AND R. T. T. FORMAN. 1984. Landscape ecology: directions and approaches. Special Publication 2. Illinois Natural History Survey, Urbana, USA.

ROSEBERRY, J. L., AND W. D. KLIMSTRA. 1984. Population ecology of the bobwhite. Southern Illinois University Press, Carbondale, USA.

SAUER, J. R., J. E. HINES, AND J. FALLON. 2002. The North American Breeding Bird Survey, results and analysis 1966–2001. Version 2002.1. U.S. Department of the Interior, Geological Survey, Patuxent Wildlife Research Center, Laurel, Maryland, USA.

SCHLEBECKER, J. T. 1975. Whereby we thrive: a history of American farming, 1607–1972. Iowa State University Press, Ames, USA.

STACEY, P. B., V. A. JOHNSON, AND M. L. TAPER. 1997. Migration within metapopulations: the impact upon local population dynamics. Pages 267–291 *in* I. A. Hanski and M. E. Gilpin, editors. Metapopulation biology: ecology, genetics and evolution. Academic Press, San Diego, California, USA.

STAIRS, G. R. 1985. Predation on overwintering codling moth populations by birds. Ornis Scandinavia 16:323–324.

STAMPS, J. A., M. BUECHNER, AND V. V. KRISHNAN. 1987. The effects of edge permeability and habitat geometry on emigration from patches of habitat. American Naturalist 129:533–552.

SWANSON, F. J., T. K. KRATZ, N. CAINE, AND R. G. WOODMANSEE. 1988. Landform effects on ecosystem patterns and processes. BioScience 38:92–98.

TURNER, M. G. 1987. Land use changes and net primary production in the Georgia, USA, landscape: 1935–1982. Environmental Management 11:237–247.

U.S. DEPARTMENT OF AGRICULTURE. 1999. Conservation corridor planning at the landscape level: managing for wildlife habitat. Natural Resources Conservation Service. National Biology Handbook Part 190. Available online at http://www.ms.nrcs.usda.gov/whmi/pdf/Corridors/cover.pdf.

———. 2001*a*. Trends in U.S. agriculture. National Agricultural Statistics Service. Available online at http://www.usda.gov/nass/pubs/trends/index.htm.

———. 2001*b*. U.S. Department of Agriculture homepage. Available online at http://www.usda.gov.

———. 2002. Conservation Reserve Program: summary for active contracts by program year. Natural Resources Conservation Service, Farm Service Agency. Available online at http://www.fsa.usda.gov/crpstorpt/08approved/.

VAN EMDEN, H. F. 1965. The role of uncultivated land in the biology of crop pests and beneficial insects. Scientific Horticulture 17:121-136.

VAN HORNE, B. 1983. Density as a misleading indicator of habitat quality. Journal of Wildlife Management 47:893–901.

VICKERY, P. D., M. L. HUNTER, JR., AND J. V. WELLS. 1992. Is density an indicator of breeding success? Auk 109:706–710.

WALK, J. W. 2001. Nesting ecology of grassland birds in an agricultural landscape. Dissertation. University of Illinois, Urbana, USA.

———, AND R. E. WARNER. 1999. Effects of habitat area on the occurrence of grassland birds in Illinois. American Midland Naturalist 141:339–344.

WARNER, R. E. 1984. Effects of changing agriculture on ring-necked pheasant brood movements in Illinois. Journal of Wildlife Management 48:1014–1018.

———. 1992. Nest ecology of grassland passerines on road rights-of-way in central Illinois. Biological Conservation 59:1–7.

———. 1994. Agricultural land use and grassland habitat in Illinois: future shock for midwestern birds? Conservation Biology 8:147–156.

———, AND S. J. BRADY. 1994. Managing farmlands for wildlife. Pages 648–662 in T. A. Bookhout, editor. Research and management techniques for wildlife and habitats. Fifth edition. The Wildlife Society, Bethesda, Maryland, USA.

———, AND S. L. ETTER. 1985. Farm conservation measures to benefit wildlife, especially pheasant populations. Transactions of the North American Wildlife and Natural Resources Conference 50:135–141.

———, AND ———. 1989. Hay cutting and the survival of pheasants: a long-term perspective. Journal of Wildlife Management 53:455–461.

———, AND S. P. HAVERA. 1989. Relationships of conservation tillage to the quality of wildlife habitat in row-crop environments of the midwestern United States. Journal of Environmental Management 29:333–343.

———, P. HUBERT, P. C. MANKIN, AND C. A. GATES. 2000. Disturbance and the survival of female ring-necked pheasants in Illinois. Journal of Wildlife Management 64:663–672.

———, P. C. MANKIN, L. M. DAVID, AND S. L. ETTER. 1999. Declining survival of ring-necked pheasant chicks in Illinois during the late 1900s. Journal of Wildlife Management 63:705–710.

WINTER, M., AND J. FAABORG. 1999. Patterns of area sensitivity in grassland-nesting birds. Conservation Biology 13:1424–1436.

———, D. H. JOHNSON, AND J. FAABORG. 2000. Evidence for edge effects on multiple levels in tallgrass prairie. Condor 102:256–266.

WOOLHOUSE, M. E. J., AND R. HARMSEN. 1987. Just how unstable are agroecosystems? Canadian Journal of Zoology 65:1577–1580.

33

MANAGING RANGELANDS FOR WILDLIFE

Vernon C. Bleich, John G. Kie, Eric R. Loft, Thomas R. Stephenson, Michael W. Oehler, Sr., and Alvin L. Medina

INTRODUCTION

Rangelands are plant communities dominated by grasses, forbs, and shrubs. Their primary use by humans worldwide is for livestock grazing, but these communities also are habitat for wildlife. Traditionally, wildlife-related concerns of range managers focused on predators of livestock and on wildlife species that are hunted. Today, managers are interested in biodiversity and a wide range of species. Management of public rangelands in the United States is constrained by federal and state laws, which require managers to address the impact of management activities on all wildlife.

The majority of rangelands used by wildlife in the United States are public lands administered by the U.S. Forest Service and Bureau of Land Management, both of which have multiple-use mandates. With existing laws such as the Endangered Species Act and Clean Water Act, and ecosystem management and ecosystem health policies of the major land management agencies in the United States, there is expanding need to address the ecology of rangelands as it relates to plants, soils, water, wildlife, and livestock.

Photographs, videos, Internet web sites, agenda-driven "science," opinion pieces, the growth of advocacy groups, legal challenges (and threat of legal challenges), and society's changing sentiments about use and condition of public rangelands have generated an abundance of confusion and uncertainty about rangeland management. What formerly was a field primarily limited to understanding livestock-big game species relationships is now open to examination of livestock impacts on all native flora and fauna, and the communities and ecosystems in which they exist.

The single greatest change influencing wildlife on western rangeland management during the 1990s has been the shift of concern from competition of livestock with big game such as deer (*Odocoileus* spp.) and elk (*Cervus elaphus*), to concern for all wildlife, and biodiversity in general. For terrestrial wildlife species, the fate of species such as the willow flycatcher (*Empidonax traillii*) and sage-grouse (*Centrocercus* spp.) now dominate livestock and wildlife issues in montane meadow-riparian systems and sagebrush (*Artemisia* spp.) steppe, respectively, in many areas of the western United States. In California for example, ungulates aren't mentioned in a recent decision to amend management of >1.7 million ha on 11 national forests (U.S. Department of Agriculture 2001). Aquatic, riparian, and meadow system rangeland management would, instead, be heavily influenced by habitat needs of the willow flycatcher, mountain yellow-legged frog (*Rana muscosa*), Yosemite toad (*Bufo canorus*), and great gray owl (*Strix nebulosa*).

Effectively managing rangelands for wildlife requires achieving a specified level of habitat structure as represented by vertical and canopy cover, food items as represented by species composition, and adequate water quality and availability. Additionally, where livestock grazing is involved, there is a need to understand and manage for interspecific and social interactions between livestock and wildlife, as well as strategies to mitigate adverse effects. These interactions may be in the form of behavioral avoidance or attraction, direct mortality caused by livestock, or habitat modifications, and indirect mortality caused by disease transmission. Wildlife-livestock interactions have greater application at a broad geographic scale rather than a site-specific study area.

Because most state and federal agencies have unique missions and mandates (Salwasser et al. 1987), management philosophies and on-the-ground techniques differ markedly among agencies. Philosophical differences can be further exacerbated when adjacent tracts of land, managed by different agencies, have their own unique designations (e.g., specially designated area). Specially designated areas come in a variety of shapes and sizes, but in the United States they are typically managed by one of a few federal agencies (e.g., U.S. Forest Service, Bureau of Land Management, National Park Service, or U.S. Fish and Wildlife Service), and include such areas as wilderness, special research areas, wildlife refuges, sanctuaries, or any other site where certain activities or management tools (e.g., aircraft, mechanical equipment) may be precluded. These areas are usually small relative to the management prescriptions of adjacent properties and, thus, exist as noncontiguous islands that must be managed differently from surrounding landscapes.

Because of the varied and unique challenges confronting managers in today's world, this chapter is not intended to be an all-encompassing treatise. Rather, it presents a discussion of selected issues and techniques in an effort to provide the reader with a general understanding and appreciation for the complexities associated with managing rangelands. An extensive literature review is included and the reader is encouraged to explore the vast quantity of information that has been published on this subject, some of which is also summarized elsewhere (e.g., Krausman 1996). It is our hope this chapter adequately (1) provides an overview of rangeland management to benefit wildlife species and natural communities, with an emphasis on western North America; (2) identifies some of the topical issues and primary rangeland systems of concern; and, (3) describes some of the techniques for accommodating wildlife and wildlife issues on rangelands.

PLANT SUCCESSION AND WILDLIFE MANAGEMENT GOALS FOR RANGELANDS

Plant succession is the gradual replacement of one assemblage of plant species with others through time until a relatively stable climax community is reached (Clements 1916). As each group of plant species is replaced, the value of the community as habitat to any particular species of wildlife changes. The result is a succession of wildlife species as plant communities and populations of primary consumers undergo successional changes altering the different trophic levels (Kie et al. 1994).

Range Condition and Wildlife Habitat

Only a portion of the vegetation biomass in a rangeland will provide adequate nutrition for an herbivore. As body size decreases, diet selectivity generally increases (Van Soest 1994); consequently, many wild herbivores (which tend to be smaller than domestic livestock) consume much less of the vegetation resource than livestock, particularly cattle. Furthermore, domestic livestock may consume a greater proportion of poorer-quality bulk forages because producers supplement diets of livestock to balance nutritional requirements for growth and reproduction at least for some portion of the year. Proper estimates of carrying capacity for wildlife on rangelands assume that all nutrients will be obtained from the range (Hobbs and Swift 1985).

Rangelands exist in many different successional stages and structural conditions because of the influence of fire, mechanical disturbance, herbicide treatment, and grazing by wild and domestic herbivores. Some plant communities respond to grazing in a predictable manner, depending on the plant species present (Dyksterhuis 1949). Some plant species are dominant in climax communities because they are superior competitors in the absence of disturbance. However, they begin to decline in vigor and abundance with increased grazing pressure (Dyksterhuis 1949). As they decline, other less palatable plants present at the climax stage become more abundant as competition is reduced. If grazing intensity is sufficiently heavy and occurs over a long period of time, new plant species, well adapted to heavy grazing, appear in the community. As a result, many exotic species of plants (e.g., spurges, thistles, brome grasses) become established and overall condition of the range is reduced.

In the past, rangelands have been managed on a concept of how close existing vegetation approximates a climax community using terms such as excellent, good, fair, and poor (Dyksterhuis 1949). This procedure cannot be used on seeded rangelands, however, or those dominated by introduced, naturalized plant species such as the annual grasslands of California (Smith 1978, 1988). Also, range condition terms including excellent, good, fair, and poor are defined in terms of providing forage for livestock–habitat is species specific and differs greatly among species. A site rated as poor may provide excellent habitat for wildlife adapted to early-seral vegetation (e.g., white-tailed deer [*Odocoileus virginianus*]), whereas a site rated as excellent on this scale (e.g., grassland) may not be used at all by that species. More appropriate terms for describing the condition of rangeland vegetation as they relate to wildlife needs are climax, late seral, mid-seral, and early seral (Pieper and Beck 1990).

Additional problems may arise when changes in livestock grazing practices do not immediately produce a change in rangeland vegetation. For example, some grassland sites in southeastern Arizona that had been converted to shrublands by heavy livestock grazing failed to revert to native grasses following 20 years without livestock (Valone et al. 2002). In contrast, other sites that were protected for up to 39 years exhibited an increase in grasses, suggesting that substantial time lags following protection from grazing were necessary (Valone et al. 2002).

Since 1990, range ecologists have been developing models of change in rangeland vegetation based on the concept of multiple steady states (Laycock 1991, 1994). These states are often portrayed as state-transition models (Westoby et al. 1989), wherein "states" are recognizable assemblages of species at a particular site that are stable over time. Such models are useful in understanding why some plant communities fail to respond immediately to changes in management practices. Parameterizing state-transition models, however, often requires large data sets on composition of rangeland vegetation collected over many years. If such data are available, state-transition models can provide more precise predictions about vegetation change (Allen-Diaz and Bartolome 1998) than the classical linear succession model developed by Clements (1916) and may be useful in restoring degraded rangelands (Chambers and Linnerooth 2001).

Models of Rangelands as Wildlife Habitat

The system of classifying wildlife habitats according to potential natural vegetation and seral stage for coniferous forests (Thomas 1979) also has been applied to rangeland vegetation in southeastern Oregon (Maser et al. 1984). Habitat data were assembled for 341 species of vertebrates assessing impacts of different range management activities on those species by equating plant communities and their structural conditions with habitat values for wildlife. The structural conditions were grass-forb, low shrub, tall shrub, tree, and tree-shrub. As a plant community progresses from grass-forb to tree-shrub conditions through succession, changes occur in environmental variables important to wildlife. For example, herbage production tends to be highest in grass-forb communities; browse production highest in low-shrub and high-shrub communities; and canopy closure, canopy volume, and structural diversity highest in tree and tree-shrub communities (Maser et al. 1984). Management actions such as brush and weed control, water development, prescribed burning, seeding and planting, and grazing also can result in changes in structural conditions (Maser et al. 1984).

Accounting for needs of large numbers of wildlife species makes land-use planning difficult. To simplify the process, wildlife can be grouped into life forms based on the relationship of the species to their habitats. In southeastern Oregon, 2 characteristics of each species (where it feeds and where it reproduces) were used to distinguish 16 life forms. For example, dark-eyed juncos (*Junco hyemalis*) and mule deer (*Odocoileus hemionus*) characterize those species that feed and reproduce on the ground. Other examples of such life forms include the long-toed salamander (*Ambystoma macrodactylum*) and western toad (*Bufo boreas*), which feed on the ground, in shrubs, or in trees, and reproduce in water (Maser et al. 1984).

Beyond generalized models of wildlife habitat associations, managers occasionally estimate nutritional carrying capacity of rangelands. Most models of range supply and animal demand sum the available nutrients supplied by forage in the habitat and then divide by the animal's nutritional requirements (Robbins 1973, Hobbs et al. 1982). However, these models are simple and fail to make predictions based on varying levels of nutritional quality required by individuals (e.g., pregnant or lactating females, breeding males, migrating adults, etc.) (Hobbs and Swift 1985). To avoid overestimating the number of animals that existing plant biomass can support, carrying capacity models should consider minimum dietary nutrient concentration (Hobbs and Swift 1985, Hanley and Rogers 1989).

The influence of grazing can also affect wildlife species richness, diversity, density, and abundance. Some conclusions, for example that grazing tends to increase abundance of common species but reduces the overall diversity of species (Bronham et al. 1999, Rambo and Faeth 1999), provide a community approach that may contribute to additional generalizations when other taxonomic groups are considered.

CONTEMPORARY ISSUES IN RANGELAND MANAGEMENT

Key Rangelands of Concern

Riparian, montane meadow, and aquatic habitats continue to remain a high priority for conservation and management on western rangelands. Minimizing soil erosion and maintaining or restoring water quality are paramount in sustaining these systems for the future. Meeting these 2 umbrella objectives may accommodate the needs of some wildlife species that inhabit these systems. Increasing concern now exists for other wildlife habitats that are rangelands. This interest has arisen largely because of growing concern for biological diversity, but also for specific wildlife species that are declining and/or are being petitioned for listing under the federal Endangered Species Act. While there are numerous other plant communities and wildlife habitats that comprise rangelands throughout the world, the following systems or habitats are currently of great issue on public rangelands in the western United States.

Sagebrush Steppe

Foremost of concern among rangeland habitats at present are the expanses of sagebrush/perennial bunchgrass range that dominate much of public land in the west (e.g., Paige and Ritter 1999). From a timing perspective, just as range livestock management has been challenged in the 1990s to work toward avoiding negative impacts to the riparian zone and to more effectively use upland range, livestock use of uplands has now come under scrutiny as well. Recent research indicating that sage-grouse are declining and that they nest most successfully when there is an herbaceous understory at least 18 cm in height (Sveum et al. 1998) has created an additional challenge for livestock managers on public lands–how to avoid impacting riparian zones while ensuring adequate herbaceous cover to meet the needs of at least one nesting species in sagebrush/grass communities. Use and management of fire, herbicides, proximity to urbanization and agriculture, use of off-road vehicles, and power lines also are contributing factors affecting quality of wildlife habitat on these rangelands.

Other habitats of concern geographically associated with sagebrush steppe are browse communities dominated by antelope bitterbrush (*Purshia tridentata*), mountain mahogany (*Cercocarpus* spp.), or saltbush (*Atriplex* spp.). Often, these communities serve as a seasonal range for wildlife, such as in winter, but are grazed by livestock in summer.

Desert

Concern about potential impacts to the desert tortoise (*Gopherus agassizii*) from livestock grazing and other uses prompted the Bureau of Land Management to recently issue a grazing decision to help protect this species in California desert systems. These systems are particularly susceptible to impacts of grazing because they require a long time for recovery of vegetation growth and vigor if they are able to recover at all (e.g., Krueger et al. 2002). Additionally, concern exists for native frogs relying on the rare and often heavily impacted riparian and aquatic areas of the desert southwest (Jennings and Hayes 1993).

Aspen

Habitats dominated by quaking aspen (*Populus tremuloides*) support a high diversity of wildlife on western ranges (Debyle 1985). These habitats also serve as valuable grazing (Sampson and Malmsten 1926) areas for livestock because of the proximity of food, cover, and usually water. There is growing concern that this community is on the decline in managed forests and ranges throughout the west because of lack of stand regeneration resulting from browsing by herbivores, fire suppression, and disease (e.g., California Department of Fish and Game 1998, Knight 2001). In turn, succession to dominance by conifers or by shrub communities (e.g., sagebrush) may result, thereby decreasing the value as wildlife habitat or as rangeland for domestic livestock grazing.

Integrating Wildlife Objectives and Range Livestock Management

Livestock grazing results in impacts on rangelands and wildlife species. It can either decrease or improve the conditions for wildlife depending on the species or community attribute of interest. A goal for public land resource managers is to identify the acceptable level of livestock impact, apply appropriate standards and guidelines, and then monitor their impacts. Implementing management decisions to meet wildlife species and habitat objectives, as well as broader goals of ecosystem health on public rangelands, often are emotionally charged socioeconomic (if not sociopolitical) decisions. These decisions often involve reducing use or eliminating livestock in the area of concern for a period of time to allow recovery. Numerous case studies and demonstration areas have illustrated that these actions are effective in some rangeland habitats such as riparian and aspen communities.

Within the field of wildlife–livestock interactions, addressing competition between livestock and large native herbivores was a primary emphasis on western public lands during the 1950s–1980s; during the 1990s the emphasis shifted to developing strategies to protect and restore riparian areas from overgrazing by livestock. Preventing livestock from negatively affecting riparian areas and achieving better distribution of grazing animals throughout upland areas were desired objectives. More recently (mid 1990s to present), there is evidence demon-

strating the importance of standing herbaceous vegetation for nesting sage-grouse, a vegetation component that could be difficult to meet without significant change in grazing management strategies. Thus, more encompassing ecosystem-landscape-biodiversity concepts for management of rangelands have evolved in recent years. These have caused further shifts in the directions of many interest groups, government agencies, and academicians.

On public rangelands, recent objectives go beyond achieving and maintaining good to excellent range conditions for livestock and wildlife. Instead, objectives have broadened to conserve biodiversity, improve ecosystem health, and meet habitat requirements of federally listed, or potentially listed, wildlife. These objectives could be represented in many cases by increased herbaceous cover, soil maintenance, reduction in invasive species, and clean water. A more general approach would be to define positive ecological changes through rangeland management actions. Across landscapes, achieving such positive changes likely would satisfy most concerns for wildlife simply because such large-scale changes have been needed for decades.

Examples of species receiving substantial attention at present are the willow flycatcher and great gray owl, which rely on high quality mountain meadow-willow (*Salix* spp.) riparian complexes, and sage-grouse that rely on a combined habitat structure of sagebrush and standing herbaceous vegetation. The former 2 species continue to represent the needs and concerns related to grazing impacts on montane meadow and riparian areas, while the burgeoning sage-grouse issue has been labeled the range equivalent of the spotted owl (*Strix occidentalis*) issue because desired herbaceous cover levels will be difficult to achieve on grazed rangelands.

Investigations of Wildlife–Livestock Relationships

Studies of wildlife and livestock interactions are typically conducted to increase understanding of direct and indirect effects of livestock (as the manipulated perturbation or stressor) on a native species and/or its habitat. Much of the existing work was retrospective, rather than experimental, in that it was conducted with livestock as part of the system rather than as an introduced perturbation with treatments and controls. This difference also reflects one of the fundamental social debates regarding livestock on public lands in the United States: are humans, and the impacts they bring, part of the biotic community or ecosystem (e.g., Box 2000)?

Unquestionably, the science on wildlife-livestock relationships varies in terms of its rigor, thoroughness, results, and applicability to real systems. It indicates the presence of large, non-native herbivores is beneficial to some species and detrimental to others. Some initial investigations of wildlife–livestock relationships examined how cattle and mule deer distributed themselves throughout a common range (Julander and Robinette 1950, Julander 1955, Julander and Jeffery 1964) instead of manipulating cattle to measure how deer responded with and without cattle in the same area. Unfortunately, the ability to conduct replicated experiments at appropriate spatial and temporal scales to assess livestock grazing impacts on a wildlife population is logistically difficult. Conclusions from retrospective studies, that deer or other wildlife species preferred the steeper slopes while livestock preferred the flatter areas, became dogma in range science and suggested that a harmonious coexistence occurs without objective experimental evidence.

Perhaps the most acceptable generalization that can be made is that increasing the grazing level (often termed heavy, uncontrolled, excessive, or severe grazing) above some site-based threshold results in impacts that are not desirable to any interest. Further confounding our ability to generalize among wildlife–livestock investigations is that stocking rates, number of grazing levels (ungrazed or grazed in some studies; none, light, moderate, or heavy grazing in others), time of year grazed, vegetation communities, time lags to examine the response (e.g., Dobkin et al. 1998), and wildlife species of interest are not consistently applied or comparable.

During the 1950s–1980s, the primary wildlife emphasis on public rangelands was competition among large ungulates and livestock. Kie et al. (1994) summarized much of the knowledge in this area, and large herbivores continue to be of interest (e.g., Austin 2000). Rangeland science, however, has broadened to include examinations of livestock impacts on nontraditional wildlife and biodiversity. The body of literature examining the impacts of livestock on taxonomic groups such as amphibians (Jennings and Hayes 1993, Denton and Beebee 1996, Bull and Hayes 2000), reptiles (Bock et al. 1990, Bostick 1990, Kazmaier et al. 2001), birds (Dobkin et al. 1998, Goguen and Mathews 1998, Sveum et al. 1998, Belanger and Picard 1999, Beck and Mitchell 2000), small mammals (Hayward et al. 1997), and invertebrates (Rambo and Faeth 1999, Bronham et al. 1999) continues to grow, as does the number of review papers on livestock grazing impacts on biological diversity and ecosystems (Fleischner 1994, Belsky and Blumenthal 1997, Larsen et al. 1998, Belsky et al. 1999, Jones 2000).

Using livestock as a tool to manage wildlife habitat has been advocated for many years and examples of how this benefits one or more wildlife species do exist (Severson 1990). For example, Leopold et al. (1951) described the benefits of livestock in opening up paths for deer and other wildlife throughout willow-dominated montane meadow systems. Other examples describe the benefits of livestock in helping maintain or enhance vegetation species diversity (Rambo and Faeth 1999, Humphrey and Patterson 2000) or enhancing forage quality for other large herbivores (Clark et al. 2000). Whether the mechanical benefits, or more importantly, ecological benefits are needed every year is rarely, but should be, asked in the context of the entire system affected. Have Leopold et al.'s (1951) willow meadows been opened up "enough," or do they need to be continually grazed summer-long in high mountain ecosystems, such as those in the Sierra Nevada?

Accommodating Wildlife and Habitat Objectives on Rangelands

A common link between the wildlife biologist and the range manager is the vegetation community and the wildlife habitats represented. From a wildlife perspective, perhaps an efficient technique would be to develop habitat objectives such as percent cover, desired plant species composition, and structural conditions of vegetation that

are desired for a species, a suite of species, or a community as a whole, rather than a targeted species population objective. This approach leaves the range or livestock manager with the task of identifying potential strategies for managing livestock to achieve wildlife objectives. Identifying how wildlife species respond to livestock grazing might be of value in assessing whether the overall effects of the grazing level are acceptable or not; this process for wildlife would be analogous to characterizing plant species as increasers, decreasers, or invaders in response to livestock grazing (e.g., Stoddart et al. 1975).

The concept of maintaining or enhancing biodiversity on multiple use rangelands should also capitalize on interjecting management diversity in terms of grazing systems used. Interjecting unpredictable changes in habitat structure by resting habitats that normally are grazed continuously adds to this kind of diversity. Additional study and information on how individual species respond would help distinguish between desirable and undesirable trends in species responses.

Historically, land use plans prepared by the U.S. Forest Service and Bureau of Land Management, in collaboration with state wildlife agencies, often developed population objectives for species such as deer, elk, or pronghorn (*Antilocapra americana*). A more measurable approach would involve moving from a specific population target and, instead, focusing on achieving a desired habitat condition across the landscape–at the scale of allotments, resource areas, districts, or entire national forests.

Role of Monitoring and Assessment in Addressing Wildlife–Livestock Issues

"The lack of biological data is, without a doubt, one of the greatest single factors in retarding development of a larger conservation program" (California Fish and Game 1926:28)

Because of the inherent controversy and often-polarized views of wildlife and livestock relationships, difficult management decisions are often tabled in the absence of adequate data on species trends or ecological condition of the system in question. Consequently, among the most valuable activities that can be undertaken for the benefit of wildlife on rangelands is the collection of scientifically defensible data on distribution, abundance, status, trend, and habitat relationships. Ranging from basic inventory, to implementation of long-term monitoring, and experimental investigation of cause-and-effect relationships, scientific data aid management decisions. A meaningful progression of actions to examine and understand wildlife and livestock relationships might involve assessing:

a) wildlife habitat requirements and preferences,
b) livestock use of habitats preferred by wildlife,
c) livestock and wildlife effects on those habitats and vegetation communities,
d) livestock effects on wildlife species, and
e) how wildlife responds over time.

The effects studied range from direct influences of livestock on species (e.g., trampling of frogs) to numerous indirect effects (e.g., effect on prey species or hiding cover). Far more likely than experimental manipulations, however, are study and characterization of habitat conditions including structure and composition of vegetation and how it influences species productivity and abundance. An adaptive element would include mechanisms to change livestock management strategies as information is gained or to test specific hypotheses with an experimental or manipulative approach.

MANAGING LIVESTOCK ON RANGELANDS

Heavy livestock grazing has been detrimental to many wildlife species in western North America (Smith 1977, Gallizioli 1979, Peek and Krausman 1996). Uncontrolled grazing clearly can affect the structure and composition of wildlife habitats. When adverse impacts occur, elimination of livestock can improve habitat conditions, although in many situations changes in livestock management practices can result in similar benefits. When properly managed, livestock grazing can be used to improve habitat for wildlife dependent on early-seral stage plant communities (Longhurst et al. 1976; Urness 1976, 1990; Kie and Loft 1990; Ohmart 1996). Information on relationships between livestock and wildlife is available in a variety of books, symposium proceedings, and review papers (Smith 1975, Townsend and Smith 1977, Schmidt and Gilbert 1978, DeGraaf 1980, Wallmo 1981, Peek and Dalke 1982, Thomas and Toweill 1982, Menke 1983, Severson and Medina 1983, Halls 1984, Severson 1990, Krausman 1996).

The relationship between grazing and wildlife habitat is complex. Livestock influence wildlife habitat by modifying plant biomass, species composition, and structural components such as vegetation height and cover. The impact of livestock grazing on wild ungulates can be classified as direct negative, indirect negative, operational, or beneficial (Mackie 1978, Wagner 1978). An example of a direct negative impact is competition between cattle and deer for a resource such as food or cover (Mackie 1978, Wagner 1978). Competition occurs when 2 organisms use a resource in short supply, or when one organism harms another in the process of seeking the resource (Birch 1957, Wagner 1978). Factors affecting impacts of livestock on wildlife include diet similarity, forage availability, animal distribution patterns, season of use, and behavioral interactions (Nelson and Burnell 1975, Severson and Medina 1983).

Indirect negative impacts of cattle grazing include: (1) gradual reductions in vigor of some plants and in amount and quality of forage produced; (2) elimination or reduction of the ability of forage plants to reproduce; (3) reduction or elimination of locally important cover types and replacement by less favorable types or communities, by direct actions over time or by changing the rate of natural succession; and (4) general alterations and reduction in the kinds, qualities, and amounts of preferred or otherwise important plants through selective grazing, browsing, or other activities (Mackie 1978).

Operational impacts are associated with livestock management (Mackie 1978) and include fence construction, water development (Evans and Kerbs 1977, Wilson 1977, Yoakum 1980), brush control (Holechek 1981), and disturbance associated with handling of livestock. For example,

deer may temporarily move from pastures when cattle roundups occur (Hood and Inglis 1974, Rodgers et al. 1978).

Small mammals also influence rangeland vegetation (Moore and Reid 1951, Wood 1969, Batzli and Pitelka 1970, Turner et al. 1973, Borchert and Jain 1978) and compete with livestock for forage (Fitch and Bentley 1949, Howard et al. 1959). Because of their size and susceptibility to predation, rodents, lagomorphs, and other small mammals are highly dependent on the structure of vegetation in their habitats (Grant et al. 1982, Parmenter and MacMahon 1983, Bock et al. 1984). Grazing by livestock influences vegetation structure in those habitats and can significantly affect small mammal populations (Reynolds and Trost 1980).

Livestock grazing adversely affects many grassland birds, although moderate grazing can be neutral or beneficial to some species (Buttery and Shields 1975). Livestock management practices also can affect birds indirectly. For example, an organophosphate insecticide externally applied to cattle to control warbles may kill American magpies (*Pica hudsonia*) and cause secondary mortality among red-tailed hawks (*Buteo jamaicensis*) eating carcasses of the poisoned magpies (Henny et al. 1985).

Livestock management practices that can affect wildlife habitats and populations include livestock numbers, timing and duration of grazing, animal distribution, livestock types, and specialized grazing systems. These practices can be modified to reduce or eliminate adverse effects on wildlife and, at times, to enhance wildlife habitats (Severson 1990).

Livestock Numbers

Livestock numbers, or stocking rates, usually are specified by animal unit months (AUMs). One AUM is one animal unit (one mature cow with a calf, or equivalent) grazed for one month (Heady 1975:117). Livestock effects on wildlife become more pronounced with increasing stocking rates. A few cattle in a pasture may have no discernible effect on wildlife, but beyond some threshold wildlife response may increase rapidly. A range manager's traditional definition of proper grazing is based on maintaining a mix of plant species valuable as livestock forage and preventing soil erosion. Optimum livestock densities for wildlife may occur at different, and often lower, stocking rates. Thus, as with most effects of livestock on wildlife, responses can be difficult to interpret because of inherent site differences (Johnson 1982), and differences in grazing intensity, timing, and duration.

Timing and Duration of Grazing

Moderate cattle grazing of riparian areas in late fall in Colorado had no detectable impact on 6 species of birds dependent on the grass-herb-shrub layer for foraging, nesting, or both (Sedgwick and Knopf 1987). However, summer grazing can eliminate habitat specialists such as willow flycatchers, Lincoln's sparrows (*Melospiza lincolnii*), and white-crowned sparrows (*Zonotrichia leucophrys*) (Knopf et al. 1988).

The time of year that livestock are present can alter the composition of plant communities. Heavy grazing during a period of rapid growth of one plant species will favor other species that grow more rapidly at other times. For

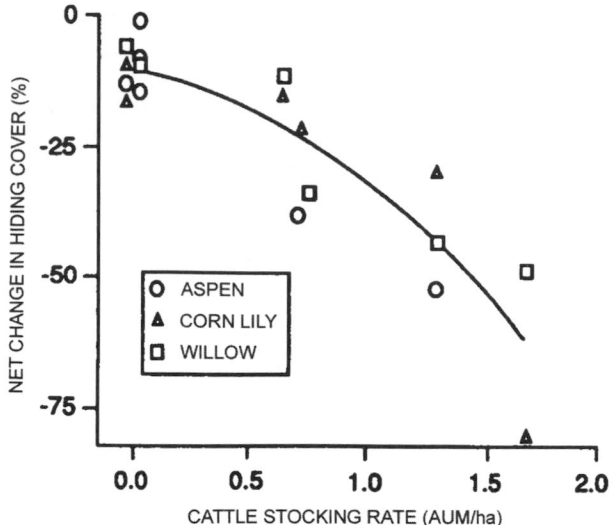

Fig. 1. Net change in mule deer hiding cover between 0 and 1 m in height from beginning of summer until mid-August as a function of cattle stocking rate (AUM/ha = animal unit months per hectare) (after Loft et al. 1987).

example, spring grazing of annual grasslands in California reduces grass cover and encourages growth of summer-maturing forbs such as turkey-mullein (*Eremocarpus setigerus*), the seeds of which are readily eaten by mourning doves (*Zenaida macroura*) (Kie 1988). Conversely, many wildlife species are most susceptible to livestock-induced changes in habitat during their reproductive seasons. Birds that nest on the ground or in shrubs can experience reproductive losses if their nests are trampled or otherwise destroyed by cattle. For example, willow flycatchers in California breed exclusively in riparian deciduous woodlands, and prefer willows as nesting substrate (Valentine et al. 1988). Flycatchers prefer to nest near the edges of willow clumps or along livestock trails (Valentine et al. 1988, Sanders and Flett 1989), where they are susceptible to physical disturbance. In one study, 4 of 20 willow flycatcher nests in a 4-year period were destroyed by cattle before young fledged, and 4 other nests were destroyed after young fledged (Valentine et al. 1988). When cattle stocking levels were reduced and 75% of the remaining cattle were confined to a fenced pasture away from willow flycatcher nest sites until 15 July, no willow flycatcher nests were lost (Valentine et al. 1988).

Excessive grazing can accelerate loss of hiding cover early in summer when mule deer fawns are young (Loft et al. 1987) (Fig. 1). These conflicts can be minimized or eliminated by delaying grazing until later in the year (Kie 1991).

Livestock Distribution

Livestock congregate around sources of water, supplemental feed, and mineral blocks; their impacts are most pronounced in those areas. Riparian zones, because of their abundant forage and water, are good examples of livestock concentration areas. Cross-fencing, developing alternative water sources, and providing feeding supplements on upland sites away from riparian areas more evenly distribute livestock. However, in certain situations, wildlife can benefit from patchy livestock distribution

because some areas are lightly grazed. For example, many species of wildlife inhabit ecotonal areas ("edges"), and patchy distribution of livestock across home ranges of those species enables selection of grazed versus ungrazed patches to serve as foraging areas or refugia.

Types of Livestock

Effects of grazing on wildlife depend on the species of livestock. Differences in diet between cattle and domestic sheep dictate the effects they have on plant species composition. Also, cattle usually range within the confines of a fenced allotment, but sheep often are herded. Herded bands of sheep may have enhanced some habitats for mule deer in California (Longhurst et al. 1976) by repeated grazing and browsing that stimulated regrowth of more palatable shrubs and herbaceous vegetation. However, transmission of diseases from domestic sheep to mountain sheep (*Ovis canadensis*) may have eliminated many populations of the latter from California (Wehausen et al. 1987). As a result, professional organizations (e.g., Desert Bighorn Council Technical Staff 1990) and federal agencies have adopted management policies that reduce the probability of contact between domestic sheep and mountain sheep (U.S. Department of Interior 1992, U.S. Department of Interior and California Department of Fish and Game 2002).

Competition between pronghorn and domestic sheep is greater than between pronghorn and cattle because of increased overlap in forage preferences. On overgrazed sheep ranges, insufficient forb growth was available for pronghorn during the critical mid-winter period, and pronghorn die-offs were common (Buechner 1950). In general, domestic sheep are more likely than cattle to affect pronghorn adversely (Autenrieth 1978, Salwasser 1980, Yoakum 1980, Kindschy et al. 1982), and even moderate use by sheep during the winter dormant period can leave range units unsuitable for pronghorn until plant regrowth in spring (Clary and Beale 1983). Cows with calves often exhibit grazing patterns different from those of steers, and differences among breeds of cattle and sheep may occur.

Specialized Grazing Systems

Many specialized grazing systems exist, although most can be classified into 3 types (Heady 1975, Stoddart et al. 1975). *Continuous grazing* allows livestock to graze season-long or year-long. *Deferred grazing* refers to delaying or deferring grazing until after most of the range plants have set seed. Deferred grazing allows plants to grow, store carbohydrates, and reproduce at high rates. *Rotational grazing* involves dividing a range unit and rotating livestock through different pastures.

Combinations of periodic deferment and rotational grazing are called *deferred-rotation* grazing systems. A common one of these is the *4-pasture deferred-rotation* system, in which 4 range units or pastures are used, with 3 being grazed year-long and the fourth being deferred for 4 months. The pastures are then rotated each year.

Rest-rotation grazing is similar to a deferred-rotation system, but the period of rest consists of a full year or more. *Short-duration* grazing systems are similar to deferred-rotation systems, except that ≥8 small pastures are used, stocking rates are high in each pasture as it is used, but livestock are present for only short periods of time. Because timing of livestock grazing is critically important to most rangeland wildlife species, rotational grazing systems designed to consider wildlife have the greatest potential to reduce adverse effects.

Rest-rotation grazing may have the most potential to provide benefits to wildlife. This system often is economically disruptive because it foregoes livestock forage, but such losses may be compensated by benefits derived from wildlife-related recreation on public lands. For example, development of a rest-rotation grazing system in a single deer-hunting zone in California might specify that each range unit would be grazed only 1 of 3 years. The value of unused livestock forage, calculated on the basis of net economic value at $12.82 per AUM, would equal about $71,000 over each 3-year grazing cycle. However, increased deer populations and additional hunting opportunities would be valued at $6.5 million over the same period (Loomis et al. 1991).

Using Livestock to Manage Wildlife Habitat

In some situations, livestock grazing can be used to manage wildlife habitat (Longhurst et al. 1976, 1982; Holechek 1980, 1982; Urness 1982, 1990; Severson 1990). Livestock grazing has been applied to the management of habitat for species as diverse as mule deer (Smith et al. 1979, Willms et al. 1979, Reiner and Urness 1982), northern bobwhites *(Colinus virginianus)* (Moore and Terry 1979), and Canada geese *(Branta canadensis)* (Glass 1988). For example, cattle grazing in late winter and spring on foothill, annual grasslands in California encourages growth of forbs that are valuable to many wildlife species.

In other situations, application of prescribed grazing has met with mixed results. Too often, the intent of using livestock grazing has been to manage habitat for a single species, whereas entire communities actually are affected. Using livestock to maintain a plant community in an early seral stage often will benefit those wildlife species dependent on such habitat, while simultaneously impacting species associated with climax communities (Kie and Loft 1990).

The prescription, or strategy, for grazing is important. Maximizing benefits to wildlife from changes in grazing will involve reductions in livestock numbers and shortening grazing seasons compared to management plans designed to maximize livestock production. Livestock grazing by itself is neither good nor bad for wildlife, but depends on a variety of factors, including wildlife species of concern, livestock numbers, timing and duration of livestock grazing, livestock distribution, and kinds of livestock (Kie and Loft 1990). Wildlife and range managers might consider avoiding generalizations and evaluate the role of livestock on wildlife and their habitats independently for each species, grazing plan, and management situation.

MANAGING RANGELAND BY ANTHROPOGENIC MANIPULATION

Fire

Rangeland species evolved under the influence of fire and, hence, many are fire adapted. The natural occurrence of fire varies among regions as a result of fuels, topography, climate, and ignition source. The effect that fires have on landscapes is further dependent upon fire size, intensity, frequency, time of year during which they occur, and resulting burn patterns (Riggs et al. 1996). The interval at which fire occurs on a landscape varies as a function of active fire suppression, prior fire regime, plant community, and geographic location (Wright and Bailey 1982).

Effects of fire on wildlife populations may be positive or negative depending upon the temporal scale under consideration (short- vs. long-term), species involved, and characteristics of the burn. Fire effects on wildlife may be characterized as those directly affecting diet and those relating to habitat structure. Although effects on forage quality tend to be rather short-lived following a fire (Hobbs and Spowart 1984), structural changes may persist for decades, as is the case when forested and shrub stands are eliminated (Bunting 1986, Everett 1986, West and Yorks 2002). Effects of fire on bird and small mammal populations tend to be related to modifications of vegetation structure (Blake 1982, Bock and Bock 1983, Niemi and Probst 1990, Riggs et al. 1996).

Diet quality may be altered by fire as a result of alterations to floristic composition of plant communities, chemical composition of plant tissues, and structure of the plant canopy (Riggs et al. 1996). Although investigators have observed increases in both crude protein (Hobbs and Spowart 1984, Cook et al. 1994) and in vitro digestibility (Hobbs and Spowart 1984) in forages following fire, some of the greatest nutritional benefits may be derived through increases in foraging efficiency (Hobbs and Spowart 1984, Canon et al. 1987). Fire removes litter and dead standing herbage of low nutritional value (Van Soest 1994) enabling herbivores to more efficiently select nutritious plant material (Hobbs and Spowart 1984). The effects of burning on forage quality and stand composition and canopy among graminoids and herbaceous species persist for 1–3 years (Hobbs and Spowart 1984). Ultimately, effects on animal condition and productivity are most definitive; Svejcar (1989) noted increases in cattle performance when feeding on burned tallgass prairie.

Grazing prior to burning proportionately reduces nitrogen losses in forage (Hobbs et al. 1991), and grazing that precedes fire in tallgrass prairie reduces spatial variability of patches and improves animal performance (Hobbs et al. 1991). However, grazing of dry prairies following fire can inhibit forage recovery, and preference for burns by cattle may require adjustments to stocking rate (Erichsen-Arychuk et al. 2002).

Riggs et al. (1996) discussed the economics of prescribed fire and reported the larger the prescribed fire, the more cost effective, because fixed costs are applied over a greater area. They cautioned, however, that beneficial effects of fire treatments on wildlife habitats and populations should outweigh issues focusing too heavily on the amount of area burned. The role of fire varies from region to region and by ecosystem. Thus, prescriptions should be tailored to specific project areas.

Other Methods of Vegetation Manipulation

In addition to burning and grazing, vegetation manipulation of rangelands may occur through use of hand tools, mechanical equipment, and chemical spraying. The goals, as well as logistic and financial constraints, will affect which method is most suitable for any given area. Mechanical treatments are used to remove undesirable overstory species that inhibit growth of understory forage species (Bleich and Holl 1981, Fulbright and Guthery 1996, Holechek et al. 1998, Stephenson et al. 1998). Herbicide application may be used to control either unwanted brush or herbaceous species.

Although there may be social and legal constraints that affect use of herbicides, their application may be appropriate in some cases. In contrast to mechanical removal of vegetation, application of herbicides over large areas is typically less expensive and time consuming. Herbicides may be applied by hand, or with sprayers mounted to tractors or aircraft (Koerth 1996). The Herbicide Handbook Committee (1994, 1998) provides a thorough review of the types of chemicals available and their known effects.

Mechanical removal of brush from rangelands for the benefit of wildlife tends to be most successful when applied to patches intermixed in a landscape mosaic (Fulbright and Guthery 1996). In contrast, extensive clearing is detrimental to species dependent on woody plants. Major techniques for large scale brush removal include use of roller choppers, shredders (e.g., rotary axe), and crushers for top growth removal or, conversely, whole plant removal by root plowing, chaining and cabling, disking, and bulldozing and power grubbing (Bleich and Holl 1981, Fulbright and Guthery 1996). Additional considerations when selecting mechanical methods include topography, extent of resprouting, soil type, and size of the area to be treated (Holechek et al. 1998).

MANAGING RANGELAND RIPARIAN AREAS

Riparian areas are important habitats for terrestrial and aquatic wildlife (Carothers and Johnson 1975; Thomas et al. 1979a,c; Platts and Raleigh 1984; Skovlin 1984; Platts 1990). Their importance is a result of being obligate habitat for many aquatic species, of the uniqueness of their soil and vegetation complexes that produce diverse vegetation structure and concomitant diverse biological communities, and of their limited extent across a diversity of landscapes. Their value for a given species of wildlife is a function of water availability (for example, mule deer in the Sonoran Desert vs. wildlife in the Prairie Pothole Region of North America), life stages, animal movements, weather, and other factors.

Riparian vegetation and its structural arrangement are important for wildlife. Many vertebrate and invertebrate species depend directly or indirectly on riparian vegetation for food, cover, or other life requisites. Some wildlife use riparian zones disproportionately more than any other habitat. For example, of 363 terrestrial species in the Great Basin of southeastern Oregon, 288 depend directly on riparian zones or use them more than other habitats (Thomas et al. 1979a). Herpetofaunas also are strongly associated with riparian areas (Jones 1988). Riparian soils and substrates are important to amphibians, reptiles, and small mammals because these wildlife forms often inhabit subsurface environments. The temperate microclimate, availability of moisture, and greater biomass production of these areas provide for complex food webs.

The value of riparian areas to wildlife is only generally described, owing to the difficulty of long-term observa-

tions. Mule (Thomas et al. 1979b) and white-tailed (Compton et al. 1988) deer select woody riparian vegetation for cover and forage. Selected bird species have demonstrated an affinity for distinct layers of vegetation (Gutzwiller and Anderson 1986). Riparian zones provide migration routes for birds, bats, deer, and elk (Wauer 1977) and are frequently used by deer and elk as travel corridors between high-elevation summer ranges and low-elevation winter ranges. Moreover, riparian habitats are strongly selected by mountain lions (*Puma concolor*) in some areas (Dickson and Beier 2002).

Riparian habitats are of further importance because they comprise only about 1% of the landscape in the United States (Knopf 1988). Further, >70% of the original riparian habitats in the United States have been lost through a variety of land use practices (Megahan and King 1985). Barclay (1978) reported that natural riparian habitats within the Oklahoma grasslands have nearly vanished, and channelization was responsible for conversion of 86% of bottomland forests to other land uses. In the southwestern United States, many historically perennial streams are largely ephemeral watercourses today (Johnson et al. 1989).

Central to development of management strategies for riparian areas are: (1) an understanding of what constitutes a riparian area, (2) their internal functions and processes, (3) the influences on riparian ecosystems, and (4) their importance to wildlife. Elmore (1989) argued that a fundamental understanding of the functioning of riparian ecosystems was initially necessary to evaluate benefits and incorporate management actions into land use plans.

Rivers and streams transport water and sediments (Jensen and Platts 1987). Thus, riparian habitats are unique products derived from the dynamic processes that a given stream produces and are influenced by the interactions of climate, geology, geomorphology, hydrology, pedogenesis, and chemical and biological processes. Little information is available, however, on wildlife/riparian interactions. As a result, wildlife management considerations frequently are excluded from land use plans (Dwyer et al. 1984, Dickson and Huntley 1987). Substantial work has been done on riverine/riparian dynamics (reviewed by Curtis and Ripley 1975; Thomas et al. 1979a,b; Brinson et al. 1981, Kauffman and Krueger 1984; Platts and Raleigh 1984; Skovlin 1984; Warner and Hendrix 1984; DeBano and Schmidt 1989; Platts 1990).

Value, Structure, and Function of Riparian Areas

Several authors have proposed riparian terminology; both Swanson et al. (1982) and Johnson and Lowe (1985) suggest that disparity exists among users. They defined riparian areas as the sum of the terrestrial and aquatic components characterized by: (1) presence of permanent or ephemeral surface or subsurface water, (2) water flowing through channels defined by the local physiography, and (3) the presence of obligate, occasionally facultative, plants requiring readily available water and rooted in aquatic soils derived from alluvium. Riparian ecosystems usually occur as an ecotone between aquatic and upland ecosystems, and have distinct and variable vegetation, soil, and water characteristics. Typically, riparian areas are viewed as riverine habitats with perennial surface flows and associated plants and soils. However, surface flows may be ephemeral or periodic, as in desert washes or arroyos of the southwestern United States.

Riparian vegetation typically functions to allow necessary sediment transport and natural erosional processes. It also effectively reduces accelerated erosion that could result in loss of riparian habitats (Miller 1987). Riparian trees supply large organic debris and function to influence the physical (morphology), chemical (nutrient cycling), and biological (flora and fauna) components of the system (Bisson et al. 1987). Changes in stream channel structure and habitat diversity can occur when large organic debris is removed (Bilby 1984). Structural diversity, an important feature of riparian vegetation (Jain 1976, Anderson and Ohmart 1977), is affected by consequences of natural or human-caused habitat disruption.

Management Problems and Strategies

Management of riparian habitats is important because of the role of these ecosystems in water quality and nutrient recycling (Stednick 1988), and because riparian vegetation is considered to be the most sensitive and productive North American wildlife habitat (Carothers and Johnson 1975). Indeed, no other habitat in North America is as important to noncolonial nesting birds; riparian areas are equally important to other terrestrial vertebrates (Szaro et al. 1985).

Riparian zones are easily affected by natural or induced changes on their watersheds, including grazing (Kauffman and Krueger 1984, Skovlin 1984, Chaney et al. 1990). Moreover, problems seemingly related to riparian habitats alone cannot be resolved by considering only that habitat. As a result, management of riparian areas should be considered both onsite (within the riparian zone) and offsite (outside the riparian zone), which accounts for all adjacent uplands that exert influence over the watershed. Onsite activities such as grazing management and vegetation treatments are performed within riparian habitats; offsite activities include logging, road construction, and slash burning. Management activities outside the riparian zone may change the quantity and quality of water entering the riparian area (Stednick 1988). A variety of range management options are available for sustaining health of riparian habitats including complete protection (Stromberg and Patten 1988), multiple-use approaches, and exclusive use.

Livestock grazing is perhaps the greatest biological threat to riparian habitats in the western United States, given that about 91% of the total rangeland is grazed (Chaney et al. 1990). Improper livestock grazing affects all 4 components of the riverine/riparian system–channel, stream banks, water column, and vegetation (Platts 1990). Livestock grazing problems usually are the result of improper distribution of cows and not simply too many (Severson and Medina 1983). Concentrated livestock use results in sparse tree or shrub stands of low vigor, generally with substantial dead material on the ground, a tight, sod-bound soil, and lack of tree or shrub reproduction. Damage occurs in several ways. One is compaction of soil, which reduces moisture infiltration and increases runoff. Another is constant removal of herbage, which allows soil temperatures to rise and increases evaporation from the soil surface. A third is physical damage to the trees or shrubs by rubbing, trampling, and browsing (Severson and Boldt 1978). The primary method for

resolving overuse of riparian areas has been modified grazing strategies, which have met with mixed results (Dwyer et al. 1984, Skovlin 1984, Chaney et al. 1990).

Isolated case studies have demonstrated that revised grazing management improved conditions, but also that condition of riparian habitats continues to decline (U.S. General Accounting Office 1988). Myers (1989) reported 74% of the grazing systems evaluated failed to positively improve rangeland health within 20 years; however, riparian vegetation usually improves from grazing relief within 4–6 years, depending on severity of use (Platts and Nelson 1989). Areas with severe overuse require greater periods of time (>15 years) for native species such as sedges (Cyperaceae) to displace species adapted to overuse (Elmore and Beschta 1987).

Conventional grazing systems (Heady 1975) were developed with consideration only for production and maintenance of forage plants, primarily graminoids. Application of these systems to maintain woody streamside vegetation and stream bank integrity likely will not be satisfactory, given the ecophysiology of shrubs and trees. Platts (1990: 6) provided an excellent description of grazing strategies designed to complement restoration objectives with livestock management, and suggested that, "the solution is to identify and develop compatible grazing methods," given our state of knowledge of the functions of riparian systems. Indeed, at least one grazing strategy is available that would provide riparian areas with the necessary rest or protection needed to restore, maintain, or enhance their productivity. The least acceptable option is "no use" by ungulates and this option may be attractive in situations where restoration is a major objective of overall riparian management. Another recommendation is to fence critical reaches of riparian habitats in an effort to maintain the integrity of the streamside zone (Platts 1990).

A good management strategy for sustaining rangeland riparian areas will: (1) maintain the productivity of the vegetation (e.g., structure, species composition), (2) maintain the integrity of stream dynamics (e.g., channel and bank stability), and (3) recognize that several factors (e.g., soils, vegetation, hydrology, and animals) interact to maintain a dynamic equilibrium within the riparian zone. Successful management of riparian areas is dependent on application of knowledge from the physical sciences, such as hydrology and geomorphology, combined with an aggressive program that provides adequate protection to the structure, composition, and diversity of vegetation in such areas.

DEVELOPING RANGELAND WATER SOURCES

Increasing the amount of water available to wildlife has been used to enhance habitat for species inhabiting arid rangelands (Kie et al. 1994). Techniques include improvement of natural springs, seeps, and waterholes, and construction of artificial devices to capture and store rainfall (Tsukamoto and Stiver 1990, Young et al. 1995, Arizona State University College of Law 1997). Recently, development of rangeland water sources has been questioned (Broyles 1995) and become controversial (e.g., Broyles and Cutler 1999, Rosenstock et al. 2001) and will require substantial effort to resolve (Rosenstock et al. 1999).

Many methods have been used to make subsurface water available to wildlife including manual techniques, explosives, prescribed fire, and chemicals. Recently, horizontal well technology has been applied to development of springs and seeps for wildlife (Kie et al. 1994). Handwork, although time consuming and costly, may be the most practical way to accomplish some types of developments (Weaver et al. 1959). Helicopters can be used to transport personnel and hand tools into remote sites, thereby allowing development of those sites (Bleich 1983).

Water sources can be improved with explosives (Weaver et al. 1959), but caution is necessary to ensure that water-yielding subsurface formations are not altered drastically and water flow is not interrupted. When such damage does occur, it is usually the result of a heavy charge opening a crack that allows water to escape. Explosives should be used only on marginal seeps where sufficient water is not immediately available and where it can be used safely. Explosives also are useful in clearing channels to allow storm flows to bypass a spring, or to lay pipe to be used for gravity flow of water to a basin (Weaver et al. 1959).

Prescribed fire can be used to remove phreatophytic vegetation, resulting in a decrease in the transpiration of subsurface water and increased surface flows (Biswell and Schultz 1958, Weaver et al. 1959). Use of prescribed fire requires extreme caution and periodic reburning may be necessary to maintain surface flows. However, the importance of small patches of desert riparian vegetation to a multitude of species makes any substantial reduction in the occurrence of such vegetation undesirable (Bleich 1992). Where prescribed fire can be used to temporarily clear a spring site or seep so that other development may proceed, its use may be desirable, but its role is limited.

Herbicides increase surface flows by eliminating vegetation responsible for evapotranspiration of subsurface water. They can be particularly useful where water is limited; loss of cover or shade may be more than offset by making a permanent water supply available to wildlife (Weaver et al. 1959). The limited distribution of native, riparian vegetation in arid areas makes widespread use of herbicides undesirable. Herbicides can, however, be used to control saltcedar or tamarisk (*Tamarix* spp.) at desert water sources (Sanchez 1975). Control of this exotic species can be successfully accomplished on a small scale by hand cutting and herbicide application (Sanchez 1975, Neill 1990).

Development of Springs

Development of springs should: (1) provide at least one escape route for wildlife to and from the site that takes advantage of the natural terrain and vegetation; (2) provide an alternate escape route where feasible; (3) protect water developments from livestock while allowing access for wildlife; (4) reduce the possibility of wildlife drowning by providing gentle basin slopes or ramps in tanks; (5) maintain or provide adequate natural cover, plantings, or brush piles around the watering area; (6) provide, where applicable, a sign to inform the public of the purpose of the development; (7) provide for development of sufficient capacity to supply water whenever it is needed for wild animals; and (8) provide livestock and public access to water outside the protected water development (Yoakum et al. 1980,

Bleich 1992, Kie et al. 1994). If shy animals are involved, water for human consumption can be piped some distance from the wildlife water source. For example, sustained camping should be discouraged within a 1-km radius of water used by mountain sheep.

Ramps or walk-in wells offer a simple and inexpensive method of making water available to wildlife (Weaver et al. 1959). Unless the ramp is cut through rock, however, the sides must be boarded to keep material from sloughing into the excavation. Ramps should be a minimum of 1 m wide to allow large animals to enter and exit easily. Ramps are also important for escape in other types of water developments such as livestock troughs (Wilson 1977) and guzzlers (Andrew et al. 2001).

Construction of small basins or pools at a water source is an effective way to conserve water and make it readily available to wildlife. Basins may be constructed with rock, cement, or masonry, or they may be gouged from solid rock near the source when small seeps originate in a rock stratum. A simple basin, constructed with hand tools, can be chiseled into solid rock and will effectively store water for years. Where appropriate, power tools and explosives may be used to create larger storage basins. When explosives are used, care must be taken not to damage the source of the water, or the rock face so that it cannot be modified to store water. A major advantage of this type of development is that they are nearly indestructible.

Rock basins can be enlarged with cement and rocks or masonry materials. Similarly, these materials may be used to construct diversions to protect a basin from debris caused by storm flows, or to create an artificial basin at a location where the development of a solid rock basin is impractical. Special masonry techniques may be necessary to ensure a bond between the mortar and rock (Gray 1974).

Many springs and seeps occur in canyon bottoms. Even when developed, such springs are subject to damage by water from storms. A method of development that often is satisfactory is to bury a length of perforated asphalt or plastic pipe packed in gravel, at the spring source, and pipe the water to a basin or trough away from the canyon bottom and danger of flooding. Placing large rocks over a source after it has been developed and capping the development with concrete increases protection. Alternatively, a redwood spring box may be installed at a water source allowing access for maintenance with water piped to a trough in a safe location.

Plastic pipe is a good choice for use because it is lightweight, durable, and not subject to rust or corrosion; further, repairs are easily accomplished. Any type of pipe should be buried sufficiently deep to prevent freezing, trampling by livestock and wild ungulates, or damage from floods. A continuous downhill grade will help prevent air locks from developing in the pipe and ensure constant flow of water. When water is to be piped away from excavated springs, a trough constructed of concrete or masonry is preferred because it will not rust. If the trough poses a potential hazard for small animals and birds, a ramp should be installed to facilitate access to the water (Bond 1947).

Horizontal Wells

Traditional techniques used to develop springs and seeps have several disadvantages: (1) flow of water from the source cannot be controlled, (2) variable flow may be inadequate to generate enough water to create a surface source, and (3) exposed spring water and the source may be susceptible to contamination (Welchert and Freeman 1973). Horizontal well technology can overcome some of these disadvantages (Coombes and Bleich 1979; Bleich 1982, 1990; Bleich et al. 1982*a*).

Horizontal wells have several advantages: (1) success rate, particularly in arid regions where historical sources may have failed, is high; (2) amount of water can be readily controlled, thus reducing waste; (3) the area is not readily subject to contamination; (4) they are relatively inexpensive to develop; and (5) maintenance requirements are low. Horizontal wells also have disadvantages: (1) the initial cost of the equipment necessary to construct them can be high (although private contractors can do the work with their own equipment), (2) transporting the necessary equipment to remote sites can be difficult, and (3) some horizontal wells require a vacuum relief valve to prevent air locks from interrupting the flow.

Site selection is the most important and difficult step in development of a horizontal well. Several factors, including presence of historical springs and seeps, distribution of phreatophytes, and presence of an appropriate geological formation, must be evaluated (Welchert and Freeman 1973). Dike formations (a tilted, impervious formation that forms a natural barrier to an aquifer) and the contact formation (a perched water table over an impervious material) are both suitable for horizontal well development. Developing a dike formation requires the impervious barrier be penetrated to tap the stored water (Fig. 2). A contact formation is developed by penetrating at or above a seep area at the boundary of an impervious layer (Fig. 2).

Tinajas

Tinajas are rock tanks created by erosion that hold water. In some desert mountain ranges, tinajas may provide the only sources of water for wildlife. The capacity of tinajas can range from a few liters to more than 100,000 L of water.

Several techniques are available to increase storage capacity of tinajas. Sunshades can be used to reduce evaporation of water (Halloran 1949; Halloran and Deming 1956, 1958; Weaver et al. 1959). Shades can be constructed by anchoring eyebolts into the canyon walls, installing cables, and attaching shading material such as sheet metal to the cables (Weaver et al. 1959). In Arizona, sunshades have been built with a framework of 5-cm pipe placed into holes drilled into bedrock, with shading material then attached to the framework (Werner 1984).

Some tinajas can be deepened or enlarged with explosives (Halloran 1949, Weaver et al. 1959), but use of this method risks damage to the tinaja. A safer, and potentially more effective, method involves constructing an impervious dam on the downstream side, combined with a pervious structure to divert debris around the tinajas but allowing water to flow into them (Werner 1984). Deep, steep-sided tinajas often pose special problems for wildlife, because individuals can become trapped when water levels are low. Pneumatic equipment or explosives can be used to chisel or blast access ramps in such situations (Halloran 1949). Mensch (1969) used explosives to create an escape ramp at a natural tinaja in which 34 mountain sheep had died within a 2-year period.

Sand Dams

Some of the earliest techniques designed to increase water availability in arid regions involved construction of sand dams or sand tanks (Sykes 1937; Halloran 1949; Halloran and Deming 1956, 1958). These devices originally were constructed by placing a concrete dam across a narrow canyon. One or more pipes that could be capped to prevent water from draining penetrated the dam. The dammed area then filled with sand and gravel washed in by floods. Water soaks into the sand and gravel, and is stored, protected from excessive evaporation (National Academy of Sciences 1974).

Sand dams must be securely anchored in bedrock, and the design and construction of the dam may be the most important aspect of the entire system (Bleich and Weaver 1983). Because seepage at the bedrock interface could be a significant source of water loss, Bleich and Weaver (1983) emphasized that techniques used must result in an efficient bond between cement and bedrock (Gray 1974).

Storage volume of sand dams can be increased in a variety of ways (Sivils and Brock 1981, Bleich and Weaver 1983), but dams should not be too large. Compounds such as calcium aluminate can be added to the concrete to decrease set-up time (Gray 1974); however, sand dams should be no more than 12 m long and 3 m high (Halloran and Deming 1956, 1958). Water stored behind sand dams

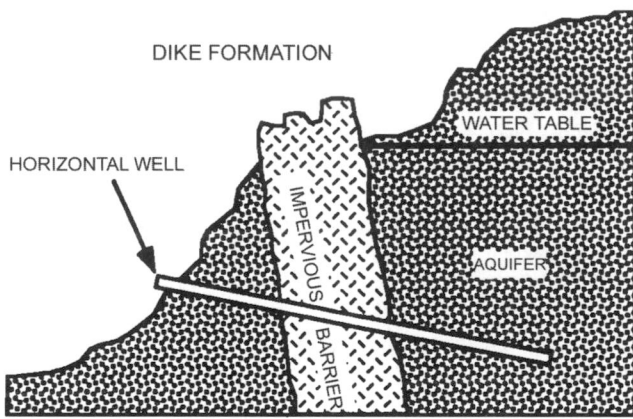

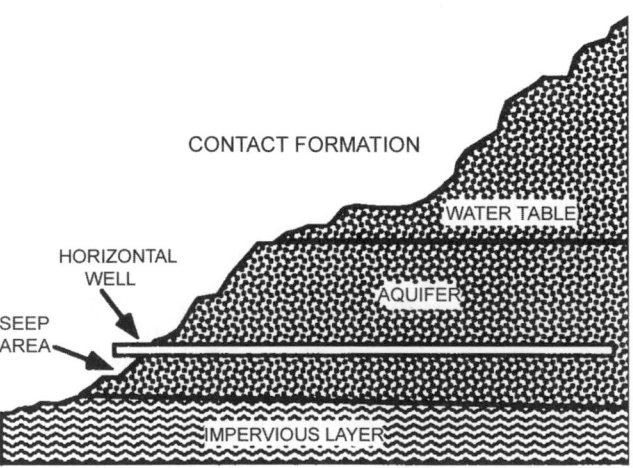

Fig. 2. Horizontal wells can be developed in dike or contact formations. The position of the well relative to the aquifer and impervious barrier is critically important to the success of the well (after Welchert and Freeman 1973).

can be piped to a trough some distance from the dam (Sivils and Brock 1981), or used to flood natural or constructed potholes downstream.

Because precipitation in arid regions often occurs as violent thunderstorms, washes and canyons often flow large amounts of water over a short period of time. These brief flows may not allow sufficient time for storm water to saturate areas behind sand dams, especially if the underground storage capability has been enhanced (Sivils and Brock 1981, Bleich and Weaver 1983). Rock-filled baskets or gabions anchored into bedrock can be placed across a wash or canyon perpendicular to the direction of flow to slow water velocity. Such structures also raise and widen the wash.

Reservoirs and Small Ponds

A reservoir consists of open water impounded behind a dam. Reservoirs can be constructed by building a dam directly across a drainage or by enclosing a depression on one side of a drainage and constructing a ditch to divert water into the resulting basin (Yoakum et al. 1980). They also recommended that reservoirs be designed to provide maximum storage with minimum surface area to reduce evaporation. Major points to consider in selection of reservoir sites include: (1) suitability of soils for dams (clays with a fair proportion of sand and gravel, i.e., 1 part clay to 2–3 parts grit); (2) the watershed area above the dam should be sufficiently large to provide water to fill the reservoir, but not so large that excessive flows will damage the spillway or wash out the dam; (3) channel width and depth with a bottom easily made watertight and channel grade immediately above the dam as flat as possible; (4) easy access for wildlife to the water; and (5) an adequate spillway naturally incorporated into the development.

The base thickness of the dam must be equal to or greater than 4.5 times the height plus the crest thickness. Slopes of the dam should be 2.5:1 on the upstream face and 2:1 on the downstream face. Minimum width of the top of all dams should be 3 m. Fill of the dam should be at least 10% higher than the required height to allow for settling. Freeboard (depth from the top of the dam to the high-water mark when the spillway is carrying the estimated peak runoff) should not be less than 60 cm, and the spillway should be designed to handle double the largest expected volume of runoff. A natural spillway is preferred and it should have a broad, relatively flat cross section. Water should be taken out through the spillway well above the fill, and then re-enter the main channel some distance downstream. Spillways should be wide, flat-bottomed, and protected by riprapping, or by facing with rocks. The entrance should be wide and smooth, and the grade of the spillway channel should be low so the water will flow through without cutting (Hamilton and Jepson 1940).

New reservoirs usually do not hold water satisfactorily for several months. Bentonite spread over the bottom and sides of the basin and face of the dam will help seal the impoundment. The basin also can be lined with polyethylene or another appropriate material, with 15–30 cm of dirt rolled evenly over the top (U.S. Department of Interior 1966). Other artificial materials such as Hypalon® (Water Saver Company, Denver, Colorado, USA) are superior to polyethylene, because of their strength and resistance to ultraviolet radiation. These liners can be custom made for reservoirs of different sizes.

Dugouts

Large earthen catchment basins built to collect water for livestock were commonly called charcos by early settlers along the Mexican border, and dugouts by pioneers in other areas (Yoakum et al. 1980). Dugouts can be placed in almost any type of topography, but are most common in areas of comparatively flat, well-drained terrain. Such areas facilitate maximum storage with minimum excavation. Dugouts can be small, rectangular excavations (Fig. 3). All sides should be sloped sufficiently to prevent sloughing (usually ≤2:1) and one or more relatively flat side slopes (≤4:1) should be provided to facilitate access for large mammals (U.S. Department of Interior 1964).

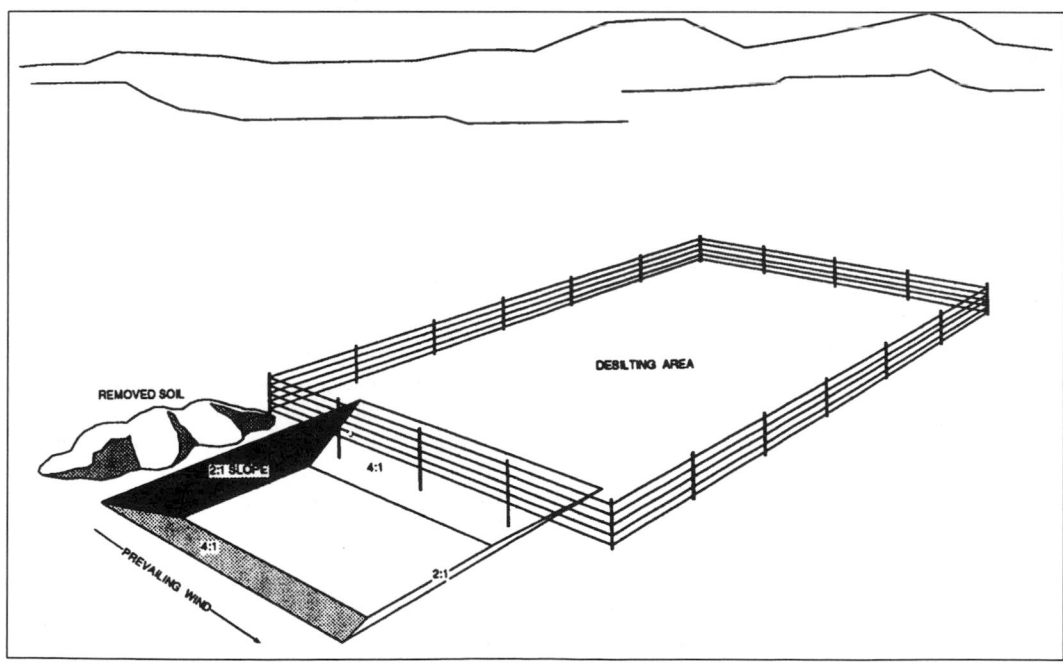

Fig. 3. Dugouts, also known as charcos, can be constructed to provide water for wildlife on rangelands (after Yoakum et al. 1980, Kindschy et al. 1982).

Fig. 4. An adit is a short tunnel that has been blasted into solid rock to store water for wildlife. The entrance to the adit must be at the same elevation as the bottom of the wash in which it is located.

Fig. 5. Contemporary underground guzzlers (Lesicka and Hervert 1995) store up to 40,000 L of water and have no moving parts. Wildlife walk down a ramp to reach stored water.

Adits

Adits (Fig. 4) are short, dead end tunnels that extend into solid rock constructed with a downward sloping floor to allow access by wildlife (Halloran and Deming 1956, 1958). Adits have been constructed in Arizona and other western states, primarily to benefit mountain sheep (Parry 1972, Weaver 1973).

Personnel skilled in hard rock blasting techniques should be used to construct adits. These water storage depots should have openings at least 2 × 3 m and be at least 4–5 m in length. The water storage depth should be at least 4 m to ensure a dependable water supply (Halloran and Deming 1956, 1958). Commercial masonry sealers should be used to prevent seepage of water through rock fractures (Halloran and Deming 1956, 1958; Gray 1974; Werner 1984).

Because the opening of an adit must be approximately the same elevation of the wash in which it is placed, it may be necessary to construct a diversion that allows flood waters to enter, yet causes debris, sand, and boulders to bypass the adit. Boulders placed on the upstream sides of adits can be used for this purpose (Halloran and Deming 1956, 1958). Another effective, but simple, technique involves construction of a rock gabion (Werner 1984).

Adits also can be designed to store water from a natural source, such as a seasonal or permanent spring (Werner 1984), and water sometimes can be diverted into adits from natural slick-rock aprons above the site. Adits also can be used to store water that normally would be unavailable, and water can be pumped from the adit into a nearby tinaja (Werner 1984). In such instances, the adit should be covered to reduce evaporation. Shade structures have been used to reduce evaporation at adits in which stored water is directly available to wildlife (Halloran and Deming 1956, 1958).

Guzzlers

Guzzlers are permanent, self-filling, structures that collect and store rainwater and make it directly available to wildlife. Guzzlers can be constructed to provide water for small animals only, or for animals of all sizes.

Several techniques can be used to collect water for guzzlers. Aprons that collect rainfall can be of manufactured or natural materials, including concrete or sheet metal, but asphalted, oiled, waxed, or otherwise treated soil aprons can be used (Glading 1947, Fink et al. 1973, Rauzi et al. 1973, Myers and Frasier 1974, Frasier et al. 1979, Johnson and Jacobs 1986, Rice 1990, Lesicka and Hervert 1995).

Guzzlers useful for wildlife generally store water in underground tanks, and wildlife walk a ramp to enter the guzzler to drink (Halloran and Deming 1956, 1958; Lesicka and Hervert 1995) (Fig. 5). However, water can also be stored in underground or aboveground concrete, plastic, metal, or fiberglass tanks (Garton 1956*a,b*; Roberts 1977; Bleich et al. 1982*b*; Remington et al. 1984; Werner 1984; Bardwell 1990; Bleich and Pauli 1990; deVos and Clarkson 1990; Gunn 1990; Lesicka and Hervert 1995). Aboveground tanks (Fig. 6) usually have a float-valve to regulate water at a drinking trough away from the water storage tanks (Roberts 1977, Werner 1984, Bleich and Pauli 1990). Underground tanks generally have no moving parts (Lesicka and Hervert 1995) and are not as subject to mechanical failures as are designs that incorporate a float valve. Moreover, guzzlers that store water for large mammals below the surface of the ground are nearly undetectable by humans more than a few meters from them (Fig. 7); current designs (Lesicka and Hervert 1995) present little risk of drowning to native vertebrates, including desert tortoise (Andrew et al. 2001).

The most important step in installation of a guzzler is locating a suitable site. A guzzler should not be placed in a wash or gully where it may collect silt or sand or be damaged by floodwaters; many guzzlers have been installed in areas lacking critical habitat components (Lewis 1973). When constructing a guzzler for small animals, Yoakum et al. (1980) recommended that: (1) size of the water-collecting apron be proportioned so the storage tank will need no water source other than rainfall to fill it, (2) a site should be chosen where digging is comparatively easy, and (3) the tank should be placed with its open end away from the

Fig. 6. Guzzlers constructed with above ground storage tanks generally have a float valve to control the water level in the drinking trough. Guzzlers of this type store up to 10,000 L of water for use by large mammals in the Mojave Desert, California.

prevailing wind and, if possible, facing in a northerly direction to reduce water temperature, evaporation, and growth of algae.

Tanks usually are made of concrete or plastic. Occasionally, steel tanks are used as are used heavy equipment tires (Elderkin and Morris 1989, Morris and Elderkin 1990). The plastic guzzler is a prefabricated tank constructed of fiberglass impregnated with plastic resin. Only washed gravel aggregates should be used for construction of concrete tanks, or the concrete may disintegrate in several years. Tanks made of steel are used for guzzlers in some areas and give satisfactory service. Use of tanks constructed of other artificial materials is relatively new.

Concrete sealed with bitumul, galvanized metal sheet roofing, glass mat and bitumul, rubber or plastic sheets,

Fig. 7. Underground guzzlers of the design by Lesicka and Hervert (1995) are nearly invisible to humans more than a few meters away, making them especially useful in designated wilderness.

asphalt, and plywood have been used successfully for water collecting surfaces. Durable materials such as concrete or metal are least expensive to maintain, although soil cement appears to be a promising material; (Rice 1990) and Lesicka and Hervert (1995) successfully used areas of native desert soil. Efficiency (percent of water collected) and life-spans (years) vary among materials: steel (98%, 25 years) is best, followed by asphalt roofing (86–92%, 8 years), plastic covered with 2.5 cm of gravel (66–87%, 8–15 years), butyl rubber (98%, 15–20 years), asphalt paving (95%, 15 years) and liquid asphalt soil water (90%, 5 years) (Fairbourn et al. 1972).

The area of the water-collecting surface needed to fill a guzzler (Fig. 8) depends on the storage capacity of the guzzler, minimum annual rainfall at the site, and type of collecting surface. Each 10 m^2 in apron surface area will result in collection of about 1 liter of water for each centimeter of rainfall. Calculations should be based on minimum precipitation expected, rather than the average or maximum, to prevent guzzler failure during drought years. When different types of aprons are used, required surface area can be calculated from the harvest efficiencies (Fairbourn et al. 1972). Leakage, evaporation, and heavy use by wildlife may also dictate a larger apron.

Big-game guzzlers are designed to collect water from either artificial (Gunn 1990) or natural aprons (Stevenson 1990, Lesicka and Hervert 1995). Using slick-rock catchments to collect runoff from bare rock areas is a common technique (Bleich et al. 1982b, deVos and Clarkson 1990, Stevenson 1990). These guzzlers take advantage of the fact that rock surfaces yield nearly 100% of the precipitation falling on them as runoff. Several authors (Bardwell 1990, Gunn 1990, Stevenson 1990, Lesicka and Hervert 1995) provide design specifications and other recommendations for construction of these catchments. Bardwell (1990), Bleich and Pauli (1990), deVos and Clarkson (1990), and Gunn (1990) provide information regarding performance of these units over time. These investigators

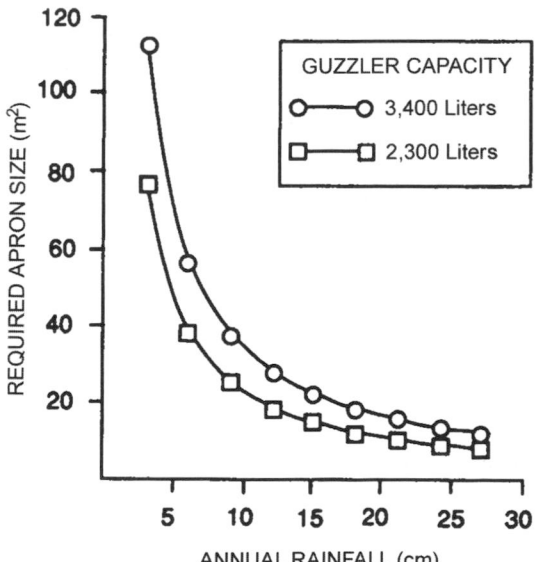

Fig. 8. Size of an apron necessary to fill a guzzler is dependent upon total annual rainfall and storage capacity of the guzzler. The relationship portrayed is based on the assumption the apron yields 100% of rainfall as runoff (after Yoakum et al. 1980).

also evaluated techniques used in the construction of big-game guzzlers and evaluated the reliability of materials.

One of the most important considerations when constructing guzzlers is that all anthropogenic devices are subject to failure; regular monitoring is an essential aspect of any maintenance program. Recently, methods of monitoring the status of water sources that incorporate remote sensing have been developed (Hill and Bleich 1999) for use in areas that are difficult to reach, or that have otherwise restricted access, such as wilderness areas. This technology does not replace biannual visits, which are necessary to detect potential failures, or correct those that already may have occurred (Bleich and Pauli 1990, Hill and Bleich 1999).

The effectiveness and performance of some big-game guzzlers depends on plumbing components. For example, Bleich and Pauli (1990) reported that frozen pipes and fittings accounted for 35 of 98 failures among 22 guzzlers over an 11-year period. Furthermore, of the 98 failures, float-valve malfunction accounted for 31, design and construction flaws for 9, and natural disasters for 6. Other problems, including rusted tanks, rusted drinker boxes, and vandalism, accounted for 17. Overall, each of the 22 guzzlers evaluated averaged 4.4 mechanical failures over an 11-year period, but each was in service an average of 87% of that time. Mechanical failures did not necessarily lead to an inoperative guzzler, but did require effort to repair them.

The most complete guide for construction of guzzlers currently available was prepared by Brigham and Stevenson (1997) and is available on request from the U.S. Department of Interior, Bureau of Land Management, National Applied Resources Sciences Center, P.O. Box 25047, Denver, Colorado, USA.

CONSTRUCTING RANGELAND FENCES

The relationship of fences and wildlife on rangelands in the western United States has been a point of contention for the past century. Fences constructed to control domestic livestock can adversely impact some wildlife species. For example, fences can be major obstacles or traps to pronghorn (Martinka 1967, Spillett et al. 1967, Oakley 1973) and mule deer (Yoakum et al. 1980, Mackie 1981). Proper fence design and use of appropriate construction materials can reduce adverse effects. Details of fence construction on rangelands used by pronghorn, mule deer, elk, bison (*Bison bison*), and collared peccary (*Pecari tajacu*) are available elsewhere (U.S. Department of Interior 1985, Karsky 1988). Preventing the movement of some wildlife species may be desirable, and specific fence designs can accomplish that goal (Longhurst et al. 1962, Messner et al. 1973, deCalesta and Cropsey 1978, Jepson et al. 1983, Karsky 1988).

Fences and Pronghorn

The severity of pronghorn-fence problems varies among areas. Fences are primarily a problem for herds moving seasonally to and from wintering areas on northern rangelands (Oakley 1973). However, seasonal movement problems also were reported in New Mexico (Russell 1964, Howard et al. 1983) and Texas (Buechner 1950, Hailey 1979), especially during drought years.

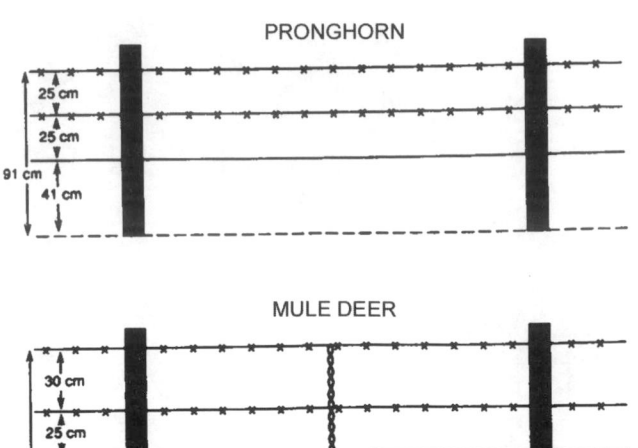

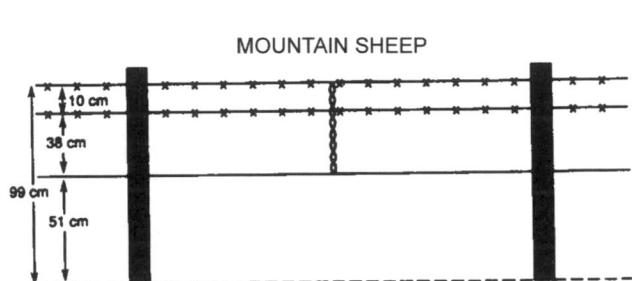

Fig. 9. Recommended specifications for wire fences constructed on ranges used by pronghorn (after Yoakum 1980, Kindschy et al. 1982, U.S. Department of Interior 1985), mule deer (after Jepson et al. 1983, U.S. Department of Interior 1985), and mountain sheep (after Hall 1985, Brigham 1990). Note the use of a smooth bottom wire on all designs and the lack of stays on fences for use on pronghorn ranges.

If fencing is necessary, only that required to provide proper livestock control and minimize hindrance to pronghorn and other wildlife should be used. Unrestricted passage for all age classes during all seasons and all weather conditions should be provided (Yoakum et al. 1980). Fencing watering areas on dry summer rangelands may be as detrimental to pronghorn as fencing migration routes. If a fenced water development is provided specifically for pronghorn, the area should encompass at least 1–2 ha of relatively level terrain (Yoakum et al. 1980).

Fence specifications to control livestock on pronghorn range have evolved over many years (Spillett et al. 1967, Autenrieth 1978, Salwasser 1980, Yoakum 1980, Kindschy et al. 1982, U.S. Department of Interior 1985). Fences should consist of 3 strands of wire, the bottom strand being smooth (Fig. 9). Four- to 6-strand barbed-wire fences limit pronghorn movements and should not be used. The bottom wire should be at least 40 cm above ground. Absence of stays between posts will facilitate the occasional movement of pronghorn through the fence (Yoakum et al. 1980, Kindschy et al. 1982, Hall 1985).

New fences should be flagged with white cloth so pronghorn can become familiar with their locations. By the time a white rag tied to the top of each fence post deteriorates, pronghorn will have become accustomed to the fence (Kindschy et al. 1982). Painting the top of steel fence posts white also helps make the fence more visible to pronghorn (Hall 1985).

Where snow accumulation restricts pronghorn movements, let-down or adjustable fences should be used (Yoakum et al. 1980). A let-down fence can consist of a wooden stay at each fence post to which the wires are attached. The stay is secured to the fence post with a wire loop at the top and either a second loop or a pivot bolt at the bottom.

Let-down fence sections may be designed to permit pulling the let-down sections back against sections of permanently standing fence. Let-down fences should provide for adjustments in wire tension. When the wire is so taut that it does not lie flat on the ground or is so loose that wire loops are formed, a hazard is created for people and animals (U.S. Department of Interior 1985). Adjustable fences (Fig. 10) that allow the movement of one or more wires can allow pronghorn passage during periods when livestock are not present (Anderson and Denton 1980). Adjustable fences are particularly useful when winter snow depths exceed 30 cm (Yoakum et al. 1980).

Pronghorn passes are structures that resemble cattle guards intersecting a fence (Spillett et al. 1967, Mapston and ZoBell 1972, Yoakum et al. 1980, Howard et al. 1983). Suitable locations for pronghorn passes make use of the tendency of individuals to parallel a fence, looking for a way to cross. The pass capitalizes on the ability of pronghorn to jump laterally over obstacles. Pronghorn passes have been built and tested under a variety of conditions (Spillett et al. 1967, Howard et al. 1983). Some adult pronghorn quickly learn to use the facilities, but others do not. Pronghorn fawns often were unable to negotiate the passes. Pronghorn passes are of limited value and should not be used as a panacea for pronghorn access problems (U.S. Department of Interior 1985).

Net-wire fences prevent the movement of pronghorn fawns in particular, and should not be used on public rangelands where pronghorn occur (Autenrieth 1978, Yoakum 1980). However, some adults may become adept at jumping a net-wire fence up to 80 cm high. Higher net-wire fences can be used where the goal is to restrict the movement of animals, such as in live-trapping, control of animals in research projects, decreasing crop depredations, or restricting access to hazardous areas such as highways.

Fences and Mule Deer

The relationship between livestock fences and mule deer has not raised the political furor that it has for pronghorn. However, throughout North America where fences have been built, they likely have caused far greater mortality to deer than to pronghorn. Deer are more apt to be trapped as individuals, whereas large numbers of pronghorn may be restricted. Also, deer frequently are caught in fences in isolated areas not readily witnessed, whereas pronghorn mortalities in open country are easy to observe.

Deer often crawl under fences when not hurried, but jump them when startled or chased (Mackie 1981). When a deer jumps a fence, its feet can become entangled between the top 2 wires, resulting in death. Limiting total fence height to 96 cm can reduce this problem (U.S. Department of Interior 1985) (Fig. 9). If the top wire is barbed, it should be separated from the next wire by 30 cm; otherwise, it should be a smooth wire (Jepson et al. 1983). Unlike fences used on pronghorn ranges, wire stays should be placed every 2.5 m between posts to keep the top wires from twisting around the leg of a deer (Yoakum et al. 1980, U.S. Department of Interior 1985).

The effective height of a fence as a barrier to deer moving uphill is increased on steep slopes. For example, a 110-cm fence on a 20% slope is equivalent to a 140-cm fence on level ground. On a 50% slope, it is equivalent to a 190-cm fence on level ground (Kerr 1979, Anderson and Denton 1980). Thus, height adjustments should be made accordingly.

Let-down fences along seasonal travel routes for deer help ensure free movement. The let-down feature of the fence also helps prevent damage from snow loading during winter. Movements of mule deer also can be aided with an adjustable fence. Net-wire fences no higher than 90 cm allow movement of adult deer but prevent passage of fawns. They should not be placed on summer and autumn migration routes used by deer.

Fences and Mountain Sheep

The construction of wire fences on ranges used by mountain sheep (for example, to exclude livestock from water developments) presents particular problems. Mountain sheep are likely to become entangled in a fence when placing their head through the top 2 wires. This problem is minimized if the 2 top wires are no more than 10 cm apart (Brigham 1990). A 3-wire fence should be used with wires spaced at 51, 38, and 10 cm intervals (Fig. 9), allowing mountain sheep movement under the bottom wire and between it and the middle wire (U.S. Department of Interior 1985, Brigham 1990). Six-wire fence designs (U.S. Department of Interior 1985) are dangerous to mountain sheep and should not be used (Brigham 1990). To minimize the probability of mountain sheep becoming entangled, fences consisting of uprights and 2 parallel rails easily can be constructed (Andrew et al. 1997) (Fig. 11).

Electric Fences

Electric fences often are used to control livestock or feral hoof stock such as burros, and some designs pose little hindrance to movement of wildlife. Electric fences are most effective on moist sites, where 2 wires may be sufficient to control cattle. On sites with at least 60 cm of rain annually, an electric fence can be made of 2 smooth wires at heights of 60 and 90 cm above ground (U.S. Department of Interior 1985, Karsky 1988). The top wire is electrified and the bottom wire serves as the ground. The wires are free running at all posts, and pose little danger of entrap-

Fig. 10. Adjustable fence modifications to facilitate movement of pronghorn and other ungulates (after Anderson and Denton 1980).

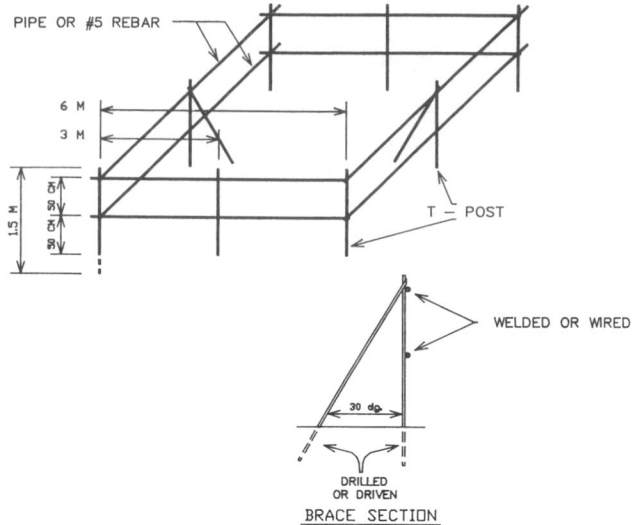

Fig. 11. A simple fence, constructed of metal t-posts and rebar spaced at appropriate intervals effectively excludes feral asses from water sources in desert ecosystems, yet allows passage by native ungulates (after Andrew et al. 1997).

ping mule deer. On drier sites, electric fences require more wires to function effectively (Karsky 1988), and the added wires can adversely affect movements by wildlife.

Wood and Steel Fences

Fences can be constructed entirely from wood posts and rails in a variety of designs with raw materials obtained at the site or manufactured materials (U.S. Department of Interior 1985, Karsky 1988, Andrew et al. 1997). Wood fences are usually expensive but can be attractive and may require less maintenance than wire fences. Construction options include post and pole, log worm, log and block, and buck and pole designs (Karsky 1988). The same principles apply to wood fences as to wire fences in minimizing hindrance to wildlife movements. The top rail or pole of a wooden fence should be kept low to allow mule deer to jump over and the bottom rail or post kept sufficiently high to allow movement of fawns. Andrew et al. (1997) designed an inexpensive rail fence using t-posts and rebar, which was totally effective in reducing access to water sources by feral asses and yet provided unimpeded access by mountain sheep and mule deer.

Rock Jacks

In many areas, soils are too shallow and rocky to allow steel fence posts to be easily driven into the ground (Hall 1985). At such sites, rock jacks are often constructed in the form of wood-rail cribs or wire baskets. The cribs or baskets are filled with rocks and serve as anchors to which wire fences can be secured. Cover and dens for small mammals are provided if the bottom rail of a rock jack is kept 10–15 cm above the ground (Hall 1985). Use of rocks at least 30 cm in diameter will also provide crevasses suitable for use by small mammals (Maser et al. 1979, Hall 1985).

Fences To Exclude Wildlife

Excluding selected wildlife species from certain areas may be desirable. Elk, mule deer, and other species often heavily depredate orchards, vineyards, and other crops;

appropriate fence designs can help alleviate such problems. Highways can be hazardous to mule deer and other ungulates that need to reach critically important seasonal ranges. Fences can be used to channel their movement to suitable underpasses and minimize collisions with vehicles. Experimental plots used in research often require exclusion of one or more species of wildlife. Finally, fencing can be used as an alternative to other control measures in reducing predation on livestock.

A 1.8-m upright net-wire fence, or one slanted at 45 degrees to a total height of about 1.3 m, can be used to exclude mule deer (Longhurst et al. 1962, Messner et al. 1973, Karsky 1988). Electric fences with 4–6 wires also discourage deer movements (Karsky 1988).

Fences can be used to reduce or eliminate the need for lethal control of coyotes (*Canis latrans*), which can be excluded from pastures by either woven wire (Thompson 1979, deCalesta and Cropsey 1978, Jepson et al. 1983) or electric fences (Gates et al. 1978, Dorrance and Bourne 1980, Karsky 1988, Nass and Theade 1988). To be effective, a woven wire fence must be at least 170 cm high, have mesh openings no larger than 10×15 cm, and have an overhang to prevent jumping and an apron to prevent digging, each at least 40 cm wide (Thompson 1979). A 7-wire electric fence (4 hot wires alternating with 3 ground wires) totaling 130 cm in height also can be used (Dorrance and Bourne 1980). Other electric fence designs are available to deter coyotes (Karsky 1988). In general, fencing to control coyotes is expensive, and probably justified only to protect small areas of high production capacity, such as irrigated pastures.

SUMMARY

Management of livestock on public rangelands has become a divisive and contentious issue. Land management agencies increasingly are criticized for failing to give appropriate consideration to grazing issues that affect wildlife, or wildlife habitat, on public lands. The single greatest change influencing conservation of wildlife on western rangelands during the 1990s has been the shift from an emphasis on competition of livestock with big game to concern for biodiversity in general.

We chose to not criticize current grazing practices but to present a reasonable review of contemporary issues related to livestock management on public lands. Further, we have attempted to: (1) provide an overview of rangeland management to benefit wildlife species and natural communities, with an emphasis on western North America; (2) identify some of the topical issues and primary rangeland systems of particular concern; and (3) describe some of the methods for accommodating wildlife and wildlife-related issues, including habitat enhancement techniques, on rangelands. Students and others making use of information in this chapter are encouraged to further explore the vast literature on management of rangelands and livestock, and to use that information to ensure the persistence of healthy and productive rangeland ecosystems, particularly as they relate to the issue of wildlife conservation.

ACKNOWLEDGMENTS

We thank G. M. Foote, P. L. Kiddoo, C. W. Milliron, B. M. Pierce, and J. T. Villepique for assistance with manuscript preparation, A. W. Stephenson for proofreading and attention to detail in checking literature citations, and 2 anonymous reviewers for helpful comments on drafts of the manuscript. This is Professional Paper 033 from the Eastern Sierra Center For Applied Population Ecology.

LITERATURE CITED

ALLEN-DIAZ, B., AND J. W. BARTOLOME. 1998. Sagebrush-grass vegetation dynamics: comparing classical and state-transition models. Ecological Applications 8:795–804.

ANDERSON, B. W., AND R. D. OHMART. 1977. Vegetation structure and bird use in the lower Colorado River valley. Pages 23–34 in R. R. Johnson and D. A. Jones, technical coordinators. Importance, preservation, and management of riparian habitat. U.S. Department of Agriculture, Forest Service, General Technical Report RM-43.

ANDERSON, L. D., AND J. W. DENTON. 1980. Adjustable wire fences for facilitating big game movement. U.S. Department of the Interior, Bureau of Land Management, Technical Note 343.

ANDREW, N. G., L. M. LESICKA, AND V. C. BLEICH. 1997. An improved fence design to protect water sources for native ungulates. Wildlife Society Bulletin 25:823–825.

——, V. C. BLEICH, A. D. MORRISON, L. M. LESICKA, AND P. J. COOLEY. 2001. Wildlife mortalities associated with artificial water sources. Wildlife Society Bulletin 29:275–280.

ARIZONA STATE UNIVERSITY COLLEGE OF LAW. 1997. Environmental, economic, and legal issues related to rangeland water developments. Center for the Study of Law, Science, and Technology, Arizona State University, Tempe, USA.

AUSTIN, D. D. 2000. Managing livestock grazing for mule deer (*Odocoileus hemionus*) on winter range in the Great Basin. Western North American Naturalist 60:198–203.

AUTENRIETH, R. 1978. Guidelines for the management of pronghorn antelope. Proceedings of the Pronghorn Antelope Workshop 8:473–526.

BARCLAY, J. S. 1978. The effects of channelization on riparian vegetation and wildlife in south-central Oklahoma. Pages 129–138 in R. R. Johnson and J. F. McCormick, technical coordinators. Strategies for protection and management of floodplain wetlands and other riparian ecosystems. U.S. Department of Agriculture, Forest Service, General Technical Report WO-12.

BARDWELL, P. P. 1990. Artificial water development design, materials, and problems encountered in the BLM, Carson City District, Nevada. Pages 133–139 in G. K. Tsukamoto and S. J. Stiver, editors. Proceedings, wildlife water development symposium. Nevada Chapter of The Wildlife Society, U.S. Department of the Interior, Bureau of Land Management, and Nevada Department of Wildlife, Reno, USA.

BATZLI, G. O., AND F. A. PITELKA. 1970. Influence of meadow mouse populations on California grasslands. Ecology 51:1027–1039.

BECK, J. L., AND D. L. MITCHELL. 2000. Influences of livestock grazing on sage grouse habitat. Wildlife Society Bulletin 28:986–992.

BELANGER, L., AND M. PICARD. 1999. Cattle grazing and avian communities of the St. Lawrence River Islands. Journal of Range Management 52:332–338.

BELSKY, A. J., AND D. M. BLUMENTHAL. 1997. Effects of livestock grazing on stand dynamics and soils in upland forests of the Interior West. Conservation Biology 12:315–327.

——, A. MATZKE, AND S. USELMAN. 1999. Survey of livestock influences on stream and riparian ecosystems in the western United States. Journal of Soil and Water Conservation 54:419–431.

BILBY, R. E. 1984. Removal of woody debris may affect stream channel stability. Journal of Forestry 82:609–613.

BIRCH, L. C. 1957. The meanings of competition. American Naturalist 91:5–18.

BISSON, P. A., R. E. BILBY, M. D. BRYAN, C. A. DOLOFF, G. B. GRETTER, R. A. HOUSE, M. L. MURPHY, K. V. KOSKY, AND J. R. SEDELL. 1987. Large woody debris in forested streams in the Pacific Northwest: past, present, and future. Pages 143–190 in E. O. Salo and T. W. Cundy, editors. Streamside management: forestry and fishery interactions. Contribution 57. Institute of Forest Resources, University of Washington, Seattle, USA.

BISWELL, H. H., AND A. M. SCHULTZ. 1958. Effects of vegetation removal on spring flow. California Fish and Game 44:211–230.

BLAKE, J. G. 1982. Influence of fire and logging on nonbreeding bird communities of ponderosa pine forests. Journal of Wildlife Management 46:404–415.

BLEICH, V. C. 1982. Horizontal wells for mountain sheep: desert bighorn "get the shaft". Transactions of the Desert Bighorn Council 26:63–64.

——. 1983. Comments on helicopter use by wildlife agencies. Wildlife Society Bulletin 11:304–306.

——. 1990. Horizontal wells for wildlife water development. Pages 51–58 in G. K. Tsukamoto and S. J. Stiver, editors. Proceedings, wildlife water development symposium. Nevada Chapter of The Wildlife Society, U.S. Department of the Interior, Bureau of Land Management, and Nevada Department of Wildlife, Reno, USA.

——. 1992. History of wildlife water developments, Inyo County, California. Pages 100–106 in C. A. Hall, Jr., V. Doyle-Jones, and B. Widawski, editors. The history of water: eastern Sierra Nevada, Owens Valley, White-Inyo Mountains. University of California, White Mountain Research Station, Bishop, USA.

——, AND S. A. HOLL. 1981. Management of chaparral habitat for mule deer and mountain sheep in southern California. Pages 247–254 in C. E. Conrad and W. C. Oechel, technical coordinators. Proceedings, symposium on dynamics and management of Mediterranean-type ecosystems. U.S. Department of Agriculture, Forest Service, General Technical Report PSW-58.

——, AND A. M. PAULI. 1990. Mechanical evaluation of artificial watering devices built for mountain sheep in California. Pages 65–72 in G. K. Tsukamoto and S. J. Stiver, editors. Proceedings, wildlife water development symposium. Nevada Chapter of The Wildlife Society, U.S. Department of the Interior, Bureau of Land Management, and Nevada Department of Wildlife, Reno, USA.

——, AND R. A. WEAVER. 1983. "Improved" sand dams for wildlife habitat management. Journal of Range Management 36:133.

——, L. J. COOMBES, AND J. H. DAVIS. 1982a. Horizontal wells as a wildlife habitat improvement technique. Wildlife Society Bulletin 10:324–328.

——, ——, AND G. W. SUDMEIER. 1982b. Volunteer participation in California wildlife habitat improvement projects. Transactions of the Desert Bighorn Council 26:56–58.

BOCK, C. E., AND J. H. BOCK. 1983. Responses of birds and deer mice to prescribed burning in ponderosa pine. Journal of Wildlife Management 47:836–840.

——, H. M. SMITH, AND J. H. BOCK. 1990. The effect of livestock grazing upon abundance of the lizard, *Sceloporus scalaris*, in southeastern Arizona. Journal of Herpetology 24:445–446.

——, J. A. BOCK, W. R. KENNEY, AND V. M. HAWTHORNE. 1984. Responses of birds, rodents, and vegetation to livestock exclosure in a semidesert grassland site. Journal of Range Management 37:239–242.

BOND, R. M. 1947. Ramps for escape of wildlife from stock troughs. Journal of Wildlife Management 7:122–123.

BORCHERT, M. I., AND S. K. JAIN. 1978. The effect of rodent seed predation on four species of California annual grasses. Oecologia 33:101–113.

BOSTICK, V. 1990. The desert tortoise in relation to cattle grazing. Rangelands 12:149–151.

BOX, T. 2000. Public rangelands without cows? Rangelands 22(4):27–30.

BRIGHAM, W. R. 1990. Fencing wildlife water developments. Pages 37–43 in G. K. Tsukamoto, and S. J. Stiver, editors. Proceedings, wildlife water development symposium. Nevada Chapter of The Wildlife Society, U.S. Department of the Interior, Bureau of Land Management, and Nevada Department of Wildlife, Reno, USA.

——, AND C. STEVENSON. 1997. Wildlife water catchment construction in Nevada. U.S. Department of the Interior, Bureau of Land Management, Technical Note 397.

BRINSON, M. M., B. L. SWIFT, R. C. PLANTICO, AND J. S. BARCLAY. 1981. Riparian ecosystems: their ecology and status. U.S. Department of the Interior, Fish and Wildlife Service, FWS/OBS-81.

BRONHAM, L., M. CARDILLO, A. F. BENNETT, AND M. A. ELGAR. 1999. Effects of stock grazing on the ground invertebrate fauna of woodland remnants. Australian Journal of Ecology 24:199–207.

BROYLES, B. 1995. Desert wildlife water developments: questioning use in the southwest. Wildlife Society Bulletin 23:663–675.

———, AND T. L. CUTLER. 1999. Effect of surface water on desert bighorn sheep in the Cabeza Prieta National Wildlife Refuge, southwestern Arizona. Wildlife Society Bulletin 27:1082–1088.

BUECHNER, H. K. 1950. Life history, ecology, and range use of the pronghorn antelope in Trans-Pecos Texas. American Midland Naturalist 43:257–354.

BULL, E. L., AND M. P. HAYES. 2000. Livestock effects on reproduction of the Columbia spotted frog. Journal of Range Management 53:291–294.

BUNTING, S. C. 1986. Use of prescribed burning in juniper and pinyon-juniper woodlands. Pages 141–145 *in* R. L. Everett, editor. Proceedings of the pinyon-juniper conference. U.S. Department of Agriculture, Forest Service, General Technical Report INT-215.

BUTTERY, R. F., AND P. W. SHIELDS. 1975. Range management practices and bird habitat values. Pages 183–189 *in* D. R. Smith, technical coordinator. Proceedings of the symposium on management of forest and range habitats for nongame birds. U.S. Department of Agriculture, Forest Service, General Technical Report WO-1.

CALIFORNIA DEPARTMENT OF FISH AND GAME. 1926. Editorial. California Fish and Game 12:28.

———. 1998. Report to the Fish and Game Commission: an assessment of mule deer and black-tailed deer habitats and populations in California. California Department of Fish and Game, Sacramento, USA.

CANON, S. K., P. J. URNESS, AND N. V. DEBYLE. 1987. Habitat selection, foraging behavior, and dietary nutrition of elk in burned aspen forest. Journal of Range Management 40:433–438.

CAROTHERS, S. W., AND R. R. JOHNSON. 1975. Water management practices and their effects on nongame birds in range habitats. Pages 210–222 *in* D. R. Smith, technical coordinator. Proceedings of the symposium on management of forest and range habitats for nongame birds. U.S. Department of Agriculture, Forest Service, General Technical Report WO-1.

CHAMBERS, J. C., AND A. R. LINNEROOTH. 2001. Restoring riparian meadows currently dominated by *Artemisia* using alternative state concepts—the establishment component. Applied Vegetation Science 4:157–166.

CHANEY, E., W. ELMORE, AND W. S. PLATTS. 1990. Livestock grazing on western riparian areas. U.S. Environmental Protection Agency, Denver, Colorado, USA.

CLARK, P. E., W. C. KRUEGER, L. D. BRYANT, AND D. R. THOMAS. 2000. Livestock grazing effects on forage quality of elk winter range. Journal of Range Management 53:97–105.

CLARY, W. P., AND D. M. BEALE. 1983. Pronghorn reactions to winter sheep grazing, plant communities, and topography in the Great Basin. Journal of Range Management 36:749–752.

CLEMENTS, F. E. 1916. Plant succession: an analysis of the development of vegetation. Carnegie Institute Publication 242.

COMPTON, B. B., R. J. MACKIE, AND G. L. DUSEK. 1988. Factors influencing distribution of white-tailed deer in riparian habitats. Journal of Wildlife Management 52:544–548.

COOK, J. G., T. J. HERSHEY, AND L. L. IRWIN. 1994. Vegetative response to burning on Wyoming mountain-shrub big game ranges. Journal of Range Management 47:296–302.

COOMBES, L. J., AND V. C. BLEICH. 1979. Horizontal wells—The DFG's new slant on water for wildlife. Outdoor California 40(6):10–12.

CURTIS, R. L., AND T. H. RIPLEY. 1975. Water management practices and their effect on nongame bird habit values in a deciduous forest community. Pages 128–141 *in* D. R. Smith, technical coordinator. Proceedings of the symposium on management of forest and range habitats for nongame birds. U.S. Department of Agriculture, Forest Service, General Technical Report WO-1.

DEBANO, L. F., AND L. J. SCHMIDT. 1989. Improving southwestern riparian areas through watershed management. U.S. Department of Agriculture, Forest Service, General Technical Report RM-182.

DEBYLE, N. V. 1985. Wildlife. Pages 135–152 *in* N. V. DeByle and R. P. Winokur, editors. Aspen: ecology and management in the western United States. U.S. Department of Agriculture, Forest Service, General Technical Report RM-119.

deCALESTA, D. S., AND M. G. CROPSEY. 1978. Field test of a coyote-proof fence. Wildlife Society Bulletin 6:256–259.

DEGRAAF, R. M., technical coordinator. 1980. Workshop proceedings—management of western forests and grasslands for nongame birds. U.S. Department of Agriculture, Forest Service, General Technical Report INT-86.

DENTON, J. S., AND T. J. C. BEEBEE. 1996. Habitat occupancy by juvenile natterjack toads (*Bufo calamita*) on grazed and ungrazed heathland. Herpetological Journal 6:49–52.

DESERT BIGHORN COUNCIL TECHNICAL STAFF. 1990. Guidelines for management of domestic sheep in the vicinity of desert bighorn habitat. Desert Bighorn Council Transactions 34:33–35.

deVos, JR., J. C., AND R. W. CLARKSON. 1990. A historic review of Arizona's water developments with discussions on benefits to wildlife, water quality, and design considerations. Pages 157–165 *in* G. K. Tsukamoto and S. J. Stiver, editors. Proceedings, wildlife water development symposium. Nevada Chapter of The Wildlife Society, U.S. Department of the Interior, Bureau of Land Management, and Nevada Department of Wildlife, Reno, USA.

DICKSON, B. G., AND P. BEIER. 2002. Home-range and habitat selection by adult cougars in southern California. Journal of Wildlife Management 66:1235–1245.

DICKSON, J. G., AND J. C. HUNTLEY. 1987. Riparian zones and wildlife in southern forests: the problem and squirrel relationships. Pages 37–39 *in* J. G. Dickson and O. E. Maughan, editors. Managing southern forests for wildlife and fish. U.S. Department of Agriculture, Forest Service, General Technical Report SO-65.

DOBKIN, D. S., A. C. RICH, AND W. H. PYLE. 1998. Habitat and avifaunal recovery from livestock grazing in a riparian meadow system of the northwestern Great Basin. Conservation Biology 12:209–221.

DORRANCE, M. J., AND J. BOURNE. 1980. An evaluation of anti-coyote electric fencing. Journal of Range Management 33:385–387.

DWYER, D. D., J. C. BUCKHOUSE, AND W. S. HUEY. 1984. Impacts of grazing intensity and specialized grazing systems on the use and value of rangeland: summary and recommendations. Pages 867–884 *in* Impacts of grazing intensity and specialized grazing systems on use and values of rangelands. National Academy of Sciences, Natural Resource Council, and U.S. Department of the Interior, Bureau of Land Management, Washington, D.C., USA.

DYKSTERHUIS, E. J. 1949. Condition and management of rangeland based on quantitative ecology. Journal of Range Management 2:104–115.

ELDERKIN, JR., R. L., AND J. MORRIS. 1989. Design for a durable and inexpensive guzzler. Wildlife Society Bulletin 17:192–194.

ELMORE, W. 1989. Rangeland riparian systems. Pages 93–95 *in* D. L. Abell, technical coordinator. Proceedings of the California riparian systems conference: protection, management, and restoration for the 1990's. U.S. Department of Agriculture, Forest Service, General Technical Report PSW-110.

———, AND R. L. BESCHTA. 1987. Riparian areas: perceptions in management. Rangelands 9:260–265.

ERICHSEN-ARYCHUK, C., E. W. BORK, AND A. W. BAILEY. 2002. Northern dry mixed prairie responses to summer wildfire and drought. Journal of Range Management 55:164–170.

EVANS, K. E., AND R. R. KERBS. 1977. Avian use of livestock watering ponds in western South Dakota. U.S. Department of Agriculture, Forest Service, General Technical Report RM-35.

EVERETT, R. L. 1986. Plant response to fire in the pinyon-juniper zone. Pages 152–157 *in* R. L. Everett, editor. Proceedings of the pinyon-juniper Conference. U.S. Department of Agriculture, Forest Service, General Technical Report INT-215.

FAIRBOURN, M. L., F. RAUZI, AND H. R. GARDNER. 1972. Harvesting precipitation for a dependable, economical water supply. Journal of Soil and Water Conservation 27:23–26.

FINK, D. H., K. R. COOLEY, AND G. W. FRASIER. 1973. Wax-treated soils for harvesting water. Journal of Range Management 26:396–398.

FITCH, H. S., AND J. R. BENTLEY. 1949. Use of California annual-plant forage by range rodents. Ecology 30:306–321.

FLEISCHNER, T. L. 1994. Ecological costs of livestock grazing in western North America. Conservation Biology 8:629–644.

FRASIER, G. W., K. R. COOLEY, AND J. R. GRIGGS. 1979. Performance evaluation of water harvesting catchments. Journal of Range Management 32:453–456.

FULBRIGHT, T. E., AND F. S. GUTHERY. 1996. Mechanical manipulation of plants. Pages 339–354 *in* P. R. Krausman, editor. Rangeland wildlife.

The Society for Range Management, Denver, Colorado, USA.

GALLIZIOLI, S. 1979. Effects of livestock grazing on wildlife. California-Nevada Wildlife Transactions 15:83–87.

GARTON, D. A. 1956a. Experimental big game watering device and detailed information on construction and costs. California Department of Fish and Game, Long Beach, USA.

———. 1956b. Experimental big game watering device and information on construction. California Department of Fish and Game, Long Beach, USA.

GATES, N. L., J. E. RICH, D. D. GODTEL, AND C. V. HULET. 1978. Development and evaluation of anti-coyote electric fencing. Journal of Range Management 31:151–153.

GLADING, B. 1947. Game watering devices for the arid southwest. Transactions of the North American Wildlife Conference 12:286–292.

GLASS, R. J. 1988. Habitat improvement costs on state-owned wildlife management areas in New York. U.S. Department of Agriculture, Forest Service, Research Paper NE-621.

GOGUEN, C. B., AND N. E. MATHEWS. 1998. Songbird community composition and nesting success in grazed and ungrazed pinyon-juniper woodlands. Journal of Wildlife Management 62:474–484.

GRANT, W. E., E. C. BIRNEY, N. R. FRENCH, AND D. M. SWIFT. 1982. Structure and productivity of grassland small mammal communities related to grazing-induced changes in vegetative cover. Journal of Mammalogy 63:248–260.

GRAY, R. S. 1974. Lasting waters for bighorn. Transactions of the Desert Bighorn Council 18:25–27.

GUNN, J. 1990. Arizona's standard rainwater catchment. Pages 19–24 in G. K. Tsukamoto and S. J. Stiver, editors. Proceedings, wildlife water development symposium. Nevada Chapter of The Wildlife Society, U.S. Department of the Interior, Bureau of Land Management, and Nevada Department of Wildlife, Reno, USA.

GUTZWILLER, K. J., AND S. H. ANDERSON. 1986. Trees used simultaneously and sequentially by breeding cavity-nesting birds. Great Basin Naturalist 46:358–360.

HAILEY, T. L. 1979. A handbook on pronghorn antelope management in Texas. Texas Parks and Wildlife Department, Austin, USA.

HALL, F. C. 1985. Wildlife habitats in managed rangelands—the Great Basin of southeastern Oregon: management practices and options. U.S. Department of Agriculture, Forest Service, General Technical Report PNW-189.

HALLORAN, A. F. 1949. Desert bighorn management. Transactions of the North American Wildlife Conference 14:527–537.

———, AND O. V. DEMING. 1956. Water development for desert bighorn sheep. U.S. Department of the Interior, Fish and Wildlife Service, Wildlife Management Service Leaflet 14.

———, AND ———. 1958. Water development for desert bighorn sheep. Journal of Wildlife Management 22:1–9.

HALLS, L. K., editor. 1984. White-tailed deer: ecology and management. Stackpole Books, Harrisburg, Pennsylvania, USA.

HAMILTON, C. L., AND H. G. JEPSON. 1940. Stock water developments: wells, springs, and ponds. U.S. Department of Agriculture, Farmer's Bulletin 1859.

HANLEY, T. A., AND J. J. ROGERS. 1989. Estimating carrying capacity with simultaneous nutritional constraints. U.S. Department of Agriculture, Forest Service, Research Note PNW-RN-485.

HAYWARD, B., E. J. HESKE, AND C. W. PAINTER. 1997. Effects of livestock grazing on small mammals at a desert cienega. Journal of Wildlife Management 61:123–129.

HEADY, H. F. 1975. Rangeland management. McGraw-Hill Book Co., New York, USA.

HENNY, C. J., L. J. BLUS, E. J. KOLBE, AND R. E. FITZNER. 1985. Organophosphate insecticide (Famphur) topically applied to cattle kills magpies and hawks. Journal of Wildlife Management 49:648–658.

HERBICIDE HANDBOOK COMMITTEE. 1994. Herbicide handbook of the Weed Science Society of America. Seventh edition. Weed Science Society of America, Champaign, Illinois, USA.

———. 1998. Supplement to the herbicide handbook, seventh edition. Weed Science Society of America, Champaign, Illinois, USA.

HILL, S. D., AND V. C. BLEICH. 1999. Monitoring wildlife water sources using low Earth orbiting satellites (LEOS). Wildlife Society Bulletin 27:25–27.

HOBBS, N. T., AND R. A. SPOWART. 1984. Effects of prescribed fire on nutrition of mountain sheep and mule deer during winter and spring. Journal of Wildlife Management 48:551–560.

———, AND D. M. SWIFT. 1985. Estimates of habitat carrying capacity incorporating explicit nutritional constraints. Journal of Wildlife Management 49:814–822.

———, D. S. SCHIMEL, C. E. OWENSBY, AND D. S. OJIMA. 1991. Fire and grazing in the tallgrass prairie: contingent effects on nitrogen budgets. Ecology 72:1374–1382.

———, D. L. BAKER, J. E. ELLIS, D. M. SWIFT, AND R. A. GREEN. 1982. Energy- and nitrogen-based estimates of elk winter-range carrying capacity. Journal of Wildlife Management 46:12–21.

HOLECHEK, J. L. 1980. Livestock grazing impacts on rangeland ecosystems. Journal of Soil and Water Conservation 35:162–164.

———. 1981. Brush control impacts on rangeland wildlife. Journal of Soil and Water Conservation 36:265–269.

———. 1982. Managing rangelands for mule deer. Rangelands 4:25–28.

———, R. D. PIEPER, AND C. H. HERBEL. 1998. Range management: principles and practices. Third edition. Prentice Hall, Englewood Cliffs, New Jersey, USA.

HOOD, R. E., AND J. M. INGLIS. 1974. Behavioral responses of white-tailed deer to intensive ranching operations. Journal of Wildlife Management 38:488–498.

HOWARD, V. W., J. L. HOLECHEK, AND R. D. PIEPER. 1983. Roswell pronghorn study. New Mexico State University, Las Cruces, USA.

HOWARD, W. E., K. A. WAGNON, AND J. R. BENTLEY. 1959. Competition between ground squirrels and cattle for range forage. Journal of Range Management 12:110–115.

HUMPHREY, J. W., AND G. S. PATTERSON. 2000. Effects of late summer cattle grazing on the diversity of riparian pasture vegetation in an upland conifer forest. Journal of Applied Ecology 37:986–996.

JAIN, S., editor. 1976. Vernal pools: their ecology and conservation. Publication 9. Institute of Ecology, University of California, Davis, USA.

JENNINGS, M. R., AND M. P. HAYES. 1993. Decline of native ranids in the desert Southwest. Pages 183–211 in P. R. Brown and J. W. Wright, editors. Proceedings: herpetology of the North American deserts. Society of Southwestern Herpetologists, Special Publication Number 5.

JENSEN, S., AND W. S. PLATTS. 1987. Processes influencing riparian ecosystems. Proceedings of the Annual Meeting of the Society of Wetland Science 8:228–232.

JEPSON, R., R. G. TAYLOR, AND D. W. MCKENZIE. 1983. Rangeland fencing systems: state-of-the-art review. U.S. Department of Agriculture, Forest Service, Equipment Development Center, San Dimas, California, USA.

JOHNSON, M. K. 1982. Response of small mammals to livestock grazing in southcentral Idaho. Journal of Range Management 35:51–53.

JOHNSON, R. R., AND C. H. LOWE. 1985. On the development of riparian ecology. Pages 112–116 in R. R. Johnson, C. D. Ziebell, D. R. Patton, P. F. Ffolliott, and R. H. Hamre, technical coordinators. Riparian ecosystems and their management: reconciling conflicting uses. U.S. Department of Agriculture, Forest Service, General Technical Report RM-120.

———, P. S. BENNETT, AND L. T. HAIGHT. 1989. Southwestern woody riparian vegetation and succession: an evolutionary approach. Pages 135–139 in D. L. Abell, technical coordinator. Proceedings of the California riparian systems conference: protection, management, and restoration for the 1990's. U.S. Department of Agriculture, Forest Service, General Technical Report PSW-110.

JOHNSON, T., AND R. A. W. JACOBS. 1986. Gallinaceous guzzlers. U.S. Department of the Army, Corps of Engineers, Wildlife Resource Management Manual, Section 5.4.1. Technical Report EL-86–8.

JONES, A. 2000. Effects of cattle grazing on North American arid ecosystems: a quantitative review. Western North American Naturalist 60:155–164.

JONES, K. B. 1988. Comparison of herpetofaunas of a natural and altered riparian ecosystem. Pages 222–227 in R. C. Szaro, K. E. Severson, and D. R. Patton, editors. Management of amphibians, reptiles, and small mammals in North America. U.S. Department of Agriculture, Forest Service, General Technical Report RM-166.

JULANDER, O., AND D.E. JEFFERY. 1964. Deer, elk, and cattle range relations on summer range in Utah. Transactions of the North American Wildlife and Natural Resources Conference 29:404–414.

————, AND W. L. ROBINETTE. 1950. Deer and cattle range relationships on Oak Creek Range in Utah. Journal of Forestry 48:410–415.

KARSKY, R. 1988. Fences. U.S. Department of the Interior, Bureau of Land Management and U.S. Department of Agriculture, Forest Service, Technology and Development Program, Missoula, Montana, USA.

KAUFFMAN, J. B., AND W. C. KRUEGER. 1984. Livestock impacts on riparian ecosystems and streamside management implications…a review. Journal of Range Management 37:430–438.

KAZMAIER, R. T., E. C. HELLGREN, D. C. RUTHVEN III, AND D. R. SYNATZSKE. 2001. Effects of grazing on the demography and growth of the Texas tortoise. Conservation Biology 15:1091–1101.

KERR, R. M. 1979. Mule deer habitat guides. U.S. Department of the Interior, Bureau of Land Management, Technical Note 336.

KIE, J. G. 1988. Annual grassland. Pages 118–119 in K. E. Mayer, and W. F. Laudenslayer, Jr., editors. A guide to the wildlife habitats of California. California Department of Forestry, Sacramento, USA.

————. 1991. Wildlife and livestock grazing alternatives in the Sierra Nevada. Transactions of the Western Section of The Wildlife Society 27:17–29.

————, AND E. R. LOFT. 1990. Using livestock to manage wildlife habitat: some examples from California annual grassland and wet meadow communities. Pages 7–24 in K. E. Severson, technical coordinator. Can livestock be used as a tool to enhance wildlife habitat? U.S. Department of Agriculture, Forest Service, General Technical Report RM-194.

————, V. C. BLEICH, A. L. MEDINA, J. D. YOAKUM, AND J. W. THOMAS. 1994. Managing rangelands for wildlife. Pages 663–688 in T. A. Bookhout, editor. Research and management techniques for wildlife and habitats. Fifth edition. The Wildlife Society, Bethesda, Maryland, USA.

KINDSCHY, R. R., C. SUNDSTROM, AND J. D. YOAKUM. 1982. Wildlife habitats in managed rangelands—the Great Basin of southeastern Oregon. Pronghorn. U.S. Department of Agriculture, Forest Service, General Technical Report PNW-145.

KNIGHT, D. H. 2001. Summary: aspen decline in the west? Pages 441–446 in W. D. Shepperd, D. Binkley, D. L. Bartos, T. J. Stohlgren, and L. G. Eskew, compilers. Sustaining aspen in western landscapes. U.S. Department of Agriculture, Forest Service, RMRS-P-18.

KNOPF, F. L. 1988. Riparian wildlife habitats: more, worth less, and under invasion. Pages 20–22 in K. M. Mutz, D. J. Cooper, M. L. Scott, and L. K. Miller, technical coordinators. Restoration, creation and management of wetlands and riparian ecosystems in the American west. PIC Technology, Denver, Colorado, USA.

————, J. A. SEDGWICK, AND R. W. CANNON. 1988. Guild structure of a riparian avifauna relative to seasonal cattle grazing. Journal of Wildlife Management 52:280–290.

KOERTH, B. H. 1996. Chemical manipulation of plants. Pages 321–337 in P. R. Krausman, editor. Rangeland wildlife. The Society for Range Management, Denver, Colorado, USA.

KRAUSMAN, P. R., editor. 1996. Rangeland wildlife. The Society for Range Management, Denver, Colorado, USA.

KRUEGER, W. C., M. A. SANDERSON, J. B. CROPPER, M. MILLER-GOODMAN, C. E. KELLEY, R. D. PIEPER, P. L. SHAVER, AND M. L. TRLICA. 2002. Environmental impacts of livestock on U.S. grazing lands. Issue Paper 22. Council for Agricultural Science and Technology, Ames, Iowa, USA.

LARSEN, R. E., W. C. KRUEGER, M. R. GEORGE, M. R. BARRINGTON, J. C. BUCKHOUSE, AND D. A. JOHNSON. 1998. Livestock influences on riparian zones and fish habitat: literature classification. Journal of Range Management 51:661–664.

LAYCOCK, W. A. 1991. Stable states and thresholds of range condition on North American rangelands: a viewpoint. Journal of Range Management 44:427–433.

————. 1994. Implications of grazing vs. no grazing on today's rangelands. Pages 250–280 in M. Vavra, W. A. Laycock, and R. D. Pieper, editors. Ecological implications of livestock herbivory in the west. The Society for Range Management, Denver, Colorado, USA.

LEOPOLD, A. S., T. RINEY, R. MCCAIN, AND L. TEVIS, JR. 1951. The Jawbone deer herd. Game Bulletin 4. California Department of Fish and Game, Sacramento, USA.

LESICKA, L. M., AND J. J. HERVERT. 1995. Low maintenance water developments for arid environments: concepts, materials, and techniques.

Pages 52–57 in D. P. Young, Jr., R. Vinzant, and M. D. Strickland, editors. Wildlife water development. Water for Wildlife Foundation, Lander, Wyoming, USA.

LEWIS, M. D. 1973. Upland game guzzler evaluation: Lassen County. Federal Aid in Wildlife Restoration Job Progress Report, Project W-26-D-29-1. California Department of Fish and Game, Sacramento, USA.

LOFT, E. R., J. W. MENKE, J. G. KIE, AND R. C. BERTRAM. 1987. Influence of cattle stocking rate on the structural profile of deer hiding cover. Journal of Wildlife Management 51:655–664.

LONGHURST, W. M., R. E. HAFENFELD, AND G. E. CONNOLLY. 1982. Deer-livestock interrelationships in the western states. Pages 409–420 in J. M. Peek and P. D. Dalke, editors. Proceedings of the wildlife-livestock relationships symposium. University of Idaho, Moscow, USA.

————, E. O. GARTON, H. F. HEADY, AND G. E. CONNOLLY. 1976. The California deer decline and possibilities for restoration. California-Nevada Wildlife Transactions 23:74–103.

————, M. B. JONES, R. R. PARKS, L. W. NEUBAUER, AND M. W. CUMMINGS. 1962. Fences for controlling deer damage. Agricultural Experimental Station Circular 514. University of California, Davis, USA.

LOOMIS, J. B., E. R. LOFT, D. R. UPDIKE, AND J. G. KIE. 1991. Cattle-deer interactions in the Sierra Nevada: a bioeconomic approach. Journal of Range Management 44:395–399.

MACKIE, R. J. 1978. Impacts of livestock grazing on wild ungulates. Transactions of the North American Wildlife and Natural Resources Conference 43:462–476.

————. 1981. Interspecific relationships. Pages 487–501 in O. C. Wallmo, editor. Mule and black-tailed deer of North America. University of Nebraska Press, Lincoln, USA.

MAPSTON, R. D., AND R. S. ZOBELL. 1972. Antelope passes: their value and use. U.S. Department of the Interior, Bureau of Land Management, Technical Note D-360.

MARTINKA, C. J. 1967. Mortality of northern Montana pronghorns in a severe winter. Journal of Wildlife Management 31:159–164.

MASER, C., J. W. THOMAS, AND R. G. ANDERSON. 1984. Wildlife habitats in managed rangelands—the Great Basin of southeastern Oregon: the relationship of terrestrial vertebrates to plant communities and structural conditions. U.S. Department of Agriculture, Forest Service, General Technical Report PNW-172.

————, J. M. GEIST, D. M. CONCANNON, R. ANDERSON, AND B. LOVELL. 1979. Wildlife habitats in managed rangelands—the Great Basin of southeastern Oregon: geomorphic and edaphic habitats. U.S. Department of Agriculture, Forest Service, General Technical Report PNW-99.

MEGAHAN, W. F., AND P. N. KING. 1985. Identification of critical areas on forest lands for control of nonpoint sources of pollution. Environmental Management 9:7–18.

MENKE, J. W., editor. 1983. Proceedings of the workshop on livestock and wildlife-fisheries relationships in the Great Basin. Special Publication 3301. University of California, Berkeley, USA.

MENSCH, J. L. 1969. Desert bighorn (*Ovis canadensis nelsoni*) losses in a natural trap tank. California Fish and Game 55:237–238.

MESSNER, H. E., D. R. DIETZ, AND E. C. GARRETT. 1973. A modification of the slanting deer fence. Journal of Range Management 26:233–235.

MILLER, E. 1987. Effects of forest practices on relationships between riparian areas and aquatic ecosystems. Pages 40–47 in J. G. Dickson and O. E. Maughan, editors. Managing southern forests for wildlife and fish. U.S. Department of Agriculture, Forest Service, General Technical Report SO-65.

MOORE, A. W., AND E. H. REID. 1951. The Dalles pocket gopher and its influence on forage production of Oregon mountain meadows. U.S. Department of Agriculture Circular 884.

MOORE, W. H., AND W. S. TERRY. 1979. Short-duration grazing may improve wildlife habitat in southeastern pinelands. Proceedings of the Annual Conference of the Southeastern Association of Fish and Wildlife Agencies 33:279–287.

MORRIS, J. E., AND R. L. ELDERKIN. 1990. A heavy equipment tire guzzler. Pages 49–50 in G. K. Tsukamoto and S. J. Stiver, editors. Proceedings, wildlife water development symposium. Nevada Chapter of The Wildlife Society, U.S. Department of the Interior, Bureau of Land Management, and Nevada Department of Wildlife,

Reno, USA.

MYERS, L. E., AND G. W. FRASIER. 1974. Asphalt-fiberglass for precipitation catchments. Journal of Range Management 27:12–15.

MYERS, L. H. 1989. Grazing and riparian management in southwestern Montana. Pages 117–120 *in* R. E. Gresswell, B. A. Barton, and J. L. Kershner, technical coordinators. Practical approaches to riparian resource management: an educational workshop. U.S. Department of the Interior, Bureau of Land Management, Billings, Montana, USA.

NASS, R. D., AND J. THEADE. 1988. Electric fences for reducing sheep losses to predators. Journal of Range Management 41:251–252.

NATIONAL ACADEMY OF SCIENCES. 1974. More water for arid lands: promising techniques and research opportunities. A report to the Advisory Committee on Technology Innovation, Board on Science and Technology for International Development. Commission on International Relations, Washington, D.C., USA.

NEILL, W. M. 1990. Control of tamarisk at desert springs. Pages 121–126 *in* G. K. Tsukamoto and S. J. Stiver, editors. Proceedings, wildlife water development symposium. Nevada Chapter of The Wildlife Society, U.S. Department of the Interior, Bureau of Land Management, and Nevada Department of Wildlife, Reno, USA.

NELSON, J. R., AND D. G. BURNELL. 1975. Elk-cattle competition in central Washington. Pages 78–83 *in* Range multiple use management. Cooperative Extension Service, Washington State University, Pullman, Oregon State University, Corvallis, and University of Idaho, Moscow, USA.

NIEMI, G. J., AND J. R. PROBST. 1990. Wildlife and fire in the upper Midwest. Pages 32–47 *in* J. M. Sweeney, editor. Management of dynamic ecosystems. North Central Section, The Wildlife Society, West Lafayette, Indiana, USA.

OAKLEY, C. 1973. The effects of livestock fencing on antelope. Wyoming Wildlife 37(12):26–29.

OHMART, R. D. 1996. Historical and present impacts of livestock grazing on fish and wildlife resources in western riparian habitats. Pages 245–279 *in* P. R. Krausman, editor. Rangeland wildlife. The Society for Range Management, Denver, Colorado, USA.

PAIGE, C., AND S. A. RITTER. 1999. Birds in a sagebrush sea: managing sagebrush habitats for bird communities. Partners in Flight Western Working Group, Boise, Idaho, USA.

PARMENTER, R. R., AND J. A. MACMAHON. 1983. Factors determining the abundance and distribution of rodents in a shrub-steppe ecosystem: the role of shrubs. Oecologia 59:145–156.

PARRY, P. L. 1972. Development of permanent wildlife water supplies, Joshua Tree National Monument. Transactions of the Desert Bighorn Council 16:92–96.

PEEK, J. M., AND P. D. DALKE, editors. 1982. Proceedings of the wildlife-livestock relationships symposium. University of Idaho, Moscow, USA.

———, AND P. R. KRAUSMAN. 1996. Grazing and mule deer. Pages 183–192 *in* P. R. Krausman, editor. Rangeland wildlife. The Society for Range Management, Denver, Colorado, USA.

PIEPER, R. D., AND R. F. BECK. 1990. Range condition from an ecological perspective: modifications to recognize multiple use objectives. Journal of Range Management 43:550–552.

PLATTS, W. S. 1990. Managing fisheries and wildlife on rangelands grazed by livestock. White Horse Association, Smithfield, Utah, USA.

———, AND R. L. NELSON. 1989. Characteristics of riparian plant communities and streambanks with respect to grazing in northeastern Utah. Pages 73–81 *in* R. E. Gresswell, B. A. Barton, and J. L. Kershner, technical coordinators. Practical approaches to riparian resource management: an educational workshop. U.S. Department of the Interior, Bureau of Land Management, Billings, Montana, USA.

———, AND R. F. RALEIGH. 1984. Impacts of grazing on wetlands and riparian habitat. Pages 1105–1117 *in* Developing strategies for rangeland management: a report. National Research Council and National Academy of Science, Westview Press, Boulder, Colorado, USA.

RAMBO, J. L., AND S. H. FAETH. 1999. Effect of vertebrate grazing on plant and insect community structure. Conservation Biology 13:1047–1054.

RAUZI, F., M. L. FAIRBOURN, AND L. LANDERS. 1973. Water harvesting efficiencies of four soil surface treatments. Journal of Range Management 26:399–403.

REINER, R. J., AND P. J. URNESS. 1982. Effect of grazing horses managed as manipulators of big game winter range. Journal of Range Management 35:567–571.

REMINGTON, R., W. E. WERNER, K. R. RAUTENSTRAUCH, AND P. R. KRAUSMAN. 1984. Desert mule deer use of a new permanent water source. Pages 92–94 *in* P. R. Krausman and N. S. Smith, editors. Deer in the Southwest: a symposium. Arizona Cooperative Wildlife Research Unit and the School of Renewable Natural Resources, University of Arizona, Tucson, USA.

REYNOLDS, T. D., AND C. H. TROST. 1980. The response of native vertebrate populations to crested wheatgrass planting and grazing by sheep. Journal of Range Management 33:122–125.

RICE, W. E. 1990. Soil cement application for wildlife developments and range developments. Pages 3–10 *in* G. K. Tsukamoto and S. J. Stiver, editors. Proceedings, wildlife water development symposium. Nevada Chapter of The Wildlife Society, U.S. Department of the Interior, Bureau of Land Management, and Nevada Department of Wildlife, Reno, USA.

RIGGS, R. A., S. C. BUNTING, AND S. E. DANIELS. 1996. Prescribed fire. Pages 295–319 *in* P. R. Krausman, editor. Rangeland wildlife. The Society for Range Management, Denver, Colorado, USA.

ROBERTS, R. F. 1977. Big game guzzlers. Rangeman's Journal 4:80–82.

ROBBINS, C. T. 1973. The biological basis for the determination of carrying capacity. Dissertation. Cornell University, Ithaca, New York, USA.

RODGERS, K. J., P. F. FFOLLIOTT, AND D. R. PATTON. 1978. Home range and movement of five mule deer in a semidesert grass-shrub community. U.S. Department of Agriculture, Forest Service, Research Note RM-355.

ROSENSTOCK, S. S., W. B. BALLARD, AND J. C. DEVOS, JR. 1999. Viewpoint: benefits and impacts of wildlife water developments. Journal of Range Management 52:302–311.

———, J. J. HERVERT, V. C. BLEICH, AND P. R. KRAUSMAN. 2001. Muddying the water with poor science: a reply to Broyles and Cutler. Wildlife Society Bulletin 29:734–738.

RUSSELL, T. P. 1964. Antelope of New Mexico. Bulletin 12. New Mexico Department of Game and Fish, Santa Fe, USA.

SALWASSER, H. 1980. Pronghorn antelope population and habitat management in northwestern Great Basin environments. Interstate Antelope Conference Guidelines, Fresno, California, USA.

———, C. SCHONEWALD-COX, AND R. BAKER. 1987. The role of interagency cooperation in managing for viable populations. Pages 159–173 *in* M. E. Soulé, editor. Viable populations for conservation. University of Cambridge Press, New York, USA.

SAMPSON, A. W., AND H. E. MALMSTEN. 1926. Grazing periods and forage production on the national forests. U.S. Department of Agriculture, Bulletin 1405.

SANCHEZ, P. G. 1975. A tamarisk fact sheet. Transactions of the Desert Bighorn Council 19:12–14.

SANDERS, S. D., AND M. A. FLETT. 1989. Montane riparian habitat and willow flycatchers: threats to a sensitive environment and species. Pages 262–266 *in* D. L. Abell, technical coordinator. Proceedings of the California riparian systems conference: protection, management, and restoration for the 1990's. U.S. Department of Agriculture, Forest Service, General Technical Report PSW-110.

SCHMIDT, J. L., AND D. L. GILBERT, editors. 1978. Big game of North America: ecology and management. Stackpole Books, Harrisburg, Pennsylvania, USA.

SEDGWICK, J. A., AND F. L. KNOPF. 1987. Breeding bird response to cattle grazing of a cottonwood bottomland. Journal of Wildlife Management 51:230–237.

SEVERSON, K. E., technical coordinator. 1990. Can livestock be used as a tool to enhance wildlife habitat? U.S. Department of Agriculture, Forest Service, General Technical Report RM-194.

———, AND C. E. BOLDT. 1978. Cattle, wildlife and riparian habitats in the western Dakotas. Pages 91–102 *in* Regional rangeland symposium on management and use of northern plains rangeland. Dickinson State University, Dickinson, North Dakota, USA.

———, AND A. L. MEDINA. 1983. Deer and elk habitat management in the southwest. Journal of Range Management Monograph 2.

SIVILS, B. E., AND J. H. BROCK. 1981. Sand dams as a feasible water development for arid regions. Journal of Range Management 34:238–239.

SKOVLIN, J. M. 1984. Impacts of grazing on wetlands and riparian habitat: a review of our knowledge. Pages 1001–1103 *in* Developing strategies for rangeland management. National Research Council and National Academy of Science, Westview Press, Boulder, Colorado, USA.

SMITH, D. R., editor. 1975. Proceedings of the symposium on management of forest and range habitats for nongame birds. U.S. Department of Agriculture, Forest Service, General Technical Report WO-1.

SMITH, E. L. 1978. A critical evaluation of the range condition concept. Pages 226–267 *in* D. N. Hyder, editor. International Rangelands Congress. The Society for Range Management, Denver, Colorado, USA.

———. 1988. Successional concepts in relation to range condition assessment. Pages 113–133 *in* P. T. Tueller, editor. Vegetation science applications for rangeland analysis and management. Kluwer Academic Publishers, Dordrecht, The Netherlands.

SMITH, M. A., J. C. MALECHECK, AND K. O. FULGHAM. 1979. Forage selection by mule deer on winter range grazed by sheep in spring. Journal of Range Management 32:40–45.

SMITH, R. J. 1977. Conclusion. Pages 117–118 *in* J. E. Townsend and R. J. Smith, editors. Proceedings of a seminar on improving fish and wildlife benefits in range management. U.S. Department of the Interior, Fish and Wildlife Service, FSW/OBS-77/01.

SPILLETT, J. J., J. B. LOW, AND D. SILL. 1967. Livestock fences—How they influence pronghorn antelope movements. Bulletin 470. Utah Agriculture Experiment Station, Utah State University, Logan, USA.

STEDNICK, J. D. 1988. The influence of riparian/wetlands systems on surface water quality. Pages 17–19 *in* K. M. Mutz, D. J. Cooper, M. L. Scott, and L. K. Miller, technical coordinators. Restoration, creation and management of wetland and riparian ecosystems in the American West. PIC Technologies, Denver, Colorado, USA.

STEPHENSON, T. R., V. VAN BALLENBERGHE, AND J. M. PEEK. 1998. Response of moose forages to mechanical cutting on the Copper River Delta, Alaska. Alces 34:479–494.

STEVENSON, C. A. 1990. Identification and construction of slickrock water developments in southern Nevada by Nevada Department of Wildlife. Pages 25–35 *in* G. K. Tsukamoto and S. J. Stiver, editors. Proceedings, wildlife water development symposium. Nevada Chapter of The Wildlife Society, U.S. Department of the Interior, Bureau of Land Management, and Nevada Department of Wildlife, Reno, USA.

STODDART, L. A., A. D. SMITH, AND T. W. BOX. 1975. Range management. Third edition. McGraw-Hill Book Co., New York, USA.

STROMBERG, J. C., AND D. T. PATTEN. 1988. Total protection: one management option. Pages 61–62 *in* K. M. Mutz, D. J. Cooper, M. L. Scott, and L. K. Miller, technical coordinators. Restoration, creation and management of wetland and riparian ecosystems in the American West. PIC Technologies, Denver, Colorado, USA.

SVEJCAR, T. J. 1989. Animal performance and diet quality as influenced by burning in tallgrass prairie. Journal of Range Management 42:11–15.

SVEUM, C. M., W. D. EDGE, AND J. A. CRAWFORD. 1998. Nesting habitat selection by sage grouse in south-central Washington. Journal of Range Management 51:265–269.

SWANSON, F. J., S. V. GREGORY, J. R. SEDELL, AND A. G. CAMPBELL. 1982. Land-water interactions: the riparian zone. Pages 267–291 *in* R. L. Edmonds, editor. Analyses of coniferous forest ecosystems in the western United States. US/IBP Synthesis Series 14. Hutchinson Ross Publishing Company, Stroudsburg, Pennsylvania, USA.

SYKES, G. 1937. Sand tanks for water storage in desert regions. U.S. Department of Agriculture, Forest Service, Southwest Forest and Range Experiment Station, Research Note 9.

SZARO, R. C., S. C. BELFIT, J. K. AITKIN, AND J. N. RINNE. 1985. Impact of grazing on a riparian garter snake. Pages 359–363 *in* R. R. Johnson, C. D. Ziebell, D. R. Patton, P. F. Ffolliott, and R. H. Hamre, technical coordinators. Riparian ecosystems and their management: reconciling conflicting uses. U.S. Department of Agriculture, Forest Service, General Technical Report RM-120.

THOMAS, J. W., editor. 1979. Wildlife habitats in managed forests-The Blue Mountains of Oregon and Washington. U.S. Department of Agriculture, Forest Service, Agriculture Handbook 553.

———, AND D. E. TOWEILL, editors. 1982. Elk of North America: ecology and management. First edition. Stackpole Books, Harrisburg, Pennsylvania, USA.

———, C. MASER, AND J. E. RODIEK. 1979a. Riparian zones. Pages 40–47 *in* J. W. Thomas, editor. Wildlife habitats in managed forests-The Blue Mountains of Oregon and Washington. U.S. Department of Agriculture, Forest Service, Agriculture Handbook 553.

———, ———, AND ———. 1979b. Wildlife habitats in managed rangelands-The Great Basin of southeastern Oregon: riparian zones. U.S. Department of Agriculture, Forest Service, General Technical Report PNW-80.

———, H. C. BLACK, JR., R. J. SCHERZINGER, AND R. J. PEDERSEN. 1979c. Deer and elk. Pages 104–127 *in* J. W. Thomas, editor. Wildlife habitats in managed forests-The Blue Mountains of Oregon and Washington. U.S. Department of Agriculture, Forest Service, Agriculture Handbook 553.

THOMPSON, B. C. 1979. Evaluation of wire fences for coyote control. Journal of Range Management 32:457–461.

TOWNSEND, J. E., AND R. J. SMITH, editors. 1977. Proceedings of a seminar on improving fish and wildlife benefits in range management. U.S. Department of the Interior, Fish and Wildlife Service, FWS/OBS-77/01.

TSUKAMOTO, G. K., AND S. J. STIVER, editors. 1990. Proceedings, wildlife water development symposium. Nevada Chapter of The Wildlife Society, U.S. Department of the Interior, Bureau of Land Management, and Nevada Department of Wildlife, Reno, USA.

TURNER, G. T., R. M. HANSEN, V. H. REID, H. P. TIETJEN, AND A. L. WARD. 1973. Pocket gophers and Colorado mountain rangeland. Experimental Station Bulletin 554S. Colorado State University, Fort Collins, USA.

URNESS, P. J. 1976. Mule deer habitat changes resulting from livestock practices. Pages 21–35 *in* G. W. Workman and J. B. Low, editors. Mule deer decline in the west: a symposium. Utah State University, Logan, USA.

———. 1982. Livestock as tools for managing big game range in the Intermountain West. Pages 20–31 *in* J. M. Peek and P. D. Dalke, editors. Proceedings of the wildlife-livestock relationships symposium. University of Idaho, Moscow, USA.

———. 1990. Livestock as manipulators of mule deer winter habitats in northern Utah. Pages 25–40 *in* K. E. Severson, technical coordinator. Can livestock be used as a tool to enhance wildlife habitat? U.S. Department of Agriculture, Forest Service, General Technical Report RM-194.

U.S. DEPARTMENT OF AGRICULTURE. 2001. Sierra Nevada forest plan amendment: final Environmental Impact Statement and Record of Decision. U.S. Department of Agriculture, Forest Service, Pacific Southwest Region, Vallejo, California, USA.

U.S. DEPARTMENT OF INTERIOR. 1964. Water development: range improvements in Nevada for wildlife, livestock, and human use. U.S. Department of the Interior, Bureau of Land Management, Reno, Nevada, USA.

———. 1966. Polyethylene liner for pit reservoir including trough and fencing. U.S. Department of the Interior, Bureau of Land Management, Technical Note P712C, Portland Service Center, Oregon, USA.

———. 1985. Fencing. U.S. Department of the Interior, Bureau of Land Management, Manual Handbook H-1741-1. Washington, D.C., USA.

———. 1992. Guidelines for domestic sheep management in bighorn sheep habitat. U.S. Department of the Interior, Bureau of Land Management, Instruction Memorandum 92–264.

———, AND CALIFORNIA DEPARTMENT OF FISH AND GAME. 2002. Recovery plan for the Sierra Nevada bighorn sheep, California. U.S. Department of the Interior, Fish and Wildlife Service, Portland, Oregon, USA.

U.S. GENERAL ACCOUNTING OFFICE. 1988. Public rangelands: some riparian areas restored, but widespread improvement will be slow: report to congressional questions. U.S. General Accounting Office, Resource and Community Economic Development Division, Report GAP/RCED-88–105.

VALENTINE, B. E., T. A. ROBERTS, S. P. BOLAND, AND A. P. WOODMAN. 1988. Livestock management and productivity of willow flycatchers in the central Sierra Nevada. Transactions of the Western Section of The Wildlife Society 24:105–114.

VALONE, T. J., M. MEYER, J. H. BROWN, AND R. M. CHEW. 2002. Timescale of perennial grass recovery in desertified arid grasslands following livestock removal. Conservation Biology 16:995–1002.

VAN SOEST, P. J. 1994. Nutritional ecology of the ruminant. Second edition. Cornell University Press, Ithaca, New York, USA.

WAGNER, F. H. 1978. Livestock grazing and the livestock industry. Pages 121–145 *in* H. P. Brokaw, editor. Wildlife and America: contribution to an understanding of American wildlife and its conservation. Council on Environmental Quality. U.S. Government Printing Office, Washington, D.C., USA.

WALLMO, O. C., editor. 1981. Mule and black-tailed deer of North America. University of Nebraska Press, Lincoln, USA.

WARNER, R. E., AND K. M. HENDRIX. 1984. California riparian systems: ecology, conservation, and productive management. University of California Press, Berkeley, USA.

WAUER, R. H. 1977. Significance of Rio Grande riparian systems upon the avifauna. Pages 165–174 *in* R. R. Johnson and D. A. Jones, technical coordinators. Importance, preservation, and management of riparian habitat: a symposium. U.S. Department of Agriculture, Forest Service, General Technical Report RM-43.

WEAVER, R. A. 1973. California's bighorn management plan. Transactions of the Desert Bighorn Council 17:22–42.

———, F. VERNOY, AND B. CRAIG. 1959. Game water development on the desert. California Fish and Game 45:333–342.

WEHAUSEN, J. D., V. C. BLEICH, AND R. A. WEAVER. 1987. Mountain sheep in California: a historical perspective on 108 years of full protection. Transactions of the Western Section of The Wildlife Society 23:65–74.

WELCHERT, W. T., AND B. N. FREEMAN. 1973. 'Horizontal' wells. Journal of Range Management 26:253–256.

WERNER, W. E. 1984. Bighorn sheep water development in southwestern Arizona. Transactions of the Desert Bighorn Council 28:12–13.

WEST, N. E., AND T. P. YORKS. 2002. Vegetation responses following wildfire on grazed and ungrazed sagebrush semi-desert. Journal of Range Management 55:171–181.

WESTOBY, M., B. WALKER, AND I. NOY-MEIR. 1989. Opportunistic management for rangelands not at equilibrium. Journal of Range Management 42:266–274.

WILLMS, W., A. MCLEAN, R. TUCKER, AND R. RITCEY. 1979. Interactions between mule deer and cattle on big sagebrush range in British Columbia. Journal of Range Management 32:299–304.

WILSON, L. O. 1977. Guidelines and recommendations for design and modification of livestock watering developments to facilitate safe use by wildlife. U.S. Department of the Interior, Bureau of Land Management, Technical Note 305.

WOOD, J. E. 1969. Rodent populations and their impact on desert rangelands. Bulletin 555. Agricultural Experiment Station, New Mexico State University, Las Cruces, USA.

WRIGHT, H. A., AND A. W. BAILEY. 1982. Fire ecology—United States and southern Canada. John Wiley and Sons, New York, USA.

YOAKUM, J. D. 1980. Habitat management guidelines for the American pronghorn antelope. U.S. Department of the Interior, Bureau of Land Management, Technical Note 347.

———, W. P. DASMANN, H. R. SANDERSON, C. M. NIXON, AND H. S. CRAWFORD. 1980. Habitat improvement techniques. Pages 329–403 *in* S. D. Schemnitz, editor. Wildlife management techniques manual. Fourth edition. The Wildlife Society, Washington, D.C., USA.

YOUNG, JR., D. P., R. VINZANT, AND M. D. STRICKLAND, editors. 1995. Wildlife water development. Water for Wildlife Foundation, Lander, Wyoming, USA.

34

MANAGING FORESTLANDS FOR WILDLIFE

Richard H. Yahner, Carolyn G. Mahan, and Amanda D. Rodewald

INTRODUCTION
Forest Definition and Types

A forest can be defined as a group of trees in a prescribed area, but what represents a forest can vary markedly, depending on geography and human perceptions. For instance, an urban woodlot in a metropolitan area, an old-growth stand in the Pacific Northwest, a midwestern shelterbelt, an eastern state forest, or a southern pine (*Pinus*) plantation can each be viewed as forests by people from different regions of the United States. Moreover, although these forests vary in characteristics, such as extent of naturalness or size, each has aesthetic, wildlife habitat, economic, recreational, educational, and other values (Yahner 2000).

Forestland in the lower 48 states can be broadly divided into coniferous forest in western states and deciduous forest in eastern states, separated by a nonforested landscape of extensive farmland, grassland, and remnant prairie in midwestern states (U.S. Department of Agriculture 1968, Patton 1992, Yahner 2000). The western coniferous forest includes 3 regions: Pacific Coast and Interior (dominated by Douglas-fir [*Pseudotsuga menziesii*], ponderosa pine

[*Pinus ponderosa*], and redwood [*Sequoia sempervirens*]), Northern Rocky Mountains (lodgepole pine [*P. contorta*], Douglas-fir, larch [*Larix* spp.), and Southern Rocky Mountains (pinyon [*Pinus* spp.]-juniper [*Juniperus* spp.], ponderosa pine, fir [*Abies* spp.]-spruce [*Picea* spp.]). The eastern deciduous forest also has 3 regions: Lake States and Northeast (aspen [*Populus* spp.]-birch [*Betula* spp.], maple [*Acer* spp.]-beech [*Fagus* spp.]-birch], Central Mountains and Plateaus (oak [*Quercus* spp.]-hickory [*Carya* spp.], oak-pine, and Southern States (loblolly pine [*P. taeda*]-shortleaf pine [*P. echinata*], longleaf pine [*P. palustris*]-slash pine [*P. elliottii*]).

History of Forests

The pre-European forest once covered about two-thirds of North America (Cutter et al. 1991). In the lower 48 states during the 17th century, approximately 50% of the landscape was forested, with 75% of this total in the eastern states (Harrington 1991, MacCleery 1992). In this pre-European era, disturbances in the forest were those resulting from natural events (e.g., wildfires and windthrows) or created by Native Americans (e.g., prescribed fires and clearings) for agriculture, fuelwood harvesting, wildlife habitat, and village establishment (e.g., Day 1953, Spurr and Barnes 1980, Delcourt and Delcourt 1997).

Subsequent to European settlement in the early 17th century and continuing into the 21st century, the original forest in the United States was dramatically reduced by human activities (reviewed by Yahner 2000). Early on, timber was harvested extensively in eastern states and exported to other countries for shipbuilding and sugar-producing industries (Perlin 1989, MacCleery 1992). Wood was used extensively in the United States for building farm fences, fuelwood to heat homes, and fuel for iron production and railroad engines (Spurr and Barnes 1980, MacCleery 1992). The distribution and abundance of certain tree species, such as eastern hemlock (*Tsuga canadensis*) and American chestnut (*Castanea dentata*), were markedly reduced by the tanning industry and disease, respectively (Spurr and Barnes 1980, Duffield 1990, Patton 1990, Yahner 2000). In addition, an estimated 47 million ha of forest in the eastern United States was cleared for agriculture by the mid-19th century (Clawson 1979, Williams 1989). As a result of historical land uses, the 400 million ha of forestland present in the lower 48 states in the 1500s were systematically reduced to about 188 million ha (53% decline) by the early 20th century (Harrington 1991).

Early-successional forest reverted to second-growth forest with regeneration, fire suppression, and abandonment of many farms in the initial decades of the 20th century (Cutter et al. 1991, Pimm and Askins 1995, Trani et al. 2001). In some instances, the composition of the forest changed, as red maple (*Acer rubrum*) replaced oak stands in some areas of the East (Abrams 1992). These changes (habitat loss or change in species composition) in the forest landscape in the lower 48 states had pronounced negative effects on distribution and abundance of some forest wildlife populations, some of which were well-documented (e.g., those of American beaver [*Castor canadensis*] and white-tailed deer [*Odocoileus virginianus*]) or strongly suspected of occurring despite a lack of data on historical population trends (e.g., those of forest and early-successional bird species) (Perlin 1989, MacCleery 1992, Litvaitis 1993, Yahner 2000, Trani et al. 2001).

Increased urbanization and suburban sprawl continue to influence the amount of forest in the United States (e.g., Robbins et al. 1989). Only about 3–5% of the original old-growth forest remains in the lower 48 states, with most confined to the Pacific Northwest (Miller 1992). As a consequence, most of today's forest is second-growth, with 54 and 81% in the Mid-Atlantic and New England States, respectively (Trani et al. 2001). Moreover, relative low amounts of early-successional forest remains in some regions of the eastern United States (e.g., 15–16% of total forestland).

Forests of Today and Their Management

Today's forestlands can be classified into 1 of 3 categories from a timber-management perspective: commercial forestland, reserved timberland, or noncommercial forestland (Hagenstein 1990, Cutter et al. 1991). Commercial forestland in the lower 48 states (66% of the total forestland) is the most common category, but its extent differs from east (95% of the total forestland) to west (<50%) (Hagenstein 1990). Private-forest landowners own the majority of commercial forestland (57%) in the United States; public agencies and forest industries control a smaller amount (28 and 15%, respectively) (Martin and Bliss 1990, Cutter et al. 1991). Over time, the amount of commercial forestland in the United States has increased 5% from the mid-1940s to the mid-1970s, whereas the amount of noncommercial forestland has increased 102% from the 1930s through the 1970s (Williams 1992).

Forestlands must be managed for other values besides timber production, including their value as wildlife habitat (e.g., Gullion 1990, Yahner 2000). Forested habitats are used by 80–90% of the vertebrate species in North America (Flather and Hoekstra 1989), making the successful management of forestlands one of the most important challenges facing wildlife biologists and natural resource managers. However, the effective management of forestlands for wildlife is contingent on a number of factors, such as land ownership and public opinion. Ownership of forestland, which totals approximately 296 million ha in the United States, has remained relatively stable since at least the middle of the 20th century (Society of American Foresters 1981, Hagenstein 1990). Private landowners control nearly 46% of the total forestland; the remaining forest (41%) consists of public lands (federal, state, and county owned) or forest-industry lands (13%) (Society of American Foresters 1981).

Forestland ownership patterns vary substantially among regions, with private ownership predominating in the eastern United States and federal ownership (e.g., U.S. Forest Service, Bureau of Land Management) in the western United States (Mannan et al. 1996, Yahner 2000). Approximately, 84 million ha of the forestland is managed by the U.S. Forest Service (USFS), 190 million ha (most of this land is rangeland) by the Bureau of Land Management, 32 million ha by the National Park Service, and 49 million ha by other governmental agencies (U.S. Fish and Wildlife Service, U.S. Army Corps of Engineers, and U.S. Department of Energy) (Bureau of Land Management 2001). Individual state governments and nongovernmental organizations, such as The Nature Conservancy and a variety of land trusts, own public-accessible forests. Because there is no adequate system to coordinate large-scale, comprehensive management activities on privately owned forests, successful management of these forests for the benefit of wildlife biodiversity can pose challenges from sociopolitical perspectives.

Management of forestlands requires an understanding of changing land uses plus support from the public. For example, with a reduction in area affected by agriculture and timber harvesting in recent decades, slightly more timber is being grown today than is being harvested (U.S. Department of Agriculture 1982, Cutter et al. 1991). The public may view this increase in total forestland, e.g., second-growth forest, as wise use of a resource, thereby leading to conflicting opinions regarding some forest-management practices (Askins 2001).

LEGISLATION RELATED TO FOREST MANAGEMENT

With the passage of the Forest Reserve Act in 1891, executive authority created the first forest reserves in

Wyoming and Colorado in response to unregulated and exploitative logging (Bolen and Robinson 1995). The Act of 1897, also known as the Organic Act, formerly established the National Forest Service, which originally was under the jurisdiction of the Department of Interior but was transferred to the U.S. Department of Agriculture. Under the leadership of Gifford Pinchot and President Theodore Roosevelt at the turn of the 20th century, 4 million ha of western forestlands were transferred into federal ownership (Miller 1992). The passage of the Weeks Law in 1911 permitted states to cooperate with Federal assistance to acquire land for forest and water conservation. Throughout the early 20th century, management of federally- and state-owned forests focused on sustained yields of timber but changed to a multiple-use approach after World War II (Bolen and Robinson 1995).

The Multiple Use and Sustained Yield Act of 1960 and subsequent amendments mandated that national forests be managed for outdoor recreation, range, timber, watershed, and wildlife and fish purposes. This act marked the first time the federal government formally acknowledged the importance of national forests for wildlife conservation. Passage of the Wilderness Act in 1964 further recognized the importance of national forestlands for uses other than timber production. Currently, wilderness designation applies to approximately 2% of all federally owned lands (Bolen and Robinson 1995).

In 1969, the federal government passed the National Environmental Policy Act (NEPA) that required federal agencies to consult with each other and systematically review and evaluate activities occurring on federally owned lands (Gilbert and Dodds 1992). Specifically, NEPA requires a detailed environmental impact statement (EIS) involving the effects of proposed activities on environment and natural resources, including wildlife (Truett et al. 2005).

With the passage of the Forest and Rangeland Renewable Resources Planning Act and the Forest and Rangeland Renewable Resources Research Act in 1974 and 1978, respectively, the federal government began the coordination of multiple-use and sustained-yield opportunities between federal and private lands. These acts called for assessment, comprehensive inventories, coordinated research, and development of land-management plans to meet specific management objectives for conservation of natural resources, including wildlife. The Sikes Act of 1974 more specifically promoted planning, development, maintenance, and coordination of wildlife conservation and rehabilitation on public lands by federal and state agencies (Mannan et al. 1996).

The National Forest Management Act of 1976 formalized governmental sale of timber on federal lands and required public comment and an EIS. Implementation of this act required that forest management maintain viable populations of existing native vertebrate species. This act also established the Salvage Timber Fund, which encouraged removal of insect-infested, dead, damaged, or downed timber for purposes of stand improvement and fire suppression. A portion of the purchase of salvaged timber was designated to fund road construction and maintenance necessary for timber harvesting and other multiple-use purposes. The Emergency Salvage Timber Act of 1995 permitted expedited reviews of requests to salvage timber to further decrease risk of fire in national forests.

In recent years, however, salvage timber sales have come under increased scrutiny, criticism, and controversy. For example, in 2002, a federal court denied a salvage timber purchase in Montana's Bitterroot National Forest because of opposition by environmental organizations (Sierra Club 2002). The controversy stems from lack of evidence that removal of salvage timber reduces fire risk. Furthermore, road building associated with salvage timber operations may cause environmental degradation of streams, and equipment necessary to remove salvaged timber may impede forest regeneration by causing compressed soils and erosion.

In 1978, 2 acts were passed that promoted and enhanced forest management of private lands for conservation of natural resources. These were the Renewable Resources Extension Act, which funded research and educational assistance directed at private-forest landowners, and the Cooperative Forestry Assistance Act, which provided cooperative forestry assistance for private landowners interested in managing their lands for timber, wildlife, and other renewable resources. The Cooperative Forestry Assistance Act specifically mentioned threatened and endangered species as resources in need of protection and management.

The Forest Resources Conservation and Shortage Relief Act of 1990 also identified threatened and endangered species as important resources. Under this act, the federal government set aside millions of hectares of otherwise harvestable timber in national forests for the sole purpose of conservation of natural resources pursuant to the objectives of the Endangered Species Act (1973) and the National Forest Management Act (1976). In addition, the Forest Resources Conservation and Shortage Relief Act restricted exports of unprocessed timber from federal lands. This act has been met with much controversy, especially in western states where logging was prohibited on millions of hectares of national forestlands.

Another controversial policy was signed into effect in 1999 when President William J. Clinton directed the USFS to protect roadless areas in national forests (Strittholt and DellaSala 2001). Under this directive, the USFS released a proposed EIS that included a rule-making process on roadless areas, prompting over one million public responses both for and against protecting roadless areas. Although road construction is permitted and often encouraged in national forests under the Forest Roads and Trails Act of 1964, it is controversial as research indicates that roads contribute to forest fragmentation, spread of exotic species, and restriction of wildlife movements (Andrews 1990, Forman 2000). A recent study of the importance of roadless areas in biodiversity conservation was conducted in the Klamath-Siskiyou ecoregion of the United States; this study indicated that roadless areas contained important ecological elements, including at-risk species, key watersheds for aquatic biodiversity, and landscape connectivity (Strittholt and DellaSala 2001).

FOREST AND WILDLIFE SUCCESSION

Successful forest management is directly linked with the concept of forest succession of both plants and animals and is critical to understanding distribution and abundance patterns of forest biota (Yahner 2000) (Fig. 1). Plant succession may be classified as primary or secondary (Spurr and Barnes 1980, Aber 1990). Primary succession occurs after a catastrophic disturbance, such as a volcanic eruption on Mount St. Helens in 1980 that left areas of bare earth and ash (Frenzen 1992). Secondary succession proceeds from the plant community that remains after a less severe disturbance, such as that created by fire or timber harvest.

Shade-intolerant species of plants (e.g., aspen and grasses) predominate in early-successional habitats, which are replaced over time with shade-tolerant, longer-lived and more competitive plant species (e.g., sugar maple [*Acer saccharum*] and hemlock [*Tsuga* spp.]) (Spurr and Barnes 1980, Patton 1992). As plant succession changes composition and structure of a forest stand, the associated animal community also changes (Yahner 2000). For instance, bird species characteristic of early-successional habitat, e.g., common yellowthroat (*Geothlypis trichas*) and chestnut-sided warbler (*Dendroica pensylvanica*), are replaced by species adapted to more mature forests, e.g., red-eyed vireo (*Vireo olivaceus*) and ovenbird (*Seiurus aurocapillus*) (Probst et al. 1992, Yahner 1997, King et al. 2001).

Because a forested landscape is dynamic and subject to both natural and human-induced perturbations, the major challenge for wildlife biologists and land managers is to provide the necessary successional stages for disturbance-dependent species while balancing the needs of other species that rely on relatively undisturbed mature forests (Thompson and DeGraaf 2001). Early-successional stages resulting from recurring disturbances, such as fire, timber harvest, and storms, must be an integral component of the ecology a forested landscape (The Wildlife Society 1993, Franklin 1997, Trani et al. 2001). Absence or scarcity of early-successional stages in some areas contributes to regional declines in many species of wildlife, such as a variety of songbirds (Askins 1993, 2001; Brawn et al. 2001), American woodcock (*Philohela minor*) (McAuley and Clugston 1998), and New England cottontail (*Sylvilagus transitionalis*) (Litvaitis 1993, 2001).

The wildlife profession is beginning to appreciate that ecological disturbances are fundamental to conservation of forest wildlife (e.g., Askins 2001, Brawn et al. 2001). For instance, forest birds comprise 60–89% of the breeding bird species in the eastern deciduous forest (Yahner 2000), and those adapted to early-successional stands more likely show dramatic population declines compared to those typ-

ical of more mature forest stands (Askins 1993, Yahner 1995, Brawn et al. 2001, Hunter et al. 2001). Hence, conservation efforts in forested landscapes need to maintain a variety of stands in different stages of plant succession with variable disturbance frequency to enhance diversity (Anglestam 1998, Brawn et al. 2001, Hunter et al. 2001, Trani et al. 2001). Two major anthropogenic disturbances or management tools that can help wildlife biologists and forest managers create a mosaic of forest stands in various successional stages are fire and silviculture (Yahner 2000, Brawn et al. 2001).

FIRE AND WILDLIFE RESPONSE

Wildfires have been a major natural anthropogenic factor affecting forests well before European settlement, but fire-suppression efforts subsequent to the 19th century have decreased number and size of fires and increased intervals between wildfires (Oliver and Larson 1996, Yahner 2000). Historically, wildfires probably occurred every 50–100 years in some areas of eastern North America but now occur every 100–400 years (Lorimer 1990*b*, Cutter et al. 1991).

Fires are important to the successful regeneration of species, like aspen and oak, (Schier 1975, Lorimer 1990*a*) (Fig. 2). Some fire-adapted tree species (e.g., *Quercus*, *Pinus*) often have thick bark or serotinous cones, and fires create favorable seedbeds for their regeneration (Lorimer 1985); conversely, fires act to control species that compete with fire-adapted species (Van Lear and Waldrop 1989). Lack of fires may contribute to decline of oak in some regions and thereby result in greater regeneration of other species (e.g., maple), which have relatively lower resistance to fire (Abrams 1992, Abrams and Ruffner 1995).

Prescribed fire has been a controversial but useful tool in managing vegetation in certain ecosystems (Jacobson et al. 2001), such as serpentine barrens in eastern North America (Arabas 1997). They also have been deliberately set and managed by foresters as a means of removing excess woody debris after a timber harvest or preparing a seedbed prior to tree planting (Lorimer 1990*a*). Prescribed fire can be used to prepare a site for planting trees or enhance natural regeneration (Mannan et al. 1996). Moreover, prescribed fires have been traditionally used to manage habitat for a variety of wildlife species, such as northern bobwhite (*Colinus virginianus*) (Stoddard 1931), ruffed grouse (*Bonasa umbellus*) (Gullion 1972),

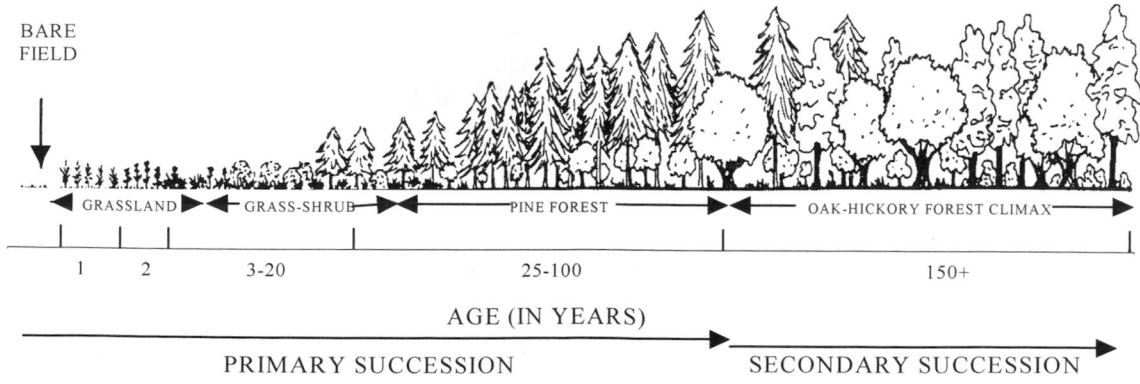

Fig. 1. Plant community succession in a hypothetical forest stand (from Mannan et al. 1996:692).

Fig. 2. A low-intensity forest fire in a northern pin oak (*Pinus palustris*) stand in northern Wisconsin (photograph by M. D. Abrams, School of Forest Resources, Pennsylvania State University; from Yahner 2000:80).

Kirtland's warbler (*Dendroica kirtlandii*) (Probst and Weinrich 1993), white-tailed deer, and elk (*Cervus elaphus*) (Masters 1991).

The role of prescribed fires in restoring or maintaining biodiversity of songbird communities in coniferous and boreal forests of the western United States and southern Canada, oak savannas of the midwestern United States, and pine savannas of the southeastern United States has been reviewed extensively by Brawn et al. (2001). For instance, the abundance of 15 bird species increased appreciably in western coniferous forests that were recently (within 1–3 years) burned (Hutto 1995). Early-successional bird species, e.g., field sparrow (*Spizella pusilla*), and woodpeckers were quite abundant in midwestern oak forests altered by fire; these burned forests were characterized by variable densities of understory vegetation, high densities of snags, and fewer trees compared to unburned oak forests (Davis et al. 2000). Habitat management using fires for a species of concern, e.g., the red-cockaded woodpecker (*Picoides borealis*), occupying southern pine forests can have direct benefits to other bird species adapted to early-successional habitats (Krementz and Christie 1999). In contrast, fires can have negative impacts on canopy feeding birds, e.g., red-eyed vireo (Davis et al. 2000).

Alteration of vegetative structure of forests by fires also can have indirect effects on other biotic communities, such as herpetofauna in southeastern forests (Russell et al. 1999). For instance, certain amphibian and reptilian species in Florida pine forests benefited by the mosaic of habitats created by frequent fires in the landscape (Campbell and Christman 1982, Mushinsky 1985). The availability of browse as food for white-tailed deer and elk can be increased by prescribed burning at regular (3 year) intervals (Masters 1991). These studies are representative of those showing that fire can have profound effects on biodiversity of biotic communities in forested habitats (Brawn et al. 2001). Hence, natural resource and wildlife managers need a better understanding of the impacts of fire as a management tool for wildlife communities and ecosystems (Russell et al. 1999). These professionals also have the challenge of informing the public about the historical role of fires in shaping structure and composition of past and current forests and the potential role of fire as a management tool.

CHEMICAL TREATMENTS

In addition to prescribed fire, chemicals can be used for site preparation prior to tree planting or to enhance natural regeneration (Gullion 1990, Mannan et al. 1996). Although controversial, herbicide applications have little or no direct toxic effect on wildlife, but the negative effects of pesticides on wildlife are well documented (Ratcliffe 1967). Herbicide application in combination with certain mechanical treatments on wooded rights-of-ways, for example, provides ideal conditions for wildlife associated with early-successional habitats (e.g., Bramble et al. 1999, Yahner et al. 2002). However, reductions in abundance of several bird species have been observed after herbicides were applied to clearcut forest stands (Savidge 1978, Morrison and Meslow 1984, Santillo et al. 1989).

FOREST MANAGEMENT AND WILDLIFE RESPONSE

Forest management consists of planting, growing, and tending a stand of trees as well as the economics associated with growing trees (Society of American Foresters 1981). Forest management can be divided into 2 general systems: uneven-aged and even-aged (Society of American Foresters 1981, Lorimer 1990*b*) (Fig. 3).

Uneven-aged Vs. Even-aged Management

Uneven-aged management retains trees of different age via selective cutting of single or small groups of trees at frequent (e.g., 5–10 years) intervals (Yahner 2000, Thompson and DeGraaf 2001). Selective cutting involves the removal of either individual trees to promote growth of preferred trees or small groups (<0.1 ha) of trees to enhance growth of shade-intolerant species (Leak and Filip 1977, Mannan et al. 1996). Because stands treated with uneven-aged techniques retain many overstory trees, shade-tolerant tree species, like maple and beech, regenerate best in these stands (Society of American Foresters 1981). Uneven-aged management may be a good strategy on small parcels of forest if landowners want to realize both timber and wildlife benefits. In contrast, even-aged management is the infrequent removal of all trees of a desired age at the same time to create regenerating stands often ranging in size from 0.5 to 20 ha (Hunter 1990, Lorimer 1990*b*, Yahner 2000, Thompson and DeGraaf 2001). Examples are clear-cuts (all trees removed), seed tree cuts (a few trees are left standing to be sources of

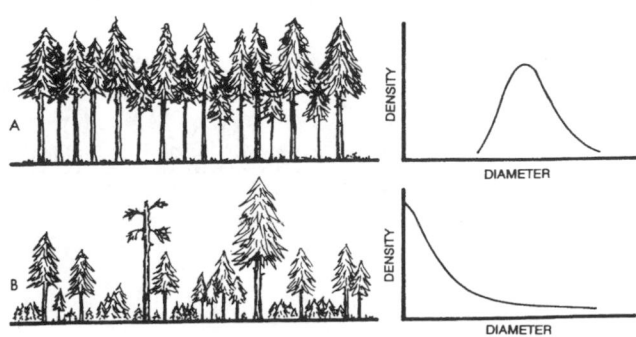

Fig. 3. Distribution of tree sizes in an even-aged forest stand (A) and an uneven-aged forest stand (from Mannan et al. 1996:694).

seeds for regeneration), and shelterwood cuts (more trees are left to provide shelter to regenerating trees). These methods work best when trying to regenerate trees that are not shade tolerant, such as oak. Choosing not to harvest also can be a good option in some situations, as when managing for late-successional wildlife species.

Even-aged and uneven-aged management approaches affect wildlife differentially by creating either early- or late-successional stands. From a wildlife perspective, the "best" approach depends on availability of nearby habitat, sensitive wildlife species in the area, and management goals. Clear-cuts will attract species, such as eastern cottontail (*Sylvilagus floridanus*) and chestnut-sided warbler, which use shrubs and saplings but will not be regularly used by species that require mature forests. Harvesting methods that retain large numbers of overstory trees provide suitable habitat for a variety of mid- to late-successional forest animals and retain much of the original plant and animal community.

Selective cutting is generally an acceptable method of forest management for landowners who wish to obtain income from timber sales without dramatically changing the structure of plant and wildlife communities. For instance, the creation of small (<0.4 ha) openings in north temperate deciduous forests had little effect on incidences of predation or parasitism of avian nests (Robinson and Robinson 2001). Similarly, selective cutting had no impact on survival or densities of adult gray (*Sciurus carolinensis*) or fox squirrel (*S. niger*) populations (Nixon et al. 1980). However, if large oak and hickory trees are selectively cut, it potentially can be detrimental to squirrels and other wildlife species that rely on mast for food (Yahner 2000). Compared to even-aged management, single- or group-tree selection can provide favorable, short-term habitat for a variety of forest bird species, such as white-breasted nuthatch (*Sitta carolinensis*), red-eyed vireo, hooded warbler (*Wilsonia citrina*), and ovenbird (Crawford et al. 1981, Annand and Thompson 1997, Rodewald and Smith 1998).

Thinning

Thinning is the selective removal of trees in advance of a scheduled, extensive harvest (Patton 1992). As many as 10–50% of the trees in a stand may be removed, thereby increasing growth rate of the remaining trees and resulting in a stand with relatively evenly-spaced trees (Crawford and Titterington 1979). This type of removal is termed a commercial thinning if trees are removed as timber or a salvage cut if unusable trees (e.g., no commercial value because of damage by insects, fire, etc.) are removed. Thinning can benefit certain species adapted to more open forested areas, e.g., hooded warblers (Crawford et al. 1981, Carey and Wilson 2001). Conversely, retention of large dying trees can have benefits to wildlife that use these substrates as nesting and foraging sites (e.g., Yahner 1987, Stribling et al. 1990), such as pileated woodpecker (*Dryocopus pileatus*) (McClelland and McClelland 1999). Selectively removing or thinning only the highest quality trees from a stand (sometimes termed high-grading) also can have detrimental effects on flora and fauna as well as on future timber production from the stand.

EVEN-AGED REGENERATION METHODS
Clear-cutting Method

Clear-cutting is a method of regenerating an even-aged forest stand in which nearly all trees in a prescribed area are harvested and seedlings become established to produce a stand with trees of similar age and size (Society of American Foresters 1981). This has been the most common method of even-aged forest regeneration, often accounting for about two-thirds of the timber harvested in the United States in the past (Gullion 1990, Miller 1992). The term clear-cut refers to stands during the time between clear-cutting and the formation of a closed-canopy sapling forest (mean stem diameter >2.5 cm). Clear-cuts provide quality early-successional wildlife habitat that generally persists for 5–20 years following cutting, depending on site quality and growth rate of seedlings. Yet despite the widespread use of clear-cutting, it has been controversial, especially as applied to relatively large stands (>100 ha) on steep slopes and adjacent to highways, which results in soil erosion and negative public reaction (Harlow et al. 1997).

The value of clear-cuts to wildlife is species-specific and can vary with size and age of the stands (reviewed by Harlow et al. 1997, Yahner 2000, Thompson and DeGraaf 2001). For instance, small (e.g., <10 ha) clear-cuts are habitat for gray catbird (*Dumetella carolinensis*), ruffed grouse, snowshoe hare (*Lepus americanus*), and white-tailed deer (Scott and Yahner 1989, Hughes and Fahey 1991, Yahner 1997). Larger clear-cuts provide habitat for populations of other early-successional species, e.g., field sparrow, yellow-breasted chat (*Icteria virens*) (Crawford et al. 1981) but are not used by species requiring older forests, e.g., ovenbird, red-cockaded woodpecker (Thompson et al. 1992, Irwin and Wigley 1993). Some studies have shown that species richness of breeding birds is greater in larger than smaller clear-cuts (Rudnicky and Hunter 1993*b*, Yohn 2002, but see Krementz and Christie 2000).

Younger (e.g., <5 years since harvest) clear-cuts generally have lower numbers of vertebrate species than older clear-cuts (e.g., Yahner 1988*b*, 1993). A major factor affecting suitability of younger clear-cuts for wildlife is the absence of key features, such as understory vegetation, snags, overstory trees, and certain types of food resources (Yahner 2000). For example, in the first 2 years after clear-cutting, aspen and mixed-oak clear-cuts in Pennsylvania were virtually devoid of bird species, including early-successional species, because of a lack of understory vegetation for nesting and foraging (Yahner 1993). Reduced understory vegetation and leaf-litter moisture in relatively young clear-cuts result in lower abundance of other vertebrates, e.g., terrestrial salamanders, compared to abundance in mature forests (Ash 1997, Rodewald and Yahner 1999, Grialou et al. 2000, Yahner et al. 2001). Gray squirrels are typically absent from clear-cuts because of the lack of overstory mast-producing trees (Nixon et al. 1980). The absence of snags in clear-cuts reduces the suitability of these areas for cavity-nesting species, e.g., woodpeckers or small mammals (Yahner 1988*b*, Stribling et al. 1990, Renken and Wiggers 1993, Shackelford and Conner 1997). Certain species rely on snags as perch sites while hunting in clear-cuts (e.g., red-tailed hawk [*Buteo jamaicensis*]). Use of perch sites by birds can be an important means of seed dispersal by the excretion of seeds while perched on these substrates (McClanahan and Wolfe 1993).

Populations of some wildlife species, like black bear (*Ursus americanus*), white-tailed deer, moose (*Alces alces*), ruffed grouse, and American woodcock, and assemblages of species (e.g., shrubland bird communities) require early-successional stages of forest development, such as those created by clear-cutting, in conjunction with features provided by proximal forest stands of differing ages, to meet their circannual resource needs (Gullion 1976, 1990; Liviaitis 2001; McDonald et al. 1994; Dessecker and McAuley 2001; Hunter et al. 2001). This necessitates a mosaic of different-aged stands in the landscape (Fig. 4). Other species, like snowshoe hare and New England cottontail, require early-successional habitats spaced relatively close to one another (e.g., <0.5 km) to sustain populations in the long term (Scott and Yahner 1989, Liviaitis 1993).

The traditional method of clear-cutting has been modified by other silvicultural methods that retain a certain number of trees in a forest stand after harvest (Society of American Foresters 1981, Lorimer 1990*b*, Yahner 2000). Retention of trees in harvested stands increases aesthetics and often improves their value to wildlife adapted to early-successional habitats (Thompson and DeGraaf 2001).

Seed-tree Method

The seed-tree method is another even-aged regeneration technique that removes the old stand in one cutting, except for a small number of seed trees (5–10 trees/ha) left singly or in small groups, and seed trees are then harvested once new trees become established in the stand (Society of American Foresters 1981, Smith et al. 1997). This method has been used extensively in management of southern pine stands. Trees retained by the seed-tree method can provide cavities for nesting birds, such as eastern bluebird (*Sialia sialis*) (Crawford et al. 1981). Somewhat similar to the seed-tree method, retention of 15–20 trees scattered within small (1 ha), even-aged oak stands in Pennsylvania creates perch sites for bird species, like cedar waxwing (*Bombycilla cedorum*) and Baltimore oriole (*Icterus galbula*) (Yahner 1993, 1997). Clusters of about 15 residual trees in even-aged aspen stands in Minnesota are used extensively by ovenbird, black-throated green warbler (*Dendroica virens*), and other forest species (Merrill et al. 1998).

Fig. 4. An aerial photo of a mosaic of clear-cuts in the Allegheny National Forest, Pennsylvania, USA (photograph by J. T. Kimmel, School of Forest Resources, Pennsylvania State University; from Yahner 2000:89).

In addition to consideration of the density of residual trees to be retained in even-aged stands, wildlife biologists and forest managers also need to consider size of residual trees (Hunter and Bond 2001). As an example, at least 5 trees/ha of Douglas-fir or redwood with a dbh of at least 91 or 122 cm, respectively, have been recommended for retention in even-aged stands of the Pacific Northwest.

Shelterwood Method

In contrast to other methods of even-aged forest management, the shelterwood method involves a series (3) of cuts spanning about 10 years (Lorimer 1990*b*). Roughly 30–50% of the trees are harvested in the first cut to permit light penetration and increase vigor of seedlings and seed production in the remaining trees; many of the trees removed may be diseased (Society of American Foresters 1981, Patton 1992). After seedlings become established, another 25% of the unharvested trees are removed followed by a final cut that removes all unharvested trees, allowing seedlings to grow to maturity and creating an even-aged stand. Depending on the wildlife species, the shelterwood method may have contrasting effects on small mammal populations (e.g., Sullivan et al. 1999). For instance, populations of white-footed mice (*Peromyscus leucopus*) may remain the same, whereas those of southern red-backed voles (*Clethrionomys gapperi*) can increase immediately after treatment of stands by the shelterwood method (Sullivan et al. 1999).

ALTERNATIVES TO CLEAR-CUTTING METHOD

Two-age Method

A recent alternative to clear-cutting is the two-age method or deferment cutting (Smith et al. 1989, Miller et al. 1997). This method involves retention of 30–49 trees/ha; after 40–80 years of sufficient regeneration, residual trees are then harvested. Bird species nesting or foraging in low-lying vegetation are more abundant in two-age cuts after the first cutting cycle compared to those in clear-cuts in West Virginia (Duguay 1997, Duguay et al. 2001). Salamander abundance was similar in two-age cuts and clear-cuts but was lower than in mature forests (Duguay and Wood 2002).

Variable-retention Systems

Variable-retention systems retain trees, snags, or small patches of trees within areas harvested; these systems are increasingly popular in North America (Franklin et al. 1997). These systems attempt to achieve harvest goals while enhancing local biodiversity. An excellent example of such a system, termed even-aged reproduction stands with guidelines, was adopted in Pennsylvania (Boardman and Yahner 1999). At least 12 trees and shrubs/ha are retained in these stands to provide vertical stratification of vegetation, enhance floral diversity, and increase aesthetics; often more than 100 trees/ha are retained in these stands (Rodewald and Yahner 2000). Trees retained were used by birds of mature forests (e.g., eastern wood-pewee [*Contopus virens*] and scarlet tanager [*Piranga olivacea*], while the stands simultaneously provided breeding habitat for a variety of early-successional birds (Boardman and Yahner 1999, Talbott 1999, Rodewald and Yahner 2000,

Talbott and Yahner 2003). These stands are most beneficial in enhancing avian diversity when between 10 and 40 ha in size (Boardman and Yahner 1999). However, because abundances of forest-breeding birds decreased and brown-headed cowbirds (*Molothrus ater*) increased with size of the harvest, managers should consider limiting size to <20 ha (Rodewald and Yahner 2000). Despite the presence of residual trees, harvests in these areas fail to provide habitat for woodland salamanders (Rodewald and Yahner 1999).

RECOMMENDATIONS FOR WILDLIFE-SENSITIVE HARVESTING

Although it is difficult to generalize about the effects of forest management on wildlife, several practices can improve the suitability of harvested stands for forest wildlife.

Protection of Unique and Important Habitat Features

Tree removal proximal to unique habitat features, such as rocky outcrops, small ponds, temporary pools (vernal pools), and seeps, can destroy valuable wildlife habitat. Rocky outcrops in forested landscapes of the Northeast, for instance, are critical habitat for conservation of the threatened Allegheny woodrat (*Neotoma magister*) (Balcom and Yahner 1996). Vernal ponds, in particular are required by many forest amphibians and should be protected from harvesting operations whenever possible.

Retention of Unharvested Buffers Along Forest Streams

Riparian zones are important to a rich diversity of flora and fauna (Naiman and Dechamps 1997). Tree removal near streams not only destroys habitat for terrestrial wildlife but also harms aquatic organisms by increasing water temperature and sedimentation (Brown and Krygier 1967, Society of American Foresters 1981, Mitsch and Gosselink 1993). Depending on slope and other site characteristics, buffer zones of 30–75 m should be unharvested near streams and other riparian zones to reduce impacts of tree removal on aquatic fauna and flora (Brazier and Brown 1973, Society of American Foresters 1981). Logging roads and skid trails should also be kept away from water, and number of stream crossings for roads should be minimized.

Retention of Overstory Trees in Harvested Areas

Live overstory trees, retained both individually and in small groups of different species and sizes, provide perching, nesting, and foraging opportunities for wildlife (Duguay 1997, Merrill et al. 1998, Boardman and Yahner 1999, Rodewald and Yahner 2000). Special efforts should be made to retain trees that produce mast (e.g., fruits, nuts, and seeds), such as that of beech, oak, cherry (*Prunus* spp.), and dogwood (*Cornus* spp.), which provide important food resources to many species of forest wildlife. Small groups of conifers (like spruce and hemlock) also can provide important cover from snow and cold temperatures during winter.

Retention of Decaying and Dead Trees (Snags)

Tree cavities provide shelter, dens, nests, and foraging sites for many wildlife species (Fig. 5). At least 85 bird species in North America use tree cavities (Scott et al. 1977). Thus, retention of standing trees and limbs of all sizes is a good management practice; in particular, large snags and large decadent trees (e.g., live trees with dead or broken tops) are valuable for cavity-nesting and cavity-roosting species that cannot use smaller cavities (Thomas et al. 1979*b*, Bonar 2000, Aubry and Raley 2002). Some trees should be as large as 46 cm dbh for larger cavity-dependent species, such as wood duck (*Aix sponsa*) and pileated woodpecker. Some damaged young trees should be reserved to provide future cavity trees. Trees with fungal conks, dead branches, old scars, and soft or decaying wood (especially heartrot) are good indicators of cavity potential. Estimates for densities of trees with cavity potential to be retained have been recommended by Thomas et al. (1979*b*).

Retention of Woody Debris

Many animals, especially salamanders and small mammals, use logs, slash, and other woody debris for cover, dens, nests, foraging sites, and even as places for courtship displays (e.g., Maser et al. 1979, Yahner 1986, Petranka et al. 1993, but see Rodewald and Yahner 1999). If possible leave large logs, which persist longer than small logs. At

Fig. 5. Snag containing a cavity for wildlife (photograph by R. H. Yahner; from Yahner 2000:92).

least 5 large logs (>12 cm diam, >2 m long) per hectare should be retained as wildlife habitat (Maser et al. 1979). Woody debris on the forest floor also mitigates soil erosion, increases moisture on the forest floor, and stores energy and nutrients (Spurr and Barnes 1980). Woody debris often impedes movements by deer, thereby improving opportunities for seedlings to regenerate in managed stands (Grisez 1960).

Creation of Feathered and Meandering Edges

An edge is the interface between 2 types of landscape elements, such as the juncture of a forest stand and a crop field (e.g., Yahner 2000). Edges can be abrupt, as with the interface of a forest and a farm field, or feathered, as with a gradual transition along a gradient from forest to old field to grassland (Fig. 6). Some wildlife, such as salamanders and certain forest birds, avoid using abrupt edges, and those that use them may experience high rates of predation and brood parasitism (Gates and Gysel 1978, Brittingham and Temple 1983, Wilcove 1985, Hoover et al. 1995). Edges are often associated with higher amounts of nest predation, fewer food resources for some species, warmer air and soil temperatures, drier conditions, and more wind than interior forest (Yahner 1988*a*). Abrupt and highly contrasting edges generally have more negative "edge effects" than gradual, low-contrast edges (Suarez et al. 1997, Yahner et al. 2001). Gradual, low-contrast edges can be made by allowing shrubs, saplings, and some overstory trees to remain along the harvest boundary.

Maximizing Forest Interior

Forest interior is unbroken forest at least 100 m from edges and usually is positively related to size of a patch of forest, assuming the patch is more circular than linear (i.e., the larger the patch size, the greater amount of forest interior) (Forman and Godron 1986). Some wildlife species occur only in forests containing adequate amounts of interior forest (e.g., Forman et al. 1976, Ambuel and Temple 1983, Blake and Karr 1987, Robbins et al. 1989). Large tracts of mature timber, for instance, are recommended as roosting habitat for forest bats, such as red bat (*Lasiurus borealis*) (Hutchinson and Lacki 2000), and for many Neotropical migratory birds, such as wood thrush (*Hylocichla mustelina*), ovenbird, and scarlet tanager (Robbins et al. 1989). The amount of interior forest can be

Fig. 6. Forest clear-cutting creates edges for wildlife (photograph by R. H. Yahner; from Yahner 2000:124).

increased by leaving a large patch of uncut forest. If harvesting is necessary in the large patch, it should be confined to the borders of a forest stand instead of within the patch, thereby fragmenting the intact forest.

Retention of Old-growth Stands

In the 1500s, about 400 million ha of forestland spanned the 48 contiguous states (Harrington 1991). Since European settlement, only about 3–5% of the original or old-growth forest remains today. Old-growth forest differs from managed, younger stands in structure, composition, and function (Thomas et al. 1988). Old-growth forests have larger trees, snags, and logs, the canopy is multi-layered, and the understory is relatively open compared to younger stands. Hence, today's managed forests cannot be expected to contain the same plant and animal communities as pristine, old-growth forests (Yahner 2000). Examples of wildlife species characteristic of old-growth forests are northern spotted owl (*Strix occidentalis caurina*), red-cockaded woodpecker, and fisher (*Martes pennanti*) (Thomas et al. 1988, Mannan et al. 1996).

Because old-growth forest is virtually gone from the United States, contiguous blocks of forest of at least 1,000 ha should be maintained for species sensitive to human-induced disturbances (e.g., Robbins 1979). Moreover, state and federal agencies, which serve as stewards of public lands, should ensure that a proportion of forestlands (e.g., 10%) be set aside in large tracts (>100 ha) for establishment of old-growth forests of the future (Yahner 2000).

FOREST FRAGMENTATION AND LANDSCAPE CONSIDERATIONS

Habitat fragmentation is one of the greatest threats to ecological communities throughout the world (Wilcox and Murphy 1985). Fragmentation is associated with several changes to a landscape, and each change can strongly affect wildlife communities (Andrén 1994). Fragmentation, such as that created by timber harvesting or urbanization, can result in habitat loss of varying permanency in a forested landscape (McIntyre and Barrett 1992, Yahner 1996). Because of the direct impact of habitat loss on native flora and fauna, fragmentation has been implicated in population declines of more species than any other human-induced influence (e.g., Terbough 1989).

As amount of forest cover declines in the landscape, the remaining forest patches generally are reduced in size and become increasingly isolated (Harris and Silva-Lopez 1992, Knight and Landres 2002). For this reason, area and isolation add to the effects of habitat loss and exacerbate negative impacts on forest-dependent, area-sensitive species in fragmented landscapes (Andrén 1994). As landscapes are fragmented, the presence of new land uses (like agriculture or urban development) increases, and these land uses can vary markedly in their effects on adjacent habitats (Friesen et al. 1995; Rodewald and Yahner 2001*a*, 2001*b*). In some respects, the extent of fragmentation falls along a continuum, with small perforations of disturbance in a relatively continuous matrix of habitat occurring at low levels of fragmentation and greater shrinkage of remaining habitat patches within an extensive disturbed matrix at high levels of fragmentation (Forman 1995) (Fig. 7).

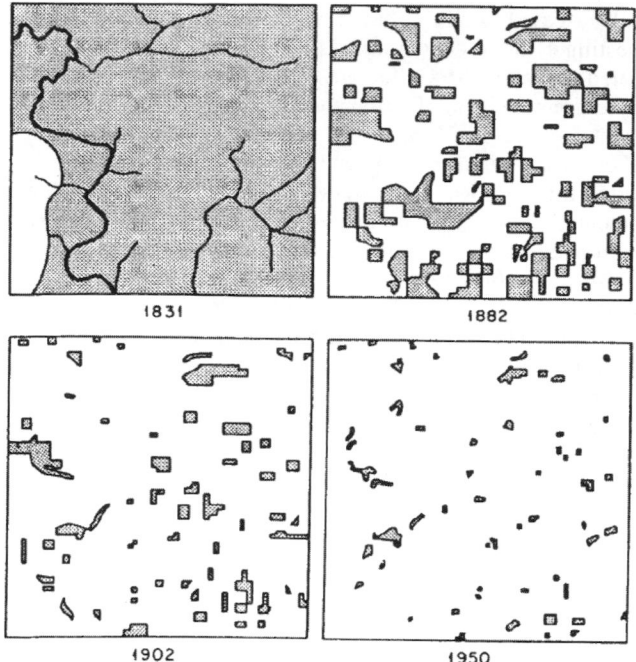

Fig. 7. Fragmentation of forests (shaded areas) in Cadiz Township, Wisconsin, from 1831 to 1950 (from Mannan et al. 1996:705).

Fig. 8. Brood parasitism by a brown-headed cowbird (2 large speckled eggs) in a chestnut-sided warbler nest (photograph by R. H. Yahner; from Yahner 2000:151).

Fragmentation and Edge Effects

Fragmentation is often related to edge because small forest patches have greater edge-to-interior ratios than large patches (Forman and Godron 1986). Edges can affect ecosystems and within-patch ecological functions through abiotic effects (e.g., alter fluxes of radiation, wind, and water), direct biological effects (e.g., promote plant growth near edges), and indirect biological effects (e.g., alter species interactions) (reviewed by Yahner 1988a and Murcia 1995). In most ornithological studies, edge effects have been largely attributed to indirect biological effects, such as higher rates of nest predation and brood parasitism (Fig. 8) nearer than farther from edges (Gates and Gysel 1978, Brittingham and Temple 1983, Wilcove 1985, Hoover et al. 1995, Brand and George 2000; but see Ratti and Reese 1988, Rudnicky and Hunter 1993a, Yahner et al. 1993, Chalfoun et al. 2002). Edges in conjunction with other landscape features, such as proximity to agricultural fields and streams, however, are preferred habitats for some wildlife species, like raccoon (*Procyon lotor*) (Dijak and Thompson 2000).

Abrupt or permanent edges are generally thought to have more severe effects than gradual edges (Suarez et al. 1997), but this is controversial based on studies conducted in forested landscapes (Ratti and Reese 1988, Yahner et al. 1989, Chalfoun et al. 2002). Studies of nest predation along edges created by silviculture have detected greater rates near edges (Small and Hunter 1988; King et al. 1996, 1998; Tittler and Hannon 2000), whereas others have failed to detect differences (Yahner and Wright 1985, Ratti and Reese 1988, Rudnicky and Hunter 1993a, Hanski et al. 1996, Morse and Robinson 1999, Yahner et al. 2001, Rodewald 2002). Most (88%) studies of edge-related nest predation in forested landscapes have failed to detect edge effects (Andrén 1995). These conflicting results may be partly explained by the role of landscape characteristics, such as amount of fragmentation (Donovan et al. 1997, Hartley and Hunter 1998) and type of land uses within fragmented landscapes (Askins 1995, Bayne and Hobson 1997, Rodewald 2002). Elevated predation rates near edges were detected less often in highly forested than in fragmented landscapes (Hartley and Hunter 1998).

Area and Isolation Effects

The importance of patch area and isolation (distance to other patches) to faunal communities became widely recognized with the development of island-biogeography theory (MacArthur and Wilson 1967), which predicted that species richness increased with increasing island size and decreasing distance to the mainland (source habitat). In the decades since, numerous studies have demonstrated that certain populations may be more abundant or communities may be more diverse (particularly vertebrates) in larger patches of habitat than in smaller ones and in less-isolated patches than more isolated ones (e.g., Forman et al. 1976, Ambuel and Temple 1983, Blake and Karr 1987, Robbins et al. 1989, Keller 2001, Crooks 2002; but see Fleishman and MacNally 2002) (Fig. 9).

Despite problems with applying island-biogeography theory to terrestrial habitat patches (e.g., habitat patches are usually surrounded by a matrix that allows some dispersal), these species-area patterns have been detected across many forest ecosystems, especially in the eastern United States.

Wildlife biologists and forest managers recognize that some taxonomic groups, e.g., many forest bird species, are area-sensitive and require large tracts of habitat to live and reproduce successfully (Whitcomb et al. 1981, Robbins et al. 1989). Good examples are Neotropical migratory birds like scarlet tanager, ovenbird, and wood thrush.

Several factors have been proposed to explain area sensitivity in forest birds. Small habitat patches may not be sufficiently large enough to accommodate a territory or provide sufficient resources for individuals (Whitcomb et al. 1981). Also, reduced habitat size can decrease probability of occurrence of large carnivores with appreciable home ranges, such as mountain lion (*Puma concolor*) and

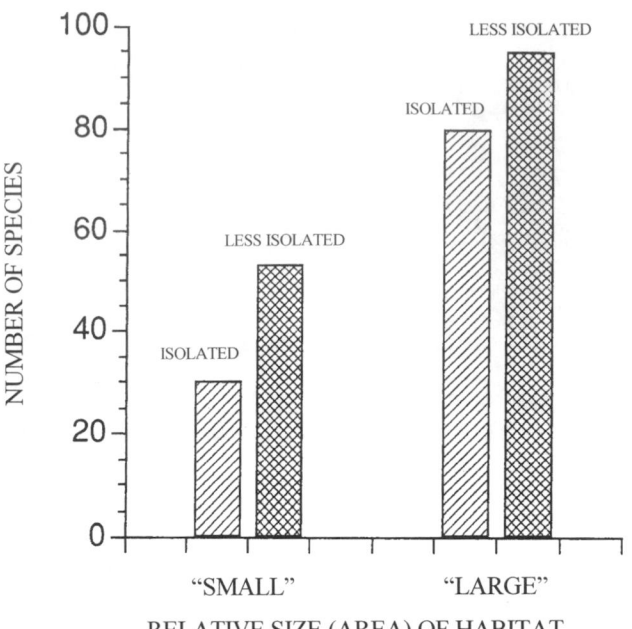

Fig. 9. A hypothetical species-area relationship in isolated versus less isolated habitats (from Yahner 2000:106).

bobcat (*Lynx rufus*), whereas the exotic domestic cat (*Felis catus*) is more apt to occur in smaller fragments than larger ones (Crooks 2002). A reduction in patch size may also reduce habitat heterogeneity (Freemark and Merriam 1986), making a species less likely to find specific habitat requirements in smaller patches. A frequently invoked explanation for area sensitivity of some bird species is that rates of nest predation and brood parasitism are much higher in small patches or fragmented landscapes than in large patches or in forested landscapes (Lynch and Whigham 1984, Wilcove 1985, Wilcove and Robinson 1990, Hoover et al. 1995, Van Horn et al. 1995). In this respect, small fragments may be viewed as "ecological traps" (Gates and Gysel 1978), where birds nest in areas that are unlikely to allow successful breeding.

The extent of isolation among patches is an important landscape consideration because it can affect the ability of organisms to successfully disperse among habitat patches (Lynch and Whigham 1984). For example, movements of eastern chipmunk (*Tamias striatus*) and eastern cottontail are restricted in intensively-farmed landscapes that lack woody corridors connecting woodlots (Swihart and Yahner 1982). As a habitat patch becomes more isolated with increased fragmentation, the less likely it will contain large carnivores, e.g., mountain lion and bobcat (Crooks 2002). Furthermore, severity of isolation effects is not necessarily a function of only juxtaposition of patches but also a function of dispersal capabilities of organisms and characteristics of the landscape matrix (area between habitat patches through which the organism disperses). A matrix containing residential developments may be more difficult and risky to traverse during dispersal by a wide-ranging, yearling bobcat compared to a matrix comprised of agricultural pasture and cropland.

Maintenance or creation of habitat corridors connecting patches is frequently proposed as a solution to mitigate isolation effects on wildlife (Noss 1987, Simberloff and Cox

1987, Vos et al. 2002) because, in theory, corridors should facilitate movement among patches (MacClintock et al. 1977, Harris and Gallagher 1989, Vos et al. 2002) and enhance gene flow (Britten and Baker 2002). For instance, American robin (*Turdus migratorius*) and brown thrasher (*Toxostoma rufum*) in agricultural landscapes moved more often between wooded patches connected by wooded corridors than between isolated wooded habitats (Haas 1995). A wooded corridor also may provide additional suitable habitat for home ranges of some wildlife species (Hodges and Krementz 1996, Yahner 1997), depending on width and landscape context (Beier and Loe 1992). However, few empirical data are available to evaluate usefulness of corridors in fragmented landscapes (Harrison 1992, Morrison et al. 1992, Vos et al. 2002). Some ecologists contend that corridors may negatively influence some wildlife by facilitating spread of disease, exotic species, or disturbances (Noss 1987, Simberloff and Cox 1987, Hess 1994). At present, though, potential benefits of corridors seem to outweigh possible negative impacts.

Landscape Matrices and Land Uses

A landscape matrix is the "background" within which habitat patches and corridors are embedded. The matrix can alter movements of individuals, serve as sources of species and individuals invading patches and corridors, and can affect severity of edge, area, and isolation effects on wildlife (Donovan et al. 1997, Hartley and Hunter 1998, Gascon et al. 1999). Both amount and type of disturbance or land use within the matrix can affect flora and fauna within adjacent habitat patches and corridors.

Land uses within landscapes can vary structurally and temporally and, hence, differ in their impact on associated wildlife (McIntyre and Barrett 1992; Yahner 1996; Rodewald and Yahner 2001a, 2001b; Rodewald 2002). For example, conversion of forest to residential developments or agriculture generally can be regarded as permanent loss to wildlife, whereas silvicultural treatments may change the forest from one developmental stage to another. Furthermore, silvicultural disturbances tend to be more structurally heterogeneous than agricultural areas and may provide more habitat structure than other types of disturbances.

Residential or urban development adjacent to woodlots, in particular, can have pronounced effects on wildlife (Friesen et al. 1995). The presence of residential homes within 100 m of woodlots, for example, decreased diversity and abundance of breeding birds, irrespective of woodlot size. Similarly, riparian forests within urban landscapes had fewer Neotropical migratory birds (e.g., Acadian flycatcher [*Empidonax virescens*]), and higher rates of nest predation than riparian forests in rural landscapes (A. D. Rodewald, unpublished data).

The characteristics of a given matrix can have profound influences on wildlife movements. Small clear-cuts (0.5–22.3 ha) in northern hardwood forests, ranging from 1 to 13 years since cutting, can impede movement of southern flying squirrels (*Glaucomys volans*) (Bendel and Gates 1987, Healy and Brooks 1988). Forests within a landscape matrix disturbed by small amounts of agricultural land uses (e.g., pasture, cropland) had fewer forest-dependent and long-distance migratory bird species but higher abundance of nest predators than forests within landscapes disturbed by similar amounts of silvicultural land uses (e.g., even-aged forest stands) (Rodewald and Yahner 2001*b*). Although other studies have shown that fragmented agricultural landscapes have greater abundances of generalist predators than silvicultural landscapes (Andrén 1992, Bayne and Hobson 1997, Pedlar et al. 1997, Saab 1999; but see Tewksbury et al. 1998), this pattern had not been established in forested landscapes (reviewed by Chalfoun et al. 2002).

Management Recommendations for Forest-reserve Design

Biologists and land managers increasingly recognize that successful conservation of forest-dependent wildlife requires management at both landscape and broader landscape scales (e.g., Yahner 2000). However, identifying the appropriate number, size, and spatial arrangement of habitat patches for a focal species or group is not easy. An optimal landscape design could vary substantially across landscapes and regions, especially when characteristics of matrices differ. In spite of apparent problems, there are several general strategies that can be used by land managers (e.g., Diamond 1975, Franklin and Forman 1987).

First, characteristics of the desired forest reserve need to be given careful consideration. Managers should retain or plan for large reserves of contiguous forest, but how large is enough (reviewed by Yahner 2000)? Minimum-area requirements for area-sensitive bird species range from several to thousands of hectares (Fig. 10) and can vary widely among species, landscapes (i.e., forested vs. fragmented), and regions (e.g., Northeast vs. Midwest). Moreover, reserves should be sufficiently large to accommodate natural disturbances (e.g., fires, floods) and still provide forest habitat for wildlife (i.e., minimum dynamic area, Pickett and Thompson 1978).

Shape of the reserve should maximize the ratio of forest interior to forest edge (i.e., square or circular in configuration) to provide more habitats for species that avoid or are negatively influenced by edges. In addition, both amount of fragmentation and type of adjacent land uses can influence minimum-area requirements. For example, minimum area required to provide high suitability for scarlet tanagers in forested landscapes (>70% forest cover in a 1,000-ha block) was 26 ha compared to 245 ha in fragmented landscapes (<40% forest) (Rosenberg et al. 1999). Thus, suitability of a reserve for wildlife may decline as the surrounding landscape becomes more fragmented.

Second, distances among habitat patches should be minimized whenever possible to facilitate movement of individual animals among patches. A challenge for wildlife biologists in the future will be to identify the appropriate distance between contiguous habitats to ensure long-term viability of metapopulations (Fig. 11), such as those of New England cottontail (Litvaitis 1993). This information is contingent on a solid understanding of the dispersal behavior and mobility of the focal species or group. Unfortunately, these data are often lacking or difficult to obtain (e.g., Yahner and Mahan 2002).

Third, when possible, efforts should be made to improve the suitability of the landscape matrix, thereby increasing probability of survival and/or successful dispersal of animals moving through the matrix. This might be accomplished in a variety of ways, e.g., from preserving "stepping stones" of forest habitat (e.g., small woodlots) to creating forested corridors, and from adopting wildlife-sensitive agricultural practices to preserving "open spaces" within the fragmented landscape. Whenever possible, the amount of urban or residential development should be limited adjacent to nature reserves and other forest habitats. Currently, appropriate distances between nature reserves and developed areas or other disturbances are poorly understood (Ambrose and Bratton 1990). Edge effects in general may extend up to 600 m from an edge into the interior of an adjacent forest stand (Wilcove et al. 1986).

Fourth, edges should be irregular rather than straight, and contrast should be reduced between habitats at edges (e.g., Thomas et al. 1979*a*). Low-contrast, gradual edges can be made by allowing shrubs, saplings, and some overstory trees to remain along the harvest or development boundary. Edges can be feathered by retaining more trees closer to the forest interior and gradually fewer trees closer to the nonforested area.

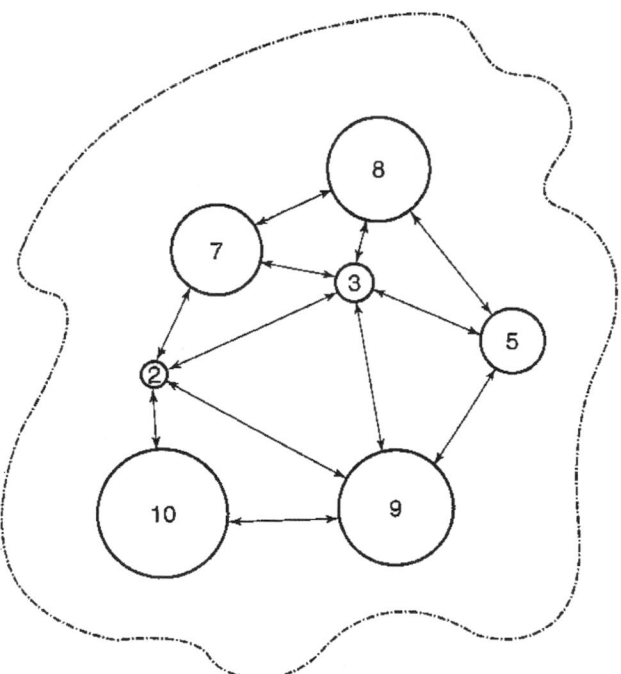

Fig. 11. A hypothetical landscape containing a metapopulation, or group of interconnected populations. Populations are indicated by circles, and relative sizes of populations are given by numbers within circles (from Yahner 2000:135)

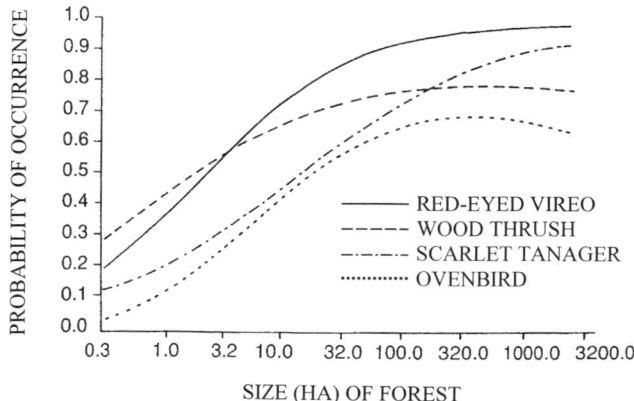

Fig. 10. The probability of occurrence of 4 songbird species in relation to size of forest stand (from Yahner 2000:117).

FOREST-MANAGEMENT MODELS

Plant-species composition, age, size, and growth dynamics of a forest stand can have important influences on habitat selection and use by wildlife. Thus, habitat models enable resource managers to predict wildlife species occurrences and adjust forest management regimes. Management regimes can be adjusted to benefit wildlife by altering forest yield and productivity, regeneration, and tree composition (Mannan et al. 1996, Roloff et al. 2001). Three general types of models are available to resource managers: silvicultural models, single-species wildlife-habitat models, and multi-species wildlife-habitat models.

For the purposes of modeling forest dynamics, a forest stand is defined as a contiguous group of trees sufficiently uniform in species composition, age class, site quality, and condition to be a distinguishable unit (Smith et al 1997). In contrast, the term "forest" connotes a more landscape-level approach and is a collection of stands administered as an integrated unit.

Silvicultural Models

Silvicultural models display and predict forest composition and structure at different levels of scale. Three types of silvicultural models exist: 1) stand-based models, 2) individual-tree models, and 3) landscape or regional models (Gadow and Hui 1999).

Stand-based Models

The stand-based model is the traditional model, which uses forest stand as the unit of management. These models estimate timber growth and potential yield (software lists in Ramm and Miner [1986] and Mannan et al. [1996]) and take into account climate, soil, and native-tree communities. Potential yield is estimated by predicting forest height and basal area that are functions of stem density within a given stand (Gadow and Hui 1999). Although these models traditionally have been used to predict timber growth and yield, these components of forest stands have important implications for wildlife. In addition, some models predict basal area as a function of stand age, initial basal area, and changes in diameter distributions within a stand. These models typically require data on tree development under natural growing conditions in response to thinning regimes, which are species-specific and vary with environmental conditions. Data on forest-stand growth are available from government research organizations (e.g., USFS) and through university research cooperatives (e.g., Loblolly Pine Growth and Yield Research Cooperative at the Virginia Polytechnic Institute and State University).

The development of an even-aged forest stand may be predicted using stand-based models that consider average stand height, basal area, and stems per ha (density). Several models recently have been used to model the development of height based upon stand age (e.g., Zeide 1993, Shvets and Zeide 1996). Other models have been developed to project stand basal area primarily for commercially valuable species, such as slash pine (Pienaar et al. 1990).

In uneven-aged, mixed-species forest stands, size-class models can be used to project the development of the stand by assuming that a representative tree of a particular diameter exhibits the attributes of all trees of that particular diameter class regardless of species (Smalley and Bailey 1974). Furthermore, size-class models assume that future diameters of trees may be predicted from known initial diameter and stand age. However, diameter growth is also influenced by crown surface area, stand density (manipulated by thinning regimes), tree height, stem quality, and competition among trees in a stand (Spurr and Barnes 1980).

Individual-tree Models

Individual tree-growth models have been developed, resulting in an increased level of modeling resolution. These models depend upon knowledge of the precise location of a tree within the stand and its relation to neighboring trees, thereby enabling the calculation of competition indices (Clutter et al. 1983, Trepl 1994) and the application of more exact growth models to a given stand. In addition, individual-tree models (also called distance-dependent models) can be used that incorporate the effects of thinning on individual trees within a stand (Gadow and Hui 1999).

Several model simulators, such as *FOREST*, developed by Ek and Monserud (1974), assume that potential growth of individual trees is reduced by competition from neighboring trees. *MOSES* estimates height and diameter growth, and changes in tree height based on spatial positioning of individual trees within the stand (Gadow and Hui 1999). *SILVA* is a growth simulator for individual trees, which was originally developed for mixed spruce-beech forests in Germany (Gadow and Hui 1999). Variables necessary to operate SILVA models include stand age, initial basal area, crown volume, and crown surface area, shading, and constriction.

Some models incorporate environmental variables, such as light and temperature, to individual tree diameter-growth equations (Roloff et al. 2001). This inclusion makes it possible to predict the response of tree growth to varying environmental conditions. For example, Pastor and Post (1985) examined effects of climate, soil moisture, nitrogen availability, and light conditions on individual tree growth. These models often require detailed information about conditions within a forest stand (Qi and Gilles 1999).

Landscape or Regional Models

Models are also available that project the estimated yield of regional timber resources based upon site-quality categories (Shvidenko et al. 1995). These regional models permit resource managers to estimate standing volume of timber for a given age assuming different harvest scenarios (Gadow and Hui 1999). Regional models have been developed to estimate yield of even-aged forest stands and managed stands with continuous cover forest (where trees are removed selectively). However, yield projections must be adjusted in stands that are not fully stocked (e.g., thinned stands). Yield projections for stands characterized by different site quality, tree species, and silvicultural practices do not exist (Gadow and Hui 1999).

Another modeling approach for regional application involves tracking the amount of land in different successional stages and forest types. For example, *FORPLAN* can be used to predict the amount of land in different forest types and growth stages over time (Kirkman et al. 1986, Mannan et al. 1996).

Silvicultural-model Application

The integration of forest and wildlife management using silvicultural models is illustrated by an approach to biodiversity conservation in western Massachusetts (DeGraaf et al. 1992, Smith et al. 1997). A mosaic of suitable forest-age classes and composition had to be created and maintained to provide appropriate habitat for an assemblage of vertebrate species that inhabit the area. Regeneration of white pine (*Pinus strobus*) and the development of vertical structure in some areas were among the specific recommendations. By collecting data on appropriate variables, resource managers could use the growth model SILVA, for instance, to predict how certain silvicultural practices affect the growth of white pine trees.

Wildlife-habitat Models

Single-species Wildlife-habitat Models

Resource managers often use correlation models or species habitat matrices to identify habitat requirements of individual forest wildlife species in a given forest stand or type (DeGraaf et al. 1992, Roloff et al. 2001). These correlation models, consisting of tables listing vegetation types or environmental conditions associated with different wildlife species, provide an efficient means of predicting presence or relative abundance of different species. Correlation models have been developed for wildlife associated with ecosystems in the Sierra Nevadas, New England, and the southern United States (Verner and Boss 1980, DeGraaf and Yamasaki 2001, Dettmers et al. 2002, respectively).

Another type of single-species wildlife-habitat model is the habitat-evaluation procedure (HEP). HEP is based on indices of habitat quality, where quality is measured by vegetation structure, composition, and spatial arrangement (Roloff et al. 2001, Anderson and Gutzwiller 2005). Habitat quantity is calculated by multiplying the quality index by the corresponding amounts of each habitat type. This model assumes that a greater quantity of habitat for a particular species will result in higher abundance of that species (Roloff and Haufler 1997). HEP has been used extensively because this type of model can be applied to a range of habitats or ecosystems and it is relatively inexpensive to develop. However, HEP has been criticized because of its relative simplicity and subjectivity (Roloff et al. 2001).

The habitat-suitability-index (HSI) model, developed by the U.S Fish and Wildlife Service, focuses on single species and generates a numeric value that assesses the capacity of a habitat to support a species as a function of vegetation structure and composition, and spatial arrangement of differing habitat types (U.S. Department of Interior 1980, Anderson and Gutzwiller 2005). A high HSI value for a particular wildlife species (based on a range of 0.0–1.0) indicates the habitat of interest likely contains that species (referenced online at http://policy.fws.gov/870fw1.html for all published HSI models).

Bayesian and pattern-recognition models also have been used to examine the relationship between forest habitat and wildlife (Roloff et al. 2001). To use these models, a researcher must classify a habitat patch into a category of habitat suitability, identify which attributes dictate habitat-suitability categories, and assign a set of Bayesian probabilities that reflect the association between habitat attributes and each suitability category (Williams et al. 1977, Kirkman et al. 1986, Mannan et al. 1996). For example, Bayesian and pattern-recognition models have been used in modeling studies involving bald eagles (*Haliaeetus leucocephalus*) (Grubb 1988) and mountain sheep (*Ovis canadensis*) (Holl 1982).

Multivariate-statistical models show potential relationships between multiple environmental characteristics and a species' abundance and distribution (Morrison et al. 1992, Roloff et al. 2001). These models identify habitat variables that have the greatest effect on the occurrence or population of wildlife of interest. Several multivariate-statistical approaches used in wildlife-modeling studies include multiple regression, principal component analysis, discriminate function analysis, regression tree analysis, and fuzzy logic (Roloff et al. 2001). Multivariate models have been developed for a variety of wildlife species because they have a low level of subjectivity (Digby and Kempton 1987), but they are limited by data availability and often are difficult to interpret and communicate (Roloff et al. 2001).

Habitat-preference models can also be used to examine how wildlife use varies among forest stands that differ in age, species composition, and structure in relation to the availability of these stands (Morrison et al. 1998, Roloff et al. 2001). Habitat preference can be examined by the amount of time a given wildlife species uses a particular habitat type relative to its availability. Often these models require use of remote methodology, such as radio or satellite tracking of individual animals, to measure habitat use.

Multi-species Wildlife-habitat Models

Multi-species wildlife-habitat models have been developed, such as gap analysis (Scott et al. 1993). A gap-analysis model is based on the geographic distribution of assemblages of wildlife species by depicting "gaps" in species distribution or by identifying areas of high species richness. Gap analysis is especially useful when portraying wildlife-habitat relationships across large areas (Roloff et al. 2001).

Multi-species wildlife-habitat models have been used to describe biodiversity based on vegetation attributes of a given area (e.g., Maurer 1994, Rosenzweig 1995, Roloff et al. 2001). These models assess wildlife community structure in terms of the number of species (e.g., species richness) or the number of individuals of each species.

Other types of multi-species models, focusing on well-defined groups of wildlife species or guilds, have been used to evaluate the effects of habitat changes on the overall functional, structural, and compositional conditions of ecosystems (Roloff et al. 2001). Guild models have been primarily developed for songbirds (e.g., O'Connell et al. 2000) but have also been applied to other taxa, e.g., salamanders (Hairston 1987). An example of a guild model, the Bird Community Index, is based on response guilds, which are defined as groups of bird species that require similar habitat, food, or other elements for survival (O'Connell et al. 2000). This model assumes that high-integrity environmental conditions will be reflected by the presence of guilds containing more specialist than generalist species. High-integrity environmental conditions are those that typify the habitat type or ecosystem in the absence of human disturbance.

Other guild models have used occurrence, abundance, and locations of ecological communities to predict animal responses. For example, Haufler et al. (1996) stratified landscapes into "ecological land units" on the basis of similar disturbance regimes and geological conditions, which were then used to describe and predict floral and faunal diversity for planning purposes. Guild models have been criticized because often the guild as an entity exhibits little response to changes in habitat condition, whereas individual species within the guild may vary in their response to the same habitat changes (Mannan et al. 1996).

Forest-fragmentation Models

Models developed from island-biogeography theory have been used to understand the effects of forest fragmentation on wildlife (MacArthur and Wilson 1967, Harris 1984, Yahner 2000). For instance, an important model, the species-area curve, predicts that species richness will increase as the size of a forest patch increases (Fig. 12). The relationship between forest patch size and species richness also is affected by the extent to which the patch is isolated from other similar habitat. Wilcox (1980) developed a model that predicted isolated, small forest patches would have lower rates of species colonization and higher rates of extinction than large, non-isolated patches. However, simulation models have indicated that forest patches connected by corridors, such as wooded fencerows, can maintain viable populations of wildlife (Merriam and Wegner 1992).

BIODIVERSITY CONSERVATION AND ECOSYSTEM MANAGEMENT

An inclusive and generally accepted definition of biological diversity, or biodiversity, is the variety of life and its processes at 4 interrelated levels: genetic, species, community and ecosystem, and landscape diversity (Keystone Center 1991, Society of American Foresters 1992, The Wildlife Society 1993, Noss and Cooperrider 1994, Yahner 2000, Knight and Landres 2002). In addition, biodiversity includes ecological structures, functions, and processes at each of these levels. The foremost goal of biological con-

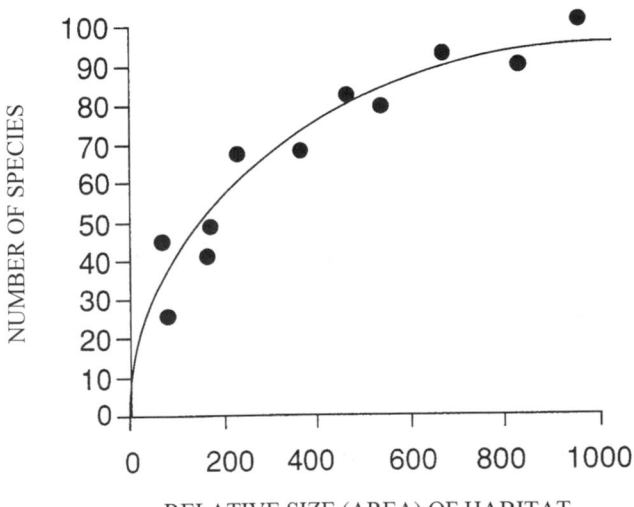

Fig. 12. A hypothetical species-area curve. Each dot represents a forest stand of a given size (from Yahner 2000:105).

servation is long-term maintenance of the world's species and other levels of biodiversity (Wiens 2002).

Biological diversity at the genetic level has been given increasing attention by wildlife biologists, as with isolated populations of black bear, which is a species of concern in some southern and eastern states (e.g., Walthen et al. 1985, Pelton and Van Manen 1994, Clark and Pelton 1999; reviewed by Yahner 2001). Species diversity has been recognized by wildlife biologists as an important measure of wildlife communities since the founding of wildlife management as a discipline by Aldo Leopold (1933). The measurement of species diversity on a local scale, i.e., alpha diversity, has been emphasized by researchers over the years in numerous studies (Samson and Knopf 1982), such as those examining bird diversity in even-aged stands (e.g., Yahner 1993). Community or ecosystem diversity is important when managing for species requiring critical habitats or features in extensive forest tracts, as with the threatened Allegheny woodrat (Balcom and Yahner 1996). Landscape diversity, which represents the largest scale of biodiversity, deals with interacting communities and ecosystems, viable populations of wildlife, and natural and human-induced disturbances to the landscape (Noss 1992). The conservation of biodiversity at the landscape level has important implications for ecosystem management (Petit et al. 1995). Moreover, a national strategy for biological conservation will require scientific information at all levels of biodiversity from genetic to landscape (Blockstein 1995).

Biodiversity conservation is closely linked with landscape ecology because the latter discipline deals with causes and consequences of the spatial configuration and the composition of landscape, such as types of land uses or presence of corridors in the landscape matrix (Wiens 2002). Furthermore, biodiversity conservation is intricately linked with ecosystem management because the latter focuses on maintenance of viable wildlife populations and perpetuation of all native ecosystems (National Ecosystem Management Forum 1993, Grumbine 1994, Petit et al. 1995, Yahner 2000). Federal agencies, including those involved with forest management, have adopted policies for ecosystem management (Grumbine 1997).

Ecosystem management applied to forests also includes consideration of values, such as safeguarding its biodiversity and ecological sustainability (Wood 1994). Moreover, sound forest or ecosystem management views a forest as an interactive system of plants, animals, soil, water, and climate (Behan 1990). Thus, ecosystem management is an attractive concept for conservation of forest wildlife because it is concerned with more than a single species and addresses a range of spatial scales from individual forest stand to landscape (Reed 1995, Franklin 1997).

The future success of implementing ecosystem management will rely on effective partnership and compromise among agencies (e.g., state and federal) concerned with biodiversity conservation (Knight and Meffe 1997). Moreover, ecosystem management will require use of scientific principles, ranging from application of biological concepts, evaluating key components of ecosystems, and establishing protocols for inventorying, monitoring, and storing ecological data obtained from ecosystems (Christensen et al. 1996, Reichman and Pulliam 1996). A key example of how ecosystem management can be viewed conceptually is in management of a taxonomic group, such as birds, and is well illustrated by Petit et al. (1995).

FORESTS FOR THE FUTURE

A major goal of natural resource managers and society concerned with forest management and wildlife must be to ensure continuation of a sustainable, productive, and healthy forest (Durning 1994). This will require a collegial and straightforward approach to enhancing forest health (DellaSala et al. 1995), which involves a management strategy for forests that encompasses a broad spectrum of resource and sociopolitical issues, and requires cooperation among environmentalists, industry, landowners, natural resource managers, and recreationists (Thorne 1993, Yahner 2000).

At least 5 issues face the future successful management of forests: biodiversity conservation and ecosystem management, forest fragmentation, education, recreation, and regional and global influences (Yahner 2000). A multi-species approach to forest wildlife management using sound principles developed by the rapidly growing disciplines of biodiversity conservation and ecosystem management, as well as landscape ecology, makes sense in today's era (after DeBell and Curtis 1993, Grumbine 1997, Wiens 2002). This is essential to the health and productivity of forests, and to the well-being and quality of life of those who enjoy outdoor experiences in forests (Scavia et al. 1996).

Forest fragmentation and habitat loss will continue to be issues confronting sound management of forests (e.g., Robbins 1988, Litvaitis 1993, Yahner 1995, Brawn et al. 2001). A balance needs to be struck between ensuring a mosaic of adequate old-growth stands and early- and mid-successional habitats for forest wildlife. The wildlife profession has embraced this challenge as witnessed by a recent, concerted focus on this issue (e.g., Lorimer and Frelich 1994, Brawn et al. 2001, Thompson and DeGraaf 2001).

Education will be key to the conservation of forests and associated resources (Yahner 2000). These forests, whether an urban woodlot or an extensive tract of national forest, can be invaluable as outdoor laboratories for introducing youth to appreciate the stewardship of our wildlands. In addition, forests serve as ideal research sites for monitoring of resources over the long term to better understand and document trends in forest wildlife in relationship to changing landscapes or other perturbations. In many parts of the country, as in the eastern United States, forests are privately owned; thus, the Forest Stewardship Program, administered by the U.S. Forest Service, is a critical program for wildlife and natural resource professionals who are mandated to conserve and manage forest wildlife.

Recreation has been identified as a major value of forests, providing the public with birding, hunting, photography, observation, and other opportunities for viewing and enjoying wildlife resources (e.g., Hammitt et al. 1993). Thus, efforts should be made to enhance wildlife-viewing experiences (Harrington 1991), but a downside is the potential impact on wildlife of these activities, e.g., via road construction (Cole and Knight 1991).

Forest management, like most other aspects of today's world, has gone global. Landscape linkages, acid deposition, ozone depletion, and global climatic change are just several issues that require interagency and, more importantly, interstate and international cooperation (Yahner 2000). The scope of these issues has gone beyond a forested tract or state forest, thereby requiring economic, social, and political considerations at a scale unprecedented in wildlife conservation.

SUMMARY

Forest types, ownership, and legislation can affect the value of forests to wildlife. Plant-forest succession resulting from fire, chemicals, or management systems can have profound effects on forest wildlife. For example, uneven-aged forest management can influence wildlife distribution and abundance differently than even-aged forest management. Several practices, e.g., retention of unique habitat features or overstory trees in harvested stands, can have positive effects on forest wildlife. The impacts of forest management, however, cannot be considered solely from the stand level (e.g., stand size) but must take into consideration landscape features (e.g., characteristics of surrounding landscape). Several types of models are available to predict wildlife species occurrences and adjust forest-management regimes. Successful forest management in the future will be contingent on biodiversity conservation and ecosystem management to ensure a sustainable, productive, and healthy forest for the benefit of wildlife while simultaneously providing educational and recreational values.

ACKNOWLEDGMENTS

Our ideas presented in this chapter are based on research funded over the years by the GPU/Penelec, Hammermill Paper Company, International Paper Company, Max McGraw Wildlife Foundation, Minnesota Agricultural Experiment Station, National Park Service, National Rifle Association, Pennsylvania Agricultural Experiment Station, Pennsylvania Game Commission, Pennsylvania Wild Resource Conservation Fund, Ruffed Grouse Society, U.S. Environmental Protection Agency, U.S. Forest Service, and Western Pennsylvania Conservancy. We thank W. M. Healy and R. W. Mannan for reviews of the manuscript and particularly C. E. Braun for his cooperation and helpful suggestions in the preparation of this manuscript.

LITERATURE CITED

ABER, J. D. 1990. Forest ecology and the forest ecosystem. Pages 119–143 *in* R. A. Young and R. L. Giese, editors. Introduction to forest science. John Wiley and Sons, Inc., New York, USA.

ABRAMS, M. D. 1992. Fire and the development of oak forests. BioScience 42:346–353.

———, AND C. M. RUFFNER. 1995. Physiographic analysis of witness-tree distribution (1765–1798) and present forest cover through north central Pennsylvania. Canadian Journal of Forest Research 25:659–668.

AMBROSE, J. P., AND S. P. BRATTON. 1990. Trends in habitat heterogeneity along the borders of Great Smoky Mountains National Park. Conservation Biology 4:135–143.

AMBUEL, B., AND S. A. TEMPLE. 1983. Area-dependent changes in the bird communities and vegetation of southern Wisconsin forests. Ecology 64:1057–1068.

ANDERSON, S. H., AND K. J. GUTZWILLER. 2005. Wildlife habitat evaluation. Pages 489–502 *in* C. E. Braun, editor. Techniques for wildlife investigations and management. Sixth edition. The Wildlife Society, Bethesda, Maryland, USA.

ANDRÉN, H. 1992. Corvid density and nest predation in relation to forest fragmentation: a landscape perspective. Ecology 73:794–804.

———. 1994. Effects of habitat fragmentation on birds and mammals in landscapes with different proportions of suitable habitat: a review. Oikos 71:355–366.

———. 1995. Effects of landscape composition on predation rates at habitat edges. Pages 225–255 in L. Hansson, L. Fahrig, and G. Merriam, editors. Mosaic landscapes and ecological processes. Chapman and Hall, London, United Kingdom.

ANDREWS, A. 1990. Fragmentation of habitat by roads and utility corridors: a review. Australian Zoology 26:130–141.

ANGLESTAM, P. 1998. Maintaining and restoring biodiversity in European boreal forests by developing natural disturbance regimes. Journal of Vegetation Science 9:593–602.

ANNAND, E. M., AND F. R. THOMPSON, III. 1997. Forest bird response to regeneration practices in central hardwood forests. Journal of Wildlife Management 61:159–171.

ARABAS, K. B. 1997. Fire and vegetation dynamics in the eastern serpentine barrens. Dissertation. Pennsylvania State University, University Park, USA.

ASH, A. N. 1997. Disappearance and return of plethodontid salamanders to clearcut plots in the southern Blue Ridge Mountains. Conservation Biology 11:983–989.

ASKINS, R. A. 1993. Population trends in grassland, shrubland, and forest birds in eastern North America. Pages 1–34 in D. M. Power, editor. Current ornithology. Volume 11. Plenum Press, New York, USA.

———. 1995. Hostile landscapes and the decline of migratory songbirds. Science 267:1956–1957.

———. 2001. Sustaining biological diversity in early successional communities: the challenge of managing unpopular habitats. Wildlife Society Bulletin 29:407–412.

AUBRY, K. B., AND C. M. RALEY. 2002. Selection of nest and roost trees by pileated woodpeckers in coastal forests of Washington. Journal of Wildlife Management 66:392–406.

BALCOM, B. J., AND R. H. YAHNER. 1996. Microhabitat and landscape characteristics associated with the threatened Allegheny woodrat. Conservation Biology 10:515–525.

BAYNE, E. M., AND K. A. HOBSON. 1997. Comparing the effects of landscape fragmentation by forestry and agriculture on predation of artificial nests. Conservation Biology 11:1418–1429.

BEHAN, R. W. 1990. Multiresource forest management: a paradigmatic challenge to professional forestry. Journal of Forestry 88(4):12–18.

BEIER, P., AND S. LOE. 1992. A checklist for evaluating impacts to wildlife movement corridors. Wildlife Society Bulletin 20:434–440.

BENDEL, P. R., AND J. E. GATES. 1987. Home range and microhabitat partitioning of the southern flying squirrel (Glaucomys volans). Journal of Mammalogy 68:243–255.

BLAKE, J. G., AND J. R. KARR. 1987. Breeding birds of isolated woodlots: area and habitat relationships. Ecology 68:1724–1734.

BLOCKSTEIN, D. E. 1995. A strategic approach for biodiversity conservation. Wildlife Society Bulletin 23:365–369.

BOARDMAN, L. A., AND R. H. YAHNER. 1999. Wildlife community structure and composition in managed forested stands of central Pennsylvania. Northern Journal of Applied Forestry 16:1–7.

BOLEN, E. G., AND W. L. ROBINSON. 1995. Wildlife ecology and management. Third edition. Prentice Hall, Englewood Cliffs, New Jersey, USA.

BONAR, R. L. 2000. Availability of pileated woodpecker cavities and use by other species. Journal of Wildlife Management 64:52–59.

BRAMBLE, W. C., R. H. YAHNER, AND W. R. BYRNES. 1999. Effect of herbicide maintenance of an electric transmission right-of-way on butterfly populations. Journal of Arboriculture 25:302–310.

BRAND, L. A., AND T. L. GEORGE. 2000. Predation risks for nesting birds in fragmented coast redwood forest. Journal of Wildlife Management 64:42–51.

BRAWN, J. D., S. K. ROBINSON, AND F. R. THOMPSON, III. 2001. The role of disturbance in the ecology and conservation of birds. Annual Review of Ecology and Systematics 32:251–276.

BRAZIER, J. R., AND G. W. BROWN. 1973. Buffer strips for stream temperature control. Research Paper 15. School of Forestry, Oregon State University, Corvallis, USA.

BRITTEN, H. B., AND R. J. BAKER. 2002. Landscape connections and genetic diversity. Pages 131–149 in K. Gutzwiller, editor. Concepts and applications of landscape ecology in biological conservation. Springer-Verlag, Inc., New York, USA.

BRITTINGHAM, M. C., AND S. A. TEMPLE. 1983. Have cowbirds caused forest songbirds to decline? BioScience 33:31–35.

BROWN, G. W., AND J. T. KRYGIER. 1967. Changing water temperature in small mountain streams. Journal of Soil and Water Conservation 22:242–244.

BUREAU OF LAND MANAGEMENT. 2001. Public land statistics 2000. Volume 185. BLM/BC/ST-01/0011.

CAMPBELL, H. W., AND S. P. CHRISTMAN. 1982. The herpetological components of Florida sandhill and sand pine scrub associations. Pages 163–171 in N. J. Scott, editor. Herpetological communities. U.S. Department of the Interior, Fish and Wildlife Service, Research Report 13.

CAREY, A. B., AND S. M. WILSON. 2001. Induced spatial heterogeneity in forest canopies: responses of small mammals. Journal of Wildlife Management 65:1014–1027.

CHALFOUN, A. D., F. R. THOMPSON III, AND M. J. RATNASWAMY. 2002. Nest predators and fragmentation: a review and meta-analysis. Conservation Biology 16:306–319.

CHRISTENSEN, N. L., A. M. BARTUSKA, J. H. BROWN, S. CARPENTER, C. D'ANTONIO, R. FRANCIS, J. F. FRANKLIN, J. A. MACMAHON, R. F. NOSS, D. J. PARSONS, C. H. PETERSON, M. G. TURNER, AND R. G. WOODMANSEE. 1996. The report of the Ecological Society of America Committee on the scientific basis for ecosystem management. Ecological Applications 6:665–691.

CLARK, J. D., AND M. R. PELTON. 1999. Management of a large carnivore: black bear. Pages 209–223 in J. D. Peine, editor. Ecosystem management for sustainability. Lewis Publishers, Boston, Massachusetts, USA.

CLAWSON, M. 1979. Forests in the long sweep of U.S. history. Science 204:1168–1174.

CLUTTER, J. L., J. C. FORTSON, L. V. PIENAAR, G. H. BRISTER, AND R. L. BAILEY. 1983. Timber management—a quantitative approach. John Wiley and Sons, Inc., New York, USA.

COLE, D. N., AND R. L. KNIGHT. 1991. Wildlife preservation and recreational use: conflicting goals of wildland management. Transactions of the North American Wildlife and Natural Resources Conference 56:233–237.

CRAWFORD, H. S., AND R. W. TITTERINGTON. 1979. Effects of silvicultural practices on bird communities in upland spruce-fir stands. Pages 110–119 in R. M. DeGraaf and K. E. Evans, editors. Proceedings of the workshop for the management of north-central and northeastern forests for nongame birds. U.S. Department of Agriculture, Forest Service, General Technical Report NC-51.

———, R. G. HOOPER, AND R. W. TITTERINGTON. 1981. Songbird population response to silvicultural practices in central Appalachian hardwoods. Journal of Wildlife Management 45:680–692.

CROOKS, K. R. 2002. Relative sensitivities of mammalian carnivores to habitat fragmentation. Conservation Biology 16:488–502.

CUTTER, S. L., H. L. RENWICK, AND W. H. RENWICK. 1991. Exploitation, conservation, preservation: a geographic perspective of natural resource use. Second edition. John Wiley and Sons, Inc., New York, USA.

DAVIS, M. A., D. W. PETERSON, P. B. REICH, M. CROZIER, T. QUERY, E. MITCHELL, J. HUNTINGTON, AND P. BAZAKAS. 2000. Restoring savanna using fire: impact on the breeding bird community. Restoration Ecology 8:30–40.

DAY, G. M. 1953. The Indian as an ecological factor in the northeastern forest. Ecology 34:329–346.

DEBELL, D. S., AND R. O. CURTIS. 1993. Silviculture and new forestry in the Pacific Northwest. Journal of Forestry 91(12):25–30.

DEGRAAF, R. M., AND M. YAMASAKI. 2001. New England wildlife: habitat, natural history, and distribution. University Press of New England, Hanover, New Hampshire, USA.

———, ———, W. B. LEAK, AND J. W. LANIER. 1992. New England wildlife: management of forested habitats. U.S. Department of Agriculture, Forest Service, General Technical Report NE-144.

DELCOURT, H. R., AND P. A. DELCOURT. 1997. Pre-Columbian Native American use of fire on southern Appalachian landscapes. Conservation Biology 11:1010–1014.

DELLASALA, D. A., D. M. OLSON, S. E. BARTH, S. L. CRANE, AND S. A. PRIMM. 1995. Forest health: moving beyond rhetoric to restore healthy landscapes in the inland Northwest. Wildlife Society Bulletin 23:346–356.

DESSECKER, D. R., AND D. G. MCAULEY. 2001. Importance of early successional habitat to ruffed grouse and American woodcock. Wildlife Society Bulletin 29:456–465.

DETTMERS, R., D. A. BUEHLER, AND K. E. FRANZREB. 2002. Testing habitat-relationship models for forest birds of the southeastern United States. Journal of Wildlife Management 66:417–424.

DIAMOND, J. M. 1975. The island dilemma: lessons of modern biogeographic studies for the design of nature reserves. Biological Conservation 7:129–146.

DIGBY, P. G. N., AND R. A. KEMPTON. 1987. Multivariate analysis of ecological communities. Chapman and Hall, London, United Kingdom.

DIJAK, W. D., AND F. R. THOMPSON, III. 2000. Landscape and edge effects on the distribution of mammalian predators in Missouri. Journal of Wildlife Management 64:209–216.

DONOVAN, T. M., P. W. JONES, E. M. ANNAND, AND F. R. THOMPSON III. 1997. Variation in local-scale edge effects: mechanisms and landscape context. Ecology 78:2064–2075.

DUFFIELD, J. W. 1990. Forest regions of North America and the world. Pages 33–65 *in* R. A. Young and R. L. Giese, editors. Introduction to forest science. John Wiley and Sons, Inc., New York, USA.

DUGUAY, J. P. 1997. Influence of two-age and clear-cut timber management practices on songbird abundance, nest success, and invertebrate biomass in West Virginia. Dissertation. West Virginia University, Morgantown, USA.

———, AND P. B. WOOD. 2002. Salamander abundance in regenerating forest stands on the Monongahela National Forest, West Virginia. Forest Science 48:331–335.

———, ———, AND J. V. NICHOLS. 2001. Songbird abundance and avian nest survival rates in forests fragmented by different silvicultural treatments. Conservation Biology 15:1405–1415.

DURNING, A. T. 1994. Redesigning the forest economy. Pages 22–40 *in* L. Starke, editor. State of the world—1994. W. W. Norton and Company, New York, USA.

EK, A. R., AND R. A. MONSERUD. 1974. FOREST: a computer model for simulating the growth and reproduction of mixed species forest stands. Research Report R2635. School of Natural Resources, University of Wisconsin, Madison, USA.

FLATHER, C. H., AND T. W. HOEKSTRA. 1989. An analysis of the wildlife and fish situation in the United States 1989–2040: a technical document supporting the 1989 USDA Forest Service RPA Assessment. U.S. Department of Agriculture, Forest Service, Fort Collins, Colorado, USA.

FLEISHMAN, E., AND R. MACNALLY. 2002. Topographic determinants of faunal nestedness in Great Basin butterfly assemblages: applications to conservation planning. Conservation Biology 16:422–429.

FORMAN, R. T. T. 1995. Some general principles of landscape and regional ecology. Landscape Ecology 10:133–142.

———. 2000. Estimate of the area affected ecologically by the road system in the United States. Conservation Biology 14:31–35.

———, AND M. GODRON. 1986. Landscape ecology. John Wiley and Sons, Inc., New York, USA.

———, A. E. GALLI, AND C. F. LECK. 1976. Forest size and avian diversity in New Jersey woodlots with some land use implications. Oecologia 26:1–8.

FRANKLIN, J. F. 1997. Ecosystem management: an overview. Pages 21–25 *in* M. A. Boyce and A. Haney, editors. Ecosystem management. Yale University, New Haven, Connecticut, USA.

———, AND R. T. T. FORMAN. 1987. Creating landscape patterns by forest cutting: ecological consequences and principles. Landscape Ecology 1:5–18.

———, D. R. BERG, D. A. THORNBURGH, AND J. C. TAPPEINER. 1997. Alternative silvicultural approaches to timber harvesting: variable retention systems. Pages 111–139 *in* K. A. Kohm and J. F. Franklin, editors. Creating a forestry for the 21st century: the science of ecosystem management. Island Press, Washington, D.C., USA.

FREEMARK, K. E., AND H. G. MERRIAM. 1986. Importance of area and habitat heterogeneity to bird assemblages in temperate forest fragments. Biological Conservation 36:115–141.

FRENZEN, P. 1992. Mount St. Helens: a laboratory for research and education. Journal of Forestry 90(5):14–18, 27.

FRIESEN, L. E., P. F. J. EAGLES, AND R. J. MACKAY. 1995. Effects of residential developments on forest-dwelling Neotropical migrant songbirds. Conservation Biology 9:1408–1414.

GADOW, K. V., AND G. HUI. 1999. Modelling forest development. Kluwer Academic Publishers, Norwell, Massachusetts, USA.

GASCON, C., T. E. LOVEJOY, R. O. BIERREGAARD, JR., J. R. MALCOLM, P. C. SOUFFER, H. L. VASCONCELOS, W. F. LAURANCE, B. ZIMMERMAN, M. TOCHER, AND S. BORGES. 1999. Matrix habitat and species richness in tropical forest remnants. Biological Conservation 91:223–229.

GATES, J. E., AND L. W. GYSEL. 1978. Avian nest dispersion and fledging success in field-forest ecotones. Ecology 59:871–883.

GILBERT, F. F., AND D. G. DODDS. 1992. The philosophy and practice of wildlife management. Second edition. R. E. Krieger Publishing Co., Malabar, Florida, USA.

GRIALOU, J. A., S. D. WEST, AND R. N. WILKINS. 2000. The effects of forest clearcut harvesting and thinning on terrestrial salamanders. Journal of Wildlife Management 64:105–113.

GRISEZ, T. J. 1960. Slash helps protect seedlings from deer browsing. Journal of Forestry 58:385–387.

GRUBB, T. G. 1988. Pattern recognition—a simple model for evaluating wildlife habitat. U.S. Department of Agriculture, Forest Service, Research Note RM-487.

GRUMBINE, R. E. 1994. What is ecosystem management? Conservation Biology 8:27–38.

———. 1997. Reflections on "what is ecosystem management?" Conservation Biology 11:41–47.

GULLION, G. W. 1972. Improving your forest lands for ruffed grouse. Miscellaneous Journal Serial Publication 1439. Minnesota Agricultural Experiment Station, St. Paul, USA.

———. 1976. Ruffed grouse habitat manipulation—Mille Lacs Wildlife Management Area, Minnesota. Minnesota Wildlife Research Quarterly 36:97–121.

———. 1990. Forest-wildlife interactions. Pages 349–383 *in* R. A. Young and R. L. Giese, editors. Introduction to forest science. Second edition. John Wiley and Sons, Inc., New York, USA.

HAAS, C. A. 1995. Dispersal and use of corridors by birds in wooded patches on an agricultural landscape. Conservation Biology 9:845–854.

HAGENSTEIN, P. 1990. Forests. Pages 78–100 *in* R. N. Sampson and D. Hair, editors. Natural resources for the 21st century. American Forestry Association, Island Press, Washington, D.C., USA.

HAIRSTON, N. G. 1987. Community ecology and salamander guilds. Cambridge University Press, New York, USA.

HAMMITT, W. E., J. N. DULIN, AND G. R. WELLS. 1993. Determinants of quality wildlife viewing in Great Smoky Mountains National Park. Wildlife Society Bulletin 21:21–30.

HANSKI, I. K., T. J. FENSKE, AND G. J. NIEMI. 1996. Lack of edge effect in nesting success of breeding birds in managed forest landscapes. Auk 113:578–585.

HARLOW, R. F., R. L. DOWNING, AND D. H. VAN LEAR. 1997. Responses of wildlife to clearcutting and associated treatments in the eastern United States. Technical Paper 19. Department of Forest Resources, Clemson University, Clemson, South Carolina, USA.

HARRINGTON, W. 1991. Wildlife: severe decline and partial recovery. Pages 205–246 *in* K. D. Frederick and R. A. Sedjo, editors. America's renewable resources: historical trends and current challenges. Resources for the Future, Washington, D.C., USA.

HARRIS, L. D. 1984. The fragmented forest: island biogeography theory and the preservation of biotic diversity. University of Chicago Press, Chicago, Illinois, USA.

———, AND P. B. GALLAGHER. 1989. New initiatives for wildlife conservation: the need for movement corridors. Pages 11–34 *in* G. Mackintosh, editor. Preserving communities and corridors. Defenders of Wildlife, Washington, D.C., USA.

———, AND G. SILVA-LOPEZ. 1992. Forest fragmentation and the conservation of biological diversity. Pages 197–237 *in* G. Mackintosh, editor. Preserving communities and corridors. Defenders of Wildlife, Washington, D.C., USA.

HARRISON, R. L. 1992. Toward a theory of inter-refuge corridor design. Conservation Biology 6:293–295.

HARTLEY, M. J., AND M. L. HUNTER, JR. 1998. A meta-analysis of forest cover, edge effects, and artificial nest predation rates. Conservation

Biology 12:465–469.

HAUFLER, J. B., C. A. MEHL, AND G. J. ROLOFF. 1996. Using a coarse-filter approach with species assessment for ecosystem management. Wildlife Society Bulletin 24:200–208.

HEALY, W. M., AND R. T. BROOKS. 1988. Small mammal abundance in northern hardwood stands in West Virginia. Journal of Wildlife Management 52:491–496.

HESS, G. R. 1994. Conservation corridors and contagious disease: cautionary note. Conservation Biology 8:256–262.

HODGES, JR., M. F., AND D. G. KREMENTZ. 1996. Neotropical migratory breeding bird communities in riparian forests of different widths along the Altamaha River, Georgia. Wilson Bulletin 108:496–506.

HOLL, S. A. 1982. Evaluation of bighorn sheep habitat. Desert Bighorn Council Transactions 26:47–49.

HOOVER, J. P., M. C. BRITTINGHAM, AND L. J. GOODRICH. 1995. Effects of forest patch size on nesting success of wood thrushes. Auk 112:146–155.

HUGHES, J. W., AND T. J. FAHEY. 1991. Availability, quantity, and selection of browse by white-tailed deer after clearcutting. Journal of Forestry 89(10):31–36.

HUNTER, J. E., AND M. L. BOND. 2001. Residual trees: wildlife associations and recommendations. Wildlife Society Bulletin 29:995–999.

HUNTER, JR., M. L. 1990. Wildlife, forests, and forestry: principles of managing forests. Prentice Hall, Englewood Cliffs, New Jersey, USA.

HUNTER, W. C., D. A. BUEHLER, R. A. CANTERBURY, J. L. CONFER, AND P. B. HAMEL. 2001. Conservation of disturbance-dependent birds in eastern North America. Wildlife Society Bulletin 29:440–455.

HUTCHINSON, J. T., AND M. J. LACKI. 2000. Selection of day roosts by red bats in mixed mesophytic forests. Journal of Wildlife Management 64:87–94.

HUTTO, R. L. 1995. Composition of bird communities following stand-replacement fires in Northern Rocky Mountain (U.S.A.) conifer forests. Conservation Biology 9:1041–1058.

IRWIN, L. L., AND T. B. WIGLEY. 1993. Toward an experimental basis for protecting forest wildlife. Ecological Applications 3:213–217.

JACOBSON, S. K., M. C. MONROE, AND S. MARYNOWSKI. 2001. Fire at the wildland interface: the influence of experience and mass media on public knowledge, attitudes, and behavioral interactions. Wildlife Society Bulletin 29:929–937.

KELLER, G. S. 2001. Community structure and distributional patterns of avifauna in isolated deciduous-forest patches in south-central Pennsylvania. Dissertation. Pennsylvania State University, University Park, USA.

KEYSTONE CENTER. 1991. Biological diversity on federal lands. The Keystone Center, Keystone, Colorado, USA.

KING, D. I., R. M. DEGRAAF, AND C. R. GRIFFIN. 1998. Edge-related nest predation in clearcut and groupcut stands. Conservation Biology 12:1412–1415.

———, ———, AND ———. 2001. Productivity of early successional shrubland birds in clearcuts and groupcuts in an eastern deciduous forest. Journal of Wildlife Management 65:345–350.

———, C. R. GRIFFIN, AND R. M. DEGRAAF. 1996. Effects of clearcutting on habitat use and reproductive success of the ovenbird in forested landscapes. Conservation Biology 10:1380–1386.

KIRKMAN, R. L., J. A. EBERLY, W. R. PORATH, AND R. R. TITUS. 1986. A process for integrating wildlife needs into forest management planning. Pages 347–350 in J. Verner, M. L. Morrison, and C. J. Ralph, editors. Wildlife 2000: modeling habitat relationships of terrestrial vertebrates. University of Wisconsin Press, Madison, USA.

KNIGHT, R. L., AND P. L. LANDRES. 2002. Central concepts and issues in biological conservation. Pages 22–33 in K. Gutzwiller, editor. Concepts and applications of landscape ecology in biological conservation. Springer-Verlag, Inc., New York, USA.

———, AND G. K. MEFFE. 1997. Ecosystem management: agency liberation from command and control. Wildlife Society Bulletin 25:676–678.

KREMENTZ, D. G., AND J. S. CHRISTIE. 1999. Scrub-successional bird community dynamics in young and mature longleaf pine-wiregrass savannahs. Journal of Wildlife Management 63:803–814.

———, AND ———. 2000. Clearcut stand size and scrub-successional bird assemblages. Auk 117:913–924.

LEAK, W. B., AND S. M. FILIP. 1977. Thirty-eight years of group selection in New England northern hardwoods. Journal of Forestry 75:641–643.

LEOPOLD, A. 1933. Game management. Chas. Scribner's Sons, New York, USA.

LITVAITIS, J. A. 1993. Response of early successional vertebrates to changes in land use. Conservation Biology 7:866–873.

———. 2001. Importance of early successional habitats to mammals in eastern forests. Wildlife Society Bulletin 29:466–473.

LORIMER, C. G. 1985. The role of fire in the perpetuation of oak forest. Pages 8–25 in J. E. Johnson, editor. Challenges in oak management and utilization. Cooperative Extension Service, University of Wisconsin, Madison, USA.

———. 1990a. Behavior and management of forest fires. Pages 427–448 in R. A. Young and R. L. Giese, editors. Introduction to forest science. John Wiley and Sons, Inc., New York, USA.

———. 1990b. Silviculture. Pages 300–325 in R. A. Young and R. L. Giese, editors. Introduction to forest science. John Wiley and Sons, Inc., New York, USA.

———, AND L. E. FRELICH. 1994. Natural disturbance regimes in old-growth northern hardwoods: implications for restoration efforts. Journal of Forestry 92(1):33–38.

LYNCH, J. F., AND D. F. WHIGHAM. 1984. Effects of forest fragmentation on breeding bird communities in Maryland, U.S.A. Biological Conservation 28:287–324.

MACARTHUR, R. H., AND E. O. WILSON. 1967. The theory of island biogeography. Princeton University Press, Princeton, New Jersey, USA.

MACCLEERY, D.W. 1992. American forests: a history of resiliency and recovery. FS-540. U.S. Department of Agriculture, Forest Service, Washington, D.C., USA.

MACCLINTOCK, L., R. F. WHITCOMB, AND B. L. WHITCOMB. 1977. Island biogeography and "habitat islands" of eastern forest. II. Evidence for the value of corridors and minimization of isolation in preservation of biotic diversity. American Birds 31:6–12.

MANNAN, R. W., R. N. CONNER, B. MARCOT, AND J. M. PEEK. 1996. Managing forestlands for wildlife. Pages 689–721 in T. A. Bookhout, editor. Fifth edition. Research and management techniques for wildlife and habitats. The Wildlife Society, Bethesda, Maryland, USA.

MARTIN, A. J., AND J. BLISS. 1990. Nonindustrial private forests. Pages 231–253 in R. A. Young and R. A. Giese, editors. Introduction to forest science. John Wiley and Sons, Inc., New York, USA.

MASER, C., R., G. ANDERSON, K. CROMACK, JR., J. T. WILLIAMS, AND R. E. MARTIN. 1979. Dead and down wood material. Pages 78–95 in J. W. Thomas, editor. Wildlife habitats in managed forests—the Blue Mountains of Oregon and Washington. U.S. Department of Agriculture, Forest Service, Handbook 553.

MASTERS, R. E. 1991. Effects of fire and timber harvest on vegetation and cervid use of oak-pine sites in Oklahoma Ouachita Mountains. Pages 168–176 in S. C. Nodvin and T. A. Waldrop, editors. Fire and the environment: ecological and cultural perspectives. U.S. Department of Agriculture, Forest Service, General Technical Report SE-69.

MAURER, B. A. 1994. Geographical population analysis: tools for the analysis of biodiversity. Blackwell Scientific Publications, Oxford, United Kingdom.

MCAULEY, D., AND D. A. CLUGSTON. 1998. American woodcock. Pages 193–197 in M. J. Mac, P. A. Opler, C. E. Puckett Haecker, and P. D. Doran, editors. Status and trends of the nation's biological resources. Volume 1. U.S. Department of the Interior, Geological Survey, Reston, Virginia, USA.

MCCLANAHAN, T. R., AND R. W. WOLFE. 1993. Accelerating forest succession in a fragmented landscape: the role of birds and perches. Conservation Biology 7:279–288.

MCCLELLAND, B. R., AND P. T. MCCLELLAND. 1999. Pileated woodpecker nest and roost trees in Montana: links with old-growth and forest "health." Wildlife Society Bulletin 27:846–857.

MCDONALD, JR., J. E., W. L. PALMER, AND G. L. STORM. 1994. Ruffed grouse population response to intensive forest management in central Pennsylvania, USA. Proceedings of the International Union of Game Biologists 21:126–131.

MCINTYRE, S., AND G. W. BARRETT. 1992. Habitat variegation, an alternative to fragmentation. Conservation Biology 6:146–147.

MERRIAM, G., AND J. WEGNER. 1992. Local extinctions, habitat fragmentation, and ecotones. Ecological studies: analysis and synthesis

92:150–169.

MERRILL, S. B., F. J. CUTHBERT, AND G. OEHLERT. 1998. Residual patches and their contribution to forest-bird diversity on northern Minnesota aspen clear-cuts. Conservation Biology 12:190–199.

MILLER, JR., G. T. 1992. Living in the environment. Seventh edition. Wadsworth, Inc., Belmont, California, USA.

MILLER, G. W., J. E. JOHNSON, AND J. E. BAUMGRAS. 1997. Deferment cutting in central Appalachian hardwoods. Forest Landowner 56(5): 28–31, 68.

MITSCH, W. J., AND J. G. GOSSELINK. 1993. Wetlands. Second edition. Van Nostrand Reinhold, New York, USA.

MOORMAN, C. E., AND B. R. CHAPMAN. 1996. Nest-site selection of red-shouldered and red-tailed hawks in a managed forest. Wilson Bulletin 108:357–368.

MORRISON, M. L., AND E. C. MENSLOW. 1984. Response of avian communities to herbicide-induced vegetation changes. Journal of Wildlife Management 48:14–22.

———, B. G. MARCOT, AND R. W. MANNAN. 1992. Wildlife-habitat relationships: concepts and applications. University of Wisconsin Press, Madison, USA.

———, ———, AND ———. 1998. Wildlife-habitat relationships: concepts and applications. Second edition. University of Wisconsin Press, Madison, USA.

MORSE, S. F., AND S. K. ROBINSON. 1999. Nesting success of a Neotropical migrant in a multiple-use, forested landscape. Conservation Biology 13:327–337.

MURCIA, C. 1995. Edge effects in fragmented forests: implications for conservation. Trends in Ecology and Evolution 10:58–62.

MUSHINSKY, H. R. 1985. Fire and the Florida sandhill herpetofaunal community: with special attention to responses of *Cnemidophorus sexlineatus*. Herpetologica 41:333–342.

NAIMAN, R. J., AND H. DECHAMPS. 1997. The ecology of interfaces: riparian zones. Annual Review of Ecology and Systematics 28:621–658.

NATIONAL ECOSYSTEM MANAGEMENT FORUM. 1993. Meeting summary. The Keystone Center, Keystone, Colorado, USA.

NIXON, C. M., S. P. HAVERA, AND L. P. HANSEN. 1980. Initial response of squirrels to forest changes associated with selective cutting. Wildlife Society Bulletin 8:298–306.

NOSS, R. F. 1987. Corridors in real landscapes: a reply to Simberloff and Cox. Conservation Biology 1:159–164.

———. 1992. Issues of scale in conservation biology. Pages 239–250 *in* P. L. Fiedler and S. K. Jain, editors. Conservation biology: the theory and practice of nature conservation, preservation, and management. Chapman and Hall, New York, USA.

———, AND A. Y. COOPERRIDER. 1994. Saving nature's legacy: protecting and restoring biodiversity. Island Press, Washington, D.C., USA.

O'CONNELL, T. J., L. E. JACKSON, AND R. P. BROOKS. 2000. Bird guilds as indicators of ecological condition in the central Appalachians. Ecological Applications 10:1706–1721.

OLIVER, C. D., AND B. C. LARSON. 1996. Forest stand dynamics. John Wiley and Sons, Inc., New York, USA.

PASTOR, J., AND W. M. POST. 1985. Development of a linked forest productivity-soil process model. Environmental Sciences Division 2455, Oak Ridge National Laboratory, Oak Ridge, Tennessee, USA.

PATTON, D. R. 1992. Wildlife habitat relationships in forested ecosystems. Timber Press, Portland, Oregon, USA.

PATTON, R. F. 1990. Diseases of forest trees. Pages 169–194 *in* R. A. Young and R. L. Giese, editors. Introduction to forest science. John Wiley and Sons, Inc., New York, USA.

PEDLAR, J. H., L. FAHRIG, AND H. G. MERRIAM. 1997. Raccoon habitat use at two spatial scales. Journal of Wildlife Management 61:102–112.

PELTON, M. R., AND F. T. VAN MANEN. 1994. Distribution of black bears in North America. Eastern Workshop on Black Bear Research and Management 12:133–138.

PERLIN, J. 1989. A forest journey: the role of wood in the development of civilization. Harvard University Press, Cambridge, Massachusetts, USA.

PETIT, L. J., D. R. PETIT, AND T. E. MARTIN. 1995. Landscape-level management of migratory birds: looking past the trees to see the forest. Wildlife Society Bulletin 23:420–429.

PETRANKA, J. W., M. E. ELDRIDGE, AND K. E. HALEY. 1993. Effects of timber harvesting on southern Appalachian salamanders.

Conservation Biology 7:363–370.

PICKETT, S. T. A., AND J. N. THOMPSON. 1978. Patch dynamics and the design of nature reserves. Biological Conservation 13:27–37.

PIENAAR, L. V., H. H. PAGE, AND J. W. RHENEY. 1990. Yield predictions for mechanically site-prepared slash pine plantations. Southern Journal of Applied Forestry 14:104–109.

PIMM, S. L., AND R. A. ASKINS. 1995. Forest losses predict bird extinctions in eastern North America. Proceedings of the National Academy of Sciences 92:9343–9347.

PROBST, J. R., AND J. WEINRICH. 1993. Relating Kirtland's warbler population to changing landscape composition and structure. Landscape Ecology 8:257–271.

———, D. S. RAKSTAD, AND D. J. RUGG. 1992. Breeding bird communities in regenerating broadleaf forests of the USA Lake States. Forest Ecology and Management 49:43–60.

QI, Y., AND J. K. GILLES. 1999. Modeling ecosystem processes and patterns for multiple-use management. Pages 14–22 *in* F. Helles, P. Holten-Andersen, and L. Wichmann, editors. Multiple use of forests and other natural resources—aspects of theory and application. Kluwer Academic Publishers, Norwell, Massachusetts, USA.

RAMM, C. W., AND C. L. MINER. 1986. Growth and yield programs used on microcomputers in the North Central Region. Northern Journal of Applied Forestry 3:44–45, 79.

RATCLIFFE, D. A. 1967. Decrease in eggshell weight in certain birds of prey. Nature 215:208–210.

RATTI, J. T., AND K. P. REESE. 1988. Preliminary test of the ecological trap hypothesis. Journal of Wildlife Management 52:484–491.

REED, J. M. 1995. Ecosystem management and an avian habitat dilemma. Wildlife Society Bulletin 23:453–457.

REICHMAN, O. J., AND H. R. PULLIAM. 1996. The scientific basis for ecosystem management. Ecological Applications 6:694–696.

RENKEN, R. B., AND E. P. WIGGERS. 1993. Habitat characteristics related to pileated woodpecker densities in Missouri. Wilson Bulletin 105:77–83.

ROBBINS, C. S. 1979. Effect of forest fragmentation on bird populations. Pages 198–212 *in* R. DeGraaf, technical coordinator. Proceedings of the workshop for the management of north central and northeastern forests for nongame birds. U.S. Department of Agriculture, Forest Service, General Technical Report NC-51.

———. 1988. Forest fragmentation and its effects on birds. Pages 61–65 *in* J. E. Johnson, editor. Managing north-central forest for nontimber values. Publication 98–04. Society of American Foresters, Bethesda, Maryland, USA.

———, D. K. DAWSON, AND B. A. DOWELL. 1989. Habitat area requirements of breeding forest birds of the Middle Atlantic States. Wildlife Monographs 103.

ROBINSON, S. K., AND W. D. ROBINSON. 2001. Avian nesting success in a selectively harvested north temperate deciduous forest. Conservation Biology 15:1763–1771.

RODEWALD, A. D. 2002. Nest predation in forested regions: landscape and edge effects. Journal of Wildlife Management 66:634–640.

———, AND R. H. YAHNER. 1999. Effects of forest management and landscape composition on woodland salamanders. Northeast Wildlife 54:45–54.

———, AND ———. 2000. Bird communities associated with harvested hardwood stands containing residual trees. Journal of Wildlife Management 64:924–932.

———, AND ———. 2001a. Avian nesting success in forested landscapes: influence of landscape composition, stand and nest-patch microhabitat, and biotic interactions. Auk 118:1018–1028.

———, AND ———. 2001b. Landscape composition in forested landscapes: influence on avian community structure and associated mechanisms. Ecology 82:3493–3504.

RODEWALD, P. G., AND K. G. SMITH. 1998. Short-term effects of understory and overstory management on breeding birds in Arkansas oak-hickory forests. Journal of Wildlife Management 62:1411–1417.

ROLOFF, G. J., AND J. B. HAUFLER. 1997. Establishing population viability planning objectives based on habitat potentials. Wildlife Society Bulletin 25:895–904.

———, G. F. WILHERE, T. QUINN, AND S. KOHLMAN. 2001. An overview of models and their role in wildlife management. Pages 512–536 *in* D. H. Johnson and T. A. O'Neil, editors. Wildlife-habitat relationships in Oregon and Washington. Oregon State University Press, Corvallis,

USA.

ROSENBERG, K. V., R. W. ROHRBAUGH, JR., S. E. BARKER, J. D. LOWE, R. S. HAMES, AND A. A. DHONDT. 1999. A land manager's guide to improving habitat for scarlet tanagers and other forest-interior birds. Cornell Lab of Ornithology, Ithaca, New York, USA.

ROSENZWEIG, M. L. 1995. Species diversity in space and time. Cambridge University Press, New York, USA.

RUDNICKY, T. C., AND M. L. HUNTER, JR. 1993a. Avian nest predation in clearcuts, forests, and edges in a forest-dominated landscape. Journal of Wildlife Management 57:358–364.

———, AND ———. 1993b. Reversing the fragmentation perspective: effects of clear-cut size on bird species richness in Maine. Ecological Applications 3:357–366.

RUSSELL, K. R., D. H. VAN LEAR, AND D. C. GUYNN, JR. 1999. Prescribed fire effects on herpetofauna: review and management implications. Wildlife Society Bulletin 27:374–384.

SAAB, V. 1999. Importance of spatial scale to habitat use by breeding birds in riparian forests: a hierarchical analysis. Ecological Applications 9:135–151.

SAMSON, F. B., AND F. L. KNOPF. 1982. In search of a diversity ethic for wildlife management. Transactions of the North American Wildlife and Natural Resources Conference 47:421–431.

SANTILLO, D. J., P. W. BROWN, AND D. M. LESLIE, JR. 1989. Response of songbirds to glyphosate-induced habitat changes on clearcuts. Journal of Wildlife Management 53:64–71.

SAVIDGE, J. A. 1978. Wildlife in a herbicide-treated Jeffrey pine plantation in eastern California. Journal of Forestry 76:476–478.

SCAVIA, D., M. RUGGIERO, AND E. HAWES. 1996. Building a scientific basis for ensuring the vitality and productivity of U.S. ecosystems. Bulletin of the Ecological Society of America 77:125–127.

SCHIER, G. A. 1975. Deterioration of aspen clones in the Middle Rocky Mountains. U.S. Department of Agriculture, Forest Service, Research Paper INT-170.

SCOTT, D. P., AND R. H. YAHNER. 1989. Winter habitat and browse use by snowshoe hares, *Lepus americanus*, in a marginal habitat in Pennsylvania. Canadian Field-Naturalist 103:560–563.

SCOTT, J. M., F. DAVIS, B. CSUTI, R. NOSS, B. BUTTERFIELD, C. GROVES, H. ANDERSON, S. CAICCO, F. D'ERCHIA, T. C. EDWARDS, JR., J. ULLIMAN, AND R. G. WRIGHT. 1993. Gap analysis: a geographic approach to protection of biological diversity. Wildlife Monographs 123.

SCOTT, V. E., K. E. EVANS, D. R. PATTON, AND C. P. STONE. 1977. Cavity-nesting birds of North American forests. U.S. Department of Agriculture, Forest Service, Agricultural Handbook 511.

SHACKELFORD, C. E., AND R. N. CONNER. 1997. Woodpecker abundance and habitat use in three forest types in eastern Texas. Wilson Bulletin 109:614–629.

SHVETS, V., AND B. ZEIDE. 1996. Investigating parameters of growth equations. Canadian Journal of Forest Research 26:1980–1990.

SHVIDENKO, A., S. VENEVSKY, G. RAILE, AND S. NILSSON. 1995. A system for evaluation of growth and mortality in Russian forests. Water, Air, and Soil Pollution 82:333–348.

SIERRA CLUB. 2002. Victory on forest protection. Press release, Sierra Club, San Francisco, California, USA.

SIMBERLOFF, D., AND J. COX. 1987. Consequences and costs of conservation corridors. Conservation Biology 1:63–71.

SMALL, M. F., AND M. L. HUNTER. 1988. Forest fragmentation and avian nest predation in forested landscapes. Oecologia 76:62–64.

SMALLEY, G. W., AND R. L. BAILEY. 1974. Yield tables and stand structure for shortleaf pine plantations in the Tennessee, Alabama and Georgia highlands. U.S. Department of Agriculture, Forest Service, Research Paper SO-97.

SMITH, D. M., B. C. LARSON, M. J. KELTY, AND P. M. S. ASHTON. 1997. The practice of silviculture: applied forest ecology. Ninth edition. John Wiley and Sons, Inc., New York, USA.

SMITH, H. C., N. I. LAMSON, AND G. W. MILLER. 1989. An esthetic alternative to clearcutting? Journal of Forestry 87(3):14–18.

SOCIETY OF AMERICAN FORESTERS. 1981. Choices in silviculture for American forests. Society of American Foresters, Bethesda, Maryland, USA.

———. 1992. Biological diversity in forest ecosystems. Journal of Forestry 90(2):42–43.

SPURR, S. H., AND B. V. BARNES. 1980. Forest ecology. Third edition.

John Wiley and Sons, Inc., New York, USA.

STODDARD, H. L. 1931. The bobwhite quail: its habits, preservation and increase. Charles Scribner's Sons, New York, USA.

STRIBLING, H. L., H. R. SMITH, AND R. H. YAHNER. 1990. Bird community response to timber stand improvement and snag retention. Northern Journal of Applied Forestry 7:35–38.

STRITTHOLT, J. R., AND D. A. DELLASALA. 2001. Importance of roadless areas in biodiversity conservation in forested ecosystems: case study of the Klamath-Siskiyou ecoregion of the United States. Conservation Biology 15:1742–1754.

SUAREZ, A. V., K. S. PFENNIG, AND S. K. ROBINSON. 1997. Nesting success of a disturbance-dependent songbird on different kinds of edges. Conservation Biology 11:928–935.

SULLIVAN, T. P., D. S. SULLIVAN, AND C. KURTA. 1999. Relations of small mammal populations to even-aged shelterwood systems: a reply. Journal of Wildlife Management 63:1381–1389.

SWIHART, R. K., AND R. H. YAHNER. 1982. Eastern cottontail use of fragmented farmland habitat. Acta Theriologica 27:257–273.

TALBOTT, S. C. 1999. Temporal and spatial use of diversity cuts by bird communities in two state forests of central Pennsylvania. Thesis. Pennsylvania State University, University Park, USA.

———, AND R. H. YAHNER. 2003. Temporal and spatial use of even-aged reproduction stands by bird communities in central Pennsylvania. Northern Journal of Applied Forestry 20:117–123.

TERBOUGH, J. 1989. Where have all the birds gone? Princeton University Press, Princeton, New Jersey, USA.

TEWKSBURY, J. J., S. J. HEJL, AND T. E. MARTIN. 1998. Breeding productivity does not decline with increasing fragmentation in a western landscape. Ecology 79:2890–2903.

THOMAS, J. W., C. MASER, AND J. E. RODIEK. 1979a. Edges. Pages 48–59 *in* J. W. Thomas, editor. Wildlife habitats in managed forest: the Blue Mountains of Oregon and Washington. U.S. Department of Agriculture, Forest Service, Agricultural Handbook 553.

———, R. G. ANDERSON, C. MASER, AND E. L. BULL. 1979b. Snags. Pages 60–77 *in* J. W. Thomas, editor. Wildlife habitats in managed forests—the Blue Mountains of Oregon and Washington. U.S. Department of Agriculture, Forest Service, Agricultural Handbook 553.

———, L. F. RUGGIERO, R. W. MANNAN, J. W. SCHOEN, AND R. A. LANCIA. 1988. Management and conservation of old-growth forests in the United States. Wildlife Society Bulletin 16:252–262.

THOMPSON, III, F. R., AND R. M. DEGRAAF. 2001. Conservation approaches for woody, early successional communities in the eastern United States. Wildlife Society Bulletin 29:483–494.

———, W. D. DIJAK, T. G. KULOWIEC, AND D. A. HAMILTON. 1992. Breeding bird populations in Missouri Ozark forests with and without clearcutting. Journal of Wildlife Management 56:23–30.

THORNE, S. G. 1993. Penn's Woods at the turning point: creating the future forest. Pages 160–168 *in* J. C. Finley and S. B. Jones, editors. Penn's Woods—changes and challenges. Proceedings of the Penn State Forest Resources Conference, Pennsylvania State University, University Park, USA.

TITTLER, R., AND S. J. HANNON. 2000. Nest predation in and adjacent to cutblocks with variable tree retention. Forest Ecology and Management 136:147–157.

TRANI, M. K., R. T. BROOKS, T. L. SCHMIDT, V. A. RUDIS, AND C. M. GABBARD. 2001. Patterns and trends of early successional forests in the eastern United States. Wildlife Society Bulletin 29:413–424.

TREPL, L. 1994. Competition and coexistence: on the historical background in ecology and the influence of economy and social science. Ecological Modelling 75:99–110.

TRUETT, J. C., M. A. ZABLAN, AND K. KUNKEL. 2005. Ecological impact assessments and habitat conservation plans. Pages 503–523 *in* C. E. Braun, editor. Techniques for wildlife investigations and management. Sixth edition. The Wildlife Society, Bethesda, Maryland, USA.

U.S. DEPARTMENT OF AGRICULTURE. 1968. Forest regions of the United States. U.S. Department of Agriculture, Forest Service, Map, Washington, D.C., USA.

———. 1982. An analysis of the timber situation in the United States 1952–2030. U.S. Department of Agriculture, Forest Service, Forest Resources Report 23.

U.S. DEPARTMENT OF INTERIOR. 1980. Habitat evaluation procedures. U.S. Department of the Interior, Fish and Wildlife Service, Division of Ecological Services, ESM 102.

VAN HORN, M. A., R. M. GENTRY, AND J. FAABORG. 1995. Patterns of ovenbird (*Seiurus aurocapillus*) pairing success in Missouri forest tracts. Auk 112:98–106.

VAN LEAR, D. H., AND T. A. WALDROP. 1989. History, uses, and effects of fire in the Appalachians. U.S. Department of Agriculture, Forest Service, General Technical Report SE-54.

VERNER, J., AND A. S. BOSS. 1980. California wildlife and their habitats: western Sierra Nevada. U.S. Department of Agriculture, Forest Service, General Technical Report PSW-37.

VOS, C. C., H. BAVECO, AND C. J. GRASHOF-BOKDAM. 2002. Corridors and species dispersal. Pages 84–104 *in* K. Gutzwiller, editor. Concepts and applications of landscape ecology in biological conservation. Springer-Verlag, Inc., New York, USA.

WATHEN, W. G., G. F. MCCRACKEN, AND M. R. PELTON. 1985. Genetic variation in black bears from the Great Smoky Mountains National Park. Journal of Mammalogy 66:564–567.

WHITCOMB, R. F., C. S. ROBBINS, J. F. LYNCH, B. L. WHITCOMB, M. K. KLIMKIEWICZ, AND D. BYSTRAK. 1981. Effects of forest fragmentation on avifauna of the eastern deciduous forest. Pages 125–205 *in* R. L. Burgess and D. M. Sharpe, editors. Forest island dynamics in man-dominated landscapes. Springer-Verlag, Inc., New York, USA.

WIENS, J. A. 2002. Central concepts and issues in landscape ecology. Pages 3–21 *in* K. Gutzwiller, editor. Concepts and applications of landscape ecology in biological conservation. Springer-Verlag, Inc., New York, USA.

WILCOVE, D. S. 1985. Nest predation in forest tracts and the decline of migratory songbirds. Ecology 66:1211–1214.

———, AND S. K. ROBINSON. 1990. The impact of forest fragmentation on bird communities in eastern North America. *In* A. Keast, editor. Biogeography and ecology of forest bird communities. SPB Academic Publishing, The Netherlands.

———, C. H. MCLELLAN, AND A. P. DOBSON. 1986. Habitat fragmentation in the temperate zone. Pages 237–256 *in* M. E. Soulé, editor. Conservation biology: the science of scarcity and diversity. Sinauer Associates, Sunderland, Massachusetts, USA.

WILCOX, B. A. 1980. Insular ecology and conservation. Pages 95–117 *in* M. E. Soulé and B. A. Wilcox, editors. Conservation biology. Sinauer Associates, Sunderland, Massachusetts, USA.

———, AND D. D. MURPHY. 1985. Conservation strategy: the effects of fragmentation on extinction. American Naturalist 125:879–887.

WILDLIFE SOCIETY, THE. 1993. Conserving biological diversity. The Wildlifer 256:3.

WILLIAMS, G. L., K. R. RUSSELL, AND W. K. SEITZ. 1977. Pattern recognition as a tool in the ecological analysis of habitat. Pages 521–531 *in* Classification, inventory, and analysis of fish and wildlife habitat. U.S. Department of the Interior, Fish and Wildlife Service, OBS-78/76.

WILLIAMS, M. 1989. Americans and their forests: historical geography. Cambridge University Press, New York, USA.

———. 1992. Americans and their forests: a historical perspective. Cambridge University Press, New York, USA.

WOOD, C. A. 1994. Ecosystem management: achieving the new land ethic. Renewable Resources Journal 12:6–12.

YAHNER, R. H. 1986. Microhabitat use by small mammals in even-aged forest stands. American Midland Naturalist 115:174–180.

———. 1987. Use of even-aged stands by winter and spring bird communities. Wilson Bulletin 99:218–232.

———. 1988*a*. Changes in wildlife communities near edges. Conservation Biology 2:333–339.

———. 1988*b*. Small mammals associated with even-aged aspen and mixed-oak forest stands in central Pennsylvania. Journal of the Pennsylvania Academy of Science 62:122–126.

———. 1993. Effects of long-term forest clear-cutting on wintering and breeding birds. Wilson Bulletin 105:239–255.

———. 1995. Forest fragmentation and avian populations in the Northeast: some regional landscape considerations. Northeast Wildlife 52:93–102.

———. 1996. Habitat fragmentation and habitat loss. Wildlife Society Bulletin 24:592.

———. 1997. Long-term dynamics of bird communities in a managed forested landscape. Wilson Bulletin 109:595–613.

———. 2000. Eastern deciduous forest: ecology and wildlife conservation. Second edition. University of Minnesota Press, Minneapolis, USA.

———. 2001. Fascinating mammals: conservation and ecology in the mid-eastern states. University of Pittsburgh Press, Pittsburgh, Pennsylvania, USA.

———, AND C. G. MAHAN. 2002. Animal behavior in fragmented landscapes. Pages 266–285 *in* K. Gutzwiller, editor. Concepts and applications of landscape ecology in biological conservation. Springer-Verlag, Inc., New York, USA.

———, AND A. L. WRIGHT. 1985. Depredation on artificial ground nests: effects of edge and plot age. Journal of Wildlife Management 49:508–513.

———, R. J. HUTNIK, AND S. A. LISCINSKY. 2002. Bird populations associated with an electric transmission right-of-way. Journal of Arboriculture 28:123–130.

———, C. G. MAHAN, AND C. A. DELONG. 1993. Dynamics of depredation on artificial ground nests in habitat managed for ruffed grouse. Wilson Bulletin 105:172–179.

———, T. E. MORRELL, AND J. S. RACHAEL. 1989. Effects of edge contrast on depredation of artificial avian nests. Journal of Wildlife Management 53:1135–1138.

———, N. H. PIERGALLINI, AND B. D. ROSS. 2001. A survey of amphibians and reptiles in two managed forests in central Pennsylvania. Journal of the Pennsylvania Academy of Science 74:48–51.

———, A. D. RODEWALD, AND S. C. TALBOTT. 2001. Edge-related nest predation associated with the retention of residual trees in harvested hardwood stands. Canadian Field-Naturalist 115:405–410.

YOHN, C. E. 2002. Comparison of breeding-bird communities associated with young even-aged stands of differing size and shape in a northern hardwood forest. Dissertation. Pennsylvania State University, University Park, USA.

ZEIDE, B. 1993. Analysis of growth equations. Forest Science 39:594–616.

INDEX

reproductive activity, 593
surveys, 115
trapping, 240
dove, ringed turtle
as bait in decoy traps, 247
dove, white-winged
age characteristics, 322
capture by nest traps, 244, 246
coo-counts, 670
dye as a marker, 351
gender characteristics, 322
HIP harvest surveys, 671
nest counts, 116
doves
age classification, 318
altricial young, 313
bands, 346
crop gland development, 600
gender identification, 318
Migratory Bird Treaty Act, 671
prolactin levels, 605
dowitcher, long-billed
foraging depth, 810
dowitchers
coastal marsh habitat, 842
dragonflies
urban abundance, 723
drainage
in coastal marsh management, 849
of wetlands, 801, 845
draining and flooding
coastal marsh impoundments, 852
drawdown
coastal marsh management, 845,846, 849
in impoundments, 727
marsh impoundments, 851, 855
plant germination, 813
wetlands, 812
DRC-1339 (avicide), 224, 225, 250, 746
dredged marsh creation
coastal marshes, 854
different vegetation, 850
marsh creation, 850
marsh plants, 850
drift fences, 262, 263, 268
drift nets, 272
drift traps, 243, 244
drive counts, 118
drive nets, 264, 265
drive traps, 243, 244
drop nets, 240, 241, 272
drowning
in guzzlers, 886
drug administration, 193
drug combinations
in immobilization, 291
drug delivery systems, 292
drug dosages, 287, 288, 296, 297
calculations, 289
definition of, 287
Drug Enforcement Administration, 287
drug
exposure, 292
synergy, 291

therapeutic index, 289
drugs
accountability, 294
antagonizing, 289
classes of, 289
euthanasia, 290
extra-label use, 287
FDA approved, 287
neuromuscular blocking, 290
use in restraint, 190
drugs, oral
as capture methods, 249
dry matter digestibility
see digestible dry matter
dual frequency measurement
GPS receivers, 430
dual-energy X-ray absorptiometry
(DXA), 563, 564
duck broods
population indices, 670
duck eggs
internal markers, 353
duck hunting regulations, 669, 670, 673
duck plague, 199, 200duck trap
design, 248
duck virus enteritis, 228
duck, American black
coastal marsh habitat, 842
wings in age identification, 319
wings in gender identification, 319
duck, black-bellied whistling
wings in age identification, 321
wings in gender identification, 321
duck, canvasback
aerial photography, 119
capture by decoy traps, 247
corral traps, 264
estradiol, 606
luteinizing hormone (LH), 606
mortality rate, 163
polychlorinated biphenyls, 606
population estimate, 118, 120
population size, 692
progesterone, 606
prolactin levels, 606
reproductive hormones, 606
wings in age identification, 320
wings in gender identification, 320
duck, Florida
coastal marsh habitat, 842
duck, fulvous whistling
wings in age identification, 321
wings in gender identification, 321
duck, harlequin
wings in age identification, 320
wings in gender identification, 320
duck, Hawaiian
wetland habitat, 829
duck, Laysan
reintroduction, 829
duck, long-tailed
wings in age identification, 321

wings in gender identification, 321
duck, Mandarin
urban populations, 721
duck, mottled
coastal marsh habitat, 842
wings in age identification, 319
wings in gender identification, 319
duck, northern shoveler
foraging depth, 810, 816
visual obstruction readings (VOR), 817
duck, redhead
capture by nest traps, 245
foraging depth, 810
wings in age identification, 320
wings in gender identification, 320
duck, ring-necked
foraging depth, 810
survival rate, 81
wings in age identification, 320
wings in gender identification, 320
duck, ruddy
foraging depth, 816
wings in age identification, 321
wings in gender identification, 321
duck, wood
brood parasitism, 618, 619
capture by drive and drift traps, 243
capture by nest traps, 244
cavities, 525, 818, 905,
clutch size, 619
dioxin toxicity, 219
marking tags, 357
nest box placement, 619
nest boxes, 618
nesting sites, 525
recoveries, 165, 166
remote marking, 342
second-cavity nesters, 618
semicoloniality breeding, 618
wings in age identification, 319
wings in gender identification, 319
ducklings
bands, 346
marking tags, 357
ducks
bait-traps, 733
banding programs, 671
blood collection, 204
botulism, 227
brackish water impoundments, 853
breeding habitat status, 670
capture by nest traps, 245
cattle grazing benefits, 854
coastal freshwater impoundments, 852
damage to crops, 744
dyes as markers, 352
food plants, 841
grassland habitat, 546
harvests, 659

hunting mortality, 669
hunting regulations, 670, 673
impoundments, 727
Migratory Bird Treaty Act, 671
nasal saddles with sensors, 386
neck collars, 343
nest counts, 125
plant use, 524
population indices, 670
productivity, 162
transmitters on bills, 386
trapping, 240
wetland habitat needs, 815
wings in age identification, 318, 319
wings in gender identification, 319
Ducks Unlimited, 436, 797
ducks, dabbling
breeding habitat, 817
coastal marsh habitat, 842
food habits, 816
foraging depth, 816
nest predation rate, 824
palustrine wetlands use, 809
botulism, 225
mortality from white phosphorus, 220
ducks, diving
breeding habitat, 818
capture by drive and drift traps, 243
coastal marsh habitat, 842
food habits, 816
foraging depth, 816
palustrine wetlands use, 809
ducks, migratory
marsh impoundments, 851
ducks, upland nesting
capture by nest traps, 245
capture by nets, 241
Duffer's traps, 253
dugouts as water source development, 885
Duncan's multiple range test, 84
dunlin
post-oil field development population status, 510
duration of behavioral states
definition of, 626
Dursban®, 263
Dycam ADC (software), 544
dyes
marking equipment, 350, 351
remote marking, 342
dye-spraying devices
remote marking, 342
dynamic animal interaction analyses, 396
dynamic mapping applications
GIS web-based, 427

E

E value
total body electrical conductivity, 563
eagle, bald, 25
backpacks, 348

944

thiram, 757, 758
thrasher, brown
  edge habitat, 719
  movements, 908
thrasher, pearly-eyed, 102
threatened species
  depredation permits, 742
  wetland habitat, 803
threshold of security
  population sizes, 661
thrush, red-legged, 102
thrush, wood
  forest habitat, 906, 907
  forest stand size, 909
thymus
  necropsy sample, 210
  tissue preservation, 232
thyroxine
  energy indices, 564
ticks
  as parasites, 203
  butyric acid, 619
  sequential behaviors, 619
tidal action
  on coastal wetlands, 839
tidal cycle
  coastal marshes, 841
tidal exchange, 847
  brackish water impoundments, 853
  in coastal marshes, 849
  marsh restoration, 850
tidal flow
  marsh restoration, 850
  restoration to impounded marshes, 849
tidal fluctuations, 840
  coastal wetlands, 808
tidal freshwater marshes, 841
tidal marshes, 840
  brackish water impoundments, 853
  salinity, 846
  sedimentary development, 848
  zonation patterns, 847, 848
tidal range
  coastal marshes, 842
tidewater
  variable flow, 842
tiger
  camera-trapped, 116
  natural marks, 341
  stripes as identification, 131
tiger, Amur
  neck collar snares, 254
tiger, Siberian
  individual recognition, 265
tile-drainage water, 868
tiletamine, 250, 290, 299, 300, 301
tiletamine-zolazepam, 291
tillage, conservation
  crop residues, 865, 866
timber
  value of, 804
timber company
  habitat conservation plans (HCPs), 514
timber harvesting, 899, 905
timber resources

regional models, 910
timber volume
  harvests, 424
timberland
  reserved, 899
time
  in population viability analysis, 698
time budgets, 626
time of detection, 126, 127
time series
  analysis, 102, 103
  population abundance, 699
time-behavioral response model, 135, 136
time-behavior-heterogeneity model, 136
time-energy budget (TEB), 577
time-heterogeneity model, 135
time-variation model, 135
timing
  recreational impacts, 791
tinajas, 807, 884, 886
tinamou, Chilean
  stocking, 669
tissue collection, 188, 189
tissue nitrogen balance (TNB), 555
tissue preservation
  ovarian analysis, 598
tissue removal methods, 360
tissue samples, 202, 203, 204
  legal acceptability, 230
  preservation for necropsy, 232
tissue sampling
  DNA extraction, 635
tissues
  dissection for sampling, 230
tit, great
  urban survival, 723
titles
  brochures, 39
TMSURVIV (software), 141
toad, golden, 35
toad, Natterjack
  genetic diversity of translocated populations, 643
toad, spadefoot
  aquatic environment, 819
toad, western, 875
toads
  blood samples, 188
  courtship behavior, 593
  dyes as markers, 352
  endangered status, 803
  follicular development, 592
  gender identification, 315
  marking tags, 357
  passive integrated transponders (PIT), 355
  radioisotopes for marking, 354
  reproductive hormones, 604
  tissue removal methods, 361
  urban abundance, 723
TOBEC®, 563
tody, Puerto Rican, 102
toe clipping, 190, 362
toenail clipping, 362
Tolazine®, 291

tolazoline, 290, 291, 298, 299
Tomahawk 206 traps, 259
Tomahawk wire cage traps, 256, 259
Tomahawk™ No. 108 wire cage traps, 260
Tomahawk™ No. 208 wire cage traps, 260
tooth removal
  ethics, 312
  for age classification, 312
tooth replacement
  age classification, 314
tooth wear, 312
tooth, standard
  cementum annuli analysis, 313
toothcup
  plant germination, 813
topi, 12
topology, 421
Tordoff bow trap, 250
tortoise conservation
  education, 518
  research, 518
tortoise, Bolson
  capture methods, 269
tortoise, desert, 876
  capture methods, 269
  core mitigation measure, 515
  digestible energy, 571
  guzzlers, 886
  habitat conservation plans (HCPs), 516, 517, 520
  incidental take permits, 516, 517
  passive integrated transponders (PIT), 355
  population model, 126
  reserve design, 517
tortoise, gopher
  capture methods, 270
tortoises
  paints as markers, 352
  reproductive hormones, 604
  testosterone, 607
total body electrical conductivity (TOBEC®), 563
total body fat
  nutritional indices, 559
total body water, 559
  related to body fat, 562
  related to body mass, fat-free, 562
  stable isotopes for estimation, 562
total collection digestibility trial, 572
total counts
  sample plots, 119
total dietary fiber method, 569
total functional redundancy
  GIS map, 419
touch, 622
  characteristics, 623
tours
  restoration projects, 730
tower collisions, 621
towhee, Inyo California
  threatened status, 695
toxic bait

rodent control, 757
  to control damage by wildlife, 746
toxic substances
  reproduction, 606
toxicants, 757, 758, 759
  assays, 204
  spills of, 201
  to control damage by wildlife, 746
toxicity
  basic, 214
  contaminants, 213
toxicology, 204
  wildlife, 234
toxins, 201, 204
  animal, 233
  fungal, 199
  natural mortality, 215, 225
  plant, 233
  risk to humans, 198
tracking
  DNA collection, 646
tracking lights, nocturnal, 348
tracks
  population indices, 116
traffic networks
  recreational disturbance, 793, 794
trail hounds
  predator tracking, 770
trailing devices
  marking equipment, 347, 349
Trailmaster® cameras, 265, 266
trails
  design of, 793, 794
  trail-use habituation, 791
trammel nets, 270
tranquilization, 189
  definition of, 287
tranquilizer trap devices (TTDs), 261, 272
tranquilizers, 290, 291
transect lines
  quadrats, 526
transect plots, 56, 58
translocated populations
  genetic diversity, 643
translocation programs
  gene flow, 640, 641
  guidelines, 705
translocations, 705
transmitter
  attachment, 384
  frequencies, 393
transmitters, 380
  basic VHF circuit, 380
  costs of, 379
  detachment of, 386
  with sensors, 383
transmitters, radio, 382
  encapsulation, 383
  in anesthetic darts, 384
  in eggs, 384
  small mammal collars, 381
  to trigger trap release devices, 384
  transmission interval, 384
  used with other markers, 378